American Casebook Series
Hornbook Series and Basic Legal Texts
Nutshell Series

of

WEST PUBLISHING COMPANY
P.O. Box 64526
St. Paul, Minnesota 55164-0526

ACCOUNTING

Faris' Accounting and Law in a Nutshell, 377 pages, 1984 (Text)

Fiflis, Kripke and Foster's Teaching Materials on Accounting for Business Lawyers, 3rd Ed., 838 pages, 1984 (Casebook)

Siegel and Siegel's Accounting and Financial Disclosure: A Guide to Basic Concepts, 259 pages, 1983 (Text)

ADMINISTRATIVE LAW

Davis' Cases, Text and Problems on Administrative Law, 6th Ed., 683 pages, 1977 (Casebook)

Davis' Basic Text on Administrative Law, 3rd Ed., 617 pages, 1972 (Text)

Gellhorn and Boyer's Administrative Law and Process in a Nutshell, 2nd Ed., 445 pages, 1981 (Text)

Mashaw and Merrill's Cases and Materials on Administrative Law–The American Public Law System, 2nd Ed., 976 pages, 1985 (Casebook)

Robinson, Gellhorn and Bruff's The Administrative Process, 3rd Ed., 978 pages, 1986 (Casebook)

ADMIRALTY

Healy and Sharpe's Cases and Materials on Admiralty, 2nd Ed., 876 pages, 1986 (Casebook)

Maraist's Admiralty in a Nutshell, 390 pages, 1983 (Text)

Sohn and Gustafson's Law of the Sea in a Nutshell, 264 pages, 1984 (Text)

AGENCY—PARTNERSHIP

Fessler's Alternatives to Incorporation for Persons in Quest of Profit, 2nd Ed., 326 pages, 1986 (Casebook)

AGENCY—PARTNERSHIP—Cont'd

Henn's Cases and Materials on Agency, Partnership and Other Unincorporated Business Enterprises, 2nd Ed., 733 pages, 1985 (Casebook)

Reuschlein and Gregory's Hornbook on the Law of Agency and Partnership, 625 pages, 1979, with 1981 pocket part (Text)

Seavey, Reuschlein and Hall's Cases on Agency and Partnership, 599 pages, 1962 (Casebook)

Selected Corporation and Partnership Statutes and Forms, 555 pages, 1985

Steffen and Kerr's Cases and Materials on Agency-Partnership, 4th Ed., 859 pages, 1980 (Casebook)

Steffen's Agency-Partnership in a Nutshell, 364 pages, 1977 (Text)

AGRICULTURAL LAW

Meyer, Pedersen, Thorson and Davidson's Agricultural Law: Cases and Materials, 931 pages, 1985 (Casebook)

ALTERNATIVE DISPUTE RESOLUTION

Kanowitz' Cases and Materials on Alternative Dispute Resolution, 1024 pages, 1986 (Casebook)

AMERICAN INDIAN LAW

Canby's American Indian Law in a Nutshell, 288 pages, 1981 (Text)

Getches and Wilkinson's Cases on Federal Indian Law, 2nd Ed., approximately 870 pages, 1986 (Casebook)

ANTITRUST LAW

Gellhorn's Antitrust Law and Economics in a Nutshell, 3rd Ed., about 425 pages, 1987 (Text)

List current as of July, 1986

ANTITRUST LAW—Cont'd

Gifford and Raskind's Cases and Materials on Antitrust, 694 pages, 1983 with 1985 Supplement (Casebook)
Hovenkamp's Hornbook on Economics and Federal Antitrust Law, Student Ed., 414 pages, 1985 (Text)
Oppenheim, Weston and McCarthy's Cases and Comments on Federal Antitrust Laws, 4th Ed., 1168 pages, 1981 with 1985 Supplement (Casebook)
Posner and Easterbrook's Cases and Economic Notes on Antitrust, 2nd Ed., 1077 pages, 1981, with 1984–85 Supplement (Casebook)
Sullivan's Hornbook of the Law of Antitrust, 886 pages, 1977 (Text)
See also Regulated Industries, Trade Regulation

ART LAW

DuBoff's Art Law in a Nutshell, 335 pages, 1984 (Text)

BANKING LAW

Lovett's Banking and Financial Institutions in a Nutshell, 409 pages, 1984 (Text)
Symons and White's Teaching Materials on Banking Law, 2nd Ed., 993 pages, 1984 (Casebook)

BUSINESS PLANNING

Painter's Problems and Materials in Business Planning, 2nd Ed., 1008 pages, 1984 (Casebook)
Selected Securities and Business Planning Statutes, Rules and Forms, 470 pages, 1985

CIVIL PROCEDURE

Casad's Res Judicata in a Nutshell, 310 pages, 1976 (text)
Cound, Friedenthal, Miller and Sexton's Cases and Materials on Civil Procedure, 4th Ed., 1202 pages, 1985 with 1985 Supplement (Casebook)
Ehrenzweig, Louisell and Hazard's Jurisdiction in a Nutshell, 4th Ed., 232 pages, 1980 (Text)
Federal Rules of Civil-Appellate Procedure—West Law School Edition, about 550 pages, 1986
Friedenthal, Kane and Miller's Hornbook on Civil Procedure, 876 pages, 1985 (Text)
Kane's Civil Procedure in a Nutshell, 2nd Ed., 306 pages, 1986 (Text)
Koffler and Reppy's Hornbook on Common Law Pleading, 663 pages, 1969 (Text)
Marcus and Sherman's Complex Litigation–Cases and Materials on Advanced Civil Procedure, 846 pages, 1985 (Casebook)
Park's Computer-Aided Exercises on Civil Procedure, 2nd Ed., 167 pages, 1983 (Coursebook)

CIVIL PROCEDURE—Cont'd

Siegel's Hornbook on New York Practice, 1011 pages, 1978 with 1985 Pocket Part (Text)
See also Federal Jurisdiction and Procedure

CIVIL RIGHTS

Abernathy's Cases and Materials on Civil Rights, 660 pages, 1980 (Casebook)
Cohen's Cases on the Law of Deprivation of Liberty: A Study in Social Control, 755 pages, 1980 (Casebook)
Lockhart, Kamisar, Choper and Shiffrin's Cases on Constitutional Rights and Liberties, 6th Ed., about 1300 pages, 1986 with 1986 Supplement (Casebook)—reprint from Lockhart, et al. Cases on Constitutional Law, 6th Ed., 1986
Vieira's Civil Rights in a Nutshell, 279 pages, 1978 (Text)

COMMERCIAL LAW

Bailey's Secured Transactions in a Nutshell, 2nd Ed., 391 pages, 1981 (Text)
Epstein and Martin's Basic Uniform Commercial Code Teaching Materials, 2nd Ed., 667 pages, 1983 (Casebook)
Henson's Hornbook on Secured Transactions Under the U.C.C., 2nd Ed., 504 pages, 1979 with 1979 P.P. (Text)
Murray's Commercial Law, Problems and Materials, 366 pages, 1975 (Coursebook)
Nordstrom and Clovis' Problems and Materials on Commercial Paper, 458 pages, 1972 (Casebook)
Nordstrom, Murray and Clovis' Problems and Materials on Sales, 515 pages, 1982 (Casebook)
Nordstrom, Murray and Clovis' Problems and Materials on Secured Transactions, about 500 pages, 1987 (Casebook)
Selected Commercial Statutes, 1389 pages, 1985
Speidel, Summers and White's Teaching Materials on Commercial and Consumer Law, 3rd Ed., 1490 pages, 1981 (Casebook)
Stockton's Sales in a Nutshell, 2nd Ed., 370 pages, 1981 (Text)
Stone's Uniform Commercial Code in a Nutshell, 2nd Ed., 516 pages, 1984 (Text)
Uniform Commercial Code, Official Text with Comments, 994 pages, 1978
UCC Article 9, Reprint from 1962 Code, 128 pages, 1976
UCC Article 9, 1972 Amendments, 304 pages, 1978
Weber and Speidel's Commercial Paper in a Nutshell, 3rd Ed., 404 pages, 1982 (Text)
White and Summers' Hornbook on the Uniform Commercial Code, 2nd Ed., 1250 pages, 1980 (Text)

COMMUNITY PROPERTY

Mennell's Community Property in a Nutshell, 447 pages, 1982 (Text)

Verrall and Bird's Cases and Materials on California Community Property, 4th Ed., 549 pages, 1983 (Casebook)

COMPARATIVE LAW

Barton, Gibbs, Li and Merryman's Law in Radically Different Cultures, 960 pages, 1983 (Casebook)

Glendon, Gordon and Osakive's Comparative Legal Traditions: Text, Materials and Cases on the Civil Law, Common Law, and Socialist Law Traditions, 1091 paqes, 1985 (Casebook)

Glendon, Gordon, and Osakwe's Comparative Legal Traditions in a Nutshell, 402 pages, 1982 (Text)

Langbein's Comparative Criminal Procedure: Germany, 172 pages, 1977 (Casebook)

COMPUTERS AND LAW

Maggs and Sprowl's Computer Applications in the Law, about 300 pages, 1986 (Text)

Mason's An Introduction to the Use of Computers in Law, 223 pages, 1984 (Text)

CONFLICT OF LAWS

Cramton, Currie and Kay's Cases-Comments-Questions on Conflict of Laws, 3rd Ed., 1026 pages, 1981 (Casebook)

Scoles and Hay's Hornbook on Conflict of Laws, Student Ed., 1085 pages, 1982 with 1986 P.P. (Text)

Scoles and Weintraub's Cases and Materials on Conflict of Laws, 2nd Ed., 966 pages, 1972, with 1978 Supplement (Casebook)

Siegel's Conflicts in a Nutshell, 469 pages, 1982 (Text)

CONSTITUTIONAL LAW

Barron and Dienes' Constitutional Law in a Nutshell, about 400 pages, 1986 (Text)

Engdahl's Constitutional Power in a Nutshell: Federal and State, 411 pages, 1974 (Text)

Lockhart, Kamisar, Choper and Shiffrin's Cases-Comments-Questions on Constitutional Law, 6th Ed., 1601 pages, 1986 with 1986 Supplement (Casebook)

Lockhart, Kamisar, Choper and Shiffrin's Cases-Comments-Questions on the American Constitution, 6th Ed., about 1200 pages, 1986 with 1986 Supplement (Casebook)—abridgment of Lockhart, et al. Cases on Constitutional Law, 6th Ed., 1986

Manning's The Law of Church-State Relations in a Nutshell, 305 pages, 1981 (Text)

Miller's Presidential Power in a Nutshell, 328 pages, 1977 (Text)

CONSTITUTIONAL LAW—Cont'd

Nowak, Rotunda and Young's Hornbook on Constitutional Law, 3rd Ed., Student Ed., approximately 1100 pages, 1986 (Text)

Rotunda's Modern Constitutional Law: Cases and Notes, 2nd Ed., 1004 pages, 1985, with 1986 Supplement (Casebook)

Williams' Constitutional Analysis in a Nutshell, 388 pages, 1979 (Text)

See also Civil Rights

CONSUMER LAW

Epstein and Nickles' Consumer Law in a Nutshell, 2nd Ed., 418 pages, 1981 (Text)

McCall's Consumer Protection, Cases, Notes and Materials, 594 pages, 1977, with 1977 Statutory Supplement (Casebook)

Selected Commercial Statutes, 1389 pages, 1985

Spanogle and Rohner's Cases and Materials on Consumer Law, 693 pages, 1979, with 1982 Supplement (Casebook)

See also Commercial Law

CONTRACTS

Calamari & Perillo's Cases and Problems on Contracts, 1061 pages, 1978 (Casebook)

Calamari and Perillo's Hornbook on Contracts, 2nd Ed., 878 pages, 1977 (Text)

Corbin's Text on Contracts, One Volume Student Edition, 1224 pages, 1952 (Text)

Fessler and Loiseaux's Cases and Materials on Contracts, 837 pages, 1982 (Casebook)

Friedman's Contract Remedies in a Nutshell, 323 pages, 1981 (Text)

Fuller and Eisenberg's Cases on Basic Contract Law, 4th Ed., 1203 pages, 1981 (Casebook)

Hamilton, Rau and Weintraub's Cases and Materials on Contracts, 830 pages, 1984 (Casebook)

Jackson and Bollinger's Cases on Contract Law in Modern Society, 2nd Ed., 1329 pages, 1980 (Casebook)

Keyes' Government Contracts in a Nutshell, 423 pages, 1979 (Text)

Schaber and Rohwer's Contracts in a Nutshell, 2nd Ed., 425 pages, 1984 (Text)

COPYRIGHT

See Patent and Copyright Law

CORPORATIONS

Hamilton's Cases on Corporations—Including Partnerships and Limited Partnerships, 3rd Ed., 1213 pages, 1986 with 1986 Statutory Supplement (Casebook)

Hamilton's Law of Corporations in a Nutshell, 379 pages, 1980 (Text)

Henn's Teaching Materials on Corporations, 2nd Ed., about 1200 pages, 1986 (Casebook)

CORPORATIONS—Cont'd

Henn and Alexander's Hornbook on Corporations, 3rd Ed., Student Ed., 1371 pages, 1983 with 1986 P.P. (Text)

Jennings and Buxbaum's Cases and Materials on Corporations, 5th Ed., 1180 pages, 1979 (Casebook)

Selected Corporation and Partnership Statutes, Regulations and Forms, 555 pages, 1985

Solomon, Stevenson and Schwartz' Materials and Problems on Corporations: Law and Policy, 1172 pages, 1982 with 1986 Supplement (Casebook)

CORPORATE FINANCE

Hamilton's Cases and Materials on Corporate Finance, 895 pages, 1984 with 1986 Supplement (Casebook)

CORRECTIONS

Krantz's Cases and Materials on the Law of Corrections and Prisoners' Rights, 3rd Ed., 855 pages, 1986 (Casebook)

Krantz's Law of Corrections and Prisoners' Rights in a Nutshell, 2nd Ed., 386 pages, 1983 (Text)

Popper's Post-Conviction Remedies in a Nutshell, 360 pages, 1978 (Text)

Robbins' Cases and Materials on Post Conviction Remedies, 506 pages, 1982 (Casebook)

CREDITOR'S RIGHTS

Bankruptcy Code, Rules and Forms, Law School and C.L.E. Ed., about 800 pages, 1986

Epstein's Debtor-Creditor Law in a Nutshell, 3rd Ed., 383 pages, 1986 (Text)

Epstein and Landers' Debtors and Creditors: Cases and Materials, 2nd Ed., 689 pages, 1982 (Casebook)

LoPucki's Player's Manual for the Debtor-Creditor Game, 123 pages, 1985 (Coursebook)

Riesenfeld's Cases and Materials on Creditors' Remedies and Debtors' Protection, 4th Ed., about 800 pages, 1987 (Casebook)

White's Bankruptcy and Creditor's Rights: Cases and Materials, 812 pages, 1985 (Casebook)

CRIMINAL LAW AND CRIMINAL PROCEDURE

Abrams', Federal Criminal Law and its Enforcement, 882 pages, 1986 (Casebook)

Carlson's Adjudication of Criminal Justice, Problems and References, about 124 pages, 1986 (Casebook)

Dix and Sharlot's Cases and Materials on Criminal Law, 2nd Ed., 771 pages, 1979 (Casebook)

CRIMINAL LAW AND CRIMINAL PROCEDURE—Cont'd

Federal Rules of Criminal Procedure—West Law School Edition, about 465 pages, 1986

Grano's Problems in Criminal Procedure, 2nd Ed., 176 pages, 1981 (Problem book)

Israel and LaFave's Criminal Procedure in a Nutshell, 3rd Ed., 438 pages, 1980 (Text)

Johnson's Cases, Materials and Text on Criminal Law, 3rd Ed., 783 pages, 1985 (Casebook)

Kamisar, LaFave and Israel's Cases, Comments and Questions on Modern Criminal Procedure, 6th Ed., about 1600 pages, 1986 with 1986 Supplement (Casebook)

Kamisar, LaFave and Israel's Cases, Comments and Questions on Basic Criminal Procedure, 6th Ed., about 800 pages, 1986 with 1986 Supplement (Casebook)—reprint from Kamisar, et al. Modern Criminal Procedure, 6th ed., 1986

LaFave's Modern Criminal Law: Cases, Comments and Questions, 789 pages, 1978 (Casebook)

LaFave and Israel's Hornbook on Criminal Procedure, Student Ed., 1142 pages, 1985 with 1985 P.P. (Text)

LaFave and Scott's Hornbook on Criminal Law, 2nd Ed., Student Ed., about 800 pages, 1986 (Text)

Langbein's Comparative Criminal Procedure: Germany, 172 pages, 1977 (Casebook)

Loewy's Criminal Law in a Nutshell, 302 pages, 1975 (Text)

Saltzburg's American Criminal Procedure, Cases and Commentary, 2nd Ed., 1193 pages, 1985 with 1986 Supplement (Casebook)

Uviller's The Processes of Criminal Justice: Investigation and Adjudication, 2nd Ed., 1384 pages, 1979 with 1979 Statutory Supplement and 1986 Update (Casebook)

Uviller's The Processes of Criminal Justice: Adjudication, 2nd Ed., 730 pages, 1979. Soft-cover reprint from Uviller's The Processes of Criminal Justice: Investigation and Adjudication, 2nd Ed. (Casebook)

Uviller's The Processes of Criminal Justice: Investigation, 2nd Ed., 655 pages, 1979. Soft-cover reprint from Uviller's The Processes of Criminal Justice: Investigation and Adjudication, 2nd Ed. (Casebook)

Vorenberg's Cases on Criminal Law and Procedure, 2nd Ed., 1088 pages, 1981 with 1985 Supplement (Casebook)

See also Corrections, Juvenile Justice

DECEDENTS ESTATES

See Trusts and Estates

DOMESTIC RELATIONS

Clark's Cases and Problems on Domestic Relations, 3rd Ed., 1153 pages, 1980 (Casebook)

Clark's Hornbook on Domestic Relations, 754 pages, 1968 (Text)

Krause's Cases and Materials on Family Law, 2nd Ed., 1221 pages, 1983 with 1986 Supplement (Casebook)

Krause's Family Law in a Nutshell, 2nd Ed., 444 pages, 1986 (Text)

Krauskopf's Cases on Property Division at Marriage Dissolution, 250 pages, 1984 (Casebook)

ECONOMICS, LAW AND

Goetz' Cases and Materials on Law and Economics, 547 pages, 1984 (Casebook)

See also Antitrust, Regulated Industries

EDUCATION LAW

Alexander and Alexander's The Law of Schools, Students and Teachers in a Nutshell, 409 pages, 1984 (Text)

Morris' The Constitution and American Education, 2nd Ed., 992 pages, 1980 (Casebook)

EMPLOYMENT DISCRIMINATION

Jones, Murphy and Belton's Cases on Discrimination in Employment, about 930 pages, 1986 (Casebook)

Player's Cases and Materials on Employment Discrimination Law, 2nd Ed., 782 pages, 1984 (Casebook)

Player's Federal Law of Employment Discrimination in a Nutshell, 2nd Ed., 402 pages, 1981 (Text)

See also Women and the Law

ENERGY AND NATURAL RESOURCES LAW

Laitos' Cases and Materials on Natural Resources Law, 938 pages, 1985 (Casebook)

Rodgers' Cases and Materials on Energy and Natural Resources Law, 2nd Ed., 877 pages, 1983 (Casebook)

Selected Environmental Law Statutes, about 850 pages, 1986

Tomain's Energy Law in a Nutshell, 338 pages, 1981 (Text)

See also Environmental Law, Oil and Gas, Water Law

ENVIRONMENTAL LAW

Bonine and McGarity's Cases and Materials on the Law of Environment and Pollution, 1076 pages, 1984 (Casebook)

Findley and Farber's Cases and Materials on Environmental Law, 2nd Ed., 813 pages, 1985 (Casebook)

Findley and Farber's Environmental Law in a Nutshell, 343 pages, 1983 (Text)

ENVIRONMENTAL LAW—Cont'd

Rodgers' Hornbook on Environmental Law, 956 pages, 1977 with 1984 pocket part (Text)

Selected Environmental Law Statutes, about 950 pages, 1986

See also Energy Law, Natural Resources Law, Water Law

EQUITY

See Remedies

ESTATES

See Trusts and Estates

ESTATE PLANNING

Kurtz' Cases, Materials and Problems on Family Estate Planning, 853 pages, 1983 (Casebook)

Lynn's Introduction to Estate Planning, in a Nutshell, 3rd Ed., 370 pages, 1983 (Text)

See also Taxation

EVIDENCE

Broun and Meisenholder's Problems in Evidence, 2nd Ed., 304 pages, 1981 (Problem book)

Cleary and Strong's Cases, Materials and Problems on Evidence, 3rd Ed., 1143 pages, 1981 (Casebook)

Federal Rules of Evidence for United States Courts and Magistrates, 337 pages, 1984

Graham's Federal Rules of Evidence in a Nutshell, 429 pages, 1981 (Text)

Kimball's Programmed Materials on Problems in Evidence, 380 pages, 1978 (Problem book)

Lempert and Saltzburg's A Modern Approach to Evidence: Text, Problems, Transcripts and Cases, 2nd Ed., 1232 pages, 1983 (Casebook)

Lilly's Introduction to the Law of Evidence, 490 pages, 1978 (Text)

McCormick, Elliott and Sutton's Cases and Materials on Evidence, 5th Ed., 1212 pages, 1981 (Casebook)

McCormick's Hornbook on Evidence, 3rd Ed., Student Ed., 1156 pages, 1984 (Text)

Rothstein's Evidence, State and Federal Rules in a Nutshell, 2nd Ed., 514 pages, 1981 (Text)

Saltzburg's Evidence Supplement: Rules, Statutes, Commentary, 245 pages, 1980 (Casebook Supplement)

FEDERAL JURISDICTION AND PROCEDURE

Currie's Cases and Materials on Federal Courts, 3rd Ed., 1042 pages, 1982 with 1985 Supplement (Casebook)

Currie's Federal Jurisdiction in a Nutshell, 2nd Ed., 258 pages, 1981 (Text)

FEDERAL JURISDICTION AND PROCEDURE—Cont'd

Federal Rules of Civil-Appellate Procedure—West Law School Edition, about 550 pages, 1986

Forrester and Moye's Cases and Materials on Federal Jurisdiction and Procedure, 3rd Ed., 917 pages, 1977 with 1985 Supplement (Casebook)

Redish's Cases, Comments and Questions on Federal Courts, 878 pages, 1983 with 1986 Supplement (Casebook)

Vetri and Merrill's Federal Courts, Problems and Materials, 2nd Ed., 232 pages, 1984 (Problem Book)

Wright's Hornbook on Federal Courts, 4th Ed., Student Ed., 870 pages, 1983 (Text)

FUTURE INTERESTS

See Trusts and Estates

IMMIGRATION LAW

Aleinikoff and Martin's Immigration Process and Policy, 1042 pages, 1985 (Casebook)

Weissbrodt's Immigration Law and Procedure in a Nutshell, 345 pages, 1984 (Text)

INDIAN LAW

See American Indian Law

INSURANCE

Dobbyn's Insurance Law in a Nutshell, 281 pages, 1981 (Text)

Keeton's Cases on Basic Insurance Law, 2nd Ed., 1086 pages, 1977

Keeton's Basic Text on Insurance Law, 712 pages, 1971 (Text)

Keeton's Case Supplement to Keeton's Basic Text on Insurance Law, 334 pages, 1978 (Casebook)

York and Whelan's Cases, Materials and Problems on Insurance Law, 715 pages, 1982, with 1985 Supplement (Casebook)

INTERNATIONAL LAW

Buergenthal and Maier's Public International Law in a Nutshell, 262 pages, 1985 (Text)

Folsom, Gordon and Spanogle's International Business Transactions – a Problem-Oriented Coursebook, 1160 pages, 1986 (Casebook)

Henkin, Pugh, Schachter and Smit's Cases and Materials on International Law, 2nd Ed., about 1200 pages, 1987 with Documents Supplement (Casebook)

Jackson and Davey's Legal Problems of International Economic Relations, 2nd Ed., about 1250 pages, 1986, with Documents Supplement (Casebook)

Kirgis' International Organizations in Their Legal Setting, 1016 pages, 1977, with 1981 Supplement (Casebook)

INTERNATIONAL LAW—Cont'd

Weston, Falk and D'Amato's International Law and World Order—A Problem Oriented Coursebook, 1195 pages, 1980, with Documents Supplement (Casebook)

Wilson's International Business Transactions in a Nutshell, 2nd Ed., 476 pages, 1984 (Text)

INTERVIEWING AND COUNSELING

Binder and Price's Interviewing and Counseling, 232 pages, 1977 (Text)

Shaffer's Interviewing and Counseling in a Nutshell, 353 pages, 1976 (Text)

INTRODUCTION TO LAW STUDY

Dobbyn's So You Want to go to Law School, Revised First Edition, 206 pages, 1976 (Text)

Hegland's Introduction to the Study and Practice of Law in a Nutshell, 418 pages, 1983 (Text)

Kinyon's Introduction to Law Study and Law Examinations in a Nutshell, 389 pages, 1971 (Text)

See also Legal Method and Legal System

JUDICIAL ADMINISTRATION

Nelson's Cases and Materials on Judicial Administration and the Administration of Justice, 1032 pages, 1974 (Casebook)

JURISPRUDENCE

Christie's Text and Readings on Jurisprudence—The Philosophy of Law, 1056 pages, 1973 (Casebook)

JUVENILE JUSTICE

Fox's Cases and Materials on Modern Juvenile Justice, 2nd Ed., 960 pages, 1981 (Casebook)

Fox's Juvenile Courts in a Nutshell, 3rd Ed., 291 pages, 1984 (Text)

LABOR LAW

Gorman's Basic Text on Labor Law—Unionization and Collective Bargaining, 914 pages, 1976 (Text)

Leslie's Labor Law in a Nutshell, 2nd Ed., 397 pages, 1986 (Text)

Nolan's Labor Arbitration Law and Practice in a Nutshell, 358 pages, 1979 (Text)

Oberer, Hanslowe, Andersen and Heinsz' Cases and Materials on Labor Law—Collective Bargaining in a Free Society, 3rd Ed., about 1200 pages, 1986 with Statutory Supplement (Casebook)

See also Employment Discrimination, Social Legislation

LAND FINANCE

See Real Estate Transactions

LAND USE

Callies and Freilich's Cases and Materials on Land Use, 1233 pages, 1986 (Casebook)

Hagman's Cases on Public Planning and Control of Urban and Land Development, 2nd Ed., 1301 pages, 1980 (Casebook)

Hagman and Juergensmeyer's Hornbook on Urban Planning and Land Development Control Law, 2nd Ed., Student Edition, approximately 580 pages, 1986 (Text)

Wright and Gitelman's Cases and Materials on Land Use, 3rd Ed., 1300 pages, 1982 (Casebook)

Wright and Wright's Land Use in a Nutshell, 2nd Ed., 356 pages, 1985 (Text)

LEGAL HISTORY

Presser and Zainaldin's Cases on Law and American History, 855 pages, 1980 (Casebook)

See also Legal Method and Legal System

LEGAL METHOD AND LEGAL SYSTEM

Aldisert's Readings, Materials and Cases in the Judicial Process, 948 pages, 1976 (Casebook)

Berch and Berch's Introduction to Legal Method and Process, 550 pages, 1985 (Casebook)

Bodenheimer, Oakley and Love's Readings and Cases on an Introduction to the Anglo-American Legal System, 161 pages, 1980 (Casebook)

Davies and Lawry's Institutions and Methods of the Law—Introductory Teaching Materials, 547 pages, 1982 (Casebook)

Dvorkin, Himmelstein and Lesnick's Becoming a Lawyer: A Humanistic Perspective on Legal Education and Professionalism, 211 pages, 1981 (Text)

Greenberg's Judicial Process and Social Change, 666 pages, 1977 (Casebook)

Kelso and Kelso's Studying Law: An Introduction, 587 pages, 1984 (Coursebook)

Kempin's Historical Introduction to Anglo-American Law in a Nutshell, 2nd Ed., 280 pages, 1973 (Text)

Kimball's Historical Introduction to the Legal System, 610 pages, 1966 (Casebook)

Murphy's Cases and Materials on Introduction to Law—Legal Process and Procedure, 772 pages, 1977 (Casebook)

Reynolds' Judicial Process in a Nutshell, 292 pages, 1980 (Text)

See also Legal Research and Writing

LEGAL PROFESSION

Aronson, Devine and Fisch's Problems, Cases and Materials on Professional Responsibility, 745 pages, 1985 (Casebook)

Aronson and Weckstein's Professional Responsibility in a Nutshell, 399 pages, 1980 (Text)

LEGAL PROFESSION—Cont'd

Mellinkoff's The Conscience of a Lawyer, 304 pages, 1973 (Text)

Mellinkoff's Lawyers and the System of Justice, 983 pages, 1976 (Casebook)

Pirsig and Kirwin's Cases and Materials on Professional Responsibility, 4th Ed., 603 pages, 1984 (Casebook)

Schwartz and Wydick's Problems in Legal Ethics, 285 pages, 1983 (Casebook)

Selected Statutes, Rules and Standards on the Legal Profession, 276 pages, Revised 1984

Smith's Preventing Legal Malpractice, 142 pages, 1981 (Text)

Wolfram's Hornbook on Modern Legal Ethics, Student Edition, 1120 pages, 1986 (Text)

LEGAL RESEARCH AND WRITING

Cohen's Legal Research in a Nutshell, 4th Ed., 450 pages, 1985 (Text)

Cohen and Berring's How to Find the Law, 8th Ed., 790 pages, 1983. Problem book by Foster, Johnson and Kelly available (Casebook)

Cohen and Berring's Finding the Law, 8th Ed., Abridged Ed., 556 pages, 1984 (Casebook)

Dickerson's Materials on Legal Drafting, 425 pages, 1981 (Casebook)

Felsenfeld and Siegel's Writing Contracts in Plain English, 290 pages, 1981 (Text)

Gopen's Writing From a Legal Perspective, 225 pages, 1981 (Text)

Mellinkoff's Legal Writing—Sense and Nonsense, 242 pages, 1982 (Text)

Rombauer's Legal Problem Solving—Analysis, Research and Writing, 4th Ed., 424 pages, 1983 (Coursebook)

Squires and Rombauer's Legal Writing in a Nutshell, 294 pages, 1982 (Text)

Statsky's Legal Research, Writing and Analysis, 2nd Ed., 167 pages, 1982 (Coursebook)

Statsky and Wernet's Case Analysis and Fundamentals of Legal Writing, 2nd Ed., 441 pages, 1984 (Text)

Teply's Programmed Materials on Legal Research and Citation, 2nd Ed., 358 pages, 1986. Student Library Exercises available (Coursebook)

Weihofen's Legal Writing Style, 2nd Ed., 332 pages, 1980 (Text)

LEGISLATION

Davies' Legislative Law and Process in a Nutshell, 2nd Ed., 346 pages, 1986 (Text)

Nutting and Dickerson's Cases and Materials on Legislation, 5th Ed., 744 pages, 1978 (Casebook)

LEGISLATION—Cont'd

Statsky's Legislative Analysis: How to Use Statutes and Regulations, 2nd Ed., 217 pages, 1984 (Text)

LOCAL GOVERNMENT

McCarthy's Local Government Law in a Nutshell, 2nd Ed., 404 pages, 1983 (Text)
Reynolds' Hornbook on Local Government Law, 860 pages, 1982 (Text)
Valente's Cases and Materials on Local Government Law, 2nd Ed., 980 pages, 1980 with 1982 Supplement (Casebook)

MASS COMMUNICATION LAW

Gillmor and Barron's Cases and Comment on Mass Communication Law, 4th Ed., 1076 pages, 1984 (Casebook)
Ginsburg's Regulation of Broadcasting: Law and Policy Towards Radio, Television and Cable Communications, 741 pages, 1979, with 1983 Supplement (Casebook)
Zuckman and Gayne's Mass Communications Law in a Nutshell, 2nd Ed., 473 pages, 1983 (Text)

MEDICINE, LAW AND

King's The Law of Medical Malpractice in a Nutshell, 2nd Ed., 342 pages, 1986 (Text)
Shapiro and Spece's Problems, Cases and Materials on Bioethics and Law, 892 pages, 1981 (Casebook)
Sharpe, Fiscina and Head's Cases on Law and Medicine, 882 pages, 1978 (Casebook)

MILITARY LAW

Shanor and Terrell's Military Law in a Nutshell, 378 pages, 1980 (Text)

MORTGAGES

See Real Estate Transactions

NATURAL RESOURCES LAW

See Energy and Natural Resources Law

NEGOTIATION

Edwards and White's Problems, Readings and Materials on the Lawyer as a Negotiator, 484 pages, 1977 (Casebook)
Williams' Legal Negotiation and Settlement, 207 pages, 1983 (Coursebook)

OFFICE PRACTICE

Hegland's Trial and Practice Skills in a Nutshell, 346 pages, 1978 (Text)
Strong and Clark's Law Office Management, 424 pages, 1974 (Casebook)
See also Computers and Law, Interviewing and Counseling, Negotiation

OIL AND GAS

Hemingway's Hornbook on Oil and Gas, 2nd Ed., Student Ed., 543 pages, 1983 with 1986 P.P. (Text)

OIL AND GAS—Cont'd

Kuntz, Lowe, Anderson and Smith's Cases and Materials on Oil and Gas Law, 857 pages, 1986 (Casebook)
Lowe's Oil and Gas Law in a Nutshell, 443 pages, 1983 (Text)
See also Energy and Natural Resources Law

PARTNERSHIP

See Agency—Partnership

PATENT AND COPYRIGHT LAW

Choate and Francis' Cases and Materials on Patent Law, 2nd Ed., 1110 pages, 1981 (Casebook)
Miller and Davis' Intellectual Property—Patents, Trademarks and Copyright in a Nutshell, 428 pages, 1983 (Text)
Nimmer's Cases on Copyright and Other Aspects of Entertainment Litigation, 3rd Ed., 1025 pages, 1985 (Casebook)

PRODUCTS LIABILITY

Noel and Phillips' Cases on Products Liability, 2nd Ed., 821 pages, 1982 (Casebook)
Noel and Phillips' Products Liability in a Nutshell, 2nd Ed., 341 pages, 1981 (Text)

PROPERTY

Bernhardt's Real Property in a Nutshell, 2nd Ed., 448 pages, 1981 (Text)
Boyer's Survey of the Law of Property, 766 pages, 1981 (Text)
Browder, Cunningham and Smith's Cases on Basic Property Law, 4th Ed., 1431 pages, 1984 (Casebook)
Bruce, Ely and Bostick's Cases and Materials on Modern Property Law, 1004 pages, 1984 (Casebook)
Burke's Personal Property in a Nutshell, 322 pages, 1983 (Text)
Cunningham, Stoebuck and Whitman's Hornbook on the Law of Property, Student Ed., 916 pages, 1984 (Text)
Donahue, Kauper and Martin's Cases on Property, 2nd Ed., 1362 pages, 1983 (Casebook)
Hill's Landlord and Tenant Law in a Nutshell, 2nd Ed., 311 pages, 1986 (Text)
Moynihan's Introduction to Real Property, 254 pages, 1962 (Text)
Uniform Land Transactions Act, Uniform Simplification of Land Transfers Act, Uniform Condominium Act, 1977 Official Text with Comments, 462 pages, 1978
See also Real Estate Transactions, Land Use

PSYCHIATRY, LAW AND

Reisner's Law and the Mental Health System, Civil and Criminal Aspects, 696 pages, 1985 (Casebooks)

REAL ESTATE TRANSACTIONS

Bruce's Real Estate Finance in a Nutshell, 2nd Ed., 262 pages, 1985 (Text)

Maxwell, Riesenfeld, Hetland and Warren's Cases on California Security Transactions in Land, 3rd Ed., 728 pages, 1984 (Casebook)

Nelson and Whitman's Cases on Real Estate Transfer, Finance and Development, 2nd Ed., 1114 pages, 1981, with 1986 Supplement (Casebook)

Nelson and Whitman's Hornbook on Real Estate Finance Law, 2nd Ed., Student Ed., 941 pages, 1985 (Text)

Osborne's Cases and Materials on Secured Transactions, 559 pages, 1967 (Casebook)

REGULATED INDUSTRIES

Gellhorn and Pierce's Regulated Industries in a Nutshell, 394 pages, 1982 (Text)

Morgan, Harrison and Verkuil's Cases and Materials on Economic Regulation of Business, 2nd Ed., 666 pages, 1985 (Casebook)

See also Mass Communication Law, Banking Law

REMEDIES

Dobbs' Hornbook on Remedies, 1067 pages, 1973 (Text)

Dobbs' Problems in Remedies, 137 pages, 1974 (Problem book)

Dobbyn's Injunctions in a Nutshell, 264 pages, 1974 (Text)

Friedman's Contract Remedies in a Nutshell, 323 pages, 1981 (Text)

Leavell, Love and Nelson's Cases and Materials on Equitable Remedies and Restitution, 4th Ed., 1111 pages, 1986 (Casebook)

McCormick's Hornbook on Damages, 811 pages, 1935 (Text)

O'Connell's Remedies in a Nutshell, 2nd Ed., 320 pages, 1985 (Text)

York, Bauman and Rendleman's Cases and Materials on Remedies, 4th Ed., 1029 pages, 1985 (Casebook)

REVIEW MATERIALS

Ballantine's Problems

Black Letter Series

Smith's Review Series

West's Review Covering Multistate Subjects

SECURITIES REGULATION

Hazen's Hornbook on The Law of Securities Regulation, Student Ed., 739 pages, 1985 (Text)

Ratner's Securities Regulation: Materials for a Basic Course, 3rd Ed., 1000 pages, 1986 (Casebook)

Ratner's Securities Regulation in a Nutshell, 2nd Ed., 322 pages, 1982 (Text)

SECURITIES REGULATION—Cont'd

Selected Securities and Business Planning Statutes, Rules and Forms, 470 pages, 1985

SOCIAL LEGISLATION

Hood and Hardy's Workers' Compensation and Employee Protection Laws in a Nutshell, 274 pages, 1984 (Text)

LaFrance's Welfare Law: Structure and Entitlement in a Nutshell, 455 pages, 1979 (Text)

Malone, Plant and Little's Cases on Workers' Compensation and Employment Rights, 2nd Ed., 951 pages, 1980 (Casebook)

SPORTS LAW

Schubert, Smith and Trentadue's Sports Law, 395 pages, 1986 (Text)

TAXATION

Dodge's Cases and Materials on Federal Income Taxation, 820 pages, 1985 (Casebook)

Dodge's Federal Taxation of Estates, Trusts and Gifts: Principles and Planning, 771 pages, 1981 with 1982 Supplement (Casebook)

Garbis and Struntz' Cases and Materials on Tax Procedure and Tax Fraud, 829 pages, 1982 with 1984 Supplement (Casebook)

Gelfand and Salsich's State and Local Taxation and Finance in a Nutshell, 309 pages, 1986 (Text)

Gunn's Cases and Materials on Federal Income Taxation of Individuals, 785 pages, 1981 with 1985 Supplement (Casebook)

Hellerstein and Hellerstein's Cases on State and Local Taxation, 4th Ed., 1041 pages, 1978 with 1982 Supplement (Casebook)

Kahn and Gann's Corporate Taxation and Taxation of Partnerships and Partners, 2nd Ed., 1204 pages, 1985 (Casebook)

Kragen and McNulty's Cases and Materials on Federal Income Taxation: Individuals, Corporations, Partnerships, 4th Ed., 1287 pages, 1985 (Casebook)

McNulty's Federal Estate and Gift Taxation in a Nutshell, 3rd Ed., 509 pages, 1983 (Text)

McNulty's Federal Income Taxation of Individuals in a Nutshell, 3rd Ed., 487 pages, 1983 (Text)

Posin's Hornbook on Federal Income Taxation of Individuals, Student Ed., 491 pages, 1983 with 1985 pocket part (Text)

Selected Federal Taxation Statutes and Regulations, about 1400 pages, 1986

Solomon and Hesch's Cases on Federal Income Taxation of Individuals, about 800 pages, 1987 (Casebook)

TAXATION—Cont'd

Sobeloff and Weidenbruch's Federal Income Taxation of Corporations and Stockholders in a Nutshell, 362 pages, 1981 (Text)

TORTS

Christie's Cases and Materials on the Law of Torts, 1264 pages, 1983 (Casebook)

Dobbs' Torts and Compensation—Personal Accountability and Social Responsibility for Injury, 955 pages, 1985 (Casebook)

Green, Pedrick, Rahl, Thode, Hawkins, Smith and Treece's Cases and Materials on Torts, 2nd Ed., 1360 pages, 1977 (Casebook)

Green, Pedrick, Rahl, Thode, Hawkins, Smith, and Treece's Advanced Torts: Injuries to Business, Political and Family Interests, 2nd Ed., 544 pages, 1977 (Casebook)—reprint from Green, et al. Cases and Materials on Torts, 2nd Ed., 1977

Keeton, Keeton, Sargentich and Steiner's Cases and Materials on Torts, and Accident Law, 1360 pages, 1983 (Casebook)

Kionka's Torts in a Nutshell: Injuries to Persons and Property, 434 pages, 1977 (Text)

Malone's Torts in a Nutshell: Injuries to Family, Social and Trade Relations, 358 pages, 1979 (Text)

Prosser and Keeton's Hornbook on Torts, 5th Ed., Student Ed., 1286 pages, 1984 (Text)

Shapo's Cases on Tort and Compensation Law, 1244 pages, 1976 (Casebook)

See also Products Liability

TRADE REGULATION

McManis' Unfair Trade Practices in a Nutshell, 444 pages, 1982 (Text)

Oppenheim, Weston, Maggs and Schechter's Cases and Materials on Unfair Trade Practices and Consumer Protection, 4th Ed., 1038 pages, 1983 with 1986 Supplement (Casebook)

See also Antitrust, Regulated Industries

TRIAL AND APPELLATE ADVOCACY

Appellate Advocacy, Handbook of, 2nd Ed., 182 pages, 1986 (Text)

Bergman's Trial Advocacy in a Nutshell, 402 pages, 1979 (Text)

Binder and Bergman's Fact Investigation: From Hypothesis to Proof, 354 pages, 1984 (Coursebook)

Goldberg's The First Trial (Where Do I Sit?, What Do I Say?) in a Nutshell, 396 pages, 1982 (Text)

Haydock, Herr and Stempel's, Fundamentals of Pre-Trial Litigation, 768 pages, 1985 (Casebook)

Hegland's Trial and Practice Skills in a Nutshell, 346 pages, 1978 (Text)

Hornstein's Appellate Advocacy in a Nutshell, 325 pages, 1984 (Text)

TRIAL AND APPELLATE ADVOCACY—Cont'd

Jeans' Handbook on Trial Advocacy, Student Ed., 473 pages, 1975 (Text)

Martineau's Cases and Materials on Appellate Practice and Procedure, about 550 pages, 1987 (Casebook)

McElhaney's Effective Litigation, 457 pages, 1974 (Casebook)

Nolan's Cases and Materials on Trial Practice, 518 pages, 1981 (Casebook)

Parnell and Shellhaas' Cases, Exercises and Problems for Trial Advocacy, 171 pages, 1982 (Coursebook)

Sonsteng, Haydock and Boyd's The Trialbook: A Total System for Preparation and Presentation of a Case, Student Ed., 404 pages, 1984 (Coursebook)

TRUSTS AND ESTATES

Atkinson's Hornbook on Wills, 2nd Ed., 975 pages, 1953 (Text)

Averill's Uniform Probate Code in a Nutshell, 425 pages, 1978 (Text)

Bogert's Hornbook on Trusts, 5th Ed., 726 pages, 1973 (Text)

Clark, Lusky and Murphy's Cases and Materials on Gratuitous Transfers, 3rd Ed., 970 pages, 1985 (Casebook)

Gulliver's Cases and Materials on Future Interests, 624 pages, 1959 (Casebook)

Gulliver's Introduction to the Law of Future Interests, 87 pages, 1959 (Casebook)—reprint from Gulliver's Cases and Materials on Future Interests, 1959

McGovern's Cases and Materials on Wills, Trusts and Future Interests: An Introduction to Estate Planning, 750 pages, 1983 (Casebook)

Mennell's Cases and Materials on California Decedent's Estates, 566 pages, 1973 (Casebook)

Mennell's Wills and Trusts in a Nutshell, 392 pages, 1979 (Text)

Powell's The Law of Future Interests in California, 91 pages, 1980 (Text)

Simes' Hornbook on Future Interests, 2nd Ed., 355 pages, 1966 (Text)

Turano and Radigan's Hornbook on New York Estate Administration, approximately 575 pages, 1986 (Text)

Uniform Probate Code, 5th Ed., Official Text With Comments, 384 pages, 1977

Waggoner's Future Interests in a Nutshell, 361 pages, 1981 (Text)

Waterbury's Materials on Trusts and Estates, 1039 pages, 1986 (Casebook)

WATER LAW

Getches' Water Law in a Nutshell, 439 pages, 1984 (Text)

WATER LAW—Cont'd

Sax and Abram's Cases and Materials on Legal Control of Water Resources in the United States, 941 pages, 1986 (Casebook)

Trelease and Gould's Cases and Materials on Water Law, 4th Ed., 816 pages, 1986 (Casebook)

See also Energy and Natural Resources Law, Environmental Law

WILLS

See Trusts and Estates

WOMEN AND THE LAW

Kay's Text, Cases and Materials on Sex-Based Discrimination, 2nd Ed., 1045 pages, 1981, with 1986 Supplement (Casebook)

Thomas' Sex Discrimination in a Nutshell, 399 pages, 1982 (Text)

See also Employment Discrimination

WORKERS' COMPENSATION

See Social Legislation

MODERN CRIMINAL PROCEDURE

CASES, COMMENTS AND QUESTIONS

Sixth Edition

By

Yale Kamisar
Henry K. Ransom Professor of Law,
University of Michigan

Wayne R. LaFave
David C. Baum Professor of Law,
University of Illinois

Jerold H. Israel
Alene and Allan F. Smith
Professor of Law, University of Michigan

AMERICAN CASEBOOK SERIES

WEST PUBLISHING CO.
ST. PAUL, MINN., 1986

Printed in the United States of America

Library of Congress Cataloging in Publication Data

Kamisar, Yale.
Modern criminal procedure.

(American casebook series)
Includes index.
1. Criminal procedure—United States—Cases.
I. LaFave, Wayne R. II. Israel, Jerold H., 1934– .
III. Title. IV. Series.

KF9618.K36 1986 345.73'05 86–11178
347.3055

ISBN 0–314–23839–5

Mod.Crim.Proc., 6th Ed. (K, L & I) ACB

UNITED STATES SUPREME COURT
SINCE 1940

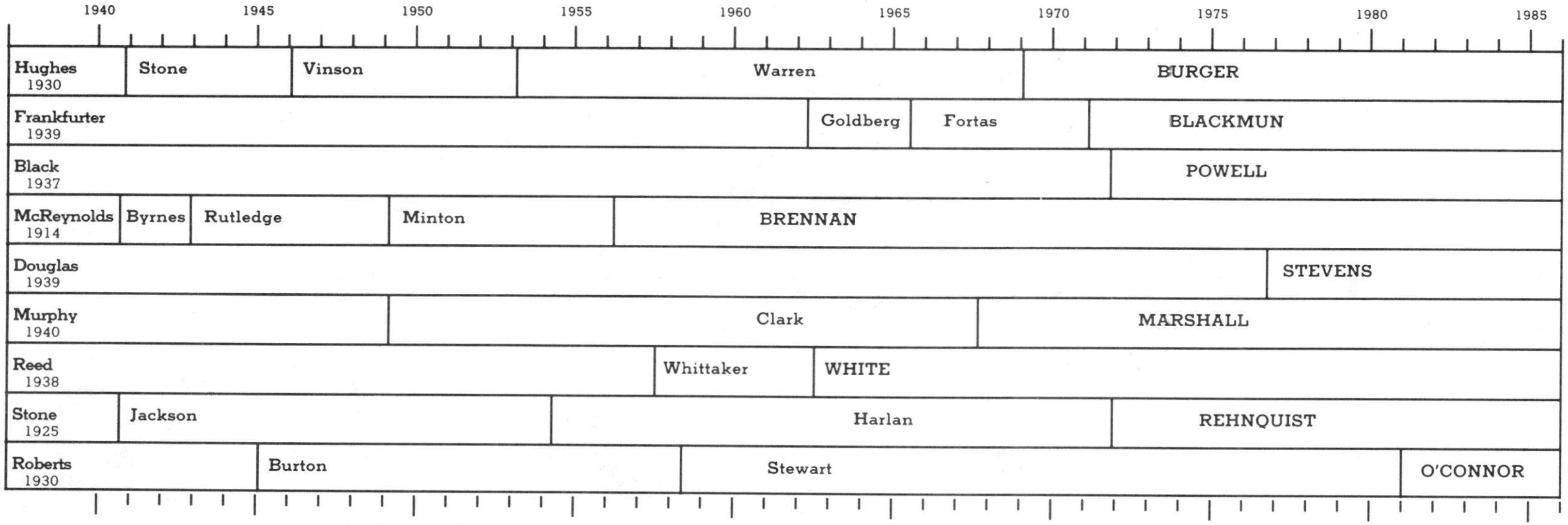

The publishers wish to acknowledge that the above chart was developed from a suggestion by Dean Joe E. Covington of the University of Missouri Law School.

Preface to the Sixth Edition

Six eventful years have passed since the publication of the fifth edition of *Modern Criminal Procedure*. Because of the need to integrate the material in a 550-page 1985 Supplement, as well as cases and other materials that have appeared since, strenuous efforts were made to compress older material to make room for the new. Every case—indeed every paragraph of every opinion—has had to "pay its way." As a result, we produced a new edition some 100 pages slimmer than its predecessor.

This is still a big book. This is so because we have taken pains to set forth the views of *all* the Justices in the leading cases; because we feel strongly that the student should see the subsequently overruled or distinguished opinion "in the original" rather than rely on the overruling or distinguishing case's version of the earlier opinion; because we have retained older cases which contribute significantly to an understanding of new trends and developments; because we have covered significant non-constitutional issues, as well as traditional constitutional matters; in treating non-constitutional issues, we have looked to state law (with its frequent variations) as well as federal law; and because, at many places, we have sought to enrich the case materials with authors' Notes & Questions or extracts from illuminating and stimulating books, reports, articles, model codes and proposed standards.

The size of this book—the result of striving both for breadth of coverage and depth of treatment—indicates clearly enough that our purpose is not to provide a volume to be taught from cover to cover in a single one term course on the subject. Rather it is to present materials that afford a teacher maximum freedom to shape his or her own course—in light of a particular teacher's own sense of priorities and interests and other related courses available at that teacher's school. For example, the authors have used these materials as a basis for three different courses: (1) a course dealing almost exclusively with police practices, based on Chapters 1–11; (2) a course placing primary emphasis on the post-"police practices" or post-"investigation" phases—from bail to post-conviction review—built mainly on Parts Three (The Commencement of Formal Proceedings), Four (The Adversary System and the Trial), and Five (Appeals, Post-Conviction Review); and (3) an alternative single course "surveying" all aspects of criminal procedure, utilizing the opening sections or introductory notes in certain chapters as "points of departure" for a discussion of various problems raised throughout the chapter. Many chapters have been reorganized to enable the instructor more easily to pick and choose among the materials. In some chapters, introductory sections provide an overview permitting the instructor to give a subject brief coverage based on that section alone.

The thorough revision has produced some restructuring of chapters. For example, the material previously contained in Chapters 11 and 12 has been combined in a single chapter on the scope of the exclusionary rule (Chapter 11) and the material on pleading, previously combined with that on discovery, now appears in a separate chapter on the charging instrument (Chapter 16).

In the main, we have followed a chronological approach in ordering the materials which appear in this book. Following the introductory materials, which include an overview of the criminal justice system and a general consideration of due process, the system is examined from arrest and search to post-conviction review. We have occasionally departed from the chronological scheme when it seemed appropriate to do so. For example, the chapter on right to counsel is included in the introductory part of the book on the premise that it is "the most pervasive right" of an accused and on the assumption that it is beneficial to the student to understand how and when an attorney becomes involved in a criminal case before examining the procedural issues which will confront the attorney. Wiretapping and other surveillance activities are discussed after search and seizure on the ground that the student must first understand the basic Fourth Amendment doctrines which have developed in the latter area, while the entrapment material is presented following the surveillance chapter because of the relationship between entrapment and other uses of secret agents.

Some teachers may prefer to cover various aspects of the right to counsel at different points in the criminal process rather than at one place. Chapter 3 is organized so that this can be done quite easily. On the other hand, some teachers may prefer to treat all self-incrimination problems at one place rather than, as we have done, at various points. Those who prefer to take what might be called a doctrinal rather than a chronological approach to Fifth Amendment problems should have no difficulty doing so. This would mean pulling together materials from Chapter 2, § 2 (e.g., *Schmerber*); Chapter 8 (e.g., *Miranda*); Chapter 9 (e.g., *Wade*); Chapter 10, §§ 2 & 3 (e.g., *Boyd* and *Fisher*); Chapter 11, §§ 3 & 4 (e.g., *Harris* and *Elstad*); and Chapter 24, § 4 (e.g., *Griffin v. California*). The index is designed so that one can immediately pick out the various materials that relate to a particular right or privilege.

In the main, we were unable to include cases handed down by the Supreme Court after January 1, 1986. These cases will appear in a supplement that will be published in August, 1986. Important developments thereafter will appear in annual supplements. The Supplement will also contain relevant federal court rules and statutory materials.

Case citations in the text and the footnotes of judicial opinions and in the writings of commentators have been omitted without so specifying. Numbered footnotes are from the original materials; lettered footnotes are ours.[1] A reference to p.___ supra or p.___ infra is to this Book. A reference to an article, supra, at p.___, is to a page in the article.

1. Abbreviations used throughout a particular chapter are indicated at the outset of the chapter. In addition, the following abbreviations have been used throughout:

One or more of the authors has been fortunate enough to participate actively in four major criminal procedure projects: the American Bar Association project on *Standards for Criminal Justice*; The American Law Institute's *Model Code of Pre-Arraignment Procedure* project; the National Conference of Commissioners on Uniform State Laws' *Uniform Rules of Criminal Procedure*; and the ongoing revision of the *Federal Rules of Criminal Procedure*. We are indebted to the members of the various committees with whom we have worked for providing us with many leads and insights. We are also indebted to many users of this book for their helpful suggestions, especially Professors Francis Allen, Paul Borman, Gerald Caplan, Ronald Carlson, Joseph Grano, Herman Schwartz, Barry Stern, James Strazzella and Welsh White.

We thank David Westup for preparing the Table of Authorities with speed, efficiency and good cheer. Our thanks go also to the student research assistants of the past and present who contributed so much to this book. We are most appreciative of the able secretarial assistance provided, too often under great stress, by Carol Haley, Carolyn Lloyd, and Faye Smoller. Finally, we should like to acknowledge the permission granted by the publishers of the secondary materials produced herein.

YALE KAMISAR
WAYNE R. LAFAVE
JEROLD H. ISRAEL

June, 1986

References to the 2d edition of the American Bar Association Project on Standards for Criminal Justice are cited as *A.B.A. Standards*, and are cited to volume with the standard treated as a § ___ e.g., *A.B.A. Standards § 3–6.1.*

References to the earlier A.B.A. Standards include the title and the date, e.g., *A.B.A. Standards Relating to Post-Conviction Remedies* (1968).

American Law Institute, Model Penal Code (Official Draft, 1962) is cited as *Model Penal Code* § ___. Citations to earlier drafts include the draft and the date.

American Law Institute, A Model Code of Prearraignment Procedure (Official Draft, 1975) is cited as *Model Pre-Arraignment Code*, § ___. Reference to earlier drafts indicate draft and date.

National Conference of Commissioners on Uniform State Laws, Proposed Final Draft of the Uniform Rules of Criminal Procedure (1974) is cited as *Unif. R. Crim. P.* ___.

The Federal Rules of Criminal Procedure are cited as *Fed. R. Crim. P.* and the proposed rules as *Proposed Fed. R. Crim. P.*

The reports of the National Advisory Commission on Criminal Justice Standards and Goals are cited as *N.A.C. Standards.*

The various task force reports of the President's Commission on Law Enforcement and Administration of Criminal Justice are cited as, e.g., *Task Force Report: Corrections* ___.

The Code of Professional Responsibility is cited as *A.B.A. Code of Prof. Resp.*, followed by the citation to the Disciplinary Rule (D.R.), Ethical Consideration (E.C.) or Canon (Can.)—e.g., *A.B.A. Code of Prof. Resp.* D.R. 4–101.

The A.B.A.'s Model Rules of Professional Conduct are cited as *A.B.A. Model R. Prof. Cond.* followed by the rule number and (comment), when citing to commentary—e.g., *A.B.A. Model R. Prof. Cond.* (comment 1.7).

LaFave, *Search and Seizure: A Treatise on the Fourth Amendment* (1978) is cited as LaFave, § ___.

LaFave & Israel, *Criminal Procedure* (1984) is cited as LaFave & Israel, § ___.

C. Wright, *Federal Practice and Procedure (Criminal)* (2d ed. 1982) is cited as Wright, § ___.

*

Summary of Contents

PART FOUR. THE ADVERSARY SYSTEM AND THE DETERMINATION OF GUILT

PART FIVE. APPEALS, POST-CONVICTION REVIEW

Table of Contents

[This Table contains main cases (in **bold**), significantly abstracted cases, major notes, and major extracts from secondary authorities.]

PART TWO

POLICE PRACTICES

PART THREE

THE COMMENCEMENT OF FORMAL PROCEEDINGS

PART FIVE

APPEALS, POST-CONVICTION REVIEW

Table of Cases

References are to pages. Principal cases are in Bold type. Nonprincipal cases are in Roman type. For Commonwealth v. ______, People v. ______, State v. ______, United States v. ______, see the name of the other party. For Ex parte ______, In re ______, In the Matter of ______, see the name of the party. For People ex rel. ______, State ex rel. ______, United States ex rel. ______, see the name of the first party. Where a case is discussed in another case, reference is made only to the first page at which it is cited. No reference is made to discussion of a principal case in the Notes and Questions that follow that case.

Table of Articles, Books, Proposed Standards, and Reports

Bold type indicates major extracts

MODERN CRIMINAL PROCEDURE

CASES, COMMENTS AND QUESTIONS

Sixth Edition

*

Part One

INTRODUCTION

Analysis

Chapter 1

AN OVERVIEW OF THE CRIMINAL JUSTICE PROCESS

The criminal justice process consists of that series of procedures through which the substantive criminal law is enforced. This chapter provides a general overview of those procedures, the persons responsible for administering those procedures, and the environment in which that administration takes place. It hopefully will serve as a useful backdrop for the discussion in later chapters of the law governing the process.

As with any description of this type, a certain degree of overgeneralization is inevitable. The reader stands forewarned that in any particular jurisdiction one is likely to find variations in procedure, personnel, and administrative environment that simply do not fit the "big picture" provided here. As one commentator noted, "There is no single criminal justice system in this country; rather there are many systems which, while similar, are individually unique." *

SECTION 1. THE STEPS IN THE PROCESS

In this section, we shall describe briefly the major steps taken in the processing of a criminal case. Not all of these steps are part of the process in all 51 jurisdictions (state and federal) and not all of those steps adopted in a particular jurisdiction are applied to all types of cases.[a] Our focus is on the processing of a "typical case" in a "typical jurisdiction" (i.e., those procedures employed by most states in processing most of their criminal cases). We cover the processing of both felony and misdemeanor cases, but our primary concentration is upon felony cases.[b]

* Bureau of Justice Statistics (B.J.S.), U.S. Department of Justice, *The American Response to Crime* 1 (1983).

a. Each state's process, and the federal process as well, must comply with federal constitutional standards, but all 51 jurisdictions retain considerable autonomy in formulating their own procedural standards within the framework of those constitutional limitations. A common grounding for the various state processes was provided initially by the English common law, but the English process was then reshaped to fit the needs of the particular jurisdiction. That restructuring was the product of gradual development over the years; the process was not designed in one piece at one time. A few of the variations from the common law were suggested by the legal systems of those other countries that also furnished our first settlers, and still others were suggested by later developments in England and other common law countries, but many more were strictly American inventions. See generally, Hughes, *English Criminal Justice: Is It Better Than Ours?,* 26 Ariz.L.Rev. 507 (1984) (comparing the current English and American processes).

b. American jurisdictions commonly use one of two different standards in distinguishing between felonies and misdemeanors. Some classify as felonies all offenses punishable by a maximum term of imprisonment of more than one year; offenses punishable by imprisonment for one year or less are then misdemeanors. Others look to the location of the possible imprisonment: if the offense is punishable by incarceration in a peni-

While we take note of most of the major distinctions that separate the processing of misdemeanors from felonies, the numerous minor distinctions are left to later chapters. Where the states are sharply divided in the treatment of a particular step in the process, we shall note the major alternatives followed by significant groups of states, but modifications adopted by only a few states are largely ignored.

While our primary objective in this section is to provide an overview of the interrelated procedural steps that constitute the total process, we have also sought to provide some indication of the significance of the different steps as measured in quantitative terms.[c] This hopefully will assist the reader in gauging the practical significance of the various legal standards discussed in the subsequent chapters. While some of those standards govern procedures employed in the vast majority of criminal prosecutions, others apply to procedures utilized only in the rarest of cases.

Step 1: The Report of the Crime. The criminal justice process usually starts when the police receive information concerning the possible commission of a crime. The police may obtain that information either through their own observations or from the reports of interested citizens. In either case, if it appears likely that a crime was committed, the offense will be recorded in the police files as a "reported" crime (and will be listed statistically as an offense "known to the police").

Surprisingly, we have only limited data on the exact distribution of reported crimes in this country.[d] That data is adequate, however, to provide a rough estimate of the likely distribution of reported offenses in a typical industrial state.[e] Ap-

tentiary, it is a felony; if punishable only by a jail term, it is a misdemeanor. See W. LaFave and A. Scott, *Criminal Law* § 26 (1972). As a matter of practice, both dividing lines frequently produce the same result since state correction codes commonly provide for imprisonment in the penitentiary if a sentence exceeds one year and for imprisonment in jail if the sentence is for one year or less.

Our discussion of the processing of misdemeanors excludes the ordinary traffic violation. In many jurisdictions, all but the most serious traffic violations (e.g., driving while intoxicated) have been decriminalized. Indeed, even in those jurisdictions in which all traffic violations are technically misdemeanors, the less serious traffic offenses often are governed by somewhat different procedures than misdemeanors generally. On the other hand, our discussion does encompass city ordinance violations in those jurisdictions in which ordinances largely duplicate in substance and penalty state misdemeanor provisions governing such offenses as assault, petty theft, etc. Such ordinances commonly are used as a basis for prosecution in lieu of the state misdemeanor provisions (often because the fines collected for ordinance violations go to the city). In jurisdictions of this type, the procedure applied to ordinance violations is basically the same as that applied to misdemeanors.

c. The data cited in this section is taken from a combination of government reports and studies of particular jurisdictions. The government reports include: B.J.S., *Sourcebook of Criminal Justice Statistics—1984;* the latest available Annual Report of the State Judicial Department, State Court Administrator, or the Judicial Conference for various states; the 1984 Annual Reports of the Attorney General of the United States and the Director of the Administrative Office of the United States Courts; F.B.I., *Uniform Crime Reports—1985;* and B.J.S., *Criminal Victimization in the United States—1982* (the National Crime Survey). The studies relied upon include: Boland, Brady, Tyson, and Bassler, *Prosecution of Felony Arrests* (1979); Brosi, *A Cross-City Comparison of Felony Case Processing* (1979); Chaiken, Greenwood, and Petersilia, *The Criminal Investigation Process* (1975); Forst, Lucianovic, and Cox, *What Happens After Arrest?* (1977); N.I.J., *Solving Crimes: The Investigation of Burglary and Robbery* (1984); Reiss, *The Police and The Public* (1971); Vera Institute, *Felony Arrests: Their Prosecution and Disposition in New York City's Courts* (1982); and Zeisel, *The Limits of Law Enforcement* (1982). See also Parisi, *Sources of National Criminal Justice Statistics* (1977).

d. The best statistical source on the number of reported crimes, the F.B.I.'s *Uniform Crime Reports,* provides data on reported offenses only for a selected group of "Index" offenses—murder, nonnegligent manslaughter, forcible rape, robbery, aggravated assault, burglary, larceny-theft, motor vehicle theft, and, since 1978, arson. As to other offenses, the F.B.I. collects data only on arrests. The National Crime Survey, which estimates the actual (i.e., reported and non-reported) crime rate based upon survey interviews of a sample of 60,000 households, measures the same Index crimes (except for homicide and arson).

e. The National Crime Survey indicates that this distribution will be somewhat different from proximately 60% of all reported crimes will relate to the taking or destruction of property. The major offenses in this group will include the various forms of theft (perhaps 50% of all property offenses), burglary (15%), and vandalism (15%). Assaults of all varieties, ranging from assaults with weapons to simple assaults, may provide an additional 10% of the reported crimes. Offenses relating to the use of alcohol and drugs (e.g., public drunkenness, possession of drugs, and driving under the influence) are likely to constitute another 10% of the reported offenses. The remaining 20% of the reported crimes will be spread over a variety of offenses. Included in this group are the most serious violent felonies, such as robbery (likely to constitute 2–4% of all reported offenses), and murder and forcible rape (each likely to fall below ½ of 1%).

Step 2: Pre-Arrest Investigation. Once the police become aware of the possible commission of a crime, they must determine (1) whether the crime actually was committed and (2) if it was, whether there is sufficient information pointing to the guilt of a particular person to justify arresting and charging that person. Pre-arrest investigative procedures are designed to answer these questions and to collect evidence that may be helpful in establishing guilt at trial.[f] The particular procedures used will vary with the circumstances of the crime. In some instances, a police officer will observe a crime being committed in his presence and will make an arrest "on the spot." In such cases, the pre-arrest investigation consists of no more than the officer's initial observation. In other cases, the officer will observe activity that is suspicious, though not necessarily criminal, and will seek further information to determine whether to make an arrest. Where an alleged offense has been called to the officer's attention by an interested citizen (usually a victim), the officer also is likely to seek information beyond that provided by the complainant.

Where additional information is sought, the officer may utilize a variety of investigatory techniques to gather that information. Perhaps the most common is to question the suspect. Pre-arrest questioning may be accompanied by the temporary detention of the suspect on the street or at home, but does not involve taking him into custody, as occurs with an arrest. The scope of the officer's questioning may range from merely asking the suspect to identify himself to asking him to respond to an accusation made by others. Where the crime investigated involved violence, or there is some other reason to believe the suspect could be armed, the officer may undertake some sort of search of the temporarily detained suspect (usually a pat-down or "frisk" of the suspect's outer clothing). In a small percentage of these police-suspect encounters, the officer also may search the car of a suspect who was stopped while driving.

Along with the police-suspect encounter, the other common pre-arrest investigatory techniques are the interviewing of poten-

the distribution of crimes actually committed. For those Index crimes examined in the Survey, the ratio of reported to actual crimes was found to vary substantially with the offense. Thus, while there may be three burglaries committed for each one reported, almost every motor vehicle theft is reported. A similar variation is likely as to other crimes not covered by the Survey. Since accidental deaths are almost always discovered, almost all negligent homicides will be reported. On the other hand, narcotics possession is likely to become a reported offense only if discovered by an arresting officer.

f. Not all pre-arrest investigations are aimed at previously committed offenses. In dealing with certain crimes, such as vice offenses, the police often use undercover agents and other investigative techniques aimed more at anticipated future crimes than at previously committed offenses. Also, not all pre-arrest investigations directed at past offenses are conducted by the police. The prosecutor, utilizing the aid of the grand jury, will conduct investigations of those offenses that are most readily solved through the use of the grand jury's investigative powers, such as its subpoena authority. Both the future-offense investigation and the grand jury investigation are exceptions to the general rule, however, and represent a very small percentage of all pre-arrest investigations.

tial witnesses and the examination of the scene of the crime.[g] In certain types of cases (e.g., homicides), that examination may include the collection of physical evidence (e.g., fingerprints) that will be subjected to scientific analysis. For other offenses, commonly those committed by specialized professional criminals, police informants may be contacted for information concerning possible offenders. Thorough searches of homes and offices, and electronic eavesdropping through wiretaps and similar devices, are also used in certain types of investigations. However, those procedures, which commonly require prior judicial authorization through the issuance of a search warrant, are used in only a very small portion of all investigations.[h] Most prearrest investigations will be completed in a relatively short period of time, whether successful or not. The vast majority of burglary and robbery cases, for example, are investigated in no more than 4 hours, although that investigation may be spread over several days.

Step 3: The Arrest. Once the officer has acquired sufficient information to justify arresting a suspect, the arrest ordinarily is the next step in the criminal justice process. An arrest generally occurs when the officer takes the suspect into custody for the purpose of transporting him to the station and then charging him with a crime.[i] Although an arrest may be authorized in advance by a judicially issued warrant, the vast majority of all arrests are made on the officer's own initiative, without a warrant.

As with reported crimes, arrests will be distributed over a variety of offenses. The distribution of arrests will differ substantially from the distribution of reported crimes, however, because some reported crimes are more likely to lead to arrests than others.[j] While the exact distribution of arrests will vary with the individual jurisdiction, a general pattern emerges that roughly fits most jurisdictions. Typically, only 20–30% of the arrests will be for felonies, with the remainder being for misdemeanors. Though the theft group of offenses constitutes the number one category of reported crimes, it will rank slightly behind the alcohol/drug offenses as a basis for arrests. A substantial percentage of the arrests, perhaps as high as 20%, will be for public disorder misdemeanors, such as simple assaults, vandalism, and disorderly conduct. Less than 10% will be for serious felony offenses against the person, with aggravated assault and robbery likely to account for 2% each and forcible rape

g. A substantial majority of all arrests, however, are likely to be made with little investigation beyond obtaining the victim's report and a suspect-police encounter. Thus, a New York sampling of 400 felony arrests for Index crimes found that 18% of those arrests were based on the officer's personal observation of the crime, 38% were made at the scene or nearby after the police arrived in response to the victim's call, 25% were made elsewhere but involved a positive identification by a victim who knew the alleged offender, 7% involved suspects who surrendered or were arrested originally for some other offense, and only 13% were based on identification through mug shots, license plate checks, or other investigative work. See Zeisel, fn. e supra, at 32.

h. Indeed, only about 650 court-authorized orders for electronic surveillance are issued annually. Approximately a third of those are issued to federal officers, with an average cost of $65,316 for installation and operation. See *Sourcebook,* fn. c. supra, at 548–54.

i. As an alternative to the traditional "custodial arrest," many jurisdictions grant the officer discretion to briefly detain a person subject to arrest and to then release him upon issuance of a citation (sometimes called an "appearance ticket"). This alternative is most commonly authorized for misdemeanor offenses, and sometimes is limited to particular types of misdemeanors.

j. The "arrest-clearance" rate for reported crimes (which is basically the percentage of reported offenses resulting in the arrest of a suspected offender) varies from over 90% for some offenses to less than 20% for others. Those crimes that tend to come to the attention of a police officer through his personal observation of the crime usually have the highest arrest-clearance rates. Substantially lower rates are found for offenses that become known to the police primarily through victim reports. Here, the most significant factor will be the victim's ability to identify the offender. Thus, the arrest-clearance rate for burglary (20%) is far less than that for aggravated assault (over 60%).

and murder for less than one-half of one percent each. The remaining arrests, approximately 10%, will be spread over a wide variety of offenses, including arson, nonviolent sex offenses, and possession of weapons.

A substantial percentage of the persons arrested (typically 20–30%) will be within the age limit for juvenile court jurisdiction. Ordinarily, juvenile arrestees will be separated from the adult arrestees shortly after their arrest. From this point on, we will assume that we are dealing only with the adult arrestees.

Step 4: Booking. Immediately after making an arrest, the arresting officer usually will search the arrestee's person and remove any weapons, contraband, or evidence relating to a crime. He then will arrange for the transportation of the arrestee to the police station, a centrally located jail, or some similar "holding" facility. It is at this facility that the arrestee will be taken through a process known as "booking." Initially, the arrestee's name, the time of his arrival, and the offense for which he was arrested are noted in the police "blotter" or "log." The arrestee then will be photographed and fingerprinted. Typically, he also will be informed of the charge on which he has been booked and will be allowed to make at least one telephone call. When booked on a minor offense, he may be able to obtain his release on "stationhouse bail," i.e., by posting cash as a security payment and promising to appear before a magistrate at a specified date. Persons arrested on serious offenses, and those arrested on minor offenses but unable to gain their release, will remain at the holding facility until ready to be presented before a magistrate (see step 8). Ordinarily, they will be placed in a "lockup," which usually is some kind of cell. Before entering the lockup, they will be subjected to another search, more thorough than that conducted at the point of arrest. This search is designed primarily to inventory the arrestee's personal belongings and to prevent the introduction of contraband into the lockup.

Step 5: Post-Arrest Investigation. The extent of the post-arrest investigation will vary with the fact situation. In some situations, such as where the arrestee was caught "red-handed," there will be little left to be done. In other situations, police will utilize many of the same kinds of investigative procedures as are used before arrest (e.g., interviewing witnesses, searching the suspect's home, and viewing the scene of the crime). Post-arrest investigation does offer one important investigative source, however, that ordinarily is not available prior to the arrest—the person of the arrestee. Thus, the arrestee may be placed in a lineup or simply taken to a place where a witness can view him individually (a "showup"). He may be required to provide handwriting or hair samples that can be compared with evidence the police have found at the scene of the crime. He also may be questioned at length about the crime for which he was arrested and any other crime thought to be related. Although we do not have precise data on these post-arrest procedures involving the arrestee, the best available estimates indicate they are not applied to the vast majority of arrestees. In most communities, they are used almost exclusively in the investigation of felony cases and even then not in most of those investigations.

Step 6: The Decision to Charge. Sometime between the booking of the arrestee and his presentation before a magistrate, there will be a review of the decision to file charges. Initially, the police officer making the arrest fills out an arrest report, which is reviewed by a higher ranking police officer. That officer may conclude either that charges should not be brought or that they should be based on a lower level offense than that for which the arrestee was booked. The decision not to charge may be based upon the officer's conclusion that there is insufficient evidence or that the particular offense can more appropriately be handled by a "stationhouse adjustment" (e.g., in the case of a fight among acquaintances, a warning and lecture may be deemed sufficient). If the officer decides against prosecution, the arrestee may be released from the lockup on the officer's direction (although some departments follow the practice of seeking prosecutor approval before releasing felony arrestees). In some jurisdictions, the police will drop as many as 10 15% of their arrests (predominantly misdemeanor arrests) at this point.

The second review of the decision to charge is usually the review by the prosecuting attorney. Prosecutors' offices vary, however, both as to the timing and extent of their review. In some jurisdictions, prosecutors regularly screen all felony and misdemeanor cases before charges are filed with the court. In other jurisdictions, pre-charge prosecutorial review is limited to exceptional cases, primarily those in which the police seek the prosecutor's advice. Here, the primary prosecutorial screening occurs sometime after charges have been filed. In the case of felonies, the prosecutor may not review the case until he is required to present it at a preliminary hearing or a grand jury screening. In misdemeanor cases, the prosecutor may not review the case until it goes to trial (and thus he may never screen misdemeanor charges to which the defendant pleads guilty). Still other jurisdictions prefer a midway position, with prosecutors undertaking a pre-charge screening of all felony cases, but utilizing a post-charge review for all but the most serious misdemeanors.

The timing of the screening is likely to have an impact upon the scope of the screening, as prosecutors tend to have less information available to them the earlier their review is undertaken. However, even among prosecutors utilizing the most prompt post-arrest screening, there is considerable variation in the sources considered in deciding whether to charge. The practice ranges from prosecutors who read only the police reports to those who regularly interview the police officer and often the victim of the crime as well.

Prosecutor offices also vary in the weight that will be given to a particular factor in determining whether to prosecute. The most significant factor, of course, is the strength of the evidence. If the evidence clearly is insufficient to gain a conviction, the case will be dropped. Similarly, if the evidence will support only a lesser offense than that suggested by the police, the charge will be reduced. Where the evidence arguably is sufficient to support the requested charge, the prosecutor will then turn to other factors that might suggest the case is inappropriate for prosecution in light of the equities of the situation and the overall caseload of the prosecutor's office. Such factors include the harm caused by the offense, the victim's attitude toward pressing the case,[k] the arrestee's criminal record, and the adequacy of alternative remedies.[l] It is in the consideration of these factors that differences between prosecutors are most likely to be significant.

Though we can hardly characterize any particular pre-charge screening program as typical of most jurisdictions, a fairly common pattern is found in the eventual re-

k. This factor is especially significant in situations in which the offender and the victim were close acquaintances. Several studies report that the high rate of dismissals in non-stranger violent crime cases (e.g., assaults) is due to the reluctance of a victim to press charges.

l. Many prosecutor offices have developed pre-charge "diversion programs" that provide a formal structure for the prosecutor's refusal to charge notwithstanding sufficient evidence. Under these programs, certain types of charges (usually misdemeanors) will not be prosecuted if the arrestee agrees to comply with specified "rehabilitative conditions" (e.g., making restitution to the victim, maintaining regular employment, etc.). Other prosecutors prefer not to tie the decision to charge to such conditions. They will bring charges and then seek to have the rehabilitative conditions imposed as conditions of probation following conviction.

sults of the overall prosecutorial screening through the entire criminal justice process. In the end, at least as to felonies, the cases against 30–60% of all arrestees will be dropped as a result of such screening.[m] If only a small percentage of the felony cases are rejected at pre-charge screening, then there will be a much higher percentage rejected at subsequent stages when the prosecutor engages in more thorough screening.

The prosecutor's post-charge screening is more likely to focus primarily upon the sufficiency of the evidence, but the prosecutor remains free to consider also all of the factors that are considered in pre-charge screening. If the prosecutor decides in his post-charge screening that the case does not merit prosecution, he will file a motion to terminate the prosecution (a *nolle prosequi* motion), which will be granted almost automatically by the court. In jurisdictions in which pre-charge screening is not extensive, post-charge screening may account for the disposition of more charges than any other step in the criminal justice process. In New York City, for example, where only a few percent of all felony arrestees are rejected for prosecution at the pre-charge stage, approximately 40% of all charges are subsequently rejected through post-charge screening, usually before the cases reach the trial court. Secondary screening also can be quite significant in jurisdictions with extensive pre-charge screening. In the District of Columbia, for example, the cases against 21% of the arrestees are rejected by an initial decision not to charge, but then an additional 29% are dismissed after charges are brought on *nolle prosequi* motions.

Statistics on charge reductions reflect a less consistent pattern than that characterizing dismissals. The percentage of reductions attributable to the screening process varies considerably, but prosecutors have been known to reduce the offense from that designated in the police booking in as many as 30% of the felony cases subjected to pre-charge screening. In many jurisdictions, certain types of felony arrests, most notably those involving non-professional thefts, are almost automatically reduced to misdemeanors (e.g., first-offense shoplifting reduced to petty theft). While most reductions occur before the initial charge is filed, a substantial number of reductions often occur later in the proceedings on the prosecutor's motion. Where plea bargaining takes the form of a charge bargain rather than a sentence bargain (see step 12), most of the later reductions are likely to be attributable to plea bargaining rather than post-charge prosecutorial screening.

Step 7: Filing the Complaint. Assuming that the pre-charge screening results in a decision to prosecute, the next step in the criminal justice process is the filing of charges with the lowest level court, the magistrate court. Typically, the initial charging instrument will be called a "complaint." In misdemeanor cases, which may be tried before the magistrate court, the complaint will serve as the charging instrument throughout the proceedings. In felony cases, on the other hand, the complaint serves to set forth the charges only before the magistrate court; felony cases may be adjudicated only in a trial court of general jurisdiction, and an information or indictment will replace the complaint as the charging instrument when the case reaches that court. The complaint ordinarily includes a brief description of the offense and is sworn to by a complainant. The complainant usually will be either the victim or the investigating officer. When an officer-complainant did not observe the offense being committed, but

m. The limited data available on the disposition of misdemeanor arrests indicates that a high percentage of misdemeanor cases also are rejected as a result of prosecutorial screening, but those figures are much more difficult to evaluate. In some jurisdictions, for example, post-charge dismissals may include situations in which defendants charged with offenses such as disorderly conduct are allowed to forfeit their bail, with the charges against them then being dismissed—a practice that amounts, in effect, to imposing a fine without a conviction record.

relied on information received from the victim or other witnesses, he will note that the facts alleged in the complaint are based on "information or belief."

In most jurisdictions, at some point between the filing of the complaint and the first appearance (see step 8), the magistrate will conduct an *ex parte* review of the case. The purpose of this review is to ensure that the arrest and complaint are supported by sufficient incriminating information to establish probable cause to believe the defendant committed the crime charged. The magistrate's review may be based on the complaint itself where the complaint alleges the facts establishing probable cause (e.g., that the complainant observed the offense). In other cases, it may be based on a police officer's affidavit setting forth available information establishing probable cause. In some jurisdictions, the magistrate also may base his determination upon a brief oral statement presented by the complainant. If the magistrate finds that probable cause has not been established, he will direct the prosecution to promptly produce more information or release the arrested person. Such instances tend to be quite rare, however.[n]

Step 8: The First Appearance. After the complaint has been filed and reviewed, the arrestee (who is now formally a defendant) is presented before the magistrate. This proceeding before the magistrate usually is described as the "first appearance," although some jurisdictions call it the "initial presentment" or the "arraignment on the warrant." Where the arrested person was released by police on a citation or stationhouse bail, the first appearance will not be scheduled until several days after the arrest. In most instances, however, the arrestee will still be in custody, and state law will require that he be brought before the magistrate without unnecessary delay. Ordinarily, the time consumed in booking, transportation, reviewing the decision to charge, and limited post-arrest investigation makes it unlikely that the arrestee will be presented before the magistrate until at least several hours after his arrest. Thus, if the magistrate court does not have an evening session, a person arrested in the afternoon or evening will not be presented before the magistrate until the next day. If arrested on a Friday or a weekend, he will not be presented until the next Monday, unless the magistrate court has a special weekend session.

The first appearance often is a quite brief proceeding. Initially, the magistrate will make certain that the person before him is the person named in the complaint. The magistrate then will inform the defendant of the charge in the complaint and will note various rights that the defendant may have in further proceedings. The range of rights mentioned will vary from one jurisdiction to another. Commonly, the magistrate will inform the defendant of his right to remain silent and warn him that anything he says in court or to the police may be used against him at trial. The magistrate also will inform the defendant of his right to be represented by counsel and his right to appointed counsel if he is indigent. Although the timing varies, most jurisdictions at least initiate the process of providing counsel for the indigent at the first appearance. The magistrate first will determine that the defendant is indigent and desires the assistance of appointed counsel. The magistrate then will either himself arrange for representation by the public defender or appointed private counsel or notify the judge in charge of appointments.

n. In many states, if the defendant was arrested without a warrant (as is usually the case), the magistrate will issue an arrest warrant after finding probable cause. Since the defendant has already been arrested, the warrant is not being used here for its traditional function of obtaining prior judicial approval for the arrest. Instead, the post-arrest warrant serves simply to provide judicial authorization for continuing to hold the arrestee in custody. In most jurisdictions, the post-arrest issuance of a warrant is viewed as an unnecessary formality, and the magistrate's finding of probable cause will combine with the complaint to authorize continuing custody.

Other aspects of the first appearance are likely to depend upon whether the defendant is charged with a felony or misdemeanor. In the felony case, the magistrate will advise the defendant of the next step in the process, the preliminary hearing, and will set a date for that hearing unless the defendant desires to waive it. If the defendant is charged with a misdemeanor, he will not be entitled to a preliminary hearing (or a subsequent grand jury review). The misdemeanor charge is triable to the magistrate,[o] and the magistrate therefore can proceed with a misdemeanor case in the same fashion as a general trial court receiving a felony case. For the misdemeanor, the first appearance becomes an arraignment on the complaint, equivalent to the arraignment on the information or indictment in a felony case (see step 12).[p]

The final function of the magistrate at the first appearance is to set bail (i.e., set the conditions under which the defendant can obtain his release from custody pending the final disposition of his case). If the defendant obtained his release previously by posting stationhouse bail, the magistrate will merely review that bail. In felony cases, the defendant ordinarily will still be in custody and the magistrate will be making the initial decision on bail. At one time, bail was limited almost entirely to the posting of cash or a secured bond, purchased from a professional bondsman. Today, the defendant may also be able to obtain his release by depositing with the court cash equal to 10% of the amount of the bond set by the magistrate. Indeed, several states make such extensive use of the 10% alternative that they have effectively eliminated the role of the professional bondsman. In addition, courts today frequently authorize release upon the defendant's unsecured promise to appear (commonly called "release on personal recognizance" or "personal bond"). In some jurisdictions, as many as 50% of all defendants are released under this procedure. Other non-financial bail conditions that may be imposed include curfews, regular reporting to a designated pretrial services agency, and avoiding contact with the victim.

While most felony arrestees will be released prior to trial, a substantial percentage will not gain their release. In some jurisdictions, preventive detention statutes allow the magistrate to deny bail upon a finding (made after a hearing) that the accused is so likely to flee, obstruct justice, or pose a threat to the community that no condition of release will be satisfactory. Most of those who fail to gain release, however, have had bail set, but have been unable to meet the financial conditions of that bail. In a jurisdiction in which liberal use is made of non-financial alternatives, the percentage of those felony defendants who fail to gain their release is likely to be in the neighborhood of 15–20%, but in other jurisdictions that figure may be twice as high. In misdemeanor cases, the per-

o. In some jurisdictions, the magistrate's trial jurisdiction does not extend to all misdemeanors, but only those punishable by no more than a certain term of imprisonment. See p. 29 infra. For the sake of brevity, our discussion will assume a dividing line between the trial authority of magistrate's and general trial court's that coincides with the misdemeanor-felony distinction (see fn. b supra).

p. The initial step in the magistrate's arraignment of the misdemeanor defendant involves an explanation of available pleas to the charge stated in the complaint and an entry of a plea to that charge. While most misdemeanor defendants eventually plead guilty, many will not do so at the first appearance since they have not yet had the opportunity to consult with counsel or others (e.g., relatives) whose advice might be sought. They will plead not guilty or will be allowed to defer entry of their plea to a later date. In a jurisdiction relying primarily on post-charge screening, a substantial percentage of the misdemeanor cases will be reviewed by the prosecutor and dismissed on his motion prior to the defendant's next scheduled court appearance. For the cases that survive this screening, the rate of guilty pleas is likely to be 80–95%. For these defendants, the next step in the process is sentencing (see step 15). For the 5–20% of the surviving cases that go to trial, the next step will be the filing of pretrial motions (see step 13).

centage remaining in custody will be much lower, very often less than 10%.

Step 9: Preliminary Hearing. Following the first appearance, the next scheduled step in a felony case ordinarily is the preliminary hearing. In many jurisdictions, however, a substantial portion of the felony caseload will be disposed of during the period (usually one or two weeks) between the first appearance and the scheduled preliminary examination. As mentioned previously, where the primary screening by the prosecutor occurs after charges are filed, a substantial number of felony charges are likely to be dismissed or reduced to a misdemeanor during this period. Even for those felony charges that remain, a preliminary hearing will not necessarily be held. The defendant ordinarily may waive his right to a preliminary hearing, and it is not unusual for a substantial percentage (e.g., 20–30%) to waive, usually because they intend to plead guilty. Also, even if the defendant desires a preliminary hearing, state law commonly allows the prosecutor to bypass the hearing by taking the case directly to the grand jury (a practice infrequently followed in some jurisdictions and very often followed in others). In those jurisdictions in which plea negotiations (see step 12) begin at this stage of the proceedings, a substantial percentage of the felony cases (e.g., 30%) may be resolved prior to a preliminary hearing upon agreement of the defendant to enter a plea of guilty before the magistrate to a charge reduced to the misdemeanor level.

Where the preliminary hearing is held, it will provide, like grand jury review, a screening of the decision to charge by a neutral body. In the preliminary hearing, that neutral body is the magistrate, who must determine whether, on the evidence presented, there is probable cause to believe that defendant committed the crime charged. Ordinarily, the magistrate will already have determined that probable cause exists as part of the *ex parte* screening of the complaint (see step 7). The preliminary hearing, however, provides screening in an adversary proceeding in which both sides are represented by counsel. Jurisdictions vary in the evidentiary rules applicable to the preliminary hearing, but most require that the parties rely primarily on live witnesses rather than affidavits. Typically, the prosecution will present its key witnesses and the defense will limit its response to the cross-examination of those witnesses. The defendant has the right to present his own evidence at the hearing, but traditional defense strategy advises against subjecting defense witnesses to prosecution cross-examination in any pretrial proceeding.

If the magistrate concludes that the evidence presented establishes probable cause, he will "bind the case over" to the next stage in the proceedings. In an indictment jurisdiction (see step 10), the case is boundover to the grand jury, and in a jurisdiction that permits the direct filing of an information (see step 11), the case is boundover directly to the general trial court. If the magistrate finds that the probable cause supports only a misdemeanor charge, he will reject the felony charge and allow the prosecutor to substitute the lower charge, which will then be set for trial in the magistrate court. If the magistrate finds that the prosecution's evidence does not support any charge, he will order that the defendant be released. The rate of dismissals at the preliminary hearing quite naturally varies with the degree of previous screening exercised by the prosecutor. In a jurisdiction with fairly extensive screening, the percentage of dismissals is likely to fall in the range of 5–15% of the cases heard.

Step 10: Grand Jury Review. Although all American jurisdictions still have provisions authorizing grand jury screening of felony charges, such screening is mandated only in those states requiring felony prosecutions to be instituted by an indictment, a charging instrument issued by the grand jury. About one-third of the states and the federal system currently require grand jury indictments for all felony prosecutions (unless waived by the defendant). If there has been a preliminary hearing, the magistrate's decision at that hearing is not binding on the grand jury. It can reject prosecution notwithstanding a preliminary hearing bindover, or reinstitute prosecution even though the magistrate concluded that the prosecution's evidence was inadequate.

The grand jury is composed of a group of private citizens who are selected to review cases presented over a term that may range from one to several months. Traditionally the grand jury consisted of 23 persons with the favorable vote of a majority needed to indict. Today, many states use a somewhat smaller grand jury (e.g., 12) and some require more than a simple majority to indict. As in the case of the magistrate at the preliminary hearing, the primary function of the grand jury is to determine whether there is sufficient evidence to justify a trial on the charge sought by the prosecution. The grand jury, however, participates in a screening process quite different from the preliminary hearing. It meets in a closed session and hears only the evidence presented by the prosecution. The defendant has no right to offer his own evidence or to be present during grand jury proceedings. If a majority of the grand jurors conclude that the prosecution's evidence is sufficient, the grand jury will issue the indictment requested by the prosecutor. The indictment will set forth a brief description of the offense charged, and the grand jury's approval of that charge will be indicated by its designation of the indictment as a "true bill." If the grand jury majority refuses to approve a proposed indictment, the charges against the defendant will be dismissed. In most indictment jurisdictions, grand juries refuse to indict in only a small percentage (e.g., 3–8%) of the cases presented before them.

Step 11: The Filing of the Indictment or Information. If an indictment is issued, it will be filed with the general trial court and will replace the complaint as the accusatory instrument in the case. Where grand jury review either is not required or has been waived in the particular case, an information will be filed with the general trial court. Like the indictment, the information is a charging instrument which replaces the complaint, but it is issued by the prosecutor rather than the grand jury. Approximately two-thirds of the states do not require prosecution by indictment, and prosecutors in these jurisdictions generally proceed by information in all but a very small portion of their prosecutions. In these "information states," the charge in the information ordinarily must be supported by a preliminary hearing bindover (unless the preliminary hearing was waived).

Step 12: Arraignment on the Information or Indictment. After the indictment or information has been filed, the defendant is arraigned—i.e., he is brought before the trial court, informed of the charges against him, and asked to enter a plea of guilty, not guilty, or, as is permitted under some circumstances, *nolo contendere.* The vast majority of the cases that reach the arraignment stage will not go to trial. Depending upon the quality of pre-arraignment screening, anywhere from 10–30% of the felony cases will be dismissed as a result of a *nolle prosequi.* Of the remaining felony cases, 70–90% will be resolved by a guilty plea in most jurisdictions.[q] Whether the guilty plea rate in a particular jurisdiction is closer to 70% or 90% depends upon several factors. One very significant varia-

q. This figure holds for the guilty-plea disposition of non-dismissed felony charges in most jurisdictions, although the proportion of pleas in the general trial court may be lower where pleas to charges reduced to a misdemeanor are entered before the magistrate (see the discussion of step 9 supra). There are judicial districts in which an even higher percentage (e.g., 95–98%) of all non-dismissed felony charges are resolved by guilty plea, and there are also districts in which prosecutors generally do not plea bargain and the percentage of pleas therefore is much lower. Jurisdictions in the latter category, however, often make more frequent use of bench trials.

ble may be the extent to which the prosecutor is willing to plea bargain—i.e., grant concessions in return for a guilty plea. While the vast majority of prosecutors make substantial use of plea bargaining, they vary markedly both as to the type of cases in which they will grant major concessions and as to the nature of those concessions. One of the most common concessions is the reduction of the offense charged in return for a guilty plea to a lesser offense. Thus, in a jurisdiction with extensive plea bargaining, it is not unusual to find that only a small percentage of the defendants plead guilty to the original charge. In other jurisdictions, prosecutors will offer concessions that deal directly with the sentence as opposed to the level of the charge. Such sentencing concessions often take the form of a prosecutorial recommendation of a lenient sentence (which will be given great weight by the sentencing judge) or the promise of a specific sentence agreed to by the judge.

Step 13: Pretrial Motions. In most jurisdictions, a broad range of objections must be raised by a pretrial motion. Those motions commonly present challenges to the institution of the prosecution (e.g., claims regarding the grand jury or the preliminary hearing), attacks upon the sufficiency of the charging instrument, requests for discovery of the prosecution's evidence, and requests for the suppression of evidence allegedly obtained through a constitutional violation. While some pretrial motions are made only by defendants who intend to go to trial, other motions are advanced almost as frequently by defendants expecting to plead guilty even if the motion succeeds. Nevertheless, pretrial motions are likely to be made in no more than 10% of all felony cases that reach the trial court. In misdemeanor cases, pretrial motions may be made in less than one percent of the cases before the magistrate court. The use of pretrial motions varies, of course, with the nature of the case. In narcotics cases, for example, motions to suppress are quite common. In the typical forgery case, on the other hand, pretrial motions of any type are quite rare.

As a group, pretrial motions are likely to result in the dismissal of not substantially more than 5% of all of the felony cases before the trial judge (and they are likely to have even less impact on the misdemeanor docket). The pretrial motion most likely to produce a dismissal is the motion to suppress. Quite frequently, if the defendant gains suppression of unconstitutionally obtained evidence, there will be insufficient remaining evidence to continue with the prosecution.

Step 14: The Trial. As noted previously, most felony and misdemeanor cases are likely to be disposed of either by a guilty plea or by a dismissal. Quite commonly, only 10–15% of the felony cases that reach the trial court actually will go to trial. Misdemeanor cases tend to have an even lower trial rate. Magistrate courts often have trials in less than 5% of the cases presented before them. Most trials will not be lengthy affairs. Misdemeanor trials typically last less than one day. Felony trials may occupy somewhat more time, particularly when tried to a jury, but most will be completed within a few days.

In all jurisdictions, the defendant will have a right to a jury trial for all felony offenses and for misdemeanors punishable by more than 6 months imprisonment (although the jury trial right in the misdemeanor cases may exist only through a trial *de novo*). Most states also provide a jury trial for lesser misdemeanors as well. Juries traditionally were composed of 12 persons, but many states now utilize 6 person juries in misdemeanor cases and several use the smaller juries in non-capital felony cases as well. Of course, the right to a jury trial can be waived, and in most jurisdictions, a significant number of defendants will waive the jury in favor of a bench trial. Over the country as a whole, however, a clear majority (perhaps 60–65%) of all felony trials are tried to a jury. In several jurisdictions, the percentage of jury trials comes close to 80%, although in one state, it often is as low as 15%. In misdemeanor cases, bench trials often are in the majority even in jurisdictions that extend the defendant's jury trial right to all misdemeanors. In all but a few jurisdictions, the jury verdict in misdemeanor and felony cases, whether for acquittal or conviction, must be unanimous. Where the jurors cannot agree, no verdict is entered and the case may be retried. Such "hung juries" occur in only a small percentage of tried cases (e.g., 3–6%).

The criminal trial resembles the civil trial in many respects. There are, however, several distinguishing features that are either unique to criminal trials or of special importance in such trials. These include (1) the presumption of defendant's innocence, (2) the requirement of proof beyond a reasonable doubt, (3) the right of the defendant not to take the stand, (4) the exclusion of evidence obtained through unconstitutional police procedures, and (5) the more frequent use of incriminating statements of defendants. In most jurisdictions, the misdemeanor trial will be almost indistinguishable from a felony trial. In some jurisdictions, however, misdemeanor trials tend to be less formal, with rules of evidence applied in a rather loose fashion.

Whether a criminal case is tried to the bench or to a jury, the odds favor conviction over acquittal. The acquittal rate for felonies generally does not exceed one-third. At the misdemeanor level, the rate of acquittals often is somewhat lower. A substantial variation exists, however, among the different types of crimes. Acquittal rates for rape and robbery tend to be considerably higher, for example, than acquittal rates for forgery or assault. Where the offense is one that is not likely to produce either an offender caught "red-handed," more than one eyewitness, or contraband discovered in the defendant's possession, the acquittal rate for the offense is likely to be higher than the average for offenses generally.

Step 15: Sentencing. If the defendant pleads guilty or is found guilty at trial, the judge will enter a judgment of conviction and set the case for sentencing. The structure of the sentence and the discretion of the judge in choosing among sentencing alternatives will be controlled by statute. For misdemeanors a judge ordinarily has discretion to impose a fine, probation, suspended sentence, or fixed jail term not to exceed a statutorily prescribed maximum. For felony offenses, the choice ordinarily is between imprisonment and probation, although the legislature is likely to have prohibited probation for some offenses. When imprisonment is imposed, most states continue to use the indeterminate sentences, i.e., the court sets a minimum and maximum term, with the parole board determining the actual release date between the minimum and maximum. State law will set the highest maximum sentence permissible for the particular crime and will also require that the minimum be no greater than a certain percentage (e.g., one-half) of the maximum. Some jurisdictions also impose other restrictions upon the trial court (e.g., compliance with sentencing guidelines) in its setting of the maximum and minimum terms. In recent years, many states have moved from indeterminate to determinate prison sentences for most felonies. Under determinate sentencing, the judge sets a single fixed term of imprisonment, which must fall within a fairly narrow range set by the legislature for the particular crime. This sentencing structure eliminates earlier parole release except for limited good-behavior credits.

In the case of misdemeanor sentences, there often is a substantial difference in the pattern of dispositions for those persons originally charged with misdemeanors and those originally charged with felonies that were reduced to misdemeanors as part of a plea bargain. The vast majority of the defendants in the former category will be fined, placed on probation, or receive a suspended sentence. Where the initial charge was a felony, the defendant is much more likely to receive a jail sentence (often combined with probation). Defendants convicted on felony charges are even more likely to be incarcerated for at least a short period. Prison sentences usually are imposed in anywhere from one-third to one-half of the felony convictions. Many jurisdictions also make extensive use of short jail sentences, combined with probation, in felony cases.

Step 16: Appeals.[r] In felony cases, initial appeals will be taken to the intermediate appellate court or to the state supreme court if there is no intermediate appellate court. Initial appeals in misdemeanor cases will be taken to the general trial court, and in some jurisdictions will consist of a trial *de novo*. Although all convicted defendants are entitled to appeal their conviction, appeals are taken predominantly by those defendants who were sentenced to imprisonment. In several states, a fairly substantial portion of felony appeals (perhaps as many as 20%) come from imprisoned defendants who pled guilty and are challenging their pleas. Most felony appeals, however, are taken by imprisoned defendants who are seeking review of a trial conviction. In some jurisdictions, as many as 90% of the defendants who were both convicted after a trial and sentenced to imprisonment will appeal their convictions. Even with almost automatic appeals by this group of defendants, however, the total number of felony appeals is still not likely to exceed 15% of all felony convictions. In misdemeanor cases, the appeal rate is much lower.

The rate of reversals on appeal varies with the particular appellate court, but tends to fall within the range of 10–20%. In many jurisdictions, the most common objection raised on appeal is the trial court's admission of evidence obtained through an allegedly unconstitutional search. That objection also provides the most common basis for reversal. Other grounds raised quite frequently (but with much less success) are the insufficiency of the evidence, the incompetency of counsel, constitutional violations in identification procedures, and challenges to the admission of defendant's incriminating statements made to the police.

Step 17: Postconviction Remedies. After the appellate process is exhausted, imprisoned defendants may be able to use postconviction remedies to challenge their convictions on limited grounds. In particular, federal postconviction remedies allow state as well as federal prisoners to challenge their convictions in the federal courts on certain constitutional grounds. The federal district courts receive roughly 9,000 such postconviction applications each year. Relief is granted on less than 4% of these petitions, however, and the relief often is limited to requiring a further hearing. In the state systems, postconviction remedies are used far less frequently.

THE CRIMINAL JUSTICE FUNNEL

If one were to draw a diagram of the criminal justice process, charting the numbers of persons processed at each stage, the shape of the diagram would be roughly that of a funnel. A great number of persons are subjected to the process at its initial stage (pre-arrest investigation), and at each subsequent stage, fewer and fewer persons are involved. There are more persons investigated as suspects than arrested, more persons arrested than charged, more persons charged than finally brought to adjudication, more persons adjudicated than found guilty, and more persons found guilty than subjected to incarceration. As the caseload moves through it, the criminal justice process sifts out

r. Our discussion of defense appeals is limited to challenges to the conviction rather than requests for appellate review of sentences. Prosecution appeals also are possible, but there are far fewer prosecution appeals than defense appeals. Most prosecution appeals must be taken prior to trial from an adverse pretrial order, although some jurisdictions permit an appeal from a dismissal at trial. Prosecution appeals may not be taken from an acquittal.

cases in much the same manner as a sieve. To provide a rough picture of the actual contours of this "funnel analogy" or "sieve effect", we offer the following "model" of the distribution of a cross-section of felony cases in a typical jurisdiction. While our model probably is not duplicated in any particular jurisdiction, available figures suggest it approximates the distribution found in various communities.

We start with 5,000 possible felonies that come to the attention of the police either through citizen complaint or officer observations. Although the investigation of some of these possible felonies will not point to any suspects, the investigation of others will require police encounters with more than one suspect. As a result, the police investigation process for 5,000 felonies can readily produce more than 5,000 police-suspect encounters. Assuming a typical mix of reported felonies (i.e., with a heavy emphasis on property crimes), the investigation of the 5,000 felonies is likely to lead to the arrest of no more than 1,500 persons. Out of this group of arrestees, approximately 400 will be juveniles. They will be transferred to the juvenile process, leaving 1,100 adult arrestees for possible criminal prosecution. After the police and prosecutor have reviewed the cases against these arrestees, about 350 will be released without any charges being pressed. In an additional 150 cases, the charges will immediately be reduced to misdemeanors. Thus, of 1,500 felony arrestees, only 600 will have felony charges filed against them.

The 600 felony charges will then be screened at preliminary hearings or grand jury proceedings, and will be subject to challenge by defense motions of various sorts. These procedures are likely to result in the dismissal of roughly 50 cases. Still another 50 cases may be dismissed by the prosecutor as a result of his review of the case once it reaches the trial court. Of the 500 felony cases that are left, approximately 400 will be resolved by guilty pleas. Perhaps half of those pleas will be to misdemeanor charges, and the others will be to the felony charged or to a lesser felony. There remain roughly 100 felony cases that will go to trial. Approximately 70 of the trials will result in convictions, although not necessarily for felonies.

In the end, of the 1,100 adult arrestees, approximately 250 will be convicted on a felony charge (including felonies lesser than that originally charged) and 300 will be convicted of misdemeanor charges. Of the 550 arrestees eventually convicted, as many as 250 may receive a sentence that includes some incarceration, but for most of the 250, incarceration will be limited to a short jail term, typically combined with probation. Approximately 100 will be sentenced to prison terms.

SECTION 2. THE AGENCIES OF THE CRIMINAL JUSTICE SYSTEM

Throughout this book, you will find both commentators and appellate judges referring to "police," "prosecutors," "defense counsel" and "judges." In this section, we hope to develop an awareness of the variety of officials that fit under these generic terms. At the same time, we will briefly describe the institutional structure within which these officials operate and the professional backgrounds they bring to their roles.

POLICE AGENCIES [a]

Fragmentation. Police agencies constitute the largest and most complex group of participants in the administration of the criminal justice system. They have the greatest volume of work, the most diverse

a. The data contained in this section is taken primarily from the F.B.I., *Uniform Crime Reports—1985;* B.J.S., *Justice Agencies in the United States—1980;* B.J.S., *Sourcebook of Criminal Justice Statistics—1984.* See also the sources cited p. 184 infra.

range of functions, and the greatest number of employees. They also clearly operate in the most decentralized fashion. Over 20,000 different governmental agencies in the United States can be classified as "police" agencies in that (1) they have been given primary responsibility for the enforcement of one or more criminal statutes, and (2) at least some of their employees have been given the special enforcement authority (e.g., special arrest powers) that distinguishes the police officer from the private citizen. Most of these 20,000 governmental agencies are units of local government (counties, cities, townships), but close to a thousand are part of a state government and about fifty are part of the federal government. Many of the agencies at the state and federal level are "specialized" police agencies; they have authority to enforce only a limited group of criminal laws (as in the case of state conservation officers) or to deal with offenses committed within a special geographic enclave (as in the case of campus police). However, the vast majority of all police agencies, including almost all of those that are part of local governments, are "general" police agencies. Such agencies have authority to enforce all of the state's criminal laws throughout the geographical limits of their particular unit of government. In 1984, 12,000 of these general police agencies, operating at the state and local level, employed approximately 467,000 police officers (roughly 2 officers per every 100,000 inhabitants).

One consequence of this fragmentation of police authority is that over 100 different police agencies may be operating within a single metropolitan area. In the tri-county area of metropolitan Detroit, for example, over 125 police agencies are separately engaged in the investigation of crime. Initially, over a dozen federal agencies have agents assigned to the area. The state adds several agencies, including the state police. Each of the three counties contributes its sheriff's department. Finally, over 100 cities and townships provide their own police departments.

Federal agencies. Leaving aside the special case of the District of Columbia police department (which is more appropriately viewed as a local government agency), all but one of the major federal police agencies are clearly specialized agencies. Most, like the Drug Enforcement Agency, are assigned to enforcement of a limited group of crimes.[b] Others, like the United States Park Police, have enforcement responsibility only within a specified enclave. The Federal Bureau of Investigation is the one federal police agency that might be classified as a "general" agency. Its enforcement responsibility extends to violations of all federal laws other than those laws assigned to specialized agencies such as the D.E.A.

Though considered a general police agency, the F.B.I. is quite unlike any local or state general police agency. With over 8,500 agents, it is larger than any other police agency except for the police departments of New York and Chicago. It insists upon educational prerequisites for its agents (generally a law degree or a bachelor's degree with expertise in accounting or other specialized field) that go beyond those found in any local or state agency. The mix and volume of the crimes it investigates are substantially different from

b. Other such federal agencies include: the Immigration and Naturalization Service (responsible for enforcing laws relating to the admission, exclusion, deportation and naturalization of aliens, and also including the Border Patrol); the Alcohol, Tobacco, and Firearms Division (enforcing various criminal laws relating to the distribution of alcohol, tobacco, firearms, and explosives); and the Secret Service (responsible for the suppression of counterfeit currency as well as its more well known function of protecting the President). These specialized federal agencies are scattered through a variety of federal departments. For example, the D.E.A., like the F.B.I., is a part of the Justice Department; the A.T.F. and Secret Service are part of the Treasury Department; the National Park Service is part of the Interior Department; and the Postal Inspection Service is part of the United States Postal Service.

those found in any other jurisdiction.[c] Finally, and most significantly, the F.B.I. does not bear the general peacekeeping, traffic control, and social service functions that occupy so much of the effort of local and state agencies.[d]

State agencies. At the state level, like the federal level, most police agencies are specialized agencies assigned to the enforcement of specific laws. These agencies typically enforce regulatory laws that have criminal sanctions (e.g., liquor laws or fish and gaming provisions). The state agency commonly known as the "state police," "state patrol" or "state troopers" is a specialized agency in some states and a general police agency in others. Where a specialized agency, its basic responsibility is to enforce state traffic laws and the authority of its officers to arrest for violations of the state's general criminal laws is tied to the state highway systems (i.e., officers can make arrests only if the offense took place on the highway, in the immediate vicinity of the highway, or in their presence). In other states, the state police have a general law enforcement responsibility that extends throughout the state in addition to their highway responsibilities. Such state police departments usually include a criminal investigative unit, a uniformed patrol force, a criminal intelligence network of some type, and a forensic science laboratory. Ordinarily, the department will limit its patrol efforts to the state highways and to rural areas that are not serviced by a local police department. Where local departments are quite small (as is often the case), the investigative unit of the state police will assist the local department in the investigation of serious crime. Even larger police departments will make use of the state police department's criminal intelligence network and forensic laboratory. Overall, the officers of the various state police agencies will provide no more than 10–20% of the total police manpower within the state. The state police department, however, especially where a general agency, may have more sworn officers than all but a handful of the local police agencies.

Local police agencies. The local police agencies perform the bulk of the police work in this country and contain approximately 85% of our law enforcement officers. At the county level, the primary police agency is the sheriff's department. While the sheriff's departments in some states are limited to the administration of the county jail and the service of process, most states grant those department full law enforcement responsibilities. To avoid overlap, sheriff's deputies commonly concentrate their efforts in those communities that lack their own police departments (usually villages and some townships) and are not patrolled by the state police.

The great majority of the local police agencies are found at the city and township level.[e] They include over 11,000 municipal police departments. Over 90%

c. These differences are reflected in the prosecutions brought by local and federal prosecutors. The total number of federal prosecutions (see fn. b, p. 21 infra), not all the product of F.B.I. investigations, is smaller than the number of prosecutions typically brought by local prosecutors in districts with police forces only half the size of the F.B.I. Those federal prosecutions, however, include a substantially greater portion of offenses involving commercial fraud and other complex transactions and a substantially smaller proportion of crimes akin to the typical "street crimes" that dominate local prosecutions.

d. However, even the F.B.I., though it is known as basically a criminal investigative agency, has numerous other obligations. It agents are used, for example, to gain background information on prospective government employees and to collect information for use in civil suits involving the government.

e. The city police department of general enforcement responsibility was not developed until the mid–1800's. During the colonial period, local governments relied on an assortment of public police officials—basically constables, marshalls, and sheriffs—assisted by the *posse commitatus.* This "hodpodge of small jurisdictions staffed by various officials with different powers, responsibilities, and legal standing" continued in the post-revolutionary period. See Bayley, *Police: History* in the Encyclopedia of Crime and Justice (Kadish, ed., 1983). In 1829, Sir Robert Peel established in London the first paid, full-time, uniformed police organization having a city-wide jurisdicof all municipalities with a population of 2,500 or more have their own police force. As might be expected, most municipal police agencies have small staffs. Close to two-thirds have less than 20 sworn officers, and over one-third employ less than 5 officers. In such departments, all officers except the chief are likely to be assigned to patrol. Standing in sharp contrast to the typical small municipal department are the roughly 100 local departments employing more than 300 sworn officers, with the largest, the New York City police department, having over 20,000 officers.

Variety of police functions. The materials in this book relating to police activities most frequently concern the investigation of serious crimes. It must be kept in mind, however, that the investigation of serious crime is only one of many aspects of police work. Indeed, in a typical local police department, a comparatively small portion of the department's total activity is spent on the investigation of serious crimes. Far more time will be spent on social service activities, traffic control, and preserving the peace. These multiple responsibilities are reflected in the typical organization of larger police departments. Those departments are divided into three major segments—patrol, services and administration, and investigation. The services and administration division is concerned with various functions, such as record-keeping and community relations, that generally are quite removed from investigation. Officers assigned to the patrol division, by far the bulk of the departmental manpower, also will spend most of their time on activities other than criminal investigation. They will be occupied primarily with such matters as the patrol itself, social service functions (e.g., helping to find a lost child), and traffic control. Of the time spent directly on criminal activities, most will be devoted to misdemeanors.[f] It is unlikely that a patrolman, over the year, will devote more than one-tenth of his time to the investigation of major crimes.[g] The detective division—the division devoted primarily to the inves-

tion. The example of London's "bobbies" was followed in Boston within the decade and by the 1870's almost all major American cities had municipal police forces. At the state level, the concept of a state police, although it had roots in the Texas Ranger organization established in the 1830's, did not get underway until the turn of the century. The F.B.I. was not established until 1924, although it was an outgrowth of a smaller Bureau of Investigation created in the Justice Department in 1908.

f. Even here, the sometimes conflicting functions of the police come into play, as evidenced by James Q. Wilson's description of three distinctive styles used by patrol officers in the exercise of their arrest discretion—the "watchman," "legalistic" and "service" styles. See Wilson, *Varieties of Police Behavior: The Management of Law and Order in Eight Communities* (1968). The watchman style emphasizes order maintenance, and seeks to control minor offenders or potentially explosive situations through informal techniques rather than arrests. The legalistic style calls for primary emphasis on law enforcement, with officers generally making a misdemeanor arrest whenever they have the basis for doing so. The service style gives highest priority to community relations. Arrest authority is more likely to be used where such action is responsive to citizen complaints, but the primary focus is upon serving the citizenry rather than law enforcement as such. Wilson found that, among larger police departments, the watchman style was preferred by departments in heterogeneous communities with significant crime problems, the legalistic style by departments seeking to project a professional image, and the service style by departments in suburban middle-class communities.

A later study, Wilson and Boland, *The Effect of Police in Crime* (1980), suggests that differences in patrol style can have a bearing on serious crime as well as misdemeanors. Cities where police employed an "aggressive," legalistic patrol strategy—making frequent "street stops" and using an above average number of traffic tickets—generally had a higher arrest rate and lower crime rate for robberies. It does not necessarily follow, however, that such a strategy will obtain what most police departments view as their primary objective, achieving "community satisfaction."

g. As a result, most officers outside the detective division do not have extensive experience in investigating and making arrests for such offenses. A District of Columbia study of 17,500 annual arrests for felonies and serious misdemeanors (those punishable by incarceration for six months or more) revealed that 46% of the 4,505 officers of the local department had not made such an arrest during the past year. Of the half that had made one or more such arrests, tigation of major crimes—commonly is no more than one-tenth of the size of the patrol division.[h] Moreover, even detectives commonly have other, non-investigative responsibilities that occupy a substantial portion of their time.

Selection and training. Better selection of personnel has always been given a high priority in efforts to improve police operations. It is recognized that police officers at the lowest level must be given largely ungovernable discretion to exercise substantial authority, and assumed that who the officer is will make a substantial difference in how he exercises that authority.[i] Initially, efforts to improve the quality of personnel focused on instituting a civil service system of selection that excluded political considerations and looked to factors evidencing integrity, intelligence, and emotional stability. Once that was achieved, the emphasis turned to raising educational standards. During the 1960's, a Presidential Commission set as a national goal the hiring of only college graduates by 1983. That goal proved impossible to reach. Many local departments do hire primarily persons who have at least one year of college experience, but for many others, particularly in large cities, a high school diploma is all that is needed.[j] The racial turmoil of late 1960's led to another hiring goal—the recruitment of a substantially greater number of minority group members, particularly in cities with large minority populations. The large urban departments found this goal easier to meet. Most large cities with substantial minority populations now have at least 15% minority officers and those major cities with the highest percentage of minority residents have 30–50% minority officers. A more recent drive to increase the hiring of women has raised the national average of female officers in state and local departments from roughly 1% in 1973 to almost 6% a decade later.

Where the new police recruit attended college (particularly if enrolled in a criminal justice program), he or she is more likely to have some grounding in the political, sociological, and psychological theories that may relate to police work. In general, the training programs provided by the departments themselves (either directly or through a state training program)

31% had not made an arrest leading to conviction. Indeed, over half of the arrests leading to felony convictions were made by only 249 officers (less than 6% of the total force). See Forst, et. al, fn. c, p. 3 supra.

h. Vice and "tactical" squads that seek out offenders through aggressive decoy programs may also be viewed as basically investigative units, but the manpower devoted to such units does not add significantly to the total percentage of officers who might be considered investigative specialists. Also, in some communities, patrol officers do somewhat more investigative work than suggested above. While patrol officers in many departments are directed to turn over immediately to detectives all investigations of serious crimes not resolved by an on-the-scene arrest, other departments expect patrol officers to look to the detectives only if a substantial initial investigation by the patrol officer has proven unsuccessful. However, in the latter departments, the detective department also is likely to be smaller than suggested above.

i. Some would modify that assumption to stress not the individual, but the group as a whole. They note the existence of a strong subculture among police officers that shapes the actions of the individual to fit the expectation of his peers. At the same time, it is generally recognized that, given the strength of this police subculture, changes in management policies in themselves are likely to have only a limited impact upon the street behavior of police. See Muir, *Police: Street Corner Politicians* (1977).

j. Several factors explain the failure of all but a small number of departments to reach the goal set by the Presidential Commission. First, while the typical compensation package for new police officers commonly exceeds the median salaries for high school graduates (and offers substantially better retirement benefits), it is far less competitive as to college graduates. Second, the push to hire more minorities conflicted to some degree with the emphasis upon higher educational requirements because there was a smaller pool of minorities who were college graduates. Finally, many departments were not convinced that a college education would substantially improve the performance of their personnel. The studies on that subject are mixed. See Sherman, *Causes of Police Behavior: The Current State of Quantitative Research,* 17 J. of Res. in Crime and Delinquency 71 (1980).

largely eschew such subjects. They concentrate instead on "how to do it" subjects like accident investigation, use of firearms, and legal standards governing search and seizure. Most states require at least 200 hours of this type of curriculum and many larger departments double that to meet the 400 hour standard recommended by the National Advisory Commission. Most departments add a few weeks of formal field training to the prescribed classroom work. After completing their initial training, officers are placed on a probationary status for periods commonly ranging from six months to a year, during which they are supposed to be under fairly close supervision. In many departments, the training process is largely completed when the probationary period is ended. In others, a certain number of hours (e.g., 40–60) of in-service continuing education is required each year.[k]

PROSECUTORS

Although the British common law tradition was one of private prosecution (i.e., the complainant hired private counsel to press the prosecution), Americans had established an office of public prosecutor even before the Revolution.[a] In most of the colonies, public prosecution was originally superimposed upon a system of private prosecution, but private prosecution was eventually seen as impracticable, too often subject to abuse, and inconsistent with the view that crimes were "acts against the state" and not simply wrongs inflicted upon an individual victim. As the office of public prosecutor grew in status and prosecutors became elected officials (a product of the Jacksonian reform movement), the public prosecutor was gradually given a virtual monopoly over criminal prosecutions with extensive discretion over both the filing and selection of criminal charges.

As in the case of police power, the authority of the public prosecutor has not been centralized, but divided among a group of officials. Initially, there is the division between state officials responsible for prosecutions under state laws (the vast majority of all prosecutions [b]), and federal officials responsible for prosecutions under federal laws. The Attorney General of the United States is the chief federal prosecutor, but federal prosecutorial authority has long been divided among a series of lesser officials (most noteably, the United States Attorneys) who are responsible to the Attorney General. At the state level, the primary recipient of prosecutorial authority is the local prosecutor, commonly known as the "prosecuting attorney,"

k. As might be expected, this training regime does not satisfy those who place greater weight on a theoretical grounding or in the detailed examination of each element of decisionmaking. Thus, the *A.B.A. Standards Relating to the Urban Police Function* 203 (1973) offered the following criticism: "A physician is an authority with the power of life and death in situations involving physical disorder. A policeman is a life and death authority in situations of social disorder. Yet physicians are trained, on the average, in 11,000 hours. The average policeman receives fewer than 200 hours of training, and in the latter instance, most of the training is irrelevant to the functions to be performed."

a. The ancestry of this "American invention" is a matter of some dispute. Some see it as an expansion of the role of the British officer known as the King's Counsel or Attorney General, who could bring prosecutions in cases of special interest to the Crown. Others note that the office had its earliest start in the Middle Atlantic colonies, where the early Dutch settlers had introduced the position of the Dutch *schout*. The office of public prosecutor has also been attributed to the influence of the French and their office of *procurer*. See generally, Jacoby, *The American Prosecutor: A Search for Identity* 3–43 (1980).

b. Federal prosecutors account for less than 2% of all felony prosecutions and an even smaller percentage of all misdemeanor prosecutions. The total number of criminal filings in the federal district courts in a given year is not likely to exceed 40,000, with approximately 60% at the felony level. *1984 Report of the Administrative Office of the United States Courts.* Criminal filings in state courts (including ordinance violations and various regulatory, non-traffic misdemeanors) exceeds 10 million. Although a fairly precise figure for the number of felony filings is difficult to come by, felony prosecutions in most states constitute anywhere from 7–12% of all criminal filings (suggesting a rough estimate of nationwide felony filings in the neighborhood of 1 million). B.J.S., *Case Filings in State Court, 1983.*

"county prosecutor," "state attorney" or "district attorney." These prosecutors represent districts consisting of a single county or a group of counties that coincide with a judicial district. While the local prosecutors tend to have virtually autonomous authority in prosecuting for crimes committed in their districts, that authority may not be exclusive. In many states, the state attorney general also may bring prosecutions for at least some crimes and the city attorney may prosecute for violations of local ordinances. The material that follows looks at all of these "prosecutors," but it focuses primarily on the local prosecutor, who is responsibile for the vast majority of prosecutions.

Federal prosecutors. The primary responsibility for federal prosecutions rests with the United States Attorney, an office created in 1789. There are 94 United States Attorneys, one for each of the federal judicial districts. Those offices range in size from one or two assistants in the sparsely populated districts to over 50 assistants in the large urban districts. By and large, political considerations play a substantial role in the selection of the U.S. Attorney, but not in the selection of their assistants. The U.S. Attorney is a presidential appointee, confirmed by the Senate. In practice, the appointee is almost invariably a member of the President's political party and is appointed on the recommendation of the Senators or Representatives from the particular state who are members of that party. When a president of a different political party takes office, the U.S. Attorney usually is replaced (tradition dictates that the U.S. Attorney, though appointed to a four year term, resign upon presidential request). The assistants are hired by the U.S. Attorney, usually without reference to their political affiliation. When a new U.S. Attorney is appointed, even after a shift in political party, the assistants no longer are replaced en masse. Nevertheless, assistants do not view their jobs as career positions, and the vast majority stay no more than several years, (usually leaving to return to private practice).

Like many state prosecutors, U.S. Attorneys have various civil enforcement responsibilities (e.g., debt collection) as well as their criminal enforcement responsibilities. However, unlike most local prosecutors, the U.S. Attorney can obtain substantial support services from beyond his local district. The U.S. Attorney's office can utilize the investigative assistance of offices of the F.B.I. located throughout the United States, the legal expertise provided by the Justice Department's Criminal Division, and the data collection and case management systems provided by other divisions within the Justice Department.

Although U.S. Attorneys are subject to the supervisory authority of the Attorney General, they are given considerable autonomy in their exercise of prosecutorial discretion. The Attorney General has set forth a series of departmental guidelines, contained in the United States Attorney's Manual, but those guidelines allow for considerable flexibility both as to prosecution priorities and practices. However, the use of certain types of litigation and investigative practices (e.g., the use of electronic surveillance or the granting of immunity to witnesses) requires the approval of the Attorney General's designated representative in Washington. Such approval is also required in several substantive areas where a national enforcement policy is deemed essential (e.g., internal security violations).

The U.S. Attorneys offices present the vast majority of the approximately 35,000 federal criminal prosecutions brought in a typical year, but various divisions within the Justice Department also exercise prosecutorial authority as to particular types of offenses. Criminal antitrust prosecutions are developed and presented by the Antitrust Division, and the Civil Rights Division often brings prosecutions within its area of expertise. The Criminal Division itself initiates prosecutions in several fields (e.g., organized crime, public corruption, and narcotics distribution), acting through its special Strike Forces and regional offices located in 25 major cities.

Local prosecutors: the rural and small suburban office. As a leading study of the office of the local prosecutor notes, the public image of that office has been shaped largely by the big city office, but "hidden behind this single image are vastly different types of offices dealing with vastly different issues and offering services distinctly different from each other." [c] There are over 2,500 local prosecutor's offices in the United States, and a substantial majority represent districts with populations under 60,000. In contrast to large urban or suburban offices, many prosecutors in these districts operate without even one full time assistant. Indeed, less than 20% of all local prosecutor's offices have four or more assistants. In districts with an especially small population, the prosecutor is likely to be a part-time official, maintaining a private practice in addition to his public office.

The criminal caseload in small districts often is fairly light, particularly as to felonies. Solo prosecutors may process no more than two felonies per month. Indeed, one national survey of the total range of local prosecutor's offices reported that 45% process fewer than 200 felony cases per year. Of course, in most of these districts, the prosecutor's responsibility is not limited to criminal prosecution. The prosecutor also handles juvenile cases and often has extensive civil responsibilities; these include advising the county board of supervisors, representing the county in civil actions, and representing the state in mental commitments and in the enforcement of health and safety regulations.

Small prosecutor's offices have no need for a bureaucratic structure. The assistants, if any, work closely with the prosecutor and should fully understand his prosecutorial policies. Dealings with defense counsel, who are likely to be known socially as well as professionally, require no formal guidelines. There is neither the resources nor the need for highly structured programs dealing with matters such as diversion or the investigation and prosecution of complex fraud or narcotics offenses. The former can be handled through relatively informal arrangements, and the latter is often best handled by turning the matter over to the state attorney general or federal authorities.

Local prosecutors: the urban and large suburban office. Prosecuting attorneys in metropolitan districts not uncommonly have a larger legal staff than even the largest of the private law firms in the community. Los Angeles County, for example, has over 600 assistant prosecutors. Notwithstanding their size, these offices commonly have extraordinarily heavy caseloads per prosecutor, often four or five times that found in smaller offices. To assist the local prosecutor in handling that caseload, some counties have relieved the prosecutor's office of most of its civil responsibilities, or provided a separate staff for civil cases. Prosecutors in metropolitan areas are also provided with various support services, including special investigators, librarians, record control clerks, and where the office is large enough to support an automated case tracking system, computer programers and systems analysts. Large offices may also support a substantial diversion program staffed by a director and several counselors.

In a large office, the assignment of prosecutors may have a substantial bearing on the operation of the office. The two most common assignment systems are the vertical or integrated system and the horizontal or process system. The vertical system is most commonly found in districts in which

c. Jacoby, fn. a supra, at 55–56. The statistics cited in this section are taken largely from surveys cited in Chapter 3 of the Jacoby study.

a complaint once filed will be assigned to a specified caseflow resulting in its eventual presentation in a particular courtroom or before a particular judge. A single assistant prosecutor or a team of assistants will then be assigned to all cases docketed for that courtroom or judge, with the assistant handling those cases from the point of filing through their final disposition. Where special units are established to handle particular types of cases (e.g., narcotics) or particular types of offenders (e.g., career criminals), the assignment will start at an even earlier point, with the prosecutor assuming responsibility for the case prior to the decision to charge and carrying it through to disposition. The horizontal assignment system, in contrast, revolves around each process step rather than the individual case. Thus, separate assistants may be assigned to intake, preliminary hearings, grand jury review, arraignments, trials, and appeals. As the case moves from one step to another, a new prosecutor will take over. Under this system, the newest assistants are commonly assigned to the preliminary steps or to misdemeanor trials, with the more seasoned prosecutors handling felony trials or supervising at one of the other stages.

Large offices also vary in the degree to which they seek to control the assistants in their exercise of discretion. Some assign experienced assistants to major areas of discretionary decisionmaking (e.g., charging and plea negotiation) and allow basically autonomous exercise of that authority by each assistant. Others utilize detailed guidelines, require assistants to justify their decision in writing by reference to those guidelines, and require all variations to be approved by one of a selected group of senior assistants. Spot checks and statistical analysis are run to ensure that all prosecutors are adhering basically to the same policies. Even here, however, individual prosecutors retain considerable flexibility, particularly in evaluating the factual elements of the case.

Local prosecutors: selection. With few exceptions, local prosecutors are elected officials. Their elected term of office is fairly short (usually 4 years, but only 2 years in approximately a dozen states). While the incumbent often has a very good chance of being reelected, elections for this post often attract a fair degree of voter attention due to the centrality of the crime issue. In part because of their limited job security, most local prosecutors do not view their office as a career position. Many see it as a stepping stone to higher political office and others view it as an opportunity to make a reputation and gain contacts that will later be helpful in private practice. Thus, studies of prosecutor career patterns report that 50% of the prosecutors in a particular state are likely to be serving their first term and close to 50% may have a current interest in seeking another government position. Of course, there are exceptions to the general pattern. In almost every state, one can find local prosecutors who have remained in office for twenty to thirty years, rejecting numerous opportunities to become judges or enter private practices.

In most jurisdictions, the assistant prosecutors also have a fairly short tenure. Like the prosecuting attorney, they do not view themselves as career public servants. In some jurisdictions, the process of their selection is so highly political that assistants are likely to lose their positions, or at least be demoted from supervisory positions, if the prosecutor hiring them is succeeded in office by a candidate from another party. Prosecutors in most larger counties, however, tend to hire on a non-partisan, merit-oriented basis. While the assistants in such offices are not protected by civil service, they do have substantial job security. Nevertheless, their turnover rate tends to be substantial. Estimates of the current annual turnover rate throughout the country range as high as 25–33%. Assistants commonly are hired at an early stage in their legal careers, often immediately upon their graduation from law school. They stay for a few years, handling a high caseload at comparatively low pay and gaining considerable practical experience. They then leave to enter various fields of private practice (including criminal defense work) where their experience in litigation will be most valuable. Various prosecutor's offices, in an effort to produce more career professionals, have sought to establish salaries for higher ranked, experienced assistants at a level only slightly below that of a trial judge.

Local prosecutors: prosecutor/police relations. The local prosecutor is commonly described as the "chief law-enforcement officer" of the local district, but this does not mean that the prosecutor has the authority to simply order the police to engage or not engage in certain investigative practices as he so directs. Police departments commonly do follow the legal advice of the prosecutor but they do so because the interaction of police and prosecutor make cooperation necessary, not because they are legally required to do so. The local prosecutor and the local police are separate agencies, often receiving their funding from separate sources. Unlike the federal system, where the U.S. Attorney and F.B.I. are both subject to the supervisory power of the Attorney General, the local police and local prosecutor are not subject to the higher authority of a single executive. Short of threatening to withdraw his power to prosecute, the prosecutor must rely on his power of persuasion to gain any changes in police practices thought to be desirable.

A complete breakdown in prosecutor/police relations is rare, but various studies have found more tensions and conflict than one might initially expect, considering their shared interest in law enforcement.[d] The lack of smoother prosecutor/police relations may often be a product of inadequate communication, but it also is attributable to the different vantage points from which police and prosecutor view the same event. Unlike the prosecutor, police see crime as it is committed in the streets rather than as reported in a law office. They are more likely to be influenced in their appraisal of a case by the extent of the victim's suffering, by the accused's subsequent reaction to his criminal behavior, and by the officer's own peril in making the arrest. Although both prosecutor and police officer are interested in effective law enforcement, their immediate goals and interests also tend to differ. The police are concerned primarily with their responsibility for keeping the streets safe, while the prosecutor is focusing upon his role as the legal representative of the state, the need to keep the court process moving, and his participation in the courtroom "work group" of prosecutor, defense counsel, and judge.[e]

State attorneys general. In all but a few states, the state attorney general also has prosecutorial authority with respect to at least some state law violations. In approximately a dozen states, that authority is limited to cases in which the governor, legislature, or some other body (e.g., a grand jury) has requested that the attorney general replace the prosecutor. In such cases, the attorney general may intervene in prosecutions already initiated by the local prosecuting attorney or initiate his own prosecutions. In approximately half

d. Police, it is said, "are often disappointed with and wary of the prosecutor's decisions; the prosecutor often distrusts and questions the actions and motives of the police. In many instances, the two work together more in an atmosphere of sullen resignation than in one of trust and cooperation." Jacoby, fn. c supra, at 110.

e. Social scientists, using organizational theory, have suggested that the criminal justice process is substantially affected by the internal group dynamics of the courtroom work group. See, e.g., Eisenstein and Jacob, *Felony Justice: An Organizational Analysis of Criminal Courts* (1977). Finding a complex network of ongoing social as well as professional relationships among judges, prosecutors, and defense attorneys who work together on a daily basis, they see as its product a considerable degree of cooperation designed to serve the shared goals of maintaining group cohesion, reducing uncertainty, disposing of the caseload, and "doing justice."

of the states, the attorney general has a general authority to intervene in pending prosecutions at his discretion. In many of those states, he also is given authority to institute prosecutions at his discretion, although this authority sometimes is limited to specific groups of offenses, such as tax fraud and criminal antitrust violations. In practice, the state attorneys general rarely exercise their authority to intervene in pending prosecutions. The authority to initiate prosecutions also is used very sparingly in most of the jurisdictions in which it exists. However, there has been a growing trend to make use of that authority with respect to certain types of criminal activity, most noteably organized crime and public corruption. In those areas, several state attorneys general have developed extensive investigative units and are frequently initiating prosecutions. Finally, notice should be taken of three states (Alaska, Delaware, and Rhode Island) in which there are no independent local prosecutors; all prosecuting authority is granted to the attorney general, who may assign particular assistants to exercise that authority in each of the judicial districts.

City attorneys. In many states, city ordinances duplicate state misdemeanor provisions and minor offenses therefore may be prosecuted either under the state law or under the local ordinances. Whether minor offenses are prosecuted as ordinance violations or as misdemeanors usually will depend upon the policy of the police department making the arrest for these offenses. If the prosecution is brought under the local ordinance, the prosecuting official will be the city attorney rather than the prosecuting attorney, whose responsibility ordinarily is limited to enforcing state law. The city attorney's primary responsibility tends to lie in the area of civil law, but a substantial portion of his staff may be assigned to ordinance enforcement. Indeed, in some communities, the number of assistant city attorneys assigned to prosecute ordinance violations will exceed the number of assistants to the local prosecuting attorney assigned to misdemeanor cases. In such situations, the ordinance division of a city attorney's office may face many of the same problems relating to internal structure, support services, and assistant autonomy that are found in a medium sized prosecutor's office.

DEFENSE COUNSEL [a]

Public defenders. In most jurisdictions, 60–70% of all felony defendants are "indigent" in the sense that they lack the funds to hire defense counsel. The percentage of misdemeanor defendants who are indigent usually is somewhat lower, but it can easily fall in the range of 30–50%. As will be seen in Chapter Three, indigent felony defendants are constitutionally entitled to defense representation paid for by the state. Indigent misdemeanor defendants have a similar right only when sentenced to incarceration, but many jurisdictions provide free representation for all indigent misdemeanor defendants charged with a misdemeanor or ordinance violation that carries a potential sentence of imprisonment. A majority of local judicial districts provide counsel for the indigent defendant through an assigned counsel system; the court makes individual appointments of private practitioners who receive compensation from the state for the work done in the particular case, usually at a rate somewhat lower than that which would be earned in private practice. In the more heavily populated districts, however, a public defender agency is likely to be the primary provider of counsel for the indigent. Only one-third of all counties have defender agencies, but those counties

a. The factual data on defender offices is taken largely from B.J.S., *Criminal Defense Systems* (1984), the sources cited there, and Wice and Pilgrim, *Meeting the Gideon Mandate: A Survey of Public Defender Programs,* 58 Judicature 400 (1975). Leading studies of both public defenders and private defense counsel are cited in Reed and Keltner, *Careers in Criminal Justice: Law* in Encyclopedia of Criminal Justice (Kadish, ed., 1983).

contain over 60% of the nation's population. In most of these districts, defender agencies are the almost exclusive provider of representation for the indigent, with private counsel being assigned only to avoid potential conflicts in cases of jointly charged codefendants. In other districtss, a "mixed system" is used, with the defender agency and appointed counsel each representing a substantial portion of the indigents (although the defender agency usually has the larger group).[b]

Public defender programs may be either statewide or local programs. Under a statewide system, a chief defender is appointed either by the governor or the judiciary and is charged with providing a system of representation for each of the counties in the state. The chief defender commonly establishes branch offices staffed by his assistants, although a contractual arrangement with a local law firm may be used for some counties. The local branches are subject to the supervisory authority of the chief defender and receive support services from the central office. Local defender agencies are organized by county or judicial district. They usually are government agencies, but some are private non-profit organizations receiving funding from the local courts (based on the number of indigents represented) or the community's charitable giving program. Where the defender agency is a governmental agency, the chief defender may be elected, but most chief defenders of such agencies are selected by the local legislative body or a governing board appointed by that body.

In many respects, local defender agencies or local branches of statewide agencies present a mirror image of a local prosecutor's office. Individual offices range in size from a single part-time defender to a staff of more than 200 lawyers. A majority of all local public defender offices employ 3 or fewer lawyers. Larger offices are likely to include such support personnel as investigators and paralegals. However, lawyers in those offices are also likely to have very heavy caseloads (e.g., close to 200 cases per year for a deputy handling felonies, and nearly 500 for the misdemeanor deputy). While most offices assign each client to a single lawyer, some use a horizontal assignment system similar to that found in prosecutor's offices. Separate deputies may handle the first appearance, preliminary hearing, pretrial motions, and the trial.

As with local prosecutor's offices, defender offices tend to hire young and relatively inexperienced attorneys and have a high employee turnover. Large offices, in particular, face a substantial problem of "burnout." Young lawyers enter the office filled with idealism and enthusiasm but frequently leave it disillusioned and cynical. Faced with a heavy caseload, judges who sometimes force them to take a backseat in scheduling to private practitioners, clients who sometimes misuse them and often suspect their motives (or at least view them as second-rate attorneys), and cases requiring infrequent use of their trial skills, deputy defenders often are ready to give up on defense work after only a few years (turning instead to a private civil practice or the prosecutor's office). Thus, a nationwide survey found that only about one-third of the deputies had more than four years service with their agency.

Private practitioners. The representation of criminal defendants is shared by a surprisingly small segment of the roughly 400,000 members of the private bar.[c] A good many general practitioners, particu-

b. The federal system uses a combination of the major assignment systems, with federal defender agencies located only in the more heavily populated judicial districts. Overall, representation of indigents in the federal courts is split almost equally between defender organizations and private attorneys.

c. See Wice, *Criminal Lawyers: An Endangered Species* 29 (1978) (estimating the total number of lawyers, excluding defenders, who "accept criminal cases 'more than occasionally'" as falling between 6,000 and 16,000); Carlin, *Lawyers' Ethics* 12 (1966) (author's sampling indicated that no more than 1% of all private practitioners in larly in smaller communities, will handle a few criminal cases each year, but studies of defense representation in medium and large cities indicate that the private bar is represented primarily by a small group of attorneys who specialize in criminal cases.[d]

A substantial majority of all lawyers either never take a criminal case or do so only on rare occasions. These lawyers commonly view criminal defense work as one of the least desirable fields of specialization. Compensation tends to be lower than that of practitioners in other fields (even defendants able to retain counsel are likely to have fairly limited financial resources), and collection of the fee is often a difficult task (leading many defense lawyers to insist upon an "up-front" payment). Perhaps even more important, the working conditions are decidedly unappealing, at least to the average practitioner. The defense counsel must expect to spend most of his time in police stations, jails, and the crowded (and often hectic) misdemeanor courts. His clients generally will be people who have committed acts which he views as questionable at best. He must be reconciled to the fact that, no matter how great his ability, he will "lose" most of his cases (in the sense that his clients will be convicted). Finally, as compared to lawyers in other fields, the defense specialist is likely to rank low in public esteem and in reputation among fellow-lawyers. Of course, many very good lawyers do make criminal law their specialty, but most lawyers with other options prefer those alternatives.

THE JUDICIARY [a]

Magistrate courts. The courts of first instance in the administration of the criminal justice process ordinarily are the courts of limited jurisdiction. These courts are known in different jurisdictions as magistrate courts, justice of the peace courts, municipal courts, district courts, police courts, and recorder's courts.[b] We will refer to them simply as magistrate courts. The magistrate courts traditionally have

Manhattan and the Bronx considered criminal law their main area of practice).

d. A specialist for this purpose is not limited to attorneys who spend all of their time in the criminal practice, but also includes those who treat it as a specialty by devoting at least 25% of their time to criminal cases. See Wood, *Criminal Lawyers* (1967). These criminal law specialists include the white collar crime experts in the large corporate firms, the high powered and sometimes flamboyant lawyers who are noted for their favorable record in highly publicized homicide cases, and the substance abuse experts who can count among their clients the rich and famous. But the specialists who handle the highest volume of cases come from two groups who rank considerably farther down the socio-economic ladder of the bar—the young lawyers who seek court appointments (in jurisdictions without public defenders) to provide a steady monetary base in the building of their practices, and the so-called "courthouse regulars" (usually having offices in a "down on the heels" district located close to the courthouse, and commonly described as the "bar" of that district, as in Detroit's "Clinton Street Bar"). The latter group take occasional assignments, but usually rely on a private clientele developed through direct solicitation of unrepresented defendants awaiting court appearances and through contacts with bailbondsmen and others who might recommend them to prospective clients.

a. The data contained in this section is taken primarily from B.J.S., *State Court Caseload Statistics* (1983); National Center for State Courts, *State Court Organization* (1984); Stille, *The Judiciary's New Look, Nat'l.L.S.,* Dec. 30, 1985, p. 1.

b. In the federal system, there is not a separate magistrate court, but United States magistrates perform the same functions as part of the District Court. The position of United States magistrate was created in 1968 to replace the former United States commissioners. Unlike the commissioners, the magistrates must be lawyers, although some may serve on a part-time basis. The full-time and part-time magistrates are selected by a majority of the judges of the District Court and serve for periods of 8 and 4 years respectively. Magistrates have trial jurisdiction over all federal misdemeanors, subject to one major limitation—the defendant can always elect a trial before the district court rather than the magistrate. Where a misdemeanor case is tried to a magistrate, a convicted defendant is then entitled to appellate review on the record before the district court. Magistrates also may perform various functions applicable to all offenses. These include issuance of search and arrest warrants, conducting the first appearances of arrested persons, and setting bail. In addition, magistrates hold preliminary examinations in felony cases and, where requested by the district court, pretrial discovery proceedings in such cases.

trial jurisdiction over lower-level criminal offenses. In some states, this trial jurisdiction extends to all misdemeanors; in other states, it is limited either to misdemeanors punishable by no more than 90 days imprisonment or to misdemeanors punishable by no more than 6 months imprisonment. In addition to their trial jurisdiction, magistrate courts have a limited jurisdiction in the processing of felonies and any misdemeanors that are beyond their trial authority. Cases involving those offenses are brought before the magistrate court for preliminary processing before they are sent to the courts of general jurisdiction where they can be tried. The preliminary matters that may be handled by the magistrate include: the issuance of search and arrest warrants; the first appearance of the arrested person before a court; the setting of bail; the appointment of counsel for indigent defendants; and a preliminary hearing review of the sufficiency of the evidence to proceed on the charge. As we shall see in later chapters, these are most important functions that can have considerable bearing on the disposition of the case. Of course, magistrate courts also handle those preliminary procedures that are applicable to the misdemeanors within their trial jurisdiction.

The structure and staffing of magistrate courts differ considerably from state to state. Perhaps the greatest variation is found in the drawing of the judicial districts served by the magistrate courts. Some states have divided the state into uniform districts with the same type of magistrate court for each district. Others have districts that coincide with different political subdivisions (city, township, village, etc.). In these states, there may be several different types of magistrate courts, each with different limits on their trial jurisdiction, different qualifications required for their judges, and even different procedures for review of their decisions. In New York state, for example, there are seven different courts that perform the traditional functions of magistrate courts. These include a special criminal court for New York City, a county court for two of the more populous counties, city courts in most cities, and justice of the peace courts in various towns and villages.

In over half of the states, at least one of the magistrate courts is a court "not of record." Historically, courts not of record lacked the capacity to prepare a fairly complete transcript of their trials. Without that record, their decisions in misdemeanor cases could not be subjected to the traditional form of appellate review. Accordingly, on appeal, the higher court simply gave the case *de novo* consideration through a new trial. Today, the magistrate courts not of record often have the facilities to provide a verbatim transcript of their proceedings, but convictions in their court remain subject to review by a trial *de novo* before a trial court of general jurisdiction. The trial *de novo* procedure has been retained, in large part, due to concern that a person convicted of a misdemeanor should be entitled to a more formal and thorough trial than is provided in courts not of record. Magistrates in such courts often are not lawyers, and they may follow the traditional rules governing trials only in a rather loose fashion.

Almost all states permit judges in at least some magistrate courts to serve as part-time jurists. Where the judges are lawyers, state law commonly restricts their private practice to avoid a conflict of interest with their judicial duties. In approximately 40 states, judges in at least some magistrate courts need not be lawyers.[c]

c. See generally, Silberman, *Non-Attorney Justice in the United States: An Empirical Study* (1979). While the number of non-lawyer judges in the United States is high (estimated at 13,000 to 14,000), their significance as measured by the population serviced is uncertain. Many serve in judicial districts confined to a single township or village, so that a substantial number of part-time lay judges may serve a population no greater than that of a single, full-time, lawyer-judge in a municipal court. Also, over one-third of all of the lay judges are found in 3 states, Georgia, New York and Texas.

Typically, a state will require that judges of magistrate courts in metropolitan areas be lawyers and serve full-time, while judges in rural magistrate courts may be nonlawyers and may serve part-time.[d] Ordinarily, lay judges sit only in courts not of record so that defendants convicted in their courts may obtain a trial *de novo* review before general trial court (which will have an attorney-judge). In most jurisdictions, judges of the magistrate court, whether lawyers or laymen, are elected to office.[e] The remaining states fill magistrate judgeships through the appointment process, with appointment made either by the governor or by local government officials.

Over the years, commentators and national commissions have repeatedly cited the importance of the magistrate courts and the need for improvement in their administration.[f] Magistrate courts in the rural areas have been criticized for their lack of legal competency and the lack of dignity and decorum in their courtrooms. Lay judges, it has been argued, too often ignore the law and reflect a local bias rather than the "good common sense" that is allegedly their strongpoint. Where prosecutors or police are not available to present the case, lay magistrates too frequently seek to prosecute the cases themselves. Their courts too often are housed in stores, fire stations, and other unsuitable quarters, and too frequently are closed when they are most needed (usually because the judge must tend to his primary occupation). Complaints as to the lack of dignity and decorum have also been leveled at the magistrate courts in metropolitan areas, where a form of "assembly line justice" too frequently prevails. In those courts, it is argued, judges tend to place greater emphasis on the speedy disposition of cases rather than assuring that the correct result is attained in the individual case. With their crowded facilities, lack of adequate staffing, and routinized procedures, big city magistrate courts create an atmosphere, critics contend, that is more appropriate for a supermarket than a court of justice.

In recent years, state legislatures have sought to respond to these criticisms, although few have undertaken the "massive overhaul" of the lower courts recommended by the critics. Lay judges have been required to participate in training programs, and even to pass examinations testing their legal knowledge. Magistrates have been required to extend their hours so that defendants arrested on weekends may be promptly presented. Various measures have been adopted to provide some relief from the pressure of the tremendously heavy caseloads typically borne by the urban courts. Traffic cases have either been removed from the court's jurisdiction or largely assigned to court personnel other than the judges. To reduce the civil docket, more cases have been brought within the range of the small claims divi-

d. In recent years, various reforms have been introduced to limit the role of lay judges. Several states have restricted the use of such judges to judicial districts with small populations. These are the districts in which it usually is most difficult to find a lawyer to fill the post. Other states have limited the lay judge's trial jurisdiction in misdemeanor cases to the acceptance of guilty pleas. Several states prohibit lay judges from imposing a sentence of imprisonment. Finally, there are approximately 10 states that either deny lay judges any criminal jurisdiction or prohibit lay judges entirely.

e. While a majority of the states still select judges at all levels through contested elections (see p. 31 infra), that selection method remains particularly popular for magistrate courts. The many jurisdictions which now select their higher court judges through the Missouri Plan (or some other method of appointment plus approval/disapproval elections) have not carried that reform over to the selection of magistrates.

f. Indeed, several distinguished commissions have argued that separate magistrate courts should be abolished and their jurisdiction transferred to the trial courts of general jurisdiction. Only a few states have adopted this recommendation, however. In these states, preliminary proceedings in felony cases and misdemeanor trials are part of the general trial court's jurisdiction, but those duties commonly are assigned to special judicial officers appointed by the court. A similar approach is taken in the federal courts. See fn. b supra.

sion of the court.[g] Decriminalization of public drunkenness (which otherwise might constitute as much as 15–20 percent of the misdemeanor docket) has helped to reduce the misdemeanor docket. Even with such reforms, however, the caseload per judge, including misdemeanors, minor civil cases, and preliminary proceedings in felony cases, can easily reach 2,000 cases a year in a busy urban court.

Trials courts of general jurisdiction. The courts that try felony cases (and any misdemeanors beyond the magistrate court's trial jurisdiction) are the basic trial courts that you have encountered in your civil law courses. In the federal system, that court is the United States District Court. In the state system, the felony trial court is the court of general jurisdiction (commonly called the superior court, circuit court, or district court). In addition to its felony trial jurisdiction, this court will also provide the first level of appellate review for misdemeanors tried in the magistrate court (although, as noted previously, that review may be by trial *de novo* in many states).

Judges of courts of general jurisdiction are selected in a variety of different ways. A few states use an appointive process similar to that found in the federal system. Many more use the Missouri Plan, and the majority use a contested election (either partisan or non-partisan). Even with an election system, however, a majority of the judges will have been initially appointed to fill an interim vacancy and then elected as an incumbent. Although many jurisdictions have statutory prerequisites of a minimum number of years in practice, this does not ensure that newly selected judges will have had any practice experience in the criminal field.[h] Even if that is not the case, however, criminal cases constitute such a substantial portion of the trial judge's workload that the newly selected judge is likely to gain such experience rather rapidly.

The criminal caseload of the general trial court typically constitutes anywhere from 15 to 40 percent of the court's docket, with the lower figure applicable primarily where that docket includes juvenile and probate cases in addition to the traditional civil cases. Moreover, when caseloads are weighted according to the time spent on the particular type of case, the significance of the criminal docket increases at least twofold. Weighted caseload formulas commonly attach a substantially higher weight to criminal cases than to almost all types of civil cases. Although, as we have seen, only a small percentage of felony cases actually go to trial, that rate is still much higher than the trial rate in civil cases. Thus, in a jurisdiction in which criminal cases constitute no more than 25% of the total docket, they can readily provide over 50% of all jury trials.

Appellate courts. Except for a few state appellate courts that hear only criminal appeals, the appellate courts reviewing decisions in criminal cases are the same courts that deal with civil appeals. In approximately two-thirds of the states, those courts are, first, an intermediate

g. Even without such a reduction, the civil docket ordinarily will be somewhat smaller than the criminal docket. For a typical court with a medium range civil jurisdiction (e.g., cases involving sums of $1,000 or less), the non-traffic docket might be divided between 20 percent civil cases, 60 percent misdemeanor cases, and 10 percent felony cases. Moreover, criminal cases are more likely to require a time-consuming hearing (a trial in a misdemeanor case and a preliminary hearing in a criminal case) than a civil case.

h. The percentage of newly selected judges with some experience in criminal cases is often greater than the comparative experience in the bar as a whole. Those persons who seek the office very often are trial lawyers who started their careers in the office of the prosecutor or public defender or took criminal cases by appointment. As with the bar generally, the percentage of racial minorities and women on the bench is disproportionate to the population, but there is considerable variation from one jurisdiction to another. Compare, e.g., Alaska (22% of the judiciary are women) with New Hampshire (less than 3% women), and Maryland (10% black) with several states without any black members of the judiciary.

court of appeals, and then the highest state court. In the remainder of the states, there is simply the state supreme court. In the federal system, appeals are taken initially to the United States Court of Appeals and then to the Supreme Court. Most of the cases reviewed by the various appellate courts involve convictions at the trial level that are being appealed by the defendant. The convicted defendant ordinarily will have an automatic right to appeal to the next highest court. Any further appellate review generally lies in the discretion of the higher appellate court. In those appellate courts as to which there is an automatic right to review, criminal cases are likely to constitute at least one-third, and often more than half, of the total docket. Among appellate courts having discretion as to the cases they review, the proportion of criminal cases may be somewhat lower, but the percentage still is not likely to dip below 25%.

SECTION 3. THE ADMINISTRATIVE ENVIRONMENT

As Roscoe Pound noted in the seminal empirical study of the twentieth century criminal justice process, an understanding of that process requires consideration not only of the legal institutions involved, but also of the "environment" in which those institutions operate.[a] That environment, however, is exceedingly complex and varied. It is the product of a broad range of political and social forces, the nature of crime itself, and the institutional structure of the agencies that administer the process. A complete description of the current administrative environment, even if one were to ignore the variations from one community to another, would take far more space than we have available. Indeed, it is hard to find any one volume that successfully presents such a description. We believe, however, that a picture somewhat distorted by a lack of completeness can nevertheless be helpful, and certainly is to be preferred to totally ignoring the influence of the administrative environment upon the operation of the process. The elements discussed below are offered not as a complete list of the most influential factors shaping that environment, but as illustrative of the type of factors that must be considered to gain a full understanding of what makes the process what it is.

Variety of offenses and offenders. The criminal justice process must deal with a tremendously large range of offenses and offenders. Actions classified as criminal include, for example, violent crimes against the person, property crimes, public-order crimes, regulatory offenses, vice offenses, and the misuse of positions of trust. Offenders include persons who act out of passion, persons acting under influence of alcohol or drugs, and persons who act in a cold and calculated attempt to gain profit. They include the young and the old (although the vast majority are under 30), the first-time offender and the recidivist, the offender who operates by himself and the offender who works with confederates (sometimes as part of a large criminal organization). Almost every crime, as defined by the legislature, will encompass significant differences in behavior and motivation. A burglary, for example, encompasses various modes of entry into different types of buildings by persons intending different ulterior crimes. Persons guilty of theft from a building will include, among others, the teenager showing off to his peers, the respectable member of the community who "can't resist the temptation," and the professional "booster." Robbery may be the work of the unemployed youth who suddenly spots a particularly vulnerable victim walking alone on a dark street, a seasoned expert who spe-

a. Pound, *Criminal Justice in the American City* in Criminal Justice in Cleveland 562 (Pound and Frankfurter, eds., 1922) (noting also the need to consider the "men by whom [the process] is administered" and the "practical limitations and practical difficulties inherent in the legal ordering of human relations").

cializes in the carefully planned hold-ups of establishments that yield the "highest score" (e.g., banks or payroll offices), or the lesser professional who looks to small business establishments that are open late at night (e.g., gas stations).

The great diversity in offenses and offenders requires that the process allow for considerable flexibility, particularly at the investigatory stage. Investigative procedures that are more than adequate in dealing with most types of crimes may be of little value in handling others. Accordingly, the process includes a broad range of investigatory tools, designed to facilitate the enforcement of the total range of offenses. Indeed, many of the investigative practices that have proven most controversial (e.g., paid informants and electronic eavesdropping) have been supported on the ground that they are essential to the successful investigation of particular types of crime.

Flexibility is also provided in the substantial discretionary authority granted to police officers, prosecutors, and judges. Through that authority, distinctions can be drawn that are not necessarily recognized in the statutes but are consistent nonetheless with the general goals of the criminal law. Consideration can be given, for example, to the character of the offender, the circumstances under which he acted, and the degree of harm caused. The availability of discretion also permits priorities to be set in use of limited resources. With a substantial portion of certain serious offenses being committed by a disproportionately small percentage of repeat offenders, it would be surprising if the criminal justice process did not provide some way in which investigatory and prosecutorial resources could be concentrated on those recidivists.

Public concern. Few legal institutions deal with a subject of greater concern to the public than the criminal justice process. Crime has for many years been viewed as one of the most serious (if not *the* most serious) social problem facing this country. This widespread public concern is reflected in public opinion polls, the speeches of public officials, and media coverage. Although some contend that numerous other social ills are more significant, that crime is a major problem in this country can hardly be denied. Every possible measuring stick establishes its extensive pernicious impact upon our daily lives.[b]

The status of crime as a primary subject of public concern is felt in various ways by the criminal justice process. The administration of the process is constantly in the spotlight, with every failing receiving media attention. Criticism and proposed reform of the process have become almost as inevitable as death and taxes.[c] The process has been the subject of continupus

b. Consider, for example, the following indicators: (1) the rate of reported crimes to population (roughly 5,000 for each 100,000 persons, counting only Index crimes); (2) the general upward trend of that crime rate over the past few decades (although there has been a shift downward in the past several years, the 1984 rate is roughly 3 times that of 1954); (3) the substantial economic losses resulting from crime (the cost of personal and household crimes alone exceeds 10 billion annually and the cost of economic crimes to the business community has been estimated as exceeding 3 or 4 times that amount); (4) the number of victimizations each year (over 40 million for just those crimes covered in the National Crime Survey); and (5) the percentage of households immediately affected (over the period 1975–84, between 32% to 26% of all households were victimized annually by one or more of the Index crimes).

c. For the most part these changes have not been billed as likely to have a substantial impact on the crime rate itself except insofar as a more efficient process may result in the incarceration of more persons who would otherwise be committing crimes. Increases in the crime rate generally have been attributed by legislative leaders to causes admittedly beyond the influence of the process. These include: (1) increased urbanization, combined with deterioration of the innercity; (2) increases in the percentage of persons who fall within the age range of those most likely to commit crimes; (3) a decline in the influence of family, school, and the church; (4) an increasingly materialistic society, with expectations heightened by the constant displays of wealth brought home through the mass media to those who have little or no opportunity to gain "their share" except through crime; (5) the increased use of drugs; and (6) racial and other prejudices that political debate, endless hearings and commission reports, and one legislative change after another. Faced with a bewildering panoply of new ideas, legislatures have been sorely tempted to try each in turn. As a result, policy often has shifted back and forth in an attempt to find the "right" answer and to convince the public that "something is being done." [d]

The public's reaction to violent crime has a special quality, somewhat distinct from the reaction to the overall problem of crime. Violent crime often generates, not simply a basic concern, but a sense of fear, frustration, and outrage. Whether the current reaction to violent crime far exceeds the true scope of the problem (as some suggest[e]), or is grounded on "the harsh reality" of today's urban communities (as others suggest[f]), it is clear that a pervasive feeling of fear and outrage has been building in this country, almost without interruption, since the mid-1960's. Perhaps the most patent reflection of that feeling is to be found in special sentencing legislation aimed at violent offenders, but it would be amazing if such a deeply felt reaction was not also reflected in less direct ways. Arguably, that state of public agitation partially explains what may be viewed as excesses in actions by police and prosecutors.[g] It surely contributes as well

have created disrespect for society and its laws among a significant segment of the population. There are those, however, who see the system itself as contributing to the increase in crime rates, arguing that the failure of the process to deliver swift and sure punishment has emboldened those who might otherwise have been deterred from committing crimes. See generally, Miller, *Ideology and Criminal Justice,* 64 J.Crim. L. & Criminology 41 (1973).

d. Thus, that "something" has included both changes designed to make the process more "humane" (e.g., liberalized pretrial release) and changes designed to make the system "tougher" (e.g., mandatory prison terms). It included both a massive influx of federal funding (through the now defunct Law Enforcement Assistant Agency grant program), used to promote statewide planning, innovative programs, and the purchase of sophisticated equipment, and substantially increased state expenditure to build more prisons.

e. See Reiss, *How Serious is Serious Crime?,* 35 Vand.L. 541 (1982). The public's fear of violence, it is argued, is largely the product of sensationalistic reporting by the press and the irresponsible rhetoric of politicians, rather than a careful evaluation of the actual likelihood of suffering death or physical injury from violent crimes. Violent crimes affect approximately 6% of all households annually, and a substantial portion of those crimes (roughly 40%) involve acquaintances rather than the stranger-crime that is so greatly feared. Of those victimized by violent strangers, only 1 in 20 receive a serious injury (i.e., a knife or gunshot wound, broken bones, or internal injury), although 1 in 4 receive some minor injury. See B.J.S., *Violent Crimes by Strangers* (1982). The chance of dying in an automobile accident is more than twice that of being a homicide victim and the chance of accidental injury is more than 5 times greater than the chance of being a victim (with or without injury) of a violent crime. See B.J.S., *Report to the Nation on Crime and Justice* 18 (1983). Of course, the risks are greater for some than others. Among black males under the age of 34, the greatest cause of death is not vehicle accidents, but homicides. Indeed, 1 nonwhite baby out of every 28 born in this country is likely to die of homicide. F.B.I., *Uniform Crime Reports* 339–41 (1981). But the groups of persons expressing the greatest fear of crime often are those least likely to be victimized.

f. See Silberman, *Criminal Violence, Criminal Justice* 5–26 (1980). The key, it argued, is not so much the injuries caused by violent crime, but the impact of the event upon the psyche. "Violence at the hands of a stranger is far more frightening than a comparable injury suffered in an automobile injury or fall"; it suggests a "fraying of the bonds of society," an inability to assume that one is safe among strangers. Ibid. Considering this special impact of violent crime, the rate of such crime in this country, though far lower than the rate for property crimes, must be viewed as exceptionally high. It far exceeds that in any other stable democracy. And while the rate of violent crime has decreased in the last several years, the overall trend over the last few decades has been sharply upward. At the same time, it is argued, there is evidence that violent offenders, particularly youths, have become more brutal and vicious.

g. Indeed, it may influence as well the reaction of the courts to those excesses. See Allen, *A Serendipitous Trek Through the Advance-Sheet Jungle: Criminal Justice in the Courts of Review,* 70 Iowa L.Rev. 311, 316 (1985): "It is inevitable, of course, that when public frustrations, fears, and outrage are widespread and reach the levels of intensity of those associated with the American crime problem during the last two decades, the same attitudes, reactions, and assumptions will be given judicial expression. * * * The judges reflect the public mood because the judges are, in the first instance, members of society and are susceptible to the same movements of thought and emotion that influence the commuto the racial tensions reflected in police/community relations in so many cities. A substantially disproportionate number of violent crimes are committed by young black males (largely against other members of their own community).[h] With the police giving the highest priority to violent crimes, those also are the persons most frequently stopped and most frequently arrested.[i]

Image of inefficiency. More and more the image of the criminal justice system in the public eye is one of inefficiency. The common complaint is that too few reported crimes result in arrests, too few arrests result in convictions, and too few convictions result in incarceration. Time and again the media cite statistics suggesting that crime indeed can be made to pay. In New York City, it is noted, "out of 550,000 reported crimes, police made 106,000 arrests, but only 13,500 suspects wound up behind bars." [j] The chance of a burglar going to jail for a single crime, it is said, is only 1 in 400. At times, it is noted, the system is almost Kafkaesque; an arrested offender may be released on stationhouse bail while his victim remains at the station, still waiting for someone to take his statement.

Many experts would argue that such criticism rests on a superficial analysis of the process. The system on the whole, they argue, is clearly efficient, given its limited resources. Aspects commonly cited as evidencing inefficiency, such as the case attrition between arrest and incarceration, actually reflect a rational allocation of those resources to matters of highest priority. Be that as it may, the image remains, and it presents a substantial threat, in particular, to the system's ability to gain citizen support. As a result, the system has sought to respond in various ways.[k] Victim/witness service programs and community relations projects have been developed to encourage citizens both to report crimes and appear as witnesses.[l] At least

nity at large. In general, the appellate opinions do not directly express the outrage and revulsion that the facts of the cases being reviewed often inspire; such indulgence in overt emotion is contrary to the dispassionate mode aspired to by most writers of appellate opinions. Occasionally, however, the inhibitions and restraints break down, and one finds a statement like that in a recent Mississippi case:

> 'The callous and senseless murders of these young people, who had the inalienable right to life and the pursuit of happiness, were atrocious and heinous beyond description. In reflecting upon the species Homo sapiens, now supposedly advanced to an enlightened and civilized age, we cannot help but wonder—how could it ever enter into the heart of man to take the lives so brutally of two such innocent young people.' "

h. The percentage of black offenders over a several year period as reported by victims in the National Crime Survey, fell within 24–44% range for rapes, 34–51% range for personal-sector robberies, and 22–31% range for aggravated assaults. See Curtis (ed.), *American Violence and Public Policy,* table 18 (1985). The percentage of blacks of those persons arrested for crimes of violence over a several year period fell within the low of 36–49% for aggravated assault to the high of 57–66% for robberies. Id. at table 17. Roughly 75% of all crimes of violence are intraracial. B.J.S., *Violent Crime in the United States* 23 (1981).

i. Indeed, "about one-half of the nonwhite males who grow up and continue to live in large cities—compared with 14% of the white males—probably will be arrested at some point in their lifetimes." Reiss, fn. e supra, at 568. With violent offenders most likely to be incarcerated, blacks constitute a disproportionate number (roughly 50%) of the inmates in prisons and jails. See B.J.S., *Violent Crime in the United States* 32 (1981).

j. *Time,* April 8, 1985, p. 29.

k. So too, the system has found it necessary to respond to other negative images, less widely shared but still accepted by sufficient numbers of people to prove troublesome. These include the views that the system is racist, that it favors certain classes of persons, that it is riddled by corruption in many communities, and that its officials are looking primarily to serve their own interests (e.g., that police are simply interested in "putting in their time and collecting their pensions," that judges are interested primarily in "getting home early," that defense counsel are willing to "shave corners" to earn larger fees, and that prosecutors are interested primarily in "having a good scoresheet").

l. Victim protection legislation, for example, permits victims to present their views to the court in sentencing, requires restitution as a condition of probation, mandates continuous prosecutor consultation with the victim, and seeks to make witness appearances less burdensome. See e.g., Fla.Stat. §§ 914.16–914.21.

some police departments and prosecutor's offices have thought it necessary to present their case to the public, to proclaim their successes and explain why they did not proceed in particular cases. So too, judges have found it desirable to devote considerable energy to obtaining the proper decorum in the courtroom and to keeping in mind the press coverage of any proceeding of special public interest. Indeed, various criminal justice agencies have found it necessary to add to their roster a public relations officer.

The impact of fragmentation. As noted in our description of police and prosecutor agencies, both police and prosecutorial authority is divided among a multitude of agencies, found primarily at the local level. This fragmentized structure is designed to serve various goals. It seeks to avoid the potential dangers of centralized power, particularly the threat to democratic institutions that might be posed by the misuse of an all powerful national police force. It seeks to preserve the values of local control (e.g., accountability to the population most immediately affected, development of a community sense of responsibility for law enforcement, and administration in accordance with local conditions). It seeks to facilitate experimentation and to allow for the diversity needed in a pluralist society. It is debatable whether or not the degree of fragmentation currently existing goes far beyond what is necessary to achieve these goals.[m] Few would suggest, however, that our current state of fragmentation does not make the task of law enforcement more costly and less efficient.[n]

Fragmentation has produced numerous prosecutor's offices and police agencies so small as to adversely effect their efficiency. Small police departments often have difficulty recruiting qualified personnel since they offer limited opportunity for advancement.[o] Unless they can work out a cooperative venture with other departments, they are likely to lack the enrollment or expertise needed to provide an effective training program. Their staffing is too limited to develop investigation specialists or experts in the use of sophisticated equipment and information systems. And while assistance in those areas may be obtained from larger agencies, such services may not be as readily utilized (or as readily available) when not provided by the department itself. Size limitations arguably are not as critical in the prosecu-

m. Over the years, various commissions have argued for consolidation of police and prosecutor agencies to produce a less fragmented structure. Indeed, the development of a centralized, statewide system of prosecution was recommended by the first of the major national commissions, the Wickersham Commission, in 1931. Although there has been some movement toward consolidation, particularly in the elimination of police forces with less than 10 officers (a proposal of the 1973 National Advisory Commission on Criminal Justice Standards and Goals), reform generally has focused on establishing new agencies that might facilitate coordination and cooperative ventures. See Skoler, *Organizing the Non-System* 249–89 (1979). At the same time, however, there has been a movement in some quarters towards decentralization of authority in larger police agencies. See Danzig, *Toward the Creation of A Complementary, Decentralized System of Criminal Justice,* 26 Stan. 1 (1973). There has been a much more substantial movement toward consolidation with respect to judicial agencies, where many jurisdictions have moved to a unified and simplified court system. See Skoler, supra, at 204–05.

n. These consequences are commonly viewed as unfortunate costs of fragmentation, although many would argue that such costs are more than offset by the benefits of localism. Still other consequences of fragmentation are considered unfortunate costs by some and desirable attributes by others. These include the inevitable inconsistencies in the administration of justice among different communities (e.g., local prosecutors in adjoining districts may differ as to whether or not similar action by similar offenders justifies prosecution), and the ability of local political groups to influence the selection of high-level officials who are not themselves elected (e.g., a police chief).

o. The turnover rate in small police departments (those with fewer than 25 officers) is almost 7 times as high (22.4%) as that in the largest departments (those with over 2,000 employees). N.I.J., *The National Manpower Survey* 64 (1978). Because police departments generally do not accept lateral entries, the officer finding his path to advancement blocked by a scarcity of openings generally must either bide his time or leave police work.

tor's office, but they are felt in special situations. Small offices, because they use part-time prosecutors, more often face serious conflict of interest difficulties. Where the prosecution of a particular crime requires special investigatory or legal expertise, or substantial manpower, the small office is likely to be at a serious disadvantage. Additionally, the prolonged illness of a prosecutor in a one or two person office can result in a logjam that sets the entire criminal docket back for months or even years.

Even where the agencies involved are sufficiently large to take advantage of economics of scale, fragmentation adds expense and administrative difficulties. The multiplicity of federal, state, and local police agencies having some law enforcement responsibilities in the same metropolitan community almost invariably produces some duplication of services and not infrequently fosters a tension between agencies that leads to competitiveness rather than cooperation. Moreover, not all crimes stop at the borders of the particular community. Where the primary responsibility for investigation or prosecution lies with local agencies, there often is a need for coordination between prosecutors of different counties or police departments of different cities that is not easily achieved. The common division of police and prosecutorial authority along different unit lines (city vs. county) also makes it difficult to achieve any substantial degree of budgetary coordination.[p]

Caseload pressures. As Professor Francis Allen has observed: "The American system of criminal justice is confronted by quantitative demands that exceed the capacities of its resources and procedures. The administration of criminal justice groans under a stifling and increasing weight of numbers—numbers of offenses, of accused persons, and of convicted offenders."[q] Of course, caseloads vary considerably from one jurisdiction or another, and many counties have quite acceptable caseloads. But in those judicial districts containing the 60 or so cities with a population over 250,000 (which alone report roughly 40% of all Index crimes) and in the districts containing the heavily populated suburbs of those cities, the vast majority of agencies have caseloads that exceed the maximum that experts consider compatible with the highest professional standards of performance. It is not uncommon, for example, for a trial judge of general jurisdiction in a metropolitan area to have a combined caseload of civil and criminal cases that exceeds 600 per year, and the magistrate's caseload can easily exceed 2,000 cases annually. In the same jurisdiction, the prosecutor's office is likely to have a caseload that equals 100 felonies and 600 misdemeanors for each assistant. In the defender's office, deputies assigned to felony cases may carry over 200 cases per year and those assigned to misdemeanor cases may well be assigned over 500 cases per year. Only the police caseload of 100 reported crimes per officer may seem fairly light, but the burden of that caseload is magnified tremendously when one considers the limited portion of police time that will be devoted to the investigation of reported crimes.

p. To some extent, all of the major agencies involved in the administration of the criminal justice process are contiguous and functionally interdependent. Each is but one component in an integrated process. To give one component additional funds to speed-up the process makes little sense if other components are not similarly assisted. Yet, the different components commonly receive their funding from different governmental units, each drawing on a separate source of revenue. Thus, a local police department will receive its funds from the city, a local prosecutor will be funded by the county, a local branch of a statewide court system will be supported by the state, and a public defender agency may be supported by a combination of local, state, and even private funds.

q. Allen, *Central Problems of American Criminal Justice,* 75 Mich.L.Rev. 813, 818 (1977). See also Nardilli, *The Caseload Controversy and the Study of Criminal Courts,* 70 J.Crim.L. & Criminology 89 (1979). Data on caseloads is taken from the sources cited in fn. c, p. 3 supra, fn. a, p. 28 supra, and fn. c, p. 23 supra.

The pressure of heavy caseloads has an impact upon almost every facet of the administration of the criminal justice process. We have already noted the assembly line approach of some magistrate courts. Other consequences, such as the emphasis upon the disposition of cases without trial (particularly through plea bargaining) and increased reliance upon routinized decisionmaking, will be seen in many of the chapters that follow. Some observers contend that the most significant impact may be upon the self-image (and hence the performance) of the prosecutors, public defenders, and judges. They tend to see themselves, it is argued, as bureaucrats struggling to stay abreast of an ever increasing caseload rather than as lawyers fulfilling their traditional roles in the adversary process.[r]

r. See Blumberg, *Criminal Justice* (1970). The attitudes of other participants may be similarly influenced. Whether innocent or guilty, a defendant is unlikely to respect a system that seems to be interested primarily in the rapid movement of cases. So too, the victim is likely to be disillusioned by a system that may require him to make several trips to the courthouse or prosecutor's office without ever testifying, and that produces a result that all too often may never be explained to him. The police officer likewise may have little faith in a process he views as dominated by an assembly line mentality that values managerial efficiency over providing "just deserts."

Chapter 2

THE NATURE AND SCOPE OF FOURTEENTH AMENDMENT DUE PROCESS; RETROACTIVITY; THE FEDERAL "SUPERVISORY POWER"; STATE RIGHTS PROTECTIONS

SECTION 1. THE "ORDERED LIBERTY"—"FUNDAMENTAL FAIRNESS," "TOTAL INCORPORATION" AND "SELECTIVE INCORPORATION" THEORIES

In *Twining v. New Jersey,* 211 U.S. 78, 29 S.Ct. 14, 53 L.Ed. 97 (1908); *Palko v. Connecticut,* 302 U.S. 319, 58 S.Ct. 149, 82 L.Ed. 288 (1937); and *Adamson v. California,* 332 U.S. 46, 67 S.Ct. 1672, 91 L.Ed. 1903 (1947), the Court rejected the "total incorporation" view of the history of the Fourteenth Amendment, the view—which has never commanded a majority—that the Fourteenth Amendment made all of the provisions of the federal Bill of Rights fully applicable to the states.[a] But *Twining* recognized that "it is possible that some of the personal rights safeguarded by the first eight Amendments against National action may also be safeguarded against state action, because a denial of them would be a denial of due process of law." And the Court early found among

a. *Palko,* which held that the Fourteenth Amendment did not encompass at least certain aspects of double jeopardy prohibition of the Fifth Amendment, was later overruled in *Benton v. Maryland,* 395 U.S. 784, 89 S.Ct. 2056, 23 L.Ed.2d 707 (1969). The position taken in *Twining* and *Adamson*—that the Fifth Amendment privilege against self-incrimination was not incorporated in the Fourteenth—was rejected in *Malloy v. Hogan* (1964), discussed below. *Griffin v. California,* Ch. 24, § 4, subsequently applied *Malloy* to overrule the specific holdings of *Twining* and *Adamson,* which had permitted comment on a state defendant's failure to take the stand. These later decisions, while overruling *Palko, Twining* and *Adamson,* were still consistent with the rejection of the "total incorporation" interpretation.

The total incorporation position had received its strongest support in the *Adamson* dissents. In the principal dissent, Justice Black, joined by Douglas, J., maintained that the history of the Fourteenth Amendment suggested its purpose was to totally incorporate the federal Bill of Rights. Dissenting separately in *Adamson,* Justice Murphy, joined by Rutledge, J., "agree[d] that the specific guarantees of the Bill of Rights should be carried over intact into [the Fourteenth but was] not prepared to say that the latter is entirely and necessarily limited by the Bill of Rights. Occasions may arise where a proceeding falls so far short of conforming to fundamental standards of procedure as to warrant constitutional condemnation in terms of a lack of due process despite the absence of a specific provision of the Bill of Rights."

Responding to the dissents, Justice Frankfurter's concurring opinion in *Adamson* stressed the "independent potency" of the Fourteenth Amendment Due Process Clause, maintaining that that Amendment "neither comprehends the specific provisions by which the founders deemed it appropriate to restrict the federal government nor is confined to them."

the procedural requirements of Fourteenth Amendment due process certain rules paralleling provisions of the first eight amendments. For example, it held in *Powell v. Alabama* (1932) (discussed at pp. 73, 78 infra) that defendants in a capital case were denied due process when a state refused them the aid of counsel. "The logically critical thing, however," pointed out Justice Harlan years later, "was not that the rights had been found in the Bill of Rights, but that they were deemed [to] be fundamental." *Duncan v. Louisiana,* Ch. 22, § 1. (dissenting opinion joined by Stewart, J.).

Particular procedural safeguards included in the Bill of Rights were said to be applicable to the states if they were "implicit in the concept of ordered liberty," Cardozo J., in *Palko;* "of the very essence of a scheme of ordered liberty," ibid.; "a fair and enlightened system of justice would be impossible without them," ibid.; required by "the 'immutable principles of justice' as conceived by a civilized society," Frankfurter, J., concurring in *Adamson;* or "fundamental to the American scheme of justice," White, J., in *Duncan v. Louisiana.*

As Justice WHITE noted (fn. 14) for the Court in DUNCAN v. LOUISIANA, 391 U.S. 145, 88 S.Ct. 1444, 20 L.Ed.2d 491 (1968) (holding the Sixth Amendment right to jury trial applicable to the states via the Fourteenth), the different phraseology is not without significance:

"Earlier the Court can be seen as having asked, when inquiring into whether some particular procedural safeguard was required of a State, if a civilized system could be imagined that would not accord the particular protection [quoting from *Palko*]. The recent cases, on the other hand, have proceeded upon the valid assumption that state criminal processes are not imaginary and theoretical schemes but actual systems bearing virtually every characteristic of the common-law system that has been developing contemporaneously in England and this country. The question thus is whether given this kind of system a particular procedure is fundamental—whether, that is, a procedure is necessary to an Anglo-American regime of ordered liberty. It is this sort of inquiry that can justify the conclusions that state courts must exclude evidence seized in violation of the Fourth Amendment, *Mapp v. Ohio* [Ch. 5] [and] that state prosecutors may not comment on a defendant's failure to testify, *Griffin v. California* [Ch. 24, § 4] * * *. [Of] each of these determinations that a constitutional provision originally written to bind the Federal Government should bind the States as well it might be said that the limitation in question is not necessarily fundamental to fairness in every criminal system that might be imagined but is fundamental in the context of the criminal processes maintained by the American States.

"When the inquiry is approached in this way the question whether the States can impose criminal punishment without granting a jury trial appears quite different from the way it appeared in the older cases opining that States might abolish jury trial. A criminal process which was fair and equitable but used no juries is easy to imagine. It would make use of alternative guarantees and protections which would serve the purposes that the jury serves in the English and American systems. Yet no American State has undertaken to construct such a system. Instead, every American State, including Louisiana, uses the jury extensively, and imposes very serious punishments only after a trial at which the defendant has a right to a jury's verdict. In every State, including Louisiana, the structure and style of the criminal process—the supporting framework and the subsidiary procedures—are of the sort that naturally complement jury trial, and have developed in connection with and in reliance upon jury trial." [b]

Although the Court has remained unwilling to accept the total incorporationists' reading of the Fourteenth Amendment, in the 1960's it "selectively" "incorporated" or "absorbed" more and more of the specifics of the Bill of Rights into the Fourteenth Amendment. As Justice White observed in *Duncan:*

"In resolving conflicting claims concerning the meaning of this spacious [Fourteenth Amendment] language, the Court has looked increasingly to the Bill of Rights for guidance; many of the rights guaranteed by the first eight Amendments to the Constitution have been held to be protected against state action by the Due Process Clause of the Fourteenth Amendment. That clause now protects [the] Fourth Amendment rights to be free from unreasonable searches and seizures and to have excluded from criminal trials any evidence illegally seized; the right guaranteed by the Fifth Amendment to be free of compelled self-incrimination; and the Sixth Amendment rights to counsel, to a speedy and public trial [*Klopfer v. North Carolina,* Ch. 19, § 1], to confrontation of opposing witnesses [*Pointer v. Texas,* Ch. 14, § 1] and to compulsory process for obtaining witnesses [*Washington v. Texas,* Ch. 24, § 3]." [c]

Moreover, the Court seemed to be "incorporating" not only the basic notion or general concept of the "selected" provision of the Bill of Rights, but applying the provision to the states *to the same extent* it applied to the federal government. As some Justices, especially Harlan, protested, the federal guarantees were being incorporated into the Fourteenth "freighted with their entire accompanying body of federal doctrine" (Harlan, J., joined by Clark, J., dissenting in *Malloy v. Hogan,* discussed below); "jot-for-jot and case-for-case" (Harlan, J., joined by Stewart, J., dissenting in *Duncan*); "bag and baggage, however securely or insecurely affixed they may be by law and precedent to federal proceedings" (Fortas, J., concurring in *Duncan*).

Thus, Justice Brennan observed for a majority of the Court in *Malloy v. Hogan,* 378 U.S. 1, 84 S.Ct. 1489, 12 L.Ed.2d 653 (1964):

b. See also Justice Powell, concurring in the companion 1972 "jury unanimity" cases of *Johnson v. Louisiana* and *Apodaca v. Oregon* (discussed below) (fn. 9):

"I agree with Mr. Justice White's analysis in *Duncan* that the departure from earlier decisions was, in large measure, a product of a change in focus in the Court's approach to due process. No longer are questions regarding the constitutionality of particular criminal procedures resolved by focusing alone on the element in question and ascertaining whether a system of criminal justice might be imagined in which a fair trial could be afforded in the absence of that particular element. Rather, the focus is, as it should be, on the fundamentality of that element viewed in the context of the basic Anglo-American jurisprudential system common to the States. That approach to due process readily accounts both for the conclusion that jury trial *is* fundamental and that unanimity *is not.*"

c. See also Justice Black, joined by Douglas, J., concurring in *Duncan:* "[I] believe as strongly as ever that the Fourteenth Amendment was intended to make the Bill of Rights applicable to the States. I have been willing to support the selective incorporation doctrine, however, as an alternative, although perhaps less historically supportable than complete incorporation [because it] keeps judges from roaming at will in their own notions of what policies outside the Bill of Rights are desirable and what are not. And, most importantly for me, the selective incorporation process has the virtue of having already worked to make most of the Bill of Rights' protections applicable to the States."

In the area of criminal procedure, the Court has indeed come very close to incorporation of all of the relevant Bill of Rights guarantees. In addition to the provisions noted above, the double jeopardy prohibition has also been made applicable to the states in *Benton,* fn. a supra. The Court has refused, however, to apply to the states the Fifth Amendment requirement that prosecution be initiated by grand jury indictment. See Ch. 15. On the application of the prohibition against excessive bail, see Ch. 12. See also Israel, *Selective Incorporation Revisited,* 71 Geo. L.J. 253 (1982), for an overview of the development and application of the selective incorporation doctrine.

"We hold that the Fourteenth Amendment guaranteed the petitioner the protection of the Fifth Amendment's privilege against self-incrimination, and that *under the applicable federal standard,* the [state court] erred in holding that the privilege was not properly invoked. [The State urges] that the availability of the federal privilege to a witness in a state inquiry is to be determined according to a less stringent safeguard than is applicable in a federal proceeding. We disagree. We have held that the guarantees of the First Amendment, the prohibition of unreasonable searches and seizures of the Fourth Amendment, *Ker v. California* [p. 329 infra], and the right to counsel guaranteed by the Sixth Amendment, *Gideon v. Wainwright* [p. 77 infra], are all to be enforced against the States under the Fourteenth Amendment *according to the same standards that protect those personal rights against federal encroachment.* [The] Court thus has rejected the notion that the Fourteenth Amendment applies to the States only a 'watered-down, subjective version of the individual guarantees of the Bill of Rights.'" (Emphasis added.)

And Justice White put it for a majority of the Court in *Duncan:* "Because we believe that trial by jury in criminal cases is fundamental to the American scheme of justice, we hold that the Fourteenth Amendment guarantees a right of jury trial in all criminal cases which—*were they to be tried in a federal court*—would come within the Sixth Amendment's guarantee." (Emphasis added.) [d]

Justice Harlan repeatedly voiced his opposition to the *Malloy-Duncan* approach to Fourteenth Amendment Due Process. "The consequence," he protested in his *Malloy* dissent, "is inevitably disregard of all relevant differences which may exist between state and federal criminal law and its enforcement. The ultimate result is compelled uniformity, which is inconsistent with the purpose of our federal system and which is achieved either by encroachment on the State's sovereign powers or by dilution in federal law enforcement of the specific protections found in the Bill of Rights."

Concurring in the result in *Pointer v. Texas,* 380 U.S. 400, 13 L.Ed.2d 923, 85 S.Ct. 1065 (1965) (holding that the Sixth Amendment's right of an accused to confront the witnesses against him applies in its entirety to the states via the Fourteenth), Justice Harlan maintained that "'selective' incorporation or 'absorption' amounts to little more than a diluted form of the full incorporation theory. Whereas it rejects full incorporation because of recognition that not all of the guarantees of the Bill of Rights should be deemed 'fundamental,' it at the same time ignores the possibility that not all phases of any given guaranty described in the Bill of Rights are necessarily fundamental." [e]

In the 1970's matters were brought to a head by the "right to jury trial" cases:[f] *Baldwin v. New York,* 399 U.S. 117, 90 S.Ct. 1914, 26 L.Ed.2d 437 (1970) (no offense can be deemed "petty," thus dispensing with the Fourteenth and Sixth Amendment rights to jury trial, where more than six months incarceration is authorized); *Williams v. Florida,* 399 U.S. 78, 90 S.Ct. 1893, 26 L.Ed.2d 446 (1970) ("that jury at common law was composed of precisely 12 is an historical accident, unnecessary to effect the purposes of the jury system"; thus 6-person jury in criminal cases does not violate Sixth Amendment, as applied to the states via Fourteenth); [g] and the 1972 *Apodaca* and *Johnson* cases, discussed below, dealing

d. See also Justice Marshall's opinion for the Court in *Benton v. Maryland,* fn. a supra, and Justice Goldberg's concurring opinion in *Pointer v. Texas* (1965), infra, responding to Justice Harlan's repeated criticism of the "selective incorporation" approach.

e. See also Justice Harlan's dissenting opinion in *Benton v. Maryland,* fn. a supra.

f. For a fuller discussion of these cases, see Ch. 22, § 1.

g. But the Court subsequently held, in *Ballew v. Georgia,* 435 U.S. 223, 98 S.Ct. 1029, 55 L.Ed.2d with whether unanimous jury verdicts are required in criminal cases.

Dissenting in *Baldwin* and concurring in *Williams,* Justice Harlan maintained:

"[*Williams*] evinces [a] recognition that the "incorporationist' view of the Due Process Clause of the Fourteenth Amendment, which underlay *Duncan* and is now carried forward into *Baldwin,* must be tempered to allow the States more elbow room in ordering their own criminal systems. With that much I agree. But to accomplish this by diluting constitutional protections within the federal system itself is something to which I cannot possibly subscribe. Tempering the rigor of *Duncan* should be done forthrightly, by facing up to the fact that at least in this area the 'incorporation' doctrine does not fit well with our federal structure, and by the same token that *Duncan* was wrongly decided.

"[Rather] than bind the States by the hitherto undeviating and unquestioned federal practice of 12-member juries, the Court holds, based on a poll of state practice, that a six-man jury satisfies the guarantee of a trial by jury in a federal criminal system and consequently carries over to the States. This is a constitutional *renvoi.* With all respect, I consider that before today it would have been unthinkable to suggest that the Sixth Amendment's right to a trial by jury is satisfied by a jury of six, or less, as is left open by the Court's opinion in *Williams,* or by less than a unanimous verdict, a question also reserved in today's decision.[h] * * *

"These decisions demonstrate that the difference between a 'due process' approach, that considers each particular case on its own bottom to see whether the right alleged is one 'implicit in the concept of ordered liberty,' and 'selective incorporation' is not an abstract one whereby different verbal formulae achieve the same results. The internal logic of the selective incorporation doctrine cannot be respected if the Court is both committed to interpreting faithfully the meaning of the federal Bill of Rights and recognizing the governmental diversity that exists in this country. The 'backlash' in *Williams* exposes the malaise, for there the Court dilutes a federal guarantee in order to reconcile the logic of 'incorporation,' the 'jot-for-jot and case-for-case' application of the federal right to the States, with the reality of federalism. Can one doubt that had Congress tried to undermine the common law right to trial by jury before *Duncan* came on the books the history today recited would have barred such action? Can we expect repeat performances when this Court is called upon to give definition and meaning to other federal guarantees that have been 'incorporated'? * * *

"[T]he best evidence of the vitality of federalism is today's decision in *Williams.* The merits or demerits of the jury system can, of course, be debated and those States that have diluted the common-law requirements evince a conclusion that the protection as known at common law is not necessary for a fair trial, or is only such marginal assurance of a fair trial that the inconvenience of assembling 12 individuals outweighs other gains in the administration of justice achieved by using only six individuals (or none at all as was the case in New York City).

"The Court rejects in *Baldwin* what would be the consistent approach, requiring affirmance, simply because New York

234 (1978), that a state trial in a non-petty criminal case to a jury of only five persons did deprive a defendant of the right to trial by jury guaranteed him by the Sixth and Fourteenth Amendments.

h. Cf. Frankfurter, J., for the Court in *Rochin v. California* (1952) (discussed in the next section): "Words being symbols do not speak without a gloss. [T]he gloss may be the deposit of history, whereby a term gains technical content. Thus the requirements of the Sixth and Seventh Amendments for trial by jury in the federal courts have a rigid meaning. No changes or chances can alter the content of the verbal symbol of 'jury'—a body of twelve men who must reach a unanimous conclusion if the verdict is to go against the defendant."

City is the single jurisdiction in the Nation that sees fit to try misdemeanants without a jury. In doing so it, in effect, holds that 'due process' is more offended by a trial without jury for an offense punishable by no more than a year in prison than it is by a trial with a jury of six or less for offenses punishable by life imprisonment. This ignores both the basic fairness of the New York procedure and the peculiar local considerations that have led the New York Legislature to conclude that trial by jury is more apt to retard than further justice for criminal defendants in New York City. * * *

" 'Incorporation' in *Duncan* closed the door on debate, irrespective of local circumstances, such as the backlogs in urban courts like those of New York City, and has, without justification, clouded with uncertainty the constitutionality of these differing states modes of proceeding pending approval by this Court; it now promises to dilute in other ways the settled meaning of the federal right to a trial by jury. Flexibility for experimentation in the administration of justice should be returned to the States here and in other areas that now have swept into the rigid mold of 'incorporation.' * * *

"It is time, I submit, for this Court to face up to the reality implicit in today's holdings and reconsider the 'incorporation' doctrine before its leveling tendencies further retard development in the field of criminal procedure by stifling flexibility in the States and by discarding the possibility of federal leadership by example."

In the companion cases of *Apodaca v. Oregon,* 406 U.S. 404, 92 S.Ct. 1628, 32 L.Ed.2d 184 (1972) and *Johnson v. Louisiana,* 406 U.S. 356, 92 S.Ct. 1620, 32 L.Ed.2d 152 (1972), upholding the constitutionality of less-than-unanimous jury verdicts in state criminal cases, eight Justices adhered to the *Duncan* position that each element of the Sixth Amendment right to jury trial applies to the states to the same extent it applies to the federal government, but split 4–4 over whether the federal guarantee *did require* jury unanimity in criminal cases. State convictions by less than unanimous votes were sustained only because the ninth member of the Court, newly appointed Justice Powell read the Sixth Amendment as requiring jury unanimity, but—taking a Harlan-type approach—concluded that *this feature* of the federal right is not "so fundamental to the essentials of jury trial" as to require unanimity in state criminal cases as a matter of Fourteenth Amendment Due Process.[i]

Observed Powell: "[I]n holding that the Fourteenth Amendment has incorporated 'jot-for-jot and case-for-case' every element of the Sixth Amendment, the Court derogates principles of federalism that are basic to our system. In the name of uniform application of high standards of due process, the Court has embarked upon a course of constitutional interpretation that deprives the States of freedom to experiment with adjudicatory processes different from the federal model. At the same time, the Court's understandable unwillingness to impose requirements that it finds unnecessarily rigid (e.g., *Williams*), has culminated in the dilution of federal rights that were, until these decisions, never seriously questioned. The doubly undesirable consequence of this reasoning process, labeled by Mr. Justice Harlan as 'constitutional schizophrenia,' may well be detrimental both to the state and federal criminal justice systems. Although it is perhaps late in the day for an expression of my views, I [believe] that, at least in defining the elements of the right to jury trial, there is no sound basis for interpreting the Fourteenth Amendment to require blind

i. But the Court subsequently held, in *Burch v. Louisiana,* Ch. 22, § 1, per Rehnquist, J. (without a dissent on this issue), that conviction by a nonunanimous *six-person* jury in a state criminal trial for a non-petty offense did violate the Sixth and Fourteenth Amendment rights to trial by jury.

adherence by the States to all details of the federal Sixth Amendment standards." [j]

Dissenting Justice Brennan, joined by Marshall, J., observed:

"Readers of today's opinions may be understandably puzzled why convictions by 11–1 and 10–2 jury votes are affirmed [when] a majority of the Court agrees that the Sixth Amendment requires a unanimous verdict in federal criminal jury trials, and a majority also agrees that the right to jury trial guaranteed by the Sixth Amendment is to be enforced against the States according to the same standards that protect that right against federal encroachment. The reason is that while my Brother Powell agrees that a unanimous verdict is required in federal criminal trials, he does not agree that the Sixth Amendment right to a jury trial is to be applied in the same way to State and Federal Governments. In that circumstance, it is arguable that the affirmance of the convictions * * * is not inconsistent with a view that today's decision is a holding that only a unanimous verdict will afford the accused in a state criminal prosecution the jury trial guaranteed him by the Sixth Amendment. In any event, the affirmance must not obscure that the majority of the Court remains of the view that, as in the case of every specific of the Bill of Rights that extends to the States, the Sixth Amendment's jury trial guarantee, however it is to be construed, has identical application against both State and Federal Governments." [k]

SECTION 2. THE PROBLEM OF BODILY EXTRACTIONS: ANOTHER LOOK AT THE "DUE PROCESS" AND "SELECTIVE INCORPORATION" APPROACHES

As noted in the previous section, dissenting in *Baldwin* and concurring in *Williams,* Justice Harlan maintained that "the difference between a 'due process' approach [and] 'selective incorporation' is not an abstract one whereby different formulae achieve the same results." But he made this observation in the context of the applicability to the states of the Sixth Amendment right to trial by jury, which had, or was thought to have, a relatively rigid meaning. Most language in the Bill of Rights, however, is rather vague and general, at least when specific problems arise under a particular phrase. In such cases, does dwelling on the literal language simply *shift the focus of broad judicial inquiry* from "due process" to, e.g., "freedom of speech," "establishment of religion," "unreasonable searches and seizures," "excessive bail," "cruel and unusual punishments," and "the assistance of counsel"? See Friendly, *The Bill of Rights as a Code of Criminal Procedure,* 53 Calif.L. Rev. 929, 937 (1965); Kadish, *Methodology and Criteria in Due Process Adjudication—A Survey and Criticism,* 66 Yale L.J. 319, (1957); Nowak, *Due Process Methodology in the Postincorporation World,* 70 J.Crim.L.&C. 397, 400–01 (1979) (arguing that decisions based on specific guarantees tend to rely on definitional analysis and fail to explore the interests at stake.)

In considering whether the right to counsel "begins" at the time of arrest, preliminary hearing, arraignment, or not

j. In his continued resistance to "jot-for-jot" or "bag and baggage" incorporation of a "selected" provision of the Bill of Rights, Justice Powell has gained two allies. See Powell, J., joined by the Chief Justice and Rehnquist, J., dissenting in *Crist v. Bretz,* Ch. 25, § 1. In *Ballew,* fn. g supra, although he concurred in the judgment, Justice Powell, again joined by the Chief Justice and Rehnquist, J., did not join Justice Blackmun's opinion because it "assumes full incorporation of the Sixth Amendment, contrary to my view in *Apodaca.*"

k. In a separate dissent, Stewart, J., joined by Brennan and Marshall, JJ., protested that "unless *Duncan* is to be overruled," "the only relevant question here is whether the Sixth Amendment [guarantees] that the verdict of the jury must be unanimous. The answer to that question is clearly 'yes,' as my Brother Powell has cogently demonstrated * * *."

until the trial itself, or includes probation and parole revocation hearings or applies to juvenile delinquency proceedings, deportation hearings or civil commitments, or, where the defendant is indigent, includes the right to *assigned* counsel or an assigned psychiatrist at state expense, how helpful is the Sixth Amendment language entitling an accused to "the assistance of counsel for his defense"? Is the specificity or direction of this language significantly greater than the "due process" clause?

To turn to another cluster of problems—which form the basis for this section—in considering whether, and under what conditions, the police may direct the "pumping" of a person's stomach to uncover incriminating evidence, or the taking of a blood sample from him, without his consent, do the "specific guarantees" in the Bill of Rights against "unreasonable searches and seizures" and against compelling a person to be "a witness against himself" free the Court from the demands of appraising and judging involved in answering these questions by interpreting the "due process" clause?

ROCHIN v. CALIFORNIA, 342 U.S. 165, 72 S.Ct. 205, 96 L.Ed. 183 (1952), arose as follows: Having "some information" that Rochin was selling narcotics, three deputy sheriffs "forced open the door of [his] room and found him sitting partly dressed on the side of the bed, upon which his wife was lying. On a 'night stand' beside the bed the deputies spied two capsules. When asked 'Whose stuff is this?' Rochin seized the capsules and put them in his mouth. A struggle ensued in the course of which the three officers 'jumped upon him' and [unsuccessfully] attempted to extract the capsules. [Rochin] was handcuffed and taken to a hospital. At the direction of one of the officers, a doctor forced an emetic solution through a tube into Rochin's stomach against his will. This 'stomach pumping' produced vomiting. In the vomited matter were found two capsules which proved to contain morphine. [Rochin was convicted of possessing morphine] and sentenced to sixty days' imprisonment. The chief evidence against him was the two capsules."

The Court, per FRANKFURTER, J., concluded that the police conduct violated fourteenth amendment due process: "This is conduct that shocks the conscience. Illegally breaking into the privacy of the petitioner, the struggle to open his mouth and remove what was there, the forcible extraction of his stomach's contents—this course of proceeding by agents of government to obtain evidence is bound to offend even hardened sensibilities. They are methods too close to the rack and the screw to permit of constitutional differentiation.

"It has long since ceased to be true that due process of law is heedless of the means by which otherwise relevant and credible evidence is obtained. [The confession] decisions [are] only instances of the general requirement that States in their prosecutions respect certain decencies of civilized conduct. Due process of law, as a historic and generative principle, precludes defining, and thereby confining, these standards of conduct more precisely than to say that convictions cannot be brought about by methods that offend 'a sense of justice.' It would be a stultification of the responsibility which the course of constitutional history has cast upon this Court to hold that in order to convict a man the police cannot extract by force what is in his mind but can extract what is in his stomach. * * *

"[E]ven though statements contained in them may be independently established as true, [c]oerced confessions offend the community's sense of fair play and decency. So here, to sanction the brutal conduct which naturally enough was condemned by the court whose judgment is before us, would be to afford brutality the cloak of law. Nothing would be more calculated to discredit law and thereby to brutalize the temper of a society."

Concurring Justice BLACK reasoned that the Fifth Amendment's protection against compelled self-incrimination applied to the states and that "a person is compelled to be a witness against himself not only when he is compelled to testify, but also when as here, incriminating evidence is forcibly taken from him by a contrivance of modern science." He maintained that "faithful adherence to the specific guarantees in the Bill of Rights insures a more permanent protection of individual liberty than that which can be afforded by the nebulous [Fourteenth Amendment due process] standards stated by the majority."

In a separate concurring opinion, Justice DOUGLAS also criticized the majority's approach. He contended that the privilege against self-incrimination applied to the states as well as the federal government and because of the privilege "words taken from [an accused's] lips, capsules taken from his stomach, blood taken from his veins are all inadmissible provided they are taken from him without his consent. [This] is an unequivocal, definite and workable rule of evidence for state and federal courts. But we cannot in fairness free the state courts from the [restraints of the Fifth Amendment privilege against self-incrimination] and yet excoriate them for flouting the 'decencies of civilized conduct' when they admit the evidence. This is to make the rule turn not on the Constitution but on the idiosyncracies of the judges who sit here."

Irvine v. California, 347 U.S. 128, 74 S.Ct. 381, 98 L.Ed. 561 (1954), limited *Rochin* to situations involving coercion, violence or brutality to the person.[a] BREITHAUPT v. ABRAM, 352 U.S. 432, 77 S.Ct. 408, 1 L.Ed.2d 448 (1957), illustrated that under the *Rochin* test state police had considerable leeway even when the body of the accused was "invaded." In *Breithaupt,* the police took a blood sample from an unconscious person who had been involved in a fatal automobile collision. A majority, per CLARK, J., affirmed a manslaughter conviction based on the blood sample (which showed intoxication), stressing that the sample was "taken under the protective eye of a physician" and that "the blood test procedure has become routine in our everyday life." "[T]he interests of society in the scientific determination of intoxication, one of the great causes of the mortal hazards of the road," outweighed "so slight an intrusion" of a person's body.

a. In *Irvine* the police made repeated illegal entries into petitioner's home, first to install a secret microphone and then to move it to the bedroom, in order to listen to the conversations of the occupants—for over a month.

Jackson, J., who announced the judgment of the Court and wrote the principal opinion, recognized that "few police measures have come to our attention that more flagrantly, deliberately, and persistently violated the fundamental principle declared by the Fourth Amendment as a restriction on the Federal Government," but adhered to the holding in *Wolf v. Colorado* (1949) (Ch. 5, § 1) that the exclusionary rule in federal search and seizure cases is not binding on the states. (*Wolf* was overruled in *Mapp v. Ohio* (1961), (Ch. 5, § 1) Nor did Justice Jackson deem *Rochin* applicable: "However obnoxious are the facts in the case before us, they do not involve coercion, violence or brutality to the person [as did *Rochin*], but rather a trespass to property, plus eavesdropping."

Because of the "aggravating" and "repulsive" police misconduct in *Irvine,* Frankfurter, J., joined by Burton, J., dissented, maintaining that *Rochin* was controlling, not *Wolf.* (He had written the majority opinions in both cases.) Black, J., joined by Douglas, J., dissented separately, arguing that petitioner had been convicted on the basis of evidence "extorted" from him in violation of the Fifth Amendment's privilege against compelled self-incrimination, which he considered applicable to the states. Douglas, J., dissenting separately, protested against the use in state prosecutions of evidence seized in violation of the Fourth Amendment.

Speaking for himself and Chief Justice Warren, Justice Jackson suggested that copies of the Court's opinion and the record in the case be sent to the U.S. Attorney General for possible federal prosecution. The FBI did conduct an investigation which revealed that the officers who placed the microphone in Irvine's home were acting under orders of the Chief of Police and with the full knowledge of the local prosecutor. Thus, concluded the Department of Justice, "it would be both useless and inadvisable to present [the] matter to the Federal grand jury." See Comment, 7 Stan.L.Rev. 76, 94, fn. 75 (1954).

Dissenting Chief Justice WARREN, joined by Black and Douglas, JJ., deemed *Rochin* controlling and argued that police efforts to curb the narcotics traffic, involved in *Rochin*, "is surely a state interest of at least as great magnitude as the interest in highway law enforcement. * * * Only personal reaction to the stomach pump and the blood test can distinguish the [two cases]."

Justice DOUGLAS, joined by Black, J., also wrote a separate dissent, maintaining that "if the decencies of a civilized state are the test, it is repulsive to me for the police to insert needles into an unconscious person in order to get the evidence necessary to convict him, whether they find the person unconscious, give him a pill which puts him to sleep, or use force to subdue him."

Nine years later, even though in the meantime the Court had held in *Mapp* that the federal exclusionary rule in search and seizure cases was binding on the states and in *Malloy v. Hogan*, supra, that the Fifth Amendment's protection against compelled self-incrimination was likewise applicable to the states, the Court still upheld the taking by a physician, at police direction, of a blood sample from an injured person, over his objection. SCHMERBER v. CALIFORNIA, 384 U.S. 757, 86 S.Ct. 1826, 16 L.Ed.2d 908 (1966).[b] In affirming the conviction for operating a vehicle while under the influence of intoxicating liquor, a 5–4 majority, per BRENNAN, J., ruled: (1) that the extraction of blood from petitioner under the aforementioned circumstances "did not offend 'that "sense of justice"' of which we spoke in *Rochin*," thus reaffirming *Breithaupt;* (2) that the privilege against self-incrimination, now binding on the states, "protects an accused only from being compelled to testify against himself, or otherwise provide the State with evidence of a testimonial or communicative nature and that the withdrawal of blood and use of the analysis in question did not involve compulsion to these ends";[c] and (3) that the protection against unreasonable search and seizure, now binding on the states, was satisfied because (a) "there was plainly probable cause" to arrest and charge petitioner and to suggest "the required relevance and likely success of a test of petitioner's blood for alcohol"; (b) the officer "might reasonably have believed that he was confronted with an emergency, in which the delay necessary to obtain a warrant, under the circumstances, threatened 'the destruction of evidence' "; and (c) "the test chosen to measure petitioner's blood-alcohol level was a reasonable one * * * performed in a reasonable manner."

Dissenting Justice BLACK, joined by Justice Douglas, expressed amazement at the majority's "conclusion that compelling a person to give his blood to help the State to convict him is not equivalent to compelling him to be a witness against himself." "It is a strange hierarchy of values that allows the State to extract a human being's blood to convict him of a crime because of the blood's content but proscribes compelled production of his lifeless papers."[d]

b. For other aspects of *Schmerber*, see p. 397 infra.

c. In fn. 7 to its opinion, the Court compared "Wigmore's view, 'that the privilege is limited to testimonial disclosure. It was directed at the employment of legal process *to extract from the person's own lips* an admission of guilt, which would thus take the place of other evidence.' 8 Wigmore, *Evidence* § 2263 (McNaughton rev. 1961)." "Our holding today," noted the Court, "is not to be understood as adopting the Wigmore formulation." But see *United States v. Wade*, Ch. 9 infra.

d. Warren, C.J., and Douglas, J., dissented in separate opinions,, each adhering to his dissenting views in *Breithaupt.* In a third dissenting opinion, Fortas, J., maintained that "petitioner's privilege against self-incrimination applies" and, moreover, "under the Due Process Clause, the State, in its role as prosecutor, has no right to extract blood from an accused or anyone else, over his protest."

Notes and Questions

1. In light of *Rochin, Breithaupt* and *Schmerber,* when courts decide constitutional questions by "looking to" the Bill of Rights, to what extent do they proceed, as Justice Black expressed it in *Adamson,* "within clearly marked constitutional boundaries"? To what extent does resort to these "particular standards" enable courts to avoid substituting their "own concepts of decency and fundamental justice" for the language of the Constitution?

2. Did *Mapp* and *Malloy,* decided in the interim between *Breithaupt* and *Schmerber,* affect any Justice's vote? Did the applicability of the "particular standards" of the Fourth and Fifth Amendments inhibit Justices Black, Douglas or Brennan from employing their own concepts of "decency" and "justice" in *Schmerber?* After *Schmerber,* how much force is there in Justice Black's view, concurring in *Rochin,* that "faithful adherence to the specific guarantees in the Bill of Rights assures a more permanent protection of individual liberty than that which can be afforded by the nebulous standards stated by the majority"?

SECTION 3. THE RETROACTIVE EFFECT OF A HOLDING OF UNCONSTITUTIONALITY [a]

LINKLETTER v. WALKER, 381 U.S. 618, 85 S.Ct. 1731, 14 L.Ed.2d 601 (1965), per CLARK, J., declined to apply *Mapp* to state convictions which had become final prior to the overruling of *Wolf.* (*Mapp,* however, had been applied to state cases still pending on direct appeal at the time it was handed down.)

"[In deciding whether to apply a decision retroactively, we must look] to the prior history of the rule in question, its purpose and effect, and whether retrospective operation will further or retard its operation. [*Mapp's*] prime purpose [was] enforcement of the Fourth Amendment through the [exclusionary rule]. This, it was found, was the only effective deterrence against lawless police action. [T]his purpose [would not] be advanced by making the rule retrospective. The misconduct of the police prior to *Mapp* has already occurred and will not be corrected by releasing the prisoners involved. Nor would it add harmony to the delicate state-federal relationship of which we have spoken as part and parcel of the purpose of *Mapp.* Finally, the ruptured privacy of the victim's homes and effects cannot be restored. Reparation comes too late.

"[To] make [*Mapp*] retrospective would tax the administration of justice to the utmost. Hearings would have to be held on the excludability of evidence long since destroyed, misplaced or deteriorated. If it is excluded, [witnesses may no longer be available] or if located their memory will be dimmed. To thus legitimate such an extraordinary procedural weapon that has no bearing on guilt would seriously disrupt the administration of justice.

"[Although we have applied *Gideon,* [p. 77 infra], *Griffin v. Illinois* [p. 105 infra] and 'coerced confession' cases retrospectively, those principles] went to the fairness of the trial—the very integrity of the fact-finding process. [Here,] the fairness of the trial is not under attack."

Dissenting, BLACK, J., joined by Douglas, J., stressed that Linkletter's offense had been committed more than a year *after* Miss Mapp's. "There is no experience of the past," maintained the dissenters, "that justifies a new Court-made rule to perpetuate a grossly invidious and unfair discrimination against Linkletter simply because he happened to be prosecuted in a State that was evidently well up with its criminal

a. This cluster of problems has generated a vast literature, starting in the 1960's. See, e.g., the articles quoted or cited at p. — infra. For fairly recent commentary see F. Allen, *The Judicial Quest for Penal Justice: The Warren Court and the Criminal Cases,* 1975 U. Ill. L.F. 518, 529–30; Beytagh, *Ten Years of Non-Retroactivity: A Critique and a Proposal,* 61 Va.L.Rev. 1557 (1975); Schaefer, *Prospective Rulings: Two Perspectives,* 1982 Sup.Ct.Rev. 1.

court docket." Nor could the dissenters accept the primary reason put forward by the majority for its refusal to give Linkletter the benefit of *Mapp*—"the repeated statement that the purpose of [the exclusionary rule] is to deter [police] from making unlawful searches and seizures. The inference [is] that the rule is not a right or privilege accorded to defendants charged with crime but is a sort of punishment against officers in order to keep them from depriving people of their constitutional rights. [If this] is the sole purpose, [and effect] of the rule, the Court's action in adopting it sounds more like law-making than construing the Constitution. [I] have been unable to find one word in [*Mapp*] to indicate that the [exclusionary rule] was intended to do nothing in the world except to deter officers of the law."

TEHAN v. UNITED STATES ex rel. SHOTT, 382 U.S. 406, 86 S.Ct. 459, 15 L.Ed. 453 (1966), declined to apply *Griffin v. California* (1965) (p. 39 fn. a supra) (holding that adverse comment by prosecutor or judge upon a defendant's failure to testify in a state criminal trial violates the federal privilege against compulsory self-incrimination) to state cases "finalized" before that decision was handed down. A 5–2 majority, per STEWART, J., observed that "the basic purposes that lie behind the privilege against self-incrimination do not relate to protecting the innocent from conviction, but rather to preserving the integrity of a judicial system in which even the guilty are not to be convicted unless the prosecution 'shoulder the entire load.' [The privilege] is not an adjunct to the ascertainment of truth [but] stands as a protection of quite different constitutional values—values reflecting the concern of our society for the right of each individual to be let alone." The majority also took cognizance of "the States' [good faith] reliance upon the *Twining* rule [p. 39 & fn. a] for more than half a century."

Warren, C.J., and Fortas, J., took no part; Black, J., joined by Douglas, J., dissented for substantially the same reasons set forth in their dissenting opinion in *Linkletter.*

JOHNSON v. NEW JERSEY, 384 U.S. 719, 86 S.Ct. 1772, 16 L.Ed.2d 882 (1966), per WARREN, C.J., held that *Escobedo* and *Miranda* affect only those cases in which *the trial began* after the date of these decisions:[b] "[T]he prime purpose of [*Escobedo* and *Miranda*] is to guarantee full effectuation of the privilege against self-incrimination. [W]hile *Escobedo* and *Miranda* guard against the possibility of unreliable statements in every instance of in-custody interrogation, they encompass situations in which the danger is not necessarily as great as when the accused is subjected to overt and obvious coercion.

"At the same time, our case law on coerced confessions is available for persons whose trials have already been completed. [They] may invoke [the voluntariness test which] has become increasingly meticulous throughout the years [and] now takes specific account of the failure to advise the accused of his privilege against self-incrimination or to allow him access to outside assistance. [Thus] while *Escobedo* and *Miranda* provide important new safeguards against the use of unreliable statements at trial, the nonretroactivity of these decisions will not preclude persons whose trials have already been completed from invoking the same safeguards as part of an involuntariness claim.

Clark, Harlan, Stewart and White, JJ., concurred in the opinion of the Court, noting continued adherence to their dissent in *Miranda.* Black and Douglas, JJ., dissented, again for substantially the same reasons stated in their *Linkletter* dissent.

b. In *Jenkins v. Delaware,* 395 U.S. 213, 89 S.Ct. 1677, 23 L.Ed.2d 253 (1969), the Court held, 7–1, that *Miranda's* standards do not apply to post-*Miranda* retrials of cases originally tried prior to that decision.

Notes and Questions

1. The *Johnson* Court points out that "our [law] on coerced confessions is available" for persons whose trials have been completed prior to *Escobedo* and *Miranda.* Weren't the "special circumstances" and "prejudice" tests available for persons convicted without counsel prior to *Gideon? Escobedo* and *Miranda,* observes *Johnson* "encompass situations in which the danger [of unreliable statements] is not necessarily as great as when the accused is subjected to overt and obvious coercion." May it not be said of *Gideon* that it encompasses situations where the danger of wrongful conviction is not necessarily as great as when the accused can show "prejudice" or "special circumstances"?

2. How can the Court say that "while *Escobedo* and *Miranda* provide *important new safeguards* against the use of *unreliable* statements at trial, the nonretroactivity of these decisions will not preclude persons whose trials have already been completed from invoking *the same safeguards* as part of an involuntariness claim"? (Emphasis added.) Do not *Escobedo* and *Miranda* indicate dissatisfaction with—and lack of confidence in—the actual operation of the voluntary-involuntary test, just as *Gideon* manifests dissatisfaction with and lack of confidence in the "special circumstances" and "prejudice" standards? If past defendants could be adequately protected by a judicial examination into whether their confessions were "voluntary," then were *Escobedo* and *Miranda* wrongly decided? See Johnson, *Retroactivity in Retrospect,* 56 Calif.L.Rev. 1612, 1617 (1968).

Unlike *Mapp,* which applied to police searches conducted *before* the date of this decision—so long as the case was still pending on appeal—and unlike *Escobedo* and *Miranda,* which applied to police questioning conducted before the dates of these decisions—so long as *the trial* began after these dates—STOVALL v. DENNO, 388 U.S. 293, 87 S.Ct. 1967, 18 L.Ed.2d 1199 (1967), held that *Wade* and *Gilbert* (see Ch. 9, § 1), the 1967 cases establishing the right to counsel at certain pretrial lineups, "affect only those cases [involving] *confrontations for identification purposes* conducted in the absence of counsel *after* [the date of these decisions]" (emphasis added.) Thus, the landmark lineup decisions were completely prospective, except that they overturned the convictions of Wade and Gilbert themselves. Selection of *the date of the police conduct,* rather than the date of the trial or some other point in the criminal process indicated that *police reliance* is a major factor in retroactivity disputes.

Similarly, DESIST v. UNITED STATES, 394 U.S. 244, 89 S.Ct. 1030, 22 L.Ed. 248 (1969), held that *Katz v. United States* (1967) (p. 237 infra) (holding that the reach of the fourth amendment "cannot turn upon the presence or absence of a physical intrusion into any given enclosure" and that electronic eavesdropping upon private conversations constitutes a search and seizure that must meet fourth amendment requirements) should only be given what the Court called "wholly prospective application," i.e., applied only to *police activity* occurring after the date of the decision. Observed the Court, per STEWART, J.:

"Ever since [*Linkletter*] the Court has viewed the retroactivity or nonretroactivity of [decisions expounding new constitutional rules] as a function of three considerations. As we most recently summarized them in *Stovall,* '[T]he criteria guiding resolution of the question implicate (a) the purpose to be served by the new standards, (b) the extent of the reliance by law enforcement authorities on the old standards, and (c) the effect on the administration of justice of a retroactive application of the new standards.'

"Foremost among these factors is the purpose to be served by the new constitutional rule. [Thus,] it was principally the Court's assessment of the purpose of *Mapp,* which led it in *Linkletter* to deny those finally convicted the benefit of *Mapp's* extension of the exclusionary rule to the States: 'We cannot say that [the deterrent purpose of *Mapp*] would be advanced by making [it] retrospective. The [police misconduct] has already occurred and will not be corrected by releasing the prisoners involved.'[14]

"We further observed that, in contrast with decisions which had been accorded retroactive effect,[15] 'there is no likelihood of unreliability or coercion present in a search-and-seizure case' * * *.

"The second and third factors—reliance of law enforcement officials, and the burden on the administration of justice that would flow from a retroactive application—also militate in favor of applying *Katz* prospectively. *Katz* for the first time explicitly overruled the 'physical penetration' and 'trespass' tests enunciated in earlier decisions of this Court. Our periodic restatements of those tests confirmed the interpretation that police and courts alike had placed on the controlling precedents and fully justified reliance on their continuing validity. * * *

"All of the reasons for making *Katz* [prospective] also undercut any distinction between final convictions and those still pending on review. Both the deterrent purpose of the exclusionary rule and the reliance of law enforcement officers focus upon the time of the search, not any subsequent point in the prosecution as the relevant date. * * * ".[24]

"Upon reflection," dissenting JUSTICE HARLAN could "no longer accept the rule first announced two years ago in *Stovall,* and reaffirmed today, which permits this Court to apply a 'new' constitutional rule entirely prospectively, while making an exception only for the particular litigant whose case was chosen as the vehicle for establishing that rule. Indeed, I have concluded that *Linkletter* was right in insisting that all 'new' rules of constitutional law must, at a minimum, be applied to all those cases which are still subject to direct review by this Court at the time the 'new' decision is handed down.

"[We release a prisoner] only because the Government has offended constitutional principle in the conduct of his case. And when another similarly situated defendant comes before us, we must grant the same relief or give a principled reason for acting differently. We depart from this basic judicial tradition when we simply pick and choose from among similarly situated defendants those who alone will receive the benefit of a 'new' rule of constitutional law.

" * * * If a 'new' constitutional doctrine is truly right, we should not reverse

14. In other areas where retroactivity has been denied the "purpose" criterion offered much weaker support. Compare *Stovall* where it was conceded that "the *Wade* and *Gilbert* rules also are aimed at avoiding unfairness at the trial by enhancing the reliability of the fact-finding process in the area of identification evidence"; *Johnson v. New Jersey,* where it was recognized that "*Escobedo* and *Miranda* guard against the possibility of unreliable statements in every instance of in-custody interrogation"; and *Tehan,* where it was stated that "the 'purpose' of the *Griffin* rule is to be found in the whole complex of values that the privilege against self-incrimination itself represents," including "our realization that the privilege, while sometimes 'a shelter to the guilty,' is often 'a protection to the innocent.'"

15. *Jackson v. Denno,* 378 U.S. 368, 84 S.Ct. 1774, 12 L.Ed.2d 908 (1964) [striking down the procedure in some 16 states whereby if the evidence presented a "fair question" as to the voluntariness of a confession, the trial court submitted that issue along with all others to the jury]; *Gideon; Griffin v. Illinois.*

24. * * * Of course, Katz himself benefited from the new principle announced on [the date of the *Katz* decision], and, as our Brother Douglas observes, to that extent the decision has not technically been given wholly prospective application. But, as we recently explained in *Stovall,* the fact that the parties involved in the decision are the only litigants so situated who receive the benefit of the new rule is "an unavoidable consequence of the necessity that constitutional adjudications not stand as mere dictum." Whatever inequity may arguably result from applying the new rule to those "chance beneficiaries" is "an insignificant cost for adherence to sound principles of decision-making."

lower courts which have accepted it; nor should we affirm those which have rejected the very arguments we have embraced. Anything else would belie the truism that it is the task of this Court, like that of any other, to do justice to each litigant on the merits of his own case. It is only if each of our decisions can be justified in terms of this fundamental premise that they may properly be considered the legitimate products of a court of law, rather than the commands of a super-legislature."[c]

In a separate dissent, Justice FORTAS protested: "[T]he Court not only denies the benefit of a fundamental constitutional provision [to] a class of persons because of the chance operation of the judicial calendar; it does so in face of the fact that the ruling at issue is neither novel nor unanticipated. * * *

"In the present cases, the Court decides that the lawfulness of wiretaps and electronic eavesdropping occurring before [the day *Katz* was announced] will be controlled by *Olmstead* [p. 423 infra], a decision that the Court agrees is a false and insupportable reading of the Constitution. The Court holds that the Fourth Amendment meant something quite different before *Katz* was decided than it means afterwards; that Katz and persons whose rights are violated after the date of that decision may have the benefit of the true meaning of the constitutional provision, but that those who were victims before *Katz* may not.

"* * * [T]here is no justification for refusing 'retroactive' application to a constitutional principle merely because of an earlier reading of the Constitution that had been widely repudiated as unsound and that this Court's own intervening opinions had discredited although not expressly overruled. *Olmstead* is in this category. *Katz* did no more than administer the *coup de grace* to its moribund doctrine. * * *

"[Today's decision awards] dunce caps to those law enforcement officers, courts, and public officials [who] generously apply the mandates of the Constitution as the developing case law elucidates them. [The] vitality of our Constitution depends upon conceptual faithfulness and not merely decisional obedience. Certainly, this Court should not encourage police or other courts to disregard the plain purport of our decisions and to adopt a let's-wait-until-it's-decided approach."

Notes and Questions

1. *Other decisions applied prospectively only. Williams v. United States,* 401 U.S. 646, 91 S.Ct. 1148, 22 L.Ed.2d 388 (1971), held *Chimel* (p. 309 infra) inapplicable to searches occurring before the date of decision in that case. White, J.'s plurality opinion, joined by Burger, C.J., and Stewart and Blackmun, JJ., "consider[ed] *Desist* [as] represent[ing] the sound approach to retroactivity claims in Fourth Amendment cases" and found "no constitutional difference between the applicability of *Chimel* to those prior convictions which are here on direct appeal and those involving collateral proceedings." *Adams v. Illinois* (1972) (Ch. 15, § 4) declined to apply *Coleman v. Alabama,* 399 U.S. 1, 90 S.Ct. 1999, 26 L.Ed.2d 387 (1970) (preliminary hearing is "critical stage" at which accused is entitled to assistance of counsel) to preliminary hearings conducted prior to the date of that decision. Brennan, J.'s plurality opinion, joined by Stewart and White, JJ., noted, inter alia, that "the lack of counsel at a preliminary hearing involves less danger to 'the integrity of the truth-determining process at trial' than the omission of counsel at the trial itself or on appeal." *North Carolina v. Pearce* (1969) (Ch. 26, § 1) imposed restrictions on resentencing in order to ensure that "vindictiveness" against a de-

c. Consider *United States v. Johnson* (1982) and *Shea v. Louisiana* (1985), both discussed infra, both relying heavily on Justice Harlan's dissent in *Desist.*

fendant for having successfully attacked his first conviction would play no part in the sentence he receives after a new trial and that apprehension of such vindictiveness would not "deter" a defendant's exercise of his right to attack the first conviction. *Michigan v. Payne,* 412 U.S. 47, 93 S.Ct. 1966, 36 L.Ed.2d 736 (1973), held the "prophylactic" due process limitations imposed by *Pearce* inapplicable to resentencing proceedings that occurred prior to the date of that decision.

2. *Other decisions given retroactive effect. Ivan v. New York,* 407 U.S. 203, 92 S.Ct. 1951, 32 L.Ed.2d 659 (1972) (per curiam) held that "the major purpose" of the constitutional requirement of proof beyond a reasonable doubt announced in *In re Winship* (Ch. 12, § 2) "was to overcome an aspect of a criminal trial that substantially impairs the truth-finding function, and *Winship* is thus to be given complete retroactive effect." *Waller v. Florida,* (1970) (Ch. 25, § 4) held that the double jeopardy clause barred two prosecutions, state and municipal, based on the same act or offense. *Robinson v. Neil,* 409 U.S. 505, 93 S.Ct. 876, 35 L.Ed.2d 29 (1973), held that *Waller* "is to be accorded full retroactive effect." The Court, per Rehnquist, J., recognized that "*Linkletter* indicated [that] only those procedural rules affecting 'the very integrity of the fact-finding process' would be given retrospective effect," but maintained that the prohibition against being placed in double jeopardy is "not readily susceptible of analysis under the *Linkletter* line of cases. [The double jeopardy clause's] practical result is to prevent a trial from taking place at all, rather than to prescribe procedural rules that govern the conduct of a trial. A number of the constitutional rules applied prospectively only under the *Linkletter* cases were found not to affect the basic fairness of the earlier trial, but to have been directed instead to collateral purposes such as the deterrence of unlawful police conduct. [But *Waller*] was squarely directed to the prevention of the second trial's taking place at all, even though it might have been conducted with a scrupulous regard for [all] constitutional procedural rights." The Court's treatment of *Waller* was anticipated in H. Schwartz, *Retroactivity, Reliability, and Due Process: A Reply to Professor Mishkin,* 33 U.Chi.L.Rev. 719, 741 (1966).

3. To a considerable extent *Linkletter, Johnson* and *Stovall* adopted the analysis of Mishkin, *The High Court, the Great Writ, and the Due Process of Time and Law,* 79 Harv.L.Rev. 56 (1965). But consider H. Schwartz, Note 2 supra, at 748–49: "Since newly declared constitutional criminal procedure rights 'are of the very essence [of] "ordered liberty," ' states should not be allowed to continue to deprive persons of their freedom on the basis of proceedings now considered contrary to 'the kind of fair trial which is this country's constitutional goal.' [I]f the accusatorial system and the privilege against self-incrimination are indeed of the essence of our system of criminal justice, was a trial which forced the accused to 'shoulder [some of the] load' any less a violation of that system merely because it happened five or even twenty-five years ago? [Has] it not always been wrong to compel a man to incriminate himself, or to allow him, because of ignorance, to waive his rights either in the police station or in court? Has there ever been a time when special handicaps imposed by poverty or race were not fundamentally wrong? * * *

"The truth is, I think, that recent decisions have not discovered or created new rights; rather, they have only granted new federal remedies for old wrongs. These remedies have been granted only recently not because the rights they protect are newly conceived or newly relevant, but rather because concern for considerations of federalism has lessened and perhaps because sensitivity to due process problems has increased. But the newness of the remedy does not eliminate the faults of the condemned proceeding, for just as we cannot tolerate the continued imprisonment of a man whose conviction was based on unreliable evidence, so we cannot tolerate the continued imprisonment of a man whose conviction failed in other respects to meet the fundamental legal standards of the community."

4. Consider Haddad, *"Retroactivity Should be Rethought": A Call for the End of the Linkletter Doctrine,* 60 J.Crim.L.C. & P.S. 417, 439 (1969): "The alternative to the prospective-only technique is a more conservative approach to constitutional criminal procedure. Deference to varying state practices would be required. Detailed federal standards such as those laid down in *Miranda* would no longer be possible. Adoption of safeguards, such as the right to counsel at lineups, which not a single state anticipated, would also be impossible. For liberals the choice is clear." See also F. Allen, *The Judicial Quest for Penal Justice: The Warren Court and the Criminal Cases,* 1975 U.Ill.L.F. 518, 530 (although "at first glance the prospectivity rule appears to be an act of judicial self-abnegation," "in reality [it] encourages the making of new law by reducing some of the social costs").

THE COURT'S RECENT RELIANCE ON JUSTICE HARLAN'S DISSENT IN *DESIST*

More than a decade after the *Desist* Court had found no valid distinction for retroactivity purposes between final convictions and those still pending on review, the Court, relying heavily on Harlan, J.'s dissent in *Desist,* deemed such a distinction persuasive and applied it in *United States v. Johnson,* 457 U.S. 537, 102 S.Ct. 2579, 73 L.Ed. 202 (1982) (per Blackmun, J.). *Johnson* applied *Payton v. New York* (1980) (p. 322 infra) (holding that police must obtain an arrest warrant when entering a suspect's home to make a routine felony arrest) to cases still pending on direct appeal at the time *Payton* was handed down. The Court pointed out that "*Payton* overturned no long-standing practice approved by a near-unanimous body of lower court authority [and thus] does not fall into that narrow class of decisions whose nonretroactivity is effectively preordained because they unmistakably signal 'a clean break with the past.' "

The *Johnson* Court "express[ed] no view on the retroactive application of decisions construing any constitutional provision other than the Fourth Amendment," but as *Shea v. Louisiana,* immediately below, soon made clear, the *Johnson* approach was not to be confined to the Fourth Amendment setting.

SHEA v. LOUISIANA, ___ U.S. ___, 105 S.Ct. 1065, 84 L.Ed.2d 38 (1985) arose as follows: Upon being read his *Miranda* rights, petitioner asserted his right to counsel and the interview was then terminated. But the next day, before petitioner had communicated with a lawyer and without any indication from him that he was willing to be questioned, the police again read petitioner the *Miranda* warnings. Petitioner agreed to talk and confessed. The confession was admitted into evidence and petitioner was convicted. While his appeal was pending, the U.S. Supreme Court ruled in *Edwards v. Arizona,* p. 613 infra, that a suspect's rights were violated by the use of his confession obtained by police-instigated interrogation—without counsel present—after he had requested a lawyer. The state supreme court held *Edwards* inapplicable to a case pending on direct appeal at the time *Edwards* was decided. The Court, per BLACKMUN, J., disagreed:

"The primary difference between *United States v. Johnson,* on the one hand, and *Solem v. Stumes,* 465 U.S. 638, 104 S.Ct. 1338, 79 L.Ed.2d 579 (1984) [holding that *Edwards* does not apply retroactively to a state-court conviction finally affirmed by the state supreme court *before Edwards* was decided], on the other, is the difference between a pending and undecided direct view of a judgment of conviction and a federal collateral attack upon a state conviction which has become final. We must acknowledge [that] *Johnson* does not directly control the disposition of the present case. * * * [a] [But] [w]e now conclude [that] there is no reason to reach in this case a result that is different from the one reached in *Johnson.* There is nothing about a Fourth Amendment rule that suggests that in this context it should be given greater retroactive effect than a Fifth Amendment rule. Indeed, a Fifth Amendment violation may be more likely to affect the truthfinding process than a Fourth Amendment violation. And Justice Harlan's reasoning—that principled decisionmaking and fairness to similarly situated petitioners requires application of a new rule to all cases pending on direct review—is applicable with equal force to the situation presently before us. We hold that our analysis in *Johnson* is relevant for petitioner's direct-review Fifth Amendment claim under *Edwards.* He is entitled to the benefit of the ruling in that case.

"[It is argued] that drawing a distinction between a case pending on direct review and a case on collateral attack produces inequities and injustices that are not any different from those that *Johnson* purported to cure. The argument is that the litigant whose *Edwards* claim will not be considered because it is presented on collateral review will be just as unfairly treated as the direct-review litigant whose claim would be by-passed were *Edwards* not the law. The distinction, however, properly rests on considerations of finality in the judicial process. The one litigant already has taken his case through the primary system. The other has not. For the latter, the curtain of finality has not been drawn. Somewhere, the closing must come. * * *

"[It is also argued] that in every case, *Edwards* alone excepted, reliance on existing law justifies the nonapplication of *Edwards.* [But], there is no difference between the petitioner in *Edwards* and the petitioner in the present case. If the *Edwards* principle is not to be applied retroactively, the only way to dispense equal justice to Edwards and to Shea would be a rule that confined the *Edwards* principle to prospective application unavailable even to Edwards himself."

WHITE, J., joined by the Chief Justice, and Rehnquist and O'Connor, JJ., dissented:

"We concluded [in *Stumes*] that the prophylactic purpose of the *Edwards* rule, the justifiable failure of police and prosecutors to foresee the Court's decision in *Edwards,* and the substantial disruption of the criminal justice system that retroactive application of *Edwards* would entail all indicated the wisdom of holding *Edwards* nonretroactive. Today, however, the majority concludes that notwithstanding the substantial reasons for restricting the application of *Edwards* to cases involving interrogations that postdate the Court's opinion in [that case], the *Edwards* rule must be applied retroactively to all cases in which the process of direct appeal had not yet been completed when *Edwards* was decided. In so holding, the majority apparently adopts a rule long advocated by a shifting minority of Justices and endorsed in limited circumstances by the majority in *Johnson*: namely, the rule that any new constitutional decision—except, perhaps, one that constitutes a 'clear break with the past'—must be applied to all cases pending on direct appeal at the time it is handed down.

"The futility of this latest attempt to use retroactivity doctrine to avoid the superlegislature difficulty is highlighted by the majority's unwillingness to commit itself to the logic of its position. For even as it

a. The Court noted that *Johnson* specifically declined to address the implications of its approach to non-Fourth Amendment cases and "also declined to address situations clearly controlled by existing retroactivity precedents, such as where the new rule of law is so clean a break with the past that it has been considered nonretroactive almost automatically. Whatever the merits of a different retroactivity rule for cases of that kind may be, [*Stumes*] recognized that *Edwards* was 'not the kind of clean break with the past that is automatically nonretroactive.' "

maintains that retroactivity is essential to the judicial function, today's majority, like the majority in *Johnson*, continues to hold out the possibility that a 'really' new rule—one that marks a clear break with the past—may not have to be applied retroactively even to cases pending on direct review at the time the new decision is handed down. Of course, if the majority were truly concerned with the super-legislature problem it would be 'clear break' decisions that would trouble it the most. Indeed, one might expect that a Court as disturbed about the problem as the majority purports to be would swear off such decisions altogether, not reserve the power both to issue them and to decline to apply them retroactively. In leaving open the possibility of an exception for 'clear break' decisions, the majority demonstrates the emptiness of its proposed solution to the super-legislature problem.

"The claim that the majority's rule serves the interest of fairness is equally hollow. Although the majority finds it intolerable to apply a new rule to one case on direct appeal but not to another, it is perfectly willing to tolerate disparate treatment of defendants seeking direct review of their convictions and prisoners attacking their convictions in collateral proceedings. [T]he attempt to distinguish between direct and collateral challenges for purposes of retroactivity is misguided. Under the majority's rule, otherwise identically situated defendants may be subject to different constitutional rules, depending on just how long ago now-unconstitutional conduct occurred and how quickly cases proceed through the criminal justice system. The disparity is no different in kind from that which occurs when the benefit of a new constitutional rule is retroactively afforded to the defendant in whose case it is announced but to no others; the Court's new approach equalizes nothing except the numbers of defendants within the disparately treated classes.

"The majority recognizes that the distinction between direct review and habeas is problematic, but justifies its differential treatment by appealing to the need to draw 'the curtain of finality' on those who were unfortunate enough to have exhausted their last direct appeal at the time *Edwards* was decided. Yet the majority offers no reasons for its conclusion that finality should be the decisive factor. When a conviction is overturned on direct appeal on the basis of an *Edwards* violation, the remedy offered the defendant is a new trial at which any inculpatory statements obtained in violation of *Edwards* will be excluded. It is not clear to me why the majority finds such a burdensome remedy more acceptable when it is imposed on the state on direct review than when it is the result of a collateral attack. The disruption attendant upon the remedy does not vary depending on whether it is imposed on direct review or habeas; accordingly, if the remedy must be granted to defendants on direct appeal, there is no strong reason to deny it to prisoners attacking their convictions collaterally. Conversely, if it serves no worthwhile purpose to grant the remedy to a defendant whose conviction was final before *Edwards*, it is hard to see why the remedy should be available on direct review.

"The underlying flaw of the majority's opinion is its failure to articulate the premises on which the retroactivity doctrine it announces actually rests. In recognizing that a decision making a clear break from the past may not be retroactive and in holding that the concern of finality trumps considerations of fairness that might otherwise dictate retroactivity in collateral proceedings, the majority implicitly recognizes that there is in fact more at issue in decisions involving retroactivity than treating like cases alike. In short, the majority recognizes that there are *reasons* why certain decisions ought not be retroactive. But the rules the majority announces fail to reflect any thoughtful inquiry into what those reasons might be. By contrast, the principles of retroactivity set forth in *Linkletter* and most recently applied in *Stumes* provide a rational framework for thinking about the question whether retroactive application of any particular decision makes sense—that is, whether the benefits of retroactivity outweigh its costs. Because the Court has already determined that the relevant considerations set forth in *Linkletter* (the purpose of the new rule, the extent of law enforcement officials' justifiable reliance on the prior rule, and the effects on the criminal justice system of retroactivity) dictate nonretroactive application of the rule in *Edwards,* I cannot join in the majority's conclusion that that rule should be applied retroactively to cases pending on direct review at the time of our decision in *Edwards.* More importantly, I cannot concur in the approach to retroactivity adopted by today's majority—an approach that, if our precedents regarding the nonretroactivity of decisions marking a clear break with the past remain undisturbed, merely adds a confusing and unjustifiable addendum to our retroactivity jurisprudence.[2] * * * [b]

SECTION 4. THE FEDERAL COURTS' "SUPERVISORY POWER" OVER THE ADMINISTRATION OF FEDERAL CRIMINAL JUSTICE

As the Court, per FRANKFURTER, J., observed in MCNABB v. UNITED STATES, 318 U.S. 332, 63 S.Ct. 608, 87 L.Ed. 819 (1943) (more extensively discussed at p. 524 infra), "while the power of this Court to undo convictions in *state* courts is limited to the enforcement of those 'fundamental principles of liberty and justice' secured by [fourteenth amendment due process]" (emphasis added), the standards of *federal* criminal justice "are not satisfied merely by observance of those minimal historic safeguards." Rather, "[i]n the exercise of its supervisory authority over the administration of criminal justice in the federal courts, [this Court has] formulated rules of evidence to be applied in federal criminal prosecutions." Thus, in *McNabb,* the Court held incriminating statements obtained during prolonged and hence unlawful detention (i.e., while the suspect was held in violation of federal statutory requirements that he be promptly taken before a committing magistrate) inadmissible in federal courts "[q]uite apart from the Constitution."

For a long, hard look at *McNabb* itself and the federal "supervisory power" generally, see Beale, *Reconsidering Supervisory Power in Criminal Cases: Constitutional and Statutory Limits on the Authority of the Federal Courts,* 84 Colum.L.Rev. 1433 (1984). Professor Beale maintains, inter alia, that "the supervisory power has blurred the constitutional and statutory limitations on the authority of the federal courts [and] fostered the erroneous view that the federal courts exercise general supervision over federal prosecutors and investigators"; and that "there is no statutory or constitutional source of authority broad enough to encompass all of the supervisory power decisions." Id. at 1434–35.

"In cases not involving questions of judicial procedure or a statutory violation," concludes Beale, id. at 1521–22, the federal courts lack the authority "to exclude evidence or to dismiss a prosecution unless the government's conduct violated the

2. After today, a decision that is foreshadowed—not new at all—is applicable both on direct review and in collateral proceedings. A decision that makes law that is somewhat new is to apply to all cases on direct review but will generally not be a basis for collateral relief. Really new decisions breaking with the past, however, will likely apply neither in collateral proceedings nor to cases on direct review other than that in which the decision is announced. The majority thus recognizes for purposes of retroactivity doctrine three categories of decisions: not new, newish, and brand new. I had hoped that after plenary review, we could do better than that.

b. Rehnquist, J., also filed a separate dissent, emphasizing that apparently the Court was unwilling to adopt "both aspects" of Justice Harlan's approach to retroactivity—according to Harlan, a new ruling would not apply, with narrow exceptions, in collateral proceedings challenging convictions that had become final before the new rule was announced.

Constitution. This analysis requires the federal courts to decide some constitutional issues they are now able to avoid—or at least defer—by grounding their rulings on supervisory power. * * * [Requiring the federal courts to ground decisions on a constitutional basis] would be likely to result in eliminating some restrictions on federal investigators and prosecutors that have been grounded solely on supervisory power. This is as it should be.

"But this approach need not straitjacket the courts. Where there has been a legislative grant of authority, such as the rules enabling legislation, the power of the courts is extensive. Amendments to the Federal Rules of Criminal Procedure may properly regulate some matters that have been the subject of highly questionable supervisory power rulings. * * * But the concept of separation of powers dictates that federal prosecutors and investigators, like their state counterparts, should perform their duties subject only to the requirements imposed by the federal Constitution and statutes, not subject to the federal judiciary's preference for particular policies and practices."

In *United States v. Russell,* 411 U.S. 423, 93 S.Ct. 1637, 36 L.Ed.2d 366 (1973) (discussed at p. 493 infra), in the course of rejecting respondent's argument that he had been "entrapped" because there had been an intolerable degree of government involvement in the criminal enterprise, the Court, per Rehnquist, J., observed:

"[Several lower federal court decisions] have undoubtedly gone beyond this Court's [precedents] in order to bar prosecutions because of what they thought to be * * * 'overzealous law enforcement.' But the [entrapment defense] was not intended to give the federal judiciary a 'chancellor's foot' veto over law enforcement practices of which it does not disapprove. The execution of the federal laws under our Constitution is confined primarily to the Executive Branch of the Government, subject to applicable constitutional and statutory limitations and to judicially fashioned rules to enforce those limitations."

When a three-justice plurality (Rehnquist, J., joined by the Chief Justice and White, J.,) quoted the "chancellor's foot" passage with approval in *Hampton v. United States,* 425 U.S. 484, 96 S.Ct. 1646, 48 L.Ed.2d 113 (1976) (discussed at p. 495 infra), concurring Justice Powell, joined by Blackmun, J., observed:

"The plurality's use of the 'chancellor's foot' passage from *Russell* may suggest that it also would foreclose reliance on our supervisory power to bar conviction of [a defendant predisposed to commit the crime] because of outrageous police conduct. * * * I do not understand *Russell* to have gone so far. There we indicated only that we should be extremely reluctant to invoke the supervisory power in cases of this kind because that power does not give the 'federal judiciary a "chancellor's foot" veto over law enforcement practices of which it [does] not approve.' * * * I therefore am unwilling to join the plurality in concluding that, no matter what the circumstances, neither due process principles nor our supervisory power could support a bar to conviction in any case where the Government is able to prove predisposition [to commit the crime]." [a]

Whatever the implications of the "chancellor's foot" passage, both in *Payner,* infra, and in *Hasting,* infra, the Court left no doubt that it took a dim view of the federal courts' exercise of their "supervisory power."

UNITED STATES v. PAYNER, 447 U.S. 727, 100 S.Ct. 2439, 65 L.Ed.2d 468 (1980), arose as follows: An IRS investi-

a. Dissenting Justice Brennan, joined by Stewart and Marshall, JJ., agreed with Justices Powell and Blackmun that "*Russell* does not foreclose imposition of a bar to conviction—based upon our supervisory power or due process principles—where the conduct of law enforcement authorities is sufficiently offensive, even though the individuals entitled to invoke such a defense might be 'predisposed.' "

gation into the financial activities of American citizens in the Bahamas focused on a certain Bahamian bank. When an official of that bank visited the United States, IRS agents stole his briefcase for a time, removed hundreds of documents from the briefcase and photographed them. As a result of this "briefcase caper," defendant Payner was convicted of federal income tax violations. Because Payner lacked "standing" to challenge the "briefcase caper" under the Court's Fourth Amendment precedents (see Ch. 11, § 1), the federal district court invoked its supervisory power to exclude the tainted evidence. The district court found, and these findings were undisturbed by the higher courts, that "the Government counsels its agents that the Fourth Amendment standing limitation permits them to purposefully conduct an unconstitutional search and seizure of one individual in order to obtain evidence against third parties who are the real targets of the government intrusion" and that IRS agents "transacted the 'briefcase caper' with a purposeful, bad faith hostility toward the Fourth Amendment rights of [the bank official] in order to obtain evidence against persons like Payner." But a 6–3 majority, per POWELL, J., held that the supervisory power "does not authorize a federal court" to exclude evidence that did not violate the defendant's Fourth Amendment rights:

"[T]he interest in deterring illegal searches does not justify the exclusion of tainted evidence at the instance of a party who was not the victim of the challenged practices. The values assigned to the competing interests do not change because a court has elected to analyze the question under the supervisory power instead of the Fourth Amendment. In either case, the need to deter the underlying conduct and the detrimental impact of excluding the evidence remain precisely the same.

"[The district court's reasoning, which the [Sixth Circuit] affirmed, amounts to a substitution of individual judgment for the controlling decisions of this Court. Were we to accept this use of the supervisory power, we would confer on the judiciary discretionary power to disregard the considered limitations of the law it is charged with enforcing. [T]he supervisory power does not extend so far."

Dissenting Justice MARSHALL, joined by Brennan and Blackmun, JJ., maintained that the Court's holding "effectively turns the standing rules created by this Court for assertions of Fourth Amendment violations into a sword to be used by the Government to permit it deliberately to invade one person's Fourth Amendment rights in order to obtain evidence against another person. Unlike the Court, I do not believe that the federal courts are unable to protect the integrity of the judicial system from such gross government misconduct." Continued the dissent:

"The Court's decision to engraft the standing limitations of the Fourth Amendment onto the exercise of supervisory powers is puzzling not only because it runs contrary to the major purpose behind the exercise of the supervisory powers—to protect the integrity of the court—but also because it appears to render the supervisory powers superfluous. In order to establish that suppression of evidence under the supervisory powers would be proper, the Court would also require Payner to establish a violation of his Fourth or Fifth Amendment rights, in which case suppression would flow directly from the Constitution. This approach is totally unfaithful to our prior supervisory power cases, which, contrary to the Court's suggestion, are not constitutional cases in disguise."

UNITED STATES v. HASTING, 461 U.S. 499, 103 S.Ct. 1974, 76 L.Ed.2d 96 (1983), arose as follows: Five defendants were convicted of kidnapping and transporting women across state lines for immoral purposes. Concluding that the prosecutor had violated *Griffin v. California*

(p. 39 fn. a supra) by, in effect, commenting on the failure of any defendant to take the stand in his own defense, the U.S. Court of Appeals for the Seventh Circuit reversed. The Seventh Circuit was motivated at least in part by what it perceived to be continuing violations of *Griffin* by the prosecutors within its jurisdiction. Although impermissible comment on a defendant's failure to take the stand is subject to a "harmless error" doctrine (See Ch. 11, § 2), the Seventh Circuit declined to apply that doctrine, stating that its application "would impermissibly compromise the clear constitutional violation of the defendants' Fifth Amendment rights." The Court, per BURGER, C.J., reversed:

"[W]e proceed on the assumption that, without so stating, the court was exercising its supervisory powers to discipline the prosecutors of its jurisdiction. The question presented is whether, on this record, in a purported exercise of supervisory powers, a reviewing court may ignore the harmless error [doctrine]. We hold that the [doctrine] may not be avoided by an assertion of supervisory power, simply to justify a reversal of these criminal convictions.

"[I]n the exercise of supervisory powers, federal courts may, within limits, formulate procedural rules not specifically required by the Constitution or the Congress. The purposes underlying use of the supervisory powers are threefold: to implement a remedy for violation of recognized rights; to preserve judicial integrity by ensuring that a conviction rests on appropriate considerations validly before the jury; and finally, as a remedy designed to deter illegal conduct.

"[These goals] are not, however, significant in the context of this case if, as the Court of Appeals plainly implied, the errors alleged are harmless. Supervisory power to reverse a conviction is not needed as a remedy when the error to which it is addressed is harmless since by definition, the conviction would have been obtained notwithstanding the asserted error. Further, in this context, the integrity of the process carries less weight, for it is the essence of the harmless error doctrine that a judgment may stand only when there is no 'reasonable possibility that the [practice] complained of might have contributed to the conviction.' *Fahy v. Connecticut.* Finally, deterence is an inappropriate basis for reversal where, as here, the prosecutor's remark is at most an attenuated violation of *Griffin* and where means more narrowly tailored to deter objectionable prosecutorial conduct are available.[5]

"To the extent that the values protected by supervisory authority are at issue here, these powers may not be exercised in a vacuum. Rather, reversals of convictions under the court's supervisory power must be approached 'with some caution,' *Payner,* and with a view toward balancing the interests involved. [T]he Court of Appeals failed in this case to give appropriate—if, indeed, any—weight to these relevant interests. It did not consider the trauma the victims of these particularly heinous crimes would experience in a new trial, forcing them to relive harrowing experiences now long past, or the practical problems of retrying these sensitive issues more than four years after the events. The conclusion is inescapable that the Court of Appeals focused exclusively on its concern that the prosecutors within its jurisdiction

5. Here, for example, the court could have dealt with the offending argument by directing the District Court to order the prosecutor to show cause why he should not be disciplined, or by asking the Department of Justice to initiate a disciplinary proceeding against him. The Government informs us that in the last three years, the Department of Justice's Office of Professional Responsibility has investigated 28 complaints of unethical conduct and that one assistant United States attorney resigned in the face of an investigation that he made improper arguments to a grand jury. The Court also could have publicly chastised the prosecutor by identifying him in its opinion.

were indifferent to the frequent admonitions of the court. The court appears to have decided to deter future similar comments by the drastic step of reversal of these convictions. But the interests preserved by the doctrine of harmless error cannot be so lightly and casually ignored in order to chastise what the court viewed as prosecutorial overreaching." [b]

Justice BRENNAN, joined by Marshall, J., concurred in part and dissented in part, observing:

"Although I would not reach the question, I do not believe that [the] fact that an error is harmless, necessarily precludes a court of appeals from exercising its supervisory powers to reverse a conviction.

"[Various cases] indicate that the policy considerations supporting the harmless error rule and those supporting the existence of an appellate court's supervisory powers are not in irreconcilable conflict. Both the harmless error rule and the exercise of supervisory powers advance the important judicial and public interest in the orderly and efficient administration of justice. Exercise of the supervisory powers also can further the strong public interest in the integrity of the judicial process. If Government prosecutors have engaged in a pattern and practice of intentionally violating defendants' constitutional rights, a court of appeals certainly might be justified in reversing a conviction, even if the error at issue is harmless, in an effort to deter future violations. If effective as a deterrent, the reversal could avert further damage to judicial integrity. Admittedly, using the supervisory powers to reverse a conviction under these circumstances appears to conflict with the public's interest in upholding otherwise valid convictions that are tainted only by harmless error. But it is certainly arguable that the public's interests in preserving judicial integrity and in insuring the Government prosecutors, as its agents, refrain from intentionally violating defendants' rights are stronger than its interest in upholding the conviction of a particular criminal defendant. Convictions are important, but they should not be protected at any cost."

Notes and Questions

1. Under the *Massiah* doctrine (p. 527 infra), an indicted defendant has a Sixth Amendment right to counsel as well as his *Miranda* safeguards. Stressing that the "strict standard" governing waiver of counsel at trial should apply to an alleged waiver of the *Massiah* right to counsel as well, in *United States v. Mohabir* (1980) (discussed more extensively at p. 636 infra), the U.S. Court of Appeals for the Second Circuit exercised its supervisory power to hold that a "valid waiver of the Sixth Amendment right to have counsel present during post-indictment interrogation must be preceded by a federal judicial officer's explanation of the content and significance of this right." Would the Supreme Court agree? Or would it deem the Second Circuit's reasoning "a substitution of individual judgment for the controlling decisions of this Court"? Cf. *Payner.*

2. The *Hastings* Court noted that, within limits, federal courts may exercise their "supervisory power [to] formulate procedural rules not specifically required by the Constitution or the Congress." After *Payner* and *Hastings,* what procedural rules? Consider Note 5, p. 705 infra and ch. 15, § 3 (Schofield) (exercise of federal supervisory power over grand juries). After *Payner* and *Hastings,* may the federal courts still *exclude evidence* or reverse a conviction based in part on inadmissible evidence if such exclusion or reversal is not required by the Constitution or the Congress?

b. Stevens, J., concurred in the judgment, deeming the prosecutor's comments "free of constitutional error." Blackmun, J., would vacate the judgment and remand the case for consideration of whether the Fifth Amendment violation it perceived was "harmless."

SECTION 5. TRENDS AND COUNTERTRENDS: THE "NEW FEDERALISM IN CRIMINAL PROCEDURE" AND NEW LIMITATIONS ON STATE RIGHTS PROTECTIONS [a]

When the Warren Court's "criminal procedure revolution" came to a halt, a number of state courts "greeted the Burger Court's retreat from activism not with submission, but with a stubborn independence that displays a determination to keep alive the Warren Court's philosophical commitment to protection of the criminal suspect." Wilkes, *More on the New Federalism in Criminal Procedure,* 63 Ky.L.J. 873 (1975). See also Howard, *State Courts and Constitutional Rights in the Day of the Burger Court,* 62 Va.L.Rev. 873, 891–907 (1976).

Typically, the state court determined to provide the accused with greater protection under state law than that said to be required by the Federal Constitution construes a state constitutional provision more expansively than the Burger Court has interpreted a *textually identical* or *parallel* provision of the Federal Bill of Rights.[b] But sometimes, as in *People v. Jackson,* 217 N.W.2d 22 (Mich.1974), the state court may rest its decision on its authority to establish rules of evidence for its own courts.[c]

Justice Brennan and Marshall, who often found themselves in a dissenting role in the 1970's, frequently pointed to—and approved and encouraged—the practice of some state courts (a distinct minority) to interpret state procedural rights more expansively than does the current U.S. Supreme Court. See especially Justice Brennan's dissenting opinions in *United States v. Miller* (p. 249 infra) and in *Michigan v. Mosley* (p. 610 infra). See also Brennan, *State Constitutions and the Protection of Individual Rights,* 90 Harv.L.Rev. 489, 502 (1977), stressing that "the decisions of the Court are not, and should not be, dispositive of questions regarding rights guaranteed by counterpart provisions of state law. * * * [A]lthough in the past it might have been safe for counsel to raise only federal constitutional issues in state courts, plainly it would be most unwise these days not also to raise the state constitutional questions."[d]

a. The phrase "new federalism in criminal procedure" was coined by Professor Donald Wilkes, Jr., in his 1974 article, *The New Federalism in Criminal Procedure: State Court Evasion of the Burger Court,* 62 Ky.L.J. 421.

b. See, e.g., *People v. Brisendine,* 531 P.2d 1099 (Cal.1975) (refusing to follow the U.S. Supreme Court's interpretation of the Fourth Amendment in *United States v. Robinson* (p. 386 infra) and *Gustafson v. Florida* (p. 393 infra) and interpreting California's virtually identical state constitutional guarantee to permit only "pat-down" searches for weapons in similar circumstances); *People v. Disbrow,* 545 P.2d 272 (Cal. 1976) (rejecting *Harris v. New York* (p. 828 infra and *Oregon v. Hass* (p. 380 infra), and holding that the California Constitution prohibits the use of incriminating statements obtained in violation of *Miranda* for impeachment purposes). See also *State v. Glass,* 583 P.2d 872 (Alaska 1978) (rejecting *United States v. White* (p. 463 infra) and holding that "participant monitoring" by law enforcement personnel must satisfy state constitutional requirements); *People v. Beavers,* 227 N.W. 2d 511 (Mich.1975) (same) *State v. Kaluna,* 520 P.2d 51 (Hawaii 1974) (rejecting *Robinson*); *State v. Santiago,* 492 P.2d 657 (Hawaii 1971) (rejecting *Harris*); *Commonwealth v. Triplett,* 341 A.2d 62 (Pa.1975) (same); *State v. Johnson,* 346 A.2d 66 (N.J.1975) (rejecting *Schneckloth v. Bustamonte,* p. 408 infra); *State v. Opperman* (p. 360 infra) (rejecting *South Dakota v. Opperman* p. 355 infra).

c. Rejecting *Kirby v. Illinois* (p. 668 infra) and *United States v. Ash* (p. 674 infra), *Jackson* held that a Michigan defendant is entitled to the assistance of counsel at a preindictment lineup and at any photographic display. *Kirby* was also rejected in *Blue v. State,* 558 P.2d 636 (Alaska 1977) and *Commonwealth v. Richman,* 320 A.2d 351 (Pa.1974).

d. See generally Abrahamson, *Criminal Law and State Constitutions: The Emergence of State Constitutional Law,* 63 Texas L.Rev. 1141 (1985); Howard, *Introduction: A Frequent Recurrence to Fundamental Principles,* in Developments in State Constitutional Law (B. McGraw ed. 1984) (hereinafter referred to as "Developments"); Linde, *E. Pluribus—Constitutional Theory and State Courts,* 18 Ga.L.Rev. 165 (1984); Mosk, *State Constitutionalism after Warren: Avoiding*

In recent years, some state courts, when applying their own state constitutional guarantee against unreasonable searches and seizures, have refused to follow the interpretation the U.S. Supreme Court has given the Fourth Amendment in several highly publicized cases. Thus, *People v. Bigelow,* 488 N.E.2d 451 (N.Y.1985), per Simons, J., and *Stringer v. State,* 477 So.2d 1335 (Miss.1985), per Robertson, J., rejected the "good faith" exception to the Fourth Amendment exclusionary rule established in *United States v. Leon* (p. 216 infra). *Stringer* "perceived no vehicle for protecting [the rights of state citizens against unreasonable searches and seizures] and assuring that issuing magistrates take seriously their responsibilities other than continued enforcement of the state's exclusionary rule."

On remand from the U.S. Supreme Court (see *Massachusetts v. Upton,* p. 278 infra), *Commonwealth v. Upton,* 476 N.E.2d 548 (Mass.1985), per Wilkins, J., concluded that Article 14 of the state's Declaration of Rights "provides more substantive protection [than] does the Fourth Amendment in the determination of probable cause." The state court then rejected the "totality of the circumstances" test for probable cause adopted by the U.S. Supreme Court in *Illinois v. Gates* (p. 264 infra), deeming that test "unacceptably shapeless and permissive."[e]

People v. Oates, 698 P.2d 811 (Colo. 1985) per Dubofsky, J., rejected the U.S. Supreme Court's reasoning in *United States v. Karo* (p. 251 infra) and held that the installation of a "beeper" in a chemical drum prior to its transfer to a buyer infringed a legitimate expectation of privacy under the Colorado constitutional analogue to the Fourth Amendment and thus constituted a "search" requiring a warrant under the state constitution. "The broader definition of what constitutes a legitimate expectation of privacy under the Colorado Constitution [Art. II, § 7]," concluded the Court, "encompasses the expectation that purchased commercial goods will be free of government surveillance devices such as beepers."

Dissenting, Erickson, C.J., joined by Rovira, J., disagreed with the majority's use of the state constitution to avoid the *Karo* analysis: "This court should not depart from U.S. Supreme Court decisions interpreting identical language in the federal constitution without principled reasons for doing so. This case illustrates the practical reason for hesitation. The DEA's activities cover the entire country. A beeper installed legally in one state may be traced to another where a warrant is required; DEA agents should not be expected to know the individual requirements in each state."[f]

Although the "new federalism in criminal procedure" became apparent more than a decade ago, "recent constitutional and statutory changes in state law * * * have imposed new restrictions on the new federalism." Wilkes, *The New Federalism*

201; Schleuter, *Federalism and Supreme Court Review of Expansive State Court Decisions: A Response to Unfortunate Impressions,* 11 Hastings Con.L.Q. 523 (1984); Wilkes, *The New Federalism in Criminal Procedure in 1984: Death of the Phoenix?,* in Developments 166; *Developments in the Law—The Interpretation of State Constitutional Rights,* 95 Harv.L.Rev. 1324, 1367–98 (1982).

e. See also *State v. Jackson,* 688 P.2d 136 (Wash.1984), rejecting the *Gates* test under the state's constitution and maintaining that the *Gates* approach "lacks sufficient specificity and analytical structure to adequately inform magistrates as to the appropriate standards required to protect the right of privacy secured by [the state constitution]."

f. See also *Sterling v. Cupp,* 625 P.2d 123 (Or. 1981) (Linde, J.) (relying on state constitutional provision to enjoin certain searches of state prisoners by guards of the opposite sex, and stressing that "the proper sequence" is to analyze the state's law before reaching a federal constitutional claim); *State v. Davis,* 666 P.2d 802 (Or.1983) (Carson, J.) (reviewing basis upon which illegally seized evidence has been held inadmissible in this state and rejecting the "deterrence rationale" or "instrumentalist approach" of recent U.S. Supreme Court decisions).

in Criminal Procedure in 1984: Death of the Phoenix?, in Developments in State Constitutional Law 166, 169 (B. McGraw ed. 1985) (hereinafter referred to as "Wilkes").

"Many of the best and brightest of the new federalism decisions have come from the California Supreme Court," Wilkes at 171, but The California Victims' Bill of Rights, often called Proposition 8, an initiative approved by the voters in 1982, "represents a major victory for the opponents of the new federalism in California, who have become increasingly vocal in their attacks since the early 1970s." Id. Proposition 8 added a new Section 28 to Article I of the California Bill of Rights. A so-called "right to truth-in-evidence" provision of the new section reads: "Except as provided by statute hereafter enacted by a two thirds vote of the membership in each house of the Legislature, relevant evidence shall not be excluded in any criminal proceeding * * *." *In re Lance W.,* 694 P.2d 744 (Cal.1985), held that this provision abrogated the vicarious exclusionary rule that was established in *People v. Martin* (1955) (p. 777 infra) and applied to both Fourth Amendment and state constitutional violations. The court observed, per Grodin, J.:

"The substance [of the state constitutional guarantees] remains unaffected by Proposition 8. What would have been an unlawful search or seizure in this state before the passage of [Proposition 8] would be unlawful today, and this is so even if it would pass muster under the federal Constitution. What Proposition 8 does is to eliminate a judicially created *remedy* for violations of the search and seizure provisions of the federal or state Constitutions, through the exclusion of evidence so obtained, except to the extent that exclusion remains federally compelled." [g]

Art. 1, § 12 of the 1968 Florida Constitution contained language that for the first time wrote the exclusionary rule into the text of the state constitutional guarantee against unreasonable search and seizure and the state supreme court subsequently held that the state guarantee provided Florida citizens with more protection against governmental intrusion than did the Fourth Amendment. See, e.g., *State v. Dodd,* 419 So.2d 333 (Fla.1982). But a 1982 amendment to Art. 1, § 12 [h] apparently requires the state guarantee to be interpreted in lockstep with the interpretation given the Fourth Amendment by the U.S. Supreme Court and "links Florida's [explicit] exclusionary rule to the federal exclusionary rule, making it also nothing more than a creature of judicial decisional policy and removing the 'independent protective force of state law.'" *State v. Lavazzoli,* 434 So.2d 321 (Fla.1983).[i]

---

g. "In light of the long history of jurisprudence in this state surrounding [the vicarious exclusionary] rule, and the vague, imprecise and inconclusive language of the assertedly relevant portion of Proposition 8," dissenting Justice Mosk, joined by Bird, C.J., and Reynoso, J., maintained that those who adopted Proposition 8 did not intend to abolish the state's vicarious exclusionary rule.

h. As amended, this section now provides: "This right shall be construed in conformity with the 4th Amendment to the United States Constitution, as interpreted by the United States Supreme Court * * *. Articles or information obtained in violation of this right shall not be admissible in evidence if [they] would be inadmissible under decisions of the United States Supreme Court construing the 4th Amendment * * *."

i. Consider, too, the 1981 statutory repeal of Maryland's short-lived version of the *McNabb-Mallory* rule (p. 524 infra), a legislative blow to the new federalism discussed in Wilkes at 169–71; and the overturning, by state constitutional amendment, of a 1975 Pennsylvania Supreme Court ruling, *Commonwealth v. Triplett* (fn. b supra), barring the use for impeachment purposes of confessions obtained in violation of *Miranda.* As amended, Art. 1, § 9 of the Pennsylvania Constitution permits "the use of a suppressed voluntary confession to impeach the credibility of a person" and provides that such use "shall not be construed as compelling a person to give evidence against himself." See generally Collins, *The New Federalism Is Thriving Despite Setbacks and Losses in 1984,* April 29, 1985, Nat'l L.J., p. 32.

As might be expected, the state courts' interpretation of state constitutional provisions so that they provide greater protection than that required by the present Supreme Court's interpretation of identical or parallel provisions of the Bill of Rights has received a chilly reception in some U.S. Supreme Court Justices' chambers. Thus, concurring in the dismissal of the writ of certiorari as improvidently granted in *Florida v. Casal,* 462 U.S. 637, 103 S.Ct. 3100, 77 L.Ed.2d 277 (1983), Chief Justice Burger expressed satisfaction with the 1982 amendment to the Florida Constitution. "As amended," he noted, Art. 1, § 12 "ensures that Florida courts will no longer be able to rely on the State Constitution to suppress evidence that would be admissible under the decisions of the Supreme Court of the United States. * * * [W]hen state courts interpret state law to require *more* than the Federal Constitution requires, the citizens of the state must be aware that they have the power to amend state law to ensure rational law enforcement."

In MICHIGAN v. LONG, 463 U.S. 1032, 103 S.Ct. 3469, 77 L.Ed.2d 1201 (1983) (also discussed at p. 382 infra), rejecting the argument that "the Michigan courts have provided greater protection from searches and seizures under the state constitution than is afforded under the Fourth Amendment, and the [state supreme court's] references to the state constitution therefore establishes an adequate and independent ground for the decision below," the Court, per O'CONNOR, J., took the occasion to "reexamine our treatment of [the] jurisdictional issue in order to achieve the consistency that is necessary" when various forms of references to state law are said to constitute adequate and independent state grounds:

"[W]hen, as in this case, a state court decision fairly appears to rest primarily on federal law, or to be interwoven with the federal law, and when the adequacy and independence of any possible state law ground is not clear from the face of the opinion, we will accept as the most reasonable explanation that the state court decided the case the way it did because it believed that federal law required it to do so. If a state court chooses merely to rely on federal precedents as it would on the precedents of all other jurisdictions, then it need only make clear by a plain statement in its judgment or opinion that the federal cases are being used only for the purpose of guidance, and do not themselves compel the result that the court has reached. In this way, both justice and judicial administration will be greatly improved. If the state court decision indicates clearly and expressly that it is alternatively based on bona fide separate, adequate, and independent grounds, we, of course, will not undertake to review the decision.

"The principle that we will not review judgments of state courts that rest on adequate and independent state grounds is based, in part, on 'the limitations of our own jurisdiction.' The jurisdictional concern is that we not 'render an advisory opinion, and if the same judgment would be rendered by the state court after we corrected its views of federal laws, our review could amount to nothing more than an advisory opinion.' Our requirement of a 'plain statement' that a decision rests upon adequate and independent state grounds does not in any way authorize the rendering of advisory opinions. Rather, in determining, as we must, whether we have jurisdiction to review a case that is alleged to rest on adequate and independent state grounds, we merely assume that there are no such grounds when it is not clear from the opinion itself that the state court relied upon an adequate and independent state ground and when it fairly appears that the state court rested its decision primarily on federal law." [j]

j. The Court then reviewed the decision below under this framework and came away "unconvinced that it rests upon an independent state ground."

Dissenting Justice STEVENS could not accept the Court's decision "to presume that adequate state grounds are intended to be dependent on federal law unless the record plainly shows otherwise." He continued:

"I am confident that all members of this Court agree that there is a vital interest in the sound management of scarce federal judicial resources. All of those policies counsel against the exercise of federal jurisdiction. They are fortified by my belief that a policy of judicial restraint—one that allows other decisional bodies to have the last word in legal interpretation until it is truly necessary for this Court to intervene—enables this Court to make its most effective contribution to our federal system of government.

"The nature of the case before us hardly compels a departure from tradition. These are not cases in which an American citizen has been deprived of a right secured by the United States Constitution or a federal statute. Rather, they are cases in which a state court has upheld a citizen's assertion of a right, finding the citizen to be protected under both federal and state law. The complaining party is an officer of the state itself, who asks us to rule that the state court interpreted federal rights too broadly and 'over-protected' the citizen. Such cases should not be of inherent concern to this Court. * * *

"In this case the State of Michigan has arrested one of its citizens and the Michigan Supreme Court has decided to turn him loose. The respondent is a United States citizen as well as a Michigan citizen, but since there is no claim that he has been mistreated by the State of Michigan, the final outcome of the state processes offended no federal interest whatever. Michigan simply provided greater protection to one of its citizens than some other State might provide or, indeed, than this Court might require throughout the country.

"I believe that in reviewing the decisions of state courts, the primary role of this Court is to make sure that persons who seek to *vindicate* federal rights have been fairly heard. That belief resonates with statements in many of our prior cases. * * *

"Until recently we had virtually no interest in cases of this type. Some time during the past decade, * * * our priorities shifted. The result is a docket swollen with requests by states to reverse judgments that their courts have rendered in favor of their citizens. I am confident that a future Court will recognize the error of this allocation of resources. When that day comes, I think it likely that the Court will also reconsider the propriety of today's expansion of our jurisdiction." [k]

See also *Florida v. Meyers,* 466 U.S. 380, 104 S.Ct. 1852, 80 L.Ed.2d 381 (1984) (per curiam), summarily reversing a state intermediate appellate court because it "either misunderstood or ignored our prior rulings with respect to the constitutionality of the warrantless search of an impounded automobile." (The state supreme court had denied discretionary review.) Respondent argued that the Court should not review the search and seizure issue because the state court had reversed the conviction on two independent grounds, one of which (restricted cross-examination) the state did not contest. But the Court found no "clear indication that the cross-examina-

k. Although he was satisfied that the Court had jurisdiction in this particular case, concurring Justice Blackmun did not join the part of the Court's opinion "fashioning a new presumption of jurisdiction over cases coming here from state courts." Brennan, J., joined by Marshall, J., agreed that the Court had jurisdiction to decide the case, but dissented on the merits of the search and seizure issue. (See p. 383 infra.)

For strong criticism of *Michigan v. Long,* see Greenhalgh, *Independent and Adequate State Grounds: The Long and the Short of It,* in Developments in State Constitutional Law (B. McGraw ed. 1985). For a discussion of how defense lawyers can protect a favorable state court ruling from possible federal court review, see Collins, *Plain Statements: The Supreme Court's New Requirements,* Mar. 1984 A.B.A.J., p. 92.

tion ruling provided an independent and adequate basis for reversal of the conviction. See *Michigan v. Long.*"

Dissenting Justice Stevens, joined by Brennan and Marshall, JJ., who saw "no reason why we cannot leave to the Florida Supreme Court the task of managing its own discretionary docket," took issue with the Court's reliance on *Long.* And he noted: "Since the beginning of the October 1981 Term, the Court has decided in summary fashion 19 cases, including this one, concerning the constitutional rights of persons accused or convicted of crimes. All 19 were decided on the petition of the warden or prosecutor, and in all he was successful in obtaining reversal of a decision upholding a claim of constitutional right. * * * [T]his pattern of results, and in particular the fact that in its last two and one-half Terms the Court has been unwilling in even a single criminal case to employ its discretionary power of summary disposition in order to uphold a claim of constitutional right, is quite striking."

Chapter 3

THE RIGHT TO COUNSEL, TRANSCRIPTS AND OTHER AIDS; POVERTY, EQUALITY AND THE ADVERSARY SYSTEM

REPORT OF THE ATTORNEY GENERAL'S COMMITTEE ON POVERTY AND THE ADMINISTRATION OF FEDERAL CRIMINAL JUSTICE 5–11 (1963) [a]

POVERTY AND CRIMINAL JUSTICE: THE NATURE OF GOVERNMENT'S OBLIGATION

* * *

a. *The Concept of "Poverty."* [The] concept proved an elusive one and the difficulties of definition substantial.[b] It is apparent that a total absence in the accused of all means and resources cannot be adequate for these purposes. Even the constitutional rights to the appointment of counsel are not conditioned on a showing of total destitution. Rather, the criterion appears to be a lack of financial resources adequate to permit the accused to hire his own lawyer.[c] Reflection led the Committee to the conclusion that the poverty must be viewed as a relative concept with the consequence that the poverty of accused must be measured in each case by reference to the particular need or service under consideration.

Thus in the criminal process a problem of poverty may arise at each stage of the proceedings. There is a problem of poverty if the defendant is unable to obtain pre-trial release by reason of financial inability to meet the bail requirements or to retain a lawyer to represent him at the trial. There is also a problem of poverty if the accused is unable to finance a pretrial investigation of the case or to obtain the services of expert witnesses when such in-

a. The Report is often called *The Allen Report,* after the Chairman of the Committee, Professor Francis A. Allen.

b. "[F]ew statutory standards are available to guide the [trial court] in its determination of indigency sufficient to warrant court-appointed counsel; as a result, the courts have utilized various criteria for determining eligibility. While some courts have limited the scope of inquiry, for example, to whether the accused is working and has money to hire a lawyer, other courts have considered the accused's assets, debts, employment, ability to post bail, and responsibility for dependents. The confusion and lack of consistency that exist in federal indigency standards are mirrored in the state courts." Note, 12 U.S.F.L.Rev. 717, 720–21 (1978). See also Zeigler & Hermann, *The Invisible Litigant: An Inside View of Pro Se Actions in the Federal Courts,* 47 N.Y.U.L.Rev. 157, 187–89 (1972).

c. Consider, *In re Smiley,* 427 P.2d 179 (Cal. 1967), defining the test of eligibility for court-appointed counsel as "whether or not a private attorney would be interested in representing the defendant in his present economic circumstances." Can this standard be applied with any uniformity?

vestigation or testimony is essential to an adequate defense.[d] So, too, in the appellate process, there is a problem of poverty if through lack of means the accused is inhibited or prevented from presenting grounds of reversal to the appellate court or from making adequate presentation.

It follows that concern with poverty and the administration of criminal justice requires attention to be extended beyond those who are unable at the outset of the proceedings to obtain release on bail or to hire counsel.[e] It requires consideration, also, of those who, although possessing means to obtain some elements of an adequate defense (such as hiring a lawyer), lack means to secure other essential elements.[f] Indeed, it requires attention be given to the plight of the accused with substantial means rendered indigent by the levy of a jeopardy assessment and thus unable to hire the services of an accountant in defense of a net-worth tax prosecution. * * *

In summary, the Committee believes that, for the purposes at hand, poverty must be conceived as a relative concept. An impoverished accused is not necessarily one totally devoid of means. A problem of poverty arises for the system of criminal justice when at any stage of the proceedings lack of means in the accused substantially inhibits or prevents the proper assertion of a right or a claim of right.

b. *The obligation of "Equal Justice."* * * *

[It] should be understood that governmental obligation to deal effectively with problems of poverty in the administration of criminal justice does not rest or depend upon some hypothetical obligation of government to indulge in acts of public charity. It does not presuppose a general commitment on the part of the federal government to relieve impoverished persons of the consequences of limited means, whenever or however manifested. It does not even presuppose that government is always required to take into account the means of the citizen when dealing directly with its citizens. * * *

The obligation of government in the criminal cases rests on wholly different considerations and reflects principles of much more limited application. The essential point is that the problems of poverty with which this Report is concerned arise in a process *initiated* by government for the achievement of basic governmental purposes. It is, moreover, a process that has as one of its consequences the imposition of severe disabilities on the persons proceeded against. Duties arise from action. When a course of conduct, however legitimate, entails the possibility of serious injury to persons, a duty on the actor to avoid the reasonably avoidable injuries is ordinarily recognized. When government chooses to exert its powers in the criminal area, its obligation is surely no less than that of taking reasonable measures to eliminate those factors that are irrelevant to just administration of the law but which, nevertheless, may occasionally affect determinations of the accused's liability or penalty. While government may not be required to relieve the accused of his poverty, it may properly be required to minimize the influence of poverty on its administration of justice.

The Committee, therefore, conceives the obligation of government less as an undertaking to eliminate "discrimination"

d. On the indigent's right to investigatory, expert and other assistance in addition to counsel, see *Ake v. Oklahoma* (p. 102 infra) and accompanying Notes.

e. I *A.B.A. Standards* § 5–6.1 provides that assigned counsel "should not be denied merely because friends or relatives have resources adequate to retain counsel or because bond has been or can be posted."

f. I *A.B.A. Standards* § 5–6.1 provides: "Supporting services necessary to an adequate defense should be available to all persons eligible for representation *and to the clients of retained counsel* who are financially unable to afford necessary supporting services." (Emphasis added.) See also the discussion of the Criminal Justice Act at p. 105 fn. a infra.

against a class of accused persons and more as a broad commitment by government to rid its processes of all influences that tend to defeat the ends a system of justice is intended to serve. Such a concept of "equal justice" does not confuse equality of treatment with identity of treatment. We assume that government must be conceded flexibility in devising its measures and that reasonable classifications are permitted. The crucial question is, has government done all that can reasonably be required of it to eliminate those factors that inhibit the proper and effective assertion of grounds relevant to the criminal liability of the accused or to the imposition of sanctions and disabilities on the accused at all stages of the criminal process?

c. *Poverty and the Adversary System.*

* * *

[The] essence of the adversary system is challenge. The survival of our system of criminal justice and the values which it advances depend upon a constant, searching, and creative questioning of official decisions and assertions of authority at all stages of the process. The proper performance of the defense function is thus as vital to the health of the system as the performance of the prosecuting and adjudicatory functions. It follows that insofar as the financial status of the accused impedes vigorous and proper challenges, it constitutes a threat to the viability of the adversary system. We believe that the system is imperiled by the large numbers of accused persons unable to employ counsel or to meet even modest bail requirements and by the large, but indeterminate, numbers of persons, able to pay some part of the costs of defense, but unable to finance a full and proper defense.[g] Persons suffering such disabilities are incapable of providing the challenges that are indispensable to satisfactory operation of the system. The loss to the interests of accused individuals, occasioned by these failures, are great and apparent. It is also clear that a situation in which persons are required to contest a serious accusation but are denied access to the tools of contest is offensive to fairness and equity. Beyond these considerations, however, is the fact that the conditions produced by the financial incapacity of the accused are detrimental to the proper functioning of the system of justice and that the loss in vitality of the adversary system, thereby occasioned, significantly endangers the basic interests of a free community.

g. Subsequent experience indicates a typical indigency rate of 60–70% for felonies and as high as 30–50% for misdemeanors. See p. 26 supra.

Notes and Questions

1. *The indigent defendant's "obligation" to repay the government for defense costs; reimbursement as a condition of probation. Rinaldi v. Yeager,* 384 U.S. 305, 86 S.Ct. 1497, 16 L.Ed.2d 577 (1966), invalidated a New Jersey statute which required only those indigent defendants who were sentenced to prison to reimburse the state for the cost of a transcript on appeal, finding an "invidious discrimination" between those convicted defendants and others sentenced only to pay fines or subject only to a suspended sentence or to probation. *James v. Strange,* 407 U.S. 128, 92 S.Ct. 2027, 32 L.Ed. 600 (1972), held that a Kansas recoupment statute (which applied whether or not the indigent defendant was convicted) violated equal protection because the indigent defendant could not avail himself of restrictions on wage garnishments and other protective exemptions afforded to other civil judgment debtors.

Fuller v. Oregon, 417 U.S. 40, 94 S.Ct. 2116, 40 L.Ed.2d 642 (1974), however, upheld an Oregon recoupment statute which, under certain circumstances, authorized repayment to the state of the costs of a free legal defense as a condition of probation. A 7–2 majority, per Stewart, J., stressed that "the recoupment statute is quite clearly directed only at those convicted defendants who are indigent at the time of the criminal proceedings against them but who subsequently gain the ability to pay the expenses of legal representation. Defendants with no likelihood of having the means to repay are not put under even a conditional obligation to do so, and those upon whom a conditional obligation is imposed are not subjected to collection procedures until their indigency has ended and no 'manifest hardship' [to defendant or his immediate family] will result."

Distinguishing *James* and *Rinaldi,* the Court rejected petitioner's equal protection challenge. It pointed out that Oregon had not denied exemptions from execution afforded to other judgment debtors. Unlike the classification struck down in *Rinaldi,* it deemed a distinction between defendants who are convicted, on the one hand, and those acquitted or whose convictions are reversed, on the other hand, "wholly noninvidious": "Oregon could surely decide with objective rationality that when a defendant has been forced to submit to a criminal prosecution that does not end in conviction, he will be freed of any potential liability to reimburse the state for the costs of his defense."

Nor was the Court impressed with the argument that a defendant's knowledge that he may be obligated to reimburse the state for expenses incurred in providing him a legal defense might lead him to reject the services of appointed counsel and thus "chill" his constitutional right to counsel: "The fact that an indigent who accepts [appointed counsel] knows that he might someday be required to repay the costs of these services in no way affects his eligibility to obtain counsel. The Oregon statute is carefully designed to insure that only those who actually become capable of repaying the State will ever be obliged to do so."

Dissenting Justice Marshall, joined by Brennan, J., protested that "the important fact which the majority ignores" is that because the repayment of the indigent defendant's debt to the state can be made a condition of his probation, as it was in this case, "[p]etitioner's failure to pay his debt can result in his being sent to prison. In this respect the indigent defendant in Oregon, like [his counterpart in *James*], is treated quite differently from other civil judgment debtors."

Notwithstanding the *Fuller* case, I *A.B.A. Standards* § 5–6.2 (commentary) "recommends that defendants be ordered to [make reimbursement] for their defense only in instances where they have made fraudulent representations for purposes of being found eligible for counsel. * * * The offer of free legal assistance is rendered hollow if defendants are required to make payments for counsel for several years following conviction. Reimbursement requirements also may serve to discourage defendants from exercising their right to counsel, and long-term duties to make payments for representation may interfere with the rehabilitation of defendants."

"Policy considerations are different if defendants with limited financial resources are required to make contributions for their defense at the time counsel is provided or during the course of the proceedings. Such contribution orders do not impose upon defendants' long-term financial debts and normally are not entered unless there is a realistic prospect that the defendants can make reasonably prompt payments. * * * [But] one very practical consideration militates against the use of either reimbursement or contribution: the amounts which can be collected under such programs are negligible. * * * Pursuant to the federal Criminal Justice Act, for example, the amounts contributed by defendants nationwide averaged approximately $9,000 per annum between 1966 and 1971. During the same period, the annual expenditures for defense services in the federal courts averaged $2,600,000."

2. *Does a conflict between the fifth and sixth amendments inhere in the process of determining indigency as it is presently conducted?* At present, an indigency determination is generally made in open court, without the protections afforded by in camera proceedings and absent any form of immunity. May a defendant's statements about his financial situation be used against him at his pending criminal trial? See *United States v. Kahan,* p. 781 fn. f infra. See generally Note, 12 U.S.F.L.Rev. 717 (1978). If eligibility information can be a source of incriminating evidence, may it be said that an indigent defendant, seeking court-appointed counsel, can be compelled to incriminate himself in order to exercise his Sixth Amendment right to counsel? If so, are there "less restrictive" alternatives available to resolve the constitutional conflicts posed by present indigency proceedings? Should indigency testimony be excluded from evidence? Should indigency proceedings be held in camera? Or should the public defender or, in counties without a public defender, public counsel appointed for this limited purpose, determine eligibility for counsel or other legal assistance? See 12 U.S.F.L.Rev. at 735–42.

SECTION 1. THE RIGHT TO APPOINTED COUNSEL AND RELATED PROBLEMS

I. THE RIGHT TO APPOINTED COUNSEL IN CRIMINAL PROCEEDINGS

BETTS v. BRADY

316 U.S. 455, 62 S.Ct. 1252, 86 L.Ed. 1595 (1942).

MR. JUSTICE ROBERTS delivered the opinion of the Court.

Petitioner, an indigent, was indicted for robbery. His request for counsel was denied because local practice permitted appointment only in rape and murder prosecutions. Petitioner then pled not guilty and elected to be tried without a jury. At the trial he chose not to take the stand. He was convicted and sentenced to eight years imprisonment.

* * * The due process clause of the Fourteenth Amendment does not incorporate, as such, the specific guarantees found in the Sixth Amendment although a denial by a state of rights or privileges specifically embodied in that and others of the first eight amendments may, in certain circumstances, or in connection with other elements, operate, in a given case, to deprive a litigant of due process of law in violation of the Fourteenth. Due process of law * * * formulates a concept less rigid and more fluid than those envisaged in other specific and particular provisions of the Bill of Rights. Its application is less a matter of rule. Asserted denial is to be tested by an appraisal of the totality of facts in a given case.

[Petitioner] says the rule to be deduced from our former decisions is that, in every case, whatever the circumstances, one charged with crime, who is unable to obtain counsel, must be furnished counsel by the state. Expressions in the opinions of this court lend color to the argument, but, as the petitioner admits, none of our decisions squarely adjudicates the question now presented.

In *Powell v. Alabama,* 287 U.S. 45, 53 S.Ct. 55, 77 L.Ed. 158 [1932], ignorant and friendless negro youths, strangers in the community, without friends or means to obtain counsel, were hurried to trial for a capital offense without effective appointment of counsel on whom the burden of preparation and trial would rest, and without adequate opportunity to consult even the counsel casually appointed to represent them. This occurred in a State whose statute law required the appointment of counsel for indigent defendants prosecuted for the offense charged. Thus the trial was conducted in disregard of every principle of fairness and in disregard of that which was declared by the law of the State a requisite of a fair trial. This court held the resulting convictions were without due process of law. It said that, in the light of all the facts, the failure of the trial court to afford the defendants reasonable time and opportunity to secure counsel was a clear denial of due process. The court stated further that "under the circumstances [the] necessity of counsel was so vital and imperative that the failure of the trial court to make an effective appointment of counsel was likewise a denial of due process," but added: "whether this would be so in other criminal prosecutions, or under other circumstances, we need not determine. All that it is necessary now to decide, as we do decide, is that in a capital case, where the defendant is unable to employ counsel, and is incapable adequately of making his own defense because of ignorance, feeble-mindedness, illiteracy, or the like, it is the duty of the court, whether requested or not, to assign counsel for him as a necessary requisite of due process of law * * *"

* * * We have construed the [Sixth Amendment] to require appointment of counsel in all [federal] cases where a defendant is unable to procure the services of an attorney, and where the right has not been intentionally and competently waived. [*Johnson v. Zerbst,* 304 U.S. 458, 58 S.Ct. 1019, 82 L.Ed. 1461 (1938)].[a] Though [the] amendment lays down no rule for the conduct of the states, the question recurs whether the constraint laid by the amendment upon the national courts expresses a rule so fundamental and essential to a fair trial, and so, to due process of law, that it is made obligatory upon the states by the Fourteenth Amendment. Relevant data on the subject are afforded by constitutional and statutory provisions subsisting in the colonies and the states prior to the inclusion of the Bill of Rights in the national Constitution, and in the constitutional, legislative, and judicial history of the states to the present date. * * *

[I]n the great majority of the states, it has been the considered judgment of the people, their representatives and their courts that appointment of counsel is not a fundamental right, essential to a fair trial. On the contrary, the matter has generally been deemed one of legislative policy. In the light of this evidence we are unable to say that the concept of due process incorporated in the Fourteenth Amendment obligates the states, whatever may be their own views, to furnish counsel in every such case. Every court has power, if it deems proper, to appoint counsel where that course seems to be required in the interest of fairness.

The practice of the courts of Maryland gives point to the principle that the states should not be straight-jacketed in this respect, by a construction of the Fourteenth Amendment. Judge Bond's opinion states, and counsel at the bar confirmed the fact, that in Maryland the usual practice is for the defendant to waive a trial by jury. This the petitioner did in the present case. Such trials, as Judge Bond remarks, are much more informal than jury trials and it is obvious that the judge can much better control the course of the trial and is in a better position to see impartial justice done than when the formalities of a jury trial are involved.

In this case there was no question of the commission of a robbery. The State's case consisted of evidence identifying the petitioner as the perpetrator. The defense was an alibi. Petitioner called and ex-

a. In holding that the Sixth Amendment required appointment of counsel, the Court, per Black, J., had reasoned: "The Sixth Amendment stands as a constant admonition that if the constitutional safeguards it provides be lost, justice will not 'still be done.' Cf. *Palko.* It embodies a realistic recognition of the obvious truth that the average defendant does not have the professional legal skill to protect himself when brought before a tribunal with power to take his life or liberty, wherein the prosecution is presented by experienced and learned counsel. * * * The Sixth Amendment withholds from federal courts, in all criminal proceedings, the power and authority to deprive an accused of his life or liberty unless he has or waives the assistance of counsel."

amined witnesses to prove that he was at another place at the time of the commission of the offense. The simple issue was the veracity of the testimony for the State and that for the defendant. As Judge Bond says, the accused was not helpless, but was a man forty-three years old, of ordinary intelligence and ability to take care of his own interests on the trial of that narrow issue. He had once before been in a criminal court, pleaded guilty to larceny and served a sentence and was not wholly unfamiliar with criminal procedure. It is quite clear that in Maryland, if the situation had been otherwise and it had appeared that the petitioner was, for any reason, at a serious disadvantage by reason of the lack of counsel, a refusal to appoint would have resulted in the reversal of a judgment of conviction. * * *

To deduce from the due process clause a rule binding upon the states in this matter would be to impose upon them, as Judge Bond points out, a requirement without distinction between criminal charges of different magnitude or in respect of courts of varying jurisdiction. As he says: "Charges of small crimes tried before justices of the peace and capital charges tried in the higher courts would equally require the appointment of counsel. Presumably it would be argued that trials in the Traffic Court would require it." * * *

As we have said, the Fourteenth Amendment prohibits the conviction and incarceration of one whose trial is offensive to the common and fundamental ideas of fairness and right, and while want of counsel in a particular case may result in a conviction lacking in such fundamental fairness, we cannot say that the amendment embodies an inexorable command that no trial for any offense, or in any court, can be fairly conducted and justice accorded a defendant who is not represented by counsel.

The judgment is affirmed.

MR. JUSTICE BLACK, dissenting, with whom MR. JUSTICE DOUGLAS and MR. JUSTICE MURPHY concur.

To hold that the petitioner had a constitutional right to counsel in this case does not require us to say that "no trial for any offense, or in any court, can be fairly conducted and justice accorded a defendant who is not represented by counsel." This case can be determined by resolution of a narrower question: whether in view of the nature of the offense and the circumstances of his trial and conviction, this petitioner was denied the procedural protection which is his right under the federal constitution. I think he was.

The petitioner [was] a farm hand, out of a job and on relief. [The] court below found that [he] had "at least an ordinary amount of intelligence." It is clear from his examination of witnesses that he was a man of little education.

If this case had come to us from a federal court, it is clear we should have to reverse it, because the Sixth Amendment makes the right to counsel in criminal cases inviolable by the federal government. I believe that the Fourteenth Amendment made the sixth applicable to the states. But this view [has] never been accepted by a majority of this Court and is not accepted today. * * * I believe, however, that under the prevailing view of due process, as reflected in the opinion just announced, a view which gives this Court such vast supervisory powers that I am not prepared to accept it without grave doubts, the judgment below should be reversed. * * *

The right to counsel in a criminal proceeding is "fundamental." *Powell v. Alabama.* [A] practice cannot be reconciled with "common and fundamental ideas of fairness and right" which subjects innocent men to increased dangers of conviction merely because of their poverty. Whether a man is innocent cannot be determined from a trial in which as here, denial of counsel has made it impossible to conclude, with any satisfactory degree of certainty, that the defendant's case was adequately presented.[b] * * *

Denial to the poor of the request for counsel in proceedings based on charges of serious crime has long been regarded as shocking to the "universal sense of justice" throughout this country. In 1854, for example, the Supreme Court of Indiana said: "It is not to be thought of, in a civilized community, for a moment, that any citizen put in jeopardy of life or liberty should be debarred of counsel because he was too poor to employ such aid. No Court could be respected, or respect itself, to sit and hear such a trial. The defence of the poor, in such cases, is a duty resting somewhere, which will be at once conceded as essential to the accused, to the Court, and to the public." *Webb v. Baird,* 6 Ind. 13, 18. And most of the other states have shown their agreement by constitutional provisions, statutes, or established practice judicially approved which assure that no man shall be deprived of counsel merely because of his poverty. Any other practice seems to me to defeat the promise of our democratic society to provide equal justice under the law.

THE AFTERMATH OF BETTS v. BRADY—NOTES AND QUESTIONS

1. *Must it be "all or nothing"?* The *Betts* majority framed the issue of the right to appointed counsel in noncapital cases as an all or nothing proposition—if granted, it would have to be granted "for any offense or in any court." Need the question have been so asked? Could stopping points have been "serious" or "major" felonies? All crimes except misdemeanors? Or petty offenses? Or offenses punishable by fine only?

2. *Was Betts "prejudiced"?* When the Court reviewed Betts' case, he had appellate counsel, but his lawyer was confident—too confident—that the Court would apply the full measure of the Sixth Amendment right to counsel to the states. Thus he did not make any analysis of the trial and present any specific examples of how Betts might have been prejudiced by the absence of counsel. For the view that a number of such examples could have been shown and that competent trial counsel could have raised many more issues than "the simple issue [of] the veracity of the testimony for the State and that for the defendant," see Kamisar, *The Right to Counsel and the Fourteenth Amendment,* 30 U.Chi.L.Rev. 1, 42–56 (1962).

3. *The "flat" requirement of counsel in capital cases.* In *Bute v. Illinois,* 333 U.S. 640, 676, 68 S.Ct. 763, 781, 92 L.Ed. 986, 1006 (1948), and subsequent noncapital cases, the Court suggested that there was a "flat" requirement of counsel in capital cases. In *Hamilton v. Alabama,* 368 U.S. 52, 55, 82 S.Ct. 157, 159, 7 L.Ed.2d 114, 117 (1961), holding that arraignment is so critical a stage in Alabama procedure that denial of counsel at that stage in a capital case violates due process, a unanimous Court declared, per Douglas, J., that "when one pleads to a capital charge without benefit of counsel, we do not stop to determine whether prejudice resulted. [T]he degree of prejudice can never be known." For an explanation and criticism of the Court's distinction between capital and noncapital cases, see Allen, *The Supreme Court, Federalism, and State Systems of Criminal Justice,* 8 DePaul L.Rev. 213, 230–31 (1959).

b. Consider Beaney, *The Right to Counsel in American Courts* 163, 185 (1955): "Surely the [*Betts*] majority, in adopting [Judge] Bond's position that counsel could have done little or nothing for the defendant was pursuing a line of reasoning which would inevitably destroy all rights. Rights are agreed upon in order to insure that justice will be done prospectively, in the ordinary run of affairs. To hold that an individual can be deprived of rights except in those cases where a retrospective view of events reveals a shocking situation is to defeat the whole rationale of the rule of law." See also Note 2 infra.

4. *The absolute right to retained counsel.* During the *Betts* reign, the Court made it clear that denying a defendant the assistance of *his own lawyer* on *any* issue in the trial of *any* case, constituted a per se violation of "fundamental fairness." Thus, in *Chandler v. Fretag,* 348 U.S. 3, 75 S.Ct. 1, 99 L.Ed. 4 (1954), the Court stamped the right of petitioner "to be heard through his own counsel" as "unqualified." And in *Ferguson v. Georgia,* 365 U.S. 570, 81 S.Ct. 756, 5 L.Ed.2d 783 (1961), held, in effect, that a state may not deny a criminal defendant the right to have his own counsel guide him on direct examination. Could these cases be reconciled with *Betts?* See Israel, *Gideon v. Wainwright: The "Art" of Overruling,* 1963 Sup.Ct.Rev. 211, 243; Kamisar, *Betts v. Brady Twenty Years Later,* 61 Mich.L.Rev. 219, 227–28, 256–60 (1962).

5. *On the eve of Gideon, what was left of the Betts rule?* The last of the *Betts* rule cases to reach the court was *Chewning v. Cunningham,* 368 U.S. 443, 82 S.Ct. 498, 7 L.Ed.2d 442 (1962), and, as was true of all such cases after 1950, the Court found "special circumstances" requiring the services of counsel. In the course of invalidating a 10 year sentence under Virginia's recidivist statute, because an habitual criminal charge is so "serious," the issues presented under the statute so "complex" and "the *potential prejudice* resulting from the absence of counsel so great" (emphasis added), the Court, per Douglas, J., suggested various issues (e.g., lack of jurisdiction, double jeopardy) that might be considered by "an *imaginative lawyer* [examining] the layer of prior convictions on which the recidivist charge rests" (emphasis added). But the Court was careful to add that it "intimate[d] no opinion" as to whether any of these possible defenses "would have merit."

Justice Harlan, who concurred in the result, explicitly rejected the Court's rationale. To him, "the bare possibility" that a lawyer could have asserted "the improbable claims" suggested by the Court did not amount to the "special circumstances" requiring the state to provide counsel for an indigent non-capital defendant.

Can an "imaginative lawyer" always think up defenses not considered by an unrepresented and untrained defendant? Is the "potential prejudice" resulting from the absence of counsel *always* great? After *Chewning,* what if anything, was left of *Betts* to overrule?

GIDEON v. WAINWRIGHT

372 U.S. 335, 83 S.Ct. 792, 9 L.Ed.2d 799 (1963).

MR. JUSTICE BLACK delivered the opinion of the Court.

Petitioner was charged in a Florida state court with having broken and entered a poolroom with intent to commit a misdemeanor. This offense is a felony under Florida law. Appearing in court without funds and without a lawyer, petitioner asked the court to appoint counsel for him, whereupon the following colloquy took place:

"The Court: Mr. Gideon, I am sorry, but I cannot appoint Counsel to represent you in this case. Under the laws of the State of Florida, the only time the Court can appoint Counsel to represent a Defendant is when that person is charged with a capital offense. * * *

"The Defendant: The United States Supreme Court says I am entitled to be represented by Counsel."

Put to trial before a jury, Gideon conducted his defense about as well as could be expected from a layman. He made an opening statement to the jury, cross-examined the State's witnesses, presented witnesses in his own defense, declined to testify himself, and made a short argument "emphasizing his innocence to the charge contained in the Information filed in this case." The jury returned a verdict of guilty, and petitioner was sentenced to serve five years in the state prison. Later, petitioner [unsuccessfully attacked his conviction and sentence in the state supreme court on the ground that the trial court's refusal to appoint counsel for him violated his constitutional rights]. Since 1942, when *Betts v. Brady* was decided by a divided Court, the problem of a defendant's federal constitutional right to counsel in a state court has been a continuing source of controversy and litigation in both state and federal courts. To give this problem another review here, we granted certiorari [and] appointed counsel to represent [petitioner].

We accept *Betts* 's assumption, based as it was on our prior cases, that a provision of the Bill of Rights which is "fundamental and essential to a fair trial" is made obligatory upon the States by the Fourteenth Amendment. We think the Court in *Betts* was wrong, however, in concluding that the Sixth Amendment's guarantee of counsel is not one of these fundamental rights. Ten years before *Betts,* this Court, after full consideration of all the historical data examined in *Betts,* had unequivocally declared that "the right to the aid of counsel is of this fundamental character." *Powell.* While the Court at the close of its *Powell* opinion did by its language, as this Court frequently does, limit its holding to the particular facts and circumstances of that case, its conclusions about the fundamental nature of the right to counsel are unmistakable. [The] fact is that in deciding as it did—that "appointment of counsel is not a fundamental right, essential to a fair trial"—the [*Betts* Court] made an abrupt break with its own well-considered precedents. In returning to these old precedents, sounder we believe than the new, we but restore constitutional principles established to achieve a fair system of justice. Not only these precedents but also reason and reflection require us to recognize that in our adversary system of criminal justice, any person haled into court, who is too poor to hire a lawyer, cannot be assured a fair trial unless counsel is provided for him. This seems to us to be an obvious truth. Governments, both state and federal, quite properly spend vast sums of money to establish machinery to try defendants accused of crime. Lawyers to prosecute are everywhere deemed essential to protect the public's interest in an orderly society. Similarly, there are few defendants charged with crime, few indeed, who fail to hire the best lawyers they can get to prepare and present their defenses. That government hires lawyers to prosecute and defendants who have the money hire lawyers to defend are the strongest indications of the widespread belief that lawyers in criminal courts are necessities, not luxuries. The right of one charged with crime to counsel may not be deemed fundamental and essential to fair trials in some countries, but it is in ours. From the very beginning, our state and national constitutions and laws have laid great emphasis on procedural and substantive safeguards designed to assure fair trials before impartial tribunals in which every defendant stands equal before the law. This noble ideal cannot be realized if the poor man charged with crime has to face his accusers without a lawyer to assist him. * * *

The Court in *Betts* departed from the sound wisdom upon which the Court's holding in *Powell* rested. Florida, supported by two other States, has asked that *Betts v. Brady* be left intact. Twenty-two States, as friends of the Court, argue that *Betts* was "an anachronism when handed down" and that it should now be overruled. We agree. * * *

Reversed.[a]

MR. JUSTICE CLARK, concurring in the result. * * *

[T]he Constitution makes no distinction between capital and noncapital cases. The Fourteenth Amendment requires due process of law for the deprival of "liberty" just as for deprival of "life," and there

a. Gideon was retried, this time with appointed counsel, and acquitted. See Lewis, *Gideon's Trumpet* 223–38 (1964).

cannot constitutionally be a difference in the quality of the process based merely upon a supposed difference in the sanction involved. How can the Fourteenth Amendment tolerate a procedure which it condemns in capital cases on the ground that deprival of liberty may be less onerous than deprival of life—a value judgment not universally accepted—or that only the latter deprival is irrevocable? * * *

MR. JUSTICE HARLAN, concurring.

I agree that *Betts* should be overruled, but consider it entitled to a more respectful burial than has been accorded, at least on the part of those of us who were not on the Court when that case was decided.

I cannot subscribe to the view that *Betts* represented "an abrupt break with its own well-considered precedents." [In *Powell*] this Court declared that under the particular facts there presented—"the ignorance and illiteracy of the defendants, their youth, the circumstances of public hostility [and] above all that they stood in deadly peril of their lives"—the state court had a duty to assign counsel for the trial as a necessary requisite of due process of law. It is evident that these limiting facts were not added to the opinion as an afterthought; they were repeatedly emphasized [and] were clearly regarded as important to the result.

Thus when this Court, a decade later, decided *Betts,* it did no more than to admit of the possible existence of special circumstances in noncapital as well as capital trials, while at the same time to insist that such circumstances be shown in order to establish a denial of due process. The right to appointed counsel had been recognized as being considerably broader in federal prosecutions, see *Johnson v. Zerbst,* but to have imposed these requirements on the States would indeed have been "an abrupt break" with the almost immediate past. The declaration that the right to appointed counsel in state prosecutions, as established in *Powell,* was not limited to capital cases was in truth not a departure from, but an extension of, existing precedent.

The principles declared in *Powell* and in *Betts,* however, had a troubled journey throughout the years that have followed first the one case and then the other. Even by the time of the *Betts* decision, dictum in at least one of the Court's opinions had indicated that there was an absolute right to the services of counsel in the trial of state capital cases. * * *

In noncapital cases, the "special circumstances" rule has continued to exist in form while its substance has been substantially and steadily eroded. In the first decade after *Betts,* there were cases in which the Court found special circumstances to be lacking, but usually by a sharply divided vote. However, no such decision has been cited to us, and I have found none, [after] 1950. At the same time, there have been not a few cases in which special circumstances were found in little or nothing more than the "complexity" of the legal questions presented, although those questions were often of only routine difficulty. The Court has come to recognize, in other words, that the mere existence of a serious criminal charge constituted in itself special circumstances requiring the services of counsel at trial. In truth the *Betts* rule is no longer a reality.

This evolution, however, appears not to have been fully recognized by many state courts, in this instance charged with the front-line responsibility for the enforcement of constitutional rights. To continue a rule which is honored by this Court only with lip service is not a healthy thing and in the long run will do disservice to the federal system.

The special circumstances rule has been formally abandoned in capital cases, and the time has now come when it should be similarly abandoned in noncapital cases, at least as to offenses which, as the one involved here, carry the possibility of a substantial prison sentence. (Whether the rule should extend to *all* criminal cases need not now be decided.)

* * * In what is done today I do not understand the Court to depart from the principles laid down in *Palko* [or] to embrace the concept that the Fourteenth Amendment "incorporates" the Sixth Amendment as such.

On these premises I join in the judgment of the Court.

Notes and Questions

1. *The significance of Powell v. Alabama and Johnson v. Zerbst.* Did the Court in *Betts* make, as Justice Black asserts in *Gideon,* "an abrupt break with its own well-considered precedents"? Did *Powell* furnish a steppingstone to either a *Betts* or a *Gideon,* depending on how far and fast the Supreme Court was willing to use the opinion's potential for expansion? Did the *Palko* doctrine constitute a clear warning that the Court would not impose the same requirements for appointed counsel upon the states as it had upon the federal government in *Johnson v. Zerbst?* See Israel, *Gideon v. Wainwright: The "Art" of Overruling,* 1963 Supreme Court Rev. 211, 234–38, 240–41.

2. *Alternative techniques of overruling available in Gideon.* Among the traditional arts of overruling are the arguments that (a) the old precedent has not withstood the "lessons of experience" and (b) that its rejection is required by later "inconsistent precedents." See e.g., *Mapp v. Ohio,* Ch. 5 infra. Were these arguments available in *Gideon?* As to (b) reconsider, for example, the *Chandler* and *Ferguson* cases, establishing the unqualified right to the assistance of counsel *one can hire;* and the post-*Betts* development of the "automatic right" to appointed counsel in capital cases and its implicit admission of the unsoundness of the "fair trial" rule. As to (a), consider how, in the two decades since *Betts,* the assumption that a lawyerless defendant would usually be able to defend himself had fared in light of the constant expansion of the "special circumstances" concept; and how the assumption that a "special circumstances" test was more consistent with the "obligations of federalism" than an "absolute rule" had stood up in the face of the proliferation of federal habeas corpus cases produced by the *Betts* rule and the resulting friction between state and federal courts. See generally Israel, supra at 242–66, 269.

3. *Why did the Gideon opinion take the route it did?* If the foregoing techniques of overruling were available in *Gideon,* why did Justice Black fail to utilize them? Would it have been most desirable to emphasize that the overruling of *Betts* was not attributable to recent changes in personnel, but that it constituted the product of a long line of Justices who, over two decades, participated in various decisions undermining *Betts?* See Israel, supra at 225, 269. Is the failure to employ the usual overruling "arts" in *Gideon* attributable to Justice Black's personal interest in vindicating his own dissenting opinion in *Betts?* Or his reluctance to admit even the *original validity* of a decision that exemplifies the evils (to him) of the "fundamental rights" interpretation of the fourteenth amendment? See id. at 270–72.

In ARGERSINGER v. HAMLIN, 407 U.S. 25, 92 S.Ct. 2006, 32 L.Ed.2d 530 (1972), the Court, per DOUGLAS, J., struck down a Florida rule (following the line marked out in the jury trial cases) requiring that counsel be appointed only "for nonpetty offenses punishable by more than six months imprisonment," and held that "absent a knowing and intelligent waiver, no person may be *imprisoned* for any offense, whether classified as petty, misdemeanor, or felony unless he was represented by counsel" (emphasis added):

"While there is historical support for limiting the [right] to trial by jury [to] 'serious criminal cases,' there is no such support for a similar limitation on the right to assistance of counsel. * * * We reject, therefore, the premise that since prosecutions for crimes punishable by imprisonment for less than six months may be tried without a jury, they may always be tried without a lawyer. * * * The requirement of counsel may well be necessary for a fair trial even in a petty offense prosecution. We are by no means convinced that legal and constitutional questions involved in a case that actually leads to imprisonment even for a brief period are any less complex than when a person can be sent off for six months or more. * * *

"Beyond the problem of trials and appeals is that of the guilty plea, a problem which looms large in misdemeanor as well as in felony cases. Counsel is needed so that the accused may know precisely what he is doing, so that he is fully aware of the prospect of going to jail or prison, and so that he is treated fairly by the prosecution.

"In addition, the volume of misdemeanor cases, far greater in number than felony prosecutions, may create an obsession for speedy dispositions, regardless of the fairness of the result. * * *

"We must conclude, therefore, that the problems associated with misdemeanor and petty offenses often require the presence of counsel to insure the accused a fair trial. [In his concurring opinion,] Mr. Justice Powell suggests that these problems are raised even in situations where there is no prospect of imprisonment. We need not consider the requirements of the Sixth Amendment as regards the right to counsel where loss of liberty is not involved, however, for here, petitioner was in fact sentenced to jail * * *.

"Under the rule we announce today, every judge will know when the trial of a misdemeanor starts that no imprisonment may be imposed, even though local law permits it, unless the accused is represented by counsel. He will have a measure of the seriousness and gravity of the offense and therefore know when to name a lawyer to represent the accused before the trial starts." [a]

Analyzing the problem in terms of general due process rather than the sixth amendment right to counsel, concurring Justice POWELL, joined by Rehnquist, J., concluded that "there is a middle course, between the extremes of Florida's six month rule and the Court's rule, which comports with the requirements of the Fourteenth Amendment"—"fundamental fairness" requires that a defendant have the assistance of counsel in petty cases when, but only when, "necessary to assure a fair trial":

"Due process, perhaps the most fundamental concept in our law, embodies principles of fairness rather than immutable line-drawing as to every aspect of a criminal trial. While counsel is often essential to a fair trial, this is by no means a universal fact. Some petty offense cases are complex; others are exceedingly simple. [The] government often does not hire lawyers to prosecute petty offenses; instead the arresting police officer presents the case. Nor does every defendant who can afford to do so hire lawyers to defend petty charges. Where the possibility of a jail sentence is remote and the probable fine seems small, or where the evidence of guilt is overwhelming, the costs of assistance of counsel may exceed the benefits. It is anomalous that the Court's opinion today will extend the right of appointed counsel to indigent defendants in cases where the right to counsel would rarely be exercised by nonindigent defendants.

"Indeed, one of the effects of this ruling will be to favor defendants classified as

a. Burger, C.J., concurred in the result. Brennan, J., joined by Douglas and Stewart, JJ., joined the Court's opinion and, in a brief concurring opinion, added the observation that "law students as well as practicing attorneys may provide an important source of legal representation for the indigent. [M]ore than 125 of the country's 147 accredited law schools have established clinical programs in which faculty-supervised students aid clients in a variety of civil and criminal matters."

indigents over those not so classified yet who are in low income groups where engaging counsel in a minor petty offense case would be a luxury the family could not afford. The line between indigency and assumed capacity to pay for counsel is necessarily somewhat arbitrary, drawn differently from State to State and often resulting in serious inequities to accused persons. The Court's new rule will accent the disadvantage of being barely self-sufficient economically. * * *

"The rule adopted today [is] limited to petty offense cases in which the sentence is some imprisonment. The thrust of the Court's position indicates, however, that when the decision must be made, the rule will be extended to all petty offense cases except perhaps the most minor traffic violations. If the Court rejects on constitutional grounds, as it has today, the exercise of any judicial discretion as to need for counsel if a jail sentence is imposed, one must assume a similar rejection of discretion in other petty offense cases. It would be illogical—and without discernible support in the Constitution—to hold that no discretion may ever be exercised where a nominal jail sentence is contemplated and at the same time endorse the legitimacy of discretion in 'non-jail' petty offense cases which may result in far more serious consequences than a few hours or days of incarceration. * * *

"The Fifth and Fourteenth Amendments guarantee that property, as well as life and liberty, may not be taken from a person without affording him due process of law. The majority opinion suggests no constitutional basis for distinguishing between deprivations of liberty and property. In fact, the majority suggests no reason at all for drawing this distinction. The logic it advances for extending the right to counsel to all cases in which the penalty of any imprisonment is imposed applies equally well to cases in which other penalties may be imposed. Nor does the majority deny that some 'non-jail' penalties are more serious than brief jail sentences.

"[The] Court's opinion foreshadows the adoption of a broad prophylactic rule applicable to all petty offenses [whether or not the defendant is actually incarcerated]. No one can foresee the consequences of such a drastic enlargement of the constitutional right to free counsel. But even today's decision could have a seriously adverse impact upon the day to day functioning of the criminal justice system. * * *

"I would hold that the right to counsel in petty offense cases is not absolute but is one to be determined by the trial courts exercising a judicial discretion on a case-by-case basis. * * *

"[T]hree general factors should be weighed. First, the court should consider the complexity of the offense charged. For example, charges of traffic law infractions would rarely present complex legal or factual questions, but charges that contain difficult intent elements or which raise collateral legal questions, such as search and seizure problems, would usually be too complex for an unassisted layman. If the offense were one where the State is represented by counsel and where most defendants who can afford to do so obtain counsel, there would be a strong indication that the indigent also needs the assistance of counsel.

"Second, the court should consider the probable sentence that will follow if a conviction is obtained. The more serious the likely consequences, the greater is the probability that a lawyer should be appointed. [I]mprisonment is not the only serious consequence the court should consider.

"Third, the court should consider the individual factors peculiar to each case. These, of course, would be the most difficult to anticipate. One relevant factor would be the competency of the individual defendant to present his own case. The attitude of the community toward a particular defendant or particular incident would be another consideration. But there might be other reasons why a defendant would have a peculiar need for a lawyer which would compel the appointment of counsel in a case where the court would normally think this unnecessary. * * *

"Such a rule is similar in certain respects to the special circumstances rule applied to felony cases in *Betts,* which this Court overruled in *Gideon.* One of the reasons for seeking a more definitive standard in felony cases was the failure of many state courts to live up to their responsibilities in determining on a case-by-case basis whether counsel should be appointed. But this Court should not assume that the past insensitivity of some state courts to the rights of defendants will continue. Certainly if the Court follows the course of reading rigid rules into the Constitution, so that the state courts will be unable to exercise judicial discretion within the limits of fundamental fairness, there is little reason to think that insensitivity will abate.

" * * * We are all strongly drawn to the ideal of extending the right to counsel, but I differ as to two fundamentals: (i) what the Constitution *requires,* and (ii) the effect upon the criminal justice system, especially in the smaller cities and the thousands of police, municipal and justice of the peace courts across the country."

Petitioner, an indigent, was charged with shoplifting merchandise valued at less than $150, punishable by as much as a $500 fine, or one year in jail, or both. He was not provided counsel. After a bench trial he was convicted of the offense and fined $50. The Supreme Court of Illinois declined to "extend *Argersinger*" to a case where one is charged with an offense for which imprisonment upon conviction is authorized but not actually imposed. A 5–4 majority of the Supreme Court, per REHNQUIST, J., agreed, SCOTT v. ILLINOIS, 440 U.S. 367, 99 S.Ct. 1158, 59 L.Ed.2d 383 (1979):

"Although the intentions of the *Argersinger* Court are not unmistakably clear from its opinion, we conclude today that *Argersinger* did indeed delimit the constitutional right to appointed counsel in state criminal proceedings. Even were the matter *res nova,* we believe that the central premise of *Argersinger*—that actual imprisonment is a penalty different in kind from fines or the mere threat of imprisonment—is eminently sound and warrants adoption of actual imprisonment as the line defining the constitutional right to appointment of counsel. * * * We therefore hold that the Sixth and Fourteenth Amendments to the United States Constitution require only that no indigent criminal defendant be sentenced to a term of imprisonment unless the State has afforded him the right to assistance of appointed counsel in his defense."

Concurring Justice POWELL noted that "the drawing of a line based on whether there is imprisonment (even for overnight) can have the practical effect of precluding provision of counsel in other types of cases in which conviction can have more serious consequences." He also thought that an "actual imprisonment" rule "tends to impair the proper functioning of the criminal justice system in that trial judges, in advance of hearing any evidence and before knowing anything about the case except the charge, all too often will be compelled to forego the legislatively granted option to impose a sentence of imprisonment upon conviction." Despite his "continuing reservations about the *Argersinger* rule," however, Justice Powell joined the opinion of the Court because "[i]t is important that this Court provide clear guidance to the hundreds of courts across the country that confront this problem daily." He hoped, however, "that in due time a majority will recognize that a more flexible rule is consistent with due process and will better serve the cause of justice."

Justice BRENNAN, joined by MARSHALL and STEVENS, JJ., dissented:

"[*Argersinger*] established a 'two dimensional' test for the right to counsel: the right attaches to any 'non-petty' offense punishable by more than six months in jail and in addition to any offense where actual incarceration is likely regardless of the maximum authorized penalty. See Duke, *The Right to Appointed Counsel: Argersinger and Beyond,* 12 Am.Crim.L.Rev. 601 (1975).

"The offense of 'theft' with which Scott was charged is certainly not a 'petty' one. It is punishable by a sentence of up to one year in jail. Unlike many traffic or other 'regulatory' offenses, it carries the moral stigma associated with common-law crimes traditionally recognized as indicative of moral depravity. The State indicated at oral argument that the services of a professional prosecutor were considered essential to the prosecution of this offense. Likewise, nonindigent defendants charged with this offense would be well advised to hire the 'best lawyers they can get.' Scott's right to the assistance of appointed counsel is thus plainly mandated by the logic of the Court's prior cases, including *Argersinger* itself.

"* * * Not only is the 'actual imprisonment' standard unprecedented as the exclusive test, but the problems inherent in its application demonstrate the superiority of an 'authorized imprisonment' standard that would require the appointment of counsel for indigents accused of any offense for which imprisonment for any time is authorized. * * *

"Perhaps the strongest refutation of respondent's alarmist prophecies that an authorized imprisonment standard would wreak havoc on the States is that the standard has not produced that result in the substantial number of States that already provide counsel in all cases where imprisonment is authorized—States that include a large majority of the country's population and a great diversity of urban and rural environments. Moreover, of those States that do not yet provide counsel in all cases where *any* imprisonment is authorized, many provide counsel when periods of imprisonment longer than 30 days, 3 months, or 6 months are authorized. In fact, Scott would be entitled to appointed counsel under the current laws of at least 33 States.

"It may well be that adoption by this Court of an authorized imprisonment standard would lead state and local governments to re-examine their criminal statutes. A state legislature or local government might determine that it no longer desired to authorize incarceration for certain minor offenses in light of the expense of meeting the requirements of the Constitution. In my view this re-examination is long overdue. In any event, the Courts actual imprisonment standard must inevitably lead the courts to make this re-examination, which plainly should more properly be a legislative responsibility."

In a separate dissent, Justice BLACKMUN maintained that the right to counsel "extends at least as far as the right to jury trial" and thus that "an indigent defendant in a state criminal case must be afforded appointed counsel whenever the defendant is prosecuted for a nonpetty criminal offense, that is, one punishable by more than six months' imprisonment, *or* whenever the defendant is actually subjected to a term of imprisonment."

Notes and Questions

1. Were Justice Powell's reasons for switching from his position in *Argersinger* to the "actual confinement" approach in *Scott*—to "provide clear guidance" to lower courts and to reach a result consistent with *Argersinger*—persuasive? Did Justice Powell explain why the "actual confinement" test provides clearer guidance than the alternative to it? Did he explain why he declined to join Justice Blackmun's dissenting opinion? Of all the opinions in *Scott,* does the Blackmun opinion diverge least from the views Powell expressed in *Argersinger?* See Herman & Thompson, *Scott v. Illinois and the Right to Counsel: A*

Decision in Search of a Doctrine? 17 Am. Crim.L.Rev. 71, 94 (1979).

2. Was the *Scott* decision "motivated primarily by an undifferentiated, and certainly undocumented, fear of the costs and burden of implementing a right to counsel broader than that explicitly recognized in *Argersinger*"? See Herman & Thompson, supra, at 71–72. Instead of speculating about the costs of expanding the right to counsel, should the Court have set *Scott* for reargument the following term and invited the state attorneys-general and the National Legal Aid and Defender Association and its affiliates to file *amicus curiae* briefs addressing the options for expanding the right to counsel and the impact that each option would have in each state? See id. at 116.

3. Are unrepresented defendants likely to waive their right to a jury trial, hoping that a judge who sits as factfinder will be able to provide assistance? If so, how in a *non-jury* case, can a judge *properly* make an intelligent pre-trial determination as to whether the sentence is likely to include incarceration, at least where he will hear the case? Isn't a considerable amount of potentially prejudicial information likely to be injected into the factfinding process? If an indigent defendant charged with an offense usually punished only by a fine is appointed counsel, would a *different* judge hearing the case assume that a colleague had found that the defendant had a "bad record" or had committed the minor offense in an egregious manner? See Commentary to Unif.R.Crim.P. 321(b); Note, 1979 U.Ill.L.F. 739, 752.

4. May the problems raised in Note 3 never be reached because of judicial reluctance to conduct pretrial inquiries about the likely sentence? Consider Note, 93 Harv.L.Rev. 82, 87 (1979): "It seems far more likely that, due to the sheer volume of misdemeanor cases, judges simply will not appoint counsel, thereby relinquishing their discretion to impose the penalty of imprisonment." If so, would this constitute improper judicial interference with the legislature's judgment concerning the appropriate range of penalties? See id.

5. *The right to assigned counsel vs. the right to trial by jury.* Does *Scott* break precedent by restricting the right to counsel more narrowly than any other Sixth Amendment right had been restricted up to this point? Consider Note, 1979 U.Ill. L.F. 739, 748–49: "Prior to *Scott* the right to a jury trial was the sole sixth amendment guarantee that was not absolute in application. [But one important factor] justifies the limit placed on the jury trial right; in the absence of a jury, the judge will be an able replacement. * * * No such secondary guarantee exists, however, for a defendant denied counsel; a defendant without counsel is defenseless. [The right to appointed counsel] is far less burdensome to the state and far more important to the defendant than the right to a jury trial. Jury trials are more expensive than appointed counsel and place larger demands on the administration of the courts."

6. *Should the Court have employed a due process methodology in Scott?* Consider Nowak, *Foreword—Due Process Methodology in the Postincorporation World,* 74 J.Crim.L. & C. 397, 408–09 (1979): "[N]othing in *Betts* indicated that there was a class of cases in which a right to appointed counsel might never attach under the concept of due process. * * * [*Scott*] means that an indigent, regardless of his individual capability to represent himself, will never have a right to counsel in any case where actual incarceration is not imposed;[a] not even if the sanction involves a severe fine with major impact on the individual's life, the loss of a license necessary for his employment, or the creation of a criminal

a. Is this clear? May *Scott* be read as holding only that an indigent defendant not sentenced to a term of imprisonment has no *automatic* right to appointed counsel, but that "special circumstances," e.g., little or no education, low intelligence, the complexity of the legal issues involved, may still entitle him to appointed counsel in a particular case?

record which may damage the individual in a variety of ways.[b] * * * That such a serious result should come about with absolutely no consideration of due process values is shocking. Even if the Court were to find the sixth amendment irrelevant, it should have examined due process values. Were this a civil case where a party was asking for some procedural safeguard, the Court, employing the *Mathews* balancing test,[c] would have examined the worth of the safeguard to the individual and its value in insuring a reliable fact determination. It would then have weighed these benefits against the societal cost imposed by the requirement. The *Scott* majority engaged in no such analysis. Use of the suggested due process methodology model would have required the Court to examine the value in a fair criminal process to both the individual and society, the chance that individual rights were endangered by the absence of counsel, and the societal worth of having the added assurance of systematic fairness and equality of treatment in the adversary process. Instead, the Court simply asserted that the sixth amendment did not require counsel in such cases."

7. *What constitutes a loss of liberty under the Argersinger-Scott rule?* If the defendant was arrested for the offense or incarcerated pending trial, is he entitled to assigned counsel? Is a loss of liberty any less a substantial deprivation before conviction than afterward? What of a misdemeanor, conviction of which constitutes a ground for revocation of probation or parole? See Duke, *The Right to Appointed Counsel: Argersinger and Beyond,* 12 Am.Crim.L.Rev. 601, 613–15 (1975).

8. *Use of a prior uncounselled misdemeanor conviction to increase imprisonment under an enhanced penalty statute.* In BALDASAR v. ILLINOIS, 446 U.S. 222, 100 S.Ct. 1585, 64 L.Ed.2d 169 (1980), a 5–4 majority held, *per curiam,* that an uncounselled misdemeanor theft conviction (valid under *Scott,* because defendant had received only a fine and probation) could not be used to elevate a subsequent conviction for a similar offense to a felony. (The maximum punishment for misdemeanor theft was one year imprisonment, but a second conviction for the same offense could be treated as a felony with a prison term of one to three years—what Baldasar actually received.) It seemed plain to concurring Justice STEWART, joined by Brennan and Stevens, JJ., that the prison sentence violated *Scott*—petitioner had been sentenced to an increased term of imprisonment "*only* because he had been convicted in a previous prosecution in which he had *not* had the assistance of counsel." In another concurring opinion, Justice MARSHALL, joined by Brennan and Stevens, JJ., "remain[ed] convinced that [*Scott*] was wrongly decided," but even under *Scott,* "that petitioner has been deprived of his liberty 'as a result of [the first] criminal trial' could not be clearer." In a third concurring opinion, BLACKMUN, J., maintained that since Baldasar was prosecuted for an offense punishable by more than six months imprisonment, he was entitled to

b. But see Note, 93 Harv.L.Rev. 82, 88 (1979): "Under *Scott,* it may still be possible for an indigent misdemeanant who was convicted without counsel to argue that just as his conviction cannot be the basis for a jail sentence, it cannot support a significant legal disability [such as the inability to obtain an occupational license or disqualification from a federal job]."

c. The issue in *Mathews v. Eldridge,* 424 U.S. 319, 96 S.Ct. 893, 47 L.Ed.2d 18 (1976), was whether a worker had a due process right to an evidentiary hearing before his Social Security disability benefits were terminated on the ground that he was no longer disabled. After taking various factors into account, such as the "private interest" affected by the official action, "the risk of an erroneous deprivation of such interest through the procedure used, and the probable value, if any, of additional or substitute procedural safeguards," and "the fiscal and administrative burdens that the additional or substitute procedural requirements would entail," the Court held that due process did not require an evidentiary hearing. Compare *Goldberg v. Kelly,* 397 U.S. 254, 90 S.Ct. 1011, 25 L.Ed. 287 (1970) (due process requires an evidentiary hearing prior to termination of welfare benefits).

counsel at the prior misdemeanor proceeding and thus his uncounselled misdemeanor conviction was "invalid and may not be used to support enhancement."

Dissenting Justice POWELL, joined by the Chief Justice and Justices White and Rehnquist, protested that the Court's holding "undermines the rationale of *Scott* and *Argersinger* and leaves no coherent rationale in its place. A constitutionally valid conviction is not constitutionally invalid if relied upon as the predicate for enhancing the sentence of a recidivist." The dissenters deemed the Court's result "logically indefensible":

"No court can predict with confidence whether a misdemeanor defendant is likely to become a recidivist. The option of not imposing a jail sentence on an uncounseled misdemeanant, expressly preserved by *Argersinger* and *Scott,* no longer exists unless the court is willing prospectively to preclude enhancement of future convictions."

See generally Note, 1979 U.Ill.L.F. 739 (criticizing Illinois courts for relying on uncounselled misdemeanor convictions to increase a second offender's term of imprisonment). Cf. I *A.B.A. Standards,* § 5–4–1.

9. *Nonlawyer judges.* Rejecting, inter alia, the argument that the right to counsel articulated in *Argersinger* and *Gideon* is meaningless without a lawyer-judge to understand the arguments of counsel, *North v. Russell,* 427 U.S. 328, 96 S.Ct. 2709, 49 L.Ed.2d 534 (1976), per Burger, C.J., held that a person subject to possible imprisonment may be tried before a nonlawyer judge where, under a state's two-tier court system, he has a right to trial *de novo* before a traditionally law-trained judge.[d] Dissenting Justice Stewart, joined by Marshall, J., protested that a trial before a judge "without any legal training or education whatever" that results in defendant's imprisonment "deprives the accused of his effective assistance of counsel. * * * The essential presupposition of [the *Argersinger-Gideon*] right is that the judge conducting the trial will be able to understand what the defendant's lawyer is talking about. [I cannot agree] that these constitutional deficiencies can all be swept under the rug and forgotten because the convicted defendant may have a trial *de novo* before a qualified judge."

d. Brennan, J., concurred in the result. Stevens, J., did not participate.

II. THE RIGHT TO APPOINTED COUNSEL IN PROCEEDINGS OTHER THAN CRIMINAL PROSECUTIONS: THE CONTINUED VITALITY OF THE *BETTS v. BRADY* APPROACH

A. THE PENO-CORRECTIONAL PROCESS

GAGNON v. SCARPELLI

411 U.S. 778, 93 S.Ct. 1756, 36 L.Ed.2d 656 (1973).

MR. JUSTICE POWELL delivered the opinion of the Court.

[Respondent Scarpelli] pleaded guilty in July, 1965, to a charge of armed robbery. The trial judge sentenced him to 15 years' imprisonment, but suspended the sentence and placed him on probation for seven years. [A month later, Scarpelli and one Fred Kleckner were apprehended] in the course of the burglary of a house. After being apprised of his constitutional rights, respondent admitted that he and Kleckner had [unlawfully] broken into the house [but] he now asserts that his statement was made under duress and is false. [Probation was revoked without a hearing on the stated grounds that:]

"1. [Scarpelli] has associated with known criminals, in direct violation of his probation regulations and his supervising agent's instructions;

"2. [Scarpelli] while associating with a known criminal, namely Fred Kleckner, was involved in, and arrested for, a burglary * * *."

[A month after the burglary, Scarpelli began serving the 15 years to which he had been sentenced].

In *Mempa v. Rhay*,[a] the Court held a probationer is entitled to be represented by appointed counsel at a combined revocation and sentencing hearing. Reasoning that counsel is required "at every stage of a criminal proceeding where substantial rights of a criminal accused may be affected," and that sentencing is one such stage, the Court concluded that counsel must be provided an indigent at sentencing even when it is accomplished as part of a subsequent, probation revocation proceeding. But this line of reasoning does not require a hearing or counsel at the time of probation revocation in a case such as the present one, where the probationer was sentenced at the time of that trial.[b]

Of greater relevance [is] *Morrissey v. Brewer,* 408 U.S. 471, 92 S.Ct. 2953, 33 L.Ed.2d 484 (1978), [holding that] even though the revocation of parole is not a part of the criminal prosecution, [the] loss of liberty entailed is a serious deprivation requiring that the parolee be accorded due process. * * * Probation revocation, like parole revocation, is not a stage of a criminal prosecution, but does result in a loss of liberty. Accordingly, we hold that a probationer, like a parolee, is entitled to a preliminary and a final revocation hearing, under the conditions specified in *Morrissey.*

The [more difficult question] is whether an indigent probationer or parolee has a due process right to be represented by appointed counsel at these hearings.[6] * * *

Because the probation or parole officer's function is not so much to compel conformance to a strict code of behavior as to supervise a course of rehabilitation, he has been entrusted traditionally with broad discretion to judge the progress of rehabilitation in individual cases, and has been armed with the power to recommend or even to declare revocation. * * *

But an exclusive focus on the benevolent attitudes of those who administer the probation/parole system when it is working successfully obscures the modification in attitude which is likely to take place once the officer has decided to recommend revocation. Even though the officer is not by this recommendation converted into a prosecutor committed to convict, his role as counsellor to the probationer or parolee is then surely compromised.

When the officer's view of the probationer's or parolee's conduct differs in this fundamental way from the latter's own view, due process requires that the difference be resolved before revocation becomes final. Both the probationer or parolee and the State have interests in the accurate finding of fact and the informed

a. In *Mempa,* 389 U.S. 128, 88 S.Ct. 254, 19 L.Ed.2d 336 (1967), petitioners' sentencing was deferred subject to probation. The prosecutor subsequently moved to have their probation revoked on the ground that petitioners had committed other crimes. At these hearings neither petitioner was represented by counsel or offered counsel. As a result of these hearings, each petitioner's probation was revoked and he was sentenced to a term of imprisonment. A unanimous Court, per Marshall, J., held that "a lawyer must be afforded at this [deferred sentencing] procedure whether it be labeled a revocation of probation or a deferred sentencing."

b. But see Cohen, *Sentencing, Probation, and the Rehabilitative Ideal,* 47 Texas L.Rev. 1, 2–6 (1968), viewing *Mempa* as "the beginning of judicial activity in the sentencing-to-final discharge area of law, and not as a rearguard mopping-up operation in the natural evolution of right-to-counsel decisions," and stressing that "[t]here is no other area of law, except perhaps the civil commitment of the mentally ill, where the lives of so many people are so drastically affected by officials who exercise a virtually absolute, unreviewed discretion."

6. * * * Since respondent did not attempt to retain counsel but asked only for appointed counsel, we have no occasion to decide in this case whether a probationer or parolee has a right to be represented at a revocation hearing by retained counsel in situations other than those where the State would be obliged to furnish counsel for an indigent.

use of discretion, the probationer or parolee to insure that his liberty is not unjustifiably taken away and the State to make certain that it is neither unnecessarily interrupting a successful effort at rehabilitation nor imprudently prejudicing the safety of the community. It was to serve all of these interests that *Morrissey* mandated preliminary and final revocation hearings. * * *

These requirements in themselves serve as substantial protection against ill-considered revocation, and petitioner argues that counsel need never be supplied. What this argument overlooks is that the effectiveness of the rights guaranteed by *Morrissey* may in some circumstances depend on the use of skills which the probationer or parolee is unlikely to possess. Despite the informal nature of the proceedings and the absence of technical rules of procedure or evidence, the unskilled or uneducated probationer or parolee may well have difficulty in presenting his version of a disputed set of facts where the presentation requires the examining or cross-examining of witnesses or the offering or dissecting of complex documentary evidence.

[While a rule] that the State is under a constitutional duty to provide counsel for indigents in all probation or parole revocation cases [has] the appeal of simplicity, it would impose direct costs and serious collateral disadvantages without regard to the need or the likelihood in a particular case for a constructive contribution by counsel. In most cases, the probationer or parolee has been convicted of committing another crime or has admitted the charges against him. And while in some cases he may have a justifiable excuse for the violation or a convincing reason why revocation is not the appropriate disposition, mitigating evidence of this kind is often not susceptible of proof or is so simple as not to require either investigation or exposition by counsel.

The introduction of counsel into a revocation proceeding will alter significantly the nature of the proceeding. If counsel is provided for the probationer or parolee, the State in turn will normally provide its own counsel; lawyers, by training and disposition, are advocates and bound by professional duty to present all available evidence and arguments in support of their clients' positions and to contest with vigor all adverse evidence and views. The role of the hearing body itself, aptly described in *Morrissey* as being "predictive and discretionary" as well as fact-finding, may become more akin to that of a judge at a trial, and less attuned to the rehabilitative needs of the individual probationer or parolee. In the greater self-consciousness of its quasi-judicial role, the hearing body may be less tolerant of marginal deviant behavior and feel more pressure to reincarcerate rather than continue nonpunitive rehabilitation. Certainly, the decision-making process will be prolonged, and the financial cost to the State—for appointed counsel, counsel for the State, a longer record, and the possibility of judicial review—will not be insubstantial.[7]

In some cases, these modifications in the nature of the revocation hearing must be endured and the costs borne because [the] probationer's or parolee's version of a disputed issue can fairly be represented only by a trained advocate. But due process is not so rigid as to require that the significant interests in informality, flexibility, and economy must always be sacrificed.

In so concluding, we are of course aware that the case-by-case approach to the right to counsel in felony prosecutions adopted in *Betts* [was] later rejected in favor of a *per se* rule. [But we do not] draw from *Gideon* and *Argersinger* the con-

7. The scope of the practical problem which would be occasioned by a requirement of counsel in all revocation cases is suggested by the fact that in the mid-1960's there were an estimated average of 20,000 adult felony parole revocations and 108,000 adult probation revocations each year. President's Commission on Law Enforcement and Administration of Justice *Task Force Report: The Courts* 56, fn. 28 (1967).

clusion that a case-by-case approach to furnishing counsel is necessarily inadequate to protect constitutional rights asserted in varying types of proceedings: there are critical differences between criminal trials and probation or parole revocation hearings, and both society and the probationer or parolee have stakes in preserving these differences.

In a criminal trial, the State is represented by a prosecutor; formal rules of evidence are in force; a defendant enjoys a number of procedural rights which may be lost if not timely raised; and, in a jury trial, a defendant must make a presentation understandable to untrained jurors. In short, a criminal trial under our system is an adversary proceeding with its own unique characteristics. In a revocation hearing, on the other hand, the State is represented not by a prosecutor but by a parole officer with the orientation described above; formal procedures and rules of evidence are not employed; and the members of the hearing body are familiar with the problems and practice of probation or parole. The need for counsel at revocation hearings derives not from the invariable attributes of those hearings but rather from the peculiarities of particular cases.

The differences between a criminal trial and revocation hearing do not dispose altogether of the argument that under a case-by-case approach there may be cases in which a lawyer would be useful but in which none would be appointed because an arguable defense would be uncovered only by a lawyer. [But] we think it a sufficient answer that we deal here not with the right of an accused to counsel in a criminal prosecution, but with the more limited due process right of one who is a probationer or parolee only because he has been convicted of a crime.

We thus find no justification for a new inflexible constitutional rule with respect to the requirement of counsel. We think, rather, that the decision as to the need for counsel must be made on a case-by-case basis in the exercise of a sound discretion by the state authority charged with responsibility for administering the probation and parole system. Although the presence and participation of counsel will probably be both undesirable and constitutionally unnecessary in most revocation hearings, there will remain certain cases in which fundamental fairness—the touchstone of due process—will require that the State provide at its expense counsel for indigent probationers or parolees.

* * * Presumptively, it may be said that counsel should be provided in cases where, after being informed of his right to request counsel, the probationer or parolee makes such a request, based on a timely and colorable claim (i) that he has not committed the alleged violation of the conditions upon which he is at liberty; or (ii) that, even if the violation is a matter of public record or is uncontested, there are substantial reasons which justified or mitigated the violation and make revocation inappropriate and that the reasons are complex or otherwise difficult to develop or present. In passing on a request for the appointment of counsel, the responsible agency also should consider, especially in doubtful cases, whether the probationer appears to be capable of speaking effectively for himself. In every case in which a request for counsel at a preliminary or final hearing is refused, the grounds for refusal should be stated succinctly in the record.

We return to the facts of the present case. Because respondent was not afforded either a preliminary hearing or a final hearing, the revocation of his probation did not meet the standards of due process prescribed in *Morrissey,* which we have here held applicable to probation revocations. Accordingly, respondent was entitled to a writ of habeas corpus. [His] admission to having committed another serious crime creates the very sort of situation in which counsel need not ordinarily be provided. But because of respondent's subsequent assertions regarding that admission, we conclude that the failure [to] provide respondent with the assistance of counsel should be reexamined in light of this opinion. The general guidelines outlined above should be applied in the first instance by those charged with conducting the revocation hearing.

Affirmed in part, reversed in part, and remanded.

MR. JUSTICE DOUGLAS, dissenting in part.

I believe that due process requires the appointment of counsel in this case because of the claim that respondent's confession of the burglary was made under coercion. See *Morrissey v. Brewer.*

Notes and Questions

1. Compare the *Gagnon* Court's views of the role and utility of counsel at revocation hearings with Kadish, *The Advocate and the Expert-Counsel in the Peno-Correctional Process,* 45 Minn.L.Rev. 803, 833–38 (1961):[a]

"[T]he determination to revoke and recommit because of conduct in violation of the conditions on which release was granted, involves, if not exclusively, then at least centrally, the fairly narrowly focused issue of what the conduct of the releasee actually was and whether it constituted a violation of a stated condition, entitling the court or agency to consider whether revocation is thereby indicated. Given the character of the issue to be determined and the fact that the continued liberty of a person depends on the outcome, it is difficult to understand the view sometimes expressed that a lawyer has no proper business in these matters. The central task of ascertaining whether the prisoner has committed the acts alleged, and measuring the acts proven against a standard to which he was obliged to conform is precisely the business of the criminal trial itself where the right to the assistance of counsel has been recognized as one of the 'immutable principles of justice.' Indeed, in many contested revocation proceedings, the conduct charged actually constitutes the commission of a criminal act. No doubt it is simpler and faster for a court or a board to make the determination by whatever means seem to it sufficient to persuade—whether it be an informal talk with the parole officer or a brief interview with the prisoner or a written report by an investigator. But it would seem patently at war with the central concept of procedural justice to deny to a person with his liberty at stake the opportunity to hear and meet the specific charge against him with the benefit of counsel. * * *

"[S]ome of the apprehension that lawyers would bog down the system is less than real, stemming from the layman's traditional distrust of lawyers as masters of the art of frustration, sworn to advance the cause of their client rather than the truth and hence prime instigators of delay and diversion. * * * The issue is not whether the lawyer's paraphernalia of technicalities appropriate to other areas are proper in parole matters; no one has seriously suggested that rules of pleading and evidence should be imported into parole hearings. The issue is whether the attorney may speak for his client, given the areas of relevance of parole and revocation proceedings and always subject to the authority of the agency to draw the ground rules. A sensible and pragmatic adaptation of the nature of legal advocacy to the needs and purposes of the inquiry is as plausible in parole as it has proven to be in such 'non-legal' areas as labor arbitration and the regulatory and adjudicative work of administrative agencies. * * *"

2. *Betts, Gideon and Gagnon compared.* How likely is it that a probationer or parolee will be able to convince a court, *without* the benefit of counsel, on the basis

a. Reprinted with permission of the publisher; copyright © 1961 by the Minnesota Law Review Foundation.

of a record made *without* the assistance of counsel, that there are "substantial reasons which justified or mitigated the violation" or that "the reasons are complex or otherwise difficult to develop or present"? How many probationers or parolees will know *what* to point to or look for and *why?* How intelligent a decision can be made as to whether "the probationer appears to be capable of speaking effectively for himself" without knowing what justifications or mitigations a competent lawyer might have raised or developed? Can *Gagnon* escape the criticism of *Betts?* Consider, e.g., Kamisar, *The Right to Counsel and the Fourteenth Amendment: A Dialogue on "the Most Pervasive Right" of an Accused,* 30 U.Chi.L.Rev. 53, 65 (1962).

3. *The A.B.A. Standards approach.* "In common [with] numerous commentators," III *ABA Standards* § 18–7.5 (commentary) "rejects [the] vague and uncertain [*Gagnon*] standard." Continues the commentary:

"Few legal inquiries could be more inherently speculative and problematic than examining a record after the event seeking to determine whether the defendant would have fared better if counsel had been present. The problem is that records made by laypersons do not reflect what a trained advocate would have seen: lines of inquiry not followed, bases for impeachment of witnesses never explored, alternative dispositions that might have been proposed. No hint of these will appear when an inexperienced and probably scared layperson is forced to defend himself or herself and has a 'fool for a client.'

"Still another reason for rejecting the case-by-case standard fashioned by *Gagnon* is that it is inefficient. It must be recognized that any denial of counsel at probation revocation will only invite an appeal or a later collateral attack, and possibly both. [Even if the denial of counsel] is ultimately sustained, more effort, expense, and appellate time will be spent than if counsel had originally been provided. Post-*Gagnon* experience in the federal courts confirms this * * *. Given a context in which only a minority of offenders can be said not to have needed the assistance of counsel, it appears far more expeditious and efficient to establish a bright-line standard that grants counsel in all cases than to litigate the hazy and narrow contours of the constitutionally permissible case in which counsel need not be provided."

B. Collateral Attack Proceedings

Although a majority of states provide for the appointment of counsel in postconviction proceedings in the discretion of the court, and in several jurisdictions appointment appears to be mandatory once an evidentiary hearing has been granted, see I *A.B.A. Standards* § 5–4.2 (commentary),[a] "[c]ourts have generally held that there is no constitutional grounding for requiring the appointment of counsel in what is basically a civil proceeding," LaFave & Israel, § 27.9(a). But "unless and until the State provides some reasonable alternative to assist inmates in the preparation of petitions for postconviction relief," it may not, holds JOHNSON v. AVERY, 393 U.S. 483, 89 S.Ct. 747, 21 L.Ed.2d 718 (1969), per FORTAS, J., prohibit inmates from furnishing such assistance to fellow-prisoners:

"There can be no doubt that Tennessee could not constitutionally adopt and enforce a rule forbidding illiterate or poorly educated prisoners to file habeas corpus petitions. Here, Tennessee has adopted a rule which, in the absence of any other source of assistance for such prisoners, effectively does just that. * * *

a. Since 1976 an indigent is automatically appointed counsel under Rule 8(c) of the rules governing § 2254 cases in the federal district courts once it is determined that an evidentiary hearing is required. This rule does not limit the authority of the court to provide counsel at an earlier stage "if the interest of justice so requires."

"In most federal courts, it is the practice to appoint counsel in postconviction proceedings only after a petition for [such relief] passes initial judicial evaluation and the court has determined that issues are represented calling for an evidentiary hearing. [Thus, the initial burden] usually rests upon the indigent prisoner himself with such help as he can obtain within the prison walls or the prison system. In the case of all except those who are able to help themselves—usually a few old hands or exceptionally gifted prisoners—the prisoner is, in effect, denied access to the courts unless such help is available."

Concurring Justice DOUGLAS deemed the "closed-shop philosophy of the legal profession that cuts down drastically active roles for layman" "utterly out of place in the modern world" where there are not enough lawyers available to handle "the almost endless paperwork," "where claims pile high and pursuing them requires the patience and wisdom of a layman rather than the legal skills of a member of the bar." He maintained that "[l]aymen—in and out of prison—should be allowed to act as 'next of kin' to any person in the preparation of any paper or claim, so long as he does not hold himself out as practicing law or being a member of the Bar. The cooperation and help of laymen, as well as of lawyers, is necessary if the right of 'reasonable access to the courts' is to be available to the indigents among us."

Dissenting Justice WHITE, joined by Black, J., voiced fears that if "jailhouse lawyers" were allowed to engage in the business of writing writs "the most aggressive and domineering personalities may predominate. And it may not be those with the best claims to relief who are served as clients, but those who are weaker and more gullible. [Those] whom the jailhouse lawyer serves may come morally under his sway as the one hope of their release, and repay him not only with obedience but with what minor gifts and other favors are available to them. When a client refuses to pay, violence may result, in which the jailhouse lawyer may be aided by his other clients."

Noting that petitioner Johnson was a convicted rapist serving a life sentence and that the state has wide discretion in regulating prison conduct, Justice White did not see why Johnson "cannot be disciplined for violating a prison rule against aiding other prisoners in seeking postconviction relief, particularly when there is no showing that [any prison inmate] has been denied access to the courts, that Johnson has confined his services to those who need it, or that Johnson is himself competent to give the advice which he offers."

Justice White agreed that the problem of the indigent and ignorant seeking postconviction relief was "substantial," but "the better course is not in effect to sanction and encourage spontaneous jailhouse lawyer systems but to decide the matter directly in the case of a man who himself needs help and in that case to rule that the State must provide access to the courts by ensuring that those who cannot help themselves have reasonably adequate assistance in preparing their postconviction papers." "Ideally, perhaps, professional help should be furnished," but Justice White was "inclined to agree" with Justice Douglas that "it is neither practical nor necessary to require the help of lawyers."

Although *Johnson v. Avery* could be, and had been, read narrowly, BOUNDS v. SMITH, 430 U.S. 817, 97 S.Ct. 1491, 52 L.Ed.2d 72 (1977), per MARSHALL, J., rejected the contention that the constitutional duty to provide "meaningful access" to the courts "merely obliges states to allow inmate 'writ writers' to function" and does not require the expenditure of state funds "to implement affirmatively the right of access." The state must do more than refrain from interfering with indigents seeking assistance from other prisoners; the right of access to the courts "requires prison authorities to assist inmates in the preparation and filing of meaningful legal papers by [furnishing] adequate law libraries or adequate assistance from persons trained in the law."

The Court noted that while adequate law libraries are "one constitutionally acceptable method" of assuring meaningful access to the courts, "our decision [today] does not foreclose alternative means to achieve that goal. Nearly half the States and the District of Columbia provide some degree of professional or quasi-professional legal assistance to prisoners. Such programs take many imaginative forms and may have a number of advantages over libraries alone. * * * Legal services plans not only result in more efficient and skillful handling of prisoner cases, but also avoid the disciplinary problems associated with writ writers. Independent legal advisors can mediate or resolve administratively many prisoner complaints that would otherwise burden the courts, and can convince inmates that other grievances against the prison or the legal system are ill-founded. [A] legal access program need not include any particular element we have discussed, [but] must be evaluated as a whole to ascertain its compliance with constitutional standards."

There were three dissenting opinions. In one, REHNQUIST, J., joined by Burger, C.J., maintained that "there is nothing in the United States Constitution which requires that a convict serving a term of imprisonment pursuant to a final judgment of a court of competent jurisdiction in a state penal institution have a 'right of access' to the federal courts in order to attack his sentence." * * * [The Court enunciates] a 'fundamental constitutional right of access to the courts,' which is found nowhere in the Constitution." Nor could Rehnquist see a bright line between entitling a prisoner (seeking collateral relief) to a law library and entitling him to state appointed counsel.

In a second dissent, STEWART, J., joined by Burger, C.J., observed that "more than 20 years of experience with *pro se* habeas corpus petitions have convinced me that 'meaningful access' to the federal courts can seldom be realistically advanced by the device of making law libraries available to prison inmates untutored in their use. [If], on the other hand, Mr. Justice Rehnquist is correct in his belief that a convict in a state prison pursuant to a final judgment of a court of competent jurisdiction has no constitutional right of 'meaningful access' to the federal courts in order to attack his sentence, then a State can be under no constitutional duty to make that access 'meaningful.' "

In a third dissent, BURGER, C.J., deemed it "a novel and doubtful proposition [that] the Federal Government can, by statute, give individuals certain rights and then require the State, as a constitutional matter, to fund the means for exercise of those rights. [A]bsent a federal constitutional right to attack convictions collaterally—and I discern no such right—I can find no basis on which a federal court may require States to fund costly law libraries for prison inmates. Proper federal-state relations preclude such intervention in the 'complex and intractable' problems of prison administration."

Notes and Questions

1. *Must inmates be afforded adequate law libraries even if legal assistance is available?* Does the right to proceed *pro se* recognized in *Faretta* (p. 122 infra) encompass the incarcerated *pro se* defendant's right to prepare for his task? If so, would the view that the availability of legal assistance relieves the state of the duty to provide legal materials for inmates obviate the *pro se* right? Is the choice afforded the states under the *Bounds* right of access, therefore, whether to provide law libraries *only* or *both* law libraries *and* legal assistance? See generally Potuto, *The Right of Prisoner Access: Does* Bounds *Have Bounds?,* 53 Ind. L.J. 207, 227–40 (1978).

2. *What constitutes an "adequate" law library?* Consider Potuto, supra, at 242: "It is difficult [to] understand how access

can be 'meaningful' when a prisoner can use a law library no more than once every three or four weeks, with no assurance that he will be able to use the books that he wants when he gets there [because only one copy of a title may be available in each library and the ratio of prisoners to copies of titles is approximately 2,000 to one]. Yet this is all that is provided by the plan found adequate [by the lower federal courts] in *Bounds.*"

3. Consider *Hooks v. Wainwright.* After eleven years of litigation, during which time three separate evidentiary hearings were held, the federal district court concluded that, "given the high level of illiteracy among Florida's prisoners" (about half could read only at or below the seventh grade level) "it would be intellectually dishonest" to say that "meaningful access" to the courts could be achieved under the state's proposed plan calling for the establishment of seven "major" law libraries and 20 "minor" ones, all operated by inmate law clerks and staff librarians. 536 F.Supp. 1330 (M.D.Fla.1982) (per Scott, J.). "[M]eaningful access to the courts on behalf of Florida's prisoners," maintained the district court, "can be realized only through the assistance of attorneys, in one form or another."

But the Court of Appeals held that the district court had erred in concluding that any state library plan devised to insure meaningful access to the courts by state inmates must include a provision for lawyer assistance, 716 F.2d 913 (11th Cir. 1985) (per Roney, J.):

"[I]t is noteworthy that *Bounds* refers to law libraries *or* other forms of legal assistance, in the disjunctive, no fewer than five times. * * * It presses credulity to contend that the [*Bounds* Court] intended there would be constitutional right to legal counsel, if it were found that some prisoners were illiterate and that nonlawyer prisoners could not use the libraries as well as lawyers.

" * * * At the time it was decided, *Bounds* was the culmination of a series of cases [that] in effect tended to place prisoners in the same position as non-prisoners and indigent prisoners in the same position as non-indigent prisoners. Having held that inmates can represent themselves, if able to do so, and can help [others] who are not so able, it was but a small step to hold that such able inmates, who presumably would have access to libraries but for imprisonment, must be given access to libraries in prison, or access to people who have access to libraries. This is a far cry from constitutionally requiring the state to provide legal counsel for the imprisoned, not available as a matter of constitutional right to the unimprisoned in civil cases.

"That state prisoners are not constitutionally entitled to have the state provide attorneys for them is most visibly manifested in the practice of both state and federal judicial systems that treat the application for appointed counsel for collateral and civil rights proceedings on a case-by-case basis. * * *

"Programs offering legal assistance * * * may have a number of advantages * * *. But all good ideas are not constitutionally required."

C. Summary Courts-Martial

MIDDENDORF v. HENRY, 425 U.S. 25, 96 S.Ct. 1281, 47 L.Ed.2d 556 (1976), held that there is no right to appointed counsel at summary courts-martial, even though the officer conducting these proceedings can impose a maximum punishment of 30 days confinement at hard labor. The summary court-martial is designed "to exercise justice promptly for relatively minor offenses" in an informal proceeding conducted by a single commissioned officer (acting as judge, fact-finder, prosecutor and defense counsel). It occupies a position between disciplinary punishment administered by the commanding officer for the most minor offenses and the courtroom-type procedures of the general and special court-martial (with lawyer counsel for both the prosecution and the defense). In rejecting even the view that counsel must be provided in "special circumstances," the Court, per REHNQUIST, J., observed:

"[E]ven were the Sixth Amendment to be held applicable to court-martial proceedings, the summary court-martial provided for in these cases was not a 'criminal prosecution' within the meaning of that Amendment. [T]he fact that the outcome of a proceeding may result in loss of liberty does not by itself, even in civilian life, mean that the Sixth Amendment's guarantee of counsel is applicable. In *Gagnon,* the respondent faced the prospect of being sent to prison as a result of the revocation of his probation, but we held that the revocation proceeding was nonetheless not a 'criminal proceeding.' * * * [In *In re Gault* [a]] the juvenile faced possible initial confinement as a result of the proceeding in question, but the Court nevertheless based its conclusion that counsel was required on [Fourteenth Amendment due process], rather than on any determination that the hearing was a 'criminal prosecution' within the meaning of the Sixth Amendment.

"[T]ogether [*Gault* and *Gagnon*] surely stand for the proposition that even in the civilian community a proceeding which may result in deprivation of liberty is nonetheless not a 'criminal proceeding' within the meaning of the Sixth Amendment if there are elements about it which sufficiently distinguish it from a traditional civilian criminal trial. The summary court-martial proceeding here is likewise different from a traditional trial in many respects, the most important of which is that it occurs within the military community. This latter factor [is] every bit as entitled to be given controlling weight, as the fact in *Gagnon* that the defendant had been previously sentenced, or the fact in *Gault* that the proceeding had a rehabilitative purpose.

" * * * Much of the conduct proscribed by the military is not 'criminal' conduct in the civilian sense of the word. Here, for example, [most] were charged with 'unauthorized absence,' an offense which has no common-law counterpart and which carries little popular opprobrium. Conviction of such an offense would likely have no [collateral consequences] unlike conviction for such civilian misdemeanors as a vagrancy or larceny which carry a stamp of 'bad character' with conviction.

"[Moreover, a summary court-martial] is not an adversary proceeding. Yet the adversary nature of civilian criminal proceedings is one of the touchstones of the Sixth Amendment's right to counsel." [b]

Dissenting Justice MARSHALL, joined by Brennan, J., maintained that "[a]pplication of the Sixth Amendment right to counsel

a. 387 U.S. 1, 87 S.Ct. 1428, 18 L.Ed.2d 527 (1967). *Gault* held that the "Due Process Clause of the Fourteenth Amendment requires that in respect to proceedings to determine [juvenile] delinquency which may result in commitment to an institution in which the juvenile's freedom is curtailed, the child and his parent must be notified of the child's right to be represented by counsel retained by them, or if they are unable to afford counsel, that counsel will be appointed to represent the child." The Court stressed the need for counsel to assure a fair hearing in a proceeding which "was comparable in seriousness to a felony prosecution." It rejected the state's suggestion that the probation officers, parents, and judge might be relied upon to "represent the child," noting that "there is no material difference in this respect between adult and juvenile proceedings of the sort involved here." *Gault* was hailed as demonstrating the Court's reluctance to be "hemmed in by such artificial labels as 'criminal,' 'civil' or 'quasi-administrative,'" and the view that "a desire to help—the rehabilitative ideal—no longer will serve as the incantation before which procedural safeguards must succumb." Cohen, *Sentencing, Probation and the Rehabilitative Ideal,* 47 Texas L.Rev. 1, 2 (1968).

b. Powell, J., joined by Blackmun, J., joined the opinion of the Court, but also wrote a separate opinion emphasizing that *Argersinger* was distinguishable on the ground that the military is a "specialized society" and that one "must ignore history, tradition, and practice for two centuries to read into the Constitution, at this late date, a requirement for counsel in the discipline of minor violations of military law."

to the military follows logically and naturally from the modern right-to-counsel decisions, in which the right has been held fully applicable in every case in which a defendant faced conviction of a criminal offense and potential incarceration. The due process right to counsel, usually applied on a case-by-case basis, extends a qualified right to counsel to persons not involved in criminal proceedings, see *Gagnon,* but has not been viewed as a replacement for the Sixth Amendment right [in] situations in which a defendant stands to be convicted of a criminal offense." No less than other courts-martial, "summary courts-martial are directed at adjudicating 'charges of criminal violations of military law,' and [conviction] can lead to confinement for one month."

"To the extent that the Court's characterization of summary court-martial as 'nonadversary' is meant to convey something about the goal or purpose of the proceeding," the dissenters found it "totally unpersuasive": The summary court-martial "is far less 'nonadversary' than the juvenile delinquency proceedings to which we held the right to counsel applicable in *In re Gault.* [Yet *Gault*] confronted the reality that, however, beneficial [the rehabilitative goal] of delinquency proceedings, they have as their potential result the confinement on an individual in an institution."

As for the second possible meaning of "nonadversary"—"the responsibility of the presiding officer to act as judge, jury, prosecutor, and defense counsel combined"—the dissenters found this argument equally unpersuasive: "The Court intimates that the presiding officer's duty to advise the accused of his rights and his ability to help the accused assemble facts, examine witnesses, and cross-examine his accusers make defense counsel unnecessary, particularly in light of the absence of a formal prosecutor in the proceeding. [But in *Powell*] we rejected the notion that a judge could 'effectively discharge the obligations of counsel for the accused,' largely because of [the judge's inability to] 'participate in those necessary conferences between counsel and accused which sometimes partake of the inviolable character of the confessional.' "[c]

D. Parental Status Termination Proceedings

LASSITER v. DEPARTMENT OF SOCIAL SERVICES, 452 U.S. 18, 101 S.Ct. 2153, 68 L.Ed.2d 640 (1981), per STEWART, J., rejected the view that due process requires the appointment of counsel in every parental status termination proceeding involving indigent parents and left the appointment of counsel in such proceedings to be determined by the state courts on a case-by-case basis:[a]

"The pre-eminent generalization that emerges from this Court's precedents on an indigent's right to appointed counsel is that such a right has been recognized to

c. Stewart, J., dissented on the ground that Fifth Amendment due process requires that a defendant be accorded the assistance of counsel in a summary court-martial. Stevens, J., did not participate.

a. In the spring of 1975, after hearing evidence that petitioner had not provided her infant son with proper medical care, a North Carolina court adjudicated him "a neglected child" and transferred him to the department of social services (the Department). A year later, Ms. Lassiter was charged with and convicted of murder. She was sentenced to a long term of imprisonment. In 1978 the Department petitioned the court to terminate Ms. Lassiter's parental rights because, inter alia, alleged the Department, she had had no contact with the child since December of 1975 and had willfully left the child in foster care for more than two years without showing that substantial progress had been made in correcting the conditions which led to the removal of the child. Although her mother had retained counsel for her in an effort to overturn her murder conviction, Ms. Lassiter never mentioned the forthcoming termination hearing to him. Because the judge concluded that she had had "ample opportunity" to seek and obtain counsel prior to the termination hearing and that her failure to do so was "without just cause," he did not postpone the proceedings so that Ms. Lassiter might have more time to obtain legal assistance. Ms. Lassiter did not allege that she was indigent, and the court did not appoint counsel for her.

exist only where the litigant may lose his physical liberty if he loses the litigation. * * * Significantly, as a litigant's interest in personal liberty diminishes, so does his right to appointed counsel. [Thus,] [*Gagnon*] declined to hold that indigent probationers have, *per se,* a right to counsel at revocation hearings, and instead left the decision whether counsel should be appointed to be made on a case-by-case basis.

"[T]he Court has refused to extend the right to appointed counsel to include prosecutions which, though criminal, do not result in the defendant's loss of personal liberty. [*Scott*], for instance, interpreted the 'central premise of *Argersinger*' to be 'that actual imprisonment is a penalty different in kind from fines or the mere threat of imprisonment,' [and] endorsed that premise as 'eminently sound and warrant[ing] adoption of actual imprisonment as the line defining the constitutional right to appointment of counsel.' "

The Court then measured "all the other elements in the due process decision" against "the presumption that an indigent litigant has a right to appointed counsel only when, if he loses, he may be deprived of his physical liberty." Employing the *Mathews v. Eldridge* balancing test (see p. 86 & fn. c supra), the Court concluded that "the *Eldridge* factors" (the private interest at stake, the government's interest, and the risk that the procedure used will lead to erroneous decisions) "did not suffice to rebut that presumption."

The Court then held that in the circumstances of this case the trial judge did not deny Ms. Lassiter due process when he failed to appoint counsel for her: The record shows that the petition to terminate parental rights contained no allegations of neglect or abuse upon which criminal charges could be based; the department was represented at the hearing by counsel, but no expert witness testified, and the case presented no specially troublesome points of law, either procedural or substantive. While hearsay evidence was no doubt admitted, and while Ms. Lassiter no doubt left incomplete her defense that the department had not adequately assisted her in rekindling her interest in her son, the weight of the evidence that she had few sparks of such an interest was sufficiently great that the presence of counsel for [her] could not have made a determinative difference." [b]

Dissenting Justice BLACKMUN, joined by Brennan and Marshall, JJ., protested: "[The Court] revives an ad hoc approach thoroughly discredited nearly 20 years ago in *Gideon.* [T]he unique importance of a parent's interest in the care and custody of his or her child cannot constitutionally be extinguished through formal judicial proceedings without the benefit of counsel.

"* * * A termination of parental rights is both total and irrevocable. Unlike other custody proceedings, it leaves the parent with no right to visit or communicate with the child, to participate in, or even to know about, any important decision affecting the child's religious, educational, emotional, or physical development. It is hardly surprising that this forced dissolution of the parent-child relationship has been recognized as a punitive sanction by courts, Congress, and commentators. * * *

"The magnitude of this deprivation is of critical significance in the due process calculus, for the process to which an individual is entitled is in part determined 'by the extent to which he may be "condemned to suffer grievous loss." ' Surely there can be few losses more grievous than the abrogation of parental rights. Yet the Court today asserts that this deprivation somehow is less serious than threatened losses deemed to require appointed counsel, because in this instance the parent's

b. Chief Justice Burger, who joined the Court's opinion, also added, in a brief concurrence responding to the dissenters, that the purpose of the parental status termination proceeding "was not 'punitive'" but "*protective* of the child's best interests."

own 'personal liberty' is not at stake. * * *

"The method chosen by North Carolina to extinguish parental rights resembles in many respects a criminal prosecution. [T]he procedure devised by the State vastly differs from the informal and rehabilitative probation revocation decision in *Scarpelli* * * *. The provision of counsel for the parent would not alter the character of the proceeding, which is already adversarial, formal, and quintessentially legal. It, however, would diminish the prospect of an erroneous termination, a prospect that is inherently substantial, given the gross disparity in power and resources between the State and the uncounseled indigent parent. * * *

"The legal issues posed by the State's petition are neither simple nor easily defined. The standard is imprecise and open to the subjective values of the judge. A parent seeking to prevail against the State must be prepared to adduce evidence about his or her personal abilities and lack of fault, as well as proof of progress and foresight as a parent that the State would deem adequate and improved over the situation underlying a previous adverse judgment of child neglect. The parent cannot possibly succeed without being able to identify material issues, develop defenses, gather and present sufficient supporting nonhearsay evidence, and conduct cross-examination of adverse witnesses.

"* * * Faced with a formal accusatory adjudication, with an adversary—the State—that commands great investigative and prosecutorial resources, with standards that involve ill-defined notions of fault and adequate parenting, and with the inevitable tendency of a court to apply subjective values or to defer to the State's 'expertise,' the defendant parent plainly is outstripped if he or she is without the assistance of 'the guiding hand of counsel.' When the parent is indigent, lacking in education, and easily intimidated by figures of authority, the imbalance may well become insuperable. * * *

"[W]here, as here, the threatened loss of liberty is severe and absolute, the State's role is so clearly adversarial and punitive, and the cost involved is relatively slight, there is no sound basis for refusing to recognize the right to counsel as a requisite of due process in a proceeding initiated by the State to terminate parental rights." [c]

In a separate dissenting opinion, Justice STEVENS maintained: "[T]he Court appears to treat this case as though it merely involved the deprivation of an interest in property that is less worthy of protection than a person's liberty. The analysis employed in *Eldridge,* in which the Court balanced the costs and benefits of different procedural mechanisms for allocating a finite quantity of material resources among competing claimants, is an appropriate method of determining what process is due in property cases. Meeting the Court on its own terms, Justice Blackmun demonstrates that the *Eldridge* analysis requires the appointment of counsel in this type of case. I agree [but] would take one further step.

"In my opinion the reasons supporting the conclusion that [due process] entitles the defendant in a criminal case to representation by counsel apply with equal force to a case of this kind. The issue is one of fundamental fairness, not of weighing the pecuniary costs against the societal benefits. Accordingly, even if the costs to the State were not relatively insignificant but rather were just as great as the costs of providing prosecutors, judges, and defense counsel to ensure the fairness of criminal

c. The dissent then examines the termination hearing in considerable detail. "In light of the unpursued avenues of defense, and of the experience petitioner underwent at this hearing," it found "virtually incredible" the Court's conclusion that the termination proceeding was fundamentally fair.

proceedings, I would reach the same result in this category of cases." [d]

III. THE "BEGINNINGS" OF THE RIGHT TO COUNSEL: HEREIN OF "CRIMINAL PROSECUTIONS" AND "CRITICAL STAGES"

The point at which the right to the assistance of counsel "begins" or first "attaches" is a question that arises in a number of different contexts and one that is considered at various parts of the book. See, e.g., *Miranda* (p. 542 infra) ("custodial interrogation"); *United States v. Wade* (p. 652 infra) (pretrial lineups); *Coleman v. Alabama* (Ch. 14, § 2) (preliminary hearing).

Compelled self-incrimination considerations aside, one only has a right to counsel at (1) a "critical stage" of (2) the "prosecution." As Justice Stewart observed, concurring in a pretrial identification case, *United States v. Ash* (p. 674 infra): [a]

"The requirement that there be a 'prosecution' means that [the] 'right to counsel attaches only at or after the time that the adversary judicial proceedings have been initiated against [an accused].' 'It is this point [that] marks the commencement of the 'criminal prosecutions' to which alone the explicit guarantees of the Sixth Amendment are applicable.' " [b]

Although at one time the *Escobedo* case (p. 529 infra) indicated otherwise, it is now clear that the right to counsel does not come into play simply because a person is or becomes the "prime suspect" or "focal point," or even when he is arrested (absent "interrogation" or its equivalent). "[A] person is entitled to the help of a lawyer"—assuming the stage of the "prosecution" is a "critical" one[c]—"at or after the time that judicial proceedings have been initiated against him—'whether by way of formal charge, preliminary hearing, indictment, information, or arraignment [presumably as early as the first appearance before a judicial officer].' " *Brewer v. Williams* (p. 626 infra) (the Court, per Stewart, J.)

As indicated by the cases dealing with the use of informants and other secret government agents to obtain incriminating statements (see, e.g., *Hoffa, Osborn* and *White,* all discussed in Ch. 6, § 3), when judicial proceedings have not been initiated against a person, the privilege against self-incrimination as interpreted in *Miranda*—and *Miranda* alone—strikes the appropriate balance. If and when the conditions surrounding or inherent in a "preformal charge" confrontation are sufficiently coercive, "interrogation" or its equivalent may

d. For varying degrees of lack of enthusiasm for *Lassiter,* see Choper, Kamisar & Tribe, *The Supreme Court: Trends and Developments 1980–81* (1982) at 171–78; Note, 95 Harv.L.Rev. 132 (1981).

a. *Ash* held that the right to counsel did not apply to a post-indictment *photographic* identification proceeding, maintaining that the right has always been limited to "trial-like confrontations" between prosecuting authorities and the accused, where the lawyer acts as "a spokesman for, or advisor to the accused." Dissenting Justice Brennan, joined by Douglas and Marshall, JJ., insisted that, regardless of whether the accused is physically present, "a 'stage' of the prosecution must be deemed 'critical' for the purpose of the Sixth Amendment if it is one at which the presence of counsel is necessary 'to protect the fairness of *the trial itself.*' "

b. Justice Stewart quoted from his four-justice plurality opinion in *Kirby v. Illinois* (p. 668 infra) (right to counsel inapplicable to identification procedures held prior to the start of adversary judicial proceedings). To the same effect is Justice Powell's opinion for the Court in *Moore v. Illinois* (p. 672 infra), also quoting from Justice Stewart's plurality opinion in *Kirby.*

c. In *Ash,* fn. a supra, the photographic display was conducted after adversary proceedings had begun, but the photographic identification was not considered a "critical stage." Compare *Coleman v. Alabama* (1970) (Ch. 15): "The inability of the indigent accused on his own to realize [the] advantages of a lawyer's assistance [at the preliminary hearing, e.g., skilled examination and cross-examination of witnesses, effective discovery of the prosecution's case, and effective arguments for the accused for an early psychiatric examination or bail] compels the conclusion that the Alabama preliminary hearing is a 'critical stage' of the State's criminal process at which the accused is 'as much entitled to [counsel] as at the trial itself.' *Powell v. Alabama.*"

bring the "*Miranda* right to counsel" into play. But the right to counsel as such, what might be called the "pure" right to counsel, is not brought into play. At the "pre-charge" stage, at least when the suspect neither has nor has expressed a desire for counsel, the right to counsel is triggered by, and dependent on, forces that "jeopardize" the privilege against compelled self-incrimination; it has no life it can call its own.

UNITED STATES v. GOUVEIA, 467 U.S. 180, 104 S.Ct. 2292, 81 L.Ed.2d 146 (1984), per REHNQUIST, J., reaffirmed that one does not become an "accused" for right to counsel purposes simply because he has been detained by government authorities who contemplate filing charges against him. During the investigation of murders of fellow inmates in a federal prison, defendants were placed in administrative detention. A disciplinary hearing held shortly thereafter led prison officials to conclude that defendants had participated in the murders. But defendants remained in administrative detention without appointed counsel for periods ranging from eight to nineteen months until their indictment on federal criminal charges. The Ninth Circuit reasoned that the administrative detention of an inmate for more than 90 days because of a pending felony investigation constitutes an "accusation" for Sixth Amendment right to counsel purposes [a] and that, in order to ensure that a prisoner or his lawyer will be able to take pre-indictment investigatory steps to preserve his defense at trial, indigent prisoners isolated in administrative detention while the subject of a felony investigation must be afforded counsel after 90 days or be released back into the prison population. The Supreme Court disagreed:

"[O]ur cases have long recognized that the right to counsel attaches only at or after the initiation of adversary proceedings against the defendant [referring to *Kirby v. Illinois* and subsequent cases]. That interpretation of the Sixth Amendment right to counsel is consistent not only with the literal language of the Amendment, which requires the existence of both a 'criminal prosecution' and an 'accused,' but also with the purposes which we have recognized that the right to counsel serves. We have recognized that the 'core purpose' of the counsel guarantee is to assure aid at trial, 'when the accused [is] confronted with both the intricacies of the law and the advocacy of the public prosecutor.' *Ash.*

"* * * Although we have extended an accused's right to counsel to certain 'critical' pre-trial proceedings, *Wade,* we have done so recognizing that at those proceedings, 'the accused [is] confronted, just as at trial, by the procedural system, or by his expert adversary, or by both,' *Ash,* in a situation where the results of the confrontation 'might well settle the accused's fate and reduces the trial itself to a mere formality.' *Wade.*

"* * * Of course, both inside and outside the prison, it may well be true that in some cases pre-indictment investigation could help a defendant prepare a better defense. [But] our cases have never suggested that the purpose of the right to counsel is to provide a defendant with a pre-indictment private investigator, and we see no reason to adopt that novel interpretation of the right to counsel in this case.

"[A]t bottom, [the Ninth Circuit's] concern is that because an inmate suspected of a crime is already in prison, the prosecution may have little incentive promptly to bring formal charges against him, and that the resulting preindictment delay may be particularly prejudicial to the inmate, given the problems inherent in investigating prison crimes, such as the transient nature of the prison population and the general reluctance of inmates to cooperate. But applicable statutes of limitations protect against the prosecution's bringing stale

a. The Ninth Circuit arrived at the 90-day figure based on its reading of federal prison regulations as permitting detention for up to 90 days for disciplinary reasons.

criminal charges against any defendant, and, beyond that protection, the Fifth Amendment requires the dismissal of an indictment, even if it is brought within the statute of limitations, if the defendant can prove that the government's delay in bringing the indictment was a deliberate device to gain an advantage over him and that it caused him actual prejudice in presenting his defense. Those protections apply to criminal defendants within and without the prison walls, and we decline to depart from our traditional interpretation of the Sixth Amendment right to counsel in order to provide additional protections for respondents here."

Concurring Justice STEVENS, joined by Brennan, J., maintained that "[i]f the authorities take a person into custody [to] interrogate him or to otherwise facilitate the process of making a case against him, then under the rationale of *Escobedo, Miranda,* and our other cases, [he] is sufficiently 'accused' to be entitled to the protections of the Sixth Amendment." He concurred in the result, however, because he agreed that defendants' administrative detention "did not serve an accusatorial function. [Under the circumstance] there can be no doubt that concern for the welfare of other inmates or respondents themselves fully justified administrative detention entirely apart from its relation to an ongoing criminal investigation. Indeed, there is no finding [that] respondents were placed in [administrative detention] at the behest of [or in order to aid] prosecutorial authorities [nor] is there a finding that their detention facilitated the investigation of the two murders at issue."

Dissenting Justice MARSHALL shared Justice Stevens' view that "the government treats an individual as an accused when that individual 'is deprived of liberty in order to aid the prosecution in its attempt to convict him, and when the deprivation is likely to have the extended effect,' " but his reading of the record led him to a different conclusion: "[The] District Court [was] justified in concluding that respondents' 'commitment to [administrative detention] was neither a form of prison discipline nor an attempt to ensure prison security,' [but] 'part and parcel of a sequence of prosecutive acts integrally related to the application of criminal sanctions.' "

IV. THE INDIGENT DEFENDANT'S RIGHT TO EXPERT SERVICES IN ADDITION TO COUNSEL

AKE v. OKLAHOMA, ___ U.S. ___, 105 S.Ct. 1087, 84 L.Ed.2d 53 (1985), held that (1) at least when a defendant has made a preliminary showing that his sanity at the time of the offense is likely to be a significant factor at trial, the state must provide access to "the psychiatric examination and assistance necessary to prepare an effective defense based on [the defendant's] mental condition" and (2) when, at a capital sentencing proceeding, the state presents psychiatric evidence of the defendant's future dangerousness, due process requires access to psychiatric assistance.

The case arose as follows: Ake, an indigent, was charged with first-degree murder. At his arraignment, Ake's behavior was so bizarre that the trial judge ordered him to be examined by a psychiatrist. The examining psychiatrist found Ake incompetent to stand trial. Six weeks after being committed to the state mental hospital, Ake was found to be competent to stand trial on the condition that he continue to be sedated with an antipsychotic drug. Petitioner's attorney informed the court that he would raise an insanity defense, but his motion for a psychiatric evaluation at state expense was denied. The jury rejected the insanity defense and petitioner was convicted of first-degree murder. At the capital sentencing proceeding, the state asked for the death penalty, relying on the examining psychiatrist's testimony to establish the likelihood of petitioner's future dangerousness. Petitioner had no expert witness to rebut this testimony or to give evidence in mitigation of his punishment, and he was sentenced to death. In reversing, the Court observed, per MARSHALL, J:

"This Court has long recognized that when a State brings its judicial power to bear on an indigent defendant in a criminal proceeding, it must take steps to assure that the defendant has a fair opportunity to present his defense. [Thus,] this court held almost 30 years ago that once a State offers to criminal defendants the opportunity to appeal their cases, it must provide a trial transcript to an indigent defendant if the transcript is necessary to a decision on the merits of the appeal. *Griffin v. Illinois* (1956) [p. 105 infra]. * * * Indeed, in *Little v. Streater*, 452 U.S. 1, 101 S.Ct. 2202, 68 L.Ed.2d 627 (1981), we extended this principle of meaningful participation to a 'quasi-criminal' proceeding and held that, in a paternity action, the State cannot deny the putative father blood grouping tests, if he cannot otherwise afford them.

"Meaningful access to justice has been the consistent theme of these cases. * * * [A] criminal trial is fundamentally unfair if the State proceeds against an individual defendant without making certain that he has access to the raw materials integral to the building of an effective defense. Thus, while the Court has not held that a State must purchase for the indigent defendant all the assistance that his wealthier counterpart might buy, see *Ross v. Moffitt* (p. 112 infra), it has often reaffirmed that fundamental fairness entitles indigent defendants to 'an adequate opportunity to present their claims fairly within the adversary system,' id. To implement this principle, we have focused on identifying the 'basic tools of an adequate defense or appeal,' and we have required that such tools be provided to those defendants who cannot afford to pay for them.

" * * * [W]ithout the assistance of a psychiatrist to conduct a professional examination on issues relevant to the defense, to help determine whether the insanity defense is viable to present testimony, and to assist in preparing the cross-examination of a State's psychiatric witnesses, the risk of an inaccurate resolution of sanity issues is extremely high. With such assistance, the defendant is fairly able to present at least enough information to the jury, in a meaningful manner, as to permit it to make a sensible determination.

"A defendant's mental condition is not necessarily at issue in every criminal proceeding, however, and it is unlikely that psychiatric assistance of the kind we have described would be of probable value in cases where it is not. The risk of error from denial of such assistance, as well as its probable value, are most predictably at their height when the defendant's mental condition is seriously in question. When the defendant is able to make an ex parte threshold showing to the trial court that his sanity is likely to be a significant factor in his defense, the need for the assistance of a psychiatrist is readily apparent. It is in such cases that a defense may be devastated by the absence of a psychiatric examination and testimony; with such assistance, the defendant might have a reasonable chance of success. In such a circumstance, where the potential accuracy of the jury's determination is so dramatically enhanced, and where the interests of the individual and the State in an accurate proceeding are substantial, the State's interest in its fisc must yield.

"We therefore hold that when a defendant demonstrates [that] his sanity at the time of the offense is to be a significant factor at trial, the State must, at a minimum, assure the defendant access to a competent psychiatrist who will conduct an appropriate examination and assist in evaluation, preparation, and presentation of the defense. This is not to say, of course, that the indigent defendant has a constitutional right to choose a psychiatrist of his personal liking or to receive funds to hire his own. Our concern is that the indigent defendant have access to a competent psychiatrist for the purpose we have discussed, and as in the case of provision of counsel we leave to the State the decision on how to implement this right.

"Ake also was denied the means of presenting evidence to rebut the State's evidence of his future dangerousness. The foregoing discussion compels a similar conclusion in the context of a capital sentencing proceeding, when the State presents psychiatric evidence of the defendants future dangerousness. * * *

"This Court has upheld the practice [in state capital sentencing proceedings] of placing before the jury psychiatric testimony on the question of future dangerousness, at least where the defendant has had access to an expert of his own. * * * Without a psychiatrist's assistance, the defendant cannot offer a well-informed expert's opposing view, and thereby loses a significant opportunity to raise in the jurors' minds questions about the State's proof of an aggravating factor. In such a circumstance, where the consequence of error is so great, the relevance of responsive psychiatric testimony so evident, and the burden on the State so slim, due process requires access to a psychiatric examination on relevant issues, to the testimony of the psychiatrist, and to assistance in preparation at the sentencing phase." [a]

Notes and Questions

1. *The breadth of the supporting services that may be needed.* "Quality legal representation," emphasizes I *A.B.A. Standards* § 5–1.4 (commentary), "cannot be rendered either by defenders or by assigned counsel unless the lawyers have available for their use adequate supporting services. These [include] expert witnesses * * *, personnel skilled in social work and related disciplines to provide assistance at pretrial release hearings and at sentencing, and trained investigators to interview witnesses and to assemble demonstrative evidence. The quality of representation at trial, for example, may be excellent and yet valueless to the defendant if the defense requires the assistance of a psychiatrist or handwriting expert and no such services are available. If the defense attorney must personally conduct factual investigations, the financial cost to the justice system is likely to be greater. Moreover, when an attorney personally interviews witnesses, [he] may be placed in the untenable position of either taking the stand to challenge their credibility if their testimony conflicts with statements previously given or withdrawing from the case."

2. *The need to make a showing of particularized need.* As pointed out in LaFave & Israel, § 11.2(d), unlike the position taken with respect to transcripts (see Sec. 2 infra), "the courts uniformly hold that the constitutional right to assistance of state-paid experts exists only upon a showing of particularized need. Thus, in seeking the assistance of an expert in scientific analysis (e.g., ballistics), the defendant must show that 'a substantial question exists over an issue requiring expert testimony for its resolution' and that the 'defendant's position cannot be fully developed without professional assistance.' Establishing sufficient need for a special investigator appears to be especially difficult, perhaps because it is assumed that investigation of the facts is ordinarily within the expertise of counsel. * * *

"In recent years, a substantial number of jurisdictions have adopted statutory provisions authorizing the appointment of a

a. Burger, C.J. concurred in the judgment, maintaining: "The facts of this case and the question presented confine the actual holding of the Court. In capital cases the finality of the sentence imposed warrants protections that may or may not be required in other cases. Nothing in the Court's opinion reaches non-capital cases." What, if anything, in the Court's opinion suggests that it is limited to capital cases? Rehnquist, J., dissented. He did not believe that "the facts of this case warrant" the establishment of the constitutional rule announced by the Court and, in any event, he thought the rule "far too broad." He would limit it to capital cases and "make clear that the entitlement is to an independent psychiatric evaluation, not to a defense consultant." Is it clear that the entitlement *is* to a "defense consultant?"

wide range of experts to assist appointed counsel. Many are modeled after [the Criminal Justice Act (CJA),] 18 U.S.C. § 3006A(e)(1), which provides for 'investigative, expert, or other services' [a] upon a court finding that the particular service is 'necessary for an adequate defense.' [67] Such provisions are frequently interpreted as requiring a less stringent showing of particularized need than the constitutional right to assistance. Neither the legislatures nor the courts have been willing, however, to totally dispense with a showing of need and thereby make experts automatically available upon defense request. * * * Both courts and legislatures fear that, [lacking the fiscal restraint operating on retained counsel], appointed counsel, if given automatic access to experts, would use them for speculative inquiries based on the slim hope that helpful evidence somehow might be uncovered."

SECTION 2. THE *GRIFFIN–DOUGLAS* "EQUALITY" PRINCIPLE

GRIFFIN v. ILLINOIS: "There Can Be No Equal Justice Where the Kind of Trial a Man Gets Depends on the Money He Has"

Prior to GRIFFIN v. ILLINOIS, 351 U.S. 12, 76 S.Ct. 585, 100 L.Ed. 891 (1956), full direct appellate review could only be had in Illinois by furnishing the appellate court with a bill of exceptions or report of the trial proceedings, certified by the trial judge. Preparation of these documents was sometimes impossible without a stenographic transcript of the trial proceedings, but such a transcript was furnished free only to indigent defendants sentenced to death. *Griffin* upheld by a 5–4 vote the contention that the due process and equal protection clauses of the fourteenth amendment require that *all* indigent defendants be furnished a transcript, at least where allegations that manifest errors occurred at the trial are not denied. See generally F. Allen, *Griffin v. Illinois: Antecedents and Aftermath,* 25 U.Chi.L.Rev. 151, 152 (1957).

There was no opinion of the Court in *Griffin.* Justice Black announced the Court's judgment in a four-justice opinion; Mr. Justice Frankfurter concurred specially. In the course of his opinion, JUSTICE BLACK observed: "In criminal trials a State can no more discriminate on account of poverty than on account of religion, race, or color. Plainly the ability to pay costs in advance bears no rational relationship to a defendant's guilt or innocence and could not be used as an excuse to deprive a defendant of a fair trial. [It] is true that a State is not required by the federal constitution to provide appellate courts or a right to appellate review at all. [But] that is not to say that a State that does grant appellate review can do so in a way that discriminates against some convicted defendants on account of their poverty. * * *

"All of the States now provide some method of appeal from criminal convic-

a. This statute authorizes payments for services other than counsel even for the clients of *retained* lawyers who are unable to afford investigators and experts. In all cases, however, unless payment in excess of that amount is certified by the court or by the federal magistrate (if services were rendered in connection with a case disposed of entirely before him), compensation to be paid to an investigator or expert is limited to a maximum of $300.

As pointed out by Judge Bazelon, dissenting in *United States v. Decoster (Decoster III),* 624 F.2d 196, 279 n. 80 (D.C.Cir.1976), despite the availability of CJA funds for hiring investigators and for compensating counsel who do such work themselves, very few court-appointed counsel make use of the Act to support investigations on behalf of their clients. One explanation suggests Judge Bazelon is the fear of court-appointed counsel, "often reinforced by comments from trial judges, that any money spent on such services will eventually be subtracted from the renumeration the attorneys themselves would otherwise receive. Moreover, the CJA itself, by compensating attorneys at rates of $30 per hour for time expended in court and only $20 per hour for out-of-court time [18 U.S.C. § 3006A(d)(1)], provides a disincentive for counsel to perform their own investigating work."

67. The finding is made in an ex parte proceeding, so that the defense is not forced to disclose the nature of its defense to the prosecution.

tions, recognizing the importance of appellate review to a correct adjudication of guilt or innocence. Statistics show that a substantial proportion of criminal convictions are reversed by state appellate courts. Thus to deny adequate review to the poor means that many of them may lose their life, liberty or property because of unjust convictions which appellate courts would set aside. Many States have recognized this and provided aid for convicted defendants who have a right to appeal and need a transcript but are unable to pay for it. A few have not. Such a denial is a misfit in a country dedicated to affording equal justice to all and special privileges to none in the administration of its criminal law. There can be no equal justice where the kind of trial a man gets depends on the amount of money he has. Destitute defendants must be afforded as adequate appellate review as defendants who have money enough to buy transcripts."

I. APPLICATION (OR EXTENSION) OF *GRIFFIN* TO MINOR OFFENSES, POST-CONVICTION PROCEEDINGS, FILING FEES, INCARCERATION FOR INABILITY TO PAY FINES; RULES CONDITIONING AVAILABILITY OF FREE TRANSCRIPTS

In the decade and a half following *Griffin,* its underlying principle was broadly applied. See *Burns v. Ohio,* 360 U.S. 252, 79 S.Ct. 1164, 3 L.Ed.2d 1209 (1959) (state cannot require indigent defendant to pay filing fee before permitting him to appeal); *Smith v. Bennett,* 365 U.S. 708, 81 S.Ct. 895, 6 L.Ed.2d 39 (1961) (extending ban on filing fees to state post-conviction proceedings); *Long v. District Court of Iowa,* 385 U.S. 192, 87 S.Ct. 362, 17 L.Ed.2d 290 (1966) (indigent must be furnished a free transcript of a state habeas corpus hearing for use on appeal from a denial of habeas corpus, although availability of transcript not a sine qua non to access to the appellate court); *Gardner v. California,* 393 U.S. 367, 89 S.Ct. 580, 21 L.Ed.2d 601 (1969) (indigent prisoner entitled to free transcript of lower court habeas proceeding for use in filing application for a new habeas proceeding before a higher state court, even though that application need contain only a "brief statement" of prior proceedings and need not assign errors or refer to testimony in the prior proceeding) (Harlan and Stewart, JJ., dissenting); *Roberts v. LaVallee,* 389 U.S. 40, 88 S.Ct. 194, 19 L.Ed.2d 41 (1967) (indigent defendant entitled to free transcript of preliminary hearing for use at trial, even though both defendant and his counsel attended preliminary hearing and no indication of use to which preliminary hearing transcript could be put—points stressed by dissenting Justice Harlan); *Williams v. Illinois,* 399 U.S. 235, 90 S.Ct. 2018, 26 L.Ed.2d 586 (1970) (defendant unable to pay fine could not be incarcerated beyond maximum term fixed by statute; equal protection requires that "statutory ceiling" on imprisonment be same for all "irrespective of their economic status"); *Tate v. Short,* 401 U.S. 395, 90 S.Ct. 668, 28 L.Ed.2d 130 (1971) (indigent convicted of offenses punishable by fine only cannot be incarcerated a sufficient time to satisfy fines); [a] *Britt v. North Carolina,* 404

a. Recently, the Court relied on *Williams* and *Tate* to hold that a sentencing court cannot "automatically revoke" probation because a defendant cannot pay his fine without determining that the defendant "had not made sufficient bona fide efforts to pay or that adequate alternative forms of punishment did not exist." *Bearden v. Georgia,* 461 U.S. 660, 103 S.Ct. 2064, 76 L.Ed.2d 221 (1983).

As a condition of his three years probation for burglary, petitioner was ordered to pay a $500 fine and $250 in restitution. He was to pay $200 within 48 hours and the $550 within the next four months. Petitioner borrowed the money from his parents to pay the first $200, but, because he was laid off from his job and could not find other work, was unable to pay the balance. The trial court then revoked probation and sentenced petitioner to serve the remaining portion or the probationary period in prison (more than two years). The Court, per O'Connor, J., viewed this as a case where a probationer had been deprived of his conditional freedom "simply because, through no fault of his own, he cannot pay

U.S. 226, 92 S.Ct. 431, 30 L.Ed.2d 400 (1972) (recognition that under ordinary circumstances indigent would be entitled to free transcript of previous trial ending with a hung jury because such a transcript would be "valuable to the defendant" as a discovery device and "as a tool at the [second] trial itself for the impeachment of prosecution witnesses").

In MAYER v. CHICAGO, 404 U.S. 189, 92 S.Ct. 410, 30 L.Ed.2d 372 (1971), a unanimous Court, per BRENNAN, J., carried the *Griffin* principle further than it ever has the *Gideon* principle by holding that an indigent appellant "cannot be denied a 'record of sufficient completeness' to permit proper consideration of his claims" because he was convicted of ordinance violations punishable by fine only. "The size of the defendant's pocketbook bears no more relationship to his guilt or innocence in a non-felony than in a felony case." Nor was the Court impressed with the argument that appellant's interest in a transcript in a case where he is not subject to imprisonment is outweighed by the State's fiscal and other interests in not burdening the appellate process:

"*Griffin* does not represent a balance between the needs of the accused and the interests of society; its principle is a flat prohibition against pricing indigent defendants out of as effective an appeal as would be available to others able to pay their own way. The invidiousness of the discrimination that exists when criminal procedures are made available only to those who can pay is not erased by any differences in the sentences that may be imposed. The State's fiscal interest is, therefore, irrelevant.

"We add that even approaching the problem in the terms the city suggests hardly yields the answer the city tenders. The practical effects of conviction of even petty offenses of the kind involved here

the fine" and thus "contrary to the fundamental fairness required by the Fourteenth Amendment":

"[I]n revocation proceedings for failure to pay a fine or restitution, a sentencing court must inquire into the reasons for the failure to pay. If the probationer willfully refused to pay or failed to make sufficient bona fide efforts legally to acquire the resources to pay, the court may revoke probation * * *. [But if] the probationer could not pay despite sufficient bona fide efforts [to do so], the court must consider alternate means of punishment other than imprisonment [such as an extension of time to make payments or some form of labor or public service]. Only if alternate measures are not adequate to meet the State's interests in punishment and deterrence may the court imprison a probationer who has made sufficient bona fide efforts to pay. To do otherwise * * * would be contrary [to] the Fourteenth Amendment.

"[In the instant case, the sentencing court, in effect,] imprison[ed] a person solely because he lacks funds to pay the fine, a practice we condemned in *Williams* and *Tate*. By sentencing petitioner to imprisonment simply because he could not pay the fine, without considering the reasons for the inability to pay or the propriety of reducing the fine or extending the time for payments or making alternative orders, the court automatically turned a fine into a prison sentence."

Justice White, joined by the Chief Justice and Powell and Rehnquist, JJ., concurred in the judgment because "the state court obviously did not find that the prison sentence was 'a rational and necessary trade-off to punish the individual who possessed no accumulated assets,' *Williams* (Harlan, J., concurring)," but found no support for the Court's "novel requirement." He observed: "Had the sentencing judge been quite sure that the defendant could not pay the fine, I cannot believe that the court would not have imposed some jail time or that either [due process or equal protection] would prevent such imposition. Poverty does not insulate those who break the law from punishment. When probation is revoked for failure to pay a fine, I find nothing in the Constitution to prevent the trial court from revoking probation and imposing a term of imprisonment if revocation does not automatically result in the imposition of a long jail term and if the sentencing court makes a good-faith effort to impose a jail sentence that in terms of the state's sentencing objectives will be roughly equivalent to the fine and restitution that the defendant failed to pay."

Responding to Justice White, the Court agreed that poverty does not insulate one from punishment or "necessarily prevent revocation of his probation for inability to pay a fine," but rejected Justice White's approach as "impractical": "Even putting to one side the question of judicial 'good faith,' we perceive no meaningful standard by which a sentencing or reviewing court could assess whether a given prison sentence has an equivalent sting to the original fine."

are not to be minimized. A fine may bear as heavily on an indigent accused as forced confinement.[b] The collateral consequences of conviction may be even more serious, as when (as was apparently a possibility in this case) the impecunious medical student finds himself barred from the practice of medicine because of a conviction he is unable to appeal for lack of funds. Moreover, the State's longterm interest would not appear to lie in making access to appellate processes from even its most inferior courts depend upon the defendant's ability to pay. * * *

"Arbitrary denial of appellate review of proceedings of the State's lowest trial courts may save the State some dollars and cents, but only at the substantial risk of generating frustration and hostility toward its courts among the most numerous consumers of justice." [c]

II. THE IMPACT OF THE "EQUALITY" PRINCIPLE ON THOSE WHO CANNOT AFFORD COUNSEL OR OTHER FORMS OF ASSISTANCE

Prior to *Gideon,* the *Griffin* case posed a challenge to *Betts:* How could the *Betts* line of cases be reconciled with the language, if not the holding, of *Griffin?* Since there was an unqualified right to have one's own paid counsel of his choosing at state trial, capital or not, did *Griffin* not imply that an indigent also has this unqualified right? By requiring *special circumstances* to exist before the indigent was entitled to appointed counsel in non-capital state cases, was the indigent not denied equal protection of the law? But see Qua, *Griffin v. Illinois,* 25 U.Chi.L.Rev. 143, 150 (1957).

When the Supreme Court finally overruled the *Betts* case, somewhat surprisingly, it did not rely on *Griffin* at all, but *Douglas v. California,* infra, decided the same day, is another story.

DOUGLAS v. CALIFORNIA

372 U.S. 353, 83 S.Ct. 814, 9 L.Ed.2d 811 (1963).

MR. JUSTICE DOUGLAS delivered the opinion of the Court.

* * * The record shows that petitioners requested, and were denied, the assistance of counsel on appeal, even though it plainly appeared they were indigents. In denying petitioners' requests, the California District Court of Appeal stated that it had "gone through" the record and had come to the conclusion that "no good whatever could be served by appointment of counsel." [The court] was acting in accordance with a California rule of criminal procedure which provides that state appellate courts, upon the request of an indigent for counsel, may make "an independent investigation of the record and determine whether it would be of advantage to the defendant or helpful to the appellate court to have counsel appointed. [After] such investigation, appellate courts should appoint counsel if in their opinion it would be helpful to the defendant or the court, and should deny the appointment of counsel only if in their judgment such appointment would be of no value to either the defendant or the court." * * *

We agree, however, with Justice Traynor of the California Supreme Court, who said that the "[d]enial of counsel on appeal [to an indigent] would seem to be a discrimination at least as invidious as that condemned in [*Griffin,*" where] we held that a State may not grant appellate review in such a way as to discriminate against some convicted defendants on account of their poverty. [Whether the issue is a transcript on appeal or the assistance of counsel on appeal] the evil is the same:

b. But cf. *Argersinger v. Hamlin,* p. 80 supra; *Scott v. Illinois,* p. 83 supra.

c. Chief Justice Burger joined the Court's opinion, but in a separate opinion emphasized that "there are alternatives in the majority of cases to a full verbatim transcript of an entire trial."

discrimination against the indigent. For there can be no equal justice where the kind of an appeal a man enjoys "depends on the amount of money he has." * * *

[Under California's] present practice the type of an appeal [one is afforded] hinges upon whether or not he can pay for the assistance of counsel. If he can the appellate court passes on the merits of his case only after having the full benefit of written briefs and oral argument by counsel. If he cannot the appellate court is forced to prejudge the merits before it can even determine whether counsel should be provided. At this stage in the proceedings only the barren record speaks for the indigent, and, unless the printed pages show that an injustice has been committed, he is forced to go without a champion on appeal. Any real chance he may have had of showing that his appeal has hidden merit is deprived him when the court decides on an *ex parte* examination of the record that the assistance of counsel is not required.

* * * We are dealing only with the first appeal, granted as a matter of right to rich and poor alike (Cal.Penal Code §§ 1235, 1237), from a criminal conviction. We need not now decide whether California would have to provide counsel for an indigent seeking [discretionary review or] whether counsel must be appointed for an indigent seeking review of an appellate affirmance of his conviction in this Court. [But] it is appropriate to observe that a State can, consistently with the Fourteenth Amendment, provide for differences so long as the result does not amount to a denial of due process or an "invidious discrimination." Absolute equality is not required; lines can be and are drawn and we often sustain them. [But] where the merits of the one and only appeal an indigent has as of right are decided without benefit of counsel, we think an unconstitutional line has been drawn between rich and poor.

When an indigent is forced to run this gantlet of a preliminary showing of merit, the right to appeal does not comport with fair procedure. [T]he discrimination is not between "possibly good and obviously bad cases," but between cases where the rich man can require the court to listen to argument of counsel before deciding on the merits, but a poor man cannot. There is lacking that equality demanded by the Fourteenth Amendment where the rich man, who appeals as of right, enjoys the benefit of counsel's examination into the record, research of the law, and marshalling of arguments on his behalf, while the indigent, already burdened by a preliminary determination that his case is without merit, is forced to shift for himself. The indigent, where the record is unclear or the errors are hidden, has only the right to a meaningless ritual, while the rich man has a meaningful appeal. * * *

Judgment of the District Court of Appeals vacated and case remanded.

MR. JUSTICE CLARK, dissenting.

* * * We all know that the overwhelming percentage of *in forma pauperis* appeals are frivolous. Statistics of this Court show that over 96% of the petitions filed here are of this variety. [California's courts] after examining the record certified that [an] appointment [of counsel] would be neither advantageous to the petitioners nor helpful to the court. It, therefore, refused to go through the useless gesture of appointing an attorney. In my view neither the Equal Protection Clause nor the Due Process Clause requires more. I cannot understand why the Court says that this procedure afforded petitioners "a meaningless ritual." To appoint an attorney would not only have been utter extravagance and a waste of the State's funds but as surely "meaningless" to petitioners.

MR. JUSTICE HARLAN, whom MR. JUSTICE STEWART joins, dissenting.

[T]he Court appears to rely both on the Equal Protection Clause and on the guarantees of fair procedure inherent in the

Due Process Clause of the Fourteenth Amendment, with obvious emphasis on "equal protection." In my view the Equal Protection Clause is not apposite, and its application to cases like the present one can lead only to mischievous results. This case should be judged solely under the Due Process Clause, and I do not believe that the California procedure violates that provision.

EQUAL PROTECTION

To approach the present problem in terms of the Equal Protection Clause is, I submit, but to substitute resounding phrases for analysis. I dissented from this approach in [*Griffin*] and I am constrained to dissent from the implicit extension of the equal protection approach here—to a case in which the State denies no one an appeal, but seeks only to keep within reasonable bounds the instances in which appellate counsel will be assigned to indigents.

The States, of course, are prohibited by the Equal Protection Clause from discriminating between "rich" and "poor" *as such* in the formulation and application of their laws. But it is a far different thing to suggest that this provision prevents the State from adopting a law of general applicability that may affect the poor more harshly than it does the rich, or, on the other hand, from making some effort to redress economic imbalances while not eliminating them entirely.

Every financial exaction which the State imposes on a uniform basis is more easily satisfied by the well-to-do than by the indigent. Yet I take it that no one would dispute the constitutional power of the State to levy a uniform sales tax, to charge tuition at a state university, to fix rates for the purchase of water from a municipal corporation, to impose a standard fine for criminal violations, or to establish minimum bail for various categories of offenses. Nor could it be contended that the State may not classify as crimes acts which the poor are more likely to commit than are the rich. And surely, there would be no basis for attacking a state law which provided benefits for the needy simply because those benefits fell short of the goods or services that others could purchase for themselves.

Laws such as these do not deny equal protection to the less fortunate for one essential reason: the Equal Protection Clause does not impose on the States "an affirmative duty to lift the handicaps flowing from differences in economic circumstances." To so construe it would be to read into the Constitution a philosophy of leveling that would be foreign to many of our basic concepts of the proper relations between government and society. The State may have a moral obligation to eliminate the evils of poverty, but it is not required by the Equal Protection Clause to give to some whatever others can afford.
* * *

* * * [I]t should be noted that if the present problem may be viewed as one of equal protection, so may the question of the right to appointed counsel at trial, and the Court's analysis of that right in *Gideon* [is] wholly unnecessary. The short way to dispose of *Gideon,* in other words, would be simply to say that the State deprives the indigent of equal protection whenever it fails to furnish him with legal services, and perhaps with other services as well, equivalent to those that the affluent defendant can obtain.[a]

The real question in this case, I submit, and the only one that permits of satisfactory analysis, is whether or not the state rule, as applied in this case, is consistent with

a. One may ask, too, why the Court failed even to discuss the applicability of the *Griffin-Douglas* "equality" principle to the issue raised in *Scott v. Illinois* p. 83 supra. Since it is plain that one charged with an offense *punishable* by incarceration may *retain* counsel for his defense, does not the "equality" principle—especially in light of its application in *Mayer*—suggest that the "actual imprisonment" standard, even if it defensibly defines the Sixth Amendment right to appointed counsel, is unsatisfactory under the equal protection clause?

the requirements of fair procedure guaranteed by the Due Process Clause. Of course, in considering this question, it must not be lost sight of that the State's responsibility under the Due Process Clause is to provide justice for all. Refusal to furnish criminal indigents with some things that others can afford may fall short of constitutional standards of fairness. The problem before us is whether this is such a case.

DUE PROCESS * * *

We have today held that in a case such as the one before us, there is an absolute right to the services of counsel at trial. *Gideon.* [But] the appellate procedures involved here stand on an entirely different constitutional footing. *First,* appellate review is in itself not required by the Fourteenth Amendment, *McKane v. Durston,* 153 U.S. 684, 14 S.Ct. 913, 38 L.Ed. 867 [1894]; see *Griffin,* and thus the question presented is the narrow one whether the State's rules with respect to the appointment of counsel are so arbitrary or unreasonable, *in the context of the particular appellate procedure that it has established,* as to require their invalidation. *Second,* the kinds of questions that may arise on appeal are circumscribed by the record of the proceedings that led to the conviction; they do not encompass the large variety of tactical and strategic problems that must be resolved at the trial. *Third,* as California applies its rule, the indigent appellant receives the benefit of expert and conscientious legal appraisal of the merits of his case on the basis of the trial record, and whether or not he is assigned counsel, is guaranteed full consideration of his appeal. It would be painting with too broad a brush to conclude that under these circumstances an appeal is just like a trial.

What the Court finds constitutionally offensive in California's procedure bears a striking resemblance to the rules of this Court and many state courts of last resort on petitions for certiorari or for leave to appeal filed by indigent defendants *pro se.* Under the practice of this Court, only if it appears from the petition for certiorari that a case merits review is leave to proceed *in forma pauperis* granted, the case transferred to the Appellate Docket, and counsel appointed. Since our review is generally discretionary, and since we are often not even given the benefit of a record in the proceedings below, the disadvantages to the indigent petitioner might be regarded as more substantial than in California. But as conscientiously committed as this Court is to the great principle of "Equal Justice Under Law," it has never deemed itself constitutionally required to appoint counsel to assist in the preparation of each of the more than 1,000 *pro se* petitions for certiorari currently being filed each Term. We should know from our own experience that appellate courts generally go out of their way to give fair consideration to those who are unrepresented.

The Court distinguishes our review from the present case on the grounds that the California rule relates to "the first appeal, granted as a matter of right." [But] I fail to see the significance of this difference. Surely, it cannot be contended that the requirements of fair procedure are exhausted once an indigent has been given one appellate review. Nor can it well be suggested that having appointed counsel is more necessary to the fair administration of justice in an initial appeal taken as a matter of right, which the reviewing court on the full record has already determined to be frivolous, than in a petition asking a higher appellate court to exercise its discretion to consider what may be a substantial constitutional claim.

I cannot agree that the Constitution prohibits a State in seeking to redress economic imbalances at its bar of justice and to provide indigents with full review, from taking reasonable steps to guard against needless expense. This is all that California has done. * * *

ROSS v. MOFFITT

417 U.S. 600, 94 S.Ct. 2437, 41 L.Ed.2d 341 (1974).

[Like many other states, the North Carolina appellate system is multitiered, providing for both an intermediate Court of Appeals and a Supreme Court. North Carolina authorizes appointment of counsel for a convicted defendant appealing to the intermediate court of appeals, but not for a defendant who seeks either discretionary review in the state supreme court or a writ of certiorari in the U.S. Supreme Court. In one case, the Mecklenburg County forgery conviction, respondent sought appointed counsel for discretionary review in the state supreme court. In another case, the Guilford County forgery conviction, respondent was represented by the public defender in the state supreme court, but sought court-appointed counsel to prepare a writ of certiorari to the U.S. Supreme Court. On federal habeas corpus, a unanimous panel of the U.S. Court of Appeals for the Fourth Circuit, per Haynsworth, C.J., held that the *Douglas* rationale required appointment of counsel in both instances. 483 F.2d 650 (4th Cir.1973).]

MR. JUSTICE REHNQUIST delivered the opinion of the Court.

[In *Griffin,* the Court struck down] an Illinois rule allowing a convicted criminal defendant to present claims of trial error to the [state supreme court] only if he procured a transcript of the testimony adduced at his trial. No exception was made for the indigent defendant, and thus one who was unable to pay the cost of obtaining such a transcript was precluded from obtaining appellate review of asserted trial error * * *.

[*Griffin* and succeeding cases, such as *Burns v. Ohio* and *Smith v. Bennett* (the filing fee cases summarized at p. 106 supra),] invalidat[ing] similar financial barriers to the appellate process, * * * stand for the proposition that a State cannot arbitrarily cut off appeal rights for indigents while leaving open avenues of appeal for more affluent persons. In *Douglas,* however, [the] Court departed somewhat from the limited doctrine of [these] cases and undertook an examination of whether an indigent's access to the appellate system was adequate. [The *Douglas* Court] concluded that a State does not fulfill its responsibility toward indigent defendants merely by waiving its own requirements that a convicted defendant procure a transcript or pay a fee in order to appeal, and held that the State must go further and provide counsel for the indigent on his first appeal as of right. It is this decision we are asked to extend today.

* * *

The precise rationale for the *Griffin* and *Douglas* lines of cases has never been explicitly stated, some support being derived from the Equal Protection Clause of the Fourteenth Amendment, and some from the Due Process Clause of that Amendment. Neither clause by itself provides an entirely satisfactory basis for the result reached, each depending on a different inquiry which emphasizes different factors. "Due process" emphasizes fairness between the State and the individual dealing with the State, regardless of how other individuals in the same situation may be treated. "Equal protection," on the other hand, emphasizes disparity in treatment by a State between classes of individuals whose situations are arguably indistinguishable. We will address these issues separately in the succeeding sections.

Recognition of the due process rationale in *Douglas* is found both in the Court's opinion and in the dissenting opinion of Mr. Justice Harlan. The Court in *Douglas* stated that "[w]hen an individual is forced to run this gantlet of a preliminary showing of merit, the right to appeal does not comport with fair procedure." Mr. Justice Harlan thought that the due process issue in *Douglas* was the only one worthy of extended consideration. * * *

We do not believe that the Due Process Clause requires North Carolina to provide respondent with counsel on his discretionary appeal to the State Supreme Court. At the trial stage of a criminal proceeding, the right of an indigent defendant to counsel [is] fundamental and binding upon the States by virtue of the Sixth and Fourteenth Amendments. But there are significant differences between the trial and appellate stages of a criminal proceeding. The purpose of the trial stage from the State's point of view is to convert a criminal defendant from a person presumed innocent to one found guilty beyond a reasonable doubt. To accomplish this purpose, the State employs a prosecuting attorney who presents evidence to the court, challenges any witnesses offered by the defendant, argues rulings of the court, and makes direct arguments to the court or jury seeking to persuade them of the defendant's guilt. Under these circumstances "* * * reason and reflection require us to recognize that in our adversary system of criminal justice, any person haled into court, who is too poor to hire a lawyer, cannot be assured a fair trial unless counsel is provided for him." *Gideon.*

By contrast, it is ordinarily the defendant, rather than the State, who initiates the appellate process, seeking not to fend off the efforts of the State's prosecutor but rather to overturn a finding of guilt made by a judge or jury below. The defendant needs an attorney on appeal not as a shield to protect him against being "haled into court" by the State and stripped of his presumption of innocence, but rather as a sword to upset the prior determination of guilt. This difference is significant for, while no one would agree that the State may simply dispense with the trial stage of proceedings without a criminal defendant's consent, it is clear that the State need not provide any appeal at all. *McKane v. Durston.* The fact that an appeal *has* been provided does not automatically mean that a State then acts unfairly by refusing to provide counsel to indigent defendants at every stage of the way. Unfairness results only if indigents are singled out by the State and denied meaningful access to that system because of their poverty. That question is more profitably considered under an equal protection analysis.

Language invoking equal protection notions is prominent both in *Douglas* and in other cases treating the rights of indigents on appeal. * * * Despite the tendency of all rights "to declare themselves absolute to their logical extreme," there are obviously limits beyond which the equal protection analysis may not be pressed without doing violence to principles recognized in other decisions of this Court. The Fourteenth Amendment "does not require absolute equality or precisely equal advantages," nor does it require the State to "equalize economic conditions." *Griffin* (Frankfurter, J., concurring). It does require [that] indigents have an adequate opportunity to present their claims fairly within the adversarial system. The State cannot adopt procedures which leave an indigent defendant "entirely cut off from any appeal at all," by virtue of his indigency, *Lane,* or extend to such indigent defendants merely a "meaningless ritual" while others in better economic circumstances have a "meaningful appeal." *Douglas.* The question is not one of absolutes, but one of degrees. In this case we do not believe that the Equal Protection Clause when interpreted in the context of these cases, requires North Carolina to provide free counsel for indigent defendants seeking to take discretionary appeals to the North Carolina Supreme Court, or to file petitions for certiorari in this Court. * * *

The facts show that respondent, in connection with his Mecklenburg County conviction, received the benefit of counsel in examining the record of his trial and in preparing an appellate brief on his behalf for the state Court of Appeals. Thus, prior to his seeking discretionary review in the State Supreme Court, his claims "had once been presented by a lawyer and passed upon by an appellate court." *Douglas.* We do not believe that it can be said, therefore, that a defendant in respondent's circumstances is denied meaningful access to the North Carolina Supreme Court simply because the State does not appoint counsel to aid him in seeking review in that court. At that stage he will have, at the very least, a transcript or other record of trial proceedings, a brief on his behalf in the Court of Appeals setting forth his claims of error, and in many cases an opinion by the Court of Appeals disposing of his case. These materials, supplemented by whatever submission respondent may make *pro se,* would appear to provide the Supreme Court of North Carolina with an adequate basis on which to base its decision to grant or deny review.

We are fortified in this conclusion by our understanding of the function served by discretionary review in the North Carolina Supreme Court. The critical issue in that court, as we perceive it, is not whether there has been "a correct adjudication of guilt" in every individual case, but rather whether "the subject matter of the appeal has significant public interest," whether "the cause involves legal principles of major significance to the jurisprudence of the state," or whether the decision below is in probable conflict with a decision of the Supreme Court. The Supreme Court may deny certiorari even though it believes that the decision of the Court of Appeals was incorrect, since a decision which appears incorrect may nevertheless fail to satisfy any of the criteria discussed above. Once a defendant's claims of error are organized and presented in a lawyerlike fashion to the Court of Appeals, the justices of the Supreme Court of North Carolina who make the decision to grant or deny discretionary review should be able to ascertain whether his case satisfies the standards established by the legislature for such review.

This is not to say, of course, that a skilled lawyer, particularly one trained in the somewhat arcane art of preparing petitions for discretionary review, would not prove helpful to any litigant able to employ him. An indigent defendant seeking review in the Supreme Court of North Carolina is therefore somewhat handicapped in comparison with a wealthy defendant who has counsel assisting him in every conceivable manner at every stage in the proceeding. But both the opportunity to have counsel prepare an initial brief in the Court of Appeals and the nature of discretionary review in the Supreme Court of North Carolina make this relative handicap far less than the handicap borne by the indigent defendant denied counsel on his initial appeal as of right in *Douglas.* And the fact that a particular service might be of benefit to an indigent defendant does not mean that the service is constitutionally required. The duty of the State under our cases is not to duplicate the legal arsenal that may be privately retained by a criminal defendant in a continuing effort to reverse his conviction, but only to assure the indigent defendant an adequate opportunity to present his claims fairly in the context of the State's appellate process. We think respondent was given that opportunity under the existing North Carolina system.

Much of the discussion in the preceding section is equally relevant to the question of whether a State must provide counsel for a defendant seeking review of his conviction in this Court. North Carolina will have provided counsel for a convicted defendant's only appeal as of right, and the brief prepared by that counsel together with one and perhaps two North Carolina appellate opinions will be available to this Court in order that it may decide whether or not to grant certiorari. This Court's review, much like that of the Supreme Court of North Carolina, is discretionary and depends on numerous factors other than the perceived correctness of the judgment we are asked to review.

There is also a significant difference between the source of the right to seek discretionary review in the Supreme Court of North Carolina and the source of the right to seek discretionary review in this

Court. The former is conferred by the statutes of the State of North Carolina, but the latter is granted by statutes enacted by Congress. Thus the argument relied upon in the *Griffin* and *Douglas* cases, that the State having once created a right of appeal must give all persons an equal opportunity to enjoy the right, is by its terms inapplicable. The right to seek certiorari in this Court is not granted by any State, and exists by virtue of federal statute with or without the consent of the State whose judgment is sought to be reviewed.

The suggestion that a State is responsible for providing counsel to one petitioning this Court simply because it initiated the prosecution which led to the judgment sought to be reviewed is unsupported by either reason or authority. It would be quite as logical under the rationale of *Douglas* and *Griffin,* and indeed perhaps more so, to require that the Federal Government or this Court furnish and compensate counsel for petitioners who seek certiorari here to review state judgments of conviction. Yet this Court has followed a consistent policy of denying applications for appointment of counsel by persons seeking to file jurisdictional statements or petitions for certiorari in this Court. In the light of these authorities, it would be odd, indeed, to read the Fourteenth Amendment to impose such a requirement on the States, and we decline to do so.

We do not mean by this opinion to in any way discourage those States which have, as a matter of legislative choice, made counsel available to convicted defendants at all stages of judicial review. Some States which might well choose to do so as a matter of legislative policy may conceivably find that other claims for public funds within or without the criminal justice system preclude the implementation of such a policy at the present time. [T]he Fourteenth Amendment leaves these choices to the State * * *.

Reversed.

MR. JUSTICE DOUGLAS, with whom MR. JUSTICE BRENNAN and MR. JUSTICE MARSHALL concur, dissenting.

[In his opinion below] Chief Judge Haynsworth could find "no logical basis for differentiation between appeals of right and permissive review procedures in the context of the Constitution and the right to counsel." More familiar with the functioning of the North Carolina criminal justice system than are we, he concluded that "in the context of constitutional questions arising in criminal prosecutions, permissive review in the state's highest court may be predictably the most meaningful review the conviction will receive." The North Carolina Court of Appeals, for example, will be constrained in diverging from an earlier opinion of the State Supreme Court, even if subsequent developments have rendered the earlier Supreme Court decision suspect. "[T]he state's highest court remains the ultimate arbiter of the rights of its citizens."

Chief Judge Haynsworth also correctly observed that the indigent defendant proceeding without counsel is at a substantial disadvantage relative to wealthy defendants represented by counsel when he is forced to fend for himself in seeking discretionary review from the State Supreme Court or from this Court. It may well not be enough to allege error in the courts below in layman's terms; a more sophisticated approach may be demanded:

"An indigent defendant is as much in need of the assistance of a lawyer in preparing and filing a petition for certiorari as he is in the handling of an appeal as of right. In many appeals, an articulate defendant could file an effective brief by telling his story in simple language without legalisms, but the technical requirement for applications for writs of certiorari are hazards which one untrained in the law could hardly be expected to negotiate.

" 'Certiorari proceedings constitute a highly specialized aspect of appellate work. The factors which [a court] deems important in connection with deciding whether to grant certiorari are certainly not within the normal knowledge of an indigent appellant.' Boskey, *The Right to Counsel in Appellate Proceedings,* 45 Minn.L.Rev. 783, 797 (1961)."

* * * The right to discretionary review is a substantial one, and one where a lawyer can be of significant assistance to an indigent defendant. It was correctly perceived below that the "same concepts of fairness and equality which require counsel in a first appeal of right, require counsel in other and subsequent discretionary appeals."

ON THE MEANING OF *ROSS v. MOFFITT*

1. Is *Mayer v. Chicago* (p. 107 supra) "good law" after *Ross?* Are *Long v. District Court, Gardner v. California, Roberts v. LaVallee,* and *Britt v. North Carolina* (all summarized at p. 106 supra) "good law" after *Ross?* Does the *Long-Gardner* line of cases (never mentioned by the *Ross* Court) constitute a significant "departure" from what the *Ross* Court calls the "limited doctrine" of *Griffin* and succeeding cases? Cf. *United States v. MacCollom,* Note 4 infra.

2. Consider Tribe, *American Constitutional Law* 1119 (1978): "[The *Ross* Court] disengaged *Griffin* from *Douglas,* deftly rewove the *Griffin* transcript and filing fee decisions together as minimal access cases rather than equal protection cases, and neatly severed *Douglas* from this newly created body of law." See also Kamisar, *Poverty, Equality, and Criminal Procedure,* in National College of District Attorneys, *Constitutional Law Deskbook* 1–97 to 1–100 (1977).

3. Does the *Ross* opinion's "equal protection analysis" closely resemble a "due process analysis"? Indeed, now that *Ross* is on the books, does the "equality" principle *add anything* to what the indigent defendant or prisoner already has in his arsenal? Consider Kamisar, supra, at 1–101 to 1–108: "[The *Ross* 'equal protection analysis'] seems to put to one side the admitted fact that an indigent seeking discretionary review is 'somewhat handicapped in comparison with a wealthy defendant who has counsel assisting him' and focuses instead on whether an indigent seeking discretionary review without counsel has a '*meaningful* opportunity' (emphasis added) to present his claims in the state supreme court—to provide the court 'with an *adequate* basis for its decision to grant or deny review' (emphasis added)—*regardless* of whether a wealthy defendant who has counsel at this stage has a *significantly better* opportunity to present his claims.

" * * * What [*Ross*] really seems to be asking, and deciding, is whether an indigent in respondent's circumstances has a *fair chance,* a *fighting chance* (or the requisite *minimum* chance), to get the attention of the state supreme court. [This] is 'due process,' not 'equal protection' reasoning.

"Pursuing this analysis, in *Douglas,* it may *now* be said, the indigent, without a lawyer and *without the materials available to an indigent on second appeal* after he has benefited from the assistance of counsel on the first appeal, lacked a *fair chance,* the requisite *minimum* opportunity, to present his claim. Moreover, the requisite minimum standard may be *significantly higher* when, as in *Douglas,* involving the first appeal as of right, 'the critical issue [is] whether there has been "a correct adjudication of guilt" in every individual case,' *Ross* [a] * * *

"So long as the indigent defendant's 'brand of justice' satisfies certain minimal standards—passes government inspection, one might say—[*Ross* tells us that] *it need not be* the same brand of justice or the same 'choice' or 'prime' grade of justice as the wealthy man's. [In some phases of the

a. The due process underpinnings of *Douglas* are emphasized in *Ake v. Oklahoma,* p. 102 supra, and *Evitts v. Lucey,* p. 119 infra.

criminal process an indigent will not have 'meaningful access' to the hearing body or an 'adequate opportunity' to present his claim], but in [such] cases 'fundamental fairness'—'due process'—will require the state to furnish counsel. In those cases where due process *does not* impose a duty on the state to provide counsel, *neither,* it seems, *will 'equal protection.'* " b

4. What light, if any, is shed on the meaning of *Ross* by UNITED STATES v. MacCOLLOM, 426 U.S. 317, 96 S.Ct. 2086, 48 L.Ed.2d 666 (1976)? Some two years after his conviction of a federal crime, from which he took an appeal, respondent moved for a free transcript of his trial, alleging that he intended to seek vacation of his sentence pursuant to 28 U.S.C. § 2255, that he was unable to afford a transcript of his trial, that without one he could not frame his arguments for fair and effective collateral review, and that the transcript would show that he had been denied effective assistance of counsel and other errors. After granting respondent leave to proceed *in forma pauperis,* appointing counsel, and holding a hearing, the district court denied relief. 28 U.S.C. § 753(f) provides for a free transcript for indigents asserting § 2255 claims if the trial judge certifies (a) that the claim is "not frivolous" and (b) that the transcript is "needed to decide the issue presented." By denying relief, the district court implicitly decided one of these issues against respondent. Where the § 753(f) conditions are not met, held the Supreme Court, expenditure of public funds is unauthorized and such conditions "comport with fair procedure." There was no opinion of the Court. The principal opinion, written by REHNQUIST, J., joined by Burger, C.J. and Stewart and Powell, JJ., observed:

"[I]t is undoubtedly true that [the conditions established in § 753(f)] place an indigent in a somewhat less advantageous position than a person of means. But * * * [t]he basic question is one of adequacy of respondent's access to procedures for review of his conviction, *Ross,* and it must be decided in the light of avenues which respondent chose not to follow as well as those he now seeks to widen. We think it enough at this collateral relief stage that Congress has provided that the transcript be paid for by public funds if one [satisfies the conditions imposed by § 753(f)]. [T]he fact that a transcript was available had respondent chosen to appeal from his conviction, and remained available on the conditions set forth in § 753 [afforded] respondent an adequate opportunity to attack his conviction. To hold otherwise would be to place the indigent defendant in a more favorable position than a similarly situated prisoner of some, but not unlimited means, who presumably would make an evaluation much like that prescribed in § 753(f) before he spent his own funds for a transcript."

Concurring Justice BLACKMUN, who provided the fifth vote for the Court's judgment, underscored the lack of any statement of "articulable facts" in respondent's claim indicating that "a transcript

b. But compare Israel, *Criminal Procedure, the Burger Court, and the Legacy of the Warren Court,* 75 Mich.L.Rev. 1319, 1334–36 (1977). After a close examination of *Douglas, Ross* and related cases, Professor Israel rejects Professor Kamisar's reading of *Ross.* Israel observes, inter alia: "Admittedly, the *Ross* majority did note that especially skilled counsel could be helpful, that the indigent therefore was disadvantaged as opposed to the wealthy, and that this differential did not violate equal protection so long as the indigent defendant still has 'an adequate opportunity to present his claim fairly.' I do not view that analysis, however, as suggesting anything more than what was acknowledged directly in *Douglas* and indirectly in *Argersinger*—that 'absolute equality is not required.' "

"[If] a state supreme court or the United States Supreme Court exercised its discretion to grant a second-or third-level review," maintains Israel, "the equal protection clause still would appear to require that the indigent defendant be provided the assistance of counsel in presenting that appeal [without regard to whether due process required the appointment of counsel], since there is much greater need for counsel to present the merits of an appeal than to perform the narrower function involved in *Ross* ".

would assist him in his § 2255 proceeding." Thus, respondent, who had been provided counsel, "has a *current* opportunity to present his claim fairly, and we need not consider the constitutional significance of what he might have done at the time a direct appeal from his conviction would have been taken."

Justice Blackmun thought it clear that "there is no constitutional requirement that the [government] provide an indigent with a transcript when that transcript is not necessary in order for him to prove his claim, or when his claim is frivolous on its face. Nor does the Constitution require that an indigent be furnished every possible legal tool, no matter how devoid of assistance it may be, merely because a person of unlimited means might choose to waste his resources in a quest of that kind."

BRENNAN, J., joined by Marshall, J., dissented, maintaining that the government's refusal to furnish a free transcript in a § 2255 proceeding "upon merely a showing of indigency" violated the "equal protection" element of fifth amendment due process: "The *Griffin* principle of equality was not limited to transcripts for purposes of direct appellate review [discussing, e.g., *Lane v. Brown, Long v. District Court, Gardner v. California*]. I reject as wholly fallacious the argument that adequacy of opportunity to present claims at trial and on direct appeal so far diminishes the importance of collateral review, that discrimination between indigent and non-indigent in post-conviction proceedings is constitutionally tolerable. That argument is implicitly if not explicitly rejected in the unbroken line of our decisions that make no distinction, for purposes of equal protection analysis, between collateral proceedings and trials and direct appeals. Any distinction must necessarily be constitutionally intolerable where the stakes are no less than the constitutionality of a criminal conviction." [a]

5. Reconsider *Bounds v. Smith,* the prison library case decided three years after *Ross.* Although the Court's opinion (per Marshall, J.) did not seem to be grounded on equal protection, it took pains to reject the argument that libraries or other forms of assistance to prisoners were not constitutionally required in light of *Ross:* "[Unlike *Ross,* in this case] we are concerned in large part with original actions seeking new trials, release from confinement or vindication of fundamental civil rights. Rather than presenting claims that have been passed on by two courts, they frequently raise heretofore unlitigated issues. [While] applications for discretionary review need only apprise an appellate court of a case's possible relevance to the development of the law, the prisoner petitions here are the first line of defense against constitutional violations. The need for new legal research or advice to make a meaningful initial presentation to a trial court in such a case is far greater than is required to file an adequate petition for discretionary review." [a]

But dissenting in *Bounds* (joined by Burger, C.J), Justice Rehnquist, the author of the *Ross* opinion, maintained that "it would seem a fortiori to follow from [*Ross*] that an incarcerated prisoner who has pursued all his avenues of direct review would have no constitutional right whatever to state appointed counsel to represent him in a collateral attack on his conviction * * *. Yet this is the logical destina-

a. In a separate dissent, Stevens, J., joined by Brennan, White and Marshall, JJ., maintained that § 753(f) should be construed to make free transcripts available as a matter of course to § 2255 petitioners, as well as to convicted defendants pursuing direct appeals. The plurality's response was that Justice Stevens' construction of § 753(f) "would do violence to the intent of Congress."

a. Nor, added the Court, is *MacCollom* inconsistent with its decision: "Without a library or legal assistance, [prisoners] will not have 'a *current* opportunity to present [their] claims fairly,' (Blackmun, J., concurring in *MacCollom*), and valid claims will undoubtedly be lost."

tion of the Court's reasoning today. If 'meaningful access' to the courts is to include law libraries, there is no convincing reason why it should not also include lawyers appointed at the expense of the State."

III. THE FAILURE OF COUNSEL TO COMPLY WITH RULES GOVERNING APPEALS OR APPLICATIONS FOR REVIEW

Consider WAINWRIGHT v. TORNA, 455 U.S. 586, 102 S.Ct. 1300, 71 L.Ed.2d 475 (1982) (per curiam). Respondent's felony convictions were affirmed by an intermediate state appellate court. But his application for a writ of certiorari was dismissed by the state supreme court on the grounds that it had not been filed timely. Respondent contended that he had been denied effective assistance of counsel by the failure of his retained counsel to file the application timely. Summarily reversing the Fifth Circuit, the U.S. Supreme Court held that the federal district court was correct in denying habeas corpus relief:

"[*Ross*] held that a criminal defendant does not have a constitutional right to counsel to pursue discretionary state appeals or applications for review in this Court. [Since] respondent had no constitutional right to counsel, he could not be deprived of the effective assistance of counsel by his retained counsel's failure to file the application timely."

Dissenting Justice MARSHALL reiterated his view that *Ross* was wrongly decided, but added:

"Even if I believed that *Ross* were correctly decided, however, I would dissent from the majority's conclusion that habeas corpus provides no recourse to a criminal defendant who has been denied his right to seek discretionary review because of his attorney's error. Although respondent's sixth amendment right to effective assistance of counsel may not have been infringed, he was denied his right to due process. * * * I would hold that when [as here] a defendant can show that he reasonably relied on his attorney's promise to seek discretionary review, due process requires the State to consider his application, even when the application is untimely. To deny the right to seek discretionary review simply because of counsel's error is fundamentally unfair." [a]

Compare *Torna* with EVITTS v. LUCEY, ___ U.S. ___, 105 S.Ct. 830, 83 L.Ed.2d 821 (1985). Because, when he filed his brief and the record on appeal, respondent's retained counsel failed to file the "statement of appeal" required by the state rule of appellate procedure, his appeal from a Kentucky drug conviction was dismissed. Respondent then sought federal habeas corpus relief, maintaining that under the circumstances the dismissal of his appeal deprived him of the right to effective assistance of counsel on appeal guaranteed by due process. A 7–2 majority of the Court, per BRENNAN, J., agreed, and upheld the district court's action in granting respondent a conditional writ, ordering his release unless the state either reinstated his appeal or retried him:

"[N]ominal representation on an appeal as of right—like nominal representation at trial—does not suffice to render the proceedings constitutionally adequate; a party whose counsel is unable to provide effective representation is in no better position than one who has no counsel at all.

"A first appeal as of right therefore is not adjudicated in accord with due process of law if the appellant does not have the effective assistance of an attorney.[7] [T]he promise of *Douglas* that a criminal defendant has a right to counsel on appeal—like

a. Brennan, J., would set the case for oral argument.

7. As *Ross* held, the considerations governing a discretionary appeal are somewhat different. Of course, the right to effective assistance of counsel is dependent on the right to counsel itself. See *Torna*.

the promise of *Gideon* that a criminal defendant has a right to counsel at trial—would be a futile gesture unless it comprehended the right to the effective assistance of counsel. * * *

"[As for the argument that counsel may disobey vital procedural rules governing appeals with impunity if the state courts cannot enforce these rules by dismissing the appeal], a State may certainly enforce a vital procedural rule by imposing sanctions against the attorney rather than against the client. Such a course may well be more effective than the alternative of refusing to decide the merits of an appeal and will reduce the possibility that a defendant who was powerless to obey the rules will serve a term of years in jail on an unlawful conviction. * * * A system of appeal as of right is established precisely to assure that only those who are validly convicted have their freedom drastically curtailed. A State may not extinguish this right because another right of the appellant—the right to effective assistance of counsel—has been violated. * * *

"[As for the argument that because a state need not establish a system of appeal as of right in the first instance, it is immune from all constitutional scrutiny when it chooses to do so], [t]he right to appeal would be unique among state actions if it could be withdrawn without consideration of applicable due process norms. * * * [W]hen a State opts to act in a field where its action has significant discretionary elements, it must nonetheless act in accord with the dictates of the Constitution—and, in particular, in accord with the Due Process Clause.

"Finally, petitioners argue that [the] Due Process Clause * * * is not offended by the [State's] refusal to decide respondent's appeal on the merits, because that Clause has no role to play in granting a criminal appellant the right to counsel—or a fortiori to the effective assistance of counsel on appeal. * * * [P]etitioners claim that [*Griffin, Douglas* and their progeny] should be understood as equal protection cases challenging the constitutional validity of the distinction made between rich and poor criminal defendants. [They] conclude that if the Due Process Clause permits criminal appeals as of right to be forfeited because the appellant has no transcript or no attorney, it surely permits such appeals to be forfeited when the appellant has an attorney who is unable to assist in prosecuting the appeal.

"Petitioners' argument rests on a misunderstanding of the diverse sources of our holdings in this area. * * * [The] rather clear statement in *Ross* that the Due Process Clause played a significant role in prior decisions is well supported by the cases themselves. In *Griffin,* for instance, the State had in effect dismissed petitioner's appeal because he could not afford a transcript. * * * Such a disposition violated equal protection principles because it distinguished between poor and rich with respect to such a vital right. But it also violated due process principles because it decided the appeal in a way that was arbitrary with respect to the issues involved. * * * See also *Douglas* (procedure whereby indigent defendant must demonstrate merit of case before obtaining counsel or appeal 'does not comport with fair procedure'). * * *

"The lesson of our cases, as we pointed out in *Ross,* is that each Clause triggers a distinct inquiry. * * * In cases like *Griffin* and *Douglas,* due process concerns were involved because the States involved had set up a system of appeals as of right but had refused to offer each defendant a fair opportunity to obtain an adjudication on the merits of his appeal. Equal protection concerns were involved because the State treated a class of defendants—indigent ones—differently for purposes of offering them a meaningful appeal. Both of these concerns were implicated in the *Griffin* and *Douglas* cases and both Clauses supported the decisions reached by this Court."

Justice REHNQUIST, joined by the Chief Justice, dissented:

"Neither the language of the Constitution nor this Court's precedents establish a right to effective assistance of counsel on appeal. The Sixth Amendment provides that: 'In all criminal *prosecutions*, the accused shall enjoy the right * * * to have the Assistance of Counsel for his *defense*' (emphasis added). [T]he words 'prosecutions' and 'defense' plainly indicate that the Sixth Amendment right to counsel applies only to trial level proceedings. At this stage, the accused needs an attorney 'as a shield to protect him against being "haled into court" by the State and stripped of his presumption of innocence.' *Ross*.

"An appeal by a convicted criminal is an entirely different matter. He has been found guilty beyond a reasonable doubt and, if sentenced to a term of imprisonment, is subject to immediate deprivation of his liberty without any constitutional requirement of further proceedings. He seeks 'to upset the prior determination of guilt' and universally is permitted to retain an attorney to serve 'as a sword' in that endeavor. * * *

"There is no constitutional requirement that a State provide an appeal at all. * * * If a State decides to confer a right of appeal, it is free to do so 'upon such terms as in its wisdom may be deemed proper.' *McKane v. Durston*. * * *

"The consequences of the Court's decision seems undesirable. Challenges to trial counsel's performance have become routine in federal habeas petitions. Now lawfully convicted criminals who have no meritorious bases for attacking the conduct of their trials will be able to tie up the courts with habeas petitions alleging defective performance by appellate counsel. * * *

"Today's decision also undermines the ability of both the state and the federal courts to enforce procedural rules on appeal. Presumably, rules which are common to almost every appellate system in our country providing for dismissal of an appeal for failure to comply with reasonable time limits can no longer be enforced against a criminal defendant on appeal. The Court's understandable sympathy with a criminal defendant who has been badly served by the lawyer whom he hired to represent him in appealing his conviction has led it to treat the Due Process Clause of the Fourteenth Amendment as a general dispensing authority, by the use of which the Court may indiscriminately free litigants from the consequences of their attorneys' neglect or malpractice. In most other areas of life and law we are bound, often to our prejudice, by the acts and omissions of our agents, and I do not believe that the Fourteenth Amendment prohibits the States from carrying over that generally recognized principle to the prosecution of appeals from a judgment of conviction."

SECTION 3. SOME BASIC CONCEPTS AND ISSUES

I. WAIVER OF THE RIGHT TO COUNSEL; THE RIGHT TO DEFEND *PRO SE*

The courts have long been concerned about the alleged waiver of constitutional rights, especially the right to the assistance of counsel. In *Johnson v. Zerbst*, 304 U.S. 458, 58 S.Ct. 1019, 82 L.Ed. 1461 (1938), in the course of remanding the case to determine whether petitioner "competently and intelligently waive[d] his right to counsel," the Court observed, per Black, J.:

" 'Courts indulge every reasonable presumption against waiver' of fundamental rights [and] we 'do not presume acquiescence in the loss of fundamental rights.' A waiver is ordinarily an intelligent relinquishment or abandonment of a known right or privilege."

In *Von Moltke v. Gillies*, 332 U.S. 708, 68 S.Ct. 316, 92 L.Ed. 309 (1948), a four-judge plurality opinion per Black, J., pointed out:

"A waiver of the constitutional right to the assistance of counsel is of no less moment to an accused who must decide whether to plead guilty than to an accused who stands trial. * * * 'The constitutional right of an accused to be represented by counsel invokes, of itself, the protection of a trial court, in which the accused—whose life or liberty is at stake—is without counsel. This protecting duty imposes the serious and weighty responsibility upon the trial judge of determining whether there is an intelligent and competent waiver by the accused' [quoting from *Johnson v. Zerbst*]. To discharge this duty properly in light of the strong presumption against waiver of the constitutional right to counsel, a judge must investigate as long and as thoroughly as the circumstances of the case before him demand. The fact that an accused may tell him that he is informed of his right to counsel and desires to waive this right does not automatically end the judge's responsibility."

The strong presumption against waiver of counsel is also manifested in *Carnley v. Cochran,* 369 U.S. 506, 82 S.Ct. 884, 8 L.Ed.2d 70 (1962), where the Court, per Brennan, J., noted that "where the assistance of counsel is a constitutional requisite, the right to be furnished counsel does not depend on a request" and pointed out:

"Presuming waiver from a silent record is impermissible. The record must show, or there must be an allegation and evidence which show, that an accused was offered counsel but intelligently and understandably rejected the offer. Anything less is not waiver."

As a general matter, appellate courts seemed justified in begrudgingly treating a claim that counsel had been waived. For where trial judges were painstakingly careful in providing counsel and explaining the important role that a defense lawyer may play, only one or two percent waived counsel. See, e.g., Kamisar & Choper, *The Right to Counsel in Minnesota: Some Field Findings and Legal-Policy Observations,* 48 Minn.L.Rev. 1, 34–38 (1963). But this "scrupulousness [was] sometimes carried to the point of simply *not permitting* a defendant to waive the assistance of counsel." *Id.* at 35 (emphasis added). Could a trial court "force" counsel upon a criminal defendant who wanted to represent himself? On the eve of *Faretta,* infra, the answer was unclear. See Commentary to Unif.R.Crim.P. 711 (approved a year before *Faretta*) at 287–88 and fn. 1; Grano, *The Right to Counsel: Collateral Issues Affecting Due Process,* 54 Minn.L.Rev. 1175, 1193–94 (1970).

FARETTA v. CALIFORNIA

422 U.S. 806, 95 S.Ct. 2525, 45 L.Ed.2d 562 (1975).

[Well before the date of his trial, Faretta, charged with grand theft, requested that he be allowed to represent himself. Questioning by the trial judge revealed that Faretta had once before represented himself in a criminal prosecution, that he had a high school education, and that he did not want to be represented by the public defender because he thought that that office had too heavy a case load. Several weeks thereafter, but still prior to trial, the judge held a hearing to inquire into Faretta's ability to conduct his own defense, in the course of which Faretta was questioned specifically about both the hearsay rule and the law governing the challenge of jurors. The judge ruled that Faretta (a) had not made an intelligent and knowing waiver of his right to counsel and (b) had no constitutional right to conduct his own defense. The judge then appointed the public defender to represent Faretta. Throughout the subsequent trial, the judge required that Faretta's defense be conducted only through the appointed lawyer. Faretta was found guilty as charged and sentenced to prison. The appellate court affirmed his conviction.]

MR. JUSTICE STEWART delivered the opinion of the Court. * * *

The Court's past recognition of the right of self-representation, the federal court authority holding the right to be of constitutional dimension, and the state constitutions pointing to the right's fundamental nature form a consensus not easily ignored. * * * This consensus is soundly premised. The right of self-representation finds support in the structure of the Sixth Amendment, as well as in the English and colonial experience from which the Amendment emerged. * * *

The Sixth Amendment does not provide merely that a defense shall be made for the accused; it grants to the accused personally the right to make his defense. It is the accused, not counsel, who must be "informed of the nature and cause of the accusation," who must be "confronted with witnesses against him," and who must be accorded "compulsory process for obtaining witnesses in his favor." [T]he right to self-representation—to make one's defense personally—is thus necessarily implied by the structure of the Amendment.[15] The right to defend is given directly to the accused; for it is he who suffers the consequences if the defense fails.

The counsel provision supplements this design. It speaks of the 'assistance' of counsel, and an assistant, however expert, is still an assistant. The language and spirit of the Sixth Amendment contemplate that counsel, like the other defense tools guaranteed by the Amendment, shall be an aid to a willing defendant—not an organ of the State interposed between an unwilling defendant and his right to defend himself personally. To thrust counsel upon the accused, against his considered wish, thus violates the logic of the Amendment. * * * It is true that when a defendant chooses to have a lawyer manage and present his case, law and tradition may allocate to the counsel the power to make binding decisions of trial strategy in many areas.[a] This allocation can only be justified, however, by the defendant's consent, at the outset, to accept counsel as his representative. An unwanted counsel "represents" the defendant only through a tenuous and unacceptable legal fiction. Unless the accused has acquiesced in such representation, the defense presented is not the defense guaranteed by the Constitution, for, in a very real sense, it is not *his* defense.

The Sixth Amendment, when naturally read, thus implies a right of self-representation. This reading is reinforced by the Amendment's roots in English legal history. [After an extensive discussion of the right of self-representation in England and the American colonies, the Court concluded:]

In sum, there is no evidence that the colonists and the Framers ever doubted the right of self-representation, or imagined that this right might be considered inferior to the right of assistance of counsel. To the contrary, [they], as well as their English ancestors, always conceived of the right to counsel as an 'assistance' for the accused, to be used at his

15. * * * The inference of rights is not, of course, a mechanical exercise. In *Singer v. United States* [Ch. 22] (1965), the Court held that an accused has no right to a bench trial, despite his capacity to waive his right to a jury trial. In so holding, the Court stated that "[t]he ability to waive a constitutional right does not ordinarily carry with it the right to insist upon the opposite of that right." But that statement was made only *after* the Court had concluded that the Constitution does not affirmatively protect any right to be tried by a judge. Recognizing that an implied right must arise independently from the design and history of the constitutional text, the Court searched for, but could not find, any "indication that the colonists considered the ability to waive a jury trial to be of equal importance to the right to demand one." Instead, the Court could locate only "isolated instances" of a right to trial by judge, and concluded that these were "clear departures from the common law."

We follow the approach of *Singer* here. Our concern is with an *independent* right of self-representation. We do not suggest that this right arises mechanically from a defendant's power to waive the right to the assistance of counsel. On the contrary, the right must be independently found in the structure and history of the constitutional text.

a. See Note 3 following this case.

option, in defending himself. The Framers selected in the Sixth Amendment a form of words that necessarily implies the right of self-representation. That conclusion is supported by centuries of history.

There can be no blinking the fact that the right of an accused to conduct his own defense seems to cut against the grain of this Court's decisions holding that the Constitution requires that no accused can be convicted and imprisoned unless he has been accorded the right to the assistance of counsel. For it is surely true that the basic thesis of those decisions is that the help of a lawyer is essential to assure the defendant a fair trial. And a strong argument can surely be made that the whole thrust of those decisions must inevitably lead to the conclusion that a State may constitutionally impose a lawyer upon even an unwilling defendant.

But it is one thing to hold that every [accused] has the right to the assistance of counsel, and quite another to say that a State may compel a defendant to accept a lawyer he does not want. The value of state-appointed counsel was not unappreciated by the Founders, yet the notion of compulsory counsel was utterly foreign to them. [W]here the defendant will not voluntarily accept representation by counsel, the potential advantage of a lawyer's training and experience can be realized, if at all, only imperfectly. To force a lawyer on a defendant can only lead him to believe that the law contrives against him. Moreover, it is not inconceivable that in some rare instances, the defendant might in fact present his case more effectively by conducting his own defense. Personal liberties are not rooted in the law of averages. The right to defend is personal. The defendant, and not his lawyer or the State, will bear the personal consequences of a conviction. It is the defendant, therefore, who must be free personally to decide whether in his particular case counsel is to his advantage. And although he may conduct his own defense ultimately to his own detriment, his choice must be honored out of "that respect for the individual which is the lifeblood of the law." [46]

When an accused manages his own defense, he relinquishes, as a purely factual matter, many of the traditional benefits associated with the right to counsel. For this reason, in order to represent himself, the accused must "knowingly and intelligently" forego those relinquished benefits. *Johnson v. Zerbst.* Although a defendant need not himself have the skill and experience of a lawyer in order competently and intelligently to choose self-representation, he should be made aware of the dangers and disadvantages of self-representation, so that the record will establish that "he knows what he is doing and his choice is made with eyes open." *Adams v. United States* ex rel. *McCann.* [b]

46. We are told that many criminal defendants representing themselves may use the courtroom for deliberate disruption of their trials. But the right of self-representation has been recognized from our beginnings by federal law and by most of the States, and no such result has thereby occurred. Moreover, the trial judge may terminate self-representation by a defendant who deliberately engages in serious and obstructionist misconduct. Of course, a State may—even over objection by the accused—appoint a 'standby counsel' to aid the accused if and when the accused requests help, and to be available to represent the accused in the event that termination of the defendant's self-representation is necessary.

The right of self-representation is not a license to abuse the dignity of the courtroom. Neither is it a license not to comply with relevant rules of procedural and substantive law. Thus, whatever else may or may not be open to him on appeal, a defendant who elects to represent himself cannot thereafter complain that the quality of his own defense amounted to a denial of "effective assistance of counsel."

b. In *Adams,* 317 U.S. 269, 63 S.Ct. 236, 87 L.Ed. 268 (1942), a mail fraud defendant who professed to have "studied law" and be "sufficiently familiar with it to defend himself," insisted on proceeding without counsel. He then waived trial by jury and was convicted after a trial by the judge alone. In holding that defendant could waive his rights to counsel and to trial by jury and that he had intelligently and competently done so, the Court, per Frankfurter, J., observed that "the Constitution does not force a lawyer upon a defendant." Assuming arguendo

Here, weeks before trial, Faretta clearly and unequivocally declared [that] he wanted to represent himself and did not want counsel. The record affirmatively shows that [defendant] was literate, competent, and understanding, and that he was voluntarily exercising his informed free will. The trial judge had warned [defendant] that he thought it was a mistake not to accept the assistance of counsel and that [defendant] would be required to follow all the 'ground rules' of trial procedure. We need make no assessment of how well or poorly [defendant] had mastered the intricacies of the hearsay rule and the California code provisions that govern challenges of potential jurors on *voir dire* [matters about which the trial judge specifically questioned defendant before ruling that he had not made an intelligent and knowing waiver of his right to the assistance of counsel]. For [defendant's] technical legal knowledge, as such was not relevant to an assessment of his knowing exercise of the right to defend himself."

MR. CHIEF JUSTICE BURGER, with whom MR. JUSTICE BLACKMUN and MR. JUSTICE REHNQUIST join, dissenting.

[This case] is another example of the judicial tendency to constitutionalize what is thought "good." That effort fails on its own terms here, because there is nothing desirable or useful in permitting every accused person, even the most uneducated and inexperienced, to insist upon conducting his own defense to criminal charges. * * *

[I]n all but an extraordinarily small number of cases an accused will lose whatever defense he may have if he undertakes to conduct the trial himself. [His needs for a lawyer] do not vary depending upon whether [he] actively desires to be represented by counsel or wishes to proceed *pro se.* Nor is it accurate to suggest [that] the quality of his representation at trial is a matter with which only the accused is legitimately concerned. [The goal of achieving justice] is ill-served, and the integrity of and public confidence in the system are undermined, when an easy conviction is obtained due to the defendant's ill-advised decision to waive counsel. [The criminal justice system] should not be available as an instrument of self-destruction.

[B]oth the "spirit and the logic" of the Sixth Amendment are that every person accused of crime shall receive the fullest possible defense; in the vast majority of cases this command can be honored only by means of the expressly-guaranteed right to counsel, and the trial judge is in the best position to determine whether the accused is capable of conducting his defense. True freedom of choice and society's interest in seeing that justice is achieved can be vindicated only if the trial court retains discretion to reject any attempted waiver of counsel and insist that the accused be tried according to the Constitution. This discretion is as critical an element of basic fairness as a trial judge's discretion to decline to accept a plea of guilty. * * *

'If we were to assume that there will be widespread exercise of the newly-discovered constitutional right to self-representation, it would almost certainly follow that there will be added congestion in the courts and that the quality of justice will suffer. Moreover, [i]t is totally unrealistic [to] suggest that an accused will always be held to the consequences of a decision to conduct his own defense. Unless [most defendants] have more wit than to insist upon [self-representation], we can expect that many expensive and good-faith prosecutions will be nullified on appeal for rea-

that a federal defendant might waive a jury trial, dissenting Justice Douglas, joined by Black and Murphy, JJ., maintained that McCann should have had the benefit of legal advice before his waiver was accepted. For otherwise the Court could not "safely assume [that] a waiver by a layman of his constitutional right to a jury trial was intelligent and competent in a case such as this."

sons that trial courts are now deprived of the power to prevent.

MR. JUSTICE BLACKMUN, with whom THE CHIEF JUSTICE and MR. JUSTICE REHNQUIST join, dissenting.

* * * [T]he Court holds that any defendant in any criminal proceeding may insist on representing himself regardless of how complex the trial is likely to be and regardless of how frivolous the defendant's motivations may be. I cannot agree that there is anything in the [Constitution] that requires the States to subordinate the solemn business of conducting a criminal prosecution to the whimsical—albeit voluntary—caprice of every accused who wishes to use his trial as a vehicle for personal or political self-gratification.

The Court seems to suggest that so long as the accused is willing to pay the consequences of his folly, there is no reason for not allowing him the right to self-representation. [That] view ignores the established principle that the interest of the State in a criminal prosecution "is not that it shall win a case, but that justice shall be done." For my part, I do not believe that any amount of *pro se* pleading can cure the injury to society of an unjust result, but I do believe that a just result should prove to be an effective balm for almost any frustrated *pro se* defendant.

* * * I note briefly the procedural problems that, I suspect, today's decision will visit upon trial courts in the future. * * * Must every defendant be advised of his right to proceed *pro se?* If so, when must that notice be given? Since the right to the assistance of counsel and the right to self-representation are mutually exclusive, how is the waiver of each right to be measured? If a defendant has elected to exercise his right to proceed *pro se,* does he still have a constitutional right to assistance of standby counsel? How soon in the criminal proceeding must a defendant decide between proceeding by counsel or *pro se?* Must he be allowed to switch in mid-trial? May a violation of the right to self-representation ever be harmless error? Must the trial court treat the *pro se* defendant differently than it would professional counsel? * * * The procedural problems spawned by an absolute right to self-representation will far outweigh whatever tactical advantage the defendant may feel he has gained by electing to represent himself.

If there is any truth to the old proverb that "one who is his own lawyer has a fool for a client," the Court by its opinion today now bestows a *constitutional* right on one to make a fool of himself.

Notes and Questions

1. *Waiver of counsel.* According to I *A.B.A. Standards* § 5–7.2, before accepting a waiver of counsel "the court should inquire whether the accused apprehends the nature of the charges, the offenses included within them, the allowable punishments, possible defenses to the charges, and circumstances in mitigation thereof, among other factors." [a] How can a judge explain all possible defenses unless he is familiar with the facts of the case? More-

a. At this point, the commentary cites Justice Black's plurality opinion in *Von Moltke v. Gillies,* 332 U.S. 708, 68 S.Ct. 316, 92 L.Ed.2d 309 (1948). Although the Court invalidated petitioner's guilty plea, there was no opinion of the Court. Speaking for four Justices who maintained that the guilty plea had to be overturned because petitioner had not competently waived counsel, Justice Black observed:

"To be valid [a waiver of the right to counsel] must be made with an apprehension of the nature of the charges, the statutory offenses included within them, the range of allowable punishments thereunder, possible defenses to the charges and circumstances in mitigation thereof, and all other facts essential to a broad understanding of the whole matter."

Some courts have not felt bound by Justice Black's formulation in *Von Moltke* since it was not supported by a majority of the Court; and have sought to shorten the list of matters with which the defendant must be familiar. The component most frequently sought to be eliminated is that requiring knowledge of "possible defenses to the charges." See generally LaFave & Israel, 11.3(b); Note, 49 Minn.L.Rev. 1133, 1142–45 (1965).

over, wouldn't literal compliance with the A.B.A. Standards require the court to give the accused a course in criminal law?

Consider Unif.R.Crim.P. (commentary): "Instead of requiring the defendant to *know* each of the included offenses, possible defenses, and circumstances in mitigation, [Rule 711(2)] requires him to understand that a defense lawyer might discover such matters and use them to the defendant's advantage. This would appear to afford sufficient protection, particularly in light of [another provision] of this Rule authorizing the court to refuse to accept a waiver until the defendant has first consulted with a lawyer, and in light of the fact that the plea provisions of these Rules require a determination of factual basis which will uncover the existence of possible defenses, circumstances in mitigation and situations where the defendant may be guilty only of a lesser included offense." [b]

I *A.B.A. Standards* § 5–7.3 provides in part: "If an accused has not seen a lawyer and indicates an intention to waive the assistance of counsel, a lawyer should be provided for consultation purposes. No waiver should be accepted unless the accused has at least once conferred with a lawyer." On the premise that an early waiver should not be held to preclude appointment of counsel at a later stage (because the value and need for legal assistance may become clear to the defendant only at a stage of the proceedings subsequent to the initial offer and waiver), Standard 5–7.3. also provides: "If a waiver is accepted, the offer should be renewed at each subsequent stage of the proceedings at which the accused appears without counsel."

2. *"Standby counsel."* McKASKLE v. WIGGINS, 465 U.S. 168, 104 S.Ct. 944, 79 L.Ed.2d 122 (1984), per O'CONNOR, J., made explicit "what is already implicit in *Faretta:* a defendant's Sixth Amendment rights are not violated when a trial judge appoints standby counsel—even over the defendant's objection—to relieve the judge of the need to explain and enforce basic rules of courtroom protocol or to assist the defendant in overcoming routine obstacles that stand in the way of the defendant's achievement of his own clearly indicated goals."

The trial court permitted Wiggins to represent himself at his state robbery trial, but designated two appointed lawyers as "standby counsel." Before and during the trial, Wiggins frequently changed his mind regarding the standby attorneys' role, objecting to their participation on some occasions, but conferring with them or expressly adopting their initiatives on other occasions. Wiggins filed and argued numerous *pro se* motions both before and during the trial. He conducted the defense's voir dire of prospective jurors, made the opening statement for the defense and, throughout the trial, selected the witnesses for the defense. He cross-examined the prosecution's witnesses freely. He also filed his own requested charges to the jury and made his own objections to the court's suggested charge. On several occasions, however he strongly opposed the initiatives of counsel and sometimes indignantly demanded that counsel not participate further without invitation. At one point, an acrimonious exchange between Wiggins and one of his standby lawyers occurred over the questioning of a witness. Wiggins was convicted and sentenced to life imprisonment as a recidivst. The U.S. Court of Appeals for the Fifth Circuit granted habeas corpus relief, concluding that Wiggin's right of self-representation had been violated by the unsolicited participation of overzealous standby counsel. The Fifth Circuit established a rule that "standby counsel is 'to be seen, but not heard' "; "his presence is

b. Did the *Von Moltke* plurality opinion cause confusion because petitioner's waiver of counsel in that case was *immediately followed* by a plea of guilty? As a result, did the plurality opinion merge, or at least blur, the procedures for waiving counsel with those for pleading guilty?

there for advisory purposes only, to be used or not used as the defendant sees fit." The Supreme Court explicitly rejected the Fifth Circuit's rule and reversed its judgment:

"A defendant's right to self-representation plainly encompasses certain specific rights to have his voice heard. The *pro se* defendant must be allowed to control the organization and content of his own defense, to make motions, to argue points of law, to participate in voir dire, to question witnesses, and to address the court and the jury at appropriate points in the trial. The record reveals that Wiggins was in fact accorded all of these rights. * * *

"Wiggins' complaint is directed not at limits placed on *his* participation in the trial, for there clearly were none. It is directed instead at the allegedly inadequate limits placed on standby counsel's participation. * * * Wiggins claims, and the Court of Appeals agreed, that the *pro se* defendant may insist on presenting his own case wholly free from interruption or other uninvited involvement by standby counsel. * * *

"In our view, [*Faretta* indicates] that no absolute bar on standby counsel's unsolicited participation is appropriate or was intended. The right to appear *pro se* exists to affirm the dignity and autonomy of the accused and to allow the presentation of what may, at least occasionally, be the accused's best possible defense. Both of these objectives can be achieved without categorically silencing standby counsel.

"In determining whether a defendant's *Faretta* rights have been respected, the primary focus must be on whether the defendant had a fair chance to present his case in his own way. *Faretta* itself dealt with the defendant's affirmative right to participate, not with the limits on standby counsel's additional involvement. The specific rights to make his voice heard that Wiggins was plainly accorded, form the core of a defendant's right of self-representation.

"We recognize, nonetheless, that the right to speak for oneself entails more than the opportunity to add one's voice to a cacophony of others. * * * Accordingly, the *Faretta* right must impose some limits on the extent of standby counsel's unsolicited participation.[8]

First, the *pro se* defendant is entitled to preserve actual control over the case he chooses to present to the jury. This is the core of the *Faretta* right. If standby counsel's participation over the defendant's objection effectively allows counsel to make or substantially interfere with any significant tactical decisions, or to control the questioning of witnesses, or to speak *instead* of the defendant on any matter of importance, the *Faretta* right is eroded.

"Second, participation by standby counsel without the defendant's consent should not be allowed to destroy the jury's perception that the defendant is representing himself. The defendant's appearance in the status of one conducting his own defense is important in a criminal trial, since the right to appear *pro se* exists to affirm

8. Since the right of self-representation is a right that when exercised usually increases the likelihood of a trial outcome unfavorable to the defendant, its denial is not amenable to "harmless error" analysis. The right is either respected or denied; its deprivation cannot be harmless.

As a corollary, however, a defendant who exercises his right to appear *pro se* "cannot thereafter complain that the quality of his own defense amounted to a denial of 'effective assistance of counsel.'" *Faretta.* Moreover, the defendant's right to proceed *pro se* exists in the larger context of the criminal trial designed to determine whether or not a defendant is guilty of the offense with which he is charged. The trial judge may be required to make numerous rulings reconciling the participation of standby counsel with a *pro se* defendant's objection to that participation; nothing in the nature of the *Faretta* right suggests that the usual deference to "judgment calls" on these issues by the trial judge should not obtain here as elsewhere.

the accused's individual dignity and autonomy. * * *

"Participation by standby counsel outside the presence of the jury engages only the first of these two limitations. A trial judge, who in any event receives a defendant's original *Faretta* request and supervises the protection of the right throughout the trial, must be considered capable of differentiating the claims presented by a *pro se* defendant from those presented by standby counsel. Accordingly, the appearance of a *pro se* defendant's self-representation will not be unacceptably undermined by counsel's participation outside the presence of the jury.

"Thus, *Faretta* rights are adequately vindicated in proceedings outside the presence of the jury if [as here] the *pro se* defendant is allowed to address the court freely on his own behalf and if [as here] disagreements between counsel and the *pro se* defendant are resolved in the defendant's favor whenever the matter is one that would normally be left to the discretion of counsel. * * *

"Though several of [the exchanges between Wiggins and standby counsel] are regrettable, we are satisfied that counsel's participation outside the presence of jury fully satisfied the first standard we have outlined. * * *

"Equally important, all conflicts between Wiggins and counsel were resolved in Wiggins' favor. The trial judge repeatedly explained to all concerned that Wiggins' strategic choices, not counsel's would prevail. Not every motion made by Wiggins was granted, but in no instance was counsel's position adopted over Wiggins' on a matter that would normally be left to the defense's discretion.

"Participation by standby counsel in the presence of the jury is more problematic. It is here that the defendant may legitimately claim that excessive involvement by counsel will destroy the appearance that the defendant is acting *pro se.* This, in turn, may erode the dignitary values that the right to self-representation is intended to promote and may undercut the defendant's presentation to the jury of his own most effective defense. Nonetheless, we believe that a categorical bar on participation by standby counsel in the presence of the jury is unnecessary. * * *

"The record in this case reveals that Wiggins' *pro se* efforts were undermined primarily by his own, frequent changes of mind regarding counsel's role. * * * The only two long appearances by counsel at Wiggins' trial, one before the jury and one outside its presence, were both initiated with Wiggins' express approval. In these circumstances it is very difficult to determine how much of counsel's participation was in fact contrary to Wiggins' desires of the moment.

"*Faretta* does not require a trial judge to permit 'hybrid' representation of the type Wiggins was actually allowed. But if a defendant is given the opportunity and elects to have counsel appear before the court or jury, his complaints concerning counsel's subsequent unsolicited participation lose much of their force. A defendant does not have a constitutional right to choreograph special appearances by counsel. Once a *pro se* defendant invites or agrees to any substantial participation by counsel, subsequent appearances by counsel must be presumed to be with the defendant's acquiescence, at least until the defendant expressly and unambiguously renews his request that standby counsel be silenced. * * *

"*Faretta* affirmed the defendant's constitutional right to appear on stage at his trial. We recognize that a *pro se* defendant may wish to dance a solo, not a *pas de deux.* Standby counsel must generally respect that preference. But counsel need not be excluded altogether, especially when the participation is outside the presence of the jury or is with the defendant's express or tacit consent. The defendant in this case was allowed to make his own appearances as he saw fit. In our judgment counsel's unsolicited involvement was held within reasonable limits." [a]

Dissenting Justice WHITE, joined by Brennan and Marshall, JJ., protested:

"Although petitioner characterizes counsel's participation as 'limited' and 'intermittent,' nothing could be further from the truth. Standby counsel intervened in a substantial manner without Wiggins' permission well over 50 times during the course of the three-day trial; many of these interruptions precipitated direct conflicts between Wiggins and counsel, often in the presence of the jury. Although the trial court appears to have resolved the conflicts calling for a ruling in Wiggins' favor, their mere existence disrupted the proceedings and turned the trial into an ordeal through which the jury was required to suffer. At several points during the trial, moreover, counsel blatantly interfered with Wiggins' attempt to present his defense in a manner not calling for a ruling from the bench, and we of course have no way of knowing the extent to which Wiggins' defense was subtly undermined or adversely affected by counsel's extensive unsolicited participation. * * *

"Under the Court's new test, it is necessary to determine whether the *pro se* defendant retained 'actual control over the case he [chose] to present to the jury' and whether standby counsel's participation 'destroy[ed] the jury's perception that the defendant [was] representing himself.' Although this test purports to protect all of the values underlying our holding in *Faretta,* it is unclear whether it can achieve this result.

"As long as the *pro se* defendant is allowed his say, the first prong of the Court's test accords standby counsel at a bench trial or any proceeding outside the presence of a jury virtually untrammeled discretion to present any factual or legal argument to which the defendant does not object. The limits placed on counsel's participation in this context by the 'actual control' test are more apparent than real. First, counsel may not 'make or substantially interfere with any significant tactical decisions.' Unless counsel directly overrides a defendant's strategy in the presence of the judge, however, it is apparent that courts will be almost wholly incapable of assessing the subtle and not-so-subtle effects of counsel's participation on the defense. Second, the court suggests that conflicts between the *pro se* defendant and standby counsel on 'matter[s] that would normally be left to the defense's discretion', will be resolved in the defendant's favor. But many disagreements will not produce direct conflicts requiring a trial court to choose one position over another. Under the Court's opinion, the burden apparently will fall on the *pro se* defendant to comprehend counsel's submissions and to create conflicts for the trial court to resolve. If applied this way, the Court's test surely will prove incapable of safeguarding the interest in individual autonomy from which the *Faretta* right derives.

"Although the Court is more solicitous of a *pro se* defendant's interests when standby counsel intervenes before a jury, the test's second prong suffers from similar shortcomings. To the extent that trial and appellate courts can discern the point at which counsel's unsolicited participation substantially undermines a *pro se* defendant's appearance before the jury, a matter about which I harbor substantial doubts, their decisions will, to a certain extent, 'affirm the accused's individual dignity and autonomy.' But they will do so incompletely, for in focusing on how the jury views the defendant, the majority opinion ignores *Faretta*'s emphasis on the defendant's own perception of the criminal justice system, and implies that the Court actually adheres to the result-oriented

a. Justice Blackmun concurred in the result without opinion.

harmless error standard it purports to reject. [See fn. 8 to the Court's opinion].

"As a guide for standby counsel and lower courts, moreover, the Court's two-part test is clearly deficient. * * * [Trial courts] clearly must prevent standby counsel from overtly muzzling their *pro se* clients and resolve certain conflicts in defendants' favor. But the Court's opinion places few, if any, other clear limits on counsel's uninvited participation; instead it requires trial courts to make numerous subjective judgments concerning the effect of counsel's actions on defendants' *Faretta* rights. Because trial courts generally will consider only isolated actions of standby counsel expressly challenged by *pro se* defendants, only appellate courts may be in a position to form impressions on the basis of the entire trial. These courts, however, also will suffer from the lack of clear standards and from their inability or unwillingness to make the factual inquiries necessitated by the Court's two-part test.

"In short, I believe that the Court's test is unworkable and insufficiently protective of the fundamental interests we recognized in *Faretta.*

"The inappropriateness of the Court's standard is made manifest by the Court's conclusion that the conduct of standby counsel in this case passes muster under that standard. In frequently and grievously exceeding the proper role of standby counsel, the more active of Wiggins' appointed attorneys distracted Wiggins and usurped his prerogatives, altered the tenor of the defense, disrupted the trial, undermined Wiggins' perception that he controlled his own fate, induced a belief—most assuredly unfounded, but sincerely held nevertheless—that 'the law contrive[d] against him,' and undoubtedly reduced Wiggins' credibility and prejudiced him in the eyes of the jury. In allowing such intervention to continue despite Wiggins' repeated requests that it cease, the trial court clearly denied Wiggins' right of self-representation. The right to present and control one's own defense means little indeed if one's 'standby' attorneys remain free to take any action they choose, whether consistent with the desired defense or inimical to it, at any point during the trial. In short, whatever advantage or satisfaction Wiggins might have hoped to derive from self-representation was surely nullified by the trial court's tolerance of counsel's conduct."

3. *Did Faretta alter the basic division of decision-making authority between counsel and client?* Prior to *Faretta* the decisions whether to plead guilty, whether to waive jury trial, and whether defendant should take the stand in his or her own defense were regarded as ultimately for the defendant to make, because of the "fundamental nature" of these decisions, "so crucial to the accused's fate." I *A.B.A. Standards* § 4–5.2 (commentary).[a] On the other

a. See also *People v. Frierson,* 705 P.2d 396 (Cal.1985), holding that a defense lawyer could not withhold the presentation of any defense (in this case, diminished capacity) at the guilt phase of a capital case "in the face of a defendant's openly expressed desire to present a defense at that stage and despite some credible evidence to support the defense." (Counsel had waited until the penalty phase of the case to offer evidence of defendant's diminished capacity.)

The court pointed out that the issue involved "is quite distinct from the question whether trial counsel provided competent representation." It assumed that counsel's decision "fell within the range of conduct that competent counsel might reasonably employ," but even so, the decision "is so fundamental, and has such serious consequences for a defendant, that it is one that cannot properly be taken from him by his counsel." Moreover, the fact that counsel's action was "motivated by strategic considerations" did not foreclose inquiry into whether the challenged decision was of such fundamental importance that the defendant's wishes should have been respected.

The court noted that it had no occasion to determine whether a defendant had a constitutional right to insist on the presentation of a defense which lacked any evidentiary support or on which no competent attorney would rely. Nor was it suggesting that in the absence of such an express conflict as was presented here (in the course of an in-chambers discussion, counsel had made clear that a conflict had developed between him and the defendant as to whether the diminished capacity defense should be presented), a hand, the power of decision in matters of trial strategy and tactics, e.g., whether to call a certain witness, cross-examine a government witness, stipulate to certain facts, whether to object to the admission of evidence on constitutional and other grounds, and whether to strike an improper jury instruction, were generally regarded as within the exclusive province of the lawyer, after consultation with the client. See id.; LaFave & Israel, § 11.6(a).[b]

But *Faretta* was thought by some to have altered the basic division between "strategic" and "personal" decisions and perhaps limited the attorney's ultimate authority only to "on-the-spot" decisions where timing considerations precluded the attorney's consultation with his client. See LaFave & Israel, supra. By holding, however, that an indigent defendant has no right "to compel appointed counsel to press nonfrivolous points requested by the client, if counsel, as a matter of professional judgment, decides not to present these points," JONES v. BARNES, 463 U.S. 745, 103 S.Ct. 3308, 77 L.Ed.2d 987 (1983), rejected this view of *Faretta.* The majority and dissenting opinions in *Barnes*, including the discussion of *Faretta*, are set forth at p. 176 infra.

4. *Must a defendant be specifically informed of his right to represent himself?* Most courts have answered in the negative, on the premise that the policy favoring the granting of a lawyer to every individual accused of a serious crime "overrides" the right to defend *pro se* or on the premise that it is only necessary to inform a defendant of those rights that are "essential to a fair trial" (and the right to self-representation is not such a right). See LaFave & Israel, § 11.5(b). Can the reasoning of the courts that do not require that an accused be advised of his right to conduct his own defense be reconciled with the spirit and logic of *Faretta?*

5. *Stage of proceedings at which counsel may be waived.* The right of self-representation may be lost if not timely asserted. Once the trial is underway, most courts are reluctant to allow the defendant to discharge counsel and proceed *pro se,* analogizing the situation to the attempt of a represented defendant to change counsel during the trial. For criticism of this view see Note, 25 Am.U.L.Rev. 897, 911–13 (1976).

6. *A right to "mixed" or "hybrid" representation?* May a defendant assert both "halves" of her Sixth Amendment right and demand *both* the assistance of a lawyer and the right to self-representation? Reconsider the last paragraph of fn. 15 to the *Faretta* opinion. If, as *Faretta* seems to say, the rights to self-representation and to the assistance of counsel are *independent* constitutional rights, why should the defendant have to chose one right to the exclusion of the other? [c]

court must obtain an on-the-record, personal waiver from the defendant whenever counsel chooses to rest without putting on a defense.

b. As pointed out in LaFave & Israel, §§ 11.6(a) and (b), "the various rulings produce a picture that is clear at many points but clouded at others." It is not easy "to distinguish the right to be tried before a jury, for example, from the right to present a particular witness or to cross-examine an opposing witness. If the fundamental nature of a right is measured by its importance, its historic tradition, or its current status in constitutional or state law, those rights would appear to be on the same plane." Moreover, "[t]he Court's emphasis upon the strategic element in those decisions subject to counsel's control also fails to distinguish the different types of decisions. Certainly the decisions to waive a jury or not have the defendant testify also involve substantial strategic considerations." LaFave & Israel suggest that the "concern of the courts that the lawyer not be forced to sacrifice his professional reputation while providing no true assistance to his client" may explain not only *Jones v. Barnes,* infra (appellate counsel need not present every nonfrivolous claim that his client wishes to press), but "much of the law governing the division of authority between counsel and client."

c. Consider also Angela Davis's criticism of the prevailing view that a defendant has no right to *both* participate in her own defense *and* enjoy the assistance of counsel, A. Davis, *If They Come in the Morning*, 253 (1971): "I consider my participation decisive for my defense. One might argue that since I am determined to play an active

Some commentators have advocated a right to "mixed" or "hybrid" representation, i.e., a mode of representation in which the defendant has active assistance of counsel, but also participates herself as co-counsel. See Chused, *Faretta and the Personal Defense: The Role of a Represented Defendant in Trial Tactics*, 65 Calif.L.Rev. 636 (1977); Notes, 57 B.U.L.Rev. 570 (1977), 12 Val.U.L. 329 (1978). In the main, however, the courts have viewed the rights to self-representation and to representation by counsel as mutually exclusive, although occasionally a trial court may permit hybrid representation as "a matter of grace." See V. Berger, *The Supreme Court and Defense Counsel: Old Roads, New Paths—A Dead End?*, 86 Colum.L.Rev. 9, 39–43 (1986). According to Professor Berger, the complexities of mixed representation and the heavy burdens it would inflict on an already overstrained system—without promoting the interests of defendants as much as does the right to defend pro se—militate strongly against giving constitutional stature to a right to hybrid representation. See id. at 42–43.[d]

7. *The right to representation by a nonattorney.* Does the individual autonomy to choose to represent oneself, constitutionally protected in *Faretta,* carry with it the right to delegate the power of self-representation to a nonlawyer? The Supreme Court has not directly addressed this question, but the lower courts have answered it in the negative. See, e.g., *United States v. Whitesel,* 543 F.2d 1176 (6th Cir.1976) (representation in tax case by accountant refused); *United States v. Jordan,* 508 F.2d 750 (7th Cir.1975) (representation by disbarred attorney refused); *United States v. Kelley,* 539 F.2d 1199 (9th Cir.1976) (representation by a friend, a roofer by trade, refused). For a criticism of the lower courts' approach and the view that the right to representation by a nonattorney "closely resembles the issue in *Faretta,*" see Note, 26 Emory L.J. 457, 462–74 (1977).

8. *Are there occasions when the government may not prohibit lay representation?* In the so-called jailhouse lawyer case, *Johnson v. Avery* (1969) (p. 92 supra), the Court struck down, as an impermissible bar on a prisoner's access to the courts, a prison regulation forbidding any inmate to advise or assist another in preparing "Writs or other legal matters." Pointing out that "jails and penitentiaries include among their inmates a high percentage of persons who are totally or functionally illiterate," and that the state provided no alternative to the assistance provided by other inmates in the preparation of petitions for post-conviction relief, the Court held that "unless and until the State provides [such an alternative], it may not validly enforce a regulation such as that here in issue, barring inmates from furnishing such assistance to other prisoners."

What is the scope of this "limited endorsement of the concept of lay represen-

role in the trial, I should fire my lawyers and assume the entire burden of the defense. This is to say, if I wish to exercise my constitutional right to defend myself, I must relinquish the right to counsel. This either/or situation in my opinion flies blatantly in the face of justice. Rigorously speaking, neither is a *right* if one must be renounced in order to exercise the other. Should I be penalized because I do not possess the legal knowledge, experience or expertise necessary to proceed entirely pro se?" In her prosecution for murder, kidnapping and conspiracy, Ms. Davis successfully argued for the right to participate in her trial as co-counsel alongside her private attorneys, but her motion was not granted on constitutional grounds, only on the basis of "a narrow finding that in her case, the cause of justice will be served and expeditious conduct of the Court's business will not be hampered." See 59 Calif.L.Rev. 1479, 1480 (1971). See also Note, 21 U.Kan.L.Rev. 47, 52, 66 (1972).

d. Does concern for the attorney's professional pride also underlie the failure of the courts to allow hybrid representation? Are courts "unwilling to relegate counsel to a subordinate role for fear that competent lawyers will refuse to take criminal cases as a result"? Is there also a concern that "allowing the defendant to participate actively in making decisions and in conducting the defense may lead to havoc in the courtroom"? See Note, 57 B.U.L.Rev. 570, 574 (1977). See also Note, 25 Am.U.L.Rev. 897, 915 (1976).

tation"? See Note, 26 Emory L.J. 457, 472 (1977). Suppose an indigent misdemeanor defendant not entitled to assigned counsel under state law or under *Scott v. Illinois* appears with a nonattorney friend and states that he wishes his friend to represent him. Can the state prohibit lay representation under such circumstances?

II. AN INDIGENT DEFENDANT'S RIGHT TO COUNSEL OF HIS CHOICE

"Almost unanimously," observes Tague, *An Indigent's Right to the Attorney of His Choice,* 27 Stan.L.Rev. 73, 79–80 (1974), "courts have held that the selection of counsel for an indigent is a matter within the sole discretion of the trial court. * * * Courts generally justify this decision on two grounds: first, judges assume that they can choose a more able attorney than the indigent because they know the abilities of the available local counsel; and, second, the right to effective representation is not interpreted to guarantee the defendant the best representation but only a certain minimal level of competence that an attorney, once appointed, is expected to provide. * * * Traditionally the courts have found that a defendant has an interest in defending himself in whatever way he considers best, using whatever resources are legitimately available to him, regardless of the consequences. For the nonindigent this has meant that the courts will not interfere with his choice of who will represent him [except if the defendant attempts to switch counsel after the trial begins or the issue of conflict of interest among clients arises]." [a]

"The importance to the indigent of choosing his attorney," observes Tague, id. at 99, "is clear: improvement in the attorney-client relationship, representation by an able attorney who will fight aggressively for him, and the likelihood of greater participation in structuring his defense. * * *

"[V]arious legitimate governmental concerns of fairness, orderliness, economy, efficiency, and protection of the bar [b] * * * justify vesting the trial judge with discretion to select the attorney if the indigent asks for no one in particular. How-

a. What Professor Tague describes as the nonindigent defendant's "interest in defending himself in whatever way he considers best" may not prevail when he desires to be represented by an out-of-state lawyer. Cf. *Leis v. Flynt,* 439 U.S. 438, 99 S.Ct. 698, 58 L.Ed.2d 717 (1979) (per curiam), viewing the matter from the perspective of *the out-of-state lawyer's* interest in pursuing his calling. In an Ohio criminal obscenity case, defendant Larry Flynt sought representation by two members of the New York bar who specialize in criminal defense and obscenity law, Harold Fahringer and Paul Cambria. The Ohio trial judge refused to allow either out-of-state lawyer to represent Flynt. Although the Supreme Court recognized that "the practice of courts in most states is to allow an out-of-state lawyer the privilege of appearing upon motion, especially when [as here] he is associated with a member of the local bar," it held that this "is not a right granted either by statute or the Constitution. Since the founding of the Republic, the licensing and regulation of lawyers has been left exclusively to the States * * *." The Court noted that it was not ruling on whether the constitutional rights of the defendant might be violated since that claim was not before it.

Justice White would grant certiorari and set the case for oral argument. Justice Stevens, joined by Brennan and Marshall, JJ., dissented: "The notion that a state trial judge has arbitrary and unlimited power to refuse a nonresident lawyer permission to appear in his courtroom is nothing but a remnant of a bygone era. * * * Because the assertion of federal claims or defenses is often unpopular, 'advice and assistance by an out-of-state lawyer may be the only means available for vindication.' [The instant case] is the classic situation in which the interests of justice would be served by allowing the defendant to be represented by counsel of his choice." As the dissenters saw it: "Either the 'nature' of the interest in *pro hac vice* admissions or the 'implicit promise' inhering in Ohio custom with respect to those admissions is sufficient to create an interest protected by the Due Process Clause."

b. As Professor Tague notes elsewhere, if the right to choose counsel is limited to situations where the chosen attorney agrees to represent the indigent, the rationale for protecting better-known attorneys from a heavy burden of appointments disappears. Id. at 97–98. "Ironically, now that appointments are compensated, there may be an economic incentive to protect lesser-known attorneys who rely upon court appointments for much of their income. But protecting the economic interests of the bar is not a favored governmental concern * * *." Id. at 98.

ever, whenever the indigent asks for a particular attorney, these concerns, with the possible exception of economy, can be protected by the less intrusive procedure of a pretrial hearing, where the attorney's qualifications and willingness to enter the case are examined, the likelihood that he will disrupt the proceedings is tested against the clear-and-present-danger standard, and the timeliness with which he could enter the case is determined. Economy remains a significant governmental interest chiefly where the public defender is available to represent the indigent; even then, however, recoupment and limitations on the amount paid for appointments could offset whatever greater costs result from appointing the requested private attorney.

"Thus, denying an indigent the right to choose his counsel fails to further in any substantial way legitimate governmental interests—interests that can be protected by less intrusive measures. The classification distinguishing indigent from nonindigent should therefore fall and an indigent should have equal opportunity to select his own counsel."

Professor Tague's strong views on the subject have not prevailed, see LaFave & Israel, § 11.4. But consider HARRIS v. SUPERIOR COURT, 567 P.2d 750 (Cal. 1977), apparently the first case to limit a trial judge's discretion to appoint counsel when the indigent can show "objective considerations" supporting the choice of appointed counsel.

Harris arose as follows: The petitioners, Emily and William Harris, were charged in municipal court with multiple felony counts in connection with the kidnapping of Patricia Hearst. Petitioners requested the municipal court to appoint attorneys Susan Jordan and Leonard Weinglass to represent them and when the public defender filed an affidavit of conflict as to both petitioners, the court did appoint the requested attorneys for purposes of the municipal court proceedings. On the same date, a grand jury charged the Harrises with multiple felony counts.

When the superior court appointed two other attorneys to represent the Harrises (Ballachey and Mintz), indicating that he had given considerable weight to their good reputation, their experience in trying capital cases and their certification as criminal law specialists by the state bar, the Harrises strenuously objected, stressing that they had developed a relationship of trust and confidence with Attorneys Jordan and Weinglass and maintaining that the "total strangers" appointed by the court could not provide as effective a defense. Attorneys Ballachey and Mintz joined in petitioners' request that Attorneys Jordan and Weinglass be appointed. After a hearing on the matter, the court reaffirmed its prior order appointing Ballachey and Mintz. The California Supreme Court, per MANUEL, J., held that the trial court had abused its discretion in denying petitioners' request:

"We reaffirm our basic holding in *Drumgo* [*v. Superior Court*].[a] An indigent defendant's preference for a particular attorney, while it is to be considered by the trial court in making an appointment, is not a determinative factor *requiring* the appointment of that attorney—even in combination with other relevant factors such as the subject attorney's competence and availability. As we have indicated,

a. *Drumgo,* 506 P.2d 1007 (Cal.1973), rejected the view that "an indigent defendant may force selection of a particular attorney who, in the defendant's opinion, can provide the best representation. We have repeatedly held that constitutional and statutory guarantees are not violated by the appointment of an attorney other than the one requested by a defendant. * * * The additional factor that requested counsel had indicated his willingness and availability to act does not raise any constitutional compulsion requiring his appointment. * * * If, as is the case, an indigent defendant who is necessarily represented by the public defender may not select the particular deputy who will represent him, then [one] for whom assigned counsel must be appointed should likewise not be entitled to be represented by a particular attorney."

the matter rests wholly within the sound discretion of the trial court. * * *

[In *Drumgo,* however] the sole basis upon which the petitioner urged the appointment of the attorney chosen by him rather than the one selected by the court was what we have [called] the 'subjective' factor—i.e., his trust and confidence in Attorney Hodge and his corresponding 'lack of knowledge' of the appointed attorney. No other factors were advanced. [W]e did not mean to indicate that in all cases, regardless of the circumstances, the appointment by the court of an individual meeting the minimum standards of competency effectively insulates the court's decision in this regard from all review.

"[In] the instant case, [the] factors before the court at the time of its decision included not only those of 'subjective' character [but] also matters of a more 'objective' nature. The most significant of these concerned petitioners' prior representation and assistance by Attorneys Jordan and Weinglass in related prosecutions arising out of petitioners' alleged activities as members of the so-called Symbionese Liberation Army. This experience, it must be concluded, not only established a close working relationship between petitioners and Attorneys Jordan and Weinglass but also served to provide those attorneys with an extensive background in various factual and legal matters which may well become relevant in the instant proceeding—a background which any other attorney appointed to the case would necessarily be called upon to acquire. * * *

"Secondly, although the appointed attorneys in this matter did not go so far as to refuse their appointment or declare their inability to act effectively on petitioners' behalf, their vigorous support of petitioners' plea that they not be appointed is here a factor of considerable significance. [T]hey placed primary emphasis upon the fact of their relative unfamiliarity with the facts and legal issues involved and the necessity for their expenditure of considerable energy and time if they were to bring their level of familiarity with those facts and issues to a point comparable with that already reached by Attorneys Jordan and Weinglass. * * *

"In summary, while we reaffirm today the basic holding of *Drumgo* * * * we hold that when [a defendant's statement of personal preference], timely made, is supported by objective considerations of the consequence here involved, and where there are no countervailing considerations of comparable weight, it is an abuse of sound judicial discretion to deny the defendant's request to appoint the counsel of his preference."

Concurring Justice MOSK, joined by Bird, C.J., disagreed with the "express reaffirmation" of *Drumgo,* maintaining that it involved "an abuse of discretion as patent as that involved herein." "When trial judges adopt an obdurate stance on appointment of counsel, as in this case and in *Drumgo,* there lurks behind their action an implication that because defendant is indigent and counsel is appointed rather than hired, the need for trust and confidence between attorney and client is less compelling." [b]

Notes and Questions

1. *"Objective" vs. "subjective" considerations.* How helpful is this distinction? Does it stem more from a desire to distinguish *Drumgo* factually than from a principled effort to provide standards guiding future trial court discretion? See Note, 66

b. Although *Harris* could readily be limited to its unusual facts, *People v. Chavez,* 605 P.2d 401 (Cal.1980) indicates that it will have a significant impact upon appointment practices in a substantial number of cases. In ruling that the trial court had erred in failing to afford defendant an opportunity to explain why he desired appointment of the lawyer who had represented him at the preliminary hearing, the *Chavez* court made clear that the trial court was at least obligated to explore the defendant's reasons for requesting a particular attorney, and suggested further that not all of the *Harris* circumstances need be present to require serious consideration of the defendant's preference.

Calif.L.Rev. 180, 309–10 (1978). Once a sufficient showing of "objective" factors has been made in support of a request for appointment of particular private counsel, may the trial court deny it without specific reason? If the court may not, is the major shortcoming of *Harris* its failure to indicate what objective considerations would be sufficient to make the threshold showing or to suggest examples of reasons that would justify denial of the request? Under what circumstances, if any, would the denial of an indigent's timely request for appointment of particular private counsel amount to an abuse of discretion when (unlike the *Drumgo* and *Harris* cases), *the public defender is available to provide representation?* See id. at 310–11.

2. *Should an indigent defendant's preference be given more weight?* Is an indigent defendant's preference for particular counsel (at least when the public defender is unavailable), although "subjective," entitled to more weight than the *Harris* court gave it? Does it indicate that a relationship of trust and confidence, important in any attorney-client relationship, already exists? Would granting such a request "enhance the appearance of fairness in the criminal justice system" and afford the indigent defendant "the opportunity, already provided to nonindigents as a matter of course, to appear and defend as he deems best"? See California Note at 309.

3. *The significance of Faretta.* In "reaffirming [the] basic holding of *Drumgo*" that the trial court's discretion in appointing counsel is not to be constrained by a defendant's "personal preference for a particular attorney," the *Harris* court found "nothing in the intervening case of *Faretta* which would lead us to reconsider this point," fn. 8. Do you agree? Recall that the *Faretta* Court observed: "To thrust counsel upon the accused, against his considered wish, * * * violates the logic of the [Sixth] Amendment. [A]n unwanted counsel 'represents' the defendant only through a tenuous and unacceptable legal fiction." Does *Faretta,* as an expression of constitutional values, at least suggest that "courts should make every reasonable effort to provide counsel of choice"? California Note at 313.

4. *Doing something about the defendant's distrust of public defenders.* Consider J. Casper, *Criminal Courts: The Defendant's Perspective* 82 (1978): "[T]he distrust of public defenders has its roots, [in considerable measure], in the lack of choice of which lawyer is to represent the client. Unlike the marketplace, where the defendant does make this choice, such freedom is usually not accorded to indigents. * * * [A public defender] office policy of giving the client the maximum choice possible—if not to choose initially, at least to select another public defender after unsatisfactory experience with one—can contribute to effective lawyer-client relationships. Some public defenders have suggested that even less is required: if public defenders make it clear at the outset that they realize that the defendant is being forced to accept their services and that this may make the defendant uncomfortable, this may be an important first step. Moreover, if the public defender tells the client that if he becomes dissatisfied the lawyer will be willing to withdraw, this may even further increase the defendant's sense of control. Such an acknowledgement of the problem and indication of willingness to deal with it may, in and of itself, be enough. Experience of some public defenders who use this strategy indicates that clients may be typically quite struck by the offer and not inclined to actually take the lawyer up on it."

MORRIS v. SLAPPY, 461 U.S. 1, 103 S.Ct. 1610, 75 L.Ed.2d 610 (1983), rejected "the novel idea that the Sixth Amendment guarantees an accused a 'meaningful attorney-client relationship.'" The case arose as follows: Slappy was charged, inter alia, with rape, robbery, and burglary, all involving the same female victim. The court appointed the Public Defender's office to represent him and

Deputy Public Defender Goldfine was assigned to defend him. Goldfine represented Slappy at the preliminary hearing and supervised an extensive investigation. Shortly before the trial, Goldfine was hospitalized for emergency surgery. Six days before the trial the Public Defender assigned Hotchkiss, a senior trial attorney in the office, to represent Slappy.

After the trial was under way, Slappy moved for a continuance, claiming his new attorney had not had enough time to prepare the case. But the attorney told the court that he was "ready" for trial. The court denied a continuance. On the third day of trial, Slappy claimed that he was unrepresented by counsel, maintaining that Goldfine, not Hotchkiss, was his attorney. The court treated this as a motion for a continuance and denied it. Slappy then announced that he would not cooperate at all in the trial. Ignoring Hotchkiss' advice, Slappy refused to take the stand. The jury returned a verdict of guilty on some counts, but failed to reach a verdict on the sexual assault counts. A week later, a second trial was held on the charges left unresolved as a result of the mistrial. Hotchkiss again represented defendant. Again, defendant ignored Hotchkiss' advice and refused to testify. Indeed, defendant refused to even speak to Hotchkiss. The second jury returned a guilty verdict on the sexual assault counts.

The Court of Appeals for the Ninth Circuit subsequently granted federal habeas corpus relief, acknowledging that "an indigent defendant does not have an unqualified right to the appointment of counsel of his own choosing," but maintaining that Slappy was "merely seeking a continuance of the trial date so that his attorney [Goldfine] would be able to represent him." The Sixth Amendment, observed the court, "would be without substance *if it did not include the right to a meaningful attorney-client relationship.*" (Emphasis added by the Supreme Court.) The Court of Appeals next stated that by failing to weigh defendant's interest in continued representation by Goldfine against the state's interest in proceeding with the scheduled trial (the trial court had not inquired about the probable length of Goldfine's absence), the trial court had ignored Slappy's Sixth Amendment right to a "meaningful attorney-client relationship" and that this violation of the right to counsel required reversal without any need to show prejudice. The Supreme Court, per BURGER, C.J., disagreed. After finding no merit to the claim that the denial of a continuance prevented Hotchkiss from being fully prepared for trial and concluding that respondent's motion on the third day of trial for a continuance to permit Goldfine to continue to represent him was not timely, the Court observed:

"[The] Court of Appeals' conclusion that the Sixth Amendment right to counsel 'would be without substance if it did not include the right to a *meaningful attorney-client relationship*' (emphasis added) is without basis in the law. * * * No court could possibly guarantee that a defendant will develop the kind of rapport with his attorney—privately retained or provided by the public—that the Court of Appeals thought part of the Sixth Amendment guarantee of counsel. Accordingly, we reject the claim that the Sixth Amendment guarantees a 'meaningful relationship' between an accused and his counsel.[6]

* * *

"In its haste to create a novel Sixth Amendment right, the court wholly failed to take into account the interest of the victim of these crimes in not undergoing the ordeal of yet a third trial in this case. Of course, inconvenience and embarrass-

6. The Court of Appeals seems to have believed that an appointed counsel with whom the accused did not have a "meaningful relationship" was the equivalent of no counsel; as a consequence, it held that no prejudice need be shown for violations of the right to a "meaningful" attorney-client relationship. Our holding that there is no Sixth Amendment right to a "meaningful attorney-client relationship" disposes of that argument.

ment to witnesses cannot justify failing to enforce constitutional rights of an accused: when prejudicial error is made that clearly impairs a defendant's constitutional rights, the burden of a new trial must be borne by the prosecution, the courts, and the witnesses; the Constitution permits nothing less. But in the administration of criminal justice, courts may not ignore the concerns of victims. Apart from all other factors, such a course would hardly encourage victims to report violations to the proper authorities; this is especially so when the crime is one calling for public testimony about a humiliating and degrading experience such as was involved here. Precisely what weight should be given to the ordeal of reliving such an experience for the third time need not be decided now; but that factor is not to be ignored by the courts. The spectacle of repeated trials to establish the truth about a single criminal episode inevitably places burdens on the system in terms of witnesses, records, and fading memories, to say nothing of misusing judicial resources."

Justice BRENNAN, joined by Marshall, J., concurred in the result, but disputed much of the Court's reasoning:

"Because [I agree with the Court that] respondent did not make a timely motion for a continuance based on Goldfine's unavailability, I concur in the Court's reversal of the Court of Appeals' judgment. We need go no further to support a reversal. * * *

"Given the importance of counsel to the presentation of an effective defense, it should be obvious that a defendant has an interest in his relationship with his attorney. As we noted in *Faretta,* '[t]he right to defend is personal.' It is the defendant's interests, and freedom, which are at stake. Counsel is provided to assist the defendant in presenting his defense, but in order to do so effectively the attorney must work closely with the defendant in formulating defense strategy. This may require the defendant to disclose embarrassing and intimate information to his attorney. In view of the importance of uninhibited communication between a defendant and his attorney, attorney-client communications generally are privileged. Moreover, counsel is likely to have to make a number of crucial decisions throughout the proceedings on a range of subjects that may require consultation with the defendant. These decisions can best be made, and counsel's duties most effectively discharged, if the attorney and the defendant have a relationship characterized by trust and confidence. * * *

"In light of the importance of a defendant's relationship with his attorney to his Sixth Amendment right to counsel, recognizing a qualified right to continue that relationship is eminently sensible. The Court of Appeals simply held that where a defendant expresses a desire to continue to be represented by counsel who already has been appointed for him by moving for a continuance until that attorney again will be available, the trial judge has an obligation to inquire into the length of counsel's expected unavailability and to balance the defendant's interest against the public's interest in the efficient and expeditious administration of criminal justice. Contrary to the Court's suggestion, this does not require a trial court 'to guarantee' attorney-defendant 'rapport.' The defendant's expressed desire in continued representation by a particular attorney is a clear indication that an attorney-client relationship has developed. The quality of that relationship, or the reasons that it developed, are of no concern to the court. The trial court's only duty is to inquire into the expected length of the attorney's unavailability and to determine whether the existing attorney-client relationship can be preserved consistent with society's interests. This is a minimal burden. It is one that we should readily impose in order to insure that a defendant's rights are not arbitrarily denied.

"The defendant's interest in preserving his relationship with a particular attorney is not afforded absolute protection. If the attorney is likely to be unavailable for an extended period, or if other factors exist that tip the balance in favor of proceeding in spite of a particular attorney's absence, the defendant's motion for a continuance clearly may be denied. Such denials would be subject to review under the traditional 'abuse of discretion' standard. As the Court of Appeals suggested, however, the balancing is critical. In the absence of a balancing inquiry a trial court cannot discharge its 'duty to preserve the fundamental rights of an accused.' * * *

"While the Court of Appeals may have misread the record, its opinion reflects a thoughtful and dedicated effort to protect the rights of an indigent criminal defendant. Despite their poverty and the fact that they stand accused of a crime, indigent defendants are entitled to the enforcement of procedural rules that protect substantive rights guaranteed by the Constitution.[10] The Court of Appeals should be commended, not criticized, for carrying out its obligation to respect this entitlement." [a]

FORFEITURE OF AN ATTORNEY'S FEES AS A THREAT TO A DEFENDANT'S RIGHT TO RETAIN COUNSEL OF HIS CHOICE

The scope of a defendant's right to retain counsel of his choice has recently been examined in a quite different context. The Comprehensive Forfeiture Act of 1984, 18 U.S.C. § 1963, provides for the forfeiture of proceeds derived from racketeering activity and the profits of drug traffickers—including, arguably, fees already paid to attorneys. These provisions, implemented by pretrial restraining orders freezing a defendant's assets, have been viewed as severely restricting a defendant's ability to obtain counsel of his choice. See *United States v. Lewis,* 759 F.2d 1316 (8th Cir.1985); *United States v. Badalamenti,* 614 F.Supp. 194 (S.D.N.Y.1985); *United States v. Rogers,* 602 F.Supp. 1332 (D.Colo. 1985); Krieger & Van Dusen, *The Lawyer, the Client and the New Law,* 22 Am.Crim.L. Rev. 737 (1985); Reed, *Criminal Forfeiture Under the Comprehensive Forfeiture Act of 1984: Raising the Stakes,* 22 Am.Crim.L. Rev. 747, 776–82 (1985).

Should a pretrial hearing be held to determine whether money intended to be used for attorney's fees is in fact forfeitable? If so, what should the standard of proof be at such a hearing? Should the government be allowed to make use of what it learns at a forfeiture hearing? See 38 Crim.L.Rptr. 2216 (Dec. 11, 1985) (summary of, and extracts from, a conference on forfeiture of attorney's fees.)

For the Justice Department's guidelines on how the department will seek to implement the new forfeiture provisions, see 38 Crim.L.Rptr. 3001 (Oct. 1, 1985). The guidelines begin with strong criticism of *Badalamenti* and *Rogers,* supra, both holding that since the forfeiture provisions interfere with a criminal defendant's right to retain counsel of his choice they must be construed to exempt legitimate attorneys' fees from forfeiture. An exemption for attorneys' fees, according to the guidelines, is "contrary to the plain language and history of the legislation."

10. [The Court] appears to suggest that the interests of a victim in a particular case should be considered by courts in determining whether to enforce the established rights of a criminal defendant. Such a suggestion finds no support in our cases.

a. Blackmun, J., joined by Stevens, J., concurred in the result agreeing with the Court that Slappy had not made a timely motion for continuance based on Goldfine's unavailability. He saw no occasion to consider the Sixth Amendment issue. "Accordingly, I find the Court's rather broad-ranging dicta about the right to counsel and the concerns of victims (deserving of sympathy as they may be) to be unnecessary in this case."

For strong criticism of the majority opinion in *Slappy*, see V. Berger, *The Supreme Court and Defense Counsel: Old Roads, New Paths—A Dead End?*, 86 Colum.L.Rev. 9, 49–55 (1986).

III. THE RIGHT TO "EFFECTIVE" ASSISTANCE OF COUNSEL

"Nearly 30 percent of the defendants who had public defenders reported that their attorney spent less than 10 minutes with them; 32 percent stated 10 to 29 minutes; 27 percent stated one-half hour to 3 hours; and only 14 percent stated more than 3 hours. To the extent that we are willing to embrace the notion that providing an adequate defense includes providing the client with a sense that he has been adequately represented, time spent with client is an important aspect of an adequate defense. In view of these findings, it is not surprising that nearly half (49 percent) of the public defender clients thought their attorney was 'on the side of the state.' "

—J. Casper, *Criminal Courts: The Defendant's Perspective* iv (1978) (abstract).

As early as the landmark case of *Powell v. Alabama* (1932), the Court pointed out that when a court is required to appoint counsel that duty "is not discharged by an assignment at such a time or under such circumstances as to preclude the giving of *effective aid* in the preparation and trial of the case." (Emphasis added.) Since the trial court in *Powell* had failed to make an "effective appointment of counsel," the defendants were denied due process. Ten years later, in *Glasser v. United States,* 315 U.S. 60, 62 S.Ct. 457, 86 L.Ed. 680 (1942), when counsel's effectiveness was limited by a conflict of interest, the Court held that a federal defendant's Sixth Amendment right was violated by judicial action that denied him his "right to have the effective assistance of counsel." More recently the Court held in *Evitts v. Lucey* (1985) (p. 119 supra) that a defendant taking his first appeal also had a constitutional right to the effective assistance of his appellate counsel. "Taken together, these rulings establish a right to effective counsel that apparently extends to all proceedings for which there would be a right to appointed counsel under either the Sixth Amendment, due process, or some other constitutional provision." LaFave & Israel, § 11.7(a) [a]

Cuyler v. Sullivan (1980) (p. 164 infra) put to rest the division among the lower courts as to whether different standards for reviewing ineffective assistance claims turned on whether counsel was appointed or privately retained. *Cuyler* rejected the government's claim that the alleged failings of retained counsel cannot provide a basis for a constitutional violation because the conduct of such counsel does not involve "state action." "Since the State's conduct of a criminal trial itself implicates the State in the defendant's conviction," the Court could "see no basis for drawing a distinction between retained and appointed counsel that would deny equal justice to defendants who must choose their own lawyers."

Until the 1970's the prevailing standard was the "mockery of justice" test under which representation was considered "ineffective" only when it was so poor as to "reduce the trial to a farce" or render it a "mockery of justice." Under this test, "employed as a short-hand recognition of the judiciary's reluctance to examine the conduct of defense counsel in depth," Erickson, *Standards of Competency for Defense Counsel in a Criminal Case*, 17 Am.Crim.L. Rev. 233, 251 (1979), lawyers could appear in court drunk or could fall asleep during trial and still not be found "ineffective." The test required "such a minimal level of performance from counsel" that it was called "a mockery of the Sixth Amendment." Bazelon, *The Defective Assistance of Counsel*, 42 U.Cin.L.Rev. 1, 28 (1973). See also Finer, *Ineffective Assistance of Counsel*, 58 Cornell L.Rev. 1077 (1973).

Among the policies or fears underlying the reluctance to find "ineffectiveness"

a. As *Wainright v. Torna* (1982) (p. 119 supra) illustrates, a different standard prevails, however in those situations in which there would be no right to appointed counsel.

(and to hold lawyers to a higher standard) are that to do so would jeopardize finality interests, force the trial judge to intervene whenever possible error is being committed, lead appellate courts to "second guess" defense tactics with the benefit of hindsight, make lawyers more reluctant to accept court assignments, and encourage lawyers with desperate cases to commit errors deliberately. See generally V. Berger, *The Supreme Court and Defense Counsel: Old Roads, New Paths—A Dead End?*, 86 Colum.L.Rev. 9, 65–66 (1986); Waltz, *Inadequacy of Trial Defense Representation as a Ground for Post-Conviction Relief in Criminal Cases*, 59 Nw.U.L.Rev. 289 (1964); Notes, 78 Harv.L.Rev. 1435 (1965), 49 Va.L.Rev. 1531 (1963). Judge Bazelon has gone so far as to say (Bazelon at 22): "I have often been told that if my court were to reverse in every case in which there was inadequate counsel, we would have to send back half the convictions in my jurisdiction." [a]

In the early 1970s, in two cases involving collateral attacks on guilty pleas, *Tollett v. Henderson* (Ch. 21, § 5), and *McMann v. Richardson* (Ch. 21, § 5), the Supreme Court approached the issue of ineffective counsel in terms of whether counsel's advice fell "within the range of competence demanded of attorneys in criminal cases." The Court's language "stirred further discomfort with the mockery and farce test," Strazzella, *Ineffective Assistance of Counsel Claims: New Uses, New Problems*, 19 Ariz.L. Rev. 443, 450 (1977), and many courts, and a majority of the U.S. Courts of Appeals soon scrapped it in favor of some "reasonable" or "normal" or "customary" competence test.

But such standards, maintained Judge Bazelon, "beg the question of what is customary or reasonable for a lawyer to do prior to or at arraignment, plea bargaining, trial, or sentencing." Bazelon, *The Realities of Gideon and Argersinger*, 64 Geo. L.J. 811, 819 (1976). "Thus far," he maintained in 1976, "the courts have failed to address these questions, with the result that the new test has made little change. * * * [W]hat matters is not developing a new verbal formulation but developing a clearer understanding of what the words mean."

Both in his judicial opinions and in his law review articles, Judge Bazelon championed what has been called the "checklist" or "categorical" approach to the ineffective counsel problem. He attempted to give substantive content to the Sixth Amendment's mandate by setting forth specific minimum requirements of competent performance—a categorization of minimum duties owed by counsel to client derived from *A.B.A. Standards Relating to the Defense Function* (1971). Dissenting in *United States v. Decoster (Decoster III)*, 624 F.2d 196, 275 (D.C.Cir.1976) (en banc), Judge Bazelon (joined by Wright, C.J.), observed: "The heart of [the 'categorical'] approach lies in defining ineffective assistance in terms of the *quality of counsel's performance*, rather than looking to the effect of counsel's actions on the outcome of the case. If the Sixth Amendment is to serve a central role in eliminating second-class justice for the poor, then it must proscribe second-class performances by

a. Is still another "practical reason" the impatience of many appellate courts with what amounts to a claim that defendant's lawyer might have, but failed to, "suppress the truth," i.e., object to illegally seized, but trustworthy evidence? What weight, if any, should the court give to the fact that the alleged error does not go to "guilt or innocence"? Compare *People v. Ibarra*, 386 P.2d 487 (Cal.1963) and *United States v. Easter*, 539 F.2d 663 (8th Cir.1976) with *Edwards v. United States*, 256 F.2d 707 (D.C.Cir.1958) and *People v. Washington*, 241 N.E.2d 425 (Ill.1968). Does adequate representation *require* that counsel contest an arguably illegal search? *Easter*, supra, so indicates. If the failure to object is not based on unawareness of applicable law (as apparently it was in *Ibarra* and *Easter*, supra), but reflects "tactics" or "judgment" of counsel, should it ever constitute "ineffective assistance of counsel"? See *United States v. Bosch*, 584 F.2d 1113 (1st Cir.1978) (counsel "ineffective" because disclosure to jury of his client's prior convictions "bore no relation, and clearly was not necessary, to implementation of [defense] strategy").

counsel, whatever the consequences in a particular case. Moreover, by focusing on the quality of representation and providing incentives in all cases for counsel to meet or exceed minimum standards, this approach reduces the likelihood that any particular defendant will be prejudiced by counsel's shortcomings. In this way, courts can safeguard the defendant's rights to a constitutionally adequate trial without engaging in the inherently difficult task of speculating about the precise effect of each error or omission by an attorney."

Although the "categorical" approach has strong supporters, see Smithburn & Springman, *Effective Assistance of Counsel: In Quest of a Uniform Standard of Review*, 17 Wake Forest L.Rev. 497 (1980); Notes, 80 Colum.L.Rev. 1053 (1980) 93 Harv.L. Rev. 752 (1980); cf. Genego, *The Future of Effective Assistance of Counsel: Performance Standards and Competent Representation,* 22 Am.Crim.L.Rev. 181, 203–12 (1984); this approach has not prevailed. Instead Judge Leventhal's plurality opinion in *Decoster* has proved highly influential.

Because a determination of whether counsel's performance amounted to ineffective assistance "cannot be divorced from consideration of the peculiar facts and circumstances that influenced counsel's judgment," Judge Leventhal concluded that a reviewing court's appraisal requires what he called a "judgmental approach"—one that looks to the totality of circumstances of the case in evaluating counsel's effectiveness—rather than a categorical approach. Speaking for four members of the D.C. Circuit, he voiced concern that Judge Bazelon's approach would "torture" the adversary system "out of shape":

"[Although Judge Bazelon] recognizes that the government can always defend by showing beyond a doubt that the violation was harmless [, the] realistic thrust [of his approach] is a rule structured toward a conclusion of prejudice from any deviation from the checklist of standards concerning preparation, whatever the likely or actual consequence. Omissions of investigation lead to new trials on the rationale that one can never be certain what might have happened had counsel performed better. A new trial is needed [even if] the fruits of the investigation would have proved neutral or even inculpatory, for defense counsel could have been in a stronger position to lead his client to prove guilty. This kind of speculation renders no error harmless. * * *

"Judge Bazelon is animated by a view of the adversary system as so impaired in practice as to warrant a thorough reordering, with extensive supervision by the trial judge through a pretrial 'checklist' to ensure that counsel has met his duties of preparation, and oversight of the conduct of the trial. The manifest consequence would be inevitable and increasing intrusion into the development and presentation of the defense case by the trial judge, and (out of self-protection) by the prosecution."

Strickland v. Washington and *United States v. Cronic*, both set forth below, left no doubt about the Supreme Court's rejection of any "checklist" or "categorical" approach and its determination to evaluate ineffectiveness claims on a case-specific basis, and one requiring a showing of prejudicial impact.

STRICKLAND v. WASHINGTON

466 U.S. 668, 104 S.Ct. 2052, 80 L.Ed.2d 674 (1984).

[During a ten-day period, respondent planned and committed three groups of crimes, including three brutal capital murders, torture, kidnapping and attempted murders. Against counsel's advice, respondent pled guilty to all charges, including the three capital murder charges.

[In the plea colloquy, respondent told the Florida trial judge that, although he had committed a string of burglaries, he had no significant prior criminal record and that at the time of his criminal spree he was under extreme stress caused by his inability to support his family. He also stated, however, that he accepted responsibility for the crimes. The trial judge told respondent that he had "a great deal of respect for people who are willing to step forward and admit their responsibility" but that he was making no statement at all about his likely sentencing decision.

[Against counsel's advice, respondent waived his state right to an advisory jury at his capital sentencing hearing and chose to be sentenced by the trial judge without a jury recommendation. In preparing for the sentencing hearing, counsel spoke on the phone with respondent's wife and mother, but did not otherwise seek out character witnesses for respondent. Nor did he request a psychiatric examination, since his conversations with his client gave no indication that respondent had psychological problems. Counsel decided not to present and hence not to look further for evidence concerning respondent's character and emotional state. This decision reflected counsel's sense of hopelessness about overcoming the impact of respondent's confessions to the gruesome crimes and his judgment that it was advisable to rely on the plea colloquy for evidence as to such matters, thus preventing the state from cross-examining respondent and from presenting psychiatric evidence of its own. Finally, counsel did not request a presentence report because it would have included respondent's criminal history and thereby undermine the claim of no significant prior criminal record.

[At the sentencing hearing, counsel's strategy was based primarily on the trial judge's remarks at the plea colloquy as well as on his reputation as a sentencing judge who thought it important for a convicted defendant to own up to his crime. However, as the U.S. Supreme Court summarized it, "the trial judge found numerous aggravating circumstances and no (or a single comparatively insignificant) mitigating circumstance." He therefore sentenced respondent to death on each of the three counts of murder. The state supreme court upheld the convictions and sentences on direct appeal.

[Respondent eventually sought federal habeas corpus relief on the ground, inter alia, that counsel had rendered ineffective assistance at the sentencing proceeding in several respects, including his failure to request a psychiatric report, to seek out and present character witnesses, and to request a presentence report. The district court concluded that, although trial counsel had made errors in judgment in failing to investigate nonstatutory mitigating evidence further than he did, no prejudice to respondent's sentence resulted from any such error. On rehearing en banc, Unit B of the former Fifth Circuit, now the Eleventh Circuit, developed its own framework for analyzing ineffective assistance claims and reversed and remanded the case for new factfinding under the newly announced standards.]

JUSTICE O'CONNOR delivered the opinion of the Court. * * *

[T]he Court has recognized that "the right to counsel is the right to the effective assistance of counsel." *McMann v. Richardson* (1970). Government violates the right to effective counsel when it interferes in certain ways with the ability of counsel to make independent decisions about how to conduct the defense. See, e.g., *Geders v. United States*, 425 U.S. 80, 96 S.Ct. 1330, 47 L.Ed.2d 592 (1976) (bar on attorney-client consultation during overnight recess); *Herring v. New York*, 422 U.S. 853, 95 S.Ct. 2550, 45 L.Ed.2d 593 (1975) (bar on summation at bench trial); *Brooks v. Tennessee*, 406 U.S. 605, 92 S.Ct. 1891, 32 L.Ed.2d 358 (1972) (requirement that defendant be first defense witness); *Ferguson v. Georgia*, 365 U.S. 570, 81 S.Ct. 756, 5 L.Ed.2d 783 (1961) (bar on direct examination of defendant). Counsel, however, can also deprive a defendant of the right to effective legal assistance, simply by failing to render "adequate legal assistance," *Cuyler v. Sullivan* [p. 164 infra] (actual conflict of interest adversely affecting lawyer's performance renders assistance ineffective).

The Court has not elaborated on the meaning of the constitutional requirement of effective assistance in the latter class of cases—that is, those presenting claims of "actual ineffectiveness." In giving meaning to the requirement, however, we must take its purpose—to ensure a fair trial—as the guide. The benchmark for judging any claim of ineffectiveness must be whether counsel's conduct so undermined the proper functioning of the adversarial process that the trial cannot be relied on as having produced a just result.

The same principle applies to a capital sentencing proceeding such as that provided by Florida law. We need not consider the role of counsel in an ordinary sentencing, which may involve informal proceedings and standardless discretion in the sentencer, and hence may require a different approach to the definition of constitutionally effective assistance. A capital sentencing proceeding like the one involved in this case, however, is sufficiently like a trial in its adversarial format and in the existence of standards for decision that counsel's role in the proceeding is comparable to counsel's role at trial—to ensure that the adversarial testing process works to produce a just result under the standards governing decision. For purposes of describing counsel's duties, therefore, Florida's capital sentencing proceeding need not be distinguished from an ordinary trial.

A convicted defendant's claim that counsel's assistance was so defective as to require reversal of a conviction or death sentence has two components. First, the defendant must show that counsel's performance was deficient. This requires showing that counsel made errors so serious that counsel was not functioning as the "counsel" guaranteed the defendant by the Sixth Amendment. Second, the defendant must show that the deficient performance prejudiced the defense. This requires showing that counsel's errors were so serious as to deprive the defendant of a fair trial, a trial whose result is reliable. Unless a defendant makes both showings, it cannot be said that the conviction or death sentence resulted from a breakdown in the adversary process that renders the result unreliable.

As all the Federal Courts of Appeals have now held, the proper standard for attorney performance is that of reasonably effective assistance. The Court indirectly recognized as much when it stated in *McMann* that a guilty plea cannot be attacked as based on inadequate legal advice unless counsel was not "a reasonably competent attorney" and the advice was not "within the range of competence demanded of attorneys in criminal cases." When a convicted defendant complains of the ineffectiveness of counsel's assistance, the defendant must show that counsel's representation fell below an objective standard of reasonableness.

More specific guidelines are not appropriate. The Sixth Amendment refers simply to "counsel," not specifying particular requirements of effective assistance. It relies instead on the legal profession's maintenance of standards sufficient to justify the law's presumption that counsel will fulfill the role in the adversary process that the Amendment envisions. The proper measure of attorney performance remains simply reasonableness under prevailing professional norms.

Representation of a criminal defendant entails certain basic duties. Counsel's function is to assist the defendant, and hence counsel owes the client a duty of loyalty, a duty to avoid conflicts of interest. From counsel's function as assistant to the defendant derive the overarching duty to advocate the defendant's cause and the more particular duties to consult with the defendant on important decisions and to keep the defendant informed of important developments in the course of the prosecution. Counsel also has a duty to bring to bear such skill and knowledge as will render the trial a reliable adversarial testing process.

These basic duties neither exhaustively define the obligations of counsel nor form a checklist for judicial evaluation of attorney performance. In any case presenting an ineffectiveness claim, the performance inquiry must be whether counsel's assistance was reasonable considering all the circumstances. Prevailing norms of practice as reflected in American Bar Association standards and the like are guides to determining what is reasonable, but they are only guides. No particular set of detailed rules for counsel's conduct can satisfactorily take account of the variety of circumstances faced by defense counsel or the range of legitimate decisions regarding how best to represent a criminal defendant. Any such set of rules would interfere with the constitutionally protected independence of counsel and restrict the wide latitude counsel must have in making tactical decisions. Indeed, the existence of detailed guidelines for representation could distract counsel from the overriding mission of vigorous advocacy of the defendant's cause. Moreover, the purpose of the effective assistance guarantee of the Sixth Amendment is not to improve the quality of legal representation, although that is a goal of considerable importance to the legal system. The purpose is simply to ensure that criminal defendants receive a fair trial.

Judicial scrutiny of counsel's performance must be highly deferential. It is all too tempting for a defendant to second-guess counsel's assistance after conviction or adverse sentence, and it is all too easy for a court, examining counsel's defense after it has proved unsuccessful, to conclude that a particular act or omission of counsel was unreasonable. A fair assessment of attorney performance requires that every effort be made to eliminate the distorting effects of hindsight, to reconstruct the circumstances of counsel's challenged conduct, and to evaluate the conduct from counsel's perspective at the time. Because of the difficulties inherent in making the evaluation, a court must indulge a strong presumption that counsel's conduct falls within the wide range of reasonable professional assistance; that is, the defendant must overcome the presumption that, under the circumstances, the challenged action "might be considered sound trial strategy." There are countless ways to provide effective assistance in any given case. Even the best criminal defense attorneys would not defend a particular client in the same way.

The availability of intrusive post-trial inquiry into attorney performance or of detailed guidelines for its evaluation would encourage the proliferation of ineffectiveness challenges. Criminal trials resolved unfavorably to the defendant would increasingly come to be followed by a second trial, this one of counsel's unsuccessful defense. Counsel's performance and even willingness to serve could be adversely affected. Intensive scrutiny of counsel and rigid requirements for acceptable assistance could dampen the ardor and impair the independence of defense counsel, discourage the acceptance of assigned cases, and undermine the trust between attorney and client.

Thus, a court deciding an actual ineffectiveness claim must judge the reasonableness of counsel's challenged conduct on the facts of the particular case, viewed as of the time of counsel's conduct. A convicted defendant making a claim of ineffective assistance must identify the acts or omissions of counsel that are alleged not to have been the result of reasonable professional judgment. The court must then determine whether, in light of all the circumstances, the identified acts or omissions were outside the wide range of professionally competent assistance. In making that determination, the court should keep in mind that counsel's function, as elaborated in prevailing professional norms, is to make the adversarial testing process work in the particular case. At the same time, the court should recognize that counsel is strongly presumed to have rendered adequate assistance and made all significant decisions in the exercise of reasonable professional judgment.

These standards require no special amplification in order to define counsel's duty to investigate, the duty at issue in this case. [S]trategic choices made after thorough investigation of law and facts relevant to plausible options are virtually unchallengeable; and strategic choices made after less than complete investigation are reasonable precisely to the extent that reasonable professional judgments support the limitations on investigation. In other words, counsel has a duty to make reasonable investigations or to make a reasonable decision that makes particular investigations unnecessary. In any ineffectiveness case, a particular decision not to investigate must be directly assessed for reasonableness in all the circumstances, applying a heavy measure of deference to counsel's judgments.

The reasonableness of counsel's actions may be determined or substantially influenced by the defendant's own statements or actions. Counsel's actions are usually based, quite properly, on informed strategic choices made by the defendant and on information supplied by the defendant. In particular, what investigation decisions are reasonable depends critically on such information. For example, when the facts that support a certain potential line of defense are generally known to counsel because of what the defendant has said, the need for further investigation may be considerably diminished or eliminated altogether. And when a defendant has given counsel reason to believe that pursuing certain investigations would be fruitless or even harmful, counsel's failure to pursue those investigations may not later be challenged as unreasonable. In short, inquiry into counsel's conversations with the defendant may be critical to a proper assessment of counsel's investigation decisions, just as it may be critical to a proper assessment of counsel's other litigation decisions.

An error by counsel, even if professionally unreasonable, does not warrant setting aside the judgment of a criminal proceeding if the error had no effect on the judgment. The purpose of the Sixth Amendment guarantee of counsel is to ensure that a defendant has the assistance necessary to justify reliance on the outcome of the proceeding. Accordingly, any deficiencies in counsel's performance must be prejudicial to the defense in order to constitute ineffective assistance under the Constitution.

In certain Sixth Amendment contexts, prejudice is presumed. Actual or constructive denial of the assistance of counsel altogether is legally presumed to result in prejudice. So are various kinds of state interference with counsel's assistance. Prejudice in these circumstances is so likely that case by case inquiry into prejudice is not worth the cost. Moreover, such circumstances involve impairments of the Sixth Amendment right that are easy to identify and, for that reason and because the prosecution is directly responsible, easy for the government to prevent.

One type of actual ineffectiveness claim warrants a similar, though more limited, presumption of prejudice. In *Cuyler v. Sullivan*, the Court held that prejudice is presumed when counsel is burdened by an actual conflict of interest. In those circumstances, counsel breaches the duty of loyalty, perhaps the most basic of counsel's duties. Moreover, it is difficult to measure the precise effect on the defense of representation corrupted by conflicting interest. Given the obligation of counsel to avoid conflicts of interest and the ability of trial courts to make early inquiry in certain situations likely to give rise to conflicts, see e.g., Fed.R.Crim.P. 44(c), it is reasonable for the criminal justice system to maintain a fairly rigid rule of presumed prejudice for conflicts of interest. Even so, the rule is not quite the *per se* rule of prejudice that exists for the Sixth Amendment claims mentioned above. Prejudice is presumed only if the defendant demonstrates that counsel "actively represented conflicting interests" and "that an actual conflict of interest adversely affected his lawyer's performance." *Cuyler v. Sullivan.*

Conflict of interest claims aside, actual ineffectiveness claims alleging a deficiency in attorney performance are subject to a general requirement that the defendant affirmatively prove prejudice. [Attorney errors] cannot be classified according to likelihood of causing prejudice. Nor can they be defined with sufficient precision to inform defense attorneys correctly just what conduct to avoid. Representation is an art, and an act or omission that is unprofessional in one case may be sound or even brilliant in another. Even if a defendant shows that particular errors of counsel were unreasonable, therefore, the defendant must show that they actually had an adverse effect on the defense.

It is not enough for the defendant to show that the errors had some conceivable effect on the outcome of the proceeding. Virtually every act or omission of counsel would meet that test, and not every error that conceivably could have influenced the outcome undermines the reliability of the result of the proceeding. Respondent suggests requiring a showing that the errors "impaired the presentation of the defense." That standard, however, provides no workable principle. Since any error, if it is indeed an error, "impairs" the presentation of the defense, the proposed standard is inadequate because it provides no way of deciding what impairments are sufficiently serious to warrant setting aside the outcome of the proceeding.

On the other hand, we believe that a defendant need not show that counsel's deficient conduct more likely than not altered the outcome in the case. This outcome-determinative standard has several strengths. It defines the relevant inquiry in a way familiar to courts, though the inquiry, as is inevitable, is anything but precise. The standard also reflects the profound importance of finality in criminal proceedings. Moreover, it comports with the widely used standard for assessing motions for new trial based on newly discovered evidence. Nevertheless, the standard is not quite appropriate.

Even when the specified attorney error results in the omission of certain evidence, the newly discovered evidence standard is not an apt source from which to draw a prejudice standard for ineffectiveness claims. The high standard for newly discovered evidence claims presupposes that all the essential elements of a presumptively accurate and fair proceeding were present in the proceeding whose result is challenged. An ineffective assistance claim asserts the absence of one of the crucial assurances that the result of the proceeding is reliable, so finality concerns are somewhat weaker and the appropriate standard of prejudice should be somewhat lower. The result of a proceeding can be rendered unreliable, and hence the proceeding itself unfair, even if the errors of counsel cannot be shown by a preponderance of the evidence to have determined the outcome.

Accordingly, the appropriate test for prejudice finds its roots in the test for materiality of exculpatory information not disclosed to the defense by the prosecution, *United States v. Agurs* [Ch. 20, § 4], and in the test for materiality of testimony made unavailable to the defense by Government deportation of a witness, *United States v. Valenzuela-Bernal* [Ch. 24, § 4]. The defendant must show that there is a reasonable probability that, but for counsel's unprofessional errors, the result of the proceeding would have been different. A reasonable probability is a probability sufficient to undermine confidence in the outcome.

In making the determination whether the specified errors resulted in the required prejudice, a court should presume, absent challenge to the judgment on grounds of evidentiary insufficiency, that the judge or jury acted according to law.

An assessment of the likelihood of a result more favorable to the defendant must exclude the possibility of arbitrariness, whimsy, caprice, "nullification," and the like. A defendant has no entitlement to the luck of a lawless decisionmaker, even if a lawless decision cannot be reviewed. The assessment of prejudice should proceed on the assumption that the decisionmaker is reasonably, conscientiously, and impartially applying the standards that govern the decision. It should not depend on the idiosyncracies of the particular decisionmaker, such as unusual propensities toward harshness or leniency. Although these factors may actually have entered into counsel's selection of strategies and, to that limited extent, may thus affect the performance inquiry, they are irrelevant to the prejudice inquiry. Thus, evidence about the actual process of decision, if not part of the record of the proceeding under review, and evidence about, for example, a particular judge's sentencing practices, should not be considered in the prejudice determination.

The governing legal standard plays a critical role in defining the question to be asked in assessing the prejudice from counsel's errors. When a defendant challenges a conviction, the question is whether there is a reasonable probability that, absent the errors, the factfinder would have had a reasonable doubt respecting guilt. When a defendant challenges a death sentence such as the one at issue in this case, the question is whether there is a reasonable probability that, absent the errors, the sentencer—including an appellate court, to the extent it independently reweighs the evidence—would have concluded that the balance of aggravating and mitigating circumstances did not warrant death.

In making this determination, a court hearing an ineffectiveness claim must consider the totality of the evidence before the judge or jury. Some of the factual findings will have been unaffected by the errors, and factual findings that were affected will have been affected in different ways. Some errors will have had a pervasive effect on the inferences to be drawn from the evidence, altering the entire evidentiary picture, and some will have had an isolated, trivial effect. Moreover, a verdict or conclusion only weakly supported by the record is more likely to have been affected by errors than one with overwhelming record support. Taking the unaffected findings as given, and taking due account of the effect of the errors on the remaining findings, a court making the prejudice inquiry must ask if the defendant has met the burden of showing that the decision reached would reasonably likely have been different absent the errors.

A number of practical considerations are important for the application of the standards we have outlined. Most important, in adjudicating a claim of actual ineffectiveness of counsel, a court should keep in mind that the principles we have stated do not establish mechanical rules. Although those principles should guide the process of decision, the ultimate focus of inquiry must be on the fundamental fairness of the proceeding whose result is being challenged. In every case the court should be concerned with whether, despite the strong presumption of reliability, the result of the particular proceeding is unreliable because of a breakdown in the adversarial process that our system counts on to produce just results.

To the extent that this has already been the guiding inquiry in the lower courts, the standards articulated today do not require reconsideration of ineffectiveness claims rejected under different standards. Cf. *Trapnell v. United States*, 725 F.2d 149 (2d Cir.1983) (in several years of applying "farce and mockery" standard along with "reasonable competence" standard, court "never found that the result of a case hinged on the choice of a particular standard"). In particular, the minor differences in the lower courts' precise formulations of the performance standard are insignificant: the different formulations are mere variations of the overarching reasonableness standard. With regard to the prejudice inquiry, only the strict outcome-determinative test, among the standards articulated in the lower courts, imposes a heavier burden on defendants than the tests laid down today. The difference, however, should alter the merit of an ineffectiveness claim only in the rarest case.

Although we have discussed the performance component of an ineffectiveness claim prior to the prejudice component, there is no reason for a court deciding an ineffective assistance claim to approach the inquiry in the same order or even to address both components of the inquiry if the defendant makes an insufficient showing on one. In particular, a court need not determine whether counsel's performance was deficient before examining the prejudice suffered by the defendant as a result of the alleged deficiencies. The object of an ineffectiveness claim is not to grade counsel's performance. If it is easier to dispose of an ineffectiveness claim on the ground of lack of sufficient prejudice, which we expect will often be so, that course should be followed. Courts should strive to ensure that ineffectiveness claims not become so burdensome to defense counsel that the entire criminal justice system suffers as a result.

The principles governing ineffectiveness claims should apply in federal collateral proceedings as they do on direct appeal or in motions for a new trial. [The] presumption that a criminal judgment is final is at its strongest in collateral attacks on that judgment. An ineffectiveness claim, however, * * * is an attack on the fundamental fairness of the proceeding whose result is challenged. Since fundamental fairness is the central concern of the writ of habeas corpus, no special standards ought to apply to ineffectiveness claims made in habeas proceedings.

Finally, in a federal habeas challenge to a state criminal judgment, a state court conclusion that counsel rendered effective assistance is not a finding of fact binding on the federal court to the extent stated by 28 U.S.C. § 2254(d). [Rather,] like the question whether multiple representation in a particular case gave rise to a conflict of interest, * * * both the performance and prejudice components of the ineffectiveness inquiry are mixed questions of law and fact.

Having articulated general standards for judging ineffectiveness claims, we think it useful to apply those standards to the facts of this case in order to illustrate the meaning of the general principles. The record makes it possible to do so. There are no conflicts between the state and federal courts over findings of fact, and the principles we have articulated are sufficiently close to the principles applied both in the Florida courts and in the District Court that it is clear that the factfinding was not affected by erroneous legal principles.

Application of the governing principles is not difficult in this case. [The facts] make clear that the conduct of respondent's counsel at and before respondent's sentencing proceeding cannot be found unreasonable. They also make clear that, even assuming the challenged conduct of counsel was unreasonable, respondent suffered insufficient prejudice to warrant setting aside his death sentence.

With respect to the performance component, the record shows that respondent's counsel made a strategic choice to argue for the extreme emotional distress mitigating circumstance and to rely as fully as possible on respondent's acceptance of responsibility for his crimes. Although counsel understandably felt hopeless about respondent's prospects, nothing in the record indicates, [that] counsel's sense of hopelessness distorted his professional judgment. Counsel's strategy choice was well within the range of professionally reasonable judgments, and the decision not to seek more character or psychological evidence than was already in hand was likewise reasonable.

The trial judge's views on the importance of owning up to one's crimes were well known to counsel. The aggravating circumstances were utterly overwhelming. Trial counsel could reasonably surmise from his conversations with respondent that character and psychological evidence would be of little help. Respondent had already been able to mention at the plea colloquy the substance of what there was to know about his financial and emotional troubles. Restricting testimony on respondent's character to what had come in at the plea colloquy ensured that contrary character and psychological evidence and respondent's criminal history, which counsel had successfully moved to exclude, would not come in. On these facts, there can be little question, even without application of the presumption of adequate performance, that trial counsel's defense, though unsuccessful, was the result of reasonable professional judgment.

With respect to the prejudice component, the lack of merit of respondent's claim is even more stark. The evidence that respondent says his trial counsel should have offered at the sentencing hearing would barely have altered the sentencing profile presented to the sentencing judge. As the state courts and District Court found, at most this evidence shows that numerous people who knew respondent thought he was generally a good person and that a psychiatrist and a psychologist believed he was under considerable emotional stress that did not rise to the level of extreme disturbance. Given the overwhelming aggravating factors, there is no reasonable probability that the omitted evidence would have changed the conclusion that the aggravating circumstances outweighed the mitigating circumstances and, hence, the sentence imposed. Indeed, admission of the evidence respondent now offers might even have been harmful to his case: his "rap sheet" would probably have been admitted into evidence, and the psychological reports would have directly contradicted respondent's claim that the mitigating circumstance of extreme emotional disturbance applied to his case. * * *

Failure to make the required showing of either deficient performance or sufficient prejudice defeats the ineffectiveness claim. Here there is a double failure. More generally, respondent has made no showing that the justice of his sentence was rendered unreliable by a breakdown in the adversary process caused by deficiencies in counsel's assistance. Respondent's sentencing proceeding was not fundamentally unfair.

We conclude, therefore, that the District Court properly declined to issue a writ of habeas corpus. * * *

JUSTICE BRENNAN, concurring in part and dissenting in part.

I join the Court's opinion but dissent from its judgment.[a] * * *

I join the Court's opinion because I believe that the standards it sets out today will both provide helpful guidance to courts considering claims of actual ineffectiveness of counsel and also permit those courts to continue their efforts to achieve progressive development of this area of the law. * * *

[T]he standards announced today can and should be applied with concern for the special considerations that must attend review of counsel's performance in a capital sentencing proceeding. In contrast to a case in which a finding of ineffective assistance requires a new trial, a conclusion that counsel was ineffective with respect to only the penalty phase of a capital trial imposes on the state the far lesser burden of reconsideration of the sentence alone. On the other hand, the consequences to the defendant of incompetent assistance at

a. Adhering to his view that the death penalty is in all circumstances forbidden cruel and unusual punishment, Justice Brennan would vacate respondent's death sentence and remand the case for further proceedings.

a capital sentencing could not, of course, be greater. * * *

JUSTICE MARSHALL, dissenting. * * *

The opinion of the Court revolves around two holdings. First, the majority ties the constitutional minima of attorney performance to a simple "standard of reasonableness." Second, the majority holds that only an error of counsel that has sufficient impact on a trial to "undermine confidence in the outcome" is grounds for overturning a conviction. I disagree with both of these rulings.

My objection to the performance standard adopted by the Court is that it is so malleable that, in practice, it will either have no grip at all or will yield excessive variation in the manner in which the Sixth Amendment is interpreted and applied by different courts. To tell lawyers and the lower courts that counsel for a criminal defendant must behave "reasonably" and must act like "a reasonably competent attorney" is to tell them almost nothing. In essence, the majority has instructed judges called upon to assess claims of ineffective assistance of counsel to advert to their own intuitions regarding what constitutes "professional" representation, and has discouraged them from trying to develop more detailed standards governing the performance of defense counsel. In my view, the Court has thereby not only abdicated its own responsibility to interpret the Constitution, but also impaired the ability of the lower courts to exercise theirs.

The debilitating ambiguity of an "objective standard of reasonableness" in this context is illustrated by the majority's failure to address important issues concerning the quality of representation mandated by the Constitution. It is an unfortunate but undeniable fact that a person of means, by selecting a lawyer and paying him enough to ensure he prepares thoroughly, usually can obtain better representation than that available to an indigent defendant, who must rely on appointed counsel, who, in turn, has limited time and resources to devote to a given case. Is a "reasonably competent attorney" a reasonably competent adequately paid retained lawyer or a reasonably competent appointed attorney? It is also a fact that the quality of representation available to ordinary defendants in different parts of the country varies significantly. Should the standard of performance mandated by the Sixth Amendment vary by locale? The majority offers no clues as to the proper responses to these questions.

* * * I agree that counsel must be afforded "wide latitude" when making "tactical decisions" regarding trial strategy, but many aspects of the job of a criminal defense attorney are more amenable to judicial oversight [than the majority indicates]. For example, much of the work involved in preparing for a trial, applying for bail, conferring with one's client, making timely objections to significant, arguably erroneous rulings of the trial judge, and filing a notice of appeal if there are colorable grounds therefor could profitably be made the subject of uniform standards. * * *

I object to the prejudice standard adopted by the Court for two independent reasons. First, it is often very difficult to tell whether a defendant convicted after a trial in which he was ineffectively represented would have fared better if his lawyer had been competent. Seemingly impregnable cases can sometimes be dismantled by good defense counsel. On the basis of a cold record, it may be impossible for a reviewing court confidently to ascertain how the government's evidence and arguments would have stood up against rebuttal and cross-examination by a shrewd, well prepared lawyer. The difficulties of estimating prejudice after the fact are exacerbated by the possibility that evidence of injury to the defendant may be missing from the record precisely because of the incompetence of defense counsel. In view of all these impediments to a fair evaluation of the probability that the outcome of a trial was affected by ineffectiveness of counsel, it seems to me senseless to impose on a defendant whose lawyer has been shown to have been incompetent the burden of demonstrating prejudice.

Second and more fundamentally, the assumption on which the Court's holding rests is that the only purpose of the constitutional guarantee of effective assistance of counsel is to reduce the chance that innocent persons will be convicted. In my view, the guarantee also functions to ensure that convictions are obtained only through fundamentally fair procedures. The majority contends that the Sixth Amendment is not violated when a manifestly guilty defendant is convicted after a trial in which he was represented by a manifestly ineffective attorney. I cannot agree. Every defendant is entitled to a trial in which his interests are vigorously and conscientiously advocated by an able lawyer. A proceeding in which the defendant does not receive meaningful assistance in meeting the forces of the state does not, in my opinion, constitute due process.

In *Chapman v. California* [p. 796 infra], we acknowledged that certain constitutional rights are "so basic to a fair trial that their infraction can never be treated as harmless error." Among these rights is "the right to the assistance of counsel at trial." [6] In my view, the right to *effective* assistance of counsel is entailed by the right to counsel, and abridgment of the former is equivalent to abridgment of the latter. I would thus hold that a showing that the performance of a defendant's lawyer departed from constitutionally prescribed standards requires a new trial regardless of whether the defendant suffered demonstrable prejudice thereby.

Even if I were inclined to join the majority's two central holdings, I could not abide the manner in which the majority elaborates upon its rulings. Particularly regrettable are the majority's discussion of the "presumption" of reasonableness to be accorded lawyers' decisions and its attempt to prejudge the merits of claims previously rejected by lower courts using different legal standards. * * * [The majority suggests] that reviewing courts should "indulge a strong presumption that counsel's conduct" was constitutionally acceptable and should "apply[ ] a heavy measure of deference to counsel's judgments".

I am not sure what these phrases mean, and I doubt that they will be self-explanatory to lower courts. If they denote nothing more than that a defendant claiming he was denied effective assistance of counsel has the burden of proof, I would agree. But the adjectives "strong" and "heavy" might be read as imposing upon defendants an unusually weighty burden of persuasion. If that is the majority's intent, I must respectfully dissent. The range of acceptable behavior defined by "prevailing professional norms" seems to me sufficiently broad to allow defense counsel the flexibility they need in responding to novel problems of trial strategy. To afford attorneys more latitude, by "strongly presuming" that their behavior will fall within the zone of reasonableness, is covertly to legitimate convictions and sentences obtained on the basis of incompetent conduct by defense counsel.

The only justification the majority itself provides for its proposed presumption is that undue receptivity to claims of ineffective assistance of counsel would encourage too many defendants to raise such claims and thereby would clog the courts with frivolous suits and "dampen the ardor" of defense counsel. I have more confidence than the majority in the ability of state and federal courts expeditiously to dispose of meritless arguments and to ensure that responsible, innovative lawyering is not inhibited. In my view, little will be

6. In cases in which the government acted in a way that prevented defense counsel from functioning effectively, we have refused to require the defendant, in order to obtain a new trial, to demonstrate that he was injured. * * *

gained and much may be lost by instructing the lower courts to proceed on the assumption that a defendant's challenge to his lawyer's performance will be insubstantial.

For many years the lower courts have been debating the meaning of "effective" assistance of counsel. Different courts have developed different standards [governing] the level of performance required by the Constitution [and] the level of prejudice necessary to compel a new trial * * *.

The Court today substantially resolves these disputes. [It] holds that the Constitution is violated when defense counsel's representation falls below the level expected of reasonably competent defense counsel and so affects the trial that there is a "reasonable probability" that, absent counsel's error, the outcome would have been different.

Curiously, though, the Court discounts the significance of its rulings, suggesting that its choice of standards matters little and that few if any cases would have been decided differently if the lower courts had always applied the tests announced today. Surely the judges in the state and lower federal courts will be surprised to learn that the distinctions they have so fiercely debated for many years are in fact unimportant.

The majority's comments on this point seem to be prompted principally by a reluctance to acknowledge that today's decision will require a reassessment of many previously rejected ineffective-assistance-of-counsel claims. The majority's unhappiness on this score is understandable, but its efforts to mitigate the perceived problem will be ineffectual. Nothing the majority says can relieve lower courts that hitherto have been using standards more tolerant of ineffectual advocacy of their obligation to scrutinize all claims, old as well as new, under the principles laid down today.

The majority suggests that, "[f]or purposes of describing counsel's duties," a capital sentencing proceeding "need not be distinguished from an ordinary trial." I cannot agree.

The Court has repeatedly acknowledged that the Constitution requires stricter adherence to procedural safeguards in a capital case than in other cases. * * *

"Reliability" in the imposition of the death sentence can be approximated only if the sentencer is fully informed of "all possible relevant information about the individual defendant whose fate it must determine." The job of amassing that information and presenting it in an organized and persuasive manner to the sentencer is entrusted principally to the defendant's lawyer. The importance to the process of counsel's efforts,[13] combined with the severity and irrevocability of the sanction at stake, require that the standards for determining what constitutes "effective assistance" be applied especially stringently in capital sentencing proceedings.

It matters little whether strict scrutiny of a claim that ineffectiveness of counsel resulted in a death sentence is achieved through modification of the Sixth Amendment standards or through especially careful application of those standards. Justice Brennan suggests that the necessary adjustment of the level of performance required of counsel in capital sentencing proceedings can be effected simply by construing the phrase, "reasonableness under prevailing professional norms," in a manner that takes into account the nature of the impending penalty. Though I would prefer a more specific iteration of counsel's duties in this special context,[15] I can accept that proposal. However, when instructing lower courts regarding the probability of impact upon the outcome that requires a

13. See Goodpaster, *The Trial for Life: Effective Assistance of Counsel in Death Penalty Cases,* 58 N.Y.U.L.Rev. 299, 303 (1983).

15. * * * For a sensible effort to formulate guidelines for the conduct of defense counsel in

resentencing, I think the Court would do best explicitly to modify the legal standard itself.[16] In my view, a person on death row, whose counsel's performance fell below constitutionally acceptable levels, should not be compelled to demonstrate a "reasonable probability" that he would have been given a life sentence if his lawyer had been competent; if the defendant can establish a significant chance that the outcome would have been different, he surely should be entitled to a redetermination of his fate.[17]

The views expressed in the preceding section oblige me to dissent from the majority's disposition of the case before us. It is undisputed that respondent's trial counsel made virtually no investigation of the possibility of obtaining testimony from respondent's relatives, friends, or former employers pertaining to respondent's character or background. Had counsel done so, he would have found several persons willing and able to testify that, in their experience, respondent was a responsible, nonviolent man, devoted to his family, and active in the affairs of his church. Respondent contends that his lawyer could have and should have used that testimony to "humanize" respondent, to counteract the impression conveyed by the trial that he was little more than a cold-blooded killer. Had this evidence been admitted, respondent argues, his chances of obtaining a life sentence would have been significantly better.

Measured against the standards outlined above, respondent's contentions are substantial. Experienced members of the death-penalty bar have long recognized the crucial importance of adducing evidence at a sentencing proceeding that establishes the defendant's social and familial connections. See Goodpaster, supra note 13. The State makes a colorable—though in my view not compelling—argument that defense counsel in this case might have made a reasonable "strategic" decision not to present such evidence at the sentencing hearing on the assumption that an unadorned acknowledgment of respondent's responsibility for his crimes would be more likely to appeal to the trial judge, who was reputed to respect persons who accepted responsibility for their actions.[19] But however justifiable such a choice might have been after counsel had fairly assessed the potential strength of the mitigating evidence available to him, counsel's failure to make any significant effort to find out what evidence might be garnered from respondent's relatives and acquaintances surely cannot be described as "reasonable." Counsel's failure to investigate is particularly suspicious in light of his candid admission that respondent's confession and conduct in the course of the trial gave him a feeling of "hopelessness" re-

capital sentencing proceedings, see Goodpaster, supra.

16. For the purposes of this and the succeeding section, I assume solely for the sake of argument, that some showing of prejudice is necessary to state a violation of the Sixth Amendment. * * *

17. As I read the opinion of the Court, it does not preclude this kind of adjustment of the legal standard. The majority defines "reasonable probability" as "a probability sufficient to undermine confidence in the outcome." In view of the nature of the sanction at issue, and the difficulty of determining how a sentencer would have responded if presented with a different set of facts, it could be argued that a lower estimate of the likelihood that the outcome of a capital sentencing proceeding was influenced by attorney error is sufficient to "undermine confidence" in that outcome than would be true in an ordinary criminal case.

19. Two considerations undercut the State's explanation of counsel's decision. First, it is not apparent why adducement of evidence pertaining to respondent's character and familial connections would have been inconsistent with respondent's acknowledgment that he was responsible for his behavior. Second, the Florida Supreme Court possesses—and frequently exercises—the power to overturn death sentences it deems unwarranted by the facts of a case. Even if counsel's decision not to try to humanize respondent for the benefit of the trial judge were deemed reasonable, counsel's failure to create a record for the benefit of the state Supreme Court might well be deemed unreasonable.

garding the possibility of saving respondent's life.

That the aggravating circumstances implicated by respondent's criminal conduct were substantial, does not vitiate respondent's constitutional claim; judges and juries in cases involving behavior at least as egregious have shown mercy, particularly when afforded an opportunity to see other facets of the defendant's personality and life. Nor is respondent's contention defeated by the possibility that the material his counsel turned up might not have been sufficient to establish a statutory mitigating circumstance under Florida law; Florida sentencing judges and the Florida Supreme Court sometimes refuse to impose death sentences in cases "in which, even though *statutory* mitigating circumstances do not outweigh statutory aggravating circumstances, the addition of nonstatutory mitigating circumstances tips the scales in favor of life imprisonment."

If counsel had investigated the availability of mitigating evidence, he might well have decided to present some such material at the hearing. If he had done so, there is a significant chance that respondent would have been given a life sentence. In my view, those possibilities, conjoined with the unreasonableness of counsel's failure to investigate, are more than sufficient to establish a violation of the Sixth Amendment and to entitle respondent to a new sentencing proceeding. * * *

Notes and Questions

1. *Dispensing with Strickland's outcome-prejudice test.* "Both because the right to effective assistance rests on concern with process as much as results and because injury is difficult to prove in many cases where it doubtless exists," V. Berger, *The Supreme Court and Defense Counsel: Old Roads, New Paths—A Dead End?*, 86 Colum.L.Rev. 9, 95–96 (1986) "reject[s] the concept of actual prejudice as an element of counsel inadequacy claims. * * * For screening out those instances where counsel's defaults surely did not damage the client, the harmless constitutional error test satisfactorily accommodates both the state's and the defendant's interests. This thoroughly familiar standard places a very heavy burden on the prosecution to demonstrate the absence of outcome effect. When society can say *with confidence* that entirely adequate representation would not have changed the result of the case, and only then, I believe that the state is justified in salvaging judgments despite the undeniable incursion on the prophylactic and dignitary values embodied in the right to effective assistance."

2. *Disposing of an ineffectiveness claim on ground of lack of prejudice.* Recall the *Strickland* Court's comments that "[t]he object of an ineffectiveness claim is not to grade counsel's performance" and that "[i]f it is easier to dispose of an ineffectiveness claim on the ground of lack of sufficient prejudice, which we expect will often be so, that course should be followed." "This injunction," protests V. Berger, Note 1 supra, at 86–87, "amounts to a blatant invitation—indeed, direction—to the lower courts to avoid refining more detailed criteria for lawyer conduct, as well as a not so subtle suggestion that virtually all challenges to counsel can be readily rejected. Each of these messages is regrettable. The latter, of a piece with the stated strong presumption of competence, reveals at best an insensitive attitude toward a very serious problem. The former evinces, perhaps even more unfortunately, blindness toward an important facet of adjudication. Decisions on the merits of claims of ineffective assistance may operate preventively, not only remedially, but determinations of lack of prejudice tell counsel nothing in the absence of any discussion of whether the lawyer erred in the first place. Maybe grading individual counsel is beside the point, as the Court stated. Surely, however, teaching the bar in general about their duties is not."

3. *The role of an attorney.* According to *Strickland,* does defense counsel provide

inadequate representation only when society cannot rely on the result as just? If so, consider Genego, *The Future of Effective Assistance of Counsel: Performance Standards and Competent Representation,* 22 Am.Crim. L.Rev. 181, 200 (1984): "The role of a [defense attorney] is not [to] see that his or her client received a fair trial and that a just outcome resulted. The attorney's role is to do everything ethically proper to see that the client receives the most favorable outcome possible—whether or not it produces an outcome which society considers just. Society relies on the adversary system to produce just results from partisan advocacy. The guiding principle in determining whether an attorney has provided effective representation must then be whether he or she discharged the role of partisan advocate faithfully and zealously, not whether the performance yielded what a court views as a just result."

4. *Would a "reasonably competent" defense attorney have performed as Washington's attorney did?* For the view that the failure of Washington's counsel to have his client examined by a psychiatrist was "unreasonable" under the circumstances and constituted deficient representation, see Genego, Note 3 supra, at 197. "The critical point," maintains Professor Genego, "is that Washington's attorney could not make a reasonable strategic decision about the utility of relying on psychiatric testimony without having his own doctor examine Washington. . . . Washington had everything to gain and nothing to lose from a defense-initiated psychiatric examination, and the defense attorney could not have known the value of a report before one was made."

Genego contends, id. at 197–98, that the *Strickland* Court was "similarly misguided about the failure of Washington's attorney to interview character witnesses. [Washington's attorney] could not have intelligently speculated about the utility of [the fourteen character witnesses'] evidence because his efforts to obtain the character evidence were limited to speaking by telephone with Washington's wife and mother. Thus, the attorney had no idea what the fourteen character witnesses could have said about Washington's request that he be allowed to live. Prevailing professional norms should obligate a 'reasonably competent' attorney representing someone in a capital sentencing proceeding at least to investigate the possible existence of favorable character evidence."

5. *Application of Strickland to guilty pleas. Hill v. Lockhart* (1985) (Ch. 21, § 5) applied the two-part *Strickland* test to challenges to guilty pleas based on ineffective assistance of counsel. In order to satisfy the second half—or "prejudice" requirement—of the test, "the defendant must show that there is a reasonable probability that, but for counsel's errors, he would not have pleaded guilty and would have insisted on going to trial."

UNITED STATES v. CRONIC

466 U.S. 648, 104 S.Ct. 2039, 80 L.Ed.2d 657 (1984).

[Respondent and two associates were indicted on federal mail fraud charges involving a "check kiting" scheme whereby checks were transferred between banks in Florida and Oklahoma. Shortly before the scheduled trial date, respondent's retained counsel withdrew. The district court appointed a young lawyer with a real estate practice who had never participated in a jury trial to represent respondent, but allowed him only 25 days for pretrial preparation, even though it had taken the government over four and one-half years to investigate the case and it had reviewed thousands of documents during that investigation. Respondent was convicted on eleven of the thirteen counts in the indictment, but the U.S. Court of Appeals for the Tenth Circuit reversed, inferring, on the basis of the circumstances surrounding the representation of defendant, that respondent's Sixth Amendment right to the effective assistance of counsel had been violated. This conclusion was not supported by a determination that respondent's trial counsel had made any specified errors or that his actual performance had prejudiced the defense or that his performance had failed to satisfy a standard of reasonably effective assistance.]

JUSTICE STEVENS delivered the opinion of the Court.

[The Court of Appeals' inference] that respondent's constitutional right to the effective assistance of counsel had been violated * * * was based on its use of five criteria: "(1) [T]he time afforded for investigation and preparation; (2) the experience of counsel; (3) the gravity of the charge; (4) the complexity of possible defenses; and (5) the accessibility of witnesses to counsel." Under [this test], reversal is required even if the lawyer's actual performance was flawless. By utilizing this inferential approach, the Court of Appeals erred. * * *

[T]he adversarial process protected by the Sixth Amendment requires that the accused have "counsel acting in the role of an advocate," *Anders v. California* [p. 175 infra]. The right to the effective assistance of counsel is thus the right of the accused to require the prosecution's case to survive the crucible of meaningful adversarial testing. When a true adversarial criminal trial has been conducted—even if defense counsel may have made demonstrable errors—the kind of testing envisioned by the Sixth Amendment has occurred.[19] But if the process loses its character as a confrontation between adversaries, the constitutional guarantee is violated. * * *[21]

While the Court of Appeals purported to apply a standard of reasonable competence, it did not indicate that there had been an actual breakdown of the adversarial process during the trial of this case. Instead it concluded that the circumstances surrounding the representation of respondent mandated an inference that counsel was unable to discharge his duties.

In our evaluation of that conclusion, we begin by recognizing that the right to the effective assistance of counsel is recognized not for its own sake, but because of the effect it has on the ability of the accused to receive a fair trial. Absent some effect of challenged conduct on the reliability of the trial process, the Sixth Amendment guarantee is generally not implicated. Moreover, because we presume that the lawyer is competent to provide the guiding hand that the defendant needs, the burden rests on the accused to demonstrate a constitutional violation. There are, however, circumstances that are so likely to prejudice the accused that the cost of litigating their effect in a particular case is unjustified.

Most obvious, of course, is the complete denial of counsel. The presumption that counsel's assistance is essential requires us to conclude that a trial is unfair if the accused is denied counsel at a critical stage of his trial.[25] Similarly, if counsel entirely fails to subject the prosecution's case

19. Of course, the Sixth Amendment does not require that counsel do what is impossible or unethical. If there is no *bona fide* defense to the charge, counsel cannot create one and may disserve the interests of his client by attempting a useless charade. At the same time, even when no theory of defense is available, if the decision to stand trial has been made, counsel must hold the prosecution to its heavy burden of proof beyond reasonable doubt. And, of course, even when there is a *bona fide* defense, counsel may still advise his client to plead guilty if that advice falls within the range of reasonable competence under the circumstances.

21. Thus, the appropriate inquiry focuses on the adversarial process, not on the accused's relationship with his lawyer as such. If counsel is a reasonably effective advocate, he meets constitutional standards irrespective of his client's evaluation of his performance. It is for this reason that we attach no weight to either respondent's expression of satisfaction with counsel's performance at the time of his trial, or to his later expression of dissatisfaction.

25. The Court has uniformly found constitutional error without any showing of prejudice when counsel was either totally absent, or prevented from assisting the accused during a critical stage of the proceedings. * * *

to meaningful adversarial testing, then there has been a denial of Sixth Amendment rights that makes the adversary process itself presumptively unreliable. * * * [26]

Circumstances of that magnitude may be present on some occasions when although counsel is available to assist the accused during trial, the likelihood that any lawyer, even a fully competent one, could provide effective assistance is so small that a presumption of prejudice is appropriate without inquiry into the actual conduct of the trial. *Powell v. Alabama,* was such a case. * * * [28]

But every refusal to postpone a criminal trial will not give rise to such a presumption. In *Avery v. Alabama,* 308 U.S. 444, 60 S.Ct. 321, 84 L.Ed. 377 (1940), counsel was appointed in a capital case only three days before trial, and the trial court denied counsel's request for additional time to prepare. Nevertheless, the Court held that since evidence and witnesses were easily accessible to defense counsel, the circumstances did not make it unreasonable to expect that counsel could adequately prepare for trial during that period of time. Similarly, in *Chambers v. Maroney,* 399 U.S. 42, 90 S.Ct. 1975, 26 L.Ed.2d 419 (1970), the Court refused "to fashion a *per se* rule requiring reversal of every conviction following tardy appointment of counsel." Thus, only when surrounding circumstances justify a presumption of ineffectiveness can a Sixth Amendment claim be sufficient without inquiry into counsel's actual performance at trial.[31] * * *

The five factors listed in the Court of Appeals' opinion are relevant to an evaluation of a lawyer's effectiveness in a particular case, but neither separately nor in combination do they provide a basis for concluding that competent counsel was not able to provide this respondent with the guiding hand that the Constitution guarantees. * * *

Neither the period of time that the Government spent investigating the case, nor the number of documents that its agents reviewed during that investigation, is necessarily relevant to the question whether a competent lawyer could prepare to defend the case in 25 days. The Government's task of finding and assembling admissible evidence that will carry its burden of proving guilt beyond a reasonable doubt is entirely different from the defendant's task in preparing to deny or rebut a criminal charge. Of course, in some cases the rebuttal may be equally burdensome and time consuming, but there is no necessary correlation between the two. In this case, the time devoted by the Government to the assembly, organization, and summarization of the thousands of written records

26. Apart from circumstances of that magnitude, however, there is generally no basis for finding a Sixth Amendment violation unless the accused can show how specific errors of counsel undermined the reliability of the finding of guilt. See *Strickland.*

28. * * * Ineffectiveness is also presumed when counsel "actively represented conflicting interests." *Cuyler v. Sullivan* [p. 164 infra].

31. The Government suggests that a presumption of prejudice is justified when counsel is subject to "external constraints" on his performance. In this case the Court of Appeals identified an "external" constraint—the District Court's decision to give counsel only 25 days to prepare for trial. The fact that the accused can attribute a deficiency in his representation to a source external to trial counsel does not make it any more or less likely that he received the type of trial envisioned by the Sixth Amendment, nor does it justify reversal of his conviction absent an actual effect on the trial process or the likelihood of such an effect. [That] is made clear by *Chambers* and *Avery.* Both cases involved "external constraints" on counsel in the form of court-imposed limitations on the length of pretrial preparation, yet in neither did the Court presume that the "constraint" had an effect on the fairness of the trial. In fact, only last Term we made it clear that with respect to a trial court's refusal to grant the defense additional time to prepare for trial, an "external constraint" on counsel, great deference must be shown to trial courts, because of the scheduling problems they face. See *Morris v. Slappy.* Conversely, we have presumed prejudice when counsel labors under an actual conflict of interest, despite the fact that the constraints on counsel in that context are entirely self-imposed. See *Cuyler v. Sullivan.*

evidencing the two streams of checks flowing between the banks in Florida and Oklahoma unquestionably simplified the work of defense counsel in identifying and understanding the basic character of the defendants' scheme.[33] When a series of repetitious transactions fit into a single mold, the number of written exhibits that are needed to define the pattern may be unrelated to the time that is needed to understand it.

The significance of counsel's preparation time is further reduced by the nature of the charges against respondent. Most of the Government's case consisted merely of establishing the transactions between the two banks. A competent attorney would have no reason to question the authenticity, accuracy or relevance of this evidence—there could be no dispute that these transactions actually occurred. As respondent appears to recognize, the only *bona fide* jury issue open to competent defense counsel on these facts was whether respondent acted with intent to defraud. When there is no reason to dispute the underlying historical facts, the period of 25 days to consider the question whether those facts justify an inference of criminal intent is not so short that it even arguably justifies a presumption that no lawyer could provide the respondent with the effective assistance of counsel required by the Constitution.

That conclusion is not undermined by the fact that respondent's lawyer was young, that his principal practice was in real estate, or that this was his first jury trial. Every experienced criminal defense attorney once tried his first criminal case. Moreover, a lawyer's experience with real estate transactions might be more useful in preparing to try a criminal case involving financial transactions than would prior experience in handling, for example, armed robbery prosecutions. The character of a particular lawyer's experience may shed light in an evaluation of his actual performance, but it does not justify a presumption of ineffectiveness in the absence of such an evaluation.[38]

The three other criteria—the gravity of the charge, the complexity of the case, and the accessibility of witnesses—are all matters that may affect what a reasonably competent attorney could be expected to have done under the circumstances, but none identifies circumstances that in themselves make it unlikely that respondent received the effective assistance of counsel.

This case is not one in which the surrounding circumstances make it unlikely that the defendant could have received the effective assistance of counsel. The criteria used by the Court of Appeals do not demonstrate that counsel failed to function in any meaningful sense as the Government's adversary. Respondent can therefore make out a claim of ineffective assistance only by pointing to specific errors made by trial counsel.[41] * * * [W]e leave that claim [for] the consideration of the Court of Appeals on remand.

The judgment is reversed and the case is remanded for further proceedings consistent with this opinion.[a]

33. It is noteworthy that only about 60 exhibits, consisting primarily of bank records and batches of checks, together with summary charts prepared by the Government, were actually introduced at trial.

38. We consider in this case only the commands of the Constitution. We do not pass on the wisdom or propriety of appointing inexperienced counsel in a case such as this. It is entirely possible that many courts should exercise their supervisory powers to take greater precautions to ensure that counsel in serious criminal cases are qualified. * * *

41. Since counsel's overall performance was the only question on which the Court of Appeals passed, and is the primary focus of respondent's arguments in this court, we have confined our analysis to a claim challenging counsel's overall performance, and not one based on particular errors or omissions. Should respondent pursue claims based on specified errors made by counsel on remand, they should be evaluated under the standards enunciated in *Strickland.*

a. Justice Marshall concurred in the judgment without opinion.

WHEN DO DEFENSE COUNSEL'S ACTIONS IN PREVENTING HER CLIENT FROM TESTIFYING FALSELY IMPERMISSIBLY COMPROMISE THE CLIENT'S RIGHT TO EFFECTIVE ASSISTANCE OF COUNSEL?

A murder defendant claimed he had killed in self-defense. Shortly before trial, defendant told his lawyer that he had seen something "metallic" in deceased's hand just before stabbing him. The state supreme court found that "counsel was convinced with good cause to believe" that his client's proposed testimony would be "deliberately untruthful" and that counsel had based this belief upon an independent investigation and prior discussions with defendant. Counsel told his client that if he insisted on testifying that he saw a metallic object in deceased's hand then counsel would move to withdraw, advise the trial judge that the testimony was perjurious and testify against defendant. At trial, defendant testified only that he thought deceased had a gun. He was convicted of second degree murder. Did counsel's threats, which prevented defendant from testifying falsely, deprive defendant of the effective assistance of counsel?

Yes, answered a three-judge panel, in WHITESIDE v. SCURR, 744 F.2d 1323 (8th Cir.1984), petition for rehearing en banc denied (5–4), 750 F.2d 713 (8th Cir. 1984), cert. granted (NIX v. WHITESIDE), ___ U.S. ___, 105 S.Ct. 2016, 85 L.Ed.2d 298 (1985). Observed the three-judge panel, per MCMILLAN, J.:

"[C]ounsel's actions in threatening to withdraw, advise the state trial judge and testify against appellant [a] if appellant testified falsely,[b] impermissibly compromised appellant's right to effective assistance of counsel. Despite counsel's legitimate ethical concerns, [his threats] were inconsistent with the obligations of confidentiality and zealous advocacy. * * * Counsel's actions, in particular the threat to testify against appellant, indicate that a conflict of interest had developed between counsel and appellant, even though this conflict was admittedly precipitated by appellant's intention to testify falsely. At this point counsel had ceased to serve as a zealous advocate of appellant's interests. * * * Counsel's actions also impermissibly compromised appellant's right to testify in his own defense by conditioning continued representation by counsel and confidentiality upon appellant's restricted testimony. * * *

"Although *Cuyler v. Sullivan* [p. 164 infra] involved an allegation of conflict of interest on the basis of multiple representation, we think that the same limited presumption of prejudice should apply to the conflict of interest between counsel and

a. The Eighth Circuit's statement of the facts is challenged by Professor Phillip Johnson, *A Distorted Record,* Nat'l L.J. Nov. 4, 1985, pp. 13, 24, who points out that defense counsel's exact words, when he testified at a motion for a new trial in the state court, were that if Whiteside testified falsely "it would be my duty to advise the court of what he was doing and that I felt he was committing perjury; also that *I probably would be allowed to attempt to impeach that particular testimony*" (emphasis added by Johnson). Continues Johnson: "I agree that one *could* construe the statement as implying a threat to take the stand in front of the jury, but I am not at all confident that the lawyer really meant to say that, or that the defendant understood what he said in that way. (The Iowa Supreme Court understood the attorney to have meant only that he would inform the judge of the proposed perjury.)

"The defendant also testified at the motion for a new trial, and he did not remember any threat to testify as a rebuttal witness, or to 'impeach' or anything of the kind. He was not even sure that there had been an explicit threat to withdraw from the case if he insisted on testifying that he saw a gun. He remembered only that it was his 'impression' that the lawyer might withdraw if he persisted. * * * Whether or not the defense attorney actually used the word 'impeach' in saying what he would do if the defendant insisted on testifying falsely, there is no evidence at all that the defendant heard such a threat. An unheard threat has no coercive effect."

b. For purposes of its analysis, the court presumed that Whiteside would have testified falsely.

client involved in this case. [A lawyer's threats to testify against her client] undermine the fundamental trust between lawyer and client that can exist only if the lawyer 'can convince the client that full and confidential disclosure [will] never result in prejudice to the client by any word or action of the lawyer.' Freedman, *Professional Responsibility of the Criminal Defense Lawyer: The Three Hardest Questions,* 64 Mich.L.Rev. 1469, 1473 (1966).[c] Thus, threats like the one here are presumptively prejudicial to the defense.

"* * * Our holding is no broader than necessary to dispose of the perhaps unique fact situation presented here. In particular, we express no view on the sixth amendment implications of a lawyer's simply moving to withdraw, with or without informing the trial court of the reason. Surely a lawyer who actually testified against his own client could not be said to be rendering effective assistance. The same is true, we think, of a lawyer who threatens to testify against his own client.

"Here, counsel went so far in his (at least initially) commendable zeal to avoid deceiving the court that he became an adversary to his own client. In this situation, we believe that appellant did not receive the effective assistance of counsel."

Judge FAGG, joined by Ross, Gibson and Bowman, JJ., dissented from the Eighth Circuit's denial of rehearing en banc, "find[ing] it hard to believe that a lawyer who nips perjury in the bud is 'ineffective' within the context of the constitutional fabric," and observing:

"In *Strickland,* the Supreme Court observed that '[t]he benchmark for judging any claim of ineffectiveness must be whether counsel's conduct so undermined the proper functioning of the adversarial process that the trial cannot be relied on as having produced a just result.' The panel opinion disregards the *Strickland* benchmark and totally ignores the lawyer's duty as an officer of the court to protect the integrity of our Nation's courts. False testimony on a crucial factual issue is not 'evidence subject to adversarial testing' within the framework of a fair trial. *Strickland.*"

Judge GIBSON "join[ed] Judge Fagg in his views on the performance component but [wrote] separately to underscore [his] concerns with the absence of prejudice, which is a sufficient ground to deny [federal habeas corpus relief]:

"Assuming that there was a [conflict of interest], the record simply does not show that it adversely affected counsel's performance. The attorney's threat produced a single effect: it persuaded Whiteside to tell the truth as a witness. The case was tried and Whiteside testified, [although] his testimony was restricted in the sense that he was prevented from testifying falsely. The record reveals that Whiteside testified that he thought [deceased] had a gun, which was precisely what he told his lawyer he would testify to, before he told

c. For a more recent statement of Professor Monroe Freedman's views, urging the Supreme Court to affirm the Eighth Circuit's decision in *Whiteside,* see Freedman, *An Important Issue,* Nat'l L.J., Nov. 4, 1985, p. 13. Freedman concludes, id. at 28:

"[T]he Supreme Court is faced with two possible models of the lawyer-client relationship. Under the traditional model, the lawyer makes every effort to be fully informed of the client's case by establishing a relationship of trust and confidence with the client. The lawyer then honors that trust, but uses it to dissuade the client from wrongful conduct, going forward with the client's perjury only in those rare instances in which disuasion is unsuccessful and withdrawal not feasible. Under the second model, the lawyer remains purposefully ignorant of potentially embarrassing facts because the lawyer warns the client (or because clients become aware in time) that lawyers are required to disclose harmful information to the court. There, too, lawyers will go forward with client's perjury—probably much more frequently—because they will be ignorant of the truth.

"It seems clear that this second model would, in a real sense, 'undermine the proper functioning of the adversary process', *Strickland,* and that only the traditional model is compatible with effective assistance of counsel and with the privilege against self-incrimination."

his lawyer that he intended to testify that he saw something metallic in [deceased's] hand just before the stabbing. I cannot justify the court's presuming that Whiteside was prejudiced when he testified fully in his defense and was restricted only in the sense that he did not testify falsely. Whiteside has not suggested that any other prejudice resulted from the threats of his counsel. The record reveals no other action during or before the trial that in any way demonstrates that counsel's performance was adversely affected by an actual conflict of interest. *Strickland* makes clear that it does not announce a *per se* presumption of prejudice in conflict of interest situations. In actuality, the court does apply such a *per se* rule to presume prejudice in this case."

Chief Judge LAY concurred in the denial of a rehearing en banc, but wrote separately to address Judge Fagg's dissenting opinion:

"Ethical standards allow a lawyer to seek withdrawal when a client insists on giving testimony the lawyer knows to be perjurious. Counsel should not, however, advise the court of his or her reason for seeking withdrawal. In this case, defendant's counsel threatened to take the stand and impeach his client. Such a threat is not only unethical, it creates a conflict of interest between the lawyer and the defendant rendering counsel ineffective in violation of defendant's sixth amendment rights.

" * * * That it is both unethical and a denial of effective counsel for an attorney to threaten to testify against [his client] as to information given in confidence by the client is uncontestable. That a lawyer must serve as a guardian of truth in the judicial process is also without doubt. The panel opinion in *Whiteside* does no more than tie the two certainties together."

IV. MULTIPLE REPRESENTATION AND CONFLICTS OF INTEREST

"An attorney appeared in a municipal court for the purpose of requesting a reduction of bail for four defendants jointly charged with possession of a large cache of drugs seized from a communal house. Referring to the first of his clients, the lawyer stated: 'The defendant should be released on his recognizance, Your Honor, because he has no rap sheet. Obviously he is not a hardened criminal and should not be locked up with others who are.' When the second defendant's case was called, counsel argued: 'No drugs were found in this defendant's bedroom, Your Honor. His chance for an acquittal is great and consequently it is highly likely that he will show up for trial.' On behalf of the third defendant, the lawyer began to argue that his client had lived in the area all of his life. The judge interrupted the lawyer, asking him if any drugs had been seized from the bedroom of defendant number three. The lawyer responded, 'No comment, Your Honor.' The judge countered with the remark: 'I suppose that this client also has a prior record, making him a hardened criminal,' evoking the response that although the defendant had a prior record, he certainly was not a hardened criminal. The fourth defendant then interrupted the proceedings by eagerly requesting to be represented by the public defender."

—Lowenthal, *Joint Representation in Criminal Cases: A Critical Appraisal,* 64 Va.L. Rev. 939, 941 (1978) [a]

When a single attorney represents two or more defendants, a conflict of interest can surface, and is likely to do so, at any stage of the criminal process—plea bargaining, the decision whether to have the defendants testify, closing argument or sentencing. The many ways that an attor-

a. This incident occurred in Professor Lowenthal's presence when he was an assistant public defender. Such incidents prompted him to write his article.

ney representing multiple defendants can find himself in the bind of a conflict and the difficulty, if not futility, of searching the record for a "lost" defense or other evidence of conflict, are discussed and documented in, e.g., Geer, *Representation of Multiple Criminal Defendants: Conflicts of Interest and the Professional Responsibilities of the Defense Attorney,* 62 Minn.L.Rev. 119, 125–35 (1978); Lowenthal, supra, at 941–50, 978–79; Tague, *Multiple Representation and Conflicts of Interest in Criminal Cases,* 67 Geo.L.J. 1075, 1077–80 (1979); *Developments—Conflicts of Interest in the Legal Profession,* 94 Harv.L.Rev. 1244, 1380–84 (1981); Comment, 68 J.Crim.L. & Crim. 226, 233–41 (1977). A summary, based on these commentaries, follows:

In the plea bargaining process, the prosecutor will often negotiate with one codefendant, offering a reduced charge, immunity or even a dismissal, in exchange for testimony against the remaining defendants or other cooperation with the government. A deal offered to one defendant and not to others puts a single counsel for multiple defendants in a most difficult, if not untenable, position.

The often crucial decision whether to put a defendant on the witness stand is greatly complicated by one attorney representing multiple defendants. One defendant's testimony might aid him but badly damage a codefendant. One defendant may make an excellent witness but another a very poor one. If both defendants take the stand, the poor witness, or one highly vulnerable to impeachment, may drag down the better witness. Putting on the stand only the defendant who makes a good witness may suggest to the jury that the defendants' own lawyer finds significant differences between them, or at least raise questions in the minds of the jurors as to why one defendant refused to testify.

When a lawyer represents only one of several defendants, in closing argument he may stress favorable comparisons between his client and the other defendants. When a single attorney represents all the defendants, however, he must approach comparisons among the defendants with the greatest caution.

Even if the dangers of multiple representation have somehow been avoided throughout the trial, any unity of interests among multiple defendants will often, perhaps inevitably, break down at the sentencing stage. More often than not, each defendant's role in the planning and the commission of the crime and each defendant's age, background and prior criminal record will vary significantly.

How can a lawyer representing multiple defendants differentiate between or among them by drawing attention to the mitigating factors in favor of each without creating a conflict of interest?

Because a single lawyer representing several defendants may impose an enforced harmony of defenses for the "benefit of all defendants," many conflicts between defendants may not even appear as part of the record. A lost plea bargaining opportunity that results from a defense lawyer's effort to protect a codefendant, for example, will not be reflected in the record. Nor will a defense strategy never pursued in court, or even investigated, because it was in conflict with another strategy available to a codefendant.

CUYLER v. SULLIVAN

446 U.S. 335, 100 S.Ct. 1708, 64 L.Ed.2d 333 (1980).

MR. JUSTICE POWELL delivered the opinion of the Court.

The question in this case is whether a state prisoner may obtain a federal writ of habeas corpus by showing that his retained counsel represented potentially conflicting interests.

I

Respondent John Sullivan was indicted with Gregory Carchidi and Anthony DiPasquale for the first-degree murders of [two persons].

Two privately retained lawyers, G. Fred DiBona and A. Charles Peruto, represented all three defendants throughout the state proceedings that followed the indictment. Sullivan had different counsel at the medical examiner's inquest, but he thereafter accepted representation from the two lawyers retained by his codefendants because he could not afford to pay his own lawyer.[1] At no time did Sullivan or his lawyers object to the multiple representation. Sullivan was the first defendant to come to trial. The evidence against him was entirely [circumstantial]. At the close of the Commonwealth's case, the defense rested without presenting any evidence. The jury found Sullivan guilty and fixed his penalty at life imprisonment. * * * Sullivan's codefendants, Carchidi and DiPasquale, were acquitted at separate trials. * * *

The Pennsylvania Supreme Court affirmed both Sullivan's original conviction and the denial of collateral relief. The court saw no basis for Sullivan's claim that he had been denied effective assistance of counsel at trial. It found that Peruto merely assisted DiBona in the Sullivan trial and that DiBona merely assisted Peruto in the trials of the other two defendants. Thus, the court concluded, there was "no dual representation in the true sense of the term." The court also found that resting the defense was a reasonable tactic which had not denied Sullivan the effective assistance of counsel.

* * *

[On federal habeas corpus, the Third Circuit] held that the participation by DiBona and Peruto in the trials of Sullivan and his codefendants established, as a matter of law, that both lawyers had represented all three defendants. * * * [It] acknowledged that resting at the close of the prosecutor's case "would have been a legitimate tactical decision if made by independent counsel." Nevertheless, the court thought that action alone raised a possibility of conflict sufficient to prove a violation of Sullivan's Sixth Amendment rights. The court found support for its conclusion in Peruto's admission that concern for Sullivan's codefendants had affected his judgment that Sullivan should not present a defense. * * *

[Noting that the state supreme court's conclusion that the lawyers did not engage in multiple representation was "a mixed determination of law and fact * * * open to review on collateral attack in a federal court," the Supreme Court then agreed with the Third Circuit that the circumstances established the existence of multiple representation.]

III

We turn next to the claim that the alleged failings of Sullivan's retained counsel cannot provide the basis for a writ of habeas corpus because the conduct of retained counsel does not involve state action. * * *

[A] proper respect for the Sixth Amendment disarms petitioner's contention that defendants who retain their own lawyers are entitled to less protection than defendants for whom the State appoints counsel. * * * [The] vital guarantee of the Sixth Amendment would stand for little if the often uninformed decision to retain a particular lawyer could reduce or forfeit the defendant's entitlement to constitutional protection. Since the State's conduct of a criminal trial itself implicates the State in the defendant's conviction, we see no basis for drawing a distinction between retained and appointed counsel that would deny equal justice to defendants who must choose their own lawyers.

IV

We come at last to Sullivan's claim that he was denied the effective assistance of counsel guaranteed by the Sixth Amend-

1. DiBona and Peruto were paid in part with funds raised by friends of the three defendants. The record does not disclose the source of the balance of their fee, but no part of the money came from either Sullivan or his family.

ment because his lawyers had a conflict of interest. The claim raises two issues expressly reserved in *Holloway v. Arkansas,* 435 U.S. 475, 98 S.Ct. 1173, 55 L.Ed.2d 426 (1978). The first is whether a state trial judge must inquire into the propriety of multiple representation even though no party lodges an objection. The second is whether the mere possibility of a conflict of interest warrants the conclusion that the defendant was deprived of his right to counsel.

In *Holloway,* a single public defender represented three defendants at the same trial. The trial court refused to consider the appointment of separate counsel despite the defense lawyer's timely and repeated assertions that the interests of his clients conflicted. This Court recognized that a lawyer forced to represent codefendants whose interests conflict cannot provide the adequate legal assistance required by the Sixth Amendment. Given the trial court's failure to respond to timely objections, however, the Court did not consider whether the alleged conflict actually existed. It simply held that the trial court's error unconstitutionally endangered the right to counsel.

Holloway requires state trial courts to investigate timely objections to multiple representation. But nothing in our precedents suggests that the Sixth Amendment requires state courts themselves to initiate inquiries into the propriety of multiple representation in every case.[10] Defense counsel have an ethical obligation to avoid conflicting representations and to advise the court promptly when a conflict of interest arises during the course of trial. Absent special circumstances, therefore, trial courts may assume either that multiple representation entails no conflict or that the lawyer and his clients knowingly accept such risk of conflict as may exist. Indeed, as the Court noted in *Holloway,* trial courts necessarily rely in large measure upon the good faith and good judgment of defense counsel. "An 'attorney representing two defendants in a criminal matter is in the best position professionally and ethically to determine when a conflict of interest exists or will probably develop in the course of a trial.'" Unless the trial court knows or reasonably should know that a particular conflict exists, the court need not initiate an inquiry.

Nothing in the circumstances of this case indicates that the trial court had a duty to inquire whether there was a conflict of interest. The provision of separate trials for Sullivan and his codefendants significantly reduced the potential for a divergence in their interests. No participant in Sullivan's trial ever objected to the multiple representation. DiBona's opening argument for Sullivan outlined a defense compatible with the view that none of the defendants was connected with the murders. The opening argument also suggested that counsel was not afraid to call witnesses whose testimony might be needed at the trials of Sullivan's codefendants. [Finally,] counsel's critical decision to rest Sullivan's defense was on its face a reasonable tactical response to the weakness of the circumstantial evidence presented by the prosecutor. On these facts, we conclude that the Sixth Amendment imposed upon the trial court no affirmative duty to inquire into the propriety of multiple representation.

Holloway reaffirmed that multiple representation does not violate the Sixth Amendment unless it gives rise to a conflict of interest. Since a possible conflict inheres in almost every instance of multiple representation, a defendant who ob-

10. In certain cases, proposed [and subsequently adopted] Fed.R.Crim.P. 44(c) provides that the federal district courts "shall promptly inquire with respect [to] joint representation and shall personally advise each defendant of his right to the effective assistance of counsel, including separate representation." Several Courts of Appeals already invoke their supervisory power to require similar inquiries. As our promulgation of Rule 44(c) suggests, we view such an exercise of the supervisory power as a desirable practice. * * *

jects to multiple representation must have the opportunity to show that potential conflicts impermissibly imperil his right to a fair trial. But unless the trial court fails to afford such an opportunity, a reviewing court cannot presume that the possibility for conflict has resulted in ineffective assistance of counsel. Such a presumption would preclude multiple representation even in cases where " '[a] common defense * * * gives strength against a common attack.' "

In order to establish a violation of the Sixth Amendment, a defendant who raised no objection at trial must demonstrate that an actual conflict of interest adversely affected his lawyer's performance. * * *

[A] defendant who shows that a conflict of interest actually affected the adequacy of his representation need not demonstrate prejudice in order to obtain relief. But until a defendant shows that his counsel actively represented conflicting interests, he has not established the constitutional predicate for his claim of ineffective assistance.

The Court of Appeals granted Sullivan relief because he had shown that the multiple representation in this case involved a possible conflict of interest. We hold that the possibility of conflict is insufficient to impugn a criminal conviction. In order to demonstrate a violation of his Sixth Amendment rights, a defendant must establish that an actual conflict of interest adversely affected his lawyer's performance. Sullivan believes he should prevail even under this standard. He emphasizes Peruto's admission that the decision to rest Sullivan's defense reflected a reluctance to expose witnesses who later might have testified for the other defendants. The petitioner, on the other hand, points to DiBona's contrary testimony and to evidence that Sullivan himself wished to avoid taking the stand. Since the Court of Appeals did not weigh these conflicting contentions under the proper legal standard, its judgment is vacated and the case is remanded for further proceedings consistent with this opinion.

So ordered.

MR. JUSTICE BRENNAN, concurring in Part III of the opinion of the Court and in the result.

I agree with the Court, in Part III, that the alleged failure of retained counsel to render effective assistance involves state action and thus provides the basis for a writ of habeas corpus. I cannot, however, join Part IV of the opinion. * * *

[As the Court observes], "a possible conflict inheres in almost every instance of multiple representation." Therefore, upon discovery of joint representation, the duty of the trial court is to ensure that the defendants have not unwittingly given up their constitutional right to effective counsel. This is necessary since it is usually the case that defendants will not know what their rights are or how to raise them. This is surely true of the defendant who may not be receiving the effective assistance of counsel as a result of conflicting duties owed to other defendants. Therefore, the trial court cannot safely assume that silence indicates a knowledgeable choice to proceed jointly. The court must at least affirmatively advise the defendants that joint representation creates potential hazards which the defendants should consider before proceeding with the representation.

Had the trial record in the present case shown that respondent made a knowing and intelligent choice of joint representation, I could accept the Court's standard for a post-conviction determination as to whether respondent in fact was denied effective assistance. Where it is clear that a defendant has voluntarily chosen to proceed with joint representation, it is fair, if he later alleges ineffective assistance growing out of a conflict, to require that he demonstrate [as the Court states] "that a conflict of interest actually affected the adequacy of his representation." Here, however, where there is no evidence that the court advised respondent about the potential for conflict or that respondent made a knowing and intelligent choice to forego his right to separate counsel, I believe that respondent, who has shown a significant possibility of conflict, is entitled to a presumption that his representation in fact suffered. Therefore, I would remand the case to allow the government an opportunity to rebut this presumption by demonstrating that respondent's representation was not actually affected by the possibility of conflict.

MR. JUSTICE MARSHALL, concurring in part and dissenting in part.

* * * I join Parts I, II, and III of the Court's opinion.

I believe, however, that the potential for conflict of interest in representing multiple defendants is "so grave," see I *A.B.A. Standards* § 4–3.5(b), that whenever two or more defendants are represented by the same attorney the trial judge must make a preliminary determination that the joint representation is the product of the defendants' informed choice. I therefore agree with Mr. Justice Brennan that the trial court has a duty to inquire whether there is multiple representation, to warn defendants of the possible risks of such representation, and to ascertain that the representation is the result of the defendants' informed choice.

I dissent from the Court's formulation of the proper standard for determining whether multiple representation has violated the defendant's right to the effective assistance of counsel. The Court holds that in the absence of an objection at trial, the defendant must show "that an actual conflict of interest adversely affected his lawyer's performance." If the Court's holding would require a defendant to demonstrate that his attorney's trial performance differed from what it would have been if the defendant had been the attorney's only client, I believe it is inconsistent with our previous cases. Such a test is not only unduly harsh, but incurably speculative as well. The appropriate question under the Sixth Amendment is whether an actual, relevant conflict of interests existed during the proceedings. If it did, the conviction must be reversed. Since such a conflict was present in this case, I would affirm the [judgment].

Because it is the simultaneous representation of conflicting interests against which the Sixth Amendment protects a defendant, he need go no further than to show the existence of an actual conflict. An actual conflict of interests negates the unimpaired loyalty a defendant is constitutionally entitled to expect and receive from his attorney.

Moreover, a showing that an actual conflict adversely affected counsel's performance is not only unnecessary, it is often an impossible task. As the Court emphasized in *Holloway:*

"[I]n a case of joint representation of conflicting interests the evil—it bears repeating—is in what the advocate finds himself compelled to *refrain* from doing * * *." (Emphasis in original).

Accordingly, in *Holloway* we emphatically rejected the suggestion that a defendant must show prejudice in order to be entitled to relief. For the same reasons, it would usually be futile to attempt to determine how counsel's conduct would have been different if he had not been under conflicting duties.

In the present case Peruto's testimony, if credited by the court, would be sufficient to make out a case of ineffective assistance by reason of a conflict of interests under even a restrictive reading of the Court's standard. In the usual case, however, we might expect the attorney to be unwilling to give such supportive testimony, thereby impugning his professional efforts. Moreover, in many cases the effects of the conflict on the attorney's performance will not be discernible from the record. It is plain to me, therefore, that in some instances the defendant will be able to show there was an actual, relevant conflict, but be unable to show that it changed his attorney's conduct.

It is possible that the standard articulated by the Court may not require a defendant to demonstrate that his attorney chose an action adverse to his interests because of a conflicting duty to another client. Arguably, if the attorney had to make decisions concerning his representation of the defendant under the constraint of inconsistent duties imposed by an actual conflict of interests, the adequacy of the representation was adversely affected. * * * [If] that is the case, the Court's view and mine may not be so far apart after all.

Notes and Questions

1. *Cuyler v. Sullivan on remand; what constitutes "adversely affecting" counsel's performances?* On remand, the Third Circuit accepted the district court's finding that defense counsel's failure to call codefendant Carchidi to testify at Sullivan's trial constituted "an actual conflict of interest that adversely affected counsel's performance." *Sullivan v. Cuyler,* 723 F.2d 1077 (3d Cir.1983) "The record establishes," observed the court, "that counsel's duty of loyalty to Sullivan to consider the sufficiency of the evidence presented and the availability of exculpatory evidence before deciding to rest his defense conflicted with [his] duty of loyalty to Carchidi to protect him against self-incrimination. In fact it indicates that the conflict could not be avoided."

The court rejected the contention that there was no adverse effect "because had Carchidi been represented by independent counsel, he would have been advised to invoke, and probably would have invoked, the fifth amendment if called as a witness": "This argument seeks to require Sullivan to demonstrate prejudice. But [a defendant need not do so] to make out a violation of his sixth amendment rights where he has already established an actual conflict of interest adversely affecting counsel's performance. Here, it was sufficient for Sullivan to show that defense counsel consciously rejected calling Carchidi as a witness in the Sullivan trial to present Carchidi's case in the best light at his subsequent trial."

Judge Adams, who wanted the Third Circuit to rehear the case en banc, was "much less certain" than the panel that decided *Cuyler* on remand "that Sullivan was adversely affected by the decision not to call Carchidi as a witness. Indeed, there is little hard evidence to suggest that Carchidi would have testified. In any case, I believe that we are bound [to] accept the findings of the Pennsylvania Supreme Court on [this point]."

2. *The confusing language in Cuyler: must the defendant show an "adverse effect" as well as an "actual conflict"? Cuyler* states that a defendant who shows that a conflict "adversely affected" or "actually affected the adequacy of his representation need not demonstrate prejudice in order to obtain relief." But are the lower courts likely to experience considerable difficulty distinguishing between a requirement that the conflict "adversely affected" a lawyer's performance and a requirement that it "prejudiced" the defendant's case in some way? Does the Supreme Court's use of the term "adverse effect" merely describe how courts can identify the existence of an "actual conflict"? Should the courts require that a defendant show only that an actual conflict existed, i.e., that during the course of the representation the codefendants' interests diverged with respect to a material factual or legal issue or to a course of action? Or, once multiple representation is established and an actual conflict of interest identified, should the courts *presume* that the conflict adversely affected the lawyer's performance, but allow the government to rebut this presumption by demonstrating the absence of adverse effect? See generally Note, 70 Geo. L.J. 1527, 1536–62 (1982) (advocating the last approach mentioned).

3. *When should the trial judge "reasonably know" that a conflict exists?* *Cuyler* held that, absent an objection by counsel or defendant, an inquiry was not required "[u]nless the trial court knows or reasonably should know that a particular conflict exists." What information would place a trial judge in a position where she "reasonably should know" that a conflict exists? Consider *Wood v. Georgia,* 450 U.S. 261, 101 S.Ct. 1097, 67 L.Ed. 220 (1981). Both at the trial which led to their conviction and at the hearing revoking their probation petitioners' counsel was paid by their employer. In the course of vacating the judgment with instructions to hold a hearing to determine whether a conflict of interest actually existed at the time of the probation revocation or earlier, the Court, per Powell, J., observed that "the record [demonstrates] that the *possibility* of a conflict of interest was sufficiently apparent at the time of the revocation hearing to impose upon the court a duty to inquire further." All of the relevant facts relating to the employer's retention of counsel, the employer's failure to pay petitioners' fines (which led to the revocation of probation), and "counsel's insistence upon pressing a constitutional attack rather than making the arguments for leniency" were known to the trial court. Any doubts were "dispelled by the fact that the state raised the conflict problem explicitly and requested that the court look into it."

Responding to the dissent's claim that its ruling went beyond *Cuyler,* the Court observed: "[N]othing in [*Cuyler*] rules out the raising of a conflict-of-interest problem that is apparent in the record. Moreover, [*Cuyler*] *mandates* a reversal when the trial court has failed to make an inquiry even though 'it knows or reasonably should know that a particular conflict exists.' "

4. *The "affirmative inquiry" approach.* What is the trial judge's responsibility if she does not know and should not reasonably know that a conflict exists? Before the enactment of Fed.R.Crim.P. 44(c), a number of federal courts had adopted an "affirmative inquiry" approach whereby, before appointing, or permitting multiple defendants to proceed with, a single attorney, the trial court is required to inform the defendants of the risks of conflict, to ensure that they understand these risks, and to explain to them their right to separate counsel if a conflict does or may exist. See especially *United States v. Garcia,* 517 F.2d 272 (5th Cir.1975) (before obtaining waiver of right to unimpaired counsel, trial court "should seek to elicit a narrative response from each defendant that he has been advised of his right to effective representation, that he understands the details of his attorney's possible conflict of interest and the potential perils of such a conflict, that he has discussed the matter with his attorney or if he wishes with outside counsel, and that he voluntarily waives his Sixth Amendment protections.") See also *United States v. Garafola,* 428 F.Supp. 620 (D.C.N.J.1977), aff'd sub nom. *United States v. Dolan,* 570 F.2d 1177 (3d Cir. 1978). See generally Geer, *Representation of Multiple Defendants,* 62 Minn.L.Rev. 119, 140–43 (1977) (hereinafter referred to as "Geer"); Hyman, *Joint Representation of Multiple Defendants in a Criminal Trial,* 5 Hofstra L.Rev. 315, 320–24 (1977) (hereinafter referred to as "Hyman"); Lowenthal, *Joint Representation in Criminal Cases,* 64 Va.L.Rev. 939, 980–83 (1978) (hereinafter referred to as "Lowenthal"); Tague, *Multiple Representation and Conflicts of Interest in Criminal Cases,* 67 Geo.L.J. 1075, 1088–91 (1979) (hereinafter referred to as "Tague").[a]

a. Fed.R.Crim.P. 44(c) is similar to the "affirmative inquiry" approach:

"Whenever two or more defendants have been jointly charged [or] have been joined for trial [and] are represented by the same retained or assigned counsel or by retained or assigned counsel who are associated in the practice of law, the court shall promptly inquire with respect to such joint representation and shall personally advise each defendant of his right to the effective assistance of counsel, including separate representation. Unless it appears that there is good cause to believe no conflict of interest is likely to arise, the court shall take such measures as may be

According to Lowenthal 981, if the trial court meets its "affirmative inquiry" responsibilities, and the multiple defendants choose to proceed with shared counsel, "the reviewing court places a 'heavy burden' on a defendant seeking to overturn his conviction to show that an actual conflict of interest appears in the record. On the other hand, if the trial court makes no affirmative inquiry, the government bears the burden on appeal of demonstrating that a prejudicial conflict of interest was improbable." But cf. Tague at 1089 ("affirmative inquiry" courts "disagree dramatically with respect to the burden required to prove that a conflict warrants reversal").

5. *Is the "affirmative inquiry" approach an effective way to deal with conflict of interest problems?* Is the "affirmative inquiry" approach likely to solve conflict of interest problems or is it merely a way for *reviewing* courts to *avoid facing* these problems? Are abstract cautions to defendants likely to be meaningful unless related to the specific problems that may arise in their particular case? How often will a judge be able to make a useful *pretrial* assessment of the possibilities for conflict? Consider Geer at 141–42: "At the start of the trial, the judge will not know the defenses to be raised on behalf of each defendant, the potential defenses to be foregone, the weight and sufficiency of the evidence to be adduced against each defendant, or each defendant's personal history and past criminal record. Without such information, the trial judge cannot impress upon a defendant the significance of waiver, nor can he evaluate the defendant's appreciation of it."

Does the privilege against self-incrimination and the attorney-client privilege severely restrict the trial judge's ability to obtain information by inquiry? Even if the trial judge could identify a potential conflict of interest and so warn the defendants, would "the social and economic pressures on defendants to share counsel—at least at the beginning of a criminal case—dilute the effectiveness of [the] warnings"? Moreover, does retained counsel have "a strong economic incentive to minimize the risk of a conflict of interest when discussing a trial court's warning with his clients"? See Lowenthal at 981–83. But cf. Hyman at 320–21.

6. *Should joint representation in criminal cases be absolutely prohibited?* Because "the potential conflict of interest in representing multiple defendants is so grave," I *A.B.A. Standards* § 4–3.5(b) provides that "ordinarily" a lawyer should decline to represent multiple defendants "except in unusual situations when, after careful investigation, it is *clear* that no conflict is likely to develop" (emphasis added), and then only when "the several defendants give an informed consent to such multiple representation; and [the consent] is made a matter of judicial record." Given the many ways in which a conflict of interest may arise at various stages of the criminal process, can it *ever* be *clear* that a single attorney can adequately represent multiple criminal defendants?

According to one study, most public defender offices have a general policy against representing multiple defendants in a criminal case and about half "follow a policy of *never* representing more than one defendant in multiple defendant cases." Lowenthal at 950. This opposition to joint representation is based primarily on a "widespread belief that the interests of the codefendants will conflict in virtually every case, requiring the lawyer to choose a course favorable to one defendant that necessarily is detrimental to another." Id at 952. Because they are convinced that conflict of interest is "generally inherent" or "inevitable" in the defense of multiple defendants, some commentators have proposed that ethical standards be interpreted,

appropriate to protect each defendant's right to counsel."

For a hard look at proposed (and subsequently adopted) Rule 44(c), extensive criticism of it and suggested changes, see Tague at 1092–1130.

or revised, to prohibit any attorney from representing more than one defendant in a criminal case. See Cole, *Time for a Change: Multiple Representation Should Be Stopped,* 2 J.Crim. Defense 149 (1976); Geer at 157–62; Lowenthal at 983–89; *Developments—Conflicts of Interest in the Legal Profession,* 94 Harv.L.Rev. 1244, 1395–96 (1981).

But consider Margolin & Coliver, *Pretrial Disqualification of Criminal Defense Counsel,* 20 Am.Crim.L.Rev. 227, 253 (1982): "Enforcement of a 'one client, one lawyer' rule would result in fundamental unfairness. Clients, even those with common defenses and interests, would be prohibited from pooling their resources to retain joint counsel. This denial would subject them to the unnecessary cost of separate attorneys and could lower the quality of representation if their pooled assets would purchase better representation. There may also be few qualified counsel available to work on these cases. Lastly, if defendants of means are required to retain their own individual lawyers, indigent defendants clearly will have to be supplied with separate appointed counsel. This would place a high price tag on the 'one client, one lawyer' requirement."

7. *Would a categorical rule forbidding joint representation of codefendants deprive a defendant of his constitutional right to representation by the attorney of his choice?* Does a defendant have such a constitutional right? Yes, answer Margolin & Coliver, Note 6 supra, at 250–51; "[j]ust as the courts must honor a request to proceed without counsel, they must respect the defendant's waiver of conflict-free counsel." But consider Geer at 158–60: "In *Faretta* the Court found an *independent* right of self-representation and stated that it did not arise mechanically from a defendant's power to waive the right to assistance of counsel. See [*Faretta* at fn. 15 and accompanying text]. Thus, if an accused has a sixth amendment right to be represented by counsel of his choice, that right must arise independently; the power to waive assistance of counsel does not in itself imply a right to constitutionally defective legal assistance.

"There is, however, no such independent, absolute right to counsel of choice. * * * An indigent defendant, for example, does not have an absolute right to be assigned counsel of his choice * * *. [N]o defendant may select an attorney in a manner that will obstruct the administration of the judicial process or frustrate the judicial function [and] courts have consistently spurned defendants' constitutional arguments that they have a sixth amendment right to be represented by laymen [or] attorneys who have been disbarred. Thus, there are many limitations upon the ability of a defendant to choose counsel under current law. [A disciplinary rule prohibiting an attorney from representing multiple criminal defendants] simply imposes one more * * *."

"Distinguishing *Faretta* from the multiple representation case," according to Moore, *Conflicts of Interest in the Simultaneous Representation of Multiple Clients,* 61 Texas L.Rev. 211, 284–85 (1985), "requires two steps. The first is to separate what is constitutionally *required* to effectuate the right to effective assistance of counsel and what is constitutionally *permitted* in the exercise of a court's supervisory power over the regulation of professional conduct. Thus while it may be true that criminal codefendants have the capacity to effectively waive the right to conflict-free counsel in the absence of an ethical rule to the contrary, this capacity does not itself render any prophylactic rule against waiver unconstitutional.

"The second step is to note that the right to self-representation cannot be infringed without being abrogated altogether, whereas the right to counsel of choice will still exist in a meaningful way even though the defendant's choices have been somewhat restricted. For instance, by having the independent attorneys cooperate in presenting a unified strategy, some of the benefits of sharing a common attorney can still be enjoyed. Similarly, if the preferred attorney has special expertise or prior knowledge, he can share his knowledge with independent counsel or even take a dominant role in the actual trial. To the extent that the preferred attorney is unwilling to cooperate, his failure to do so only provides additional evidence that the conflicts would have impaired his ability to effectively represent both codefendants in the absence of a requirement for separate counsel."

Consider, too, Tague at 1113–14: "*Faretta* assumes that the court can explain to the defendant the risks of *pro se* representation and the benefit of having an attorney. [The Advisory Committee which drafted proposed Rule 44(c)] implicitly challenges such an assumption in the context of multiple representation. Because the judge cannot always determine whether a conflict exists or may arise, he cannot adequately inform the defendants of the peril they face in proceeding with the same attorney; if the defendants are not informed of that peril, their waiver is not intelligently given. This chain of reasoning results in an invalid waiver; therefore, according to the Advisory Committee, the court can impose separate representation.

"Assuming that the Advisory Committee is correct in its interpretation of *Faretta,* its position leads to a remarkable result. Although the court can impose separate representation whenever the judge cannot gather enough information to assess fully the source and effect of a conflict, the court cannot impose separate representation if the conflict is so blatant that the judge perceives it. In the latter situation, the court could provide enough information to allow an intelligent waiver. Thus, in the only situation in which the courts of appeals have exercised their supervisory power to impose separate representation, they arguably have acted unconstitutionally.

"Obviously, courts may recoil at this result * * *. Of course, when faced with [an obvious conflict], counsel on his own may elect to withdraw. If [not], [the court might conclude that] it could disqualify any attorney whose continued representation would violate the Code of Professional Responsibility. Less grandly, the court might decide it could remove appointed counsel even if its power did not reach retained counsel. * * * Or, [if] the defendants refused to provide whatever information the court demanded to determine the extent of their understanding, the court could conclude that it was unable to inform the defendants adequately of the risks they faced.[249]"

8. *Imposing separate counsel over a defendant's objection. United States v. Dolan,* 570 F.2d 1177 (3d Cir.1978), is apparently the first case holding that a court may disqualify counsel (because his continual representation of two defendants would violate his ethical obligations) even when the defendant objects and executes an informed waiver.[b] *Dolan* involved an actual conflict, but Fed.R.Crim.P. 44(c) can be read as going beyond actual conflict situations by authorizing the court to require separate representation when there is a clear potential for conflict.

Consider *Flanagan v. United States,* 679 F.2d 1072 (3d Cir.1982), rev'd on procedural grounds, 465 U.S. 259, 104 S.Ct. 1051, 79 L.Ed.2d 288 (1984). Although

249. This analysis is based on an analogy to forfeiture rather than waiver. The defendant can forfeit a right by not asserting it, and the court is not required independently to inform him of that right. Cf. *Wainwright v. Sykes* [Ch. 27, § 2] * * * In contrast, a defendant can waive a specific right only after an intelligent and voluntary relinquishment. To use an analysis based on forfeiture rather than waiver makes sense when the defendant wants to choose an option that will probably hurt him more than it will help. * * *

b. Other courts of appeals have taken the position that the defendant has the right to conflict-laden counsel as long as he waives any objection, and believe that *Faretta* requires such a conclusion. See LaFave & Israel, § 11.9(c).

no actual conflict had yet developed and the federal district court had found that petitioners had voluntarily, knowingly, and intelligently waived their right to conflict-free representation, the court nevertheless granted the government's motion to disqualify a law firm from its multiple representation of petitioners. The court concluded that it had the authority—and, indeed, the obligation—under Rule 44(c) to disqualify counsel when "the likelihood is great that a potential conflict may escalate into an actual conflict." The Third Circuit sustained the disqualification order because an actual conflict of interest was very likely to arise. The Supreme Court reversed on the ground that a pretrial order disqualifying a law firm on conflict grounds from representing multiple defendants was not immediately appealable. (See Ch. 26, § 2.) Thus the Court never reached the merits of petitioners' contention that disqualification of counsel of their choice after they had knowingly waived conflict-free representation deprived them of their Sixth Amendment right to counsel and of their due process right to present a common defense through counsel of their choice.

9. *Should separate counsel be appointed for indigent defendants at the first appearance and nonindigent defendants be required to retain separate counsel at the outset, or at least be required to discuss the matter of conflict with a separate attorney?* Although no court has yet condemned multiple representation per se, *Ford v. United States,* 379 F.2d 123 (D.C.Cir.1967), has "approached this position by exercising its supervisory power to require initial appointment of separate counsel for each indigent defendant." Tague at 1081. Under the practice of the District of Columbia Circuit, if after consulting with his client and investigating the case, the attorneys conclude that the defendants would benefit from joint representation, they must explain their reasons to the court, which then takes what it considers appropriate action. Recently, the California Supreme Court adopted this approach as a judicially declared rule of procedure. *People v. Mroczko,* 672 P.2d 835 (Cal. 1983). Patterning his proposal after this practice, Professor Tague has suggested two "possible improvements" to Rule 44(c), id. at 116–17:

"First, the magistrate or judge should appoint separate counsel at the first appearance of the indigent defendants and the court should require that nonindigent defendants retain separate counsel or at least discuss the matter of conflict with a separate attorney. Second, if the defendants nonetheless insist upon a single attorney, the court could require them to satisfy the burden of proving an intelligent waiver. This second change might include demanding that the defendants themselves discuss with the court—or at least permit counsel to discuss—the facts of the case and the reasons why each wants a single attorney as a way of determining whether each understands the significance of his choice.

"The first suggested change * * * should all but eliminate multiple representation for several reasons. First, it would prevent the defendants from coming to trust the single attorney who represented them before the court informed each of the right to separate representation. The defendants might fear the entry of a new attorney after indictment more than the prospect of a conflict that could divide the loyalty of a trusted attorney. Second, defendants unaware of the opportunity for joint representation would not be tempted to ask for it. It would be rare that an indigent defendant would request that he and his codefendant be represented by a single attorney. Furthermore, the indigent may not have the right to demand representation by codefendant's counsel."

"SUCCESSIVE REPRESENTATION" AND CONFLICTS OF INTEREST

Another source of potential conflict of interest arises from the defense lawyers' prior representations of individuals who are witnesses for the prosecution. On the one hand, defense counsel may use confidential information obtained from her former client to impeach him; on the other hand she may fail to cross-examine her former client rigorously for fear of misusing confidential information. For an empirical study of the frequency with which criminal defense lawyers confront former clients as government witnesses, a nationwide survey of public defender offices to ascertain how lawyers actually handle the problem, a discussion of judicial treatment of the problem, and a suggested approach, see Lowenthal, *Successive Representation by Criminal Lawyers,* 93 Yale L.J. 1 (1983). See also Margolin & Coliver, *Pretrial Disqualification of Criminal Defense Counsel,* 20 Am.Crim.L.Rev. 227, 236–51 (1982); *Developments—Conflict of Interest in the Legal Profession,* 94 Harv.L.Rev. 1244, 1376–78 (1981).

SECTION 4. THE ROLE OF APPOINTED COUNSEL; SYSTEMS OF DEFENSE REPRESENTATION

If court appointed counsel believes an appeal should not be filed because it lacks any merit, how should he proceed? ANDERS v. CALIFORNIA, 386 U.S. 738, 87 S.Ct. 1396, 18 L.Ed.2d 493 (1967), per CLARK, J., held a "no-merit letter"—counsel had stated in a letter to the state appellate court that he would not file a brief because he was "of the opinion that there is no merit to the appeal"—insufficient because it "affords neither the client nor the court any aid. The former must shift entirely for himself while the court has only the cold record which it must review without the help of an advocate." If, after a "conscientious examination" of his case, counsel finds an appeal to be "wholly frivolous," he should so advise the court and request permission to withdraw. "That request must, however, be accompanied by a brief referring to anything in the record that might arguably support the appeal. A copy of counsel's brief should be furnished the indigent and time allowed him to raise any points that he chooses; the court—not counsel—then proceeds, after a full examination of all the proceedings, to decide whether the case is wholly frivolous. If it so finds it may grant counsel's request to withdraw and dismiss the appeal insofar as federal requirements are concerned, or proceed to a decision on the merits, if state law so requires. On the other hand, if it finds any of the legal points arguable on their merits (and therefore not frivolous) it must, prior to decision, afford the indigent the assistance of counsel to argue the appeal."

Dissenting Justice STEWART, joined by Black and Harlan, JJ., expressed puzzlement as to why an appointed lawyer who considers an appeal "wholly frivolous" should be required to file "a brief reference to anything in the record that might arguably support the appeal." "[I]f the record did present any such 'arguable' issues, the appeal would not be frivolous and counsel would not have filed a 'non-merit' letter in the first place."

See also *Suggs v. United States,* 391 F.2d 971 (D.C.Cir.1968) (Leventhal, J.), stressing that appointed counsel should not ask to withdraw "unless in the same circumstances he would insist on withdrawal if he had been retained. As a general rule, the court will be greatly aided if appointed counsel remains in a case, even though he may be subjectively unimpressed with the merits of the available points." Adequate representation of an indigent appellant should include personal interviews "if in the same circumstances [they would be considered] useful or desirable were [counsel] representing a private client. Ordinarily at least one interview by counsel would appear to be useful." [a]

a. Cf. *Commonwealth v. Moffett,* 418 N.E.2d 585 (Mass.1981), prohibiting appointed counsel from withdrawing solely on the ground that the appeal is frivolous even when she files an "*Anders* brief" demonstrating that all possible arguments in favor of her client lack any merit: "As long as counsel must research and prepare an advocate's brief, he or she may as well submit it

Notes and Questions

1. *Anders* has been sharply criticized by an assistant public defender who maintains that "it offers counsel the choice of filing a schizophrenic motion to withdraw (accompanied by a formal brief opposing the motion), or the alternative of writing the brief and not moving to withdraw. Human nature will force the selection of the latter alternative. [If tax-supported] groups of lawyers are forced to brief frivolous appeals, the people who will suffer the most are the indigent prisoners who have been *unjustly* convicted; they will languish in prison while the lawyers devote time and energy to hopeless causes on a first come-first served basis." Doherty, *Wolf! Wolf!—The Ramifications of Frivolous Appeals,* 59 J.Crim.L.C. & P.S. 1, 2 (1968).

2. The egalitarian pronouncement in *Suggs* that appointed counsel should not seek to withdraw "unless in the same circumstances he would insist on withdrawal if he had been retained" has been criticized on the ground that it "glosses over the possibility that the two situations may not be comparable. It is likely that the need to pay a lawyer's fee and expenses is some deterrent to frivolous criminal appeals.[a] Retained counsel can also withdraw more readily and informally—usually by substitution of other counsel—than can assigned counsel and further, can more readily avoid prejudicing the defendant by alerting the court, and in some circuits the Government, to the weaknesses of the case." Hermann, *Frivolous Criminal Appeals,* 47 N.Y.U.L.Rev. 701, 706 (1972). But compare the remarks of Judge Jack Day, *Proceedings of the National Conference on Standards for the Administration of Criminal Justice* (1972), 57 F.R.D. 303, 309 (1973): "I can never remember a case, really never, in a long life at the Bar, [where] if the money was there the appeal was so frivolous that the lawyer couldn't make it. I'm not suggesting nobody ever stood up and said grandly, 'Take away that $10,000; there's nothing to this case; I will not appeal it.' Maybe that happened, but maybe there are angels in the balcony, too. [Moreover,] there is always the probability that unless there's an excellent reason, beyond being busy, the lawyer at least ought to be told that he might try to present what the client wanted. He doesn't have to argue as his own points matters that are stupid or ridiculous, but at least there ought to be some effort made to present the point the client believes important." [b]

3. *Does an indigent defendant have a right to compel appointed counsel to argue all nonfrivolous points?* No, if counsel, "as a matter of professional judgment," decides not to do so, answered JONES v. BARNES, 463

for the purpose of an ordinary appeal. Even if the appeal is frivolous, less time and energy will be spent directly reviewing the case on the merits. If the appeal is not frivolous, [prohibiting] withdrawal would also obviate any need to substitute counsel to argue the appeal." See also *State v. McKenney,* 568 P.2d 1213 (Idaho 1977) *State v. Gates,* 466 S.W.2d 681 (Mo.1971). See generally Mendelson, *Frivolous Criminal Appeals: The Anders Brief or the Idaho Rule,* 19 Crim.L.Bull. 22 (1983).

a. A major reason for "hopeless appeals," observe Carrington, Meador & Rosenberg, *Justice on Appeal* 91–95 (1976), is that unlike the non-indigent convicted of crime, who has incentives *not* to appeal (he must balance benefit against cost), the indigent defendant is in "a no-lose situation, which provides every inducement to appeal, however forlorn the hope." In order to give the indigent "something to lose in the appeal similar to that which the non-indigent has," the authors propose establishing a fund, supplied out of tax money, that will cause the indigent to decide, with the aid of counsel, "whether there are any appealable issues that make the appeal worthwhile when balanced against the economic loss that will be involved." The indigent would be given an option: "he could purchase his appeal at public expense (as he can now) or he could elect instead to take a specified amount of money from the fund [at least several hundred dollars], either for himself [or for] persons he would designate [e.g., his spouse, children or bona fide creditors]. This plan would force the defendant to think about his case as a non-indigent must."

b. See also Carrington, et. al., fn. a supra at 77: "Several judges have reported to us the disheartening experience of reversing convictions after appointed counsel has filed an '*Anders*' brief explaining that his client's cause was entirely hopeless."

U.S. 745, 103 S.Ct. 3308, 77 L.Ed.2d 987 (1983).

The case arose as follows: After Barnes was convicted of robbery and assault in a New York state court, Melinger was appointed to represent him on appeal. Barnes sent Melinger a letter listing several issues he thought should be raised. Barnes also enclosed a *pro se* brief that he had written. Melinger rejected most of the suggested claims, stating they would be of no aid and that they could not be raised because not based on evidence in the record. Melinger's brief to the state appellate court and his argument before that court concentrated on three points. But he did not argue a number of points Barnes felt should be raised. Barnes' own *pro se* briefs, however, were filed with the court. When his convictions were affirmed, Barnes sought federal habeas corpus relief on the ground that he had been denied effective counsel on appeal.

The Court of Appeals for the Second Circuit granted relief, concluding that, under *Anders,* when an appellant insists that his attorney raise additional colorable points, the attorney "*must argue the additional points to the full extent of his professional ability.*" (emphasis added by the Supreme Court). Since *Anders* bars counsel from abandoning a nonfrivolous appeal, reasoned the Second Circuit, it also bars counsel from abandoning a nonfrivolous issue.[a] The Supreme Court, per BURGER, C.J., disagreed:

"[B]y promulgating a *per se* rule that the client, not the professional advocate, must be allowed to decide what issues are to be pressed, the Court of Appeals seriously undermines the ability of counsel to present the client's case in accord with counsel's professional evaluation. Experienced advocates [have long] emphasized the importance of winnowing out weaker arguments on appeal and focusing on one central issue if possible, or at most on a few key issues. * * * A brief that raises every colorable issue runs the risk of burying good arguments—those [that] 'go for the jugular.'[b]

"[F]ar from giving support to the new *per se* rule announced by the Court of Appeals, [*Anders*] is to the contrary. *Anders* recognized that the role of the advocate 'requires that he support his client's appeal to the best of his ability.' Here the appointed counsel did just that. For judges to second-guess reasonable professional judgments and impose on appointed counsel a duty to raise every 'colorable' claim suggested by a client would disserve the very goal of vigorous and effective advocacy that underlies *Anders.*"[c]

Dissenting Justice BRENNAN, joined by Marshall, J., relied heavily on *Faretta* and *Anders:*

"[To] satisfy the Constitution, counsel must function as an advocate for the defendant, as opposed to a friend of the court. Admittedly, the question in this case requires us to look beyond those clear guar-

a. The Second Circuit concluded that Melinger had failed to press at least two nonfrivolous issues. That Barnes had raised these issues in his own briefs did not cure the error, for a *pro se* brief is "no substitute for the advocacy of experienced counsel."

b. The Court recognized [fn. 6] that "the *ABA Standards for Criminal Appeals* [IV *A.B.A. Standards* § 21–3.2, discussed in the dissent] appear to indicate that counsel should accede to a particular contention on appeal." But it pointed out that "the *ABA Defense Function Standards* [I *A.B.A. Standards* § 4–5.2] provide that [except for the client's decision whether to enter a guilty plea, waive jury trial, and testify in his or her own behalf] "strategic and tactical decisions are the exclusive province of [defense counsel] after consultation with the client." In any event, concluded the Court, "the fact that the ABA may have chosen to recognize a given practice as desirable or appropriate does not mean that the practice is required by the Constitution."

c. Blackmun, J., who concurred in the judgment, agreed with the dissent that "as an *ethical* matter" an attorney should argue "all nonfrivolous claims upon which his client insists," but agreed with Court that this view was not a constitutional requirement. Although the Court did not reach the question, Justice Blackmun expressed the view that counsel's refusal to raise requested nonfrivolous constitutional claims on appeal must constitute "cause" for a petitioner's default within the meaning of *Wainwright v. Sykes,* Ch. 27, § 2.

antees. What is at issue here is the relationship between lawyer and client—who has ultimate authority to decide which nonfrivolous issues should be presented on appeal? I believe the right to 'the assistance of counsel' carries with it a right, personal to the defendant, to make that decision, against the advice of counsel if he chooses.

"If all the Sixth Amendment protected was the State's interest in substantial justice, it would not include such a right. However, in *Faretta,* we decisively rejected that view of the Constitution * * *. [And even] when appointed counsel believes an appeal has no merit, he must furnish his client a brief covering all arguable grounds for appeal so that the client may 'raise any points that he chooses.' *Anders.*

"The right to counsel as *Faretta* and *Anders* conceive it is not an all-or-nothing right, under which a defendant must choose between forgoing the assistance of counsel altogether or relinquishing control over every aspect of his case beyond its most basic structure (i.e., how to plead, whether to present a defense, whether to appeal). A defendant's interest in his case clearly extends to other matters. * * * He may want to press the argument that he is innocent, even if other stratagems are more likely to result in the dismissal of charges or in a reduction of punishment. He may want to insist on certain arguments for political reasons. He may want to protect third parties. This is just as true on appeal as at trial, and the proper role of counsel is to *assist* him in these efforts, insofar as that is possible consistent with the lawyer's conscience, the law, and his duties to the court.

"I find further support for my position in the legal profession's own conception of its proper role. The American Bar Association has taken the position that

> '[W]hen, in the estimate of counsel, the decision of the client to take an appeal, *or the client's decision to press a particular contention on appeal,* is incorrect[, c]ounsel has the professional duty to give to the client fully and forcefully an opinion concerning the case and its probable outcome. *Counsel's role, however, is to advise. The decision is made by the client.*' IV *A.B.A. Standards* § 21–3.2 (commentary) (emphasis added).

"The Court disregards this clear statement of how the profession defines the 'assistance of counsel' at the appellate stage of a criminal defense by referring to standards governing the allocation of authority between attorney and client at trial. [See fn. b supra.] In the course of a trial, however, decisions must often be made in a matter of hours, if not minutes or seconds. From the standpoint of effective administration of justice, the need to confer decisive authority on the attorney is paramount with regard to the hundreds of decisions that must be made quickly in the course of a trial. Decisions regarding which issues to press on appeal, in contrast, can and should be made more deliberately, in the course of deciding whether to appeal at all.

" * * * It should take little or no persuasion to get a wise client to understand that, if staying out of prison is what he values most, he should encourage his lawyer to raise only his two or three best arguments on appeal, and he should defer to his lawyer's advice as to which are the best arguments. The Constitution, however, does not require clients to be wise, and other policies should be weighed in the balance as well.

"[T]oday's ruling denigrates the values of individual autonomy and dignity central to many constitutional rights, especially those Fifth and Sixth Amendment rights that come into play in the criminal process. [U]ntil his conviction becomes final and he has had an opportunity to appeal, any restrictions on [a defendant's] individual autonomy and dignity should be limited to the minimum necessary to vindicate the State's interest in a speedy, effective prosecution. The role of the defense lawyer should be above all to function as the instrument and defender of the client's autonomy and dignity in all phases of the criminal process. * * *

"I cannot accept the notion that lawyers are one of the punishments a person receives merely for being accused of a crime. Clients, if they wish, are capable of making informed judgments about which issues to appeal, and when they exercise that prerogative their choices should be respected unless they would require lawyers to violate their consciences, the law, or their duties to the court."

4. *New counsel on appeal.* Should trial counsel be required to remain on the criminal defense for purposes of arguing the appeal? Presumably the trial counsel is already intimately familiar with the case and sometimes, at least, can start writing a brief even before a trial transcript is prepared. Thus, much time might be lost by a change in counsel. On the other hand, how, on appeal, can trial counsel be expected to explore the possibility of ineffective counsel? Moreover, might a good trial lawyer turn out to be a very poor appellate lawyer? See generally Carrington, et. al., fn. a supra, at 83–84 and authorities cited therein.

When an appellate court denies defense counsel's motion to be relieved because he is of the opinion that the appeal is frivolous, should the court continue present counsel's appointment or assign new counsel? See Hermann, Note 2 supra, at 714.

SYSTEMS OF DEFENSE REPRESENTATION

HAZEL B. KERPER—INTRODUCTION TO THE CRIMINAL JUSTICE SYSTEM

279–80 (Israel rev. 1979).[a]

Methods of Appointing Counsel. There are essentially three systems used for the appointment of counsel to assist the indigent: the assigned counsel system, the public defender system, and a mixed system which uses elements of both of the other systems. Under the assigned counsel system, an individual attorney is selected by the court (often by the magistrate) to represent a particular indigent defendant. * * * The public defender system relies upon a state-funded legal office which is, in many respects, the defense counterpart of the prosecutor's office. * * * The mixed system is basically an assigned counsel system except that some cases are assigned to individual attorneys and others are assigned to a defender office. * * *

There are advantages and disadvantages to each of the systems. A major difficulty of the assigned counsel system has been the misuse of the appointment process. Some judges have been known to appoint friends or political supporters who are not faring well in the practice of law and can use the additional business. Others have looked primarily to young, inexperienced lawyers who also are grateful for the additional income. In either instance, the lawyers may not be familiar with criminal practice. Some jurisdictions have avoided this difficulty by appointing counsel, largely in rotation, from a list of all of the criminal lawyers in the community. This system produces more experienced counsel, but not all are pleased to work for a lesser fee than they would receive in pri-

a. Reprinted by permission; copyright © 1979 by the West Publishing Co. See also Blumberg, *Criminal Justice* (1967); Casper, *American Criminal Justice: The Defendant's Perspective* (1972) (especially ch. 4); Carrington, Meador & Rosenberg, *Justice on Appeal* 79–81 (1976); Oaks, *The Criminal Justice Act in the Federal District Courts* (1969) (published by Subcommittee on Constitutional Rights of U.S. Senate Judiciary Committee); Comments, 50 Texas L.Rev. 60 (1971).

[See pp. 26–28 supra for a further description of the three systems of free representation.]

vate practice. The mixed system, by permitting appointment of the defender office to the less serious cases, tends to alleviate the burden on private counsel while still providing experienced private counsel in significant cases.

The public defender system offers the advantages of expertise and efficiency. The public defender's office, like the prosecutor's office, is solely engaged in criminal practice. Its staff can take advantage of their specialization and familiarity with local court practice. The office often has a sufficient caseload to hire investigators and other para-professionals to assist in preparing cases. Since they are full time government employees, paid a regular salary, public defender attorneys do not have the incentive of trying to quickly dispose of a case so as to earn a fee as rapidly as possible. On the other hand, it has been suggested that clients may view a public defender with distrust. They know that they are being prosecuted by the state and that their attorney is an employee of the state rather than a "private attorney." [b] Also, most defender offices carry huge caseloads, and some commentators suggest that defenders therefore are inclined to "trade off" their cases, encouraging guilty pleas in the hopeless cases so they will have more time for the stronger cases.[c] On the other hand, because they are handling criminal cases constantly, defenders

b. Consider Casper, *Criminal Courts: The Defendant's Perspective* 31, 81 (1978): "[T]here does not appear to be any difference between defendants' evaluations of assigned counsel versus public defenders. * * * [A]pparently the fact that both are paid by the state and not by the client leads to a general lumping of them into a single category as defendants see it.

"Public defenders—whether assigned counsel or employed by organizations devoted to defense of indigents—begin at a disadvantage. Clients come to such relationships with a chip on their shoulder, with a willingness to believe that things are not going to go particularly well. * * * [T]his client distrust presents a challenge both to the attorneys and to the criminal justice system as a whole.

"* * * [T]hose involved with criminal courts—whether attorneys, prosecutors, judges, probation officers, etc.—might begin with the recognition that this defendant distrust is not, in its fundamental sense, anything to be surprised about, nor does it indicate either a psychological quirk or a desire to blame others for the defendant's own misdeeds. Rather, [the] source of this distrust lies in part in a set of general values or beliefs about the operation of the marketplace that are deeply rooted in our culture.

"* * * Many defendants believe—rightly or wrongly—that privately retained attorneys are 'real' lawyers, and that appointed counsel are somehow inferior substitutes. This belief, I have suggested, stems from the fact that there is a marketplace in which one *can* 'buy' the services of attorneys. [Indigent] defendants realize that they cannot participate in it but believe that what is available there is somehow superior to what is 'given' them free of charge. Thus, those who serve as public defenders might well pay attention to making sure that they do not contribute to the notion that they are not 'real' lawyers. * * *

"Not only do defendants wonder whether public defenders are the 'real thing'; they are also made suspicious by the fact that their 'enemy'—the state—is not only paying the prosecutor and judge, but also paying 'their' lawyer. Thus the notion that the public defender is somewhere in the middle, or even on the state's side, arises."

c. Consider Skolnick, *Social Control in the Adversary System,* 11 J. Conflict Res. 52, 60–68 (1967): "[Critics such as noted defense lawyer Edward Bennett Williams and sociologist David Sudnow tend] to draw conclusions [about the public defender (PD)] that are partly false or misleading, because of a fundamental flaw in the assumptions underlying their analysis. This consists in taking given institutional categories—such as 'public defender'—at face value. A better understanding of the system is achieved, however, by considering the PD to represent a more general phenomenon, that of the 'cooperative' defense attorney. [To] the prosecutor, it matters not so much whether a defendant is being represented by a PD as whether the defense attorney, regardless of his institutional base, can be counted upon as a 'cooperative' defense attorney, a category that usually includes leading private defense attorneys and only some of the members of the PD's office. * * *

"[C]ritics of the public defender have tended to underestimate the quality of defense provided by the public defender, in part because they have failed to take into account the socioeconomic differences between the public defender's clients and those of the private defense attorney, and in part because they have neglected to make distinctions among personnel in the public defender's office.

"They also fail to make two important distinctions among private defense attorneys when they make implied comparisons between the PD as an institution and the class of private defense attorneys. Both Williams and Sudnow, for example, become accustomed to police practices and therefore may be more familiar with investigative deficiencies that might help their clients. Also, since the defenders automatically represent all indigent defendants, they often can begin representing defendants at an earlier stage than would be permitted under an assigned counsel system. Thus, a defender ordinarily will be available in the courtroom at the first appearance and can be of immediate assistance in such matters as the setting of bail. Under an assigned system, the appointment usually will not be made until after the first appearance.

seem to have as their model of the private defense attorney someone very much like Edward Bennett Williams. That is, when they compare the public defender as an institution with the private defense attorney as an institution, the comparison is with the most able private defense attorney. Thus, when interviewed regarding their opinion of the public defender, other criminal attorneys might indicate the top men in the office, and conclude that the public defender is 'just as good' as the private attorney, or they might consider a particular case that had been handled poorly by a member of the PD's staff, and conclude that the public defender was not so able.

"Second, critics tend to confound ability with 'hostility' when in fact the most able private defense attorneys, who operate on the local level, are no less 'partners' of the district attorney than the public defender. The problem of the adversary system is maintaining the ethic of individuality and challenge in a system where the professionals will see greater advantage in cooperativeness than in conflict."

*

Part Two

POLICE PRACTICES

Analysis

Chapter 4

SOME GENERAL REFLECTIONS ON THE POLICE, THE COURTS AND THE CRIMINAL PROCESS

HAZEL B. KERPER—INTRODUCTION TO THE CRIMINAL JUSTICE SYSTEM

415–20 (Israel rev. 1979).

Reprinted with permission of the publisher; copyright © 1979 by West Publishing Co. In addition to authorities cited infra, see 1 *A.B.A. Standards* Ch. 1 (Urban Police Function); Chevigny, *Police Power* (1969); K.C. Davis, *Police Discretion* (1975); H. Goldstein, *Policing a Free Society* (1977); Niederhoffer & Blumberg, *The Ambivalent Force* (2d ed. 1976) (esp. ch. 1); Reiss, *The Police and the Public* (1971); Silberman, *Criminal Violence, Criminal Justice* (1978) (esp. ch. 7); Skolnick, *Justice Without Trial* (1966); Skolnick, *The Police and the Urban Ghetto* (1968); Livermore, *Policing,* 55 Minn.L.Rev. 649 (1971); Symposium, *Police Practices,* 36 Law & Contemp.Prob. 445–588 (1971).

THE ROLE OF A POLICE OFFICER

The traditional image of police work—the image conveyed over the years in countless television dramas, comic strips, and newspaper articles—is that of the officer who outwits or outwrestles a dangerous criminal in the course of investigating serious crimes. The investigation of serious crime is, however, only one of many aspects of police work. Indeed, in a typical police department, a comparatively small portion of the department's total activity is spent on the investigation of major felonies. Far more time will be spent on general patrol or even on performing various social services. Police are responsible for directing traffic, issuing licenses, and handling various emergencies, both minor and major. If a city gas main springs a leak, the police cordon off the area, and go from house to house warning the residents. If a child's pet can't get down out of the tree, the police are called to help. Police aid the sick, free passengers from stalled elevators, and comfort lost children. They also are expected to perform an essentially social service function in dealing with various minor offenses. * * *

The detective division is the only major [police] division devoted primarily to the investigation of crimes. Where the offender is not apprehended in the act or immediately identified, the case ordinarily will be turned over to a detective unit for further investigation. * * * The detective division is a comparatively small division (commonly no more than one-tenth the size of the patrol division) operating with a caseload which experts invariably view as too heavy. Ordinarily, the key to a successful investigation by detectives is the presence of a "lead" pointing to a specific person. Without it, the chances of a successful investigation are very slim.[a]

The multiple functions of the police department tend, in several ways, to restrict the effectiveness of the police in the investigation of crime and the enforcement of the law. First, the resources available to the police must be spread over all of its responsibilities; police manpower cannot be concentrated solely on law enforcement functions. Second, the diversity of police responsibilities may require some compromise in the selection of officers. The qualities needed in criminal investigation are not necessarily the same qualities required to perform other police functions. It often is difficult, for example, to find people who will act effectively and courageously in apprehending a felon, yet have the ability to endure the long periods of monotony involved in routine patrol. Similarly, the social-service functions of the police may not always be compatible with the investigation functions. Officers servicing people in times of stress may develop an informality and flexibility in approach that is somewhat inconsistent with their adherence to the formalistic legal requirements often imposed in the area of criminal investigation.[b]

In various situations, the officer also may be torn between his social service and law enforcement responsibilities. Consider, for example, the role of an officer called to the scene of a family altercation. Is it the function of the officer to arrest the family member who obviously has committed an assault? If the officer makes an arrest, he may be destroying all possibilities of reconciliation. In some instances, the strong family ties make it likely that an arrest will cause the family members to redirect their anger toward the police officer, possibly leading to even more violence. Many argue that the proper police role in dealing with family disturbances is first to restore and maintain order and then to act as mediator. The test of success, they argue, is not whether the officer makes a successful arrest, but whether he can assist in restoring family harmony so as to avoid further violence.

In recent years, various proposals have been advanced to eliminate some of the multiple functions of police departments. These proposals seek to make the police department a streamlined law enforcement agency and not a community service organization. The proposals suggest that offenses such as drunkenness and drug abuse be handled in detoxification centers and drug abuse clinics, removing police responsibility for these offenders. It also is suggested that many domestic disputes be turned over to trained social workers, and that various existing offenses, such as homosexual conduct between consenting adults, be removed from the criminal code. Special traffic departments could be staffed with persons trained for traffic control but not trained for criminal investigation; only when a traffic offense required

a. See fn. g, p. 5 supra. Consider also the views of Patrick Murphy, the former head of the New York City, Detroit and District of Columbia police departments, in Murphy & Plate, *Commissioner: A View from the Top of American Law Enforcement* 185–87 (1977):

"The [detective] mystique was promoted by the popular entertainments of our time. The image of the detective working his leads, dusting for prints, pumping informants, hitting the case from every angle until it cracked, was a pretty picture, but it was also an unforgivably misleading one."

b. Because the police spend relatively so little time investigating and apprehending criminals, are police departments recruiting and promoting the wrong people? See Terris, *The Role of the Police,* The Annals, Nov. 1967, pp. 58, 67–69:

"The point is that the situations in which police officers most frequently find themselves do not require the expert aim of a marksman, the cunningness of a private eye, or the toughness of a stereotyped Irish policeman. Instead, they demand knowledge of human beings and the personal, as opposed to official, authority to influence people without the use or even threat of force. "These characteristics are not commonly found in police officers because police departments do not consider these values as paramount. As a result, persons with these abilities are not attracted to police work nor rewarded by promotion or other incentive if they happen to enter a department."

See also pp. 21–22 supra as to the selection and training of police officers.

more than routine investigation would the fully trained police officer be called. Parking meters could be monitored by metermaids, and school crossings could be protected by men and women hired for that service. Several of these proposals have been instituted, but the change in the role of the police has not been dramatic. Public drunkenness is no longer a crime in many jurisdictions, but it is still the police who pick up the drunks and take them to the detoxification centers rather than the jails.

Aside from reconciling its social service and law enforcement responsibilities, the police department must deal with various complexities presented by the law enforcement system alone. First among these is the obvious need to exercise discretion in determining the extent to which various criminal laws will be enforced. The officer must deal with the fact that we pass many laws that we do not expect to be enforced at all, or at least not to their full extent. The speed limit may be 70 miles an hour, but the officer is not supposed to give a ticket to the citizen doing 72 on the freeway. Gambling and prostitution are forbidden, but red light districts flourish and are tacitly accepted by the community. Stealing is illegal, but the police officer is not supposed to arrest the conventioner who takes a couple of towels from the motel.[c]

Where the offense involved is one that society clearly wants enforced, the police role is filled with other complexities. We do not simply tell the police to enforce the law in the most effective and efficient manner possible. We do not approach law enforcement as a "war against crime" with "no holds barred." The law enforcement officer must abide by legal restrictions designed to protect the rights of individuals. Although police officers are not lawyers and often must make quick decisions under tense and rapidly changing conditions, we require that they adhere to legal standards that sometimes are so unclear that they produce a 5–4 division among the justices of the Supreme Court. Some have suggested that the difficulties faced by the police in adhering to legal standards are partly of their own making. The National Advisory Commission has suggested, for example, that police would have far less difficulty in understanding and applying legal standards if they made an effort to formulate specific operational rules, relating to arrests, searches, and other activities, that are based upon the various judicial decisions. Even with such guidelines, however, there will be many areas in which police officers will be dealing with legal uncertainties.

The police are expected not only to adhere to the law, but to do so in a manner that does not alienate the community. They are expected to act with fairness, but without "throwing their weight around." They are given discretion to arrest or not arrest, to release on a citation or retain in custody, and to use or not use deadly force, but we expect them to exercise that discretion on the basis of sound judgment that gives no weight to personal

c. Consider Morris & Hawkins, *The Honest Politician's Guide to Crime Control* 91 (1970). Citing the "funnel effect" noted at p. 15 supra, the authors conclude that the police, through their exercise of discretion as to whether to arrest, "are deciding more largely than are the judges whether the criminal justice system should be invoked."

See also Wilson, *Varieties of Police Behavior* 8–9 (1968), observing that, although discretion is exercised in almost every public organization, "the police department has the special property [that] within it discretion increases as one moves *down* the hierarchy. [T]he lowest-ranking police officer—the patrolman—has the greatest discretion and thus his behavior is of greatest concern to the police administrator. The patrolman is almost solely in charge of enforcing those laws that are the least precise, most ambiguous (those dealing with disorderly conduct, for example), or whose application is most sensitive to the availability of scarce resources and the policies of the administrator (those governing traffic offenses, for example.)" Professor Wilson's characterization of different patrol "styles," as they relate to this use of police discretion, is summarized at fn. f, p. 19 supra.

prejudices. Persons are to be treated the same way without regard to their race, ethnic background, or general life style. Police officers are told that they must display the same even-handed approach in communities that welcome them and communities that resent them. The police are asked to maintain their calm while dealing with persons who are often angry, desperate, and violent. These are not easy tasks, and in many respects, they require personality traits that are not readily found in persons who fill the other image we have of the effective law enforcement officer—that of the aggressive, individualistic man of action who views law enforcement as more than "just another job." Indeed, very often, the officer is forced to deal with conflicting public images of the police officer's role as well as the competing values reflected in the governing law.

Over the years, the police have had their good periods and their bad periods in terms of public esteem. During the late 1960's, for example [when the police had their difficulties making marijuana "busts," responding to racial disturbances, and arresting persons engaged in civil disobedience], the public image of police hit a distinct low. It was, perhaps, the worst period for that image since the pre-civil war days when police jobs were distributed as part of political patronage. Many of the factors that have contributed to an adverse police image flow from specific police actions, but an unrealistic public view of the role and responsibility of the police has also been a contributing factor. Too frequently, antagonism toward specific laws is carried over to antagonism toward the police, although they have no special responsibility for those laws. In some instances, the police become the focus for a general discontent with the policies of the community. Police difficulties in the ghettoes, for example, arise in part from the fact that the police are the most visible symbol of the middle class society that ghetto residents view as largely ignoring their problems.

Similarly, the police image will almost certainly suffer during periods when crime appears to be rising rapidly and disrespect for the law appears widespread. Unfortunately, most people tend to overestimate the role of the police in crime prevention. The police do not create and they cannot resolve the social conditions that stimulate crime. They do not start, nor can they control, the dramatic social changes that so often result in widespread challenges to laws that fail to keep up with these changes. Yet, because the police are the most visible element of the criminal justice process, they tend to bear the responsibility for the difficulties suffered by the criminal justice system as a result of these factors.

Finally, the police image is subject to the high standards of responsibility that flow from the special role of police in our society. One of the factors that has plagued the police community over the years has been the occurrence of police scandals in many major cities. Bribery and misuse of authority for personal profit is not unique to the police profession. Corporate businessmen and union leaders also have had their share of scandals. But crime by people who are themselves engaged in the law enforcement process causes special public concern. It is viewed as undermining respect for the law itself. Similarly, misuse of authority to trample on individual rights causes far more concern when the misuse is by the police rather than by some other governmental agency. During the 1960's, when there was a great clamor for civilian review boards that could investigate citizen complaints against government officials, the focus was primarily on complaints against the police.[d] In a democratic society, there is special concern as to misuse of police

d. "The fights over the establishment [or repeal] of civilian police review boards [which occurred in the 1960s largely took] the form of a struggle between the liberal political forces which favor creating such checks over the power of police departments to discipline their own memauthority because only the police have such direct control over individual liberty. While the police are our official protectors, they also are the possessors of the kind of authority as to which there is the greatest fear of misuse.

FRANCIS A. ALLEN—THE JUDICIAL QUEST FOR PENAL JUSTICE: THE WARREN COURT AND THE CRIMINAL CASES

1975 U.Ill.L.F. 518, 521–25.

[T]he performance of the Warren Court in the criminal cases has both prologue and epilogue. * * * Although the origins of a complex body of constitutional doctrine can rarely be fully identified, for practical purposes the modern law of constitutional criminal procedure begins, not in 1953 when the Warren judicial tenure commenced or even when the Warren Court began to speak in its own distinctive tones, but rather in 1932 with the decision in the great case of *Powell v. Alabama.* In *Powell* the Court for the first time interpreted the due process clause of the fourteenth amendment to include rights of counsel in state criminal proceedings.

One of the intriguing questions of our constitutional history is why the Court in the 1930's, under the aegis of the due process clause, first undertook to impose limitations on state power in the administration of criminal justice. The *Powell* case, after all, was decided more than 60 years after the fourteenth amendment became part of the Constitution. * * *

The reasons for the Court's new conception of the uses of the due process clause as it emerged in *Powell* and in scores of cases that followed have invited speculation. If the question is put more broadly, however, the modern concern with problems of criminal justice appears natural and even inevitable. A crisis in freedom has afflicted western societies since the First World War, and anxiety about the proper containment of the public force exerted through systems of criminal justice has been widely felt. The *Powell* case was decided in a period when totalitarian regimes were forming in western Europe. It is an interesting coincidence that *Powell v. Alabama* was decided within a few months of Hitler's rise to power in Germany. The European dictatorships, once installed, taught graphic lessons in the uses of the institutions of criminal justice as instrumentalities for the systematic destruction of political values upon which free societies rest. The impact of these events was felt in the United States. One can safely assume that some public officials, including judges, were led to view the regulation of criminal justice functions not as a matter of local concern, but rather as part of the essential strategy of freedom.

Since the Second World War the involvement of criminal justice in the central concerns of American life has increased rather than abated. To a remarkable degree the issues that have divided and agi-

bers and the conservatives who oppose these. In the best-publicized case, [the 1966 New York City referendum], the ideological lineup was clearcut." Lipset, *Why Cops Hate Liberals—and Vice Versa,* The Atlantic, Mar. 1969, pp. 76, 80.

Civilian review boards never gained wide acceptance. Presently complaints against the police commonly are subject to a police review board or a board composed of representatives of higher-level city officials. See National Advisory Commission on Criminal Justice Standards and Goals, *Report on Police* 469–91 (1973); Quick, *Attitudinal Aspects of Police Compliance with Procedural Due Process,* 6 Am.J.Crim.L. 25, 45 (1978).

For an extensive discussion of efforts to establish efficient and responsive review boards in New York and Philadelphia—and the difficulty, generally, of establishing a review mechanism acceptable to both the community and the police involved—see Hudson, *Police Review Boards and Police Accountability,* 36 Law & Contemp.Prob. 515 (1971). For a discussion of "additional defects," aside from their unpopularity with the police and large segments of the public, "that argue against [the] viability" of civilian review boards, see Quick, supra, at 45–46. But see L.B. Schwartz & S. Goldstein, *Law Enforcement Handbook* 56–58 (2d ed.1980).

tated us in the past two decades have assumed their most concrete forms and have appeared in sharpest focus within the context of the criminal law and its applications. Fundamental questions about the nature of political obligation, fidelity to law, and the emancipation of conscience from legal restraints reappeared in the 1960's. These questions were made inescapable by criminal prosecutions of those who set themselves against the Viet Nam War or involved themselves in racial militancy. Closely related to these issues are the allegations of inequalities and inequities in American society. These charges have not been confined to the criminal law, but, on the contrary, have encompassed nearly every aspect of our social arrangements. But charges of inequality possess an even sharper bite when they are hurled at a system that employs as its sanctions the deprivation of property, of liberty, and, on occasion, of life itself.

Finally, the administration of criminal justice has held a place of central concern in the modern world because of the insecurity and apprehensions produced by the widespread conviction that serious crime is increasing in this country. We have again seen that fears of crime and of the collapse of public order are a powerful political dynamic in American society, a perception that appears to have sometimes eluded practitioners of liberal politics.

An argument can thus be stated for the importance of the criminal justice process in the 20th century world. Less clear, however, is the reason why problems of regulating the uses of governmental power in the criminal process have become so predominantly a matter of judicial concern in the United States. In no other western society has the regulation of police and prosecutorial officials, as well as the functioning of the courts, been understood in comparable degree to be a function of judges. In no other nation has so large and intricate a corpus of constitutional doctrine emerged relating to the functioning of criminal justice as that created or influenced by the Supreme Court of the United States. The reasons surely do not reside in any peculiar qualifications of American judges or any unusual adaptability of American courts for the task, especially that part of the task that relates to the oversight of nonjudicial officers performing official functions outside of Court. On the contrary, the courts operate under severe and inherent limitations of means and resources for the task. One devising institutions for Utopia would not likely delegate so large a responsibility for maintaining the integrity of the criminal justice process to the courts. * * * One is tempted to say that the Court has taken the initiative in regulating the exercise of government power in systems of criminal justice because of an American propensity to delegate to courts the resolution of great public issues that are agitating society at any particular moment. Given the breadth and adaptability of the great moral imperatives of our Constitution such as due process of law and the equal protection of the laws, few significant public issues cannot be restated in a form apparently consistent with constitutional adjudication. This phenomenon was noted by de Tocqueville almost a century and one half ago and was once again demonstrated in the Watergate crisis.

Part of the reason for the high degree of judicial involvement in the regulation of the criminal process, however, may stem from certain aspects of the criminal justice system in the United States. One of the outstanding characteristics of American criminal justice is the remarkable fragmentation of the system.[a] In a large metropolitan area as many as 100 separate police systems operate, each largely independent of the other. Although the powers of regulation over local prosecution possessed by the state attorney general vary from

a. See pp. 16–17 and 21–22 supra, discussing the fragmentation of police and prosecutor agencies, and pp. 36–37 supra, discussing the impact of fragmentation upon police and prosecutor "efficiency."

jurisdiction to jurisdiction, the local prosecutor is typically a publicly elected official with an independent power base who is consequently able to resist efforts at meaningful scrutiny and direction from above. In these circumstances no state prosecutory policy exists, except as may accidentally arise out of the like-mindedness of the officials involved. In addition, some jurisdictions have failed to establish centralized supervision of local jails and lockups even though the interests of public health and safety require it. Admittedly, local police forces are expected to be accountable to the agencies of local government that create and maintain them. In reality, however, one of the striking characteristics of American police agencies, both at the state and federal level, is the degree to which they have succeeded at eluding genuine accountability to civil authority. Indeed, the upper levels of the police hierarchy itself are often unable to maintain effective supervision over the lower levels.

All of this is in sharp contrast to the situation existing in some countries. The ministry of justice, with its broad powers of supervision and coordination, is familiar to continental nations, but is unknown in the United States. Nothing comparable to the Home Secretary in Great Britain exists here.[33] These institutions may, of course, be wholly inappropriate to American conditions. Some persons have assumed that the fragmentation of American law enforcement avoids the threat to political liberty implicit in a centralized system of internal police. Whether we are in fact free of these dangers is less clear in the light of post-Watergate inquiries into the operations of national police and intelligence agencies. Apart from that controversy, the salient fact remains that in the United States no person or agencies possess political or administrative responsibility for the decency and efficiency of criminal justice as a whole. We have not been ingenious in devising institutions that subject criminal justice functions to scrutiny and test. This failure to devise alternative institutions charged with such responsibilities explains in part the willingness of American courts to enter these areas. The same fact helps explain the particular forms that judicial intervention has taken.

33. Great Britain's Home Secretary is a cabinet officer with broad responsibilities over law enforcement functions. The Secretary's role nevertheless allows for considerable local autonomy and initiative. * * *

HERBERT L. PACKER—THE COURTS, THE POLICE AND THE REST OF US

57 J.Crim.L.C. & P.S. 238, 239 (1966).

Reprinted by special permission of the Journal of Criminal Law, Criminology and Police Science; copyright © 1966 by the Northwestern University School of Law. See also Packer, *The Limits of the Criminal Sanction* 239–46 (1968).

As I have elaborated elsewhere,[6] the kind of criminal process that we have is profoundly affected by a series of competing value choices which, consciously or unconsciously, serve to resolve tensions that arise in the system. These values represent polar extremes which, in real life, are subject to almost infinite modulation and compromise. But the extremes can be identified. The choice, basically, is between what I have termed the Crime Control and the Due Process models. The Crime Control model see the efficient, expeditious and reliable screening and disposition of persons suspected of crime as the central value to be served by the criminal process. The Due Process model sees that function as limited by and subordinate to the maintenance of the dignity and autonomy of the individual. The Crime Control model is administrative and managerial; the Due Process model is adversary and judicial. The Crime Control model may be analogized to an assembly line, the Due Process model to an obstacle course.[a]

6. Packer, *Two Models of the Criminal Process,* 118 U.Pa.L.Rev. 1–68 (1964).

a. But cf. Griffiths, *Ideology in Criminal Procedure,* or *A Third "Model" of the Criminal Process,* 79 Yale L.J. 359 (1970), for the view that

What we have at work today is a situation in which the criminal process as it actually operates in the large majority of cases probably approximates fairly closely the dictates of the Crime Control model. The real-world criminal process tends to be far more administrative and managerial than it does adversary and judicial. Yet, the officially prescribed norms for the criminal process, as laid down primarily by the Supreme Court, are rapidly providing a view that looks more and more like the Due Process model.[b] This development [has] been in the direction of "judicializing" each stage of the criminal process, of enhancing the capacity of the accused to challenge the operation of the process, and of equalizing the capacity of all persons to avail themselves of the opportunity for challenge so created.

The nature of the trend is obvious enough. What has brought it about and how durable is it? A definitive answer to this question would comprehend a large slice of the history of our times, but I should like to venture a few tentative and speculative observations on the point. Let us start with the Supreme Court itself. To some extent, the Court's decisions are not simply evidence of the trend but are in themselves a contributor to it. Typically, the Court's intervention in any given phase of the criminal process has started with a highly particularistic decision dealing on a narrow basis with the facts of a particularly flagrant or shocking case brought before it. That was true of the first right to counsel case, *Powell v. Alabama,* and it was true also of the first confession case, *Brown v. Mississippi.* The confession cases are particularly instructive on this issue. For approximately twenty years following *Brown v. Mississippi,* a number of confession cases came before the court. As the standards it sought to lay down emerged, they placed great emphasis on the "special circumstances" of the cases. A given confession was deemed involuntary because of the defendant's personal characteristics—illiterate, a low intelligence, immature, a member of a disadvantaged minority group—or because of coercive forces at work in the interrogation process, or because of some conbination of these factors. In those decisions, the Court tried, among other things, to influence police behavior by dealing, in its traditional way, with the facts of the specific case before it. But the gap between aspiration and reality proved too great to bridge in the court's traditional way. And so, the movement has been to ever increasing generality of statement: from *this* confession was coerced for the following par-

Professor Packer "has given us only one 'Model'—the Battle Model." Starting from "an assumption of reconcilable—even mutually supportive—interests, a state of love," Professor Griffiths offers "a 'Family Model' of the criminal process," in which perspective "much of the special vocabulary and underlying assumptions which Packer (reflecting all of us, rather well, I think) uses in discussing the criminal process, would undoubtedly seem cramped, or distorted, or simply irrelevant." For criticism of both the Packer and Griffiths "Models" and the presentation of still another approach, see Duffee & O'Leary, *Models of Correction: An Entry in the Packer-Griffiths Debate,* 7 Crim.L.Bull. 329 (1971).

b. Consider Blumberg, *Criminal Justice: Issues and Ironies* 70–71 (2d ed. 1979): "[T]he police officer's sense of frustration is ultimately produced by the fact that he is held to a due process standard by agencies that review his work, whereas the crime control model is demanded by his superiors because of the cross-pressures of production norms and political demands. * * * Although he is unable to control the input in his work situation, he is nevertheless held responsible for any of the negative features of the end product of the criminal process. He thereby becomes a suitable target of displaced hostility on the part of the public he serves because of their chronic dissatisfaction with ever-increasing crime rates which are often erroneously attributed to defects in policing and law enforcement."

See also Quick, *Attitudinal Aspects of Police Compliance with Procedural Due Process,* 6 Am.J. Crim.L. 25, 26–27 (1978): "[The police officer's] perception of himself as a crime-fighting craftsman is outwardly manifested by a general hostility toward concepts of due process and those institutions that are identified with securing individual rights—the courts and the liberal elements of society. The policeman identifies the liberal voices as his natural adversaries because they seek to impose checks upon his official power."

ticularistic reasons unique to this case, to *all* confessions are bad when they are obtained from an arrestee who has not been promptly brought before a magistrate, as in the famous *Mallory* rule [p. 525 infra] announced for the federal criminal courts in 1957. *Escobedo* [p. 529 infra] may perhaps turn out to mark the beginning of a similar line of generalized development for the state courts.[c] The great criminal procedure decisions of the last few years can all be regarded as exemplifying this movement toward increasingly generalized statement, sparked by the court's despair over the prospect of significantly affecting police practices through its more traditional activity. The court has sensed a lawmaking vacuum into which, rightly or wrongly, it has seen itself as having to rush. *Mapp v. Ohio,* in extending the exclusionary rule on unreasonable searches and seizures to the state courts, was explicitly based on the proposition that no other presently available means of control held out any hope for deterring police disregard for the dictates of the Fourth Amendment (which had been held applicable to the states in *Wolf v. Colorado,* in 1949). *Gideon* substituted a blanket rule on right to counsel explicitly because the earlier case-by-case approach of *Betts v. Brady* had failed to bring about universal compliance with what the court perceived as needed reform in the provision of counsel to indigent defendants.

Moves of this sort by the Supreme Court are, in my view, moves of desperation. Nobody else is exerting control over the law enforcement process, so the justices think that they must. But they can do so, in state cases, at any rate, only in the discharge of their duty to construe the Constitution in cases that come before them. And so, the rules of the criminal process, which ought to be the subject of flexible inquiry and adjustment by lawmaking bodies having the institutional capacity to deal with them, are evolved through a process that its warmest defenders recognize as to some extent awkward and inept: the rules become "constitutionalized." The Bill of Rights becomes, as Judge Henry Friendly's gibe has it, a code of criminal procedure.[d]

It is easy enough to poke holes in, not to say fun at, this development. But what it represents is an increased consciousness that our criminal process in its everyday functioning does not live up to minimum standards of fairness or, for that matter, of efficiency. That increased consciousness comes from a number of sources, of which I shall mention only two.

Perhaps the most powerful propellant of the trend toward the Due Process Model has been provided by the Negro's struggle for his civil rights and the response to that struggle by law enforcement in the Southern states—as well, it needs to be said, by law enforcement in some Northern cities. What we have seen in the South is the perversion of the criminal process into an instrument of official oppression. The discretion which, we are reminded so often, is essential to the healthy operation of law enforcement agencies has been repeatedly abused in the South: by police, by prosecutors, by judges and juries. * * * We have had many reminders from abroad that law enforcement may be used for evil as well as for beneficent purposes; but the experience in the South during the last decade has driven home the lesson that law enforcement unchecked by law is tyrannous. * * *

As we all know, the Negro's plight is also, and at least as importantly, a problem of urban poverty in the large cities of the North and West. Our heightened national consciousness about the problems of urban poverty likewise contribute to and sustain the trend in the direction of the Due Process model. The urban Negro's plight is joined to that of the Puerto Rican, the Mexican-American, and other sub-

c. This paper was delivered prior to the decision in *Miranda,* p. 542 infra.

d. Friendly, *The Bill of Rights as a Code of Criminal Procedure,* 53 Calif.L.Rev. 929 (1965).

merged groups. Law enforcement may not be a cause of social injustice, but it must reckon with the consequences of social injustice. It is broadly recognized that the urban poor, and particularly those who belong to minority groups, provide most of the raw material for the criminal process. As the idea develops and is promoted by governmental programs that the legal rights of the poor require special attention, politically and economically muscular pressure for reforms in the criminal process continues to make itself felt.

It is far from clear that this powerful trend is going to continue at anything like the velocity that it has exhibited in the past few years. * * * However, the trend may well be in its broad outlines irreversible, if for no other reason than that once the problems have become visible, it is unlikely that the national sense of injustice, (to borrow Edmond Cahn's phrase), whether manifested by the Supreme Court or by other agencies of government, will be easily turned off.

FRANCIS A. ALLEN—THE JUDICIAL QUEST FOR PENAL JUSTICE: THE WARREN COURT AND THE CRIMINAL CASES

1975 U.Ill.L.F. 518, 525–42.

Reprinted with permission of the publisher; copyright © 1975 by the Board of Trustees of the University of Illinois. See also Graham, *The Self-Inflicted Wound* (1970); Levy, *Against the Law* (1974); Chase, *The Burger Court, the Individual and the Criminal Process: Directions and Misdirections,* 52 N.Y.U.L.Rev. 518 (1977); Elson, *Balancing Costs in Constitutional Construction: The Burger Court's Expansive New Approach,* 17 Am.Crim.L.Rev. 160 (1979); Rosen, *Contemporary Winds and Currents in Criminal Law with Special Reference to Constitutional Criminal Procedure: A Defense and Appreciation,* 27 Md.L.Rev. 103 (1967).

For a good sampling of the mixed reaction to the Warren Court's "revolution" in American criminal procedure, compare Friendly, *The Bill of Rights as a Code of Criminal Procedure,* 53 Calif.L.Rev. 929 (1965) with Pye, *The Warren Court and Criminal Procedure,* 67 Mich.L.Rev. 249 (1968). For differing views on the Burger Court's "counter-revolution" in criminal procedure, compare Israel, *Criminal Procedure, The Burger Court, and the Legacy of the Warren Court,* 75 Mich.L.Rev. 1319 (1977); Saltzburg, *The Flow and Ebb of Constitutional Criminal Procedure in the Warren and Burger Courts,* 69 Geo.L.J. 151 (1980); and Kamisar, *The Warren Court (Was It Really So Defense Minded?), the Burger Court (Is It Really So Prosecution-Oriented?), and Police Investigatory Practices,* in The Burger Court: The Counter-Revolution that Wasn't 62 (Blasi ed. 1983) with Arenella, *Rethinking the Functions of Criminal Procedure: The Warren and Burger Courts' Competing Ideologies,* 72 Geo.L.J. 185 (1983) and the comments of Paul Bender and David Rudovsky in *Our Endangered Rights* (Dorsen ed. 1984) at 203–18, 243–46.

* * * The history of the Warren Court may be taken as a case study of a court that for a season determined to employ its judicial resources in an effort to alter significantly the nature of American criminal justice in the interest of a larger realization of the constitutional ideal of liberty under the law. So viewed, this is surely a history worthy of attention. * * *

The heart of the problem for judicial activism in the criminal area is not simply that of effecting an expansion of doctrine relating to the rights and immunities of persons against whom the state proceeds. The problem also encompasses the question of how, given the limitations of judicial remedies and devices, judicial power may be effectively exerted to achieve the desired objectives. Stated more graphically: how can a court, however exalted its authority, that stands at the apex of a complex judicial structure exercise its powers so as to achieve a genuine impact on the day-by-day behavior of police, prosecutory, judicial, and correctional officials throughout a nation of two hundred million inhabitants? Anyone who studies carefully the judicial expressions of the Warren Court in the criminal cases comes to the realization that this concern with implementation is never far below the surface. One is unlikely to understand the phenomenon of the Warren Court until he perceives that the persistent motive of the

Court is not only to declare the rights of persons confronting state power in the criminal arena, but also to enlarge the exercise of its judicial authority in such fashion as most likely to render those declarations effective. This is surely not to say that concern with remedies and implementation is peculiar to fourteenth amendment law relating to criminal justice or even to constitutional adjudication generally. Such concerns impinge upon and condition judicial law-making whenever it occurs. Such problems assumed particularly large proportions for the Court, however, as it considered its role in the criminal cases during the early years of the 1960's and before. * * *

Perhaps the most interesting influence of the exigencies of judicial supervision in criminal cases on the kinds of judicial law-making in which the Court is engaged is revealed in the tendency of the Court to turn to broad, legislative-like directives, sometimes called "flat" or "per se" rules. Such a rule is one in which a given fact, circumstances, or a limited set of facts is taken as the requisite ground for reversal in a criminal case or the barring of evidence from court. These rules avoid or lessen the occasions that require consideration of the "totality of the circumstances" presented by the record and the concomitant determination whether, on balance, the defendant received a fair trial in the particular case. * * * [S]uch rules give relatively certain guidance to the lower courts, and thus avoid the confusions and uncertainties associated with precedents that weigh a multitude of factors, some of which may be unique to the particular case at hand. Second, such rules are applicable to a great mass of cases at the trial court levels without direct involvement of the Supreme Court, thereby minimizing the consequences of the Court's lack of time and resources to adjudicate more than the smallest fraction of criminal cases presenting constitutional issues. Justice Black was merely articulating long-held concerns when, in the oral argument of the *Miranda* case, he said: "[I]f you are going to determine [the admissibility of the confession] each time on the circumstances . . . [if] the Court will take them one by one . . . it is more than we are capable of doing." * * *

The reasons for the loss of impetus by the Warren Court in the closing years of the Chief Justice's tenure are worth a moment's speculation. Sooner or later, of course, a decline in the rate of innovation was inevitable. Throughout the Court's expansionist phase substantial opposition existed within the Court to the course of decisions. Some members opposed most of the principal holdings in this era, and few important cases were decided without sharp dissent. *Gideon* is one conspicuous exception. A determined minority on the Court, even when it does not prevail, may succeed in reducing the momentum of the majority. There is another possibility considerably more conjectural than the first. Perhaps the late history of the Warren Court suggests that something inherent in the judicial process or the traditions of court adjudication renders it difficult for a court to formulate and to adhere to broad categorical rules that demand the judge to ignore apparently substantial social costs in the form of frustrations of law enforcement in the particular cases under scrutiny. Assurances that the categorical rules do by and large constitute a proper restraint on police activity may often appear remote, speculative, and insufficient to justify the losses sustained in the concrete case.

But surely the most fundamental reasons for the Court's loss of impetus lies in the social and political context of the Court in the late 1960's.[106] That period was a time of social upheaval, violence in the ghettos, and disorder on the campuses. Fears of the breakdown of public order were widespread. Inevitably, the issue of

106. Graham, *The Self-Inflicted Wound* (1970).

law and order was politically exploited. In the presidential campaign of 1968 the bewildering problems of crime in the United States were represented simply as a war between the "peace forces" and the "criminal forces." The decision in *Miranda* evoked a chorus of criticism of the Court, ranging from the excited to the psychotic.[108] Congress responded with the Omnibus Crime Control and Safe Streets Act of 1968,[109] some provisions of which were obviously retaliatory. These events combined to create an atmosphere that, to say the least, was unfavorable to the continued vitality of the Warren Court's mission in criminal cases.

How is the record of the Warren Court in the criminal cases to be appraised? What is its continuing influence likely to be? One cannot give final answers to these questions because the impact of that Court is part of a still evolving history. Undoubtedly it was an important phenomenon. Whatever diversions or retreats from the precedents of the Warren era are achieved by the Burger Court or future Courts, one can be sure that the status quo ante will not be restored. By reason of what the Warren Court said and did, we now perceive as problems what too often were not seen as problems before. This is the dynamic of change, and that fact may well be more significant than many of the solutions proposed by the Warren Court. The critique of American criminal justice implicit in the opinions of the Warren era was essentially ethical. Barring cataclysmic upheavals in American life even more devastating than those we anticipate, one expects this ethical insight to persist and to provide guidance in the years ahead.

It is important, however, not to canonize the Warren Court and not to regard its works as sacrosanct. It was often wrong and wrongheaded. It frequently failed to articulate its decisions adequately and sometimes appeared to doubt the importance of adequate articulation. It was frequently self-righteous and intolerant of competing considerations. At times it flouted the Court conventions when adherence to them would have cost little and might have marshalled greater support for the innovations it was effecting.[111] Strangely enough, one of the most serious criticisms of the Court is that often, having embarked upon a problem it did not go far enough. This was true not only in *Miranda*. The Warren Court failed to realize its opportunity to place the law of entrapment on a more satisfactory footing and left the way open for the Burger Court to halt promising developments in the Courts of Appeals that might well have led to more reasonable outcomes.[112] Having struggled its way to a new and more useful approach to the fourth amendment in *Katz v. United States* [p. 237 infra], it failed to pursue the implications of its insight. Sometimes its conflicting motivations appeared paradoxical. In the same period that it was pursuing innovations in the area of pretrial interrogation that many warned were threatening the effectiveness of law enforcement, it stubbornly defended in the name of law enforcement the use of undercover agents and resisted efforts to restrict and regulate their activities.[b]

* * * The Warren Court enjoyed its greatest successes when it advanced solutions that were supported by a broad ethical consensus, as in cases involving the right of impoverished defendants to coun-

108. Id. at 184–93; Harris, *The Fear of Crime* 22–29 (1969). Among the other important factors contributing to the temper of the times was undoubtedly the assassination of Robert Kennedy in the spring of 1968.

109. [See provisions of the Act set forth at pp. 573 and 668 infra.]

111. Thus, in *Mapp*, the Court overruled *Wolf*, even though the latter case was not cited in the appellant's brief. Justice Harlan charged that the majority had "simply 'reached out' " to obtain their result.

112. See *United States v. Russell* (1973) [p. 494 infra]; *Sherman v. United States* (1958) [p. 481 infra].

b. See the *Lopez, Lewis and Hoffa* cases, all discussed in Ch. 6, infra.

sel in the courtroom. When it moved beyond this consensus in the areas of police behavior it was confronted by resistance that was real and seriously constricting. The opposition to *Miranda* represented more than an inflamed and deluded public opinion. The heart of the matter was identified by Justice White when in his dissent he said: "I see nothing wrong or immoral [in] the police's asking a suspect . . . whether or not he killed his wife. . . ." However incomplete this statement of the underlying ethical issue may be, Justice White's proposition clearly expressed the convictions of a significant fraction of the population.

The central problem of the Warren Court's activism in the criminal area was not that it threatened serious abuses of power by politically irresponsible judges. Rather, it was simply that, despite the Court's ingenious, persistent, and, some may feel, heroic efforts to overcome the inherent limitations of judicial power, the Court attempted more than it could possibly achieve. Moreover, the attempt incurred costs. The Court was unable to see the problems of criminal justice in their full complexity. While concentrating on the vindication of individual rights, the Court was unable to offer any contributions to the staggering problems created for the system of criminal justice by the weight of numbers—both numbers of crimes and numbers of persons processed by the system. Indeed, much of what it did exacerbated those problems. This is not to suggest that the Warren Court should have ignored the issues of rights and immunities that confronted it pending administrative housekeeping. Rather, it suggests that until we simultaneously attack the full range of problems afflicting criminal justice, the outcome of our efforts is likely to be partial and unsatisfactory. This, in turn, suggests the necessity of a greater role for legislative and administrative expertise in the approach to these issues.

In the final analysis, the Court will not succeed unless it stimulates a constructive response from the localities and the other branches of government. To a degree frequently overlooked, the Warren Court and those that immediately preceded it produced that response. Legislatures have enacted scores of innovations relating to criminal and juvenile justice. Court rules adopted in the states often responded even more clearly and rapidly to the Court's new directions. Private professional groups like the American Law Institute,[117] the American Bar Association,[118] and the National Commissioners on Uniform State Laws [119] are providing invaluable impetus to legislative reform. The Court has stimulated by far the larger part of this activity. The prospects of a continuing impact of the Warren Court on our institutions depends most importantly on the continuation and enlargement of similar efforts.

Nevertheless, the slowness and perversity of legislative response to the problems of criminal justice is often disheartening. The attitudes revealed by Congress in the Omnibus Crime Control Bill of 1968 are illustrative. One example will suffice. In the closing years of the Warren tenure the Court decided several cases extending the right to counsel to police line-up identification procedures. The Court was wholly right in recognizing the problem of misidentification as a central one in the administration of criminal justice. The problem here is not that of releasing an obviously guilty defendant because of the system's failure to respect his rights. On the contrary, the problem is one of convicting the innocent. Studies reveal that misidentification may well be the greatest peril confronting the innocent person caught up in the criminal process. What-

117. A.L.I., *A Model Code of Pre-Arraignment Procedure* (1975).

118. A.B.A., *Standards for Criminal Justice* (1973).

119. *Uniform Rules of Criminal Procedure* (1974).

ever the values of the right to counsel in these procedures—and opinions differ—no one is likely to regard it as a sufficient solution to these problems. Alternative devices, possibly including the removal of identification procedures entirely from the police and placing them in the hands of an expert and neutral administrative agency, are required. Congress' rejection of the Court's solution is not surprising. The fact that it contented itself with simply attempting a legislative repeal of the Court's decision without offering anything to deal with the critical problem the Court had identified is deplorable. Yet this is what occurred.[123]

A new allocation of responsibilities is required. The role of the Court will remain critical. It has shown its capacity to identify and dramatize problems in criminal justice administration; this role is an essential catalyst for reform. The Court will have to make the ultimate decisions on the constitutional validity of the solutions devised. Nevertheless, its role is better adapted to review than to initiation. If categorical rules for the system are needed, it is better that other institutions formulate most rules. * * *

ANTHONY G. AMSTERDAM—THE SUPREME COURT AND THE RIGHTS OF SUSPECTS IN CRIMINAL CASES

45 N.Y.U.L.Rev. 785–94, 810–14 (1970), reprinted in *The Rights of Americans* 401 (Dorsen ed. 1971).

 In addition to authorities cited infra, see also I *A.B.A. Standards* Ch. 1 (Urban Police Function); Davis, *Discretionary Justice: A Preliminary Inquiry* (1969); Davis, *Police Discretion* (1975) (study of police discretion in selective enforcement based on Chicago police practices); H. Goldstein, *Police Policy Formulation: A Proposal for Improving Police Performance,* 65 Mich. L.Rev. 1123 (1967); LaFave & Remington, *Controlling the Police: The Judge's Role in Making and Reviewing Enforcement Decisions,* 63 Mich. L.Rev. 987 (1965); Quinn, *The Effect of Police Rulemaking on the Scope of Fourth Amendment Rights,* 52 J.Urban Law 25 (1974).

The impression is widespread that decisions of the Supreme Court of the United States during the past decade have vastly enlarged the rights of criminal suspects and defendants. That impression is not wholly unfounded, but the broad form in which it is generally entertained ignores very significant limitations upon what the Supreme Court can do, and what it has in fact done, to create and enforce such rights. * * *

According to Pär Lagerkvist, the role of the Pythia or priestess of the Oracle at Delphi was of incomparable grandeur and futility. This young maiden was periodically lashed to a tripod above a noisome abyss, where her god dwelt and from which nauseating odors rose and assaulted her. There, the god entered her body and soul, so that she thrashed madly and uttered inspired, incomprehensible cries. The cries were interpreted by the corps of professional priests of the Oracle, and their interpretations were, of course, for mere mortals the words of the god. The Pythia experienced incalculable ecstasy and degradation; she was viewed with utmost reverence and abhorrence; to her every utterance, enormous importance attached; but, from the practical point of view, what she said did not matter much.

On its tripod atop the system of American criminal justice, the Supreme Court of the United States performs in remarkably Pythian fashion. Occasional ill-smelling cases are wafted up to it by the fortuities of litigation, evoking its inspired and spasmodic reaction. Neither the records nor the issues presented by these cases give the Court a comprehensive view—or even a reliably representative view—of the doings in the dark pit in which criminal suspects, police and the functionaries of the criminal courts wrestle with each other in the sight-

123. See 18 U.S.C. § 3502 (1970) [set forth at p. 668 infra].

less ooze. It is not surprising, then, that in these cases the Court should be incapable of announcing judgments which respond coherently to the real problems of the pit. No matter. The significance of the Court's pronouncements—their power to shake the assembled faithful with awful tremors of exultation and loathing—does not depend upon their correspondence with reality. Once uttered, these pronouncements will be interpreted by arrays of lower appellate courts, trial judges, magistrates, commissioners and police officials. *Their* interpretation of the Pythia, for all practical purposes, will become the word of god.

To some extent this Pythian metaphor describes the Supreme Court's functioning in all the fields of law with which the Court deals. But the metaphor has special cogency with regard to the field of criminal procedure and particularly procedure that regulates the rights of suspects in their dealings with police prior to the time of the suspect's first court appearance. Let me explain why this is so and some of the implications of that fact.

First, the Supreme Court, like any other court, lacks the sort of supervisory power over the practices of the police that is possessed by the chief of police or the district attorney. The Court can only review those practices, and thus can only define the rights of suspects subject to those practices, when the practices become an issue in a lawsuit. There are several ways in which police practices may become the subject of a lawsuit. An individual who thinks that he has been mistreated by the police may file a civil action for damages or, in limited circumstances, for an injunction, complaining of false arrest or false imprisonment or assault or the violation of his constitutional rights. But such lawsuits are very rare, and until recently were so rare as to be insignificant, because the obstacles to their maintenance are formidable. Most persons mistreated by the police are marginal types who are quite happy, once out of police clutches, to let well enough alone. Few have the knowledge or resources to obtain the services of a lawyer. Many lawyers who might otherwise be available to them cannot afford to tangle with the police because these lawyers depend upon the good will of the police in other cases (e.g., to protect a divorce client who is being badgered by her estranged husband or to reduce charges against a criminal client) or upon police testimony in other cases (e.g., motor vehicle accident cases) or upon more dubious police services (e.g., referrals).

Juries are not sympathetic to suits against the police; policemen are seldom sufficiently solvent to make verdicts against them worth the trouble to obtain; even fairly solid citizens who sue policemen may have to fear reprisals in the form of traffic tickets, refusals to give needed aid and similar harassments. As a result, civil suits seldom bring police practices under judicial scrutiny. And for reasons too obvious to detail, criminal charges against policemen for mistreatment of citizens are even rarer than civil suits.

So, to date the Supreme Court has had occasion to review the conduct of police almost exclusively in criminal cases where the defendant is the asserted victim of police misconduct. The way in which the issue of police misconduct is presented in such cases almost invariably involves the application of the "exclusionary rule"—that is, an evidentiary rule which disallows the admission against a criminal defendant, at his trial, of certain kinds of evidence obtained in violation of his rights. This exclusionary rule, whose scope and utility in enforcing various constitutional guarantees has been considerably expanded by the Supreme Court in the past decade, is today the principal instrument of judicial control of the police and the principal vehicle for announcement by the courts of the rights of suspects in their dealings with the police.

This last point, in itself, has important implications. Certain police practices (for example, the "booking" and "mugging" of suspects and the assorted minor or major indignities that attend stationhouse detention of suspects, ranging from the taking of a suspect's belt and shoelaces to vicious beatings) will virtually never become the subjects of judicial scrutiny because they virtually never produce evidence against the suspect. Since there can arise no exclusionary rule challenges to these practices, there have been no significant judicial decisions concerning them; and since (as I shall develop shortly) judicial decisions are almost the only source of legal rights of suspects, suspects do not now have legal rights against or in connection with such practices.

Other police practices (for example, refusing arrested suspects the right to use the telephone or detaining them in pigsty cells) may or may not come under judicial consideration, depending upon whether they do or do not produce evidentiary consequences such as confessions. For several reasons, judicial control of the latter practices and judicial definition of a suspect's rights in connection with those practices must remain an imprecise, haphazard business. Under the exclusionary rule, judicial attention is focused upon an evidentiary product of the practices rather than upon the practices themselves. For example, a confession will ordinarily be the product of several such practices and of other adventitious circumstances such as the suspect's age and psychological makeup, the nature of police interrogation, etc. Consequently, a judicial ruling admitting or excluding it will seldom give occasion for a clear-cut pronouncement concerning the legality of any one of the underlying practices. Moreover, because these practices themselves are not the focus of the litigation, they will usually be imperfectly explained and explored in the record made before the courts. Courts which pass judgment on them may do so half-sightedly; or, realizing this danger, the courts may strive to avoid passing judgment upon practices that they know they do not understand. The result, once again, is that courts are unable to speak clearly concerning any particular or specific rights of a criminal suspect. Still less are they able to develop systematically any comprehensive canon or register of suspects' rights in the context of the entire range of police practices that affect the suspect.

Second, the Supreme Court of the United States is uniquely unable to take a comprehensive view of the subject of suspects' rights. In part its inability is simply a function of the Court's workload. Saddled with a back-breaking docket and properly occupied with other matters of grave national importance, the Court can only hear three or four cases a year involving the treatment of criminal suspects by the police.

Workload is not the Court's only problem. I have said earlier that fortuities determine which criminal cases reach the Supreme Court. Because police practices are ordinarily challengeable only through the exclusionary rule and because the exclusionary rule ordinarily comes into play only at trial following a plea of not guilty, police treatment of a suspect is effectively insulated against Supreme Court review in that large percentage of criminal convictions (as many as 90 per cent in some jurisdictions) that rest upon a guilty plea.

Guilty pleas may be entered for many reasons in cases that involve serious questions of violations of a suspect's rights in the precourt phases. The arguable violations may have had no evidentiary consequences. The prosecution may have sufficient evidence for conviction apart from that obtained through the arguable violations. The defendant may be detained pending trial in default of bail on a charge for which a probationary or "time-served" sentence is likely, so that he will be imprisoned longer awaiting trial on a plea of not guilty than he would as a result of a quick guilty plea. The prosecutor may offer an attractive plea bargain, or the known sentencing practices of the trial judge may promise similar consideration for a guilty plea. Obviously, these factors that determine the entry of a guilty plea do not systematically send to trial a selection of cases which present the courts with any comprehensive set of issues relative to suspects' rights.

Additional selective factors prevent many of the cases that are tried from being appealed or from being carried all the way to the Supreme Court. Factual findings by the trial judge concerning contested police conduct frequently obscure or entirely obstruct the presentation to appellate courts of issues relating to that conduct. A convicted defendant cannot challenge on appeal any treatment by the police that the trial court, crediting incredible police denials, finds did not occur. (For example, suspects invariably "trip" and strike their heads while entering their cells; they are never shoved against the bars by police.) Also, the trial court may admit the police conduct but credit incredible explanations of it. (For example, the humiliating anal examinations to which some suspects are subjected in police stations are justified as "weapons searches" on police testimony that such suspects are known to conceal razor blades between their buttocks.) Finally, the trial court may admit and resolve against the defendant an issue relating to the legality of police conduct, then sentence him so lightly that an appeal is not worthwhile. (Some trial judges will impose light sentences in cases in which they have made dubious evidentiary rulings, thereby "buying off" appeals.) In any event the presentation of a convicted defendant's appeal—still more, the taking of his case to the Supreme Court—depends upon the energy, dedication and painstaking care of his lawyer, commodities understandably scarce on the part of overworked public defenders or private lawyers conscripted without compensation to represent the indigents who constitute the bulk of convicted persons.

For these reasons, the Supreme Court simply never gets to see many of the police practices that raise the most pervasive and significant issues of suspects' rights. The cases which do come to the Court are selected by a process that can only be described as capricious insofar as it may be relied upon to present the Court any opportunity for systematic development of a body of legal rights of individuals in the police, or precourt, phases of criminal proceedings. Therefore, the Court's ability to serve as architect of such a body of rights is woefully slight.[a]

Third, the Court is further disabled by the fact that almost the only law relating to police practices or to suspects' rights is the law that the Court itself makes by its judicial decisions. Statutes and administrative regulations governing these matters are virtually nonexistent. The ubiquitous lack of legislative and executive attention to the problems of police treatment of suspects both forces the Court into the role of lawmaker in this area and makes it virtually impossible for the Court effectively to play that role.

This point has been largely ignored by the Court's conservative critics. The judicial "activism" that they deplore, usually citing the Court's "handcuffing" of the police, has been the almost inevitable consequence of the failure of other agencies

a. Consider McGowan, *Rulemaking and the Police,* 70 Mich.L.Rev. 659, 679–80 (1972) (hereinafter cited as "McGowan"):

"Over and above the advantages which have been thought to exist in the administrative process in all contexts, there are considerations peculiar to the functioning of the police which argue for its merits in this narrower setting. The points of contact between the police and the citizen are of infinite variety. Many of them—indeed most—are neither directed towards gathering evidence of specific crimes, nor do they eventuate in prosecutions. There is a wide range of police practices, with potentially severe impact upon the citizen, which never come to the notice of the courts. The promulgation of formal rules relating to these operations offers the prospect of greater control of police activities presently unrestrained by external scrutiny."

of law to assume responsibility for regulating police practices. In most areas of constitutional law the Supreme Court of the United States plays a back-stopping role, reviewing the ultimate permissibility of dispositions and policies guided in the first instance by legislative enactments, administrative rules or local common-law traditions. In the area of controls upon the police, a vast abnegation of responsibility at the level of each of these ordinary sources of legal rulemaking has forced the Court to construct *all* the law regulating the everyday functioning of the police. Of course, the Court has responded by being "activist"; it has had to. Its decisions have seemed wildly "liberal" because the only other body of principles operating in the field, against which the Court's principles may be measured, are the principles under which individual policemen act in the absence of any legal restraint.

This same subconstitutional lawlessness which forces the Court to act also prevents it from acting informedly. When the Court reviews the operation of legislation or of administrative regulations or of common-law rules governing, for example, criminal trial procedure, its consideration of the constitutional issues raised is informed and greatly assisted by the very fact that it *is* legislation or a regulation or a rule of some sort that is in question. Because the rule is articulated in more or less general terms, its contour is more or less visible; its relations and interactions with other rules are more or less perceptible, and some of the judgments and policies that underlie or oppose its acceptance are more or less intelligible. However, when the Court reviews conduct, such as police conduct, that is essentially rule-less, it is seriously impeded in understanding the nature, purposes and effects of what it is reviewing. Its view of the questioned conduct is limited to the appearance of the conduct on a particular trial record or records—records which may not even isolate or focus precisely upon that conduct. The Court cannot know whether the conduct before it is typical or atypical, unconnected or connected with a set of other practices or—if there is some connection—what is the comprehensive shape of the set of practices involved, what are their relations, their justifications, their consequences.

Operating thus darkly, the Court is obviously deprived of the ability to make any coherent response to, or to develop any organized regulation of, police conduct. Nor can the Court predict or understand the implications of any rule of constitutional law that it may itself project into this well of shadows. If the Court announces a decision striking down or modifying, for example, some rule of criminal trial practice, it can reasonably foresee how a trial will be conducted following its decision since the decision will operate within a system governed by other visible and predictable rules. But if the Court strikes down a police practice, announces a "right" of a criminal suspect in his dealings with the police, God only knows what the result will be. Out there in the formless void, some adjustment will undoubtedly be made to accommodate the new "right," but what the product of this whole exercise will be remains unfathomable. So, again, the Court is effectively disarmed.

Fourth, when and if the Supreme Court ventures to announce some constitutional right of a suspect, that "right" filters down to the level of flesh and blood suspects only through the refracting layers of lower courts, trial judges, magistrates and police officials. All pronouncements of the Supreme Court undergo this filtering process, but in few other areas of law are the filters as opaque as in the area of suspects' rights.

Let there be no mistake about it. To a mind-staggering extent—to an extent that conservatives and liberals alike who are not criminal trial lawyers simply cannot conceive—the entire system of criminal justice below the level of the Supreme

Court of the United States is solidly massed against the criminal suspect. Only a few appellate judges can throw off the fetters of their middle-class backgrounds—the dimly remembered, friendly face of the school crossing guard, their fear of a crowd of "toughs," their attitudes engendered as lawyers before their elevation to the bench, by years of service as prosecutors or as private lawyers for honest, respectable business clients—and identify with the criminal suspect instead of with the policeman or with the putative victim of the suspect's theft, mugging, rape or murder. Trial judges still more, and magistrates beyond belief, are functionally and psychologically allied with the police, their co-workers in the unending and scarifying work of bringing criminals to book.[b]

These trial judges and magistrates are the human beings that must find the "facts" when cases involving suspects' rights go into court (that is, when police treatment of a suspect is not conclusively masked behind a guilty plea or ignored by a defense lawyer too overworked or undercompensated to develop the issues adequately). Their factual findings resolve the inevitable conflict between the testimony of the police and the testimony of the suspect—usually a down-and-outer or a bad type, and often a man with a record. The result is about what one would expect. Even when the cases go to court, a suspect's rights as announced by the Supreme Court are something he has, not something he gets.

But, of course, for the reasons mentioned previously, most cases do not go to court. In these cases, the "rights" of the suspect are defined by how the police are willing to treat him. With regard to matters of treatment that have no evidentiary consequences and hence will not be judicially reviewable in exclusionary rule proceedings, the police have no particular reason to obey the law, even if the Supreme Court has had occasion to announce it. With regard to police practices that may have evidentiary consequences, the police are motivated to obey the law only to the extent that (1) they are more concerned with securing a conviction than with some other police purpose which is served by disobeying the law (in this connection, it is worth noting that police departments almost invariably measure their own efficiency in terms of "clearances by arrest," not by conviction), and (2) they think that they can secure the evidence necessary for conviction within the law.

Police work is hard work; it is righteous work; it is combative work, and competitive. Policemen are undereducated, they are scandalously underpaid, and their personal advancement lies in producing results according to the standards of the police ethic. When they go to the com-

b. But see Israel, *Criminal Procedure, the Burger Court, and the Legacy of the Warren Court,* 75 Mich.L.Rev. 1319, 1422 fn. 433 (1977), "find[ing] Professor Amsterdam's characterization deficient at several points":

"First, * * * the difficulties that police encountered in the 1960s frequently altered the attitudes not only of [those who were then] teenagers and college students, but of their parents as well. Skepticism as to police efficiency, motive, etc., spread beyond those immediately involved and obviously included a significant group of those 'middle-class' lawyers who are now on the bench. Second, the bench itself, at least in the large cities, comes from a far more diversified background than Amsterdam acknowledges. [See fn. h, p. 31 supra.] * * * Third, insofar as these judges are functionally allied with anyone on a day-to-day basis, it is not so much with the police as the prosecutor *and* the public defender or defense 'regulars' who appear in their courtrooms. [See fn. e, p. 25 supra.] Obviously the pressure of high volume may lead some judges to want to 'push past' preliminary motions and 'get to the case.' [See pp. 37–38 supra.] Also, many may take the position, perhaps correctly, that as between a defendant and a police officer, the defendant is more likely to lie, having a greater interest in the outcome. This is not the equivalent, however, of the almost inevitable bias that Amsterdam suggests. The substantial rate of defense success on suppression motions in narcotics cases, as documented in cities like Chicago and Washington, certainly suggests that a fair portion of judges in many overburdened courts will quickly dispose of matters against, as well as for, the police. *See* Oaks, *Studying the Exclusionary Rule in Search and Seizure,* 37 U.Ch.L.Rev. 665, 681–89 (1970)."

mander's office or to court, their conformity to this ethic is almost always vindicated. Neither their superiors nor the judges whom they know nor the public find it necessary to impede the performance of their duties with fettering rules respecting rights of suspects. If the Supreme Court finds this necessary, it must be that the Court is out of step. So its decisions—which are difficult to understand anyway—cannot really be taken seriously.

* * * The idealist would conclude from what I have said that the priests surrounding the Pythia are unfaithful to their priesthood. The cynic would conclude that the whole damned system is corrupt. I forgo such judgments and conclude only that Supreme Court power to enlarge the rights of suspects is very, very limited.

By what I have said so far, I do not mean to suggest that Supreme Court decisions respecting suspects' and defendants' rights are unimportant. Like the Pythia's cries, they have vast mystical significance. They state our aspirations. They give a few good priests something to work with. They give some of the faithful the courage to carry on and reason to improve the priesthood instead of tearing down the temple.

Also, they have *some* practical significance. With the Pythia shrieking underground, the priests may pervert the word of the god, but they cannot ignore it entirely, nor entirely silence those who offer interpretations of it different from their own. Indeed, fear lest these alternative explanations gain popular support may cause the priests to bend a little in their direction. * * *

So we cannot rely upon the Supreme Court in the 1970's to provide adequate definition and protection of the rights of suspects. That job is beyond the power of the Court in the best of times, and present times are not the best. If the job is to be done, it must be done by others. But, by whom?

I think that it must be done, and that sooner or later it will be done, by local legislators, executives, the police command structure and citizens in their communities.[c] * * *

MACKLIN FLEMING—OF CRIMES AND RIGHTS

150–59 (1978).

Reprinted with permission of the author and W. W. Norton & Co.; copyright © 1978 by Macklin Fleming. See also Caplan, *Questioning Miranda*, 38 Vand.L.Rev. 1417 (1985) (extensively extracted at p. 810 infra) and R. Morgan, *Disabling America: The "Rights Industry" in Our Time* 74–106 (1984).

Factual inquiry presupposes investigation capable of collecting evidence relevant to crime and bringing criminal suspects to court. A failure in investigation will gut criminal process at its outset. In today's world of specialization we need full-time government investigators and police to protect primary personal right by making it possible to teach the lesson that crime does not pay. But with creation of permanent investigative and police forces comes the need for further protection—this time not against invasions by criminal suspects but against invasions by the police themselves. To secure this further protection we limit police authority by requiring that their interrogations be free from compulsion, their searches and seizures be rea-

c. Judge McGowan believes that utilization by the police of formal rule-making procedures might secure the advantages normally characterizing the administrative process in a number of respects: "the provision of *flexibility*"; "the application of *expertise on a continuous and systematic basis*"; and *"visibility,"* in the last analysis, the "greatest virtue" of the administrative rule-making process: "Without [the visibility of the rule-making process], the police have never been compelled to recognize the degree to which their daily operations involve policy decisions of the greatest significance to the community. Nor have they been obliged to reach a conscious decision as to whether familiar ways of doing things, which appeal to them as effective, are compatible with overriding values generally comprehended within our own concept of government of laws." See McGowan at 677–81.

sonable, and their arrests be based on probable cause.

During the past twenty years we have constructed a cathedral of constitutional law, elaborating restrictions on the authority of police to deal with criminal suspects. The mass of this edifice has become so immense that it obscures the secondary and derivative nature of the rights these rules are designed to protect. Patently, we restrict police activity to keep it within lawful bounds, not to curtail the effectiveness of criminal investigation. But our preoccupation with restrictions on police activity has become so great that an impression circulates that the chief end of criminal law is to prevent invasions by police rather than invasions by criminals. Unquestionably, this preoccupation has led to the release of patently guilty criminals and thereby weakened the deterrent effect of criminal law. Supreme Court Justice Hugo L. Black, a staunch advocate of civil rights, has commented, in an opinion joined by Justice White:

> For me the importance of bringing guilty criminals to book is a far more crucial consideration than the desirability of giving defendants every possible assistance in their attempts to invoke an evidentiary rule which itself can result in the exclusion of highly relevant evidence. . . . The consequence of the Court's holding . . . is but to permit lawless people to play ducks and drakes with the basic principles of the administration of criminal law.[2]

[In another dissenting opinion, Justice Black, joined by Chief Justice Burger, observed:]

> [This decision] may well be classified as one of those calculated to make many good people believe our Court actually enjoys frustrating justice by unnecessarily turning professional criminals loose to prey upon society with impunity . . . I consider it a travesty of justice to turn this man out of jail or give him a new trial six years after he was convicted.[5]

Black's comments were directed against court-adopted rules requiring suppression of evidence obtained unlawfully by those conducting criminal investigations, rules initially designed to prevent police misconduct, but which have expanded their scope to include lack of compliance with any technical procedural requirement of law. Under these suppressionary rules chastisement of the police for misconduct receives priority over prosecution of the criminal for crime. Promptness and reliability of criminal investigation suffer alike—promptness because investigation is diverted into tangential issues, reliability because evidence relevant to crime is suppressed.

Two separate but related factors have fueled the impetus for these suppressionary rules. First, is fear of a police state, a fear periodically inflamed by well-publicized instances of police corruption or police misconduct. Those who fear the police argue that criminal investigators periodically get out of control and become lawless or corrupt, that with loss of control police contribute more to the growth of crime than to its suppression. Police efficiency is equated with police tyranny, and it is concluded we can avoid tyranny only through sacrifice of efficiency. This argument assumes that periodic loss of control over a police force is inevitable and that it is easier to regain control over an inefficient than over an efficient police force. Undoubtedly, loss of control over criminal investigators and police can occur, especially within police forces of large metropolitan areas, and loss of control can lead to pernicious consequences that range from physical coercion of suspects to police burglaries, false arrests, and fabrication of evidence. But the existence of many fine investigative and police forces functioning without corruption and lawlessness is proof that loss of control need not oc-

2. *Simmons v. United States* (1968), 390 U.S. 377, at 397–98 (dissenting opinion).

5. *Whiteley v. Warden* (1971), 401 U.S. 560 at 570, 574.

cur. And because it is easier to control an efficient organization than an inefficient one, when loss of control does occur, the remedy is to regain control of the organization, not to make it ineffective and ineffectual.

The second impetus to suppressionary rules of evidence comes from tacit assumption that criminal investigation should not be too efficient, because excessive investigative efficiency detracts from our basic social values. If we were to punish all crime, the argument runs, we would all find ourselves criminals, living in a rigidly regimented community of informers. Therefore, criminal investigation should remain at a modest level of efficiency to keep prosecutions within tolerable bounds. This argument derives its strength from the indiscriminate mingling of true crime with public offenses in one undifferentiated body of crime. Significantly, many of the leading cases establishing rules for suppression of illegally obtained evidence involved conduct of debatable criminality—gambling, prostitution, pornography, bootlegging, possession of marijuana and dangerous drugs—conduct we may not wish to see policed too closely or too effectively. We recognize that excessive efficiency of investigation into certain regulatory offenses may be socially undesirable. For example, were we to attack noise pollution in a large city by arming a regiment of investigators with appropriate devices and instructing them to cite all violators of noise regulations, the resulting inconvenience to numerous legitimate activities would far outweigh the benefits of a reduced level of noise. We therefore limit the number of our investigators and force them to concentrate their activities on those violations that are most noxious and troublesome. Similar considerations apply to enforcement of traffic laws, gambling laws, and sexual solicitation laws. In traffic enforcement, we may even limit use of radar devices to identify and catch speeders, not because these devices are unreliable but because they are overly effective. Yet the fact that we may not desire to pursue relentlessly every public offense and penalize every public offender provides no argument against prompt and reliable investigation of each instance of homicide, rape, robbery, and other true crime in order to protect our lives, our property, and our persons through identification, arrest, and prosecution of criminals. Once we correctly identify true crime, the argument to keep criminal investigation ineffective in order to make it tolerable is seen as specious. * * *

* * * Our reaction to abuse of authority by criminal investigators and police has taken a curiously convoluted and byzantine turn. In suppressing evidence and undertaking to immunize judicial process against abuse, we have sought to turn back the clock and reconstruct events as though the evidence never existed. Thus, we suppress the incriminating letter, eyewitness identification, discovery of the murder weapon, even discovery of the corpse, if those items of evidence are found to have been illegally obtained, and we solemnly conduct our factual hearing under the legal fiction that those events never happened. As so-called fruit of the poisonous tree, we erase entire chains of events by pretending they never took place.[a]

Such widespread adoption of conventional rules as essentials of due process seriously distorts factual hearing and weakens the protection of primary personal right that criminal law should provide. Invasion of the victim's primary right goes unprosecuted as a consequence of police invasion of the criminal's civil right, which likewise goes unprosecuted. We have set fire to the house of criminal law in our attempt to roast the police pig. Defenders

a. But consider *Nix v. Williams,* p. 810 infra, applying the "inevitable discovery" exception to the exclusionary rule and admitting the body of the victim on the ground that the search teams would have found the body even if the defendant's rights had not been violated and he had not led the police to the body.

of the practice of suppressing evidence argue that criminal process provides an appropriate forum for correction of its own abuses and, therefore, suppression of evidence is both permissible and desirable. The abuses, however, are not those of courts but of government agents—investigators and police—and our corrective efforts should be directed against them, not against reliability of criminal hearing. Professor Wigmore has pointed out that the exclusionary rule "regards the over-zealous officer of the law as a greater danger to the community than the unpunished murderer," [9] and Justice Cardozo observed that under the rule, "[t]he criminal is to go free because the constable has blundered . . . [t]he privacy of the home has been infringed, and the murderer goes free." [10]

* * * The exclusionary rules introduce into factual hearing much uncertainty of outcome, for in almost every criminal cause we have shuffled a number of wild cards into the deck, and if an accused is lucky enough to draw one of these jokers he may forestall prosecution and evade the consequences of his act. The uncertainty is so great that even skilled criminal lawyers cannot predict with accuracy the application of exclusionary rules in a particular hearing. As a consequence, factual hearing has suffered losses in effectiveness and credibility, for it often finds itself unable to prove in court facts that are demonstrably true. Artificial restrictions on factual hearing may bring about the following consequences: the criminal escapes public examination and self-scrutiny of his conduct; the victim and potential victim see criminal law as helpless to protect them; the potential criminal comes to look on the restraint of criminal law as ineffectual. The wrong lesson is taught, and the inevitable sequel is encouragement of rational criminal intent, emotional criminal intent, and apparent profitability of crime. By reducing *reliability* of factual hearing, we erode criminal law's ability to protect through deterrence, and we foster the impression that criminal law is aimed more at the process of criminal prosecution than at crime itself.

The subject of promptness in factual hearing touches a nerve sensitive in Shakespeare's time and before that in St. Paul's. The root cause of the law's delay is that one litigant wants delay and can employ conventional rules to get it. In a criminal cause almost invariably it is the accused who seeks delay, for he has little to gain and much to lose from prompt factual hearing. An accused, therefore, is apt to claim that promptness of hearing subverts reliability of hearing and hence is hostile to due process. By manipulating the myriad of conventional rules that have become encrusted upon essential procedures of due process an accused can normally secure substantial and repeated delay in factual hearing.

Delay in criminal process also results from procedural duplication, which comes about through addition of new procedures to criminal process without subtraction of old ones. To illustrate, we have long insisted on the best and most elaborate techniques possible to ensure perfectibility of *criminal trial,* since trial puts the accused's life or liberty at risk. For almost as long a time we have insisted upon the best possible *preliminary examination,* at which everything of importance to accusation is presented to a judicial body in advance of trial. More recently, we have extended the same elaborate methods to issuance of warrant for arrest, and we require nearly the same procedures and showing for *issuance of a warrant* as for accusation. We have now extended the same ideal of perfectibility to *opening an investigation,* and we seek to surround interrogation, issuance of subpoenas, temporary

9. 8 Wigmore, *Evidence* 37–40 (3d ed. 1940).

10. *People v. DeFore,* 150 N.E. 585, 587–88 (N.Y.1926).

detention, even surveillance, with the safeguards of criminal prosecution. Each step in this expanded criminal process appears good in itself. But the cumulative result of this multiplication of legal safeguards leads not to perfectibility of criminal procedure but to its paralysis, where, in the words of Voltaire, "the best is the enemy of the good."

A companion obstacle to promptness of factual hearing is procrastination, a way of life in criminal law, the common sin of lawyers, trial judges, clerks, reporters, and appellate judges. As does multiple factual inquiry, procrastination relies on the terminology of due process for its justification. Accusations must be allowed to ripen. There must be no rush to judgment. In time, continuously tolerated procrastination takes on the appearance of a right to procrastinate, which when denied amounts to denial of due process. Procrastination can be monumental. The trial of the San Quentin Six, convicts charged with the murder of three guards and two convicts in August 1971, was still in progress five years later. Delay, like law and order, becomes a good in itself. And as in the Scottish Church, we come to equate holiness of proceedings with length and repetitiveness of services.

The vice of repetitiveness and dilatoriness in factual hearing lies in its corrosive effect on criminal law's protection through deterrence. Promptness of factual hearing need not threaten reliability, an assertion we make with confidence after examining modes of criminal procedure used in England, the nation that pioneered the concept of due process. What we require to slay the dragon of procrastination is simple adherence to time schedules we now possess, adherence for a sufficient period of time to allow promptness to take hold and become habitual.

One further point on factual hearing. We jeopardize its reliability when we use criminal prosecution to litigate tangential issues—conduct of police, composition of grand jury, qualifications of trial jurors, operation of jail systems, availability of law libraries for prisoners, racial discrimination in law enforcement, indeed almost any issue an accused cares to raise. A criminal prosecution is not the proper forum to litigate general issues of court organization, government operation, penal administration, and public policy. Criminal process cannot perpetually question its own legitimacy and at the same time effectively carry out its designated function of criminal adjudication, for it is not a process of general inquest but one of criminal adjudication. An analogous situation would be that of a legislative body which, in the course of consideration of individual enactments and appropriations, allows perpetual challenge to the legitimacy of its creation, its composition, its membership, and its authority. When we routinely annex tangential issues to specific criminal process, the latter, like an electrical system overloaded with attachments, becomes unable to function. Uniformity, certainty, and reliability of treatment all suffer from this overload of factual hearing, and Bentham's sporting theory of criminal law (the fox must be given a chance to escape) becomes our daily reality. * * *

Chapter 5

ARREST, SEARCH AND SEIZURE [a]

SECTION 1. THE EXCLUSIONARY RULE [b]

WOLF v. COLORADO

338 U.S. 25, 69 S.Ct. 1359, 93 L.Ed. 1782 (1949).

MR. JUSTICE FRANKFURTER delivered the opinion of the Court.

The precise question for consideration is this: Does a conviction by a State court for a State offense deny the "due process of law" required by the Fourteenth Amendment, solely because evidence that was admitted at the trial was obtained under circumstances which would have rendered it inadmissible in a prosecution for violation of a federal law in a court of the United States because there deemed to be an infraction of the Fourth Amendment as applied in *Weeks v. United States,* 232 U.S. 383, 34 S.Ct. 341, 58 L.Ed. 652 [1914]? * * *

The security of one's privacy against arbitrary intrusion by the police—which is at the core of the Fourth Amendment—is basic to a free society. It is therefore implicit in "the concept of ordered liberty" and as such enforceable against the States through the Due Process Clause. * * *

Accordingly, we have no hesitation in saying that were a State affirmatively to sanction such police incursion into privacy it would run counter to the guaranty of the Fourteenth Amendment. But the ways of enforcing such a basic right raise questions of a different order. How such arbitrary conduct should be checked, what remedies against it should be afforded, the means by which the right should be made effective, are all questions that are not to be so dogmatically answered as to preclude the varying solutions which spring from an allowable range of judgment on issues not susceptible of quantitative solution.

In *Weeks v. United States,* this Court held that in a federal prosecution the Fourth Amendment barred the use of evidence secured through an illegal search and seizure. This ruling * * * was not derived from the explicit requirements of the Fourth Amendment; it was not based on legislation expressing Congressional policy in the enforcement of the Constitution. The decision was a matter of judicial impli-

a. For detailed treatment of this subject and reference to other secondary sources, consult LaFave, *Search and Seizure: A Treatise on the Fourth Amendment* (1978) [cited herein as LaFave].

b. Although the concern here is with the exclusion of evidence obtained in violation of the Fourth Amendment, it should be noted that an arrest or search which passes Fourth Amendment muster may nonetheless violate state law. The exclusionary sanction is also used when state constitutional provisions similar to the Fourth Amendment have been violated. As for violations of statutes, court rules and administrative regulations, it is customary to require exclusion if the violation significantly affected the defendant's substantial rights.

cation. Since then it has been frequently applied and we stoutly adhere to it. But the immediate question is whether the basic right to protection against arbitrary intrusion by the police demands the exclusion of logically relevant evidence obtained by an unreasonable search and seizure because, in a federal prosecution for a federal crime, it would be excluded. As a matter of inherent reason, one would suppose this to be an issue as to which men with complete devotion to the protection of the right of privacy might give different answers. When we find that in fact most of the English-speaking world does not regard as vital to such protection the exclusion of evidence thus obtained, we must hesitate to treat this remedy as an essential ingredient of the right. The contrariety of views of the States is particularly impressive in view of the careful reconsideration which they have given the problem in the light of the *Weeks* decision.

* * * As of today 30 States reject the *Weeks* doctrine, 17 States are in agreement with it. * * * Of 10 jurisdictions within the United Kingdom and the British Commonwealth of Nations which have passed on the question, none has held evidence obtained by illegal search and seizure inadmissible. * * *

The jurisdictions which have rejected the *Weeks* doctrine have not left the right to privacy without other means of protection. Indeed, the exclusion of evidence is a remedy which directly serves only to protect those upon whose person or premises something incriminating has been found. We cannot, therefore, regard it as a departure from basic standards to remand such persons, together with those who emerge scatheless from a search, to the remedies of private action and such protection as the internal discipline of the police, under the eyes of an alert public opinion, may afford. Granting that in practice the exclusion of evidence may be an effective way of deterring unreasonable searches, it is not for this Court to condemn as falling below the minimal standards assured by the Due Process Clause a State's reliance upon other methods which, if consistently enforced, would be equally effective. * * * There are, moreover, reasons for excluding evidence unreasonably obtained by the federal police which are less compelling in the case of police under State or local authority. The public opinion of a community can far more effectively be exerted against oppressive conduct on the part of police directly responsible to the community itself than can local opinion, sporadically aroused, be brought to bear upon remote authority pervasively exerted throughout the country.

We hold, therefore, that in a prosecution in a State court for a State crime the Fourteenth Amendment does not forbid the admission of evidence obtained by an unreasonable search and seizure. * * *

MR. JUSTICE BLACK, concurring.

* * * I agree with what appears to be a plain implication of the Court's opinion that the federal exclusionary rule is not a command of the Fourth Amendment but is a judicially created rule of evidence which Congress might negate. * * *

MR. JUSTICE MURPHY, with whom MR. JUSTICE RUTLEDGE joins, dissenting.

[T]here is but one alternative to the rule of exclusion. That is no sanction at all.

* * * Little need be said concerning the possibilities of criminal prosecution. Self-scrutiny is a lofty ideal, but its exaltation reaches new heights if we expect a District Attorney to prosecute himself or his associates for well-meaning violations of the search and seizure clause during a raid the District Attorney or his associates have ordered. But there is an appealing ring in another alternative. A trespass action for damages is a venerable means of securing reparation for unauthorized invasion of the home. Why not put the old writ to a new use? When the Court cites cases permitting the action, the remedy seems complete.

But what an illusory remedy this is, if by "remedy" we mean a positive deterrent to police and prosecutors tempted to violate the Fourth Amendment. The appealing ring softens when we recall that in a trespass action the measure of damages is simply the extent of the injury to physical property. If the officer searches with care, he can avoid all but nominal damages—a penny, or a dollar. Are punitive damages possible? Perhaps. But a few states permit none, whatever the circumstances. In those that do, the plaintiff must show the real ill will or malice of the defendant, and surely it is not unreasonable to assume that one in honest pursuit of crime bears no malice toward the search victim. If that burden is carried, recovery may yet be defeated by the rule that there must be physical damages before punitive damages may be awarded. In addition, some states limit punitive damages to the actual expenses of litigation. * * * Even assuming the ill will of the officer, his reasonable grounds for belief that the home he searched harbored evidence of crime is admissible in mitigation of punitive damages. * * * The bad reputation of the plaintiff is likewise admissible. * * * If the evidence seized was actually used at a trial, that fact has been held a complete justification of the search, and a defense against the trespass action. * * * And even if the plaintiff hurdles all these obstacles, and gains a substantial verdict, the individual officer's finances may well make the judgment useless—for the municipality, of course, is not liable without its consent. Is it surprising that there is so little in the books concerning trespass actions for violation of the search and seizure clause? * * *

MR. JUSTICE DOUGLAS, dissenting.

* * * I agree with MR. JUSTICE MURPHY that * * * in absence of [an exclusionary] rule of evidence the Amendment would have no effective sanction. * * *

MAPP v. OHIO

367 U.S. 643, 81 S.Ct. 1684, 6 L.Ed.2d 1081 (1961).

MR. JUSTICE CLARK delivered the opinion of the Court. * * *

On May 23, 1957, three Cleveland police officers arrived at appellant's residence in that city pursuant to information that "a person [was] hiding out in the home who was wanted for questioning in connection with a recent bombing, and that there was a large amount of policy paraphernalia being hidden in the home." Miss Mapp and her daughter by a former marriage lived on the top floor of the two-family dwelling. Upon their arrival at that house, the officers knocked on the door and demanded entrance but appellant, after telephoning her attorney, refused to admit them without a search warrant. * * *

The officers again sought entrance some three hours later when four or more additional officers arrived on the scene. When Miss Mapp did not come to the door immediately, at least one of the several doors to the house was forcibly opened and the policemen gained admittance. Meanwhile Miss Mapp's attorney arrived, but the officers, having secured their own entry, and continuing in their defiance of the law, would permit him neither to see Miss Mapp nor to enter the house. [When the officers broke into the hall, Miss Mapp] demanded to see the search warrant. A paper, claimed to be a warrant, was held up by one of the officers. She grabbed the "warrant" and placed it in her bosom. A struggle ensued in which the officers recovered the piece of paper and as a result of which they handcuffed appellant because she had been "belligerent" in resisting their official rescue of the "warrant" from her person. * * * Appellant, in handcuffs, was then forcibly taken upstairs to her bedroom where the officers searched a dresser, a chest of drawers, a closet and some suitcases. * * * The search spread to the rest of the second floor * * *. The basement of the building and a trunk found therein were also searched. The obscene materials for possession of which she was ultimately convicted were discovered in the course of that widespread search.

At the trial no search warrant was produced by the prosecution, nor was the failure to produce one explained or accounted for. At best [as the Ohio Supreme Court, which affirmed the conviction, expressed it], "there is, in the record, considerable doubt as to whether there ever was any warrant for the search of defendant's home." * * *

The State says that even if the search were made without authority, or otherwise unreasonably, it is not prevented from using the unconstitutionally seized evidence at trial, citing *Wolf v. Colorado*, * * *. On this appeal, * * * it is urged once again that we review that holding.[3]

Seventy-five years ago, in *Boyd v. United States* [p. 706 infra], considering the Fourth and Fifth Amendments as running "almost into each other" on the facts before it, this Court held that the doctrines of those Amendments "apply to all invasions on the part of the government and its employes of the sanctity of a man's home and the privacies of life. It is not the breaking of his doors, and the rummaging of his drawers, that constitutes the essence of the offense; but it is the invasion of his indefeasible right of personal security, personal liberty and private property * * *. Breaking into a house and opening boxes and drawers are circumstances of aggravation; but any forcible and compulsory extortion of a man's own testimony or of his private papers to be used as evidence to convict him of crime or to forfeit his goods, is within the condemnation * * * [of those Amendments]." * * *

[I]n the *Weeks* case, this Court "for the first time" held that "in a federal prosecution the Fourth Amendment barred the use of evidence secured through an illegal search and seizure." * * * This Court has ever since required of federal law officers a strict adherence to that command which this Court has held to be a clear, specific, and constitutionally required—even if judicially implied—deterrent safeguard without insistence upon which the Fourth Amendment would have been reduced to "a form of words." Holmes, J., *Silverthorne Lumber Co. v. United States*, 1920, 251 U.S. 385, 392, 40 S.Ct. 182, 183, 64 L.Ed. 319. It meant, quite simply, that "conviction by means of unlawful seizures and enforced confessions * * * should find no sanction in the judgments of the courts * * *" * * * and that such evidence "shall not be used at all." * * *

In 1949, 35 years after *Weeks* was announced, this Court, in *Wolf v. Colorado*, again for the first time, discussed the effect of the Fourth Amendment upon the States through the operation of the Due Process Clause of the Fourteenth Amendment. * * *

The Court in *Wolf* first stated that "[t]he contrariety of views of the States" on the adoption of the exclusionary rule of *Weeks* was "particularly impressive" * * * While in 1949, prior to the *Wolf* case, almost two-thirds of the States were opposed to the use of the exclusionary rule, now, despite the *Wolf* case, more than half of those since passing upon it, by their own legislative or judicial decision, have wholly or partly adopted or adhered to the *Weeks* rule. * * * Significantly, among those now following the rule is California which, according to its highest court, was "compelled to reach that conclusion because other remedies have completely failed to secure compliance with the constitutional provisions * * *." In connection with this California case, we note that

3. Other issues have been raised on this appeal but, in the view we have taken of the case, they need not be decided. Although appellant chose to urge what may have appeared to be the surer ground for favorable disposition and did not insist that *Wolf* be overruled, the *amicus curiae*, who was also permitted to participate in the oral argument, did urge the Court to overrule *Wolf*.

the second basis elaborated in *Wolf* in support of its failure to enforce the exclusionary doctrine against the States was that "other means of protection" have been afforded "the right to privacy." The experience of California that such other remedies have been worthless and futile is buttressed by the experience of other States.

Likewise, time has set its face against what *Wolf* called the "weighty testimony" of *People v. Defore,* 1926, 242 N.Y. 13, 150 N.E. 585. There Justice (then Judge) Cardozo, rejecting adoption of the *Weeks* exclusionary rule in New York, had said that "[t]he Federal rule as it stands is either too strict or too lax." However the force of that reasoning has been largely vitiated by later decisions of this Court. These include the recent discarding of the "silver platter" doctrine, *Elkins v. United States;* [a] the relaxation of the formerly strict requirements as to standing to challenge the use of evidence thus seized, * * * and finally, the formulation of a method to prevent state use of evidence unconstitutionally seized by federal agents, *Rea v. United States.* [b] * * *

It, therefore, plainly appears that the factual considerations supporting the failure of the *Wolf* Court to include the *Weeks* exclusionary rule when it recognized the enforceability of the right to privacy against the States in 1949, while not basically relevant to the constitutional consideration, could not, in any analysis, now be deemed controlling.

Some five years after *Wolf,* in answer to a plea made here Term after Term that we overturn its doctrine on applicability of the *Weeks* exclusionary rule, this Court indicated that such should not be done until the States had "adequate opportunity to adopt or reject the [*Weeks*] rule." Today we once again examine *Wolf's* constitutional documentation of the right to privacy free from unreasonable state intrusion, and, after its dozen years on our books, are led by it to close the only courtroom door remaining open to evidence secured by official lawlessness in flagrant abuse of that basic right, reserved to all persons as a specific guarantee against that very same unlawful conduct. We hold that all evidence obtained by searches and seizures in violation of the Constitution is, by that same authority, inadmissible in a state court.

Since the Fourth Amendment's right of privacy has been declared enforceable against the States through the Due Process Clause of the Fourteenth, it is enforceable against them by the same sanction of exclusion as is used against the Federal Government. Were it otherwise then just as without the *Weeks* rule the assurance against unreasonable federal searches and seizures would be "a form of words," valueless and

a. 364 U.S. 206, 80 S.Ct. 1437, 4 L.Ed.2d 1669 (1960). Under the "silver platter" doctrine, evidence of a federal crime seized by state police in the course of an illegal search while investigating a state crime could be turned over to federal authorities and used in a federal prosecution so long as federal agents had not participated in the illegal search but had simply received the evidence on a "silver platter." In rejecting the doctrine, the Court pointed out that the determination in *Wolf* that Fourteenth Amendment Due Process prohibited illegal searches and seizures by state officers, marked the "removal of the doctrinal underpinning" for the admissibility of state-seized evidence in federal prosecutions.

Elkins must be distinguished from the situation in which the search by the state officers was in violation of state law but not unconstitutional. In such a case, even if the evidence would be excluded in the state where the search occurred (see fn. b supra), it is admissible in the federal courts, or the courts of another state.

b. 350 U.S. 214, 76 S.Ct. 292, 100 L.Ed. 233 (1956), where the Court held that a federal law enforcement agent who seized evidence on the basis of an invalid search warrant should be enjoined from turning over such evidence to state authorities for use in a state prosecution and from giving testimony concerning the evidence: "The District Court is not asked to enjoin state officials nor in any way to interfere with state agencies in enforcement of state law. * * * The only relief asked is against a federal agent, who obtained the property as a result of the abuse of process issued by a United States Commissioner. * * * In this posture we have then a case that raises not a constitutional question but one concerning our supervisory powers over federal law enforcement agencies."

undeserving of mention in a perpetual charter of inestimable human liberties, so too, without that rule the freedom from state invasions of privacy would be so ephemeral and so neatly severed from its conceptual nexus with the freedom from all brutish means of coercing evidence as not to merit this Court's high regard as a freedom "implicit in 'the concept of ordered liberty.' "

* * * [I]n extending the substantive protections of due process to all constitutionally unreasonable searches—state or federal—it was logically and constitutionally necessary that the exclusion doctrine—an essential part of the right to privacy—be also insisted upon as an essential ingredient of the right newly recognized by the *Wolf* case. In short, the admission of the new constitutional right by *Wolf* could not consistently tolerate denial of its most important constitutional privilege, namely, the exclusion of the evidence which an accused had been forced to give by reason of the unlawful seizure. To hold otherwise is to grant the right but in reality to withhold its privilege and enjoyment. Only last year the Court itself recognized that the purpose of the exclusionary rule "is to deter—to compel respect for the constitutional guaranty in the only effectively available way—by removing the incentive to disregard it." *Elkins v. United States.*

Indeed, we are aware of no restraint, similar to that rejected today, conditioning the enforcement of any other basic constitutional right. The right to privacy, no less important than any other right carefully and particularly reserved to the people, would stand in marked contrast to all other rights declared as "basic to a free society." * * * [N]othing could be more certain than that when a coerced confession is involved, "the relevant rules of evidence" are overridden without regard to "the incidence of such conduct by the police," slight or frequent. Why should not the same rule apply to what is tantamount to coerced testimony by way of unconstitutional seizure of goods, papers, effects, documents, etc.? We find that, as to the Federal Government the Fourth and Fifth Amendments and, as to the States, the freedom from unconscionable invasions of privacy and the freedom from convictions based upon coerced confessions do enjoy an "intimate relation" in their perpetuation of "principles of humanity and civil liberty * * *." They express "supplementing phases of the same constitutional purpose—to maintain inviolate large areas of personal privacy." The philosophy of each Amendment and of each freedom is complementary to, although not dependent upon, that of the other in its sphere of influence—the very least that together they assure in either sphere is that no man is to be convicted on unconstitutional evidence.

Moreover, our holding * * * is not only the logical dictate of prior cases, but it also makes very good sense. There is no war between the Constitution and common sense. Presently, a federal prosecutor may make no use of evidence illegally seized, but a State's attorney across the street may, although he supposedly is operating under the enforceable prohibitions of the same Amendment. Thus the State, by admitting evidence unlawfully seized, serves to encourage disobedience to the Federal Constitution which it is bound to uphold. * * *

There are those who say, as did Justice (then Judge) Cardozo, that under our constitutional exclusionary doctrine "[t]he criminal is to go free because the constable has blundered." *People v. Defore.* In some cases this will undoubtedly be the result. But, as was said in *Elkins,* "there is another consideration—the imperative of judicial integrity." The criminal goes free, if he must, but it is the law that sets him free. Nothing can destroy a government more quickly than its failure to observe its own laws, or worse, its disregard of the charter of its own existence. As Mr. Justice Brandeis, dissenting, said in *Olmstead v. United States* [p. 423 infra]: "Our government is the potent, the omnipresent teacher. For good or for ill, it teaches the whole people by its example. * * * If the government becomes a lawbreaker, it breeds contempt for law; it invites every man to become a law unto himself; it invites anarchy." Nor can it lightly be assumed that, as a practical matter, adoption of the exclusionary rule fetters law enforcement. Only last year this Court expressly considered that contention and found that "pragmatic evidence of a sort" to the contrary was not wanting. *Elkins v. United States* * * *. The Court noted that:

"The federal courts themselves have operated under the exclusionary rule of *Weeks* for almost half a century; yet it has not been suggested either that the Federal Bureau of Investigation has thereby been rendered ineffective, or that the administration of criminal justice in the federal courts has thereby been disrupted. Moreover, the experience of the states is impressive * * *. The movement toward the rule of exclusion has been halting but seemingly inexorable."

The ignoble shortcut to conviction left open to the State tends to destroy the entire system of constitutional restraints on which the liberties of the people rest. Having once recognized that the right to privacy embodied in the Fourth Amendment is enforceable against the States, and that the right to be secure against rude invasions of privacy by state officers is, therefore, constitutional in origin, we can no longer permit that right to remain an empty promise. Because it is enforceable in the same manner and to like effect as other basic rights secured by the Due Process Clause, we can no longer permit it to be revocable at the whim of any police officer who, in the name of law enforcement itself, chooses to suspend its enjoyment. Our decision, founded on reason and truth, gives to the individual no more than that which the Constitution guarantees him, to the police officer no less than that to which honest law enforcement is entitled, and, to the courts, that judicial integrity so necessary in the true administration of justice. * * *

Reversed and remanded.

MR. JUSTICE BLACK, concurring. * * *

I am still not persuaded that the Fourth Amendment, standing alone, would be enough to bar the introduction into evidence against an accused of papers and effects seized from him in violation of its commands. For the Fourth Amendment does not itself contain any provision expressly precluding the use of such evidence, and I am extremely doubtful that such a provision could properly be inferred from nothing more than the basic command against unreasonable searches and seizures. Reflection on the problem, however, in the light of cases coming before the Court since *Wolf,* has led me to conclude that when the Fourth Amendment's ban against unreasonable searches and seizures is considered together with the Fifth Amendment's ban against compelled self-incrimination, a constitutional basis emerges which not only justifies but actually requires the exclusionary rule. * * *

MR. JUSTICE DOUGLAS, concurring.

* * * I believe that this is an appropriate case in which to put an end to the asymmetry which *Wolf* imported into the law. * * * The question was raised in the notice of appeal, the jurisdictional statement and in appellant's brief on the merits. It is true that argument was mostly directed to another issue in the case, but that is often the fact. * * *

Memorandum of MR. JUSTICE STEWART.

Agreeing fully with Part I of MR. JUSTICE HARLAN'S dissenting opinion, I express no view as to the merits of the constitutional issue which the Court today decides. * * *

MR. JUSTICE HARLAN, whom MR. JUSTICE FRANKFURTER and MR. JUSTICE WHITTAKER join, dissenting. * * *

I.

From the Court's statement of the case one would gather that the central, if not controlling, issue on this appeal is * * * the need for re-examining *Wolf.* However, such is not the situation. For, although that question was indeed raised here and below among appellant's subordinate points, the new and pivotal issue brought to the Court by this appeal is whether * * * making criminal the *mere* knowing possession or control of obscene material, * * * is consistent with the rights of free thought and expression assured against state action by the Fourteenth Amendment. That was the principal issue which was decided by the Ohio Supreme Court, which was tendered by appellant's Jurisdictional Statement, and which was briefed and argued in this Court.

In this posture of things, I think it fair to say that five members of this Court have simply "reached out" to overrule *Wolf.* * * * I can perceive no justification for regarding this case as an appropriate occasion for re-examining *Wolf.* * * *

II. * * *

I would not impose upon the States this federal exclusionary remedy. The reasons given by the majority for now suddenly turning its back on *Wolf* seem to me notably unconvincing.

First, it is said that "the factual grounds upon which *Wolf* was based" have since changed, in that more States now follow the *Weeks* exclusionary rule than was so at the time *Wolf* was decided. While that is true, a recent survey indicates that at present one half of the States still adhere to the common-law non-exclusionary rule, and one, Maryland, retains the rule as to felonies. * * * But in any case surely all this is beside the point, as the majority itself indeed seems to recognize. Our concern here, as it was in *Wolf,* is not with the desirability of that rule but only with the question whether the States are Constitutionally free to follow it or not as they may themselves determine, and the relevance of the disparity of views among the States on this point lies simply in the fact that the judgment involved is a debatable one. Moreover, the very fact on which the majority relies, instead of lending support to what is now being done, points away from the need of replacing voluntary state action with federal compulsion.

The preservation of a proper balance between state and federal responsibility in the administration of criminal justice demands patience on the part of those who might like to see things move faster among the States in this respect. Problems of criminal law enforcement vary widely from State to State. One State, in considering the totality of its legal picture, may conclude that the need for embracing the *Weeks* rule is pressing because other remedies are unavailable or inadequate to secure compliance with the substantive Constitutional principle involved. Another, though equally solicitous of Constitutional rights, may choose to pursue one purpose at a time, allowing all evidence relevant to guilt to be brought into a criminal trial, and dealing with Constitutional infractions by other means. Still another may consider the exclusionary rule too rough and ready a remedy, in that it reaches only unconstitutional intrusions which eventuate in criminal prosecution of the victims. Further, a State after experimenting with the *Weeks* rule for a time may, because of unsatisfactory experience with it, decide to revert to a non-exclusionary rule. And so on. * * * For us the question remains, as it has always been, one of state power, not one of passing judgment on the wisdom of one state course or another. In my view this Court should continue to forbear from fettering the States with an adamant rule which may embarrass them in coping with their own peculiar problems in criminal law enforcement. * * *

* * * Our role in promulgating the *Weeks* rule and its extensions * * * was quite a different one than it is here.

There, in implementing the Fourth Amendment, we occupied the position of a tribunal having the ultimate responsibility for developing the standards and procedures of judicial administration within the judicial system over which it presides. Here we review State procedures whose measure is to be taken not against the specific substantive commands of the Fourth Amendment but under the flexible contours of the Due Process Clause. I do not believe that the Fourteenth Amendment empowers this Court to mould state remedies effectuating the right to freedom from "arbitrary intrusion by the police" to suit its own notions of how things should be done * * *.

Finally, it is said that the overruling of *Wolf* is supported by the established doctrine that the admission in evidence of an involuntary confession renders a state conviction constitutionally invalid. Since such a confession may often be entirely reliable, and therefore of the greatest relevance to the issue of the trial, the argument continues, this doctrine is ample warrant in precedent that the way evidence was obtained and not just its relevance, is constitutionally significant to the fairness of a trial. I believe this analogy is not a true one. The "coerced confession" rule is certainly not a rule that any illegally obtained statements may not be used in evidence. I would suppose that a statement which is procured during a period of illegal detention is, as much as unlawfully seized evidence, illegally obtained, but this Court has consistently refused to reverse state convictions resting on the use of such statements. * * *

The point, then, must be that in requiring exclusion of an involuntary statement of an accused, we are concerned not with an appropriate remedy for what the police have done, but with something which is regarded as going to the heart of our concepts of fairness in judicial procedure. The operative assumption of our procedural system is that "ours is the accusatorial as opposed to the inquisitorial system. * * *." * * * The pressures brought to bear against an accused leading to a confession, unlike an unconstitutional violation of privacy, do not, apart from the use of the confession at trial, necessarily involve independent Constitutional violations. What is crucial is that the trial defense to which an accused is entitled should not be rendered an empty formality by reason of statements wrung from him, for then "a prisoner * * * [has been] made the deluded instrument of his own conviction." That this is a *procedural right,* and that its violation occurs at the time his improperly obtained statement is admitted at trial, is manifest. * * *

This, and not the disciplining of the police, as with illegally seized evidence, is surely the true basis for excluding a statement of the accused which was unconstitutionally obtained. In sum, I think the coerced confession analogy works strongly *against* what the Court does today. * * *

UNITED STATES v. LEON

— U.S. —, 104 S.Ct. 3405, 82 L.Ed.2d 677 (1984).

JUSTICE WHITE delivered the opinion of the Court. * * *

This case presents the question whether the Fourth Amendment exclusionary rule should be modified so as not to bar the use in the prosecution's case-in-chief of evidence obtained by officers acting in reasonable reliance on a search warrant issued by a detached and neutral magistrate but ultimately found to be unsupported by probable cause. * * *

The Fourth Amendment contains no provision expressly precluding the use of evidence obtained in violation of its commands, and an examination of its origin and purposes makes clear that the use of fruits of a past unlawful search or seizure "work[s] no new Fourth Amendment wrong." The wrong condemned by the Amendment is "fully accomplished" by the unlawful search or seizure itself, and the exclusionary rule is neither intended nor able to "cure the invasion of the defendant's rights which he has already suffered." The rule thus operates as "a judicially created remedy designed to safeguard Fourth Amendment rights generally through its deterrent effect, rather than a personal constitutional right of the person aggrieved."

Whether the exclusionary sanction is appropriately imposed in a particular case, our decisions make clear, is "an issue separate from the question whether the Fourth Amendment rights of the party seeking to invoke the rule were violated by police conduct." Only the former question is currently before us,[a] and it must be resolved by weighing the costs and benefits of preventing the use in the prosecution's case-in-chief of inherently trustworthy tangible evidence obtained in reliance on a search warrant issued by a detached and neutral magistrate that ultimately is found to be defective.

The substantial social costs exacted by the exclusionary rule for the vindication of Fourth Amendment rights have long been a source of concern. "Our cases have consistently recognized that unbending application of the exclusionary sanction to enforce ideals of governmental rectitude would impede unacceptably the truth-finding functions of judge and jury." An objectionable collateral consequence of this interference with the criminal justice system's truth-finding function is that some guilty defendants may go free or receive reduced sentences as a result of favorable plea bargains.[6] Particularly when law enforcement officers have acted in objective good faith or their transgressions have been minor, the magnitude of the benefit conferred on such guilty defendants offends basic concepts of the criminal justice system. Indiscriminate application of the exclusionary rule, therefore, may well "generat[e] disrespect for the law and the administration of justice." Accordingly, "[a]s with any remedial device, the application of the rule has been restricted to those areas where its remedial objectives are thought most efficaciously served."

Close attention to those remedial objectives has characterized our recent decisions concerning the scope of the Fourth Amendment exclusionary rule. The Court has, to be sure, not seriously questioned, "in the absence of a more efficacious sanction, the continued application of the rule to suppress evidence from the [prosecution's] case where a Fourth Amendment violation has been substantial and deliber-

a. A large quantities of drugs were suppressed on the ground the warrant had not issued on probable cause, in that the affidavit reported only the allegations of an untested informant and limited corroboration by police surveillance of events themselves "as consistent with innocence as * * * with guilt." The Court earlier noted that whether this warrant would pass muster under the less demanding test of *Illinois v. Gates,* p. 264, infra, "has not been briefed or argued," and thus chose "to take the case as it comes to us."

6. Researchers have only recently begun to study extensively the effects of the exclusionary rule on the disposition of felony arrests. One study suggests that the rule results in the nonprosecution or nonconviction of between 0.6% and 2.35% of individuals arrested for felonies. Davies, *A Hard Look at What We Know (and Still Need to Learn) About the "Costs" of the Exclusionary Rule: The NIJ Study and Other Studies of "Lost" Arrests,* 1983 A.B.F.Res.J. 611, 621. The estimates are higher for particular crimes the prosecution of which depends heavily on physical evidence. Thus, the cumulative loss due to nonprosecution or nonconviction of individuals arrested on felony drug charges is probably in the range of 2.8% to 7.1%. Davies' analysis of California data suggests that screening by police and prosecutors results in the release because of illegal searches or seizures of as many as 1.4% of all felony arrestees, id., at 650, that 0.9% of felony arrestees are released because of illegal searches or seizures at the preliminary hearing or after trial, *id.,* at 653, and that roughly 0.5% of all felony arrestees benefit from reversals on appeal because of illegal searches. * * *

Many of these researchers have concluded that the impact of the exclusionary rule is insubstantial, but the small percentages with which they deal mask a large absolute number of felons who are released because the cases against them were based in part on illegal searches or seizures. * * * Because we find that the rule can have no substantial deterrent effect in the sorts of situations under consideration in this case, we conclude that it cannot pay its way in those situations.

ate * * *." Nevertheless, the balancing approach that has evolved in various contexts—including criminal trials—"forcefully suggest[s] that the exclusionary rule be more generally modified to permit the introduction of evidence obtained in the reasonable good-faith belief that a search or seizure was in accord with the Fourth Amendment." *Illinois v. Gates* (White, J., concurring in the judgment). * * *

As yet, we have not recognized any form of good-faith exception to the Fourth Amendment exclusionary rule. But the balancing approach that has evolved during the years of experience with the rule provides strong support for the modification currently urged upon us. As we discuss below, our evaluation of the costs and benefits of suppressing reliable physical evidence seized by officers reasonably relying on a warrant issued by a detached and neutral magistrate leads to the conclusion that such evidence should be admissible in the prosecution's case-in-chief. * * *

Only [when a warrant is grounded upon an affidavit knowingly or recklessly false] has the Court set forth a rationale for suppressing evidence obtained pursuant to a search warrant;[b] in the other areas, it has simply excluded such evidence without considering whether Fourth Amendment interests will be advanced. To the extent that proponents of exclusion rely on its behavioral effects on judges and magistrates in these areas, their reliance is misplaced. First, the exclusionary rule is designed to deter police misconduct rather than to punish the errors of judges and magistrates. Second, there exists no evidence suggesting that judges and magistrates are inclined to ignore or subvert the Fourth Amendment or that lawlessness among these actors requires application of the extreme sanction of exclusion.[14]

Third, and most important, we discern no basis, and are offered none, for believing that exclusion of evidence seized pursuant to a warrant will have a significant deterrent effect on the issuing judge or magistrate. Many of the factors that indicate that the exclusionary rule cannot provide an effective "special" or "general" deterrent for individual offending law enforcement officers apply as well to judges or magistrates. And, to the extent that the rule is thought to operate as a "systemic" deterrent on a wider audience, it clearly can have no such effect on individuals empowered to issue warrants. Judges and magistrates are not adjuncts to the law enforcement team; as neutral judicial officers, they have no stake in the outcome of particular criminal prosecutions. The threat of exclusion thus cannot be expected significantly to deter them. Imposition of the exclusionary sanction is not necessary meaningfully to inform judicial officers of their errors, and we cannot conclude that admitting evidence obtained pursuant to a warrant while at the same time declaring that the warrant was somehow defective will in any way reduce judicial officers' professional incentives to comply with the Fourth Amendment, encourage them to repeat their mistakes, or lead to the granting of all colorable warrant requests.[18]

If exclusion of evidence obtained pursuant to a subsequently invalidated warrant is

b. The reference is to the *Franks* case, p. 281 infra, where the Court declared "it would be an unthinkable imposition upon [the magistrate's] authority if a warrant affidavit, revealed after the fact to contain a deliberately or recklessly false statement, were to stand beyond impeachment."

14. Although there are assertions that some magistrates become rubber stamps for the police and others may be unable effectively to screen police conduct, we are not convinced that this is a problem of major proportions.

18. Limiting the application of the exclusionary sanction may well increase the care with which magistrates scrutinize warrant applications. We doubt that magistrates are more desirous of avoiding the exclusion of evidence obtained pursuant to warrants they have issued than of avoiding invasions of privacy.

Federal magistrates, moreover, are subject to the direct supervision of district courts. They may be removed for "incompetency, misconduct, neglect of duty, or physical or mental disability." 28 U.S.C. § 631(i). If a magistrate serves merely to have any deterrent effect, therefore, it must alter the behavior of individual law enforcement officers or the policies of their departments. One could argue that applying the exclusionary rule in cases where the police failed to demonstrate probable cause in the warrant application deters future inadequate presentations or "magistrate shopping" and thus promotes the ends of the Fourth Amendment. Suppressing evidence obtained pursuant to a technically defective warrant supported by probable cause also might encourage officers to scrutinize more closely the form of the warrant and to point out suspected judicial errors. We find such arguments speculative and conclude that suppression of evidence obtained pursuant to a warrant should be ordered only on a case-by-case basis and only in those unusual cases in which exclusion will further the purposes of the exclusionary rule.[19]

We have frequently questioned whether the exclusionary rule can have any deterrent effect when the offending officers acted in the objectively reasonable belief that their conduct did not violate the Fourth Amendment. "No empirical researcher, proponent or opponent of the rule, has yet been able to establish with any assurance whether the rule has a deterrent effect * * *." But even assuming that the rule effectively deters some police misconduct and provides incentives for the law enforcement profession as a whole to conduct itself in accord with the Fourth Amendment, it cannot be expected, and should not be applied, to deter objectively reasonable law enforcement activity. * * *[20]

This is particularly true, we believe, when an officer acting with objective good faith has obtained a search warrant from a judge or magistrate and acted within its scope. In most such cases, there is no police illegality and thus nothing to deter. It is the magistrate's responsibility to determine whether the officer's allegations establish probable cause and, if so, to issue a warrant comporting in form with the requirements of the Fourth Amendment. In the ordinary case, an officer cannot be expected to question the magistrate's probable-cause determination or his judgment that the form of the warrant is technically sufficient. "[O]nce the warrant issues, there is literally nothing more the policeman can do in seeking to comply with the law." Penalizing the officer for the magistrate's error, rather than his own, cannot logically contribute to the deterrence of Fourth Amendment violations.[22]

as a "rubber stamp" for the police or is unable to exercise mature judgment, closer supervision or removal provides a more effective remedy than the exclusionary rule.

19. Our discussion of the deterrent effect of excluding evidence obtained in reasonable reliance on a subsequently invalidated warrant assumes, of course, that the officers properly executed the warrant and searched only those places and for those objects that it was reasonable to believe were covered by the warrant. * * *

20. We emphasize that the standard of reasonableness we adopt is an objective one. Many objections to a good-faith exception assume that the exception will turn on the subjective good faith of individual officers. "Grounding the modification in objective reasonableness, however, retains the value of the exclusionary rule as an incentive for the law enforcement profession as a whole to conduct themselves in accord with the Fourth Amendment." The objective standard we adopt, moreover, requires officers to have a reasonable knowledge of what the law prohibits. As Professor Jerold Israel has observed:

"The key to the [exclusionary] rule's effectiveness as a deterrent lies, I believe, in the impetus it has provided to police training programs that make officers aware of the limits imposed by the fourth amendment and emphasize the need to operate within those limits. [An objective good-faith exception] * * * is not likely to result in the elimination of such programs, which are now viewed as an important aspect of police professionalism. Neither is it likely to alter the tenor of those programs; the possibility that illegally obtained evidence may be admitted in borderline cases is unlikely to encourage police instructors to pay less attention to fourth amendment limitations. Finally, [it] * * * should not encourage officers to pay less attention to what they are taught, as the requirement that the officer act in 'good faith' is inconsistent with closing one's mind to the possibility of illegality."

22. * * * Our cases establish that the question whether the use of illegally obtained evidence in judicial proceedings represents judicial participation in a Fourth Amendment violation and offends the integrity of the courts "is essen-

We conclude that the marginal or nonexistent benefits produced by suppressing evidence obtained in objectively reasonable reliance on a subsequently invalidated search warrant cannot justify the substantial costs of exclusion. We do not suggest, however, that exclusion is always inappropriate in cases where an officer has obtained a warrant and abided by its terms. [T]he officer's reliance on the magistrate's probable-cause determination and on the technical sufficiency of the warrant he issues must be objectively reasonable,[23] and it is clear that in some circumstances the officer [24] will have no reasonable grounds for believing that the warrant was properly issued.

Suppression therefore remains an appropriate remedy if the magistrate or judge in issuing a warrant was misled by information in an affidavit that the affiant knew was false or would have known was false except for his reckless disregard of the truth. The exception we recognize today will also not apply in cases where the issuing magistrate wholly abandoned his judicial role in the manner condemned in *Lo-Ji Sales, Inc. v. New York,* [p. 289, infra][c], in such circumstances, no reasonably well-trained officer should rely on the warrant. Nor would an officer manifest objective good faith in relying on a warrant based on an affidavit "so lacking in indicia of probable cause as to render official belief in its existence entirely unreasonable." Finally, depending on the circumstances of the particular case, a warrant may be so facially deficient—i.e., in failing to particularize the place to be searched or the things to be seized—that the executing officers cannot reasonably presume it to be valid.

In so limiting the suppresion remedy, we leave untouched the probable-cause standard and the various requirements for a valid warrant. Other objections to the modification of the Fourth Amendment exclusionary rule we consider to be insubstantial. The good-faith exception for searches conducted pursuant to warrants is not intended to signal our unwillingness strictly to enforce the requirements of the Fourth Amendment, and we do not believe that it will have this effect. As we have already suggested, the good-faith exception, turning as it does on objective reasonableness, should not be difficult to apply in practice. When officers have acted pursuant to a warrant, the prosecution should ordinarily be able to establish objective good faith without a substantial expenditure of judicial time.

Nor are we persuaded that application of a good-faith exception to searches conducted pursuant to warrants will preclude review of the constitutionality of the search or seizure, deny needed guidance

tially the same as the inquiry into whether exclusion would serve a deterrent purpose." * * * Absent unusual circumstances, when a Fourth Amendment violation has occurred because the police have reasonably relied on a warrant issued by a detached and neutral magistrate but ultimately found to be defective, "the integrity of the courts is not implicated."

23. [O]ur good-faith inquiry is confined to the objectively ascertainable question whether a reasonably well-trained officer would have known that the search was illegal despite the magistrate's authorization. In making this determination, all of the circumstances—including whether the warrant application had previously been rejected by a different magistrate—may be considered.

24. References to "officer" throughout this opinion should not be read too narrowly. It is necessary to consider the objective reasonableness, not only of the officers who eventually executed a warrant, but also of the officers who originally obtained it or who provided information material to the probable-cause determination. Nothing in our opinion suggests, for example, that an officer could obtain a warrant on the basis of a "bare bones" affidavit and then rely on colleagues who are ignorant of the circumstances under which the warrant was obtained to conduct the search.

c. There the magistrate was held not to have "manifest[ed] that neutrality and detachment demanded of a judicial officer when presented with a warrant application," where he went to the scene and made judgments there about what should be seized as obscene, as he "allowed himself to become a member, if not the leader of the search party which was essentially a police operation."

from the courts, or freeze Fourth Amendment law in its present state.[25] There is no need for courts to adopt the inflexible practice of always deciding whether the officers' conduct manifested objective good faith before turning to the question whether the Fourth Amendment has been violated. Defendants seeking suppression of the fruits of allegedly unconstitutional searches or seizures undoubtedly raise live controversies which Article III empowers federal courts to adjudicate. * * *

If the resolution of a particular Fourth Amendment question is necessary to guide future action by law enforcement officers and magistrates, nothing will prevent reviewing courts from deciding that question before turning to the good-faith issue.[26] Indeed, it frequently will be difficult to determine whether the officers acted reasonably without resolving the Fourth Amendment issue. Even if the Fourth Amendment question is not one of broad import, reviewing courts could decide in particular cases that magistrates under their supervision need to be informed of their errors and so evaluate the officers' good faith only after finding a violation. In other circumstances, those courts could reject suppression motions posing no important Fourth Amendment questions by turning immediately to a consideration of the officers' good faith. We have no reason to believe that our Fourth Amendment jurisprudence would suffer by allowing reviewing courts to exercise an informed discretion in making this choice. * * *

In the absence of an allegation that the magistrate abandoned his detached and neutral role, suppression is appropriate only if the officers were dishonest or reckless in preparing their affidavit or could not have harbored an objectively reasonable belief in the existence of probable cause. Only respondent Leon has contended that no reasonably well-trained police officer could have believed that there existed probable cause to search his house; significantly, the other respondents advance no comparable argument. Officer Rombach's application for a warrant clearly was supported by much more than a "bare bones" affidavit. The affidavit related the results of an extensive investigation and, as the opinions of the divided panel of the Court of Appeals make clear, provided evidence sufficient to create disagreement among thoughtful and competent judges as to the existence of probable cause. Under these circumstances, the officers' reliance on the magistrate's determination of probable cause was objectively reasonable, and application of the extreme sanction of exclusion is inappropriate.

Accordingly, the judgment of the Court of Appeals is *reversed.*

JUSTICE BLACKMUN, concurring. * * *

As the Court's opinion in this case makes clear, the Court has narrowed the scope of the exclusionary rule because of an empirical judgment that the rule has little appreciable effect in cases where officers act in objectively reasonable reliance on search warrants. Because I share the view that the exclusionary rule is not a constitutionally compelled corollary of the Fourth Amendment itself, I see no way to avoid making an empirical judgment of this sort, and I am satisfied that the Court has made the correct one on the information before it. * * *

25. The argument that defendants will lose their incentive to litigate meritorious Fourth Amendment claims as a result of the good-faith exception we adopt today is unpersuasive. Although the exception might discourage presentation of insubstantial suppression motions, the magnitude of the benefit conferred on defendants by a successful motion makes it unlikely that litigation of colorable claims will be substantially diminished.

26. It has been suggested, in fact, that "the recognition of a 'penumbral zone,' within which an inadvertent mistake would not call for exclusion, * * * will make it less tempting for judges to bend fourth amendment standards to avoid releasing a possibly dangerous criminal because of a minor and unintentional miscalculation by the police."

What must be stressed, however, is that any empirical judgment about the effect of the exclusionary rule in a particular class of cases necessarily is a provisional one. * * * If it should emerge from experience that, contrary to our expectations, the good faith exception to the exclusionary rule results in a material change in police compliance with the Fourth Amendment, we shall have to reconsider what we have undertaken here. The logic of a decision that rests on untested predictions about police conduct demands no less. * * *

JUSTICE BRENNAN, with whom JUSTICE MARSHALL joins, dissenting. * * *

[The majority's reading of the Fourth Amendment] appears plausible, because, as critics of the exclusionary rule never tire of repeating, the Fourth Amendment makes no express provision for the exclusion of evidence secured in violation of its commands. A short answer to this claim, of course, is that many of the Constitution's most vital imperatives are stated in general terms and the task of giving meaning to these precepts is therefore left to subsequent judicial decision-making in the context of concrete cases. The nature of our Constitution, as Chief Justice Marshall long ago explained, "requires that only its great outlines should be marked, its important objects designated, and the minor ingredients which compose those objects be deduced from the nature of the objects themselves."

A more direct answer may be supplied by recognizing that the Amendment, like other provisions of the Bill of Rights, restrains the power of the government as a whole; it does not specify only a particular agency and exempt all others. The judiciary is responsible, no less than the executive, for ensuring that constitutional rights are respected.

When that fact is kept in mind, the role of the courts and their possible involvement in the concerns of the Fourth Amendment comes into sharper focus. Because seizures are executed principally to secure evidence, and because such evidence generally has utility in our legal system only in the context of a trial supervised by a judge, it is apparent that the admission of illegally obtained evidence implicates the same constitutional concerns as the initial seizure of that evidence. Indeed, by admitting unlawfully seized evidence, the judiciary becomes a part of what is in fact a single governmental action prohibited by the terms of the Amendment. Once that connection between the evidence-gathering role of the police and the evidence-admitting function of the courts is acknowledged, the plausibility of the Court's interpretation becomes more suspect. Certainly nothing in the language or history of the Fourth Amendment suggests that a recognition of this evidentiary link between the police and the courts was meant to be foreclosed. It is difficult to give any meaning at all to the limitations imposed by the Amendment if they are read to proscribe only certain conduct by the police but to allow other agents of the same government to take advantage of evidence secured by the police in violation of its requirements. The Amendment therefore must be read to condemn not only the initial unconstitutional invasion of privacy—which is done, after all, for the purpose of securing evidence—but also the subsequent use of any evidence so obtained. * * *

Such a conception of the rights secured by the Fourth Amendment was unquestionably the original basis of what has come to be called the exclusionary rule when it was first formulated in *Weeks v. United States.* * * *

[T]he question whether the exclusion of evidence would deter future police misconduct was never considered a relevant concern in the early cases from *Weeks* to *Olmstead.* In those formative decisions, the Court plainly understood that the exclusion of illegally obtained evidence was compelled not by judicially fashioned remedial purposes, but rather by a direct constitutional command. * * *

* * * Indeed, no other explanation suffices to account for the Court's holding in *Mapp*, since the only possible predicate for the Court's conclusion that the States were bound by the Fourteenth Amendment to honor the *Weeks* doctrine is that the exclusionary rule was "part and parcel of the Fourth Amendment's limitation upon [governmental] encroachment of individual privacy."

Despite this clear pronouncement, however, the Court since *Calandra* has gradually pressed the deterrence rationale for the rule back to center stage. The various arguments advanced by the Court in this campaign have only strengthened my conviction that the deterrence theory is both misguided and unworkable. First, the Court has frequently bewailed the "cost" of excluding reliable evidence. In large part, this criticism rests upon a refusal to acknowledge the function of the Fourth Amendment itself. If nothing else, the Amendment plainly operates to disable the government from gathering information and securing evidence in certain ways. In practical terms, of course, this restriction of official power means that some incriminating evidence inevitably will go undetected if the government obeys these constitutional restraints. It is the loss of that evidence that is the "price" our society pays for enjoying the freedom and privacy safeguarded by the Fourth Amendment. Thus, some criminals will go free *not*, in Justice (then Judge) Cardozo's misleading epigram, "because the constable has blundered," but rather because official compliance with Fourth Amendment requirements makes it more difficult to catch criminals. Understood in this way, the Amendment directly contemplates that some reliable and incriminating evidence will be lost to the government; therefore, it is not the exclusionary rule, but the Amendment itself that has imposed this cost.

In addition, the Court's decisions over the past decade have made plain that the entire enterprise of attempting to assess the benefits and costs of the exclusionary rule in various contexts is a virtually impossible task for the judiciary to perform honestly or accurately. Although the Court's language in those cases suggests that some specific empirical basis may support its analyses, the reality is that the Court's opinions represent inherently unstable compounds of intuition, hunches, and occasional pieces of partial and often inconclusive data. * * * To the extent empirical data is available regarding the general costs and benefits of the exclusionary rule, it has shown, on the one hand, as the Court acknowledges today, that the costs are not as substantial as critics have asserted in the past, and, on the other hand, that while the exclusionary rule may well have certain deterrent effects, it is extremely difficult to determine with any degree of precision whether the incidence of unlawful conduct by police is now lower than it was prior to *Mapp*. The Court has sought to turn this uncertainty to its advantage by casting the burden of proof upon proponents of the rule. "Obviously," however, "the assignment of the burden of proof on an issue where evidence does not exist and cannot be obtained is outcome determinative. [The] assignment of the burden is merely a way of announcing a predetermined conclusion."

By remaining within its redoubt of empiricism and by basing the rule solely on the deterrence rationale, the Court has robbed the rule of legitimacy. A doctrine that is explained as if it were an empirical proposition but for which there is only limited empirical support is both inherently unstable and an easy mark for critics. The extent of this Court's fidelity to Fourth Amendment requirements, however, should not turn on such statistical uncertainties. * * *

Even if I were to accept the Court's general approach to the exclusionary rule, I could not agree with today's result. * * *

At the outset, the Court suggests that society has been asked to pay a high price—in terms either of setting guilty persons free or of impeding the proper functioning of trials—as a result of excluding relevant physical evidence in cases where the police, in conducting searches and seizing evidence, have made only an "objectively reasonable" mistake concerning the constitutionality of their actions. But what evidence is there to support such a claim?

Significantly, the Court points to none, and, indeed, as the Court acknowledges, recent studies have demonstrated that the "costs" of the exclusionary rule—calculated in terms of dropped prosecutions and lost convictions—are quite low. Contrary to the claims of the rule's critics that exclusion leads to "the release of countless guilty criminals," these studies have demonstrated that federal and state prosecutors very rarely drop cases because of potential search and seizure problems. For example, a 1979 study prepared at the request of Congress by the General Accounting Office reported that only 0.4% of all cases actually declined for prosecution by federal prosecutors were declined primarily because of illegal search problems. If the GAO data are restated as a percentage of *all* arrests, the study shows that only 0.2% of all felony arrests are declined for prosecution because of potential exclusionary rule problems.[11] Of course, these data describe only the costs attributable to the exclusion of evidence in all cases; the costs due to the exclusion of evidence in the narrower category of cases where police have made objectively reasonable mistakes must necessarily be even smaller. The Court, however, ignores this distinction and mistakenly weighs the aggregated costs of exclusion in *all* cases, irrespective of the circumstances that led to exclusion, against the potential benefits associated with only those cases in which evidence is excluded because police reasonably but mistakenly believe that their conduct does not violate the Fourth Amendment. When such faulty scales are used, it is little wonder that the balance tips in favor of restricting the application of the rule.

What then supports the Court's insistence that this evidence be admitted? Apparently, the Court's only answer is that even though the costs of exclusion are not very substantial, the potential deterrent effect in these circumstances is so marginal that exclusion cannot be justified. The key to the Court's conclusion in this respect is its belief that the prospective deterrent effect of the exclusionary rule operates only in those situations in which police officers, when deciding whether to go forward with some particular search, have reason to know that their planned conduct will violate the requirements of the Fourth Amendment. If these officers in fact understand (or reasonably should understand because

11. In a series of recent studies, researchers have attempted to quantify the actual costs of the rule. A recent National Institute of Justice study based on data for the four year period 1976–1979 gathered by the California Bureau of Criminal Statistics showed that 4.8% of all cases that were declined for prosecution by California prosecutors were rejected because of illegally seized evidence. However, if these data are calculated as a percentage of all arrests that were declined for prosecution, they show that only 0.8% of all arrests were rejected for prosecution because of illegally seized evidence.

In another measure of the rule's impact—the number of prosecutions that are dismissed or result in acquittals in cases where evidence has been excluded—the available data again show that the Court's past assessment of the rule's costs has generally been exaggerated. For example, a study based on data from 9 mid-sized counties in Illinois, Michigan and Pennsylvania reveals that motions to suppress physical evidence were filed in approximately 5% of the 7,500 cases studied, but that such motions were successful in only 0.7% of all these cases. The study also shows that only 0.6% of all cases resulted in acquittals because evidence had been excluded. In the GAO study, suppression motions were filed in 10.5% of all federal criminal cases surveyed, but of the motions filed, approximately 80–90% were denied. Evidence was actually excluded in only 1.3% of the cases studied, and only 0.7% of all cases resulted in acquittals or dismissals after evidence was excluded. And in another study based on data from cases during 1978 and 1979 in San Diego and Jacksonville, it was shown that only 1% of all cases resulting in nonconviction were caused by illegal searches.

the law is well-settled) that their proposed conduct will offend the Fourth Amendment and that, consequently, any evidence they seize will be suppressed in court, they will refrain from conducting the planned search. In those circumstances, the incentive system created by the exclusionary rule will have the hoped-for deterrent effect. But in situations where police officers reasonably (but mistakenly) believe that their planned conduct satisfies Fourth Amendment requirements—presumably either (a) because they are acting on the basis of an apparently valid warrant, or (b) because their conduct is only later determined to be invalid as a result of a subsequent change in the law or the resolution of an unsettled question of law—then such officers will have no reason to refrain from conducting the search and the exclusionary rule will have no effect.

* * * But what the Court overlooks is that the deterrence rationale for the rule is not designed to be, nor should it be thought of as, a form of "punishment" of individual police officers for their failures to obey the restraints imposed by the Fourth Amendment. Instead, the chief deterrent function of the rule is its tendency to promote institutional compliance with Fourth Amendment requirements on the part of law enforcement agencies generally. Thus, as the Court has previously recognized, "over the long term, [the] demonstration [provided by the exclusionary rule] that our society attaches serious consequences to violation of constitutional rights is thought to encourage those who formulate law enforcement policies, and the officers who implement them, to incorporate Fourth Amendment ideals into their value system." It is only through such an institution-wide mechanism that information concerning Fourth Amendment standards can be effectively communicated to rank and file officers.[13]

If the overall educational effect of the exclusionary rule is considered, application of the rule to even those situations in which individual police officers have acted on the basis of a reasonable but mistaken belief that their conduct was authorized can still be expected to have a considerable long-term deterrent effect. If evidence is consistently excluded in these circumstances, police departments will surely be prompted to instruct their officers to devote greater care and attention to providing sufficient information to establish probable cause when applying for a warrant, and to review with some attention the form of the warrant that they have been issued, rather than automatically assuming that whatever document the magistrate has signed will necessarily comport with Fourth Amendment requirements.

After today's decision, however, that institutional incentive will be lost. Indeed, the Court's "reasonable mistake" exception to the exclusionary rule will tend to put a premium on police ignorance of the law. Armed with the assurance provided by today's decision that evidence will always be admissible whenever an officer has "reasonably" relied upon a warrant, police departments will be encouraged to train officers that if a warrant has simply been signed, it is reasonable, without more, to rely on it. Since in close cases there will no longer be any incentive to err on the side of constitutional behavior, police would have every reason to adopt a "let's-wait-until-its-decided" approach in situations in which there is a question about a warrant's validity or the basis for its issuance.[14]

13. * * * A former United States Attorney and now Attorney General of Maryland, Stephen Sachs, has described the impact of the rule on police practices in similar terms: "I have watched the rule deter, routinely, throughout my years as a prosecutor * * *. [P]olice-prosecutor consultation is customary in all our cases when Fourth Amendment concerns arise * * *. In at least three Maryland jurisdictions, for example, prosecutors are on twenty-four hour call to field search and seizure questions presented by police officers."

14. The authors of a recent study of the warrant process in seven cities concluded that application of a good faith exception where an officer

Although the Court brushes these concerns aside, a host of grave consequences can be expected to result from its decision to carve this new exception out of the exclusionary rule. A chief consequence of today's decision will be to convey a clear and unambiguous message to magistrates that their decisions to issue warrants are now insulated from subsequent judicial review. Creation of this new exception for good faith reliance upon a warrant implicitly tells magistrates that they need not take much care in reviewing warrant applications, since their mistakes will from now on have virtually no consequence: If their decision to issue a warrant was correct, the evidence will be admitted; if their decision was incorrect but the police relied in good faith on the warrant, the evidence will also be admitted. Inevitably, the care and attention devoted to such an inconsequential chore will dwindle. Although the Court is correct to note that magistrates do not share the same stake in the outcome of a criminal case as the police, they nevertheless need to appreciate that their role is of some moment in order to continue performing the important task of carefully reviewing warrant applications. Today's decision effectively removes that incentive.

Moreover, the good faith exception will encourage police to provide only the bare minimum of information in future warrant applications. The police will now know that if they can secure a warrant, so long as the circumstances of its issuance are not "entirely unreasonable," all police conduct pursuant to that warrant will be protected from further judicial review. The clear incentive that operated in the past to establish probable cause adequately because reviewing courts would examine the magistrate's judgment carefully, has now been so completely vitiated that the police need only show that it was not "entirely unreasonable" under the circumstances of a particular case for them to believe that the warrant they were issued was valid. The long-run effect unquestionably will be to undermine the integrity of the warrant process.

Finally, even if one were to believe, as the Court apparently does, that police are hobbled by inflexible and hypertechnical warrant procedures, today's decision cannot be justified. This is because, given the relaxed standard for assessing probable cause established just last Term in *Illinois v. Gates*, the Court's newly fashioned good faith exception, when applied in the warrant context, will rarely, if ever, offer any greater flexibility for police than the *Gates* standard already supplies. In *Gates*, the Court held that "the task of an issuing magistrate is simply to make a practical, common-sense decision whether, given all the circumstances set forth in the affidavit before him, * * * there is a fair probability that contraband or evidence of a crime will be found in a particular place." The task of a reviewing court is confined to determining whether "the magistrate had a 'substantial basis' for concluding that probable cause existed." Given such a relaxed standard, it is virtually inconceivable that a reviewing court, when faced with a defendant's motion to suppress, could first find that a warrant was invalid under the new *Gates* standard, but then, at the same time, find that a police officer's reliance on such an invalid warrant was nevertheless "objectively reasonable" under the test announced today. * * *

JUSTICE STEVENS, * * * dissenting * * *.

* * * It is probable, though admittedly not certain, that the Court of Appeals would now conclude that the warrant in *Leon* satisfied the Fourth Amendment if it were given the opportunity to reconsider the issue in the light of *Gates*. Adherence

relies upon a warrant "would further encourage police officers to seek out the less inquisitive magistrates and to rely on boilerplate formulae, thereby lessening the value of search warrants overall. * * *

to our normal practice following the announcement of a new rule would therefore postpone, and probably obviate, the need for the promulgation of the broad new rule the Court announces today.

[W]hen the Court goes beyond what is necessary to decide the case before it, it can only encourage the perception that it is pursuing its own notions of wise social policy, rather than adhering to its judicial role. I do not believe the Court should reach out to decide what is undoubtedly a profound question concerning the administration of criminal justice before assuring itself that this question is actually and of necessity presented by the concrete facts before the Court. * * * [d]

Notes and Questions

1. In the companion case of MASSACHUSETTS v. SHEPPARD, 468 U.S. 981, 104 S.Ct. 3424, 82 L.Ed.2d 737 (1984), a detective prepared an affidavit for a search warrant to search for various specified items of evidence of a homicide but, because it was Sunday, could only find a warrant form for controlled substances. He presented his affidavit and that form to a judge at his home and pointed out the problem to him, and the judge, unable to locate a more suitable form, told the detective that he would make the necessary changes to make it a proper warrant. He made some changes, but failed to change that part of the warrant which authorized a search only for controlled substances and related paraphernalia. The detective took the two documents and he and other officers then executed the warrant, seizing evidence of the homicide. That evidence was suppressed in the state court because the warrant failed to particularly describe the items to be seized, as required by the Fourth Amendment. The Supreme Court, per White, J., held this situation fell within *Leon* because "there was an objectively reasonable basis for the officers' mistaken belief" that "the warrant authorized the search that they conducted." As for defendant's objection that the detective knew when he went to the judge that the warrant was defective, the Court stated: "Whatever an officer may be required to do when he executes a warrant without knowing beforehand what items are to be seized,[6] we refuse to rule that an officer is required to disbelieve a judge who has just advised him, by word and by action, that the warrant he possesses authorizes him to conduct the search he has requested." [e]

What if the detective who obtained the warrant had simply turned it over to another officer for execution and that officer,

d. For commentary on *Leon* and related cases, see Alschuler, *"Close Enough for Government Work:" The Exclusionary Rule after Leon,* 1984 Sup.Ct.Rev. 309; Baker, *Rights, Remedies and the Exclusionary Rule after U.S. v. Leon,* May-June 1984 Benchmark at 23; Bloom, *United States v. Leon and Its Ramifications,* 56 U.Colo. L.Rev. 247 (1985); Bradley, *The "Good Faith" Exception Cases: Reasonable Exercises in Futility,* 60 Ind.L.J. 287 (1985); LaFave, *"The Seductive Call of Expediency": U.S. v. Leon, Its Rationale and Ramifications,* 1984 U.Ill.L.Rev. 895 (1984); Wald, *The Unreasonable Reasonableness Test for Fourth Amendment Searches,* 4 Crim.Just. Ethics 2 (Winter/Spring, 1985); Wasserstrom & Mertens, *The Exclusionary Rule on the Scaffold: But Was It A Fair Trial?,* 22 Am.Crim.L.Rev. 85 (1984); *The Supreme Court, 1983 Term,* 98 Harv. L.Rev. 87, 108 (1984).

6. Normally, when an officer who has not been involved in the application stage receives a warrant, he will read it in order to determine the object of the search. In this case, Detective O'Malley, the officer who directed the search, knew what items were listed in the affidavit presented to the judge, and he had good reason to believe that the warrant authorized the seizure of those items. Whether an officer who is less familiar with the warrant application or who has unalleviated concerns about the proper scope of the search would be justified in failing to notice a defect like the one in the warrant in this case is an issue we need not decide. We hold only that it was not unreasonable for the police in this case to rely on the judge's assurances that the warrant authorized the search they had requested.

e. Brennan and Marshall, JJ., dissented for the same reasons as in *Leon.* Stevens, J., concurring, argued there had been no Fourth Amendment violation because the particularity requirement was intended to prohibit general searches, which had been accomplished here because "the judge who issued the warrant, the police officers who executed it, and the reviewing courts all were able easily to ascertain the precise scope of the authorization provided by the warrant."

after a careful reading of the warrant, had made a search for and found drugs within an envelope, a place he would not have been entitled to look had he been aware that the warrant should have described certain larger items which could not be concealed in the envelope?

2. What result under *Leon* and *Sheppard* on the following facts, essentially those in *People v. Deitchman,* 695 P.2d 1146 (Colo. 1985)? Four teenage girls were sexually assaulted in the same area over a 10-day span, and they gave a similar general description of their assailant. One said he wore distinctively marked shoes; one said he had a red bandana; and two said his car license was CN–4714. Those facts were put into a search warrant affidavit, along with a statement that investigation "revealed that CN–4714 lists to Jerry M. Deitchman of 1755 South Pecos Street." The affidavit asserted, without explanation, that there was "reason to believe" that the shoes and bandana were at 3300 West Ohio Avenue; the magistrate issued a warrant to search that location for the shoes and bandana, which were found there in execution of the warrant. Police had earlier been unable to locate Deitchman until his employer said he had moved to 3300 West Ohio, and police arrested him there prior to obtaining the warrant, but those facts were not reported to the magistrate.

3. Will (should) *Leon* be extended to warrantless arrests and searches? In *Lopez-Mendoza,* p. 232 infra, involving a warrantless arrest, White, J., dissenting, asserted *Leon* was applicable, so that "if the agents neither knew nor should have known that they were acting contrary to the dictates of the Fourth Amendment, evidence will not be suppressed even if it is held that their conduct was illegal." If that is wrong, then does it follow, as concluded in *People v. Ciraolo,* 208 Cal.Rptr. 93 (App.1984), cert. granted, ___ U.S. ___, 105 S.Ct. 2672, 86 L.Ed.2d 691 (1985), that *Leon* is also inapplicable to the magistrate's apparent determination, when issuing a search warrant, that a warrantless surveillance included in the affidavit was lawful and thus is properly considered in deciding whether there was probable cause?

4. Are there other "limitations" which might well be imposed upon the exclusionary rule? Consider the two proposals made in Kaplan, *The Limits of the Exclusionary Rule,* 26 Stan.L.Rev. 1027 (1974). One is that "the rule not apply in the most serious cases—treason, espionage, murder, armed robbery, and kidnapping by organized groups," where exclusion would occur only under the *Rochin* [p. 46 supra] test. In support, it is said that "the political costs of the rule, the possibility of releasing serious and dangerous offenders into the community, and the disproportion between the magnitude of the policeman's constitutional violation and the crime in which the evidence is to be suppressed are sufficient reasons to modify the rule."

The second proposal is "to hold the exclusionary rule inapplicable to cases where the police department in question has taken seriously its responsibility to adhere to the fourth amendment. Specifically, departmental compliance would require a set of published regulations giving guidance to police officers as to proper behavior in situations such as the one under litigation, a training program calculated to make violations of the fourth amendment rights isolated occurrences, and, perhaps most importantly, a history of taking disciplinary action where such violations are brought to its attention."

5. Should the Court instead abolish the exclusionary rule entirely on the ground that the deterrence function stressed in *Leon* is more generally not served by exclusion? Consider Burger, C.J., dissenting in *Bivens v. Six Unknown Named Agents,* p. 235 infra, asserting a lack of deterrent efficacy because: (i) "The rule does not apply any direct sanction to the individual official whose illegal conduct results in the exclusion of evidence in a criminal trial." (ii) Police "have no * * * stake in successful prosecutions," and "the prosecutor

who loses his case because of police misconduct is not an official in the police department; he can rarely set in motion any corrective action or administrative penalties." (iii) "Policemen do not have the time, inclination, or training to read and grasp the nuances of the appellate opinions that ultimately define the standards of conduct they are to follow." (iv) "[T]here are large areas of police activity which do not result in criminal prosecutions—hence the rule has virtually no applicability and no effect in such situations." Would such abolition be more palliatable if, as the Chief Justice also suggested in *Bivens*, Congress were to "develop an administrative or quasi-judicial remedy against the government itself to afford compensation and restitution for persons whose Fourth Amendment rights have been violated"? Consider also Posner, *Excessive Sanctions for Governmental Misconduct in Criminal Cases,* 57 Wash.L.Rev. 635 (1982), applying an economic analysis to the problem and concluding it should suffice if the government were required to compensate the victim of an illegal search for his "cleanup costs."

6. In MICHIGAN v. DeFILLIPPO, 443 U.S. 31, 99 S.Ct. 2627, 61 L.Ed.2d 343 (1979), the defendant was arrested for violating a Detroit ordinance making it a violation for a person lawfully stopped by police to refuse to produce evidence of his identity, after which drugs were found on his person. His conviction of the drug offense was reversed by the Michigan court of appeals, which held that the ordinance was unconstitutionally vague and that consequently the arrest and search were invalid. The Supreme Court, per THE CHIEF JUSTICE, reversed, reasoning: "A prudent officer, in the course of determining whether respondent had committed an offense under all the circumstances shown by this record, should not have been required to anticipate that a court would later hold the ordinance unconstitutional.

"Police are charged to enforce laws until and unless they are declared unconstitutional. The enactment of a law forecloses speculation by enforcement officers concerning its constitutionality—with the possible exception of a law so grossly and flagrantly unconstitutional that any person of reasonable prudence would be bound to see its flaws. Society would be ill served if its police officers took it upon themselves to determine which laws are and which are not constitutionally entitled to enforcement." [f]

The Chief Justice added that this result was not inconsistent with the Court's earlier holdings "that the exclusionary rule required suppression of evidence obtained in searches carried out pursuant to statutes" subsequently held unconstitutional, as those "decisions involved statutes which, by their own terms, authorized searches under circumstances which did not satisfy the traditional warrant and probable cause requirements of the Fourth Amendment." Does *Leon* affect those earlier holdings?

7. Should the fruits of constitutional but yet illegal arrests and searches be excluded? Reconsider fn. b, p. 208 supra, and consider UNITED STATES v. CACERES, 440 U.S. 741, 99 S.Ct. 1465, 59 L.Ed.2d 733 (1979), holding that the failure of an IRS agent to follow IRS electronic surveillance regulations did not require suppression. STEVENS, J., for the majority, reasoned:

f. Brennan, J., joined by Marshall and Stevens, JJ., objected: "Since the State is responsible for the actions of its legislative bodies as well as for the actions of its police, the State can hardly defend against this charge of unconstitutional conduct by arguing that the constitutional defect was the product of legislative action and that the police were merely executing the laws in good faith." Blackmun, J., concurring, cautioned: "If a defendant in a proper case showed that the police habitually arrest, but do not prosecute, under a Stop and Identify ordinance, then I think this would suffice to rebut any claim that the police were acting in reasonable, good-faith reliance on the constitutionality of the ordinance."

"Regulations governing the conduct of criminal investigations are generally considered desirable, and may well provide more valuable protection to the public at large than the deterrence flowing from the occasional exclusion of items of evidence in criminal trials. Although we do not suggest that a suppression order in this case would cause the Internal Revenue Service to abandon or modify its electronic surveillance regulations, we cannot ignore the possibility that a rigid application of an exclusionary rule to every regulatory violation could have a serious deterrent impact on the formulation of additional standards to govern prosecutorial and police procedures. Here, the Executive itself has provided for internal sanctions in cases of knowing violations of the electronic surveillance regulations. To go beyond that, and require exclusion in every case, would take away from the Executive Department the primary responsibility for fashioning the appropriate remedy for the violation of its regulations. But since the content, and indeed the existence, of the regulations would remain within the Executive's sole authority, the result might well be fewer and less protective regulations. In the long run, it is far better to have rules like those contained in the IRS Manual, and to tolerate occasional erroneous administration of the kind displayed by this record, than either to have no rules except those mandated by statute, or to have them framed in a mere precatory form."

NOTES ON THE "DIMENSIONS" OF THE EXCLUSIONARY RULE

1. *Evidence obtained by government agents, used as basis for questions to grand jury witness.* In UNITED STATES v. CALANDRA, 414 U.S. 338, 94 S.Ct. 613, 38 L.Ed.2d 561 (1974), the Court, per POWELL, J., held that a grand jury witness may not refuse to answer questions on the ground that they are based on evidence obtained from him in an earlier unlawful search. After observing that a contrary holding would unduly interfere with the effective and expeditious discharge of the grand jury's duties [see p. 723 infra], the Court asserted: "Whatever deterrence of police misconduct may result from the exclusion of illegally-seized evidence from criminal trials, it is unrealistic to assume that application of the rule to grand jury proceedings would significantly further that goal. Such an extension would deter only police investigation consciously directed toward the discovery of evidence solely for use in a grand jury investigation. The incentive to disregard the requirement of the Fourth Amendment solely to obtain an indictment from a grand jury is substantially negated by the inadmissibility of the illegally-seized evidence in a subsequent criminal prosecution of the search victim. For the most part, a prosecutor would be unlikely to request an indictment where a conviction could not be obtained. We therefore decline to embrace a view that would achieve a speculative and undoubtedly minimal advance in the deterrence of police misconduct at the expense of substantially impeding the role of the grand jury."

BRENNAN, J., joined by Douglas and Marshall, JJ., dissenting, quoted from *Weeks* to show that "the twin goals of enabling the judiciary to avoid the taint of partnerships in official lawlessness and of assuring the people * * * that the government would not profit from its lawless behavior, * * * not the rule's possible deterrent effect, were uppermost in the minds of the framers of the rule," and then argued:

"It is no answer, as the Court suggests, that the grand jury witnesses' Fourth Amendment rights will be sufficiently protected 'by the inadmissibility of the illegally-seized evidence in a subsequent criminal prosecution of the search victim.' This, of course, is no alternative for Calandra, since he was granted transactional immunity and cannot be criminally prosecuted. But the fundamental flaw of the alternative is that to compel Calandra to testify in the first place under penalty of contempt necessarily 'thwarts' his Fourth Amendment protection and 'entangle the courts in the illegal acts of Government agents' * * *."

2. *Evidence obtained by government agents, used in criminal case after conviction.* Should illegally seized evidence be admissible after conviction for consideration by the judge in determining the sentence to be imposed? *Verdugo v. United States,* 402 F.2d 599 (9th Cir.1968), holding no, was distinguished in *United States v. Schipani,* 315 F.Supp. 253 (E.D.N.Y.1970), aff'd, 435 F.2d 26 (2d Cir.1970), in that the decision in *Verdugo* was "predicated upon the fact that the search which had produced the improper evidence was conducted outside the course of the regular criminal investigation. It was undertaken, not to obtain evidence to support an indictment and conviction, but to recover contraband and thus to enhance the possibility of a heavier sentence after the basic investigation had been completed. [Under these circumstances,] law enforcement officials would have little to lose, but much to gain, in violating the Fourth Amendment." That situation was not present in *Schipani,* and thus the court concluded that "no appreciable increment in deterrence would result from applying a second exclusion at sentencing after the rule has been applied at the trial itself."

Should the exclusionary rule be applied at probation or parole revocation proceedings? Is a negative answer justified on the ground that such application "would tend to obstruct the parole system in accomplishing its remedial purposes," as stated in *United States ex rel. Sperling v. Fitzpatrick,* 426 F.2d 1161 (2d Cir.1970)? On the ground that "the bungling police officer is not likely to be halted by the thought that his unlawful conduct will prevent the termination of parole," as stated in *In re Martinez,* 463 P.2d 734 (Cal.1970)? Should a contrary result obtain when "illegal acts of a government agent were directed specifically at a probationer," as concluded in *Thompson v. United States,* 444 A.2d 972 (D.C.App.1982)? Or, should the exclusionary rule *always* apply because police "know of the high probability that any suspect in a new crime may be a probationer or parolee," as concluded in *State v. Burkholder,* 466 N.E.2d 176 (Ohio 1984)?

3. *Evidence obtained by government agents, used in "quasi-criminal" or civil case.* In ONE 1958 PLYMOUTH SEDAN v. PENNSYLVANIA, 380 U.S. 693, 85 S.Ct. 1246, 14 L.Ed.2d 170 (1965), a unanimous Court held that the *Weeks-Mapp* exclusionary rule applies to forfeiture proceedings. *Boyd v. United States,* "the leading case on the subject of search and seizure * * * itself was not a criminal case," pointed out the majority, "but was a proceeding by the United States to forfeit 35 cases of plate glass which had allegedly been imported without payment of the customs duty * * *. [As] pointed out in *Boyd,* a forfeiture proceeding is quasi-criminal in character. Its object, like a criminal proceeding, is to penalize for the commission of an offense against the law. In this case * * * the driver and owner of the automobile was arrested and charged with a criminal offense against the Pennsylvania liquor laws. * * * In this forfeiture proceeding he was subject to the loss of his automobile, which at the time involved had an estimated value of approximately $1,000, a higher amount than the maximum fine in the criminal proceeding. It would be anomalous indeed, under these circumstances, to hold that in the criminal proceeding the illegally seized evidence is excludable, while in the forfeiture proceeding, requiring the determination that the criminal law has been violated, the same evidence would be admissible."

Los Angeles police seized wagering records and $4,940 in cash pursuant to a search warrant, and then notified the IRS, which made an assessment against Janis for wagering taxes and levied upon the seized cash in partial satisfaction. After Janis' motion to suppress was granted in the state criminal proceedings, he sued for refund of the money and to quash the assessment because it was based upon illegally seized evidence. The federal district court ruled for Janis, and the court of appeals affirmed. In UNITED STATES v. JANIS, 428 U.S. 433, 96 S.Ct. 3021, 49 L.Ed.2d 1046 (1976), the Court, per BLACKMUN, J., reversed: "Working, as we must, with the absence of convincing empirical data, common sense dictates that the deterrent effect of the exclusion of relevant evidence is highly attenuated when the 'punishment' imposed upon the offending criminal enforcement officer is the removal of that evidence from a civil suit by or against a different sovereign. In *Elkins* [p. 212 supra] the Court indicated that the assumed interest of criminal law enforcement officers in the criminal proceedings of another sovereign counterbalanced this attenuation sufficiently to justify an exclusionary rule. Here, however, the attenuation is further augmented by the fact that the proceeding is one to enforce only the civil law of the other sovereign.

"This attenuation coupled with the existing deterrence effected by the denial of use of the evidence by either sovereign in the criminal trials with which the searching officer is concerned, creates a situation in which the imposition of the exclusionary rule sought in this case is unlikely to provide significant much less substantial, additional deterrence. It falls outside the offending officer's zone of primary interest."

Brennan and Marshall, JJ., dissented on the basis of their *Calandra* dissent. Stewart, J., dissenting, argued that the majority's deterrence theory compelled the opposite result in light of the fact that "federal and local law enforcement personnel regularly provide federal tax officials with information, obtained in criminal investigations, indicating liability under the wagering tax. The pattern is one of mutual cooperation and coordination, with the federal wagering tax provisions buttressing state and federal criminal sanctions." He noted that it was admitted by the local police officer in the instant case that he notified the IRS whenever he uncovered a gambling operation involving a substantial amount of cash.

Utilizing the *Janis* cost-benefit approach, the Court held 5–4 in I.N.S. v. LOPEZ-MENDOZA, 468 U.S. 1032, 104 S.Ct. 3479, 82 L.Ed.2d 778 (1984), that the exclusionary rule is inapplicable in a civil deportation hearing. O'Connor, J., explained that the deterrent value of the exclusionary rule in this context was reduced because (i) "deportation will still be possible when evidence not derived directly from the arrest is sufficient to support deportation," (ii) INS agents know "that it is highly unlikely that any particular arrestee will end up challenging the lawfulness of his arrest," (iii) "the INS has its own comprehensive scheme for deterring Fourth Amendment violations" by training and discipline, and (iv) "alternative remedies" including the "possibility of declaratory relief" are available for institutional practices violating the Fourth Amendment. On the cost side, the Court continued, are these factors: (i) that application of the exclusionary rule "in proceedings that are intended not to punish past transgressions but to prevent their continuance or renewal would require courts to close their eyes to ongoing violations of the law," (ii) that invocation of the exclusionary rule at deportation hearings, where "neither the hearing officers nor the attorneys * * * are likely to be well versed in the intricacies of Fourth Amendment law," "might significantly change and complicate the character of these proceedings," and (iii) that because many INS arrests "occur in crowded and confused circumstances," application of the exclusionary rule "might well result in the suppression of large amounts of information that had been obtained entirely lawfully." White, J., dissenting, objected that "unlike the situation in *Janis,* the conduct challenged here falls within 'the offending officer's zone of primary interest,'" and concluded that "the costs and benefits of applying the exclusionary rule in civil deportation proceedings do not differ in any significant way from the costs and benefits of applying the rule in ordinary criminal proceedings."

4. *Evidence obtained by private persons, used in criminal proceedings.* In *Burdeau v. McDowell,* 256 U.S. 465, 41 S.Ct. 574, 65 L.Ed.2d 1048 (1921), the exclusionary rule was characterized "as a restraint upon the activities of sovereign authority and * * * not * * * a limitation upon other than governmental agencies," and on this basis courts have declined to exclude evidence in criminal cases when obtained by private persons.

The result is otherwise if the private person is acting on behalf of the police, as in *Stapleton v. Superior Court,* 447 P.2d 967 (Cal.1968). Agents of a credit card company sought the aid of police in arresting the defendant, who was wanted for credit card fraud. The defendant was arrested in his home, and a search of the premises was then undertaken. In the presence of the police, one of the credit card agents learned that the defendant's car had not yet been searched and left the house with defendant's keys for the purpose of conducting such a search. Tear-gas cannisters were found in the car, and the defendant sought to exclude them from evidence. The court concluded:

"The search of petitioner's car was clearly part of a joint operation by police and the credit card agents aimed at arresting petitioner and obtaining evidence against him. This official participation in the planning and implementation of the overall operation is sufficient without more to taint with state action the subsequent acts of such credit card agents. * * * [T]he police need not have requested or directed the search in order to be guilty of 'standing idly by'; knowledge of the illegal search coupled with a failure to protect the petitioner's rights against such a search suffices."

What result, then, upon the following facts: FBI agents who suspected that defendant was shipping obscene films in interstate commerce advised an airline's customer service manager that they believed the air waybill for defendant's packages, left with the airline for shipment, contained a nonexistent return address and a false description of the contents. The agents did not tell the manager what they believed the packages contained, nor did they ask the manager to open the packages. After the agents departed, the manager opened the packages, found obscene films, and notified the FBI agents of his discovery. Consider Comment, 119 U.Pa. L.Rev. 163 (1970), arguing that in such cases private action taken in response to a police notification, bulletin, or request "warrants a finding of police agency when the activity would not have occurred but for the bulletin and could reasonably have been expected by the police."

One issue which frequently arises with respect to private person searches is whether, if that person then summons the police, police activity with respect to the same object is a separate "search" subject to Fourth Amendment constraints. For example, in UNITED STATES v. JACOBSEN, 466 U.S. 109, 104 S.Ct. 1652, 80 L.Ed.2d 85 (1984), Federal Express employees opened a damaged box and found newspapers covering a tube which, when cut open, was found to contain plastic bags of white powder. Federal drug agents were summoned, but before their arrival the bags had been put back into the tube and the tube and newspapers back into the box, which was left open. A federal agent reopened the packaging to the extent necessary to expose the powder, which he field tested and found to be cocaine. The Court, per STEVENS, J., concluded the agent's actions were not a significant expansion of the earlier private search and that consequently no warrant was required. "Respondents could have no privacy interest in the contents of the package, since it remained unsealed and since the Federal Express employees had just examined the package and had, of their own accord, invited the federal agent to their offices for the express purpose of viewing its contents. The agent's viewing of what a private party had freely made available for his inspection did not violate the Fourth Amendment.

"Similarly, the removal of the plastic bags from the tube and the agent's visual inspection of their contents enabled the agent to learn nothing that had not previously been learned during the private search. It infringed no legitimate expectation of privacy and hence was not a 'search' within the meaning of the Fourth Amendment." [a]

Three members of the Court rejected that reasoning. WHITE, J., objected:

"The majority opinion is particularly troublesome when one considers its logical implications. I would be hard-pressed to distinguish this case, which involves a private search, from (1) one in which the private party's knowledge, later communicated to the government, that a particular container concealed contraband and nothing else arose from his presence at the time the container was sealed; (2) one in which the private party learned that a container concealed contraband and nothing else when it was previously opened in his presence; or (3) one in which the private party knew to a certainty that a container concealed contraband and nothing else as a result of conversations with its owner. In each of these cases, the approach adopted by the Court today would seem to suggest that the owner of the container has no legitimate expectation of privacy in its contents and that government agents opening that container without a warrant on the strength of information provided by the private party would not violate the Fourth Amendment."

6. *Evidence obtained by foreign officials, used in domestic criminal proceedings.* Would any purpose be served by applying the exclusionary rule in such circumstances? What if American authorities requested or participated in the actions of the foreign police?

NOTES ON OTHER REMEDIES

1. *The "constitutional tort" by state officers. Monroe v. Pape*, 365 U.S. 167, 81 S.Ct. 473, 5 L.Ed.2d 492 (1961), concerned an action for damages under 42 U.S.C. § 1983 [b] against the City of Chicago and 13 Chicago police officers. The complaint alleged that the officers broke into petitioners' home in the early morning, routed them from bed, made them stand naked in the living room, and ransacked every room in the house, after which Mr. Monroe was taken to the station and interrogated incommunicado about a murder. The Court rejected the respondents' argument that the suit was barred because no "statute, ordinance, regulation, custom or usage" of Illinois made a state remedy unavailable: "It is no answer that the State has a law which if enforced would give relief. The federal remedy is supplementary to the state remedy, and the latter need not be first sought and refused before the federal one is invoked. Hence the fact that Illinois by its constitution and laws outlaws unreasonable searches and seizures is no barrier to the present suit in the federal court."

In *Pierson v. Ray,* 386 U.S. 547, 87 S.Ct. 1213, 18 L.Ed.2d 288 (1967), involving arrests under a breach of the peace statute thereafter found unconstitutional, the Court held that "if the jury found that the officers reasonably believed in good faith that the arrest was constitutional, then a verdict for the officers would follow even

a. As for the field test, see p. 245 infra.

b. "Every person who, under color of any statute, ordinance, regulation, custom, or usage, of any State or Territory, subjects, or causes to be subjected, any citizen of the United States or other person within the jurisdiction thereof to the deprivation of any rights, privileges, or immunities secured by the Constitution and laws, shall be liable to the party injured in an action at law, suit in equity, or other proper proceeding for redress."

though the arrest was in fact unconstitutional." But on the ground that "substantial costs attend the litigation of the subjective good faith of government officials," this defense was later reformulated by the Court as a purely objective standard. *Harlow v. Fitzgerald,* 457 U.S. 800, 102 S.Ct. 2727, 73 L.Ed.2d 396 (1982).

Although *Monroe* also held that the City of Chicago was properly dismissed as a party because "Congress did not undertake to bring municipal corporations within the ambit" of the statute, the Court took another look at the legislative history in *Monell v. New York City Dep't of Social Services,* 436 U.S. 658, 98 S.Ct. 2018, 56 L.Ed.2d 611 (1978), and ruled otherwise. The Court in *Monell* cautioned that the statute did not "impose liability vicariously on governing bodies solely on the basis of the existence of an employer-employee relationship with a tortfeasor," and thus concluded "that a local government may not be sued for an injury inflicted solely by its employees or agents. Instead, it is when execution of a government's policy or custom, whether made by its lawmakers or by those whose edicts or acts may fairly be said to represent official policy, inflicts the injury that the government as an entity is responsible under § 1983."

In *Owen v. City of Independence,* 445 U.S. 662, 100 S.Ct. 1398, 63 L.Ed.2d 673 (1980), the Court held, 5–4, that the statute did not confer upon municipalities the tort law immunities for "governmental" functions and "discretionary" activities, and also that a municipality may not assert as a defense the good faith of its officers.

2. *The "constitutional tort" by federal officers.* Section 1983 applies only to persons acting under color of state law, thus excluding federal officers acting under color of their authority. In BIVENS v. SIX UNKNOWN NAMED AGENTS, 403 U.S. 388, 91 S.Ct. 1999, 29 L.Ed.2d 619 (1971), the Court held that, although Congress had not provided a tort remedy under such circumstances, a complaint alleging that the Fourth Amendment had been violated by federal agents acting under color of their authority gives rise to a federal cause of action for damages.

The government argued that petitioner could obtain damages to redress invasion of Fourth Amendment rights only by means of a state law tort suit and that in this scheme the Fourth Amendment would merely limit the extent to which the agents could defend the suit by asserting their actions were a valid exercise of federal power: if the agents had violated the Fourth Amendment, such a defense would be lost to them and they would be viewed merely as private individuals. The Court rejected this contention as resting upon "an unduly restrictive view of the Fourth Amendment's protection" and upon the misconception that "the relationship between a citizen and a federal agent unconstitutionally exercising his authority" is "no different from the relationship between two private citizens." The Court pointed out: (1) the Amendment proscribes more conduct than that which, if engaged in by private persons, would be condemned by state law; (2) interests protected by state law and those protected by the Amendment "may be inconsistent or even hostile"; (3) "historically, damages have been regarded as the ordinary remedy for an invasion of personal interests in liberty." [c]

As for liability of the federal government, the Court in *Bivens* stated this issue was better left to Congress because "the federal purse was involved." In 1974 Congress amended the Federal Tort

c. On remand, 456 F.2d 1339 (2d Cir.1972), it was held that federal police officers "have no immunity to protect them from damage suits charging violations of constitutional rights," but "that it is a valid defense to such charges to allege and prove that the federal agent or other federal police officer acted in the matter complained of in good faith and with a reasonable belief in the validity of the arrest and search and in the necessity for carrying out the arrest and search in the way the arrest was made and the search was conducted."

Claims Act to make it applicable "to acts or omissions of investigative or law enforcement officers of the United States Government" on any subsequent claim arising "out of assault, battery, false imprisonment, false arrest, abuse of process, or malicious prosecution. For the purpose of this subsection, 'investigative or law enforcement officer' means any officer of the United States who is empowered by law to execute searches, to seize evidence, or to make arrests for violations of Federal law." 28 U.S.C. § 2680(h). The "effect of this provision is to deprive the Federal Government of the defense of sovereign immunity in cases * * * [involving] the same kind of conduct that is alleged to have occurred in *Bivens.*" S.Rep.No. 93–588, 93d Cong., 2d Sess., 1974 *U.S.Code Cong. & Ad.News* 2789, 2791 (1974).

The availability of a FTCA remedy against the government does not bar a *Bivens* suit against the offending officer, as the latter is "a more effective deterrent." *Carlson v. Green,* 446 U.S. 14, 100 S.Ct. 1468, 64 L.Ed.2d 15 (1980).

3. *Injunction and mandamus.* RIZZO v. GOODE, 423 U.S. 362, 96 S.Ct. 598, 46 L.Ed.2d 561 (1976), involved two class actions brought under 42 U.S.C. § 1983 against the Mayor of Philadelphia, the Police Commissioner, and others, alleging a pervasive pattern of unconstitutional police mistreatment of minority citizens in particular and Philadelphia residents in general. The district court found in one suit that two policemen, not named as parties, had violated complainants' constitutional rights on three occasions, and in the other found that in two incidents police conduct amounting to a deprivation of federal rights had occurred. The court also found that the evidence did not establish the existence of any policy by the Mayor or Police Commissioner to violate constitutional rights, but did find evidence of departmental discouragement of complaints and a tendency to minimize the consequences of police misconduct. In addition, the court found that only a small percentage of police commit violations of the rights of Philadelphia residents, but that such violations could "not be dismissed as rare, isolated instances." The district court ordered the preparation of "a comprehensive program for dealing adequately with civilian complaints" in accordance with the court's "guidelines," and the court of appeals affirmed.

The Supreme Court, per Rehnquist, J., reversed on two grounds: (1) There was no Article III case or controversy, as the individually named complainants claim to "real and immediate" injury rested not on what the Mayor or Police Commissioner might do to them in the future, but upon what one of a small, unnamed minority of police might do to them in light of that officer's perception of departmental disciplinary procedures; this "hypothetical" was too "attenuated" to constitute the requisite "personal stake in the outcome" regarding overhauling police disciplinary procedures. (2) The district court's judgment constituted an unwarranted federal judicial intrusion into the discretionary authority of petitioners to perform their official functions as prescribed by state and local law, and thus the court exceeded its authority under 42 U.S.C. § 1983.

The Court distinguished *Lankford v. Gelston,* 364 F.2d 197 (4th Cir.1966) (enjoining the Baltimore Police Department from searching private homes to arrest nonresidents without probable cause the person to be arrested is present there, upon a showing over 300 homes had been entered on the basis of anonymous tips), in that there the wholesale raids were the effectuation of a plan conceived by high ranking police officials, and also distinguished *Allee v. Medrano,* 416 U.S. 802, 94 S.Ct. 2191, 40 L.Ed.2d 566 (1974), also involving federal injunctive relief against state police, in that there "a persistent pattern of police misconduct" had been established.

4. *Dismissal of criminal charges.* Although an illegal arrest or other unreason-

able seizure of the person is itself a violation of the Fourth and Fourteenth Amendments, the exclusionary sanction comes into play only when the police have obtained evidence as a result of the unconstitutional seizure. It is no defense to a state or federal criminal prosecution that the defendant was illegally arrested or forcibly brought within the jurisdiction of the court. The trial of such a defendant violates neither Fifth nor Fourteenth Amendment Due Process nor any federal legislation. *Frisbie v. Collins,* 342 U.S. 519, 72 S.Ct. 509, 96 L.Ed. 541 (1952); *Ker v. Illinois,* 119 U.S. 436, 7 S.Ct. 225, 30 L.Ed. 421 (1886). In *Gerstein v. Pugh,* p. 306 infra, the Court declined to "retreat from the established rule that illegal arrest or detention does not void a subsequent conviction." See also *United States v. Crews,* p. 808 infra, holding an illegally arrested defendant "is not himself a suppressible 'fruit' and the illegality of his detention cannot deprive the Government of the opportunity to prove his guilt through the introduction of evidence wholly untainted by the police misconduct."

6. *Self-help.* Many statutes provide that a person is not authorized to use force to resist an arrest by one known to be a police officer, even if he believes that the arrest is unlawful and it is in fact. Such deviations from the common law rule that reasonable force may be used to resist an unlawful arrest have generally been upheld. Compare the view of Justice Douglas, dissenting from the dismissal of the writ of certiorari in *Wainwright v. New Orleans,* 392 U.S. 598, 88 S.Ct. 2243, 20 L.Ed.2d 1322 (1968), that one has "the right to offer some resistance to an unconstitutional 'seizure' or 'search'" under "the principle that a citizen can defy an unconstitutional act," and consider Chevigny, *The Right to Resist an Unlawful Arrest,* 78 Yale L.J. 1128, 1141 (1969): "The impairment of fourth amendment rights, however, is not enough to justify resistance to an unlawful arrest. The problem is to determine the circumstances under which such a seizure becomes so provocative as to make unfair the imposition of a criminal penalty for resisting it."

SECTION 2. PROTECTED AREAS AND INTERESTS

KATZ v. UNITED STATES

389 U.S. 347, 88 S.Ct. 507, 19 L.Ed.2d 576 (1967).

MR. JUSTICE STEWART delivered the opinion of the Court.

The petitioner was convicted [of] transmitting wagering information by telephone from Los Angeles to Miami and Boston in violation of a federal statute. At trial the Government was permitted, over the petitioner's objection, to introduce evidence of the petitioner's end of telephone conversations, overheard by FBI agents who had attached an electronic listening and recording device to the outside of the public telephone booth from which he had placed his calls. In affirming his conviction, the Court of Appeals rejected the contention that the recordings had been obtained in violation of the Fourth Amendment, because "[t]here was no physical entrance into the area occupied by [the petitioner]." We granted certiorari in order to consider the constitutional questions thus presented.

The petitioner has phrased those questions as follows:

> "A. Whether a public telephone booth is a constitutionally protected area so that evidence obtained by attaching an electronic listening recording device to the top of such a booth is obtained in violation of the right to privacy of the user of the booth.
>
> "B. Whether physical penetration of a constitutionally protected area is necessary before a search and seizure can be said to be violative of the Fourth Amendment to the United States Constitution."

We decline to adopt this formulation of the issues. In the first place the correct solution of Fourth Amendment problems is not necessarily promoted by incantation of the phrase "constitutionally protected area." Secondly, the Fourth Amendment cannot be translated into a general constitutional "right to privacy." That Amendment protects individual privacy against certain kinds of governmental intrusion, but its protections go further, and often have nothing to do with privacy at all. Other provisions of the Constitution protect personal privacy from other forms of governmental invasion. But the protection of a person's *general* right to privacy—his right to be let alone by other people—is, like the protection of his property and of his very life, left largely to the law of the individual States.

Because of the misleading way the issues have been formulated, the parties have attached great significance to the characterization of the telephone booth from which the petitioner placed his calls. The petitioner has strenuously argued that the booth was a "constitutionally protected area." The Government has maintained with equal vigor that it was not. But this effort to decide whether or not a given "area," viewed in the abstract, is "constitutionally protected" deflects attention from the problem presented by this case. For the Fourth Amendment protects people, not places. What a person knowingly exposes to the public, even in his own home or office, is not a subject of Fourth Amendment protection. * * * But what he seeks to preserve as private, even in an area accessible to the public, may be constitutionally protected. * * *

The Government stresses the fact that the telephone booth from which the petitioner made his calls was constructed partly of glass, so that he was as visible after he entered it as he would have been if he had remained outside. But what he sought to exclude when he entered the booth was not the intruding eye—it was the uninvited ear. He did not shed his right to do so simply because he made his calls from a place where he might be seen. No less than an individual in a business office, in a friend's apartment, or in a taxicab, a person in a telephone booth may rely upon the protection of the Fourth Amendment. One who occupies it, shuts the door behind him, and pays the toll that permits him to place a call, is surely entitled to assume that the words he utters into the mouthpiece will not be broadcast to the world. To read the Constitution more narrowly is to ignore the vital role that the public telephone has come to play in private communication.

The Government contends, however, that the activities of its agents in this case should not be tested by Fourth Amendment requirements, for the surveillance technique they employed involved no physical penetration of the telephone booth from which the petitioner placed his calls.

* * * [A]lthough a closely divided Court supposed in *Olmstead* [p. 423 infra] that surveillance without any trespass and without the seizure of any material object fell outside the ambit of the Constitution, we have since departed from the narrow view on which that decision rested. Indeed, we have expressly held that the Fourth Amendment governs not only the seizure of tangible items, but extends as well to the recording of oral statements overheard without any "technical trespass under * * * local property law." *Silverman v. United States.* Once this much is acknowledged, and once it is recognized that the Fourth Amendment protects people—and not simply "areas"—against unreasonable searches and seizures it becomes clear that the reach of that Amendment cannot turn upon the presence or absence of a physical intrusion into any given enclosure.

We conclude that the underpinnings of *Olmstead* and *Goldman* [p. 426 infra] have been so eroded by our subsequent decisions that the "trespass" doctrine there enunciated can no longer be regarded as controlling. The Government's activities in electronically listening to and recording the petitioner's words violated the privacy upon which he justifiably relied while using the telephone booth and thus constituted a "search and seizure" within the meaning of the Fourth Amendment. The fact that the electronic device employed to achieve that end did not happen to penetrate the wall of the booth can have no constitutional significance.

The question remaining for decision, then, is whether the search and seizure conducted in this case complied with constitutional standards. In that regard, the Government's position is that its agents acted in an entirely defensible manner: They did not begin their electronic surveillance until investigation of the petitioner's activities had established a strong probability that he was using the telephone in question to transmit gambling information to persons in other States, in violation of federal law. Moreover, the surveillance was limited, both in scope and in duration to the specific purpose of establishing the contents of the petitioner's unlawful telephonic communications. The agents confined their surveillance to the brief periods during which he used the telephone booth, and they took great care to overhear only the conversations of the petitioner himself.

Accepting this account of the Government's actions as accurate, it is clear that this surveillance was so narrowly circumscribed that a duly authorized magistrate, properly notified of the need for such investigation, specifically informed of the basis on which it was to proceed, and clearly apprised of the precise intrusion it would entail, could constitutionally have authorized, with appropriate safeguards, the very limited search and seizure that the Government asserts in fact took place. Only last Term we sustained the validity of such an authorization, holding that, under sufficiently "precise and discriminate circumstances" a federal court may empower government agents to employ a concealed electronic device, "for the narrow and particularized purpose of ascertaining the truth of the * * * allegations" of a "detailed factual affidavit alleging the commission of a specific criminal offense." *Osborn v. United States* [p. 428 infra]. Discussing that holding, the Court, in *Berger v. New York* [p. 427 infra], said that "the order authorizing the use of the electronic device" in *Osborn* "afforded similar protections to those * * * of conventional warrants authorizing the seizure of tangible evidence." * * * Here, too, a similar judicial order could have accommodated "the legitimate needs of law enforcement" by authorizing the carefully limited use of electronic surveillance. * * *

The Government * * * urges the creation of a new exception to cover this case.[23] It argues that surveillance of a telephone booth should be exempted from the usual requirement of advance authorization by a magistrate upon a showing of probable cause. We cannot agree. Omission of such authorization "bypasses the safeguards provided by an objective predetermination of probable cause, and substitutes instead the far less reliable procedure of an after-the-event justification for the * * * search, too likely to be subtly influenced by the familiar shortcomings of hindsight judgment." And bypassing a neutral predetermination of the *scope* of a search leaves individuals secure from Fourth Amendment violations "only in the discretion of the police."

These considerations do not vanish when the search in question is transferred from the setting of a home, an office, or a hotel room, to that of a telephone booth. Wherever a man may be, he is entitled to know that he will remain free from unreasonable searches and seizures. The government agents here ignored "the proce-

23. Whether safeguards other than prior authorization by a magistrate would satisfy the Fourth Amendment in a situation involving the national security is a question not presented by this case.

dure of antecedent justification * * * that is central to the Fourth Amendment," procedure that we hold to be a constitutional precondition of the kind of electronic surveillance involved in this case. * * *

Judgment reversed.

MR. JUSTICE MARSHALL took no part in the consideration or decision of this case.

MR. JUSTICE DOUGLAS, with whom MR. JUSTICE BRENNAN joins, concurring.

While I join the opinion of the Court, I feel compelled to reply to the separate concurring opinion of my Brother White, which I view as a wholly unwarranted green light for the Executive Branch to resort to electronic eavesdropping without a warrant in cases which the Executive Branch itself labels "national security" matters.

Neither the President nor the Attorney General is a magistrate. In matters where they believe national security may be involved they are not detached, disinterested, and neutral as a court or magistrate must be. Under the separation of powers created by the Constitution, the Executive Branch is not supposed to be neutral and disinterested. Rather it should vigorously investigate and prevent breaches of national security and prosecute those who violate the pertinent federal laws. The President and Attorney General are properly interested parties, cast in the role of adversary, in national security cases. They may even be the intended victims of subversive action. Since spies and saboteurs are as entitled to the protection of the Fourth Amendment as suspected gamblers like petitioner, I cannot agree that where spies and saboteurs are involved adequate protection of Fourth Amendment rights is assured when the President and Attorney General assume both the position of adversary-and-prosecutor and disinterested, neutral magistrate.

There is, so far as I understand constitutional history, no distinction under the Fourth Amendment between types of crimes. Article III, § 3, gives "treason" a very narrow definition and puts restrictions on its proof. But the Fourth Amendment draws no lines between various substantive offenses. * * *

MR. JUSTICE HARLAN, concurring. * * *

As the Court's opinion states, "The Fourth Amendment protects people, not places." The question, however, is what protection it affords to those people. Generally, as here, the answer to that question requires reference to a "place." My understanding of the rule that has emerged from prior decisions is that there is a twofold requirement, first that a person have exhibited an actual (subjective) expectation of privacy and, second, that the expectation be one that society is prepared to recognize as "reasonable." Thus a man's home is, for most purposes, a place where he expects privacy, but objects, activities, or statements that he exposes to the "plain view" of outsiders are not "protected" because no intention to keep them to himself has been exhibited. On the other hand, conversations in the open would not be protected against being overheard, for the expectation of privacy under the circumstances would be unreasonable. * * *

The critical fact in this case is that "[o]ne who occupies it, [a telephone booth] shuts the door behind him, and pays the toll that permits him to place a call, is surely entitled to assume" that his conversation is not being intercepted. The point is not that the booth is "accessible to the public" at other times, but that it is a temporarily private place whose momentary occupants' expectations of freedom from intrusion are recognized as reasonable. * * *

Finally, I do not read the Court's opinion to declare that no interception of a conversation one-half of which occurs in a public telephone booth can be reasonable in the absence of a warrant. As elsewhere under the Fourth Amendment, warrants are the general rule, to which the legitimate needs of law enforcement may demand specific exceptions. It will be time enough to consider any such exceptions when an appropriate occasion presents itself, and I agree with the Court that this is not one.

MR. JUSTICE WHITE, concurring.

* * * **

* * * In joining the Court's opinion, I note the Court's acknowledgment that there are circumstances in which it is reasonable to search without a warrant. In this connection, in footnote 23 the Court points out that today's decision does not reach national security cases. Wiretapping to protect the security of the Nation has been authorized by successive Presidents. The present Administration would apparently save national security cases from restrictions against wiretapping. * * * We should not require the warrant procedure and the magistrate's judgment if the President of the United States or his chief legal officer, the Attorney General, has considered the requirements of national security and authorized electronic surveillance as reasonable.

MR. JUSTICE BLACK, dissenting.

* * *

Tapping telephone wires, of course, was an unknown possibility at the time the Fourth Amendment was adopted. But eavesdropping (and wiretapping is nothing more than eavesdropping by telephone) was, as even the majority opinion in *Berger,* supra, recognized, "an ancient practice which at common law was condemned as a nuisance. In those days the eavesdropper listened by naked ear under the eaves of houses or their windows, or beyond their walls seeking out private discourse." There can be no doubt that the Framers were aware of this practice, and if they had desired to outlaw or restrict the use of evidence obtained by eavesdropping, I believe that they would have used the appropriate language to do so in the Fourth Amendment. They certainly would not have left such a task to the ingenuity of language-stretching judges. * * *

I do not deny that common sense requires and that this Court often has said that the Bill of Rights' safeguards should be given a liberal construction. This principle, however, does not justify construing the search and seizure amendment as applying to eavesdropping or the "seizure" of conversations. The Fourth Amendment was aimed directly at the abhorred practice of breaking in, ransacking and searching homes and other buildings and seizing peoples' personal belongings without warrants issued by magistrates. The Amendment deserves, and this Court has given it, a liberal construction in order to protect against warrantless searches of buildings and seizures of tangible personal effects. But until today this Court has refused to say that eavesdropping comes within the ambit of Fourth Amendment restrictions.

* * *

** In previous cases, which are undisturbed by today's decision, the Court has upheld, as reasonable under the Fourth Amendment, admission at trial of evidence obtained (1) by an undercover police agent to whom a defendant speaks without knowledge that he is in the employ of the police, *Hoffa v. United States* [p. 459 infra]; (2) by a recording device hidden on the person of such an informant, *Lopez v. United States* [p. 455 infra]; *Osborn v. United States* [p. 428 infra]; and (3) by a policeman listening to the secret microwave transmissions of an agent conversing with the defendant in another location, *On Lee v. United States* [p. 455 infra]. When one man speaks to another he takes all the risks ordinarily inherent in so doing, including the risk that the man to whom he speaks will make public what he has heard. The Fourth Amendment does not protect against unreliable (or law-abiding) associates. *Hoffa v. United States.* It is but a logical and reasonable extension of this principle that a man take the risk that his hearer, free to memorize what he hears for later verbatim repetitions, is instead recording it or transmitting it to another. The present case deals with an entirely different situation, for as the Court emphasizes the petitioner "sought to exclude * * * the uninvited ear," and spoke under circumstances in which a reasonable person would assume that uninvited ears were not listening.

[Note: In connection with this footnote by Justice White, see *United States v. White,* p. 463 infra.]

* * * By clever word juggling the Court finds it plausible to argue that language aimed specifically at searches and seizures of things that can be searched and seized may, to protect privacy, be applied to eavesdropped evidence of conversations that can neither be searched nor seized. Few things happen to an individual that do not affect his privacy in one way or another. Thus, by arbitrarily substituting the Court's language, designed to protect privacy, for the Constitution's language, designed to protect against unreasonable searches and seizures, the Court has made the Fourth Amendment its vehicle for holding all laws violative of the Constitution which offend the Court's broadest concept of privacy. * * *

The Fourth Amendment protects privacy only to the extent that it prohibits unreasonable searches and seizures of "persons, houses, papers and effects." No general right is created by the Amendment so as to give this Court the unlimited power to hold unconstitutional everything which affects privacy. Certainly the Framers, well acquainted as they were with the excesses of governmental power, did not intend to grant this Court such omnipotent lawmaking authority as that. The history of governments proves that it is dangerous to freedom to repose such powers in courts. * * *

ANTHONY G. AMSTERDAM—PERSPECTIVES ON THE FOURTH AMENDMENT

58 Minn.L.Rev. 349, 383–85, 387–88, 393–94 (1974).

The [*Katz*] case is, of course, now generally recognized as seminal and has rapidly become the basis of a new formula of fourth amendment coverage. The formula is that "wherever an individual may harbor a reasonable 'expectation of privacy,' * * * he is entitled to be free from unreasonable governmental intrusion." [330] Notwithstanding the Supreme Court's several repetitions of this formula or variations of it, and notwithstanding even its apparent acceptance by Mr. Justice Stewart (the author of the *Katz* opinion),[332] I believe that it destroys the spirit of *Katz* and most of *Katz's* substance.

Let us start with the seemingly harmless substitution of the phrase "governmental intrusion" for the finding in *Katz* that the government had "violated" *Katz's* interests. If the word "intrusion" is used, as "violated" plainly was, to mean only that interests protected by the fourth amendment have been defeated by the "Government's activities," I have no quarrel with it. The problem with the word lies in its subtle suggestion that a particular kind or sort of government activity, labeled an "intrusion," is necessary to trigger the fourth amendment. But this, in my view, was precisely the approach to fourth amendment coverage that *Katz* decisively rejected.

The entire thrust of the opinion is that it is needless to ask successively whether an individual has the kind of interest that the fourth amendment protects and whether that interest is invaded by a kind of governmental activity characterizable by its attributes as a "search." Rather, a "search" is anything that invades interests protected by the amendment. * * *

Now let us consider the word "expectation" in the "reasonable expectation of privacy" formula to which *Katz* is speedily being reduced. "Expectation" is not a term used in Mr. Justice Stewart's majority opinion in *Katz;* it has been lifted by subsequent cases from Mr. Justice Harlan's concurring opinion, where it is used to mean "an actual (subjective) expectation of privacy * * * that society is prepared to recognize as 'reasonable.'" But Mr. Justice Harlan himself later expressed sec-

330. *Terry v. Ohio,* [p. 361 infra].

332. See *United States v. Dionisio,* [p. 715 infra].

ond thoughts about this conception,[345] and rightly so. An actual, subjective expectation of privacy obviously has no place in a statement of what *Katz* held or in a theory of what the fourth amendment protects. It can neither add to, nor can its absence detract from, an individual's claim to fourth amendment protection. If it could, the government could diminish each person's subjective expectation of privacy merely by announcing half-hourly on television * * * that we were all forthwith being placed under comprehensive electronic surveillance. * * *

Finally, it is plainly wrong to capsulate *Katz* into a comprehensive definition of fourth amendment coverage in terms of "privacy." *Katz* holds that the fourth amendment protects certain privacy interests, but not that those interests are the only interests which the fourth amendment protects. To the contrary, the *Katz* opinion says in so many words that "its protections go further, and often have nothing to do with privacy at all." In short, the common formula for *Katz* fails to capture *Katz* at any point because the *Katz* decision was written to resist captivation in any formula. An opinion which sets aside prior formulas with the observation that they cannot "serve as a talismanic solution to every Fourth Amendment problem" should hardly be read as intended to replace them with a new talisman.

* * * In *Katz* the government argued that even if its electronic surveillance were held to be a search or seizure within the purview of the amendment, it was not an *unreasonable* search or seizure. [But] the Court held their surveillancc unconstitutional for want of a warrant. This, of course, is nothing more or less than the familiar fourth amendment warrant requirement, but I hope that its familiarity will not cause you to overlook the implications of its imposition here. Having once held that a coin telephone booth was protected by the fourth amendment against non-trespassory electronic surveillance, the Court proceeded to require the same justifications for that surveillance as would be required before an officer could go barging into Katz's bedroom. * * *

The fourth amendment, then, is ordinarily treated as a monolith: wherever it restricts police activities at all, its subjects them to the same extensive restrictions that it imposes upon physical entries into dwellings. To label any police activity a "search" or "seizure" within the ambit of the amendment is to impose those restrictions upon it. On the other hand, if it is not labeled a "search" or "seizure," it is subject to no significant restrictions of any kind. It is only "searches" or "seizures" that the fourth amendment requires to be reasonable: police activities of any other sort may be as unreasonable as the police please to make them. * * *

A sliding scale approach would considerably ease the strains that the present monolithic model of the fourth amendment almost everywhere imposes on the process of defining the amendment's outer boundaries. It would obviously be easier and more likely for a court to say that a patrolman's shining of a flashlight into the interior of a parked car was a "search" if that conclusion did not encumber the flashlight with a warrant requirement but simply required, for example, that the patrolman "be able to point to specific and articulable facts" supporting a reasonable inference that something in the car required his attention. It would be easier and more sensible for a court to say that some "constitutionally adequate, reasonable grounds" must exist before a policeman can enter the common hallways of a tenement house and listen at apartment doors, than to say either that this kind of activity is not a search or that it requires a search

345. *United States v. White,* [p. 463 infra] (dissenting opinion): "The analysis must, in my view, transcend the search for subjective expectations or legal attribution of assumptions of risk. Our expectations, and the risks we assume, are in large part reflections of the laws that translate into rules the customs and values of the past and present."

warrant. As a general matter, courts working with a graduated model of the fourth amendment would and should approach questions of its coverage with the disposition to extend it so as to find in the amendment—as Mr. Justice Brennan once urged in dissent—"nothing less than a comprehensive right of personal liberty in the face of governmental intrusion." The question of what constitutes a covered "search" or "seizure" would and should be viewed with an appreciation that to exclude any particular police activity from coverage is essentially to exclude it from judicial control and from the command of reasonableness, whereas to include it is to do no more than say that it must be conducted in a reasonable manner. With the question put in this fashion the answer should seldom be delivered against coverage.

The problem with the graduated model, of course, is [that] it converts the fourth amendment into one immense Rorschach blot. The complaint is being voiced now that fourth amendment law is too complicated and confused for policemen to understand or to obey. Yet present law is a positive paragon of simplicity compared to what a graduated fourth amendment would produce. The varieties of police behavior and of the occasions that call it forth are so innumerable that their reflection in a general sliding scale approach could only produce more slide than scale. * * * If there are no fairly clear rules telling the policeman what he may and may not do, courts are seldom going to say that what he did was unreasonable.

NOTES ON THE IMPACT OF *KATZ* ON THE LAW OF SEARCH AND SEIZURE

1. *Open view.* Generally speaking, it is fair to say that it is not a search for an officer, lawfully present at a certain place, to detect something by one of his natural senses. *United States v. Fisch,* 474 F.2d 1071 (9th Cir.1973) (no search to overhear conversations in adjoining motel room, as they "were audible by the naked ear"). The result ordinarily is the same when common means of enhancing the senses, such as a flashlight or binoculars, are used. But consider *Raettig v. State,* 406 So.2d 1273 (Fla.App.1981) (use of flashlight to look into camper through half-inch wide crack a search, as "a minute crack on the surface of such area can hardly be regarded as an implied invitation to any curious passerby to take a look"); *State v. Ward,* 617 P.2d 568 (Hawaii 1980) (use of binoculars to see crap game in 7th story apartment from closest vantage point an eighth of a mile away a search, as "the constitution does not require that in all cases a person, in order to protect his privacy, must shut himself off from fresh air, sunlight and scenery").

In UNITED STATES v. PLACE, dealing with a temporary seizure of luggage (see p. 379) at an airport so that it could be brought into contact with a drug detection dog, the majority declared "that a person possesses a privacy interest in the contents of personal luggage that is protected by the Fourth Amendment. A 'canine sniff' by a well-trained narcotics detection dog, however, does not require opening the luggage. It does not expose noncontraband items that otherwise would remain hidden from public view, as does, for example, an officer's rummaging through the contents of the luggage. Thus, the manner in which information is obtained through this investigative technique is much less intrusive than a typical search. Moreover, the sniff discloses only the presence or absence of narcotics, a contraband item. Thus, despite the fact that the sniff tells the authorities something about the contents of the luggage, the information obtained is limited. This limited disclosure also ensures that the owner of the property is not subjected to the embarrassment and inconvenience entailed in less discriminate and more intrusive investigative methods.

"In these respects, the canine sniff is *sui generis.* We are aware of no other investigative procedure that is so limited both in the manner in which the information is obtained and in the content of the information revealed by the procedure. Therefore, we conclude that the particular course of investigation that the agents intended to pursue here—exposure of respondent's luggage, which was located in a public place, to a trained canine—did not constitute a 'search' within the meaning of the Fourth Amendment." [a]

Is the notion that "the fourth amendment exists to protect the innocent and may normally be invoked by the guilty only when necessary to protect the innocent," so that "if a device could be invented that accurately detected weapons and did not disrupt the normal movement of people, there could be no fourth amendment objection to its use"? Loewy, *The Fourth Amendment as a Device for Protecting the Innocent,* 81 Mich.L.Rev. 1229, 1246, 1248 (1983). Is the use of these dogs nonetheless objectionable because people have a right to be free of unwanted suspicion, Gardner, *Sniffing for Drugs in the Classroom,* 74 Nw.U.L.Rev. 803, 844–47 (1980), or is the answer that the innocent are benefited by "the dog that freed them from the unwarranted suspicion which otherwise would have continued"? Loewy, supra, at 1247. What then of other concerns about the use of such dogs: "To the extent that the dog is less than perfectly accurate, innocent people run the risk of being searched. Additionally, the very act of being subjected to a body sniff by a German Shepherd may be offensive at best or harrowing at worst to the innocent sniffee." Id. at 1246–47. Finally, what if a dog were utilized to ascertain that there were drugs inside a particular dwelling? [b]

Place was relied upon in *United States v. Jacobsen,* p. 233 supra, holding that where police lawfully came upon a white powder in a package originally opened by private parties, an on-the-spot chemical test of a trace of the powder which would reveal only whether or not it was cocaine was not a search. "Here, as in *Place,* the likelihood that official conduct of the kind disclosed by the record will actually compromise any legitimate interest in privacy seems much too remote to characterize the testing as a search subject to the Fourth Amendment." Brennan and Marshall, JJ., dissenting, objected that "under the Court's analysis in these cases, law enforcement officers could release a trained cocaine-sensitive dog * * * to roam the streets at random, alerting the officers to people carrying cocaine. Or, if a device were developed that, when aimed at a person, would detect instantaneously whether the person is carrying cocaine, there would be no Fourth Amendment bar, under the Court's approach, to the police setting up such a device on a street corner and scanning all passersby. In fact, the Court's analysis is so unbounded that if a device were developed that could detect, from the outside of a building, the presence of cocaine inside, there would be no constitutional obstacle to the police cruising through a residential neighborhood and using the device to identify all homes in which the drug is present."

2. *Residential premises.* Consider which of the following investigative activities constitutes a search under *Katz:*

(a) Though the entrance to an apartment building was locked and could be opened only by a key or by someone within activating a buzzer, an officer en-

a. Brennan and Marshall, JJ., concurring in the result, objected that this issue, neither reached by the court of appeals nor briefed and argued in the Supreme Court, should not be decided in "a discussion unnecessary to the judgment." Blackmun, J., concurring separately, expressed the same concern and added: "While the Court has adopted one plausible analysis of the issue, there are others. For example, a dog sniff may be a search, but a minimally intrusive one that could be justified in this situation under *Terry* upon mere reasonable suspicion."

b. See *United States v. Thomas,* 757 F.2d 1359 (2d Cir.1985), reading *Place* with *United States v. Karo,* p. 251 infra, and concluding such use of those dogs is a search.

tered by catching the door as someone exited the building; once inside he saw an exchange of drugs in a third-floor hallway.

(b) An officer, unable to see into a house from the street or adjacent driveway, crossed a 10-foot strip of land on a side of the house where there were no doors or defined pathways and took a position beneath a window; because the shade was two inches from the bottom of the window, he was able to see drugs inside. See *Lorenzana v. Superior Court,* 511 P.2d 33 (Cal.1973) (is a search). Compare *Moody v. State,* 295 So.2d 272 (Ala.App.1974) (no search to look through blinds on motel room window from area immediately outside the window).

(c) "Suppose that two men drive into Minneapolis and rent a hotel room, paying in advance for three nights. During the first night, they plan a bank robbery which they execute the next day. Following the robbery, they drive directly out of town, never returning to the hotel. Late that same evening, policemen go the rounds of the local cheap hotels, armed with a police artist's sketch of the unmasked half of one bank robber's face drawn from a bystander's description. The night manager tells the officers that the sketch looks like one of the guys in room 212. From outside the hotel, the officers observe that the lights in 212 are lit. The night manager informs them that the occupants checked in yesterday afternoon for three days. After obtaining the manager's permission, the officers break the door of room 212 in force with drawn guns. No one is there, of course; but the officers find and take away a penciled map of the bank area, parts cut from a stocking to make a stocking mask, and other items that are later sought to be used in evidence to connect the former occupants of the room with the bank robbery after their apprehension." Amsterdam, supra, at 368.

3. *Other premises.* Consider:

(a) *Business and commercial premises* are covered by the Fourth Amendment. As stated in *See v. City of Seattle,* p. 399 infra, "[t]he businessman, like the occupant of a residence, has a constitutional right to go about his business free from unreasonable official entries upon his private commercial property." But consider *Dow Chemical Co. v. United States,* 749 F.2d 307 (6th Cir. 1984), cert. granted, ___ U.S. ___, 105 S.Ct. 2700, 86 L.Ed.2d 716 (1985) (company had no justified expectation of privacy against aerial surveillance, given plant's size and location in urban area within flight pattern for nearby airport).

(b) *Private areas in public places.* What if a police officer, positioned at an overhead vent above a rest room, looks down into an individual closed stall and observes criminal conduct? See *State v. Bryant,* 177 N.W.2d 800 (Minn.1970) (is a search). What, however, if the stalls had no doors? What if the observed conduct had not occurred within a stall?

(c) *Detention facilities.* In *Hudson v. Palmer,* 468 U.S. 517, 104 S.Ct. 3194, 82 L.Ed.2d 393 (1984), involving a § 1983 action brought by a state prison inmate who alleged a prison guard had conducted a "shakedown" search of his cell and had destroyed his noncontraband property for purposes of harassment, the Court held, 5–4, "that the Fourth Amendment has no applicability to a prison cell." The Chief Justice reasoned: "The two interests here are the interest of society in the security of its penal institutions and the interest of the prisoner in privacy within his cell. The latter interest, of course, is already limited by the exigencies of the circumstances: A prison 'shares none of the attributes of privacy of a home, an automobile, an office, or a hotel room.' We strike the balance in favor of institutional security, which we have noted is 'central to all other correctional goals.' A right of privacy in traditional Fourth Amendment terms is fundamentally incompatible with the close and continual surveillance of inmates and their cells required to ensure institutional security and internal order. We are satisfied that society would insist that the prisoner's expectation of privacy always yield to what must be considered the paramount interest in institutional security. We believe that it is accepted by our society that '[l]oss of freedom of choice and privacy are inherent incidents of confinement.'' The Court added that for "the same reasons" the seizure and destruction of a prisoner's effects did not fall within the protections of the Fourth Amendment. It is unclear whether *Hudson* applies to the search of the person of a prisoner [c] or, in any event, to a pretrial detention facility.[d]

4. *"Open fields" and other lands.* In OLIVER v. UNITED STATES, 466 U.S. 170, 104 S.Ct. 1735, 80 L.Ed.2d 214 (1984), the Court, per POWELL, J., held that the "open fields" doctrine of *Hester v. United States,* 265 U.S. 57, 44 S.Ct. 445, 68 L.Ed. 898 (1924), by which police entry and examination of a field is free of any Fourth Amendment restraints, had not been implicitly overruled by *Katz.* This was because the *Hester* rule "was founded upon the explicit language of the Fourth Amendment. That Amendment indicates with some precision the places and things encompassed by its protections. As Justice Holmes explained for the Court in his characteristically laconic style: '[T]he special protection accorded by the Fourth Amendment to the people in their "persons, houses, papers, and effects," is not extended to the open fields. The distinction between the latter and the house is as old as the common law.' "

The Court in *Oliver* reasoned that this interpretation of the Amendment was consistent with *Katz,* as "open fields do not provide the setting for those intimate activities that the Amendment is intended to shelter from government interference or surveillance. There is no societal interest in protecting the privacy of those activities, such as the cultivation of crops, that occur in open fields. Moreover, as a practical matter these lands usually are accessible to the public and the police in ways that a home, an office or commercial structure would not be. It is not generally true that fences or no trespassing signs effectively bar the public from viewing open fields in rural areas. And both petitioner Oliver and respondent Thornton concede that the public and police lawfully may survey lands from the air. For these reasons, the asserted expectation of privacy in open fields is not an expectation that 'society recognizes as reasonable.'

"The historical underpinnings of the 'open fields' doctrine also demonstrate that the doctrine is consistent with respect for 'reasonable expectations of privacy.' As Justice Holmes, writing for the Court, observed in *Hester,* the common law distinguished 'open fields' from the 'curtilage,' the land immediately surrounding and associated with the home. The distinction implies that only the curtilage, not the neighboring open fields, warrants the Fourth Amendment protections that attach to the home. At common law, the curtilage is the area to which extends the intimate activity associated with the 'sanctity of a man's home and the privacies of life,' and therefore has been considered part of home itself for Fourth Amendment purposes. Thus, courts have extended Fourth Amendment protection to the curtilage; and they have defined the curtilage, as did the common law, by reference to the factors that determine whether an individual

c. As the dissenters noted, the majority "appears to limit its holding to a prisoner's 'papers and effects' located in his cell" and apparently "believes that at least a prisoner's 'person' is secure from unreasonable search and seizure." In *Bell v. Wolfish,* 441 U.S. 520, 99 S.Ct. 1861, 60 L.Ed.2d 447 (1979), where the Court declared that at best prisoners have a "reasonable expectation of privacy * * * of a diminished scope," it was held that neither strip searches nor body cavity inspections of pretrial detainees after contact visits with outsiders were unreasonable.

d. Much, but certainly not all, of the Court's analysis in *Hudson* has to do with circumstances existing in facilities housing those convicted of crime. But O'Connor, J., concurring, stated the broader proposition that the "fact of arrest and incarceration abates all legitimate Fourth Amendment privacy and possessory interests in personal effects."

reasonably may expect that an area immediately adjacent to the home will remain private. Conversely, the common law implies, as we reaffirm today, that no expectation of privacy legitimately attaches to open fields.[11] "

As for the contention of Oliver and Thornton that the circumstances may sometimes show the existence of a reasonable expectation of privacy, the Court said it was answered by the "language of the Fourth Amendment," but added that such a case-by-case approach would in any event be unworkable because "police officers would have to guess before every search whether landowners had erected fences sufficiently high, posted a sufficient number of warning signs, or located contraband in an area sufficiently secluded to establish a right of privacy." The *Oliver* majority also asserted that it rejected "the suggestion that steps taken to protect privacy establish that expectations of privacy in an open field are legitimate. It is true, of course, that petitioner Oliver and respondent Thornton, in order to conceal their criminal activities, planted the marijuana upon secluded land and erected fences and no trespassing signs around the property. And it may be that because of such precautions, few members of the public stumbled upon the marijuana crops seized by the police. Neither of these suppositions demonstrates, however, that the expectation of privacy was *legitimate* in the sense required by the Fourth Amendment. The test of legitimacy is not whether the individual chooses to conceal assertedly 'private' activity. Rather, the correct inquiry is whether the government's intrusion infringes upon the personal and societal values protected by the Fourth Amendment. As we have explained, we find no basis for concluding that a police inspection of open fields accomplishes such an infringement."

MARSHALL, J., joined by Brennan and Stevens, JJ., dissenting, argued (1) that the Court's first ground could not be squared with earlier decisions, including *Katz* itself, for "neither a public telephone booth nor a conversation conducted therein can fairly be described as a person, house, paper, or effect"; and (2) that society *is* prepared to recognize as reasonable the expectations of Oliver and Thornton, which were supported by the law of criminal trespass, the private uses to which privately owned lands could be put, and the precautions which they had taken to manifest their privacy interest to others. From this the dissenters posited this "clear, easily administrable rule": "Private land marked in a fashion sufficient to render entry thereon a criminal trespass under the law of the state in which the land lies is protected by the Fourth Amendment's proscription of unreasonable searches and seizures."

Compare *People v. Ciraolo,* 208 Cal.Rptr. 93 (App.1985), cert. granted, ___ U.S. ___, 105 S.Ct. 2672, 86 L.Ed.2d 691 (1985) (because *Oliver* reaffirmed open fields-curtilage distinction, it follows that aerial surveillance at 1000 ft. which revealed marijuana plants in defendant's back yard, surrounded by 6-ft. outer fence and 10-ft inner fence, was a search).

5. *Vehicles.* Consider:

(a) In *Cardwell v. Lewis,* 417 U.S. 583, 94 S.Ct. 2464, 41 L.Ed.2d 325 (1974), police seized a car from a public parking lot and later took a small paint sample off the car and matched the tire tread with tracks at a crime scene. The Court divided on the propriety of the seizure of the

11. Neither petitioner Oliver nor respondent Thornton has contended that the property searched was within the curtilage. Nor is it necessary in this case to consider the scope of the curtilage exception to the open fields doctrine or the degree of Fourth Amendment protection afforded the curtilage, as opposed to the home itself. It is clear, however, that the term "open fields" may include any unoccupied or undeveloped area outside of the curtilage. An open field need be neither "open" nor a "field" as those terms are used in common speech. For example, contrary to respondent Thornton's suggestion, a thickly wooded area nonetheless may be an open field as that term is used in construing the Fourth Amendment.

car, but the plurality opinion seemed to view the later activity as no search: "With the 'search' limited to the examination of the tire on the wheel and the taking of paint scraping from the exterior of the vehicle left in the public parking lot, we fail to comprehend what expectation of privacy was infringed."

(b) Agents came onto defendant's property for the legitimate purpose of questioning him, and while there detected a suspicious odor coming from his truck. One agent then looked through a small crack between the rear doors and saw incriminating evidence. See *United States v. Bradshaw,* 490 F.2d 1097 (4th Cir.1974) (viewing was a search; smelling was not).

(c) What if an officer opens the door or raises the hood of a car in order to determine the auto's vehicle identification number? Compare *United States v. Forrest,* 620 F.2d 446 (5th Cir.1980) (no search); with *People v. Class,* 472 N.E.2d 1009 (N.Y.1984), cert. granted, ___ U.S. ___, 105 S.Ct. 1863, 85 L.Ed.2d 157 (1985) (is a search).

6. *Effects.* Consider:

(a) An officer squeezed the locked luggage which defendant had checked with an airline and smelled the odor of marijuana in the escaping air. See *Hernandez v. United States,* 353 F.2d 624 (9th Cir.1966) (is a search).

(b) An officer entered the open back yard area of defendant's residence and looked in three trash cans located 2–3 feet from the back door and found a bag with a small amount of marijuana. See *People v. Edwards,* 458 P.2d 713 (Cal.1969) (is a search). What if (i) the trash barrel was also used by others; (ii) the police go through the defendant's trash after it has been placed out on the street for collection; (iii) the police examine the trash after it has been placed out on the public way, but a local ordinance prohibits anyone except authorized collectors from rummaging into or otherwise interfering with garbage so placed; or (iv) the defendant's trash was picked up by an authorized collector at the regular time, but by prearrangement with the police the collector kept that trash segregated from other garbage collected and turned it over to the police?

7. *Surveillance of relationships and movements.*

(a) *Examining financial records.* In *United States v. Miller,* 425 U.S. 435, 96 S.Ct. 1619, 48 L.Ed.2d 71 (1976), the respondent contended that "the combination of the recordkeeping requirements of the [Bank Secrecy] Act [requiring banks to make and keep microfilm copies of checks and similar instruments] and the issuance of a subpoena to obtain those records permits the Government to circumvent the requirements of the Fourth Amendment by allowing it to obtain a depositor's private records without complying with the legal requirements that would be applicable had it proceeded against him directly." The Court, per Powell, J., disagreed, concluding that the respondent had no expectation of privacy as to the checks and deposit slips which he "voluntarily conveyed to the banks and exposed to their employees in the ordinary course of business." "The depositor," said the Court, "takes the risk, in revealing his affairs to another, that the information will be conveyed by that person to the government." Thus, there was no need to consider respondent's claim "that a subpoena issued to a bank to obtain records maintained pursuant to the Act is subject to more stringent Fourth Amendment requirements than is the ordinary subpoena."

Brennan, J., dissenting, relied upon *Burrows v. Superior Court,* 529 P.2d 590 (Cal. 1974), a unanimous holding that a "bank customer's reasonable expectation is that, absent compulsion by legal process, the matters he reveals to the bank will be utilized by the bank only for internal banking purposes." (In *Burrows,* the bank turned papers over to the police merely upon their request.) Marshall, J., also dissented.[e]

(b) *Pen registers.* What if the police, with the assistance of the phone company, install and use a pen register, i.e., place a mechanical device on defendant's phone line which records all numbers dialed from his phone and the times the numbers were dialed, but does not overhear oral communications nor indicate whether calls are actually completed? In SMITH v. MARYLAND, 442 U.S. 735, 99 S.Ct. 2577, 61 L.Ed. 220 (1979), the Court, per BLACKMUN, J., held in a 5–3 decision (Powell, J., not participating) that no "search" had occurred, and thus no warrant was required, "conclud[ing] that petitioner in all probability entertained no actual expectation of privacy in the phone numbers he dialed, and that, even if he did, his expectation was not 'legitimate' ":

"Although petitioner's conduct may have been calculated to keep the *contents* of his conversation private, his conduct was not and could not have been calculated to preserve the privacy of the number he dialed. Regardless of his location, petitioner had to convey that number to the telephone company in precisely the same way if he wished to complete his call. The fact that he dialed the number on his home phone rather than on some other phone could make no conceivable difference, nor could any subscriber rationally think that it would.

"[E]ven if petitioner did harbor some subjective expectation that the phone numbers he dialed would remain private, this expectation is not 'one that society is prepared to recognize as "reasonable." ' This Court consistently has held that a person has no legitimate expectation of privacy in information he voluntarily turns over to third parties [referring to *Miller,* supra, and the consensual eavesdropping cases, *White, Hoffa* and *Lopez,* all discussed in Ch. 6, § 3].

"[The analysis of *Miller*] dictates that petitioner can claim no legitimate expectation of privacy here. When he used his phone, petitioner voluntarily conveyed numerical information to the telephone company and 'exposed' that information to its equipment in the ordinary course of business. In so doing, petitioner assumed the risk that the company would reveal to police the numbers he dialed."

There were two dissenting opinions, one by Justice Stewart (joined by Brennan, J.), the other by Justice Marshall (also joined by Brennan, J.). MARSHALL, J., objected: "Privacy is not a discrete commodity, possessed absolutely or not at all. Those who disclose certain facts to a bank or phone company for a limited business purpose need not assume that this information will be released to other persons for other purposes. * * *

"Implicit in the concept of assumption of risk is some notion of choice. At least in the third-party consensual surveillance cases, which first incorporated risk analysis into Fourth Amendment doctrine, the defendant presumably had exercised some discretion in deciding who should enjoy his confidential communications. By contrast here, unless a person is prepared to forego use of what for many has become a personal or professional necessity, he cannot help but accept the risk of surveillance. It is idle to speak of 'assuming' risks in contexts where, as a practical matter, individuals have no realistic alternative.

"More fundamentally, to make risk analysis dispositive in assessing the reasonableness of privacy expectations would allow the Government to define the scope of Fourth Amendment protections. For example, law-enforcement officials could, simply by announcing their intent to moni-

e. In response to *Miller,* Congress enacted the "Right to Financial Privacy Act of 1978," Pub.L. No. 95–630, which requires that a copy of any federal subpoena or summons for financial records be served on the customer with full notice of his right to challenge the subpoena or summons in court prior to its execution 10 days hence, unless a "protective order" is obtained upon a showing that such notice would seriously jeopardize the investigation.

tor the content of random samples of first class mail or private phone conversations, put the public on notice of the risks they would thereafter assume in such communications. [W]hether privacy expectations are legitimate within the meaning of *Katz* depends not on the risks an individual can be presumed to accept when imparting information to third parties, but on the risks he should be forced to assume in a free and open society."

STEWART, J., the author of the *Katz* opinion, protested that the *Smith* majority had forgotten the teachings of *Katz* :

"[The *Katz* case] held that the user of even a public telephone is entitled 'to assume that the words he utters into the mouthpiece will not be broadcast to the world.' " [T]he central question in this case is whether a person who makes telephone calls from his home is entitled to make a similar assumption about the numbers he dials. What the telephone company does or does not do with those numbers is no more relevant to this inquiry than it would be in a case involving the conversation itself. It is simply not enough to say, after *Katz,* that there is no legitimate expectation of privacy in the numbers dialed because the caller assumes the risk that the telephone company will disclose them to the police."

(c) *Mail covers.* What if, at the request of the police, postal authorities record all information (e.g., postmarks, return addresses) on mail received by the defendant? In *United States v. Choate,* 576 F.2d 165 (9th Cir.1978), the court relied on *Miller* in asserting: "While the Supreme Court has not expressly passed on the mail cover device, recent analogous opinions lead us to conclude that it would not hold mail covers unconstitutional even though neither the addressee nor the sender is aware that the exterior data is being used for purposes other than the proper routing of the mail."

(d) *Electronic tracking.* With the consent of a chemical company, police installed a "beeper," a battery operated radio transmitter, into a container of chloroform, a chemical used to manufacture illicit drugs, prior to its purchase by suspect Armstrong. By a combination of visual surveillance and monitoring of the beeper signal the police tracked the container as it was carried in Petschen's automobile to a cabin in a rural area. On that evidence and other information obtained during surveillance of those premises, a search warrant for the cabin was issued, and an illicit drug lab was discovered within. Knotts, the owner of the cabin, was one of those convicted of conspiracy to manufacture controlled substances. In *United States v. Knotts,* 460 U.S. 276, 103 S.Ct. 1081, 75 L.Ed.2d 55 (1983), the Court, per Rehnquist, J., held that the use of the "beeper" did not constitute a Fourth Amendment search:

"Visual surveillance from public places along Petschen's route or adjoining Knotts' premises would have sufficed to reveal all of these facts to the police. The fact that the officers in this case relied not only on visual surveillance, but on the use of the beeper to signal the presence of Petschen's automobile to the police receiver, does not alter the situation. Nothing in the Fourth Amendment prohibited the police from augmenting the sensory faculties bestowed upon them at birth with such enhancement as science and technology afforded them in this case."

To Knotts' objection that under such a view "twenty-four hour surveillance of any citizen of this country will be possible, without judicial knowledge or supervision," the Court responded that "if such dragnet type law enforcement practices as respondent envisions should eventually occur, there will be time enough then to determine whether different constitutional principles may be applicable."

In UNITED STATES v. KARO, 468 U.S. 705, 104 S.Ct. 3296, 82 L.Ed.2d 530 (1984), the Court was "called upon to address two questions left unresolved in *Knotts:* (1) whether installation of a beeper in a container of chemicals with the consent of the original owner constitutes a search or seizure within the meaning of the Fourth Amendment when the container is delivered to a buyer having no knowledge of the presence of the beeper, and (2) whether monitoring of a beeper falls within the ambit of the Fourth Amendment when it reveals information that could not have been obtained through visual surveillance." The Court, per White, J., answered the first question in the negative, reasoning that the mere transfer of the can containing an unmonitored beeper "infringed no privacy interest" because it "conveyed no information that [the recipient] wished to keep private, for it conveyed no information at all," and thus was no search, and that "it cannot be said that anyone's possessory interest was interfered with in a meaningful way," and thus there was no seizure. (Stevens, Brennan and Marshall, JJ., dissenting on this branch of the case, argued that by "attaching the beeper and using the container to conceal it, the Government in the most fundamental sense was asserting 'dominion and control' over the property," which "is a 'seizure' in the most basic sense of the term.")

The Court answered the second question in the affirmative, first noting that unquestionably it would be an unreasonable search to surreptitiously enter a residence without a warrant to verify that the container was there. "For purpose of the Amendment, the result is the same where, without a warrant, the Government surreptitiously employs an electronic device to obtain information that it could not have obtained by observation from outside the curtilage of the house. The beeper tells the agent that a particular article is actually located at a particular time in the private residence and is in the possession of the person or persons whose residence is being surveilled. Even if visual surveillance has revealed that the article to which the beeper is attached has entered the house, the later monitoring not only verifies the officers' observations but also establishes that the article remains on the premises." The Court next concluded that absent "truly exigent circumstances" such use of the beeper was governed by "the general rule that a search of a house should be conducted pursuant to a warrant." [f] Such monitoring was characterized by the Court as "less intrusive than a full-scale search," but the Court did not have occasion to decide whether as a consequence such a warrant could issue upon reasonable suspicion rather than probable cause.[g]

In *Gouled v. United States,* 255 U.S. 298, 41 S.Ct. 261, 65 L.Ed. 647 (1921), the Court held that search warrants "may not be used as a means of gaining access to a man's house or office and papers solely for the purpose of making search to secure evidence to be used against him in a criminal or penal proceeding." The Court derived from *Boyd v. United States,* p. 706 infra, the proposition that warrants may be resorted to "only when a primary right to such search and seizure may be found in the interest which the public or the complainant may have in the property to be seized, or in the right to the possession of it, or when a valid exercise of the police power renders possession of the property by the accused unlawful and provides that it may be taken," that is, when the proper-

f. In response to the government's claim that a warrant should not be required because of the difficulty in satisfying the particularity requirement of the Fourth Amendment, in that it is usually not known in advance to what place the container with the beeper in it will be taken, the Court concluded that it would suffice if the warrant were "to describe the object into which the beeper is to be placed, the circumstances that led agents to wish to install the beeper, and the length of time for which beeper surveillance is requested."

g. See Fishman, *Electronic Tracking Devices and the Fourth Amendment: Knotts, Karo, and the Questions Still Unanswered,* 34 Cath.U.L.Rev. 277 (1985).

ty is an instrumentality or fruit of crime or contraband. This "mere evidence" rule, as it came to be called, was finally repudiated in *Warden v. Hayden,* 387 U.S. 294, 87 S.Ct. 1642, 18 L.Ed.2d 782 (1967). Stressing that "the principal object of the Fourth Amendment is the protection of privacy rather than property," the Court noted that "privacy 'would be just as well served by a restriction on search to the even-numbered days of the month. * * * And it would have the extra advantage of avoiding hair-splitting questions.' " The government need not have a property interest in the property to be seized, as "government has an interest in solving crime," and that interest and the protection of privacy are best accommodated, the Court reasoned, by merely requiring probable cause that "the evidence sought will aid in a particular apprehension or conviction." But the Court cautioned:

"The items of clothing involved in this case are not 'testimonial' or communicative' in nature, and their introduction therefore did not compel respondent to become a witness against himself in violation of the Fifth Amendment. This case thus does not require that we consider whether there are items of evidential value whose very nature precludes them from being the object of a reasonable search and seizure."

ANDRESEN v. MARYLAND

427 U.S. 463, 96 S.Ct. 2737, 49 L.Ed.2d 627 (1976).

MR. JUSTICE BLACKMUN delivered the opinion of the Court.

[State authorities obtained search warrants to search petitioner's law office and also corporate offices for specified documents pertaining to a fraudulent sale of land. The papers found in the execution of the warrants were admitted against the petitioner at his trial, and he was convicted.]

The Fifth Amendment * * * provides that "[n]o person * * * shall be compelled in any criminal case to be a witness against himself." * * * The "historic function" of the privilege has been to protect a " 'natural individual from compulsory incrimination through his own testimony or personal records.' " There is no question that the records seized from petitioner's offices and introduced against him were incriminating. Moreover, it is undisputed that some of these business records contain statements made by petitioner. The question, therefore, is whether the seizure of these business records, and their admission into evidence at his trial, compelled petitioner to testify against himself in violation of the Fifth Amendment. This question may be said to have been reserved in *Warden v. Hayden.*

Petitioner contends that "the Fifth Amendment prohibition against compulsory self-incrimination applies as well to personal business papers seized from his offices as it does to the same papers being required to be produced under a subpoena." He bases his argument, naturally, on dicta in a number of cases which imply, or state, that the search for and seizure of a person's private papers violate the privilege against self-incrimination. Thus, in *Boyd v. United States* the Court said: "[W]e have been unable to perceive that the seizure of a man's private books and papers to be used in evidence against him is substantially different from compelling him to be a witness against himself." And in *Hale v. Henkel* [p. 712 infra], it was observed that "the substance of the offense is the compulsory production of private papers, whether under a search warrant or a *subpoena duces tecum,* against which the person * * * is entitled to protection."

We do not agree, however, that these broad statements compel suppression of this petitioner's business records as a violation of the Fifth Amendment. In the very recent case of *Fisher v. United States* [p. 757 infra], the Court held that an attorney's production, pursuant to a lawful summons, of his client's tax records in his hands did not violate the Fifth Amendment privilege of the taxpayer "because enforcement against a taxpayer's lawyer would not 'compel' the taxpayer to do anything—and certainly would not compel him to be a 'witness' against himself." We recognized that the continued validity of the broad statements contained in some of the Court's earlier cases had been discredited by later opinions. In those earlier cases, the legal predicate for the inadmissibility of the evidence seized was a violation of the Fourth Amendment; the unlawfulness of the search and seizure was thought to supply the compulsion of the accused necessary to invoke the Fifth Amendment. Compulsion of the accused was also absent in *Couch v. United States,* 409 U.S. 322, 93 S.Ct. 611, 34 L.Ed.2d 548 (1973), where the Court held that a summons served on a taxpayer's accountant requiring him to produce the taxpayer's personal business records in his possession did not violate the taxpayer's Fifth Amendment rights.

Similarly, in this case, petitioner was not asked to say or to do anything. The records seized contained statements that petitioner had voluntarily committed to writing. The search for and seizure of these records were conducted by law enforcement personnel. Finally, when these records were introduced at trial, they were authenticated by a handwriting expert, not by petitioner. Any compulsion of petitioner to speak, other than the inherent psychological pressure to respond at trial to unfavorable evidence, was not present.

This case thus falls within the principle stated by Mr. Justice Holmes: "A party is privileged from producing the evidence but not from its production." * * * Thus, although the Fifth Amendment may protect an individual from complying with a subpoena for the production of his personal records in his possession because the very act of production may constitute a compulsory authentication of incriminating information, a seizure of the same materials by law enforcement officers differs in a crucial respect—the individual against whom the search is directed is not required to aid in the discovery, production, or authentication of incriminating evidence.

A contrary determination that the seizure of a person's business records and their introduction into evidence at a criminal trial violates the Fifth Amendment, would undermine the principles announced in earlier cases. * * * These cases recognize a general rule: "There is no special sanctity in papers, as distinguished from other forms of property, to render them immune from search and seizure, if only they fall within the scope of the principles of the cases in which other property may be seized, and if they be adequately described in the affidavit and warrant."

Moreover, a contrary determination would prohibit the admission of evidence traditionally used in criminal cases and traditionally admissible despite the Fifth Amendment. For example, it would bar the admission of an accused's gambling records in a prosecution for gambling; a note given temporarily to a bank teller during a robbery and subsequently seized in the accused's automobile or home in a prosecution for bank robbery; and incriminating notes prepared, but not sent, by an accused in a kidnapping or blackmail prosecution. * * *

Finally we do not believe that permitting the introduction into evidence of a person's business records seized during an otherwise lawful search would offend or undermine any of the policies undergirding the privilege.

In this case, petitioner, at the time he recorded his communication, at the time of the search, and at the time the records were admitted at trial, was not subjected to "the cruel trilemma of self-accusation, perjury or contempt." Indeed, he was never required to say or to do anything under penalty of sanction. Similarly, permitting the admission of the records in question does not convert our accusatorial system of justice into an inquisitorial system. * * * Further, the search for and seizure of business records pose no danger greater than that inherent in every search that evidence will be "elicited by inhumane treatment and abuses." In this case, the statements seized were voluntarily committed to paper before the police arrived to search for them, and petitioner was not treated discourteously during the search. Also, the "good cause" to "disturb," petitioner was independently determined by the judge who issued the warrants; and the State bore the burden of executing them. Finally, there is no chance in this case, of petitioner's statements being self-deprecatory and untrustworthy because they were extracted from him—they were already in existence and had been made voluntarily. * * *

MR. JUSTICE BRENNAN, dissenting. * * *

The matter cannot be resolved on any simplistic notion of compulsion. Search and seizure is as rife with elements of compulsion as subpoena. The intrusion occurs under the lawful process of the State. The individual is not free to resist that authority. * * *

And compulsion does not disappear merely because the individual is absent at the time of search and seizure. The door to one's house, for example, is as much the individual's resistance to the intrusion of outsiders as his personal physical efforts to prevent the same. To refuse recognition to the sanctity of that door and, more generally, to confine the dominion of privacy to the mind compels an unconstitutional disclosure by denying to the individual a zone of physical freedom necessary for conducting one's affairs. * * *

Until today, no decision by this Court had held that the seizure of testimonial evidence by legal process did not violate the Fifth Amendment. Indeed, with few exceptions, the indications were strongly to the contrary. * * * These cases all reflect the root understanding of *Boyd v. United States:* "It is not the breaking of his doors, and the rummaging of his drawers, that constitutes the essence of the offence [to the Fifth Amendment]; but it is the invasion of his indefeasible right of personal security, personal liberty and private property. * * * [A]ny forcible and compulsory extortion of a man's own testimony or his private papers to be used as evidence to convict him of crime * * *, is within the condemnation of [the Amendment]. In this regard the fourth and fifth amendments run almost into each other." [a]

Notes and Questions

1. If the item to be seized was a diary instead of the business records in *Andresen,* would there be a stronger Fourth Amendment [b] or Fifth Amendment [c] argument against permitting the seizure? Consider *Model Pre-Arraignment Code* § SS 210.3(2): "With the exception of handwriting samples, and other writings or recordings of evidentiary value for reasons other than their testimonial content, things subject to seizure * * * shall not include personal diaries, letters, or other writings or recordings, made solely for private use or communication to an individual occupying a family, personal, or other confidential relation, other than a relation in criminal en-

a. Marshall, J., dissented on other grounds and thus found it unnecessary to reach the Fifth Amendment issue.

b. In *Fisher,* relied upon in *Andresen,* the Court, after stating that the taxpayers "have not raised arguments of a Fourth Amendment nature * * * and could not be successful if they had," cautioned that the "[s]pecial problems of privacy which might be presented by subpoena of a personal diary * * * are not involved here." See also fn. a, p. 759.

c. "[I]t has been thought that a diary in which its author has recited his criminal conduct, seized in an otherwise lawful search, should not be used against him, just as any other kind of involuntary confession is unusable under the Fifth Amendment." *United States v. Boyette,* 299 F.2d 92 (4th Cir.1962). But see Note 5, p. 770 infra.

terprise, unless such things have served or are serving a substantial purpose in furtherance of a criminal enterprise."

2. Given the *Andresen* holding about the inapplicability of the Fifth Amendment in a search case and the very slight Fourth Amendment protection available in a subpoena duces tecum case, see p. 713 infra, what should the result be when the prosecutor resorts to what the court in *United States v. Howell,* 466 F.Supp. 835 (D.Or. 1979), characterized as "the 'one-two' punch"? There, the prosecutor subpoenaed six black books in the possession of Howell and they were produced *in camera* so that the judge could rule on his Fifth Amendment claim, and when the court ruled in his favor but before the books could be returned, the prosecutor sought a search warrant for those books.

ZURCHER v. STANFORD DAILY

436 U.S. 547, 98 S.Ct. 1970, 56 L.Ed.2d 525 (1978).

MR. JUSTICE WHITE delivered the opinion of the Court.

[Nine policemen were injured by demonstrators at Stanford University Hospital. Two days later the Stanford Daily carried articles and photos devoted to the demonstration and attack; the photos by a staff member indicated he had been located where he could have photographed the assailants. A warrant was obtained to search the Daily's offices for negatives, film and pictures relevant to identification of the assailants. Executing officers searched photo labs, filing cabinets and desks, but found no evidence. The Daily later brought a civil action in district court, where declaratory relief was granted. That court held (i) that the Fourth Amendment forbade the issuance of a warrant to search for materials in the possession of one not suspected of crime except upon a showing of probable cause a subpoena *duces tecum* would be impracticable; and (ii) that the First Amendment bars search of newspaper offices except upon a clear showing that important materials would otherwise be destroyed or removed and that a restraining order would be futile.]

It is an understatement to say that there is no direct authority in this or any other federal court for the District Court's sweeping revision of the Fourth Amendment. Under existing law, valid warrants may be issued to search *any* property, whether or not occupied by a third party, at which there is probable cause to believe that fruits, instrumentalities, or evidence of a crime will be found. Nothing on the face of the Amendment suggests that a third-party search warrant should not normally issue. * * *

Against this background, it is untenable to conclude that property may not be searched unless its occupant is reasonably suspected of crime and is subject to arrest. * * * The Fourth Amendment has itself struck the balance between privacy and public need, and there is no occasion or justification for a court to revise the Amendment and strike a new balance by denying the search warrant in the circumstances present here and by insisting that the investigation proceed by subpoena *duces tecum,* whether on the theory that the latter is a less intrusive alternative, or otherwise. * * *

In any event, the reasons presented by the District Court and adopted by the Court of Appeals for arriving at its remarkable conclusion do not withstand analysis. First, as we have said, it is apparent that whether the third-party occupant is suspect or not, the State's interest in enforcing the criminal law and recovering the evidence remains the same; and it is the seeming innocence of the property owner that the District Court relied on to foreclose the warrant to search. But as respondents themselves now concede, if the third party knows that contraband or other illegal materials are on his property, he is sufficiently culpable to justify the issuance of a search warrant. Similarly, if his ethical stance is the determining factor, it seems to us that whether or not he knows that the sought-after articles are secreted on his property and whether or not he knows that the articles are in fact the fruits, instrumentalities, or evidence of crime, he will be so informed when the search warrant is served, and it is doubtful that he should then be permitted to object to the search, to withhold, if it is there, the evidence of crime reasonably believed to be possessed by him or secreted on his property, and to forbid the search and insist that the officers serve him with a subpoena *duces tecum.*

Second, we are unpersuaded that the District Court's new rule denying search warrants against third parties and insisting on subpoenas would substantially further privacy interests without seriously undermining law enforcement efforts. As the District Court understands it, denying third-party search warrants would not have substantial adverse effects on criminal investigations because the nonsuspect third party, once served with a subpoena, will preserve the evidence and ultimately, lawfully respond. The difficulty with this assumption is that search warrants are often employed early in an investigation, perhaps before the identity of any likely criminal and certainly before all the perpetrators are or could be known. The seemingly blameless third party in possession of the fruits or evidence may not be innocent at all; and if he is, he may nevertheless be so related to or so sympathetic with the culpable that he cannot be relied upon to retain and preserve the articles that may implicate his friends, or at least not to notify those who would be damaged by the evidence that the authorities are aware of its location. In any event, it is likely that the real culprits will have access to the property, and the delay involved in employing the subpoena *duces tecum,* offering as it does the opportunity to litigate its validity, could easily result in the disappearance of the evidence, whatever the good faith of the third party. * * * [8]

We are also not convinced that the net gain to privacy interests by the District Court's new rule would be worth the candle.[9] In the normal course of events, search warrants are more difficult to obtain than subpoenas, since the latter do not involve the judiciary and do not require proof of probable cause. Where, in the real world, subpoenas would suffice, it can be expected that they will be employed by the rational prosecutor. On the other hand, when choice is available under local law and the prosecutor chooses to use the search warrant, it is unlikely that he has needlessly selected the more difficult course. His choice is more likely to be based on the solid belief, arrived at through experience but difficult, if not impossible, to sustain a specific case, that

8. It is also far from clear, even apart from the dangers of destruction and removal, whether the use of the subpoena *duces tecum* under circumstances where there is probable cause to believe that a crime has been committed and that the materials sought constitute evidence of its commission will result in the production of evidence with sufficient regularity to satisfy the public interest in law enforcement. Unlike the individual whose privacy is invaded by a search, the recipient of a subpoena may assert the Fifth Amendment privilege against self-incrimination in response to a summons to produce evidence or give testimony. See *Maness v. Meyers,* 419 U.S. 449, 95 S.Ct. 584, 42 L.Ed.2d 574 (1975). This privilege is not restricted to suspects. We have construed it broadly as covering any individual who might be incriminated by the evidence in connection with which the privilege is asserted. *Hoffman v. United States,* 341 U.S. 479, 71 S.Ct. 814, 95 L.Ed. 1118 (1951). The burden of overcoming an assertion of the Fifth Amendment privilege, even if prompted by a desire not to cooperate rather than any real fear of self-incrimination, is one which prosecutors would rarely be able to meet in the early stages of an investigation despite the fact they did not regard the witness as a suspect. Even time spent litigating such matters could seriously impede criminal investigations.

9. We reject totally the reasoning of the District Court that additional protections are required to assure that the Fourth Amendment rights of third parties are not violated because of the unavailability of the exclusionary rule as a deterrent to improper searches of premises in the control of nonsuspects. * * * It is probably seldom that police during the investigatory stage when most searches occur will be so convinced that no potential defendant will have standing to exclude evidence on Fourth Amendment grounds that they will feel free to ignore constitutional restraints. * * *

the warranted search is necessary to secure and to avoid the destruction of evidence.

[The Framers] did not forbid warrants where the press was involved, did not require special showings that subpoenas would be impractical, and did not insist that the owner of the place to be searched, if connected with the press, must be shown to be implicated in the offense being investigated. Further, the prior cases do no more than insist that the courts apply the warrant requirements with particular exactitude when First Amendment interests would be endangered by the search. As we see it, no more than this is required where the warrant requested is for the seizure of criminal evidence reasonably believed to be on the premises occupied by a newspaper. Properly administered, the pre-conditions for a warrant—probable cause, specificity with respect to the place to be searched and the things to be seized, and overall reasonableness—should afford sufficient protection against the harms that are assertedly threatened by warrants for searching newspaper offices.

There is no reason to believe, for example, that magistrates cannot guard against searches of the type, scope, and intrusiveness that would actually interfere with the timely publication of a newspaper. Nor, if the requirements of specificity and reasonableness are properly applied, policed, and observed, will there be any occasion or opportunity for officers to rummage at large in newspaper files or to intrude into or to deter normal editorial and publication decisions. The warrant issued in this case authorized nothing of this sort. Nor are we convinced, * * * that confidential sources will disappear and that the press will suppress news because of fears of warranted searches. Whatever incremental effect there may be in this regard if search warrants, as well as subpoenas, are permissible in proper circumstances, it does not make a constitutional difference in our judgment.

The fact is that respondents and *amici* have pointed to only a very few instances in the entire United States since 1971 involving the issuance of warrants for searching newspaper premises. This reality hardly suggests abuse; and if abuse occurs, there will be time enough to deal with it. Furthermore, the press is not only an important, critical, and valuable asset to society, but it is not easily intimidated—nor should it be. * * *

* * * Of course, the Fourth Amendment does not prevent or advise against legislative or executive efforts to establish nonconstitutional protections against possible abuses of the search warrant procedure,[a] but we decline to reinterpret the Amendment to impose a general constitutional barrier against warrants to search newspaper premises, to require resort to subpoenas as a general rule, or to demand prior notice and hearing in connection with the issuance of search warrants. * * *

MR. JUSTICE BRENNAN took no part in the consideration or decision of this case.

MR. JUSTICE POWELL, concurring.

* * * Even aside from the difficulties involved in deciding on a case-by-case basis whether a subpoena can serve as an adequate substitute,[1] I agree with the Court that there is no constitutional basis for such a reading. * * *

a. Consider the Privacy Protection Act of 1980, Supp. App. B.

1. For example, respondent had announced a policy of destroying any photographs that might aid prosecution of protestors. While this policy probably reflected the deep feelings of the Vietnam era, and one may assume that under normal circumstances few, if any, press entities would adopt a policy so hostile to law enforcement, respondent's policy at least illustrates the possibility of such hostility. Use of a subpoena, as proposed by the dissent would be of no utility in face of a policy of destroying evidence. And unless the policy were publicly announced, it probably would be difficult to show the impracticality of a subpoena as opposed to a search warrant.

MR. JUSTICE STEWART, with whom MR. JUSTICE MARSHALL joins, dissenting.
* * *

It seems to me self-evident that police searches of newspaper offices burden the freedom of the press. The most immediate and obvious First Amendment injury caused by such a visitation by the police is physical disruption of the operation of the newspaper. Policemen occupying a newsroom and searching it thoroughly for what may be an extended period of time will inevitably interrupt its normal operations, and thus impair or even temporarily prevent the processes of newsgathering, writing, editing, and publishing. By contrast, a subpoena would afford the newspaper itself an opportunity to locate whatever material might be requested and produce it.

But there is another and more serious burden on a free press imposed by an unannounced police search of a newspaper office: the possibility of disclosure of information received from confidential sources, or of the identity of the sources themselves. Protection of those sources is necessary to ensure that the press can fulfill its constitutionally designated function of informing the public, because important information can often be obtained only by an assurance that the source will not be revealed. * * *

Today the Court does not question the existence of this constitutional protection, but says only that it is not "convinced . . . that confidential sources will disappear and that the press will suppress news because of fears of warranted searches." This facile conclusion seems to me to ignore common experience. It requires no blind leap of faith to understand that a person who gives information to a journalist only on condition that his identity will not be revealed will be less likely to give that information if he knows that, despite the journalist's assurance his identity may in fact be disclosed. And it cannot be denied that confidential information may be exposed to the eyes of police officers who execute a search warrant by rummaging through the files, cabinets, desks and wastebaskets of a newsroom. Since the indisputable effect of such searches will thus be to prevent a newsman from being able to promise confidentiality to his potential sources, it seems obvious to me that a journalist's access to information, and thus the public's will thereby be impaired.

A search warrant allows police officers to ransack the files of a newspaper, reading each and every document until they have found the one named in the warrant,[7] while a subpoena would permit the newspaper itself to produce only the specific documents requested. A search, unlike a subpoena, will therefore lead to the needless exposure of confidential information completely unrelated to the purpose of the investigation. The knowledge that police officers can make an unannounced raid on a newsroom is thus bound to have a deterrent effect on the availability of confidential news sources. The end result, wholly inimical to the First Amendment, will be a diminishing flow of potentially important information to the public. * * *

MR. JUSTICE STEVENS, dissenting.
* * *

In the pre-*Hayden* era warrants were used to search for contraband, weapons and plunder, but not for "mere evidence." The practical effect of the rule prohibiting the issuance of warrants to search for mere evidence was to narrowly limit not only the category of objects, but also the cate-

7. The Court says that "if the requirements of specificity and reasonableness are properly applied, policed, and observed" there will be no opportunity for the police to "rummage at large in newspaper files." But in order to find a particular document, no matter how specifically it is identified in the warrant, the police will have to search every place where it might be—including, presumably, every file in the office—and to examine each document they find to see if it is the correct one. I thus fail to see how the Fourth Amendment would provide an effective limit to these searches.

gory of persons and the character of the privacy interests that might be affected by an unannounced police search.

Just as the witnesses who participate in an investigation or a trial far outnumber the defendants, the persons who possess evidence that may help to identify an offender, or explain an aspect of a criminal transaction, far outnumber those who have custody of weapons or plunder. Countless law abiding citizens—doctors, lawyers, merchants, customers, bystanders—may have documents in their possession that relate to an ongoing criminal investigation. The consequences of subjecting this large category of persons to unannounced police searches are extremely serious. The *ex parte* warrant procedure enables the prosecutor to obtain access to privileged documents that could not be examined if advance notice gave the custodian an opportunity to object. The search for the documents described in a warrant may involve the inspection of files containing other private matter. The dramatic character of a sudden search may cause an entirely unjustified injury to the reputation of the persons searched. * * *

A showing of probable cause that was adequate to justify the issuance of a warrant to search for stolen goods in the 18th century does not automatically satisfy the new dimensions of the Fourth Amendment in the post-*Hayden* era. * * * The only conceivable justification for an unannounced search of an innocent citizen is the fear that, if notice were given, he would conceal or destroy the object of the search. Probable cause to believe that the custodian is a criminal, or that he holds a criminal's weapons, spoils, or the like, justifies that fear, and therefore such a showing complies with the Clause. But if nothing said under oath in the warrant application demonstrates the need for an unannounced search by force, the probable cause requirement is not satisfied. In the absence of some other showing of reasonableness, the ensuing search violates the Fourth Amendment. * * *

Notes and Questions

1. Compare *O'Connor v. Johnson,* 287 N.W.2d 400 (Minn.1979), involving a warrant issued for an attorney's office to search for and seize a certain client's business records:

"Even the most particular warrant cannot adequately safeguard client confidentiality, the attorney-client privilege, the attorney's work product, and the criminal defendant's constitutional right to counsel of all of the attorney's clients. It is unreasonable, in any case, to permit law enforcement officers to peruse miscellaneous documents in an attorney's office while attempting to locate documents listed in a search warrant. Even if it were possible to meet the particularity requirement regarding the place to be searched, the file would still contain some confidential information that is immune from seizure under the attorney-client privilege or the work product doctrine. Once that information is revealed to the police, the privileges are lost, and the information cannot be erased from the minds of the police. * * *

"It will not unreasonably burden prosecutors' offices and effective law enforcement to require officers to proceed by subpoena duces tecum in seeking documents held by an attorney. Attorneys are required by statute, the Code of Professional Responsibility, and the oath of admission to the bar to preserve and protect the judicial process. Thus, attorneys must respond faithfully and promptly, while still being allowed the opportunity to assert applicable privileges by a motion to quash."

2. It is noted in 67 A.B.A.J. 33 (1981) "that California's legislative response to the problem of surprise searches of offices of 'privilege-holders' may serve as a model for other states. The law calls for appointment of a special master to spearhead the search. * * *

"The California solution hasn't satisfied everyone, however. John Cleary, head of the federal public defender office in San

Diego, said the law is 'unhealthy. There is an illusion of protection.' Robert Philibosian, chief assistant California attorney general, said: 'We vigorously opposed [the law].' He said it impairs law enforcement, especially in the white-collar crime area: 'We have to jump through hoops [to obtain evidence].' "

3. Compare *Model Pre-Arraignment Code* §§ 220.5(2) & (3) providing that if the documents to be seized "cannot be searched for or identified without examining the contents of other documents, or if they constitute items or entries in account books, diaries, or other documents containing matter not specified in the warrant, the executing officer shall not examine the documents but shall either impound them under appropriate protection where found, or seal and remove them for safekeeping pending further proceedings." At a later adversary judicial hearing, a motion may be made for return of the documents or for "specification of such conditions and limitations on the further search for the documents to be seized as may be appropriate to prevent unnecessary or unreasonable invasion of privacy." If return is not ordered, "the search shall proceed under such conditions and limitations as the order shall prescribe."

SECTION 3. "PROBABLE CAUSE"

SPINELLI v. UNITED STATES

393 U.S. 410, 89 S.Ct. 584, 21 L.Ed.2d 637 (1969).

MR. JUSTICE HARLAN delivered the opinion of the Court.

William Spinelli was convicted * * of traveling to St. Louis, Missouri, from a nearby Illinois suburb with the intention of conducting gambling activities proscribed by Missouri law. At every appropriate stage in the proceedings in the lower courts, the petitioner challenged the constitutionality of the warrant which authorized the FBI search that uncovered the evidence necessary for his conviction. * * * Believing it desirable that the principles of [*Aguilar v. Texas,* 378 U.S. 108, 84 S.Ct. 1509, 12 L.Ed.2d 723 (1964)] should be further explicated, we granted certiorari * * *.

In *Aguilar,* a search warrant had issued upon an affidavit of police officers who swore only that they had "received reliable information from a credible person and do believe" that narcotics were being illegally stored on the described premises. While recognizing that the constitutional requirement of probable cause can be satisfied by hearsay information, this Court held the affidavit inadequate for two reasons. First, the application failed to set forth any of the "underlying circumstances" necessary to enable the magistrate independently to judge of the validity of the informant's conclusion that the narcotics were where he said they were. Second, the affiant-officers did not attempt to support their claim that their informant was " 'credible' or his information 'reliable.' " The Government is, however, quite right in saying that the FBI affidavit in the present case is more ample than that in *Aguilar.* Not only does it contain a report from an anonymous informant, but it also contains a report of an independent FBI investigation which is said to corroborate the informant's tip. We are, then, required to delineate the manner in which *Aguilar's* two-pronged test should be applied in these circumstances.

In essence, the affidavit * * * contained the following allegations:

1. The FBI had kept track of Spinelli's movements on five days during the month of August 1965. On four of these occasions, Spinelli was seen crossing one of two bridges leading from Illinois into St. Louis, Missouri, between 11 a.m. and 12:15 p.m. On four of the five days, Spinelli was also seen parking his car in a lot used by residents of an apartment house at 1108 Indian Circle Drive in St. Louis, between 3:30 p.m. and 4:45 p.m. On one day, Spinelli was followed further

and seen to enter a particular apartment in the building.

2. An FBI check with the telephone company revealed that this apartment contained two telephones listed under the name of Grace P. Hagen, and carrying the numbers WYdown 4–0029 and WYdown 4–0136.

3. The application stated that "William Spinelli is known to this affiant and to federal law enforcement agents and local law enforcement agents as a bookmaker, an associate of bookmakers, a gambler, and an associate of gamblers."

4. Finally, it was stated that the FBI "has been informed by a confidential reliable informant that William Spinelli is operating a handbook and accepting wagers and disseminating wagering information by means of the telephones which have been assigned the numbers WYdown 4–0029 and WYdown 4–0136."

There can be no question that the last item mentioned, detailing the informant's tip, has a fundamental place in this warrant application. Without it, probable cause could not be established. The first two items reflect only innocent-seeming activity and data. Spinelli's travels to and from the apartment building and his entry into a particular apartment on one occasion could hardly be taken as bespeaking gambling activity; and there is surely nothing unusual about an apartment containing two separate telephones. Many a householder indulges himself in this petty luxury. Finally, the allegation that Spinelli was "known" to the affiant and to other federal and local law enforcement officers as a gambler and an associate of gamblers is but a bald and unilluminating assertion of suspicion that is entitled to no weight in appraising the magistrate's decision. *Nathanson v. United States,* 290 U.S. 41, 46, 54 S.Ct. 11, 12, 78 L.Ed. 159 (1933).

So much indeed the Government does not deny. Rather, following the reasoning of the Court of Appeals, the Government claims that the informant's tip gives a suspicious color to the FBI's reports detailing Spinelli's innocent-seeming conduct and that, conversely, the FBI's surveillance corroborates the informant's tip, thereby entitling it to more weight. * * * We believe, however, that the "totality of circumstances" approach taken by the Court of Appeals paints with too broad a brush. Where, as here, the informer's tip is a necessary element in a finding of probable cause, its proper weight must be determined by a more precise analysis.

The informer's report must first be measured against *Aguilar's* standards so that its probative value can be assessed. If the tip is found inadequate under *Aguilar,* the other allegations which corroborate the information contained in the hearsay report should then be considered. At this stage as well, however, the standards enunciated in *Aguilar* must inform the magistrate's decision. He must ask: Can it fairly be said that the tip, even when certain parts of it have been corroborated by independent sources, is as trustworthy as a tip which would pass *Aguilar's* tests without independent corroboration? * * *

Applying these principles to the present case, we first consider the weight to be given the informer's tip when it is considered apart from the rest of the affidavit. It is clear that a Commissioner could not credit it without abdicating his constitutional function. Though the affiant swore that his confidant was "reliable," he offered the magistrate no reason in support of this conclusion. Perhaps even more important is the fact that *Aguilar's* other test has not been satisfied. The tip does not contain a sufficient statement of the underlying circumstances from which the informer concluded that Spinelli was running a bookmaking operation. We are not told how the FBI's source received his information—it is not alleged that the informant personally observed Spinelli at work or that he had ever placed a bet with him. Moreover, if the informant came by the information indirectly, he did not explain why his sources were reliable. In the absence of a statement detailing the manner in which the information was gathered, it is especially important that the tip describe the accused's criminal activity in sufficient detail so that the magistrate may know that he is relying on something more substantial than a casual rumor circulating in the underworld or an accusation based merely on an individual's general reputation.

The detail provided by the informant in *Draper v. United States,* 358 U.S. 307, 79 S.Ct. 329, 3 L.Ed.2d 327 (1959), provides a suitable benchmark. While Hereford, the FBI's informer in that case, did not state the way in which he had obtained his information, he reported that Draper had gone to Chicago the day before by train and that he would return to Denver by train with three ounces of heroin on one of two specified mornings. Moreover, Hereford went on to describe, with minute particularity, the clothes that Draper would be wearing upon his arrival at the Denver station. A magistrate, when confronted with such detail, could reasonably infer that the informant had gained his information in a reliable way. Such an inference cannot be made in the present case. Here, the only facts supplied were that Spinelli was using two specified telephones and that these phones were being used in gambling operations. This meager report could easily have been obtained from an off-hand remark heard at a neighborhood bar.

Nor do we believe that the patent doubts *Aguilar* raises as to the report's reliability are adequately resolved by a consideration of the allegations detailing the FBI's independent investigative efforts. At most, these allegations indicated that Spinelli could have used the telephones specified by the informant for some purpose. This cannot by itself be said to support both the inference that the informer was generally trustworthy and that he had made his charge against Spinelli on the basis of information obtained in a reliable way. Once again, *Draper* provides a relevant comparison. Independent police work in that case corroborated much more than one small detail that had been provided by the informant. There, the police, upon greeting the inbound Denver train on the second morning specified by informer Hereford, saw a man whose dress corresponded precisely to Hereford's detailed description. It was then apparent that the informant had not been fabricating his report out of whole cloth; since the report was of the sort which in common experience may be recognized as having been obtained in a reliable way, it was perfectly clear that probable cause had been established.

We conclude, then, that in the present case the informant's tip—even when corroborated to the extent indicated—was not sufficient to provide the basis for a finding of probable cause. * * *

The judgment of the Court of Appeals is reversed * * *.

MR. JUSTICE WHITE, concurring.

* * *

The tension between *Draper* and the *Nathanson-Aguilar* line of cases is evident from the course followed by the majority opinion. * * * Since [the informant's] specific information about Spinelli using two phones with particular numbers had been verified, did not his allegation about gambling thereby become sufficiently more believable if the *Draper* principle is to be given any scope at all? I would think so, particularly since the information from the informant which was verified was not neutral, irrelevant information but was material to proving the gambling allegation: two phones with different numbers in an apartment used away from home indicates a business use in an operation, like bookmaking, where multiple phones are needed. The *Draper* approach would reasonably justify the issuance of a warrant in this case, particularly since the police had some awareness of Spinelli's past activities. The majority, however, while seemingly embracing *Draper,* confines that case to its own facts. Pending full scale reconsideration of that case, on the one hand, or of the *Nathanson-Aguilar* cases on the other, I join the opinion of the Court and the judgment of reversal especially since a vote to affirm would produce an equally divided Court.[a]

ILLINOIS v. GATES

462 U.S. 213, 103 S.Ct. 2317, 76 L.Ed.2d 527 (1983).

JUSTICE REHNQUIST delivered the opinion of the Court.

* * * A chronological statement of events usefully introduces the issues at stake. Bloomingdale, Ill., is a suburb of Chicago located in DuPage County. On May 3, 1978, the Bloomingdale Police Department received by mail an anonymous handwritten letter which read as follows:

> "This letter is to inform you that you have a couple in your town who strictly make their living on selling drugs. They are Sue and Lance Gates, they live on Greenway, off Bloomingdale Rd. in the condominiums. Most of their buys are done in Florida. Sue his wife drives their car to Florida, where she leaves it to be loaded up with drugs, then Lance flys down and drives it back. Sue flys back after she drops the car off in Florida. May 3 she is driving down there again and Lance will be flying down in a few days to drive it back. At the time Lance drives the car back he has the trunk loaded with over $100,000.00 in drugs. Presently they have over $100,000.00 worth of drugs in their basement.
>
> They brag about the fact they never have to work, and make their entire living on pushers.
>
> I guarantee if you watch them carefully you will make a big catch. They are friends with some big drugs dealers, who visit their house often.
>
> Lance & Susan Gates
> Greenway
> in Condominiums"

a. Black, Fortas, and Stewart, JJ., dissented separately; Marshall, J., took no part in the case.

The letter was referred by the Chief of Police of the Bloomingdale Police Department to Detective Mader, who decided to pursue the tip. Mader learned, from the office of the Illinois Secretary of State, that an Illinois driver's license had been issued to one Lance Gates, residing at a stated address in Bloomingdale. He contacted a confidential informant, whose examination of certain financial records revealed a more recent address for the Gates, and he also learned from a police officer assigned to O'Hare Airport that "L. Gates" had made a reservation on Eastern Airlines flight 245 to West Palm Beach, Fla., scheduled to depart from Chicago on May 5 at 4:15 p.m.

Mader then made arrangements with an agent of the Drug Enforcement Administration for surveillance of the May 5 Eastern Airlines flight. The agent later reported to Mader that Gates had boarded the flight, and that federal agents in Florida had observed him arrive in West Palm Beach and take a taxi to the nearby Holiday Inn. They also reported that Gates went to a room registered to one Susan Gates and that, at 7:00 a.m. the next morning, Gates and an unidentified woman left the motel in a Mercury bearing Illinois license plates and drove northbound on an interstate frequently used by travelers to the Chicago area. In addition, the DEA agent informed Mader that the license plate number on the Mercury registered to a Hornet station wagon owned by Gates. The agent also advised Mader that the driving time between West Palm Beach and Bloomingdale was approximately 22 to 24 hours.

Mader signed an affidavit setting forth the foregoing facts, and submitted it to a judge of the Circuit Court of DuPage County, together with a copy of the anonymous letter. The judge of that court thereupon issued a search warrant for the Gates' residence and for their automobile. The judge, in deciding to issue the warrant, could have determined that the *modus operandi* of the Gates had been substantially corroborated. As the anonymous letter predicted, Lance Gates had flown from Chicago to West Palm Beach late in the afternoon of May 5th, had checked into a hotel room registered in the name of his wife, and, at 7:00 a.m. the following morning, had headed north, accompanied by an unidentified woman, out of West Palm Beach on an interstate highway used by travelers from South Florida to Chicago in an automobile bearing a license plate issued to him.

At 5:15 a.m. on May 7th, only 36 hours after he had flown out of Chicago, Lance Gates, and his wife, returned to their home in Bloomingdale, driving the car in which they had left West Palm Beach some 22 hours earlier. The Bloomingdale police were awaiting them, searched the trunk of the Mercury, and uncovered approximately 350 pounds of marijuana. A search of the Gates' home revealed marijuana, weapons, and other contraband. The Illinois Circuit Court ordered suppression of all these items, on the ground that the affidavit submitted to the Circuit Judge failed to support the necessary determination of probable cause to believe that the Gates' automobile and home contained the contraband in question. This decision was affirmed in turn by the Illinois Appellate Court and by a divided vote of the Supreme Court of Illinois.

The Illinois Supreme Court concluded—and we are inclined to agree—that, standing alone, the anonymous letter sent to the Bloomingdale Police Department would not provide the basis for a magistrate's determination that there was probable cause to believe contraband would be found in the Gates' car and home. The letter provides virtually nothing from which one might conclude that its author is either honest or his information reliable; likewise, the letter gives absolutely no indication of the basis for the writer's predictions regarding the Gates' criminal activities. Something more was required, then, before a magistrate could conclude that there was probable cause to believe that contraband would be found in the Gates' home and car.

The Illinois Supreme Court also properly recognized that Detective Mader's affidavit might be capable of supplementing the anonymous letter with information sufficient to permit a determination of probable cause. In holding that the affidavit in fact did not contain sufficient additional information to sustain a determination of probable cause, the Illinois court applied a "two-pronged test," derived from our decision in *Spinelli v. United States.* The Illinois Supreme Court, like some others, apparently understood *Spinelli* as requiring that the anonymous letter satisfy each of two independent requirements before it could be relied on. According to this view, the letter, as supplemented by Mader's affidavit, first had to adequately reveal the "basis of knowledge" of the letter writer—the particular means by which he came by the information given in his report. Second, it had to provide facts sufficiently establishing either the "veracity" of the affiant's informant, or, alternatively, the "reliability" of the informant's report in this particular case.

The Illinois court, alluding to an elaborate set of legal rules that have developed among various lower courts to enforce the "two-pronged test,"[4] found that the test

4. In summary, these rules posit that the "veracity" prong of the *Spinelli* test has two "spurs"—the informant's "credibility" and the "reliability" of his information. Various interpretations are advanced for the meaning of the "reliability" spur of the "veracity" prong. Both the "basis of knowledge" prong and the "veracity" prong are treated as entirely separate requirements, which must be independently satisfied in every case in order to sustain a

had not been satisfied. First, the "veracity" prong was not satisfied because, "there was simply no basis [for] * * * conclud[ing] that the anonymous person [who wrote the letter to the Bloomingdale Police Department] was credible." The court indicated that corroboration by police of details contained in the letter might never satisfy the "veracity" prong, and in any event, could not do so if, as in the present case, only "innocent" details are corroborated. In addition, the letter gave no indication of the basis of its writer's knowledge of the Gates' activities. The Illinois court understood *Spinelli* as permitting the detail contained in a tip to be used to infer that the informant had a reliable basis for his statements, but it thought that the anonymous letter failed to provide sufficient detail to permit such an inference. Thus, it concluded that no showing of probable cause had been made.

We agree with the Illinois Supreme Court that an informant's "veracity," "reliability" and "basis of knowledge" are all highly relevant in determining the value of his report. We do not agree, however, that these elements should be understood as entirely separate and independent requirements to be rigidly exacted in every case, which the opinion of the Supreme Court of Illinois would imply. Rather, as detailed below, they should be understood simply as closely intertwined issues that may usefully illuminate the common sense, practical question whether there is "probable cause" to believe that contraband or evidence is located in a particular place.

This totality of the circumstances approach is far more consistent with our prior treatment of probable cause than is any rigid demand that specific "tests" be satisfied by every informant's tip. Perhaps the central teaching of our decisions bearing on the probable cause standard is that it is a "practical, nontechnical conception." *Brinegar v. United States,* 338 U.S. 160, 69 S.Ct. 1302, 93 L.Ed. 1879 (1949). "In dealing with probable cause, * * * as the very name implies, we deal with probabilities. These are not technical; they are the factual and practical considerations of everyday life on which reasonable and prudent men, not legal technicians, act." Our observation in *United States v. Cortez,* [p. 372 infra], regarding "particularized suspicion," is also applicable to the probable cause standard:

> The process does not deal with hard certainties, but with probabilities. Long before the law of probabilities was articulated as such, practical people formulated certain common-sense conclusions about human behavior; jurors as factfinders are permitted to do the same—and so are law enforcement officers. Finally, the evidence thus collected must be seen and weighed not in terms of library analysis by scholars, but as understood by those versed in the field of law enforcement.

As these comments illustrate, probable cause is a fluid concept—turning on the assessment of probabilities in particular factual contexts—not readily, or even usefully, reduced to a neat set of legal rules. Informants' tips doubtless come in many shapes and sizes from many different types of persons. * * * Rigid legal rules are ill-suited to an area of such diversity. "One simple rule will not cover every situation." [7]

Moreover, the "two-pronged test" directs analysis into two largely independent

determination of probable cause. Some ancillary doctrines are relied on to satisfy certain of the foregoing requirements. For example, the "self-verifying detail" of a tip may satisfy the "basis of knowledge" requirement, although not the "credibility" spur of the "veracity" prong. Conversely, corroboration would seem not capable of supporting the "basis of knowledge" prong, but only the "veracity" prong. * * *

7. The diversity of informants' tips, as well as the usefulness of the totality of the circumstances approach to probable cause, is reflected in our prior decisions on the subject. In *Jones v. United States,* 362 U.S. 257, 80 S.Ct. 725, 4 L.Ed.2d 697 (1960), we held that probable cause to search petitioners' apartment was established by an affidavit based principally on an informant's tip. The unnamed informant claimed to have pur-

channels—the informant's "veracity" or "reliability" and his "basis of knowledge." There are persuasive arguments against according these two elements such independent status. Instead, they are better understood as relevant considerations in the totality of circumstances analysis that traditionally has guided probable cause determinations: a deficiency in one may be compensated for, in determining the overall reliability of a tip, by a strong showing as to the other, or by some other indicia of reliability.

If, for example, a particular informant is known for the unusual reliability of his predictions of certain types of criminal activities in a locality, his failure, in a particular case, to thoroughly set forth the basis of his knowledge surely should not serve as an absolute bar to a finding of probable cause based on his tip. Likewise, if an unquestionably honest citizen comes forward with a report of criminal activity—which if fabricated would subject him to criminal liability—we have found rigorous scrutiny of the basis of his knowledge unnecessary. Conversely, even if we entertain some doubt as to an informant's motives, his explicit and detailed description of alleged wrongdoing, along with a statement that the event was observed first-hand, entitles his tip to greater weight than might otherwise be the case. Unlike a totality of circumstances analysis, which permits a balanced assessment of the relative weights of all the various indicia of reliability (and unreliability) attending an informant's tip, the "two-pronged test" has encouraged an excessively technical dissection of informants' tips, with undue attention being focused on isolated issues that cannot sensibly be divorced from the other facts presented to the magistrate. * * *

We also have recognized that affidavits "are normally drafted by non-lawyers in the midst and haste of a criminal investigation. Technical requirements of elaborate specificity once exacted under common law pleading have no proper place in this area." Likewise, search and arrest warrants long have been issued by persons who are neither lawyers nor judges, and who certainly do not remain abreast of each judicial refinement of the nature of "probable cause." The rigorous inquiry into the *Spinelli* prongs and the complex superstructure of evidentiary and analytical rules that some have seen implicit in our *Spinelli* decision, cannot be reconciled with

chased narcotics from petitioners at their apartment; the affiant stated that he had been given correct information from the informant on a prior occasion. This, and the fact that petitioners had admitted to police officers on another occasion that they were narcotics users, sufficed to support the magistrate's determination of probable cause.

Likewise, in *Rugendorf v. United States,* 376 U.S. 528, 84 S.Ct. 825, 11 L.Ed.2d 887 (1964), the Court upheld a magistrate's determination that there was probable cause to believe that certain stolen property would be found in petitioner's apartment. The affidavit submitted to the magistrate stated that certain furs had been stolen, and that a confidential informant, who previously had furnished confidential information, said that he saw the furs in petitioner's home. Moreover, another confidential informant, also claimed to be reliable, stated that one Schweihs had stolen the furs. Police reports indicated that petitioner had been seen in Schweihs' company and a third informant stated that petitioner was a fence for Schweihs.

Finally, in *Ker v. California,* [p. 329 infra], we held that information within the knowledge of officers who searched the Ker's apartment provided them with probable cause to believe drugs would be found there. The officers were aware that one Murphy had previously sold marijuana to a police officer; the transaction had occurred in an isolated area, to which Murphy had led the police. The night after this transaction, police observed Ker and Murphy meet in the same location. Murphy approached Ker's car, and, although police could see nothing change hands, Murphy's *modus operandi* was identical to what it had been the night before. Moreover, when police followed Ker from the scene of the meeting with Murphy he managed to lose them after performing an abrupt U-turn. Finally, the police had a statement from an informant who had provided reliable information previously, that Ker was engaged in selling marijuana, and that his source was Murphy. We concluded that "To say that this coincidence of information was sufficient to support a reasonable belief of the officers that Ker was illegally in possession of marijuana is to indulge in understatement."

the fact that many warrants are—quite properly—issued on the basis of nontechnical, common-sense judgments of laymen applying a standard less demanding than those used in more formal legal proceedings. Likewise, given the informal, often hurried context in which it must be applied, the "built-in subtleties" of the "two-pronged test" are particularly unlikely to assist magistrates in determining probable cause.

Similarly, we have repeatedly said that after-the-fact scrutiny by courts of the sufficiency of an affidavit should not take the form of *de novo* review. A magistrate's "determination of probable cause should be paid great deference by reviewing courts." "A grudging or negative attitude by reviewing courts toward warrants" is inconsistent with the Fourth Amendment's strong preference for searches conducted pursuant to a warrant "court should not invalidate * * * warrant[s] by interpreting affidavit[s] in a hypertechnical, rather than a common-sense, manner."

If the affidavits submitted by police officers are subjected to the type of scrutiny some courts have deemed appropriate, police might well resort to warrantless searches, with the hope of relying on consent or some other exception to the warrant clause that might develop at the time of the search. In addition, the possession of a warrant by officers conducting an arrest or search greatly reduces the perception of unlawful or intrusive police conduct, by assuring "the individual whose property is searched or seized of the lawful authority of the executing officer, his need to search, and the limits of his power to search." Reflecting this preference for the warrant process, the traditional standard for review of an issuing magistrate's probable cause determination has been that so long as the magistrate had a "substantial basis for * * * conclud[ing]" that a search would uncover evidence of wrongdoing, the Fourth Amendment requires no more. We think reaffirmation of this standard better serves the purpose of encouraging recourse to the warrant procedure and is more consistent with our traditional deference to the probable cause determinations of magistrates than is the "two-pronged test."

Finally, the direction taken by decisions following *Spinelli* poorly serves "the most basic function of any government": "to provide for the security of the individual and of his property. The strictures that inevitably accompany the "two-pronged test" cannot avoid seriously impeding the task of law enforcement. If, as the Illinois Supreme Court apparently thought, that test must be rigorously applied in every case, [anonymous tips would be] of greatly diminished value in police work. Ordinary citizens, like ordinary witnesses, generally do not provide extensive recitations of the basis of their everyday observations. Likewise, as the Illinois Supreme Court observed in this case, the veracity of persons supplying anonymous tips is by hypothesis largely unknown, and unknowable. As a result, anonymous tips seldom could survive a rigorous application of either of the *Spinelli* prongs. Yet, such tips, particularly when supplemented by independent police investigation, frequently contribute to the solution of otherwise "perfect crimes." While a conscientious assessment of the basis for crediting such tips is required by the Fourth Amendment, a standard that leaves virtually no place for anonymous citizen informants is not.

For all these reasons, we conclude that it is wiser to abandon the "two-pronged test" established by our decisions in *Aguilar* and *Spinelli*.[11] In its place we reaffirm the totality of the circumstances analysis

11. * * *

Whether the allegations submitted to the magistrate in *Spinelli* would, under the view we now take, have supported a finding of probable cause, we think it would not be profitable to decide. There are so many variables in the probable cause equation that one determination will seldom be a useful "precedent" for another. Suffice it to say that while we in no way abandon *Spinelli's* concern for the trustworthiness of informers that traditionally has informed probable cause determinations. The task of the issuing magistrate is simply to make a practical, common-sense decision whether, given all the circumstances set forth in the affidavit before him, including the "veracity" and "basis of knowledge" of persons supplying hearsay information, there is a fair probability that contraband or evidence of a crime will be found in a particular place. And the duty of a reviewing court is simply to ensure that the magistrate had a "substantial basis for * * * conclud[ing]" that probable cause existed. We are convinced that this flexible, easily applied standard will better achieve the accommodation of public and private interests that the Fourth Amendment requires than does the approach that has developed from *Aguilar* and *Spinelli.*

Our earlier cases illustrate the limits beyond which a magistrate may not venture in issuing a warrant. A sworn statement of an affiant that "he has cause to suspect and does believe that" liquor illegally brought into the United States is located on certain premises will not do. *Nathanson v. United States.* An affidavit must provide the magistrate with a substantial basis for determining the existence of probable cause, and the wholly conclusory statement at issue in *Nathanson* failed to meet this requirement. An officer's statement that "affiants have received reliable information from a credible person and believe" that heroin is stored in a home, is likewise inadequate. *Aguilar v. Texas.* As in *Nathanson,* this is a mere conclusory statement that gives the magistrate virtually no basis at all for making a judgment regarding probable cause. Sufficient information must be presented to the magistrate to allow that official to determine probable cause; his action cannot be a mere ratification of the bare conclusions of others. In order to ensure that such an abdication of the magistrate's duty does not occur, courts must continue to conscientiously review the sufficiency of affidavits on which warrants are issued. But when we move beyond the "bare bones" affidavits present in cases such as *Nathanson* and *Aguilar,* this area simply does not lend itself to a prescribed set of rules, like that which had developed from *Spinelli.* Instead, the flexible, common-sense standard articulated in *Jones, Ventresca,* and *Brinegar* better served the purposes of the Fourth Amendment's probable cause requirement.

Justice Brennan's dissent suggests in several places that the approach we take today somehow downgrades the role of the neutral magistrate, because *Aguilar* and *Spinelli* "preserve the role of magistrates as independent arbiters of probable cause * * *." Quite the contrary, we believe, is the case. Nothing in our opinion in any way lessens the authority of the magistrate to draw such reasonable inferences as he will from the material supplied to him by applicants for a warrant; indeed, he is freer than under the regime of *Aguilar* and *Spinelli* to draw such inferences, or to refuse to draw them if he is so minded.

The real gist of Justice Brennan's criticism seems to be a second argument, somewhat at odds with the first, that magistrates should be restricted in their authority to make probable cause determinations by the standards laid down in *Aguilar* and *Spinelli* and that such findings "should not be authorized unless there is some assurance that the information on which they are based has been obtained in a reliable way by an honest or credible person." However, under our opinion magistrates remain perfectly free to exact such assurances as they deem necessary, as well as those required by this opinion, in making probable cause determinations. Justice Brennan would apparently prefer that magistrates be restricted in their findings of probable cause by the development of an elaborate body of case law dealing with the "veracity" prong of the *Spinelli* test,

and for the principle that it is the magistrate who must ultimately make a finding of probable cause, we reject the rigid categorization suggested by some of its language.

which in turn is broken down into two "spurs"—the informant's "credibility" and the "reliability" of his information, together with the "basis of knowledge" prong of the *Spinelli* test. That such a labyrinthine body of judicial refinement bears any relationship to familiar definitions of probable cause is hard to imagine. * * *

Justice Brennan's dissent also suggests that "words such as 'practical,' 'nontechnical,' and 'common sense,' as used in the Court's opinion, are but code words for an overly permissive attitude towards police practices in derogation of the rights secured by the Fourth Amendment." * * * "Fidelity" to the commands of the Constitution suggests balanced judgment rather than exhortation. The highest "fidelity" is achieved neither by the judge who instinctively goes furthest in upholding even the most bizarre claim of individual constitutional rights, any more than it is achieved by a judge who instinctively goes furthest in accepting the most restrictive claims of governmental authorities. The task of this Court, as of other courts, is to "hold the balance true," and we think we have done that in this case.

Our decisions applying the totality of circumstances analysis outlined above have consistently recognized the value of corroboration of details of an informant's tip by independent police work.

Our decision in *Draper v. United States,* however, is the classic case on the value of corroborative efforts of police officials. There, an informant named Hereford reported that Draper would arrive in Denver on a train from Chicago on one of two days, and that he would be carrying a quantity of heroin. The informant also supplied a fairly detailed physical description of Draper, and predicted that he would be wearing a light colored raincoat, brown slacks and black shoes, and would be walking "real fast." Hereford gave no indication of the basis for his information.[12]

On one of the stated dates police officers observed a man matching this description exit a train arriving from Chicago; his attire and luggage matched Hereford's report and he was walking rapidly. We explained in *Draper* that, by this point in his investigation, the arresting officer "had personally verified every facet of the information given him by Hereford except whether petitioner had accomplished his mission and had the three ounces of heroin on his person or in his bag. And surely with every other bit of Hereford's information being thus personally verified, [the officer] had 'reasonable grounds' to believe that the remaining unverified bit of Hereford's information—that Draper would have the heroin with him—was likewise true."

The showing of probable cause in the present case was fully as compelling as that in *Draper.* Even standing alone, the facts obtained through the independent investigation of Mader and the DEA at least suggested that the Gates were involved in drug trafficking. In addition to being a popular vacation site, Florida is well-known as a source of narcotics and other illegal drugs. Lance Gates' flight to Palm Beach, his brief, overnight stay in a motel, and apparent immediate return north to Chicago in the family car, conveniently awaiting him in West Palm Beach, is as suggestive of a prearranged drug run, as it is of an ordinary vacation trip.

In addition, the magistrate could rely on the anonymous letter, which had been corroborated in major part by Mader's ef-

12. The tip in *Draper* might well not have survived the rigid application of the "two-pronged test" that developed following *Spinelli.* The only reference to Hereford's reliability was that he had "been engaged as a 'special employee' of the Bureau of Narcotics at Denver for about six months, and from time to time gave information to [the police] for small sums of money, and that [the officer] had always found the information given by Hereford to be accurate and reliable." Likewise, the tip gave no indication of how Hereford came by his information. At most, the detailed and accurate predictions in the tip indicated that, however Hereford obtained his information, it was reliable.

forts—just as had occurred in *Draper*.[13] The Supreme Court of Illinois reasoned that *Draper* involved an informant who had given reliable information on previous occasions, while the honesty and reliability of the anonymous informant in this case were unknown to the Bloomingdale police. While this distinction might be an apt one at the time the police department received the anonymous letter, it became far less significant after Mader's independent investigative work occurred. The corroboration of the letter's predictions that the Gates' car would be in Florida, that Lance Gates would fly to Florida in the next day or so, and that he would drive the car north toward Bloomingdale all indicated, albeit not with certainty, that the informant's other assertions also were true. "Because an informant is right about some things, he is more probably right about other facts," *Spinelli, supra* (White, J., concurring)—including the claim regarding the Gates' illegal activity. This may well not be the type of "reliability" or "veracity" necessary to satisfy some view of the "veracity prong" of *Spinelli,* but we think it suffices for the practical, common-sense judgment called for in making a probable cause determination. It is enough, for purposes of assessing probable cause, that "corroboration through other sources of information reduced the chances of a reckless or prevaricating tale," thus providing "a substantial basis for crediting the hearsay."

Finally, the anonymous letter contained a range of details relating not just to easily obtained facts and conditions existing at the time of the tip, but to future actions of third parties ordinarily not easily predicted. The letter writer's accurate information as to the travel plans of each of the Gates was of a character likely obtained only from the Gates themselves, or from someone familiar with their not entirely ordinary travel plans. If the informant had access to accurate information of this type a magistrate could properly conclude that it was not unlikely that he also had access to reliable information of the Gates' alleged illegal activities.[14] Of course, the

13. The Illinois Supreme Court thought that the verification of details contained in the anonymous letter in this case amounted only to "the corroboration of innocent activity," and that this was insufficient to support a finding of probable cause. We are inclined to agree, however, with the observation of Justice Moran in his dissenting opinion that "In this case, just as in *Draper,* seemingly innocent activity became suspicious in the light of the initial tip." And it bears noting that *all* of the corroborating detail established in *Draper, supra,* was of entirely innocent activity—a fact later pointed out by the Court in both *Jones v.* United States, *and* Ker v. California.

This is perfectly reasonable. As discussed previously, probable cause requires only a probability or substantial chance of criminal activity, not an actual showing of such activity. By hypothesis, therefore, innocent behavior frequently will provide the basis for a showing of probable cause; to require otherwise would be to *sub silentio* impose a drastically more rigorous definition of probable cause than the security of our citizens demands. We think the Illinois court attempted a too rigid classification of the types of conduct that may be relied upon in seeking to demonstrate probable cause. In making a determination of probable cause the relevant inquiry is not whether particular conduct is "innocent" or "guilty," but the degree of suspicion that attaches to particular types of non-criminal acts.

14. The dissent seizes on one inaccuracy in the anonymous informant's letter—its statement that Sue Gates would fly from Florida to Illinois, when in fact she drove—and argues that the probative value of the entire tip was undermined by this allegedly "material mistake." We have never required that informants used by the police be infallible, and can see no reason to impose such a requirement in this case. Probable cause, particularly when police have obtained a warrant, simply does not require the perfection the dissent finds necessary.

Likewise, there is no force to the dissent's argument that the Gates' action in leaving their home unguarded undercut the informant's claim that drugs were hidden there. Indeed, the line-by-line scrutiny that the dissent applies to the anonymous letter is akin to that we find inappropriate in reviewing magistrate's decisions. The dissent apparently attributes to the magistrate who issued the warrant in this case the rather implausible notion that persons dealing in drugs always stay at home, apparently out of fear that to leave might risk intrusion by criminals. If accurate, one could not help sympathizing with the self-imposed isolation of people so situated. In reality, however, it is scarcely likely that the magistrate ever thought that the anonymous tip "kept one spouse" at home, much less that he relied on the theory advanced by the dissent. The letter simply says that Sue would fly from Florida to

Gates' travel plans might have been learned from a talkative neighbor or travel agent; under the "two-pronged test" developed from *Spinelli,* the character of the details in the anonymous letter might well not permit a sufficiently clear inference regarding the letter writer's "basis of knowledge." But, as discussed previously, probable cause does not demand the certainty we associate with formal trials. It is enough that there was a fair probability that the writer of the anonymous letter had obtained his entire story either from the Gates or someone they trusted. And corroboration of major portions of the letter's predictions provides just this probability. It is apparent, therefore, that the judge issuing the warrant had a "substantial basis for * * * conclud[ing]" that probable cause to search the Gates' home and car existed. The judgment of the Supreme Court of Illinois therefore must be

Reversed.

JUSTICE WHITE, concurring in the judgment.[a]

* * * Although I agree that the warrant should be upheld, I reach this conclusion in accordance with the *Aguilar-Spinelli* framework.

For present purposes, the *Aguilar-Spinelli* rules can be summed up as follows. First, an affidavit based on an informer's tip, standing alone, cannot provide probable cause for issuance of a warrant unless the tip includes information that apprises the magistrate of the informant's basis for concluding that the contraband is where he claims it is (the "basis of knowledge" prong), *and* the affiant informs the magistrate of his basis for believing that the informant is credible (the "veracity" prong).[20] Second, if a tip fails under either or both of the two prongs, probable cause may yet be established by independent police investigatory work that corroborates the tip to such an extent that it supports "both the inference that the informer was generally trustworthy and that he made his charge on the basis of information obtained in a reliable way." In instances where the officers rely on corroboration, the ultimate question is wheth-

Illinois, without indicating whether the Gates' made the bitter choice of leaving the drugs in their house, or those in their car, unguarded. The magistrate's determination that there might be drugs or evidence of criminal activity in the Gates' home was well-supported by the less speculative theory, noted in text, that if the informant could predict with considerable accuracy the somewhat unusual travel plans of the Gates, he probably also had a reliable basis for his statements that the Gates' kept a large quantity of drugs in their home and frequently were visited by other drug traffickers there.

a. In an omitted portion of his opinion, Justice White argued for adoption of a "good-faith" exception to the exclusionary rule.

20. The "veracity" prong is satisfied by a recitation in the affidavit that the informant previously supplied accurate information to the police, see *McCray v. Illinois,* [p. 282 infra], or by proof that the informant gave his information against his penal interest, see *United States v. Harris,* 403 U.S. 573, 91 S.Ct. 2075, 29 L.Ed.2d 723 (1971) (plurality opinion). [Editor's Note: In *Harris,* the informant said that he had purchased illicit whiskey from defendant for two years, most recently within the past two weeks, and had often seen defendant get the whiskey for him and others from a certain building. The plurality opinion concluded that because "people do not lightly admit a crime and place critical evidence in the hands of the police in the form of their own admissions," such admissions "carry their own indicia of credibility—sufficient at least to support finding of probable cause to search" when, as here, the basis of knowledge is also indicated (as almost inevitably will be the case when there is such an admission). The four dissenters objected that "the effect of adopting such a rule would be to encourage the Government to prefer as informants participants in criminal enterprises rather than ordinary citizens, a goal the Government specifically eschews in its brief in this case upon the explicit premise that such persons are often less reliable than those who obey the law."] The "basis of knowledge" prong is satisfied by a statement from the informant that he personally observed the criminal activity, or, if he came by the information indirectly, by a satisfactory explanation of why his sources were reliable, or, in the absence of a statement detailing the manner in which the information was gathered, by a description of the accused's criminal activity in sufficient detail that the magistrate may infer that the informant is relying on something more substantial than casual rumor or an individual's general reputation. *Spinelli v. United States.*

er the corroborated tip "is as trustworthy as a tip which would pass *Aguilar's* tests without independent corroboration."

In the present case, it is undisputed that the anonymous tip, by itself, did not furnish probable cause. The question is whether those portions of the affidavit describing the results of the police investigation of the respondents, when considered in light of the tip, "would permit the suspicions engendered by the informant's report to ripen into a judgment that a crime was probably being committed." * * *

In my view, the lower court's characterization of the Gates' activity here as totally "innocent" is dubious. In fact, the behavior was quite suspicious. I agree with the Court that Lance Gates' flight to Palm Beach, an area known to be a source of narcotics, the brief overnight stay in a motel, and apparent immediate return North, suggest a pattern that trained law-enforcement officers have recognized as indicative of illicit drug-dealing activity.

Even, however, had the corroboration related only to completely innocuous activities, this fact alone would not preclude the issuance of a valid warrant. The critical issue is not whether the activities observed by the police are innocent or suspicious. Instead, the proper focus should be on whether the actions of the suspects, whatever their nature, give rise to an inference that the informant is credible and that he obtained his information in a reliable manner.

Thus, in *Draper v. United States* an informant stated on Sept. 7 that Draper would be carrying narcotics when he arrived by train in Denver on the morning of Sept. 8 or Sept. 9. The informant also provided the police with a detailed physical description of the clothes Draper would be wearing when he alighted from the train. The police observed Draper leaving a train on the morning of Sept. 9, and he was wearing the precise clothing described by the informant. The Court held that the police had probable cause to arrest Draper at this point, even though the police had seen nothing more than the totally innocent act of a man getting off a train carrying a briefcase. As we later explained in *Spinelli,* the important point was that the corroboration showed both that the informant was credible, *i.e.* that he "had not been fabricating his report out of whole cloth," and that he had an adequate basis of knowledge for his allegations, "since the report was of the sort which in common experience may be recognized as having been obtained in a reliable way." The fact that the informer was able to predict, two days in advance, the exact clothing Draper would be wearing dispelled the possibility that his tip was just based on rumor or "an off-hand remark heard at a neighborhood bar." Probably Draper had planned in advance to wear these specific clothes so that an accomplice could identify him. A clear inference could therefore be drawn that the informant was either involved in the criminal scheme himself or that he otherwise had access to reliable, inside information.[22]

22. Thus, as interpreted in *Spinelli,* the Court in *Draper* held that there was probable cause because "the kind of information related by the informant [was] not generally sent ahead of a person's arrival in a city except to those who are intimately connected with making careful arrangements for meeting him." *Spinelli* (White, J., concurring). As I said in *Spinelli,* the conclusion that *Draper* itself was based on this fact is far from inescapable. Prior to *Spinelli, Draper* was susceptible to the interpretation that it stood for the proposition that "the existence of the tenth and critical fact is made sufficiently probable to justify the issuance of a warrant by verifying nine other facts coming from the same source." *Spinelli* (White, J., concurring). But it now seems clear that the Court in *Spinelli* rejected this reading of *Draper.*

Justice Brennan erroneously interprets my *Spinelli* concurrence as espousing the view that "corroboration of certain details in a tip may be sufficient to satisfy the veracity, but not the basis of knowledge, prong of *Aguilar.*" I did not say that corroboration could *never* satisfy the basis of knowledge prong. My concern was, and still is, that the prong might be deemed satisfied on the basis of corroboration of information that does

As in *Draper*, the police investigation in the present case satisfactorily demonstrated that the informant's tip was as trustworthy as one that would alone satisfy the *Aguilar* tests. The tip predicted that Sue Gates would drive to Florida, that Lance Gates would fly there a few days after May 3, and that Lance would then drive the car back. After the police corroborated these facts, the magistrate could reasonably have inferred, as he apparently did, that the informant, who had specific knowledge of these unusual travel plans, did not make up his story and that he obtained his information in a reliable way. It is theoretically possible, as respondents insist, that the tip could have been supplied by a "vindictive travel agent" and that the Gates' activities, although unusual, might not have been unlawful. But *Aguilar* and *Spinelli*, like our other cases, do not require that certain guilt be established before a warrant may properly be issued. "[O]nly the probability, and not a prima facie showing, of criminal activity is the standard of probable cause." I therefore conclude that the judgment of the Illinois Supreme Court invalidating the warrant must be reversed.

The Court agrees that the warrant was valid, but, in the process of reaching this conclusion, it overrules the *Aguilar-Spinelli* tests and replaces them with a "totality of the circumstances" standard. As shown above, it is not at all necessary to overrule *Aguilar-Spinelli* in order to reverse the judgment below. Therefore, because I am inclined to believe that, when applied properly, the *Aguilar-Spinelli* rules play an appropriate role in probable cause determinations, and because the Court's holding may foretell an evisceration of the probable cause standard, I do not join the Court's holding.

The Court reasons that the "veracity" and "basis of knowledge" tests are not independent, and that a deficiency as to one can be compensated for by a strong showing as to the other. Thus, a finding of probable cause may be based on a tip from an informant "known for the unusual reliability of his predictions" or from "an unquestionably honest citizen," even if the report fails thoroughly to set forth the basis upon which the information was obtained. If this is so, then it must follow *a fortiori* that "the affidavit of an officer, known by the magistrate to be honest and experienced, stating that [contraband] is located in a certain building" must be acceptable. It would be "quixotic" if a similar statement from an honest informant, but not one from an honest officer, could furnish probable cause. But we have repeatedly held that the unsupported assertion or belief of an officer does not satisfy the probable cause requirement. Thus, this portion of today's holding can be read as implicitly rejecting the teachings of these prior holdings.

The Court may not intend so drastic a result. Indeed, the Court expressly reaffirms the validity of cases such as *Nathanson* that have held that, no matter how reliable the affiant-officer may be, a warrant should not be issued unless the affidavit discloses supporting facts and circumstances. The Court limits these cases to situations involving affidavits containing only "bare conclusions" and holds that, if an affidavit contains anything more, it should be left to the issuing magistrate to decide, based solely on "practical[ity]" and "common-sense," whether there is a fair probability that contraband will be found in a particular place.

Thus, as I read the majority opinion, it appears that the question whether the

not in any way suggest that the informant had an adequate basis of knowledge for his report. If, however, as in *Draper*, the police corroborate information from which it can be inferred that the informant's tip was grounded on inside information, this corroboration is sufficient to satisfy the basis of knowledge prong. *Spinelli* (White, J., concurring). The rules would indeed be strange if, as Justice Brennan suggests, the basis of knowledge prong could be satisfied by detail in the tip alone, but not by independent police work.

probable cause standard is to be diluted is left to the common-sense judgments of issuing magistrates. I am reluctant to approve any standard that does not expressly require, as a prerequisite to issuance of a warrant, some showing of facts from which an inference may be drawn that the informant is credible and that his information was obtained in a reliable way. The Court is correctly concerned with the fact that some lower courts have been applying *Aguilar-Spinelli* in an unduly rigid manner. I believe, however, that with clarification of the rule of corroborating information, the lower courts are fully able to properly interpret *Aguilar-Spinelli* and avoid such unduly-rigid applications. I may be wrong; it ultimately may prove to be the case that the only profitable instruction we can provide to magistrates is to rely on common sense. But the question whether a particular anonymous tip provides the basis for issuance of a warrant will often be a difficult one, and I would at least attempt to provide more precise guidance by clarifying *Aguilar-Spinelli* and the relationship of those cases with *Draper* before totally abdicating our responsibility in this area. Hence, I do not join the Court's opinion rejecting the *Aguilar-Spinelli* rules.

JUSTICE BRENNAN, with whom JUSTICE MARSHALL joins, dissenting.

Although I join Justice Stevens' dissenting opinion and agree with him that the warrant is invalid even under the Court's newly announced "totality of the circumstances" test, I write separately to dissent from the Court's unjustified and ill-advised rejection of the two-prong test for evaluating the validity of a warrant based on hearsay announced in *Aguilar v. Texas,* and refined in *Spinelli v. United States.*

* * * In *Spinelli,* the Court reviewed a search warrant based on an affidavit that was "more ample" than the one in *Aguilar.* The affidavit in *Spinelli* contained not only a tip from an informant, but also a report of an independent police investigation that allegedly corroborated the informant's tip. Under these circumstances, the Court stated that it was "required to delineate the manner in which *Aguilar's* two-pronged test should be applied * * *."

The Court held that the *Aguilar* test should be applied to the tip, and approved two additional ways of satisfying that test. First, the Court suggested that if the tip contained sufficient detail describing the accused's criminal activity it might satisfy *Aguilar's* basis of knowledge prong. Such detail might assure the magistrate that he is "relying on something more substantial than a casual rumor circulating in the underworld or an accusation based merely on an individual's general reputation." Although the tip in the case before it did not meet this standard, "[t]he detail provided by the informant in *Draper v. United States* provide[d] a suitable benchmark" because "[a] magistrate, when confronted with such detail, could reasonably infer that the informant had gained his information in a reliable way."

Second, the Court stated that police corroboration of the details of a tip could provide a basis for satisfying *Aguilar.* The Court's opinion is not a model of clarity on this issue since it appears to suggest that corroboration can satisfy both the basis of knowledge and veracity prongs of *Aguilar.* Justice White's concurring opinion, however, points the way to a proper reading of the Court's opinion. After reviewing the Court's decision in *Draper v. United States,* Justice White concluded that "[t]he thrust of *Draper* is not that the verified facts have independent significance with respect to proof of [another unverified fact]." In his view, "[t]he argument instead relates to the reliability of the source: because an informant is right about some things, he is more probably right about other facts, usually the critical, unverified facts." Justice White then pointed out that prior cases had rejected "the notion that the past reliability of an officer is sufficient reason for believing his current assertions." Justice White went on to state:

"Nor would it suffice, I suppose, if a reliable informant states there is gambling equipment in Apartment 607 and then proceeds to describe in detail Apartment 201, a description which is verified before applying for the warrant. He was right about 201, but that hardly makes him more believable about the equipment in 607. But what if he states that there are narcotics locked in a safe in Apartment 300, which is described in detail, and the apartment manager verifies everything but the contents of the safe? I doubt that the report about the narcotics is made appreciably more believable by the verification. The informant could still have gotten his information concerning the safe from others about whom nothing is known or could have inferred the presence of narcotics from circumstances which a magistrate would find unacceptable."

I find this reasoning persuasive. Properly understood, therefore, *Spinelli* stands for the proposition that corroboration of certain details in a tip may be sufficient to satisfy the veracity, but not the basis of knowledge, prong of *Aguilar.* As noted, *Spinelli* also suggests that in some limited circumstances considerable detail in an informant's tip may be adequate to satisfy the basis of knowledge prong of *Aguilar.* * * *

In rejecting the *Aguilar-Spinelli* standards, the Court * * * relies on * * * the "practical, nontechnical" nature of probable cause.

[O]ne can concede that probable cause is a "practical, nontechnical" concept without betraying the values that *Aguilar* and *Spinelli* reflect. As noted, *Aguilar* and *Spinelli* require the police to provide magistrates with certain crucial information. They also provide structure for magistrates' probable cause inquiries. In so doing, *Aguilar* and *Spinelli* preserve the role of magistrates as independent arbiters of probable cause, insure greater accuracy in probable cause determinations, and advance the substantive value of precluding findings of probable cause, and attendant intrusions, based on anything less than information from an honest or credible person who has acquired his information in a reliable way. Neither the standards nor their effects are inconsistent with a "practical, nontechnical" conception of probable cause. Once a magistrate has determined that he has information before him that he can reasonably say has been obtained in a reliable way by a credible person, he has ample room to use his common sense and to apply a practical, nontechnical conception of probable cause. * * *

The Court also insists that the *Aguilar-Spinelli* standards must be abandoned because they are inconsistent with the fact that non-lawyers frequently serve as magistrates. To the contrary, the standards help to structure probable cause inquiries and, properly interpreted, may actually help a non-lawyer magistrate in making a probable cause determination. * * *

At the heart of the Court's decision to abandon *Aguilar* and *Spinelli* appears to be its belief that "the direction taken by decisions following *Spinelli* poorly serves 'the most basic function of any government: to provide for the security of the individual and of his property.' " This conclusion rests on the judgment that *Aguilar* and *Spinelli* "seriously imped[e] the task of law enforcement," and render anonymous tips valueless in police work. Surely, the Court overstates its case. But of particular concern to all Americans must be that the Court gives virtually no consideration to the value of insuring that findings of probable cause are based on information that a magistrate can reasonably say has been obtained in a reliable way by an honest or credible person. * * *

The Court's complete failure to provide any persuasive reason for rejecting *Aguilar* and *Spinelli* doubtlessly reflects impatience with what it perceives to be "overly technical" rules governing searches and seizures under the Fourth Amendment.

Words such as "practical," "nontechnical," and "commonsense," as used in the Court's opinion, are but code words for an overly permissive attitude towards police practices in derogation of the rights secured by the Fourth Amendment. Everyone shares the Court's concern over the horrors of drug trafficking, but under our Constitution only measures consistent with the Fourth Amendment may be employed by government to cure this evil. We must be ever mindful of Justice Stewart's admonition in *Coolidge v. New Hampshire*, [p. 296 infra], that "[i]n times of unrest, whether caused by crime or racial conflict or fear of internal subversion, this basic law and the values that it represents may appear unrealistic or 'extravagant' to some. But the values were those of the authors of our fundamental constitutional concepts." * * *

Rights secured by the Fourth Amendment are particularly difficult to protect because their "advocates are usually criminals." But the rules "we fashion [are] for the innocent and guilty alike." By replacing *Aguilar* and *Spinelli* with a test that provides no assurance that magistrates, rather than the police, or informants, will make determinations of probable cause; imposes no structure on magistrates' probable cause inquiries; and invites the possibility that intrusions may be justified on less than reliable information from an honest or credible person, today's decision threatens to "obliterate one of the most fundamental distinctions between our form of government, where officers are under the law, and the police-state where they are the law."

JUSTICE STEVENS, with whom JUSTICE BRENNAN joins, dissenting.

* * * The informant had indicated that "Sue drives their car to Florida *where she leaves it to be loaded up with drugs * * *. Sue flies back after she drops the car off in Florida.*" (emphasis added). Yet Detective Mader's affidavit reported that she "left the West Palm Beach area driving the Mercury northbound."

The discrepancy between the informant's predictions and the facts known to Detective Mader is significant for three reasons. First, it cast doubt on the informant's hypothesis that the Gates already had "over $100,000 worth of drugs in their basement." The informant had predicted an itinerary that always kept one spouse in Bloomingdale, suggesting that the Gates did not want to leave their home unguarded because something valuable was hidden within. That inference obviously could not be drawn when it was known that the pair was actually together over a thousand miles from home.

Second, the discrepancy made the Gates' conduct seem substantially less unusual than the informant had predicted it would be. It would have been odd if, as predicted, Sue had driven down to Florida on Wednesday, left the car, and flown right back to Illinois. But the mere facts that Sue was in West Palm Beach with the car,[1] that she was joined by her husband at the Holiday Inn on Friday,[2] and that the couple drove north together the next morning [3] are neither unusual nor probative of criminal activity.

1. The anonymous note suggested that she was going down on Wednesday, but for all the officers knew she had been in Florida for a month.

2. Lance does not appear to have behaved suspiciously in flying down to Florida. He made a reservation in his own name and gave an accurate home phone number to the airlines. And Detective Mader's affidavit does not report that he did any of the other things drug couriers are notorious for doing, such as paying for the ticket in cash, dressing casually, looking pale and nervous, improperly filling out baggage tags, carrying American Tourister luggage, not carrying any luggage, or changing airlines en route.

3. Detective Mader's affidavit hinted darkly that the couple had set out upon "that interstate highway commonly used by travelers to the Chicago area." But the same highway is also commonly used by travelers to Disney World, Sea World, and Ringling Brothers and Barnum and Bailey Circus World. It is also the road to Cocoa Beach, Cape Canaveral, and Washington, D.C. I would venture that each year dozens of perfectly

Third, the fact that the anonymous letter contained a material mistake undermines the reasonableness of relying on it as a basis for making a forcible entry into a private home.

Of course, the activities in this case did not stop when the magistrate issued the warrant. The Gates drove all night to Bloomingdale, the officers searched the car and found 400 pounds of marijuana, and then they searched the house. However, none of these subsequent events may be considered in evaluating the warrant, and the search of the house was legal only if the warrant was valid. I cannot accept the Court's casual conclusion that, *before the Gates arrived in Bloomingdale,* there was probable cause to justify a valid entry and search of a private home. No one knows who the informant in this case was, or what motivated him or her to write the note. Given that the note's predictions were faulty in one significant respect, and were corroborated by nothing except ordinary innocent activity, I must surmise that the Court's evaluation of the warrant's validity has been colored by subsequent events. * * *[b]

Notes and Questions

1. In MASSACHUSETTS v. UPTON, 466 U.S. 727, 104 S.Ct. 2085, 80 L.Ed.2d 721 (1984), police Lt. Beland assisted in the execution of a search warrant for a motel room reserved by one Richard Kelleher, which produced several items of identification belonging to two persons whose homes had recently been burglarized. Other items taken in the burglaries, such as jewelry, silver and gold, were not found. A few hours later Beland received a call from an unidentified female who told him that there was "a motor home full of stolen stuff," including jewelry, silver and gold, at George Upton's premises. After verifying that a motor home was parked there, Beland prepared an application for a search warrant, to which he attached the police reports on the two prior burglaries, along with lists of the stolen property, and his affidavit with the above information and the following:

"She further stated that George Upton was going to move the motor home any time now because of the fact that Ricky Kelleher's motel room was raided and that George Upton had purchased these stolen items from Ricky Kelleher. This unidentified female stated that she had seen the stolen items but refused to identify herself because "he'll kill me," referring to George Upton. I then told this unidentified female that I knew who she was, giving her the name of Lynn Alberico, who I had met on May 16, 1980, at George Upton's repair shop off Summer St., in Yarmouthport. She was identified to me by George Upton as being his girlfriend, Lynn Alberico. The unidentified female admitted that she was the girl that I had named, stating that she was surprised that I knew who she was. She then told me that she'd broken up with George Upton and wanted to burn him. She also told me that she wouldn't give me her address or phone number but that she would contact me in the future, if need be."

innocent people fly to Florida, meet a waiting spouse, and drive off together in the family car.

b. For criticism of *Gates,* see Kamisar, *Gates, "Probable Cause," "Good Faith," and Beyond,* 69 Iowa L.Rev. 557 (1984); LaFave, *Fourth Amendment Vagaries (of Improbable Cause, Imperceptible Plain View, Notorious Privacy, and Balancing Askew),* 74 J.Crim.L. & C. 1171, 1186–99 (1983); Loewy, *Protecting Citizens from Cops and Crooks: An Assessment of the Supreme Court's Interpretation of the Fourth Amendment During the 1982 Term,* 62 N.C.L.Rev. 329, 336–45 (1984) (criticizing the Court's handling of "probable cause," but not its abandonment of the "two-pronged test"); Wasserstrom, *The Incredible Shrinking Fourth Amendment,* 21 Am.Crim.L. Rev. 257, 274–75, 329–40 (1984) (same). Cf. Moylan, *Illinois v. Gates: What It Did and Did Not Do,* 20 Crim.L.Bull. 93 (1984) (criticizing the Court's "rhetoric," but maintaining that, on its facts, *Gates* is an exceedingly narrow holding). For a strong defense of *Gates,* see Grano, *Probable Cause and Common Sense: A Reply to the Critics of Illinois v. Gates,* 17 U.Mich.J.L.Ref. 465 (1984).

A magistrate issued the warrant, and a subsequent search of the motor home produced the described items. The Massachusetts Supreme Court, viewing *Gates* as not making "a significant change in the appropriate Fourth Amendment treatment of applications for search warrants," held probable cause was lacking because (i) the basis of the informant's knowledge was not "forcefully apparent"; (ii) "none of the common bases for determining the credibility of an informant or the reliability of her information is present here"; and (iii) the corroboration was insufficient because each item of corroboration either related to innocent, nonsuspicious conduct or to an event in a public place. The Supreme Court, per curiam, asserting that the state court had erred in reading *Gates* as only refining the two-pronged test and in failing to grant deference to the magistrate's decision as contemplated by the *Gates* "substantial basis" test, reversed:

"Examined in light of Gates, Lt. Beland's affidavit provides a substantial basis for the issuance of the warrant. No single piece of evidence in it is conclusive. But the pieces fit neatly together and, so viewed, support the magistrate's determination that there was 'a fair probability that contraband or evidence of crime' would be found in Upton's motor home. The informant claimed to have seen the stolen goods and gave a description of them which tallied with the items taken in recent burglaries. She knew of the raid on the motel room—which produced evidence connected to those burglaries—and that the room had been reserved by Kelleher. She explained the connection between Kelleher's motel room and the stolen goods in Upton's motor home. And she provided a motive both for her attempt at anonymity—fear of Upton's retaliation—and for furnishing the information—her recent breakup with Upton and her desire 'to burn him.'

"The Massachusetts court dismissed Lt. Beland's identification of the caller as a mere 'unconfirmed guess.' * * * It is of course possible that the caller merely adopted Lt. Beland's suggestion as 'a convenient cover for her true identity.' But given the caller's admission, her obvious knowledge of who Alberico was and how she was connected with Upton, and her explanation of her motive in calling, Lt. Beland's inference appears stronger than a mere uninformed and unconfirmed guess. It is enough that the inference was a reasonable one and conformed with the other pieces of evidence making up the total showing of probable cause." [c]

2. It is apparent from the language of the Fourth Amendment that a valid arrest warrant or search warrant may only be issued upon facts establishing probable cause. However, as we will see later, police are often permitted to make arrests and searches without first obtaining a warrant, to which the Fourth Amendment's protection against "unreasonable searches and seizures" applies. But, because a "principal incentive" for the procurement of warrants would be destroyed if police needed less evidence when acting without a warrant, the requirements in such instances "surely cannot be less stringent" than when a warrant is obtained. *Wong Sun v. United States*, 371 U.S. 471, 83 S.Ct. 407, 9 L.Ed.2d 441 (1963). Thus probable cause is also required for warrantless arrests and searches.[d]

3. It is generally assumed that the same quantum of evidence is required whether one is concerned with probable cause to arrest or probable cause to search. How-

c. Brennan and Marshall, JJ., dissented from the summary disposition of the case and would have denied the petition for certiorari. After remand, *Commonwealth v. Upton*, 476 N.E.2d 548 (Mass.1985), held that *Aguilar* and *Spinelli* "provide a more appropriate structure for probable cause inquiries" under the *state* constitution, and concluded that the affidavit failed to establish probable cause.

d. However, as discussed in §§ 7, 9 of this chapter, certain kinds of searches and seizures, because they involve a lesser degree of intrusion or interference, are permitted upon less than the traditional amount of probable cause.

ever, probable cause for search requires a somewhat different kind of conclusion than probable cause for arrest. For arrest, there must be a substantial probability that a crime has been committed and that the person to be arrested committed it; for search, there must be a substantial probability that certain items are the fruits, instrumentalities or evidence of crime and that these items are presently to be found at a certain place.

Because the latter type of probable cause has to do with the *present* location of certain objects, it may be found to be lacking because the time of the facts relied upon is unknown or highly uncertain. See, e.g., *Commonwealth v. Simmons,* 301 A.2d 819 (Pa.1973) (no probable cause to search for drugs at defendant's residence where affidavit merely said that informant "had purchased" drugs from defendant there, as this purchase "could have been a day, a week or months prior to the date of the affidavit"). For the same reason, when the time of the facts is given probable cause will sometimes be lacking because that information has become "stale."[e] See, e.g., *United States v. Steeves,* 525 F.2d 33 (8th Cir.1975) (warrant to search for clothing, ski mask, hand gun, money and money bag, all sought as evidence of bank robbery which occupant of premises participated in three months earlier; held, there was no probable cause the money or bag would still be there, but there was probable cause the other items would be there, as "a highly incriminating or consumable item of personal property is less likely to remain in one place as long as an item of property which is not consumable or which is innocuous in itself or not particularly incriminating"). Finally, even if no such problems are present, it must be remembered that to have probable cause to search there must be a sufficient connection of the items sought with a particular place. Thus, while a valid search warrant can sometimes issue even when the perpetrator of the crime is unknown, it does not necessarily follow that probable cause to arrest a person will likewise constitute probable cause to search that person's residence for evidence of that crime. See, e.g., *Commonwealth v. Kline,* 335 A.2d 361 (Pa.Super.1975) (affidavit stating that defendant had recently made a street sale of LSD to two young girls did not provide probable cause to search his apartment for drugs, as there "is no indication of where the transaction took place, how long it took, how long [the defendant] was gone, or what led the girls to conclude that he had gone to his apartment").

4. When the police act without a warrant, they initially make the probable cause decision themselves, although it is subject to after-the-fact review by a judicial officer upon a motion to suppress evidence found because of the arrest or search. When the police act with a warrant, the probable cause decision is made by a magistrate in the first instance, but his decision may likewise be challenged in an adversary setting upon a motion to suppress (except insofar as the question is avoided entirely by reliance on *United States v. Leon,* p. 216 supra). In a warrant case, the issue upon the motion to suppress is usually cast in terms of whether the facts set out in the complaint or affidavit upon which the warrant was issued establish probable cause.[f] However, the dissenters in *Aguilar* suggested that a defective affidavit might be cured by what the judge was told at the

e. In contrast to the "stale" information problem, the question is sometimes raised whether the information is premature, in the sense that it only shows that certain goods are to be at a certain place at some future time. Most courts agree with *People v. Glen,* 282 N.E.2d 614 (N.Y.1972), noted in 19 Wayne L.Rev. 1339 (1973) (search warrant issued on information that package containing narcotics would arrive at designated premises on future date; held: "as long as the evidence creates substantial probability that the seizable property will be on the premises when searched, the warrant should be sustained").

f. But consider *United States v. Marin-Buitrago,* 734 F.2d 889 (2d Cir.1984), holding that police are required "to report [to the magistrate who issued the warrant] any material changes in the facts contained in a warrant affidavit that occur before the warrant is executed."

time the warrant was sought, and they would also resuscitate the affidavit on the basis of the officer's subsequent testimony on the motion to suppress.

As to the first possibility, consider *Frazier v. Roberts*, 441 F.2d 1224 (8th Cir. 1971) (Fourth Amendment only requires that probable cause be "supported by Oath or affirmation," and thus *sworn* testimony may be considered; "preferable procedure is to preserve a written record" of this testimony); *United States v. Anderson*, 453 F.2d 174 (9th Cir.1971) (under Fed.R. Crim.P. 41(c), affidavit must be self-sufficient, a requirement which ensures "that the reviewing court may determine whether the constitutional requirements have been met without reliance upon faded and often confused memories"). As to the second possibility, consider *Whiteley v. Warden*, 401 U.S. 560, 91 S.Ct. 1031, 28 L.Ed.2d 306 (1971): "Under the cases of this Court, an otherwise insufficient affidavit cannot be rehabilitated by testimony concerning information possessed by the affiant when he sought the warrant but not disclosed to the issuing magistrate. * * * A contrary rule would, of course, render the warrant requirements of the Fourth Amendment meaningless." [g]

5. Does it follow that the defendant may not challenge an affidavit which is sufficient on its face? No, the Court answered in FRANKS v. DELAWARE, 438 U.S. 154, 98 S.Ct. 2674, 57 L.Ed.2d 667 (1978). Reasoning that (i) "a flat ban on impeachment of veracity could denude the probable cause requirement of all real meaning," (ii) "the hearing before the magistrate not always will suffice to discourage lawless or reckless misconduct," (iii) "the alternative sanctions of a perjury prosecution, administrative discipline, contempt, or a civil suit are not likely to fill the gap," (iv) "allowing an evidentiary hearing, after a suitable preliminary proffer of material falsity, will not diminish the importance and solemnity of the warrant-issuing process," (v) "the claim that a post-search hearing will confuse the issue of the defendant's guilt with the issue of the State's possible misbehavior is footless," and (vi) allowing impeachment does not really extend the exclusionary rule "to a 'new' area," the Court, per Blackmun, J., held "that, where the defendant makes a substantial preliminary showing that a false statement knowingly and intentionally, or with reckless disregard for the truth, was included by the affiant in the warrant affidavit, and if the allegedly false statement is necessary to the finding of probable cause, the Fourth Amendment requires that a hearing be held at the defendant's request. In the event that at that hearing the allegation of perjury or reckless disregard is established by the defendant by a preponderance of the evidence, and, with the affidavit's false material set to one side, the affidavit's remaining content is insufficient to establish probable cause, the search warrant must be voided and the fruits of the search excluded to the same extent as if probable cause was lacking on the face of the affidavit." [h]

Shouldn't the same result obtain if the false statement was negligently made, as reasoned in *Theodor v. Superior Court*, 501 P.2d 234 (Cal.1972), given "the overriding principle of reasonableness which governs the application of the Fourth Amendment"? Shouldn't the same result follow even as to innocently made falsehoods, where "[a]n honestly-erring individual

g. Compare the concurring opinion in *State v. Rice*, 199 N.W.2d 480 (Neb.1972): "At the time of making the affidavit for the search warrant, the police department had ample information to constitute probable cause for the issuance of the warrant, but much of the information was omitted from the affidavit. To apply the exclusionary rule under such circumstances exalts form over substance."

h. Rehnquist, J., joined by the Chief Justice, dissenting, argued: "If the function of the warrant requirement is to obtain the determination of a neutral magistrate as to whether sufficient grounds have been urged to support the issuance of a warrant, that function is fulfilled at the time the magistrate concludes that the requirement has been met."

* * * has substituted his erroneous judgment for that of the magistrate," as argued in Comment, 19 U.C.L.A.L.Rev. 96, 140 (1971)? If there was a deliberate false statement, then why shouldn't this *always* invalidate the warrant because, as stated in *United States v. Carmichael,* 489 F.2d 983 (7th Cir.1973), "[t]he fullest deterrent sanctions of the exclusionary rule should be applied to such serious and deliberate government wrongdoing"?

Should *Franks* apply where defendant's objection is that the police left out of the affidavit some additional information which would have put into question the probable cause shown by the information included? If so, what constitutes a material omission for this purpose, and what is the applicable mental state regarding the affiant's failure to include that information?

NOTES ON THE INFORMER'S PRIVILEGE

1. In McCRAY v. ILLINOIS, 386 U.S. 300, 87 S.Ct. 1056, 18 L.Ed.2d 62 (1967), petitioner was arrested and found to have heroin on his person. At the suppression hearing, the arresting officers testified that an informant who had supplied reliable information in about 20 previous cases told them that he had observed McCray selling narcotics at a certain corner and then accompanied them to that corner and pointed him out. Both officers were asked for the name and address of the informant, but objections to these questions were sustained. Petitioner's motion was denied, and he was subsequently convicted. The Court, per STEWART, J., affirmed:

"When the issue is not guilt or innocence, but, as here, the question of probable cause for an arrest or search, the Illinois Supreme Court has held that police officers need not invariably be required to disclose an informant's identity if the trial judge is convinced, by evidence submitted in open court and subject to cross-examination, that the officers did rely in good faith upon credible information supplied by a reliable informant. This Illinois evidentiary rule is consistent with the law of many other States. * * *

"The reasoning of the Supreme Court of New Jersey in judicially adopting the same basic evidentiary rule was instructively expressed by Chief Justice Weintraub in *State v. Burnett,* 42 N.J. 377, 201 A.2d 39 [1964]:

" 'If a defendant may insist upon disclosure of the informant in order to test the truth of the officer's statement that there is an informant or as to what the informant related or as to the informant's reliability, we can be sure that every defendant will demand disclosure. He has nothing to lose and the prize may be the suppression of damaging evidence if the State cannot afford to reveal its source, as is so often the case. And since there is no way to test the good faith of a defendant who presses the demand, we must assume the routine demand would have to be routinely granted. The result would be that the State could use the informant's information only as a lead and could search only if it could gather adequate evidence of probable cause apart from the informant's data. Perhaps that approach would sharpen investigatorial techniques, but we doubt that there would be enough talent and time to cope with crime upon that basis. Rather we accept the premise that the informer is a vital part of society's defensive arsenal. The basic rule protecting his identity rests upon that belief. * * *

" 'We must remember also that we are not dealing with the trial of the criminal charge itself. There the need for a truthful verdict outweighs society's need for the informer privilege. Here, however, the accused seeks to avoid the truth. The very purpose of a motion to suppress is to escape the inculpatory thrust of evidence in hand, not because its probative force is diluted in the least by the mode of seizure, but rather as a sanction to compel enforcement officers to respect the constitutional security of all of us under the Fourth Amendment. * * *

If the motion to suppress is denied, defendant will still be judged upon the untarnished truth. * * *

" 'The Fourth Amendment is served if a judicial mind passes upon the existence of probable cause. Where the issue is submitted upon an application for a warrant, the magistrate is trusted to evaluate the credibility of the affiant in an *ex parte* proceeding. As we have said, the magistrate is concerned, not with whether the informant lied, but with whether the affiant is truthful in his recitation of what he was told. If the magistrate doubts the credibility of the affiant, he may require that the informant be identified or even produced. It seems to us that the same approach is equally sufficient where the search was without a warrant, that is to say, that it should rest entirely with the judge who hears the motion to suppress to decide whether he needs such disclosure as to the informant in order to decide whether the officer is a believable witness.' * * *

"[W]e are now asked to hold that the Constitution somehow compels Illinois to abolish the informer's privilege from its law of evidence, and to require disclosure of the informer's identity in every such preliminary hearing where it appears that the officers made the arrest or search in reliance upon facts supplied by an informer they had reason to trust. The argument is based upon the Due Process Clause of the Fourteenth Amendment, and upon the Sixth Amendment right of confrontation, applicable to the States through the Fourteenth Amendment. * * *

"Nothing in the Due Process Clause of the Fourteenth Amendment requires a state court judge in every such hearing to assume the arresting officers are committing perjury. * * *

"The petitioner does not explain precisely how he thinks his Sixth Amendment right to confrontation and cross-examination was violated by Illinois' recognition of the informer's privilege in this case. If the claim is that the State violated the Sixth Amendment by not producing the informer to testify against the petitioner, then we need no more than repeat the Court's answer to that claim a few weeks ago: 'Petitioner also presents the contention here that he was unconstitutionally deprived of the right to confront a witness against him, because the State did not produce the informant to testify against him. This contention we consider absolutely devoid of merit.'

"On the other hand, the claim may be that the petitioner was deprived of his Sixth Amendment right to cross-examine the arresting officers themselves, because their refusal to reveal the informer's identity was upheld. But it would follow from this argument that no witness on cross-examination could ever constitutionally assert a testimonial privilege, including the privilege against compulsory self-incrimination guaranteed by the Constitution itself. We have never given the Sixth Amendment such a construction, and we decline to do so now."

DOUGLAS, J., joined by The Chief Justice, and Justices Brennan and Fortas, dissented:

"There is no way to determine the reliability of Old Reliable, the informer, unless he is produced, at the trial and cross-examined. Unless he is produced, the Fourth Amendment is entrusted to the tender mercies of the police. What we do today is to encourage arrests and searches without warrants. The whole momentum of criminal law administration should be in precisely the opposite direction, if the Fourth Amendment is to remain a vital force. Except in rare and emergency cases, it requires magistrates to make the findings of 'probable cause.' We should be mindful of its command that a judicial mind should be interposed between the police and the citizen. We should also be mindful that 'disclosure, rather than suppression, of relevant materials ordinarily promotes the proper administration of criminal justice.' "

2. How valid is the following criticism of *McCray* by Irving Younger, a former federal prosecutor, in *The Perjury Routine,* The Nation, May 8, 1967, pp. 596–97:

"[The *McCray* majority] said that 'nothing in the Due Process Clause of the Fourteenth Amendment requires a state court judge in every such hearing to assume the arresting officers are committing perjury.' Why not? Every lawyer who practices in the criminal courts knows that police perjury is commonplace.

"The reason is not hard to find. Policemen see themselves as fighting a two-front war—against criminals in the street and against 'liberal' rules of law in court. All's fair in this war, including the use of perjury to subvert 'liberal' rules of law that might free those who 'ought' to be jailed. * * *

"Far from adopting a presumption of perjury, the *McCray* case almost guarantees wholesale police perjury. When his conduct is challenged as constituting an unreasonable search and seizure, all the policeman need say is that an unnamed 'reliable informant' told him that the defendant was committing a crime. Henceforth, every policeman will have a genie-like informer to legalize his master's arrests."

3. Appellate decisions reversing a trial judge's denial of disclosure are extremely rare, and typically involve a situation in which the court could have simply said that probable cause had not been shown. But a growing number of cases are to be found along the lines of *People v. Darden,* 313 N.E.2d 49 (N.Y.1974), concluding it is "fair and wise, in a case such as this, where there is insufficient evidence to establish probable cause apart from the testimony of the arresting officer as to communications received from an informer, when the issue of identity of the informer is raised at the suppression hearing, for the suppression judge then to conduct an in camera inquiry. The prosecution should be required to make the informer available for interrogation before the Judge. The prosecutor may be present but not the defendant or his counsel. Opportunity should be afforded counsel for defendant to submit in writing any questions which he may desire the Judge to put to the informer. The Judge should take testimony, with recognition of the special need for protection of the interests of the absent defendant, and make a summary report as to the existence of the informer and with respect to the communications made by the informer to the police to which the police testify. That report should be made available to the defendant and to the People and the transcript of testimony should be sealed to be available to the appellate courts if the occasion arises. At that stage of the procedure, of course, every reasonable precaution should be taken to assure that the anonymity of the informer is protected to the maximum degree possible."

4. In *United States ex rel. Pugh v. Pate,* 401 F.2d 6 (7th Cir.1968), involving a search warrant affidavit signed with a fictitious name by a police informant, the court held that "the fourth amendment itself, in requiring an oath or affirmation, precludes hiding the identity of affiant or affirmant by use of a false name." The dissent noted that petitioner had not questioned the existence of probable cause and had not alleged that the magistrate was unaware of the informant's true identity, and distinguished *King v. United States,* 282 F.2d 398 (4th Cir.1960), where "the affiant used a quality fictitious name to add reliability to the application, and * * * the issuing magistrate was deceived."

NOTES ON OTHER SOURCES OF PROBABLE CAUSE

The probable cause decisions of the United States Supreme Court, almost exclusively concerned with when information from an informant, with or without some corroborating facts, is sufficient for arrest or search, are not fairly representative of the full range of probable cause issues confronted by the police. Consider these situations:

1. *Information from an alleged victim of, or witness to, a crime.* A major distinction between the victim-witness cases and the informant cases is that prior reliability need not be shown as to the former. As explained in *State v. Paszek,* 184 N.W.2d 836 (Wis.1971): "Information supplied to officers by the traditional police informer is not given in the spirit of a concerned citizen, but often is given in exchange for some concession, payment, or simply out of revenge against the subject. The nature of these persons and the information which they supply convey a certain impression of unreliability, and it is proper to demand that some evidence of their credibility and reliability be shown. * * *

"However, an ordinary citizen who reports a crime which has been committed in his presence, or that a crime is being or will be committed, stands on much different ground than a police informer. He is a witness to criminal activity who acts with an intent to aid the police in law enforcement because of his concern for society or for his own safety. He does not expect any gain or concession in exchange for his information. An informer of this type usually would not have more than one opportunity to supply information to the police, thereby precluding proof of his reliability by pointing to previous accurate information which he has supplied."

In the victim-witness cases, the critical question usually is whether the general description given by the victim or witness is sufficient to justify the arrest of any one person. For example, in *Brown v. United States,* 365 F.2d 976 (D.C.Cir.1966), the police received a radio report at 4:30 a.m. of a recent armed robbery, and were told to be on the lookout for a heavily built black male driving a maroon 1954 Ford. Shortly thereafter, 20 blocks from the robbery scene, the police saw what they thought to be such a car (actually, it was a 1952 Ford), and radioed for details about the robber. They were told that the robber was about five feet five inches, and that he was wearing a brown jacket and cream-colored straw hat. The suspect was about five feet eleven inches, was wearing blue, and had only a felt hat, but he was nonetheless arrested. Held: "These discrepancies, which can be the result of the victim's excitement or poor visibility or of the suspect's changing clothes, did not destroy the ascertainment made on the basis of the accurate portion of the identification, which was by itself enough to constitute probable cause."

2. *Direct observations by police.* Most troublesome, because the situations are so varied, are those cases in which the probable cause determination must be made solely upon suspicious conduct observed by police. For example, in *Brooks v. United States,* 159 A.2d 876 (D.C.Mun.App. 1960), an officer observed two men, both known to have prior convictions for larceny, carrying a console-type record player in the commercial area at 6:30 p.m. The officer noted that the player was new and still bore store tags. Upon questioning, one of the suspects said the machine belonged to his mother and that he was taking it in to be repaired. When the officer pointed out the tags, the suspect changed his story and said that the machine had been given to him by an unknown person, whom he was unable to describe. The officer then placed the two men under arrest. The court, noting that "the probabilities must be measured by the standards of the reasonable, cautious and prudent peace officer as he sees them, and not those of the casual passerby," held that the officer had acted on probable cause.

What if the officer had not known of the suspects' past records? What if the suspects had refused to answer any questions? Or, what if the suspect had not changed his first story? If the officer had been aware of the fact that larcenies were common in that area, would this be relevant?[a] What if the suspects had taken flight upon

a. Consider *United States v. Davis,* 458 F.2d 819 (D.C.Cir.1972): "Although no presumption of guilt arises from the activities of inhabitants of an area in which the police know that narcotics being stopped? What if they had engaged in "furtive gestures" upon seeing the police? To what extent, if at all, should account be taken of the expertise of the police in ascertaining what is probably criminal conduct?[b]

The police sometimes confront the question of how many persons may be arrested, as in *United States v. Hill,* 340 F.Supp. 344 (E.D.Pa.1972). In response to a radio report that someone had observed suspicious activity possibly involving narcotics, police went to the scene and observed two cars parked together. The rear car was empty and the front car contained the driver (*A*) and a passenger (*B*) in the front seat and two passengers (*C* and *D*) in the rear; a fifth person (*E*) was leaning in the front passenger-side window. When the police approached, *C, D,* and *E* attempted to flee, and *C* dropped a gun while exiting the car. When *B* was directed to get out of the car, he surreptitiously attempted to place paper bags in the gutter by the car; the police found counterfeit money in one of the bags. How many of those present could be lawfully arrested?

3. *Information and orders from official channels.* In *Whiteley v. Warden,* 401 U.S. 560, 91 S.Ct. 1031, 28 L.Ed.2d 306 (1971), Laramie, Wyoming police arrested two men fitting a description given in a police bulletin emanating from the office of the Carbon County Sheriff and transmitted over the state police radio network, indicating that the two described men were wanted for breaking and entering and that a warrant had been issued for their arrest. Although the warrant had not issued on probable cause, the state claimed that the arrests made by the Laramie officers were nonetheless legal because "they reasonably assumed that whoever authorized the bulletin had probable cause to direct Whiteley's and Daley's arrest." The Court, per Justice Harlan, disagreed: "We do not of course question that the Laramie police were entitled to act on the strength of the radio bulletin. Certainly police officers called upon to aid other officers in executing arrest warrants are entitled to assume that the officers requesting aid offered the magistrate the information requisite to support an independent judicial assessment of probable cause. Where, however, the contrary turns out to be true, an otherwise illegal arrest cannot be insulated from challenge by the decision of the instigating officer to rely on fellow officers to make the arrest." [c]

In *Commonwealth v. Riley,* 425 A.2d 813 (Pa.Super.1981), an officer lawfully stopped defendant for investigation and upon obtaining his identification checked his name through the National Crime Information Center, which reported that defendant was wanted on an outstanding ar-

offenses frequently occur, the syndrome of criminality in those areas cannot realistically go unnoticed by the judiciary. It too is a valid consideration when coupled with other reliable indicia or suspicious circumstances. We make this statement warily, for it is all too clear that few live in these areas by choice."

Compare Skolnick, *Justice Without Trial* 217–18 (1966): "If an honest citizen resides in a neighborhood heavily populated by criminals, just as the chances are high that he might be one, so too are the chances high that he might be mistaken for one. The probabilities, from the point of view of the individual, are always the same—either he is or is not culpable. Thus, behavior which seems 'reasonable' to the police because of the character of the neighborhood is seen by the honest citizen in it as irresponsible and unreasonable. About *him,* more errors will necessarily be made under a 'reasonableness' standard."

b. Compare *United States v. 1964 Ford Thunderbird,* 445 F.2d 1064 (3d Cir.1971) ("The standard is not what a police officer trained in a particular field would conclude, but rather it is what a reasonable prudent man would conclude"); with *United States v. McClard,* 333 F.Supp. 158 (E.D.Ark.1971) ("a Magistrate passing on the question of probable cause in connection with an affidavit for a search warrant presented by an experienced officer has a right to give at least some weight to the officer's presumed expertise").

c. Compare *United States v. Webster,* 750 F.2d 307 (5th Cir.1984) (arrest illegal notwithstanding probable cause at the source of the request, as defendant was arrested in response to a request which merely asked that anyone discovered in the area of the crime be picked up).

rest warrant and juvenile detainer. Based on that information, the officer arrested defendant, but it was later determined that the NCIC computer was incorrect in that the warrant and detainer had been satisfied four days earlier. The court held the arrest was lawful because, though "made in reliance upon the misinformation from the NCIC, the arresting officer did not know, and could not have known, that the information was wrong when he made the arrest." Can this result be squared with *Whiteley?* Should it make any difference how long the erroneous information was in the computer or why it was that it was not corrected? See Note, 28 Hastings L.J. 509 (1976).

NOTES ON HOW "PROBABLE" THE PROBABLE CAUSE MUST BE

If there is very good reason to believe that *A* has stolen property concealed *either* in his home *or* in his office, are there grounds for issuance of a search warrant for either or both places? If there is very good reason to believe that either *B* or *C* (but not both) has committed a certain crime, may either or both be arrested? Consider:

1. *Johnson v. United States,* 333 U.S. 10, 68 S.Ct. 367, 92 L.Ed. 436 (1948), where officers smelled burning opium outside a hotel room, knocked on the door and then arrested petitioner after she was found to be alone, and the Court held that the entry could not be justified as a step toward a lawful *arrest* [a] because "the arresting officer did not have probable cause to arrest petitioner until he had entered her room and found her to be the sole occupant."

2. *Mallory v. United States,* p. 525 infra, involving a rape by a masked black man, where the three blacks who had access to the basement where the rape occurred and who fit the general description of the rapist were arrested: "Presumably, whomever the police arrest they must arrest on 'probable cause.' It is not the function of the police to arrest, as it were, at large and to use an interrogating process at police headquarters in order to determine whom they should charge before a committing magistrate on 'probable cause.'"

3. *Wong Sun v. United States,* p. 803 infra, where an informant had said that an individual named "Blackie Toy," the proprietor of a laundry on Leavenworth Street, had sold an ounce of heroin; there were several Chinese laundries on this street, and apparently more than one Toy; and the arrest of one of them was held unlawful because there was no showing that the officers "had some information of some kind which had narrowed the scope of their search to this particular Toy."

4. *Restatement (Second) of Torts* § 119, comment *j* (1965): "A sees B and C bending over a dead man, D. B and C each accuse the other of murdering D. A is not sure that either B or C did the killing, but he has a reasonable suspicion that either B or C killed D. A is privileged to arrest either or both."

5. *Model Pre-Arraignment Code* § 120.1, Comment: "If the 'more probable than not' standard were adopted and taken seriously, many arrests made, for instance, on the basis of a victim's or a witness's description would be illegal. The description which a victim gives of an assailant will very rarely justify an officer in believing that a person who appears to correspond to that description is more probably than not guilty of the assault. To approach this degree of certainty, the victim needs an opportunity to identify the suspect, perhaps even in the carefully controlled context of a lineup. If, however, such a description is not sufficient basis for arrest, an officer in the field must allow

a. There was probable cause to *search,* but the entry could not be justified on that basis because the officers did not have a search warrant.

the suspect to disappear, and allow to disappear with him a possibility for solving the particular case and for imprisoning a dangerous offender. Present law does not require this conclusion,[b] and the Code also would not."

6. *Mistaken identity.* Are those situations distinguishable from the case in which the "probable cause" was not precise enough, as it turns out, to prevent arrest of the wrong person? In *Hill v. California,* 401 U.S. 797, 91 S.Ct. 1106, 28 L.Ed.2d 484 (1971), two men driving Hill's car admitted that they and Hill had committed a robbery which produced the property found in the car. Based upon the description of Hill given by the two men and verified by police records, police arrested a man found in Hill's apartment who "fit the description exactly" but who claimed (correctly, it was later determined) to be one Miller. The Court, per Justice White, upheld the arrest: "[A]liases and false identifications are not uncommon. Moreover, there was a lock on the door and Miller's explanation for his mode of entry was not convincing. He also denied knowledge of firearms in the apartment although a pistol and loaded ammunition clip were in plain view in the room. The upshot was that the officers in good faith believed Miller was Hill and arrested him. They were quite wrong as it turned out, and subjective good-faith belief would not in itself justify either the arrest or the subsequent search. But sufficient probability, not certainty, is the touchstone of reasonableness under the Fourth Amendment and on the record before us the officers' mistake was understandable and the arrest a reasonable response to the situation facing them at the time."

SECTION 4. SEARCH WARRANTS

A. Issuance of the Warrant

1. *The "neutral and detached magistrate" requirement.* In *Coolidge v. New Hampshire,* 403 U.S. 443, 91 S.Ct. 2022, 29 L.Ed.2d 564 (1971), the State Attorney General (authorized by state law to issue search warrants as a justice of the peace) issued a search warrant for the defendant's car in the course of a murder investigation of which he had taken personal charge and for which he later served as chief prosecutor at trial. The Court, per Stewart, J., held that this procedure "violated a fundamental premise of both the Fourth and Fourteenth Amendments" because "the state official who was the chief investigator and prosecutor in this case * * * was not the neutral and detached magistrate required by the Constitution," and summarily rejected "the proposition that the existence of probable cause renders noncompliance with the warrant procedure an irrelevance." Justice Black, joined by Chief Justice Burger and Justice Blackmun, dissented: "In the first place, there is no language in the Fourth Amendment which provides any basis for disqualification of the state attorney general to act as a magistrate. * * * In the second place, * * * the state attorney general's participation in the investigation of the case at the time he issued the search warrant was 'harmless error' if it was error at all" because "a refusal to issue a warrant on the showing of probable cause made in this case would have been an abuse of discretion."

Compare *Shadwick v. City of Tampa,* 407 U.S. 345, 92 S.Ct. 2119, 32 L.Ed.2d 783 (1972), where a unanimous Court, per

b. E.g., *Browne v. State,* 129 N.W.2d 175 (Wis. 1964), stating that "it is not necessary that the evidence * * * be sufficient to prove that guilt is more probable than not. It is only necessary that the information lead a reasonable officer to believe that guilt is more than a possibility."

Reconsider *Brown v. United States,* Note 1 at p. 285 supra, where the court reasoned: "The total number of 1954 Fords meeting that description being driven in 1964 was limited; still smaller was the total number being driven at 4:30 on a Monday morning, and yet smaller those driven in that immediate neighborhood at that time by heavy Negro males. Ordinary human experience alone, without resort to the precise factors of the law of probability, tells us this."

Powell, J., upheld a city charter provision authorizing municipal court clerks to issue *arrest* warrants for municipal ordinance violations. Rejecting the notion "that all warrant authority must reside exclusively in a lawyer or judge" (and noting that "even within the federal system warrants were until recently widely issued by nonlawyers"), the Court concluded that "an issuing magistrate must meet two tests. He must be neutral and detached, and he must be capable of determining whether probable cause exists for the requested arrest or search." The clerk possesses the requisite detachment, as he "is removed from prosecutor or police and works within the judicial branch subject to the supervision of the municipal court judge." [a] As to capacity: "We presume from the nature of the clerk's position that he would be able to deduce from the facts on an affidavit before him whether there was probable cause to believe a citizen guilty of impaired driving, breach of peace, drunkenness, trespass or the multiple other common offenses covered by a municipal code. There has been no showing that this is too difficult a task for a clerk to accomplish. Our legal system has long entrusted nonlawyers to evaluate more complex and significant factual data than that in the case at hand. Grand juries daily determine probable cause prior to rendering indictments, and trial juries assess whether guilt is proved beyond a reasonable doubt." On the basis of *Shadwick,* could court clerks be authorized to issue arrest warrants in all cases? To issue search warrants?

In *Connally v. Georgia,* 429 U.S. 245, 97 S.Ct. 546, 50 L.Ed.2d 444 (1977), a unanimous Court held that the search warrant had not been issued by a "neutral and detached magistrate" where the issuing justice of the peace was unsalaried and, so far as search warrants were concerned, was paid a fee of $5 if he issued a warrant but nothing if he denied the application.

In *Rooker v. Commonwealth,* 508 S.W.2d 570 (Ky.App.1974), the court, in ruling that evidence obtained in execution of a search warrant must be suppressed, held: "Where a judge issues a search warrant based upon an affidavit which he does not read, he makes no determination of probable cause but merely serves as a rubber stamp for the police. Such action is improper even though the affidavit actually shows probable cause for the issuance of the warrant."

United States v. Davis, 346 F.Supp. 435 (S.D.Ill.1972), involved these facts: A Treasury agent, accompanied by an assistant U.S. attorney, went to Magistrate Ghiglieri and presented an affidavit for a search warrant. The agent did not swear to the affidavit, but the magistrate dated and signed the affidavit and indicated that it was denied. The following day the agent, again accompanied by the assistant, went to Magistrate Giffin and presented the same affidavit. Giffin, after being apprised of the proceedings before Ghiglieri, issued a search warrant. The court found this procedure to be "highly improper" and concluded: "Magistrate Ghiglieri's decision was final and binding, and his denial of the application * * * equitably estopped Magistrate Giffin from issuing a search warrant on the exact same showing." Is this a desirable result, in that it limits magistrate-shopping? If the first magistrate was in error, what recourse should be open to the affiant-officer?

2. *Particular description of the place to be searched.* As for the Fourth Amendment requirement of particularity in the description of the place to be searched, it "is enough if the description is such that the officer with a search warrant can, with reasonable effort ascertain and identify the place intended." *Steele v. United States,*

a. Is the magistrate sufficiently detached from the police if it is his practice to assist the police in the preparation of search warrant affidavits? See *United States v. Steed,* 465 F.2d 1310 (9th Cir.1972); *Albitez v. Beto,* 465 F.2d 954 (5th Cir.1972). If he assists the police in execution of the warrant? See *Lo-Ji Sales, Inc. v. New York,* 442 U.S. 319, 99 S.Ct. 2319, 60 L.Ed.2d 920 (1979).

267 U.S. 498, 45 S.Ct. 414, 69 L.Ed. 757 (1925). The common practice is to identify premises in an urban area by street address, which is sufficient. Less particularity is required for rural premises; for example, description of a farm by the name of the owner and general directions for reaching the farm is adequate.

Most of the problems which arise concerning the particularity of description occur not because the warrant description is facially vague, but rather because upon execution it proves to be not as certain as theretofore assumed. One possibility is that the description will turn out not to be sufficiently precise, as where the warrant refers to apartment 3 in a certain building but the officers find apartments with that number on each floor. In this kind of case, courts are receptive to a showing that the executing officers had other information (e.g., the occupant's name), via the affidavit or otherwise, which made it apparent which place was intended.

Another type of case is that in which the executing officers find that some but not all of the descriptive facts fit the same place. Illustrative is *State v. Blackburn,* 511 P.2d 381 (Or.1973), where the apartment in a particular building was said to be apartment number 2 with "the letters ECURB on the door," but the officer found one apartment with the numeral 2 on the door and another with no numeral but the letters ECURB on the door. In upholding the search of the latter apartment, the court held that "there could be no real doubt as to which of the premises was intended" because "[n]o one could have made a mistake or been confused about a word like ECURB, but anyone could easily have made a mistake about a numeral."

In the absence of a probable cause showing as to all the separate living units in a multiple-occupancy structure, the warrant for such a building must describe the particular unit to be searched. But, if the building in question from its outward appearance would be taken to be a single-occupancy structure and neither the affiant nor other investigating officers nor the executing officers knew or had reason to know otherwise until execution of the warrant was under way, then the warrant is not defective for failure to specify a unit within the building.

3. *Particular description of the things to be seized.* The Fourth Amendment requirement of particularity in the description of the things to be seized is intended to prevent general searches, to prevent the seizure of objects on the mistaken assumption that they fall within the magistrate's authorization, and to prevent "the issuance of warrants on loose, vague or doubtful bases of fact." *Go-Bart Importing Co. v. United States,* 282 U.S. 344, 51 S.Ct. 153, 75 L.Ed. 374 (1931). As noted in LaFave, § 4.6:

"Consistent with these three purposes are certain general principles which may be distilled from the decided cases in this area. They are: (1) A greater degree of ambiguity will be tolerated when the police have done the best that could be expected under the circumstances, by acquiring all the descriptive facts which reasonable investigation of this type of crime could be expected to uncover and by ensuring that all of those facts were included in the warrant.[13] (2) A more general type of description will be sufficient when the nature of the objects to be seized are such that they could not be expected to have more specific characteristics.[14] (3) A less precise description is required of prop-

13. * * * Compare *State v. Withers,* 8 Wash. App. 123, 504 P.2d 1151 (1972), approving a general description of stolen property when no accurate inventory of what was taken was possible, with *Lockridge v. Superior Court,* 275 Cal.App.2d 612, 80 Cal.Rptr. 223 (1969), not permitting general description of stolen property because there was no showing that an inventory was unavailable.

14. *State v. Salsman,* 112 N.H. 138, 290 A.2d 618 (1972) (description of 42 sheets of plywood sufficient, "considering the nature of these items"); * * *

erty which is, because of its particular character, contraband. (4) Failure to provide all of the available descriptive facts is not a basis for questioning the adequacy of the description when the omitted facts could not have been expected to be of assistance to the executing officer.[16] (5) An error in the statement of certain descriptive facts is not a basis for questioning the adequacy of the description if the executing officer was nonetheless able to determine, from the other facts provided, that the object seized was that intended by the description.[17] (6) Greater care in description is ordinarily called for when the type of property sought is generally in lawful use in substantial quantities.[18] (7) A more particular description than otherwise might be necessary is required when other objects of the same general classification are likely to be found at the particular place to be searched.[19] (8) The greatest care in description is required when the consequences of a seizure of innocent articles by mistake is most substantial, as when the objects to be seized are books or films."

4. *Neutrality, particularity, and "good faith."* Consider the impact of *United States v. Leon,* p. 216 supra, and *Massachusetts v. Sheppard,* p. 227 supra, in this context.

B. Execution of the Warrant

1. *Time of execution.* Statutes and court rules commonly provide that a search warrant must be executed within a certain time, such as 10 days. Execution within that time is proper, "provided that the probable cause recited in the affidavit continues until the time of execution, giving consideration to the intervening knowledge of the officers and the passage of time." *United States v. Nepstead,* 424 F.2d 259 (9th Cir.1970) (execution of warrant, for seizure of equipment used to manufacture LSD, 6 days after issuance timely, as premises under daily surveillance and no activity noted until after first 5 days).[b] Compare Fed.R.Crim.P. 41(c), which requires the issuing magistrate to direct the officer to search "within a specified period of time, not to exceed 10 days."

Also, in many jurisdictions a search warrant may be served only in the daytime unless it expressly states to the contrary, and a warrant so stating often can be obtained only by meeting special requirements—e.g., obtaining the concurrence of two magistrates, showing that the property is definitely in the place to be searched, or showing some need for prompt action. In GOODING v. UNITED STATES, 416 U.S. 430, 94 S.Ct. 1780, 40 L.Ed.2d 250 (1974), holding that the federal statute relating to searches for controlled substances required no special showing for a nighttime search other than that the contraband is likely to be on the property at that time, Justice Marshall, joined by Douglas and Brennan, JJ., noted in dissent that while the "constitutional question is not presented in this case and need not be resolved here," the principle that nighttime searches "involve a greater intrusion

16. *United States v. Scharfman,* 448 F.2d 1352 (2d Cir.1971) (any effort to describe more particularly which furs in fur stores were stolen "would have required a legion of fur experts" to execute the warrant).

17. *United States v. Rytman,* 475 F.2d 192 (5th Cir.1973) (compressor of described brand and with serial number approximating that stated in the warrant could be seized); * * *

18. *People v. Prall,* 314 Ill. 518, 145 N.E. 610 (1924) (thus description of "certain automobile tires and tubes" insufficient); * * *

19. *People v. Einhorn,* 75 Misc.2d 183, 346 N.Y.S.2d 986 (1973) (search warrant for drug store permitted search for "drugs, invoices, prescription pills, freight and shipment records, * * * canceled checks, journals, ledgers, and other business records," among other things; held, "the particulars are so broad as to make them indistinguishable from a general warrant authorizing a search and seizure of everything in the drug store with the possible exception of aspirin and toothpaste"). Compare *United States v. Scharfman,* supra note 16.

b. See also *United States v. Marin-Buitrago,* fn. f at p. 280 supra.

than ordinary searches and therefore require a greater justification * * * may well be a constitutional imperative. It is by now established Fourth Amendment doctrine that increasingly severe standards of probable cause are necessary to justify increasingly intrusive searches. In *Camara v. Municipal Court* [p. 399 infra], after holding that search warrants were required to authorize administrative inspections, we held that the quantum of probable cause required for issuance of an inspection warrant must be determined in part by the reasonableness of the proposed search. As Mr. Justice White stated, 'there can be no ready test for determining reasonableness other than by balancing the need to search against the invasion which the search entails.' The Court in *Camara* thus approved the issuance of area inspection warrants in part because such searches 'involve a relatively limited invasion of the urban citizen's privacy.' I do not regard this principle as a one-way street, to be used only to water down the requirement of probable cause when necessary to authorize governmental intrusions. In some situations—and the search of a private home during nighttime would seem to be a paradigm example—this principle requires a showing of additional justification for a search over and above the ordinary showing of probable cause."

In *United States v. Gervato,* 474 F.2d 40 (3d Cir.1973), the court emphasized the various protections provided by Fed.R. Crim.P. 41 in rejecting the district court's holding "that a search warrant executed in the absence of the occupant constitutes an unreasonable search because there exists the possibility of a general search and 'pilferage by officers of the law.' "

2. *Gaining entry.* In STATE v. GASSNER, 488 P.2d 822 (Or.App.1971), the defendant argued that the narcotics obtained in the execution of a search warrant should be suppressed because the police entered the premises by use of a pass key without first giving notice of their authority and purpose. The court, per SCHWAB, C.J., agreed: "[*Ker v. California,* p. 329 infra] held that it was constitutionally permissible to make an unannounced search when it was likely that evidence would otherwise be destroyed. The major battle in the state courts since *Ker* has been over the proper scope of this exception.

"To better understand the area of disagreement, we first review the areas of agreement. Under the destruction-of-the-evidence exception all courts agree that announcement is not required if, before arriving to search, the police have particular reasons to reasonably believe in a particular case that evidence will be destroyed. Such situations might occur, for example, if a reliable informant advises the police that betting slips are kept on "flash paper," or that a small amount of narcotics is always kept near a toilet. There is further agreement that if the police knock and announce and then hear indications that evidence is being destroyed, they are justified in making an immediate forcible entry. Also, if police observe persons within a house in possession of easily disposable amounts of narcotics, or other evidence, announcement is not required.

"The split in authority has arisen in cases where none of these clearly exigent circumstances are present. One group of cases has held that since certain evidence, for example, of gambling and narcotics offenses, is, by its very nature easily destroyed or disposed of, unannounced searches are always constitutionally permissible in these contexts. On the other hand, a more substantial body of authority has rejected this blanket rule, and concluded that the police must have a particular reason in each case to make an unannounced search. * * * The leading case for this latter point of view is *People v. Gastelo.*[c] * * *

c. 432 P.2d 706 (Cal.1967): "Under the Fourth Amendment, a specific showing must always be made to justify any kind of police action tending to disturb the security of the people in their homes. Unannounced forcible entry is in itself a serious disturbance of that security and cannot

"[W]e are not persuaded that the standard adopted by the California court in *Gastelo* is constitutionally required by *Ker v. California.* There is an intermediate position with regard to preventing the destruction of evidence which we believe adequate to meet the requirements of *Ker.* It is: the minimum showing necessary to invoke the destruction-of-the-evidence exception to the constitutional announcement requirement is that (1) before making the search the police have probable cause to believe there to be a small, readily disposable amount of evidence at the premises to be searched, *or do not know the amount,* and (2) reasonably believe there is likelihood that the evidence might be destroyed if announcement is given.

"Such minimum showing has not been made in this case. The affidavit in support of the search warrant reveals the police had probable cause to believe they would find "scored pills" in the form of "1,000 'whites', a slang term for benzedrine." Nothing in the record suggests this is an easily disposable amount of narcotics. Also, there is no showing the police were reasonably concerned that the evidence sought would be destroyed."

A few jurisdictions have adopted legislation permitting magistrates to issue search warrants specifically authorizing entry without prior announcement upon a sufficient showing to the magistrate of a need to do so, either to prevent destruction of evidence or to prevent harm to the executing officer. In *Parsley v. Superior Court,* 513 P.2d 611 (Cal.1973), holding magistrates in that state were without authority to issue such warrants, the court commented: "While a search warrant must necessarily rest upon previously obtained information, unannounced entry is excused only on the basis of exigent circumstances existing at the time an officer approaches a site to make an arrest or execute a warrant. Facts existing at the time of obtaining a warrant may no longer exist at the time of entry. Such an emergency, therefore, can be judged only in light of circumstances of which the officer is aware at the latter moment."

3. *Detention and search of persons on the premises.* On the basis of information from an informant that he had frequently and recently observed tinfoil packets of heroin behind the bar and on the person of the bartender of a certain tavern and that the bartender told him he would that day have heroin for sale, a warrant authorizing search of the tavern and bartender for heroin was issued. The warrant was executed during the late afternoon by 7–8 officers, who proceeded to pat down each of the 9–13 customers then present. A cigarette package was located and retrieved from customer Ybarra's pocket, and tinfoil packets of heroin were found therein. State courts held the heroin admissible because found in a search authorized by a statute [d] deemed constitutional as applied in the instant case. In YBARRA v. ILLINOIS, 444 U.S. 85, 100 S.Ct. 338, 62 L.Ed.2d 238 (1979), the Court, in a 6–3 decision, reversed. STEWART, J., for the majority, stated:

"There is no reason to suppose that, when the search warrant was issued on March 1, 1976, the authorities had probable cause to believe that any person found on the premises of the Aurora Tap Tavern, aside from [bartender] 'Greg,' would be violating the law. The Complaint for Search Warrant did not allege that the bar was frequented by persons illegally purchasing drugs. It did not state that the

be justified on a blanket basis. Otherwise the constitutional test of reasonableness would turn only on practical expediency, and the amendment's primary safeguard—the requirement of particularity—would be lost. Just as the police must have sufficiently particular reason to enter at all, so must they have some particular reason to enter in the manner chosen."

d. This statute, Ill.Rev.Stat. ch. 38, § 108–9, reads: "In the execution of the warrant the person executing the same may reasonably detain to search any person in the place at the time: (a) To protect himself from attack, or (b) To prevent the disposal or concealment of any instruments, articles or things particularly described in the warrant."

informant had ever seen a patron of the tavern purchase drugs from 'Greg' or from any other person. Nowhere, in fact, did the complaint even mention the patrons of the Aurora Tap Tavern.

"Not only was probable cause to search Ybarra absent at the time the warrant was issued; it was still absent when the police executed the warrant. Upon entering the tavern, the police did not recognize Ybarra and had no reason to believe that he had committed, was committing or was about to commit any offense under state or federal law. Ybarra made no gestures indicative of criminal conduct, made no movements that might suggest an attempt to conceal contraband, and said nothing of a suspicious nature to the police officers. * * *

"It is true that the police possessed a warrant based on probable cause to search the tavern in which Ybarra happened to be at the time the warrant was executed. But, a person's mere propinquity to others independently suspected of criminal activity does not, without more, give rise to probable cause to search that person. * * * [4]"

As for the state's claim "that the first patdown search of Ybarra constituted a reasonable frisk for weapons under the doctrine of *Terry v. Ohio,* " p. 361 infra, the Court responded that the frisk was "not supported by a reasonable belief that he was armed and presently dangerous, a belief which this Court has invariably held must form the predicate to a patdown of a person for weapons. * * * Upon seeing Ybarra, [the police] neither recognized him as a person with a criminal history nor had any particular reason to believe that he might be inclined to assault them. Moreover, as police agent Johnson later testified, Ybarra, whose hands were empty, gave no indication of possessing a weapon, made no gestures or other actions indicative of an intent to commit an assault, and acted generally in a manner that was not threatening."

Emphasizing "the ease with which the evidence of narcotics possession may be concealed or moved around from person to person," the State next contended that the *Terry* standard "should be made applicable to aid the evidence-gathering function of the search warrant." The Court answered: "The 'long prevailing' constitutional standard of probable cause embodies ' "the best compromise that has been found for accommodating the [ ] often opposing interests" in "safeguard[ing] citizens from rash and unreasonable interferences with privacy" and in "seek[ing] to give fair leeway for enforcing the law in the community's protection." ' "

REHNQUIST, J., for the dissenters, reasoned that the *Terry* individualized suspicion standard, "important in the case of an on-the-street stop, where the officer must articulate some reason for singling the person out of the general population, was of "less significance in the present situation" for two reasons: (i) "in place of the requirement of 'individualized suspicion' as a guard against arbitrary exercise of authority, we have here the determination of a neutral and detached magistrate that a search was necessary"; and (ii) "the task performed by the officers executing a search warrant is inherently more perilous than is a momentary encounter on the street."

4. *Detention of persons on the premises.* MICHIGAN v. SUMMERS, 452 U.S. 692, 101 S.Ct. 2587, 69 L.Ed.2d 340 (1981), involved these facts: "As Detroit police officers were about to execute a warrant to search a house for narcotics, they encountered respondent descending the front steps. They requested his assistance in gaining entry and detained him while they searched the premises. After

4. [W]e need not consider situations where the warrant itself authorizes the search of unnamed persons in a place and is supported by probable cause to believe that persons who will be in the place at the time of the search will be in possession of illegal drugs.

finding narcotics in the basement and ascertaining that respondent owned the house, the police arrested him, searched his person, and found in his coat pocket an envelope containing 8.5 grams of heroin." The Court, per STEVENS, J., upheld the seizure on the basis of the principle derived from *Terry* and related cases, namely, that "some seizures * * * constitute such limited intrusions on the personal security of those detained and are justified by such substantial law enforcement interests that they may be made on less than probable cause, so long as police have an articulable basis for suspecting criminal activity":

"Of prime importance in assessing the intrusion is the fact that the police had obtained a warrant to search respondent's house for contraband. A neutral and detached magistrate had found probable cause to believe that the law was being violated in that house and had authorized a substantial invasion of the privacy of the persons who resided there. The detention of one of the residents while the premises were searched, although admittedly a significant restraint on his liberty, was surely less intrusive than the search itself. Indeed, we may safely assume that most citizens—unless they intend flight to avoid arrest—would elect to remain in order to observe the search of their possessions. Furthermore, the type of detention imposed here is not likely to be exploited by the officer or unduly prolonged in order to gain more information, because the information the officers seek normally will be obtained through the search and not through the detention. Moreover, because the detention in this case was in respondent's own residence, it could add only minimally to the public stigma associated with the search itself and would involve neither the inconvenience nor the indignity associated with a compelled visit to the police station. * * *

"In assessing the justification for the detention of an occupant of premises being searched for contraband pursuant to a valid warrant, both the law enforcement interest and the nature of the "articulable facts" supporting the detention are relevant. Most obvious is the legitimate law enforcement interest in preventing flight in the event that incriminating evidence is found. Less obvious, but sometimes of greater importance, is the interest in minimizing the risk of harm to the officers. Although no special danger to the police is suggested by the evidence in this record, the execution of a warrant to search for narcotics is the kind of transaction that may give rise to sudden violence or frantic efforts to conceal or destroy evidence. The risk of harm to both the police and the occupants is minimized if the officers routinely exercise unquestioned command of the situation. Finally, the orderly completion of the search may be facilitated if the occupants of the premises are present. Their self-interest may induce them to open locked doors or locked containers to avoid the use of force that is not only damaging to property but may also delay the completion of the task at hand.

"It is also appropriate to consider the nature of the articulable and individualized suspicion on which the police base the detention of the occupant of a home subject to a search warrant. We have already noted that the detention represents only an incremental intrusion on personal liberty when the search of a home has been authorized by a valid warrant. The existence of a search warrant, however, also provides an objective justification for the detention. A judicial officer has determined that police have probable cause to believe that someone in the home is committing a crime. Thus a neutral magistrate rather than an officer in the field has made the critical determination that the police should be given a special authorization to thrust themselves into the privacy of a home. The connection of an occupant to that home gives the police officer an easily identifiable and certain basis for determining that suspicion of criminal activity justifies a detention of that occupant."

STEWART, J., joined by Brennan and Marshall, JJ., dissenting, objected that *Terry* and related cases required "some governmental interest independent of the ordinary interest in investigating crime and apprehending suspects," which was not present here, and also that the majority's "view that the detention here is of the limited, unintrusive sort" required under *Terry* was in error, as "a detention 'while a proper search is being conducted' can mean a detention of several hours."

5. *Intensity and duration of the search.* Although a search under a search warrant may extend to all parts of the premises described in the warrant, it does not follow that the executing officers may look everywhere within the described premises; they may only look where the items described in the warrant might be concealed. For example, if a search warrant indicated that the items sought were stolen television sets, the officer would not be authorized to rummage through desk drawers and other places too small to hold these items. Once the items named in the search warrant have been found, the search must cease.

6. *Seizure of items not named in the search warrant.* In *Coolidge v. New Hampshire,* 403 U.S. 443, 91 S.Ct. 2022, 29 L.Ed.2d 564 (1971), in the context of a broad-ranging discussion of the "plain view" doctrine, the Court, per Stewart, J., indicated that the seizure of unnamed items was sometimes permissible. "An example of the applicability of the 'plain view' doctrine," said the Court, "is the situation in which the police have a warrant to search a given area for specific objects, and in the course of the search come across some other article of incriminating character." Permitting seizure of that article does not conflict with the warrant requirement, as the police do have a warrant and (for there to be a valid plain view) have limited their search to the areas authorized by the warrant. "Where, once an otherwise lawful search is in progress, the police inadvertently come upon a piece of evidence, it would often be a needless inconvenience, and sometimes dangerous—to the evidence or to the police themselves—to require them to ignore it until they have obtained a warrant particularly describing it." Over the strong dissent of the Chief Justice and Justices Black, Blackmun and White, Justice Stewart asserted, however, that "the discovery of evidence in plain view must be inadvertent": "If the initial intrusion is bottomed upon a warrant which fails to mention a particular object, though the police know its location and intend to seize it, then there is a violation of the express constitutional requirement of 'warrants * * * particularly describing * * * [the] things to be seized.' "

Of course, the mere fact that an item is found in plain view while a search warrant naming other items is being executed does not justify seizure of that item. As noted in *Coolidge,* it must be an "article of incriminating character." Compare *Commonwealth v. Wojcik,* 266 N.E.2d 645 (Mass. 1971) (unnamed stolen property suppressed because police did not have probable cause to believe the articles were stolen at the time they seized them); with *Commonwealth v. DeMasi,* 283 N.E.2d 845 (Mass.1972) (unnamed stolen property properly seized, as police kept up with teletypes and knew kinds of property recently stolen).

In determining whether the discovered article is incriminating in nature, how carefully may the police examine it? See *Stanley v. Georgia,* 394 U.S. 557, 89 S.Ct. 1243, 22 L.Ed.2d 542 (1969) (obscene films suppressed where police found reels of film while searching for gambling paraphernalia and then viewed the film on a projector and screen found in another room); *Commonwealth v. Hawkins,* 280 N.E.2d 665 (Mass.1972) (government bonds with name other than that of occupant found while executing search warrant for narcotics, officer called named person and found that bonds had been stolen from him, held: bonds suppressed, as police did not have probable cause to believe bonds were stolen at moment of discovery, and police may not take them from defendant's "possession, even momentarily, in order to establish their ownership").

C. THE "PREFERENCE" FOR WARRANTS

1. The Supreme Court has long expressed a strong preference for searches made pursuant to a search warrant, e.g., *United States v. Ventresca*, 380 U.S. 102, 85 S.Ct. 741, 13 L.Ed.2d 684 (1965), and on occasion has even asserted "that the police must, whenever practicable, obtain advance judicial approval of searches and seizures." *Terry v. Ohio*, p. 361 infra. But this is far from being an accurate portrayal of current law or practice; the fact of the matter is that a great majority of police seizures and searches are made and upheld notwithstanding the absence of a warrant.

This is so because, as is elaborated upon in the following sections in this Chapter, the Supreme Court has recognized a considerable variety of circumstances in which the police may lawfully make a search or a seizure without the prior approval of a magistrate. A warrant is excused in situations other than those in which there existed genuine exigent circumstances making it unfeasible for the police to utilize the often time-consuming warrant process. Sometimes this is explained by the Court on the ground that the police activity being permitted without a warrant intrudes only upon lesser Fourth Amendment values. Illustrative is *California v. Carney*, p. 330, allowing warrantless search of vehicles because of the "diminished expectation of privacy" in them. Sometimes warrant excusal is rationalized on the ground that the permitted police activity is merely "routine," as with the inventory allowed in *South Dakota v. Opperman*, p. 355 infra. On other occasions the Supreme Court has recognized an exception to the warrant requirement because of a purported need for "bright lines" in the rules governing police conduct. Illustrative is *United States v. Watson*, p. 298 infra, holding a warrant is never needed to arrest in a public place because a contrary holding would "encumber criminal prosecutions with endless litigation with respect to the existence of exigent circumstances, whether it was practicable to get a warrant, whether the suspect was about to flee, and the like." The tension between these and other considerations has not always produced predictable or consistent results in the Court's decisions concerning what is permissible warrantless police action.

2. This state of affairs has prompted the following comments, which should be considered in assessing the cases which follow in this Chapter. Bradley, *Two Models of the Fourth Amendment*, 83 Mich.L.Rev. 1468, 1471–72 (1985), suggests "that current fourth amendment law, complete with the constant tinkering which it necessarily entails, should be abandoned altogether. Instead, there are two, and only two, ways of looking at the fourth amendment which will provide the police with reasonably coherent direction as to how they must proceed and the courts with a consistent basis for decision.

"The two models, briefly, may be called the 'no lines' and the 'bright line' approaches. Model I, no lines, uses tort law as a guide in proposing that the hopeless quest of establishing detailed guidelines for police behavior in every possible situation be abandoned. It suggests that the Court adopt the following view of the fourth amendment: A search or seizure must be reasonable, considering all relevant factors on a case-by-case basis. If it is not, the evidence must be excluded. Factors to be considered include, but are not limited to, whether probable cause existed, whether a warrant was obtained, whether exigent circumstances existed, the nature of the intrusion, the quantum of evidence possessed by the police, and the seriousness of the offense under investigation. This model enjoys support from the history of the fourth amendment and is (roughly) the current practice in Germany and other European countries. Moreover, in most cases it reflects the result, though not the reasoning, of current Supreme Court cases.

"The second model may be as shocking at first glance to 'law and order' advocates as the first model is to civil libertarians. It is, basically, that the Supreme Court should actually enforce the warrant doctrine to which it has paid lip service for so many years. That is, a warrant is *always* required for *every* search and seizure when it is practicable to obtain one. However, in order that this requirement be workable and not be swallowed by its exception, the warrant need not be in writing but rather may be phoned or radioed into a magistrate (where it will be tape recorded and the recording preserved) who will authorize or forbid the search orally. By making the procedure for obtaining a warrant less difficult (while only marginally reducing the safeguards it provides), the number of cases where 'emergencies' justify an exception to the warrant requirement should be very small.

"These models are the only two possibilities because they are the only two ways of dealing with fourth amendment problems that do not force the Court into the clear rule/flexible response dilemma. Model I, by presenting an unabashedly *unclear* rule that provides no guidelines, will never have to be modified to suit an unusual fact situation. While not an ideal solution, it will, it is argued, work considerably better than the present system where the Court purports to set forth clear rules but does not actually do so. Model II presents a clear rule which can be lived with. If the Court required a modified, easily obtainable warrant to be used in all but true emergencies, the police would know what is expected of them and would be able to conform their conduct to the requirement of the law, much as they have accommodated their behavior to the *Miranda* requirements. Any other approach which tries to set forth rules which the Court is unwilling to enforce strictly will necessarily become mired in exceptions and modifications (with resultant confusion) as has occurred in the current law."

SECTION 5. WARRANTLESS ARRESTS

UNITED STATES v. WATSON

423 U.S. 411, 96 S.Ct. 820, 46 L.Ed.2d 598 (1976).

MR. JUSTICE WHITE delivered the opinion of the Court.

[Reliable informant Khoury told a federal postal inspector that Watson had supplied him with a stolen credit card and had agreed to furnish additional cards at their next meeting, scheduled for a few days later. At that meeting, which occurred in a restaurant, Khoury signaled the inspector that Watson had the cards, at which point the inspector arrested Watson without a warrant, as he was authorized to do under 18 U.S.C. § 3061 and applicable postal regulations. The court of appeals held the arrest unconstitutional because the inspector had failed to secure an arrest warrant although he concededly had time to do so, and this was a significant factor in the court's additional holding that Watson's consent to a search of his car was not voluntary.]

* * * Section 3061 represents a judgment by Congress that it is not unreasonable under the Fourth Amendment for postal inspectors to arrest without a warrant provided they have probable cause to do so. This was not an isolated or quixotic judgment of the legislative branch. Other federal law enforcement officers have been expressly authorized by statute for many years to make felony arrests on probable cause but without a warrant. * * *

Because there is a "strong presumption of constitutionality due to an Act of Congress, especially when it turns on what is 'reasonable,' * * * [o]bviously the Court should be reluctant to decide that a search thus authorized by Congress was unreasonable and that the Act was therefore unconstitutional." Moreover, there is nothing in the Court's prior cases indicating that under the Fourth Amendment a warrant is required to make a valid arrest for a felony. Indeed, the relevant prior decisions are uniformly to the contrary. * * *[a]

The cases construing the Fourth Amendment thus reflect the ancient common-law rule that a peace officer was permitted to arrest without a warrant for a misdemeanor or felony committed in his presence as well as for a felony not committed in his presence if there was reasonable grounds for making the arrest. This has also been the prevailing rule under state constitutions and statutes. * * *

Because the common-law rule authorizing arrests without warrant generally prevailed in the States, it is important for present purposes to note that in 1792 Congress invested United States Marshals and their deputies with "the same powers in executing the laws of the United States, as sheriffs and their deputies in their several states have by law, in executing the laws of their respective states." The Second Congress thus saw no inconsistency between the Fourth Amendment and giving United States Marshals the same power as local peace officers to arrest for a felony without a warrant.[8] * * *

The balance struck by the common law in generally authorizing felony arrests on probable cause, but without a warrant, has survived substantially intact. It appears in almost all of the States in the form of express statutory authorization. * * *

This is the rule Congress has long directed its principal law enforcement officers to follow. Congress has plainly decided against conditioning warrantless arrest power on proof of exigent circumstances. Law enforcement officers may find it wise to seek arrest warrants where practicable to do so, and their judgments about probable cause may be more readily accepted where backed by a warrant issued by a magistrate. But we decline to transform this judicial preference into a constitutional rule when the judgment of the Nation and Congress has for so long been to authorize warrantless public arrests on probable cause rather than to encumber criminal prosecutions with endless litigation with respect to the existence of exigent circumstances, whether it was practicable to get a warrant, whether the suspect was about to flee, and the like. * * *

Reversed.

MR. JUSTICE STEVENS took no part in the consideration or decision of this case.

MR. JUSTICE POWELL, concurring.

* * * Today's decision is the first square holding that the Fourth Amendment permits a duly authorized law enforcement officer to make a warrantless arrest in a public place even though he had adequate opportunity to procure a warrant after developing probable cause for arrest.

On its face, our decision today creates a certain anomaly. There is no more basic constitutional rule in the Fourth Amendment area than that which makes a warrantless search unreasonable except in a few "jealously and carefully drawn" exceptional circumstances. * * * In short, the course of judicial development of the Fourth Amendment with respect to searches has remained true to the principles so well expressed by Mr. Justice Jackson:

> "Any assumption that evidence sufficient to support a magistrate's disinterested determination to issue a search

a. The Court noted by way of footnote that because the arrest here was in a public place, it did not have to resolve the "still unsettled question" of whether a warrant is needed to enter private premises to make an arrest. This issue is considered at p. 322 infra.

8. Of equal import is the rule recognized by this Court that even in the absence of a federal statute granting or restricting the authority of federal law enforcement officers, "the law of the state where an arrest without warrant takes place determines its validity." *United States v. Di Re,* 332 U.S. 581, 68 S.Ct. 222, 92 L.Ed. 210 (1948). * * *

warrant will justify the officers in making a search without a warrant would reduce the Amendment to a nullity and leave the people's homes secure only in the discretion of police officers. * * * When the right of privacy must reasonably yield to the right of search is, as a rule, to be decided by a judicial officer, not by a policeman or Government enforcement agent." *Johnson v. United States*, 333 U.S. 10, 14, 68 S.Ct. 367, 369, 92 L.Ed. 436 (1948).

Since the Fourth Amendment speaks equally to both searches and seizures, and since an arrest, the taking hold of one's person, is quintessentially a seizure, it would seem that the constitutional provision should impose the same limitations upon arrests that it does upon searches. Indeed, as an abstract matter an argument can be made that the restrictions upon arrest perhaps should be greater. A search may cause only annoyance and temporary inconvenience to the law-abiding citizen, assuming more serious dimension only when it turns up evidence of criminality. An arrest, however, is a serious personal intrusion regardless of whether the person seized is guilty or innocent. Although an arrestee cannot be held for a significant period without some neutral determination that there are grounds to do so, no decision that he should go free can come quickly enough to erase the invasion of his privacy that already will have occurred. Logic therefore would seem to dictate that arrests be subject to the warrant requirement at least to the same extent as searches.

But logic sometimes must defer to history and experience. The Court's opinion emphasizes the historical sanction accorded warrantless felony arrests. * * *

The historical momentum for acceptance of warrantless arrests, already strong at the adoption of the Fourth Amendment, has gained strength during the ensuing two centuries. * * * Given the revolutionary implications of such a holding, a declaration at this late date that warrantless felony arrests are constitutionally infirm would have to rest upon reasons more substantial than a desire to harmonize the rules for arrest with those governing searches.

Moreover, a constitutional rule permitting felony arrests only with a warrant or in exigent circumstances could severely hamper effective law enforcement. Good police practice often requires postponing an arrest, even after probable cause has been established, in order to place the suspect under surveillance or otherwise develop further evidence necessary to prove guilt to a jury. Under the holding of the Court of Appeals such additional investigative work could imperil the entire prosecution. Should the officers fail to obtain a warrant initially, and later be required by unforeseen circumstances to arrest immediately with no chance to procure a last-minute warrant, they would risk a court decision that the subsequent exigency did not excuse their failure to get a warrant in the interim since they first developed probable cause. If the officers attempted to meet such a contingency by procuring a warrant as soon as they had probable cause and then merely held it during their subsequent investigation, they would risk a court decision that the warrant had grown stale by the time it was used.[5] Law enforcement personnel caught in this squeeze could ensure validity of their arrests only by obtaining a warrant and arresting as soon as probable cause existed, thereby foreclosing the possibility of gathering vi-

5. The probable cause to support issuance of an arrest warrant normally would not grow stale as easily as that which supports a warrant to search a particular place for particular objects. This is true because once there is probable cause to believe that someone is a felon the passage of time often will bring new supporting evidence. But in some cases the original grounds supporting the warrant could be disproved by subsequent investigation that at the same time turns up wholly new evidence supporting probable cause on a different theory. In those cases the warrant could be stale because based upon discredited information.

tal additional evidence from the suspect's continued actions. * * *

MR. JUSTICE STEWART, concurring in the result. * * *

MR. JUSTICE MARSHALL, with whom MR. JUSTICE BRENNAN joins, dissenting. * * *

The signal of the reliable informant that Watson was in possession of stolen credit cards gave the postal inspectors probable cause to make the arrest. This probable cause was separate and distinct from the probable cause relating to the offense six days earlier, and provided an adequate independent basis for the arrest. Whether or not a warrant ordinarily is required prior to making an arrest, no warrant is required when exigent circumstances are present. When law enforcement officers have probable cause to believe that an offense is taking place in their presence and that the suspect is at that moment in possession of the evidence, exigent circumstances exist. Delay could cause the escape of the suspect or the destruction of the evidence. Accordingly, Watson's warrantless arrest was valid under the recognized exigent circumstances exception to the warrant requirement, and the Court has no occasion to consider whether a warrant would otherwise be necessary. * * *

Since, for reasons it leaves unexpressed, the Court does not take this traditional course, I am constrained to express my views on the issues it unnecessarily decides. The Court reaches its conclusion that a warrant is not necessary for a police officer to make an arrest in a public place, so long as he has probable cause to believe a felony has been committed, on the basis of its views of precedent and history. As my Brother Powell correctly observes, the precedent is spurious. None of the cases cited by the Court squarely confronted the issue decided today. * * *

The Court next turns to history. It relies on the English common-law rule of arrest and the many state and federal statutes following it. There are two serious flaws in this approach. First, as a matter of factual analysis, the substance of the ancient common-law rule provides no support for the far-reaching modern rule that the Court fashions on its model. Second, as a matter of doctrine, the longstanding existence of a Government practice does not immunize the practice from scrutiny under the mandate of our Constitution.

* * * Only the most serious crimes were felonies at common law, and many crimes now classified as felonies under federal or state law were treated as misdemeanors. * * * To make an arrest for any of these crimes at common law, the police officer was required to obtain a warrant, unless the crime was committed in his presence. Since many of these same crimes are commonly classified as felonies today however, under the Court's holding a warrant is no longer needed to make such arrests, a result in contravention of the common law.

* * * As a matter of substance, the balance struck by the common law in accommodating the public need for the most certain and immediate arrest of criminal suspects with the requirement of magisterial oversight to protect against mistaken insults to privacy decreed that only in the most serious of cases could the warrant be dispensed with. This balance is not recognized when the common-law rule is unthinkingly transposed to our present classifications of criminal offenses. Indeed, the only clear lesson of history is contrary to the one the Court draws: the common law considered the arrest warrant far more important than today's decision leaves it.

I do not mean by this that a modern warrant requirement should apply only to arrests precisely analogous to common-law misdemeanors, and be inapplicable to analogues of common-law felonies. Rather, the point is simply that the Court's unblinking literalism cannot replace analysis of the constitutional interests involved. * * *

Lastly, the Court relies on the numerous state and federal statutes codifying the common-law rule. But this, too, is no substitute for reasoned analysis. * * *

The Court has typically engaged in a two-part analysis in deciding whether the presumption favoring a warrant should be given effect in situations where a warrant has not previously been clearly required. Utilizing that approach we must now consider (1) whether the privacy of our citizens will be better protected by ordinarily requiring a warrant to be issued before they may be arrested; and (2) whether a warrant requirement would unduly burden legitimate governmental interests.

The first question is easily answered. Of course the privacy of our citizens will be better protected by a warrant requirement. We have recognized that "the Fourth Amendment protects people, not places." Indeed, the privacy guaranteed by the Fourth Amendment is quintessentially personal. Thus a warrant is required in search situations not because of some high regard for property, but because of our regard for the individual, and *his* interest in his possessions and person. * * *

We come then to the second part of the warrant test: whether a warrant requirement would unduly burden legitimate law enforcement interests. [T]he argument that a warrant requirement for arrests would be an onerous chore for the police seems somewhat anomalous in light of the Government's concession that "it is the standard practice of the Federal Bureau of Investigation [FBI] to present its evidence to the United States Attorney, and to obtain a warrant, before making an arrest."

The Government's assertion that a warrant requirement would impose an intolerable burden stems, in large part, from the specious supposition that procurement of an arrest warrant would be necessary as soon as probable cause ripens. There is no requirement that a search warrant be obtained the moment police have probable cause to search. The rule is only that present probable cause be shown and a warrant obtained before a search is undertaken. The same rule should obtain for arrest warrants, where it may even make more sense. Certainly, there is less need for prompt procurement of a warrant in the arrest situation. Unlike probable cause to search, probable cause to arrest, once formed will continue to exist for the indefinite future, at least if no intervening exculpatory facts come to light.

This sensible approach obviates most of the difficulties that have been suggested with an arrest warrant rule. Police would not have to cut their investigation short the moment they obtain probable cause to arrest, nor would undercover agents be forced suddenly to terminate their work and forfeit their covers. Moreover, if in the course of the continued police investigation exigent circumstances develop that demand an immediate arrest, the arrest may be made without fear of unconstitutionality, so long as the exigency was unanticipated and not used to avoid the arrest warrant requirement. Likewise, if in the course of the continued investigation police uncover evidence tying the suspect to another crime, they may immediately arrest him for that crime if exigency demands it, and still be in full conformity with the warrant rule. This is why the arrest in this case was not improper.[15] Other than where police attempt to evade the warrant requirement, the rule would invalidate an arrest only in the obvious situation: where police, with probable cause but without exigent circumstances, set out to arrest a suspect. Such an arrest must be void, even if exigency develops in the course of the arrest that would ordina-

15. Although the postal inspectors here anticipated the occurrence of the second crime, they could not have obtained a warrant for Watson's arrest for that crime until probable cause formed, just moments before the arrest. A warrant based on anticipated facts is premature and void. *United States v. Roberts,* 333 F.Supp. 786 (ED Tenn. 1971).

rily validate it; otherwise the warrant requirement would be reduced to a toothless prescription. * * *

It is suggested, however, that even if application of this rule does not require police to secure a warrant as soon as they obtain probable cause, the confused officer would nonetheless be prone to do so. If so, police "would risk a court decision that the warrant had grown stale by the time it was used." (Powell, J., concurring). This fear is groundless. First, as suggested above, the requirement that police procure a warrant before an arrest is made is rather simple of application. Thus, there is no need for the police to find themselves in this "squeeze." Second, the "squeeze" is nonexistent. Just as it is virtually impossible for probable cause for an arrest to grow stale between the time of formation and the time a warrant is procured, it is virtually impossible for probable cause to become stale between procurement and arrest. Delay by law enforcement officers in executing an arrest warrant does not ordinarily affect the legality of the arrest. * * *

Notes and Questions

1. Consider LaFave, § 5.1: "A study conducted for the President's Commission on Law Enforcement and Administration of Justice indicated that, while nearly fifty percent of all arrests are made within two hours of the crime as a result of a 'hot' search of the crime scene or a 'warm' search of the general vicinity of the crime, very few additional arrests occur immediately thereafter. Rather, there is a delay while further investigation is conducted; about 45 percent of all arrests occur more than a day after the crime, and nearly 35 percent of all arrests are made after the passage of over a week. In these latter instances, * * * the risk is negligible that the defendant will suddenly flee between the time the police solve the case and the time which would be required to obtain and serve an arrest warrant. Indeed, in such cases the need to arrest before an arrest warrant can be obtained is likely to be considerably less apparent than the need to search before a search warrant can be acquired and executed; the defendant is unlikely suddenly to decide to flee or go into hiding at that point, but he well might have reached the stage where he is about to dispose of the fruits of his crime or destroy or abandon items of physical evidence which might link him with the crime."

2. As for the *Watson* dissenters' conclusion that "the privacy of our citizens will be better protected by ordinarily requiring a warrant to be issued before they may be arrested," consider Barrett, *Criminal Justice: The Problem of Mass Production,* in The American Assembly, Columbia University, The Courts, the Public, and the Law Explosion 85, 117–18 (H.W. Jones ed. 1965): "How can a magistrate be more than a 'rubber stamp' in signing warrants unless he devotes at least some minutes in each case to reading the affidavits submitted to him in support of the request for a warrant, and inquiring into the background of the conclusions stated therein? And where is the judicial time going to be found to make such inquiries in the generality of cases? The Los Angeles Municipal Court with annual filings of about 130,000 (excluding parking and traffic) *finds itself so pressed that in large areas of its caseload it averages but a minute per case in receiving pleas and imposing sentence.* How could it cope with the added burden that would be involved in the issuance of warrants to govern the approximately 200,000 arrests made per year in Los Angeles for offenses other than traffic"?

3. Is the "preference" for arrest warrants nonetheless justified on the ground that, at least the police must make a record before the event of the basis for their actions? Consider Skolnick, *Justice Without Trial* 214–15 (1966): "[T]he policeman perceives * * * the need to be able to reconstruct a set of complex happenings in such a way that, subsequent to the arrest, probable cause can be found according to

appellate court standards. In this way, as one district attorney expressed it, 'the policeman fabricates probable cause.' By saying this, he did not mean to assert that the policeman is a liar, but rather that he finds it necessary to construct an *ex post facto* description of the preceding events so that these conform to legal arrest requirements, whether in fact the events actually did so or not at the time of the arrest. Thus, the policeman respects the necessity for 'complying' with the arrest laws. His 'compliance,' however, may take the form of *post hoc* manipulation of the facts rather than before-the-fact behavior."

4. Given the concern regarding "*post hoc* manipulation of the facts," may the arrest of a person booked for one offense be upheld on the ground that the police actually had sufficient evidence of a quite different offense? No, argued Chief Justice Warren, dissenting from the dismissal of the writ of certiorari in *Wainwright v. New Orleans,* 392 U.S. 598, 88 S.Ct. 2243, 20 L.Ed.2d 1322 (1968): "I see no more justification for permitting the State to disregard its own booking record than for permitting any other administrative body to disregard its own records. Quite the contrary. In the 'low-visibility' sphere of police investigatory practices, there are obvious and compelling reasons why official records should prevail over the second guessing of lawyers and judges. Nor would holding the police to official records frustrate any legitimate interest of society. If the police in this case really believed that petitioner was the murder suspect, and if they had probable cause to so believe, all they had to do was to arrest and book him for murder."

That view has not prevailed, although courts are not in complete agreement as to how much leeway should be permitted. Compare *United States v. Atkinson,* 450 F.2d 835 (5th Cir.1971) (court will not "indulge in *ex post facto* extrapolation of all crimes that might have been charged" because "such an exercise might permit an arrest that was really a sham or fraud at the outset"; but if crime initially charged and crime now relied upon to show probable cause "are in some fashion related," this is permissible, as "any other rule would force police officers to routinely charge every citizen taken into custody with every offense they thought he could be held for in order to increase the chances that at least one charge would survive the test for probable cause"); with *Hatcher v. State,* 410 N.E.2d 1187 (Ind.1980) ("public policy in detecting and prosecuting criminal offenders outweighs the value of having arresting officers choose and enunciate the correct legal theory for the arrest").[b]

5. The common law "in presence" requirement for a warrantless misdemeanor arrest has sometimes caused the courts difficulties. Consider *People v. Burdo,* 223 N.W.2d 358 (Mich.App.1974) (officer could not arrest for misdemeanor of driving under influence of liquor when he came on scene of auto accident and found defendant there, even though defendant obviously was intoxicated and admitted he had been driving); *People v. Dixon,* 222 N.W.2d 749 (Mich.1974) (after stopping noisy vehicle, officer could arrest driver for misdemeanor of driving without a license after being advised via police radio that defendant's license had been suspended).

6. In *Street v. Surdyka,* 492 F.2d 368 (4th Cir.1974), it was held that the Fourth Amendment should not "be interpreted to prohibit warrantless arrests for misdemeanors committed outside an officer's presence." Is this so after *Watson?* Consider that some states now use the felony-arrest rule for *all* offenses, while some have rede-

b. A somewhat different problem arises when the booking entry indicates that the defendant was arrested "on suspicion of" or "for investigation of" a certain offense. A few courts have taken the position that such an entry makes the arrest illegal, although in practice such entries are often made solely as a means of identifying those cases which require the attention of the detective division.

fined the misdemeanor arrest power in terms of need, as in Neb.Rev.Stat. § 29-404.02, which permits an officer to arrest a person without a warrant if he "has reasonable cause to believe that such person has committed * * * [a] misdemeanor, and the officer has reasonable cause to believe that such person either (a) will not be apprehended unless immediately arrested; (b) may cause injury to himself or others or damage to property unless immediately arrested; (c) may destroy or conceal evidence of the commission of such misdemeanor; or (d) has committed a misdemeanor in the presence of the officer."

7. Rejecting the contention that if the *Watson* probable cause "requirement is satisfied the Fourth Amendment has nothing to say about *how* that seizure is made," the Court in TENNESSEE v. GARNER, ___ U.S. ___, 105 S.Ct. 1694, 85 L.Ed.2d 1 (1985), held that the use of deadly force to arrest a fleeing felon is sometimes unreasonable under the Fourth Amendment. WHITE, J., stated for the majority:

"The use of deadly force to prevent the escape of all felony suspects, whatever the circumstances, is constitutionally unreasonable. It is not better that all felony suspects die than that they escape. Where the suspect poses no immediate threat to the officer and no threat to others, the harm resulting from failing to apprehend him does not justify the use of deadly force to do so. It is no doubt unfortunate when a suspect who is in sight escapes, but the fact that the police arrive a little late or are a little slower afoot does not always justify killing the suspect. A police officer may not seize an unarmed, nondangerous suspect by shooting him dead. The Tennessee statute is unconstitutional insofar as it authorizes the use of deadly force against such fleeing suspects.

"It is not, however, unconstitutional on its face. Where the officer has probable cause to believe that the suspect poses a threat of serious physical harm, either to the officer or to others, it is not constitutionally unreasonable to prevent escape by using deadly force. Thus, if the suspect threatens the officer with a weapon or there is probable cause to believe that he has committed a crime involving the infliction or threatened infliction of serious physical harm, deadly force may be used if necessary to prevent escape, and if, where feasible, some warning has been given. As applied in such circumstances, the Tennessee statute would pass constitutional muster."

O'CONNOR, J., joined by the Chief Justice and Rehnquist, J., dissenting, objected:

"A proper balancing of the interests involved suggests that use of deadly force as a last resort to apprehend a criminal suspect fleeing from the scene of a nighttime burglary is not unreasonable within the meaning of the Fourth Amendment. Admittedly, the events giving rise to this case are in retrospect deeply regrettable. No one can view the death of an unarmed and apparently nonviolent 15-year old without sorrow, much less disapproval. Nonetheless, the reasonableness of Officer Hymon's conduct for purposes of the Fourth Amendment cannot be evaluated by what later appears to have been a preferable course of police action. The officer pursued a suspect in the darkened backyard of a house that from all indications had just been burglarized. The police officer was not certain whether the suspect was alone or unarmed; nor did he know what had transpired inside the house. He ordered the suspect to halt, and when the suspect refused to obey and attempted to flee into the night, the officer fired his weapon to prevent escape. The reasonableness of this action for purposes of the Fourth Amendment is not determined by the unfortunate nature of this particular case; instead, the question is whether it is constitutionally impermissible for police officers, as a last resort, to shoot a burglary suspect fleeing the scene of the crime."

8. In GERSTEIN v. PUGH, 420 U.S. 103, 95 S.Ct. 854, 43 L.Ed.2d 54 (1975), the Court, per POWELL, J., held:

"[A] policeman's on-the-scene assessment of probable cause provides legal justification for arresting a person suspected of crime, and for a brief period of detention to take the administrative steps incident to arrest. Once the suspect is in custody, however, the reasons that justify dispensing with the magistrate's neutral judgment evaporate. There no longer is any danger that the suspect will escape or commit further crimes while the police submit their evidence to a magistrate. And, while the State's reasons for taking summary action subside, the suspect's need for a neutral determination of probable cause increases significantly. The consequences of prolonged detention may be more serious than the interference occasioned by arrest. Pretrial confinement may imperil the suspect's job, interrupt his source of income, and impair his family relationships. Even pretrial release may be accompanied by burdensome conditions that effect a significant restraint on liberty. When the stakes are this high, the detached judgment of a neutral magistrate is essential if the Fourth Amendment is to furnish meaningful protection from unfounded interference with liberty. Accordingly, we hold that the Fourth Amendment requires a judicial determination of probable cause as a prerequisite to extended restraint on liberty following arrest.[c]

"This result has historical support in the common law that has guided interpretation of the Fourth Amendment. At common law it was customary, if not obligatory, for an arrested person to be brought before a justice of the peace shortly after arrest. The justice of the peace would 'examine' the prisoner and the witnesses to determine whether there was reason to believe the prisoner had committed a crime. If there was, the suspect would be committed to jail or bailed pending trial. If not, he would be discharged from custody. The initial determination of probable cause also could be reviewed by higher courts on a writ of habeas corpus. This practice furnished the model for criminal procedure in America immediately following the adoption of the Fourth Amendment, and there are indications that the Framers of the Bill of Rights regarded it as a model for a 'reasonable' seizure."

The Court then concluded the Court of Appeals had erred in holding "that the determination of probable cause must be accompanied by the full panoply of adversary safeguards—counsel, confrontation, cross-examination, and compulsory process for witnesses." The Court of Appeals had required that the state provide, in effect, a "full preliminary hearing * * * modeled after the procedure used in many States to determine whether the evidence justifies going to trial under an information or presenting the case to a grand jury." The Fourth Amendment, the Court noted, did not require such an adversary proceeding:

"The sole issue is whether there is probable cause for detaining the arrested person pending further proceedings. This issue can be determined reliably without an adversary hearing. That standard—probable cause to believe the suspect has committed a crime—traditionally has been decided by a magistrate in a nonadversary proceeding on hearsay and written testimony, and the Court has approved these

c. In a subsequent footnote, the Court indicated that a grand jury determination to indict would provide such a "judicial determination." In distinguishing the prosecutor's determination that probable cause exists, the Court noted: "By contrast, the Court has held that an indictment, 'fair upon its face,' and returned by a 'properly constituted grand jury' conclusively determines the existence of probable cause and requires issuance of an arrest warrant without further inquiry. The willingness to let a grand jury judgment substitute for that of a neutral and detached magistrate is attributable to the grand jury's relationship to the courts and its historical role of protecting individuals from unjust prosecution."

informal modes of proof. * * * The use of an informal procedure is justified not only by the lesser consequences of a probable cause determination but also by the nature of the determination itself. It does not require the fine resolution of conflicting evidence that a reasonable-doubt or even a preponderance standard demands, and credibility determinations are seldom crucial in deciding whether the evidence supports a reasonable belief in guilt. This is not to say that confrontation and cross-examination might not enhance the reliability of probable cause determinations in some cases. In most cases, however, their value would be too slight to justify holding, as a matter of constitutional principle, that these formalities and safeguards designed for trial must also be employed in making the Fourth Amendment determination of probable cause." [d]

"* * * There is no single preferred pretrial procedure, and the nature of the probable cause determination usually will be shaped to accord with a State's pretrial procedure viewed as a whole. * * * It may be found desirable, for example, to make the probable cause determination at the suspect's first appearance before a judicial officer,[24] the determination may be incorporated into the procedure for setting bail or fixing other conditions of pretrial release. * * * Whatever procedure a State may adopt, it must provide a fair and reliable determination of probable cause as a condition for any significant pretrial restraint on liberty,[26] and this determination must be made by a judicial officer either before or promptly after arrest.[27] "

9. Is it clear from *Gerstein* which defendants are entitled to a prompt judicial review of probable cause? Consider *In re*

d. Stewart, J., joined by Douglas, Brennan and Marshall, JJ., refused to join this portion of the Court's opinion. Justice Stewart noted: "I see no need in this case for the Court to say that the Constitution extends less procedural protection to an imprisoned human being than is required to test the propriety of garnishing a commercial bank account, *North Georgia Finishing, Inc. v. DiChem, Inc.*, 419 U.S. 601, 95 S.Ct. 719, 42 L.Ed.2d 751 [(1975)], the custody of a refrigerator, *Mitchell v. W. T. Grant Co.*, 416 U.S. 600, 94 S.Ct. 1895, 40 L.Ed.2d 406 [(1975)], the temporary suspension of a public school student, *Goss v. Lopez*, 419 U.S. 565, 95 S.Ct. 729, 42 L.Ed.2d 725 [(1975)], or the suspension of a driver's license, *Bell v. Burson*, 402 U.S. 535, 91 S.Ct. 1586, 29 L.Ed.2d 90 [(1971)]. Although it may be true that the Fourth Amendment's 'balance between individual and public interests always has been thought to define the "process that is due" for seizures of person or property in criminal cases,' this case does not involve an initial arrest, but rather the continuing incarceration of a presumptively innocent person. Accordingly, I cannot join the Court's effort to foreclose any claim that the traditional requirements of constitutional due process are applicable in the context of pretrial detention."

24. Several States already authorize a determination of probable cause at this stage or immediately thereafter. This Court has interpreted the Federal Rules of Criminal Procedure to require a determination of probable cause at the first appearance.

26. Because the probable cause determination is not a constitutional prerequisite to the charging decision, it is required only for those suspects who suffer restraints on liberty other than the condition that they appear for trial. There are many kinds of pretrial release and many degrees of conditional liberty. We cannot define specifically those that would require a prior probable cause determination, but the key factor is significant restraint on liberty.

27. In his concurring opinion, Mr. Justice Stewart objects to the Court's choice of the Fourth Amendment as the rationale for decision and suggests that the Court offers less procedural protection to a person in jail than it requires in certain civil cases. Here we deal with the complex procedures of a criminal case and a threshold right guaranteed by the Fourth Amendment. The historical basis of the probable cause requirement is quite different from the relatively recent application of variable procedural due process in debtor-creditor disputes and termination of government-created benefits. The Fourth Amendment was tailored explicitly for the criminal justice system, and its balance between individual and public interests always has been thought to define the "process that is due" for seizures of person or property in criminal cases, including the detention of suspects pending trial. Moreover, the Fourth Amendment probable cause determination is in fact only the *first* stage of an elaborate system, unique in jurisprudence, designed to safeguard the rights of those accused of criminal conduct. The relatively simple civil procedures (e.g., prior interview with school principal before suspension) presented in the cases cited in the concurring opinion are inapposite and irrelevant in the wholly different context of the criminal justice system. * * *

Walters, 543 P.2d 607 (Cal.1975): "As the posting of bail may impose an unwarranted burden on an accused if probable cause to detain is lacking, the accused is entitled to have that determination made prior to electing to post or not to post bail."

10. Under *Gerstein,* how promptly must the probable cause determination be made? Compare *Lively v. Cullinane,* 451 F.Supp. 1000 (D.D.C.1978) ("the police can justify each delay before presentment only by a strong showing that it is necessitated by a substantial administrative need," so any "individuals who require more than one-and-a-half hours to be processed may have a constitutional claim that they were not processed and presented as quickly as possible"); with *Sanders v. Houston,* 543 F.Supp. 694 (S.D.Tex.1982), aff'd, 741 F.2d 1379 (5th Cir.1984) ("administrative steps" in *Gerstein* "include more than transportation, booking, and filing charges," and thus include conducting lineups, fingerprinting and photographing, but yet probable cause determination must always be made within 24 hours of arrest). Statutes or court rules typically provide that the arrestee must be presented before a magistrate "without unnecessary delay" or "forthwith," though some set an outside limit such as 24 or 48 hours.

11. In *People v. Doran,* 258 N.W.2d 406 (Mich.1977), the governor of Michigan issued an arrest warrant for Doran pursuant to a request for extradition from the governor of Arizona. Attached to the Arizona requisition were an arrest warrant for theft, two supporting affidavits, and the original complaint on which the charge was based. Relying upon *Gerstein* and language of the Uniform Criminal Extradition Act that the "indictment, information, or affidavit made before the magistrate must substantially charge the person demanded with having committed a crime," the court held that Doran could not be extradited because the "complaint and arrest warrant are both phrased in conclusory language" and "the two supporting affidavits fail to set out facts which could justify a Fourth Amendment finding of probable cause."

But in MICHIGAN v. DORAN, 439 U.S. 282, 99 S.Ct. 530, 58 L.Ed.2d 521 (1978), the Court, per BURGER, C.J., held "that once the governor of the asylum state has acted on a requisition for extradition based on the demanding state's judicial determination that probable cause existed, no further judicial inquiry may be had on that issue in the asylum state." Emphasizing that the Extradition Clause [e] "was intended to enable each state to bring offenders to trial as swiftly as possible in the state where the alleged offense was committed," the Court concluded that to "allow plenary review in the asylum state of issues that can be fully litigated in the charging state would defeat the plain purposes of the summary and mandatory procedure authorized by" the Clause.

BLACKMUN, J., joined by Brennan and Marshall, JJ., concurred in the result. After noting the absence of any discussion in the majority opinion of the significance of the Fourth Amendment, they reasoned: "The extradition process involves an 'extended restraint of liberty following arrest' even more severe than that accompanying detention within a single State. Extradition involves, at a minimum, administrative processing in both the asylum State and the demanding State, and forced transportation in between. It surely is a 'significant restraint on liberty.' For me, therefore, the Amendment's language and the holding in *Gerstein* mean that, even in the extradition context, where the demanding State's 'charge' rests upon something less than an indictment, there must be a determination of probable cause by a detached and neutral magistrate, and that the asylum

e. U.S. Const., Art. IV, § 2: "A Person charged in any State with Treason, Felony, or other Crime, who shall flee from Justice, and be found in another State, shall on Demand of the executive Authority of the State from which he fled, be delivered up, to be removed to the State having Jurisdiction of the Crime."

State need not grant extradition unless that determination has been made. The demanding State, of course, has the burden of so demonstrating." They concluded that this burden had been met in the instant case because the Arizona arrest warrant declared that a probable cause finding had been made.

SECTION 6. WARRANTLESS SEARCHES OF PREMISES, VEHICLES, AND CONTAINERS

CHIMEL v. CALIFORNIA

395 U.S. 752, 89 S.Ct. 2034, 23 L.Ed.2d 685 (1969).

MR. JUSTICE STEWART delivered the opinion of the Court. * * *

The relevant facts are essentially undisputed. Late in the afternoon of September 13, 1965, three police officers arrived at the Santa Ana, California, home of the petitioner with a warrant authorizing his arrest for the burglary of a coin shop. The officers knocked on the door, identified themselves to the petitioner's wife, and asked if they might come inside. She ushered them into the house, where they waited 10 or 15 minutes until the petitioner returned home from work. When the petitioner entered the house, one of the officers handed him the arrest warrant and asked for permission to "look around." The petitioner objected, but was advised that "on the basis of the lawful arrest," the officers would nonetheless conduct a search. No search warrant had been issued.

Accompanied by the petitioner's wife, the officers then looked through the entire three-bedroom house, including the attic, the garage, and a small workshop. In some rooms the search was relatively cursory. In the master bedroom and sewing room, however the officers directed the petitioner's wife to open drawers and "to physically move contents of the drawers from side to side so that [they] might view any items that would have come from [the] burglary." After completing the search, they seized numerous items—primarily coins, but also several medals, tokens, and a few other objects. The entire search took between 45 minutes and an hour.

At the petitioner's subsequent state trial on two charges of burglary, the items taken from his house were admitted into evidence against him, over his objection that they had been unconstitutionally seized. He was convicted, and the judgments * * * affirmed * * *.

Without deciding the question, we proceed on the hypothesis that the California courts were correct in holding that the arrest of the petitioner was valid under the Constitution. This brings us directly to the question whether the warrantless search of the petitioner's entire house can be constitutionally justified as incident to that arrest. The decisions of this Court bearing upon that question have been far from consistent, as even the most cursory review makes evident.[a]

a. In an omitted portion of the opinion, the Court described how dictum on search incident to arrest broadened from search of the "person," *Weeks v. United States,* 232 U.S. 383, 34 S.Ct. 341, 58 L.Ed. 652 (1914), to search for what is "upon his person or in his control," *Carroll v. United States,* 267 U.S. 132, 45 S.Ct. 280, 69 L.Ed. 543 (1925), to search of "persons lawfully arrested" and "the place where the arrest is made," *Agnello v. United States,* 269 U.S. 20, 46 S.Ct. 4, 70 L.Ed. 145 (1925). Then, in *Marron v. United States,* 275 U.S. 192, 48 S.Ct. 74, 72 L.Ed. 231 (1927), concerning seizure of evidence at a place where illegal liquor sales were occurring, the Court held that because the police had made an arrest on the premises they "had a right without a warrant contemporaneously to search the place in order to find and seize the things used to carry on the criminal enterprise." But in *Go-Bart Importing Co. v. United States,* 282 U.S. 344, 51 S.Ct. 153, 75 L.Ed. 374 (1931), *Marron* was limited to where the items seized "were visible and accessible and in the offender's immediate custody" and there "was no threat of force or general search or rummaging of the place." This limitation was reiterated in *United States v. Lefkowitz,* 285 U.S. 452, 52 S.Ct. 420, 76 L.Ed. 877 (1932), which, like *Go-Bart,* held unlawful a search of a desk despite the fact the search had accompanied a lawful arrest, but was abandoned in *Harris v. United States,* 331 U.S. 145, 67 S.Ct. 1098, 91 L.Ed. 1399 (1947), upholding the search of a four-room apart-

In 1950 * * * came *United States v. Rabinowitz,* 339 U.S. 56, 70 S.Ct. 430, 94 L.Ed. 653 (1950), the decision upon which California primarily relies in the case now before us. In *Rabinowitz,* federal authorities had been informed that the defendant was dealing in stamps bearing forged overprints. On the basis of that information they secured a warrant for his arrest, which they executed at his one-room business office. At the time of the arrest, the officers "searched the desk, safe, and file cabinets in the office for about an hour and a half," and seized 573 stamps with forged overprints. The stamps were admitted into evidence at the defendant's trial, and this Court affirmed his conviction, rejecting the contention that the warrantless search had been unlawful. The Court held that the search in its entirety fell within the principle giving law enforcement authorities "[t]he right 'to search the place where the arrest is made in order to find and seize things connected with the crime * * *.'" * * * The test, said the Court, "is not whether it is reasonable to procure a search warrant, but whether the search was reasonable."

Rabinowitz has come to stand for the proposition, inter alia, that a warrantless search "incident to a lawful arrest" may generally extend to the area that is considered to be in the "possession" or under the "control" of the person arrested. And it was on the basis of that proposition that the California courts upheld the search of the petitioner's entire house in this case. That doctrine, however, at least in the broad sense in which it was applied by the California courts in this case, can withstand neither historical nor rational analysis.

Even limited to its own facts, the *Rabinowitz* decision was, as we have seen, hardly founded on an unimpeachable line of authority. * * *

Nor is the rationale by which the State seeks here to sustain the search of the petitioner's house supported by a reasoned view of the background and purpose of the Fourth Amendment. Mr. Justice Frankfurter wisely pointed out in his *Rabinowitz* dissent that the Amendment's proscription of "unreasonable searches and seizures" must be read in light of "the history that gave rise to the words"—a history of "abuses so deeply felt by the Colonies as to be one of the potent causes of the Revolution * * *." The Amendment was in large part a reaction to the general warrants and warrantless searches that had so alienated the colonists and had helped speed the movement for independence. In the scheme of the Amendment, therefore, the requirement that "no Warrants shall issue, but upon probable cause," plays a crucial part. * * * Even in the *Agnello* case the Court relied upon the rule that "[b]elief, however well founded, that an article sought is concealed in a dwelling house furnishes no justification for a search of that place without a warrant. And such searches are held unlawful notwithstanding facts unquestionably showing probable cause." Clearly, the general requirement that a search warrant be obtained is not lightly to be dispensed with, and "the burden is on those seeking [an] exemption [from the requirement] to show the need for it * * *."

* * * When an arrest is made, it is reasonable for the arresting officer to search the person arrested in order to remove any weapons that the latter might seek to use in order to resist arrest or effect his escape. Otherwise, the officer's safety might well be endangered, and the arrest itself frustrated. In addition, it is entirely reasonable for the arresting officer to search for and seize any evidence on the arrestee's person in order to prevent its concealment or destruction. And the area into which an arrestee might reach in or-

ment as "incident to arrest." But *Harris* was not followed in *Trupiano v. United States,* 334 U.S. 699, 68 S.Ct. 1229, 92 L.Ed. 1663 (1948), declaring that "law enforcement agents must secure and use search warrants wherever reasonably practicable."

der to grab a weapon or evidentiary items must, of course, be governed by a like rule. A gun on a table or in a drawer in front of one who is arrested can be as dangerous to the arresting officer as one concealed in the clothing of the person arrested. There is ample justification, therefore, for a search of the arrestee's person and the area "within his immediate control"—construing that phrase to mean the area from within which he might gain possession of a weapon or destructible evidence.

There is no comparable justification, however, for routinely searching rooms other than that in which an arrest occurs—or, for that matter, for searching through all the desk drawers or other closed or concealed areas in that room itself. Such searches, in the absence of well-recognized exceptions, may be made only under the authority of a search warrant. The "adherence to judicial processes" mandated by the Fourth Amendment requires no less. * * *

It is argued in the present case that it is "reasonable" to search a man's house when he is arrested in it. But that argument is founded on little more than a subjective view regarding the acceptability of certain sorts of police conduct, and not on considerations relevant to Fourth Amendment interests. Under such an unconfined analysis, Fourth Amendment protection in this area would approach the evaporation point. It is not easy to explain why, for instance, it is less subjectively "reasonable" to search a man's house when he is arrested on his front lawn—or just down the street—than it is when he happens to be in the house at the time of arrest. * * *

It would be possible, of course, to draw a line between *Rabinowitz* and *Harris* on the one hand, and this case on the other. For *Rabinowitz* involved a single room, and *Harris* a four-room apartment, while in the case before us an entire house was searched. But such a distinction would be highly artificial. The rationale that allowed the searches and seizures in *Rabinowitz* and *Harris* would allow the searches and seizures in this case. No consideration relevant to the Fourth Amendment suggests any point of rational limitation, once the search is allowed to go beyond the area from which the person arrested might obtain weapons or evidentiary items. The only reasoned distinction is one between a search of the person arrested and the area within his reach on the one hand, and more extensive searches on the other.[12]

The petitioner correctly points out that one result of decisions such as *Rabinowitz* and *Harris* is to give law enforcement officials the opportunity to engage in searches not justified by probable cause, by the simple expedient of arranging to arrest suspects at home rather than elsewhere. We do not suggest that the petitioner is necessarily correct in his assertion that such a strategy was utilized here, but the fact remains that had he been arrested

12. It is argued in dissent that so long as there is probable cause to search the place where an arrest occurs, a search of that place would be permitted even though no search warrant has been obtained. This position seems to be based principally on two premises: first, that once an arrest has been made, the additional invasion of privacy stemming from the accompanying search is "relatively minor"; and second, that the victim of the search may "shortly thereafter" obtain a judicial determination of whether the search was justified by probable cause. With respect to the second premise, one may initially question whether all of the States in fact provide the speedy suppression procedures the dissent assumes. More fundamentally, however, we cannot accept the view that Fourth Amendment interests are vindicated so long as "the rights of the criminal" are "protect[ed] * * * against introduction of evidence seized without probable cause." The Amendment is designed to prevent, not simply to redress, unlawful police action. In any event, we cannot join in characterizing the invasion of privacy that results from a top-to-bottom search of a man's house as "minor." And we can see no reason why, simply because some interference with an individual's privacy and freedom of movement has lawfully taken place, further intrusions should automatically be allowed despite the absence of a warrant that the Fourth Amendment would otherwise require.

earlier in the day, at his place of employment rather than at home, no search of his house could have been made without a search warrant. In any event, even apart from the possibility of such police tactics, the general point so forcefully made by Judge Learned Hand in *United States v. Kirschenblatt,* 16 F.2d 202 [2d Cir.1926], remains:

> "After arresting a man in his house, to rummage at will among his papers in search of whatever will convict him, appears to us to be indistinguishable from what might be done under a general warrant; indeed, the warrant would give more protection, for presumably it must be issued by a magistrate. True, by hypothesis the power would not exist, if the supposed offender were not found on the premises; but it is small consolation to know that one's papers are safe only so long as one is not at home."

Rabinowitz and *Harris* have been the subject of critical commentary for many years, and have been relied upon less and less in our own decisions. It is time, for the reasons we have stated, to hold that on their own facts, and insofar as the principles they stand for are inconsistent with those that we have endorsed today, they are no longer to be followed.

Application of sound Fourth Amendment principles to the facts of this case produces a clear result. The search here went far beyond the petitioner's person and the area from within which he might have obtained either a weapon or something that could have been used as evidence against him. There was no constitutional justification, in the absence of a search warrant, for extending the search beyond that area. The scope of the search was, therefore, "unreasonable" under the Fourth and Fourteenth Amendments, and the petitioner's conviction cannot stand.

Reversed.

MR. JUSTICE HARLAN, concurring.

* * *

The only thing that has given me pause in voting to overrule *Harris* and *Rabinowitz* is that as a result of *Mapp v. Ohio,* every change in Fourth Amendment law must now be obeyed by state officials facing widely different problems of local law enforcement. We simply do not know the extent to which cities and towns across the Nation are prepared to administer the greatly expanded warrant system which will be required by today's decision; nor can we say with assurance that in each and every local situation, the warrant requirement plays an essential role in the protection of those fundamental liberties protected against state infringement by the Fourteenth Amendment. * * *

MR. JUSTICE WHITE, with whom MR. JUSTICE BLACK joins, dissenting.

* * * The Court has always held, and does not today deny, that when there is probable cause to search and it is "impracticable" for one reason or another to get a search warrant, then a warrantless search may be reasonable. This is the case whether an arrest was made at the time of the search or not.

This is not to say that a search can be reasonable without regard to the probable cause to believe that seizable items are on the premises. But when there are exigent circumstances, and probable cause, then the search may be made without a warrant, reasonably. An arrest itself may often create an emergency situation making it impracticable to obtain a warrant before embarking on a related search. Again assuming that there is probable cause to search premises at the spot where a suspect is arrested, it seems to me unreasonable to require the police to leave the scene in order to obtain a search warrant when they are already legally there to make a valid arrest, and when there must almost always be a strong possibility that confederates of the arrested man will in the meanwhile remove the items for which the police have probable cause to search. * * *

This case provides a good illustration of my point that it is unreasonable to require police to leave the scene of an arrest in order to obtain a search warrant when they already have probable cause to search and there is a clear danger that the items for which they may reasonably search will be removed before they return with a warrant. Petitioner was arrested in his home after an arrest whose validity will be explored below, but which I will now assume was valid. There was doubtless probable cause not only to arrest petitioner, but to search his house. He had obliquely admitted both to a neighbor, and to the owner of the burglarized store, that he had committed the burglary. In light of this, and the fact that the neighbor had seen other admittedly stolen property in petitioner's house, there was surely probable cause on which a warrant could have issued to search the house for the stolen coins. Moreover, had the police simply arrested petitioner, taken him off to the station house, and later returned with a warrant,[5] it seems very likely that petitioner's wife, who in view of petitioner's generally garrulous nature must have known of the robbery, would have removed the coins. For the police to search the house while the evidence they had probable cause to search out and seize was still there cannot be considered unreasonable.

This line of analysis, supported by the precedents of this Court, hinges on two assumptions. One is that the arrest of petitioner without a valid warrant[7] was constitutional as the majority assumes; the other is that the police were not required to obtain a search warrant in advance, even though they knew that the effect of the arrest might well be to alert petitioner's wife that the coins had better be removed soon. Thus it is necessary to examine the constitutionality of the arrest since if it was illegal, the exigent circumstances which it created may not, as the consequences of a lawless act, be used to justify the contemporaneous warrantless search. But for the arrest, the warrantless search may not be justified.[8] And if circumstances can justify the warrantless arrest, it would be strange to say that the Fourth Amendment bars the warrantless search, regardless of the circumstances, since the invasion and disruption of a man's life and privacy which stem from his arrest are ordinarily far greater than the relatively minor intrusions attending a search of his premises. * * *

In light of the uniformity of judgment of the Congress, past judicial decisions, and common practice rejecting the proposition that arrest warrants are essential wherever it is practicable to get them, the conclusion is inevitable that such arrests and accompanying searches are reasonable, at least until experience teaches the contrary. It must very often be the case that by the time probable cause to arrest a man is accumulated, the man is aware of police interest in him or for other good reasons is on the verge of flight. Moreover, it will likely be very difficult to determine the probability of his flight. Given this situation, it may be best in all cases simply to allow the arrest if there is probable cause, especially

5. There were three officers at the scene of the arrest, one from the city where the coin burglary had occurred, and two from the city where the arrest was made. Assuming that one policeman from each city would be needed to bring the petitioner in and obtain a search warrant, one policeman could have been left to guard the house. However, if he not only could have remained in the house against petitioner's wife's will, but followed her about to assure that no evidence was being tampered with, the invasion of her privacy would be almost as great as that accompanying an actual search. Moreover, had the wife summoned an accomplice, one officer could not have watched them both.

7. An arrest warrant was in fact issued, but it was issued on an inadequate supporting affidavit and was therefore invalid, so that the case must be considered as though no warrant had issued.

8. This in turn assumes that where it is practicable to obtain a search warrant and the search is not contemporaneous with an arrest, a warrant must be obtained to validate the search. This is the holding of past cases and I do not question it.

since that issue can be determined very shortly after the arrest. * * *

If circumstances so often require the warrantless arrest that the law generally permits it, the typical situation will find the arresting officers lawfully on the premises without arrest or search warrant. * * * [W]here as here the existence of probable cause is independently established and would justify a warrant for a broader search for evidence, I would follow past cases and permit such a search to be carried out without a warrant, since the fact of arrest supplies an exigent circumstance justifying police action before the evidence can be removed, and also alerts the suspect to the fact of the search so that he can immediately seek judicial determination of probable cause in an adversary proceeding, and appropriate redress. * * *

NOTES ON SEARCH OF PREMISES INCIDENT TO AND AFTER ARREST THEREIN

1. Is the *Chimel* dissent strengthened or weakened by the Court's later decision in *Watson?*

2. Some of the cases which have applied the *Chimel* "immediate control" test seem to assume that defendants maintain control over a considerable area even after they have been arrested. See, e.g., *People v. Perry,* 266 N.E.2d 330 (Ill.1971) (4 officers broke into a 10 by 12 foot motel room, saw defendant place something in a dresser drawer, handcuffed him, and took him out into the corridor; their immediately subsequent search of the partially open dresser drawer and a purse on the bed was within *Chimel* rule, "since it was within the area from which defendant could have obtained a weapon or something that could have been used as evidence against him"). May these cases be explained on the ground that, as asserted in *People v. Fitzpatrick,* 300 N.E.2d 139 (N.Y.1973), "it is not at all clear that the 'grabbing distance' authorized in the *Chimel* case is conditioned upon the arrested person's continued capacity 'to grab' "?

3. *Chimel* also requires attention to the question of when, if ever, officers may look into other areas of the defendant's home *after* the defendant has been placed under arrest there. Consider:

(a) *when it is necessary for the arrestee to put on street clothes.* See, e.g., *Giacalone v. Lucas,* 445 F.2d 1238 (6th Cir.1971) (defendant arrested at front door went into bedroom to change into street clothes; held, police could look into dresser drawer defendant was about to open, and gun found therein admissible; dissent argues defendant initially told police he was ready to go immediately, thereby expressing "his desire to limit the officers' intrusion into the privacy of his home," and that he went to get dressed upon order of the police).

(b) *when the officers are acting for their own protection.* Compare *United States v. Briddle,* 436 F.2d 4 (8th Cir.1970) (defendant arrested in hallway of apartment, after which one officer entered nearby bedroom and found shotgun; held, gun was found in plain view while officer was exercising "his conceded right to conduct a quick and cursory viewing of the apartment area for the presence of other persons who might present a security risk"); with *United States v. Gamble,* 473 F.2d 1274 (7th Cir.1973) (police have no right to make "protective sweep" through apartment where defendant arrested for armed robbery, given fact his two accomplices were in custody).

(c) *when the officers are seeking other offenders.* See, e.g., *People v. Block,* 491 P.2d 9 (Cal.1971) (officers knocked on door to check out tip concerning narcotics suspect, when door was opened they detected smell of burning marijuana, five persons in living room and two in dining room with odor of marijuana on their breath were arrested, after which one of the officers went upstairs and looked into bedrooms, where he found marijuana; held, in view of "undetermined number of participants" and fact upstairs light was on, officers had "reasonable cause to believe" other participants might be present; dissent objects there was not probable cause here and distinguishes *Guevara v. Superior Court,* 86 Cal.Rptr. 657 (App.1970), where informant had told police confederates were probably present). If a "potential accomplice" is located, should the police then be allowed to search areas within *his* immediate control?

4. In some circumstances, the Court concluded in WASHINGTON v. CHRISMAN, 455 U.S. 1, 102 S.Ct. 812, 70 L.Ed.2d 778 (1982), a warrantless *entry* of premises will be permissible incident to and following an arrest elsewhere. There, a campus policeman arrested an apparently underage student as he left a campus dormitory carrying a half-gallon bottle of gin, accompanied the student back to his room so that he could obtain his identification, and there observed marijuana seeds and a marijuana pipe. The state court had held that the entry was unlawful, but the Supreme Court, per CHIEF JUSTICE BURGER, disagreed:

" * * * The absence of an affirmative indication that an arrested person might have a weapon available or might attempt to escape does not diminish the arresting officer's authority to maintain custody over the arrested person. Nor is that authority altered by the nature of the offense for which the arrest was made.

"Every arrest must be presumed to present a risk of danger to the arresting officer. Cf. *United States v. Robinson,* [p. 386], n. 5. There is no way for an officer to predict reliably how a particular subject will react to arrest or the degree of the potential danger. Moreover, the possibility that an arrested person will attempt to escape if not properly supervised is obvious. Although the Supreme Court of Washington found little likelihood that Overdahl could escape from his dormitory room, an arresting officer's custodial authority over an arrested person does not depend upon a reviewing court's after-the-fact assessment of the particular arrest situation. Cf. *New York v. Belton* [p. 349].

"We hold, therefore, that it is not 'unreasonable' under the Fourth Amendment for a police officer, as a matter of routine, to monitor the movements of an arrested person, as his judgment dictates, following the arrest."

As for respondent's argument that in fact the officer had made the observation from the hallway and then entered to seize the objects, contrary to established doctrine that warrantless entry to seize evidence requires both probable cause and exigent circumstances, the majority in *Chrisman* responded that this "argument, if accepted, would have the perverse effect of penalizing the officer for exercising more restraint than was required under the circumstances."

WHITE, Brennan and Marshall, JJ., dissenting, could "perceive no justification for what is in effect a per se rule that an officer in Daugherty's circumstances could always enter the room and stay at the arrestee's elbow," and concluded that the instant case was one "where the record before us does not demonstrate that it was necessary for the officer to enter the room as an incident to his custodial arrest," and where entry was in fact made for the purpose of more closely scrutinizing the suspicious items the officer had seen from the doorway. Thus, they concluded, the holding was inconsistent with the rule "that the plain view doctrine applies only after a lawful search is in progress or the officer was otherwise legally present at the place of the seizure."

NOTES ON WARRANTLESS SEIZURES WHILE IN PREMISES TO ARREST

1. If an officer is lawfully present within premises to make an arrest, he may observe certain items not within the "immediate control" of the arrestee which will nonetheless be subject to warrantless seizure under the so-called "plain view"

doctrine. But, as cautioned in *Coolidge v. New Hampshire,* 403 U.S. 443, 91 S.Ct. 2022, 29 L.Ed.2d 564 (1971), such "extension of the original justification is legitimate only where it is immediately apparent [a] to the police that they have evidence before them; the 'plain view' doctrine may not be used to extend a general exploratory search from one object to another until something incriminating at last emerges."

2. Does this mean that a closer scrutiny of what is in plain view in order to determine if it *is* evidence of crime is prohibited? Compare *Eiseman v. Superior Court,* 98 Cal.Rptr. 342 (App.1971) (policeman who arrested defendant in his room for a past marijuana sale saw some vials on the dresser in the midst of a clutter of bottles, walked across the room, picked up the vials and examined them, and concluded they contained contraband; held, the contents of the vials should be suppressed, as the officer was not justified in examining them); with *State v. Bruzzese,* 463 A.2d 320 (N.J.1983) (where defendant, arrested on contempt charge, was prime suspect as to burglary at which distinctive footprints found, officer could pick up defendant's boots and check the soles).

3. The *Coolidge* plurality opinion [b] also asserts that a "second limitation is that the discovery of evidence in plain view must be inadvertent. The rationale of the exception to the warrant requirement, as just stated, is that a plain view seizure will not turn an initially valid (and therefore limited) search into a 'general' one, while the inconvenience of procuring a warrant to cover an inadvertent discovery is great. But where the discovery is anticipated, where the police know in advance the location of the evidence and intend to seize it, the situation is altogether different. The requirement of a warrant to seize imposes no inconvenience whatever, or at least none which is constitutionally cognizable in a legal system that regards warrantless searches as 'per se unreasonable' in the absence of 'exigent circumstances.'

" * * * The initial intrusion may, of course, be legitimated * * * by one of the exceptions to the warrant requirement, such as hot pursuit or search incident to lawful arrest. But to extend the scope of such an intrusion to the seizure of objects—not contraband nor stolen nor dangerous in themselves—which the police know in advance they will find in plain view and intend to seize, would fly in the face of the basic rule that no amount of probable cause can justify a warrantless seizure."

White, J., joined by the Chief Justice, objected: "[T]he areas of permissible search incident to arrest are strictly circumscribed by *Chimel.* Excluding evidence seen from within those areas can hardly be effective to operate to prevent wider, unauthorized searches. If the police stray outside the scope of an authorized *Chimel* search they are already in violation of the Fourth Amendment, and evidence so seized will be excluded; adding a second reason for excluding evidence hardly seems worth the candle. Perhaps the Court is concerned that officers, having the right to intrude upon private property to make arrests, will use that right as a

a. In *Texas v. Brown,* p. 345, the plurality opinion asserted that this phrase "was very likely an unhappy choice of words, since it can be taken to imply that an unduly high degree of certainty as to the incriminating character of evidence is necessary for an application of the 'plain view' doctrine," and then concluded it was intended to be merely a "statement of the rule * * * requiring probable cause for seizure in the ordinary case."

b. In *Texas v. Brown,* p. 345, four members of the Court stated that because "the *Coolidge* plurality's discussion of 'plain view' * * * has never been expressly adopted by a majority of this Court," it was "not a binding precedent" but "should obviously be the point of reference for further discussion of the issue." Two other members of the Court saw "no reason at this late date to imply criticism of [*Coolidge's*] articulation of this exception" because it "has been accepted generally for over a decade." The remaining three Justices, without addressing this point, cited *Coolidge* as a precedent on the plain view doctrine.

pretext to obtain entry to search for objects in plain sight, cf. *Chimel,* but, if so, such a concern is unfounded. The reason is that under *Chimel* the police can enter only into those portions of the property into which entry is necessary to effect the arrest. Given the restrictions of *Chimel,* the police face a substantial risk that in effecting an arrest and a search incident thereto they will never enter into those portions of the property from which they can plainly see the objects for which they are searching and that, if they do not, those objects will be destroyed before they can return and conduct a search of the entire premises pursuant to a warrant. If the police in fact possess probable cause to believe that weapons, contraband or evidence of crime is in plain view on the premises, it will be far safer to obtain a search warrant than to take a chance that in making an arrest they will come into plain view of the object they are seeking. It is only when they lack probable cause for a search—when, that is, discovery of objects in plain view from a lawful vantage point is inadvertent—that entry to make an arrest might, as a practical matter, assist the police in discovering an object for which they could not have obtained a warrant. But the majority in that circumstance would uphold their authority to seize what they see. I thus doubt that the Court's new rule will have any measurable effect on police conduct. It will merely attach undue consequences to what will most often be an unintended mistake or a misapprehension of some of this Court's probable cause decisions, a failing which, I am afraid, we all have."

4. Is inadvertence exactly the same as absence of probable cause? Does it make any difference whether the police had time to obtain a search warrant following their acquiring of knowledge as to the location of the items in question? Is the inadvertence rule workable, considering that it "will foster an anomalous situation in which police contend they did not have probable cause to seize the object before they made their entry, while the defendant contends probable cause existed and the police could have obtained a warrant"? *The Supreme Court, 1970 Term,* 85 Harv.L. Rev. 3, 245 (1971).

NOTES ON WARRANTLESS SEARCH OF PREMISES UNDER EXIGENT CIRCUMSTANCES

1. In VALE v. LOUISIANA, 399 U.S. 30, 90 S.Ct. 1969, 26 L.Ed.2d 409 (1970), officers possessing two warrants for Vale's arrest and having information that he was residing at a specified address set up a surveillance of the house in an unmarked car. After about 15 minutes they observed a car drive up and sound the horn twice. A man they recognized as Vale then came out of the house and walked up to the car, had a brief conversation with the driver, looked up and down the street and then returned to the house. A few minutes later he reappeared on the porch, looked cautiously up and down the street, and then proceeded to the car and leaned through the window. Convinced that a narcotics sale had just occurred, the officers approached. Vale retreated toward the house while the driver of the car began driving off. The police blocked the car and saw the driver, one Saucier, place something in his mouth. Vale was then arrested on his front steps and the police advised him they were going to search the house. An officer made a cursory inspection of the house to ascertain if anyone else was present, after which Vale's mother and brother entered the house and were told of the arrest and impending search. A quantity of narcotics were found in a rear bedroom. The Court, per STEWART, J., concluded (without deciding whether *Chimel* should be accorded retroactive effect [a]) that "no precedent of this Court can sustain the constitutional validity of the search in the case before us":

a. *Chimel* was later held not to be retroactive in *Williams v. United States,* p. 53 supra.

"A search may be incident to an arrest 'only if it is substantially contemporaneous with the arrest and is confined to the *immediate* vicinity of the arrest.' If a search of a house is to be upheld as incident to an arrest, that arrest must take place *inside* the house, not somewhere outside—whether two blocks away, twenty feet away, or on the sidewalk near the front steps. 'Belief, however well founded, that an article sought is concealed in a dwelling house furnishes no justification for a search of that place without a warrant.' That basic rule 'has never been questioned in this Court.'

"The Louisiana Supreme Court thought the search independently supportable because it involved narcotics, which are easily removed, hidden, or destroyed. It would be unreasonable, the Louisiana court concluded, 'to require the officers under the facts of the case to first secure a search warrant before searching the premises, as time is of the essence inasmuch as the officers never know whether there is anyone on the premises to be searched who could very easily destroy the evidence.' Such a rationale could not apply to the present case, since by their own account the arresting officers satisfied themselves that no one else was in the house when they first entered the premises. But entirely apart from that point, our past decisions make clear that only in 'a few specifically established and well-delineated' situations, may a warrantless search of a dwelling withstand constitutional scrutiny, even though the authorities have probable cause to conduct it. The burden rests on the State to show the existence of such an exceptional situation. And the record before us discloses none.
* * *

"The officers were able to procure two warrants for the appellant's arrest. They also had information that he was residing at the address where they found him. There is thus no reason, so far as anything before us appears, to suppose that it was impracticable for them to obtain a search warrant as well. We decline to hold that an arrest on the street can provide its own 'exigent circumstance' so as to justify a warrantless search of the arrestee's house."

JUSTICE BLACK, joined by The Chief Justice, dissented:

"[When Vale and Saucier were arrested,] the police had probable cause to believe that Vale was engaged in a narcotics transfer, and that a supply of narcotics would be found in the house, to which Vale had returned after his first conversation, from which he had emerged furtively bearing what the police could readily deduce was a supply of narcotics, and toward which he hurried after seeing the police. But the police did not know then who else might be in the house. Vale's arrest took place near the house, and anyone observing from inside would surely have been alerted to destroy the stocks of contraband which the police believed Vale had left there. The police had already seen Saucier, the narcotics addict, apparently swallow what Vale had given him. Believing that some evidence had already been destroyed and that other evidence might well be, the police were faced with the choice of risking the immediate destruction of evidence or entering the house and conducting a search. I cannot say that their decision to search was unreasonable. Delay in order to obtain a warrant would have given an accomplice just the time he needed.

"That the arresting officers did, in fact, believe that others might be in the house is attested to by their actions upon entering the door left open by Vale. The police at once checked the small house to determine if anyone else was present. Just as they discovered the house was empty, however, Vale's mother and brother arrived. Now what had been a suspicion became a certainty: Vale's relatives were in possession and knew of his arrest. To have abandoned the search at this point, and left the house with Vale, would not have been the action of reasonable police officers. * * *

"Moreover, the circumstances here were sufficiently exceptional to justify a search, even if the search was not strictly 'incidental' to an arrest. The Court recognizes that searches to prevent the destruction or removal of evidence have long been held reasonable by this Court. Whether the 'exceptional circumstances' justifying such a search exist or not is a question which may be, as it is here, quite distinct from whether or not the search was incident to a valid arrest. It is thus unnecessary to determine whether the search was valid as incident to the arrest * * *.

"[T]he Court seems to argue that the search was unreasonable because the police officers had time to obtain a warrant. I agree that the opportunity to obtain a warrant is one of the factors to be weighed in determining reasonableness. But the record conclusively shows that there was no such opportunity here. As I noted above, once the officers had observed Vale's conduct in front of the house they had probable cause to believe that a felony had been committed and that immediate action was necessary. At no time after the events in front of Mrs. Vale's house would it have been prudent for the officers to leave the house in order to secure a warrant.

"The Court asserts, however, that because the police obtained two warrants for Vale's arrest there is 'no reason * * * to suppose that it was impracticable for them to obtain a search warrant as well.' The difficulty is that the two arrest warrants on which the Court seems to rely so heavily were not issued because of any present misconduct of Vale's; they were issued because the bond had been increased for an earlier narcotics charge then pending against Vale. When the police came to arrest Vale, they knew only that his bond had been increased. There is nothing in the record to indicate that, absent the increased bond, there would have been probable cause for an arrest, much less a search. Probable cause for the search arose for the first time when the police observed the activity of Vale and Saucier in and around the house."

2. What *should* the officers have done in *Vale?* Consider *United States v. Grummel,* 542 F.2d 789 (9th Cir.1976) (defendant picked up package known to contain heroin at post office; 10 minutes after taking the package into his home he was arrested there; because his mother was home, agent gave her the option of leaving the premises or remaining inside with him while another agent left to get a search warrant; held, it was proper on these facts to "secure the premises to the extent necessary to prevent destruction of the evidence until a warrant could be obtained"). Consider, in assessing the reasonableness of this alternative, the possibility of obtaining a warrant very promptly via telephone, as authorized in some jurisdictions (see, e.g., Fed.R.Crim.P. 41(c)(2)).

In SEGURA v. UNITED STATES, 468 U.S. 796, 104 S.Ct. 3380, 82 L.Ed.2d 599 (1984), the police, upon confirming that they had in fact observed a drug sale by Colon and Segura, went to their apartment building. Segura was arrested in the lobby, and when Colon answered a knock on the door she was also arrested. Police made a warrantless entry of the apartment and remained there until a search warrant was issued, which occurred some 19 hours later because of "administrative delay." The Court held "that where officers, having probable cause, enter premises, and with probable cause, arrest the occupants who have legitimate possessory interests in its contents and take them into custody and, for no more than the period here involved, secure the premises from within to preserve the status quo while others, in good faith, are in the process of obtaining a warrant, they do not violate the Fourth Amendment's proscription against unreasonable seizures." The Court also held that the evidence first discovered in execution of the warrant was not a fruit of the illegal entry. (See p. 808.) The first holding was explicated in a portion of an opinion by THE CHIEF JUSTICE in which only O'Connor, J., joined. Without deciding whether the petitioners were correct in characterizing the police action as a seizure of the entire contents of the apartment, they concluded any such seizure was not unreasonable. Noting that in other contexts the Court had approved warrantless seizures in circumstances where a warrantless search could not have been held (see the *Chadwick* and *Sanders* cases, discussed in *United States v. Ross,* p. 336), they could see "no reason * * * why the same principle should not apply when a dwelling is involved." These two Justices continued:

"In this case, the agents entered and secured the apartment from within. Arguably, the wiser course would have been to depart immediately and secure the premises from the outside by a 'stakeout' once the security check revealed that no one other than those taken into custody were in the apartment. But the method actually employed does not require a different result under the Fourth Amendment, insofar as the *seizure* is concerned. As the Court of Appeals held, absent exigent circumstances, the entry may have constituted an illegal *search,* or interference with petitioners' privacy interests, requiring suppression of all evidence observed during the entry. Securing of the premises from within, however, was no more an interference with the petitioners' possessory interests in the contents of the apartment than a perimeter 'stakeout.' In other words, the initial entry—legal or not—does not affect the reasonableness of the seizure. Under either method—entry and securing from within or a perimeter stakeout—agents control the apartment pending arrival of the warrant; both an internal securing and a perimeter stakeout interfere to the same extent with the possessory interests of the owners. * * *

"Of course, a seizure reasonable at its inception because based upon probable cause may become unreasonable as a result of its duration or for other reasons. Here, because of the delay in securing the warrant, the occupation of the apartment continued throughout the night and into the next day. Such delay in securing a warrant in a large metropolitan center unfortunately is not uncommon; this is not, in itself, evidence of bad faith. And there is no suggestion that the officers, in bad faith, purposely delayed obtaining the warrant. The asserted explanation is that the officers focused first on the task of processing those whom they had arrested before turning to the task of securing the warrant. It is not unreasonable for officers to believe that the former should take priority, given, as was the case here, that the proprietors of the apartment were in the custody of the officers throughout the period in question.

"There is no evidence that the agents in any way exploited their presence in the apartment; they simply awaited issuance of the warrant. Moreover, more than half of the 19-hour delay was between 10 p.m. and 10 a.m. the following day, when it is reasonable to assume that judicial officers are not as readily available for consideration of warrant requests. Finally, and most important, we observed in *United States v. Place,* [p. 379 infra], that '[t]he intrusion on possessory interests occasioned by a seizure * * * can vary both in its nature and extent. The seizure may be made after the owner has relinquished control of the property to a third party or * * * from the immediate custody and control of the owner.' Here, of course, Segura and Colon, whose possessory interests were interfered with by the occupation, were under arrest and in the custody of the police throughout the entire period the agents occupied the apartment. The actual interference with their possessory interests in the apartment and its contents was, thus, virtually nonexistent. We are not prepared to say under these limited circumstances that the seizure was unreasonable under the Fourth Amendment."

The four dissenters, per STEVENS, J., argued that the occupation was an unreasonable search, infringing upon a reasonable expectation of privacy, and an unreasonable seizure, involving exercise of "complete dominion and control over the apartment and its contents"; that the Fourth Amendment protects possessory interests in a residence even when the occupants are in custody; and that "what is even more strange about the Chief Justice's conclusion is that it permits the authorities to benefit from the fact that they had unlawfully arrested" an occupant of the apartment.[b]

3. Although in *Vale* the Court noted in passing that "the goods ultimately seized were not in the process of destruction," many lower courts have not taken that language too seriously in light of the Court's assumption that not even a threat of destruction was present. In *United States v. Rubin,* 474 F.2d 262 (3d Cir. 1973), the court upheld a warrantless search [c] pursuant to this test:

"When Government agents, however, have probable cause to believe contraband is present and, in addition, based on the surrounding circumstances or the information at hand, they reasonably conclude that the evidence will be destroyed or removed before they can secure a search warrant, a warrantless search is justified. The emergency circumstances will vary from case to case, and the inherent necessities of the situation at the time must be scrutinized. Circumstances which have seemed relevant to courts include (1) the degree of urgency involved and the amount of time necessary to obtain a warrant * * *; (2) reasonable belief that the contraband is about to be removed * * *; (3) the possibility of danger to police officers guarding the site of the contraband while a search warrant is sought * * *; (4) information indicating the possessors of the contraband are aware that the police are on their trail * * *; and (5) the ready destructibility of the contraband and the knowledge 'that efforts to dispose of narcotics and to escape are characteristic behavior of persons engaged in the narcotics traffic.' "

4. Although several courts had held that when the police are summoned to the scene of a homicide they may remain on those premises without a warrant (and, perhaps, return after a brief absence) to conduct a general investigation into the cause of the death, in *Mincey v. Arizona,* 437 U.S. 385, 98 S.Ct. 2408, 57 L.Ed.2d 290 (1978), the Court, confronted with a rather broad variation of the so-called homicide scene exception to the warrant requirement (the criminal nature and perpetrator of the homicide were known from the outset, no occupant of the premises had summoned the police, and the searches upheld by the lower court continued for four days), "decline[d] to hold that the seriousness of the offense under investigation itself creates exigent circumstances of the kind that under the Fourth Amendment justify a warrantless search." *Mincey* was later applied in *Thompson v. Louisiana,* 469 U.S. 17, 105 S.Ct. 409, 83 L.Ed.2d 246 (1984), to invalidate a two-hour general search of premises to which police were summoned because of defendant's attempt to get medical assistance after

b. For criticism of *Segura,* see Dressler, *A Lesson in Incaution, Overwork, and Fatigue: The Judicial Miscraftsmanship of Segura v. United States,* 26 Wm. & Mary L.Rev. 375 (1985).

c. The facts in *Rubin* were as follows: Customs agents received reliable information that a bronze statute containing a large shipment of illicit drugs would be shipped to a hospital in a certain area. Agents were posted at the airport and waterfront, and finally a crate answering the general description given by the informant arrived at the airport from abroad. It was inspected and found to contain narcotics. Agents observed one Agnes pick up the crate and take it to a certain address, where it was unloaded at about 5 p.m. After one agent was dispatched to secure a search warrant, Agnes left the premises in his car but without the crate. He was tailed for a short distance, but when his evasive actions led agents to believe he was aware of the tail, they arrested him. When he was placed under arrest about six blocks from the house in question, he yelled to spectators to call his brother. At this point the agents, fearing disposal of the narcotics if they waited for the search warrant, entered the house and searched for and seized the narcotics.

shooting her husband. The Court noted the authorities, "while they were in petitioner's house to offer her assistance," could have seized evidence in plain view and could also have made a limited search for a suspect or for other victims.

5. The question is sometimes raised as to whether evidence of criminal conduct discovered by the police without a warrant while performing certain other functions is admissible. Compare *State v. Sanders,* 506 P.2d 892 (Wash.App.1973) ("police officers may enter a dwelling without a warrant to render emergency aid and assistance to a person whom they reasonably believe to be in distress and in need of that assistance," and thus properly entered apartment of distressed person who made partially completed phone call to police); with *People v. Smith,* 496 P.2d 1261 (Cal. 1972) (where police were called to scene because small child was crying in the street, it was not reasonable for officer to enter apartment where child lived for purported reason of seeing if mother was there and if she needed help, as child had told officer her mother was not home and there was no evidence to support the assumption that the mother had returned unnoticed and was in need of assistance).

PAYTON v. NEW YORK

445 U.S. 573, 100 S.Ct. 1371, 63 L.Ed.2d 639 (1980).

MR. JUSTICE STEVENS delivered the opinion of the Court. * * *

On January 14, 1970, after two days of intensive investigation, New York detectives had assembled evidence sufficient to establish probable cause to believe that Theodore Payton had murdered the manager of a gas station two days earlier. At about 7:30 a.m. on January 15, six officers went to Payton's apartment in the Bronx, intending to arrest him. They had not obtained a warrant. Although light and music emanated from the apartment, there was no response to their knock on the metal door. They summoned emergency assistance and, about 30 minutes later, used crowbars to break open the door and enter the apartment. No one was there. In plain view, however, was a 30-caliber shell casing that was seized and later admitted into evidence at Payton's murder trial. * * *

On March 14, 1974, Obie Riddick was arrested for the commission of two armed robberies that had occurred in 1971. He had been identified by the victims in June of 1973 and in January 1974 the police had learned his address. They did not obtain a warrant for his arrest. At about noon on March 14, a detective, accompanied by three other officers, knocked on the door of the Queens house where Riddick was living. When his young son opened the door, they could see Riddick sitting in bed covered by a sheet. They entered the house and placed him under arrest. Before permitting him to dress, they opened a chest of drawers two feet from the bed in search of weapons and found narcotics and related paraphernalia. Riddick was subsequently indicted on narcotics charges. * * *

The New York Court of Appeals, in a single opinion, affirmed the convictions of both Payton and Riddick. * * *

Before addressing the narrow question presented by these appeals, we put to one side other related problems that are *not* presented today. Although it is arguable that the warrantless entry to effect Payton's arrest might have been justified by exigent circumstances, none of the New York courts relied on any such justification. The Court of Appeals majority treated both *Payton's* and *Riddick's* cases as involving routine arrests in which there was ample time to obtain a warrant, and we will do the same. Accordingly, we have no occasion to consider the sort of emergency or dangerous situation, described in our cases as "exigent circumstances," that would justify a warrantless entry into a home for the purpose of either arrest or search.

Nor do these cases raise any question concerning the authority of the police, without either a search or arrest warrant, to enter a third party's home to arrest a suspect. The police broke into Payton's apartment intending to arrest Payton and they arrested Riddick in his own dwelling. We also note that in neither case is it argued that the police lacked probable cause to believe that the suspect was at home when they entered. Finally, in both cases we are dealing with entries into homes made without the consent of any occupant. In *Payton,* the police used crowbars to break down the door and in *Riddick,* although his three-year-old son answered the door, the police entered before Riddick had an opportunity either to object or to consent. * * *

It is a "basic principle of Fourth Amendment law" that searches and seizures inside a home without a warrant are presumptively unreasonable. Yet it is also well-settled that objects such as weapons or contraband found in a public place may be seized by the police without a warrant. The seizure of property in plain view involves no invasion of privacy and is presumptively reasonable, assuming that there is probable cause to associate the property with criminal activity. * * *

As the late Judge Leventhal recognized, this distinction has equal force when the seizure of a person is involved. Writing on the constitutional issue now before us for the United States Court of Appeals for the District of Columbia Circuit sitting en banc, *Dorman v. United States,* 435 F.2d 385 (D.C.Cir.1970), Judge Leventhal first noted the settled rule that warrantless arrests in public places are valid. He immediately recognized, however, that

> "[a] greater burden is placed [ ] on officials who enter a home or dwelling without consent. Freedom from intrusion into the home or dwelling is the archetype of the privacy protection secured by the Fourth Amendment."

His analysis of this question then focused on the long-settled premise that, absent exigent circumstances, a warrantless entry to search for weapons or contraband is unconstitutional even when a felony has been committed and there is probable cause to believe that incriminating evidence will be found within. He reasoned that the constitutional protection afforded to the individual's interest in the privacy of his own home is equally applicable to a warrantless entry for the purpose of arresting a resident of the house; for it is inherent in such an entry that a search for the suspect may be required before he can be apprehended. Judge Leventhal concluded that an entry to arrest and an entry to search for and to seize property implicate the same interest in preserving the privacy and the sanctity of the home, and justify the same level of constitutional protection. * * * We find this reasoning to be persuasive and in accord with this Court's Fourth Amendment decisions.

The majority of the New York Court of Appeals, however, suggested that there is a substantial difference in the relative intrusiveness of an entry to search for property and an entry to search for a person. It is true that the area that may legally be searched is broader when executing a search warrant than when executing an arrest warrant in the home. See *Chimel v. California,* [p. 309 supra]. This difference may be more theoretical than real, however, because the police may need to check the entire premises for safety reasons, and sometimes they ignore the restrictions on searches incident to arrest.

But the critical point is that any differences in the intrusiveness of entries to search and entries to arrest are merely ones of degree rather than kind. The two intrusions share this fundamental characteristic: the breach of the entrance to an individual's home. * * * In terms that apply equally to seizures of property and to seizures of persons, the Fourth Amendment has drawn a firm line at the entrance to the house. Absent exigent circumstances, that threshold may not reasonably be crossed without a warrant. * * * [a]

The parties have argued at some length about the practical consequences of a warrant requirement as a precondition to a felony arrest in the home. In the absence of any evidence that effective law enforcement has suffered in those States that already have such a requirement, we are inclined to view such arguments with skepticism. More fundamentally, however, such arguments of policy must give way to a constitutional command that we consider to be unequivocal.

Finally, we note the State's suggestion that only a search warrant based on probable cause to believe the suspect is at home at a given time can adequately protect the privacy interests at stake, and since such a warrant requirement is manifestly impractical, there need be no warrant of any kind. We find this ingenious argument unpersuasive. It is true that an arrest warrant requirement may afford less protection than a search warrant requirement, but it will suffice to interpose the magistrate's determination of probable cause between the zealous officer and the citizen. If there is sufficient evidence of a citizen's participation in a felony to persuade a judicial officer that his arrest is justified, it is constitutionally reasonable to require him to open his doors to the officers of the law. Thus, for Fourth Amendment purposes, an arrest warrant founded on probable cause implicitly carries with it the limited authority to enter a dwelling in which the suspect lives when there is reason to believe the suspect is within.

Because no arrest warrant was obtained in either of these cases, the judgments must be reversed * * *.

MR. JUSTICE BLACKMUN, concurring. * * *

MR. JUSTICE WHITE, with whom THE CHIEF JUSTICE and MR. JUSTICE REHNQUIST join, dissenting. * * *

Today's decision ignores the carefully crafted restrictions on the common-law power of arrest entry and thereby overestimates the dangers inherent in that practice. At common law, absent exigent circumstances, entries to arrest could be made only for felony. Even in cases of felony, the officers were required to announce their presence, demand admission, and be refused entry before they were entitled to break doors. Further, it seems generally accepted that entries could be made only during daylight hours. And, in my view, the officer entering to arrest must have reasonable grounds to believe, not only that the arrestee has committed a crime, but also that the person suspected is present in the house at the time of the entry.[13]

a. At this point, Stevens, J., observed that New York argued that "the reasons supporting the *Watson* [p. 298 supra] holding require a similar result here. In *Watson* the Court relied on (a) the well-settled common-law rule that a warrantless arrest in a public place is valid if the arresting officer had probable cause to believe the suspect is a felon; (b) the clear consensus among the States adhering to that well-settled common-law rule; and (c) the expression of the judgment of Congress that such an arrest is 'reasonable.' We consider each of these reasons as it applies to a warrantless entry into a home for the purpose of making a routine felony arrest."

In an extended analysis, the *Payton* majority concluded (a) that "the relevant common law does not provide the same guidance that was present in *Watson*," as there is "no direct authority supporting forcible entries into a home to make a routine arrest and the weight of the scholarly opinion is somewhat to the contrary"; (b) that presently 24 states permit such warrantless entries, 15 prohibit them, and 11 have taken no position, with "a significant decline during the last decade in the number of States permitting warrantless entries for arrest"; and (c) that "no congressional determination that warrantless entries into the home are 'reasonable' has been called to our attention." While the majority then concluded from this that "neither history nor this Nation's experience" lent support to the New York position, the *Payton* dissenters read essentially the same data as supporting their position.

13. I do not necessarily disagree with the Court's discussion of the quantum of probable cause necessary to make a valid home arrest. The Court indicates that only an arrest warrant, and not a search warrant, is required. To obtain the warrant, therefore, the officers need only show probable cause that a crime has been committed and that the suspect committed it. How-

These four restrictions on home arrests—felony, knock and announce, daytime, and stringent probable cause—constitute powerful and complementary protections for the privacy interests associated with the home. The felony requirement guards against abusive or arbitrary enforcement and ensures that invasions of the home occur only in case of the most serious crimes. The knock and announce and daytime requirement protect individuals against the fear, humiliation and embarrassment of being aroused from the beds in states of partial or complete undress. And these requirements allow the arrestee to surrender at his front door, thereby maintaining his dignity and preventing the officers from entering other rooms of the dwelling. The stringent probable cause requirement would help ensure against the possibility that the police would enter when the suspect was not home, and, in searching for him, frighten members of the family or ransack parts of the house, seizing items in plain view. In short, these requirements, taken together, permit an individual suspected of a serious crime to surrender at the front door of his dwelling and thereby avoid most of the humiliation and indignity that the Court seems to believe necessarily accompany a house arrest entry. Such a front door arrest, in my view, is no more intrusive on personal privacy than the public warrantless arrests which we found to pass constitutional muster in *Watson.*[14]

All of these limitations on warrantless arrest entries are satisfied on the facts of the present cases. The arrests here were for serious felonies—murder and armed robbery—and both occurred during daylight hours. The authorizing statutes required that the police announce their business and demand entry; neither Payton nor Riddick makes any contention that these statutory requirements were not fulfilled. And it is not argued that the police had no probable cause to believe that both Payton and Riddick were in their dwellings at the time of the entries. Today's decision, therefore, sweeps away any possibility that warrantless home entries might be permitted in some limited situations other than those in which exigent circumstances are present. The Court substitutes, in one sweeping decision, a rigid constitutional rule in place of the common-law approach, evolved over hundreds of years, which achieved a flexible accommodation between the demands of personal privacy and the legitimate needs of law enforcement.

A rule permitting warrantless arrest entries would not pose a danger that officers would use their entry power as a pretext to justify an otherwise invalid warrantless search. A search pursuant to a warrantless arrest entry will rarely, if ever, be as complete as one under authority of a search warrant. If the suspect surrenders at the door, the officers may not enter other rooms. Of course, the suspect may flee or hide, or may not be at home, but the officers cannot anticipate the first two of these possibilities and the last is unlikely given the requirement of probable cause to believe that the suspect is at home. Even when officers are justified in searching other rooms, they may seize only items within the arrestee's position [sic] or immediate control or items in plain view discovered during the course of a search reasonably directed at discovering a hiding suspect. Hence a warrantless home entry is likely to uncover far less evidence than a search conducted under authority of a search warrant. Furthermore, an arrest entry will inevitably tip off the suspects

ever, under today's decision, the officers apparently need an extra increment of probable cause when executing the arrest warrant, namely grounds to believe that the suspect is within the dwelling.

14. If the suspect flees or hides, of course, the intrusiveness of the entry will be somewhat greater; but the policeman's hands should not be tied merely because of the possibility that the suspect will fail to cooperate with legitimate actions by law enforcement personnel.

and likely result in destruction or removal of evidence not uncovered during the arrest. I therefore cannot believe that the police would take the risk of losing valuable evidence through a pretextual arrest entry rather than applying to a magistrate for a search warrant.

While exaggerating the invasion of personal privacy involved in home arrests, the Court fails to account for the danger that its rule will "severely hamper effective law enforcement." The policeman on his beat must now make subtle discriminations that perplex even judges in their chambers. As Mr. Justice Powell noted, concurring in *United States v. Watson,* police will sometimes delay making an arrest, even after probable cause is established, in order to be sure that they have enough evidence to convict. Then, if they suddenly have to arrest, they run the risk that the subsequent exigency will not excuse their prior failure to obtain a warrant. This problem cannot effectively be cured by obtaining a warrant as soon as probable cause is established because of the chance that the warrant will go stale before the arrest is made.

Further, police officers will often face the difficult task of deciding whether the circumstances are sufficiently exigent to justify their entry to arrest without a warrant. This is a decision that must be made quickly in the most trying of circumstances. If the officers mistakenly decide that the circumstances are exigent, the arrest will be invalid and any evidence seized incident to the arrest or in plain view will be excluded at trial. On the other hand, if the officers mistakenly determine that exigent circumstances are lacking, they may refrain from making the arrest, thus creating the possibility that a dangerous criminal will escape into the community. The police could reduce the likelihood of escape by staking out all possible exits until the circumstances become clearly exigent or a warrant is obtained. But the costs of such a stakeout seem excessive in an era of rising crime and scarce police resources.

The uncertainty inherent in the exigent circumstances determination burdens the judicial system as well. In the case of searches, exigent circumstances are sufficiently unusual that this Court has determined that the benefits of a warrant outweigh the burdens imposed, including the burdens on the judicial system. In contrast, arrests recurringly involve exigent circumstances, and this Court has heretofore held that a warrant can be dispensed with without undue sacrifice in Fourth Amendment values. The situation should be no different with respect to arrests in the home. Under today's decision, whenever the police have made a warrantless home arrest there will be the possibility of "endless litigation with respect to the existence of exigent circumstances, whether it was practicable to get a warrant, whether the suspect was about to flee, and the like."

* * * It would be far preferable to adopt a clear and simple rule: after knocking and announcing their presence, police may enter the home to make a daytime arrest without a warrant when there is probable cause to believe that the person to be arrested committed a felony and is present in the house. * * * [b]

Notes and Questions

1. The Supreme Court has approved of warrantless entries to arrest under some circumstances. In *Warden v. Hayden,* 387 U.S. 294, 87 S.Ct. 1642, 18 L.Ed.2d 782 (1967), where police were reliably informed that an armed robbery had taken place and that the perpetrator had entered a certain house five minutes earlier, the Court concluded they "acted reasonably when they entered the house and began to search for a man of the description they

b. See Harbaugh & Faust, *"Knock on Any Door"—Home Arrests After Payton and Steagald,* 86 Dick.L.Rev. 191 (1982).

had been given and for weapons which he had used in the robbery or might use against them.[c] The Fourth Amendment does not require police officers to delay in the course of an investigation if to do so would gravely endanger their lives or the lives of others." And in *United States v. Santana,* 427 U.S. 38, 96 S.Ct. 2406, 49 L.Ed.2d 300 (1976), it was held that *United States v. Watson,* p. 298 supra, permitted the police to attempt a warrantless arrest of the defendant when she was found "standing directly in the doorway—one step forward would have put her outside, one step backward would have put her in the vestibule of her residence." The Court reasoned that she "was in a public place," as she "was not merely visible to the public but was exposed to public view, speech, hearing and touch as if she had been standing completely outside her house." Thus, under the *Hayden* "hot pursuit" rule the police could pursue her without a warrant when she sought refuge within upon their approach.

What then if the person to be arrested answers a knock on the door by the police but does not step onto or over the threshhold? What if he does because of a police request or subterfuge which conceals their purpose in being there? Or, what if the police use such tactics to gain entry into the premises?

2. In *Dorman,* relied upon in *Payton,* the court found that exceptional circumstances were present by assessing these considerations:

"First, that a grave offense is involved, particularly one that is a crime of violence. * * *

"Second, * * * that the suspect is reasonably believed to be armed. * * *

"Third, that there exists not merely the minimum of probable cause, that is requisite even when a warrant has been issued, but beyond that a clear showing of probable cause, including 'reasonably trustworthy information,' to believe that the suspect committed the crime involved.

"Fourth, strong reason to believe that the suspect is in the premises being entered.

"Fifth, a likelihood that the suspect will escape if not swiftly apprehended.

"Sixth, the circumstance that the entry, though not consented, is made peaceably. * * *

"Another factor to be taken into account, though it works in more than one direction, relates to time of entry—whether it is made at night. On the one hand, as we shall later develop, the late hour may underscore the delay (and perhaps impracticability of) obtaining a warrant and hence serve to justify proceeding without one. On the other hand, the fact that an entry is made at night raises a particular concern over its reasonableness * * * and may elevate the degree of probable cause required, both as implicating the suspect, and as showing that he is in the place entered."

Judge Wright, disagreed: "The police, while waiting for a judicial officer to authorize entry into the home, could simply stake out the apartment."

3. The Supreme Court focused upon the first *Dorman* factor in WELSH v. WISCONSIN, 466 U.S. 740, 104 S.Ct. 2091, 80 L.Ed.2d 732 (1984), where Welsh was arrested within his own home minutes after a witness had seen him nearby driving erratically and then departing on foot in an apparently inebriated condition after driving off the road into a field. The Court, per BRENNAN, J., held "that an important factor to be considered when determining whether any exigency exists is the gravity of the underlying offense for which the arrest is being made. Moreover, although no exigency is created simply because there is probable cause to believe that a

c. Thus, the Court held admissible clothing found in a washing machine, where an officer looked for weapons "prior to or immediately contemporaneous with Hayden's arrest."

serious crime has been committed, see *Payton,* application of the exigent-circumstances exception in the context of a home entry should rarely be sanctioned when there is probable cause to believe that only a minor offense, such as the kind at issue in this case, has been committed.

"Application of this principle to the facts of the present case is relatively straightforward. The petitioner was arrested in the privacy of his own bedroom for a noncriminal, traffic offense. The State attempts to justify the arrest by relying on the hot-pursuit doctrine, on the threat to public safety, and on the need to preserve evidence of the petitioner's blood-alcohol level. On the facts of this case, however, the claim of hot pursuit is unconvincing because there was no immediate or continuous pursuit of the petitioner from the scene of a crime. Moreover, because the petitioner had already arrived home, and had abandoned his car at the scene of the accident, there was little remaining threat to the public safety. Hence, the only potential emergency claimed by the State was the need to ascertain the petitioner's blood-alcohol level.

"Even assuming, however, that the underlying facts would support a finding of this exigent circumstance, mere similarity to other cases involving the imminent destruction of evidence is not sufficient. The State of Wisconsin has chosen to classify the first offense for driving while intoxicated as a noncriminal, civil forfeiture offense for which no imprisonment is possible. This is the best indication of the state's interest in precipitating an arrest, and is one that can be easily identified both by the courts and by officers faced with a decision to arrest. Given this expression of the state's interest, a warrantless home arrest cannot be upheld simply because evidence of the petitioner's blood-alcohol level might have dissipated while the police obtained a warrant. To allow a warrantless home entry on these facts would be to approve unreasonable police behavior that the principles of the Fourth Amendment will not sanction."

WHITE, J., joined by Rehnquist, J., dissenting, agreed that the gravity of the offense is "a factor to be considered," but asserted that "if, under all the circumstances of a particular case, an officer has probable cause to believe that the delay involved in procuring an arrest warrant will gravely endanger the officer or other persons or will result in the suspect's escape, I perceive no reason to disregard those exigencies on the ground that the offense for which the suspect is sought is a 'minor' one." By like reasoning, they concluded that "nothing in our previous decisions suggests that the fact that a State has defined an offense as a misdemeanor for a variety of social, cultural, and political reasons necessarily requires the conclusion that warrantless in-home arrests designed to prevent the imminent destruction or removal of evidence of that offense are always impermissible. * * * A test under which the existence of exigent circumstances turns on the perceived gravity of the crime would significantly hamper law enforcement and burden courts with pointless litigation concerning the nature and gradation of various crimes."

4. In STEAGALD v. UNITED STATES, 451 U.S. 204, 101 S.Ct. 1642, 68 L.Ed.2d 38 (1981), police entered Steagald's home in an effort to find one Lyons, for whom they had an arrest warrant; they did not find Lyons but did find drugs in plain view, resulting in Steagald's prosecution and conviction. In reversing the conviction, the Court, per MARSHALL, J., reasoned that "whether the arrest warrant issued in this case adequately safeguarded the interests protected by the Fourth Amendment depends upon what the warrant authorized the agents to do. To be sure, the warrant embodied a judicial finding that there was probable cause to believe that Ricky Lyons had committed a felony, and the warrant therefore authorized the officers to seize Lyons. Howev-

er, the agents sought to do more than use the warrant to arrest Lyons in a public place or in his home; instead, they relied on the warrant as legal authority to enter the home of a third person based on their belief that Ricky Lyons might be a guest there. Regardless of how reasonable this belief might have been, it was never subjected to the detached scrutiny of a judicial officer. Thus, while the warrant in this case may have protected Lyons from an unreasonable seizure, it did absolutely nothing to protect petitioner's privacy interest in being free from an unreasonable invasion and search of his home. Instead, petitioner's only protection from an illegal entry and search was the agent's personal determination of probable cause. In the absence of exigent circumstances, we have consistently held that such judicially untested determinations are not reliable enough to justify an entry into a person's home to arrest him without a warrant, or a search of a home for objects in the absence of a search warrant. We see no reason to depart from this settled course when the search of a home is for a person rather than an object.

"A contrary conclusion—that the police, acting alone and in the absence of exigent circumstances, may decide when there is sufficient justification for searching the home of a third party for the subject of an arrest warrant—would create a significant potential for abuse. Armed solely with an arrest warrant for a single person, the police could search all the homes of that individual's friends and acquaintances. See, e.g., *Lankford v. Gelston,* 364 F.2d 197 (CA4 1966) (enjoining police practice under which 300 homes searched pursuant to arrest warrants for two fugitives). Moreover, an arrest warrant may serve as the pretext for entering a home in which the police have a suspicion, but not probable cause to believe, that illegal activity is taking place."

Though the majority went on to conclude that this result was not contrary to common law precedent and "will not significantly impede effective law enforcement efforts," in that "the situations in which a search warrant will be necessary are few" and in those situations "the inconvenience incurred by the police is simply not that significant," REHNQUIST and WHITE, JJ., dissenting, argued that "the common law as it existed at the time of the framing of the Fourth Amendment" did not support such a result, and concluded:

"The genuinely unfortunate aspect of today's ruling is not that fewer fugitives will be brought to book, or fewer criminals apprehended, though both of these consequences will undoubtedly occur; the greater misfortune is the increased uncertainty imposed on police officers in the field, committing magistrates, and trial judges, who must confront variations and permutations of this factual situation on a day-to-day basis. They will, in their various capacities, have to weigh the time during which a suspect for whom there is an outstanding arrest warrant has been in the building, whether the dwelling is the suspect's home, how long he has lived there, whether he is likely to leave immediately, and a number of related and equally imponderable questions. Certainty and repose, as Justice Holmes said, may not be the destiny of man, but one might have hoped for a higher degree of certainty in this one narrow but important area of the law than is offered by today's decision."

5. In KER v. CALIFORNIA, 374 U.S. 23, 83 S.Ct. 1623, 10 L.Ed.2d 726 (1963), police entered defendant's premises without first demanding admittance and explaining their purpose, and arrested defendant for possession of marijuana. The California courts concluded that the police were excused from the state statutory demand-notice requirements because of the need to prevent the destruction of contraband. JUSTICE CLARK, writing for only four members of the Court on this point, upheld the entry: "Here justification for the officers' failure to give notice is uniquely present. In addition to the

officers' belief that Ker was in possession of narcotics, which could be quickly and easily destroyed, Ker's furtive conduct in eluding them shortly before the arrest was ground for the belief that he might well have been expecting the police."

JUSTICE HARLAN concurred in the result on the ground that state searches and seizures should be judged by "concepts of fundamental fairness." JUSTICE BRENNAN, joined by the remaining three members of the Court, argued that under the Fourth Amendment the only exceptions to demand-notice requirements are "where such circumstances as an escape and hot pursuit by the arresting officer leave no doubt that the fleeing felon is aware of the officer's presence and purpose" and "possibly where the officers are justified in the belief that someone within is in immediate danger of bodily harm."

6. Many states have statutes which expressly provided that an officer may not enter for purposes of arrest unless he has been denied admittance after giving "notice of his office and purpose," but these statutes have generally been interpreted as codifying the common law exception for "exigent circumstances." The prevailing but not unanimous view, as stated in *People v. Rosales,* 437 P.2d 489 (Cal.1968), is that entry without notice is proper "when the officer acts on a reasonable and good faith belief that compliance would increase his peril, frustrate an arrest, or permit the destruction of evidence. Such a belief, however, must be based on the facts of the particular case. It cannot be justified by a general assumption that certain classes of persons subject to arrest are more likely than others to resist arrest, attempt to escape, or destroy evidence."

CALIFORNIA v. CARNEY

— U.S. —, 105 S.Ct. 2066, 85 L.Ed.2d 406 (1985).

CHIEF JUSTICE BURGER delivered the opinion of the Court. * * *

On May 31, 1979, Drug Enforcement Agency Agent Robert Williams watched respondent, Charles Carney, approach a youth in downtown San Diego. The youth accompanied Carney to a Dodge Mini Motor Home parked in a nearby lot. Carney and the youth closed the window shades in the motor home, including one across the front window. Agent Williams had previously received uncorroborated information that the same motor home was used by another person who was exchanging marihuana for sex. Williams, with assistance from other agents, kept the motor home under surveillance for the entire one and one-quarter hours that Carney and the youth remained inside. When the youth left the motor home, the agents followed and stopped him. The youth told the agents that he had received marijuana in return for allowing Carney sexual contacts.

At the officers' request, the youth returned to the motor home and knocked on its door; Carney stepped out. The agents identified themselves as law enforcement officers. Without a warrant or consent, one agent entered the motor home and observed marihuana, plastic bags, and a scale of the kind used in weighing drugs on a table. Agent Williams took Carney into custody and took possession of the motor home. A subsequent search of the motor home at the police station revealed additional marihuana in the cupboards and refrigerator.

Respondent was charged with possession of marihuana for sale. At a preliminary hearing, he moved to suppress the evidence discovered in the motor home. The Magistrate denied the motion, [but later the state supreme court reversed the conviction, holding the search was unreasonable because no warrant was obtained.]

* * * There are, of course, exceptions to the general rule that a warrant must be secured before a search is undertaken; one is the so-called "automobile exception" at issue in this case. This ex-

ception to the warrant requirement was first set forth by the Court 60 years ago in *Carroll v. United States,* 267 U.S. 132, 45 S.Ct. 280, 69 L.Ed. 543 (1925). There, the Court recognized that the privacy interests in an automobile are constitutionally protected; however, it held that the ready mobility of the automobile justifies a lesser degree of protection of those interests. The Court rested this exception on a long-recognized distinction between stationary structures and vehicles:

> "[T]he guaranty of freedom from unreasonable searches and seizures by the Fourth Amendment has been construed, practically since the beginning of Government, as recognizing a necessary difference between a search of a store, dwelling house or other structure in respect of which a proper official warrant readily may be obtained, and a search of a ship, motor boat, wagon or automobile, for contraband goods, where it is not practicable to secure a warrant because the vehicle can be *quickly moved* out of the locality or jurisdiction in which the warrant must be sought."

The capacity to be "quickly moved" was clearly the basis of the holding in *Carroll,* and our cases have consistently recognized ready mobility as one of the principal bases of the automobile exception. * * *

However, although ready mobility alone was perhaps the original justification for the vehicle exception, our later cases have made clear that ready mobility is not the only basis for the exception. The reasons for the vehicle exception, we have said, are twofold. "Besides the element of mobility, less rigorous warrant requirements govern because the expectation of privacy with respect to one's automobile is significantly less than that relating to one's home or office."

Even in cases where an automobile was not immediately mobile, the lesser expectation of privacy resulting from its use as a readily mobile vehicle justified application of the vehicular exception. In some cases, the configuration of the vehicle contributed to the lower expectations of privacy; for example, we held in *Cardwell v. Lewis,* 417 U.S. [583], 94 S.Ct. [2464, 41 L.Ed. 2d 325 (1974)], that, because the passenger compartment of a standard automobile is relatively open to plain view, there are lesser expectations of privacy. But even when enclosed "repository" areas have been involved, we have concluded that the lesser expectations of privacy warrant application of the exception. We have applied the exception in the context of a locked car trunk, *Cady v. Dombrowski,* [413 U.S. 433, 93 S.Ct. 2523, 37 L.Ed.2d 706 (1973)], a sealed package in a car trunk, *United States v. Ross,* [p. 336], a closed compartment under the dashboard, *Chambers v. Maroney,* [p. 335], the interior of a vehicle's upholstery, *Carroll, supra,* or sealed packages inside a covered pickup truck, *United States v. Johns,* [p. 347].

These reduced expectations of privacy derive not from the fact that the area to be searched is in plain view, but from the pervasive regulation of vehicles capable of traveling on the public highways. As we explained in *South Dakota v. Opperman,* an inventory search case:

> "Automobiles, unlike homes, are subjected to pervasive and continuing governmental regulation and controls, including periodic inspection and licensing requirements. As an everyday occurrence, police stop and examine vehicles when license plates or inspection stickers have expired, or if other violations, such as exhaust fumes or excessive noise, are noted, or if headlights or other safety equipment are not in proper working order."

The public is fully aware that it is accorded less privacy in its automobiles because of this compelling governmental need for regulation. Historically, "individuals always [have] been on notice that movable vessels may be stopped and searched on facts giving rise to probable cause that the vehicle contains contraband, without the protection afforded by a magistrate's prior evaluation of those facts." In short, the pervasive schemes of regulation, which necessarily lead to reduced expectations of privacy, and the exigencies attendant to ready mobility justify searches without prior recourse to the authority of a magistrate so long as the overriding standard of probable cause is met.

When a vehicle is being used on the highways, or if it is readily capable of such use and is found stationary in a place not regularly used for residential purposes—temporary or otherwise—the two justifications for the vehicle exception come into play. First, the vehicle is obviously readily mobile by the turn of a switch key, if not actually moving. Second, there is a reduced expectation of privacy stemming from its use as a licensed motor vehicle subject to a range of police regulation inapplicable to a fixed dwelling. At least in these circumstances, the overriding societal interests in effective law enforcement justify an immediate search before the vehicle and its occupants become unavailable.

While it is true that respondent's vehicle possessed some, if not many of the attributes of a home, it is equally clear that the vehicle falls clearly within the scope of the exception laid down in *Carroll* and applied in succeeding cases. Like the automobile in *Carroll,* respondent's motor home was readily mobile. Absent the prompt search and seizure, it could readily have been moved beyond the reach of the police. Furthermore, the vehicle was licensed to "operate on public streets; [was] serviced in public places; * * * and [was] subject to extensive regulation and inspection." And the vehicle was so situated that an objective observer would conclude that it was being used not as a residence, but as a vehicle.

Respondent urges us to distinguish his vehicle from other vehicles within the exception because it was *capable of functioning as a home.* In our increasingly mobile society, many vehicles used for transportation can be and are being used not only for transportation but for shelter, i.e., as a "home" or "residence." To distinguish between respondent's motor home and an ordinary sedan for purposes of the vehicle exception would require that we apply the exception depending upon the size of the vehicle and the quality of its appointments. Moreover, to fail to apply the exception to vehicles such as a motor home ignores the fact that a motor home lends itself easily to use as an instrument of illicit drug traffic and other illegal activity. In *United States v. Ross,* we declined to distinguish between "worthy" and "unworthy" containers, noting that "the central purpose of the Fourth Amendment forecloses such a distinction." We decline today to distinguish between "worthy" and "unworthy" vehicles which are either on the public roads and highways, or situated such that it is reasonable to conclude that the vehicle is not being used as a residence.

Our application of the vehicle exception has never turned on the other uses to which a vehicle might be put. The exception has historically turned on the ready mobility of the vehicle, and on the presence of the vehicle in a setting that objectively indicates that the vehicle is being used for transportation.[3] These two requirements for application of the exception ensure that law enforcement officials are not unnecessarily hamstrung in their efforts to detect and prosecute criminal activity, and that the legitimate privacy interests of the public are protected. Applying the

3. We need not pass on the application of the vehicle exception to a motor home that is situated in a way or place that objectively indicates that it is being used as a residence. Among the factors that might be relevant in determining whether a warrant would be required in such a circumstance is its location, whether the vehicle is readily mobile or instead, for instance, elevated on blocks, whether the vehicle is licensed, whether it is connected to utilities, and whether it has convenient access to a public road.

vehicle exception in these circumstances allows the essential purposes served by the exception to be fulfilled, while assuring that the exception will acknowledge legitimate privacy interests. * * *

This search was not unreasonable; it was plainly one that the magistrate could authorize if presented with these facts. * * *

The judgment of the California Supreme Court is reversed * * *.

JUSTICE STEVENS, with whom JUSTICE BRENNAN and Justice MARSHALL join, dissenting. * * *

In *United States v. Ross,* the Court reaffirmed the primary importance of the general rule condemning warrantless searches, and emphasized that the exception permitting the search of automobiles without a warrant is a narrow one. * * *

As we explained in *Ross,* the automobile exception is the product of a long history:

> "since its earliest days Congress had recognized the impracticability of securing a warrant in cases involving the transportation of contraband goods. It is this impracticability, viewed in historical perspective, that provided the basis for the *Carroll* decision. Given the nature of an automobile in transit, the Court recognized that an immediate intrusion is necessary if police officers are to secure the illicit substance. In this class of cases, the Court held that a warrantless search of an automobile is not unreasonable."

The automobile exception has been developed to ameliorate the practical problems associated with the search of vehicles that have been stopped on the streets or public highways because there was probable cause to believe they were transporting contraband. Until today, however, the Court has never decided whether the practical justifications that apply to a vehicle that is stopped in transit on a public way apply with the same force to a vehicle parked in a lot near a court house where it could easily be detained while a warrant is issued.[15]

In this case, the motor home was parked in an off-the-street lot only a few blocks from the courthouse in downtown San Diego where dozens of magistrates were available to entertain a warrant application.[16] The officers clearly had the element of surprise with them, and with curtains covering the windshield, the motor home offered no indication of any imminent departure. The officers plainly had probable cause to arrest the petitioner and search the motor home, and on this record, it is inexplicable why they eschewed the safe harbor of a warrant.

In the absence of any evidence of exigency in the circumstances of this case, the

15. In *Coolidge v. New Hampshire,* 403 U.S. 443, 91 S.Ct. 2045, 99 L.Ed.2d 564 (1971), a plurality refused to apply the automobile exception to an automobile that was seized while parked in the driveway of the suspect's house, towed to a secure police compound, and later searched:

"The word 'automobile' is not a talisman in whose presence the Fourth Amendment fades away and disappears. And surely there is nothing in this case to invoke the meaning and purpose of the rule of *Carroll v. United States*—no alerted criminal bent on flight, no fleeting opportunity on an open highway after a hazardous chase, no contraband or stolen goods or weapons, no confederates waiting to move the evidence, not even the inconvenience of a special police detail to guard the immobilized automobile. In short, by no possible stretch of the legal imagination can this be made into a case where 'it is not practicable to secure a warrant,' and the 'automobile exception' despite its label, is simply irrelevant." (opinion of Stewart, J., joined by Douglas, Brennan and Marshall, JJ.).

In *Cardwell v. Lewis,* 417 U.S. 583, 94 S.Ct. 2464, 41 L.Ed.2d 325 (1974), a different plurality approved the seizure of an automobile from a public parking lot, and a later examination of its exterior. (opinion of Blackmun, J.). Here, of course, we are concerned with the reasonableness of the search, not the seizure. Even if the diminished expectations of privacy associated with an automobile justify the warrantless search of a parked automobile notwithstanding the diminished exigency, the heightened expectations of privacy in the interior of motor home require a different result.

16. In addition, a telephonic warrant was only 20 cents and the nearest phone booth away.

Court relies on the inherent mobility of the motor home to create a conclusive presumption of exigency. This Court, however, has squarely held that mobility of the place to be searched is not a sufficient justification for abandoning the warrant requirement. In *United States v. Chadwick,* 433 U.S. 1, 97 S.Ct. 2476, 53 L.Ed. 2d 538 (1977), the Court held that a warrantless search of a footlocker violated the Fourth Amendment even though there was ample probable cause to believe it contained contraband. The Government had argued that the rationale of the automobile exception applied to movable containers in general, and that the warrant requirement should be limited to searches of homes and other "core" areas of privacy. We categorically rejected the Government's argument observing that there are greater privacy interests associated with containers than with automobiles, and that there are less practical problems associated with the temporary detention of a container than with the detention of an automobile.

We again endorsed that analysis in *Ross.* * * * It is perfectly obvious that the citizen has a much greater expectation of privacy concerning the interior of a mobile home than of a piece of luggage such as a footlocker. If "inherent mobility" does not justify warrantless searches of containers, it cannot rationally provide a sufficient justification for the search of a person's dwelling place.

Unlike a brick bungalow or a frame Victorian, a motor home seldom serves as a permanent lifetime abode. The motor home in this case, however, was designed to accommodate a breadth of ordinary everyday living. Photographs in the record indicate that its height, length and beam provided substantial living space inside: stuffed chairs surround a table; cupboards provide room for storage of personal effects; bunk-beds provide sleeping space; and a refrigerator provides ample space for food and beverages. Moreover, curtains and large opaque walls inhibit viewing the activities inside from the exterior of the vehicle. The interior configuration of the motor home establishes that the vehicle's size, shape, and mode of construction should have indicated to the officers that it was a vehicle containing mobile living quarters.

The State contends that officers in the field will have an impossible task determining whether or not other vehicles contain mobile living quarters. It is not necessary for the Court to resolve every unanswered question in this area in a single case, but common English usage suggests that we already distinguish between a "motor home" which is "equipped as a self-contained traveling home," a "camper" which is only equipped for "casual travel and camping," and an automobile which is "designed for passenger transportation." Surely the exteriors of these vehicles contain clues about their different functions which could alert officers in the field to the necessity of a warrant.[21] * * *

In my opinion, searches of places that regularly accommodate a wide range of private human activity are fundamentally different from searches of automobiles which primarily serve a public transportation function. Although it may not be a castle, a motor home is usually the functional equivalent of a hotel room, a vacation and retirement home, or a hunting and fishing cabin. These places may be as spartan as a humble cottage when compared to the most majestic mansion, but the highest and most legitimate expectations of privacy associated with these temporary abodes should command the re-

21. In refusing to extend the California Supreme Court's decision in *Carney* beyond its context, the California Courts of Appeals have had no difficulty in distinguishing the motor home involved there from a Ford van and a cab-high camper shell on the back of a pick-up truck. There is no reason to believe that trained officers could not make similar distinctions between different vehicles, especially when state vehicle laws already require them to do so.

spect of this Court. In my opinion, a warrantless search of living quarters in a motor home is "presumptively unreasonable absent exigent circumstances."

I respectfully dissent.

Notes and Questions

1. As the Court's earlier cases make clear, the "ready mobility" language in *Carney* does *not* refer to the actual likelihood that the vehicle would be moved if a search warrant were sought. In *Chambers v. Maroney,* police stopped a station wagon on probable cause the occupants had just committed a robbery; the occupants were arrested and the car was driven to the police station, where a thorough search revealed a revolver under the dashboard and other evidence. Although Harlan, J., dissenting, reasoned that there was no need for a warrantless search because the car could simply be held in police custody until a warrant was obtained, the majority, per White, J., responded with this syllogism: (i) "the blue station wagon could have been searched on the spot when it was stopped since there was probable cause to search and it was a fleeting target for a search"; (ii) it "was not unreasonable * * * to take the car to the station house," as the arrests were made "in a dark parking lot in the middle of the night"; (iii) once the car was at the station, "there is little to choose in terms of practical consequences between an immediate search without a warrant and the car's immobilization until a warrant is obtained." But in *Texas v. White,* 423 U.S. 67, 96 S.Ct. 304, 46 L.Ed.2d 209 (1975), *Chambers* was deemed applicable to an at-the-station vehicle search though, as the two dissenters noted, "the arrest took place at 1:30 in the afternoon, and there is no indication that an immediate search would have been either impractical or unsafe for the arresting officers."

Consider also *Colorado v. Bannister,* 449 U.S. 1, 101 S.Ct. 42, 66 L.Ed.2d 1 (1980) (unanimous Court concludes that where probable cause to search developed after the car was stopped for a traffic violation, "it would be especially unreasonable to require a detour to a magistrate before the unanticipated evidence could be lawfully seized"); *Michigan v. Thomas,* 458 U.S. 259, 102 S.Ct. 3079, 73 L.Ed.2d 750 (1982) (Court stresses that "the justification to conduct such a warrantless search does not vanish once the car has been immobilized; nor does it depend upon a reviewing court's assessment of the likelihood in each particular case that the car would have been driven away, or that its contents would have been tampered with, during the period required for the police to obtain a warrant"); *Florida v. Meyers,* 466 U.S. 380, 104 S.Ct. 1852, 80 L.Ed.2d 381 (1984) (Court holds on authority of *Thomas* that lower court erred in concluding warrantless search of car improper where, as here, the car had been impounded eight hours earlier and was presently stored in a secure area).

2. In *Chambers* the Court stated that what is required, even if no warrant need first be obtained, is "probable cause to search a particular auto for particular articles." Consider the following cases, both holding that the facts stated justified a warrantless search of the car under *Chambers: United States v. Jones,* 452 F.2d 884 (8th Cir.1971) (defendant was stopped after he made illegal turn and ran red light while driving car without plates, as officer approached he saw defendant tear paper into small pieces and push them between seat and back cushions, defendant was arrested and placed in squad car after he displayed driver's license of another person, officer then retrieved the pieces of paper, which turned out to be stolen welfare check); *People v. Hering,* 327 N.E.2d 583 (Ill.App.1975) (trooper stopped car because one headlight out, as he was writing ticket defendant drove off and, when overtaken, could not explain why he did so, trooper then searched the car).

Compare *United States v. Coleman,* 322 F.Supp. 550 (E.D.Pa.1971) (officer checking out two suspicious persons obtained consent to look in trunk of car owned by one of them and found a gun, after which the two were arrested; later a detective came to scene of arrests and searched the car and seized a revolver, two ski masks and two shopping bags; held, evidence suppressed: "Knowing all this, we have no idea what [the detective] reasonably expected to find inside the car other than its interior").

3. The probable cause to search must also be assessed in order to ascertain whether an otherwise lawful warrantless search of a vehicle was properly limited in scope and intensity, as is illustrated by *Maldonado v. State,* 528 S.W.2d 234 (Tex. Crim.1975) (truck searched on probable cause it was stolen, officers pulled up flooring and found false compartment containing 650 packages of marijuana; held, that part of search illegal because it "could not reasonably be expected that evidence of theft might be uncovered by these means"); *Wimberly v. Superior Court,* 547 P.2d 417 (Cal.1976) (after vehicle stopped for traffic violation, officer saw pipe and 12 marijuana seeds on floor and smelled odor of marijuana, passenger compartment was searched and bag with very small amount of marijuana was found in jacket pocket, trunk of car then searched and several pounds of marijuana found there; held, latter search illegal, as police had probable cause occupants of car were occasional users rather than dealers, and thus "it was not reasonable to infer that petitioners had additional contraband hidden in the trunk").

4. Assuming grounds to make a warrantless search of a car, but the absence of grounds to arrest some occupant of the car, may that occupant also be searched if the items sought are of such a nature that they could be concealed on his person? No, the Supreme Court held in *United States v. DiRe* [p. 299 supra]. However, *Model Pre-Arraignment Code* § SS 260.3 provides otherwise (except as to passengers in a common carrier) if the officer has not found the items sought in the vehicle and has "reason to suspect that one or more of the occupants of the vehicle may have the things subject to seizure so concealed." The Reporters argue that "it seems absurd to say that the occupants can take the narcotics out of the glove compartment and stuff them in their pockets, and drive happily away after the vehicle has been fruitlessly searched." Can that position be squared with *Ybarra v. Illinois,* p. 293 supra?

UNITED STATES v. ROSS

456 U.S. 798, 102 S.Ct. 2157, 72 L.Ed.2d 572 (1982).

JUSTICE STEVENS delivered the opinion of the Court. * * *

[On the basis of information from an informant that Ross had just made a narcotics sale and had more drugs in the trunk of his car, police stopped the vehicle and, after arresting Ross, located a closed paper bag in the trunk which upon examination was found to contain heroin. At the station, after a more thorough search of the car, a zippered leather pouch was also found in the trunk, and it was opened and $3,200 in cash was discovered therein. Ross moved to suppress the heroin and money, but the motion was denied and he was convicted of possession of heroin with intent to distribute. A panel of the court of appeals held that the police had probable cause to search the car and that under *Chambers* no search warrant was needed, but then concluded that a warrantless search may not extend to a container in the car when the owner has a reasonable expectation of privacy in its contents, which was deemed to be the case as to the pouch but not as to the paper bag. On rehearing en banc, the court rejected the conclusion that a distinction of constitutional significance existed between the two containers and held the police should not have opened either of them without a warrant.]

We begin with a review of the decision in *Carroll* itself. * * *

The Court explained at length the basis for [the automobile exception]. The Court noted that historically warrantless searches of vessels, wagons, and carriages—as opposed to fixed premises such as a home or other building—had been considered reasonable by Congress. * * *

Thus, since its earliest days Congress had recognized the impracticability of securing a warrant in cases involving the transportation of contraband goods. It is this impracticability, viewed in historical perspective, that provided the basis for the *Carroll* decision. Given the nature of an automobile in transit, the Court recognized that an immediate intrusion is necessary if police officers are to secure the illicit substance. In this class of cases, the Court held that a warrantless search of an automobile is not unreasonable. * * *

The rationale justifying a warrantless search of an automobile that is believed to be transporting contraband arguably applies with equal force to any movable container that is believed to be carrying an illicit substance. That argument, however, was squarely rejected in *United States v. Chadwick,* 433 U.S. 1, 97 S.Ct. 2476, 53 L.Ed.2d 538 (1977).

Chadwick involved the warrantless search of a 200-pound footlocker secured with two padlocks. Federal railroad officials in San Diego became suspicious when they noticed that a brown footlocker loaded onto a train bound for Boston was unusually heavy and leaking talcum powder, a substance often used to mask the odor of marijuana. Narcotics agents met the train in Boston and a trained police dog signaled the presence of a controlled substance inside the footlocker. The agents did not seize the footlocker, however, at this time; they waited until respondent Chadwick arrived and the footlocker was placed in the trunk of Chadwick's automobile. Before the engine was started, the officers arrested Chadwick and his two companions. The agents then removed the footlocker to a secured place, opened it without a warrant, and discovered a large quantity of marijuana.

In a subsequent criminal proceeding, Chadwick claimed that the warrantless search of the footlocker violated the Fourth Amendment. In the District Court, the Government argued that as soon as the footlocker was placed in the automobile a warrantless search was permissible under *Carroll.* The District Court rejected that argument, and the Government did not pursue it on appeal. Rather, the Government contended in this Court that the warrant requirement of the Fourth Amendment applied only to searches of homes and other "core" areas of privacy. The Court unanimously rejected that contention. Writing for the Court, The Chief Justice stated:

> "[I]f there is little evidence that the Framers intended the Warrant Clause to operate outside the home, there is no evidence at all that they intended to exclude from protection of the Clause all searches occurring outside the home. The absence of a contemporary outcry against warrantless searches in public places was because, aside from searches incident to arrest, such warrantless searches were not a large issue in colonial America. Thus, silence in the historical record tells us little about the Framers' attitude toward application of the Warrant Clause to the search of respondents' footlocker. What we do know is that the Framers were men who focused on the wrongs of that day but who intended the Fourth Amendment to safeguard fundamental values which would far outlast the specific abuses which gave it birth."

The Court in *Chadwick* specifically rejected the argument that the warrantless search was "reasonable" because a footlocker has some of the mobile characteristics that support warrantless searches of automobiles. The Court recognized that "a person's expectations of privacy in personal luggage are substantially greater than in an automobile," and noted that the practical problems associated with the temporary detention of a piece of luggage during the period of time necessary to obtain a warrant are significantly less than those associated with the detention of an automobile. In ruling that the warrantless search of the footlocker was unjustified, the Court reaffirmed the general principle that closed packages and containers may not be searched without a warrant. In sum, the Court in *Chadwick* declined to extend the rationale of the "automobile exception" to permit a warrantless search of any movable container found in a public place.[16]

The facts in *Arkansas v. Sanders,* 442 U.S. 753, 99 S.Ct. 2586, 61 L.Ed.2d 235 (1979), were similar to those in *Chadwick.* In *Sanders,* a Little Rock police officer received information from a reliable informant that Sanders would arrive at the local airport on a specified flight that afternoon carrying a green suitcase containing marijuana. The officer went to the airport. Sanders arrived on schedule and retrieved a green suitcase from the airline baggage service. Sanders gave the suitcase to a waiting companion who placed it in the trunk of a taxi. Sanders and his companion drove off in the cab; police officers followed and stopped the taxi several blocks from the airport. The officers opened the trunk, seized the suitcase, and searched it on the scene without a warrant. As predicted, the suitcase contained marijuana.

The Arkansas Supreme Court ruled that the warrantless search of the suitcase was impermissible under the Fourth Amendment, and this Court affirmed. As in *Chadwick,* the mere fact that the suitcase had been placed in the trunk of the vehicle did not render the automobile exception of *Carroll* applicable; the police had probable cause to seize the suitcase before it was placed in the trunk of the cab and did not have probable cause to search the taxi itself. Since the suitcase had been placed in the trunk, no danger existed that its contents could have been secreted elsewhere in the vehicle. As The Chief Justice noted in his opinion concurring in the judgment:

> "Because the police officers had probable cause to believe that respondent's green suitcase contained marijuana before it was placed in the trunk of the taxicab, their duty to obtain a search warrant before opening it is clear under *United States v. Chadwick.*
>
> * * *
>
> Here, as in *Chadwick,* it was the *luggage* being transported by respondent at the time of the arrest, not the automobile in which it was being carried, that was the suspected locus of the contraband. The relationship between the automobile and the contraband was purely coincidental, as in *Chadwick.* The fact that the suitcase was resting in the trunk of the automobile at the time of respondent's arrest does not turn this into an 'automobile' exception case. The Court need say no more."

The Court in *Sanders* did not, however, rest its decision solely on the authority of *Chadwick.* In rejecting the State's argument that the warrantless search of the suitcase was justified on the ground that it had been taken from an automobile lawfully stopped on the street, the Court broadly suggested that a warrantless search of a container found in an automobile could never be sustained as part of a warrantless

16. The Court concluded that there is a significant difference between the seizure of a sealed package and a subsequent search of its contents; the search of the container in that case was "a far greater intrusion into Fourth Amendment values than the impoundment of the footlocker." A temporary seizure of a package or piece of luggage often may be accomplished without as significant an intrusion upon the individual—and without as great a burden on the police—as in the case of the seizure of an automobile.

search of the automobile itself.[19] The Court did not suggest that it mattered whether probable cause existed to search the entire vehicle. It is clear, however, that in neither *Chadwick* nor *Sanders* did the police have probable cause to search the vehicle or anything within it except the footlocker in the former case and the green suitcase in the latter.

Robbins v. California, 453 U.S. 420, 101 S.Ct. 2841, 69 L.Ed.2d 744 (1981), however, was a case in which suspicion was not directed at a specific container. In that case the Court for the first time was forced to consider whether police officers who are entitled to conduct a warrantless search of an automobile stopped on a public roadway may open a container found within the vehicle. In the early morning of January 5, 1975, police officers stopped Robbins' station wagon because he was driving erratically. Robbins got out of the car, but later returned to obtain the vehicle's registration papers. When he opened the car door, the officers smelled marijuana smoke. One of the officers searched Robbins and discovered a vial of liquid; in a search of the interior of the car the officer found marijuana. The police officers then opened the tailgate of the station wagon and raised the cover of a recessed luggage compartment. In the compartment they found two packages wrapped in green opaque plastic. The police unwrapped the packages and discovered a large amount of marijuana in each.

Robbins was charged with various drug offenses and moved to suppress the contents of the plastic packages. The California Court of Appeal held that "[s]earch of the automobile was proper when the officers learned that appellant was smoking marijuana when they stopped him" and that the warrantless search of the packages was justified because "the contents of the packages could have been inferred from their outward appearance, so that appellant could not have held a reasonable expectation of privacy with respect to the contents."

This Court reversed. Writing for a plurality, Justice Stewart rejected the argument that the outward appearance of the packages precluded Robbins from having a reasonable expectation of privacy in their contents. He also squarely rejected the argument that there is a constitutional distinction between searches of luggage and searches of "less worthy" containers. Justice Stewart reasoned that all containers are equally protected by the Fourth Amendment unless their contents are in plain view. The plurality concluded that the warrantless search was impermissible because *Chadwick* and *Sanders* had established that "a closed piece of luggage found in a lawfully searched car is constitutionally protected to the same extent as are closed pieces of luggage found anywhere else."

In a concurring opinion Justice Powell, the author of the Court's opinion in *Sanders,* stated that "[t]he plurality's approach strains the rationales of our prior cases and imposes substantial burdens on law enforcement without vindicating any significant values of privacy."[21] He noted that possibly "the controlling question should

19. The Court stated that "the extent to which the Fourth Amendment applies to containers and other parcels depends not at all upon whether they are seized from an automobile." This general rule was limited only by the observation that "[n]ot all containers and packages found by police during the course of a search will deserve the full protection of the Fourth Amendment. Thus, some containers (for example a kit of burglar tools or a gun case) by their very nature cannot support any reasonable expectation of privacy because their contents can be inferred from their outward appearance. Similarly, in some cases the contents of a package will be open to 'plain view,' thereby obviating the need for a warrant."

21. "While the plurality's blanket warrant requirement does not even purport to protect any privacy interest, it would impose substantial new burdens on law enforcement. Confronted with a cigar box or a Dixie cup in the course of a probable cause search of an automobile for narcotics, the conscientious policeman would be required to take the object to a magistrate, fill out the appropriate forms, await the decision, and be the scope of the automobile exception to the warrant requirement," and explained that under that view

> "when the police have probable cause to search an automobile, rather than only to search a particular container that fortuitously is located in it, the exigencies that allow the police to search the entire automobile without a warrant support the warrantless search of every container found therein. This analysis is entirely consistent with the holdings in *Chadwick* and *Sanders,* neither of which is an 'automobile case,' because the police there had probable cause to search the double-locked footlocker and the suitcase respectively before either came near an automobile."

The parties in *Robbins* had not pressed that argument, however, and Justice Powell concluded that institutional constraints made it inappropriate to re-examine basic doctrine without full adversary presentation. He concurred in the judgment, since it was supported—although not compelled—by the Court's opinion in *Sanders,* and stated that a future case might present a better opportunity for thorough consideration of the basic principles in this troubled area.

That case has arrived. Unlike *Chadwick* and *Sanders,* in this case police officers had probable cause to search respondent's entire vehicle. Unlike *Robbins,* in this case the parties have squarely addressed the question whether, in the course of a legitimate warrantless search of an automobile, police are entitled to open containers found within the vehicle. We now address that question. Its answer is determined by the scope of the search that is authorized by the exception to the warrant requirement set forth in *Carroll.*

In *Carroll* itself, the whiskey that the prohibition agents seized was not in plain view. It was discovered only after an officer opened the rumble seat and tore open the upholstery of the lazyback. The Court did not find the scope of the search unreasonable. Having stopped Carroll and Kiro on a public road and subjected them to the indignity of a vehicle search—which the Court found to be a reasonable intrusion on their privacy because it was based on probable cause that their vehicle was transporting contraband—prohibition agents were entitled to tear open a portion of the roadster itself. The scope of the search was no greater than a magistrate could have authorized by issuing a warrant based on the probable cause that justified the search. Since such a warrant could have authorized the agents to open the rear portion of the roadster and to rip the upholstery in their search for concealed whiskey, the search was constitutionally permissible.

In *Chambers v. Maroney* the police found weapons and stolen property "concealed in a compartment under the dashboard." No suggestion was made that the scope of the search was impermissible. It would be illogical to assume that the outcome of *Chambers* —or the outcome of *Carroll* itself—would have been different if the police had found the secreted contraband enclosed within a secondary container and had opened that container without a warrant. If it was reasonable for prohibition agents to rip open the upholstery in *Carroll,* it certainly would have been reasona-

finally obtain a warrant. Suspects or vehicles normally will be detained while the warrant is sought. This process may take hours removing the officer from his normal police duties. Expenditure of such time and effort, drawn from the public's limited resources for detecting or preventing crimes, is justified when it protects an individual's reasonable privacy interests. In my view, the plurality's requirement cannot be so justified. The aggregate burden of procuring warrants whenever an officer has probable cause to search the most trivial container may be heavy and will not be compensated by the advancement of important Fourth Amendment values."

The substantial burdens on law enforcement identified by Justice Powell would, of course, not be affected by the character of the container found during an automobile search. No comparable practical problems arise when the official suspicion is confined to a particular piece of luggage, as in *Chadwick* and *Sanders.*

ble for them to look into a burlap sack stashed inside; if it was reasonable to open the concealed compartment in *Chambers,* it would have been equally reasonable to open a paper bag crumpled within it. A contrary rule could produce absurd results inconsistent with the decision in *Carroll* itself.

In its application of *Carroll,* this Court in fact has sustained warrantless searches of containers found during a lawful search of an automobile. In *Husty v. United States,* 282 U.S. 694, 51 S.Ct. 240, 75 L.Ed. 629 (1931), the Court upheld a warrantless seizure of whiskey found during a search of an automobile, some of which was discovered in "whiskey bags" that could have contained other goods. In *Scher v. United States,* 305 U.S. 251, 59 S.Ct. 174, 83 L.Ed. 151 (1938), federal officers seized and searched packages of unstamped liquor found in the trunk of an automobile searched without a warrant. As described by a police officer who participated in the search: "I turned the handle and opened the trunk and found the trunk completely filled with packages wrapped in brown paper, and tied with twine; I think somewhere around thirty packages, each one containing six bottles." In these cases it was not contended that police officers needed a warrant to open the whiskey bags or to unwrap the brown paper packages. These decisions nevertheless "have much weight, as they show that this point neither occurred to the bar or the bench." The fact that no such argument was even made illuminates the profession's understanding of the scope of the search permitted under *Carroll.* Indeed, prior to the decisions in *Chadwick* and *Sanders,* courts routinely had held that containers and packages found during a legitimate warrantless search of an automobile also could be searched without a warrant.

As we have stated, the decision in *Carroll* was based on the Court's appraisal of practical considerations viewed in the perspective of history. It is therefore significant that the practical consequences of the *Carroll* decision would be largely nullified if the permissible scope of a warrantless search of an automobile did not include containers and packages found inside the vehicle. Contraband goods rarely are strewn across the trunk or floor of a car; since by their very nature such goods must be withheld from public view, they rarely can be placed in an automobile unless they are enclosed within some form of container. The Court in *Carroll* held that "contraband goods *concealed* and illegally transported in an automobile or other vehicle may be searched for without a warrant." As we [later] noted, the decision in *Carroll* "merely relaxed the requirements for a warrant on grounds of impracticability." It neither broadened nor limited the scope of a lawful search based on probable cause.

A lawful search of fixed premises generally extends to the entire area in which the object of the search may be found and is not limited by the possibility that separate acts of entry or opening may be required to complete the search. Thus, a warrant that authorizes an officer to search a home for illegal weapons also provides authority to open closets, chests, drawers, and containers in which the weapon might be found. A warrant to open a footlocker to search for marijuana would also authorize the opening of packages found inside. A warrant to search a vehicle would support a search of every part of the vehicle that might contain the object of the search. When a legitimate search is under way, and when its purpose and its limits have been precisely defined, nice distinctions between closets, drawers, and containers, in the case of a home, or between glove compartments, upholstered seats, trunks, and wrapped packages, in the case of a vehicle, must give way to the interest in the prompt and efficient completion of the task at hand.[28]

28. The practical considerations that justify a warrantless search of an automobile continue to apply until the entire search of the automobile and its contents has been completed. Arguably,

This rule applies equally to all containers, as indeed we believe it must. One point on which the Court was in virtually unanimous agreement in *Robbins* was that a constitutional distinction between "worthy" and "unworthy" containers would be improper. Even though such a distinction perhaps could evolve in a series of cases in which paper bags, locked trunks, lunch buckets, and orange crates were placed on one side of the line or the other,[30] the central purpose of the Fourth Amendment forecloses such a distinction. For just as the most frail cottage in the kingdom is absolutely entitled to the same guarantees of privacy as the most majestic mansion, so also may a traveler who carries a toothbrush and a few articles of clothing in a paper bag or knotted scarf claim an equal right to conceal his possessions from official inspection as the sophisticated executive with the locked attaché case.

[A]n individual's expectation of privacy in a vehicle and its contents may not survive if probable cause is given to believe that the vehicle is transporting contraband. Certainly the privacy interests in a car's trunk or glove compartment may be no less than those in a movable container. An individual undoubtedly has a significant interest that the upholstery of his automobile will not be ripped or a hidden compartment within it opened. These interests must yield to the authority of a search, however, which—in light of *Carroll*—does not itself require the prior approval of a magistrate. The scope of a warrantless search based on probable cause is no narrower—and no broader—than the scope of a search authorized by a warrant supported by probable cause. Only the prior approval of the magistrate is waived; the search otherwise is as the magistrate could authorize.

The scope of a warrantless search of an automobile thus is not defined by the nature of the container in which the contraband is secreted. Rather, it is defined by the object of the search and the places in which there is probable cause to believe that it may be found. Just as probable cause to believe that a stolen lawnmower may be found in a garage will not support a warrant to search an upstairs bedroom, probable cause to believe that undocumented aliens are being transported in a van will not justify a warrantless search of a suitcase. Probable cause to believe that a container placed in the trunk of a taxi contains contraband or evidence does not justify a search of the entire cab.

* * * We hold that the scope of the warrantless search authorized by [the automobile] exception is no broader and no narrower than a magistrate could legitimately authorize by warrant. If probable cause justifies the search of a lawfully stopped vehicle, it justifies the search of every part of the vehicle and its contents that may conceal the object of the search.

* * *

JUSTICE BLACKMUN, concurring.

My dissents in prior cases have indicated my continuing dissatisfaction and discontent with the rationale supporting the decisions in *Carroll* and *Chambers*.

the entire vehicle itself (including its upholstery) could be searched without a warrant, with all wrapped articles and containers found during that search then taken to a magistrate. But prohibiting police from opening immediately a container in which the object of the search is most likely to be found and instead forcing them first to comb the entire vehicle would actually exacerbate the intrusion on privacy interests. Moreover, until the container itself was opened the police could never be certain that the contraband was not secreted in a yet undiscovered portion of the vehicle; thus in every case in which a container was found, the vehicle would need to be secured while a warrant was obtained. Such a requirement would be directly inconsis-

30. If the distinction is based on the proposition that the Fourth Amendment protects only those containers that objectively manifest an individual's reasonable expectation of privacy, however, the propriety of a warrantless search necessarily would turn on much more than the fabric of the container. A paper bag stapled shut and marked "private" might be found to manifest a reasonable expectation of privacy, as could a cardboard box stacked on top of two pieces of heavy luggage. The propriety of the warrantless search seemingly would turn on an objective appraisal of all the surrounding circumstances.

fort with the Court's vacillation in what is rightly described as "this troubled area."

I adhere to the views expressed in those dissents. * * * In order to have an authoritative ruling, I join the Court's opinion and judgment.

JUSTICE POWELL, concurring.

* * * It is fair also to say that, given *Carroll v. United States* and *Chambers v. Maroney,* the Court's decision does not depart substantially from Fourth Amendment doctrine in automobile cases. Moreover, in enunciating a readily understood and applied rule, today's decision is consistent with the similar step taken last Term in *New York v. Belton* [p. 349 infra].

I join the Court's opinion.

JUSTICE WHITE, dissenting:

I would not overrule *Robbins v. California.* For the reasons stated by Justice Stewart in that case, I would affirm the judgment of the Court of Appeals. I also agree with much of Justice Marshall's dissent in this case.

JUSTICE MARSHALL, with whom JUSTICE BRENNAN joins, dissenting.

* * *

Our cases do recognize a narrow exception to the warrant requirement for certain automobile searches. Throughout our decisions, two major considerations have been advanced to justify the automobile exception to the warrant requirement. We have upheld only those searches that are actually justified by those considerations.

First, these searches have been justified on the basis of the exigency of the mobility of the automobile. This "mobility" rationale is something of a misnomer, since the police ordinarily can remove the car's occupants and secure the vehicle on the spot. However, the inherent mobility of the vehicle often creates situations in which the police's only alternative to an immediate search may be to release the automobile from their possession.[2] This alternative creates an unacceptably high risk of losing the contents of the vehicle, and is a principal basis for the Court's automobile exception to the warrant requirement.

In many cases, however, the police will, prior to searching the car, have cause to arrest the occupants and bring them to the station for booking. In this situation, the police can ordinarily seize the automobile and bring it to the station. Because the vehicle is now in the exclusive control of the authorities, any subsequent search cannot be justified by the mobility of the car. Rather, an immediate warrantless search of the vehicle is permitted because of the second major justification for the automobile exception: the diminished expectation of privacy in an automobile.

* * * By focusing on the defendant's reasonable expectation of privacy, this Court has refused to require a warrant in situations where the process of obtaining such a warrant would be more intrusive than the actual search itself. A defendant may consider the seizure of the car a greater intrusion than an immediate search. Therefore, even where police *can* bring both the defendants and the automobile to the station safely and can house the car while they seek a warrant, the police are permitted to decide whether instead to conduct an immediate search of the car. In effect, the warrantless search is permissible because a warrant requirement would not provide significant protection of the defendant's Fourth Amendment interests.

The majority's rule is flatly inconsistent with these established Fourth Amendment principles * * *.

The practical mobility problem—deciding what to do with both the car and the

2. The fact that the police are able initially to remove the occupants from the car does not remove the justification for an immediate search. If police could not conduct an immediate search of a stopped automobile, they would often be left with the difficult task of deciding what to do with the occupants while a warrant is obtained. In the case of a parked automobile, by contrast, if the automobile is unoccupied, this problem is not presented.

occupants if an immediate search is not conducted—is simply not present in the case of movable containers, which can easily be seized and brought to the magistrate. The lesser expectation of privacy rationale also has little force. A container, as opposed to the car itself, does not reflect diminished privacy interests. Moreover, the practical corollary that this Court has recognized—that depriving occupants of the use of a car may be a greater intrusion than an immediate search—is of doubtful relevance here, since the owner of a container will rarely suffer significant inconvenience by being deprived of its use while a warrant is being obtained. * * *

Here, because appellant Ross had placed the evidence in question in a closed paper bag, the container could be seized, but not searched, without a warrant. No practical exigencies required the warrantless searches on the street or at the station: Ross had been arrested and was in custody when both searches occurred, and the police succeeded in transporting the bag to the station without inadvertently spilling its contents. * * *

[T]he Court's argument that allowing warrantless searches of certain integral compartments of the car in *Carroll* and *Chambers,* while protecting movable containers within the car, would be "illogical" and "absurd," ignores the reason why this Court has allowed warrantless searches of automobile compartments. Surely an integral compartment within a car is just as mobile, and presents the same practical problems of safekeeping, as the car itself. This cannot be said of movable containers located within the car. The fact that there may be a high expectation of privacy in both containers and compartments is irrelevant, since the privacy rationale is not, and cannot be, the justification for the warrantless search of compartments.

The Court's second argument, which focuses on the practical advantages to police of the *Carroll* doctrine, fares no better. The practical considerations which concerned the *Carroll* Court involved the difficulty of immobilizing a vehicle while a warrant must be obtained. The Court had no occasion to address whether *containers* present the same practical difficulties as the car itself or integral compartments of the car. They do not. *Carroll* hardly suggested, as the Court implies, that a warrantless search is justified simply because it assists police in obtaining more evidence.

Although it can find no support for its rule in this Court's precedents or in the traditional justifications for the automobile exception, the majority offers another justification. In a footnote [28], the majority suggests that "practical considerations" militate against securing containers found during an automobile search and taking them to the magistrate. * * *

This explanation is unpersuasive. As this Court explained in *Sanders* and as the majority today implicitly concedes, the burden to police departments of seizing a package or personal luggage simply does not compare to the burden of seizing and safeguarding automobiles. Other aspects of the Court's explanation are also implausible. The search will not always require a "combing" of the entire vehicle, since police may be looking for a particular item and may discover it promptly. If, instead, they are looking more generally for evidence of a crime, the immediate opening of the container will not protect the defendant's privacy; whether or not it contains contraband, the police will continue to search for new evidence. Finally, the defendant, not the police, should be afforded the choice whether he prefers the immediate opening of his suitcase or other container to the delay incident to seeking a warrant. The more reasonable presumption, if a presumption is to replace the defendant's consent, is surely that the immediate search of a closed container will be a greater invasion of the defendant's privacy interests than a mere temporary seizure of the container.

Finally, the majority's new rule is theoretically unsound and will create anomalous and unwarranted results. These consequences are readily apparent from the Court's attempt to reconcile its new rule with the holdings of *Chadwick* and *Sanders.* The Court suggests that probable cause to search only a container does not justify a warrantless search of an automobile in which it is placed, absent reason to believe that the contents could be secreted elsewhere in the vehicle. This, the majority asserts, is an indication that the new rule is carefully limited to its justification, and is not inconsistent with *Chadwick* and *Sanders.* But why is such a container more private, less difficult for police to seize and store, or in any other relevant respect more properly subject to the warrant requirement, than a container that police discover in a probable cause search of an entire automobile? [10] This rule plainly has peculiar and unworkable consequences: the Government "must show that the investigating officer knew enough but not too much, that he had sufficient knowledge to establish probable cause but insufficient knowledge to know exactly where the contraband was located."

Alternatively, the majority may be suggesting that *Chadwick* and *Sanders* may be explained because the connection of the container to the vehicle was incidental in these two cases. That is, because police had preexisting probable cause to seize and search the containers, they were not entitled to wait until the item was placed in a vehicle to take advantage of the automobile exception. I wholeheartedly agree that police cannot employ a pretext to escape Fourth Amendment prohibitions and cannot rely on an exigency that they could easily have avoided. This interpretation, however, might well be an exception that swallows up the majority's rule. In neither *Chadwick* nor *Sanders* did the Court suggest that the delay of the police was a pretext for taking advantage of the automobile exception. For all that appears, the Government may have had legitimate reasons for not searching as soon as they had probable cause. In any event, asking police to rely on such an uncertain line in distinguishing between legitimate and illegitimate searches for containers in automobiles hardly indicates that the majority's approach has brought clarification to this area of the law.[11]

Notes and Questions [a]

1. In TEXAS v. BROWN, 460 U.S. 730, 103 S.Ct. 1535, 75 L.Ed.2d 502 (1983), after a car stopped at a routine driver's license checkpoint, an officer

10. In a footnote, the Court appears to suggest a more pragmatic rationale for distinguishing *Chadwick* and *Sanders*—that no practical problems comparable to those engendered by a general search of a vehicle would arise if the official suspicion is confined to a particular piece of luggage. This suggestion is illogical. A general search might disclose only a single item worth searching; conversely, pre-existing suspicion might attach to a number of items later placed in a car. Surely the protection of the warrant requirement cannot depend on a numerical count of the items subject to search.

11. Unless one of these alternative explanations is adopted, the Court's attempt to distinguish the holdings in *Chadwick* and *Sanders* is not only unpersuasive but appears to contradict the Court's own theory. The Court suggests that in each case, the connection of the container to the vehicle was simply coincidental, and notes that the police did not have probable cause to search the entire vehicle. But the police assuredly did have probable cause to search the vehicle *for the container.* The Court states that the scope of the permitted warrantless search is determined only by what a magistrate could authorize. Once police found that container, according to the Court's own rule, they should have been entitled to search at least the container without a warrant. There was probable cause to search and the car was mobile in each case.

a. For a close examination of *Ross,* see Gardner, *Searches and Seizures of Automobiles and Their Contents: Fourth Amendment Considerations in a Post-Ross World,* 62 Neb.L.Rev. 1 (1983); L. Katz, *United States v. Ross: Evolving Standards for Warrantless Searches,* 74 J.Crim.L. & C. 172 (1983). Professor Katz voices concern that the *Ross* decision may evolve into a "public place-probable cause exception to the warrant requirement." "Ultimately," he maintains, "only the legal fiction surrounding automobiles allows police to conduct warrantless searches of containers found in vehicles but requires a warrant when the container is seized elsewhere."

shined a flashlight into the car and saw in the driver's hand an opaque party balloon knotted about one-half inch from the tip. The officer, aware narcotics were frequently packaged in such balloons, also saw several plastic vials, a quantity of loose white powder, and an open bag of balloons in the glove compartment. The officer then ordered the driver out of the car, seized the balloon and noted a powdery substance within the tied-off portion, and arrested the driver. A police chemist later examined the balloon's contents without a warrant and determined that it contained heroin.

A four-Justice plurality, per REHNQUIST, J., concluded that the police action in seizing and searching the balloon was authorized under the plain view doctrine of *Coolidge v. New Hampshire,* p. 296 supra, as (i) the officer was lawfully positioned when he saw the balloon; (ii) the officer had probable cause that the balloon contained an illicit substance; and (iii) the discovery of the drugs was "inadvertent" because the roadblock was not a pretext to obtain evidence of narcotics violations, there was no prior belief this particular car would contain drugs, and there was at best a "generalized suspicion" some of the stopped cars would contain drugs.

Powell and Blackmun, JJ., concurring, declined to join the plurality opinion because "it appears to accord less significance to the Warrant Clause of the Fourth Amendment than is justified by the language and purpose of that Amendment." STEVENS, J., joined by Brennan and Marshall, JJ., concurring, objected that the "plurality's explanation" was "incomplete" because it "gives inadequate consideration to our cases holding that a closed container may not be opened without a warrant, even when the container is in plain view and the officer has probable cause to believe contraband is concealed within." Added Justice Stevens:

"If a movable container is in plain view, seizure does not implicate any privacy interests. Therefore, if there is probable cause to believe it contains contraband, the owner's possessory interest in the container must yield to society's interest in making sure that the contraband does not vanish during the time it would take to obtain a warrant. The item may be seized temporarily. It does not follow, however, that the container may be opened on the spot. Once the container is in custody, there is no risk that evidence will be destroyed. Some convenience to the officer is entailed by requiring him to obtain a warrant before opening the container, but that alone does not excuse the duty to go before a neutral magistrate. * * * Exigent circumstances must be shown before the Constitution will entrust an individual's privacy to the judgment of a single police officer.

"In this case, I have no doubt concerning the propriety of the officer's warrantless seizure of the balloon. For the reasons stated by Justices Powell and Rehnquist, I agree that the police officer invaded no privacy interest in order to see the balloon, and that when he saw it he had probable cause to believe it contained drugs. But before the balloon's contents could be used as evidence against the respondent, the state also had to justify opening it without a warrant. I can perceive two potential justifications. First, it is entirely possible that what the officer saw in the car's glove compartment, coupled with his observation of respondent and the contents of his pockets, provided probable cause to believe that contraband was located somewhere in the car—and not merely in the one balloon at issue. If so, then under *Ross* * * * it was permissible to examine the contents of any container in the car, including this balloon.

"Alternatively, the balloon, could be one of those rare single-purpose containers which 'by their very nature cannot support any reasonable expectation of privacy because their contents can be inferred from their outward appearance.' [*Ross* at n. 19.] Whereas a suitcase or a paper bag may contain an almost infinite variety of items, a balloon of this kind might be used only to transport drugs. Viewing it where he did could have given the officer a degree of certainty that is equivalent to the plain view of the heroin itself. If that be true, I would conclude that the plain view doctrine supports the search as well as the seizure even though the contents of the balloon were not actually visible to the officer.[4]

"This reasoning leads me to the conclusion that the Fourth Amendment would not require exclusion of the balloon's contents in this case if, but only if, there was probable cause to search the entire vehicle or there was virtual certainty that the balloon contained a controlled substance.[5] Neither of these fact-bound inquiries was made by the Texas courts, and neither should be made by this Court in the first instance. Moreover, it may be that on remand the Texas Court of Criminal Appeals will find those inquiries unnecessary because the respondent may have waived his right to demand them. I therefore concur in the judgment."

2. Just how difficult is it, as a general matter, to determine when *Ross* rather than *Sanders* applies? What information, at what point in time and from what source, is to be considered? Compare *State v. Jaso,* 648 P.2d 1 (Kan.1982) (police surveillance of apartment where wholesaler to supply drugs for retailer to sell to undercover agent, wholesaler seen to enter with blue suitcase and later exit without it, but when apartment raided suitcase not there and police discovered rear exit of which they previously unaware; other police contacted and they stopped wholesaler and searched blue suitcase in his car without a warrant; held, search lawful, as "there was no specific reason to be searching only for the blue suitcase and the searching officer had no knowledge as to any specific container"); with *State v. Grinier,* 659 P.2d 550 (Wash.App.1983) (*Ross* does not permit warrantless search of suitcase defendant put in car upon leaving place he believed to be at to purchase biweekly marijuana supply, as "the police focused their suspicion and search solely on defendant's suitcase").

Consider in this connection UNITED STATES v. JOHNS, ___ U.S. ___, 105 S.Ct. 881, 83 L.Ed.2d 890 (1985). Pursuant to an investigation of a suspected drug smuggling operation, customs officers by ground and air surveillance saw two pickup trucks as they traveled to a remote private airstrip and the arrival and departure there of two small airplanes. The officers smelled the odor of marijuana as they approached the trucks and saw in the back of the trucks packages wrapped in dark green plastic and sealed with tape, a common method of packaging marijuana. The trucks were seized and taken to headquarters, where the packages were removed and thereafter opened without a search warrant. The defendants claimed that *Ross* was inapplicable because there was only probable cause as to the packages, but the Supreme Court, per O'CONNOR, J., did not agree:

" * * * The events surrounding the rendezvous of the aircraft and the pickup trucks at the isolated desert airstrip indicated that the vehicles were involved in

4. Conversely, the fact that an object is visible does not automatically mean that it is in plain view in the sense that no invasion of privacy is required to seize it. This case does not require elaboration of what the Fourth Amendment demands before an officer may seize a visible item that he could not reach without, for example, entering a private home or destroying a valuable container.

5. Sometimes there can be greater certainty about the identity of a substance within a container than about the identity of a substance that is actually visible. One might actually see a white powder without realizing that it is heroin, but be virtually certain a balloon contains such a substance in a particular context. It seems to me that in evaluating whether a person's privacy interests are infringed, "virtual certainty" is a more meaningful indicator than visibility.

smuggling activity. The Customs officers on the ground were unable to observe the airplanes after they landed, and consequently did not see the packages loaded into the pickup trucks. After the officers came closer and detected the distinct odor of marijuana, they had probable cause to believe that the vehicles contained contraband. Given their experience with drug smuggling cases, the officers no doubt suspected that the scent was emanating from the packages that they observed in the back of the pickup trucks. The officers, however, were unaware of the packages until they approached the trucks, and contraband might well have been hidden elsewhere in the vehicles. We agree with the Court of Appeals that the Customs officers had probable cause to believe that not only the packages but also the vehicles themselves contained contraband."

The Court added it made no difference "that the officers did not search the vehicles more extensively," that is, that the officers merely removed the packages and searched them but did not otherwise search the trucks.

3. However, "the central issue" in *Johns* was whether the warrantless search was permissible in light of the fact that the packages were not opened until three days after they had been removed from the trucks. The majority answered in the affirmative, relying upon the conclusions that the *Carroll* line of vehicle-search cases would allow such a deferred search and that *Ross* was grounded in the notion that "the fact that a container is involved does not in itself either expand or contract the well-established exception to the warrant requirement recognized in *Carroll.* * * *

"We do not suggest that police officers may indefinitely retain possession of a vehicle and its contents before they complete a vehicle search. Nor do we foreclose the possibility that the owner of a vehicle or its contents might attempt to prove that delay in the completion of a vehicle search was unreasonable because it adversely affected a privacy or possessory interest. We note that in this case there was probable cause to believe that the trucks contained contraband and there is no plausible argument that the object of the search could not have been concealed in the packages. Respondents do not challenge the legitimacy of the seizure of the trucks or the packages, and they never sought return of the property. Thus, respondents have not even alleged, much less proved, that the delay in the search of packages adversely affected legitimate interests protected by the Fourth Amendment."

BRENNAN and MARSHALL, JJ., dissenting, objected that "no exigency precluded reasonable efforts to obtain a warrant prior to the search of the packages in the warehouse."

4. After customs agents found marijuana inside a table shipped into the country, it was repackaged and delivered to defendant by police posing as delivery men. Surveilling police saw defendant pull the container into his apartment, and when he reemerged with it 30 to 45 minutes later he was arrested and the package searched without a warrant. The state court, relying upon *Sanders* and *Chadwick,* held the marijuana inadmissible, but the Supreme Court, in ILLINOIS v. ANDREAS, 463 U.S. 765, 103 S.Ct. 3319, 77 L.Ed.2d 1003 (1983), disagreed. The Court, per THE CHIEF JUSTICE, first addressed the threshold question of "whether an individual has a legitimate expectation of privacy in the contents of a previously lawfully searched container. It is obvious that the privacy interest in the contents of a container diminishes with respect to a container that law enforcement authorities have already lawfully opened and found to contain illicit drugs. No protected privacy interest remains in contraband in a container once government officers lawfully have opened that container and identified its contents as illegal. The simple act of resealing the container to enable the police to make a controlled delivery does

not operate to revive or restore the lawfully invaded privacy rights.

"This conclusion is supported by the reasoning underlying the 'plain view' doctrine. The plain view doctrine authorizes seizure of illegal or evidentiary items visible to a police officer whose access to the object has some prior Fourth Amendment justification and who has probable cause to suspect that the item is connected with criminal activity. The plain view doctrine is grounded on the proposition that once police are lawfully in a position to observe an item first-hand, its owner's privacy interest in that item is lost; the owner may retain the incidents of title and possession but not privacy. That rationale applies here; once a container has been found to a certainty to contain illicit drugs, the contraband becomes like objects physically within the plain view of the police, and the claim to privacy is lost. Consequently the subsequent opening is not a 'search' within the intendment of the Fourth Amendment."

The Court then noted that "perfect" controlled deliveries are often impossible, so that there may result "a gap in surveillance" during which "it is possible that the container will be put to other uses—for example, the contraband may be removed or other items may be placed inside." On the resulting question of "at what point after an interruption of control or surveillance, courts should recognize the individual's expectation of privacy in the container as a legitimate right protected by the Fourth Amendment," the Court adopted the "workable," "reasonable" and "objective" standard of "whether there is a substantial likelihood that the contents of the container have been changed during the gap in surveillance. We hold that absent a substantial likelihood that the contents have been changed, there is no legitimate expectation of privacy in the contents of a container previously opened under lawful authority." The Court then concluded there was no substantial likelihood in the instant case. "The unusual size of the container, its specialized purpose, and the relatively short break in surveillance, combine to make it substantially unlikely that the respondent removed the table or placed new items inside the container while it was in his apartment."

BRENNAN and MARSHALL, JJ., dissenting, objected that while after the customs search "any reasonable expectation respondent may have had that the existence of the contraband would remain secret was lost, and could not be regained," he still had a Fourth Amendment right "to be 'let alone' " which "is, at the very least, the right not to have one's repose and possessions disturbed" without a warrant. That the Fourth Amendment protects both secrecy and security, they noted, is suggested by the limits on the plain view doctrine, under which "the fact that a person displays incriminating evidence in his living room window (or allows it to pass through customs inspection) is *not* enough by itself to authorize a search and seizure of that evidence." Moreover, "if a person has no reasonable expectation of privacy in a package whose contents are already legally known to the authorities, a reasonable expectation of privacy should reattach if the person has unobserved access to the package and any opportunity to change its contents." Stevens, J., dissenting separately, would remand for reconsideration under his "virtual certainty" test in *Texas v. Brown.*

NEW YORK v. BELTON

453 U.S. 454, 101 S.Ct. 2860, 69 L.Ed.2d 768 (1981).

JUSTICE STEWART delivered the opinion of the Court. * * *

On April 9, 1978, Trooper Douglas Nicot, a New York State policeman driving an unmarked car on the New York Thruway, was passed by another automobile travelling at an excessive rate of speed. Nicot gave chase, overtook the speeding vehicle, and ordered its driver to pull it over to the side of the road and stop. There were four men in the car, one of whom was Roger Belton, the respondent in this case. The policeman asked to see the driver's license and automobile registration, and discovered that none of the men owned the vehicle or was related to its owner. Meanwhile, the policeman had smelled burnt marihuana and had seen on the floor of the car an envelope marked "Supergold" that he associated with marihuana. He therefore directed the men to get out of the car, and placed them under arrest for the unlawful possession of marihuana. He patted down each of the men and "split them up into four separate areas of the Thruway at this time so they would not be in physical touching area of each other." He then picked up the envelope marked "Supergold" and found that it contained marihuana. After giving the arrestees the warnings required by *Miranda v. Arizona,* the state policeman searched each one of them. He then searched the passenger compartment of the car. On the back seat he found a black leather jacket belonging to Belton. He unzipped one of the pockets of the jacket and discovered cocaine. Placing the jacket in his automobile, he drove the four arrestees to a nearby police station.

Belton was subsequently indicted for criminal possession of a controlled substance. In the trial court he moved that the cocaine the trooper had seized from the jacket pocket be suppressed. The court denied the motion. Belton then pleaded guilty to a lesser included offense, but preserved his claim that the cocaine had been seized in violation of the Fourth and Fourteenth Amendments. The Appellate Division of the New York Supreme Court upheld the constitutionality of the search and seizure, reasoning that "[o]nce defendant was validly arrested for possession of marihuana, the officer was justified in searching the immediate area for other contraband."

The New York Court of Appeals reversed, holding that "[a] warrantless search of the zippered pockets of an unaccessible jacket may not be upheld as a search incident to a lawful arrest where there is no longer any danger that the arrestee or a confederate might gain access to the article." * * *

It is a first principle of Fourth Amendment jurisprudence that the police may not conduct a search unless they first convince a neutral magistrate that there is probable cause to do so. This Court has recognized, however, that "the exigencies of the situation" may sometimes make exemption from the warrant requirement "imperative." Specifically, the Court held in *Chimel v. California* [p. 309 supra], that a lawful custodial arrest creates a situation which justifies the contemporaneous search without a warrant of the person arrested and of the immediately surrounding area. Such searches have long been considered valid because of the need "to remove any weapons that [the arrestee] might seek to use in order to resist arrest or effect his escape" and the need to prevent the concealment or destruction of evidence.

The Court's opinion in *Chimel* emphasized the principle that, "The scope of [a] search must be 'strictly tied to and justified by' the circumstances which rendered its initiation permissible." Thus while the Court in *Chimel* found "ample justification" for a search of "the area from within which [an arrestee] might gain possession of a weapon or destructible evidence," the Court found "no comparable justification * * * for routinely searching any room other than that in which an arrest occurs—or, for that matter, for searching through all the desk drawers or other closed or concealed areas in that room itself."

Although the principle that limits a search incident to a lawful custodial arrest may be stated clearly enough, courts have discovered the principle difficult to apply in specific cases. Yet, as one commentator has pointed out, the protection of the Fourth and Fourteenth Amendments "can only be realized if the police are acting under a set of rules which, in most instances, makes it possible to reach a correct determination beforehand as to whether an invasion of privacy is justified in the interest of law enforcement." LaFave, *"Case-by-Case Adjudication" versus "Standardized Procedures": The Robinson Dilemma,* 1974 Sup.Ct.Rev. 127, 142. This is because

> "Fourth Amendment doctrine, given force and effect by the exclusionary rule, is primarily intended to regulate the police in their day-to-day activities and thus ought to be expressed in terms that are readily applicable by the police in the context of the law enforcement activities in which they are necessarily engaged. A highly sophisticated set of rules, qualified by all sorts of ifs, ands, and buts and requiring the drawing of subtle nuances and hairline distinctions, may be the sort of heady stuff upon which the facile minds of lawyers and judges eagerly feed, but they may be 'literally impossible of application by the officer in the field.'" Id., at 141.

In short, "A single, familiar standard is essential to guide police officers, who have only limited time and expertise to reflect on and balance the social and individual interests involved in the specific circumstances they confront." *Dunaway v. New York* [p. 385 infra].

So it was that, in *United States v. Robinson* [p. 386 infra], the Court hewed to a straightforward rule, easily applied, and predictably enforced: "[I]n the case of a lawful custodial arrest a full search of the person is not only an exception to the warrant requirement, but it is also a 'reasonable' search under that amendment." In so holding, the Court rejected the suggestion "that there must be litigated in each case the issue of whether or not there was present one of the reasons supporting the authority for a search of the person incident to a lawful arrest."

But no straightforward rule has emerged from the litigated cases respecting the question involved here—the question of the proper scope of a search of the interior of an automobile incident to a lawful custodial arrest of its occupants. The difficulty courts have had is reflected in the conflicting views of the New York judges who dealt with the problem in the present case, and is confirmed by a look at even a small sample drawn from the narrow class of cases in which courts have decided whether, in the course of a search incident to the lawful custodial arrest of the occupants of an automobile, police may search inside the automobile after the arrestees are no longer in it. * * *

When a person cannot know how a court will apply a settled principle to a recurring factual situation, that person cannot know the scope of his constitutional protection, nor can a policeman know the scope of his authority. While the *Chimel* case established that a search incident to an arrest may not stray beyond the area within the immediate control of the arrestee, courts have found no workable definition of "the area within the immediate control of the arrestee" when that area arguably includes the interior of an automobile and the arrestee is its recent occupant. Our reading of the cases suggests the generalization that articles inside the relatively narrow compass of the passenger compartment of an automobile are in fact generally, even if not inevitably, within "the area into which an arrestee might reach in order to grab a weapon or evidentiary item." In order to establish the workable rule this category of cases requires, we read *Chimel* 's definition of the limits of the area that may be searched in light of that generalization. Accordingly, we hold that when a policeman has made a lawful custodial arrest of the occupant of an automobile, he may, as a contemporaneous incident of that arrest, search the passenger compartment of that automobile.[3]

3. Our holding today does no more than determine the meaning of *Chimel* 's principles in this particular and problematic content. It in no way alters the fundamental principles established in

It follows from this conclusion that the police may also examine the contents of any containers found within the passenger compartment, for if the passenger compartment is within reach of the arrestee, so also will containers in it be within his reach.[4] Such a container may, of course, be searched whether it is open or closed, since the justification for the search is not that the arrestee has no privacy interest in the container, but that the lawful custodial arrest justifies the infringement of any privacy interest the arrestee may have. Thus, while the Court in *Chimel* held that the police could not search all the drawers in an arrestee's house simply because the police had arrested him at home, the Court noted that drawers within an arrestee's reach could be searched because of the danger their contents might pose to the police.

It is true, of course, that these containers will sometimes be such that they could hold neither a weapon nor evidence of the criminal conduct for which the suspect was arrested. However, in *United States v. Robinson,* the Court rejected the argument that such a container—there a "crumpled up cigarette package"—located during a search of Robinson incident to his arrest could not be searched: "The authority to search the person incident to a lawful custodial arrest, while based upon the need to disarm and to discover evidence, does not depend on what a court may later decide was the probability in a particular arrest situation that weapons or evidence would in fact be found upon the person of the suspect. A custodial arrest of a suspect based on probable cause is a reasonable intrusion under the Fourth Amendment; that intrusion being lawful, a search incident to the arrest requires no additional justification."

The New York Court of Appeals relied upon *United States v. Chadwick,* [p. 337 supra], and *Arkansas v. Sanders,* [p. 338 supra], in concluding that the search and seizure in the present case were constitutionally invalid.[5] But neither of those cases involved an arguably valid search incident to a lawful custodial arrest. * * *

It is not questioned that the respondent was the subject of a lawful custodial arrest on a charge of possessing marihuana. The search of the respondent's jacket followed immediately upon that arrest. The jacket was located inside the passenger compartment of the car in which the respondent had been a passenger just before he was arrested. The jacket was thus within the area which we have concluded was "within the arrestee's immediate control" within the meaning of the *Chimel* case.[6] The search of the jacket, therefore, was a search incident to a lawful custodial arrest, and it did not violate the Fourth and Fourteenth Amendments. Accordingly, the judgment is reversed.

JUSTICE REHNQUIST, concurring.

Because it is apparent that a majority of the Court is unwilling to overrule *Mapp v. Ohio,* and because the Court does not find it necessary to consider the "automobile

the *Chimel* case regarding the basic scope of searches incident to lawful custodial arrests.

4. "Container" here denotes any object capable of holding another object. It thus includes closed or open glove compartments, consoles, or other receptacles located anywhere within the passenger compartment, as well as luggage, boxes, bags, clothing, and the like. Our holding encompasses only the interior of the passenger compartment of an automobile and does not encompass the trunk.

5. It seems to have been the theory of the Court of Appeals that the search and seizure in the present case could not have been incident to the respondent's arrest, because Trooper Nicot, by the very act of searching the respondent's jacket and seizing the contents of its pocket, had gained "exclusive control" of them. But under this fallacious theory no search or seizure incident to a lawful custodial arrest would ever be valid; by seizing an article even on the arrestee's person, an officer may be said to have reduced that article to his "exclusive control."

6. Because of this disposition of the case, there is no need here to consider whether the search and seizure were permissible under the so-called "automobile exception."

exception" in its disposition of this case, I join the opinion of the Court.

JUSTICE STEVENS, concurring in the judgment.

For the reasons stated in my dissenting opinion in *Robbins v. California,* I agree [that] this judgment should be reversed. [That opinion follows.—ed.]

The Court's careful and repeated use of the term "lawful custodial arrest" seems to imply that a significant distinction between custodial arrests and ordinary arrests exists. I am familiar with the distinction between a "stop," see, e.g., *Terry v. Ohio,* [p. 361 infra], and an "arrest," but I am not familiar with any difference between custodial arrests and any other kind of arrest. It is, of course, true that persons apprehended for traffic violations are frequently not required to accompany the arresting officer to the police station before they are permitted to leave on their own recognizance or by using their driver's licenses as a form of bond. It is also possible that state law or local regulations may in some cases forbid police officers from taking persons into custody for violation of minor traffic laws. As a matter of constitutional law, however, any person lawfully arrested for the pettiest misdemeanor may be temporarily placed in custody.[11] Indeed, as the Court has repeatedly held, every arrest is a seizure of the person within the meaning of the Fourth Amendment. The rule of constitutional law the Court fashions today therefore potentially applies to every arrest of every occupant of an automobile.[12]

After the vehicle in which respondent was riding was stopped, the officer smelled marihuana and thereby acquired probable cause to believe that the vehicle contained contraband. A thorough search of the car was therefore reasonable. But if there were no reason to believe that anything more than a traffic violation had occurred, I should think it palpably unreasonable to require the driver of a car to open his briefcase or his luggage for inspection by the officer. The driver so compelled, however, could make no constitutional objection to a decision by the officer to take the driver into custody and thereby obtain justification for a search of the entire interior of the vehicle. Indeed, under the Court's new rule, the arresting officer may find reason to follow that procedure whenever he sees an interesting looking briefcase or package in a vehicle that has been stopped for a traffic violation. That decision by a police officer will therefore provide the constitutional predicate for broader vehicle searches than any neutral magistrate could authorize by issuing a warrant. * * *

JUSTICE BRENNAN, with whom JUSTICE MARSHALL joins, dissenting.

* * *

11. Justice Stewart apparently believes that the Fourth and Fourteenth Amendments might provide some impediment to police taking a defendant into custody for violation of a "minor traffic offense." See *Gustafson v. Florida* (Stewart, J. concurring). Although I agree that a police officer's authority to restrain an individual's liberty should be limited in the context of stops for routine traffic violations, the Court has not directly considered the question whether "there are constitutional limits upon the use of 'custodial arrests' as the means for invoking the criminal process when relatively minor offenses are involved." See 2 W. LaFave, *Search and Seizure* § 5.2, p. 290 (1978); see also id. § 5.1, p. 256–260, § 5.2, p. 281–291. To the extent that the Court has considered the scope of an officer's authority in making routine traffic stops, the Court has not imposed constitutional restrictions on that authority. Thus the Court may be assuming that its new rule will be limited by a constitutional restriction that does not exist.

12. After today, the driver of a vehicle stopped for a minor traffic violation must look to state law for protection from unreasonable searches. Such protection may come from two sources. Statutory law may provide some protection. Legislatures in some states permit officers to take traffic violators into custody only for certain violations. In some states, however, the police officer has the discretion to make a "custodial arrest" for violation of any motor vehicle law. Additionally, the failure to produce a satisfactory bond will often justify "detention and custodial arrest." Given the incomplete protection afforded by statutory law, drivers in many States will have to persuade state supreme courts to interpret their state constitution's equivalent to the Fourth Amendment to prohibit the unreasonable searches permitted by the Court here.

By approving the constitutionality of the warrantless search in this case, the Court carves out a dangerous precedent that is not justified by the concerns underlying *Chimel.* Disregarding the principle "that the scope of a warrantless search must be commensurate with the rationale that excepts the search from the warrant requirement," the Court for the first time grants police officers authority to conduct a warrantless "area" search under circumstances where there is no chance that the arrestee "might gain possession of a weapon or destructible evidence." Under the approach taken today, the result would presumably be the same even if Officer Nicot had handcuffed Belton and his companions in the patrol car before placing them under arrest, and even if his search had extended to locked luggage or other inaccessible containers located in the back seat of the car. * * *

The Court seeks to justify its departure from the principles underlying *Chimel* by proclaiming the need for a new bright line rule to guide the officer in the field. As we pointed out in *Mincey v. Arizona,* [p. 321 supra], however, "the mere fact that law enforcement may be made more efficient can never by itself justify disregard of the Fourth Amendment." Moreover, the Court's attempt to forge a "bright line" rule fails on its own terms. * * * The Court's new approach leaves open too many questions and, more important, it provides the police and the courts with too few tools with which to find the answers.

Thus, although the Court concludes that a warrantless search of a car may take place even though the suspect was arrested outside the car, it does not indicate how long after the suspect's arrest that search may validly be conducted. Would a warrantless search incident to arrest be valid if conducted five minutes after the suspect left his car? Thirty minutes? Three hours? Does it matter whether the suspect is standing in close proximity to the car when the search is conducted? Does it matter whether the police formed probable cause to arrest before or after the suspect left his car? And *why* is the rule announced today necessarily limited to searches of cars? What if a suspect is seen walking out of a house where the police, peering in from outside, had formed probable cause to believe a crime was being committed? Could the police then arrest that suspect and enter the house to conduct a search incident to arrest? Even assuming today's rule is limited to searches of the "interior" of cars—an assumption not demanded by logic—what is meant by "interior"? Does it include locked glove compartments, the interior of door panels, or the area under the floorboards? Are special rules necessary for station wagons and hatchbacks, where the luggage compartment may be reached through the interior, or taxicabs, where a glass panel might separate the driver's compartment from the rest of the car? Are the only containers that may be searched those that are large enough to be "capable of holding another object"? Or does the new rule apply to any container, even if it "could hold neither a weapon nor evidence of the criminal conduct for which the suspect was arrested"?

The Court does not give the police any "bright line" answers to these questions. More important, because the Court's new rule abandons the justifications underlying *Chimel, it offers no guidance to the police officer seeking to work out these answers for himself.* * * *

The standard announced in *Chimel* is not nearly as difficult to apply as the Court suggests. To the contrary, I continue to believe that *Chimel* provides a sound, workable rule for determining the constitutionality of a warrantless search incident to arrest. Under *Chimel,* searches incident to arrest may be conducted without a warrant only if limited to the person of the arrestee, or to the area within the arrestee's "immediate control." While it may be difficult in some cases to measure the exact scope of the arrestee's immediate control, relevant factors would surely include the relative number of police officers and arrestees, the manner of restraint placed on the arrestee, and the ability of the arrestee to gain access to a particular area or container.[5] Certainly there will be some close cases, but when in doubt the police can always turn to the rationale underlying *Chimel*—the need to prevent the arrestee from reaching weapons or contraband—before exercising their judgment. A rule based on that rationale should provide more guidance than the rule announced by the Court today. Moreover, unlike the Court's rule, it would be faithful to the Fourth Amendment.

JUSTICE WHITE, with whom JUSTICE MARSHALL joins, dissenting.

In *Robbins v. California,* it was held that a wrapped container in the trunk of a car could not be searched without a warrant even though the trunk itself could be searched without a warrant because there was probable cause to search the car and even though there was probable cause to search the container as well. This was because of the separate interest in privacy with respect to the container. The Court now holds that as incident to the arrest of the driver or any other person in an automobile, the interior of the car and any container found therein, whether locked or not, may not only be seized but also searched even absent probable cause to believe that contraband or evidence of crime will be found. As to luggage, briefcases or other containers, this seems to me an extreme extension of *Chimel* and one to which I cannot subscribe. * * *[a]

SOUTH DAKOTA v. OPPERMAN

428 U.S. 364, 96 S.Ct. 3092, 49 L.Ed.2d 1000 (1976).

MR. CHIEF JUSTICE BURGER, delivered the opinion of the Court.

[After a vehicle had accumulated two tickets while continuously illegally parked at least seven hours, it was towed to the city impound lot. A police officer, who saw a watch on the dashboard and other property on the back seat, unlocked the door and, pursuant to standard police procedures, inventoried the contents of the car.[b] A plastic bag of marijuana was found in the unlocked glove compartment. Defendant was convicted of marijuana possession, but the conviction was reversed by the state supreme court on the ground the search had been illegal.]

This Court has traditionally drawn a distinction between automobiles and homes

5. The Court sets up a straw man when it claims that under the "exclusive control" approach taken by the Court of Appeals, "no search or seizure incident to a lawful custodial arrest would ever be valid; by seizing an article even on the arrestee's person, an officer may be said to have reduced that article to his 'exclusive control.' "

If a police officer could obtain exclusive control of an article by simply holding it in his hand, I would certainly agree with the Court. But as we recognized in *United States v. Chadwick,* exclusive control means more than that. It means sufficient control such that there is no significant risk that the arrestee or his confederates "might gain possession of a weapon or destructible evidence." *Chimel v. California.* The issue of exclusive control presents a question of fact to be decided under the circumstances of each case, just as the New York Court of Appeals has decided it here.

a. For close analyses of *Belton,* see Grano, *Rethinking the Fourth Amendment Warrant Requirement,* 19 Am.Crim.L.Rev. 603 (1982); L. Katz, *Automobile Searches and Diminished Expectations in the Warrant Clause,* 19 Am.Crim.L. Rev. 557 (1982); Rudstein, *The Search of an Automobile Incident to an Arrest: An Analysis of New York v. Belton,* 67 Marq.L.Rev. 205 (1984).

b. The Court noted that at trial, the officer who conducted the inventory testified as follows:

"Q. And why did you inventory the car?

"A. Mainly for safekeeping, because we have had a lot of trouble in the past of people getting into the impound lot and breaking into cars and stealing stuff out of them.

"Q. Do you know whether the vehicles that were broken into . . . were locked or unlocked?

"A. Both of them were locked, they would be locked."

In describing the impound lot, the officer stated:

"A. It's the old county highway yard. It has a wooden fence partially around part of it, and kind of a dilapidated wire fence, a makeshift fence."

or offices in relation to the Fourth Amendment. * * *

The reason for this well-settled distinction is twofold. First, the inherent mobility of automobiles creates circumstances of such exigency that, as a practical necessity, rigorous enforcement of the warrant requirement is impossible. * * * Besides the element of mobility, less rigorous warrant requirements govern because the expectation of privacy with respect to one's automobile is significantly less than that relating to one's home or office. * * *

In the interests of public safety and as part of what the Court has called "community caretaking functions," automobiles are frequently taken into police custody. Vehicle accidents present one such occasion. To permit the uninterrupted flow of traffic and in some circumstances to preserve evidence, disabled or damaged vehicles will often be removed from the highways or streets at the behest of police engaged solely in caretaking and traffic-control activities. Police will also frequently remove and impound automobiles which violate parking ordinances and which thereby jeopardize both the public safety and the efficient movement of vehicular traffic. The authority of police to seize and remove from the streets vehicles impeding traffic or threatening public safety and convenience is beyond challenge.

When vehicles are impounded, local police departments generally follow a routine practice of securing and inventorying the automobiles' contents. These procedures developed in response to three distinct needs: the protection of the owner's property while it remains in police custody; the protection of the police against claims or disputes over lost or stolen property; and the protection of the police from potential danger. The practice has been viewed as essential to respond to incidents of theft or vandalism. In addition, police frequently attempt to determine whether a vehicle has been stolen and thereafter abandoned.

These caretaking procedures have almost uniformly been upheld by the state courts, which by virtue of the localized nature of traffic regulation have had considerable occasion to deal with the issue. Applying the Fourth Amendment standard of "reasonableness," [5] the state courts have overwhelmingly concluded that, even if an inventory is characterized as a "search," the intrusion is constitutionally permissible. * * *

The majority of the federal Courts of Appeals have likewise sustained inventory procedures as reasonable police intrusions. * * * These cases have recognized that standard inventories often include an examination of the glove compartment, since it is a customary place for documents of ownership and registration, as well as a place for the temporary storage of valuables. * * *

In applying the reasonableness standard adopted by the Framers, this Court has consistently sustained police intrusions into automobiles impounded or otherwise in lawful police custody where the process is aimed at securing or protecting the car and its contents. In *Cooper v. California,* 386

5. In analyzing the issue of reasonableness *vel non* the courts have not sought to determine whether a protective inventory was justified by "probable cause." The standard of probable cause is peculiarly related to criminal investigations, not routine, noncriminal procedures. The probable-cause approach is unhelpful when analysis centers upon the reasonableness of routine administrative caretaking functions, particularly when no claim is made that the protective procedures are a subterfuge for criminal investigations.

In view of the noncriminal context of inventory searches, and the inapplicability in such a setting of the requirement of probable cause, courts have held—and quite correctly—that search warrants are not required, linked as the warrant requirement textually is to the probable-cause concept. We have frequently observed that the warrant requirement assures that legal inferences and conclusions as to probable cause will be drawn by a neutral magistrate unrelated to the criminal investigative-enforcement process. With respect to noninvestigative police inventories of automobiles lawfully within governmental custody, however, the policies underlying the warrant requirement, to which Mr. Justice Powell refers, are inapplicable.

U.S. 58, 87 S.Ct. 788, 17 L.Ed.2d 730 (1967), the Court upheld the inventory of a car impounded under the authority of a state forfeiture statute. Even though the inventory was conducted in a distinctly criminal setting [7] and carried out a week after the car had been impounded, the Court nonetheless found that the car search, including examination of the glove compartment where contraband was found, was reasonable under the circumstances. This conclusion was reached despite the fact that no warrant had issued and probable cause to search for the contraband in the vehicle had not been established. The Court said in language explicitly applicable here:

> "It would be unreasonable to hold that the police, having to retain the car in their custody for such a length of time, had no right, even for their own protection, to search it." [8]

In the following Term, the Court in *Harris v. United States,* 390 U.S. 234, 88 S.Ct. 992, 19 L.Ed.2d 1067 (1968), upheld the introduction of evidence, seized by an officer who, after conducting an inventory search of a car and while taking means to safeguard it, observed a car registration card lying on the metal stripping of the car door. Rejecting the argument that a warrant was necessary, the Court held that the intrusion was justifiable since it was "taken to protect the car while it was in police custody." [9]

Finally, in *Cady v. Dombrowski,* 413 U.S. 433, 93 S.Ct. 2523, 37 L.Ed.2d 706 (1973), the Court upheld a warrantless search of an auto towed to a private garage even though no probable cause existed to believe that the vehicle contained fruits of a crime. The sole justification for the warrantless incursion was that it was incident to the caretaking function of the local police to protect the community's safety. Indeed, the protective search was instituted solely because the local police "were under the impression" that the incapacitated driver, a Chicago police officer, was required to carry his service revolver at all times; the police had reasonable grounds to believe a weapon might be in the car, and thus available to vandals. The Court carefully noted that the protective search was carried out in accordance with *standard procedures* in the local police department, a factor tending to ensure that the intrusion would be limited in scope to the extent necessary to carry out the caretaking function. * * *

The Vermillion police were indisputably engaged in a caretaking search of a lawfully impounded automobile. The inventory was conducted only after the car had been impounded for multiple parking violations. The owner, having left his car illegally parked for an extended period, and thus subject to impoundment, was not present to make other arrangements for the safekeeping of his belongings. The inventory itself was prompted by the presence in plain view of a number of valuables inside the car. As in *Cady,* there is no suggestion whatever that this standard procedure, essentially like that followed throughout the

7. In *Cooper,* the owner had been arrested on narcotics charges, and the car was taken into custody pursuant to the state forfeiture statute. The search was conducted several months before the forfeiture proceedings were actually instituted.

8. There was, of course, no certainty at the time of the search that forfeiture proceedings would ever be held. Accordingly, there was no reason for the police to assume automatically that the automobile would eventually be forfeited to the State. Indeed, as the California Court of Appeal stated, "[T]he instant record nowhere discloses that forfeiture proceedings were instituted in respect to defendant's car * * *." No reason would therefore appear to limit *Cooper* to an impoundment pursuant to a forfeiture statute.

9. The Court expressly noted that the legality of the inventory was not presented, since the evidence was discovered at the point when the officer was taking protective measures to secure the automobile from the elements. But the Court clearly held that the officer acted properly in opening the car for protective reasons.

country, was a pretext concealing an investigatory police motive.[10]

On this record we conclude that in following standard police procedures, prevailing throughout the country and approved by the overwhelming majority of courts, the conduct of the police was not "unreasonable" under the Fourth Amendment. * * *

MR. JUSTICE POWELL, concurring.

* * * As the Court's opinion emphasizes, the search here was limited to an inventory of the unoccupied automobile and was conducted strictly in accord with the regulations of the Vermillion Police Department. Upholding searches of this type provides no general license for the police to examine all the contents of such automobiles.[7] * * *

The routine inventory search under consideration in this case does not fall within any of the established exceptions to the warrant requirement. But examination of the interests which are protected when searches are conditioned on warrants issued by a judicial officer reveals that none of these is implicated here. A warrant may issue only upon "probable cause." In the criminal context the requirement of a warrant protects the individual's legitimate expectation of privacy against the overzealous police officer. * * * Inventory searches, however, are not conducted in order to discover evidence of crime. The officer does not make a discretionary determination to search based on a judgment that certain conditions are present. Inventory searches are conducted in accordance with established police department rules or policy and occur whenever an automobile is seized. There are thus no special facts for a neutral magistrate to evaluate. * * *

MR. JUSTICE MARSHALL, with whom MR. JUSTICE BRENNAN and MR. JUSTICE STEWART join, dissenting. * * *

To begin with, the Court appears to suggest by reference to a "diminished" expectation of privacy, that a person's constitutional interest in protecting the integrity of closed compartments of his locked automobile may routinely be sacrificed to governmental interests requiring interference with that privacy that are less compelling than would be necessary to justify a search of similar scope of the person's home or office. This has never been the law. The Court correctly observes that some prior cases have drawn distinctions between automobiles and homes or offices in Fourth Amendment cases; but even as the Court's discussion makes clear, the reasons for distinction in those cases are not present here. Thus, *Chambers v. Maroney,* * * * reaffirmed that the standard of probable cause necessary to authorize such a search was no less than the standard applicable to search of a home or office. In other contexts the Court has recognized that automobile travel sacrifices some privacy interests to the publicity of plain view. But this recognition, too, is inapposite here, for there is no question of plain

10. The inventory was not unreasonable in scope. Respondent's motion to suppress in state court challenged the inventory only as to items inside the car not in plain view. But once the policeman was lawfully inside the car to secure the personal property in plain view, it was not unreasonable to open the unlocked glove compartment, to which vandals would have had ready and unobstructed access once inside the car.

The "consent" theory advanced by the dissent rests on the assumption that the inventory is exclusively for the protection of the car owner. It is not. The protection of the municipality and public officers from claims of lost or stolen property and the protection of the public from vandals who might find a firearm, *Cady v. Dombrowski,* supra, or as here, contraband drugs, are also crucial.

7. As part of their inventory search the police may discover materials such as letters or checkbooks that "touch upon intimate areas of an individual's personal affairs," and "reveal much about a person's activities, associations, and beliefs." In this case the police found, *inter alia,* "miscellaneous papers," a checkbook, an installment loan book, and a social security status card. There is, however, no evidence in the record that in carrying out their established inventory duties the Vermillion police do other than search for and remove for storage such property without examining its contents.

view in this case. Nor does this case concern intrusions of the scope [the] Court apparently assumes would ordinarily be permissible in order to insure the running safety of a car. * * *

The Court's opinion appears to suggest that its result may in any event be justified because the inventory search procedure is a "reasonable" response to

> "three distinct needs: the protection of the owner's property while it remains in police custody * * *; the protection of the police against claims or disputes over lost or stolen property * * *; and the protection of the police from potential danger."

This suggestion is flagrantly misleading, however, because the record of this case explicitly belies any relevance of the last two concerns. In any event it is my view that none of these "needs," separately or together, can suffice to justify the inventory search procedure approved by the Court.

First, this search cannot be justified in any way as a safety measure, for—though the Court ignores it—the sole purpose given by the State for the Vermillion police's inventory procedure was to secure *valuables*. Nor is there any indication that the officer's search in this case was tailored in any way to safety concerns, or that ordinarily it is so circumscribed. Even aside from the actual basis for the police practice in this case, however, I do not believe that any blanket safety argument could justify a program of routine searches of the scope permitted here. As Mr. Justice POWELL recognizes, ordinarily "there is little danger associated with impounding unsearched automobiles." Thus, while the safety rationale may not be entirely discounted when it is actually relied upon, it surely cannot justify the search of every car upon the basis of undifferentiated possibility of harm; on the contrary, such an intrusion could ordinarily be justified only in those individual cases where the officer's inspection was prompted by specific circumstances indicating the possibility of a particular danger.

Second, the Court suggests that the search for valuables in the closed glove compartment might be justified as a measure to protect the police against lost property claims. Again, this suggestion is belied by the record, since—although the Court declines to discuss it—the South Dakota Supreme Court's interpretation of state law explicitly absolves the police, as "gratuitous depositors," from any obligation beyond inventorying objects in plain view and locking the car. Moreover, * * * it may well be doubted that an inventory procedure would in any event work significantly to minimize the frustrations of false claims.

Finally, the Court suggests that the public interest in protecting valuables that may be found inside a closed compartment of an impounded car may justify the inventory procedure. I recognize the genuineness of this governmental interest in protecting property from pilferage. But even if I assume that the posting of a guard would be fiscally impossible as an alternative means to the same protective end, I cannot agree with the Court's conclusion. The Court's result authorizes—indeed it appears to require—the routine search of nearly every [12] car impounded. In my view, the Constitution does not permit such searches as a matter of routine; absent specific consent, such a search is permissible only in exceptional circumstances of particular necessity.

It is at least clear that any owner might prohibit the police from executing a pro-

12. The Court makes clear that the police may not proceed to search an impounded car if the owner is able to make other arrangements for the safekeeping of his belongings. Additionally, while the Court does not require consent before a search, it does not hold that the police may proceed with such a search in the face of the owner's denial of permission. In my view, if the owner of the vehicle is in police custody or otherwise in communication with the police, his consent to the inventory is prerequisite to an inventory search.

tective search of his impounded car, since by hypothesis the inventory is conducted for the owner's benefit. Moreover, it is obvious that not everyone whose car is impounded would want it to be searched. * * * Nevertheless, according to the Court's result the law may presume that each owner in respondent's position consents to the search. I cannot agree. In my view, the Court's approach is squarely contrary to the law of consent; it ignores the duty, in the absence of consent, to analyze in each individual case whether there is a need to search a particular car for the protection of its owner which is sufficient to outweigh the particular invasion. It is clear to me under established principles that in order to override the absence of explicit consent, such a search must at least be conditioned upon the fulfillment of two requirements. First, there must be specific cause to believe that a search of the scope to be undertaken is necessary in order to preserve the integrity of particular valuable property threatened by the impoundment * * *. Second, even where a search might be appropriate, such an intrusion may only follow the exhaustion and failure of reasonable efforts under the circumstances to identify and reach the owner of the property in order to facilitate alternative means of security or to obtain his consent to the search, for in this context the right to refuse the search remains with the owner.[16] * * *

Statement of MR. JUSTICE WHITE.

Although I do not subscribe to all of my Brother Marshall's dissenting opinion, particularly some aspects of his discussion concerning the necessity for obtaining the consent of the car owner, I agree with most of his analysis and conclusions and consequently dissent from the judgment of the Court.

Notes and Questions

1. A narrower view is taken in some jurisdictions. For example, the South Dakota Supreme Court held on remand that the inventory search of Opperman's automobile violated his rights under the search and seizure guarantee of the South Dakota Constitution, the language of which "is almost identical to that found in the Fourth Amendment." *State v. Opperman,* 247 N.W.2d 673 (S.D.1976). Under the state constitutional provision, warrantless inventory searches of automobiles "must be restricted to safeguarding those articles which are within plain view of the officer's vision."

2. Consider the dissent of Ely, J., in *United States v. Mitchell,* 458 F.2d 960 (9th Cir.1972), suggesting that an "effective compromise" would be "to permit extensive inventory searches of seized vehicles, so as fully to protect the police, but to forbid, over the objection of one having standing, the use of any item seized in the search as evidence against the objector."

3. Evidence found in an otherwise lawful inventory must be suppressed if the prior impoundment of the vehicle was not justified. See, e.g., *Dyke v. Taylor Implement Mfg. Co.,* 391 U.S. 216, 88 S.Ct. 1472, 20 L.Ed.2d 538 (1968) (search of car outside courthouse while driver, arrested for reckless driving, inside to post bond was improper, as "there is no indication that the police had purported to impound or to hold the car [or] that they were authorized by any state law to do so"); *State v. Simpson,* 622 P.2d 1199 (Wash. 1980) (where defendant arrested at home, impoundment of his truck lawfully parked in front of house illegal).

4. What, then, if the car was impounded because the driver of the car was arrested for a serious offense while driving

16. Additionally, although not relevant on this record, since the inventory procedure is premised upon benefit to the owner, it cannot be executed in any case in which there is reason to believe the owner would prefer to forego it. This principle, which is fully consistent with the Court's result today, requires, for example, that when the police harbor suspicions (amounting to less than probable cause) that evidence or contraband may be found inside the automobile, they may not inventory it, for they must presume that the owner would refuse to permit the search.

the car on the public way? Compare *State v. Goodrich,* 256 N.W.2d 506 (Minn.1977) (when arrestee specifically requests that his car be lawfully parked in the vicinity of the arrest or turned over to a friend, and it feasible to do so, impoundment improper); and *State v. Lunsford,* 655 S.W.2d 921 (Tenn.1983) (police must advise defendant of alternative of leaving car at scene); with *Cabbler v. Superintendent,* 374 F.Supp. 690 (E.D.Va.1974), rev'd on other grounds, 528 F.2d 1142 (4th Cir.1975) ("officers are not required to take time out from their immediate purpose to allow their suspect to put his affairs in order"); and *State v. Shorney,* 524 P.2d 69 (Okla. Crim.1974) ("an arresting officer has no mandatory legal duty to advise an arrestee of any administrative regulation authorizing the release of his automobile to a third party").

5. If the owner or possessor of the car is at hand at the time of a lawful impoundment, under *Opperman* must he be given the option of inventory or no inventory? Should he be?

What if the *Opperman* inventory had extended to the locked trunk? To examination of the contents of containers in the car? Consider *Illinois v. Lafayette,* p. 394 infra, rejecting the notion that police must utilize the "less intrusive means" of sealing, rather than inventorying, an arrestee's shoulder bag.

SECTION 7. STOP AND FRISK

TERRY v. OHIO

392 U.S. 1, 88 S.Ct. 1868, 20 L.Ed.2d 889 (1968).

MR. CHIEF JUSTICE WARREN delivered the opinion of the court.

[Officer McFadden, a Cleveland plainclothes detective, became suspicious of two men standing on a street corner in the downtown area at about 2:30 in the afternoon. One of the suspects walked up the street, peered into a store, walked on, started back, looked into the same store, and then joined and conferred with his companion. The other suspect repeated this ritual, and between them the two men went through this performance about a dozen times. They also talked with a third man, and then followed him up the street about ten minutes after his departure. The officer, thinking that the suspects were "casing" a stickup and might be armed, followed and confronted the three men as they were again conversing. He identified himself and asked the suspects for their names. The men only mumbled something, and the officer spun Terry around and patted his breast pocket. He felt a pistol, which he removed. A frisk of Terry's companion also uncovered a pistol; a frisk of the third man did not disclose that he was armed, and he was not searched further. Terry was charged with carrying a concealed weapon, and he moved to suppress the weapon as evidence. The motion was denied by the trial judge, who upheld the officer's actions on a stop-and-frisk theory. The Ohio court of appeals affirmed, and the state supreme court dismissed Terry's appeal.]

* * * The question is whether in all the circumstances of this on-the-street encounter, [Terry's] right to personal security was violated by an unreasonable search and seizure.

We would be less than candid if we did not acknowledge that this question thrusts to the fore difficult and troublesome issues regarding a sensitive area of police activity—issues which have never before been squarely presented to this Court. * * *

On the one hand, it is frequently argued that in dealing with the rapidly unfolding and often dangerous situations on city streets the police are in need of an escalating set of flexible responses, graduated in relation to the amount of information they possess. For this purpose it is urged that distinctions should be made between a "stop" and an "arrest" (or a "seizure" of a person), and between a "frisk" and a "search." Thus, it is argued, the police should be allowed to "stop" a person and detain him briefly for questioning upon suspicion that he may be connected with criminal activity. Upon suspicion that the person may be armed, the police should have the power to "frisk" him for weapons. If the "stop" and the "frisk" give rise to probable cause to believe that the suspect has committed a crime, then the police should be empowered to make a formal "arrest," and a full incident "search" of the person. This scheme is justified in part upon the notion that a "stop" and a "frisk" amount to a mere "minor inconvenience and petty indignity," which can properly be imposed upon the citizen in the interest of effective law enforcement on the basis of a police officer's suspicion.

On the other side the argument is made that the authority of the police must be strictly circumscribed by the law of arrest and search as it has developed to date in the traditional jurisprudence of the Fourth Amendment. It is contended with some force that there is not—and cannot be—a variety of police activity which does not depend solely upon the voluntary cooperation of the citizen and yet which stops short of an arrest based upon probable cause to make such an arrest. The heart of the Fourth Amendment, the argument runs, is a severe requirement of specific justification for any intrusion upon protected personal security, coupled with a highly developed system of judicial controls to enforce upon the agents of the State the commands of the Constitution. * * *

* * * The State has characterized the issue here as "the right of a police officer * * * to make an on-the-street stop, interrogate and pat down for weapons (known in the street vernacular as 'stop and frisk')." But this is only partly accurate. For the issue is not the abstract propriety of the police conduct, but the admissibility against petitioner of the evidence uncovered by the search and seizure. * * * [I]n our system evidentiary rulings provide the context in which the judicial process of inclusion and exclusion approves some conduct as comporting with constitutional guarantees and disapproves other actions by state agents. A ruling admitting evidence in a criminal trial, we recognize, has the necessary effect of legitimizing the conduct which produced the evidence, while an application of the exclusionary rule withholds the constitutional imprimatur.

The exclusionary rule has its limitations, however, as a tool of judicial control. It cannot properly be invoked to exclude the products of legitimate police investigative techniques on the ground that much conduct which is closely similar involves unwarranted intrusions upon constitutional protections. Moreover, in some contexts the rule is ineffective as a deterrent. Street encounters between citizens and police officers are incredibly rich in diversity. They range from wholly friendly exchanges of pleasantries or mutually useful information to hostile confrontations of armed men involving arrests, or injuries, or loss of life. Moreover, hostile confrontations are not all of a piece. Some of them begin in a friendly enough manner, only to take a different turn upon the injection of some unexpected element into the conversation. Encounters are initiated by the police for a wide variety of purposes, some of which are wholly unrelated to a desire to prosecute for crime. Doubtless some police "field interrogation" conduct violates the Fourth Amendment. But a stern refusal by this Court to condone such activity does not necessarily render it responsive to the exclusionary rule. Regardless of how effective the rule may be where obtaining convictions is an important objective of the police, it is powerless to deter invasions of constitutionally guaranteed rights where the police either have no interest in prosecuting or are willing to forego successful prosecution in the interest of serving some other goal.

Proper adjudication of cases in which the exclusionary rule is invoked demands a constant awareness of these limitations.

The wholesale harassment by certain elements of the police community, of which minority groups, particularly Negroes, frequently complain, will not be stopped by the exclusion of any evidence from any criminal trial. Yet a rigid and unthinking application of the exclusionary rule, in futile protest against practices which it can never be used effectively to control, may exact a high toll in human injury and frustration of efforts to prevent crime. No judicial opinion can comprehend the protean variety of the street encounter, and we can only judge the facts of the case before us. * * *

[W]e turn our attention to the quite narrow question posed by the facts before us: whether it is always unreasonable for a policeman to seize a person and subject him to a limited search for weapons unless there is probable cause for an arrest.

* * * It is quite plain that the Fourth Amendment governs "seizures" of the person which do not eventuate in a trip to the station house and prosecution for crime—"arrests" in traditional terminology. It must be recognized that whenever a police officer accosts an individual and restrains his freedom to walk away, he has "seized" that person. And it is nothing less than sheer torture of the English language to suggest that a careful exploration of the outer surfaces of a person's clothing all over his or her body in an attempt to find weapons is not a "search." Moreover, it is simply fantastic to urge that such a procedure performed in public by a policeman while the citizen stands helpless, perhaps facing a wall with his hands raised, is a "petty indignity."[13] It is a serious intrusion upon the sanctity of the person, which may inflict great indignity and arouse strong resentment, and it is not to be undertaken lightly.

* * * We therefore reject the notions that the Fourth Amendment does not come into play at all as a limitation upon police conduct if the officers stop short of something called a "technical arrest" or a "full-blown search."

In this case there can be no question, then, that Officer McFadden "seized" petitioner and subjected him to a "search" when he took hold of him and patted down the outer surfaces of his clothing. We must decide whether at that point it was reasonable for Officer McFadden to have interfered with petitioner's personal security as he did.[16] And in determining whether the seizure and search were "unreasonable" our inquiry is a dual one—whether the officer's action was justified at its inception, and whether it was reasonably related in scope to the circumstances which justified the interference in the first place.

If this case involved police conduct subject to the Warrant Clause of the Fourth Amendment, we would have to ascertain whether "probable cause" existed to justify the search and seizure which took place. However, that is not the case. We do not retreat from our holdings that the police must, whenever practicable, obtain advance judicial approval of searches and seizures through the warrant procedure, * * * or that in most instances failure

13. Consider the following apt description:

"[T]he officer must feel with sensitive fingers every portion of the prisoner's body. A thorough search must be made of the prisoner's arms and armpits, waistline and back, the groin and area about the testicles, and entire surface of the legs down to the feet." Priar & Martin, *Searching and Disarming Criminals,* 45 J.Crim.L.C. & P.S. 481 (1954).

16. We thus decide nothing today concerning the constitutional propriety of an investigative "seizure" upon less than probable cause for purposes of "detention" and/or interrogation. Obviously, not all personal intercourse between policemen and citizens involves "seizures" of persons. Only when the officer, by means of physical force or show of authority, has in some way restrained the liberty of a citizen may we conclude that a "seizure" has occurred. We cannot tell with any certainty upon this record whether any such "seizure" took place here prior to Officer McFadden's initiation of physical contact for purposes of searching Terry for weapons, and we thus may assume that up to that point no intrusion upon constitutionally protected rights had occurred.

to comply with the warrant requirement can only be excused by exigent circumstances. * * * But we deal here with an entire rubric of police conduct—necessarily swift action predicated upon the on-the-spot observations of the officer on the beat—which historically has not been, and as a practical matter could not be, subjected to the warrant procedure. Instead, the conduct involved in this case must be tested by the Fourth Amendment's general proscription against unreasonable searches and seizures.

Nonetheless, the notions which underlie both the warrant procedure and the requirement of probable cause remain fully relevant in this context. In order to assess the reasonableness of Officer McFadden's conduct as a general proposition, it is necessary "first to focus upon the governmental interest which allegedly justifies official intrusion upon the constitutionally protected interests of the private citizen," for there is "no ready test for determining reasonableness other than by balancing the need to search [or seize] against the invasion which the search [or seizure] entails." *Camara v. Municipal Court* [p. 399 infra]. And in justifying the particular intrusion the police officer must be able to point to specific and articulable facts which, taken together with rational inferences from those facts, reasonably warrant that intrusion. The scheme of the Fourth Amendment becomes meaningful only when it is assured that at some point the conduct of those charged with enforcing the laws can be subjected to the more detached, neutral scrutiny of a judge who must evaluate the reasonableness of a particular search or seizure in light of the particular circumstances. And in making that assessment it is imperative that the facts be judged against an objective standard: would the facts available to the officer at the moment of the seizure or the search "warrant a man of reasonable caution in the belief" that the action taken was appropriate? * * * Anything less would invite intrusions upon constitutionally guaranteed rights based on nothing more substantial than inarticulate hunches, a result this Court has consistently refused to sanction. * * *

Applying these principles to this case, we consider first the nature and extent of the governmental interests involved. One general interest is of course that of effective crime prevention and detection; it is this interest which underlies the recognition that a police officer may in appropriate circumstances and in an appropriate manner approach a person for purposes of investigating possibly criminal behavior even though there is no probable cause to make an arrest. It was this legitimate investigative function Officer McFadden was discharging when he decided to approach petitioner and his companions. He had observed Terry, Chilton, and Katz go through a series of acts, each of them perhaps innocent in itself, but which taken together warranted further investigation. There is nothing unusual in two men standing together on a street corner, perhaps waiting for someone. Nor is there anything suspicious about people in such circumstances strolling up and down the street, singly or in pairs. Store windows, moreover, are made to be looked in. But the story is quite different where, as here, two men hover about a street corner for an extended period of time, at the end of which it becomes apparent that they are not waiting for anyone or anything; where these men pace alternately along an identical route, pausing to stare in the same store window roughly 24 times; where each completion of this route is followed immediately by a conference between the two men on the corner; where they are joined in one of these conferences by a third man who leaves swiftly; and where the two men finally follow the third and rejoin him a couple of blocks away. It would have been poor police work indeed for an officer of 30 years' experience in the detection of thievery from stores in this same neighborhood to have failed to investigate this behavior further.

The crux of this case, however, is not the propriety of Officer McFadden's taking steps to investigate petitioner's suspicious behavior, but rather, whether there was justification for McFadden's invasion of Terry's personal security by searching him for weapons in the course of that investigation. We are now concerned with more than the governmental interest in investigating crime; in addition, there is the more immediate interest of the police officer in taking steps to assure himself that the person with whom he is dealing is not armed with a weapon that could unexpectedly and fatally be used against him. Certainly it would be unreasonable to require that police officers take unnecessary risks in the performance of their duties. American criminals have a long tradition of armed violence, and every year in this country many law enforcement officers are killed in the line of duty, and thousands more are wounded. Virtually all of these deaths and a substantial portion of the injuries are inflicted with guns and knives.

In view of these facts, we cannot blind ourselves to the need for law enforcement officers to protect themselves and other prospective victims of violence in situations where they may lack probable cause for an arrest. When an officer is justified in believing that the individual whose suspicious behavior he is investigating at close range is armed and presently dangerous to the officer or to others, it would appear to be clearly unreasonable to deny the officer the power to take necessary measures to determine whether the person is in fact carrying a weapon and to neutralize the threat of physical harm. * * *

Petitioner * * * does not say that an officer is always unjustified in searching a suspect to discover weapons. Rather, he says it is unreasonable for the policeman to take that step until such time as the situation evolves to a point where there is probable cause to make an arrest. * * *

There are two weaknesses in this line of reasoning however. First, it fails to take account of traditional limitations upon the scope of searches, and thus recognizes no distinction in purpose, character, and extent between a search incident to an arrest and a limited search for weapons. The former, although justified in part by the acknowledged necessity to protect the arresting officer from assault with a concealed weapon, is also justified on other grounds, and can therefore involve a relatively extensive exploration of the person. A search for weapons in the absence of probable cause to arrest, however, must, like any other search, be strictly circumscribed by the exigencies which justify its initiation. Thus it must be limited to that which is necessary for the discovery of weapons which might be used to harm the officer or others nearby, and may realistically be characterized as something less than a "full" search, even though it remains a serious intrusion.

A second, and related, objection to petitioner's argument is that it assumes that the law of arrest has already worked out the balance between the particular interests involved here—the neutralization of danger to the policeman in the investigative circumstance and the sanctity of the individual. But this is not so. An arrest is a wholly different kind of intrusion upon individual freedom from a limited search for weapons, and the interests each is designed to serve are likewise quite different. An arrest is the initial stage of a criminal prosecution. It is intended to vindicate society's interest in having its laws obeyed, and it is inevitably accompanied by future interference with the individual's freedom of movement, whether or not trial or conviction ultimately follows. The protective search for weapons, on the other hand, constitutes a brief, though far from inconsiderable intrusion upon the sanctity of the person. It does not follow that because an officer may lawfully arrest a person only when he is apprised of facts sufficient to warrant a belief that the person has committed or is committing a crime, the officer is equally unjustified, absent that kind of evidence, in making any intrusions short of an arrest. Moreover, a perfectly reasonable apprehension of danger may arise long before the officer is possessed of adequate information to justify taking a person into custody for the purpose of prosecuting him for a crime. * * *

Our evaluation of the proper balance that has to be struck in this type of case leads us to conclude that there must be a narrowly drawn authority to permit a reasonable search for weapons for the protection of the police officer, where he has reason to believe that he is dealing with an armed and dangerous individual, regardless of whether he has probable cause to arrest the individual for a crime. The officer need not be absolutely certain that the individual is armed; the issue is whether a reasonably prudent man in the circumstances would be warranted in the belief that his safety or that of others was in danger. * * * And in determining whether the officer acted reasonably in such circumstances, due weight must be given, not to his inchoate and unparticularized suspicion or "hunch", but to the specific reasonable inferences which he is entitled to draw from the facts in light of his experience.

We must now examine the conduct of Officer McFadden in this case to determine whether his search and seizure of petitioner were reasonable, both at their inception and as conducted. He had observed Terry, together with Chilton and another man, acting in a manner he took to be preface to a "stick-up." We think on the facts and circumstances Officer McFadden detailed before the trial judge a reasonably prudent man would have been warranted in believing petitioner was armed and thus presented a threat to the officer's safety while he was investigating his suspicious behavior. The actions of Terry and Chilton were consistent with McFadden's hypothesis that these men were contemplating a daylight robbery—which, it is reasonable to assume, would be likely to involve the use of weapons—and nothing in their conduct from the time he first noticed them until the time he confronted them and identified himself as a police officer gave him sufficient reason to negate that hypothesis. Although the trio had departed the original scene, there was nothing to indicate abandonment of an intent to commit a robbery at some point. Thus, when Officer McFadden approached the three men gathered before the display window at Zucker's store he had observed enough to make it quite reasonable to fear that they were armed; and nothing in their response to his hailing them, identifying himself as a police officer, and asking their names served to dispel that reasonable belief. We cannot say his decision at that point to seize Terry and pat his clothing for weapons was the product of a volatile or inventive imagination, or was undertaken simply as an act of harassment; the record evidences the tempered act of a policeman who in the course of an investigation had to make a quick decision as to how to protect himself and others from possible danger, and took limited steps to do so.

The manner in which the seizure and search were conducted is, of course, as vital a part of the inquiry as whether they were warranted at all. The Fourth Amendment proceeds as much by limitations upon the scope of governmental action as by imposing preconditions upon its initiation. The entire deterrent purpose of the rule excluding evidence seized in violation of the Fourth Amendment rests on the assumption that "limitations upon the fruit to be gathered tend to limit the quest itself." * * * Thus, evidence may not be introduced if it was discovered by means of a seizure and search which were not reasonably related in scope to the justification for their initiation.

[A protective search for weapons,] unlike a search without a warrant incident to a lawful arrest, is not justified by any need to prevent the disappearance or destruction of evidence of crime. The sole justification of the search in the present situation is the protection of the police officer and others nearby, and it must therefore be confined in scope to an intrusion reasonably designed to discover guns, knives, clubs, or other hidden instruments for the assault of the police officer.

The scope of the search in this case presents no serious problem in light of these standards. Officer McFadden patted down the outer clothing of petitioner and his two companions. He did not place his hands in their pockets or under the outer surface of their garments until he had felt weapons, and then he merely reached for and removed the guns. He never did invade Katz's person beyond the outer surfaces of his clothes, since he discovered nothing in his pat down which might have been a weapon. Officer McFadden confined his search strictly to what was minimally necessary to learn whether the men were armed and to disarm them once he discovered the weapons. He did not conduct a general exploratory search for whatever evidence of criminal activity he might find.

We conclude that the revolver seized from Terry was properly admitted in evidence against him. At the time he seized petitioner and searched him for weapons, Officer McFadden had reasonable grounds to believe that petitioner was armed and dangerous, and it was necessary for the protection of himself and others to take swift measures to discover the true facts and neutralize the threat of harm if it materialized. The policeman carefully restricted his search to what was appropriate to the discovery of the particular items which he sought. Each case of this sort will, of course, have to be decided on its own facts. We merely hold today that where a police officer observes unusual conduct which leads him reasonably to conclude in light of his experience that criminal activity may be afoot and that the persons with whom he is dealing may be armed and presently dangerous; where in the course of investigating this behavior he identifies himself as a policeman and makes reasonable inquiries; and where nothing in the initial stages of the encounter serves to dispel his reasonable fear for his own or others' safety, he is entitled for the protection of himself and others in the area to conduct a carefully limited search of the outer clothing of such persons in an attempt to discover weapons which might be used to assault him. Such a search is a reasonable search under the Fourth Amendment, and any weapons seized may properly be introduced in evidence against the person from whom they were taken.

Affirmed.

MR. JUSTICE HARLAN, concurring.

* * * The holding has * * * two logical corollaries that I do not think the Court has fully expressed.

In the first place, if the frisk is justified in order to protect the officer during an encounter with a citizen, the officer must first have constitutional grounds to insist on an encounter, to make a *forcible* stop. Any person, including a policeman, is at liberty to avoid a person he considers dangerous. If and when a policeman has a right instead to disarm such a person for his own protection, he must first have a right not to avoid him but to be in his presence. That right must be more than the liberty (again, possessed by every citizen) to address questions to other persons, for ordinarily the person addressed has an equal right to ignore his interrogator and walk away; he certainly need not submit to a frisk for the questioner's protection. I would make it perfectly clear that the right to frisk in this case depends upon the reasonableness of a forcible stop to investigate a suspected crime.

Where such a stop is reasonable, however, the right to frisk must be immediate and automatic if the reason for the stop is, as here, an articulable suspicion of a crime of violence. Just as a full search incident to a lawful arrest requires no additional justification, a limited frisk incident to a lawful stop must often be rapid and routine. There is no reason why an officer, rightfully but forcibly confronting a person suspected of a serious crime, should have to ask one question and take the risk that the answer might be a bullet. * * *

MR. JUSTICE WHITE, concurring.

* * * I think an additional word is in order concerning the matter of interrogation during an investigative stop. There is nothing in the Constitution which prevents a policeman from addressing questions to anyone on the streets. Absent special circumstances, the person approached may not be detained or frisked but may refuse to cooperate and go on his way. However, given the proper circumstances, such as those in this case, it seems to me the person may be briefly detained against his will while pertinent questions are directed to him. Of course, the person stopped is not obliged to answer, answers may not be compelled, and refusal to answer furnishes no basis for an arrest, although it may alert the officer to the need for continued observation. * * *

MR. JUSTICE DOUGLAS, dissenting.

* * * Had a warrant been sought, a magistrate would, therefore, have been unauthorized to issue one, for he can act only if there is a showing of "probable cause." We hold today that the police have greater authority to make a "seizure" and conduct a "search" than a judge has to authorize such action. We have said precisely the opposite over and over again. * * *

The infringement on personal liberty of any "seizure" of a person can only be "reasonable" under the Fourth Amendment if we require the police to possess "probable cause" before they seize him. Only that line draws a meaningful distinction between an officer's mere inkling and the presence of facts within the officer's personal knowledge which would convince a reasonable man that the person seized has committed, is committing, or is about to commit a particular crime. * * *

THE SIGNIFICANCE OF THE STOP-AND-FRISK CASES

A. THE UTILITY OF THE BALANCING TEST

1. Is Barrett, *Personal Rights, Property Rights and the Fourth Amendment,* 1960 Supreme Court Rev. 46, 63, correct in asserting that "the policy of the Fourth Amendment [would] be better served by an approach which determines the reasonableness of each investigative technique by balancing the seriousness of the suspected crime and the degree of reasonable suspicion possessed by the police against the magnitude of the invasion of the personal security and property rights of the individual involved?" Compare H. Schwartz, *Stop and Frisk (A Case Study in Judicial Control of the Police),* 58 J.Crim.L.C. & P.S. 433, 448–49 (1967): "Are all of these subtle considerations to be balanced by the policeman on the spot, in a matter of seconds or minutes, subject to second guessing by the courts? If the policeman's 'balancing' turns out to produce evidence of crime, how many courts will be ready to find that he balanced wrongly, that there was not enough suspicion for the crime suspected?"

2. What qualifies a particular police practice for assessment under the balancing test? In *Michigan v. Summers,* p. 294 supra, Stewart, J., joined by Brennan and Marshall, JJ., dissenting, objected to the majority's use of the balancing test in holding that a warrant to search premises for contraband authorizes police to detain the occupants while the warrant is executed. They reasoned "that before a court can uphold a detention on less than probable cause on the ground that it is 'reasonable' in the light of the competing interests, the government must demonstrate an important purpose beyond the normal goals of criminal investigation, or must demonstrate an extraordinary obstacle to such investigation," which they believed had not been done in the instant case.

3. Should the balancing test also be used to keep the evidentiary requirements for a given police practice "flexible," so that, for example, less evidence would be required when the crime being investigated is a serious one? Consider Justice Jackson, dissenting in *Brinegar v. United States,* 338 U.S. 160, 69 S.Ct. 1302, 93 L.Ed. 1879 (1949): "If we assume, for example, that a child is kidnapped and the officers throw a roadblock about the neighborhood and search every outgoing car, it would be a drastic and undiscriminating use of the search. The officers might be unable to show probable cause for searching any particular car. However, I should candidly strive hard to sustain such an action, executed fairly and in good faith, because it might be reasonable to subject travelers to that indignity if it was the only way to save a threatened life and detect a vicious crime. But I should not strain to sustain such a roadblock and universal search to salvage a few bottles of bourbon and catch a bootlegger." [a]

B. POLICE ACTION SHORT OF A SEIZURE

1. In UNITED STATES v. MENDENHALL, 446 U.S. 544, 100 S.Ct. 1870, 64 L.Ed.2d 497 (1980), where the court of appeals had held defendant's consent to a search of her person was the fruit of her illegal detention at an airport by federal drug agents, STEWART, J., announcing the judgment of the Court,[b] stated:

"We conclude that a person has been 'seized' within the meaning of the Fourth Amendment only if, in view of all of the circumstances surrounding the incident, a reasonable person would have believed that he was not free to leave.[6] Examples of circumstances that might indicate a seizure, even where the person did not attempt to leave, would be the threatening presence of several officers, the display of a weapon by an officer, some physical touching of the person of the citizen, or the use of language or tone of voice indicating that compliance with the officer's request might be compelled. See 3 LaFave, *Search and Seizure* 53–55 (1978). In the absence of some such evidence, otherwise inoffensive contact between a member of the public and the police cannot, as a matter of law, amount to a seizure of that person.

"On the facts of this case, no 'seizure' of the respondent occurred. The events took place in the public concourse. The agents wore no uniforms and displayed no weapons. They did not summon the respondent to their presence, but instead approached her and identified themselves as federal agents. They requested, but did not demand to see the respondent's identification and ticket. Such conduct without more, did not amount to an intrusion upon any constitutionally protected interest.

a. Compare *Dunaway v. New York,* p. 385 infra.

On the use of roadblocks, consider *Model Pre-Arraignment Code* § 110.2, providing in part:

"(2) *Stopping of Vehicles at Roadblock.* A law enforcement officer may, if

"(a) he has reasonable cause to believe that a felony has been committed; and

"(b) stopping all or most vehicles moving in a particular direction or directions is reasonably necessary to permit a search for the perpetrator or victim of such felony in view of the seriousness and special circumstances of such felony,

order the drivers of such vehicles to stop, and may search such vehicles to the extent necessary to accomplish such purpose. Such action shall be accomplished as promptly as possible under the circumstances."

b. Rehnquist, J., joined in this part of the Stewart opinion. Powell, J., joined by the Chief Justice and Blackmun, J., concurring, noted they did "not necessarily disagree" with the Stewart analysis, but preferred to uphold the action on the ground that reasonable suspicion was present. White, J., joined by Brennan, Marshall and Stevens, JJ., dissenting, objected the government should not be allowed to raise the no-seizure issue for the first time before the Supreme Court.

6. We agree with the District Court that the subjective intention of the DEA agent in this case to detain the respondent, had she attempted to leave, is irrelevant except insofar as that may have been conveyed to the respondent.

The respondent was not seized simply by reason of the fact that the agents approached her, asked her if she would show them her ticket and identification, and posed to her a few questions. Nor was it enough to establish a seizure that the person asking the questions was a law enforcement official. In short, nothing in the record suggests that the respondent had any objective reason to believe that she was not free to end the conversation in the concourse and proceed on her way, and for that reason we conclude that the agents' initial approach to her was not a seizure.

"Our conclusion that no seizure occurred is not affected by the fact that the respondent was not expressly told by the agents that she was free to decline to cooperate with their inquiry, for the voluntariness of her responses does not depend upon her having been so informed. We also reject the argument that the only inference to be drawn from the fact that the respondent acted in a manner so contrary to her self-interest is that she was compelled to answer the agents' questions. It may happen that a person makes statements to law enforcement officials that he later regrets, but the issue in such cases is not whether the statement was self-protective, but rather whether it was made voluntarily.

"The Court's decision last Term in *Brown v. Texas,* 443 U.S. 47, 99 S.Ct. 2637, 61 L.Ed.2d 357 (1979), on which the respondent relies, is not apposite. It could not have been plainer under the circumstances there presented that Brown was forcibly detained by the officers. In that case, two police officers approached Brown in an alley, and asked him to identify himself and to explain his reason for being there. Brown 'refused to identify himself and angrily asserted that the officers had no right to stop him.' Up to this point there was no seizure. But after continuing to protest the officers' power to interrogate him, Brown was first frisked, and then arrested for violation of a state statute making it a criminal offense for a person to refuse to give his name and address to an officer 'who has lawfully stopped him and requested the information.' * * *

"The Court's decisions involving investigatory stops of automobiles do not point in any different direction. * * * [S]topping or diverting an automobile in transit, with the attendant opportunity for a visual inspection of areas of the passenger compartment not otherwise observable, is materially more intrusive than a question put to a passing pedestrian, and the fact that the former amounts to a seizure tells very little about the constitutional status of the latter."

2. Compare FLORIDA v. ROYER, 460 U.S. 491, 103 S.Ct. 1319, 75 L.Ed.2d 229 (1983), where detectives at an airport, suspecting Royer was a drug courier, approached and asked to speak with him and requested his ticket and driver's license and noted the former, like the tags, bore the name "Holt" while the latter carried the name "Royer." The detectives then asked Royer to accompany them to a nearby room (an aspect of the case discussed in Note 2, p. 376). The *Royer* plurality [c] concluded that as of that moment there was a seizure under Justice Stewart's test in *Mendenhall:* "Asking for and examining Royer's ticket and his driver's license were no doubt permissible in themselves, but when the officers identified themselves as narcotics agents, told Royer that he was suspected of transporting narcotics, and asked him to accompany them to the police room, while retaining his ticket and driver's license and without indicating in any way that he was free to depart, Royer was effectively seized for the purposes of the Fourth Amendment. These circumstances surely amount to a

c. White, J., joined by Marshall, Powell and Stevens, JJ.

show of official authority such that 'a reasonable person would have believed he was not free to leave.' " [d]

3. IMMIGRATION AND NATURALIZATION SERV. v. DELGADO, 466 U.S. 210, 104 S.Ct. 1758, 80 L.Ed.2d 247 (1984), concerned the constitutionality of "factory surveys," where with the employer's consent or pursuant to a warrant issued on a showing of probable cause that numerous illegal aliens were employed at a particular factory, numerous INS agents would survey the work force. Moving through the factory, the agents would ask a few questions of workers at their work stations and, if the response was unsatisfactory or alienage was admitted, ask for immigration papers. The court of appeals held (1) that the entire work force was seized during the duration of each survey, lasting one to two hours, because the stationing of agents at the doors meant that "a reasonable worker 'would have believed that he was not free to leave' "; and (2) that questioning of individual workers was a seizure requiring individualized reasonable suspicion. The Supreme Court, per REHNQUIST, J., rejected both holdings by relying upon the *Mendenhall-Royer* test, said to support the conclusion "that police questioning, by itself, is unlikely to result in a Fourth Amendment violation."

As for the first holding below, the Court stressed not only that "when people are at work their freedom to move about has been meaningfully restricted, not by the actions of law enforcement officials, but by the workers' voluntary obligations to their employers," but also that the agents at the doors did not prevent anyone from leaving but merely ensured that all persons in the factories were questioned. "The presence of agents by the exits posed no reasonable threat of detention to these workers while they walked through the factories on job assignments. Likewise, the mere possibility that they would be questioned if they sought to leave the buildings should not have resulted in any reasonable apprehension by any of them that they would be seized or detained in any meaningful way." As for the second holding below, the Court concluded that the individual respondents had not been seized because they had been subjected to "nothing more than a brief encounter" while at their work station or while moving about the factory, and "it was obvious from the beginning of the surveys that the INS agents were only questioning people." Thus the respondents' "description of the encounters with the INS agents satisfies us that the encounters were classic consensual encounters rather than Fourth Amendment seizures."

BRENNAN and MARSHALL, JJ., dissenting in part, disputed the second conclusion. "Although none of the respondents was physically restrained by the INS agents during the questioning, it is nonetheless plain beyond cavil that the manner in which the INS conducted these surveys demonstrated a 'show of authority' of sufficient size and force to overbear the will of any reasonable person." [e]

d. Brennan, J., concurring, concluded it was "wholly unnecessary to reach" the questions concerning "the legality of the officers' initial stop." Blackmun, J., dissenting, concurred "in the plurality's adoption of the Fourth Amendment 'seizure' standard proposed by Justice Stewart in *Mendenhall*" and "with the plurality's conclusion that at some point in this encounter that threshold was passed." Rehnquist, J., joined by the Chief Justice and O'Connor, J., dissenting, expressed agreement "with the plurality's intimation that when the detectives first approached and questioned Royer, no seizure occurred and thus the constitutional safeguards of the Fourth Amendment were not involved."

e. Powell, J., concurring, relied upon *Martinez-Fuerte*, p. 403 infra. "The government's interest in using factory surveys is as great if not greater" than in using the fixed checkpoint traffic stops permitted there, and the intrusion upon the employees "is about the same as it was in *Martinez-Fuerte*."

C. Grounds for Temporary Seizure for Investigation

1. Under *Terry,* what grounds are needed for a stop, and how do they differ from those needed for a full-fledged arrest? Shortly after *Terry,* one commentator suggested that for arrest it must be "more probable than not that the person is the offender," while for a *Terry* stop "it should be sufficient that there is a substantial possibility that a crime has been or is about to be committed and that the suspect is the person who committed or is planning the offense." [f] Compare the Court's later elaboration in UNITED STATES v. CORTEZ, 449 U.S. 411, 101 S.Ct. 690, 66 L.Ed.2d 621 (1981):

"Courts have used a variety of terms to capture the elusive concept of what cause is sufficient to authorize police to stop a person. Terms like 'articulable reasons' and 'founded suspicion' are not self-defining; they fall short of providing clear guidance dispositive of the myriad factual situations that arise. But the essence of all that has been written is that the totality of the circumstances—the whole picture—must be taken into account. Based upon that whole picture the detaining officers must have a particularized and objective basis for suspecting the particular person stopped of criminal activity.

"The idea that an assessment of the whole picture must yield a particularized suspicion contains two elements, each of which must be present before a stop is permissible. First, the assessment must be based upon all the circumstances. The analysis proceeds with various objective observations, information from police reports, if such are available, and consideration of the modes or patterns of operation of certain kinds of lawbreakers. From these data, a trained officer draws inferences and makes deductions—inferences and deductions that might well elude an untrained person.

"The process does not deal with hard certainties, but with probabilities. Long before the law of probabilities was articulated as such, practical people formulated certain common sense conclusions about human behavior; jurors as factfinders are permitted to do the same—and so are law enforcement officers. Finally, the evidence thus collected must be seen and weighed not in terms of library analysis by scholars, but as understood by those versed in the field of law enforcement.

"The second element contained in the idea that an assessment of the whole picture must yield a particularized suspicion is the concept that the process just described must raise a suspicion that the particular individual being stopped is engaged in wrongdoing."

2. In SIBRON v. NEW YORK, 392 U.S. 40, 88 S.Ct. 1889, 20 L.Ed.2d 917 (1968), a companion case to *Terry,* the facts as stated by the Court were as follows: "At the hearing on the motion to suppress, Officer Martin testified that while he was patrolling his beat in uniform on March 9, 1965, he observed Sibron 'continually from the hours of 4:00 P.M. to 12:00, midnight * * * in the vicinity of 742 Broadway.' He stated that during this period of time he saw Sibron in conversation with six or eight persons whom he (Patrolman Martin) knew from past experience to be narcotics addicts. The officer testified that he did not overhear any of these conversations, and that he did not see anything pass between Sibron and any of the others. Late in the evening Sibron entered a restaurant. Patrolman

f. LaFave, *"Street Encounters" and the Constitution: Terry, Sibron, Peters and Beyond,* 67 Mich.L.Rev. 40, 73–75 (1968). An excellent illustration is provided by *Luckett v. State,* 182 N.E.2d 738 (Ind.1972), where an officer stopped for investigation a green car bearing a license plate prefix 82J upon information that such a car had been used by persons fleeing from a burglary earlier in the evening. The court concluded that the officer had "probable cause to stop the automobile" even though it was "readily apparent" that he "did not have probable cause to stop every green automobile with an 82J license prefix and formally arrest its occupants."

Martin saw Sibron speak with three more known addicts inside the restaurant. Once again, nothing was overheard and nothing was seen to pass between Sibron and the addicts. Sibron sat down and ordered pie and coffee, and as he was eating, Patrolman Martin approached him and told him to come outside. Once outside, the officer said to Sibron, 'You know what I am after.' According to the officer, Sibron 'mumbled something and reached into his pocket.' Simultaneously, Patrolman Martin thrust his hand into the same pocket, discovering several glassine envelopes, which, it turned out, contained heroin."

Though the Court, per WARREN, C.J., focused primarily upon the lack of grounds for and the improper manner of the frisk (see Notes 1 and 2, p. 381 infra), it was intimated that there were not even grounds for a stop:

"It must be emphasized that Patrolman Martin was completely ignorant regarding the content of these conversations, and that he saw nothing pass between Sibron and the addicts. So far as he knew, they might indeed 'have been talking about the World Series.' The inference that persons who talk to narcotics addicts are engaged in the criminal traffic in narcotics is simply not the sort of reasonable inference required to support an intrusion by the police upon an individual's personal security."

Do you believe that Officer Martin was less certain of what Sibron was up to than Officer McFadden was as to what Terry and his companions were up to? Are there other considerations at play here? HARLAN, J., concurring in *Sibron,* observed:

"[I]n *Terry,* the police officer judged that his suspect was about to commit a violent crime and that he had to assert himself in order to prevent it. Here there was no reason for Officer Martin to think that an incipient crime, or flight, or the destruction of evidence would occur if he stayed his hand; indeed, there was no more reason for him to intrude upon Sibron at the moment when he did than there had been four hours earlier, and no reason to think the situation would have changed four hours hence. While no hard-and-fast rule can be drawn, I would suggest that one important factor, missing here, that should be taken into account in determining whether there are reasonable grounds for a forcible intrusion is whether there is any need for immediate action."

3. In ADAMS v. WILLIAMS, 407 U.S. 143, 92 S.Ct. 1921, 32 L.Ed.2d 612 (1972), Sgt. Connolly, on patrol in a high crime area, was approached at 2:15 a.m. by a person known to him and informed that an individual in a nearby car was carrying narcotics and had a gun at his waist. Connolly approached the vehicle to investigate, tapped on the window and asked the occupant, Williams, to open the door. Williams instead rolled down the window, and Connolly then reached into the car and removed a fully loaded revolver from Williams' waistband. Williams was then arrested for unlawful possession of the gun, and a search incident thereto uncovered heroin on his person. The Court, per REHNQUIST, concluded "that Sgt. Connolly acted justifiably in responding to his informant's tip. The informant was known to him personally and had provided him with information in the past. This is a stronger case than obtains in the case of an anonymous telephone tip.[g] The informant here came forward personally to give information that was immediately verifiable at the scene. Indeed, under Connecticut law, the informant herself might have been subject to immediate arrest for making a false complaint had Sgt. Connolly's investigation proven the tip in-

g. What then if an anonymous telephone caller tells the police that a youth of a certain description is standing on a certain corner and that he "had a loaded 32 calibre revolver in his left hand jacket pocket," and an officer proceeds to the location and sees the described person standing in the middle of a group of children, as in *People v. Taggart,* 229 N.E.2d 581 (N.Y.1967)?

correct.[2] Thus, while the Court's decisions indicate that this informant's unverified tip may have been insufficient for a narcotics arrest or search warrant, the information carried enough indicia of reliability to justify the officer's forcible stop of Williams.

"In reaching this conclusion, we reject respondent's argument that reasonable cause for a stop and frisk can only be based on the officer's personal observation, rather than on information supplied by another person. Informants' tips, like all other clues and evidence coming to a policeman on the scene, may vary greatly in their value and reliability. One simple rule will not cover every situation. Some tips, completely lacking in indicia of reliability, would either warrant no police response or require further investigation before a forcible stop of a suspect would be authorized. But in some situations—for example, when the victim of a street crime seeks immediate police aid and gives a description of his assailant, or when a credible informant warns of a specific impending crime—the subtleties of the hearsay rule should not thwart an appropriate police response."

DOUGLAS, J., joined by Marshall, J., dissenting, expressed a concern that the easy extension of *Terry v. Ohio,* to "possessory offenses" is a serious intrusion on Fourth Amendment safeguards. "If it is to be extended to the latter at all, this should be only where observation by the officer himself or well authenticated information shows 'that criminal activity may be afoot.' "

MARSHALL, J., joined by Douglas, J., dissenting, objected that "the officer had no idea how long respondent had been in the car, how long the car had been parked, or to whom the car belonged. With respect to the gun,[5] the officer did not know if or when the informant had ever seen the gun, or whether the gun was carried legally, as Connecticut law permitted, or illegally. And with respect to the narcotics, the officer did not know what kind of narcotics respondent allegedly had, whether they were legally or illegally possessed, what the basis of the informant's knowledge was, or even whether the informant was capable of distinguishing narcotics from other substances.

"Unable to answer any of these questions, the officer nevertheless determined that it was necessary to intrude on respondent's liberty. I believe that his determination was totally unreasonable. As I read *Terry,* an officer may act on the basis of *reliable* information short of probable cause to make a stop, and ultimately a frisk, if necessary; but, the officer may not use unreliable, unsubstantiated, conclusory hearsay to justify an invasion of liberty." [h]

4. Should either the seriousness of the suspected crime or the time of its apparent commission have any bearing on whether a *Terry* stop is permissible? In UNITED STATES v. HENSLEY, 469 U.S. 221, 105 S.Ct. 675, 83 L.Ed.2d 604 (1985), the Court, per O'CONNOR, J., held by analogy to *Whiteley v. Warden,* p. 286 supra, "that, if a flyer or bulletin has been issued on the basis of articulable facts supporting a reasonable suspicion that the

2. Section 53–168 of the Connecticut General Statutes, in force at the time of these events, provided that a "person who knowingly makes to any police officer * * * a false report or a false complaint alleging that a crime or crimes have been committed" is guilty of a misdemeanor.

5. The fact that the respondent carried his gun in a high crime area is irrelevant. In such areas it is more probable than not that citizens would be more likely to carry weapons authorized by the State to protect themselves.

h. Brennan, J., dissenting separately, expressed similar concerns. Consider in this regard *The Supreme Court, 1971 Term,* 86 Harv.L.Rev. 50, 178 (1972): "Probable cause is determined both by the quantum and content of the information an officer possesses and by the degree of its reliability. The two are nevertheless distinct concepts and a case can certainly be made that the standard of cause to stop should be less than probable cause only in the sense that the officer may stop on less or different information than probable cause would require and *not* in the sense that he may act on information that is received in a manner less reliable than probable cause would require."

wanted person has committed an offense, then reliance on that flyer or bulletin justifies a stop to check identification, to pose questions to the person, or to detain the person briefly while attempting to obtain further information." But the Court first rejected the lower court's position that *Terry* is limited to ongoing criminal activity:

"* * * The precise limits on investigatory stops to investigate past criminal activity are more difficult to define. The proper way to identify the limits is to apply the same test already used to identify the proper bounds of intrusions that further investigations of imminent or ongoing crimes. That test, which is grounded in the standard of reasonableness embodied in the Fourth Amendment, balances the nature and quality of the intrusion on personal security against the importance of the governmental interests alleged to justify the intrusion. When this balancing test is applied to stops to investigate past crimes, we think that probable cause to arrest need not always be required.

"The factors in the balance may be somewhat different when a stop to investigate past criminal activity is involved rather than a stop to investigate ongoing criminal conduct. This is because the governmental interest and the nature of the intrusions involved in the two situations may differ. As we noted in *Terry,* one general interest present in the context of ongoing or imminent criminal activity is 'that of effective crime prevention and detection.' A stop to investigate an already completed crime does not necessarily promote the interest of crime prevention as directly as a stop to investigate suspected ongoing criminal activity. Similarly, the exigent circumstances which require a police officer to step in before a crime is committed or completed are not necessarily as pressing long afterwards. Public safety may be less threatened by a suspect in a past crime who now appears to be going about his lawful business than it is by a suspect who is currently in the process of violating the law. Finally, officers making a stop to investigate past crimes may have a wider range of opportunity to choose the time and circumstances of the stop.

"Despite these differences, where police have been unable to locate a person suspected of involvement in a past crime, the ability to briefly stop that person, ask questions, or check identification in the absence of probable cause promotes the strong government interest in solving crimes and bringing offenders to justice. Restraining police action until after probable cause is obtained would not only hinder the investigation, but might also enable the suspect to flee in the interim and to remain at large. Particularly in the context of felonies or crimes involving a threat to public safety, it is in the public interest that the crime be solved and the suspect detained as promptly as possible. The law enforcement interests at stake in these circumstances outweigh the individual's interest to be free of a stop and detention that is no more extensive than permissible in the investigation of imminent or ongoing crimes.

"We need not and do not decide today whether *Terry* stops to investigate all past crimes, however serious, are permitted. It is enough to say that, if police have a reasonable suspicion, grounded in specific and articulable facts, that a person they encounter was involved in or is wanted in connection with a completed felony, then a *Terry* stop may be made to investigate that suspicion." [i]

i. But, what if the stop is made other than at a crime scene because the individual is thought to have information about the criminal activity of others? A stop for such a purpose was involved in *United States v. Ward,* 488 F.2d 162 (9th Cir. 1973), where FBI agents used their siren to stop a person driving a car, after which he displayed a false draft card. The court held that the seizure was improper because there was no emergency requiring the interview of that person at that particular time, and went on to note that *Terry* "cannot be stretched so far as to allow detentive stops for generalized criminal inquiries."

5. *Terry* relied upon the *Camara* case, p. 399 infra, allowing safety inspections of buildings without such individualized suspicion when pursuant to an established scheme or plan. And in *Brown v. Texas,* 443 U.S. 47, 99 S.Ct. 2637, 61 L.Ed.2d 357 (1979), a unanimous Court declared that the Fourth Amendment requires that a brief detention for investigation "be based on specific, objective facts indicating that society's legitimate interests require the seizure of the particular individual, or that the seizure must be carried out pursuant to a plan embodying explicit, neutral limitations on the conduct of individual officers." Does this mean that such a plan is a sufficient substitute for individualized suspicion? How might such a plan be drafted?

D. PERMISSIBLE EXTENT OF TEMPORARY SEIZURE

1. Assuming that the police only have grounds to make a temporary seizure on the street for purposes of investigation, what limits must be observed by them to prevent the seizure from becoming illegal? What if the officer approaches with a drawn gun and orders the suspect to raise his hands? What if the officer asserts that the suspect is under arrest? And what of the length of detention? Compare *United States v. Jennings,* 468 F.2d 111 (9th Cir. 1972) (25 minutes too long where suspect cooperated fully and no greater suspicion developed); with *United States v. Richards,* 500 F.2d 1025 (9th Cir.1974) (1 hour not too long where suspects gave implausible responses to questions, thereby adding to initial suspicion, and police diligently pursued the most plausible means of clarifying the situation). What if the suspect was transported to a nearby crime scene for possible identification as the perpetrator, held impermissible in *People v. Harris,* 540 P.2d 632 (Cal.1975), whenever the witnesses could be transported to the detention scene? [j] As for detention at the police station, see pp. 383–386 infra.

2. In FLORIDA v. ROYER, p. 370 supra, the detectives asked Royer to accompany them to a small room about 40 feet away. His luggage was retrieved from the airline and brought to that room, and Royer was then asked to consent to a search of the suitcases, which he did. About 15 minutes had elapsed since the initial encounter. The *Royer* plurality [k] first commented:

"The predicate permitting seizures on suspicion short of probable cause is that law enforcement interests warrant a limited intrusion on the personal security of the suspect. The scope of the intrusion permitted will vary to some extent with the particular facts and circumstances of each case. This much, however, is clear: an investigative detention must be temporary and last no longer than is necessary to effectuate the purpose of the stop. Similarly, the investigative methods employed should be the least intrusive means reasonably available to verify or dispel the officer's suspicion in a short period of time. It is the State's burden to demonstrate that the seizure it seeks to justify on the basis of a reasonable suspicion was sufficiently limited in scope and duration to satisfy the conditions of an investigative seizure."

The plurality then concluded "that at the time Royer produced the key to his suitcase, the detention to which he was then subjected was a more serious intrusion on his personal liberty than is allowable on mere suspicion of criminal activity." They stressed: (i) that the situation "had escalated into an investigatory procedure in a police interrogation room," so that

j. Compare *People v. Bloyd,* 331 N.W.2d 447 (Mich.1982), concluding that because transportation of a suspect even a short distance is more intrusive than a mere stop, it "should be dependent upon knowledge that a crime has been committed" and impermissible when the defendant's conduct was suspicious but "there has not been any report of a crime" recently in the vicinity.

k. White, J., joined by Marshall, Powell and Stevens, JJ.

"[a]s a practical matter, Royer was under arrest"; and (ii) that "the officers' conduct was more intrusive than necessary to effectuate an investigative detention otherwise authorized by the *Terry* line of cases," as while "there are undoubtedly reasons of safety and security that would justify moving a suspect from one location to another during an investigatory detention, such as from an airport concourse to a more private area," there was "no indication in this case that such reasons prompted the officers to transfer the site of the encounter from the concourse to the interrogation room. It appears, rather, that the primary interest of the officers was not in having an extended conversation with Royer but in the contents of his luggage, a matter which the officers did not pursue orally with Royer until after the encounter was relocated to the police room. The record does not reflect any facts which would support a finding that the legitimate law enforcement purposes which justified the detention in the first instance were furthered by removing Royer to the police room prior to the officer's attempt to gain his consent to a search of his luggage. As we have noted, had Royer consented to a search on the spot, the search could have been conducted with Royer present in the area where the bags were retrieved by Officer Johnson and any evidence recovered would have been admissible against him. If the search proved negative, Royer would have been free to go much earlier and with less likelihood of missing his flight, which in itself can be a very serious matter in a variety of circumstances.

"Third, the State has not touched on the question whether it would have been feasible to investigate the contents of Royer's bags in a more expeditious way. The courts are not strangers to the use of trained dogs to detect the presence of controlled substances in luggage. There is no indication here that this means was not feasible and available. If it had been used, Royer and his luggage could have been momentarily detained while this investigative procedure was carried out. Indeed, it may be that no detention at all would have been necessary. A negative result would have freed Royer in short order; a positive result would have resulted in his justifiable arrest on probable cause." [l]

Brennan, J., concurring, addressed this point in a footnote reading as follows: "I interpret the plurality's requirement that the investigative methods employed pursuant to a *Terry* stop be 'the least intrusive means reasonably available to verify or dispel the officer's suspicion in a short period of time,' to mean that the availability of a less intrusive means may make an otherwise reasonable stop unreasonable. I do not interpret it to mean that the absence of a less intrusive means can make an otherwise unreasonable stop reasonable."

Blackmun, J., dissenting because he believed that Royer consented to go to the room, added that he could not "accept the 'least intrusive' alternative analysis the plurality would impose on the law of the Fourth Amendment." Rehnquist, J., joined by the Chief Justice and O'Connor, J., dissenting, also found no support in prior cases for the plurality's "least intrusive means" principle and concluded that the plurality's analysis "adds up to little more than saying that if my aunt were a man, she would be my uncle. The officers might have taken different steps than they did to investigate Royer, but the same may be said of virtually every investigative encounter that has more than one step to it. The question we must decide is what was *unreasonable* about the steps which *these officers* took with respect to *this* suspect in the Miami Airport on this particular day."

l. The plurality then concluded "that probable cause to arrest Royer did not exist at the time he consented to the search of his luggage," so that the consent was the fruit of an illegal arrest. The dissenters, believing the detention in the room was permissible under *Terry,* found it unnecessary to address the probable cause issue.

3. What limits, if any, does *Royer* place upon *Terry* stops? Does the case justify the conclusion (i) that such a stop may not extend as long as 15 minutes? (ii) that the person detained may never be moved to another location? (iii) that the person detained may not be moved from a public area to a private one? (iv) that the police must opt for the most expeditious means of investigation? Consider UNITED STATES v. SHARPE, ___ U.S. ___, 105 S.Ct. 1568, 84 L.Ed.2d 605 (1985). There, a federal drug agent, patrolling in an unmarked car in a highway area under surveillance for drug trafficking, saw an apparently overloaded camper truck traveling in tandem with a Pontiac. He radioed for assistance, and when a highway patrolman responded they attempted to stop the two vehicles. The Pontiac pulled over, but the truck continued on, pursued by the patrolman. Once the drug agent obtained identification from the driver of the Pontiac, he sought without success to reach the patrolman by radio. He then radioed for more assistance, and when local police appeared he left them with the Pontiac and drove ahead to where the patrolman had stopped the truck. After smelling the odor of marijuana coming from the vehicle, he opened it and saw bales of marijuana and then arrested the driver of the truck, one Savage. The Court of Appeals held that the 20-minute detention of Savage "failed to meet the [Fourth Amendment's] requirement of brevity," but the Supreme Court, per CHIEF JUSTICE BURGER, disagreed:

"* * * Obviously, if an investigative stop continues indefinitely, at some point it can no longer be justified as an investigative stop. But our cases impose no rigid time limitation on *Terry* stops. * * * Much as a 'bright line' rule would be desirable, in evaluating whether an investigative detention is unreasonable, common sense and ordinary human experience must govern over rigid criteria.[m]

"In assessing whether a detention is too long in duration to be justified as an investigative stop, we consider it appropriate to examine whether the police diligently pursued a means of investigation that was likely to confirm or dispel their suspicions quickly, during which time it was necessary to detain the defendant. A court making this assessment should take care to consider whether the police are acting in a swiftly developing situation, and in such cases the court should not indulge in unrealistic second-guessing. A creative judge engaged in *post hoc* evaluation of police conduct can almost always imagine some alternative means by which the objectives of the police might have been accomplished. But '[t]he fact that the protection of the public might, in the abstract, have been accomplished by "less intrusive" means does not, in itself, render the search unreasonable.' The question is not simply whether some other alternative was available, but whether the police acted unreasonably in failing to recognize or to pursue it."

Stressing that the "delay in this case was attributable almost entirely to the evasive actions of Savage," that most of the 20 minutes was consumed by the agent trying to reach the patrolman and to obtain additional assistance, and that when the agent reached Savage "he proceeded expeditiously," the majority in *Sharpe* concluded the delay was not unreasonable. Marshall, J., though concurring because the "prolonged encounter" was attributable to "the evasive actions" of Savage, argued that "fidelity to the rationales that justify *Terry* stops require that the intrusiveness of the stop be measured independently of law enforcement needs. A stop must first be found not unduly intrusive, particularly in its length, before it is proper to consider whether law enforcement aims warrant

m. Compare *Model Code of Pre-Arraignment Procedure* § 110.2(1), recommending a maximum of 20 minutes for a *Terry* stop.

limited investigation." Brennan, J., dissenting, objected that record did not clearly show that Savage had tried to elude the police, and that the government had not met its burden under *Royer* to "show at a minimum that the 'least intrusive means reasonably available' were used in carrying out the stop."

4. Will the most common investigative technique, interrogation, ordinarily be the most expeditious? Does that depend upon the significance which can be attached to noncooperation? Cf. KOLENDER v. LAWSON, 461 U.S. 352, 103 S.Ct. 1855, 75 L.Ed.2d 903 (1983), where the Court overturned on void for vagueness grounds a statute which, as construed, made it a criminal offense for a person lawfully stopped under *Terry* to fail to provide "credible and reliable" identification and to account for his presence, as the statute "contains no standard for determining what a suspect has to do in order to satisfy the requirement to provide a 'credible and reliable' identification." The majority thus found it unnecessary to address other issues, but Brennan, J., concurring, asserted that "under the Fourth Amendment, police officers with reasonable suspicion that an individual has committed or is about to commit a crime may detain that individual, using some force if necessary, for the purpose of asking investigative questions. They may ask their questions in a way calculated to obtain an answer. But they may not *compel* an answer, and they must allow the person to leave after a reasonably brief period of time unless the information they have acquired during the encounter has given them probable cause sufficient to justify an arrest." [4]

E. TEMPORARY SEIZURE OF EFFECTS

1. In *United States v. Van Leeuwen,* 397 U.S. 249, 90 S.Ct. 1029, 25 L.Ed.2d 282 (1970) a postal clerk in Mt. Vernon, Washington, advised a policeman that he was suspicious of two packages of coins just mailed. The policeman immediately noted that the return address was fictitious and that the individual who mailed the packages had Canadian license plates, and later investigation disclosed that the addressees (one in California, the other in Tennessee) were under investigation for trafficking in illegal coins. Upon this basis a search warrant for both packages was obtained, but not until the packages had been held for slightly more than a day. A unanimous Court, although acknowledging that "detention of mail could at some point become an unreasonable seizure of 'papers' or 'effects' within the meaning of the Fourth Amendment," cited *Terry* in upholding this "detention, without a warrant, while an investigation was made." The Court emphasized that the investigation was conducted promptly and that most of the delay was attributable to the fact that because of the time differential the Tennessee authorities could not be reached until the following day.

2. In UNITED STATES v. PLACE, 462 U.S. 696, 103 S.Ct. 2637, 77 L.Ed.2d 110 (1983), federal agents stopped respondent, a suspected drug courier, at LaGuardia Airport, seized his luggage for the purported purpose of taking it to a judge while a warrant was sought, and then allowed respondent to go his way. They took the bags to Kennedy Airport, where a trained narcotics dog reacted positively to one of them and ambiguously to the other, but because it was late Friday afternoon held the bags until Monday morning, when a warrant was obtained for the first

4. * * * In some circumstances it is even conceivable that the mere fact that a suspect refuses to answer questions once detained, viewed in the context of the facts that gave rise to reasonable suspicion in the first place, would be enough to provide probable cause. A court confronted with such a claim, however, would have to evaluate it carefully to make certain that the person arrested was not being penalized for the exercise of his right to refuse to answer.

bag and cocaine was found in execution of the warrant. The Court, per O'CONNOR, J., first recognized "the reasonableness under the Fourth Amendment of warrantless seizures of personal luggage from the custody of the owner on the basis of less than probable cause for the purpose of pursuing a limited course of investigation, short of opening the luggage, that would quickly confirm or dispel the authorities' suspicion." Applying the *Terry* balancing of interests approach, the Court concluded that "the governmental interest in seizing the luggage briefly to pursue further investigation is substantial," and that because "seizures of property can vary in intrusiveness, some brief detentions of personal effects may be so minimally intrusive of Fourth Amendment interests that strong countervailing governmental interests will justify a seizure based only on specific articulable facts that the property contains contraband or evidence of a crime.

"* * * Particularly in the case of detention of luggage within the traveler's immediate possession, the police conduct intrudes on both the suspect's possessory interest in his luggage as well as his liberty interest in proceeding with his itinerary. The person whose luggage is detained is technically still free to continue his travels or carry out other personal activities pending release of the luggage. Moreover, he is not subjected to the coercive atmosphere of a custodial confinement or to the public indignity of being personally detained. Nevertheless, such a seizure can effectively restrain the person since he is subjected to the possible disruption of his travel plans in order to remain with his luggage or to arrange for its return.[8] Therefore, when the police seize luggage from the suspect's custody, we think the limitations applicable to investigative detentions of the person should define the permissible scope of an investigative detention of the person's luggage on less than probable cause. Under this standard, it is clear that the police conduct here exceeded the permissible limits of a *Terry*-type investigative stop.

"The length of the detention of respondent's luggage alone precludes the conclusion that the seizure was reasonable in the absence of probable cause. Although we have recognized the reasonableness of seizures longer than the momentary ones involved in *Terry,* the brevity of the invasion of the individual's Fourth Amendment interests is an important factor in determining whether the seizure is so minimally intrusive as to be justifiable on reasonable suspicion. Moreover, in assessing the effect of the length of the detention, we take into account whether the police diligently pursue their investigation. We note that here the New York agents knew the time of Place's scheduled arrival at LaGuardia, had ample time to arrange for their additional investigation at that location, and thereby could have minimized the intrusion on respondent's Fourth Amendment interests. Thus, although we decline to adopt any outside time limitation for a permissible *Terry* stop, we have never approved a seizure of the person for the prolonged 90-minute period involved here and cannot do so on the facts presented by this case.

"Although the 90-minute detention of respondent's luggage is sufficient to render the seizure unreasonable, the violation was exacerbated by the failure of the agents to accurately inform respondent of the place to which they were transporting his luggage, of the length of time he might be dispossessed, and of what arrangements would be made for return of the luggage if the investigation dispelled the suspicion."

8. "At least when the authorities do not make it absolutely clear how they plan to reunite the suspect and his possessions at some future time and place, seizure of the object is tantamount to seizure of the person. This is because that person must either remain on the scene or else seemingly surrender his effects permanently to the police." 3 W. LaFave, *Search and Seizure* § 9.6, p. 61 (1982 Supp.).

BRENNAN, J., joined by Marshall, J., concurring in the result, objected that the majority's approval of brief detention of luggage was "unnecessary to the Court's judgment" and "finds no support in *Terry* or its progeny and significantly dilutes the Fourth Amendment's protections against government interference with personal property." They contended that when the officers "did not develop probable cause to arrest respondent during their encounter with him," "they had to let him go" and could not then subject him "to an independent dispossession of his personal effects based simply on reasonable suspicion." They argued that the *Terry* "balancing inquiries should not be conducted except in the most limited circumstances," while BLACKMUN, J., concurring separately, similarly expressed concern "with what appears to me to be an emerging tendency on the part of the Court to convert the *Terry* decision into a general statement that the Fourth Amendment requires only that any seizure be reasonable."

F. PROTECTIVE SEARCH

1. After *Terry,* what is the test for determining whether an officer may conduct a "frisk"? Consider *Sibron,* p. 372 supra, where the Court stated: "In the case of the self-protective search for weapons, [the officer] must be able to point to particular facts from which he reasonably inferred that the individual was armed and dangerous. Patrolman Martin's testimony reveals no such facts. The suspect's mere act of talking with a number of known narcotics addicts over an eight-hour period no more gives rise to reasonable fear of life or limb on the part of the police officer than it justifies an arrest for committing a crime. Nor did Patrolman Martin urge that when Sibron put his hand in his pocket, he feared that he was going for a weapon and acted in self-defense. His opening statement to Sibron—'You know what I am after'—made it abundantly clear that he sought narcotics, and his testimony at the hearing left no doubt that he thought there were narcotics in Sibron's pocket."

Compare *Adams v. Williams,* p. 373 supra, where the majority concluded that "Sgt. Connolly had ample reason to fear for his safety." [n] Marshall, J., joined by Douglas, J., dissenting, objected: "The fact remains that Connecticut specifically authorizes persons to carry guns so long as they have a permit. Thus, there was no reason for the officer to infer from anything that the informant said that the respondent was dangerous."

2. As for the requisite search procedure, the Court in *Sibron* stated: "The search for weapons approved in *Terry* consisted solely of a limited patting of the outer clothing of the suspect for concealed objects which might be used as instruments of assault. Only when he discovered such objects did the officer in *Terry* place his hands in the pockets of the men he searched. In this case, with no attempt at an initial limited exploration for arms, Patrolman Martin thrust his hand into Sibron's pocket and took from him envelopes of heroin. His testimony shows that he was looking for narcotics, and he found them. The search was not reasonably limited in scope to the accomplishment of the only goal which might conceivably have justified its inception—the protection of the officer by disarming a potentially dangerous man."

Compare *Adams v. Williams,* where the officer immediately reached into the car and removed a theretofore concealed gun

n. The Court footnoted that statement with the following:

"Figures reported by the Federal Bureau of Investigation indicate that 125 policemen were murdered in 1971, with all but five of them having been killed by gunshot wounds. Federal Bureau of Investigation *Law Enforcement Bulletin,* February 1972, p. 33. According to one study, approximately 30% of police shootings occurred when a police officer approached a suspect seated in an automobile. Bristow, *Police Officer Shootings—A Tactical Evaluation,* 54 J.Crim.L.C. & P.S. 93 (1963)."

from defendant's waistband. The Court stated: "When Williams rolled down his window, rather than complying with the policeman's request to step out of the car so that his movements could more easily be seen, the revolver allegedly at Williams' waist became an even greater threat. Under these circumstances the policeman's action in reaching to the spot where the gun was thought to be hidden constituted a limited intrusion designed to insure his safety, and we conclude that it was reasonable."

3. Assuming that there are grounds for a protective search, how extensive a "patting down" of the suspect is permissible? Consider the description quoted in note 13 of *Terry.* Is the right to make a protective search limited to the person of the suspect? What if the suspect is carrying an attache case, a shopping bag, a purse, or similar object?

4. In MICHIGAN v. LONG, 463 U.S. 1034, 103 S.Ct. 3469, 77 L.Ed.2d 1201 (1983), two deputies saw a car swerve into a ditch and stopped to investigate. Long, the only occupant of the car, met the deputies at the rear of the car, supplied his driver's license upon demand, and started back toward the open door when asked for his vehicle registration. The officers saw a large hunting knife on the floorboard, so Long was frisked and one officer then entered the vehicle and found an open pouch of marijuana under an armrest. The Supreme Court, per O'CONNOR, J., held:

"Our past cases indicate then that protection of police and others can justify protective searches when police have a reasonable belief that the suspect poses a danger, that roadside encounters between police and suspects are especially hazardous, and that danger may arise from the possible presence of weapons in the area surrounding a suspect. These principles compel our conclusion that the search of the passenger compartment of an automobile, limited to those areas in which a weapon may be placed or hidden, is permissible if the police officer possesses a reasonable belief based on 'specific and articulable facts which, taken together with the rational inferences from those facts, reasonably warrant' the officers in believing that the suspect is dangerous and the suspect may gain immediate control of weapons. * * *

"The circumstances of this case clearly justified Deputies Howell and Lewis in their reasonable belief that Long posed a danger if he were permitted to reenter his vehicle. The hour was late and the area rural. Long was driving his automobile at excessive speed, and his car swerved into a ditch. The officers had to repeat their questions to Long, who appeared to be 'under the influence' of some intoxicant. Long was not frisked until the officers observed that there was a large knife in the interior of the car into which Long was about to reenter. The subsequent search of the car was restricted to those areas to which Long would generally have immediate control, and that could contain a weapon. The trial court determined that the leather pouch containing marijuana could have contained a weapon. It is clear that the intrusion was 'strictly circumscribed by the exigencies which justifi[ed] its initiation.' * * *

"The Michigan Supreme Court appeared to believe that it was not reasonable for the officers to fear that Long could injure them, because he was effectively under their control during the investigative stop and could not get access to any weapons that might have been located in the automobile. This reasoning is mistaken in several respects. During any investigative detention, the suspect is 'in the control' of the officers in the sense that he 'may be briefly detained against his will * * *.' Just as a *Terry* suspect on the street may, despite being under the brief control of a police officer, reach into his clothing and retrieve a weapon, so might a *Terry* suspect in Long's position break away from police control and retrieve a weapon from his automobile. In addition, if the suspect is not placed under arrest, he will be permitted to reenter his automobile, and he will then have access to any weapons inside. Or, as here, the suspect may be permitted to reenter the vehicle before the *Terry* investigation is over, and again, may have access to weapons. In any event, we stress that a *Terry* investigation, such as the one that occurred here, involves a police investigation 'at close range,' when the officer remains particularly vulnerable in part *because* a full custodial arrest has not been effected, and the officer must make a 'quick decision as to how to protect himself and others from possible danger * * *.' In such circumstances, we have not required that officers adopt alternate means to ensure their safety in order to avoid the intrusion involved in a *Terry* encounter."

BRENNAN and Marshall, JJ., dissenting, objected: "Putting aside the fact that the search at issue here involved a far more serious intrusion than that 'involved in a *Terry* encounter,' and as such might suggest the need for resort to 'alternate means,' the Court's reasoning is perverse. The Court's argument in essence is that the *absence* of probable cause to arrest compels the conclusion that a broad search, traditionally associated in scope with a search incident to arrest, must be permitted based on reasonable suspicion. But *United States v. Robinson, supra,* stated: 'It is scarcely open to doubt that the danger to an officer is far greater in the case of the extended exposure which follows the taking of a suspect into custody and transporting him to the police station than in the case of the relatively fleeting contact resulting from the typical *Terry*-type stop.' In light of *Robinson*'s observation, today's holding leaves in grave doubt the question of whether the Court's assessment of the relative dangers posed by given confrontations is based on any principled standard."

5. Can a limited search for any other reason ever be undertaken incident to a lawful stop? In *State v. Flynn,* 285 N.W.2d 710 (Wis.1979), one of two suspects lawfully stopped for investigation of a just-completed burglary admitted he had identification in his wallet but refused to identify himself, so the officer removed the wallet and examined it to the extent necessary to find the suspect's name and then arrested the suspect when a radio check revealed he was wanted for an earlier crime. Reasoning that "unless the officer is entitled to at least ascertain the identity of the suspect, the right to stop him can serve no useful purpose at all," that the search was a very limited one, and "that defendant could himself have substantially avoided the intrusion simply by producing the identification himself as his companion did," the court held the officer's actions reasonable under the *Terry* balancing test. Compare *People v. Williams,* 234 N.W.2d 541 (Mich.App.1975) (even though officer had good reason to believe lawfully stopped suspect was lying when he said he had no identification, looking in his wallet at driver's license violated the Fourth Amendment).

What then of on-the-scene fingerprinting? In *Hayes v. Florida,* ___ U.S. ___, 105 S.Ct. 1643, 84 L.Ed.2d 705 (1985), the majority in dictum opined this would be permissible "if there is reasonable suspicion that the suspect has committed a criminal act, if there is a reasonable basis for believing that fingerprinting will establish or negate the suspect's connection with that crime, and if the procedure is carried out with dispatch." Brennan and Marshall, JJ., concurring, responded "that onsite fingerprinting (apparently undertaken in full view of any passerby) would involve a singular intrusion on the suspect's privacy, an intrusion that would not be justifiable (as was the patdown in *Terry*) as necessary for the officer's protection."

G. OTHER BRIEF DETENTION FOR INVESTIGATION

1. In DAVIS v. MISSISSIPPI, 394 U.S. 721, 89 S.Ct. 1394, 22 L.Ed.2d 676

(1969), petitioner and 24 other black youths were detained for questioning and fingerprinting in connection with a rape for which the only leads were a general description given by the victim and a set of fingerprints around the window through which the assailant entered. Petitioner's prints were found to match those at the scene of the crime, and this evidence was admitted at his trial. The Court, per BRENNAN, J., held that the prints should have been excluded as the fruits of a seizure of petitioner in violation of the Fourth Amendment, but intimated that a detention for such a purpose might sometimes be permissible on evidence insufficient for arrest:

"Detentions for the sole purpose of obtaining fingerprints are no less subject to the constraints of the Fourth Amendment. It is arguable, however, that because of the unique nature of the fingerprinting process, such detentions might, under narrowly defined circumstances, be found to comply with the Fourth Amendment even though there is no probable cause in the traditional sense. Detention for fingerprinting may constitute a much less serious intrusion upon personal security than other types of police searches and detentions. Fingerprinting involves none of the probing into an individual's private life and thoughts which marks an interrogation or search. Nor can fingerprint detention be employed repeatedly to harass any individual, since the police need only one set of each person's prints. Furthermore, fingerprinting is an inherently more reliable and effective crime-solving tool than eyewitness identifications or confessions and is not subject to such abuses as the improper line-up [o] and the 'third degree.' Finally, because there is no danger of destruction of fingerprints, the limited detention need not come unexpectedly or at an inconvenient time. For this same reason, the general requirement that the authorization of a judicial officer be obtained in advance of detention would seem not to admit of any exception in the fingerprinting context.

"We have no occasion in this case, however, to determine whether the requirements of the Fourth Amendment could be met by narrowly circumscribed procedures for obtaining, during the course of a criminal investigation, the fingerprints of individuals for whom there is no probable cause to arrest. For it is clear that no attempt was made here to employ procedures which might comply with the requirements of the Fourth Amendment: the detention at police headquarters of petitioner and the other young Negroes was not authorized by a judicial officer; petitioner was unnecessarily required to undergo two fingerprinting sessions; and petitioner was not merely fingerprinted during the December 3 detention but also subjected to interrogation." [p]

2. *United States v. Dionisio,* p. 715 infra, holds that the Fourth Amendment was not violated by subpoenaing witnesses to appear before a grand jury to give voice exemplars. No preliminary showing of "probable cause" or "reasonableness" is required in such a case, as: (a) "a subpoena to appear before a grand jury is not a 'seizure' in the Fourth Amendment sense," and thus "*Davis* is plainly inapposite"; and (b) the requirement that the witness give exemplars does not infringe upon Fourth Amendment rights, as "the physical characteristics of a person's voice, its tone and manner, as opposed to the content of a specific conversation, are constantly exposed to the public," so that "no person

o. In *Wise v. Murphy,* 275 A.2d 205 (D.C.App. 1971), the court noted the negative reference in *Davis* was only to an "improper line-up" and thus concluded that upon a proper showing, lacking in the instant case, a court could order a person to appear in a lineup even if grounds for arrest were lacking, at least for investigation of "serious felonies involving grave personal injuries."

p. *Davis* was reaffirmed in *Hayes v. Florida,* Supp. p. 383 supra, where the Court again suggested "the Fourth Amendment might permit the judiciary to authorize the seizure of a person on less than probable cause and his removal to the police station for the purpose of fingerprinting."

can have a reasonable expectation that others will not know the sound of his voice." *United States v. Mara,* p. 718 infra, reached the same result as to the subpoenaing of a witness to give handwriting exemplars.

3. A few jurisdictions have adopted statutes or rules of court which authorize brief detention at the station (usually pursuant to court order), on less than the grounds needed to arrest, for the purpose of conducting certain identification procedures. Such provisions have been upheld by the courts, and some other cases have upheld similar procedures even absent such a provision. For example, in *In re Fingerprinting of M.B.,* 309 A.2d 3 (N.J. Super.1973), the court affirmed an order requiring all 22 male members of the eighth grade class of a particular school to submit to fingerprinting. A ring of that elementary school's graduating class was found near the body of a homicide victim, and later the victim's car was located. Fingerprints other than those of the victim were found both inside and outside the vehicle. Upon request of the prosecutor, the court ordered all male members of that graduating class to submit to fingerprinting; the order permitted the pupils to be accompanied by a parent, guardian or attorney, directed that the prints be used only in the investigation of the homicide, and specified further that upon completion of the investigation the prints should be destroyed. The appellate court, in affirming commented:

"[T]here [is] a substantial basis to suspect that a member of the school class in question may have had some implication in or material knowledge of the homicide such that fingerprinting of all the male members of the class was reasonable, having in mind the protective provision of the order for destruction of the prints after completion of the investigation. Under all the circumstances extant and the terms of the order below we find the existence of such 'narrowly circumscribed procedures' as render the order reasonable within the view of the Fourth Amendment adumbrated in *Davis.*"

4. In DUNAWAY v. NEW YORK, 442 U.S. 200, 99 S.Ct. 2248, 60 L.Ed.2d 824 (1979), the police, lacking grounds to arrest petitioner but suspecting he was implicated in an attempted robbery and homicide, had him "picked up" for questioning. He was placed in an interrogation room at police headquarters, where he was questioned by officers after being given the *Miranda* warnings. Petitioner waived counsel and within an hour gave incriminating statements. His conviction following a trial at which those statements were admitted was affirmed by the state court on the ground that officers "may detain an individual upon reasonable suspicion for questioning for a reasonable and brief period of time under carefully controlled conditions which are ample to protect the individual's Fifth and Sixth Amendment Rights." The Supreme Court, per BRENNAN, J., reversed:

"In contrast to the brief and narrowly circumscribed intrusions involved in [*Terry* and its progeny], the detention of petitioner was in important respects indistinguishable from a traditional arrest. Petitioner was not questioned briefly where he was found. Instead, he was taken from a neighbor's home to a police car, transported to a police station, and placed in an interrogation room. He was never informed that he was 'free to go'; indeed, he would have been physically restrained if he had refused to accompany the officers or had tried to escape their custody. The application of the Fourth Amendment's requirement of probable cause does not depend on whether an intrusion of this magnitude is termed an 'arrest' under state law. The mere facts that petitioner was not told he was under arrest, was not 'booked,' and would not have had an arrest record if the interrogation had proved fruitless, * * * obviously do not make petitioner's seizure even roughly analogous to the narrowly defined intrusions involved in *Terry* and its progeny. Indeed, any 'exception' that could cover a seizure as intrusive as that in this case would threaten to swallow the general rule that Fourth Amendment seizures are 'reasonable' only if based on probable cause. * * *

"In effect, respondents urge us to adopt a multifactor balancing test of 'reasonable police conduct under the circumstances' to cover all seizures that do not amount to technical arrests. But the protections intended by the Framers could all too easily disappear in the consideration and balancing of the multifarious circumstances presented by different cases, especially when that balancing may be done in the first instance by police officers engaged in the 'often competitive enterprise of ferreting out crime.' A single, familiar standard is essential to guide police officers, who have only limited time and expertise to reflect on and balance the social and individual interests involved in the specific circumstances they confront. Indeed, our recognition of these dangers, and our consequent reluctance to depart from the proven protections afforded by the general rule, is reflected in the narrow limitations emphasized in the cases employing the balancing test. For all but those narrowly defined intrusions, the requisite 'balancing' has been performed in centuries of precedent and is embodied in the principle that seizures are 'reasonable' only if supported by probable cause."

Justice Brennan then concluded "that the treatment of petitioner, whether or not it is technically characterized as an arrest, must be supported by probable cause" because "detention for custodial interrogation—regardless of its label—intrudes so severely on interests protected by the Fourth Amendment as necessarily to trigger the traditional safeguards against illegal arrest."

WHITE, J., concurring, cautioned that the majority opinion should not be read to mean that *Terry*" is an almost unique exception to a hard-and-fast standard of probable cause," and added that it was "enough, for me, that the police conduct here is similar enough to an arrest that the normal level of probable cause is necessary before the interests of privacy and personal security must give way." REHNQUIST, J., joined by the Chief Justice in dissent, indicated he "would have little difficulty joining" the opinion of the Court but for his conclusion that no Fourth Amendment seizure had occurred: "After learning that the person who answered the door was petitioner, the officer asked him if he would accompany the officers to police headquarters for questioning, and petitioner responded that he would. Petitioner was not told that he was under arrest or in custody and was not warned not to resist or flee. No weapons were displayed and petitioner was not handcuffed. Each officer testified that petitioner was not touched or held during the trip downtown; his freedom of action was not in any way restrained by the police. In short, the police behavior in this case was entirely free of 'physical force or show of authority.'"

SECTION 8. OTHER WARRANTLESS SEARCHES OF THE PERSON

UNITED STATES v. ROBINSON

414 U.S. 218, 94 S.Ct. 467, 38 L.Ed.2d 427 (1973).

MR. JUSTICE REHNQUIST delivered the opinion of the Court.

Respondent Robinson was convicted in United States District Court for the District of Columbia of the possession and facilitation of concealment of heroin. * * * [T]he Court of Appeals *en banc* reversed the judgment of conviction, holding that the heroin introduced in evidence against respondent had been obtained as a result of a search which violated the Fourth Amendment to the United States Constitution.

On April 23, 1968, at approximately 11 o'clock p.m., Officer Richard Jenks, a 15-

year veteran of the District of Columbia Metropolitan Police Department, observed the respondent driving a 1965 Cadillac near the intersection of 8th and C Streets, Southeast, in the District of Columbia. Jenks, as a result of previous investigation following a check of respondent's operator's permit four days earlier, determined there was reason to believe that respondent was operating a motor vehicle after the revocation of his operator's permit. This is an offense defined by statute in the District of Columbia which carries a mandatory minimum jail term, a mandatory minimum fine, or both.

Jenks signaled respondent to stop the automobile, which respondent did, and all three of the occupants emerged from the car. At that point Jenks informed respondent that he was under arrest for "operating after revocation and obtaining a permit by misrepresentation." It was assumed by the majority of the Court of Appeals, and is conceded by the respondent here, that Jenks had probable cause to arrest respondent, and that he effected a full custody arrest.

In accordance with procedures prescribed in Police Department instructions,[2] Jenks then began to search respondent. He explained at a subsequent hearing that he was "face to face" with the respondent, and "placed [his] hands on [the respondent], my right hand to his left breast like this (demonstrating) and proceeded to pat him down thus (with the right hand)." During this patdown, Jenks felt an object in the left breast pocket of the heavy coat respondent was wearing, but testified that he "couldn't tell what it was" and also that he "couldn't actually tell the size of it." Jenks then reached into the pocket and pulled out the object, which turned out to be a "crumpled up cigarette package." Jenks testified that at this point he still did not know what was in the package:

> "As I felt the package I could feel objects in the package but I couldn't tell what they were. * * * I knew they weren't cigarettes."

The officer then opened the cigarette pack and found 14 gelatin capsules of white powder which he thought to be, and which later analysis proved to be, heroin. Jenks then continued his search of respondent to completion, feeling around his waist and trouser legs, and examining the remaining pockets. The heroin seized from the respondent was admitted into evidence at the trial which resulted in his conviction in the District Court. * * *

It is well settled that a search incident to a lawful arrest is a traditional exception to the warrant requirement of the Fourth Amendment. This general exception has historically been formulated into two distinct propositions. The first is that a search may be made of the *person* of the arrestee by virtue of the lawful arrest. The second is that a search may be made of the area within the control of the arrestee.

Examination of this Court's decisions in the area show that these two propositions have been treated quite differently. The validity of the search of a person incident to a lawful arrest has been regarded as settled from its first enunciation, and has

2. The government introduced testimony at the evidentiary hearing upon the original remand by the Court of Appeals as to certain standard operating procedures of the Metropolitan Police Department. Sergeant Dennis C. Donaldson, a Training Division Instructor, testified that when a police officer makes "a full custody arrest" which he defined as where an officer "would arrest a subject and subsequently transport him to a police facility for booking," the officer is trained to make a full "field type search" * * *. Sergeant Donaldson testified that officers are instructed to examine the "contents of all of the pockets" of the arrestee in the course of the field search. * * * Those regulations also provide that in the case of some traffic offenses, including the crime of operating a motor vehicle after revocation of an operator's permit, the officer shall make a summary arrest of the violator and take the violator, in custody, to the stationhouse for booking. D.C.Metropolitan Police Department General Order No. 3, series 1959 (April 24, 1959). Such operating procedures are not, of course, determinative of the constitutional issues presented by this case.

remained virtually unchallenged until the present case. The validity of the second proposition, while likewise conceded in principle, has been subject to differing interpretations as to the extent of the area which may be searched. * * *

Throughout the series of cases in which the Court has addressed the second proposition relating to a search incident to a lawful arrest—the permissible area beyond the person of the arrestee which such a search may cover—no doubt has been expressed as to the unqualified authority of the arresting authority to search the person of the arrestee. * * *

Thus the broadly stated rule, and the reasons for it, have been repeatedly affirmed in the decisions of this Court since *Weeks v. United States* nearly 60 years ago. Since the statements in the cases speak not simply in terms of an exception to the warrant requirement, but in terms of an affirmative authority to search, they clearly imply that such searches also meet the Fourth Amendment's requirement of reasonableness. * * *

Virtually all of the statements of this Court affirming the existence of an unqualified authority to search incident to a lawful arrest are dicta. We would not therefore be foreclosed by principles of *stare decisis* from further examination into history and practice in order to see whether the sort of qualifications imposed by the Court of Appeals in this case were in fact intended by the Framers of the Fourth Amendment or recognized in cases decided prior to *Weeks.* Unfortunately such authorities as exist are sparse. * * *

While these earlier authorities are sketchy, they tend to support the broad statement of the authority to search incident to arrest found in the successive decisions of this Court, rather than the restrictive one which was applied by the Court of Appeals in this case. * * *

The Court of Appeals in effect determined that the *only* reason supporting the authority for a *full* search incident to lawful arrest was the possibility of discovery of evidence or fruits. Concluding that there could be no evidence or fruits in the case of an offense such as that with which respondent was charged, it held that any protective search would have to be limited by the conditions laid down in *Terry* for a search upon less than probable cause to arrest. Quite apart from the fact that *Terry* clearly recognized the distinction between the two types of searches, and that a different rule governed one than governed the other, we find additional reason to disagree with the Court of Appeals.

The justification or reason for the authority to search incident to a lawful arrest rests quite as much on the need to disarm the suspect in order to take him into custody as it does on the need to preserve evidence on his person for later use at trial. The standards traditionally governing a search incident to lawful arrest are not, therefore, commuted to the stricter *Terry* standards by the absence of probable fruits or further evidence of the particular crime for which the arrest is made.

Nor are we inclined, on the basis of what seems to us to be a rather speculative judgment, to qualify the breadth of the general authority to search incident to a lawful custodial arrest on an assumption that persons arrested for the offense of driving while their license has been revoked are less likely to be possessed of dangerous weapons than are those arrested for other crimes.[5] It is scarcely open to

5. Such an assumption appears at least questionable in light of the available statistical data concerning assaults on police officers who are in the course of making arrests. The danger to the police officer flows from the fact of the arrest, and its attendant proximity, stress and uncertainty, and not from the grounds for arrest. One study concludes that approximately 30% of the shootings of police officers occur when the officer approaches a person seated in a car. Bristow, *Police Officer Shootings—A Tactical Evaluation,* 54 J.Crim.L.C. & P.S. 93 (1963). The Government in its brief notes that the Uniform Crime Reports, prepared by the Federal Bureau of Investigation, indicate that a significant percentage of police officers murders occur when the officers

doubt that the danger to an officer is far greater in the case of the extended exposure which follows the taking of a suspect into custody and transporting him to the police station than in the case of the relatively fleeting contact resulting from the typical *Terry*-type stop. This is an adequate basis for treating all custodial arrests alike for purposes of search justification.

But quite apart from these distinctions, our more fundamental disagreement with the Court of Appeals arises from its suggestion that there must be litigated in each case the issue of whether or not there was present one of the reasons supporting the authority for a search of the person incident to a lawful arrest. We do not think the long line of authorities of this Court dating back to *Weeks,* nor what we can glean from the history of practice in this country and in England, requires such a case by case adjudication. A police officer's determination as to how and where to search the person of a suspect whom he has arrested is necessarily a quick *ad hoc* judgment which the Fourth Amendment does not require to be broken down in each instance into an analysis of each step in the search. The authority to search the person incident to a lawful custodial arrest, while based upon the need to disarm and to discover evidence, does not depend on what a court may later decide was the probability in a particular arrest situation that weapons or evidence would in fact be found upon the person of the suspect. A custodial arrest of a suspect based on probable cause is a reasonable intrusion under the Fourth Amendment; that intrusion being lawful, a search incident to the arrest requires no additional justification. It is the fact of the lawful arrest which establishes the authority to search, and we hold that in the case of a lawful custodial arrest a full search of the person is not only an exception to the warrant requirement of the Fourth Amendment, but is also a "reasonable" search under that Amendment.

The search of respondent's person conducted by Officer Jenks in this case and the seizure from him of the heroin, were permissible under established Fourth Amendment law. * * * Since it is the fact of custodial arrest which gives rise to the authority to search, it is of no moment that Jenks did not indicate any subjective fear of the respondent or that he did not himself suspect that respondent was armed.[7] Having in the course of a lawful search come upon the crumpled package of cigarettes, he was entitled to inspect it; and when his inspection revealed the heroin capsules, he was entitled to seize them as "fruits, instrumentalities, or contraband" probative of criminal conduct. The judgment of the Court of Appeals holding otherwise is reversed.

Reversed.

MR. JUSTICE MARSHALL, with whom MR. JUSTICE DOUGLAS and MR. JUSTICE BRENNAN join, dissenting.

Certain fundamental principles have characterized this Court's Fourth Amendment jurisprudence over the years. Perhaps the most basic of these was expressed by Mr. Justice Butler, speaking for a unanimous Court in *Go-Bart Co. v. United States,* 282 U.S. 344, 51 S.Ct. 153, 75 L.Ed. 374 (1931): "There is no formula for the determination of reasonableness. Each case is to be decided on its own facts and circumstances." * * *

The majority's attempt to avoid case-by-case adjudication of Fourth Amendment issues is not only misguided as a matter of

are making traffic stops. Brief for the United States, at 23. Those reports indicate that during January-March, 1973, 35 police officers were murdered; 11 of those officers were killed while engaged in traffic stops. Ibid.

7. The United States concedes that "in searching respondent, [Officer Jenks] was not motivated by a feeling of imminent danger and was not specifically looking for weapons." Brief for the United States. Officer Jenks testified, "I just searched him [Robinson]. I didn't think about what I was looking for. I just searched him." Officer Jenks also testified that upon removing the cigarette package from the respondent's custody, he was still unsure what was in the package, but that he knew it was not cigarettes.

principle, but is also doomed to fail as a matter of practical application. As the majority itself is well aware, the powers granted the police in this case are strong ones, subject to potential abuse. Although, in this particular case, Officer Jenks was required by Police Department regulation to make an in-custody arrest rather than to issue a citation, in most jurisdictions and for most traffic offenses the determination of whether to issue a citation or effect a full arrest is discretionary with the officer. There is always the possibility that a police officer, lacking probable cause to obtain a search warrant, will use a traffic arrest as a pretext to conduct a search. I suggest this possibility not to impugn the integrity of our police, but merely to point out that case-by-case adjudication will always be necessary to determine whether a full arrest was effected for purely legitimate reasons or, rather, as a pretext for searching the arrestee.

The majority states that "A police officer's determination as to how and where to search the person of a suspect whom he has arrested is necessarily a quick *ad hoc* judgment which the Fourth Amendment does not require to be broken down in each instance into an analysis of each step in the search." No precedent is cited for this broad assertion—not surprisingly, since there is none. Indeed, we only recently rejected such "a rigid all-or-nothing model of justification and regulation under the Amendment, [for] it obscures the utility of limitations upon the scope, as well as the initiation, of police action as a means of constitutional regulation. This Court has held in the past that a search which is reasonable at its inception may violate the Fourth Amendment by virtue of its intolerable intensity and scope." *Terry v. Ohio.* As we there concluded, "in determining whether the seizure and search were 'unreasonable' our inquiry is a dual one—whether the officer's action was justified at its inception, and whether it was reasonably related in scope to the circumstances which justified the interference in the first place."

As I view the matter, the search in this case divides into three distinct phases: the patdown of respondent's coat pocket; the removal of the unknown object from the pocket; and the opening of the crumpled up cigarette package.

No question is raised here concerning the lawfulness of the patdown of respondent's coat pocket. The Court of Appeals unanimously affirmed the right of a police officer to conduct a limited frisk for weapons when making an incustody arrest, regardless of the nature of the crime for which the arrest was made. As it said,

> "it would seem clearly unreasonable to expect a police officer to place a suspect in his squad car for transportation to the station house without first taking reasonable measures to insure that the suspect is unarmed. We therefore conclude that whenever a police officer, acting within the bounds of his authority, makes an in-custody arrest, he may also conduct a limited *frisk* of the suspect's outer clothing in order to remove any weapons the suspect may have in his possession."

With respect to the removal of the unknown object from the coat pocket, * * * Officer Jenks had no reason to believe and did not in fact believe that the object in respondent's coat pocket was a weapon. He admitted later that the object did not feel like a gun. * * *

Since the removal of the object from the pocket cannot be justified as part of a limited *Terry* weapons frisk, the question arises whether it is reasonable for a police officer, when effecting an in-custody arrest of a traffic offender, to make a fuller search of the person than is permitted pursuant to *Terry.* * * *

The Government does not now contend that the search of respondent's pocket can be justified by any need to find and seize evidence in order to prevent its concealment or destruction, for as the Court of

Appeals found, there are no evidence or fruits of the offense with which respondent was charged. The only rationale for a search in this case, then, is the removal of weapons which the arrestee might use to harm the officer and attempt an escape. This rationale, of course, is identical to the rationale of the search permitted in *Terry*. * * *

Since the underlying rationale of a *Terry* search and the search of a traffic violator are identical, the Court of Appeals held that the scope of the searches must be the same. * * *

The problem with this approach, however, is that it ignores several significant differences between the context in which a search incident to arrest for a traffic violation is made, and the situation presented in *Terry*. Some of these differences would appear to suggest permitting a more thorough search in this case than was permitted in *Terry*; other differences suggest a narrower, more limited right to search than was there recognized.

The most obvious difference between the two contexts relates to whether the officer has cause to believe that the individual he is dealing with possesses weapons which might be used against him. *Terry* did not permit an officer to conduct a weapons frisk of anyone he lawfully stopped on the street, but rather, only where "he has reason to believe that he is dealing with an armed and dangerous individual. * * *" While the policeman who arrests a suspected rapist or robber may well have reason to believe he is dealing with an armed and dangerous person, certainly this does not hold true with equal force with respect to persons arrested for motor vehicle violations of the sort involved in this case.

Nor was there any particular reason in this case to believe that respondent was dangerous. He had not attempted to evade arrest, but had quickly complied with the police both in bringing his car to a stop after being signalled to do so and in producing the documents Officer Jenks requested. In fact, Jenks admitted that he searched respondent face-to-face rather than in spread-eagle fashion because he had no reason to believe respondent would be violent.

While this difference between the situation presented in *Terry* and the context presented in this case would tend to suggest a lesser authority to search here than was permitted in *Terry*, other distinctions between the two contexts suggest just the opposite. As the Court of Appeals noted, a crucial feature distinguishing the in-custody arrest from the *Terry* context "is not the greater likelihood that a person taken into custody is armed, but rather the increased likelihood of danger to the officer *if* in fact the person is armed." A *Terry* stop involves a momentary encounter between officer and suspect, while an in-custody arrest places the two in close proximity for a much longer period of time. If the individual happens to have a weapon on his person, he will certainly have much more opportunity to use it against the officer in the in-custody situation. The prolonged proximity also makes it more likely that the individual will be able to extricate any small hidden weapon which might go undetected in a weapons frisk, such as a safety pin or razor blade. In addition, a suspect taken into custody may feel more threatened by the serious restraint on his liberty than a person who is simply stopped by an officer for questioning, and may therefore be more likely to resort to force.

Thus, in some senses there is less need for a weapons search in the in-custody traffic arrest situation than in a *Terry* context, while in other ways, there is a greater need. Balancing these competing considerations in order to determine what is a reasonable warrantless search in the traffic arrest context is a difficult process, one for which there may be no easy analytical guideposts. We are dealing in factors not easily quantified and, therefore, not easily weighed one against the other. And the competing interests we are protecting—the individual's interest in remaining free from unnecessarily intrusive invasions of privacy and society's interest that police officers not take unnecessary risks in the performance of their duties—are each deserving of our most serious attention and do not themselves tip the balance in any particular direction. * * *

The majority relies on statistics indicating that a significant percentage of police officer murders occur when the officers are making traffic stops. But these statistics only confirm what we recognized in *Terry*—that "American criminals have a long tradition of armed violence, and every year in this country many law enforcement officers are killed in the line of duty, and thousands more are wounded." As the very next sentence in *Terry* recognized, however, "Virtually all of these deaths and a substantial portion of the injuries are inflicted with guns and knives." The statistics relied on by the Government in this case support this observation. Virtually all of the killings are caused by guns and knives, the very type of weapons which will not go undetected in a properly conducted weapons frisk.[5] * * *

The majority opinion fails to recognize that the search conducted by Officer Jenks did not merely involve a search of respondent's person. It also included a separate search of effects found on his person. And even were we to assume, *arguendo,* that it was reasonable for Jenks to remove the object he felt in respondent's pocket, clearly there was no justification consistent with the Fourth Amendment which would authorize his opening the package and looking inside.

To begin with, after Jenks had the cigarette package in his hands, there is no indication that he had reason to believe or did in fact believe that the package contained a weapon. More importantly, even if the crumpled up cigarette package had in fact contained some sort of small weapon, it would have been impossible for respondent to have used it once the package was in the officer's hands. Opening the package therefore did not further the protective purpose of the search. * * *

It is suggested, however, that since the custodial arrest itself represents a significant intrusion into the privacy of the person, any additional intrusion by way of opening or examining effects found on the person is not worthy of constitutional protection. But such an approach was expressly rejected by the Court in *Chimel.* There it was suggested that since the police had lawfully entered petitioner's house to effect an arrest, the additional invasion of privacy stemming from an accompanying search of the entire house was inconsequential. The Court answered: "[W]e see no reason why, simply because some interference with an individual's privacy and freedom of movement has lawfully taken place, further intrusions should automatically be allowed despite the absence of a warrant that the Fourth Amendment would otherwise require." * * *

The Government argues that it is difficult to see what constitutionally protected "expectation of privacy" a prisoner has in the interior of a cigarette pack. One wonders if the result in this case would have been the same were respondent a businessman who was lawfully taken into custody for driving without a license and whose wallet was taken from him by the police. Would it be reasonable for the police officer, because of the possibility that a razor blade was hidden somewhere in the wallet, to open it, remove all the contents, and examine each item carefully? Or suppose a lawyer lawfully arrested for a traffic offense is found to have a sealed envelope on his person. Would it be permissible

5. The Uniform Crime Reports prepared by the Federal Bureau of Investigation which are relied on by the majority, see ante, at 476 n. 5, indicate that 112 police officers were killed nationwide in 1972. Of these, 108 were killed by firearms. Two of the remaining four were killed with knives, and the last two cases involved a bomb and an automobile.

for the arresting officer to tear open the envelope in order to make sure that it did not contain a clandestine weapon—perhaps a pin or a razor blade? Would it not be more consonant with the purpose of the Fourth Amendment and the legitimate needs of the police to require the officer, if he has any question whatsoever about what the wallet or letter contains, to hold onto it until the arrestee is brought to the precinct station?

I, for one, cannot characterize any of these intrusions into the privacy of an individual's papers and effects as being negligible incidents to the more serious intrusion into the individual's privacy stemming from the arrest itself. Nor can any principled distinction be drawn between the hypothetical searches I have posed and the search of the cigarette package in this case. The only reasoned distinction is between warrantless searches which serve legitimate protective and evidentiary functions and those that do not.

Notes and Questions

1. In the companion case of GUSTAFSON v. FLORIDA, 414 U.S. 260, 94 S.Ct. 488, 38 L.Ed.2d 456 (1973), petitioner was arrested for failure to have an operator's license after the car he was driving was observed weaving across the center line several times, and was then searched, resulting in the discovery of a cigarette box within which the arresting officer found marijuana cigarettes. Petitioner contended his case was different from *Robinson* in that (a) he had experienced no previous encounters with the officer; (b) the offense for which he was arrested was "benign or trivial in nature," carrying with it no mandatory minimum sentence; and (c) there were no police regulations which required the officer to take petitioner into custody or which required full scale body searches upon arrest in the field. The Court, per Rehnquist, J., did "not find these differences determinative of the constitutional issue," and thus upheld the search on the basis of *Robinson.*

Marshall, Douglas, and Brennan, JJ., dissented for the reasons stated in *Robinson.* Stewart, J., concurring, noted "that a persuasive claim might have been made in this case that the custodial arrest of the petitioner for a minor traffic offense violated his rights under the Fourth and Fourteenth Amendments," but since petitioner had "fully conceded the constitutional validity of his custodial arrest," the search of his person should be accepted as incidental to that arrest. Powell, J., concurring in both cases, emphasized that for him the "essential premise" of both decisions was "that an individual lawfully subjected to a custodial arrest retains no significant Fourth Amendment interest in the privacy of his person."

2. In what sense could a "persuasive claim" have been made in *Gustafson* that the arrest violated the Fourth Amendment? A few cases are to be found suppressing evidence upon a showing, of what the *Robinson* dissenters called a "pretext" arrest. See e.g., *Blazak v. Eyman,* 339 F.Supp. 40 (D.Ariz.1971) (where police knew for some time that defendant's driver's license had been revoked, but did not arrest him for driving without a license until they suspected he was carrying narcotics, arrest was a pretext and narcotics not admissible). But more typical is *State v. Tucker,* 595 P.2d 1364 (Or.1979), declaring it is not "practical or desirable," when an officer arrests or stops for a minor offense but suspects a greater one, to determine the validity thereof "on the basis of the officer's purpose, or primary purpose, in making it."

3. Does this suggest that the "persuasive claim," to be effective, must have some other rationale? Does Stewart, J., mean that the *Gustafson* arrest, unlike the *Robinson* arrest, was subject to attack on Fourth Amendment grounds because no

statute[a] or police regulations guided the officer as to when a "custodial arrest" was to be employed instead of a citation? Compare the "standard police procedures" requirement in *South Dakota v. Opperman,* p. 355 supra. Or, does Stewart mean the *Gustafson* arrest was subject to attack because it was unnecessary in the sense that the "lesser intrusion" of a citation would have sufficed? Does *Zurcher v. Stanford Daily,* p. 256 supra, foreclose such a contention?

4. Full searches of an arrested person are more typically made when that person has been delivered to the place of his forthcoming detention. These searches are typically upheld on two bases: (1) as a delayed *Robinson* search incident to arrest; and (2) as an inventory incident to booking to safeguard the property of the accused and to ensure that weapons and contraband are not introduced into the jail. However, some jurisdictions have rejected the *Robinson* rule and have also limited the extent of permissible inventory. See, e.g., *State v. Kaluna,* 520 P.2d 51 (Hawaii 1974) (police matron subjected female arrested for armed robbery to strip search, resulting in discovery of packet of drugs in her bra; held, not a valid search incident to arrest because no reason to believe weapons or evidence of the crime there, and not valid inventory because the packet could have been inventoried without opening it). Also, in some jurisdictions a search at the station is deemed unlawful if the defendant was not afforded a sufficient opportunity to gain his release. See, e.g., *Zehrung v. State,* 569 P.2d 189 (Alaska 1977), on rehearing, 573 P.2d 858 (1978) ("when one is arrested and brought to a jail for a minor offense for which bail has already been set in a bail schedule, he should be allowed a reasonable opportunity to attempt to raise bail before being subjected to remand and booking procedures and the incidental inventory search"; but on rehearing court admits state may be correct in saying this impractical in smaller communities with no separate holding cells in unsecured area, and that there the search may be proper unless defendant presently has the bail money).

5. ILLINOIS v. LAFAYETTE, 462 U.S. 604, 103 S.Ct. 2605, 77 L.Ed.2d 65 (1983), concerned the admissibility of amphetamines found in respondent's shoulder bag during an at-the-station inventory of his effects following his arrest for disturbing the peace. The Court, per BURGER, C.J., concluded:

"The governmental interests underlying a stationhouse search of the arrestee's person and possessions may in some circumstances be even greater than those supporting a search immediately following arrest. Consequently, the scope of a stationhouse search will often vary from that made at the time of arrest. Police conduct that would be impractical or unreasonable—or embarrassingly intrusive—on the street can more readily—and privately—be performed at the station. For example, the interests supporting a search incident to arrest would hardly justify disrobing an arrestee on the street, but the practical necessities of routine jail administration may even justify taking a prisoner's clothes before confining him, although that step

a. Note, in this regard, the variation in state law governing traffic "arrests." Some states require that persons halted for violations of misdemeanor traffic laws be released upon issuance of a citation unless they fall within certain exceptions. The exceptions usually are divided into two categories: (1) persons who must be arrested and taken before a magistrate—usually those violating several specified laws (e.g., driving with a suspended license, or driving under the influence of alcohol); and (2) person who may be released on citation or taken before a magistrate at the option of the police officer—e.g., those who have violated several other specified laws (e.g., reckless driving or failure to submit to vehicle inspection), who fail to have a license in their possession, or who fail to furnish satisfactory evidence of identification. Other states require that persons in certain categories be taken into custody, but grant the officer discretion as to whether to take other misdemeanor violators into custody or to release them upon issuance of a citation. Special requirements are often imposed for release of nonresident drivers.

would be rare. This was made clear in *United States v. Edwards,* * * *.[2]

"At the stationhouse, it is entirely proper for police to remove and list or inventory property found on the person or in the possession of an arrested person who is to be jailed. A range of governmental interests support an inventory process. It is not unheard of for persons employed in police activities to steal property taken from arrested persons; similarly, arrested persons have been known to make false claims regarding what was taken from their possession at the stationhouse. A standardized procedure for making a list or inventory as soon as reasonable after reaching the stationhouse not only deters false claims but also inhibits theft or careless handling of articles taken from the arrested person. Arrested persons have also been known to injure themselves—or others—with belts, knives, drugs or other items on their person while being detained. Dangerous instrumentalities—such as razor blades, bombs, or weapons—can be concealed in innocent-looking articles taken from the arrestee's possession. The bare recital of these mundane realities justifies reasonable measures by police to limit these risks—either while the items are in the police possession or at the time they are returned to the arrestee upon his release. Examining all the items removed from the arrestee's person or possession and listing or inventorying them is an entirely reasonable administrative procedure. It is immaterial whether the police actually fear any particular package or container; the need to protect against such risks arises independent of a particular officer's subjective concerns. Finally, inspection of an arrestee's personal property may assist the police in ascertaining or verifying his identity. In short, every consideration of orderly police administration benefiting both police and the public points toward the appropriateness of the examination of respondent's shoulder bag prior to his incarceration.

"Our prior cases amply support this conclusion. In *South Dakota v. Opperman,* [p. 355 supra], we upheld a search of the contents of the glove compartment of an abandoned automobile lawfully impounded by the police. We held that the search was reasonable because it served legitimate governmental interests that outweighed the individual's privacy interests in the contents of his car. Those measures protected the owner's property while it was in the custody of the police and protected police against possible false claims of theft. We found no need to consider the existence of less intrusive means of protecting the police and the property in their custody—such as locking the car and impounding it in safe storage under guard. Similarly, standardized inventory procedures are appropriate to serve legitimate governmental interests at stake here.

"The Illinois court held that the search of respondent's shoulder bag was unreasonable because 'preservation of the defendant's property and protection of police from claims of lost or stolen property, 'could have been achieved in a less intrusive manner.' For example, * * * the defendant's shoulder bag could easily have been secured by sealing it within a plastic bag or box and placing it in a secured locker.' Perhaps so, but the real question is not what 'could have been achieved,' but whether the Fourth Amendment *requires* such steps; it is not our function to write a manual on administering routine, neutral procedures of the stationhouse. Our role is to assure against violations of the Constitution.

" * * * We are hardly in a position to second-guess police departments as to what practical administrative method will best deter theft by and false claims against its employees and preserve the security of the stationhouse. It is evident that a sta-

2. We were not addressing in *Edwards,* and do not discuss here, the circumstances in which a strip search of an arrestee may or may not be appropriate.

tionhouse search of every item carried on or by a person who has lawfully been taken into custody by the police will amply serve the important and legitimate governmental interests involved.

"Even if less intrusive means existed of protecting some particular types of property, it would be unreasonable to expect police officers in the everyday course of business to make fine and subtle distinctions in deciding which containers or items may be searched and which must be sealed as a unit.[b] * * * "[3]

6. UNITED STATES v. EDWARDS, 415 U.S. 800, 94 S.Ct. 1234, 39 L.Ed.2d 711 (1974), concerned the admissibility of paint chips obtained from defendant's clothing, taken from him without a warrant while he was in jail about 10 hours after his arrest for attempted breaking and entering. The clothing was seized because investigation subsequent to the arrest showed that paint had been chipped from a window when entry was attempted with a pry bar. The Court, per WHITE, J., concluded "that once the defendant is lawfully arrested and is in custody, the effects in his possession at the place of detention that were subject to search at the time and place of his arrest may lawfully be searched and seized without a warrant even though a substantial period of time has elapsed between the arrest and subsequent administrative processing on the one hand and the taking of the property for use as evidence on the other. This is true where the clothing or effects are immediately seized upon arrival at the jail, held under the defendant's name in the 'property room' of the jail and at a later time searched and taken for use at the subsequent criminal trial. The result is the same where the property is not physically taken from the defendant until sometime after his incarceration."[c] The Court added it was not holding "that the warrant clause of the Fourth Amendment is never applicable to postarrest seizures of the effects of an arrestee," and by footnote to that caveat stated it was expressing no view "concerning those circumstances surrounding custodial searches incident to incarceration which might 'violate the dictates of reason either because of their number or their manner of perpetration.' "

STEWART, J., joined by Douglas, Brennan, and Marshall, JJ., dissented, arguing that they could "see no justification for dispensing with the warrant requirement here. The police had ample time to seek a warrant, and no exigent circumstances were present to excuse their failure to do so," as the government "has not even suggested that [the defendant] was aware of the presence of the paint chips on his clothing."

7. After *Robinson, Lafayette* and *Edwards,* is a person in custody following a lawful arrest "fair game" for a search for evidence of crimes other than the crime for which the arrest was made? Compare *People v. Trudeau,* 187 N.W.2d 890 (Mich. 1971) (defendant was under arrest for breaking and entering, in recent attempted burglary with similar modus operandi watchman was killed and heel print was left at scene, police subsequently took defendant's shoe and matched it with heel

b. Marshall and Brennan, JJ., concurring, asserted: "A very different case would be presented if the State had relied solely on the fact of arrest to justify the search of respondent's shoulder bag."

3. The record is unclear as to whether respondent was to have been incarcerated after being booked for disturbing the peace. That is an appropriate inquiry on remand.

c. Of course, if the search incident to arrest is made at the station, it will be unlawful if the grounds for the arrest have dissipated prior to the time of the search. See *United States v. Coughlin,* 338 F.Supp. 1328 (E.D.Mich.1972) (defendant arrested upon leaving house at which mailman had just delivered package containing narcotics; at the station, police put his hands under flourescent light and determined that defendant had handled the narcotics which the police had previously dusted with flourescent powder; held, search illegal because promptly after arrest police learned that defendant was not the addressee of the package, so that there was not probable cause for further detention).

print; held, seizure illegal because police "had no probable cause to believe that the seized shoes were evidence linked to the crime").

8. Given the fact that probable cause is not needed to search under *Robinson,* does it follow that probable cause is likewise not required for seizure of the items uncovered? In *State v. Elkins,* 422 P.2d 250 (Or.1966), the defendant was arrested for public intoxication, and a search of his person uncovered "an unlabeled bottle containing three kinds of capsules and pills." The officer seized them, and a later examination established that some of them were methadone, but at the hearing on the motion to suppress the officer conceded that he seized them merely because he was suspicious of them and not because he recognized them as contraband. The court held that the seizure was unlawful on the ground that "before the officer had the right to seize the implements of a crime committed in his presence, other than that for which the arrest was made, he must have reasonable grounds to believe that the article he has discovered is contraband." Compare *Wright v. Edwards,* 343 F.Supp. 792 (N.D.Miss.1972), where following defendant's arrest for drunkenness and disturbing the peace the police found what they suspected (and what turned out to be) marijuana cigarettes on his person, holding: "A lawful arrest having been made, the law imposes no requirement of probable cause to seize contraband."

9. In SCHMERBER v. CALIFORNIA, [the facts and other aspects of which are discussed at p. 48 supra], the Court per BRENNAN, J., observed:

"Although the facts which established probable cause to arrest in this case also suggested the required relevance and likely success of a test of petitioner's blood for alcohol, the question remains whether the arresting officer was permitted to draw these inferences himself, or was required instead to procure a warrant before proceeding with the test. Search warrants are ordinarily required for searches of dwellings, and, absent an emergency, no less could be required where intrusions into the human body are concerned. * * *

"The officer in the present case, however, might reasonably have believed that he was confronted with an emergency, in which the delay necessary to obtain a warrant, under the circumstances, threatened 'the destruction of evidence' * * *. We are told that the percentage of alcohol in the blood begins to diminish shortly after drinking stops, as the body functions to eliminate it from the system. Particularly in a case such as this, where time had to be taken to bring the accused to a hospital and to investigate the scene of the accident, there was no time to seek out a magistrate and secure a warrant. Given these special facts, we conclude that the attempt to secure evidence of blood-alcohol content in this case was an appropriate incident to petitioner's arrest." [d]

10. Applying the *Schmerber* balancing test, the Court in WINSTON v. LEE, ___ U.S. ___, 105 S.Ct. 1611, 84 L.Ed.2d 662 (1985), held that the proposed court-ordered surgery on defendant, for the purpose of removing a bullet expected to show that defendant was the robber hit by the victim's gunfire, would constitute an unreasonable search. "The reasonableness of surgical intrusions beneath the skin," the Court stated per Brennan, J., "depends on a case-by-case approach, in which the individual's interests in privacy and security are weighed against society's interests in conducting the procedure." Taking into account medical evidence that the operation would require a general anesthetic, might last over two hours, and could re-

d. Is it essential that this be characterized as a search incident to arrest? What if the defendant had not been arrested and the blood sample was taken while he was in the emergency room of the hospital for treatment of injuries he received in an accident in which he was involved, because it reasonably appeared to the police investigating the accident that he was intoxicated? Is this issue resolved by *Cupp v. Murphy,* discussed infra?

quire probing of muscle tissue which might cause injury to the muscle as well as to nerves, blood vessels and other tissue, the Court concluded the "operation sought will intrude substantially on respondent's protected interests." Such an intrusion would not be reasonable, the Court then decided, given the state's failure "to demonstrate a compelling need for it." No such need was deemed to be present, as the state had considerable other evidence connecting defendant with the robbery, including a prompt identification of him by the victim and his location near the robbery shortly after it occurred.

11. In light of *Schmerber* and *Winston,* what about other scientific tests and intrusions into the body after arrest? See *United States v. Smith,* 470 F.2d 377 (D.C.Cir. 1972) (following arrest for assault with intent to rape, warrantless benzidine test to determine presence of blood on penis proper); and compare *Ewing v. State,* 310 N.E.2d 571 (Ind.App.1974) (warrantless taking of urine sample proper, as it a "routine bodily function"); with *People v. Williams,* 557 P.2d 399 (Colo.1976) (contra). Consider also *United States ex rel. Guy v. McCauley,* 385 F.Supp. 193 (E.D.Wis. 1974), concerning a stationhouse search of the vagina of an incarcerated female which resulted in the discovery of a packet of narcotics. The court held the search violated due process because not conducted "by skilled medical technicians." But what if it had been so conducted? In *Guy,* the defendant also objected that the search was not made upon probable cause, but the court, while noting that the search was apparently prompted by "vague information several years old that [she] was known to carry heroin in her vagina," asserted that this objection "missed the mark" in light of *Robinson* and *Edwards.* Is that so?

12. In *Robinson,* the Court did not have occasion to consider what kind of search could be made incident to an arrest which was not "custodial." The court of appeals did, 471 F.2d 1082 (D.C.Cir.1972), and concluded that because "the dangers presented in that situation are to some extent similar to, and certainly no greater than, those presented in the stop-and-frisk situations involved in *Terry,* * * * the permissible scope of searches incident to routine traffic arrests, where there is no evidentiary basis for a search and where the officer intends simply to issue a notice of violation and to allow the offender to proceed, must be governed by the teachings of the Supreme Court as set forth in *Terry.*"

In *Pennsylvania v. Mimms,* 434 U.S. 106, 98 S.Ct. 330, 54 L.Ed.2d 331 (1977), officers stopped a vehicle with an expired license plate for the purpose of issuing a traffic summons and then ordered the driver out of the car, which resulted in the observation of a large bulge under his pocket, and this prompted a frisk and discovery of a gun. Rejecting the state court's holding that the driver could be directed to get out of the car only upon a reasonable suspicion he "posed a threat to police safety," the Court reasoned that "this additional intrusion can only be described as de minimus" and was justified because it "reduces the likelihood that the officer will be the victim of an assault." Under *Mimms,* may the officer also order passengers to get out of the vehicle?

13. As for search of the person without any arrest at all, consider CUPP v. MURPHY, 412 U.S. 291, 93 S.Ct. 2000, 36 L.Ed.2d 900 (1973). The Court, per Stewart, J., held that where Murphy voluntarily appeared at the station for questioning concerning the strangulation of his wife, at which time the police noticed what appeared to be blood on his finger, and the police had probable cause to arrest him but did not formally place him under arrest,[e] the warrantless taking of scrapings

e. Murphy was not arrested until over a month later, and thus the case is unlike those in which the arrest followed the search by a matter of minutes. The prevailing view is that a search "incident" to arrest may actually come before the formal making of an arrest if the police had from his fingernails "was constitutionally permissible." Noting that Murphy was aware of the police suspicion and tried to wipe his fingers clean, the Court concluded that "the rationale of *Chimel* * * * justified the police in subjecting him to the very limited search necessary to preserve the highly evanescent evidence they found under his fingernails." But, because a person not under formal arrest "might well be less hostile to the police and less likely to take conspicuous, immediate steps to destroy incriminating evidence on his person," the Court emphasized it was *not* holding "that a full *Chimel* search would have been justified in this case without a formal arrest and without a warrant." Marshall, J., concurring, noted that the police could not have preserved the evidence by "close surveillance" and that detaining Murphy while a warrant was sought "would have been as much a seizure as detaining him while his fingernails were scraped." Douglas, J., dissenting, argued: "There was time to get a warrant; Murphy could have been detained while one was sought; and that detention would have preserved the perishable evidence the police sought."

SECTION 9. ADMINISTRATIVE INSPECTIONS AND REGULATORY SEARCHES: MORE ON BALANCING THE NEED AGAINST THE INVASION OF PRIVACY

1. *Safety inspections of dwellings.* In CAMARA v. MUNICIPAL COURT, 387 U.S. 523, 87 S.Ct. 1727, 18 L.Ed.2d 930 (1967), the Court, per WHITE, J., held that appellant could not be convicted of an ordinance violation for his refusal to permit a warrantless inspection of his residence by an inspector of the municipal Department of Health.

"Under the present system, when the inspector demands entry, the occupant has no way of knowing whether enforcement of the municipal code involved requires inspection of his premises, no way of knowing the lawful limits of the inspector's power to search, and no way of knowing whether the inspector himself is acting under proper authorization. These are questions which may be reviewed by a neutral magistrate without any reassessment of the basic agency decision to canvass an area. Yet, only by refusing entry and risking a criminal conviction can the occupant at present challenge the inspector's decision to search. * * * The practical effect of this system is to leave the occupant subject to the discretion of the official in the field. This is precisely the discretion to invade private property which we have consistently circumscribed by a requirement that a disinterested party warrant the need to search. * * *

"The final justification suggested for warrantless administrative searches is that the public interest demands such a rule. * * * But we think this argument misses the mark. The question is not, at this stage at least, whether these inspections may be made, but whether they may be made without a warrant. * * * It has nowhere been urged that fire, health, and housing code inspection programs could not achieve their goals within the confines of a reasonable search warrant requirement." [a]

grounds to arrest at the time the search was made. As stated in *Rawlings v. Kentucky* (other aspects of which are discussed at p. 792 infra), the Court stated: "Where the formal arrest followed quickly on the heels of the challenged search of petitioner's person, we do not believe it particularly important that the search preceded the arrest rather than vice versa."

a. Clark, J., joined by Harlan and Stewart, JJ., dissented in *Camara* and the companion case of *See v. City of Seattle,* 387 U.S. 541, 87 S.Ct. 1737, 18 L.Ed.2d 943 (1967) (applying *Camara* to similar inspections of commercial structures not open to the public), objecting: "This boxcar warrant will be identical as to every dwelling in the area, save the street number itself. I daresay they will be printed up in pads of a thousand or more—with space for the street number to be inserted—and issued by magistrates in broadcast fashion as a matter of course. I ask: Why go through such an exercise, such a pretense?"

The Court then turned to the question of whether such warrants could issue only on the traditional criminal law quantum of probable cause: "Unfortunately, there can be no ready test for determining reasonableness other than by balancing the need to search against the invasion which the search entails. But we think that a number of persuasive factors combine to support the reasonableness of area code-enforcement inspections. First, such programs have a long history of judicial and public acceptance. Second, the public interest demands that all dangerous conditions be prevented or abated, yet it is doubtful that any other canvassing technique would achieve acceptable results. Many such conditions—faulty wiring is an obvious example—are not observable from outside the building and indeed may not be apparent to the inexpert occupant himself. Finally, because the inspections are neither personal in nature nor aimed at the discovery of evidence of crime, they involve a relatively limited invasion of the urban citizen's privacy. * * *

"Having concluded that the area inspection is a 'reasonable' search of private property within the meaning of the Fourth Amendment, it is obvious that 'probable cause' to issue a warrant to inspect must exist if reasonable legislative or administrative standards for conducting an area inspection are satisfied with respect to a particular dwelling. Such standards, which will vary with the municipal program being enforced, may be based upon the passage of time, the nature of the building (e.g., a multi-family apartment house), or the condition of the entire area, but they will not necessarily depend upon specific knowledge of the condition of the particular dwelling."

2. *Inspection of business premises.* In *Marshall v. Barlow's Inc.*, 436 U.S. 307, 98 S.Ct. 1816, 56 L.Ed.2d 305 (1978), the Court, per White, J., held unconstitutional a provision in the Occupational Safety and Health Act which empowered agents to search without a warrant the work area of any employment facility within OSHA's jurisdiction for safety hazards. Noting the absence of "a long tradition of close government supervision" in this area, the Court declared that only in "the most fictional sense" can "voluntary consent to later searches be found in the single fact that one conducts a business affecting interstate commerce," which is all it takes to come within OSHA's jurisdiction. Thus, what is required is a *Camara*-type "warrant showing that a specific business has been chosen for an OSHA search on the basis of a general administrative plan for the enforcement of the Act derived from neutral sources such as, for example, dispersion of employees in various types of industries across a given area, and the desired frequency of searches in any of the lesser division of the area." Requiring such warrants, the Court concluded, would not "impose serious burdens on the inspection system or the courts, * * * prevent inspections necessary to enforce the statute, or * * * make them less effective," as (i) most businessmen will consent to inspection without a warrant; and (ii) the advantages of surprise would not be lost "if, after being refused entry, procedures were available for the Secretary to seek an *ex parte* warrant and to reappear at the premises without further notice to the establishment being inspected."

But in DONOVAN v. DEWEY, 452 U.S. 594, 101 S.Ct. 2534, 69 L.Ed.2d 262 (1981), the Court, per MARSHALL, J., concluded "that the warrantless inspections required by the Mine Safety and Health Act do not offend the Fourth Amendment. * * * In enacting the statute, Congress was plainly aware that the mining industry is among the most hazardous in the country and that the poor health and safety record of this industry has significant deleterious effects on interstate commerce. Nor is it seriously contested that Congress in this case could reasonably determine * * * that a system of warrantless inspections was necessary 'if the law is to be properly enforced and inspection made effective.' * * * We see no reason not to defer to this legislative determination. * * * Congress could properly conclude that 'if inspection is to be effective and serve as a credible deterrent, unannounced, even frequent, inspections are essential. In this context, the prerequisite of a warrant could easily frustrate inspection.'

"Because a warrant requirement clearly might impede the 'specific enforcement needs' of the Act, the only real issue before us is whether the statute's inspection program, in terms of the certainty and regularity of its application, provides a constitutionally adequate substitute for a warrant. We believe that it does. * * * First, the Act requires inspection of *all* mines and specifically defines the frequency of inspection. * * * Second, the standards with which a mine operator is required to comply are all specifically set forth in the Act or in Title 30 of the Code of Federal Regulations. Indeed, the Act requires that the Secretary inform mine operators of all standards proposed pursuant to the Act. Thus, rather than leaving the frequency and purpose of inspections to the unchecked discretion of government officers, the Act establishes a predictable and guided federal regulatory presence. [T]he operator of a mine 'is not left to wonder about the purposes of the inspector or the limits of his task.'

"Finally, the Act provides a specific mechanism for accommodating any special privacy concerns that a specific mine operator might have. The Act prohibits forcible entries, and instead requires the Secretary, when refused entry onto a mining facility, to file a civil action in federal court to obtain an injunction against future refusals. This proceeding provides an adequate forum for the mine owner to show that a specific search is outside the federal regulatory authority, or to seek from the District Court an order accommodating any unusual privacy interests that the mine owner might have. * * *

"Appellees contend, however, that [the statute] violates the Fourth Amendment as applied to authorize warrantless inspections of stone quarries * * * because [they] do 'not have a long tradition of government regulation.' * * * But if the length of regulation were the only criteria, absurd results would occur. Under appellees' view, new or emerging industries, including ones such as the nuclear power industry that pose enormous potential safety and health problems, could never be subject to warrantless searches even under the most carefully structured inspection program simply because of the recent vintage of regulation." [b]

3. *Fire investigations.* In *Michigan v. Clifford,* 464 U.S. 287, 104 S.Ct. 641, 78 L.Ed.2d 477 (1984), a fire was extinguished at defendants' home, and six hours

b. Stevens, J., concurring because he agreed that *Dewey* was distinguishable from *Barlow's,* concluded he "need not confront the more difficult question whether *Camara* represented such a fundamental misreading of the Fourth Amendment that it should be overruled. I would merely observe that that option is more viable today than when some of the reasoning that would support it could only be found in dissenting opinions, or in the earlier Court opinion in *Frank* that had itself been overruled in *Camara.*"

Rehnquist, J., concurring on an "open fields" theory, objected to the Court's rationale "that warrantless searches of stone quarries are permitted because the mining industry has been pervasively regulated. But I have no doubt that had Congress enacted a criminal statute similar to that involved here—authorizing for example unannounced warrantless searches of property reasonably thought to house unlawful drug activity—the warrantless search would be struck down under our existing Fourth Amendment line of decisions. This Court would invalidate the search despite the fact that Congress has a strong interest in regulating and preventing drug related crime and has in fact pervasively regulated such crime for a longer period of time than it has regulated mining."

Stewart, J., dissenting, objected that the warrant exception applies to businesses that are both pervasively regulated *and* have a long history of regulation because "the very rationale for the exception—that the 'businessman * * * in effect consents to the restrictions placed upon him'—disappears without it."

later a fire investigator entered the home without a warrant or consent as it was being boarded up pursuant to the absent owners' instructions. He found evidence of arson in the basement, where the fire originated, and in upper rooms found evidence that the owners had before the fire removed much valuable personal property. The four-Justice plurality accepted and followed the rule in *Michigan v. Tyler,* 436 U.S. 499, 98 S.Ct. 1942, 56 L.Ed.2d 486 (1978), namely, that a burning building creates exigent circumstances justifying authorities to enter to fight the blaze and to remain a reasonable time to investigate the cause of the fire, but that later entries without consent require a warrant—an administrative warrant "to determine the cause and origin of a recent fire" on a showing "that a fire of undetermined origin has occurred on the premises, that the scope of the proposed search is reasonable and will not intrude unnecessarily on the fire victim's privacy, and that the search will be executed at a reasonable and convenient time"; or a conventional search warrant on probable cause if the "primary objective of the search is to gather evidence of criminal activity." Stevens, J., concurring, disagreed as to the administrative warrant requirement, stating he "would require the fire investigator to obtain a traditional criminal search warrant in order to make an unannounced entry, but would characterize a warrantless entry as reasonable whenever the inspector had either given the owner sufficient advance notice to enable him or an agent to be present or had made a reasonable effort to do so." The four dissenters agreed that a conventional warrant was required to search the balance of the home, but declared that a warrantless inspection of the fire scene was permissible because "the utility of requiring a magistrate to evaluate the grounds for a search following a fire is so limited that the incidental protection of an individual's privacy interests simply does not justify imposing a warrant requirement."

4. *Inspection of international mail.* In UNITED STATES v. RAMSEY, 431 U.S. 606, 97 S.Ct. 1972, 52 L.Ed.2d 617 (1977), a customs inspector found in the same bag of incoming mail from Thailand (a known source of narcotics) eight letter-size airmail envelopes, apparently addressed with the same typewriter, all of which were bulky (weighing 3 to 6 times as much as normal international airmail). He opened the envelopes and found them to contain heroin. The Court, per REHNQUIST, J., held: (1) that the inspector had met the requirements of 19 U.S.C. § 482, which authorizes a search of an incoming "envelope" in which "he may have reasonable cause to suspect there is merchandise which was imported contrary to law"; (2) that the search would be constitutional under the rule generally applicable to border searches, namely, that such searches are "considered to be 'reasonable' by the single fact that the person or item in question had entered into our country from outside"; (3) that the general rule was applicable to incoming mail as well as persons and vehicles because (contrary to the view of the court of appeals, which concluded that a search warrant was required for mail because of the lack of exigent circumstances) "the 'border search' exception is not based on the doctrine of 'exigent circumstances' at all"; and (4) that greater Fourth Amendment protection of letters was not necessary because of First Amendment considerations, especially in light of the fact that postal regulations prohibited the reading of correspondence unless a search warrant is first obtained.[c]

5. *Searches at the border.* In *Henderson v. United States,* 390 F.2d 805 (9th Cir.1967), the court held that a border search of appellant, by which she was compelled to submit to a procedure whereby a medical doctor removed two packets of heroin

c. Stevens, J., joined by Brennan and Marshall, JJ., concluded that Congress, in using the word "envelope" in the statute, had not intended to refer to items traveling via mail.

from her vagina, was unreasonable where based solely upon her resemblance to a woman found to have narcotics in her purse in a border inspection three to four weeks earlier: "[E]very person crossing our border may be required to disclose the contents of his baggage, and of his vehicle, if he has one. The mere crossing of the border is sufficient cause for such a search. Even 'mere suspicion' is not required. We assume that the same rule would apply to the contents of his or her purse, wallet, or pockets. If, however, the search of the person is to go further, if the party, male or female, is to be required to strip, we think that something more, at least a real suspicion, directed specifically to that person, should be required. And if there is to be a more than casual examination of the body, if in the course of the search of a woman there is to be a requirement that she manually open her vagina for visual inspection to see if she has something concealed there, we think that we should require more than a mere suspicion. * * * Surely, in such a case, to be warranted, the official's action should be backed by at least the 'clear indication', the 'plain suggestion', required in [*Schmerber v. California,* p. 48 supra].[d]

In *United States v. Montoya de Hernandez,* ___ U.S. ___, 105 S.Ct. 3304, 87 L.Ed.2d 381 (1985), the Court, per Rehnquist, J., held (i) "that the detention of a traveler at the border, beyond the scope of a routine customs search and inspection, is justified at its inception if customs agents, considering all the facts surrounding the traveler and her trip, reasonably suspect that the traveler is smuggling contraband in her alimentary canal"; and (ii) that such a detention is "reasonably related in scope to the circumstances which justified it initially" if the suspect is held so long as is "necessary to either verify or dispel the suspicion." This means that if, as in *de Hernandez,* the suspect declines to submit to an x-ray, then the detention on reasonable suspicion may continue until a bowel movement occurs.[e]

6. *Inspections for alien traffic not at the border.* UNITED STATES v. MARTINEZ-FUERTE, 428 U.S. 543, 96 S.Ct. 3074, 49 L.Ed.2d 1116 (1976), concerned whether a vehicle may be stopped at a fixed checkpoint away from the international border, for the purpose of briefly questioning its occupants, without reason to believe the vehicle contains illegal aliens. The Court, per POWELL, J., reasoned:

"The Fourth Amendment imposes limits on search and seizure powers in order to prevent arbitrary and oppressive interference by enforcement officials with the privacy and personal security of individuals. In delineating the constitutional safeguards applicable in particular contexts, the Court has weighed the public interest against the Fourth Amendment interest of the individual, a process evident in our previous cases dealing with Border Patrol traffic-checking operations.

"In *Almeida-Sanchez v. United States* [413 U.S. 266, 93 S.Ct. 2535, 37 L.Ed.2d 596 (1973)], the question was whether a roving-patrol unit constitutionally could search a vehicle for illegal aliens simply because it was in the general vicinity of the border. We recognized that important law enforcement interests were at stake

d. As for whether the border search rules apply after a person has crossed the border and travelled some distance into the country, this depends, says *Alexander v. United States,* 362 F.2d 379 (9th Cir.1966) on "whether the totality of the surrounding circumstances, including the time and distance elapsed as well as the manner and extent of surveillance, are such as to convince the fact finder of a reasonable certainty that any contraband which might be found in or on the vehicle at the time of search was aboard the vehicle at the time of entry into the jurisdiction of the United States."

e. Stevens, J., concurring, unlike the majority, made it explicit that the authorities must opt for the x-ray alternative except when, as here, the suspect declined to be x-rayed. Brennan, J., joined by Marshall, J., dissenting, asserted that "Government officials may no more confine a person at the border under such circumstances for purposes of criminal investigation than they may within the interior of the country."

but held that searches by roving patrols impinged so significantly on Fourth Amendment privacy interests that a search could be conducted without consent only if there was probable cause to believe that a car contained illegal aliens, at least in the absence of a judicial warrant authorizing random searches by roving patrols in a given area. We held in *United States v. Ortiz* [422 U.S. 891, 95 S.Ct. 2585, 45 L.Ed.2d 623 (1975)], that the same limitations applied to vehicle searches conducted at a permanent checkpoint.

"In *United States v. Brignoni-Ponce,* [422 U.S. 873, 95 S.Ct. 2574, 45 L.Ed.2d 607 (1975)], however, we recognized that other traffic-checking practices involve a different balance of public and private interests and appropriately are subject to less stringent constitutional safeguards. The question was under what circumstances a roving patrol could stop motorists in the general area of the border for brief inquiry into their residence status. We found that the interference with Fourth Amendment interests involved in such a stop was 'modest,' while the inquiry served significant law enforcement needs. We therefore held that a roving-patrol stop need not be justified by probable cause and may be undertaken if the stopping officer is 'aware of specific articulable facts, together with rational inferences from those facts, that reasonably warrant suspicion' that a vehicle contains illegal aliens. * * *

"Routine checkpoint stops do not intrude similarly on the motoring public. First, the potential interference with legitimate traffic is minimal. Motorists using these highways are not taken by surprise as they know, or may obtain knowledge of, the location of the checkpoints and will not be stopped elsewhere. Second, checkpoint operations both appear to and actually involve less discretionary enforcement activity. The regularized manner in which established checkpoints are operated is visible evidence, reassuring to law-abiding motorists, that the stops are duly authorized and believed to serve the public interest. The location of a fixed checkpoint is not chosen by officers in the field, but by officials responsible for making overall decisions as to the most effective allocation of limited enforcement resources. We may assume that such officials will be unlikely to locate a checkpoint where it bears arbitrarily or oppressively on motorists as a class. And since field officers may stop only those cars passing the checkpoint, there is less room for abusive or harassing stops of individuals than there was in the case of roving-patrol stops. Moreover, a claim that a particular exercise of discretion in locating or operating a checkpoint is unreasonable is subject to post-stop judicial review.

"The defendants arrested at the San Clemente checkpoint suggest that its operation involves a significant extra element of intrusiveness in that only a small percentage of cars are referred to the secondary inspection area, thereby 'stigmatizing' those diverted and reducing the assurances provided by equal treatment of all motorists. We think defendants overstate the consequences. Referrals are made for the sole purpose of conducting a routine and limited inquiry into residence status that cannot feasibly be made of every motorist where the traffic is heavy. * * * Moreover, selective referrals—rather than questioning the occupants of every car—tend to advance some Fourth Amendment interests by minimizing the intrusion on the general motoring public.

"The defendants note correctly that to accommodate public and private interests some quantum of individualized suspicion is usually a prerequisite to a constitutional search or seizure. But the Fourth Amendment imposes no irreducible requirement of such suspicion. In *Camara* * * * the Court examined the government interests advanced to justify such routine intrusions 'upon the constitutionally protected interests of the private citizen,' and concluded that under the circumstances the government interests outweighed those of the private citizen.

"We think the same conclusion is appropriate here, where we deal neither with searches nor with the sanctity of private dwellings, ordinarily afforded the most stringent Fourth Amendment protection. As we have noted earlier, one's expectation of privacy in an automobile and of freedom in its operation are significantly different from the traditional expectation of privacy and freedom in one's residence. And the reasonableness of the procedures followed in making these checkpoint stops makes the resulting intrusion on the interests of motorists minimal. On the other hand, the purpose of the stops is legitimate and in the public interest, and the need for this enforcement technique is demonstrated by the records in the cases before us. Accordingly, we hold that the stops and questioning at issue may be made in the absence of any individualized suspicion at reasonably located checkpoints.

"We further believe that it is constitutional to refer motorists selectively to the secondary inspection area at the San Clemente checkpoint on the basis of criteria that would not sustain a roving-patrol stop. Thus, even if it be assumed that such referrals are made largely on the basis of apparent Mexican ancestry, we perceive no constitutional violation. As the intrusion here is sufficiently minimal that no particularized reason need exist to justify it, we think it follows that the Border Patrol officers must have wide discretion in selecting the motorists to be diverted for the brief questioning involved.

"Sifuentes' alternative argument is that routine stops at a checkpoint are permissible only if a warrant has given judicial authorization to the particular checkpoint location and the practice of routine stops. A warrant requirement in these circumstances draws some support from *Camara* * * *.

"We do not think, however, that *Camara* is an apt model. It involved the search of private residences, for which a warrant traditionally has been required. As developed more fully above, the strong Fourth Amendment interests that justify the warrant requirement in that context are absent here. The degree of intrusion upon privacy that may be occasioned by a search of a house hardly can be compared with the minor interference with privacy resulting from the mere stop for questioning as to residence. Moreover, the warrant requirement in *Camara* served specific Fourth Amendment interests to which a warrant requirement here would make little contribution. The Court there said:

> '[W]hen [an] inspector [without a warrant] demands entry, the occupant has no way of knowing whether enforcement of the municipal code involved requires inspection of his premises, no way of knowing the lawful limits of the inspector's power to search, and no way of knowing whether the inspector himself is acting under proper authorization.'

A warrant provided assurance to the occupant on these scores. We believe that the visible manifestations of the field officers' authority at a checkpoint provide substantially the same assurances in this case.

"Other purposes served by the requirement of a warrant also are inapplicable here. One such purpose is to prevent hindsight from coloring the evaluation of the reasonableness of a search or seizure. The reasonableness of checkpoint stops, however, turns on factors such as the location and method of operation of the checkpoint, factors that are not susceptible to the distortion of hindsight, and therefore will be open to post-stop review notwithstanding the absence of a warrant. Another purpose for a warrant requirement is to substitute the judgment of the magistrate for that of the searching or seizing officer. But the need for this is reduced when the decision to 'seize' is not entirely in the hands of the officer in the field, and deference is to be given to the administrative decisions of higher ranking officials."

Brennan, J., joined by Marshall, J., dissenting, objected that "the governmental interests relied on as warranting intrusion here are the same as those in *Almeida-Sanchez* and *Ortiz,* which required a showing of probable cause for roving-patrol and fixed checkpoint searches, and *Brignoni-Ponce,* which required at least a showing of reasonable suspicion based on specific articulable facts to justify roving-patrol stops. Absent some difference in the nature of the intrusion, the same minimal requirement should be imposed for checkpoint stops."

7. *Driver's license, vehicle registration and DWI checks.* In DELAWARE v. PROUSE, 440 U.S. 648, 99 S.Ct. 1391, 59 L.Ed.2d 660 (1979), the Court held "that except in those situations in which there is at least articulable and reasonable suspicion that a motorist is unlicensed or that an automobile is not registered, or that either the vehicle or an occupant is otherwise subject to seizure for violation of law, stopping an automobile and detaining the driver in order to check his driver's license and the registration of the automobile are unreasonable under the Fourth Amendment." Justice White for the majority, in balancing the intrusion against the need, reasoned that: (i) it could not be assumed "that the physical and psychological intrusion visited upon the occupants of a vehicle by a random stop to check documents is of any less moment than that occasioned by a stop by border patrol agents on roving patrol"; (ii) "the States have a vital interest in ensuring that only those qualified to do so are permitted to operate motor vehicles, that these vehicles are fit for safe operation, and hence that licensing, registration, and vehicle inspection requirements are being observed"; and (iii) "the discretionary spot check [is not] a sufficiently productive mechanism to justify the intrusion," as compared to "the alternative mechanisms available, both those in use and those that might be adopted," in that purely random selection could not be expected to uncover many violations.[f] The Court stressed that it was not precluding states "from developing methods for spot checks that involve less intrusion or that do not involve the unconstrained exercise of discretion." [g]

f. Neither *Prouse* nor *Martinez-Fuerte,* the Court concluded in *United States v. Villamonte-Marquez,* 462 U.S. 579, 103 S.Ct. 2573, 77 L.Ed.2d 22 (1983), bars customs officers from exercising their statutory authority to board any vessel at any time and place to examine the vessel's manifest and other documents. As Rehnquist, J., explained: "The nature of waterborne commerce in waters providing ready access to the open sea is sufficiently different from the nature of vehicular traffic on highways as to make possible alternatives to the sort of 'stop' made in this case less likely to accomplish the obviously essential governmental purposes involved. The system of prescribed outward markings used by States for vehicle registration is also significantly different than the system of external markings on vessels, and the extent and type of documentation required by federal law is a good deal more variable and more complex than are the state vehicle registration laws. The nature of the governmental interest in assuring compliance with documentation requirements, particularly in waters where the need to deter or apprehend smugglers is great, are substantial; the type of intrusion made in this case, while not minimal, is limited." Brennan and Marshall, JJ., dissented.

g. The majority listed as "one possible alternative" the "questioning of all oncoming traffic at roadblock-type stops," and also declared that the holding did not "cast doubt on the permissibility of roadside truck weigh-stations and inspection checkpoints, at which some vehicles may be subject to further detention for safety and regulatory inspection than are others.

Blackmun and Powell, JJ., concurring, assumed "that the Court's reservation also includes other not purely random stops (such as every 10th car to pass a given point) that equate with, but are less intrusive than, a 100% roadblock stop. And I would not regard the present case as a precedent that throws any constitutional shadow upon the necessarily large random examinations by game wardens in the performance of their duties. In a situation of that type, it seems to me, the Court's balancing process, and the value factors under consideration, would be quite different."

Rehnquist, J., dissenting, objected that the majority had elevated "the adage 'misery loves company' to a novel role in Fourth Amendment jurisprudence" by allowing the stopping of all motorists on a particular thoroughfare but not less than all motorists.

Police sometimes establish so-called DWI checkpoints, where many or all vehicles are stopped at a roadblock.[h] Based upon brief contact with each driver, some vehicles are further detained on suspicion the driver is intoxicated, and he is then required to undergo some sort of sobriety test. Appellate courts are split on the constitutionality of this practice, although the results in these cases have often turned upon the precise manner in which the checkpoint was established and conducted. In light of *Prouse* and *Martinez-Fuerte,* what are the most important considerations?

8. *Airport inspections.* At a time when airport hijacker detection searches were conducted selectively, depending upon whether the traveler fit the government's hijacker "profile," such searches were upheld by reliance upon *Terry v. Ohio,* p. 361 supra. Now that *all* passengers and their carry-on luggage are checked, the program is upheld as a form of administrative search. For example, applying *Camara*-type reasoning, it was held in *United States v. Davis,* 482 F.2d 893 (9th Cir.1973), that "airport screening searches of the person and immediate possessions of potential passengers for weapons and explosives are reasonable under the Fourth Amendment provided each prospective boarder retains the right to leave rather than submit to the search."

9. *Supervision of parolees and probationers.* The Fourth Amendment rights of probationers and parolees are not of precisely the same scope and dimension as those of the public at large. As to parolees, it has often been held that their residences and vehicles may be searched and their persons seized without a warrant or even without probable cause. There is some disagreement as to whether a probationer's Fourth Amendment rights are diminished to the same extent, but clearly probationers may lawfully be subjected to searches which, absent their probation status, would be deemed unlawful because of the absence of probable cause or a search warrant or both.

A variety of theories have been articulated by the courts in purported justification for these holdings. With respect to parolees, one notion commonly relied upon is that such persons are in the "constructive custody" of the government during the period of their parole and thus are in essentially the same position, in terms of their Fourth Amendment rights, as those persons who have not obtained parole release and are still serving time in prison. Some courts instead stress that parole or probation is an "act of grace," from which it is concluded that such beneficence may be attended by whatever restrictions upon privacy the government may deem appropriate. Or, particularly when such a "waiver" is expressly set out and agreed to by the probationer or parolee at the time of his conditional release, it is frequently concluded that searches of such persons are proper because consented to as a part of the "contract" of release.

Are these theories sound? What then of the approach which some courts have taken recently, namely, to view searches conducted within the framework of probation and parole supervision as yet another type of "administrative search" governed by the balancing test of *Camara*? What results should be reached under the latter approach, based on what considerations? Is it important, for example, whether the extent of the authority to search is determined on an individual basis at the time of the conditional release and is spelled out in the conditions of release? Whether the search is instigated by the police or by correctional personnel?

h. For analysis of this practice, see Grossman, *Sobriety Checkpoints: Roadblocks to Fourth Amendment Protections,* 12 Am.J.Crim.L. 123 (1984); Jacobs & Stroessen, *Mass Investigations Without Individualized Suspicion: A Constitutional and Policy Critique of Drunk Driving Roadblocks,* 18 U.C.Davis L.Rev. 595 (1985); Rogers, *The Drunk-Driving Roadblock: Random Seizure or Minimal Intrusion?,* 21 Crim.L.Bull. 197 (1985).

10. *Search of students.* Utilizing the *Camara* balancing test, the Court in NEW JERSEY v. T.L.O., ___ U.S. ___, 105 S.Ct. 733, 83 L.Ed.2d 720 (1985), struck "the balance between the school child's legitimate expectations of privacy and the school's equally legitimate needs to maintain an environment in which learning can take place" by holding: (i) "that school officials need not obtain a warrant before searching a student who is under their authority"; (ii) that ordinarily "a search of a student by a teacher or other school official will be 'justified at its inception' when there are reasonable grounds for suspecting that the search will turn up evidence that the student has violated or is violating either the law or the rules of the school"; and (iii) that such a search "will be permissible in its scope when the measures adopted are reasonably related to the objectives of the search and not excessively intrusive in light of the age and sex of the student and the nature of the infraction." The *T.L.O.* case involved the search of the purse of a student suspected of violating the school's smoking regulations, and the Court noted it was not passing upon various other school-search issues, such as "whether a schoolchild has a legitimate expectation of privacy in lockers, desks, or other school property provided for the storage of school supplies"; whether there is a different "standard for assessing the legality of searches connected by school officials in conjunction with or at the behest of law enforcement agencies"; and "whether individualized suspicion is an essential element of the reasonableness standard we adopt for searches by school authorities" so as to bar general searches of students or lockers.

SECTION 10. CONSENT SEARCHES

Consent searches are frequently relied upon by the police because they involve no time-consuming paper work and offer an opportunity to search even when probable cause is lacking. Thus, the constitutional protection against unreasonable search and seizure widens or narrows, depending on the difficulty or ease with which the prosecution can establish that the defendant (or some other authorized person) has "consented" to what would otherwise be an unconstitutional invasion of his privacy.

A. THE NATURE OF "CONSENT"

SCHNECKLOTH v. BUSTAMONTE

412 U.S. 218, 93 S.Ct. 2041, 36 L.Ed.2d 854 (1973).

MR. JUSTICE STEWART delivered the opinion of the Court. * * *

While on routine patrol in Sunnyvale, California, at approximately 2:40 in the morning, Police Officer James Rand stopped an automobile when he observed that one headlight and its license plate light were burned out. Six men were in the vehicle. Joe Alcala and the respondent, Robert Bustamonte, were in the front seat with Joe Gonzales, the driver. Three older men were seated in the rear. When, in response to the policeman's question, Gonzales could not produce a driver's license, Officer Rand asked if any of the other five had any evidence of identification. Only Alcala produced a license, and he explained that the car was his brother's. After the six occupants had stepped out of the car at the officer's request and after two additional policemen had arrived, Officer Rand asked Alcala if he could search the car. Alcala replied, "Sure, go ahead." Prior to the search no one was threatened with arrest and, according to Officer Rand's uncontradicted testimony, it "was all very congenial at this time." Gonzales testified that Alcala actually helped in the search of the car, by opening the trunk and glove compartment. In Gonzales' words: ". . . the police officer asked Joe [Alcala], he goes, 'Does the trunk open?' And Joe said, 'Yes.' He went to the car and got the keys and opened up the trunk." Wadded up under the left rear seat, the police officers found three checks that had previously been stolen from a car wash.

The trial judge denied the motion to suppress, and the checks in question were admitted in evidence at Bustamonte's trial. On the basis of this and other evidence he was convicted, and the California Court of Appeal for the First Appellate District affirmed the conviction. * * * The California Supreme Court denied review.

Thereafter, the respondent sought a writ of habeas corpus in a federal district court. It was denied. On appeal, the Court of Appeals for the Ninth Circuit set aside the District Court's order. * * *

The precise question in this case, then, is what must the state prove to demonstrate that a consent was "voluntarily" given. * * *

The most extensive judicial exposition of the meaning of "voluntariness" has been developed in those cases in which the Court has had to determine the "voluntariness" of a defendant's confession for purposes of the Fourteenth Amendment. * * * It is to that body of case law to which we turn for initial guidance on the meaning of "voluntariness" in the present context. * * *

The significant fact about all of these decisions is that none of them turned on the presence or absence of a single controlling criterion; each reflected a careful scrutiny of all the surrounding circumstances. In none of them did the Court rule that the Due Process Clause required the prosecution to prove as part of its initial burden that the defendant knew he had a right to refuse to answer the questions that were put. While the state of the accused's mind, and the failure of the police to advise the accused of his rights, were certainly factors to be evaluated in assessing the "voluntariness" of an accused's responses, they were not in and of themselves determinative.

Similar considerations lead us to agree with the courts of California that the question whether a consent to a search was in fact "voluntary" or was the product of duress or coercion, express or implied, is a question of fact to be determined from the totality of all the circumstances. While knowledge of the right to refuse consent is one factor to be taken into account, the government need not establish such knowledge as the *sine qua non* of an effective consent. As with police questioning, two competing concerns must be accommodated in determining the meaning of a "voluntary" consent—the legitimate need for such searches and the equally important requirement of assuring the absence of coercion.

In situations where the police have some evidence of illicit activity, but lack probable cause to arrest or search, a search authorized by a valid consent may be the only means of obtaining important and reliable evidence. In the present case for example, while the police had reason to stop the car for traffic violations, the State does not contend that there was probable cause to search the vehicle or that the search was incident to a valid arrest of any of the occupants. Yet, the search yielded tangible evidence that served as a basis for a prosecution, and provided some assurance that others, wholly innocent of the crime, were not mistakenly brought to trial. And in those cases where there is probable cause to arrest or search, but where the police lack a warrant, a consent search may still be valuable. If the search is conducted and proves fruitless, that in itself may convince the police that an arrest with its possible stigma and embarrassment is unnecessary, or that a far more extensive search pursuant to a warrant is not justified. In short a search pursuant to consent may result in considerably less inconvenience for the subject of the search, and, properly conducted, is a constitutionally permissible and wholly legitimate aspect of effective police activity.

But the Fourth and Fourteenth Amendments require that a consent not be coerced, by explicit or implicit means, by implied threat or covert force. For, no matter how subtly the coercion were applied, the resulting "consent" would be no more than a pretext for the unjustified police intrusion against which the Fourth Amendment is directed. * * *

The problem of reconciling the recognized legitimacy of consent searches with the requirement that they be free from any aspect of official coercion cannot be resolved by an infallible touchstone. To approve such searches without the most careful scrutiny would sanction the possibility of official coercion; to place artificial restrictions upon such searches would jeopardize their basic validity. Just as was true with confessions, the requirement of a "voluntary" consent reflects a fair accommodation of the constitutional requirements involved. In examining all the surrounding circumstances to determine if in fact the consent to search was coerced, account must be taken of subtly coercive police questions, as well as the possibly vulnerable subjective state of the person who consents. Those searches that are the product of police coercion can thus be filtered out without undermining the continuing validity of consent searches. In sum, there is no reason for us to depart in the area of consent searches, from the traditional definition of "voluntariness."

The approach of the Court of Appeals for the Ninth Circuit finds no support in any of our decisions that have attempted to define the meaning of "voluntariness." Its ruling, that the State must affirmatively prove that the subject of the search knew that he had a right to refuse consent, would, in practice, create serious doubt whether consent searches could continue to be conducted. There might be rare cases where it could be proved from the record that a person in fact affirmatively knew of his right to refuse—such as a case where he announced to the police that if he didn't sign the consent form, "you [police] are going to get a search warrant;" or a case where by prior experience and training a person had clearly and convincingly demonstrated such knowledge. But more commonly where there was no evidence of any coercion, explicit or implicit, the prosecution would nevertheless be unable to demonstrate that the subject of the search in fact had known of his right to refuse consent.

The very object of the inquiry—the nature of a person's subjective understanding—underlines the difficulty of the prosecution's burden under the rule applied by the Court of Appeals in this case. Any defendant who was the subject of a search authorized solely by his consent could effectively frustrate the introduction into evidence of the fruits of that search by simply failing to testify that he in fact knew he could refuse to consent. And the near impossibility of meeting this prosecutorial burden suggests why this Court has never accepted any such litmus-paper test of voluntariness. * * *

One alternative that would go far towards proving that the subject of a search did know he had a right to refuse consent would be to advise him of that right before eliciting his consent. That, however, is a suggestion that has been almost universally repudiated by both federal and state courts, and, we think, rightly so. For it would be thoroughly impractical to impose on the normal consent search the detailed requirements of an effective warning. Consent searches are part of the standard investigatory techniques of law enforcement agencies. They normally occur on the highway, or in a person's home or office, and under informal and unstructured conditions. The circumstances that prompt the initial request to search may develop quickly or be a logical extension of investigative police questioning. The police may seek to investigate further suspicious circumstances or to follow up leads developed in questioning persons at the scene of a crime. These situations are a far cry from the structured atmosphere of a trial where, assisted by counsel if he chooses, a defendant is informed of his trial rights. And, while surely a closer question, these situations are still immeasurably far removed from "custodial interrogation" where, in *Miranda v. Arizona* [p. 542 infra], we found that the Constitution required certain now familiar warnings as a prerequisite to police interrogation. * * *

It is said, however, that a "consent" is a "waiver" of a person's rights under the Fourth and Fourteenth Amendments. The argument is that by allowing the police to conduct a search, a person "waives" whatever right he had to prevent the police from searching. It is argued that under the doctrine of *Johnson v. Zerbst,* 304 U.S. 458, 58 S.Ct. 1019, 82 L.Ed. 1461 (1938), to establish such a "waiver" the state must demonstrate "an intentional relinquishment or abandonment of a known right or privilege." * * *

Almost without exception the requirement of a knowing and intelligent waiver has been applied only to those rights which the Constitution guarantees to a criminal defendant in order to preserve a fair trial. Hence, and hardly surprisingly in view of the facts of *Johnson* itself, the standard of a knowing and intelligent waiver has most often been applied to test the validity of a waiver of counsel, either at trial, or upon a guilty plea. And the Court has also applied the *Johnson* criteria to assess the effectiveness of a waiver of other trial rights such as the right to confrontation, to a jury trial, and to a speedy trial, and the right to be free from twice being placed in jeopardy. Guilty pleas have been carefully scrutinized to determine whether the accused knew and understood all the rights to which he would be entitled at trial, and that he had intentionally chosen to forgo them. And the Court has evaluated the knowing and intelligent nature of the waiver of trial rights in trial-type situations, such as the waiver of the privilege against compulsory self-incrimination before an administrative agency or a congressional committee, or the waiver of counsel in a juvenile proceeding.

The guarantees afforded a criminal defendant at trial also protect him at certain stages before the actual trial, and any alleged waiver must meet the strict standard of an intentional relinquishment of a "known" right. But the "trial" guarantees that have been applied to the "pretrial" stage of the criminal process are similarly designed to protect the fairness of the trial itself. * * * [a]

The standards of *Johnson* were, therefore, found to be a necessary prequisite to a finding of a valid waiver.[29] * * *

A strict standard of waiver has been applied to those rights guaranteed to a criminal defendant to insure that he will be accorded the greatest possible opportunity to utilize every facet of the constitutional model of a fair criminal trial. Any trial conducted in derogation of that model leaves open the possibility that the trial reached an unfair result precisely because all the protections specified in the Constitution were not provided. A prime example is the right to counsel. For without that right, a wholly innocent accused faces the real and substantial danger that

a. At this point, the Court noted that "the standard of a knowing and intelligent waiver" applies to waiver of counsel at a lineup under *United States v. Wade,* p. 652 infra, and *Gilbert v. California,* p. 654 infra, because counsel is provided to protect the right of cross-examination at trial; and that the same standard applies to waiver of counsel at custodial interrogation under *Miranda v. Arizona,* p. 542 infra, because counsel is provided to ensure that the safeguards concerning the giving of testimony at trial do not "become empty formalities."

29. As we have already noted, *Miranda* itself involved interrogation of a suspect detained in custody and did not concern the investigatory procedures of the police in general on-the-scene questioning. By the same token, the present case does not require a determination of the proper standard to be applied in assessing the validity of a search authorized solely by an alleged consent that is obtained from a person after he has been placed in custody. We do note, however, that other courts have been particularly sensitive to the heightened possibilities for coercion when the "consent" to a search was given by a person in custody.

simply because of his lack of legal expertise he may be convicted. * * *

The protections of the Fourth Amendment are of a wholly different order, and have nothing whatever to do with promoting the fair ascertainment of truth at a criminal trial. Rather, as Mr. Justice Frankfurter's opinion for the Court put it in *Wolf v. Colorado* [p. 208 supra], the Fourth Amendment protects the "security of one's privacy against arbitrary intrusion by the police. . . ." * * *

Nor can it even be said that a search, as opposed to an eventual trial, is somehow "unfair" if a person consents to a search. While the Fourth and Fourteenth Amendments limit the circumstances under which the police can conduct a search, there is nothing constitutionally suspect in a person voluntarily allowing a search. The actual conduct of the search may be precisely the same as if the police had obtained a warrant. And, unlike those constitutional guarantees that protect a defendant at trial, it cannot be said every reasonable presumption ought to be indulged against voluntary relinquishment. We have only recently stated: "[I]t is no part of the policy underlying the Fourth and Fourteenth Amendments to discourage citizens from aiding to the utmost of their ability in the apprehension of criminals." *Coolidge v. New Hampshire,* [p. 296 supra]. Rather the community has a real interest in encouraging consent, for the resulting search may yield necessary evidence for the solution and prosecution of crime, evidence that may insure that a wholly innocent person is not wrongly charged with a criminal offense.

Those cases that have dealt with the application of the *Johnson v. Zerbst* rule make clear that it would be next to impossible to apply to a consent search the standard of "an intentional relinquishment or abandonment of a known right or privilege." To be true to *Johnson* and its progeny, there must be examination into the knowing and understanding nature of the waiver, an examination that was designed for a trial judge in the structured atmosphere of a courtroom. * * * It would be unrealistic to expect that in the informal, unstructured context of a consent search, a policeman, upon pain of tainting the evidence obtained, could make the detailed type of examination demanded by *Johnson.* And, if for this reason a diluted form of "waiver" were found acceptable, that would itself be ample recognition of the fact that there is no universal standard that must be applied in every situation where a person forgoes a constitutional right.[33]

Similarly, a "waiver" approach to consent searches would be thoroughly inconsistent with our decisions that have approved "third party consents." In *Coolidge v. New Hampshire,* where a wife surrendered to the police guns and clothing belonging to her husband, we found nothing constitutionally impermissible in the admission of that evidence at trial since the wife had not been coerced. *Frazier v. Cupp,* [p. 422 infra], held that evidence seized from the defendant's duffel bag in a search authorized by his cousin's consent was admissible at trial. We found that the defendant had assumed the risk that his cousin with whom he shared the bag would allow the police to search it. And in *Hill v. California,* [p. 288 supra], we held that the police had validly seized evidence from the petitioner's apartment incident to the arrest of a third party, since the police had probable cause to arrest the petitioner and reasona-

33. It seems clear that even a limited view of the demands of "an intentional relinquishment or abandonment of a known right or privilege" standard would inevitably lead to a requirement of detailed warnings before any consent search—a requirement all but universally rejected to date. As the Court stated in *Miranda* with respect to the privilege against compulsory self-incrimination: "[W]e will not pause to inquire in individual cases whether the defendant was aware of his rights without a warning being given. Assessments of the knowledge the defendant possessed, based on information as to his age, education, intelligence, or prior contact with authorities, can never be more than speculation; a warning is a clearcut fact."

bly though mistakenly believed the man they had arrested was he. Yet it is inconceivable that the Constitution could countenance the waiver of a defendant's right to counsel by a third party, or that a waiver could be found because a trial judge reasonably though mistakenly believed a defendant had waived his right to plead not guilty. * * *

Much of what has already been said disposes of the argument that the Court's decision in the *Miranda* case requires the conclusion that knowledge of a right to refuse is an indispensable element of a valid consent. The considerations that informed the Court's holding in *Miranda* are simply inapplicable in the present case. In *Miranda* the Court found that the techniques of police questioning and the nature of custodial surroundings produce an inherently coercive situation. The Court concluded that "[u]nless adequate protective devices are employed to dispel the compulsion inherent in custodial surroundings, no statement obtained from the defendant can truly be the product of his free choice." And at another point the Court noted that "without proper safeguards the process of in-custody interrogation of persons suspected or accused of crime contains inherently compelling pressures which work to undermine the individual's will to resist and to compel him to speak where he would not otherwise do so freely."

In this case there is no evidence of any inherently coercive tactics—either from the nature of the police questioning or the environment in which it took place. Indeed, since consent searches will normally occur on a person's own familiar territory, the spectre of incommunicado police interrogation in some remote station house is simply inapposite. There is no reason to believe, under circumstances such as are present here, that the response to a policeman's question is presumptively coerced; and there is, therefore, no reason to reject the traditional test for determining the voluntariness of a person's response. *Miranda,* of course, did not reach investigative questioning of a person not in custody, which is most directly analogous to the situation of a consent search, and it assuredly did not indicate that such questioning ought to be deemed inherently coercive.

It is also argued that the failure to require the Government to establish knowledge as a prerequisite to a valid consent, will relegate the Fourth Amendment to the special province of "the sophisticated, the knowledgeable, and the privileged." We cannot agree. The traditional definition of voluntariness we accept today has always taken into account evidence of minimal schooling, low intelligence, and the lack of any effective warnings to a person of his rights; and the voluntariness of any statement taken under those conditions has been carefully scrutinized to determine whether it was in fact voluntarily given.

Our decision today is a narrow one. We hold only that when the subject of a search is not in custody and the State attempts to justify a search on the basis of his consent, the Fourth and Fourteenth Amendments require that it demonstrate that the consent was in fact voluntarily given, and not the result of duress or coercion, express or implied. Voluntariness is a question of fact to be determined from all the circumstances, and while the subject's knowledge of a right to refuse is a factor to be taken into account, the prosecution is not required to demonstrate such knowledge as a prerequisite to establishing a voluntary consent.[b]

b. Powell, J., joined by the Chief Justice and Rehnquist, J., concurred on the ground "that federal collateral review of a state prisoner's Fourth Amendment claims—claims which rarely bear on innocence—should be confined solely to the question of whether the petitioner was provided a fair opportunity to raise and have adjudicated the question in state courts." Blackmun, J., concurred to express substantial agreement with the Powell opinion. Douglas, J., dissenting, would have remanded for a determination of whether Alcala knew he had the right to refuse. Brennan, J., dissenting, declared: "It wholly escapes me how our citizens can meaningfully be

MR. JUSTICE MARSHALL, dissenting.

* * *

The Court assumes that the issue in this case is, what are the standards by which courts are to determine that consent is voluntarily given? It then imports into the law of search and seizure standards developed to decide entirely different questions about coerced confessions.

The Fifth Amendment, in terms, provides that no person "shall be compelled in any criminal case to be a witness against himself." Nor is the interest protected by the Due Process Clause of the Fourteenth Amendment any different. The inquiry in a case where a confession is challenged as having been elicited in an unconstitutional manner is, therefore, whether the behavior of the police amounted to compulsion of the defendant. * * *

In contrast, this case deals not with "coercion," but with "consent," a subtly different concept to which different standards have been applied in the past. Freedom from coercion is a substantive right, guaranteed by the Fifth and Fourteenth Amendments. Consent, however, is a mechanism by which substantive requirements, otherwise applicable, are avoided. In the context of the Fourth Amendment, the relevant substantive requirements are that searches be conducted only after evidence justifying them has been submitted to an impartial magistrate for a determination of probable cause. There are, of course, exceptions to these requirements based on a variety of exigent circumstances that make it impractical to invalidate a search simply because the police failed to get a warrant. But none of the exceptions relating to the overriding needs of law enforcement are applicable when a search is justified solely by consent. On the contrary, the needs of law enforcement are significantly more attenuated, for probable cause to search may be lacking but a search permitted if the subject's consent has been obtained. Thus, consent searches are permitted not because such an exception to the requirements of probable cause and warrant is essential to proper law enforcement, but because we permit our citizens to choose whether or not they wish to exercise their constitutional rights. Our prior decisions simply do not support the view that a meaningful choice has been made solely because no coercion was brought to bear on the subject. * * *

My approach to the case is straightforward and, to me, obviously required by the notion of consent as a relinquishment of Fourth Amendment rights. I am at a loss to understand why consent "cannot be taken literally to mean a 'knowing' choice." In fact, I have difficulty in comprehending how a decision made without knowledge of available alternatives can be treated as a choice at all.

If consent to search means that a person has chosen to forego his right to exclude the police from the place they seek to search, it follows that his consent cannot be considered a meaningful choice unless he knew that he could in fact exclude the police. * * * I would therefore hold, at a minimum, that the prosecution may not rely on a purported consent to search if the subject of the search did not know that he could refuse to give consent. Where the police claim authority to search yet in fact lack such authority, the subject does not know that he may permissibly refuse them entry, and it is this lack of knowledge that invalidates the consent. * * *

The burden on the prosecutor would disappear, of course, if the police, at the time they requested consent to search, also told the subject that he had a right to refuse consent and thus his decision to refuse would be respected. The Court's assertions to the contrary notwithstanding,

said to have waived something as precious as a constitutional guarantee without ever being aware of its existence."

there is nothing impractical about this method of satisfying the prosecution's burden of proof. * * *

The Court contends that if an officer paused to inform the subject of his rights, the informality of the exchange would be destroyed. I doubt that a simple statement by an officer of an individual's right to refuse consent would do much to alter the informality of the exchange, except to alert the subject to a fact that he surely is entitled to know. It is not without significance that for many years the agents of the Federal Bureau of Investigation have routinely informed subjects of their right to refuse consent, when they request consent to search. The reported cases in which the police have informed subject of their right to refuse consent show, also, that the information can be given without disrupting the casual flow of events. What evidence there is, then, rather strongly suggests that nothing disastrous would happen if the police, before requesting consent, informed the subject that he had a right to refuse consent and that his refusal would be respected.[12]

I must conclude, with some reluctance, that when the Court speaks of practicality, what it really is talking of is the continued ability of the police to capitalize on the ignorance of citizens so as to accomplish by subterfuge what they could not achieve by relying only on the knowing relinquishment of constitutional rights. Of course it would be "practical" for the police to ignore the commands of the Fourth Amendment, if by practicality we mean that more criminals will be apprehended, even though the constitutional rights of innocent people also go by the boards. But such a practical advantage is achieved only at the cost of permitting the police to disregard the limitations that the Constitution places on their behavior, a cost that a constitutional democracy cannot long absorb. * * *

12. The Court's suggestion that it would be "unrealistic" to require the officers to make "the detailed type of examination" involved when a court considers whether a defendant has waived a trial right, deserves little comment. The question before us relates to the inquiry to be made in court when the prosecution seeks to establish that consent was given. I therefore do not address the Court's strained argument that one may waive constitutional rights without making a knowing and intentional choice so long as the rights do not relate to the fairness of a criminal trial. I would suggest, however, that that argument is fundamentally inconsistent with the law of unconstitutional conditions.

NOTES ON THE RELEVANT FACTORS IN DETERMINING THE VALIDITY OF A CONSENT

1. Consider Weinreb, *Generalities of the Fourth Amendment,* 42 U.Chi.L.Rev. 47, 57–58 (1974). "When the police do rely on consent, either (1) they could not have obtained a warrant because a constitutional requirement like probable cause was not met; or (2) they could have obtained a warrant but did not; or (3) the constitutional requirements were met, but the police could not obtain a warrant for other reasons, such as the unavailability of a magistrate.

"In the first two situations, the courts should place a heavy burden of proving consent on the police: in the first case because the Constitution explicitly prefers the private person's interest to society's and in the second because the police could have avoided the dispute by obtaining a warrant. Also, being professionally involved and having initiated the incident, the police are better able than the private person to plan the encounter so that if consent is given, proof of it will be available. In the third situation, the police stand on firmer ground. They can plausibly argue that if a warrant that would ordinarily and properly have been issued was unobtainable, the situation was an emergency. If the police also do what they reasonably can to minimize their use of force and authority, and if consent to the search is not explicitly withheld, the search should be sustained on that basis."

2. *What is the issue?* Some courts, as did the court of appeals in *Bustamonte,* 448 F.2d 699 (9th Cir.1971), characterize a consent to search as "a waiver of a constitutional right" and thus focus upon the state of mind of the person allegedly giving the consent. Some other courts look instead to the state of mind of the officer seeking the consent; the question is said to be whether "the officers, as reasonable men, could conclude that defendant's consent was given," e.g., *People v. Henderson,* 210 N.E.2d 483 (Ill.1965).[a] The assumption is that waiver of a constitutional right is not involved, in that the Fourth Amendment does not confer a right not to be searched or not to be searched without a warrant, but rather only provides protection against unreasonable searches. Does *Bustamonte* clearly indicate a choice of either of these theories?

An illustration of how the choice of one of these theories over the other can affect the outcome is provided by *United States v. Elrod,* 441 F.2d 353 (5th Cir.1971), holding: "No matter how genuine the belief of the officers is that the consenter is apparently of sound mind and deliberately acting, the search depending upon his consent fails if it is judicially determined that he lacked mental capacity. It is not that the actions of the officers were imprudent or unfounded. It is that the key to validity—consent—is lacking for want of mental capacity, no matter how much concealed."

In considering the balance of the material in this section, assess the issues and principles discussed in terms of the two theories.

3. *Claim or show of authority.* In *Bumper v. North Carolina,* 391 U.S. 543, 88 S.Ct. 1788, 20 L.Ed.2d 797 (1968), defendant's grandmother allowed the police to search her house after one of them announced, "I have a search warrant to search your house." At the hearing on the motion to suppress the rifle found therein, the prosecutor did not rely upon a warrant to justify the search. The Supreme Court was advised that the officers did have a warrant, but none was ever returned and nothing was known about the conditions under which it was issued. The Court held, 7–2, per Stewart, J., that a search cannot be justified on the basis of consent "when that 'consent' has been given only after the official conducting the search has asserted that he possesses a warrant":

"When a prosecutor seeks to rely upon consent to justify the lawfulness of a search, he has the burden of proving that the consent was, in fact, freely and voluntarily given. This burden cannot be discharged by showing no more than acquiescence to a claim of lawful authority. A search conducted in reliance upon a warrant cannot later be justified on the basis of consent if it turns out that the warrant was invalid. The result can be no different when it turns out that the State does not even attempt to rely upon the validity of the warrant, or fails to show that there was, in fact, any warrant at all.

"When a law enforcement officer claims authority to search a home under a warrant, he announces in effect that the occupant has no right to resist the search. The situation is instinct with coercion—albeit colorably lawful coercion. Where there is coercion there cannot be consent."

What if the grandmother had responded to the police, "You don't need a search warrant, go ahead"? What if the officer

a. Query, does this approach make more sense in those cases in which, at the time the police received what they believed was consent, they had probable cause to obtain a search warrant? In *Leavitt v. Howard,* 462 F.2d 992 (1st Cir.1972), it is noted: "If the police have over-reached and obtained oral admissions, they have received something they otherwise would not have. As to a search, on the other hand, if the only result of the apparent consent is a premature search, suppressing the evidence because of police reliance on a faulty consent has the effect of suppressing for all time what, but for misplaced reliance on an apparent consent, the police would have been entitled to find later. [This] calls for what might seem a highly disproportionate penalty upon the state under such circumstances."

in *Bumper* had merely threatened to obtain a search warrant? Consider *United States v. Boukater,* 409 F.2d 537 (5th Cir.1969) (coercive unless the officer actually had grounds to obtain a warrant or he merely said he would seek a search warrant). The "claim of lawful authority" referred to in *Bumper* need not involve mention of a search warrant; a flat assertion by the police that they have come to search will suffice. *Amos v. United States,* 255 U.S. 313, 41 S.Ct. 266, 65 L.Ed. 654 (1921).

4. *Prior illegal police action.* Under the "fruit of the poisonous tree" doctrine of *Wong Sun,* p. 803, infra, a consent may be held ineffective because obtained in exploitation of a prior illegal arrest.

5. *Mental or emotional state of the person.* See *United States v. Elrod,* Note 2 supra; *Commonwealth v. Angivoni,* 417 N.E.2d 422 (Mass.1981) (voluntary consent of defendant in hospital emergency room with dislocated hip not established, as "defendant's understanding and ability to reason reflectively may have been impaired by intoxication or as a result of his injuries or an emotional trauma attendant to his just having been in an accident").

6. *Cooperation or lack thereof.* Courts sometimes find that a consent to search was valid because of the generally cooperative attitude of the defendant. What then of the defendant's lack of cooperation? Consider *Higgins v. United States,* 209 F.2d 819 (D.C.Cir.1954): "No sane man who denies his guilt would actually be willing that policemen search his room for contraband which is certain to be discovered." [b]

7. *Custody; Warning of Fourth Amendment rights.* In *United States v. Watson,* p. 298 supra, the majority concluded that the failure to give the defendant Fourth Amendment warnings "is not to be given controlling significance" where, as there, the defendant "had been arrested and was in custody, but his consent was given while on a public street, not in the confines of the police station." Marshall and Brennan, JJ., dissenting, objected that the case should be remanded for reconsideration of the consent issue by the court of appeals in light of the fact that the "lack of custody was of decisional importance in *Schneckloth,* which repeatedly distinguished the case before it from one involving a suspect in custody."

In *Gentile v. United States,* 419 U.S. 979, 95 S.Ct. 241, 42 L.Ed.2d 191 (1974), where consent was obtained from the defendant during stationhouse custodial interrogation after the giving of the *Miranda* warnings but without Fourth Amendment warnings, Douglas and Marshall, JJ., dissenting from the denial of certiorari, noted: "When a suspect is in custody the situation is in control of the police. The pace of events will not somehow deny them an opportunity to give a warning, as the [*Schneckloth*] Court apparently feared would happen in noncustodial settings. Moreover, the custodial setting will permit easy documentation of both the giving of a warning and the arrestee's response."

8. *Warning of Fifth Amendment rights.* It has sometimes been held that "a consent to search, given during custodial interrogation must, as a matter of law, be preceded by a proper *Miranda* warning," *Schorr v. State,* 499 P.2d 450 (Okla.Crim.1972), because "the request to search is a request that defendant be a witness against himself which he is privileged to refuse under the Fifth Amendment." *State v. Williams,* 432 P.2d 679 (Or.1967). The prevailing view, however, is to the contrary. As

b. The *Higgins* rationale was expressly rejected in *Leavitt v. Howard,* 462 F.2d 992 (1st Cir. 1972): "To hold, as did the district court, that expressions of consent relieve officers of the need of obtaining a warrant only when the speaker is not aware that the search will disclose damaging evidence, would place the police in an especially poignant dilemma. The officers may not be in a position to know beforehand whether a search will produce incriminating evidence, or whether the suspect is aware that it will. As the Second Circuit has observed, such a ruling would therefore 'enable experienced criminals to lay traps for officers who, relying on the words of consent, failed to secure a search warrant that would have been theirs for the asking.' "

stated in *People v. Thomas,* 91 Cal.Rptr. 867 (App.1970), obtaining defendant's consent does not violate "a value which *Miranda* was designed to protect."

9. *Right to counsel.* In *Tidwell v. Superior Court,* 95 Cal.Rptr. 213 (App.1971), the police asked petitioner, who was in jail, if they could search his car, which had been impounded. Petitioner allegedly replied, "Go ahead and search." The court held that petitioner's consent was ineffective since at the time he had been arraigned on a burglary charge and counsel had been appointed, yet the police had asked him to consent to the search without notifying his lawyer. Rejecting the argument that *Massiah* [p. 527 infra] should apply only to "statements elicited and not to consents given," the court observed: "This distinction is very thin considering the incriminating effect a consent to search may have. The reasoning of [the cases protecting] defendants' right to effective aid of counsel applies equally to a consent given at the instigation of the police."

10. *"Consent" by deception.* In contrast to the type of deception allegedly used in *Bumper,* Note 3 supra, the police sometimes obtain evidence of criminal activity by acting in an undercover capacity and obtaining a "consent" which the defendant would not have given had he known the officer's true identity; see *Lewis v. United States,* p. 457 infra, upholding this practice upon the facts presented. A third situation is that in which the officer's true identity is known but he misleads the suspect as to his intentions. Compare *Graves v. Beto,* 424 F.2d 524 (5th Cir.1970) (rape defendant's consent to blood test which resulted in matching his blood with that at crime scene not freely and intelligently given where his acquiescence was obtained by intimating that test was to be taken simply to determine whether he had a sufficient quantity of alcohol in his blood stream to be detained on a charge of public drunkenness); with *United States v. Andrews,* 746 F.2d 247 (5th Cir.1984) (federal agents asked to see shotgun on ruse they were trying to connect it with robberies, actual purpose was to establish defendant's crime of illegal possession of firearm by convicted felon; consent voluntary, *Graves* distinguished because "there is no evidence indicating that Andrews was assured his production of the guns would only be used to investigate the robberies").

11. *Scope of the consent.* Assuming a valid consent, the police may not exceed the physical bounds of the area to which consent was granted. See, e.g., *United States v. Dichiarinte,* 445 F.2d 126 (7th Cir. 1971) (where defendant told police they could search his house for narcotics, police could not open and examine private papers found in the house). If the search is so limited and there is no subterfuge involved, evidentiary items other than those the police said they were looking for may be seized.

Does a consent, voluntary when given, justify a second search of the same place at a later time after a fruitless first search? Compare *People v. Nawrocki,* 148 N.W.2d 211 (Mich.App.1967) (defendant's consent to search his car construed as "permission to search the car at any time," thus justifying second search hours later after the car was impounded and the defendant was in jail); with *State v. Brochu,* 237 A.2d 418 (Me.1967) (contra where passage of time was greater, second search involved re-entry of defendant's home, and defendant's status had changed from suspect to accused in interim).

B. Third Party Consent

UNITED STATES v. MATLOCK, 415 U.S. 164, 94 S.Ct. 988, 39 L.Ed.2d 242 (1974), involved these facts: Matlock was arrested for bank robbery in the front yard of a house in which he lived with a Mrs. Graff and others. The arresting officers were then admitted to the house by Mrs. Graff and, with her consent, searched the house, including a bedroom she said was jointly occupied by Matlock and herself, where the officers seized money taken in the robbery. The district court suppressed the evidence, holding (1) that in a third party consent situation the government must show that it reasonably appeared to the police that the person had authority to consent *and* that the person had actual authority to consent, and (2) that Mrs. Graff's statements to the officers that she and Matlock occupied the bedroom and her statements to others at various times that she and Matlock were married were hearsay and thus inadmissible to prove her actual authority to consent. The court of appeals affirmed, but the Supreme Court, per WHITE, J., reversed. The Court first noted "that when the prosecution seeks to justify a warrantless search by proof of voluntary consent, it is not limited to proof that consent was given by the defendant, but may show that permission to search was obtained from a third party who possessed common authority over or other sufficient relationship to the premises or effect sought to be inspected.[7]" The majority in *Matlock* then concluded that "the rules of evidence normally applicable in criminal trials do not operate with full force at hearings before the judge to determine the admissibility of evidence" and that the judge "should not have excluded Mrs. Graff's statements in the circumstances present here," namely, where "the court was quite satisfied that the statements had in fact been made" and "there is nothing in the record to raise serious doubts about the truthfulness of the statements themselves." The Court emphasized that "Mrs. Graff's statements were against her penal interest and they carried their own indicia of reliability," and that "she was available for cross-examination, and the risk of prejudice, if there was any, from the use of hearsay was reduced." The Court thus found it unnecessary to "reach another major contention here: that the Government in any event had only to satisfy the District Court that the searching officers reasonably believed that Mrs. Graff had sufficient authority over the premises to consent to the search."

DOUGLAS, J., dissenting, objected: "This was not a case where a grave emergency, such as the imminent loss of evidence or danger to human life, might excuse the failure to secure a warrant. Mrs. Graff's permission to the police to invade the house, simultaneously violating the privacy of Matlock and the [other occupants], provides a sorry and wholly inadequate substitute for the protections which inhere in a judicially granted warrant. It is inconceivable that a search conducted without a warrant can give more authority than a search conducted with a warrant. But here the police procured without a warrant all the authority which they had under the feared general warrants, hatred of which led to the passage of the Fourth Amendment." Brennan, J., joined by Marshall, J., dissented for the reasons set forth in their dissents in *Schneckloth v. Bustamonte.*

NOTES ON WHO MAY CONSENT

1. *Husband-wife.* It is generally agreed that a spouse who has an equal right to the use and occupation of the family premises may give consent to a search there which will be effective against the other spouse.

2. *Parent-child.* If a child is living at the home of his parents, the courts are in agreement that the head of the household may give consent to a search of the child's living quarters. A contrary result is sometimes reached if the "child" living with his parents has reached adulthood. A child

7. Common authority is, of course, not to be implied from the mere property interest a third party has in the property. The authority which justifies the third-party consent does not rest upon the law of property, with its attendant historical and legal refinements, see *Chapman v. United States,* [p. 420 infra], *Stoner v. California,* [p. 420 infra], but rests rather on mutual use of the property by persons generally having joint access or control for most purposes, so that it is reasonable to recognize that any of the co-inhabitants has the right to permit the inspection in his own right and that the others have assumed the risk that one of their number might permit the common area to be searched.

may not give consent to a full search of the parent's house. However, where it is not unusual or unauthorized for the child to admit visitors into the home, the mere entry of police on the premises with the consent of the child is not improper.

3. *Landlord-tenant; co-tenants.* A landlord may not consent to a search of his tenant's premises (as compared to areas of common usage), and this is so even though the landlord may have some right of entry for purposes of inspecting or cleaning the premises. *Chapman v. United States,* 365 U.S. 610, 81 S.Ct. 776, 5 L.Ed.2d 828 (1961). Hotel employees may not consent to the search of a particular room during the period in which it has been rented by a guest. *Stoner v. California,* 376 U.S. 483, 84 S.Ct. 889, 11 L.Ed.2d 856 (1964). But "where two or more persons occupy a dwelling place jointly, the general rule is that a joint tenant can consent to police entry and search of the entire house or apartment, even though they occupy separate bedrooms." *State v. Thibodeau,* 317 A.2d 172 (Me.1974).

4. *Employer-employee.* As to consent by defendant's employer, compare *Gillard v. Schmidt,* 579 F.2d 825 (3d Cir.1978) (consent invalid as to search of defendant's desk; protection of the Fourth Amendment "does not turn on the nature of the property interest in the searched premises, but on the reasonableness of the person's privacy expectation," and defendant had a high expectation concerning his desk because he worked "in an office secured by a locked door and a desk containing psychological profiles and other confidential student records"); with *Commonwealth v. Glover,* 405 A.2d 945 (Pa.Super.1979) (factory owner could consent to search of items on top of work bench, as it not an area assigned to defendant or used exclusively by him).

Whether an employee can give a valid consent to a search of his employer's premises depends upon the scope of his authority. Generally, the courts have been of the view that the average employee, such as a clerk, janitor, driver, or other person temporarily in charge, may not give consent. However, if the employee is a manager or other person of considerable authority who is left in complete charge for a substantial period of time, then the prevailing view is that such a person can waive his employer's rights.

5. *Bailor-bailee.* If a person leaves his car at a garage for repairs, does he assume the risk that the repairman might permit police to look inside the car to determine whether it is stolen, as held in *State v. Baker,* 310 S.E.2d 101 (N.C.App.1983)? If so, is a different result called for if the repairman turns the vehicle over to the police so that they can inspect it more closely at another location, as in *State v. Farrell,* 443 A.2d 438 (R.I.1982)?

6. *Apparent authority.* In *People v. Gorg,* 291 P.2d 469 (Cal.1955), defendant (a law student!) was arrested for shoplifting. Police went to the house of one Stevens, where the defendant occupied a room in exchange for doing the gardening, and "Stevens gave them permission to enter and requested that they search the entire house." The court, per Traynor, J., upheld the search: "Defendant was living in the Stevens home, and it is clear that whether he was in fact a tenant, servant, or guest, Stevens believed that he had at least joint control over his quarters and the right to enter them, * * * and authorize a search thereof. Under these circumstances the officers were justified in concluding that Stevens had the authority over his home that he purported to have, and there was nothing unreasonable in their acting accordingly. In this proceeding we are not concerned with enforcing defendant's rights under the law of trespass and landlord and tenant, but was discouraging unreasonable activity on the part of law enforcement officers."

Compare *People v. Miller,* 238 N.E.2d 407 (Ill.1968) (where owner of home consented to search of car in garage, and police previously determined that license plates on that car were registered in name of home owner, but it turned out that car was in fact owned by defendant, abortion tools found in car must be suppressed under *Stoner* "regardless of the officer's good faith in making the search"); and *People v. Rodriguez,* 223 N.E.2d 414 (Ill. App.1967) (where woman in defendant's hotel room, earlier identified by defendant as his wife but who told police "she was living with the defendant but was not married to him," consented to search of room, consent would not be effective against defendant under rule that joint occupant of premises can give effective consent, where it was later ascertained that the woman was not in fact a full-time resident there).

In *Stoner v. California*, Note 3 supra, where police searched a hotel room they knew was rented by defendant, it was argued that the police "had a reasonable basis for the belief that the clerk had authority to consent to the search" of a guest's room. The Court responded that "the rights protected by the Fourth Amendment are not to be eroded * * * by unrealistic doctrines of 'apparent authority.'" Does *Stoner* indicate that *Gorg* was wrongly decided and that *Miller* and *Rodriguez* could not have been decided otherwise?

NOTES ON LIMITS ON THIRD-PARTY CONSENT

Even if the consent was given by a third party who, at least in some circumstances, could give effective consent, it may still be questioned whether other circumstances of the particular case made that person's consent ineffective vis-a-vis the defendant. Consider:

1. *Antagonism.* What if, for example, a wife calls the police into the house and points out incriminating evidence because she is angry at her husband? Compare *State v. Gonzalez-Valle,* 385 So.2d 681 (Fla. App.1980) (where "the motive of the defendant's wife in consenting to the search was clearly one of spite," she "had no right to waive her husband's protection against unreasonable searches and seizures"); with *Commonwealth v. Martin,* 264 N.E.2d 366 (Mass.1970) ("while they are both living in the premises the equal authority does not lapse and revive with the lapse and revival of amicable relations between the spouses").

2. *Defendant's instructions.* If the defendant had previously instructed the third party not to allow a search, should those instructions be controlling? In *People v. Fry,* 76 Cal.Rptr. 718 (App.1969), the court held: "When the officers solicited consent of the wife to enter for the purpose of seizing property they knew her husband had instructed her not to consent and, under these circumstances, were not entitled to rely upon her consent as justification for their conduct" in searching the family home. *Fry* was distinguished in *People v. Reynolds,* 127 Cal.Rptr. 561 (App. 1976), because in the later case the police were unaware of the husband's instructions to his wife. Is *Matlock* relevant on this issue?

3. *Defendant's prior or contemporaneous refusal to consent.* In *People v. Mortimer,* 361 N.Y.S.2d 955 (1974), defendant was arrested for drug possession, and after he declined to consent to a search of his room the police went to the home of his parents and obtained their consent to search defendant's bedroom there. The court held that consent could not be "binding upon an absent defendant who has been requested by the police to consent to a search of his property and who has refused that permission." Contra: *United States v. Baldwin,* 644 F.2d 381 (5th Cir.1981). Which view can be more readily squared with *Matlock?* What if the defendant had been present at the premises and had objected to the search at the time it was made on the consent of another occupant, as in *People v. Haskett,* 640 P.2d 776 (Cal. 1982)?

4. *Police failure to seek defendant's consent.* Note that in *Matlock* the police, though they arrested defendant in the front yard, never sought his consent to search his room. Should that invalidate the consent obtained from Mrs. Graff? Consider Swygert, J., dissenting in *United States v. Stone,* 471 F.2d 170 (7th Cir.1972):

"Basic to the third party consent rationale is the premise that the absent party might, were he present, consent to the search, in which event no constitutional rights would be violated. Therefore the whereabouts of the absent party is highly important, as is the cause of his absence. When the person who could waive his right to privacy is absent from his dwelling by reason of flight or hiding from law enforcement officers for fear of arrest, a strong case for third party consent to search is presented. The suspect has consciously made himself unavailable to the police, and it is entirely his fault that they cannot obtain his answer to their request to search. If, on the other hand, his absence is not in response to a fear of arrest, but simply the result of an errand or other everyday activity, the case becomes less clear.

"In the present case, the defendant was not 'absent' in any sense in which that term should be used in the context of a third party consent search. He was in official custody at the scene of the search only minutes prior to the consent of his wife and, after that, was in custody in transit to and at the police station. Without the slightest difficulty, the arresting officers could have requested his consent to search. They did not, perhaps in fear of a negative reply, and it is now contended that his wife's consent was valid on the basis of a rule which rests, as I see it, on the actual impossibility of presenting the suspect with a request to search. I reject this contention."

5. *Exclusive control by defendant of effects or areas within shared premises or objects.* In *State v. Evans,* 372 P.2d 365 (Hawaii 1962), the court held the wife could not consent to a search of personal items found in a cuff link case located in her husband's dresser drawer. Is this holding consistent with *Matlock?* Consider also the relevance of *Frazier v. Cupp,* 394 U.S. 731, 89 S.Ct. 1420, 22 L.Ed.2d 684 (1969), where the Court concluded that one of petitioner's contentions, namely, that the police illegally searched and seized clothing from his duffel bag, could "be dismissed rather quickly":

"This duffel bag was being used jointly by petitioner and his cousin Rawls and it had been left in Rawls' home. The police, while arresting Rawls, asked him if they could have his clothing. They were directed to the duffel bag and both Rawls and his mother consented to its search. During this search, the officers came upon petitioner's clothing and it was seized as well. Since Rawls was a joint user of the bag, he clearly had authority to consent to its search. The officers therefore found evidence against petitioner while in the course of an otherwise lawful search. * * * Petitioner argues that Rawls only had actual permission to use one compartment of the bag and that he had no authority to consent to a search of the other compartments. We will not, however, engage in such metaphysical subleties in judging the efficacy of Rawls' consent. Petitioner, in allowing Rawls to use the bag and in leaving it in his house, must be taken to have assumed the risk that Rawls would allow someone else to look inside."

Chapter 6

WIRETAPPING, ELECTRONIC EAVESDROPPING, THE USE OF SECRET AGENTS TO OBTAIN INCRIMINATING STATEMENTS, AND THE FOURTH AMENDMENT [a]

SECTION 1. HISTORICAL BACKGROUND

A. CONSTITUTIONAL PERMISSION

OLMSTEAD v. UNITED STATES, 277 U.S. 438, 48 S.Ct. 564, 72 L.Ed. 944 (1928), held (5–4), per Chief Justice TAFT, that wiretapping did not amount to a search and seizure for reasons that have since been rejected by the Court. The Fourth Amendment itself, observed Taft, "shows that the search is to be of material things—the person, the house, his papers or his effects. The description of the warrant necessary to make the proceeding lawful, is that it must specify the place to be searched and the person or *things* to be seized." Moreover, not only did the police fail to violate the amendment by tapping, as such, but neither did they do so at any point along the way, in the course of gaining access to the wiretap evidence: "The evidence was secured by the use of the sense of hearing and that only. There was no entry of the houses or offices of the defendants."

Although the evidence which led to the conviction for conspiracy to violate the National Prohibition Act was obtained by federal prohibition agents in violation of a statute of the state of Washington, which made it a misdemeanor to "intercept" telegraphic or telephonic messages, the Chief Justice pointed out that "this statute does not declare that evidence obtained by such interception shall be inadmissible, and by the common law [it] would not be." Moreover, "clearly a [state statute] cannot affect the rules of evidence applicable in courts of the United States." [b]

In an exhaustive dissenting opinion, Justice BRANDEIS observed:

a. This chapter does not attempt to cover in detail Title III of the Crime Control Act of 1968 and the extensive litigation it has generated. For a comprehensive analysis of Title III and the cases decided thereunder see Carr, *The Law of Electronic Surveillance* (1977); Fishman, *Wiretapping and Eavesdropping* (1978); Goldsmith, *The Supreme Court and Title III: Rewriting the Law of Electronic Surveillance*, 74 J.Crim. L. & C. 1 (1983).

b. "Taft did not challenge the fourth amendment exclusionary rule; he *confined* it. Rejecting the argument that 'unethically,' as well as unconstitutionally, secured evidence should be barred, he concluded that 'the exclusion of evidence should be confined to cases where *rights under the Constitution* would be violated by *admitting* it' [emphasis added.] Kamisar, *Does (Did) (Should) the Exclusionary Rule Rest on a "Principled Basis" Rather than an "Empirical*

"The progress of science in furnishing the government with means of espionage is not likely to stop with wire tapping. Ways may some day be developed by which the government, without removing papers from secret drawers, can reproduce them in court, and by which it will be enabled to expose to a jury the most intimate occurrences of the home. Advances in the psychic and related sciences may bring means of exploring unexpressed beliefs, thoughts and emotions. * * * Can it be that the Constitution affords no protection against such invasions of individual security? * * *

"In *Ex parte Jackson,* 96 U.S. 727, 24 L.Ed. 877 [1877], it was held that a sealed letter intrusted to the mail is protected by the amendments. The mail is a public service furnished by the government. The telephone is a public service furnished by its authority. There is, in essence, no difference between the sealed letter and the private telephone message. * * *

"The evil incident to invasion of the privacy of the telephone is far greater than that involved in tampering with the mails. Whenever a telephone line is tapped, the privacy of the persons at both ends of the line is invaded, and all conversations between them upon any subject, and although proper, confidential, and privileged, may be overheard. Moreover, the tapping of one man's telephone line involves the tapping of the telephone of every other person whom he may call, or who may call him. As a means of espionage, writs of assistance and general warrants are but puny instruments of tyranny and oppression when compared with wire tapping.

"Time and again this court, in giving effect to the principle underlying the Fourth Amendment, has refused to place an unduly literal construction upon it. * * * No court which looked at the words of the amendment rather than at its underlying purpose would hold, as this court did in *Ex parte Jackson,* that its protection extended to letters in the mails. * * *

"The makers of our Constitution * * * conferred, as against the government, the right to be let alone—the most comprehensive of rights and the right most valued by civilized men. To protect that right, every unjustifiable intrusion by the government upon the privacy of the individual, whatever the means employed, must be deemed a violation of the Fourth Amendment. And the use, as evidence in a criminal proceeding, of facts ascertained by such intrusion must be deemed a violation of the Fifth. * * *

"Independently of the constitutional question, I am of opinion that the judgment should be reversed. By the laws of Washington, wire tapping is a crime. To prove its case, the government was obliged to lay bare the crimes committed by its officers on its behalf. A federal court should not permit such a prosecution to continue. * * *

"Decency, security, and liberty alike demand that government officials shall be subjected to the same rules of conduct that are commands to the citizen. In a government of laws, existence of the government will be imperiled if it fails to observe the law scrupulously. Our government is the potent, the omnipresent teacher. For good or for ill, it teaches the whole people by its example. Crime is contagious. If the government becomes a lawbreaker, it breeds contempt for law; it invites every man to become a law unto himself; it invites anarchy. To declare that in the administration of the criminal law the end justifies the means—to declare that the government may commit crimes in order to secure the conviction of a private criminal—would bring terrible retribution. Against that pernicious doctrine this court should resolutely set its face."

Proposition"?, 16 Creighton L.Rev. 565, 603 (1983).

In a brief separate dissent, Justice HOLMES commented:

"While I do not deny it I am not prepared to say that the penumbra of the Fourth and Fifth Amendments covers the defendants, although I fully agree that courts are apt to err by sticking too closely to the words of a law where these words import a policy that goes beyond them. [But] I think, as Mr. Justice Brandeis says, that apart from the Constitution the government ought not to use evidence obtained and only obtainable by a criminal act. * * * It is desirable that criminals should be detected, and to that end that all available evidence should be used. It also is desirable that the government should not itself foster and pay for other crimes, when they are the means by which the evidence is to be obtained. * * * We have to choose, and for my part I think it is a less evil that some criminals should escape than that the government should play an ignoble part.

"For those who agree with me no distinction can be taken between the government as prosecutor and the government as judge. If the existing code does not permit district attorneys to have a hand in such dirty business it does not permit the judge to allow such iniquities to succeed. [And] if all that I have said so far be accepted it makes no difference that in this case wire tapping is made a crime by the law of the state, not by the law of the United States. * * * I am aware of the often-repeated statement that in a criminal proceeding the court will not take notice of the manner in which papers offered in evidence have been obtained. But that somewhat rudimentary mode of disposing of the question has been overthrown by *Weeks.* [T]he reason for excluding evidence obtained by violating the Constitution seems to me logically to lead to excluding evidence obtained by a crime of the officers of the law." [c]

B. STATUTORY PROHIBITION: § 605 OF THE 1934 FEDERAL COMMUNICATIONS ACT [a]

Chief Justice Taft noted in his *Olmstead* opinion that "Congress may of course protect the secrecy of telephone messages by making them when intercepted, inadmissible in evidence in federal criminal trials, by direct legislation, and thus depart from the common law of evidence." Such a development occurred with the passage of the Federal Communications Act of 1934. Section 605 of the Act read in part: "[N]o person not being authorized by the sender shall intercept any communication and divulge or publish the existence, contents, substance, purport, effect, or meaning of such intercepted communication to any person * * *." This wording was held to cover wiretapping by state or federal officers as well as by private persons, *Nardone v. United States,* 302 U.S. 379, 82 L.Ed. 314, 58 S.Ct. 275 (1937), 308 U.S. 338, 84 L.Ed. 307, 60 S.Ct. 266 (1939); *Benanti v. United States,* 355 U.S. 96, 2 L.Ed.2d 126, 78 S.Ct. 155 (1957); and to apply to intrastate as well as interstate communications, *Weiss v. United States,* 308 U.S. 321, 84 L.Ed. 298, 60 S.Ct. 269 (1939).

The Department of Justice and the FBI took the position that Section 605 did not

c. Consider Kamisar, fn. b supra, at 603–04: "Although often invoked by proponents of the fourth amendment exclusionary rule, the most famous passages in the Holmes-Brandeis dissents [were] actually arguments for extending the [exclusionary rule] to situations where the federal government had not violated the Constitution, or even federal law, but only a state anti-wiretapping statute. * * * Nevertheless, these famous dissents shed light on the original bases and purposes of the exclusionary rule. [They] underscore that the exclusionary rule is [or at least was thought to be] based on principle—one might also say that it has an important symbolic quality—not on estimates of how substantially the exclusion of evidence affects police behavior."

a. Section 605 of the 1934 Act was "amended" by Title III of the Crime Control Act of 1968, permitting court-approved wiretapping and electronic eavesdropping by federal and state law enforcement officials in the investigation of many listed offenses.

prohibit wiretapping *alone,* only tapping *followed by* "divulgence," and, further, that it was not a "divulgence" when one member of the government communicated to another, but only when he communicated outside the government, e.g., sought to introduce the wiretap information into evidence. See e.g., Rogers, *The Case for Wire Tapping,* 63 Yale L.J. 792, 793 (1954). For sharp criticism of this view see, e.g., E.B. Williams, *The Wiretapping-Eavesdropping Problem; A Defense Counsel's View,* 44 Minn.L.Rev. 855, 860 (1960).

C. Wiretapping, § 605 and Federal-State Relations

Since it involved the use of state-gathered wiretap evidence in a state prosecution, *Schwartz v. Texas,* 344 U.S. 199, 73 S.Ct. 232, 97 L.Ed. 231 (1952), posed the wiretapping counterpart of *Wolf v. Colorado.* Although the Court recognized that "the problem under § 605 is somewhat different [than *Wolf*] because the introduction of the intercepted communication would itself be a violation of the statute," i.e., a prohibited "divulgence," it nevertheless relied on *Wolf* to hold the evidence admissible. Only Douglas, J., dissented.

More weight was given to the Federal Communication Act's "built-in" exclusionary rule in *Benanti v. United States,* supra, which barred state-gathered wiretap evidence proffered in a *federal* prosecution, even though at the time the great weight of authority (later overruled in *Elkins,* p. 212 supra) allowed federal prosecutors to use evidence obtained by illegal state searches so long as there was no "collusion" between the two "sovereignties."

Two days before the electronic surveillance provisions of the Crime Control Act of 1968 were signed into law, *Schwartz* was overruled by *Lee v. Florida,* 392 U.S. 378, 88 S.Ct. 2096, 20 L.Ed.2d 1168 (1968): "*Schwartz* cannot survive the demise of *Wolf.* [*Mapp*] imposed a judicially devised exclusionary rule. [In] the present case the federal law itself explicitly protects intercepted communications from divulgence, in a court or any other place."

D. Non-Telephonic Electronic Eavesdropping

1. *Brandeis' fears become a reality.* Several studies, e.g., Dash, Knowlton & R. Schwartz, *The Eavesdroppers* 339–79 (1959); Westin, *Privacy and Freedom* 69–89 (1967); indicate that modern developments in electronic eavesdropping have made the prophetic fears voiced by Justice Brandeis in his *Olmstead* dissent a reality. According to these studies: Tiny microphones can be secreted behind a picture or built into a coat button. Highly directive microphones known as "parabolic microphones" are capable of eavesdropping on a conversation taking place in an office on the *opposite side of a busy street* or on a park bench or outdoor restaurant terrace hundreds of feet away. Laser beams can pick sound waves off closed windows. A small, continuously operating transmitter can be placed beneath the fender of an automobile and its signal picked up by a receiver in another car or in a fixed plant. A special gun developed for American military authorities can shoot a small dart containing a wireless radio microphone into a tree, window pane, awning or any other object near the subject of investigation.

However, while electronic eavesdropping looms as "the ultimate invasion of privacy," E.B. Williams, supra, at 866, for decades the law furnished much less protection against this danger than it did against wiretapping. The Federal Communications Act applied only when telephone, telegraph, or radiotelegraph conversations were overheard and until the 1960's the constitutional protection against unreasonable search and seizure applied only when electronic snooping was accomplished by a physical invasion or "trespass". No such "trespass" occurred in *Olmstead* (the taps from house lines were made in the streets near the house) or in *Goldman v. United States,* 316 U.S. 129, 62

S.Ct. 993, 86 L.Ed. 1322 (1942) (where federal officers placed a detectaphone *against the wall* of a private office) or in *On Lee v. United States* (1952) (Sec. 3, infra) (where incriminating statements were picked up via a "wired for sound" former acquaintance of petitioner).

That the Constitution does furnish *some* protection against the electronic seizure of conversations as well as the seizure of "papers and effects" was made plain by *Silverman v. United States,* 365 U.S. 505, 81 S.Ct. 679, 5 L.Ed.2d 734 (1961). There, a unanimous Court, per Stewart, J., held that listening to incriminating conversations within a house by inserting an electronic device (a so-called "spike mike") into a party wall and making contact with a heating duct serving the house occupied by petitioners, "thus converting their entire heating system into a conductor of sound," amounted to an illegal search and seizure.

Justice Douglas concurred, maintaining: "The depth of the penetration of the electronic device—even the degree of its remoteness from the inside of the house—is not measure of the injury. * * * Our concern should not be with the trivialities of the local law of trespass, as the opinion of the Court indicates. But neither should the command of the Fourth Amendment be limited by nice distinctions turning on the kind of electronic equipment employed. Rather our sole concern should be with whether the privacy of the home was invaded."

Silverman not only established that conversations could be "seized" within the meaning of the Fourth Amendment, but suggested that a Fourth Amendment "search" for them might occur without any trespass. This seemed even more certain when three years later, in *Clinton v. Virginia,* 377 U.S. 158, 84 S.Ct. 1186, 12 L.Ed.2d 213 (1964) (per curiam), the Court summarily rejected the state court's holding that *Silverman* did not apply where the spike mike "was not driven into the wall but was 'stuck in' it." Any lingering doubts were dispelled by *Katz v. United States* (p. 237 supra).

SECTION 2. *BERGER AND KATZ*; THE WISDOM AND CONSTITUTIONALITY OF TITLE III OF THE CRIME CONTROL ACT

A. THE IMPLICATIONS OF *Berger* and *Katz*

BERGER v. NEW YORK, 388 U.S. 41, 87 S.Ct. 1873, 18 L.Ed.2d 1040 (1967),[a] left the dissenting Justices (and many others) wondering whether *any* wiretapping or electronic eavesdropping statute could pass constitutional muster. The Court, per CLARK, J., struck down a New York electronic surveillance statute,[b] calling it a "blanket grant of permission to

a. The case grew out of a state investigation of alleged bribery of state liquor authority officials. Pursuant to the challenged New York statute, a court order was obtained permitting the installation of a recording device in a lawyer's office for up to 60 days. On the basis of information gathered from this eavesdrop, a second order was obtained, authorizing the installation of a recording device in another person's office. As a result of evidence obtained from the second eavesdrop, petitioner was indicted for, and convicted of, conspiracy to bribe the chairman of the state liquor authority.

b. The statute, N.Y.Code Crim.P. § 813–a, provided in part: "An ex parte order for eavesdropping * * * may be issued by any justice of the supreme court [a trial court in New York] or judge of a county court * * * upon oath or affirmation of a district attorney [or police officer above the rank of sergeant] that there is reasonable ground to believe that evidence of crime may be thus obtained, and particularly describing the person or persons whose communications, conversations or discussions are to be overheard or recorded and the purpose thereof * * *. Any such order shall be effective for the time specified therein but not for a period of more than two months unless extended or renewed by [the judge who issued the original order] upon satisfying himself that such extension or renewal is in the public interest. Any such order, together with the papers upon which the application was based, shall be delivered to and retained by the applicant as authority for the eavesdropping authorized therein. A true copy of such order [or denial of any application for such an order] shall at all times be retained [by the judge issuing the order or denying the application]."

eavesdrop * * * without adequate supervision or protective procedures."

The statute, observed Justice Clark, (1) permitted a court order to issue merely on reasonable grounds to believe that evidence of crime may be obtained, without specifying what crime has been or is being committed and without describing what conversations are to be overheard—thus failing to "particularly [describe] the place to be searched, and the person or things to be seized," as required by the Fourth Amendment [c]—(2) permitted installation and operation of surveillance equipment for 60 days—"the equivalent of a series of intrusions, searches and seizures pursuant to a single showing of probable cause"—(3) permitted renewal of the order on the basis of the original grounds on which the initial order was issued—"this we believe insufficient without a showing of present probable cause for continuance of the eavesdrop"—(4) placed no termination on the eavesdrop once the conversation sought is seized—"this is left entirely to the discretion of the officer"—and (5) did not provide for a return on the warrant—"thereby leaving full discretion in the officer as to the use of seized conversations of innocent as well as guilty parties."

The Court contrasted the New York statute's "broadside authorization" of electronic surveillance with the "precise and discriminate" procedures followed in *Osborn v. United States.* 385 U.S. 323, 87 S.Ct. 429, 17 L.Ed.2d 394 (1966), where two federal judges authorized a tape recorder to be concealed on the person of an attorney's "employee" (actually a secret government agent) for a specific meeting with the attorney. There was a detailed factual affidavit alleging the commission of a specific offense, bribing a juror, to justify the order. Furthermore, "the order authorized one limited intrusion rather than a series or a continuous surveillance." Moreover, a new order was issued for the tape recording of a second meeting and probable cause was shown for the second order. And the government agent "was required to and did make a return on the order showing how it was executed and what was seized." [d] Because *Osborn* involved such a rare fact situation, one atypical of police investigations, the Court's reference to this case raised further doubts about the constitutionality of most electronic surveillance.[e]

DOUGLAS, J., concurred in the result, maintaining that electronic surveillance is "a search for 'mere evidence,' " which is a violation of the Fourth and Fifth Amendments regardless of "the nicety and precision with which a warrant may be drawn." [f] "If a statute were to authorize placing a policeman in every home or

c. The statute did require the naming of "the person or persons whose communications, conversations or discussions are to be overheard or recorded," but, said the Court, "this does no more than identify the person whose constitutionally protected area is to be invaded rather than 'particularly describing' the communications, conversations, or discussions to be seized. As with general warrants, this leaves too much to the discretion of the officer executing the order."

d. Is there a "certain irony" in the *Berger* Court's approval of *Osborn?* If the *Osborn* order was properly issued without any statutory authorization, why didn't the *Berger* Court consider the particularity of the order issued in this case without regard to the constitutionality of the New York statute? See Greenawalt, *The Consent Problem in Wiretapping and Eavesdropping,* 68 Colum.L.Rev. 189, 201–02 (1968).

e. Consider Dash, *Katz—Variations on a Theme by Berger,* 17 Catholic L.Rev. 296, 311–13 (1968): "If [*Osborn*] is to be the guideline for the type of eavesdropping cases which will qualify for court order supervision, then the interpretation that *Berger* eliminates nearly all police electronic surveillance is compelling. * * * The probable explanation for the Court's [reference] to *Osborn* is, frankly, that it is the only available case which on its facts can demonstrate to governmental authorities the kind of investigative situation where the nature of the conversation was fully known in advance and could be described to a magistrate with the specificity required by *Berger.*" See also Enker, *Controls on Electronic Eavesdropping—A Basic Distinction,* 2 Israel L.Rev. 461, 469 (1967); Pitler, *Eavesdropping and Wiretapping—The Aftermath of Katz and Kaiser,* 34 Brooklyn L.Rev. 223, 225–37 (1968).

f. Since *Berger* was briefed and argued prior to *Warden v. Hayden* (p. 253 supra), petitioner argued at some length that the New York statute authorized "general searches" for "mere evioffice where it was shown that there was probable cause to believe that evidence would be obtained," he observed, "there is little doubt that it would be struck down as a bald invasion of privacy, far worse than the general warrants prohibited by the Fourth Amendment. I can see no difference between such a statute and one authorizing electronic surveillance, which, in effect, places an invisible policeman in the home. If anything, the latter is more offensive because the homeowner is completely unaware of the invasion of privacy." [g]

STEWART, J., concurred in the result. He fully agreed with the dissenters that the challenged New York law was constitutional, but he concluded that "the affidavits on which the judicial order issued in this case did not constitute a showing of probable cause adequate to justify the authorizing order." The standard of reasonableness embodied in the Fourth Amendment," he observed, "demands that the showing of justification match the degree of intrusion. By its very nature electronic eavesdropping for a 60-day period, even of a specified office, involves a broad invasion of a constitutionally protected area. Only the most precise and rigorous standard of probable cause should justify an intrusion of this sort." The affidavits "might be enough to satisfy the standards of the Fourth Amendment for a conventional search or arrest," but not "an intrusion of the scope and duration that was permitted in this case."

Dissenting Justice HARLAN responded to the contentions that court-ordered electronic surveillance fails to specify with adequate particularity the conversations to be seized and allows a general and indiscriminate search and seizure as follows:

"If listening alone constitutes a seizure, it would be virtually impossible [to] describe with particularity the seizures which would later be made during extended eavesdropping; correspondingly, seizures would unavoidably be made which lacked any sufficient nexus with the offenses for which the order was first issued. * * * [But] conversations are not 'seized' either by eavesdropping alone, or by their recording so that they may later be heard at the eavesdropper's convenience. Just as some exercise of dominion, beyond mere perception, is necessary for the seizure of tangibles, so some use of the conversation beyond the initial listening process is required for the seizure of the spoken word."

Dissenting Justice WHITE maintained that an electronic surveillance that is continued over a span of time is no more a "general search" barred by the Fourth Amendment than the typical execution of a search warrant over a described area:

"Petitioner suggests that the search is inherently overbroad because the eavesdropper will overhear conversations which do not relate to criminal activity. But the same is true of almost all searches of private property which the Fourth Amendment permits. In searching for seizable matters, the police must necessarily see or hear, and comprehend, items which do not relate to the purpose of the search. That this occurs, however, does not render the search invalid, so long as it is authorized by a suitable search warrant and so long as the police, in executing that warrant, limit themselves to searching for items which may constitutionally be seized. Thus,

dence." But the Court, per Clark, J., rejected the contention in a brisk footnote (fn. 2), stating that it had been "disposed of in *Hayden* adversely to petitioner's assertion here." For the view that it had not, that *Hayden* had been careful to leave open the possibility of some "testimonial limit" on the permissible objects of seizure, see Taylor, *Two Studies in Constitutional Interpretation* 68–71, 101–03 (1969).

g. How can this argument be met? Could a police officer lawfully hide in the closet of a suspect's home for 30 days? Ten? Twenty-four hours? Does it matter whether the officer looks through the keyhole as well as listens? As you limit the area of the search, may the time be increased? May a tap be distinguished from a bug on the ground that the former is a "search" of a much narrower "area"?

while I would agree with petitioner that individual searches of private property through surreptitious eavesdropping with a warrant must be carefully circumscribed to avoid excessive invasion of privacy and security, I cannot agree that all such intrusions are constitutionally impermissible general searches."

A short time after *Berger,* the Court, per STEWART, J. made plain in KATZ v. UNITED STATES (p. 237 supra) that the "trespass" doctrine enunciated in *Olmstead* and *Goldman* was no longer viable and that the "penetration" of the governmental intrusion "can have no constitutional significance." But the *Katz* Court thought it "clear that [the surveillance involved in this case] was so narrowly circumscribed that a duly authorized magistrate, properly notified of the need for such investigation, specifically informed of the basis on which it was to proceed, and clearly apprised of the precise intrusion it would entail, could constitutionally have authorized, with appropriate safeguards, the very limited search and seizure that the Government asserts in fact took place." [a]

The Court likened the "discriminate circumstances" of the electronic surveillance in *Katz* to those in *Osborn* where, the *Berger* Court had said, the court order "afforded similar protections to those [of] conventional warrants authorizing the seizure of tangible evidence." "Here, too," observed the *Katz* Court, "a similar judicial order could have accommodated 'the legitimate needs of law enforcement' by authorizing the carefully limited use of electronic surveillance."

Although he dissented in *Katz,* Justice BLACK was encouraged: "[T]oday's opinion differs sharply from *Berger,* [which] set up what appeared to be insuperable obstacles to the valid passage [of] wiretapping laws * * *. The Court's opinion [in] this case [removes] the doubts about state power in this field and abates to a large extent the confusion and near paralyzing effect of the *Berger* holding."

The basis for Justice Black's view that the *Katz* opinion "differs sharply from *Berger* " is unclear. *Both opinions* referred to *Osborn* with approval. And the surveillance in *Katz* itself, as well as in *Osborn,* was very narrowly circumscribed. But the Congress seemed to read *Katz* the same way Justice Black did. Within seven months of *Katz,* in Title III of the Omnibus Crime Control and Safe Streets Act of 1968 (commonly referred to as Title III), discussed immediately below, Congress adopted legislation granting law enforcement officials extensive powers to conduct wiretapping and electronic surveillance.

B. TITLE III: AN OVERVIEW

The text of Title III is set forth in Supp. App. B. For useful summaries of Title III, on which the following brief discussion relies heavily, see LaFave & Israel, § 4.2; Goldsmith, *The Supreme Court and Title III: Rewriting the Law of Electronic Surveillance,* 74 J.Crim.L. & C. 1, 39–56 (1983) (hereinafter referred to as Goldsmith).

Title III was designed to regulate all "*nonconsensual* " electronic surveillance (i.e., electronic surveillance when *none* of the parties overheard have consented to

a. FBI agents had attached an electronic listening and recording device to the outside of the public phone booth from which petitioner had placed his calls. The agents "did not begin their electronic surveillance until investigation had established a strong possibility that he was using the telephone in question to transmit gambling information [in] violation of federal law. Moreover, the surveillance was limited, both in scope and in duration, to the specific purpose of establishing the contents of the petitioner's unlawful telephone communications. The agents confined their surveillance to the brief periods during which he used the telephone booth, and they took great care to overhear only the conversations of the petitioner himself."

the interception),[a] except "national security" eavesdropping.[b] The states are free to adopt laws of their own authorizing court-ordered electronic surveillance, but compliance with federal statutory standards is essential. See § 2516(2).[c]

Title III is concerned only with orders "authorizing or approving the *interception* of a wire or oral communication," § 2518(1) (emphasis added), and the statute defines "intercept" to mean "the *aural* acquisition of the contents of any wire or oral *communication* through the use of any electronic, mechanical, or other device." § 2410(4) (emphasis added). Thus, "pen register" surveillance (the use of a device that does not record phone conversations, but only makes a record of the phone numbers dialed from a given phone and of the times the number was dialed) is not governed by Title III; "pen registers do not accomplish the 'aural acquisition' of anything." [d] Nor, the Seventh Circuit held recently, is surreptitious *television* surveillance (without a soundtrack) of persons inside a house an "interception" of wire or oral communications: "A man televised while silently making a bomb is not engaged in any form of communication, let alone 'wire or oral communication.'" And "[a] visual observation is in no possible sense an 'aural acquisition' * * * of a 'wire or oral communication.'" [e]

a. Section 2511(2)(c) provides that "it shall not be unlawful under this chapter for a person acting under color of law to intercept a wire or oral communication where such person is a party to the communication or *one of the parties* to the communication has given prior consent to such interception." (Emphasis added.) Consensual electronic surveillance is not restricted by the Fourth Amendment. See *Lopez v. United States* (1963) (p. 455 infra); *United States v. White* (1971) (p. 463 infra).

The National Wiretap Commission, *Majority Report* (1976) found that consensual electronic surveillance "is especially vital for the investigation of certain criminal activities, particularly official corruption, extortion, and loan-sharking," and that "it also serves to protect police officers, informants, and complainants, or whoever is the consenting participant to the conversation." The Majority Report deemed court authorization for such surveillance "unnecessary for the protection of privacy because it is not a 'search' within the meaning of the Fourth Amendment" and because "it serves not to intercept conversations, but merely to corroborate them, improving the accuracy of evidence for use in court."

b. Section 2511(3) states that nothing in Title III "shall limit the constitutional power of the President to take such measures as he deems necessary to protect the Nation against actual or potential attack or other hostile acts of a foreign power, to obtain foreign intelligence information deemed essential to the security of the United States, or to protect national security information against foreign intelligence activities. Nor shall anything contained in this chapter be deemed to limit the constitutional power of the President to take such measures as he deems necessary to protect the United States against the overthrow of the Government by force or other unlawful means, or against any other clear and present danger to the structure or existence of the Government." *United States v. United States District Court* (1972) (p. 440 infra) held that the President lacked power to conduct warrantless surveillance in "domestic security" cases, but left open the question whether there could be warrantless surveillance of foreign powers or their agents. In response, Congress enacted the Foreign Intelligence Surveillance Act of 1978. The Act, inter alia, provides that under certain circumstance the President, through the Attorney General, may authorize electronic surveillance for periods up to one year to acquire foreign intelligence information. For further discussion of the Act, see p. 442 infra.

c. For a list of state statutes (1) enacted to conform with Title III requirements and (2) modeled after Title III, and a brief comparison of these statutes with federal law, see I *A.B.A. Standards* Ch. 2 (Electronic Surveillance) (App. 2.1).

d. *United States v. New York Telephone Co.,* 434 U.S. 159, 98 S.Ct. 364, 54 L.Ed.2d 376 (1977) (White, J.). The Court also held that the District Court had power to authorize the installation of pen registers under Fed.R.Crim.P. 41(b), which is "broad enough to encompass a 'search' designed to ascertain the use which is being made of a telephone suspected of facilitating a criminal venture and the 'seizure' of evidence which the 'search' of the telephone produces."

The Court subsequently held, *Smith v. Maryland* (1979) (p. 250 supra), that the use of a pen register did not constitute a "search" within the meaning of the Fourth Amendment, observing, inter alia: "[P]etitioner in all probability entertained no actual expectation of privacy in the phone numbers he dialed [and] even if he did, his expectation was not 'legitimate.'" Although his conduct "may have been calculated to keep the *contents* of his conversation private, his conduct was not and could not have been calculated to preserve the privacy of the number he dialed."

e. *United States v. Torres,* 751 F.2d 875 (7th Cir.1984) (Posner, J.) The Court also held that

Criminal penalties and civil remedies are available against one who willfully intercepts, uses or discloses information in violation of the statute. See §§ 2511(a), 2520. Violations of Title III are also enforced by "a broad statutory exclusionary rule that transcends its constitutional counterpart by being applicable to all governmental judicial, quasi-judicial, and administrative proceedings." Goldsmith at 40, referring to § 2515.[f] Thus, "the Title III exclusionary rule may be invoked by a party in a bail hearing, a parole revocation proceeding, or a police department disciplinary proceeding." LaFave & Israel at 406.

Suppression of the evidence, however, is not the consequence of *every* failure to follow the provisions of Title III. Suppression is required only when the particular statutory provision violated "directly and substantially implement[s]" the congressional intention to restrict the use of electronic surveillance or "was intended to play a central role in the statutory scheme." *United States v. Giordano* (1974) (p. 443 infra).

the District Court had authority—under both Fed.R.Crim.P. 41(b) and its inherent judicial power to issue warrants—to issue a warrant authorizing the television surveillance of the interior of a house allegedly used by a terrorist group to assemble bombs. The videotapes had no soundtracks, but at the same time that the FBI was televising the interior of the house it was recording the sounds on different equipment. (The admissibility of these sound tapes was not an issue in this appeal.) "The FBI wanted to see as well as hear," pointed out Judge Posner, "because it had reason to believe that the [suspects], concerned that they might be bugged, would play the radio loudly when they were speaking to each other and also would speak in code, and that the actual assembly of bombs would be carried out in silence."

Although the court concluded that Title III neither authorized nor forbid television surveillance (with no soundtrack), it "made clear" its view that "because television surveillance is potentially so menacing to personal privacy," a warrant for television surveillance that did not satisfy [as the government did in this case] the [provisions] of Title III that implement the Fourth Amendment's requirement of particularity would violate the Fourth Amendment."

Federal applications may be authorized only by the Attorney General or a specially designated Assistant Attorney General, see § 2516(1), a requirement designed to ensure that discretion is exercised by a senior and politically accountable executive official before a court is asked to pass on an application. (When authorized by state law, the "principal prosecuting attorney of any state or political subdivision thereof" may apply to a state judge for an electronic surveillance order. The state provisions are thus less centralized, but this was deemed necessitated by realities of state law enforcement systems.) Only federal district and appellate judges and their state counterparts may issue surveillance orders. See § 2510(9).

Except for "emergencies"—§ 2518(7) permits warrantless electronic surveillance when "an emergency situation exists with respect to conspiratorial activities threatening the national security interest or to conspiratorial activities characteristic of organized crime" [g]—no electronic surveillance is permitted without a properly authorized application. See § 2518(1).

f. *Calandra* (1974) (p. 230 supra), it will be recalled, refused to allow a grand jury witness to invoke the Fourth Amendment exclusionary rule, reasoning that a contrary result "would achieve a speculative and undoubtedly minimal advance in the deterrence of police misconduct at the expense of substantially impeding the role of the grand jury." In *Gelbard v. United States,* 408 U.S. 41, 92 S.Ct. 2357, 33 L.Ed.2d 179 (1972), however, a 5–4 majority, per Brennan, J., held that grand jury witnesses may refuse to testify where their testimony is sought on the basis of illegal electronic surveillance. For such testimony would constitute "evidence derived" from violations of Title III, whose use is prohibited by § 2515.

g. There must be "grounds upon which an order could be entered under this chapter to authorize such interception"; the situation must require an interception before a court order "can with due diligence be obtained"; and, within 48 hours after the interception has begun to occur, an application must be filed seeking retroactive approval for such interception.

The emergency provision has been criticized on the ground that it is too broad and too ambiguous. See Goldsmith at 47–49; Lapidus, *Eavesdropping on Trial* 6, 93–95 (1974); H. Schwartz,

Each application must be in writing and under oath; disclose the identify of the officer making the application and the officer authorizing it (see *United States v. Chavez* (1974), p. 443 infra); and include a "full and complete" statement of the circumstances justifying the belief that an order should be issued, including (i) details as to the particular offense, (ii) a particular description of the communication facility, (iii) a particular description of "the type of communication" sought to be intercepted, and (iv) "the identity of the person, if known, committing the offense, and whose conversation is to be intercepted."[h] "In other words," comments Goldsmith at 42, "there must be probable cause to believe that a particular person involved in a designated crime will have discussion pertinent to that crime using a particular phone (or at a particular place) during a specified time period."

Moreover, to discourage routine use of tapping or electronic eavesdropping, the application must include "full and complete" statements as to "whether or not other investigative procedures have been tried or failed or why they reasonably appear to be unlikely to succeed if tried or to be too dangerous"[i] and of the facts concerning all previous applications "involving any of the same persons, facilities or places specified in the application, and the action taken by the judge on each such application." See § 2518(1)(c), (e).

The judge may enter an order as requested or as modified upon determining, on the basis of the facts submitted, that "normal investigative procedures" are not a viable alternative and that there is probable cause for believing three things: an individual has committed or is about to commit a particular offense enumerated in the statute; "particular communications concerning that offense will be obtained through such interception"; and the facilities or place where the communications are to be intercepted are being, or about to be, used in connection with the offense or "are leased to, listed in the name of, or commonly used by such person." See § 2518(3).

The court order must designate the personnel authorized to conduct the surveillance, identify both the person (if known) and the facilities or place targeted for interception, specify the period of surveillance, and furnish a "particular description of the type of communication sought to be intercepted, and a statement of the particular offense to which it relates."[j] See § 2518(4). In addition, each order must provide, § 2518(5), that the authorization to intercept "shall be executed as soon as practicable, shall be conducted in such a way as to *minimize the interception of communications not otherwise subject to interception*" (emphasis added),[k] and "must terminate upon attainment of the authorized objective, or in any event in thirty days."

The Legitimation of Electronic Eavesdropping: The Politics of "Law and Order," 67 Mich.L.Rev. 455, 486–90 (1969). For example, neither "organized crime" nor "national security" is statutorily defined. Moreover, *Katz* indicated that warrantless electronic surveillance could not be justified on traditional emergency search grounds. On the other hand, as pointed out in Goldsmith, supra, the "emergency situation" provision seems unduly *narrow* in one respect: it fails to allow emergency surveillance in life-endangering situations (e.g., kidnapping, hostage-taking) *not* involving organized crime or national security interests.

"There has been virtually no use of this emergency power," report LaFave & Israel at 374, "with the consequence that the courts have not been called upon to assess its constitutionality."

h. What is the obligation of the government to discover and name the persons to be heard? See *United States v. Kahn* (1974), p. 445 infra. What are the consequences of noncompliance with this provision? See *United States v. Donovan,* (1977), p. 446 infra.

i. In practice, maintains Carr, *The Law of Electronic Surveillance* 179 (1977), this requirement has been watered down to "one of investigatory utility, rather than necessity."

j. What was intended by "type of communication" is unclear. It now "appears to be generally accepted that [this requirement] can be fulfilled by indicating the offense under investigation, without further details about the anticipated conversations," Carr, fn. i supra, at 173.

k. But see *Scott v. United States* (1978) (p. 448 infra), rejecting the contention that the failure of

Title III does meet at least some of the objections voiced by the *Berger* Court when it invalidated the state law involved in that case. The federal statute requires that surveillance cease once "the objective of the authorization" is achieved, § 2815(5), and it permits electronic surveillance extensions only upon a new showing of probable cause and only by resort to the procedures required in obtaining the initial order. (See id.) But Title III does allow continued electronic surveillance for up to 30 days on the basis of a single showing of probable cause, id., and it permits an unlimited number of 30 day extensions, albeit on renewed showings of probable cause. See id.

"Allowing such lengthy surveillance, possibly for years," argues a leading critic of police electronic eavesdropping, H. Schwartz, fn. g supra, at 461, "conflicts sharply with *Berger's* clear disapproval of the two-month authorization permitted by the New York statute. Moreover, sections 2518(1)(d) and 4(e) of the Act do not limit the eavesdropping to specific points in time, unlike the [situation] in *Katz* and the cases approvingly cited in *Berger,* but rather allow uninterrupted eavesdropping over a 'period of time.' Under such a provision, officers may install a tap or a bug which will be in *continuous* operation throughout the days or months for which the interception is authorized. This would seem to pose a rather clear conflict with the Supreme Court's holding in *Berger,* which disapproved the uninterrupted interception as allowing 'indiscriminate' seizure and approved the *Osborn* interception because 'the order authorized one limited intrusion rather [than] a continuous surveillance'." [l]

the surveilling officers to make any effort to comply with a minimization requirement was alone a basis for suppression. The Court took the position that "subjective intent alone does not make otherwise lawful conduct illegal," meaning that the officers' presumed failure to make even a good-faith effort to comply with the requirement was not itself a reason for excluding the evidence obtained.

Section 2518(8)(d) provides that "within a reasonable period but not later than ninety days" after the filing of an application has been denied or the authorized surveillance terminated, the issuing or denying judge shall serve on "the persons *named* in the order or the application, and *such other parties* to intercepted communication as the judge *may determine in his discretion that is in the interest of justice* " (emphasis added) an "inventory" including (1) the fact of the entry of the order or the application; (2) the date of the entry and the period of interception, or the denial of the application; and (3) the fact that during the period communications were or were not intercepted. However, upon "an ex parte showing of good cause," the serving of the inventory may be postponed.[m]

That only "named" individuals are guaranteed statutory notice, comments Goldsmith at 55, "is not constitutionally objectionable. * * * Congress realized that at times notice of interception might be a source of considerable distress. For example, eavesdropping targets could be embarrassed if their innocent conversations resulted in disclosure of the surveillance to uninvolved parties. The possibility also existed that notice mailed to one's home or business could cause domestic or professional discomfiture respectively. Accordingly, Congress decided to give notice to those most obviously affected by the investigation; others would receive it upon a proper exercise of judicial discretion."

C. The Facial Validity of Title III

Surprisingly, the Supreme Court has never explicitly considered the facial valid-

l. But see *United States v. Cafero* (3d Cir. 1973), p. 435 infra.

m. "The 'reasonable time' requirement has been broadly construed. As for the 'good cause' for postponement, it has been held to include such reasons as protecting the integrity of an ongoing investigation or ensuring that persons would not flee to avoid arrest." LaFave & Israel at 399.

ity of Title III. But there is no hint in the Court's many decisions interpreting various provisions of Title III that the statute is facially invalid. And the lower federal courts have consistently upheld the statute against constitutional challenge.

Lower court decisions reconciling continuing electronic surveillance up to 30 days, permitted by Title III, with the Fourth Amendment "rely upon the analysis of Justices Harlan and White, [both of whom] dissented in *Berger*. [See p. 429 supra.] Their contention was that an electronic surveillance which is continued over a span of time is no more a general search than the typical execution of a search warrant over a described area." LaFave & Israel 369.

Illustrative of the lower federal courts' rejection of constitutional challenges to Title III is UNITED STATES v. CAFERO, 473 F.2d 489 (3d Cir.1973), where the court, per ALDISERT, J., observed:

"Implicit in [the constitutional objection] to the thirty-day maximum requirement of § 2518(5) is an unspoken premise that a shorter time might have passed constitutional muster. A good case can be presented, however, that a fifteen-day period would also not [satisfy the Fourth Amendment]. This day-counting approach to constitutional acceptability, however, misses the mark because it overlooks what we perceive to be the clear congressional intent that: (1) the length of interception in each case be determined by judicial decision on a case-by-case basis; (2) the interception be terminated automatically, not on a predetermined calendar date, but when the objective of the authorization is achieved, § 2518; and (3) while there is a maximum statutory life span of thirty days for each approval order, each interception has the very real potential of earlier extinction, § 2518(6).

"The thirty-day period contemplated by Title III is a statutory *maximum,* not an automatic authorization for continuous interception for thirty days." The court then interpreted § 2518(5) "as requiring automatic termination" of the surveillance "upon interception of the first sought communication on the achievement of the interception's objective unless the judge finds probable cause to justify continued surveillance" regardless "of whether a statement to this effect has been included by the authorizing judge."

"Thus, the offensive autocracy of the calendar condemned in *Berger* has been supplanted by judicial authority in the first instance, by the right of *sua sponte* judicial review at any time, and by the expiration of statutory authority to continue the interception once the objective has been achieved. Carte blanche is given to no one. Executing officers are not free to intercept beyond attainment of their objective for an hour, a day, seven days, or twenty-nine day. They are allotted time to achieve an objective, period. Should they intercept beyond this time, they have violated the Act."

As for the argument that Title III is fatally defective because it fails to require prompt notice to those people whose conversations have been intercepted after authorized surveillance has been completed: "We find it difficult to accept the proposition that a search may be deemed reasonable, and therefore constitutional, during the various stages of application for authorization, execution, supervision of the interception, and termination, only to be invalidated *ab initio* because of the operation of some condition subsequent, to wit, a failure to give notice of the items seized. In the context of traditional search warrants, a failure to comply with certain procedural requirements of Fed.R.Crim.P. 41 [e.g., a failure to deliver promptly a copy of the warrant to the party whose premises were searched] has been held not to amount to deprivation of Fourth Amendment rights necessitating suppression. * * *[a]

a. Cf. United States v. Donovan, p. 446 infra.

"[Nor do we believe that the inventory procedure set forth in § 2518(8)(d)] lacks the degree of promptness required by the Constitution. * * * Only unreasonable searches and seizures are beyond the constitutional pale. A statute which requires an inventory to be filed within 'a reasonable time' cannot, without more, offend this test. If, in a given case, there is undue delay, that contention may be pressed in an appropriate averment alleging non-compliance with the statute. * * *

"The same analysis should apply to inspection of the contents of the interception, [which § 2518(8)(d)] leaves to the discretion of the issuing court "as the judge determines to be in the interest of justice." * * * The parameters of 'the interest of justice' within the statutory schema and the Federal Constitution remain to be fashioned on a case-by-case basis. For our immediate purpose we decide only that the Congressional decision to entrust this inspection to the judicial process is not offensive to the Fourth Amendment.

"The New York procedure condemned in *Berger* did not 'provide for a return on the warrant, thereby leaving full discretion in the officer as to the use of seized conversations of innocent as well as guilty parties.' We conclude that this objection has been adequately negated by the provisions of Title III."

It will be recalled that, concurring in the result in *Berger,* Justice Stewart concluded that although the evidence might have been adequate "for a conventional search or arrest," it was "constitutionally insufficient to constitute probable cause to justify an intrusion of the scope and duration that was permitted in this case." (See p. 429 supra) This argument, however, has not prevailed. Illustrative is *United States v. Falcone,* 505 F.2d 478 (3d Cir.1974): "Probable cause is not a matter of degree. Although *Berger* and *Katz* call for extra vigilance in the supervision of electronic eavesdropping, neither case separates probable cause into degrees. Moreover, no special probable cause requirement can be found in the statutory scheme." [b]

D. The Need for, and Utility of, Title III

As pointed out in Goldsmith, at 35–37: "[A year before Title III was enacted into law, the President's Crime Commission's task force on organized crime had] noted that traditional evidence gathering techniques are relatively ineffectual in organized crime cases. * * * To illustrate the potential utility of electronic surveillance, the Commission provided several examples of successful New York organized crime prosecutions that purportedly could not have been made without electronic surveillance. Indeed, the Commission observed that only in New York,

b. But cf. Posner, J., in *United States v. Torres* (p. 431 fn. e) (upholding warrant for *television* surveillance):

"The usual way in which judges interpreting the Fourth Amendment take account of the fact that searches vary in the degree to which they invade personal privacy is by requiring a higher degree of probable cause (to believe that the search will yield incriminating evidence), and by being more insistent that a warrant be obtained if at all feasible, the more intrusive the search is. See * * * *United States v. Karo* [p. 251 supra]. But maybe in dealing with so intrusive a technique as television surveillance, other methods of control as well, such as banning the technique outright from use in the home in connection with minor crimes, will be required, in order to strike a proper balance between public safety and personal privacy. That question is not before us, but we mention it to make clear that in declining to hold television surveillance unconstitutional per se we do not suggest that the Constitution must be interpreted to allow it to be used as generally as less intrusive techniques can be used. The first clause of the Fourth Amendment guarantees the right of the American people to be free from unreasonable searches * * * and a search could be unreasonable, though conducted pursuant to an otherwise valid warrant, by intruding on personal privacy to an extent disproportionate to the likely benefits from obtaining fuller compliance with the law. '[T]here can be no ready test for determining reasonableness other than by balancing the need to search against the invasion which the search entails.' *Camara v. Municipal Court* [p. 399 supra]."

where electronic surveillance had been used for more than two decades, 'have law enforcement officials achieved some level of success in bringing prosecutions against organized crime.' It was these findings, together with a concern for controlling abuses, which prompted a majority of the Commission members to recommend the adoption of legislation authorizing electronic surveillance under a system of strict controls.

"* * * [T]he drafters of Title III relied heavily upon the Commission's analysis in determining that such legislation was necessary for modern law enforcement. The legislative history noted that crime was a 'national catastrophe' and that organized crime, in particular, had a pervasive influence upon American society which previous law enforcement efforts had been unable to control. * * * Congress suggested that police misconduct had been responsible for few unlawful invasions of privacy, and implicitly concluded that providing the police with a carefully controlled, lawful means for conducting electronic surveillance would remove the incentive for abuse. * * *

"It has been suggested that Title III was the product of a hysterical Congress responding to conservative political pressure during a national climate of fear. No doubt the debate over electronic surveillance was at times emotional, and it is probably true that the assassination of Martin Luther King and Robert F. Kennedy contributed somewhat to Title III's expedited approval. Overall, however, the measure appears to have been a bipartisan effort designed to accommodate the demands of modern society's need for privacy and law enforcement." [a]

The wisdom, as well as the constitutionality, of various provisions of Title III are forcefully challenged in H. Schwartz, *The Legitimation of Electronic Eavesdropping: The Politics of "Law and Order,"* 67 Mich.L.Rev. 455 (1969).[b] Professor Schwartz observes, inter alia, at 481–82:

"[S]ection 2516 allows federal officials to tap and bug not only for such common activities of organized crime as extortion, corruption, interstate gambling, loan sharking, labor racketeering, and the like, but also for any offense involving marijuana, riots, obstruction of a criminal investigation, counterfeiting, and theft from interstate shipments.

"State officers are treated even more generously, despite the fact that the states have a far smaller role than the federal government in fighting organized crime. Indeed, one of the greatest problems in fighting organized crime is [that] few state or local law enforcement agencies show any interest in the enterprise. Yet states are given authority to use electronic surveillance for [a practically unlimited number of offenses, referring to § 2516(2)].[c] * * * Yet even with respect to certain

a. But see H. Schwartz, *Taps, Bugs, and Fooling the People* 13 (1977): "[Title III was enacted at a time when] Americans were frightened as rarely before in a time of official peace. They feared street crime, black rebellions, radicals, young people, organized crime. Overhanging everything was Vietnam.

"Congress had a pretty good idea of how bad the bill was. As Richard Harris reported, 'all those who voted against it, many of those who voted for it, and most of those who didn't vote at all [believed] the bill was a piece of demagoguery, devised out of malevolence and enacted in hysteria.' Nevertheless, records Harris, 'in the House, only 17 members voted against it, and in the Senate only four.' "

Professor Schwartz's reference to Harris is to a detailed, critical account of the political and legislative history of Title III, Harris, *Annals of Legislation—The Turning Point,* New Yorker, Dec. 14, 1968, pp. 68, 152–63.

b. See also Spritzer, *Electronic Surveillance by Leave of the Magistrate: The Case in Opposition,* 118 U.Pa.L.Rev. 169 (1969); Notes, 23 Rutgers L.Rev. 319 (1969); 11 Am.Crim.L.Rev. 639, 674–92 (1973). But see Burpo, *Electronic Surveillance by Leave of the Magistrate: The Case for the Prosecution,* 38 Tenn.L.Rev. 14 (1970).

c. Section 2516(2) of Title III invites the states to pass legislation modeled on the federal act, but many states have not done so and thus their law enforcement officials lack statutory authority to apply for an electronic surveillance order. As to the division of court-authorized wiretap orders between federal and state officials (and the numserious offenses, the case for eavesdropping authority is feeble, for the technique is of little use in solving murder cases and of almost no use in investigating robbery, rape, or any other crimes of violence that usually involved sudden, nonrepetitive encounters. [Thus] Title III grants authority to use eavesdropping almost as freely as any other standard investigative tool. In this respect, it is not very different from the New York statute which allows eavesdropping for any crime, and under which some eighty per cent of police wiretapping was for the investigation of minor gambling and vice offenses."

Professor Schwartz also maintains that Title III "will turn out to be either a provision of relatively little value in the struggle against organized crime or a verbal smoke screen for continuing illegality" (id. at 468–69, 471–72):

"According to its proponents, the special advantage of electronic surveillance is that it is a valuable tool for gathering strategic intelligence about organized crime and that it thus enables law enforcement officials to obtain 'a look at the overall picture' for 'prevention' purposes. The techniques of fighting organized crime differ from those used in ordinary criminal investigation. The former involves accumulating a great deal of superficially irrelevant information which is then collated. Furthermore, in investigating organized crime the police do not work from a known crime to an unknown or suspected criminal, but 'backwards' from a 'known criminal' to a hoped-for discovery of an as-yet-unknown crime. * * *

"The fact is that searches for strategic intelligence, without a specific crime as the objective, cannot be squared with *Berger, Katz,* and *Osborn.* Judging by the language used by the Court, the facts at issue in those cases, and the kinds of permissible electronic surveillance cited in the various opinions, it would seem that gathering tactical intelligence is the only kind of surveillance that is justifiable under present theories of the fourth amendment. And in this respect, [Title III] is verbally consistent with the cases in limiting eavesdropping to such tactical intelligence purposes * * *.

"This is surely an odd result, for if the war against organized crime—the justification for Title III—really requires strategic intelligence, how will that war be advanced by legislation which seems to permit the acquisition of only tactical intelligence? And if the Act does not grant law enforcement officers the power to obtain allegedly crucial strategic information, will we not again experience the same kind of widespread flouting of clear legal limitations that has recently come to light? In sum, even the very loose Title III is too restrictive to accomplish the purposes advanced by its proponents, and this raises serious questions about the reasons for their support of the legislation, and about how meaningful they expect its ostensible limitations to be."[d]

But see National Wiretap Commission, *Majority Report* (1976),[e] "vigorously reaffirm[ing] the findings and statements of policy made by Congress in 1968 that organized criminals make extensive use of

ber of such orders issued annually), see fn. h, p. 5 supra.

d. Professor Goldsmith maintains, however, Goldsmith at 52 n. 322, that Professor Schwartz's contention that Title III's limitation on surveillance for purely strategic intelligence is inconsistent with its drafters' goal of providing a means to combat organized crime on a long term basis "overlooks [that] strategic intelligence is often legitimately overheard during the course of actual surveillance."

e. Title III was enacted as a compromise of various conflicting views of the form any legislation regulating electronic surveillance should take. The National Commission for the Review of Federal and State Laws Relating to Wiretapping and Electronic Surveillance (National Wiretap Commission) was created, as part of the compromise, to, among other duties, conduct a comprehensive study and review of the operation of Title III in the first six years after its enactment. The majority and minority reports issued in 1976 were the result of two years of work by the Commission.

wire and oral communications in their criminal activities" and that "the interception of such communications to obtain evidence of the commission of crimes or to prevent their commission is an indispensable aid to law enforcement and the administration of justice."

"We have, for example," reports the Commission, "seen much of the major organized criminal activity in an entire state—New Jersey—weeded out through the astute use of electronic surveillance in coordination with other investigative techniques. Notable in the use of Title III by the New Jersey Attorney General's office is the technique of 'working up the ladder' of an organized crime group through successive wiretaps, each based on probable cause, each leading to higher echelons of criminality, each being promptly shut down when it achieved its object. * * * In Washington, D.C., we have seen how the Capital City's major narcotics dealer, who had survived all conventional efforts to gather evidence for his apprehension, was finally convicted by the use of wiretap evidence. * * *

"[On the other hand], the inability of Illinois investigators to use court-authorized electronic surveillance [because they lacked such authority][f] foreclosed the possibility of identifying and indicting the top leaders of [a large theft and fencing ring].[g] There is no doubt that the use of court-authorized electronic surveillance has accomplished a great deal for law enforcement that could not have been done without it."

The Majority Report called for *more* extensive use of electronic surveillance, "particularly in the investigation of narcotics importation and distribution and theft and fencing." It also found that "federal officials responsible for administering wiretap application review procedures have shown a commendable concern for adhering to the requirements of Title III." Indeed, "it appears that these review procedures for authorizing an electronic-surveillance application have in some instances been *too* time-consuming" (emphasis added).[h]

SECTION 3. THE APPLICATION OF TITLE III

After considerable discussion, Professor Goldsmith concludes that Title III is constitutional on its face, Goldsmith at 55, but he quickly adds: "The real question today * * * is not Title III's facial validity, but the manner in which it has been applied. Congress intended that the statute be strictly enforced under careful judicial supervision. Indeed, given the many questions raised about its facial validity, the law's ultimate constitutionality was said by some to depend upon such enforcement. Yet, ironically, the Supreme Court, which originally took the initiative in ad-

f. See fn. c supra.

g. But see H. Schwartz, fn. a supra, at 33, urging an end to state authority for electronic surveillance because "the results are meager, the abuses are great, judicial scrutiny is poor and not likely to improve, and few states are really eager for the authority."

h. A minority of the Commission differed sharply on the conclusions to be drawn from the evidence. The Minority Report observed, for example, that "in seven years Title III has been responsible, directly or indirectly, for only nine federal convictions and three pending indictments against leading Organized Crime figures. The actual impact of these cases on an organization with over 5,000 known members nationwide must be regarded as minimal at best."

The Minority Report also noted that "electronic surveillance has been used since 1968 against a very great number of low-level gamblers with very little success in reaching up into the hierarchy of any major gambling or related Organized Crime operation. Despite seven years of court-ordered electronic surveillance, illegal gambling continues to flourish in every major city in the country and in many rural areas as well. * * * [E]ven if convicted, the gambler virtually never receives a prison sentence * * *. Finally, the Commission found no evidence to support the theory, advanced by some, that gambling wiretaps lead the authorities to more serious crimes."

See also H. Schwartz, fn. a supra, at 33, urging that "[e]lectronic surveillance in gambling and drug cases should be stopped, if only for fiscal reasons. This alone would eliminate more than 80% of the taps and bugs."

vising Congress as to the drafting of electronic surveillance legislation, has since failed to enforce Title III in a consistently scrupulous manner." It is to the "Title III enforcement" cases that we now turn.

A. The "Domestic Security" Exception to Court Order Requirements

Section 2511(3) of Title III provides that none of the electronic surveillance requirements of the Act shall "limit the constitutional power of the President to take such measures as he deems necessary to protect the United States against the overthrow of the Government by force or other unlawful means, or against any other clear and present danger to the structure or existence of the Government." In UNITED STATES v. UNITED STATES DISTRICT COURT, 407 U.S. 297, 92 S.Ct. 2125, 32 L.Ed.2d 752 (1972) (often called *Keith,* after then District Judge Damon Keith), a case involving a conspiracy to destroy federal government property, the government relied on this provision to justify taps without a court order. The Court, per POWELL, J., held, without a dissent, that neither § 2511(3) nor the inherent powers of the President to defend the government "justify departure * * * [from] the customary Fourth Amendment requirement of judicial approval prior to initiation of a search or surveillance":

"[Section 2511(3)] merely provides that the Act shall not be interpreted to limit or disturb such power as the President may have under the Constitution. * * * Congress simply left presidential powers where it found them. Congress only intended to make clear that the Act simply did not legislate with respect to national security surveillances.

" * * * Though the investigative duty of the executive may be stronger in [national security] cases, so also is there greater jeopardy to constitutionally protected speech. 'Historically the struggle for freedom of speech and press in England was bound up with the issue of the scope of the search and seizure power.' * * * Fourth Amendment protections become the more necessary when the targets of official surveillance may be those suspected of unorthodoxy in their political beliefs. The danger to political dissent is acute where the Government attempts to act under so vague a concept as the power to protect 'domestic security.'

" * * * Fourth Amendment freedoms cannot properly be guaranteed if domestic security surveillances may be conducted solely within the discretion of the executive branch. The Fourth Amendment does not contemplate the executive officers of Government as neutral and disinterested magistrates. * * * The historical judgment, which the Fourth Amendment accepts, is that unreviewed executive discretion may yield too readily to pressures to obtain incriminating evidence and overlook potential invasions of privacy and protected speech. * * *

"We cannot accept the Government's argument that internal security matters are too subtle and complex for judicial evaluation. * * * Certainly courts can recognize that domestic security surveillance involves different considerations from the surveillance of ordinary crime. If the threat is too subtle or complex for our senior law enforcement officers to convey its significance to a court, one may question whether there is probable cause for surveillance.

"Nor do we believe prior judicial approval will fracture the secrecy essential to official intelligence gathering. The investigation of criminal activity has long involved imparting sensitive information to judicial officers who have respected the confidentialities involved. Judges may be counted upon to be especially conscious of security requirements in national security cases. * * * Moreover, a warrant application involves no public or adversary proceedings: it is an ex parte request before a magistrate or judge."

"Thus, we conclude that the Government's concerns do not justify departure in this case from the customary Fourth Amendment requirement of judicial approval prior to initiation of a search or surveillance. Although some added burden will be imposed upon the Attorney General, this inconvenience is justified in a free society to protect constitutional values. * * *

"[W]e do not hold that the same type of standards and procedures prescribed by Title III are necessarily applicable to this case. We recognize that domestic security surveillance may involve different policy and practical considerations from the surveillance of 'ordinary crime.' The gathering of security intelligence is often long range and involves the interrelation of various sources and types of information. The exact targets of such surveillance may be more difficult to identify than in surveillance operations against many types of crime specified in Title III. Often, too, the emphasis of domestic intelligence gathering is on the prevention of unlawful activity or the enhancement of the Government's preparedness for some possible future crisis or emergency. Thus, the focus of domestic surveillance may be less precise than that directed against more conventional types of crimes.

"Given these potential distinctions between Title III criminal surveillances and those involving the domestic security, Congress may wish to consider protective standards for the latter which differ from those already prescribed for specified crimes in Title III. Different standards may be compatible with the Fourth Amendment if they are reasonable both in relation to the legitimate need of Government for intelligence information and the protected rights of our citizens. For the warrant application may vary according to the governmental interest to be enforced and the nature of citizen rights deserving protection [quoting *Camara,* p. 399 supra]. It may be that Congress, for example, would judge that the application and affidavit showing probable cause need not follow the exact requirements of § 2518 but should allege other circumstances more appropriate to domestic security cases; that the request for prior court authorization could, in sensitive cases, be made to any member of a specially designated court * * * and that the time and reporting requirements need not be so strict as those in § 2518."

Justice DOUGLAS joined in the opinion of the Court and also wrote a concurring opinion, observing: * * *

"[The Fourth Amendment's] Warrant Clause has stood as a barrier against intrusions by officialdom into the privacies of life. But if that barrier were lowered now to permit suspected subversives' most intimate conversations to be pillaged then why could not their abodes or mail be secretly searched by the same authority? To defeat so terrifying a claim of inherent power we need only stand by the enduring values served by the Fourth Amendment."

Justice WHITE concurred in the result on statutory grounds, finding it "unnecessary, and therefore improper," to reach the constitutional questions. As he saw it, the challenged wiretaps did not fall within the § 2511(3) exception, for the government's affidavit (stating that the taps were designed to obtain information "necessary to protect the nation from attempts of domestic organizations to attack and subvert the existing structure of the Government") "utterly fails to assume responsibility for the judgment that Congress demanded"—it "makes no reference to force or unlawfulness [nor concludes] the attempts involved any clear and present danger to the existence or structure of the Government." Moreover, under § 2511 (3) the contents of any communication "intercepted by authority of the President" may be received in evidence " '*only* where such interception was reasonable, and shall not be otherwise used or disclosed except as is necessary to implement that power.' (Emphasis added.) There has been no determination by the District Court that it would be reasonable to use the fruits of the wiretap [or] necessary to do so to implement the purposes for which the tap was authorized." [b]

NOTE ON THE FOREIGN INTELLIGENCE ACT OF 1978

Because, as the Court stressed, *District Court* dealt with the electronic surveillance of a "domestic organization," one that had "no significant connection" with a foreign power or its agents, the Court had no occasion to address the meaning or validity of the "foreign affairs" disclaimer that, at the time, was also contained in § 2511(3): "Nothing [in this statute] shall limit the constitutional power of the President to take such measures as he deems necessary to protect the Nation against actual or potential attack or other hostile acts of a foreign power, to obtain foreign intelligence information deemed essential to the security of the United States, or to protect national security information against foreign intelligence activities." This matter is now dealt with by another statute, the Federal Intelligence Surveillance Act (FISA) of 1978, 50 U.S.C. § 1801 et seq., upheld in *United States v. Belfield,* 692 F.2d 141 (D.C.Cir.1982) and *United States v. Truong Dinh Hung,* 629 F.2d 908 (4th Cir. 1980). See generally Senate Select Committee on Intelligence, *The Foreign Surveillance Act of 1978: The First Five Years,* S.Doc. No 660, 98th Cong., 2d Sess. 3 (1984); Note, 71 Mich.L.Rev. 1116 (1980).

The FISA provides that the Chief Justice of the United States shall publicly designate seven district judges from seven of the federal judicial circuits "who shall constitute a court which shall have jurisdiction to hear applications for and grant orders approving electronic surveillance anywhere within the United States under the procedures set forth in this Act" (§ 1803(a)), and also provides that the Chief Justice shall publicly designate three judges from the federal district courts or courts of appeals who shall "comprise a court of review which shall have jurisdiction to review the denial of any application made under this Act" (§ 1803(b)).

Section 1805 authorizes the existence of an electronic surveillance order if "there is probable cause to believe" that "the target" is "a foreign power or an agent of a foreign power" (both defined in § 1801). The President, through the Attorney General, provides § 1802, may authorize warrantless electronic surveillance up to one year "to acquire foreign intelligence information" if, inter alia, the Attorney General certifies that the surveillance is "solely directed at" the acquisition of information "transmitted by means of communications used exclusively between or among foreign powers" and that there is "no substantial likelihood that the surveillance will acquire the contents of any communication to which a United States person is a party."

Section 1806 provides for the suppression, in any federal trial or proceeding, of unlawfully obtained evidence. However, if the Attorney General files an affidavit that "disclosure or an adversary hearing would harm the national security of the United States," the trial court must review *in camera* and ex parte the application, order and such other matters relating to the surveillance as may be necessary to determine the legality of the surveillance.

According to the Director of the FBI, Webster, *Sophisticated Surveillance—Intolerable Intrusion or Prudent Protection?,* 63 Wash. U.L.Q. 351, 359 n. 10 (1985): "The [FISA] covers four categories of electronic surveillance: (1) wiretaps; (2) radio intercepts; (3) monitoring devices, such as

b. Chief Justice Burger concurred in the Court's result without opinion, Rehnquist, J., did not participate.

microphones, closed-circuit television, transmitters that track vehicle movement, and other techniques; and (4) watch listing—acquiring wire or radio communications of a particular individual. * * *

"Proposals for electronic surveillance under FISA receive a thorough review beginning with an FBI Headquarters supervisor. * * * [M]y special assistants and I evaluate the proposal. Once I approve it, I send it to the Justice Department for approval by the Attorney General. Finally, the application is reviewed by the FISA court.

"One important purpose served by all of these steps is to ensure that we do not direct electronic surveillance against people because of lawful political activities * * *. We want to be confident that when we approve a FISA application, as well as any proposal for use of electronic surveillance techniques, we are using these tools in not only a *legal,* but an *appropriate* manner."

B. PRESCRIBED INTERNAL GOVERNMENTAL PROCEDURES IN APPLYING FOR ELECTRONIC SURVEILLANCE ORDERS; DOES EVERY FAILURE TO COMPLY FULLY WITH TITLE III REQUIRE SUPPRESSION?

Section 2516(1) provides that "the Attorney General or any Assistant Attorney General specially designated by the Attorney General," may authorize an application for an interception order. UNITED STATES v. GIORDANO, 416 U.S. 505, 94 S.Ct. 1820, 40 L.Ed.2d 341 (1974), per WHITE, J., held that the provision did not permit the Attorney General's Executive Assistant to authorize a wiretap application and that the intercepted communication and "evidence derived therefrom" must be excluded because "unlawfully intercepted" within the meaning of § 2518(10)(a)(i).[a] Rejecting the government's contention that the communications had not been "unlawfully intercepted" because approval by the wrong official is merely a statutory violation and § 2518(10)(a)(i) should be construed to reach constitutional violations only, the Court observed:

"The words 'unlawfully intercepted' are themselves not limited to constitutional violations, and we think Congress intended to require suppression where there is failure to satisfy any of those statutory requirements that directly and substantially implement the Congressional intention to limit the use of intercept procedures to those situations clearly calling for the employment of this extraordinary investigative device. * * * We are confident that the provision for pre-application control was intended to play a central role in the statutory scheme and that suppression must follow when it is shown that this statutory requirement has been ignored."[b]

But compare the companion case of UNITED STATES v. CHAVEZ, 416 U.S. 562, 94 S.Ct. 1849, 40 L.Ed.2d 380 (1974). The Court proceeded on the premise, as had the lower federal courts, that the Attorney General had personally approved the application for a court order, but the application and hence, the court order as well, incorrectly identified Assistant Attorney General Wilson as the authorizing official. Thus the Justice Department violated the "identification requirement" of § 2518(1)(a) (each appli-

a. The failure of the Attorney General properly to authorize wiretap applications involved 60 cases and over 600 defendants. The failure to identify the Attorney General as the authorizing official when he had in fact authorized the applications, discussed in *Chavez,* infra, involved an additional 99 cases and over 800 defendants.

b. The Court was unanimous that the authorization by the Attorney General's Executive Assistant violated § 2516(1) and that the statutory remedy is suppression of all evidence obtained under such an order, but there were four dissents from the Court's conclusion that evidence obtained under extension orders also had to be suppressed.

cation "shall include [the] identity of [the] officer authorizing the application") and, because of the misinformation supplied the court, the wiretap order violated § 2518(4)(d) (interception orders "shall specify [the identity of the official] authorizing the application"). But a 5–4 majority, per WHITE, J., held that Title III did not require suppression under the circumstances.

"[I]t cannot be seriously contended that had the Attorney General been identified as the person authorizing the application, rather than his subordinate [the] district judge would have had any greater hesitation in issuing the interception order. The same could not be said, of course, if as in *Giordano,* the correct information had revealed that none of the individuals in whom Congress reposed the responsibility for authorizing interception applications had satisfied this preliminary step. * * *

"Though we rejected, in *Giordano,* the Government's claim that Congress intended 'unlawfully intercepted' communications to mean only those intercepted in violation of constitutional requirements, we did not go so far as to suggest that every failure to comply fully with any requirement provided in Title III would render the interception ['unlawful.'] [The identification requirements] do not establish a substantive role to be played in the regulatory system. Nor is there any legislative history concerning these sections [suggesting] that they were meant, by themselves, to occupy a central, or even functional role, in guarding against unwarranted use of wiretapping or electronic surveillance."

Dissenting Justice DOUGLAS, joined by Brennan, Stewart, and Marshall, JJ., protested that Title III does not authorize "the courts to pick and choose among various statutory provisions, suppressing evidence only when they determine that a provision is 'substantive,' 'central,' or 'directly and substantially' related to the Congressional scheme." Moreover, maintained the dissenters, the requirements of §§ 2518(1)(a) and (4)(d) *do* "significantly implement the congressional intention to limit the use of electronic surveillance procedures":

"[The] personal responsibility and political accountability, relied on by Congress to check the reckless use of electronic surveillance, is rendered a mere chimera when the official actually authorizing a wiretap application is not identified until years after the tap has occurred, when he might already be out of office, when the usefulness of the tap is already established, when it is clear that the surveillance was not abusive, and then only through voluntary admissions or the sifting of potentially contradictory affidavits. Responsibility is hardly 'focused,' and the 'lines of responsibility' are gossamer at best. This is why Congress added the demand that responsibility be immediately *fixed.*"[c]

Notes and Questions

1. Did the Court uncritically assume that Attorney General Mitchell had actually authorized the *Chavez* application, rather than merely having designated Assistant Attorney General Wilson to perform this function? In any event, why did the Court give virtually no weight to the apparently intentional nature of the violation? See Pulaski, *Authorizing Wiretap Applications under Title III: Another Dissent to Giordano and Chavez,* 123 U.Pa.L.Rev. 750, 789–802 (1975). The author voices concern, id. at 818–21, that "the lower courts will accept the Supreme Court's invitation 'to pick and choose' among the different provisions of Title III, suppressing evidence in some cases and refusing suppression in others"—thus "further weaken[ing] the ability of the statute to

c. See also *United States v. Donovan,* p. 446 infra, concluding that neither violation of the "naming" provision nor violation of the "inventory notice" provision required suppression of the evidence.

protect individual privacy in the manner Congress intended."

2. The "centrality test" established in *Giordano* and applied in *Chavez*, observes Carr, *The Law of Electronic Surveillance* 355 (1977), amounts to acceptance of the "harmless error concept proposed by a 1968 draft of the American Bar Association's *Standards Relating to Electronic Surveillance* but discarded prior to final adoption." But, maintains Goldsmith at 82, "a sound basis existed for applying a harmless error analysis to electronic surveillance litigation—albeit a basis not recognized by the Supreme Court in *Giordano* and *Chavez*. Although Title III was intended to be exclusive with regard to electronic surveillance, it did not restrict the independent operation of the federal harmless error statute [28 USC § 2111]." However, adds Goldsmith, id. at 84, the harmless error statute "was not mentioned, and no explicit consideration was given to questions of prejudice and willfulness, both factors which should normally be important in determining whether substantial rights have been violated."

C. WHAT CONSTITUTES A FAILURE TO COMPLY WITH THE "NAMING" AND "INVENTORY NOTICE" PROVISIONS OF TITLE III? DOES A VIOLATION OF THESE PROVISIONS REQUIRE SUPPRESSION?

UNITED STATES v. KAHN, 415 U.S. 143, 94 S.Ct. 977, 39 L.Ed.2d 225 (1974), grew out of the following facts: A federal judge approved an application to intercept wire communications of Irving Kahn "and others as yet unknown," in order to obtain information about gambling offenses. The order authorized FBI agents to "intercept wire communications of Irving Kahn and others as yet unknown" to and from two named telephones. When subsequently indicted for gambling offenses along with her husband, *Mrs.* Kahn moved to suppress all conversations between her and her husband and between her and a third party on the ground they were outside the scope of the wiretap order. The motion was granted and affirmed by the Seventh Circuit, which held that all intercepted conversations had to satisfy two requirements under the wiretap order: "(1) that Irving Kahn be a party to the conversations, and (2) that his conversations intercepted be with 'others as yet unknown.'" The court then construed the statutory requirements that the person whose communications are to be intercepted be identified, "if known," [a] as excluding from the term "others as yet unknown" any persons, such as Mrs. Kahn, "whom careful investigation by the government would disclose were probably using the Kahn telephones in conversations for illegal activities." The Supreme Court reversed, Justice STEWART observing for a 6–3 majority:

"In effect, the Court of Appeals read [the provisions quoted in fn. c requiring identity of the person] as if they required that the application and order identify 'all persons, known or discoverable, who are committing the offense and whose communications are to be intercepted.' But that is simply not what the statute says: identification is required only of those 'known' to be 'committing the offense.' * * *

"Moreover, the Court of Appeals' interpretation of § 2518 would have a broad impact. A requirement that the Government fully investigate the possibility that any likely user of a telephone was engaging in criminal activities before applying for an interception order would greatly subvert the effectiveness of the law enforcement mechanism that Congress constructed. * * * [T]he statute as actually drafted contains no intimation of such total investigative demands.

a. Title III provides that each application for a court order shall, inter alia, include "the identity of the person, if known, committing the offense and whose communications are to be intercepted," § 2518(1)(b)(iv); and that each order authorizing interception shall specify, inter alia, "the identity of the person, if known, whose communications are to be intercepted," § 2518(4)(a).

"* * * Since it is undisputed that the Government had no reason to suspect [Mrs.] Kahn of complicity in the gambling business before the wire interceptions here began, it follows that under the statute she was among the class of persons 'as yet unknown' covered by [the wiretap] order."

Nor could the Court read either the actual language of the wiretap order or the underlying provisions of Title III as limiting the admissibility of the intercepted conversations to those to which Irving Kahn himself was a party. "The order does not refer to conversations *between* Irving Kahn and others; rather, it describes 'communications *of* Irving Kahn and others as yet unknown' to and from the target telephones." As for Title III, "the clear implication" of the statutory language quoted in fn. a that the person be identified only "if known" is that "when there is probable cause to believe that a particular telephone is being used to commit an offense but no particular person is identifiable, a wire interception order may, nevertheless, properly issue under the statute. It necessarily follows that Congress could not have intended that the authority to intercept must be limited to those conversations *between* a party named in the order and others, since at least in some cases, the order might not name any specific party at all."

In the course of his dissent, Justice DOUGLAS, joined by Brennan and Marshall, JJ., maintained:

"In light of the prejudice against general warrants which I believe Congress shared, I would not allow Mrs. Kahn's conversations to be impliedly covered by the warrant, for to do so allows a search of the entire list of outgoing and incoming calls to the Kahn telephones, even though no showing of probable cause has been made concerning any member of the household other than Mr. Kahn. I cannot believe that Congress sanctioned that practice. * * *

"Under today's decision a wiretap warrant apparently need specify but one name and a national dragnet becomes operative. Members of the family of the suspect, visitors in his home, doctors, ministers, merchants, teachers, attorneys, and everyone having any possible connection with the Kahn household are caught up in this web."

UNITED STATES v. DONOVAN, 429 U.S. 413, 97 S.Ct. 658, 50 L.Ed.2d 652 (1977), per POWELL, J., concluded that the government had failed to comply with two provisions of Title III—the "naming" [§ 2518 (1)(b)(iv)] and postintercept "inventory notice" [§ 2518(8)(d)] requirements—but went on to hold that neither violation required suppression of the evidence.

Rejecting the contention that the "naming" provision required the government to name only the interception's "principal target" (usually the person whose phone is monitored), the Court ruled that the provision required the government to name *all* individuals who it has probable cause to believe are engaged in the criminal activity under investigation and whose conversations it expects will be intercepted over the target phone. But the failure to satisfy this provision did not warrant suppression. For the identification of all those likely to be overheard in incriminating statements does not play "a 'substantive role' with respect to judicial authorization of intercept orders":

"Here, [the] statutorily imposed preconditions to judicial authorization were satisfied, and the issuing judge was simply unaware that additional persons might be overheard engaging in incriminating conversations. In no meaningful sense can it be said that the presence of that information as to additional targets would have precluded judicial authorization of the intercept. Rather, this case resembles *Chavez* * * *. The *Chavez* intercept was lawful because the Justice Department had performed its task of prior approval, and the instant intercept is lawful because the application provided sufficient information to enable the issuing judge to determine that the statutory preconditions were satisfied. * * * [N]othing in the legislative history suggests that Congress intended this broad identification requirement to play 'a central, or even functional, role in guarding against unwarranted use [of] electronic surveillance.' *Chavez.*"

The Court reached the same conclusion with respect to the government's failure to satisfy the "inventory notice" requirement, providing that the issuing judge shall cause an "inventory" to be served "on the persons named in the order or the application, and such other parties to intercepted communications as the judge may determine in his discretion that is in the interest of justice." Since two defendants had not, and need not have, been named in the application and order, inventory notice to them was discretionary. The Court agreed, however, that the government had violated their Title III rights by failing to provide the judge with sufficient information with which to exercise inventory notice discretion. But the Court deemed the inventory requirement peripheral to the statutory scheme:

"Nothing in the structure of the Act or [its] legislative history suggests that incriminating statements are 'unlawfully intercepted' [within the meaning of the suppression provision, § 2518(10)(a)] whenever parties to those conversations do not receive discretionary inventory notice as a result of the Government's failure to inform the District Court of their identities. At the time inventory notice was served on the other identifiable persons, the intercept had been completed and the conversations had been 'seized' under a valid intercept order. The fact that discretionary notice reached 39 rather than 41 identifiable persons does not in itself mean that the conversations were unlawfully intercepted. * * * [W]e do not think that postintercept notice was intended to serve as an independent restraint on resort to the wiretap procedure."

MARSHALL, J., joined by Brennan and Stevens, JJ., dissented in part, agreeing that the "naming" and "inventory notice" requirements had been violated, but maintaining that these requirements played a "substantive" or "central" role in the congressional scheme:

"The Court ignores the [naming] requirement's function as a statutory 'trigger'. * * * Section 2518(1)(e) requires that the Government disclose to the court the history of all prior applications to intercept the communications of anyone named in a warrant application. A history of recent applications would at least cause a judge to consider whether the application before him was an attempt to circumvent the restrictive rulings of another judge or to continue an unjustified invasion of privacy. The decision whether to issue the warrant would certainly be affected by such consideration. * * *

"Moreover, even where there is no prior interception or application to disclose, as is apparently the case here, the naming requirement plays a vital role in the system designed by Congress. For unless that requirement is complied with from the first interception, no judge will know that a later interception is not the first. In addition, the naming requirement triggers the mandatory notification provision of [the postintercept inventory notice requirement], another important component of the congressional design. * * *

"[The Court also] takes too narrow a view of the ['inventory notice' provision], ignoring its place in the [congressional system.] That system involves not only direct restraints on applying for a warrant, but also restraints which reduce wiretaps by providing sanctions for misuse of surveillance techniques. * * * Congress designed the ['inventory notice' provision] to provide the information necessary to make the civil sanctions of [Title III] meaningful."

"Together," concludes Goldsmith at 97, *Kahn* and *Donovan* "reduced the identification requirement from a constitutional precept to an insignificant statutory chore. Ironically, the *Donovan* Court once again called for strict enforcement of the statute, and for the first time intimated that intentional violations would be treated more severely. Despite this, just a year later, in *Scott v. United States* [immediately below] the Court would decline to suppress even for purposeful misconduct."

D. "MINIMIZ[ING] THE INTERCEPTION OF COMMUNICATIONS NOT OTHERWISE SUBJECT TO INTERCEPTION"; WHAT WEIGHT, IF ANY, SHOULD BE GIVEN TO THE OFFICER'S UNDERLYING INTENT OR MOTIVATION?

One of the limiting provisions of Title III is found in § 2518(5), requiring every order to contain a provision that the authorization to intercept "be conducted in such a way as to minimize the interception of communications not otherwise subject to interception." In SCOTT v. UNITED STATES, 436 U.S. 128, 98 S.Ct. 1717, 56 L.Ed.2d 168 (1978), pursuant to a court wiretap order requiring "minimization," government agents intercepted for a one-month period virtually all conversations over a particular telephone suspected of being used in furtherance of a conspiracy to import and distribute narcotics. Only forty percent of the conversations were shown to be narcotics related and the Special Agent who conducted the wiretap testified that "he and the agents working under him knew of the minimization requirement but made no attempt to comply therewith." Rejecting petitioners' argument that the failure to make good-faith efforts to comply with the minimization requirement is itself a violation of § 2518(5), a 7–2 majority per REHNQUIST, J., agreed with the Court of Appeals that an evaluation of compliance with the minimization requirement, like evaluation of all alleged violations of the Fourth Amendment, should "be based on the reasonableness of the actual interceptions and not on whether the agents subjectively intended to minimize their interceptions." Observed the Court:

"The Government [contends] that petitioners' argument fails to properly distinguish between what is necessary to establish a statutory or constitutional violation and what is necessary to support a suppression remedy once a violation has been established. In view of the deterrent purposes of the exclusionary rule, consideration of official motives may play some part in determining whether application of the exclusionary rule is appropriate *after* a statutory or constitutional violation has been established. But the existence *vel non* of such a violation turns on an objective assessment of the officer's actions in light of the facts and circumstances confronting him at the time. Subjective intent alone, the Government contends, does not make otherwise lawful conduct illegal or unconstitutional.

"We think the Government's position, which also served as the basis for decision in the Court of Appeals, embodies the proper approach for evaluating compliance with the minimization requirement. [A]lmost without exception in evaluating alleged violations of the Fourth Amendment the Court has first undertaken an objective assessment of an officer's actions in light of the facts and circumstances then known to him. The language of the Amendment itself proscribes only 'unreasonable' searches and seizures.

"[Petitioners' argument that, regardless of the search-and-seizure analysis conducted under the Fourth Amendment, the agents' failure to make good-faith efforts at minimization is itself a violation of Title III which requires suppression] fails for more than one reason. In the first place, in the very section in which it directs minimization, Congress, by its use of the word 'conducted,' made it clear that the focus was to be on the agents' actions, not their motives. Any lingering doubt is dispelled by the legislative history [which declares that] § 2515 was not 'intended generally to press the scope of the suppression role beyond present search and seizure law.' " 13

Analyzing the reasonableness of the agents' conduct, the Court observed:

"[B]lind reliance on the percentage of nonpertinent calls intercepted is not a sure guide to the correct answer. Such percentages may provide assistance, but there are surely cases, such as the one at bar, where the percentage of nonpertinent calls is relatively high and yet their interception was still reasonable. The reasons for this may be many. Many of the nonpertinent calls may have been very short. Others may have been one-time only calls. Still others may have been ambiguous in nature or involve guarded or coded language. In all these circumstances agents can hardly be expected to know that their calls are not pertinent prior to their termination.

"[W]hen the investigation is focusing on what is thought to be a widespread conspiracy more extensive surveillance may be justified in an attempt to determine the precise scope of the enterprise. [The] type of use to which the telephone is normally put may also have some bearing on the extent of minimization required. For example, if the agents are permitted to tap a public telephone because one individual is thought to be placing bets over the phone, substantial doubts as to minimization may arise if the agents listen to every call which goes out over that phone regardless of who places the call. On the other hand, if the phone is located [as in the case at bar] in the residence of a person who is thought to be the head of a major drug ring, a contrary conclusion may be indicated.

"Other factors may also play a significant part in a particular case. For example, it may be important to determine at exactly what point during the authorized period the interception was made. During the early stages of surveillance the agents may be forced to intercept all calls to establish categories of nonpertinent calls which will not be intercepted thereafter.

"[W]e find nothing to persuade us that the Court of Appeals was wrong in its rejection of [the minimization] claims. Forty percent of the calls were clearly narcotics related * * *. Many of the remaining calls were very short, such as wrong number calls [and] calls to persons who were not available to come to the phone. [In] a case such as this, involving a wide-ranging conspiracy with a large number of participants, even a seasoned listener would have been hard pressed to determine with any precision the relevancy of many of the calls before they were completed. A large number were ambiguous in nature, making characterization virtually impossible until the completion of these calls. And some of the non-pertinent conversations were one-time conversations. Since these calls did not give the agents an opportunity to develop a category of innocent calls which should not have been intercepted, their interception cannot be viewed as a violation of the minimization requirement.

"We are thus left with the seven calls between [petitioner] Jenkins and her

13. This is not to say, of course, that the question of motive plays absolutely no part in the suppression inquiry. On occasion, the motive with which the officer conducts an illegal search may have some relevance in determining the propriety of applying the exclusionary rule. * * * This focus on intent, however, becomes relevant only after it has been determined that the Constitution was in fact violated. We also have little doubt that as a practical matter the judge's assessment of the motives of the officers may occasionally influence his judgment regarding the credibility of the officers' claims with respect to what information was or was not available to them at the time of the incident in question. But the assessment and use of motive in this limited manner is irrelevant to our analysis of the questions at issue in this case.

mother. [After pointing out that most of the calls were intercepted at the beginning of the surveillance and that several indicated that the mother may have known of the conspiracy, the Court concluded that] [a]lthough none of these conversations turned out to be material to the investigation at hand, we cannot say that the Court of Appeals was incorrect in concluding that the agents did not act unreasonably at the time they made these interceptions."

Dissenting Justice BRENNAN, joined by Marshall, J., maintained that the Court's reasoning "is thrice flawed":

"First, and perhaps most significant, it totally disregards the explicit congressional command that the wiretap be *conducted* so as to minimize interception of communications not subject to interception. Second, it blinks reality by accepting as a substitute for the good-faith exercise of judgment as to which calls should not be intercepted by the agent most familiar with the investigation, the *post hoc* conjectures of the Government as to how the agent would have acted had he exercised his judgment. Because it is difficult to know with any degree of certainty whether a given communication is subject to interception prior to its interception, there necessarily must be a margin of error permitted. But we do not enforce the basic premise of the Act that intrusions of privacy must be kept to the minimum by excusing the failure of the agent to make the good-faith effort to minimize which Congress mandated. In the nature of things it is impossible to know how many fewer interceptions would have occurred had a good-faith judgment been exercised, and it is therefore totally unacceptable to permit the failure to exercise the congressionally imposed duty to be excused by the difficulty in predicting what might have occurred had the duty been exercised. Finally, the Court's holding permits government agents deliberately to flout the duty imposed upon them by Congress. In a linguistic *tour de force* the Court converts the mandatory language that the interception shall be conducted to a precatory suggestion. Nor can the Court justify its disregard of the statute's language by any demonstration that it is necessary to do so to effectuate Congress' purpose as expressed in the legislative history. On the contrary, had the Court been faithful to the congressional purpose, it would have discovered in § 2518(10)(a) and its legislative history the unambiguous congressional purpose to have enforced the several limitations on interception imposed by the statute. Section 2518(10)(a) requires suppression of evidence intercepted in violation of the statute's limitations on interception and the legislative history emphasizes Congress' intent that the exclusionary remedy serve as a deterrent against the violation of those limitations by law enforcement personnel. * * *

"Moreover, today's decision does not take even a sidelong glance at *United States v. Kahn,* whose reasoning it undercuts and which may now require overruling. * * * To support its holding [that naming a person in the application or interception order is required only when the government has probable cause to believe that the person is committing the offense] against the argument that it would, in effect, approve a general warrant, [the *Kahn* Court] relied on the minimization requirement as an adequate safeguard to prevent such unlimited invasions of personal privacy."

Notes and Questions

1. Consider the criticism of *Scott* in Burkoff, *The Court that Devoured the Fourth Amendment: The Triumph of an Inconsistent Exclusionary Doctrine,* 58 Or.L.Rev. 151, 187–88 (1979): "In the fourth amendment exclusionary context, since there is only one effective remedy for violation of fourth amendment rights, the distinction between right and remedy is semantic, not substantive. * * *

"Ironically, the *Scott* Court's use of one test for determining the existence of a fourth amendment violation and a second test for application of an exclusionary remedy appears to have as its casuistic end the exclusion of deterrence from the first test although deterrence is the key element of the second test. After all, law enforcement deterrence is the issue that raises the question of the ill-motivated subjective intent of law enforcement agents; for unintended unlawful acts cannot be deterred, whereas if any unlawful acts can be deterred, consciously undertaken ones can be. Given, however, the objection to distinguishing right from remedy in this context, the real issue is not whether deterrence should be part of the test for one, but not the other; rather, the issue is whether deterrence should be a part of both elements of fourth amendment analysis or neither. Since deterrence is the keystone of the Burger Court exclusionary doctrine, and since the Court indicated in *Scott* that 'the deterrent purposes of the exclusionary rule' dictate that 'consideration of official motives may play some part in determining whether application of the exclusionary rule is appropriate,' then simply as a matter of doctrinal consistency deterrence should be one, if not the primary, element of the test for gauging the existence of fourth amendment violations. On this ground, the *Scott* case was wrongly decided."

2. Compare Burkoff, supra, with LaFave, § 1.2(g) (Supp.1986), taking the view that *Scott* properly rejected the contention that "lack of good faith efforts" required suppression even if no minimization would have been feasible in this case. As a general matter, maintains LaFave, deciding the Fourth Amendment claim, as the *Scott* Court did, by "an objective assessment of an officer's action in the light of the facts and circumstances then known to him," without regard to the officer's underlying intent or motivation, is a sound approach.

3. But consider Goldsmith at 108–09: "[Whatever the rule should be with respect to conventional searches], [g]iven the greater intrusion occasioned by electronic surveillance, [the] fourth amendment's reasonableness clause would seem to require such searches to be undertaken in good faith. Moreover, from a statutory perspective [*Scott*] directly contravened basis Title III principles. Section 2518(5) requires that execution of the order be '*conducted* in such a way as to minimize the interception of [nonpertinent] communications' [emphasis supplied by Goldsmith]. Given the broad deterrent purpose underlying Title III, there is no reason to read the term 'conducted' as excluding subjective intent. * * * [P]rovision for criminal prohibitions in section 2511(1), outlawing willful misconduct, demonstrates that intent was an integral aspect of the overall statutory scheme—indeed by 'willfully' intercepting or 'endeavor[ing]' to intercept in a manner unauthorized by Title III, the agents [in *Scott*] appear to have committed statutory felonies."

Adds Goldsmith (at 109): "Certainly, conformance to a court order should be evaluated in subjective terms. For example, assume that, for the sake of efficiency, surveillance agents decide to put their equipment on 'automatic record,' thereby allowing them to devote their energies to other aspects of the investigation. Even if all the resulting interceptions could be justified subsequently under prevailing minimization standards, would any judge be satisfied that the authorization had been conducted in compliance with his order?"

4. *Should the minimization provision be amended?* Consider Fishman, *The "Minimization" Requirement in Electronic Surveillance: Title III, the Fourth Amendment and the Dread Scott Decision,* 28 Am.U.L.Rev. 315, 354–55 (1979):

"Even before *Scott,* several courts had held that in complex cases, it is reasonable for monitors to intercept every conversation in full until patterns of innocent conversations emerge. Because the practice of initial, total interception tends to become self-perpetuating and self-justifying, the minimization requirement often has received little more than lip service. In concluding that the monitor's good faith or lack thereof is irrelevant in assessing whether the minimization provision has been adhered to, *Scott* suggests that even lip service is no longer necessary.

"* * * A purely objective analysis of reasonableness may be adequate to decide whether an officer was justified in making an isolated arrest, stop, frisk, search or seizure. Such an analysis, however, is wholly inadequate when several weeks of continuous, surreptitious interceptions of otherwise private conversations are at issue. Particularly in complex investigations, where the government, with superficial plausibility can retroactively defend total interception, it is unlikely that any minimization will be achieved unless a good-faith effort is made to do so.

"* * * The minimization provision should be amended to read: 'Every order and extension thereof shall contain a provision that the authorization to intercept * * * shall be conducted in a *good faith and reasonable manner in order to* minimize the interception of communications not otherwise subject to interception under this chapter. * * *'"

E. ELECTRONIC SURVEILLANCE WHICH INVOLVES COVERT ENTRY INTO PRIVATE PREMISES TO INSTALL EQUIPMENT; HAS THE COURT'S STATUTORY PERSPECTIVE UNDERGONE A FUNDAMENTAL CHANGE?

DALIA v. UNITED STATES, 441 U.S. 238, 99 S.Ct. 1682, 60 L.Ed.2d 177 (1979), arose as follows: Finding reasonable cause to believe that petitioner was conspiring to steal goods being shipped in interstate commerce and that his business office was being used by petitioner and others in connection with the alleged conspiracy, a federal district court authorized the interception of all oral communications concerning the conspiracy at petitioner's office. Although the court order did not explicitly authorize entry into petitioner's office, FBI agents secretly entered the office one midnight by prying open a window and spent three hours in the building installing a listening device in the ceiling. All electronic surveillance of petitioner ended some six weeks later, at which time the agents secretly re-entered petitioner's office and removed the bug. Partly on the basis of conversations intercepted pursuant to this order, petitioner was convicted of receiving stolen goods and related charges. The Court, per POWELL, J., upheld the electronic surveillance:

First, "[t]he Fourth Amendment does not prohibit *per se* a covert entry performed for the purpose of installing otherwise legal electronic bugging equipment." *Second,* the Court rejected the contention that, even if it could have constitutionally done so, Congress had not given the courts statutory authority to approve covert entries for electronic surveillance purposes: "In the face of [the legislative history of Title III], one simply cannot assume that Congress, aware that most bugging requires covert entry, nonetheless wished to except surveillance requiring such entries from the broad authorization of Title III, and that it resolved to do so by remaining silent on the subject. On the contrary, the language and history of Title III convey quite a different explanation for Congress' failure to distinguish between surveillance that requires covert entry and that which does not. Those considering the surveillance legislation understood that, by authorizing electronic interception of oral communications in addition to wire communications, they were necessarily authorizing surreptitious entries."

Third, the Court rejected the contention that, because the authorizing court did not explicitly set forth its approval of covert entries, the entry violated petitioner's Fourth Amendment privacy rights: The Warrant Clause of the Fourth Amendment requires only that warrants be issued by "neutral, disinterested magistrates"; that they be based on probable cause to believe that " 'the evidence sought will aid in a particular apprehension or conviction' for a particular offense"; and that they "particularly describe" the things to be seized as well as the place to be searched. Nothing in the language of the Fourth Amendment or the Court's decisions "suggests that, in addition to [these three requirements], search warrants also must include a specification of the precise manner in which they are to be executed. On the contrary, it is generally left to the discretion of the executing officers to determine the details of how best to proceed with the performance of a search authorized by warrant—subject of course to the general Fourth Amendment protection 'against unreasonable searches and seizures.' "

To require, whenever it is reasonably likely that Fourth Amendment rights may be affected in more than one way, that the authorizing court must set forth precisely the procedures to be followed by the executing officers "would extend the warrant clause to the extreme. [W]e would promote empty formalism were we to require magistrates to make explicit what unquestionably is implicit in bugging authorizations: that a covert entry, with its attendant interference with Fourth Amendment interests, may be necessary for the installation of the surveillance equipment."

Dissenting Justice STEVENS, joined by Brennan and Marshall, JJ., thought the majority's conclusion that Title III implicitly authorizes breaking and entering "especially anomalous because the statutory scheme in all other respects is exhaustive and explicit * * * Only one relevant conclusion can be drawn from a review of the entire legislative history of Title III. The legislators never even considered the possibility that they were passing a statute that would authorize federal agents to break into private premises without any finding of necessity by a neutral and detached magistrate. * * *

"Because it is not supported by either the text of the statute or the scraps of relevant legislative history, I fear that the Court's holding may reflect an unarticulated presumption that national police officers have the power to carry out a surveillance order by whatever means may be necessary unless explicitly prohibited by the statute or by the Constitution.

"But surely the presumption should run the other way. Congressional silence should not be construed to authorize the Executive to violate state criminal laws or to encroach upon constitutionally protected privacy interests. Before confronting the serious constitutional issues raised by the Court's reading of Title III, we should insist upon an unambiguous statement by Congress that this sort of police conduct may be authorized by a court and that a specific showing of necessity, or at least probable cause, must precede such authorization. Without a legislative mandate that is both explicit and specific, I would presume that this flagrant invasion of the citizen's privacy is prohibited."

In a separate opinion, concurring in part and dissenting in part, Justice BRENNAN, joined by Stewart, J., maintained that "even reading Title III to authorize covert entries, the Justice Department's present practice of securing specific authorization for covert entries is not only preferable, but also constitutionally required":

"Breaking and entering into private premises for the purpose of planting a bug cannot be characterized as a mere mode of warrant execution to be left to the discretion of the executing officer. The practice entails an invasion of privacy of constitutional significance distinct from that which attends nontrespassory surveillance; indeed, it is tantamount to an independent search and seizure. First, rooms may be bugged without the need for surreptitious entry and physical invasion of private premises. Second, covert entry, a practice condemned long before we condemned unwarranted eavesdropping, breaches physical as well as conversational privacy. Third, the practice is particularly intrusive and susceptible to abuse since it leaves naked to the hands and eyes of government agents items beyond the reach of simple eavesdropping.

"Because of these additional intrusions attendant to covert entries, the Constitution requires that government agents who wish to break into private premises first secure specific judicial authorization for the surreptitious entry. Authority for the physical invasion cannot be derived from a Title III order authorizing only electronic surveillance.

"[A] warrant that describes only the seizure of conversations cannot be read expansively to authorize constitutionally distinct physical invasions of privacy at the discretion of the executing officer. Rather, the Constitution demands that the necessity for home invasion be decided 'by a neutral and detached magistrate instead of being judged by the officer engaged in the often competitive enterprise of ferreting out crimes.'

"[Since] premises may be bugged through means less drastic than home invasion, requiring police to secure prior approval for covert entries may well prevent unnecessary and improper intrusions."

Notes and Questions

1. Consider Note, 67 Geo.L.J. 1429, 1446 (1979): "The [*Dalia*] Court's failure to require separate authorization for [entry into private premises] violates the spirit of Title III, which was designed to create a series of procedures to safeguard individual privacy. It is reasonable to assume that a Congress which put the judge so squarely between the public and the police in matters of electronic surveillance would generally wish to extend that concept to the specifics of entry. In the Foreign Intelligence Surveillance Act [FISA] of 1978, * * * Congress provided that applications for eavesdropping orders must state the anticipated means of entry, including a statement whether physical entry is required. Furthermore, the electronic surveillance order itself must specify the means of entry and whether physical entry will be used. It thus appears that Congress intended a magistrate to authorize covert entry to eavesdrop on foreign powers. The FISA follows Title III by a decade; comparisons between the two acts should not be overdrawn. Nevertheless, it is difficult to imagine that the Congress intended to provide less protection for United States citizens than for foreign nationals and their agents."

2. Consider, Comment, 70 J.Crim.L. & C. 510, 526–27 (1979): "[The *Dalia* majority's approach] is inconsistent with the overall emphasis of Title III—an emphasis upon minimizing the intrusiveness of an intercept order. According to sections 2518(1)(c), and 2518(3)(c), electronic surveillance is 'not to be routinely employed as the initial step in a criminal investigation.' Additionally, such methods are not to be 'resorted to in situations where traditional investigative techniques would suffice to expose the crime.' As such, the application must contain a complete statement as to why normal investigative procedures are not being used. * * *

"By construing the statutory language—or the absence thereof—so as to require that breaking and entering be employed only when alternative means have been tried and have failed or else reasonably appear too unlikely to succeed if tried, the Supreme Court would merely have been extending the express requirement of sections 2518(1)(c) and 2518(3)(c). Moreover, such a position would have substantially minimized the potential for abuse, the threat to personal security, and the invasion of personal privacy [posed by covert entries]. Only when efforts to minimize the intrusion have proven unacceptable would breaking and entering to plant listening devices be authorized." [a]

3. "In all likelihood," observes Goldsmith at 116–18, the [*Dalia*] majority's pragmatic analysis more closely reflected congressional intent; * * * it is inconceivable that, after years of debate, Congress would have failed to realize that most bugs necessitate covert entries. * * * Nevertheless, as enacted the statute contained a potential defect which had to be remedied. Ultimately, in *Dalia,* judicial process was used to rectify this legislative interstice. "Hence, the true significance of *Dalia* lay not in the Court's holding that Title III conferred authority to effect covert entries, but in the manner in which this decision was made. * * * *Dalia* abandoned the mode of analysis adopted in *District Court* to remedy what Congress might otherwise have made explicit. In the process, the Court's statutory perspective seems to have undergone a fundamental change; although Title III had been designed to constitute a blanket prohibition against electronic surveillance, subject to narrowly tailored statutory exceptions, Justice Powell's analysis now suggested that the law conferred a general grant of authority subject to narrowly tailored prohibitions. Thus, analytically and perhaps philosophically, *Dalia* symbolized the extent to which the Supreme Court had changed direction since 1968 when Title III was enacted."

a. See also Notes, 57 B.U.L.Rev. 587 (1977); 47 Ford.L.Rev. 203 (1978).

SECTION 4. THE USE OF SECRET AGENTS (WITH AND WITHOUT ELECTRONIC DEVICES) TO OBTAIN INCRIMINATING STATEMENTS

In LOPEZ v. UNITED STATES, 373 U.S. 427, 83 S.Ct. 1381, 10 L.Ed.2d 462 (1963), petitioner made an unsolicited bribe offer to Davis, an IRS agent, who, following his superiors' instructions to "pretend to play along with the scheme," met petitioner in the latter's office and recorded his subsequent bribe offers by means of a concealed wire recorder. Relying heavily on *On Lee v. United States* [a] and *Rathbun v. United States,* [b] the Court, per HARLAN, J., rejected the argument that considering the agent's falsification of his mission, he gained access to Lopez's office by misrepresentation and consequently illegally "seized" Lopez's words:

"[T]his case involves no 'eavesdropping' whatever in any proper sense of that term. The Government did not use an electronic

a. In *On Lee,* 343 U.S. 747, 72 S.Ct. 967, 96 L.Ed. 1270 (1952), Chin Poy, an old acquaintance and former employee of defendant, entered the latter's laundry and engaged him in conversation, in the course of which defendant made incriminating statements. Unknown to defendant, Chin Poy was a "wired for sound" secret government agent, and the microphone concealed on his person transmitted all sounds to a narcotics agent stationed outside. Chin Poy was not called to testify about defendant's incriminating statements—probably because "the very defects of character and blemishes of record which [led defendant to confide in him] would make a jury distrust his testimony"—but the narcotics agent was allowed to relate the conversations he overheard. A 5–4 majority, per Jackson, J., rejected the claim that Chin Poy had committed a trespass because consent to enter defendant's laundry was obtained by fraud. And the Court dismissed as "verging on the frivolous" the further contention that the agent stationed outside the laundry was "a trespasser" because, by virtue of the microphone concealed on Chin Poy, he overheard what went on inside. "It would be a dubious service to the genuine liberties protected by the Fourth Amendment," observed the Court, "to make them bedfellows with spurious liberties improvised by farfetched analogies which would liken eavesdropping on a conversation, with the connivance of one of the parties, to an unreasonable search and seizure."

b. In *Rathbun,* 355 U.S. 107, 78 S.Ct. 161, 2 L.Ed.2d 134 (1957), the Court held, per Warren, C.J., that the overhearing of a conversation on a regularly used telephone extension with the consent of one party to the conversation was not a violation of § 605 of the Federal Communications Act: "Each party to a telephone conversation takes the risk that the other party may have an extension telephone and may allow another to overhear the conversation. When such takes place there has been no violation of any privacy of which the parties may complain. Consequently, one element of Section 605, *interception,* has not occurred." See generally Hodgson, *United States v. Rathbun: A Fourteen Year Critique,* 13 U.S.A.F.J.A.G.L.Rev. 224 (1971).

device to listen in on conversations it could not otherwise have heard. Instead, the device was used only to obtain the most reliable evidence possible of a conversation in which the Government's own agent was a participant and which that agent was fully entitled to disclose. And the device was not planted by means of an unlawful physical invasion of petitioner's premises under circumstances which would violate the Fourth Amendment. It was carried in and out by an agent who was there with petitioner's assent, and it neither saw nor heard more than the agent himself. * * *

"Stripped to its essentials, petitioner's argument amounts to saying that he has a constitutional right to rely on possible flaws in the agent's memory, or to challenge the agent's credibility without being beset by corroborating evidence that is not susceptible of impeachment. For no other argument can justify excluding an accurate version of a conversation that the agent could testify to from memory. We think the risk that petitioner took in offering a bribe to Davis fairly included the risk that the offer would be accurately reproduced in court, whether by faultless memory or mechanical recording."

Chief Justice WARREN concurred separately, agreeing with the *Lopez* dissenters that *On Lee* was wrongly decided, but finding *On Lee* and the instant case "quite dissimilar constitutionally":

"The only purpose the recording served [in the instant case] was to protect the credibility of [Agent] Davis against that of a man who wished to corrupt a public servant in the performance of his public trust. I find nothing unfair in this procedure. * * *

The use and purpose of the transmitter in *On Lee* was substantially different from the use of the recorder here. Its advantage was not to corroborate the testimony of Chin Poy, but rather, to obviate the need to put him on the stand. * * Had Chin Poy been available for cross-examination, [the defense could have explored] the possibility of entrapments, police pressure brought to bear to persuade Chin Poy to turn informer, and Chin Poy's own recollection of the contents of the conversation. His testimony might not only have seriously discredited the prosecution, but might also have raised questions of constitutional proportions."

Justice BRENNAN, joined by Douglas and Goldberg, JJ., dissented, finding *On Lee* indistinguishable from the instant case and maintaining that the evidence should have been excluded in both cases:

"[Not] all communications are privileged. On Lee assumed the risk that his acquaintance would divulge their conversation; Lopez assumed the same risk *vis-à-vis* Davis. The risk inheres in all communications which are not in the sight of the law privileged. It is not an undue risk to ask persons to assume, for it does no more than compel them to use discretion in choosing their auditors, to make damaging disclosures only to persons whose character and motives may be trusted. But the risk which both *On Lee* and today's decision impose is of a different order. It is the risk that third parties, whether mechanical auditors like the Minifon or human transcribers of mechanical transmissions as in *On Lee*—third parties who cannot be shut out of a conversation as conventional eavesdroppers can be, merely by a lowering of voices, or withdrawing to a private place—may give independent evidence of any conversation. There is only one way to guard against such a risk, and that is to keep one's mouth shut on all occasions. * * *

"[The Government argues that] 'if the agent's relatively innocuous conduct here is found offensive, *a fortiori,* the whole gamut of investigatorial techniques involving more serious deception must also be condemned. Police officers could then no longer employ confidential informants, act as undercover agents, or even wear "plain clothes."' But this argument misses the point. It is not Agent Davis' deception that offends constitutional principles, but his use of an electronic device to probe and record words spoken in the privacy of a man's office. For there is a qualitative difference between electronic surveillance, [and] conventional police stratagems such as eavesdropping and disguise. The latter do not so seriously intrude upon the right of privacy. The risk of being overheard by an eavesdropper or betrayed by an informer or deceived as to the identity of one with whom one deals is probably inherent in the conditions of human society. It is the kind of risk we necessarily assume whenever we speak. But as soon as electronic surveillance comes into play, the risk changes crucially. There is no security from that kind of eavesdropping, no way of mitigating the risk, and so not even a residuum of true privacy.

"Furthermore, the fact that the police traditionally engage in some rather disreputable practices of law enforcement is no argument for their extension. Eavesdropping was indictable at common law and most of us would still agree that it is an unsavory practice. The limitations of human hearing, however, diminish its potentiality for harm. Electronic aids add a wholly new dimension to eavesdropping. They make it more penetrating, more indiscriminate, more truly obnoxious to a free society. Electronic surveillance, in fact, makes the police omniscient; and police omniscience is one of the most effective tools of tyranny."

Notes and Questions

1. If conversations are within the protection of the Fourth Amendment, why should it matter whether the conversation was "seized" by an electronic device? Was the police practice involved in *On Lee* any dirtier business than it would have been had the defendant's old acquaintance simply elicited the incriminating admissions and then testified? Why does the fact that On Lee would have been better able to attack the acquaintance's credibility than he was to challenge that of the narcotics bureau agent make the original deceit more moral? See Greenawalt, *The Consent Problem in Wiretapping and Eavesdropping,* 68 Colum.L.Rev. 189, 193 (1968); Kitch, *Katz v. United States: The Limits of the Fourth Amendment,* 1968 Supreme Court Rev. 133, 141–42.

2. Is the issue not whether secret agents and informers can be monitored, but whether a warrant is necessary for such monitoring? To what extent is Justice Brennan's position based on the premise that "the warrant procedure can be adapted to electronic surveillance of specific persons at specific places for a limited period of time," but—inasmuch as informers and secret agents "must be developed or placed over a long period of time and the objectives of their 'search' will almost always be broad and impossible to delineate with any precision in advance"—the Fourth Amendment warrant requirement would "prevent altogether the use of informers and secret agents"? See Kitch, supra, at 142.

3. In considering whether participant monitoring should be controlled or prohibited, how significant are the following factors: the relationship between the parties, e.g., monitoring by a relative or close friend vs. monitoring by a government official; who has initiated the subject of the conversation; "offensive" monitoring vs. "defensive" monitoring; the place of conversation, e.g., a person's own home or office vs. a restaurant; the amount and nature of the material likely to be monitored; monitoring of phone conversations vs. monitoring in person? See Greenawalt, Note 1 supra at 223–25.

In LEWIS v. UNITED STATES, 385 U.S. 206, 87 S.Ct. 424, 17 L.Ed.2d 312 (1966), decided the same day as *Hoffa,* infra, a federal narcotics agent, by misrepresenting his identity as "Jimmy the Pollack [sic]" and expressing a willingness to purchase narcotics, was invited into petitioner's home where an unlawful narcotics transaction took place. At petitioner's trial, the agent testified as to what occurred in petitioner's home and the narcotics were introduced. Petitioner relied on *Gouled v. United States,* 255 U.S. 298, 41 S.Ct. 261, 65 L.Ed. 647 (1921) (other aspects of which are discussed at p. 252 supra), which excluded incriminating documents obtained when, acting under federal officers' orders, a business acquaintance of defendant obtained entry into defendant's office by pretending that he intended only to pay a social visit, but in defendant's absence searched the office. A unanimous Court held: [W]hether entrance to the home or office of a [suspect] be obtained by a [government agent] by stealth or through social acquaintance, or in the guise of a business call, and whether the owner be present or not when he enters, any search and seizure subsequently and secretly made in his absence falls within the scope of the prohibition of the Fourth Amendment * * * "

Distinguishing *Gouled,* the Court, per WARREN, C.J., stressed that "in the instant case [the] petitioner invited the undercover agent to his home for the specific purpose of executing a felonious sale of narcotics. * * * During neither of his visits to petitioner's home did the agent see, hear, or take anything that was not contemplated and in fact intended by petitioner as a necessary part of his illegal business. Were we to hold the deceptions of the agent in this case constitutionally prohibited, we would come near to a rule that the use of undercover agents in any manner is virtually unconstitutional per se.[a] [W]hen, as here, the home is converted into a commercial center to which outsiders are invited for purposes of transacting unlawful business, that business is entitled to no greater sanctity than if it were carried on in a store, a garage, a car or on the street. [This case has been well summarized by the Government as follows:] '[T]he only statements repeated were those that were willingly made to the agent and the only things taken were the packets of marihuana voluntarily transferred to him. The pretense resulted in no breach of privacy; it merely encouraged the suspect to say things which he was willing and anxious to say to anyone who would be interested in purchasing marihuana.' "[b]

Why didn't the *Lewis* Court dismiss petitioner's argument out of hand with a citation to *Lopez?* Why instead, in a case in which no electronic device was used, did the Court assume, without any reference either to *On Lee* or *Lopez,* that the use of a secret agent raised a serious Fourth Amendment problem. See Kitch, *Katz v.*

a. Consider Rotenberg, *The Police Detection Practice of Encouragement: Lewis v. United States and Beyond,* 4 Houston L.Rev. 609, 614 (1967): "To say that public encouragement [the author defines 'encouragement' as the activity of police or their agents acting in the capacity of 'victims' and communicating this feigned willingness to be a victim to the suspect, see p. 476 infra] is proper, but private encouragement is not, is to tell narcotics sellers to 'move indoors.' [Where] the *modus operandi* of the criminal includes both public and private places, the encouraging officer, if he is to complete the encouragement detection, has no choice except to enter the defendant's private quarters. Observations of the practices of prostitutes show that some of them operate out of hotel rooms or private residences using the telephone to make appointments. If a policeman is to detect the prostitute's commission of a solicitation he must, playing the role of a client, enter her private room or residence and encourage her. It follows that, if the narcotics seller were, in effect, told to 'move indoors,' he would. Copying the homosexual [in a jurisdiction where only public solicitation by a homosexual is criminal] and prostitute, he would use the telephone to set up sales, or would roam the streets locating buyers and then retreat into privacy before making the outlawed sale. The [*Lewis*] Court obviously appreciated the inseparable relationship of public and private encouragement."

As Professor Rotenberg has observed, id. at 612, "the practice [of police encouragement], although not the label," was before the Court in *Lewis,* but what significance, if any, the case has for police encouragement and the defense of entrapment is unclear for, as the Court noted, "petitioner does not argue that he was entrapped, as he could not on the facts of this case." See generally Ch. 7, infra.

b. Only Justice Douglas dissented. See p. 460 infra.

United States: The Limits of the Fourth Amendment, 1968 Supreme Court Rev. 133, 143–45.

James Hoffa was convicted for endeavoring to bribe members of a jury, during the so-called Test Fleet trial, which ended in a hung jury. A substantial element in the government's proof was the testimony of one Partin, a local union official. After being released from jail where he had been held pending state and federal charges, Partin had made frequent visits to the Hoffa hotel suite, on which occasions he was continually in the company of Hoffa and his associates. Proceeding upon the premise that Partin was a "governmental informer" from the time he first arrived on the scene in the Test Fleet and that the government had compensated him for his services as such, the Court nevertheless affirmed the conviction, HOFFA v. UNITED STATES, 385 U.S. 293, 87 S.Ct. 408, 17 L.Ed.2d 374 (1966),[a] in an opinion by Justice STEWART:

"The argument is that Partin's failure to disclose his role as a government informer vitiated the consent that the petitioner gave to Partin's repeated entries into [Hoffa's hotel] suite, and that by listening to the petitioner's statements Partin conducted an illegal 'search' for verbal evidence. [Where] the argument falls is in its misapprehension of the fundamental nature and scope of Fourth Amendment protection. What the Fourth Amendment protects is the security a man relies upon when he places himself or his property within a constitutionally protected area, be it his home or his office, his hotel room or his automobile.[b] * * *

"In the present case, however, it is evident that no interest legitimately protected by the Fourth Amendment is involved. [Partin] was in the suite by invitation, and every conversation which he heard was either directed to him or knowingly carried on in his presence. The petitioner, in a word, was not relying on the security of the hotel room; he was relying upon his misplaced confidence that Partin would not reveal his wrongdoing. * * * Neither this Court nor any member of it has ever expressed the view that the Fourth Amendment protects a wrongdoer's misplaced belief that a person to whom he voluntarily confides his wrongdoing will not reveal it. Indeed, the Court unanimously rejected that very contention less than four years ago in *Lopez.* [The] Court was divided [on the admissibility of the surreptitious recording]. But there was no dissent from the view that testimony about the conversation by Davis himself was clearly admissible. [In] the words of the dissenting opinion in *Lopez,* 'the risk of being overheard by an eavesdropper or betrayed by an informer or deceived to the identity of one with whom one deals is probably inherent in the conditions of human society. It is the kind of risk we necessarily assume whenever we speak.' "[c]

Chief Justice WARREN dissented, deeming it unnecessary to reach the fourth amendment and other constitutional questions "for the affront to the quality and fairness of federal law which this case presents is sufficient to require an exercise of our supervisory powers":

"Here, Edward Partin, a jailbird languishing in a Louisiana jail under indictments for such state and federal crimes as embezzlement, kidnapping, and man-

a. *Hoffa* was decided the same day as *Lewis* and *Osborn* (p. 428 supra), where, on the basis of a tape recorded meeting between defendant and his "employee" (a secret government agent), one of Hoffa's lawyers was convicted of attempting to bribe a juror.

b. But compare the same Justice's analysis for the Court a year later in *Katz,* p. 237 supra.

c. Note well that at the time the meetings at which Partin was present occurred Hoffa had not been indicted for bribing a juror nor had judicial proceedings otherwise commenced against him with respect to this crime. If they had, Hoffa would have had the benefit of the *Massiah* doctrine. Cf. *United States v. Henry,* p. 633 infra.

slaughter (and soon to be charged with perjury and assault), contacted federal authorities and told them he was willing to become, and would be useful as, an informer against Hoffa who was then about to be tried in the Test Fleet case. A motive for his doing this is immediately apparent—namely, his strong desire to work his way out of jail and out of his various legal entanglements with the State and Federal Governments. And it is interesting to note that, if this was his motive, he has been uniquely successful in satisfying it. In the four years since he first volunteered to be an informer against Hoffa he has not been prosecuted on any of the serious federal charges for which he was at that time jailed, and the state charges have apparently vanished into thin air. * * *

"This type of informer and the uses to which he was put in this case evidence a serious potential for undermining the integrity of the truth-finding process in the federal courts. Given the incentives and background of Partin, no conviction should be allowed to stand when based heavily on his testimony. And that is exactly the quicksand upon which these convictions rest * * *.

I do not say that the Government may never use as a witness a person of dubious or even bad character. In performing its duty to prosecute crime the Government must take the witnesses as it finds them. [But here] the Government reaches into the jailhouse to employ a man who was himself facing indictments far more serious (and later including one for perjury) than the one confronting the man against whom he offered to inform. It employed him not for the purpose of testifying to something that had already happened, but rather for the purpose of infiltration to see if crimes would in the future be committed. * * * Certainly if a criminal defendant insinuated his informer into the prosecution's camp in this manner he would be guilty of obstructing justice. * * *"

Justice Clark, joined by Justice Douglas, would have dismissed the writs of certiorari as improvidently granted for the reason that the district court's finding that the government did *not* "place" Partin in the defendant's midst could not be regarded "clearly erroneous." However, in the companion case of *Osborn,* fn. a supra, Justice DOUGLAS, the lone dissenter in that case, made it plain that if he had been satisfied in *Hoffa* that the government had "placed" Partin in Hoffa's councils he would have voted to reverse the conviction: "[A] person may take the risk that a friend will turn on him and report to the police. But that is far different from the Government's 'planting' a friend in a person's entourage so that he can secure incriminating evidence. In the one case the Government has merely been the willing recipient of information supplied by a fickle friend. In the other, the Government has actively encouraged and participated in a breach of privacy by sending in an undercover agent. [T]he Government unlawfully enters a man's home when its agent crawls through a window, breaks down a door, enters surreptitiously, or, as alleged here, gets in by trickery and fraud." d

d. Justices Fortas and White took no part in the case.

Notes and Questions

1. Had Hoffa opened his hotel suite for the conduct of any business? Did any specificity of purpose or duration limit Partin's presence there? Why "while so carefully limiting its holding in *Lewis,*" did the Court "at the same time approve the extensive intrusion in *Hoffa* without even acknowledging the substantial differences in the breadth of the searches involved in the two cases"? See *The Supreme Court, 1966 Term,* 81 Harv.L.Rev. 69, 192–93 (1967).

2. Was Hoffa, as the majority put it, "relying upon his misplaced confidence that Partin would not reveal his wrongdoing" or also on the assumption that the government would not attempt to spy on him in the privacy of his hotel room? Was Partin a friend who later "revealed wrongdoing" or was he working for the government at the very time Hoffa spoke? Must people take the risk that their "friends" or associates are "government agents," i.e., have been "planted" by the government or have already promised to report whatever they see or hear to the government? See Kitch, *Katz v. United States: The Limits of the Fourth Amendment,* 1968 Supreme Court, Rev. 133, 151–52; Note, 76 Yale L.J. 994, 1009–13 (1967).

If so, then why does one using the phone not "assume the risk" that the police will be tapping the wire? And why does one using the mails not assume that the police will be reading his letters? Are these other risks small only because the Court has made them so? Should the inquiry be not whether a person has "assumed the risk," but what risks of governmental intrusion citizens of a free society *should have to assume?* Is the view that one "assumes the risk" that the friend in whom he confides is a "government agent" anything more than a conclusion that the probability of accomplishing some social good by such a tactic outweighs the invasion of privacy and therefore the risk is tolerable in a free society? See Notes, 37 Geo.Wash.L.Rev. 634, 655–58 (1969); 81 Harv.L.Rev. 69, 193–94 (1967); cf. Greenawalt, *The Consent Problem in Wiretapping and Eavesdropping,* 68 Colum.L.Rev. 189, 221–25 (1968); Josephson, *Book Review,* 15 U.C.L.A.L.Rev. 1586, 1597–98 (1968). See also Harlan, J., dissenting in *United States v. White,* p. 466 infra.

3. Consider Note, 76 Yale L.J. 994, 1010 (1967):

"Though rejected by the Court in Lopez, Brennan's dichotomy between bugging and secret agents became in *Hoffa* the basis of the Court's decision that secret agents do not threaten privacy enough to merit Fourth Amendment limitation. But it is difficult to accept, at least without explanation, [this reasoning]. Consider, for example, the likely reactions of the citizenry if asked to rank the offensiveness of three practices:

"(1) the police will be allowed to search your home, without force during daylight hours;

"(2) the police will be allowed to offer your friends very strong inducements to report to them any illegal activities on your part;

"(3) the police will be allowed to employ agents, who may be strangers, business associates or friends, to invite or encourage you to take part in a criminal venture.

"The clear state of the constitutional law after *Hoffa* and its companion cases is that (1) represents an invasion of privacy abhorrent to the American way of life, but (2) and (3) are quite proper. The average citizen would hardly agree."

Does an undercover agent's participation in a pretrial meeting between defendant and his lawyer constitute a *per se* violation of defendant's right to the effective assistance of counsel with respect to the pending criminal action? If not, under what circumstances does such governmental activity fatally taint the trial? Consider WEATHERFORD v. BURSEY, 429 U.S. 545, 97 S.Ct. 837, 51 L.Ed.2d 30 (1977): Bursey and Weatherford (a state undercover agent) vandalized a selective service office. Weatherford reported the incident to the police, but in order to maintain his undercover status and his usefulness on other current matters in that capacity, he was arrested and charged along with Bursey. Both were released on bond and retained separate attorneys. Then, at the request of Bursey's attorney, who sought Weatherford's presence in order to discuss his client's defense, Weatherford attended two pretrial meetings with Bursey and his attorney. Weatherford had no discussions either with his superiors or the prosecution concerning anything said at the attorney-client meetings. Although Weatherford had not expected to be a witness at the trial, and had so told Bursey, on the day of the trial (because Weatherford had been seen in the company of police officers shortly before and his effectiveness as an undercover agent thus impaired), the prosecution decided to call him as a witness.[a] Weatherford's testimony related only to events prior to the meetings with Bursey and his lawyer and did not refer to anything said at these meetings. Nor was there any evidence that any of Weatherford's testimony was the product of anything said at these meetings. Bursey was convicted. After he had served his sentence, he brought an action against Weatherford under 42 U.S.C. § 1983, alleging that the latter's participation in the pretrial meetings had deprived him of the effective assistance of counsel as well as his right to a fair trial. The Court, per WHITE, J., held that Bursey's constitutional rights were not violated and that the right to counsel establishes no *per se* rule forbidding an undercover agent to meet with a defendant's counsel:

"[The argument that Weatherford, a dutiful agent, surely communicated Bursey's defense plans and strategy to the prosecution] founders on the District Court's express finding that [he did not]. The Court of Appeals did not disturb this finding, but sought to surmount it by declaring Weatherford himself to have been a member of the prosecuting team. [But] this reasoning is not a realistic assessment of the relationship of Weatherford to the prosecuting staff or of the potential for detriment to Bursey or benefit to the Government that Weatherford's uncommunicated knowledge might pose. If the fact was, [as found], that Weatherford communicated nothing about the two meetings to anyone else, we are quite unconvinced that a constitutional claim under the Sixth and Fourteenth Amendments was made out.

"[As] long as the information possessed by Weatherford remained uncommunicated, he posed no substantial threat to Bursey's Sixth Amendment rights. Nor do we believe [that] prosecutors will be so prone to lie or the difficulties of proof so great that we must always assume not only that an informant communicates what he learns from an encounter with the defendant and his counsel but also that what he communicates has the potential for detriment or benefit to the prosecutor's case.

"Moreover, [Weatherford went to the attorney-client meeting], not to spy, but because he was asked and because the State was interested in retaining his undercover services on other matters and it was therefore necessary to avoid raising the suspicion that he was in fact the informant whose existence [was] already suspected.

"That [a *per se* rule] would operate prophylactically and effectively is very likely true; but it would require the informant to refuse to participate in attorney-client meetings, even though invited, and thus for all practical purposes to unmask himself. Our cases, however, have recognized the unfortunate necessity of undercover work and the value it often is to effective law enforcement. * * *

"There being no tainted evidence in this case, no communication of defense strategy to the prosecution, and no purposeful intrusion by Weatherford, there was no violation of the Sixth Amendment insofar as it is applicable to the States by virtue of the Fourteenth Amendment. The proof in this case thus fell short of making out a § 1983 claim * * *."

Justice MARSHALL, joined by Brennan, J., dissented, unable to "join in providing

a. Bursey's contention that the government was constitutionally forbidden to conceal Weatherford's identity from him during his trial preparation and to permit Weatherford to "deny" that he would testify against him is treated in Ch. 21, § 5.

even the narrowest of openings to the practice of spying upon attorney-client communications." After stressing that "two independent constitutional values" are "jeopardized" by governmental intrusions into private attorney-client communications—"the integrity of the adversary system and the fairness of trials" and the defendant's "right to the effective assistance of counsel"—the dissent continued:

"[E]ven if I could agree that unintended and undisclosed interceptions by government witness-employers [violate no constitutional rights], I still could not join in upholding the practice. For [the] precious constitutional rights at stake here, like other constitutional rights, need 'breathing space to survive' and a prophylactic prohibition on all intrusions of this sort is therefore essential. A rule that offers defendants relief only when they can prove 'intent' or 'disclosure' is, I fear, little better than no rule at all. Establishing [an intent or desire to spy] will seldom be possible, since the State can always argue plausibly that its sole purpose was to continue to enjoy the legitimate services of the undercover agent. Proving that an informer reported to the prosecution on defense strategy will be equally difficult, not only because such proof requires an informer or prosecutor to admit his own wrongdoing (and open the door to damage suits and attacks on convictions), but also because an informer's failure to make a report after overhearing a lawyer-client session often-times can be an effective means of communicating to the prosecutor that nothing surprising was uncovered. Given these problems of proof, the only way to assure that defendants will feel free to communicate candidly with their lawyers is to prohibit the government from intercepting such confidential communications, at least absent a compelling justification for doing so."[5]

UNITED STATES v. WHITE

401 U.S. 745, 91 S.Ct. 1122, 28 L.Ed.2d 453 (1971).

[On numerous occasions a government informer, carrying a concealed radio transmitter, engaged defendant in conversations which were electronically overheard by federal narcotics agents. The conversations in a restaurant, defendant's home and in the informer's car were overheard by the use of radio equipment. A number of conversations in the informer's home were not only electronically overheard by an agent stationed outside the house but by another agent who, with the informer's consent, concealed himself in the latter's kitchen closet.[a] At no time did the agents obtain a warrant or court order. The informer was not produced at the trial, but the testimony of the "eavesdropping" agents was admitted and led to defendant's conviction of narcotics violations. The U.S. Court of Appeals for the Seventh Circuit read *Katz* as overruling *On Lee* and interpreted the Fourth Amendment as prohibiting testimony about the electronically overheard statements.]

MR. JUSTICE WHITE announced the judgment of the Court and an opinion in which THE CHIEF JUSTICE, MR. JUSTICE STEWART, and MR. JUSTICE BLACKMUN join. * * *

Hoffa, which was left undisturbed by *Katz,* held that however strongly a defendant may trust an apparent colleague, his expectations in this respect are not protected by the Fourth Amendment when it turns out that the colleague is a govern-

5. There is no evidence in this record that Weatherford's life would have been jeopardized or any ongoing investigations compromised had Weatherford given up his cover [after] the crime was committed, rather than [after] trial began. To the contrary, the fact that Weatherford felt no need for police protection after trial, suggests that there was no danger at any time. And [Weatherford's chief] conceded that Weatherford was not working on "anything particular" between the time of the crime and the time of the trial. Indeed the Chief admitted that he "wasn't concerned" about losing Weatherford's cover because after breaking the case "his identity was going to be known anyway." * * *

a. No testimony by this agent was offered at trial. See Note 6 following this case.

ment agent regularly communicating with the authorities. * * *

Conceding that *Hoffa, Lewis,* and *Lopez* remained unaffected by *Katz,* the Court of Appeals nevertheless read both *Katz* and the Fourth Amendment to require a different result if the agent not only records his conversations with the defendant but instantaneously transmits them electronically to other agents equipped with radio receivers. * * *

To reach this result it was necessary for the Court of Appeals to hold that *On Lee* was no longer good law. In that case, which involved facts very similar to the case before us, the Court first rejected claims of a Fourth Amendment violation because the informer had not trespassed when he entered the defendant's premises and conversed with him. To this extent the Court's rationale cannot survive *Katz.* But the Court announced a second and independent ground for its decision; for it went on to say that overruling *Olmstead* and *Goldman* [which the Court subsequently did in *Katz*] would be of no aid to On Lee since he "was talking confidentially and indiscreetly with one he trusted, and he was overheard. * * *" We see no indication in *Katz* that the Court meant to disturb that understanding of the Fourth Amendment or to disturb the result reached in the *On Lee* case, nor are we now inclined to overturn this view of the Fourth Amendment.

Concededly a police agent who conceals his police connections may write down for official use his conversations with a defendant and testify concerning them, without a warrant authorizing his encounters with the defendant and without otherwise violating the latter's Fourth Amendment rights. *Hoffa.* For constitutional purposes, no different result is required if the agent instead of immediately reporting and transcribing his conversations with defendant, either (1) simultaneously records them with electronic equipment which he is carrying on his person, *Lopez;* (2) or carries radio equipment which simultaneously transmits the conversations either to recording equipment located elsewhere or to other agents monitoring the transmitting frequency. *On Lee.* If the conduct and revelations of an agent operating without electronic equipment do not invade the defendant's constitutionally justifiable expectations of privacy, neither does a simultaneous recording of the same conversations made by the agent or by others from transmissions received from the agent to whom the defendant is talking and whose trustworthiness the defendant necessarily risks.

Our problem is not what the privacy expectations of particular defendants in particular situations may be or the extent to which they may in fact have relied on the discretion of their companions. Very probably, individual defendants neither know nor suspect that their colleagues have gone or will go to the police or are carrying recorders or transmitters. Otherwise, conversation would cease and our problem with these encounters would be nonexistent or far different from those now before us. Our problem, in terms of the principles announced in *Katz,* is what expectations of privacy are constitutionally "justifiable"—what expectations the Fourth Amendment will protect in the absence of a warrant. So far, the law permits the frustration of actual expectations of privacy by permitting authorities to use the testimony of those associates who for one reason or another have determined to turn to the police, as well as by authorizing the use of informants in the manner exemplified by *Hoffa* and *Lewis.* If the law gives no protection to the wrongdoer whose trusted accomplice is or becomes a police agent, neither should it protect him when that same agent has recorded or transmitted the conversations which are later offered in evidence to prove the State's case.

Inescapably, one contemplating illegal activities must realize and risk that his companions may be reporting to the police. If he sufficiently doubts their trustworthiness, the association will very probably end or never materialize. But if he has no doubts, or allays them, or risks what doubt he has, the risk is his. In terms of what his course will be, what he will or will not do or say, we are unpersuaded that he would distinguish between probable informers on the one hand and probable informers with transmitters on the other. * * *

[It is] untenable to consider the activities and reports of the police agent himself, though acting without a warrant, to be a "reasonable" investigative effort and lawful under the Fourth Amendment but to view the same agent with a recorder or transmitter as conducting an "unreasonable" and unconstitutional search and seizure. Our opinion is currently shared by Congress and the Executive Branch, Title III, Omnibus Crime Control and Safe Streets Act of 1968, and the American Bar Association. Standards, *Electronic Surveillance* § 4.1 (1971). * * *

No different result should obtain where, as in *On Lee* and the instant case, the informer disappears and is unavailable at trial; for the issue of whether specified events on a certain day violate the Fourth Amendment should not be determined by what later happens to the informer. * * * Judgment of Court of Appeals reversed.[b]

MR. JUSTICE DOUGLAS, dissenting.

The issue in this case is clouded and concealed by the very discussion of it in legalistic terms. What the ancients knew as "eavesdropping," we now call "electronic surveillance"; but to equate the two is to treat man's first gunpowder on the same level as the nuclear bomb. Electronic surveillance is the greatest leveler of human privacy ever known. How most forms of it can be held "reasonable" within the meaning of the Fourth Amendment is a mystery. [The] concepts of privacy which the Founders enshrined in the Fourth Amendment vanish completely when we slavishly allow an all-powerful government, proclaiming law and order, efficiency, and other benign purposes, to penetrate all the walls and doors which men need to shield them from the pressures of a turbulent life around them and give them the health and strength to carry on. * * *

On Lee and *Lopez* are of a vintage opposed to *Berger* and *Katz*. However they may be explained, they are products of the old common-law notions of trespass. *Katz*, on the other hand, emphasized that with few exceptions "searches conducted outside the judicial process, without prior approval by judge or magistrate, are *per se* unreasonable under the Fourth Amendment. * * *"

Monitoring, if prevalent, certainly kills free discourse and spontaneous utterances. Free discourse—a First Amendment value—may be frivolous or serious, humble or defiant, reactionary or revolutionary, profane or in good taste; but it is not free if there is surveillance. Free discourse liberates the spirit, though it may produce only froth. The individual must keep some facts concerning his thoughts within a small zone of people. At the same time he must be free to pour out his woes or inspirations or dreams to others. He remains the sole judge as to what must be said and what must remain unspoken. This is the essence of the idea of privacy

b. The plurality opinion also upheld the admissibility of the evidence of defendant's incriminating statements on another ground: the events in question took place long prior to *Katz* and *Desist v. United States*, p. 51 supra, had held that *Katz* applied only to those electronic surveillances which occurred subsequent to the date of that decision. Justice Brennan, whose concurring opinion is summarized infra, concurred in the result, agreeing that *Desist* required affirmance, but differing on the issue of the continued viability of *On Lee*. Justice Black concurred in the result for the reasons set forth in his *Katz* dissent, but adhered to his view that *Katz* should be applied retroactively. Dissenting Justices Douglas, Harlan and Marshall would apply *Katz* retroactively and viewed it as overruling *On Lee*.

implicit in the First and Fifth Amendments as well as in the Fourth. * * *

MR. JUSTICE HARLAN, dissenting. * * *

The plurality opinion seeks to erase the crucial distinction between the facts before us and [the holdings in *Lopez, Lewis* and *Hoffa*] by the following reasoning: if A can relay verbally what is revealed to him by B (as in *Lewis* and *Hoffa*), or record and later divulge it (as in *Lopez*), what difference does it make if A conspires with another to betray B by contemporaneously transmitting to the other all that is said? The contention is, in essence, an argument that the distinction between third-party monitoring and *other* undercover techniques is one of form and not substance. The force of the contention depends on the evaluation of two separable but intertwined assumptions: first, that there is no greater invasion of privacy in the third-party situation, and, second, that uncontrolled consensual surveillance in an electronic age is a tolerable technique of law enforcement, given the values and goals of our political system.

The first of these assumptions takes as a point of departure the so-called "risk analysis" approach of *Lewis,* and *Lopez,* and to a lesser extent *On Lee,* or the expectations approach of *Katz.* While these formulations represent an advance over the unsophisticated trespass analysis of the common law, they too have their limitations and can, ultimately, lead to the substitution of words for analysis. The analysis must, in my view, transcend the search for subjective expectations or legal attribution of assumptions of risk. Our expectations, and the risks we assume, are in large part reflections of laws that translate into rules the customs and values of the past and present.

Since it is the task of the law to form and project, as well as mirror and reflect, we should not, as judges, merely recite the expectations and risks without examining the desirability of saddling them upon society. The critical question, therefore, is whether under our system of government, as reflected in the Constitution, we should impose on our citizens the risks of the electronic listener or observer without at least the protection of a warrant requirement.

This question must, in my view, be answered by assessing the nature of a particular practice and the likely extent of its impact on the individual's sense of security balanced against the utility of the conduct as a technique of law enforcement. For those more extensive intrusions that significantly jeopardize the sense of security which is the paramount concern of Fourth Amendment liberties, I am of the view that more than self-restraint by law enforcement officials is required and at the least warrants should be necessary.

The impact of the practice of third-party bugging, must, I think, be considered such as to undermine that confidence and sense of security in dealing with one another that is characteristic of individual relationships between citizens in a free society. It goes beyond the impact on privacy occasioned by the ordinary type of "informer" investigation upheld in *Lewis* and *Hoffa.* The argument of the plurality opinion, to the effect that it is irrelevant whether secrets are revealed by the mere tattletale or the transistor, ignores the differences occasioned by third-party monitoring and recording which insures full and accurate disclosure of all that is said, free of the possibility of error and oversight that inheres in human reporting.

Authority is hardly required to support the proposition that words would be measured a good deal more carefully and communication inhibited if one suspected his conversations were being transmitted and transcribed. Were third-party bugging a prevalent practice, it might well smother that spontaneity—reflected in frivolous, impetuous, sacrilegious, and defiant discourse—that liberates daily life. Much offhand exchange is easily forgotten and one may count on the obscurity of his remarks, protected by the very fact of a limited audience, and the likelihood that the listener will either overlook or forget what is said, as well as the listener's inability to reformulate a conversation without having to contend with a documented record. All these values are sacrificed by a rule of law that permits official monitoring of private discourse limited only by the need to locate a willing assistant. * * *

[I]t is too easy to forget—and, hence, too often forgotten—that the issue here is whether to interpose a search warrant procedure between law enforcement agencies engaging in electronic eavesdropping and the public generally. By casting its "risk analysis" solely in terms of the expectations and risks that "wrongdoers" or "one contemplating illegal activities" ought to bear, the plurality opinion, I think, misses the mark entirely. *On Lee* does not simply mandate that criminals must daily run the risk of unknown eavesdroppers prying into their private affairs; it subjects each and every law-abiding member of society to that risk. The very purpose of interposing the Fourth Amendment warrant requirement is to redistribute the privacy risks throughout society in a way that produces the results the plurality opinion ascribes to the *On Lee* rule. Abolition of *On Lee* would not end electronic eavesdropping. It would prevent public officials from engaging in that practice unless they first had probable cause to suspect an individual of involvement in illegal activities and had tested their version of the facts before a detached judicial officer. The interest *On Lee* fails to protect is the expectation of the ordinary citizen, who has never engaged in illegal conduct in his life, that he may carry on his private discourse freely, openly, and spontaneously without measuring his every word against the connotations it might carry when instantaneously heard by others unknown to him and unfamiliar with his situation or analyzed in a cold, formal record played days, months, or years after the conversation. Interposition of a warrant requirement is designed not to shield "wrongdoers," but to secure a measure of privacy and a sense of personal security throughout our society.

The Fourth Amendment does, of course, leave room for the employment of modern technology in criminal law enforcement, but in the stream of current developments in Fourth Amendment law I think it must be held that third-party electronic monitoring, subject only to the self-restraint of law enforcement officals, has no place in our society.

I reach these conclusions notwithstanding seemingly contrary views espoused by both Congress and an American Bar Association study group. Both the ABA study and Title III appear to reflect little more than this Court's prior decisions. * * * While individual Congressmen expressed concern about and criticized the provisions for unsupervised consensual electronic surveillance contained in § 2511, the Senate Committee Report comment, to the effect that "[i]t [§ 2511(2)(c)] largely reflects existing law," followed by citations to *On Lee* and *Lopez*, strongly suggests that the provisions represent not intractable approval of these practices, but rather an intention to adopt these holdings and to leave to the courts the task of determining their viability in light of later holdings such as *Berger*, *Osborn*, and *Katz*.

I find in neither the ABA study nor Title III any justification for ignoring the identifiable difference—albeit an elusive one in the present state of knowledge—between the impact on privacy of single-party informer bugging and third-party bugging, which in my opinion justifies drawing the constitutional line at this juncture between the two as regards the necessity for obtaining a warrant. Recognition of this difference is, at the very least, necessary to preserve the openness which is at the core of our traditions and is secure only in a society that tolerates official invasion of privacy simply in circumscribed situations. * * *

MR. JUSTICE MARSHALL, dissenting.

I am convinced that the correct view of the Fourth Amendment in the area of electronic surveillance is one that brings the safeguards of the warrant requirement to bear on the investigatory activity involved in this case. In this regard I agree with the dissents of Mr. Justice DOUGLAS and Mr. Justice HARLAN. In short, I believe that *On Lee* cannot be considered viable in light of the constitutional principles articulated in *Katz* and other cases.

* * *

[JUSTICE BRENNAN concurred in the result, agreeing that *Katz* should not be applied retroactively but emphasizing that on the issue of the viability of *On Lee*, neither the dissenters' views nor Justice White's "commands the support of a majority of the Court."[c] He would "go further" than the dissenters; their reasoning "compels the conclusion" that *Lopez*, as well as *On Lee*, is "no longer sound law. [C]urrent Fourth Amendment jurisprudence interposes a warrant requirement not only in cases of third-party electronic monitoring (the situation in *On Lee* and in this case) but also in cases of electronic recording by a government agent of a face-to-face conversation with a criminal suspect, which was the situation in *Lopez*." As he viewed it, *Katz* had adopted the "doctrinal basis" of his *Lopez* dissent and that meant that both *On Lee* and *Lopez*, which presented "rationally indistinguishable" situations,[d] should now be regarded as overruled.[e]]

Notes and Questions

1. After *White*, what, if anything, is left of anyone's "justifiable reliance" on the privacy of his conversation (*Katz*)? Did *Katz* mean that a citizen must adjust his expectations of privacy to new laws and electronic techniques or that these new laws and techniques should conform to present expectations? Did *Katz* mean, or should it be read as meaning, that the individual only "assumes the risk" that he objectively perceives and no more? That *reasonable* reliance on the privacy of one's conversation suffices to invoke the protection of the Fourth Amendment? See Note, 52 B.U.L.Rev. 831, 838–44 (1972).

Didn't defendant White take reasonable steps to protect against governmental intrusion by choosing the locations he did for his private conversations? Didn't federal agents employ an informer and conceal a radio transmitter on his person for the very reason that they anticipated defendant White would make reasonable efforts to avoid being overheard? Does the *White* plurality opinion mean the privacy of one's conversation is unprotected if one can anticipate *any* risk that his words might be disclosed to third parties? If so, how does the Fourth Amendment protect the privacy of one's conversations unless one *completely stops* communicating to others? See Note, 85 Harv.L.Rev. 250, 254 (1971). See also Hufstedler, J., dissenting in *Holmes v. Burr*, 486 F.2d 55, 61, 71–76 (9th Cir.1973).

2. Did the *White* plurality opinion refuse to recognize normal expectations of privacy because to do so would restrict a

c. Aren't there "five votes" in *White* sustaining *On Lee?* Recall that the "fifth Justice," Black, concurred in the *White* result for the reasons advanced in his *Katz* dissent, where he viewed Fourth Amendment protection of privacy as extending only to "unreasonable searches and seizures of 'persons, houses, papers and effects.'" Recall, too, Justice Black's *Berger* dissent, where he could not read the Fourth Amendment as applying to "the spoken word" as well as "tangible things." Justice Black did dissent in *On Lee*—solely on the ground that the Court should reject the evidence in the exercise of its supervisory authority over federal criminal justice. Why didn't he make that argument in *White?*

d. Did they? Consider Note 5 following this case.

e. On the government's duty to retain tapes of conversations for the defense's use in *White*-type situations, see *United States v. Bryant*, Ch. 20, § 2.

"normal" police stratagem? Is the "reasonableness" of privacy expectations to be measured by how the average person views a given situation or by whether affording Fourth Amendment protection would "unreasonably" impede the police? See 52 B.U.L.Rev. at 838; Note, Harv.L. Rev. 63, 192–93 (1968).

3. Are the privacy interests subordinated to the government's use of electronic surveillance in *White* distinguishable from those subordinated to the government's use of informers in *Hoffa*? Why should assuming the risk that the listener will disclose the substance of one's conversations to third parties "trigger" the risks of being electronically overheard? Why should an individual be viewed as giving a government informer "a proxy on his privacy," including the right to record or broadcast his conversation? Why must there be an "all-or-nothing" approach when expectations that privacy will be maintained may differ significantly according to the investigative technique being used? See 52 B.U.L.Rev. at 842–44; 85 Harv.L.Rev. at 254.

4. The *White* plurality opinion observes that "the law gives no protection to the wrongdoer whose trusted accomplice [*unequipped* with an electronic device] *is* or *becomes* a police agent." (Emphasis added.) Should the law distinguish between (1) a "trusted accomplice" who, absent prior arrangements with the police, *subsequently* supplies them with evidence; and (2) a "trusted accomplice" who was a "police agent" all along, who was "planted" by the government to secure incriminating evidence? Reconsider Chief Justice Warren's dissenting opinion in *Hoffa*, p. 459 supra; and Justice Douglas' dissenting opinion in *Osborn* and *Lewis*, p. 460 supra.

Might the *White* dissenters have read *Katz* more broadly than they did? Might they have argued, alternatively, that if, as the *White* plurality opinion maintains, "the difference between the electronically equipped [governmental 'plant'] and the unequipped [governmental 'plant'] is [not] substantial enough to require discrete constitutional recognition," then *Katz* should be read as overruling *Hoffa* as well as *On Lee*? May it be said of *Hoffa* that the government's use of a "trusted friend," to whom defendant had always been loyal and helpful, to secure evidence against defendant "violated the privacy upon which he justifiably relied [and] thus constituted a 'search and seizure'" (*Katz*)? Compare Kitch, *Katz v. United States: The Limits of the Fourth Amendment*, 1968 Sup. Ct.Rev. 133, 150 with Note, 52 B.U.L. Rev. 831, 84–41 (1972).

5. Wasn't the *Hoffa* defendant's reliance on the privacy of his conversations more "justifiable" or "reasonable" than the *Lopez* defendant's because Hoffa, like defendants On Lee and White, was dealing with a *secret* agent, but Lopez was trying to corrupt a *known* government agent? Shouldn't Lopez have reasonably calculated that the agent he was attempting to bribe would report the attempt to his superiors? Shouldn't one, such as Lopez, who willfully invites direct government participation in his criminal fraud assume the risk of being electronically overheard or be deemed to have "waived" all expectations of privacy with respect to his scheme? See 52 B.U.L.Rev. at 844–45.

6. Both the Seventh Circuit and Supreme Court opinions in *White* dealt only with the use of *electronically* overheard conversations because only such evidence was offered at trial. If the *White* dissenters had prevailed, would their reasoning also have led to the exclusion of the testimony of the narcotics agent (not equipped with an electronic device) who had overheard defendant's conversations from his hiding place in the informer's kitchen closet? Why (not)?

In *Marshall v. Barlow's* (p. 400 supra), the government maintained that the pervasiveness of state and national safety regulations refuted the view that an employer can have a "realistic privacy interest" in employee work areas. Rejecting this argument, the Court, per White, J., observed:

"Employees are not prohibited from reporting OSHA violations. What they observe in their daily functions is undoubtedly beyond the employer's reasonable expectation of privacy. The Government inspector, however, is not an employee. Without a warrant he stands in no better position than a member of the public. [That] an employee is free to report, and the Government is free to use, any evidence of noncompliance with OSHA that the employee observes furnishes no justification for federal agents to enter a place of business from which the public is restricted and to conduct their own warrantless search."

Does *Barlow's* raise serious questions and renewed doubts about the validity of *White, Hoffa* and other cases dealing with participant monitoring? Consider Grano, infra:

JOSEPH D. GRANO—PERPLEXING QUESTIONS ABOUT THREE BASIC FOURTH AMENDMENT ISSUES: FOURTH AMENDMENT ACTIVITY, PROBABLE CAUSE AND THE WARRANT REQUIREMENT

69 J.Crim.L. & C. 425, 435–38 (1978).

Participant Monitoring Reconsidered

* * *

The ultimate, difficult question * * * is whether the fourth amendment should speak at all to the issue of participant monitoring. * * * While *Barlow's* states that expectations of privacy must be analyzed vis-á-vis the government, it nowhere provides guidelines for determining what expectations against government are reasonable. In fact, *Barlow's* fails to specify the exact interest or expectation that an unwanted OSHA inspection would violate. On one plausible reading, the unwanted entry upon private property constituted the evil in *Barlow's.* That is, *Barlow's* may be read as holding that one may invite others onto private property without opening the door to government. Under this limited reading, expectations of privacy would be defined vis-á-vis government when property interests are at stake, but in the context of informational privacy, voluntary disclosure to others would be tantamount to relinquishment of fourth amendment interests: *Katz* cannot preclude such a "property" reading of *Barlow's,* for *Katz* held only that property concepts do not limit the fourth amendment's ultimate reach, not that property concepts are irrelevant altogether to fourth amendment analysis. Indeed, the fourth amendment must have something to do with property, because it explicitly protects against the unreasonable seizure of things. Moreover, only a property analysis can explain *Alderman v. United States,*[102] which held, two years after *Katz,* that a wiretap of a phone in a defendant's home implicates his fourth amendment interests, even when the tap intrudes upon the conversations of others while the defendant is away.

While thus permissible, a property reading of *Barlow's* would nevertheless render the fourth amendment functionally trivial in that case and at the same time ignore the significance of *Katz.* It seems frivolous to suggest that the employer's only interest in *Barlow's* was in keeping government agents from trespassing upon his premises. Certainly what the employer found offensive was not mere presence, but presence for the purpose of seeking out information. Indeed, the search warrant's function of defining the legitimate scope of an OSHA inspection addresses this very concern. While *Katz* does not dictate this broader reading of *Barlow's,* it clearly supports it. In *Katz,* the uninvited

102. [See p. 778 infra.]

ear intruded upon the privacy of a conversation without trespassing onto property.[103] By applying the fourth amendment to that situation, the Court made clear that informational privacy, as well as property-privacy, is a valid fourth amendment concern.

If *Barlow's* thus stands for the proposition that expectations of informational privacy must be considered vis-á-vis the government, the planted spy becomes a ready subject of fourth amendment interest. Nevertheless, a rejoinder may still be attempted. Conceding that expectations of informational privacy must be defined against government, it may be argued that the case still has not been made for concluding that a presumably innocent person has a justifiable expectation that government will not be planting spies to see what he will voluntarily expose. After all, the difference between the OSHA inspection in *Barlow's* and the spying activity in *Lewis, Hoffa,* [and *White*] is that the defendants in the latter either authorized entry or voluntarily disclosed information. This counter-argument, however, misses the point. Once informational privacy is recognized as an appropriate fourth amendment interest, and once this interest is defined vis-á-vis government, the voluntary disclosure rationale breaks down. By talking to a confidant, the defendant in *White* no more consented to governmental information-gathering than did the defendant in *Barlow's,* who permitted employees to observe his premises. Indeed, if all else fails, the spy hypothetical should make the point. From the view of informational privacy interests against government, one would have a heavy burden explaining why the fourth amendment addresses the inspector's attempt to enter at the front door to gather evidence and yet stands oblivious to the government's undercover entry in the rear for the same purpose.[106]

An obvious tension exists, therefore, between cases like *Barlow's* and *Katz* on the one hand and cases like *Lewis, Hoffa,* and *White* on the other. Barring a reconsideration of the *Katz* doctrine, which now seems basic to fourth amendment law, it is submitted that the latter cases, with the possible exception of *Lewis,*[107] should be overruled. This suggestion should not cause great consternation if it is remembered, as it too often is not, that the issue is whether spying for information is a search under the fourth amendment and not whether a search warrant or full traditional probable cause should be required.

The possible exception for *Lewis* requires explanation. Situations may arise in which government is seeking information

103. The bugging device in *Katz* was outside the phone booth used by the defendant.

106. Cf. Amsterdam, *Perspectives on the Fourth Amendment,* 58 Minn.L.Rev. 349, 365 (1974) ("I can conceive of no rational system of concerns and values that restricts the government's power to rifle my drawers or tap my telephone but not its power to infiltrate my home or my life with a legion of spies."). Amsterdam also suggested that the government's use of spies may be more intrusive than its use of third-party electronic surveillance. Id. at 407–09.

107. * * * Interestingly, Professor Weinreb would overrule *Lewis* but not *White.*

[Professor Weinreb suggests that the Fourth Amendment protects the "privacy of presence" and the "privacy of place." The former refers to privacy interests against government as long as people are in a private place; the latter refers to privacy interests in a place whether or not people are present. Weinreb, *Generalities of the Fourth Amendment,* 42 U.Chi.L.Rev. 47, 69 (1974).

[Comments Grano at fn. 94: This interpretation of the fourth amendment can explain both *Katz* and *White.* The defendant in *Katz* had the privacy of presence while he was using the phone booth, but the defendant in *White,* at least while in the informant's home and in the restaurant, had the privacy of neither presence nor place. Weinreb at 69, fn. 65.

[Continues Grano: "Professor Weinreb's interpretation ties the fourth amendment to property concepts. For example, he sees no fourth amendment issue when an undercover agent buys narcotics from a defendant on the street, but he sees a violation of the privacy of place when, as in *Lewis,* the same agent enters the defendant's home to complete the purchase. Surely, however, the fourth amendment is concerned with more than property-privacy. What *Katz* and the spy cases have in common is a governmental intrusion upon informational privacy in situations where the individual is seeking to make only a limited disclosure."]

and yet an informational privacy interest against government is not justifiable.[109] Not every government quest for evidence or information is, or need be, a subject of fourth amendment interest. For example, undercover fencing operations—popularly known as "sting" operations—should not raise fourth amendment concerns. What distinguishes the deception in such an operation from the deception in *Hoffa?* The answer must be that one, unlike the other, involves no threat to justifiable expectations of informational privacy. The reason for this assertion is the difficult part. As a tentative reason, the implications of which need further study, it is submitted that such operations can only induce individuals to acknowledge guilt or commit a crime. Merely to ask someone to acknowledge wrongdoing (e.g., "Do you have any radios you would like to fence?") or to commit a crime (e.g., "I'll pay you ten dollars for a stolen clock radio.") does not seem to implicate privacy at all. In any event, expectations that government will not engage in such activity hardly seem reasonable or justifiable and thus should not be encompassed within the area of fourth amendment concern.

* * * This is not to say that the guilty do not deserve fourth amendment protection. The question at issue is what kind of police conduct implicates fourth amendment concerns, and once this conduct is identified, the appropriate fourth amendment restraints apply in cases involving the guilty and innocent alike. In taking the first step of defining the activity that constitutes a search it suffices, in a free society, to ask whether the conduct at issue could ever threaten or intrude upon informational privacy expectations unrelated to criminal conduct.[111] The spying in *Hoffa* [and] the inspection [in *Barlow's*] could intrude upon innocent privacy expectations, for not only could the individuals affected have been innocent of wrongdoing, but the police intrusion, by its very nature, had to uncover more than unlawful conduct.[112] The spy in *Hoffa,* for example, necessarily intruded upon both lawful and unlawful conversations.[113]

109. For example, it is not a search for the government deliberately to observe what the defendant discloses to the general public.

111. [T]he proffered rationale for cases like *Lewis* is tentative. * * * For example, suppose the government develops a sensor that detects narcotics but nothing else. Would the use of such a sensor, at airports for example, constitute fourth amendment activity? To the extent the text suggests that this conduct would not be a search because it can only detect unlawful activity, the analysis does not seem satisfactory.

In Kamisar, Grano & Haddad, *Sum and Substance of Criminal Procedure* 122–25 (1977), the thesis is proffered that cases like *Lewis* are based upon the defendant's voluntary decision to disclose his illegal activity to "anyone" interested in participating in it. This thesis would satisfactorily account for Professor Weinreb's concern of a "squad of government agents posing as gas and electric company inspectors" to enter houses. See note 114 infra. The difficulty, however, is that defendants in cases like *Lewis* are not willing to make disclosures to the general public but only to those segments of the public willing to engage in the illegal enterprise. The same, of course, could be said for the defendant in *White.* If cases like *White* and *Lewis* are to be distinguished, therefore, as this article suggests they should, the rationale set forth in the cited book also seems incomplete.

112. The hypothesis suggested in the text provides a rationale for the statement by Professor Kitch that a burglar cannot complain about governmental monitoring of the burglarized house without the owner's consent. Kitch, *Katz v. United States: The Limits of the Fourth Amendment,* 1968 Sup.Ct.Rev. 133, 136. With respect to the burglar, such monitoring, like a "sting" operation, could not intrude upon any privacy expectations concerning lawful activity. But see note 111 supra.

Professor Kitch's hypothetical, however, really raises a question of standing, not one of fourth amendment activity. Secret monitoring poses a threat to legitimate informational privacy interests and thus is a search, but without either a property interest or a justifiable privacy interest, the burglar lacks standing to raise the issue.

113. Similarly, it would be a search for an undercover agent to give a defendant a television with a hidden radio transmitter in exchange for a delivery of narcotics. Although the transmitter would be imposed on an obviously guilty person, it, like the spy in *Hoffa,* would intrude upon conversations of both the defendant and third parties having nothing to do with wrongdoing. It bears emphasis that the hypothesis in the text

The proffered hypothesis, then, is that the fourth amendment's concern for the security of persons is exceeded when justifiable expectations of privacy include expectations that relate to nothing more than a propensity for wrongful conduct. A "sting" operation can only uncover a person's propensity to commit crime. Similarly, it would seem that the police conduct in *Lewis,* unlike that in *Hoffa,* did not constitute a threat to any justifiable expectation of privacy. Barring persistent entreaties that smack of entrapment, a simple request for an individual to sell narcotics can only ascertain whether that individual is willing to do so. The request in *Lewis,* unlike the spying in *Hoffa,* posed no threat to justifiable expectations of informational privacy.[114]

It may be hard to draw a line between spying activities that necessarily intrude broadly and indiscriminately upon informational privacy on the one hand and undercover activities or decoy operations that only give an individual an opportunity to acknowledge or commit wrongdoing on the other. Yet not to attempt to draw it, or to draw some other satisfactory line, results in either too little fourth amendment protection, as in *White,* or too much.

does not deny justifiable expectations of privacy to guilty people; rather, the hypothesis suggests that expectations of privacy that relate only to wrongful conduct are not justifiable. Most governmental quests for information necessarily pose a threat to both justifiable and unjustifiable expectations of privacy. Such quests, therefore, would be considered searches under the hypothesis in the text.

Changing the facts somewhat, it should likewise be a search if the agent attached a hidden "beeper"—a tracking device that emits an electronic signal but does not transmit conversation—to the television. Again, it cannot matter that the defendant must be guilty. The information disclosed by a beeper encompasses more than criminal conduct. * * * Of course, it is another thing altogether to suggest that individuals, whether guilty or innocent, cannot have privacy expectations in their comings and goings because such matters are necessarily observable by the general public. The fourth amendment requirements should apply unless the government uses the same means as the general public to observe the defendant.

[Reconsider *Karo,* p. 251 supra; and *Knotts,* p. 251 supra; both decided years after Professor Grano wrote this article.]

114. In arguing that *Lewis* should be overruled, Professor Weinreb posits the hypothetical of a squad of government agents posing as gas and electric company inspectors. Weinreb at 67. The Weinreb hypothetical, however, is clearly distinguishable from *Lewis.* The agent in *Lewis* only provided an opportunity for the defendant to commit a crime; the agents in Professor Weinreb's hypothetical would obviously intrude upon the justifiable privacy expectations of innocent and guilty people alike. For another explanation, see note 111 supra.

Chapter 7

POLICE "ENCOURAGEMENT" AND THE DEFENSE OF ENTRAPMENT

"The mode adopted [to] bring to light the malfeasance of the defendant, had no necessary connection with his violation of law. He exercised his own volition * * *. Even if inducements to commit crime could be assumed to exist in this case, the allegation of the defendant would be but the repetition of the plea as ancient as the world, and first interposed in Paradise: 'The serpent beguiled me and I did eat.' That defence was overruled by the great Lawgiver, and whatever estimate we may form, or whatever judgment pass upon the character or conduct of the tempter, this plea has never since availed to shield crime or give indemnity to the culprit, and it is safe to say that under any code of civilized, not to say christian ethics, it never will."

—Bacon, J., in *Board of Commissioners v. Backus,* 29 How.Pr. 33, 42 (N.Y.Sup. Ct.1864).

"[T]wo deeply seated and widely shared intuitive judgments [explain the creation and survival of the entrapment defense]. The first is that a person is somewhat less culpable if tempted into crime by certain kinds of inducements. The second is that it is extremely dangerous to allow government the power to stress test the morality of ordinary citizens by dangling substantial inducements before them. * * * But where do [these] intuitions come from?

—Seidman, *The Supreme Court, Entrapment, and Our Criminal Justice Dilemma,* 1981 Sup.Ct.Rev. 111, 146.

"The central evil of entrapment is discriminatory law enforcement, whether the police zero in on a 'politician' or a 'drug dealer.' The act of selecting a subject for temptation is always, even at a minor level, a political act."

—Chevigny, *A Rejoinder,* The Nation, Feb. 23, 1980, p. 205.

"Our national integrity has been on a downhill slide for seven years; we really don't need the FBI to grease the skids with Operation ABSCAM.[a] Where no crime

a. "Abscam" is an acronym combining the first two letters of Abdul Enterprises, a fictitious Middle Eastern corporation, and "scam," a slang term for swindle or confidence game. Abscam began as a standard "sting" operation, i.e., an FBI undercover scheme to recover stolen securities and paintings. In 1978, the operation shifted to political corruption in the New Jersey area. A year later, it had turned its attention to the "Asylum Scenario"; unsuspecting "middlemen" (private persons unaware that they were part of a government undercover operation) passed the word to various Congressmen, or to their aides and acquaintances, that wealthy Arabs were willing to bribe members of Congress in order to ensure that they would introduce private immigration bills on the Arabs' behalf if and when necessary. In early 1980, shortly before shutting has been contemplated, the FBI has, through entrapment, induced to crime men who were previously involved in no wrongdoing. Aren't there enough naturally encouraging crimes to keep the FBI busy? Must they spend astronomical sums creating crime?"

—Letter to the Editor, Newsweek, Mar. 1, 1980, p. 5.

"House Speaker Thomas P. (Tip) O'Neill may have thundered that '[Operation ABSCAM] was a setup, a goddam setup,' but a crook is a crook is a crook. Whether set up or not, honest people do not take bribes."

—Letter to the Editor, Newsweek Mar. 1, 1980, p. 5.

SECTION 1. THE NEED FOR, AND NATURE OF, POLICE AND INFORMER "ENCOURAGEMENT"

SIR A.P. HERBERT—UNCOMMON LAW

pp. 77–81 (1952).

(13) REX *v.* THE COMMISSIONER OF METROPOLITAN POLICE, CHIEF INSPECTOR CHARLES, INSPECTOR SMART, SERGEANT OLIPHANT, AND CONSTABLE BOOT

EXPLOITS OF BOOT

At the Old Bailey the hearing of this case approached its conclusion to-day when Mr. Justice SWALLOW began his address to the jury. He said:

[The] prisoners are officers in the London Police Force, and, at the instigation of a public-minded citizen, Mr. Albert Haddock, they are accused of conspiring to do certain unlawful acts.

[By] the wise ordinances of our land it is unlawful to buy or sell chocolates after the hour of half-past nine o'clock in the evening or to buy cigarettes, cigars, or matches after the hour of eight. * * *

Now, the evidence for the prosecution is that at eight-five p.m. on April 14th the defendant Boot, being in plain clothes, entered the bar of the Folliseum Theatre and asked the barmaid for a packet of Anódyne cigarettes. Miss Perceval, as she has told you, replied that the magic hour was past; but Boot pleaded with her, and, no one else being present except the vigilant Haddock, who happened, it appears, to be preparing his mind for the performance, Miss Perceval at last relented. As you have seen, Boot has a pleasant countenance and manly figure, and Miss Perceval liked the look of him. [At] nine-thirty-five the defendant Boot again entered the bar and asked for a box of chocolates. Miss Perceval, who had just refused a number of similar requests, was moved by the spectacle of this strong man pleading for sweetmeats, and as a personal favour made him a surreptitious sale at the end of the interval, when every one had left the bar except, as it happened, Mr. Haddock. That gentleman was refreshing his mind for the second act, and had been intensely irritated by Miss Perceval's refusal to sell him chocolates, of which, as he told you, he is passionately fond.

Boot then took Miss Perceval's name and address and informed her that a

down, the operation shifted to political corruption in Philadelphia.

As a result of Abscam, a U.S. Senator, six U.S. Representatives and a number of other public officials and lawyers were convicted of various corrupt acts. Although many of the defendants (and many critics of the operation both in and out of Congress) charged that the FBI's methods constituted entrapment and/or violated the due process rights of the individuals caught in the operation, not a single Abscam defendant prevailed in the courts. See, e.g., *United States v. Kelly* (D.C. Cir.1983), p. 499 infra, which discusses one phase of the Abscam operation at considerable length.

charge would be made. The management was prosecuted and fined, and the tender-hearted Miss Perceval was dismissed from their employment. There is no doubt upon the evidence that Boot deliberately broke or procured a breach of the law * * *.

Now, this is only one of a number of similar episodes. In recent years, it appears, there has entered for the first time, systematically and unashamed, into the administration of British justice the repellant figure of the *agent provocateur,* which is a French expression signifying an official spy who causes an offence to secure a conviction; and I use that phrase partly to impress upon you your own profound ignorance and partly because there is no other. There is no other phrase, and for a very good reason; the idea is so repugnant to British notions of fair play and decency that it has never found expression in our language. [This] loathsome practice [is] not employed for the suppression of the major crimes,[a] where official dishonour might be forgiven in a noble cause; no constable causes himself to be murdered or robbed for the protection of the public by the apprehension of a dangerous person. But it is the constant support of small prosecutions for small offences wisely invested by righteous people for the hindrance or prevention of public enjoyment.

The defendant Boot has been prominent in many of these. [He] is always in disguise. [He] lurks in theatres and in public-houses, in sweetshops and nightclubs, in borrowed overalls or chartered evening dress as the occasion demands; he endears himself to women, is affable to men, and at last, by a shameless exploitation of his personality, demands and is granted, at the public expense, tobacco, chocolates, matches, beer, snuff, champagne, and barley-sugar, or whatever other commodity it may be unlawful at that time and place to purchase. The ordinary citizen, however rich, contents himself with an occasional lapse, but Boot is constantly breaking the law. And this is the more shocking from the honest aspect of the man. If the evidence is to be believed, seldom in the history of wrongdoing can a countenance so open and engaging have been associated with so much duplicity.

It is urged for the defence that these officers have broken the law for the law's good; but this is as much as to say that the police may break a man's head if he complains of headache. * * * [S]o long as I am on this Bench I shall do what I can to discourage the hateful practices of the *agent provocateur.* If the public cannot be prevented from enjoying themselves in an honest and straightforward manner they had better be allowed to enjoy themselves. And if you find, as you had better find, that these officers, high and low, have been guilty of conspiring together to do things which the good Mr. Haddock is not allowed to do, then you will return a verdict of "Guilty." If, on the other hand, you find that [they] have not been guilty of the acts alleged, then you will return a verdict of "Not Guilty"; and I shall ignore your verdict. Now, gentlemen, I have done my duty. Do yours.

The jury retired.

DANIEL ROTENBERG—THE POLICE DETECTION PRACTICE OF ENCOURAGEMENT

49 Va.L.Rev. 871, 874–79 (1963).

 See also Tiffany, McIntyre & Rotenberg, *Detection of Crime* 273–82 (Remington ed. 1967)

II. The Practice of Encouragement

"Encouragement" is descriptive of an intentional technique of police agencies

a. "Some large police departments, such as New York and Chicago, are using encouragement to detect crimes of personal violence. Police officers dressed as 'decoys'—women, drunks, or other likely victims—roam the streets in locations where crimes of personal violence are known to occur." Tiffany, McIntyre and Rotenberg, *Detection of Crime* 280 n. 12 (Remington ed. 1967).

used in the detection of a certain class of crimes.[8] In this article it denotes activity of the police or their agent: (1) acting in the capacity of a victim,[10] (2) intending by his actions to suggest his willingness to be a victim, (3) actually communicating this feigned willingness to the suspect, and (4) thereby having some influence upon his commission of the crime. It is not necessarily a single act; it usually consists of a series of acts by the officer which are part of the normal interplay between victim and suspect in the specific crime. It is utilized as a device in dealing with certain crimes having the common element of vice [12]—prostitution, homosexuality, liquor sales, narcotics, and gambling. The reason that the same technique is adapted to all these crimes is suggested by the "vice" label applicable to all of them, that these offenses are committed privately with a willing victim who will not complain, making normal detection virtually impossible. "Encouragement," to state it more succinctly, is a process of persuasion.

An example may be helpful in understanding the process: An officer of a state vice squad suspected that a tavern in a rural community was a front for prostitution in quarters at the rear of the tavern. In order to acquire sufficient evidence to support an arrest and conviction, the officer decided to encourage. He prepared a false story to explain his presence in the rural area generally and at the tavern-brothel specifically. He dressed appropriately for his assumed role. Upon arriving at the tavern he ordered a drink and engaged in small talk. He neither hurried nor lingered. At the appropriate time, he asked for a woman. After convincing the madam of his good faith, he was allowed to select a prostitute from several available. They settled the terms of the contract in private, and she examined him for venereal disease. She requested that he pay her, and he did. At that point the arrest was made.

This example fairly typifies the process and characteristics of the practice; further observations concerning encouragement may be profitably oriented to it.

It is significant to note that the officer "suspected" that the tavern was a front for prostitution. Leaving aside the corrupt and incompetent police officer and excepting narcotic sales cases,[15] in all or almost all instances of encouragement, the police officer or unit has a reasonable suspicion that the person or institution [16] encouraged has engaged in, is currently engaged in, or is about to engage in the crime to be detected. Further, such suspicion is held by the officer or unit before the encouragement process begins. The nature of the process demands this,[a] for it

8. It should be noted that the word "encourages" is used in the entrapment provision of the Model Penal Code; however, as used there it does not denote police impropriety. On the contrary, it is only a descriptive term and thus is consistent with the use of "encouragement" in this article. See *Model Penal Code* § 2.13(1) (1962).

10. The word "victim" is not intended to imply that the willing participant is not a party to the crime, for he may be. Because of his willingness, the participant is not a victim in the sense that the crime is *against* him. However, he is the vehicle which carries the crime to society, the ultimate victim.

12. Although the "vice" label unifies these crimes, the unity does not extend to specifics. For example, social and legal attitudes toward these crimes differ greatly. "Prostitution solicitations" may be misdemeanors, whereas "narcotics sales" are serious felonies, and, of course, the elements comprising the offenses differ.

15. This exception is necessary because in about 90% of narcotics sales detections, the suspect is selected and encouraged by an informer rather than by the police and, seemingly, in most instances the police do not verify that the seller is a suspect at that stage. This and other questionable aspects of the "agency system," such as an addict's being maintained on the narcotics habit as long as he serves as an agent, lead to the conclusion that the system needs reappraisal.

* * *

16. A tavern selling liquor after hours is an example of an institutional crime. In such cases, the individual who sells—bartender, waitress, etc.—is not important except as an instrument of the institution. The suspicion held by the encouraging officer is usually about the tavern and not the individual to whom he makes his request for the after-hours purchase.

a. Does the law, or should the law, *require* it on the ground that the policies underlying the is too complex and time-consuming a technique to be used on a hit-or-miss basis.

This raises a challenging question: If the police are able to acquire information to support a reasonable suspicion, why can they not do a little more detective work, acquire evidence of "probable cause," and then utilize the more conventional detection techniques of search, or arrest and search? This would avoid the controversial encouragement practice. A single answer has not been isolated. [The] difference between "suspicion" and "probable cause" may be not in the *quantity* of evidence but in the *quality,* and this different kind of evidence may not be easily obtained. If this is so, then it may mean that sometimes encouragement is necessarily conducted when the officer is not *sure* of the criminal propensities of his suspect until sometime during the process, at which time the officer makes the decision to abandon the process or proceed with it until the suspect commits the crime. A second explanation is that the officer *can* acquire the evidence to bridge the gap from "suspicion" to "probable cause" and make a valid arrest or conduct a valid search, but these techniques would not produce the evidence necessary to satisfy the higher standard of guilt beyond a reasonable doubt necessary for conviction. For example, if the goal is to achieve a conviction for the illegal sale of narcotics, evidence that a suspect is in possession of a large quantity of narcotics and that known narcotic users are seen visiting his home may be "probable cause" for arrest, and search may reveal evidence sufficient to convict the suspect of possession, but this evidence may not be sufficient to prove a sale. Whatever the reason may be that the police cannot transcend the suspicion standard, the pervasive use of encouragement by enforcement agencies at city, state and national levels is itself highly persuasive that alternative detection methods are simply inadequate.

As illustrated in the example, the encouraging officer seeks out the institution or individual under suspicion, not vice versa. Further, the officer actually initiates the process by hinting, suggesting, or requesting the criminal act. Precisely how he initiates it depends upon the crime and the requirements of reality. Thus if he is seeking to be solicited by a prostitute, he must not be so aggressive as to legally preclude the solicitation by her. If he is seeking a drink after hours in a tavern, he must be aggressive enough, at minimum, to order it. This does not preclude the illegal sale and is necessary to achieve the appearance of reality. Thus it is that the police role in the initiation of encouragement is not, and cannot be, passive. The confrontation of "victim" and suspect is police-planned and arranged.

The decisions which the officer must make after the process is initiated are extremely difficult. They involve questions such as: Is the suspect really innocent or just wary? What types of inducement are improper? How far may I go without legally precluding the commission of the crime by the suspect? Of course, in certain instances decision-making may be minimal. Thus if the officer is firmly convinced of the suspect's criminal propensities, he need not be on guard for indications of the suspect's innocence. He interprets reluctance and delay as signs of wariness. He does not face a decision of stopping or going on. Similarly, in the same situation, there may be no decisions concerning the propriety of inducements to be made. However, he cannot ignore the problems of simulating reality and permitting the suspect the opportunity to commit the crime. On the other hand, if the officer entertains only a suspicion that the suspect is guilty, he must reassess his evaluation of the innocence or guilt of the

Fourth Amendment qualify the state's power to solicit crime no less than its power to detect crime? See p. 504 infra.

suspect at every turn and make decisions concerning the type of inducement he should use—one that would induce the criminal but not the innocent. The obvious danger is that the encouragement will be so realistic and persistent that a weak but innocent party may succumb and commit a crime only because of police inducement.

In all cases, the officer is faced with unanticipated decisions. In the example, the officer had to submit to being inspected for veneral disease before the prostitute would give her consent to intercourse. Other examples are readily conjured by the imagination. Thus, suppose the prostitute was a masochist and insisted upon being physically beaten before consenting. Suppose at the particular bawdy house it was customary to smoke marijuana, and the officer is invited to participate. The difficulty of such decisions, serious under ideal conditions, is compounded by the conditions of the encouragement process because of several factors: there is no one to consult; the officer, being enmeshed in the process, is hardly able to make an objective evaluation of the unfolding scene; the decisions must be made instantaneously; and they must comport with reality in terms of timing, result, language, and physical reaction.

The example makes it clear that encouragement is by no means a wholesome police practice. It is founded upon deception. Not only must the participating officer deliberately deceive, but he must often say and do things that are vulgar, profane and indecent.[b] However, to condemn the characteristics is to condemn the practice, because deception, vulgarity, profanity, and indecency are often essential to the simulation of reality which encouragement attempts to achieve. When to these characteristics is added the unfortunate fact that on occasion encouragement induces persons to commit crime who ordinarily would not, it is understandable that the practice is roundly criticized.[17] But if there is no way to protect society effectively from certain criminal harms except through detection by encouragement, then it is as idle to criticize the practice continually as it would be to criticize surgery for its efforts to eliminate disease because the surgical method, of necessity, cuts and hurts the body. The fact should not be overlooked that the fault lies more with the social harm and the human hurt and their causes than with the methods of eradication.

In onc large city it was observed that several of the trial judges determined the propriety of police encouragement by reference to the duration of the process. If

b. See *United States v. Owens,* 228 F.Supp. 300 (D.D.C.1964), where Judge Youngdahl left no doubt he thought that, in endeavoring to become "accepted" by a group of suspected narcotics violaters, the narcotics undercover agent had overdone it: "It is shocking to this Court that in order to obtain evidence of a sale of narcotics, the undercover agent, with the approval of his superior officers, participated with others at [50 or 60] 'after-hours parties' [covering a period of five months] in open and conceded violation of the local laws against gambling, the illegal sale of liquor, and the illegal possession and use of cocaine. [W]e have arrived at a low level of appropriate law enforcement when in order to secure evidence of narcotics violations Federal Narcotics agents themselves have to violate the law and thus be in *particeps criminis* with the very criminals they are trying to detect."

17. Because "encouragement" is not a recognized detection practice, the criticisms are not directed to it, but rather to entrapment, which is encouragement extended to the point of illegality. However, many of the criticisms are applicable as well to encouragement, for some commentators' attacks are leveled against any such police action:

> There is scarcely a case sustaining the defense of entrapment in which such words as "detestation," "indecent," "to be deplored," "intolerable" do not occur to describe the acts of the officer in luring the defendant into the crime * * *.
>
> Certainly the whole practice, whether it consists in the mere "laying of a trap or decoy" or of a scheme whereby the officer "conceives and plans" the offense, is a "dirty business" and should be ended.

Mikell, *The Doctrine of Entrapment in the Federal Courts,* 90 U.Pa.L.Rev. 245, 263–64 (1942).

the process took longer than the presiding judge considered proper, the case would be dismissed. Apparently it was believed that a lengthy encouragement process is consistent only with the inducement of innocent persons to commit crimes. Although this may be partially true, a lengthy process is also explicable on other grounds. As the example suggests, time is to a great extent a function of simulating reality and thus is beyond the control of the officer. Furthermore, the more criminally-sophisticated the suspect, the greater his awareness of the police use of encouragement and the greater his caution. Thus a lengthy process is as consistent with the detection of crime committed by a confirmed criminal as it is with the detection of crime committed by an "innocent" person.[19] Finally, because at times the officer's goal is not only to establish the requisite probability of guilt for arrest but also to establish the greater probability of guilt for conviction, he must continue the process until sufficient evidence to convict is acquired. This, of course, may lengthen the process.

[Encouragement] is an unsavory, time-consuming process of persuasion calling for adherence to reality and spur-of-the-moment decisions; it is a process rooted in necessity * * *.

RICHARD C. DONNELLY—JUDICIAL CONTROL OF INFORMANTS, SPIES, STOOL PIGEONS AND AGENT PROVOCATEURS

60 Yale L.J. 1091, 1093–94 (1951).

Notwithstanding such euphemistic characterizations as "confidential informant" and "special employee," the informant, the police spy, the stool pigeon, and the agent provocateur have been generally regarded with aversion and nauseous disdain. Nevertheless, these characters are used widely by police forces the world over. They are particularly effective in the enforcement of [of] [v]ice suppression laws, [laws that] create special problems for the police. Except, perhaps, for the narcotics laws they do not command the general and convinced support of public opinion. A considerable segment of the community regards them as an unnecessary interference with the lives of individual citizens or as penalizing behavior that is not the legitimate concern of government. Others insist upon rigid enforcement while still a third group, often the most numerous, views them with complete indifference. * * *

The task of the police is thus one of great difficulty. If rigorous enforcement is attempted, public sympathy is apt to be shown detected offenders and expressed by the failure of juries to convict. Criticism, which should be directed at the law itself, is aimed at the police. If, on the other hand, a tolerant attitude is adopted, another section of the community inveighs against police inactivity or even hints at collusion or corrupt dealing between the offenders and the police.

Furthermore, there is a marked difference between the enforcement of social and economic regulatory statutes, of which vice legislation is an example, and the traditional type of criminal law, such as the law of murder, rape, larceny, robbery, arson, and the like. The regulatory statutes condemn behavior directed, not against particular individuals, but against public order. Violation is deemed a wrong against society as a whole and is generally unattended with any particular harm to a definite person. These offenses are car-

19. A relevant observation was made by Mr. Justice Jackson, concurring in part in *Watts v. Indiana,* 338 U.S. 49, 69 S.Ct. 1347, 93 L.Ed. 1801 (1949), concerning the extent of police interrogation designed to elicit confessions or admissions: "The duration of an interrogation may well depend on the temperament, shrewdness and cunning of the accused and the competence of the examiner. But, assuming a right to examine at all, the right must include what is made reasonably necessary by the facts of the particular case." Id. at 61.

ried on in secret and the violators resort to many devices and subterfuges to evade detection. It is rare for any member of the public, whatever his attitude may be in principle towards these offenses, to be willing to assist in the enforcement of the law. It is necessary, therefore, that government in detecting and punishing violations of these statutes, rely, not upon the voluntary action of aggrieved individuals, but upon the diligence of its own officials. This means that the police must be present at the time the offenses are committed either in an undercover capacity or through spies and stool pigeons.

Though considered essential by the police in enforcing vice legislation, the stool pigeon system breeds abominable abuse. Frequently a person who will accept payment from the police to assist in the apprehension of prostitutes, gamblers, and liquor or narcotics violators will also accept payment from these persons to deceive the police. The stool pigeon himself may be a drug addict, pickpocket, pimp, or other petty criminal. The spectacle of government secretly mated with the underworld and using underworld characters to gain its end is not an ennobling one. The employment of stool pigeons by the police probably arouses more resentment and hatred than any other non-violent abuse. Even confirmed lawbreakers have their standards of "squareness." To them the stool pigeon situation is the outstanding proof that law enforcement is not square. Contempt for law is thus encouraged. In addition, the temptation to "frame" a case is great.[12] * * *

SECTION 2. THE TESTS FOR ENTRAPMENT [a]

SHERMAN v. UNITED STATES

356 U.S. 369, 78 S.Ct. 819, 2 L.Ed.2d 848 (1958).

MR. CHIEF JUSTICE WARREN delivered the opinion of the Court.

[In] late August 1951, Kalchinian, a government informer, first met petitioner at a doctor's office where apparently both were being treated to be cured of narcotics addiction. * * * From mere greetings, conversation progressed to a discussion of mutual experiences and problems, including their attempts to overcome addiction to narcotics. Finally Kalchinian asked petitioner if he knew of a good source of narcotics. He asked petitioner to supply him with a source because he was not responding to treatment. From the first, petitioner tried to avoid the issue. Not until after a number of repetitions of the request, predicated on Kalchinian's presumed suffering, did petitioner finally acquiesce. Several times thereafter he obtained a quantity of narcotics which he shared with Kalchinian. Each time petitioner told Kalchinian that the total cost of narcotics he obtained was twenty-five dollars and that Kalchinian owed him fifteen dollars. The informer thus bore the cost of his share of the narcotics plus the taxi and other expenses necessary to obtain the drug. After several such sales Kalchinian informed agents of the Bureau of Narcotics that he had another seller for them. On three occasions during November 1951, government agents observed petitioner give narcotics to Kalchinian in return for money supplied by the Government.

12. For example, of 150 prostitution cases in which a stool pigeon named Chile Acuna assisted the Vice Squad in New York, 40 were admittedly framed. Hopkins, *Our Lawless Police* 105 (1931).

a. "Entrapment" is sometimes confused with, but should be distinguished from, "estoppel," which occurs when defendants rely on the assurances of government authorities that their contemplated conduct is lawful only to be prosecuted for such conduct. See *Cox v. Louisiana,* 379 U.S. 559, 85 S.Ct. 476, 13 L.Ed.2d 487 (1965) (to sustain appellant's conviction "for demonstrating where [public officials] told him he could 'would be to sanction an indefensible sort of entrapment by the State * * * ' "); *Raley v. Ohio,* 360 U.S. 423, 79 S.Ct. 1257, 3 L.Ed.2d 1344 (1959); *People v. Donovan,* 279 N.Y.S.2d 404 (Ct.Spec.Sess.1967), 81 Harv.L.Rev. 895 (1968).

At the trial the factual issue was whether the informer had convinced an otherwise unwilling person to commit a criminal act or whether petitioner was already predisposed to commit the act [a] and exhibited only the natural hesitancy of one acquainted with the narcotics trade. The issue of entrapment went to the jury, and a conviction resulted. Petitioner was sentenced to imprisonment for ten years. [The Second Circuit affirmed.]

In *Sorrells v. United States,* 287 U.S. 435, 53 S.Ct. 210, 77 L.Ed. 413 [1932], this Court firmly recognized the defense of entrapment in the federal courts. The intervening years have in no way detracted from the principles underlying that decision. The function of law enforcement is the prevention of crime and the apprehension of criminals. Manifestly, that function does not include the manufacturing of crime. Criminal activity is such that stealth and strategy are necessary weapons in the arsenal of the police officer. However, "A different question is presented when the criminal design originates with the officials of the government, and they implant in the mind of an innocent person the disposition to commit the alleged offense and induce its commission in order that they may prosecute." Then stealth and strategy become as objectionable police methods as the coerced confession and the unlawful search. Congress could not have intended that its statutes were to be enforced by tempting innocent persons into violations.

However, the fact that government agents "merely afford opportunities or facilities for the commission of the offense does not" constitute entrapment. Entrapment occurs only when the criminal conduct was "the product of the *creative* activity" of law-enforcement officials. (Emphasis supplied.) To determine whether entrapment has been established a line must be drawn between the trap for the unwary innocent and the trap for the unwary criminal. The principles by which the courts are to make this determination were outlined in *Sorrells.* On the one hand, at trial the accused may examine the conduct of the government agent; and on other hand, the accused will be subjected to an "appropriate and searching inquiry into his own conduct and predisposition" as bearing on his claim of innocence.

We conclude from the evidence that entrapment was established as a matter of law. [It] is patently clear that petitioner was induced by Kalchinian. * * * One request was not enough, for Kalchinian tells us that additional ones were necessary to overcome, first, petitioner's refusal, then his evasiveness, and then his hesitancy in order to achieve capitulation. Kalchinian not only procured a source of narcotics but apparently also induced petitioner to return to the habit. Finally, assured of a catch, Kalchinian informed the authorities so that they could close the net. * * * Although he was not being paid, Kalchinian was an active government informer who had but recently been the instigator of at least two other prosecutions. Undoubtedly the impetus for such achievements was the fact that in 1951 Kalchinian was himself under criminal charges for illegally selling narcotics and had not yet been sentenced.[3] [In] his testimony the

a. What does it mean to say that the defendant was "already predisposed" to commit the criminal act? When it speaks of "disposition" does the Court really mean "temperament" or "character" rather than "tendency"? If so, does this explain "the Court's otherwise baffling insistence on separating the concept of predisposition from that of inducement"? See Seidman, *The Supreme Court, Entrapment, and our Criminal Justice Dilemma,* 1981 Sup.Ct. 111, 124–25.

3. "Q. But you had made a promise, an agreement, though, to cooperate with the Federal Bureau of Narcotics before you received a suspended sentence from the court?

"A. [Kalchinian]. I had promised to co-operate in 1951.

"Q. And that was before your sentence?

"A. Yes, that was before my sentence." R. 99.

Kalchinian received a suspended sentence in 1952 after a statement by the United States Attorney to the Judge that he had been cooperative with the Government.

federal agent in charge of the case admitted that he never bothered to question Kalchinian about the way he had made contact with petitioner. The Government cannot make such use of an informer and then claim disassociation through ignorance.

The Government sought to overcome the defense of entrapment by claiming that petitioner evinced a "ready complaisance" to accede to Kalchinian's request. Aside from a record of past convictions, which we discuss in the following paragraph, the Government's case is unsupported. There is no evidence that petitioner himself was in the trade. When his apartment was searched after arrest, no narcotics were found. There is no significant evidence that petitioner even made a profit on any sale to Kalchinian. The Government's characterization of petitioner's hesitancy to Kalchinian's request as the natural wariness of the criminal cannot fill the evidentiary void.

The Government's additional evidence in the second trial to show that petitioner was ready and willing to sell narcotics should the opportunity present itself was petitioner's record of two past narcotics convictions. In 1942 petitioner was convicted of illegally selling narcotics; in 1946 he was convicted of illegally possessing them. However, a nine-year-old sales conviction and a five-year-old possession conviction are insufficient to prove petitioner had a readiness to sell narcotics at the time Kalchinian approached him, particularly when we must assume from the record he was trying to overcome the narcotics habit at the time.

The case at bar illustrates an evil which the defense of entrapment is designed to overcome. The government informer entices someone attempting to avoid narcotics not only into carrying out an illegal sale but also into returning to the habit of use. Selecting the proper time, the informer then tells the government agent. The set-up is accepted by the agent without even a question as to the manner in which the informer encountered the seller. Thus the Government plays on the weaknesses of an innocent party and beguiles him into committing crimes which he otherwise would not have attempted. Law enforcement does not require methods such as this.

It has been suggested that in overturning this conviction we should reassess the doctrine of entrapment according to principles announced in the separate opinion of Mr. Justice Roberts in *Sorrells.* To do so would be to decide the case on grounds rejected by the majority in *Sorrells* [and] not raised here or below by the parties before us. We do not ordinarily decide issues not presented by the parties and there is good reason not to vary that practice in this case.

At least two important issues of law enforcement and trial procedure would have to be decided without the benefit of argument by the parties, one party being the Government. Mr. Justice Roberts asserted that although the defendant could claim that the Government had induced him to commit the crime, the Government could not reply by showing that the defendant's criminal conduct was due to his own readiness and not to the persuasion of government agents. The handicap thus placed on the prosecution is obvious. Furthermore, it was the position of Mr. Justice Roberts that the factual issue of entrapment—now limited to the question of what the government agents did—should be decided by the judge, not the jury. Not only was this rejected by the Court in *Sorrells,* but [since then, by all the Courts that have addressed the issue].

To dispose of this case on the ground suggested would entail both overruling a leading decision of this Court and brushing aside the possibility that we would be creating more problems than we would supposedly be solving.

[The judgment] is reversed and the case [remanded] with instructions to dismiss the indictment. * * *

MR. JUSTICE FRANKFURTER, whom MR. JUSTICE DOUGLAS, MR. JUSTICE HARLAN, and MR. JUSTICE BRENNAN join, concurring in the result.

Although agreeing with the Court that the undisputed facts show entrapment as a matter of law, I reach this result by a route different from the Court's. * * *

It is surely sheer fiction to suggest that a conviction cannot be had when a defendant has been entrapped by government officers or informers because "Congress could not have intended that its statutes were to be enforced by tempting innocent persons into violations." In these cases raising claims of entrapment, the only legislative intention that can with any show of reason be extracted from the statute is the intention to make criminal precisely the conduct in which the defendant has engaged. That conduct includes all the elements necessary to constitute criminality. Without compulsion and "knowingly," where that is requisite, the defendant has violated the statutory command. If he is to be relieved from the usual punitive consequences, it is on no account because he is innocent of the offense described. In these circumstances, conduct is not less criminal because the result of temptation, whether the tempter is a private person or a government agent or informer.

The courts refuse to convict an entrapped defendant, not because his conduct falls outside the proscription of the statute, but because, even if his guilt be admitted, the methods employed on behalf of the Government to bring about conviction cannot be countenanced. [The] federal courts have an obligation to set their face against enforcement of the law by [offensive or objectionable means]. They do this in the exercise of a recognized jurisdiction to formulate and apply "proper standards for the enforcement of the federal criminal law in the federal courts," *McNabb v. United States,*[b] an obligation that goes beyond the conviction of the particular defendant before the court. Public confidence in the fair and honorable administration of justice, upon which ultimately depends the rule of law, is the transcending value at stake.

The formulation of these standards does not in any way conflict with the statute the defendant has violated, or involve the initiation of a judicial policy disregarding or qualifying that framed by Congress. A false choice is put when it is said that either the defendant's conduct does not fall within the statute or he must be convicted. The statute is wholly directed to defining and prohibiting the substantive offense concerned and expresses no purpose, either permissive or prohibitory, regarding the police conduct that will be tolerated in the detection of crime. A statute prohibiting the sale of narcotics is as silent on the question of entrapment as it is on the admissibility of illegally obtained evidence. It is enacted, however, on the basis of certain presuppositions concerning the established legal order and the role of the courts within that system in formulating standards for the administration of criminal justice when Congress itself has not specifically legislated to that end. Specific statutes are to be fitted into an antecedent legal system. * * *

The crucial question, not easy of answer, to which the court must direct itself is whether the police conduct revealed in the particular case falls below standards, to which common feelings respond, for the proper use of governmental power. For answer it is wholly irrelevant to ask if the "intention" to commit the crime originated with the defendant or government officers, or if the criminal conduct was the product of "the creative activity" of law-enforcement officials. Yet in the present case the Court repeats and purports to apply these unrevealing tests. Of course

b. For a brief discussion of *McNabb* and the federal courts' supervisory power over criminal justice generally, see p. 58 supra.

in every case of this kind the intention that the particular crime be committed originates with the police, and without their inducement the crime would not have occurred. But it is perfectly clear [as] where the police [simply furnish] the opportunity for the commission of the crime, that this is not enough to enable the defendant to escape conviction.

The intention referred to, therefore, must be a general intention or predisposition to commit, whenever the opportunity should arise, crimes of the kind solicited, and in proof of such a predisposition evidence has often been admitted to show the defendant's reputation, criminal activities, and prior disposition. The danger of prejudice in such a situation, particularly if the issue of entrapment must be submitted to the jury and disposed of by a general verdict of guilty or innocent, is evident. The defendant must either forego the claim of entrapment or run the substantial risk that, in spite of instructions, the jury will allow a criminal record or bad reputation to weigh in its determination of guilt of the specific offense of which he stands charged.[c] Furthermore, a test that looks to the character and predisposition of the defendant rather than the conduct of the police loses sight of the underlying reason for the defense of entrapment. No matter what the defendant's past record and present inclinations to criminality, or the depths to which he has sunk in the estimation of society, certain police conduct to ensnare him into further crime is not to be tolerated by an advanced society. And in the present case it is clear that the Court in fact reverses the conviction because of the conduct of the informer Kalchinian, and not because the Government has failed to draw a convincing picture of petitioner's past criminal conduct. Permissible police activity does not vary according to the particular defendant concerned; surely if two suspects have been solicited at the same time in the same manner, one should not go to jail simply because he has been convicted before and is said to have criminal disposition. No more does it vary according to the suspicions, reasonable or unreasonable, of the police concerning the defendant's activities. Appeals to sympathy, friendship, the possibility of exorbitant gain, and so forth, can no more be tolerated when directed against a past offender than against an ordinary law-abiding citizen. A contrary view runs afoul of fundamental principles of equality under law, and would espouse the notion that when dealing with the criminal classes anything goes. * * * Past crimes do not forever outlaw the criminal and open him to police practices, aimed at securing his repeated conviction, from which the ordinary citizen is protected. The whole ameliorative hopes of modern penology and prison administration strongly counsel against such a view.

[This means] that in holding out inducements [the police] should act in such a manner as is likely to induce to the commission of crime only these persons and not others who would normally avoid crime and through self-struggle resist ordinary temptations. This test shifts attention from the record and predisposition of the particular defendant to the conduct of the police and the likelihood, objectively considered, that it would entrap only those ready and willing to commit crime. It is as objective a test as the subject matter permits, and will give guidance in regulating police conduct that is lacking when the reasonableness of police suspicions must be judged or the criminal disposition of the defendant retrospectively appraised. * * *

As Mr. Justice Roberts convincingly urged in the *Sorrells* case, [the judgment as to what police conduct is to be condemned, because likely to induce those not otherwise ready and willing to commit

c. See Note 3, p. 487 infra.

crime,] [d] is appropriate for the court and not the jury.[e] "The protection of its own functions and the preservation of the purity of its own temple belongs only to the court. It is the province of the court and of the court alone to protect itself and the government from such prostitution of the criminal law. * * *" Equally important is the consideration that a jury verdict [cannot provide] significant guidance for official conduct for the future. Only the court, through the gradual evolution of explicit standards in accumulated precedents, can do this with the degree of certainty that the wise administration of criminal justice demands.

COMMENTARY ON THE "SUBJECTIVE" AND "OBJECTIVE" TESTS

1. *Support for the "hypothetical person" or "objective" test.* As pointed out in LaFave & Israel, § 5.2(b), "the objective test is favored by a majority of the commentators, and is reflected in the formulation of the entrapment defense appearing in the [*Model Penal Code* § 2.13]. Its first authoritative acceptance came by judicial decision in Alaska [*Grossman v. State,* 457 P.2d 226 (Alaska 1969)], and now at least ten other states have adopted it either by statute or judicial decision."

See, e.g., PEOPLE v. BARRAZA, 591 P.2d 947 (Cal.1979), per MOSK, J., holding that the proper test of entrapment in California is: "was the [police conduct] likely to induce a normally law-abiding person to commit the offense?" Observed the court:

"[W]e presume that [a normally law-abiding] person would resist the temptation to commit a crime presented by the simple opportunity to act unlawfully. [But] it is impermissible for the police or their agents to pressure the suspect by overbearing conduct such as badgering, cajoling, importuning, or other affirmative acts likely to induce a normally law-abiding person to commit the crime."

"[G]uidance will generally be found in the application of one or both of two principles. First, if the [police conduct] would generate in a normally law-abiding person a motive for the crime other than ordinary criminal intent, entrapment will be established. An example of such conduct would be an appeal by the police that would induce such a person to commit the act because of friendship or sympathy, instead of a desire for personal gain or other typical criminal purpose. Second, affirmative police conduct that would make commission of the crime unusually attractive to a normally law-abiding person will likewise constitute entrapment. Such conduct would include, for example, a guarantee that the act is not illegal or the offense will go undetected, an offer of exorbitant consideration, or any similar enticement." [a]

2. *Doubts about the efficacy of the "objective" test.* Consider DeFeo, *Entrapment as a Defense to Criminal Responsibility,* 1 U.S.F.L. Rev. 243, 275–76 (1967): "[T]he tavern keeper selling to minors, the bellboy or taxi driver taking bets [and] the escort furnishing prostitutes require reassurance, gratuities, and lies to overcome their criminal caution, all of which would be outlawed [under the objective test] because tempting to some situational violator with inhibitions weakened by drink or financial need. I cannot but feel that those things which would attract professional criminals *and no others* are so few as to make enforcement of legislation against consensual crime [under the objective test] nearly impossible. * * * [I]t seems an excess of sympathy to design a [test] protecting all but the most reckless of criminals, those who require no persuasion or inducement. There is proverbially a little larceny in each of us, and a great deal in some. To

d. For examples of such police conduct, see Note 1, this page.

e. See Note 4, p. 492 infra.

a. Under this test, emphasized the court, "the character of the suspect, his predisposition to commit the offense, and his subjective intent are irrelevant." On this point, see Note 3 infra.

deny the police use of certain tactics solely because they might tempt those with only a little larceny, even though said tactics are necessary to catch the more larcenous, is inferior to judging those techniques by a standard of reasonableness, or under the orthodox test allowing a jury to express a community judgment on whether the defendant deserved protection from such entrapping tactics."

See also Park, *The Entrapment Controversy,* 60 Minn.L.Rev. 163, 270–71 (1976), doubting that the "hypothetical person" test could control the conduct of police and informers: "Standardized procedures cannot govern the sundry and unpredictable events that occur during encounters between target and temptor. Moreover, even if such procedures could be formulated and somehow taught to the army of addicts and criminals used by police to set up controlled offenses, it is doubtful that they would be followed—particularly since the rules would inevitably become known to targets as well as police agents.

" * * * Because many targets are professional criminals, judges will be reluctant to rule that entrapment has occurred simply because an agent found it necessary to appeal to friendship, make multiple requests, or offer a substantial profit. Yet approval of such conduct would lead to unfair results in cases where the target was law-abiding but ductile. For example, conviction of someone who has been solicited by a friend may be fair enough in the general run of cases, but unfair if the target was a nondisposed person who would not have committed the type of crime charged but for a request from that particular friend.

"The danger of acquitting wolves and convicting lambs would be ameliorated if courts following the hypothetical-person test allow predisposition evidence to be introduced for its bearing on the propriety of the agent's inducement. The degree of persistence permitted would then depend upon whether the agent had sound reasons to believe that his target was already engaged in criminal enterprise. However, this approach would create even greater uncertainty about the boundaries of permissible inducement and further limit the defense's utility as a guide to police conduct. * * *

"[The federal defense] attempts to distinguish between persons who are blameworthy and persons who are not. In the absence of extraordinary circumstances, that should be the goal of our law of crimes."

3. *Should the "subjective" test be retained, but stripped of its indiscriminate attitude toward "predisposition" evidence?* The "subjective" test, protested Stewart, J., dissenting in *United States v. Russell* (p. 494 infra), permits the use of otherwise inadmissible "hearsay, suspicion and rumor" to prove defendant's predisposition.[b] The defendant, in effect, is "put on trial for his past offenses and character." *Grossman v. State,* 457 P.2d 226, 229 (Alaska 1969) (adopting the objective test).

But, maintains Park, supra, at 272, "the indiscriminate attitude toward predisposition evidence"—"the greatest fault" of the subjective test—"is by no means a necessary feature of the subjective test. If the accused was already engaged in a course of criminal conduct, the prosecution should be able to develop an arsenal of reliable predisposition evidence. If it cannot, the danger of wrongful acquittal is outweighed by the danger of convicting a person whose only real vice is a bad reputation. Reputation and other hearsay evidence should not become admissible merely because the accused has raised the defense of entrapment. If construed to exclude such testimony, the subjective defense should present more reliable evidence to the fact-

b. Not only prior convictions, but prior arrests, acts of prior misconduct, "reputation testimony" and "suspicious conduct" have been admitted on this issue. See, e.g., LaFave & Israel, § 5.2(c); Notes, 49 J.Crim.L.C. & P.S. 447, 450–52 (1959); 37 Mo.L.Rev. 633, 648–50 (1972).

finder than the hypothetical-person defense. The latter focuses upon the nature of the inducement offered; consequently, trials are likely to be reduced to a swearing match between unreliable witnesses about words said in private."

4. *Is the distinction between the objective and subjective approaches overstated?* Consider Seidman, *The Supreme Court, Entrapment, and Our Criminal Justice Dilemma,* 1981 Sup.Ct.Rev. 111, 118–20:

"The [subjective test] is premised on the notion that it is possible to isolate the class of 'unwary criminals' who are 'ready and willing' to engage in crime apart from the inducements offered by the government. But whether a person is 'ready and willing' to break the law depends on what the person expects to get in return—that is, on the level of inducement. Like the rest of us, criminals do not generally work for free. Their willingness to take the risks of crime varies with the incentive which is provided. To be sure, the less cynical among us may believe that there is still a class of people who 'have no price' * * *. But even if one concedes that such people can be found somewhere, they are, by definition, not among the ranks of entrapped defendants, since such defendants must have succumbed to some inducement in order to be entrapped.

"Consequently, so long as one equates 'predisposition' with a readiness to commit crime, no definition of 'predisposition' can be complete without an articulation of the level of inducement to which a 'predisposed' defendant would respond. Furthermore, the 'predisposed' cannot be distinguished from the 'nondisposed' without focusing on the propriety of the government's conduct—the very factor that the subjective approach professes to ignore. This is true because a defendant who responds favorably to a 'proper' inducement has thereby conclusively demonstrated that he is disposed to crime when such an inducement is offered.[c] It would seem, then, that so long as government agents restrict themselves to 'proper' inducements, they run no risk of violating the entrapment rules. The entrapment test is 'subjective' only in the sense that even if the government offers an 'excessive' inducement, the defendant may nonetheless be convicted under such a test if he would have responded favorably to a proper one.

"Even this formulation, however, overstates the distinction between the objective and subjective approaches for two reasons.

"First, the objective test in theory avoids analysis of the defendant's predisposition and focuses, instead, exclusively on the propriety of the inducement.[29] That question, in turn, is determined 'by the likelihood, objectively considered, that it would entrap only those ready and willing to commit crime.'[30] But plainly that likelihood depends in large measure on the group to whom the inducement is targeted. So long as the police direct their attention toward only those likely to be predisposed, the risk of entrapment, objectively considered, is small, and the inducement is, therefore, presumably permissible. Thus, in most cases, both the objective and subjective approaches would permit an inducement, so long as the defendant is predisposed. The two approaches would reach different results only in the rare case where the police reasonably, but incorrectly, believe the defendant to be predisposed at the time the inducement is offered.

c. In the Abscam cases, observes Gershman, *Abscam, the Judiciary, and the Ethics of Entrapment,* 91 Yale L.J. 1565, 1581 (1982), "the jury was allowed to infer predisposition simply from the defendant's affirmative response to the government's inducements. For instance, that [two defendants] readily accepted cash payments was found to constitute sufficient evidence that they had a *preexisting* intention to take a bribe. In other words, the defendant is said to be predisposed because he committed the act, and then is held responsible for the act because he was predisposed. The pernicious circularity of this approach is obvious."

29. See, e.g., Sherman (Frankfurter, J., concurring).

30. Id.

"Second, most courts adopting an objective approach have supplemented it with a causation requirement.[33] This requirement means that the defendant must demonstrate not only the impropriety of the inducement, but also that the inducement caused him to commit the crime. If the requirement is taken literally, the distinction between the objective and subjective approaches collapses completely. A defendant who is predisposed and who would have responded to a proper inducement cannot claim that his conduct was caused by an improper inducement, because he would have committed the same crime even if the inducement had been proper. He therefore fares no differently under the objective and subjective tests. Conversely, if the defendant responds favorably to a proper inducement, he cannot claim that he was not predisposed, because his favorable response *ipso facto* demonstrates predisposition. The result is, therefore, again the same whether an objective or subjective standard is utilized."

5. *Was the distinction between the subjective and objective tests smudged in the DeLorean case?* Because John DeLorean was prosecuted for drug violations in federal court, the judge instructed the jury to consider the entrapment claim in accordance with the subjective test. However, points out Whelan, *Lead Us Not Into (Unwarranted) Temptation: A Proposal to Replace the Entrapment Defense with a Reasonable Suspicion Requirement,* 133 U.Pa. 1193, 1199–1200 (1985), "it seems from the jurors' remarks" after the acquittal that "they followed the objective approach instead. Those jurors who discussed the entrapment issue with reporters emphasized the impropriety of the operation, not DeLorean's character. One juror expressed the view that the FBI went after DeLorean only because he was an influential person. There were several indications that the agents viewed DeLorean as a highly desirable arrest. * * * It was undoubtedly the spirit of the hunt that led [one agent] to report to FBI headquarters that DeLorean was 'involved in large scale narcotics transactions, in addition to the laundering [of] large amounts of illegally received income,' although he knew it wasn't true. His explanation for this message? 'I thought it sounded pretty good.' "[d]

6. *Can the subjective and objective tests for entrapment coexist?* Yes, answered CRUZ v. STATE, 465 So.2d 516 (Fla.1985). The case arose as follows: Tampa police undertook a decoy operation in a high-crime area. An officer posed as an inebriated indigent, smelling of alcohol and pretending to drink wine from a bottle. Plainly displayed from the decoy officer's rear pants pocket was $150 in currency, paper-clipped together. Cruz and a companion happened upon the scene as passersby, then returned about fifteen minutes later, at which point Cruz took the money

33. See, e.g., *Grossman v. State,* 457 P.2d 226, 229 (Alaska 1969) (misconduct by government must be shown to have induced crime); *State v. Mullen,* 216 N.W.2d 375, 382 (Iowa 1974) (same).

d. According to newspaper accounts of the DeLorean trial, summarized in Whelan, supra, at 1197–99, by 1980 DeLorean desperately needed ten million dollars to save his automobile company. About this time, he was invited to participate in a major cocaine transaction by FBI informant James Hoffman, a former neighbor of DeLorean and an admitted perjurer and occasional drug dealer. The FBI had no reason to believe that DeLorean was involved in drugs in any way until Hoffman came forward with his allegation that DeLorean wanted to make money quickly in a big narcotics deal and hoped that Hoffman could arrange something.

According to the original scenario, DeLorean would invest two million dollars toward the purchase of the cocaine and make as much as sixty million dollars. When DeLorean reported that he would have to withdraw from the operation because of his inability to raise the money, either Hoffman or an FBI agent proposed an alternative: simply put up two million dollars of collateral, which included various property. DeLorean also signed over the entire voting stock of his company to the federal agents who were posing as drug dealers. An FBI agent recommended that DeLorean "launder" any profits from the operation through one of his companies.

The jury's acquittal of DeLorean was based both on disapproval of the FBI's methods and the conclusion that the government had failed to prove that DeLorean had committed a crime.

from the decoy's pocket without harming him in any way. Other officers arrested Cruz as he walked from the scene. The decoy situation did not involve the same modus operandi as any of the unsolved crimes which had occurred in the area. The police were not seeking a particular individual, nor were they aware of any prior criminal acts by the defendant. In holding that the police activity constituted entrapment as a matter of law under its threshold test, the court observed, per EHRLICH, J.:

"Although the United States Supreme Court implies the objective and subjective views of entrapment are mutually exclusive, we find that they are not. The objective view is a statement of judicially cognizable considerations worthy of being given as much weight as the subjective view. * * *

"We find, like the New Jersey court,[a] that the subjective and objective entrapment doctrines can coexist. The subjective test is normally a jury question. The objective test is a matter of law for the trial court to decide.

"The effect of a threshold objective test is to require the state to establish initially whether 'police conduct revealed in the particular case falls below standards, to which common feelings respond, for the proper use of governmental power.' *Sherman* (Frankfurter, J., concurring). Once the state has established the validity of the police activity, the question remains whether 'the criminal design originates with the officials of the government, and they implant in the mind of an innocent person the disposition to commit the alleged offense and induce its commission in order that they may prosecute.' *Sorrells.* This question is answered by deciding whether the defendant was predisposed, and is properly for the jury to decide. In other words, the court must first decide whether the police have cast their nets in permissible waters, and, if so, the jury must decide whether the particular defendant was one of the guilty the police may permissibly ensnare.

"To guide the trial courts, we propound the following threshold test of an entrapment defense: Entrapment has not occurred as a matter of law where police activity (1) has as its end the interruption of a specific ongoing criminal activity; and (2) utilizes means reasonably tailored to apprehend those involved in the ongoing criminal activity.

"The first prong of this test addresses the problem of police 'virtue testing,' that is, police activity seeking to prosecute crime where no such crime exists but for the police activity engendering the crime. * * *

"The second prong of the threshold test addresses the problem of inappropriate techniques. Considerations in deciding whether police activity is permissible under this prong include whether a government agent 'induces or encourages another person to engage in conduct constituting such offense by either: (a) making knowingly false representations designed to induce the belief that such conduct is not prohibited; or (b) employing methods of persuasion or inducement which create a substantial risk that such an offense will be committed by persons other than those who are ready to commit it.' *Model Penal Code* § 2.13 (1962).

"Applying this test to the case before us, we find that the drunken bum decoy operation fails. [O]ne of the undisputed facts was that 'none of the unsolved crimes occuring [sic] near this location involved the same modus operandi as the simulated

a. See *State v. Molnar,* 410 A.2d 37 (N.J.1980). Subsequent to its *Molnar* decision, the New Jersey court held that statutory law had superseded the common law, placing the decision on both the subjective and objective aspects of entrapment in the hands of the trier of fact. *State v. Rockholt,* 476 A.2d 1236 (N.J.1984). The Florida Supreme Court noted that "[t]here is no parallel to the New Jersey legislative action in Florida, and we conclude that the policy considerations of the *Molnar* decision remain valid in this case."

situation created by the officers.' * * * This lack of focus is sufficient for the scenario to fail the first prong of the test. However, even if the police were seeking to catch persons who had been 'rolling' drunks in the area, the criminal scenario here, with $150 (paper-clipped to ensure more than $100 was taken, making the offense a felony) enticingly protruding from the back pocket of a person seemingly incapable of noticing its removal, carries with it the 'substantial risk that such an offense will be committed by persons other than those who are ready to commit it.' *Model Penal Code* § 2.13."

OTHER ISSUES RAISED BY THE ENTRAPMENT DEFENSE [a]

1. *Contingent fee arrangements.* In *Williamson v. United States,* 311 F.2d 441 (5th Cir.1962), the informer had been promised $200 and $100, respectively, for producing legally admissible evidence that two specified persons were engaged in illicit liquor dealings. Using its supervisory powers over the administration of federal criminal justice,[b] the court held that absent a special justification for its use in a particular case, a conviction is invalid if it rests on evidence of informants hired on such a basis. *Williamson* "could have been construed to limit the widespread practice of offering leniency to arrested persons who agree to incriminate others by making purchases of contraband," but the case "has had virtually no impact. Courts faced with a defense based on it have almost invariably found a way to distinguish it." Park, *The Entrapment Controversy,* 60 Minn.L.Rev. 163, 175 (1976).

Williamson was, in effect, disapproved in *United States v. Grimes,* 438 F.2d 391 (6th Cir.1971), reasoning that a contingent fee informer is "no more likely to [lie and manufacture crimes] than witnesses acting for other, more common reasons," such as a codefendant hoping for leniency or an informant who feels that his future employment may depend upon success on this occasion. But are not contingent fee informers likely to be more desperate then informers generally? Are they not likely to have a stronger incentive for overreaching and falsification? See LaFave & Israel, § 5.4(a). However, aside from *Williamson's* cool reception in subsequent Fifth Circuit cases, *Grimes* finds support in the Supreme Court's expressed unwillingness in *United States v. Russell* (p. 493 infra) to establish "fixed rules" of due process in the entrapment or give the federal court "a 'chancellor's foot' veto" over law enforcement practices it disapproves. Park, supra, at 196.

2. *The availability of the entrapment defense in administrative proceedings.* Ordinarily, the entrapment defense is interposed in the context of a criminal prosecution, but some states have recognized the defense in proceedings to revoke or suspend a license to practice a profession or trade. See LaFave & Israel, § 5.1(c). See, e.g., *Patty v. Board of Medical Examiners,* 508 P.2d 1121 (Cal.1973), discussed in Note, 62 Calif.L.Rev. 408 (1974), where the court observed: " 'Sound public policy' and 'good morals' are incompatible with entrapment of an innocent person [in] order to revoke his professional license as clearly as they are incompatible with entrapment in order to obtain a criminal conviction. [The] public's concern with the fair administration of justice applies equally to administrative as to judicial proceedings."

3. *"Inconsistent" defenses.* The traditional view has been that the defense of entrapment is not available to one who denies commission of the criminal act with

a. Because two issues—(1) when a private person should be considered a "government agent" for purposes of the entrapment defense and (2) whether a government agent should be allowed to solicit an offense absent "probable cause" or at least "reasonable suspicion" that his target is engaged in criminal activity—received prominent attention as a result of the Abscam cases, treatment of these issues is postponed until the Notes and Questions following *United States v. Kelly,* p. 499 infra.

b. See generally pp. 58–62 supra.

which he is charged, for the reason that the denial is inconsistent with the assertion of such a defense. See generally Groot, *The Serpent Beguiled Me and I (Without Scienter) Did Eat—Denial of Crime and the Entrapment Defense,* 1973 U.Ill.F. 254.[c] Does this rule, in effect compel a defendant to incriminate himself and require him to surrender his presumption of innocence in order to plead entrapment? See Groot, supra, at 269–78.

Constitutional arguments aside, is a defendant not entitled to an instruction on any issue fairly raised by the evidence, whether or not consistent with his testimony or his trial theory? Are not logically inconsistent claims generally allowed in criminal cases? See Groot, supra, at 259, citing cases allowing a defendant to deny the criminal act and claim self-defense or insanity, or to make an alibi defense and also claim provocation or intoxication. See also Note, 4 Sw.U.L.Rev. 121, 123 (1972).

Consider Gershman, *Abscam, the Judiciary, and the Ethics of Entrapment,* 91 Yale L.J. 1565, 1583 (1982): "Where a transaction is unambiguous, as in drug cases, the rule precluding inconsistent defenses is not problematic. In such cases, claims of entrapment and lack of involvement would be difficult to reconcile.[d] In a corruption case, on the other hand, the transaction that is the gravamen of the crime often is ambiguous; while money may have been exchanged, its characterization as a bribe, a consulting fee, or a campaign contribution may be the critical issue. To require from a defendant who wishes to claim entrapment an admission that the payment was a bribe forces him to make a Hobson's choice."

4. *Triable by court or jury.* Recall that *Sorrells* rejected, and *Sherman* declined to reconsider, the argument that the issue of entrapment should be tried separately to the court without a jury. Although most commentators favor a judicial determination of the issue, the defense has traditionally been regarded as a matter for the jury, except in those unusual cases where entrapment is established as a matter of law. It has been argued, in support of this position, that a jury has special, or at least traditional, competence to judge matters of credibility and motivation and to assess the subjective response to the stimulus of police encouragement. Moreover, if the matter is placed in the hands of the jury, there is an opportunity for "jury nullification" if the police conduct evokes "moral revulsion." See generally LaFave & Israel § 5.3(b).

On the other hand, it has been said that where the subjective test prevails "the most urgent considerations" support judicial determination of the issue—to avoid the great impact on the jury of prior convictions, prior arrests and "reputation testimony"—but that in those jurisdictions that follow the objective approach "the case for separate trial to the court is more evenly balanced." See Comment to *Model Penal Code* § 2.10(2) (Tent. Draft No. 9, 1959). It has been argued, however, that here, too, the case for having the matter decided by the court is a strong one: It is the function of the court to preserve its own purity; to the extent that the objective approach is based on a deterrence-of-police rationale, this is the function of the court, just as it is when the court rules on suppression motions; and, as Frankfurter, J., maintained in *Sherman,* only the court can

c. But LaFave & Israel, § 5.3(c), report that "a trend in the opposite direction appears to be developing." See, e.g., *United States v. Demma,* 523 F.2d 981 (9th Cir.1975); *People v. Perez,* 401 P.2d 934 (Cal.1965); *State v. McBride,* 599 P.2d 449 (Or.1979).

d. Moreover, in most such cases, since scienter is not required, will proof that the defendant committed the act be virtually insurmountable? Thus, even if the rule against inconsistent defenses were inoperative, would it not be poor tactics for the defendant to deny that the act was committed? Would not such a denial in the face of overwhelming proof often destroy whatever credibility the defendant might have had on the entrapment issue? See Groot, supra, at 263.

provide government agents with the necessary guidance. See LaFave & Israel, supra.

5. *Burden of proof.* In those jurisdictions following the subjective approach, it is generally agreed that the defendant must establish the fact of inducement by a government agent. Once the defendant satisfies this threshold requirement (and it is unclear whether he need only produce "some evidence" of inducement or sustain a burden of persuasion by a preponderance of the evidence), the burden is then on the government to negate the defense by establishing the defendant's "predisposition" beyond a reasonable doubt. See LaFave & Israel, § 5.3(d).

In states where the objective test prevails, entrapment is viewed as an "affirmative defense" rather than something that negates the existence of an element of the crime charged, and the entire burden of production and persuasion is on the defendant. The defendant must establish the defense by a preponderance of the evidence. The *Model Penal Code* § 2.13(2) also takes this position. For criticism of this approach, see Park, Note 1 supra, at 265–67, suggesting that the real basis for placing the burden of persuasion on the defendant is that entrapment is a disfavored defense.

SECTION 3. THE DUE PROCESS DEFENSE TO GOVERNMENT "OVERINVOLVEMENT" IN A CRIMINAL ENTERPRISE [a]

UNITED STATES v. RUSSELL, 411 U.S. 423, 93 S.Ct. 1637, 36 L.Ed.2d 366 (1973), arose as follows: An undercover narcotics agent told respondent and his two codefendants that he represented an organization interested in controlling the manufacture and distribution of methamphetamine ("speed"). In return for one-half of the drug produced, the agent offered to supply the defendants with the chemical propanone, an essential ingredient in the manufacture of "speed." There was testimony that propanone was difficult to obtain—at the request of the Narcotics Bureau, some chemical firms had stopped selling it. The agent made the offer on the condition that he be shown a sample of the drug which defendants were making and the laboratory where it was being produced. One of the defendants gave the agent a quantity of "speed" that he represented as being from "the last batch that we made." The agent was then shown defendants' laboratory. The agent subsequently supplied defendants with 100 grams of propanone, which was used to produce two batches of "speed." The agent was then given one-half of the drug. Respondent was subsequently convicted of unlawfully manufacturing and selling "speed" which he had been producing by using the propanone supplied by the government agent. On appeal, respondent conceded that the jury could have found him predisposed to commit the offense, but contended that the level of the undercover agent's involvement in the criminal enterprise was so high that his prosecution violated fundamental principles of due process. REHNQUIST, J., disagreed:

"[Respondent] contends that the same factors that led this Court to apply the exclusionary rule to illegal searches and seizures should be considered here. But he would have the Court go further in deterring undesirable official conduct by requiring that any prosecution be barred absolutely because of the police involvement in criminal activity. The analogy is imperfect in any event, for the principal reason behind the adoption of the exclusionary rule was the government's 'failure to observe its own laws.' *Mapp.* Unlike the situations giving rise to the holdings in

a. Although the claim that the government has unduly "dominated" or become impermissibly "overinvolved" in the criminal activity has been viewed as a species of the objective test for entrapment, it seems preferable to view it as the basis for a separate test for entrapment or as a due process defense independent of general entrapment theory. See Note 1 following *Russell,* infra; and Note 2 following *Hampton,* infra.

Mapp and *Miranda*, the government's conduct here violated no independent constitutional right of the respondent. Nor did [the agent] violate any federal statute or rule or commit any crime in infiltrating the respondent's drug enterprise.

"Respondent would overcome this basic weakness in his analogy to the exclusionary rule cases by having the Court adopt a rigid constitutional rule that would preclude any prosecution when it is shown that the criminal conduct would not have been possible had not an undercover agent 'supplied an indispensable means to the commission of the crime that could not have been obtained otherwise, through legal or illegal channels.' Even if we were to surmount the difficulties attending the notion that due process of law can be embodied in fixed rules, and those attending respondent's particular formulation, the rule he proposes would not appear to be of significant benefit to him. For [the record] discloses that although the propanone was difficult to obtain it was by no means impossible. [The record also shows] that the propanone used in the illicit manufacture of methamphetamine not only *could* have been obtained without the intervention of [the undercover agent] but was in fact obtained by these defendants.

"While we may some day be presented with a situation in which the conduct of law enforcement agents is so outrageous that due process principles would absolutely bar the government from invoking judicial process to obtain a conviction, cf. *Rochin*, the instant case is distinctly not of that breed. [The undercover agent's] contribution of propanone to the criminal enterprise already in process was scarcely objectionable. The chemical is by itself a harmless substance and its possession is legal. * * *

"Several [lower federal court decisions] have undoubtedly gone beyond this Court's [precedents] in order to bar prosecutions because of what they thought to be for want of a better term 'overzealous law enforcement.' But the defense of entrapment enunciated in those opinions was not intended to give the federal judiciary a 'chancellor's foot' veto over law enforcement practices of which it did not approve. The execution of the federal laws under our Constitution is confided primarily to the Executive Branch of the Government, subject to applicable constitutional and statutory limitations and to judicially fashioned rules to enforce those limitations. We think that the decision [below] quite unnecessarily introduces an unmanageably subjective standard which is contrary to the holdings of this Court in *Sorrells* and *Sherman*.

"[In the light of *Sorrells* and *Sherman*, respondent's concession] that the jury finding as to predisposition was supported by the evidence [is] fatal to his claim of entrapment. He was an active participant in an illegal drug manufacturing enterprise which began before the government agent appeared on the scene, and continued after the government agent had left the scene. He was, in the words of *Sherman*, not an 'unwary innocent' but an 'unwary criminal.' "

Dissenting Justice STEWART, joined by Brennan and Marshall, JJ., urged adoption of the "objective" test for entrapment and maintained that the undercover agent's involvement in the criminal enterprise was "precisely the type of conduct that the entrapment defense is meant to prevent":

"[W]hen the agents' involvement in [a criminal enterprise] is of a kind that could induce or instigate the commission of a crime by one not ready and willing to commit it,[a] then—regardless of the character or propensities of the particular person

a. But how would adoption of the "objective" test aid Russell? Is an offer to supply propanone likely to induce a normally law-abiding person to manufacture and to sell "speed"? See Note 1, infra.

induced—I think entrapment has occurred. For in that situation, the Government has engaged in the impermissible manufacturing of crime, and the federal courts should bar the prosecution in order to preserve the institutional integrity of the system of federal criminal justice. * * *

"In this case, the chemical ingredient [provided by the undercover agent was an essential ingredient in the manufacture of 'speed,' is not used for any other purpose,] was available only to licensed persons, and the Government itself had requested suppliers not to sell that ingredient even to people with a license. Yet the government agent readily offered and supplied that ingredient to an unlicensed person and asked him to make a certain illegal drug with it. The Government then prosecuted that person for making the drug produced *with the very ingredient* which its agent had so helpfully supplied. This strikes me as the very pattern of conduct that should be held to constitute entrapment as a matter of law." [b]

Notes and Questions

1. *How helpful is the objective approach to entrapment in dealing with complaints that the government played too dominant a role or became too "involved" or "enmeshed" in the criminal enterprise to permit a conviction?* Consider Kamisar, Grano & Haddad, *Sum and Substance of Criminal Procedure* 172–73 (1977): "Proponents of the 'objective' test have often assumed that if their approach is adopted, the entrapment defense must prevail in cases where the government has 'dominated' or become 'over-involved' in the unlawful activity, but this is by no means clear. It seems highly unlikely that a normally law-abiding citizen would be very tempted to engage in the counterfeiting business simply because a government agent offered to supply him the requisite kind of paper (or ink). Only a person with the know-how, equipment and contacts, only someone already engaged in the counterfeiting business or ready and willing to do so, would be likely to find an offer to supply him with special materials very attractive. Thus, the objection to government 'over-involvement' in a criminal enterprise seems to be not that such government activity will cause an otherwise law-abiding citizen to turn to crime but that such government activity is unseemly or offensive or shocking. Consequently, it seems preferable to view the concern over excessive government enmeshment in a criminal activity as [the basis for a] separate test for entrapment."

2. *Supplying materials "wholly unobtainable from other sources."* "It cannot be doubted," observed Justice Stewart in his *Russell* dissent, that if propanone "had been wholly unobtainable from other sources," the undercover agent's offer to supply it in return for part of the illicit "speed" "would be precisely the type of governmental conduct that constitutes entrapment under any definition. For the agent's conduct in that situation would make possible the commission of an otherwise totally impossible crime * * *" Under the circumstances hypothesized by Justice Stewart, would the government's conduct constitute entrapment under any definition? Should it? Cf. *Hampton v. United States,* infra.

HAMPTON v. UNITED STATES, 425 U.S. 484, 96 S.Ct. 1646, 48 L.Ed.2d 113 (1976), grew out of the following facts: Petitioner was convicted of distributing heroin in violation of federal law. The district court refused to give petitioner's

b. In a separate dissent, Justice Douglas, joined by Brennan, J., dismissed the fact that the chemical ingredient supplied by the undercover agent might have been obtained from other sources as "quite irrelevant. Supplying [the ingredient] made the United States an active participant in the unlawful activity. * * * Federal agents play a debased role when they become the instigators of the crime, or partners in its commission, or the creative brain behind the illegal scheme. That is what the federal agent did here when he furnished the accused with one of the chemical ingredients needed to manufacture the unlawful drug."

requested instruction that if it were found, as he claimed, that the narcotics he sold to government agents (posing as narcotics buyers) had been supplied to him by a government informant [a] he must be acquitted as a matter of law regardless of his predisposition to commit the offense charged. On appeal, petitioner conceded that he was "predisposed." A majority of the Court rejected petitioner's contention, but there was no opinion of the Court. Justice REHNQUIST, who announced the judgment of the Court in an opinion in which Burger, C.J., and White, J., joined, observed:

"In view of [*Sorrells, Sherman* and *Russell*], petitioner correctly recognized that his case does not qualify as one involving 'entrapment' at all, [but] relies on the language in *Russell* that 'we may some day be presented with a situation in which the conduct of law enforcement agents is so outrageous that due process principle would absolutely bar the government from invoking judicial processes to obtain a conviction * * *'

"In urging that this [is such a case], petitioner misapprehends the meaning of the quoted language in *Russell.* Admittedly petitioner's case is different from Russell's but the difference is one of degree, not of kind. In *Russell* the ingredient supplied by the government agent was a legal drug which the defendants demonstrably could have obtained from other sources besides the Government. Here the drug which the government informant allegedly supplied [was] both illegal and constituted the *corpus delicti* for the sale of which the petitioner was convicted. The Government obviously played a more significant role in enabling petitioner to sell contraband in this case than it did in *Russell.*

"But in each case the government agents were acting in concert with the defendant, and in each case either the jury found or the defendant conceded that he was predisposed to commit the crime for which he was convicted. The remedy of the criminal defendant with respect to the acts of government agents, which, far from being resisted, are encouraged by him, lies solely in the defense of entrapment. But, as noted, petitioner's conceded predisposition rendered this defense unavailable to him.

"To sustain petitioner's contention here would run directly contrary to our statement in *Russell* that the defense of entrapment is not intended 'to give the federal judiciary a "chancellor's foot" veto over law enforcement practices of which it did not approve. * * * ' "

Concurring Justice POWELL, joined by Blackmun, J., agreed that "this case is controlled completely by *Russell,*" but was "unwilling to join the plurality in concluding that, no matter what the circumstances, neither due process principles nor our supervisory power could support a bar to conviction in any case where the Government is able to prove disposition":

"The plurality [says, in effect,] that the concept of fundamental fairness inherent in the guarantee of due process would never prevent the conviction of a predisposed defendant, regardless of the outrageousness of police behavior in light of the

a. According to petitioner's version of the events, the informant not only supplied the narcotics but was the first to propose the criminal enterprise. Petitioner alleged that when he stated that he was short of cash, the informant responded by proposing they sell drugs that he could get from a pharmacist friend. Evidently, petitioner did not deem this particular aspect of his version of the facts significant. Evidently, too, a majority of the Court considered it irrelevant so long as petitioner was "predisposed" to commit the offense and the governmental activity had not "implant[ed] in the mind of an *innocent* person the disposition to commit the alleged offense." (Emphasis added.) No member of the majority disputed dissenting Justice Brennan's characterization of the case as one where "the two sales for which petitioner was convicted were allegedly instigated by Government agents." See also Judge Adams's dissent in *United States v. Twigg* (p. 498 fn. a infra) (describing *Hampton* as a case where the government "suggested the operation"). But see the majority opinion in *Twigg* and Note, 67 Geo.L.J. 1455, 1464 & fn. 73, 1466 (1979).

surrounding circumstances. I do not understand *Russell* or earlier cases [to] have gone so far, and there was no need for them to do so. [Disposition of the claims in those cases] did not require the Court to consider whether overinvolvement of government agents in contraband offenses could ever reach such proportions as to bar conviction of a predisposed defendant as a matter of due process. Nor have we had occasion yet to confront Government overinvolvement in areas outside the realm of contraband offenses. In these circumstances, I am unwilling to conclude that an analysis other than one limited to predisposition would never be appropriate under due process principles.[b]

"The plurality's use of the 'chancellor's foot' passage from *Russell* may suggest that it also would foreclose reliance on our supervisory power to bar conviction of a predisposed defendant because of outrageous police conduct. Again, I do not understand *Russell* to have gone so far."

Justice BRENNAN, joined by Stewart and Marshall, JJ., dissented, urging that conviction be "barred as a matter of law where the subject of the criminal charge is the sale of contraband provided to the defendant by a Government agent."[c] The dissenters reiterated their support for the "objective" approach to entrapment, under which, they maintained, petitioner's claims "would plainly be held to constitute entrapment as a matter of law," but considered reversal compelled even "for those who follow the 'subjective' approach." Continued the dissent:

"Two facts sufficiently distinguish this case from *Russell.* First, the chemical supplied in that case was not contraband. [In] contrast, petitioner claims that the very narcotic he is accused of selling was supplied by an agent of the Government.

"Second, [Russell] 'was an active participant in an illegal drug manufacturing enterprise which began before the Government agent appeared on the scene, and continued after the Government agent had left the scene.' [H]is crime was participation in an ongoing operation. In contrast, the two sales for which petitioner was convicted were allegedly instigated by Government agents and completed by the Government's purchase. The beginning and end of this crime thus coincided exactly with the Government's entry into and withdrawal from the criminal activity involved in this case * * *.

"Whether the differences from the *Russell* situation are of degree or of kind, I think they clearly require a different result. Where the Government's agent deliberately sets up the accused by supplying him with contraband and then bringing him to another agent as a potential purchaser, the Government's role has passed the point of toleration. The Government is doing nothing less than buying contraband from itself through an intermediary and jailing the intermediary. There is little, if any, law enforcement interest promoted by such conduct; plainly it is not designed to discover ongoing drug traffic. Rather, such conduct deliberately entices an individual to commit a crime. That the accused is 'predisposed' cannot possibly justify the action of government officials in purposefully creating the crime. No one would suggest that the police could round up and jail all 'predisposed' individuals, yet that is precisely what set-ups like the instant one are intended to accomplish."[d]

b. At this point Justice Powell quotes from Judge Friendly's view in *United States v. Archer,* 486 F.2d 670, 676 (2d Cir.1973), that "it would be unthinkable, for example, to permit government agents to instigate robberies and beatings merely to gather evidence to convict other members of a gang of hoodlums."

c. The dissent deemed it sufficient "for present purposes" to adopt this rule "under our supervisory power and leave to another day whether it ought to be made applicable to the States under the Due Process Clause." For a general discussion of the federal court's supervisory power over criminal justice, see pp. 58–62 supra.

d. Stevens, J., took no part in the consideration or decision of the case.

Notes and Questions

1. "The depth of our confusion concerning the proper limits on government power in this area," observes Seidman, *The Supreme Court, Entrapment, and Our Criminal Justice Dilemma,* 1981 Sup.Ct.Rev. 111, 116 n. 20, "is illustrated by comparing the intuitions of Justice Powell with those of the authors of the Model Penal Code. Justice Powell hints that his objective, due process test would be violated if the government induced beatings or armed robberies. [See fn. b to his concurring opinion in *Hampton.*] Yet the Model Penal Code [§ 2.13(3)] makes an entrapment defense unavailable in precisely those cases where the defendant causes or threatens bodily injury."

2. Abramson & Lindeman, *Entrapment and Due Process in the Federal Courts,* 8 Am. J.Crim.Law 139, 180–82 (1980), concludes, inter alia: "Many courts treat the constitutional due process defense as an illegitimate offspring of entrapment, and recognize the issue reluctantly when it is presented in the pleadings. It is then granted only cursory review. The better approach, therefore, is to plead the defense independently of the general entrapment defense, with police misconduct as the exclusive basis. In that case, the due process defense cannot later be dismissed by a finding of predisposition, because a defendant can prove police misconduct and overreaching without having to disprove his own predisposition. The trial court can then decide the due process question as a matter of law. * * *

"[M]ost of the due process cases following *Russell* and *Hampton* concern the sale or manufacture of drugs. Police tactics for combatting the narcotics traffic frequently require law enforcement officers to supply 'some item of value that the drug ring requires' *[Russell].* In apprehending suspects, the police must establish a rapport with dealers and pushers. The 'relationship' between an informer and a pusher, or a government agent and a defendant, demands that the agent use tactics which might 'shock the conscience' of a lay person. The nature of the crime, however, makes the gathering of evidence an all but impossible task. Police techniques in drug cases tend to differ from other crimes. It may therefore be that the very nature of the crime accounts for the general reluctance of the courts to adopt the objective and due process approaches. In a typical drug transaction, the individual's due process rights are generally thought to be outweighed by society's interest in controlling the drug traffic. Accordingly, most courts apply the subjective test that focuses exclusively on the defendant's predisposition. * * *

"The due process defense requires a stricter scrutiny of government conduct than the traditional entrapment defense. Possibly, as in *United States v. Twigg,*[a] low-

a. In *Twigg,* 588 F.2d 373 (3d Cir.1978), apparently the first case since *Hampton* in which a defendant has prevailed on a due process defense, the informant contacted an old acquaintance, defendant Neville, and proposed that they set up a "speed" laboratory. Neville assumed responsibility for raising the capital and arranging for distribution of the product. The informant assumed responsibility for acquiring the necessary equipment, raw materials, and a production site. The DEA assisted the informant in carrying out his part of the operation by providing two and one-half gallons of the essential and hard to obtain ingredient, propanone; some of the glassware needed; and a rented farmhouse for the laboratory site. Defendant Twigg joined the operation, at the invitation of Neville. The laboratory operated for one week, producing about six pounds of speed. The informant alone had the expertise to manufacture the drug and thus was completely in charge of the laboratory.

Neville and Twigg were convicted of conspiracy to manufacture speed. On appeal, a 2–1 majority, per Rosenn, J., reversed. Distinguishing *Russell* as a case in which the defendant was an active participant before the government agent arrived on the scene, and *Hampton* as concerned with the sale of an illegal drug—"a much more fleeting and elusive crime to detect than the operation of an illicit drug laboratory"—the *Twigg* majority concluded that the government involvement was so "overreaching," "egregious" and "outrageous" as to bar prosecution as a matter of due process. The court emphasized (a) that the "illicit plan did not originate with the crimier courts will soon accept the need for a constitutional due process defense independent of the general entrapment theory. To protect the constitutional rights of an individual does not necessarily require application of a 'chancellor's foot.' "

UNITED STATES v. KELLY

707 F.2d 1460 (D.C.Cir.1983).

[The phase of the Abscam operation that resulted in the indictment of Kelly and other Congressmen was conceived by convicted confidence man Weinberg and approved by the FBI. It was to spread the word that wealthy Arabs were willing to bribe members of Congress to ensure that they would introduce private immigration legislation on the Arabs' behalf if and when necessary.

[Among those to whom the word was passed was codefendant Ciuzio, an acquaintance of Congressman Kelly. At a November, 1979 meeting, Ciuzio told Kelly that he had some Arab clients with immigration difficulties and asked Kelly if he could help them. Kelly indicated that he would be glad to do so, particularly since Ciuzio indicated the Arabs might invest in his district. Ciuzio told Kelly that he—Ciuzio—would receive a large fee if Kelly helped the Arabs. Kelly replied that the fee would cause no difficulties. Ciuzio then told codefendant Weisz, who was a business associate of Rosenberg (who was helping Weinberg locate politicians willing to assist the latter's "Arab-employers"), that Kelly would be happy to help the Arabs. The word was passed via the Abscam "middlemen" to Weinberg that a "candidate" was available who would assist with the Arabs' immigration problems and that he wanted $250,000. Weinberg suggested that the Congressman be paid $25,000 down, with the balance paid when legislation was required.

[At a December 19 meeting among Ciuzio, Weinberg and FBI agent Amoroso (Weinberg's immediate supervisor), Ciuzio was told what assistance would be expected of the Congressman. Ciuzio indicated that the Congressman was Kelly and intimated that he and Kelly had had previous dealings of a similar nature. Ciuzio suggested that he had told Kelly of the offer and claimed that Kelly had left the arrangements to him. But Ciuzio opposed direct payment to Kelly and suggested that the money instead be escrowed through Weisz.

[A January 8, 1980 meeting was arranged between Kelly and the "Arabs' representatives" at the FBI's townhouse in Washington, D.C. Soon after his arrival, Ciuzio, in a private meeting with Wein-

nal defendants"; (b) that the informant's expertise was "an indispensable requisite to this criminal enterprise"; and (c) that Neville was "lawfully and peacefully minding his own affairs" until approached by the defendant.

As dissenting Judge Adams read the relevant Supreme Court cases, due process analysis "was not intended simply to reestablish the objective approach to entrapment under a new name." He dissented because he did not believe that "this situation presents the intolerable set of circumstances necessary to warrant resort to the due process clause." He thought the facts less persuasive for reversal than were those in *Hampton* because none of the chemicals, equipment or skill provided by the governemnt "was itself contraband." The government, through its agent, did suggest the operation, "but that is the situation in many undercover operations, and was the case in *Hampton.*"

Twigg suggests that the oft-proposed but rarely applied "reasonable suspicion" requirement (see p. 504 infra) "may on occasion emerge as an aspect of the due process limits upon encouragement activity. The point seems to be that over-involvement by the government to the extent reflected in *Twigg* is permissible, if at all, only against a person who is 'reasonably suspected of criminal conduct or design.' " LaFave & Israel, § 5.4(c). See also Note, 67 Geo.L.J. 1455, 1461, 1467 (1979).

Another important principle recognized in *Twigg* is that "the practicalities of combatting" a certain type of criminal activity must be considered in determining whether "more extreme methods of investigation" are constitutionally permissible. But *Twigg* may have misapplied this principle. Consider Note, 67 Geo.L.J. at 1463: "[A] drug laboratory, which by nature is sophisticated and covert, arguably is *more* difficult to detect than the sale of drugs."

berg and Amoroso, sought to dissuade them from attempting to bribe Kelly directly. It was ultimately agreed that Kelly would acknowledge that the money was in exchange for his agreement to assist the Arabs, but that Ciuzio would actually take the money from the meeting.

[Finally, later that evening, Congressman Kelly met with Amoroso alone. When Amoroso proposed a payoff, Kelly told him that he was interested in the investment in his district, that he didn't "know anything about" Amoroso's arrangement with Ciuzio and others—"I'm not involved with it"—but that Amoroso's arrangement with Ciuzio and others was "fine."

[After Amoroso received a phone call from an Assistant United States Attorney who was monitoring the meeting and who told Amoroso that Kelly was "being cute," Amoroso sought to clarify Kelly's position. Kelly maintained that he wanted the money given to Ciuzio. Amoroso indicated that all of the money was supposed to go to Kelly, that Ciuzio would be compensated separately, and that giving the money directly to Kelly would avoid witnesses, thus protecting Kelly. The Congressman then agreed that that was "the best way of doing it." Amoroso then gave Kelly $25,000 in packets of $100 bills and Kelly stuffed the money in the pockets of his suit.]

PER CURIAM: Judge MacKinnon files an opinion in Parts I, II, III(A), and IV of which Chief Judge Robinson concurs.[a] Judge Ginsburg files an opinion in which Chief Judge Robinson concurs. Thus Parts I, II, III(A) and IV of Judge MacKinnon's opinion together with Judge Ginsburg's opinion constitute the opinion of the court. * * *

MACKINNON, CIRCUIT JUDGE. * * * On January 8, 1980, Congressman Richard Kelly accepted $25,000 from an agent of the FBI who was posing as a representative of two wealthy Arabs as part of the FBI's elaborate Abscam investigation. In return, Kelly agreed to use his position in Congress to assist the Arabs to become permanent residents of the United States. Unbeknownst to Kelly, the FBI recorded the entire illegal transaction on video tape.

On the basis of this and other evidence, Kelly and [Ciuzio and Weisz] were charged with [bribery and other federal offenses]. A jury found each defendant guilty on all counts. However, the district court granted Kelly's motion to dismiss the indictment, entering a judgment of acquittal in his favor, because it concluded that the FBI's actions in furtherance of Abscam were so outrageous that prosecution of Kelly was barred by principles of due process. * * *

III. ANALYSIS

A. THE DUE PROCESS DEFENSE

* * *

"[Our task] is to assess whether the FBI's conduct in Abscam reached a "demonstrable level of outrageousness" [Powell, J., concurring in *Hampton*], while keeping in mind the difficulties inherent in detecting corrupt public officials. Measured against this standard, the FBI's conduct did not violate due process.

B. ABSCAM

[S]tripped of [its] trappings of wealth, Abscam was no more than an "opportunity for the commission of crime by those willing to do so." *United States v. Myers,* 692 F.2d 823, 837 (2d Cir.1982). Amoroso and Weinberg let it be known that they would pay substantial sums of money to congressmen willing to promise to assist the wealthy Arabs with their immigration difficulties. Thereafter, the FBI operatives simply waited for the grapevine to work

a. Part I, a detailed discussion of the facts, and Part II, a discussion of the district court opinion dismissing the indictment, are omitted.

and to see who appeared to take bribes. No congressmen were targeted for investigation; rather, Abscam pursued all who were brought to the operation by the grapevine.[50] In essence, then, Abscam was *not* significantly different from an undercover drug or fencing operation offering to buy from all who appear at its door.[51] Instead of buying stolen goods or contraband drugs, Abscam bought corrupt official influence in Congress. Such government involvement in crime does not violate principles of due process.

We need not determine the exact limits on government involvement in crime imposed by the due process clause for it is clear that the FBI's involvement in Abscam was less than that government involvement found unobjectionable by the Supreme Court.[52] * * *

In [*Russell* and *Hampton*] the government not only provided an *opportunity* to commit a crime, but also provided the *means* to commit that crime. Nevertheless, in each case the Supreme Court concluded that the government's conduct did

50. However, not all officials brought to Abscam were offered bribes. The Abscam operatives recognized that they had no control over the representations made by intermediaries such as Ciuzio, Rosenberg, and Weisz. Accordingly, the FBI *always* discussed the asylum scenario with the officials prior to the offer of a bribe. That was certainly the case with Kelly; Amoroso carefully discussed the details of the asylum scenario with Kelly *before* any bribe money was paid. See discussion infra. In one instance, where this discussion revealed that the official was unaware of the corrupt nature of the proposal, the FBI terminated the meeting.

51. The district court concluded that Abscam was unlike ordinary, "passive" undercover operations because it used "recruiting agents" to spread the word that bribes were available. I disagree. I seriously doubt that the government would establish an undercover drug or fencing operation without spreading the word, through informants and criminal elements (labeled "recruiting agents" by the district court), that its services were available. The Abscam investigators did no more.

My colleagues term Abscam an extraordinary operation. It was extraordinary only in the positions of some of the individuals involved and in the intangible nature of the "commodity" purchased. Otherwise, it is strikingly similar to ordinary undercover operations. To conclude otherwise suggests lack of familiarity with changes in the law enforcement activities of the FBI since the death of J. Edgar Hoover in 1972. *Final Report of the Select Committee to Study Undercover Activities of Components of the Department of Justice,* S.Rep. No. 682, 97th Cong., 2d Sess. 39 (1982). Hoover was an advocate of keeping FBI activities "of an open character not in any manner subject to criticism." He resisted efforts to get the FBI into drug enforcement because it would have required that FBI agents become involved in "unsavory" undercover operations, but was forced by presidential directive to allow undercover FBI activities in defense intelligence matters during World War II. Following Hoover's death his successor, Clarence M. Kelly, with the support of Congress, and pursuant to widespread public demand, began to move the FBI into "big cases" involving *white-collar* and organized crime.

Initially, the FBI, in cooperation with local law enforcement authorities, established undercover fencing operations, gaining valuable experience in undercover techniques "that avoided claims of entrapment." Thereafter, the FBI's undercover activities have expanded to include "investigations of white-collar crimes, political corruption, personal and property crimes, and racketeering crimes." The FBI now also has responsibility to investigate violations of the criminal drug laws of the United States. Unfortunately, the government cannot select the nature of the crimes that will be committed and the detection of many of these "big" crimes require highly sophisticated undercover operations. Congressional appropriations for such undercover activity have increased substantially, from $1 million for 53 operations in 1977 to $4.5 million for 463 operations in 1981. Thus, although large FBI undercover operations might once have been characterized as extraordinary, such operations are now clearly part of the FBI's routine activities and their legality is not destroyed by their imaginative character.

My colleagues also criticize the failure of the FBI to closely supervise the Abscam operation. To the extent that this criticism extends to the non-FBI middlemen, such as Ciuzio, Rosenberg and Weisz, involved in Abscam, their activities could hardly be "supervised" because they did not know Abscam was an undercover investigation. The FBI took considerable precautions to compensate for its inability to control the representations of the middlemen. See note 50 supra.

* * *

52. For this reason, we need not decide the validity of the due process test formulated by the district court—whether the temptation offered is "one which the individual is likely to encounter in the ordinary course." It is suggested, however, that criminal conduct being as highly varied as it is that such test is unduly speculative.

not violate due process. Where, as in Abscam, the government simply provides the opportunity to commit a crime, prosecution of a defendant does not violate principles of due process. This conclusion is in accord with decisions of the Second and Third Circuits upholding Abscam convictions challenged on due process grounds. *United States v. Williams,* (2d Cir. Apr. 5, 1983); *Meyers,* supra; *United States v. Alexandro,* 675 F.2d 34 (2d Cir.); *United States v. Jannotti,* 673 F.2d 578 (3d Cir.) (en banc).[53]

C. Specific Claims

1. *Reasonable Suspicion* [b]

Nor do any of the specifically challenged FBI actions in furtherance of Abscam reach that "demonstrable level of outrageousness" which would bar Kelly's prosecution. The district court stressed that Abscam's asylum scenario was not triggered by any suspicion of corruption in government. [But] prior to the January 8 meeting with Kelly, the Abscam operatives had evidence from which they could conclude that Kelly was, in fact, corrupt. Ciuzio stated as much in his meeting with Amoroso and Weinberg on December 19. Furthermore, *Ciuzio told Weinberg on December 20 that he asked Kelly to call him from a "safe" phone booth to discuss the transaction; that Kelly did so was strong evidence for the Abscam operatives that Kelly was fully aware that he was participating in an illicit transaction.* Thus, the FBI had ample suspicion of corruption to justify pursuing the asylum scenario and Kelly, if such suspicion was necessary.[58] * * *

2. *Utilization of Weinberg*

[The] argument that the FBI violated due process by utilizing the services of an admitted confidence man, Melvin Weinberg, in Abscam should likewise be rejected. Successful creation of an "elaborate hoax" such as Abscam may well *require* employment of "experts" such as Weinberg to give the operation an aura of "credibility" and "contacts" with criminal elements. The employment of a convicted confidence man in Abscam is analogous to the entirely proper employment of a convicted seller of drugs to purchase drugs from a suspected distributor. * * *

4. *Multiple Bribe Offers*

Finally, Kelly contends that the FBI operatives violated due process when they persisted in offering a bribe after what he characterizes as his initial rejection. *Kelly asserts that he rejected the bribe at his meeting with Ciuzio on December 23, that Ciuzio informed Amoroso and Weinberg of that fact at the townhouse on January 8, and that he rejected the bribe several times in his meeting with Amoroso.* Kelly argues, and the district court agreed, that under these circumstances Amoroso's several bribe offers to Kelly were outrageous and violated due process. I cannot agree.

The evidence in this case clearly demonstrates that at no time did Kelly reject Abscam's corrupt immigration proposal. On both December 23 and January 8, Kelly agreed to assure the wealthy Arabs that he would help them with their immigration problems as a favor to Ciuzio, despite the fact that Kelly knew that in return the Arabs would pay substantial sums to Ciuzio [and others]. It is also clear that Kelly understood that part of the arrangement was that the Arabs would

53. The Third Circuit's decision in *Jannotti* is particularly significant because it held that *Twigg,* the only post-*Hampton* case to uphold a due process challenge to prosecution because of excessive government involvement, did not control its consideration of Abscam. Thus Kelly's reliance on *Twigg* is misplaced.

b. See Note 1 following this case.

58. Although we need not decide the question, both the Second and Third Circuits have rejected the argument that the government must have reasonable suspicion of wrongdoing before proceeding with an undercover operation such as Abscam.

make substantial investments in his district. Such agreements, which would benefit Kelly indirectly, constitute violations of the bribery statute. Furthermore, the discussions between Ciuzio, Kelly, and the Abscam operatives at the townhouse of January 8 focused on the *manner* in which the bribe would be paid, not on whether it would be paid. Ciuzio told Weinberg not to bribe Kelly directly, but agreed that he would take the money for Kelly. After agreeing that Amoroso was going to give him some money at the meeting, Kelly asked Amoroso to pay the bribe to Ciuzio—to "deal with [Ciuzio] about it." In my view, Congressman Kelly "did not reject a bribe, he [initially] rejected its payment under circumstances he feared would be incriminating." *Myers.*

I likewise reject Kelly's characterization of his conversation with Amoroso on January 8 as a *series* of bribe offers. Although the terms of the corrupt Abscam proposal were mentioned several times during that conversation, Amoroso's discussion reflects the evasive and circumspect negotiation to be expected of a person seeking to corrupt a public official. In my view, Amoroso's conversation with Kelly on January 8 can be fairly characterized only as a *single offer* of a corrupt proposal to Kelly. For these reasons I reject Kelly's contention that he initially rejected a bribe, that the Abscam agents persisted in offering him a bribe, and that they thus violated due process.

IV. CONCLUSION * * *

The Supreme Court has made it clear that "a successful due process defense must be predicated on *intolerable government conduct* which goes beyond that necessary to sustain an entrapment defense." *Jannotti* (emphasis added). Considering the genuine need to detect corrupt public officials, as well as the difficulties inherent in doing so, we conclude that the FBI's conduct in furtherance of its Abscam operation, insofar as it involved Kelly, simply did not reach intolerable levels. * * *

GINSBURG, CIRCUIT JUDGE: ["Abscam"] was an extraordinary operation. The investigation was steered in large part by a convicted swindler; it relied upon con men to identify and attract targets, to whom legitimate as well as illegitimate inducements were offered; it proceeded without close supervision by responsible officials.[1] * * *

The District Court stated and attempted to apply an objective test to determine when government investigation exceeds tolerable limits: Was the crime-inducing conduct in which the government engaged, the temptation presented to the target, modeled on reality? This test, the District Court indicated, should apply when the government had no knowledge of prior wrongdoing by the target and no reason to believe the target was about to commit a crime; it would serve as a check against government creation (rather than apprehension) of criminals by offers or importuning that would never occur in the real world.

The real-world test, as applied by the District Court, is speculative. The District Judge assumed that a person who offers a bribe would retreat upon encountering an initial rejection and would not "have the audacity" to press on "for fear of being

1. * * * We do not share Judge MacKinnon's view that, apart from "trappings of wealth," Abscam "was *not* significantly different from" run-of-the-mill "passive" undercover operations. As the District Court's opinion sets out in painstaking detail, the Abscam actors did a good deal more than simply "spread the word." Nor can we agree with Judge MacKinnon that the FBI "had ample suspicion of corruption to justify pursuing * * * Kelly." That suspicion, as Judge MacKinnon recites, was based on Ciuzio's report to Amoroso and Weinberg that "Kelly was, in fact, corrupt." But as the District Court observed:

"Ciuzio went to great lengths to make it appear that he had virtual control over the Congressman, indicating at the time that Kelly was dishonest and was already taking money and had various other weaknesses. He indicated that he had known and cultivated Kelly for about 2½ years. None of this was true. No attempt was made to verify it; and there is no indication that Weinberg and Amoroso believed it."

reported." But the first overture renders the party offering the bribe vulnerable to prosecution. "In for a calf," such a person might press on if he perceives any chance of ultimate success.[9] Nonetheless, were the slate clean, we might be attracted to an approach similar to the District Court's, and would perhaps ask whether, in real-world circumstances, the person snared would ever encounter bait as alluring as the offer the government tendered.

However, our slate contains references that lower courts are not positioned to erase. We may not alter the contours of the entrapment defense under a due process cloak,[11] and we lack authority, where no *specific* constitutional right of the defendant has been violated, to dismiss indictments as an exercise of supervisory power over the conduct of federal law enforcement agents. *See United States v. Payner* [p. 59 supra]. Precedent dictates that we refrain from applying the general due process constraint to bar a conviction except in the rare instance of "[p]olice overinvolvement in crime" that reaches "a demonstrable level of outrageousness." *Hampton* (Powell, J., concurring) * * *; *Russell.*

The requisite level of outrageousness, the Supreme Court has indicated, is not established merely upon a showing of obnoxious behavior or even flagrant misconduct on the part of the police; the broad "fundamental fairness" guarantee, it appears from High Court decisions, is not transgressed absent "coercion, violence or brutality to the person." * * *

The importuning of Congressman Kelly and the offers made to him, extraordinary and in excess of real-world opportunities as they appear to have been, did not involve the infliction of pain or physical or psychological coercion. We are therefore constrained to reverse, although we share the District Court's grave concern that the Abscam drama, both in its general tenor, and in "the [particular] manner in which Kelly was handled," unfolded as "an unwholesome spectacle."

9. As the government points out, parties to real-world transactions could readily adjust to a one-refusal rule: the bribe taker would always resist the first overture.

11. See *Twigg* (Adams, J., dissenting).

Notes and Questions

1. *The "reasonable suspicion" requirement.* A number of commentators have maintained that the government should not be permitted to solicit an offense absent "probable cause" or at least "reasonable suspicion" that the target is engaged in criminal activity, but current lower federal court authority "overwhelmingly holds that no 'reasonable cause' requirement exits." Note, 67 Geo.L.J. 1455, 1467 (1979). Moreover, "*Russell* seems to have sapped [this theory] of any remaining vitality by indicating that the entrapment defense is intended to protect nondisposed defendants rather than to control police conduct." Park, *The Entrapment Controversy,* 60 Minn.L.Rev. 163, 197 (1976). See generally Dix, *Undercover Investigations and Police Rulemaking,* 53 Texas L.Rev. 203, 249–54 (1975); Rotenberg, *The Police Detection Practice of Encouragement,* 4 Houston L.Rev. 609, 615–20 (1967).

Operation Abscam, however, has prompted renewed interest in this issue, for there a convicted swindler and other "middlemen," themselves under investigation, decided which politicians would be offered bribes. Congressman Don Edwards, a former FBI agent, voiced concern about "free-floating surveyors, middlemen, who work with the FBI and are the ones who finger people," and his colleague, Representative John Seiberling, balked at "the idea of giving some people of dubious ethical standards free rein to entice anyone they can entice to commit a crime." See N.Y. Times, Feb. 17, 1980, pp. 1, 20. Indeed, Professor Paul Chevigny maintains that "Abscam shows [that the] central evil of entrapment is discriminatory law enforcement, whether the police zero in on a 'politician' or a 'drug dealer.' " *A Rejoinder,* The Nation, Feb. 23, 1980, p. 205 [a] Consider Gershman, *Abscam, the Judiciary, and the Ethics of Entrapment,* 91 Yale L.J. 1565, 1584–85 (1982):

"The excessive inducements used in Abscam become even more objectionable when viewed in light of the means by which the government chose the targets at which Abscam was aimed. Prior to the investigation the government lacked any factual basis to suspect any public official of engaging in criminal activity. The presence of some factual justification—perhaps not even reaching the level of probable cause or reasonable suspicion—would have suggested that the government was using its scarce resources properly, not arbitrarily, and was offering inducements only to those persons who either had shown a willingness to engage in crime or were currently engaged in crime or about to commit a crime. The absence of any factual basis naturally raises questions about the bona fides of such law enforcement tactics.

"The government's ability gratuitously to generate crime through random honesty checks clearly involves unjustified intrusion into citizens' privacy and autonomy. Such interference, however, is ordinarily restricted by procedural safeguards such as the requirement of a warrant. Ironically, however, the Abscam operation, an intrusion of greater duration and intensity, was not subject to such safeguards. Government agents secretly monitored the Abscam defendants for many months, recorded their intimate conversations and surreptitiously videotaped meetings they attended. No judge authorized such procedures; indeed it is unlikely that any judge would have authorized this type of surveillance absent prior suspicion."

Professor Gershman proposes a federal entrapment statute that, inter alia, requires government agents to offer inducements "only to individuals currently engaged in, or reasonably suspected of engaging in, criminal activity." Id. at 1588. Such a requirement would allow courts "to dispense with the predisposition inquiry and to use instead the concept of 'reasonable suspicion' to test whether an individual is 'nondisposed.' " Id.

See also Whelan, *Lead Us Not Into (Unwarranted) Temptation: A Proposal to Replace the Entrapment Defense with a Reasonable-Suspicion Requirement,* 133 U.Pa.L.Rev. 1193, 1217–18 (1985), proposing that before testing an individual's penchant for illegal transactions or setting up an operation creating an environment in which criminal activities will be encouraged, investigators should obtain a warrant from a "neutral and detached magistrate" for the authorization of any inducement. Observes Whelan, id. at 1220–21:

"The reasonable-suspicion inquiry required for issuance of the warrant improves on the test for predisposition under the current subjective approach to entrapment in two important respects. First, the inquiry will be conducted by a magistrate *before* the commencement of the undercover operation. Unless government officials can show that they reasonably suspect that the target is involved in ongoing criminal activities, and that it will be difficult to catch the suspect without undercover inducement, there will be no sting or scam at all. The antecedent judicial inquiry reduces the likelihood that overzealous agents will lure wary innocents into crime. Moreover, because the magistrate's reasonable-suspicion inquiry will be held prior to commencement of the operation, evidence of the target's ready complaisance in committing the offense will not be considered. The 'evidentiary bootstrapping' that be-

a. But compare the views of Chevigny's colleague, Professor Stephen Gillers, *In Defense of Abscam: Entrapment, Where is Thy Sting?,* The Nation, Feb. 23, 1980, p. 203.

devils the present inquiry into predisposition will therefore be eliminated.

"Second, the magistrate will consider evidence only of a *current* criminal career. * * * [T]he mere fact of prior criminality would not suffice to establish reasonable suspicion. * * * Because the reasonable-suspicion inquiry obviates reliance on evidence of the target's ready complaisance or past conduct, it is less circular, tenuous, and unfair than the inquiry into predisposition used under the present subjective approach to entrapment."

2. *When is a private person a "government agent" for entrapment purposes? The use of "unwitting agents."* Defending Operation Abscam, then Assistant Attorney General Heymann emphasized: "No one associated with the United States ever picked any politician for the investigation. The middlemen did all that." N.Y. Times, Mar. 5, 1980 p. 18. But this raises another problem. Many of the people involved in Abscam were "unsuspecting middlemen," i.e., private persons who were unaware that they were working with, or for, government agents. But because entrapment is ultimately concerned with government conduct, it offers no defense to those who succumb to the inducements of private individuals acting alone. For entrapment purposes, should "unsuspecting middlemen," such as those utilized in Abscam, be regarded as agents of the government, albeit "unwitting agents"?

When government agents have persuaded a "middleman" to induce *a particular target selected by the agents* to commit a crime, the courts generally extend the entrapment defense to the ultimate targets. See, e.g., *People v. McIntire,* 591 P.2d 527 (Cal.1979), where a narcotics agent, posing as a high school student, importuned a classmate, the brother of the defendant, to obtain marijuana from his sister. Rejecting the prosecution's argument that entrapment cannot be effected through an "unwitting agent" (in this case, the defendant's brother), the court, per Mosk, J., observed: "The purposes of the entrapment defense can be fulfilled only if it is understood that one can act as a [government agent] without realizing the identity of his principal; the unwitting agent, though he may not appreciate the true nature of his role, is nonetheless being manipulated as the officer's tool in a plan to foster a crime and entrap its perpetrator."

However, when investigations are not aimed at a specific target, even though there is "substantial certainty that the person solicited by the police for the commission of a crime will seek the participation of another," such as when the agent requests the middleman to seek unidentified public officials who will accept bribes, the federal courts have "sharply disagreed" on how to apply the law of entrapment. See Note, 95 Harv.L.Rev. 1122, 1126–27 (1982). "Whenever it is reasonable to expect that the investigation will result in a secondary target's committing an offense," maintains the Harvard Note, "whether the secondary target was selected by [a government agent] or [the unsuspecting middleman], the additional offense must be considered 'the creature of [the agent's] purpose' unless the government can prove that the defendant was predisposed to commit a similar crime." Id. at 1128.

Moreover, "even when the government has no reason to expect that [the initial target] of an investigation will induce a nonessential [third party] to join in criminal activity, the third party should still be able to plead entrapment if it is found that the initial target was himself entrapped. If the original target was entrapped, the government has by definition created the actions that the initial target took in pursuing the illegal activity." Id. at 1129.

3. The Abscam cases have generated a considerable literature. In addition to the material cited above, see e.g., Blecker, *Beyond 1984: Undercover in America—Serpico to Abscam,* 28 N.Y.L.S.L.Rev. 823 (1984); Note, 25 B.C.L.Rev. 351 (1984).

For a multi-dimensional view, see *ABSCAM Ethics: Moral Issues and Deception in Law Enforcement* (G. Caplan ed. 1982). Contributors are: Wayne Kerstetter, a criminal justice professor and former law enforcement official; constitutional law professor Sanford Levinson; sociologists Gary Marx and Lawrence Sherman; Mark Moore, a professor of criminal justice policy and management; Irvin Nathan, the Department of Justice lawyer who coordinated the ABSCAM investigations when he served as deputy assistant attorney general; and economist Peter Reutre.

Chapter 8

POLICE INTERROGATION AND CONFESSIONS

SECTION 1. SOME DIFFERENT PERSPECTIVES

FRED E. INBAU: POLICE INTERROGATION—A PRACTICAL NECESSITY

52 J.Crim.L.C. & P.S. 16 (1961), reprinted in Police Power and Individual Freedom 147 (Sowle ed. 1962).

One completely false assumption accounts for most of the legal restrictions on police interrogations. It is this, and the fallacy is certainly perpetuated to a very considerable extent by mystery writers, the movies, and TV: whenever a crime is committed, if the police will only look carefully at the crime scene they will almost always find some clue that will lead them to the offender and at the same time establish his guilt; and once the offender is located, he will readily confess or disclose his guilt by trying to shoot his way out of the trap. But this is pure fiction; in actuality the situation is quite different. As a matter of fact, the art of criminal investigation has not developed to a point where the search for and the examination of physical evidence will always, or even in most cases, reveal a clue to the identity of the perpetrator or provide the necessary proof of his guilt. In criminal investigations, even of the most efficient type, there are many, many instances where physical clues are entirely absent, and the only approach to a possible solution of the crime is the interrogation of the criminal suspect himself, as well as others who may possess significant information. Moreover, in most instances these interrogations, particularly of the suspect himself, must be conducted under conditions of privacy and for a reasonable period of time; and they frequently require the use of psychological tactics and techniques that could well be classified as "unethical," if we are to evaluate them in terms of ordinary, everyday social behavior.

To protect myself from being misunderstood, I want to make it unmistakably clear that I am not an advocate of the so-called "third degree," for I am unalterably opposed to the use of any interrogation tactic or technique that is apt to make an innocent person confess. I am opposed, therefore, to the use of force, threats, or promises of leniency—all of which might well induce *an innocent person* to confess; but I do approve of such psychological tactics and techniques as trickery and deceit that are not only helpful but frequently necessary in order to secure incriminating information from the guilty, or investigate leads from otherwise uncooperative witnesses or informants.

My position, then, is this, and it may be presented in the form of three separate points, each accompanied by case illustrations:

1. *Many criminal cases, even when investigated by the best qualified police departments, are capable of solution only by means of an admission or confession from the guilty individual or upon the basis of information obtained from the questioning of other criminal suspects.*

As to the validity of this statement, I suggest that consideration be given to the situation presented by cases such as these. A man is hit on the head while walking home late at night. He did not see his assailant, nor did anyone else. A careful and thorough search of the crime scene reveals no physical clues. Then take the case of a woman who is grabbed on the street at night and dragged into an alley and raped. Here, too, the assailant was unaccommodating enough to avoid leaving his hat or other means of identification at the crime scene; and there are no other physical clues. All the police have to work on is the description of the assailant given by the victim herself. She described him as about six feet tall, white, and wearing a dark suit. Or consider this case, an actual recent one in Illinois. Three women are vacationing in a wooded resort area. Their bodies were found dead alongside a foot trail, the result of physical violence, and no physical clues are present.

In cases of this kind—and they all typify the difficult investigation problem that the police frequently encounter—how else can they be solved, if at all, except by means of the interrogation of suspects or of others who may possess significant information?

There are times, too, when a police interrogation may result not only in the apprehension and conviction of the guilty, but also in the release of the innocent from well-warranted suspicion. Here is one such actual case within my own professional experience.

The dead body of a woman was found in her home. Her skull had been crushed, apparently with some blunt instrument. A careful police investigation of the premises did not reveal any clues to the identity of the killer. No fingerprints or other significant evidence were located; not even the lethal instrument itself could be found. None of the neighbors could give any helpful information. Although there was some evidence of a slight struggle in the room where the body lay, there were no indications of a forcible entry into the home. The deceased's young daughter was the only other resident of the home and she had been away in school at the time of the crime. The daughter could not give the police any idea of what, if any, money or property had disappeared from the home.

For several reasons the police considered the victim's husband a likely suspect. He was being sued for divorce; he knew his wife had planned on leaving the state and taking their daughter with her; and the neighbors reported that the couple had been having heated arguments, and that the husband was of a violent temper. He also lived conveniently near—in a garage adjoining the home. The police interrogated him and although his alibi was not conclusive his general behavior and the manner in which he answered the interrogator's questions satisfied the police of his innocence. Further investigation then revealed that the deceased's brother-in-law had been financially indebted to the deceased; that he was a frequent gambler; that at a number of social gatherings which he had attended money disappeared from some of the women's purses; that at his place of employment there had been a series of purse thefts; and that on the day of the killing he was absent from work. The police apprehended and questioned him. As the result of a few hours of competent interrogation—unattended by any abusive methods, but yet conducted during a period of delay in presenting the suspect before a committing magistrate as required by state statute—the suspect confessed to the murder. * * *

Without an opportunity for interrogation the police could not have solved this case. The perpetrator of the offense would have remained at liberty, perhaps to repeat his criminal conduct.

2. *Criminal offenders, except, of course, those caught in the commission of their crimes, ordinarily will not admit their guilt unless questioned under conditions of privacy, and for a period of perhaps several hours.*

* * * Self-condemnation and self-destruction not being normal behavior characteristics, human beings ordinarily do not utter unsolicited, spontaneous confessions. They must first be questioned regarding the offense. In some instances, a little bit of information inadvertently given to a competent interrogator by the suspect may suffice to start a line of investigation which might ultimately establish guilt. Upon other occasions, a full confession, with a revelation of details regarding a body, the loot, or the instruments used in the crime, may be required to prove the case. But whatever the possible consequences may be, it is impractical to expect any but a very few confessions to result from a guilty conscience unprovoked by an interrogation. It is also impractical to expect admissions or confessions to be obtained under circumstances other than privacy. Here again recourse to our everyday experience will support the basic validity of this requirement. For instance, in asking a personal friend to divulge a secret, or embarrassing information, we carefully avoid making the request in the presence of other persons, and seek a time and place when the matter can be discussed in private. The very same psychological factors are involved in a criminal interrogation, and even to a greater extent. For related psychological considerations, if an interrogation is to be had at all, it must be one based upon an unhurried interview, the necessary length of which will in many instances extend to several hours, depending upon various factors such as the nature of the case situation and the personality of the suspect. * * *

If the right to counsel arises only at the time of trial, or even when the judicial process begins, as at a preliminary hearing or at the time of indictment, the police have at least some opportunity for an interrogation. On the other hand, if the right is considered to exist immediately upon arrest, the interrogation opportunity, for all practical purposes, is gone—because of the prevailing concept that the role of defense counsel is to advise his client, "keep your mouth shut; don't say anything to anybody." * * *

In my judgment the right to counsel at the time of trial, or even at the very start of the judicial process, should be accorded *and provided* to all indigent defendants, insofar as practicable, regardless of whether the case involves a capital or non-capital offense, or even if it amounts only to a misdemeanor. What I do object to is an extension of the right to arrestees, indigent or non-indigent, prior to the start of the judicial process. It is not constitutionally required, and practical considerations will not tolerate such an extension, and particularly so if the extension is supplemented by a rule of court that would nullify, as a violation of due process, a confession obtained during a period of police detention before the start of the judicial process. Moreover, sometime in the near future we will have to come to grips with this interrogation problem and consider the passage of legislation, by all the states as well as the federal government, which will specifically provide for a reasonable period of police detention for the interrogation of suspects who are not otherwise unwilling to talk. * * *

Regarding the routine advice of counsel to an arrestee to remain silent and refuse to answer questions put to him by the police, it is my suggestion that the legal profession give serious consideration to the adoption of an alternative practice, which would require counsel to say to his client, the arrestee: "Although you do not have to say anything, my advice to you is that you discuss this matter with the police and that you tell them the truth; I'll stand by to protect you from any harm or abuse." With the advent of such a change in the ethical concept of the role of counsel, we might then be able to say that all arrestees should be entitled to counsel from the time of their arrest. As matters now stand, however, public protection and safety require that we adhere to the present viewpoint that there is no right to counsel during the investigative, non-judicial stage of the case.

3. *In dealing with criminal offenders, and consequently also with criminal suspects who may actually be innocent, the interrogator must of necessity employ less refined methods than are considered appropriate for the transaction of ordinary, everyday affairs by and between law-abiding citizens.*

To illustrate this point, permit me to revert to the previously discussed case of the woman who was murdered by her brother-in-law. His confession was obtained largely as a result of the interrogator adopting a friendly attitude in questioning the suspect, when concededly no such genuine feeling existed; by pretending to sympathize with the suspect because of his difficult financial situation; by suggesting that perhaps the victim had done or said something which aroused his anger and which would have aroused the anger of anyone else similarly situated to such an extent as to provoke a violent reaction; and by resorting to other similar expressions, or even overtures of friendliness and sympathy such as a pat on the suspect's shoulder or knee. In all of this, of course, the interrogation was "unethical" according to the standards usually set for professional, business and social conduct. But the pertinent issue in this case was no ordinary, lawful, professional, business or social matter. It involved the taking of a human life by one who abided by no code of fair play toward his fellow human beings. The killer would not have been moved one bit toward a confession by subjecting him to a reading or lecture regarding the morality of his conduct. It would have been futile merely to give him a pencil and paper and trust that his conscience would impel him to confess. Something more was required—something which was in its essence an "unethical" practice on the part of the interrogator. But, under the circumstances involved in this case, how else would the murderer's guilt have been established? Moreover, let us bear this thought in mind. From the criminal's point of view, *any* interrogation of him is objectionable. To *him* it may be a "dirty trick" to be talked into a confession, for surely it was not done for his benefit. Consequently, any interrogation of him might be labeled as deceitful or unethical.

Of necessity, criminal interrogators must deal with criminal offenders on a somewhat lower moral plane than that upon which ethical, law-abiding citizens are expected to conduct their everyday affairs. That plane, in the interest of innocent suspects need only be subject to the following restriction: Although both "fair" and "unfair" interrogation practices are permissible, nothing shall be done or said to the subject that will be apt to make an innocent person confess.

If all this be so, why then the withholding of this essential interrogation opportunity from the police? And we do, insofar as the stated law is concerned. It comes in the form of statutes or rules that require the prompt delivery of an arrested person before a magistrate for a preliminary hearing or arraignment. Moreover, the United States Supreme Court has decreed that in federal cases no confession is to be received in evidence, regardless of its voluntariness or trustworthiness, if it was obtained during a period of unnecessary delay in delivering the arrestee to a federal commissioner or judge for arraignment. In the federal jurisdiction of Washington, D.C., which must cope with a variety of criminal offenses and problems similar to any other city of comparable size, this federal court rule has had a very crippling effect on police investigations.[6]

One incongruity of the prompt arraignment rule is this. It is lawful for the police to arrest upon *reasonable belief* that the arrestee has committed the offense, following which they must take him before a magistrate, without unnecessary delay, and charge him with the crime; but for legal proof of the charge, his guilt at the time of trial must be established *beyond reasonable doubt.* Moreover, when the accused gets into the hands of a magistrate for the preliminary hearing, the opportunity for an effective interrogation is ended, many times because of the advice he receives from his attorney to keep his mouth shut.

If we view this whole problem realistically, we must come to the conclusion that an interrogation opportunity is necessary and that legislative provision ought to be made for a privately conducted police interrogation, covering a reasonable period of time, of suspects who are not unwilling to be interviewed, and that the only tactics or techniques that are to be forbidden are those which are apt to make an innocent person confess. * * *

The only real, practically attainable protection we can set up for ourselves against police interrogation abuses (just as with respect to arrest and detention abuses) is to see to it that our police are selected and promoted on a merit basis, that they are properly trained, adequately compensated, and that they are permitted to remain substantially free from politically inspired interference. In the hands of men of this competence there will be a minimum degree of abusive practices. And once again I suggest that the real interest that should be exhibited by the legislatures and the courts is with reference to the protection of the innocent from the hazards of tactics and techniques that are apt to produce confessions of guilt or other false information. Individual civil liberties can survive in such an atmosphere, alongside the protective security of the public.[a]

6. In addition, some concern should be exhibited over the risk involved in freeing obviously guilty offenders as a result of the courts' efforts to discipline the police. For instance, following the Supreme Court's reversal of his rape conviction, and his release from custody, the defendant in *Mallory* [p. 525 infra] committed two other offenses against female victims. For the latest one he was found guilty and sentenced to the penitentiary by a Pennsylvania Court. * * *

a. See also Inbau, Reid & Buckley, *Criminal Interrogation and Confessions* xiii (3d ed. 1986) (introduction).

YALE KAMISAR—EQUAL JUSTICE IN THE GATEHOUSES AND MANSIONS OF AMERICAN CRIMINAL PROCEDURE

In Kamisar, Inbau & Arnold, Criminal Justice in Our Time 19–36 (Howard ed.1965).

THE SHOW IN THE "GATEHOUSE" VS. THE SHOW IN THE "MANSION" * * *

The courtroom is a splendid place where defense attorneys bellow and strut and prosecuting attorneys are hemmed in at many turns. But what happens before an accused reaches the safety and enjoys the comfort of this veritable mansion? Ah, there's the rub. Typically he must first pass through a much less pretentious edifice, a police station with bare back rooms and locked doors.

In this "gatehouse" of American criminal procedure—through which most defendants journey and beyond which many never get—the enemy of the state is a depersonalized "subject" to be "sized up" and subjected to "interrogation tactics and techniques most appropriate for the occasion";[55] he is "game" to be stalked and cornered.[56] Here, ideals are checked at

55. Inbau & Reid, *Criminal Interrogation and Confessions* 20 (1962).

56. "[T]he interrogator's task is somewhat akin to that of a hunter stalking his game. Each must patiently maneuver himself into a position from which the desired objective may be attained; and in the same manner that the hunter may

the door, "realities" faced, and the prestige of law enforcement vindicated. Once he leaves the "gatehouse" and enters the "mansion"—if he ever gets there—the enemy of the state is repersonalized, even dignified, the public invited, and a stirring ceremony in honor of individual freedom from law enforcement celebrated.

I suspect it is not so much that society knows and approves of the show in the gatehouse, but that society does not know or care. "[S]ociety, by its insouciance, has divested itself of a moral responsibility and unloaded it on to the police. Society doesn't want to know about criminals, but it does want them put away, and it is incurious how this can be done provided it is done. Thus society, in giving the policeman power and wishing to ignore what his techniques must be, has made over to him part of its own conscience." [57]

True, the man in the street would have considerable difficulty explaining why the Constitution requires so much in the courtroom and means so little in the police station, but that is not his affair. "The task of keeping the two shows going at the same time without losing the patronage or the support of the Constitution for either," as Thurman Arnold once observed, is "left to the legal scholar." [58] Perhaps this is only fitting and proper, for as Thomas Reed Powell used to say, if you can think about something that is related to something else without thinking about the thing to which it is related, then you have the legal mind.

That the legal mind passes by or shuts out the *de facto* inquisitorial system which has characterized our criminal procedure for so long is bad enough. What is worse is that such an attitude leads many—perhaps requires many—to recoil with horror and dismay at any proposal which recognizes the grim facts of the criminal process and seeks to do something about them.

[At this point, the author discusses suggestions in the late 1920's that (rather than a police officer) a magistrate, or a prosecutor in the presence of a magistrate, do the interrogation, and a proposal in the early 1940's that in federal cases a commissioner do the interrogation at preliminary hearings, but only after advising the suspect of his right to counsel and his right to remain silent. Both proposals were "beaten down to the accompaniment of cries" that they were "opposed to our traditions of fair play," "contrary to the basic traditions of Anglo-American procedure" and violative of the constitutional guarantee against self-incrimination.]

Evidently, so long as neither the proceedings nor the presiding officer is "judicial," basic traditions are honored and self-incrimination problems avoided. * * *

Four score years ago, Sir James Fitzjames Stephen noted with pride that the fact that "the prisoner is absolutely protected against all judicial questioning before or at the trial * * * contributes greatly to the dignity and apparent humanity of a criminal trial. It effectually avoids the appearance of harshness, not to say cruelty, which often shocks an English spectator in a French court of justice." Whatever the case then, one would have to underscore the "apparent" and "the appearance" in that statement today. Stephen also told us that "the fact that the prisoner cannot be questioned stimulates the search for independent evidence." Whatever the case then, one cannot but wonder today how often the only thing "stimulated" by the inability of judicial officers to question a prisoner is questioning by police officers. One cannot but wonder how often the availability of the

lose his game by a noisy dash through the bush, can the interrogator fail by not exercising the proper degree of patience." Inbau & Reid, *Lie Detection and Criminal Interrogation* 185 (3d ed. 1953). The authors have dropped this graphic language from their later work.

57. MacInnes, *The Criminal Society,* in The Police and the Public 101 (Rolph ed. 1962).

58. Arnold, *The Symbols of Government* 156 (Harbinger ed. 1962).

privilege (or, perhaps more aptly, the inability of the State to undermine the privilege), once the accused reaches the safety and comfort of the mansion, only furnishes the State with an *additional incentive* for proving the charge against him out of his own mouth before he leaves the gatehouse.

Is the Privilege Checked at the "Gatehouse" Door?

* * *

[O]ne who would apply the privilege to the police station may select from the vast conglomerate of determinants which form its history the fact that the maxim "no man shall be compelled to accuse himself" first meant (and until the seventeenth century probably only meant) that no man shall be compelled to make the *first charge* against himself, to submit to a "fishing" interrogation about his crimes, to furnish his own indictment from his own lips. Until the 1600's all parties concerned seemed to have operated on the premise that *after* pleading to the indictment, the accused could be compelled to incriminate himself. * * * When we apply the privilege to "arrests for investigation" or "routine pickups," do we disguise a revolutionary idea in the garb of the past or do we restore the privilege to its primordial state?

Nor should it be forgotten that for many centuries there were simply no "police interrogators" to whom the privilege could be applied. Although what Dean Wigmore calls "the first part" of the history of the privilege, the opposition to the ex officio oath of the ecclesiastical courts, began in the 1200's "criminal investigation by the police, with its concomitant of police interrogation, is a product of the late nineteenth century"; [82] in eighteenth-century America as in eighteenth-century England "there were no police [in the modern sense] and, though some states seem to have had prosecutors, private prosecution was the rule rather than the exception." [83] In fact as well as in theory, observes Professor Edmond M. Morgan, "there can be little question that the modern American police have taken over the functions performed originally by the English committing magistrates [and at least by some colonial magistrates]; they are in a real sense administrative officers and their questioning of the person under arrest is an investigative proceeding in which testimony is taken." If modern police are permitted to interrogate under the coercive influence of arrest and secret detention, then, insists Professor Albert R. Beisel, "they are doing the very same acts which historically the judiciary was doing in the seventeenth century but which the privilege against self-incrimination abolished."

I do not contend that "the implications of a tangled and obscure history" dictate that the privilege apply to the police station, only that they permit it. I do not claim that this long and involved history displaces judgment, only that it liberates it. I do not say that the distinct origins of the confession and self-incrimination rules are irrelevant, only that it is more important (if we share Dean Charles T. McCormick's views) that "the kinship of the two rules is too apparent for denial" and that "such policy as modern writers are able to discover as a basis for the self-incrimination privilege * * * pales to a flicker beside the flaming demands of justice and humanity for protection against extorted confessions."

Those who applaud the show in the mansion without hissing the show in the gatehouse may also:

Find refuge in the notion that compulsion to testify means *legal* compulsion. Since he is threatened neither with perjury for testifying falsely nor contempt for re-

82. Note, *An Historical Argument for the Right to Counsel During Police Interrogation,* 73 Yale L.J. 1000, 1034 (1964).

83. Id. at 1041. See also Barrett, *Police Practices and the Law—From Arrest to Release or Charge,* 50 Calif.L.Rev. 11, 16–19 (1962). * * *

fusing to testify at all, it cannot be said, runs the argument, that the man in the back room of the police station is being "compelled" to be a "witness against himself" within the meaning of the privilege. Since the police have no legal right to make him answer, "there is no legal obligation to which a privilege in the technical sense can apply."[91]

Can we accept this analysis without forgetting as lawyers and judges what we know as men? Without permitting logic to triumph over life? So long as "what on their face are merely words of request take on color from the officer's badge, gun and demeanor";[94] so long as his interrogators neither advise him of his rights nor permit him to consult with a lawyer who will; can there be any doubt that many a "subject" will *assume* that the police have a legal right to an answer? That many an incriminating statement will be extracted under "color" of law? So long as the interrogator is instructed to "get the idea across * * * that [he] has 'all the time in the world' "; so long as "the power [legal or otherwise] to extract answers begets a forgetfulness of the just limitations of the power" and "the simple and peaceful process of questioning breeds a readiness to resort to bullying and to physical force"; can there be any doubt that many a subject will assume that there is an *illegal* sanction for contumacy?

If these inferences are unfair, if very few "subjects" are misled to believe that there is either a legal obligation to talk or unlimited time and illegal means available to make them do so—if, in short, they know they can "shut up"—why are the police so bent on preventing counsel from telling them what they already know? Why, at least, don't the officers themselves tell their "subjects" plainly and emphatically that they need not and cannot be made to answer? That they will be permitted to consult with counsel, or be brought before a magistrate in short order? And why is the "subject" questioned in *secret?* Why does the modest proposal that a suspect be interrogated by or before an impartial functionary immediately after arrest "meet with scant favor in police circles, even from the most high-minded and highly respected elements in those circles"?[99]

Finally, those who have learned to live with the widespread practices in the gatehouse may take the "waiver" tack. They may:

Concede that the privilege against self-incrimination exists in the police station, but maintain that when (instead of exercising his right to remain silent or to make only self-serving remarks) a suspect "volunteers" damaging statements he has *waived* his rights. This is not much of a concession for "if the privilege is easily waived, there is really no privilege at all."[100] However, if "when the state is putting questions, the answers to which will disclose criminal activities by the witness, there is likely to be an especially high insistence checked by an especially high reluctance," then there is likely to be an especially low incidence of valid waiving of the privilege.

So long as "the classic definition of waiver enumerated in *Johnson v. Zerbst*—'an intelligent relinquishment or abandonment of a known right or privilege'—furnishes the controlling standard,"[102] so long as the courts "indulge every reasonable presumption against [such] waiver," it is difficult to see how the contention that an unadvised suspect waives the privilege simply by talking even presents a substantial question. "The Fourteenth Amend-

91. See Mayers, *Shall We Amend the Fifth Amendment?* 82–83, 223–33 (1959); 8 Wigmore, *Evidence* 329 n. 27 (McNaughton rev. 1961). But both authors are quick to marshal the contrary arguments.

94. Foote, *The Fourth Amendment: Obstacle or Necessity in the Law of Arrest?* in Police Power and Individual Freedom 29, 30 (Sowle ed. 1962).

99. Mayers 90.

100. Note, 5 Stan.L.Rev. 459, 477 (1953).

102. *Fay v. Noia* [Ch. 27, § 2].

ment," announced the Supreme Court only a year ago, "secures against state invasion the same privilege that the Fifth Amendment guarantees against federal infringement—the right of a person to remain silent unless he chooses to speak in the unfettered exercise of his own will." [104] Can it seriously be said of the routine police interrogation that the suspect so speaks? Again, only a year ago, the Court pointed out that "no system of criminal justice can, or should, survive if it comes to depend for its continued effectiveness on the citizens' abdication through unawareness of their constitutional rights." [105] On what else does the existing system depend? * * *

The trouble with both the "waiver" and "no legal compulsion" rationalizations of the existing *de facto* inquisitorial system is this: when we expect the police dutifully to notify a suspect of the very means he may utilize to frustrate them—when we rely on them to advise a suspect unbegrudgingly and unequivocally of the very rights he is being counted on *not* to assert—we demand too much of even our best officers. As Dean Edward L. Barrett has asked: "[I]s it the duty of the police to persuade the suspect to talk or persuade him not to talk? They cannot be expected to do both." [110]

Suspects there are who feel in a "pleading guilty" mood, for some of the many reasons most defendants do plead guilty. Suspects there are who would intentionally relinquish their rights for some hoped-for favor from the state. I do not deny this. I do deny that such suspects do not need a lawyer.

Surely the man who, in effect, is pleading guilty in the gatehouse needs a lawyer no less than one who arrives at the same decision only after surviving the perilous journey through that structure.

* * *

104. *Malloy v. Hogan* [p. 536 infra].

105. *Escobedo v. Illinois* [p. 529 infra.]

110. Brief Amicus Curiae, p. 9, *People v. Dorado*, 42 Cal.Rep. 169, 398 P.2d 361 (1965) (on rehearing).

JOSEPH D. GRANO—RHODE ISLAND v. INNIS: A NEED TO RECONSIDER THE CONSTITUTIONAL PREMISES UNDERLYING THE LAW OF CONFESSIONS

17 Am.Crim.L.Rev. 1, 25–28 (1979).

[T]he right to counsel's shield function * * * cannot apply at either [the stage of an investigation when attention has begun to focus on a particular suspect or at the stage when a suspect is taken into custody]. By default, the only point left for attachment of sixth amendment rights is at some stage of the *judicial* process. Argument by default, however, is often unsatisfactory, especially in constitutional law. For this reason, I attempt [to] develop the arguments in favor of drawing the sixth amendment line at the start of adversary judicial proceedings [by way of indictment, information, or preliminary arraignment, sometimes called the initial appearance].

[At this point, Professor Grano quotes from Justice Stewart's dissenting opinion in *Escobedo* (p. 529 infra) and from his plurality opinion in *Kirby* (p. 668 infra) to the effect that the initiation of judicial criminal proceedings marks the point at which a criminal investigation has ended and the "criminal prosecution"—to which alone the right to counsel and other Sixth Amendment guarantees are applicable—has commenced.]

To determine whether Justice Stewart has proven his case, it helps first to emphasize his major points: (1) the constitutional guarantees at issue are those that pertain to a criminal trial; (2) historically these guarantees applied only after the onset of formal prosecutorial proceedings; (3) the accused faces the intricacies of substantive and procedural law only after the onset of formal judicial proceedings; (4) police investigation of an unsolved crime cannot be analogized to a judicial trial; and (5) to attempt such an analogy is to threaten society's vital interest in successful law enforcement.

Each of these points, with the possible exception of the third, has considerable force behind it. The third is cryptic. If Justice Stewart meant that only after the judicial process has begun does the accused face formal legal decisions, such as what defense to raise or whether to waive the preliminary examination, then he is basically correct. But legal issues may affect an accused's extra-judicial decisions before the judicial process begins. For example, Escobedo might have avoided revealing any knowledge of the crime had he known that mere complicity was sufficient for full criminal liability. In deciding whether to cooperate or how much to reveal, the legal ramifications of one's answers cannot be ignored.

Even if the third point is weak, however, the other points are sufficient to preclude application of the sixth amendment before the start of formal judicial proceedings. Sixth amendment guarantees *are* trial guarantees. Trials are supposed to be speedy and public. The rights of confrontation and compulsory process apply at trial, or trial-like proceedings such as the preliminary examination. History, moreover, reinforces what the sixth amendment's language makes plain. Indeed, from an historical perspective, application of even the fifth amendment protection against compulsory self-incrimination beyond the judicial context—and especially to police interrogation—is dubious. The historical support for application of sixth amendment rights outside the judicial context is even weaker.

The fourth and fifth points summarized above also support Justice Stewart's thesis. * * * [P]olice interrogation is basically an inquisitorial institution. It cannot be analogized to the trial process. Its purpose is to get the guilty to confess, not to ensure that the defendant makes the choices that will best enhance his chances for acquittal at trial. At trial, the accusatorial-adversary process demands rough equality between the contending parties. In the police station, however, society wants the advantage to lie with the police and, at least until *Escobedo* and *Miranda*, the Court had always been sympathetically cognizant of this desire. To bring the attributes of the judicial trial to police interrogation is really to say that police interrogation, as it has existed, should be abolished. It is simply disingenuous to say that this institution can perform its inquisitorial function under the rules of an adversary trial.

[Application of the right to counsel to the "focus" or "custody" stages] would seriously undermine legitimate law enforcement interests in areas including police interrogation. For over a century, society's sentiment, frequently expressed in Supreme Court decisions, has been that police interrogation is not only desirable but essential to successful law enforcement. Given the constitutional language referring to judicial proceedings and the lack of historical proceedings and the lack of historical support for a broader interpretation, it would be remarkable indeed were police interrogation now found to violate the Constitution under a right to counsel argument.

The system described in this article may seem schizophrenic in its rigid insistence on accusatorial protections during the judicial process and its complacent tolerance of inquisitorial procedures, which frequently assure conviction, before the judicial process begins. The dichotomy, however, between the show in the "mansion" and the one in the "gatehouse" is a product not of schizophrenia but of historical compromise. Building from scratch, we could construct a system that more consistently and more rationally accommodates these competing tensions. We might, for example, as Professor Kauper once suggested, remove the interrogation process from police control, where it is largely invisible and often abused, and place it in the sunlight of open court.[165] Such reforms, however, are precluded by the evolutionary development of constitutional doctrine, now too ingrained to be altered. Even judicial examination of the accused at the preliminary examination, which persisted in New York in the mid-nineteenth century, is now everywhere recognized as unacceptable. The tightening of constitutional controls on the judicial process, however, occurred simultaneously with the development of extra-judicial procedures to perform the needed investigatory function. Indeed, the possibility cannot be dismissed that the judicial process became more rigid only because the system became more flexible in its prejudicial stages. The system we have today reflects the historic resolution of competing forces. Though another system, such as Professor Kauper's, would perhaps be preferable, such a system would now require the Constitution to be amended. That we cannot have what would be preferable, however, is hardly a satisfactory argument against what we do have.

SECTION 2. HISTORICAL BACKGROUND [a]

A. THE INTERESTS PROTECTED BY THE DUE PROCESS "VOLUNTARINESS" TEST FOR ADMITTING CONFESSIONS

The first rules governing the admissibility of confessions were laid down in the eighteenth and nineteenth centuries, a time when illegal police methods were relevant only insofar as they affected the trustworthiness of the evidence. Whatever the meaning of the elusive terms "involuntary" and "coerced" confessions since 1940, for centuries the rule that a confession was admissible so long as it was "voluntary" was more or less an alternative statement of the rule that a confession was admissible so long as it was free of influence which made it untrustworthy or "probably untrue." See generally McCormick, *Evidence* 226 (1954); 3 Wigmore, *Evidence* § 822 (3d ed. 1940).

Indeed, Dean Wigmore condemned the use of the "voluntary" terminology for the reason that "there is nothing in the mere circumstance of compulsion to speak in general * * * which creates any risk of untruth." 3 Wigmore, § 843. But the courts' continued reference to the term "voluntariness" in enunciating the requisites for the admissibility of a confession under the due process clause was defended by Dean McCormick, who suggested that it might be prompted "not only by a liking for its convenient brevity, but also by a recognition that there is an interest here to be protected closely akin to the interest of a witness or of an accused person which is protected by the privilege against compulsory self-incrimination." McCormick, *The Scope of Privilege in the Law of Evidence,* 16 Texas L.Rev. 447, 453 (1938).

At least in its advanced stage (the early 1960s), it became fairly clear that the "due process" or "voluntariness" test had *three* underlying values or goals. It barred admission of confessions (a) which were of doubtful reliability because of the police methods used to obtain them; (b) which were produced by offensive police methods even though the reliability of the con-

165. See Kauper, *Judicial Examination of the Accused—A Remedy for the Third Degree,* 30 Mich.L.Rev. 1224 (1932), reprinted in 73 Mich.L. Rev. 39 (1974).

a. For a much more detailed treatment of the subject matter of this Note, see Stephens, *The Supreme Court and Confessions of Guilt* 17–119 (1973). See also the discussion in LaFave & Israel, § 6.2; McCormick, *Evidence* § 147 (Cleary 3d ed. 1984); 3 Wigmore, Evidence §§ 817–26 (Chadbourn rev. 1970); Amsterdam, *The Supreme Court and the Rights of Suspects in Criminal Cases,* 45 N.Y.U.L.Rev. 785, 803–10 (1970), reprinted in *The Rights of Americans* 401, 418–24 (Dorsen ed. 1971); Caplan, *Questioning Miranda,* 38 Vand.L.Rev. 1417, 1427–43 (1985); Grano, *Voluntariness, Free Will, and the Law of Confessions,* 65 Va.L.Rev. 859 (1979); Kamisar, *What is an "Involuntary" Confession?,* 17 Rutgers L.Rev. 728 (1963), reprinted in Kamisar, *Police Interrogation and Confessions* (1980); *Developments in the Law—Confessions,* 79 Harv.L.Rev. 935, 954–96 (1966).

fession was not in question; and (c) which were obtained from a person whose volitional power was seriously impaired (e.g., a drugged person), even though the confession was entirely trustworthy and not the product of conscious police wrongdoing.[b]

At the outset, however, the primary (and perhaps the exclusive) basis for excluding confessions under the due process "voluntariness" test was the "untrustworthiness" rationale, the view that the confession rule was designed merely to protect the integrity of the fact-finding process. This rationale sufficed to explain the exclusion of the confession in *Brown v. Mississippi,* 297 U.S. 278, 56 S.Ct. 461, 80 L.Ed. 682 (1936), the first fourteenth amendment due process confession case (where the deputy who had presided over the beating of the defendants conceded that one prisoner had been whipped but "not too much for a Negro; not as much as I would have done if it were left to me"), and the cases which immediately followed for they, too, were pervaded by threats of, or outright, physical violence. "But when cases involving the more subtle 'psychological' pressures began to appear—usually instances of prolonged interrogation * * * it was no longer possible easily to assume that the confessions exacted were unreliable as evidence of guilt. [In *Ashcraft v. Tennessee,* 322 U.S. 143, 64 S.Ct. 921, 88 L.Ed. 1192 (1944)] a conviction was reversed where a confession had been obtained after some thirty-six hours of continuous interrogation of the defendant by the police. In effect, the Court ruled that the extended questioning raised a conclusive presumption of 'coercion.' Considering the facts as revealed in the record of the *Ashcraft* case, it is fair to suggest that the result reached by the Court reflected less a concern with the reliability of the confession as evidence of guilt in the particular case than disapproval of police methods which a majority of the

b. As for the third underlying value, see *Townsend v. Sain,* 372 U.S. 293, 83 S.Ct. 745, 9 L.Ed.2d 770 (1963), excluding a confession obtained from one given a drug with the properties of a truth serum, even though the police were unaware of the drug's effect and had engaged in no conscious wrongdoing, and even though the confession was apparently reliable. "Any questioning by police officers which *in fact* produces a confession which is not the product of free intellect," observed the Court, "renders that confession inadmissible."

Now that the principal basis for the inadmissibility of a confession is the Fifth Amendment privilege against compulsory self-incrimination, see *Miranda,* infra, it is unclear whether the courts would or should exclude a confession that is neither untrustworthy nor the product of coercive, offensive or otherwise improper police tactics. Consider *United States v. Bernett,* 495 F.2d 943 (D.C.Cir.1974), where a 2–1 majority, per Wilkey, J., upheld the admissibility of a confession taken from an intoxicated person, observing, inter alia, that "the language of the self-incrimination clause * * * demonstrates that some form of government *compulsion* is a basic element of an involuntary confession. [The relevant decisions] treat of 'voluntariness' as an *absence of compulsion.*" Robinson, J., dissenting, maintained that "[w]hen evidence of mental illness, drug use, physical or psychological duress, or intoxication indicates an inculpatory statement was not understandably and volitionally made, [due process requires] that the statement and its fruits be excluded."

Compare *Bernett* with *People v. Connelly,* 702 P.2d 722 (Colo.1985), cert. granted, ___ U.S. ___, 106 S.Ct. 785, 88 L.Ed.2d 763 (1986), where defendant, a mentally ill person, approached an officer and volunteered that "he had killed someone" and wanted to tell the police about it. According to expert testimony, "God's voice" told defendant that he had only two options: confess his crime or commit suicide. At that point he spoke to the first officer he could find. The trial court found that defendant did not exercise free will in choosing to speak to the police, but was "compelled by his illness" to confess. In upholding the trial court on this issue, the Colorado Supreme Court, per Quinn, C.J., observed: "[T]he absence of police coercion or duress does not foreclose a finding of involuntariness. One's capacity for rational judgment and free choice may be overborne as much by certain forms of severe mental illness as by external pressure."

Dissenting Justice Rovira, joined by Erickson, J. protested that "[t]he majority opinion essentially requires police officers to close their eyes and ears when openly approached with evidence that a crime has been committed." "A statement can be suppressed as involuntary," maintained the dissent, "only if it has been extracted by police questioning or obtained through improper external force. * * * While the defendant's mental condition may be introduced at trial to attack the credibility of his confession * * * [his] mental illness should not preclude a finding that his statement was voluntary for purposes of the fifth amendment."

Court conceived as generally dangerous and subject to serious abuse." Allen, *The Supreme Court, Federalism, and State Systems of Criminal Justice,* 8 DePaul L.Rev. 213, 235 (1959). See also Paulsen, *The Fourteenth Amendment and the Third Degree,* 6 Stan.L.Rev. 411, 418–19 (1954).

In *Watts v. Indiana,* 338 U.S. 49, 69 S.Ct. 1347, 93 L.Ed. 1801 (1949) and the companion cases of *Harris v. South Carolina,* 338 U.S. 68, 69 S.Ct. 1354, 93 L.Ed. 1815 (1949) and *Turner v. Pennsylvania,* 338 U.S. 62, 69 S.Ct. 1352, 93 L.Ed. 1810 (1949), the Court reversed three convictions resting on coerced confessions without disputing the accuracy of Justice Jackson's observation (concurring in *Watts* and dissenting in the other cases) that "checked with external evidence they [the confessions in each case] are inherently believable and were not shaken as to truth by anything that occurred at the trial."

The majority, per Frankfurter, J., commented: "In holding that the Due Process Clause *bars police procedure* which violates the basic notions of our accusatorial mode of prosecuting crime and vitiates a conviction based on the fruits of such procedure, we apply the Due Process Clause to its historic function of *assuring appropriate procedure* before liberty is curtailed or life is taken." (Emphasis added.) And three years later, in the famous "stomach-pumping" case of *Rochin v. California,* p. 46 supra, the Court, again speaking through Justice Frankfurter, viewed the coerced confession cases as "only instances of the general requirement that States in their prosecutions respect certain decencies of civilized conduct," pointing out: "Use of involuntary verbal confessions in State criminal trials is constitutionally obnoxious not only because of their unreliability. They are inadmissible under the Due Process Clause even though statements contained in them may be independently established as true. Coerced confessions offend the community's sense of fair play and decency."

That the Court was applying a "police methods"—as well as a "trustworthiness"—test was made clear by *Spano v. New York,* 360 U.S. 315, 79 S.Ct. 1202, 3 L.Ed.2d 1265 (1959); *Blackburn v. Alabama,* 361 U.S. 199, 80 S.Ct. 274, 4 L.Ed. 2d 242 (1960) and *Rogers v. Richmond,* 365 U.S. 534, 81 S.Ct. 735, 5 L.Ed.2d 760 (1961). Thus, the Court, per Warren, C.J., pointed out in *Spano* that the ban against "involuntary" confessions turns not only on their reliability but on the notion that "the police must obey the law while enforcing the law." And the Court, again speaking through the Chief Justice, acknowledged in *Blackburn* that "a *complex of values* underlies the strictures against use by the state of confessions which, by way of *convenient shorthand,* this Court terms involuntary." (Emphasis added.)

Perhaps the most emphatic statement of the point that the untrustworthiness of a confession was not (or no longer) the principal reason for excluding it appears in one of Justice Frankfurter's last opinions on the subject. Writing for the Court in *Rogers,* he observed: "Our decisions under [the Fourteenth Amendment] have made clear that convictions following the admission into evidence of [involuntary confessions] cannot stand * * * not so much because such confessions are unlikely to be true but because the methods used to extract them offend an underlying principle in the enforcement of our criminal law: that ours is an accusatorial and not an inquisitorial system. * * * Indeed, in many of the cases [reversing] state convictions involving the use of confessions obtained by impermissible methods, independent corroborating evidence left little doubt of the truth of what the defendant had confessed." [c]

c. In admitting the confession, the *Rogers* trial court had found that the interrogation tactics "had no tendency to produce a confession that was not in accord with the truth." The Supreme Court did not consider the finding *unwarranted,* but *irrelevant.* The admissibility of the confession had been decided "by reference to a legal standard which took into account the circumstance of probable truth or falsity"—"and this is not a permissible standard under the Due

Although, theoretically, the "police methods" and "trustworthiness" standards for admitting confessions are to be applied independently of each other, in practice they often overlap. Even though it might be conclusively demonstrated that "offensive" police interrogation methods did not produce an "untrustworthy" confession *in the particular case* before the Court, the continued use of such methods is likely to create a substantial risk that other suspects subjected to similar tactics would falsely confess. See Kamisar, *What is an "Involuntary" Confession?,* 17 Rutgers L.Rev. 728, 754–55 (1963), reprinted in Kamisar, *Police Interrogation and Confessions* 1, 20–22 (1980).

What *are* the objectionable police methods which render a resulting confession "involuntary"? In the advanced stages of the test, at least, the use or threatened use of physical violence or the kind of protracted relay interrogation that occurred in *Ashcraft,* supra, rendered any resulting confession inadmissible *per se.* In the main, however, it is difficult to isolate any particular interrogation tactic and say that, standing alone, it is so "coercive" or so "offensive" that it requires the exclusion of any resulting confession. For the significant fact about the great bulk of the "involuntary confessions" cases is that "none of them turned on the presence or absence of a single controlling criterion; each reflected a careful scrutiny of all the surrounding circumstances" *Schneckloth v. Bustamonte* (p. 408 supra) at 226. And the totality of the surrounding circumstances included "both the characteristics of the accused [many of whom were uneducated, of low mentality or emotionally unstable] and the details of the interrogation." Ibid.

Nevertheless, the pre-*Escobedo,* pre-*Miranda* cases reveal numerous police practices which, if not impermissible *per se,* certainly militate heavily against the "voluntariness" of any resulting confession: stripping off defendant's clothes and keeping him naked for several hours, *Malinski v. New York,* 324 U.S. 401, 65 S.Ct. 781, 89 L.Ed. 1029 (1945); informing defendant that state financial aid for her infant children would be cut off, and her children taken from her, if she failed to "cooperate" with police, *Lynumn v. Illinois,* 372 U.S. 528, 83 S.Ct. 917, 9 L.Ed.2d 922 (1963); after defendant persisted in his denial of guilt, pretending to "bring in" defendant's wife (who suffered from arthritis) for questioning, *Rogers v. Richmond,* supra; repeatedly rejecting defendant's requests to phone his wife and repeatedly informing him that he would not be able to call her or anyone else unless and until he gave the police a statement, *Haynes v. Washington,* 373 U.S. 503, 83 S.Ct. 1336, 10 L.Ed.2d 513 (1963); removing defendant from jail to a distant place in order to thwart the efforts of his friends or relatives to secure his release, or at least to contact him, *Ward v. Texas,* 316 U.S. 547, 62 S.Ct. 1139, 86 L.Ed. 1663 (1942); utilization of a state-employed psychiatrist, with considerable knowledge of hypnosis, who posed as a "general practitioner" who would provide defendant with the medical relief he needed and succeeded in obtaining a confession from defendant by skillful and suggestive questioning, *Leyra v. Denno,* 347 U.S. 556, 74 S.Ct. 716, 98 L.Ed. 948 (1954); utilization of defendant's "childhood friend," then a fledgling police officer, who, pursuant to his superiors' instructions, pretended that defendant's phone call had gotten his "friend" "in a lot of trouble," so much so that his "friend's" job was in jeopardy, and loss of his job would prove disastrous to his "friend's" wife and children, *Spano v. New York,* supra.

B. THE SHORTCOMINGS OF THE "VOLUNTARINESS" TEST

Although the Supreme Court customarily used the terms "voluntariness" and "involuntariness" in explaining and applying

Process Clause." See Schulhofer, *Confessions and the Court,* 79 Mich.L.Rev. 865, 867 (1981).

the due process test for the admissibility of confessions, the "voluntariness" concept seems to be at once too wide and too narrow. In one sense, in the sense of wanting to confess, or doing so in a completely spontaneous manner, "in the sense of a confession to a priest merely to rid one's soul of a sense of guilt" (Jackson, J., dissenting in *Ashcraft v. Tennessee*), few criminal confessions reviewed by the courts, if any, had been "voluntary." On the other hand, in the sense that the situation always presents a "choice" between two alternatives, either one disagreeable, to be sure, *all* confessions are "voluntary." See 3 Wigmore, § 824.

Moreover, as the rationales for the Court's coerced confession cases evolved, it became increasingly doubtful that terms such as "voluntariness," "coercion," and "breaking the will" were very helpful in resolving the issue. For such terms do not focus directly on either the risk of untrue confessions or the offensiveness of police interrogation methods employed in eliciting the confession. See Paulsen, supra at 429–30.

As the Court, per O'Connor, J., recently observed in *Miller v. Fenton,* ___ U.S. ___, 106 S.Ct. 445, 88 L.Ed.2d 405 (1985) (holding that the "voluntariness" of a confession is not a "factual issue" but "a legal question meriting independent consideration in a federal habeas corpus proceeding"): "[T]he admissibility of a confession turns as much on whether the techniques for extracting the statements, as applied to *this* suspect, are compatible with a system that presumes innocence and assures that a conviction will not be secured by inquisitorial means as on whether the defendant's will was in fact overborne. * * * [The] hybrid quality of the voluntariness inquiry, subsuming, as it does, a 'complex of values,' *Blackburn,* itself militates against treating the question as one of simple historical fact." As the *Miller* Court also noted, "[t]he voluntariness rubric has been variously condemned as 'useless,' 'perplexing,' and 'legal "double-talk." ' "

Nor was "the elusive, measureless standard of psychological coercion heretofore developed in this Court by accretion on almost an ad hoc, case-by-case basis," as Justice Clark described it, dissenting in *Reck v. Pate,* 367 U.S. 433, 81 S.Ct. 1541, 6 L.Ed.2d 948 (1961); a test which seemed to permit constitutionally permissible police interrogation to vary widely according to how dull or alert or soft or tough the particular suspect, see e.g., Maguire, *Evidence of Guilt* 134 fn. 5 (1959); likely to guide or to shape police conduct very much, if at all.

As pointed out in Schulhofer, fn. c supra, at 869–70, the vagueness of the voluntariness test "impaired the effectiveness and the legitimacy of judicial review": "Not only were conscientious trial judges left without guidance for resolving confession claims but they were virtually invited to give weight to their subjective preferences when performing the elusive task of balancing. * * * The ambiguity of the due process test and its subtle mixture of factual and legal elements discouraged active review even by the most conscientious appellate judges. Moreover, when higher courts did attempt to address confession questions, they found themselves so wholly at sea that the appearance of principled judicial decision-making inevitably suffered, whether or not they chose to hold the confession inadmissible." [a]

a. But consider Caplan, *Questioning Miranda,* 38 Vand.L.Rev. 1417, 1433–34 (1985): "[The voluntariness test] allowed the Court to move carefully, to feel its way, and to make its judgments without fear of prematurely constitutionalizing interrogation practices.

"* * * The Court's failure to state the basis for a particular decision or its blurring of a holding in the veiled attire of the 'totality of the circumstances' can be seen as shrewd and responsible pragmatism. Pragmatism may have been preferable to principles at a time when there was little general agreement on the principles to be applied. * * * If the development of the voluntariness test had not come to a near end with the advent of *Miranda,* perhaps the test would have continued to achieve definition and improved serviceability."

As police interrogators made greater use of "psychological" techniques over the years, the always difficult problems of proof confronting the alleged victims of improper interrogation practices became increasingly arduous. Disputes over whether physical violence occurred are not always easy to resolve, but evidence of "mental" or "psychological" coercion is especially elusive. Frequently, the defendant was inarticulate, which aggravated the difficulties of recreating the tenor and atmosphere of the police questioning or the *manner* in which the appropriate advice about the suspect's rights might have been given or, if properly given, subsequently undermined.

Moreover, the local courts almost always resolved the almost inevitable "swearing contest" over what happened behind the closed doors in favor of the police, perhaps for the reasons suggested by Justice Schaefer, *Federalism and State Criminal Procedure,* 70 Harv.L.Rev. 1, 7 (1956): "In the field of criminal procedure [a] strong local interest competes only against an ideal. Local interest is concerned with the particular case and with the guilt or innocence of the particular individual. * * * While it is hard indeed for any judge to set apart the question of the guilt or innocence of a particular defendant and focus solely upon the procedural aspect of the case, it becomes easier [in] a reviewing court where the impact of the evidence is diluted. The more remote the court, the easier it is to consider the case in terms of a hypothetical defendant accused of crime, instead of a particular man whose guilt has been established." [b]

Under the old case-by-case approach, however, the defendant could not often avail himself of the "remoteness" of the U.S. Supreme Court. In the thirty years since *Brown v. Mississippi,* the Court had taken an average of about one state confession case per year and *two-thirds of these* had been "death penalty" cases. Indeed, the Court's workload was so great that it even denied a hearing in most "death penalty"

b. This may help to explain the strikingly different reactions of the state courts and the U.S. Supreme Court to the situation in *Mincey v. Arizona,* 437 U.S. 385, 98 S.Ct. 2408, 57 L.Ed.2d 290 (1978) (other aspects of which are discussed at pp. 321, 796). Just a few hours before the interrogation occurred, Mincey had been seriously wounded during a narcotics raid which resulted in the death of a police officer. According to the attending physician, Mincey had arrived at the hospital "depressed almost to the point of coma." At the time Detective Hust questioned him, Mincey's condition was still sufficiently serious that he was in the intensive care unit. Lying on his back on a hospital bed, encumbered by tubes, needles and breathing apparatus, Mincey (according to the Supreme Court) clearly and repeatedly expressed his wish not to be interrogated, but Hust continued to question him. Unable to speak because of the tube in his mouth, Mincey responded to Hust's questions by writing answers on pieces of paper provided by the hospital, at one point writing: "This is all I can say without a lawyer." (In a written report dated about a week later, Hust transcribed Mincey's answers and added the questions he believed he had asked.)

Under these circumstances, the trial court found "with unmistakable clarity" that Mincey's statements were "voluntary" and thus, despite being obtained in violation of *Miranda,* admissible for impeachment purposes. (On this point, see Ch. 11, § 4 infra). The state supreme court unanimously affirmed. On the basis of its independent evaluation of the record, the Court, per Stewart, J., reversed. It noted, inter alia, that "the reliability of Hust's report [reconstructing the interrogation] is uncertain." It concluded that "the undisputed evidence makes clear that Mincey wanted *not* to answer Detective Hust" but that—"weakened by pain and shock, isolated from family, friends and legal counsel, and barely conscious"—Mincey's "will was simply overborne."

Rehnquist, J., dissented from the holding that Mincey's statements were involuntary and—as was true of so many of the older "involuntariness" cases—disputed the Court's reading of the record: "[The Court] ignores entirely some evidence of voluntariness and distinguishes away yet other testimony. * * * Despite the contrary impression given by the Court, [the state supreme court's] opinion casts no doubt on the testimony or report of Detective Hust. The Court is thus left solely with its own conclusions as to the reliability of various witnesses based on a re-examination of the record on appeal. * * * I believe that the trial court was entitled to conclude that, notwithstanding Mincey's medical condition, his statements in the intensive care unit were admissible. [T]hat the same court might have been equally entitled to reach the opposite conclusion does not justify this Court's adopting the opposite conclusion."

cases. See Kamisar, *A Dissent from the Miranda Dissents,* 65 Mich.L.Rev. 59, 102–03 (1966), reprinted in Kamisar, *Police Interrogation and Confessions* 41, 75 (1980). Almost no garden-variety criminal defendant who cried "coerced confession" but lost the "swearing contest" below was likely to survive the winnowing process above. Not surprisingly, Justice Black remarked in the course of the oral arguments in *Miranda:* "[I]f you are going to determine [the admissibility of the confession] each time on the circumstances, [if] this Court will take them one by one [it] is more than we are capable of doing."

Although the 1964 *Massiah* and *Escobedo* cases and the 1966 *Miranda* case (all discussed infra) were to catch heavy criticism, "[g]iven the Court's inability to articulate a clear and predictable definition of 'voluntariness,' the apparent persistence of state courts in utilizing the ambiguity of the concept to validate confessions of doubtful constitutionality, and the resultant burden on its own workload, it seemed inevitable that the Court would seek 'some automatic device by which the potential evils of incommunicado interrogation [could] be controlled.'" Stone, *The Miranda Doctrine in the Burger Court,* 1977 Sup.Ct.Rev. 102–03 (quoting from Schaefer, *The Suspect and Society* 10 (1967)).[c]

C. THE *McNabb-Mallory* RULE: SUPERVISORY AUTHORITY OVER FEDERAL CRIMINAL JUSTICE VS. FOURTEENTH AMENDMENT DUE PROCESS

As Justice FRANKFURTER pointed out for the majority in the famous case of McNABB v. UNITED STATES, 318 U.S. 332, 63 S.Ct. 608, 87 L.Ed. 819 (1943), while the power of the Court to upset *state* convictions is limited to the enforcement of fourteenth amendment due process, the standards of *federal* criminal justice "are not satisfied merely by observance of those minimal historic safeguards." Rather, the Court can, and has, formulated rules of evidence in the exercise of its "supervisory authority" over the administration of federal criminal justice which go well beyond due process requirements.[a] A good exam-

c. *The continued vitality of the pre-Miranda voluntariness test.* Since the landmark *Miranda* case, the police must give a suspect the now familiar warnings and obtain a waiver of his rights before subjecting him to "custodial interrogation." However, as pointed out in Schulhofer, supra, at 877, in a number of important situations "the primary criterion of admissibility under *current* law is [still] the 'old' due process voluntariness test." These situations, observes Professor Schulhofer, include police questioning of suspects not in "custody" (e.g., *Oregon v. Mathiason,* p. 586 infra); "questioning by private parties even when suspects are in a custody-like situation" (e.g., *Commonwealth v. Mahnke,* 335 N.E.2d 660 (Mass.1975)); and the use of confessions to impeach a defendant's trial testimony (e.g., *Harris v. New York,* p. 828 infra; *Mincey v. Arizona,* fn. b supra). See also Grano, *Voluntariness, Free Will, and the Law of Confessions,* 65 Va.L.Rev. 859, 864–65 n. 33 (1979), pointing out, inter alia, that "improper use of an involuntary confession seems to require automatic reversal on appeal while use of a confession obtained in violation of *Miranda* may be subject to the harmless error rule" (see generally Ch. 11, & § 2) and that "the fruit of the poisonous tree doctrine may require different results depending on whether a traditional voluntariness or a *Miranda* violation is found" (see generally Ch. 11, § 3).

Thus, "[c]areful attention to the voluntariness issue remains an imperative, though sometimes overlooked, obligation of court and counsel," Schulhofer 878. To illustrate his point, Professor Schulhofer points to *United States v. Mesa,* discussed at pp. 583, 596 infra. The *Mesa* court's rejection of a *Miranda* challenge, observes Schulhofer, id. at 878 n. 58, was "based on particularities of *Miranda's* rationale and would by no means preclude a voluntariness claim. Yet the defense never argued, and so the [Third Circuit] never considered, whether the statements made by this psychologically distraught suspect, on the verge of suicide, [who had barricaded himself in a motel room and threatened that he would not surrender peacefully], in the course of a three-and-one-half-hour conversation [with an FBI crisis negotiator] under highly charged circumstances, were admissible under the due process test."

a. For a long, hard look at the federal courts' exercise of "supervisory powers" over the administration of federal criminal justice generally and a look back at *McNabb,* regarded by many as the first supervisory power decision, see Beale, *Reconsidering Supervisory Power in Criminal Cases: Constitutional and Statutory Limits on the Authority of the Federal Courts,* 84 Colum.L.Rev.

ple was the significance given to the fact that incriminating statements were obtained during illegal detention, i.e., while the suspect was held in violation of federal statutory requirements that he be promptly taken before a committing magistrate to ascertain whether good cause exists to hold him for trial. Although, during this period, an otherwise voluntary confession was not rendered inadmissible in a *state* prosecution solely because it was elicited during prolonged and hence illegal precommitment detention (this was only *one* of many factors in determining whether a confession was voluntary), the 1943 *McNabb* case, although hardly free from ambiguity, seemed to hold that such a confession had to be excluded from *federal* prosecutions.

The *McNabb* rule was heavily criticized by law enforcement spokesmen and many members of Congress and begrudgingly interpreted by most lower federal courts. See generally Hogan & Snee, *The McNabb-Mallory Rule: Its Rise, Rationale and Rescue,* 47 Geo.L.J. 1 (1958). However, it was emphatically reaffirmed in MALLORY v. UNITED STATES, 354 U.S. 449, 77 S.Ct. 1356, 1 L.Ed.2d 1479 (1957), where, speaking for a unanimous Court, Justice FRANKFURTER observed:

"We cannot sanction this extended delay [some seven hours], resulting in confession, without subordinating [Fed.R.Crim. P. 5(a), requiring that an arrestee be taken 'without unnecessary delay' to the nearest available committing officer] to the discretion of arresting officers in finding exceptional circumstances for its disregard. [There is no escape] from the constraint laid upon the police by that Rule in that two other suspects were involved for the same crime. Presumably, whomever the police arrest they must arrest on 'probable cause.' It is not the function of the police to arrest, as it were, at large and to use an interrogating process at police headquarters in order to determine whom they should charge before a committing magistrate on 'probable cause.' "

Only a handful of states adopted the *McNabb-Mallory* rule or its equivalent on their own initiative.[b] But many hoped (any many others feared) that some day the Court would apply the rule to the states as a matter of fourteenth amendment due process. The Court never did. Instead, in the years since the 1957 *Mallory* decision, the last of the *McNabb* line of cases, the Court closed in on the state confession problem by making increasing resort to the right to counsel and the privilege against self-incrimination. By such means the state confession rules were

1433 (1984). Extracts from Professor Beale's article appear at p. 58 supra.

b. It was not until 1960 that the states' unanimity in refusing to follow the Supreme Court's lead in the *McNabb-Mallory* line of cases was broken. See *People v. Hamilton,* 102 N.W.2d 738, 741–43 (Mich.1960); Rothblatt & Rothblatt, *Police Interrogation: The Right to Counsel and to Prompt Arraignment,* 27 Brooklyn L.Rev. 24, 40–44 (1960). On the eve of *Miranda,* two more states adopted an equivalent of the rule, Delaware, see *Webster v. State,* 213 A.2d 298, 301 (Del. 1965); and Connecticut, by legislation, see *State v. Vollhardt,* 244 A.2d 601, 607 (Conn.1968) (subsequent case construing statute). In recent years at least three more state courts—Maryland, Montana, and Pennsylvania—adopted some equivalent of the rule. See *Johnson v. State,* 384 A.2d 709, 714–18 (Md.1978); *State v. Benbo,* 570 P.2d 894, 899–900 (Mont.1977); *Commonwealth v. Davenport,* 370 A.2d 301, 306 (Pa.1977); *Commonwealth v. Futch,* 290 A.2d 417, 418–19 (Pa.1972).

The life of Maryland's version of the *McNabb-Mallory* rule, adopted in the 1978 *Johnson* case, "was short and unhappy." Wilkes, *The New Federalism in Criminal Procedure in 1984: Death of the Phoenix?,* in Developments in State Constitutional Law 166, 170 (B. McGraw ed. 1985). The *Johnson* rule was usually interpreted begrudgingly and—in a "legislative blow to the new federalism"—repealed by statute in 1981. See id. at 169–171.

For a close examination and strong criticism of the recent "state court revival" of the *McNabb-Mallory* rule, see Note, 72 J.Crim.L. & C. 204 (1981). The Note maintains, id. at 241, that "current constitutional law addresses many of the original concerns underlying delay statutes, obviating the need for reliance on a doctrine of implied statutory exclusion."

eventually to *go beyond* the *McNabb-Mallory* doctrine in a number of respects.[c]

D. The Right to Counsel and the Analogy to the Accusatorial, Adversary Trial

CROOKER v. CALIFORNIA, 357 U.S. 433, 78 S.Ct. 1287, 2 L.Ed.2d 1448, (1958), involved a petitioner who attended one year of law school, during which time he studied criminal law, and who indicated in his dealings with the police that he was fully aware of his right to remain silent. On the basis of a challenged confession, he was convicted of murder of his paramour and sentenced to death. He contended that by persisting in interrogating him after denying his specific request to contact his lawyer the police violated his due process right to legal representation and advice and that therefore use of any confession obtained from him under these circumstances should be barred even though "freely" and "voluntarily" made under traditional standards. Such a rule retorted the Court, per CLARK, J., "would have [a] devastating effect on enforcement of criminal law, for it would effectively preclude police questioning—*fair as well as unfair*—until the accused was afforded opportunity to call his attorney. Due process, a concept 'less rigid and more fluid than those envisaged in other specific and particular provisions of the Bill of Rights,' *Betts v. Brady,* demands no such rule."

In his dissenting opinion, Justice DOUGLAS, with whom Warren, C.J., and Black and Brennan, JJ., joined, insisted: "The right to have counsel at the pretrial stage is often necessary to give meaning and protection to the right to be heard at the trial itself. It may also be necessary as a restraint on the coercive power of the police. * * * The demands of our civilization expressed in the Due Process Clause require that the accused who wants a counsel should have one at any time after the moment of arrest."

In the companion case of CICENIA v. LA GAY, 357 U.S. 504, 78 S.Ct. 1297, 2 L.Ed.2d 1523 (1958), not only did petitioner unsuccessfully ask to see his lawyer while he was being questioned by the police, but his lawyer, who arrived at the police station while petitioner was being interrogated, repeatedly (and unsuccessfully) asked to see his client. Moreover, petitioner was not well educated as was Crooker. Nevertheless, the Court affirmed the murder conviction (which led to a life sentence), disposing of petitioner's contention that he had a constitutional right to confer with counsel on the authority of *Crooker.* With the exception of Justice Brennan, who took no part in the case, the Court split along the same lines it had in *Crooker.*

The following year, however, by virtue of SPANO v. NEW YORK, it appeared that the Court had reached the view that once a person was *formally charged* by indictment or information his constitutional right to counsel had "begun"—at least his right to the assistance of counsel he himself had retained. Four concurring Justices took this position in *Spano:* Justices Black, Douglas and Brennan, all of whom had dissented in *Crooker;* and newly appointed Justice Stewart, who had replaced Justice Burton.

In separate concurring opinions both Justice Douglas (joined by Black and Brennan, JJ.) and Justice Stewart (joined by Douglas and Brennan, JJ.) stressed that *Spano* was not a case where the police were questioning a suspect in the course of investigating an unsolved crime but one where the subject of interrogation was already under indictment for murder when he surrendered to the authorities. Both concurring opinions also measured the

c. Title II of the Omnibus Crime Control and Safe Streets Act of 1968 purports to repeal (among other judicial doctrines) the *McNabb-Mallory* rule. Because the possible constitutional vulnerability of this 1968 provision turns in part on an appraisal of *Miranda,* treatment of this point is postponed until p. 573 infra.

proceedings in the "interrogation" room against the standard of a public trial and formal judicial proceedings. Thus Justice STEWART observed: "Under our system of justice an indictment is supposed to be followed by an arraignment and a trial. * * * What followed the petitioner's surrender in this case was not arraignment in a court of law, but an all-night inquisition in a prosecutor's office, a police station, and an automobile. * * * Our Constitution guarantees the assistance of counsel to a man on trial for his life in an orderly courtroom, presided over by a judge, open to the public, and protected by all the procedural safeguards of the law. Surely a Constitution which promises that much can vouchsafe no less to the same man under midnight inquisition in the squad room of a police station."

As we have already seen, a majority of the *Spano* Court did not go off on "right to counsel" grounds, finding the confession inadmissible on straight "coerced confession" grounds, but the Chief Justice, who wrote the majority opinion, had taken the position, a year earlier in *Crooker,* that the right to counsel should "begin" even earlier than at the point of indictment. Thus, counting heads, it appeared that by 1959 the view of the concurring Justices in *Spano* commanded a majority of the Court.

E. *Massiah and Escobedo*: THE COURT CLOSES IN ON THE "CONFESSION PROBLEM"

"There is a case in the Supreme Court now from Illinois, *People v. Escobedo,* that involves this very issue [of when the right to counsel begins] and I am scared that the Court is going to hold that this right exists from the time of arrest—if a person asks for counsel and he is not given counsel, anything you get from him after that has to be excluded."

—Fred E. Inbau, *A Forum on the Interrogation of the Accused,* 49 Corn.L.Q. 382, 401 (January 31, 1964).

Five years after *Spano,* in MASSIAH v. UNITED STATES, 377 U.S. 201, 84 S.Ct. 1199, 12 L.Ed.2d 246 (1964), a 6–3 majority (consisting of the four concurring Justices in *Spano,* Chief Justice Warren, and newly appointed Justice Goldberg) adopted the view advanced in the *Spano* concurring opinions. *Massiah* arose as follows: After he had been indicted for federal narcotics violations, Massiah retained a lawyer, pled not guilty, and was released on bail. A codefendant, Colson, invited him to discuss the pending case in Colson's car, parked on a city street. Unknown to Massiah, Colson had decided to cooperate with federal agents in their continuing investigation of the case. A radio transmitter was installed under the front seat of Colson's car, enabling a nearby agent (Murphy), who was equipped with a recording device, to overhear the Massiah-Colson conversation. As expected, Massiah made several damaging admissions.

It is hardly surprising that the *Massiah* dissenters considered the facts of the case a "peculiarly inappropriate" setting for a major breakthrough on the "police interrogation"–"confession" front. Even if the *Spano* concurring opinions had come to represent the majority view, argued then Solicitor General Archibald Cox, Massiah's statements should still be admissible because at the time he made them he was neither in "custody"—not even in the loosest sense—nor undergoing "police interrogation." He was under no "official pressure" to answer questions or even to engage in conversation; his conversation "was not affected by even that degree of constraint which may result from a suspect's knowledge that he is talking to a law enforcement officer." [e] Moreover, Colson, a layman unskilled in the art of interrogation, did not and probably could not

e. Extensive extracts from the Government's brief and oral argument in *Massiah* appear in Kamisar, *Police Interrogation and Confessions: Essays in Law and Policy* 171–73 (1980) (hereinafter referred to as Kamisar essays).

utilize any of the standard techniques to induce Massiah to incriminate himself.[f]

Nevertheless, as the *Massiah* majority, per STEWART, J., saw it, the decisive feature of the case was that after he had been indicted—"and therefore at a time when he was clearly entitled to a lawyer's help" and at a time when he was awaiting trial "in an orderly courtroom, presided over by a judge, open to the public, and protected by all the procedural safeguards of the law"—Massiah had been subjected to a "completely extrajudicial" police-orchestrated proceeding designed to obtain incriminating statements from him. Besides, if in one respect—the lack of an inherently or potentially "coercive atmosphere"—Massiah had been less seriously imposed upon than the average "confession" defendant, he was more seriously imposed upon in another respect—he did not, and could not be expected to, keep his guard up because he was not even aware that he was dealing with a government agent[g]: "We hold that the petitioner was denied the basic protections of [the right to counsel] when there was used against him at his trial evidence of his own incriminating words, which federal agents had deliberately elicited from him after he had been indicted and in the absence of his counsel. It is true that in the *Spano* case the defendant was interrogated in a police station, while here the damaging testimony was elicited from [him] without his knowledge while he was free on bail. But, as Judge Hays pointed out in his dissent in the [Second Circuit], 'if such a rule is to have any efficacy it must apply to indirect and surreptitious interrogations as well as those conducted in the jailhouse. In this case, Massiah was more seriously imposed upon * * * because he did not even know that he was under interrogation by a government agent.' * * *

"We do not question that in this case, as in many cases, it was entirely proper to continue an investigation of the suspected criminal activities of the defendant and his alleged confederates, even though the defendant had already been indicted. All that we hold is that the defendant's own incriminating statements, obtained by federal agents under the circumstances here disclosed, could not constitutionally be used by the prosecution as evidence against *him* at his trial."

Dissenting Justice WHITE, joined by Clark and Harlan, JJ., protested: "[H]ere there was no substitution of brutality for brains, no inherent danger of police coercion justifying the prophylactic effect of another exclusionary rule. Massiah was not being interrogated in a police station, was not surrounded by numerous officers or questioned in relays, and was not forbidden access to others. Law enforcement may have the elements of a contest about it, but it is not a game."

The dissenters were "unable to see how this case presents an unconstitutional interference with Massiah's right to counsel. Massiah was not prevented from consulting with counsel as often as he wished. No meetings with counsel were disturbed or spied upon. Preparation for trial was in no way obstructed. It is only a sterile syllogism—an unsound one besides—to

f. The Massiah-Colson conversation was not only broadcast to a nearby federal agent, but secretly tape-recorded by Colson. In the district court, however, Massiah successfully objected to the admission of these tapes on the ground that they implicated other defendants and contained privileged matters. The Government maintained that the recording confirmed the testimony of Agent Murphy that Colson did not coerce Massiah into making any incriminating statements or even induce him by appeals to talk in the guise of friendship and filed the recording with the clerk of the Court. Colson did not testify himself. Massiah did not testify either or otherwise contradict Murphy's testimony about the meeting. See Kamisar essays at 278 n. 202.

g. Massiah's unawareness that he was, in effect, talking to the police, and thus his inability to protect himself, "was a nice point (or counterpoint), but it was hardly the decisive one." Kamisar essays at 174. Any doubts that the *Massiah* doctrine also applies when the suspect realizes he is in the presence of the police were removed in *Brewer v. Williams* (1977), p. 626 infra.

say that because Massiah had a right to counsel's aid before and during the trial, his out-of-court conversations and admissions must be excluded if obtained without counsel's consent or presence."

"This case," maintained the dissenters, "cannot be analogized to [Canon 9 of the ABA's Canons of Professional Ethics] forbidding an attorney to talk to the opposing party litigant outside the presence of his counsel. Aside from the fact that [the canons] are not of constitutional dimensions, [Canon 9] deals with the conduct of lawyers and not with the conduct of investigators.[h] Lawyers are forbidden to interview the opposing party because of the supposed imbalance of legal skill and acumen between the lawyer and the party litigant; the reason for the rule does not apply to nonlawyers and certainly not to Colson, Massiah's codefendant."

Were the *Massiah* dissenters right when they observed that "the reason given for the result here—the admissions were obtained in the absence of counsel—would seem equally pertinent to statements obtained at any time after the right to counsel attaches, whether there has been an indictment or not"? Does the subject of police interrogation who has not yet been indicted need "a lawyer's help" every bit as much as one who has been formally charged? By drawing the line at the institution of formal judicial proceedings, had Justice Stewart (author of *Massiah,* but a dissenter in *Escobedo,* infra) "painted himself into a corner [from] which he could extricate himself only by a highly formalistic reading of the Sixth Amendment"? See Herman, *The Supreme Court and Restrictions on Police Interrogation,* 25 Ohio St.L.J. 449, 491 (1964).

As made plain a short five weeks later in the same Term, ESCOBEDO v. ILLINOIS, 378 U.S. 478, 84 S.Ct. 1758, 12 L.Ed.2d 977 (1964), a majority of the Court was not about to give the Sixth Amendment a formalistic reading. Escobedo's interrogation had occurred before "judicial" or "adversary" proceedings had commenced against him, but, as dissenting Justice Stewart characterized the *Escobedo* majority's reasoning, "[t]he Court disregards this basic difference between the present case and Massiah's, with the bland assertion that 'that fact should make no difference.' "

Escobedo arose as follows: On the night of January 19, petitioner's brother-in-law was fatally shot. A few hours later petitioner was taken into custody for questioning, but he made no statement and was released the following afternoon pursuant to a writ of habeas corpus obtained by his retained counsel. On January 30, one Di Gerlando, was was then in police custody and who was later indicted for the murder along with petitioner, stated that petitioner had fired the shots which killed his brother-in-law. That evening petitioner was again arrested and taken to police headquarters. En route to the police station he was told that Di Gerlando had named him as the one who fired the fatal shots and that he might as well admit it, but petitioner replied (probably because his attorney had obtained his release from police custody only 11 days earlier or because he had consulted with his attorney in the meantime): "I am sorry but I would like to have advice from my lawyer." Shortly after petitioner reached police headquarters, his retained lawyer arrived and spent the next three or four hours trying unsuccessfully to speak to his client. He talked

h. But consider Breitel, C.J., in *People v. Hobson,* 348 N.E.2d 894, 898 (N.Y.1976): "[I]t would not be rational, logical, moral or realistic to make any distinction between a lawyer acting for the State who [by seeking a waiver of the right to counsel from a suspect in the absence of, and without notification to, his lawyer] violates [the Code of Professional Responsibility] directly and one who indirectly uses the admissions improperly obtained by a police officer, who is the badged and uniformed representative of the State." See also *United States v. Springer,* 460 F.2d 1344, 1354–55 (7th Cir.1972) (Judge (now Justice) Stevens, dissenting); *People v. Patterson,* 198 N.W.2d 175, 181 (Mich.1971) (Levin, J., dissenting). See generally Note, 53 Ind.L.J. 313, 320 N. 42 (1978).

to every officer he could find, but was repeatedly told that he could not see his client and that he would have to get a writ of habeas corpus. In the meantime, petitioner repeatedly but unsuccessfully asked to speak to his lawyer. Instead, the police arranged a confrontation between petitioner and Di Gerlando. Petitioner denied that he had fired the fatal shots, claiming that Di Gerlando had done so, but thereby implicated himself in the murder plot. Petitioner's subsequent statement, "taken" by an assistant prosecutor who asked carefully framed questions, was admitted into evidence and he was convicted of murder. The Supreme Court of Illinois affirmed.

When certiorari was granted, the lawyers involved were well aware, as were close students of the problem, that *Escobedo* might be a momentous case. Bernard Weisberg, author of one of the most provocative and influential articles ever written on police interrogation, *Police Interrogation of Arrested Persons: A Skeptical View,* 52 J.Crim.L. & P.S. 21 (1961), in *Police Power and Individual Freedom* 153 (Sowle ed. 1962), argued the case for the ACLU, as *amicus curiae.* Because he thought it "playing Hamlet without the ghost to discuss police questioning without knowing what such questioning is really like," in his article Weisberg had made very extensive use of the interrogation manuals. He did the same in his *Escobedo* brief. He "urge[d] the Court to examine these books [which he extracted at considerable length in his brief]. They are not exhibits in a museum of third degree horrors. Indeed they carefully advise the police interrogator to avoid tactics which are clearly coercive under prevailing law. They are invaluable because they vividly describe the kind of interrogation practices which are accepted as lawful and proper under the best current standards of professional police work."

"What the police interrogation manuals reveal," argued Weisberg, "is that 'fair and reasonable' and 'effective' interrogation" is basically unfair and inherently coercive. "The type of 'fair and reasonable' and 'effective' police interrogation which has been described in the brief and in effect sanctioned by the Illinois Supreme Court in this case," he maintained, "adds a stage to criminal prosecutions which is not described in the statutes or judicial decisions relating to criminal procedure—a preliminary, secret and informal examination by interrogators whose actions are not governed by judicial standards and are essentially unsupervised. * * * Assertions that the police would be 'handcuffed' by the protective rule urged here cannot justify the virtually unlimited discretionary power which is at issue in this case, a power which effectively nullifies the basic and historic right to fairness in a criminal proceeding." [i]

Former Northwestern University law professor (now Governor) James Thompson argued the *Escobedo* case for the State of Illinois. He warned the Court:

"[A decision that the right to counsel begins at the moment of arrest] means the end of confessions as a tool of law enforcement. It cannot be stated more plainly than that. For once this petitioner's claim with Illinois is settled, the inevitable progression of the law must follow:

"*First,* if the right to counsel attaches at the moment of arrest [as the dissent in *Crooker* maintained], then it can hardly be denied that this right must be available to the poor as well as to the rich. * * * If

i. Weisberg' article on confessions, apparently the first to make extensive use of the interrogation manuals, and his *Escobedo* brief set the fashion for civil libertarians. The ACLU brief in *Miranda,* primarily the work of Professors Anthony Amsterdam and Paul Mishkin, reprinted a full chapter from one interrogation manual. In turn, Chief Justice Warren's opinion for the Court in *Miranda,* infra, devoted six full pages to extracts from various police manuals and texts "document[ing] procedures employed with success in the past, [and] recommend[ing] various other effective tactics." Many of the examples selected by the *Miranda* Court in 1966 were the same ones Weisberg used in his 1961 article and his 1964 *Escobedo* brief.

petitioner was entitled to counsel immediately upon being taken into custody on January 30, then so is every other defendant. Any other conclusion is foreclosed [by] *Gideon* and *Griffin*.

"*Second*, if indigent criminal defendants are entitled to counsel from the moment of arrest, then already established law makes it clear that such a right does not depend upon a request. [N]ot only must the state furnish counsel to the indigent defendant at this stage of the criminal proceeding, it must make sure that he does not waive the right through ignorance of its existence, for 'it is settled that where the assistance of counsel is a constitutional requisite, the right to be furnished counsel does not depend upon a request.' *Carnley v. Cochran*, 369 U.S. 506, 513, 82 S.Ct. 884, 888, 8 L.Ed.2d 70, 75 [1962].[j]

" * * * We believe, with Justice Walter Schaefer of the Supreme Court of Illinois, that due process 'includes those procedures that are fair and feasible in the light of then existing values and capabilities.'[36] Extension of the right to counsel back to the moment of arrest is neither fair nor feasible at this moment in the administration of criminal justice in the fifty states. * * *

"Criminal defendants, rich as well as poor, enjoy more protection from unjust conviction today than at any time in our history. 'The terrible engine' of the criminal law has been repeatedly braked by this Court, by state courts and legislatures and by fair and honest administration of the law by prosecutors and police. We need to guard against its derailment. * * * "

A 5–4 majority of the Court, per GOLDBERG, J., struck down Escobedo's confession, but, until *Miranda* moved *Escobedo* off center stage two years later, the scope and meaning of the decision was a matter of strong and widespread disagreement. In large part this was due to the accordion-like quality of the *Escobedo* opinion. At some places the opinion launches so broad an attack on the use of confessions in general and rejects the arguments for an "effective interrogation opportunity" so forcefully that it threatens (or promises) to eliminate virtually all police interrogation. At other places, however, the language of the opinion is quite confining, so much so that it arguably limits the case to its special facts:

"The interrogation here was conducted before petitioner was formally indicted. But in the context of this case, that fact should make no difference. When petitioner requested, and was denied, an opportunity to consult with his lawyer, the investigation had ceased to be a general investigation of 'an unsolved crime.' Petitioner had become the accused, and the purpose of the interrogation was to 'get him' to confess his guilt despite his constitutional right not to do so. At the time of his arrest and throughout the course of the interrogation, the police told petitioner that they had convincing evidence that he had fired the fatal shots. Without informing him of his absolute right to remain silent in the face of this accusation, the police urged him to make a statement. * * *

"Petitioner, a layman, was undoubtedly unaware that under Illinois law an admission of 'mere' complicity in the murder

j. Thompson's discussion of "the inevitable progression of the law" was, of course, the statement of an advocate; Illinois deemed it advantageous to underscore the extent to which the rule espoused by its adversaries would "cripple" law enforcement. But Escobedo's lawyers were advocates, too, and they could not, or at least did not try to, minimize the impact of the rule they sought. Neither the ACLU brief nor the brief filed by Escobedo's own lawyers ever cited *Gideon, Douglas, Griffin*, or *Carnley*. Moreover, shortly after *Escobedo* was decided, Thompson continued to view the case essentially the same way, now not as an advocate, but as assistant director of the Northwestern University Law School's Criminal Law Program. See fn. *l* infra.

36. Schaefer, *Federalism and State Criminal Procedure*, 70 Harv.L.Rev. 1, 6 (1956).

plot was legally as damaging as an admission of firing of the fatal shots. The 'guiding hand of counsel' was essential to advise petitioner of his rights in this delicate situation. This was the 'stage when legal aid and advice' were most critical to petitioner. *Massiah.* * * * What happened at this interrogation could certainly 'affect the whole trial,' since rights 'may be as irretrievably lost, if not then and there asserted, as they are when an accused represented by counsel waives a right for strategic purposes.' It would exalt form over substance to make the right to counsel, under these circumstances, depend on whether at the time of the interrogation, the authorities had secured a formal indictment. Petitioner had, for all practical purposes, already been charged with murder. * * *

"It is argued that if the right to counsel is afforded prior to indictment, the number of confessions obtained by the police will diminish significantly, because most confessions are obtained during the period between arrest and indictment, and 'any lawyer worth his salt will tell the suspect in no uncertain terms to make no statement to police under any circumstances.' This argument, of course, cuts two ways. The fact that many confessions are obtained during this period points up its critical nature as a 'stage when legal aid and advice' are surely needed. *Massiah.* The right to counsel would indeed be hollow if it began at a period when few confessions were obtained. There is necessarily a direct relationship between the importance of a stage to the police in their quest for a confession and the criticalness of that stage to the accused in his need for legal advice. Our Constitution, unlike some others, strikes the balance in favor of the right of the accused to be advised by his lawyer of his privilege against self-incrimination.

"We have learned the lesson of history, ancient and modern, that a system of criminal law enforcement which comes to depend on the 'confession' will, in the long run, be less reliable and more subject to abuses than a system which depends on extrinsic evidence independently secured through skillful investigation. * * *

"We have also learned the companion lesson of history that no system of criminal justice can, or should, survive if it comes to depend for its continued effectiveness on the citizens' abdication through unawareness of their constitutional rights. No system worth preserving should have to *fear* that if an accused is permitted to consult with a lawyer, he will become aware of, and exercise, these rights. If the exercise of constitutional rights will thwart the effectiveness of a system of law enforcement, then there is something very wrong with that system.[k]

"We hold, therefore, that where, as here, the investigation is no longer a general inquiry into an unsolved crime but has begun to focus on a particular suspect, the suspect has been taken into police custody, the police carry out a process of interrogations that lends itself to eliciting incriminating statements, the suspect has requested and been denied an opportunity to consult with his lawyer, and the police have not effectively warned him of his absolute constitutional right to remain silent, the accused has been denied 'the Assistance of Counsel' in violation of the Sixth Amendment to the Constitution as 'made obligatory upon the States by the Fourteenth Amendment,' *Gideon,* and that no statement elicited by the police during the interrogation may be used against him at a criminal trial. * * *

"Nothing we have said today affects the power of the police to investigate 'an unsolved crime' by gathering information from witnesses and by other 'proper inves-

k. But consider Caplan, *Questioning Miranda,* 38 Vand.L.Rev. 1417, 1440 (1985): "This statement is misleading because the right that the Court was defending, far from being of long standing, was newly discovered, indeed created, in this very opinion. What may have been 'very wrong' was not the extant 'system,' but the right the Court just announced."

tigative efforts.' We hold only that when the process shifts from investigatory to accusatory—when its focus is on the accused and its purpose is to elicit a confession—our adversary system begins to operate, and, under the circumstances here, the accused must be permitted to consult with his lawyer." *l*

Dissenting Justice STEWART protested:

"*Massiah* is not in point here. * * * Putting to one side the fact that the case now before us is not a federal case, the vital fact remains that this case does not involve the deliberate interrogation of a defendant after the initiation of judicial proceedings against him. The Court disregards this basic difference between the present case and Massiah's, with the bland assertion that that fact should make no difference.'

"It is 'that fact,' I submit, which makes all the difference. Under our system of criminal justice the institution of formal, meaningful judicial proceedings, by way of indictment, information, or arraignment, marks the point at which a criminal investigation has ended and adversary litigative proceedings have commenced. It is at this point that the constitutional guarantees attach which pertain to a criminal trial. * * *

"Supported by no stronger authority than its own rhetoric, the Court today converts a routine police investigation of an unsolved murder into a distorted analogue of a judicial trial. It imports into this investigation constitutional concepts historically applicable only after the onset of formal prosecutorial proceedings."

In a separate dissent, Justice WHITE, joined by Stewart and Clark, JJ., observed:

"[*Massiah*] held that as of the date of the indictment the prosecution is disentitled to secure admissions from the accused. The Court now moves that date back to the time when the prosecution begins to 'focus' on the accused. Although the opinion purports to be limited to the facts of this case, it would be naive to think that the new constitutional right announced will depend upon whether the accused has retained his own counsel, or has asked to consult with counsel in the course of interrogation. At the very least the Court holds that once the accused becomes a suspect and, presumably, is arrested, any admission made to the police thereafter is inadmissible in evidence unless the accused has waived his right to counsel. The decision is thus another major step in the direction of the goal which the Court seemingly has in mind—to bar from evidence all admissions obtained from an individual suspected of crime, whether involuntarily made or not. * * * I reject this step and the invitation to go farther which the Court has now issued. * * *

"It is incongruous to assume that the provision for counsel in the Sixth Amendment was meant to amend or supersede

l. As to whether *Escobedo* extended the constitutional role of counsel to the preindictment stage "when the process shifts from investigatory to accusatory—when its focus is on the accused and its purpose is to elicit a confession"—or when the process so shifts *and* one or some combination or all of the limiting facts in *Escobedo* are also present, see the summary of the wide disagreement over the probable meaning of the case in Kamisar essays at 161 n. 26.

Although many lower courts construed *Escobedo* quite narrowly, James Thompson, who had the distinction of making the losing argument in the case, read it quite broadly. He told a group of prosecuting attorneys attending a criminal law program that "in all cases where the police desire to obtain a confession from a suspect under circumstances like those in *Escobedo* [and] the suspect does not have retained counsel and does not request counsel, the police should, before interrogation, (a) inform him of his right not to say anything; and (b) inform him that anything he does say might be used against him." He also observed: "*Escobedo* does not, by its explicit language, require a *warning of the right to counsel,* but in that case the defendant concededly knew of, and attempted to exercise, that right. [I]n dealing with an accused who has not expressly indicated that he is aware of his right to counsel, absolute compliance with the *Escobedo* rule may well require a warning of the right to counsel along with the warning of the privilege against self-incrimination." See the extensive extracts from Thompson's analysis of *Escobedo* in Kamisar, supra, at 66–68.

the self-incrimination provision of the Fifth Amendment, which is now applicable to the States. That amendment addresses itself to the very issue of incriminating admissions of an accused and resolves it by proscribing only compelled statements. * * *

"The Court chooses [to] rely on the virtues and morality of a system of criminal law enforcement which does not depend on the 'confession.' No such judgment is to be found in the Constitution. * * * The only 'inquisitions' the Constitution forbids are those which compel incrimination. Escobedo's statements were not compelled and the Court does not hold that they were. * * *

"The Court may be concerned with a narrower matter: the unknowing defendant who responds to police questioning because he mistakenly believes that he must and that his admissions will not be used against him. But this worry hardly calls for the broadside the Court has now fired. * * * If an accused is told he must answer and did not know better, it would be very doubtful that the resulting admissions could be used against him. When the accused has not been informed of his rights at all the Court characteristically and properly looks very closely at the surrounding circumstances. I would continue to do so. But, in this case Danny Escobedo knew full well that he need not answer and knew full well that his lawyer had advised him not to answer." [m]

ON THE MEANING OF *ESCOBEDO*

1. *What right comes into play?* Once the investigation has ceased to be "a general inquiry of an unsolved crime but has begun to focus on a particular suspect," what right comes into play? The right of the suspect to consult with his lawyer before resuming the interrogation or the right to enjoy his attorney's *continued presence* and *constant advice* from that point on, as a protection in the face of any further police interrogation? Cf. *Massiah.*

2. *The role of counsel.* Consider Caplan, *Questioning Miranda,* 38 Vand.L.Rev. 1417, 1440–41 (1985): "Danny Escobedo's lawyer had advised him not to say anything to the police. If the homicide detectives had granted Escobedo's request to see his attorney again, there would have been nothing additional for his attorney to communicate. Escobedo had already been given all the assistance his counsel could provide without actually being present to assist his client on a question-by-question basis. Was Escobedo's attorney seeking the right to be present during the interrogation? Probably not. His intent in seeking entry to the homicide bureau was most likely to bring the interrogation to a close. Given that a defense attorney's usual objective is to stop the interrogation, it is hard to understand why the Court was so certain that 'no system worth preserving should have to fear that if an accused person is permitted to consult with a lawyer, he will become aware of, and exercise [his] rights,' unless the Court simply believed that there was no social utility in police interrogation. The *Escobedo* opinion contains no hint of anxiety that harm may accrue from a right to counsel: that there may be fewer confessions, and more crime."

3. *The "right to remain silent."* Until *Escobedo,* it seemed that the Constitution only entitled a suspect to refrain from incriminating himself, not from answering any and all questions (as opposed to a defendant in a criminal trial who need not "take the stand"), and that the suspect's "right" to remain absolutely silent in the face of police interrogation—perhaps more aptly characterized as his "immunity" from being required to answer any question—stemmed not from the Constitution as

m. In a brief separate dissent, Justice Harlan agreed with Justice White that "the rule announced today is most ill-conceived and that it seriously and unjustifiably fetters perfectly legitimate methods of criminal law enforcement."

such, but from the police department's lack of legislative authorization to compel an answer. That is to say, until *Escobedo* was decided, at any rate, the Constitution did not appear to prohibit legislatures from investing police with the power to compel non-incriminating answers, although the legislatures had not seen fit to do so.

As we have seen, *Escobedo* refers to a suspect's "absolute constitutional right to remain silent." Does this "right" now attach the moment a person is taken into custody or only when the investigation has ceased to be a general one and begun to "focus" on him "in particular"? Or does the Court merely mean that if, *in the absence of counsel,* a person chooses not to incriminate himself, the only practical way he can assure that he will not do so is to remain completely silent?

F. A Late Arrival on the Scene: The Privilege Against Self-Incrimination

"[Despite] a great deal of emotional writing which elevates the privilege against self-incrimination to 'one of the great landmarks in man's struggle to make himself civilized,' [the] most abundant proof [that it does not prohibit pretrial interrogation] is to be found in the United States. There the privilege is in the Federal Constitution and in [forty-eight state constitutions]. But in none of the forty-nine jurisdictions does it apply to what happens in the police station. The police interrogate freely, sometimes for seven to eight hours on end. The statements thus extracted are given in evidence. [O]nly statements made voluntarily may be given in evidence, but that seems to be interpreted rather liberally, judged by our standards."

—Judge V.G. Hiemstra of the Supreme Court of South Africa, *Abolition of the Right Not to be Questioned,* 80 South African L.J. 187, 194–95 (1963).

As long ago as 1931, Ernest Hopkins, a member of the Wickersham Commission staff, forcefully argued that the "third degree"—indeed, all secret police interrogation as typically practiced—was fundamentally in violation of the privilege against self-incrimination. E. Hopkins, *Our Lawless Police,* 193–95 (1931). As we have seen, however, the concurring justice in *Spano* and the majorities in *Massiah* and *Escobedo* relied primarily on the right to counsel, not the privilege against self-incrimination—the other essential mainstay of the accusatorial, adversary system. But the "prime suspect"—focal point—"accusatory state" test(s) of *Escobedo* threatened the admissibility of even "volunteered" statements. There was reason to think that the Court might be in the process of shaping "a novel right not to confess except knowingly and with the tactical assistance of counsel," Enker & Elsen, *Counsel for the Suspect: Massiah v. United States and Escobedo v. Illinois,* 49 Minn.L.Rev. 47, 60–61, 69, 83 (1964). Thus *critics* of *Escobedo* turned to the privilege against self-incrimination as a less restrictive alternative. Dissenting in *Escobedo,* Justice White, joined by Clark and Stewart, JJ., observed:

"It is incongruous to assume that the provision for counsel in the Sixth Amendment was meant to amend or supersede the self-incrimination provision of the Fifth Amendment which is now applicable to the States. [*Malloy v. Hogan,* infra.] That amendment addresses itself to the very issue of incriminating admissions and resolves it by proscribing only compelled statements. [That amendment provides no support] for the idea that an accused has an absolute constitutional right not to answer even in the absence of compulsion, [no support for the view that he has] the constitutional right not to incriminate himself by making voluntary disclosures."

Even as Justice White spoke, there was reason to think that, at long last, the privilege against self-incrimination was knocking on the door of the interrogation room. Only a few months before *Escobedo* had been decided, the Court, in MALLOY v. HOGAN, 378 U.S. 1, 84 S.Ct. 1489, 12 L.Ed.2d 653 (1964) (per Brennan, J.), had performed "what might have seemed to some a shotgun wedding of the privilege [against self-incrimination] to the confession rule," Herman, *The Supreme Court and Restrictions on Police Interrogation,* 25 Ohio St.L.J. 449, 465 (1965), by declaring that "today the admissibility of a confession in a state criminal prosecution is tested by the same standard applied in federal prosecutions since 1897, when in *Bram v. United States,* 168 U.S. 532, 18 S.Ct. 183, 42 L.Ed. 568, the Court held that '[i]n criminal trials, in the courts of the United States, wherever a question arises whether a confession is incompetent because not voluntary, the issue is controlled by [the self-incrimination] portion of the Fifth Amendment.' "

Whether or not this approach to police interrogation and confessions makes good sense it constitutes very questionable history—at least since *Brown v. Mississippi* (1936). The old *Bram* case might well have furnished a steppingstone to the standard advanced in *Malloy,* but until *Escobedo,* at any rate, it only seemed to amount to an early excursion from the prevailing multifactor or "totality of circumstances" approach. In none of the dozens of federal *or* state confession cases decided by the Court in the 1930's, 1940's and 1950's had the privilege against self-incrimination, certainly not as it applied to judicial proceedings, been the basis for judgment (although it had occasionally been mentioned in an opinion). If the privilege against self-incrimination had been the way to resolve the confession problem, then all the state courts and lower federal courts that had admitted confessions would have been reversed *per curiam.* For it was plain that law enforcement officers could, and without hesitation did, resort to methods they would never consider utilizing at the trial, that they had much greater power over a suspect or defendant away from the restraining influence of a public trial in an open courtroom.

Although certain factors, such as the length of pre-arraignment detention, had been taking on increasing significance, as Justice Frankfurter described the situation in *Culombe v. Connecticut* (1961), neither the privilege against self-incrimination nor any other "single litmus-paper test for constitutionally impermissible interrogation [had] been evolved: neither extensive cross-questioning—deprecated by the English judges; nor undue delay in arraignment—proscribed by *McNabb;* nor failure to caution a prisoner—enjoined by the [English] Judges' Rules; nor refusal to permit communication with friends and legal counsel at stages in the proceedings when the prisoner is still only a suspect—prohibited by several state statutes." That was why, as Justice Goldberg put it for a majority in *Haynes v. Washington,* 373 U.S. 503, 83 S.Ct. 1336, 10 L.Ed.2d 513 (1963) (only a year before he wrote the opinion of the Court in *Escobedo*), "the line between proper and permissible police conduct and techniques and methods offensive to due process is, at best, a difficult one to draw, particularly in cases such as this where it is necessary to make fine judgments as to the effect of psychologically coercive pressures and inducements on the mind and will of an accused."

Why had the privilege against self-incrimination been excluded from the stationhouse all these years? The legal reasoning was that compulsion to testify meant *legal* compulsion. Since he is threatened neither with perjury for testifying falsely nor contempt for refusing to testify at all, it cannot be said, ran the argument, that the subject of police interrogation is being "compelled" to be "a witness against himself" within the meaning of the privilege—even though he may assume or be led to believe that there *are* legal (or extralegal) sanctions for contumacy. Since the police have no *legal right* to make a suspect answer, there is no legal obligation to answer to which a privilege in the technical sense can apply. For an appraisal of this argument, see Mayers, *Shall We Amend the Fifth Amendment?,* 82–83, 223–33 (1959); Schaefer, *The Suspect and Society* 16–18 (1967); 8 Wigmore, *Evidence,* 329 fn. 27 (McNaughton rev. 1961).

It has been suggested that the reasoning above "had a great deal more to commend it than merely the inherent force of its 'logic' or the self-restraint and tenderness of the exempted class of interrogators," Kamisar essays 59–60; and that among the forces at work were *"necessity"*—the conviction that police interrogation without advising the suspect of his rights was "indispensable" in law enforcement—and the *invisibility* of the process, which made it easy for society to be complacent about what was really going on and to readily accept police-prosecution "sanitized" versions of what was going on. Id. at 60–63.

How the *Malloy* opinion looked back, however, was not as important as how it looked forward. Whatever one thought of the manner in which *Malloy* had recorded the recent past, one could not treat lightly the way it anticipated the near future.

SECTION 3. THE *MIRANDA* REVOLUTION

ORAL ARGUMENTS IN *MIRANDA* AND COMPANION CASES [a]

* * *

MR. DUANE R. NEDRUD, on behalf of the National District Attorneys Association. *Amicus Curiae.* * * *

THE CHIEF JUSTICE: May I ask you this, please, Mr. Nedrud: if you agree on the facts that *Escobedo* should not be overruled, what would you say as to the man who did not have a lawyer, but who said he wanted a lawyer before he talked?

MR. NEDRUD: If he asked for a lawyer, and he does not waive his right to counsel, I think that he should have a lawyer. [I] would go so far as to say that I think the state should appoint a lawyer if he asks for a lawyer. I do not think, however, that we should in effect encourage him to have a lawyer.

THE CHIEF JUSTICE: Why do you say we should not encourage him to have a lawyer? Are lawyers a menace? * * *

MR. NEDRUD: I think [a lawyer] is not a menace at the trial level. He is not a menace, per se, but he is, in doing his duty, going to prevent a confession from being obtained. * * *

MR. JUSTICE DOUGLAS: * * * [A lawyer] needs time to prepare for the trial, so the appointment must be at some point anterior to the trial. Our question here is how far anterior. * * *

MR. NEDRUD: The question comes down I think, Mr. Justice Douglas, to whether or not we are going to allow the trial court to determine guilt or innocence—or the defense counsel. If the defense counsel comes in at the arrest stage, he will, as he should, prevent the defendant from confessing to his crime, and you will have fewer convictions. If this is what is wanted, this is what will occur.

MR. JUSTICE BLACK: I guess there is no doubt, is there, as to the effect of the provision which provides for protection against compelling him to give testimony. Is is not fewer convictions?

MR. NEDRUD: [I believe] there is a point of diminishing returns and at some stage the police must be in a position to protect us.

MR. JUSTICE BLACK: * * * Can you think of any time when [a person]

a. These extracts from the oral arguments are not taken from an "official transcript"—no such transcript is available—but from a transcript the Institute of Criminal Law and Procedure of the Georgetown University Law Center and several private parties, including the editors of this book, arranged to have made. Substantial extracts from the oral arguments also appear in Medalie, *From Escobedo to Miranda: The Anatomy of a Supreme Court Decision* (1966) (Inst. of Crim.L. & P., Geo.U.).

needs a lawyer more than [at] the point of detention?

MR. NEDRUD: Mr. Justice Black, again, the question is are we interested in convicting the defendant, or are we interested in protecting or acquitting him? This is the only point that I can, in effect, make, if you say that this defendant needs counsel at this time.

For example, if I may use this illustration, I worked when I was a professor of law, which I was prior to taking this position, I worked on the defense project for the American Bar Association. In the questionnaire there was a statement, "When is the ideal time for counsel to be appointed for the defendant?"

Actually, the question is, "When is the ideal time for whom, the people or the defendant?" If it is for the defendant, then it is the earliest possible opportunity; if it is for the people, it should not be until a critical stage. * * *

MR. JUSTICE BLACK: I have found out over many years a very critical stage is when a person is taken to the police headquarters. * * *

A person is taken to police headquarters and placed under arrest or detention. He can't leave, if he wants to, unless they let him. Would you call that voluntary for him, then, for [the police] to have him there in that situation and probe him about probable conviction of crime? Would you think of that as voluntary?

MR. NEDRUD: As being voluntarily in the police station, no. * * *

MR. VICTOR M. EARLE, III on behalf of the petitioner in VIGNERA v. NEW YORK. * * *

MR. JUSTICE FORTAS: [Are you saying] that when the point of time comes where it appears that the police have enough information to satisfy themselves that the fellow really did the act, then the right to arrange for counsel or to give the warning attaches?

MR. EARLE: I think that is correct, although we don't have to look into the mind of the police necessarily to be able to determine that. * * * If in doubt, push it out on the other side of the warning. That is why I don't see that it should pose so much of a problem. I think the FBI Agents give warnings on this proceeding.

MR. JUSTICE STEWART: What should this warning contain? What should this warning be?

MR. EARLE: The Chief of Police in the District of Columbia last August promulgated a warning which, I understand, is now being given by all police officials in the District. It goes something like this: You have been placed under arrest. You are not required to say anything to us any time or to answer any questions. Anything you say may be used as evidence in court. You may call a lawyer or a relative or a friend. Your lawyer may be present here, and you may talk with him. If you cannot obtain a lawyer, one will be appointed for you when your case first goes to court.

I might have a little quibble with that third point, because it suggests a little bit that you might not be able to get a lawyer now.

MR. JUSTICE FORTAS: Much more than a little bit of quibble on the basis of what you have argued so far—that he has an absolute right for a lawyer to be appointed for him at that point, unless he waives it.

MR. EARLE: Yes, sir, unless he waives it. The question might come up of how do the police, or what do the police do when the fellow says, "Thanks. I would like a lawyer now that you mention it, but I don't happen to have any money." They have a choice. They can give him ten cents and the number of a legal aid society.

They have another alternative—just stop interrogating. That alternative was never mentioned. * * *

MR. JUSTICE WHITE: They give him the warning, and he nods his head, yes. (laughter)

MR. JUSTICE WHITE: What happens?

MR. EARLE: It takes a conscious relinquishing of his known rights, those rights I have been telling you about, Justice White.

MR. JUSTICE WHITE: I thought that is what you would say. What happens then if the fellow just nods his head and just looks at him?

MR. EARLE: If we can believe he nodded his head, it is possible that he waives it. I would be very reluctant to come to that conclusion on [that] hypothesis.

MR. JUSTICE WHITE: What else besides giving a warning and right to counsel?

MR. EARLE: I think if he writes down in his own handwriting, "I have been warned, I understand that I have a right to a lawyer now, to talk to him this minute, if I want to, or the right to say nothing if I want to. I understand that. I would like to go ahead and cooperate with the police. Signed: Michael Vignera." That would be enough.

MR. JUSTICE WHITE: That is just barely the first stage.

MR. EARLE: That is what the police have to say.

MR. JUSTICE WHITE: Sure, but if they want to rely on a waiver at any time, is this the only ground that you would accept for a lawyer not being present, a written waiver? Isn't that right?

MR. EARLE: I think that is right. It should be definitely recorded.

MR. JUSTICE WHITE: It should be a written waiver?

MR. EARLE: Absolutely. It shouldn't be something he is conned into giving. * * *

MR. JUSTICE WHITE: What if he doesn't waive? He says, "I do want counsel," and the state says, "Fine. Here is a dime, and there is the legal aid number," and the fellow calls him. He talks to the lawyer, and he comes back and sits down, and you ask him some questions, and he answers them.

MR. EARLE: Without his lawyer being present, for example?

MR. JUSTICE WHITE: Yes.

MR. EARLE: I take it that would be a decision made by his lawyer, and the lawyer can waive rights for his client.

MR. JUSTICE WHITE: Is that a waiver in your book? What is it, a waiver of the right to consult counsel or a waiver of the right to have counsel present?

MR. EARLE: I think it is a waiver to have a counsel in all the ways it is meant. The lawyer can make the determination of whether he should be present or not. Lawyers have waived many rights, like not filing the 30th day and the notice of appeal and the like * * *

MR. JUSTICE WHITE: My question is really going to what you think the scope of the right is. You think the scope of the right is to have counsel present and that you must waive not only the right to consult counsel, but the right to have counsel present?

MR. EARLE: I think that is right, Mr. Justice White. I want to elaborate on it, if I might. In a deposition in a civil case, for example, customarily, the plaintiff and the defendant can have counsel present. I can certainly conceive that one lawyer will not be present. The client, through him, would, therefore, waive that right. It would seem that the only way we could distinguish this case from *Escobedo* is the fact that Vignera did not make a request. What we have been talking about is doing that.

Obviously, it wasn't the request of the individual that made the right attach. The significance of the request, I think, in *Escobedo* was that it was a subjective piece of evidence to show that a stage had been reached. * * *

MR. JUSTICE STEWART: How can there be a waiver, if these are Constitutional rights and are important? How can anybody waive them without the consent of counsel or without the advice of counsel? Doesn't he need a lawyer before he can waive them, if you are right?

MR. EARLE: You are entitled to waive in other situations. It is true in court when they want to plead guilty, for example, the judge will decline assignment of counsel, and the judge will, typically, interrogate him to some length to realize the significance of his act, and that is a lot more advisable a situation than—and more conducive to our being receptive to the idea of a waiver than the police station. I agree that is the worst place for waiver. The party alleging waiver has control of the party alleged to have waived.

MR. JUSTICE STEWART: It seems to follow that he needs a lawyer before he can waive his right to a lawyer.

MR. EARLE: I wouldn't be unhappy to have lawyers in the police station.

MR. JUSTICE STEWART: It follows naturally.

MR. EARLE: It doesn't follow naturally, because a majority of the court in *Escobedo* said these rights can be waived. I think we do have to recognize some of the realities of law enforcement. They do have to investigate. They do have the public duty of—if crimes are being committed by the minute, they do have to operate out of the police station. * * *

MR. JUSTICE HARLAN: Is there a claim that the confession was coerced?

MR. EARLE: In no sense. I don't think it was coerced at all. Mr. Justice White asked yesterday a question about compelling someone to give up his Fifth Amendment privilege. I think there is a substantial difference between that and coercing a confession. I mean, it wasn't until 1964 that the Fifth Amendment privilege applied to the states, and so * * * all through until the '60's, really, state convictions were overturned only by looking to the generality of the totality of the circumstances under the due process clause.

Now, we have specific Constitutional guarantees that are applied in branch to the states, of both the Fifth and Sixth Amendment rights. It is true that the word "compel" is used in the Fifth Amendment with respect to the privilege, but it is quite different to say that the privilege is cut down and impaired by detention and to say a man's will has been so overborne a confession is forced from him. * * *

I hate to sound cynical, but if we go back to the totality of circumstances, that means this Court will sit all by itself as it has so many years to overturn the few confessions it can take, necessarily, by the bulk of the work. The lower courts won't do their job. We need some specific guidelines as *Escobedo* to help them along the way. * * *

MR. WILLIAM I. SIEGEL, on behalf of the respondent in VIGNERA v. NEW YORK. * * *

MR. JUSTICE FORTAS: Mr. Siegel, [the problem presented by these cases] really affects the basic relationship of the individual and the state. It really goes beyond the administration of justice, and that has been the history of mankind. * * *

MR. SIEGEL: [T]here is an immediate objective, also, and the immediate objective is to protect society; because, if society isn't protected, it, in one degree or another, lapses into anarchy because of crime and then the opportunity to reach this beautiful ideal is gone. It is the function of the police—.

MR. JUSTICE FORTAS: (Interrupting) * * * The problem is to reconcile a good many objectives that are not totally consonant.

I am a little troubled, I must say, when I sit here and hear so much reference to this problem as if it were merely a pragmatic problem of convicting people who did a crime, because there are many more dimensions, I suggest, to the problem than just that simple statement.

MR. SIEGEL: * * * The problem that is before this Court, it seems to me is just how to keep the balance between the ultimate necessity of the civilized, peaceful society and the constitutional rights of a specific defendant.

MR. JUSTICE BLACK: Don't you think that the Bill of Rights has something to do with making that balance?

MR. SIEGEL: Yes, sir.

MR. JUSTICE BLACK: There is not any doubt, is there, that no person should be convicted on evidence he has been compelled to give? Why do we have to get into a discussion of society or the beauties of the ideal civilization when that is the issue before us?

MR. SIEGEL: Because the Bill of Rights only says that [one] shall not be compelled, but the word "compelled" is not self-defining. We, for many, many years, were told [by] a great majority of Your Honors' predecessors, that compelled meant that which couldn't make a man talk by the exercise of process.

MR. JUSTICE BLACK: By what?

MR. SIEGEL: By the exercise of process. You couldn't subpoena him into a court and, under pain of punishment, make him talk. * * *

SOLICITOR GENERAL THURGOOD MARSHALL, on behalf of the government in WESTOVER v. UNITED STATES. * * *

MR. JUSTICE BLACK: [As] I understand you to say, of course, any person that has a lawyer or has the money to get a lawyer could get one immediately. This man has no lawyer and has no money to get one. The only reason he doesn't have a lawyer is for that reason. Does that raise any principles as to what an indigent is entitled to? He is certainly not getting treated like a man who has the money to get a lawyer.

MR. MARSHALL: He is not being denied anything. The state is not affirmatively denying anything. The state is just not furnishing him anything. * * *

MR. JUSTICE BLACK: I understood you to say if he had the money he would have the right to have the lawyer but the man that has no money has no chance to. That is the situation that we had in *Griffin.*

MR. MARSHALL: *Griffin* was a different point. You can't equalize the whole thing. I don't believe that we can. * * *

"I was introduced for my accomplishments primarily as being of counsel in *Miranda,* and consistently I must disabuse everyone of the accomplishment * * *. When certiorari was granted and we were asked by the ACLU to prepare and file the brief, we had a meeting in our law office in which we agreed that the briefs should be written with the entire focus on the Sixth Amendment [right to counsel] because that is where the Court was headed after *Escobedo,* and, as you are all aware, in the very first paragraph [of the *Miranda* opinion] Chief Justice Warren said, 'It is the Fifth Amendment to the Constitution that is at issue today.' That was Miranda's effective use of counsel."

—John J. Flynn, *Panel Discussion on the Exclusionary Rule,* 61 F.R.D. 259, 278 (1972).

MIRANDA v. ARIZONA (No. 759) *

384 U.S. 436, 86 S.Ct. 1602, 16 L.Ed.2d 694 (1966).

MR. CHIEF JUSTICE WARREN delivered the opinion of the Court.

* * * [W]e deal with the admissibility of statements obtained from an individual who is subjected to custodial police interrogation and the necessity for procedures which assure that the individual is accorded his privilege under the Fifth Amendment to the Constitution not to be compelled to incriminate himself. * * *

We start here, as we did in *Escobedo* with the premise that our holding is not an innovation in our jurisprudence, but is an application of principles long recognized and applied in other settings. We have undertaken a thorough re-examination of the *Escobedo* decision and the principles it announced, and we reaffirm it. That case was but an explication of basic rights that are enshrined in our Constitution—that "No person * * * shall be compelled in any criminal case to be a witness against himself," and that "the accused [shall] have the Assistance of Counsel"—rights which were put in jeopardy in that case through official overbearing. * * *

Our holding will be spelled out with some specificity in the pages which follow but briefly stated it is this: the prosecution may not use statements, whether exculpatory or inculpatory, stemming from custodial interrogation of the defendant unless it demonstrates the use of procedural safeguards effictive to secure the privilege against self-incrimination. By custodial interrogation, we mean questioning initiated by law enforcement officers after a person has been taken into custody or otherwise deprived of his freedom of action in any significant way.[4] As for the procedural safeguards to be employed, unless other fully effective means are devised to inform accused persons of their right of silence and to assure a continuous opportunity to exercise it, the following measures are required. Prior to any questioning, the person must be warned that he has a right to remain silent, that any statement he does make may be used as evidence against him, and that he has a right to the presence of an attorney, either retained or appointed. The defendant may waive effectuation of these rights, provided the waiver is made voluntarily, knowingly and intelligently. If, however, he indicates in any manner and at any stage of the process that he wishes to consult with an attorney before speaking there can be no questioning. Likewise, if the individual is alone and indicates in any manner that he does not wish to be interrogated, the police may not question him. The mere fact that he may have answered some questions or volunteered some statements on his own does not deprive him of the right to refrain from answering any further inquiries until he has consulted with an attorney and thereafter consents to be questioned.

The constitutional issue we decide in each of these cases is the admissibility of statements obtained from a defendant questioned while in custody and deprived of his freedom of action in any significant way. In each, the defendant was questioned by police officers, detectives, or a prosecuting attorney in a room in which he was cut off from the outside world. In none of these cases was the defendant given a full and effective warning of his rights at the outset of the interrogation process. In all the cases, the questioning elicited oral admissions, and in three of them, signed statements as well which were admitted at their trials. They all thus share salient features—incommunicado interrogation of individuals in a police-dominated atmosphere, resulting in self-incriminating statements without full warnings of constitutional rights. * * *

* Together with No. 760, *Vignera v. New York* [and] No. 761, *Westover v. United States* [and] No. 584, *California v. Stewart* * * *.

4. This is what we meant in *Escobedo* when we spoke of an investigation which had focused on an accused.

Again we stress that the modern practice of in-custody interrogation is psychologically rather than physically oriented. * * * Interrogation still takes place in privacy. Privacy results in secrecy and this in turn results in a gap in our knowledge as to what in fact goes on in the interrogation rooms. A valuable source of information about present police practices, however, may be found in various police manuals and texts which document procedures employed with success in the past, and which recommend various other effective tactics. These texts are used by law enforcement agencies themselves as guides.[9] It should be noted that these texts professedly present the most enlightened and effective means presently used to obtain statements through custodial interrogation. By considering these texts and other data, it is possible to describe procedures observed and noted around the country. * * *

To highlight the isolation and unfamiliar surroundings, the manuals instruct the police to display an air of confidence in the suspect's guilt and from outward appearance to maintain only an interest in confirming certain details. The guilt of the subject is to be posited as a fact. The interrogator should direct his comments toward the reasons why the subject committed the act, rather than court failure by asking the subject whether he did it. Like other men, perhaps the subject has had a bad family life, had an unhappy childhood, had too much to drink, had an unrequited desire for women. The officers are instructed to minimize the moral seriousness of the offense, to cast blame on the victim or on society. These tactics are designed to put the subject in a psychological state where his story is but an elaboration of what the police purport to know already—that he is guilty. Explanations to the contrary are dismissed and discouraged.

The texts thus stress that the major qualities an interrogator should possess are patience and perseverance. * * *

[When other techniques] prove unavailing, the texts recommend they be alternated with a show of some hostility. One ploy often used has been termed the "friendly-unfriendly" or the "Mutt and Jeff" act:

> ". . . In this technique, two agents are employed. Mutt, the relentless investigator, who knows the subject is guilty and is not going to waste any time. He's sent a dozen men away for this crime and he's going to send the subject away for the full term. Jeff, on the other hand, is obviously a kindhearted man. He has a family himself. He has a brother who was involved in a little scrape like this. He disapproves of Mutt and his tactics and will arrange to get him off the case if the subject will cooperate. He can't hold Mutt off for very long. The subject would be wise to make a quick decision. The technique is applied by having both investigators present while Mutt acts out his role. Jeff may stand by quietly and demur at some of Mutt's tactics. When Jeff makes his plea for cooperation, Mutt is not present in the room."

The interrogators sometimes are instructed to induce a confession out of trickery. The technique here is quite effective in crimes which require identification or which run in series. In the identification

9. The methods described in Inbau and Reid, *Criminal Interrogation and Confessions* (1962), are a revision and enlargement of material presented in three prior editions of a predecessor text, *Lie Detection and Criminal Interrogation* (3d ed. 1953). The authors and their associates are officers of the Chicago Police Scientific Crime-Detection Laboratory and have had extensive experience in writing, lecturing and speaking to law enforcement authorities over a 20-year period. They say that the techniques portrayed in their manuals reflect their experiences and are the most effective psychological strategems to employ during interrogations. Similarly, the techniques described in O'Hara, *Fundamentals of Criminal Investigation* (1959), were gleaned from long service as observer, lecturer in police science, and work as a federal criminal investigator. All these texts have had rather extensive use among law enforcement agencies and among students of police science, with total sales and circulation of over 44,000.

situation, the interrogator may take a break in his questioning to place the subject among a group of men in a line-up. "The witness or complainant (previously coached, if necessary) studies the line-up and confidently points out the subject as the guilty party." Then the questioning resumes "as though there were now no doubt about the guilt of the subject." A variation on this technique is called the "reverse line-up":

> "The accused is placed in a line-up, but this time he is identified by several fictitious witnesses or victims who associated him with different offenses. It is expected that the subject will become desperate and confess to the offense under investigation in order to escape from the false accusations."

The manuals also contain instructions for police on how to handle the individual who refuses to discuss the matter entirely, or who asks for an attorney or relatives. The examiner is to concede him the right to remain silent. "This usually has a very undermining effect. First of all, he is disappointed in his expectation of an unfavorable reaction on the part of the interrogator. Secondly, a concession of this right to remain silent impresses the subject with the apparent fairness of his interrogator." After this psychological conditioning, however, the officer is told to point out the incriminating significance of the suspect's refusal to talk:

> "Joe, you have a right to remain silent. That's your privilege and I'm the last person in the world who'll try to take it away from you. If that's the way you want to leave this, O.K. But let me ask you this. Suppose you were in my shoes and I were in yours and you called me in to ask me about this and I told you, 'I don't want to answer any of your questions.' You'd think I had something to hide, and you'd probably be right in thinking that. That's exactly what I'll have to think about you, and so will everybody else. So let's sit here and talk this whole thing over."

Few will persist in their initial refusal to talk, it is said, if this monologue is employed correctly.

In the event that the subject wishes to speak to a relative or an attorney, the following advice is tendered:

> "[T]he interrogator should respond by suggesting that the subject first tell the truth to the interrogator himself rather than get anyone else involved in the matter. If the request is for an attorney, the interrogator may suggest that the subject save himself or his family the expense of any such professional service, particularly if he is innocent of the offense under investigation. The interrogator may also add, 'Joe, I'm only looking for the truth, and if you're telling the truth, that's it. You can handle this by yourself.' "

From these representative samples of interrogation techniques, the setting prescribed by the manuals and observed in practice becomes clear. In essence, it is this: To be alone with the subject is essential to prevent distraction and to deprive him of any outside support. The aura of confidence in his guilt undermines his will to resist. He merely confirms the preconceived story the police seek to have him describe. Patience and persistence, at times relentless questioning, are employed. To obtain a confession, the interrogator must "patiently maneuver himself or his quarry into a position from which the desired object may be obtained." When normal procedures fail to produce the needed result, the police may resort to deceptive stratagems such as giving false legal advice. It is important to keep the subject off balance, for example, by trading on his insecurity about himself or his surroundings. The police then persuade, trick, or cajole him out of exercising his constitutional rights.

Even without employing brutality, the "third degree" or the specific stratagems described above, the very fact of custodial interrogation exacts a heavy toll on individual liberty and trades on the weakness of individuals. * * *

In the cases before us today, given this background, we concern ourselves primarily with this interrogation atmosphere and the evils it can bring. In *Miranda v. Arizona,* the police arrested the defendant and took him to a special interrogation room where they secured a confession. In *Vignera v. New York,* the defendant made oral admissions to the police after interrogation in the afternoon, and then signed an inculpatory statement upon being questioned by an assistant district attorney later the same evening. In *Westover v. United States,* the defendant was handed over to the Federal Bureau of Investigation by local authorities after they had detained and interrogated him for a lengthy period, both at night and the following morning. After some two hours of questioning, the federal officers had obtained signed statements from the defendant. Lastly, in *California v. Stewart,* the local police held the defendant five days in the station and interrogated him on nine separate occasions before they secured his inculpatory statement.

In these cases, we might not find the defendants' statements to have been involuntary in traditional terms. Our concern for adequate safeguards to protect precious Fifth Amendment rights is, of course, not lessened in the slightest. In each of the cases, the defendant was thrust into an unfamiliar atmosphere and run through menacing police interrogation procedures. The potentiality for compulsion is forcefully apparent, for example, in *Miranda,* where the indigent Mexican defendant was a seriously disturbed individual with pronounced sexual fantasies, and in *Stewart,* in which the defendant was an indigent Los Angeles Negro who had dropped out of school in the sixth grade. To be sure, the records do not evince overt physical coercion or patented psychological ploys. The fact remains that in none of these cases did the officers undertake to afford appropriate safeguards at the outset of the interrogation to insure that the statements were truly the product of free choice.

It is obvious that such an interrogation environment is created for no purpose other than to subjugate the individual to the will of his examiner. This atmosphere carries its own badge of intimidation. To be sure, this is not physical intimidation, but it is equally destructive of human dignity. The current practice of incommunicado interrogation is at odds with one of our Nation's most cherished principles—that the individual may not be compelled to incriminate himself. Unless adequate protective devices are employed to dispel the compulsion inherent in custodial surroundings, no statement obtained from the defendant can truly be the product of his free choice.

From the foregoing, we can readily perceive an intimate connection between the privilege against self-incrimination and police custodial questioning. It is fitting to turn to history and precedent underlying the Self-Incrimination Clause to determine its applicability in this situation.

[W]e may view the historical development of the privilege as one which groped for the proper scope of governmental power over the citizen. As a "noble principle often transcends its origins," the privilege has come rightfully to be recognized in part as an individual's substantive right, a "right to a private enclave where he may lead a private life. That right is the hallmark of our democracy." We have recently noted that the privilege against self-incrimination—the essential mainstay of our adversary system—is founded on a complex of values. All these policies point to one overriding thought: the constitutional foundation underlying the privilege is the respect a government—state or federal—must accord to the dignity and integrity of its citizens. To maintain a "fair state-individual balance," to require the government "to shoulder the entire load," 8 Wigmore, *Evidence* (McNaughton rev., 1961), 317, to respect the inviolability of the human personality, our accusatory system of criminal justice demands that the government seeking to punish an individual produce the evidence against him by its own independent labors, rather than by the cruel, simple expedient of compelling it from his own mouth. In sum, the privilege is fulfilled only when the person is guaranteed the right "to remain silent unless he chooses to speak in the unfettered exercise of his own will." *Malloy v. Hogan* [536 supra].

* * * We are satisfied that all the principles embodied in the privilege apply to informal compulsion exerted by law-enforcement officers during in-custody questioning. An individual swept from familiar surroundings into police custody, surrounded by antagonistic forces, and subjected to the techniques of persuasion described above cannot be otherwise than under compulsion to speak. As a practical matter, the compulsion to speak in the isolated setting of the police station may well be greater than in courts or other official investigations, where there are often impartial observers to guard against intimidation or trickery. * * *

Because of the adoption by Congress of Rule 5(a) of the Federal Rules of Criminal Procedure, and this Court's effectuation of that Rule in *McNabb* and *Mallory,* we have had little occasion in the past quarter century to reach the constitutional issues in dealing with federal interrogations. These supervisory rules, requiring production of an arrested person before a commissioner "without unnecessary delay" and excluding evidence obtained in default of that statutory obligation, were nonetheless responsive to the same considerations of Fifth Amendment policy that unavoidably face us now as to the States. In [the *McNabb* and *Mallory* cases] we recognized both the dangers of interrogation and the appropriateness of prophylaxis stemming from the very fact of interrogation itself.[32]

Our decision in *Malloy v. Hogan* necessitates an examination of the scope of the privilege in state cases as well. In *Malloy,* we squarely held the privilege applicable to the States, and held that the substantive standards underlying the privilege applied with full force to state court proceedings. [T]he reasoning in *Malloy* made clear what had already become apparent—that the substantive and procedural safeguards surrounding admissibility of confessions in state cases had become exceedingly exacting, reflecting all the policies embedded in the privilege. The voluntariness doctrine in the state cases, as *Malloy* indicates, encompasses all interrogation practices which are likely to exert such pressure upon an individual as to disable him from making a free and rational choice. The implications of this proposition were elaborated in our decision in *Escobedo,* decided one week after *Malloy* applied the privilege to the States. * * *

[In *Escobedo*], as in the cases today, we sought a protective device to dispel the compelling atmosphere of the interrogation. In *Escobedo,* however, the police did not relieve the defendant of the anxieties which they had created in the interrogation rooms. Rather, they denied his request for the assistance of counsel.[35] This heightened his dilemma, and made his later statements the product of this compulsion. * * * The denial of the defendant's request for his attorney thus undermined his ability to exercise the privilege—to remain silent if he chose or to

32. Our decision today does not indicate in any manner, of course, that these rules can be disregarded. When federal officials arrest an individual, they must as always comply with the dictates of the congressional legislation and cases thereunder. * * *

35. The police also prevented the attorney from consulting with his client. Independent of any other constitutional proscription, this action constitutes a violation of the Sixth Amendment right to the assistance of counsel and excludes any statement obtained in its wake. See *People v. Donovan,* 13 N.Y.2d 148, 243 N.Y.S.2d 841, 193 N.E.2d 628 (N.Y.1963) (Fuld, J.).

speak without any intimidation, blatant or subtle. The presence of counsel, in all the cases before us today, would be the adequate protective device necessary to make the process of police interrogation conform to the dictates of the privilege. His presence would insure that statements made in the government-established atmosphere are not the product of compulsion.

It was in this manner that *Escobedo* explicated another facet of the pre-trial privilege, noted in many of the Court's prior decisions: the protection of rights at trial. That counsel is present when statements are taken from an individual during interrogation obviously enhances the integrity of the fact-finding processes in court. The presence of an attorney, and the warnings delivered to the individual, enable the defendant under otherwise compelling circumstances to tell his story without fear, effectively, and in a way that eliminates the evils in the interrogation process. Without the protections flowing from adequate warnings and the rights of counsel, "all the careful safeguards erected around the giving of testimony, whether by an accused or any other witness, would become empty formalities in a procedure where the most compelling possible evidence of guilt, a confession, would have already been obtained at the unsupervised pleasure of the police." *Mapp v. Ohio* (Harlan, J., dissenting).

Today, then, there can be no doubt that the Fifth Amendment privilege is available outside of criminal court proceedings and serves to protect persons in all settings in which their freedom of action is curtailed from being compelled to incriminate themselves. We have concluded that without proper safeguards the process of in-custody interrogation of persons suspected or accused of crime contains inherently compelling pressures which work to undermine the individual's will to resist and to compel him to speak where he would not otherwise do so freely. In order to combat these pressures and to permit a full opportunity to exercise the privilege against self-incrimination, the accused must be adequately and effectively apprised of his rights and the exercise of those rights must be fully honored.

It is impossible for us to foresee the potential alternatives for protecting the privilege which might be devised by Congress or the States in the exercise of their creative rule-making capacities. Therefore we cannot say that the Constitution necessarily requires adherence to any particular solution for the inherent compulsions of the interrogation process as it is presently conducted. Our decision in no way creates a constitutional straitjacket which will handicap sound efforts at reform, nor is it intended to have this effect. We encourage Congress and the States to continue their laudable search for increasingly effective ways of protecting the rights of the individual while promoting efficient enforcement of our criminal laws. However, unless we are shown other procedures which are at least as effective in apprising accused persons of their right of silence and in assuring a continuous opportunity to exercise it, the following safeguards must be observed.

At the outset, if a person in custody is to be subjected to interrogation, he must first be informed in clear and unequivocal terms that he has the right to remain silent. For those unaware of the privilege, the warning is needed simply to make them aware of it—the threshold requirement for an intelligent decision as to its exercise. More important, such a warning is an absolute prerequisite in overcoming the inherent pressures of the interrogation atmosphere. It is not just the subnormal or woefully ignorant who succumb to an interrogator's imprecations, whether implied or expressly stated, that the interrogation will continue until a confession is obtained or that silence in the face of accusation is itself damning and will bode ill when presented to a jury.[37] Further, the warning will show the individual that his interrogators are prepared to recognize his privilege should he choose to exercise it.

The Fifth Amendment privilege is so fundamental to our system of constitutional rule and the expedient of giving an adequate warning as to the availability of the privilege so simple, we will not pause to inquire in individual cases whether the defendant was aware of his rights without a warning being given. Assessments of the knowledge the defendant possessed, based on information as to his age, education, intelligence, or prior contact with authorities, can never be more than speculation;[38] a warning is a clearcut fact. More important, whatever the background of the person interrogated, a warning at the time of the interrogation is indispensable to overcome its pressures and to insure that the individual knows he is free to exercise the privilege at that point in time.

The warning of the right to remain silent must be accompanied by the explanation that anything said can and will be used against the individual in court. This warning is needed in order to make him aware not only of the privilege, but also of the consequences of forgoing it. It is only through an awareness of these consequences that there can be any assurance of real understanding and intelligent exercise of the privilege. Moreover, this warning may serve to make the individual more acutely aware that he is faced with a phase of the adversary system—that he is not in the presence of persons acting solely in his interest.

The circumstances surrounding in-custody interrogation can operate very quickly to overbear the will of one merely made aware of his privilege by his interrogators. Therefore, the right to have counsel present at the interrogation is indispensable to the protection of the Fifth Amendment privilege under the system we delineate today. Our aim is to assure that the individual's right to choose between silence and speech remains unfettered throughout the interrogation process. A once-stated warning, delivered by those who will conduct the interrogation, cannot itself suffice to that end among those who most require knowledge of their rights. A mere warning given by the interrogators is not alone sufficient to accomplish that end. Prosecutors themselves claim that the admonishment of the right to remain silent without more "will benefit only the recidivist and the professional." Brief for the National District Attorneys Association as *amicus curiae.* Even preliminary advice given to the accused by his own attorney can be swiftly overcome by the secret interrogation process. Thus, the need for counsel to protect the Fifth Amendment privilege comprehends not merely a right to consult with counsel prior to questioning but also to have counsel present during any questioning if the defendant so desires.

The presence of counsel at the interrogation may serve several significant subsidiary functions as well. If the accused decides to talk to his interrogators, the assistance of counsel can mitigate the dangers of untrustworthiness. With a lawyer present the likelihood that the police will practice coercion is reduced, and if coercion is nevertheless exercised the lawyer can testify to it in court. The presence of a lawyer can also help to guarantee that the accused gives a fully accurate statement to the police and that the statement is rightly reported by the prosecution at trial. See *Crooker v. California* (Douglas, J., dissenting).

37. * * * In accord with this decision, it is impermissible to penalize an individual for exercising his Fifth Amendment privilege when he is under police custodial interrogation. The prosecution may not, therefore, use at trial the fact that he stood mute or claimed his privilege in the face of accusation. Cf. *Griffin v. California* [Ch. 24, § 5].

38. Cf. *Betts v. Brady,* and the recurrent inquiry into special circumstances it necessitated. * * *

An individual need not make a preinterrogation request for a lawyer. While such request affirmatively secures his right to have one, his failure to ask for a lawyer does not constitute a waiver. No effective waiver of the right to counsel during interrogation can be recognized unless specifically made after the warnings we here delineate have been given. The accused who does not know his rights and therefore does not make a request may be the person who most needs counsel. * * *

Accordingly we hold that an individual held for interrogation must be clearly informed that he has the right to consult with a lawyer and to have the lawyer with him during interrogation under the system for protecting the privilege we delineate today. As with the warnings of the right to remain silent and that anything stated can be used in evidence against him, this warning is an absolute prerequisite to interrogation. No amount of circumstantial evidence that the person may have been aware of this right will suffice to stand in its stead. Only through such a warning is there ascertainable assurance that the accused was aware of this right.

If an individual indicates that he wishes the assistance of counsel before any interrogation occurs, the authorities cannot rationally ignore or deny his request on the basis that the individual does not have or cannot afford a retained attorney. The financial ability of the individual has no relationship to the scope of the rights involved here. The privilege against self-incrimination secured by the Constitution applies to all individuals. The need for counsel in order to protect the privilege exists for the indigent as well as the affluent. In fact, were we to limit these constitutional rights to those who can retain an attorney, our decisions today would be of little significance. The cases before us as well as the vast majority of confession cases with which we have dealt in the past involve those unable to retain counsel. While authorities are not required to relieve the accused of his poverty, they have the obligation not to take advantage of indigence in the administration of justice.[41] Denial of counsel to the indigent at the time of interrogation while allowing an attorney to those who can afford one would be no more supportable by reason or logic than the similar situation at trial and on appeal struck down in *Gideon* and *Douglas v. California*.

In order fully to apprise a person interrogated of the extent of his rights under this system then, it is necessary to warn him not only that he has the right to consult with an attorney, but also that if he is indigent a lawyer will be appointed to represent him. Without this additional warning, the admonition of the right to consult with counsel would often be understood as meaning only that he can consult with a lawyer if he has one or has the funds to obtain one. The warning of a right to counsel would be hollow if not couched in terms that would convey to the indigent—the person most often subjected to interrogation—the knowledge that he too has a right to have counsel present. As with the warnings of the right to remain silent and of the general right to counsel, only by effective and express explanation to the indigent of this right can there be assurance that he was truly in a position to exercise it.[43]

Once warnings have been given, the subsequent procedure is clear. If the indi-

41. See Kamisar, *Equal Justice in the Gatehouses and Mansions of American Criminal Procedure*, in Criminal Justice in Our Time (1965), 64–81; * * * Report of the Attorney General's Committee on *Poverty and the Administration of Federal Criminal Justice* (1963), p. 9 * * *.

43. While a warning that the indigent may have counsel appointed need not be given to the person who is known to have an attorney or is known to have ample funds to secure one, the expedient of giving a warning is too simple and the rights involved too important to engage in *ex post facto* inquiries into financial ability when there is any doubt at all on that score.

vidual indicates in any manner, at any time prior to or during questioning, that he wishes to remain silent, the interrogation must cease.[44] At this point he has shown that he intends to exercise his Fifth Amendment privilege; any statement taken after the person invokes his privilege cannot be other than the product of compulsion, subtle or otherwise. Without the right to cut off questioning, the setting of in-custody interrogation operates on the individual to overcome free choice in producing a statement after the privilege has been once invoked. If the individual states that he wants an attorney, the interrogation must cease until an attorney is present. At that time, the individual must have an opportunity to confer with the attorney and to have him present during any subsequent questioning. If the individual cannot obtain an attorney and he indicates that he wants one before speaking to police, they must respect his decision to remain silent.

This does not mean, as some have suggested, that each police station must have a "station house lawyer" present at all times to advise prisoners. It does mean, however, that if police propose to interrogate a person they must make known to him that he is entitled to a lawyer and that if he cannot afford one, a lawyer will be provided for him prior to any interrogation. If authorities conclude that they will not provide counsel during a reasonable period of time in which investigation in the field is carried out, they may do so without violating the person's Fifth Amendment privilege so long as they do not question him during that time.

If the interrogation continues without the presence of an attorney and a statement is taken, a heavy burden rests on the Government to demonstrate that the defendant knowingly and intelligently waived his privilege against self-incrimination and his right to retained or appointed counsel. This Court has always set high standards of proof for the waiver of constitutional rights, *Johnson v. Zerbst,* and we reassert these standards as applied to in-custody interrogation. Since the State is responsible for establishing the isolated circumstances under which the interrogation takes place and has the only means of making available corroborated evidence of warnings given during incommunicado interrogation, the burden is rightly on its shoulders.

An express statement that the individual is willing to make a statement and does not want an attorney followed closely by a statement could constitute a waiver. But a valid waiver will not be presumed simply from the silence of the accused after warnings are given or simply from the fact that a confession was in fact eventually obtained. A statement we made in *Carnley v. Cochran,* 369 U.S. 506, 82 S.Ct. 884, 8 L.Ed.2d 70 (1962), is applicable here:

> "Presuming waiver from a silent record is impermissible. The record must show, or there must be an allegation and evidence which show, that an accused was offered counsel but intelligently and understandably rejected the offer. Anything less is not waiver."

* * * Moreover, where in-custody interrogation is involved, there is no room for the contention that the privilege is waived if the individual answers some questions or gives some information on his own prior to invoking his right to remain silent when interrogated.[45]

44. If an individual indicates his desire to remain silent, but has an attorney present, there may be some circumstances in which further questioning would be permissible. In the absence of evidence of overbearing, statements then made in the presence of counsel might be free of the compelling influence of the interrogation process and might fairly be construed as a waiver of the privilege for purposes of these statements.

45. Although this Court held in *Rogers v. United States,* 340 U.S. 367, 71 S.Ct. 438, 95 L.Ed. 344 (1951), over strong dissent, that a witness before a grand jury may not in certain circumstances decide to answer some questions and then refuse to answer others that decision has no application to the interrogation situation we deal with today. No legislative or judicial fact-finding authority is involved here, nor is there a possibili-

Whatever the testimony of the authorities as to waiver of rights by an accused, the fact of lengthy interrogation or incommunicado incarceration before a statement is made is strong evidence that the accused did not validly waive his rights. In these circumstances the fact that the individual eventually made a statement is consistent with the conclusion that the compelling influence of the interrogation finally forced him to do so. It is inconsistent with any notion of a voluntary relinquishment of the privilege. Moreover, any evidence that the accused was threatened, tricked, or cajoled into a waiver will, of course, show that the defendant did not voluntarily waive his privilege. The requirement of warnings and waiver of rights is a fundamental with respect to the Fifth Amendment privilege and not simply a preliminary ritual to existing methods of interrogation.

The warnings required and the waiver necessary in accordance with our opinion today are, in the absence of a fully effective equivalent, prerequisites to the admissibility of any statement made by a defendant. No distinction can be drawn between statements which are direct confessions and statements which amount to "admissions" of part or all of an offense. The privilege against self-incrimination protects the individual from being compelled to incriminate himself in any manner; it does not distinguish degrees of incrimination. Similarly, for precisely the same reason, no distinction may be drawn between inculpatory statements and statements alleged to be merely "exculpatory." If a statement made were in fact truly exculpatory it would, of course, never be used by the prosecution. In fact, statements merely intended to be exculpatory by the defendant are often used to impeach his testimony at trial or to demonstrate untruths in the statement given under interrogation and thus to prove guilt by implication. These statements are incriminating in any meaningful sense of the word and may not be used without the full warnings and effective waiver required for any other statement. In *Escobedo* itself, the defendant fully intended his accusation of another as the slayer to be exculpatory as to himself.

The principles announced today deal with the protection which must be given to the privilege against self-incrimination when the individual is first subjected to police interrogation while in custody at the station or otherwise deprived of his freedom of action in any significant way. It is at this point that our adversary system of criminal proceedings commences, distinguishing itself at the outset from the inquisitorial system recognized in some countries. Under the system of warnings we delineate today or under any other system which may be devised and found effective, the safeguards to be erected about the privilege must come into play at this point.

Our decision is not intended to hamper the traditional function of police officers in investigating crime. When an individual is in custody on probable cause, the police may, of course, seek out evidence in the field to be used at trial against him. Such investigation may include inquiry of persons not under restraint. General on-the-scene questioning as to facts surrounding a crime or other general questioning of citizens in the fact-finding process is not affected by our holding. It is an act of responsible citizenship for individuals to give whatever information they may have to aid in law enforcement. In such situations the compelling atmosphere inherent in the process of in-custody interrogation is not necessarily present.[46]

ty that the individual might make self-serving statements of which he could make use at trial while refusing to answer incriminating statements.

46. The distinction and its significance has been aptly described in the opinion of a Scottish court:

"In former times such questioning, if undertaken, would be conducted by police officers visiting the

In dealing with statements obtained through interrogation, we do not purport to find all confessions inadmissible. Confessions remain a proper element in law enforcement. Any statement given freely and voluntarily without any compelling influences is, of course, admissible in evidence. The fundamental import of the privilege while an individual is in custody is not whether he is allowed to talk to the police without the benefit of warnings and counsel, but whether he can be interrogated. There is no requirement that police stop a person who enters a police station and states that he wishes to confess to a crime, or a person who calls the police to offer a confession or any other statement he desires to make. Volunteered statements of any kind are not barred by the Fifth Amendment and their admissibility is not affected by our holding today.

To summarize, we hold that when an individual is taken into custody or otherwise deprived of his freedom by the authorities in any significant way and is subjected to questioning, the privilege against self-incrimination is jeopardized. Procedural safeguards must be employed to protect the privilege, and unless other fully effective means are adopted to notify the person of his right of silence and to assure that the exercise of the right will be scrupulously honored, the following measures are required. He must be warned prior to any questioning that he has the right to remain silent, that anything he says can be used against him in a court of law, that he has the right to the presence of an attorney, and that if he cannot afford an attorney one will be appointed for him prior to any questioning if he so desires. Opportunity to exercise these rights must be afforded to him throughout the interrogation. After such warnings have been given, and such opportunity afforded him, the individual may knowingly and intelligently waive these rights and agree to answer questions or make a statement. But unless and until such warnings and waiver are demonstrated by the prosecution at trial, no evidence obtained as a result of interrogation can be used against him.[48] * * *

If the individual desires to exercise his privilege, he has the right to do so. This is not for the authorities to decide. An attorney may advise his client not to talk to police until he has had an opportunity to investigate the case, or he may wish to be present with his client during any police questioning. In doing so an attorney is merely exercising the good professional judgment he has been taught. This is not cause for considering the attorney a menace to law enforcement. He is merely carrying out what he is sworn to do under his oath—to protect to the extent of his ability the rights of his client. In fulfilling this responsibility the attorney plays a vital role in the administration of criminal justice under our Constitution.

In announcing these principles, we are not unmindful of the burdens which law enforcement officials must bear, often under trying circumstances. We also fully recognize the obligation of all citizens to aid in enforcing the criminal laws. This Court, while protecting individual rights, has always given ample latitude to law enforcement agencies in the legitimate exercise of their duties. The limits we have placed on the interrogation process should not constitute an undue interference with a proper system of law enforcement. As we have noted, our decision does not in any way preclude police from carrying out their traditional investigatory functions. Although confessions may play an important role in some convictions, the cases before us present graphic examples of the

house or place of business of the suspect and there questioning him, probably in the presence of a relation or friend. However convenient the modern practice may be, it must normally create a situation very unfavorable to the suspect." *Chalmers v. H. M. Advocate*, [1954] Sess.Cas. 66, 78 (J.C.).

48. In accordance with our holdings today and in *Escobedo*, *Crooker* and *Cicenia* are not to be followed.

overstatement of the "need" for confessions. In each case authorities conducted interrogations ranging up to five days in duration despite the presence, through standard investigating practices, of considerable evidence against each defendant.[51] Further examples are chronicled in our prior cases.[52]

It is also urged that an unfettered right to detention for interrogation should be allowed because it will often redound to the benefit of the person questioned. When police inquiry determines that there is no reason to believe that the person has committed any crime, it is said, he will be released without need for further formal procedures. The person who has committed no offense, however, will be better able to clear himself after warnings, with counsel present than without. It can be assumed that in such circumstances a lawyer would advise his client to talk freely to police in order to clear himself.

Custodial interrogation, by contrast, does not necessarily afford the innocent an opportunity to clear themselves. A serious consequence of the present practice of the interrogation alleged to be beneficial for the innocent is that many arrests "for investigation" subject large numbers of innocent persons to detention and interrogation. In one of the cases before us, *California v. Stewart,* police held four persons, who were in the defendant's house at the time of the arrest, in jail for five days until defendant confessed. At that time they were finally released. Police stated that there was "no evidence to connect them with any crime." Available statistics on the extent of this practice where it is condoned indicate that these four are far from alone in being subjected to arrest, prolonged detention, and interrogation without the requisite probable cause. * * *

The experience in some other countries * * * suggests that the danger to law enforcement in curbs on interrogation is overplayed. The English procedure since 1912 under the Judge's Rules is significant. As recently strengthened, the Rules require that a cautionary warning be given an accused by a police officer as soon as he has evidence that affords reasonable grounds for suspicion; they also require that any statement made be given by the accused without questioning by police.[57]

51. Miranda, Vignera, and Westover were identified by eyewitnesses. Marked bills from the bank robbed were found in Westover's car. Articles stolen from the victim as well as from several other robbery victims were found in Stewart's home at the outset of the investigation.

52. Dealing as we do here with constitutional standards in relation to statements made, the existence of independent corroborating evidence produced at trial is, of course, irrelevant to our decisions. * * *

57. [1964] Crim.L.Rev. 166–170. These Rules provide in part:

"II. As soon as a police officer has evidence which would afford reasonable grounds for suspecting that a person has committed an offence, he shall caution that person or cause him to be cautioned before putting to him any questions, or further questions, relating to that offence.

"The caution shall be in the following terms:

"'You are not obliged to say anything unless you wish to do so but what you say may be put into writing and given in evidence.'

"When after being cautioned a person is being questioned, or elects to make a statement, a record shall be kept of the time and place at which any such questioning or statement began and ended and of the persons present.

. . .

"(b) It is only in exceptional cases that questions relating to the offence should be put to the accused person after he has been charged or informed that he may be prosecuted.

. . .

"IV. All written statements made after caution shall be taken in the following manner:

"(a) If a person says that he wants to make a statement he shall be told that it is intended to make a written record of what he says.

"He shall always be asked whether he wishes to write down himself what he wants to say; if he says that he cannot write or that he would like someone to write it for him, a police officer may offer to write the statement for him. * * *

"(b) Any person writing his own statement shall be allowed to do so without any prompting as distinct from indicating to him what matters are material.

. . .

"(d) Whenever a police officer writes the statement, he shall take down the exact words spoken

The right of the individual to consult with an attorney during this period is expressly recognized. * * *

Because of the nature of the problem and because of its recurrent significance in numerous cases, we have to this point discussed the relationship of the Fifth Amendment privilege to police interrogation without specific concentration on the facts of the cases before us. We turn now to these facts to consider the application to these cases of the constitutional principles discussed above. In each instance, we have concluded that statements were obtained from the defendant under circumstances that did not meet constitutional standards for protection of the privilege.

No. 759. *Miranda v. Arizona.*

On March 13, 1963, petitioner, Ernesto Miranda, was arrested at his home and taken in custody to a Phoenix police station. He was there identified by the complaining witness. The police then took him to "Interrogation Room No. 2" of the detective bureau. There he was questioned by two police officers. The officers admitted at trial that Miranda was not advised that he had a right to have an attorney present. Two hours later, the officers emerged from the interrogation room with a written confession signed by Miranda. At the top of the statement was a typed paragraph stating that the confession was made voluntarily, without threats or promises of immunity and "with full knowledge of my legal rights, understanding any statement I make may be used against me." 67

[Miranda] was found guilty of kidnapping and rape. [On] appeal, the Supreme Court of Arizona held that Miranda's constitutional rights were not violated in obtaining the confession and affirmed the conviction. In reaching its decision, the court emphasized heavily the fact that Miranda did not specifically request counsel.

We reverse. From the testimony of the officers and by the admission of respondent, it is clear that Miranda was not in any way apprised of his right to consult with an attorney and to have one present during the interrogation, nor was his right not to be compelled to incriminate himself effectively protected in any other manner. Without these warnings the statements were inadmissible. The mere fact that he signed a statement which contained a typed-in clause stating that he had "full knowledge" of his legal rights does not approach the knowing and intelligent waiver required to relinquish constitutional rights. * * *

No. 760. *Vignera v. New York.*

Petitioner, Michael Vignera, was picked up by New York police on October 14, 1960, in connection with the robbery three days earlier of a Brooklyn dress shop. They took him to the 17th Detective Squad headquarters in Manhattan. Sometime thereafter he was taken to the 66th Detective Squad. There a detective questioned Vignera with respect to the robbery. Vignera orally admitted the robbery to the detective. [T]he defense was precluded from making any showing that warnings had not been given. While at

by the person making the statement, without putting any questions other than such as may be needed to make the statement coherent, intelligible and relevant to the material matters: he shall not prompt him." * * *

[Ed. Note—*The Police and Criminal Evidence 1984* grants British police new powers. E.g., the police are permitted to detain a person without charge for questioning for 24 hours and under certain circumstances to detain a person arrested for a "serious arrestable offense" (e.g., treason, terrorism, murder and kidnapping) up to 36 hours when authorized by a police officer of at least superintendent rank. To counterbalance these additional police powers, the Act contains new safeguards. E.g., a person detained in custody has a right to have this fact notified to a friend or relative and a person detained for an offense other than a "serious arrestable offense" has an absolute right to consult a solicitor at any time. See generally S. Jones, *The Police and Criminal Evidence Act 1984,* 48 Modern L.Rev. 679 (1985).]

67. One of the officers testified that he read this paragraph to Miranda. Apparently, however, he did not do so until after Miranda had confessed orally.

the 66th Detective Squad, Vignera was identified by the store owner and a saleslady as the man who robbed the dress shop. At about 3:00 p.m. he was formally arrested. The police then transported him to still another station, the 70th Precinct in Brooklyn, "for detention". At 11:00 p.m. Vignera was questioned by an assistant district attorney in the presence of a hearing reporter who transcribed the questions and Vignera's answers. This verbatim account of these proceedings contains no statement of any warnings given by the assistant district attorney. * * *

Vignera was [convicted of first degree robbery]. We reverse. The foregoing indicates that Vignera was not warned of any of his rights before the questioning by the detective and by the assistant district attorney. No other steps were taken to protect these rights. Thus he was not effectively apprised of his Fifth Amendment privilege or of his right to have counsel present and his statements are inadmissible.

No. 761. *Westover v. United States.*

At approximately 9:45 p.m. on March 20, 1963, petitioner, Carl Calvin Westover, was arrested by local police in Kansas City as a suspect in two Kansas City robberies. A report was also received from the FBI that he was wanted on a felony charge in California. The local authorities took him to a police station and placed him in a line-up on the local charges, and at about 11:45 p.m. he was booked. Kansas City police interrogated Westover on the night of his arrest. He denied any knowledge of criminal activities. The next day local officers interrogated him again throughout the morning. Shortly before noon they informed the FBI that they were through interrogating Westover and that the FBI could proceed to interrogate him. There is nothing in the record to indicate that Westover was ever given any warning as to his rights by local police. At noon, three special agents of the FBI continued the interrogation in a private interview room of the Kansas City Police Department, this time with respect to the robbery of a savings and loan association and a bank in Sacramento, California. After two or two and one-half hours, Westover signed separate confessions to each of these two robberies which had been prepared by one of the agents during the interrogation. At trial one of the agents testified, and a paragraph on each of the statements states, that the agents advised Westover that he did not have to make a statement, that any statement he made could be used against him, and that he had the right to see an attorney.

Westover was tried by a jury in federal court and convicted of the California robberies. * * *

We reverse. On the facts of this case we cannot find that Westover knowingly and intelligently waived his right to remain silent and his right to consult with counsel prior to the time he made the statement. At the time the FBI agents began questioning Westover, he had been in custody for over 14 hours and had been interrogated at length during that period. The FBI interrogation began immediately upon the conclusion of the interrogation by Kansas City police and was conducted in local police headquarters. Although the two law enforcement authorities are legally distinct and the crimes for which they interrogated Westover were different, the impact on him was that of a continuous period of questioning. There is no evidence of any warning given prior to the FBI interrogation nor is there any evidence of an articulated waiver of rights after the FBI commenced their interrogation. The record simply shows that the defendant did in fact confess a short time after being turned over to the FBI following interrogation by local police. Despite the fact that the FBI agents gave warnings at the outset of their interview, from Westover's point of view the warnings came at the end of the interrogation process. In these circumstances an intelligent waiver of constitutional rights cannot be assumed.

We do not suggest that law enforcement authorities are precluded from questioning any individual who has been held for a period of time by other authorities and interrogated by them without appropriate warnings. A different case would be presented if an accused were taken into custody by the second authority, removed both in time and place from his original surroundings, and then adequately advised of his rights and given an opportunity to exercise them. But here the FBI interrogation was conducted immediately following the state interrogation in the same police station—in the same compelling surroundings. Thus, in obtaining a confession from Westover the federal authorities were the beneficiaries of the pressure applied by the local in-custody interrogation. In these circumstances the giving of warnings alone was not sufficient to protect the privilege.

No. 584. *California v. Stewart.*

In the course of investigating a series of purse-snatch robberies in which one of the victims had died of injuries inflicted by her assailant, respondent, Roy Allen Stewart, was pointed out to Los Angeles police as the endorser of dividend checks taken in one of the robberies. At about 7:15 p.m., January 31, 1963, police officers went to Stewart's house and arrested him. One of the officers asked Stewart if they could search the house, to which he replied, "Go ahead." The search turned up various items taken from the five robbery victims. At the time of Stewart's arrest, police also arrested Stewart's wife and three other persons who were visiting him. These four were jailed along with Stewart and were interrogated. Stewart was taken to the University Station of the Los Angeles Police Department where he was placed in a cell. During the next five days, police interrogated Stewart on nine different occasions. Except during the first interrogation session, when he was confronted with an accusing witness, Stewart was isolated with his interrogators.

During the ninth interrogation session, Stewart admitted that he had robbed the deceased and stated that he had not meant to hurt her. Police then brought Stewart before a magistrate for the first time. Since there was no evidence to connect them with any crime, the police then released the other four persons arrested with him.

Nothing in the record specifically indicates whether Stewart was or was not advised of his right to remain silent or his right to counsel. In a number of instances, however, the interrogating officers were asked to recount everything that was said during the interrogations. None indicated that Stewart was ever advised of his rights.

[The] jury found Stewart guilty of robbery and first degree murder and fixed the penalty as death. On appeal, the Supreme Court of California reversed. It held that under this Court's decision in *Escobedo,* Stewart should have been advised of his right to remain silent and of his right to counsel and that it would not presume in the face of a silent record that the police advised Stewart of his rights.

We affirm. In dealing with custodial interrogation, we will not presume that a defendant has been effectively apprised of his rights and that his privilege against self-incrimination has been adequately safeguarded on a record that does not show that any warnings have been given or that any effective alternative has been employed. Nor can a knowing and intelligent waiver of these rights be assumed on a silent record. Furthermore, Stewart's steadfast denial of the alleged offenses through eight of the nine interrogations over a period of five days is subject to no other construction than that he was compelled by persistent interrogation to forgo his Fifth Amendment privilege.

Therefore, in accordance with the foregoing, [*Miranda,*[a] *Vignera,* and *Westover* are reversed and *Stewart* is affirmed].[b]

MR. JUSTICE CLARK, dissenting in [*Miranda, Vignera,* and *Gilbert,* and concurring in the result in *Stewart.*]

[I cannot] agree with the Court's characterization of the present practices of police and investigatory agencies as to custodial interrogation. The materials referred to as "police manuals" are not shown by the record here to be the official manuals of any police department, much less in universal use in crime detection. Moreover, the examples of police brutality mentioned by the Court are rare exceptions to the thousands of cases that appear every year in the law reports. * * *

[The Court's] strict constitutional specific inserted at the nerve center of crime detection may well kill the patient. Since there is at this time a paucity of information and an almost total lack of empirical knowledge on the practical operation of requirements truly comparable to those announced by the majority, I would be more restrained lest we go too far too fast. * * *

Rather than employing the arbitrary Fifth Amendment rule which the Court lays down I would follow the more pliable dictates of Due Process Clauses of the Fifth and Fourteenth Amendments which we are accustomed to administering and which we know from our cases are effective instruments in protecting persons in police custody. In this way we would not be acting in the dark nor in one full sweep changing the traditional rules of custodial interrogation which this Court has for so long recognized as a justifiable and proper tool in balancing individual rights against the rights of society. It will be soon enough to go further when we are able to appraise with somewhat better accuracy the effect of such a holding. * * *

MR. JUSTICE HARLAN, whom MR. JUSTICE STEWART and MR. JUSTICE WHITE join, dissenting. * * *

While the fine points of [the Court's new constitutional code of rules for confessions] are far less clear than the Court admits, the tenor is quite apparent. The new rules are not designed to guard against police brutality or other unmistakably banned forms of coercion. Those who use third-degree tactics and deny them in court are equally able and destined to lie as skillfully about warnings and waivers. Rather, the thrust of the new rules is to negate all pressures, to reinforce the nervous or ignorant suspect, and ultimately to discourage any confession at all. The aim in short is toward "voluntariness" in a utopian sense, or to view it from a different angle, voluntariness with a vengeance.

To incorporate this notion into the Constitution requires a strained reading of history and precedent and a disregard of the very pragmatic concerns that alone may on occasion justify such strains. I believe that reasoned examination will show that the Due Process Clauses provide an adequate tool for coping with confessions and that, even if the Fifth Amendment privilege against self-incrimination be invoked, its precedents taken as a whole do not sustain the present rules. Viewed as a choice based on pure policy, these new rules prove to be a highly debatable if not one-sided appraisal of the competing interests, imposed over wide-spread objection, at the very time when judicial restraint is most called for by the circumstances. * * *

[The] Court's asserted reliance on the Fifth Amendment [is] an approach which I

a. On retrial, *Miranda* was again convicted of kidnapping and rape. The conviction was affirmed in *State v. Miranda,* 450 P.2d 364 (Ariz. 1969). For a rich narrative of *Miranda* from arrest to reconviction, see L. Baker, *Miranda: Crime, Law & Politics* (1983). See also Caplan, *Miranda Revisited* (Book Review), 93 Yale L.J. 1375 (1984); Kamisar, *Miranda: The Case, the Man, and the Players* (Book Review), 82 Mich.L. Rev. 1074 (1984).

b. A week later, the Court ruled that *Escobedo* and *Miranda* applied only to trials begun after the decisions were announced.

frankly regard as a *trompe l' oeil.* The Court's opinion in my view reveals no adequate basis for extending the Fifth Amendment's privilege against self-incrimination to the police station. Far more important, it fails to show that the Court's new rules are well supported, let alone compelled, by Fifth Amendment precedents. Instead, the new rules actually derive from quotation and analogy drawn from precedents under the Sixth Amendment, which should properly have no bearing on police interrogation. * * *

Having decided that the Fifth Amendment privilege does apply in the police station, the Court reveals that the privilege imposes more exacting restrictions than does the Fourteenth Amendment's voluntariness test. It then emerges from a discussion of *Escobedo* that the Fifth Amendment requires for an admissible confession that it be given by one distinctly aware of his right not to speak and shielded from "the compelling atmosphere" of interrogation. From these key premises, the Court finally develops the safeguards of warning, counsel, and so forth. I do not believe these premises are sustained by precedents under the Fifth Amendment.[9]

The more important premise is that pressure on the suspect must be eliminated though it be only the subtle influence of the atmosphere and surroundings. The Fifth Amendment, however, has never been thought to forbid *all* pressure to incriminate one's self in the situations covered by it. * * *

A closing word must be said about the Assistance of Counsel Clause of the Sixth Amendment, which is never expressly relied on by the Court but whose judicial precedents turn out to be linchpins of the confession rules announced today. * * *

The only attempt in this Court to carry the right to counsel into the station house occurred in *Escobedo,* the Court repeating several times that that stage was no less "critical" than trial itself. * * * This is hardly persuasive when we consider that a grand jury inquiry, the filing of a certiorari petition, and certainly the purchase of narcotics by an undercover agent from a prospective defendant may all be equally "critical" yet provision of counsel and advice on that score have never been thought compelled by the Constitution in such cases. The sound reason why this right is so freely extended for a criminal trial is the severe injustice risked by confronting an untrained defendant with a range of technical points of law, evidence, and tactics familiar to the prosecutor but not to himself. This danger shrinks markedly in the police station where indeed the lawyer in fulfilling his professional responsibilities of necessity may become an obstacle to truthfinding. See infra, n. 12. * * *

The Court's new rules aim to offset [the] minor pressures and disadvantages intrinsic to any kind of police interrogation. The rules do not serve due process interests in preventing blatant coercion since, as I noted earlier, they do nothing to contain the policeman who is prepared to lie from the start. The rules work for reliability in confessions almost only in the Pickwickian sense that they can prevent some from being given at all.[12] * * *

What the Court largely ignores is that its rules impair, if they will not eventually serve wholly to frustrate, an instrument of law enforcement that has long and quite

9. I lay aside *Escobedo* itself; it contains no reasoning or even general conclusions addressed to the Fifth Amendment and indeed its citation in this regard seems surprising in view of *Escobedo's* primary reliance on the Sixth Amendment.

12. The Court's vision of a lawyer "mitigat[ing] the dangers of untrustworthiness" by witnessing coercion and assisting accuracy in the confession is largely a fancy; for if counsel arrives, there is rarely going to be a police station confession. *Watts v. Indiana* (separate opinion of Jackson, J.): "[A]ny lawyer worth his salt will tell the suspect in no uncertain terms to make no statement to police under any circumstances." See Enker & Elsen, *Counsel for the Suspect,* 49 Minn.L.Rev. 47, 66–68 (1964).

reasonably been thought worth the price paid for it. There can be little doubt that the Court's new code would markedly decrease the number of confessions. To warn the suspect that he may remain silent and remind him that his confession may be used in court are minor obstructions. To require also an express waiver by the suspect and an end to questioning whenever he demurs must heavily handicap questioning. And to suggest or provide counsel for the suspect simply invites the end of the interrogation. See supra, n. 12. * * *

While passing over the costs and risks of its experiment, the Court portrays the evils of normal police questioning in terms which I think are exaggerated. Albeit stringently confined by the due process standards interrogation is no doubt often inconvenient and unpleasant for the suspect. However, it is no less so for a man to be arrested and jailed, to have his house searched, or to stand trial in court, yet all this may properly happen to the most innocent given probable cause, a warrant, or an indictment. Society has always paid a stiff price for law and order, and peaceful interrogation is not one of the dark moments of the law.

This brief statement of the competing considerations seems to me ample proof that the Court's preference is highly debatable at best and therefore not to be read into the Constitution. However, it may make the analysis more graphic to consider the actual facts of one of the four cases reversed by the Court. *Miranda* serves best, being neither the hardest nor easiest of the four under the Court's standards.[15]

On March 3, 1963, an 18-year-old girl was kidnapped and forcibly raped near Phoenix, Arizona. Ten days later, on the morning of March 13, petitioner Miranda was arrested and taken to the police station. At this time Miranda was 23 years old, indigent, and educated to the extent of completing half the ninth grade. He had "an emotional illness" of the schizophrenic type, according to the doctor who eventually examined him; the doctor's report also stated that Miranda was "alert and oriented as to time, place, and person", intelligent within normal limits, competent to stand trial, and sane within the legal definition. At the police station, the victim picked Miranda out of a lineup, and two officers then took him into a separate room to interrogate him, starting about 11:30 a.m. Though at first denying his guilt, within a short time Miranda gave a detailed oral confession and then wrote out in his own hand and signed a brief statement admitting and describing the crime. All this was accomplished in two hours or less without any force, threats or promises and—I will assume this though the record is uncertain * * *—without any effective warnings at all.

Miranda's oral and written confessions are now held inadmissible under the Court's new rules. One is entitled to feel astonished that the Constitution can be read to produce this result. These confessions were obtained during brief, daytime questioning conducted by two officers and unmarked by any of the traditional indicia of coercion. They assured a conviction for a brutal and unsettling crime, for which the police had and quite possibly could obtain little evidence other than the victim's identifications, evidence which is frequently unreliable. There was, in sum, a legitimate purpose, no perceptible unfairness, and certainly little risk of injustice in the interrogation. Yet the resulting confessions, and the responsible course of police practice they represent, are to be sacrificed to the Court's own finespun conception of fairness which I seriously doubt is shared by many thinking citizens in this country. * * *

15. In *Westover*, a seasoned criminal was practically given the Court's full complement of warnings and did not heed them. The *Stewart* case, on the other hand, involves long detention and successive questioning. In *Vignera*, the facts are complicated and the record somewhat incomplete.

[It is] instructive to compare the attitude in this case of those responsible for law enforcement with the official views that existed when the Court undertook three major revisions of prosecutorial practice prior to this case, *Johnson v. Zerbst, Mapp*, and *Gideon*. In *Johnson*, which established that appointed counsel must be offered the indigent in federal criminal trials, the Federal Government all but conceded the basic issue, which had in fact been recently fixed as Department of Justice policy. In *Mapp*, which imposed the exclusionary rule on the States for Fourth Amendment violations, more than half of the States had themselves already adopted some such rule. In *Gideon*, which extended *Johnson v. Zerbst* to the States, an *amicus* brief was filed by 22 States and Commonwealths urging that course; only two States beside the respondent came forward to protest. By contrast, in this case new restrictions on police questioning have been opposed by the United States and in an *amicus* brief signed by 27 States and Commonwealths, not including the three other States who are parties. No State in the country has urged this Court to impose the newly announced rules, nor has any State chosen to go nearly so far on its own. * * *

The law of the foreign countries described by the Court * * * reflects a more moderate conception of the rights of the accused as against those of society when other data is considered. Concededly, the English experience is most relevant. In that country, a caution as to silence but not counsel has long been mandated by the "Judges' Rules," which also place other somewhat imprecise limits on police cross-examination of suspects. However, in the court's discretion confessions can be and apparently quite frequently are admitted in evidence despite disregard of the Judges' Rules, so long as they are found voluntary under the common-law test. Moreover, the check that exists on the use of pretrial statements is counter-balanced by the evident admissibility of fruits of an illegal confession and by the judge's often-used authority to comment adversely on the defendant's failure to testify. * * *

[S]ome reference must be made to [the] ironic untimeliness [of these confession rules]. There is now in progress in this country a massive re-examination of criminal law enforcement procedures on a scale never before witnessed. Participants in this undertaking include a Special Committee of the American Bar Association, under the chairmanship of Chief Judge Lumbard of the Court of Appeals for the Second Circuit; a distinguished study group of the American Law Institute, headed by Professor Vorenberg of the Harvard Law School; and the President's Commission on Law Enforcement and Administration of Justice, under the leadership of the Attorney General of the United States. Studies are also being conducted by [other groups] equipped to do practical research. * * *

It is no secret that concern has been expressed lest long-range and lasting reforms be frustrated by this Court's too rapid departure from existing constitutional standards. Despite the Court's disclaimer, the practical effect of the decision made today must inevitably be to handicap seriously sound efforts at reform, not least by removing options necessary to a just compromise of competing interests. [T]he legislative reforms when they came would have the vast advantage of empirical data and comprehensive study, they would allow experimentation and use of solutions not open to the courts, and they would restore the initiative in criminal law reform to those forums where it truly belongs. * * *

MR. JUSTICE WHITE, with whom MR. JUSTICE HARLAN and MR. JUSTICE STEWART join, dissenting.

The proposition that the privilege against self-incrimination forbids in-custody interrogation without the warnings specified in the majority opinion and without a clear waiver of counsel has no significant support in the history of the privilege or in the language of the Fifth Amendment. As for the English authorities and the common-law history, the privilege, firmly established in the second half of the seventeenth century, was never applied except to prohibit compelled judicial interrogations. The rule excluding coerced confessions matured about 100 years later, "[b]ut there is nothing in the reports to suggest that the theory has its roots in the privilege against self-incrimination. And so far as the cases reveal, the privilege, as such, seems to have been given effect only in judicial proceedings, including the preliminary examinations by authorized magistrates." Morgan, *The Privilege Against Self-Incrimination,* 34 Minn.L.Rev. 1, 18 (1949). * * *

That the Court's holding today is neither compelled nor even strongly suggested by the language of the Fifth Amendment, is at odds with American and English legal history, and involves a departure from a long line of precedent does not prove either that the Court has exceeded its powers or that the Court is wrong or unwise in its present reinterpretation of the Fifth Amendment. It does, however, underscore the obvious—that the Court has not discovered or found the law in making today's decision, nor has it derived it from some irrefutable sources; what it has done is to make new law and new public policy in much the same way that it has in the course of interpreting other great clauses of the Constitution. This is what the Court historically has done. Indeed, it is what it must do and will continue to do until and unless there is some fundamental change in the constitutional distribution of governmental powers.

But if the Court is here and now to announce new and fundamental policy to govern certain aspects of our affairs, it is wholly legitimate to examine the mode of this or any other constitutional decision in this Court and to inquire into the advisability of its end product in terms of the long-range interest of the country. At the very least the Court's text and reasoning should withstand analysis and be a fair exposition of the constitutional provision which its opinion interprets. Decisions like these cannot rest alone on syllogism, metaphysics or some ill-defined notions of natural justice, although each will perhaps play its part. * * *

[The Court] extrapolates a picture of what it conceives to be the norm from police investigatorial manuals, published in 1959 and 1962 or earlier, without any attempt to allow for adjustments in police practices that may have occurred in the wake of more recent decisions of state appellate tribunals or this Court. But even if the relentless application of the described procedures could lead to involuntary confessions, it most assuredly does not follow that each and every case will disclose this kind of interrogation or this kind of consequence.[2] Insofar as it appears from the Court's opinion, it has not examined a single transcript of any police interrogation, let alone the interrogation that took place in any one of these cases which it decides today. Judged by any of the standards for empirical investigation utilized in the social sciences the factual basis for the Court's premises is patently inadequate.

Although in the Court's view in-custody interrogation is inherently coercive, it says that the spontaneous product of the coercion of arrest and detention is still to be deemed voluntary. An accused, arrested on probable cause, may blurt out a confes-

2. In fact, the type of sustained interrogation described by the Court appears to be the exception rather than the rule. A survey of 399 cases in one city found that in almost half of the cases the interrogation lasted less than 30 minutes. Barrett, *Police Practices and the Law—From Arrest to Release or Charge,* 50 Calif.L.Rev. 11, 41–45 (1962). Questioning tends to be confused and sporadic and is usually concentrated on confrontations with witnesses or new items of evidence, as these are obtained by officers conducting the investigation. See generally LaFave, *Arrest: The Decision to Take a Suspect into Custody* 386 (1965); ALI, *Model Pre-Arraignment Procedure Code,* Commentary § 5.01, at 170, n. 4 (Tent.Draft No. 1, 1966).

sion which will be admissible despite the fact that he is alone and in custody, without any showing that he had any notion of his right to remain silent or of the consequences of his admission. Yet, under the Court's rule, if the police ask him a single question such as "Do you have anything to say?" or "Did you kill your wife?" his response, if there is one, has somehow been compelled, even if the accused has been clearly warned of his right to remain silent. Common sense informs us to the contrary. While one may say that the response was "involuntary" in the sense the question provoked or was the occasion for the response and thus the defendant was induced to speak out when he might have remained silent if not arrested and not questioned, it is patently unsound to say the response is compelled. * * *

If the rule announced today were truly based on a conclusion that all confessions resulting from custodial interrogation are coerced, then it would simply have no rational foundation. * * * Even if one were to postulate that the Court's concern is not that all confessions induced by police interrogation are coerced but rather that some such confessions are coerced and present judicial procedures are believed to be inadequate to identify the confessions that are coerced and those that are not, it would still not be essential to impose the rule that the Court has now fashioned. Transcripts or observers could be required, specific time limits, tailored to fit the cause, could be imposed, or other devices could be utilized to reduce the chances that otherwise indiscernible coercion will produce an inadmissible confession.

On the other hand, even if one assumed that there was an adequate factual basis for the conclusion that all confessions obtained during in-custody interrogation are the product of compulsion, the rule propounded by the Court would still be irrational, for, apparently, it is only if the accused is also warned of his right to counsel and waives both that right and the right against self-incrimination that the inherent compulsiveness of interrogation disappears. But if the defendant may not answer without a warning a question such as "Where were you last night?" without having his answer be a compelled one, how can the court ever accept his negative answer to the question of whether he wants to consult his retained counsel or counsel whom the court will appoint? And why if counsel is present and the accused nevertheless confesses, or counsel tells the accused to tell the truth, and that is what the accused does, is the situation any less coercive insofar as the accused is concerned? The court apparently realizes its dilemma of foreclosing questioning without the necessary warnings but at the same time permitting the accused, sitting in the same chair in front of the same policemen, to waive his right to consult an attorney. It expects, however, that not too many will waive the right; and if it is claimed that he has, the State faces a severe, if not impossible burden of proof.

All of this makes very little sense in terms of the compulsion which the Fifth Amendment proscribes. That amendment deals with compelling the accused himself. It is his free will that is involved. Confessions and incriminating admissions, as such, are not forbidden evidence; only those which are compelled are banned. I doubt that the Court observes these distinctions today. By considering any answers to any interrogation to be compelled regardless of the content and course of examination and by escalating the requirements to prove waiver, the Court not only prevents the use of compelled confessions but for all practical purposes forbids interrogation except in the presence of counsel. That is, instead of confining itself to protection of the right against compelled self-incrimination the Court has created a limited Fifth Amendment right to counsel—or, as the Court expresses it, a "right to counsel to protect the Fifth Amendment privilege * * *." The focus then is not on the will of the accused but on the will of counsel and how much influence he can have on the accused. Obviously there is no warrant in the Fifth Amendment for thus installing counsel as the arbiter of the privilege.

In sum, for all the Court's expounding on the menacing atmosphere of police interrogation procedures it has failed to supply any foundation for the conclusions it draws or the measures it adopts.

Criticism of the Court's opinion, however, cannot stop at a demonstration that the factual and textual bases for the rule it propounds are, at best, less than compelling. Equally relevant is an assessment of the rule's consequences measured against community values. The Court's duty to assess the consequences of its action is not satisfied by the utterance of the truth that a value of our system of criminal justice is "to respect the inviolability of the human personality" and to require government to produce the evidence against the accused by its own independent labors. More than the human dignity of the accused is involved; the human personality of others in the society must also be preserved. Thus the values reflected by the privilege are not the sole desideratum; society's interest in the general security is of equal weight.

The obvious underpinning of the Court's decision is a deep-seated distrust of all confessions. As the Court declares that the accused may not be interrogated without counsel present, absent a waiver of the right to counsel, and as the Court all but admonishes the lawyer to advise the accused to remain silent, the result adds up to a judicial judgment that evidence from the accused should not be used against him in any way, whether compelled or not. This is the not so subtle overtone of the opinion—that it is inherently wrong for the police to gather evidence from the accused himself. And this is precisely the nub of this dissent. I see nothing wrong or immoral, and certainly nothing unconstitutional, with the police asking a suspect whom they have reasonable cause to arrest whether or not he killed his wife or with confronting him with the evidence on which the arrest was based, at least where he has been plainly advised that he may remain completely silent. * * * Particularly when corroborated, as where the police have confirmed the accused's disclosure of the hiding place of implements or fruits of the crime, such confessions have the highest reliability and significantly contribute to the certitude with which we may believe the accused is guilty. * * *

The rule announced today [is] a deliberate calculus to prevent interrogations, to reduce the incidence of confessions and pleas of guilty and to increase the number of trials. * * * Under the present law, the prosecution fails to prove its case in about 30% of the criminal cases actually tried in the federal courts. But it is something else again to remove from the ordinary criminal case all those confessions which heretofore have been held to be free and voluntary acts of the accused and to thus establish a new constitutional barrier to the ascertainment of truth by the judicial process. There is, in my view, every reason to believe that a good many criminal defendants, who otherwise would have been convicted on what this Court has previously thought to be the most satisfactory kind of evidence, will now, under this new version of the Fifth Amendment, either not be tried at all or acquitted if the State's evidence, minus the confession, is put to the test of litigation.

I have no desire whatsoever to share the responsibility for any such impact on the present criminal process. * * *

There is another aspect to the effect of the Court's rule on the person whom the police have arrested on probable cause. The fact is that he may not be guilty at all and may be able to extricate himself quickly and simply if he were told the circumstances of his arrest and were asked to explain. This effort, and his release, must now await the hiring of a lawyer or his appointment by the court, consultation with counsel and then a session with the police or the prosecutor. Similarly, where probable cause exists to arrest several suspects as where the body of the victim is discovered in a house having several residents, it will often be true that a suspect may be cleared only through the results of interrogation of other suspects. Here too the release of the innocent may be delayed by the Court's rule.

Much of the trouble with the Court's new rule is that it will operate indiscriminately in all criminal cases, regardless of the severity of the crime or the circumstances involved. It applies to every defendant whether the professional criminal or one committing a crime of momentary passion who is not part and parcel of organized crime. It will slow down the investigation and the apprehension of confederates in those cases where time is of the essence, such as kidnapping, [those] involving the national security, [and] some organized crime situations. In the latter context the lawyer who arrives may also be the lawyer for the defendants' colleagues and can be relied upon to insure that no breach of the organization's security takes place even though the accused may feel that the best thing he can do is to cooperate.

At the same time, the Court's *per se* approach may not be justified on the ground that it provides a "bright line" permitting the authorities to judge in advance whether interrogation may safely be pursued without jeopardizing the admissibility of any information obtained as a consequence. Nor can it be claimed that judicial time and effort, assuming that is a relevant consideration, will be conserved because of the ease of application of the new rule. Today's decision leaves open such questions as whether the accused was in custody, whether his statements were spontaneous or the product of interrogation, whether the accused has effectively waived his rights, and whether nontestimonial evidence introduced at trial is the fruit of statements made during a prohibited interrogation, all of which are certain to prove productive of uncertainty during investigation and litigation during prosecution. For all these reasons, if further restrictions on police interrogation are desirable at this time, a more flexible approach makes much more sense than the Court's constitutional strait-jacket which forecloses more discriminating treatment by legislative or rule-making pronouncements. * * *

GERALD M. CAPLAN: QUESTIONING MIRANDA

38 Vand.L.Rev. 1417, 1455–76 (1985).

In the fourth amendment area, the Supreme Court has held that a suspect may validly waive his right to refuse to allow the police to conduct a warrantless search of his premises or property even though he is unaware of his constitutional right to deny the police access. The government need not prove that there was "an intentional relinquishment or abandonment of a known right" [187] by the suspect. The government need only prove that the consent was given "voluntarily" under the totality of the circumstances. The Court has stated that this test represents a balance between competing concerns: "the legitimate need for such searches and the equally important requirement of assuring the absence of coercion." By adopting this balance, the Supreme Court refused to follow the lead of *Miranda.* The *Miranda* approach—that a suspect is irrebuttably presumed to be ignorant of his rights unless the police inform him of them, and that such ignorance renders any statement made in response to questions coerced—ignores the competing values at stake.[190]

Thus, the *Miranda* approach reflects a bias against self-accusation on principle. This bias has roots in the desire to treat suspects equally. Suspects who do not know their rights, or do not assert them as

187. *Schneckloth v. Bustamonte* [p. 408 supra].

190. See *Michigan v. Summers* [p. 294 supra] (characterizing "the balance of competing interests" as "the key principle of the Fourth Amendment"). * * *

a consequence of some handicap—poverty, lack of education, emotional instability—should not, it is felt, fare worse than more accomplished suspects who know and have the capacity to assert their rights. This "equal protection" appeal finds its way repeatedly into judicial opinions and legal commentary. * * *

[To the extent that observations about the need for "equal protection" in the administration of criminal justice are true], they suggest two lines of remedy. One would be to make it more difficult to convict those who are most vulnerable; the other would be to develop ways to bring those hardier, more knowledgeable persons—the hired killer, the calculating embezzler, the experienced burglar—to justice. The critics [of the pre-*Miranda* state of affairs] have preferred the former. They do not see the lack of stamina and professionalism of the suspect as conferring a benefit on society by facilitating the identification of wrongdoers.[196]

But guilt is personal. That another, equally guilty, person got away with murder because of some fortuitous factor—he was more experienced in dealing with the police, he had a poorly developed sense of guilt, he had a smart lawyer, he knew his rights—or even because of discrimination, does not make the more vulnerable murderer less guilty. To hold otherwise is to confuse justice with equality. * * * Since sophisticated suspects ordinarily will choose not to confess (with or without knowledge of their rights), "to strive for equality" is to "strive to eliminate confessions."[199] Thus, the *Miranda* Court elected to let one person get away with murder because of the advantage possessed by another.

* * * [T]he early empirical studies on the influence of *Miranda* clearly document that, where opportunity permitted, post-*Miranda* interrogators chose to "persuade the subject to talk" rather than "persuade him not to talk." [a] The studies reveal that, contrary to the intent of the Court, suspects more often have surrendered their rights than exercised them. These studies conclude that *Miranda* has done little to promote the exercise of the right to silence or the right to have counsel at the police station.[218]

To be truly protective of the suspect's decision to invoke or forego his rights would require making the right to counsel not waivable, so that prior professional advice would always be available, or granting the suspect a cooling-off period. * * * A cooling-off period might make for more dispassionate judgment, but if we believe in the justness of our prohibitions and punishments, what social value is promoted?

* * * Although [the empirical] studies are often cited for the proposition that *Miranda* has had little effect on police efficiency, this characterization is inaccurate. This interpretation makes sense only in a historical context as a reply to the hyperbolic assertions of those who predicted that installing a right to counsel at the stationhouse would maim criminal investi-

196. Nicholas Katzenbach, [the U.S. Attorney General at the time, stated on the eve of *Miranda*]: "I never understood why the gangster should be made the model and all others raised, in the name of equality, to his level of success in suppressing evidence." [For the full text of Katzenbach's remarks and for commentary on these remarks, see Kamisar, *Has the Court left the Attorney General Behind?—The Bazelon-Katzenbach Letters on Poverty, Equality and the Administration of Criminal Justice,* 54 Ky.L.J. 464 (1966), and the spirited responses of Dean Edward Barrett, Richard Kuh, Professor Gerhard Mueller and Justice Walter Schaefer.]

199. Grano, *Voluntariness, Free Will and the Law of Confessions,* 65 Va.L.Rev. 785, 914 (1979) [noting that equality is not the proper standard for measuring fairness in the interrogation context].

a. At this point, as he notes, Professor Caplan is borrowing language from Dean Barrett. See p. 516 n. 110 supra.

218. Special Project, *Interrogations in New Haven: The Impact of Miranda,* 76 Yale L.J. 1519, 1615 (1967); Leiken, *Police Interrogation in Colorado: The Implementation of Miranda,* 47 Den.L.J. 1, 47–49 (1970). [Professor Caplan also refers to Grisso, *Juveniles' Waiver of Rights* 147 (1981) and Stephens, *The Supreme Court and Confessions of Guilt* 200 (1973).]

gation. This perspective notwithstanding, the studies indicate that *Miranda* took a toll.

The study that best measures *Miranda's* impact on crime detection was conducted in Pittsburgh, a medium-sized city with a significant crime problem.[223] The researchers compare the difference in the confession rate before and after the *Miranda* decision for all offenses investigated by the detective division: homicide, robbery, burglary, auto larceny, and forcible sex. The results are striking. Before *Miranda,* the detective division obtained confessions in 54.5% of all cases. After *Miranda* confessions were secured in 37.5% of all cases, an overall decline of 31%. For robbery and burglary cases, the drop is sharper, from a 60% confession rate prior to *Miranda* to a 40% rate after *Miranda.* In homicide cases, the decline in confessions is even steeper. The researchers further estimate that in "approximately 20% of all cases a confession is probably necessary to obtain a conviction," and that in 25% of the cases in which the suspect confessed, the confession probably was necessary to obtain the conviction. * * *

Prior to *Miranda* [the rules governing confessions] were a compromise among competing considerations, only one of which was the protection of the suspect's interest in avoiding the discomforts of interrogation and escaping punishment. The suspect's determination whether cooperation would earn lenient treatment, whether "fast talk" would divert suspicion, or whether a steadfast refusal to answer questions might contribute to the prosecutor's decision to "throw the book at him" was considered an appropriate dilemma. That some suspects were no match for the police, did not grasp their rights, and unwisely tried to talk their way out of trouble was seen as a benefit to society, as long as the police were not too harsh or the suspect under too great a handicap. * * *

The *Miranda* majority saw interrogation quite differently. The Court viewed as unfair a suspect's inadequacies in confronting his interrogators on an equal basis or in possessing the same fortitude as other suspects. The Court wanted to place all of the participants on equal ground. To accomplish this objective, the Court sought to provide counsel to the suspect before the police could take advantage of the suspect's particular shortcomings. Thus with one stroke, the Court boldly and improperly resolved the contradictions in the law of confessions by giving it a single focus—protection of the suspect.

In retrospect, *Miranda* seems most understandable as an exaggerated response to the times rather than as an enunciation of a natural right mined at last from the Constitution. *Miranda* was a child of the racially troubled nineteen sixties and our tragic legacy of slavery. * * * *Miranda* itself was decided not only in the shadow of the police practices exposed in [the early Fourteenth Amendment due process confession cases], but also in the more recent past of the third degree applied particularly to southern blacks. To many, the government itself seemed the cause of racism and poverty, and those apprehended by the police, armed robbers as well as civil rights protesters, were seen as victims rather than offenders. Crime was not understood as the offshoot of individual will, but as a byproduct of one's status as poor or black or both. * * *

In this setting, *Miranda* stood out like a crown jewel. It spoke to the disadvantaged and the discontented. It conferred status on the accused. As such, it infused vitality into larger social and political movements and it contributed to a climate of greater respect for suspects. *Miranda* popularized the principle of warning one's

223. Seeburger & Wettick, *Miranda in Pittsburgh—A Statistical Story,* 29 U.Pitt.L.Rev. 1 (1967).

adversary, of assisting him in defending himself, and of envisioning the criminal not as a foreigner, but as a neighbor down on his luck. Criminals, *Miranda* suggested, were not wicked; they were unfortunate.

* * * There is something attractive about a legal system that insists that suspects have a right to refuse to answer police inquiries, that imposes on the police an obligation to communicate that right and that provides counsel to the indigent. The fifth amendment, as much as any constitutional provision, illustrates that ours is a limited government. It reflects a historic distrust of authority. It reveals an unwillingness to wage all-out war on crime, even heinous crime, lest other values be demeaned.

But the root idea of *Miranda*, as well as earlier decisions [such as *Escobedo*] is quite different and more ominous. These decisions do more than suggest that the government must be restricted in the means it employs in criminal investigation. They impose a serious handicap on the government, which arises not merely from a desire to curb historic police abuses, but also from an ambivalence about criminality itself and a confusion concerning the purpose behind the rules of criminal procedure. The result blurs the traditional and theoretical distinction between the police and the criminal: one is useful, the other noxious.

This blurring arose, in part, because we lost sight of the values implicated by confession. Confession should be understood as an endorsement of the prevailing order. When a person confesses against himself, he speaks for the law. * * *

When *Miranda* was decided in 1966, it was popular to see the criminal as a type of victim; he was caught in the role assigned to persons in his circumstances, a member of the underclass. One spoke not of volition but of status or condition. The idea of individual guilt and remorse for wrongful deeds was out of fashion. The causal factors of criminality were thought to lay outside the individual in the deeper, corrupt foundations of the society—the so-called "root causes."

This perspective on criminal process was perhaps but a special case of "authority under siege" during the decade of the 1960's and early 1970's, an understandable reaction to a history of racial prejudice and perhaps to Vietnam and Watergate as well, but a reaction in need of tempering nonetheless. * * *

We know from the experience of other countries that the rules can be drawn to make the police far more effective than they are in this country; and there may be nations where the police in some particulars operate under greater restraint than our own. A fair state-individual balance can be achieved, it would seem, through a variety of arrangements as long as it is conceded at the outset that society has a stake in the outcome of police efforts to investigate crime.[b] * * *

There is no neutral position. One must lean toward the government or subversion. With respect to criminal investigations, we should not require the government to provide information that would discourage a suspect's participation when the lawful character of the interrogation can otherwise be guaranteed; the concern for accuracy runs too high and the public interest in identifying and segregating dan-

b. At this point Professor Caplan suggests that the Warren Court might have required the government to prove voluntariness beyond a reasonable doubt rather than by a preponderance of the evidence; "could have added teeth to the voluntariness test by establishing *per se* rules forbidding certain practices"; might have set time limits for questioning suspects; and "could have mandated compliance with the prompt arraignment statutes in effect in about three quarters of the states. * * * Finally, current technology makes videotaped interrogations practical. A rule mandating recording would confine extensive questioning to those cases in which it mattered most and would provide an accurate record by which the judiciary could evaluate the police pressure on the suspect."

gerous persons is too great. The ultimate issue is whether the government proceeded fairly, in a proper manner, not whether the suspect knew his rights. When the interrogation is noncoercive and the answers voluntary, the Constitution should be satisfied. The privilege against self-incrimination is best understood as a denial to the government of the power to extract confessions forcibly and indecently, not as a denial of the value of confession. * * *[c]

WELSH W. WHITE—DEFENDING MIRANDA: A REPLY TO PROFESSOR CAPLAN

39 Vand.L.Rev. 2, 7–9, 17–22 (1986).

[Professor Caplan] objects to *Miranda's* holding and analysis but does not specify whether his objections primarily center on the Court's conclusion that the fifth amendment privilege applies to police questioning at the station house or to the Court's determination that the *Miranda* warnings are necessary to protect that privilege.[5] Professor Caplan does criticize the specific warnings required and intimates that the much maligned voluntariness test provides a preferable way to control police interrogations. After examining the empirical data relating to *Miranda's* operation and finding that *Miranda's* adverse effect on law enforcement is much greater than generally has been recognized, he concludes that the rule established in *Miranda* is not an appropriate compromise between the competing interests of protecting individual rights and promoting the interests of law enforcement. * * *

* * * Professor Caplan praises the voluntariness test in part because "its inquiry was a search of existential fact, an attempt to capture what actually happened at the police station." But long before *Miranda* it was widely recognized that, in most cases, the adversary process was not equipped to give anything close to an accurate picture of what happened at the police station. The problem was not simply one of resolving the "swearing contest" in which the police officers and the defendant gave differing versions of the interrogation.[33] * * * [E]ven if the officers gave an accurate account of the facts, including the length of questioning, the number of officers involved, and a description of any tricks that were used, this account would still not begin to describe the interrogation process experienced by the suspect. The police manuals indicate that interrogation techniques are sophisticated. The police tactics are designed to have subtle effects that may not easily be described. Thus, a verbal account of what the police said or did to a suspect does not reflect the atmosphere created in the interrogation room. * * *

c. For additional criticism of *Miranda,* see Frey, *Modern Police Interrogation Law: The Wrong Road Taken,* 42 U.Pitt.L.Rev. 731 (1981); Gangi, *The Inbau-Kamisar Debate: Time for Round 2?,* 12 Western State U.L.Rev. 117 (1984); Inbau, *Over-reaction—The Mischief of Miranda v. Arizona, 73 J.Crim.L. & C. 797 (1982);* and three articles by Professor Grano: *Prophylactic Rules in Criminal Procedure: A Question of Article III Legitimacy,* 80 Nw.U.L.Rev. 100 (1985); *Rhode Island v. Innis: A Need to Reconsider the Constitutional Premises underlying the Law of Confessions,* 17 Am.Crim.L.Rev. 1 (1979); *Voluntariness, Free Will and the Law of Confessions,* 65 Va.L. Rev. 859 (1979).

5. In this respect Professor Caplan is similar to other critics of *Miranda.* For example, [in the summer of 1985] Attorney General Edwin Meese complained that *Miranda* was "a wrong decision," [but] went on to say, "I think that if a person doesn't want to answer, that's [his] right, but you have had * * * all these ridiculous situations in which the police are precluded from asking the one person who knows the most about the crime what happened." * * * By admitting that the defendant has a right to remain silent, the Attorney General implicitly suggested that he does not object to *Miranda's* holding that the fifth amendment privilege applies to the police station.

33. For an incisive discussion of the implications of this "swearing contest," see Amsterdam, *The Supreme Court and the Rights of Suspects in Criminal Cases,* 45 N.Y.U.L.Rev. 785, 806–808 (1970). See also Schulhofer, *Confessions and the Court,* 79 Mich.L.Rev. 865, 870–71 (1981).

[T]he *Miranda* rule was necessary in part because the litigation process was incapable of "captur[ing] what actually happened at the police station." Based on this perception of the realities of police interrogation, the Court believed that the warnings generally would be necessary to dissipate the coercive atmosphere at the station house. Moreover, based on the Court's awareness of the inherent limitations of the litigation process, it also believed that the warnings were appropriate because, in their absence, the objective of determining whether a particular confession was coerced would be elusive at best. Finally, the Court implicitly believed that, by providing the defendant an opportunity to exercise his rights, the warnings largely would eliminate the need for future litigation relating to the circumstances of the interrogation process.

Thus, *Miranda* rests on a legitimate constitutional basis. The *Miranda* rule represents an effort to apply the fifth amendment privilege to a vital stage of the adversary process. Moreover, the Court was justified in believing that the *Miranda* rule would alleviate some of the principal problems associated with the Court's earlier efforts to control police interrogation at the police station. * * *

In arguing that *Miranda* fails to strike an appropriate balance between government and individual interests, Professor Caplan quotes extensively from Justice Jackson's opinion in *Watts v. Indiana.* [83] After observing that police interrogation of suspects in the absence of counsel "presents a real dilemma in a free society," Jackson posited a stark contrast between allowing the police to question a suspect without his attorney present and allowing the suspect to have counsel present during the custodial interrogation. Anticipating the views of the dissenters in *Miranda,* Jackson indicated that the choice is between police questioning that may lead to effective law enforcement and requiring that the "police stand by helplessly while those suspected of murder prowl about unmolested." * * *

Despite Justice Jackson's perception of the consequences involved, he, nevertheless, acknowledged that the issue of the suspect's right to have counsel present during police questioning was a difficult one. He noted that, under any interpretation, our constitutional system "comes close" to requiring that a suspect be convicted only on the basis of "such evidence as he cannot conceal from the authorities, who cannot compel him to testify in court and also cannot question him before." After presenting his view of the extreme costs to law enforcement that this requirement would impose, he concludes with the following famous passage:

> Is it a necessary price to pay for the fairness which we know as "due process of law"? And if not a necessary one, should it be demanded by this Court? I do not know the ultimate answer to these questions; but, for the present, I should not increase the handicap on society.

Miranda does not, of course answer the questions Justice Jackson posed, but the post-*Miranda* experience suggests that the questions should perhaps be posed in different terms. The empirical data on *Miranda's* impact suggest that, contrary to the dissenters' expectations, the Court's decision to provide suspects with the *Miranda* protections has not substantially "increase[d] the handicap on society." Surprisingly, the studies show that *Miranda* has had relatively little effect on law enforcement. These results suggest perhaps that the dilemma Justice Jackson posited does not really exist. Maybe criminal suspects can be afforded protections that are fully consistent with the spirit of our constitutional system without significantly impairing the interests of law enforcement.

Professor Caplan would disagree with this assessment. He asserts that the *Miran-*

83. 338 U.S. 49 (1949).

da studies show that it is inaccurate to conclude that "*Miranda* has had little effect on police efficiency." He relies particularly on the Pittsburgh study, in which the researchers determined that the detective division, which investigated homicide, robbery, burglary, auto larceny, and forcible sex, obtained confessions in 54.4% of all cases before *Miranda* but only in 37.5% of all cases after *Miranda* —an overall decline of 17%. A decline of 17% in the confession rate does appear to be significant, but in order to determine the effect of this decline on police efficiency, one would also want to investigate the conviction rate. The authors of the Pittsburgh study in fact made this investigation. They concluded that the conviction rate for major crimes in Allegheny County during this period "remained steady." * * * While the conviction rate is not the only indication of police efficiency, these figures certainly suggest that the 17% decline in the confession rate did not produce a dramatic impact on law enforcement.

Professor Caplan asserts that the Pittsburgh study "best measures *Miranda's* impact on crime detection." Apparently, Professor Caplan based this assertion on the fact that the Pittsburgh study presented pre-*Miranda* and post-*Miranda* data obtained from "a medium-sized city with a significant crime problem." In fact, the Pittsburgh study is not the only one to meet these criteria. A much more extensive study, conducted by the Institute of Criminal Law and Procedure, Georgetown University Law Center, examined the effect of *Miranda* on people arrested for felony and serious misdemeanor cases in Washington, D.C.. By questioning defendants subjected to arrest procedures in the District of Columbia during 1965 and 1966, the Institute obtained figures showing the frequency with which defendants asserted their rights before and after *Miranda.* The study's overall conclusion is that little has changed since *Miranda* was decided.[97] The rate of statements reported to have been given to the police was "remarkably uniform" at around forty percent in both the pre- and post-*Miranda* periods.

I have no basis for asserting that either of these studies is superior to the other. Of all the post-*Miranda* studies, however, the Pittsburgh study was the only one to find that *Miranda* effected a significant decrease in the confession rate.[99] [That] study focused on a detective branch composed of highly professional officers who may have been particularly conscientious in complying with *Miranda.* Moreover, Professor Richard Seeburger, one of the study's authors, recently commented that the study's "central finding was that law enforcement's effectiveness was not significantly impaired as a result of *Miranda.*" Professor Seeburger added that, at the time of the study, Pittsburgh law enforcement officials expressed the opinion that *Miranda* would ultimately benefit law enforcement by prompting the police to de-

97. See Medalie, Zeitz & Alexander, *Custodial Interrogation in Our Nation's Capitol: The Attempt to Implement Miranda,* 66 Mich.L.Rev. 1347 (1968).

99. The great weight of empirical evidence supports the conclusion that *Miranda's* impact on the police's ability to obtain confessions has not been significant. [At this point, in addition to discussing the Georgetown study and the studies cited at p. 565 n. 218 supra, Professor White refers to, and briefly summarizes, e.g. Neubaner, *Confessions in Prairie City,* 65 J.Crim.L. & C. 103, 111 (1974) (1968 data for medium sized central Illinois city indicated that "police are fairly successful in obtaining statements from suspects; over 45% of the felony defendants made a confession."); Robinson, *Police and Prosecutor Practices and Attitudes Relating to Interrogation as Revealed by Pre- and Post-Miranda Questionnaires,* 1968 Duke L.J. 425, 464–65; Witt, *Non Coercive Interrogation and The Administration of Criminal Justice,* 64 J.Crim.L. & C. 320, 325 (1973) (interrogations conducted in "Seaside City," a pseudonymous subdivision of the Los Angeles metropolitan area, were successful in 69% of pre-*Miranda* cases and 67% of post-Miranda cases); Younger, *Interrogation of Criminal Defendants—Some Views on Miranda v. Arizona,* 35 Fordham L.Rev. 255 (1966–67) (confession rate for a sample of Los Angeles county felony cases increased from 40% to 50% after *Miranda*).]

velop more effective investigatory techniques.

Since Professor Caplan obviously is a skilled advocate, his emphasis on the Pittsburgh study is itself significant. If there were any hard data to support the conclusion that *Miranda* has had an adverse impact on law enforcement, critics of *Miranda* certainly would have unearthed it by now.[a] The strongest evidence that Professor Caplan can cite, however, is a study that shows a 17% decline in the confession rate and no decline in the conviction rate. This in itself provides striking confirmation of the widely shared perception that Miranda's effect on law enforcement has been negligible.[104]

Professor Caplan concludes his discussion of the empirical data by pointing out that, because the studies were conducted shortly after the *Miranda* decision, they fail "to conclusively tell us what *Miranda* would mean if followed in letter *and* spirit' or if extended." The simple answer to this point is that Professor Caplan is neither arguing against a different implementation of *Miranda* nor against its extension. According to his thesis, the decision should be overruled because it strikes an inappropriate accommodation between individual and law enforcement interests. The *Miranda* decision as it presently stands, however, seems to strike an excellent accommodation between those interests. The criminal suspect is afforded constitutional protection, but the interests of law enforcement are not impaired. Why should *Miranda* be overruled? It gives us the best of all possible worlds.

My last statement could be challenged by those who feel that the *Miranda* warnings do not effectively safeguard the individual's fifth amendment privilege at the station house. If the empirical studies indicate that *Miranda* has made little difference, perhaps the goal of providing constitutional protections at the station house has not been realized. If *Miranda* merely provides the illusion that we can avoid the dilemma arising from our simultaneous commitments to the fifth amendment privilege and to a system of law enforcement that relies heavily upon police interrogation, what is the value of retaining it? Indeed, Professor Schulhofer suggests that *Miranda* is inferior to the voluntariness test in one respect because "[*Miranda* 's] technique for denying this dilemma, for insuring that we can have our cake and eat it, is infinitely less candid than the due process balancing analysis."

In my opinion, *Miranda* does have value as a symbol of our commitment to maintaining a fair system of criminal procedure that seeks to implement the protections embodied in the federal constitution. As Professor Caplan admits, *Miranda* "contributed to a climate of greater respect for suspects [and] is a gesture of government's willingness to treat the lowliest antagonist as worthy of respect and consideration." Thus *Miranda's* symbolic value not only has produced a better atmosphere for people who come in contact with the police, but also may have made a tangible contri-

a. At this point Professor White notes that when, shortly after *Miranda,* Evelle Younger, then the Los Angeles District Attorney, reported that a study conducted by his office revealed that *Miranda* had had no appreciable adverse effect on law enforcement in his jurisdiction—indeed, the conviction rate had increased—many of Younger's colleagues showed "resentment" toward him "for having broken ranks with them on *Miranda.*" According to a news story covering the 1967 annual convention of prosecuting attorneys, some of Youngers' colleagues "buttonholed" him and urged him to review his statistics and change his conclusions, but Younger stated that, in the face of the data, he could not do so. See Kamisar, *How to Use, Abuse—and Fight Back With—Crime Statistics,* 25 Okla.L.Rev. 239, 255 (1972).

104. See generally LaFave & Israel, Criminal Procedure 285–286 (1985); see also Israel, *Criminal Procedure, the Burger Court, and the Legacy of the Warren Court,* 75 Mich.L.Rev. 1320, 1383 (1977) ("The police officers with whom I have spoken generally acknowledge that announcement of the *Miranda* warnings cause little difficulty if the warnings requirement is limited to interrogation of arrested persons at the police station or in similar settings (e.g., a patrol car).)

bution toward curbing abusive police practices. Retaining *Miranda* symbolizes the Court's approval of the direction in which our system of justice has moved since the time when, in the words of Justice Harlan, [dissenting in *Miranda*], the police were allowed to exert "quite significant pressures" to extract confessions from suspects.

Conversely, overruling *Miranda* would send a very different message. In reference to the fourth amendment's prohibition upon unreasonable searches, Justice Jackson once said, "We must remember that the extent of any privilege [that] we sustain, the officers interpret and apply themselves and will push to the limit." [109] Just as overruling the fourth amendment exclusionary rule likely would suggest to the police that they no longer must comply with the fourth amendment, overruling *Miranda* would convey the message that restraints on police interrogation have been largely abandoned. Undoubtedly, this decision would change the relationship between the police and the criminal suspect. In light of our commitment to maintaining a fair system of criminal justice, however, it seems doubtful whether this new relationship would be preferable to the present one.

TITLE II OF THE OMNIBUS CRIME CONTROL AND SAFE STREETS ACT OF 1968—ADMISSIBILITY OF CONFESSIONS [a]

Title II of the Crime Control Act of 1968, which purports to "repeal" *Miranda* and the *McNabb-Mallory* rule in federal prosecutions, amends Chapter 223, title 18, United States Code, by adding the following new sections:

"§ 3501. Admissibility of confessions

"(a) In any criminal prosecution brought by the United States or by the District of Columbia, a confession, as defined in subsection (e) hereof, shall be admissible in evidence if it is voluntarily given. Before such confession is received in evidence, the trial judge shall, out of the presence of the jury, determine any issue as to voluntariness. If the trial judge determines that the confession was voluntarily made it shall be admitted in evidence and the trial judge shall permit the jury to hear relevant evidence on the issue of voluntariness and shall instruct the jury to give such weight to the confession as the jury feels it deserves under all the circumstances.

"(b) The trial judge in determining the issue of voluntariness shall take into consideration all the circumstances surrounding the giving of the confession, including (1) the time elapsing between arrest and arraignment of the defendant making the confession, if it was made after arrest and before arraignment, (2) whether such defendant knew the nature of the offense with which he was charged or of which he was suspected at the time of making the confession, (3) whether or not such defendant was advised or knew that he was not required to make any statement and that any such statement could be used against him, (4) whether or not such defendant had been advised prior to questioning of his right to the assistance of counsel; and (5) whether or not such defendant was without the assistance of counsel when questioned and when giving such confession.

"The presence or absence of any of the above-mentioned factors to be taken into consideration by the judge need not be

109. *Brinegar v. United States,* 338 U.S. 160, 182 (1949) (Jackson, J., dissenting).

a. For a detailed account of congressional reaction to *Miranda* and related decisions, see Breckenridge, *Congress Against the Court* (1970). For other accounts of congressional, and Presidential Candidate Nixon's, hostility to *Miranda,* see Graham, *The Self-Inflicted Wound* 305–32 (1970); Kamisar, *How to Use, Abuse—and Fight Back with—Crime Statistics,* 25 Okla.L.Rev. 239 (1972).

conclusive on the issue of voluntariness of the confession.

"(c) In any criminal prosecution by the United States or by the District of Columbia, a confession made or given by a person who is a defendant therein, while such person was under arrest or other detention in the custody of any law-enforcement officer or law-enforcement agency, shall not be inadmissible solely because of delay in bringing such person before a commissioner or other officer empowered to commit persons charged with offenses against the laws of the United States or of the District of Columbia if such confession is found by the trial judge to have been made voluntarily and if the weight to be given the confession is left to the jury and if such confession was made or given by such person within six hours immediately following his arrest or other detention: *Provided,* That the time limitation contained in this subsection shall not apply in any case in which the delay in bringing such person before such commissioner or other officer beyond such six-hour period is found by the trial judge to be reasonable considering the means of transportation and the distance to be traveled to the nearest available such commissioner or other officer.

"(d) Nothing contained in this section shall bar the admission in evidence of any confession made or given voluntarily by any person to any other person without interrogation by anyone, or at any time at which the person who made or gave such confession was not under arrest or other detention.

"(e) As used in this section, the term 'confession' means any confession of guilt of any criminal offense or any self-incriminating statement made or given orally or in writing."

Is there any basis for a constitutional attack on § 3501(c), which badly cripples the *McNabb-Mallory rule?* Is the rule only a rule of evidence subject to congressional control or do its roots run deeper than the Court's supervisory powers? Even if a confession can no longer be excluded on *McNabb-Mallory* grounds, in light of *Miranda's* discussion of the impact of lengthy interrogation or incommunicado incarceration on the issue of waiver [see language immediately following reference to fn. 45], might the interrogation conditions permitted by § 3501(c) render a suspect's waiver of his *Miranda* rights invalid? See *Frazier v. United States,* 419 F.2d 1161 (D.C.Cir.1969); Wright, *Federal Practice and Procedure: Criminal,* § 72 at 91–92 (2d ed. 1982); Note, 57 Geo.L.J. 438, 451–54 (1968).

On signing the Crime Control Act into law on June 19, 1968, President Johnson commented that "the provisions of Title II, vague and ambiguous as they are, can, I am advised by the Attorney General, be interpreted in harmony with the Constitution." (N.Y. Times, June 20, 1968, p. 23, col. 1.) Insofar as the Act attempts to repeal *Massiah, Escobedo* and *Miranda,*[b] how?

b. Consider Judge Friendly, *The Constitution* 24–25 (U.S. Dep't. Justice Bicentennial Lecture Series, 1976): "Fortunately, [the federal statute which purports to overrule *Miranda*] has not provoked the head-on collision that might have been predicted, principally because of a statesmanslike effort [by the executive branch] to avoid a battle that could only be damaging to our institutions. The Attorney General in office when the statute was passed instructed his subordinates not to rely on it where it differed from *Miranda,* and although a later Attorney General changed this as official policy, most United States Attorneys appear in practice to have continued to take the restrained position initially directed. Nevertheless, the conflict was bound to surface, and [recently] a federal appeals court did hold [although the holding was unnecessary since the court ruled, alternatively, that *Miranda* had not been violated] that the statute was constitutional. [*United States v. Crocker,* 510 F.2d 1129 (10th Cir. 1975), discussed in Note, 47 U.Colo.L.Rev. 279 (1976).] While I need not discuss the merits of that issue, I can say that the spectacle of Congress feeling compelled to enact a law intended to overrule a constitutional opinion of the Supreme Court and then having the law ignored by those who are charged with a duty to enforce it raises a question whether the Court acted wisely in endeavoring, by a slender majority, to impose for all

Are the *Miranda* warnings "constitutional rules" or congressionally reversible "constitutionally inspired common law"? Compare Monaghan, *The Supreme Court, 1974 Term—Foreword: Constitutional Common Law,* 89 Harv.L.Rev. 1, 18–23, 30–34, 42n. 217 (1975) with Schrock, Welsh & Collins, *Interrogational Rights: Reflections on Miranda v. Arizona,* 52 So.Cal.L.Rev. 1 (1978). See also Burt, *Miranda and Title II: A Morganatic Marriage,* 1967 Sup.Ct. Rev. 81; Cox, *The Role of Congress in Constitutional Determinations,* 40 U.Cinn.L.Rev. 199 (1971). May Congress repeal *Miranda* by discrediting *Miranda's* factual underpinning, i.e., by establishing that custodial interrogation is not "inherently coercive"? Is the *Massiah* doctrine less subject to congressional repeal or revision than *Miranda* because *Massiah* turns on issues of "law" rather than "fact"? If so, how much sense does this make? Are there plausible premises for the *Miranda* warnings requirement other than the "inherently coercive" nature of custodial interrogation? See Schrock, Welsh & Collins, supra, at 5–8.

Even if *Miranda* is subject to congressional revision, e.g., may be displaced by a statute that provides an adequate alternative to the now-familiar warnings, is Title II of the Crime Control Act nevertheless invalid because it "does little more than turn the clock back to the 'voluntariness' doctrine of prior decisions espoused by the *Miranda* dissents?" See Cox, supra, at 252. But consider Caplan, *Questioning Miranda,* 38 Vand.L.Rev. 1417, 1474 (1985), maintaining that because the 1968 Crime Control Act requires the federal trial court "to take into consideration" whether the defendant had been advised or knew of his rights, it "admirably blended the traditional voluntariness test with the fourfold warnings."

In the years since the Crime Control Act was enacted, the Supreme Court has repeatedly called the *Miranda* warnings not constitutional commands but "prophylactic" rules designed to secure or reinforce constitutional rights. (See the cases discussed under the next heading). Does this make *Miranda* especially susceptible to congressional "repeal"? See Caplan, supra, at 1474 n. 271; Grano, *Prophylactic Rules in Criminal Procedure: A Question of Article III Legitimacy,* 80 Nw.U.L.Rev. 100 (1985).

IS A VIOLATION OF *MIRANDA* A VIOLATION OF THE PRIVILEGE AGAINST SELF-INCRIMINATION AS SUCH OR ARE THE *MIRANDA* WARNINGS ONLY "PROPHYLACTIC" RULES?

MICHIGAN v. TUCKER, 417 U.S. 433, 94 S.Ct. 2357, 41 L.Ed.2d 182 (1974), dealt with the admissibility of the testimony of a witness whose identity had been learned by questioning defendant without giving him the full *Miranda* warnings.[a] The questioning occurred before *Miranda* was decided, but defendant's trial took place afterwards. Thus, *Miranda* was applicable to the case [b] and, accordingly, defendant's own statements to the police were excluded; but the witness' testimony was not. In the course of holding that under the circumstances the witness' testimony was admissible,[c] the Court, per

future time such an extensive set of dicta which the country was not prepared to accept." See also Gandara, *Admissibility of Confessions in Federal Prosecutions,* 63 Geo.L.J. 305 (1974).

a. Defendant had been told that he had a right to the presence of counsel, but had not been informed that if he could not afford a lawyer but desired one, a lawyer would be appointed for him prior to any questioning.

b. The Court held, a week after *Miranda,* that *Miranda* affects only those cases in which *the trial* began after the date of that decision. Should the Court have held that *Miranda* only applies to *police interrogations* conducted after the date of that decision? See generally Ch. 2, § 3.

c. The Court noted, *inter alia,* that since the police action "was pursued in complete good faith," the deterrent purpose of the exclusionary rule "loses much of its force"; and deemed it "significant [that] the officers' failure to advise

REHNQUIST, J., viewed the *Miranda* warnings as "not themselves rights protected by the Constitution" but only "prophylactic standards" designed to "safeguard" or to "provide practical reinforcement" for the privilege against self-incrimination:

"[T]he Court in *Miranda,* for the first time, expressly declared that the Self-Incrimination Clause was applicable to state interrogations at a police station, and that a defendant's statements might be excluded at trial despite their voluntary character under traditional principles.

"To supplement this new doctrine, and to help police officers conduct interrogations without facing a continued risk that valuable evidence would be lost, the [*Miranda* Court] established a set of specific guidelines, now commonly known as the *Miranda* rules. * * *

"The [*Miranda* Court] recognized that these procedural safeguards were not themselves rights protected by the Constitution but were instead measures to insure that the right against compulsory self-incrimination was protected. As [it] remarked: '[W]e cannot say that the Constitution necessarily requires adherence to any particular solution for the inherent compulsions of the interrogation process as it is presently conducted.' The suggested safeguards were not intended to 'create a constitutional straitjacket,' *Miranda,* but rather to provide practical reinforcement for the right against compulsory self-incrimination.[d]

"A comparison of the facts in this case with the historical circumstances underlying the privilege against compulsory self-incrimination strongly indicates that the police conduct here did not deprive [Tucker] of his privilege against self-incrimination as such, but rather failed to make available to him the full measure of procedural safeguards associated with that right since *Miranda.* Certainly no one could contend that the interrogation faced by [Tucker] bore any resemblance to the historical practices at which the right against compulsory self-incrimination was aimed. * * * [H]is statements could hardly be termed involuntary as that term has been defined in the decisions of this Court. * * *

"Our determination that the interrogation in this case involved no compulsion sufficient to breach the right against compulsory self-incrimination does not mean there was not a disregard, albeit an inadvertent disregard, of the procedural rules later established in *Miranda.* The question for decision is how sweeping the judicially imposed consequences of this disregard shall be." [e]

[defendant] of his right to appointed counsel occurred prior [to] *Miranda*."

d. But as Justice Douglas observed in his *Tucker* dissent, the Court, per Rehnquist, J., overlooked other language in the *Miranda* opinion. For example, in the same paragraph from *Miranda* quoted by Justice Rehnquist in *Tucker,* the *Miranda* Court added: "However, unless we are shown other procedures which are at least as effective in apprising accused persons of their right of silence and in assuring a continuous opportunity to exercise it, the following safeguards [the *Miranda* warnings] must be observed." Moreover, later in the opinion, the *Miranda* Court reiterated: "The warnings required and the waiver necessary in accordance with our opinion today are, in the absence of a fully effective equivalent, prerequisites to the admissibility of any statements made by a defendant. * * * Procedural safeguards must be employed to protect the privilege, and unless other fully effective means are adopted to notify the person of his right of silence and to assure that the exercise of the right will be scrupulously honored, the following measures [the *Miranda* warnings] are required."

e. Consider, also *Brown v. Illinois* (p. 805 infra) where the Court, per Blackmun, J., observed: "This Court has described the *Miranda* warnings as a 'prophylactic rule' and as a 'procedural safeguard' employed to protect Fifth Amendment rights against 'the compulsion inherent in custodial surroundings.' The function of the warnings relates to the Fifth Amendment's guarantee against coerced self-incrimination, and the exclusion of a statement made in the absence of the warnings, it is said, serves to deter the taking of an incriminating statement without first informing the individual of his Fifth Amendment rights." Note, too, that dissenting in *Brewer v. Williams* (p. 635 infra), Justice Blackmun, joined by White and Rehnquist, JJ., described *Miranda* as "this Court's procedural (as distinguished from constitutional) ruling."

A decade later, first in NEW YORK v. QUARLES (1984) (p. 599 infra), and then in OREGON v. ELSTAD (1985) (p. 817 infra), the Court reiterated *Tucker's* way of looking at, and thinking about, *Miranda*. *Quarles* recognized a "public safety" exception to the *Miranda* warnings and thus held both the suspect's statement, "the gun is over there," and the gun found as a result admissible. *Elstad* ruled that the fact that the police had earlier obtained a statement from defendant in violation of his *Miranda* rights (when they questioned him in his home) did not bar the admissibility of a subsequent confession (at the station house) when, this time, the police complied with *Miranda*. In both cases the Court underscored the distinction between statements that are *actually* "coerced" or "compelled" and those obtained *merely* in violation of *Miranda's* "procedural safeguards" or "prophylactic rules."

In *Quarles,* the Court, per REHNQUIST, J., relied heavily on Justice Rehnquist's opinion for the Court in *Tucker:*

"The prophylactic *Miranda* warnings * * * are 'not themselves rights protected by the Constitution but [are] instead measures to insure that the right against compulsory self-incrimination [is] protected' *Tucker.* Requiring *Miranda* warnings before custodial interrogation provides 'practical reinforcement' for the Fifth Amendment right. *Tucker.*

"In this case we have before us no claim that [Quarles'] statements were actually compelled by police conduct which overcame his will to resist. Thus the only issue before us is whether [the officer] was justified in failing to make available to [Quarles] the procedural safeguards associated with the privilege against compulsory self-incrimination since *Miranda.* * * *

"We conclude that the need for answers to questions in a situation posing a threat to the public safety outweighs the need for the prophylactic rule protecting the Fifth Amendment's privilege against self-incrimination."

In *Elstad,* defendant contended that the second confession, although immediately preceded by *Miranda* warnings and a waiver of rights, should be excluded as the "fruit" of the earlier *Miranda* violations. The Court's reply was that defendant's "fruit of the poisonous tree" argument assumed the existence of an underlying constitutional right, but a failure to give the *Miranda* warnings, when called for, is not in itself a violation of the fifth amendment. Observed the Court per O'CONNOR, J.:

"If errors are made by law enforcement officers in administering the prophylactic *Miranda* procedures, they should not breed the same irremediable consequences as police infringement of the Fifth Amendment itself. * * * There is a vast difference between the direct consequences flowing from coercion of a confession by physical violence or other deliberate means calculated to break the suspect's will and the uncertain consequences of disclosure of a 'guilty secret' freely given in response to an unwarned but noncoercive question, as in this case. * * * [A]bsent deliberately coercive or improper tactics in obtaining the initial statement, the mere fact that a suspect has made an unwarned admission does not warrant a presumption of compulsion. A subsequent administration of *Miranda* warnings to a suspect who has given a voluntary but unwarned statement ordinarily should suffice to remove the conditions that precluded admission of the earlier statement."

THE IMPLICATIONS OF THE *TUCKER–QUARLES–ELSTAD* WAY OF THINKING ABOUT *MIRANDA:* HAS THE COURT PREPARED THE WAY FOR OVERRULING *MIRANDA*? IS *MIRANDA* AN "ILLEGITIMATE" DECISION?

By equating "compulsion" within the meaning of the self-incrimination clause with "coercion" or "involuntariness" under the pre-*Miranda* due process "totality of the circumstances" test for admitting confessions, does the present Court overlook that in pre-*Miranda* days the terms "coercion" and "involuntariness" were not used in their ordinary sense, but as terms of art? Does it overlook, too, that *much greater* pressures were necessary to render a confession "coerced" or "involuntary" under the old test for admitting confessions than are needed (or were deemed needed at the time of *Miranda*) to render a confession "compelled" within the meaning of the privilege? Was that not a principal reason for abandoning the old test in favor of *Miranda?* If, as the present Court seems to say, a violation of the self-incrimination clause *itself* occurs only when a confession is "involuntary" under traditional standards, is this "an outright rejection of the core premise of *Miranda*"? See Stone, *The Miranda Doctrine in the Burger Court,* 1977 Sup.Ct.Rev. 99, 118.

Since the Court has no "supervisory power" over *state* criminal justice, if *Miranda* warnings are not constitutional requirements (but only "second-class" prophylactic safeguards) and *Miranda* violations not constitutional violations (but only "second-class" wrongs) where did the Court get the authority to impose *Miranda* on the states? Consider Stone, supra, at 123: "The [*Tucker* opinion] deprived *Miranda* of a constitutional basis but did not explain what other basis for it there might be. Thus, *Tucker* seems certainly to have laid the groundwork to overrule *Miranda.* Moreover, even if *Tucker* did not entirely dismantle *Miranda,* it clearly severed it from the privilege against compelled self-incrimination. As a result, the Court in future cases need not face the inherent command of the privilege that evidence obtained in violation of its dictates is *per se* inadmissible. The Court is now free to balance at will."

After an extensive examination of the legitimacy of the *Miranda* rules and other "prophylactic constitutional rules"—"what distinguishes a prophylactic rule from a true constitutional rule is the possibility of violating the former without actually violating the Constitution"—Professor Grano concludes that *Miranda,* as the Court *now understands* what it did in that case,[a] is "illegitimate," i.e., outside the scope of the federal courts' Article III lawmaking authority. *Miranda,* he maintains, does not conform to the *Marbury v. Madison* model of judicial review; the Supreme Court has no constitutional authority to reverse state convictions when the Constitution has not actually been violated. See Grano, *Prophylactic Rules in Criminal Procedure: A Question of Article III Legitimacy,* 80 Nw.U.L.Rev. 100 (1985).

TWENTY YEARS WITH *MIRANDA:* AN OVERVIEW

Because *Miranda* was the centerpiece of the Warren Court's "revolution in American criminal procedure" and the prime target of those who thought the courts were "soft" on criminals, almost everyone expected the so-called Burger Court to treat *Miranda* unkindly. And it did—at first. But it must also be said that the new Court has interpreted *Miranda* fairly generously in some important respects.

The first blows the Burger Court dealt *Miranda* were the impeachment cases, *Harris v. New York* (1971) (Ch. 11, § 4) and *Oregon v. Hass* (1975) (Ch. 11, § 4). *Harris* held that statements preceded by defective warnings, and thus inadmissible to establish the prosecution's case-in-chief, could nevertheless be used to impeach the defendant's credibility if he chose to take

a. Professor Grano recognizes that "the *Miranda* opinion itself was somewhat ambiguous" on this score—some language indicates that without the prescribed warnings, or an effective alternative, a statement produced by custodial interrogation actually has been "compelled" within the meaning of the self-incrimination clause, but other portions of the opinion "suggest that the Court was promulgating a prophylactic rule."

the stand in his own defense. The Court noted, but seemed unperturbed by the fact, that some language in the *Miranda* opinion could be read as barring the use of statements obtained in violation of *Miranda* for *any* purpose.

The Court went a step beyond *Harris* in the *Hass* case. In this case, after being advised of his rights, the defendant *asserted* them. Nevertheless, the police refused to honor the defendant's request for a lawyer and continued to question him. The Court ruled that here, too, the resulting incriminating statements could be used for impeachment purposes. Since many suspects make incriminating statements even after the receipt of complete *Miranda* warnings, *Harris* might have been explained—and contained—on the ground that permitting impeachment use of statements acquired without complete warnings would not greatly encourage the police to violate *Miranda.* But now that *Hass* is on the books, when a suspect asserts his rights, it seems the police have virtually nothing to lose and everything to gain by continuing to question him.[a]

Although language in *Miranda* could be read as establishing a *per se* rule against any further questioning of one who has asserted his "right to silence" (as opposed to his *right to counsel,* discussed below), *Michigan v. Mosley* (1975) (p. 610 infra) held that under certain circumstances (and what they are is unclear), if they cease questioning on the spot, the police may "try again," and succeed at a later interrogation session. At the very least, it seems, the police must promptly terminate the original interrogation, resume questioning after the passage of a significant period of time, and give the suspect a fresh set of warnings at the outset of the second session. Whether *Mosley* requires more is a matter of dispute.

The Court has read "custody" or "*custodial* interrogation" rather narrowly. *Oregon v. Mathiason* (1977) (p. 586 infra) and *California v. Beheler* (1983) (p. 587 infra) illustrate that even *police station* questioning designed to produce incriminating statements is not necessarily "custodial interrogation." The result in *Mathiason* is more easily defensible because the suspect went down to the station house on his own after an officer had requested that he meet him there at a convenient time and he had agreed to do so. In *Beheler,* however, the suspect went to the station house in the company of the police. (He was said to have "voluntarily agreed" to accompany the police.)

In *Brown v. Illinois* (1975) (Ch. 11, § 3), the Court declined an invitation to do serious damage to the Fourth Amendment by making the *Miranda* warnings, in effect, a "cure-all." The Court rejected the contention that the giving of the warnings should purge the taint of any preceding illegal arrest—a view that would have permitted the admissibility at trial of any resulting incriminating statements to be considered without regard to the illegal arrest and thus would have encouraged such arrests.[b]

In the early 1980's *Miranda* seemed to enjoy a "second honeymoon." Considering the alternatives (e.g., a mechanical approach to "interrogation," one limited to situations where the police directly address a suspect), the Court gave the key term "interrogation" a fairly generous reading in *Rhode Island v. Innis* (1980) (p. 588 infra). Although the *Innis* case itself in-

a. More recently, the Court held that a defendant's prior silence could be used to impeach him when he testified in his own defense, *Jenkins v. Anderson* (1980) (Ch. 11, § 4), and that even a defendant's *post*arrest silence (so long as he was not given the *Miranda* warnings) could be used for impeachment purposes, *Fletcher v. Weir* (1982) (Ch. 11, § 4). Both *Jenkins* and *Weir* distinguished *Doyle v. Ohio* (1976) (Ch. 11, § 4), which deemed it a violation of due process to use a defendant's silence for impeachment purposes when the defendant remained silent *after* being given *Miranda* warnings.

b. *Brown* was reaffirmed and fortified in *Dunaway v. New York* (1979) and *Taylor v. Alabama* (1982), both discussed in Ch. 11, § 3.

volved police "speech," the Court's definition of "interrogation" embraces interrogation techniques that do not. The following year, in *Edwards v. Arizona* (1981) (p. 613 infra), the Court reinvigorated *Miranda* in an important respect. In effect, it added a "bright line" test to the "bright line" *Miranda* rules. Sharply distinguishing *Mosley*, the *Edwards* Court held that when a suspect asserts his right to counsel (as opposed to his right to remain silent), the police *cannot* "try again." Under these circumstances, a suspect cannot be questioned anew "*until* counsel has been made available to him, *unless* [he] himself *initiates* further communication, exchanges or conversations with the police" (emphasis added).[c]

But then, as discussed earlier, Justice Rehnquist's way of thinking about *Miranda*, which had first surfaced in *Michigan v. Tucker* (1974), reappeared—first in *New York v. Quarles* (1984) and then, more prominently, in Justice O'Connor's opinion for the Court in *Oregon v. Elstad* (1985). This left defenders of *Miranda* with the distinct feeling that "the honeymoon was over."

MORE ON THE MEANING *OF MIRANDA*

1. *Is there a basic ambiguity in the Miranda opinion with respect to waiver?* Reconsider Justice Stewart's question during the *Miranda* oral arguments, p. 540 supra: "[If a person possesses important constitutional rights when taken into custody], doesn't he need a lawyer before he can waive them?" Consider Commentary to *Model Pre-Arraignment Code* (Study Draft No. 1, 1968) at 39–40: [If, as the *Miranda* Court maintains, one's choice] to cooperate with the police cannot be voluntary if one is confronted with it by the police without the guidance of counsel, how can the choice to dispense with counsel be voluntary in the same circumstances? And won't it be precisely the persons who are most likely to be 'compelled' to cooperate by the subtle coercion of custody who will be 'compelled' by the same subtle coercion to waive the right to counsel itself? Thus if this tendency of the opinion is extrapolated to its extreme, does it not suggest that waiver of counsel by one in police custody should not be permitted at all?" See also remarks of Professor Louis Schwartz and Paul Bator in *Criminal Justice in the Mid-Sixties: Escobedo Revisited*, 42 F.R.D. 463, 469, 472 (1967); Kamisar, *Police Interrogation and Confessions: Essays in Law and Policy* 49 n. 11 (1980) (hereinafter referred to as Kamisar essays).

2. *Can a waiver in police custody which is a preliminary to the making of incriminating statements ever really be an "intelligent" one?* No, maintains Kuh, *Some Views on Miranda v. Arizona*, 35 Fordham L.Rev. 233, 234–35 (1966). Adds Kuh: "Had [the] Supreme Court recognized what I think is clear—at least the improbability, if not the impossibility, of an intelligent waiver of the Fifth Amendment privilege—the Justices might have squarely wrestled with the issue and said: 'Confessions are *no longer usable* in our adversary system.' I think this would have resulted in a much more adverse public reaction, but I also believe that, had the Supreme Court done this, it would have been intellectually honest, and we would have had clarity."

Assuming arguendo that a guilty person can only "hurt himself" by talking to the police, is the waiver of his rights nevertheless "intelligent" *within the meaning* of *Miranda* so long as he understands that he has the right to remain silent and thereby to avoid the risk of self-incrimination? Consider *State v. McKnight*, 243 A.2d 240 (N.J.1968), per Weintraub, C.J.: "[I]f a defendant was given the *Miranda* warnings, if the coercion of custodial interrogation was thus dissipated, his 'waiver' was no less 'voluntary' and 'knowing' and 'in-

c. But *Oregon v. Bradshaw* (1983) (p. 617 infra) may have sapped *Edwards* of a good deal of its vitality.

telligent' because he misconceived the inculpatory thrust of the facts he admitted, or because he thought what he said could not be used because it was only oral (or because he had his fingers crossed) or because he could well have used a lawyer. A man need not have the understanding of a lawyer to waive one. * * * [When] the coercion of custodial interrogation has been dispelled by the *Miranda* warnings * * * the essential fact remains that the defendant understood he had the right to remain silent and thereby to avoid the risk of self-incrimination. That is what the Fifth Amendment privilege is about."

See also *Collins v. Brierly,* 492 F.2d 735 (3d Cir.1974) (en banc): "*Miranda* speaks of 'intelligent' waiver [in the sense] that the individual must know of his available options before deciding what he thinks best suits his particular situation. In this context intelligences is not equated with wisdom."

3. *Adequacy of warnings.* Alleged misleading or ambiguous advice with respect to the right to the presence of an attorney, especially assigned counsel, *before or during* police questioning constitutes the basis for the most frequent challenge to the adequacy of the warnings. Consider *CALIFORNIA v. PRYSOCK,* 453 U.S. 355, 101 S.Ct. 2806, 69 L.Ed.2d 696 (1981) (per curiam). A police sergeant told a juvenile suspect, inter alia, that "you have the right to talk to a lawyer before you are questioned, have him present with you while you are being questioned, and all during the questioning" and that "[you] have the right to have a lawyer appointed to represent you at no cost to yourself." The state court excluded the resulting confession, concluding that "the minor was not given the crucial information that the services of the free attorney were available *prior to the impending questioning.*" The Supreme Court summarily reversed: "This Court has never indicated that the 'rigidity' of *Miranda* extends to the precise formulation of the warnings given a criminal defendant. * * * Quite the contrary, *Miranda* itself indicates that no talismanic incantation was required to satisfy its strictures. * * * [The challenged] warnings conveyed to respondent his right to have a lawyer appointed if he could not afford one prior to and during interrogation."

STEVENS, J. joined by Brennan and Marshall, JJ., dissented: "The warning recited by the police sergeant is sufficiently ambiguous on its face to provide adequate support for the California court's finding. That court's conclusion is at least reasonable, and is clearly not so patently erroneous as to warrant summary reversal. * * * Because lawyers are normally 'appointed' by judges, and not by law enforcement officers, the reference to appointed counsel could reasonably have been understood to refer to *trial* counsel." (Emphasis added.)

United States v. Contreras, 667 F.2d 976 (11th Cir.1981), relied on *Prysock* to uphold a *Miranda* warning which stated in part: "You have the right to consult *your attorney* before making any statement or answering any question, and you can have *your attorney* present while we interrogate you. [Emphasis added.] If you want an attorney but cannot pay for one on your own, the *United States Magistrate* in this city or *in the Federal Court* will assign you an attorney free of charge." [Emphasis added.]

Are these warnings significantly more "deficient" than the warnings sustained in *Prysock*? Why shouldn't the police be required to phrase the warnings as simply and directly as possible, e.g., "If you cannot afford to pay for a lawyer but want one, we shall see that you are provided one (or given one) free of charge before we ask you any questions." Do *Prysock* and *Contreras* invite the police to "play a game" whose object is to see how far the police may depart from the standard *Miranda* warning and still "get away with it"?

4. *Need for police admonitions in addition to the four Miranda warnings.*

(a) *The right to cut off questioning (the "fifth warning").* At various places, *Miranda* admonishes *police interrogators* that "[o]pportunity to exercise these rights must be afforded to [a suspect] *throughout* the interrogation" (emphasis added); that a suspect may cut off questioning "at any time prior to *or during* questioning" (emphasis added); and that "[t]he mere fact that [a suspect] may have answered some questions or volunteered some statements on his own *does not deprive him of the right to refrain from answering any further inquiries* until he has consulted with an attorney and thereafter consents to be questioned" (emphasis added). But "[n]owhere in the Court's opinion is there to be found a directive to the police that this right had to be incorporated as a warning to the suspect himself. * * * Since the fifth warning was not required it should be eliminated, unless a state * * * specifically requires it." Inbau, Reid & Buckley, *Criminal Interrogation and Confessions* 221–22 (3d ed. 1986). Do you agree? For many years the U.S. Drug Enforcement Administration directed its agents to advise suspects that they could cut off further questioning, but it revised its policy regarding *Miranda* in 1984, eliminating the "fifth warning" as a requirement. See id. at 222.

(b) *The consequences of silence.* If, as *Miranda* points out, many suspects will assume that "silence in the face of accusation is itself damning and will bode ill when presented to a jury" (text at fn. 37), should the suspect be explicitly advised not only that any statement he makes may be used against him but that his silence may *not* be used against him? Isn't a suspect likely to ask himself most urgently: "How do I get out of this mess and avoid looking guilty?" Absent assurance on this point, are many suspects likely to stand by their *Miranda* rights? An interrogator can truthfully tell a suspect that once the police advise him of his right to remain silent the prosecution may not comment at trial on his reliance on that right, but can he truthfully tell him that his silence will not be used against him *in any way?* For example, won't the suspect's silence affect the decision to prosecute? See Elsen & Rosett, *Protections for the Suspect under Miranda v. Arizona,* 67 Colum.L.Rev. 645, 654–55 (1967).

(c) *Nature and seriousness of crime.* Must the police give a suspect notice of the charge which will be filed against him or, if such information is not known, at least inform him of the nature and seriousness of the crime they are investigating? (The problem commonly arises when the police fail to inform a suspect that the victim of his alleged assault has died and thus the suspect is now facing or likely to face murder or manslaughter charges). Most courts have not required a warning about the nature of the crime or the penalty it carries. See, e.g., *Collins v. Brierly,* Note 2 supra. But both *Unif.R.Crim.* P. 241 and *Model Pre-Arraignment Code* § 130.1(2) provide that a suspect shall be informed of the offense for which he has been arrested. See also W. White, *Police Trickery in Inducing Confessions,* 127 U.Pa.L.Rev. 581, 613 (1979).

5. *Warnings at points other than custodial interrogation: arrest, removal from scene, arrival at police station.* Recall the comment of Justice White in his *Miranda* dissent: "[Although the majority considers custodial interrogation] inherently coercive, it says that the spontaneous product of the coercion of arrest and detention is still to be deemed voluntary. [A suspect] may blurt out [an admissible] confession despite the fact that he is alone and in custody, without any showing that he had any notion of his right to remain silent or of the consequences of his admission." Is this a significant weakness in the *Miranda* protections? In order to neutralize the confusion and pressures generated by an arrest, removal from the scene of arrest, and transportation to a police station, should a suspect be given certain advice at these stages whether or not any questioning is attempted? Aside from *Miranda* warnings, should he

be told, for example, where he is being taken, how long the police can hold him and with whom he will be able to communicate when he arrives? Consider Rules 211–212 and 241 of the *Uniform Rules;* §§ 120.8, 130.1 of the *Model Code.*

6. *"Custody" vs. "focus."* After defining "custodial interrogation" in the text, the *Miranda* Court, as one commentator put it, Graham, *What Is "Custodial Interrogation"?,* 14 U.C.L.A.L.Rev. 59, 114 (1966), dropped an "obfuscating footnote [4]": "This is what we meant in *Escobedo* when we spoke of an investigation which has focused on an accused." This footnote led some to think that "custody" and "focus" were alternative grounds for requiring the warnings, but these are different events and they have very different consequences.[a] The likely explanation for footnote 4 was the *Miranda* Court's understandable effort to maintain some continuity with a recent precedent. Despite that footnote, however, *Miranda* actually marked a fresh start in describing the circumstances under which constitutional protections first come into play. See Kamisar, *"Custodial Interrogation" within the Meaning of Miranda,* in *Criminal Law and the Constitution* 335, 338–51 (1968); Smith, *The Threshold Question in Applying Miranda,* 25 S.Car.L.Rev. 699, 707–10 (1974); Stone, *The Miranda Doctrine in the Burger Court,* 1977 Sup.Ct.Rev. 99, 149.

The "focus" test, as it had generally been understood at the time of *Escobedo* was expressly rejected in BECKWITH v. UNITED STATES, 425 U.S. 341, 96 S.Ct. 1612, 48 L.Ed.2d 1 (1976). Agents of the Intelligence Division of the IRS did not arrest petitioner, but met with him in a private home where he occasionally stayed. Petitioner argued that the "interview," which produced incriminating statements, should have been preceded by full *Miranda* warnings (instead of the modified *Miranda* warning which petitioner received) because the taxpayer is clearly the "focus" of a criminal investigation when a case is assigned to the Intelligence Division and such a confrontation "places the taxpayer under 'psychological restraints' which are the functional, and therefore, the legal equivalent of custody." The Court per BURGER, C.J., was "not impressed with this argument in the abstract nor as applied to the particular facts of [petitioner's] interrogation":

"An interview with government agents in a situation such as [this one] simply does not present the elements which the *Miranda* Court found so inherently coercive as to require its holding. Although the 'focus' of an investigation may indeed have been on [petitioner] at the time of the interview in the sense that it was his tax liability which was under scrutiny, he hardly found himself in the custodial situation described by the *Miranda* Court as the basis for its holding. *Miranda* specifically defined 'focus,' for its purposes, as 'questioning initiated by law enforcement officers *after* a person has been taken into custody or otherwise deprived of his freedom of action in any significant way.' "[b]

7. *What constitutes "custody" or "custodial interrogation"?* According to Israel, *Criminal Procedure, the Burger Court and the Legacy of the Warren Court,* 75 Mich.L.Rev. 1320, 1383–84 (1977), "difficulties [with

a. *Hoffa v. United States,* p. 459 supra, emphasized, albeit not in a *Miranda* context, that "there is no constitutinal right to be arrested" and that the police "are under no constitutional duty to call a halt to a criminal investigation the moment they have the minimum evidence to establish probable cause."

b. See also Chief Justice Burger's plurality opinion in *United States v. Mandujano,* p. 771 infra, rejecting the argument that a "putative" or "virtual" defendant called before the grand jury is entitled to full *Miranda* warnings and stressing that the *Miranda* warnings "were aimed at the evils seen by the Court as endemic to police interrogation of a person in custody. [*Miranda*] recognized that many official investigations, such as grand jury questioning, take place in a setting wholly different from custodial police interrogation. * * * To extend [*Miranda*] concepts to questioning before a grand jury inquiring into criminal activity under the guidance of a judge is an extravagant expansion [of that case]." But see Justice Brennan's concurring opinion in *Mandujano,* p. 772 infra.

Miranda] have arisen primarily in situations involving questioning 'on the street.' [P]olice can easily identify what constitutes 'custodial interrogation' where that concept is limited to questioning at the police station or a similar setting." In the main, the concept has been so limited. (Indeed, as discussed below, the Court has made it plain that *Miranda* may not apply even when police questioning *does* take place in the station house.)

The great majority of lower courts, often relying on language in *Miranda* that "general-on-the-scene questioning * * * is not affected by our holding," have concluded that absent special circumstances (such as arresting a suspect at gunpoint or forcibly subduing him),[c] police questioning "on the street," in a public place or in a person's home or office is not "custodial." See LaFave & Israel, § 6.6 (e), (f); cf. *Schneckloth v. Bustamonte* (p. 408 supra) (warning requirement need not

c. See *Orozco v. Texas,* 394 U.S. 324, 89 S.Ct. 1095, 22 L.Ed.2d 311 (1969) (applying *Miranda* to a situation where defendant was questioned in his bedroom by four police officers at 4:00 a.m., circumstances that produced a "potentiality for compulsion" equivalent to police station interrogation); *New York v. Quarles* (1984) (p. 599 infra) (defendant in "custody" when questioned in a supermarket minutes after arrested at gunpoint, surrounded by four officers, "frisked" and handcuffed, but "public safety" exception to *Miranda* applied).

The "custodial interrogation" issue arose in a unique setting in *United States v. Mesa,* 638 F.2d 582 (3d Cir.1980). After shooting and wounding both his wife and daughter, Mesa barricaded himself in a motel room. FBI agents cleared the area and repeatedly called to him, through a bullhorn, to surrender. Mesa did not respond. Believing that Mesa was armed (he was) and not knowing whether he had hostages (he did not), the FBI brought in a "hostage negotiator." Mesa agreed to take a mobile phone into his room. Before Mesa finally surrendered peacefully, the negotiator and Mesa conversed over the mobile phone for three and a half hours. The conversation consisted mainly of long narrative monologues by Mesa, but in the course of his exchange of remarks with the negotiator Mesa did make some incriminating statements about the shootings. At no time was he given the *Miranda* warnings. A 2–1 majority of the Third Circuit held that Mesa's statements were admissible, but because one judge decided the case solely on the ground that the exchange between Mesa and the negotiator did not constitute "interrogation" (see p. 596 infra), there was no majority opinion on the "custody" issue.

Maintaining that *Miranda's* description of the custodial setting "demonstrates that, at a minimum, the police must have immediate control over the suspect," Chief Judge Seitz concluded that Mesa had not been subjected to *custodial* interrogation: "Mesa successfully had barricaded himself [in] such a way that he prevented [the police] from exercising immediate control over his actions. They could not compel [him] even to listen to any questions they might want to ask, much less subject him to the interviewing techniques or 'tricks' that concerned the *Miranda* Court. They had no power to handcuff him or [otherwise] confine him in such a manner that he had no choice but to listen. * * * Furthermore, implicit in [*Miranda*] is the notion that the police are in a position to give a suspect his warnings. [But here] no one would suggest that [the negotiator] should have given Mesa [the warnings]. [*Miranda*] should not be expanded to encompass the present situation where the giving of warnings could have disastrous effects on the suspect and perhaps on others in the vicinity."

Dissenting Judge Weiner appraised the situation quite differently: "Mesa was isolated in his room and in communication only with law enforcement officers. * * * In a very real sense, therefore, he was under the direct and immediate control of the authorities and was effectively being restrained by them in his freedom of movement. [He] could have left the room in only one of three possible ways: dead, injured and under arrest, or uninjured and under arrest. It is thus of little import that he was not actually placed under arrest. * * * [Although a person barricaded in a motel room with a gun retains some ability to 'call the shots,' the overall 'balance of power' was with the authorities surrounding the motel, who were clearly in command of the situation. * * * The mere ability to terminate [police questioning] does not abrogate one's rights under the Fifth Amendment and the *Miranda* rule; rather it is the need to assure that those who in fact possess Fifth Amendment rights are actually informed of their rights and ability to exercise them that gives rise to the required [warnings]."

Did the judges who addressed the "custody" issue in *Mesa* make the "logical error" of assuming that exclusion of the incriminating statements would somehow *require* the police to give *Miranda* warnings in such situations? Is the best resolution of "standoff situations" for the police "simply [to] decide, as they probably did here, that it [is] better to withhold the *Miranda* warnings and do without the evidence obtained during the conversation"? See Gibbons, J., dissenting from the denial of a petition for rehearing en banc in *Mesa.* See also Note, 91 Yale L.J. 344 (1981).

be imposed on "normal consent searches" because they occur on highways, homes or offices and "under informal and unstructured conditions" "immeasurably far removed from 'custodial interrogations.' ") [d]

BERKEMER v. McCARTY, 468 U.S. 420, 104 S.Ct. 3138, 82 L.Ed.2d 317 (1984) (also discussed at p. 625 infra), per MARSHALL, J., held that "roadside questioning" of a motorist detained pursuant to a traffic stop does not constitute "custodial interrogation" for *Miranda* purposes and made plain that an officer who stops a person on the street to "investigate the circumstances that provoke suspicion" is not subject to the dictates of *Miranda.*

The case arose as follows: after observing respondent McCarty's car weaving in and out of a highway lane, Trooper Williams forced him to stop and asked him to get out of the car. Noticing that McCarty had difficulty standing, the officer concluded that he would be charged with a traffic offense and not allowed to leave the scene. But the officer did not tell McCarty this. When asked to perform a field sobriety test, commonly known as a "balancing test," McCarty could not do so without falling. The officer then asked McCarty whether he had been using intoxicants. McCarty replied that he had consumed two beers and smoked marijuana a short time before. Moreover, his speech was slurred. The officer then formally arrested McCarty and drove him to a county jail where questioning resumed and McCarty made more incriminating statements. At no point in this sequence of events did Williams or anyone else give McCarty the *Miranda* warnings. McCarty's statements were admitted into evidence and he was convicted of operating a motor vehicle while under the influence of alcohol and/or drugs, a first-degree misdemeanor under Ohio law. On federal habeas corpus, the Supreme Court concluded, without a dissent, that, although McCarty had been "seized" within the meaning of the Fourth Amendment when the police had stopped his car and detained him, he had not been taken into "custody" for *Miranda* purposes until Williams had formally arrested him. Thus the statements McCarty made prior to that point were admissible against him:

"Two features of an ordinary traffic stop mitigate the danger that a person questioned will be induced 'to speak where he would not otherwise do so freely,' *Miranda.* First, detention of a motorist pursuant to a traffic stop is presumptively temporary and brief. The vast majority of roadside detentions last only a few minutes. A motorist's expectations, when he sees a

d. Consider *Minnesota v. Murphy,* 465 U.S. 420, 104 S.Ct. 1136, 79 L.Ed. 409 (1984). Murphy, a probationer, arranged to meet with his probation officer in her office as she had requested. He then admitted, in response to her questioning, that he had committed a rape and a murder a number of years earlier. Although the terms of his probation required Murphy to report to his probation officer periodically and to respond truthfully to all her questions, and although the officer had substantial reason to believe that Murphy's answers to her questions were likely to be incriminating, a 6–3 majority, per White, J., concluded that Murphy could not claim the "in custody" exception to the general rule that the privilege against self-incrimination is not self-executing:

"Custodial arrest is said to convey to the suspect a message that he has no choice but to submit to the officers' will and to confess. It is unlikely that a probation interview, arranged by appointment at a mutually convenient time, would give rise to a similar impression. Moreover, custodial arrest thrusts an individual [into] 'an interrogation environment * * * created for no purpose other than to subjugate the individual to the will of his examiner.' Many of the psychological ploys discussed in *Miranda* capitalize on the suspect's unfamiliarity with the officers and the environment. Murphy's regular meetings with his probation officer should have served to familiarize him with her and her office and to insulate him from psychological intimidation that might overbear his desire to claim the privilege. Finally, the coercion inherent in custodial interrogation derives in large measure from an interrogator's insinuations that the interrogation will continue until a confession is obtained. [Since] Murphy was not physically restrained and could have left the office, any compulsion he might have felt from the possibility that terminating the meeting would have led to revocation of probation was not comparable to the pressure on a suspect who is painfully aware that he literally cannot escape a persistent custodial interrogator."

policeman's light flashing behind him, are that he will be obliged to spend a short period of time answering questions and waiting while the officer checks his license and registration, that he may then be given a citation, but that in the end he most likely will be allowed to continue on his way. In this respect, questioning incident to an ordinary traffic stop is quite different from stationhouse interrogation, which frequently is prolonged, and in which the detainee often is aware that questioning will continue until he provides his interrogators the answers they seek.

"Second, circumstances associated with the typical traffic stop are not such that the motorist feels completely at the mercy of the police. To be sure, the aura of authority surrounding an armed, uniformed officer and the knowledge that the officer has some discretion in deciding whether to issue a citation, in combination, exert some pressure on the detainee to respond to questions. But other aspects of the situation substantially offset these forces. Perhaps most importantly, the typical traffic stop is public, at least to some degree. [This] exposure to public view both reduces the ability of an unscrupulous policeman to use illegitimate means to elicit self-incriminating statements and diminishes the motorist's fear that, if he does not cooperate, he will be subjected to abuse. The fact that the detained motorist typically is confronted by only one or at most two policemen further mutes his sense of vulnerability. In short, the atmosphere surrounding an ordinary traffic stop is substantially less 'police dominated' than that surrounding the kinds of interrogation at issue in *Miranda* itself and in the subsequent cases in which we have applied *Miranda*.

"In both of these respects, the usual traffic stop is more analogous to a so-called '*Terry* stop' than to a formal arrest. Under the Fourth Amendment, we have held, a policeman who lacks probable cause but whose 'observations lead him reasonably to suspect' that a particular person has committed, is committing, or is about to commit a crime, may detain that person briefly in order to 'investigate the circumstances that provoke suspicion.' * * * Typically, this means that the officer may ask the detainee a moderate number of questions to determine his identity and to try to obtain information confirming or dispelling the officer's suspicions. But the detainee is not obliged to respond. And, unless the detainee's answers provide the officer with probable cause to arrest him, he must then be released. The comparatively nonthreatening character of detentions of this sort explains the absence of any suggestion in our opinions that *Terry* stops are subject to the dictates of *Miranda*. The similarly noncoercive aspect of ordinary traffic stops prompts us to hold that persons temporarily detained pursuant to such stops are not 'in custody' for the purposes of *Miranda*. * * *

"Turning to the case before us, we find nothing in the record that indicates that respondent should have been given *Miranda* warnings at any point prior to the time Trooper Williams placed him under arrest. At no point [during the short period of time between the stop and the formal arrest] was respondent informed that his detention would not be temporary. Although Trooper Williams apparently decided as soon as respondent stepped out of his car that respondent would be taken into custody and charged with a traffic offense, Williams never communicated his intention to respondent. A policeman's unarticulated plan has no bearing on the question whether a suspect was 'in custody' at a particular time; the only relevant inquiry is how a reasonable man in the suspect's position would have understood his situation." [e]

e. Prior to *Berkemer v. McCarty,* it was unclear what test should apply in determining when questioning becomes "custodial": (a) the *subjective intention* of the questioning officer to take the suspect into custody; (b) the *subjective belief* of the suspect that he was in custody; or (c)

The *Miranda* warnings are not required, the Court made plain in OREGON v. MATHIASON, 429 U.S. 492, 97 S.Ct. 711, 50 L.Ed.2d 714 (1977) (per curiam), "simply because the questioning takes place in the station house." About a month after a burglary, defendant, a parolee and a suspect in the burglary, agreed over the phone to meet with a police officer at a convenient time and place (the state patrol office only two blocks from defendant's apartment). Defendant went to the patrol office on his own. When he arrived the officer told him he was not under arrest. The officer then said he wanted to talk to defendant about a burglary and that his truthfulness might be considered by the prosecutor or judge. A few minutes later, when the officer stated his belief that defendant was involved in the burglary and told him that his fingerprints had been found at the scene (which was not true), defendant confessed. The Court held that defendant was not being subjected to "custodial interrogation" at the time he confessed:

"[T]here is no indication that the questioning took place in a context where respondent's freedom to depart was restricted in any way. He came voluntarily to the police station where he was immediately informed that he was not under arrest. [He left] the police station without hindrance.[f]

" * * * Any interview of one suspected of a crime by a police officer will have coercive effects to it, simply by virtue of the fact that the police officer is part of a law enforcement system which may ultimately cause the suspect to be charged with a crime. But police officers are not required to administer *Miranda* warnings to everyone whom they question. Nor is the requirement of warnings to be imposed simply because the questioning takes place in the station house, or because the questioned person is one whom the police suspect. *Miranda* warnings are required only where there has been such a restriction on a person's freedom as to render him 'in custody.' It was *that* sort of coercive environment to which *Miranda* by its terms was made applicable, and to which it is limited."

"At the very least," observed dissenting Justice MARSHALL, if Mathiason "entertained an objectively reasonable belief that he was not free to leave during the questioning, then he was 'deprived of his freedom of action in a significant way.' Plainly, [he] could have so believed, after being told by the police that they thought he was involved in a burglary and that his fingerprints had been found at the scene."

"More fundamentally," maintained Marshall, "even if [Mathiason] were not in custody, the coercive elements in the instant case were so pervasive as to require *Miranda*-type warnings. Respondent was interrogated in 'privacy' and in 'unfamiliar surroundings,' factors on which *Miranda* places great stress." [g]

whether *a reasonable person* in the suspect's situation would believe he was in custody. Some language in *Orozco*, fn. c supra, and in *Oregon v. Mathiason*, this Note infra, indicated that the Court might have been applying an intent-of-the-officer approach.

The objective standard expressly adopted in *McCarty* is the approach that had been taken by most of the lower courts. They regarded this test as the most sensible and the most consistent with *Miranda's* underlying concerns. It avoids reliance on self-serving statements by the police or the suspect, avoids the need to determine the officer's state of mind, and frees the police of responsibility for the idiosyncracies of various suspects. See Judge Friendly's much-quoted opinion in *United States v. Hall*, 421 F.2d 540 (2d Cir.1969). See also the discussion in *Hunter v. State*, 590 P.2d 888 (Alaska 1979).

f. *After* defendant's initial confession, the officer advised him of his rights and took a taped confession. Defendant was then released to go about his job and return to his family until the prosecutor decided how to treat the case. But why is it significant, or even relevant, that *after* he confessed defendant was allowed to leave? Was the Court applying the "subjective intent of the officer" approach to "custody" in this case? Cf. *Berkemer v. McCarty*, supra.

g. Stevens, J., dissented from the Court's summary disposition, believing the issues presented too important for the case to be so decided. "Of particular importance is the fact that respondent was on parole at the time of his interrogation."

If the so-called "invitation" to come to the police station involves doing so *in the company of the police,* a finding of "custody" is more likely. *Dunaway v. New York* (1979) (p. 385 supra), although not involving a *Miranda* issue is illustrative. Rejecting the contention of dissenting Justice Rehnquist, joined by Burger, C.J., that petitioner had "voluntarily accompanied the police to the station to answer their questions," the Court per Brennan, J., concluded that petitioner's detention "was in important respects indistinguishable from a traditional arrest":

"[Petitioner] was taken from a neighbor's home to a police car, transported to a police station, and placed in an interrogation room. He was never informed that he was 'free to go'; indeed, he would have been physically restrained if he had refused to accompany the officers * * *. The mere fact that he was not told he was under arrest, was not 'booked,' and would not have an arrest record if the interrogation had proved fruitless, while not insignificant for all purposes, obviously do not make petitioner's seizure ['custody' for *Miranda* purposes?] even roughly analogous to the narrowly defined intrusions involved in *Terry* and its progeny."

After *Dunaway,* there was some reason to think that *Mathiason* might be limited to situations where suspects went to the station house *unaccompanied* by police officers. But CALIFORNIA v. BEHELER, 463 U.S. 1121, 103 S.Ct. 3517, 77 L.Ed.2d 1275 (1983) (per curiam) made it plain that *Mathiason* could not be read that narrowly. Some hours after the murder weapon (which defendant claimed others had hidden) was found in his backyard, defendant, as the Court described it, "voluntarily agreed to accompany police to the station house, although the police specifically told [him] that he was not under arrest." At the station house, Beheler agreed to talk about the murder, but the police did not advise him of his *Miranda* rights. The incriminating statements made at the station house, ruled the Court, were not the product of "custodial interrogation." Although the California Court of Appeals had concluded that the instant case differed from *Mathiason* in a number of significant respects, the Supreme Court considered the two cases "remarkably similar":

"The court below believed incorrectly that *Mathiason* could be distinguished from the present case because [the defendant in the former case] was not questioned by police until some 25 days after the burglary [whereas] Beheler was interviewed shortly after the crime was committed [and] was emotionally distraught. In addition, the court observed that the police had a great deal more information about Beheler before their interview than did the police in *Mathiason* and that Mathiason was a parolee who knew that 'it was incumbent upon him to cooperate with police.'

"* * * That the police knew more about Beheler before his interview than they did about Mathiason before his is irrelevant [referring to *Beckwith*], especially because it was Beheler himself who had initiated the earlier communication with police. Moreover, the length of time that elapsed between the commission of the crime and the police interview has no relevance to the inquiry." [h]

Brennan, J., also dissented from the summary disposition and "would set the case for oral argument."

In a case such as *Mathiason,* should the police be required to clarify an ambiguous situation by informing a person "requested" to appear at the station house that he is not *obliged* to do so? For such a requirement, see *Model Pre-Arraignment Code* § 120.5(2).

h. Dissenting Justice Stevens, joined by Brennan and Marshall, JJ., maintained that a summary reversal on the merits was improper since state courts "are far better equipped than this Court" to make the kind of factual study that must precede a determination of whether a suspect is "in custody."

8. *What constitutes "interrogation" within the meaning of Miranda?*

RHODE ISLAND v. INNIS

446 U.S. 291, 100 S.Ct. 1682, 64 L.Ed.2d 297 (1980).

MR. JUSTICE STEWART delivered the opinion of the Court.

[*Miranda*] held that, once a defendant in custody asks to speak with a lawyer, all interrogation must cease until a lawyer is present. The issue in this case is whether the respondent was "interrogated" in violation [of *Miranda*].[a]

[At approximately 4:30 a.m., a patrolman arrested respondent, suspected of robbing a taxicab driver and murdering him with a shotgun blast to the back of the head. Respondent was unarmed. He was advised of his rights. Within minutes a sergeant (who advised respondent of his rights) and then a captain arrived at the scene of the arrest. The captain also gave respondent the *Miranda* warnings, whereupon respondent asked to speak with a lawyer. The captain then directed that respondent be placed in a police vehicle with a wire screen mesh between the front and rear seats and be driven to the police station. Three officers were assigned to accompany the arrestee. Although the record is somewhat unclear, it appears that Patrolman Williams was in the back seat with respondent and that Patrolmen Gleckman and McKenna were in front.]

While enroute to the central station, Patrolman Gleckman initiated a conversation with Patrolman McKenna concerning the missing shotgun.[1] As Patrolman Gleckman later testified:

> "A. At this point, I was talking back and forth with Patrolman McKenna stating that I frequent this area while on patrol and [that because a school for handicapped children is located nearby,] there's a lot of handicapped children running around in this area, and God forbid one of them might find a weapon with shells and they might hurt themselves."

Patrolman McKenna apparently shared his fellow officer's concern:

> "A. I more or less concurred with him [Gleckman] that it was a safety factor and that we should, you know, continue to search for the weapon and try to find it."

* * *

[Respondent then interrupted the conversation, stating that he would show the officers where the gun was located. The police vehicle then returned to the scene of the arrest where a search for the shotgun was in progress. There, the captain again advised respondent of his rights. He replied that he understood his rights, but "wanted to get the gun out of the way because of the kids in the area in the school." He then led the police to a nearby field, where he pointed out the shotgun under some rocks.

[Respondent was convicted of murder. The trial judge admitted the shotgun and testimony related to its discovery. On appeal, the Rhode Island Supreme Court concluded that the police had "interrogated" respondent without a valid waiver of his right to counsel; the conversation in the police vehicle had constituted "subtle coercion" that was the equivalent of *Miranda* "interrogation."]

a. Why is *this* the issue? Since respondent asserted his right to counsel, why isn't the issue whether the police "scrupulously honored" the exercise of that right? Cf. *Michigan v. Mosley* (p. 610 infra). Or why isn't the issue (a) whether the police impermissibly "prompted" respondent to change his mind after he invoked his right to counsel or (b) whether respondent "*himself initiate[d]* further communication, exchanges or conversations with the police," *Edwards v. Arizona* (p. 613 infra) (emphasis added), after initially invoking his right to counsel?

1. Although there was conflicting testimony about the exact seating arrangements, it is clear that everyone in the vehicle heard the conversation.

[Since the parties agree that respondent was fully informed of his *Miranda* rights, that he asserted his right to counsel, and that he was "in custody" while being driven to the police station, the issue is whether he was "interrogated" in violation of *Miranda.*] In resolving this issue, we first define the term "interrogation" under *Miranda* before turning to a consideration of the facts of this case.

[Various references throughout the *Miranda* opinion] to "questioning" might suggest that the *Miranda* rules were to apply only to those police interrogation practices that involve express questioning of a defendant while in custody.

We do not, however, construe the *Miranda* opinion so narrowly. The concern of the Court in *Miranda* was that the "interrogation environment" created by the interplay of interrogation and custody would "subjugate the individual to the will of his examiner" and thereby undermine the privilege against compulsory self-incrimination. The police practices that evoked this concern included several that did not involve express questioning [such as] the so-called "reverse lineup" in which a defendant would be identified by coached witnesses as the perpetrator of a fictitious crime, [to induce] him to confess to the actual crime of which he was suspected in order to escape the false prosecution. * * * It is clear that these techniques of persuasion, no less than express questioning, were thought, in a custodial setting, to amount to interrogation.[3]

This is not to say, however, that all statements obtained by the police after a person has been taken into custody are to be considered the product of interrogation. * * * It is clear [that the *Miranda* warnings] are required not where a suspect is simply taken into custody, but rather where a suspect in custody is subjected to interrogation. "Interrogation," as conceptualized [in *Miranda*], must reflect a measure of compulsion above and beyond that inherent in custody itself.[4]

We conclude that the *Miranda* safeguards come into play whenever a person in custody is subjected to either express questioning or its functional equivalent. That is to say, the term "interrogation" under *Miranda* refers not only to express questioning, but also to any words or actions on the part of the police (other than those normally attendant to arrest and custody)[a] that the police should know are reasonably likely to elicit an incriminating

3. To limit the ambit of *Miranda* to express questioning would "place a premium on the ingenuity of the police to devise methods of indirect interrogation, rather than to implement the plain mandate of *Miranda.*" *Commonwealth v. Hamilton,* 445 Pa. 292, 297, 285 A.2d 172, 175 [(1971)].

4. There is language in the opinion of the Rhode Island Supreme Court in this case suggesting that the definition of "interrogation" under *Miranda* is informed by this Court's decision in *Brewer v. Williams,* [p. 626 infra, reaffirming and expansively interpreting the *Massiah* doctrine]. This suggestion is erroneous. Our decision in *Brewer* rested solely on the Sixth and Fourteenth Amendment right to counsel. That right, as we held in *Massiah,* prohibits law enforcement officers from "deliberately elicit[ing]" incriminating information from a defendant in the absence of counsel after a formal charge against the defendant has been filed. Custody in such a case is not controlling; indeed, the petitioner in *Massiah* was not in custody. By contrast, the right to counsel at issue in the present case is based not on the Sixth and Fourteenth Amendments, but rather on the Fifth and Fourteenth Amendments as interpreted in the *Miranda* opinion. The definitions of "interrogation" under the Fifth and Sixth Amendments, if indeed the term "interrogation" is even apt in the Sixth Amendment context, are not necessarily interchangeable, since the policies underlying the two constitutional protections are quite distinct. See Kamisar, *Brewer v. Williams, Massiah and Miranda: What is "Interrogation"? When Does it Matter?,* 67 Geo.L.J. 1, 41–55 (1978).

a. In *South Dakota v. Neville* (1983) (p. 832 infra), the Court noted (fn. 15) that "in the context of an arrest for driving while intoxicated, a police inquiry of whether the suspect will take a blood-alcohol test is not an interrogation within the meaning of *Miranda.* " Recalling that *Innis* had excluded "police words or actions 'normally attendant to arrest and custody' " from the definition of "interrogation," the *Neville* Court added: "The police inquiry here is highly regulated by state law, and is presented in virtually the same words to all suspects. It is similar to a police request to submit to fingerprinting or photography. Respondent's choice of refusal thus enjoys no prophylactic *Miranda* protection response from the suspect.[6] The latter portion of this definition focuses primarily upon the perceptions of the suspect, rather than the intent of the police. This focus reflects the fact that the *Miranda* safeguards were designed to vest a suspect in custody with an added measure of protection against coercive police practices, without regard to objective proof of the underlying intent of the police. A practice that the police should know is reasonably likely to evoke an incriminating response from a suspect thus amounts to interrogation.[7] But, since the police surely cannot be held accountable for the unforeseeable results of their words or actions, the definition of interrogation can extend only to words or actions on the part of police officers that they *should have known* were reasonably likely to elicit an incriminating response.[8]

B

Turning to the facts of the present case, we conclude that the respondent was not "interrogated" within the meaning of *Miranda.* It is undisputed that the first prong of the definition of "interrogation" was not satisfied, for the [Gleckman-McKenna conversation] included no express questioning of the respondent. Rather, that conversation was, at least in form, nothing more than a dialogue between the two officers to which no response from the respondent was invited.

Moreover, it cannot be fairly concluded that the respondent was subjected to the "functional equivalent" of questioning. It cannot be said, in short, that [the officers] should have known that their conversation was reasonably likely to elicit an incriminating response from the respondent. There is nothing in the record to suggest that the officers were aware that the respondent was peculiarly susceptible to an appeal to his conscience concerning the safety of handicapped children [or that] the police knew that the respondent was unusually disoriented or upset at the time of his arrest.[9]

The case thus boils down to whether, in the context of a brief conversation, the officers should have known that the respondent would suddenly be moved to make a self-incriminating response. Given the fact that the entire conversation appears to have consisted of no more than a few off-hand remarks, we cannot say that the officers should have known that it was reasonably likely that Innis would so respond. This is not a case where the police carried on a lengthy harangue in the presence of the suspect. Nor does the record support the respondent's contention that, under the circumstances, the officers' comments were particularly "evocative." * * *

The Rhode Island Supreme Court erred, in short, in equating "subtle compulsion" with interrogation. That the officers' comments struck a responsive cord is readily apparent. Thus, it may be said, as the Rhode Island Supreme Court did say, that

outside the basic Fifth Amendment protection. See generally Arenella, *Schmerber and the Privilege Against Self-Incrimination: A Reappraisal,* 20 Am.Crim.L.Rev. 31, 56–58 (1982)."

6. One of the dissenting opinions seems totally to misapprehend this definition in suggesting that it "will almost certainly exclude every statement [of the police] that is not punctuated with a question mark."

7. This is not to say that the intent of the police is irrelevant, for it may well have a bearing on whether the police should have known that their words or actions were reasonably likely to evoke an incriminating response. In particular, where a police practice is designed to elicit an incriminating response from the accused, it is unlikely that the practice will not also be one which the police should have known was reasonably likely to have that effect.

8. Any knowledge the police may have had concerning the unusual susceptibility of a defendant to a particular form of persuasion might be an important factor in determining whether the police should have known that their words or actions were reasonably likely to elicit an incriminating response from the suspect.

9. The record in no way suggests that the officers' remarks were *designed* to elicit a response. It is significant that the trial judge, after hearing the officers' testimony, concluded that it was "entirely understandable that [the officers] would voice their concern [for the safety of the handicapped children] to each other."

the respondent was subjected to "subtle compulsion." But that is not the end of the inquiry. It must also be established that a suspect's incriminating response was the product of words or actions on the part of the police that they should have known were reasonably likely to elicit an incriminating response.[10] This was not established in the present case. * * *

MR. CHIEF JUSTICE BURGER, concurring in the judgment.

Since the result is not inconsistent with *Miranda*, I concur in the judgment.

The meaning of *Miranda* has become reasonably clear and law enforcement practices have adjusted to its strictures; I would neither overrule *Miranda*, disparage it, nor extend it at this late date. I fear, however, that [the Court's opinion] may introduce new elements of uncertainty; under the Court's test, a police officer, in the brief time available, apparently must evaluate the suggestibility and susceptibility of an accused. Few, if any, police officers are competent to make the kind of evaluation seemingly contemplated; even a psychiatrist asked to express an expert opinion on these aspects of a suspect in custody would very likely employ extensive questioning and observation to make the judgment now charged to police officers. * * *

MR. JUSTICE MARSHALL, with whom MR. JUSTICE BRENNAN joins, dissenting.

I am substantially in agreement with the Court's definition of "interrogation" within the meaning of *Miranda*. In my view, the *Miranda* safeguards apply whenever police conduct is intended or likely to produce a response from a suspect in custody. As I read the Court's opinion, its definition of "interrogation" for *Miranda* purposes is equivalent, for practical purposes, to my formulation, since it contemplates that "where a police practice is designed to elicit an incriminating response from the accused, it is unlikely that the practice will not also be one which the police should have known was reasonably likely to have that effect" [fn. 7]. Thus, the Court requires an objective inquiry into the likely effect of police conduct on a typical individual, taking into account any special susceptibility of the suspect to certain kinds of pressure of which the police know or have reason to know.

I am utterly at a loss, however, to understand how this objective standard as applied to the facts before us can rationally lead to the conclusion that there was no interrogation. * * *

One can scarcely imagine a stronger appeal to the conscience of a suspect—*any* suspect—than the assertion that if the weapon is not found an innocent person will be hurt or killed. And not just any innocent person, but an innocent child—a little girl—a helpless, handicapped little girl on her way to school. The notion that such an appeal could not be expected to have any effect unless the suspect were known to have some special interest in handicapped children verges on the ludicrous. As a matter of fact, the appeal to a suspect to confess for the sake of others, to "display some evidence of decency and honor," is a classic interrogation technique.

Gleckman's remarks would obviously have constituted interrogation if they had been explicitly directed to petitioner, and the result should not be different because they were nominally addressed to McKenna. This is not a case where police officers speaking among themselves are accidentally overheard by a suspect. These officers were "talking back and forth" in close quarters with the handcuffed sus-

10. By way of example, if the police had done no more than to drive past the site of the concealed weapon while taking the most direct route to the police station, and if the respondent, upon noticing for the first time the proximity of the school for handicapped children, had blurted out that he would show the officers where the gun was located, it could not seriously be argued that this "subtle compulsion" would have constituted "interrogation" within the meaning of the *Miranda* opinion.

pect,* traveling past the very place where they believed the weapon was located. They knew petitioner would hear and attend to their conversation, and they are chargeable with knowledge of and responsibility for the pressures to speak which they created.

I firmly believe that this case is simply an aberration, and that in future cases the Court will apply the standard adopted today in accordance with its plain meaning.

MR. JUSTICE STEVENS, dissenting.

* * *

As the Court recognizes, *Miranda* makes it clear that, once respondent requested an attorney, he had an absolute right to have any type of interrogation cease until an attorney was present. As it also recognizes, *Miranda* requires that the term "interrogation" be broadly construed to include "either express questioning or its functional equivalent." In my view any statement that would normally be understood by the average listener as calling for a response is the functional equivalent of a direct question, whether or not it is punctuated by a question mark. The Court, however, takes a much narrower view. It holds that police conduct is not the "functional equivalent" of direct questioning unless the police should have known that what they were saying or doing was likely to elicit an incriminating response from the suspect.[5] This holding represents a plain departure from the principles set forth in *Miranda*.

In *Miranda* the Court required the now-familiar warnings to be given to suspects prior to custodial interrogation in order to dispel the atmosphere of coercion that necessarily accompanies such interrogations. In order to perform that function effectively, the warnings must be viewed by both the police and the suspect as a correct and binding statement of their respective rights. Thus, if, after being told that he has a right to have an attorney present during interrogation, a suspect chooses to cut off questioning until counsel can be obtained, his choice must be "scrupulously honored" by the police. At the least this must mean that the police are prohibited from making deliberate attempts to elicit statements from the suspect.[7] Yet the Court is unwilling to characterize all such attempts as "interrogation," noting only that "where a police practice is designed to elicit an incriminating response from the accused, it is unlikely that the practice will not also be one which the police should have known was reasonably likely to have that effect" [fn. 7].[8]

From the suspect's point of view, the effectiveness of the warnings depends on whether it appears that the police are scrupulously honoring his rights. Apparent attempts to elicit information from a suspect after he has invoked his right to cut off questioning necessarily demean that

* [Although the record is unclear], Gleckman may even have been riding in the back seat beside [Innis].

5. * * * In limiting its test to police statements "likely to elicit an incriminating response," the Court confuses the scope of the exclusionary rule with the definition of "interrogation." Of course, any incriminating statement as defined in *Miranda*, must be excluded from evidence if it is the product of impermissible interrogation. But I fail to see how this rule helps in deciding whether a particular statement or tactic constitutes "interrogation." After all, *Miranda* protects a suspect in Innis' position not simply from interrogation that is likely to be successful, but from any interrogation at all.

7. In *Brewer* the Court applied the "deliberately elicited" standard in determining that statements were extracted from Williams in violation of his Sixth Amendment right to counsel. Although this case involves Fifth Amendment rights and the *Miranda* rules designed to safeguard those rights, respondent's invocation of his right to counsel makes the two cases indistinguishable. In both cases the police had an unqualified obligation to refrain from trying to elicit a response from the suspect in the absence of his attorney. See Kamisar, *Brewer v. Williams, Massiah,* and *Miranda: What is "Interrogation"? When Does it Matter?* 67 Geo.L.J. 1, 73 (1978).

8. This factual assumption is extremely dubious. I would assume that police often interrogate suspects without any reason to believe that their efforts are likely to be successful in the hope that a statement will nevertheless be forthcoming.

right and tend to reinstate the imbalance between police and suspect that the *Miranda* warnings are designed to correct.[9] Thus, if the rationale for requiring those warnings in the first place is to be respected, any police conduct or statements that would appear to a reasonable person in the suspect's position to call for a response must be considered "interrogation." [10]

In short, in order to give full protection to a suspect's right to be free from any interrogation at all, the definition of "interrogation" must include any police statement or conduct that has the same purpose or effect as a direct question. Statements that appear to call for a response from the suspect, as well as those that are designed to do so, should be considered interrogation. By prohibiting only those relatively few statements or actions that a police officer should know are likely to elicit an incriminating response, the Court today accords a suspect considerably less protection. Indeed, since I suppose most suspects are unlikely to incriminate themselves even when questioned directly, this new definition will almost certainly exclude every statement that is not punctuated with a question mark from the concept of "interrogation." [11]

The difference between the approach required by a faithful adherence to *Miranda* and the stinted test applied by the Court today can be illustrated by comparing three different ways in which Officer Gleckman could have communicated his fears about the possible dangers posed by the shotgun to handicapped children. He could have:

(1) directly asked Innis:

> Will you please tell me where the shotgun is so we can protect handicapped schoolchildren from danger?

(2) announced to the other officers in the wagon:

> If the man sitting in the back seat with me should decide to tell us where the gun is, we can protect handicapped children from danger.

or (3) stated to the other officers:

> It would be too bad if a little handicapped girl would pick up the gun that this man left in the area and maybe kill herself.

In my opinion, all three of these statements should be considered interrogation because all three appear to be designed to elicit a response from anyone who in fact knew where the gun was located.[12] Under the Court's test, on the other hand, the form of the statements would be critical. Statement # 3 would not be interrogation because in the Court's view there was no reason for Officer Gleckman to believe that Innis was susceptible to this type of an implied appeal; therefore, the statement would not be reasonably likely to elicit an incriminating response. Assuming that this is true, then it seems to me that the first two statements, which would be just as unlikely to elicit such a response, should also not be considered interrogation. But, because the first statement is clearly an express question, it *would* be considered interrogation under the Court's test. The

9. See White, *Police Trickery in Inducing Confessions*, 127 U.Pa.L.Rev. 581, 609–611 (1979). As Mr. Justice White pointed out in his concurring opinion in *Mosley*, when a suspect invokes his right to an attorney, he is expressing "his own view that he is not competent to deal with the authorities without legal advice." Under these circumstances, continued interrogation is likely to produce the same type of coercive atmosphere that the *Miranda* warnings are supposed to dispel.

10. I would use an objective standard both to avoid the difficulties of proof inherent in a subjective standard and to give police adequate guidance in their dealings with suspects who have requested counsel.

11. The Court's suggestion [that] I totally misapprehend the import of its definition is belied by its application of the new standard to the facts of this case.

12. See White, *Rhode Island v. Innis: The Significance of a Suspect's Assertion of His Right to Counsel*, 17 Amer.Crim.L.Rev. 53, 68 (1979), where the author proposes the same test and applies it to the facts of this case * * *.

second statement, although just as clearly a deliberate appeal to Innis to reveal the location of the gun, would presumably not be interrogation because (a) it was not in form a direct question and (b) it does not fit within the "reasonably likely to elicit an incriminating response" category that applies to indirect interrogation.

As this example illustrates, the Court's test creates an incentive for police to ignore a suspect's invocation of his rights in order to make continued attempts to extract information from him. If a suspect does not appear to be susceptible to a particular type of psychological pressure, the police are apparently free to exert that pressure on him despite his request for counsel, so long as they are careful not to punctuate their statements with question marks. And if, contrary to all reasonable expectations, the suspect makes an incriminating statement, that statement can be used against him at trial. The Court thus turns *Miranda* 's unequivocal rule against any interrogation at all into a trap in which unwary suspects may be caught by police deception.

* * * I think the Court is clearly wrong in holding, as a matter of law, that Officer Gleckman should not have realized that his statement was likely to elicit an incriminating response. The Court implicitly assumes that, at least in the absence of a lengthy harangue, a criminal suspect will not be likely to respond to indirect appeals to his humanitarian impulses. * * *

[This assumption] is directly contrary to the teachings of police interrogation manuals, which recommend appealing to a suspect's sense of morality as a standard and often successful interrogation technique. Surely the practical experience embodied in such manuals should not be ignored in a case such as this in which the record is devoid of any evidence—one way or the other—as to the susceptibility of suspects in general or of Innis in particular.

Moreover, there is evidence in the record to support the view that Officer Gleckman's statement was intended to elicit a response from Innis. Officer Gleckman, who was not regularly assigned to the caged wagon, was directed by a police captain to ride with respondent to the police station. Although there is a dispute in the testimony, it appears that Gleckman may well have been riding in the back seat with Innis. The record does not explain why, notwithstanding the fact that respondent was handcuffed, unarmed, and had offered no resistance when arrested by an officer acting alone, the captain ordered Officer Gleckman to ride with respondent. It is not inconceivable that two professionally trained police officers concluded that a few well-chosen remarks might induce respondent to disclose the whereabouts of the shotgun.[18] This conclusion becomes even more plausible in light of the emotionally charged words chosen by Officer Gleckman ("God forbid" that a "little girl" should find the gun and hurt herself).[19]

III

Under my view of the correct standard, the judgment of the Rhode Island Supreme Court should be affirmed because the statements made within Innis' hearing were as likely to elicit a response as a direct question. However, even if I were to agree with the Court's much narrower standard, I would disagree with its disposition of this particular case because the Rhode Island courts should be given an

18. Although Officer Gleckman testified that the captain told him not to interrogate, intimidate or coerce respondent on the way back, this does not rule out the possibility that either or both of them thought an indirect psychological ploy would be permissible.

19. In his article [fn. 12,] Professor White also points out that the officers were probably aware that the chances of a handicapped child finding the weapon at a time when police were not present were relatively slim. Thus, he concluded that it was unlikely that the true purpose of the conversation was to voice a genuine concern over the children's welfare. [See also Note 5, following this case].

opportunity to apply the new standard to the facts of this case.

Notes and Questions

(a) If Officer Gleckman's remarks had been explicitly directed to Innis, would they have constituted "interrogation" regardless of whether they were reasonably likely—or at all likely—to elicit an incriminating response? If so, why should words or actions that are the "functional equivalent" of express questioning have to satisfy a "reasonable likelihood" or "apparent probability" of success standard? Why isn't it sufficient that the police speech or conduct—unlike "administrative questioning" (routine questions asked of all arrestees "booked" or otherwise processed) and unlike casual conversation in no way related to the case—would normally be understood as *calling for* a response about the merits of the case or be *likely to be viewed* as *having the same force and effect* as a question about the merits of the case? See Choper, Kamisar & Tribe, *The Supreme Court: Trends and Developments, 1979–80* at 88–89, 92–95 (1981) (remarks of Professor Kamisar); W. White, *Interrogation without Questions,* 78 Mich.L.Rev. 1209, 1227–36 (1980).

(b) If Gleckman *had admitted* that his remarks to McKenna were *designed* to get Innis to make incriminating statements, would (should) they have constituted "interrogation" regardless of Gleckman's apparent likelihood of success? Why (not)? Reconsider fns. 7 & 9 to the majority opinion. But see fn. 6 to *New York v. Quarles,* p. 600 infra. Did it (should it) matter whether the "Christian burial speech" delivered in *Brewer v. Williams,* p. 626 infra, was reasonably likely to elicit an incriminating response from Williams? Why (not)?

(c) Consider White, supra, at 1231: "In order to preserve both the majority's objective focus and a close correlation between the officer's purpose and the 'reasonably likely' standard, the best reading of the *Innis* test is that it focuses on the *objective* purpose *manifested* by the police. Thus, an officer 'should know' that his speech or conduct will be 'reasonably likely to elicit an incriminating response' when he should realize that the speech or conduct will probably be viewed by the suspect as designed to achieve this purpose. To put it more precisely: if an objective observer (with the same knowledge of the suspect as the officer) would, on the sole basis of hearing the officer's remarks, infer that the remarks were designed to elicit an incriminating response, then the remarks should constitute 'interrogation.' Additional portions of the Court's opinion provide further support for this reading of the majority's test. Drawing from the language of a Pennsylvania Supreme Court case, the Court stated [fn. 3] that '[to] limit the ambit of *Miranda* to express questioning would "place a premium on the ingenuity of the police to devise methods of indirect interrogation, rather than to implement the plain mandate of *Miranda.*"' By suggesting that *Miranda*'s prohibition against 'interrogation' must not be thwarted by the 'ingenuity of the police,' the Court indicates that 'interrogation' within the meaning of *Miranda* should be defined to include at least all situations where the police are plainly seeking to elicit incriminating evidence."

(d) To what extent does the *Innis* result turn on the fact that "the officers involved were ordinary patrolmen as opposed to detectives specifically trained in the art of interrogation"? That their "only assignment" was to transport the suspect? That "indeed, they had specific instructions not to question him during the trip"? See White, at 1235 fn. 161. To what extent does the result turn on the fact that there was a *plausible basis* for believing that Gleckman's remarks were made for a purpose *other than* that of eliciting an incriminating response? See id. at 1234–35.

(e) *The import of the officers' dialogue.* By characterizing the officers' conversation as "no more than a few off-hand remarks," did the *Innis* majority "cavalierly dismiss" the import of the officers' dialogue? Consider Collins & Welsh, *Miranda's Fate in the Burger Court,* The Center Magazine, Sept./Oct. 1980, pp. 43, 44–45:

"The terms 'God forbid' and 'Gee' are not the kind of language that seasoned officers typically employ in casual conversation. But, as the leading police manuals on interrogation attest, such remarks can be an effective way to appeal to a suspect's conscience and thus weaken his resolve to assert his rights.

"In effect, the defendant was made an unwitting participant in a police-directed morality play. Innis was led to believe that his assistance in locating the murder weapon was crucial in order to prevent some handicapped child from untoward harm. That such a stratagem was allowed to succeed flies in the face of *Miranda* 's declaration that 'any evidence that an accused was threatened, tricked, or cajoled into a waiver will, of course, show that the defendant did not voluntarily waive his privilege.'

"* * * *Miranda* seeks to foster among custodial suspects the awareness that they must decide between asserting their rights to silence and to counsel or waiving their rights and admitting their guilt. This decision is exclusively the suspect's. It may not be made for him by the police, nor may the police, as in *Innis,* attempt to disguise the reality of the choice by leading the suspect to believe that the choice involves something else."

(f) *Application (or misapplication) of Innis.* Consider *Harryman v. Estelle,* 616 F.2d 870 (5th Cir.1980, en banc; 24 judges): After defendant, a burglary suspect was arrested, a search of his person turned up a condom containing a white powdered substance. At this point, without reciting the *Miranda* warnings and alleging that he acted out of shock and surprise, the officer asked, "What is this?" The defendant replied that it was heroin. Rejecting the argument that the officer's question "was not an attempt to elicit an answer of any sort, much less evidence of a crime, [but] an exclamation of surprise," the court, per Frank Johnson, J., held that *Miranda* had been violated: "The rigidity of the *Miranda* rules and the way in which they are to be applied was conceived of and continues to be recognized as the decision's greatest strength. * * * [T]he factual difficulties inherent in [an inquiry as to whether a police question was asked in an attempt to elicit incriminating statements or asked out of shock and surpise] are of the very sort [the *Miranda* Court] thought essential to avoid."

Nine judges dissented, likening the officer's question to inquiries made during booking and inventorying. Three of these judges also dissented on the ground that *Miranda* did not apply to "the excited utterance of a police officer"; "the type of interrogation forbidden by *Miranda* does not occur where [the question] does not have an investigatory purpose."

In *United States v. Mesa,* discussed at p. 583 fn. c supra, involving a lengthy conversation between a barricaded suspect and a "hostage negotiator," Judge Adams concurred in the result on the ground that "Mesa's statements were made in the course of a colloquy that is not an 'interrogation,' as that term was recently defined in *Innis* ": the conversation was "nonadversarial and noninquisitive in nature"; the negotiator "acted not as a questioner, but primarily as a listener"; and the comments interjected by the negotiator "were not designed to elicit an incriminating response, [but] calculated to convey sympathy and understanding, to indicate that [the negotiator] was still listening, and to keep Mesa from dwelling on thoughts of suicide."

But dissenting Judge Weiner maintained that the negotiator's comments were "frequently investigatory" and "appear[ed] calculated to both bring about a peaceful end to the standoff [and] to elicit incriminating statements about the shootings.

* * * [I]t seems inconceivable that [the negotiator] could not have known that the entire conversation itself, as well as the specific questions related to the shootings, would be reasonably likely to elicit an incriminating response."

For sharp disagreement over the import of *Innis,* see *United States v. Thierman,* 678 F.2d 1331 (9th Cir.1982). Thierman was arrested and brought to his apartment at 3:00 a.m., where he was advised of his rights. After being allowed to talk to his lawyer over the phone, Thierman told the police that he was not going to talk to the police until the next day. At that point, a detective left the apartment to interrogate Thierman's girlfriend, as he had threatened to do earlier. The officers who remained behind then discussed in Thierman's presence the need to contact the defendant's friends about the case and one officer stated that it was "too bad" that defendant's girlfriend had to get involved. Thierman then told the officer that he would like to talk to the detective again. When the police brought the detective back to the apartment, Thierman made incriminating statements.

Although the officer testified at the suppression hearing that the conversation about defendant's girlfriend occurred in defendant's presence, that he looked at defendant while speaking, and that he "guessed" that he was trying to get defendant to respond, a 2–1 majority, per Choy, J., held that Thierman's rights had not been violated, finding "nothing in the record to compel a finding that the police conversation was more evocative than the one in *Innis.*"

Dissenting Judge Wallace argued that the officer's admissions that "he spoke in Thierman's presence, while looking at him and intending for him to hear [and that he] intended to induce a confession from Thierman" "decisively sets this case apart from *Innis.* [There] the conversation was 'nothing more than a dialogue between the two officers to which no response [was] intended,' [and] there was no suggestion in the record that the police intended their conversation to elicit an incrimination response. Here there is."

Consider, too, *People v. Ferro,* 472 N.E.2d 13 (N.Y.1984), which grew out of the following facts: Defendant was suspected of murdering a woman in the course of a fur robbery. When advised of his rights, he invoked his right to remain silent. He was then placed in a detention cell. He asked to speak to a district attorney, but abandoned that attempt when told he first had to reveal to Detective Hudson what he wanted to talk about. Detective Hudson then left the police station and returned shortly thereafter with the stolen furs (obtained from a codefendant). Without any verbal communication with defendant, the furs "were placed right in front of the cell a foot away from [Ferro]." Ferro then implicated himself in the robbery-murder.

A 5–1 majority, per Meyer, J., held that the statements Ferro made subsequently to viewing the furs were inadmissible: "On [the aforementioned facts] objectively considered, no other conclusion is possible than that, in causing the decedent's furs to be placed where defendant could not help but see them, [Detective] Hudson should have known, in light of defendant's prior request to speak to a District Attorney, that doing so was reasonably likely to elicit [an] incriminating response."

Jasen, J., dissenting, maintained that "[t]o construe the mere placing of evidence before defendant—little more than a simple disclosure of information which might, in fact, contribute to an intelligent exercise of his judgment—as an impermissible interrogation is to attribute to that police conduct the qualities of coercion and overbearing of defendant's will which it certainly was not. Such a construction, in my view, gives a tortured and unintended interpretation to the *Miranda* safeguards and the underlying privilege against compulsory self-incrimination."[a]

Should *Ferro* have been treated as a *Mosley* case, not an *Innis* case? See *Michigan v. Mosley,* p. 610 infra. Should *Thierman* have been treated as an *Edwards* case, not an *Innis* case? See *Edwards v. Arizona,* p. 613 infra. In other words, should the question in a *Ferro* -type case be whether the police "scrupulously honored" the suspect's right to remain silent? And should the question in a *Thierman* -type case be: Did the police induce the suspect to change his mind after he asserted his right to counsel or did the suspect change his mind on his own initiative?

9. *The "jail plant" situation; "surreptitious interrogation."* Suppose a secret government agent is placed in the same cell with a defendant and induces him to discuss the crime for which he has been arrested? Does this constitute "custodial interrogation"? Confinement does increase a suspect's anxiety and make him more likely to relieve this anxiety by discussing his situation with another. See Dix, *Undercover Investigations and Police Rulemaking,* 53 Texas L.Rev. 203, 230 (1975). Moreover, unlike the *Hoffa* situation (see p. 459 supra), an incarcerated suspect's ability to select people with whom he can confide is completely within the control of the police and thus they have a "unique opportunity to exploit [his] vulnerability," W. White, *Police Trickery in Inducing Confessions,* 127 U.Pa.L.Rev. 581, 605 (1979). But consider Kamisar essays at 195–96:

"[U]nless a person *realizes* he is dealing with the police, their efforts to elicit incriminating statements from him do not constitute 'police interrogation' within the meaning of *Miranda.* * * * It is the impact on the suspect's mind of the *interplay* between police interrogation and police custody—each condition *reinforcing* the pressures and anxieties produced by the other—that, as the *Miranda* Court correctly discerned, makes 'custodial police interrogation' so devastating. [But in the 'jail plant' situation] there is no *integration* of 'custody' and 'interrogation,' no *interplay* between the two, at least none where it counts—in the suspect's mind. * * *

"One can deliberately elicit incriminating statements from a person without having him realize it—that is what happened in *Massiah.*[a] But how can one envelop someone in a 'police-dominated atmosphere' without having him realize it? * * * That is why, I submit, whatever may lurk in the heart or mind of the fellow prisoner (or apparent friend or colleague), if it is not 'custodial police interrogation' *in the eye of the beholder,* then it is not such interrogation within the meaning of *Miranda.*"

10. *"Volunteered" statements and "follow-up" questioning.* "Volunteered statements of any kind," observed the *Miranda* Court, "are not barred by the Fifth Amendment and their admissibility is not affected by our holding today." Indeed, a statement may qualify as "volunteered" even though made by one in custody (because *Miranda* deemed only custody *plus* interrogation inherently coercive) or by one who had

a. Although the *Innis* case involved police "speech," the Court's definition of "interrogation" embraces police tactics that do not. Thus, the Court seems to have repudiated the position taken by a number of courts prior to *Innis* that *confronting* a suspect with physical or documentary evidence (e.g., a ballistics report or a bank surveillance photograph) or *arranging a meeting* between an arrestee and an accomplice who has already confessed is not "interrogation" because it does not involve verbal conduct on the part of the police. For criticism of these pre-*Innis* cases, see Kamisar essays at 156–58 n. 21.

a. See especially *United States v. Henry,* p. 638 infra. The *Massiah* doctrine does prevent the government from "eliciting" or "inducing" incriminating statements from a suspect whether or not he is aware that he is dealing with a government agent (indeed, whether or not he is in custody), but *only when* "adversary judicial proceedings" have already commenced against that person, e.g., he has been indicted or has appeared before a judicial officer.

previously asserted his *Miranda* rights (because one can always change his mind).

But to what extent may the police "follow up" a volunteered statement with some questions? Should statements made in response to follow-up questions be regarded a "continuation" of the initial volunteered statement only if questions are "neutral efforts" to clarify what has already been said (e.g. "did what?" in response to "I did it") rather than attempts to enhance the defendant's guilt or raise the offense to a higher degree? For an affirmative answer, see LaFave & Israel, § 6.7(d), who add:

"The underlying rationale of *Innis* is that *Miranda* covers only police conduct likely to be coercive when coupled with defendant's custody, which cannot be said of a question that does nothing more than seek clarification of what the defendant has already volunteered. Here again, however, the *Innis* Court's unfortunate 'likely to elicit an incriminating response' language may prove a source of difficulty. If applied literally, it would seem to foreclose even a clarifying question."

11. *Questioning prompted by concern for "public safety."*

NEW YORK v. QUARLES

467 U.S. 649, 104 S.Ct. 2626, 81 L.Ed.2d 550 (1984).

[At approximately 12:30 a.m., police apprehended respondent in the rear of a supermarket. He matched the description of the man who had just raped a woman. The woman had told the police that the rapist had just entered the supermarket and that he was carrying a gun. Apparently upon seeing Officer Kraft enter the store, respondent turned and ran toward the rear. Officer Kraft pursued him with a drawn gun and, upon regaining sight of him, ordered him to stop and put his hands over his head. Although several other officers had arrived at the scene by then, Kraft was the first to reach respondent. He frisked him and discovered he was wearing an empty shoulder holster. After handcuffing him, the officer asked where the gun was. Respondent nodded in the direction of some empty cartons and responded, "the gun is over there." At that time, emphasized the New York Court of Appeals, respondent was surrounded by four officers whose guns had been returned to their holsters because, as one testified, the situation was under control.

[The gun was not visible, but Officer Kraft reached into one of the cartons and retrieved a loaded revolver. Respondent was then formally placed under arrest and advised of his *Miranda* rights. Respondent waived his rights. In response to questions, he then stated that he owned the revolver and had purchased it in Miami.

[In the subsequent prosecution of respondent for criminal possession of a weapon (the record does not reveal why the state failed to pursue the rape charge), the New York courts suppressed the statement "the gun is over there" as well as the gun itself because they had been obtained in violation of respondent's *Miranda* rights. Respondent's statements about his ownership of the gun and the place of purchase were also excluded as having been fatally tainted by the seizure of the gun and the prewarning response as to its location.]

JUSTICE REHNQUIST delivered the opinion of the Court.

* * * We conclude that under the circumstances involved in this case, overriding considerations of public safety justify the officer's failure to provide *Miranda* warnings before he asked questions devoted to locating the abandoned weapon. * * *

The Fifth Amendment itself does not prohibit all incriminating admissions; "[a]bsent some officially *coerced* self-accusation, the Fifth Amendment privilege is not violated by even the most damning admissions." *United States v. Washington* [p. 743

infra] (emphasis added). The *Miranda* Court, however, presumed that interrogation in certain custodial circumstances is inherently coercive and held that statements made under those circumstances are inadmissible unless the suspect is specifically informed of his *Miranda* rights and freely decides to forgo those rights. The prophylactic *Miranda* warnings therefore are "not themselves rights protected by the Constitution but [are] instead measures to insure that the right against compulsory self-incrimination [is] protected." *Michigan v. Tucker.* * * *

In this case we have before us no claim that respondent's statements were actually compelled by police conduct which overcame his will to resist. Thus the only issue before us is whether Officer Kraft was justified in failing to make available to respondent the procedural safeguards associated with the privilege against compulsory self-incrimination since *Miranda.*[5]

The New York Court of Appeals was undoubtedly correct in deciding that the facts of this case come within the ambit of the *Miranda* decision as we have subsequently interpreted it. * * * As the New York Court of Appeals observed, [when the questioning at issue took place] there was nothing to suggest that any of the officers were any longer concerned for their own physical safety. The New York Court of Appeals' majority declined to express an opinion as to whether there might be an exception to the *Miranda* rule if the police had been acting to protect the public, because the lower courts in New York had made no factual determination that the police had acted with that motive.

We hold that on these facts there is a "public safety" exception to the requirement that *Miranda* warnings be given before a suspect's answers may be admitted into evidence, and that the availability of that exception does not depend upon the motivation of the individual officers involved. In a kaleidoscopic situation such as the one confronting these officers, where spontaneity rather than adherence to a police manual is necessarily the order of the day, the application of the exception which we recognize today should not be made to depend on *post hoc* findings at a suppression hearing concerning the subjective motivation of the arresting officer.[6] Undoubtedly most police officers, if placed in Officer Kraft's position, would act out of a host of different, instinctive, and largely unverifiable motives—their own safety, the safety of others, and perhaps as well the desire to obtain incriminating evidence from the suspect.

Whatever the motivation of individual officers in such a situation, we do not believe that the doctrinal underpinnings of *Miranda* require that it be applied in all its rigor to a situation in which police officers ask questions reasonably prompted by a concern for the public safety. * * *

The police in this case, in the very act of apprehending a suspect, were confronted with the immediate necessity of ascertaining the whereabouts of a gun which they had every reason to believe the suspect had just removed from his empty holster and discarded in the supermarket. So long as the gun was concealed somewhere in the supermarket, with its actual whereabouts unknown, it obviously posed more

5. The dissent curiously takes us to task for "endors[ing] the introduction of coerced self-incriminating statements in criminal prosecutions" * * * Of course our decision today does nothing of the kind. * * * [R]espondent is certainly free on remand to argue that his statement was coerced under traditional due process standards. Today we merely reject the only argument that respondent has raised to support the exclusion of his statement, that the statement must be *presumed* compelled because of Officer Kraft's failure to read him his *Miranda* warnings.

6. Similar approaches have been rejected in other contexts. See *Innis* (officer's subjective intent to incriminate not determinative of whether "interrogation" occurred); *Mendenhall,* (opinion of Stewart, J.) (officer's subjective intent to detain not determinative of whether a "seizure" occurred within the meaning of the Fourth Amendment); *Robinson,* (officer's subjective fear not determinative of necessity for "search incident to arrest" exception to the Fourth Amendment warrant requirement).

than one danger to the public safety: an accomplice might make use of it, a customer or employee might later come upon it.

In such a situation, if the police are required to recite the familiar *Miranda* warnings before asking the whereabouts of the gun, suspects in Quarles' position might well be deterred from responding. Procedural safeguards which deter a suspect from responding were deemed acceptable in *Miranda* in order to protect the Fifth Amendment privilege; when the primary social cost of those added protections is the possibility of fewer convictions, the *Miranda* majority was willing to bear that cost. Here, had *Miranda* warnings deterred Quarles from responding to Officer Kraft's question about the whereabouts of the gun, the cost would have been something more than merely the failure to obtain evidence useful in convicting Quarles. Officer Kraft needed an answer to his question not simply to make his case against Quarles but to insure that further danger to the public did not result from the concealment of the gun in a public area.

We conclude that the need for answers to questions in a situation posing a threat to the public safety outweighs the need for the prophylactic rule protecting the Fifth Amendment's privilege against self-incrimination. We decline to place officers such as Officer Kraft in the untenable position of having to consider, often in a matter of seconds, whether it best serves society for them to ask the necessary questions without the *Miranda* warnings and render whatever probative evidence they uncover inadmissible, or for them to give the warnings in order to preserve the admissibility of evidence they might uncover but possibly damage or destroy their ability to obtain that evidence and neutralize the volatile situation confronting them.[7]

* * * [W]e recognize [the] importance of a workable rule "to guide police officers, who have only limited time and expertise to reflect on and balance the social and individual interests involved in the specific circumstances they confront." *Dunaway.* [But] we believe that the exception which we recognize today lessens the necessity of that on-the-scene balancing process. The exception will not be difficult for police officers to apply because in each case it will be circumscribed by the exigency which justifies it. We think police officers can and will distinguish almost instinctively between questions necessary to secure their own safety or the safety of the public and questions designed solely to elicit testimonial evidence from a suspect.

The facts of this case clearly demonstrate that distinction and an officer's ability to recognize it. Officer Kraft asked only the question necessary to locate the missing gun before advising respondent of his rights. It was only after securing the loaded revolver and giving the warnings that he continued with investigatory questions about the ownership and place of purchase of the gun. The exception which we recognize today, far from complicating the thought processes and the on-the-scene judgments of police officers, will simply free them to follow their legitimate instincts when confronting situations presenting a danger to the public safety.[8]

7. The dissent argues that a public safety exception to *Miranda* is unnecessary because in every case an officer can simply ask the necessary questions to protect himself or the public, and then the prosecution can decline to introduce any incriminating responses at a subsequent trial. But absent actual coercion by the officer, there is no constitutional imperative requiring the exclusion of the evidence that results from police inquiry of this kind; and we do not believe that the doctrinal underpinnings of *Miranda* require us to exclude the evidence, thus penalizing officers for asking the very questions which are the most crucial to their efforts to protect themselves and the public.

8. Although it involves police questions in part relating to the whereabouts of a gun, *Orozco v. Texas,* 394 U.S. 324, 89 S.Ct. 1095, 22 L.Ed.2d 311 (1969), is in no sense inconsistent with our disposition of this case. [In *Orozco,*] the questions about the gun were clearly investigatory; they did not in any way relate to an objectively reasonable need to protect the police or the public

We hold that the Court of Appeals in this case erred in excluding the statement, "the gun is over there," and the gun because of the officer's failure to read respondent his *Miranda* rights before attempting to locate the weapon. Accordingly we hold that it also erred in excluding the subsequent statements as illegal fruits of a *Miranda* violation.[9] * * *

JUSTICE O'CONNOR, concurring in part in the judgment and dissenting in part. * * *

[Justice O'Connor would suppress the respondent's initial statement, "the gun is over there"—but not the gun itself because "nothing in *Miranda* or the privilege itself requires exclusion of nontestimonial evidence derived from informal custodial interrogation." Justice O'Connor's views on why *Miranda* requires that respondent's initial statement be suppressed are set forth below. Her views on the admissibility of the gun itself and her thoughts about the statements elicited after the *Miranda* warnings were given are set forth at p. 816 infra.]

In my view, a "public safety" exception unnecessarily blurs the edges of the clear line heretofore established and makes *Miranda's* requirements more difficult to understand. In some cases, police will benefit because a reviewing court will find that an exigency excused their failure to administer the required warnings. But in other cases, police will suffer because, though they thought an exigency excused their noncompliance, a reviewing court will view the "objective" circumstances differently and require exclusion of admissions thereby obtained. The end result will be a finespun new doctrine on public safety exigencies incident to custodial interrogation, complete with the hair-splitting distinctions that currently plague our Fourth Amendment jurisprudence. * * *

The justification the Court provides for upsetting the equilibrium that has finally been achieved—that police cannot and should not balance considerations of public safety against the individual's interest in avoiding compulsory testimonial self-incrimination—really misses the critical question to be decided. *Miranda* has never been read to prohibit the police from asking questions to secure the public safety. Rather, the critical question *Miranda* addresses is who shall bear the cost of securing the public safety when such questions are asked and answered: the defendant or the State. *Miranda,* for better or worse, found the resolution of that question implicit in the prohibition against compulsory self-incrimination and placed the burden on the State. When police ask custodial questions without administering the required warnings, *Miranda* quite clearly requires that the answers received be presumed compelled and that they be excluded from evidence at trial. * * *

JUSTICE MARSHALL, with whom JUSTICE BRENNAN and JUSTICE STEVENS join, dissenting * * *.

The majority's entire analysis rests on the factual assumption that the public was at risk during Quarles' interrogation. This assumption is completely in conflict with the facts as found by New York's highest court. Before the interrogation began, Quarles had been "reduced to a condition of physical powerlessness." Contrary to the majority's speculations, Quarles was not believed to have, nor did he in fact have, an accomplice to come to his rescue. When the questioning began, the arresting

from any immediate danger associated with the weapon. In short there was no exigency requiring immediate action by the officers beyond the normal need expeditiously to solve a serious crime.

Innis also involved the whereabouts of a missing weapon, but our holding in that case depended entirely on our conclusion that no police interrogation took place so as to require consideration of the applicability of the *Miranda* prophylactic.

9. Because we hold that there is no violation of *Miranda* in this case, we have no occasion to [decide whether] the gun is admissible either because it is nontestimonial or because the police would inevitably have discovered it absent their questioning.

officers were sufficiently confident of their safety to put away their guns. * * *

The New York court's conclusion that neither Quarles nor his missing gun posed a threat to the public's safety is amply supported by the evidence presented at the suppression hearing. * * * Although the supermarket was open to the public, Quarles' arrest took place during the middle of the night when the store was apparently deserted except for the clerks at the checkout counter. The police could easily have cordoned off the store and searched for the missing gun. Had they done so, they would have found the gun forthwith. [As] the State acknowledged before the New York Court of Appeals: "After Officer Kraft had handcuffed and frisked the defendant in the supermarket, *he knew with a high degree of certainty that the defendant's gun was within the immediate vicinity of the encounter.* He undoubtedly would have searched for it in the carton a few feet away without the defendant having looked in that direction and saying that it was there." (Emphasis added.) * * *

This case is illustrative of the chaos the "public-safety" exception will unleash. The circumstances of Quarles' arrest have never been in dispute. [T]he New York Court of Appeals concluded that there was "no evidence in the record before us that there were exigent circumstances posing a risk to the public safety." Upon reviewing the same facts and hearing the same arguments, a majority of this Court has come to precisely the opposite conclusion * * *.

If after plenary review two appellate courts so fundamentally differ over the threat to public safety presented by the simple and uncontested facts of this case, one must seriously question how law enforcement officers will respond to the majority's new rule in the confusion and haste of the real world. * * * Not only will police officers have to decide whether the objective facts of an arrest justify an unconsented custodial interrogation; they will also have to remember to interrupt the interrogation and read the suspect his *Miranda* warnings once the focus of the inquiry shifts from protecting the public's safety to ascertaining the suspect's guilt. Disagreements of the scope of the "public-safety" exception and mistakes in its application are inevitable.[4] * * *

Though unfortunate, the difficulty of administering the "public-safety" exception is not the most profound flaw in the majority's decision. The majority has lost sight of the fact that *Miranda* and our earlier custodial-interrogation cases all implemented a constitutional privilege against self-incrimination. The rules established in these cases were designed to protect criminal defendants against prosecutions based on coerced self-incriminating statements. The majority today turns its back on these constitutional considerations, and invites the government to prosecute through the use of what necessarily are coerced statements.

The majority's error stems from a serious misunderstanding of *Miranda* and of the Fifth Amendment upon which that decision was based. The majority implies that *Miranda* consisted of no more than a judicial balancing act in which the benefits of "enlarged protection for the Fifth Amendment privilege" were weighed against "the cost to society in terms of fewer convictions of guilty suspects." Supposedly because the scales tipped in favor of the privilege against self-incrimination, the *Miranda* Court erected a prophylactic barrier around statements made during custodial interrogations. The ma-

4. One of the peculiarities of the majority's decision is its suggestion that police officers can "distinguish almost instinctively" questions tied to public safety and questions designed to elicit testimonial evidence. Obviously, these distinctions are extraordinarily difficult to draw. In many cases—like this one—custodial questioning may serve both purposes. It is therefore wishful thinking for the majority to suggest that the intuitions of police officers will render its decision self-executing.

jority now proposes to return to the scales of social utility to calculate whether *Miranda* 's prophylactic rule remains cost-effective when threats to public's safety are added to the balance. * * *

The majority misreads *Miranda.* Though the *Miranda* dissent prophesized dire consequences, the *Miranda* Court refused to allow such concerns to weaken the protections of the Constitution * * *.

Whether society would be better off if the police warned suspects of their rights before beginning an interrogation or whether the advantages of giving such warnings would outweigh their costs did not inform the *Miranda* decision. On the contrary, the *Miranda* Court was concerned with the proscriptions of the Fifth Amendment, and, in particular, whether the Self-Incrimination Clause permits the government to prosecute individuals based on statements made in the course of custodial interrogations. * * *

In fashioning its "public-safety" exception to *Miranda,* the majority makes no attempt to deal with the constitutional presumption established by that case. The majority does not argue that police questioning about issues of public safety is any less coercive than custodial interrogations into other matters. The majority's only contention is that police officers could more easily protect the public if *Miranda* did not apply to custodial interrogations concerning the public's safety.[7] But *Miranda* was not a decision about public safety; it was a decision about coerced confessions. Without establishing that interrogations concerning the public's safety are less likely to be coercive than other interrogations, the majority cannot endorse the "public-safety" exception and remain faithful to the logic of *Miranda.* * * *

That the application of the "public-safety" exception in this case entailed coercion is no happenstance. The majority's *ratio decidendi* is that interrogating suspects about matters of public safety *will* be coercive. In its cost-benefit analysis, the Court's strongest argument in favor of a public-safety exception to *Miranda* is that the police would be better able to protect the public's safety if they were not always required to give suspects their *Miranda* warnings. The crux of this argument is that, by deliberately withholding *Miranda* warnings, the police can get information out of suspects who would refuse to respond to police questioning were they advised of their constitutional rights. The "public-safety" exception is efficacious precisely because it permits police officers to coerce criminal defendants into making involuntary statements. * * *

[The] irony of the majority's decision is that the public's safety can be perfectly well protected without abridging the Fifth Amendment. If a bomb is about to explode or the public is otherwise imminently imperiled, the police are free to interrogate suspects without advising them of their constitutional rights. * * * If trickery is necessary to protect the public, then the police may trick a suspect into confessing. While the Fourteenth Amendment sets limits on such behavior, nothing in the Fifth Amendment or our decision in *Miranda* proscribes this sort of emergency questioning. All the Fifth Amendment

7. The majority elsewhere attempts to disguise its decision as an effort to cut back on the overbreadth of *Miranda* 's prophylactic standard. The disguise is transparent. Although *Miranda* was overbroad in that its application excludes some statements made during custodial interrogations that are not in fact coercive, the majority is not dealing with a class of cases affected by *Miranda* 's overbreadth. The majority is exempting from *Miranda* 's prophylactic rule incriminating statements that were elicited to safeguard the public's safety. As is discussed below, the majority supports the "public safety" exception because "public-safety" interrogations can be coercive. In this respect, the Court's decision differs greatly from *Michigan v. Tucker,* in which the Court sanctioned the admission of the fruits of a *Miranda* violation, but only because the violation was technical and the interrogation itself noncoercive.

forbids is the introduction of coerced statements at trial.

* * * [The] policies underlying the Fifth Amendment's privilege against self-incrimination are not diminished simply because testimony is compelled to protect the public's safety. The majority should not be permitted to elude the Amendment's absolute prohibition simply by calculating special costs that arise when the public's safety is at issue. Indeed, were constitutional adjudication always conducted in such an *ad hoc* manner, the Bill of Rights would be a most unreliable protector of individual liberties.[b]

Notes and Questions

(a) If a case like *Innis* or *Mesa* (the "hostage negotiator" case) arose today, would the courts quickly dispose of it under the "public safety" exception to *Miranda* without ever reaching the question whether the suspect had been subjected to "custodial interrogation" in violation of *Miranda*?

(b) Is the *Quarles* Court's attempt to distinguish *Orozco* (see fn. 8) convincing? In *Orozco,* the police entered a sleeping defendant's room and questioned him about a gun used in a murder several hours earlier. They had ample cause to believe that defendant was the murderer and, as it turned out, the murder weapon *was* hidden in his room. There was no need to protect *the public* from immediate danger, but why wasn't there a need to protect *the police*? Does the Court's treatment of *Orozco* mean that, at least where there is no threat to members of the public, *Quarles* only permits the police to ask about the location of a gun when they come upon the scene in "hot pursuit?"

(c) *The "rescue doctrine."* Somewhat similar to the "public safety" exception is the "rescue doctrine." Should statements obtained in violation of *Miranda* be admissible if police interrogation of a suspected kidnapper is motivated primarily by a desire to save the victim's life? Yes, answer *People v. Dean,* 114 Cal.Rptr. 555 (Cal. App.1974) and *People v. Krom,* 461 N.E.2d 276 (N.Y.1984). How can a court ever tell what the police's *primary* motivation was? Does (should) it matter?

Are there (should there be) any limits on what a police officer may do to a suspected kidnapper in order to get him to reveal the location of a kidnap victim? Cf. *Leon v. State,* 410 So.2d 201 (Fla.App. 1982), holding, over a forceful dissent, that the use of police threats and physical violence at the scene of arrest in order to ascertain the kidnap victim's whereabouts "did not constitutionally infect the later confessions." But cf. *People v. Knapp,* 441 N.E.2d 1057 (N.Y.1982), rejecting the contention that the police should be allowed to use an informant to obtain information from a person represented by counsel when the police are trying to find and possibly rescue a missing person.

12. *Meeting the "heavy burden" of demonstrating waiver: should written records and sound recordings be required?* Recall that *Miranda* states that "if the interrogation continues without the presence of an attorney, and a statement is taken, a *heavy burden* rests on the government to demonstrate that the defendant knowingly and intelligently waived his [rights]" and that "since the State is responsible for establishing the isolated circumstances under which the interrogation takes place and has the only means of making available *corroborated evidence* of warnings given during incommunicado interrogation, the burden is rightly on its shoulders." (Emphasis added). Does this language mean that, whenever feasible, law enforcement officers must record on audio or video tape the warning, any waiver and any questioning and statements made in response?

Emphasizing that sound recordings (and written records covering actions taken

b. For the portion of Justice Marshall's dissenting opinion dealing with the admissibility of the gun discovered as a result of Quarles' statement, see p. 817 infra.

with respect to each arrestee) will avoid a "swearing contest" between police and defendant and "allow the court to make its own independent interpretation, based on an accurate picture of what really happened" (Commentary), *Model Pre-Arraignment Code* § 130.4 requires sound recordings and written records. To the same effect is *Unif.R.Crim.P.* 243. A number of commentators have also underscored the need to record all police "interviews" with a suspect, whenever feasible and all warnings and "waiver transactions" as well. See, e.g., Enker & Elsen, *Counsel for the Suspect,* 49 Minn.L.Rev. 47, 87 (1964); Kamisar essays at 132–37; Pye, *Some Views on Miranda v. Arizona,* 35 Fordham L.Rev. 199, 21–15 (1966).[a]

Despite the references to "heavy burden" and "corroborated evidence" in the *Miranda* opinion and the strong support for sound recording safeguards in the literature, most courts have held that the testimony of an officer that he gave complete *Miranda* warnings and obtained a waiver is sufficient and need not be corroborated. See Commentary to *Model Pre-Arraignment Code* § 130.4.

A striking recent exception is STEPHAN v. STATE, 711 P.2d 1156 (Alaska 1985), holding that "an unexcused failure to electronically record a custodial interrogation conducted in a place of detention violates a suspect's right to due process, under the Alaska Constitution, and that any statement thus obtained is generally inadmissible." Observed the court, per BURKE, J.:

"We reach this conclusion because we are convinced that recording, [when feasible], is now a reasonable and necessary safeguard, essential to the adequate protection of the accused's right to counsel, his right against self incrimination and, ultimately, his right to a fair trial. * * *

"The recording of custodial interrogations is not, however, a measure intended to protect only the accused; a recording also protects the public's interest in honest and effective law enforcement, and the individual interests of those police officers wrongfully accused of improper tactics. A recording, in many cases, will aid law enforcement efforts, by confirming the content and the voluntariness of a confession, when a defendant changes his testimony or claims falsely that his constitutional rights were violated. In any case, a recording will help trial and appellate courts to ascertain the truth. * * *

"In both of the cases before us, the police were engaged in custodial interrogations of suspects in a place of detention. A working recording device was readily available, but was used to record only part of the questioning. Compliance with the recording rule is not unduly burdensome under these circumstances. Turning the recorder on a few minutes earlier entails minimal cost and effort. In return, less time, money and resources would have been consumed in resolving the disputes that arose over the events that occurred during the interrogations.

"The only real reason advanced by police for their frequent failure to electronically record an entire interrogation is their claim that recordings tend to have a 'chilling effect' on a suspect's willingness to talk. Given the fact that an accused has a constitutional right to remain silent, under both the state and federal constitutions,

a. For a powerful statement of the need for such safeguards by a leading British commentator, see G. Williams, *The Authentication of Statements to the Police,* 1979 Crim.L.Rev. (Brit.) 1. Professor Williams wonders "whether the real objection of the police to tape-recording (although it is never avowed) is their fear of the consequences of police inspection of what happens in the interviewing of suspects." Id. at 22. He points out, however, how a sound recording "can work to the advantage of the police as well as against them." Id. at 13.

If procedures relating to sound recordings are established, should the police interrogator inform the suspect that what he says is being recorded? Would such a requirement inhibit too many from talking? On the other hand, would it bring home to suspects the "seriousness of their situations"? See Kamisar essays at 133 n. 22; G. Williams at 21–22.

and that he must be clearly warned of that right prior to any custodial interrogation, this argument is not persuasive." Moreover, added the court, when a person knows that he is speaking to a police officer, there is no constitutional requirement that he be informed that the interview is being recorded.

13. *An implied waiver of Miranda rights may suffice.* Although a waiver is not established merely by showing that a defendant was given complete *Miranda* warnings and thereafter made an incriminating statement, *Tague v. Louisiana,* 444 U.S. 469, 100 S.Ct. 652, 62 L.Ed.2d 622 (1980), this does not mean that a waiver of *Miranda* rights will never be recognized unless "specifically made" after the warnings are given. As the Court, per STEWART, J., observed in NORTH CAROLINA v. BUTLER, 441 U.S. 369, 99 S.Ct. 1755, 60 L.Ed.2d 286 (1979):

"The question is not one of form, but rather whether the defendant knowingly and voluntarily waived [his *Miranda* rights]. [Although] mere silence is not enough [that] does not mean that the defendant's silence, coupled with an understanding of his rights and a course of conduct indicating waiver, may never support a conclusion that a defendant has waived his rights. The courts must presume that a defendant did not waive his rights; the prosecution's burden is great; but in at least some cases waiver can be clearly inferred from the actions and words of the person interrogated." [b]

Dissenting Justice BRENNAN, joined by Marshall and Stevens, JJ., protested: "[The Court] shrouds in half-light the question of waiver, allowing courts to construct inferences from ambiguous word and gestures. But the very premise of *Miranda* requires that ambiguity be interpreted against the interrogator. [Under the conditions inherent in custodial interrogation], only the most explicit waiver of rights can be considered knowingly and freely given. * * * [S]ince the Court agrees that *Miranda* requires the police to obtain some kind of waiver—whether express or implied—the requirement of an express waiver would impose no burden on the police not imposed by the Court's interpretation. It would merely make that burden explicit. Had [the agent] simply elicited a clear answer to the question, 'Do you waive your right to a lawyer?' this journey through three courts would not have been necessary."

14. *"Qualified" waiver.* As *North Carolina v. Butler* itself illustrates (see fn. b supra), a suspect may refuse to sign a waiver but nonetheless indicate that he is willing to talk.[c] Or he may object to any notetaking by an officer but agree to talk about the case or indicate that he will talk only if a tape recorder is turned off. Are oral waivers effective in the face of such objections? A number of courts have held that they are. See, e.g., *United States v. Frazier,* 476 F.2d 891 (D.C.Cir.1973) (en banc) (*Frazier II*), ruling—over a forceful dissent that "capacity to understand the warnings does not by any means guarantee that they will actually be understood"—that since the suspect who objected to the police "writing anything down" had the capacity to comprehend the warnings the officer questioning him was not required

b. After reading the FBI's "Advice of Rights" form, defendant was asked whether he understood his rights. He replied that he did, but refused to sign the waiver at the bottom of the form. He was then told that he need neither speak nor sign the form, but that the agents would like him to talk to them. He replied, "I will talk to you but I am not signing any form." He then made incriminating statements. Because defendant had said nothing when advised of his right to counsel, and because the state supreme court read *Miranda* as requiring a specific waiver of each right, it concluded that defendant had not waived his right to counsel. The U.S. Supreme Court disagreed: "By creating an inflexible rule that no implicit waiver [of *Miranda* rights] can ever suffice, the [state court] has gone beyond the requirements of federal organic law."

c. The *Butler* Court did not hold that this constituted a valid waiver, but only rejected the state court's view that nothing short of an express waiver would satisfy *Miranda.*

to "place a legal interpretation on the language of the *Miranda* warnings he was required to give." But consider LaFave & Israel, § 6.9(f):

"An objective view of the [*Frazier* facts] strongly suggests that the defendant acted as he did because of a mistaken impression that an oral confession which was not contemporaneously recorded could not be used against him.[d] Similarly, the *Butler* facts certainly suggest that the defendant misperceived the effect of a waiver which was oral rather than written. Under such circumstances, there is much to be said for the view that the police are under an obligation to clear up misunderstandings of this nature which are apparent to any reasonable observer."

15. *If a suspect has not requested a lawyer, but, unbeknownst to him, somebody else has retained one for him, does the failure to inform the suspect that a lawyer is trying to see him vitiate the waiver of his Miranda rights?* This question is raised in *Burbine v. Moran,* 753 F.2d 178 (1st Cir.1985), cert. granted, ___ U.S. ___, 105 S.Ct. 2319, 85 L.Ed.2d 838 (1985).[e] The Rhode Island Supreme Court, per *Weisberger, J.,* 451 A.2d 22 (R.I.1982), held that defendant had waived his rights knowingly, intelligently and voluntarily, observing:

"Nothing in [*Miranda* indicates] that the right to counsel may be asserted by anyone other than the accused. * * * [The] principles of *Miranda* place the assertion of the right to remain silent and the right to counsel upon the accused, and not upon benign third parties, whether or not they happen to be attorneys. * * *

"[*Miranda* holds] that the failure to honor the *accused's* right to consult with an attorney constituted a denial of the *accused's* right to assistance of counsel * * *. To modify this right [so] that it may be invoked by family members or any third party who happens to be a member of the bar would badly upset the balance between the societal interests and those of the accused. The next logical step would be to ban confessions altogether on the theory that a person should not be denied his right to counsel on the fortuitous circumstance that someone might not see fit to call the station."

On federal habeas corpus, however, the First Circuit, per Coffin, J., ruled that the failure to inform defendant that a lawyer was trying to see him vitiated the waiver of his *Miranda* rights:

"[W]e can do no better than repeat Justice Linde's statement: 'To pass up an abstract offer to call some unknown lawyer is very different from refusing to talk with an identified attorney actually available to provide at least initial assistance and advice, whatever might be arranged in the long run. A suspect indifferent to the first offer may well react differently to the second.' *State v. Haynes,* 602 P.2d 272, 278 (Or.1979).

"* * * We do not subscribe to the New York rule, based on that state's constitution, that a suspect may never waive his privilege against self-incrimination in

d. One study indicates that 45 percent of post-*Miranda* defendants mistakenly believed that oral statements could not be used against them. See Leiken, *Police Interrogation in Colorado: The Implementation of Miranda,* 47 Denver L.J. 1, 15–16, 33 (1970). If so many people do not realize the significance of an oral statement, should the warning take this form: "You have a right to remain silent and anything you say, *orally or* in writing, may (will) be used against you"? *Unif.R. Crim.P.* 212(b) and 243 so provide.

e. In *Burbine,* defendant's sister called the office of the public defender (without defendant's knowledge) to seek help for her brother, who had previously been represented by a member of the defender's office in another matter. An assistant public defender then called the police and stated that she would represent defendant in the event that the police intended to question him that night. The police said they would not question defendant; that they were "through with him for the night." This was not true. Defendant signed a waiver-of-rights form and then made incriminating statements. Thus the Supreme Court could conceivably dispose of the case on the ground that the police "deceived" or "misled" the lawyer, without reaching the broader question.

the absence of his attorney.[f] We also acknowledge that a person in custody [may] speak if he chooses, and without a lawyer's advice. The crucial point is that it must be a knowing choice * * *."

16. *What constitutes an invocation of Miranda rights?* In FARE v. MICHAEL C., 442 U.S. 707, 99 S.Ct. 2560, 61 L.Ed.2d 197 (1979), after being fully advised of his *Miranda* rights, a juvenile, who had been taken into custody on suspicion of murder, asked, "Can I have my probation officer here?" The police officer replied that he was "not going to call [the probation officer] right now," then continued: "If you want to talk to us without an attorney present, you can. If you don't want to, you don't have to." The juvenile then agreed to talk to the police without an attorney being present and made incriminating statements. The Court, per BLACKMUN, J., held the statements admissible, deeming the request to see a probation officer not a *per se* invocation of *Miranda* rights—not the equivalent of asking for a lawyer. The admissibility of the statements on the basis of waiver turned on "the totality of the circumstance surrounding the interrogation." (e.g., evaluation of the juvenile's age, experience, background and intelligence).

"The *per se* aspect of *Miranda,*" emphasized the Court, was "based on the unique role the lawyer plays in the adversarial system of criminal justice in this country. * * * A probation officer is not in the same posture with regard to either the accused or the system of justice as a whole. * * * Moreover, [he] is the employee of the State which seeks to prosecute the alleged offender. He is a peace officer, and as such is allied, to a greater or lesser extent, with his fellow peace officers. * * * It is [the] pivotal role of legal counsel [in the administration of criminal justice] that justifies the *per se* rule established in *Miranda* and that distinguishes the request for counsel from the request for a probation officer, a clergyman, or a close friend."

Justice MARSHALL, joined by Brennan and Stevens, JJ., dissented. Noting that the California Supreme Court had "determined that probation officers have a statutory duty to represent minors' interests and, indeed, are 'trusted guardian figure[s]' to whom a juvenile would likely turn for assistance," the dissenters maintained that "*Miranda* requires that interrogation cease whenever a juvenile requests an adult who is obligated to represent his interests." Such request "constitutes both an attempt to obtain advice and a general invocation of the right to silence. For, as the California Supreme Court recognized, 'it is fatuous to assume that a minor in custody will be in a position to call an attorney for assistance,' or that he will trust the police to obtain an attorney for him. A juvenile in these circumstances will likely turn to his parents, or another adult responsible for his welfare, as the only means of securing legal counsel. Moreover, a request for such adult assistance is surely inconsistent with a present desire to speak freely." [a]

Does *Fare v. Michael C.* stand for the broad proposition that a request by any suspect (with the possible exception of a young, inexperienced juvenile; Michael C. was an "experienced" 16½ year old) to see anyone *other than an attorney,* whether

f. The New York rule prohibits the police from questioning a suspect, absent an affirmative waiver *in the presence of his attorney,* once a defense attorney "enters the picture." See, e.g. *People v. Hobson,* 348 N.E.2d 894 (N.Y.1976). A lawyer's phoning the police department central switchboard and informing the civilian operators that he wished to speak to his client and did not want him questioned has been held sufficient to invoke the rule. See *People v. Pinzon,* 377 N.E.2d 721 (N.Y.1978). The rule has received a very cold reception elsewhere. See *State v. Smith,* 241 S.E.2d 674, 680 (N.C.1978) (collecting cases). For criticism of the rule, see Kamisar essays at 220–22.

a. Justice Powell wrote a separate dissent, "not satisfied that this particular 16-year-old boy, in this particular situation was subjected to a fair interrogation free from inherently coercive circumstances."

it be a parent, spouse or best friend, does not *per se* constitute an assertion or invocation of *Miranda* rights? If so, is this because neither parent, spouse or best friend has the "unique ability to protect the Fifth Amendment rights" of a suspect undergoing custodial interrogation? How much weight, if any, should be given to the fact that the mother, father or husband requested by the suspect plays a "unique role" in the life of the particular suspect?

17. *Resumption of questioning following the exercise of the right to remain silent; "scrupulously honoring" the "right to cut off questioning."* Consider MICHIGAN v. MOSLEY, 423 U.S. 96, 96 S.Ct. 321, 46 L.Ed. 313 (1975): Mosley was arrested in connection with certain robberies. The arresting officer, Detective Cowie of the Robbery Section of the Detroit Police Department, brought Mosley to the Robbery Bureau, located on the fourth floor of the headquarters building. After being given *Miranda* warnings, Mosley declined to discuss the robberies. Detective Cowie promptly ceased the questioning and made no effort to persuade Mosley to reconsider his position. (At no time during this session did Mosley request a lawyer.) Mosley was then taken to a cell block in the ninth floor of the building. After an interval of some two hours, another officer from another bureau, Homicide Detective Hill, brought Mosley from the cell block to the Homicide Bureau, located on the fifth floor of the same building, for questioning about "the Williams murder," characterized by a majority of the Court as "an unrelated holdup murder." Williams had been killed during a holdup other than those for which Mosley had been arrested and questioned by Robbery Detective Cowie, but the original tip to Cowie had implicated Mosley in this murder.

Mosley was again given complete *Miranda* warnings at the outset of this second session. This time he made an incriminating statement. This second interrogation session lasted about 15 minutes and at no time during its course did Mosley ask to consult with a lawyer or indicate to Detective Hill, that he did not want to discuss the murder. The Court, per STEWART, J., held the statement obtained by Detective Hill admissible:

"Resolution of the question [whether the Detroit police violated the *Miranda* 'guidelines'] turns almost entirely on the interpretation of a single passage in the *Miranda* opinion upon which this Michigan appellate court relied in finding a *per se* violation of *Miranda:*

" 'Once warnings have been given, the subsequent procedure is clear. If the individual indicates in any manner, at any time prior to or during questioning, that he wishes to remain silent, the interrogation must cease. At this point he has shown that he intends to exercise his Fifth Amendment privilege; any statement taken after the person invokes his privilege cannot be other than the product of compulsion, subtle or otherwise. Without the right to cut off questioning, the setting of in-custody interrogation operates on the individual to overcome free choice in producing a statement after the privilege has been once invoked.'

"The passage could be literally read to mean that a person who has invoked his 'right to silence' can never again be subjected to custodial interrogation by any police officer at any time or place on any subject. Another possible construction of the passage would characterize 'any statement taken after the person invokes his privilege' as 'the product of compulsion' and would therefore mandate its exclusion from evidence, even if it were volunteered by the person in custody without any further interrogation whatever. Or the passage could be interpreted to require only the immediate cessation of questioning, and to permit a resumption of interrogation after a momentary respite.

"It is evident that any of these possible literal interpretations would lead to absurd and unintended results. To permit the continuation of custodial interrogation after a momentary cessation would clearly frustrate the purposes of *Miranda* by allowing repeated rounds of questioning to undermine the will of the person being questioned. At the other extreme, a blanket prohibition against the taking of voluntary statements or a permanent immunity from further interrogation, regardless of the circumstances, would transform the *Miranda* safeguards into wholly irrational obstacles to legitimate police investigative activity, and deprive suspects of an opportunity to make informed and intelligent assessments of their interests. Clearly, therefore, [*Miranda* cannot] sensibly be read to create a *per se* proscription of indefinite duration upon any further questioning by any police officer on any subject, once the person in custody has indicated a desire to remain silent.[a]

"A reasonable and faithful interpretation of the *Miranda* opinion must rest on the intention of the Court in that case to adopt 'fully effective means [to] notify the person of his right of silence and to assure that the exercise of the right will be scrupulously honored.' The critical safeguard identified in the passage at issue is a person's 'right to cut off questioning.' Through the exercise of his option to terminate questioning he can control the time at which questioning occurs, the subjects discussed, and the duration of the interrogation. The requirement that law enforcement authorities must respect a person's exercise of that option counteracts the coercive pressures of the custodial setting. We therefore conclude that the admissibility of statements obtained after the person in custody has decided to remain silent depends under *Miranda* on whether his 'right to cut off questioning' was 'scrupulously honored.'

"[Mosley's] 'right to cut off questioning' was fully respected in this case. [When he stated at the first interrogation session that he] did not want to discuss the robberies, Detective Cowie immediately ceased the interrogation and did not try either to resume the questioning or in any way to persuade Mosley to reconsider his position. After an interval of more than two hours, Mosley was questioned by another police officer at another location about an unrelated holdup murder. He was given full and complete *Miranda* warnings at the outset of the second interrogation. * * * The subsequent questioning [by Detective Hill] focused exclusively on [a] crime different in nature and in time and place of occurrence from the robberies for which Mosley had been arrested and interrogated by Detective Cowie. [Hill's] questioning of Mosley about an unrelated homicide was quite consistent with a reasonable interpretation of Mosley's earlier refusal to answer any questions about the robberies.

"This is not a case, therefore, where the police failed to honor a decision of a person in custody to cut off questioning, either by refusing to discontinue the interrogation upon request or by persisting in repeated efforts to wear down his resistance and make him change his mind. In contrast to such practices, the police here immediately ceased the interrogation, resumed questioning only after the passage of a significant period of time and the provision of a fresh set of warnings, and restricted the second interrogation to a crime that had not been a subject of the earlier interrogation."[b]

a. But see *Model Pre-Arraignment Code* § 140.8(2)(d), providing that no waiver shall be sought at any time from an arrestee once he has asserted one of his rights. "[E]ven a seemingly voluntary waiver given after a person has once indicated he does not wish to cooperate," notes the Commentary to the Model Code, "may be the product of subtle coercion; the very passage of time while a person continues to be in police detention will create fears and pressures undermining the will to insist on one's right to silence and right to counsel."

b. The Court also distinguished *Westover,* a companion case to *Miranda* discussed at p. 555 supra. Observed Stewart, J.: "The cardinal fact of *Westover*—the failure of the police officers to give any warnings whatever to the person in

Justice WHITE concurred in the result "and in much of the majority's reasoning," but added:

"The majority seems to say that a statement obtained within some unspecified time after an assertion by an individual of his 'right to silence' is always inadmissible, even if it was the result of an informed and voluntary decision—following, for example, a disclosure to such an individual of a piece of information bearing on his waiver decision which the police had failed to give him prior to his assertion of the privilege but which they gave him immediately thereafter. Indeed, the majority characterizes as 'absurd' any contrary rule. I disagree.[c] I do not think the majority's conclusion is compelled by *Miranda,* and I suspect that in the final analysis the majority will adopt voluntariness as the standard by which to judge the waiver of the right to silence by a properly informed defendant. I think the Court should say so now.

" * * * I am no more convinced that *Miranda* was required by the United States Constitution than I was when it was decided. However, there is at least some support in the law both before and after *Miranda* for the proposition that some rights will never be deemed waived unless the defendant is first expressly advised of their existence. There is little support in the law or in common-sense for the proposition that an *informed* waiver of a right may be ineffective even where voluntarily made. Indeed, the law is exactly to the contrary. Unless an individual is incompetent, we have in the past rejected any paternalistic rule protecting a defendant from his intelligent and voluntary decisions about his own criminal case. *Faretta.* * * * I am very reluctant to conclude that *Miranda* stands for such a proposition.

"The language of *Miranda* no more compels such a result than does its basic rationale. As the majority points out, the statement in *Miranda* requiring interrogation to *cease* after an assertion of the 'right to silence' tells us nothing because it does not indicate how soon this interrogation may resume. The Court showed in the very next paragraph, moreover, that when it wanted to create a *per se* rule against further interrogation after assertion of a right, it knew how to do so. The Court there said 'if the individual states that he wants an attorney, the interrogation must cease *until an attorney is present.*' [2] However, when the individual indicates that *he* will decide unaided by counsel whether or not to assert his 'right to silence' the situation is different. * * *

"In justifying the implication that questioning must inevitably cease for some unspecified period of time following an exercise of the 'right to silence,' the majority says only that such a requirement would be necessary to avoid 'undermining' 'the will of the person being questioned.' [d] Yet, surely a waiver of the 'right to silence' obtained by 'undermining the will'

their custody before embarking on an intense and prolonged interrogation of him—was simply not present in [*Mosley*]."

c. Is Justice White saying, in effect, that *immediately after* a suspect has asserted his rights, the interrogator may attempt to persuade the suspect to reconsider his position by revealing that a ballistics report indicates that the suspect's weapon fired the fatal bullet or that an accomplice has confessed, implicating the suspect? Is disclosure of such information to one who has just asserted his rights "scrupulously honor[ing]" the exercise of these rights? Is disclosure of such information itself a form of "interrogation"?

2. The question of the proper procedure following expression by an individual of his desire to consult counsel is not presented in this case. It is sufficient to note that the reasons to keep the lines of communication between the authorities and the accused open when the accused has chosen to make his own decisions are not present when he indicates instead that he wishes legal advice with respect thereto. The authorities may then communicate with him through an attorney. More to the point, the accused having expressed his own view that he is not competent to deal with the authorities without legal advice, a later decision at the authorities' insistence to make a statement without counsel's presence may properly be viewed with skepticism.

d. Is such a requirement necessary to avoid "undermining" the *Miranda* warnings?

of the person being questioned would be considered an involuntary waiver. Thus, in order to achieve the majority's only stated purpose, it is sufficient to exclude all confessions which are the result of involuntary waivers. To exclude any others is to deprive the factfinding process of highly probative information for no reason at all. * * *

Dissenting Justice BRENNAN, joined by Marshall, J., protested:

"[S]crupulously honoring exercises of the right to cut off questioning is only meaningful insofar as the suspect's will to exercise that right remains wholly unfettered. The Court's formulation thus assumes the very matter at issue here: whether renewed questioning following a lengthy period of detention acts to overbear the suspect's will, irrespective of giving the *Miranda* warnings a second time (and scrupulously honoring them), thereby rendering inconsequential any failure to exercise the right to remain silent. For the Court it is enough conclusorily to assert that '[t]he subsequent questioning did not undercut Mosley's previous decision not to answer Detective Cowie's inquiries.' Under *Miranda,* however, Mosley's failure to exercise the right upon renewed questioning is presumptively the consequence of an overbearing in which detention and that subsequent questioning played a central role. * * *

"The fashioning of guidelines for this case is an easy task. Adequate procedures are readily available. Michigan law requires that the suspect be arraigned before a judicial officer 'without unnecessary delay,' certainly not a burdensome requirement. Alternatively, a requirement that resumption of questioning should await appointment and arrival of counsel for the suspect would be an acceptable and readily satisfied precondition to resumption. *Miranda* expressly held that '[t]he presence of counsel [would] be the adequate protective device necessary to make the process of police interrogation conform to the dictates of the privilege [against self-incrimination].' The Court expediently bypasses this alternative in its search for circumstances where renewed questioning would be permissible.

"* * * Today's decision virtually empties *Miranda* of principle, for plainly the decision encourages police asked to cease interrogation to continue the suspect's detention until the police station's coercive atmosphere does its work and the suspect responds to resumed questioning."

How significant is it that the second interrogation in *Mosley* was restricted to a separate and "unrelated" crime, one "different in nature and in time and place of occurrence from the robberies for which Mosley had been [earlier] interrogated"? Is this fact "critical," because without it "one is left only with a renewed effort to question by a different member of the same police force, in a different room in the same building, only two hours after Mosley's assertion of his right not to be questioned"? See Stone, *The Miranda Doctrine in the Burger Court,* 1977 Sup.Ct. Rev. 99, 134. Is "a fresh set of warnings" at the outset of the second interrogation session "sufficient to dissipate the coercion inherent in the continuing custody and the renewed questioning"? See Chase, *The Burger Court, the Individual and the Criminal Process: Directions and Misdirections,* 52 N.Y.U.L.Rev. 518, 559 (1977).

---

18. *Resumption of questioning following assertion of the right to counsel; initiating further communication with the police.* Distinguishing the *Mosley* case, EDWARDS v. ARIZONA, 451 U.S. 477, 101 S.Ct. 1880, 68 L.Ed.2d 378 (1981), held that once a suspect has invoked his right to counsel "a valid waiver of that right cannot be established by showing only that he responded to further police-initiated custodial interrogation even if he has been advised of his right"; under such circum-

stances the suspect "is not subject to further interrogation [until] counsel has been made available to him, unless [he] himself initiates further communication, exchanges or conversations with the police."

The case arose as follows: On January 19, 1976, Edwards was arrested for burglary, robbery and first-degree murder. At the police station, after waiving his *Miranda* rights, Edwards was told that another suspect had implicated him in the crime. Edwards sought to "make a deal," but the interrogating officer said he lacked authority to negotiate a deal. At some point thereafter, Edwards said, "I want an attorney before making a deal." At that point questioning ceased and Edwards was taken to jail. The following morning two detectives visited Edwards, stated they wanted to talk to him, and informed him of his *Miranda* rights.[a] Edwards was willing to talk, but only after hearing the taped statement of the alleged accomplice who had implicated him. After listening to the tape, Edwards said he would make a statement so long as it was not tape recorded. After being informed that whether or not his statement was recorded, the detectives could still testify to what he said, Edwards replied: "I'll tell you anything you want to know, but I don't want it on tape." He then incriminated himself. The Arizona Supreme Court held that although Edwards had invoked his rights the day before, he waived them the following morning when he voluntarily gave his statement to the detectives after again being advised of his *Miranda* rights. In reversing, the Court, per WHITE, J., observed:

"[T]he Arizona Supreme Court applied an erroneous standard for determining waiver where the accused has specifically invoked his right to counsel. [W]aivers of counsel must not only be voluntary, but constitute a knowing and intelligent relinquishment or abandonment of a known right or privilege, a matter which depends in each case 'upon the particular facts and circumstances surrounding that case, including the background, experience and conduct of the accused.' *Johnson v. Zerbst.*

"Considering the proceedings in the state courts in the light of this standard, we note [that] the trial court found [Edwards' waiver and confession] to have been 'voluntary' without separately focusing on whether [he] had knowingly and intelligently relinquished his right to counsel. [The Arizona Supreme Court] stated that the issue of [the 'voluntariness' of a confession] should be determined based on the totality of the circumstances as it related to whether an accused's action was 'knowing and intelligent and whether his will was overborne.' [It] then upheld the trial court's finding that the 'waiver and confession was voluntarily and knowingly made.'

" * * * [H]owever sound the conclusion of the state courts as to the voluntariness of Edwards' admissions may be, [they did not undertake] to focus on whether Edwards understood his right to counsel and intelligently and knowingly relinquished it. It is thus apparent that the decision below misunderstood the requirement for finding a valid waiver of the right to counsel, once invoked.[b]

"[When an accused asks for counsel, a] valid waiver of that right cannot be established by showing only that he responded to further police-initiated custodial interrogation even if he has been advised of his right. We further hold that an accused, such as Edwards, having expressed his de-

a. When the detention officer informed Edwards that two detectives wanted to talk to him, he replied that he did not want to talk to anyone. But the guard told him that "he had" to talk to the detectives and then took him to meet with them. The opinion of the Court, however, seems to be written without regard to these particular facts. But see the concurring opinions of Burger, C.J., and Powell, J., infra.

b. For a discussion of the distinction between "voluntariness" and "rationality," see Schrock, Welsh & Collins, *Interrogational Rights: Reflections on Miranda v. Arizona,* 52 So.Cal.L.Rev. 1, 33–56 (1978).

sire to deal with the police only through counsel, is not subject to further interrogation by the authorities until counsel has been made available to him, unless the accused himself initiates further communication, exchanges or conversations with the police.

" * * * Had Edwards initiated the meeting on January 20, [nothing] would prohibit the police from merely listening to his voluntary, volunteered statements and using them against him at the trial. [Absent any custodial interrogation], there would have been no infringement of the right that Edwards invoked and there would be no occasion to determine whether there had been a valid waiver. *Rhode Island v. Innis* makes this sufficiently clear.

"But this is not what the facts of this case show. * * *. We think it is clear that Edwards was subjected to custodial interrogation on January 20 within the meaning of *Innis* and that this occurred at the instance of the authorities. His statement, made without having had access to counsel, did not amount to a valid waiver and hence was inadmissible." 10

BURGER, C.J., concurred "only in the judgment because I do not agree that either any constitutional standard or the holding of *Miranda*—as distinguished from its dicta—calls for a special rule as to how an accused in custody may waive the right to be free from interrogation."

Concurring Justice POWELL, joined by Rehnquist, J., did not join the Court's opinion "because I am not sure what it means." He observed:

"I have thought it settled law, as [*Zerbst* and other] cases tell us, that one accused of crime may waive *any* of the constitutional safeguards * * *. Whatever the right, the standard for waiver is whether the actor fully understands the right in question and voluntarily intends to relinquish it. * * *

"In view of the emphasis placed on 'initiation' [of further communication with the police], I find the Court's opinion unclear. If read to create a new *per se* rule, requiring a threshold inquiry as to precisely who opened any conversation between an accused and state officials, I cannot agree. I would not superimpose a new element of proof on the established doctrine of waiver of counsel. * * *

"[O]nce warnings have been given and the right to counsel has been invoked, the relevant inquiry—whether the suspect now desires to talk to police without counsel—is a question of fact to be determined in light of all of the circumstances. Who 'initiated' a conversation may be relevant to the question of waiver, but it is not the *sine qua non* to the inquiry. The ultimate question is whether there was a free and knowing waiver of counsel before interrogation commenced.

"If the Court's opinion does nothing more than restate these principles, I am in agreement with it. I hesitate to join the opinion only because of what appears to be an undue, and undefined, emphasis on a single element: 'initiation.' * * * My concern is that the Court's opinion today may be read as 'constitutionalizing' not the generalized *Zerbst* standard but a *single element of fact* among the various facts that may be relevant to determining whether there has been a valid waiver." c

10. We need not decide whether there would have been a valid waiver of counsel had the events of January 20 been the first and only interrogation to which Edwards had been subjected. Cf. *North Carolina v. Butler.*

c. Relying heavily on *Edwards,* a panel of the U.S. Court of Appeals for the District of Columbia Circuit (Robinson, C.J., and Wright and Wald, JJ.) upheld the suppression of all information obtained during a 25-minute "background" interview of John W. Hinckley, Jr., immediately after his attempted assassination of the President. *United States v. Hinckley,* 672 F.2d 115 (D.C.Cir. 1982) (per curiam). As the FBI agents who conducted the interview knew, when Hinckley was still in the custody of the Metropolitan Police he had asked to confer with an attorney before answering any questions. "[H]e did not initiate further communication, but rather responded to police-initiated questioning undertaken in the face of [his] expressed desire to remain silent until he had an attorney." Moreover, while in

19. *The tension between Mosley and Edwards.* Consider the remarks of Professor Kamisar in Choper, Kamisar & Tribe, *The Supreme Court: Trends and Developments 1982–83* (1984) at 153–57:

The *Miranda* opinion states (384 U.S. at 473–74): If the individual indicates in any manner, at any time prior to or during questioning, that he wishes to remain silent, the interrogation must cease. * * * If the individual states that he wants an attorney, the interrogation must cease until an attorney is present. * * * If the individual cannot obtain an attorney and he indicates that he wants one before speaking to the police, they must respect his decision to remain silent.'

"I find it baffling that the Court has interpreted [the above language] to give the police *greater* leeway to resume interrogation when a suspect has exercised his right to remain silent rather than his right to counsel. If anything, the language *seems* to cut the other way: (1) once a suspect asserts his right to remain silent *the police* may not resume interrogation *period* (but the *suspect* may change his mind and 'initiate' reinterrogation); (2) once the suspect invokes his right to counsel the police may not resume interrogation (again, this doesn't mean the suspect can't change his mind [if he does so without any prompting by the police] and initiate reinterrogation) *unless and until* an attorney arrives and meets with his client.

"Another possible interpretation, and perhaps a more plausible interpretation, of the [*Miranda* language above] is that *regardless of which right the suspect asserts,* police interrogation may resume in the presence of counsel. This view finds support in a footnote [44] to [the instruction in *Miranda*] that if a suspect asserts his right to remain silent 'the interrogation must cease.' The footnote states: 'In the absence of evidence of overbearing, statements then made *in the presence of counsel* might be free of the compelling influence of the interrogation process and might fairly be construed as a waiver of the privilege for purposes of these statements.' [Emphasis added.]

"It is worth noting that *Model Pre-Arraignment Code* § 104.8(2)(d), [adopted only six months before *Mosley*], makes no distinction between invocation of the right to remain silent and the right to consult with counsel. If *either* right is asserted, [explains the Model Code Commentary], 'no law enforcement officer shall seek a waiver or interrogate the suspect in any way *until the suspect meets with counsel.*' [Emphasis added.] * * *

"[E]ither *Mosley* was wrongly decided or *Edwards* was. If it is inherently coercive—if it is inconsistent with *Miranda*—to renew interrogation after a suspect has invoked his right to counsel, I think it is equally wrong for the police to do so if the suspect has asserted his right to remain silent. The average person has no idea that different procedural safeguards are triggered by saying 'I want to see a lawyer' (or 'I don't want to say anything until I see a lawyer') rather than 'I don't want to say anything' (or 'I don't want to talk to you.') If after being advised [of his *Miranda* rights], a suspect replies that he wishes to remain silent, he may *really* be saying that he wants to remain silent *until he sees a lawyer.* Indeed, I would argue that if, immediately after being informed of [both rights], the suspect responds 'I don't want to say anything' he is invoking *both* rights.

"Moreover, as the [prosecution] argued in [*Oregon v. Bradshaw,* p. 617 infra], [the *Miranda* right to counsel] 'was intended to further the basic right to remain silent during custodial interrogation. Logically, waiver of the derivative right to counsel

the custody of the FBI, and after he had provided some background information, Hinckley had renewed his request for an attorney, but the FBI had continued to seek, and did obtain, additional "background" information. The *Hinckley* case is criticized in Inbau, *Over-Reaction—The Mischief of Miranda v. Arizona,* 73 J.Crim.L. & C. 101 (1982), but defended in Choper, Kamisar & Tribe, *The Supreme Court: Trends and Developments 1981–82* at 232–34 (1983) (remarks of Kamisar).

should not be treated by more stringent safeguards than those used to judge waiver of the basic right to remain silent.' "

20. *What constitutes "initiating" further communication with the police? Edwards* was deemed inapplicable in OREGON v. BRADSHAW, 462 U.S. 1039, 103 S.Ct. 2830, 77 L.Ed.2d 405 (1983), which arose as follows: Reynolds' body had been found in his wrecked pickup truck, in which he appeared to have been a passenger at the time the vehicle left the road. Bradshaw, suspected of being responsible for Reynolds' death, was brought to the police station. There he was advised of his *Miranda* rights. Bradshaw admitted that he had furnished liquor to Reynolds, a minor, but denied involvement in the traffic accident that apparently killed Reynolds. Bradshaw was then placed under arrest for furnishing liquor to Reynolds and again advised of his rights. An officer suggested that Bradshaw had been behind the wheel of the truck when Reynolds died, but Bradshaw again denied his involvement, and added: "I do want an attorney before it goes much further." The officer immediately terminated the conversation.

A few minutes thereafter, either while still at the police station or enroute to the jail, Bradshaw asked the officer: "Well, what is going to happen to me now?" As the plurality opinion described it, the officer responded: "You do not have to talk to me. You have requested an attorney and I don't want you talking to me unless you so desire because anything you say—because—since you have requested an attorney, you know, it has to be at your own free will." [a] Bradshaw said he understood. General conversation followed, in the course of which there was a discussion about where Bradshaw was being taken and the offense with which he would be charged. The officer then suggested that Bradshaw take a lie detector test in order to "clean the matter up." Bradshaw agreed.

The next day, just before he took the lie detector test, Bradshaw was given another set of *Miranda* warnings and he signed a written waiver of these rights. At the conclusion of the test, the polygraph examiner told Bradshaw that he had not been truthful in response to certain questions. Bradshaw then admitted that he had been driving the vehicle in which Reynolds was killed, that he had consumed a considerable amount of alcohol, and that he had passed out at the wheel before the vehicle left the roadway. Bradshaw was convicted of first degree manslaughter, but, relying on *Edwards,* the Oregon Court of Appeals reversed, concluding that Bradshaw's incriminating statements had been obtained in violation of his Fifth Amendment rights. The Supreme Court disagreed, but there was no opinion of the Court. Justice REHNQUIST, joined by Burger, C.J., and White and O'Connor, JJ., observed:

"[*Edwards*] was in effect a prophylactic rule, designed to protect an accused in police custody from being badgered by police officers in the manner in which the defendant in *Edwards* was. We recently restated the requirement in *Wyrick v. Fields,* 459 U.S. 42, 103 S.Ct. 394, 74 L.Ed.2d 214 (1982) (per curiam), to be that before a suspect in custody can be subjected to further interrogation after he requests an attorney there must be a showing that the 'suspect himself initiates dialogue with the authorities.' [b]

a. As the dissent pointed out, the officer also said: "I can't prevent you from talking, but you understand where your place—you know, where your standing is here?"

b. *Fields* arose as follows: After discussing the matter with his private counsel and with a military attorney, Fields, a soldier charged with rape, requested a polygraph examination. Prior to undergoing the examination, Fields signed a waiver-of-rights form. He was also told: "If you are now going to discuss the offense under investigation, which is rape, with or without a lawyer present, you have a right to stop answering questions at any time or speak to a lawyer before answering further, even if you sign a waiver certificate. Do you want a lawyer at this time?" Fields answered: "No."

"But even if a conversation taking place after the accused has 'expressed his desire to deal with the police only through counsel,' is initiated by the accused, where reinterrogation follows, the burden remains upon the prosecution to show that subsequent events indicated a waiver of the Fifth Amendment right to have counsel present during the interrogation. * * *

"There can be no doubt in this case that in asking, 'Well, what is going to happen to me now?', respondent 'initiated' further conversation in the ordinary dictionary sense of that word. * * * There are some inquiries, such as a request for a drink of water or a request to use a telephone that are so routine that they cannot be fairly said to represent a desire on the part of an accused to open up a more generalized discussion relating directly or indirectly to the investigation. Such inquiries or statements, by either an accused or a police officer, relating to routine incidents of the custodial relationship, will not generally 'initiate' a conversation in the sense in which that word was used in *Edwards.*

"Although ambiguous, the respondent's question in this case as to what was going to happen to him evinced a willingness and a desire for a generalized discussion about the investigation; it was not merely a necessary inquiry arising out of the incidents of the custodial relationship. It could reasonably have been interpreted by the officer as relating generally to the investigation. That the police officer so understood it is apparent from the fact that he immediately reminded the accused that 'you do not have to talk to me,' and only after the accused told him that he 'understood' did they have a generalized conversation. On these facts we believe that there was not a violation of the *Edwards* rule.

"[The next inquiry, therefore] was 'whether a valid waiver of the right to counsel and the right to silence had occurred, that is, whether the purported waiver was knowing and intelligent and found to be so under the totality of the circumstances, including the necessary fact that the accused, not the police, reopened the dialogue with the authorities.' *Edwards.* * * *

"The state trial court [found that a valid waiver of defendant's rights did occur and] we have no reason to dispute these conclusions * * *."

At the conclusion of the polygraph examination, which took less than two hours, a CID agent told Fields that there had been some deceit and asked him if he could explain why his answers were bothering him. Fields then made some incriminating statements. On federal habeas corpus, the Eighth Circuit found that the State had failed to satisfy its burden of proving that Fields knowingly and intelligently waived his right to have counsel present at the *post*-test interrogation. The Supreme Court disagreed:

"The only plausible explanation for the [Eighth Circuit's] holding is that, encouraged by what it regarded as a *per se* rule established in *Edwards,* it fashioned another rule of its own: that, notwithstanding a voluntary, knowing, and intelligent waiver of the right to have counsel present at a polygraph examination, and notwithstanding clear evidence that the suspect understood that right and was aware of his power to stop questioning at any time or to speak to an attorney at any time, the police again must advise the suspect of his rights before questioning him at the same interrogation about the results of the polygraph. [This approach] certainly finds no support in *Edwards,* which emphasizes that the totality of the circumstances, including the fact that the suspect initiated the questioning, is controlling. Nor is the rule logical; the questions put to Fields after the examination would not have caused him to forget the rights of which he had been advised and which he had understood moments before. The rule is simply an unjustifiable restriction on reasonable police questioning."

Dissenting Justice Marshall underscored the distinction between "an agreement to submit to a polygraph examination" and "the initiation of an ordinary conversation with the authorities": "[A] polygraph examination is a discrete test. It has a readily identifiable beginning and end. An individual who submits to such an examination does not necessarily have any reason whatsoever to expect that he will be subjected to a post-examination interrogation." In any event, Justice Marshall did "not believe that this substantial constitutional question should be disposed of summarily."

Concurring Justice POWELL agreed that defendant had knowingly and intelligently waived his right to counsel, but deemed a two-step analysis unnecessary:

"[Justice Rehnquist and dissenting Justice Marshall] agree in one respect. They view the 'initiation' question as the first step of a two-step analysis, the second step being the application of the *Zerbst* standard that requires examination of the 'totality of the circumstances.'

"[S]ince Justice Marshall concludes that Bradshaw had not initiated the dialogue, he does not [get to the second step.] Justice Rehnquist, however, moves from the first to the second step to conclude that the facts and circumstances, when viewed in their entirety, clearly establish a valid waiver of the right to counsel. To this extent, I agree with his plurality opinion.

"My concern is that a two-step analysis could confound the confusion evident from the differing views expressed by other courts and indeed evidenced by the conflicting reading of *Edwards* by Justices Marshall and Rehnquist. The *Zerbst* standard is one that is widely understood and followed. It also comports with common sense. Fragmenting the standard into a novel two-step analysis—if followed literally—often would frustrate justice as well as common sense. Courts should engage in more substantive inquiries than 'who said what first.' The holding of the Court in *Edwards* cannot in my view fairly be reduced to this."

Justice MARSHALL, joined by Brennan, Blackmun and Stevens, JJ., dissented:

" * * * When this Court in *Edwards* spoke of 'initiat[ing] further communication' with the police and 'reopen[ing] the dialogue with the authorities,' it obviously had in mind communication or dialogue *about the subject matter of the criminal investigation.* The rule announced in *Edwards* was designed to ensure that any interrogation subsequent to an invocation of the right to counsel be at the instance of the accused, not the authorities. Thus, a question or statement which does not invite further interrogation before an attorney is present cannot qualify as 'initiation' under *Edwards.* To hold otherwise would drastically undermine the safeguards that *Miranda* and *Edwards* carefully erected around the right to counsel in the custodial setting. * * * [2]

"I agree with the plurality that, in order to constitute 'initiation' under *Edwards,* an accused's inquiry must demonstrate a desire to discuss the subject matter of the criminal investigation. I am baffled, however, at the plurality's application of that standard to the facts of this case. The plurality asserts that respondent's question, 'What is going to happen to me now?', evinced both 'a willingness and a desire for a generalized discussion about the investigation.' If respondent's question had been posed by Jean-Paul Sartre before a class of philosophy students, it might well have evinced a desire for a 'generalized' discussion. But under the circumstances of this case, it is plain that respondent's only 'desire' was to find out where the police were going to take him. As the Oregon Court of Appeals stated, respondent's query came only minutes after his invocation of the right to counsel and was simply 'a normal reaction to being taken from the police station and placed in a police car, obviously for transport to some destination.' * * * On these facts, I fail to see how respondent's question can be considered 'initiation' of a conversation about the subject matter of the criminal investigation.

2. In his opinion concurring in the judgment, Justice Powell suggests that there is confusion as to whether *Edwards* announced a *per se* rule. In my view, *Edwards* unambiguously established such a rule. In any event, no confusion on this point can remain after today's decision for eight Justices manifestly agree that *Edwards* did create a *per se* rule. * * * The *only* dispute between the plurality and the dissent in this case concerns the meaning of "initiation" for purposes of *Edwards' per se* rule.

"To hold that respondent's question in this case opened a dialogue with the authorities flies in the face of the basic purpose of the *Miranda* safeguards. When someone in custody asks, 'What is going to happen to me now?', he is surely responding to his custodial surroundings. The very essence of custody is the loss of control over one's freedom of movement. The authorities exercise virtually unfettered control over the accused. To allow the authorities to recommence an interrogation based on such a question is to permit them to capitalize on the custodial setting. Yet *Miranda's* procedural protections were adopted precisely in order 'to dispel the compulsion inherent in custodial surroundings.' "

21. *Does the Bradshaw case sap Edwards of much of its vitality? Should a "natural response" to arrest or transportation to a police station be viewed as the suspect's counterpart to "administrative questioning"?* Consider the remarks of Professor Kamisar in Choper, Kamisar & Tribe, *The Supreme Court: Trends and Developments 1982–83* (1984), at 159–60, 165–66:

"According to the 'statement of the case' in Oregon's brief, there was considerable conversation [in the police vehicle] and before [suggesting] that Bradshaw take a polygraph examination [the officer reiterated] his own theory of the auto accident, * * * the very theory that the officer had announced earlier just before Bradshaw invoked his right to counsel.

"Now, when an officer handcuffs you or orders you into a police vehicle it is hard to think of a more normal or a more natural response than asking, 'What is going to happen to me now?' Nothing prevented the officer from answering *that* question. But *Miranda* and *Edwards,* I submit, prevented the officer from doing what he did, 'going to work' on Bradshaw—picking up where he left off when Bradshaw had first invoked his [right to counsel] and once again advancing the theory that Bradshaw had been behind the wheel when the fatal accident occurred."

"True, *the next day,* the day Bradshaw had agreed to take a polygraph examination, he was given a fresh set of *Miranda* warnings just before the polygraph test was administered—and Bradshaw did sign a written waiver of his rights. But [the] second set of *Miranda* warnings came too late—a day too late. * * *

"The critical moment occurs when a suspect who has invoked his right to counsel is induced to change his mind—when he agrees to submit himself to further interrogation—regardless of whether the further interrogation *takes place then or later.* The suspect needs the *Miranda* warnings at that critical moment, not at the time the interrogation is actually renewed.

"According to *Miranda* and *Edwards,* the suspect who invokes his right to counsel is supposed to *change his own mind,* not have it changed for him by the police. To give the suspect the *Miranda* warnings the next day, when the authorities have *already* succeeded in changing [his] mind, when the suspect has *already* been pressured, prompted or conned into agreeing to undergo another interrogation session, is to engage in an empty ceremony. * * *

"When the [*Innis* Court defined 'police interrogation'] it *excluded* police words or actions 'normally attendant to arrest and custody' and properly so. Such statements, often called 'administrative questioning,' e.g., the routine questions asked of all persons 'booked' or otherwise processed, do not enhance the pressures and anxiety generated by arrest and detention. Thus, any incriminating statements in response to administrative questioning is, and should be, viewed as a 'volunteered' statement.

"The suspect's counterpart to 'administrative questioning' [is] an expression of fear, anxiety or confusion *normally attendant* to arrest, removal from the scene of arrest, or transportation to the stationhouse or jail. These expressions, such as, Where am I being taken? When can I call my lawyer? and, yes, What's going to happen to me? should not count as "initiation of dialogue" for *Edwards* purposes.

"Of course, if the officer *answers* one of the arrestee's questions about what's going to happen to him by *telling him* where he is being taken [or] when he will be able to meet with an attorney * * * that should not count either. But when the officer's response to the suspect's expression of concern or confusion clearly goes beyond the scope of the suspect's question—when the officer exploits the situation, as he did in the *Bradshaw* case, [by] pressuring, challenging, prompting or 'sweet-talking' the suspect into discussing the case without a lawyer—that *should* count as 'police interrogation.' * * * Under such circumstances, the suspect did not 'invite' or 'initiate' conversation about the merits of the case—the officer 'initiated' a *new* conversation."

22. *What constitutes an "unambiguous" request for counsel for purposes of Edwards?*

Once a suspect has clearly requested the assistance of counsel, holds SMITH v. ILLINOIS, 469 U.S. 91, 105 S.Ct. 490, 83 L.Ed.2d 488 (1984) (per curiam), his responses to further reading, or discussion of, the *Miranda* warnings "may not be used to cast retrospective doubt on the clarity of the initial request itself." The case arose as follows: Shortly after his arrest, 18-year-old Smith was taken to an interrogation room for questioning. A detective began reading Smith his rights in the usual order. According to a tape transcript, when the detective came to the part of the warnings dealing with the right to consult with a lawyer, the following occurred:

"Q. * * * You have a right to consult with a lawyer and to have a lawyer present with you when you're being questioned. Do you understand that?

"A. *Uh, yeah. I'd like to do that.*

"Q. Okay."

"Q. * * * If you want a lawyer and you're unable to pay for one a lawyer will be appointed to represent you free of cost, do you understand that?

"A. Okay.

"Q. Do you wish to talk to me at this time without a lawyer being present?

"A. *Yeah and no, uh, I don't know what's what, really.*

"Q. *Well. You either have to talk to me this time without a lawyer being present* and if you do agree to talk with me without a lawyer being present you can stop at any time you want to.

"Q. All right. I'll talk to you then."

Smith then admitted his involvement in the robbery. The state supreme court affirmed Smith's robbery conviction, maintaining that "Smith's statements, *considered in total,* were ambiguous, and did not effectively invoke his right to counsel" (emphasis added). But a 6–3 majority of the U.S. Supreme Court pointed out that Smith's initial request for counsel could be considered ambiguous "*only* by looking to [his] *subsequent* responses to continued police questioning" and that this approach was unacceptable.

"Our decision is a narrow one," the Court pointed out. "We do not decide the circumstances in which an accused's request for counsel may be characterized as ambiguous or equivocal as a result of events preceding the request or of nuances inherent in the request itself, nor do we decide the consequences of such ambiguity or equivocation. We hold only [that] an accused's *post-request* responses to further interrogation may not be used to cast retrospective doubt on the clarity of the initial request itself. Such subsequent statements are relevant only to the distinct question of waiver."

Justice REHNQUIST, joined by The Chief Justice, and Powell, J., dissented:

"* * * It may be that a crystal clear statement could not be rendered ambiguous by subsequent responses to questions seeking clarification. But statements are rarely that clear; differences between certainty and hesitancy may well turn on the inflection with which words are spoken, especially where, as here, a seven-word statement is isolated from the statements surrounding it. But in the ordinary give and take of statement and response in a colloquy such as this, I see no reason why the entire flavor of the colloquy—lasting less than five minutes—cannot be considered by the trier of fact.

"* * * [I]t simply slices a legal abstraction thinner than common sense will permit to conclude on the basis of this colloquy that it may not be used in its entirety to determine whether petitioner 'clearly asserted' his right to counsel. * * *

"Common sense suggests that the police should both complete reading petitioner his rights and then ask him to state clearly what he elects to do, even if he indicated a tentative desire while he was being informed of his rights. This is entirely consistent with applicable language in *Miranda* itself. * * * The reading of this short colloquy between petitioner and the police officer satisfies me that the police were faithfully attempting to follow our *Miranda* decision. The Court's opinion gives the impression that it is concerned about overreaching, badgering, and wearing down a suspect; but no fair reading of this five-minute transcript can lead to the conclusion that those factors were present here." [a]

23. *What kinds of trickery or deception, if any, may the police engage in after a suspect waives his rights?* Is *Miranda's* prohibition against police deception and trickery confined to their use *in obtaining a waiver* of *Miranda* rights or does it also bar such techniques by the police *after* a person has validly waived his rights? Suppose a suspect truly waives his rights. May the police then display apparent sympathy? Pretend that an accomplice has confessed? Subject him first to a friendly, gentle interrogator and then a hostile, short-tempered one (the "Mutt and Jeff" routine)? Although such techniques seemed to have

a. May a suspect invoke his right to counsel for *Edwards* purposes *before* he is subjected to "custodial interrogation"? Consider *United States v. Goodson,* 18 M.J. 243 (Ct.Mil.App.1984), vacated and remanded for further consideration in light of *Smith v. Illinois.* Goodson was one of nine soldiers arrested for drug violations and taken to a military police station for interrogation by Military Police Investigator Allinder. While waiting his turn to be interrogated (Allinder didn't get around to him until nine hours later), Goodson asked a sergeant whether he could contact a lawyer. But when his turn came to be questioned and he was advised of his rights by Allinder, Goodson signed a waiver-of-rights form. He then made an incriminating statement. Goodson never indicated to Allinder that he wanted, or had previously requested, counsel. And Allinder did not recall anyone telling him that Goodson had requested counsel.

In upholding the admissibility of Goodson's statement, a 2–1 majority, per Cook, J., distinguished *Edwards* on the ground that "Goodson made all of his requests for counsel *before* he was advised of his rights and while the case was still in the investigatory state. * * * [T]he right to appointed counsel does not arise until in-custody interrogation has begun. The corollary is that a waiver of the *Miranda* rights cannot occur unless there has been a full advisement of rights. * * * To exclude evidence taken after the proper advisement of rights and the waiver of those rights solely because a person, at some earlier point to another person, had requested counsel would unduly paralyze the government and the society it represents in a criminal prosecution."

Dissenting Chief Judge Everett rejected the view that "a request for counsel may be ignored unless it is made after in-custody interrogation has begun and the [*Miranda* warnings] given."

"[E]ven if a waiver of *Miranda* rights cannot proceed without full advisement of those rights," it does not follow, maintained the dissent, "that a request for counsel which precedes this advice can be ignored, as was done here." Moreover, the Court's approach "is an invitation to hair-splitting. [If a suspect] requests counsel a moment before his *Miranda* rights are explained, he may thereafter be interrogated by the police without counsel, so long as the request is not repeated; but if the *Miranda* warning is given and then the suspect asks for a lawyer, interrogation must halt indefinitely. I cannot believe that important constitutional rights * * * hinge on such temporal distinctions."

By vacating the judgment and remanding the case for further consideration in light of *Smith v. Illinois,* did the Supreme Court indicate support for dissenting Chief Judge Everett's views?

"vented Chief Justice Warren's judicial ire" in *Miranda,* see Broderick, Book Review, 53 Cornell L.Rev. 737, 741 (1968), *Miranda* "did not condemn any specific techniques as such or hold that evidence obtained by use of them would be admissible. Reliance was placed on warning and counsel to protect the suspect." Elsen & Rosett, *Protections for the Suspect under Miranda v. Arizona,* 67 Colum.L.Rev. 645, 667 (1967). A decade after *Miranda* was decided, the issue is still largely unresolved.[a]

In the post-*Miranda* edition of their leading interrogation manual, *Criminal Interrogation and Confessions* 1 (2d ed. 1967), Professor Inbau and Mr. Reid take the position that "all but a very few of the interrogation techniques presented in our earlier [pre-*Escobedo,* pre-*Miranda*] publication are still valid if used after the recently prescribed warnings have been given to the suspect under interrogation, and after he has waived his self-incriminating privilege and his right to counsel." See also Inbau, Reid & Buckley, *Criminal Interrogation and Confessions* 216 (3d ed. 1986), maintaining that, although the Court did not explicitly address the issue in *Frazier v. Cupp,* fn. a supra, that case "implicitly recognized" the essentiality of interrogation practices involving trickery or deceit, and approved of them. [Moreover,] there are many appellate court cases holding that a confession is admissible even when it was obtained by trickery and deceit, [provided that the trickery does not] 'shock the conscience' [or is not] apt to induce a false confession."

But see W. White, *Police Trickery in Inducing Confessions,* 127 U.Pa.L.Rev. 581–90, 599–600, 628–29 (1979), maintaining that, because they are likely to render a resulting confession involuntary *or* because they distort the meaning or vitiate the effect of the *Miranda* warnings *or* because they "undermine [a] suspect's independent right to an attorney," "several widely employed interrogation tactics * * * should be absolutely prohibited." Among the techniques Professor White considers "impermissible per se" are deception that distorts the seriousness of the matter under investigation (e.g., falsely informing a murder suspect that the victim is still alive), the "assumption of non-adversary roles" by interrogating officers (e.g., assuming the role of a father figure or religious counselor), repeated assurances that the suspect is known to be guilty, and the "Mutt and Jeff" routine.

24. *Use of a pretrial psychiatric examination at a capital sentencing proceeding.* ESTELLE v. SMITH, 451 U.S. 454, 101 S.Ct. 1866, 68 L.Ed.2d 359 (1981), arose as follows: Respondent was indicted for murder. The state announced its intention to seek the death penalty. Thereafter, although defense counsel had not put into issue his client's competency to stand trial or his sanity at the time of the offense, a judge informally ordered the prosecution to arrange a psychiatric examination of respondent by Dr. Grigson to determine respondent's capacity to stand trial. But Dr. Grigson did not merely report to the court on the issue of competence to stand trial; after respondent was convicted of murder the doctor also testified—indeed, he was the prosecution's only witness—at the penalty phase of the capital case. On the basis of his pretrial examination of respondent, Dr. Grigson testified as to respondent's "future dangerousness," one of the critical issues to be resolved by a jury at the capital sentencing proceeding.[a]

a. Cf. *Frazier v. Cupp,* 394 U.S. 731, 89 S.Ct. 1420, 22 L.Ed.2d 684 (1969) (admitting a confession in a pre-*Miranda* case although the police had falsely told the defendant that another had confessed and had also "sympathetically" suggested that the victim's homosexual advances may have started the fight). See also *Oregon v. Mathiason* (p. 586 supra) (interrogator's false statement to defendant that his fingerprints were found at scene may have bearing on other issues in case, but "has nothing to do with whether [defendant] was in custody for [*Miranda*] purposes").

a. In Texas, if the defendant is found guilty of a capital offense, a separate proceeding is held to

The jury answered the "future dangerousness" question and other requisite questions in the affirmative and, thus, under Texas law, the death penalty for respondent was mandatory.

Dr. Grigson did not obtain permission from respondent's attorneys to examine him. Nor was respondent advised before the pretrial psychiatric examination that he had a right to remain silent or that any statement he made could be used against him at a sentencing proceeding. The state argued, however, that the privilege against self-incrimination was inapplicable because (a) Dr. Grigson's testimony was used only to determine punishment after conviction, not to establish guilt; and (b) respondent's communications to Dr. Grigson were "nontestimonial" in nature. Rejecting these contentions, the Court held, per BURGER, C.J., that both respondent's Fifth and Sixth Amendment rights were violated by the use of Dr. Grigson's testimony at the penalty phase of the case: [b]

"In this case, the ultimate penalty of death was a potential consequence of what respondent told the examining psychiatrist. Just as the Fifth Amendment prevents a criminal defendant from being made 'the deluded instrument of his own conviction,' it protects him as well from being made the 'deluded instrument' of his own execution.

"We can discern no basis to distinguish between the guilt and penalty phases of respondent's capital murder trial so far as the protection of the Fifth Amendment privilege is concerned. Given the gravity of the decision to be made at the penalty phase, the State is not relieved of the obligation to observe fundamental constitutional guarantees."

As for the argument that respondent's communications to the examining psychiatrist were "nontestimonial" in nature, "Dr. Grigson's prognosis as to future dangerousness rested on statements respondent made and remarks he omitted, in reciting the details of the crime. The Fifth Amendment privilege, therefore, is directly involved here because the State used as evidence against respondent the substance of his disclosures during the pretrial psychiatric examination."

The Court distinguished (a) sanity examination occasioned by a defendant's plea of not guilty by reason of insanity and (b) examinations restricted to ensuring that a defendant is competent to stand trial. But "[w]hen Dr. Grigson went beyond simply reporting to the court on the issue of competence and testified for the prosecution at the penalty phase on the crucial issue of respondent's future dangerousness, his role changed and became essentially like that of an agent of the State recounting unwarned statements made in a post-arrest custodial setting. * * * If, upon being adequately warned, respondent had indicated that he would not answer Dr. Grigson's questions, the validly ordered competency examination nevertheless could have proceeded upon the condition that the results would be applied solely for that purpose. In such circumstances, the proper conduct and use of competency and sanity examinations are not frustrated, but the State must make its case on future dangerousness in some other way." [c]

determine the punishment. If, at the penalty phase, the jury affirmatively answers three questions on which the state has the burden of proof beyond a reasonable doubt, the judge must impose the death sentence. One of the three critical questions is "whether there is a probability that the defendant would commit criminal acts of violence that would constitute a continuing threat to society."

b. The *Massiah* aspect of the case is discussed at p. 637 infra.

c. Because respondent had been indicted and assigned counsel before Dr. Grigson examined him and the examination had taken place without notice to respondent's counsel, Stewart, J., joined by Powell, J., concurred in the judgment on *Massiah* grounds "without reaching the other issues discussed by the Court." In a separate opinion, Rehnquist, J., also concurred in the result on *Massiah* grounds, but he dissented, in effect, on the *Miranda* issue.

25. *Questioning about minor offenses.* In BERKEMER v. McCARTY, whose facts are set forth at p. 584 supra, the Court, per MARSHALL, J., rejected the argument that *Miranda* does not apply to misdemeanor traffic offenses and held that one subjected to custodial interrogation is entitled to the *Miranda* warnings "regardless of the nature or severity of the offense of which he is suspected or for which he was arrested":

"One of the principle advantages of the doctrine that suspects must be given warnings before being interrogated while in custody is the clarity of that rule. [The 'misdemeanor traffic offense'] exception to *Miranda* proposed by petitioner would substantially undermine this crucial advantage of the doctrine. The police often are unaware when they arrest a person whether he may have committed a misdemeanor or a felony. [For example, under] Ohio law, both driving while under the influence of intoxicants and negligent vehicular homicides are misdemeanors, while reckless vehicular homicide is a felony. When arresting a person for causing a collision, the police may not know which of these offenses he may have committed. * * *

"Equally importantly, the doctrinal complexities that would confront the courts if we accepted petitioner's proposal would be byzantine. Difficult questions quickly spring to mind: For instance, investigations into seemingly minor offenses sometimes escalate gradually into investigations into more serious matters; at what point in the evolution of an affair of this sort would the police be obliged to give *Miranda* warnings to a suspect in custody? What evidence would be necessary to establish that an arrest for a misdemeanor offense was merely a pretext to enable the police to interrogate the suspect (in hopes of obtaining information about a felony) without providing him the safeguards prescribed by *Miranda?* The litigation necessary to resolve such matters would be time-consuming and disruptive of law enforcement. And the end result would be an elaborate set of rules, interlaced with exceptions and subtle distinctions, discriminating between different kinds of custodial interrogations. Neither the police nor criminal defendants would benefit from such a development.

"* * * There can be no question that respondent was 'in custody' at least as of the moment he was formally placed under arrest and instructed to get into the police car. Because he was not informed of his constitutional rights at that juncture, respondent's subsequent admissions should not have been used against him."

26. *Confessions by juveniles.* Although some states require a parent to be present at any interrogation of a juvenile before a confession or waiver can be valid, apparently on the assumption that the presence of a parent would benefit the child, a recent study, Grisso, *Juveniles' Waiver of Rights* 187, 200 (1981), and the case law itself—"replete with instances of parents coercing their children into confession to the police"—indicate that "[r]ather than mitigating the pressures of interrogation, parents appear disposed to coercing their children to waive the right to silence." Feld, *Criminalizing Juvenile Justice,* 69 Minn.L.Rev. 141, 181–82 (1984).

27. *Questioning by private citizens and private security personnel.* It is plain that *Miranda* does not govern questioning by private citizens acting on their own, but a plausible case can be made for applying *Miranda* to questioning by private security personnel, e.g., a department store security guard, for such personnel "also utilize detention, privacy, the appearance of authority, and psychologically coercive methods to facilitate fruitful interrogation. * * * [But] the courts have rather consistently held that such persons as security officers, railroad detectives, insurance investigators, and private investigators are not required to comply with the *Miranda* procedures." LaFave & Israel, § 6.10(b). See, e.g., *People v. Deborah C.,* 635 P.2d

446 (Cal.1981). See generally Inbau, Aspen & Spiotto, *Protective Security Law* (1983) (Ch. 4).

28. *Other Miranda problems.* If a defendant takes the stand in his own defense, may the prosecution impeach him by using statements obtained from him in violation of Miranda? See Ch. 11, § 4, infra. May a defendant's *prior silence,* even his *post*arrest silence, be used to impeach his credibility when he chooses to testify at his trial? See id.

Suppose, after a suspect is illegally arrested, he is advised of his rights, waives them, and confesses? Do the *Miranda* warnings "cure" the illegality of the arrest? See Ch. 11, § 3, infra.

Suppose, a couple of hours after the police obtain an incriminating statement from a suspect in violation of *Miranda,* they give him the complete warnings and the suspect waives his rights and confesses? Is the "second confession" admissible or is it "the fruit" of the first inadmissible statement? See Ch. 11, § 3, infra. Suppose, as the result of a statement obtained in violation of *Miranda,* the police find the murder weapon or locate an important witness. Is the testimony of the witness or the murder weapon admissible? Or is it the "fruit of the poisonous tree"? See id.

SECTION 4. *MASSIAH* REVISITED: *MASSIAH* AND *MIRANDA* COMPARED AND CONTRASTED

BREWER v. WILLIAMS (WILLIAMS I)

430 U.S. 387, 97 S.Ct. 1232, 51 L.Ed.2d 424 (1977).

MR. JUSTICE STEWART delivered the opinion of the Court. * * *

On the afternoon of December 24, 1968, a 10-year-old girl named Pamela Powers went with her family to the YMCA in Des Moines, Iowa * * *. When she failed to return from a trip to the washroom, a search for her began. The search was unsuccessful.

Robert Williams, who had recently escaped from a mental hospital, was a resident of the YMCA. Soon after the girl's disappearance Williams was seen in the YMCA lobby carrying some clothing and a large bundle wrapped in a blanket. He obtained help from a 14-year-old boy in opening the street door of the YMCA and the door to his automobile parked outside. When Williams placed the bundle in the front seat of his car the boy "saw two legs in it and they were skinny and white." Before anyone could see what was in the bundle Williams drove away. His abandoned car was found the following day in Davenport, Iowa, roughly 160 miles east of Des Moines. A warrant was then issued in Des Moines for his arrest on a charge of abduction.

On the morning of December 26, a Des Moines lawyer named Henry McKnight went to the Des Moines police station and informed the officers present that he had just received a long distance call from Williams, and that he had advised Williams to turn himself in to the Davenport police. Williams did surrender that morning to the police in Davenport, and they booked him on the charge specified in the arrest warrant and gave him the [*Miranda* warnings]. The Davenport police then telephoned their counterparts in Des Moines to inform them that Williams had surrendered. McKnight, the lawyer, was still at the Des Moines police headquarters, and Williams conversed with McKnight on the telephone. In the presence of the Des Moines Chief of Police and a Police Detective named Leaming [a captain and 20-year veteran of the Des Moines police department], McKnight advised Williams that Des Moines police officers would be driving to Davenport to pick him up, that the officers would not interrogate him or mistreat him, and that Williams was not to talk to the officers about Pamela Powers until after consulting with McKnight upon his return to Des Moines. As a result of these conversations, it was agreed between McKnight and the Des Moines police officials that Detective Leaming and a fellow officer would drive to Davenport to pick up Williams, that they would bring him directly back to Des Moines, and that they would not question him during the trip.

In the meantime Williams was arraigned before a judge in Davenport on the outstanding arrest warrant. The judge advised him of his *Miranda* rights and committed him to jail. Before leaving the courtroom, Williams conferred with a lawyer named Kelly, who advised him not to make any statements until consulting with McKnight back in Des Moines.

Detective Leaming and his fellow officer arrived in Davenport about noon to pick up Williams and return him to Des Moines. Soon after their arrival they met with Williams and Kelly, who, they understood, was acting as Williams' lawyer. Detective Leaming repeated the *Miranda* warnings, and told Williams:

> "* * * we both know that you're being represented here by Mr. Kelly and you're being represented by Mr. McKnight in Des Moines, and * * * I want you to remember this because we'll be visiting between here and Des Moines."

Williams then conferred again with Kelly alone, and after this conference Kelly reiterated to Detective Leaming that Williams was not to be questioned about the disappearance of Pamela Powers until after he had consulted with McKnight back in Des Moines. When Leaming expressed some reservations, Kelly firmly stated that the agreement with McKnight was to be carried out—that there was to be no interrogation of Williams during the automobile journey to Des Moines. Kelly was denied permission to ride in the police car back to Des Moines with Williams and the two officers.

The two Detectives, with Williams in their charge, then set out on the 160-mile drive. At no time during the trip did Williams express a willingness to be interrogated in the absence of an attorney. Instead, he stated several times that "[w]hen I get to Des Moines and see Mr. McKnight, I am going to tell you the whole story." Detective Leaming knew that Williams was a former mental patient, and knew also that he was deeply religious.

The Detective and his prisoner soon embarked on a wide-ranging conversation covering a variety of topics, including the subject of religion. Then, not long after leaving Davenport and reaching the interstate highway, Detective Leaming delivered what has been referred to [as] the "Christian burial speech." Addressing Williams as "Reverend," the Detective said:

> "I want to give you something to think about while we're traveling down the road. * * * Number one, I want you to observe the weather conditions, it's raining, it's sleeting, it's freezing, driving is very treacherous, visibility is poor, it's going to be dark early this evening. They are predicting several inches of snow for tonight, and I feel that you yourself are the only person that knows where this little girl's body is, that you yourself have only been there once, and if you get a snow on top of it you yourself may be unable to find it. And, since we will be going right past the area on the way into Des Moines, I feel that we could stop and locate the body, that the parents of this little girl should be entitled to a Christian burial for the little girl who was snatched away from them on Christmas Eve and murdered. And I feel we should stop and locate it on the way in rather than waiting until morning and trying to come back out after a snow storm and possibly not being able to find it at all." [a]

a. Although no member of the Supreme Court discussed, or even noted, this point, Captain Leaming offered two different versions of the "Christian burial speech." The captain's first version was given at a pretrial hearing to suppress evidence; his second version, the only one

Williams asked Detective Leaming why he thought their route to Des Moines would be taking them past the girl's body, and Leaming responded that he knew the body was in the area of Mitchellville—a town they would be passing on the way to Des Moines.[1] Leaming then stated: "I do not want you to answer me. I don't want to discuss it further. Just think about it as we're riding down the road."

As the car approached Grinell, a town approximately 100 miles west of Davenport, Williams asked whether the police had found the victim's shoes. When Detective Leaming replied that he was unsure, Williams directed the officers to a service station where he said he had left the shoes; a search for them proved unsuccessful. As they continued towards Des Moines, Williams asked whether the police had found the blanket, and directed the officers to a rest area where he said he had disposed of the blanket. Nothing was found. The car continued towards Des Moines, and as it approached Mitchellville, Williams said that he would show the officers where the body was. He then directed the police to the body of Pamela Powers.

[The trial judge admitted all evidence relating to or resulting from statements Williams made in the car ride. He found that "an agreement" had been made between defense counsel and the police that Williams would not be questioned on the return trip to Des Moines, but ruled that Williams had waived his rights before giving such information.]

[On federal habeas corpus, the] District Court made findings of fact as summarized above, and concluded as a matter of law that the evidence in question had been wrongly admitted at Williams' trial. This conclusion was based on three alternative and independent grounds: (1) that Williams had been denied his constitutional right to the assistance of counsel; (2) that he had been denied [his *Miranda* rights]; and (3) that in any event, [his] statements [had] been involuntarily made.

* * * The Court of Appeals appears to have affirmed the judgment on [the first two] grounds. We have concluded that only one of them need be considered here.

Specifically, there is no need to review the [*Miranda* doctrine] [or the] the ruling of the District Court that Williams' self-incriminating statements were, indeed, involuntarily made. For it is clear that the judgment before us must in any event be affirmed upon the ground that Williams was deprived of a different constitutional right—the right to the assistance of counsel.

* * * Whatever else it may mean, the right to counsel * * * means at least that a person is entitled to the help of a lawyer at or after the time that judicial proceedings have been initiated against him—"whether by way of formal charge, preliminary hearing, indictment, information, or arraignment." *Kirby v. Illinois* [p. 668 infra].

There can be no doubt in the present case that judicial proceedings had been initiated against Williams before the start of the automobile ride from Davenport to

quoted and discussed by the Supreme Court and lower federal courts, was given four weeks later at the trial. See Kamisar, *Foreword: Brewer v. Williams—A Hard Look at a Discomfiting Record,* 66 Geo.L.J. 209, 215–18 (1977). For the view that these two versions are significantly different, see id. at 218–33.

Justice Stewart notes that the captain addressed Williams as "Reverend," and then gives the captain's *second* version of the speech and related testimony *in its entirety.* But Captain Leaming did not testify that he addressed Williams as "Reverend" in the second version, only in the first. Justice Stewart may have called attention to the "Reverend" address because the Attorney General of Iowa was sufficiently troubled by it to go outside the record to explain in his brief why Captain Leaming employed it. See Kamisar, supra, at 223. For a discussion of the significance of the " 'Reverend' ploy," see id. at 221–23.

1. The fact of the matter, of course, was that Detective Leaming possessed no such knowledge.

Des Moines. A warrant had been issued for his arrest, he had been arraigned on that warrant before a judge in a Davenport courtroom, and he had been committed by the court to confinement in jail. The State does not contend otherwise.

There can be no serious doubt, either, that Detective Leaming deliberately and designedly set out to elicit information from Williams just as surely as—and perhaps more effectively than—if he had formally interrogated him. Detective Leaming was fully aware before departing for Des Moines that Williams was being represented in Davenport by Kelly and in Des Moines by McKnight. Yet he purposely sought during Williams' isolation from his lawyers to obtain as much incriminating information as possible. Indeed, Detective Leaming conceded as much when he testified at Williams' trial:

> "Q. In fact, Captain, whether he was a mental patient or not, you were trying to get all the information you could before he got to his lawyer, weren't you?
>
> "A. I was sure hoping to find out where that little girl was, yes, sir.
>
> * * *
>
> "Q. Well, I'll put it this way: You [were] hoping to get all the information you could before Williams got back to McKnight, weren't you?
>
> "A. Yes, sir." [6]

The state courts clearly proceeded upon the hypothesis that Detective Leaming's "Christian burial speech" had been tantamount to interrogation. Both courts recognized that Williams had been entitled to the assistance of counsel at the time he made the incriminating statements. Yet no such constitutional protection would have come into play if there had been no interrogation.

The circumstances of this case are thus constitutionally indistinguishable from those presented in *Massiah* [p. 527 supra]. * * * That the incriminating statements were elicited surreptitiously in [*Massiah*], and otherwise here, is constitutionally irrelevant. Rather, the clear rule of *Massiah* is that once adversary proceedings have commenced against an individual, he has a right to legal representation when the government interrogates him.[b] It thus requires no wooden or technical application of the *Massiah* doctrine to conclude that Williams was entitled to the assistance of counsel guaranteed to him by the Sixth and Fourteenth Amendments.

The Iowa courts recognized that Williams had been denied the constitutional right to the assistance of counsel. They held, however, that he had waived that right during the course of the automobile trip from Davenport to Des Moines. The state trial court explained its determination of waiver as follows:

> "The time element involved on the trip, the general circumstances of it, and more importantly the absence on the Defendant's part of any assertion of his right or desire not to give information absent the presence of his attorney, are the main foundations for the Court's conclusion that he voluntarily waived such right." * * *

The District Court and the Court of Appeals were correct in the view that the question of waiver was not a question of historical fact, but one [that], requires "application of constitutional principles to the facts as found."

The [lower federal courts] were also correct in their understanding of the prop-

6. Counsel for the State, in the course of oral argument in this Court, acknowledged that the "Christian burial speech" was tantamount to interrogation * * *.

b. Isn't the clear rule of *Massiah* that once adversary proceedings have commenced against an individual, he has a right to counsel when the government *deliberately elicits* incriminating information from him (whether or not the government's efforts to obtain information constitute "interrogation' within the meaning of *Miranda*)? Did Justice Stewart, in effect, correct himself three years later in fn. 4 to his opinion in *Rhode Island v. Innis* (p. 589 supra)?

er standard to be applied in determining the question of waiver as a matter of federal constitutional law—that it was incumbent upon the State to prove "an intentional relinquishment or abandonment of a known right or privilege." *Johnson v. Zerbst.* [That] strict standard applies equally to an alleged waiver of the right to counsel whether at trial or at a critical stage of pretrial proceedings.

We conclude, finally that the Court of Appeals was correct in holding that, judged by these standards, the record in this case falls far short of sustaining the State's burden. It is true that Williams had been informed of and appeared to understand his right to counsel. But waiver requires not merely comprehension but relinquishment, and Williams' consistent reliance upon the advice of counsel in dealing with the authorities refutes any suggestion that he waived that right. * * * His statements while in the car that he would tell the whole story *after* seeing McKnight in Des Moines were the clearest expressions by Williams himself that he desired the presence of an attorney before any interrogation took place. But even before making these statements, Williams had effectively asserted his right to counsel by having secured attorneys at both ends of the automobile trip, both of whom, acting as his agents, had made clear to the police that no interrogation was to occur during the journey. Williams knew of that agreement and, particularly in view of his consistent reliance on counsel, there is no basis for concluding that he disavowed it.

Despite Williams' express and implicit assertions of his right to counsel, Detective Leaming proceeded to elicit incriminating statements from Williams. Leaming did not preface this effort by telling Williams that he had a right to the presence of a lawyer, and made no effort at all to ascertain whether Williams wished to relinquish that right. The circumstances of record in this case thus provide no reasonable basis for finding that Williams waived his right to the assistance of counsel.

The Court of Appeals did not hold, nor do we, that under the circumstances of this case Williams *could not,* without notice to counsel, have waived his rights under the Sixth and Fourteenth Amendments. It only held, as do we, that he did not.

* * * Although we do not lightly affirm the issuance of a writ of habeas corpus in this case, so clear a violation of the Sixth and Fourteenth Amendments as here occurred cannot be condoned. * * *

The judgment of the Court of Appeals is affirmed.[12]

MR. JUSTICE MARSHALL, concurring.

I concur wholeheartedly in my Brother Stewart's opinion for the Court, but add these words in light of the dissenting opinions filed today. The dissenters have, I believe, lost sight of the fundamental constitutional backbone of our criminal law. They seem to think that Detective Leaming's actions were perfectly proper, indeed laudable, examples of "good police work." In my view, good police work is something far different from catching the crimi-

12. The District Court stated that its decision "does not touch upon the issue of what evidence, if any, beyond the incriminating statements themselves must be excluded as 'fruit of the poisonous tree.'" We too have no occasion to address this issue, and in the present posture of the case there is no basis for the view of our dissenting Brethren [that] any attempt to retry the respondent would probably be futile. While neither Williams' incriminating statements themselves nor any testimony describing his having led the police to the victim's body can constitutionally be admitted into evidence, evidence of where the body was found and of its condition might well be admissible on the theory that the body would have been discovered in any event, even had incriminating statements not been elicited from Williams. In the event that a retrial is instituted, it will be for the state courts in the first instance to determine whether particular items of evidence may be admitted.

[On retrial, the state court ruled that the body of Pamela Powers "would have been found in any event" and Williams was again convicted of murder. The U.S. Supreme Court upheld the state court's use of the "inevitable discovery" exception. See *Williams II,* p. 810 infra.]

nal at any price. It is equally important that the police, as guardians of the law, fulfill their responsibility to obey its commands scrupulously. * * *

In this case, there can be no doubt that Detective Leaming consciously and knowingly set out to violate Williams' Sixth Amendment right to counsel and his Fifth Amendment privilege against self-incrimination, as Leaming himself understood those rights. * * * Leaming surely understood, because he had overheard McKnight tell Williams as much, that the location of the body would be revealed to police. Undoubtedly Leaming realized the way in which that information would be conveyed to the police: McKnight would learn it from his client and then he would lead police to the body. Williams would thereby be protected by the attorney-client privilege from incriminating himself by directly demonstrating his knowledge of the body's location, and the unfortunate Powers child could be given a "Christian burial."

Of course, this scenario would accomplish all that Leaming sought from his investigation except that it would not produce incriminating statements or actions from Williams. Accordingly, Leaming undertook his charade to pry such evidence from Williams. After invoking the no-passengers rule to prevent attorney Kelly from accompanying the prisoner, Leaming had Williams at his mercy: during the three- or four-hour trip he could do anything he wished to elicit a confession.

* * * If Williams is to go free—and given the ingenuity of Iowa prosecutors on retrial or in a civil commitment proceeding, I doubt very much that there is any chance a dangerous criminal will be loosed on the streets, the blood-curdling cries of the dissents notwithstanding—it will hardly be because he deserves it. It will be because Detective Leaming, knowing full well that he risked reversal of Williams' conviction, intentionally denied Williams the right of *every* American under the Sixth Amendment to have the protective shield of a lawyer between himself and the awesome power of the State.

* * *

MR. JUSTICE POWELL, concurring.

* * *

The critical factual issue is whether there had been a voluntary waiver, and this turns in large part upon whether there was interrogation. * * *

Prior to the automobile trip from Davenport to Des Moines, Williams had been arrested, booked, and carefully given *Miranda* warnings. It is settled constitutional doctrine that he then had the right to the assistance of counsel. His exercise of this right was evidenced uniquely in this case. * * * Significantly, the recognition by the police of the status of counsel was evidenced by the *express agreement* between McKnight and the appropriate police officials that the officers who would drive Williams to Des Moines would not interrogate him in the absence of counsel.

The incriminating statements were made by Williams during the long ride while in the custody of two police officers, and in the absence of his retained counsel. The dissent of the Chief Justice concludes that prior to these statements, Williams had "made a valid waiver" of his right to have counsel present. This view disregards the record evidence clearly indicating that the police engaged in interrogation of Williams. * * *

The dissenting opinion of the Chief Justice states that the Court's holding today "conclusively presumes a suspect is legally incompetent to change his mind and tell the truth until an attorney is present." I find no justification for this view. On the contrary, the opinion of the Court is explicitly clear that the right to assistance of counsel may be waived, after it has attached, without notice to or consultation with counsel. We would have such a case here if the State had proved that the police officers refrained from coercion and interrogation, as they have agreed, and that

Williams freely on his own initiative had confessed the crime. * * * [c]

MR. CHIEF JUSTICE BURGER, dissenting.

The result in this case ought to be intolerable in any society which purports to call itself an organized society. It continues the Court—by the narrowest margin—on the much-criticized course of punishing the public for the mistakes and misdeeds of law enforcement officers, instead of punishing the officer directly, if in fact he is guilty of wrongdoing. It mechanically and blindly keeps reliable evidence from juries whether the claimed constitutional violation involves gross police misconduct or honest human error.

Williams is guilty of the savage murder of a small child; no member of the Court contends he is not. While in custody, and after no fewer than *five* warnings of his rights to silence and to counsel, he led police to the concealed body of his victim. The Court concedes Williams was not threatened or coerced and that he spoke and acted voluntarily and with full awareness of his constitutional rights. In the face of all this, the Court now holds that because Williams was prompted by the detective's statement—not interrogation but a statement—the jury must not be told how the police found the body. * * *

Under well-settled precedents which the Court freely acknowledges, it is very clear that Williams had made a valid waiver of his Fifth Amendment right to silence and his Sixth Amendment right to counsel when he led police to the child's body. Indeed, even under the Court's analysis I do not understand how a contrary conclusion is possible. * * *

The evidence is uncontradicted that Williams had abundant knowledge of his right to have counsel present and of his right to silence. Since the Court does not question his mental competence, it boggles the mind to suggest that Williams could not understand that leading police to the child's body would have other than the most serious consequences. * * *

One plausible but unarticulated basis for the result reached is that once a suspect has asserted his right not to talk without the presence of an attorney, it becomes legally impossible for him to waive that right until he has seen an attorney. But constitutional rights are *personal,* and an otherwise valid waiver should not be brushed aside by judges simply because an attorney was not present. * * * [2]

* * * Mr. Justice Powell suggests that the result in this case turns on whether Detective Leaming's remarks constituted "interrogation," as he views them, or whether they were "statements" intended to prick the conscience of the accused. I find it most remarkable that a murder case should turn on judicial interpretation that a statement becomes a question simply because it is followed by an incriminating disclosure from the suspect. The Court seems to be saying that since Williams said he would "tell the whole story" at Des Moines, the police should have been content and waited; of course, that would have been the wiser course, especially in light of the nuances of constitutional jurisprudence applied by the Court, but a murder case ought not turn on such tenuous strands.

In any case, the Court assures us, this is not at all what it intends, and that a valid waiver was *possible* in these circumstances,

c. Stevens, J., joined the opinion of the Court, but also added a brief comment concluding: "If, in the long run, we are seriously concerned about the individual's effective representation by counsel, the State cannot be permitted to dishonor its promise to this lawyer."

2. [A] paternalistic rule is particularly anomalous in the Sixth Amendment context, where this Court has only recently discovered an independent constitutional right of self-representation, allowing an accused the absolute right to proceed without a lawyer at trial, once he is aware of the consequences. *Faretta,* p. 122 supra.

but was not quite made. Here of course Williams did not confess to the murder in so many words; it was his conduct in guiding police to the body, not his words, which incriminated him. And the record is replete with evidence that Williams knew precisely what he was doing when he guided police to the body. The human urge to confess wrongdoing is, of course, normal in all save hardened, professional criminals, as psychiatrists and analysts have demonstrated.

Even if there was no waiver, and assuming a technical violation occurred, the Court errs gravely in mechanically applying the exclusionary rule without considering whether that draconian judicial doctrine should be invoked in these circumstances, or indeed whether any of its conceivable goals will be furthered by its application here.

* * * Today's holding interrupts what has been a more rational perception of the constitutional and social utility of excluding reliable evidence from the truth-seeking process. In its Fourth Amendment context, we have now recognized that the exclusionary rule is in no sense a *personal* constitutional right, but a judicially conceived remedial device designed to safeguard and effectuate guaranteed legal rights generally [referring to *Stone v. Powell,* Ch. 27, § 1; *United States v. Janis,* p. 232 supra; and *United States v. Calandra,* p. 230 supra]. We have repeatedly emphasized that deterrence of unconstitutional or otherwise unlawful police conduct is the only valid justification for excluding reliable and probative evidence from the criminal factfinding process.

Accordingly, unlawfully obtained evidence is not automatically excluded from the factfinding process in all circumstances. In a variety of contexts we inquire whether application of the rule will promote its objectives sufficiently to justify the enormous cost it imposes on society. * * *

Against this background, it is striking that the Court fails even to consider whether the benefits secured by application of the exclusionary rule in this case outweigh its obvious social costs. Perhaps the failure is due to the fact that this case arises not under the Fourth Amendment, but under *Miranda,* and the Sixth Amendment right to counsel. The Court apparently perceives the function of the exclusionary rule to be so different in these varying contexts that it must be mechanically and uncritically applied in all cases arising outside the Fourth Amendment. * * *

[W]hether considered under *Miranda* or the Sixth Amendment, there is no more reason to exclude the evidence in this case than there was in *Stone* * * * [and] in other Fourth Amendment cases suggesting a balancing approach toward utilization of the exclusionary sanction. Rather than adopting a formalistic analysis varying with the constitutional provision invoked, we should apply the exclusionary rule on the basis of its benefits and costs, at least in those cases where the police conduct at issue is far from being outrageous or egregious. * * *

MR. JUSTICE WHITE, with whom MR. JUSTICE BLACKMUN and MR. JUSTICE REHNQUIST join, dissenting.

* * * The issue in this case is whether respondent—who was entitled not to make any statements to the police without consultation with and/or presence of counsel [1]—validly waived those rights. * * *

[I disagree with the majority's finding that no waiver was proved in this case.] That respondent knew of his right not to say anything to the officers without advice and presence of counsel is established on

1. It does not matter whether the right not to make statements in the absence of counsel stems from *Massiah,* or *Miranda.* In either case the question is one of waiver. Waiver was not addressed in *Massiah* because there the statements were being made to an informant and the defendant had no way of knowing that he had a right not to talk to him without counsel.

this record to a moral certainty. He was advised of the right by three officials of the State—telling at least one that he understood the right—and by two lawyers.[4] Finally, he further demonstrated his knowledge of the right by informing the police that he would tell them the story in the presence of McKnight when they arrived in Des Moines. The issue in this case, then, is whether respondent relinquished that right intentionally.

Respondent relinquished his right not to talk to the police about his crime when the car approached the place where he had hidden the victim's clothes. Men usually intend to do what they do and there is nothing in the record to support the proposition that respondent's decision to talk was anything but an exercise of his own free will. Apparently, without any prodding from the officers, respondent—who had earlier said that he would tell the whole story when he arrived in Des Moines—spontaneously changed his mind about the timing of his disclosures when the car approached the places where he had hidden the evidence. However, even if his statements were influenced by Detective Leaming's above-quoted statement, respondent's decision to talk in the absence of counsel can hardly be viewed as the product of an overborn will. The statement by Leaming was not coercive; it was accompanied by a request that respondent not respond to it; and it was delivered hours before respondent decided to make any statement. Respondent's waiver was thus knowing and intentional.

The majority's contrary conclusion seems to rest on the fact that respondent "asserted" his right to counsel by retaining and consulting with one lawyer and by consulting with another. How this supports the conclusion that respondent's later relinquishment of his right not to talk in the absence of counsel was unintentional is a mystery. The fact that respondent consulted with counsel on the question whether he should talk to the police in counsel's absence makes his later decision to talk in counsel's absence *better* informed and, if anything, more intelligent.

The majority recognizes that even after this "assertion" of his right to counsel, it would have found that respondent waived his right not to talk in counsel's absence if his waiver had been express—i.e., if the officers had asked him in the car whether he would be willing to answer questions in counsel's absence and if he had answered "yes." But waiver is not a formalistic concept. Waiver is shown whenever the facts establish that an accused knew of a right and intended to relinquish it. Such waiver, even if not express, was plainly shown here. The only other conceivable basis for the majority's holding is the implicit suggestion that the right involved in *Massiah,* as distinguished from the right involved in *Miranda,* is a right not to be *asked* any questions in counsel's absence rather than a right not to *answer* any questions in counsel's absence, and that the right not to be *asked* questions must be waived *before* the questions are asked. Such wafer thin distinctions cannot determine whether a guilty murderer should go free.[d] The only conceivable purpose for the presence of counsel during questioning is to protect an accused from making incriminating *answers.* Questions, unanswered, have no significance at all. Absent coercion—no matter how the right involved is defined—an accused is amply

4. Moreover, he in fact received advice of counsel on at least two occasions on the question whether he should talk to the police on the trip to Des Moines.

d. But see Grano, *Rhode Island v. Innis: A Need to Reconsider the Constitutional Premises Underlying the Law of Confessions,* 17 Am.Crim. L.Rev. 1, 34 (1979): "Justice White could not be more wrong in his criticism. The whole point of *Massiah* is the prevention of the state from taking advantage of an uncounseled defendant once Sixth Amendment rights attach. The Christian burial speech case was an attempt to take advantage of Williams. The attempt itself is what *Massiah* prohibits. The attempt itself violates the constitutional mandate that the system proceed, after some point, only in an accusatorial manner."

protected by a rule requiring waiver before or simultaneously with the giving by him of an answer or the making by him of a statement.

* * *

MR. JUSTICE BLACKMUN, with whom MR. JUSTICE WHITE and MR. JUSTICE REHNQUIST join, dissenting. * * *

What the Court chooses to do here, and with which I disagree, is to hold that respondent Williams' situation was in the mold of *Massiah,* that is, that it was dominated by a denial to Williams of his Sixth Amendment right to counsel after criminal proceedings had been instituted against him. The Court rules that the Sixth Amendment was violated because Detective Leaming "purposely sought during Williams' isolation from his lawyers to obtain as much incriminating information as possible." I cannot regard that as unconstitutional *per se.*

First, the police did not deliberately seek to isolate Williams from his lawyers so as to deprive him of the assistance of counsel. Cf. *Escobedo.* The isolation in this case was a necessary incident of transporting Williams to the county where the crime was committed.

Second, Leaming's purpose was not solely to obtain incriminating evidence. The victim had been missing for only two days, and the police could not be certain that she was dead. Leaming, of course, and in accord with his duty, was "hoping to find out where that little girl was," but such motivation does not equate with an intention to evade the Sixth Amendment.[e]

* * *

Third, not every attempt to elicit information should be regarded as "tantamount to interrogation." I am not persuaded that Leaming's observations and comments, made as the police car traversed the snowy and slippery miles between Davenport and Des Moines that winter afternoon, were an interrogation, direct or subtle, of Williams. Williams, after all, was counseled by lawyers, and warned by the arraigning judge in Davenport and by the police, and yet it was he who started the travel conversations and brought up the subject of the criminal investigation.

* * *

In summary, it seems to me that the Court is holding that *Massiah* is violated whenever police engage in any conduct, in the absence of counsel, with the subjective desire to obtain information from a suspect after arraignment. Such a rule is far too broad. Persons in custody frequently volunteer statements in response to stimuli other than interrogation. * * *

Notes and Questions

1. *Was it constitutionally irrelevant whether the "Christian burial speech" constituted "interrogation"?* Did the Court deem it necessary (or at least important) to classify Leaming's speech as a "form of interrogation" or "tantamount to interrogation"? If so, why? Once the Court chose the "Sixth Amendment-*Massiah*" route over a "Fifth Amendment-*Miranda*" approach, did the question whether Leaming engaged in "interrogation" become, or should it have become, constitutionally irrelevant? Did the secret government agent engage in "interrogation" in *Massiah* (p. 527 supra)? In *United States v. Henry* (p. 638 infra)?

2. *Even if Brewer v. Williams were deemed a "Miranda case," would whether Leaming engaged in "interrogation" still be the wrong question?* Since Williams had asserted both his right to remain silent and his right to

e. But see Kamisar, *Police Interrogation and Confessions* 146–47 (1980), maintaining that although at one point Leaming did testify that he was "hoping to find out where that little *girl* was," in light of the entire record he apparently meant the girl's *body.* Leaming testified that he heard Williams' lawyer say to him over the phone that he would have to tell the police "where *the body* is" when he got back. Leaming also testified that before he drove to Davenport to pick up Williams, Williams' lawyer told him that the girl "was dead when [Williams] left the YMCA with her."

counsel *several times* before he was driven back to Des Moines, should the relevant question have been whether Leaming "fully respected" or "scrupulously honored" Williams' *Miranda* rights? Cf. *Michigan v. Mosley,* p. 610 supra. How could it be said that Leaming did, when he "deliberately and designedly set out to elicit information" from *Williams?*

Brewer v. Williams was decided four years before *Edwards v. Arizona,* p. 613 supra. Looking back at *Williams* in light of *Edwards,* if *Williams* were a "*Miranda* case," should the relevant question have been whether, after expressing his unwillingness to talk to the police without his lawyer, Williams changed his mind on his own initiative or whether Leaming "persuaded" or "prompted" him to change his mind?

3. *One reason the Court may have preferred the Massiah route over Miranda in the Williams case.* *Williams* reached the Court in a federal habeas corpus proceeding eight months after the Court, emphasizing that illegally seized evidence is typically reliable and maintaining that the additional contribution, if any, of the consideration of search-and-seizure claims on collateral review is small in relation to its costs, had ruled in *Stone v. Powell,* Ch. 27, § 1, that Fourth Amendment claims may not be raised on federal habeas if the state has provided an opportunity for "full and fair litigation" of the claim. Observes Schulhofer, *Confessions and the Court,* 79 Mich.L.Rev. 865, 887–90:

"The majority opinion in *Williams* omits any mention of *Stone,* presumably because the parties had not fully briefed the issue, but it seems reasonable to speculate that at least some members of the Court would have had difficulty ignoring *Stone* 's implications, if reliance had been placed on *Miranda.* The Court's decision in *Williams* to avoid that route thus could be read as darkening the shadow cast by *Stone* over the continued availability of *Miranda* claims on habeas.

"* * * Admittedly, a *Massiah* violation will typically cast no doubt on the trustworthiness of the defendant's statements. * * * But the *Massiah* 'exclusionary rule' is not merely a prophylactic device; it is not designed to reduce the *risk* of actual constitutional violations and is not intended to deter any pretrial behavior whatsoever. * * * When the government has made an 'end run' around counsel, or effected pretrial discovery in disregard of the norms of legitimate adversary procedure it is wholly beside the point to claim that the evidence obtained by such tactics was reliable. Use of the evidence taints the judicial proceedings in a fundamental way, and relief on habeas must remain open.

"*Miranda* claims seem much closer to search and seizure claims for purposes of applying *Stone* and denying habeas review. * * * Moreover, the Court has repeatedly characterized *Miranda* as a set of prophylactic rules designed to deter unacceptable police behavior and to reduce the risk of actual constitutional violations. Given the Court's assumption in *Stone* that habeas relief is not useful in furthering such deterrence goals, the Court may consider the value of habeas relief in *Miranda* to be similarly outweighed by its costs." [a]

4. *What constitutes a valid waiver of the "Sixth Amendment-Massiah" right?* Even though the warnings satisfied *Miranda* and defendant's statements were admissible under *Miranda,* UNITED STATES v. MOHABIR, 624 F.2d 1140 (2d Cir. 1980), per FEINBERG, J., barred statements an Assistant United States Attorney had elicited from defendant after he had obtained counsel. For "the central issue before us is whether [defendant] waived his rights under the Sixth, rather than the Fifth, Amendment. The distinction is a crucial one * * *. [A] number of cases

a. But Professor Schulhofer goes on to say that the Court should reject the search and seizure analogy and reaffirm the availability of *Miranda* claims in habeas cases. See Ch. 27, § 1.

in this court have made clear that waiver of Sixth Amendment rights must be measured by a 'higher standard' than are waivers of Fifth Amendment rights." The court went on to say:

"The Supreme Court has stressed [that] the 'strict standard [applied in determining the question of waiver] applies equally to an alleged waiver of the right to counsel whether at trial or at a critical stage of pretrial proceedings.' *Brewer v. Williams.* * * * [W]e conclude, in the exercise of our supervisory power, that a valid waiver of the Sixth Amendment right to have counsel present during postindictment interrogation must be preceded by a federal judicial officer's explanation of the content and significance of this right. * * * [Moreover], a defendant arrested after indictment should be shown the indictment and told by the judicial officer that he has been indicted, the significance of an indictment, that he has a right to counsel, and the seriousness of his situation in the event he should decide to answer questions of any law enforcement officers in the absence of counsel.

"The advantages of such a rule are clear.[a] If advice is given by a judicial officer, disputes as to what occurred will be rare and legal battles as to whether the defendant's comprehension of his Sixth Amendment right was sufficient to support a finding of waiver will be less likely * * *. We realize that the number of confessions obtained under the present practice from uncounseled, indicted defendants may decrease, but this is the price of defining in a more precise way the 'higher standard' that must be met for waiver of the Sixth Amendment right."

5. *Application of Massiah to bar use of a pretrial psychiatric examination at a capital sentencing proceeding.* ESTELLE v. SMITH (p. 623 supra) held, per BURGER, C.J., without a dissent on this issue, that the use at the penalty phase of a capital case of a pretrial psychiatric examination—which took place after respondent had been indicted and been appointed counsel, but without previous notice to respondent's counsel—violated respondent's Sixth Amendment right to the assistance of counsel:

"Here, respondent's Sixth Amendment right to counsel clearly had attached when Dr. Grigson examined him[14] [and] their interview proved to be a 'critical stage' of the aggregate proceeding against respondent. Defense counsel, however, were not notified in advance that the psychiatric examination would encompass the issue of their client's future dangerousness[15] [one of the critical issues at the penalty phase], and respondent was denied the assistance of his attorneys in making the significant

a. Are not "the advantages of such a rule" equally clear for the waiver of *Fifth* Amendment rights? At one point in the *Mohabir* opinion, the court emphasizes that "warnings that might satisfy '*Miranda*'s less stringent requirements'" do not "necessarily satisfy the 'higher standard' our precedents require in examining alleged waivers once the Sixth Amendment attaches." How much support, if any, does *Miranda* provide for the view that requirements for the waiver of Fifth Amendment rights in custodial settings are "less stringent" than those for the waiver of other constitutional rights? Reconsider *Miranda* at p. 550 supra: "This Court has always set high standards of proof for the waiver of constitutional rights, *Johnson v. Zerbst,* and we re-assert these standards as applied to in-custody interrogation."

14. Because psychiatric examinations of the type at issue here are conducted after adversary proceedings have been instituted, we are not concerned in this case with the limited right to the appointment and presence of counsel recognized as a Fifth Amendment safeguard in *Miranda.* Rather, the issue before us is whether a defendant's Sixth Amendment right to the assistance of counsel is abridged when the defendant is not given prior opportunity to consult with counsel about his participation in the psychiatric examination.

Respondent does not assert, and the [Fifth Circuit] did not find, any constitutional right to have counsel actually present during the examination. In fact, the [Fifth Circuit] recognized that "an attorney present during the psychiatric interview could contribute little and might seriously disrupt the examination."

15. It is not clear that defense counsel were even informed prior to the examination that Dr. Grigson had been appointed by the trial judge to determine respondent's competency to stand trial.

decision of whether to submit to the examination and to what end the psychiatrist's findings could be employed."

UNITED STATES v. HENRY

447 U.S. 264, 100 S.Ct. 2183, 65 L.Ed.2d 115 (1980).

MR. CHIEF JUSTICE BURGER delivered the opinion of the Court.

[In November, 1972, respondent was indicted for robbing the Janaf branch bank and] held pending trial in the Norfolk City Jail. Counsel was appointed on November 27.

On November 21, 1972, shortly after Henry was incarcerated, government agents working on the Janaf robbery contacted one Nichols, an inmate at the Norfolk City jail, who [had been providing confidential information to the FBI as a paid informant.] The record does not disclose whether the agent contacted Nichols specifically to acquire information about Henry or the Janaf robbery.[1]

Nichols informed the agent that he was housed in the same cellblock with several federal prisoners awaiting trial, including Henry. The agent told him to be alert to any statements made by the federal prisoners, but not to initiate any conversation with or question Henry regarding the bank robbery. In early December, after Nichols had been released from jail, the agent again contacted Nichols, who reported that he and Henry had engaged in conversation and that Henry had told him about the robbery of the Janaf bank. Nichols was paid for furnishing the information. * * *

Nichols testified at trial that he had "an opportunity to have some conversations with Mr. Henry while he was in the jail," and that Henry told him that on several occasions he had gone to the Janaf branch to see which employees opened the vault. Nichols also testified that Henry described to him the details of the robbery and stated that the only evidence connecting him to the robbery was the rental receipt. The jury was not informed that Nichols was a paid government informant.

On the basis of this testimony, Henry was convicted of bank robbery and sentenced to [prison]. [After his conviction was affirmed, Henry filed a § 2255 petition, seeking to vacate his sentence. As requested by the district court, an affidavit was submitted by a federal agent] describing [his] relationship with Nichols and relating the following conversation:

> "I recall telling Nichols at this time to be alert to any statements made by these individuals [the federal prisoners] regarding the charges against them. I specifically recall telling Nichols that he was not to question Henry or these individuals about the charges against them, however, if they engaged him in conversation or talked in front of him, he was requested to pay attention to their statements. I recall telling Nichols not to initiate any conversations with Henry regarding the bank robbery charges against Henry, but that if Henry initiated the conversations with Nichols, I requested Nichols to pay attention to the information furnished by Henry."

The agent's affidavit also stated that he never requested anyone affiliated with the Norfolk City Jail to place Nichols in the same cell with Henry.

[The district court denied Henry's § 2255 motion, but the Fourth Circuit reversed, holding that the government had violated respondent's *Massiah* rights.]

* * * The question here is [whether] a government agent "deliberately elicited" incriminating statements from Henry within the meaning of *Massiah*. Three factors are important. First, Nichols was acting under instructions as a paid informant for the government; second Nichols was os-

1. The record does disclose that [the] same day the agent contacted Nichols, the agent's supervisor interrogated Henry at the jail. After denying participation in the robbery, Henry exercised his right to terminate the interview.

tensibly no more than a fellow inmate of Henry; and third, Henry was in custody and under indictment at the time he was engaged in conversation by Nichols.

The Court of Appeals viewed the record as showing that Nichols deliberately used his position to secure incriminating information from Henry when counsel was not present and held that conduct attributable to the government. Nichols had been a paid government informant for more than a year; moreover, the FBI agent was aware that Nichols had access to Henry and would be able to engage him in conversations without arousing Henry's suspicion. The arrangement between Nichols and the agent was on a contingent fee basis; Nichols was to be paid only if he produced useful information. This combination of circumstances is sufficient to support the Court of Appeals' determination. Even if the agent's statement is accepted that he did not intend that Nichols would take affirmative steps to secure incriminating information, he must have known that such propinquity likely would lead to that result.

The Government argues that the federal agents instructed Nichols not to question Henry about the robbery.[8] Yet according to his own testimony, Nichols was not a passive listener; rather, he had "some conversations with Mr. Henry" while he was in jail and Henry's incriminatory statements were "the product of this conversation." * * *[9]

* * * It is undisputed that Henry was unaware of Nichols' role as a government informant. The Government argues that this Court should apply a less rigorous standard under the Sixth Amendment where the accused is prompted by an undisclosed undercover informant than where the accused is speaking in the hearing of persons he knows to be government officers. That line of argument, however, seeks to infuse Fifth Amendment concerns against compelled self-incrimination into the Sixth Amendment protection of the right to the assistance of counsel. An accused speaking to a known government agent is typically aware that his statements may be used against him. The adversary positions at that stage are well established; the parties are then "arms length" adversaries.

When the accused is in the company of a fellow inmate who is acting by prearrangement as a government agent, the same cannot be said. Conversation stimulated in such circumstances may elicit information that an accused would not intentionally reveal to persons known to be government agents. Indeed, the *Massiah* Court noted that if the Sixth Amendment "is to have any efficacy it must apply to indirect and surreptitious interrogations as well as those conducted in the jailhouse." The Court pointedly observed that Massiah was more seriously imposed upon because he did not know that his codefendant was a government agent.

Moreover, the concept of a knowing and voluntary waiver of Sixth Amendment rights does not apply in the context of communications with an undisclosed undercover informant acting for the government. In that setting, Henry, being unaware that Nichols was a government agent

8. Two aspects of the agent's affidavit are particularly significant. First, it is clear that the agent in his discussions with Nichols singled out Henry as the inmate in whom the agent had a special interest. * * * Second, the agent only instructed Nichols not to question Henry or to initiate conversations regarding the bank robbery charges. Under these instructions, Nichols remained free to discharge his task of eliciting the statements in myriad less direct ways.

9. The situation where the "listening post" is an inanimate electronic device differs; such a device has no capability of leading the conversation into any particular subject or prompting any particular replies. See, e.g., *United States v. Hearst,* 563 F.2d 1331 (9th Cir.1977). However, that situation is not presented in this case, and there is no occasion to treat it; nor are we called upon to pass on the situation where an informant is placed in close proximity but makes no effort to stimulate conversations about the crime charged.

expressly commissioned to secure evidence, cannot be held to have waived his right to the assistance of counsel.

Finally, Henry's incarceration at the time he was engaged in conversation by Nichols is also a relevant factor.[11] As a ground for imposing the prophylactic requirements in *Miranda*, this Court noted the powerful psychological inducements to reach for aid when a person is in confinement. While the concern in *Miranda* was limited to custodial police interrogation, the mere fact of custody imposes pressures on the accused; confinement may bring into play subtle influences that will make him particularly susceptible to the ploys of undercover government agents.

* * * By intentionally creating a situation likely to induce Henry to make incriminating statements without the assistance of counsel, the government violated Henry's Sixth Amendment right to counsel. This is not a case where, in Justice Cardozo's words, "the constable blundered"; rather, it is one where the "constable" planned an impermissible interference with the right to the assistance of counsel. * * *

Affirmed.

[JUSTICE POWELL joined the Court's opinion on the understanding that it "rests on a conclusion that the informant deliberately elicited incriminating information" from respondent. He could not join the opinion "if it held that the mere presence or incidental conversation of an informant in a jail cell would violate *Massiah*." The *Massiah* rule, observed Justice Powell, "serves the salutary purpose of preventing police interference with the relationship between a suspect and his counsel once formal proceedings have been initiated. But *Massiah* does not prohibit the introduction of spontaneous statements that are not elicited by governmental action. Thus, the Sixth Amendment is not violated when a passive listening device collects, but does not induce, incriminating comments. See *Hearst* [fn. 9 of the Court's opinion]."]

MR. JUSTICE BLACKMUN, with whom MR. JUSTICE WHITE joins, dissenting.

In this case the Court, I fear, cuts loose from the moorings of *Massiah*[1] and overlooks or misapplies significant facts to reach a result that is not required by the Sixth Amendment, by established precedent, or by sound policy. * * *

Massiah mandates exclusion only if a federal agent "deliberately elicited" statements from the accused in the absence of counsel. The word "deliberately" denotes intent. *Massiah* ties this intent to the act of elicitation, that is, to conduct that draws forth a response. Thus *Massiah*, by its own terms, covers only action undertaken with the specific intent to evoke an inculpatory disclosure.

Faced with agent Coughlin's unequivocal expression of an intent *not* to elicit statements from respondent Henry, but merely passively to receive them, the Court, in its decision to affirm the judgment of the Court of Appeals, has no choice but to depart from the natural meaning of the *Massiah* formulation. * * *

[W]hile claiming to retain the "deliberately elicited" test, the Court really forges a new test that saps the word "deliberately" of all significance. The Court's extension of *Massiah* would cover even a "negligent" triggering of events resulting in reception of disclosures. This approach,

11. This is not to read a "custody" requirement, which is a prerequisite to the attachment of *Miranda* rights, into this branch of the Sixth Amendment. Massiah was in no sense in custody at the time of his conversation with his codefendant. Rather, we believe the fact of custody bears on whether the government "deliberately elicited" the incriminating statements from Henry.

1. For purposes of this case, I see no need to abandon *Massiah*, as Mr. Justice Rehnquist does.

in my view, is unsupported and unwise. * * *[5]

* * * While not out of line with the Court's prior right-to-counsel cases, *Massiah* certainly is the decision in which Sixth Amendment protections have been extended to their outermost point. I simply do not perceive any good reason to give *Massiah* the expansion it receives in this case.

In my view, the Court not only missteps in forging a new *Massiah* test; it proceeds to misapply the very test it has created. The new test requires a showing that the agent created a situation "likely to induce" the production of incriminatory remarks, and that the informant in fact "prompted" the defendant. Even accepting the most capacious reading of both this language and the facts, I believe that neither prong of the Court's test is satisfied.

A. *"Likely to Induce."* In holding that Coughlin's actions were likely to induce Henry's statements, the Court relies on three facts: a contingent fee arrangement; Henry's assumption that Nichols was just a cellmate; and Henry's incarceration.

[The District Court made no finding that Nichols was operating on a contingent fee basis] and I am unconvinced that the evidence of record establishes such an understanding. In any event, I question whether the existence of a contingent fee arrangement is at all significant. The reasonable conclusion of an informant like Nichols would be that, whatever the arrangement, he would *not* be remunerated if he breached his promise; yet the Court asks us to infer that Coughlin's conversation with Nichols "likely would lead" Nichols to engage in the very conduct which Coughlin told him to avoid.

The Court also emphasizes that Henry was "unaware that Nichols was a government agent." One might properly assign this factor some importance, were it not for *Brewer v. Williams,* [which] explicitly held that the fact "[t]hat the incriminating statements were elicited surreptitiously in the *Massiah* case, and otherwise here, is *constitutionally irrelevant.*" (Emphasis added.) The Court's teeter-tottering with this factor in *Massiah* analysis can only induce confusion.

It merits emphasis that the Court's resurrection of the unawareness factor is indispensable to its holding. For, in [*Williams*], substantial contact and conversation with a confined defendant preceded delivery of the "Christian burial speech." Yet the Court clearly deemed the speech critical in finding a *Massiah* violation; it thus made clear that mere "association" and "general conversation" did not suffice to bring *Massiah* into play. Since nothing more transpired here, principled application of [*Williams*] mandates reversal of the judgment in this case.

Finally, the Court notes that Henry was incarcerated when he made his statements to Nichols. * * * [E]ven assuming that "subtle influences" might encourage a detaineee to talk about his crime, there are certainly counterbalances of at least equal weight. Since, in jail, "official surveillance has traditionally been the order of the day," and a jailmate has obvious incentives to assist authorities, one may expect a detainee to act with corresponding circumspection. * * *

B. *"Prompting."* All Members of the Court agree that Henry's statements were properly admitted if Nichols did not

5. Mr. Justice Powell observes [that] "*Massiah* serves the salutary purpose of preventing police interference with the relationship between a suspect and his counsel once formal proceedings have been initiated." I fail to see any greater "interference" on the facts of this case than in a case where an inmate is permitted to have a conversation with a trusted visitor, but with an electronic listening device in place, a practice Mr. Justice Powell finds unobjectionable. Indeed, bugging might be said to present an even stronger case for finding "deliberate elicitation." There is, after all, a likelihood that the inmate will place added confidence in a relative or longtime friend who visits him. Nichols, in contrast, had not known Henry previously. Moreover, with bugging, a defendant cannot know what he is dealing with. He lacks the ability intelligently to gauge the probability that his confidences will be "reported" back to government agents.

"prompt" him. The record, however, gives no indication that Nichols "stimulated" Henry's remarks with "affirmative steps to secure incriminating information." * * * I cannot believe that *Massiah* requires exclusion when a cellmate previously unknown to the defendant and asked only to keep his ears open says: "It's a nice day," and the defendant responds: "It would be nicer if I hadn't robbed that bank." The Court of Appeals, however, found it necessary to swallow that bitter pill in order to decide this case the way it did, and this Court does not show that anything more transpired. * * *

MR. JUSTICE REHNQUIST, dissenting.

* * * The exclusion of respondent's statements has no relationship whatsoever to the reliability of the evidence, and it rests on a prophylactic application of the Sixth Amendment right to counsel that in my view entirely ignores the doctrinal foundation of that right. * * * [While] the decision today sets forth the factors that are "important" in determining whether there has been a *Massiah* violation, I think that *Massiah* constitutes such a substantial departure from the traditional concerns that underlie the Sixth Amendment guarantee that its language, if not its actual holding, should be re-examined.

* * * [N]either [the Fifth nor Sixth Amendment] suggests by its terms a rigid dichotomy between the types of police activities that are permissible before commencement of formal criminal proceedings and those that are subsequently permissible. More specifically, there is nothing in the Sixth Amendment to suggest, nor does it follow from the general accusatory nature of our criminal scheme, that once the adversary process formally begins the government may not make any effort to obtain incriminating evidence from the accused when counsel is not present. The role of counsel in an adversary system is to offer advice and assistance in the preparation of a defense and to serve as a spokesman for the accused in technical legal proceedings. And the Sixth Amendment, of course, protects the confidentiality of communications between the accused and his attorney. But there is no constitutional or historical support for concluding that an accused has a right to have his attorney serve as a sort of guru who must be present whenever an accused has an inclination to reveal incriminating information to anyone who acts to elicit such information at the behest of the prosecution. To the extent the accused is protected from revealing evidence that may be incriminatory, the focus must be on the Fifth Amendment privilege against compulsory self-incrimination.

The objectives that underlie the exclusionary rule also suggest that the results reached in *Massiah* and the decision today are incorrect. Although the exclusion of reliable, probative evidence imposes tremendous costs on the judicial process and on society, this Court has nonetheless imposed a rule for the exclusion of such evidence in some contexts in order to deter unlawful police activity. In cases in which incriminating statements made by the accused are entirely voluntary, however, and the government has merely encouraged a third party to talk to the accused and report any incriminating information that the accused might reveal, there is in my view no valid justification for the exclusion of such evidence from trial. * * *

In cases such as this one and *Massiah,* the effect of the governmental action is to encourage an informant to reveal information to the authorities that the ordinary citizen most likely would reveal voluntarily. While it is true that the informants here and in *Massiah* were encouraged to "elicit" the information from the accused, I doubt that most people would find this type of elicitation reprehensible. It involves merely engaging the accused in conversation about his criminal activity and thereby encouraging him voluntarily to make incriminating remarks. There is absolutely no element of coercion, nor is there any interference whatsoever with the attorney-client relationship. Anything the accused might reveal to the informant should, as with revelations he might make to the ordinary citizen, be available for use at trial. This Court has never held that an accused is constitutionally protected from his inability to keep quiet, whether or not he has been encouraged by third party citizens to voluntarily make incriminating remarks. I do not think the result should be different merely because the government has encouraged a third party informant to report remarks obtained in this fashion. When an accused voluntarily chooses to make an incriminatory remark in these circumstances, he knowingly assumes the risk that his confidant may be untrustworthy.[7]

Notes and Questions

1. For criticism of the *Henry* court for extending *Massiah* "despite that decision's doctrinal emptiness" and for giving *Massiah* "a firmer place in the law than it deserves," see Saltzburg, *Foreword: The Flow and Ebb of Constitutional Criminal Procedure in the Warren and Burger Courts,* 69 Geo.L.J. 151, 206–08 (1980).

2. *"Prompting."* *Do* all the Justices agree, as dissenting Justice Blackmun states, "that Henry's statements were properly admitted if Nichols did not 'prompt' him"? Is the Court's effort to distinguish "[t]he situation where the 'listening post' is an inanimate electronic device" (fn. 9) persuasive? Why isn't installing a listening device in an indicted defendant's cell "intentionally creating a situation likely to induce [the defendant] to make incriminating statements without the assistance of counsel" (Burger, C.J.)? Why shouldn't it be viewed as *permitting* "police interference with the relationship between a suspect and his counsel once formal proceedings have been initiated" (Powell, J.)?

3. *"Active" versus "passive" secret agents.* Does (should) *Massiah*, as Justice Powell maintains, prohibit the government only from "eliciting" or "inducing" incriminating statements from a defendant, not simply gathering the information? Consider the remarks of Professor Kamisar in Choper, Kamisar & Tribe, *The Supreme Court: Trends and Developments, 1979–80* at 107–08 (1981): "[W]ould it not make more sense and be a lot simpler—would the *[Massiah]* doctrine not offer the police more guidance and make the trial judges' task more manageable—to say that once adverse positions have 'solidified' and the parties have become ' "arms length" adversaries' the government should not *approach* the defendant in the absence of his counsel? If once the 'criminal prosecution' has begun, as it had in *Henry,* the defendant is supposed to be entitled to essentially the same Sixth Amendment protections he would have at the trial itself *[Massiah],* why should it matter whether *the government's efforts to obtain incriminating statements* are 'active' or 'passive'? But even if the passive agent/active agent distinction were tenable *in theory,* would it not break down in practice?

"* * * [W]hen two persons share the same cell for days or even weeks, they *both* talk and they talk back and forth. A police informant or other secret agent has to exchange remarks with the defendant if only to avoid 'alerting' the defendant that something is amiss. Even if the secret agent can honestly remember that the defendant 'initiated' a particular conversation on Wednesday night, isn't the agent likely to forget that he may have said something to the defendant Wednesday morning or Tuesday afternoon that 'stimulated' the defendant to confide in him Wednesday night?

"How much incentive does the informant really have to recall and to report carefully the flow of conversation and the progression of various conversations? Is it not fair to say that in many instances, if not most, the informant will be more strongly motivated to 'deliver' the defendant than

7. Cf. *United States v. White* * * *.

to recall exactly how he managed to do so? If ever a situation called for 'prophylactic standards,' isn't this such a case?"

4. *Known government agents, undisclosed government agents, and the Massiah doctrine.* Recall dissenting Justice Blackmun's point that *Williams* "made clear that mere 'association' and 'general conversation' did not suffice to bring *Massiah* into play." Was mere "association" and "general conversation" sufficient to trigger the *Massiah* doctrine in *Henry?* If so, why? Consider the remarks of Kamisar, supra, at 105–06: "[Unlike Henry,] Williams, of course, was well aware that he was in the company of police. If, without any 'Christian burial speech' prompting, he had blurted out an incriminating statement, this probably would have constituted—despite the preceding substantial contact and conversation—a valid waiver of his '*Massiah* right to counsel.' As the *Henry* Court pointed out, however, 'the concept of a knowing and voluntary waiver of Sixth Amendment rights does not apply in the context of communication with an undisclosed undercover informant.' Thus, whether one views it in terms of imposing stricter standards on secret government agents or in terms of showing greater solicitude for defendants who are 'more seriously imposed upon' because they do not know they are dealing with government agents, the 'unawareness factor' makes a difference—it renders the *Massiah* doctrine more awesome."

MAINE v. MOULTON

__ U.S. __, 106 S.Ct. 477, 88 L.Ed.2d 481 (1985).

JUSTICE BRENNAN delivered the opinion of the Court.

The question presented [is] whether respondent's Sixth Amendment right to the assistance of counsel was violated by the admission [of] incriminating statements made by him to his codefendant [Colson], a secret Government informant, after indictment and at a meeting of the two to plan defense strategy for the upcoming trial. [On April 7, 1982, a grand jury returned indictments charging Colson and Moulton with four charges of theft. Two days later, both defendants, represented by retained counsel, pled not guilty and were released on bail. On November 4, Colson complained to the police that he had received anonymous threatening phone calls regarding the charges against him and Moulton. He told the police he wanted to talk to them about the charges. He was told to speak with his lawyer and to call back. On November 6, Colson met with Moulton to plan for their upcoming trial. At this meeting, according to Colson, Moulton suggested the possibility of killing a state witness (Elwell), and they discussed how to commit the murder.

[On November 9 and 10, Colson, accompanied by his lawyer, met with the police. At these meetings, Colson admitted that he and Moulton had committed the crimes for which they had been indicted as well as a number of other thefts. The police offered Colson a deal. No further charges would be brought against him if he would cooperate in the prosecution of Moulton on the pending charges. Colson agreed to cooperate. At Chief Keating's request, Colson consented to have a recording device placed on his phone. He was instructed to use the device if there were threats from the anonymous caller or calls from Moulton.

[The recording device was on Colson's phone for over a month. He received no threats, but had three phone conversations with Moulton. The tapes of these calls were turned over to the police. In the course of the third phone conversation, Moulton asked Colson to set aside a day so that the two of them could meet and plan their defense. They agreed to meet on December 26.

[Colson consented to be equipped with a body wire transmitter to record what was said at the December 26 meeting. Chief Keating testified that he did this for Colson's safety, in case Moulton realized that his codefendant was cooperating with the police, and to record any further conversation concerning threats to witnesses. At the meeting, the idea of eliminating witnesses was briefly discussed, but quickly dismissed by Moulton as unworkable. The remainder of the lengthy meeting was spent discussing the case. Moulton and Colson decided to create false alibis as their defense. Apologizing for his poor memory, Colson repeatedly asked Moulton to remind him about the details of what had happened. This led Moulton to make numerous incriminating statements. Each of these statements was later admitted into evidence against Moulton at trial.

[The trial court denied Moulton's motion to suppress recorded statements made at the December 26 meeting, finding that the recordings were made to "gather information concerning the anonymous threats Colson had been receiving, to protect Colson and to gather information concerning [Moulton's] plan to kill [witness] Elwell." After Colson's role as an informant had been revealed to Moulton, the state dismissed the pending indictments and obtained seven new ones against Moulton. The new indictments realleged the pending charges, and charged Moulton with more crimes. The state introduced portions of the tapes of the December 26 meeting and Moulton was convicted of some of the original charges.

[The Supreme Judicial Court of Maine reversed and remanded for a new trial. The court agreed that there was "ample evidence" to support the trial court's finding that the police wired Colson for legitimate purposes, but held that the state could not use against Moulton recordings of conversations where it "knew, or should have known" that Moulton would incriminate himself regarding crimes as to which charges were already pending.]

* * * [A]fter the initiation of adversary criminal proceedings, " 'the government has committed itself to prosecute, and . . . the adverse positions of government and defendant have solidified. It is then that the defendant finds himself faced with the prosecutorial forces of organized society, and immersed in the intricacies of substantive and procedural criminal law.' " *United States v. Gouveia* [p. 101 supra].

Once the right to counsel has attached and been asserted, the State must of course honor it. This means more than simply that the State cannot prevent the accused from obtaining the assistance of counsel. The Sixth Amendment also imposes on the State an affirmative obligation to respect and preserve the accused's choice to seek this assistance. We have on several occasions been called upon to clarify the scope of the State's obligation in this regard, and have made clear that, at the very least, the prosecutor and police have an affirmative obligation not to act in a manner that circumvents and thereby dilutes the protection afforded by the right to counsel. * * *

We applied this principle most recently in *Henry.* Henry was arrested and indicted for bank robbery. * * * The Government argued that it should not be held responsible for Nichols' conduct because its agent had instructed Nichols not to question Henry and had not intended that Nichols take affirmative steps to obtain incriminating statements. We rejected this argument, finding that, under the circumstances, the agent "must have known" that Nichols would take affirmative steps to secure incriminating information. Consequently, the Court held, "[b]y intentionally creating a situation likely to induce Henry to make incriminating statements without the assistance of counsel, the Government violated Henry's Sixth Amendment right to counsel."

The State contends that the decisive fact in *Massiah* and *Henry* was that the police set up the confrontation between the accused and a police agent at which incriminating statements were elicited. * * * Because Moulton rather than Colson initiated the recorded telephone conversations and requested the December 26 meeting, the State concludes that Moulton's Sixth Amendment rights were not violated here.

In the first place, the identity of the party who instigated the meeting at which the Government obtained incriminating statements was not decisive or even important to our decisions in *Massiah* or *Henry.* * * * Moreover, four years after *Massiah,* the Court summarily reversed a conviction where the defendant requested the meeting and initiated and led the conversation in which incriminating statements were made to an undercover informant. *Beatty v. United States,* 389 U.S. 45, 88 S.Ct. 234, 19 L.Ed.2d 48 (1967) (*per curiam*). In that case, the Solicitor General made the same argument that he and the State make today; we rejected this argument in an opinion that simply cited *Massiah.* Finally, in *Henry,* we deemed it "irrelevant that in *Massiah* the agent had to arrange the meeting between Massiah and his codefendant while here the agents were fortunate enough to have an undercover informant already in close proximity to the accused."

Beyond this, the State's attempt to limit our holdings in *Massiah* and *Henry* fundamentally misunderstands the nature of the right we recognized in those cases. The Sixth Amendment guarantees the accused, at least after the initiation of formal charges, the right to rely on counsel as a "medium" between him and the State. [T]his guarantee includes the State's affirmative obligation not to act in a manner that circumvents the protections accorded the accused by invoking this right. The determination whether particular action by state agents violates the accused's right to the assistance of counsel must be made in light of this obligation. Thus, the Sixth Amendment is not violated whenever—by luck or happenstance—the State obtains incriminating statements from the accused after the right to counsel has attached. However, knowing exploitation by the State of an opportunity to confront the accused without counsel being present is as much a breach of the State's obligation not to circumvent the right to the assistance of counsel as is the intentional creation of such an opportunity. Accordingly, the Sixth Amendment is violated when the State obtains incriminating statements by knowingly circumventing the accused's right to have counsel present in a confrontation between the accused and a state agent.[12]

Applying this principle to the case at hand, it is clear that the State violated Moulton's Sixth Amendment right when it arranged to record conversations between Moulton and its undercover informant, Colson. It was the police who suggested to Colson that he record his telephone conversations with Moulton. Having learned from these recordings that Moulton and Colson were going to meet, the police asked Colson to let them put a body wire transmitter on him to record what was said. Police Chief Keating admitted that, when they made this request, the police knew—as they must have known from the recorded telephone conversations—that Moulton and Colson were meeting for the express purpose of discussing the pending charges and planning a defense for the trial.[13] The police thus

12. Direct proof of the State's knowledge will seldom be available to the accused. However, as *Henry* makes clear, proof that the State "must have known" that its agent was likely to obtain incriminating statements from the accused in the absence of counsel suffices to establish a Sixth Amendment violation.

13. Because Moulton thought of Colson only as his codefendant, Colson's engaging Moulton in active conversation about their upcoming trial was certain to elicit statements that Moulton would not intentionally reveal—and had a constitutional right not to reveal—to persons known to be police agents. Under these circumstances, Colson's merely participating in this conversation was "the functional equivalent of interrogation." *Henry* (Powell, J., concurring). In addition, the tapes disclose and the Supreme Judicial Court of Maine found that Colson "frequently pressed Moulton for details of various thefts and in so doing elicited much incriminating information that the State later used at trial." Thus, as in

knew that Moulton would make statements that he had a constitutional right not to make to their agent prior to consulting with counsel. As in *Henry*, the fact that the police were "fortunate enough to have an undercover agent already in close proximity to the accused" does not excuse their conduct under these circumstances. By concealing the fact that Colson was an agent of the State, the police denied Moulton the opportunity to consult with counsel and thus denied him the assistance of counsel guaranteed by the Sixth Amendment.[14]

The Solicitor General argues that the incriminating statements obtained by the Maine police nevertheless should not be suppressed because the police had other, legitimate reasons for listening to Moulton's conversations with Colson, namely, to investigate Moulton's alleged plan to kill Elwell and to insure Colson's safety. In *Massiah*, the Government also contended that incriminating statements obtained as a result of its deliberate efforts should not be excluded because law enforcement agents had "the right, if not indeed the duty, to continue their investigation of [Massiah] and his alleged criminal associates." * * * We rejected this argument, and held:

"We do not question that in this case, as in many cases, it was entirely proper to continue an investigation of the suspected criminal activities of the defendant and his alleged confederates, even though the defendant had already been indicted. All that we hold is that the defendant's own incriminating statements, obtained by federal agents under the circumstances here disclosed, could not constitutionally be used by the prosecution as evidence against him at his trial." (Emphasis omitted.)

We reaffirm this holding, which states a sensible solution to a difficult problem. The police have an interest in the thorough investigation of crimes for which formal charges have already been filed. They also have an interest in investigating new or additional crimes. Investigations of either type of crime may require surveillance of individuals already under indictment. Moreover, law enforcement officials investigating an individual suspected of committing one crime and formally charged with having committed another crime obviously seek to discover evidence useful at a trial of either crime. In seeking

Henry, we need not reach the situation where the "listening post" cannot or does not participate in active conversation and prompt particular replies.

14. The State argues that it took steps to prevent Colson from inducing Moulton to make incriminating admissions by instructing Colson to "be himself," "act normal," and "not interrogate" Moulton. In *Henry*, we rejected this same argument although the likelihood that the accused would talk about the pending charges to a cellmate was less than here, where the accused invited his co-defendant to discuss the upcoming trial, and although the instructions to the agent were far more explicit. More importantly, under the circumstances of this case, the instructions given to Colson were necessarily inadequate. The Sixth Amendment protects the right of the accused not to be confronted by an agent of the State regarding matters as to which the right to counsel has attached without counsel being present. This right was violated as soon as the State's agent engaged Moulton in conversation about the charges pending against him. Because these charges were the only subject to be discussed at Colson's December 26 meeting with Moulton, a Sixth Amendment violation was inevitable once Colson agreed to this meeting with Moulton.

In any event, we reject the State's suggestion that these instructions were designed to protect Moulton's constitutional rights. The instructions were obviously motivated by the police's concern that Colson, who had never before served as an undercover agent, might behave unnaturally or ask too many questions, thereby tipping Moulton off to the fact that Colson was cooperating with the police. Thus, rather than explain to Colson that actively questioning Moulton might taint any evidence obtained, the police simply told Colson to "be himself," and to "act normal." In addition, the instructions were not limited to questions concerning the pending charges, the only matters as to which active questioning might create problems. On the contrary, according to Chief Keating, Colson was instructed that he could engage Moulton in a conversation but should not try to draw him out on "elimination of witnesses or anything."

evidence pertaining to pending charges, however, the Government's investigative powers are limited by the Sixth Amendment rights of the accused. To allow the admission of evidence obtained from the accused in violation of his Sixth Amendment rights whenever the police assert an alternative, legitimate reason for their surveillance invites abuse by law enforcement personnel in the form of fabricated investigations and risks the evisceration of the Sixth Amendment right recognized in *Massiah.* On the other hand, to exclude evidence pertaining to charges as to which the Sixth Amendment right to counsel had not attached at the time the evidence was obtained, simply because other charges were pending at that time, would unnecessarily frustrate the public's interest in the investigation of criminal activities. Consequently, incriminating statements pertaining to pending charges are inadmissible at the trial of those charges, not withstanding the fact that the police were also investigating other crimes, if, in obtaining this evidence, the State violated the Sixth Amendment by knowingly circumventing the accused's right to the assistance of counsel.[16]

Because we hold that the Maine police knowingly circumvented Moulton's right to have counsel present at a confrontation between Moulton and a police agent, the fact that the police had additional reasons for recording Moulton's meeting with Colson is irrelevant. [Affirmed.]

CHIEF JUSTICE BURGER, with whom JUSTICE WHITE and JUSTICE REHNQUIST join, and with whom JUSTICE O'CONNOR joins [except for Part II], dissenting.

Today the Court holds that the Sixth Amendment prohibits the use at trial of post-indictment statements made to a government informant, even where those statements were recorded as part of a good faith investigation of entirely separate crimes. Nothing whatever in the Constitution or our prior opinions supports this bizarre result, which creates a new "right" only for those possibly habitual offenders who persist in criminal activity even while under indictment for other crimes. I dissent and would reverse. * * *

II

The Court today concludes that "[t]o allow the admission of evidence obtained from an accused in violation of his Sixth Amendment rights whenever the police assert an alternative, legitimate reason for their surveillance * * * risks the evisceration of the Sixth Amendment right recognized in *Massiah.*" With all deference I am bound to state that this conclusion turns the Sixth Amendment on its head by first positing a constitutional violation and then asking whether "alternative, legitimate reasons" for the police surveillance are sufficient to justify that constitutional violation. As I see it, if "alternative, legitimate reasons" motivated the surveillance, then no Sixth Amendment violation has occurred. Indeed, if the police had failed to take the steps they took here knowing that Colson was endangering his life by talking to them, in my view they would be subject to censure.

Analysis of this issue must begin with *Hoffa,* not cited in the Court's opinion. In *Hoffa,* the Court held that post-indictment statements obtained by a government informant "relat[ing] to the commission of a quite separate offense" were properly admitted at a subsequent trial for the separate crime. Other courts have also held that *Massiah,* viewed in light of the later-decided *Hoffa* case, does not prohibit the introduction of incriminating statements obtained in good faith by the government even after an indictment at a trial involving an offense different from that covered by the indictment.

Applying *Hoffa* to the facts of this case, it is clear that the statements obtained by Colson could have been introduced against

16. Incriminating statements pertaining to other crimes, as to which the Sixth Amendment right has not yet attached, are, of course, admissible at a trial of those offenses.

respondent at a subsequent trial for crimes apart from those for which respondent had already been indicted, such as conspiracy to commit murder or to obstruct justice. The majority concedes as much [quoting fn. 16]. It follows from this that the State engaged in no impermissible conduct in its investigation of respondent based on Colson's revelations. By recording conversations between respondent and Colson [the police obtained] evidence that the Court's opinion concedes could have been used to convict respondent of further crimes. In fact [the] State was able to obtain additional indictments against respondent for burglary, arson, and three more thefts. * * *

Courts ought to applaud the kind of careful and diligent efforts of the police shown by this record. Indeed, the Court's opinion does not suggest that the police should have—or could have—conducted their investigation in any other way. Yet, inexplicably, the Court holds that the highly probative and reliable evidence produced by this wholly legitimate investigation must be excluded from respondent's trial for theft. The anomaly of this position, then, is that the evidence at issue in this case should have been excluded from respondent's theft trial even though the *same evidence* could have been introduced against *respondent himself* at a trial for separate crimes. Far from being "a sensible solution to a difficult problem," as the Court modestly suggests, it is a judicial aberration conferring a windfall benefit to those who are the subject of criminal investigations for one set of crimes while already under indictment for another. I can think of no reason to turn the Sixth Amendment into a "magic cloak," to protect criminals who engage in multiple offenses that are the subject of separate police investigations.

We have held that no Sixth Amendment violation occurs unless the State "deliberately elicit[s]" comments from the defendant. * * * In using the phrase "deliberate elicitation," we surely must have intended to denote elicitation for the purpose of using such statements against the defendant in connection with charges for which the Sixth Amendment right to counsel had attached. Here the State indeed set out to elicit information from a defendant, but it was an investigation with respect to crimes other than those for which the defendant then stood indicted. As two courts found, the State recorded the conversations "for legitimate purposes not related to the gathering of evidence concerning the crime for which [respondent] had been indicted." * * *

The Court's opinion seems to rest on the notion that the evidence here is excludable because "the State 'must have known' that its agent was likely to obtain incriminating statements from the accused" with respect to the crimes for which he was already indicted. But the inquiry mandated by our holdings is whether the State recorded the statements not merely *in spite of,* but *because of* that consequence. If the State is not seeking to elicit information with respect to the crime for which the defendant is already indicted, it cannot rationally be said that the State has "planned an impermissible interference with the right to the assistance of counsel."

This case is a particularly inappropriate one for invoking the right to counsel. The right to counsel recognized in *Massiah* was designed to preserve the integrity of the trial. Here respondent was under investigation because of his plans to obstruct justice by killing an essential witness. There is no right to consult an attorney for advice on committing crimes. Indeed, any attorney who undertook to offer such advice would undoubtedly be subject to sanction. * * * Thus there is no warrant for vindicating respondent's right to consult counsel. * * *

Even though the *Massiah* rule is inapplicable to situations where the government is gathering information related to a separate crime, police misconduct need not be countenanced. Accordingly, evidence obtained through a separate crimes investigation should be admitted only "so long as investigating officers show no bad faith and do not institute the investigation of the separate offense as a pretext for avoiding the dictates of *Massiah.*" *United States v. Darwin,* 757 F.2d 1193, 1199 (11th Cir.1985). Here the careful actions of [the police] steered well clear of these prohibitions.

Until today, the clearly prevailing view in the federal and state courts was that *Massiah* and its successors did not protect a defendant from the introduction of post-indictment statements deliberately elicited when the police undertook an investigation of separate crimes. * * * Rather than expand *Massiah* beyond boundaries currently recognized, I would take note of the observation that "*Massiah* certainly is the decision in which Sixth Amendment protections have been extended to their outermost point." *Henry* (Blackmun, J., dissenting). I would not expand them more and well beyond the limits of precedent and logic.

III

Even if I were prepared to join the Court in this enlargement of the protections of the Sixth Amendment, I would have serious doubts about also extending the reach of the exclusionary rule to cover this case. * * * Application of the exclusionary rule here makes little sense, as demonstrated by "weighing the costs and benefits of preventing the use in the prosecution's case-in-chief of inherently trustworthy tangible evidence." *United States v. Leon.*

With respect to the costs, applying the rule to cases where the State deliberately elicits statements from a defendant in the course of investigating a separate crime excludes evidence that is "typically reliable and often the most probative information bearing on the guilt or innocence of the defendant." *Stone v. Powell.* Moreover, because of the trustworthy nature of the evidence, its admission will not threaten "the fairness of a trial [or] the integrity of the factfinding process." *Brewer v. Williams* (Powell, J., concurring). Hence, application of the rule to cases like this one "deflects the truthfinding process," "often frees the guilty," and may well "generat[e] disrespect for the law and [the] administration of justice." *Stone v. Powell.*

Against these costs, applying the rule here appears to create precious little in the way of offsetting "benefits." Like searches in violation of the Fourth Amendment, the "wrong" that the Court condemns was "fully accomplished" by the elicitation of comments from the defendant and "the exclusionary rule is neither intended nor able to cure the invasion of the defendant's rights which he has already suffered." *Leon.*

The application of the exclusionary rule here must therefore be premised on deterrence of certain types of conduct by the police. We have explained, however, that "[t]he deterrent purpose of the exclusionary rule necessarily assumes that the police have engaged in willful, or at the very least negligent, conduct which has deprived the defendant of some right." Here the trial court found that the State obtained statements from respondent "for legitimate purposes not related to the gathering of evidence concerning the crime for which [respondent] had been indicted." Since the State was not trying to build its theft case against respondent in obtaining the evidence, excluding the evidence from the theft trial will not affect police behavior at all. The exclusion of evidence "cannot be expected, and should not be applied, to deter objectively reasonable law enforcement activity." *Leon.* Indeed, as noted above, it is impossible to identify any police "misconduct" to deter in this case. In fact, if anything, actions by the police of the type at issue here should be encouraged. The diligent investigation of the police in this case may have saved the lives of several potential witnesses and certainly led to the prosecution and conviction of respondent for additional serious crimes.

It seems, then, that the Sixth Amendment claims at issue here "closely parallel claims under the Fourth Amendment," *Williams* (Powell, J., concurring), where we have found the exclusionary rule to be inapplicable by weighing the costs and benefits of its applications. * * * If anything, the argument for admission of the evidence here is even stronger because "[t]his is not a case [where] 'the constable * * * blundered.' " * * *

Chapter 9

LINEUPS, SHOWUPS AND OTHER PRE-TRIAL IDENTIFICATION PROCEDURES

SECTION 1. *WADE* AND *GILBERT*: CONSTITUTIONAL CONCERN ABOUT THE DANGERS INVOLVED IN EYEWITNESS IDENTIFICATIONS

UNITED STATES v. WADE

388 U.S. 218, 87 S.Ct. 1926, 18 L.Ed.2d 1149 (1967).

MR. JUSTICE BRENNAN delivered the opinion of the Court.

The question here is whether courtroom identifications of an accused at trial are to be excluded from evidence because the accused was exhibited to the witnesses before trial at a post-indictment lineup conducted for identification purposes without notice to and in the absence of the accused's appointed counsel.

The federally insured bank in Eustace, Texas, was robbed on September 21, 1964. A man with a small strip of tape on each side of his face entered the bank, pointed a pistol at the female cashier and the vice president, the only persons in the bank at the time, and forced them to fill a pillowcase with the bank's money. The man then drove away with an accomplice who had been waiting in a stolen car outside the bank. On March 23, 1965, an indictment was returned against respondent, Wade, and two others for conspiring to rob the bank, and against Wade and the accomplice for the robbery itself. Wade was arrested on April 2, and counsel was appointed to represent him on April 26. Fifteen days later [after counsel was appointed] an FBI agent, without notice to Wade's lawyer, arranged to have the two bank employees observe a lineup made up of Wade and five or six other prisoners and conducted in a courtroom of the local county courthouse. Each person in the line wore strips of tape such as allegedly worn by the robber and upon direction each said something like "put the money in the bag," the words allegedly uttered by the robber. Both bank employees identified Wade in the lineup as the bank robber.

At trial the two employees, when asked on direct examination if the robber was in the courtroom, pointed to Wade. The prior lineup identification was then elicited from both employees on cross-examination. At the close of testimony, Wade's counsel moved [to] strike the bank officials' courtroom identifications on [self-incrimination and right to counsel grounds]. The motion was denied, and Wade was convicted. The Court of Appeals for the Fifth Circuit reversed the conviction and ordered a new trial at which the in-court identification evidence was to be excluded, holding that [conducting the lineup in the absence of Wade's appointed counsel violated his Sixth Amendment rights].

The fact that the lineup involved no violation of Wade's privilege against self-incrimination [a] does not, however, dispose of his contention that the courtroom identifications should have been excluded because the lineup was conducted without notice to and in the absence of his counsel. Our rejection of the right to counsel claim in *Schmerber* rested on our conclusion in that case that "[n]o issue of counsel's ability to assist petitioner in respect of any rights he did possess is presented." In contrast, in this case it is urged that the assistance of counsel at the lineup was indispensable to protect Wade's most basic right as a criminal defendant—his right to a fair trial at which the witnesses against him might be meaningfully cross-examined. * * *

Of course, nothing decided or said in [*Powell v. Alabama, Escobedo, Miranda* and other cases] links the right to counsel only to protection of Fifth Amendment rights. * * * It is central to [the constitutional] principle that in addition to counsel's presence at trial, the accused is guaranteed that he need not stand alone against the State at any stage of the prosecution, formal or informal, in court or out, where counsel's absence might derogate from the accused's right to a fair trial. * * * The presence of counsel at such critical confrontations as at the trial itself, operates to assure that the accused's interests will be protected consistently with our adversary theory of criminal prosecution. * * *

[T]he principle of *Powell v. Alabama* and succeeding cases requires that we scrutinize *any* pretrial confrontation of the accused to determine whether the presence of his counsel is necessary to preserve the defendant's basic right to a fair trial as affected by his right meaningfully to cross-examine the witnesses against him and to have effective assistance of counsel at the trial itself. It calls upon us to analyze whether potential substantial prejudice to defendant's rights inheres in the particular confrontation and the ability of counsel to help avoid that prejudice.

The Government characterizes the lineup as a mere preparatory step in the gath-

a. On this issue, the Court held, 5–4 that "[n]either the lineup itself nor anything shown by this record that Wade was required to do in the lineup violated his privilege against self-incrimination." For "the privilege 'protects an accused only from being compelled to testify against himself, or otherwise provide the State with evidence of a testimonial or communicative nature' *Schmerber v. California* [p. 48 supra]," and thus " 'offers no protection against compulsion to submit to fingerprinting, photography, or measurements, to write or speak for identification, to appear in court, to stand, to assume a stance, to walk or to make a particular gesture.' " Compelling Wade to speak the words purportedly uttered by the robber "was not compulsion to utter statements of a 'testimonial' nature; he was required to use his voice as an identifying physical characteristic, not to speak his guilt."

Dissenting on this issue, Justice Fortas, joined by Warren, C.J. and Douglas, J., agreed with the Court that the exhibition of the person of the accused at a lineup is not itself a violation of the privilege, but maintained that "the accused may not be compelled in a lineup to speak the words uttered by the person who committed the crime. [This] is the kind of volitional act—the kind of forced cooperation by the accused—which is within the historical perimeter of the privilege against compelled self-incrimination." *Schmerber,* argued Justice Fortas, is distinguishable, for "the forced extraction of blood from the veins of an unwilling human being did not compel the person actively to cooperate—to accuse himself by a volitional act which differs only in degree from compelling him to act out the crime, which, I assume, would be rebuffed by the Court."

In a separate opinion, Justice Black also dissented from the Court's resolution of the self-incrimination issue, adhering to his dissent in *Schmerber.* He thought it "quite plain" that the privilege "was designed to bar the Government from forcing any person to supply proof of his own crime, precisely what [Schmerber and Wade were] forced to do * * *."

In the companion case of *Gilbert v. California,* infra, the Court, by the same 5–4 vote on this issue, upheld the admission of handwriting exemplars taken from petitioner after his arrest, observing that "[a] mere handwriting exemplar, in contrast to the content of what is written, like the voice or body itself, is an identifying physical characteristic outside [the privilege's] protection."

ering of the prosecution's evidence, not different—for Sixth Amendment purposes—from various other preparatory steps, such as systematized or scientific analyzing of the accused's fingerprints, blood sample, clothing, hair, and the like. We think there are differences which preclude such stages being characterized as critical stages at which the accused has the right to the presence of his counsel. Knowledge of the techniques of science and technology is sufficiently available, and the variables in techniques few enough, that the accused has the opportunity for a meaningful confrontation of the Government's case at trial through the ordinary processes of cross-examination of the Government's expert witnesses and the presentation of the evidence of his own experts. The denial of a right to have his counsel present at such analyses does not therefore violate the Sixth Amendment; they are not critical stages since there is minimal risk that his counsel's absence at such stages might derogate from his right to a fair trial.[b]

But the confrontation compelled by the State between the accused and the victim or witnesses to a crime to elicit identification evidence is peculiarly riddled with innumerable dangers and variable factors which might seriously, even crucially, derogate from a fair trial. The vagaries of eyewitness identification are well-known; the annals of criminal law are rife with instances of mistaken identification. * * * A major factor contributing to the high incidence of miscarriage of justice from mistaken identification has been the degree of suggestion inherent in the manner in which the prosecution presents the suspect to witnesses for pretrial identification. A commentator has observed that "[t]he influence of improper suggestion upon identifying witnesses probably accounts for more miscarriages of justice than any other single factor—perhaps it is responsible for more such errors than all other factors combined." Wall, *Eye-Witness Identification in Criminal Cases* 26 [1965]. Suggestion can be created intentionally or unintentionally in many subtle ways. And the dangers for the suspect are particularly grave when the witness' opportunity for observation was insubstantial, and thus his susceptibility to suggestion the greatest.

Moreover, "[i]t is a matter of common experience that, once a witness has picked out the accused at the line-up, he is not likely to go back on his word later on, so that in practice the issue of identity may (in the absence of other relevant evidence) for all practical purposes be determined there and then, before the trial."

The pretrial confrontation for purpose of identification may take the form of a lineup, also known as an "identification parade" or "showup," as in the present case, or presentation of the suspect alone

b. Consider, too, the companion case of *Gilbert v. California,* where the Court held, 5–4 on this issue, that the taking of handwriting exemplars from petitioner "was not a 'critical' stage of the criminal proceedings entitling petitioner to the assistance of counsel" for "there is minimal risk that the absence of counsel might derogate from his right to a fair trial. * * * If, for some reason, an unrepresentative exemplar is taken, this can be brought out and corrected through the adversary process at trial since the accused can make an unlimited number of additional exemplars for analysis and comparison by government and defense handwriting experts."

Justice Black dissented on this issue in *Gilbert,* maintaining that "the handwriting exemplars were just as important as the lineup and perhaps more so, for handwriting analysis, [being] 'scientific' and 'systematized,' [may] carry much more weight with the jury than any kind of lineup identification. The Court, however, suggests that absence of counsel when handwriting exemplars are obtained will not impair the right of cross-examination at trial. But just as nothing said in our previous opinions 'links the right to counsel only to protection of Fifth Amendment rights,' *Wade,* nothing has been said which justifies linking the right to counsel only to the protection of other Sixth Amendment rights."

In a separate opinion, Justice Fortas, joined by Warren, C.J., agreed with Justice Black that the giving of a handwriting exemplar "is a 'critical stage' as much as is a lineup." Justice Douglas also agreed with Justice Black and Fortas on this phase of the case.

to the witness, as in *Stovall v. Denno.*[c] It is obvious that risks of suggestion attend either form of confrontation and increase the dangers inhering in eyewitness identification. But as is the case with secret interrogations, there is serious difficulty in depicting what transpires at lineups and other forms of identification confrontations. * * * For the same reasons, the defense can seldom reconstruct the manner and mode of lineup identification for judge or jury at trial. Those participating in a lineup with the accused may often be police officers; in any event, the participants' names are rarely recorded or divulged at trial. The impediments to an objective observation are increased when the victim is the witness. Lineups are prevalent in rape and robbery prosecutions and present a particular hazard that a victim's understandable outrage may excite vengeful or spiteful motives. In any event, neither witnesses nor lineup participants are apt to be alert for conditions prejudicial to the suspect. And if they were, it would likely be of scant benefit to the suspect since neither witnesses nor lineup participants are likely to be schooled in the detection of suggestive influences.[13] Improper influences may go undetected by a suspect, guilty or not, who experiences the emotional tension which we might expect in one being confronted with potential accusers. Even when he does observe abuse, if he has a criminal record he may be reluctant to take the stand and open up the admission of prior convictions. Moreover any protestations by the suspect of the fairness of the lineup made at trial are likely to be in vain; the jury's choice is between the accused's unsupported version and that of the police officers present. In short, the accused's inability effectively to reconstruct at trial any unfairness that occurred at the lineup may deprive him of his only opportunity meaningfully to attack the credibility of the witness' courtroom identification. * * *

The potential for improper influence is illustrated by the circumstances, insofar as they appear, surrounding the prior identifications in the three cases we decide today. In the present case, the testimony of the identifying witnesses elicited on cross-examination revealed that those witnesses were taken to the courthouse and seated in the courtroom to await assembly of the lineup. The courtroom faced on a hallway observable to the witnesses through an open door. The cashier testified that she saw Wade "standing in the hall" within sight of an FBI agent. Five or six other prisoners later appeared in the hall. The vice president testified that he saw a person in the hall in the custody of the agent who "resembled the person that we identified as the one that had entered the bank."

The lineup in *Gilbert* was conducted in an auditorium in which some 100 witnesses to several alleged state and federal robberies charged to Gilbert made wholesale identifications of Gilbert as the robber in each other's presence, a procedure said to be fraught with dangers of suggestion. And the vice of suggestion created by the identification in *Stovall* was the presentation to the witness of the suspect alone handcuffed to police officers. It is hard to imagine a situation more clearly conveying the suggestion to the witness that the one presented is believed guilty by the police.

The few cases that have surfaced therefore reveal the existence of a process attended with hazards of serious unfairness to the criminal accused and strongly suggest the plight of the more numerous defendants who are unable to ferret out suggestive influences in the secrecy of the confrontation. We do not assume that

c. See pp. 667 and 680 infra.

13. An additional impediment to the detection of such influences by participants, including the suspect, is the physical conditions often surrounding the conduct of the lineup. In many, lights shine on the stage in such a way that the suspect cannot see the witness. [In] some a one-way mirror is used and what is said on the witness' side cannot be heard. * * *

these risks are the result of police procedures intentionally designed to prejudice an accused. Rather we assume they derive from the dangers inherent in eyewitness identification and the suggestibility inherent in the context of the pretrial identification. Williams & Hammelmann, in one of the most comprehensive studies of such forms of identification, said, "[T]he fact that the police themselves have, in a given case, little or no doubt that the man put up for identification has committed the offense, and that their chief pre-occupation is with the problem of getting sufficient proof, because he has not 'come clean,' involves a danger that this persuasion may communicate itself even in a doubtful case to the witness in some way * * *." *Identification Parades, Part I,* [1963] Crim. L.Rev. 479, 483.

Insofar as the accused's conviction may rest on a courtroom identification in fact the fruit of a suspect pretrial identification which the accused is helpless to subject to effective scrutiny at trial, the accused is deprived of that right of cross-examination which is an essential safeguard to his right to confront the witnesses against him. *Pointer v. Texas* [p. 42 supra]. And even though cross-examination is a precious safeguard to a fair trial, it cannot be viewed as an absolute assurance of accuracy and reliability. Thus in the present context, where so many variables and pitfalls exist, the first line of defense must be the prevention of unfairness and the lessening of the hazards of eyewitness identification at the lineup itself. The trial which might determine the accused's fate may well not be that in the courtroom but that at the pretrial confrontation, with the State aligned against the accused, the witness the sole jury, and the accused unprotected against the overreaching, intentional or unintentional, and with little or no effective appeal from the judgment there rendered by the witness—"that's the man."

Since it appears that there is grave potential for prejudice, intentional or not, in the pretrial lineup, which may not be capable of reconstruction at trial, and since presence of counsel itself can often avert prejudice and assure a meaningful confrontation at trial,[d] there can be little doubt that for Wade the post-indictment lineup was a critical stage of the prosecution at which he was "as much entitled to such aid [of counsel] * * * as at the trial itself." *Powell v. Alabama.* Thus both Wade and his counsel should have been notified of the impending lineup, and counsel's presence should have been a requisite to conduct of the lineup, absent an "intelligent waiver." No substantial countervailing policy considerations have been advanced against the requirement of the presence of counsel. Concern is expressed that the requirement will forestall prompt identifications and result in obstruction of the confrontations. As for the first, we note that in the two cases in which the right to counsel is today held to apply, counsel had already been appointed and no argument is made in either case that notice to counsel would have prejudicially delayed the confrontations. Moreover, we leave open the question whether the presence of substitute counsel might not suffice where notification and presence of the suspect's own counsel would result in prejudicial delay.[27] And to refuse to recognize the right to counsel for fear that counsel will obstruct the course of justice is contrary to the basic assumptions upon which this Court has operated in Sixth Amendment cases. We rejected similar logic in *Miran-*

d. At this point, the Court refers to and describes a model statute proposed in Murray, *The Criminal Lineup at Home and Abroad,* 1966 Utah L.Rev. 610, 627–28, a statute providing not only for counsel, but other safeguards as well.

27. Although the right to counsel usually means a right to the suspect's own counsel, provision for substitute counsel may be justified on the ground that the substitute counsel's presence may eliminate the hazards which render the lineup a critical stage for the presence of the suspect's *own* counsel.

da, concerning presence of counsel during custodial interrogation. * * *

In our view counsel can hardly impede legitimate law enforcement; on the contrary, for the reasons expressed, law enforcement may be assisted by preventing the infiltration of taint in the prosecution's identification evidence. That result cannot help the guilty avoid conviction but can only help assure that the right man has been brought to justice.[29]

Legislative or other regulations, such as those of local police departments, which eliminate the risks of abuse and unintentional suggestion at lineup proceedings and the impediments to meaningful confrontation at trial may also remove the basis for regarding the stage as "critical." [30] But neither Congress nor the federal authorities have seen fit to provide a solution. What we hold today "in no way creates a constitutional strait-jacket which will handicap sound efforts at reform, nor is it intended to have this effect." *Miranda*.

We come now to the question whether the denial of Wade's motion to strike the courtroom identification by the bank witnesses at trial because of the absence of his counsel at the lineup required, as the Court of Appeals held, the grant of a new trial at which such evidence is to be excluded. We do not think this disposition can be justified without first giving the Government the opportunity to establish by clear and convincing evidence that the in-court identifications were based upon observations of the suspect other than the lineup identification. * * * Where, as here, the admissibility of evidence of the lineup identification itself is not involved, a *per se* rule of exclusion of courtroom identification would be unjustified.[e] * * * A rule limited solely to the exclusion of testimony concerning identification at the lineup itself, without regard to admissibility of the courtroom identification, would render the right to counsel an empty one. The lineup is most often used, as in the present case, to crystallize the witnesses' identification of the defendant for future reference. We have already noted that the lineup identification will have that effect. The State may then rest upon the witnesses' unequivocal courtroom identification, and not mention the pretrial identification as part of the State's case at trial. Counsel is then in the predicament in which Wade's counsel found himself—realizing that possible unfairness at the lineup may be the sole means of attack upon the unequivocal courtroom identification, and having to probe in the dark in an attempt to discover and reveal unfairness, while bolstering the government witness'

29. Many other nations surround the lineup with safeguards against prejudice to the suspect. In England the suspect must be allowed the presence of his solicitor or a friend; Germany requires the presence of retained counsel; France forbids the confrontation of the suspect in the absence of his counsel; Spain, Mexico, and Italy provide detailed procedures prescribing the conditions under which confrontation must occur under the supervision of a judicial officer who sees to it that the proceedings are officially recorded to assure adequate scrutiny at trial. Murray, [fn. d supra at 621–627].

30. Thirty years ago Wigmore suggested a "scientific method" of pretrial identification "to reduce the risk of error hitherto inherent in such proceedings." Wigmore, *The Science of Judicial Proof* 541 (3d ed. 1937). Under this approach, at least 100 talking films would be prepared of men from various occupations, races, etc. Each would be photographed in a number of stock movements, with and without hat and coat, and would read aloud a standard passage. The suspect would be filmed in the same manner. Some 25 of the films would be shown in succession in a special projection room in which each witness would be provided an electric button which would activate a board backstage when pressed to indicate that the witness had identified a given person. Provision would be made for the degree of hesitancy in the identification to be indicated by the number of presses. Id., at 540–541. Of course, the more systematic and scientific a process or proceeding, including one for purposes of identification, the less the impediment to reconstruction of the conditions bearing upon the reliability of that process or proceeding at trial. * * *

e. In *Gilbert,* however, the Court did apply a *per se* exclusionary rule to the testimony of various prosecution witnesses that they had also identified petitioner at a pretrial lineup. See fn. f infra.

courtroom identification by bringing out and dwelling upon his prior identification. Since counsel's presence at the lineup would equip him to attack not only the lineup identification but the courtroom identification as well, limiting the impact of violation of the right to counsel to exclusion of evidence only of identification at the lineup itself disregards a critical element of that right.

We think it follows that the proper test to be applied in these situations is that quoted in *Wong Sun v. United States* [p. 803 infra], " '[W]hether, granting establishment of the primary illegality the evidence to which instant objection is made has been come at by exploitation of that illegality or instead by means sufficiently distinguishable to be purged of the primary taint.' Maguire, *Evidence of Guilt* 221 (1959)." Application of this test in the present context requires consideration of various factors; for example, the prior opportunity to observe the alleged criminal act, the existence of any discrepancy between any pre-lineup description and the defendant's actual description, any identification prior to lineup of another person, the identification by picture of the defendant prior to the lineup, failure to identify the defendant on a prior occasion, and the lapse of time between the alleged act and the lineup identification. It is also relevant to consider those facts which, despite the absence of counsel, are disclosed concerning the conduct of the lineup.[33] * * *

On the record now before us we cannot make the determination whether the in-court identifications had an independent origin. [T]he appropriate procedure to be followed is to vacate the conviction pending a hearing to determine whether the in-court identifications had an independent source, or whether, in any event, the introduction of the evidence was harmless error, *Chapman v. California* [p. 796 infra], and for the District Court to reinstate the conviction or order a new trial, as may be proper.[f] * * *

Judgment of Court of Appeals vacated and case remanded with direction.

MR. JUSTICE BLACK, dissenting in part and concurring in part. * * *

I would reverse Wade's conviction without further ado had the prosecution at trial made use of his lineup identification either in place of courtroom identification or [as it did in *Gilbert*] to bolster in a harmful manner crucial courtroom identification. But the prosecution here did neither of these things. After prosecution witnesses under oath identified Wade in the court-

33. Thus it is not the case that "[i]t matters not how well the witness knows the suspect, whether the witness is the suspect's mother, brother, or long-time associate, and no matter how long or well the witness observed the perpetrator at the scene of the crime" [quoting from Justice White's opinion in *Wade*]. Such factors will have an important bearing upon the true basis of the witness' in-court identification. Moreover, the State's inability to bolster the witness' courtroom identification by introduction of the lineup identification itself, see *Gilbert,* will become less significant the more the evidence of other opportunities of the witness to observe the defendant. Thus where the witness is a "kidnap victim who has lived for days with his abductor" [again quoting from Justice White] the value to the State of admission of the lineup identification is indeed marginal, and such identification would be a mere formality.

f. Compare *Gilbert,* where various witnesses who identified petitioner in the courtroom also testified, on direct examination by the prosecution, that they had identified petitioner at a prior lineup. "That [pretrial lineup] testimony," ruled the Court, "is the direct result of the illegal lineup 'come at by exploitation of [the primary] illegality.' *Wong Sun.* The State is therefore not entitled to an opportunity to show that that testimony had an independent source. Only a *per se* exclusionary rule as to such testimony can be an effective sanction to assure that law enforcement authorities will respect the accused's constitutional right to the presence of his counsel at the critical lineup. * * * That conclusion is buttressed by the consideration that the witness' testimony of his lineup identification will enhance the impact of his in-court identification on the jury and seriously aggravate whatever derogation exists of the accused's right to a fair trial. Therefore, unless the [state supreme court] is 'able to declare a belief that it was harmless beyond a reasonable doubt,' *Chapman,* Gilbert will be entitled on remand to a new trial * * *."

room, it was the defense, and not the prosecution, which brought out the prior lineup identification. While stating that "a *per se* rule of exclusion of courtroom identification would be unjustified," the Court, nevertheless remands this case for "a hearing to determine whether the in-court identifications had an independent source," or were the tainted fruits of the invalidly conducted lineup. From this holding I dissent.

In the first place, even if this Court has power to establish such a rule of evidence, I think the rule fashioned by the Court is unsound. The "tainted fruit" determination required by the Court involves more than considerable difficulty. I think it is practically impossible. How is a witness capable of probing the recesses of his mind to draw a sharp line between a courtroom identification due exclusively to an earlier lineup and a courtroom identification due to memory not based on the lineup? What kind of "clear and convincing evidence" can the prosecution offer to prove upon what particular events memories resulting in an in-court identification rest? * * * In my view, the Fifth and Sixth Amendments are satisfied if the prosecution is precluded from using lineup identification as either an alternative to or corroboration of courtroom identification. If the prosecution does neither and its witnesses under oath identify the defendant in the courtroom, then I can find no justification for stopping the trial in midstream to hold a lengthy "tainted fruit" hearing. The fact of and circumstances surrounding a prior lineup identification might be used by the defense to impeach the credibility of the in-court identifications, but not to exclude them completely. * * *

MR. JUSTICE WHITE whom MR. JUSTICE HARLAN and MR. JUSTICE STEWART join, dissenting in part and concurring in part.

The Court has again propounded a broad constitutional rule barring the use of a wide spectrum of relevant and probative evidence, solely because a step in its ascertainment or discovery occurs outside the presence of defense counsel. * * *

The Court's opinion is far-reaching. It proceeds first by creating a new *per se* rule of constitutional law: a criminal suspect cannot be subjected to a pretrial identification process in the absence of his counsel without violating the Sixth Amendment. If he is, the State may not buttress a later courtroom identification of the witness by any reference to the previous identification. Furthermore, the courtroom identification is not admissible at all unless the State can establish by clear and convincing proof that the testimony is not the fruit of the earlier identification made in the absence of defendant's counsel—admittedly a heavy burden for the State and probably an impossible one. To all intents and purposes, courtroom identifications are barred if pretrial identifications have occurred without counsel being present.

The rule applies to any lineup, to any other techniques employed to produce an identification and *a fortiori* to a face-to-face encounter between the witness and the suspect alone, regardless of when the identification occurs, in time or place, and whether before or after indictment or information. It matters not how well the witness knows the suspect, whether the witness is the suspect's mother, brother, or long-time associate, and no matter how long or well the witness observed the perpetrator at the scene of the crime. The kidnap victim who has lived for days with his abductor is in the same category as the witness who has had only a fleeting glimpse of the criminal. Neither may identify the suspect without defendant's counsel being present. The same strictures apply regardless of the number of other witnesses who positively identify the defendant and regardless of the corroborative evidence showing that it was the defendant who had committed the crime.

The premise for the Court's rule is not the general unreliability of eyewitness identifications nor the difficulties inherent in observation, recall, and recognition. The Court assumes a narrower evil as the basis for its rule—improper police suggestion which contributes to erroneous identifications. The Court apparently believes that improper police procedures are so widespread that a broad prophylactic rule must be laid down, requiring the presence of counsel at all pretrial identifications, in order to detect recurring instances of police misconduct.[1] I do not share this pervasive distrust of all official investigations. None of the materials the Court relies upon supports it. Certainly, I would bow to solid fact, but the Court quite obviously does not have before it any reliable, comprehensive survey of current police practices on which to base its new rule. Until it does, the Court should avoid excluding relevant evidence from state criminal trials.

[The] Court goes beyond assuming that a great majority of the country's police departments are following improper practices at pretrial identifications. To find the lineup a "critical" stage of the proceeding and to exclude identifications made in the absence of counsel the Court must also assume that police "suggestion," if it occurs at all, leads to erroneous rather than accurate identifications and that reprehensible police conduct will have an unavoidable and largely undiscoverable impact on the trial. This in turn assumes that there is now no adequate source from which defense counsel can learn about the circumstances of the pretrial identification in order to place before the jury all of the considerations which should enter into an appraisal of courtroom identification evidence. But these are treacherous and unsupported assumptions[3] resting as they do on the notion that the defendant will not be aware, that the police and the witnesses will forget or prevaricate, that defense counsel will be unable to bring out the truth and that neither jury, judge, nor appellate court is a sufficient safeguard against unacceptable police conduct occurring at a pretrial identification procedure. I am unable to share the Court's view of the willingness of the police and the ordinary citizen-witness to dissemble, either with respect to the identification of the defendant or with respect to the circumstances surrounding a pretrial identification.

There are several striking aspects to the Court's holding. First, the rule does not bar courtroom identifications where there have been no previous identifications in the presence of the police, although when identified in the courtroom, the defendant is known to be in custody and charged with the commission of a crime.[g] Second, the Court seems to say that if suitable legislative standards were adopted for the conduct of pretrial identifications, thereby lessening the hazards in such confrontations, it would not insist on the presence

1. Yet in *Stovall v. Denno* [p. 667 infra] the Court recognizes that improper police conduct in the identification process has not been so widespread as to justify full retroactivity for its new rule.

3. The instant case and its companions, *Gilbert* and *Stovall* certainly lend no support to the Court's assumptions. The police conduct deemed improper by the Court in the three cases seems to have come to light at trial in the ordinary course of events. One can ask what more counsel would have learned at the pretrial identifications that would have been relevant for truth determination at trial. * * *

g. Consider Grano, *Kirby, Biggers, and Ash: Do Any Constitutional Safeguards Remain Against the Danger of Convicting the Innocent?*, 72 Mich.L.Rev. 717, 785 (1974): "[A]n identification more unreliable than the witness's familiar selection of the conspicuous defendant, frequently after scanning the courtroom for dramatic effect, is difficult to imagine. In effect, [these identifications are] one-man showups, albeit in the courtroom." Consider, too, Uviller, *The Role of the Defense Lawyer at a Lineup in Light of the Wade, Gilbert and Stovall Decisions*, 4 Crim.L.Bull. 273, 284 (1968): "[T]alk about suggestion—what witness sitting on the stand has such a dim brain that he does not know where in the courtroom to look when he is asked whether he sees the defendant in the courtroom?"

How can defense counsel avoid or minimize the impact of a suggestive confrontation between a witness and defendant in the courtroom? See Note 7 following this case.

of counsel. But if this is true, why does not the Court simply fashion what it deems to be constitutionally acceptable procedures for the authorities to follow? Certainly the Court is correct in suggesting that the new rule will be wholly inapplicable where police departments themselves have established suitable safeguards.

Third, courtroom identification may be barred, absent counsel at a prior identification, regardless of the extent of counsel's information concerning the circumstances of the previous confrontation between witness and defendant—apparently even if there were recordings or sound-movies of the events as they occurred. But if the rule is premised on the defendant's right to have his counsel know, there seems little basis for not accepting other means to inform. A disinterested observer, recordings, photographs—any one of them would seem adequate to furnish the basis for a meaningful cross-examination of the eyewitness who identifies the defendant in the courtroom. * * *

Finally, I think the Court's new rule is vulnerable in terms of its own unimpeachable purpose of increasing the reliability of identification testimony.

Law enforcement officers have the obligation to convict the guilty and to make sure they do not convict the innocent. They must be dedicated to making the criminal trial a procedure for the ascertainment of the true facts surrounding the commission of the crime. To this extent, our so-called adversary system is not adversary at all; nor should it be. But defense counsel has no comparable obligation to ascertain or present the truth. Our system assigns him a different mission. He must be and is interested in preventing the conviction of the innocent, but, absent a voluntary plea of guilty, we also insist that he defend his client whether he is innocent or guilty. The State has the obligation to present the evidence. Defense counsel need present nothing, even if he knows what the truth is. * * * If he can confuse a witness, even a truthful one, or make him appear at a disadvantage, unsure or indecisive, that will be his normal course. * * *

I would not extend this system, at least as it presently operates, to police investigations and would not require counsel's presence at pretrial identification procedures. Counsel's interest is in not having his client placed at the scene of the crime, regardless of his whereabouts. Some counsel may advise their clients to refuse to make any movements or to speak any words in a lineup or even to appear in one. [Others] will hover over witnesses and begin their cross-examination then, menacing truthful factfinding as thoroughly as the Court fears the police now do. Certainly there is an implicit invitation to counsel to suggest rules for the lineup and to manage and produce it as best he can.[h] I therefore doubt that the Court's new rule, at least absent some clearly defined limits on counsel's role, will measurably contribute to more reliable pretrial identifications. My fears are that it will have precisely the opposite result. * * * In my view, the State is entitled to investigate and develop its case outside the presence of defense counsel. This includes the right to have private conversations with identification witnesses, just as defense counsel may have his own consultations with these and other witnesses without having the prosecutor present. * * *

h. But see Note 4 following this case.

ON THE MEANING OF THE LINEUP DECISIONS

1. *Waiver.* If *Wade* seeks to protect the reliability of the identification process and to make available testimony about the conditions under which such process is carried out, why should the right to counsel at the lineup be subject to waiver? Permitting waiver of *Miranda* rights may be defended on the ground that an important, legitimate object is served by permit-

ting suspects to bear witness to the truth under conditions which safeguard the exercise of responsible choice, but what comparable value is served by allowing suspects to waive counsel at the identification process?

2. *Waiver; adequacy of warning.* Rule 404 of Project on Law Enforcement Policy and Rulemaking, *Model Rules for Law Enforcement: Eyewitness Identification* (1972) (hereinafter referred to as *Model Rules*) provides that a suspect entitled to a lawyer at a lineup "must be told that he has the right to have a lawyer present to observe the lineup procedure"; that if he cannot afford a lawyer, one will be provided for him free of charge; and—"although apparently this additional warning about delay is rarely, if ever, given in practice"—that "the lineup will be delayed for a reasonable time after the lawyer is notified, in order to allow the lawyer to appear." The warning about delay is recommended "because it precludes the claim that the suspect waived his right to counsel because of his belief that the lawyer could not appear in time" and "also puts the suspect on notice to inform counsel of the need for promptness." Supporting Memorandum for *Model Rules* at 49. On the prosecutor's burden of establishing waiver, see Note 12, p. 842 infra. Cf. *Lego v. Twomey,* p. 840 infra.

3. *Counsel's presence at the "moment of identification."* Although some courts have ruled to the contrary, viewing a viewer's conclusion as part of a police investigation to which the right to counsel does not attach, *Model Rule* 409(c) adopts the position taken in *People v. Williams,* 478 P.2d 942 (Cal.1971) that "exclusion of counsel from the moment of actual identification frustrated [a main purpose of *Wade* and *Gilbert*], namely to safeguard against the inherent risks of suggestion which are present at that time." The *Williams* case observes further: "It is not the moment of viewing alone, but rather the whole 'procedure' by which [a suspect] is identified that counsel must be able to effectively reconstruct at trial. If defense counsel is to be able to intelligently cross-examine the witness, he cannot be excluded from the moment of identification any more than he can be excluded from the lineup itself." See also Sobel, *Eye-Witness Identification: Legal and Practical Problems* 119 (1972).

If defense counsel is entitled to be present at the "moment of identification," is he also entitled to be present at a post-lineup conference between the prosecutor and the witness who has viewed the lineup? Cf. *United States v. Ash,* Sec. 2 infra.

4. *The role of counsel; consequences of counsel's ineffective performance at the pretrial identification proceeding.* (a) What is the role of defense counsel at the lineup? Compare H.R. Uviller, *The Role of the Defense Lawyer at a Line-up in Light of the Wade, Gilbert and Stovall Decisions,* 4 Crim. L.Bull. 273, 278, 285–86 (1968) (panel discussion with, inter alia, D. Chapman and A.J. Davis) (defense counsel is "merely to be a witness"; he is not there "to give legal advice, because there is nothing virtually that he can give legally as advice"; thus *Wade* "demeans the role of defense counsel") with D. Chapman, id. at 296 (the defense attorney at the lineup is not "a wax dummy"; he has a right to question the witnesses, to find out whether they have been shown photographs and whether anybody made any suggestions to them prior to viewing the lineup; "I would demand a chance to talk to the witnesses afterwards as to what their conclusions were"). Consider Commentary to the *Model Pre-Arraignment Code* at 429–33:

"The two extreme positions might be stated thus:

"(1) Counsel is to be present merely as an observer to assure against abuse and bad faith by law enforcement officers, and to provide the basis for any attack he might wish to make on the identification at trial.

"(2) The lineup procedure is to be a fully adversary proceeding in which the counsel for the suspect may make objections and proposals, which if they are proper or even reasonable must be respected.

"The cases and commentaries, as well as the practice since *Wade* would indicate that the first interpretation of the counsel's role comes closer to describing the general interpretation of the constitutional requirement and to describing the practice under it. The major difficulty with this interpretation is that by forcing counsel into the role of a merely passive observer it gives him a job which at best can be accomplished in a large variety of ways including video recording and at worst is uncomfortable or demeaning. * * *

"On the other hand, any attempt to give counsel at identification a more active role is fraught with difficulties not only for the police but for counsel himself. For the police the difficulty is that a procedure which is often under the supervision not of lawyers but of police officers will be subject to manipulation and objection by a trained legal counsel for one side only. * * *

"The assigning of a more active role to counsel has perils for counsel as well. If he is entitled to make objections at the lineup procedure, will he be held to have waived these objections if he does not make them at the procedure and he wishes later to question the fairness or accuracy of the identification at trial? If such a possibility of waiver exists will he not almost be under an obligation to raise every conceivable objection? Moreover, this hard choice would be imposed on a lawyer at a very early stage of his contact with the case. Indeed the lawyer who did this work is often likely to be a junior member of the public defender's staff assigned on rotation to do 'lineup work,' and thus would not likely be the lawyer to handle the case at trial. * * *

"[Thus, where] a lawyer is present he should not be obliged to make his objections or be deemed to have waived them. Similarly, there does not appear to be any reason to require the police to abide by any objections or suggestions that the lawyer makes. All the Code would require is that any objections that the lawyer might have be made part of the record of the identification procedure. In this way if something has taken place to which defense counsel objects and which the record might not otherwise clearly show, the fact of the lawyer's objection will make this issue prominently available for use at the trial. At the same time, the police in hearing the objection would have the opportunity to remedy the situation if they chose. To be sure, the absence of any objection might possibly carry some factual implication that the defendant and his counsel acquiesced in an identification procedure to which they then find themselves subsequently objecting at trial. This possibility may be thought to provide just the right degree of incentive for defense counsel to make reasonable objections which the police might heed, rather than sitting back and hoping to trap the police in error." [a]

(b) Suppose the government insures that a defense lawyer is present at a pretrial lineup and does nothing to interfere with counsel's functioning, but counsel performs ineffectively. Should a witness' identification at this lineup be automatically excluded from jury consideration? Most of the few courts confronting the issue have at least assumed that, if proven, the ineffectiveness of counsel at the identification proceeding would require exclusion of the identification evidence, see

a. See also *Model Rule* 409; Sobel, supra, at 115–20; Read, *Lawyers at Lineups: Constitutional Necessity or Avoidable Extravagance,* 17 U.C.L.A.L.Rev. 339 (1969); Sanford, *Eyewitness Identification in Criminal Cases,* 46 Fla.B.J. 412 (1972); Strazzella, *Ineffective Identification Counsel: Cognizability under the Exclusionary Rule,* 48 Temple L.Q. 241, 253–58 (1975); Notes, 69 Colum.L.Rev. 1296 (1969); 29 U.Pitt.L.Rev. 65 (1967); 77 Yale L.J. 390 (1967).

Strazzella, *Ineffective Identification Counsel: Cognizability under the Exclusionary Rule,* 48 Temple L.Q. 241, 244–45 (1975), but Professor Strazzella disagrees, id. at 279–80: "Given the *Wade-Gilbert* rationale, deprivation of the right to counsel by pretrial identification counsel [performing ineffectively] ought not normally be cognizable as a means of excluding the confrontation identification. Contrary to the assumption made by the courts, except for limited exceptions, the significant judicial expenditure necessary to take cognizance of the claim and decide it is not warranted, and the suppression of the important evidence would be unjustified. * * * [N]ot every stated right to counsel which fails due to counsel's inadequate performance will trigger the same consequence as an outright state denial of the right to counsel. Each stage at which counsel is required should be investigated in order to assess the circumstances in which counsel's ineffectiveness might be equated with ordinary state denial of counsel."

5. *Refusals to cooperate; obstructionist efforts.* Since the lineup or the taking of exemplars is not protected by the privilege against self-incrimination, the prosecution may comment on the suspect's refusal to cooperate. The refusal is considered circumstantial evidence of consciousness of guilt. On occasion, courts have utilized civil or criminal contempt to coerce or punish the suspect who refuses to comply with a court order to participate in some identification proceeding. Still another possibility is for the police to proceed to conduct the identification proceeding over the suspect's objection. See LaFave & Israel, § 7.2(c); *Model Rules* 407, 408.

What may be done in response to a suspect's drastic alteration of his appearance between the time of arrest (or the occurrence of the crime) and his appearance in a lineup? [b] One possibility is to bring this alteration to the attention of the jury for consideration as evidence of defendant's consciousness of guilt. Another possibility is to conduct the identification procedure in such a way as to simulate the defendant's prior appearance. See LaFave & Israel, § 7.2(d). But see Seidelson, *The Right to Counsel: From Passive to Active Voice,* 30 Geo.Wash.L.Rev. 849 (1970).

Consider *People v. Cwikla,* 386 N.E.2d 1070 (N.Y.1979), where defendant appeared at a pretrial identification procedure with his head and face newly shaved (allegedly for medical reasons). The defendant was required to don a wig and false beard for purposes of the identification proceeding. "It was not error," ruled the court, "to compel defendant to conform his appearance at the lineup to his appearance at the time of the crime."

6. *Invalid pre-trial identification procedures and the "independent origin" of in-court identifications.* Reconsider Justice Black's complaint in *Wade* about the difficulties involved in determining whether or not an in-court identification is the "tainted fruit" of an improperly conducted lineup. Does it follow, as Justice Black maintained, that therefore *every* courtroom identification made subsequent to an illegal police lineup (so long as not supplemented or corroborated by the earlier lineup) should be admitted? Or do the very reasons advanced by Justice Black—the great difficulties, if not impossibility of ascertaining the "taint" or lack of it—suggest that *no* courtroom identification preceded by an illegal police lineup should be allowed? [c]

b. What ethical questions, if any, are raised by a defense lawyer who encourages his client to "disguise himself" prior to a lineup?

c. The difficulties of determining whether there is an "independent source" for in-court identifications following invalid pre-trial lineups are illustrated by *Clemons v. United States,* 408 F.2d 1230 (D.C.Cir.1968) and explored in Pitler, *"The Fruit of the Poisonous Tree" Revisited and Shepardized,* 56 Calif.L.Rev. 579, 636–41 (1968); Note 45 Wash.L.Rev. 202 (1970). See generally Levine & Tapp, *The Psychology of Criminal Identifications: The Gap from Wade to Kirby,* 121 U.Pa.L.Rev. 1079 (1973). The difficulties are compounded when a courtroom identification is preceded by a corporeal identification which, in

Is the requirement that the prosecution establish by clear and convincing proof that the courtroom testimony is untainted by the earlier illegal identification a "heavy" and "probably an impossible" burden, as Justice White maintained in *Wade?* If pre-trial identifications are held in violation of the suspect's right to counsel, does the *Wade-Gilbert* rule, as Justice White claimed, bar all courtroom identifications "to all intents and purposes"? Consider the remarks of A.J. Davis of the Philadelphia District Attorney's Office, Note 4 supra at 294–95, a year after the lineup cases were decided:

"How [is the defense lawyer] going to prove that the in-court identification that the victim is about to make is the fruit of [the invalid police lineup]? The Supreme Court may say the burden of proof is on the prosecution, but you know and I know that the attitude of the trial judge is going to be that the burden of proof is on [the defense lawyer] as a practical matter to convince that judge. He is not going to be terribly sympathetic to these cases.

"What is the prosecution going to do? The prosecution is going to put the victim on the stand and the victim is going to say, 'When this robber came to me and put that gun in my face, I looked at him and I formed a mental picture * * *. Then, I had this lineup and I compared this portrait in my mind with the people in the lineup and I picked out that defendant. Now I am in court and what am I doing? I am not paying any attention to the lineup. I am again conjuring up that [mental picture] which I evolved in my mind at the time of the robbery, and I am taking that [picture] and putting it next to this defendant at the counsel table and I am saying that they are precisely the same,' and the judge is going to say, 'Whoopie, there's an independent origin,' and you can attempt to prove from today to tomorrow that the pre-trial identification was unfair, but the trial court has a finding of fact to make here, and nine times out of ten, unless you have a very exceptional trial court, he is going to find against you on this issue."

Mr. Davis has turned out to be a better prognosticator than Justice White. The cases support the conclusions of commentators that when confronted with invalid pre-trial identifications the lower courts have "easily found an 'independent source' for an in-court identification," Note, 55 Minn.L.Rev. 779, 818 (1971), and have "readily avoided reversing convictions by stretching, often beyond reason and logic, the doctrines of independent source and harmless error," Grano, p. 660 fn. g supra, at 722. See also Levine & Tapp, fn. c supra at 1083; Quinn, *In the Wake of Wade: The Dimensions of the Eyewitness Identification Cases,* 42 U.Colo.L.Rev. 135, 140–43 (1970); Comment, 36 U.Chi.L.Rev. 830, 833 n. 14 (1969).[d]

7. *Defendant's right to a lineup or other identification procedure.* Reconsider fn. g, p. 660 supra. Should a defendant be allowed to sit among spectators or with nonsuspects at counsel table? Should he be entitled to an in-court lineup, or a pretrial lineup, before being required to confront witnesses in the courtroom?

Consider *Moore v. Illinois,* 434 U.S. 220, 98 S.Ct. 458, 54 L.Ed.2d 424 (1977) (also discussed at p. 672 infra). In rejecting the contention that because the corporeal identification occurred "in the course of a judicial proceeding" (a preliminary hearing to determine whether petitioner should be

turn, is preceded by a photographic identification. For the corporeal identification "may be based not upon the witness's recollection of the features of the guilty party, but upon his recollection of the photograph. Thus, although a witness who is asked to attempt a corporeal identification of a person whose photograph he has previously identified may say, 'That's the man that did it,' what he may actually mean is, 'That's the man whose photograph I identified.'" Wall, *Eye-Witness Identification in Criminal Cases* 68 (1965).

d. For a discussion of factors and circumstances supporting a finding of independent source and negating such a finding, see Sobel, supra, at 122–38; Note, 55 Minn.L.Rev. 779, 815–17 (1971).

bound over to the grand jury and to set bail) petitioner had no *Wade-Gilbert* right to counsel at the identification procedure, the Court, per Powell, J., pointed out that the identification, "a one-on-one confrontation," had been made under highly suggestive circumstances and that "[h]ad petitioner been represented by counsel, some or all of this suggestiveness could have been avoided." It then noted, 434 U.S. at 230 n. 5, 98 S.Ct. at 465 n. 5:

"For example, counsel could have requested that the hearing be postponed until a lineup could be arranged at which the victim would view petitioner in a less suggestive setting. Short of that, counsel could have asked that the victim be excused from the courtroom while the charges were read and the evidence against petitioner was recited, and that petitioner be seated with other people in the audience when the victim attempted an identification. * * * Because it is in the prosecution's interest as well as the accused's that witnesses' identifications remain untainted, we cannot assume that such requests would have been in vain. Such requests are usually addressed to the sound discretion of the court; we express no opinion as to whether the preliminary hearing court would have been required to grant any such requests."

Although such requests are occasionally granted, trial judges, in their discretion, often deny them. See generally LaFave & Israel, § 7.4(g); Grano, supra, at 784–86. A leading case on this point is *Evans v. Superior Court,* 522 P.2d 681 (Cal.1974), holding that due process requires that in an appropriate case defendant should be afforded a pretrial lineup, but that such a right arises "only when eyewitness identification is shown to be in material issue and there exists a reasonable likelihood of a mistaken identification which a lineup would tend to resolve." See also *United States v. Archibald,* 734 F.2d 938 (2d Cir. 1984), per Oakes, J., pointing out that defendant's request that he be seated away from the defense table and that other black men be seated in the courtroom "should not have been dismissed so quickly or so absolutely by the trial court. * * * While it was not necessary for the court to conduct a true *Wade*-type lineup, these relatively minor steps were required to ensure that the identification was not unfair. The in-court identification procedure utilized here was so clearly suggestive as to be impermissible, however traditional it may be." [e]

Model Pre-Arraignment Code § 170.2 permits a person "arrested for or charged with an offense or a person who shows a reasonable basis for believing he may be so charged" to request a nontestimonial identification order requiring persons *other than himself* to appear (presumably to "clear" himself by shifting suspicion to another) or to request an identification procedure involving himself.[f]

8. *The use of "blank" lineups.* To guard against the danger that an eyewitness will assume that the suspect is present in the lineup and thus tend to identify the person who *most nearly resembles* his recollection of the perpetrator of the crime, some commentators have urged the use of "blank" lineups. See, e.g., Sobel at 100–01; Jonakait, *Reliable Identification; Could the*

e. On petition for rehearing, 756 F.2d 223 (5th Cir.1984), *Archibald* was modified to make it clear that special in-court identification procedures are necessary "only when (1) identification is a contested issue; (2) the defendant has moved in a timely manner prior to trial for a lineup; and (3) despite that defense request, the witness has not had an opportunity to view a fair out-of-court lineup prior to his trial testimony."

f. Perhaps because trial judges frequently deny requests, to hold an in-court lineup or to seat the defendant in the courtroom audience before and during the testimony of the prosecution's identification witnesses, defense attorneys have sometimes resorted to "self-help," i.e., substituted another person for the defendant at counsel table without the court's permission or knowledge. This "has been viewed as a violation of ethical standards and an obstruction of justice punishable by criminal contempt." LaFave & Israel, § 7.5(g).

Supreme Court Tell in Manson v. Brathwaite?, 52 U.Colo.L.Rev. 511, 525 (1981); Lefcourt, *The Blank Lineup: An Aid to the Defense,* 14 Crim.L.Bull. 428 (1978). "The procedure of a blank lineup entails the viewing by the eyewitness of two separate line-ups. The witness should be told that the suspect may or may not appear in the room being viewed. Thereafter, the suspect is not in the first line-up but is presented in the second. Thus, if the witness is one who has a tendency to make an identification because of an assumption that the suspect is present, this tendency would be brought out during the course of the first line-up. On the other hand, if the witness [is] able to identify the suspect [in the second lineup], that identification will carry even greater weight, as it should." Lefcourt, supra, at 430.

9. *A "per se exclusionary rule" vs. jury instructions.* In *Gilbert* the Court ruled that unlike the case with in-court identifications, which the prosecution may be able to establish were not tainted by a lineup held in the absence of counsel but of "independent origin," "only a per se exclusionary rule as to [testimony about a lineup identification made in the absence of counsel] can be an effective sanction to assure that law enforcement authorities will respect the accused's constitutional right * * *." *Why?* Consider Grano, supra, at 791: "In the fourth amendment context, years of fervent debate preceded the Court's conclusion that the exclusionary rule provides the most effective safeguard against police illegality. Yet, in establishing a right to counsel at lineups, a right not presaged in a single jurisdiction, the Court, without the benefit of debate, apparently assumed that no other remedy would suffice. The Court did not even specify the possible alternatives being rejected as it had done in the search and seizure area. Since criminal prosecutions without identification evidence are difficult to imagine, the Court's rulings understandably generated substantial antipathy, usually and unfortunately directed at the counsel requirement rather than at the remedy."

Professor Grano proposes, id. at 798, "the gradual abolition of the exclusionary rule" for *Wade-Gilbert* violations and their replacement with jury instructions. "This recommendation is subject to two provisos. First, the efficacy of the instructions would have to be tested empirically. Second, to free itself of the exclusionary remedy, a jurisdiction would have to adopt regulations demonstrating adherence to the prophylactic constitutional rules."

THE DUE PROCESS "BACK-UP" TEST

STOVALL v. DENNO, 388 U.S. 293, 87 S.Ct. 1967, 18 L.Ed.2d 1199 (1967) (a federal habeas corpus proceeding collaterally attacking a state criminal conviction) (discussed more extensively in § 3, infra), held that the newly announced *Wade-Gilbert* principles would not be applied retroactively but would affect only those identification procedures conducted in the absence of counsel after the date the *Wade* and *Gilbert* decisions were handed down.[a] The court did consider, however, whether "the confrontation conducted in this case was so unnecessarily suggestive and conducive to irreparable mistaken identification" that petitioner was denied due process of law—"a recognized ground of attack upon a conviction independent of any right to counsel claim," but one that must be evaluated in light of the totality of surrounding circumstances. Since the record revealed that the showing of petitioner to a victim of the assault "in an immediate hospital confrontation was imperative," the due process claim was denied. As *Stovall* illustrates, and as the Court later articulated the due process test when it applied it to a pretrial identification by photograph, the

a. For a general discussion of the retroactive effect of a new constitutional decision in the criminal procedure field, see p. 49 supra.

question is whether the identification procedure "was so *impermissibly* suggestive as to give rise to a very substantial likelihood of irreparable misidentification." *Simmons v. United States,* 390 U.S. 377, 88 S.Ct. 967, 19 L.Ed.2d 1247 (1968). (Emphasis added.)

THE EYE-WITNESS TESTIMONY PROVISIONS OF THE 1968 CRIME CONTROL ACT

Consider the constitutionality of Title II of the Omnibus Crime Control and Safe Streets Act of 1968, 18 U.S.C. § 3502, designed to "repeal" the *Wade-Gilbert* rule in federal prosecutions: "The testimony of a witness that he saw the accused commit or participate in the commission of the crime for which the accused is being tried shall be admissible in evidence in a criminal prosecution in any trial court ordained and established under article III of the Constitution of the United States."

Consider Judge McGowan, *Constitutional Interpretation and Criminal Identification,* 12 Wm. & Mary L.Rev. 235, 249–50 (1970): "As a practical matter, the Congressional [response to *Wade-Gilbert-Stovall*] has proved to be meaningless. The inferior federal courts have considered themselves bound by the Supreme Court's reading of the Constitution rather than that of the Congress and have appeared to ignore the new statute. It exists on the books more as the expression of a legislative hope than as a binding rule of decision, and it will presumably continue in this posture until the Supreme Court, if it ever does, overrules or modifies its identification decision. * * * [Congress] appeared to overlook completely the threat to the conviction rate inherent in the impatience of juries with prosecution cases limited to incourt identification. It showed no awareness of the values that may reside, for the prosecution as well as the defense, in tightening up pretrial identification procedures so that impressively credible identification evidence can be adduced." See also Commentary to *Model Pre-Arraignment Code* at 427 & n. 15; Notes, 57 Geo.L.J. 438 (1968); 82 Harv.L.Rev. 1392 (1969); 40 Miss.L.J. 257 (1969).

In light of its sparse legislative history, may § 3502 be read as excepting from its language lineups conducted in violation of due process, which *Stovall* recognized as a basis for attacking identification testimony independent of any right to counsel claim? See *United States v. Johnson,* 461 F.2d 1165, 1170 (5th Cir.1972); *United States v. King,* 321 F.Supp. 614 (W.D.Tex.1970); Note, 57 Geo.L.J. 438, 455–60 (1968).

SECTION 2. THE COURT RETREATS: *KIRBY* AND *ASH*

KIRBY v. ILLINOIS

406 U.S. 682, 92 S.Ct. 1877, 32 L.Ed.2d 411 (1972).

MR. JUSTICE STEWART announced the judgment of the Court in an opinion in which THE CHIEF JUSTICE, MR. JUSTICE BLACKMUN, and MR. JUSTICE REHNQUIST join.

* * * In the present case we are asked to extend the *Wade-Gilbert* per se exclusionary rule to identification testimony based upon a police station show-up that took place *before* the defendant had been indicted or otherwise formally charged with any criminal offense.

On February 21, 1968, [one] Willie Shard reported to the Chicago police that the previous day two men had robbed him on a Chicago street of a wallet containing, among other things, travellers checks and a Social Security card. On February 22, two police officers [investigating an unrelated crime] stopped petitioner and a companion, [Bean], [on a Chicago street]. When asked for identification, the petitioner produced a wallet that contained three travellers checks and a Social Security card, all bearing the name of Willie Shard. * * *

Only after arriving at the police station, and checking the records there, did the arresting officers learn of the Shard robbery. A police car * * * picked up Shard and brought him to the police station. Immediately upon entering the room [where petitioner and Bean were seated], Shard positively identified them as [his robbers].[a] No lawyer was present [and neither suspect had asked for] or been advised of any right to the presence of counsel. [At the trial Shard] described his identification of the two men at the police station [and] identified them again in the courtroom as the men who had robbed him * * *.

In a line of constitutional cases in this Court stemming back to the Court's landmark opinion in *Powell v. Alabama,* it has been firmly established that a person's Sixth and Fourteenth Amendment right to counsel attaches only at or after the time that adversary judicial proceedings have been initiated against him.

This is not to say that a defendant in a criminal case has a constitutional right to counsel only at the trial itself. * * * But the point is [that] *all* of [the right to counsel cases] have involved points of time at or after the initiation of adversary judicial criminal proceedings—whether by way of formal charge, preliminary hearing, indictment, information, or arraignment.

The only seeming deviation from this long line of constitutional decisions was *Escobedo* [which] is not apposite here for two distinct reasons. First, the Court in retrospect perceived that the "prime purpose" of *Escobedo* was not to vindicate the constitutional right to counsel as such, but, like *Miranda,* "to guarantee full effectuation of the privilege against self-incrimination. * * *" *Johnson v. New Jersey* [p. 50 supra]. Secondly, and perhaps even more important for purely practical purposes, the Court has limited the holding of *Escobedo* to its own facts, and those facts are not remotely akin to the facts of the case before us.

The initiation of judicial criminal proceedings is far from a mere formalism. It is the starting point of our whole system of adversary criminal justice. For it is only then that the Government has committed itself to prosecute, and only then that the adverse positions of Government and defendant have solidified. It is then that a defendant finds himself faced with the prosecutorial forces of organized society, and immersed in the intricacies of substantive and procedural criminal law. It is this point, therefore, that marks the commencement of the "criminal prosecutions" to which alone the explicit guarantees of the Sixth Amendment are applicable.

In this case we are asked to import into a routine police investigation an absolute constitutional guarantee historically and rationally applicable only after the onset of formal prosecutorial proceedings. We decline to do so. Less than a year after *Wade* and *Gilbert* were decided, the Court explained the rule of those decisions as follows: "The rationale of those cases was that an accused is entitled to counsel at any 'critical stage of the *prosecution,*' and that a post-indictment lineup is such a 'critical stage.'" (Emphasis supplied.) *Simmons v. United States,* [p. 685 infra]. We decline to depart from that rationale today by imposing a per se exclusionary rule upon testimony concerning an identification that took place long before the commencement of any prosecution whatever.

What has been said is not to suggest that there may not be occasions during the course of a criminal investigation when the police do abuse identification procedures. Such abuses are not beyond the reach of the Constitution. * * * The Due Process Clause of the Fifth and Fourteenth Amendments forbids a lineup that is unnecessarily suggestive and conducive to irreparable mistaken identification.[8] When a person has not been formally charged

a. According to dissenting Justice Brennan, Shard testified that he identified petitioner and Bean only after the officers who brought him to the room asked him if they were the robbers.

8. In view of our limited grant of certiorari, we do not consider whether there might have been a deprivation of due process in the particularized circumstances of this case. That question with a criminal offense, *Stovall* strikes the appropriate constitutional balance between the right of a suspect to be protected from prejudicial procedures and the interest of society in the prompt and purposeful investigation of an unsolved crime.

The judgment is affirmed.[b]

MR. JUSTICE BRENNAN, with whom MR. JUSTICE DOUGLAS and MR. JUSTICE MARSHALL join, dissenting. * * *

While it should go without saying, it appears necessary, in view of the plurality opinion today, to re-emphasize that *Wade* did not require the presence of counsel at pretrial confrontations for identification purposes simply on the basis of an abstract consideration of the words "criminal prosecutions" in the Sixth Amendment, [but] in order to safeguard the accused's constitutional rights to confrontation and the effective assistance of counsel at his trial.

In view of *Wade,* it is plain, and the plurality today does not attempt to dispute it, that there inhere in a confrontation for identification conducted after arrest[5] the identical hazards to a fair trial that inhere in such a confrontation conducted "after the onset of formal prosecutorial proceedings." The plurality apparently considers an arrest, which for present purposes we must assume to be based upon probable cause, to be nothing more than part of "a routine police investigation," and thus not "the starting point of our whole system of adversary criminal justice." * * * An arrest evidences the belief of the police that the perpetrator of a crime has been caught. A post-arrest confrontation for identification is not "a mere preparatory step in the gathering of the prosecution's evidence." *Wade.* A primary, and frequently sole, purpose of the confrontation for identification at that stage is to accumulate proof to buttress the conclusion of the police that they have the offender in hand. The plurality offers no reason, and I can think of none, for concluding that a post-arrest confrontation for identification, unlike a post-charge confrontation, is not among those "critical confrontations of the accused by the prosecution at pretrial proceedings where the results might well settle the accused's fate and reduce the trial itself to a mere formality."

The highly suggestive form of confrontation employed in this case underscores the point. This showup was particularly fraught with the peril of mistaken identification. In the setting of a police station squad room where all present except petitioner and Bean were police officers, the danger was quite real that Shard's understandable resentment might lead him too readily to agree with the police that the pair under arrest, and the only persons exhibited to him, were indeed the robbers. * * * On direct examination, Shard identified petitioner and Bean not as the alleged robbers on trial in the courtroom, but as the pair he saw at the police station. * * *

The plurality [might have] discovered a different "rationale" for *Wade* and *Gilbert* [than the one it found and "decline[d] to depart from"] had it examined *Stovall,* decided the same day, [where], in the plurality's terms today, the confrontation was held "before the commencement of any prosecution." Yet in that circumstance the Court in *Stovall* stated that the accused raised "the same alleged constitutional errors in the admission of allegedly tainted identification evidence that were before us" in *Wade* and *Gilbert.* * * * [A]t one point [in *Stovall*] the Court summa-

remains open for inquiry in a federal habeas corpus proceeding.

[Following the U.S. Supreme Court's decision, the denial of Kirby's petition for federal habeas corpus relief was affirmed by the Seventh Circuit in *United States ex rel. Kirby v. Sturges,* 510 F.2d 397 (1975).]

b. As he "would not extend the *Wade-Gilbert* exclusionary rule," Powell, J., concurred in the result.

5. This case does not require me to consider confrontations that take place before custody, nor accidental confrontations not arranged by the police, nor on-the-scene encounters shortly after the crime.

rized *Wade* as holding "that the confrontation [for identification] is a 'critical stage,' and that counsel is required at *all* confrontations." (Emphasis added).

Wade and *Gilbert*, of course, happened to involve post-indictment confrontations. Yet even a cursory perusal of the opinions in those cases reveals that nothing at all turned upon that particular circumstance. In short, it is fair to conclude that rather than "declin[ing] to depart from [the] rationale" of *Wade* and *Gilbert*, the plurality today, albeit purporting to be engaged in "principled constitutional adjudication," refuses even to recognize that "rationale." * * * Because Shard testified at trial about his identification of petitioner at the police station showup, the exclusionary rule of *Gilbert* requires reversal.

MR. JUSTICE WHITE, dissenting.

Wade and *Gilbert* govern this case and compel reversal of the judgment below.

Notes and Questions

1. *Wade and Escobedo.* Does the "reinterpretation" of *Escobedo* (as designed not to vindicate the right to counsel as such but to effectuate the privilege against self-incrimination) support Justice Stewart's holding in *Kirby?* Consider Grano at 728: "*Wade*, like *Escobedo* in its new guise, did not vindicate the right to counsel as such, but rather vindicated the rights of cross-examination, confrontation, and fair trial. *Escobedo* still suggests that counsel must be provided at *any* pretrial stage when necessary to protect other constitutional rights."

2. *Wade and Powell.* Did the early right to counsel precedents, as Justice Stewart indicates, mandate the result in *Kirby?* Consider Grano at 727: "*Powell v. Alabama* [and its pre-*Gideon* progeny] relied on the fourteenth amendment due process clause rather than on the sixth amendment. Since the protections under the fourteenth amendment are not limited to any particular stage of a criminal proceeding, the fact that the defendants in these cases had already been charged is irrelevant."

3. *"Custody" vs. "the initiation of adversary judicial criminal proceedings.* Is it sound to view (as does Justice Stewart for the plurality in *Kirby*) the "initiation of judicial criminal proceedings [as] the starting point of our whole system of adversary criminal justice"? Is it realistic to say, (as Justice Stewart does for the *Kirby* plurality) that "it is only then * * * that the adverse positions of Government and defendant have solidified"? Is the postcustody police attitude supposed to be "neutral" or merely "investigative" rather than "accusatory"? Didn't the Court explicitly recognize in *Miranda* that the accusatory function begins very soon after the defendant is taken into custody? Again, see Grano at 726–27. Recall the statement in *Escobedo* —over Justice Stewart's strong dissent—that "it would exalt form over substance to make the right to counsel, under these circumstances, depend on whether at the time of the interrogation the authorities had secured a formal indictment. Petitioner had, for all practical purposes, already been charged * * *."

But consider Israel, *Criminal Procedure, the Burger Court, and the Legacy of the Warren Court,* 75 Mich.L.Rev. 1320, 1368 n. 224 (1977): "[A]ccepting the premise that the need for counsel is often equivalent in the post-indictment and pre-indictment lineup, it does not necessarily follow that appointment of counsel is constitutionally required in both situations. The sixth amendment, it can be argued, does not provide for counsel at every stage in which counsel's assistance is helpful. Rather, by its history, language, and function, the amendment sought to draw a starting point after which counsel's assistance is generally required as an element of our adversary system. That point, Justice Stewart argues, is the initiation of judicial criminal proceedings. Before that point, counsel may be constitutionally required only if essential to the protection of some other constitutional right, as in *Miranda. Kirby* obviously concluded that it was not so essential as to be required to implement the right of confronting the eyewitness at trial. After the sixth amendment starting point takes effect, however, assistance of counsel need not be essential to a fair trial to be constitutionally required. Once the judicial criminal proceedings have been initiated, counsel is necessary at all ' "critical stages" ' of the proceedings; but a critical stage simply is one in which counsel's assistance will be helpful, though not necessarily so important as to be required under the more rigorous standard of due process applicable before the sixth amendment takes effect. Cf. *Coleman v. Alabama* [p. 100 supra, and Ch. 14 infra] * * *."

4. *Alley confrontations.* To what extent did *Kirby* reject the "custody" approach because such an approach would pose a serious threat to the common police practice of conducting "alley confrontations," i.e., prompt confrontations with the victim or an eyewitness at the scene of the crime? See Grano at 731. Prior to *Kirby* most courts exempted these identifications from the right to counsel requirement. See, e.g., *Russell v. United States,* 408 F.2d 1280 (D.C.Cir.1969) (Bazelon, C.J.).

For the view that all the psychological assumptions on which *Russell* and similar cases are premised—(a) the victim or witness to a crime can be counted on to form an accurate mental image of the offender; (b) this image will be more accurate on the scene immediately after the crime than at the police station some hours later; and (c) the suggestion inherent in one-man confrontations is insignificant in light of the other factors—are speculative and questionable, see Grano at 734–38.

5. *When are adversary judicial criminal proceedings "initiated"?* In MOORE v. ILLINOIS, 434 U.S. 220, 98 S.Ct. 458, 54 L.Ed.2d 424 (1977), a police officer accompanied the victim to a courtroom where petitioner, a rape suspect, was to appear for his preliminary hearing to determine whether he should be bound over to the grand jury and to set bail. Petitioner was not represented by counsel at this hearing, nor offered appointed counsel. After petitioner's name was called and he was led before the bench, and after the prosecutor had recited evidence believed to implicate petitioner, the victim was asked by the prosecutor where she saw her assailant in the courtroom and she pointed at petitioner. At trial, the victim testified on direct that she had identified petitioner at the preliminary hearing. In reversing the judgment of the federal court of appeals denying habeas corpus relief, the Court, per POWELL, J., rejected, inter alia, the contention that evidence of a corporeal identification conducted in the absence of defense counsel must be excluded only if the identification is made after the defendant is indicted:

"The prosecution in this case was commenced under Illinois law when the victim's complaint was filed in court. The purpose of the preliminary hearing was to determine whether there was probable cause to bind petitioner over to the grand jury and to set bail. Petitioner had the right to oppose the prosecution at that hearing by moving to dismiss the charges and to suppress the evidence against him. He faced counsel for the State * * *. It is plain that '[t]he government ha[d] committed itself to prosecute,' and that petitioner found 'himself faced with the prosecutorial forces of organized society, and immersed in the intricacies of substantive and procedural criminal law.' *Kirby.* The State candidly concedes that the preliminary hearing marked the 'initiation of adversary judicial criminal proceedings' against petitioner, and it hardly could contend otherwise." [a]

a. The Court also rejected the view that petitioner had no right to counsel at this identification procedure because "it was conducted in the course of a judicial proceeding": "The reasons supporting *Wade's* holding that a corporeal identification is a critical stage of a criminal prosecution for Sixth Amendment purposes apply with equal force to this identification. It is difficult to

Section 160.3(2) of the *Model Code* "codifies" *Kirby* by granting a suspect a right to counsel at corporeal identification procedures "if a complaint has been filed charging a person with crime, or a person has been indicted for crime." Rule 403 of the *Model Rules* reads *Kirby* as giving a suspect "the right to a lawyer for any lineup connected with an arrest for which he was arrested or charged—and to have a lawyer appointed for this purpose if he cannot afford one—*if* the lineup is held following the start of criminal proceedings against him" (emphasis in the original) and provides further: "Criminal proceedings may be begun by any one of the following: a formal charge (sworn complaint); a preliminary hearing; an indictment; an arraignment; an initial appearance for a magistrate." See also Grano at 788–89.

Consider Israel, Note 3 supra at 1368–69 n. 226: "Most defendants are arrested without warrants and are placed in lineups prior to their appearance before a magistrate—i.e., before a formal charge or a complaint has been filed against them. Where the individual has been arrested pursuant to a warrant, the complaint will have been filed before his arrest, but the lineup still is likely to be held prior to his first appearance before a magistrate. Arguably, *Wade* also would not apply in that situation. Even though a complaint has been filed in the process of obtaining a warrant, adversary judicial criminal proceedings may be viewed as being initiated only after the accused is brought before a magistrate on that complaint. * * * This starting point would make sense from an administrative standpoint because counsel for the indigent ordinarily would not be appointed until the defendant has appeared before the magistrate." [b]

6. *Do adversary judicial proceedings commence at the same time for Massiah and Kirby purposes?* Consider Kamisar, *Brewer v. Williams, Massiah, and Miranda: What is "Interrogation"? When Does it Matter?,* 67 Geo.L.J., 86 n. 503 (1978): "Although the Supreme Court and courts generally seem to have treated the question of when judicial proceedings commence within the meaning of (1) *Massiah* and (2) *Kirby* as the same question, the different procedural contexts may have at least a strong subliminal impact on some courts. As a policy matter, it seems considerably more difficult to resist the presence of counsel at a lineup than in the interrogation room. When he can do so, a defense lawyer will usually prevent all police questioning, but he is unlikely—indeed, not empowered—to disrupt pretrial identification proceedings. Moreover, unlike the Warren Court 'confession' cases, which arguably 'furthered societal values not usually related to guilt or innocence,' the Warren Court pretrial identification cases 'explicitly sought to protect the innocent from wrongful conviction.' (Grano at 722.)"

7. *Due Process protection.* The *Kirby* plurality opinion notes that a person "not * * * formally charged with a criminal offense" still has the protection of "the

imagine a more suggestive manner in which to present a suspect to a witness for their critical first confrontation than was employed in this case. * * * Had petitioner been represented by counsel, some or all of this suggestiveness could have been avoided."

b. Professor Israel adds: "The English apparently use a similar starting point with respect to counsel at lineups. The Parade Rules provide that the 'suspect should be informed that if he so desires he may have his solicitor or friend present at the identification parade.' *Home Office Circular on Identification Parades* ¶ 10, reprinted in Report to the Secretary of State for the Home Department of the Departmental Committee on Evidence of Identification in Criminal Cases 158, 159 (1976) [hereinafter cited as the Devlin Report (for the committee chairman, Lord Devlin)]. * * * The Devlin Report states, however, that, for the overwhelming majority of suspects, the solicitor has to be provided by legal aid, and if the 'parade' is arranged 'before a suspect is brought before the magistrates,' legal aid assistance most often is unavailable. Devlin Report at ¶ 5.39. Accordingly, solicitors are not provided for many lineups conducted before the defendant's first appearance, notwithstanding the Parade Rules. The Devlin Report considered but rejected requiring counsel in all such cases."

Due Process of the Fifth and Fourteenth Amendments [which] forbids a lineup that is unnecessarily suggestive and conducive to irreparable mistaken identification." But see Sobel at 35: "This is something but not much. For without the presence of counsel at the pre-arraignment confrontation, counsel will be compelled at the suppression hearing and at the trial to probe in the dark in an attempt to discover 'unfairness' before, during and after the confrontation." Consider also Steele, *Kirby v. Illinois: Counsel at Lineups,* 9 Crim. Law Bull. 49, 54–55 (1973).

UNITED STATES v. ASH

413 U.S. 300, 93 S.Ct. 2568, 37 L.Ed.2d 619 (1973).

MR. JUSTICE BLACKMUN delivered the opinion of the Court.

In this case the Court is called upon to decide whether the Sixth Amendment grants an accused the right to have counsel present whenever the Government conducts a post-indictment photographic display, containing a picture of the accused, for the purpose of allowing a witness to attempt an identification of the offender. * * *

On the morning of August 26, 1965, a man with a stocking mask entered a bank in Washington, D.C., and began waving a pistol. He ordered an employee to hang up the telephone and instructed all others present not to move. Seconds later a second man, also wearing a stocking mask, entered the bank, scooped up money from tellers' drawers into a bag, and left. The gunman followed, and both men escaped through an alley. The robbery lasted three or four minutes.

A Government informer, Clarence McFarland, told authorities that he had discussed the robbery with Charles J. Ash, Jr., the respondent here. Acting on this information, an FBI agent, in February 1966, showed five black-and-white mug shots, of Negro males of generally the same age, height, and weight, one of which was of Ash, to four witnesses. All four made uncertain identifications of Ash's picture. At this time Ash was not in custody and had not been charged. On April 1, 1966, an indictment was returned charging Ash and a codefendant, John L. Bailey, in five counts related to this bank robbery * * *.

Trial was finally set for May 1968, almost three years after the crime. In preparing for trial, the prosecutor decided to use a photographic display to determine whether the witnesses he planned to call would be able to make in-court identifications. Shortly before the trial, an FBI agent and the prosecutor showed five color photographs to the four witnesses who previously had tentatively identified the black-and-white photograph of Ash. Three of the witnesses selected the picture of Ash, but one was unable to make any selection. None of the witnesses selected the picture of Bailey which was in the group. This post-indictment identification provides the basis for respondent Ash's claim that he was denied the right to counsel at a "critical stage" of the prosecution. * * *

The five-member majority of the Court of Appeals held that Ash's right to counsel, guaranteed by the Sixth Amendment, was violated when his attorney was not given the opportunity to be present at the photographic displays conducted in May 1968 before the trial. The majority did not reach the issue of suggestiveness; their opinion implies, however, that they would order a remand for additional findings by the District Court. The majority refrained from deciding whether the in-court identifications could have independent bases, but expressed doubt that the identifications at the trial had independent origins. * * *

[The historical background of the counsel guarantee] suggests that [its] core purpose * * * was to assure "Assistance" at trial, when the accused was confronted with both the intricacies of the law and the advocacy of the public prosecutor. Later developments have led this Court to recognize that "Assistance" would be less than meaningful if it were limited to the formal trial itself. * * *

Throughout this expansion of the counsel guarantee to trial-like confrontations, the function of the lawyer has remained essentially the same as his function at trial. In all cases considered by the Court, counsel has continued to act as a spokesman for, or advisor to, the accused. The accused's right to the "Assistance of Counsel" has meant just that, namely, the right of the accused to have counsel acting as his assistant. * * * In *Massiah* counsel could have advised his client on the benefits of the Fifth Amendment and could have sheltered him from the overreaching of the prosecution. * * *

The function of counsel in rendering "Assistance" continued at the lineup under consideration in *Wade* and its companion cases. Although the accused was not confronted there with legal questions, the lineup offered opportunities for prosecuting authorities to take advantage of the accused. Counsel was seen by the Court as being more sensitive to, and aware of, suggestive influences than the accused himself, and as better able to reconstruct the events at trial. Counsel present at lineup would be able to remove disabilities of the accused in precisely the same fashion that counsel compensated for the disabilities of the layman at trial. * * *

The structure of *Wade,* viewed in light of the careful limitation of the Court's language to "confrontations," makes it clear that lack of scientific precision and inability to reconstruct an event are not the tests for requiring counsel in the first instance. These are, instead, the tests to determine whether confrontation with counsel at trial can serve as a substitute for counsel at the pretrial confrontation. If accurate reconstruction is possible, the risks inherent in any confrontation still remain, but the opportunity to cure defects at trial causes the confrontation to cease to be "critical." * * *

The Court of Appeals considered its analysis complete after it decided that a photographic display lacks scientific precision and ease of accurate reconstruction at trial. That analysis, under *Wade,* however, merely carries one to the point where one must establish that the trial itself can provide no substitute for counsel if a pretrial confrontation is conducted in the absence of counsel. Judge Friendly, writing for the Second Circuit in *United States v. Bennett,* 409 F.2d 888 (1969), recognized that the "criticality" test of *Wade,* if applied outside the confrontation context, would result in drastic expansion of the right to counsel:

> "None of the classical analyses of the assistance to be given by counsel . . . suggests that counsel must be present when the prosecution is interrogating witnesses in the defendant's absence even when, as here, the defendant is under arrest; counsel is rather to be provided to prevent the defendant himself from falling into traps devised by a lawyer on the other side and to see to it that all available defenses are proffered. Many other aspects of the prosecution's interviews with a victim or a witness to a crime afford just as much opportunity for undue suggestion as the display of photographs; so, too, do the defense's interviews, notably with alibi witnesses." * * *

A substantial departure from the historical test would be necessary if the Sixth Amendment were interpreted to give Ash a right to counsel at the photographic identification in this case. Since the accused himself is not present at the time of the photographic display, and asserts no right to be present, no possibility arises that the accused might be misled by his lack of familiarity with the law or overpowered by his professional adversary. Similarly, the counsel guarantee would not be used to produce equality in a trial-like adversary confrontation. Rather, the guarantee was used by the Court of Appeals to produce confrontation at an event that previously was not analogous to an adversary trial.

Even if we were willing to view the counsel guarantee in broad terms as a generalized protection of the adversary process, we would be unwilling to go so far as to extend the right to a portion of the prosecutor's trial-preparation interviews with witnesses. Although photography is relatively new, the interviewing of witnesses before trial is a procedure that predates the Sixth Amendment. In England in the 16th and 17th centuries counsel regularly interviewed witnesses before trial. The traditional counterbalance in the American adversary system for these interviews arises from the equal ability of defense counsel to seek and interview witnesses himself.

That adversary mechanism remains as effective for a photographic display as for other parts of pretrial interviews. No greater limitations are placed on defense counsel in constructing displays, seeking witnesses, and conducting photographic identifications than those applicable to the prosecution. Selection of the picture of a person other than the accused, or the inability of a witness to make any selection, will be useful to the defense in precisely the same manner that the selection of a picture of the defendant would be useful to the prosecution. In this very case, for example, the initial tender of the photographic display was by Bailey's counsel, who sought to demonstrate that the witness had failed to make a photographic identification. Although we do not suggest that equality of access to photographs removes all potential for abuse, it does remove any inequality in the adversary process itself and thereby fully satisfies the historical spirit of the Sixth Amendment's counsel guarantee.

The argument has been advanced that requiring counsel might compel the police to observe more scientific procedures or might encourage them to utilize corporeal rather than photographic displays. This Court has recognized that improved procedures can minimize the dangers of suggestion. Commentators have also proposed more accurate techniques.

Pretrial photographic identifications, however, are hardly unique in offering possibilities for the actions of the prosecutor unfairly to prejudice the accused. Evidence favorable to the accused may be withheld; testimony of witnesses may be manipulated; the results of laboratory tests may be contrived. In many ways the prosecutor, by accident or by design, may improperly subvert the trial. The primary safeguard against abuses of this kind is the ethical responsibility of the prosecutor, who, as so often has been said, may "strike hard blows" but not "foul ones." If that safeguard fails, review remains available under due process standards. These same safeguards apply to misuse of photographs.

We are not persuaded that the risks inherent in the use of photographic displays are so pernicious that an extraordinary system of safeguards is required.

We hold, then, that the Sixth Amendment does not grant the right to counsel at photographic displays conducted by the Government for the purpose of allowing a witness to attempt an identification of the offender. * * *

Reversed and remanded.

MR. JUSTICE STEWART, concurring in the judgment. * * *

Since the photographic identification in the present case occurred after the accused had been indicted, and thus clearly after adversary judicial proceedings had been initiated, the only question is whether that procedure was such a "critical stage" that the Constitution required the presence of counsel. * * *

The [*Wade* Court held] that counsel was required at a lineup, primarily as an observer, to ensure that defense counsel could effectively confront the prosecution's evidence at trial. Attuned to the possibilities of suggestive influences, a lawyer could see any unfairness at a lineup, question the witnesses about it at trial, and effectively reconstruct what had gone on for the benefit of the jury or trial judge.*

A photographic identification is quite different from a lineup, for there are substantially fewer possibilities of impermissible suggestion when photographs are used, and those unfair influences can be readily reconstructed at trial. It is true that the defendant's photograph may be markedly different from the others displayed, but this unfairness can be demonstrated at trial from an actual comparison of the photographs used or from the witness' description of the display. Similarly, it is possible that the photographs could be arranged in a suggestive manner, or that by comment or gesture the prosecuting authorities might single out the defendant's picture. But these are the kinds of overt influence that a witness can easily recount and that would serve to impeach the identification testimony. In short, there are few possibilities for unfair suggestiveness—and those rather blatant and easily reconstructed. Accordingly, an accused would not be foreclosed from an effective cross-examination of an identification witness simply because his counsel was not present at the photographic display. For this reason, a photographic display cannot fairly be considered a "critical stage" of the prosecution.[a] * * *

Preparing witnesses for trial by checking their identification testimony against a photographic display is little different, in my view, from the prosecutor's other interviews with the victim or other witnesses before trial. While these procedures can be improperly conducted, the possibility of irretrievable prejudice is remote, since any unfairness that does occur can usually be flushed out at trial through cross-examination of the prosecution witnesses. The presence of defense counsel at such pretrial preparatory sessions is neither appropriate nor necessary under our adversary system of justice "to preserve the defendant's basic right to a fair trial as affected by his right meaningfully to cross-examine the witnesses against him and to have effective assistance of counsel at the trial itself." *Wade.*

MR. JUSTICE BRENNAN, with whom MR. JUSTICE DOUGLAS and MR. JUSTICE MARSHALL join, dissenting.

* * * In my view, today's decision is wholly unsupportable in terms of such considerations as logic, consistency and, indeed, fairness. As a result, I must reluctantly conclude that today's decision marks simply another step towards the complete evisceration of the fundamental constitutional principles established by this Court, only six years ago, in *Wade, Gilbert* and *Stovall.* * * *

To the extent that misidentification may be attributable to a witness' faulty memory or perception, or inadequate opportunity for detailed observation during the crime, the risks are obviously as great at a photographic display as at a lineup. But "[b]ecause of the inherent limitations of photography, which presents its subject in two dimensions rather than the three dimensions of reality, [a] photographic identification, even when properly obtained, is clearly inferior to a properly obtained corporeal identification." P.

* I do not read *Wade* as requiring counsel because a lineup is a "trial-type" situation, nor do I understand that the Court required the presence of an attorney because of the advice or assistance he could give to his client at the lineup itself. Rather, I had thought the reasoning of *Wade* was that the right to counsel is essentially a protection for the defendant at trial, and that counsel is necessary at a lineup in order to ensure a meaningful confrontation and the effective assistance of counsel at trial.

a. Is a post-indictment corporeal lineup recorded on video tape and played for the trial court at the suppression hearing a "critical stage" within the meaning of *Wade? Bruce v. State,* 375 N.E.2d 1042, 1086 (Ind.1978), answers in the negative.

Wall, *Eye-Witness Identification in Criminal Cases* 70 (1965). * * *

Moreover, as in the lineup situation, the possibilities for impermissible suggestion in the context of a photographic display are manifold. * * *

[A]s is the case with lineups, "[i]mproper photographic identification procedures, [by] exerting a suggestive influence upon the witnesses, can often lead to an erroneous identification." P. Wall, at 89. And "[r]egardless of how the initial misidentification comes about, the witness thereafter is apt to retain in his memory the image of the photograph rather than of the person actually seen." *Simmons.* As a result, " 'the issue of identity may (in the absence of other relevant evidence) for all practical purposes be determined there and then, before the trial.' " *Wade.*

Moreover, as with lineups, the defense can "seldom reconstruct" at trial the mode and manner of photographic identification. It is true, of course, that the photographs used at the pretrial display might be preserved for examination at trial. But "it may also be said that a photograph can preserve the record of a lineup; yet this does not justify a lineup without counsel." [b] Indeed, in reality, preservation of the photographs affords little protection to the unrepresented accused. For although retention of the photographs may mitigate the dangers of misidentification due to the suggestiveness of the photographs themselves, it cannot in any sense reveal to defense counsel the more subtle, and therefore more dangerous, suggestiveness that might derive from the manner in which the photographs were displayed or any accompanying comments or gestures. Moreover, the accused cannot rely upon the witnesses themselves to expose these latter sources of suggestion, for the witnesses are not "apt to be alert for conditions prejudicial to the suspect. And if they were, it would be of scant benefit to the suspect" since the witnesses are hardly "likely to be schooled in the detection of suggestive influences." *Wade.*

Finally, and *unlike* the lineup situation, the accused himself is not even present at the photographic identification, thereby reducing the likelihood that irregularities in the procedures will ever come to light. * * *

[B]oth photographic and corporeal identifications create grave dangers that an innocent defendant might be convicted simply because of his inability to expose a tainted identification. This being so, considerations of logic, consistency and, indeed, fairness compel the conclusion that a pretrial photographic identification, like a pretrial corporeal identification, is a "critical stage of the prosecution at which [the accused is] 'as much entitled to such aid [of counsel] as at the trial itself.' " *Wade,* quoting *Powell.*

Ironically, the Court does not seriously challenge the proposition that presence of counsel at a pretrial photographic display is essential to preserve the accused's right to a fair trial on the issue of identification. Rather, in what I can only characterize a triumph of form over substance, the Court seeks to justify its result by engrafting a wholly unprecedented—and wholly unsupportable—limitation on the Sixth Amendment right [to counsel]. Although apparently conceding that the right to counsel attaches, not only at the trial itself, but at

b. Doesn't it, at least after *Ash?* Suppose defense counsel was not notified of or in attendance at either a post-indictment lineup viewed by witness A or at the subsequent exhibition of a photograph of the lineup viewed by witness B. Would *Wade* prevent witness A from testifying that he had identified the accused at the uncounselled lineup or would the fact that the lineup was photographed and thus "preserved" for the trial court mean that it was not a "critical stage"? Cf. *Bruce v. State,* fn. a, supra. Consider, too, *People v. Lawrence,* 481 P.2d 212 (Cal. 1971) (4–3) (upholding an identification from photographs taken of a *simulated* lineup conducted earlier that day). Assuming arguendo that *Wade* would bar witness A from testifying that he had identified the accused at the uncounselled lineup, wouldn't *Ash* allow witness B to testify that he had identified the accused at the subsequent showing of the photograph of the lineup?

all "critical stages" of the prosecution, the Court holds today that, in order to be deemed "critical," the particular "stage of the prosecution" under consideration must, at the very least, involve the physical "presence of the accused," at a "trial-like confrontation" with the Government, at which the accused requires the "guiding hand of counsel." A pretrial photographic identification does not, of course, meet these criteria. * * *

The fundamental premise underlying *all* of this Court's decisions holding the right to counsel applicable at "critical" pretrial proceedings, is that a "stage" of the prosecution must be deemed "critical" for the purposes of the Sixth Amendment if it is one at which the presence of counsel is necessary "to protect the fairness of *the trial itself.*" *Schneckloth v. Bustamonte* (emphasis added). * * *

This established conception of the Sixth Amendment guarantee is, of course, in no sense dependent upon the physical "presence of the accused," at a "trial-like confrontation" with the Government, at which the accused requires the "guiding hand of counsel." On the contrary, in *Powell,* the seminal decision in this area, we explicitly held the right to counsel applicable at a stage of the pretrial proceedings involving *none* of the three criteria set forth by the Court today. * * *

[C]ontrary to the suggestion of the Court, the conclusion in *Wade* that a pretrial lineup is a "critical stage" of the prosecution did not in any sense turn on the fact that a lineup involves the physical "presence of the accused" at a "trial-like confrontation" with the Government. And that conclusion most certainly did not turn on the notion that presence of counsel was necessary so that counsel could offer legal advice or "guidance" to the accused at the lineup. On the contrary, *Wade* envisioned counsel's function at the lineup to be primarily that of a trained observer, able to detect the existence of any suggestive influences and capable of understanding the legal implications of the events that transpire. Having witnessed the proceedings, counsel would then be in a position effectively to reconstruct at trial any unfairness that occurred at the lineup, thereby preserving the accused's fundamental right to a fair trial on the issue of identification.

There is something ironic about the Court's conclusion today that a pretrial lineup identification is a "critical stage" of the prosecution because counsel's presence can help to compensate for the accused's deficiencies as an observer, but that a pretrial photographic identification is not a "critical stage" of the prosecution because the accused is not able to observe at all. * * *

Notes and Questions

1. *Wade, Kirby and Ash.* The *Ash* majority, per Blackmun, J., looks back on *Wade* as concluding that "the lineup constituted a trial-like confrontation" requiring counsel in order "to render 'Assistance' [to a suspect] in counterbalancing any 'overreaching' by the prosecution," implying that counsel is to be an active adversary at this stage. Was the *Ash* majority compelled to so interpret *Wade* because its historical analysis led it to the conclusion that the lawyer's assistance is limited to the *immediate* aid he can give his client? See Note, 64 J.Crim.L.C. & P.S. 428 (1973). Does concurring Justice Stewart disclaim this reading of *Wade?* If so, which interpretation is more consistent with the cases, commentaries and practice since *Wade?* Reconsider Note 4, p. 662 supra. Consider, too, 64 J.Crim.L.C. & P.S. at 433 & n. 40.

2. *Massiah and Ash.* According to the *Ash* majority, "in *Massiah* [p. 527 supra] counsel could have advised his client on the benefits of the Fifth Amendment and could have sheltered him from the overreaching of the prosecution." Was the defendant in *Massiah* entitled to Fifth Amendment protection? Was he com-

pelled to speak? How would the presence of counsel in *Massiah* have provided "assistance" at the "confrontation" unless counsel were aware the meeting was a confrontation? And if counsel were so aware, wouldn't he have *prevented* the confrontation from occurring? See Grano at 762 & n. 285.

3. *The significance of defendant's right to be personally present.* As noted by the Court, the defendant in *Ash* did not claim the right to be personally present at the photographic display. But does the right to counsel *only* exist when the defendant is entitled to be personally present? Voluntary absence or contumacious conduct (see *Illinois v. Allen,* Ch. 24, § 3 infra) may cause a defendant to lose his right to be present at trial, but does it follow that he also loses his right to counsel? Defendants on appeal have the right to counsel, but do they have the right to be personally present? See generally Grano at 764–67.

4. *Justice Stewart's concurring opinion.* All of the distinctions Justice Stewart made between photographic displays and lineups—photographic displays are less vulnerable to improper suggestion, are easier to reconstruct at trial and are less indelible in their effect upon a witness—are sharply challenged in Grano at 767–70.

5. *Photographic displays and other pretrial interviews of prospective witnesses.* Both the majority and concurring opinions in *Ash* indicated concern that granting a right to counsel at photographic displays might lead to the extension of the right to counsel to all pretrial interviews of prospective witnesses. But consider Note, 26 Stan.L. Rev. 399, 416–17 (1974): "Under the traditional analysis, the right to counsel does not apply unless a lack of counsel at the stage in question might make the right to counsel at trial meaningless. The fact that photographic identifications were found to be 'critical' would not necessarily lead to a finding that other interviews between the prosecutor and his witnesses were 'critical.' * * * The basis for extending the right to counsel to the identification context was that identifications by eyewitnesses—like confessions—are such damning evidence that they may completely decide the guilt or innocence of the accused. Photographic identifications can be just as critical to the future outcome of a trial as can corporeal identifications. Routine interviews between the prosecutor and his witnesses, on the other hand, do not have the potential for such damaging results, at least assuming good faith on the part of the prosecutor." See also Grano at 770, noting that "the trend is to recognize a special hearsay exception for testimony referring to pretrial identifications" which "obviously reinforces any in-court identification, thus compounding the risk of wrongful conviction in the event of mistakes." But "except for impeachment purposes, most jurisdictions exclude testimony concerning pretrial identification interviews."

SECTION 3. DUE PROCESS AND OTHER LIMITATIONS

As already pointed out, see p. 667 supra, one unable to make a *Wade-Gilbert* right to counsel argument may still establish that the identification procedure conducted in his case "was so unnecessarily suggestive and conducive to irreparable mistaken identification that he was denied due process of law." STOVALL v. DENNO, 388 U.S. 293, 87 S.Ct. 1967, 18 L.Ed.2d 1199 (1967). In this case, the stabbing victim (Mrs. Behrendt), was hospitalized for major surgery. Without affording petitioner time to retain counsel (an arraignment had been promptly held but then postponed until petitioner could retain counsel), the police, with the cooperation of the victim's surgeon, arranged a confrontation between petitioner and the victim in her hospital room. Petitioner was handcuffed to one of the seven law enforcement officials who brought him to the hospital room. He was the only black person in the room. After being asked by an officer whether petitioner "was the man," the victim identified him from her hospital bed. Both Mrs. Behrendt and the police then testified at the trial to her identification in the hospital. Despite the suggestiveness of the confrontation, the Court, per BRENNAN, J., affirmed the Second Circuit's denial of federal habeas corpus relief, observing:

"The practice of showing suspects singly to persons for the purpose of identification, and not as part of a lineup has been widely condemned. However, a claimed violation of due process of law in the conduct of a confrontation depends on the totality of the circumstances surrounding it, and the record in the present case reveals that the showing of Stovall to Mrs. Behrendt in an immediate hospital confrontation was imperative. The Court of Appeals en banc, stated [355 F.2d 731, 735 (2d Cir.1966) (per Moore, J.)]:

"'Here was the only person in the world who could possibly exonerate Stovall. Her words, and only her words, "He is not the man" could have resulted in freedom for Stovall. The hospital was not far distant from the courthouse and jail. No one knew how long Mrs. Behrendt might live. Faced with the responsibility of identifying the attacker, with the need for immediate action and with the knowledge that Mrs. Behrendt could not visit the jail, the police followed the only feasible procedure and took Stovall to the hospital room. Under these circumstances, the usual police station line-up, which Stovall now argues he should have had, was out of the question.'" [a]

MANSON v. BRATHWAITE

432 U.S. 98, 97 S.Ct. 2243, 53 L.Ed.2d 140 (1977).

MR. JUSTICE BLACKMUN delivered the opinion of the Court. * * *

[Several minutes before sunset, Glover, a black undercover police officer, purchased heroin from a seller through the open doorway of an apartment while standing for two or three minutes within two feet of the seller in a hallway illuminated by natural light. A few minutes later, Glover described the seller to a back-up officer, D'Onofrio, as being "a colored man, approximately five feet eleven inches tall, dark complexion, black hair, short Afro style, and having high cheekbones, and of heavy build. He was wearing at the time blue pants and a plaid shirt."

[On the basis of the description, D'Onofrio thought that respondent might be the heroin seller. He obtained a single photograph of respondent from police files and left it at Glover's office. Two days later, while alone, Glover viewed the photograph and identified it as that of the seller. At respondent's trial, Glover testified that there was "no doubt whatsoever" that the person shown in the photograph was respondent. Glover also made a posi-

a. But consider Judge Friendly, joined by Waterman, J., dissenting below, 355 F.2d at 744–45:

"[The argument that law enforcement officials were confronted with an emergency] ignores the huge amount of circumstantial identification the excellent police investigation had produced; moreover, if the state officials were motivated [by] solicitude [for Stovall], the natural course would have been to ask Stovall whether he wanted to go. The emergency argument fails both on the facts and on the law. * * * If Mrs. Behrendt's condition had been as serious as my brothers suppose, nothing prevented the prosecutor from informing the state district judge at the preliminary hearing that Stovall had to be taken immediately before her, and suggesting that counsel be assigned forthwith for the limited purpose of advising him in that regard—rather than standing silent when Stovall told the judge of his desire to have counsel and then carting him off to a confrontation by the victim which counsel might have done something to mitigate."

Lower courts have not only followed *Stovall* in similar cases of serious injury to the victim or a witness but have applied it to situations where the *suspect* is seriously injured. See Commentary to § 160.5 of the *Model Pre-Arraignment Code* at 451–52. Is a "showup" in such cases necessary? Could a photographic array be utilized? If the suspect is hospitalized for an extended period, could the witness be taken to several hospital rooms? See *Model Code* at 452; *Model Rules* at 20–21.

tive in-court identification. No explanation was offered by the prosecution for the failure to utilize a photographic array or to conduct a lineup.

[After the Connecticut Supreme Court affirmed respondent's conviction, he sought federal habeas corpus relief. The Second Circuit, per Friendly, J., held that because the showing of the single photograph was "suggestive" and concededly "unnecessarily so," evidence pertaining to it was subject to a *per se* rule of exclusion.]

Neil v. Biggers, 409 U.S. 188, 93 S.Ct. 375, 34 L.Ed. 401 (1972), concerned a respondent who had been convicted [of] rape, on evidence consisting in part of the victim's visual and voice identification of Biggers at a [one-person] station-house showup seven months after the crime. * * * The Court expressed concern about the lapse of seven months between the crime and the confrontation, [but pointed out that the] "central question" [was] "whether under the 'totality of the circumstances' the identification was reliable even though the confrontation procedure was suggestive." Applying that test, the Court found "no substantial likelihood of misidentification. The evidence was properly allowed to go to the jury." [a]

Biggers well might be seen to provide an unambiguous answer to the question before us: The admission of testimony concerning a suggestive and unnecessary identification procedure does not violate due process so long as the identification possesses sufficient aspects of reliability.[9] In one passage, however, the Court observed that the challenged procedure occurred pre-*Stovall* and that a strict rule would make little sense with regard to a confrontation that preceded the Court's first indication that a suggestive procedure might lead to the exclusion of evidence. One perhaps might argue that, by implication, the Court suggested that a different rule could apply post-*Stovall.* The question before us, then, is simply whether the *Biggers* analysis applies to post-*Stovall* confrontations as well to those pre-*Stovall.* * * *

Petitioner at the outset acknowledges that "the procedure in the instant case was suggestive [because only one photograph was used] and unnecessary" [because there

a. The *Biggers* Court, per Powell, J., observed:

"The victim spent a considerable period of time with her assailant, up to half an hour. She was with him under adequate artificial light in her house and under a full moon outdoors, and at least twice, once in the house and later in the woods, faced him directly and intimately. * * * Her description to the police, which included the assailant's approximate age, height, weight, complexion, skin texture, build, and voice [was] more than ordinarily thorough. She had 'no doubt' that respondent was the person who raped her. [The] victim here, a practical nurse by profession, had an unusual opportunity to observe and identify her assailant. She testified at the habeas corpus hearing that there was something about his face 'I don't think I could ever forget.'

"There was, to be sure, a lapse of seven months between the rape and the confrontation. This would be a seriously negative factor in most cases. Here, however, the testimony is undisputed that the victim made no previous identification at any of the showups, lineups, or photographic showings. Her record for reliability was thus a good one, as she had previously resisted whatever suggestiveness inheres in a showup. Weighing all the factors, we find no substantial likelihood of misidentification."

9. Mr. Justice Marshall argues in dissent that our cases have "established two different due process tests for two very different situations." Pretrial identifications are to be covered by *Stovall,* which is said to require exclusion of evidence concerning unnecessarily suggestive pretrial identifications without regard to reliability. In-court identifications, on the other hand, are to be governed by *Simmons [v. United States,* 390 U.S. 377, 88 S.Ct. 967, 19 L.Ed.2d 1247 (1968)] and admissibility turns on reliability. The Court's cases are sorted into one category or the other. *Biggers,* which clearly adopts the reliability of the identification as the guiding factor in the admissibility of both pre-trial and in-court identifications, is condemned for mixing the two lines and for adopting a uniform rule.

[Our cases] hardly suggest the formal structure the dissent would impose on them. If our cases truly established two different rules, one might expect at some point at least passing reference to the fact. There is none. And if *Biggers* departed so grievously from the past cases, it is surprising that there was not at least some mention of the point in Mr. Justice Brennan's dissent. * * * *Biggers* is not properly seen as a departure from the past cases, but as a synthesis of them.

was no emergency or exigent circumstance]. The respondent, in agreement with the Court of Appeals, proposes a *per se* rule of exclusion that he claims is dictated by the demands of the Fourteenth Amendment's guarantee of due process. He rightly observes that this is the first case in which this Court has had occasion to rule upon strictly post-*Stovall* out-of-court identification evidence of the challenged kind.

Since the decision in *Biggers,* the Courts of Appeals appear to have developed at least two approaches to such evidence. See Pulaski, *Neil v. Biggers: The Supreme Court Dismantles the Wade Trilogy's Due Process Protection,* 26 Stan.L.Rev. 1097, 1111–1114 (1974). The first, or *per se* approach, employed by the Second Circuit in the present case, focuses on the procedures employed and requires exclusion of the out-of-court identification evidence, without regard to reliability, whenever it has been obtained through unnecessarily suggested confrontation procedures.[10] The justifications advanced are the elimination of evidence of uncertain reliability, deterrence of the police and prosecutors, and the stated "fair assurance against the awful risks of misidentification."

The second, or more lenient, approach is one that continues to rely on the totality of the circumstances. It permits the admission of the confrontation evidence if, despite the suggestive aspect, the out-of-court identification possesses certain features of reliability. This second approach, in contrast to the other, is ad hoc and serves to limit the societal costs imposed by a sanction that excludes relevant evidence from consideration and evaluation by the trier of fact. * * *

There are, of course, several interests to be considered and taken into account. The driving force behind [*Wade, Gilbert* and *Stovall*] was the Court's concern with the problems of eyewitness identification. Usually the witness must testify about an encounter with a total stranger under circumstances of emergency or emotional stress. The witness' recollection of the stranger can be distorted easily by the circumstances or by later actions of the police. Thus, *Wade* and its companion cases reflect the concern that the jury not hear eyewitness testimony unless that evidence has aspects of reliability. It must be observed that both approaches before us are responsive to this concern. The *per se* rule, however, goes too far since its application automatically and peremptorily, and without consideration of alleviating factors, keeps evidence from the jury that is reliable and relevant.

The second factor is deterrence. Although the *per se* approach has the more significant deterrent effect, the totality approach also has an influence on police behavior. The police will guard against unnecessarily suggestive procedures under the totality rule, as well as the *per se* one, for fear that their actions will lead to the exclusion of identifications as unreliable.

The third factor is the effect on the administration of justice. Here the *per se* approach suffers serious drawbacks. Since it denies the trier reliable evidence, it may result, on occasion, in the guilty going free. Also, because of its rigidity, the *per se* approach may make error by the trial judge more likely than the totality approach. And in those cases in which the admission of identification evidence is error under the *per se* approach but not under the totality approach—cases in which the identification is reliable despite an unnecessarily suggestive identification procedure—reversal is a Draconian sanction. Certainly, inflexible rules of exclusion that may frustrate rather than promote

10. Although the *per se* approach demands the exclusion of testimony concerning unnecessarily suggestive identifications, it does permit the admission of testimony concerning a subsequent identification, including an in-court identification, if the subsequent identification is determined to be reliable. The totality approach, in contrast, is simpler: if the challenged identification is reliable, then testimony as to it and any identification in its wake is admissible.

justice have not been viewed recently by this Court with unlimited enthusiasm. * * *

We therefore conclude that reliability is the linchpin in determining the admissibility of identification testimony for both pre- and post-*Stovall* confrontations. The factors to be considered are set out in *Biggers*. These include the opportunity of the witness to view the criminal at the time of the crime, the witness' degree of attention, the accuracy of his prior description of the criminal, the level of certainty demonstrated at the confrontation, and the time between the crime and the confrontation. Against these factors is to be weighed the corrupting effect of the suggestive identification itself.

We turn, then, to the facts of this case and apply the analysis:

1. The opportunity to view. Glover testified that for two to three minutes he stood at the apartment door, within two feet of the respondent. The door opened twice, and each time the man stood at the door. * * * Natural light from outside entered the hallway through a window. There was natural light, as well, from inside the apartment.

2. The degree of attention. Glover was not a casual or passing observer, [but] a trained police officer on duty—and specialized and dangerous duty—when he [made the heroin purchase]. Glover himself was a Negro and unlikely to perceive only general features of [black males].

3. The accuracy of the description. Glover's description was given to D'Onofrio within minutes after the transaction. It included the vendor's race, his height, his build, the color and style of his hair, and the high cheekbone facial feature. It also included clothing the vendor wore. No claim has been made that respondent did not possess the physical characteristics so described. * * *

4. The witness' level of certainty. There is no dispute that the photograph in question was that of respondent. Glover, in response to a question whether the photograph was that of the person from whom he made the purchase, testified: "There is no question whatsoever." This positive assurance was repeated.

5. The time between the crime and the confrontation. Glover's description of his vendor was given to D'Onofrio within minutes of the crime. The photographic identification took place only two days later. We do not have here the passage of weeks or months between the crime and the viewing of the photograph.

These indicators of Glover's ability to make an accurate identification are hardly outweighed by the corrupting effect of the challenged identification itself. Although identifications arising from single-photograph displays may be viewed in general with suspicion, we find in the instant case little pressure on the witness to acquiesce in the suggestion that such a display entails. D'Onofrio had left the photograph at Glover's office and was not present when Glover first viewed it two days after the event. There thus was little urgency and Glover could view the photograph at his leisure. And since Glover examined the photograph alone, there was no coercive pressure to make an identification arising from the presence of another. The identification was made in circumstances allowing care and reflection. * * *

Surely, we cannot say that under all the circumstances of this case there is "a very substantial likelihood of irreparable misidentification." Short of that point, such evidence is for the jury to weigh. We are content to rely upon the good sense and judgment of American juries, for evidence with some element of untrustworthiness is customary grist for the jury mill. Juries are not so susceptible that they cannot measure intelligently the weight of identification testimony that has some questionable feature.

Of course, it would have been better had D'Onofrio presented Glover with a photographic array * * *. But we are not disposed to view D'Onofrio's failure as one of constitutional dimension to be enforced by a rigorous and unbending exclusionary rule. The defect, if there be one, goes to weight and not to substance.

We conclude that the criteria laid down in *Biggers* are to be applied in determining the admissibility of evidence offered by the prosecution concerning a post-*Stovall* identification, and that those criteria are satisfactorily met and complied with here.

[Reversed].[b]

MR. JUSTICE MARSHALL, with whom MR. JUSTICE BRENNAN joins, dissenting.

Today's decision can come as no surprise to those who have been watching the Court dismantle the protections against mistaken eyewitness testimony erected a decade ago in [*Wade, Gilbert* and *Stovall*]. But it is still distressing to see the Court virtually ignore the teaching of experience embodied in those decisions and blindly uphold the conviction of a defendant who may well be innocent. * * *

The development of due process protections against mistaken identification evidence, begun in *Stovall,* was continued in *Simmons v. United States* (1968). There, the Court developed a different rule to deal with the admission of in-court identification testimony that the accused claimed had been fatally tainted by a previous suggestive confrontation. In *Simmons,* the exclusionary effect of *Stovall* had already been accomplished, since the prosecution made no use of the suggestive confrontation. *Simmons,* therefore, did not deal with the constitutionality of the pretrial identification procedure. The only question was the impact of the Due Process Clause on an in-court identification that was not itself unnecessarily suggestive. *Simmons* held that due process was violated by the later identification if the pretrial procedure had been "so impermissibly suggestive as to give rise to a very substantial likelihood of irreparable misidentification." This test focused, not on the necessity for the challenged pretrial procedure, but on the degree of suggestiveness that it entailed. In applying this test, the Court understandably considered the circumstances surrounding the witnesses' initial opportunity to view the crime. Finding that any suggestion in the pretrial confrontation had not affected the fairness of the in-court identification, *Simmons* rejected petitioner's due process attack on his conviction. * * *

Thus, *Stovall* and *Simmons* established two different due process tests for two very different situations. Where the prosecution sought to use evidence of a questionable pretrial identification, *Stovall* required its exclusion, because due process had been violated by the confrontation, unless the necessity for the unduly suggestive procedure outweighed its potential for generating an irreparably mistaken identification. The *Simmons* test, on the other hand, was directed to ascertaining due process violations in the introduction of in-court identification testimony that the defendant claimed was tainted by pretrial procedures. In the latter situation, a court could consider the reliability of the identification under all the circumstances. * * *

The Court inexplicably seemed to erase the distinction between *Stovall* and *Simmons* situations in *Biggers,* [dealing with] a pretrial confrontation that was clearly both suggestive and unnecessary. Evidence of this, together with an in-court identification, was admitted at trial. *Biggers* was, in short, a case plainly cast in the *Stovall* mold. Yet the Court, without explanation or apparent recognition of the distinction,

b. Stevens, J., concurring, joined the Court's opinion, but emphasized that although "the arguments in favor of fashioning new rules to minimize the danger of convicting the innocent on the basis of unreliable eyewitness testimony carry substantial force * * * this rulemaking function can be performed 'more effectively by the legislative process than by somewhat clumsy judicial fiat,' and that the Federal Constitution does not foreclose experimentation by the States in the development of such rules."

applied the *Simmons* test. The Court stated: "[T]he primary evil to be avoided is 'a very substantial likelihood of irreparable misidentification.' *Simmons*. [It] is the likelihood of misidentification which violates a defendant's right to due process." While this statement accurately describes the lesson of *Simmons,* it plainly ignores the teaching of *Stovall* [that] an unnecessarily suggestive pretrial confrontation itself violates due process.

But the Court did not simply disregard the due process analysis of *Stovall.* It went on to take the *Simmons* standard for assessing the constitutionality of an in-court identification—" 'a very substantial likelihood of irreparable misidentification' "—and transform it into the "standard for the admissibility of testimony concerning [an] out-of-court identification." It did so by deleting the word "irreparable" from the *Simmons* formulation. This metamorphosis could be accomplished, however, only by ignoring the fact that *Stovall* [had] established a test for precisely the same situation that focused on the need for the suggestive procedure. It is not surprising that commentators almost unanimously mourned the demise of *Stovall* in the *Biggers* decision.[7]

* * * The Court weighs three factors in deciding that the totality approach, which is essentially the test used in *Biggers,* should be applied. In my view, the Court wrongly evaluates the impact of these factors.

First, the Court acknowledges that one of the factors, deterrence of police use of unnecessarily suggestive identification procedures, favors the *per se* rule. Indeed, it does so heavily, for such a rule would make it unquestionably clear to the police they must never use a suggestive procedure when a fairer alternative is available. I have no doubt that conduct would quickly conform to the rule.

Second, the Court gives passing consideration to the dangers of eyewitness identification recognized in the *Wade* trilogy. It concludes, however, that the grave risk of error does not justify adoption of the *per se* approach because that would too often result in exclusion of relevant evidence. In my view, this conclusion totally ignores the lessons of *Wade.* The dangers of mistaken identification are, as *Stovall* held, simply too great to permit unnecessarily suggestive identifications. Neither *Biggers* nor the Court's opinion today points to any contrary empirical evidence. Studies since *Wade* have only reinforced the validity of its assessment of the dangers of identification testimony. While the Court is "content to rely on the good sense and judgment of American juries," the impetus for *Stovall* and *Wade* was repeated miscarriages of justice resulting from juries' willingness to credit inaccurate eyewitness testimony.

Finally, the Court errs in its assessment of the relative impact of the two approaches on the administration of justice. The Court relies most heavily on this factor, finding that "reversal is a Draconian sanction" in cases where the identification is reliable despite an unnecessarily suggestive procedure used to obtain it. Relying on little more than a strong distaste for "inflexible rules of exclusion," the Court rejects the *per se* test. In so doing, the Court disregards two significant distinctions between the *per se* rule advocated in this case and the exclusionary remedies for certain other constitutional violations.

First, the *per se* rule here is not "inflexible." Where evidence is suppressed, for example, as the fruit of an unlawful search, it may well be forever lost to the prosecution. Identification evidence, however, can by its very nature be readily and effectively reproduced. The in-court identification, permitted under *Wade* and *Simmons* if it has a source independent of an uncoun-

7. [See, e.g.] Grano, *Kirby, Biggers, and Ash: Do Any Constitutional Safeguards Remain Against the Danger of Convicting the Innocent?,* 72 Mich.L.Rev. 717 (1974) * * *.

seled or suggestive procedure, is one example. Similarly, when a prosecuting attorney learns that there has been a suggestive confrontation, he can easily arrange another lineup conducted under scrupulously fair conditions. * * *

Second, other exclusionary rules have been criticized for preventing jury consideration of relevant and usually reliable evidence in order to serve interest unrelated to guilt or innocence, such as discouraging illegal searches or denial of counsel. Suggestively obtained eyewitness testimony is excluded, in contrast, precisely because of its unreliability and concomitant irrelevance. Its exclusion both protects the integrity of the truth-seeking function of the trial and discourages police use of needlessly inaccurate and ineffective investigatory methods. * * *

For these reasons, I conclude that adoption of the *per se* rule would enhance, rather than detract from, the effective administration of justice. In my view, the Court's totality test will allow seriously unreliable and misleading evidence to be put before juries. Equally important, it will allow dangerous criminals to remain on the streets while citizens assume that police action has given them protection. According to my calculus, all three of the factors upon which the Court relies point to acceptance of the *per se* approach.

Even more disturbing than the Court's reliance on the totality test, however, is the analysis it uses, which suggests a reinterpretation of the concept of due process of law in criminal cases. The decision suggests that due process violations in identification procedures may not be measured by whether the government employed procedures violating standards of fundamental fairness. By relying on the probable accuracy of a challenged identification, instead of the necessity for its use, the Court seems to be ascertaining whether the defendant was probably guilty. * * *

Despite my strong disagreement with the Court over the proper standards to be applied in this case, I am pleased that its application of the totality test does recognize the continuing vitality of *Stovall*. In assessing the reliability of the identification, the Court mandates weighing "the corrupting effect of the suggestive identification itself" against the "indicators of [a witness'] ability to make an accurate identification." The Court holds, as *Biggers* failed to, that a due process identification inquiry must take account of the suggestiveness of a confrontation and the likelihood that it led to mis-identification, as recognized in *Stovall* and *Wade*. Thus, even if a witness did have an otherwise adequate opportunity to view a criminal, the later use of a highly suggestive identification procedure can render his testimony inadmissible. Indeed, it is my view that, assuming applicability of the totality test enunciated by the Court, the facts of the present case require that result.

I consider first the opportunity that Officer Glover had to view the suspect. Careful review of the record shows that he could see the heroin seller only for the time it took to speak three sentences of four or five short words, to hand over some money, and later after the door reopened, to receive the drugs in return. The entire face-to-face transaction could have taken as little as 15 or 20 seconds. But during this time, Glover's attention was not focused exclusively on the seller's face. He observed that the door was opened 12 to 18 inches, that there was a window in the room behind the door, and, most importantly, that there was a woman standing behind the man. Glover was, of course, also concentrating on the details of the transaction—he must have looked away from the seller's face to hand him the money and receive the drugs. The observation during the conversation thus may have been as brief as 5 or 10 seconds.

As the Court notes, Glover was a police officer trained in and attentive to the need for making accurate identifications. [But] the mere fact that he has been so trained is no guarantee that he is correct in a specific case. * * * Moreover, "identifications made by policemen in highly competitive activities, such as undercover narcotic [work], should be scrutinized with special care." P. Wall, *Eye-Witness Identification in Criminal Cases* 14 (1965). Yet it is just such a searching inquiry that the Court fails to make here.

Another factor on which the Court relies—the witness' degree of certainty in making the identification—is worthless as an indicator that he is correct.[10] Even if Glover had been unsure initially about his identification of respondent's picture, by the time he was called at trial to present a key piece of evidence for the State that paid his salary, it is impossible to imagine his responding negatively to such questions as "is there any doubt in your mind whatsoever" that the identification was correct. * * *

Next, the Court finds that because the identification procedure took place two days after the crime, its reliability is enhanced. While such temporal proximity makes the identification more reliable than one occurring months later, the fact is that the greatest memory loss occurs within hours after an event. After that, the drop-off continues much more slowly.[11] * * *

Finally, the Court makes much of the fact that Glover gave a description of the seller to D'Onofrio shortly after the incident. [But the description] was actually no more than a general summary of the seller's appearance. We may discount entirely the seller's clothing, for that was of no significance later in the proceeding. Indeed, to the extent that Glover noticed clothes, his attention was diverted from the seller's face. * * * Conspicuously absent is any indication that the seller was a native of the West Indies, certainly something which a member of the black community could immediately recognize from both appearance and accent.[12]

From all of this, I must conclude that the evidence of Glover's ability to make an accurate identification is far weaker than the Court finds it. In contrast, the procedure used to identify respondent was both extraordinarily suggestive and strongly conducive to error. In dismissing "the corrupting effect of the suggestive identification" procedure here, the Court virtually grants the police license to convict the innocent. By displaying a single photograph of respondent to the witness Glover under the circumstances in this record almost everything that could have been done wrong was done wrong. * * *

The use of a single picture (or the display of a single live suspect, for that matter) is a grave error, of course, because it dramatically suggests to the witness that the person shown must be the culprit. Why else would the police choose the person? And it is deeply ingrained in human nature to agree with the expressed opinions of others—particularly others who should be more knowledgeable—when making a difficult decision. In this case, moreover, the pressure was not limited to that inherent in the display of a single photograph. Glover, the identifying witness, was a state police officer on special assignment. He knew that D'Onofrio, an [experienced] narcotics detective, presumably familiar with local drug operations, believed respondent to be the seller. There was at work, then, both loyalty to another police officer and deference to a better-informed colleague.

10. See, e.g., P. Wall, supra, at 15–16 * * *.

11. See, e.g., Levine & Tapp, *The Psychology of Criminal Identification: The Gap From Wade to Kirby,* 12 U.Pa.L.Rev. 1079, 1100–01 (1973) * * *.

12. Brathwaite had come to the United States from his native Barbados as an adult. It is also noteworthy that the informant who witnessed the transaction and was described by Glover as "trustworthy," disagreed with Glover's recollection of the event. The informant testified that it was a woman in the apartment who took the money from Glover and gave him the drugs in return.

Finally, of course, there was Glover's knowledge that without an identification and arrest, government funds used to buy heroin had been wasted. * * *

I must conclude that this record presents compelling evidence that there was "a very substantial likelihood of misidentification" of respondent Brathwaite. The suggestive display of respondent's photograph to the witness Glover likely erased any independent memory that Glover had retained of the seller from his barely adequate opportunity to observe the criminal. * * *

Notes and Questions

1. *Deterrence.* Will the *Manson* approach significantly deter the use of suggestive identification procedures? Consider Jonakait, *Reliable Identification: Could the Supreme Court Tell in Manson v. Brathwaite?*, 52 U.Colo.L.Rev. 511, 515 n. 15 (1981): "[R]egardless of how specifically opinions define what is unnecessarily suggestive, a police officer can never know whether he is violating a suspect's constitutional rights when he is conducting an identification procedure. That can be determined only when the indicia of reliability are examined. These factors may not be known to the officer and certainly cannot be controlled by him. The Court's approach leaves the officer without any firm rules as to what conduct violates the Constitution. If the officer has no way of knowing what actions are forbidden, he can hardly be deterred from those actions."

See also Grossman, *Suggestive Identifications: The Supreme Court's Due Process Test Fails to Meet Its Own Criteria,* 11 Baltimore L.Rev. 53, 59–60 (1981): "The uniformly condemned procedures of displaying a suspect standing alone to a witness, commonly called a show-up, and the non-corporeal equivalent of showing the witness only one photograph are flourishing under the totality of circumstances approach. Rather than deterring such conduct, the effect of *Biggers* and *Manson* has been to provide the police with a fairly clear signal that absent extremely aggravating circumstances, the one-on-one presentation of suspects to witnesses will result in no suppression. The use, therefore, of the preferable techniques of the lineup or photographic array is left to the discretion of the investigating officer, and their use can almost be considered a gratuitous act."

2. *"The other side of the scale": suggestiveness.* Although the *Manson* Court offered guidelines to determine reliability, "it failed," comments Grossman, supra, at 80, 96–97, "to articulate such criteria in evaluating the other side of the scale, suggestiveness. Police and lower courts were not given examples of what types of identification procedures were objectionable and, perhaps more important in a weighing process, what forms of suggestive behavior were more likely than others to result in an unreliable identification. * * * As a result, many courts have come to regard suggestion as a monolithic concept devoid of gradations or merely as a prerequisite to be met prior to analyzing the [*Biggers-Manson*] reliability factors. * * * Clearly, some identification procedures are worse than others and more conducive to misidentifications. The Supreme Court can [provide guidance] by indicating what types of suggestive conduct are more likely to result in unreliable identification testimony. As to these extreme forms of suggestive procedures [e.g., informing a witness that the suspect has confessed, having several witnesses view a display at the same time, presenting the suspect with a distinguishing trait or item also possessed by the perpetrator], a higher degree of reliability need be shown than that necessary to overcome nominal or less severe types of suggestive practices."

3. *Do the assumptions of the Manson majority find support in psychological research?* Drawing upon such works as Loftus, *Eyewitness Testimony* (1979) and Yarmey, *The Psychology of Eyewitness Testimony* (1979), Jonakait, supra, at 519–22, maintains that

many of the assumptions made by the *Manson* majority are unwarranted. E.g., "studies do not support the idea that police make more reliable witnesses than civilians or that their training in any way improves their ability to make identifications"; dangerous police work generates great stress and, although the Court may think that danger heightens awareness, "psychologists have known for some time that stress does not aid perception and learning, but inhibits them"; research indicates no relationship between the expressed confidence of an eyewitness and the accuracy of his or her identification. See also Grossman, supra, at 72–79.

DETENTION FOR IDENTIFICATION PROCEDURES IN THE ABSENCE OF PROBABLE CAUSE

1. *The dictum in Davis v. Mississippi that detention for the sole purpose of obtaining fingerprints might satisfy the Fourth Amendment even in the absence of traditional "probable cause."* In DAVIS v. MISSISSIPPI, 394 U.S. 721, 89 S.Ct. 1394, 22 L.Ed. 676 (1969), petitioner and 24 other black youths were detained for questioning and fingerprinting in connection with a rape for which the only leads were a general description given by the victim and a set of fingerprints around the window through which the assailant entered. Petitioner's prints were found to match those at the scene of the crime, and this evidence was admitted at his trial. The Court, per BRENNAN, J., held that the prints should have been excluded as the fruits of a seizure of petitioner in violation of the Fourth Amendment [see p. 383 infra], but intimated that a detention for such a purpose might sometimes be permissible on evidence insufficient for arrest:

"Detentions for the sole purpose of obtaining fingerprints are no less subject to the constraints of the Fourth Amendment. It is arguable, however, that because of the unique nature of the fingerprinting process, such detentions might, under narrowly defined circumstances, be found to comply with the Fourth Amendment even though there is no probable cause in the traditional sense. See *Camara v. Municipal Court* [p. 399 supra]. Detention for fingerprinting may constitute a much less serious intrusion upon personal security than other types of police searches and detentions. Fingerprinting involves none of the probing into an individual's private life and thoughts which marks an interrogation or search. Nor can fingerprint detention be employed repeatedly to harass any individual, since the police need only one set of each person's prints. Furthermore, fingerprinting is an inherently more reliable and effective crime-solving tool than eyewitness identifications or confessions and is not subject to such abuses as the improper line-up and the 'third degree.' Finally, because there is no danger of destruction of fingerprints, the limited detention need not come unexpectedly or at an inconvenient time. For this same reason, the general requirement that the authorization of a judicial officer be obtained in advance of detention would seem not to admit of any exception in the fingerprinting context.

"We have no occasion in this case, however, to determine whether the requirements of the Fourth Amendment could be met by narrowly circumscribed procedures for obtaining, during the course of a criminal investigation, the fingerprints of individuals for whom there is no probable cause to arrest. For it is clear that no attempt was made here to employ procedures which might comply with the requirements of the Fourth Amendment: the detention at police headquarters of petitioner and the other young Negroes was not authorized by a judicial officer; petitioner was unnecessarily required to undergo two fingerprinting sessions; and petitioner was not merely fingerprinted during the December 3 detention but also subjected to interrogation."

Justice HARLAN, concurring, noted: "There may be circumstances, falling short of the 'dragnet' procedures employed in this case, where compelled submission to fingerprinting would not amount to a violation of the Fourth Amendment even in the absence of a warrant, and I would leave that question open."

2. *The Model Code proposal.* On the basis of the *Davis* dictum, Art. 170 of the *Model Pre-Arraignment Code* delineates a court order procedure for detaining persons for nontestimonial identification purposes on less than "probable cause" and several states have passed similar legislation. See Commentary to Art. 170 at 475–77; Note, 45 Fordham L.Rev. 124, 130 (1976) (hereafter referred to as "Fordham Note").

Section 170.2 of the Model Code provides that a nontestimonial identification court order may issue when: (a) there is "reasonable cause" to believe that an offense has been committed; (b) there are "reasonable grounds to suspect" that the person named has committed the offense [b] "and it is reasonable in view of the seriousness of the offense to subject him to the specific identification procedures set forth in the application"; (c) the results will be "of material aid" in determining whether the person committed the offense; and (d) such evidence "cannot practicably be obtained" from another public agency. According to the Commentary (462), "a strict adherence to the standard of probable cause for detentions to conduct identification procedures not only hinders the police in their efforts to gather evidence, but also encourages them to use arrest in cases where there may not be reasonable cause." [c]

3. *Other Fourth Amendment problems.* Although the most serious Fourth Amendment question would seem to be whether, when the police lack "probable cause" to arrest a person *for any offense,* they may detain him for identification purposes, with or without a court order, Fourth Amendment problems also arise in other contexts.

Courts have generally found no Fourth Amendment violation when a person *lawfully in custody for one crime* is ordered into a lineup for other crimes for which there is no probable cause to arrest him. But some courts have indicated that even under these circumstances there must be a "reasonable suspicion" that the person committed the other crimes. See generally Fordham Note at 125–32.[d] In *United States v. Anderson,* 490 F.2d 785 (D.C.Cir. 1974), where a suspect charged with one

b. The Model Code article covers many "identification procedures," e.g., procedures to obtain identification by fingerprints, footprints, dental impressions, procedures to obtain specimens or samples of blood, urine or hair, and procedures to obtain witness identification through lineups and handwriting exemplars. To what extent should the requisite basis for the detention vary with the kind of identification involved? For example, since eyewitness identifications are a less reliable form of evidence than fingerprints, should Fourth Amendment requirements of detentions for lineup purposes be significantly more stringent? Or would it be more logical to ensure the absence of suggestiveness at a lineup held without probable cause by requiring the presence of counsel. See Fordham Note at 128–29.

c. The Commentary notes (at 460) that the police may also want to conduct identification procedures when a person is lawfully arrested for one crime but free on bail, and suspected of a second crime for which there is insufficient evidence to arrest him. If the person is unable to raise bail and thus is detained pending trial, the police may have him viewed by witnesses to "open crimes," i.e., unsolved crimes other than the one(s) for which the person was arrested. In such situations, however, the claim has been raised (and supported by a minority of the cases) that the participation of the person awaiting trial in these other identification procedures constitutes an equal protection violation since a person who could afford to raise bail could not be subjected to such procedures. See authorities collected in Commentary, supra, at 460–61 n. 3. Utilization of the nontestimonial order would eliminate such a claim, "since the order may be issued at any time, regardless of whether the person is free on bail or in custody awaiting trial." Ibid.

d. It has been argued that when a person is lawfully incarcerated, not even "reasonable suspicion" need exist to expose him to lineup viewing for "other crimes" on the ground that *the viewing* of suspects by witnesses—as opposed to *the detention* necessary to permit the viewing—should raise no Fourth Amendment problems—"the viewing of one's outward appearance may hardly be said to infringe on one's expectation of privacy." Fordham Note at 125–26.

crime was identified at a lineup by victims of another crime and convicted of that second crime, the court distinguished *Davis v. Mississippi* on the ground that Anderson was lawfully in custody (albeit for a different crime) and implied that that fact disposed of all Fourth Amendment problems. But see the separate statement of McGowan, J., joined by Bazelon, C.J., Wright, Leventhal and Robinson, JJ., in *United States v. Perry,* 504 F.2d 180 (D.C. Cir.1975).

When a defendant has been released on bail, he is generally subject to the control of the court which is empowered to order his appearance.[e] A number of courts have exercised this power to order defendant's appearance in a lineup for an unrelated crime, but again it is unclear whether this may be done indiscriminately or only when there is at least "reasonable suspicion" that the defendant committed the unrelated crimes under investigation. See Fordham Note at 127.

4. *Developments without specific statutory authorization or court-adopted rules; "Adams orders."* Although *Adams v. United States,* 399 F.2d 574 (D.C.Cir. 1968), barred evidence from lineups conducted during an unnecessary delay in bringing defendants before a magistrate,[f] the court suggested that if defendants had been promptly presented to the magistrate, the police could have invoked "the aid of that authority to make the [defendants] reasonably available for line-up identification in respect of other crimes [than the one for which they were arrested] for which there is less than probable cause * * *." Soon afterwards, the District of Columbia police began utilizing a procedure known as the "Adams order." See, e.g., *United States v. Allen,* 408 F.2d 1287 (D.C.Cir. 1969), upholding a magistrate's order compelling a person arrested for one robbery to participate in lineups viewed by witnesses to other similar modus operandi robberies. As the Commentary to the *Model Code* points out, at 472–73, "the 'Adams order' was originally designed to deal with persons already lawfully arrested. Later developments, however, have extended the use of such court orders to situations where there is reasonable suspicion to believe that a person committed the crime under investigation, but where the person is not in custody for any offense." See *Wise v. Murphy,* 275 A.2d 205 (D.C.App.1971) (en banc), noted in 18 Wayne L.Rev. 827 (1972).

Cf. *United States v. Dionisio,* 410 U.S. 1, 93 S.Ct. 764, 35 L.Ed.2d 67 (1973), holding that no preliminary showing of "probable cause" or "reasonableness" is needed to subpoena witnesses before a grand jury to give voice exemplars: (a) "a subpoena to appear before a grand jury is not a 'seizure' in the Fourth Amendment sense," and thus "*Davis* is plainly inapposite"; and (b) requiring one to furnish exemplars does not violate Fourth Amendment rights, as "the physical characteristics of a person's voice" "as opposed to the content of a specific conversation, are constantly exposed to the public," so that "no person can have a reasonable expectation that others will not know the sound of his voice." In the companion case of *United States v. Mara,* 410 U.S. 19, 93 S.Ct. 774, 35 L.Ed.2d 99 (1973), the same result was reached with respect to the subpoenaing of a witness to give handwriting exemplars. Both *Dionisio* and *Mara* are also discussed in Ch. 10, § 2.

e. *Beightol v. Kunowski,* 486 F.2d 293 (3d Cir. 1973) stresses that absent explicit legislative authority (which the state police lacked), a court order or a warrant, the police may not arrest or detain a person free on bail solely for nontestimonial identification purposes (in this instance, to obtain fingerprints and a "mug shot").

f. For the relationship between *Wade* and the *McNabb-Mallory* rule, see *Williams v. United States,* 419 F.2d 740 (D.C.Cir. 1969); Judge (now Chief Justice) Burger, concurring in *Adams v. United States,* 399 F.2d 574, 580 (D.C.Cir. 1968). If the adversary system commences, for purposes of *Kirby,* with the "preliminary arraignment," should the *McNabb-Mallory* rule be "exhumed" and applied in the context of eyewitness identifications? Otherwise, will the police "be able to violate prompt-arraignment statutes and court rules in order to avoid the constitutional right to counsel at post-arraignment lineups"? See Grano at 786–90.

Chapter 10

GRAND JURY INVESTIGATIONS

SECTION 1. THE ROLE OF THE INVESTIGATIVE GRAND JURY [a]

I. THE INVESTIGATIVE AUTHORITY OF THE GRAND JURY

1. *Dual functions.* The grand jury has been described as serving both as "the shield" and "the sword" of the criminal justice process. It is said to provide a "shield" against mistaken and vindictive prosecutions in deciding whether or not to issue an indictment. In making that determination, its function is to "screen" the prosecution's decision to charge, issuing indictments only where the available evidence is sufficient to justify a prosecution. On the other side, the grand jury is said to act as a "sword," combating crime, in the use of its investigative authority. Here, the grand jury's role is to uncover evidence not previously available to the government and thereby secure convictions that might otherwise not be obtained. The shielding function of the grand jury will be discussed in Chapter Fifteen.[b] In this Chapter we will concentrate upon the operation of the grand jury in its investigatory role. It should be kept in mind, however, that the two functions of the grand jury commonly are performed by the same grand jury. In particular, once a grand jury investigation is complete, the same group of grand jurors ordinarily will then be called upon to determine whether the evidence produced is sufficient to issue an indictment.

2. *Historical development.*[c] The English origins of the grand jury are traced to the Assize of Clarendon, created in 1166 during the reign of Henry II. The Assize established juries of 12 persons, selected from each community, who were charged with accusing those persons in the community believed to have committed crimes. It was assumed initially that the jurors would accuse based on their own knowledge, but they soon sought out informa-

a. For citations to relevant source materials, as well as a more detailed discussion of the subject, see LaFave and Israel, §§ 8.1–8.6; National Lawyers Guild, *Representation of Witnesses Before Federal Grand Juries* (3d ed. 1985).

b. The organization and operation of the grand jury are described briefly in Chapter 1, at p. 11 supra. Various aspects of the grand jury's procedure and structure relate both to its screening and investigatory functions. Those aspects that have a major impact upon its investigatory performance (e.g., grand jury secrecy) are discussed in this Chapter. Others that have a less significant bearing on investigations are discussed in Chapter 15. The composition of the grand jury, because it arguably has a greater impact on the screening function, is discussed in Chapter 15. For the purpose of this chapter, it is sufficient to note that the grand jurors will be selected in much the same manner as the petit jury, the grand jury will be somewhat larger than the petit jury (e.g., 16 to 23 in the federal system), and the grand jury will have a substantially longer term (e.g., 6 to 18 months), which often will have a bearing on its composition. For additional material on the structure of the grand jury, see LaFave and Israel, § 8.4.

c. See LaFave and Israel, § 8.2 for both citations and a further description of these developments.

tion from others. The Assize was designed not to protect against improper prosecutions by the Crown, but rather to lend assistance to government officials in the apprehension of criminals. The jurors were familiar with the local scene and could present charges that otherwise might not be known by the Crown's representatives. Any hesitancy the jurors might have in bringing accusations against their neighbors would be overcome by the substantial fines the jurors faced for failing to bring forward any known offense.

By the end of the fourteenth century the English had turned to trial by jury rather than by ordeal and the original jury had been divided into two separate juries. The trial of guilt was before a twelve-person petit jury, and the accusatory jury was expanded to a 23 person group, chosen from the entire county, which became known as "*le graunde inquest.*" At this point, the grand jury remained essentially a body designed to assist the Crown in ferreting out criminals. Accusations were either initiated by the jurors themselves, acting on the basis of community knowledge, or were initiated by a representative of the Crown, typically a justice of the peace, who produced witnesses to testify before the grand jury in support of a particular charge. When the accusation was initiated by the jury itself, its formal charge was described as a "presentment." When the accusation stemmed from a case placed before the jury by the Crown's representative, the grand jury's charging document was described as an "indictment."

Over the next few centuries, the grand jury began to assume a significant degree of independence, as evidenced by its occasional refusal to issue indictments sought by the Crown's representative. In the late seventeenth century, it established its reputation as a "bailiwick against the oppression and despotism of the Crown" when it refused to indict various supporters of the Protestant cause (including, most notably, Stephen Colledge and the Earl of Shaftesbury). During the same period, the grand jury also achieved some prominence in fighting governmental corruption, as various presentments were issued based upon grand jury inquiries into the misconduct of minor officials in matters of local administration.

In this country, the colonial grand juries expanded upon the use of grand jury inquiries and issued not only presentments but also reports criticizing actions of local officials that fell short of criminal misconduct. The colonial grand juries achieved even greater prestige, however, when they refused to issue indictments requested by Crown officials. Thus, the infamous prosecution of John Peter Zenger for seditious libel was brought by a prosecutor's information because colonial grand juries twice refused to issue requested indictments. In light of such actions, it was not surprising that the constitutions of the original states generally required that all felony prosecutions be brought by grand jury indictment or presentment, and once it was decided to add a Bill of Rights to the federal constitution, the inclusion of a similar provision in the Fifth Amendment was accepted without controversy.

During the period before the Civil War, grand juries, particularly in the western states, actively reviewed a wide range of grievances presented by citizens, and often conducted "searching investigations into corruption in government or widespread evasion of the laws." While grand juries thus achieved a considerable reputation as a "public watchdog," the value and cost of grand jury screening of cases developed by local prosecutors came under sharp attack. In 1859, Michigan became the first state to grant prosecutors the option of proceeding either by grand jury indictment or by a prosecutor's information. It is noteworthy that neither Michigan nor the many states that adopted similar option provisions abolished the grand jury, as the English eventually did. The grand jury was still viewed as a valuable instrument for occasional cases requiring the use of its investigatory authority.

Over the period between the Civil War and the mid-1900's, a majority of the states moved to allow prosecution by information. At the same time, however, grand juries remained active in both those "information" states and in the remaining "indictment" states in the investigation of corruption in local government. In several instances, the resulting indictments were so widespread as to unseat entire municipal administrations. As might be expected, local prosecutors were sometimes less than enthusiastic in cooperating with such investigations. Grand juries responded by seeking outside help (usually through court appointment of a special prosecutor) or by simply pushing forward against the wishes of a reluctant prosecutor. The most famous of these "runaway" grand jury investigations was the mid-1930's New York investigation of "racketeering" offenses, which led to the appointment of special prosecutor Thomas E. Dewey. The exploits of Dewey and his "racket busters" inspired a series of runaway grand jury investigations throughout the country and established the reputation of the grand jury as the nation's "number one instrument of discovery against organized crime."

3. *Current status.* While it was the shielding function that was responsible for the reference to the grand jury in the Fifth Amendment, the grand jury's investigatory role has proven to have the greater staying power in the approximately two-thirds of our states which no longer require prosecution by indictment. The practice in those states, as described in Chapter 15, is to bring the vast majority of prosecutions by information rather than indictment. Grand juries are still used to conduct investigations where the police investigatory authority is thought to be less helpful, and that use explains most of the cases in those jurisdictions that are prosecuted by indictment. In those states that still require prosecution by indictment, the vast majority of grand juries are engaged simply in screening cases that the prosecution presents to the grand jury as fully investigated and ready for indictment. However, in a small percentage of the cases presented to grand juries in indictment states, extensive use is made of the grand jury's investigatory authority. The federal system, because of the nature of the crimes it prosecutes, makes more extensive use of the grand jury's investigatory authority. But as in other "indictment jurisdictions," the vast majority of the cases presented to federal grand juries require only screening.

The grand jury's investigative authority continues to be recognized as a major tool in the prosecution of organized crime and government corruption. In recent years, federal grand jury investigations of white collar crime have added further luster to the grand jury's reputation as an investigative force. On the other hand, the grand jury's reputation has been sullied, at least in some quarters, by investigations that might suggest that its investigative authority had been used for partisan political ends. Several highly publicized investigations of public figures have produced damaging accusations that were supported at trial by clearly insufficient evidence, and investigations of the alleged criminal activities of "radical" groups seemed to many to be directed more toward harassment than producing supportable indictments. See Deutsch, *The Improper Uses of the Federal Grand Jury: An Instrument for the Internment of Political Activists,* 75 J.Crim.L. & Criminology 1159 (1984).

II. INVESTIGATIVE ADVANTAGES

Compared to police investigations, grand jury investigations are expensive, time consuming, and logistically cumbersome. Accordingly, the grand jury ordinarily is used to investigate only when it has a distinct investigative advantage over the police. It usually has such an advantage where investigators must unravel a complex criminal structure, deal with victims reluctant to cooperate, obtain information contained in extensive business records, or keep a continuing investigative effort from the public gaze. Criminal activities presenting such investigative problems include public corruption (e.g., bribery), misuse of economic power (e.g., price-fixing), and widespread distribution of illegal services and goods (e.g., gambling or narcotics distribution), and most grand jury investigations are directed at such activities. The grand jury's advantages in investigating this type of criminal activity stem primarily from five elements of its investigatory processes—(1) the use of subpoena authority, (2) the psychological pressure imposed by the grand jury setting, (3) the use of immunity grants, (4) grand jury secrecy requirements, and (5) public confidence attributable to lay participation.

1. *Subpoena authority.* The basic investigative advantage of the grand jury stems from its ability to use the subpoena authority of the court that impaneled it. The grand jury may utilize the subpoena duces tecum to obtain tangible evidence and the subpoena ad testificandum to obtain testimony. Both subpoenas are supported by the court's authority to hold in contempt any person who willfully refuses, without legal justification, to comply with a subpoena's directive.[a]

The contempt sanction makes the grand jury subpoena particularly useful in obtaining statements from persons who will not voluntarily furnish information to the police. While those persons have the right to refuse to cooperate with the police, their refusal to comply with a grand jury subpoena invokes the threat of a possible jail sentence. Faced with that threat, a recalcitrant witness often will have a change of heart and will give to the grand jury information that he previously refused to give to the police. Of course, if the information sought could be incriminating, the witness (unless granted immunity) may still refuse to cooperate by relying on his privilege against self-incrimination. Many persons, however, are unwilling to furnish information to the police, yet will testify before the grand jury without regard to the availability of the privilege. Thus, the victim of a fraudulent gambling operation or a loansharking operation may be either too embarrassed or too fearful to voluntarily furnish information to the police, yet be willing to testify before the grand jury when faced with the threat of contempt. Similarly, an employee may wish to avoid the appearance of voluntarily assisting officials investigating his employer, yet testify freely under the compulsion of a subpoena.

The grand jury subpoena ad testificandum also has the advantage of requiring witnesses to testify under oath. If a witness fails to tell the truth, he may be prosecuted for perjury. Generally, a person who gives false information to a police officer will not have committed a crime (though there is such a crime as to federal officials). Accordingly, where a witness

a. The contemnor may be held in either civil or criminal contempt. Civil contempt is used to coerce the contemnor into complying with the subpoena. The contemnor is sentenced to imprisonment or to a fine (which may increase daily), but he may purge himself of the sentence by complying with the subpoena. As courts have frequently noted, he "carries the keys to the prison in his pocket." The civil contemnor who refuses to purge himself will remain under sentence until the grand jury completes its term and is discharged. Moreover, if the information the contemnor possesses is still needed, he may be subpoenaed by a successor grand jury and held in contempt again if he continues to refuse to supply that information. Assuming there is a continuing need for the information sought by subpoena, most jurisdictions require that the court first utilize civil contempt unless it clearly will not be successful. If civil contempt fails or appears likely to fail, the court may then utilize criminal contempt. Here the court simply seeks to impose punishment for violation of its order in the same manner in which punishment is imposed for violation of the Penal Code. While many jurisdictions do not prescribe a specific maximum sentence for criminal contempt, the sentences imposed commonly fall in the range of several months to a few years imprisonment.

might be willing to talk to the police, but also is likely to "shade his story," requiring him to testify before a grand jury may produce more complete and truthful statements. Even where a witness is willing to give an entirely truthful statement to the police, there may be value in requiring him to testify before the grand jury. Arguably, a person who has testified under oath before the grand jury will be somewhat more hesitant to "change his story" when he testifies at trial. Also, if the witness does change his story and his prior statement is used to impeach him, the petit jurors may give greater weight to his grand jury testimony than they would to a statement he made to the police.

Finally, the grand jury subpoena duces tecum offers certain advantages over the primary device available to the police for obtaining records and physical evidence—the search pursuant to a warrant. Unlike the search warrant, the subpoena duces tecum can issue without a showing of probable cause. See *United States v. Dionisio,* p. 715 infra. Moreover, even where probable cause could be established, there are times when the subpoena will be more appropriate. For example, there may be a need to seize so many records from various locations that a search would be impractical. At other times, there may be a need to obtain records from uninvolved third parties (e.g., a bank) and a subpoena will be preferred because it is far less disruptive to the third party's operations.

2. *Psychological pressure.* In addition to the compulsion of the subpoena, the psychological pressure of grand jury interrogation also is cited as a factor that frequently enables the grand jury to obtain statements from witnesses unwilling to cooperate with the police. Proponents of grand jury investigations claim that this pressure stems from the moral force exerted by the grand jury. Thus, two prosecuting attorneys note:

> "Most witnesses before grand juries feel a moral compulsion to be honest and forthright in discharging their duties as citizens, because their peers, the members of the grand jury, have also been taken away from their jobs, businesses, and private pursuits, and have accepted the inconvenience of becoming involved. The grand jurors manifest a serious purpose and are persons with whom witnesses can identify. Thus, even though their associates may be determined not to cooperate, certain witnesses may be ashamed to engage or persist in deceitful or obstreperous conduct to deny the grand jury the information it needs." Keeney and Walsh, *The American Bar Association's Grand Jury Principles: A Critique From A Federal Criminal Justice Perspective,* 14 Idaho L.Rev. 545, 579 (1978).

On the other side, critics of grand jury investigations claim the psychological pressure stems from what they describe as the "star chamber setting" of grand jury interrogation. "In all of the United States legal system," they note, "no person stands more alone than a witness before a grand jury; in a secret hearing he faces an often hostile prosecutor and 23 strangers with no judge present to guard his rights, no lawyer present to counsel him, and sometimes no indication of why he is being questioned."

3. *Immunity grants.* An immunity grant is a court order granting a witness sufficient immunity from future prosecution to supplant the witness' self-incrimination privilege. Once the recalcitrant witness has been granted immunity, he may no longer rely upon the privilege. Since immunity grants are tied to the exercise of the privilege by a person under a legal obligation to testify, they are not available to persons who simply refuse to give a statement to the police. At the investigatory stage, almost the only way the prosecution can make use of an immunity grant is in conjunction with a subpoena directing the uncooperative witness to testify before the grand jury. The immunity grant may be needed to gain information from various

types of recalcitrant witnesses. For example, immunity quite frequently is given to a lower-level participant in organized crime in order to obtain testimony against higher-level participants. It also often is used to force testimony from witnesses who are not themselves involved in criminal activities, but desire not to give testimony that may hurt others. Although the privilege is not available simply to protect others (see Note 2, p. 737 infra), witnesses who do not actually fear personal incrimination have been known to falsely claim that they do in order to avoid testifying against their friends. Since such claims are difficult to dispute, the prosecutor may simply prefer to grant the witness immunity.

4. *Secrecy.* Grand jury secrecy requirements vary among jurisdictions, but it generally is agreed that even the weakest of those requirements adds to the grand jury's effectiveness as an investigative agency. All jurisdictions prohibit the prosecutor, the prosecutor's staff, the grand jurors, and the grand jury stenographer from disclosing grand jury testimony except when authorized by court order. In several jurisdictions, a grand jury witness is subject to a similar limitation, disclosure being permitted only to his counsel. Most jurisdictions, however, do not impose an obligation of secrecy upon grand jury witnesses. A witness may disclose, publicly or privately, both his own testimony and whatever information was revealed to him in the course of his examination before the grand jury. Where the witness desires not to disclose, however, his decision, combined with the obligations of secrecy imposed upon the other participants, usually keeps his testimony secret—at least until an indictment is issued.[b]

In *United States v. Procter & Gamble Co.,* 356 U.S. 677, 78 S.Ct. 983, 2 L.Ed.2d

b. During the pendency of the investigation, every effort is made to assist the witness who wants to keep his testimony secret. Thus jurisdictions commonly provide that the names of persons to whom subpoenas have been issued shall be kept under seal. So too, a hearing relating to the investigation may be closed to the public where necessary to prevent disclosure of grand jury matters. See Fed.R.Crim.P. 6(e)(5) (noting, however, that such power is "subject to any right to an open hearing in contempt proceedings"). Of course, even during the pendency of the investigation, the court has authority, upon a special showing of need, to order disclosure to a third party (e.g., a civil litigant who is familiar with the general subject matter of the investigation and believes that the testimony may be critical to presenting a defense in a related civil case). However, courts are extemely reluctant to exercise that authority while the investigation is ongoing. See *Douglas Oil Co. v. Petrol Stops Northwest,* 441 U.S. 211, 99 S.Ct. 1667, 60 L.Ed.2d 156 (1979).

Once the investigation has ended, there is a somewhat greater likelihood of court-ordered disclosure to a litigant in a related civil case, but the court here still will give considerable weight to the grand jury witness' interest in keeping his testimony secret. Consider, e.g., *Douglas Oil,* supra, where the Court (in discussing the "particularized need" standard that must be met by the civil litigant to gain disclosure) noted:

"Parties seeking grand jury transcripts under Rule 6(e) must show that the material they seek is needed to avoid a possible injustice in another judicial proceeding, that the need for disclosure is greater than the need for continued secrecy, and that their request is structured to cover only material so needed. Such a showing must be made even when the grand jury whose transcripts are sought has concluded its operations * * *. For in considering the effects of disclosure on grand jury proceedings, the courts must consider not only the immediate effects upon a particular grand jury, but also the possible effect upon the functioning of future grand juries. Persons called upon to testify will consider the likelihood that their testimony may one day be disclosed to outside parties. Fear of future retribution or social stigma may act as powerful deterrents to those who would come forward and aid the grand jury in the performance of its duties. Concern as to the future consequences of frank and full testimony is heightened where the witness is an employee of a company under investigation. Thus, the interests in grand jury secrecy, although reduced, are not eliminated merely because the grand jury has ended its activities."

By far the greatest likelihood of court ordered disclosure occurs where the investigation ends in an indictment and the defendant seeks to examine the grand jury testimony. Where the grand jury witness will also be a trial witness, most jurisdictions grant automatic disclosure of the witness' grand jury testimony, either pretrial or after the witness testifies at trial. See Ch. 20, § 1, pt. II. Indeed, in some jurisdictions, defendants may gain pretrial disclosure of all grand jury testimony, including that of grand jury witnesses who will not testify at trial. See Ch. 15, § 3, pt. C.

1077 (1958), the Supreme Court noted five objectives of grand jury secrecy requirements:

> "(1) to prevent the escape of those whose indictment may be contemplated; (2) to insure the utmost freedom to the grand jury in its deliberations, and to prevent persons subject to indictment or their friends from importuning the grand jurors; (3) to prevent subornation of perjury or tampering with the witnesses who may testify before grand jury and later appear at the trial of those indicted by it; (4) to encourage free and untrammeled disclosures by persons who have information with respect to the commission of crimes; (5) to protect the innocent accused who is exonerated from disclosure of the fact that he has been under investigation, and from the expense of standing trial where there was no probability of guilt."

While the second objective cited by the Court relates primarily to the screening function of the grand jury, the remaining four promote the grand jury's effectiveness as an investigative agency. The first objective—preventing the flight of the person being investigated—depends, of course, upon the cooperation of the grand jury witness. Since he is not sworn to secrecy, the witness may lawfully warn the target of the investigation. However, if the witnesses cooperate, grand jury secrecy requirements generally should deter the leaks that accompany most other types of investigation. If the target is kept unaware of the investigation until after the indictment is issued, the third objective cited by the Court also is served. When the witnesses against him have already testified, it is too late for the target to try to influence their grand jury testimony and it will be more difficult for him to successfully influence their trial testimony.

The fourth objective noted in *Procter & Gamble* probably is the most significant for investigatory success. Witnesses often are much more willing to testify if they know that their identity will be kept from the target of the investigation. Of course, if an indictment is issued, and the witness testifies at trial, the target (now the defendant) eventually will learn that the particular person furnished evidence against him (see fn. b supra). However, the witness may not necessarily be called to testify at trial. Grand jury witnesses often are subpoenaed simply to obtain leads to more crucial evidence. Moreover, if the witness can be assured that his identity will be revealed only if an indictment is issued, he may have fewer qualms about cooperating. He may be less wary of being criticized as an "informer" if he knows that his role will be revealed only after a grand jury has supported his judgment and veracity by issuing an indictment.

The fifth objective noted in *Procter & Gamble* can be of special significance in the decision to institute an investigation. Where the person being investigated occupies a position of public prominence, public disclosure of the investigation may cause irreparable damage to the person's career even though the investigation eventually reveals no basis for a prosecution. Accordingly, a prosecutor may hesitate to initiate a police investigation unless the currently available evidence makes it most likely that the investigation will result in a prosecution. On the other hand, if grand jury secrecy requirements can provide reasonable assurance that the investigation will be kept secret if an indictment is not issued, the prosecutor may feel less reluctant to initiate a grand jury investigation. In particular, when he has a strong suspicion that rumors of illegal activities are well founded, he may be willing to pursue the investigation of a public figure even though the evidence currently available is fairly flimsy.[c]

c. Of course, the prosecutor can never be absolutely certain of achieving preindictment secrecy since grand jury secrecy requirements may not work to perfection, even when the witnesses are

5. *Maintaining public confidence.* Where the subject to be investigated is a matter of public knowledge (as in the case of investigations into matters already given considerable media coverage), grand jury participation often helps in maintaining community confidence in the integrity of the investigatory process. This is especially important where the person under investigation is a public official. The community tends to be suspicious of partisan influences in such investigations, especially where the investigation results in a decision not to prosecute. As one court noted: "Where corruption is charged, it is desirable to have someone outside the administration [i.e., the grand jury] act, so that the image, as well as the fact of impartiality in the investigation can be preserved and allegations of cover-up or white-wash can be avoided." *Losavio v. Kikel,* 529 P.2d 306 (Colo.1974). The prosecutor may also look to the grand jury to help allay other public concerns, as in cases in which investigated parties are almost certain to claim police and prosecutor harassment.

6. *Grand jury reports.* Another potential investigative advantage, also relating to maintaining public confidence, lies in the grand jury's authority to issue reports in those situations in which an investigation reveals transactions that are of questionable propriety, though not criminal. A substantial number of states permit a grand jury to issue a report summarizing the evidence found on non-indictable activities thought to merit public attention.[d] Such reports have been issued on a variety of topics ranging from improper conflicts of interest to clearly fraudulent business schemes that escaped criminal liability only because of the inadequate coverage of state law. Though obviously of less significance to the prosecutor than those grand jury powers that facilitate development of a successful prosecution, the alternative of issuing a report, if a crime is not found, may be helpful in maintaining the image of the prosecutor's office as an effective "public watchdog."

7. *Alternative investigative agencies.* Several states have established alternative investigative agencies which seek to furnish at least some of the investigative advantages of the grand jury in a "less cumbersome" structure. Thus, Michigan provides for investigating magistrates, sometimes called "one-man grand juries." See Mich.Comp.L. § 767.3. A single judge is assigned by the local court to serve as a one-man grand jury upon presentation of a petition establishing sufficient grounds to justify an investigation—usually probable cause to believe a crime has been committed by unidentified persons. The investigating magistrate may then utilize basically the same tools as the traditional "citizens grand jury"—i.e., subpoena authority, immunity grants, and secrecy. The magistrate is assisted by a specially appointed prosecutor, who may

fully cooperative. Although violations of secrecy provisions by grand jurors, stenographers, or assistant prosecutors constitute contempt or a criminal offense, the threat of contempt sanctions has not proven a particularly effective deterrent against "leaks" to the press in some jurisdictions. See Frankel and Naftalis, *The Grand Jury: An Institution on Trial* 85–86 (1975).

d. State courts have divided as to whether the grand jury has a "common law authority" to issue reports in the absence of specific legislative authorization. See LaFave and Israel, § 8.3. The issue has been mooted in a substantial number of jurisdictions by the adoption of legislation clearly authorizing the grand jury to issue reports on specified subjects. Recently adopted statutes have sought both to limit the scope of reports critical of specific individuals and to provide certain safeguards for those individuals. The New York provision is illustrative. It authorizes reports as to the "misconduct, non-feasance or neglect" of public officials, but requires that: (1) the report be supported by the preponderance of "credible and legally admissible evidence," as determined by the court; (2) the public official be allowed to testify before the grand jury; and (3) the public official be given an opportunity to prepare an answer, which is to be appended to the report. N.Y.Crim.P. Law §§ 190.85–90. In the Organized Crime Control Act of 1970, Congress adopted a somewhat similar reporting provision for the special federal grand juries impaneled under that Act. 18 U.S.C. § 3333. See Note, 4 Mich.J.L.Ref. 549 (1971).

be the local prosecutor, the Attorney General, or a member of the local bar. If the investigation develops sufficient evidence to initiate prosecution, the magistrate will issue an indictment or complaint and the assistant prosecutor will then represent the state in the ensuing prosecution. Critics contend that the one-man grand jury (1) places too much authority in the hands of a single person; (2) imposes non-judicial duties upon a member of the judicial branch; (3) offers too much temptation for the judge/juror to use highly publicized investigations for political gain and self-aggrandizement; and (4) fails to provide a constantly available investigatory process that allows the initiation of an investigation without a showing of cause (and the resulting publicity that usually attends that showing).

Several states authorize the prosecutor to use subpoenas in conducting investigations apart from the grand jury. See Unif. R.Crim.P. 432 (commentary) (listing various state provisions). Under these provisions, a person may be subpoenaed to appear at the prosecutor's office to testify under oath or present records concerning possible criminal violations. In some jurisdictions, the prosecutor's investigative subpoena issues automatically upon the prosecutor's request, while others require court approval. The witness may appear with counsel and may exercise traditional witness' privileges, but an unlawful refusal to comply with the subpoena will constitute contempt. A few states authorize immunity grants for persons subject to office subpoenas, but none impose a secrecy requirement similar to that applied to the grand jury. See Unif.R.Crim.P. 432 (recommending use of immunity grants and the imposition of secrecy requirements upon request of the prosecutor or witness).

The National Advisory Commission recommended that more states grant the prosecutor investigatory subpoena authority. See N.A.C., *Courts* § 12.8 (1973). Noting that subpoena authority is a necessary investigative tool and that use of grand jury subpoenas is "cumbersome," the Commission commentary urged the more "straight forward approach of a subpoena issued directly by the prosecutor." Opponents of prosecutorial investigative subpoenas contend that (1) it bypasses important institutional safeguards derived from juror participation, and (2) is more likely to be subjected to judicial controls that restrict investigatory flexibility and effectiveness (e.g., requiring open proceedings and showings of materiality).

III. JUDICIAL REGULATION: SOME DIFFERING PERSPECTIVES

1. *LaFave and Israel, § 8.2(c) ("The Relevance of History"):*

"The grand jury investigation is frequently described as introducing an 'inquisitorial element' into a criminal justice system that is basically accusatorial. Critics argue that the grand jury's investigative authority should therefore be viewed as an anomaly and kept within narrow confines by close judicial supervision. They recognize that this position faces difficulties if history reveals that the grand jury inquest was accepted from the outset as an institution that coexisted with the accusatorial elements of the Anglo-American criminal justice process. The critics argue, however, that a careful reading of the history of the grand jury reveals no such accommodation. First, they note, the early grand juries did not frequently exercise the basic element of its modern investigative authority—its power to compel testimony—but instead relied primarily upon information known to the jurors or the voluntary testimony of aggrieved persons. Secondly, they argue, the investigative role of the grand jury was not critical to its initial acceptance in this country. It was the shielding role of the grand jury that earned it a place in the Bill of Rights and the early state constitutions. The grand jury's investigatory role was then viewed as entirely secondary and not necessarily distinct from its screening role. Today, it is argued, the significance of the two roles has been reversed. As one critic put it, 'the protective function has been trivialized and the investigatory function expanded to the point where the institution is almost precisely the opposite of what the Founding Fathers intended.'

"Supporters of the grand jury respond that the early history of the grand jury clearly establishes the legitimacy of its extensive investigative authority. The power of the grand jury to compel testimony was recognized well before the adoption of the Constitution and was used in some of the most notable grand jury inquests. At the time of the Constitution's adoption, the grand jury was a revered institution not simply because it served as a buffer between the state and the individual, but equally for its service as a watchdog against public corruption and its capacity to ferret out criminal activity that local officials either chose to ignore or were unable to investigate. The importance of this investigative authority was implicitly recognized, it is argued, in constitutional and statutory provisions authorizing the institution of prosecution by presentment as well as indictment.

"With few exceptions, American courts have accepted the position that the history of the grand jury provides a solid foundation for its broad investigative authority. The Supreme Court's discussion of that authority in *Blair v. United States* [see Note 2 infra] is typical. The Court there noted that the grand jury's authority to resort to compulsory process had been recognized in England as early as 1612, and the inquisitorial function of the grand jury was well established at the time of the Constitution's adoption. Both the Fifth Amendment and the earliest federal statutes recognized an investigative authority of the grand jury that included the 'same powers that pertained to its British prototype.' The Supreme Court would not view that authority with suspicion and subject it to new limitations. * * *

"Critics of the grand jury also contend that even if a broad investigative authority is sanctioned by history, the same historical sources also indicate that that authority was tied to an assumption of substantial grand jury independence. * * * Today, the critics argue, the sweeping powers of the grand jury are exercised in reality by the prosecutor alone. Working with the police, the prosecutor determines what witnesses will be called and when they will appear. He examines the witnesses and advises the grand jury on the validity of any legal objections the witnesses might present. If a witness refuses to comply with a subpoena, it is the prosecutor who seeks a contempt citation. If a witness refuses to testify on grounds of self-incrimination, it is the prosecutor who determines whether an immunity grant will be obtained. The grand jury must, almost of necessity, rely upon the prosecutor's leadership.[a] Few investigations can succeed

a. In large part, the prosecutor's control over the matters noted above is attributable to "the grand jury's voluntary deference, rather than the prosecutor's legal authority over the proceedings." See LaFave and Israel, § 8.4. In all but a few jurisdictions, the prosecutor is viewed as the primary "legal advisor" to the grand jury. This position is limited, however, to informing the grand jury of applicable legal standards (and even there, the grand jury is free to obtain further advice from the court). The role of legal advisor does not carry with it authority to control the direction of an investigation.

In some jurisdictions, the prosecutor's authority to subpoena witnesses is derived from the grand jury and that body can, if it so chooses, negate a subpoena issued on its behalf by the prosecutor. In others, the prosecutor has an independent right to subpoena witnesses, and the grand jury apparently has a corresponding duty to hear those witnesses. The grand jury remains free, however, to insist that additional witnesses be subpoenaed and to pursue through this power entirely new areas of investigation. Once a witness is subpoenaed, whether at the directive of the prosecutor or grand jury, most jurisdictions give the prosecutor a right to be present and to examine that witness. Several jurisdictions, however, continue to recognize the common law authority of the grand jury to exclude the prosecutor during the questioning of any witness. The jurors in all jurisdictions have a right to ask their own questions of any witness (though the prosecutor often will ask to screen those questions to without the investigative work, skillful interrogation, legal advice, and even the secretarial assistance, provided by the prosecutor and his staff. Moreover, grand jurors are neophytes in the field of criminal investigation and are participating only on a part-time basis; it is only natural that they are disposed to rely upon the prosecutor—the 'professional' who commands the resources necessary to their venture.

"Critics argue that this change in the nature of the investigative grand jury, which [they say] has converted it into the 'prosecutor's puppet,' requires a corresponding change in judicial attitudes. The courts should not, they argue, feel bound by precedent that was developed during an era when grand juries were independent bodies. Instead, they should 'pull back the veil of history and view the investigating grand jury as one would view any other investigatory instrument of government.' [b] The power of the grand jury should be subject to the same kinds of limitations as are imposed upon other weapons in the prosecutor's investigative arsenal.

"Supporters of the grand jury readily acknowledge that the prosecutor plays a substantial role in directing today's grand jury investigations. They suggest that this is a beneficial development that makes the investigatory authority more effective and helps to ensure that it is not misused. Moreover, it is noted, this development dates back over one hundred years, preceding many of the decisions that speak most eloquently of the necessary breadth of the grand jury's investigative authority. The key to the historical grant of that authority, they argue, was a legal structure that rendered the government's use of the grand jury's investigative powers subject to the veto of the jurors, who sat as community representatives. That structure has not been substantially altered, and its very presence, the argument continues, serves to hold the prosecutor in check and to distinguish grand jury investigations from investigatory tools granted directly to the prosecutor or the police. The fact that the grand jury only occasionally exercises its power to override the prosecutor does not detract from the significance of that power. The prosecutor must respect the existence of that power and act in a way that he knows, from past experience, will be acceptable to the jurors."

2. BLAIR v. UNITED STATES, 250 U.S. 273, 39 S.Ct. 468, 63 L.Ed. 979 (1919). Responding to a grand jury witness' challenge to a subpoena on the ground that the federal government lacked constitutional authority to regulate, and the federal grand jury therefore lacked jurisdiction to investigate, the campaign practices of a candidate in a state

ensure that they are proper as to form and content). If a witness refuses to answer on grounds of self-incrimination, the granting of immunity will be dependent upon the decision of the prosecutor.

In sum, the grand jury has at least shared authority over all investigatory decisions to grant immunity, and in various jurisdictions it will have exclusive authority over many of those decisions. Moreover, the grand jury always retains the authority to petition the court for the appointment of a new prosecutor when it believes that the prosecutor is not performing satisfactorily. While such a request need not be granted, it will place considerable pressure upon the prosecutor and force the court to review the prosecutor's performance.

b. Note, 7 Harv.C.R.-C.L.L.Rev. 432, 498-99 (1972). The author concludes: "[T]he investigatory grand jury—a twentieth century creation—[should be] judged by twentieth century constitutional principles. * * * [Courts should] pull back the veil of history and view the investigatory grand jury as one would view any other investigatory instrument of government. Searches are customarily required to meet a standard of reasonableness; grand jury 'searches' should be no different. Investigations that encroach on the sensitive areas of political expression and association are usually not permitted to proceed unless there is a compelling governmental interest; grand juries should also be required to respect the first amendment. Congress had decided to withhold the subpoena power from the F.B.I.; there is no reason why the Bureau should be able to circumvent that decision by working through the grand jury. A prospective defendant is entitled to counsel at other critical stages in the criminal process; the grand jury should not be an exception."

primary election for U.S. Senator, PITNEY, J., speaking for a unanimous Court, noted:

"[T]he giving of testimony and the attendance upon court or grand jury in order to testify are public duties which every person within the jurisdiction of the Government is bound to perform upon being properly summoned, and for performance of which he is entitled to no further compensation than that which the statutes provide. The personal sacrifice involved is a part of the necessary contribution of the individual to the welfare of the public. The duty, so onerous at times, yet so necessary to the administration of justice according to the forms and modes established in our system of government is subject to mitigation in exceptional circumstances; there is a constitutional exemption from being compelled in any criminal case to be a witness against oneself, entitling the witness to be excused from answering anything that will tend to incriminate him; some confidential matters are shielded from considerations of policy, and perhaps in other cases for special reasons a witness may be excused from telling all that he knows.

"But, aside from exceptions and qualifications—and none such is asserted in the present case—the witness is bound not only to attend but to tell what he knows in answer to questions framed for the purpose of bringing out the truth of the matter under inquiry. He is not entitled to urge objections of incompetency or irrelevancy, such as a party might raise, for this is no concern of his. On familiar principles, he is not entitled to challenge the authority of the court or of the grand jury, provided they have a *de facto* existence and organization. He is not entitled to set limits to the investigation that the grand jury may conduct. * * * It is a grand inquest, a body with powers of investigation and inquisition, the scope of whose inquiries is not to be limited narrowly by questions of propriety or forecasts of the probable result of the investigation, or by doubts whether any particular individual will be found properly subject to an accusation of crime."

3. IN RE GRAND JURY PROCEEDINGS (SCHOFIELD I), 486 F.2d 85 (3d Cir.1973). Rejecting the government's claim that a grand jury witness should be held in contempt for failing to respond to a grand jury subpoena with no more showing as to the grounding of the subpoena than "what appears on the face of the subpoena" (see Note 2, p. 729 infra), the Third Circuit (per GIBBONS, J.) noted:

"[I]t is well to start with some fundamental propositions. First, although federal grand juries are called into existence by order of the district court, Fed.R. Crim.P. 6(a), they are 'basically . . . a law enforcement agency.' They are for all practical purposes an investigative and prosecutorial arm of the executive branch of government. Second, although like all federal court subpoenas grand jury subpoenas are issued in the name of the district court over the signature of the clerk, they are issued pro forma and in blank to anyone requesting them. Fed.R. Crim.P. 17(a). The court exercises no prior control whatsoever upon their use. Third, although grand jury subpoenas are occasionally discussed as if they were the instrumentalities of the grand jury, they are in fact almost universally instrumentalities of the United States Attorney's office or of some other investigative or prosecutorial department of the executive branch. Grand jury subpoenas then, when they are brought before the federal courts for enforcement, for all practical purposes are exactly analogous to subpoenas issued by a federal administrative agency on the authority of a statute * * *. [A] court's determination under 28 U.S.C. § 1826(a) [the civil contempt enforcement provision] of the existence or nonexistence of just cause for refusing to obey a subpoena entails the same full judicial consideration as in the administrative subpoena cases." c

4. BLACK, J., dissenting in IN RE GROBAN, 352 U.S. 330, 77 S.Ct. 510, 1 L.Ed.2d 376 (1957). Commenting on the distinction between a grand jury proceeding (where Justice Black agreed that "a witness cannot insist, as a matter of constitutional right, on being represented by counsel") and a fire marshall's closed inquiry (where Justice Black, disagreeing with the *Groban* majority, argued that the witness had a constitutional right to be accompanied by counsel), Justice Black emphasized the special role of the grand jurors:

"They bring into the grand jury room the experience, knowledge and viewpoint of all sections of the community. They have no axes to grind and are not charged personally with the administration of the law. No one of them is a prosecuting attorney or law-enforcement officer ferreting out crime. It would be very difficult for officers of the state seriously to abuse or deceive a witness in the presence of the grand jury. Similarly the presence of the jurors offers a substantial safeguard against the officers' misrepresentation, unintentional or otherwise, of the witness statements and conduct before the grand jury."

5. Beale, *Reconsidering Supervisory Power in Criminal Cases: Constitutional and Statutory Limits on the Authority of the Federal Courts,* 84 Colum.L.Rev. 1433, 1458–60 (1984):

"The lower courts have frequently employed their supervisory authority in connection with federal grand jury proceedings. For example, in cases known as *Schofield* I and II [Note 3 supra, and Notes 2–4, pp. 729–32 infra], the Third Circuit exercised its supervisory authority to require the government to make a three-part preliminary showing to get enforcement of grand jury subpoenas. Many of the grand jury cases have involved allegations of prosecutorial abuse of the grand jury; and the Second, Third, and Ninth Circuits have all approved use of supervisory power to dismiss an indictment as a sanction for serious government misconduct in connection with grand jury proceedings. [See Ch. 15, § 4]. The Third Circuit has expressly approved the use of supervisory authority to dismiss an indictment as a prophylactic sanction 'for "entrenched and flagrant misconduct," ' even if no actual prejudice can be shown. And in *United States v. Jacobs* [547 F.2d 772 (2d Cir. 1976)], in which the Supreme Court twice heard oral arguments before dismissing the writ of certiorari as improvidently granted, the Second Circuit employed its supervisory power to dismiss a perjury indictment because a federal [strike force] prosecutor had not followed the local United States Attorney's practice of giving targets of a grand jury investigation warnings before they testified. The court of appeals stated that its order was not intended to require that warnings be given, but rather to act 'as an ad hoc sanction . . . to enforce "consistent performance" one way or another.'

"The lower courts have recognized, however, that grand jury proceedings are not equivalent in all respects to judicial

c. At a later point in the *Schofield* opinion, Judge Gibbons, explaining why two recent Supreme Court opinions should not be read as suggesting a contrary conclusion, noted: "The limited role that the Government would have the district court play in the enforcement process is illuminated by a colloquy which took place at the oral argument of this appeal. Hypothesizing an instance in which a United States attorney concluded that it might be in the interest of national security to have in the government files mug shots, fingerprints and handwriting exemplars of all members of a radical student organization at a local university, and proceeded to obtain them by the use of subpoenas identical to that issued here, a member of the court asked the United States attorney if the district court's inquiry in an enforcement proceeding should be as limited as he suggested. As might be expected, the reply was that no United States attorney ever would do such a thing—which perhaps is true—but that in order to prevent delay in the grand jury process the scope of inquiry in all cases should be the same. Clearly the Supreme Court in *Dionisio* and *Mara* did not so intend * * *."

proceedings. Cases involving the use of supervisory power to control grand jury proceedings present a potential for 'conflict between the Executive and Judicial branches of the federal government over their respective relationships to the federal grand jury.' Moreover, the grand jury is an independent institution predating the Constitution, whose continued existence is guaranteed by the fifth amendment. Unlike other institutions created by the Constitution, the grand jury is not assigned to any one of the three branches of government. Although the lower court decisions reflect increasing agreement that supervisory power should not be exercised in a way that encroaches upon the 'constitutionally-based independence' of the grand jury itself or upon the prerogatives of the prosecutor, no consensus has been reached regarding what constitutes improper encroachment." [d]

SECTION 2. CHALLENGES TO THE INVESTIGATION

I. FOURTH AMENDMENT OBJECTIONS

BOYD v. UNITED STATES

116 U.S. 616, 6 S.Ct. 524, 29 L.Ed. 746 (1886).

[Customs officials seized 35 cases of glass, imported by the partnership of Boyd and Sons, and instituted a forfeiture proceeding. That proceeding was brought under a statute providing that any importer who defrauded the government and thereby avoided payment of customs revenue was subject to fine, incarceration, and forfeiture of the imported merchandise. Utilizing an 1874 statute, the government's attorney obtained a court order directing Boyd to produce an invoice covering 29 of the cases of glass. That statute provided:

> "In all suits and proceedings other than criminal, arising under any of the revenue laws of the United States, the attorney representing the government, whenever in his belief any business book, invoice, or paper * * * will tend to prove any allegation made by the United States, may make a written motion, particularly describing such book, invoice, or paper, and setting forth the allegation which he expects to prove; and thereupon the court in which suit or proceeding is pending may, at its discretion, issue a notice to the defendant or claimant to produce such book, invoice, or paper in court * * *; and if the defendant or claimant shall fail or refuse to produce such book, invoice, or paper in obedience to such notice, the allegations stated in the said motion shall be taken as confessed, unless his failure or refusal to produce the same shall be explained to the satisfaction of the court."

The defendants produced the invoice in compliance with the notice, but objected to the validity of the court's order, and objected again when the invoice was offered as evidence. The jury subsequently found for the United States, and a judgment of forfeiture against the 35 cases was granted.]

d. Professor Beale, at a later point in her article, sharply questioned the legitimacy of the use of the supervisory power in cases like *Schofield* and *Jacobs*. "Grand jury proceedings," she notes, "are a gray area in the margin of the federal courts' ancillary authority to establish procedural rules." Since grand jury subpoenas are issued pursuant to Fed.R.Crim.P. 17, the issue posed in *Schofield* might be resolved as an "interpretation or application of Rule 17" (which authorizes the district court to quash a subpoena found to be unreasonable or oppressive) or an application of the principle that "federal courts have implied authority to prevent misuse of their own processes." Where the limitations are adopted by the Circuit Court, however, the "difficult question [is raised] of the source of the appellate courts' authority to establish procedural rules for the district courts." *Jacobs* use of supervisory power was "even more difficult to justify" because it "was not directly related to the district court's authority to subpoena witness" but an attempt to supervise the relationship of attorneys within the executive branch. See also pp. 58–59 supra.

BRADLEY, J.,

* * * [I]n regard to Fourth Amendment, it is contended that * * * [the Act of 1874], under which the order in the present case was made, is free from constitutional objection, because it does not authorize the search and seizure of books and papers, but only requires the defendant or claimant to produce them. That is so; but it declares that if he does not produce them, the allegations which it is affirmed they will prove shall be taken as confessed. This is tantamount to compelling their production; for the prosecuting attorney will always be sure to state the evidence expected to be derived from them as strongly as the case will admit of. It is true that certain aggravating incidents of actual search and seizure, such as forcible entry into a man's house and searching amongst his papers, are wanting, and to this extent the proceeding under the act of 1874 is a mitigation of that which was authorized by the former acts; but it accomplishes the substantial object of those acts in forcing from a party evidence against himself. It is our opinion, therefore, that a compulsory production of a man's private papers to establish a criminal charge against him, or to forfeit his property, is within the scope of the Fourth Amendment to the Constitution, in all cases in which a search and seizure would be; because it is a material ingredient, and effects the sole object and purpose of search and seizure.

The principal question, however, remains to be considered. Is a search and seizure, or, what is equivalent thereto, a compulsory production of a man's private papers, to be used in evidence against him in a proceeding to forfeit his property for alleged fraud against the revenue laws—is such a proceeding for such a purpose an "*unreasonable* search and seizure" within the meaning of the Fourth Amendment of the Constitution? or, is it a legitimate proceeding? It is contended by the counsel for the government, that it is a legitimate proceeding, sanctioned by long usage, and the authority of judicial decision. No doubt long usage, acquiesced in by the courts, goes a long way to prove that there is some plausible ground or reason for it in the law, or in the historical facts which have imposed a particular construction of the law favorable to such usage. * * * But we do not find any long usage, or any contemporary construction of the Constitution, which would justify any of the acts of Congress now under consideration. As before stated, the [predecessor] act of 1863 was the first act in this country, and, we might say, either in this country or in England, so far as we have been able to ascertain, which authorized the search and seizure of a man's private papers, or the compulsory production of them, for the purpose of using them in evidence against him in a criminal case, or in a proceeding to enforce the forfeiture of his property. Even the act under which the obnoxious writs of assistance were issued did not go as far as this, but only authorized the examination of ships and vessels, and persons found therein, for the purpose of finding goods prohibited to be imported or exported, or on which the duties were not paid, and to enter into and search any suspected vaults, cellars, or warehouses for such goods. The search for and seizure of stolen or forfeited goods, or goods liable to duties and concealed to avoid the payment thereof, are totally different things from a search for and seizure of a man's private books and papers for the purpose of obtaining information therein contained, or of using them as evidence against him. The two things differ toto coelo. In the one case, the government is entitled to the possession of the property; in the other it is not. * * *

In order to ascertain the nature of the proceedings intended by the Fourth Amendment to the Constitution under the terms "unreasonable searches and seizures," it is only necessary to recall the contemporary or then recent history of the controversies on the subject, both in this country and in England. * * * Prominent and principal among these was the practice of issuing general warrants by the Secretary of State, for searching private houses for the discovery and seizure of books and papers that might be used to convict their owner of the charge of libel. Certain numbers of the *North Briton,* particularly No. 45, had been very bold in denunciation of the government, and were esteemed heinously libelous. By authority of the secretary's warrant Wilkes' house was searched, and his papers were indiscriminately seized. For this outrage he sued the perpetrators and obtained a verdict of £1,000 against Wood, one of the party who made the search, and £4,000 against Lord Halifax, the secretary of state who issued the warrant. The case, however, which will always be celebrated as being the occasion of Lord Camden's memorable discussion of the subject, was that of *Entick v. Carrington and Three Other King's Messengers,* reported at length in 19 Howell's State Trials, 1029. The action was trespass for entering the plaintiff's dwelling-house in November, 1762, and breaking open his desks, boxes, &c., and searching and examining his papers. The jury rendered a special verdict, and the case was twice solemnly argued at the bar. Lord Camden pronounced the judgment of the court in Michaelmas Term, 1765, and the law as expounded by him has been regarded as settled from that time to this, and his great judgment on that occasion is considered as one of the landmarks of English liberty. It was welcomed and applauded by the lovers of liberty in the colonies as well as in the mother country. It is regarded as one of the permanent monuments of the British Constitution, and is quoted as such by the English authorities on that subject down to the present time. As every American statesmen, during our revolutionary and formative period as a nation, was undoubtedly familiar with this monument of English freedom, and considered it as the true and ultimate expression of constitutional law, it may be confidently asserted that its propositions were in the minds of those who framed the Fourth Amendment to the Constitution, and were considered as sufficiently explanatory of what was meant by unreasonable searches and seizures. * * *

After describing the power claimed by the Secretary of State for issuing general search warrants, and the manner in which they were executed, Lord Camden says [in *Entick*]:

> * * * By the laws of England, every invasion of private property, be it ever so minute, is a trespass. No man can set his foot upon my ground without my license, but he is liable to an action though the damage be nothing; which is proved by every declaration in trespass where the defendant is called upon to answer for bruising the grass and even treading upon the soil. If he admits the fact, he is bound to show, by way of justification, that some positive law has justified or excused him. The justification is submitted to the judges, who are to look into the books, and see if such a justification can be maintained by the text of the statute law, or by the principles of the common law. If no such excuse can be found or produced, the silence of the books is an authority against the defendant, and the plaintiff must have judgment. According to this reasoning, it is now incumbent upon the defendants to show the law by which this seizure is warranted. If that cannot be done, it is a trespass.
>
> Papers are the owner's goods and chattels; they are his dearest property; and are so far from enduring a seizure, that they will hardly bear an inspection; and though the eye cannot by the laws of England be guilty of a trespass, yet where private papers are removed and carried away the secret nature of those goods will be an aggravation of the trespass, and demand more considerable damages in that respect. Where is the written law that gives any magistrate

such a power? I can safely answer, there is none; and therefore, it is too much for us, without such authority, to pronounce a practice legal which would be subversive of all the comforts of society. * * *

Lastly, it is urged as an argument of utility, that such a search is a means of detecting offenders by discovering evidence. I wish some cases had been shown, where the law forceth evidence out of the owner's custody by process. There is no process against papers in civil causes. It has been often tried, but never prevailed. Nay, where the adversary has by force or fraud got possession of your own proper evidence, there is no way to get it back but by action. In the criminal law such a proceeding was never heard of; and yet there are some crimes, such, for instance, as murder, rape, robbery, and house-breaking, to say nothing of forgery and perjury, that are more atrocious than libelling. But our law has provided no paper-search in these cases to help forward the conviction. Whether this proceedeth from the gentleness of the law towards criminals, or from a consideration that such a power would be more pernicious to the innocent than useful to the public, I will not say. It is very certain that the law obligeth no man to accuse himself; because the necessary means of compelling self-accusation, falling upon the innocent as well as the guilty, would be both cruel and unjust; and it would seem, that search for evidence is disallowed upon the same principle. Then, too, the innocent would be confounded with the guilty.

* * * The principles laid down in this opinion affect the very essence of constitutional liberty and security. They reach farther than the concrete form of the case then before the court, with its adventitious circumstances; they apply to all invasions on the part of the government and its employees of the sanctity of a man's home and the privacies of life. It is not the breaking of his doors, and the rummaging of his drawers, that constitutes the essence of the offence; but it is the invasion of his indefeasible right of personal security, personal liberty and private property, where that right has never been forfeited by his conviction of some public offence,—it is the invasion of this sacred right which underlies and constitutes the essence of Lord Camden's judgment. Breaking into a house and opening boxes and drawers are circumstances of aggravation; but any forcible and compulsory extortion of a man's own testimony or of his private papers to be used as evidence to convict him of crime or to forfeit his goods, is within the condemnation of that judgment. In this regard the Fourth and Fifth Amendments run almost into each other. * * *

Reverting then to the peculiar phraseology of this act, and to the information in the present case, which is founded on it, we have to deal with an act which expressly excludes criminal proceedings from its operation (though embracing civil suits for penalties and forfeitures), and with an information not technically a criminal proceeding, and neither, therefore, within the literal terms of the Fifth Amendment to the Constitution any more than it is within the literal terms of the Fourth. Does this relieve the proceedings or the law from being obnoxious to the prohibitions of either? We think not; we think they are within the spirit of both.

We have already noticed the intimate relation between the two amendments. They throw great light on each other. For the "unreasonable searches and seizures" condemned in the Fourth Amendment are almost always made for the purpose of compelling a man to give evidence against himself, which in criminal cases is condemned in the Fifth Amendment; and compelling a man "in a criminal case to be a witness against himself," which is condemned in the Fifth Amendment, throws light on the question as to what is an "unreasonable search and seizure" within the meaning of the Fourth Amendment. And we have been unable to perceive that the seizure of a man's private books and papers to be used in evidence against him is substantially different from compelling him to be a witness against himself. * * * We are also clearly of opinion that proceedings instituted for the purpose of declaring the forfeiture of a man's property by reason of offences committed by him, though they may be civil in form, are in their nature criminal. In this very case, the ground of forfeiture * * * consists of certain acts of fraud committed against the public revenue in relation to imported merchandise, which are made criminal by the statute * * *. As, therefore, suits for penalties and forfeitures incurred by the commission of offences against the law, are of this quasi-criminal nature, we think that they are within the reason of criminal proceedings for all the purposes of the Fourth Amendment of the Constitution, and of that portion of the Fifth Amendment which declares that no person shall be compelled in any criminal case to be a witness against himself; and we are further of opinion that a compulsory production of the private books and papers of the owner of goods sought to be forfeited in such a suit is compelling him to be a witness against himself, within the meaning of the Fifth Amendment to the Constitution, and is the equivalent of a search and seizure—and an unreasonable search and seizure—within the meaning of the Fourth Amendment.

Though the proceeding in question is divested of many of the aggravating incidents of actual search and seizure, yet, as before said, it contains their substance and essence, and effects their substantial purpose. It may be that it is the obnoxious thing in its mildest and least repulsive form; but illegitimate and unconstitutional practices get their first footing in that way, namely, by silent approaches and slight deviations from legal modes of procedure. This can only be obviated by adhering to the rule that constitutional provisions for the security of person and property should be liberally construed. A close and literal construction deprives them of half their efficacy, and leads to gradual depreciation of the right, as if it consisted more in sound than in substance. It is the duty of courts to be watchful for the constitutional rights of the citizen, and against any stealthy encroachments thereon. Their motto should be *obsta principiis.* * * *

MR. JUSTICE MILLER, with whom was THE CHIEF JUSTICE concurring:

I concur in the judgment of the court * * * and in so much of the opinion of this court as holds the 5th section of the act of 1874 void as applicable to the present case. * * * The order of the court under the statute is in effect a subpoena duces tecum, and, though the penalty for the witness's failure to appear in court with the criminating papers is not fine and imprisonment, it is one which may be made more severe, namely, to have charges against him of a criminal nature, taken for confessed, and made the foundation of the judgment of the court. That this is within the protection which the Constitution intended against compelling a person to be a witness against himself, is, I think, quite clear.

But this being so, there is no reason why this court should assume that the action of the court below, in requiring a party to produce certain papers as evidence on the trial, authorizes an unreasonable search or seizure of the house, papers, or effects of that party. There is in fact no search and no seizure authorized by the statute. No order can be made by the court under it which requires or permits anything more than service of notice on a party to the suit. * * *

Nothing in the nature of a search is here hinted at. Nor is there any seizure, because the party is not required at any time to part with the custody of the papers. They are to be produced in court, and, when produced, the United States attorney is permitted, under the direction of the court, to make examination in presence of the claimant, and may offer in evidence such entries in the books, invoices, or papers as relate to the issue. The act is careful to say that "the owner of said books and papers, his agent or attorney, shall have, subject to the order of the court, the custody of them, except pending their examination in court as aforesaid."

. . .

The things . . . forbidden [by the Fourth Amendment] are two—search and seizure. * * * But what search does this statute authorize? If the mere service of a notice to produce a paper to be used as evidence, which the party can obey or not as he chooses is a search, then a change has taken place in the meaning of words, which has not come within my reading, and which I think was unknown at the time the Constitution was made. The searches meant by the Constitution were such as led to seizure when the search was successful. But the statute in this case uses language carefully framed to forbid any seizure under it, as I have already pointed out. * * *

Notes and Questions

1. *The significance of Boyd.* *Boyd* was subsequently praised by commentators and courts as the landmark civil liberties case of its era, and its statement on the need for liberal construction of constitutional safeguards [see the last paragraph of the majority's opinion] has been quoted with approval in numerous Supreme Court opinions. Nonetheless, *Boyd*'s precise holding was soon subjected to question, and would be viewed today as clearly inconsistent with applicable precedent (see, e.g., *Bellis*, p. 749 infra, and Note 4 infra). Moreover, much of its underlying analysis of the Fourth Amendment, the Fifth Amendment, and the relationship between the two, has been rejected. While that analysis reflects what might be described as a "false start," the Court has struggled with that start ever since. See, e.g., *Fisher v. United States,* p. 757 infra. Consider also Note, 76 Mich.L.Rev. 212 (1977) ("*Boyd* is dead," but a case which Justice Brandeis described as one "that will be remembered as long as civil liberty lives in the United States" deserves the "decent burial" that the Court has never given it).

2. *Boyd* has been described as a product of "nineteenth century legal formalism" that was founded on "the view that adjudication proceeds by deduction from virtually absolute legal principles rooted in natural law and enshrined in both the common law and the Constitution." Note, 90 Harv.L.Rev. 943 (1977). It is said to have rested on "two fundamental principles which formed an impenetrable boundary around the individual's sphere of privacy as defined by his common law property rights and his privilege against self-incrimination. The Fourth Amendment prohibited the government from seizing and using as evidence the defendant's personal books and papers because they are articles of personal property; the Fifth Amendment added a second layer of protection for books and papers which might tend to incriminate the owner." Id. at 955. As suggested by the same author, the jurisprudential approach of *Boyd* contrasts with the "more pragmatic and relativist vision of the law" associated with constitutional developments since the 1930's. Do the Court's subsequent decisions (discussed below as to the Fourth Amendment and in section 3 as to the Fifth Amendment) simply reflect this difference in approach or do they suggest a more basic disagreement with the substantive values that *Boyd* sought to protect? See also J.B. White, *Forgotten Points in the "Exclusionary Rule" Debate,* 81 Mich.L.Rev. 1273 (1983) (contrasting the "deterrence rationale" stressed in recent exclusionary rule decisions with *Boyd*'s view of exclusion as a necessary consequence of the Fourth Amendment's protection of private property).

3. *Hale v. Henkel (the introduction of the overbreadth doctrine).* Insofar as *Boyd* suggested that the Fourth Amendment prohib-

ited searches for property the defendant was entitled to possess (i.e., property other than the fruits or instrumentalities of crime), that aspect of *Boyd* was flatly rejected in *Warden v. Hayden* [p.253 supra] decided in 1967. Insofar as *Boyd* read the Fourth Amendment as prohibiting a search for documents, that interpretation was overturned in *Andresen v. Maryland* [p. 253 supra] decided in 1976. But long before these decisions, the Court restructured *Boyd* 's view of the bearing of the Fourth Amendment upon a subpoena duces tecum. In HALE v. HENKEL, 201 U.S. 43, 26 S.Ct. 370, 50 L.Ed. 652 (1906), the Court had before it a challenge to a subpoena directing the petitioner to produce before a grand jury (which was conducting an investigation into possible violations of the antitrust laws) various corporate documents. Petitioner's challenge was based on the combined impact of the Fourth and Fifth Amendments, but the Court initially separated those claims. Cases subsequent to *Boyd,* it noted, had "treated the Fourth and Fifth Amendments as quite distinct, having different histories, and performing separate functions." Turning first to the petitioner's self-incrimination claim, the Court found that claim clearly failed since the statute authorizing the subpoena granted petitioner immunity from prosecution (see p. 745 infra) and the corporation itself had no self-incrimination privilege (see p. 750 infra). The petitioner's Fourth Amendment claim did have merit, but for reasons other than what might have been assumed from *Boyd.* Speaking for the Court, BROWN, J., noted:

"Although * * * we are of the opinion that an officer of a corporation * * * cannot refuse to produce the books and papers of such corporation, we do not wish to be understood as holding that a corporation is not entitled to immunity, under the Fourth Amendment, against *unreasonable* searches and seizures. A corporation is, after all, but an association of individuals under an assumed name and with a distinct legal entity. In organizing itself as a collective body it waives no constitutional immunities appropriate to such body. * * * We are also of opinion that an order for the production of books and papers may constitute an unreasonable search and seizure within the Fourth Amendment. While a search ordinarily implies a quest by an officer of the law, and a seizure contemplates a forcible dispossession of the owner, still, as was held in the *Boyd* case, the substance of the offense is the compulsory production of private papers, whether under a search warrant or a subpoena duces tecum, against which the person, be he individual or corporation, is entitled to protection. Applying the test of reasonableness to the present case, we think the subpoena duces tecum is far too sweeping in its terms to be regarded as reasonable. It does not require the production of a single contract, or of contracts with a particular corporation, or a limited number of documents, but all understandings, contracts, or correspondence between the MacAndrews & Forbes Company, and no less than six different companies, as well as all reports made, and accounts rendered by such companies from the date of the organization of the MacAndrews & Forbes Company, as well as all letters received by that company since its organization from more than a dozen different companies, situated in seven different States in the Union.

"If the writ had required the production of all the books, papers and documents found in the office of the MacAndrews & Forbes Company, it would scarcely be more universal in its operation, or more completely put a stop to the business of that company. Indeed, it is difficult to say how its business could be carried on after it had been denuded of this mass of material, which is not shown to be necessary in the prosecution of this case, and is clearly in violation of the general principle of law with regard to the particularity required in the description of documents necessary to a search warrant or subpoena. Doubtless many, if not all, of these documents may ultimately be required, but some necessity should be shown, either from an examination of the witnesses orally, or from the known transactions of these companies with the other companies implicated, or some evidence of their materiality produced, to justify an order for the production of such a mass of papers. A general subpoena of this description is equally indefensible as a search warrant would be if couched in similar terms."

McKENNA, J., concurring separately in *Hale,* questioned the Court's Fourth Amendment analysis: "It is said 'a search implies a quest by an officer of the law; a seizure contemplates a forcible dispossession of the owner.' Nothing can be more direct and plain; nothing more expressive to distinguish a subpoena from a search warrant. Can a subpoena lose this essential distinction from a search warrant by the generality or speciality of its terms? I think not. The distinction is based upon what is authorized or directed to be done—not upon the form of words by which the authority or command is given. 'The quest of an officer' acts upon the things themselves—may be secret, intrusive, accompanied by force. The service of a subpoena is but the delivery of a paper to a party—is open and aboveboard. There is no element of trespass or force in it. It does not disturb the possession of property. It cannot be finally enforced except after challenge, and a judgment of the court upon the challenge. This is a safeguard against abuse the same as it is of other processes of the law, and it is all that can be allowed without serious embarrassment to the administration of justice. Of course, it constrains the will of parties, subjects their property to the uses of proof. But we are surely not prepared to say that such uses are unreasonable or are sacrifices which the law may not demand."

4. *Explaining the overbreadth doctrine.* As Judge Friendly noted in *In re Horowitz,* 482 F.2d 72 (2d Cir.1973), "the Fourth Amendment portion of the *Boyd* decision was surely not based on the overbreadth of the Government's demand; the Government [there] sought only a single invoice of unquestionable relevance." Although relying on *Boyd, Hale v. Henkel*

> left the applicability of the Fourth Amendment to subpoena duces tecum in a most confusing state. None of the Justices seemed to think that such a subpoena could be issued only "upon probable cause, supported by oath or affirmation," as would be required for a search warrant. Nevertheless, except for Mr. Justice McKenna, all were of the view that an overbroad subpoena duces tecum against an individual would be an unreasonable search and seizure.

Judge Friendly suggested in *Horowitz* that the overbreadth doctrine of *Hale* might find firmer support in the due process clause than in the Fourth Amendment. Although a due process grounding for the doctrine is suggested in *Oklahoma Press Publishing Co. v. Walling,* 327 U.S. 186, 66 S.Ct. 494, 90 L.Ed. 614 (1946) (a leading case on the application of the overbreadth doctrine to administrative agency subpoena [a]), later cases have referred to the doctrine as based on the Fourth Amendment. See e.g., *United States v. Dionisio,* p. 716 infra.

Accepting the Court's premise that the Fourth Amendment does apply to the subpoena duces tecum, why should the overbreadth doctrine be the sole Fourth

a. Speaking to petitioner's claim that enforcement of the subpoena duces tecum would violate rights secured by the Fourth Amendment, Justice Rutledge noted that the "short answer" to this contention was that "these cases present no question of actual search and seizure" as they involved no attempt by government officials "to enter petitioners' premises against their will, to search them, or to seize or examine their books." He later added: "The primary source of misconception concerning the Fourth Amendment's function lies perhaps in the identification of cases involving so-called 'figurative' or 'constructive' search with cases of actual search and seizure. Only in this analogical sense can any question related to search and seizure be thought to arise in situations which, like the present ones, involve only the validity of authorized judicial orders."

Amendment limitation as to the subpoena duces tecum? Does *Hale* reflect a determination that the requirements of the Fourth Amendment's warrant clause were inapplicable in light of the long history of subpoenas issued without regard to probable cause (particularly in the trial context, see Fed.R.Crim.P. 17) and the lesser intrusion upon privacy (as compared to the traditional search), thereby leaving applicable only the Fourth Amendment's general mandate of reasonableness? See LaFave, § 4.13(e). If so, *Hale* would be the forerunner of the various regulatory search cases that have eliminated the probable cause requirements for such searches. See Ch. 5, § 9. Consider also the suggestion that "the Court may have viewed a subpoena as falling within the Fourth Amendment only when it was clearly overbroad and thereby had the effect of a physical search in allowing the government to sift through a mass of documents while looking for the few that might be relevant." LaFave and Israel, § 8.7(a).

5. *Applying the overbreadth doctrine.* Lower courts applying the overbreadth doctrine in the grand jury setting frequently note that the doctrine requires a fact-specific judgment, with each ruling tied to the circumstances of the individual case. At the same time, they have sought to develop some general criteria to guide their judgment. Initially, the subpoena carries with it a presumption of regularity that will be called into question only if the subpoena has "sufficient breadth to suggest either that compliance will be burdensome or that the subpoena's scope may not have been shaped to the purposes of the inquiry." LaFave and Israel, § 8.7(c). If it has such breadth, the courts will then examine its scope in light of three criteria: (1) whether it "commands only the production of documents relevant to the investigation being pursued"; (2) whether the specification of the documents is made with "reasonable particularity" (measured in terms of both the subpoenaed party's ability to identify what "he is being asked to produce" and any "unreasonable business detriment" flowing from the quantity and range of the documents requested [b]); and (3) whether the documents to be produced cover "only a reasonable period of time." See *In re Grand Jury Subpoena Duces Tecum (Corrado Brothers),* 367 F.Supp. 1126 (D.Del.1973). Applying these criteria, Courts have upheld subpoenas requiring production of as much as 50 tons of documents. See *Petition of Borden,* 75 F.Supp. 857 (N.D.Ill.1948); yet they also have rejected requests for records that presumably could have occupied no more than a single filing cabinet, see *In re Certain Chinese Family Benevolent Assoc.,* 19 F.R.D. 97 (N.D.Cal.1956) (rejecting subpoenas requiring various Chinese family associations to produce available membership lists, income records, and membership photographs, dating back to the association's origin, for use in an investigation of immigration fraud). Much depends upon the nature of the investigation, as courts recognize that certain types of investigations, such as antitrust, necessarily demand a broader range of documents since the violation may be reflected in many aspects of a company's business. See also *Corrado Brothers,* supra (where the grand jury was investigating a kickback scheme involving the government highway department, all financial records were relevant since "cash for kickbacks can be readily generated by padding the * * * accounting records relating to a totally unrelated party").

b. Consider, however, LaFave and Israel, § 8.7(c): "Objections to a subpoena duces tecum based solely upon the burden and expense of assembling a large quantity of records are almost always doomed to failure. With the advent of photocopying, the possibility that the subpoenaed party will be unable to carry on its business without the relinquished records—a major concern in *Hale*—is largely mooted. Courts commonly have viewed the expense of assembling and duplicating the materials as simply another cost of doing business, particularly where the subpoenaed party is a large corporation. Moreover, in cases where the expense imposes a true financial hardship, the government may respond by offering reimbursement of all costs."

Courts recognize also that "some exploration or fishing necessarily is inherent" since the grand jury will not ordinarily have a "catalogue of what books or papers exist" nor any basis for knowing what their character or contents immediately are." *Schwimmer v. United States,* 232 F.2d 855 (8th Cir.1956).

6. *The subpoena ad testificandum.* The overbreadth doctrine is generally viewed as limited to subpoena duces tecum. If a person subpoenaed to testify is examined on a wide range of subjects, he may not raise a Fourth Amendment objection to the scope of the examination. Why the difference? Consider *United States v. Dionisio,* infra.

UNITED STATES v. DIONISIO

410 U.S. 1, 93 S.Ct. 764, 35 L.Ed.2d 67 (1973).

MR. JUSTICE STEWART delivered the opinion of the Court.

A special grand jury was convened in the Northern District of Illinois in February 1971, to investigate possible violations of federal criminal statutes relating to gambling. In the course of its investigation the grand jury received in evidence certain voice recordings that had been obtained pursuant to court orders. The grand jury subpoenaed approximately 20 persons, including the respondent Dionisio, seeking to obtain from them voice exemplars for comparison with the recorded conversations that had been received in evidence. Each witness was advised that he was a potential defendant in a criminal prosecution. Each was asked to examine a transcript of an intercepted conversation, and to go to a nearby office of the United States Attorney to read the transcript into a recording device. The witnesses were advised that they would be allowed to have their attorneys present when they read the transcripts. Dionisio and other witnesses refused to furnish the voice exemplars, asserting that these disclosures would violate their rights under the Fourth and Fifth Amendments. The Government then filed separate petitions in the District Court to compel Dionisio and the other witnesses to furnish the voice exemplars to the grand jury. * * * Following a hearing, the district judge rejected the witnesses' constitutional arguments and ordered them to comply with the grand jury's request. * * * When Dionisio persisted in his refusal to respond to the grand jury's directive, the District Court adjudged him in civil contempt and ordered him committed to custody. * * *

The Court of Appeals for the Seventh Circuit reversed. * * * The court found that the Fourth Amendment applied to the grand jury process * * *. Equating the procedures followed by the grand jury in the present case to the fingerprint detentions in *Davis v. Mississippi* [p. 383 supra], the Court of Appeals reasoned that "[t]he dragnet effect here, where approximately 30 persons were subpoenaed for purposes of identification, has the same invidious effect on fourth amendment rights as the practice condemned in *Davis.*" The Court of Appeals held that the Fourth Amendment required a preliminary showing of reasonableness before a grand jury witness could be compelled to furnish a voice exemplar, and that in this case the proposed "seizures" of the voice exemplars would be unreasonable because of the large number of witnesses summoned by the grand jury and directed to produce such exemplars. We disagree. * * *

As [this] Court made clear in *Schmerber v. California* [p. 397 supra], the obtaining of physical evidence from a person involves a potential Fourth Amendment violation at two different levels—the "seizure" of the "person" necessary to bring him into contact with government agents, see *Davis v. Mississippi,* and the subsequent search for and seizure of the evidence. * * * The constitutionality of the compulsory production of exemplars from a grand jury witness necessarily turns on the same dual inquiry—whether either the initial compulsion of the person to appear before the grand jury, or the subsequent directive to make a voice recording is an unreasonable "seizure" within the meaning of the Fourth Amendment.

It is clear that a subpoena to appear before a grand jury is not a "seizure" in the Fourth Amendment sense, even though that summons may be inconvenient or burdensome. Last Term we again acknowledged what has long been recognized, that "[c]itizens generally are not constitutionally immune from grand jury subpoenas. . . . " *Branzburg v. Hayes* [p. 724 infra]. * * * [*Branzburg* and other decisions] are recent reaffirmations of the historically grounded obligations of every person to appear and give his evidence before the grand jury. "The personal sacrifice involved is a part of the necessary contribution of the individual to the welfare of the public." *Blair v. United States.*

The compulsion exerted by a grand jury subpoena differs from the seizure effected by an arrest or even an investigative "stop" in more than civic obligation. For, as Judge Friendly wrote for the Court of Appeals for the Second Circuit:

> "The latter is abrupt, is effected with force or the threat of it and often in demeaning circumstances, and, in the case of arrest, results in a record involving social stigma. A subpoena is served in the same manner as other legal process; it involves no stigma whatever; if the time for appearance is inconvenient, this can generally be altered; and it remains at all times under the control and supervision of a court." *United States v. Doe (Schwartz)* 457 F.2d 895, 898 (1972).

Thus, the Court of Appeals for the Seventh Circuit correctly recognized in a case subsequent to the one now before us, that a "grand jury subpoena to testify is not that kind of governmental intrusion on privacy against which the Fourth Amendment affords protection, once the Fifth Amendment is satisfied." *Fraser v. United States,* 452 F.2d 616, 620 (1972).

This case is thus quite different from *Davis v. Mississippi,* on which the Court of Appeals primarily relied. For in *Davis* it was the initial seizure—the lawless dragnet detention—that violated the Fourth and Fourteenth Amendments—not the taking of the fingerprints. * * * *Davis* is plainly inapposite to a case where the initial restraint does not itself infringe the Fourth Amendment.

This is not to say that a grand jury subpoena is some talisman that dissolves all constitutional protections. The grand jury cannot require a witness to testify against himself. It cannot require the production by a person of private books and records that would incriminate him. See *Boyd v. United States.* The Fourth Amendment provides protection against a grand jury subpoena *duces tecum* too sweeping in its terms "to be regarded as reasonable." *Hale v. Henkel.* And last Term, in the context of a First Amendment claim, we indicated that the Constitution could not tolerate the transformation of the grand jury into an instrument of oppression: "Official harassment of the press undertaken not for purposes of law enforcement but to disrupt a reporter's relationship with his news sources would have no justification. Grand juries are subject to judicial control and subpoenas to motions to quash. We do not expect courts will forget that grand juries must operate within the limits of the First Amendment as well as the Fifth." *Branzburg v. Hayes.*

But we are here faced with no such constitutional infirmities in the subpoena to appear before the grand jury or in the order to make the voice recordings. There is * * * no valid Fifth Amendment claim. There was no order to produce private books and papers, and no sweeping subpoena *duces tecum.* And even if *Branzburg* be extended beyond its First Amendment moorings and tied to a more generalized due process concept, there is still no indication in this case of the kind of harassment that was of concern there.

The Court of Appeals found critical significance in the fact that the grand jury had summoned approximately 20 witnesses to furnish voice exemplars. We think that fact is basically irrelevant to the constitutional issues here. The grand jury may have been attempting to identify a number of voices on the tapes in evidence, or it might have summoned the 20 witnesses in an effort to identify one voice. But whatever the case, "[a] grand jury's investigation is not fully carried out until every available clue has been run down and all witnesses examined in every proper way to find if a crime has been committed . . . ." *United States v. Stone,* 429 F.2d 138, 140 (2d Cir.1970). * * * The grand jury may well find it desirable to call numerous witnesses in the course of an investigation. It does not follow that each witness may resist a subpoena on the ground that too many witnesses have been called. Neither the order to Dionisio to appear, nor the order to make a voice recording was rendered unreasonable by the fact that many others were subjected to the same compulsion.

But the conclusion that Dionisio's compulsory appearance before the grand jury was not an unreasonable "seizure" is the answer to only the first part of the Fourth Amendment inquiry here. Dionisio argues that the grand jury's subsequent directive to make the voice recording was itself an infringement of his rights under the Fourth Amendment. We cannot accept that argument. In *Katz v. United States* [p. 237 supra], we said that the Fourth Amendment provides no protection for what "a person knowingly exposes to the public, even in his home or office . . . ." The physical characteristics of a person's voice, its tone and manner, as opposed to the content of a specific conversation, are constantly exposed to the public. Like a man's facial characteristics, or handwriting, his voice is repeatedly produced for others to hear. No person can have a reasonable expectation that others will not know the sound of his voice, any more than he can reasonably expect that his face will be a mystery to the world. * * *

Since neither the summons to appear before the grand jury, nor its directive to make a voice recording infringed upon any interest protected by the Fourth Amendment, there was no justification for requiring the grand jury to satisfy even the minimal requirement of "reasonableness" imposed by the Court of Appeals. A grand jury has broad investigative powers to determine whether a crime has been committed and who has committed it. The jurors may act on tips, rumors, evidence offered by the prosecutor, or their own personal knowledge. *Branzburg v. Hayes.* No grand jury witness is "entitled to set limits to the investigation that the grand jury may conduct." *Blair v. United States.* And a sufficient basis for an indictment may only emerge at the end of the investigation when all the evidence has been received. * * * Since Dionisio raised no valid Fourth Amendment claim, there is no more reason to require a preliminary showing of reasonableness here than there would be in the case of any witness who, despite the lack of any constitutional or statutory privilege, declined to answer a question or comply with a grand jury request. Neither the Constitution nor our prior cases justify any such interference with grand jury proceedings.[14]

14. Mr. Justice Marshall in dissent suggests that a preliminary showing of "reasonableness" is required where the grand jury subpoenas a witness to appear and produce handwriting or voice exemplars, but not when it subpoenas him to appear and testify. Such a distinction finds no support in the Constitution. The dissent argues that there is a potential Fourth Amendment violation in the case of a subpoenaed grand jury witness because of the asserted intrusiveness of the initial subpoena to appear—the possible stigma from a grand jury appearance and the inconvenience of the official restraint. But the initial directive to appear is as intrusive if the witness is called simply to testify as it is if he is summoned to produce physical evidence.

The Fifth Amendment guarantees that no civilian may be brought to trial for an infamous crime "unless on a presentment or indictment of a Grand Jury." This constitutional guarantee presupposes an investigative body "acting independently of either prosecuting attorney or judge," *Stirone v. United States,* 361 U.S. 212, 218, 80 S.Ct. 270, 273, 4 L.Ed.2d 252 (1960), whose mission is to clear the innocent, no less than to bring to trial those who may be guilty. Any holding that would saddle a grand jury with minitrials and preliminary showing would assuredly impede its investigation and frustrate the public's interest in the fair and expeditious administration of the criminal laws.[16] The grand jury may not always serve its historic role as a protective bulwark standing solidly between the ordinary citizen and an overzealous prosecutor, but if it is even to approach the proper performance of its constitutional mission, it must be free to pursue its investigations unhindered by external influence or supervision so long as it does not trench upon the legitimate rights of any witness called before it. * * *

MR. JUSTICE MARSHALL, dissenting.[a]

* * * There can be no question that investigatory seizures effected by the police are subject to the constraints of the Fourth and Fourteenth Amendments. *Davis v. Mississippi.* * * * Like *Davis,* the present cases involve official investigatory seizures which interfere with personal liberty. The Court considers dispositive, however, the fact that the seizures were effected by the grand jury, rather than the police. I cannot agree. * * * [I]n *Hale v. Henkel,* the Court held that a subpoena *duces tecum* ordering "the production of books and papers [before a grand jury] may constitute an unreasonable search and seizure within the Fourth Amendment," and on the particular facts of the case, it concluded that the subpoena was "far too sweeping in its terms to be regarded as reasonable." Considered alone, *Hale* would certainly seem to carry a strong implication that a subpoena compelling an individual's personal appearance before a grand jury, like a subpoena ordering the production of private papers, is subject to the Fourth Amendment standard of reasonableness. The protection of the Fourth Amendment is not, after all, limited to personal "papers," but extends also to "persons," "houses," and "effects." It would seem a strange hierarchy of constitutional values that would afford papers more protection from arbitrary governmental intrusion than people.

The Court, however, offers two interrelated justifications for excepting grand jury subpoenas directed at "persons," rather than "papers," from the constraints of the Fourth Amendment. These are an "historically grounded obligation of every person to appear and give his evidence before the grand jury" [p. 716 supra], and the relative unintrusiveness of the grand jury subpoena on an individual's liberty.

In my view, the Court makes more of history than is justified. The Court treats the "historically grounded obligation" which it now discerns as extending to all "evidence," whatever its character. Yet, so far as I am aware, the obligation "to appear and give evidence" has heretofore been applied by this Court only in the context of testimonial evidence, either oral or documentary. Certainly the decisions

16. The possibilities for delay caused by requiring initial showings of "reasonableness" are illustrated by the Court of Appeals' subsequent decision in *In re September 1971 Grand Jury,* 7 Cir., 454 F.2d 580, rev'd *sub nom United States v. Mara,* 410 U.S. 19, 93 S.Ct. 774, 35 L.Ed.2d 99, where the Court held that the Government was required to show in an adversary hearing that its request for exemplars was reasonable, and "reasonableness" included proof that the exemplars could not be obtained from other sources.

a. In the companion case of *United States v. Mara,* n. 16 supra, the Court applied *Dionisio* to reject a lower court ruling that a preliminary showing of reasonableness was needed to justify a grand jury subpoena directing a witness to produce handwriting exemplars for the purpose of determining whether he was the author of certain writings. Justice Marshall's dissent was to both rulings. The separate dissents of Justices Douglas and Brennan are omitted.

relied upon by the Court, despite some dicta, have not recognized an obligation of a broader sweep. * * * In the present case, * * * it was not testimony that the grand jury sought from respondents, but physical evidence. The Court glosses over this important distinction from its prior decisions, however, by artificially bifurcating its analysis of what is taking place in these cases—that is, by effectively treating what is done with individuals once they are before the grand jury as irrelevant in determining what safeguards are to govern the procedures by which they are initially compelled to appear. Nonetheless, the fact remains that the historic exception to which the Court resorts is not necessarily as broad as the context in which it is now employed. Hence, I believe that the question we must consider is whether an extension of that exception is warranted, and if so, under what conditions. * * *

The Court seems to reason that the exception to the Fourth Amendment for grand jury subpoenas directed at persons is justified by the relative unintrusiveness of the grand jury process on an individual's liberty. * * * It may be that service of a grand jury subpoena does not involve the same potential for momentary embarrassment as does an arrest or investigatory "stop." But this difference seems inconsequential in comparison to the substantial stigma which—contrary to the Court's assertion—may result from a grand jury appearance as well as from an arrest or investigatory seizure. Public knowledge that a man has been summoned by a federal grand jury investigating, for instance, organized criminal activity can mean loss of friends, irreparable injury to business, and tremendous pressures on one's family life. Whatever nice legal distinctions may be drawn between police and prosecutor, on the one hand, and the grand jury, on the other, the public often treats an appearance before a grand jury as tantamount to a visit to the station house. Indeed, the former is frequently more damaging than the latter, for a grand jury appearance has an air of far greater gravity than a brief visit "downtown" for a "talk." The Fourth Amendment was placed in our Bill of Rights to protect the individual citizen from such potentially disruptive governmental intrusion into his private life unless conducted reasonably and with sufficient cause.

Nor do I believe that the constitutional problems inherent in such governmental interference with an individual's person are substantially alleviated because one may seek to appear at a "convenient time." In *Davis v. Mississippi,* it was recognized that an investigatory detention effected by the police "need not come unexpectedly or at an inconvenient time." But this fact did not suggest to the Court that the Fourth Amendment was inapplicable * * *. No matter how considerate a grand jury may be in arranging for an individual's appearance, the basic fact remains that his liberty has been officially restrained for some period of time. In terms of its effect on the individual, this restraint does not differ meaningfully from the restraint imposed on a suspect compelled to visit the police station house. Thus, the nature of the intrusion on personal liberty caused by a grand jury subpoena cannot, without more, be considered sufficient basis for denying respondents the protection of the Fourth Amendment.

Of course, the Fourth Amendment does not bar all official seizures of the person, but only those that are unreasonable and are without sufficient cause. With this in mind, it is possible at least to explain, if not justify, the failure to apply the protection of the Fourth Amendment to grand jury subpoenas requiring individuals to appear and *testify.* Thus, while it is true that we have traditionally given the grand jury broad investigatory powers, particularly in terms of compelling the appearance of persons before it, *Blair v. United States,* it must be understood that we have done so in heavy reliance on certain essential assumptions.

Certainly the most celebrated function of the grand jury is to stand between the Government and the citizen and thus to protect the latter from harassment and unfounded prosecution. The grand jury does not shed those characteristics which give it insulating qualities when it acts in its investigative capacity. Properly functioning, the grand jury is to be the servant of neither the Government nor the courts, but of the people. As such, we assume that it comes to its task without bias or self-interest. Unlike the prosecutor or policeman, it has no election to win or executive appointment to keep. The anticipated neutrality of the grand jury, even when acting in its investigative capacity, may perhaps be relied upon to prevent unwarranted interference with the lives of private citizens and to ensure that the grand jury's subpoena powers over the person are exercised in only a reasonable fashion. Under such circumstances, it may be justifiable to give the grand jury broad personal subpoena powers that are outside the purview of the Fourth Amendment, for—in contrast to the police—it is not likely that it will abuse those powers.

Whatever the present day validity of the historical assumption of neutrality which underlies the grand jury process, it must at least be recognized that if a grand jury is deprived of the independence essential to the assumption of neutrality—if it effectively surrenders that independence to a prosecutor—the dangers of excessive and unreasonable official interference with personal liberty are exactly those which the Fourth Amendment was intended to prevent. So long as the grand jury carries on its investigatory activities only through the mechanism of testimonial inquiries, the danger of such official usurpation of the grand jury process may not be unreasonably great. Individuals called to testify before the grand jury will have available their Fifth Amendment privilege against self-incrimination. Thus, at least insofar as incriminating information is sought directly from a particular criminal suspect, the grand jury process would not appear to offer law enforcement officials a substantial advantage over ordinary investigative techniques.

But when we move beyond the realm of grand jury investigations limited to testimonial inquiries, as the Court does today, the danger increases that law enforcement officials may seek to usurp the grand jury process for the purpose of securing incriminating evidence from a particular suspect through the simple expedient of a subpoena. * * * Thus, if the grand jury may summon criminal suspects [to obtain handwriting and voice exemplars] without complying with the Fourth Amendment, it will obviously present an attractive investigative tool to prosecutor and police. For what law enforcement officers could not accomplish directly themselves after our decision in *Davis v. Mississippi,* they may now accomplish indirectly through the grand jury process.

Thus, the Court's decisions today can serve only to encourage prosecutorial exploitation of the grand jury process, at the expense of both individual liberty and the traditional neutrality of the grand jury. * * * [B]y holding that the grand jury's power to subpoena these respondents for the purpose of obtaining exemplars is completely outside the purview of the Fourth Amendment, the Court fails to appreciate the essential difference between real and testimonial evidence in the context of these cases, and thereby hastens the reduction of the grand jury into simply another investigative device of law enforcement officials. By contrast, the Court of Appeals, in proper recognition of these dangers, imposed narrow limitations on the subpoena power of the grand jury which are necessary to guard against unreasonable official interference with individual liberty but which would not impair significantly the traditional investigatory powers of that body.

The Court of Appeals did not impose a requirement that the Government establish probable cause to support a grand jury's request for exemplars. It correctly recognized that "examination of witnesses by a grand jury need not be preceded by a formal charge against a particular individual," since the very purpose of the grand jury process is to ascertain probable cause. See *Blair v. United States.* * * * [It] ruled only that the request for physical evidence such as exemplars should be subject to a showing of reasonableness. This "reasonableness" requirement has previously been explained by this Court, albeit in a somewhat different context, to require a showing by the Government that: (1) "the investigation is authorized by Congress"; (2) the investigation "is for a purpose Congress can order"; (3) the evidence sought is "relevant"; and (4) the request is "adequate, but not excessive, for the purposes of the relevant inquiry." See *Oklahoma Press Pub. Co. v. Walling* [p. 713 supra]. This was the interpretation of the "reasonableness" requirement properly adopted by the Court of Appeals. And, in elaborating on the requirement that the request not be "excessive," it added that the Government would bear the burden of showing that it was not conducting "a mere general fishing expedition under grand jury sponsorship." These are not burdensome limitations to impose on the grand jury when it seeks to secure physical evidence, such as exemplars, that has traditionally been gathered directly by law enforcement officials. * * *

Notes and Questions

1. *Subpoenas and "seizures."* Are there any circumstances under which a grand jury subpoena might be viewed as producing "a 'seizure' in the Fourth Amendment sense" (see *Dionisio* at p. 716 supra)? What if the subpoena directs the petitioner to appear in a lineup? See *In re Melvin,* 550 F.2d 674 (1st Cir.1977) (while a lineup appearance may be more "inconvenient and burdensome" than providing a handwriting or voice exemplar, *Dionisio* nevertheless applies). But cf. *In re Kelley,* Note 2 infra. What if the subpoena requires that the individual subpoenaed appear "forthwith" before the grand jury? Consider *United States v. Re,* 313 F.Supp. 442 (S.D.N.Y.1970) (direction of a subpoena duces tecum "to produce documents forthwith" is not "*per se* invalid"; use of "forthwith" subpoena justified where witness was relative of the investigation's target and allowing more time to comply might permit alteration of the documents); *In re Nwamu,* 421 F.Supp. 1361 (S.D.N.Y. 1976) (where an F.B.I. agent, upon serving a "forthwith" subpoena duces tecum, demanded that the subpoenaed items be surrendered immediately to him, the agent's taking of the items constituted an unreasonable search and seizure; the crucial quality of a subpoena—that it permit an opportunity to challenge it in court—had been foreclosed by agent's demands).

2. *Dionisio and police investigations.* In *In re Kelley,* 433 A.2d 704 (D.C.App. 1981) (en banc), appellant had been subpoenaed to appear before a grand jury investigating an alleged arson. While there, he was served to appear in a lineup at police headquarters, but refused to do so in the absence of a prosecution showing of a reasonable basis for linking him with the arson. Finding his objection well taken, the court, per GALLAGHER, J., reasoned:

"In earlier years in this jurisdiction, and others as well, in order to obtain a lineup order the investigating officer was required to have probable cause to arrest. With the advent of *Wise v. Murphy,* 275 A.2d 205 (D.C.App.1971), that standard was lessened. Wise held that in order to obtain a lineup order the government need only articulate, as in *Terry v. Ohio* [p. 361 supra], reasons why a lineup order is reasonable. Thus, it was no longer necessary to display probable cause to arrest but only reason to suspect. Now, we must decide whether no showing whatsoever need be made by the government to obtain judicial enforcement of a lineup order emanating from the grand jury. This is a large leap to make in one decade—to move from a required showing of probable cause to arrest to no showing at all.

"The government candidly told us at oral argument that it has put our decision in *Wise v. Murphy,* supra, in 'mothballs.' The *Wise v. Murphy* procedure has been invoked when police investigators sought a lineup order in aid of their investigation of a crime. As related at oral argument, due to the intervening Supreme Court decisions in *United States v. Dionisio* and *United States v. Mara,* the government ignores the *Wise v. Murphy* procedure. The government now passes such police requests through the grand jury and thereby obtains grand jury lineup directives. By this grand jury 'pass-through' technique, the government avoids making even the moderate showing on the reasonableness of the lineup order required by our decision in *Wise v. Murphy.* The government essentially contends that this 'pass-through' procedure was validated by *United States v. Dionisio.* We do not think so. * * * [T]hose cases held only that the Fourth Amendment is not infringed upon by a summons to appear before a grand jury nor by any order to supply it with evidence of physical characteristics. * * * A lineup appearance is not simply showing one's face to the public. It involves considerable social stigma and personal risk. It entails the humiliation of standing on a stage under floodlights, removed from counsel, subject to being compelled to speak certain words and perform actions directed by the police, all at considerably more risk of mistake and misidentification than the more scientifically grounded fingerprinting and, to some extent, voiceprinting techniques involved in *Dionisio* and *Mara.* * * *

"We conclude, however, that this issue should be decided on non-constitutional grounds. Instead, we invoke our inherent supervisory power over the Superior Court, which in turn supervises the grand jury. The government acknowledges that subsequent to the Supreme Court decisions in *Dionisio* and *Mara,* it has utilized the grand jury process to obtain lineup orders, thus avoiding the moderate showing of reasonableness required by *Wise* when the prosecutor alone seeks a lineup order. We are concerned here, therefore, with avoiding the appearance of, or the potential for, abuse of the grand jury system which may result from a commingling of the separate responsibilities of grand jury, prosecutor, and judge. Consequently, to insure that the prosecutor and the grand jury are acting in good faith and not arbitrarily or to harass putative defendants, we hold that a prosecutor seeking judicial enforcement of a grand jury directive to appear in a lineup must, by affidavit of law enforcement officer or a formal representative of an Assistant United States Attorney, make a minimal factual showing sufficient to permit the judge to conclude that there is a reason for the lineup which is consistent with the legitimate function of the grand jury."

3. Compare with *Kelley,* the varying responses of lower federal courts to claims that special standards are needed to insure that grand jury subpoenas requiring identification exemplars are used to further a grand jury inquiry rather than to assist an independent police investigation. Several federal courts have held that a subpoena is not subject to attack provided the prosecutor expects to present the resulting evidence before the grand jury. Moreover, they hold, the subpoenaed party may be offered the opportunity to provide the exemplars voluntarily, in the offices of the prosecutor or an assisting law enforcement agency, rather than through the more cumbersome procedures specified in the subpoena—provided he is also informed of his right to contest the subpoena. See, e.g., *United States v. Smith,* 687 F.2d 147 (6th Cir. 1982). Other federal courts have held that identification exemplar subpoenas should not issue unless first approved by the grand jury. In justifying such a requirement (which is contrary to the usual

rule applicable to grand jury subpoenas), one court turned to the rationale of *Dionisio.* While that case had allowed the issuance of a voice exemplar subpoena without requiring a preliminary showing even as to reasonable suspicion, it had done so only because of the grand jury's "unique investigative power." If the element of juror participation which justified that power was to be "meaningful," the use of its power to impose a "major intrusion upon personal liberty" (here participation in a lineup) could not be assumed to have been automatically delegated to the prosecutor. *In re Melvin,* 546 F.2d 1 (1st Cir.1976).

4. *Underlying Fourth Amendment violations.* In UNITED STATES v. CALANDRA, 414 U.S. 338, 94 S.Ct. 613, 38 L.Ed.2d 561 (1974), grand jury witness Calandra was asked questions about certain records (evidencing "loan-sharking" activities) that had been seized by federal agents in connection with a search of Calandra's office. Calandra initially invoked his privilege against self-incrimination, but subsequently was granted immunity. He then requested and received a postponement of the grand jury proceedings so that he could present a pre-charge motion for return and suppression of the seized evidence under Federal Rule 41(e). The district court granted the motion, holding that the search had been unconstitutional. The district court also held that "Calandra need not answer any of the grand jury's questions based on suppressed evidence," since such questions constituted the fruit of the poisonous tree. A divided Supreme Court (6–3), per POWELL, J., reversed.

"In deciding whether to extend the exclusionary rule to grand jury proceedings, we must weigh the potential injury to the historic role and functions of the grand jury against the potential benefits of the rule as applied in this context. It is evident that this extension of the exclusionary rule would seriously impede the grand jury. Because the grand jury does not finally adjudicate guilt or innocence, it has traditionally been allowed to pursue its investigative and accusatorial functions unimpeded by the evidentiary and procedural restrictions applicable to a criminal trial. Permitting witnesses to invoke the exclusionary rule before a grand jury would precipitate adjudication of issues hitherto reserved for the trial on the merits and would delay and disrupt grand jury proceedings. Suppression hearings would halt the orderly progress of an investigation and might necessitate extended litigation of issues only tangentially related to the grand jury's primary objective. The probable result would be 'protracted interruptions of grand jury proceedings,' effectively transforming them into preliminary trials on the merits. In some cases the delay might be fatal to the enforcement of the criminal law. Just last Term we reaffirmed our disinclination to allow litigious interference with grand jury proceedings. *United States v. Dionisio.*

"Against this potential damage to the role and functions of the grand jury, we must weigh the benefits to be derived from this proposed extension of the exclusionary rule. * * * Any incremental deterrent effect which might be achieved by extending the rule to grand jury proceedings is uncertain at best.[a] Whatever deterrence of police misconduct may result from the exclusion of illegally seized evidence from criminal trials, it is unrealistic to assume that application of the rule to grand jury proceedings would significantly further that goal. * * * We decline to embrace a view that would achieve a speculative and undoubtedly minimal advance in the deterrence of police misconduct at

a. For further discussion of the Court's reasoning on this point, see Note 1, p. 230 supra. Dissenting in *Calandra,* Justice Brennan, joined by Justices Douglas and Marshall, stressed that the considerations underlying the exclusionary rule were equally applicable to the grand jury [see Note 1, p. 230 supra]. Consider also *In re Weir,* 495 F.2d 879 (9th Cir.1974) (*Calandra* forecloses witness challenge to grand jury questioning based upon a coerced confession).

the expense of substantially impeding the role of the grand jury." [b]

II. "CHILLING EFFECT" OBJECTIONS

1. *First Amendment claims.* In certain other investigative settings in which a special showing of need is not ordinarily required to subpoena records or testimony, the Supreme Court has held that such a showing is required to obtain information relating to the exercise of First Amendment rights. See, e.g., *Gibson v. Florida Legislative Investigation Committee,* 372 U.S. 539, 83 S.Ct. 889, 9 L.Ed.2d 929 (1963) (legislative investigation). Does the First Amendment require imposition of a similar requirement for grand jury investigations? BRANZBURG v. HAYES, 408 U.S. 665, 92 S.Ct. 2646, 33 L.Ed.2d 626 (1972), cited in *Dionisio* as reaffirming the extensive authority of the grand jury [see p. 716 supra], rejecting such a claim.

The petitioners in *Branzburg* were newspaper reporters, subpoenaed to testify before grand juries, who argued that they should not be compelled to reveal the identity of confidential sources or relevant facts obtained from those sources unless the grand jury first established a "compelling need" to obtain such information. A divided Court (5–4) rejected this contention. Justice White's opinion for the Court acknowledged that requiring the reporters to testify might deter future confidential sources, but noted that the extent of that deterrence was "unclear." Moreover, even if there would be some negative impact upon newsgathering, that impact did not outweigh the interest of the public in the grand jury's investigation of crime. The majority noted (and Justice Powell's concurring opinion stressed in particular) that judicial control of the grand jury process always was available to provide an appropriate remedy if the grand jury process was misused to harass the press. [See p. 716 supra, quoting from this portion of the *Branzburg* opinion]. The dissenting justices argued that the First Amendment interest in protecting the "confidential relationships between a reporter and his source" should not be so readily offset by "society's interest in the use of the grand jury."

2. How far does Branzburg carry? Consider *Bursey v. United States,* 466 F.2d 1059 (9th Cir.1972), rehearing denied, 466 F.2d 1090 (9th Cir.1972). The court there required the government to make a special showing of need in support of the grand jury's demand for various information relating to the publication of *The Black Panther* (a newspaper which was being investigated in connection with a reported speech in which a party leader said, "We will kill Richard Nixon"). Relying upon compulsory disclosure cases arising in other settings, including *Gibson v. Florida Legislative Investigation Committee,* supra, the court held that a grand jury inquiry which "collides with First Amendment rights," would be upheld only if the prosecutor could establish that "the Government's interest in the subject matter of the investigation is immediate, substantial, and

b. In *Gelbard v. United States,* 408 U.S. 41, 92 S.Ct. 2357, 33 L.Ed.2d 199 (1972), the Court held that the broad exclusionary remedy of the Omnibus Crime Control Act (see p. 432 supra) gave grand jury witnesses the right to object to the grand jury's use of information derived from illegal electronic surveillance. Since the witness ordinarily will not know whether there was an illegal wiretap, protection of the *Gelbard* right requires a sometimes complicated (and time consuming) procedure. Initially a witness will refuse to answer questions on a particular topic alleging some basis for believing that the questions were based on information derived from wiretaps. The government then bears the responsibility to respond, noting that a check of its records reveals that there was no wiretap or that any wiretap was valid. See also LaFave and Israel, § 8.9(b), discussing those issues that have attracted the most attention in this process: (1) the nature of the allegation that must be made by the witness to trigger a government obligation to check its files for possible wiretaps; (2) the nature of the showing that must be made by the government in a response denying the existence of wiretaps; and (3) the consequences of a government response that a wiretap was used, but that it was a court ordered wiretap permitted under the Crime Control Act.

subordinating, that there is a 'substantial connection' between the information it seeks to have the witness compelled to supply and the overriding governmental interest in the subject matter of the investigation, and that the means of obtaining the information is not more drastic than necessary to forward the asserted governmental interest." On petition for rehearing, the *Bursey* court rejected the government's contention that the standard it had applied was inconsistent with *Branzburg*. It noted that *Branzburg* was concerned with the press function of newsgathering which did not relate as directly to protected First Amendment interests as the activities involved in the case before it.

3. Did the Supreme Court in *Branzburg* provide adequate protection for First Amendment interests in noting its expectation that lower courts would act, in individual cases, to bar grand jury "harassment" of groups exercising First Amendment rights? What circumstances will establish the existence of such harassment? Consider *Ealy v. Littlejohn,* 569 F.2d 219 (5th Cir.1978). After a state grand jury failed to return an indictment in a case involving a police shooting of a black youth, the local United League, an association of black citizens, published a leaflet which described the grand jury proceeding as a "farce" and accused the local prosecuting attorney of "acting as a defense attorney" rather than a prosecutor. The supervising judge then called the grand jury back into session and directed it to interrogate all persons who "might have knowledge of any improper activities." Grand jury subpoenas were issued to several League officials and League records were also subpoenaed. While the grand jury attempted to ascertain if the subpoenaed witnesses had any personal knowledge of the shooting, it also questioned the witnesses "about the internal and financial operations and activities of their organization." Upon conclusion of its investigation, the grand jury issued a report which included a recommendation that the transcript of its proceedings be released to the news media and various officials, including the Mississippi Tax Commission. The League then brought a 42 U.S.C. § 1983 action in federal court seeking equitable relief relating to further publication and use of the transcript. In finding such relief appropriate, the Federal Court of Appeals noted: "Absent a plausible explanation—and we find the record barren of one—we are forced to conclude that the questions directed to League witnesses about purely League business having no arguable or colorable relationship to the [shooting] were posed in bad faith for the purpose of harassing those who, in the exercise of their First Amendment rights, had criticized [prosecutor] Littlejohn and had called the grand jury proceeding a farce."

Critics have charged that federal grand juries were used during the Nixon Administration to harass leftist opponents of the Vietnam War and that federal courts generally were unable (or unwilling) to protect the victims of that harassment. See, Clark, *The Grand Jury* (1975); Note, 7 Harv.C.R.—C.L.L.Rev. 432 (1972). A special unit of the Justice Department, it is alleged, was using the grand jury to build intelligence dossiers on the living patterns of the political dissidents of the "new left." It also allegedly was trying to force those persons into a position where they either had to testify about innocent activities of their friends or be held in contempt. These objectives allegedly were being achieved by initiating investigations of actual crimes (e.g., the U.S. Capitol bombing), calling before the grand jury persons who had any contact whatsoever with persons suspected of committing those crimes, granting those persons immunity when they relied on the Fifth Amendment, and then asking the most far ranging questions—e.g., "Tell the grand jury every place you went after you returned to your apartment from Cuba, every city you visited, with whom and by what means of transportation you traveled and who you visited at all of the places you went during the times of your travels after you left your apartment in Ann Arbor, Michigan, in May of 1970." Courts failed to prevent such tactics, it is argued, because it was almost impossible for the objecting witness to establish that such questions were asked in bad faith. See, Clark, supra, at 48 ("a judge would have to see the full mosaic of grand jury operations across the country"). Would the *Bursey* standard make it easier to obtain relief against such grand jury abuses?

4. *Attorney subpoenas.* In IN RE GRAND JURY SUBPOENA SERVED UPON DOE, 759 F.2d 968 (2d Cir. 1985), rehearing granted, ___ F.2d ___ (2d Cir.1985), a grand jury investigating an "organized crime family" sought to determine whether the target of the investigation had arranged for the legal representation of members of his "crew" who were apprehended during the commission of illegal activity. Accordingly, a subpoena was served upon the target's attorney calling for the production of records concerning fees and sources of fees, a subject not ordinarily encompassed by the attorney-client privilege. See Glanzer and Tasker, *Attorneys Before the Grand Jury: Assertion of the Attorney-Client Privilege to Protect a Client's Identity,* 73 J.Crim.L. & Criminology 1070 (1984). The *Doe* court assumed that the impact of the subpoena would be to have the attorney give testimony contrary to the interests of his client, thereby creating a conflict of interest that would result in the disqualification of the attorney from further representation of the client. Relying on its supervisory power, the court concluded that the subpoena therefore could be sustained only upon a special showing by the government. Speaking for the majority, ROSENN, J., reasoned:

"[W]e hold that when a subpoena is issued to an attorney to testify before a grand jury investigating his client whom he has theretofore represented, and where the attorney will be disqualified if he testifies, the Government should make a preliminary showing of relevance and reasonable need. * * * In reaching this conclusion, we are necessarily faced with the task of balancing two competing interests—the desire to present in the public interest all relevant information to the grand jury and the interest, under our adversary system of criminal law, in maintaining the integrity of the attorney-client relationship. In carefully weighing these important interests, two points support additional protection for the attorney-client relationship. First, the unbridled use of the subpoena would potentially allow the Government, in this and future cases, to decide unilaterally that an attorney will not represent his client. Such a power of disqualification can undermine and debilitate our legal system by subjecting the criminal defense bar to the subservience of a governmental agent. * * * Second, as noted earlier, the right to have counsel of one's choosing in the defense of a criminal charge is of constitutional dimensions. Thus, any potential infringement of this right must only be as a last resort. It should be noted, however, that the 'protection [provided by the right] goes no further than preventing arbitrary dismissal of the chosen attorney.' *United States v. Flanagan* [p. 726 supra]. Still, a requirement that the Government make a preliminary showing of need and relevance is consistent with this analysis and is not unduly burdensome. Requiring adequate justification will prevent the arbitrary dismissal of an attorney and still protect the grand jury's access to information if the Government can demonstrate that the attorney's testimony is not only relevant but that there is a need for it that cannot reasonably be met in some other fashion. The right to choose one's counsel is thus afforded sufficient protection without being accorded excessive deference."

Dissenting in *Doe,* Judge Timbers argued that: (1) the information sought here admittedly fell outside of the attorney-client privilege, which provides adequate protection of the attorney-client relationship; (2) the majority was adopting the "same kind of preliminary showing of which the Supreme Court has disapproved as causing undesirable delays in grand jury investigations"; (3) the impact upon any Sixth Amendment right to counsel was entirely too speculative since it existed only if the target was eventually indicted and counsel was eventually disqualified; and (4) if "any additional protection of the attorney-client relationship is required," a "more appropriate test for all concerned would be to require the party seeking to quash the subpoena * * * to show that the information sought is irrelevant to any legitimate objective of investigation by the grand jury, or that the information may be obtained from another source that would avoid the risk of disqualification."

See also *In the Matter of Klein,* 776 F.2d 628 (7th Cir.1985) (*Doe* criticized as assuming too readily that the disclosure of unprivileged information would lead to the lawyer's disqualification; a grand jury investigation should not be "stopped dead in its tracks" because of abstract possibilities). Also rejecting a general requirement of a preliminary showing, the First Circuit has stressed that granting appropriate relief from a subpoena having an overly chilling impact upon the lawyer-client relationship lies in the district court's supervisory authority. See *In re Grand Jury Matters,* 751 F.2d 13 (1st Cir.1984) (upholding district court's authority to quash subpoenas issued to attorneys who were currently serving as defense counsel for the same persons in state criminal prosecutions); *In re Grand Jury Proceedings (Wilson),* 760 F.2d 26 (1st Cir.1985) (upholding district court authority to enforce subpoena requiring an attorney to testify as to unprivileged matters relating to a target whom he formerly had represented in a civil matter).

III. SUBJECT MATTER CHALLENGES

1. After commenting generally upon the scope of the grand jury's investigative authority and the corresponding obligations and rights of grand jury witnesses [see Note 2, p. 703 supra], the Court in BLAIR v. UNITED STATES, 250 U.S. 273, 39 S.Ct. 468, 63 L.Ed. 979 (1919), quickly disposed of the petitioners' claim that their refusal to testify was justified because the subject under investigation (possible violations of the Federal Corrupt Practices Act in the course of a primary election) was beyond the regulatory authority of the federal government. JUSTICE PITNEY noted for the Court: "And, for the same reasons, witnesses are not entitled to take exception to the jurisdiction of the grand jury or the court over the particular subject-matter that is under investigation. In truth it is in the ordinary case no concern of one summoned as a witness whether the offense is within the jurisdiction of the court or not. At least, the court and grand jury have authority and jurisdiction to investigate the facts in order to determine the question whether the facts show a case within their jurisdiction. The present cases are not exceptional, and for the reasons that have been outlined we are of opinion that appellants were not entitled to raise any question about the constitutionality of the statutes under which the grand jury's investigation was conducted."

2. Does *Blair* preclude consideration of a challenge in which the witness contends not only that the subject is beyond constitutional regulation, but that the inquiry infringed upon the exercise of the witness' constitutional rights. Consider *Levinson v. Attorney General,* 321 F.Supp. 984 (E.D.Pa.1970), where the subject of the investigation was alleged mail fraud committed by the "International Committee to Defend Eldridge Cleaver." The court issued a declaratory judgment prohibiting the questioning of witnesses with respect to the truth or falsity of statements in a Committee newspaper advertisement alleging that "certain" invalid and unconstitutional "proceedings were being taken against Cleaver." It

reasoned that any such inquiry was prohibited by the First Amendment since prior decisions indicated that a prosecution based upon the alleged falsity of expressions of political philosophy would violate that amendment. See also *In re Grand Jury Matter (Gronowicz),* 764 F.2d 983 (3d Cir.1985) (en banc) (court acknowledges target-witness' right to challenge the grand jury investigation on the ground that prosecution would be prohibited under the First Amendment, but majority holds that the First Amendment does not bar prosecution of an author for allegedly false representations to his publisher concerning his sources, notwithstanding that prosecution will necessarily inquire into the truth of statements in the book).

3. Does *Blair* bar a witness' objection to an inquiry as concerned with criminal activity that clearly occurred outside the district in which the grand jury sits? (The grand jury may indict only for offenses committed within the jurisdiction of the court that impaneled it). Compare *United States v. Girgenti,* 197 F.2d 218 (3d Cir.1952) (holding that *Blair* precluded a witness objection on such a ground, but also noting that where the grand jury had not completed its investigation the court could not be certain that activities in one district might not relate to an offense in another, particularly conspiracy); *In re Grand Jury Impaneled January 21, 1975 (Freedman),* 529 F.2d 543 (3d Cir.1976) (rejecting the government's contention that the witness could not raise such an objection, but finding the objection there "not forceful" since the parties being investigated resided in the grand jury's district and their participation in illegal transactions outside the district may have related to tax returns filed within the district).

4. Insofar as the subject of the investigation may be open to challenge, how may the witness establish what that subject might be? In light of *Blair,* is the grand jury required to identify the subject even in very general terms? See *In re Black,* 47 F.2d 542 (2d Cir.1931) (upholding, on the reasoning of *Blair,* a subpoena entitled "in the matter of John Doe"); *United States v. Neff,* 212 F.2d 297 (3d Cir.1954) ("an investigation * * * need not be preceded by any definition whatever of the crime to be investigated or the persons against whom an accusation is sought"). The Justice Department's internal regulations, contained in the United States Attorneys Manual (§ 9–11.250), provide that a witness should be informed of "the general subject matter of the grand jury's inquiry (to the extent that such disclosure does not compromise the progress of the investigation or otherwise inimically affect the administration of justice)." Consider also principal No. 13 of the American Bar Association's "legislative principles" for grand jury reform legislation (adopted August 9, 1977): "A grand jury subpoena should indicate the statute or general subject area that is the concern of the grand jury inquiry. The return of an indictment in a subject area not disclosed by the grand jury subpoena shall not be a basis for dismissal."

5. While most states follow *Blair,* there is precedent in several states suggesting that they may be more lenient in permitting witness objections to the subject matter of the grand jury inquiry. See, e.g., *People v. Polk,* 174 N.E.2d 393 (Ill.1961); *Koota v. Colombo,* 216 N.E.2d 568 (N.Y. 1966). However, those states also hold that grand jury proceedings operate under a "presumption of regularity" and the objecting witness must clearly show that the subject matter was barred from grand jury investigation. *People v. Polk,* supra. Successful objections to the subject matter are most likely to be established where state law limits an investigative grand jury to particular types of investigations. See, e.g., Ariz.Stat. § 21–422(B) (limiting the statewide grand jury to investigating specified activities, such as the operations of banks and labor unions).

IV. RELEVANCY OBJECTIONS

1. *Blair* noted [see p. 704 supra] that a grand jury witness, like a trial witness is "not entitled to urge objections of incompetency or relevancy." Relying on this statement, lower federal courts generally have held that they will not consider a relevancy objection apart from the relevancy element of an overbreadth objection to a subpoena duces tecum. See, e.g., *United States v. Doe (Popkin),* 460 F.2d 328 (1st Cir.1972).[a] The Second Circuit has suggested that a relevancy objection would be sustained if the witness could show that the information sought bears "no conceivable relevance to any legitimate object of investigation," but it has consistently found that the witness has failed to meet that very stringent standard. *In re Liberatore,* 574 F.2d 78 (2d Cir.1978). The Third Circuit, on the other hand, has squarely recognized a relevancy objection and imposed a preliminary showing requirement to meet that objection. See *Schofield,* discussed below.

2. In IN RE GRAND JURY PROCEEDINGS (SCHOFIELD I), 486 F.2d 85 (3d Cir.1973), petitioner had been held in civil contempt for refusing to comply with a court order directing her to provide handwriting samples, photographs, and fingerprints to the grand jury. In seeking that court order, the government had alleged only that petitioner had been subpoenaed to furnish such matter and had refused to comply without legal justification. The Third Circuit held that the petitioner could not be found in contempt since the government had failed to show that the items sought were "relevant to the grand jury's investigation of an offense falling within its jurisdiction." The court (per GIBBONS, J.) reasoned from the premise that "[g]rand jury subpoenas, when they are brought before the federal courts for enforcement, for all practical purposes are exactly analogous to subpoenas issued by a federal administrative agency." [See Note 3, p. 704 supra]. A long line of precedent established that administrative agency subpoenas were subject to challenge on various grounds, including the subpoena's request for "irrelevant information" and the agency's use of the subpoena for an unauthorized purpose. In raising such challenges, the witness objecting to an administrative subpoena could utilize discovery proceedings to overcome the "presumption of regularity" that attaches to the subpoena. In the grand jury setting, the court noted, the secrecy requirements of Fed.R.Crim.P. 6(e) "complicat[es] the discovery problem." Accordingly, it would require the government, in seeking enforcement of a subpoena, to make a preliminary showing as to the subpoena's validity. In describ-

a. Distinguishing Supreme Court rulings allowing relevancy objections in legislative inquiry cases, see e.g., *Watkins v. United States,* 354 U.S. 178, 77 S.Ct. 1173, 1 L.Ed.2d 1273 (1957), *Popkin* offered the following explanation as to why it would not depart from the "longstanding doctrine of *Blair*" barring such objections in grand jury cases: "The concept of relevance to the legislative purpose is necessary to preserve the boundary between the legislative and the individual, and can ordinarily be enforced by reference to statements of purpose and prior testimony which are already matters of public record. A grand jury generally has a much smaller object in view, but one in which society has intense interest. At least when inquiring into specific crimes, a grand jury paints with a small brush and necessarily with painstaking detail. Its purpose is to see if there is probable cause to believe that particular crimes have been committed by particular persons, although further crimes and perpetrators may be discovered in the course of taking evidence. In either case, the number of facts which would help to identify the crime and the criminal may well be few, and the relevance of one fact may only become apparent after another is uncovered. Thus while the public product of a grand jury is a limited number of indictments, its processes may include the pursuit of numerous strands of evidence, many of which may ultimately be of no use, but none of which can safely be abandoned. From another perspective, even where a grand jury is working on the clear hypothesis of a prosecutor, its success may often depend upon its ability to offer to witnesses a guarantee of secrecy and to suspects the protection of secrecy unless probable cause is found to indict. Any meaningful statement of relevance in response to a witness's request would entail the naming of suspects and the description of prior testimony."

ing the nature of the required showing (and the basis for its ruling), the court stated:

"We need not in this case lay down inflexible procedures to govern all challenges to enforcement of any grand jury procedure, for the information here sought is both limited and unique. The Government wants only handwriting exemplars, fingerprints and a mug shot. It has no general right to any of these things. Authority for obtaining them exists, if at all, solely because they are somehow relevant to the grand jury's investigation of an offense falling within its jurisdiction. In view of the fact that information which would justify obtaining the handwriting exemplars, fingerprints, and a mug shot, is in the Government's sole possession, we think it reasonable that the Government be required to make some preliminary showing by affidavit that each item is at least relevant to an investigation being conducted by the grand jury and properly within its jurisdiction, and is not sought primarily for another purpose. We impose this requirement both pursuant to the federal courts' supervisory power over grand juries and pursuant to our supervisory power over civil [contempt] proceedings brought in the district court pursuant to 28 U.S.C. § 1826(a). We do not rule out the possibility that the Government's affidavit may be presented to the court *in camera,* but we do hold that Rule 6(e) does not require *in camera* presentation. * * * [U]nless extraordinary circumstances appear, the nature of which we cannot anticipate, the Government's supporting affidavit should be disclosed to the witness in the enforcement proceeding. If after such disclosure the witness makes application to the district court for additional discovery in the enforcement proceeding, the court must in deciding that request weigh the quite limited scope of an inquiry into abuse of the subpoena process, and the potential for delay, against any need for additional information which might cast doubt upon the accuracy of the Government's representations."[b]

The *Schofield* Court rejected the contention that the preliminary showing required under its opinion was inconsistent with *Dionisio* and its companion case, *United States v. Mara.* In discussing those cases, the court noted:

"Both [cases] hold that the fourth amendment does not require any preliminary showing for the issuance of a grand jury subpoena, either to compel testimony, or to compel production of voice or handwriting exemplars. Neither, however, involves any question as to the propriety of the grand jury's investigation, the legitimacy of the purpose for issuing the subpoena, or any nonconstitutional objection to its enforcement. Indeed Justice Stewart's opinion for the Court in *Dionisio* quite carefully circumscribes its holding by explicitly reiterating the power of the district courts to control the use of grand jury subpoenas referred to in Justice Powell's concurring opinion in *Branzburg v. Hayes.*"

3. *Schofield* has been criticized as being inconsistent with the general approach of *Dionisio* and the decisions *Dionisio* relied upon, if not the precise ruling in those cases. See, e.g., Braun, *The Grand Jury—Spirit of the Community?,* 15 Ariz.L.Rev. 893, 911–13 (1973). Is there a significant distinction, as *Schofield* suggests, between the challenge rejected in *Dionisio* and the relevancy challenge accepted in *Schofield?* Can one justify a rule holding that a witness cannot challenge a subpoena on the ground that the grand jury lacks a

b. *Schofield* subsequently was applied to refusals to testify, as well as to refusals to produce physical evidence. However, where the witness cited for contempt refuses to give testimony, *Schofield* 's relevancy element requires a governmental showing of relevancy only as to the general subject matter of the total group of questions, rather than as to specific questions. See *In re Grand Jury Investigation (Bruno),* 545 F.2d 385 (3d Cir.1976); *United States v. Weiner,* 418 F.Supp. 941 (M.D.Pa.1976), aff'd, 546 F.2d 420 (3d Cir.1976). Compare *Ex parte Jennings,* Note 5 infra, permitting relevancy objections to individual questions.

reasonable basis for requesting certain information from him, but that a witness can challenge the subpoena on the ground that the information sought has no rational relationship to a legitimate subject of investigation? Does the combination of *Dionisio* and *Schofield* produce such a rule? See Braun, supra, at 912.

Does *Schofield* run the risk, warned against in *Dionisio,* of impeding the grand jury process by saddling it with "minitrials"? Compare *In re Grand Jury Investigation (McLean),* 565 F.2d 318 (5th Cir. 1977) (suggesting that *Schofield* has that impact); *In re Grand Jury Subpoena Served Upon John Doe,* Note 4, p. 726 supra (noting that "actual experience" suggests that requiring a preliminary showing will not impede the grand jury and citing a House Committee's staff analysis which concluded that the *Schofield* decision "has not caused any serious disruption in grand jury proceedings" in the Third Circuit; the staff analysis suggested that witnesses informed in advance of the subject of investigation are more likely to be prepared and therefore will save time and provide more complete answers).[c] In a concurring opinion in *Schofield,* Judge Seitz suggested that the witness should be limited to challenging the government's preliminary showing of relevancy on its face, with no evidentiary hearing allowed. In *In re Grand Jury Proceedings (Schofield II),* 507 F.2d 963 (3d Cir. 1975), the court noted that where a district court is "not satisfied with the government's affidavits, whether because the matters set forth challenge the court's credibility or because the witness has some colorable challenge to the affidavits," it can pursue "various avenues of inquiry," including requiring "discovery, *in camera* inspection, additional affidavits and a hearing." Reported cases suggest that hearings have not been held.

4. What constitutes an adequate preliminary showing under *Schofield?* Consider *In re Grand Jury Proceedings (Schofield II),* Note 3 supra (government affidavit adequate where it alleged (1) the government was investigating possible perjury before the grand jury (the witness had testified previously before the grand jury after having been granted immunity on a forgery charge) and (2) the requested handwriting exemplars would be used "solely as a standard of comparison to determine whether or not the witness uttered any forged * * * checks"); *In re Grand Jury Impaneled January 21, 1975 (Freedman),* 529 F.2d 543 (3d Cir.1976) (subpoena of 26 categories of documents dealing with financial affairs of a law firm over a 10 year period was not adequately supported by a prosecutor's affidavit which simply noted that the government was investigating criminal violations by officers of a particular union and that there had been "allegations" in the course of the investigation of "wrongdoings" by members of the law firm; some of the documents requested related to such matters as the firm's purchase of office supplies, which had no obvious relevance); *In re Pilliteri,* 420 F.Supp. 913 (W.D.Pa.1976) (affidavit satisfactory where it alleged (1) that the grand jury was investigating a conspiracy to defraud the United States, (2) during the investigation, "said witness has come to the attention of the United States," and (3) based on "his familiarity with the case," the U.S. attorney "knows that the testimony of the said witness is relevant to the Grand Jury's investigation"). Courts applying *Schofield* have uniformly rejected the contention that a subpoena may be quashed because

c. Consider also *Statement of the Coalition to End Grand Jury Abuse,* reprinted in the same Hearings (1977 Judiciary Comm. Hearings on H.R. 94) at p. 94: "Two observations are in order here. The first is that 'delay' is in the eyes of the beholder. Any due process safeguard can be attacked on the grounds that it causes delay. * * * More fundamentally, however, we question the prosecutorial assumption that the current grand jury system operates efficiently without delay. While apologists for the grand jury status quo continually raise the spectre of a reformed grand jury system sinking in the quicksand of procedural litigation, the reality is that the grand jury system is already neck-deep in litigation."

the information or evidence sought could be obtained from another source. See, e.g., *United States v. Weiner,* fn. b supra (government will not be required to search through witness' military records to obtain his fingerprints; moreover, the government is entitled to "competent, fresh-evidence"). Consider also *In re Sinadinos,* 760 F.2d 167 (7th Cir.1985) (witness may not demand that the government establish that the information sought was not already within the grand jury's possession, absent "extreme circumstances" suggesting a governmental purpose of harassment).

5. Other federal circuits generally have refused to adopt the preliminary showing requirement of *Schofield.* Some have noted, however, that "the presiding judge always has authority to require a *Schofield* showing when there is some basis for believing that the grand jury process is being misused." LaFave and Israel, § 8.8(b). Most state courts also generally bar relevancy objections. Several states, however, follow either the *Schofield* requirement or a procedure very close to it. See, e.g., *In re January, 1974, Special Investigating Grand Jury (Salvitti),* 357 A.2d 622 (Pa.Super. 1976) (following *Schofield*); *Ex parte Jennings,* 240 S.W. 942 (Tex.Cr.App.1922) (to establish contempt, prosecutor must establish compliance with the statutory requirement that he first announced the "subject matter under investigation" and then asked "pertinent questions relative to the transaction in general terms"); *Koota v. Colombo,* 216 N.E.2d 568 (N.Y.1966) (to establish contempt, prosecutor must show that the "evidence demanded is relevant and proper"; but relevancy is established if "the bearing [of the question asked] on the subject of the investigation was susceptible of 'intelligent estimate' or if there was a 'justifiable suspicion that the former is related to the latter' ").

V. MISUSE OBJECTIONS

1. *Use for civil discovery.* In *United States v. Procter & Gamble,* 356 U.S. 677, 78 S.Ct. 983, 2 L.Ed.2d 1077 (1958), the district court granted broad disclosure of grand jury testimony to defendants in a civil antitrust action, with its ruling apparently influenced by the belief that the government had used the grand jury process "to elicit evidence" for that civil action. The Supreme Court rejected the disclosure order as not supported by a showing of particularized need [see Note 2 infra], but it also acknowledged that the alleged government subversion of the criminal process could constitute "good cause" warranting such extensive disclosure. There had been no finding, however, that the grand jury proceeding had in fact "been used as a short cut to [civil discovery] goals otherwise barred or more difficult to reach." If the grand jury had been employed in that fashion, the Court noted, the government clearly would have been guilty of "flouting the policy of the law," both as to the grand jury's proper function and the prescribed procedures for civil discovery.

Does *Procter & Gamble* provide a basis for challenge to a subpoena by a target of a grand jury? Consider IN RE GRAND JURY SUBPOENAS, APRIL, 1978, AT BALTIMORE, 581 F.2d 1103 (4th Cir. 1978), where the appellate court denied a petition for a writ of mandamus "directing the district court to hold an evidentiary hearing into allegations that the grand jury process has been abused by the Internal Revenue Service (IRS) and the Justice Department." The court, per WINTERS, J., stated:

"Petitioner contends that the powers of the grand jury have been purposely abused by the government and that, because of the government's improper motives, petitioner should not be subjected to the grand jury's process and the grand jury's investigation should be terminated. Briefly stated, petitioner alleges that IRS has had a history of using grand jury powers to further administrative investigations that have otherwise become stymied. Coupled with its allegation of historical abuse, petitioner points out that, in the instant case,

IRS was conducting a joint civil and criminal investigation during which petitioner was served with a number of administrative summons with which it refused to comply, and this refusal was subsequently vindicated in an enforcement action in the district court.[a] Shortly after IRS lost its court battle to enforce the summons, the grand jury investigation began, with several agents previously involved in the administrative investigation being deputized for the grand jury probe. The subpoenas then served by the grand jury sought the same materials which the IRS had unsuccessfully attempted to obtain administratively. Petitioner's inference, which it wants the district court to investigate, is that the grand jury is being used as a subterfuge for gaining access to documents IRS needs in its pending civil and criminal investigation of petitioner.[10]

"The district court refused to conduct the investigation into the government's motives and purposes which petitioner sought. Instead it relied on an affidavit by a Department of Justice attorney attesting to the government's good faith in utilizing the grand jury. * * * A grand jury is convened to determine 'if there is probable cause to believe that a crime has been committed . . . ' *Branzburg v. Hayes.* If the powers of the grand jury, including the power to subpoena documents, are used, not for the purpose of criminal investigation but rather to gather evidence for civil enforcement, there exists an abuse of the grand jury process. *United States v. Procter & Gamble.* This is the abuse alleged by petitioner. The precise question for decision is whether a district court is obliged to conduct a full evidentiary hearing at the time such abuse is alleged or whether it is sufficient during the course of the grand jury proceedings to rely on the government's own affirmation of good faith.

"We begin with the well-recognized principle that courts should not intervene in the grand jury process absent compelling reason. *United States v. Dionisio.* Clearly, to hold an evidentiary hearing into prosecutorial motivation with an eye toward quashing otherwise lawfully issued subpoenas and even terminating the entire process would be substantial judicial intervention. Nonetheless, such intervention might well be required if it were the only means of protecting petitioner from the abuse he alleges. There is, however, a less drastic remedy in Fed.R.Crim.P. 6(e). The district court made clear that it considered Rule 6(e) to be adequate protection of petitioner's interest. We agree.

"Rule 6(e), as recently amended, provides generally that materials secured by the grand jury in the course of its investigation shall not be disclosed except as authorized in subsection (2). As relevant here, subsection (2) allows disclosure to 'an attorney for the government for use in the performance of [his] duty' [b] and to

a. The IRS administrative summons gives the IRS investigative discovery authority that extends to both documents and testimony. As noted in *United States v. Powell,* 379 U.S. 48, 85 S.Ct. 248, 13 L.Ed.2d 112 (1964), the "Commissioner need not meet any standard of probable cause to obtain enforcement of his summons, * * * [but] he must show that the investigation will be conducted pursuant to a legitimate purpose, that the inquiry may be relevant to the purpose, that the information sought is not already within the Commissioner's possession, and that the administrative steps required by the Code have been followed." The relevancy standard commonly employed for this purpose is "whether the documents at issue 'might have thrown light upon the correctness of the return.'" *United States v. Arthur Young Co.,* 465 U.S. 936, 104 S.Ct. 1495, 79 L.Ed.2d 826 (1984).

10. "The government denies any illicit motivation, explaining the decision to initiate a grand jury investigation by pointing to the imminence of the bar of the statute of limitations. A prosecution for fraud, if any, for the taxable year 1971 will be barred by limitations unless instituted before an undisclosed date in September, 1978."

b. In *United States v. Sells Engineering,* 463 U.S. 418, 103 S.Ct. 3133, 77 L.Ed.2d 743 (1983), the Court held that the "automatic access" allowed under this provision (i.e., access without court approval) was designed solely to facilitate performance of "prosecutorial duties." Accordingly, automatic disclosure can be given only to attorneys who are "members of the prosecutorial team." Judicial approval, granted under Rule 6(e)(2)(C) (discussed infra), is required for disclosure to other government lawyers (e.g., lawyers 'such government personnel as are deemed necessary by an attorney for the government to assist an attorney for the government in the performance of such attorney's duty to enforce Federal criminal law.' In the instant case, the government attorney in charge of the grand jury investigation deemed it necessary to secure the assistance of several [IRS] special agents with some knowledge of petitioner's business and tax affairs. Subsection (2) also imposes certain obligations with respect to disclosure to these necessary government personnel. * * * Each is under a duty not to 'utilize that grand jury material for any purpose other than assisting the attorney for the government in the performance of such attorney's duty to enforce Federal criminal law.' Rule 6(e)(2)(B). Each of the special agents involved in the instant case has been advised of his duty not to disclose grand jury material and that a breach of this duty is punishable by contempt.

"This is not to say that the [IRS'] Audit Division, which is charged with civil enforcement of federal tax law, has no legitimate interest in the materials secured by the grand jury. * * * [The court here noted that the IRS might subsequently seek disclosure of the grand jury materials under the Rule 6(e)(2)(C) provision authorizing disclosure 'when so directed by a court preliminary to or in connection with a judicial proceeding.'[c]] Very recently one of the district courts in this circuit had occasion to supervise such a disclosure and in so doing developed certain criteria which the government must meet in order to secure a disclosure order under Rule 6(e)(2)(C), where the purpose of such disclosure is to aid civil tax enforcement. First, the government must provide a general description of the materials sought in order to allow the court intelligently to determine if such materials are rationally related to an existing or contemplated civil proceeding. Second, and of particular importance to the instant case, the government must satisfy the court that 'the grand jury proceeding has not been used as a subterfuge for obtaining records for a civil investigation or proceeding.' *In re December 1974 Term Grand Jury Investigation,* 449 F.Supp. 743, 751 (D.Md.1978).

"We fully agree that the government should be required to demonstrate its bona fides prior to obtaining a Rule 6(e)(2)(C) order. This showing is particularly important where the grand jury fails to return an indictment. In such case, the likelihood of improper use of the grand jury process is substantially greater, and an evidentiary hearing of the type now sought by petitioner might be necessary before disclosure is ordered. In sum, we are of the opinion that petitioner's legitimate interests are fully protected by Rule 6(e). Disclosure to the IRS for civil enforcement purposes requires a court order predicated on a demonstration of good faith. Unauthorized disclosure is deterred by the threat of contempt.[16] * * * If there does exist evidence of criminal liability, it is in society's interest that this be made available to the grand jury before limita-

in the Justice Department's civil division), even though these lawyers happen to fall within the Rule 54(c) definition of "attorneys for the government."

c. As the Supreme Court noted in *United States v. Baggot,* 463 U.S. 476, 103 S.Ct. 3164, 77 L.Ed.2d 785 (1983), the Rule 6(e)(2)(C) requirement that court ordered disclosure be "preliminary to or in connection with a judicial proceeding" contemplates that disclosure be granted only for "uses related fairly directly to some identifiable litigation, pending or anticipated." *Baggot* held that disclosure for use in an IRS audit of civil tax liability did not fall within the Rule since the agency's determination of tax liability and its collection of any deficiency did not require judicial action. If the taxpayer challenged the agency's non-judicial means of enforcing its deficiency determination, there then would be pending litigation, but the mere possibility of such a challenge did not make the agency process "preliminary to a judicial proceeding."

16. "While we do not decide the issue, it may well be argued in an appropriate case that fairness would require exclusion of any evidence in a civil proceeding which had been improperly obtained from the grand jury. See S.Rep. No. 95–354."

tions have run. Any abuse of the grand jury process can be dealt with effectively at another time and in another manner."[d]

2. *Use for post-indictment criminal discovery.* Compare with *Baltimore Subpoenas,* Note 1 supra, the ruling in IN RE GRAND JURY SUBPOENA DUCES TECUM DATED JANUARY 2, 1985 (SIMELS), 775 F.2d 499 (2d Cir.1985). The petitioner there was originally indicted for violations of the federal narcotics laws. Prior to trial his counsel, when forced to withdraw because of a conflict of interest, mentioned to the prosecutor that he had expected to receive a fee of $250,000 in the case. The grand jury at the time apparently was continuing its inquiry, and it shortly thereafter returned a superseding indictment charging petitioner with engaging in a continuous criminal narcotics enterprise and seeking forfeiture of all profits as provided in 21 U.S.C. § 848. A week later the district court issued a trial subpoena directing petitioner's new lawyer (Simels) to produce for use at trial various documents relating to the fees paid or promised to him by petitioner. The subpoena provoked opposition from the criminal defense bar, which warned of its potential widespread impact upon the "attorney/client relationship and the defendant's right to effective assistance of counsel of his choice." Shortly thereafter, the trial subpoena was withdrawn, and Simels received a grand jury subpoena directing that he produce the same documents for grand jury consideration. Petitioner then moved to intervene as of right and to quash the grand jury subpoena. Reversing the district court's refusal to grant that motion, the Second Circuit, per FEINBERG, J., noted:

"The law is settled in this circuit and elsewhere that '[i]t is improper to utilize a Grand Jury for the sole or dominating purpose of preparing an already pending indictment for trial,' *United States v. Dardi,* 330 F.2d 316 (2d Cir. [1964]). The district court specifically found that the subpoena here was 'within the scope of the Grand Jury's investigatory power and does not constitute an abuse of the grand jury process.' But while this finding must be accorded considerable deference, we do not believe that our review must be limited to the 'clearly erroneous' standard usually applied to judicial determinations of intent. The question of a grand jury's dominant purpose is not the typical question of historical fact nor even the typical inquiry as to the state of mind of a witness or a party. It is the application of a legal standard designed to ensure that the grand jury, a body operating peculiarly under court supervision, is not misused by the prosecutor for trial preparation. In applying that standard, we therefore must give more scrutiny than would be appropriate under the 'clearly erroneous' standard. Moreover, it is not at all clear that the district judge applied the correct legal standard in refusing to quash the subpoe-

d. To obtain disclosure of grand jury testimony "preliminary to" a civil proceeding, a government agency, like any third party civil litigant seeking disclosure, also must establish a "particularized need" that outweighs the "public interest" in secrecy. See fn. b, p. 733 supra. Should the possible misuse of grand jury authority to facilitate civil litigation by the government also be taken into consideration in applying that particularized need standard? Consider Israel and LaFave, § 8.5(g): "The [Supreme] Court has noted * * * that 'the district court may weigh the public interest, if any, served by disclosure to a government body—along with the requisite particularized need—in determining whether the need for disclosure is greater than the need for continued secrecy.' While lower courts commonly cite the public purpose served by the agency, they vary in the extent to which they will allow it to soften the need standard that would be applied to a private party. Some have been willing to grant government agencies disclosure for general discovery purposes, and to give at least limited weight to the agency's interest in saving 'time and effort' in its investigation. Others, however, have refused to grant agency requests where the agency might be able to obtain the underlying information through the use of its own investigative authority. One court has suggested that federal agencies especially should receive 'no special treatment,' noting that such a position provides 'a safeguard for the grand jury because it tends to prevent it from being used as an instrument for explorations in aid of [federal agency] civil proceedings.' "

na, since the judge implied that the dominant purpose rule might be applicable only when the defendant was subpoenaed.

"The timing of the subpoena casts significant light on its purposes. Simels' evidence was initially sought in October 1984 through a trial, not a grand jury, subpoena. In a letter defending the issuance of the trial subpoena, the government asserted:

> The trial subpoena was served solely for evidentiary purposes. Proof of 'substantial income or resources' from the drug enterprise is an element of a Section 848 offense. If [defendant] Payden, who purportedly has relatively small legitimate means of support, had cash or other assets from which Mr. Simels was paid a substantial fee (as we have reason to believe), that fact would be plainly admissible to help meet the Government's burden of proof on the element.

Yet when the trial subpoena was issued, we assumed that the government knew that Simels' evidence might bear on matters relevant to the grand jury's investigation, such as the identification of co-conspirators. Nevertheless, no grand jury subpoena was issued in October 1984.[e] The adjournment of the trial subpoena and the substitution of a grand jury subpoena in January 1985 might have represented a laudable attempt to alleviate the concerns raised by Simels and representatives of the organized bar, but we see no reason to believe that this concession signified a shift in the uses to which the government intended to put the information sought. In addition, since not a single witness was called to the grand jury between October 10, 1984 and January 29, 1985, claims that the grand jury desired Simels' evidence as part of an active investigation seem particularly weak. * * *

"We are well aware that the rule barring use of the grand jury to gather evidence to prepare for trial on an already pending indictment 'is difficult, if not impossible, to enforce.' 8 J. Moore, *Federal Practice* § 6.04[5]. Even where we have found clear violations, we have often been reluctant to go beyond a simple rebuke. See *United States v. Fahey,* 510 F.2d 302 (2d Cir.1974). But if the rule is to have any meaning, we believe that the subpoena here must be quashed as an abuse of the grand jury process. In some circumstances, it may be appropriate to enforce the rule against using a grand jury subpoena predominantly for trial preparation simply by barring use at trial of evidence obtained pursuant to the subpoena, thereby leaving the grand jury's access to the evidence unimpaired. See *United States v. Doe (Application of Ellsberg)* 455 F.2d 1297 (1st Cir.1972). In the circumstances of this case, however, we conclude that quashing is the appropriate remedy."

SECTION 3. APPLICATION OF THE PRIVILEGE AGAINST SELF-INCRIMINATION

I. GRAND JURY TESTIMONY[a]

1. *Application of the privilege. Counselman v. Hitchcock,* 142 U.S. 547, 12 S.Ct. 195, 35 L.Ed. 1110 (1892), put to rest any doubts as to whether the privilege against self-incrimination was available to a

e. A series of cases have held that where the primary purpose of the continuing grand jury investigation is to determine whether others not indicted were involved in the same criminal activity, or whether the indicted party committed still other crimes, the inquiry may go forward even though one result may be the production of evidence that could be used at the trial of the indicted party. See LaFave and Israel, § 8.8(d).

a. The grand jury witness may also utilize any other testimonial privilege recognized in the particular jurisdiction. Thus, the privileges applicable before federal grand juries are those generally recognized in federal courts. See Fed.R. Evid. 1101(d)(2), 501. We have focused here on the privilege against self-incrimination because it provides "what is undoubtedly [the witness'] most significant safeguard in responding to a subpoena ad testificandum." LaFave and Israel, § 8.10(a).

grand jury witness. The Court there rejected the contention that the privilege did not apply because the grand jury witness was not being compelled to incriminate himself "in a criminal case." The reference in the Fifth Amendment to compelled testimony "in a criminal case," the Court noted, was to the eventual use of testimony and not to the nature of the proceeding in which the testimony was compelled. The Fifth Amendment, it concluded, applies to a witness "in any proceeding" who is being compelled to give testimony that might be incriminating in a subsequent criminal prosecution. In support of this interpretation, the Court noted that "the privilege must have a broad construction in favor of the right it was intended to secure," and that its objective was to "insure that a person should not be compelled, when acting as a witness in any investigation, to give testimony which might tend to show that he himself had committed a crime." Does this reasoning follow from *Boyd*?

2. *The nature of "incriminating" testimony.* As *Counselman* noted, the privilege only applies to testimony which is "incriminating"—i.e., to testimony which may "tend to show" that the witness himself "had committed a crime." What standard is applied in determining whether particular testimony has that tendency and who makes that determination? The leading case on both questions is HOFFMAN v. UNITED STATES, 341 U.S. 479, 71 S.Ct. 814, 95 L.Ed. 1118 (1951). In that case, a witness subpoenaed before a federal grand jury relied on the privilege in refusing to answer questions as to his current occupation and his contacts with a fugitive witness. The district court found that there was "no real and substantial danger of incrimination" and the privilege therefore was inapplicable. When the witness persisted in his claim, he was held in contempt. In reversing that conviction, the Supreme Court (per CLARK, J.) set forth the following guidelines for the district courts:

"The privilege afforded not only extends to answers that would in themselves support a conviction under a federal criminal statute but likewise embraces those which would furnish a link in the chain of evidence needed to prosecute the claimant for a federal crime. But this protection must be confined to instances where the witness has reasonable cause to apprehend danger from a direct answer. The witness is not exonerated from answering merely because he declares that in so doing he would incriminate himself—his say-so does not of itself establish the hazard of incrimination. It is for the court to say whether his silence is justified, and to require him to answer if 'it clearly appears to the court that he is mistaken.' However, if the witness, upon interposing his claim, were required to prove the hazard in the sense in which a claim is usually required to be established in court, he would be compelled to surrender the very protection which the privilege is designed to guarantee. To sustain the privilege, it need only be evident from the implications of the question, in the setting in which it is asked, that a responsive answer to the question or an explanation of why it cannot be answered might be dangerous because injurious disclosure could result."

It has been suggested that under the *Hoffman* guidelines, it will be a "rare case" in which a court can reject a witness' assertion of the privilege. See LaFave and Israel, § 8.10(a). Consider in this connection the *Hoffman* case itself, where the Court had no difficulty in concluding that district erred in denying petitioner's claim of the privilege. The Court reasoned that, since the district court was aware that the grand jury was investigating racketeering, it should have recognized that questions concerning Hoffman's current occupation might require answers relating to violations of federal gambling laws. It also should have recognized that the questions concerning Hoffman's contacts with the fugitive witness might relate to efforts to hide that witness. See also *Malloy v. Ho-*

gan, 378 U.S. 1, 84 S.Ct. 1489, 12 L.Ed. 2d 653 (1964) (lower court erred in refusing to recognize self-incrimination claim by witness who had pled guilty to a gambling charge and was asked about the circumstances surrounding his arrest and plea; the questions were designed to determine the identity of the witness' employer in the gambling operation, and "if this person were still engaged in unlawful activity, disclosure of his name might furnish a link in a chain of evidence sufficient to connect the petitioner with a more recent crime for which he might still be prosecuted").

3. *Incrimination under the laws of another sovereign.* For many years, American courts took the position that the privilege protected only against incrimination under the laws of the sovereign which was attempting to compel the incriminating testimony. However, in *Murphy v. Waterfront Comm.,* 378 U.S. 52, 84 S.Ct. 1594, 12 L.Ed.2d 678 (1964), the Supreme Court rejected this "separate sovereign" limitation as applied to state and federal inquiries. Noting that a "separate sovereign" limitation would permit a witness to be "whip-sawed into incriminating himself under both state and federal law," the Court concluded that the "policies and purposes" of the Fifth Amendment required that the privilege protect "a state witness against incrimination under federal as well as state law and a federal witness against incrimination under state as well as federal law." Does it follow from *Murphy* that the privilege should be available where the witness' testimony would be incriminating only in a foreign country? See *Zicarelli v. New Jersey Investigation Commission*, 406 U.S. 472, 92 S.Ct. 1670, 32 L.Ed.2d 234 (1972) (issue left open, as it would be properly presented only where there was a "real danger" of foreign prosecution).

4. *Waiver.* Once a grand jury witness begins to provide incriminating information on a particular subject, does that action bar raising the privilege as to subsequent questions dealing with the same subject? If the answer might be incriminating as to a different offense, the privilege clearly is available, but that may not be the case where the only potential for incrimination is to the same offense suggested by the earlier testimony. Here the applicable standard is that set forth in *Rogers v. United States,* 340 U.S. 367, 71 S.Ct. 438, 95 L.Ed. 344 (1951). The Court there noted that "disclosure of [an incriminating] fact waives the privilege as to details" as the further disclosure does not then present "a reasonable danger of further incrimination in light of all the circumstances, including [the] previous disclosures." To allow a claim of the privilege as to details "would [only] open the way to distortion of facts by permitting a witness to select any stopping point in the testimony."

Application of the *Rogers* standard is not always easy, as the division of the Court in *Rogers* itself suggests. In that case, a grand jury was seeking various records of the Communist Party branch in Denver. The witness Rogers admitted that she had been treasurer of the branch, but stated that she had turned the records over to another person. When asked to name that person, she initially refused to do so on the ground that she would not subject other persons to "the same thing that I'm going through." After consulting with counsel, she shifted to reliance on her privilege against self-incrimination. A divided Supreme Court (5–3) rejected that claim (described by the Court majority as a "pure afterthought"). The majority noted that the privilege was "purely personal" and could not be utilized to protect others. Rogers had already incriminated herself by admitting her party membership and her prior possession and transfer of the records; the "mere disclosure of the name of the recipient of the books" presented no more than an "imaginary possibility" of "increasing the danger of her prosecution" for a possible conspiracy to violate the Smith Act. While it was true that "at least two persons are required to constitute a conspiracy, * * * the identity of the other members * * * is not needed inasmuch as one person can be convicted of conspiring with persons whose names are unknown." The dissenters saw the matter quite differently. There was a clear potential for additional incrimination, they noted, since petitioner's conviction could well "depend on testimony of the witnesses she was * * * asked to identify." The Court's analysis, they contended, made the "protection [of the privilege] dependent on timing that was so refined that lawyers, let alone laymen, will have difficulty in knowing when to claim it."

5. *Compelling the target to appear.* The self-incrimination privilege has long been held to prohibit the prosecution from forcing a defendant to appear as a witness at his own trial. Should the prosecutor similarly be prohibited from forcing the target of an investigation to appear before the grand jury, or is the Fifth Amendment satisfied by simply allowing the target-witness, like any other witness, to refuse to respond to individual questions where his answer might be incriminating? Several state courts have argued that the target of an investigation is, in effect, a "putative" or "de facto" defendant, and he therefore should be allowed to exercise his privilege in much the same manner as a "de jure defendant" at trial. They hold that, unless the target expressly waives his self-incrimination privilege, the prosecution cannot use the grand jury's subpoena authority to force him to appear. See LaFave and Israel, § 8.10(c). On the other side, the federal courts and most state courts have taken the position that the Fifth Amendment, as to the target as well as any other grand jury witness, presents only an "option of refusal and not a prohibition of inquiry." *O'Connell v. United States,* 40 F.2d 201 (2d Cir.1930). The "obligation to appear," the Supreme Court noted in *Dionisio* [p. 715 supra], is "no different for a person who may himself be the subject of the grand jury inquiry."

What justifies the different treatment of the trial defendant and the grand jury target, even when that target is so close to indictment that the court will refer to him as a "putative" defendant? Consider the following arguments: (1) the defendant's right of silence grew out of the early common law rule on the incompetency of parties to testify, which had a bearing only on the trial; (2) the right not to take the stand at trial seeks to protect the defendant from being placed in a position where he may be forced to refuse to answer questions on self-incrimination grounds in the presence of the jury (who may conclude that he therefore has something to hide), but that protective feature has less significance in the grand jury setting since that body docs no more than charge and its proceedings therefore need not be conducted "with the assiduous regard for the preservation of procedural safeguards which normally attends the ultimate trial of the issues"; (3) the grand jury, having an obligation to "run down every clue," cannot ignore the possibility that the target's testimony may lead to the identification of others who also participated in the criminal enterprise; (4) the grand jury, having an obligation to "shield the innocent," must be able to seek the target's own testimony to determine whether it might not "explain away" the evidence against him; and (5) determining whether a witness was a "target" is not easy under any standard for establishing that status [see Note 8, p. 743 infra], and a prohibition against compelling a target to testify would lead to after-the-fact disputes as to whether a witness who gave incriminating testimony was actually a target.

6. Should a jurisdiction, as a matter of appropriate supervision of grand jury proceedings, bar the grand jury and prosecutor from insisting upon the appearance of a target when that person has previously informed the prosecutor that he will exercise the privilege as to all questions that relate to the subject under inquiry? The American Bar Association has urged adop-

tion of such a prohibition, arguing that to compel a witness to appear under such circumstances serves only to "prejudice the witness in the eyes of the grand jury." I A.B.A. Standards § 3–3.6. The Justice Department, in rejecting the A.B.A. position, argued that it rests upon an unwarranted assumption "that the witness knows the precise questions to be asked of him, and also is an accurate judge as to the availability, as to those questions, of a Fifth Amendment privilege." Internal Justice Department guidelines provide that a subpoenaed target "ordinarily" should be excused if he has given advance notice of his intention to exercise the privilege, but they also authorize the grand jury and U.S. Attorney to jointly agree to "insist on the appearance" in exceptional cases. In making that determination, the grand jury and U.S. Attorney are directed to give "careful attention" to the importance of the testimony sought from the target, whether the substance of that testimony could be provided by other witnesses, and whether the "questions the prosecutor and the grand jurors intend to ask * * * would be protected by a valid claim of the privilege." U.S. Attorney's Manual 9–11.254.

7. *Self-incrimination warnings.* It generally is agreed that the Fifth Amendment does not demand that a non-target witness be advised of his privilege against self-incrimination. Lower courts are divided as to whether such advice must be given to a target, with most of the more recent rulings holding that self-incrimination warnings are constitutionally required. See LaFave and Israel, § 8.10(d). In UNITED STATES v. MANDUJANO, 425 U.S. 564, 96 S.Ct. 1768, 48 L.Ed.2d 212 (1976), there was considerable discussion bearing on that question although the Court found it unnecessary to resolve the issue. The defendant Mandujano, known by the prosecutor to be a narcotics user, was called before the grand jury in the hope that he would furnish information about significant dealers. Instead, he steadfastly denied any involvement in the sale of narcotics and specifically disclaimed having sought within the year to make a purchase for a third-party for $650.00. The latter statement was a lie since (as the prosecutor already knew) Mandujano had recently tried to make such a purchase for a person who was actually an undercover agent. Subsequently prosecuted for perjury, Mandujano moved to suppress the grand jury testimony which was the basis of the charge. The trial court granted the motion on the ground that Mandujano had not been given full *Miranda* warnings prior to testifying. He had been informed of his privilege against self-incrimination and had been advised that he could have a retained lawyer located outside the grand jury room for the purpose of consultation. However, he had not been told that a lawyer could be appointed at state expense even though he had informed the prosecutor that he could not afford to hire a lawyer. The Court unanimously concluded that, even if adequate warnings had not been given, that failure could not constitute a defense to a perjury charge. Six of the justices went on, however, to speak to the adequacy of the warnings.

Burger, C.J., joined by Justices White, Powell, and Rehnquist, concluded that the warnings here clearly were adequate. As the Chief Justice noted, since the witness had been informed of his privilege against self-incrimination, there was no need to decide whether that warning was required constitutionally. Nevertheless, both in his comments on the lower court's reasoning and in his discussion of the witness' responsibility to invoke the privilege, the Chief Justice suggested that warning would not be required. Speaking initially to the witness' responsibility, Chief Justice BURGER noted:

"The very availability of the Fifth Amendment privilege to grand jury witnesses suggests that occasions will often arise when potentially incriminating questions will be asked in the ordinary course of the jury's investigation. * * * This is true whether the grand jury embarks upon an inquiry focused upon individuals suspected of wrongdoing, or is directed at persons suspected of no misconduct but who may be able to provide links in a chain of evidence relating to criminal conduct of others, or is centered upon broader problems of concern to society. * * * Since the subject matter of the inquiry is crime, and often organized, systematic crime—as is true with drug traffic—it is unrealistic to assume that all of the witnesses capable of providing useful information will be pristine pillars of the community untainted by criminality. * * * [T]he witness can, of course, stand on the privilege, assured that its protection 'is as broad as the mischief against which it seeks to guard.' *Counselman v. Hitchcock* [Note 1 supra]. The witness must invoke the privilege however, as the 'Constitution does not forbid the asking of criminative questions.' *United States v. Monia,* 317 U.S., at 433, 63 S.Ct., at 413, 87 L.Ed., at 383 [1943] (Frankfurter, J., dissenting).

> The [Fifth] Amendment speaks of compulsion. It does not preclude a witness from testifying voluntarily in matters which may incriminate him. If, therefore, he desires the protection of the privilege, he must claim it or he will not be considered to have been "compelled" within the meaning of the Amendment.

Absent a claim of the privilege, the duty to give testimony remains absolute."

Turning to the lower court's reasoning, the Chief Justice found *Miranda* clearly distinguishable. That case, he noted, "addressed extra-judicial confessions or admissions procured in a hostile, unfamiliar environment which lacked procedural safeguards." The *Miranda* warnings "sought to negate the 'compulsion' thought to be inherent in police interrogation." *Miranda* itself recognized "that many official investigations, such as grand jury questioning, take place in a setting wholly different from custodial police interrogation." To extend a standard devised to combat "police coercion" found in such practices as the "third degree" to "questioning before a grand jury inquiry into criminal activity under the guidance of a judge" would be "an extravagant expansion never remotely contemplated by this Court in *Miranda.*"

BRENNAN, J., joined by Marshall, J., responded to what he viewed as a "denigration of the privilege against self-incrimination" in the Chief Justice's opinion. Justice Brennan did not challenge the Chief Justice's efforts to distinguish *Miranda,* but criticized instead the Chief Justice's "mechanical" reliance upon *United States v. Monia.* Justice Brennan argued:

"In my view, the conception of the Fifth Amendment privilege expressed in the *Monia* dictum is explainable only by reference to the facts and circumstances of the only case cited in support by *Monia*—*Vajtauer v. Commissioner of Immigration,* 273 U.S. 103, 47 S.Ct. 302, 71 L.Ed. 560 (1927). That case involved questions concerning the Fifth Amendment privilege in a deportation proceeding. In holding that the prospective deportee's privilege against compulsory self-incrimination had not been violated in the circumstances, the Court rested on the failure to assert any claim of privilege in the proceeding. Essential to the Court's holding was the observation that

> [i]t is for the tribunal conducting the trial to determine what weight should be given to the contention of the witness that the answer sought will incriminate him, * * * a determination which it cannot make if not advised of the contention. * * * The privilege may not be relied on and must be deemed waived if not in some manner fairly brought to the attention of the tribunal which must pass upon it.

It is only in a context where this 'lack of notice on the part of the government' rationale has significance that we can possibly justify the *Monia* dictum that a witness testifying under judicial compulsion—that classic form of compulsion to which the Fifth Amendment is centrally addressed—must claim the privilege or else, without any further analysis, 'he will not be considered to have been "compelled" within the meaning of the Amendment.'

"* * * Indeed, in the situation where a prior claim is excused and a knowing and completely voluntary waiver of the privilege is required—the situation of the *Miranda*-type custodial interrogation—the reason is that 'the inquiring government is *acutely aware* of the potentially incriminating nature of the disclosures sought.' *Garner v. United States,* 424 U.S. 648, 96 S.Ct. 1178, 47 L.Ed.2d 370 (1976). * * * I submit that this more discriminating analysis is also required in the situation in which a putative or *de facto* defendant is called to testify under judicial compulsion before a grand jury; otherwise we countenance a serious erosion of fundamental guarantees of the Constitution.

"It is clear that the government may not in the absence of an intentional and knowing waiver call an indicted defendant before a grand jury and there interrogate him concerning the subject matter of a crime for which he already stands formally charged. * * * Given the prosecutor's authority to choose the precise timing of a criminal indictment, it is not surprising that commentary uniformly decries the attempted distinction between a *de facto* and *de jure* defendant in the determination of the amount of protection accorded by the Fifth Amendment privilege. * * * Indeed, it seems obvious that a *de facto* defendant's privilege is placed in much greater jeopardy than that of a *de jure* defendant, who has at least been informed of the charges against him and is more likely to have consulted with counsel and thereby have been made aware of his privilege. * * *

"Thus, I would hold that, in the absence of an intentional and intelligent waiver by the individual of his known right to be free from compulsory self-incrimination, the Government may not call before a grand jury one whom it has probable cause—as measured by an objective standard [15]—to suspect committed a crime and by use of judicial compulsion compel him to testify with regard to that crime. In the absence of such a waiver, the Fifth Amendment requires that any testimony obtained in this fashion be unavailable to the Government for use at trial. Such a waiver could readily be demonstrated by proof that the individual was warned prior to questioning that he is currently subject to possible criminal prosecution for the commission of a stated crime, that he has a constitutional right to refuse to answer any and all questions that may tend to incriminate him, and by record evidence that the individual understood the nature of his situation and privilege prior to giving testimony. * * *

"[T]he requirements of an effective warning and an intelligent waiver by a putative defendant prior to attempts to elicit potentially incriminating information impose no onerous duty on the prosecutor. The reported decisions of the lower federal courts are replete with examples of prosecuting officials proffering such warnings as an essential element of our fundamental liberties. Where uncertain whether the situation requires it, the prosecutor may

15. Others have argued for a rule which would combine objective elements with the prosecutor's subjective intent subsequently to charge the individual by indictment. See *United States v. Scully,* 225 F.2d [113], at 117 [2d Cir.1955] (Frank, J., concurring in the judgment). But this subjective intent requirement may pose grave administrative difficulties, see *United States v. Grossman,* 154 F.Supp. 813 (N.J.1957), whereas the purely objective standard is easily manageable both for the prosecutor at the point of decision to call an individual suspect before the grand jury, and for the reviewing court. Clearly it costs the prosecutor nothing in terms of constitutionally permissible criteria to resolve any doubts in favor of warning the witness. I would at present leave open the proper answer to the case of a witness called to testify in the absence of probable cause, but whose testimony thereafter develops a case of probable cause.

safely err on the side of ensuring the knowing and intentional nature of the waiver, for he does no more than discharge his responsibility to safeguard a constitutional guarantee calculated to ensure the liberty of us all. Only when these safeguards are afforded a putative defendant called and interrogated before a grand jury may we truthfully proclaim that the Fifth Amendment 'privilege * * * is as broad as the mischief against which it seeks to guard.' "[b]

8. *Prospective defendant standard.* Assuming a jurisdiction requires that warnings be given to witnesses characterized as "targets" or "putative defendants," what standard should be applied to determine whether a witness falls within that category? Is Justice Brennan correct in assuming that a standard which considers subjective intent poses greater administrative difficulties than a purely objective standard? See fn. 15 at p. 742 supra. Consider Enker and Elsen, *Counsel for the Suspect,* 49 Minn. L.Rev. 47, 74 (1964): "The existence of probable cause may conceivably be determined after analysis of a lengthy record, but when the grand jurors or prosecutors have not yet analyzed their record, or have done so only tentatively or hastily, or have made an error—as happens in any large human enterprise—they may not realize it. Yet hindsight, * * * particularly if the test is to be objective, could serve to vitiate much of their work by suppressing testimony taken after what later appears to be the crucial point."

Would it be preferable, from the viewpoint of legislative policy, to require that all witnesses be given warnings? Several states have adopted such a requirement as matter of state law, and the Justice Department has done likewise as an internal guideline. See Note 10 infra. To ensure that the witness is aware of his rights before he even appears before the grand jury, federal prosecutors and prosecutors in various states follow the practice of attaching a notification of rights to the grand jury subpoena. Those opposed to the practice of giving warnings to non-target witnesses argue that (1) "improvidently given warnings may unduly frighten the [non-target] witness" and deter him from testifying freely; (2) warnings may lead the non-target witness to obtain counsel, causing him unnecessary expense; and (3) giving non-target witness warnings would be inconsistent with the treatment of trial witnesses, who are not given such warnings. See House Hearings, p. 731 supra, at 208, 472. Compare id. at 718 (statement of Assistant Attorney General Civiletti): "[The] truth-engendering atmosphere of the grand jury is sufficient in our view to dispel the concern that the giving of such a warning will frighten the non-target witness and lead to grand juries being deprived of testimony that otherwise would be offered. Such warnings, moreover, serve the public's perception of fundamental fairness."

9. *Target warnings.* In UNITED STATES v. WASHINGTON, 431 U.S. 181, 97 S.Ct. 1814, 52 L.Ed.2d 238 (1977), the Court answered one of the issues left open in *Mandujano:* a witness need not be warned that he is a target of the grand jury investigation. Defendant Washington had been questioned by police concerning a stolen motorcycle found in his truck. He subsequently was questioned by a prosecuting attorney, who served him with a subpoena to testify before a grand jury. When he appeared before the grand jury, the prosecuting attorney had not informed Washington that he might be indicted in connection with the stolen motorcycle charge (Washington had been

b. In *Minnesota v. Murphy,* p. 584 supra, the Supreme Court drew an analogy to the grand jury setting in holding that a probationer questioned by his probation officer was not entitled to *Miranda* warnings. The interview setting in *Murphy,* the Court noted, subjected the probationer to "less intimidating pressure than is imposed upon a grand jury witness." Accordingly, since the Court had "never held that [warnings] must be given to the grand jury witness," it would "decline to require them here."

called because both the prosecutor and police had been "more than a little skeptical" of his explanation of the presence of the motorcycle in his truck). The prosecutor had given Washington full *Miranda*-type warnings prior to any questioning, and Washington had stated that he understood those rights and was prepared to answer questions relating to the stolen motorcycle. He then proceeded to again explain that the motorcycle had been placed in the truck by an unknown motorist he had stopped to help. Washington subsequently was indicted for theft by the grand jury. The trial court suppressed his grand jury testimony on the ground that his privilege against self-incrimination had been violated by the prosecutor's failure to advise him that he was a potential defendant. The Supreme Court rejected that ruling in an opinion by Chief Justice BURGER:

"After being sworn, respondent was explicitly advised that he had a right to remain silent and that any statements he did make could be used to convict him of crime. It is inconceivable that such a warning would fail to alert him to his right to refuse to answer any questions which might incriminate him. * * * Even in the presumed psychologically coercive atmosphere of police custodial interrogation, *Miranda* does not require that any additional warnings be given simply because the suspect is a potential defendant; indeed, such suspects are potential defendants more often than not. Respondent points out that unlike one subject to custodial interrogation, whose arrest should inform him only too clearly that he is a potential criminal defendant, a grand jury witness may well be unaware that he is targeted for possible prosecution. While this may be so in some situations, it is an overdrawn generalization. In any case, events here clearly put respondent on notice that he was a suspect in the motorcycle theft. * * *

"However, all of this is largely irrelevant, since we do not understand what constitutional disadvantage a failure to give potential defendant warnings could possibly inflict on a grand jury witness, whether or not he has received other warnings. * * * Because target witness status neither enlarges nor diminishes the constitutional protection against compelled self-incrimination, potential defendant warnings add nothing of value to protection of Fifth Amendment rights."

Justice Brennan, joined by Justice Marshall, dissented, relying in substantial part on his discussion of the need for warnings in *Mandujano.*

10. *Federal practice.* In December 1977, a revision of the United States Attorney's Manual included the following guidelines on grand jury practice:

"*Section* 9–11.250. * * * Notwithstanding the lack of a clear constitutional imperative, it is the internal policy of the Department to advise grand jury witnesses of the following matters: * * * (2) that the witness may refuse to answer any question if a truthful answer to the question would tend to incriminate him; (3) that anything that the witness does say may be used against him; and (4) that the grand jury will permit the witness the reasonable opportunity to step outside the grand jury room to consult with counsel if he desires. * * * Moreover, although the Court in *United States v. Washington,* held that 'targets' of the grand jury's investigation are entitled to no special warnings relative to their status as 'potential defendant(s) in danger of indictment,' we will continue the long-standing internal practice of the Department to advise witnesses who are known 'targets' of the investigation * * * that their conduct is being investigated for possible violation of federal criminal law. * * * A 'target' is a person as to whom the prosecutor or the grand jury has substantial evidence linking him to the commission of a crime and who, in the judgment of the prosecutor, is a putative defendant."

II. IMMUNITY GRANTS

1. *Constitutionality.* The use of an immunity grant to preclude reliance upon the self-incrimination privilege dates back to the English practice known as providing "indemnity" against prosecution. See *Kastigar v. United States,* Note 2 infra (also noting the use of immunity grants in the American Colonies). Immunity grants were first upheld under the federal constitution in *Brown v. Walker,* 161 U.S. 591, 16 S.Ct. 644, 40 L.Ed. 819 (1896). A divided Court (5–4) noted that the Fifth Amendment could not be "construed literally as authorizing the witness to refuse to disclose any fact which might tend to incriminate, disgrace, or expose him to unfavorable comments." The history of the Amendment, the majority noted, indicated that its object was only to "secure the witness against criminal prosecution." Thus, the self-incrimination privilege had been held inapplicable where the witness' compelled testimony would relate only to an offense as to which he had been pardoned or as to which the statute of limitations had run. So too, the privilege did not apply where the witness' response might tend to "disgrace him or bring him into disrepute" but would furnish no information relating to a criminal offense. The majority reasoned that once it was accepted that the object of the privilege was limited to protecting the witness against criminal prosecution, the constitutionality of the immunity grant necessarily followed. Since the grant removed the danger against which the privilege protected the witness, the witness could no longer rely upon the privilege.[a]

2. *Scope of the Immunity. Counselman v. Hitchcock,* 142 U.S. 547, 12 S.Ct. 195, 35 L.Ed. 1110 (1892), struck down a federal immunity statute that granted the witness protection only against the use of his immunized testimony as evidence in any subsequent prosecution. The Supreme Court concluded that such limited protection immunity was not sufficient to replace the Fifth Amendment privilege. The Court stressed that there was no protection against derivative use of the witness' testimony. Thus, the statute "could not, and would not, prevent the use of his testimony to search out other testimony to be used in evidence against him." At the conclusion of its opinion, however, the Court spoke in terms of even broader protection. "To be valid," it noted, an immunity grant "must afford absolute immunity against future prosecution for the offense to which the question relates." This statement was read as indicating that the immunity grant must absolutely bar prosecution for any transaction noted in the witness' testimony. Accordingly, Congress adopted a new immunity statute providing for "transactional immunity." It provided that a witness directed to testify or produce documentary evidence pursuant to an immunity order could not be prosecuted "for or on account of any transaction, matter, or thing concerning which he may testify or produce evidence." The constitutionality of this provision was upheld in *Brown v. Walker,* supra, and subsequent state and federal immunity statutes

a. Although the Court was sharply divided in *Brown,* that division focused on whether the immunity had to extend to both federal and state prosecutions. The position of the dissenters that immunity must extend to both sovereigns was eventually adopted in *Murphy v. Waterfront Commission,* discussed at Note 3, p. 738 supra. The basic analysis which led *Brown* to accept the immunity grant as consistent with the purpose of the privilege was put to a challenge in *Ullmann v. United States,* 350 U.S. 422, 76 S.Ct. 497, 100 L.Ed. 511 (1956). Ullmann argued that immunity from prosecution should not supplant the Fifth Amendment when the resulting testimony (here, acknowledgement of membership in the Communist party) could lead to a wide range of legal disabilities as well as public opprobrium. A function of the privilege, petitioner argued, was to protect political and religious deviants, and immunity from prosecution failed to provide that protection. The Court (over the vigorous dissents of Justices Douglas and Black) rejected that claim. It noted that *Brown* had correctly defined the total purpose of the privilege and characterized the immunity grant as having become "part of our constitutional fabric."

were largely patterned upon the *Brown* statute.

Subsequent decisions—and the language of later statutes—recognized two limitations on the scope of transactional immunity. First, transactional immunity does not preclude a prosecution for perjury based on the immunized testimony. Second, transactional immunity does not extend to an event described in an answer totally unresponsive to the question asked. Thus, the witness cannot gain immunity from prosecution for all previous criminal acts by simply including a reference to those acts in his testimony without regard to the subject on which he was asked to testify.

In *Murphy v. Waterfront Commission,* Note 3, p. 738 supra, the Court first upheld immunity that was not as broad in scope as the traditional transactional immunity. After rejecting the separate sovereign doctrine as a limitation on the privilege's availability in either federal or state proceedings, *Murphy* turned to the scope of the immunity that must be granted to supplant the privilege as it related to prosecution in another jurisdiction. It concluded that the immunity granted in one jurisdiction (federal or state) need not absolutely bar prosecution in the other; it was sufficient to bar both use and derivative use of the witness' testimony in the other jurisdiction.

Following *Murphy,* Congress adopted a general immunity provision that granted federal witnesses protection only against use and derivative use as to federal as well as state prosecution. The statute provided that "no testimony or other information compelled under the [immunity] order (or any information directly or indirectly derived from such testimony or other information) may be used against the witness in any criminal case, except a prosecution for perjury, giving a false statement, or otherwise failing to comply with the order." 18 U.S.C. § 6002. In KASTIGAR v. UNITED STATES, 406 U.S. 441, 92 S.Ct. 1653, 32 L.Ed.2d 212 (1972), a divided Court (5–2) upheld the new federal provision.

Justice POWELL's opinion for the *Kastigar* majority discounted the "broad language in *Counselman,*" which suggested the need for transactional immunity, as inconsistent with the "conceptual basis" of the *Counselman* ruling. The crucial question, as *Counselman* noted, was whether the immunity granted was "coextensive with the scope of the privilege against self-incrimination." Both *Murphy* and the cases applying the exclusionary rule to evidence obtained through Fifth Amendment violations indicated that the constitutional privilege required no more than a prohibition against use and derivative use. The new federal statute clearly met that standard: "The statute provides a sweeping proscription of any use, direct or indirect, of the compelled testimony and any information derived therefrom. This total prohibition on use provides a comprehensive safeguard, barring the use of compelled testimony as an 'investigatory lead,' and also barring the use of any evidence obtained by focusing investigation on a witness as a result of his compelled disclosures."

The *Kastigar* majority rejected the argument, relied on by the dissenters, that the bar against derivative use could not be enforced effectively. Appropriate procedures for "taint hearings" could ensure that derivative use was not made of immunized testimony. Those procedural safeguards were described as follows: "As stated in *Murphy:* 'Once a defendant demonstrates that he has testified, under a state grant of immunity to matters related to the federal prosecution, the federal authorities have the burden of showing that their evidence is not tainted by establishing that they had an independent, legitimate source for the disputed evidence.' This burden of proof, which we reaffirm as appropriate, is not limited to a negation of taint; rather, it imposes on the prosecution the affirmative duty to prove that the evidence it proposes to use is derived from a legitimate source wholly independent of the compelled testimony. This is very substantial protection, commensurate with that resulting from invoking the privilege itself. * * * [Indeed], a defendant against whom incriminating evidence has been obtained through a grant of immunity may be in a stronger position at trial than a defendant who asserts a Fifth Amendment coerced-confession claim. One raising a claim under this statute need only show that he testified under a grant of immunity in order to shift to the government the heavy burden of proving that all of the evidence it proposes to use was derived from legitimate independent sources. On the other hand, a defendant raising a coerced-confession claim under the Fifth Amendment must first prevail in a voluntariness hearing before his confession and evidence derived from it become inadmissible."

3. In a companion case to *Kastigar, Zicarelli v. New Jersey State Comm. of Investigation,* 406 U.S. 472, 92 S.Ct. 1670, 32 L.Ed. 2d 234 (1972), the Court upheld a state immunity statute providing for use/derivative-use immunity. Since *Zicarelli* was decided, a substantial number of states have moved from transactional to use/derivative-use immunity. The A.B.A. and N.C.C.U. S.L. have urged retention of transactional immunity, however, and a majority of the states continue to provide the broader immunity. The debate between the proponents of the two types of immunity has tended to focus on three issues—the adequacy of taint hearings in preventing derivative use of immunized testimony, the comparative effectiveness of the two types of immunity in achieving witness cooperation, and the practical significance of the prosecutor's ability to bring a subsequent prosecution under use/derivative-use immunity. See e.g., Symposium, *The Granting of Witness Immunity,* 67 J.Crim.L. & C. 129–180 (1976) (articles by Carlson, Bauer, Thornburg, and Wolfson).

With respect to taint hearings, proponents and opponents of use/derivative-use immunity largely disagree on the effectiveness of even the strictest standards in ensuring that a prosecutor will not make some indirect use of the testimony and thereby derive an advantage that it would not have had if the witness had been allowed to refuse to testify on the basis of his self-incrimination privilege. As to the effectiveness of the immunity in gaining truthful and complete testimony from a recalcitrant witness, each side claims advantages for the type of immunity it favors. Proponents of transactional immunity claim that witnesses given use/derivative-use immunity are less likely to be open in testifying because they lack confidence that the prosecutor will be prevented from making use of their testimony in any subsequent prosecution. Proponents of use/derivative-use immunity, on the other hand, see such immunity as encouraging the witness to provide as much detail as possible so as to make it more difficult for the government to establish that no use was made of that testimony in any subsequent prosecution. They also contend that the absence of an absolute protection against subsequent prosecution makes the immunized witness' testimony more credible to the jury.

As to the practical significance of loosing subsequent prosecutions based upon independent sources where the witness is granted transactional immunity, proponents of transactional immunity argue that "the small number of actual successful prosecutions of immunized witnesses with 'use' immunity indicates that a return to transactional immunity will not remove a significant weapon against organized crime." *A.B.A. Legislative Principles for Grand Jury Reform* (August 9, 1977) (commentary to principle # 17). Proponents of use/derivative-use immunity acknowledge that the prosecutions of immunized witnesses can be characterized as rare occurrences in the federal system and at least as an infrequent occurrence in the states. They argue, however, that there are substantial reasons for such prosecutions, and the interests of justice would suffer if the witnesses involved, though small in number, were given the "gratuity of absolute immunity." There is no reason, they note, to run the "risk that a witness, who is subsequently and independently found to be more deserving of prosecution than originally thought, will be absolutely immune from a prosecution despite the existence of such independent evidence." House Hearings, p. 731 supra, at 713. Subsequent prosecution is also important, they argue, where the prosecution from the outset has sufficient evidence to prosecute and would ordinarily prosecute, convict, and then grant immunity, but lacks the time to do so because the witness-defendant's testimony is needed immediately in investigating other participants.

4. *Establishing an independent source.* How extensive is the prohibition against derivative use? Consider *United States v. Smith,* 580 F.Supp. 1418 (D.N.J.1984):

"The government's burden is not limited to a showing that it will not use the testimony directly (for example, introducing it into evidence) or indirectly (for example, as a means to other evidence). It also has the 'affirmative duty' of showing that it did not and will not exploit the immunized testimony in more subtle, elusive ways. In *United States v. Semkiw,* 712 F.2d 891 (3d Cir.1983), the Third Circuit warned that '[s]uch use could conceivably include . . . refusing to plea-bargain, interpreting evidence, planning cross-examination, and otherwise planning trial strategy.' The court has even suggested that the use of immunized testimony as a morale booster or to provide additional confidence to federal prosecutors in preparing for trial may be an impermissible use of immunized testimony. Cf. Note, 82 Yale L.J. 171, 181 (1972) ('No one . . . can accurately estimate the subjective effect of knowledge of the witness's guilt on the investigator's zeal in pursuing new evidence')."

If one accepts such an extensive view of derivative use, does it follow that the government must establish that the prosecution operated within a "Chinese Wall" (i.e., that the investigative and prosecutorial staff responsible for the prosecution did not read the immunized testimony or received information from those who had read it)? If it can be shown that a Chinese Wall existed, must the prosecution nevertheless also cite the specific independent sources which led it to the discovery of each piece of evidence it uses. See *United States v. Smith,* supra (so holding). If the prosecution can establish that it had each item of evidence in its possession before the witness was immunized, would that be sufficient? See *Semkiw,* supra (pre-immunization knowledge of evidence used does not preclude the possibility that the immunized testimony was employed in interpreting previously received evidence or planning cross-examination). Since a pretrial taint hearing will undoubtedly give the defendant extensive discovery, can the taint issue properly be reserved for a post-trial proceeding? See *Smith,* supra (pretrial hearing preferred so to ensure proper exclusion of tainted evidence and thereby avoid a wasted trial).

5. *Immunity procedures.* In most jurisdictions, the prosecutor may not grant immunity on his own authority, but must obtain a court order. Ordinarily, however, the scope of judicial review of an immunity application is quite limited. Under the federal immunity statute, for example, the court is directed to issue the immunity order provided the prosecutor has followed specified procedural requirements. Those requirements are: (1) that the request for an immunity order be approved by the Attorney General, Deputy Attorney General, or a designated Assistant Attorney General; and (2) that the U.S. Attorney making the request state that, "in his judgment," (i) the "testimony or other information * * * [sought from the witness] may be necessary to the public interest," and (ii) the witness "has refused or is likely to refuse to testify or provide other information on the basis of his privilege against self-incrimination." 18 U.S.C.

§ 6003. If the U.S. Attorney has complied with these requirements, the court may not refuse to grant the order on the ground, for example, that it disagrees with the conclusion that the grant may be necessary to the public interest. See *In re Santiago,* 533 F.2d 727 (1st Cir.1976).[b] Once the immunity order is granted, the witness must either testify or face contempt sanctions, unless he has some legal justification (e.g., the attorney-client privilege) for refusing to respond. The witness may not refuse to testify because his answers will subject him to substantial civil liability. See, e.g., *Patrick v. United States,* 524 F.2d 1109 (7th Cir.1975) (federal tax liability). Nor may he refuse to testify because he is fearful of physical or economic retaliation by associates or others. See LaFave and Israel, § 8.11(c). Assume that a prosecutor knows that members of a certain criminal organization will stand in contempt and take a jail sentence rather than risk retaliation for testifying against the group. Is it improper to give some of those persons immunity and thereby raise the "cost" of belonging to such a group? What if the prosecutor is willing to provide protection against retaliation through a program such as the Federal Witness Protection program?

III. THE PRODUCTION OF DOCUMENTS: DETERMINING THE SCOPE OF THE PRIVILEGE

BELLIS v. UNITED STATES

417 U.S. 85, 94 S.Ct. 2179, 40 L.Ed.2d 678 (1974).

MR. JUSTICE MARSHALL delivered the opinion of the Court.

The question presented in this case is whether a partner in a small law firm may invoke his personal privilege against self-incrimination to justify his refusal to comply with a subpoena requiring production of the partnership's financial records.

[The petitioner Bellis had been the senior partner in a three partner law firm from the period 1956–69. In addition to the three partners, the firm had six employees (associate attorneys, secretaries, and a receptionist). When the firm dissolved in 1969, Bellis maintained possession of its records. In 1973, he was served with a subpoena directing him to appear before a federal grand jury and to bring with him "all partnership records currently in your possession * * * for the years 1968 and 1969." Petitioner refused to produce the records, relying on his self-incrimination privilege. After that claim was denied, petitioner persisted in his refusal and was held in civil contempt, with the district court releasing him on his own recognizance pending an expedited appeal.]

It has long been established, of course, that the Fifth Amendment privilege against compulsory self-incrimination protects an individual from compelled production of his personal papers and effects as well as compelled oral testimony. In *Boyd v. United States* [p. 706 supra], we held that "any forcible and compulsory extortion of a man's own testimony, or of his private papers to be used as evidence to convict him of crime" would violate the Fifth Amendment privilege. [This] privilege applies to the business records of the sole proprietor or sole practitioner as well as to personal documents containing more intimate information about the individual's private life. *Boyd v. United States.* As the Court explained in *United States v. White,* [322 U.S. 694, 64 S.Ct. 1248, 88 L.Ed.

b. Does it follow from the legislative authorization of immunity grants under these procedures that the prosecutor should not be allowed to employ informal grants of immunity (i.e., promises as to the exercise of prosecutorial authority made in exchange for the witness testimony)? Very often those grants, where used, will not only bypass the statutory procedure but contain promises that are either substantially narrower or broader than the statutory immunity. While such informal grants are dependent upon witness acceptance (i.e., the court will not force a witness to testify in response to such a non-statutory promise), if the witness does accept and testify, the court will require the prosecution to live up to its promise. See LaFave and Israel, § 8.12.

1542 (1944),] "[t]he constitutional privilege against self-incrimination . . . is designed to prevent the use of legal process to force from the lips of the accused individual the evidence necessary to convict him or to force him to produce and authenticate any personal documents or effects that might incriminate him."

On the other hand, an equally long line of cases has established that an individual cannot rely upon the privilege to avoid producing the records of a collective entity which are in his possession in a representative capacity, even if these records might incriminate him personally. This doctrine was first announced in a series of cases dealing with corporate records. In *Wilson v. United States,* [221 U.S. 361, 31 S.Ct. 538, 55 L.Ed. 771 (1911),] the Court held that an officer of a corporation could not claim his privilege against compulsory self-incrimination to justify a refusal to produce the corporate books and records in response to a grand jury subpoena *duces tecum* directed to the corporation. A companion case, *Dreier v. United States,* 221 U.S. 394, 31 S.Ct. 550, 55 L.Ed. 784 (1911), held that the same result followed when the subpoena requiring production of the corporate books was directed to the individual corporate officer. * * * To some extent, these decisions were based upon the particular incidents of the corporate form, the Court observing that a corporation has limited powers granted to it by the State in its charter, and is subject to the retained "visitorial power" of the State to investigate its activities. But any thought that the principle formulated in these decisions was limited to corporate records was put to rest in *United States v. White,* supra. In *White,* we held that an officer of an unincorporated association, a labor union, could not claim his privilege against compulsory self-incrimination to justify his refusal to produce the union's records pursuant to a grand jury subpoena. * * * Relying on *White,* we have since upheld compelled production of the records of a variety of organizations over individuals' claims of Fifth Amendment privilege. See, e.g., *United States v. Fleischman,* 339 U.S. 349, 357–358, 70 S.Ct. 739, 743–744, 94 L.Ed. 906 (1950) (Joint Anti-Fascist Refugee Committee).

These decisions reflect the Court's consistent view that the privilege against compulsory self-incrimination should be "limited to its historic function of protecting only the natural individual from compulsory incrimination through his own testimony or personal records." *United States v. White.* * * * [As] Mr. Justice Murphy reasoned, "individuals, when acting as representatives of a collective group, cannot be said to be exercising their personal rights and duties nor to be entitled to their purely personal privileges. Rather they assume the rights, duties and privileges of the artificial entity or association of which they are agents or officers, and they are bound by its obligations." Ibid.

Since no artificial organization may utilize the personal privilege against compulsory self-incrimination, the Court found that it follows that an individual acting in his official capacity on behalf of the organization may likewise not take advantage of his personal privilege. In view of the inescapable fact that an artificial entity can only act to produce its records through its individual officers or agents, recognition of the individual's claim of privilege with respect to the financial records of the organization would substantially undermine the unchallenged rule that the organization itself is not entitled to claim any Fifth Amendment privilege, and largely frustrate legitimate governmental regulation of such organizations. Mr. Justice Murphy put it well:

> "The scope and nature of the economic activities of incorporated and unincorporated organizations and their representatives demand that the constitutional power of the federal and state governments to regulate those activities be correspondingly effective. The greater portion of evidence of wrongdoing by

an organization or its representatives is usually to be found in the official records and documents of that organization. Were the cloak of the privilege to be thrown around these impersonal records and documents, effective enforcement of many federal and state laws would be impossible. The framers of the constitutional guarantee against compulsory self-disclosure, who were interested primarily in protecting individual civil liberties, cannot be said to have intended the privilege to be available to protect economic or other interests of such organizations so as to nullify appropriate governmental regulations." *United States v. White* (citations omitted).

The Court's decisions holding the privilege inapplicable to the records of a collective entity also reflect a second, though obviously interrelated, policy underlying the privilege, the protection of an individual's right to a " 'private enclave where he may lead a private life.' " *Murphy v. Waterfront Comm'n* [p. 756 infra]. We have recognized that the Fifth Amendment "respects a private inner sanctum of individual feeling and thought"—an inner sanctum which necessarily includes an individual's papers and effects to the extent that the privilege bars their compulsory production and authentication—and "proscribes state intrusion to extract self-condemnation." *Couch v. United States,* [409 U.S. 322, 93 S.Ct. 611, 34 L.Ed.2d 548 (1973)]. Protection of individual privacy was the major theme running through the Court's decision in *Boyd,* and it was on this basis that the Court in *Wilson* distinguished the corporate records involved in that case from the private papers at issue in *Boyd.* But a substantial claim of privacy or confidentiality cannot often be maintained with respect to the financial records of an organized collective entity. Control of such records is generally strictly regulated by statute or by the rules and regulations of the organization, and access to the records is generally guaranteed to others in the organization. * * *

The analysis of the Court in *White,* of course, only makes sense in the context of what the Court described as "organized, institutional activity." This analysis presupposes the existence of an organization which is recognized as an independent entity apart from its individual members. The group must be relatively well organized and structured and not merely a loose, informal association of individuals. It must maintain a distinct set of organizational records, and recognize rights in its members of control and access to them. And the records subpoenaed must in fact be organizational records held in a representative capacity. In other words, it must be fair to say that the records demanded are the records of the organization rather than those of the individual under *White.*

The Court in *White* had little difficulty in concluding that the demand for production of the official records of a labor union, whether national or local, in the custody of an officer of the union, met these tests. * * * We think it is similarly clear that partnerships may and frequently do represent organized institutional activity so as to preclude any claim of Fifth Amendment privilege with respect to the partnership's financial records. Some of the most powerful private institutions in the Nation are conducted in the partnership form. Wall Street law firms and stock brokerage firms provide significant examples. These are often large, impersonal, highly structured enterprises of essentially perpetual duration. * * *

In this case, however, we are required to explore the outer limits of the analysis of the Court in *White.* Petitioner argues that in view of the modest size of the partnership involved here, it is unrealistic to consider the firm as an entity independent of its three partners; rather, he claims, the law firm embodies little more than the personal legal practice of the individual partners. Moreover, petitioner argues that he has a substantial and direct ownership interest in the partnership records, and does not hold them in a representative capacity.[2]

Despite the force of these arguments, we conclude that the lower courts properly applied the *White* rule in the circumstances of this case. While small, the partnership here did have an established institutional identity independent of its individual partners. This was not an informal association or a temporary arrangement for the undertaking of a few projects of short-lived duration. Rather, the partnership represented a formal institutional arrangement organized for the continuing conduct of the firm's legal practice. The partnership was in existence for nearly 15 years prior to its voluntary dissolution. Although it may not have had a formal constitution or bylaws to govern its internal affairs, state partnership law [adopting the Uniform Partnership Act] imposed on the firm a certain organizational structure in the absence of any contrary agreement by the partners; for example, it guaranteed to each of the partners the equal right to participate in the management and control of the firm, and prescribed that majority rule governed the conduct of the firm's business. The firm maintained a bank account in the partnership name, had stationery using the firm name on its letterhead, and, in general, held itself out to third parties as an entity with an independent institutional identity. It employed six persons in addition to its partners, including two other attorneys who practiced law on behalf of the firm, rather than as individuals on their own behalf. It filed separate partnership returns for federal tax purposes, as required by Internal Revenue Code. State law permitted the firm to be sued, and to hold title to property, in the partnership name and generally regarded the partnership as a distinct entity for numerous other purposes.

Equally important, we believe it is fair to say that petitioner is holding the subpoenaed partnership records in a representative capacity. The documents which petitioner has been ordered to produce are merely the financial books and records of the partnership.[9] These reflect the receipts and disbursements of the entire firm, including income generated by and salaries paid to the employees of the firm, and the financial transactions of the other partners. Petitioner holds these records subject to the rights granted to the other partners by state partnership law. * * * Indeed, Pennsylvania law specifically provides that "every partner shall at all times have access to and may inspect and copy any of [the partnership books]."

Petitioner relies heavily on language in the Court's opinion in *White* which suggests that the "test" for determining the applicability of the Fifth Amendment privilege in this area is whether the organization "has a character so impersonal in the scope of its membership and activities that it cannot be said to embody or represent the purely private or personal interests of its constituents, but rather to embody their common or group interests only." We must admit our agreement with the Solicitor General's observation that "it is difficult to know precisely what situations the formulation in *White* was intended to include within the protection of the privilege." The Court in *White,* after stating its test, did not really apply it, nor has any of the subsequent decisions of this Court.

2. Petitioner also argues that we have already decided the issue presented in this case, and held that the Fifth Amendment privilege could be claimed with respect to partnership records, in the *Boyd* case. It is true that the notice to produce involved in *Boyd* was in fact issued to E.A. Boyd & Sons, a partnership. However, at this early stage in the development of our Fifth Amendment jurisprudence, the potential significance of this fact was not observed by either the parties or the Court. * * *

9. Significantly, the District Court here excluded any client files from the scope of its order. A different case might be presented if petitioner had been ordered to produce files containing work which he had personally performed on behalf of his clients, even if these files might for some purposes be viewed as those of the partnership.

On its face, the test is not particularly helpful in the broad range of cases, including this one, where the organization embodies neither "purely . . . personal interests" nor "group interests only," but rather some combination of the two.

In any event, we do not believe that the Court's formulation in *White* can be reduced to a simple proposition based solely upon the size of the organization. It is well settled that no privilege can be claimed by the custodian of corporate records, regardless of how small the corporation may be. Every State has now adopted laws permitting incorporation of professional associations, and increasing numbers of lawyers, doctors, and other professionals are choosing to conduct their business affairs in the corporate form rather than the more traditional partnership. Whether corporation or partnership, many of these firms will be independent entities whose financial records are held by a member of the firm in a representative capacity. In these circumstances, the applicability of the privilege should not turn on an insubstantial difference in the form of the business enterprise.

This might be a different case if it involved a small family partnership, see *United States v. Slutsky,* 352 F.Supp. 1105 (S.D. N.Y.1972); *In re Subpoena Duces Tecum,* 81 F.Supp. [418,] at 421, [(N.D.Cal. 1948)] or, as the Solicitor General suggests, if there were some other pre-existing relationship of confidentiality among the partners. But in the circumstances of this case, petitioner's possession of the partnership's financial records in what can be fairly said to be a representative capacity compels our holding that his personal privilege against compulsory self-incrimination in inapplicable.

MR. JUSTICE DOUGLAS dissenting.

I think [this] case is clearly controlled by *Boyd v. United States,* and thus I dissent. * * * I would treat a partnership as *Boyd* treated it. This partnership is as different from a labor union or the run of corporations as black is from white. By the Court's opinion a man and wife who form a law partnership or medical partnership or dental partnership are treated as some kind of new "entity" so as to expand the power of government into an area from which the Fifth Amendment excludes it. * * * The majority refers to large law firms or brokerage houses as examples of partnerships which take on the characteristics of independent entities in the manner of corporations. None that I know could properly be considered an organization with "a character so impersonal in the scope of its membership and activities that it cannot be said to embody or represent the purely private or personal interests of its contituents," *White,* supra. That certainly is not the case presented here. At times the law may treat unlikes as if they were alike; but it surpasses understanding when a two- or three-man partnership is treated the same as members or officers of a giant corporation or a giant union. * * *

Notes and Questions

1. *The "small family partnership."* Consider in light of *Bellis,* IN RE GRAND JURY SUBPOENA DUCES TECUM DATED NOVEMBER 13, 1984 (DOE), 605 F.Supp. 174 (E.D.N.Y.1985). The court there considered a self-incrimination objection of one of two partners of a New York consulting firm to a grand jury subpoena directing the production of various partnership records. The partnership consisted of petitioner and his wife, had no employees, and produced an annual gross receipts of $85,000. Distinguishing *Bellis,* MCLAUGHLIN, D.J., reasoned:

"[A] ritualistic, mechanical application of the *Bellis* test will almost invariably result in a holding that partnership records are never privileged. The reasons for this are clear. The rights and obligations of partners under New York law, discussed above, are enumerated in the Uniform Partnership Act. The Act is presently in effect in 48 States as well as the District of

Columbia, and its provisions were discussed at length in *Bellis.* * * * Similarly, all partnerships, no matter their size, must file income tax returns *qua* partnership, 26 U.S.C. § 6301. * * * Finally, it is impossible to imagine a partner who will be able to demonstrate, under the *Bellis* test, that he holds subpoenaed records in a personal capacity. As discussed above, and as was emphasized in *Bellis,* partnership records are partnership property; access to them, and control over them, is regulated by state partnership law. This, coupled with an artfully drawn subpoena, effectively precludes any partner from claiming he holds subpoenaed records in a personal capacity. * * * Nonetheless, it cannot be gainsaid that the *Bellis* Court envisioned some partners who could invoke the Fifth Amendment with respect to partnership records. Indeed, the Court cited *United States v. Slutsky,* 352 F.Supp. 1105 (S.D.N.Y.1972) as an illustration of such a partnership. In *Slutsky,* the government subpoenaed the business records of a two-man family partnership. The partners were brothers who operated a resort country club, where they lived and which they managed full-time with their sons. The business had a $1,000,000 payroll, gross receipts of $4,000,000, and owned buildings worth $4,400,000. Among the full-time employees were an accountant and a bookkeeper. The [district] court quashed the subpoena, emphasizing that '[t]his small family partnership is not so impersonal in the scope of its membership and activities that it cannot represent the purely private or personal interests of its constituents.'

"If, as *Bellis* suggests, there exists a partnership whose records are protected by the Fifth Amendment from compelled disclosure, petitioner's husband-wife consulting firm is it. The two criteria suggested in *Bellis* for the exception, a small family partnership, or one with a pre-existing relationship of confidentiality between partners, are both satisfied here. There are no employees, and no office outside the partners' home. * * * It seems clear that the *Bellis* Court contemplated that individual owners of the proverbial 'Mom and Pop' stores would continue to enjoy the protection of the Fifth Amendment even though they elected to conduct business as a partnership. If the *Bellis* Court intended to hold that no partners could ever invoke the Fifth Amendment with respect to partnership records, it would easily have said so. * * * Accordingly, I hold that *Bellis* is no bar to petitioner's assertion of the Fifth Amendment in opposition to this subpoena."

2. *Scope of the entity agent's obligation.*[a] In *Curcio v. United States,* 354 U.S. 118, 77 S.Ct. 1145, 1 L.Ed.2d 1225 (1957), the custodian of a union's books and records, having established that he no longer possessed the documents encompassed by the grand jury subpoena,[b] refused on self-incrimination grounds to answer questions relating to the whereabouts of those documents. Sustaining that claim, a unanimous Court (per Burton, J.) distinguished *Wilson* and *White* (discussed in *Bellis* at p. 750 supra) as cases holding only that the custodian may not invoke his personal privilege to prevent production of the entity's records. There "is no hint in these decisions that a custodian of corporate or association books waives his constitutional privilege as to oral testimony by assuming the duties of his office." By, "accepting custodianship of records, [petitioner] voluntarily assumed a duty which overrides his claim of privilege *only* with respect to the production of the records them-

a. Consider also Note 4, p. 769 infra.

b. Compare *United States v. Rylander,* 460 U.S. 752, 103 S.Ct. 1548, 75 L.Ed.2d 521 (1983) (*Curcio* does not relieve the agent who fails to produce records of the obligation of establishing that he no longer possesses the record; while the defendant could rely upon the privilege in refusing to submit to cross-examination with reference to his inability to comply with the subpoena, the district court was not thereby precluded from holding him in contempt on the ground that he had not carried the burden of establishing that he could not produce the records).

selves." [c] Lower court rulings had held that "a corporate officer who has been required by subpoena to produce corporate records may also be required, by oral testimony, to identify them," but those cases were "distinguishable" and the Court had no need "to pass on their validity." Requiring the custodian "to identify or authenticate the documents * * * merely makes explicit what is implicit on the production itself"; here, the government was seeking to compel the witness to "do more," to provide information that was "more than 'auxiliary to the production' of unprivileged corporate or association records."

3. *Personal documents.* What characteristics that should be considered in classifying records kept by a corporate employee as personal and therefore not subject to the entity doctrine? Consider *In re Grand Jury Subpoena Duces Tecum Dated April 23, 1981,* 522 F.Supp. 977 (S.D.N.Y.1981) (discussing a series of cases dealing with the status of desk calendars): "More often than not, desk calendars have been found to be corporate documents. That conclusion has been reached where the calendars were used in the company's office and left on the officer's desk while in use, where they were useful as records of corporate activity and were in fact used for that purpose, and where the officer's secretary, if not others, had access to the calendars. The courts * * * have found it barely or not at all significant that the company did not supply the calendars, or did not require calendars to be used, filed, or retained; that no one but the secretary had access to them; that the calendars contained a significant number of personal notations; or that the calendars are in the officer's possession at the time they are sought by subpoena."

4. *"Required records." Shapiro v. United States,* 335 U.S. 1, 68 S.Ct. 1375, 92 L.Ed. 1787 (1948), expanding upon some dictum in *Wilson,* held that the self-incrimination clause is not violated by requiring a person to keep records of certain business activities and to make those records available for government inspection. Accordingly, a grand jury subpoena requiring the production of required records may not be successfully challenged on self-incrimination grounds even though the records are those of a business conducted as an individual proprietorship rather than an entity. See e.g., *United States v. LaPage,* 441 F.Supp. 824 (N.D.N.Y.1977) (holding the privilege inapplicable to a grand jury subpoena duces tecum requiring production of various records relating to cattle purchases and sales that licensed cattlemen were required to keep as part of a government program for controlling communicable diseases in domestic animals). Business records will not be classified as required records under *Shapiro* unless three prerequisites are met: (1) the governmental requirement that records be kept must be "essentially regulatory" in nature; (2) the records must be "of a kind which the regulated party has customarily kept," and (3) the records "must have assumed some 'public aspects' which render them at least analogous to public documents." *Grosso v. United States,* 390 U.S.

c. Must the custodian, even though personally served with the subpoena, himself produce the records? Consider *In re Two Grand Jury Subpoena Duces Tecum,* 769 F.2d 52 (2d Cir.1985): "When a corporation is asked to produce records, some individual, of course, must act on the corporation's behalf. Usually this will not create any self-incrimination problem, for an employee who produces his corporation's records 'would not be attesting to his personal possession of them but to their existence and possession by the corporation.' Yet even if the situation is unusual and a corporation's custodian of records would incriminate himself if he were to act to produce the company's records, this still does not relieve the corporation of its continuing obligation to produce the subpoenaed documents. In such a situation the corporation must appoint some other employee to produce the records, and if no existing employee could produce records without incriminating himself by such an act, then the corporation may be required to produce the records by supplying an entirely new agent who has no previous connection with the corporation that might place him in a position where his testimonial act of production would be self-incriminating." See also Note 4, p. 769 infra.

62, 88 S.Ct. 709, 19 L.Ed.2d 906 (1968).[d]

5. *The transformation of Boyd.* In *Murphy v. Waterfront Comm'n,* Note 3, p. 738 supra, Justice Goldberg, in listing the values underlying the self-incrimination privilege, included what has been described as a "privacy interest"—the right of each individual to a "private enclave where he may lead a private life."[e] Can it be said that opinions such as *Bellis* and *Shapiro* transformed *Boyd* 's Fifth Amendment analysis [in much the same way as other cases transformed its Fourth Amendment analysis, see Notes 2–4, pp. 711–713 supra] from a rationale focusing on the interrelation of compelled incrimination and "property rights" to a rationale stressing the interrelation of compelled incrimination and the preservation of individual "privacy"? See Heidt, *The Fifth Amendment Privilege and Documents—Cutting Fisher's Tangled Line,* 49 Mo.L.Rev. 440 (1984) (citing, inter alia, *Bellis'* emphasis "on the accessibility of partnership documents under state law" and *Shapiro*'s reference to the "public aspects" of required records). If so, those cases posed a rationale that was sharply questioned by commentators, not only as to the correctness of its reading of *Boyd,* but also as to its support in the structure and function of the self-incrimination privilege. See e.g., Heidt, supra. In any event, the transformation (or reinterpretation) of *Boyd* was not complete, as the next two cases, *Fisher* and *Doe,* clearly indicate.

d. The Court has also upheld a series of other statutes requiring disclosure of information in a regulatory setting notwithstanding that such information "could well be 'a link in the chain' of evidence leading to prosecution." *California v. Byers,* 402 U.S. 424, 91 S.Ct. 1535, 29 L.Ed.2d 9 (1971). Thus *Byers* upheld a state "hit and run" statute which required the driver of a motor vehicle involved in an accident to stop at the scene and give his name and address. The Court noted that, in judging the constitutionality of regulatory schemes imposing disclosure requirements, it was required "to balance the public need on the one hand, and the individual claim to constitutional protections on the other." The former had prevailed in cases like *Shapiro* and in rulings rejecting a taxpayer's claim that he must be excused from filing an income tax return because his source of income was unlawful and his claim of the privilege in response to particular questions on the return (which is allowed) would suggest that illegality. On the other hand, it had upheld self-incrimination objections to a statute requiring registration by individual members of a Communist organization, statutes imposing disclosure requirements pursuant to gambling tax and registration requirements, and a statute requiring registration of certain types of firearms. See e.g., *Grosso v. United States,* supra (federal statute requiring registration by professional gamblers in all states, including those in which gambling was illegal). In the latter cases, the *Byers* Court noted, "the disclosures condemned were only those extracted from a 'highly selective group inherently suspect of criminal activities,' and the privilege was applied only in 'an area permeated with criminal statutes'—not in 'an essentially noncriminal and regulatory area of inquiry.'" The hit and run statutes did not fit that characterization. These were regulatory measures, "not intended to facilitate criminal convictions," and they were directed to all persons who drove automobiles. There was no disclosure of inherently illegal activity as "most automobile accidents occur without creating criminal liability."

e. The complete passage stated: "The privilege against self-incrimination * * * reflects many of our fundamental values and most noble aspirations: our unwillingness to subject those suspected of crime to the cruel trilemma of self-accusation, perjury to contempt; our preference for an accusatorial rather than an inquisitorial system of criminal justice; our fear that self-incriminating statements will be elicited by inhumane treatment and abuses; our sense of fair play which dictates 'a fair state-individual balance by requiring the government to leave the individual alone until good cause is shown for disturbing him and by requiring the government in its contest with the individual to shoulder the entire load'; our respect for the inviolability of the human personality and of the right of each individual 'to a private enclave where he may lead a private life'; and our realization that the privilege, while sometimes 'a shelter to the guilty,' is often 'a protection to the innocent.'" See also O'Brien, *The Fifth Amendment: Fox Hunters, Old Woman, Hermits, and the Burger Court,* 54 Notre Dame L.Rev. 26 (1978) (compressing these values into three basic rationales: the "fox hunter" rationale of discouraging torture and browbeating and assuring the accused a "fair chance"; the "old woman" rationale of respecting human dignity by refusing to force the individual into the "perilous moral and legal consequences" created by the "cruel trilemma"; and the "hermit" rationale seeking to protect the important "substantive value" of protecting the individual's "private enclave").

FISHER v. UNITED STATES

425 U.S. 391, 96 S.Ct. 1569, 48 L.Ed.2d 39 (1976).

MR. JUSTICE WHITE delivered the opinion of the Court.

In these two cases we are called upon to decide whether a summons directing an attorney to produce documents delivered to him by his client in connection with the attorney-client relationship is enforceable over claims that the documents were constitutionally immune from summons in the hands of the client and retained that immunity in the hands of the attorney. In each case, an Internal Revenue agent visited the taxpayer or taxpayers and interviewed them in connection with an investigation of possible civil or criminal liability under the federal income tax laws. Shortly after the interviews * * *, the taxpayers obtained from their respective accountants certain documents relating to the preparation by the accountant of their tax returns. Shortly after obtaining the documents * * *, the taxpayers transferred the documents to their lawyers—each of whom was retained to assist the taxpayer in connection with the investigation. Upon learning of the whereabouts of the documents, the Internal Revenue Service served summonses on the attorneys directing them to produce documents listed therein. [Those documents were accountants' work sheets, retained copies of income tax returns, and the accountants' copies of correspondence between the accounting firm and the taxpayer]. * * * In each case, the lawyer declined to comply with the summons directing production of the documents, and enforcement actions were commenced by the Government. * * *

II

All of the parties in these cases and the Court of Appeals have concurred in the proposition that if the Fifth Amendment would have excused a *taxpayer* from turning over the accountant's papers had he possessed them, the *attorney* to whom they are delivered for the purpose of obtaining legal advice should also be immune from subpoena. Although we agree with this proposition for the reasons set forth in Part III, infra, we are convinced that, under our decision in *Couch v. United States,* 409 U.S. 322, 93 S.Ct. 611, 34 L.Ed.2d 548 (1973), it is not the taxpayer's Fifth Amendment privilege that would excuse the *attorney* from production.

The relevant part of that Amendment provides:

> "No person . . . shall be *compelled* in any criminal case to be a *witness against himself.*" (Emphasis added.)

The taxpayer's privilege under this Amendment is not violated by enforcement of the summonses involved in these cases because enforcement against a taxpayer's lawyer would not "compel" the taxpayer to do anything—and certainly would not compel him to be a "witness" against himself. The Court has held repeatedly that the Fifth Amendment is limited to prohibiting the use of "physical or moral compulsion" exerted on the person asserting the privilege. In *Couch v. United States,* supra, we recently ruled that the Fifth Amendment rights of a taxpayer were not violated by the enforcement of a documentary summons directed to her accountant and requiring production of the taxpayer's own records in the possession of the accountant. We did so on the ground that in such a case "the ingredient of personal compulsion against an accused is lacking." Here, the taxpayers are compelled to do no more than was the taxpayer in *Couch.* The taxpayers' Fifth Amendment privilege is therefore not violated by enforcement of the summonses directed toward their attorneys. This is true whether or not the Amendment would have barred a subpoena directing the taxpayer to produce the documents while they were in his hands.

The fact that the attorneys are agents of the taxpayers does not change this result. *Couch* held as much, since the accountant there was also the taxpayer's agent, and in this respect reflected a longstanding view. * * * "It is extortion of information from the accused which offends our sense of justice." *Couch v. United States.* Agent or no, the lawyer is not the taxpayer. The taxpayer is the "accused," and nothing is being extorted from him. Nor is this one of those situations, which *Couch* suggested might exist, where constructive possession is so clear or relinquishment of possession so temporary and insignificant as to leave the personal compulsion upon the taxpayer substantially intact. * * *

The Court of Appeals suggested that because legally and ethically the attorney was required to respect the confidences of his client, the latter had a reasonable expectation of privacy for the records in the hands of the attorney and therefore did not forfeit his Fifth Amendment privilege with respect to the records by transferring them in order to obtain legal advice. It is true that the Court has often stated that one of the several purposes served by the constitutional privilege against compelled testimonial self-incrimination is that of protecting personal privacy. See, e.g., *Murphy v. Waterfront Comm'n* [fn. e, p. 756 supra]. But the Court has never suggested that every invasion of privacy violates the privilege. Within the limits imposed by the language of the Fifth Amendment, which we necessarily observe, the privilege truly serves privacy interests; but the Court has never on any ground, personal privacy included, applied the Fifth Amendment to prevent the otherwise proper acquisition or use of evidence which, in the Court's view, did not involve compelled testimonial self-incrimination of some sort.

The proposition that the Fifth Amendment protects private information obtained without compelling self-incriminating testimony is contrary to the clear statements of this Court that under appropriate safeguards private incriminating statements of an accused may be overheard and used in evidence, if they are not compelled at the time they were uttered, *Katz v. United States* [p. 237 supra], and that disclosure of private information may be compelled if immunity removes the risk of incrimination. *Kastigar v. United States* [p. 746 supra]. If the Fifth Amendment protected generally against the obtaining of private information from a man's mouth or pen or house, its protections would presumably not be lifted by probable cause and a warrant or by immunity. * * * We cannot cut the Fifth Amendment completely loose from the moorings of its language, and make it serve as a general protector of privacy—a word not mentioned in its text and a concept directly addressed in the Fourth Amendment. We adhere to the view that the Fifth Amendment protects against "compelled self-incrimination, not [the disclosure of] private information." *United States v. Nobles,* 422 U.S. 225, 95 S.Ct. 2160, 45 L.Ed.2d 141 (1975). * * *

III

* * * [While the] taxpayers have erroneously relied on the Fifth Amendment without urging the attorney-client privilege in so many words, they have nevertheless invoked the relevant body of law and policies that govern the attorney-client privilege. In this posture of the case, we feel obliged to inquire whether the attorney-client privilege applies to documents in the hands of an attorney which would have been privileged in the hands of the client by reason of the Fifth Amendment. * * * This Court and the lower courts have * * * uniformly held that pre-existing documents which could have been obtained by court process from the client when he was in possession may also be obtained from the attorney by similar process following transfer by the client in order to obtain more informed legal advice. * * * It is otherwise if the documents are not obtainable by subpoena duces tecum or summons while in the exclusive possession of the client, for the client will then be reluctant to transfer possession to the lawyer unless the docu-

ments are also privileged in the latter's hands. Where the transfer is made for the purpose of obtaining legal advice, the purposes of the attorney-client privilege would be defeated unless the privilege is applicable. * * *

Since each taxpayer [here] transferred possession of the documents in question from himself to his attorney in order to obtain legal assistance in the tax investigations in question, the papers, if unobtainable by summons from the client, are unobtainable by summons directed to the attorney by reason of the attorney-client privilege. We accordingly proceed to the question whether the documents could have been obtained by summons addressed to the taxpayer while the documents were in his possession. The only bar to enforcement of such summons asserted by the parties or the courts below is the Fifth Amendment's privilege against self-incrimination. * * *

The proposition that the Fifth Amendment prevents compelled production of documents over objection that such production might incriminate stems from *Boyd v. United States* * * *.

Several of *Boyd's* express or implicit declarations have not stood the test of time. The application of the Fourth Amendment to subpoenas was limited by *Hale v. Henkel,* [p. 712 supra] and more recent cases. Purely evidentiary (but "nontestimonial") materials, as well as contraband and fruits and instrumentalities of crime, may now be searched for and seized under proper circumstances, *Warden v. Hayden* [p. 253 supra].[a] Also, any notion that "testimonial" evidence may never be seized and used in evidence is inconsistent with [various cases] approving the seizure under appropriate circumstances of conversations of a person suspected of crime. See *Katz v. United States [p. 237 supra].* It is also clear that the Fifth Amendment does not independently proscribe the compelled production of every sort of incriminating evidence but applies only when the accused is compelled to make a *testimonial* communication that is incriminating. See *Schmerber v. California* [p. 48 supra]. * * * Furthermore, despite *Boyd,* neither a partnership nor the individual partners are shielded from compelled production of partnership records on self-incrimination grounds. *Bellis v. United States.* It would appear that under that case the precise claim sustained in *Boyd* would now be rejected for reasons not there considered.

The pronouncement in *Boyd* that a person may not be forced to produce his private papers has nonetheless often ap-

a. Consider also *Andresen v. Maryland,* p. 253 supra, a post-*Fisher* decision upholding a search for business documents conducted pursuant to a warrant. In an earlier portion of the *Fisher* opinion, the Court had noted, in its footnote 7, that the "special problems of privacy which might be presented by a subpoena of a personal diary, *United States v. Bennett,* 409 F.2d 888, 897 (2d Cir.1969) (Friendly, J.) are not involved here." That footnote also noted that "First Amendment values are also plainly not implicated in these cases." In *Bennett,* Judge Friendly, relying on *Warden v. Hayden,* supra, upheld the seizure of a letter from a co-conspirator that had been discovered in the course of a search incident to defendant's arrest. Judge Friendly noted that "while the demise of the 'mere evidence rule' may well require the development of some new restriction on allowable search and seizure in its place, we suggest with deference that an approach geared to the objective of the Fourth Amendment to secure privacy would seem more promising than one based on the testimonial character of what was seized." The key from this perspective, he added, was the "vice of the unlimited search" rather than the nature of the item seized. He then commented on the search for a personal diary (in the passage apparently cited in *Fisher's* footnote 7): "The reason why we shrink from allowing a personal diary to be the object of a search is that the entire diary must be read to discover whether there are incriminating entries; most of us would feel rather differently with respect to a 'diary' whose cover page bore the title 'Robberies I Have Performed.' Similarly the abhorrence generally felt with respect to 'rummaging' through the contents of a desk to find an incriminating letter would not exist in the same measure if the letter were lying in plain view [the approximate situation in *Bennett*]." In *Andresen,* which involved a search through various records to find specified documents, *Bennett* was again cited but no reference was made to this part of Judge Friendly's opinion. See also Note 1, p. 255 supra.

peared as dictum in later opinions of this Court. * * * To the extent, however, that the rule against compelling production of private papers rested on the proposition that seizures of or subpoenas for "mere evidence," including documents, violated the Fourth Amendment and therefore also transgressed the Fifth, the foundations for the rule have been washed away. In consequence, the prohibition against forcing the production of private papers has long been a rule searching for a rationale consistent with the proscriptions of the Fifth Amendment against compelling a person to give "testimony" that incriminates him. Accordingly, we turn to the question of what, if any, incriminating testimony within the Fifth Amendment's protection, is compelled by a documentary summons.

A subpoena served on a taxpayer requiring him to produce an accountant's workpapers in his possession without doubt involves substantial compulsion. But it does not compel oral testimony; nor would it ordinarily compel the taxpayer to restate, repeat, or affirm the truth of the contents of the documents sought. Therefore, the Fifth Amendment would not be violated by the fact alone that the papers on their face might incriminate the taxpayer, for the privilege protects a person only against being incriminated by his own compelled testimonial communications. *Schmerber v. California,* supra. The accountant's workpapers are not the taxpayer's. They were not prepared by the taxpayer, and they contain no testimonial declarations by him. Furthermore, as far as this record demonstrates, the preparation of all of the papers sought in these cases was wholly voluntary, and they cannot be said to contain compelled testimonial evidence, either of the taxpayers or of anyone else. The taxpayer cannot avoid compliance with the subpoena merely by asserting that the item of evidence which he is required to produce contains incriminating writing, whether his own or that of someone else.

The act of producing evidence in response to a subpoena nevertheless has communicative aspects of its own, wholly aside from the contents of the papers produced. Compliance with the subpoena tacitly concedes the existence of the papers demanded and their possession or control by the taxpayer. It also would indicate the taxpayer's belief that the papers are those described in the subpoena. The elements of compulsion are clearly present, but the more difficult issues are whether the tacit averments of the taxpayer are both "testimonial" and "incriminating" for purposes of applying the Fifth Amendment. These questions perhaps do not lend themselves to categorical answers; their resolution may instead depend on the facts and circumstances of particular cases or classes thereof. In light of the records now before us, we are confident that however incriminating the contents of the accountant's workpapers might be, the act of producing them—the only thing which the taxpayer is compelled to do—would not itself involve testimonial self-incrimination.

It is doubtful that implicitly admitting the existence and possession of the papers rises to the level of testimony within the protection of the Fifth Amendment. The papers belong to the accountant, were prepared by him, and are the kind usually prepared by an accountant working on the tax returns of his client. Surely the Government is in no way relying on the "truthtelling" of the taxpayer to prove the existence of or his access to the documents. The existence and location of the papers are a foregone conclusion and the taxpayer adds little or nothing to the sum total of the Government's information by conceding that he in fact has the papers. Under these circumstances by enforcement of the summons "no constitutional rights are touched. The question is not of testimony but of surrender." *In re Harris,* 221 U.S. 274, 279, 31 S.Ct. 557, 558, 55 L.Ed. 732, 735 (1911).

When an accused is required to submit a handwriting exemplar he admits his ability to write and impliedly asserts that the exemplar is his writing. But in common experience, the first would be a near truism and the latter self-evident. In any event, although the exemplar may be incriminating to the accused and although he is compelled to furnish it, his Fifth Amendment privilege is not violated because nothing he has said or done is deemed to be sufficiently testimonial for purposes of the privilege.[b] This Court has also time and again allowed subpoenas against the custodian of corporate documents or those belonging to other collective entities such as unions and partnerships and those of bankrupt businesses over claims that the documents will incriminate the custodian despite the fact that producing the documents tacitly admits their existence and their location in the hands of their possessor. *E.g., Wilson v. United States* [p. 750 supra]. The existence and possession or control of the subpoenaed documents being no more in issue here than in the above cases, the summons is equally enforceable.

Moreover, assuming that these aspects of producing the accountant's papers have some minimal testimonial significance, surely it is not illegal to seek accounting help in connection with one's tax returns or for the accountant to prepare workpapers and deliver them to the taxpayer. At this juncture, we are quite unprepared to hold that either the fact of existence of the papers or of their possession by the taxpayer poses any realistic threat of incrimination to the taxpayer.

As for the possibility that responding to the subpoena would authenticate the workpapers, production would express nothing more than the taxpayer's belief that the papers are those described in the subpoena. The taxpayer would be no more competent to authenticate the accountant's workpapers or reports by producing them than he would be to authenticate them if testifying orally. The taxpayer did not prepare the papers and could not vouch for their accuracy. The documents would not be admissible in evidence against the taxpayer without authenticating testimony. Without more, responding to the subpoena in the circumstances before us would not appear to represent a substantial threat of self-incrimination. Moreover, in *Wilson v. United States,* supra * * * [and various other cases], the custodian of corporate, union or partnership books or those of a bankrupt business was ordered to respond to a subpoena for the business' books even though doing so involved a "representation that the documents produced are those demanded by the subpoena," *Curcio v. United States* [p. 754 supra].[14]

Whether the Fifth Amendment would shield the taxpayer from producing his own tax records in his possession is a question not involved here; for the papers demanded here are not his "private papers," see *Boyd v. United States,* supra. We do hold that compliance with a summons directing the taxpayer to produce the accountant's documents involved in this case would involve no incriminating testimony within the protection of the Fifth Amendment.

b. Consider also *California v. Byers,* fn. d, p. 756 supra, where Chief Justice Burger's plurality opinion, in upholding a state hit and run statute, argued as an alternative ground for constitutionality that the "act of stopping is no more testimonial" than providing a handwriting sample or speaking in a lineup. The Chief Justice acknowledged defendant's contention that the driver's action in stopping "gives rise to an inference that he believes he was the 'driver of a vehicle involved in an accident,' but responded that this was no more testimonial than the display of characteristics or abilities in an identification proceeding." Justice Harlan, providing the fifth vote for the majority, concluded that the driver's self-identification as a person involved in an accident clearly was testimonial. He stressed, however, "the context of the state collection of data for purposes essentially unrelated to criminal prosecutions."

14. In these cases compliance with the subpoena is required even though the books have been kept by the person subpoenaed and his producing them would itself be sufficient authentication to permit their introduction against him.

MR. JUSTICE STEVENS took no part in the consideration or disposition of these cases.

MR. JUSTICE BRENNAN, concurring in the judgment.

Given the prior access by accountants retained by the taxpayers to the papers involved in these cases and the wholly business rather than personal nature of the papers, I agree that the privilege against compelled self-incrimination did not in either of these cases protect the papers from production in response to the summonses. I do not join the Court's opinion, however, because of the portent of much of what is said of a serious crippling of the protection secured by the privilege against compelled production of one's private books and papers. Like today's decision in *United States v. Miller* [p. 249 supra], it is but another step in the denigration of privacy principles settled nearly 100 years ago in *Boyd v. United States.* * * *

Expressions are legion in opinions of this Court that the protection of personal privacy is a central purpose of the privilege against compelled self-incrimination. * * * The Court pays lip-service to this bedrock premise of privacy in the statement that "[w]ithin the limits imposed by the language of the Fifth Amendment, which we necessarily observe, the privilege truly serves privacy interests." But this only makes explicit what elsewhere highlights the opinion, namely, the view that protection of personal privacy is merely a byproduct and not, as our precedents and history teach, a factor controlling in part the determination of the scope of the privilege. This cart-before-the-horse approach is fundamentally at odds with the settled principle that the scope of the privilege is not constrained by the limits of the wording of the Fifth Amendment but has the reach necessary to protect the cherished value of privacy which it safeguards. * * * History and principle, not the mechanical application of its wording, have been the life of the amendment. * * *

History and principle teach that the privacy protected by the Fifth Amendment extends not just to the individual's immediate declarations, oral or written, but also to his testimonial materials in the form of books and papers. * * * The common-law and constitutional extension of the privilege to testimonial materials, such as books and papers, was inevitable. An individual's books and papers are generally little more than an extension of his person. They reveal no less than he could reveal upon being questioned directly. Many of the matters within an individual's knowledge may as easily be retained within his head as set down on a scrap of paper. I perceive no principle which does not permit compelling one to disclose the contents of one's mind but does permit compelling the disclosure of the contents of that scrap of paper by compelling its production. Under a contrary view, the constitutional protection would turn on fortuity, and persons would, at their peril, record their thoughts and the events of their lives. The ability to think private thoughts, facilitated as it is by pen and paper, and the ability to preserve intimate memories would be curtailed through fear that those thoughts or the events of those memories would become the subjects of criminal sanctions however invalidly imposed. Indeed, it was the very reality of those fears that helped provide the historical impetus for the privilege. * * *

The Court's treatment of the privilege falls far short of giving it the scope required by history and our precedents. * * * [The Court's] analysis is patently incomplete: the threshold inquiry is whether the taxpayer is compelled to produce incriminating papers. That inquiry is not answered in favor of production merely because the subpoena requires neither oral testimony from nor affirmation of the papers' contents by the taxpayer. To be sure, the Court correctly observes that "[t]he taxpayer cannot avoid compliance with the subpoena *merely* by asserting that the item of evidence which he is required to produce contains incriminating writing, whether his own or that of someone else." For it is not enough that the production of a writing, or books and papers, is compelled. Unless those materials are such as to come within the zone of privacy recognized by the Amendment, the privilege against compulsory self-incrimination does not protect against their production.

We are not without guideposts for determining what books, papers, and writings come within the zone of privacy recognized by the Amendment. In *Wilson v. United States,* * * * [t]he Court recognized that the Amendment "[u]ndoubtedly . . . protected [the corporate president] against the compulsory production of his private books and papers," but with respect to corporate records, the Court held:

> "[T]hey are of a character which subjects them to the scrutiny demanded. . . . Thus, in the case of public records and official documents, made or kept in the administration of public office, the fact of actual possession or of lawful custody would not justify the officer in resisting inspection, even though the record was made by himself and would supply the evidence of his criminal dereliction."

Couch v. United States expressly held that the Fifth Amendment protected against the compelled production of testimonial evidence only if the individual resisting production had a reasonable expectation of privacy with respect to the evidence. * * * Under *Couch,* therefore, one criterion is whether or not the information sought to be produced has been disclosed to or was within the knowledge of a third party. That is to say, one relevant consideration is the degree to which the paper holder has sought to keep private the contents of the papers he desires not to produce. * * *

A precise cataloguing of private papers within the ambit of the privacy protected by the privilege is probably impossible. Some papers, however, do lend themselves to classification. Production of documentary materials created or authenticated by a State or the Federal Government, such as automobile registrations or property deeds, would seem ordinarily to fall outside the protection of the privilege. They hardly reflect an extension of the person. Economic and business records may present difficulty in particular cases. The records of business entities generally fall without the scope of the privilege. But, as noted, the Court has recognized that the privilege extends to the business records of the sole proprietor or practitioner. Such records are at least an extension of an aspect of a person's activities, though concededly not the more intimate aspects of one's life. Where the privilege would have protected one's mental notes of his business affairs in a less complicated day and age, it would seem that that protection should not fall away because the complexities of another time compel one to keep business records.

Nonbusiness economic records in the possession of an individual, such as canceled checks or tax records, would also seem to be protected. They may provide clear insights into a person's total lifestyle. They are, however, like business records and the papers involved in these cases, frequently, though not always, disclosed to other parties; and disclosure, in proper cases, may foreclose reliance upon the privilege. Personal letters constitute an integral aspect of a person's private enclave. And while letters, being necessarily interpersonal, are not wholly private, their peculiarly private nature and the generally narrow extent of their disclosure would seem to render them within the scope of the privilege. Papers in the nature of a personal diary are *a fortiori* protected under the privilege.

The Court's treatment in the instant cases of the question whether the evidence involved here is within the protection of the privilege is, with all respect, most inadequate. The gaping hole is in the omission of any reference to the taxpayer's privacy interests and to whether the subpoenas impermissibly invade those interests. * * *[c] For the reasons I have stated at the outset, however, I do not believe that the evidence involved in these cases falls within the scope of privacy protected by the Fifth Amendment. * * *

MR. JUSTICE MARSHALL, concurring in the judgment.

Today the Court adopts a wholly new approach for deciding when the Fifth Amendment privilege against self-incrimination can be asserted to bar production of documentary evidence. * * * The Fifth Amendment basis for resisting production of a document pursuant to subpoena, the Court tells us today, lies not in the document's contents, as we previously have suggested, but in the tacit verification inherent in the act of production itself that the document exists, is in the possession of the producer, and is the one sought by the subpoena.

* * * I would have preferred it had the Court found some room in its theory for recognition of the import of the contents of the documents themselves. See *Couch v. United States,* supra (Marshall, J., dissenting). Nonetheless, I am hopeful that the Court's new theory, properly understood and applied, will provide substantially the same protection as our prior focus on the contents of the documents. * * * Indeed, there would appear to be a precise inverse relationship between the private nature of the document and the permissibility of assuming its existence. Therefore, under the Court's theory, the admission through production that one's diary, letters, prior tax returns, personally maintained financial records, or canceled checks exist would ordinarily provide substantial testimony. The incriminating nature of such an admission is clear, for while it may not be criminal to keep a diary, or write letters or checks, the admission that one does and that those documents are still available may quickly—or simultaneously—lead to incriminating evidence. If there is a "real danger" of such a result, that is enough under our cases to make such testimony subject to the claim of privilege. Thus, in practice, the Court's approach should still focus upon the private nature of the papers subpoenaed and protect those about which *Boyd* and its progeny were most concerned. * * * For the reasons stated by Mr. Justice Brennan, I concur in the judgment of the Court.

UNITED STATES v. DOE

465 U.S. 605, 104 S.Ct. 1237, 79 L.Ed.2d 552 (1984).

JUSTICE POWELL delivered the opinion of the Court.

This case presents the issue whether, and to what extent, the Fifth Amendment privilege against compelled self-incrimination applies to the business records of a sole proprietorship. * * *

[Respondent, the owner of several sole proprietorships had objected to a series of five subpoenas directing him to produce a broad range of business records, including billings, ledgers, cancelled checks, telephone records, contracts, and paid bills. The district court sustained the respondent's Fifth Amendment challenge, noting that the act of producing the documents

c. Justice Brennan's opinion also added: "I also question the Court's treatment of the question whether the act of producing evidence is 'testimonial.' I agree that the act of production implicitly admits the existence of the evidence requested and possession or control of that evidence by the party producing it. It also implicitly authenticates the evidence as that identified in the order to compel. I disagree, however, that implicit admission of the existence and possession or control of the papers in this case is not 'testimonial' merely because the Government could readily have otherwise proved existence and possession or control in these cases. I know of no Fifth Amendment principle which makes the testimonial nature of evidence and, therefore, one's protection against incriminating himself, turn on the strength of the Government's case against him."

had "communicative aspects" which could prove incriminating since the respondent would thereby be required to "admit that the records exist, that they are in his possession, and that they are authentic." On appeal, the Third Circuit agreed with the district court, but also added another self-incrimination ground justifying the quashing of the subpoenas. Following *Fisher,* that circuit had held, relying on *Boyd,* that an individual's private papers, though created voluntarily, were still privileged under the self-incrimination clause. That analysis, the Third Circuit reasoned, was also applicable to the business records of a sole proprietor.]

We granted certiorari to resolve the apparent conflict between the Court of Appeals holding and the reasoning underlying this Court's holding in *Fisher.* We now affirm in part, reverse in part, and remand for further proceedings. * * *

The Court in *Fisher* expressly declined to reach the question whether the Fifth Amendment privilege protects the contents of an individual's tax records in his possession. The rationale underlying our holding in that case is, however, persuasive here. As we noted in *Fisher,* the Fifth Amendment only protects the person asserting the privilege only from *compelled* self-incrimination. Where the preparation of business records is voluntary, no compulsion is present.[8] A subpoena that demands production of documents "does not compel oral testimony; nor would it ordinarily compel the taxpayer to restate, repeat, or affirm the truth of the contents of the documents sought." Id. * * * This reasoning applies with equal force here. Respondent does not contend that he prepared the documents involuntarily or that the subpoena would force him to restate, repeat, or affirm the truth of their contents. The fact that the records are in respondent's possession is irrelevant to the determination of whether the creation of the records was compelled. We therefore hold that the contents of those records are not privileged. * * *

Although the contents of a document may not be privileged, the act of producing the document may be. *Fisher v. United States.* A government subpoena compels the holder of the document to perform an act that may have testimonial aspects and an incriminating effect. * * * In *Fisher,* the Court explored the effect that the act of production would have on the taxpayer [there] and determined that the act of production would have only minimal testimonial value and would not operate to incriminate the taxpayer. Unlike the Court in *Fisher,* we have the explicit finding of the District Court that the act of producing the documents would involve testimonial self-incrimination.[11] The Court of Appeals agreed.[12] The District

8. Respondent's principal argument is that the Fifth Amendment should be read as creating a "zone of privacy which protects an individual and his personal records from compelled production." This argument derives from language in *Boyd v. United States.* This Court addressed substantially the same argument in Fisher: "Within the limits imposed by the language of the Fifth Amendment, which we necessarily observe, the privilege truly serves privacy interests; but the Court has never on any ground, personal privacy included, applied the Fifth Amendment to prevent the otherwise proper acquisition or use of evidence which, in the Court's view, did not involve compelled testimonial self-incrimination of some sort."

In *Andresen v. Maryland* [p. 253 supra], the petitioner also relied on *Boyd.* In rejecting his argument, we observed that "the continued validity of the broad statements contained in some of the Court's earlier cases [has] been discredited by later opinions."

11. The District Court stated: "With few exceptions, enforcement of the subpoenas would compel [respondent] to admit that the records exist, that they are in his possession, and that they are authentic. These communications, if made under compulsion of a court decree, would violate [respondent's] Fifth Amendment rights. . . . The government argues that the existence, possession and authenticity of the documents can be proved without [respondent's] testimonial communication, but it cannot satisfy this court as to how that representation can be implemented to protect the witness in subsequent proceedings." 541 F.Supp., at 3.

12. The Court of Appeals stated: "In the matter sub judice, however, we find nothing in the record that would indicate that the United States

Court's finding essentially rests on its determination of factual issues. Therefore, we will not overturn that finding unless it has no support in the record. Traditionally, we also have been reluctant to disturb findings of fact in which two courts below have concurred. *Rogers v. Lodge,* 458 U.S. 613, 102 S.Ct. 3272, 73 L.Ed.2d 1012, (1982). We therefore decline to overturn the finding of the District Court in this regard, where, as here, it has been affirmed by the Court of Appeals.[13]

* * * The Government, as it concedes, could have compelled respondent to produce the documents listed in the subpoena. Sections 6002 and 6003 of Title 18 provide for the granting of use immunity with respect to the potentially incriminating evidence. The Court upheld the constitutionality of the use immunity statute in *Kastigar v. United States* [p. 746 supra]. The Government did state several times before the District Court that it would not use respondent's act of production against him in any way. But counsel for the Government never made a statutory request to the District Court to grant respondent use immunity. We are urged to adopt a doctrine of constructive use immunity. Under this doctrine, the courts would impose a requirement on the Government not to use the incriminatory aspects of the act of production against the person claiming the privilege even though the statutory procedures have not been followed.

We decline to extend the jurisdiction of courts to include prospective grants of use immunity in the absence of the formal request that the statute requires. As we stated in *Pillsbury Co. v. Conbody,* 459 U.S. 248, 103 S.Ct. 608, 74 L.Ed.2d 430 (1983), in passing the use immunity statute, "Congress gave certain officials in the Department of Justice exclusive authority to grant immunities." "Congress foresaw the courts as playing only a minor role in the immunizing process: . . . " Id. The decision to seek use immunity necessarily involves a balancing of the Government's interest in obtaining information against the risk that immunity will frustrate the Government's attempts to prosecute the subject of the investigation. See *United States v. Mandujano,* 425 U.S. 564, 96 S.Ct. 1768, 48 L.Ed.2d 212 (1976) (plurality opinion). Congress expressly left this decision exclusively to the Justice Department. If, on remand, the appropriate official concludes that it is desirable to compel respondent to produce his business records, the statutory procedure for requesting use immunity will be available.[17]

knows, as a certainty, that each of the myriad documents demanded by the five subpoenas in fact is in the appellee's possession or subject to his control. The most plausible inference to be drawn from the broad-sweeping subpoenas is that the Government, unable to prove that the subpoenaed documents exist—or that the appellee even is somehow connected to the business entities under investigation—is attempting to compensate for its lack of knowledge by requiring the appellee to become, in effect, the primary informant against himself." 680 F.2d, at 335.

13. The Government concedes that the act of producing the subpoenaed documents might have had some testimonial aspects, but it argues that any incrimination would be so trivial that the Fifth Amendment is not implicated. * * * On the basis of the findings made in this case we think it clear that the risk of incrimination was "substantial and real" and not "trifling or imaginary." [See Note 2, p. 737 supra]. Respondent did not concede in the District Court that the records listed in the subpoena actually existed or were in his possession. Respondent argued that by producing the records, he would tacitly admit their existence and his possession. Respondent also pointed out that if the Government obtained the documents from another source, it would have to authenticate them before they would be admissible at trial. See Fed.R.Evid. 901. By producing the documents, respondent would relieve the Government of the need for authentication. These allegations were sufficient to establish a valid claim of the privilege against self-incrimination. This is not to say that the Government was foreclosed from rebutting respondent's claim by producing evidence that possession, existence, and authentication were a "foregone conclusion." *Fisher.* In this case, however, the Government failed to make such a showing.

17. Respondent argues that any grant of use immunity must cover the contents of the documents as well as the act of production. We find this contention unfounded. To satisfy the requirements of the Fifth Amendment, a grant of

We conclude that the Court of Appeals erred in holding that the contents of the subpoenaed documents were privileged under the Fifth Amendment. The act of producing the documents at issue in this case is privileged and cannot be compelled without a statutory grant of use immunity pursuant to 18 U.S.C. §§ 6002 and 6003. The judgment of the Court of Appeals is, therefore, affirmed in part, reversed in part, and the case is remanded to the District Court for further proceedings in accordance with this decision.[d]

JUSTICE O'CONNOR, concurring.

I concur in both the result and reasoning of Justice Powell's opinion for the Court. I write separately, however, just to make explicit what is implicit in the analysis of that opinion: that the Fifth Amendment provides absolutely no protection for the contents of private papers of any kind. The notion that the Fifth Amendment protects the privacy of papers originated in *Boyd v. United States,* but our decision in *Fisher v. United States,* sounded the death-knell for *Boyd.* "Several of Boyd's express or implicit declarations [had] not stood the test of time," *Fisher,* and its privacy of papers concept "had long been a rule searching for a rationale. . . . " Id. Today's decision puts a long-overdue end to that fruitless search.

JUSTICE MARSHALL, with whom JUSTICE BRENNAN joins, concurring in part and dissenting in part.

* * * Contrary to what Justice O'Connor contends, I do not view the Court's opinion in this case as having reconsidered whether the Fifth Amendment provides protection for the contents of "private papers of any kind." This case presented nothing remotely close to the question that Justice O'Connor eagerly poses and answers. First, as noted above, the issue whether the Fifth Amendment protects the contents of the documents was obviated by the Court of Appeals' rulings relating to the act of production and statutory use immunity. Second, the documents at stake here are business records which implicate a lesser degree of concern for privacy interests than, for example, personal diaries.

Were it true that the Court's opinion stands for the proposition that "the Fifth Amendment provides absolutely no protection for the contents of private papers of any kind," (O'Connor, J.), I would assuredly dissent. I continue to believe that under the Fifth Amendment "there are certain documents no person ought to be compelled to produce at the Government's request." *Fisher v. United States* (Justice Marshall, concurring).

Notes and Questions

1. As Justice Brennan notes in *Fisher* (see fn. c, p. 764 supra), in determining whether a witness' testimony might be viewed as incriminatory under the *Hoffman* standard (see Note 2, p. 737 supra), courts do not look to whether the facts conveyed in that testimony, even though potentially damaging, might be established by the government at trial through other sources. Does *Fisher's* holding that the privilege does not apply when "possession, existence and authentication" are a "foregone conclusion" (see *Doe* at n. 13) do exactly that for the act of production? If so, why this special treatment for the act of production? Does the answer lie in the special character of the admissions implied from

immunity need be only as broad as the privilege against self-incrimination. *Murphy v. Waterfront Commission* [p. 746 supra]. As discussed above, the privilege in this case extends only to the act of production. Therefore, any grant of use immunity need only protect respondent from the self-incrimination that might accompany the act of producing his business records.

d. Justice Stevens, in a separate opinion, argued that the judgment below should simply be affirmed. Since the Court agreed with the district court's reasoning, which was also accepted by the Court of Appeals, there was no reason to review any suggestion in the Third Circuit opinion as to the protection of the contents of the documents. Justice Marshall's separate opinion (see infra) also argued that there was no reason to consider that aspect of the Third Circuit's opinion.

that act that led the *Fisher* Court also to question whether those admissions could be deemed "sufficiently testimonial for purposes of the privilege" [see pp. 760–761 supra].

2. What must be shown to establish that possession, existence, and authentication are a foregone conclusion? Consider the following cases as they relate to both *Doe* and *Fisher:*

(a) *Butcher v. Bailey,* 753 F.2d 465 (6th Cir.1985). A trustee in bankruptcy subpoenaed the debtor to produce all personal records relating to the property of his estate. Sustaining the debtor's self-incrimination claim, the court noted: "The instant case is a hybrid of the situations in *Fisher* and *Doe.* As in *Fisher,* there is no serious doubt that personal records of debtor [e.g., check stubs] exist. Further, it is a foregone conclusion, bordering on a tautology, that debtor has control of his personal records. As in *Doe,* however, and unlike *Fisher,* debtor's production of these records would be sufficient to authenticate them as his personal records. See Fed.R.Evid. 901(b)(1).[a] In any future criminal prosecution, therefore, the government would be relieved of the need to authenticate these records. We conclude that debtor's production of his personal records would be testimonial."

(b) *In re Grand Jury Subpoena Duces Tecum Dated November 13, 1984,* 616 F.Supp. 1159 (E.D.N.Y.1985). The challenged subpoena here demanded the production of records of a two-person consulting firm [see Note 1, p. 753 supra], including "cash receipts and disbursements, general ledgers, cancelled checks, [and] bank statements." Upholding the challenge in part, the court noted:

"If the government can demonstrate with reasonable particularity that it knows of the existence and location of subpoenaed documents, no privilege to refuse production on [that] * * * ground exists. *United States v. Fox,* [721 F.2d 1187 (2d Cir.1983)]. The government's preproduction knowledge must be sufficient 'to eliminate any possibility that . . . production would constitute an incriminating testimonial act.' *United States v. Fox.*[b] A blunderbuss subpoena, such as that issued here, creates an inference that the government is seeking to compensate for its lack of knowledge by compelling petitioner 'to become the primary informant against himself.' Notwithstanding the broad subpoena and the inference arising therefrom, the government's ex parte affidavit establishes that much is known about this petitioner's activities. The government is aware that he keeps a set of partnership books, and is aware of two bank accounts—one in the name of the partnership and the other in the name of the petitioner and his wife. Petitioner cannot refuse to comply with the subpoena on the ground that the existence and location of the documents are unknown.

"Although the existence and location of the subpoenaed documents are known, petitioner may still refuse to produce them if by so doing he would 'implicitly authenticate' them for the government. * * * If a government official will one day be able to testify that he knows the documents in question belong to petitioner because petitioner produced them when

a. Fed.R.Evid. 901 provides that authentication " is satisfied by evidence sufficient to support a finding that the matter in question is what its proponent claims." The Rule offers various illustrations of sufficient evidence, including (1) testimony of a witness with knowledge, (2) expert and nonexpert testimony as to the genuineness of handwriting, and (3) distinctive characteristics of the document as contained on its "appearance, contents, substance, internal patterns, or other distinctive characteristics, taken in conjunction with circumstances."

b. The court in *Fox* rejected the sufficiency of the testimony of a revenue agent detailing his experience as an auditor as to records found in similar businesses. The court noted that "the government's awareness of the practice of other taxpayers has nothing to do with the proper focus of this inquiry—i.e., what the act of production would reveal to the IRS about this taxpayer." (Emphasis added).

asked, then by that very act of production petitioner will have made a self-incriminating testimonial admission. His act of production will provide a necessary link to incriminating evidence contained in the documents by removing the government's need to authenticate them by other means. *United States v. Fox.* Conversely, when the government can authenticate the documents without relying on any act by petitioner, then production by petitioner does not implicate the Fifth Amendment. * * * With respect to most of the documents demanded by the subpoena, petitioner's production of them will not constitute authentication implicating the Fifth Amendment. For example, production of the partnership's cancelled checks will not provide the government with authentication that would otherwise be lacking; the checks are self-authenticating. Fed.R. Evid. 902(9). Additionally, the bank statements demanded were not prepared by petitioner; and the government can authenticate them through the testimony of bank personnel without relying upon any testimonial act petitioner may perform by producing the statements. As to partnership ledgers, cash receipts, and records of disbursements, however, a different situation exists. Compelled production of these documents would provide the government with just what it needs for authentication—'an admission (by petitioner) that the subpoenaed documents are records pertaining to his business.' Petitioner may invoke his Fifth Amendment privilege to block production of these records if he can establish that the act of production would be incriminatory. [The court concluded that, in light of the petitioner's status as the target of the grand jury and the fact that the government 'had declined to confer immunity upon petitioner—even limited solely to the act of production—,' it could conclude that production would be incriminatory]."

3. Where the government contends that it could otherwise establish existence, possession, and authentication, why wouldn't it simply grant immunity as to production alone? Heidt, p. 756 supra, argues that the government would face a difficult hurdle in later establishing that it had made no derivative use of the act of production. See also Note 4, p. 748 supra. But compare Comisky and Comisky, *Supreme Court in Doe Limits Fifth Amendment Protection,* 60 J. of Tax 66 (August 1984): "Where previously business or personal records (such as a second set of books) could be protected from disclosure, now, the grant of limited use immunity coopted, for example, with handwriting exemplars from the taxpayer, will permit the Government to obtain tremendously damaging documents and to properly introduce them at trial."

4. Does the *Fisher-Doe* act of production rationale require reconsideration of decisions holding that the custodian of corporate records cannot rely on the privilege to refuse either to produce (see *Bellis,* p. 749 supra) or to authenticate (see Note 2, p. 754 supra) those records. Consider IN RE GRAND JURY MATTER (BROWN), 768 F.2d 525 (3d Cir.1985) (en banc). There the government sought to require the petitioner, the sole shareholder of a Professional Corporation, to produce and authenticate certain corporate records. Petitioner claimed that he could not be compelled to comply absent an assurance that his act of production would not be used in evidence against him. A divided Third Circuit agreed. Reasoned the majority (per GIBBONS, J.):

"The government urges that the holding in *United States v. Doe* does not control because in *Doe* the records were those of a sole proprietorship, while in this case they belong to a professional corporation. That argument misses the whole point of the Court's analysis in *Fisher* and *Doe.* Those cases, * * * make the significant factor, for the privilege against self-incrimination, neither the nature of the entity which owns documents, nor the contents of documents, but rather the communicative or noncommunicative nature of the arguably incriminating disclosures sought to be compelled. Our holding that a witness may not be held in contempt for refusing to authenticate records absent either a finding that there is no likelihood of self-incrimination or a grant of use immunity casts no doubt on the continued vitality of the rules of *Hale v. Henkel* and *United States v. White,* that neither corporations nor other collective entities may assert a privilege against self-incrimination. * * * Records of collective entities still must be maintained, and their production can be compelled by a subpoena *duces tecum* addressed to the entity. In situations where authentication is required, Fed.R. Evid. 901(a) [see fn. a supra] indicates that the requirement can be satisfied by the submission of 'sufficient evidence to support a finding that the matter in question is what its proponent claims.' This is particularly true in the case of business records which, more often than not, can be authenticated without resort to extrinsic evidence.

"Where a witness is required to authenticate records, most business entities will have agents who can provide the testimony without self-incrimination [see fn. c, p. 755 supra]. The grant of use immunity pursuant to 18 U.S.C. §§ 6002 and 6003 is always a possibility. * * * In the present case the government never explored alternate means of production or authentication of the documents, and it never considered the possibility of a grant of use immunity before moving to have Brown held in contempt. Indeed, it candidly concedes that what it wants amounts to compelled authentication testimony which may later be used against a target of the grand jury investigation. * * *"

Dissenting in *Brown,* Judge Garth argued that the majority erred initially in treating the case as one involving verbal testimony of authentication; the petitioner had refused to even produce the documents so the proceedings had not reached the point where such testimony was sought. The majority's second error, the dissent concluded, rested on its analysis of the collective entity doctrine. In barring assertions of the personal privilege by corporate representatives past cases had not failed to recognize that the act of production could personally incriminate those representatives. Rather, the doctrine was adopted because those courts "realiz[ed] that, were the personal privilege to apply, a corporation could avoid production of evidence of its criminal activity so long as the act of production would also incriminate those representatives capable of producing and authenticating the documents." It accordingly treated the corporate officer as having waived his personal privilege upon accepting the corporate office. Under the majority's holding, Judge Garth maintained, where the only corporate officials capable of producing and authenticating the records are those who prepared them (as in the case of minutes kept by participants in a pricefixing meeting), the corporation could well gain a defacto privilege in the absence of a grant of immunity to those officials.[c]

5. Assume that the government serves a subpoena duces tecum upon the target of a grand jury investigation directing him to present his diary. The government notes that it has compelled the testimony of the target's roommate who watched the target make entries in the diary and can identify that volume. It also is prepared by use of a handwriting expert to show that the writing therein is that of the target. Should the question of whether the government may obtain the document most

c. Consider also *In re Grand Jury Proceedings (Morganstern),* 771 F.2d 143 (6th Cir.1985) (en banc) where a divided court held that *Fisher-Doe* had in no way altered the rule that a custodian of partnership records cannot rely on his personal privilege to refuse to produce these records. The majority added, however, that it was "well settled that if the government later attempts to implicate the custodian on the basis of the act of production, evidence of that fact is subject to a motion to suppress" since "such proof would seek to add testimonial value to the otherwise testimony free act of production."

appropriately be resolved under the Fifth Amendment? Consider Heidt, p. 756 supra (arguing that the issue is more appropriately framed in terms of the First Amendment and its protection of private thoughts): "There are many advantages in not basing such a right in the fifth amendment. Traditional fifth amendment rules derived to deal with testimony, but often inappropriate for documents, may be jettisoned. One such rule provides that the claimant need not turn over allegedly privileged information in camera so the court can determine whether the privilege applies. Another fifth amendment rule gives the claimant the benefit of any doubt about whether the information is privileged. * * * Under a new [First Amendment] privilege the courts need not be hampered by these rules and thus will be better able to apply whatever test is developed to protect privacy interests. For example, the claimant can be required not only to submit the documents in camera, but to show he has authored them and has sufficiently restricted their circulation. He can also be required to show the extent to which their subject matter is personal rather than business. In short, he can be required to meet whatever standards for a first amendment privilege are developed by the courts." See also fn. a, p. 759 supra.

SECTION 4: THE WITNESS' RIGHT TO COUNSEL

1. *A constitutional right?* Although the Supreme Court has not ruled directly on whether a grand jury witness has a constitutional right to the assistance of counsel, two cases present significant discussions of the issue. IN RE GROBAN, 352 U.S. 330, 77 S.Ct. 510, 1 L.Ed.2d 376 (1957), involved a special investigative proceeding of a state fire marshall at which the witness was not allowed to be accompanied by counsel. In finding that the exclusion of counsel from that proceeding did not violate due process, the Court majority drew an analogy to the grand jury proceeding. There, it noted, the law was clear that "a witness cannot insist, as a matter of constitutional right, on being represented by counsel." Justice Black, in dissent, agreed that there was no constitutional right to counsel in the grand jury proceeding, but viewed the fire marshall's proceeding as not truly analogous. The witness before the grand jury had protection of "the presence of jurors," which offered a "substantial safeguard" against abuse. See Note 4, p. 705 supra.

UNITED STATES v. MANDUJANO, described at Note 7, p. 740 supra, presented a more extensive discussion of the counsel issue, although only six members of the Court spoke to that issue. In that case, the grand jury witness had been told that "he could have a lawyer outside the room with whom he could consult," but he was not offered the assistance of an appointed attorney, although he claimed to be indigent. The lower courts held that, as a "putative" or "virtual" defendant, he was in a position akin to an arrestee and should have been given complete *Miranda* warnings, including advice as to appointed counsel. The Court found it unnecessary to uphold or reject that ruling, since any constitutional violation would not have excused the witness' perjury (see Note 7, p. 740 supra), but Chief Justice BURGER's plurality opinion did add that the advice given to the witness was consistent with any constitutional requirements. Initially, the Chief Justice rejected the contention that the "*Miranda* right to counsel, fashioned to secure the suspect's Fifth Amendment privilege, was applicable." That right was premised upon an "inherently coercive" interrogation setting, clearly distinguishable from grand jury questioning. Turning next to alternative sources of a constitutional right to counsel, the Chief Justice found no support for the lower court's ruling. He noted:

"Respondent was * * * informed that if he desired he could have the assistance of counsel, but that counsel could not be inside the grand jury room. That statement was plainly a correct recital of the law. No criminal proceedings had been instituted against respondent, hence the Sixth Amendment right to counsel had not come into play. *Kirby v. Illinois* [p. 668 supra]. A witness 'before a grand jury cannot insist, as a matter of constitutional right, on being represented by his counsel * * *.' *In re Groban.* Under settled principles the witness may not insist upon the presence of his attorney in the grand jury room. Fed.Rule Crim.Proc. 6(d)."

JUSTICE BRENNAN, joined by Marshall, J., was critical of the Chief Justice's analysis. He argued:

"A * * * disturbing facet of the plurality opinion today is its statement that '[n]o criminal proceedings had been instituted against respondent, hence, the Sixth Amendment right to counsel had not come into play.' It will not do simply to cite, as does the plurality opinion, *Kirby v. Illinois,* for this proposition. *Kirby*'s premise, so fundamental that it was 'note[d] at the outset,' was that 'the constitutional privilege against compulsory self-incrimination is in no way implicated here.' In sharp contrast, the privilege against compulsory self-incrimination is inextricably involved in this case since a putative defendant is called and interrogated before a grand jury. Clearly in such a case a defendant is 'faced with the prosecutorial forces of organized society, and immersed in the intricacies of substantive and procedural criminal law.' *Kirby.*

"It is true that dictum in *In re Groban,* denied there is any constitutional right of a witness to be represented by counsel when testifying before a grand jury. But neither *Groban* nor any other case in this Court has squarely presented the question. Moreover, more recent decisions, e.g., *Miranda v. Arizona,* and *Escobedo v. Illinois,* recognizing the 'substantive affinity' and therefore the 'coextensive[ness]' in certain circumstances of the right to counsel and the privilege against compulsory self-incrimination, have led many to question the continuing vitality of such older dicta. * * *

"Given the inherent danger of subversion of the adversary system in the case of a putative defendant called to testify before a grand jury, and the peculiarly critical role of the Fifth Amendment privilege as the bulwark against such abuse, it is plainly obvious that some guidance by counsel is required. This conclusion entertains only the 'realistic recognition of the obvious truth that the average [putative] defendant does not have the professional legal skill to protect himself when brought before a tribunal * * * wherein the prosecution is [represented] by experienced and learned counsel.' *Johnson v. Zerbst* [p. 74 supra]. * * *

"It may be that a putative defendant's Fifth Amendment privilege will be adequately preserved by a procedure whereby, in addition to warnings, he is told that he has a right to consult with an attorney prior to questioning, that if he cannot afford an attorney one will be appointed for him, that during the questioning he may have that attorney wait outside the grand jury room, and that he may at any and all times during questioning consult with the attorney prior to answering any question posed.[22] At least if such minimal protections were present, a putative defendant would be able to consult with counsel prior to answering any question that he might in any way suspect may incriminate him. * * *

"It is of course unnecessary in this case to define the exact dimensions of the right to counsel since the testimony obtained by the grand jury interrogation was not introduced as evidence at respondent's trial on

22. Contra, arguing that the presence of counsel inside the grand jury room is required, * * * [here citing several articles]. Certainly there is no viable argument that allowing counsel to be present in the grand jury room for purposes of consultation regarding testimonial privileges would subvert the nature or functioning of the grand jury proceeding. Such a procedure is sanctioned by statute in several States.

the charge concerning which he was questioned. I write only to make plain my disagreement with the implication in the plurality opinion that constitutional rights to counsel are not involved in a grand jury proceeding, and my disagreement with the further implication that there is a right to have counsel present for consultation outside the grand jury room but that it is not constitutionally derived and therefore may be enjoyed only by those wealthy enough to hire a lawyer. I cannot accede to a return to the regime of 'squalid discrimination,' where the justice 'a man gets depends on the amount of money he has.' *Griffin v. Illinois* [p. 105 supra]. * * *"

2. *Federal practice.* Pursuant to internal guidelines, all federal grand jury witnesses are advised that they may retain counsel (who may be located in the anteroom) and "that the grand jury will permit the witness the reasonable opportunity to step outside the grand jury room to consult with counsel if he so desires." U.S. Attorney's Manual, § 9–11.250. Where the witness requests the assistance of counsel, but notes that he cannot afford to retain counsel, that request is often conveyed to the district judge, who may then appoint counsel (usually a federal public defender) to assist the witness. Lawyers representing grand jury witnesses often urge their clients to consult after each question, which allows the lawyer to construct a complete record of the questions asked. Although federal prosecutors contend that this practice demands more than a "reasonable opportunity" to consult, it very frequently has not been contested. A few federal courts have stated that, at least where the witness has been granted immunity (and therefore does not need self-incrimination advice), the witness can be limited to consultations on a less regular basis (e.g., after every few questions). See National Lawyer's Guild, *Representation of Witnesses Before Federal Grand Juries* § 6.5(c) (3d ed. 1985).

3. *State practice.* Most states follow a practice similar to the federal practice, although they may be somewhat less liberal in allowing the witness to leave the grand jury room for consultations.[a] Those states that are less liberal commonly justify that position on two grounds—avoidance of "undue delay" and restricting counsel to his proper role. If witnesses are allowed to consult after each question, no matter what its nature, they may, it is argued, simply "wear down the grand jury." Moreover, if the attorney's advice properly is limited to counseling the witnesses on the exercise of testimonial privileges, there simply is no reason to allow consultation when the question clearly poses no such difficulty. See e.g., *People v. Ianniello,* 235 N.E.2d 439 (N.Y.1968) (where witness had been immunized and had previous opportunity to consult with counsel on the same line of questioning, grand jury appropriately refused to allow him to leave for the obvious purpose of obtaining "strategic advice" rather than counseling as to any legal right that would allow him to refuse to answer). Jurisdictions allowing an unlimited opportunity to consult with counsel in the anteroom respond that: (1) it is too difficult to determine when a witness will or will not be seeking the advice of counsel relating to the exercise of privilege—particularly in light of the possibility of "unintentionally waiving"

a. Indeed, the Pennsylvania courts have stated that the witness does not have a right to leave the grand jury room for the purpose of consulting with counsel, but should be advised that, where "doubtful as to whether he can properly refuse to answer a particular question, the witness can come before the court accompanied by counsel and obtain a ruling as to whether he should answer the question." *Commonwealth v. McCloskey,* 277 A.2d 764 (Pa.1971). Of course, the witness would be able to follow the Pennsylvania procedure even without specific authorization since a grand jury witness will not be held in contempt unless first ordered by the court to answer the question. Once before the court, the witness should face no difficulties in consulting with counsel. Indeed, a witness charged with civil or criminal contempt, has a constitutional right to the assistance of counsel on that charge, including appointed counsel if the witness is indigent. See e.g., *In re Di Bella,* 518 F.2d 955 (2d Cir.1975).

the self-incrimination privilege [see Note 4, p. 738 supra]; and (2) more delay will result from litigation relating to refusals to permit the witness to consult than will result from freely permitting consultation.

Slightly more than a dozen states have statutes permitting at least certain witnesses to be assisted by counsel located within the grand jury room. See LaFave and Israel, § 8.13(b). Most of these provisions apply to all witnesses, but a few are limited to targets. The statutes commonly contain provisions limiting the role of counsel while before the grand jury. Several state that the lawyer may "advise the witness," but "may not otherwise take any part in the proceeding." One jurisdiction also allows counsel to "interpose objections on behalf of the witness." Several of the statutes provide for the appointment of counsel where the witness is indigent. In other jurisdictions, (including those in which the lawyer is restricted to the anteroom) the public defender office is available to assist indigent witnesses and witnesses are so informed as a matter of local practice.

4. *The location of counsel.* Does providing even the most liberal right to consult with counsel outside the grand jury room adequately protect the witness' rights before the grand jury? Proponents of counsel within the grand jury room, including the A.B.A. and the A.L.I., argue that it does not. They contend: (1) witnesses are reluctant to leave repeatedly for fear the grand jury will believe they have "something to hide"; (2) because witnesses will not leave after every question, they often must rely on very general advice from counsel, based on speculation as to the precise phrasing of the next series of questions; (3) even where the witness does report each question to counsel before responding, it often is difficult for a lawyer who does not himself hear the question to judge the "flow of the questioning"; (4) since witnesses before the grand jury are under considerable stress, many have difficulty following their counsel's directions; (5) since counsel does not hear the witness' precise testimony, he cannot assist the witness in correcting unintentional factual errors or misleading statements; and (6) the presence of the lawyer within the grand jury room, as opposed to the anteroom, serves as a far superior deterrent to improper questioning and harassment of the witness.

Opponents of the A.L.I. and A.B.A. position acknowledge that the need to leave the grand jury room poses certain difficulties for the witness, but argue that those difficulties are not so great as to undermine the witness' ability to exercise his rights, particularly as to the privilege against self-incrimination. They see any additional protection of witness rights as clearly outweighed by the detrimental effect that counsel's presence would have upon the grand jury's capacity to conduct effective investigations. They argue that, notwithstanding statutory prohibitions, counsel accompanying witnesses would find techniques, such as stage whispers and objections presented through the witness, for challenging the prosecutor's questions and conveying their arguments to the jurors. With no judge present to put an immediate stop to such tactics, the end result would be disruption and delay of the investigation. They further argue that with counsel at the witness' side, more witnesses will reply to questions by merely parroting responses formulated by counsel—responses that too often furnish as little information as possible or are purposely ambiguous so as to avoid potential perjury charges. The critics draw an analogy to the trial, where the defendant, once taking the stand, is not allowed to interrupt his testimony for further discussions with counsel. Finally, it is noted that, in some instances, the witness may not be entirely trustful of counsel and therefore prefer not to have counsel present. The witness may be forced to accept counsel provided by others (e.g., his employer) and fear retaliation if the full scope of his testimony is carried back to such persons.

Once the law permits counsel to be present, the witness will be under pressure to allow counsel to accompany him, and will lose the capacity to be selective in the disclosure of his testimony to counsel.

5. *Multiple representation.* In recent years, many state and federal prosecutors have pursued a policy of seeking disqualification of counsel who are simultaneously representing more than one grand jury witness or a witness and a potential target. Such motions for disqualification have been based on two grounds: (1) precluding joint representation of clients with conflicting interests and (2) maintaining grand jury effectiveness in the investigatory process. As between the two grounds, the courts generally have been far more receptive to the former. See LaFave and Israel, § 8.13(d).

Should the standard applied to a disqualification motion based on an alleged conflict of interest among jointly represented clients be the same at the grand jury stage as the standard applied to counsel representing codefendants at the trial stage? Many federal courts view their function in ruling upon such motions as roughly comparable to their role in considering possible disqualification under Rule 44(c). See Notes 4–8, pp. 170–74 supra. Commentators and some courts have suggested, however, that certain differences in the two settings should lead to a somewhat different approach. They point, in particular, to the following differences: (1) the criminal defendant's claim to the assistance of counsel of his choice rests squarely on the Sixth Amendment, whereas the grand jury witness' right to counsel, if it has any constitutional base, may rest on a "more flexible due process right to seek legal advice"; (2) qualities of the grand jury proceeding, particularly its secrecy and its focus on uncovering adverse evidence, offer tactical advantages to joint representation at this stage (e.g., increased discovery) that are not so readily obtained at the trial stage; (3) criminal codefendants, aware of the charges against them, can readily anticipate where their interests may be in conflict, but the relative status of different clients at the grand jury stage is uncertain (e.g., today's witness may be tomorrow's target) and even when an indictment is expected, the exact scope of the charge is unclear; (4) because of grand jury secrecy, the government, in urging disqualification, has greater difficulty in setting forth precisely why it believes the interests of counsel's clients may come into conflict; and (5) grand jury counsel plays a "less active" role than trial counsel since grand jury counsel does not participate in the proceedings. To what extent are the above distinctions more formalistic than substantive? For example, is grand jury counsel's role, though "less active," equally significant because at this early stage the possibility often exists that one client can gain immunity by offering to testify against the others. Insofar as the distinctions are relevant and substantial, where do they lead? For example, should courts be more or less willing to accept client waivers as the answer to conflicts at the grand jury stage as opposed to the trial stage? See Tague, *Multiple Representation of Targets and Witnesses During A Grand Jury Investigation,* 17 Amer.Crim.L.Rev. 301 (1980); Moore, *Disqualification of the Attorney Representing Multiple Witnesses Before A Grand Jury,* 27 U.C.L.A.L.Rev. 1 (1979).

6. In determining whether disqualification is justified at the grand jury level, courts seek to distinguish between "actual" and "potential" conflicts. An actual conflict is often said to require disqualification without regard to the client's willingness to accept the conflict. A potential conflict generally is said to require only that a hearing be held to ensure that the clients are aware of the difficulty and are willing to accept it. See LaFave and Israel, § 8.13(d) (also noting several contrary rulings). Consider also pp. 166–67 supra and Note 8, p. 173 supra (distinction between actual and potential conflicts in representation at trial).

7. Does the government establish that an actual conflict exists when it shows that the lawyer is representing targets and non-targets, or must the government also show that the non-target will be required (through an immunity grant, if necessary) to give testimony against the target? Compare *Matter of Investigative Grand Jury Proceedings,* 480 F.Supp. 162 (N.D.Ohio 1979) (representation of targets and non-targets creates a "substantial danger" for both classes, requiring disqualification); *In re Special Grand Jury (Gimbell),* 480 F.Supp. 174 (E.D.Wis.1979) (even immunization of one client does not create conflict with a target-client absent showing that immunized client would actually testify against the target). So too, does a target employer's payment of the fee for the representation of its employees (target or non-target) create an "actual" or "potential" conflict? See LaFave and Israel, § 8.13(d) (decisions divided).

8. Where there is no more than a potential conflict, can the government support disqualification by showing that joint representation is hindering the "effective operation of the grand jury"? This argument has been advanced most frequently in cases where a series of witnesses represented by a single attorney have adopted a "stonewalling strategy" with all witnesses claiming the self-incrimination privilege. In such cases, the government also argues that counsel is not effectively representing each client individually since that approach would suggest that at least some would seek a better accommodation for themselves (e.g., immunity). Disqualification motions have been granted in such "stonewalling" cases, but each also involved facts suggesting that the clients were not in a similar position with respect to the investigation. Other courts, rejecting such motions, have noted that "discomfort to the grand jury process, without more, is not sufficient to vitiate an individual's important right to counsel of his own choosing." See LaFave and Israel, § 8.13(c).

9. Would it be an appropriate resolution of the problems presented by client access to counsel and multiple representation to (1) provide counsel for the indigent witness, (2) allow counsel to appear with the witness, and (3) prohibit multiple representation? In *People ex rel. Losavio v. J.L.,* 580 P.2d 23 (Colo.1978), the court upheld a statutory provision which authorized counsel to appear within the grand jury room, but prohibited such counsel from representing "more than one witness in the same criminal investigation, except with the permission of the grand jury." In support of its conclusion, the *Losavio* court noted: (1) the witness did not have a constitutional right to be accompanied by counsel or to leave the grand jury room to consult with counsel (a practice no longer authorized in Colorado); (2) the attorney representing a witness was sworn to secrecy and therefore could not convey to one witness what he had learned in representing another witness; as a "practical matter," however, attorneys representing multiple witnesses "would rarely be able to totally eliminate what has been discovered in a prior grand jury appearance when offering counsel to a subsequent witness"; (3) society had an interest in the grand jury's effectiveness as an investigative body, which could be undermined by representation that encouraged a witness to act upon more than his own individual interest; and (4) a balance had to be struck between society's interest in "grand jury secrecy and effectiveness" and the witness' choice of his own counsel and the legislature's solution was reasonable in providing a statutory right to representation by some attorney within the grand jury room, while also prohibiting multiple representation. Three dissenting judges argued that, at the least, a witness should still be allowed to leave the grand jury room to consult with an attorney located in the anteroom and that attorney should not be subject to the statutory prohibition against multiple representation.

Chapter 11

THE SCOPE OF THE EXCLUSIONARY RULES

SECTION 1. "STANDING" TO OBJECT TO THE ADMISSION OF EVIDENCE

A. Historical Background and Overview

1. *Must the person asserting a Fourth Amendment claim have been the victim of the challenged search or seizure?* Long before the Supreme Court authoritatively resolved the issue, the lower courts had developed the doctrine that a defendant lacked "standing" to challenge evidence seized in violation of a third party's constitutional rights. The early basis for this doctrine seems to have been "the joint foundation of the Fourth Amendment and the self-incrimination clause of the Fifth," Comment, 58 Yale L.J. 144, 156 (1948). The rule was also "based on the theory that the evidence is excluded to provide a remedy for a wrong done to the defendant, and that accordingly, if the defendant has not been wronged he is entitled to no remedy." *People v. Martin,* 290 P.2d 855, 857 (Cal.1955) (Traynor, J.).

Six years before *Mapp,* the California Supreme Court's emphasis on the deterrence rationale for the exclusionary rule led it to abolish the "standing" requirement. *People v. Martin,* supra. "Such a limitation," observed the California court, "virtually invites law enforcement officers to violate the rights of third parties and to trade the escape of a criminal whose rights are violated for the conviction of others by the use of the evidence illegally obtained against them." Id.[a]

California's abolition of the "standing" requirement was "enthusiastically endorsed by most commentators." LaFave, § 11.3(j) at 609 (citing thirteen commentators), and when, in *Linkletter v. Warden* (1965) (p. 49 supra), the U.S. Supreme Court seemed to explain and to justify the Fourth Amendment exclusionary rule as "the only effective deterrent to lawless

a. *In re Lance,* 694 P.2d 744 (Cal.1985) (discussed at p. 65 supra), held that Proposition 8, an initiative approved by California voters in 1982, had abolished *Martin's* "vicarious exclusionary rule."

The California Supreme Court had ruled earlier, *People v. Varnum,* 427 P.2d 772 (1967), that *Martin* did not apply to *Escobedo-Miranda* violations. The majority, per Traynor, J., reasoned: "Noncoercive questioning is not in itself unlawful [and the rights] protected by *Escobedo* [and] *Miranda* are violated only when evidence obtained without the required warnings and waiver is introduced against the person whose questioning produced the evidence. The basis for the [*Miranda* warnings] is the privilege against self-incrimination [which] is not violated when the information elicited from an unwarned suspect is not used against him. [Unlike unreasonable searches and seizures], there is nothing unlawful in questioning an unwarned suspect so long as the police refrain [from tactics] condemned by due process and do not use against the suspect any evidence obtained."

For criticism of *Varnum,* see Notes, 37 U.Cin.L. Rev. 234 (1968); 15 U.C.L.A.L.Rev. 1060 (1968).

police action," there was reason to think that the High Court, too, might scrap the "standing" requirement. Thus, two years after *Linkletter* and two years before *Alderman* infra, one commentator pointed out that "a system of classification based on 'victimness' provides no deterrence" against "searches that turn up evidence against persons other than the victim" and concluded that "the standing requirement is inconsistent with the presently accepted general deterrence theory of the exclusionary rule." Note, 34 U.Chi.L.Rev. 342, 358 (1967).

However, in ALDERMAN v. UNITED STATES, 394 U.S. 165, 89 S.Ct. 961, 22 L.Ed.2d 176 (1969), the Court, per WHITE, J., reaffirmed "the established principle [that] suppression of the product of a Fourth Amendment violation can be successfully urged only by those whose rights were violated by the search itself, not by those who are aggrieved solely by the introduction of damaging evidence. Coconspirators and codefendants have been accorded no special standing." The Court was unmoved by the ascendancy of the deterrence rationale. "The necessity" for the limitation, it maintained, "was not eliminated by recognizing and acknowledging the deterrent aim of the [exclusionary] rule." Why not? Because "we are not convinced that the additional benefits of extending the exclusionary rule to other defendants would justify further encroachment upon the public interest in prosecuting those accused of crime and having them acquitted or convicted on the basis of all the evidence which exposes the truth."

Concurring in part and dissenting in part, FORTAS, J., argued that there was much to be said for abolishing the "standing" requirement: "The Fourth Amendment, unlike the Fifth, is couched in terms of a guarantee that the Government will not engage in unreasonable searches and seizures. It is a general prohibition[,] * * * not merely a privilege accorded to him whose domain has been lawlessly invaded. It grants the individual a personal right, not to privacy, but to insist that the State utilize only lawful means of proceeding against him. And it is an assurance to all that the Government will exercise its formidable powers to arrest and to investigate only subject to the rule of law." [b]

2. *"Target" standing; the use of the federal courts' "supervisory power" to overcome the "standing" requirement.* In *Alderman,* supra, Justice Fortas, joined by Douglas, J., on this point, maintained that at the very least the "target" of police misconduct should have "standing": "Such a person is surely 'the victim of an invasion of privacy' and a 'person aggrieved,' even though it is not his property that was searched or seized. [U]nless we are to insist upon property concepts, it is enough to give him 'standing' to object that the government agents conducted their unlawful search and seizure in order to obtain evidence to use against him."

Many commentators have maintained that the "targets" of third party searches should have "standing" to challenge the legality of the evidence so obtained. See e.g., Burkoff, *The Court that Devoured the Fourth Amendment: The Triumph of an Inconsistent Exclusionary Doctrine,* 58 Ore.L. Rev. 151, 176–77 (1979); Doernberg, fn. b supra, at 262; White & Greenspan, *Standing to Object to Search and Seizure,* 118 U.Pa.L.Rev. 333, 349–54 (1970). See also the *Model Pre-Arraignment Code* position, Note 3, infra. But this view apparently commands no support on the Court today. In *Rakas v. Illinois,* p. 783 infra, even the dissenters agreed with the Court's rejection of petitioners' "target standing" theory. "If there has ever been a fact situation which cried out for recogni-

b. Justice Fortas' view is supported in Doernberg, *"The Right of the People": Reconciling Collective and Individual Interests under the Fourth Amendment,* 58 N.Y.U.L.Rev. 259 (1983); Kuhns, *The Concept of Personal Aggrievement in Fourth Amendment Standing Cases,* 65 Iowa L.Rev. 493 (1980).

tion of target standing," LaFave, § 11.3(h) (1986 Supp.), it was UNITED STATES v. PAYNER, 447 U.S. 727, 100 S.Ct. 2439, 65 L.Ed.2d 468 (1980) (more fully extracted at p. 59 supra). Nevertheless, a 6–3 majority, per POWELL, J. held that a federal court could not invoke its "supervisory power" to bar the evidence.

Payner arose as follows: An IRS investigation into the financial activities of American citizens in the Bahamas focused on a certain Bahamian bank. When an official of that bank visited the United States, IRS agents stole his briefcase for a time, removed hundreds of documents from the briefcase, and photographed them. As a result of this "briefcase caper," Payner—precisely the kind of offender the IRS agents were seeking when they violated the bank official's rights—was convicted of federal income tax violations. Hemmed in by the standing requirement, but outraged by the government's "purposefully" illegal tactics, the federal district court invoked its supervisory power to exclude the tainted evidence.

But the Supreme Court rejected the federal court's "substitution of individual judgment for the controlling decisions of this Court." "The values assigned to the competing interests do not change," pointed out Justice Powell, "because a court has elected to analyze the question under the supervisory power instead of the Fourth Amendment. In either case, the need to deter the underlying conduct and the detrimental impact of excluding the evidence remain precisely the same." [c]

The *Payner* Court cautioned that exclusion of evidence in every case of illegality must be "weighed against the considerable harm that would flow from *indiscriminate application* of an exclusionary rule" (emphasis added), and that "*unbending application* of the exclusionary sanction * * * would impede unacceptably the truthfinding functions of judge and jury" (emphasis added). But consider Kamisar, *Does (Did) (Should) the Exclusionary Rule Rest on a "Principled Basis" Rather than an "Empirical" Proposition*"?, 16 Creighton L.Rev. 565, 638 (1983):

"The relevant question in *Payner* [was] not whether the exclusionary rule should *always* be applied when police illegality is somewhere in the picture, but whether it should *ever* be applied—taking into account the seriousness or flagrancy of the illegality—when the defendant lacks 'standing.' The question was not whether the exclusionary rule should be given 'unbending application,' but whether *the 'standing' requirement* should be. By deciding that even in a case like *Payner* a federal court is *unable* to exercise its supervisory powers to bar the evidence—by holding that 'judicial impotency is *compelled* in the face of such scandalous conduct' [LaFave, § 11.3(h) (1986 Supp.)]—the Court gave us its answer.

"* * * The *Payner* Court seemed content [to rely on] the balance it had struck in the early standing cases. But because it grew out of special and outrageous circumstances, the interests to be balanced in *Payner* were different. The question presented was[:] When the government has *intentionally manipulated* the standing requirement of the fourth amendment—when it has *deliberately and patently* violated the constitutional rights of a third party in order to obtain evidence against its real targets, and defendant is one of those targets—does the interest in discouraging (or reducing the incentive) to make *such* searches justify the exclusion of tainted evidence at the instance of a party who

c. "The Court's decision to engraft the standing limitations of the Fourth Amendment onto the exercise of supervisory powers," protested dissenting Justice Marshall, joined by Brennan and Blackmun, JJ., "appears to render the supervisory powers superfluous. In order to establish that suppression of evidence under the supervisory powers would be proper, the Court would also require Payner to establish a violation of his [constitutional rights] * * *. This approach is totally unfaithful to our prior supervisory power cases [see generally pp. 58–62 supra], which, contrary to the Court's suggestion, are not constitutional cases in disguise."

was not the [direct] victim of the challenged practice? The *Payner* Court never really spoke to this issue because it never really asked this question."

3. *The Model Code's approach.* A defendant cannot establish standing "merely by showing that the search was of his spouse or a business associate, for 'interpersonal relationships cannot make a "victim" of one who is not otherwise "one against whom the search or seizure is directed."'" LaFave, § 11.3(i), at 605–06. But consider *Model Pre-Arraignment Code* § SS290.1(5), which provides that a defendant has standing with respect to items obtained by a search of or seizure from:

"(a) the defendant; or

"(b) a spouse, parent, child, brother, or sister of the defendant, or any member of his household; or

"(c) any person with whom the defendant resides or sojourns; or

"(d) a co-defendant, co-conspirator * * * or

"(e) any person with whom the defendant conducts a business; or

"(f) any other person if, from the circumstances, it appears that the search or seizure was intended to avoid the application of [search and seizure rules] to any of the persons described in clauses (a) to (e) inclusive."

Is the Model Code approach—a compromise between the A.L.I. Council's view that the traditional "standing" requirement be preserved and the Reporters' and the membership's view that "standing" be eliminated—"both too narrow and too broad"? Does the Code fail to extend standing to all situations in which a defendant's "zone of privacy" is invaded? On the other hand, why should a defendant have standing with respect to a sister or spouse when she is vacationing in a hotel 500 miles away? See *1972 Proceedings of American Law Institute* at 65–73 (remarks of Judge Leventhal), 72–73 (remarks of Professor Kamisar).

But see LaFave, § 11.3 at 607: "In defense of the [Model Code] provision, it might be said that it (i) constitutes a substantially broader definition of standing than exists in current law; (ii) avoids for the most part the more troublesome results which can come about from total abolition of any requirement of standing;[d] (iii) identifies the most common situations in which it is likely that the search or seizure *either* intruded into a zone of privacy rightly shared to some extent by the defendant *or* was made with the defendant as the target of the investigation; and (iv) avoids for the most part the necessity for difficult case-by-case determinations as to what the defendant's privacy expectations were and what the actual motives of the police were."

4. *"Automatic" standing.* In *Jones v. United States,* 362 U.S. 257, 80 S.Ct. 725, 4 L.Ed.2d 697 (1960), the defendant was charged with selling and distributing narcotics and facilitating the concealment and sale of the same narcotics, which permitted conviction largely on proof of unexplained possession of narcotics. The lower court denied standing because defendant had failed either to assert a sufficient interest in the apartment where the search occurred[e] or to allege ownership or possession of the narcotics, although doing so would have "forced" him to allege facts that would tend to convict him. The Supreme Court reversed: The "same element in this prosecution which has caused a dilemma, i.e., that possession both convicts and confers standing, eliminates any necessity for a preliminary showing of an interest in the premises searched or the property seized, which ordinarily is required when standing

d. Elsewhere, Professor LaFave notes, id. at 610–11, that "the *Martin* rule can produce results which are themselves difficult to swallow, such as that a criminal must go free because his crime was detected by conduct which only infringed the Fourth Amendment rights of that criminal's *victim,*" citing *People v. Jager,* 303 P.2d 115 (Cal.App.1956).

e. For this aspect of *Jones,* see Note 5 infra.

is challenged." To hold otherwise "would be to permit the Government to have the advantage of contradictory positions as a basis of conviction."

However, the Court subsequently held, in *Simmons v. United States,* 390 U.S. 377, 88 S.Ct. 967, 19 L.Ed.2d 1247 (1968), that testimony given by a defendant in order to establish his "standing" "may not thereafter be used against him at trial on the issue of guilt." Were it otherwise, "a defendant who wishes to establish standing must do so at the risk that the words which he utters may later be used to incriminate him."

On the basis of *Simmons,* the Court subsequently abolished the *Jones* "automatic standing" rule and held that "defendants charged with crimes of possession may only claim the benefits of the exclusionary rule if their own Fourth Amendment rights have in fact been violated." UNITED STATES v. SALVUCCI, 448 U.S. 83, 100 S.Ct. 2547, 65 L.Ed.2d 619 (1980). Observed the Court, per REHNQUIST, J.: "The 'dilemma' identified in *Jones* * * * was eliminated [by] *Simmons,* [which] not only extends protection against [the] risk of self-incrimination in all of the cases covered by *Jones,* but also grants a form of 'use' immunity to those defendants charged with nonpossessory crimes." [f]

As for the vice of prosecutorial contradiction, the Court stated it need not decide whether that "could alone support a rule countenancing the exclusion of probative evidence on the grounds that someone other than the defendant was denied a Fourth Amendment right," for at least after *Rakas* [p. 783 infra] it is clear that "a prosecutor may simultaneously maintain that a defendant criminally possessed the seized good, but was not subject to a Fourth Amendment deprivation, without legal contradiction." For a "person in legal possession of a good seized during an illegal search has not necessarily been subject to a Fourth Amendment deprivation. * * * We simply decline to use possession of a seized good as a substitute for a factual finding that the owner of the good has a legitimate expectation of privacy in the area searched." [g]

5. *Residential premises.* It has long been true, and is still so under the current expectation-of-privacy approach discussed in the next subsection, that one with a present possessory interest in the premises searched, e.g., a member of the family regularly residing in a home, may challenge that search even though not present when the search was conducted. As the Court explained in *Alderman,* Note 1 supra: "If the police make an unwarranted search of a house and seize tangible prop-

f. Dissenting Justice Marshall, joined by Brennan, J., disagreed that "*Simmons* provides complete protection against the 'self-incriminating dilemma,'" for "the prosecutor may still be permitted to use the defendant's testimony [at the suppression hearing] to impeach him at trial." The *Salvucci* majority managed to sidestep this argument, but somewhat misleadingly it asserted that "the Court has held that 'the protective shield of *Simmons* is not to be converted into a license for false representations,'" quoting from *United States v. Kahan,* 415 U.S. 239, 94 S.Ct. 1179, 39 L.Ed.2d 297 (1974). But *Kahan* involved the impeachment use of false testimony given at a pretrial hearing to establish defendant's eligibility for appointed counsel and the *Kahan* Court pointed out: "We are not dealing, as was the Court in *Simmons,* with what was 'believed' by the claimant to be a 'valid' constitutional claim. Respondent was not, therefore, faced with the type of intolerable choice *Simmons* sought to relieve. The protective shield of *Simmons* is not to be converted into a license for false representations *on the issue of indigency* free from the risk that the claimant will be held accountable for his falsehood." (Emphasis added.)

Consider LaFave & Israel, § 9.2(a): "The best analogy here is * * * *New Jersey v. Portash* [440 U.S. 450, 99 S.Ct. 1292, 59 L.Ed.2d 501 (1979)], holding that testimony given before a grand jury following a grant of use testimony could not be used for impeachment purposes at the subsequent criminal trial. * * * It would seem that defendant's testimony at a suppression hearing [is] 'compelled' in the *Portash* sense, for, as *Simmons* teaches, the defendant is confronted with the choice 'either to give up what he believed, with advice of counsel, to be a valid Fourth Amendment claim or, in effect, to waive his Fifth Amendment privilege against self-incrimination.'"

g. See also *Rawlings v. Kentucky,* p. 792 infra.

erty belonging to third parties * * * the home owner may object to its use against him, not because he had any interest in the seized items [but] because they were the fruits of an unauthorized search of his house, which is itself expressly protected by the Fourth Amendment." The *Alderman* majority thus concluded that a person should have standing to challenge the legality of electronically overheard conversations in which he participated "or *conversations occurring on his premises,* whether or not he was present or participated in those conversations" (emphasis added).[h]

In *Jones v. United States,* Note 4 supra, the Court held that "anyone legitimately on premises where a search occurs may challenge its legality." The defendant not only had permission to use the apartment of his friend, but had a key to the apartment with which he admitted himself on the day of the search. He also kept some possessions in the apartment. In the more recent *Rakas* case (p. 783 infra), the Court rejected the *Jones* "legitimately on premises" *formulation*—this phrase "creates too broad a gauge for measurement of Fourth Amendment rights"—but it did not question *the result* in that case. The *Jones* holding "can best be explained," observed the *Rakas* Court, "by the fact that Jones had a legitimate expectation of privacy in the premises he was using * * * even though his 'interest' in those premises might not have been a recognized property interest at common law."

What about the defendant who claims standing with respect to a search of *his* personal privacy at a place which is not his and at a time when he was not there? Standing has frequently been recognized in such circumstances, often by reliance on *United States v. Jeffers,* 342 U.S. 48, 72 S.Ct. 93, 96 L.Ed. 59 (1951). In that case police entered the hotel room of defendant's two aunts (a room for which defendant had a key and permission to enter at will) and found his stash of drugs. The Court summarily rejected the government's argument that "the search did not invade [defendant's] privacy," but the scope of the holding is unclear. The Court expressly rejected the contention that defendant's interest in the drugs must be disregarded because it was illegal to possess such property, but it was unclear whether (a) that interest alone conferred standing or (b) defendant's continuing access to the room was essential to the outcome.

The meaning and continued vitality of *Jeffers* has been put in doubt as a result of *Rawlings v. Kentucky* (p. 792 infra), where police searched the purse of defendant's female companion and found therein the drugs she was carrying for him. Emphasizing that defendant did not "have any right to exclude other persons from access to [the woman's] purse"—a harsh threshold requirement—the Court ruled that defendant lacked standing because he had no reasonable expectation of privacy as to the purse.

6. *Business premises.* In *Mancusi v. DeForte,* 392 U.S. 364, 88 S.Ct. 2120, 20 L.Ed.2d 1154 (1968), where state police seized records belonging to a union local from an office defendant shared with several other union officials, the Court viewed the "crucial issue" as "whether the area was one in which there was a reasonable expectation of freedom from governmental intrusion." The Court answered in the affirmative. Even though defendant shared an office with others, he "still could reasonably have expected that only those persons and [their guests] would ever enter the office, and that records would not be touched except with their permission or that of union higherups."

h. Justice Harlan, joined by Stewart, J., argued that this should not be so when the eavesdropped occurred without physical penetration, for then the absent householder's property interest has not been disturbed, and he can claim no privacy interest in conversations in which he did not participate.

"Consistent with *Mancusi,* courts have held that a corporate or individual defendant in possession of the business premises searched has standing, and that an officer or employee of the business enterprise has standing if 'there was a demonstrated nexus between the area searched and the work space of the defendant.' Exclusive use would seem clearly to establish standing, but (as *Mancusi* teaches) there can be a justified expectation of privacy even absent exclusivity." LaFave & Israel, § 9.1(c).

7. *Vehicles.* Although a number of lower courts—relying on the *Jones* "legitimately on premises" formula—had reached a contrary result, in *Rakas* (p. 783 infra), where police stopped what they believed to be a robbery getaway car, ordered the occupants out, and then searched the vehicle, finding a rifle under the seat and shells in the glove compartment, the Court concluded that the passengers (who claimed no ownership of the seized items) lacked standing. For they had "made no showing that they had any legitimate expectation of privacy in the glove compartment or area under the seat of the car. * * * [T]hese are areas in which a passenger *qua* passenger simply would not normally have a legitimate expectation of privacy."

It is important to note, however, that the *Rakas* defendants neither challenged the legality of the police conduct in stopping the car in which they were riding nor complained of being made to get out of the vehicle. A majority of the *Rakas* Court indicated that a passenger *does* have standing to challenge police action which intrudes upon his Fourth Amendment protection against unreasonable seizure of *his person.* It is important to note, too, that the *Rakas* passengers disclaimed ownership of the gun and shells. *Rawlings* does not seem to bar a passenger's standing to challenge any search into *his* effects in the car, although it puts in doubt whether standing can be gained by a *non* passenger whose effects in the car are searched.

B. THE CURRENT APPROACH

RAKAS v. ILLINOIS

439 U.S. 128, 99 S.Ct. 421, 58 L.Ed. 387 (1978).

[Petitioners were convicted of armed robbery and their convictions affirmed on appeal. Suspecting that the vehicle might have been the "getaway car" in a recent robbery, police stopped the car in which petitioners were riding. After the occupants of the car (petitioners and two female companions) were ordered out, the police searched the interior of the vehicle and discovered a sawed-off rifle under the front passenger seat and a box of rifle shells in the glove compartment (which had been locked). Petitioners never asserted a property interest in the items seized. As the dissent noted, the items were useful to the prosecution solely on the theory that petitioners' possession of them was probative of their identity as the robbers. Because they did not assert ownership of the rifle or the shells and because they conceded that they did not own the automobile, but were simply passengers (the owner of the vehicle had been driving it at the time of the search), the trial court ruled that petitioners lacked "standing" to contest the search and seizure. Thus the judge denied their motions to suppress the evidence, without ever reaching the question whether the police conduct involved was lawful.

[The Supreme Court rejected petitioners' secondary theory, the so-called "target" theory, whereby any defendant at whom a search was "directed" would have "standing" to contest the legality of that search; and also their primary theory, that they had "standing" to object to the search under *Jones,* supra, because they were "legitimately on [the] premises" at the time of the search.]

MR. JUSTICE REHNQUIST delivered the opinion of the Court.

Conferring standing to raise vicarious Fourth Amendment claims would necessarily mean a more widespread invocation of the exclusionary rule during criminal trials. * * * Each time the exclusionary rule is applied it exacts a substantial social cost for the vindication of Fourth Amendment rights. Relevant and reliable evidence is kept from the trier of fact and the search for truth at trial is deflected. Since our cases generally have held that one whose Fourth Amendment rights are violated may successfully suppress evidence obtained in the course of an illegal search and seizure, misgivings as to the benefit of enlarging the class of persons who may invoke that rule are properly considered when deciding whether to expand standing to assert Fourth Amendment violations.

[H]aving rejected petitioners' target theory and reaffirmed the principle that the "rights assured by the Fourth Amendment are personal rights, [which] may be enforced by exclusion of evidence only at the instance of one whose own protection was infringed by the search and seizure," *Simmons,* the question necessarily arises whether it serves any useful analytical purpose to consider this principle a matter of standing, distinct from the merits of a defendant's Fourth Amendment claim. We can think of no decided cases of this Court that would have come out differently had we concluded, as we do now, that the type of standing requirement discussed in *Jones* and reaffirmed today is more properly subsumed under substantive Fourth Amendment doctrine. Rigorous application of the principle that the rights secured by this Amendment are personal, in place of a notion of "standing," will produce no additional situations in which evidence must be excluded. The inquiry under either approach is the same. But we think the better analysis forthrightly focuses on the extent of a particular defendant's rights under the Fourth Amendment, rather than on any theoretically separate, but invariably intertwined concept of standing. * * *

Analyzed in these terms, the question is whether the challenged search or seizure violated the Fourth Amendment rights of a criminal defendant who seeks to exclude the evidence obtained during it. That inquiry in turn requires a determination of whether the disputed search and seizure has infringed an interest of the defendant which the Fourth Amendment was designed to protect. * * *

Here petitioners, who were passengers occupying a car which they neither owned nor leased, seek to analogize their position to that of the defendant in *Jones.* In *Jones,* petitioner was present at the time of the search of an apartment which was owned by a friend. The friend had given Jones permission to use the apartment and a key to it, with which Jones had admitted himself on the day of the search. He had a suit and shirt at the apartment and had slept there "maybe a night," but his home was elsewhere. At the time of the search, Jones was the only occupant of the apartment because the lessee was away for a period of several days. Under these circumstances, this Court stated that while one wrongfully on the premises could not move to suppress evidence obtained as a result of searching them, "anyone legitimately on premises where a search occurs may challenge its legality." Petitioners argue that their occupancy of the automobile in question was comparable to that of Jones in the apartment and that they therefore have standing to contest the legality of the search—or as we have rephrased the inquiry, that they, like Jones, had their Fourth Amendment rights violated by the search.

We do not question the conclusion in *Jones* that the defendant in that case suffered a violation of his personal Fourth Amendment rights if the search in question was unlawful. Nonetheless, we believe that the phrase "legitimately on premises" coined in *Jones* creates too broad a gauge for measurement of Fourth Amendment rights. For example, applied literally, this statement would permit a casual visitor who has never seen, or been permitted to visit the basement of another's house to object to a search of the basement if the visitor happened to be in the kitchen of the house at the time of the search.[a] Likewise, a casual visitor who walks into a house one minute before a search of the house commences and leaves one minute after the search ends would be able to contest the legality of the search. The first visitor would have absolutely no interest or legitimate expectation of privacy in the basement, the second would have none in the house, and it advances no purpose served by the Fourth Amendment to permit either of them to object to the lawfulness of the search.[11]

We think that *Jones* on its facts merely stands for the unremarkable proposition that a person can have a legally sufficient interest in a place other than his own home so that the Fourth Amendment protects him from unreasonable governmental intrusion into that place. In defining the scope of that interest, we adhere to the view expressed in *Jones* and echoed in later cases that arcane distinctions developed in property and tort law between guests, licensees, invitees, and the like, ought not to control. But the *Jones* statement that a person need only be "legitimately on premises" in order to challenge the validity of the search of a dwelling place cannot be taken in its full sweep beyond the facts of that case.

Katz provides guidance in defining the scope of the interest protected by the Fourth Amendment. [The *Katz* Court] held that capacity to claim the protection of the Fourth Amendment depends not upon a property right in the invaded place but upon whether the person who claims the protection of the Amendment has a legitimate expectation of privacy in the invaded place. Viewed in this manner, the holding in *Jones* can best be explained by the fact that Jones had a legitimate expectation of privacy in the premises he was using and therefore could claim the protection of the Fourth Amendment with respect to a governmental invasion of those premises, even though his "interest" in those premises might not have been a recognized property interest at common law.

* * * In abandoning "legitimately on premises" for the doctrine that we announce today, we are not forsaking a time-tested and workable rule, which has produced consistent results when applied, solely for the sake of fidelity to the values underlying the Fourth Amendment. Rather, we are rejecting blind adherence to a phrase which at most has superficial clarity and which conceals underneath that thin veneer all of the problems of line drawing which must be faced in any conscientious effort to apply the Fourth Amendment. Where the factual premises for a rule are so generally prevalent that little would be lost and much would be gained by abandoning case-by-case analysis, we have not hesitated to do so. But the phrase "legitimately on premises" has not been shown to be an easily applicable measure of Fourth Amendment rights so much as it has proved to be simply a label placed by the courts on results which have not been subjected to careful analysis. We would not wish to be understood as saying that legitimate presence on the premises is irrelevant to one's expectation of privacy, but it cannot be deemed controlling.

Judged by the foregoing analysis, petitioners' claims must fail. They asserted neither a property nor a possessory interest in the automobile, nor an interest in the property seized.[b] And as we have previously indicated, the fact that they were "legitimately on [the] premises" in the

a. What if the casual visitor had had his privacy intruded upon in the course of a search which led to the discovery of evidence in the basement? See Note 2 following this case.

11. This is not to say that such visitors could not contest the lawfulness of the seizure of evidence or the search if their own property were seized during the search.

b. Why didn't petitioners assert a property interest in the rifle and the shells? See Note 4 following this case. What if they had? See Note 3 following this case.

sense that they were in the car with the permission of its owner is not determinative of whether they had a legitimate expectation of privacy in the particular areas of the automobile searched. It is unnecessary for us to decide here whether the same expectations of privacy are warranted in a car as would be justified in a dwelling place in analogous circumstances. We have on numerous occasions pointed out that cars are not to be treated identically with houses or apartments for Fourth Amendment purposes. But here petitioners' claim is one which would fail even in an analogous situation in a dwelling place, since they made no showing that they had any legitimate expectation of privacy in the glove compartment or area under the seat of the car in which they were merely passengers. Like the trunk of an automobile, these are areas in which a passenger *qua* passenger simply would not normally have a legitimate expectation of privacy.

Jones and *Katz* involved significantly different factual circumstances. Jones not only had permission to use the apartment of his friend, but had a key to the apartment with which he admitted himself on the day of the search and kept possessions in the apartment. Except with respect to his friend, Jones had complete dominion and control over the apartment and could exclude others from it. Likewise in *Katz,* the defendant occupied the telephone booth, shut the door behind him to exclude all others and paid the toll, which "entitled [him] to assume that the words he utter[ed] into the mouthpiece [would] not be broadcast to the world." Katz and Jones could legitimately expect privacy in the areas which were the subject of the search and seizure each sought to contest. No such showing was made by these petitioners with respect to those portions of the automobile which were searched and from which incriminating evidence was seized.[17]

* * * Since [the search of the car] did not violate any rights of these petitioners, their judgment of conviction is

Affirmed.

MR. JUSTICE POWELL, with whom CHIEF JUSTICE BURGER joins, concurring.

I concur in the opinion of the Court, and add these thoughts. * * *

The petitioners do not challenge the constitutionality of the police action in stopping the automobile in which they were riding; nor do they complain of being made to get out of the vehicle. Rather, petitioners assert that their constitutionally protected interest in privacy was violated when the police, after stopping the automobile and making them get out, searched the vehicle's interior, where they discovered a sawed-off rifle under the front seat and rifle shells in the locked glove compartment. The question before the Court, therefore, is a narrow one: Did the search of their friend's automobile after they had left it violate any Fourth Amendment right of the petitioners?

* * * Whatever the application of [the Court's] standard may lack in ready administration, it is more faithful to the purposes of the Fourth Amendment than a test focusing solely or primarily on wheth-

17. For reasons which they do not explain, our dissenting Brethren repeatedly criticize our "holding" that unless one has a common-law property interest in the premises searched, one cannot object to the search. We have rendered no such "holding," however. To the contrary, we have taken pains to reaffirm the statements in *Jones* and *Katz* that "arcane distinctions developed in [property law] * * * ought not to control." In a similar vein, the dissenters repeatedly state or imply that we now "hold" that a passenger lawfully in an automobile "may not invoke the exclusionary rule and challenge a search of that vehicle unless he happens to own or have a possessory interest in it." [The] case before us involves the search of and seizure of property from the glove compartment and area under the seat of a car in which petitioners were riding as passengers. [Petitioners] did not claim that they had any legitimate expectation of privacy in the areas of the car which were searched. We cannot, therefore, agree with the dissenters' insistence that our decision will encourage the police to violate the Fourth Amendment.

er the defendant was legitimately present during the search.[1] * * *

We are concerned here with an automobile search. Nothing is better established in Fourth Amendment jurisprudence than the distinction between one's expectation of privacy in an automobile and one's expectation when in other locations. We have repeatedly recognized that this expectation in "an automobile * * * [is] significantly different from the traditional expectation of privacy and freedom in one's residence."

A distinction also properly may be made in some circumstances between the Fourth Amendment rights of passengers and the rights of an individual who has exclusive control of an automobile or of its locked compartments. * * * Here there were three passengers and a driver in the automobile searched. None of the passengers is said to have had control of the vehicle or the keys. It is unrealistic—as the shared experience of us all bears witness—to suggest that these passengers had any reasonable expectation that the car in which they had been riding would not be searched after they were lawfully stopped and made to get out. The minimal privacy that existed simply is not comparable to that, for example, of an individual in his place of abode, of one who secludes himself in a telephone booth, or of the traveler who secures his belongings in a locked suitcase or footlocker.[4]

This is not an area of the law in which any "bright line" rule would safeguard both Fourth Amendment rights and the public interest in a fair and effective criminal justice system. The range of variables in the fact situations of search and seizure is almost infinite. Rather than seek facile solutions, it is best to apply principles broadly faithful to Fourth Amendment purposes. I believe the Court has identified these principles.

MR. JUSTICE WHITE, with whom MR. JUSTICE BRENNAN, MR. JUSTICE MARSHALL, and MR. JUSTICE STEVENS join, dissenting.

The Court today holds that the Fourth Amendment protects property, not people, and specifically that a legitimate occupant of an automobile may not invoke the exclusionary rule and challenge a search of

1. Allowing anyone who is legitimately on the premises searched to invoke the exclusionary rule extends the rule far beyond the proper scope of Fourth Amendment protections, as not all who are legitimately present invariably have a reasonable expectation of privacy. And, as the Court points out, the dissenters' standard lacks even the advantage of easy application.

I do not share the dissenters' concern that the Court's ruling will "invit[e] police to engage in patently unreasonable searches every time an automobile contains more than one occupant." A police officer observing an automobile carrying several passengers will not know the circumstances surrounding each occupant's presence in the automobile, and certainly will not know whether an occupant will be able to establish that he had a reasonable expectation of privacy. Thus, there will continue to be a significant incentive for the police to comply with the requirements of the Fourth Amendment, lest otherwise valid prosecutions be voided. Moreover, any marginal diminution in this incentive that might result from the Court's decision today is more than justified by society's interest in restricting the scope of the exclusionary rule to those cases where in fact there is a reasonable expectation of privacy.

4. The sawed-off rifle in this case was merely pushed beneath the front seat, presumably by one of the petitioners. In that position, it could have slipped into full or partial view in the event of an accident, or indeed upon any sudden stop. As the rifle shells were in the locked glove compartment, this might have presented a closer case if it had been shown that one of the petitioners possessed the keys or if a rifle had not been found in the automobile.

The dissenting opinion suggests that the petitioners here took the same actions to preserve their privacy as did the defendant in *Katz:* Just as Katz closed the door to the telephone booth after him, petitioners closed the doors to their automobile. Last Term, this Court determined in *Pennsylvania v. Mimms* [p. 398 supra], that passengers in automobiles have no Fourth Amendment right not to be ordered from their vehicle, once a proper stop is made. The dissenting opinion concedes that there is no question here of the propriety of the stopping of the automobile in which the petitioners were riding. Thus, the closing of the doors of a vehicle, even if there were only one occupant, cannot have the same significance as it might in other contexts.

that vehicle unless he happens to own or have a possessory interest in it.[1] Though professing to acknowledge that the primary purpose of the Fourth Amendment's prohibition of unreasonable searches is the protection of privacy—not property—the Court nonetheless effectively ties the application of the Fourth Amendment and the exclusionary rule in this situation to property law concepts. Insofar as passengers are concerned, the Court's opinion today declares an "open season" on automobiles. However unlawful stopping and searching a car may be, absent a possessory or ownership interest, no "mere" passenger may object, regardless of his relationship to the owner.[c] Because the majority's conclusion has no support in the Court's controlling decisions, in the logic of the Fourth Amendment, or in common sense, I must respectfully dissent. If the Court is troubled by the practical impact of the exclusionary rule, it should face the issue of that rule's continued validity squarely instead of distorting other doctrines in an attempt to reach what are perceived as the correct results in specific cases. * * * [d]

It is true that the Court asserts that it is not limiting the Fourth Amendment bar against unreasonable searches to the protection of property rights, but in reality it is doing exactly that.[14] Petitioners were in a private place with the permission of the owner, but the Court states that that is not sufficient to establish entitlement to a legitimate expectation of privacy. But if that is not sufficient, what would be? We are not told, and it is hard to imagine anything short of a property interest that would satisfy the majority. Insofar as the Court's rationale is concerned, no passenger in an automobile, without an ownership or possessory interest and regardless of his relationship to the owner, may claim Fourth Amendment protection against illegal stops and searches of the automobile in which he is rightfully present. The Court approves the result in *Jones,* but it fails to give any explanation why the facts in *Jones* differ, in a fashion material to the Fourth Amendment, from the facts here.[15] More importantly, how is the Court able to avoid answering the question why presence in a private place with the owner's permission is insufficient? * * *

The Court's holding is contrary not only to our past decisions and the logic of the Fourth Amendment but also to the everyday expectations of privacy that we all share. Because of that, it is unworkable in all the various situations that arise in real life. If the owner of the car had not only

1. For the most part, I agree with the Court's rejection, which was implicit in *Alderman,* of petitioners' secondary theory of target standing.

c. Is this what *Rakas* holds? See Note 2 following this case and fn. 17 of the opinion for the Court.

d. The dissenters then noted that "petitioners of course have standing to challenge the legality of the stop, and the evidence found may be a fruit of that stop. Petitioners have not argued that theory here, perhaps because the justification necessary for such a stop is less than that needed for a search." The dissenters also noted that "petitioners never asserted a right in the items seized from the automobile."

14. The Court's reliance on property law concepts is additionally shown by its suggestion that visitors could "contest the lawfulness of the seizure of evidence or the search if their own property were seized during the search." [n. 11]. What difference should that property interest make to constitutional protection against unreasonable searches, which is concerned with privacy? Contrary to the Court's suggestion, a legitimate passenger in a car expects to enjoy the privacy of the vehicle whether or not he happens to carry some item along for the ride. We have never before limited our concern for a person's privacy to those situations in which he is in possession of personal property. Even a person living in a barren room without possessions is entitled to expect that the police will not intrude without cause.

15. * * * [T]he only distinguishing fact is that Jones could exclude others from the apartment by using his friend's key. But petitioners and their friend the owner had excluded others by entering the automobile and shutting the doors. Petitioners did not need a key because the owner was present. Similarly, the Court attempts to distinguish *Katz* on the theory that Katz had "shut the door behind him to exclude all others," but petitioners here did exactly the same. The car doors remained closed until the police ordered them opened at gunpoint.

invited petitioners to join her but had said to them, "I give you a temporary possessory interest in my vehicle so that you will share the right to privacy that the Supreme Court says that I own," then apparently the majority would reverse. But people seldom say such things, though they may mean their invitation to encompass them if only they had thought of the problem. If the non-owner were the spouse or child of the owner,[20] would the Court recognize a sufficient interest?[e] If so, would distant relatives somehow have more of an expectation of privacy than close friends? What if the nonowner were driving with the owner's permission? Would non-owning drivers have more of an expectation of privacy than mere passengers?[f] What about a passenger in a taxicab? *Katz* expressly recognized protection for such passengers. Why should Fourth Amendment rights be present when one pays a cabdriver for a ride but be absent when one is given a ride by a friend?

The distinctions the Court would draw are based on relationships between private parties, but the Fourth Amendment is concerned with the relationship of one of those parties to the government. Divorced as it is from the purpose of the Fourth Amendment, the Court's essentially property-based rationale can satisfactorily answer none of the questions posed above. That is reason enough to reject it. The *Jones* rule is relatively easily applied by police and courts; the rule announced today will not provide law enforcement officials with a bright line between the protected and the unprotected. Only rarely will police know whether one private party has or has not been granted a sufficient possessory or other interest by another private party. Surely in this case the officers had no such knowledge. The Court's rule will ensnare defendants and police in needless litigation over factors that should not be determinative of Fourth Amendment rights.

More importantly, the ruling today undercuts the force of the exclusionary rule in the one area in which its use is most certainly justified—the deterrence of bad-faith violations of the Fourth Amendment. This decision invites police to engage in patently unreasonable searches every time an automobile contains more than one occupant. Should something be found, only the owner of the vehicle, or of the item, will have standing to seek suppression, and the evidence will presumably be usable against the other occupants. The danger of such bad faith is especially high in cases such as this one where the officers are only after the passengers and can usually infer accurately that the driver is the owner. The suppression remedy for those owners in whose vehicles something is found and who are charged with crime is small consolation for all those owners *and* occupants whose privacy will be needlessly invaded by officers following mistaken hunches not rising to the level of probable cause but operated on in the knowledge that someone in a crowded car will probably be unprotected if contraband or incriminating evidence happens to be found. After this decision, police will have little to lose by unreasonably searching vehicles occupied by more than one person.

Of course, most police officers will decline the Court's invitation and will continue to do their jobs as best they can in accord with the Fourth Amendment. But the very purpose of the Bill of Rights was to answer the justified fear that governmental agents cannot be left totally to their own devices, and the Bill of Rights is enforceable in the courts because human experience teaches that not all such officials will otherwise adhere to the stated

20. In fact, though it was not brought out at the suppression hearing, one of the petitioners is the former husband of the owner and driver of the car. He did testify at the suppression hearing that he was with her when she purchased it.

e. See Note 5 following this case.

f. See Note 6 following this case.

precepts. Some policemen simply do act in bad faith, even if for understandable ends, and some deterrent is needed. In the rush to limit the applicability of the exclusionary rule somewhere, anywhere, the Court ignores precedent, logic, and common sense to exclude the rule's operation from situations in which, paradoxically, it is justified and needed.[g]

ON THE MEANING OF *RAKAS*

1. *"Standing" and "the merits" of a Fourth Amendment claim.* Consider LaFave, § 11.3 (1986 Supp.): "[The *Rakas* Court] asked 'whether it serves any useful analytical purpose to consider [the principle that Fourth Amendment rights are personal rights] a matter of standing, distinct from the merits of a defendant's Fourth Amendment claim.' The Court, per Rehnquist, J., then proceeded to answer that inquiry in the negative, concluding that 'the better analysis forthrightly focuses on the extent of a particular defendant's rights under the Fourth Amendment, rather than on any theoretically separate, but invariably intertwined concept of standing.' This may be so at least in the sense that the expectation-of-privacy analysis utilized with respect to so-called standing issues is also used for other purposes, most notably to determine whether any search for Fourth Amendment purposes has occurred. Yet, it is important to keep in mind that the question traditionally labelled as standing (did the police intrude upon *this defendant's* justified expectation of privacy?) is not identical to, for example, the question of whether any Fourth Amendment search has occurred (did the police intrude upon *anyone's* justified expectation of privacy?), and that therefore the particular issues discussed herein are still rather discrete and deserving of separate attention, no matter what label is put on them." Cf. Note, 93 Harv.L.Rev. 171, 176 (1979).

2. *When, if ever, does a "mere passenger" in a vehicle have "standing"?* Does *Rakas* hold, as the dissenters claim, that "[h]owever unlawful stopping and searching a car may be, absent a possessory or ownership interest, no 'mere' passenger may object"? As both the four dissenting and the two concurring Justices noted, petitioners challenged neither the legality of the police action in stopping the vehicle nor their being ordered out of the vehicle. What if they had? Consider Kamisar, remarks on *Rakas,* in Choper, Kamisar & Tribe, *The Supreme Court: Trends and Developments 1978–1979* (1979) (hereinafter called "Kamisar") at 160–61: "[T]he passenger in a car shares with the driver a privacy interest in continuing his travels. If the search of the vehicle is a product of the prior illegal stopping, then the passenger should be able to challenge the search because it was brought about as a consequence or fruit of the prior invasion of his personal liberty." See also LaFave, § 11.3(b) (1986 Supp.): "If the police, without required notice or without probable cause or without a required search warrant, burst into B's home and disrupt a dinner party at which A is present as a guest, then certainly A should be deemed to have standing to object—just as passengers in a car may object to its illegal stopping. Dinner guest A has had *his* freedom, privacy and solitude intruded upon by the police, and thus he has standing to object to that encroachment upon *his* rights, even if it led to the discovery of evidence in B's basement, a place A (in Justice Rehnquist's language) 'has never seen, or been permitted to visit.' On the other hand, it is fully consistent with the *Rakas* reasoning and result to say that if the intrusion itself was lawful, then A's lawful presence would not alone give him standing as to any subsequent illegalities [e.g., a search of B's person or minor

g. For strong criticism of *Rakas,* see Doernberg, "The Right of the People": Reconciling Collective and Individual Interest under the Fourth Amendment, 58 N.Y.U.L. Rev. 259 (1983); Kuhns, *The Concept of Personal Aggrievement in Fourth Amendment Standing Cases,* 65 Iowa L.Rev. 493 (1980).

deviations from the scope limits of the search warrant] which did not increase appreciably the interference with A's personal freedom."

However, a number of lower courts have ignored the distinction drawn by LaFave and held that casual visitors lack standing to object to an unconstitutional entry as well as an unconstitutional search of the premises. See, e.g., *United States v. Adamo,* 742 F.2d 927 (6th Cir.1984); *United States v. Underwood,* 717 F.2d 482 (9th Cir.1983); *Lee v. State,* 419 N.E.2d 825 (Ind.App.1981).

3. *Does one have "standing" by virtue of the fact that effects taken from the car belong to him?* Both Justice Rehnquist and the dissenters note that petitioners never asserted a property interest in the *items taken* from the vehicle. What if they had? Would they have derived standing to object to a seizure of the items, albeit from another person's car, by virtue of the fact that these effects belonged to them, even though they had no privacy right in the car as such? See Kamisar, at 162 (answering yes, relying heavily on the pre-*Rakas* discussion in LaFave, § 11.3(e) at 577–79). See also Israel and LaFave, *Criminal Procedure in a Nutshell* § 36(B) (3d ed. 1980).

Recall that although Justice Rehnquist asserted that a casual visitor who walks into a house a minute before it is searched could not contest the legality of the search, he added (fn. 11): "This is not to say that such visitors could not contest the lawfulness of the seizure of evidence or the search *if their own property were seized during the search.*" (Emphasis added.) But compare Justice Rehnquist's opinion in *Rawlings,* p. 792 infra.

4. *Why didn't petitioners ever assert a property interest in the rifle or the shells?* Consider Kamisar, at 163–65: "[A]t the suppression hearing [the lawyer for Rakas and his codefendant] maintained that his clients did not 'have to admit' that the items seized were theirs. The way he put that suggests that perhaps the defense lawyer was unaware that testimony given to establish standing to object to illegally seized evidence may not be used against the defendant at his trial on the question of guilt or innocence. On the other hand, perhaps the defense lawyer was thinking of putting his clients on the stand at the trial and was painfully aware that in a few jurisdictions, including Illinois, a defendant's testimony at his pretrial [suppression hearing] [is] admissible for impeachment purposes [at least unless and until the U.S. Supreme Court rules otherwise]."

5. *Family members.* The *Rakas* dissenters wonder whether "if the non-owner [of the car] were the spouse or child of the owner" he would be able to challenge the legality of a search of the car. Consider LaFave, § 11.3 at 550, 577: "It would seem that all members of a family [living together] should be deemed [to have] 'a personal and constitutionally protected interest in the integrity and security of the [home],' so that [a child or grandchild living in a home] should be entitled to object to any search which was a consequence of an illegal entry of the premises. * * * Just as family members living with the owner or tenant of premises share with him an expectation of privacy in that residence, it would seem that they likewise share a protected interest in vehicles used by the family." See the post-*Rakas* case of *Pollard v. State,* 388 N.E.2d 496 (Ind. 1979) (appellant had a "legitimate expectation of privacy" in parked car belonging to his wife).

6. *Non-owning drivers vs. "mere passengers."* "Would non-owning drivers," ask the *Rakas* dissenters, "have more of an expectation of privacy than mere passengers"? Prior to *Rakas,* at least, the answer seemed clear: "If the owner of a vehicle has turned it over to another person for some period of time, then surely this latter person has standing vis-a-vis the car during the duration of the bailment. The bailee certainly has a broader expectation of privacy than a mere passenger, and thus he would not have to be actually present in

the car at the time of the objected-to-intrusion. The same may be said of those who share the vehicle with the owner on a regular and recurring basis." LaFave, § 11.3(e) at 576–77.

RAWLINGS v. KENTUCKY, 448 U.S. 98, 100 S.Ct. 2556, 65 L.Ed.2d 633 (1980), arose as follows: On the day of the challenged police conduct, petitioner and Ms. Cox, who had been his companion for several days, were visitors at the house of one Marquess. Shortly before six police officers arrived, armed with a warrant for the arrest of Marquess, petitioner, who had been carrying a large quantity of illegal drugs, dumped them into the purse of Ms. Cox. Although there was a dispute about their discussion, petitioner testified that he had asked Ms. Cox "if she would carry this for me, and she said, 'yes.'" (Although unclear, one plausible inference is that petitioner had put the contraband in the purse because he had seen police approaching the house.)

While unsuccessfully searching for Marquess in his house, the police came upon evidence of drug violations. Two of the officers then left to obtain a warrant to search the house, while the remaining officers detained the occupants, including petitioner and Cox, allowing them to leave only if they consented to a body search. Upon returning with the search warrant some 45 minutes later, the officers read the warrant to the occupants, gave them the "*Miranda* warnings," and then ordered Cox to empty her purse onto a table. As she poured out the contents of her purse, Cox told petitioner "to take what was his" and petitioner immediately claimed ownership of the drugs. Considering the "totality of the circumstances," including petitioner's admission at the suppression hearing that he did not believe that Cox's purse would be free from governmental intrusion, the state supreme court concluded that petitioner had no "standing" because he had failed to make "a sufficient showing that his legitimate or reasonable expectations of privacy were violated by the search of the purse." The Court, per REHNQUIST, J., found no reason to overturn that conclusion:

"At the time petitioner dumped thousands of dollars worth of illegal drugs into Cox's purse, he had known her for only a few days. According to Cox's uncontested testimony, petitioner had never sought or received access to her purse prior to that sudden bailment. Nor did petitioner have any right to exclude other persons from access to Cox's purse. In fact, [a third person] a longtime acquaintance and frequent companion of Cox's, had free access to her purse and on the very morning of the arrest had rummaged through its contents in search of a hair brush. Moreover, even assuming that petitioner's version of the bailment is correct[,the] precipitous nature of the transaction hardly supports a reasonable inference that petitioner took normal precautions to maintain his privacy. [Moreover,] the record also contains a frank admission by petitioner that he had no subjective expectation that Cox's purse would remain free from governmental intrusion * * *.

"Petitioner contends nevertheless that, because he claimed ownership of the drugs in Cox's purse, he should be entitled to challenge the search regardless of his expectation of privacy. We disagree. While petitioner's ownership of the drugs is undoubtedly one fact to be considered in this case, *Rakas* emphatically rejected the notion that 'arcane' concepts of property law ought to control the ability to claim the protections of the Fourth Amendment. Had petitioner placed his drugs in plain view, he would still have owned them, but he could not claim any legitimate expectation of privacy. Prior to *Rakas,* petitioner might have been given 'standing' in such a case to challenge a 'search' that netted those drugs but probably would have lost his claim on the merits. After *Rakas,* the two inquiries merge into one: whether governmental officials violated any legitimate expectation of privacy held by petitioner."

BLACKMUN, J., joined the Court's opinion, but also wrote separately. He did not read the Court's decisions "to hold that property interests cannot [sometimes be] weighty factors in establishing the existence of Fourth Amendment rights. Not every concept of ownership or possession is 'arcane.'" In his view, "[the] 'right to exclude' often may be a principal determinant in the establishment of a legitimate Fourth Amendment interest." Accordingly, he "would confine analysis to the facts of this case" and on those facts petitioner's possessory interest in the drugs "is not sufficient to create a privacy interest in [the] purse"; nor was such an interest "otherwise conferred by any agreement between petitioner and Cox."

Dissenting Justice MARSHALL, joined by Brennan, J., protested:

"[The Court's] holding cavalierly rejects the fundamental principle, unquestioned until today, that an interest in either the place searched or the property seized is sufficient to invoke the Constitution's protection against unreasonable searches and seizures.

"The Court's examination of previous Fourth Amendment cases begins and ends—as it must if it is to reach its desired conclusion—with *Rakas.* [But] [n]o Fourth Amendment claim based on an interest in the property seized was before the [*Rakas*] Court, and, consequently, the Court did not and could not have decided whether such a claim could be maintained. In fact, the Court expressly disavowed any intention to foreclose such a claim.

"[The] decision today, then, is not supported by the only case directly cited in its favor. Further, the Court has ignored a long tradition embodying the opposite view. *United States v. Jeffers,* 342 U.S. 48, 72 S.Ct. 93, 96 L.Ed. 59 (1951), for example, involved a seizure of contraband alleged to belong to the defendant from a hotel room occupied by his two aunts. The Court * * * held that standing to object to the seizure could not be separated from standing to object to the search, for '[t]he search and seizure [are] incapable of being untied.' Similarly, *Jones v. United States* is quite plainly premised on the understanding that an interest in the seized property is sufficient to establish that the defendant 'himself was the victim of an invasion of privacy.' * * *

"The Court's decision today is not wrong, however, simply because it is contrary to our previous cases. It is wrong because it is contrary to the Fourth Amendment, [which] provides in plain language that if one's security in one's 'effects' is disturbed by an unreasonable search and seizure, one has been the victim of a constitutional violation; and so it has always been understood. * * *

"In holding that the Fourth Amendment protects only those with a privacy interest in the place searched, and not those with an ownership or possessory interest in the things seized, the Court had turned the development of the law of search and seizure on its head. The history of the Fourth Amendment shows that it was designed to protect property interests as well as privacy interests; in fact, until *Jones* the question whether a person's Fourth Amendment rights had been violated turned on whether he had a property interest in the place searched or the items seized. *Jones* and *Katz* expanded our view of the protections afforded by the Fourth Amendment by recognizing that privacy interests are protected even if they do not arise from property rights. But that recognition was never intended to exclude interests that had historically been sheltered by the Fourth Amendment from its protection. * * *

"In fact, the Court rather inconsistently denies that property rights may, by themselves, entitle one to the protection of the Fourth Amendment, but simultaneously suggests that a person may claim such protection only if his expectation of privacy in the premises searched is so strong that he may exclude all others from that place. Such a harsh threshold requirement was not imposed even in the heyday of a property rights oriented Fourth Amendment."

Is *Rawlings* a sound application of the expectation-of-privacy approach? Which of the various points, if any, made by Justice Rehnquist are persuasive? Consider Professor LaFave's seriatim discussion of these points, below:

WAYNE R. LaFAVE—SEARCH AND SEIZURE: A TREATISE ON THE FOURTH AMENDMENT

(1986 Supp. to § 11.3)

(1) It is somehow thought relevant that Rawlings had known Cox "for only a few days," but that hardly establishes the absence of a justified expectation of privacy. Even assuming one might question how strong a privacy expectation there would be if a person thrust his effects upon a perfect stranger, it hardly follows that privacy attends a bailment relationship *only* if the bailment was undertaken because of a longstanding relationship of trust existing between the bailor and bailee. In *Rawlings* the defendant had met Cox shortly after he arrived in town and had "spent at least two nights of the next week" in her house, so the two were hardly strangers. Certainly the relationship was long enough and close enough that when defendant asked Cox if she would carry the controlled substances in her purse during their anticipated departure together from Marquess' house and she agreed, he could have justifiably concluded his effects were now in a private place at least as long as they remained together.

(2) Next, it is said to be significant that Rawlings had not before "sought or received access to her purse." But that added fact casts no doubt on the above-stated conclusion that Rawlings would have been justified in viewing that purse as a private place. Were this not so, then we would be left with the curious notion that a first-time bailment or, indeed, any bailment contemplating storage of the bailor's effects at a place to which the bailor had not theretofore had access, would not carry with it a justified expectation that one's goods are secure in the hands of the bailee.

(3) It is thought important that the defendant in *Rawlings* did not "have any right to exclude other persons from access to Cox's purse." Here again, the cited facts have little if anything to do with the matter at issue. * * * [W]hile a "right to exclude" may be an easy way to establish the requisite legitimate expectation of privacy, it hardly follows that it is the *only* way; as the *Rawlings* dissenters note, "such a harsh threshold requirement was not imposed even the heyday of a property rights oriented Fourth Amendment." A bailor's "right to exclude" others, even as against the later wishes of the bailee, *is* important in Fourth Amendment law, but for another purpose, namely, in deciding the lawfulness of a search into the bailor's effects with consent of the bailee. To now utilize the same approach in the law of Fourth Amendment standing would produce the incredible result that whenever police could conduct a lawful search with the bailee's consent, they may then proceed to make that search without the bailee's consent because the bailor will not have standing to object. This is not only wrong, but inconsistent with the Court's prior pronouncements on the law of standing. In *Mancusi,* for example, where the Court held an office worker had standing as to a search of records in an office used by him and his coworkers, it was properly said to be "irrelevant" that his employer and fellow employees "might validly have consented to a search of the area where the records were kept."

(4) It is also stressed in *Rawlings* that one "Stallons, a longtime acquaintance and frequent companion of Cox's, had free access to her purse" * * *. But this is

also not relevant. For one thing, this prior access by Stallons was described by Cox at the suppression hearing; there is no indication this was known by Rawlings at the time of the bailment, and thus it should not enter into an assessment of how someone in the defendant's shoes should have perceived the situation. Secondly, even if Rawlings was aware of Stallons' access on prior occasions, this still does not show a privacy expectation in the purse would be unjustified. Stallons was not present in the Marquess home and thus would not have been in a position to intrude again during this brief bailment. Moreover, the fact a third party might have access to the place in question is not decisive in any event. The issue before the Court in *Rawlings* was not whether defendant reasonably believed he was free from intrusion by *anyone*, but rather, as the Court correctly put it in *Mancusi*, "whether the area was one in which there was a reasonable expectation of freedom from *governmental* intrusion."

(5) It is next asserted that "the precipitous nature of the transaction hardly supports a reasonable inference that petitioner took normal precautions to maintain his privacy." * * * [But the Court] has ruled that a container does not have to be locked to give rise to that especially strong expectation of privacy which makes the warrant clause of the Fourth Amendment applicable, and thus it can hardly be said that an unlocked container carries with it no justified privacy expectation at all. The purse in *Rawlings*, after all, was a closed container of the type frequently used to carry intimate personal effects. If it can be said that Rawlings' act in putting his effects into such a closed container with the owner's consent does not amount to the "normal precautions" necessary to establish a Fourth Amendment privacy expectation in him, then surely Ms. Cox likewise had no justified expectation of privacy in the same purse because she did not better safeguard her effects in that purse. To require more of Rawlings in this regard than of Ms. Cox makes no sense, and again is best explainable in terms of the Court's inability to keep straight the law of standing and the law of consent searches in bailment situations.

(6) Finally, the Court in *Rawlings* makes much of the fact that "the record also contains a frank admission by petitioner that he had no subjective expectation that Cox's purse would remain free from governmental intrusion." [But] inquiry into the particular defendant's subjective state of mind has *no* place in the application of the *Katz* expectation of privacy standard. Were there ever any doubt on the soundness of this point, a careful examination of the *Rawlings* facts should remove it. The "frank admission" touted by Justice Rehnquist, he admits in a footnote, is defendant's answer of "No, sir" when he was asked at the suppression hearing: "Did you feel that Vanessa Cox's purse would be free from the intrusion of the officers as you sat there?" The question quite obviously asks the defendant what he thought was going to happen *after* the police were on the scene and *after* they had told him and the others that a warrant was being sought and that they could leave prior to the warrant execution only by submitting to a personal search. It is hardly remarkable that Rawlings thought at that time that search of the purse was inevitable, as that is exactly what the officers thought and had conveyed to him by their words and actions. But if one can be deprived of Fourth Amendment standing by being informed in advance by the police of the intrusion they intend to make, then it is certainly correct, as the *Rawlings* dissenters complained, that the majority "has turned the development of the law of search and seizure on its head." This would mean, for example, that Rawlings likewise had no standing with respect to his own person, which he also expected would be intruded upon by the police * * *.

Because *Rawlings* is based upon a series of notions which, if taken seriously, would reduce the Fourth Amendment to nothing more than "a form of words," it is to be hoped that the decision will have a short life. *Rawlings* is best viewed as an unusual case in which the result is more attributable to certain undercurrents in the case [a] than to the reasoning offered by the Court. Notwithstanding *Rawlings,* then, ordinary bailment relationships still deserve to be recognized as establishing a justified expectation of privacy upon which Fourth Amendment standing may be grounded.[b]

SECTION 2. HARMLESS CONSTITUTIONAL ERROR

Prior to the 1960's, there was reason to think that no error of constitutional dimension could ever be regarded as "harmless." But the Warren Court's dramatic expansion of federal constitutional rights cast new light on the subject.

Soon after *Mapp,* four Justices in *Fahy v. Connecticut,* 375 U.S. 85, 84 S.Ct. 229, 11 L.Ed.2d 171 (1963), indicated they would apply a "harmless error" rule to the erroneous admission of evidence obtained in violation of the Fourth Amendment.[a] But a 5–4 majority saw no need to reach this question because in its view the admission of the evidence was "prejudicial." The crucial issue, as the majority perceived it, was not "whether there was sufficient evidence on which the petitioner could have been convicted without the evidence complained of, but whether there is a reasonable possibility that [the erroneously committed evidence] might have contributed to the conviction."

In CHAPMAN v. CALIFORNIA, 386 U.S. 18, 87 S.Ct. 824, 17 L.Ed.2d 705 (1967), a case involving a violation of defendant's privilege against self-incrimination by commenting on his failure to take the stand in his own defense, the Court, per BLACK, J., announced for the first time that some constitutional errors, such as comment on a defendant's failure to testify, could be harmless.

The Court recognized that "there are some constitutional rights so basic to a fair trial that their infraction could never be treated as harmless error"—citing as examples *Tumey v. Ohio* (1927) (Chp. 22, § 2) (violation of defendant's right to an impartial judge); a case involving the use of a coerced confession: [b] and *Gideon* [c]—but observed that "there may be some constitutional errors which in the setting of a particular case are so unimportant and insignificant that they may, consistent with the Federal Constitution, be deemed harmless."

Chapman presents a two-step analysis for an appellate court dealing with a constitu-

a. At this point, LaFave notes: "Though 'none of the lower courts specifically found that Cox did not consent to the bailment,' the trial court was somewhat 'skeptical about petitioner's version of events' and seemed to think that Rawlings probably saw the police approaching the premises and then thrust the controlled substances onto Cox over her objection. The thrust of the majority opinion in *Rawlings* strongly suggests the Court was influenced by an assumption that this latter version was correct."

b. *Rawlings* is also criticized in Choper, Kamisar & Tribe, *The Supreme Court: Trends and Developments, 1979–80* at 129–31 (1981); Note, 94 Harv.L.Rev. 196 (1980). But cf. Note, 71 J.Crim.L. & C. 567 (1980).

a. This view eventually prevailed. See *Chambers v. Maroney* (1970), p. 801 infra.

b. In *Mincey v. Arizona* (1978) (p. 523 supra), the Court reaffirmed its pre-*Miranda* view that any criminal trial use of an "involuntary" or "coerced" confession requires "automatic reverse." But compare the treatment of *Massiah* and *Miranda* violations, Note 3, p. 802 infra.

c. It is plain that the Court meant that at least when a defendant is denied the right to the assistance of counsel *at trial* this infraction can never be treated as harmless error. But the rule is otherwise with respect to a violation of the right to counsel at a pretrial lineup, see Note 2, p. 801 infra; or a violation of the *Massiah* doctrine, see Note 3, p. 802 infra. See also *Coleman v. Alabama* (1970) (Ch. 15, § 2) (even where preliminary hearing is a "critical stage" of state's criminal process, violation of right to counsel at this stage may be "harmless error"). Cf. *Rushen v. Spain,* 464 U.S. 114, 104 S.Ct. 453, 78 L.Ed. 267 (1983) (unrecorded *ex parte* communication between trial judge and juror assumed to be violation of both defendant's right to be present during all critical stages of the proceedings and right to counsel, but under the circumstances constituted "harmless error").

tional error. First, the court must determine whether the error falls in that category of violations subject to the harmless error rule or that category requiring automatic reversal. Second, if the harmless error rule is applicable, the court must determine the impact of the error in the case before it under a federal standard laid down in *Chapman.* The appropriate federal rule, said the Court, is that before constitutional error can be deemed harmless, the "beneficiary of [the] constitutional error," the state, must "prove beyond a reasonable doubt that the error complained of did not contribute to the verdict obtained." The *Chapman* Court saw "little, if any, difference" between this articulation and the *Fahy* formulation. Applying the foregoing standard, the Court had little difficulty concluding that the error in the instant case was not harmless.[d]

Notes and Questions

1. *The trouble with a harmless constitutional error doctrine.* S. Goldberg, *Harmless Error: Constitutional Sneak Thief,* 71 J.Crim. L. & C. 421, 431, 436 (1980) maintains that, although the harmless error doctrine "unfortunately * * * enjoys great popularity with appellate courts as a mechanism for reducing the strict enforcement of criminal constitutional procedure rules," it is "unmatched for the secret theft of constitutional rights. A finding that constitutional error is harmless is almost beyond question on review. While there are some fact circumstance and trial situations so obvious that it is incredible that any appellate judge would make a harmless error finding, most such findings are based upon long and relatively inaccessible records. Further, the majority opinion will generally reflect those portions of the record which support the 'harmless' determination."

Professor Goldberg finds "something disquieting about the admission that constitutional rights are so often abrogated that we need a separate doctrine to excuse some of them so that our decision making system will not break down. Finally, there is some shame in trying to explain how the loss of a constitutional guarantee is harmless beyond a reasonable doubt—five to four."

2. *Is an inherent difficulty of a harmless-error rule that the erroneous admission of evidence may have significantly affected the strategies of both sides?* Consider Saltzburg, *The Harm of Harmless Error,* 59 Va.L.Rev. 988, 990 (1973): "[Decisions to call a certain witness or pursue a certain theory] are based on a careful but often subjective assessment of risk and the chances of success. They must be made with an eye to the governing law, and particularly to the rules of evidence. But when an evidentiary error occurs in the course of a trial, it disturbs this delicately balanced decision-making process. The abnegation of a particular rule upon which the defense relied may inflict more damage than initially appears. A meritorious line of defense may be dropped, an important witness held back, or entire strategies abandoned even though they should prevail."

3. *Knowing misconduct by the prosecution.* Because of the special sensitivity of prosecutors to a rule of automatic reversal, should the Court apply such a rule at least to those cases where an element of the constitutional error itself is the *knowing* misconduct of the prosecution? See Mause, *Harmless Constitutional Error: The Implications of Chapman v. California,* 53 Minn.L.Rev. 519, 553–54 (1969).

d. Dissenting Justice Harlan "regard[ed] the Court's assumption of what amounts to a general supervisory power over the trial of federal constitutional issues in state courts as a startling constitutional development that is wholly out of keeping with out federal system and completely unsupported by the Fourteenth Amendment where the source of such a power must be found." "A state appellate court's reasonable application of a constitutionally proper state harmless error rule to sustain a state conviction," maintained Harlan, "constitutes an independent and adequate state ground of judgment."

Should a prosecutor's comment, or at least repeated comments, on a defendant's failure to testify be regarded as *knowing* misconduct?

4. *May a federal court ignore the harmless error doctrine and exercise its "supervisory powers" to "discipline" prosecutors?* In *United States v. Hasting* (1983) (p. 60 supra), the Court of Appeals, motivated at least in part by what it perceived to be continuing prosecutorial violations of the prohibition against commenting on a defendant's failure to testify, the very violation involved in *Chapman,* declined to apply the harmless error doctrine. Instead, the court exercised its "supervisory power" over federal criminal justice (see generally pp. 58–62 supra) to overturn the conviction. The Supreme Court reversed, holding that the harmless error doctrine "cannot be so lightly and casually ignored in order to chastise what the Court below viewed as prosecutorial overreaching."

5. *The trouble with the Fahy-Chapman formulation.* Read literally, does the *Fahy-Chapman* harmless error test seem so extraordinarily difficult to satisfy that it amounts to a rule of "automatic reversal"? See Traynor, *The Riddle of Harmless Error* 43–44 (1970). Does the very severity of the test invite "giv[ing] the test lip service while tacitly discounting it" in order to "preclude well-nigh automatic reversal"? See Traynor, supra, contending that "[a]ppellate review would gain in forthrightness as well as reason if appellate courts could judge it highly probable, rather than almost certain, that an error did not affect the judgment." Did *Harrington v. California,* immediately below, depart from *Chapman* in favor of Justice Traynor's "high probability" test?

In HARRINGTON v. CALIFORNIA, 395 U.S. 250, 89 S.Ct. 1726, 23 L.Ed.2d 284 (1969), a 5–3 majority, per DOUGLAS, J., held that although the introduction at petitioner's trial of the confessions of two codefendants who did not take the stand violated *Bruton v. United States,* Ch. 18, § 3, it constituted "harmless error" under *Chapman.*

Petitioner and three codefendants were convicted of felony-murder. The confessions of the two codefendants placed petitioner at the scene of the crime, but so did petitioner's own statements and several eyewitnesses (although two of them had previously told the police that "four Negroes committed the crime," and petitioner, unlike his codefendants, was a Caucasian). Moreover the third codefendant (Rhone), who did take the stand and was cross-examined by petitioner, placed him in the store with a gun at the time of the murder.

Thus, as the majority saw it, the evidence supplied by the confessions of the two codefendants who did not take the stand was merely "cumulative" and, apart from this erroneously admitted evidence, the case against petitioner "so overwhelming [that] this violation of *Bruton* was harmless beyond a reasonable doubt, unless we adopt the minority view in *Chapman* that a departure from constitutional procedures should result in an automatic reversal, no matter the weight of the evidence." Continued Justice Douglas:

"It is argued that we must reverse if we can imagine a single juror whose mind might have been made up because of [the erroneously admitted codefendants'] confessions and who otherwise would have remained in doubt and unconvinced. We of course do not know the jurors who sat. Our judgment must be based on our own reading of the record and on what seems to us to have been the probable impact of the two confessions on the minds of an average jury. We admonished in *Chapman* against giving too much emphasis to 'overwhelming evidence' of guilt, stating that constitutional errors affecting the substantial rights of the aggrieved party could not be considered to be harmless. By that test we cannot impute reversible weight to the other two confessions.

"We do not depart from *Chapman;* nor do we dilute it by inference. We reaffirm it. We do not suggest that, if evidence bearing on all the ingredients of the crime is tendered, the use of cumulative evidence, though tainted, is harmless error. Our decision is based on the evidence in this record. [The case against Harrington] is so overwhelming that unless we say that no violation of *Bruton* can constitute harmless error, we must leave this state conviction undisturbed."

Dissenting Justice BRENNAN, joined by Chief Justice Warren and Justice Marshall, charged that "the Court today overrules *Chapman* [where] we left no doubt that for an error to be 'harmless' it must have made *no* contribution to a criminal conviction. *Chapman,* then, meant no compromise with the proposition that a conviction cannot constitutionally be based to any extent on constitutional error. The Court today by shifting the inquiry from whether the constitutional error contributed to the conviction to whether the untainted evidence provided 'overwhelming' support for the conviction puts aside the firm resolve of *Chapman* and makes that compromise. As a result, the deterrent effect of such cases as *Mapp, Griffin v. California, Miranda, Wade,* and *Bruton,* on the actions of both police and prosecutors, not to speak of trial courts, will be significantly undermined.

"The Court holds that constitutional error in the trial of a criminal offense may be held harmless if there is 'overwhelming' untainted evidence to support the conviction. This approach, however, was expressly rejected in *Chapman,* and with good reason. For, where the inquiry concerns the extent of accumulation of untainted evidence rather than the impact of tainted evidence on the jury's decision, convictions resulting from constitutional error may be insulated from attack. By its nature, the issue of substantiality of evidence admits of only the most limited kind of appellate review. Thus, the Court's rule will often effectively leave the vindication of constitutional rights solely in the hands of trial judges. If, instead, the task of appellate courts is to appraise the impact of tainted evidence on a jury's decision, as *Chapman* required, these courts will be better able to protect against deprivations of constitutional rights of criminal defendants. The focus of appellate inquiry should be on the character and quality of the tainted evidence as it relates to the untainted evidence and not just on the amount of untainted evidence.[a]

"The instant case illustrates well the difference in application between the approach adopted by the Court today and the approach set down in *Chapman.* At issue is the evidence going to Harrington's participation in the crime of attempted robbery, not the evidence going to his presence at the scene of the crime. Without the admittedly unconstitutional evidence against Harrington provided by the confessions of [the two codefendants who did not take the stand], the prosecutor's proof of Harrington's participation in the crime consisted of the testimony of two victims of the attempted robbery and of codefendant Rhone. The testimony of the victims was weakened by the fact that they had earlier told the police that all the participants in the attempted robbery were Negroes. Rhone's testimony against Harrington was self-serving in certain aspects. * * * Thus, although there was more than ample evidence to establish Harrington's participation in the attempted robbery, a jury might still have concluded that the case was not proved beyond a reasonable doubt. The confessions of the other two codefendants implicating Harrington in the crime were less self-serving and might well have tipped the balance in the jurors' minds in favor of conviction. Certainly, the State has not carried its burden of demonstrating beyond a reasonable

a. Does this language suggest not the *Chapman* test, but a distinctly different one, the "cumulative evidence" approach? See Notes 1 and 2 following this case.

doubt that these two confessions did not contribute to Harrington's conviction." [b]

Notes and Questions

1. *Confusion regarding "harmless error"; did the Harrington Court apply a "cumulative evidence" test?* Consider Field, *Assessing the Harmlessness of Federal Constitutional Error—A Process in Need of a Rationale,* 125 U.Pa.L. Rev. 15, 38–39, 58–60 (1976): "*Harrington* provides a good example both of the confusion regarding harmless error generally and of the Court's failure to differentiate between various processes of determining harmlessness even though those processes can lead to different results. [Although the *Harrington* opinion] says that the overwhelming evidence test should not be given 'too much emphasis,' much of the opinion reads as if the reason for the finding of harmlessness is the overwhelming nature of the evidence against Harrington.

[But the opinion also] suggests that there may be something about the way the tainted evidence relates to the untainted evidence that is pertinent to the finding of harmlessness, not simply the quantity or weight of the untainted evidence. This suggests a third variant by which harmless error might be determined, a variant I will refer to as the cumulative evidence test [an approach which asks whether the tainted evidence is merely cumulative—that is, merely duplicative of some remaining admissible evidence].

"[The Brennan dissent in *Harrington*] has the same difficulty as the majority opinion. * * * [At one point,] [in] a way that suggests the cumulative evidence test, [Justice Brennan] examines the difference between the untainted evidence against Harrington and the tainted evidence, which he believes is fuller and more probative. Yet his discussion has not recognized the cumulative evidence test as a distinct means of assessing harmlessness. Like the majority, therefore, Justice Brennan does not differentiate clearly between the separate ways of assessing harmlessness."

2. *Distinguishing the "cumulative evidence" approach from other tests.* Consider Field, supra, at 39–40: "Whether or not a cumulative evidence test explains the result in *Harrington,* this test does represent a distinct approach to harmless error. That there is a difference between this test and the [*Chapman*] approach is clear. Applying the latter approach to the facts of *Harrington,* one could not find harmlessness; examining the nontestifying codefendants' confessions, one would conclude that they incriminated Harrington. The cumulative evidence test, on the other hand, is like the overwhelming evidence test in that it allows a finding of harmlessness despite the conclusion that the error itself is prima facie incriminating as long as it is somewhat cumulative with other untainted evidence in the case. * * *

"The cumulative evidence test differs also from the overwhelming evidence test, as the following example illustrates. Suppose a defendant in a criminal case has on five occasions made identical statements to the police. The first four were volunteered and spontaneous. The police solicited the fifth under circumstances requiring *Miranda* warnings, which were not given. All five statements are introduced

b. See also *Milton v. Wainwright* (1972) (applying harmless-error rule to *Massiah* violation) (also discussed at p. 802 infra), where four dissenters—Justice Stewart plus the three *Harrington* dissenters—protested that the Court had shifted the inquiry from whether "the states had proved beyond a reasonable doubt that the [error] did not contribute to the verdict obtained" to whether "the untainted evidence provided 'overwhelming' support for the conviction." However, in *Brown v. United States,* 411 U.S. 223, 93 S.Ct. 1565, 36 L.Ed.2d 208 (1973), a *unanimous* Court, per Burger, C. J., utilized the test articulated by the *Harrington* majority in finding *Bruton* errors harmless: "The testimony erroneously admitted was merely cumulative of other overwhelming and largely uncontroverted evidence properly before the jury. In this case, as in *Harrington,* the independent evidence 'is so overwhelming that unless we say that no violation of *Bruton* can constitute harmless error, we must [affirm].'"

at trial, the fifth unconstitutionally. None of the statements admits guilt; they all deny it. But each is incriminating because it places the defendant at the scene of the crime * * *. The cumulative evidence test clearly would deem harmless the error in admitting the fifth statement, because by hypothesis it is identical in content to the four previously obtained, untainted statements. The overwhelming evidence test, standing alone, would allow a finding of harmlessness only if the untainted evidence was compelling, as opposed to simply sufficient to support the jury's verdict. That might or might not be true in the hypothetical above.[a] [One can also] hypothesize a case in which the overwhelming evidence test leads to a conclusion of harmlessness, but no untainted evidence is strictly 'cumulative' with the tainted evidence, so that if that test stood alone, a finding of harmlessness would not be possible."

APPLICATION OF THE HARMLESS-ERROR RULE TO OTHER CONSTITUTIONAL VIOLATIONS

1. *Fourth Amendment violations.* In *Chambers v. Maroney* (1970) (other aspects of which are discussed at p. 340 supra) the Court resolved the issue left open in *Fahy*—and did so, surprisingly, without discussion or dissent. Disposing quickly of petitioner's subsidiary search and seizure claim the Court, per White, J., observed: "Both [lower federal courts] found that if there was error in admitting the ammunition [seized in the course of a search of petitioner's house], the error was harmless beyond a reasonable doubt. Having ourselves studied this record, we are not prepared to differ with the two courts below. See *Harrington.*" How significant is it that the Court cited *Harrington* and omitted any reference to *Chapman?*

Should Fourth Amendment violations be subject to a rule of harmless-error? Is the added threat of reversal if the trial judge errs in ruling that certain evidence was legally obtained likely to serve as a significant additional deterrent? Even if not, to what extent will a prosecutor, counting on the pressure generated by a "harmless error" doctrine, be tempted to introduce questionably obtained evidence, "gambling" that appellate liberality in applying the harmless error rule will save the conviction?

2. *Wade-Gilbert invalid lineup identifications.* In the landmark lineup cases of *Wade* and *Gilbert,* Ch. 9 supra, decided shortly after *Chapman,* the Court afforded the government an opportunity to establish that testimony based on invalid lineup identifications was "harmless error"—without any discussion of why this consti-

a. Cf. *People v. Jacobson,* 405 P.2d 555 (Cal. 1965), discussed in Field at 55–58; Note, 65 Mich. L.Rev. 563 (1967). Of ten confessions admitted in evidence, only the last two, no more detailed than the others, were inadmissible on *Escobedo* grounds. The court deemed their admission "merely cumulative" and "harmless error." But cf. *State v. Slobodian,* 268 A.2d 849 (N.J.1970).

If, in a given "multiple confession" case, it is established that one or more unconstitutionally obtained confessions are "merely cumulative," should it make any difference *why* they were constitutionally inadmissible? More generally, can the rule of automatic reversal for erroneously admitted *involuntary* or *coerced* statements, recently reaffirmed in *Mincey,* p. 796 fn. b supra, be reconciled with the "overwhelming evidence" or "cumulative evidence" approaches? Consider Field, at 30–31:

"[It would be consistent] with the overwhelming evidence test to have a rule requiring automatic reversal whenever the constitutional error was such that by its nature it affected the entire trial process [such as denial of the right to counsel at trial or forcing an incompetent person to stand trial or, arguably, trial by a biased tribunal]. Coerced confessions, however, are clearly inconsistent with the defining principle for a category of automatically reversible errors. The only sense in which a coerced confession may be said to affect the entire trial process is that it may be so incriminating in the mind of the factfinder that it effectively forecloses the defense. To allow that rationale to support automatic reversal is to define that category according to the degree of prejudice inherent in the particular type of constitutional error—the explanation that is inconsistent with retention of the overwhelming evidence test."

tutional violation should be subject to such a rule.

3. *Miranda and Massiah violations.* Although the U.S. Supreme Court has never clearly resolved the question whether *Miranda* violations are subject to a harmless-error rule, in *Milton v. Wainwright,* 407 U.S. 371, 92 S.Ct. 2174, 33 L.Ed.2d 1 (1972), a 5–4 majority, per Burger, C.J., did hold that assuming arguendo that a post-indictment confession petitioner made to a police officer posing as his "cellmate" should have been excluded on *Massiah* grounds, any error was "harmless." In addition to hearing the arguably inadmissible testimony, observed the Court, the jury was presented with "overwhelming evidence of petitioner's guilt, including no less than three full [admissible] confessions that were made by petitioner prior to his indictment." The dissenters could find "no basis" for the Court's holding that the post-indictment statement to the "cellmate" was harmless, but operated on the premise that *Massiah* violations were subject to a *Chapman*-type harmless-error rule.

In *Harryman v. Estelle,* 616 F.2d 870 (5th Cir.1980) (en banc), the court, per Frank Johnson, J., deemed it "well established that the admission of statements obtained in violation of *Miranda* may be said to constitute harmless error." None of the 24 judges who participated in the case challenged this statement.

In determining whether a particular constitutional violation should be subject to the "harmless error" rule, how much weight should be given to the history and purposes of the underlying constitutional decision and the impact that a "harmless error" rule would have on its administration and implementation? Was not a major purpose of *Miranda* to relieve the Supreme Court of the burdensome obligation of examining the record on a case-by-case basis to determine whether the "voluntariness"-"totality of the circumstances" test had been violated in a particular instance? Was not a major purpose to displace the elusive, unruly "voluntariness" test with a set of relatively specific and more easily administered and reviewable guidelines? By committing the Court once again to a case-by-case examination of (a) whether a statement introduced at the trial was inadmissible solely on *Miranda* grounds or because it was "involuntary" or "coerced," and (b) if the former, whether in light of the whole record, the *Miranda* violation was harmless beyond a reasonable doubt, would a "harmless error" rule collide with a main thrust of the *Miranda* decision? [b]

SECTION 3. THE "FRUIT OF THE POISONOUS TREE"

A. Historical Background and Overview

"In the simplest of exclusionary rule cases," observe LaFave & Israel, § 9.3(a), "the challenged evidence is quite clearly 'direct' or 'primary' in its relationship to the prior arrest, search, interrogation [or lineup] [e.g., a confession made in response to impermissible interrogation or physical evidence obtained by an illegal search]." Not infrequently, however, point out LaFave & Israel, "challenged evidence is 'secondary' or 'derivative' in character. This occurs when, for example, a confession is obtained after an illegal arrest [a] [or] physical evidence is located after an illegally obtained confession [b] * * *. In these situations, it is necessary to determine whether the derivative evidence is 'tainted' by the prior constitutional or other violation. To use the phrase coined by Justice Frankfurter, it

b. For criticism of the application of the harmless error rule to *Miranda* violations and the conclusion that "a rule of automatic reversal seems to be both the appropriate and necessary solution if the protections and general viability of *Miranda* are to be retained," see Note, 69 Mich.L. Rev. 941 (1971). But see Notes, 1968 Utah L.Rev. 144, 151; 20 Vand.L.Rev. 1157, 1160 (1967).

a. See, e.g., *Brown v. Illinois,* p. 805 infra.

b. See, e.g., *New York v. Quarles,* p. 816 infra.

must be decided whether that evidence is 'the fruit of the poisonous tree.' " [c]

1. *Genesis of the rule; the doctrine of "attenuation."* (a) The genesis of the "taint" or "fruit of the poisonous tree" doctrine, as it came to be called, appears in *Silverthorne Lumber Co. v. United States,* 251 U.S. 385, 40 S.Ct. 182, 64 L.Ed. 319 (1920), where, in holding that the government could not use information obtained during an illegal search to subpoena the very documents illegally viewed, the Court, per Holmes, J., pointed out: "The essence of a provision forbidding the acquisition of evidence in a certain way is that not merely evidence so acquired shall not be used before the Court but that it shall not be used at all. Of course this does not mean that the facts thus obtained become sacred and inaccessible. If knowledge of them is gained from an independent source they may be proved like any others, but the knowledge gained by the Government's own wrong cannot be used by it in the way proposed."

Did *Silverthorne* mean that illegally seized *evidence* may never be used by the government although the *facts* revealed by that evidence may be obtained from an independent source? See Pitler, *"The Fruit of the Poisonous Tree" Revisited and Shepardized,* 56 Calif.L.Rev. 579, 589 (1968).

(b) In *Nardone v. United States,* 308 U.S. 338, 60 S.Ct. 266, 84 L.Ed. 307 (1939), which first used the phrase "fruit of the poisonous tree," the Court, per Frankfurter, J., refused to permit the prosecution to avoid an inquiry into its use of information gained by illegal wiretapping, observing that "to forbid the direct use of methods [but] to put no curb on their full indirect use would only invite the very methods deemed 'inconsistent with ethical standards and destructive of personal liberty.' " [a] The case also established the "attenuation" doctrine, being the first to authoritatively recognize that even where the challenged evidence did not have an "independent source" it might still be admissible: "Sophisticated argument may prove a causal connection between information obtained through illicit wire-tapping and the Government's proof. As a matter of good sense, however, such connection may have become so attenuated as to dissipate the taint."

2. *Verbal evidence as the "fruit" of illegal search and seizure.* In WONG SUN v. UNITED STATES, 371 U.S. 471, 83 S.Ct. 407, 9 L.Ed.2d 441 (1963) (other aspects of which are discussed at p. 287 supra), six federal narcotics agents illegally broke into Toy's laundry, chased him into the living quarters at the back of his shop, where Toy's wife and child were sleeping, and handcuffed him. Toy then told the agents that Yee had been selling narcotics. The agents immediately went to Yee, who surrendered heroin to them and implicated Toy and a third party, Wong Sun. A 5–4 majority, per BRENNAN, J., held that both Toy's declarations, upon being handcuffed in his bedroom, *and* "the narcotics taken from Yee, to which [Toy's] declarations led the police" had to be excluded as the "fruits" of the agents' unlawful entry into Toy's bedroom and the "bedroom arrest."

The Court recognized that "traditionally" the exclusionary rule had barred only "physical, tangible materials," but concluded that "verbal evidence which derives so immediately from an unlawful entry and an unauthorized arrest [as here] is no less the 'fruit' of official illegality than the more common tangible fruits of the unwarranted intrusion." [b] Not "all evidence

c. *Nardone v. United States,* Note 1(b) infra.

a. But cf. *United States v. Calandra,* p. 230 supra, holding that a witness may not refuse to answer grand jury questions on the ground that they are based on evidence obtained from him in an earlier unlawful search.

b. The dissenters, Clark, J., joined by Harlan, Stewart and White, JJ., did not challenge the manner in which the Court applied the "fruits" doctrine, but maintained that Toy's arrest was lawful and thus provided "no 'poisonous tree' whose fruits we must evaluate."

is 'fruit of the poisonous tree' simply because it would not have come to light but for the illegal actions of the police. Rather, the more apt question in such a case is 'whether, granting establishment of the primary illegality [the evidence] has been come at by exploitation of that illegality or instead by means sufficiently distinguishable to be purged of the primary taint.' J. Maguire, *Evidence of Guilt* 221 (1959). We think it clear that the narcotics [taken from Yee] were 'come at by the exploitation of that illegality [the lawless search and seizure of Toy]' and hence that they may not be used against Toy."

On the other hand, although Wong Sun had also been unlawfully arrested, his confession was not the "fruit" of his illegal arrest. Since he had been released on his own recognizance after a lawful arraignment and had returned voluntarily several days later to make the statement, "the connection between [Wong Sun's] arrest and [his] statement had 'become so attenuated as to dissipate the taint.'"

Notes and Questions

(a) *The relevant question.* Does the *Wong Sun* Court's talk of "purging the primary taint" obfuscate the relevant question—whether the admission of the secondary evidence will significantly encourage police misconduct in the future? See Pitler, supra, at 588–89; Note, 115 U.Pa.L.Rev. 1136, 1147 (1967).

(b) *"Purging the taint" of Fourth Amendment violations.* Are there events short of release from custody (which occurred in *Wong Sun*) which operate to "purge the taint" of an illegal arrest or search? Can the mere passage of time suffice? Or would such a rule only "postpone the testing" of the fruit but "not diminish its temptation"? See *Collins v. Beto,* 348 F.2d 823, 828 (5th Cir.1965). Would *Miranda* warnings purge the taint of an illegal arrest? See *Brown v. Illinois,* p. 805 infra.

3. *"Independent source"; "inevitable discovery."* The *Wong Sun* Court quoted from *Silverthorne,* supra, the proposition that the exclusionary rule has no application when "the Government learned of the evidence 'from an independent source.'" This means that if not even a "but for" test can be satisfied, the challenged evidence is not a fruit of the prior violation—a violation of a person's rights should not put him beyond the law's reach if his guilt can be established by evidence unconnected with or "untainted" by the violation.

A variation of the "independent source" exception is the "inevitable discovery" or "hypothetical independent source" rule, a doctrine long utilized by many lower courts and recently accepted by the U.S. Supreme Court.[a] This doctrine differs from the "independent source" exception in that the question is not whether the police *actually* acquired certain evidence by reliance upon an untainted source, but whether evidence in fact obtained illegally would inevitably or eventually or probably have been discovered lawfully.

The doctrine is most palatable, and has been most frequently applied, when the police misconduct occurred "while an investigation was already in progress and resulted in the discovery of evidence that would have eventually have been obtained through routine police investigatory procedure. The illegalities in such cases, therefore, had the effect of simply accelerating the discovery." Note, 74 Colum.L.Rev. 88, 90 (1974).

Because mechanical application of the "inevitable discovery" doctrine would seem to encourage unconstitutional shortcuts, and one purpose of the exclusionary rule is to discourage such shortcuts, it has been argued that the doctrine should be permitted only when the police have not acted in "bad faith" to accelerate the discovery of the challenged evidence. See, e.g., LaFave, § 11.4(a) at 624. But the Court rejected such a limitation in the

a. See *Nix v. Williams,* p. 810 infra.

recent case of *Nix v. Williams,* p. 810 infra.

4. *Confession as the "fruit" of an illegal arrest.* BROWN v. ILLINOIS, 422 U.S. 590, 95 S.Ct. 2254, 45 L.Ed.2d 416 (1975), arose as follows: Following his illegal arrest, petitioner, a murder suspect, was taken to a police station where, after being given the *Miranda* warnings and waiving his rights, he made incriminating statements within two hours of the arrest. The state supreme court affirmed the murder conviction, taking the view that "the *Miranda* warnings in and of themselves" purged the taint of the prior illegal arrest. The Court, per BLACKMUN, J., reversed:

"The exclusionary rule, [when] utilized to effectuate the Fourth Amendment, serves interests and policies that are distinct from those it serves under the Fifth. [E]xclusion of a confession made without *Miranda* warnings might be regarded as necessary to effectuate the Fifth Amendment, but it would not be sufficient fully to protect the Fourth. *Miranda* warnings, and the exclusion of a confession made without them, do not alone sufficiently deter a Fourth Amendment violation. * * *

"If *Miranda* warnings, by themselves, were held to attenuate the taint of an unconstitutional arrest, regardless of how wanton and purposeful the Fourth Amendment violation, the effect of the exclusionary rule would be substantially diluted. [Illegal arrests] would be encouraged by the knowledge that evidence derived therefrom hopefully could be made admissible at trial by the simple expedient of giving *Miranda* warnings. Any incentive to avoid Fourth Amendment violations would be eviscerated by making the warnings, in effect, a 'cure-all' * * *."

Although the Court rejected the *per se* rule of the Illinois court whereunder the *Miranda* warnings were deemed to break the causal connection between the arrest and confession, it declined to adopt a *per se* or "but for" rule running in the other direction. It concluded instead that such taint issues "must be answered on the facts of each case. No single fact is dispositive. [The] *Miranda* warnings are an important factor, to be sure, in determining whether the confession is obtained by exploitation of an illegal arrest. But they are not the only factor to be considered. The temporal proximity of the arrest and the confession, the presence of intervening circumstances and, particularly, the purpose and flagrancy of the official misconduct, are all relevant. The voluntariness of the statement is a threshold requirement. And the burden of showing admissibility rests, of course, on the prosecution."

The Court then concluded that the prosecution had failed to sustain its burden: "[Petitioner's] first statement was separated from his illegal arrest by less than two hours, and there was no intervening event of significance whatsoever. * * * We could hold [petitioner's] first statement admissible only if we overrule *Wong Sun.* We decline to do so. * * *

"The illegality here, moreover, had a quality of purposefulness. The impropriety of the arrest was obvious * * *. [The] detectives embarked upon this expedition for evidence in the hope that something might turn up."

Justice WHITE expressed agreement with the Court insofar as it "holds (1) that despite *Miranda* warnings the Fourth and Fourteenth Amendments require the exclusion from evidence of statements obtained as the fruit of an arrest which the arresting officers *knew or should have known* was without probable cause and unconstitutional, and (2) that the statements obtained in this case were in this category" (emphasis added), and therefore concurred in the judgment.

Justice POWELL, joined by Rehnquist, J., joined the Court insofar as it rejected the Illinois courts' *per se* rule, but "would remand the case for reconsideration under the general standards articulated in the Court's opinion."

In Justice Powell's view, "the flagrantly abusive violations of Fourth Amendment rights, on the one hand, and 'technical' Fourth Amendment violations, [on the other] call for significantly different judicial responses":

"I would require the clearest indication of attenuation in cases in which official conduct was flagrantly abusive of Fourth Amendment rights. * * * [In such cases] I would consider the equalizing potential of *Miranda* warnings rarely sufficient to dissipate the taint. * * *

"At the opposite end of the spectrum lie 'technical' violations of Fourth Amendment rights where, for example, officers in good faith arrest an individual in reliance on a warrant later invalidated or pursuant to a statute that subsequently is declared unconstitutional. * * * [In such cases] the deterrence rationale of the exclusionary rule does not obtain, and I can see no legitimate justification for depriving the prosecution of reliable and probative evidence. Thus, with the exception of statements given in the immediate circumstances of the illegal arrest—a constraint I think is imposed by existing exclusionary rule law—I would not require more than proof that effective *Miranda* warnings were given and that the ensuing statement was voluntary in the Fifth Amendment sense."

In *Dunaway v. New York,* other aspects of which are discussed at p. 385 supra, the Court, per Brennan, J., reaffirmed the view that *Miranda* warnings, by themselves, are insufficient to attenuate the taint of an unconstitutional arrest: "The situation in this case is virtually a replica of the situation in *Brown.* Petitioner was also admittedly seized without probable cause in the hope that something might turn up, and confessed without any intervening event of significance. * * * To admit petitioner's confession in such a case would allow 'law enforcement officers to violate the Fourth Amendment with impunity, safe in the knowledge that they could wash their hands in the "procedural safeguards" of the Fifth' [Comment, 25 Emory L.J. 227, 238 (1976)]."

Justice Stevens joined the Court's opinion but added a comment on "the significance of two factors that may be considered when determining whether a confession has been obtained by exploitation of an illegal arrest":

"The temporal relationship between the arrest and the confession may be an ambiguous factor. If there are no relevant intervening circumstances, a prolonged detention may well be a more serious exploitation of an illegal arrest than a short one. Conversely, even an immediate confession may have been motivated by a prearrest event such as a visit with a minister.

"The flagrancy of the official misconduct is relevant, in my judgment, only insofar as it has a tendency to motivate the defendant. A midnight arrest with drawn guns will be equally frightening whether the police acted recklessly or in good faith. Conversely, a courteous command has the same effect on the arrestee whether the officer thinks he has probable cause or knows that he does not. In either event, if the Fourth Amendment is violated, the admissibility question will turn on the causal relationship between that violation and the defendant's subsequent confession." [a]

In *Taylor v. Alabama,* 457 U.S. 687, 102 S.Ct. 2664, 73 L.Ed.2d 314 (1982), a 5–4 majority, per Marshall, J., held that petitioner's confession was the impermissible fruit of his illegal arrest even though (a) six hours had elapsed between the illegal

a. Rehnquist, J., joined by Burger, C.J., dissented, maintaining that the police had acted in "good faith and not in a flagrant manner" and that in such cases "no more [should be required] than that proper *Miranda* warnings [be] given and that the statement be voluntary within the meaning of the Fifth Amendment."

arrest and the time petitioner confessed; (b) petitioner was advised of his rights three times; and (c) he was allowed to visit briefly with his girlfriend and his neighbor shortly before he confessed.

While in both *Brown* and *Dunaway* the incriminating statements were obtained within two hours, the Court did not deem "a difference of a few hours * * * significant where, as here, petitioner was in police custody, unrepresented by counsel, and he was questioned on several occasions, fingerprinted, and subjected to a lineup." As for the state's argument that petitioner's visit with his friends constituted an "intervening circumstance": "[T]hese two visitors were outside the interrogation room where petitioner was being questioned. After petitioner signed a waiver-of-rights form, he was allowed to meet with these visitors. The State fails to explain how this five to ten minute visit, after which petitioner immediately recanted his former statements that he knew nothing about the robbery and signed the confession, could possibly have contributed to his ability to consider carefully and objectively his options and to exercise his free will. This suggestion is particularly dubious in light of petitioner's uncontroverted testimony that his girlfriend was emotionally upset at the time of his visit. If any inference could be drawn, it would be that this visit had just the opposite effect." [b]

Compare the *Brown-Dunaway-Taylor* line of cases with *Rawlings v. Kentucky* (1980), discussed at length at p. 792 supra. Petitioner argued that his admission of the ownership of drugs which had been found in Ms. Cox's purse (after the contents of the purse had been emptied, pursuant to a police order) was the fruit of an illegal detention. The Court, per Rehnquist, J., disagreed. Assuming that Rawlings and others were illegally detained in a house for 45 minutes while the police obtained a search warrant for the premises, the Court noted, inter alia, that the detention was in a "congenial atmosphere," that petitioner's admissions were "apparently spontaneous reactions to the discovery of his drugs in Cox's purse" and not the product of the initial illegality, and that the police action "does not rise to the level of conscious or flagrant misconduct requiring prophylactic exclusion of petitioner's statements. Contrast *Brown.*" [c]

The Court has never directly addressed a situation in which a confession is said to be the fruit of a prior illegal *search and seizure.* But because confronting a suspect with illegally seized evidence tends to induce incriminating statements by demonstrating the futility of remaining silent, and thus the warnings have even less of an impact in such a situation than in the case of an illegal arrest, LaFave, § 11.4(c) at 640, deems it "crystal clear that giving the defendant the *Miranda* warnings will not break the causal chain between an illegal search and a subsequent confession. * * * [The] essential fact [is that the *Miranda* warnings] 'do not advise [a suspect] whether the evidence he is confronted with is unlawfully obtained or whether it will be admissible at trial.' [But] if the police, a magistrate or counsel unequivocally and clearly 'advised the suspect that the evidence had been illegally seized and neither it nor its fruits could be used against him,' this would dissipate the taint of the illegal search."

b. Dissenting Justice O'Connor, joined by the Chief Justice, and Powell and Rehnquist, JJ., maintained that *Brown* and *Dunaway* required a contrary result. As the dissent saw it, "[t]he petitioner's confession was not proximately caused by his illegal arrest, but was the product of a decision based both on knowledge of his constitutional rights and on the discussion with his friends."

c. Dissenting Justice Marshall, joined by Brennan, J., maintained that "petitioner's admissions were obviously the fruit of the illegal detention."

5. *Identification of a person as a "fruit" of an illegal arrest. United States v. Crews,* 445 U.S. 463, 100 S.Ct. 1244, 63 L.Ed.2d 537 (1980), arose as follows: Immediately after being assaulted and robbed in a public restroom, the victim gave the police a full description of her assailant. Crews, who matched the suspect's description, was illegally taken into custody, photographed, and then released. Thereafter, when shown an array of eight photographs, the victim selected Crews' photograph as that of the man who had robbed her. At a court-ordered lineup, Crews was again positively identified. Finally, Crews was identified at the trial. Crews was convicted of robbery, but the District of Columbia Court of Appeals held the victim's in-court identification inadmissible, viewing it as obtained by official "exploitation" of the "primary illegality"—Crews' unlawful arrest.[a] The Court, per Brennan, J., disagreed:

A victim's in-court identification has "three distinct elements": "[1], the victim is present at trial to testify as to what transpired between her and the offender, and to identify the defendant as the culprit. [2], the victim possesses knowledge of and the ability to reconstruct the prior [crime] and to identify the defendant from her observations of him at the time of the crime. And [3], the defendant is also physically present in the courtroom, so that the victim can observe him and compare his appearance to that of the offender. In the present case, none of these three elements 'has been come at by exploitation' of the defendant's Fourth Amendment rights."

As for (1), the victim's presence and cooperation were "surely not the product of any police misconduct"; as for (3), because an "illegal arrest, without more, has never been viewed as a bar to subsequent prosecution," the defendant was "not himself a suppressible 'fruit,' and the illegality of his detention cannot deprive the Government of the opportunity to prove his guilt through the introduction of evidence wholly untainted by the police misconduct."

As for (2): "Nor did the illegal arrest infect the victim's ability to give accurate identification testimony. Based upon her observations at the time of the robbery, [she] constructed a mental image of her assailant. At trial, she retrieved this mnemonic representation, compared it [to] defendant, and positively identified him as the robber. No part of this process was affected by [the] illegal arrest."

Because it was clear that prior to his illegal arrest, the police both knew defendant's identity and had some reason to believe he was involved in the robbery, Justice Brennan would have reserved judgment as to whether a defendant's face could ever be considered a suppressible "fruit" of an illegal arrest.[b] But a majority of the Court, in two separate concurring opinions, explicitly rejected this possibility.

6. *A warrant search as the fruit of an illegal entry and occupation of the premises. Segura v. United States* (1984) (also discussed at p. 319 supra) arose as follows: When Segura, a suspected narcotics violator, entered his apartment building one evening, he was immediately arrested and taken to his apartment. The agents entered the apartment without requesting or obtaining permission. Four other people were there. The agents told them that Segura was under arrest and that a search warrant for the premises was being obtained.

The agents then conducted a limited security check of the apartment, in the process observing drug paraphernalia.

a. The trial court had excluded both the photographic and lineup identifications as the "fruits" of Crews' illegal arrest and on appeal the government conceded that both were inadmissible. Why? Wasn't *the lineup identification* admissible for the same reasons the Supreme Court held that the in-court identification was?

b. As Justice Brennan noted, this part of his opinion was joined only by Stewart and Stevens, JJ.

They then took Segura and the other occupants of the apartment to headquarters. Two agents remained in the apartment awaiting the warrant. Because of "administrative delay," the search warrant was not issued until some 19 hours after the initial entry. When the agents executed the warrant they discovered narcotics and records of narcotics transactions.

Since the government did not dispute the rulings below that the initial entry and security search were unlawful, "the only issue" before the Court was whether items "not observed during the illegal entry and first discovered by the agents the day after the entry, under an admittedly valid search warrant, should have been suppressed."[a] A 5–4 majority, per Burger, C.J., answered in the negative. The legality of the initial entry had no bearing on the admissibility of the challenged evidence "because there was an independent source for the warrant under which that evidence was seized": "No information obtained during the initial entry or occupation of the apartment was needed or used by the agents to secure the warrant. * * * The valid warrant search was a 'means sufficiently distinguishable' to purge the evidence of any 'taint' arising from the entry."

The argument was made that had the agents not entered and impounded the premises, the occupants might have removed or destroyed the evidence. But the Court dismissed this contention as "pure speculation." "Even more important," added the Court, "we decline to extend the exclusionary rule, which already exacts an enormous price from society and our system of justice, to further 'protect' criminal activity, as the dissent would have us do."

Dissenting Justice Stevens, joined by Brennan, Marshall and Blackmun, JJ., contended that the fact that the challenged evidence was the product of a valid warrant search, wholly unrelated to the entry the previous day, did not dispose of the claim "that the agents' *access* to the fruits of the authorized search, rather that the *information* which led to that search, was a product of illegal conduct. On this question, the length of the delay in obtaining the warrant is surely relevant." The dissent emphasized that the District Court had found "a distinct, nonspeculative possibility" that "the evidence's availability when the warrant was executed hinged solely on the illegal impoundment."

For Justice Stevens, "the controlling question" was "whether the deterrent purposes of the exclusionary rule would be served or undermined by the suppression of this evidence." He thought the deterrence rationale "plainly applicable": "The agents impounded the apartment precisely because they wished to avoid risking a loss of access to the evidence within it. Thus, the unlawful benefit they acquired * * * was exactly the benefit [that] motivated [them] in the case to violate the Constitution. * * * Under the majority's approval, the agents could have remained indefinitely—impounding the apartment for a week or a month—without being deprived of the advantage derived from the unlawful impoundment. We cannot expect such an approach to prevent similar violations of the Fourth Amendment in the future."

7. *The "tainted" witness. United States v. Ceccolini,* 435 U.S. 268, 98 S.Ct. 1054, 55 L.Ed.2d 268 (1978), grew out of the following facts: An officer in a flower shop on a social visit illegally picked up an envelope and found it to contain money and policy slips. He then learned from his friend, Mr. Hennessey, an employee of the shop (who did not notice his discovery),

a. Such illegal entries, observed the Court, are sufficiently deterred by the officers' realization that "whatever evidence they discover as a direct result of the entry may be suppressed." The four dissenters found the suggested distinction a puzzling one: "If the execution of a valid warrant takes the poison out of the hidden fruit, I should think that it would also remove the taint from the fruit in plain view."

that the envelope belonged to the defendant, the owner of the shop.

The information reached the FBI four months later. An agent questioned Hennessey about defendant, without specifically mentioning the illegally discovered policy slips. Hennessey told the agent she was willing to help, and she testified against defendant both before the grand jury and at his trial for perjury.

A 6–2 majority of the Court (Blackmun, J., not participating) held Hennessey's testimony admissible. Although it declined to adopt a *per se* rule that the testimony of a live witness should always be admissible,[a] the Court, per Rehnquist, J., pointed out that various factors indicate that "the exclusionary rule should be invoked with much greater reluctance where the claim is based on a causal relationship between a constitutional violation and the discovery of a live witness than when a similar claim is advanced to support suppression of an inanimate object":

"The greater the willingness of the witness to freely testify, the greater the liklihood that he or she will be discovered by legal means and, concomitantly, the smaller the incentive to conduct an illegal search to discover the witness. Witnesses are not like guns or documents which remain hidden from view until one turns over a sofa or opens a filing cabinet. Witnesses can, and often do, come forward and offer evidence entirely of their own volition. And evaluated properly, the degree of free will necessary to dissipate the taint will very likely be found more often in the case of live-witness testimony than other kinds of evidence."

"Moreover, exclusion of testimony "would perpetually disable a witness from testifying about relevant and material facts, regardless of how unrelated such testimony might be to the purpose of the originally illegal search or the evidence discovered thereby. * * * [S]ince the cost of excluding live-witness testimony often will be greater, a closer, more direct link between the illegality and that kind of testimony is required."

Dissenting Justice Marshall, joined by Brennan, J., did not see how "the same tree, having its roots in an unconstitutional search or seizure, can bear two different kinds of fruit, with one kind less susceptible than the other to exclusion on Fourth Amendment grounds." The dissent charged the majority with "judicial 'double counting'": The majority allows a court to consider whether the witness came forward and then, if he did not, to consider that generally (but not in this case) witnesses come forward." As for the majority's argument that often the exclusion of live-witness testimony will be very costly to society, "at least as often the exclusion of physical evidence * * * will be as costly to the same societal interest."

a. Concurring Chief Justice Burger would adopt such a rule.

B. THE "INEVITABLE DISCOVERY" DOCTRINE: THE SEQUEL TO *BREWER V. WILLIAMS*

NIX v. WILLIAMS (WILLIAMS II)

467 U.S. 431, 104 S.Ct. 2501, 81 L.Ed.2d 377 (1984)

CHIEF JUSTICE BURGER delivered the opinion of the Court. * * *

At Williams' second trial in 1977 in the Iowa court, the prosecution did not offer Williams' statements into evidence, nor did it seek to show that Williams had directed the police to the child's body. However, evidence of the condition of her body as it was found, articles and photographs of her clothing, and the results of post mortem medical and chemical tests on the body were admitted. The trial court concluded that the State had proved by a preponderance of the evidence that, if the search had not been suspended and Williams had not led the police to the victim, her body would have been discovered "*within a short time*" in essentially the same condition as it was actually found. The trial court also ruled that if the police had not located the body, "the search would clearly have been taken up again where it left off, given the extreme circumstances of this case and the body would [have] been found *in short order*" (emphasis added).

In finding that the body would have been discovered in essentially the same condition as it was actually found, the court noted that freezing temperatures had prevailed and tissue deterioration would have been suspended. The challenged evidence was admitted and the jury again found Williams guilty of first-degree murder; he was sentenced to life in prison.

[Both the Supreme Court of Iowa, which affirmed the conviction, and the U.S. District Court, which denied habeas relief, adopted the "inevitable discovery" exception to the exclusionary rule and sustained the conviction on that basis. Both courts concluded that the body would have been discovered in any event and that the police had not acted in bad faith in obtaining the excluded statements from Williams. But the U.S. Court of Appeals for the Eighth Circuit reversed the District Court's denial of habeas relief because, assuming an inevitable discovery exception, such an exception requires proof that the police did not act in "bad faith" and the record could not support such a finding.]

* * * The core rationale consistently advanced by this Court for extending the Exclusionary Rule to evidence that is the fruit of unlawful police conduct has been that this admittedly drastic and socially costly course is needed to deter police from violations of constitutional and statutory protections. * * * On this rationale, the prosecution is not to be put in a better position than it would have been in if no illegality had transpired.

By contrast, the derivative evidence analysis ensures that the prosecution is not put in a *worse* position simply because of some earlier police error or misconduct. The independent source doctrine allows admission of evidence that has been discovered by means wholly independent of any constitutional violation. That doctrine, although closely related to the inevitable discovery doctrine, does not apply here; Williams' statements to Leaming indeed led police to the child's body, but that is not the whole story. The independent source doctrine teaches us that the interest of society in deterring unlawful police conduct and the public interest in having juries receive all probative evidence of a crime are properly balanced by putting the police in the same, not a *worse,* position than they would have been in if no police error or misconduct had occurred.[4] When the challenged evidence has an independent source, exclusion of such evidence would put the police in a worse position than they would have been in absent any error or violation. There is a functional similarity between these two doctrines in that exclusion of evidence that would inevitably have been discovered would also put the government in a worse position, because the police would have obtained that evidence if no misconduct had taken place. Thus, while the independent source exception would not justify admission of evidence in this case, its rationale is wholly consistent with and justifies our adoption of the ultimate or inevitable discovery exception to the Exclusionary Rule.

It is clear that the cases implementing the Exclusionary Rule "begin with the pre-

4. The ultimate or inevitable discovery exception to the Exclusionary Rule is closely related in purpose to the harmless-error rule of *Chapman.* The harmless-constitutional-error rule "serve[s] a very useful purpose insofar as [it] block[s] setting aside convictions for small errors or defects that have little, if any, likelihood of having changed the result of the trial." The purpose of the inevitable discovery rule is to block setting aside convictions that would have been obtained without police misconduct.

mise that the challenged evidence is *in some sense* the product of illegal governmental activity." *United States v. Crews* (emphasis added). Of course, this does not end the inquiry. If the prosecution can establish by a preponderance of the evidence that the information ultimately or inevitably would have been discovered by lawful means—here the volunteers' search—then the deterrence rationale has so little basis that the evidence should be received.[5] Anything less would reject logic, experience, and common sense.

The requirement that the prosecution must prove the absence of bad faith, imposed here by the Court of Appeals, would place courts in the position of withholding from juries relevant and undoubted truth that would have been available to police absent any unlawful police activity. Of course, that view would put the police in a *worse* position than they would have been in if no unlawful conduct had transpired. And, of equal importance, it wholly fails to take into account the enormous societal cost of excluding truth in the search for truth in the administration of justice. Nothing in this Court's prior holdings supports any such formalistic, pointless, and punitive approach.

The Court of Appeals concluded, without analysis, that if an absence of bad faith requirement were not imposed, "the temptation to risk deliberate violations of the Sixth Amendment would be too great, and the deterrent effect of the Exclusionary Rule reduced too far." We reject that view. A police officer who is faced with the opportunity to obtain evidence illegally will rarely, if ever, be in a position to calculate whether the evidence sought would inevitably be discovered. * * *

On the other hand, when an officer is aware that the evidence will inevitably be discovered, he will try to avoid engaging in any questionable practice. In that situation, there will be little to gain from taking any dubious "shortcuts" to obtain the evidence. Significant disincentives to obtaining evidence illegally—including the possibility of departmental discipline and civil liability—also lessen the likelihood that the ultimate or inevitable discovery exception will promote police misconduct. In these circumstances, the societal costs of the Exclusionary Rule far outweigh any possible benefits to deterrence that a good-faith requirement might produce.

Williams contends that because he did not waive his right to the assistance of counsel, the Court may not balance competing values in deciding whether the challenged evidence was properly admitted. He argues that, unlike the Exclusionary Rule in the Fourth Amendment context, the essential purpose of which is to deter police misconduct, the Sixth Amendment Exclusionary Rule is designed to protect

5. As to the quantum of proof, we have already established some relevant guidelines. In *United States v. Matlock* (1974) [p. 418 supra] (emphasis added), we stated that "the controlling burden of proof at suppression hearings should impose *no greater burden* than proof by a preponderance of the evidence." In *Lego v. Twomey* (1972) [p. 840 infra] we observed "from our experience [that] no substantial evidence has accumulated that federal rights have suffered from determining admissibility by a preponderance of the evidence" and held that the prosecution must prove by a preponderance of the evidence that a confession sought to be used at trial was voluntary. We are unwilling to impose added burdens on the already difficult task of proving guilt in criminal cases by enlarging the barrier to placing evidence of unquestioned truth before juries.

Williams argues that the preponderance of the evidence standard used by the Iowa courts is inconsistent with *United States v. Wade* [p. 652 supra]. In requiring clear and convincing evidence of an independent souce for an in-court identification, the Court gave weight to the effect an uncounseled pre-trial identification has in "crystalliz[ing] the witnesses' identification of the defendant for the future reference." The Court noted as well that possible unfairness at the lineup "may be the sole means of attack upon the unequivocal courtroom identification," and recognized the difficulty of determining whether an in-court identification was based on independent recollection unaided by the lineup identification. By contrast, inevitable discovery involves no speculative elements but focuses on demonstrated historical facts capable of ready verification or impeachment and does not require a departure from the usual burden of proof at suppression hearings.

the right to a fair trial and the integrity of the factfinding process. Williams contends that, when those interests are at stake, the societal costs of excluding evidence obtained from responses presumed involuntary are irrelevant in determining whether such evidence should be excluded. We disagree.

Exclusion of physical evidence that would inevitably have been discovered adds nothing to either the integrity or fairness of a criminal trial. The Sixth Amendment right to counsel protects against unfairness by preserving the adversary process in which the reliability of proffered evidence may be tested in cross-examination. Here, however, Detective Leaming's conduct did nothing to impugn the reliability of the evidence in question—the body of the child and its condition as it was found, articles of clothing found on the body, and the autopsy. * * *

Nor would suppression ensure fairness on the theory that it tends to safeguard the adversary system of justice. * * * Fairness can be assured by placing the State and the accused in the same positions they would have been in had the impermissible conduct not taken place. However, if the government can prove that the evidence would have been obtained inevitably and, therefore, would have been admitted regardless of any over-reaching by the police, there is no rational basis to keep that evidence from the jury in order to ensure the fairness of the trial proceedings. In that situation, the State has gained no advantage at trial and the defendant has suffered no prejudice. Indeed, suppression of the evidence would operate to undermine the adversary system by putting the State in a *worse* position than it would have occupied without any police misconduct. Williams' argument that inevitable discovery constitutes impermissible balancing of values is without merit. * * *

The Court of Appeals did not find it necessary to consider whether the record fairly supported the finding that the volunteer search party would ultimately or inevitably have discovered the victim's body. However, three courts independently reviewing the evidence have found that the body of the child inevitably would have been found by the searchers. * * *

When [this finding was challenged] at the suppression hearing preceding Williams' second trial, the prosecution offered the testimony of Agent Ruxlow of the Iowa Bureau of Criminal Investigation. Ruxlow had organized and directed some 200 volunteers who were searching for the child's body. The searchers were instructed "to check all the roads, the ditches, any culverts * * *." Ruxlow testified that he marked off highway maps of Poweshiek and Jasper Counties in grid fashion, divided the volunteers into teams of four to six persons, and assigned each team to search specific grid areas. Ruxlow also testified that, if the search had not been suspended because of Williams' promised cooperation, it would have continued into Polk County, using the same grid system. Although he had previously marked off into grids only the highway maps of Poweshiek and Jasper Counties, Ruxlow had obtained a map of Polk County, which he said he would have marked off in the same manner had it been necessary for the search to continue.

* * * The search was not resumed once it was learned that Williams had led the police to the body, which was found two and one-half miles from where the search had stopped in what would have been the easternmost grid to be searched in Polk County. There was testimony that it would have taken an additional three to five hours to discover the body if the search had continued; the body was found near a culvert, one of the kinds of places the teams had been specifically directed to search.

On this record it is clear that the search parties were approaching the actual location of the body and we are satisfied, along with three courts earlier, that the volunteer search teams would have resumed the search had Williams not earlier led the police to the body and the body inevitably would have been found. * * *[7]

JUSTICE WHITE, concurring.

I join fully in the opinion of the Court. I write separately only to point out that many of Justice Stevens' remarks are beside the point when it is recalled that *Brewer v. Williams* was a 5–4 decision and that four members of the Court, including myself, were of the view that Officer Leaming had done nothing wrong at all, let alone anything unconstitutional. * * *

JUSTICE STEVENS, concurring in the judgment.

* * * It was the majority in *Williams I* that recognized that "evidence of where the body was found and of its condition might well be admissible on the theory that the body would have been discovered in any event, even had incriminating statements not been elicited from Williams." It was the author of today's opinion of the Court who characterized this rule of law as a "remarkable" and "unlikely theory." (Burger, C.J., dissenting).

* * * *Williams I* held that Detective Leaming had violated "the clear rule of *Massiah*" by deliberately eliciting incriminating statements from respondent during the pendency of the adversarial process and outside of that process. [The] Christian burial speech was nothing less than an attempt to substitute an *ex parte,* inquisitorial process for the clash of adversaries commanded by the Constitution.[5] Thus the now-familiar plaint that "[t]he criminal is to go free because the constable has blundered" is entirely beside the point. * * *

The majority is correct to insist that any rule of exclusion not provide the authorities with an incentive to commit violations of the Constitution. If the inevitable discovery rule provided such an incentive by permitting the prosecution to avoid the uncertainties inherent in its search for evidence, it would undermine the constitutional guarantee itself, and therefore be inconsistent with the deterrent purposes of the Exclusionary Rule. But when the burden of proof on the inevitable discovery question is placed on the prosecution, *it* must bear the risk of error in the determination made necessary by its constitutional violation. The uncertainty as to whether the body would have been discovered can be resolved in its favor here only because, as the Court explains, petitioner adduced evidence demonstrating that at the time of the constitutional violation an investigation was already under way which, in the natural and probable course of events, would have soon discovered the body. This is not a case in which the prosecution can escape responsibility for a constitutional violation through speculation; to the extent uncertainty was created by the constitutional violation the prosecution was required to resolve that uncertainty through proof.[8] Even if Detective Leaming acted

7. In view of our holding that the challenged evidence was admissible under the inevitable discovery exception to the Exclusionary Rule, we find it unnecessary to decide whether *Stone v. Powell* [Ch. 27, § 1] should be extended to bar federal habeas corpus review of Williams' Sixth Amendment claim and we express no view on that issue.

5. "The whole point of *Massiah* is the prevention of the state from taking advantage of an uncounseled defendant once sixth amendment rights attach. The Christian burial speech was an attempt to take advantage of Williams. The attempt itself *is* what *Massiah* prohibits. The attempt violates the constitutional mandate that the system proceed, after some point, only in an accusatorial manner." Grano, *Rhode Island v. Innis: A Need to Reconsider the Constitutional Premises Underlying the Law of Confessions,* 17 Am.Crim.L.Rev. 1, 35 (1979) (emphasis in original).

8. I agree with the majority's holding that the prosecution must prove that the evidence would have been inevitably discovered by a preponderance of the evidence rather than by clear and convincing evidence. An inevitable discovery finding is based on objective evidence concerning the scope of the ongoing investigation which can be objectively verified or impeached. Hence an extraordinary burden of proof is not needed in

in bad faith in the sense that he deliberately violated the Constitution in order to avoid the possibility that the body would not be discovered, the prosecution ultimately does not avoid that risk; its burden of proof forces it to assume the risk. The need to adduce proof sufficient to discharge its burden, and the difficulty in predicting whether such proof will be available or sufficient, means that the inevitable discovery rule does not permit state officials to avoid the uncertainty they would have faced but for the constitutional violation.

The majority refers to the "societal cost" of excluding probative evidence. In my view, the more relevant cost is that imposed on society by police officers who decide to take procedural shortcuts instead of complying with the law. What is the consequence of the shortcut that Detective Leaming took when he decided to question Williams in this case and not to wait an hour or so until he arrived in Des Moines?[9] * * * Instead of having a 1969 conviction affirmed in routine fashion, the case is still alive 15 years later. Thanks to Detective Leaming, the State of Iowa has expended vast sums of money and countless hours of professional labor in his defense. That expenditure surely provides an adequate deterrent to similar violations; the responsibility for that expenditure lies not with the Constitution, but rather with the constable. * * *

JUSTICE BRENNAN, with whom JUSTICE MARSHALL joins, dissenting. * * *

[T]he Court concludes that unconstitutionally obtained evidence may be admitted at trial if it inevitably would have been discovered in the same condition by an independent line of investigation that was already being pursued when the constitutional violation occurred. As has every federal Court of Appeals previously addressing this issue, I agree * * *.

The inevitable discovery exception necessarily implicates a hypothetical finding that differs in kind from the factual finding that precedes application of the independent source rule. To ensure that this hypothetical finding is narrowly confined to circumstances that are functionally equivalent to an independent source, and to protect fully the fundamental rights served by the exclusionary rule, I would require clear and convincing evidence before concluding that the government had met its burden of proof on this issue. Increasing the burden of proof serves to impress the factfinder with the importance of the decision and thereby reduces the risk that illegally obtained evidence will be admitted. Because the lower courts did not impose such a requirement, I would remand this case for application of this heightened burden of proof by the lower courts in the first instance. * * *

Notes and Questions

1. In his dissent, Justice Brennan describes the *Williams II* majority as "conclud[ing] that unconstitutionally obtained evidence may be admitted at trial if it inevitably would have been discovered in the same condition by an independent line of investigation *that was already being pursued* when the constitutional violation occurred." (Emphasis added.) Consider also concurring Justice Stevens' observation that "[t]he uncertainty as to whether the body would have been discovered can be resolved in [the prosecution's] favor here *only because* [the prosecution demonstrated] that at the time of the constitutional violation an investigation *was already under way which, in the natural and probable course of events, would have soon discovered the body.*"

order to preserve the defendant's ability to subject the prosecution's case to the meaningful adversarial testing required by the Sixth Amendment.

9. In this connection, it is worth noting, as Justice Marshall did in *Williams I,* that in light of the assistance that respondent's attorney had provided to the Des Moines police, it seems apparent that the lawyer intended to learn the location of the body from his client and then reveal it to the police. Thus, the need for a shortcut was practically nonexistent.

Is *Williams II* limited along the lines indicated by Justices Brennan and Stevens? Should it be?

2. Recall that, as did Justice Marshall in *Williams I,* Justice Stevens, concurring in *Williams II,* thought it "apparent" that Williams' Des Moines lawyer "intended to learn the location of the body and then reveal it to the police" [fn. 9]. At Williams' first trial, both Detective Leaming and Des Moines Police Chief Nichols testified that Williams' Des Moines lawyer told him over the phone in their presence that Williams would "have to tell" the officers where the body was or tell his lawyer, who would then tell the officers. See Y. Kamisar, *Police Interrogation and Confessions* 126–27 & n. 17 (1980). Moreover, Williams' Davenport lawyer testified that it was his "understanding," as he told Leaming, that Williams or his Des Moines lawyer would reveal the location of the body to the officers after Williams returned to Des Moines. Ibid.

Suppose it was undisputed that the searching party had given up all efforts to find the body *before* Williams had decided to show Leaming where the body was located. Would the body nevertheless have been admissible under the "inevitable discovery" exception because it was "apparent" that once Williams returned to Des Moines, his Des Moines lawyer planned to tell, or have his client tell, the officers where the body was?

3. For an in-depth analysis of the Supreme Court's opinion in *Williams II,* see Wasserstrom & Mertens, *The Exclusionary Rule on the Scaffold: But Was it a Fair Trial?,* 22 Am.Crim.L.Rev. 85, 130–79 (1984). For an incisive treatment of the "fruit of the poisonous tree" problems raised by the second *Williams* case prior to the Supreme Court's decision in that case, see Johnson, *The Return of the "Christian Burial Speech" Case,* 32 Emory L.J. 349 (1983).

C. IS A CONFESSION OBTAINED IN VIOLATION OF *MIRANDA* A "POISONOUS TREE"?

Because a majority of the Court held that there was no violation of *Miranda* in NEW YORK v. QUARLES, (1984), p. 599 supra, it had no occasion to reach the question whether, even if Quarles' initial statement should have been suppressed, the gun was nevertheless admissible because it was "nontestimonial" evidence or because the police would inevitably have discovered it absent their questioning. But Justice O'CONNOR, concurring in part and dissenting in part, devoted much of her opinion to a discussion of why she believed that the gun itself was admissible even though the statement that led to its discovery was not:

"* * * Only the introduction of a defendant's own *testimony* is proscribed by the Fifth Amendment's mandate that no person 'shall be compelled in any criminal case to be a witness against himself.' That mandate does not protect an accused from being compelled to surrender *nontestimonial* evidence against himself.

"The distinction between testimonial and nontestimonial evidence was explored in some detail in *Schmerber v. California* [p. 48 supra], a decision this Court handed down within a week of deciding *Miranda.* [The blood tests at issue in *Schmerber* were held] admissible because they were neither testimonial nor communicative in nature. * * *

"[W]hatever case can be made for suppression evaporates when the statements themselves are not admitted, given the rationale of the *Schmerber* line of cases. Certainly interrogation which provides leads to other evidence does not offend the values underlying the Fifth Amendment privilege any more than the compulsory taking of blood samples, fingerprints, or voice exemplars, all of which may be compelled in an 'attempt to discover evidence that might be used to prosecute [a defendant] for a criminal offense.' *Schmer-*

ber. Use of a suspect's answers 'merely to find other evidence establishing his connection with the crime [simply] differs only by a shade from the permitted use for that purpose of his body or his blood.' H. Friendly, *Benchmarks* 280 (1967). The values underlying the privilege may justify exclusion of an unwarned person's out-of-court statements, as perhaps they may justify exclusion of statements and derivative evidence compelled under the threat of contempt. But when the only evidence to be admitted is derivative evidence such as a gun—derived not from actual compulsion but from a statement taken in the absence of *Miranda* warnings—those values simply cannot require suppression, at least no more so than they would for other such nontestimonial evidence.[4] * * *[a]

Dissenting Justice MARSHALL, joined by Brennan and Stevens, JJ., considered Justice O'Connor's treatment of derivative evidence "a much more radical departure from precedent than that opinion acknowledges." "Having determined that the Fifth Amendment renders inadmissible Quarles' response to Officer Kraft's questioning," Justice Marshall had "no doubt that our precedents require that the gun discovered as a direct result of Quarles' statement must be presumed inadmissible as well." Continued Justice Marshall:

"The gun was the direct product of a coercive custodial interrogation. In *Silverthorne* and *Wong Sun* this Court held that the Government may not introduce incriminating evidence derived from an illegally obtained source. * * * When they ruled on the issue, the New York courts were entirely correct in deciding that Quarles' gun was the tainted fruit of a nonconsensual interrogation and therefore was inadmissible under our precedents.

"However, since the New York Court of Appeals issued its opinion, [this Court, in *Nix v. Williams,* has accepted the 'inevitable discovery' doctrine.] [The State] has argued that the 'inevitable-discovery' rule, if applied to this case, would permit the admission of Quarles' gun. [Under the circumstances] I believe that the proper disposition of the matter is to vacate the state court order suppressing Quarles' gun and remand the matter [for] further consideration in light of *Nix v. Williams.*"

OREGON v. ELSTAD

— U.S. —, 105 S.Ct. 1285, 84 L.Ed.2d 222 (1985).

JUSTICE O'CONNOR delivered the opinion of the Court.

This case requires us to decide whether an initial failure of law enforcement officers to administer the warnings required by *Miranda,* without more, "taints" subsequent admissions made after a suspect has been fully advised of and has waived his *Miranda* rights. [Respondent was convicted of burglary.] The Oregon Court of Appeals reversed, holding that respondent's signed confession, although voluntary, was rendered inadmissible by a prior remark made in response to questioning without benefit of *Miranda* warnings. [We] reverse.

[When the Gross home was burglarized, a witness contacted the sheriff's office, implicating respondent Elstad, an 18-year-old neighbor and friend of the Grosses' teenage son. Officers Burke and McAllister went to Elstad's home, with a warrant for his arrest for the aforementioned burglary. Elstad's mother led the officers to his

4. In suggesting that *Wong Sun* requires exclusion of the gun, Justice Marshall fails to acknowledge this Court's holding in *Michigan v. Tucker* [p. 574 supra]. In *Tucker,* the Court very clearly held that *Wong Sun* is inapplicable in cases involving mere departures from *Miranda.* *Wong Sun* and its "fruit of the poisonous tree" analysis lead to exclusion of derivative evidence only where the underlying police misconduct infringes a "core" constitutional right. Failure to administer *Miranda* warnings violates only a nonconstitutional prophylactic. * * *

a. Compare Justice O'Connor's opinion for the Court in *Oregon v. Elstad,* this page infra.

room. The officers asked Elstad to get dressed and to accompany them to the living room. Officer Burke sat down with Elstad in the living room and, without telling him that the police had a warrant for his arrest, stated that he "felt" Elstad was involved in the Gross burglary. Elstad replied, "Yes, I was there."

[Elstad was then transported to sheriff headquarters and, approximately an hour later, Officer McAllister, in the presence of Officer Burke, advised Elstad of his *Miranda* rights for the first time. Elstad agreed to talk to the police and made a statement detailing his involvement in the burglary. The statement was typed, reviewed by Elstad, read back to him for correction and signed by him.

[The trial judge excluded the incriminating remark Elstad made in his living room, but admitted the statement made at the sheriff's office. Following his conviction of burglary, Elstad appealed. The state conceded that Elstad had been in custody when he replied, "Yes, I was there," and thus that this statement was obtained in violation of *Miranda,* but maintained that any conceivable "taint" had been dissipated prior to Elstad's written confession by Officer McAllister's careful administration of the *Miranda* warnings. The Oregon Court of Appeals disagreed.

[In reversing Elstad's conviction, the Oregon court identified the crucial constitutional inquiry as whether there was "a sufficient break in the stream of events" between the inadmissible statement in respondent's living room and the written confession in the sheriff's office "to insulate the latter statement from the effect of what went before." It concluded that, because of the brief period separating the two incidents, the "cat was sufficiently out of the bag to exert a coercive impact on [respondent's] later admissions."]

* * * The Oregon court assumed and respondent here contends that a failure to administer *Miranda* warnings necessarily breeds the same consequences as police infringement of a constitutional right, so that evidence uncovered following an unwarned statement must be suppressed as "fruit of the poisonous tree." We believe this view misconstrues the nature of the protections afforded by *Miranda* warnings and therefore misreads the consequences of police failure to supply them.

[A]s we explained in *Quarles* and *Tucker,* a procedural *Miranda* violation differs in significant respects from violations of the Fourth Amendment, which have traditionally mandated a broad application of the "fruits" doctrine. The purpose of the Fourth Amendment exclusionary rule is to deter unreasonable searches, no matter how probative their fruits. * * *

The *Miranda* exclusionary rule, however, serves the Fifth Amendment and sweeps more broadly than the Fifth Amendment itself. It may be triggered even in the absence of a Fifth Amendment violation.[1] The Fifth Amendment prohibits use by the prosecution in its case in chief only of *compelled* testimony. Failure to administer *Miranda* warnings creates a presumption of compulsion. * * *

But the *Miranda* presumption, though irrebutable for purposes of the prosecution's case in chief, does not require that the statements and their fruits be discarded as inherently tainted [discussing *Harris v. New York,* (p. 828 infra) (permitting the use of statements obtained in violation of *Miranda* for impeachment purposes) and

1. Justice Stevens expresses puzzlement at our statement that a simple failure to administer *Miranda* warnings is not in itself a violation of the Fifth Amendment. Yet the Court so held in *Quarles* and *Tucker.* The *Miranda* Court itself recognized this point when it disclaimed any intent to create a "constitutional straight-jacket" and invited Congress and the States to suggest "potential alternatives for protecting the privilege." A *Miranda* violation does not *constitute* coercion but rather affords a bright-line, legal presumption of coercion, requiring suppression of all unwarned statements. It has never been remotely suggested that any statement taken from Mr. Elstad without benefit of *Miranda* warnings would be admissible.

Tucker]. Where an unwarned statement is preserved for use in situations that fall outside the sweep of the *Miranda* presumption, "the primary criterion of admissibility [remains] the 'old' due process voluntariness test." Schulhofer, *Confessions and the Court,* 79 Mich.L.Rev. 865, 877 (1981).

* * * In deciding "how sweeping the judicially imposed consequences" of a failure to administer *Miranda* warnings should be, the *Tucker* Court noted that neither the general goal of deterring improper police conduct nor the Fifth Amendment goal of assuring trustworthy evidence would be served by suppression of the witness' testimony. The unwarned confession must, of course, be suppressed, but the Court ruled that introduction of the third-party witness' testimony did not violate Tucker's Fifth Amendment rights.

We believe that this reasoning applies with equal force when the alleged "fruit" of a noncoercive *Miranda* violation is neither a witness nor an article of evidence but the accused's own voluntary testimony. As in *Tucker,* the absence of any coercion or improper tactics undercuts the twin rationales—trustworthiness and deterrence—for a broader rule. Once warned, the suspect is free to exercise his own volition in deciding whether or not to make a statement to the authorities.

* * * If errors are made by law enforcement officers in administering the prophylactic *Miranda* procedures, they should not breed the same irremediable consequences as police infringement of the Fifth Amendment itself. It is an unwarranted extension of *Miranda* to hold that a simple failure to administer the warnings, unaccompanied by any actual coercion or other circumstances calculated to undermine the suspect's ability to exercise his free will so taints the investigatory process that a subsequent voluntary and informed waiver is ineffective for some indeterminate period. Though *Miranda* requires that the unwarned admission must be suppressed, the admissibility of any subsequent statement should turn in these circumstances solely on whether it is knowingly and voluntarily made. * * *

There is a vast difference between the direct consequences flowing from coercion of a confession by physical violence or other deliberate means calculated to break the suspect's will and the uncertain consequences of disclosure of a "guilty secret" freely given in response to an unwarned but noncoercive question, as in this case. Justice Brennan's contention that it is impossible to perceive any causal distinction between this case and one involving a confession that is coerced by torture is wholly unpersuasive.[3] Certainly, in respondent's case, the causal connection between any psychological disadvantage created by his admission and his ultimate decision to cooperate is speculative and attenuated at best. It is difficult to tell with certainty what motivates a suspect to speak. * * * We must conclude that, absent deliberately coercive or improper tactics in obtaining the initial statement, the mere fact that a suspect has made an unwarned admission does not warrant a presumption of compulsion. A subsequent administration of *Miranda* warnings to a suspect who has given a voluntary but unwarned statement ordinarily should suffice to remove the conditions that precluded admission of the earlier statement. In such circumstances, the finder of fact may

3. Most of the 50 cases cited by Justice Brennan in his discussion of consecutive confessions concern an initial unwarned statement obtained through overtly or inherently coercive methods which raise serious Fifth Amendment and Due Process concerns [discussing many cases].

Justice Brennan cannot seriously mean to equate such situations with the case at bar. Likewise inapposite are the cases the dissent cites concerning suspects whose invocation of their rights to remain silent and to have counsel present were flatly ignored while police subjected them to continued interrogation. * * *

reasonably conclude that the suspect made a rational and intelligent choice whether to waive or invoke his rights.

Though belated, the reading of respondent's rights was undeniably complete. [There] is no question that respondent knowingly and voluntarily waived his right to remain silent before he described his participation in the burglary. It is also beyond dispute that respondent's earlier remark was voluntary, within the meaning of the Fifth Amendment. Neither the environment nor the manner of either "interrogation" was coercive. The initial conversation took place at midday, in the living room area of respondent's own home, with his mother in the kitchen area, a few steps away. Although in retrospect the officers testified that respondent was then in custody, at the time he made his statement he had not been informed that he was under arrest. The arresting officers' testimony indicates that the brief stop in the living room before proceeding to the station house was not to interrogate the suspect but to notify his mother of the reason for his arrest.

The state has conceded the issue of custody and thus we must assume that Burke breached *Miranda* procedures in failing to administer *Miranda* warnings before initiating the discussion in the living room. * * * [But] the incident had none of the earmarks of coercion. Nor did the officers exploit the unwarned admission to pressure respondent into waiving his right to remain silent.

Respondent, however, has argued that he was unable to give a fully *informed* waiver of his rights because he was unaware that his prior statement could not be used against him. Respondent suggests that Deputy McAllister, to cure this deficiency, should have added an additional warning to those given him at the Sheriff's office. Such a requirement is neither practicable nor constitutionally necessary. In many cases, a breach of *Miranda* procedures may not be identified as such until long after full *Miranda* warnings are administered and a valid confession obtained. The standard *Miranda* warnings explicitly inform the suspect of his right to consult a lawyer before speaking. Police officers are ill equipped to pinch-hit for counsel, construing the murky and difficult questions of when "custody" begins or whether a given unwarned statement will ultimately be held admissible.

When police ask questions of a suspect in custody without administering the required warnings, *Miranda* dictates that the answers received be presumed compelled and that they be excluded from evidence at trial in the State's case in chief. The Court has carefully adhered to this principle, permitting a narrow exception only where pressing public safety concerns demanded. See *Quarles.* The Court today in no way retreats from the bright line rule of *Miranda.* * * * [But] where the suspect's initial inculpatory statement, though technically in violation of *Miranda,* was voluntary, [the] relevant inquiry is whether, in fact, the second statement was also voluntarily made. As in any such inquiry, the finder of fact must examine the surrounding circumstances and the entire course of police conduct with respect to the suspect in evaluating the voluntariness of his statements. The fact that a suspect chooses to speak after being informed of his rights is, of course, highly probative. We find that the dictates of *Miranda* and the goals of the Fifth Amendment proscription against use of compelled testimony are fully satisfied in the circumstances of this case by barring use of the unwarned statement in the case in chief. No further purpose is served by imputing "taint" to subsequent statements obtained pursuant to a voluntary and knowing waiver. We hold today that a suspect who has once responded to unwarned yet uncoercive questioning is not thereby disabled from waiving his rights and confessing after he has been given the requisite *Miranda* warnings. * * *

JUSTICE BRENNAN, with whom JUSTICE MARSHALL joins, dissenting.

* * * [Today's decision] delivers a potentially crippling blow to *Miranda* and the ability of courts to safeguard the rights of persons accused of crime. For at least with respect to successive confessions, the Court today appears to strip remedies for *Miranda* violations of the "fruit of the poisonous tree" doctrine prohibiting the use of evidence presumptively derived from official illegality.[2]

Two major premises undergird the Court's decision. The Court rejects as nothing more than "speculative" the long-recognized presumption that an illegally extracted confession causes the accused to confess again out of the mistaken belief that he already has sealed his fate, and it condemns as " 'extravagant' " the requirement that the prosecution affirmatively rebut the presumption before the subsequent confession may be admitted. The Court instead adopts a new rule that, so long as the accused is given the usual *Miranda* warnings before further interrogation, the taint of a previous confession obtained in violation of *Miranda* "ordinarily" must be viewed as *automatically* dissipated.

In the alternative, the Court asserts that neither the Fifth Amendment itself nor the judicial policy of deterring illegal police conduct requires the suppression of the "fruits" of a confession obtained in violation of *Miranda,* reasoning that to do otherwise would interfere with "legitimate law enforcement activity." As the Court surely understands, however, "[t]o forbid the direct use of methods [but] to put no curb on their full indirect use would only invite the very methods deemed 'inconsistent with ethical standards and destructive of personal liberty.' " *Nardone.* * * *

The threshold question is this: What effect should an admission or confession of guilt obtained in violation of an accused's *Miranda* rights be presumed to have upon the voluntariness of subsequent confessions that are preceded by *Miranda* warnings? * * *

This Court has had long experience with the problem of confessions obtained after an earlier confession has been illegally secured. Subsequent confessions in these circumstances are not *per se* inadmissible, but the prosecution must demonstrate facts "sufficient to insulate the [subsequent] statement from the effect of all that went before." *Clewis v. Texas,* 386 U.S. 707, 87 S.Ct. 1338, 18 L.Ed.2d 423 (1967). * * * [The] question in each case is whether the accused's will was "overborne at the time he confessed," and the prosecution must demonstrate that the second confession "was an act independent of the [earlier] confession." *Reck v. Pate,* 367 U.S. 433, 81 S.Ct. 1541, 6 L.Ed.2d 948 (1961).

* * * Although we have thus rejected a *per se* rule forbidding the introduction of subsequent statements in these circumstances, we have emphasized that the psychological impact of admissions and confessions of criminal guilt nevertheless can have a decisive impact in undermining the voluntariness of a suspect's responses to continued police interrogation and must be accounted for in determining their admissibility. * * *

Our precedents did not develop in a vacuum. They reflect an understanding of the realities of police interrogation * * *. Standard interrogation manuals advise that "[t]he securing of the first admission is the biggest stumbling block. . . . " A. Aubry & R. Caputo, *Criminal Interrogation* 290 (3d ed.1980). If this first admission can be obtained, "there is every reason to expect that the first admission will lead to others and eventually to the full confession." * * *

2. The Court repeatedly casts its analysis in terms of the "fruits" of a *Miranda* violation, but its dicta nevertheless surely should not be read as necessarily foreclosing application of derivative-evidence rules where the *Miranda* violation produces evidence other than a subsequent confession by the accused. See n. 29, infra.

Interrogators describe the point of the first admission as the "breakthrough" and the "beachhead," R. Royal & S. Schutt, *The Gentle Art of Interviewing and Interrogation* 143 (1976), which once obtained will give them enormous "tactical advantages," F. Inbau & J. Reid, *Criminal Interrogation and Confessions* 82 (2d ed.1967). Thus "[t]he securing of incriminating admissions might well be considered as the beginning of the final stages in crumbling the defenses of the suspect," and the process of obtaining such admissions is described as "the spadework required to motivate the subject into making the full confession." Aubry & Caputo, supra.

* * * Expert interrogators and experienced lower-court judges will be startled, to say the least, to learn that the connection between multiple confessions is "speculative" and that a subsequent rendition of *Miranda* warnings "ordinarily" enables the accused in these circumstances to exercise his "free will" and to make "a rational and intelligent choice whether to waive or invoke his rights." * * *

* * * Where an accused believes that it is futile to resist because the authorities already have elicited an admission of guilt, the mere rendition of *Miranda* warnings does not convey the information most critical at that point to ensuring his informed and voluntary decision to speak again: that the earlier confession may not be admissible and thus that he need not speak out of any feeling that he already has sealed his fate. The Court therefore is flatly wrong in arguing, as it does repeatedly, that the mere provision of *Miranda* warnings prior to subsequent interrogation supplies the accused with "the relevant information" and ensures that a subsequent confession "ordinarily" will be the product of "a rational and intelligent choice" and "an act of free will."

The Court's new approach is therefore completely at odds with established dissipation analysis. A comparison of the Court's analysis with the factors most frequently relied on by lower courts in considering the admissibility of subsequent confessions demonstrates the practical and legal flaws of the new rule.

Advice that earlier confession may be inadmissible. The most effective means to ensure the voluntariness of an accused's subsequent confession is to advise the accused that his earlier admissions may not be admissible and therefore that he need not speak solely out of a belief that "the cat is out of the bag." Many courts have required such warnings in the absence of other dissipating factors, and this Court has not uncovered anything to suggest that this approach has not succeeded in the real world. The Court, however, believes that law enforcement authorities could never possibly understand "the murky and difficult question" of when *Miranda* warnings must be given, and therefore that they are "ill equipped" to make the decision whether supplementary warnings might be required.

This reasoning is unpersuasive for two reasons. First, the whole point of *Miranda* and its progeny has been to prescribe "bright line" rules for the authorities to follow. * * * Second, even where the authorities are not certain that an earlier confession has been illegally obtained, courts and commentators have recognized that a supplementary warning merely advising the accused that his earlier confession *may* be inadmissible can dispel his belief that he has nothing to lose by repetition.

Proximity in time and place. Courts have frequently concluded that a subsequent confession was so removed in time and place from the first that the accused most likely was able fully to exercise his independent judgment in deciding whether to speak again. As in the instant case, however, a second confession frequently follows immediately on the heels of the first and is obtained by the same officials in the same or similar coercive surroundings. In such situations, it is wholly unreasonable to assume that the mere rendition of *Miranda* warnings will safeguard the accused's freedom of action. * * *

Intervening factors. Some lower courts have found that because of intervening factors—such as consultation with a lawyer or family members, or an independent decision to speak—an accused's subsequent confession could not fairly be attributed to the earlier statement taken in violation of *Miranda.* On the other hand, where as here an accused has continuously been in custody and there is no legitimate suggestion of an intervening event sufficient to break the impact of the first confession, subsequent confessions are inadmissible. The Court reasons, however, that because "[a] suspect's confession *may* be traced to * * * an intervening event," it "*must* [be] conclude[d]" that subsequent *Miranda* warnings presumptively enable the suspect to make "a rational and intelligent choice" whether to repeat his confession (emphasis added). [The] only proper inquiry is whether a meaningful intervening event *actually* occurred, not whether a court simply chooses to shut its eyes to human nature and the realities of custodial interrogation.

* * * [The Court's] analysis is wholly at odds with established dissipation analysis. To begin with, the Court repeatedly suggests that a confession may be suppressed only if the police have used "improper tactics"; this obscure reasoning overlooks the fact that a violation of *Miranda* is obviously *itself* an "improper tactic," one frequently used precisely to undermine the voluntariness of subsequent confessions. The Court's negative implication that *Miranda* violations are *not* "improper tactics" is, to say the least, disquieting. Second, the Court reasons that the fact that the accused gave a subsequent confession is *itself* "highly probative" evidence that he was able to exercise his free will. This inaccurate premise follows from the Court's erroneous rejection of the "cat out of the bag" presumption in these circumstances and its inexplicable assertion that the previous extraction of a "guilty secret" neither constitutes compulsion nor compromises the voluntariness of later confessions. Finally, the foundation of the derivative-evidence doctrine has always been that, where the authorities have acted illegally, *they* must bear the "ultimate burden" of proving that their misconduct did not "taint" subsequently obtained evidence. That is precisely the point of the derivative-evidence presumption. By rejecting this presumption in *Miranda* cases, the Court today appears to adopt a "go ahead and try to prove it" posture toward citizens whose Fifth Amendment *Miranda* rights have been violated, an attitude that marks a sharp break from the Court's traditional approach to official lawlessness. * * *

In sum, today's opinion marks an evisceration of the established fruit of the poisonous tree doctrine, but its reasoning is sufficiently obscure and qualified as to leave state and federal courts with continued authority to combat obvious flouting by the authorities of the privilege against self-incrimination. I am confident that lower courts will exercise this authority responsibly, as they have for the most part prior to this Court's intervention.

Not content merely to ignore the practical realities of police interrogation and the likely effects of its abolition of the derivative-evidence presumption, the Court goes on to assert that nothing in the Fifth Amendment or the general judicial policy of deterring illegal police conduct "ordinarily" requires the suppression of evidence derived proximately from a confession obtained in violation of *Miranda.* The Court does not limit its analysis to successive confessions, but recurrently refers generally to the "fruits" of the illegal confession. Thus the potential impact of the Court's reasoning might extend far beyond the "cat out of the bag" context to include the discovery of physical evidence and other derivative fruits of *Miranda* violations as well.[29]

Twice in the last ten years, [first in *Tucker,* then in *Quarles,* the] Court has suggested that the *Miranda* safeguards are not themselves rights guaranteed by the Fifth Amendment. * * * [The assertions in these cases] are erroneous. *Miranda's* requirement of warnings and an effective waiver was not merely an exercise of supervisory authority over interrogation practices. * * * *Miranda* clearly emphasized that warnings and an informed waiver are essential to the Fifth Amendment privilege itself. * * * The Court in *Tucker* omitted to mention that in *Miranda,* after concluding that no "particular solution" is required, we went on to emphasize that "unless we are shown other procedures which are at least as effective in apprising accused persons of their right of silence and in assuring a continuous opportunity to exercise it, the [prescribed] safeguards must be observed." Thus "the use of [any] admissions obtained in the absence of the required warnings [is] a flat violation of the Self-Incrimination Clause of the Fifth Amendment * * *." *Orozco.*

The Court today finally recognizes these flaws in the logic of *Tucker* and *Quarles.*[30] Although disastrous in so many other respects, today's opinion at least has the virtue of rejecting the inaccurate assertion in *Quarles* that confessions extracted in violation of *Miranda* are not presumptively coerced for Fifth Amendment purposes. Instead, the Court holds squarely that there is an "irrebuttable" presumption that such confessions are indeed coerced and are therefore inadmissible under the Fifth Amendment except in narrow circumstances.

Unfortunately, the Court takes away with one hand far more than what it has given with the other. Although the Court concedes, as it must, that a confession obtained in violation of *Miranda* is irrebuttably presumed to be coerced and that the Self-Incrimination Clause therefore prevents its use in the prosecution's case-in-chief, the Court goes on to hold that nothing in the Fifth Amendment prevents the introduction at trial of evidence proximately derived from the illegal confession. It contends, for example, that the Fifth Amendment prohibits introduction "only" of the "compelled testimony," and that this constitutional guarantee "is not concerned with nontestimonial evidence."

This narrow compass of the protection against compelled self-incrimination does not accord with our historic understanding of the Fifth Amendment. Although the Self-Incrimination Clause "protects an accused only from being compelled to testify against himself, or otherwise provide the State with evidence of a testimonial or communicative nature," *Schmerber,* it prohibits the use of such communications "against" the accused in any way. The Fifth Amendment therefore contains a self-executing rule commanding the exclusion of evidence derived from such communications. It bars "the use of compelled testimony, as well as evidence derived directly and indirectly therefrom," and "prohibits the prosecutorial authorities from using the compelled testimony in *any* respect." *Kastigar v. United States* [p. 746 supra] (emphasis in original). If a coerced statement leads to "sources of information

29. Notwithstanding the sweep of the Court's language, today's opinion surely ought not be read as also foreclosing application of the traditional derivative-evidence presumption to physical evidence obtained as a proximate result of a *Miranda* violation. The Court relies heavily on individual "volition" as an insulating factor in successive-confession cases. Although the Court's reliance on this factor is clearly misplaced, the factor is altogether missing in the context of inanimate evidence. As they have in successive-confession cases, most courts considering the issue have recognized that physical evidence proximately derived from a *Miranda* violation is presumptively inadmissible. * * *

30. For an incisive critique of *Tucker,* see Stone, *The Miranda Doctrine in the Burger Court,* 1977 S.Ct.Rev. 99, 115–125.

which may supply other means of convicting" the accused, those sources must also be suppressed. *Counselman v. Hitchcock* [p. 745 supra]. Under this constitutional exclusionary rule, the authorities are thus "prohibited from making any * * * use of compelled testimony *and its fruits* * * * in connection with a criminal prosecution against" the accused. *Murphy v. Waterfront Comm'n* [p. 746 supra] (emphasis added). * * *

Even if I accepted the Court's conclusion that the Fifth Amendment does not command the suppression of evidence proximately derived from a *Miranda* violation, I would nevertheless dissent from the Court's refusal to recognize the importance of deterring *Miranda* violations in appropriate circumstances. * * *

The Court today refuses to apply the derivative-evidence rule even to the extent necessary to deter objectively unreasonable failures by the authorities to honor a suspect's *Miranda* rights. Incredibly, faced with an obvious violation of *Miranda,* the Court asserts that it will not countenance suppression of a subsequent confession in such circumstances where the authorities have acted "legitimate[ly]" and have not used "improper tactics." One can only respond: whither went *Miranda?*

* * * How can the Court possibly expect the authorities to obey *Miranda* when they have every incentive now to interrogate suspects without warnings or an effective waiver, knowing that the fruits of such interrogations "ordinarily" will be admitted, that an admissible subsequent confession "ordinarily" can be obtained simply by reciting the *Miranda* warnings shortly after the first has been procured and asking the accused to repeat himself, and that unless the accused can demonstrate otherwise his confession will be viewed as an "act of free will" in response to "legitimate law enforcement activity"? By condoning such a result, the Court today encourages practices that threaten to reduce *Miranda* to a mere "form of words," and it is shocking that the Court nevertheless disingenuously purports that it "in no way retreats" from the *Miranda* safeguards. * * *

JUSTICE STEVENS dissenting.

* * * I find nothing objectionable in [the Court's] holding. Moreover, * * * because the Court places so much emphasis on the special facts of this case, I am persuaded that the Court intends its holding to apply only to a narrow category of cases in which the initial questioning of the suspect was made in a totally uncoercive setting and in which the first confession obviously had no influence on the second. I nevertheless dissent because even such a narrowly confined exception is inconsistent with the Court's prior cases, because the attempt to identify its boundaries in future cases will breed confusion and uncertainty in the administration of criminal justice, and because it denigrates the importance of one of the core constitutional rights that protects every American citizen from the kind of tyranny that has flourished in other societies.

The desire to achieve a just result in this particular case has produced an opinion that is somewhat opaque and internally inconsistent. If I read it correctly, its conclusion rests on two untenable premises: (1) that the respondent's first confession was not the product of coercion; and (2) that no constitutional right was violated when respondent was questioned in a tranquil, domestic setting.

Even before the decision in *Miranda,* it had been recognized that police interrogation of a suspect who has been taken into custody is presumptively coercive. That presumption had its greatest force when the questioning occurred in a police station, when it was prolonged, and when there was evidence that the prisoner had suffered physical injury. * * *

The decision in *Miranda* clarified the law in three important respects. First, it provided the prosecutor with a simple method of overcoming the presumption of coercion. If the police interrogation is preceded by the warning specified in that opinion, the usual presumption does not attach. Second, it provided an important protection to the accused by making the presumption of coercion irrebuttable if the prescribed warnings are not given. Third, the decision made it clear that a self-incriminatory statement made in response to custodial interrogation was always to be considered "compelled" within the meaning of the Fifth Amendment to the Federal Constitution if the interrogation had not been preceded by appropriate warnings. Thus the irrebuttable presumption of coercion that applies to such a self-incriminatory statement, like a finding of actual coercion, renders the resulting confession inadmissible as a matter of federal constitutional law.[9]

In my opinion, the Court's attempt to fashion a distinction between actual coercion "by physical violence or other deliberate means calculated to break the suspect's will" and irrebuttably presumed coercion cannot succeed. The presumption is only legitimate if it is assumed that there is always a coercive aspect to custodial interrogation that is not preceded by adequate advice of the constitutional right to remain silent. Although I would not support it, I could understand a rule that refused to apply the presumption unless the interrogation took place in an especially coercive setting—perhaps only in the police station itself—but if the presumption arises whenever the accused has been taken into custody or his freedom has been restrained in any significant way, it will surely be futile to try to develop subcategories of custodial interrogation. Indeed, a major purpose of treating the presumption of coercion as irrebuttable is to avoid the kind of fact-bound inquiry that today's decision will surely engender.

* * * [S]urely the fact that an earlier confession was obtained by unlawful methods should add force to the presumption of coercion that attaches to subsequent custodial interrogation and should require the prosecutor to shoulder a heavier burden of rebuttal than in a routine case. Simple logic, as well as the interest in not providing an affirmative incentive to police misconduct, requires that result. I see no reason why the violation of a rule that is as well recognized and easily administered as the duty to give *Miranda* warnings should not also impose an additional burden on the prosecutor.[13] If we are faithful to the holding in *Miranda* itself, when we are considering the admissibility of evidence in the prosecutor's case-in-chief, we should not try to fashion a distinction between police misconduct that warrants a finding of actual coercion and police misconduct that establishes an irrebuttable presumption of coercion.

For me, the most disturbing aspect of the Court's opinion is its somewhat opaque characterization of the police misconduct in this case. The Court appears ambiva-

9. * * * Obviously, the Court's power to reverse Miranda's conviction rested entirely on the determination that a violation of the Federal Constitution had occurred.

The constitutional violation was established without any evidence that the police actually coerced Miranda in any way. The fact that Miranda had confessed while he was in custody and without having been adequately advised of his right to remain silent was sufficient to establish the constitutional violation. To phrase it another way, the absence of an adequate warning plus the fact of custody created an irrebuttable presumption of coercion. * * *

13. In view of the Court's holding, it is not necessary to consider how that additional burden should be discharged in all cases. In general, however, I should think that before the second session of custodial interrogation begins, the prisoner should be advised that his earlier statement is, or may be, inadmissible. I am not persuaded that the *Miranda* rule is so "murky" that the law-enforcement profession would be unable to identify the cases in which a supplementary warning would be appropriate. *Miranda* was written, in part, "to give concrete constitutional guidelines for law enforcement agencies and courts to follow." * * * Nearly two decades after that disposition, it is undisputed that the *Miranda* rule—now so deeply embedded in our culture that most schoolchildren know not only the warnings, but also when they are required—has given that clarity. * * *

lent on the question whether there was any constitutional violation.[14] This ambivalence is either disingenuous or completely lawless. This Court's power to require state courts to exclude probative self-incriminatory statements rests entirely on the premise that the use of such evidence violates the Federal Constitution.[15] The same constitutional analysis applies whether the custodial interrogation is actually coercive or irrebuttably presumed to be coercive. If the Court does not accept that premise, it must regard the holding in the *Miranda* case itself, as well as all of the Federal jurisprudence that has evolved from that decision, as nothing more than an illegitimate exercise of raw judicial power. * * *

Notes and Questions

1. *The role of the police officer vs. the role of the defense lawyer.* During the oral argument in *Elstad,* one Justice suggested that it would not be unduly burdensome for the police to tell a suspect that they had treated him improperly at an earlier session and that therefore the incriminating statement(s) obtained at the earlier session would not be used against him. Such a requirement, responded the Attorney General of Oregon, "might do a great deal of mischief because it confuses the role of the police officer with that of the criminal defense attorney." Does this argument come pretty late in the day? Doesn't *Miranda* itself "confuse the role of the police officer with that of the criminal defense lawyer"?

Should the police at least be able to tell whether there is a *substantial question* about the admissibility of an earlier statement? Should they at least be required to give a supplementary warning that the earlier statement is or *may be* inadmissible? Or that it is *unclear* whether the earlier statement is admissible and that the suspect is entitled to the advise of counsel on this point? If the police are "ill equipped" to do even this much, then when they obtain a statement from a person without advising him of his rights and want to question him again, instead of asking or expecting them to "pinch-hit" for counsel, should we require them to let defense counsel "bat for himself"?

2. *Does Elstad permit the use of physical evidence obtained as a result of a "mere" Miranda violation?* Dissenting in *Elstad,* Justice Brennan maintains that the language in the majority opinion should not be read as foreclosing application of the "fruit of the poisonous tree" doctrine to *physical evidence* derived from a *Miranda* violation. (See fns. 2 & 29.) Why not? If neither *Tucker* nor *Elstad* were controlled by the "fruit of the poisonous tree" doctrine because each case involved a "mere" *Miranda* violation rather than an "actual infringement of a suspect's constitutional rights," why should *any* "fruit" of a "mere" *Miranda* violation be controlled by the "fruit of the poisonous tree doctrine"?

In *Elstad,* Justice O'Connor quotes extensively from *Tucker* with approval and then adds that "the reasoning" of *Tucker*—that neither the general goal of deterring police misconduct nor the Fifth Amendment goal of assuring trustworthy evidence would be served by suppressing the testimony of a witness "tainted" by a "mere" *Miranda* violation—"applies with equal force when the alleged 'fruit' of a noncoercive *Miranda* violation is *neither* a witness *nor* an article of evidence but the accused's own voluntary testimony [i.e., his second confession]." (Emphasis added.) Isn't this sentence written as if the Court had *already held* that the "fruit of the poisonous tree" doctrine does not apply to "fruits" that are witnesses *or* articles of evidence

14. * * * Indeed, the Court's holding rests on its view that there were no "improper tactics in obtaining the initial statement."

15. At least that is my view. In response to this dissent, however, the Court has added a fn. 1, implying that whenever the Court commands exclusion of a presumptively coerced confession, it is standing—not on a constitutional predicate—but merely on its own shoulders.

and is now *extending that approach* to a suspect's second confession?

SECTION 4. USE OF ILLEGALLY OBTAINED EVIDENCE FOR IMPEACHMENT PURPOSES

A. THE EXPANSION OF A ONCE-NARROW EXCEPTION

1. In *Walder v. United States,* 347 U.S. 62, 74 S.Ct. 354, 98 L.Ed. 503 (1954), defendant, charged with various illegal narcotics transactions, asserted early on his direct examination that he had never possessed any narcotics or sold or given any narcotics to anyone in his life. The Court held, per Frankfurter, J., that this assertion "opened the door," for purposes of attacking the defendant's credibility, to evidence of heroin seized from the defendant's home, in his presence, in an earlier, unrelated case. "Of his own accord," observed the Court, "the defendant went beyond a mere denial of complicity in the crimes of which he was charged and made the sweeping claim that he had never dealt in or possessed any narcotics. [A defendant] must be free to deny all the elements of the case against him without thereby giving leave to the Government to introduce by way of rebuttal evidence illegally secured by it, and thereby not available for its case in chief. Beyond that, however, there is hardly justification for letting the defendant affirmatively resort to perjurious testimony in reliance on the Government's disability to challenge his credibility."

The instant situation, emphasized the *Walder* Court, is to be "sharply contrasted" with that presented by *Agnello v. United States,* 269 U.S. 20, 46 S.Ct. 4, 70 L.Ed. 145 (1925). There, the government sought to "smuggle in" the tainted evidence on cross-examination by asking the defendant whether he had ever seen narcotics before, and eliciting the expected denial. In *Agnello,* the defendant "did nothing" to waive his constitutional protection or to justify cross-examination with respect to the illegally seized evidence.

2. HARRIS v. NEW YORK, 401 U.S. 222, 91 S.Ct. 643, 28 L.Ed.2d 1 (1971), often called the first blow the Burger Court struck *Miranda,* arose as follows: Petitioner, charged with selling heroin to an undercover officer, took the stand in his own defense. He admitted knowing the officer, but denied making a sale of heroin. Statements made by petitioner immediately following his arrest which partially contradicted his direct trial testimony were used to impeach his credibility. According to the Court, petitioner made no claim that the statements were coerced or involuntary,[a] but they were preceded by defective *Miranda* warnings, and thus inadmissible to establish the prosecution's case in chief. A 5–4 majority, per BURGER, C.J., held that under the circumstances "petitioner's credibility was appropriately impeached by use of his earlier conflicting statements."

The Court noted that "[s]ome comments in the *Miranda* opinion can indeed be read as indicating a bar to use of [a statement obtained in violation of *Miranda*] for any purpose," but dismissed this discussion as "not at all necessary to the Court's holding" and not "controlling." [b] The Court noted, but also seemed untroubled by the fact, "that Walder was impeached as to collateral matters included in his direct examination, whereas petition-

a. According to Dershowitz & Ely, *Harris v. New York: Some Anxious Observations on the Candor and Logic of the Emerging Nixon Majority,* 80 Yale L.J. 1198, 1201 (1971), "the record is clear" that he did.

b. But consider Stone, *The Miranda Doctrine in the Burger Court,* 1977 Sup.Ct.Rev. 99, 107–08: "Rightly or wrongly, *Miranda* was deliberately structured to canvass a wide range of problems, many of which were not directly raised by the cases before the Court. This approach was thought necessary in order to 'give concrete constitutional guidelines for law enforcement agencies and courts to follow.' Thus, a technical reading of *Miranda,* such as that employed in *Harris,* would enable the Court to label many critical aspects of the decision mere dictum and therefore not 'controlling,' " er here was impeached as to testimony bearing more directly on the crimes charged." The Court next observed:

"The impeachment process here undoubtedly provided valuable aid to the jury in assessing petitioner's credibility, and the benefits of this process should not be lost * * * because of the speculative possibility that impermissible police conduct will be encouraged thereby. Assuming that the exclusionary rule has a deterrent effect * * * sufficient deterrence flows when the evidence in question is made unavailable to the prosecution in its case in chief.

"[The privilege to testify in one's defense] cannot be construed to include the right to commit perjury. Having voluntarily taken the stand, petitioner was under an obligation to speak truthfully and accurately, and the prosecution here did no more than utilize the traditional truth-testing devices of the adversary process. * * * The shield provided by *Miranda* cannot be perverted into a license to use perjury by way of a defense, free from the risk of confrontation with prior inconsistent utterances."

Dissenting Justice BRENNAN, joined by Douglas and Marshall, JJ., criticized the majority for disregarding language in *Miranda* and for selectively quoting from *Walder.* The dissent emphasized that "*Walder* was not a case where tainted evidence was used to impeach an accused's direct testimony on matters directly related to the case against him," but only such testimony "on matters *collateral* to the crime charged." Continued the dissent:

"While *Walder* did not identify the constitutional specifics that guarantee 'a defendant the fullest opportunity to meet the accusation against him [and permit him to be free to deny all the elements of the case against him,' in my view *Miranda* identified the Fifth Amendment's privilege against self-incrimination as one of those specifics. [It] is fulfilled only when an accused is guaranteed the right 'to remain silent unless he chooses to speak in the *unfettered* exercise of his own will' (emphasis added). The choice of whether to testify in one's own defense must therefore be 'unfettered' * * *. [But] the accused is denied an 'unfettered' choice when the decision whether to take the stand is burdened by the risk that an illegally obtained prior statement may be introduced to impeach his direct testimony denying complicity in the crime charged against him."[c]

3. *The Fourth Amendment vs. the Fifth.* Should the Court have considered the significance of *Miranda's* Fifth Amendment underpinning before applying (or extending) the Fourth Amendment *Walder* case to *Harris?* Is impeachment by means of evidence obtained in violation of the Fourth Amendment more defensible than such use of evidence obtained in violation of the Self-Incrimination Clause of the Fifth because the Fourth's "exclusionary rule" is a court-created device designed to deter the police and as the link between police illegality and subsequent evidence becomes more attenuated it becomes less likely that exclusion would affect future police conduct? On the other hand, is the essence of the constitutional wrong under the Fifth the *use* against him of a defendant's compelled testimony, not the mere act of compelling him to speak (otherwise no immunity statute would be constitutional)? Doesn't the Self-Incrimination Clause by its own terms seem to prohibit the use of statements obtained in violation of its command? See Dershowitz & Ely, fn. a supra, at 1214–15; Stone, fn. b supra, at 110–111; Notes, 73 Colum.L.Rev. 1476, 1482 (1973); 82 Harv.L.Rev. 63, 221–22 (1968); 82 Yale L.J. 171, 176–78 (1972). Moreover, may not illegally seized tangible evidence be said to be intrinsically more reliable than statements obtained without *Miranda* warnings?

c. Black, J., also dissented, without opinion.

4. The Court went a step beyond *Harris* in *Oregon v. Hass,* 420 U.S. 714, 95 S.Ct. 1215, 43 L.Ed.2d 570 (1975). In *Hass,* after being advised of his rights, the defendant *asserted* them—he asked for a lawyer. But the police refused to honor his request and continued to question him. A 6–2 majority, per Blackmun, J., ruled that here, too, the resulting statements could be used for impeachment purposes. "One might concede," wrote the Court, "that when proper *Miranda* warnings have been given, and the officer then continues his interrogation after the suspect asks for an attorney, the officer may be said to have little to lose and perhaps something to gain by way of possibly uncovering impeachment material. This speculative possibility, however, is even greater where the warnings are defective and the defect is not known to the officers. In any event, the balance was struck in *Harris,* and we are not disposed to change it now."

But wasn't a *different* balance struck in *Hass?* Dissenting Justice Brennan, joined by Marshall, J., thought so: "Even after *Harris,* police had some incentive for following *Miranda* by warning an accused of his [rights]. If the warnings were given, the accused might still make a statement which could be used in the prosecution's case-in-chief. Under today's holding, however, once the warnings are given, police have almost no incentive for following *Miranda's* requirement that '[i]f the individual states that he wants an attorney, the interrogation must cease until an attorney is present.' If the requirement is followed there will almost surely be no statement since the attorney will advise the accused to remain silent. If, however, the requirement is disobeyed, the police may obtain a statement which can be used for impeachment if the accused has the temerity to testify in his own defense."

5. In UNITED STATES v. HAVENS, 446 U.S. 620, 100 S.Ct. 1912, 64 L.Ed.2d 559 (1980), what had "started out in *Walder* as a narrow and reasonable exception" to the exclusionary rule took on "awesome proportions," LaFave & Israel, § 9.6(a) at 772. On direct examination, defendant denied being involved with his codefendant in the transportation of cocaine and on cross-examination denied being involved in sewing a pocket (in which drugs were found) into his codefendant's clothing or having in his own suitcase cloth from which the swatch was cut to make the pocket. Defendant's testimony was impeached by admitting the illegally seized cloth, but the Fifth Circuit reversed, maintaining that illegally seized evidence could be used for impeachment only if it contradicts a defendant's direct testimony. A 5–4 majority, per WHITE, J., disagreed:

"Neither *Harris* nor *Hass* involved the impeachment of asserted false testimony first given on cross-examination, but the reasoning of those cases controls this one. * * * [In] terms of impeaching a defendant's seemingly false statements with his prior inconsistent utterances or with other reliable evidence available to the government, we see no difference of constitutional magnitude between the defendant's statements on direct examination and his answers to questions put to him on cross-examination that are plainly within the scope of the defendant's direct examination. Without this opportunity, the normal function of cross-examination would be severely impeded.

"We also think that the policies of the exclusionary rule no more bar impeachment here than they did in *Walder, Harris,* and *Hass.* * * * [The] incremental furthering of [the ends of the exclusionary rules] by forbidding impeachment of the defendant who testifies was deemed insufficient to permit or require that false testimony go unchallenged, with the resulting impairment of the integrity of the fact-finding goals of the criminal trial. We reaffirm this assessment of the competing interests, and hold that a defendant's statements made in response to proper cross-examination reasonably suggested by the defendant's direct examination are subject to otherwise proper impeachment by the government, albeit by evidence that has been illegally obtained."

Dissenting Justice BRENNAN, joined by Stewart, Marshall and Stevens, JJ., on this point, protested: "The identical issue was confronted in *Agnello,* which determined—contrary to the instant decision—that it was constitutionally impermissible to admit evidence obtained in violation of the Fourth Amendment to rebut a defendant's response to a matter first raised during the Government's cross-examination. * * * The exclusionary rule exception established by *Harris* and *Hass* may be fairly easily cabined by defense counsel's unwillingness to forego certain areas of questioning. But [today's holding] passes control of the exception to the Government, since the prosecutor can lay the predicate for admitting otherwise suppressible evidence with his own questioning. * * * In practical terms * * * today's holding allows even the moderately talented prosecutor to 'work [in] evidence on cross-examination [as it would] in its case in chief,' *Walder.* To avoid this consequence, a defendant will be compelled to forego testifying on his own behalf."

Justice Brennan (joined only by Marshall, J., on this point) then voiced "a more fundamental difference with the Court's holding here, which culminates the approach taken in *Harris* and *Hass* ":

"[T]he Court has undertaken to strike a 'balance' between the 'policies' it finds in the Bill of Rights and the 'competing interest' in accurate trial determinations. This balancing effort is completely freewheeling. Far from applying criteria intrinsic to the Fourth and Fifth Amendments, the Court resolves succeeding cases simply by declaring that so much exclusion is enough to deter police misconduct. That hardly conforms to the disciplined analytical method described as 'legal reasoning,' through which judges endeavor to formulate or derive principles of decision that can be applied consistently and predictably.

"* * * More disturbingly, by treating Fourth and Fifth Amendment privileges as mere incentive schemes, the Court denigrates their unique status as *constitutional* protections. Yet the efficacy of the Bill of Rights as the bulwark of our national liberty depends precisely upon public appreciation of the special character of constitutional prescriptions."

B. WHAT KINDS OF CONSTITUTIONAL OR OTHER VIOLATIONS ARE ENCOMPASSED WITHIN THE IMPEACHMENT EXCEPTION?

1. *New Jersey v. Portash,* 440 U.S. 450, 99 S.Ct. 1292, 59 L.Ed.2d 501 (1979) held, per Stewart, J. that testimony given by a person in response to a grant of legislative immunity could not be used to impeach him at his subsequent trial for extortion and misconduct in office. "Central to the decisions" in *Harris* and *Hass,* emphasized the Court, was the fact that the defendant made no claim that the statements were coerced. But testimony before a grand jury in response to a grant of use immunity "is the essence of coerced testimony." Balancing of interests was thought to be necessary in *Harris* and *Hass* 'when the attempt to deter unlawful police conduct collided with the need to prevent perjury. Here, by contrast, we deal with the constitutional privilege against compulsory self-incrimination in its most pristine form. Balancing, therefore, is not simply unnecessary. It is impermissible."

2. In *Mincey v. Arizona* (1978) p. 523 supra), the Court also distinguished *Harris* and *Hass* and made clear that the use of an "involuntary" or "coerced" statement even for impeachment purposes would constitute "a denial of due process of law." But the Court's discussion seemed to overlook the possibility that an "involuntary" statement may be trustworthy in a particular case.

3. *United States v. Brown,* 699 F.2d 585 (2d Cir.1983), prohibited the use of a

statement obtained in violation of the *Massiah* doctrine for impeachment purposes, distinguishing between "a clear violation of a *constitutional* right" and a mere violation of the "prophylactic" rules of *Miranda.* Is the Supreme Court likely to accept such a distinction for impeachment purposes?

C. USE OF DEFENDANT'S PRIOR SILENCE FOR IMPEACHMENT PURPOSES

1. After being arrested for selling marijuana to an informant, defendants were given the *Miranda* warnings and chose to remain silent. At trial, each defendant claimed that he had been "framed" by narcotics agents. In an effort to undercut their testimony, the prosecution was allowed to ask each defendant why he had not told this story to the arresting officer. In *Doyle v. Ohio,* 426 U.S. 610, 96 S.Ct. 2240, 49 L.Ed.2d 91 (1976), a 6–3 majority, per Powell, J., held such use of a defendant's post-arrest silence, after receiving the *Miranda* warnings, impermissible. Not only is "every post-arrest silence * * * insolubly ambiguous because of what the State is required to advise the person arrested," but use of the silence to impeach would be "fundamentally unfair" given the fact that the *Miranda* warnings contain the "implicit" "assurance" that "silence will carry no penalty." [a] But *Doyle* has been distinguished in three subsequent impeachment cases.

2. *Impeachment by prior inconsistent statements after receiving Miranda warnings.* After being arrested while driving a stolen car and given the *Miranda* warnings, defendant agreed to talk to the police. But he gave a different version of the auto theft than he subsequently did when he testified in his own defense. On cross-examination, he was asked why he gave a different story at the time of his arrest. *Anderson v. Charles,* 447 U.S. 404, 100 S.Ct. 2180, 65 L.Ed.2d 222 (1980) (per curiam), had little difficulty in permitting such cross-examination: "[*Doyle*] does not apply to cross-examination that merely inquires into prior inconsistent statements. Such questioning makes no unfair use of silence, because a defendant who voluntarily speaks after receiving *Miranda* warnings has not been induced to remain silent."

3. *Use of defendant's prearrest silence for impeachment purposes.* In *Jenkins v. Anderson,* 447 U.S. 231, 100 S.Ct. 2124, 65 L.Ed.2d 86 (1980), where at his murder trial petitioner claimed self-defense, the prosecutor was allowed to question him about the fact that he had not surrendered to the authorities until two weeks after the killing. In closing argument, the prosecutor again referred to petitioner's prearrest silence, noting that he had "waited" at least two weeks before "reporting" the stabbing to anyone, suggesting that he would have spoken out if he had truly killed in self-defense. The Court, per Powell, J., held (1), relying heavily on *Raffel v. United States,* 271 U.S. 494, 46 S.Ct. 566, 70 L.Ed. 1054 (1926), that the Self-Incrimination Clause is not violated by the use of prearrest silence to impeach a defendant's credibility; [a] and (2) *Doyle* presents no obstacle for "no governmental action induced petitioner to remain silent before arrest. The failure to speak oc-

a. But cf. *South Dakota v. Neville* (1983) (also discussed at p. 589 fn. a supra), upholding a statute permitting a person suspected of driving while intoxicated to refuse to submit to a blood-alcohol test, but authorizing revocation of the driver's license of a person so refusing the test and also allowing such refusal to be used against him at trial. Although the defendant in *Neville* had not been told of the latter possibility, the Court thought it "unrealistic to say that the warnings given here implicitly assure a suspect that no consequences other than those mentioned will occur. Importantly, the warning that he could lose his driver's license made it clear that refusing the test was not a 'safe harbor' free of adverse consequences."

a. For strong criticism of this portion of the opinion, see Saltzburg, *Foreword: The Flow and Ebb of Constitutional Criminal Procedure in the Warren and Burger Courts,* 69 Geo. L.J. 151, 204–05 (1980).

curred before petitioner was taken into custody and given *Miranda* warnings." [b]

Dissenting Justice Marshall, joined by Brennan, J., contended that the Court's holding "has three patent—and in my view, fatal—defects": (1) Considering the various possible explanations for silence (e.g., Jenkins' story would have implicated him in the homicide), "the mere fact of prearrest silence is so unlikely to be probative of the falsity of the defendant's trial strategy that its use for impeachment is contrary to [due process]." (2) "[T]he drawing of an adverse inference from the failure to volunteer incriminating statements impermissibly infringes the privilege against self-incrimination." (3) "[T]he availability of the inference for impeachment purposes impermissibly burdens the decision to exercise the constitutional right to testify in one's own defense."

4. *Use of defendant's post-arrest silence for impeachment purposes.* When arrested, Weir, a murder suspect, said nothing, but the "significant difference" between this case and *Doyle* is that Weir did not receive any *Miranda* warnings during the period in which he remained silent immediately after his arrest. When Weir testified at his trial that he had acted in self-defense, the prosecutor cross-examined him as to why, when arrested, he had not offered this exculpatory explanation. *Fletcher v. Weir,* 455 U.S. 603, 102 S.Ct. 1309, 71 L.Ed.2d 490 (1982) (per curiam), held that "in the absence of the sort of affirmative assurances embodied in the *Miranda* warnings" a state may permit cross-examination about post-arrest silence when a defendant chooses to take the stand. The Court rejected the argument that an arrest, by itself, is "governmental action which implicitly induces a defendant to remain silent," deeming such "broadening of *Doyle* * * * unsupported by the reasoning of that case and contrary to our post-*Doyle* decisions."

Notes and Questions

(a) Suppose, when arrested, Weir had said, "I believe I have a perfectly valid defense, but I don't think I should talk to you until I first have a chance to talk to my lawyer." Could that statement and/or the subsequent post-arrest silence be used for impeachment purposes?

(b) Suppose, when being driven to the station house, a suspect asks the arresting officer, "Do I have a right to remain silent?" Or, "Do I have a right to discuss my situation with a lawyer before saying anything about it to a police officer?" How should the officer respond?

(c) Suppose, when being driven to the station house, a suspect asks the arresting officer whether he has a right to remain silent or whether his silence can be used against him at the trial and the officer meets such questions with a stony silence? What result if the suspect then says nothing during the rest of the drive? What result if the suspect then starts talking and makes incriminating statements?

D. Use of Post-*Miranda* Warnings Silence or Assertion of Rights to Rebut Defense of Insanity

May a defendant's post-*Miranda* warnings silence or request for counsel be offered not to impeach but as substantive evidence to rebut defendant's defense of insanity at the time of the offense? No, answers *Wainwright v. Greenfield,* ___ U.S. ___, 106 S.Ct. 634, 88 L.Ed.2d 623 (1986). On three occasions shortly after his arrest in Florida for sexual battery, Greenfield was given the *Miranda* warn-

b. But see Bradley, *Havens, Jenkins, and Salvucci, and the Defendant's "Right" to Testify,* 18 Am.Crim.L.Rev. 419, 434–35 (1981), maintaining that the silence in *Jenkins* was just as equivocal as that in *Doyle* for "an individual's reluctance to hand himself over to the police and admit a stabbing, in self-defense or otherwise," is not probative of guilt. "Anyone who believes that volunteering information to police is 'natural' for a resident of Detroit's inner-city has an unusually optimistic view of human nature." See also Note, 94 Harv.L.Rev. 77, 84–85 (1980).

ings. In each instance he exercised his right to remain silent and stated that he wished to speak with an attorney before answering any questions. Greenfield later pled guilty by reason of insanity. At his trial two police officers described the occasions on which Greenfield had exercised his right to remain silent and had expressed a desire to consult with counsel. In his closing argument, the prosecutor reviewed this police testimony and suggested that Greenfield's responses to the warnings demonstrated a degree of comprehension inconsistent with his claim of insanity.

The jury found Greenfield guilty and the judge sentenced him to life imprisonment. The Florida appellate courts affirmed and Greenfield sought federal habeas corpus relief. Florida argued that an insanity defense should be viewed as an "affirmative defense" and that the use of silence to overcome the defense should thus be regarded as impeachment. "Without accepting that argument, or its characterization of the insanity defense," the Court, per Stevens, J., held that *Doyle* prevented the use of post-*Miranda* warnings silence to overcome an insanity defense:

"The point of the *Doyle* holding is that it is fundamentally unfair to promise an arrested person that his silence will not be used against him and thereafter to breach that promise by using the silence to impeach his trial testimony. It is equally unfair to breach that promise by using silence to overcome a defendant's plea of insanity. In both situations, the state gives warnings to protect constitutional rights and implicitly promises that any exercise of these rights will not be penalized. In both situations, the State then seeks to make use of the defendant's exercise of those rights in obtaining his conviction. The implicit promise, the breach, and the consequent penalty are identical in both situations." [a]

SECTION 5. ALLOCATION OF THE BURDENS OF PROOF

PEOPLE v. BERRIOS

270 N.E.2d 709 (N.Y.1971).

SCILEPPI, JUDGE.

In each of these * * * appeals, the defendants have been charged with possession of heroin and arresting officers have testified that glassine envelopes containing narcotics were dropped on the ground as the defendants were approached by the police.[a] We have been called upon to

a. The Court pointed out (fn. 13), apparently in response to the concurring opinion, that "post-*Miranda* warnings 'silence'" "means not only muteness" but "includes the statement of a desire to remain silent, as well as of a desire to remain silent until attorney has been consulted."

Rehnquist, J., joined by the Chief Justice, concurred in the result because one of the prosecutor's remarks was "an improper comment on respondent's silence." But he maintained that "a request for a lawyer may be highly relevant where the plea is based on insanity"—"there is no 'insoluble ambiguity' in the request; it is a perfectly straightforward statement tending to show that an individual is able to understand his rights and is not incoherent or obviously confused or unbalanced"—and he did not read the advice *as to counsel* "as containing any promise, express or implied, that the words used in responding to notice of the right to a lawyer will not be used by the State to rebut a claim of insanity."

a. In New York, as in most jurisdictions, challenges to the admissibility of evidence on the ground that it was illegally obtained must be presented by a pretrial motion to suppress. The motion must set forth the objection with sufficient particularity, which usually requires that the defense specify the nature of the alleged illegality in the acquisition of evidence (e.g., that a statement was obtained in violation of *Miranda,* or that the search in question was incident to an arrest not supported by probable cause). See LaFave and Israel, § 10.1(b). Assuming the form of the motion is correct, the trial judge will then hold a pretrial hearing at which both sides can offer its testimony regarding the acquisition of the evidence and cross-examine the other side's witnesses. Denial of the pretrial motion does not allow an immediate appeal by the defense, but the prosecution often can appeal the granting of the motion. See Ch. 26, § 3.

In those jurisdictions that do not require a pretrial motion, an objection may be made at trial, contemporaneously with the introduction of the evidence. An objection at this point ordinarily requires the trial court to recess the trial in order to conduct a hearing on the suppression objection. Whether a state requires a pretrial decide whether, in these "dropsy" cases, or for that matter whenever a warrantless search is presented, it is the People who must bear the burden of proving the legality of the search and seizure. [In each of the cases before the court, an officer testified that as he made a movement toward the defendant—leaving his car in one case, instructing the defendant to stop in another—the defendant dropped a glassine envelope containing narcotics. The officer was undercover in one case and in uniform in another.] * * *

Simply stated, [defendants] have contended that the police testimony in these cases is inherently untrustworthy and the product of fabrication; hence, the argument is advanced that we should require that the People bear the burden of proving admissibility and depart from our present rule which places the burden of showing inadmissibility on the defendant. No argument is proffered that this departure is required by either the State or Federal Constitutions; rather, it is asserted that the change in burden of proof is necessary to alleviate the possibility of perjured police testimony. It is noted by this court that the District Attorney of New York County has joined defense counsel in [one] case in suggesting the change in burden of proof. This concession does not, however, relieve us from the performance of our judicial function and does not require us to adopt the proposal urged upon us. * * * [W]e are not persuaded that a change in burden of proof is indicated.

Thus far, we have made it clear that where a defendant challenges the admissibility of physical evidence or makes a motion to suppress, he bears the ultimate burden of proving that the evidence should not be used against him. Indeed the very words employed by the Legislature in fashioning the motion to suppress suggest no other rational conclusion. Section 813–c of the Code of Criminal Procedure provides that "[*a*] *person claiming to be aggrieved* by an unlawful search and seizure and having reasonable grounds to believe that the property * * * *claimed to have been unlawfully obtained* may be used as evidence against him * * * may move for the return * * * or * * * suppression of its use as evidence." (Emphasis supplied). Since such a person makes the claim because he contends that he is aggrieved and requests the court to give redress to an alleged wrong, it is most reasonable to require him to bear the burden of proof of that wrong. The People must, of course, always show that police conduct was reasonable. Thus, though a defendant who challenges the legality of a search and seizure has the burden of proving illegality, the People are nevertheless put to "the burden of *going forward* to show the legality of the police conduct in the first instance". *People v. Whitehurst,* 250 N.E.2d 62 (N.Y.1969). These considerations require that the People show that the search was made pursuant to a valid warrant, consent, incident to a lawful arrest or, in cases such as those here, that no search at all occurred because the evidence was dropped by the defendant in the presence of the police officer.

The appellants * * * [have] argued that the present rule is inadequate to cope with the problem of perjured testimony * * *. We have been told that with the advent of *Mapp v. Ohio,* there has been a great incidence of "dropsy" testimony by police officers. Hence, this court has been asked to infer that the police are systematically evading the mandate of *Mapp* by fabricating their testimony. We cannot embrace this *post hoc ergo propter hoc* reasoning for, as the then Judge Warren Burger observed in *Bush v. United States,* 375 F.2d 602, 604 (D.C.Cir.1967), "[i]t would be a dismal reflection on society to say that when the guardians of its security are called to testify in court under oath, their

motion or a contemporaneous objection, failure to make a timely objection can result in the procedural forfeiture of the objection. See *Wainwright v. Sykes,* Ch. 27, § 2; and LaFave and Israel, § 10.2(a).

testimony must be viewed with suspicion." Thus, we reject this frontal attack on the integrity of our entire law enforcement system. In so doing, we are not oblivious to the problem that there is always a possibility that a witness will perjure himself. Indeed, this is why credibility is usually a crucial issue whenever facts are in dispute and courts have traditionally addressed themselves to the resolution of this basic question as a part of the fact-finding process. * * * Some police officers, as well as some in other callings may be tempted to tamper with the truth. But there is no valid proof that all members of law enforcement agencies or that all other citizens who testify are perjurers. Therefore, all policemen should not be singled out as suspect as a matter of law.

The fact that some witnesses may lie does not require a change in the burden of proof for it is our view that the proposal made in this appeal is no more effective in preventing perjury than the present burden of proof. Under both the suggested change and the present system, the defendant must still refute the testimony of the police officer. Thus, even where the officer testifies that glassine envelopes were dropped by the defendant or to facts which would sustain a warrantless search, the court would still be faced with the same credibility question. Since a change in the burden of proof would be ineffective to combat the alleged evil about which the defendants herein complain, principles of *stare decisis* do not allow a departure from our present rule of burden of proof.

Moreover, it is our view that the present system, which gives the accused the protection of the Trial Judge and appellate courts on review effectively and adequately addresses itself to the basic credibility problem which is always presented. Where the Judge at the suppression hearing determines that the testimony of the police officer is unworthy of belief, he should conclude that the People have not met their burden of coming forward with sufficient evidence and grant the motion to suppress. Similarly, appellate courts by a careful exercise of their jurisdiction, in reviewing the evidence, can effectively curtail the alleged abuses.

Additionally, there are more appropriate methods of dealing with the abuses about which the defendants complain. For example, as the District Attorney of Bronx County has suggested a possible solution to the problem of some police fabrication can be found within the several police departments of this State. They can effectively formulate internal procedures and policies within the department to eliminate any such abuses. This should at the very least take the form of training and official action to prevent fabrication. Lastly, the district attorneys of this State should evaluate the testimony of police officers, as they do the testimony of all witnesses, in determining what proof will be offered in the prosecution of a case. * * *

FULD, CHIEF JUDGE (dissenting).

I, of course, agree with the court that "there is no valid proof that all members of law enforcement agencies * * * who testify are perjurers" and that "all policemen should not be singled out as suspect as a matter of law," for it must be acknowledged that those possessed of drugs or gambling slips not infrequently seek to rid themselves of such incriminating items by attempting to drop them unnoticed when they see a police officer. However, the District Attorney of New York County informs us * * * that: "For the last ten years participants in the system of justice—judges, prosecutors, defense attorneys and police officials—have privately and publicly expressed the belief that in some substantial but indeterminable percentage of dropsy cases, the testimony [that a defendant dropped narcotics or gambling slips to the ground as a police officer approached him] is tailored to meet the requirements of search-and-seizure rulings" and "it is very difficult in many [such] cases to distinguish between fact and fiction." When so able and dedicated a prosecutor as District Attorney Frank Hogan believes that there is basis for questioning the truthfulness of the testimony in a "substantial * * * percentage of dropsy cases," the conclusion seems to me inescapable * * * that the integrity of the judicial process demands that there be a reallocation of the burden of proof. * * *

Underlying the Fourth and Fourteenth Amendments is the basic proposition that "no man is to be convicted on unconstitutional evidence." In light of the situation as it today exists, the present rule—which imposes upon the accused the burden of proving the illegality of a seizure on a motion to suppress—subverts this principle by making it possible for some defendants to be convicted on evidence obtained in violation of constitutional guarantees. This follows from the fact that a trial judge who is unsure whether the prosecution's account of the seizure is credible must, nevertheless, resolve his doubt in favor of the People and admit the evidence. To thus increase the likelihood of a conviction on proof of dubious constitutionality must be stamped as highly unreasonable and unfair. A change in the rule will help assure that a defendant's constitutional rights will not be violated since, by placing the burden on the People, the judge will be permitted to suppress evidence in cases where, for instance, he finds the testimony of each side evenly balanced on the scales of credibility and is unable to make up his mind as to who is telling the truth.

* * * It is noteworthy that commentators and judges—in addition to the New York County District Attorney—have noted the existence of possible fabrication, and the studies which have been made, based on research into arrest files and interviews with law enforcement officials, persuasively negate the court's charge that this conclusion is based on "*post hoc ergo propter hoc* reasoning." Those who recognize the problem and favor a change in the burden of proof rule do not, contrary to the majority's assertion, intend an "attack on the integrity of our entire law enforcement system." Rather, their concern is solely to promote adherence to the principles articulated in *Mapp v. Ohio.* * * *

In point of fact, the suggested modification of the rule is not without support in the decisions. Thus, Federal courts and the courts of California hold that the prosecution should bear the burden of justifying a warrantless seizure of evidence. And, indeed, our court has already engrafted one exception on the present rule; "[w]hen a search and seizure is based upon consent," we declared, "the burden of proof rests heavily upon the People to establish the voluntariness of that waiver of a constitutional right." *People v. Whitehurst,* supra; see, to same effect, *Bumper v. North Carolina,* [p. 416 supra].

In short, reason and the imperative of judicial integrity, as well as substantial authority, dictate that the burden of proving the lawfulness of a search or seizure should be cast on the People in all narcotics and gambling cases when the search or seizure has been effected without a warrant. To do less, to shift the burden of proof to the People only in the classic dropsy situation, seems to me, as it does to the New York County District Attorney, "unrealistic." This is so, as he observes, not only because an "untruthful officer fearing rejection of tailored dropsy testimony could easily shift to the other scenarios which are familiar in narcotics and gambling cases in the lower courts" but also because "it is the experience of many prosecutors and judges that the problems of credibility and fact-finding raised * * * are not limited to literal dropsy cases * * * but appear in all types of possessory narcotics and gambling cases."

BURKE, JASEN and GIBSON, JJ., concur with SCILEPPI, J. FULD, C.J., dissents and votes to reverse in a separate opinion in which BERGAN and BREITEL, JJ., concur.

Notes and Questions

1. *State variations.* Aside from the justification of a search on the basis of consent—where the burden universally is placed on the prosecution—, states vary considerably in the allocation of both the burden of going forward and the ultimate burden of proof (persuasion) on Fourth Amendment claims. Ignoring minor variations, the state's position on these burdens usually will fall within one of four general categories:

(a) Under the New York approach, as noted in *Berrios*, the prosecution has the burden of going forward—i.e., introducing evidence that, if accepted, would establish the legality of the search. See *People v. Whitehurst*, supra. Thus, in a case involving a search incident to arrest, the prosecution would initially introduce the testimony of an officer showing that probable cause for the arrest existed and that the search was within the scope permitted incident to an arrest. The ultimate burden of proof is then placed upon the defendant to rebut this evidence and prove that the search was invalid.

(b) Several states put both the initial burden of going forward and the ultimate burden of proof upon the defendant. This position has been justified on several grounds: "(a) the burden should be upon the moving party, (b) there is a presumption of regularity attending the actions of law enforcement officials, (c) relevant evidence is generally admissible and thus exceptions must be justified by those claiming the exception, and (d) [this allocation] will deter spurious allegations wasteful of court time." LaFave, § 11.2(b).

(c) A majority of the states follow the pattern of allocation adopted in the federal courts. Under this pattern, if the search was pursuant to a warrant, the defendant has the burden of proof, but if the police acted without a warrant, the burden is on the prosecution. The burden of going forward follows the burden of proof. Where there was a search without a warrant, the defendant must make a prima facie showing of that fact before the prosecution is put to its burdens. Very often, however, the parties will agree as to how the evidence was obtained and an allegation of seizure without a warrant will be sufficient. But note *People v. Carson*, 84 Cal.Rptr. 699 (App.1970) (defense could not rely on an oral motion that was "not supported by any affidavit or offer of stipulation").

As noted in LaFave, § 11.2(b), the federal pattern's "warrant-no-warrant dichotomy is typically explained on the ground that when the police have acted with a warrant 'an independent determination on the issue of probable cause has already been made by a magistrate, thereby giving rise to a presumption of legality,' while when they have acted without a warrant 'the evidence comprising probable cause is particularly within the knowledge and control of the arresting agencies.' Moreover, it is said that '[w]ithout such a rule there would be little reason for law enforcement agencies to bother with the formality of a warrant.' "

(d) In several jurisdictions, the prosecution has both the burden of going forward and the burden of proof on all Fourth Amendment objections. As noted in LaFave, § 11.2(b), the reason most frequently advanced for placing the burden on the state in all cases is "that the state is the party which seeks to use the evidence and thus ought to bear the burden of establishing that it was lawfully come by."

2. *Practical consequences of the allocation.* Of what practical significance is the allocation of the ultimate burden of proof on Fourth Amendment claims? Consider in this connection the views of the majority and dissent in *Berrios* on the relation of the burden of proof to judicial treatment of police testimony in "dropsy" cases. Assuming one shared the objective of the dissent, would a more satisfactory solution have been a direction to the lower courts that they should subject such testimony to

"close scrutiny," in much the same way that a jury is directed that testimony of an accomplice or paid informer should be "scrutinized and received with care"? See Comment, 60 Geo.L.J. 507, 519–20 (1971).

Comments of defense counsel suggest that the allocation of the burden of going forward, and even the specificity required in the motion to suppress, may be more significant than the allocation of the ultimate burden of proof. Thus, Amsterdam, *Trial Manual for the Defense of Criminal Cases* § 252 (4th ed.1984), notes that a basic tactical objective of the defense is to avoid first disclosing its factual theories, lest the police "conform their testimony" to evade those theories. If defendant is required to go forward with the evidence, he often must, as a practical matter, first take the stand to tell "his side of the story." Although the officers, as prospective witnesses, usually may be excluded from the courtroom while this testimony is given, the defendant still is not in as good a position to rebut their testimony as he would be if he testified last. The defense bearing the burden of production may also seek to satisfy this burden without using the defendant's testimony, by calling the officers as its own witnesses; but this tactic may backfire if the court is unwilling to treat the officers as "adverse" witnesses subject to impeachment. Ibid. at § 253.

3. *Policy considerations.* What bearing, if any, should the following principles, often advanced in general discussions of the allocation of the burdens of proof and evidence production, have upon the allocation of those burdens with respect to Fourth Amendment claims: (1) that the burdens should be placed on the party who has the best access to the relevant facts; (2) that the burdens should be placed "on the party desiring change"; (3) that the burdens should be allocated so as to avoid providing an incentive for use of the objection primarily to gain general discovery of the other side's case, particularly where discovery otherwise is quite limited; (4) that the burdens should be allocated so as to have "one party proving a limited ground [rather than] the other party disproving many grounds"; (5) that the burdens should be allocated in accordance with the best judicial estimate of the probabilities of the particular event having occurred; (6) that the burdens should be used to "handicap" disfavored contentions? See LaFave, § 11.2(b).

4. *Constitutional requirements.* Why was it that the defendants in *Berrios* failed to argue that the federal constitution required the prosecution to bear the burden of proof? *Bumper v. North Carolina,* p. 416 supra, generally is viewed as requiring, as a matter of constitutional law, that the prosecution bear the "burden of proving that consent [to a search] was, in fact, freely and voluntarily given." See LaFave, § 11.2(b). If the Fourth Amendment requires that the prosecution bear the burden on this issue, why not on others? The Supreme Court has stated in various opinions that the Fourth Amendment generally requires a search warrant, and "the burden is on those seeking [an] exemption from [that] requirement to show the need for it." See, e.g., *Chimel v. California,* p. 310 supra. Do such statements imply that, where a search is conducted without a warrant, the prosecution must bear the burden of proving facts that justify the search under one of the recognized exceptions to the warrant requirement, or do the statements refer only to the state's burden in appellate argument of justifying any request that the Supreme Court recognize a new or expanded exception to the warrant requirement? See LaFave, § 11.2(b) (noting that the former interpretation "would seem to be closer to the mark").

5. *Confessions. Miranda* clearly places the burden on the prosecution to respond to a *Miranda* objection by showing that the "defendant knowingly and intelligently waived his privilege against self-incrimination and his right to retained or appointed counsel" (p. 550 supra). Most jurisdic-

tions also place upon the prosecution the burdens of production and persuasion in responding to a claim that a confession was involuntary. A few states, however, place the burden of proving involuntariness on the defendant. *Lego v. Twomey,* discussed at Note 9 infra, raises serious doubts as to the constitutionality of this practice. Though concerned primarily with the applicable standard of proof, *Lego* indicated that it was the constitutional obligation of the prosecution to meet that standard of proof. See, e.g., 404 U.S. at 489, 92 S.Ct. at 627 ("the prosecution must prove at least by a preponderance of the evidence that the confession was voluntary").

6. *Identification testimony. United States v. Wade,* p. 652 supra, indicates that, once the Sixth Amendment is shown to be applicable, the prosecution carries the burden of establishing that defendant intelligently waived his right to counsel at a lineup. See *Wade,* p. 656 supra. But what is the proper allocation of the burden on an objection that a lineup or other identification procedure was so unfairly conducted as to violate due process? Several courts have assumed, without extensive discussion, that the defendant, as the moving party, bears the burden of establishing the due process violation. LaFave and Israel, § 10.4(d). But compare *People v. Young,* 176 N.W.2d 420 (Mich.App.1970), holding that the prosecution bears the burdens of production and persuasion whenever the identification procedure was conducted "out of the presence of defendant's attorney." In support of that holding the *Young* court stressed that the defendant may not even be aware that witnesses were seeking to identify him (e.g., where a "showup" was conducted through a one-way mirror), and even if aware, he still may be unable to know "who was present, * * * what was said or what facts existed that might make the [identification procedure] unnecessarily suggestive." Does the position taken in *Young* constitute an open invitation to defense "fishing expeditions," that will be "automatically available in all lineup-cases"? See *State v. Bishop,* 183 N.W.2d 536 (Minn.1971).

7. *Entrapment.* Reconsider Note 5 at p. 493 supra.

8. *Exclusionary rule limitations.* Once a constitutional violation is established, does the burden of proof necessarily lie with the prosecution to establish that its evidence is not the fruit of the poisonous tree? See e.g., *United States v. Wade,* at p. 657 supra (as to proof that the in-court identification was not tainted by the unconstitutional lineup); *Nardone v. United States,* p. 425 supra (once illegal wiretap established, government must "convince the trial court that its proof had an independent origin). Consider also *Nix v. Williams,* at p. 810 supra, as to the government's burden in establishing that the same evidence would have inevitably been discovered by lawful means.

9. *Standards of proof.* Assuming that the prosecution bears the ultimate burden of proof on a particular exclusionary rule objection, what standard of proof should apply? In LEGO v. TWOMEY, 404 U.S. 477, 92 S.Ct. 619, 30 L.Ed.2d 618 (1972), the Court rejected the contention that the voluntariness of a confession must be established by proof beyond a reasonable doubt. The state there was held not to have violated due process by applying a preponderance of the evidence standard. Justice White's opinion for the Court reasoned that *In re Winship,* 397 U.S. 358, 90 S.Ct. 1068, 25 L.Ed.2d 368 (1970), requiring proof beyond a reasonable doubt at trial, was not controlling: "Since the purpose that a voluntariness hearing is designed to serve has nothing whatever to do with improving the reliability of jury verdicts, we cannot accept the charge that judging the admissibility of a confession by a preponderance of the evidence undermines the mandate of *In re Winship.* * * * *Winship* was not concerned with standards for determining the admissibility of evidence or with the prosecution's burden of proof at a suppression hearing

when evidence is challenged on constitutional grounds. *Winship* went no further than to confirm the fundamental right that protects 'the accused against conviction except upon proof beyond a reasonable doubt of every fact necessary to constitute the crime with which he is charged.' A high standard of proof is necessary, we said, to ensure against unjust convictions by giving substance to the presumption of innocence. A guilty verdict is not rendered less reliable or less consonant with *Winship* simply because the admissibility of a confession is determined by a less stringent standard."

Lego also rejected the contention that application of a reasonable doubt standard was necessary "to give adequate protection to those values that the exclusionary rules are designed to serve." Justice White's opinion noted: [W]e are unconvinced that merely emphasizing the importance of the values served by exclusionary rules is itself sufficient demonstration that the Constitution also requires admissibility to be proved beyond reasonable doubt. Evidence obtained in violation of the Fourth Amendment has been excluded from federal criminal trials for many years. The same is true of coerced confessions offered in either federal or state trials. But, from our experience over this period of time no substantial evidence has accumulated that federal rights have suffered from determining admissibility by a preponderance of the evidence. Petitioner offers nothing to suggest that admissibility rulings have been unreliable or otherwise wanting in quality because not based on some higher standard. Without good cause, we are unwilling to expand currently applicable exclusionary rules by erecting additional barriers to placing truthful and probative evidence before state juries and by revising the standards applicable in collateral proceedings. Sound reason for moving further in this direction has not been offered here nor do we discern any at the present time. This is particularly true since the exclusionary rules are very much aimed at deterring lawless conduct by police and prosecution and it is very doubtful that escalating the prosecution's burden of proof in Fourth and Fifth Amendment suppression hearings would be sufficiently productive in this respect to outweigh the public interest in placing probative evidence before juries for the purpose of arriving at truthful decisions about guilt or innocence." [b]

10. Is *Lego* inconsistent with the philosophy underlying *Chapman v. California,* p. 796 supra? Cf. Note, 7 Harv.C.R.–C.L.L. Rev. 651 (1972), suggesting that the reasoning that led the *Lego* majority to conclude that implementation of a constitutional right did not require proof beyond a reasonable doubt could just as readily have led the Court in *Chapman* to conclude that there was no need to require the especially stringent harmless error standard imposed there. The dissent in *Lego* (see fn. b supra) also argued that the majority's position there was inconsistent with "the rule that automatically reverses a conviction when an involuntary confession was admitted at trial." Cf. Saltzburg, *Standards of Proof and Preliminary Questions of Fact,* 27 Stan.L.Rev. 271 (1975), arguing that a reasonable doubt standard should have been required in *Lego* because, inter alia, the test of involuntariness (as opposed to

b. Powell and Rehnquist, JJ., did not participate in the *Lego* decision. Justice Brennan dissented, joined by Justices Douglas and Marshall. The dissent argued that "the preponderance standard does not provide sufficient protection against the danger that involuntary confessions will be employed at trial." It noted that the preponderance standard was accepted in civil cases on the assumption that it was no more serious an error to have an erroneous decision in favor of one party or another. The same could not be said, the dissent argued, as to errors relating to the admission of confessions: "If we permit the prosecution to prove by a preponderance of the evidence that a confession was voluntary, then * * * we must be prepared to justify the view that it is no more serious in general to admit involuntary confessions than it is to exclude voluntary confessions. * * * Compelled self-incrimination is so alien to the American sense of justice that I see no way that such a view could ever be justified."

other exclusionary rule standards) is designed to exclude unreliable evidence and the admission of unreliable confessions is especially dangerous because juries give such great weight to confessions.

11. The Supreme Court noted in *Lego* that, while due process was satisfied by application of the preponderance standard, the states were always "free, pursuant to their own law, to adopt a higher standard." Several states have done exactly that. See LaFave and Israel, § 10.4. On the other hand, the states uniformly have held that the standard of proof applicable to Fourth Amendment claims, except on the issue of consent, will be the preponderance standard. Ibid. In a jurisdiction that has adopted the reasonable doubt standard for the determination of the voluntariness of confession, why shouldn't the same standard apply to search and seizure claims? See Saltzburg, supra, citing inter alia, the differences in (1) the justifications for excluding involuntary confessions as opposed to illegally seized evidence and (2) the capacity of the police to keep records and to otherwise prepare to meet a higher standard of proof in establishing the events surrounding a custodial interrogation as opposed to a typical warrantless search. The few appellate decisions considering the standard of proof applicable to due process challenges to identification procedures (a claim as to which defendant usually carries the burden, see Note 6 supra) also have adopted the preponderance standard. See, e.g., *Commonwealth v. Clifford,* 372 N.E.2d 1267 (Mass.1978).

12. Does a preponderance of the evidence standard comply with the "heavy burden" that rests upon the Government to demonstrate waiver under *Miranda* (see p. 550 supra)? It generally is assumed that it does not. The same assumption also has been made with respect to the government's burden in establishing consent to a search. See LaFave and Israel, § 10.4(c), but also noting that, since *Schneckloth* (p. 408 supra) "teaches that the test to be applied in determining the validity of the consent is 'voluntariness,'" as developed in the confession cases, *Lego* may suggest a preponderance standard also is satisfactory on this issue. Does the discussion in *Nix v. Williams* (see p. 812 supra) as to why a preponderance standard was satisfactory there, cast any light as to what standard should be applied to the consent issue in the Fourth Amendment context?

Where a heavier standard is required by Supreme Court precedent, what standard will be sufficient? Cases dealing with consent to a search generally have applied a "clear and convincing" evidence standard. In *Wade,* the Supreme Court specifically referred to the "clear and convincing" evidence standard is describing the prosecution's burden in establishing that an in-court identification was not tainted by an unconstitutional lineup identification. See *Wade* at p. 657 supra.

13. *The trier of fact.* The factfinder on the constitutionality of a search has traditionally been the judge, but prior to *Jackson v. Denno,* 378 U.S. 368, 84 S.Ct. 1774, 12 L.Ed.2d 908 (1964), many states followed one of two procedures that give factfinding responsibility to the jury in judging the voluntariness of a confession. In states following the "Massachusetts rule," the trial court initially ruled on the admissibility of the confession. If the judge concluded that the confession was involuntary, that ruling excluding the confession was final. If the judge found that the confession was voluntary, it was then admitted subject to the jury's independent determination of voluntariness. The jury received evidence of the circumstances surrounding the confession, was charged as to the voluntariness standard, and was instructed that it could not consider the confession unless it first found it to be voluntary. In states following the "New York rule," the determination of voluntariness was left primarily to the jury. The judge would make an initial determination as to whether reasonable persons could differ on the issue of voluntariness, as where

testimony was in conflict or different inferences could be drawn from undisputed facts. Unless there were "no circumstances" under which the confession could be voluntary, the voluntariness issue was passed along to the jury. The jury was instructed on the voluntariness standard and told to consider the confession only if it found it to be voluntary.

In *Jackson,* a divided (5–4) Supreme Court overruled an 11 year old precedent and held the New York procedure unconstitutional. The crux of the majority's reasoning in *Jackson* was subsequently summarized in *Lego v. Twomey,* Note 9 supra: "We concluded that the New York procedure was constitutionally defective because at no point along the way did a criminal defendant receive a clear-cut determination that the confession used against him was in fact voluntary. The trial judge was not entitled to exclude a confession merely because he himself would have found it involuntary, and, while we recognized that the jury was empowered to perform that function, we doubted it could do so reliably. Precisely because confessions of guilt, whether coerced or freely given, may be truthful and potent evidence, we did not believe a jury could be called upon to ignore the probative value of a truthful but coerced confession; it was also likely, we thought, that in judging voluntariness itself the jury would be influenced by the reliability of a confession it considered an accurate account of the facts. * * *" [c]

14. As the Court noted in *Lego, Jackson* "cast no doubt upon" the Massachusetts procedure,[d] and many states continue to use that procedure (although most follow the "orthodox" procedure of having voluntariness determined initially and finally by the judge). Why should a defendant be given a "second crack" at the voluntariness issue, before the jury, where no such opportunity is given as to Fourth Amendment or other constitutional violations?

15. Does it follow from *Lego,* that it would be improper for a trial court to hear testimony on a constitutional challenge to the admissibility of evidence without first excluding the jury? Consider WATKINS v. SOWDERS, 449 U.S. 341, 101 S.Ct. 654, 66 L.Ed.2d 549 (1981). *Watkins* involved two state cases in which hearings on the admissibility of identification testimony were held in the presence of the jury. In each case, the defense counsel, in challenging an in-court identification, sought to establish that the identification was based on a pretrial identification procedure that was so suggestive as to violate due process. Over defense objection, the challenge was heard in the presence of the jury, and was rejected by the trial judge. A divided (7–2) Supreme Court found no constitutional error. Noting that various lower courts had emphasized the prudence of holding a suppression hearing outside the presence of the jury, the majority stressed that it was concerned only with whether that practice was constitutionally required. On this issue, STEWART, J., noted for the Court:

"The Court in *Jackson* did reject the usual presumption that a jury can be relied upon to determine issues according to the trial judge's instructions, but the Court did so because of the peculiar problems the issue of the voluntariness of a confession

c. The dissenting judges in *Jackson* stressed the prior precedent upholding the New York procedure and the Court's "repeated rejection," in various contexts, of "speculation" that jurors would disregard their instructions. See also fn. d infra.

d. In distinguishing the Massachusetts procedure, the Court stressed that the judge there "himself resolves evidentiary conflicts and gives his own answer to the coercion issue" and the jury therefore only considers those confessions the judge believes to be voluntary. The dissenters responded that the acceptance of the Massachusetts rule revealed the "hollowness" of the Court's holding. They argued that the distinction between the New York and Massachusetts rule was more theoretical than real. They suggested, in particular, that in "cases of doubt," a judge operating under the Massachusetts rule was likely to "resolve the doubt in favor of admissibility, relying on the final determination by the jury."

presents. * * * Where identification evidence is at issue, however, no such special considerations justify a departure from the presumption that juries will follow instructions. It is the reliability of identification evidence that primarily determines its admissibility. *Manson v. Brathwaite* [p. 681 supra]. And the proper evaluation of evidence under the instructions of the trial judge is the very task our system must assume juries can perform. * * *

"The petitioners argue, however, * * * that the presence of the jury deterred their lawyers from cross-examining the witnesses vigorously and fully as to the possible improprieties of the pretrial identifications in these cases. The petitioners point to no specific instances in the trial when their counsel were thus deterred, and the record reveals that the cross-examination on the identity issues was, if not always effective, both active and extended. Nonetheless, the petitioners rely on a passage from *United States v. Wade* [p. 652 supra], which referred to, 'the predicament in which Wade's counsel found himself—realizing that possible unfairness at the lineup may be the sole means of attack upon the unequivocal courtroom identification, and having to probe in the dark in an attempt to discover and reveal unfairness, while bolstering the government witness' courtroom identification by bringing out and dwelling upon his prior identification.' * * * The petitioners, however, attribute undue significance to this passage. The 'predicament' described in *Wade* was no more than part of the Court's demonstration that, if identification stemming from an improperly conducted lineup was to be excluded, a courtroom identification based on such a lineup logically had to be excluded as well. A 'predicament,' if one chooses to call it that, is always presented when a lawyer decides on cross-examination to ask a question that may produce an answer unfavorable to his client. Yet, under our adversary system of justice, cross-examination has always been considered a most effective way to ascertain truth. We decline in these cases to hold that the Due Process Clause of the Fourteenth Amendment inevitably requires the abandonment of the time-honored process of cross-examination as the device best suited to determine the trustworthiness of testimonial evidence.

"A judicial determination outside the presence of the jury of the admissibility of identification evidence may often be advisable. In some circumstances, not presented here, such a determination may be constitutionally necessary. But it does not follow that the Constitution requires a *per se* rule compelling such a procedure in every case." [e]

e. The dissenting justices (Brennan, J., joined by Marshall, J.) argued that "the powerful impact that such eyewitness identification evidence has on juries, regardless of its reliability, virtually mandates that, when such evidence is inadmissible, the jury should know nothing about the evidence."

Part Three

THE COMMENCEMENT OF FORMAL PROCEEDINGS

Analysis

Chapter 12

PRETRIAL RELEASE

SECTION 1. THE RIGHT TO BAIL; PRETRIAL RELEASE PROCEDURES

MARY A. TOBORG—PRETRIAL RELEASE: A NATIONAL EVALUATION OF PRACTICES AND OUTCOMES

6–18 (National Institute of Justice, 1981).

Of the 3,488 defendants in the eight-site sample,[a] 85 percent of them secured release at some point before trial. Release rates ranged from 73 percent to 92 percent in individual sites * * *.

Viewed in historical perspective, these findings suggest a continuation of a trend toward higher release rates of defendants prior to trial. An analysis by Wayne Thomas of release rates in 20 cities in 1962 and 1971 found major increases over the time period: release rates for felony defendants increased from 48 percent to 67 percent and for misdemeanor defendants, from 60 percent to 72 percent. Nevertheless, at the end of the period, in 1971, only about half of the cities released as many as 70 percent of the defendants before trial. In contrast, each of the eight sites [in this study] had a release rate of more than 70 percent between 1976 and 1978; indeed, in all sites except one the release rates exceeded 80 percent.

Despite the increase in release rates, the detention of defendants remains a serious problem in many jurisdictions and often has contributed to jail overcrowding. Many of the defendants detained until trial were jailed for relatively long time periods: one-third of them for more than 30 days and 20 percent for more than 90 days. Additionally, defendants who secured release before trial sometimes did so only after a substantial jail term: about 3 percent of the released defendants had been jailed for 30 days or more prior to release.

The major reason for the detention of defendants was inability to post bond. Only a very small percentage of defendants were detained outright, with no possibility of release provided to them.

In general as the bond amount increased, so did the percentage of defendants detained until trial. Forty percent of the defendants with bonds of $5,000–$9,999 and 65 percent of the persons with bonds of $10,000 or more were jailed the entire pretrial period, as compared with detention rates of 25 percent for defendants with bonds of $1,001–$4,999 and 29 percent for persons with bonds of $1,000 or less.

Although bond played an important role in the detention of defendants, its impact on release was considerably less: most de-

a. The 8 sites were: Baltimore City, Md.; Baltimore Co., Md.; Washington, D.C.; Dade Co., Fla.; Louisville, Ky.; Pima Co., Ariz.; Santa Cruz Co., Cal.; and Santa Clara Co., Cal.

fendants were released *without* any conditions involving money. * * * 61.4 percent of all defendants in the sample were released on "nonfinancial" conditions (i.e., on conditions that did not involve money); for individual sites the percentage of defendants released on nonfinancial conditions ranged from 35.2 percent to 76.0 percent.

Again, these data reflect the apparent continuation of a trend documented earlier for the 1962–71 period, toward higher rates of nonfinancial release. Wayne Thomas' study of 20 cities found that rates of nonfinancial release for felony defendants increased from 5 percent in 1962 to 23 percent in 1971; for misdemeanor defendants, the increase was from 10 percent to 30 percent.

Today, a wide variety of release mechanisms are used around the country. * * * After arrest there were several ways for a defendant to secure release without appearing before a judge, bail commissioner or other magistrate of the court. First, the arresting officer could make a *field release* of the defendant. This procedure, a form of "citation release" used for minor charges, is similar to issuing a traffic ticket and does not require taking the defendant into custody. If the person is taken to a police station or jail for booking, *stationhouse release* (another type of citation release) may be approved at that time, again by law enforcement officials. * * *

Additionally, some jurisdictions had *bail schedules*, listing bail amounts for various charges. Defendants in those sites could secure release at any time by posting the bond amounts shown.

Altogether, more than one-fifth of the sample obtained release prior to an appearance before a court official. Although most of these defendants were released on nonfinancial conditions, about one-third of them posted bond, based on a bail schedule.

The remaining defendants in the sample usually appeared before a judge, bail commissioner or other magistrate within a few hours. In most of the sites studied, the magistrate received information from the local pretrial release program [b] about the defendants' community ties, criminal history and other pertinent factors.

A variety of release conditions were set by the magistrates in the sites studies. *Own recognizance* (O.R.) release was initially authorized for 35 percent of the sample. Such release usually required only a defendant's promise to appear for court. Although some jurisdictions attached other conditions to O.R. release, such as a requirement to call the pretrial release program periodically or to reside within the area until trial, defendants were rarely prosecuted for violating those conditions.

Supervised release sometimes entailed the defendant's reporting to a social service agency for treatment (for drug, alcohol or mental health problems) or employment assistance. Often, however, supervision consisted only of more frequent reporting to the pretrial release program than was required for defendants released on their own recognizance.

Under *third party custody* release, a third party was formally charged with responsibility for the defendant and could, if necessary, return the person to court for reconsideration of release conditions. The third party was usually a relative, social service agency or pretrial release program.

Instead of the nonfinancial release conditions discussed above, magistrates could

b. Typically these programs (1) interview defendants in custody to obtain information about their backgrounds and ties to the community, (2) verify the information provided by the defendants, (3) determine (often by a point system, e.g., + 3 for a steady job, + 1 for continued local residence, - 1 for prior violent felony conviction) which defendants qualify for nonfinancial release, (4) submit release recommendations to the court, and (5) attempt to ensure that persons released return to court as scheduled. For an assessment of these functions, see Thomas, *Pretrial Release Programs* (Law Enforcement Assistance Administration, 1977).

require the posting or promise of money bond. The least restrictive financial release condition was *unsecured bond*: in this case the bond amount had to be paid to the court only if the defendant failed to appear. Both deposit bond and full bond required the defendant to raise money before release could be obtained. Under *deposit bond* a percentage (usually 10 percent) of the bail amount was posted with the court, and most of that "deposit" was returned if the defendant appeared for all court dates. Failure to appear, however, made the person who posted the deposit liable for the full face value of the bond. * * *

Full bond was usually arranged through a surety, or bondsman, who required payment of a nonrefundable fee for this service. Typically, bondsmen's fees were about ten percent of the face value of the bond. * * *

Most jurisdictions have a formal process for reconsidering the bond amounts of defendants detained because they cannot make bail. At this reconsideration, or "bail review," any type of release may be ordered: nonfinancial release may be set; or the bond may be lowered, remain unchanged or even be raised. For the sample studied, approximately half of all defendants for whom bail was set by a magistrate had their bonds reconsidered. As a result of this reconsideration, about one-half of the defendants were released on nonfinancial conditions.

Any defendant who had a bond set but was not released at bail review could, of course, secure release prior to trial by raising the bond amount or, more commonly, the bondsman's fee. About one-fourth of the defendants whose bonds were reconsidered secured release after posting the revised bond amount, which was usually a lower sum than had been set initially.

Thus, * * * the release process involved a variety of criminal justice officials and provided a number of release options. The process encompassed several stages at which a defendant could secure release, including arrest, booking, initial appearance in court and bail review. This process can be viewed as a sorting mechanism, which at each stage permitted additional defendants to secure release. The net result of the process was to separate defendants into two groups: released and detained. Additionally, released defendants could be divided into those who secured release on nonfinancial conditions and those for whom money was involved.

The release outcomes of defendants varied along many characteristics. * * * When compared with released defendants, detained defendants were more likely to have been charged with crimes against persons, economic crimes, crimes against public morality and miscellaneous crimes; they were less likely to have been charged with drug crimes and crimes against public order. When compared with persons released nonfinancially, defendants released on financial conditions were more likely to have been accused of crimes against persons and less likely to have been charged with crimes against public order; the incidence of the other charge categories was very similar for both groups.

In addition to charge differences, release outcomes varied by the defendant's prior record. Detained defendants had an average of 9.5 prior arrests, while persons released on financial conditions averaged 5.2 prior arrests and defendants released on nonfinancial conditions had 2.9 prior arrests. Comparisons based on the average number of prior convictions were similar: 4.0 for detained defendants, 2.0 for persons released on financial conditions and 1.3 for individuals released on nonfinancial conditions.

[D]etained defendants were less likely than released defendants to have been living with spouses when arrested and were more likely to have been living alone or with unreleased persons. Detained defendants were also much more likely than released defendants to have been unemployed when arrested: 59 percent of detained defendants were unemployed, as compared with 38 percent of released defendants. [But] there were no important differences in the length of local residence for defendants with different release outcomes.

Release outcomes varied along many dimensions besides charge, prior record and community ties. To identify the most important factors associated with release outcomes, multivariate analyses were conducted. * * *

The results of all three analyses were striking similar in terms of the variables that were found to have the greatest effect on release outcomes and release decisions. *Program recommendations* had an expecially strong impact. In particular, a program recommendation of bail release was importantly associated with the detention of defendants, with their release on financial conditions when released, and with their having had financial release conditions set by court magistrates. Program recommendations for deposit bail, conditional release and denial of own recognizance release were also associated with detention or financial release, as was the lack of a release recommendation.

Other variables importantly related to release outcomes and release decisions included charges of crimes against persons, a larger number of arrest charges, involvement with the criminal justice system at the time of arrest (i.e., on probation, parole, or pretrial release for another charge) and a record of prior failure to appear. Defendants with these characteristics were more likely to have had financial release conditions set by magistrates and to have secured release, if at all, through financial mechanisms.

For most defendants in most jurisdictions the legal basis of release decisions is whether the person will appear for court. Consequently, restrictions on release or the imposition of conditions that must be met to secure release can occur only if these are needed to prevent the defendant's flight. * * *

The overwhelmingly majority of the defendants studied appeared for court: in the eight-site sample, 87.4 percent of all released defendants appeared for every required court date. Conversely, 12.6 percent of the released defendants missed at least one court appearance. * * *

Many defendants who miss court appearances may have no intention of trying to evade justice. Instead, they have forgotten the court date, have become ill and neglected to notify the court or in some cases have been jailed on another charge.

Twenty-nine percent of the defendants who missed a court appearance returned to court of their own volition within 30 days, and an additional 16 percent returned voluntarily after that time. Approximately one-third of the defendants were returned to court as a result of an arrest, usually for another charge. Moreover, six percent of the defendants who missed court dates were tried in absentia or forfeited bail in lieu of appearance (a type of fine). Consequently, 17 percent of the defendants who failed to appear for court were still at large at the time data were collected for the National Evaluation of Pretrial Release. This is a "fugitive" rate of two percent of all released defendants. * * *

Altogether, the released defendants in the sample were required to make 8,896 appearances (for all charges associated with the original arrest) and showed up for 8,361, or 94 percent, of them. Thus, only six percent of all court appearances were missed.

The overall rate of release was not systematically related to the rate of court appearance across the eight sites. The jurisdiction with the highest release rate also had one of the highest court appearance rates. The site with the lowest release rate had a court appearance rate roughly in the middle of the rate range for all sites.

Nor were there systematic differences in court appearance rates for defendants released on nonfinancial versus financial conditions across the eight sites. * * *

The evaluation also compared defendants who appeared for all court dates with persons who missed at least one court date, to determine whether the two groups had very different characteristics. By charge category, defendants who failed to appear were more likely than other released defendants to have been charged with economic crimes and less likely to have been charged with crimes against persons or drug crimes * * *.[c]

In terms of prior record, defendants who missed court appearances had more serious criminal records than persons who reliably showed up for court. Defendants who failed to appear had an average of 5.8 prior arrests and 2.4 prior convictions, as compared with 3.2 prior arrests and 1.3 prior convictions for defendants who always appeared for court.

There were also differences in community ties. Defendants who missed court dates were less likely than other released defendants to have been living with spouses and were more likely to have been living with unrelated persons. They were also more likely to have been unemployed: 49 percent of the defendants who failed to appear were unemployed, as compared with 37 percent of the released defendants who made all their court appearances. Additionally, defendants who missed court appearances had lived in the local area a shorter time; nevertheless, their average length of local residence was almost 19 years.

As was the case for the release outcomes discussed [earlier], court appearance outcomes varied along many dimensions besides charge, prior record and community ties. To identify the most important factors associated with failure to appear, multivariate analyses were conducted, similar in nature to those performed for release outcomes and decisions. * * *

The analyses did not identify a set of characteristics that could be used to predict with reasonable accuracy the defendants who would fail to appear. This inability to develop accurate predictors reflects the difficulty of trying to predict an event that is relatively rare and experienced by persons with diverse characteristics. Only a relatively small percentage (12.6 percent) of defendants failed to appear, and those individuals did not have strikingly different characteristics from other defendants.

Under the Bail Reform Act of 1984, set out in Supp. App. B, "release of the person on his personal recognizance, or upon execution of an unsecured appearance bond in an amount specified by the court" is the preferred form of release, as it is to be utilized "unless the judicial officer determines that such release will not reasonably assure the appearance of the person as required."[d] Otherwise, the judicial officer may release the person "on a condition or combination of conditions," but he must select "the least restrictive * * * condition or combination of conditions, that he determines will reasonably assure the appearance of the person as required." The Act lists many possible conditions, including that the person "execute a bail bond" or that he do various things while

c. But consider Clarke, Freeman & Koch, *The Effectiveness of Bail Systems* 34–35 (1976), a study of 756 defendants released on bail in Charlotte, North Carolina, concludes that there is "no significant relationship between the type of offense charged and bail risk," and that "the amount of time elapsing from the defendant's release until the disposition of his case by the court * * * must be considered the variable of greatest importance."

d. Here, as elsewhere, another consideration is whether release "will endanger the safety of any other person or the community." This preventive detention aspect of the Act is considered in § 2 of this Chapter.

on release (e.g., maintain employment, comply with a curfew, return to custody during evening hours). However, the judicial officer "may not impose a financial condition that results in the pretrial detention of the person." [e] A person may be detained pending trial in certain situations (e.g., where there is "a serious risk that the person will flee") when "no condition or combination of conditions will reasonably assure the appearance of the person as required." [f]

CONSTITUTIONAL LIMITS ON THE PRETRIAL RELEASE PROCESS

1. In STACK v. BOYLE, 342 U.S. 1, 72 S.Ct. 1, 96 L.Ed. 3 (1951), indictments had been returned charging the 12 petitioners with conspiring to violate the Smith Act (which made it a crime to advocate the overthrow of the government by force or violence). Bail was fixed in the district court in the uniform amount of $50,000 for each petitioner. Petitioners then moved to reduce bail on the ground that the bail as fixed was excessive under the Eighth Amendment, and in support submitted statements as to their financial resources, family relationships, health, prior criminal records, and other information. The only evidence offered by the government was a certified record showing that four persons previously convicted under the Smith Act had forfeited bail. Though the petitioners' factual statements were uncontroverted at the hearing on the motion, the motion was denied. The same district court thereafter denied writs of habeas corpus applied for by the petitioners, and the court of appeals affirmed. The Supreme Court granted the petition for certiorari, and held that bail had "not been fixed by proper methods" and that "petitioners' remedy is by [a renewed] motion to reduce bail" in the district court. VINSON, C.J., stated for the Court:

"From the passage of the Judiciary Act of 1789, to the present * * *, federal law has unequivocally provided that a person arrested for a non-capital offense *shall* be admitted to bail. This traditional right to freedom before conviction permits the unhampered preparation of a defense, and serves to prevent the infliction of punishment prior to conviction. * * * Unless this right to bail before trial is preserved, the presumption of innocence, secured only after centuries of struggle, would lose its meaning.

"The right to release before trial is conditioned upon the accused's giving adequate assurance that he will stand trial and submit to sentence if found guilty. * * * Like the ancient practice of securing the oaths of responsible persons to stand as sureties for the accused, the modern practice of requiring a bail bond or the deposit of a sum of money subject to forfeiture serves as additional assurance of the presence of an accused. Bail set at a figure higher than an amount reasonably calculated to fulfill this purpose is 'excessive' under the Eighth Amendment.

e. In *United States v. Szott,* 768 F.2d 159 (7th Cir.1985), declining to reduce defendant's $1 million cash bail on "his bare say-so that he cannot post the bail," the court noted: "The statute does not require that a defendant be able to post the bail 'readily.' The purpose of bail is not served unless losing the sum would be a deeply-felt hurt to the defendant and his family; the hurt must be so severe that defendant will return for trial rather than flee. This implies that a court must be able to induce a defendant to go to great lengths to raise the funds without violating the condition in § 3142(c) that bail may not be used to deny release altogether."

f. In *United States v. Orta,* 760 F.2d 887 (8th Cir.1985), the court stated: "In this case, the district court erred in interpreting the 'reasonably assure' standard set forth in the statute as a requirement that release conditions 'guarantee' community safety and the defendant's appearance. Such an interpretation contradicts both the framework and the intent of the pretrial release and detention provisions of the 1984 Act. Congress envisioned the pretrial detention of only a fraction of accused individuals awaiting trial. The district court's interpretation, however, virtually mandates the detention of almost every pretrial defendant: no other safeguards can 'guarantee' the avoidance of the statutory concerns."

"Since the function of bail is limited, the fixing of bail for any individual defendant must be based upon standards relevant to the purpose of assuring the presence of that defendant. The traditional standards as expressed in the Federal Rules of Criminal Procedure[a] are to be applied in each case to each defendant. In this case petitioners are charged with offenses under the Smith Act and, if found guilty, their convictions are subject to review with the scrupulous care demanded by our Constitution. * * * Upon final judgment of conviction, petitioners face imprisonment of not more than five years and a fine of not more than $10,000. It is not denied that bail for each petitioner has been fixed in a sum much higher than that usually imposed for offenses with like penalties and yet there has been no factual showing to justify such action in this case. The Government asks the courts to depart from the norm by assuming, without the introduction of evidence, that each petitioner is a pawn in a conspiracy and will, in obedience to a superior, flee the jurisdiction. To infer from the fact of indictment alone a need for bail in an unusually high amount is an arbitrary act. Such conduct would inject into our own system of government the very principles of totalitarianism which Congress was seeking to guard against in passing the statute under which petitioners have been indicted.

"If bail in an amount greater than that usually fixed for serious charges of crimes is required in the case of any of the petitioners, that is a matter to which evidence should be directed in a hearing so that the constitutional rights of each petitioner may be preserved. In the absence of such a showing, we are of the opinion that the fixing of bail before trial in these cases cannot be squared with the statutory and constitutional standards for admission to bail."

As the Supreme Court noted in *Schilb v. Kuebel,* p. 856 infra, "the Eighth Amendment's proscription of excessive bail has been assumed to have application to the States through the Fourteenth Amendment."

2. Justice Jackson, in a separate opinion in *Stack v. Boyle,* declared it would not be correct to say "that every defendant is entitled to such bail as he can provide." Compare the observations of Justice Douglas in *Bandy v. United States,* 81 S.Ct. 197, 5 L.Ed.2d 218 (1960): "To continue to demand a substantial bond which the defendant is unable to secure raises considerable problems for the equal administration of the law. We have held that an indigent defendant is denied equal protection of the law if he is denied an appeal on equal terms with other defendants, solely because of his indigence. *Griffin v. Illinois* [p. 105 supra]. Can an indigent be denied freedom, where a wealthy man would not, because he does not happen to have enough property to pledge for his freedom?[b]

"It would be unconstitutional to fix excessive bail to assure that a defendant will not gain his freedom. *Stack v. Boyle.* Yet in the case of an indigent defendant, the fixing of bail in even a modest amount may have the practical effect of denying him release. * * * The wrong done by denying release is not limited to the denial of freedom alone. That denial may have other consequences. In case of reversal, he will have served all or part of a sentence under an erroneous judgment. Imprisoned, a man may have no opportunity to investigate his case, to cooperate with his counsel, to earn the money that is still

a. The reference is to Rule 46(c), which then stated: "Amount. If the defendant is admitted to bail, the amount thereof shall be such as in the judgment of the commissioner or court or judge or justice will insure the presence of the defendant, having regard to the nature and circumstances of the offense charged, the weight of the evidence against him, the financial ability of the defendant to give bail and the character of the defendant."

b. Consider, in this regard, *Tate v. Short,* p. 106 supra; and *Williams v. Illinois,* p. 106 supra.

necessary for the fullest use of his right to appeal."[c]

3. Under a traditional bail system relying exclusively upon financial conditions, what amount of bail would be permissible under *Stack v. Boyle* in the following situations? What should the disposition be in each instance if the 1984 federal Act were applicable?

(a) "Golding, with a previous narcotics conviction, is now indicted on four counts of narcotics law violations (and one count of passport law violation), upon which he faces a maximum exposure of imprisonment of not less than ten years to life imprisonment, forfeiture, plus fines in excess of $170,000. Golding had been a fugitive for approximately two years before his arrest, had received three passports under various aliases, was currently unemployed, and had infrequent family contacts (he had not seen his parents for over two years), and had no significant community ties. A drug enforcement agency officer testified as to a government showing that Golding had dealt in multi-hundred thousand dollar cocaine deals, and was known to have several hundred thousand dollars in banks around the country and in foreign accounts." *United States v. Golding,* 742 F.2d 840 (5th Cir.1984).

(b) "It was shown that appellant voluntarily surrendered to the police officers following the shooting and had 'cooperated' with them to the extent of confessing to the shooting of deceased, the confession being found in our record.

"Appellant testified that he was a lifelong resident of the City of Amarillo and had attended school there; that he had never been convicted of any offense other than traffic violations and had never received a probated sentence. He was nineteen years of age at the time of the hearing. His father had been employed in the sanitation department of the City of Amarillo for twenty-five years as a truck driver; his mother also worked but her occupation was not disclosed. He was a part-time dishwasher and hay hauler.

"Appellant also testified that he had no money, credit, property, assets or savings of his own; but, that his father had obtained $500 (the inference in our record being that he borrowed it from a credit union), but that was all the funds he had to procure a bond to secure his release." *Ex parte Walton,* 583 S.W.2d 786 (Tex.Crim. App.1979).

(c) Defendant was charged with five counts of delivery of a controlled substance, carrying maximum penalties totalling 220 years. A report of the pretrial release officer "showed that the defendant: 1. Resides at his present home with his wife and daughter, where he has lived for six and one-half years; 2. Has three children, two of whom are in college in Indi-

c. Are there yet other consequences? Consider *Bellamy v. Judges and Justices,* 342 N.Y.S.2d 137 (1973), in which the bail system was challenged on the basis of the results of a study of 857 closed cases by the Legal Aid Society in conjunction with the Columbia University Bureau of Applied Social Research. As noted in the Plaintiffs' Memorandum: "The study, explained at length in the text, shows in essence the following: Those people who must wait in jail for the disposition of the criminal charges against them because they do not have enough money to purchase their freedom are far more often convicted, far more often given a prison term, and far more often given a long prison term than those people who obtain their release during this time. This disparity in treatment between those detained and those released is not accounted for by any factor related to the merits of the cases, such as the seriousness and nature of the charges, the weight of the evidence and the presence or absence of aggravated circumstances, prior criminal record, family and community ties, or the amount of bail. For example, a first offender who is detained in lieu of bail is more than three times as likely to be convicted and almost twice as likely to get a prison sentence as a recidivist with more than ten prior arrests who is released. The differences in outcome between the two groups of people, the detained and the released, are accounted for only by the fact of pre-trial detention itself."

The court upheld the constitutionality of the bail system, reasoning: "It is not because bail is required that the defendant is later convicted. It is because he is likely to be convicted that bail may be required." Thus, the statistics indicating that "those denied bail are more likely to be convicted * * * shows the system is working."

ana, and one of whom is in high school in Elkhart; 3. Has been married for twenty-five years and is buying his home, mortgaged through a local bank; 4. Has been a resident of Elkhart for twelve and one-half years; 5. Holds a Masters Degree in Biophysics and has completed work toward a Ph.D.; 6. Is Chairman of the Board and fifty percent (50%) shareholder in Geocel Corporation, located in Elkhart; 7. Has no prior criminal history; and that he 8. Has no assets outside the Elkhart area. Those assets which are available to him include equity in a home worth approximately $160,000–$180,000, a third interest in a Piper Cub airplane being financed through a local bank, and stock in his corporation worth approximately $800,000 but which is subject to buy-sell agreements, in accordance with which the stock may not be encumbered or pledged." *Sherelis v. State,* 452 N.E.2d 411 (Ind.App.1983).

4. In PUGH v. RAINWATER, 557 F.2d 1189 (5th Cir.1977), involving a challenge to the Florida bail system, the court, per SIMPSON, J., first concluded that money bail is not necessary to promote the state's interest in assuring the accused's appearance, as in the event of nonappearance only the bondsman loses money, and the defendant loses the money he posts with the bondsman whether or not he appears. The court then continued:

"These valid criticisms of the professional bondsman system persuade us to the view that, in the case of indigents, money bail is irrelevant in promoting the state's interest in assuring appearance. The indigent cannot on his own pay the amount of bail upon which his release has been conditioned. Unless a friend or relative qualifies as surety * * * and is willing to post bond, the indigent must resort to the professional bondsman. Even if the bondsman deems him an acceptable risk, he is unable to pay the bondsman's fee. The incongruity of a bail system premised on the risk of forfeiting property is apparent: Those who can afford to pay a bondsman do so and thus avoid risking forfeiture of their property; indigents, who cannot afford to pay a bondsman, have no property to forfeit in the first place.

"The real assurance of appearance under the present system is the risk of forfeiture assumed by the bondsman. Because the bondsman does not want to lose money, he has a powerful incentive to make sure that the defendant for whom he is surety appears at trial. Thus, the bondsman has long enjoyed legal protection as a modern day bounty hunter, entitled to arrest his principal 'even under extreme circumstances.' In this sense, the accused pays the bondsman to perform a police function—apprehension of a person who has jumped bail. An indigent defendant released on his own recognizance would face similar consequences. Presumably, then, the deterrence factor is comparable regardless of whether money bail has been posted.

"Even though it is manifest to us that money bail is not always necessary to assure a defendant's appearance, it is necessary to consider whether other 'less drastic' alternatives are available to the State. The Supreme Court of Florida in amending its rule regarding pretrial release, has in effect conceded that many alternatives to money bail are available. It has adopted five additional forms of release,[d] none of which is conditioned on a defendant's ability to pay. * * *

"While the new Florida rule expands the options available for pretrial release, it does not provide that indigent defendants will be required to pay money bail only in the event that no other form of release will

d. Namely, (i) release on personal recognizance or unsecured bond, (ii) release into the custody of a designated person or organization, (iii) release with restrictions on travel, association or place of abode, (iv) release upon deposit of 10% of the amount specified in an appearance bond, or (v) release on some other condition, such as that defendant return to custody after specified hours.

reasonably assure their appearance at trial. Because it gives the judge essentially unreviewable discretion to impose money bail, the rule retains the discriminatory vice of the former system: When a judge decides to set money bail, the indigent will be forced to remain in jail. We hold that equal protection standards are not satisfied unless the judge is required to consider less financially onerous forms of release before he imposes money bail. Requiring a presumption in favor of non-money bail accommodates the State's interest in assuring the defendant's appearance at trial as well as the defendant's right to be free pending trial, regardless of his financial status. * * *

"Our holding is not that money bail may never be imposed on an indigent defendant. The record before us does not justify our telling the State of Florida that in no case will money bail be necessary to assure a defendant's appearance. We hold only that equal protection standards require a presumption against money bail and in favor of those forms of release which do not condition pretrial freedom on an ability to pay."

Upon rehearing en banc, 572 F.2d 1053 (5th Cir.1978), the Court, per Vance, J., expressed "no doubt that in the case of an indigent, whose appearance at trial could reasonably be assured by one of the alternative forms of release, pretrial confinement for inability to post money bail would constitute imposition of an excessive restraint." But the new Florida rule (because it mandates that "all relevant factors" be considered in determining "what form of release is necessary to assure the defendant's appearance") does not require such a result, and therefore is not unconstitutional on its face. "Further adjudication of the merits of a constitutional challenge addressed to it should await presentation of a proper record reflecting application by the courts of the State of Florida." [e]

Clark, J., specially concurring, noted: "I voted for en banc reconsideration because I thought that the panel opinion approach had the inevitable effect of rendering monetary bail unconstitutional, and because I considered that analysis misfocused and wrong. I cannot read the Constitution to either prohibit monetary bail or require a hierarchy of assurances of appearance. The Constitution's only explicit limitation on the imposition of bail is the eighth amendment's command that it may not be excessive. This constitutional imperative does not prevent a state from continuing to maintain a system for pretrial release of all persons based on monetary bail alone. That a state may also permit persons incarcerated pending trial to obtain their freedom through other means should not create a constitutional requirement that a priority order be developed among the means permitted."

5. *Kinney v. Lenon,* 425 F.2d 209 (9th Cir.1970), involved a 17-year-old detained in a juvenile detention home pending trial in juvenile court on charges arising out of a schoolyard fight. He alleged that there were many potential witnesses to the fight, that he could not identify them by name but would recognize them by sight, that his attorneys were white though he and the potential witnesses were black, that his attorneys would consequently have great practical difficulty in interviewing and lining up the witnesses, and that he was the sole person who could do so. The court concluded:

"We * * * are of the opinion that, in the peculiar circumstances of this case, failure to permit appellant's release for the purpose of aiding the preparation of his defense unconstitutionally interfered with his due-process right to a fair trial.

"The ability of an accused to prepare his defense by lining up witnesses is fundamental, in our adversary system, to his

e. Simpson, J., joined by three other members of the court, dissenting, saw no reason for abstention, arguing that the 1977 Florida rule "ensconced the practice which the [state officials], in 1971, swore they followed" and which was the basis of the panel decision.

chances of obtaining a fair trial. Recognition of this fact of course underlies the bail system. But it is equally implicit in the requirements that trial occur near in time, and place (U.S.Const.Amend. VI) to the offense, and that the accused have compulsory process to obtain witnesses in his behalf. Indeed, compulsory process as a practical matter would be of little value without an opportunity to contact and screen potential witnesses before trial.

"This is not a case where release from detention is sought simply for the convenience of the appellant. There is here a strong showing that the appellant is the only person who can effectively prepare his own defense. We may take notice, as judges and lawyers, of the difficulties often encountered, even by able and conscientious counsel, in overcoming the apathy and reluctance of potential witnesses to testify. It would require blindness to social reality not to understand that these difficulties may be exacerbated by the barriers of age and race. Yet the alternative to some sort of release for appellant is to cast the entire burden of assembling witnesses onto his attorneys, with almost certain prejudice to appellant's case." [f]

6. SCHILB v. KUEBEL, 404 U.S. 357, 92 S.Ct. 479, 30 L.Ed.2d 502 (1971), upheld against a due process and equal protection challenge an Illinois statute which provided for the pretrial release of an eligible accused by: (1) personal recognizance; (2) execution of a bail bond and deposit of cash equal to 10% of the bond, in which event 10% of the amount deposited (i.e., 1% of the amount of the bond) was retained by the state as "bail bond costs"; or (3) execution of bail bond and deposit of the full amount of the bail, in which event there is no charge or retention. Appellant Schilb had utilized the 10% provision, depositing $75 on a $750 bond, and his challenge was directed to the $7.50 that was retained by the state after he was subsequently acquitted on one charge and convicted on another. Justice Blackmun's opinion for the majority noted:

"Prior to 1964 the professional bail bondsman system with all its abuses was in full and odorous bloom in Illinois. Under that system the bail bondsman customarily collected the maximum fee (10% of the amount of the bond) permitted by statute, and retained that entire amount even though the accused fully satisfied the conditions of the bond. Payment of this substantial 'premium' was required of the good risk as well as of the bad. The results were that a heavy and irretrievable burden fell upon the accused, to the excellent profit of the bondsman, and that professional bondsmen, and not the courts, exercised significant control over the actual workings of the bail system. One of the stated purposes of the new bail provisions in the 1963 Code was to rectify this offensive situation.[g] The purpose appears to have been accomplished. It is said that

f. See also *United States v. Reese,* 463 F.2d 830 (D.C.Cir.1972), holding that where limited custodial release offered the only means by which the defendant could present a viable defense to a murder charge, a good faith representation by the defendant that there were witnesses who could exculpate him, but that he knew them by sight and not by name, constituted a sufficient showing of "good cause" under D.C.Code § 23–1321(h)(2) to warrant defendant's release in custody of a U.S. marshal in order to obtain witnesses.

g. Although the maximum fee that may be charged by a professional bondsman is ordinarily regulated by state law, the bondsman is not required to provide a bond for every person willing to pay that fee. In some instances, the bondsman may insist that the person also provide an interest in real property or stock as collateral. In others, as a matter of local practice, the bondsman may refuse to provide bonds in certain types of cases or for certain types of defendants. By demanding additional security or refusing to provide a bond, the bondsman may deny release to a person even though the court, in setting bail, may have assumed that the person would obtain his release by paying the standard premium. On the other side, if the court miscalculates and assumes that a person will not be able to obtain a bond of a certain amount without posting substantial security, the bondsman may provide release on more lenient terms than the court anticipated if he only demands the standard fee. For these and other reasons various commentators have argued that the role of the bondsman be the bail bondsman abruptly disappeared in Illinois 'due primarily to the success of the ten percent bail deposit provision.'

"Bail, of course, is basic to our system of law, and the Eighth Amendment's proscription of excessive bail has been assumed to have application to the States through the Fourteenth Amendment. But we are not at all concerned here with any fundamental right to bail or with any Eighth Amendment-Fourteenth Amendment question of bail excessiveness. Our concern, instead, is with the 1% cost-retention provision. This smacks of administrative detail and of procedure and is hardly to be classified as a 'fundamental' right or as based upon any suspect criterion. The applicable measure, therefore, must be the traditional one: Is the distinction drawn by the statutes invidious and without rational basis?

"[Appellant argues] * * * that [the 1% charge] is imposed on the poor and nonaffluent and not on the rich and affluent * * *. But it is by no means certain, as the appellants suggest, that the 10% deposit provision under § 110–7 is a provision for the benefit of the poor and the less affluent and that the full-deposit provision of § 110–8 is one for the rich and the more affluent. It should be obvious that the poor man's real hope and avenue for relief is the personal recognizance provision of § 110–2. We do not presume to say, as the appellants in their brief intimate, that § 110–2 is not utilized by Illinois judges and made available for the poor and the less affluent. Neither is it assured, as the appellants also suggest, that the affluent will take advantage of the full-deposit provision of § 110–8 with no retention charge, and that the less affluent are relegated to the 10% deposit provision of § 110–7 and the 1% retention charge. The record is silent, but the flow indeed may be the other way. The affluent, more aware of and more experienced in the marketplace, may see the advantage, in these days of high interest rates, in retaining the use of 90% of the bail amount. A 5% or greater return on this 90% in a short period of time more than offsets the 1% retention charge. In other words, it is by no means clear that the route of § 110–8 is more attractive to the affluent defendant than the § 110–7 route.[h] The situation, therefore, wholly apart from the fact that appellant Schilb himself has not pleaded indigency, is not one where we may assume that the Illinois plan works to deny relief to the poor man merely because of his poverty."[i]

7. *Ackies v. Purdy,* 322 F.Supp. 38 (S.D.Fla.1970), was a class action challenging the use of master bond schedules for the setting of bail. It was shown that the booking officer in the sheriff's department set bail pursuant to a schedule which only took account of the nature of the offense, and did not involve consideration of the defendant's background, community ties, or financial ability. A defendant who could not obtain release remained in jail from three days to three weeks before he was brought before a judge. The court held: (1) that "since procedural due pro-

eliminated. Bondsmen argue, however, that they are needed since various aspects of their practice—e.g., keeping contact with persons released on bail, and their known "effectiveness" in recapturing defendants who jump bail—serve to encourage prompt appearance by persons released on bond. Opponents argue that bondsmen do not in fact serve these functions, and, in any event, these functions may be more ably provided by public agencies.

h. As noted in Snouffer, *An Article of Faith Abolishes Bail in Oregon,* 53 Or.L.Rev. 273, 313 (1974): "While a number of jurisdictions now permit defendants to deposit ten per cent of the security amount, * * * Illinois and Oregon leave to the defendant the right to decide whether to deposit ten per cent. Most other jurisdictions permit the magistrate to decide whether the defendant is required to deposit the full amount. These provisions usually have the effect of forcing the defendant to rely upon a bondsman."

i. Justices Stewart and Brennan dissented on other grounds relating to the state's failure to impose a similar retention fee upon persons who utilized the full-deposit provision. Justice Douglas dissented on the ground that the fee actually amounted to the imposition of court costs upon persons subsequently acquitted.

cess requires a hearing in various administrative proceedings [citing *Goldberg v. Kelly,* 397 U.S. 254, 90 S.Ct. 1011, 25 L.Ed.2d 287 (1970), holding an evidentiary hearing is required before welfare payments may be discontinued], a fortiori, it requires a hearing before depriving a person of his liberty for periods of days, weeks, or months"; and (2) that the procedure also violated the equal protection clause because it is based upon an irrelevant classification, as "a poor man with strong ties in the community may be more likely to appear than a man with some cash and no community involvement."

8. Is a bail hearing a "critical stage" at which there is a constitutional right to counsel? Cf. *Coleman v. Alabama* at p. 943 infra (preliminary hearing is a critical stage because, inter alia, "counsel can also be influential * * * in making effective arguments for the accused on such matters as * * * bail").

9. Who should have the burden of producing evidence and the burden of proof at the bail hearing? Consider *Van Atta v. Scott,* 613 P.2d 210 (Cal.1980), holding (1) that the burden of *producing evidence* to establish defendant's ties to the community is on the defendant, as he "is clearly the best source for this information and for names of individuals who could verify such information" and "has a substantial incentive to cooperate in providing this information"; (2) that the burden of *producing evidence* regarding defendant's prior appearances or flight and the severity of the sentence he faces is on the prosecution, as "this information should be relatively easy and inexpensive for the prosecution to secure"; and (3) that "due process requires the burden of *proof* concerning the detainee's likelihood of appearing for future court proceedings to be borne by the prosecution," as so placing the burden "helps to preserve the respect for the individual's liberty and for the presumption of innocence that lies at the foundation of our judicial system, to maintain the respect and confidence of the community in the uniform application of the law and to systematically correct certain biases inherent in the OR decision-making process." With respect to the uniformity point, the court noted that because "the decision being made is predictive in nature" it is "peculiarly subject to abuse." On the matter of inherent biases, the court reasoned that anti-defendant distortion can easily occur because defendant's "incarceration prevents him from effectively locating witnesses or gathering other evidence to establish his local contacts and personal reliability" and because the "not infrequent practice" of overcharging "gives an inaccurate picture to the trial court of the detainee's likelihood of fleeing the jurisdiction."

10. In *State v. Williams,* 343 A.2d 29 (N.H.1975), the court held: "Defendant's own testimony regarding the crime may be critical to a court's determination whether he should be set free pending trial. Since the 'law favors the release of defendants pending determination of guilt or innocence', a defendant should be encouraged to testify at a hearing on a motion to set bail without the fear that what he says may later be used to incriminate him." [j]

Compare *United States v. Dohm,* 618 F.2d 1169 (5th Cir.1980), holding that defendant's statements at his bail hearing were inadmissible at trial because "the magistrate failed to accurately advise Dohm of his *Miranda* rights." But, the court rejected the broader claim by Dohm that in any event "he was compelled to forfeit his fifth amendment right to remain silent, in order to safeguard his eighth amendment right to reasonable bail." The defendant's

j. If the defendant makes incriminating statements to the bail agency interviewer, should these be admissible against the defendant at trial? See *State v. Winston,* 219 N.W.2d 617 (Minn.1974), holding such a statement inadmissible where the agency manual prohibits asking the defendant about "the offense with which he is charged," as it is "appropriate to require that the state honor such an agreement."

analogy to *Simmons v. United States,* p. 781 supra, was rejected by the court because in *Simmons* the Supreme Court stressed that "at one time, a defendant who wished to assert a fourth amendment objection was required to show that he was the owner or possessor of the seized property or that he had a possessory interest in the searched premises," while by contrast "a defendant at a bail bond hearing need not divulge the facts in his case in order to receive the benefits of the eighth amendment right to bail." A dissent questioned the latter conclusion, noting that the constitutional guarantee was "not just the right to bail, but the right to non-excessive bail," and that in the instant case "the defendant not unreasonably concluded that the recommended amount of bail would be determined to be appropriate for him unless he rebutted the government testimony portraying him as a big-time drug dealer." See also Note, 94 Harv.L.Rev. 426, 437 (1980), concluding that "*Dohm* represents a clearly impermissible compelled election."

11. In *Harris v. United States,* 404 U.S. 1232, 92 S.Ct. 10, 30 L.Ed.2d 25 (1971), Justice Douglas, acting as Circuit Justice on an application for bail pending appeal, noted: "While there is no automatic right to bail after convictions, 'The command of the Eighth Amendment that "Excessive bail shall not be required * * *" *at the very least* obligates judges passing on the right to bail to deny such relief only for the strongest of reasons.' "

Most state constitutions guarantee the right to bail in noncapital cases, but only "before conviction." Consequently, state statutes tend to limit the opportunities for release on appeal or, in some instances, deny bail entirely in certain specified circumstances. But once the state makes provision for release on bail during appeal, under the Eighth and Fourteenth Amendments it may not be arbitrarily denied.

The seemingly strict federal provision, 18 U.S.C. § 3143(b), in Supp. App. B, has not been applied literally. For example, *United States v. Powell,* 761 F.2d 1227 (8th Cir.1985), holds "that a defendant who wishes to be released on bail after the imposition of a sentence including a term of imprisonment must first show that the question presented by the appeal is substantial, in the sense that it is a close question or one that could go either way. It is not sufficient to show simply that reasonable judges could differ (presumably every judge who writes a dissenting opinion is still 'reasonable') or that the issue is fairly debatable and not frivolous. On the other hand, the defendant does not have to show that it is likely or probable that he or she will prevail on the issue on appeal. If this part of the test is satisfied, the defendant must then show that the substantial question he or she seeks to present is so integral to the merits of the conviction that it is more probable than not that reversal or a new trial will occur if the question is decided in the defendant's favor. In deciding whether this part of the burden has been satisfied, the court or judge to whom application for bail is made must assume that the substantial question presented will go the other way on appeal and then assess the impact of such assumed error on the conviction."

NOTES ON BAIL FOR CAPITAL (OR, FORMERLY CAPITAL) OFFENSES

1. Forty states have provisions in their constitutions limiting the right to bail in capital cases. The typical provision reads: "All prisoners shall, before conviction, be bailable by sufficient sureties, except for capital offenses, where the proof is evident, or the presumption great." There is a split of authority concerning the significance of such provisions where the legislature has declared a certain crime to be a capital offense but the death penalty provisions are not constitutional. One view is that the "underlying gravity of those offenses endures and the determination of

their gravity for the purpose of bail continues unaffected by the decision" that the death penalty provision is unconstitutional. *People v. Anderson,* 493 P.2d 880 (Cal. 1972).[a] The other is that these provisions are based upon the "strong flight urge because of the possibility of an accused forfeiting his life," and thus are inapplicable once that possibility is removed. *Commonwealth v. Truesdale,* 296 A.2d 829 (Pa. 1972).

2. In STATE v. ENGEL, 493 A.2d 1217 (N.J.1985), the court first noted it was "well settled" that "the burden is on the State to persuade the trial court that a case involves capital murder and that a defendant charged with the murder may consistent with the Constitution be denied bail." As to the precise nature of this burden, the court explained that the prosecutor must first show a "fair likelihood" that the defendant would be convicted of capital murder. But, because the jury may sentence to death only if one of the statutorily-declared aggravating factors is found to be present, the prosecutor must also establish "reasonable grounds to believe that the death penalty may be imposed"; that is, "the court must determine whether an aggravating factor exists that, if credited and accepted by a jury at the sentencing phase of the capital murder trial, would allow it to impose the death penalty." As for the evidentiary standards applicable in this context, the court concluded "that strict application of the conventional rules of evidence" was unnecessary, as courts elsewhere had usually but not unanimously concluded. This is because the proceedings are preliminary in nature, and, more importantly, because there "is an important qualitative difference in the threat to liberty that is posed by a bail hearing and that occasioned by the criminal trial itself. The denial of liberty in the former is not attended by a determination of criminal guilt, and, therefore, is not permanent or indefinite. Liberty may be restored by admission to bail upon an adequate showing. At the trial, however, the defendant's loss of liberty is based upon a criminal conviction and is permanent."

The central issue in *Engel* concerned whether a co-defendant's confession, implicating the defendant, could be considered at the bail hearing even though it would be inadmissible at trial (see *Bruton v. United States,* p. 1074 infra). After concluding that the constitutional right of confrontation was inapplicable in such "ancillary criminal proceedings," the court continued:

"Our task then is to determine whether it is possible to develop adequate standards that can guarantee that hearsay evidence proffered at a bail hearing is sufficiently reliable to constitute a reasonable substitute for the right of confrontation and an appropriate protection of the defendant's liberty. * * *

"We now hold that at a bail hearing involving a defendant's admission to bail a codefendant's confession can be considered if (1) the confession is more probative on the point for which it is offered than any other evidence that the State can procure through diligent efforts under all

a. Query, is the *Anderson* approach subject to constitutional attack? Consider *United States ex rel. Covington v. Coparo,* 297 F.Supp. 203 (S.D. N.Y.1969), holding: "New York's recent elimination of the death penalty upon conviction of murder in the first degree, following a course adopted in other states, manifests an enlightened policy which should not be deterred by a legislative concern that reduction of the penalty must automatically result in the granting of bail as a matter of constitutional right. The penalty that may be imposed in the event of a conviction should not be the sole determinant on the issue whether bail is a matter of right."

Compare *Escandar v. Ferguson,* 441 F.Supp. 53 (S.D.Fla.1977): "In Florida, a defendant charged with a capital or life felony who cannot himself show that the proof is not evident nor the presumption great is presumed, as a matter of law without rebuttal, to be an unreasonable bail risk. The defendant may, in fact, be a perfectly good bail risk who would never fail to appear but, under the procedure Florida has adopted, he will not even be heard. Such an irrebuttable presumption sweeps too broadly, and thereby violates the Due Process Clause of the Fourteenth Amendment."

of the circumstances; and (2) the confession itself is sufficiently trustworthy or circumstantial corroboration of the confession renders it sufficiently trustworthy.

"In applying these tests to determine whether a hearsay statement in the form of a codefendant's confession sought to be admitted is sufficiently trustworthy for the limited purposes of a bail hearing, judicial discretion must be exercised cautiously. Several considerations should guide the exercise of this discretion. The main factor that would tend to support a finding of trustworthiness is whether, considering the confession as a whole, a comparison of the strengths of the declarant's self-serving interest and the disserving interest shows that the disserving interest preponderates. * * *

"A statement's internal consistency may also suggest that it is true. * * *

"If a confession reflects such factors, which enhance its probative worth, a court may reasonably conclude it is sufficiently trustworthy to be used as evidence for bail hearing purposes. However, if the court is not satisfied upon a consideration of these factors that the confession is sufficiently trustworthy, it may allow or require the prosecutor to establish or bolster the trustworthiness of the confession through circumstantial corroboration. Corroborating evidence may be offered to substantiate various parts of a statement and thereby reduce the doubt that may otherwise attend its veracity. * * *

" * * * We hold further that the State must make a reasonable showing that the substance of the proffered hearsay will in some competent form be available for use at the defendant's trial. In the absence of some showing that there is a likelihood that the substance of the proffered hearsay can be used against the defendant at trial, it is hard to fathom how the State will have sustained its burden of demonstrating that the defendant is in genuine danger of being convicted. To allow hearsay that could not in any likelihood be used at the defendant's trial to be introduced and considered at the bail hearing to deny the defendant his liberty would be unfair.

"We determine therefore that the prosecutor will have the burden at the bail hearing to show that there is a likelihood that the substance of the hearsay evidence, by virtue of an exception to the hearsay rule or in some other competent form, will be admitted and used at the trial. This may be done by testimony or credible representations to the court through responsible representatives authorized to advance the State's position in terms of the handling of the criminal prosecution. The court should consider such testimony or representations in the context of the entire criminal investigation and prosecution. In this connection, it must consider the timing of the bail hearing, the reasons for the prosecutor not producing the affiant or declarant or other persons with direct knowledge of the contents of the hearsay evidence, and the steps that the prosecutor has taken or will be taking to overcome the nonproduction of such witnesses and to provide for their availability at trial."

3. What if the prosecutor, to show that "the proof is evident or the presumption great," offers a statement signed by the defendant, who objects that the statement was obtained in violation of *Miranda?* Or, what if the prosecutor offers physical evidence the defendant claims was illegally seized? Cf. *United States v. Calandra,* p. 230 supra.

SECTION 2. PREVENTIVE DETENTION

The term "preventive detention" is ordinarily used to describe pretrial detention of a defendant to protect other persons or the community at large from criminal conduct by that defendant. Even in bail systems which in theory have the single legitimate function of assuring the defendant's appearance at trial, the preventive detention function is often served sub rosa. But in recent years the preventive detention concept has been more openly discussed, and in several jurisdictions some form of preventive detention is now expressly authorized by law.

Such is the case with the federal Bail Reform Act of 1984, set out in Supp. App. B. For one thing, in determining the manner and conditions of release (discussed on p. 850 supra), the Act makes ensuring "the safety of any other person or the community" a relevant consideration. Moreover, a detention hearing is to be held, upon motion of the attorney for the government, where the case involves a crime of violence, an offense for which the maximum penalty is death or life imprisonment, certain serious drug offenses, or any felony by one with two or more convictions of the aforementioned type offenses. Also, such a hearing is to be held on motion of either the attorney for the government or the judicial officer asserting the case involves a serious risk that the person will flee or will obstruct or attempt to obstruct justice or interfere with a prospective witness or juror. If at the hearing the judicial officer "finds that no condition or combination of conditions will reasonably assure the appearance of the person as required and the safety of any other person and the community," then detention is to be ordered. (A rebuttable presumption in support of such a finding exists in certain circumstances.) The Act also makes nonviolation of any federal, state or local crime a condition of any release under the Act, and upon violation of that condition revocation of the release is required upon a finding of probable cause that such a crime was committed while on release, if there is also a finding that the person is unlikely to abide by any conditions of release or that there is no combination of release conditions that will assure the person will not flee or pose a danger. A person ordered detained may obtain review of the order from the court with original jurisdiction over the offense charged, and may appeal from the detention order.

Riley, *Preventive Detention Use Grows—But Is It Fair?*, Nat'l L.J., March 24, 1986, p. 1, 32–33, reports (i) a Justice Department claim "that at least 2,853 detention hearings were held in the first 16 months after the bill was passed" and that "prosecutors have had a success rate of about 80 percent—with 1,114 detentions on risk-of-flight grounds, 381 on dangerousness grounds, and 705 on both"; (ii) that "U.S. Magistrates reported * * * 4,178 detention hearings, or 835 per month, during a five-month period last year"; and (iii) that the "U.S. Marshal's Service says the new bail law was primarily responsible for a 32 percent increase in prisoner population and an 11 percent increase in total jail days during the first year after its passage."

No state has yet adopted such a full-scale preventive detention scheme, but nearly half the states presently permit some consideration of the defendant's dangerousness in the pretrial release determination. In addition, many states permit revocation of release because of commission of a crime or other misconduct. Preventive detention objectives are also served by state laws which permit the denial of bail to defendants charged with certain serious noncapital offenses.

The case which follows concerns the District of Columbia preventive detention law, which applies only to District of Columbia offenses and not to federal crimes committed in the District. D.C. Code 1981, § 23–1322 provides in part:

"(a) Subject to the provisions of this section, a judicial officer may order pretrial detention of—

"(1) a person charged with a dangerous crime, as defined in section 23–1331(3),[a]

a. "The term 'dangerous crime' means (A) taking or attempting to take property from another by force or threat of force, (B) unlawfully entering or attempting to enter any premises if the Government certifies by motion that based on such person's pattern of behavior consisting of his past and present conduct, and on the other factors set out in section 23–1321(b),[b] there is no condition or combination of conditions which will reasonably assure the safety of the community;

"(2) a person charged with a crime of violence, as defined in section 23–1331(4),[c] if (i) the person has been convicted of a crime of violence within the ten-year period immediately preceding the alleged crime of violence for which he is presently charged; or (ii) the crime of violence was allegedly committed while the person was, with respect to another crime of violence, on bail or other release or on probation, parole, or mandatory release pending completion of a sentence; or

"(3) a person charged with any offense if such person, for the purpose of obstructing or attempting to obstruct justice, threatens, injures, intimidates, or attempts to threaten, injure, or intimidate any prospective witness or juror.

"(b) No person described in subsection (a) of this section shall be ordered detained unless the judicial officer—

"(1) holds a pretrial detention hearing in accordance with the provisions of subsection (c) of this section;

"(2) finds—

"(A) that there is clear and convincing evidence that the person is a person described in paragraph (1), (2), or (3) of subsection (a) of this section;

"(B) that—

"(i) in the case of a person described only in paragraph (1) of subsection (a), based on such person's pattern of behavior consisting of his past and present conduct, and on the other factors set out in section 23–1321(b), or

"(ii) in the case of a person described in paragraph (2) or (3) of such subsection, based on the factors set out in section 23–1321(b),

there is no condition or combination of conditions of release which will reasonably assure the safety of any other person or the community; and

"(C) that, except with respect to a person described in paragraph (3) of subsection (a) of this section, on the basis of information presented by proffer or otherwise to the judicial officer there is a substantial probability that the person committed the offense for which he is present before the judicial officer; and

"(3) issues an order of detention accompanied by written findings of fact and the reasons for its entry." [d]

adapted for overnight accommodation of persons or for carrying on business with the intent to commit an offense therein, (C) arson or attempted arson of any premises adaptable for overnight accommodation of persons or for carrying on business, (D) forcible rape, or assault with intent to commit forcible rape, or (E) unlawful sale or distribution of a narcotic or depressant or stimulant drug (as defined by any Act of Congress) if the offense is punishable by imprisonment for more than one year."

b. These factors are: "the nature and circumstances of the offense charged, the weight of the evidence against such person, his family ties, employment, financial resources, character and mental conditions, past conduct, length of residence in the community, record of convictions, and any record of appearance at court proceedings, flight to avoid prosecution, or failure to appear at court proceedings."

c. "The term 'crime of violence' means murder, forcible rape, carnal knowledge of a female under the age of sixteen, taking or attempting to take immoral, improper, or indecent liberties with a child under the age of sixteen years, mayhem, kidnaping, robbery, burglary, voluntary manslaughter, extortion or blackmail accompanied by threats of violence, arson, assault with intent to commit any offense, assault with a dangerous weapon, or an attempt or conspiracy to commit any of the foregoing offenses as defined by any Act of Congress or any State law, if the offense is punishable by imprisonment for more than one year."

d. Subsection (c) says that a hearing shall be held upon oral motion of the U.S. Attorney when the defendant is before a judicial officer or on his ex parte written motion when the person has already been released; that the hearing is to be held "immediately" unless a continuance is

UNITED STATES v. EDWARDS

430 A.2d 1321 (D.C.App. en banc 1981).

NEWMAN, CHIEF JUDGE: [The government moved for pretrial detention, pursuant to § 23–1322(a)(1), of Edwards, who had an extensive record and was charged with armed rape. Judge Bowers denied the motion because the government declined to produce the complainant for cross-examination, and the government appealed. Edwards was later charged with burglary, robbery and sodomy arising out of another incident, and the government again moved for preventive detention under § 23–1322(a)(1). Judge Norman granted the motion, and Edwards appealed. The two appeals were consolidated.]

II. CONSTITUTIONAL RIGHT TO BAIL

Appellant attacks the constitutionality of the pretrial detention statute on its face as contrary to an asserted constitutional right to bail. The source for this asserted right is the "excessive bail" clause of the Eighth Amendment. Whether this clause grants a right to bail in a criminal case has never been decided in the federal courts. Before the adoption of the pretrial detention statute, Congress had always provided a statutory right to pretrial bail for federal detainees in noncapital cases. Appellant concedes that the literal language of the excessive bail clause does not encompass a right to bail, but would have us find such a right implied in the clause on the basis of the history of the adoption of the clause and its constitutional context. The history of the Eighth Amendment, however, is generally unilluminating and falls short of supporting, let alone compelling, the conclusion that a right to bail must be found by implication. * * *

In the same session in which Congress considered the proposals and finally approved a Bill of Rights, it also drafted and passed the Judiciary Act of 1789. The latter act established a statutory right to bail in noncapital cases. Although the Eighth Amendment and the statutory right to bail may have developed from two distinct sources, and there is nothing in the congressional record to suggest that the implications of the differing language were addressed, it must be presumed that Congress recognized the clear difference in scope of the clauses. The alternative explanation, that the clearly differing language was fortuitous, cannot be simply inferred without any evidence that Congress intended the differing language to carry the same meaning. Moreover, the right to bail in the 1879 Act would have been a redundancy if the excessive bail language meant the same thing even in capital cases.

The Supreme Court has never ruled on whether the excessive bail clause imports a right to bail. The government cites the Court's language in *Carlson v. Landon,* 342 U.S. 524, 72 S.Ct. 525, 96 L.Ed. 547 (1952), that "the very language of the Amendment fails to say all arrests are bailable." *Carlson* involved the denial of bail to alien Communists pending deportation proceedings. The Court concluded that the Eighth Amendment does not apply to such civil proceedings. Accordingly, the *Carlson* holding does not directly concern criminal cases, particularly as the Court emphasized Congress' broad powers to

granted on motion of the defendant not to exceed 5 days "unless there are extenuating circumstances" or on motion of the U.S. Attorney "granted upon good cause shown" not to exceed 3 days; that defendant is "entitled to representation by counsel and shall be entitled to present information by proffer or otherwise, to testify, and to present witnesses in his own behalf"; that the rules of evidence are inapplicable; and that defendant's testimony at the hearing is inadmissible at trial "on the issue of guilt" except "in perjury proceedings, and for the purpose of impeachment." Subsection (d) says if the defendant is ordered detained his case "shall be placed on an expedited calendar" and that the preventive detention shall cease in 60 days "unless the trial is in progress or the trial has been delayed at the request of the person other than by the filing of timely motions (excluding motions for continuances)," or whenever a judicial officer "finds that a subsequent event has eliminated the basis for such detention."

deal with aliens. Moreover, the *Carlson* dictum regarding the scope of an Eighth Amendment right to bail conflicts with the tenor of *Stack v. Boyle* [p. 851 supra], decided the same term. *Stack v. Boyle,* although concerned with the excessiveness of the bail orders under review there, recognized the "traditional right to freedom before conviction [which] permits the unhampered preparation of a defense, and serves to prevent the infliction of punishment prior to conviction."[24] Lower courts have relied, alternatively, on the dicta of both *Carlson* and *Stack* to find or deny a constitutional right to bail, but without any convincing resolution.[a]

Apart from the asserted support in the history of the development and adoption of the excessive bail clause, appellant argues that the apparent anomaly of the excessive bail clause can only be explained by construing it to grant a right to bail. The core of this argument is that the excessive bail clause, insofar as it operates as a limit on congressional power, is a futility if Congress is prohibited from requiring excessively high bail but is free to deny bail altogether by making some or all crimes nonbailable. The only explanation for prohibiting excessively high bail but allowing the denial of all bail would be a concern for economic equality between the rich and the poor, which the historical evidence clearly negates. To avoid rendering the excessive bail clause "surplusage," the argument runs, it must be broadly interpreted to grant a right to bail.

This argument presumes, however, that the excessive bail clause was intended primarily to limit the legislative power of Congress rather than to limit the discretion of the judiciary in setting individual bail. The historical origins of the excessive bail clause, as well as its narrow language, indicate that its primary purpose is to limit the judiciary. The major reason advanced for construing the clause as directed to Congress (and thus as a broader limitation on its powers) is the constitutional context of the Bill of Rights itself. The Bill of Rights, it is argued, had as its "central concern * * * protection against abuse by Congress." *See also Ingraham v. Wright,* 430 U.S. 651, 97 S.Ct. 1401, 51 L.Ed.2d 711 (1977) (history of adoption of Eighth Amendment indicates that cruel and unusual punishment clause was intended to restrict Congress as well as the judiciary). A cursory examination of other provisions contained in the Bill of Rights, however, reveals that the conduct of the judicial branch was an important, if not the chief,

24. The Court in *Stack* added that "[u]nless this right to bail before trial is preserved, the presumption of innocence, secured only after centuries of struggle, would lose its meaning." More recently, however, the Court has stated that the presumption of innocence has "no application to a determination of the rights of a pretrial detainee. * * *"

a. The conflict in the cases persists, as reflected by the recent decisions in *Sistrunk v. Lyons,* 646 F.2d 64 (3d Cir.1981), and *Hunt v. Roth,* 648 F.2d 1148 (8th Cir.1981), agreeing that the Eighth Amendment's prohibition against excessive bail applies to the states but disagreeing as to the scope of this constitutional protection. As the Third Circuit saw it, because "the Eighth Amendment does not delimit the denial of bail to capital offenses, Congress as well as the states could provide that other serious noncapital crimes are similarly not entitled to bail—subject, of course to due process constraints." But the Eighth Circuit, in striking down a Nebraska provision that bars bail for a defendant charged with a forcible sexual offense in which "the proof is evident or the presumption great," reasoned that "if legislative bodies are free to define any and all offenses as nonbailable, they may deprive the amendment of any force." The court in *Hunt* concluded that the "fatal flaw in the Nebraska constitutional amendment is that the state has created an irrebuttable presumption that every individual charged with this particular offense is incapable of assuring his appearance by conditioning it upon reasonable bail or is too dangerous to be granted release," and rejected the state's analogy to the capital offense exception because "there is a historical basis for the capital crimes exception" and "the concept of denial of bail in capital cases is at least arguably consistent with one of the purposes of bail," namely, "to provide reasonable assurance the accused would appear for trial and sentencing if convicted." The Supreme Court declined to resolve the conflict in *Murphy v. Hunt,* 455 U.S. 478, 102 S.Ct. 1181, 71 L.Ed.2d 353 (1982), concluding instead that defendant's claim became moot after his conviction.

concern. The indictment, double jeopardy, and due process clauses of the Fifth Amendment, and the Sixth Amendment's criminal trial rights, clearly were intended to curtail the powers of the courts as well as those of Congress in legislating for the courts.

A second related argument is that while an unlimited legislative power to define the boundaries of the citizen's rights, such as the right to bail, is consistent with the English theory of civil liberties in which Parliament is the ultimate authority, it is generally inconsistent with a constitutional form of government like ours. This reasoning requires, however, an antecedent finding that the right to bail is a fundamental right that the framers of the Bill of Rights meant to protect against congressional encroachment, because plainly not all asserted rights are constitutionally protected. While the history of the development of bail reveals that it is an important right, and bail in noncapital cases has traditionally been a federal statutory right, neither the historical evidence nor contemporary fundamental values implicit in the criminal justice system requires recognition of the right to bail as a "basic human right," which must then be construed to be of constitutional dimensions.

III. Due Process

Appellant attacks the statutory procedure for pretrial detention on multiple grounds as violative of his Fifth Amendment due process rights. Chief among these complaints are the contentions (1) that pretrial detention is punishment that cannot be imposed "prior to an adjudication of guilt in accordance with due process of law", (2) that the hearing, at a minimum, must provide rights of confrontation, cross-examination, and compulsory process, and (3) that the notice of the past acts that would support a finding of "dangerousness" was deficient. Appellant also contends that the statutory burden of proof is inadequate, and that the statute as a whole is violative of substantive due process and is both facially overbroad and unconstitutionally vague. We address these contentions in the order presented.

A. Detention as Punishment

* * *

The distinction between penal and regulatory sanctions is often elusive, but the compilation of traditional tests set out by the Court in *Bell v. Wolfish,* provides authoritative guidance:

> Whether the sanction involves an affirmative disability or restraint, whether it has historically been regarded as a punishment, whether it comes into play only on a finding of *scienter,* whether its operation will promote the traditional aims of punishment—retribution and deterence, whether the behavior to which it applies is already a crime, whether an alternative purpose to which it may rationally be connected is assignable for it, and whether it appears excessive in relation to the alternative purpose assigned are all relevant to the inquiry, and may often point in differing directions.

As this test explicitly recognizes, the various factors may point in differing directions, and there can be no mechanical application of the test. Characterization of pretrial detention is a particularly close question. Nevertheless, we conclude, after considering all of the relevant factors, that pretrial detention is regulatory rather than penal in nature. Although detention pending trial invokes an affirmative restraint, historically it has not been regarded as punishment where the purpose has been to prevent flight or to prevent the coercion or intimidation of witnesses. The critical question is whether detention pending trial for the purpose of protecting the community from the detainee's established dangerousness is an "alternative purpose" contemplated by the [above] factors. The traditional reasons for pretrial detention, preventing flight or the intimidation of witnesses, serve the "alternative purpose" of preserving the integrity of the judicial process, and thus are preventive and forward-looking. Similarly, pretrial detention to prevent repetition of dangerous acts under § 23–1322(a)(1) by incapacitating the detainee seeks to curtail reasonably predictable conduct, not to punish for prior acts. * * *

The statutory history makes clear that pretrial detention was intended to protect the safety of the community until it can be determined whether society may properly punish the defendant. Pretrial detention was not intended to promote either of the "traditional aims of punishment—retribution and deterrence." * * *

B. Procedural Due Process

Appellant next contends that even if pretrial detention is not found to be a penal sanction which would trigger the full procedural protections of a criminal trial under the Fifth and Sixth Amendments, the statutory provisions nonetheless are violative of the Due Process Clause by not providing the minimal procedural framework necessary to a fair hearing. In particular, appellant asserts that due process requires that a defendant in a pretrial detention hearing be afforded rights of confrontation, cross-examination, and compulsory process, and that the government must prove each required finding by proof beyond a reasonable doubt. * * *

Although pretrial detention is not punishment, it clearly implicates a liberty interest that requires a fair hearing within the mandates of procedural due process. See *Gagnon v. Scarpelli,* [p. 87 supra] (due process protections attach to probation revocation); *Morrissey v. Brewer* [p. 88 supra] (parole revocation implicates protected liberty interest). Due process is a flexible concept, however, and "not all situations calling for procedural safeguards call for the same kind of procedure." The question therefore remains "what process is due," and whether the procedures provided by statute meet the minimum due process requirements. * * *

Guidance in determining "what process is due" in a pretrial detention hearing may be derived from the Supreme Court's decision in *Gerstein v. Pugh,* [p. 306 supra], and *Morrissey v. Brewer. Gerstein* held that an arrestee is entitled to a timely hearing before a magistrate for a "judicial determination of probable cause as a prerequisite to extended restraint of liberty following arrest." The Court further held that "the full panoply of adversary safeguards—counsel, confrontation, cross-examination, and compulsory process for witnesses," which the District Court and Court of Appeals had held was mandatory, is not constitutionally required. *Morrissey,* on the other hand, held that a preliminary hearing must be held, with certain procedural safeguards, to determine whether there is probable cause to believe the parolee has committed a parole violation. The hearing must be held before a neutral magistrate and the parolee given notice and an opportunity to present evidence. The parolee also is given a right to confront and cross-examine "person[s] who [have] given adverse information on which parole revocation is to be based," unless the hearing officer specifically finds that the witness "would be subjected to a risk of harm if his identity were disclosed." The preliminary hearing is to be followed by the revocation hearing at which there is notice, an opportunity to present evidence, and a right to confront and cross-examine adverse witnesses ("unless the hearing officer specifically finds good cause for not allowing confrontation").

Appellant contends that, at a minimum, the rights of confrontation and cross-examination of adverse witnesses required in a preliminary parole revocation hearing by *Morrissey* should be similarly required in a pretrial detention hearing. Because "due process is flexible and calls for such procedural protections as the particular situation demands," an independent examination must be made of the due process requirements for pretrial detention. In determining the scope of procedural protections required, we must consider the individual's interest affected by the official action, the nature of the governmental function involved, and the probable value of and enhanced accuracy from additional procedural safeguards. * * *

The effect of the findings in a detention hearing and a preliminary (*Gerstein*) hearing is the same: each hearing determines whether the accused may be detained pending trial. The individual's liberty interest affected by each proceeding is accordingly the same. * * *

Turning to a comparison of the nature of the government's interest in the two proceedings, we find that they are also similar in scope. At the outset, the government has an obvious interest in not conducting a full-blown criminal proceeding twice, once for pretrial detention and a second time for the trial on the charges. Indeed, the individual's and the government's mutual interest in holding the hearing soon after the time of the arrest necessarily precludes the full-scale preparation and investigation that is commensurate with a criminal trial. Conversely, the limited function of a pretrial detention hearing, i.e., to determine the appropriateness of detention for a maximum of 60 days pending a trial on the charges with the full panoply of criminal trial rights, weighs in favor of a simplified hearing. The *Gerstein* Court distinguished the greater procedural formalities required by *Morrissey* in part on the basis of the overall procedural protections otherwise afforded by the criminal justice system. In addition, the Court distinguished the preliminary revocation proceeding in *Morrissey,* to be held near the place of the alleged parole violation, by its broader function of "gathering and preserving live testimony," which function is shared by neither a probable cause preliminary hearing nor a pretrial detention hearing.

With regard to the specific procedural protections of confrontation and cross-examination, which Judge Bowers ruled were constitutionally required and which Judge Norman imposed in part, we hold that the government may proceed by the use of proffer and hearsay, subject to the discretion of the judge as to the nature of the proffer and the need for admissible evidence. * * *

Appellant contends that the burden of proof required in a criminal trial, i.e., proof beyond a reasonable doubt, see *In re Winship,* [p. 840 supra], is the required standard under the dictates of procedural due process for a pretrial detention hearing. We cannot agree. The Supreme Court has consistently held that significant restraints on liberty may be imposed upon a finding of probable cause of a violation, including cases of parole violations, *Morrissey v. Brewer,* probation violations, *Gagnon v. Scarpelli;* and pretrial detention, *Gerstein v. Pugh.* The statute requires that the judicial officer find by "a substantial probability" that the accused committed the offense for which he is charged. The legislative history indicates that this standard, higher than probable cause was intended to be equivalent to the standard required "to secure a civil injunction—likelihood of success on the merits." H.R.Rep. No. 91–907, 91st Cong., 2d Sess. 182 (1970).[b]

C. Notice

Advance notice of the specific allegations against the accused is a fundamental component of procedural due process. Notice is necessary for the individual to understand the charges and the proceedings and to give him a meaningful opportunity "to marshal the facts in his defense." The pretrial detention statute does not contain any provision regarding notice but does provide for a continuance on the accused's motion which "shall not

b. By like analysis (i.e., by deeming *Gerstein* rather than *Morrissey* to be the better analogy), the procedure in the Bail Reform Act of 1984 has been held sufficient. *United States v. Delker,* 757 F.2d 1390 (3d Cir.1985).

exceed five calendar days, unless there are extenuating circumstances." Appellant availed himself of a three-day continuance in the proceeding before Judge Norman. Although appellant claims this was a constitutionally insufficient time to prepare, we find no merit in this contention. * * *

D. Substantive Due Process, Vagueness, and Overbreadth

Appellant also asserts that the pretrial detention statute violates substantive due process by denying bail pending trial and is both unconstitutionally vague and overbroad. These contentions have no merit and may be dismissed with little discussion.

1. Substantive Due Process

Substantive due process requires that when "fundamental rights" are involved, the state may limit such rights by regulation only upon a showing of a "compelling state interest." * * *

Regardless of whether the right to bail is characterized as fundamental or not, the legislative history provides ample support for a compelling state interest in the pretrial detention of the narrow class of persons covered by the statute. Congress considered (1) the alarming increase in street crime in the District of Columbia since 1966; (2) statistical studies involving recidivism by persons while on pretrial release; (3) recommendations by the President's Commission on Crime in the District of Columbia (1966), and the Judicial Council Committee to Study the Operation of the Bail Reform Act in the District of Columbia (1969); and (4) pretrial release and detention practices in England and other countries. H.R.Rep. No. 91–907, 91st Cong., 2d Sess. 87–94 (1970). Appellant attempts to litigate what are essentially legislative findings, i.e., the extent of crime committed by persons released pending trial and the predictability of criminal conduct, citing studies which reached different statistical results [45] than those relied upon by Congress. These are matters properly committed to the legislative process. Pretrial detention clearly has a substantial relation to preventing injury to the public and thus falls within the scope of Congress' power to legislate for the District of Columbia.

2. Overbreadth

In support of his contention that the pretrial detention statute is impermissibly overbroad, appellant also cites statistical studies concluding that criminal conduct generally cannot be predicted. The doctrine of constitutional overbreadth applies to statutes that sweep unnecessarily broadly and thereby substantially impinge on constitutionally-protected conduct as well as conduct subject to governmental regulation. The doctrine has no application to the pretrial detention statute as it applies only to conduct which is constitutionally regulable, i.e., the detainee must be charged with the commission of a dangerous crime or a crime of violence, which the judicial officer finds with substantial probability was committed by the accused. Moreover, the statute also requires a finding that "there is no condition or combination of conditions of release which will reasonably assure the safety of any other person or the community," which thus prohibits pretrial detention if less restrictive alternatives are available in the individual case to effect the government's interest in protecting the community. Prediction of the likelihood of certain conduct necessarily involves a margin of error, but is an established component of our pretrial release system. Trial judges have been engaged in predicting the likelihood of flight for all defendants, capital and noncapital, and have predicted the likelihood of recidivism for capital offenses

45. E.g., Note, *Preventive Detention: An Empirical Analysis,* 6 Harv.C.R.-C.L.L.Rev. 289 (1971).

since the Judiciary Act of 1789. Appellant's argument relies on the assumptions, which we do not share, that the judicial prediction of dangerousness, as distinguished from the prediction of likelihood of flight, is both a denial of a fundamental right and the imposition of punishment. Accordingly, we decline to find the statute unconstitutionally overbroad.

3. Vagueness

Appellant also asserts that the statute is impermissibly vague. The Supreme Court stated: "[A] statute which either forbids or requires the doing of an act in terms so vague that men of common intelligence must necessarily guess at its meaning and differ as to its application, violates the first essential of due process of law." * * * It is true that Congress left the meaning of "past conduct" supporting a finding of dangerousness to the sound judgment of the judicial officer. However, the crimes with which appellant was charged and the crimes which he admits he committed in the space of four months preceding his arrest—a rape, a sodomy, two burglaries, and seventeen robberies—as well as the adjudication of his juvenile social file, are all prohibited conduct under concededly valid criminal laws. Nor can there be any doubt as to the meaning of "safety of the community" in this context.

In sum, we hold that the challenged provisions of the District of Columbia pretrial detention statute are constitutional. * * *

FERREN, ASSOCIATE JUDGE, concurring in part and dissenting in part: * * * While I concur in Chief Judge Newman's Eighth Amendment analysis in Part II of his opinion for the court, I cannot accept his treatment of due process in Part III. * * *

In applying due process to probation and parole revocation, the Supreme Court imposed certain procedural safeguards to protect conditional liberty. See *Gagnon*, supra; *Morrissey*, supra. "*A fortiori*, pretrial detainees, who have not been convicted of any crimes, retain at least those constitutional rights that we have held are enjoyed by convicted prisoners." *Bell*, supra. By apparently providing pretrial detainees with *less* protection than probationers and parolees receive (as we shall see), the majority has set the constitutional hurdle for pretrial detention decidedly too low. * * *

1. Notice

The majority's discussion of the right to notice is incomplete. Any person accused of a "dangerous crime" needs to know the precise instances of "past and present conduct" on which the government proposes to rely to demonstrate a threat to the community. Timely notice is vital if the accused is to have a meaningful opportunity to defend at the pretrial detention hearing. Even when lesser liberty interests are at stake, the Supreme Court has held that notice of the specific charge is essential to due process. See *Wolff v. McDonnell*, 418 U.S. 539, 94 S.Ct. 2963, 41 L.Ed.2d 935 (1974) (prison disciplinary proceeding); *Gagnon*, supra (probation revocation); *Morrissey*, supra (parole revocation); cf. *Goldberg v. Kelly*, 397 U.S. 254, 90 S.Ct. 1011, 25 L.Ed.2d 287 (1970) (notice required before preliminary suspension of welfare benefits).

Furthermore, the government has no interest in declining to reveal the charges it will allege at the hearing, although the expedited nature of the proceeding naturally will preclude notice much in advance. Because the accused is held pending the hearing, however, the government ordinarily will not have a strong interest in denying a defense continuance if the accused wants additional time to evaluate the government's allegations. I conclude that due process requires the right to advance (even if short) notice of all charges, facilitated by the right to a reasonable continuance. The statute should be so interpreted.

2. Confrontation and Cross-Examination

* * * To save the constitutionality of the statute, I would * * * allow the government to proceed by proffer or hearsay only when it can show good cause why a witness should not be called to give live testimony.

"In almost every setting where important decisions turn on questions of fact, due process requires an opportunity to confront and cross-examine adverse witnesses." *Goldberg,* supra. Although the pretrial detention hearing does not necessitate the comprehensive examination of witnesses required when the court or the jury must resolve guilt or innocence, credibility and veracity remain at issue. In *Goldberg,* for example, the Court held that even the temporary loss of welfare benefits pending a more complete hearing was severe enough to require confrontation rights. In the case of pretrial detention, where the accused has so much more at stake, I do not believe we should downplay such a basic, due process right—as the majority does—by presumptively authorizing proffer and other hearsay to sustain the necessary showing.

The public's interest in pretrial detention, however, on occasion will justify an exception to the general right of confrontation. In *Morrissey,* supra, although recognizing that individuals faced with preliminary revocation of parole have a basic confrontation right, the Supreme Court articulated a limitation: when "the hearing officer determines that an informant would be subjected to risk of harm if his identity were disclosed, he need not be subjected to confrontation and cross-examination." Thus, concerns for the safety or well-being of government witnesses and their ability to testify both before and at trial dictate a similar limitation for pretrial detention hearings. If, for example, the government can present evidence, such as a doctor's testimony, that a rape victim would suffer emotional harm when forced to testify so soon after the event, this reason probably should suffice to justify a proffer of her testimony instead. * * *

3. The Burden of Proof * * *

We accept a relatively high risk of error in a probable cause determination because the intrusion—arrest—is limited. We even accept that high risk of error (discounted by post-arrest information) for the greater pretrial restraint of the imposition of bail. In my judgment, however, before the state can jail someone for two months without even a right to bail, the Fifth Amendment compels much greater accuracy. The injustice of a mere probable cause standard for 60-day pretrial detention is sharply reflected by the fact that this is the same standard required for the *preliminary* hearing and detention of alleged parole and probation violators who—by virtue of a criminal conviction—stand to lose only conditional liberty. See *Gagnon,* supra; *Morrissey,* supra. The final decision on revocation of this conditional liberty can come only after the alleged violator has had an opportunity for a second hearing, which "must be the basis *for more than determining probable cause;* it must lead to a final evaluation of any contested relevant facts and consideration of whether the facts as determined warrant revocation." In contrast, a potential pretrial detainee stands to lose presumptively unconditional liberty because of criminal charges yet to be proved. This substantially greater liberty interest requires substantially greater protection.

I would hold that the burden of proof for all findings under § 23–1322(b)(2) is greater than a preponderance of the evidence but less than proof beyond a reasonable doubt. In so holding, I would rely on the approach in *Addington* [*v. Texas,* 439 U.S. 908, 99 S.Ct. 276, 58 L.Ed.2d 254 (1979)], where the Supreme Court held that clear and convincing evidence is sufficient for imposing involuntary civil commitment. The Court reasoned that although only "punitive" (criminal) proceedings demand proof beyond a reasonable doubt, the risk of erroneous involuntary civil commitment is significant enough, and its consequences severe enough, to require more than a preponderance standard. Weighing the liberty and public interests at stake, I believe that the risk and consequences of erroneous pretrial detention are similarly grave and thus mandate a similar standard of proof. * * *

Having compared the private and public interests at stake, evaluated the risk of error, and considered the corrective value of additional safeguards, I conclude that § 23–1322 can survive constitutional scrutiny by the trial court's strict enforcement of specified defense rights to notice, confrontation, and cross-examination and by the imposition of a burden on the government to prove each statutory requirement by clear and convincing evidence. In failing to make clear that these requirements are inherent in a constitutional pretrial detention scheme, my colleagues in the majority implicitly have compromised the Fifth Amendment right to due process of law. * * *

MACK, ASSOCIATE JUDGE, dissenting:

[I]n my view the majority's analysis of the scope of the Eighth Amendment does not pass muster. The reasoning is not clinical—nor could it be. The conclusion is reached that the Eighth Amendment in commanding that "Excessive bail shall not be required * * " means only that, and does not grant a right to bail. I presume that the majority is saying that only the Congress can grant a right to bail, and once that right has been granted, the Constitution takes over and mandates that the bail not be excessive. This is a classic example of the cart pulling the horse since the Congress could abrogate the right to bail altogether, making the Eighth Amendment absolutely meaningless. Surely the framers of our Bill of Rights did not intend to fashion illusory protection—leaving open the possibility that a subsequent act of a legislature could empty a *critical* provision of the federal Constitution of all content. * * *

In this country, until recently, there was little doubt that the Eighth Amendment, by necessary implication, guaranteed the right to bail before trial, except in capital cases. * * *

Perhaps the reluctance of my colleagues to follow this traditional view of the Eighth Amendment's mandate stems from the phrasing of the claimed right in "absolute" terms. There is very little in the world in which we live that is absolute. Yet because the Constitution was written for the ages, judges must resist the temptation to interpret it restrictively, in the expediency of the moment, with the problems of their life span in mind. Perhaps a better solution for the majority would have been to suggest as did Justice Burton that the Eighth Amendment prohibits, along with excessive bail, the "unreasonable denial of bail." See *Carlson v. Landon*, supra. The legislative scheme here at issue then could have been evaluated as to reasonableness.

* * * One cannot question that the right to liberty is a fundamental right or that the state has a compelling interest in curtailing street crime. One can and does question whether the statute in question promotes the compelling state interest and whether it does so in a manner least restrictive of the fundamental right.

Underlying the statutory classification of "dangerous" persons is a presumption that the state can predict those persons who are dangerous. I have reviewed defense counsel's exhaustive treatment of this presumption and I am convinced by the authorities relied upon that the presumption is not a valid one. Moreover, I am likewise convinced that the utilization of this presumption for the asserted purpose will result in pretrial detention of persons who pose no threat to the community. In my view, therefore, this classification of "dangerousness" is arbitrary and invalid under due process and equal protection principles.

Without dwelling at length on the sources relied upon by defense counsel, it is interesting to note that at congressional hearings on the legislation, experts both in and out of government expressed concern with the ability of the authorities to predict dangerousness.[15] These concerns have been echoed in the results of empirical studies.[16]

The American Psychiatric Association has suggested that "[n]either psychiatrists nor anyone else have reliably demonstrated an ability to predict future violence or 'dangerousness'."[17] The American Bar Association, has deemed detention under our statute "constitutionally dubious at best",[18] noting that ten years of experience had demonstrated that the experts' doubts as to the inability to predict dangerousness were well founded. Moreover, the Bar Association has noted that the statute is virtually useless in reducing recidivism.[20]

In a like vein * * * the language of § 23–1322 poses serious problems with respect to unconstitutional vagueness. Nowhere in the statute is "past and present conduct" defined. Neither does the

15. Thus Ms. Patricia Wald, formerly of the Department of Justice and now a Judge of the United States Court of Appeals for the District of Columbia Circuit, stated that

> despite the fact that preventive detention has been talked about for years, we have as yet no empirical study, no predictable study, which shows the factors which go into recidivis[m] on bail and which the judge could use in order to single out one man in 10 who might commit the crime.

Former Chief Judge Harold Greene of the Superior Court, now Judge of the United States District Court for the District of Columbia, also testified as to the anticipated overinclusiveness of the proposed legislation:

> Statistics indicate that future criminal behavior is not easily predictable. Eight, ten, or perhaps even more suspects who would not commit crimes while out on bail would have to be detained in order to be sure to keep off the streets the one defendant who will. It is perhaps for that reason that preventive detention has been outside the mainstream of Anglo-American jurisprudence from Magna Carta to the present day.

16. The American Bar Endowment sponsored a Harvard study of the rearrest rate of persons in the Boston area during a six-month period in 1968. *Preventive Detention: An Empirical Analysis,* 6 Harv.Civ.Rights—Civ.Lib.L.Rev. 289 (1971). Using the District of Columbia preventive detention statute as a framework, the researchers focused on 427 released defendants charged with violent or dangerous crimes who would have been eligible for preventive detention had the District of Columbia law been in effect in Boston in 1968.

Of the 427 defendants in the sample, 41 were rearrested and convicted of crimes committed during the pretrial period. Twenty-two of the 41 convictions were for violent or dangerous crimes as defined by the act.

The researchers used a "dangerous scale" model which considered the factors set out in § 1321(b) with the exception of the weight of the evidence in the instant arrest (the factors set out in § 1321(b) were originally designed to predict default—i.e., flight from prosecution) and incorporated by reference into § 1322(b)(2)(B). They concluded that in order to prevent all 41 offenses it would be necessary to detain 357 persons—that is, for every one recidivist detained eight nonrecidivists would also have to be detained. Such a ratio "amounts to little less than a dragnet."

17. American Psychiatric Association, *Task Force Report on the Clinical Aspects of Violent Individuals* 28 (1974). See also Rubin, *Prediction of Dangerousness in Mentally Ill Criminals,* 27 Arch.General Psychiatry 397 (1972) (no empirical evidence to support the belief that psychiatrists can accurately predict dangerous behavior).

18. Commentary to the *American Bar Association Standards Relating to Pretrial Release* (2d ed. Approved Draft, 1979, following Standard 10–5.9) at 10–106.

20. "The chief finding of the first ten months of observation has been the virtual non-use of the preventive detention law." *Id.* at 10–105, *quoting* Vera Institute of Justice, *Preventive Detention in the District of Columbia* 72–73 (1972). See also House Committee on the District of Columbia, H.R.Rep. No. 1419, 94th Cong., 2d Sess. 4 (1976):

> [F]rom the date of enactment until [1976], pretrial detention was rarely requested (only about 60 times during the entire 5 year period.) Various explanations were given for such non-use, but nearly all agree that the 1970 Act's detention provisions have been a complete failure as a tool for dealing with the hard core group of repeat offenders. [Footnote omitted.]

statute define the "safety" of the community. * * *

I would hold this statute unconstitutional as violative of both substantive and procedural due process and I would look to more feasible and less restrictive alternatives for combating pretrial crime. [Defense counsel has suggested use and enforcement of stringent pretrial release conditions, with prosecution for violation and revocation of release in cases of noncompliance; expedited proceedings for persons deemed likely to commit crime while on bail; and extensive filing of "release papers" which enhance penalties for offenses committed by persons on pretrial release. See also American Bar Association Standards Relating to Pretrial Release, supra Standard 10–5.9 which characterize a defendant as a danger to the community *if* he has "(b)(ii)(A) * * * committed a criminal offense since release, or * * * (B) violated conditions of release designed to protect the community and no additional conditions of release are sufficient to protect the safety of the community * * *."] * * *

Notes and Questions

1. In SCHALL v. MARTIN, 467 U.S. 253, 104 S.Ct. 2403, 81 L.Ed.2d 207 (1984), the Court upheld, 6–3, a New York statute, similar to that to be found in all states, authorizing pretrial detention of an accused juvenile delinquent on a finding that there is a "serious risk" that the child "may before the return date commit an act which if committed by an adult would constitute a crime." As for whether the statute served a legitimate state interest, the Court, per REHNQUIST, J., asserted that the " 'legitimate and compelling state interest' in protecting the community from crime cannot be doubted," and that it outweighed the "juvenile's countervailing interest in freedom" because "that interest must be qualified by the recognition that juveniles, unlike adults, are always in some form of custody," for they "are assumed to be subject to the control of their parents, and if parental control falters, the State must play its part as *parens patriae.*" The Court next decided that the preventive detention authorized under the statute was neither used nor intended as a punishment, as it was "strictly limited in time" (a maximum of 17 days if a serious crime, a maximum of 6 days otherwise) and the "conditions of confinement * * * reflect the regulatory purposes" in that absent extraordinary circumstances the juvenile may not be kept in a jail.

As for the remaining question of "whether the procedures afforded juveniles detained * * * sufficient protection against erroneous and unnecessary deprivations of liberty," the Court answered in the affirmative, noting the juvenile was entitled to a prompt adversarial determination of probable cause of a prior delinquent act and that a serious risk of criminal conduct in the future existed. In response to the argument that these procedural protections were unavailing "because the ultimate decision is intrinsically arbitrary and uncontrolled," the Court declared that "from a legal point of view there is nothing inherently unattainable about a prediction of future criminal conduct," for such "a judgment forms an important element in many decisions" regarding sentencing and probation and parole release and revocation. Moreover, it was not necessary that the statute enumerate the factors to be taken into account by the juvenile court judge, as "a prediction of future criminal conduct is 'an experienced prediction based on a host of variables' which cannot be readily codified."

Compare Feld, *Criminalizing Juvenile Justice: Rules of Procedure for the Juvenile Court,* 69 Minn.L.Rev. 141, 197–98 (1984), objecting that "the majority's position that such predictions occur often ignores the important issue of whether those predictions can be made with acceptable accuracy, particularly where the subjects of the prediction have not yet been found guilty of any criminal offense."

2. To what extent does *Schall* shed light upon the question of what kind of preventive detention scheme, if any, would pass constitutional muster in criminal cases? Can (should) *Schall* be contained on the ground that the *parens patriae* rationale allowed the Court to treat the liberty interests of juveniles as less substantial than those of adults?

SECTION 3. PREVENTING DETENTION: USE OF THE CITATION AND SUMMONS

NATIONAL ADVISORY COMMISSION ON CRIMINAL JUSTICE STANDARDS AND GOALS—CORRECTIONS

pp. 116–17 (1973).

4.3 Alternatives to arrest.

Each criminal justice jurisdiction, State or local as appropriate, should immediately develop a policy, and seek enabling legislation where necessary, to encourage the use of citations in lieu of arrest and detention. This policy should provide:

1. Enumeration of minor offenses for which a police officer should be required to issue a citation in lieu of making an arrest or detaining the accused unless:

a. The accused fails to identify himself or supply required information;

b. The accused refuses to sign the citation;

c. The officer has reason to believe that the continued liberty of the accused constitutes an unreasonable risk of bodily injury to himself or others;

d. Arrest and detention are necessary to carry out additional legitimate investigative action;

e. The accused has no ties to the jurisdiction reasonably sufficient to assure his appearance, and there is a substantial risk that he will refuse to respond to the citation; or

f. It appears the accused has previously failed to respond to a citation or a summons or has violated the conditions of any pretrial release program.

2. Discretionary authority for police officers to issue a citation in lieu of arrest in all cases where the officer has reason to believe that the accused will respond to the citation and does not represent a clear threat to himself or others.

3. A requirement that a police officer making an arrest rather than issuing a citation specify the reason for doing so in writing. Superior officers should be authorized to reevaluate a decision to arrest and to issue a citation at the police station in lieu of detention.

4. Criminal penalties for willful failure to respond to a citation.

5. Authority to make lawful search incident to an arrest where a citation is issued in lieu of arrest.

Similar steps should be taken to establish policy encouraging the issuance of summons in lieu of arrest warrants where an accused is not in police custody. This policy should provide:

1. An examination of minor offenses for which a judicial officer should be required to issue a summons in lieu of an arrest warrant unless he finds that:

a. The accused has previously willfully failed to respond to a citation or summons or has violated the conditions of any pretrial release program.

b. The accused has no ties to the community and there is a reasonable likelihood that he will fail to respond to a summons.

c. The whereabouts of the accused is unknown or the arrest warrant is necessary to subject him to the jurisdiction of the court.

d. Arrest and detention are necessary to carry out additional legitimate investigative action.

2. Discretionary authority for judicial officers to issue a summons in lieu of an arrest warrant in all cases where the officer has reason to believe that the accused will respond to the summons.

3. A requirement that a judicial officer issuing a warrant instead of a summons state his reason for doing so in writing.

4. Criminal penalties for willful failure to respond to a summons.

To facilitate the use of citations and summons in lieu of arrests, police agencies should:

1. Develop through administrative rules specific criteria for police officers for determining whether to issue citations or to request issuance of a summons in lieu of arrest.

2. Develop training programs to instruct their officers in the need for and use of the citation and summons in lieu of arrest.

3. Develop a method of quickly verifying factual information given to police officers which if true would justify the issuance of a citation in lieu of arrest.

4. Develop a method of conducting a reasonable investigation concerning the defendant's ties to the community to present to the judicial officer at the time of application for a summons or an arrest warrant.

Notes and Questions

1. The number of states with statutes or court rules authorizing police to issue citations for other than traffic offenses has increased dramatically in recent years. With few exceptions, however, these provisions do not require the police to utilize the citation alternative in certain circumstances or for specified nontraffic offenses.[a] Although citations are extensively used in some localities, nationwide there has been little implementation of this reform measure.

2. Legislation authorizing issuance of a summons by a magistrate in lieu of an arrest warrant is on the books of about half of the states, but it has had little impact in decreasing the number of arrests. The occasion for choosing between a summons and a warrant rarely arises, as the great majority of arrests are made without warrant. Moreover, in those few cases in which a complaint is brought before a magistrate, he usually relies upon the prosecutor or police officer to ask for a summons, and such a request is seldom made.[b]

3. Is an arrest, even if made on probable cause, unreasonable under the Fourth Amendment if it is apparent that a citation or summons would suffice? Cf. *Bacon v. United States,* 449 F.2d 933 (9th Cir.1971) (Fourth Amendment relied upon in holding that a person may be arrested as a material witness only if it is shown "that it may become impracticable to secure his presence by subpoena")[c]; *State v. Klinker,* 537 P.2d 268 (Wash.1975) (use of arrest warrant in civil filiation proceedings violated Fourth Amendment "where the defendant was a long-time resident of the trial court's jurisdiction, presumably highly unlikely to flee to avoid service of process"). But, in *Klinker* the court assumed that such a ruling would be inappropriate with respect to a defendant in a criminal case: "Where grounds exist to believe a person has committed a crime, the public interest in law enforcement is assumed to outweigh

a. Compare Minn.R.Crim.P. 6.01: "Law enforcement officers acting without a warrant, who have decided to proceed with prosecution, shall issue citations to persons subject to lawful arrest for misdemeanors, unless it reasonably appears to the officer that arrest or detention is necessary to prevent bodily harm to the accused or another or further criminal conduct, or that there is a substantial likelihood that the accused will fail to respond to a citation."

b. In some jurisdictions the magistrate may issue a summons only if the prosecutor so requests. Many other provisions merely indicate that the magistrate may opt for either a summons or an arrest warrant, while some provide a standard for making this choice, e.g., Alaska R.Crim.P. 4(a)(2) (summons shall issue unless magistrate "has reason to believe that the defendant will not appear in response to a summons"); Ariz.R.Crim.P. 3.1(b) (magistrate may not issue summons unless he has "reason to believe that the defendant will respond to it").

c. On the constitutionality and wisdom of the statutes to be found in all jurisdictions permitting the state to severely restrict the liberty of persons needed as witnesses in criminal proceedings, see Carlson & Voepel, *Material Witness and Material Injustice,* 58 Wash.U.L.Q. 1 (1980).

the individual's interest in liberty and to justify an arrest of that person, just as the same public interest outweighs the right of privacy invaded by a criminally-related search warrant." [d]

4. Why should the policy, as stated in Standard 4.3, include "[a]uthority to make lawful search incident to an arrest where a citation is issued in lieu of arrest"? Would such a policy be constitutional? Reconsider *United States v. Robinson,* p. 386 supra, and Notes 12 and 13, p. 398 supra.

d. As to the search warrant analogy, reconsider *Zurcher v. Stanford Daily,* p. 256 supra.

Chapter 13

THE DECISION WHETHER TO PROSECUTE

SECTION 1. THE OFFICE OF PROSECUTOR AND THE NATURE OF THE DECISION WHETHER TO PROSECUTE

1. *The office of prosecutor.* Reconsider the material on the prosecutor at pp. 21–26 supra.

2. *Turnover.* "Political factors and noncareer tenure of prosecutors have certain advantages. Local election increases the likelihood that the prosecutor will be responsive to the dominant law enforcement views and demands of the community. Since he is not dependent on another official for reappointment, the prosecutor possesses a degree of political independence that is desirable in an officer charged with the investigation and prosecution of charges of bribery and corruption. The frequency of election, the turnover in the job, and the noncareer attitude toward it all have affirmative values. A new man is likely to come to the office without a comfortable acceptance of the status quo; turnover reduces the dangers of stultification.

"But many of these same factors interfere with the full development of the prosecutor's office. Political considerations make some prosecutors overly sensitive to what is safe, expedient, and in conformity with law enforcement views that are popular rather than enlightened. Political ambition does not encourage a prosecutor to take the risks that frequently inhere in reasoned judgments. In dealing with offenders, with the police and other law enforcement agencies, and with the courts, the prosecutor is safer sticking to the familiar and most limited connotation of his job." [a]

3. *Coordination.* "Although each State has a single code of criminal laws, the State prosecutorial function, like the police and the courts, is fragmented among a number of independent agencies. The States are geographically divided into districts or counties, each of which has a prosecutor's office headed by an elected or appointed official. * * * Each of these prosecutors' offices is virtually autonomous. Apart from informal communication there is often little or no coordination among them. * * *

"The existing system is not without advantages. A local prosecutor is usually a product of the community which he serves. He is locally elected and is likely to be responsive to his constituency. Most important, since marked variation in the crime problem and in community resources may exist from area to area within a State, he is in a position to adjust prosecutorial policy to local conditions.

a. *Task Force Report: The Courts* 73 (1967).

"But division of the prosecutorial function and lack of coordination among local offices within a single State is also likely to have deleterious consequences. A strict enforcement policy in one county may simply divert criminal activity into neighboring areas. A community's effort to deal with crime will be limited if criminal groups can operate from a nearby jurisdiction with relative impunity. This may be seen in large metropolitan areas where prostitution, gambling, and bootlegging become exceedingly difficult to suppress when they are operated from a nearby haven. * * *

"The prevailing pattern * * * is that most of the State attorneys general do possess formal authority to coordinate local law enforcement activity; that in most States this authority has not been exercised; and that even in those States where some coordination is attempted, much more could be done.

"The lack of coordination of local prosecutors in the States may be compared with the organization of the prosecutorial function in the Federal system. * * * Efforts have been made to coordinate and supervise the prosecutorial activities of U.S. Attorneys' offices by the Department of Justice Criminal Division, which furnishes research and manpower assistance, performs certain training functions, and establishes major prosecutorial policy for the entire country." [b]

4. *Removal.* "Various removal mechanisms are employed by different states. Impeachment is the most usual method of removal. Removal by the Governor is another common method. Other methods of removal include removal by a court, removal on recommendation of the Attorney General, impeachment by the legislature, or recall provisions.

"Grounds for removal also vary among the different states. Grounds for removal include such causes as 'malfeasance, misfeasance, nonfeasance, or nonadministration in office', 'incompetency, neglect of duty or misuse of office when such incompetency, neglect of duty or misuse of office has a material adverse effect upon the conduct of such office', and 'incompetency, corruption, malfeasance or delinquency in office, or other sufficient cause'. Disbarment and conviction of a serious crime are other common grounds for removal. Removal proceedings, however, are seldom utilized: 'The district attorney need fear ouster only for criminal activity, and even where evidence of such conduct exists, ouster proceedings are seldom employed.' " [c]

5. *The charging decision: in general.* "The decision whether to file formal charges is a vitally important stage in the criminal process. It provides an opportunity to screen out cases in which the accused is apparently innocent, and it is at this stage that the prosecutor must decide in cases of apparent guilt whether criminal sanctions are appropriate." [d] In making this decision, the prosecutor must decide: (1) whether there is sufficient evidence to support a prosecution; (2) if so, whether there are nonetheless reasons for not subjecting the defendant to the criminal process; (3) if so, whether nonprosecution should be conditioned upon the defendant's participation in a diversion program; and (4) if prosecution is to be undertaken, with what offense or offenses the defendant should be charged.

"Apart from the borderline business, family, sex, and personal injury cases, the large percentage of cases come to the attention of the prosecutor only after the police have instituted the criminal process by arresting a suspect. * * * As a consequence, the police exercise a very important influence over the initial decision as to whether to invoke the criminal process.

b. Id. at 75–76.

c. *N.D.A.A. National Prosecution Standards* 16 (1977). This document contains citations to many other authorities on the matters discussed in this Chapter.

d. *Task Force Report,* supra, at 5.

Where a decision is made to arrest, there are procedures for review by the prosecutor and, ultimately, the court. Where, however, the police decide not to invoke the criminal process, effective methods of review and control are largely lacking, and this issue of the proper scope and function of police discretion is of great, current importance and difficulty." [e]

"A prosecutor should have several kinds of information if he is to make sound charge decisions. He must evaluate the strength of his case. Police reports usually provide him with some facts about the offense, but often he needs more. Before a prosecutor decides whether to charge or dismiss in any case that is not elementary, he should review the case file to determine whether more evidence and witnesses are available than the police have uncovered. In addition, the prosecutor needs to know enough about the offender to determine whether he should be diverted from the criminal track. * * * Often the prosecutor needs to know whether there are facilities in the community for treating such medical or behavioral problems as the offender may have and whether those facilities will accept him. * * *

"Defense counsel has an important role to play at this stage, and he should be involved wherever an intrusive disposition or significant penalty is likely. Counsel can assist in gathering information and formulating a treatment program; he can help persuade the prosecutor of the appropriateness of a noncriminal disposition." [f]

6. *Charging: evidence sufficiency.* It is not possible to state categorically how much evidence is required before the prosecutor is justified in charging a suspect with a crime, as the law does not expressly provide a distinct probability of guilt standard for the charging decision.[g] Although the prosecutor's decision to charge is reflected in the post-arrest issuance of a warrant in most jurisdictions, and though it is clear that an arrest warrant may issue only upon "probable cause," this phrase has been interpreted by courts only in cases where the warrant was challenged as a basis for arrest rather than as a basis for the decision to charge. If a lawful arrest has been made, it does not necessarily follow that charging would be proper on the same evidence, as the arrest may be based upon "the factual and practical considerations of everyday life on which reasonable and prudent men, not legal technicians, act." *Brinegar v. United States,* 338 U.S. 160, 69 S.Ct. 1302, 93 L.Ed. 1879 (1949).

The prosecutor, as a legal technician, will of course have to consider whether his decision to charge will withstand review at the preliminary hearing and before the grand jury, assuming such steps are required and are not waived by the defendant. See Chapters 14 and 15 of this Book. As a practical matter, the prosecu-

e. Miller & Remington, *Procedures Before Trial,* 339 Annals 111, 115 (1962).

f. *Task Force Report,* supra, at 7. Consider, in this regard, Frampton, *Some Practical and Ethical Problems of Prosecuting Public Officials,* 36 Md.L.Rev. 5, 21 (1976): "If the Watergate prosecutors were inclined to recommend an indictment based on a reasonable certainty of obtaining a conviction, they invited the prospective defendant's lawyer to come (with his client, if he desired) into the office to present an oral argument against indictment. Permitting an accused to make a pre-indictment 'presentation' to the prosecutors is not unheard of in white collar cases, but the Special Prosecutor's Office carried the policy to unusual lengths, making it into the equivalent of an informal adversary hearing on the indictment decision itself. * * *

"Certainly it is reasonable to suggest that every prosecutor ought to be under an affirmative ethical obligation to ensure that both he and the grand jury are exposed to both sides of a prospective criminal case, and whenever possible the defendant should also have some opportunity for input into the charging decision, even if the opportunity falls short of a full adversary hearing. However, present ethical standards do not even touch on this subject."

g. But consider *A.B.A. Code of Prof. Resp.* D.R. 7–103(A): "A public prosecutor or other government lawyer shall not institute or cause to be instituted criminal charges when he knows or it is obvious that the charges are not supported by probable cause."

tor is likely to require admissible evidence showing a high probability of guilt, that is, sufficient evidence to justify confidence in obtaining a conviction. This, however, may vary from case to case, based upon the prosecutor's experience with juries in that district. For example, one former federal prosecutor has reported that in his office it was the practice to require a higher quantum of proof in receipt of stolen goods cases, where the prosecution witnesses were usually admitted thieves and the defendant would usually come from the middle class and not have a prior criminal record. By comparison, less than the normal amount of proof was found to be adequate in narcotics cases, where jury acquittals were rare and defendants were usually persons of lower class.[h] Even in the latter category of cases, however, it was the practice to insist upon a higher quantum of evidence in order to continue the 100% conviction record for these offenses and thereby induce pleas of guilty. Thus, the prosecutor "developed a vested interest in the principle that a jury acquittal in a narcotics case was impossible and hence tended to avoid prosecuting cases where this might happen." [i]

7. *Charging: screening out cases.* "In some cases invocation of the criminal process against marginal offenders seems to do more harm than good. Labeling a person a criminal may set in motion a course of events which will increase the probability of his becoming or remaining one. The attachment of criminal status itself may be so prejudicial and irreversible as to ruin the future of a person who previously had successfully made his way in the community, and it may foreclose legitimate opportunities for offenders already suffering from social, vocational, and educational disadvantages. Yet a criminal code has no way of describing the difference between a petty thief who is on his way to becoming an armed robber and a petty thief who succumbs once to a momentary impulse. The same criminal conduct may be the deliberate act of a professional criminal or an isolated abberation in the behavior of a normally law abiding person. The criminal conduct describes the existence of a problem, but not its nature or source. The system depends on prosecutors to recognize these distinctions when bringing charges.

"Among the types of cases in which thoughtful prosecutors commonly appear disinclined to seek criminal penalties are domestic disturbances; assaults and petty thefts in which victim and offender are in a family or social relationship; statutory rape when both boy and girl are young; first offense car thefts that involve teenager taking a car for a short joyride; checks that are drawn upon insufficient funds; shoplifting by first offenders, particularly when restitution is made; and criminal acts that involve offenders suffering from emotional disorders short of legal insanity." [j]

8. *Charging: diversion.* "One alternative available to prosecutors in the processing of a criminal complaint is that of diversion, 'the channeling of criminal defendants into programs that may not involve incarceration'. * * * Diversion commonly operates in the following manner:

"The pretrial diversion concept typically calls for stopping the prosecution clock on less serious or first felony complaints before or after arrest and prior to the arraignment stage, although there is no indication that more serious alleged offenders, could not be successfully diverted. Those selected for the program are offered counseling, career development, education and

h. Kaplan, *The Prosecutorial Discretion—A Comment,* 60 Nw.U.L.Rev. 174, 184–85 (1965).

i. Id. at 185. See also Skolnick, *Social Control in the Adversary System,* 11 J. Conflict Resolution 52, 57–58 (1967), noting that the prosecutor cares "less about winning than about *not losing,*" as "not only does the prosecutor desire to maintain a respectable record, but more than that, he seeks to maintain, insofar as possible, a reputation for utter credibility, inevitable truth, almost of invincibility."

j. *Task Force Report,* supra, at 5.

supportive treatment services. If the participant responds for a measurable period (e.g. 3–6 months), either the court or the prosecutor or both, depending on the authorization of the project, are asked to approve dismissal of the case prior to trial and adjudication. If the participant fails to meet program obligations, prosecution is resumed on the referral criminal charge." [k]

"In most places there is little liaison between the prosecutor and community agencies which could assist an offender. The prosecutor, frequently overworked, has difficulty searching out noncriminal dispositions, and it is open to question whether he is the appropriate official to perform this searching function. He may have few professional qualifications to decide what treatment alternatives are appropriate for particular offenders. Consultative services to analyze the offender's medical, psychiatric, and social situation; to consider that situation in light of available community resources; and to make appropriate recommendations are at best limited and in many places are not available. But the basic problem is that in many communities the resources for dealing with offenders and their problems are totally inadequate. The development of such resources is clearly essential * * *." [l]

9. *Charging: selection of the charge.* "Once the prosecutor is personally convinced of the guilt of the accused, he then must determine the charge. * * * There is seldom difficulty in the heinous murder or simple petty theft. But what of the case where the offense could be aggravated battery, aggravated assault, battery, or simple assault? Should a charge be burglary, felonious theft, or petty theft? Should a 16-year old boy be charged with a technical burglary or should he be handled as a juvenile before the family court? [m] These are the situations that pose a real test to prosecutorial discretion. Further, evidence may be insufficient, witnesses may be unavailable, the complaining witness may not wish to prosecute, the evidence may have been illegally seized, witnesses may lack credibility, or the case may appear too weak to justify prosecution on the major, technical, or primary offense under the statute. Perhaps the offender has no previous criminal record; perhaps the injuries were too slight; perhaps the offense was the result of mutual combat; perhaps it was a domestic squabble; perhaps there was a considerable delay by the prosecuting witness in reporting the crime; perhaps identification witnesses are weak and unsure of themselves; perhaps the witnesses themselves are convicted criminals and subject to im-

k. *Standards,* fn. c. supra, at 152. For more on diversion, see N.D.A.A., *Deferred Prosecution* (1976); R. Nimmer, *Diversion* (1974); Notes, 50 Ind.L.J. 783 (1975); 28 Rutgers L.Rev. 1203 (1975), and sources cited therein.

l. *Task Force Report,* supra at 7. Other criticisms have been voiced. Zimring, *Measuring the Impact of Pretrial Diversion from the Criminal Justice System,* 41 U.Chi.L.Rev. 224, 238 (1974), notes that most diversion projects have focused upon "defendants who will represent the lowest risk to the community," although "treatment cannot greatly improve this group," because of pressure on the projects to "look good" by "reducing rearrests in the treated group to the bare minimum." Note, 83 Yale L.J. 827, 835 (1974), observes: "One of the often stated advantages of pretrial diversion is the reduction of court docket congestion. This goal seems more ideal than real. Pretrial diversion saves court time only if, in its absence, the accused would go to trial. But most pretrial diversion cases, given the nonserious nature of the charges, would have been disposed of by negotiation and plea rather than trial on the merits."

m. See Mlyniec, *Juvenile Delinquent or Adult Convict—The Prosecutor's Choice,* 14 Am.Crim. L.Rev. 29 (1976), discussing and criticizing the discretion given to prosecutors in 16 states to decide whether a juvenile goes to criminal court or juvenile court. In *Russell v. Parratt,* 543 F.2d 1214 (8th Cir.1976), the court rejected defendant's claim, on habeas corpus, "that since, under the law of Nebraska at the time of his trial, the County Attorney had 'unbridled' discretion to proceed against him either as an adult or a juvenile offender, he has been denied due process in that such decision was made upon the County Attorney's authority alone and without evidentiary hearing." The court held that this is a part of the prosecutor's discretion.

peachment. These are some of the factors which must be weighed and given proper consideration by the prosecutor * * *." [n]

"Very often, an offender's conduct violates more than one criminal statute. This may be the situation because: (1) the offender has committed a series of offenses prior to apprehension, as, for example, a number of burglaries; (2) the offender may, by a single course of criminal conduct, violate more than one criminal statute of the jurisdiction where his conduct occurred, as, for example, in a situation where conduct may constitute both forgery and theft; (3) the offender may violate both state and federal law, as, for example, where theft of an automobile may violate a state statute and a federal statute if the vehicle is driven across a state line. In these situations, prosecutors must decide whether the offender's conduct is to be subjected to a single prosecution for more than one offense or to more than one prosecution.

"There is variation in practice, and there is, therefore, risk of oversimplification in generalizing. There is adequate evidence to show that charging more than one offense is routine practice in many jurisdictions. This gives to the sentencing judge the power to impose consecutive sentences, which occurs frequently in some jurisdictions and rarely in others where, typically, sentences for all of the offenses are made to run concurrently. It is apparent that the processes of charging, convicting, and sentencing the multiple offender are so closely interrelated as to make it impossible to understand completely the one without understanding the other. Charging a single offense may be the practice where the sentencing range available to the judge is adequate to deal with the offender taking cognizance of the totality of his criminal conduct. Charging a number of offenses may be the practice where the penalty for one offense is thought to be disproportionately low in relation to the conduct involved. Also, here, as in relation to the selection of charge, the willingness of the defendant to plead guilty may be reflected in the number of offenses for which he is prosecuted." [o]

SECTION 2. SOME VIEWS ON DISCRETION IN THE CRIMINAL PROCESS AND THE PROSECUTOR'S DISCRETION IN PARTICULAR

WAYNE R. LaFAVE—THE PROSECUTOR'S DISCRETION IN THE UNITED STATES

18 Am.J.Comp.L. 532, 533–39 (1970).

The American prosecutor has traditionally exercised considerable discretion in deciding whether or not to prosecute, that is, in determining whether prosecution is called for in a given case as a matter of enforcement policy. Insufficient attention has been given to the question of precisely why this is so, but the most common explanations are these:

(1) Because of legislative "overcriminalization." As one commentator has said, "The criminal code of any jurisdiction tends to make a crime of everything that people are against, without regard to enforceability, changing social concepts, etc. The result is that the criminal code becomes society's trash bin." Examination of the typical state code of criminal law supports this judgment. Included therein are likely to be crimes which are overdefined for administrative convenience (e.g., the gambling statute which bars *all* forms of gambling so as "to confront the professional gambler with a statutory facade that is wholly devoid of loopholes"); crimes which merely constitute "state-declared ideals" (e.g., the crime of

n. Mills, *The Prosecutor: Charging and "Bargaining,"* 1966 U.Ill.L.F. 511, 514–15.

o. Miller & Remington, supra, at 118–20.

adultery, which is "unenforced because we want to continue our conduct, and unrepealed because we want to preserve our morals"); and now outdated crimes which found their way into the law because of "the mood that dominated a tribunal or legislature at strategic moments in the past, a flurry of public excitement on some single matter."

(2) Because of limitations in available enforcement resources. No prosecutor has available sufficient resources to prosecute all of the offenses which come to his attention. To deny the authority to exercise discretion under these circumstances, it is said, is "like directing a general to attack the enemy on all fronts at once." Thus, so the argument goes, the prosecutor must remain free to exercise his judgment in determining what prosecutions will best serve the public interest.

(3) Because of a need to individualize justice. A criminal code can only deal in general categories of conduct. As Roscoe Pound observed:

> "No lawmaker has been able to foresee more than the broad outlines of the clash of interests or more than the main lines of the courses of conduct to which the law even of his own time must be applied. Moreover, a legal system which seeks to cover everything by a special provision becomes cumbrous and unworkable."

Individualized treatment of offenders, based upon the circumstances of the particular case, has long been recognized in sentencing, and it is argued that such individualized treatment is equally appropriate at the charging stage so as to relieve deserving defendants of even the stigma of prosecution. Were it otherwise, so that the prosecutor acted "in strict accordance with rules of law, precisely and narrowly laid down, the criminal law would be ordered but intolerable."

The current practice, as set forth in a recently-published empirical study of the charging decision, clearly reflects these three considerations. * * *

A full appreciation of the extent of the prosecutor's power, however, requires consideration of the fact that his discretion may be exercised in the other direction; a particular individual may be selected out for prosecution notwithstanding the fact that the case is one which ordinarily would not result in an affirmative charging decision. Sometimes the purpose is to benefit the offender in some way,[20] but usually it is not. Such selection may occur in response to press and public pressure for "law and order," to rid society of certain "bad actors" who are thought to have committed more serious crimes, and for similar reasons.

Should this aspect of the prosecutor's discretion be a matter of concern? Some would undoubtedly say no, on the ground that only acts of leniency are involved, but there are two answers to this. For one thing, not all leniency is consistent with the public interest in effective law enforcement. Moreover, as Professor Kenneth Davis has aptly pointed out:

> "A fundamental fact about the discretionary power to be lenient is extremely simple and entirely clear and yet is usually overlooked: *The discretionary power to be lenient is an impossibility without a concomitant discretionary power not to be lenient, and injustice from the discretionary power not to be lenient is especially frequent; the power to be lenient is the power to discriminate.*"

The discretion of the American prosecutor to decide, as a matter of policy, when to prosecute and when not to prosecute is clearly recognized in the case law. It is said, for example, that the prosecutor must

20. See, e.g., Allen, *The Borderland of Criminal Justice* 5–6 (1964), describing the practice of prosecution and conviction of prospective mothers for some offense relating to extramarital sexual relations when they are without the financial resources to pay for the medical expenses of childbirth or the subsequent care of their offspring.

be allowed to consider whether "a prosecution will promote the ends of justice, instill a respect for law, and advance the cause of ordered liberty," and to take into account "the degree of criminality, the weight of the evidence, the credibility of witnesses, precedent, policy, the climate of public opinion, timing, and the relative gravity of the offense." Indeed, it would hardly make sense to contend that the prosecutor should have *no* discretion; full enforcement would be neither possible nor tolerable. The issue is not discretion versus no discretion, but rather how discretion should be confined, structured, and checked. As Davis notes: "Half the problem is to cut back *unnecessary* discretionary power. The other half is to find effective ways to control *necessary* discretionary power."

1. *Confining the prosecutor's discretion to decide when to prosecute.* A significant part of the discretion currently exercised by American prosecutors is "unnecessary," in the sense that adequate reform of the substantive criminal law would eliminate, as a matter of law, many cases now screened out only at the option of the prosecutor. Clearly, "one of the major consequences of the state of penal law today is that administration has so largely come to dominate the field without effective guidance from the law."

No one would seriously contend that the prosecutor's discretion could be eliminated by penal law reform. It is clear, however, from even the most casual inspection of the typical state criminal code, that some significant portion of that discretion would be unnecessary if many obsolete or largely unenforceable statutes were repealed and if other statutes were more narrowly drawn. The principal benefit of such reform would be that it would eliminate that part of the prosecutor's discretion which carries with it the greatest potential for misuse:

"The worst abuses of discretion in enforcement occur in connection with those offenses that are just barely taken seriously, like most consensual sex offenses. Here, especially in the case of fornication and adultery, enforcement is so sporadic as to be just one step short of complete cessation. And it is here that the greatest danger exists of using enforcement discretion in an abusive way: to pay off a score, to provide a basis for extortion, to stigmatize an otherwise deviant or unpopular figure."

2. *Structuring the prosecutor's discretion to decide when to prosecute.* Nearly forty years ago, Thurman Arnold noted that "the idea that a prosecuting attorney should be permitted to use his discretion concerning the laws which he will enforce and those which he will disregard appears to the ordinary citizen to border on anarchy." This may be the reason why this particular aspect of the prosecutor's discretion has traditionally been exercised sub rosa and on an ad hoc basis, and has thus remained largely unstructured.

The President's Commission on Law Enforcement and Administration of Justice identified three basic needs which must be met before the prosecutor's charging discretion may become more structured and thus more rational. They are:

(a) The need for more information. More detailed background information about the offender is needed so that it may be determined whether he is a dangerous or only marginal offender. (In the absence of any information, or only the limited information provided by a brief police report, the temptation is great to resort to rule-of-thumb policies based only upon the nature of the crime.) In addition, most prosecutors lack sufficient information about alternative treatment facilities and programs in the community to be able to make a rational determination of whether there exists some better course than prosecution.

(b) The need for established standards. "Standards should pertain to such matters as the circumstances that properly can be considered mitigating or aggravating, or the kinds of offenses that should be most vigorously prosecuted in view of the community's law enforcement needs." In large offices, the absence of such standards often results in a lack of uniformity in decision-making by the several assistant prosecutors. But even in a one-man office, consistency would seem more likely if the prosecutor had beforehand attempted to articulate general enforcement standards.

(c) The need for established procedures. These procedures might include a "precharge conference" at which the prosecutor and defense counsel could discuss the appropriateness of a noncriminal disposition. At least in serious cases, a decision not to prosecute should be supported by a written statement of the underlying reasons, and this statement should become a public record.

3. *Checking the prosecutor's discretion to decide when to prosecute.* Although the American criminal justice system has reasonably effective controls to ensure that the prosecutor does not abuse his power by prosecuting upon less than sufficient evidence, there are—as a practical matter—no comparable checks upon his discretionary judgment of whether or not to prosecute one against whom sufficient evidence exists. * * *

While it may be apparent that this is an unfortunate state of affairs, it is not so apparent how the situation might be best remedied. A system of close administrative review, perhaps modeled after the practice in West Germany, would seem to require a hierarchical arrangement quite different from the present structure of most state governments. Whether such a significant change in structure would be an improvement is not readily apparent. As for judicial review, it is probably true that courts have exercised undue restraint in responding to challenges of prosecutorial discretion. Yet, there may be something to the contention that courts are ill-equipped to make enforcement policy. Finally, greater control by the electorate could readily be achieved by exposing the prosecutor's nonenforcement decisions to the public, but it is by no means clear that the soundest enforcement policies are those which would draw approval from the "silent majority."

THURMAN W. ARNOLD—LAW ENFORCEMENT—AN ATTEMPT AT SOCIAL DISSECTION

42 Yale L.J. 1, 7–8, 17–18 (1932).

The fact that prosecuting attorneys are compelled to [use discretion] is generally ignored, or when attention is called to it, regarded as evidence of some kind of social degeneration which must be preached away in public speech and judicial utterance. * * * Disorder must be curbed by law enforcement. If laws are not enforced, disorder will be conclusively presumed. Therefore failure to enforce laws is disorder in itself. The idea is essentially a religious one, and we are acclimated to a wide conflict between practice and utterance in the realm of such notions. Even those who regard the ideal as impracticable so far as their own conduct is concerned consider it good for the public in general. * * *

[An] important effect of the creed of Law Enforcement on legal theory is found in the contradictions in which it is continually involving the judicial system. These are reflected constantly in the complicated distinctions and reconciliations of the Criminal Law with the "law in action" which proceed under that elaborately embroidered verbal cloak. It is impossible to understand the "principles" of the Criminal Law without analyzing these contradictions. A few of them may be stated as follows: * * * (2) *Assumption.* Criminal Law is a body of governing rules, protecting certain social interests which are generally known and guide the ordinary citizen in his conduct. *Contradiction.* Substantive criminal law for the most part consists, not in a set of rules to be enforced, but in an arsenal of weapons to be used against such persons as the police or prosecutor may deem to be a menace to public safety. The choice of weapons is sufficiently elastic that the prosecutor may select a large number of offenses with different penalties to cover any single course of conduct.[a] (3) *Assumption.* It is the duty of the prosecuting attorney to enforce all criminal laws regardless of his own judgment of public convenience or safety. Compromises and "bargain days" in criminal courts lead to disrespect for law because this process conflicts with enforcement of law. *Contradiction.* It is the duty of the prosecuting attorney to solve the problem of public order and safety using the criminal code as an instrument rather than as a set of commands. This makes it proper and necessary that some laws should be enforced, others occasionally enforced, and others ignored according to the best judgment of the enforcing agency. The criminal problem must be looked at as a war on dangerous individuals and not as a law enforcement problem, unless we want to escape from reality by taking refuge in an ideal world of false assumptions concerning both criminal codes and criminals.[b]

A.B.A. STANDARDS

2d ed., 1980.

3–2.5 Prosecutor's handbook; policy guidelines and procedures.

(a) Each prosecutor's office should develop a statement of (i) general policies to guide the exercise of prosecutorial discretion, and (ii) procedures of the office. The objectives of these policies as to discretion and procedures should be to achieve a fair, efficient, and effective enforcement of the criminal law.

(b) In the interest of continuity and clarity, such statement of policies and procedures should be maintained in an office handbook. This handbook should be available to the public, except for subject matters declared "confidential," when it is reasonably believed that public access to their contents would adversely affect the prosecution function.[c]

a. Compare Jackson, *The Federal Prosecutor,* 31 J.Crim.L. & Crimin. 3, 5 (1940):

"If the prosecutor is obliged to choose his cases, it follows that he can choose his defendants. Therein is the most dangerous power of the prosecutor: that he will pick people that he thinks he should get, rather than pick cases that need to be prosecuted. With the law books filled with a great assortment of crimes, a prosecutor stands a fair chance of finding at least a technical violation of some act on the part of almost anyone. In such a case, it is not a question of discovering the commission of a crime and then looking for the man who has committed it, it is a question of picking the man and then searching the law books, or putting investigators to work, to pin some offense on him. It is in this realm—in which the prosecutor picks some person whom he dislikes or desires to embarrass, or selects some group of unpopular persons and then looks for an offense, that the greatest danger of abuse of prosecuting power lies. It is here that law enforcement becomes personal and the real crime becomes that of being unpopular with the predominant or governing group, being attached to the wrong political views, or being personally obnoxious to or in the way of the prosecutor himself."

b. Compare Packer, *The Limits of the Criminal Sanction* 290–91 (1968): "[T]o admit the need for discretion is not to make a virtue of it. And it is far from being a virtue in the enforcement of the criminal sanction. The basic trouble with discretion is simply that it is lawless, in the literal sense of that term. If police or prosecutors find themselves free (or compelled) to pick and choose among known or knowable instances of criminal conduct, they are making a judgment which in a society based on law should be made only by those to whom the making of law is entrusted. For the rough approximation of community values that emerges from the legislative process there is substituted the personal and often idiosyncratic values of the law enforcer."

c. Similarly, Abrams, *Internal Policy: Guiding the Exercise of Prosecutorial Discretion,* 19 U.C.L.A.L.Rev. 1, 34 (1971), concludes that "policy should be regularly published in a medium readily available to the defense bar and other interested persons." What then of the arguments, noted in Abrams, that the publication of policy will (a) encourage litigation on issues not

3–3.8 Discretion as to noncriminal disposition.

(a) The prosecutor should explore the availability of noncriminal disposition, including programs of rehabilitation, formal or informal, in deciding whether to press criminal charges. Especially in the case of a first offender, the nature of the offense may warrant noncriminal disposition.

(b) Prosecutors should be familiar with the resources of social agencies which can assist in the evaluation of cases for diversion from the criminal process.

3–3.9 Discretion in the charging decision.

(a) It is unprofessional conduct for a prosecutor to institute, or cause to be instituted, or to permit the continued pendency of criminal charges when it is known that the charges are not supported by probable cause. A prosecutor should not institute, cause to be instituted, or permit the continued pendency of criminal charges in the absence of sufficient admissible evidence to support a conviction.

(b) The prosecutor is not obliged to present all charges which the evidence might support. The prosecutor may in some circumstances and for good cause consistent with the public interest decline to prosecute, notwithstanding that sufficient evidence may exist which would support a conviction. Illustrative of the factors which the prosecutor may properly consider in exercising his or her discretion are:

(i) the prosecutor's reasonable doubt that the accused is in fact guilty;

(ii) the extent of the harm caused by the offense;

(iii) the disproportion of the authorized punishment in relation to the particular offense or the offender;

(iv) possible improper motives of a complainant;

(v) reluctance of the victim to testify;

(vi) cooperation of the accused in the apprehension or conviction of others; and

(vii) availability and likelihood of prosecution by another jurisdiction.

(c) In making the decision to prosecute, the prosecutor should give no weight to the personal or political advantages or disadvantages which might be involved or to a desire to enhance his or her record of convictions.

(d) In cases which involve a serious threat to the community, the prosecutor should not be deterred from prosecution by the fact that in the jurisdiction juries have tended to acquit persons accused of the particular kind of criminal act in question.

(e) The prosecutor should not bring or seek charges greater in number or degree than can reasonably be supported with evidence at trial.

presently the subject of judicial scrutiny; (b) give defense counsel more leverage and issues to raise; (c) tend to freeze the policy in its then-existing form; (d) improperly modify the deterrent effect of the criminal law; (e) weaken the standards set by the criminal law; (f) make the appearance of impartiality difficult to achieve and breed disrespect for the law; and (g) result in prosecutors being hesitant to articulate policy, particularly as to controversial issues?

Under current practices, guidelines usually are contained primarily in manuals, such as the U.S. Attorney's Manual, that ordinarily are not made available to the public generally nor the bar. Beck, *The Administrative Law of Criminal Prosecution: The Development of Prosecutorial Policy,* 27 Am.U.L.Rev. 310, 314 n. 10 (1978), points out that now the "nine-volume *Manual* is available under the disclosure requirements of the Freedom of Information Act." But a recent Justice Department survey established that 83 of the 94 U.S. Attorneys also have their own individual written guidelines under which they regularly decline to prosecute, and that the criteria "vary substantially from one prosecutor's office to another." The Department refused to release the text of or even excerpts from these guidelines on the ground "that the guidelines, if released, would provide a 'road map' showing where crimes could be committed with the least chance of being prosecuted." *N.Y. Times,* Jan. 7, 1980, at Al, col. 1.

H. RICHARD UVILLER—THE VIRTUOUS PROSECUTOR IN QUEST OF AN ETHICAL STANDARD: GUIDANCE FROM THE A.B.A.

71 Mich.L.Rev. 1145, 1150–53 (1973).

[T]he standards leave me with an uneasy feeling that the issue has not been squarely met. The reason for my disquiet, I think, is that the proponents of the standards embrace the principle of unequal justice (if they will forgive the use of that abrasive term) upon a consideration of only the easy side of the question: leniency and mitigation. Few, looking at the meritorious case in which the prosecutor has interposed a discretionary choice to spare the deserving offender the full harshness of the law's penalty, would call the result unjust. However, the standards leave two related questions to resolution largely by negative pregnant.

First, are we to read the standards to require that the ethical prosecutor turn resolutely away from any contrary impulse and prosecute to the fullest extent any hapless soul who falls into his hands without sufficient mercy points? * * * Let us remember that the legislature, in defining crimes and their degrees—with commensurate punishments—necessarily conceived of aggravated instances, prescribing maximum sanctions suitable for the worst cases in the range embraced by the crime category. May not the prosecutor, like the judge, consider most cases to be less than the worst manifestations of the conduct described by law and recommend lenient or alternative treatment of the offender accordingly? If so, what we need from those who would voice ethical criteria are standards that inform the prosecutor when he should treat a case as unworthy of reduced penalty: In which instances should the full fury of the law be expressed by the ethical prosecutor? Here, on the ugly side, we may expect to find the unjust effects of personal prejudice, anger, inappropriate moralism, and similar unhealthy extraneous considerations counterpointing those that might impel the prosecutor toward leniency. Properly drafted, then, the standard should imply no preference for either full or moderated prosecutions, but rather suggest the appropriate factors for consideration in making the choice.

Second, the standards fail to address the question that worries Professor Freedman: [d] When should the prosecutor pursue a selected target, seeking evidence for prosecution? Standard 3.1(a) simply states that the prosecutor "has an affirmative responsibility to investigate suspected illegal activity when it is not adequately dealt with by other agencies." Passing with wonder, but without comment, the implied deference to "other agencies" which the section's limitation imposes on the prosecutor, we discern no guidance for the exercise of this "affirmative responsibility." Perhaps it is enough for some jurisdictions to call upon the prosecutor to bend his investigative efforts to every case of suspected crime, regardless of the girth of the reed of suspicion or the nature of the crime or criminal to be pursued. But for others, surely, the decision to investigate—that is, to undertake the long, arduous task of building a case when no clear

d. The reference is to Freedman, *The Professional Responsibility of the Prosecuting Attorney*, 55 Geo.L.J. 1030, 1034–35 (1967): "If the government cannot successfully prosecute a notorious criminal for the numerous serious offenses he is suspected of having committed, some prosecutors consider it to be proper to subject him to prosecutions for a variety of other crimes, ranging from traffic offenses to tax evasion, for which he would not be investigated and charged were it not for his notoriety. In support of such practices, it is argued that if the individual is in fact guilty of the crime with which he is charged, the motive of the prosecutor is immaterial. This contention overlooks the fact that there are few of us who have led such unblemished lives as to prevent a determined prosecutor from finding some basis for an indictment or an information. Thus, to say that the prosecutor's motive is immaterial, is to justify making virtually every citizen the potential victim of arbitrary discretion."

evidence pokes through the surface—must, by necessity, be selective, and it requires one of the more significant exercises of discretion in the prosecutor's arsenal. Do the framers of the standards agree with Professor Freedman that it is unethical for the prosecutor to decide to investigate a person because he suspects that the person is engaged in one of a variety of criminal activities, and to seek to make a case against him for any crime he can support with evidence? Do the ethics of the choice dictate a prior resolve to investigate certain activity, *qua* activity, to catch whoever might be involved in it? If the framers feel—as I do—that the distinction between these two is an artificial one, unwarranted by any rational policy, then how should the prosecutor select his target, be it crime or criminal? * * *

As a matter of ethics, the problem sounds to be in tones of motivation. It is less important to me that a prosecutor spends his efforts bringing to bar a notorious pimp, while doing nothing to discover evidence of police corruption, than why this election was made. If a plea to the reduced crime of manslaughter is accepted by the prosecutor from a defendant who murdered a clerk during a holdup, while in another case the prosecutor offers no lesser plea to a man who kills a cop who interrupted a robbery, the important question is why the prosecutor insists on the full measure of guilt for the cop-killer and not for the clerk-killer. The ethical objective, it seems to me, is to keep the exercise of this important discretionary power of the prosecutor free of improper motivation.

I recognize the significance of my disparagement of objective consequences. Unequal results are unequal regardless of the motivation of the official who achieved them. * * * The prosecutor who senses the outrage of his constituency against the aggressive and unsightly hordes of prostitutes infesting the streets may ethically respond by stricter application of valid laws against prostitution. More questionable, it seems to me, is the same campaign waged by the prosecutor as self-appointed custodian of community morality, impelled by personal distaste generated by his own values. I do not suggest that the honorable prosecutor be the slave of his electorate. Indeed, in many matters his duty clearly lies in the defiance of community pressures. But, within the confines of law, I would rather see his discretion guided by an honest effort to discern public needs and community concerns than by personal pique or moralistic impertinence.

KENNETH CULP DAVIS—DISCRETIONARY JUSTICE

188–90, 224–25 (1969).

* * * Why should a prosecutor—say, a county prosecutor—have discretionary power to decide not to prosecute even when the evidence of guilt is clear, perhaps partly on the basis of political influence, without ever having to state to anyone what evidence was brought to light by his investigation and without having to explain to anyone why he interprets a statute as he does or why he chooses a particular position on a difficult question of policy? Why should the discretionary power be so unconfined that, of half a dozen potential defendants he can prove guilty, he can select any one for prosecution and let the other five go, making his decision, if he chooses, on the basis of considerations extraneous to justice? If he finds that A and B are equally guilty of felony and equally deserving of prosecution, why should he be permitted to prosecute B for felony but to let A off with a plea of guilty to a misdemeanor, unless he has a rational and legal basis for his choice, stated on an open record? Why should the vital decisions he makes be immune to review by other officials and immune to review by the courts, even though our legal and governmental system elsewhere

generally assumes the need for checking human frailties? Why should he have a complete power to decide that one statute duly enacted by the people's representatives shall not be enforced at all, that another statute will be fully enforced, and that a third will be enforced only if, as, and when he thinks that it should be enforced in a particular case? Even if we assume that a prosecutor has to have a power of selective enforcement, why do we not require him to state publicly his general policies and require him to follow those policies in individual cases in order to protect evenhanded justice? Why not subject prosecutors' decisions to a simple and general requirement of open findings, open reasons, and open precedents, except when special reason for confidentiality exists? Why not strive to protect prosecutors' decisions from political or other ulterior influence in the same way we strive to protect judges' decisions? * * *

The seeming unanimity of American prosecutors that their discretionary power must be completely uncontrolled is conclusively contradicted by the experience of West Germany, where the discretionary power of prosecutors is so slight as to be almost nonexistent, and where almost all they do is closely supervised.[e]

I think we Americans should learn from other nations that the huge discretionary power of prosecutors need not be unconfined, unstructured, and unchecked. We should reexamine the assumptions to which our drifting has led us—that a prosecutor should have uncontrolled discretion to choose one out of six cases to prosecute, without any requirement that the one most deserving of prosecution be chosen, or to trade a lesser charge for a plea of guilty in one case but not in another, with no guiding rules or standards, without disclosing findings or reasons, without any requirement of consistency, without supervision or check, and without judicial review.

Prosecutors, in my opinion, should be required to make and to announce rules that will guide their choices, stating as far as practicable what will and what will not be prosecuted, and they should be required otherwise to structure their discretion.

---

e. At pp. 194–95, Professor Davis contrasts the German and American systems:

"The most important difference between the German system and the American system is this: *Whenever the evidence that the defendant has committed a serious crime is reasonably clear and the law is not in doubt, the German prosecutor, unlike the American prosecutor, is without discretionary power to withhold prosecution. This means that selective enforcement, a major feature of the American system, is almost wholly absent from the German system.* The German prosecutor does not withhold prosecution for such reasons as that he thinks the statute overreaches, that justice requires withholding enforcement because of special circumstances, that the statute ought to be enforced against some violators and not others, that he lacks time for bringing a marginal prosecution, or that he finds political advantage in not prosecuting. Hence the German prosecutor never has discretionary power to engage in plea bargaining.

"The German and American systems also differ when the evidence or the law or both seem to the prosecutor to be doubtful. When a doubt seems to require a discretionary choice, the German prosecutor does not resolve the doubt; he almost always presents a doubtful case to the judge, who determines the sufficiency of the evidence and the proper interpretation of the law. Of course, in America the prosecutor makes a discretionary determination in every doubtful case, either to prosecute or not to prosecute.

"Even when the prosecutor finds prosecution of a suspect clearly inappropriate, the German system, unlike the American system, provides protection against abuse of power. When a crime is reported by the police or by a private party, a file is opened and registered; the file can be traced at any time. A German prosecutor can never simply forget about the case as his American counterpart may do. The file cannot be closed without a statement of written reasons, which in important cases must be approved by the prosecutor's superior, and which must be reported to any victim of the crime and to any suspect who was interrogated. Every prosecutor is supervised by a superior in a hierarchical system headed by the Minister of Justice, who is himself responsible to the cabinet. The supervision is real, not merely a threat; files are in fact often reviewed. Availability to victims of crimes of procedure to compel prosecution constitutes still another check."

The commentators are not in agreement as to the correctness of the Davis characterization of the German system. Goldstein & Marcus, *The Myth of Judicial Supervision in Three "Inquisitorial" Systems: France, Italy, and Germany,* 87 Yale L.J. 240, 275–76 (1977), state: "Though prosecutors deny that they use evidentiary grounds to conceal policy-motivated dismissals, the denials lose much of their force when we consider the large number of cases dropped for lack of evidence. In 1970, of 3.3 million reported cases, sixty-eight percent were terminated by the prosecutor on such grounds. Even though these figures include crimes reported to the police but not solved, they point plainly to the exercise of some charging discretion by the prosecutor. In Germany, as in Italy, discretion may perhaps be exercised by finding the evidence insufficient by concluding too casually that witnesses are not credible, or by terminating investigations prematurely.

"If, however, it is true that German prosecutors exercise no discretion * * *, the effect may be to shift charging discretion to the police. A recent study by the Max Planck Institute of Freiburg indicates that prosecutors usually accept the view of the police that a case or a charge is not worth pursuing, even where further investigation might produce both a suspect and enough evidence to support a prosecution. And the police, secure in the knowledge that they can 'predict' what the prosecutor will do, often decide that the case will not be solved, that they will be unable to gather sufficient evidence against a suspect, or that the prosecutor should or will drop the prosecution for other reasons. In expectation of that outcome, they may not investigate the matter at all and will instead send the file to the prosecutor with nothing more than the complaint and an officer's brief remarks. The prosecutor routinely accepts the judgment of the police by closing the case."

Langbein & Weinreb, *Continental Criminal Procedure: "Myth" and Reality,* 87 Yale L.J. 1549, 1564 (1978), reply: "Goldstein and Marcus present no evidence at all that these statistics represent anything other than what they purport to be, unsolved and preponderantly petty crimes. Yet the authors rely on these figures for the proposition that German prosecutors are disobeying the rule requiring them to prosecute all *provable* cases of *serious* crime.

"Goldstein and Marcus then shift the finger of suspicion back to the police. * * * But the authors do not mention any case in which the police have pretended that evidence was unobtainable when they in fact knew better."

NOTES ON THE PROSECUTOR'S DISCRETION

1. Should the prosecutor have the sole responsibility for determining when, on policy grounds, an offender should not be subjected to the criminal process, or should the police also be expected to make such decisions, as they frequently do when they decide not to arrest an offender who is lawfully subject to arrest? "It has been traditional to give explicit recognition to the propriety of discretion on the part of the prosecutor and either to deny or, more commonly, to ignore the issue of police discretion. [There is apparently an] assumption that the average municipal police agency lacks any special competence to make policy decisions * * *. For example, the United States Supreme Court held it proper for the Federal Trade Commission to follow a policy of proceeding criminally against only major violators because there were insufficient resources to proceed against all violators.[a] This kind of judgment was said to be within the expertness of the enforcement agency, which is familiar with the economic problems being dealt with. Under similar circumstances, a Philadelphia court held an

a. *Moog Industries, Inc. v. FTC,* 355 U.S. 411, 78 S.Ct. 377, 2 L.Ed.2d 370 (1958).

identical policy of the Philadelphia Police Commissioner to be improper.[b] The Philadelphia court gave no indication that it believed that the police commissioner was particularly qualified to decide how best to allocate the limited enforcement resources made available to him." [c]

"Although the prosecutor is legally accorded a wider area of discretion than the policeman, the setting of the policeman's role offers greater opportunity to behave inconsistently with the rule of law. Police discretion is 'hidden' insofar as the policeman often makes decisions in direct interaction with the suspect. * * * By contrast, prosecutorial discretion frequently takes place at a later stage in the system, after the initial charge has been made public. The public character of the charge may restrict the prosecutor's discretion in practice more than the policeman's, even though the scope of the prosecutor's discretion is far wider in theory." [d]

Does this mean "the police should operate in an atmosphere which exhorts and commands them to invoke impartially all criminal laws within the bounds of *full enforcement,*" so that "[r]esponsibility for the enactment, amendment, and repeal of the criminal laws will not, then, be abandoned to the whim of each police officer or department, but retained where it belongs in a democracy—with elected representatives"? [e]

2. The prosecutor's decision not to prosecute is often based upon the expectation that the judge or jury would refuse to convict notwithstanding proof of guilt beyond a reasonable doubt. The jury in a criminal case has uncontrolled discretion to acquit the guilty. An empirical study has shown that juries acquit the guilty because: (a) they sympathize with the defendant as a person; (b) they apply personal attitudes as to when self-defense should be recognized; (c) they take into account the contributory fault of the victim; (d) they believe the offense is *de minimus;* (e) they take into account the fact that the statute violated is an unpopular law; (f) they feel the defendant has already been punished enough; (g) they feel the defendant was subjected to improper police or prosecution practices; (h) they refuse to apply strict liability statutes to inadvertent conduct; (i) they apply their own standards as to when mental illness or intoxication should be a defense; and (j) they believe the offense is accepted conduct in the subculture of the defendant and victim. See Kalven & Zeisel, *The American Jury* chs. 15–27 (1966).

3. Because there is not agreement on whether such discretionary action by a jury is a desirable safety valve in the criminal justice system or an unavoidable evil, it is a debatable point whether it is proper for the trial judge to act in a similar fashion when a case is tried before him without a jury. The *Model Penal Code* would give the trial judge discretion to acquit the guilty under certain circumstances,[f] and an empirical study has established that judges acquit guilty defendants for the same rea-

b. *Bargain City U.S.A., Inc. v. Dilworth,* 29 U.S.L. Week 2002 (Pa.C.P., June 10, 1960), aff'd, 407 Pa. 129, 179 A.2d 439 (1962).

c. LaFave, *Arrest: The Decision to Take a Suspect Into Custody* 72–73 (1965).

d. Skolnick, *Justice Without Trial* 233–34 (1966)

e. J. Goldstein, *Police Discretion Not to Invoke the Criminal Process,* 69 Yale L.J. 543, 586 (1960). For more on police discretion, see Symposium, 47 Law & Contemp.Prob. 1 (1984).

f. When "the defendant's conduct:

"(1) was within a customary license or tolerance, neither expressly negatived by the person whose interest was infringed nor inconsistent with the purpose of the law defining the offense; or

"(2) did not actually cause or threaten the harm or evil sought to be prevented by the law defining the offense or did so only to an extent too trivial to warrant the condemnation of conviction; or

"(3) presents such other extenuations that it cannot reasonably be regarded as envisaged by the legislature in forbidding the offense." *Model Penal Code* § 2.12

sons that juries do. See Newman, *Conviction: The Determination of Guilt or Innocence Without Trial* chs. 9–12, 14 (Remington ed. 1966).[g]

Should the trial judge, even in a jury case, be recognized as possessing authority essentially the same as that of the prosecutor, so that he might dismiss or reduce charges? Consider *United States v. Weinstein,* 452 F.2d 704 (2d Cir.1971) (nothing in the federal rules "gives the judge an overriding power to terminate a criminal prosecution in which the Government's evidence has passed the test of legal sufficiency simply because he thinks that course would be most consonant with the interests of justice"); *People v. McAlonan,* 99 Cal.Rptr. 733 (App.1972) (judge's dismissal of possession of marijuana charge because he believed defendant's rehabilitation would thereby be better served was improper, given "society's interest that justice be dispensed with an even hand and in accordance with statutory authority").

4. To what extent, if at all, should the prosecutor's discretion be exercised only subject to the wishes of the crime victim? The federal Victim and Witness Protection Act of 1982 provides that "the victim of a serious crime, or in the case of a minor child or a homicide, the family of the victim, shall be consulted by the attorney for the Government in order to obtain the views of the victim or family about the disposition of any Federal criminal case brought as a result of such crime, including the views of the victim or family about * * * dismissal [or referral to a] pretrial diversion program." Section 6(a)(5) of the Act, in note to 18 U.S.C. § 1512. The Act requires the Justice Department to develop guidelines on "consultation with the victim," and these guidelines require consultation also with respect to "the decision not to seek an indictment or otherwise commence prosecution."

Although "it will be a long while before the results are in" on this "major experiment in criminal justice," some speculations are possible: "This approach is a long way from requiring the prosecutor to accept the victim's views and an even longer distance from judicial acceptance of those views. Indeed, there is the risk that such consultation will be perceived by victims as so plainly 'cosmetic' in nature that they will not be moved at all to increase their cooperation and confidence in law enforcement.

"Yet matters are never quite so simple. If victims must be consulted, prosecutors are likely to feel the pull towards doing so in good faith—because of their fidelity to the requirements of law and their fear of adverse publicity. The same is true of disagreement with the victim's views. Prosecutors and judges will be pressed to be responsive to an interest now being separated from the amorphous 'public' interest and urged on them more often as deserving special consideration. Even so, Congress and the victims' movement must not expect too much. In the end, the victim's views, even when he appears personally, will be only one element in a wide variety of interests which prosecutor and judge—each in his respective sphere—must take into account. The distinctive thing about the victim is that he (like the defendant) is strategically located and motivated to watch closely how the law is being applied in a particular case—and to call attention to inaccuracy, illegality, and inequality in the administration of criminal justice."[h]

g. If the trial judge exercises his discretion to acquit a guilty defendant, it appears that the state is just as powerless to object as when a jury so acts. See *State v. Evjue,* 37 N.W.2d 50 (Wis. 1949), where, notwithstanding a statutory provision permitting appeal by the state in a criminal case as to questions of law, the court refused to review the merits of an acquittal clearly contrary to the evidence. Cf. *Fong Foo v. United States,* 369 U.S. 141, 82 S.Ct. 671, 7 L.Ed.2d 629 (1962), holding that if a federal judge directs a verdict of acquittal before all of the government's evidence is in, a subsequent trial for the same offense would constitute double jeopardy.

h. A. Goldstein, *The Victim and Prosecutorial Discretion: The Federal Victim and Witness Protection Act of 1982,* 47 Law & Contemp.Prob. 225, 247 (1984).

5. What decision would you, as prosecuting attorney, reach in the following cases? What additional facts, if any, would you desire in each case prior to making a decision?

(a) A man lured several 14-year-old boys to a mountain cabin, bound them up, and sexually molested them. One of the lads managed to free himself and the others, found a rifle in the cabin, and then shot and killed their abductor upon his later return to the cabin. The juvenile court law of the state gives the criminal courts exclusive jurisdiction over juveniles when they are charged with murder. The law of self-defense in the jurisdiction only permits the use of deadly force "to prevent imminent death or great bodily harm to himself or another," which was not the case here. See Sax, *Civil Disobedience,* Saturday Review, Sept. 28, 1968, p. 22.

(b) A woman returned home from work a few hours late in a disheveled condition and told her husband that she had been kidnapped and raped. The husband called the police, and on the basis of the information given by the woman two suspects were arrested the next day. Upon questioning the woman in more detail the following day, the police discovered some discrepancies in her story, and she finally admitted that she was carrying on an affair with a man and that she had fabricated the story in order to explain her absence to her husband. Filing a false felony report is a criminal offense punishable by a fine of up to $500 and imprisonment up to six months. See LaFave, *Arrest: The Decision to Take a Suspect Into Custody* 140 (Remington ed. 1965).

(c) The three-year-old daughter of a married couple disappeared while the family was riding on a train. About 15 minutes later, she was located seated on the lap of an elderly gentleman in his compartment. Upon questioning the child, the parents learned that the man had fondled the child. The man, a respected community leader with no police record, was visibly shaken by the situation and explained that he had not thought he was doing anything wrong, that he liked children, and that he had grandchildren of his own. See LaFave, supra, at 141–42.

(d) A man called the prosecutor's office to ask that his next door neighbor be prosecuted for tearing down part of his fence, which ran between their properties. Investigation disclosed that the offense of criminal damage to property had in fact occurred, but also that this was merely the latest incident in a longstanding feud between the two men concerning the boundaries of their respective properties. See LaFave, supra, at 119.

(e) A man lawfully arrested concerning another matter, as to which he was subsequently cleared, was found to have a small amount of heroin in his apartment. At the suggestion of his counsel, he was permitted to take a lie detector test, which indicated that he was unaware that the heroin was there. The test also indicated that the man was not telling the truth when he denied being involved in the narcotics traffic. See Kaplan, *The Prosecutorial Discretion—A Comment,* 60 Nw.U.L.Rev. 174, 179 (1965).

(f) A landlord was owed a debt of $240 by his former tenant, who had moved out of the city without paying his rent. The landlord, upon seeing a tax refund check arrive at his tenant's former address, signed his debtor's name to the check (for $180) and cashed the check. This is a violation of the federal statute on forgery of government obligations, 18 U.S.C. § 471, punishable by a fine of up to $5,000 and imprisonment up to fifteen years. See Kaplan, supra, at 188–89.

(g) An applicant for temporary employment as a mail carrier during the Christmas season completed a government employment application form in which he falsely denied ever having been arrested. A subsequent investigation disclosed that he had a record of several arrests for such offenses as drunkenness and vagrancy. This, however, did not become known until the man had been hired and had completed his temporary service for the post office department. His false statements were in violation of 18 U.S.C. § 1001, and are punishable by a fine of not more than $10,000 and imprisonment for five years. See Kaplan, supra, at 189–90.

SECTION 3. CHALLENGING THE PROSECUTOR'S DISCRETION

I. THE DECISION NOT TO PROSECUTE

In INMATES OF ATTICA CORRECTIONAL FACILITY v. ROCKEFELLER, 477 F.2d 375 (2d Cir.1973), the inmates and others brought a class action seeking to require federal and state officials to investigate and prosecute persons who allegedly had violated certain federal and state criminal statutes in connection with treatment of inmates during and following the Attica prison uprising. The district court dismissed the complaint, and the court of appeals, per MANSFIELD, J., affirmed:

"With respect to the defendant United States Attorney, plaintiffs seek mandamus to compel him to investigate and institute prosecutions against state officers, most of whom are not identified, for alleged violations of 18 U.S.C. §§ 241 and 242. Federal mandamus is, of course, available only 'to compel an officer or employee of the United States * * * to perform a duty owned to the plaintiff.' 28 U.S.C. § 1361. And the legislative history of § 1361 makes it clear that ordinarily the courts are 'not to direct or influence the exercise of discretion of the officer or agency in the making of the decision.' More particularly, federal courts have traditionally and, to our knowledge, uniformly refrained from overturning, at the instance of a private person, discretionary decisions of federal prosecuting authorities not to prosecute persons regarding whom a complaint of criminal conduct is made.

"This judicial reluctance to direct federal prosecutions at the instance of a private party asserting the failure of United States officials to prosecute alleged criminal violations has been applied even in cases such as the present one where, according to the allegations of the complaint, which we must accept as true for purposes of this appeal, serious questions are raised as to the protection of the civil rights and physical security of a definable class of victims of crime and as to the fair administration of the criminal justice system.

"The primary ground upon which this traditional judicial aversion to compelling prosecutions has been based is the separation of powers doctrine. * * *

"In the absence of statutorily defined standards governing reviewability, or regulatory or statutory policies of prosecution, the problems inherent in the task of supervising prosecutorial decisions do not lend themselves to resolution by the judiciary. The reviewing courts would be placed in the undesirable and injudicious posture of becoming 'superprosecutors.' In the normal case of review of executive acts of discretion, the administrative record is open, public and reviewable on the basis of what it contains. The decision not to prosecute, on the other hand, may be based upon the insufficiency of the available evidence, in which event the secrecy of the grand jury and of the prosecutor's file may serve to protect the accused's reputation from public damage based upon insufficient, improper, or even malicious charges. *In camera* review would not be meaningful without access by the complaining party to the evidence before the grand jury or U.S. Attorney. Such interference with the normal operations of criminal investigations, in turn, based solely upon allegations of criminal conduct, raises serious questions of potential abuse by persons seeking to have other persons prosecuted. Any person, merely by filing a complaint containing allegations in general terms (permitted by the Federal Rules) of unlawful failure to prosecute, could gain access to the prosecutor's file and the grand jury's minutes, notwithstanding the secrecy normally attaching to the latter by law. See Rule 6(e), F.R.Cr.P.

"Nor is it clear what the judiciary's role of supervision should be were it to undertake such a review. At what point would the prosecutor be entitled to call a halt to further investigation as unlikely to be productive? What evidentiary standard would be used to decide whether prosecution should be compelled? How much judgment would the United States Attorney be allowed? Would he be permitted to limit himself to a strong 'test' case rather than pursue weaker cases? What collateral factors would be permissible bases for a decision not to prosecute, e.g., the pendency of another criminal proceeding elsewhere against the same parties? What sort of review should be available in cases like the present one where the conduct complained of allegedly violates state as well as federal laws? With limited personnel and facilities at his disposal, what priority would the prosecutor be required to give to cases in which investigation or prosecution was directed by the court?

"These difficult questions engender serious doubts as to the judiciary's capacity to review and as to the problem of arbitrariness inherent in any judicial decision to order prosecution. On balance, we believe that substitution of a court's decision to compel prosecution for the U.S. Attorney's decision not to prosecute, even upon an abuse of discretion standard of review and even if limited to directing that a prosecution be undertaken in good faith, would be unwise.

"Plaintiffs urge, however, that Congress withdrew the normal prosecutorial discretion for the kind of conduct alleged here by providing in 42 U.S.C. § 1987 that the United States Attorneys are 'authorized *and required* * * * to institute prosecutions against all persons violating any of the provisions of [18 U.S.C. §§ 241, 242]' (emphasis supplied), and, therefore, that no barrier to a judicial directive to institute prosecutions remains. This contention must be rejected. The mandatory nature of the word 'required' as it appears in § 1987 is insufficient to evince a broad Congressional purpose to bar the exercise of executive discretion in the prosecution of federal civil rights crimes. * * *

"Such language has never been thought to preclude the exercise of prosecutorial discretion. Indeed the same contention made here was specifically rejected in *Moses v. Kennedy,* 219 F.Supp. 762, 765 (D.D.C.1963), aff'd 342 F.2d 931 (1965), where seven black residents and one white resident of Mississippi sought mandamus to compel the Attorney General of the United States and the Director of the F.B.I. to investigate, arrest, and prosecute certain individuals, including state and local law enforcement officers, for willfully depriving the plaintiffs of their civil rights. There the Court noted that 'considerations of judgment and discretion apply with special strength to the area of civil rights, where the Executive Department must be largely free to exercise its considered judgment on questions of whether to proceed by means of prosecution, injunction, varying forms of persuasion, or other types of action.' * * *

"With respect to the state defendants, plaintiffs also seek prosecution of named and unknown persons for the violation of state crimes. However, they have pointed to no statutory language even arguably creating any mandatory duty upon the state officials to bring such prosecutions. To the contrary, New York law reposes in its prosecutors a discretion to decide whether or not to prosecute in a given case, which is not subject to review in the state courts." [a]

---

a. Many comparable decisions are to be found concerning the discretion of state prosecutors. See, e.g., *Manning v. Municipal Court,* 361 N.E.2d 1274 (Mass.1977) (spectator at Fenway Park, allegedly struck by baseball thrown from visiting team's bullpen by Ross Grimsley, cannot compel prosecutor to undertake assault and battery prosecution).

UNITED STATES v. COX, 342 F.2d 167 (5th Cir.1965), concerned the refusal of a United States Attorney, upon instructions from the Acting Attorney General, to prepare or sign indictments for a federal grand jury in the Southern District of Mississippi charging with perjury two Negroes who had testified in a civil rights action brought by the United States against a county voting registrar. A federal judge held the United States Attorney in contempt and also ordered that the Acting Attorney General show cause why he should not also be adjudged guilty of contempt. Three members of the court took the view that the United States Attorney was not obligated to either prepare or sign the indictments, three others that he was obligated to do both, and the seventh (who determined the majority) that he must prepare but need not sign the indictments.

JUDGE JONES, in the first group, wrote: "The role of the grand jury is restricted to a finding as to whether or not there is probable cause to believe that an offense has been committed. The discretionary power of the attorney for the United States in determining whether a prosecution shall be commenced or maintained may well depend upon matters of policy wholly apart from any question of probable cause. Although as a member of the bar, the attorney for the United States is an officer of the court, he is nevertheless an executive official of the Government, and it is as an officer of the executive department that he exercises a discretion as to whether or not there shall be a prosecution in a particular case. It follows, as an incident of the constitutional separation of powers, that the courts are not to interfere with the free exercise of the discretionary powers of the attorneys of the United States in their control over criminal prosecutions. The provision of Rule 7, requiring the signing of the indictment by the attorney for the Government, is a recognition of the power of Government counsel to permit or not to permit the bringing of an indictment. * * * [S]ince the United States Attorney cannot be required to give validity to an indictment by affixing his signature, he should not be required to indulge in an exercise of futility by the preparation of the form of an indictment which he is unwilling to vitalize with his signature."

JUDGES RIVES, GEWIN and BELL explained their vote to compel the United States Attorney to both prepare and sign the indictments in this way:

"The grand jury may be permitted to function in its traditional sphere, while at the same time enforcing the separation of powers doctrine as between the executive and judicial branches of the government. This can best be done, indeed, it is mandatory, by requiring the United States Attorney to assist the grand jury in preparing indictments which they wish to consider or return, and by requiring the United States Attorney to sign any indictment that is to be returned. Then, once the indictment is returned, the Attorney General or the United States Attorney can refuse to go forward. That refusal will, of course, be in open court and not in the secret confines of the grand jury room. To permit the district court to compel the United States Attorney to proceed beyond this point would invest prosecutorial power in the judiciary, power which under the Constitution is reserved to the executive branch of the government. It may be that the court, in the interest of justice, may require a showing of good faith, and a statement of some rational basis for dismis-

Compare *State ex rel. Ginsberg v. Naum*, 318 S.E.2d 454 (W.Va.1984) (court grants mandamus, on petition of Dep't of Human Services, for prosecution of welfare fraud cases; court relies on statute declaring it to be duty of every prosecutor "when he has information of the violation *of any penal law* committed within such county" to "institute and prosecute all necessary and proper proceedings against the offender," which makes it a prosecutor's non-discretionary duty to institute proceedings against persons when he has information giving him probable cause to believe that *any* penal law has been violated," even if the prosecutor has insufficient manpower).

sal. In the unlikely event of bad faith or irrational action, not here present, it may be that the court could appoint counsel to prosecute the case. In brief, the court may have the same inherent power to administer justice to the government as it does to the defendant. That question is not now before us and may never arise. Except for a very limited discretion, however, the court's power to withhold leave to dismiss an indictment is solely for the protection of the defendant."

JUDGE BROWN noted that his conclusion that the United States Attorney must prepare but need not sign the indictments "lacks logical consistency," but thought there were sound reasons for both positions. Since the signature of the federal prosecutor, together with that of the jury's foreman, "is a formal, effective initiation of a prosecution," so that "what was previously an unfettered discretionary right on the part of the executive not to initiate prosecution has now been set in motion and can be stopped only on the executive taking affirmative action for dismissal with all of the uncertainties which F.R.Crim.P. 48(a) generates," the signature should not be required. However, Judge BROWN concluded, the grand jury should be entitled to the legal assistance of the U.S. Attorney in the preparation of the indictment so that the document, as drafted, "would clearly reflect the conscientious conclusion of the Grand Jury itself" and "reveal the difference of view as between the Grand Jury and the prosecuting attorney."

Notes and Questions

1. *The court as a check on the prosecutor's decision not to prosecute.* Although all jurisdictions recognize that the prosecutor has a substantial range of discretion in deciding whether or not to prosecute, many have placed some controls on his discretion after initial steps toward prosecution have been taken. There is a split of authority, for example, on the question whether a prosecutor may nol pros (from the Latin phrase *nolle prosequi*—an entry on the record by the prosecutor declaring that he will not prosecute) after the magistrate has sent the case to the grand jury but before the grand jury has had an opportunity to make a formal accusation. When the law permits the prosecutor to forego indictment and prosecute by information (a formal charge prepared by the prosecutor), almost all jurisdictions permit the prosecutor to nol pros after the preliminary hearing and before an information has been filed, although some states require that he file a statement of his reasons with the court. After formal accusation by indictment or information, a few states still recognize the power which the prosecutor possessed in the common law to nol pros on his own. Some other states, however, have now placed this authority entirely within the discretion of the court, while others require the court's approval for entry of a nol pros.[b] Which system is preferable?

If court approval is required for dismissal of a charge, as in Fed.R.Crim.P. 48(a), what standard should the court apply in assessing the prosecutor's request? See *United States v. Cowan,* 524 F.2d 504 (5th Cir.1975), concluding that the "exercise of [the prosecutor's] discretion with respect to the termination of pending prosecutions should not be judicially disturbed unless clearly contrary to manifest public interest," and consider *United States v. Biddings,* 416 F.Supp. 673 (N.D.Ill.1976) (though after-discovered witnesses friendly to defendant stated robbery which led to kidnapping was committed by another person,

b. But in these jurisdictions it is sometimes held that the uncontrolled power of the prosecutor revives following return of the verdict and continues until judgment is entered and sentence is imposed. Compare *State ex rel. Norwood v. Drumm,* 691 S.W.2d 238 (Mo.1985), requiring court approval on the ground the court should take into account the fact that "the verdict rendered reveals that the jury, after hearing the evidence, found it sufficient to support the charge the prosecutor now seeks to dismiss."

indictment would not be dismissed where kidnap victims did not recant their identification of defendant; to dismiss "would delegate to the prosecutor the right to decide between conflicting evidence and make a mockery of the grand jury system and of the law of identification").

2. *The grand jury as a check.* Most jurisdictions permit the grand jury to initiate prosecution by indictment even though the prosecutor opposes prosecution. Some require only that the foreman, acting on behalf of the grand jury, sign the indictment. Others have provisions similar to Rule 7 requiring the prosecutor's signature, but they view that requirement as mandating essentially a "clerical act" by the prosecutor. It takes a most unusual case, however, for a grand jury to act as a "runaway" and indict notwithstanding the prosecutor's opposition. See pp. 695, 702–03 supra, and pp. 977–80 infra.

3. *The state attorney general as a check.* At common law, the attorney general exercised wide powers of supervision over all criminal prosecutions, and in states in which he retains these powers he may initiate and prosecute criminal cases and may, at his discretion, supersede and replace the local prosecutor. Also, many states by statute confer upon the attorney general the power to initiate prosecution in cases where the local prosecutor has failed to act. In practice, however, attorneys general have seldom exercised much control over local prosecuting attorneys.

4. *Private prosecution when the prosecutor does not act.* Noting that some foreign jurisdictions permit private criminal prosecution when the public prosecutor fails to act, Comment, 65 Yale L.J. 209, 233 (1955), recommends that state legislatures "enact statutes providing substantially as follows:

"1. A trial court may in its discretion, upon petition of any person, substitute an attorney hired by the petitioner to replace a public prosecutor for any criminal prosecution if (a) the public prosecutor fails or refuses to prosecute the defendant or proceeds improperly, and (b) the crime charged is open and notorious or the petitioner has a cause of action against the defendant in tort on the facts alleged.

"2. A trial court shall not grant a petition without notifying the public prosecutor of the petition and allowing him reasonable time to answer it.

"3. A private prosecution shall not be discontinued without permission of the trial court. At any stage of the proceedings the public prosecutor may present evidence showing why the private prosecution should be dismissed.

"4. A private prosecutor shall receive reasonable compensation for legal services from county funds unless the trial court determines that the prosecution is malicious, in which case the petitioner shall pay the defendant reasonable compensation for legal services plus trial costs."

Compare *Tonkin v. Michael,* 349 F.Supp. 78 (D.Virgin Islands 1972), holding that notwithstanding a court rule permitting private prosecution when the prosecutor "does not appear," the court should not allow private prosecution over the objection of the prosecutor, as "in the context of law enforcement, it is desirable to seek uniformity of prosecutorial policy," and the prosecutor's discretion should not "be controlled by any interested individual or individuals seeking redress by the use of criminal process for alleged wrongs committed against them." Consider also *People v. Municipal Court,* 103 Cal.Rptr. 645 (App.1972), holding that an individual cannot institute criminal proceedings without the prosecutor's approval because: (1) for a court to accept such a complaint is in violation of the separation of powers provision of the state constitution, as it "encroaches upon the executive power"; and (2) the due process clauses of the United States and state constitutions prohibit it, as "all persons should be protected from having to defend against frivolous prosecutions and * * * one major safeguard against such prosecutions is the function of the district attorney in screening criminal cases prior to instituting a prosecution." [c]

5. *Removal; substitution of special prosecutor.* As observed in Note 4, p. 879, supra, proceedings to permanently remove a prosecutor are seldom utilized, and are most unlikely absent a charge of criminal activity.

"There appear to be three areas where the need for the services of a special prosecutor arises: 1. Conflict: The prosecuting attorney is legally precluded from proceeding due to a conflict of interest; 2. Complexity: The prosecutor is faced with a difficult case beyond his investigative and legal abilities; 3. Public trust: There is corruption within the judicial/governmental system, and public confidence requires an 'uninvolved' outsider to investigate and prosecute." Taylor, *A Needed Legal Specialty: The Special Prosecutor,* 61 Judicature 220, 221 (1977).

In *Venhaus v. Brown,* 691 S.W.2d 141 (Ark.1985), the trial court appointed a special prosecutor because the prosecutor had failed to charge an attorney with complicity in the murder of the attorney's wife notwithstanding statements by the sheriff that he had evidence sufficient for conviction. The sheriff asserted that the prosecutor was giving favorable treatment to another lawyer, while the prosecutor asserted he failed to file charges because he believed the attorney was innocent. The appointment was held invalid as an improper interference with the prosecutor's discretion.

II. THE DECISION TO PROSECUTE

WAYTE v. UNITED STATES

___ U.S. ___, 105 S.Ct. 1524, 84 L.Ed.2d 547 (1985).

JUSTICE POWELL delivered the opinion of the Court. * * *

I

On July 2, 1980, pursuant to his authority under § 3 of the Military Selective Service Act, 62 Stat. 605, as amended, 50 U.S.C.App. § 453, the President issued Presidential Proclamation No. 4771, 3 CFR 82 (1981). This proclamation directed male citizens and certain male residents born during 1960 to register with the Selective Service System during the week of July 21, 1980. Petitioner fell within that class but did not register. Instead, he wrote several letters to Government officials, including the President, stating that he had not registered and did not intend to do so.

Petitioner's letters were added to a Selective Service file of young men who advised that they had failed to register or who were reported by others as having failed to register. For reasons we discuss, infra, Selective Service adopted a policy of passive enforcement under which it would investigate and prosecute only the cases of nonregistration contained in this file. In furtherance of this policy, Selective Service sent a letter on June 17, 1981 to each reported violator who had not registered and for whom it had an address. The letter explained the duty to register, stated that Selective Service had information that the person was required to register but

c. Cf. *Anderson v. Norfolk & Western Ry.,* 349 F.Supp. 121 (W.D.Va.1972), holding that a private citizen could not bring a *qui tam* action for pollution, as the informer fee provided by statute is derived from sanctions imposed after conviction, and U.S. Attorneys "are immune from interference by private citizens" in exercising discretion whether to prosecute. On *qui tam* actions, see Comment, 20 U.C.L.A.L.Rev. 778 (1973).

Private prosecution must be distinguished from the practice, permitted in several states, of having private counsel retained by the victim assist the prosecutor in a criminal trial. See Comment, 25 Am.U.L.Rev. 754, 755 (1976), asserting "that the practice is outdated, unnecessary, unethical, and perhaps unconstitutional"; *State v. Berg,* 694 P.2d 427 (Kan.1985) (notwithstanding statute allowing prosecution witness to provide at own expense attorney to assist the prosecutor, that private attorney may not prosecute over wishes of prosecutor; "the person representing the state in a criminal proceeding must be a law-trained, independent public prosecutor rather than a vengeful persecutor").

had not done so, requested that he either comply with the law by filling out an enclosed registration card or explain why he was not subject to registration, and warned that a violation could result in criminal prosecution and specified penalties. Petitioner received a copy of this letter but did not respond.

On July 20, 1981, Selective Service transmitted to the Department of Justice, for investigation and potential prosecution, the names of petitioner and 133 other young men identified under its passive enforcement system—all of whom had not registered in response to the Service's June letter. At two later dates, it referred the names of 152 more young men similarly identified. After screening out the names of those who appeared not to be in the class required to register, the Department of Justice referred the remaining names to the Federal Bureau of Investigation for additional inquiry and to the United States Attorneys for the districts in which the nonregistrants resided. Petitioner's name was one of those referred.

Pursuant to Department of Justice policy, those referred were not immediately prosecuted. Instead, the appropriate United States Attorney was required to notify identified nonregistrants by registered mail that, unless they registered within a specified time, prosecution would be considered. In addition, an FBI agent was usually sent to interview the nonregistrant before prosecution was instituted. This effort to persuade nonregistrants to change their minds became known as the "beg" policy. Under it young men who registered late were not prosecuted, while those who never registered were investigated further by the Government. Pursuant to the "beg" policy, the United States Attorney for the Central District of California sent petitioner a letter on October 15, 1981 urging him to register or face possible prosecution. Again petitioner failed to respond.

On December 9, 1981, the Department of Justice instructed all United States Attorneys not to begin seeking indictments against nonregistrants until further notice. On January 7, 1982, the President announced a grace period to afford nonregistrants a further opportunity to register without penalty. This grace period extended until February 28, 1982. Petitioner still did not register.

Over the next few months, the Department decided to begin prosecuting those young men who, despite the grace period and "beg" policy, continued to refuse to register. It recognized that under the passive enforcement system those prosecuted were "liable to be vocal proponents of nonregistration" or persons "with religious or moral objections." It also recognized that prosecutions would "undoubtedly result in allegations that the [case was] brought in retribution for the nonregistrant's exercise of his first amendment rights." The Department was advised, however, that Selective Service could not develop a more "active" enforcement system for quite some time. Because of this, the Department decided to begin seeking indictments under the passive system without further delay. On May 21, 1982, United States Attorneys were notified to begin prosecution of nonregistrants. On June 28, 1982, FBI agents interviewed petitioner and he continued to refuse to register. Accordingly, on July 22, 1982, an indictment was returned against him for knowingly and willfully failing to register with the Selective Service. This was one of the first indictments returned against any individual under the passive policy.

II

Petitioner moved to dismiss the indictment on the ground of selective prosecution. He contended that he and the other indicted nonregistrants [3] were "vocal" op-

3. The record indicates that only 13 of the 286 young men Selective Service referred to the Department of Justice had been indicted at the time the District Court considered this case. As of

ponents of the registration program who had been impermissibly targeted (out of an estimated 674,000 nonregistrants) for prosecution on the basis of their exercise of First Amendment rights. After a hearing, the District Court for the Central District of California granted petitioner's broad request for discovery and directed the Government to produce certain documents and make certain officials available to testify. The Government produced some documents and agreed to make some Government officials available but, citing executive privilege, it withheld other documents and testimony. On October 29, 1982, the District Court ordered the Government to produce the disputed documents and witness. The Government declined to comply and on November 5, 1982 asked the District Court to dismiss the indictment in order to allow an appeal challenging the discovery order. Petitioner asked for dismissal on several grounds, including discriminatory prosecution.

On November 15, 1982, the District Court dismissed the indictment on the ground that the Government had failed to rebut petitioner's prima facie case of selective prosecution. Following precedents of the Court of Appeals for the Ninth Circuit, the District Court found that in order to establish a prima facie case petitioner had to prove that (i) others similarly situated generally had not been prosecuted for conduct similar to petitioner's and (ii) the Government's discriminatory selection was based on impermissible grounds such as race, religion, or exercise of First Amendment rights. Petitioner satisfied the first requirement, the District Court held, because he had shown that all those prosecuted were "vocal" nonregistrants and because "[t]he inference is strong that the Government could have located non-vocal non-registrants, but chose not to." The District Court found the second requirement satisfied for three reasons. First, the passive enforcement program was " 'inherently suspect' " because " 'it focuse[d] upon the vocal offender * * * [and was] vulnerable to the charge that those chosen for prosecution [were] being punished for their expression of ideas, a constitutionally protected right.' " Second, the Government's awareness that a disproportionate number of vocal nonregistrants would be prosecuted under the passive enforcement system indicated that petitioner was prosecuted because of his exercise of First Amendment rights. Finally, the involvement of high Government officials in the prosecution decisions "strongly suggest[ed] impermissible selective prosecution." The District Court then held that the Government had failed to rebut the prima facie case.

The Court of Appeals reversed. Applying the same test, it found the first requirement satisfied but not the second. The first was satisfied by petitioner's showing that out of the estimated 674,000 nonregistrants the 13 indicted had all been vocal nonregistrants. As to the second requirement the Court of Appeals held that petitioner had to show that the Government focused its investigation on him *because of* his protest activities. Petitioner's evidence, however, showed only that the Government was aware that the passive enforcement system would result in prosecutions primarily of two types of men—religious and moral objectors and vocal objectors—and that the Government recognized that the latter type would probably make claims of selective prosecution. Finding no evidence of impermissible governmental motivation, the court held that the District Court's finding of a prima facie case of selective prosecution was clearly erroneous. The Court of Appeals also found two legitimate explanations for the Government's passive enforcement system: (i) the identities of nonreported nonregistrants were not known, and (ii)

March 31, 1984, three more men had been indicted. The approximately 270 not indicted either registered, were found not to be subject to registration requirements, could not be found, or were under continuing investigation. The record does not indicate how many fell into each category.

nonregistrants who expressed their refusal to register made clear their willful violation of the law. * * *

III

In our criminal justice system, the Government retains "broad discretion" as to whom to prosecute. "[S]o long as the prosecutor has probable cause to believe that the accused committed an offense defined by statute, the decision whether or not to prosecute, and what charge to file or bring before a grand jury, generally rests entirely in his discretion." This broad discretion rests largely on the recognition that the decision to prosecute is particularly ill-suited to judicial review. Such factors as the strength of the case, the prosecution's general deterrence value, the Government's enforcement priorities, and the case's relationship to the Government's overall enforcement plan are not readily susceptible to the kind of analysis the courts are competent to undertake. Judicial supervision in this area, moreover, entails systemic costs of particular concern. Examining the basis of a prosecution delays the criminal proceeding, threatens to chill law enforcement by subjecting the prosecutor's motives and decisionmaking to outside inquiry, and may undermine prosecutorial effectiveness by revealing the Government's enforcement policy. All these are substantial concerns that make the courts properly hesitant to examine the decision whether to prosecute.

As we have noted in a slightly different context, however, although prosecutorial discretion is broad, it is not " 'unfettered.' Selectivity in the enforcement of criminal laws is * * * subject to constitutional constraints." In particular, the decision to prosecute may not be " 'deliberately based upon an unjustifiable standard such as race, religion, or other arbitrary classification,' " including the exercise of protected statutory and constitutional rights.

It is appropriate to judge selective prosecution claims according to ordinary equal protection standards.[9] Under our prior cases, these standards require petitioner to show both that the passive enforcement system had a discriminatory effect and that is was motivated by a discriminatory purpose.[10] All petitioner has shown here is

9. Although the Fifth Amendment, unlike the Fourteenth, does not contain an equal protection clause, it does contain an equal protection component. "[Our] approach to Fifth Amendment equal protection claims has * * * been precisely the same as to equal protection claims under the Fourteenth Amendment."

10. A showing of discriminatory intent is not necessary when the equal protection claim is based on an overtly discriminatory classification. See *Strauder v. West Virginia,* 10 Otto 303, 100 U.S. 303, 25 L.Ed. 664 (1880). No such claim is presented here, for petitioner cannot argue that the passive policy discriminated on its face.

The dissent argues that Wayte made a nonfrivolous showing of all three elements of a prima facie case as established in the context of grand jury selection. *Castaneda v. Partida,* 430 U.S. 482, 97 S.Ct. 1272, 51 L.Ed.2d 498 (1977). Neither the parties nor the courts below, however, discussed the prima facie case in these terms. Rather, they used the phrase to refer to whether Wayte had made a showing, which, if unrebutted, would directly establish discriminatory effect and purpose. Even applying standards from the grand jury selection context, however, we believe that Wayte has failed to establish a prima facie case. For example, although the dissent describes the first element as merely whether the individual "is a member of a recognizable, distinct class," it is clear for reasons we discuss that Wayte has not established the first element as actually defined by *Castaneda:* whether the individual is a member of an "identifiable group" that is "a recognizable, distinct class, *singled out for different treatment under the laws, as written or as applied.*" (emphasis added). For these same reasons, we believe Wayte has failed to establish the other *Casteneda* elements, particularly the third. Furthermore, even assuming that Wayte did make out this kind of prima facie case, the "beg" policy would rebut it.

The dissent also argues that *Yick Wo v. Hopkins,* 118 U.S. 356, 6 S.Ct. 1064, 30 L.Ed. 220 (1886), would have been decided differently under the approach we take today. This misunderstanding stems from its belief that "the Government intentionally discriminated in defining the pool of potential prosecutees" in this case. This premise, however, mistakes the facts. The prosecution pool consisted of all reported nonregistrants, not just "vocal" nonregistrants, and there is no evidence of government intent to prosecute individuals because of their exercise of First Amendment rights.

that those eventually prosecuted, along with many not prosecuted, reported themselves as having violated the law. He has not shown that the enforcement policy selected nonregistrants for prosecution on the basis of their speech. Indeed, he could not have done so given the way the "beg" policy was carried out. The Government did not prosecute those who reported themselves but later registered. Nor did it prosecute those who protested registration but did not report themselves or were not reported by others. In fact, the Government did not even investigate those who wrote letters to Selective Service criticizing registration unless their letters stated affirmatively that they had refused to comply with the law. The Government, on the other hand, did prosecute people who reported themselves or were reported by others but who did not publicly protest. These facts demonstrate that the Government treated all reported nonregistrants similarly. It did not subject vocal nonregistrants to any special burden. Indeed, those prosecuted in effect selected themselves for prosecution by refusing to register after being reported and warned by the Government.

Even if the passive policy had a discriminatory effect, petitioner has not shown that the Government intended such a result. The evidence he presented demonstrated only that the Government was aware that the passive enforcement policy would result in prosecution of vocal objectors and that they would probably make selective prosecution claims. As we have noted, however, " '[d]iscriminatory purpose' * * * implies more than * * * intent as awareness of consequences. It implies that the decisionmaker * * * selected or reaffirmed a particular course of action at least in part 'because of,' not merely 'in spite of,' its adverse effects upon an identifiable group." In the present case, petitioner has not shown that the Government prosecuted him *because of* his protest activities. Absent such a showing, his claim of selective prosecution fails.

IV

Petitioner also challenges the passive enforcement policy directly on First Amendment grounds. In particular, he claims that "[e]ven though the [Government's passive] enforcement policy did not overtly punish protected speech as such, it inevitably created a content-based regulatory system with a concomitantly disparate, content-based impact on nonregistrants." This Court has held that when, as here, " 'speech' and 'nonspeech' elements are combined in the same course of conduct, a sufficiently important governmental interest in regulating the nonspeech element can justify incidental limitations on First Amendment freedoms." *United States v. O'Brien,* 391 U.S. 367, 376, 88 S.Ct. 1673, 1678, 20 L.Ed.2d 672 (1968). Government regulation is justified

> "if it is within the constitutional power of the Government; if it furthers an important or substantial governmental interest; if the governmental interest is unrelated to the suppression of free expression; and if the incidental restriction on alleged First Amendment freedoms is no greater than is essential to the furtherance of that interest." Id.

In the present case, neither the first nor third condition is disputed.

There can be no doubt that the passive enforcement policy meets the second condition. Few interests can be more compelling than a nation's need to ensure its own security. * * * With these principles in mind, the three reasons the Government offers in defense of this particular enforcement policy are sufficiently compelling to satisfy the second *O'Brien* requirement—as to either those who reported themselves or those who were reported by others.

First, by relying on reports of nonregistration, the Government was able to identify and prosecute violators without further delay. Although it still was necessary to investigate those reported to make sure that they were required to register and had not, the Government did not have to search actively for the names of these likely violators. Such a search would have been difficult and costly at that time. Indeed, it would be a costly step in any "active" prosecution system involving thousands of nonregistrants. The passive enforcement program thus promoted prosecutorial efficiency. Second, the letters written to Selective Service provided strong, perhaps conclusive evidence of the nonregistrant's intent not to comply—one of the elements of the offense. Third, prosecuting visible nonregistrants was thought to be an effective way to promote general deterrence, especially since failing to proceed against publicly known offenders would encourage others to violate the law.

The passive enforcement policy also meets the final requirement of the *O'Brien* test, for it placed no more limitation on speech than was necessary to ensure registration for the national defense. Passive enforcement not only did not subject "vocal" nonregistrants to any special burden, but also was intended to be only an interim enforcement system. Although Selective Service was engaged in developing an active enforcement program when it investigated petitioner, it had by then found no practicable way of obtaining the names and current addresses of likely nonregistrants. Eventually, it obtained them by matching state driver's license records with Social Security files. It took some time, however, to obtain the necessary authorizations and to set up this system. Passive enforcement was the only effective interim solution available to carry out the Government's compelling interest.

We think it important to note as a final matter how far the implications of petitioner's First Amendment argument would extend. Strictly speaking, his argument does not concern passive enforcement but self-reporting. The concerns he identifies would apply to all nonregistrants who report themselves even if the Selective Service engaged only in active enforcement. For example, a nonregistrant who wrote a letter informing Selective Service of his failure to register could, when prosecuted under an active system, claim that the Selective Service was prosecuting him only because of his "protest." Just as in this case, he could have some justification for believing that his letter had focused inquiry upon him. Prosecution in either context would equally "burden" his exercise of First Amendment rights. Under the petitioner's view, then, the Government could not constitutionally prosecute a self-reporter—even in an active enforcement system—unless perhaps it could prove that it would have prosecuted him without his letter. On principle, such a view would allow any criminal to obtain immunity from prosecution simply by reporting himself and claiming that he did so in order to "protest" the law. The First Amendment confers no such immunity from prosecution. * * *

JUSTICE MARSHALL, with whom JUSTICE BRENNAN joins, dissenting.

The Court decides today that petitioner "has not shown that the Government prosecuted him *because of* his protest activities," and it remands to permit his prosecution to go forward. However interesting the question decided by the Court may be, it is not necessary to the disposition of this case. Instead, the issue this Court must grapple with is far less momentous but no less deserving of thoughtful treatment. What it must decide is whether Wayte has earned the right to discover Government documents relevant to his claim of selective prosecution.

The District Court ordered such discovery, the Government refused to comply, and the District Court dismissed the indictment. The Court of Appeals reversed on the grounds that Wayte had failed to prevail on the merits of his selective prosecution claim, and that the discovery order was improper. If Wayte is entitled to obtain evidence currently in the Government's possession, the Court cannot dismiss his claim on the basis of only the evidence now in the record. To prevail here, then, all that Wayte needs to show is that the District Court applied the correct legal standard and did not abuse its discretion in determining that he had made a nonfrivolous showing of selective prosecution entitling him to discovery. * * *

A two-part inquiry leads to the resolution of the narrow discovery question before this Court: (1) what showing must a defendant make to obtain discovery on a claim of selective prosecution, and (2) under what standard does an appellate court review a district court's finding that the required showing was made.

The Courts of Appeals have adopted a standard under which a defendant establishes his right to discovery if he can show that he has a "colorable basis" for a selective prosecution claim. To make this showing, a defendant must allege sufficient facts in support of his selective prosecution claim "to take the question past the frivolous state." In general, a defendant must present "some evidence tending to show the existence of the essential elements of the defense."

This standard, which the District Court applied in this case, is consistent with our exhortation that "[t]he need to develop all relevant facts in the adversary system is both fundamental and comprehensive. The ends of criminal justice would be defeated if judgments were to be founded on a partial or speculative presentation of the facts." It also recognizes that most of the relevant proof in selective prosecution cases will normally be in the Government's hands. At the same time, the standard adequately protects the Government from attempts by the defense to seek discovery as a means of harassment or of delay.

With respect to the second determination, which concerns the appropriate scope of review, there is no doubt that trial judges should enjoy great deference in discovery matters. District court decisions on discovery are therefore not subject to plenary review on appeal, but are instead reviewed under an abuse of discretion standard. * * *

The Court of Appeals below, however, did not even mention the appropriate standard of review, much less explain how to apply it. To the extent that its conclusory statements shed any light on the basis for its decision, it appears that the Court of Appeals performed a *de novo* inquiry. Such review is especially inappropriate in this case, given the painstaking care that the District Court took in supervising the discovery process, and the narrowly tailored scope of its rulings.

The proper starting point, then, is to consider whether the District Court abused its discretion in determining that Wayte had presented sufficient facts to support a nonfrivolous claim of selective prosecution. I believe that the District Court acted well within the scope of its discretion.

To evaluate the merit of Wayte's claim, I consider the elements of a *prima facie* case of selective prosecution and ascertain whether Wayte has made a nonfrivolous showing as to the existence of these elements. It is important to bear in mind at this stage that Wayte need not have made out a full *prima facie* case in order to be entitled to discovery. A *prima facie* case, of course, is one that if unrebutted will lead to a finding of selective prosecution. It shifts to the Government the burden of rebutting the presumption of unconstitutional action. But a defendant need not meet this high burden just to get discovery; the standard for discovery is merely nonfrivolousness. * * *

To make out a *prima facie* case, Wayte must show first that he is a member of a recognizable, distinct class. Second, he must show that a disproportionate number of this class was selected for investigation and possible prosecution. Third, he must show that this selection procedure was subject to abuse or was otherwise not neutral. The inquiry then is whether Wayte has presented sufficient evidence as to each of the elements to show that the claim is not frivolous.

Wayte has clearly established the first element of a *prima facie* case. The record demonstrates unequivocally that Wayte is a member of a class of vocal opponents to the Government's draft registration program. All members of that class exercised a First Amendment right to speak freely and to petition the Government for a redress of grievances, and either reported themselves or were reported by others as having failed to register for the draft.

To establish the second element, Wayte must show that the "passive" enforcement policy identified for investigation and possible prosecution a disproportionate number of vocal opponents of draft registration. The record, as it stands given the Government's refusal to comply with the District Court's discovery order, does not contain a breakdown of how many of the approximately 300 young men referred by Selective Service to the Justice Department were "vocal." However, the record suggests that responsible officials in the Justice Department were aware that the vast majority of these individuals would be vocal opponents of draft registration. * * *

Perhaps, by itself, this evidence would not suffice to establish the second element of a *prima facie* case. However, it is more than adequate to make nonfrivolous the claim that the "passive" enforcement scheme identified for possible prosecution a disproportionate number of vocal opponents of draft registration.

As to the third element, the decision to implement the "passive" enforcement system was certainly a decision susceptible to abuse. "This is indeed an exceptional area of national life where conscientious opposition to government policy has been intertwined with violations of the laws which implement the policy." The correlation between vocal opposition and violations of the law makes it relatively easy to punish speech under the guise of enforcing the laws.

Here, the enforcement scheme was implemented with full knowledge that its effects would be particularly harsh on vocal opponents of the Government's policies. Such knowledge makes the scheme directly vulnerable to the charge that its purpose was to punish individuals for the exercise of their First Amendment rights. This Court has recognized that "[a]dherence to a particular policy or practice, 'with full knowledge of the predictable effects of such adherence * * * is one factor among others which may be considered by a court' " in determining whether a decision was based on an impermissible ground.

Thus, Wayte has established the first and third elements of a *prima facie* case, and has presented a colorable claim as to the second. As a result, there can thus be no doubt that the District Court did not abuse its discretion when it found that Wayte's equal protection claim was not frivolous.

The Court, of course, has not viewed this case through the same lens. Instead of focusing on the elements of a *prima facie* case, and on whether Wayte presented sufficient evidence as to the existence of each of these elements to earn the right to discover relevant information in the Government's possession, the Court leaps over these two issues and proceeds directly to the merits of the equal protection claim. The Court's analysis is flawed in two respects. First, as I have shown, the Court ignores the simple fact that, if Wayte is entitled to discovery, his claim cannot be rejected on the merits for lack of evidence.

Second, and of equal importance, the Court errs in the manner in which it analyzes the merits of the equal protection claim. It simply focuses on the wrong problem when it states that "the Government treated all reported nonregistrants similarly" and that "those prosecuted in effect selected themselves for prosecution by refusing to register after being reported and warned by the Government." Those issues are irrelevant to the correct disposition of this case.

The claim here is not that the Justice Department discriminated among *known* violators of the draft registration law either in its administration of the "beg" policy, which gave such individuals the option of registering to avoid prosecution, or in prosecuting only some reported nonregistrants. Instead, the claim is that the system by which the Department defined the class of possible prosecutees—the "passive" enforcement system—was designed to discriminate against those who had exercised their First Amendment rights. Such Governmental action cannot stand if undertaken with discriminatory intent. As this Court has clearly stated, "for an agent of the State to pursue a course of action whose objective is to penalize a person's reliance on his legal rights is 'patently unconstitutional.'" If the Government intentionally discriminated in defining the pool of potential prosecutees, it cannot immunize itself from liability merely by showing that it used permissible methods in choosing whom to prosecute from this previously tainted pool.

Under the Court's flawed approach, there would have been no equal protection violation in *Yick Wo v. Hopkins*, this Court's seminal selective prosecution decision. In *Yick Wo*, the Court reversed a conviction under a municipal ordinance that prohibited the construction of wooden laundries without a license. The Court held that such a conviction could not stand because the municipal licensors had discriminatorily denied licenses to individuals of Chinese origin. If the Court then had focused only on the prosecutions themselves, as it does now, it would have found no discrimination in the choice, among violators of the ordinance, of the individuals to be prosecuted. Indeed, all but one of these violators were of Chinese origin. Instead, the Court properly focused on the official action that led to those prosecutions. In *Yick Wo*, that prior action was the discriminatory denial of licenses, which affected the definition of the class from which prosecutees were chosen. In this case, the referrals made by Selective Service to the Justice Department for investigation and possible prosecution played a similar role and may also have been discriminatory. It is to that issue that the Court should have directed its attention.

I do not suggest that all prosecutions undertaken pursuant to passive enforcement schemes warrant evidentiary hearings on the question of selective prosecution. But where violations of the law are so closely intertwined with political activity, where the speech at issue is so unpalatable to the Government, and where the discriminatory effect is conceded, the need for a hearing is significant and in no way opens the door to an onslaught of such hearings in less compelling contexts.

* * *

Notes and Questions

1. *Equal protection for the criminal.* Some courts (generally in earlier cases) have taken the view that a defendant in a criminal case may not raise a discriminatory prosecution claim. Should this be so? Is the point that "the needs of society demand that persons perpetrating intrinsically harmful acts be punished whenever apprehended, even if the punishment is the product of unequal enforcement, while the needs of society do not require that acts not harmful in themselves be punished if discriminatory enforcement is involved"? Comment, 61 Colum.L.Rev. 1103, 1107 (1961). Or, is the point that "court injunction against the discriminatory enforcement would tend to bolster the 'necessary' law by compelling enforcement officials either to generalize their operations or face inquiry and discipline at the hands of an exasperated legislature." Note, 59 Yale L.J. 354, 359 (1950).

2. *The "arbitrary classification" requirement.* (a) What is an arbitrary classification? Is the enforcement policy proper if

the distinction being drawn in practice is one which the legislature could have drawn? See *Taylor v. City of Pine Bluff*, 289 S.W.2d 679 (Ark.1956), holding that enforcement of a Sunday blue law only against groceries was not a violation of equal protection because the legislature could have so limited the statute. Is this view incorrect, in that it is not the function of enforcement officials "to make the broad policy judgments that may require such classification"? Comment, supra, at 1118. Or, does this position not go far enough, in that a prosecutor must be free "to choose whom to prosecute after weighing such factors as the likelihood of successful prosecution, the social value of obtaining a conviction as against the time and expense to the state, and his own sense of justice in the particular case," id. at 1119, which are factors which could not be expressed in legislation?

(b) In *United States v. Ojala*, 544 F.2d 940 (8th Cir.1976), defendant, a state legislator, established that he was targeted for prosecution for his failure to file income tax returns (while many others were not) because he publicly announced his refusal to comply with the filing requirements in order to protest the Vietnam war. Said the court: "It is difficult to conceive of a more legitimate object of prosecution than one who exploits his own public office and reputation to urge a political position by announcing publicly that he had gone on strike against the tax laws of the nation." Is this so? What then of the IRS's "Project ACE," which gave "special priorities" to the prosecution of tax crimes by attorneys and accountants because of their "special obligation and responsibility to the tax laws"? See *United States v. Swanson*, 509 F.2d 1205 (8th Cir.1975).

(c) After more traditional efforts to curb vice in the Times Square area had failed, city officials obtained federal funding for the Midtown Enforcement Project. A task force of fire, safety and health inspectors made frequent inspections only of "sex related" businesses in that area. Defendants, operators of an adult book store, sought dismissal of the charges of health and building code violations brought against them. In *People v. Mantel*, 388 N.Y.S.2d 565 (1976), the court declared that the test is "whether a particular classification bears a rational relationship to the broad purposes of the criminal law and is reasonably related to law enforcement objectives," and then concluded: "It cannot be seriously doubted that this concentrated effort, even assuming it is aimed at sex related establishments, is rationally related to legitimate law enforcement objectives. Any area of activity that carries with it a high incidence of crime is an appropriate choice for strenuous law enforcement."

(d) What if it is the policy to prosecute prostitutes but not their customers? What if the prosecution of prostitutes but not customers is merely a consequence of the fact that prostitutes are apprehended by undercover police posing as potential customers, but little or no effort is made to catch potential customers by using undercover female police posing as prostitutes?

(e) It is the prosecutor's policy to prosecute for violations of the Sunday closing law only upon receipt of a citizen complaint, but for many years he never received one. Then the business manager of the meatcutters' union filed complaints against all supermarkets in the county but not against any so-called "Mom and Pop" groceries. What result if the supermarkets defend on equal protection grounds? Are the private complainant's reasons (concern over union members working on Sunday) relevant, or are they irrelevant because the prosecutor proceeds on all complaints without regard to what motivated them? If they are relevant, is this "an unseemly state of affairs openly inviting discrimination and harassment of one group by another," or may it be said that the complaints were designed "to achieve exactly what the statute intends"? See *People v. Acme Markets, Inc.*, 334 N.E.2d 555 (N.Y.1975).

(f) If, as has been recommended,[a] the prosecutor has a handbook setting out guidelines for the exercise of his discretion, is any deviation from them a denial of equal protection? If not, should a deviation from published policies be a defense anyway? Consider *Delay v. United States,* 602 F.2d 173 (8th Cir.1979) (relying upon *United States v. Caceres,* p. 229 supra, court concludes that "a criminal defendant has no rights under the internal policy of the Justice Department to limit dual federal-state prosecutions" and thus may not object to the prosecutor's deviation from that policy).

3. *Selective enforcement vs. selective nonenforcement.* If a certain statute is generally enforced except as to a certain identifiable group, does a defendant not in that group have a valid equal protection claim? See *United States v. Robinson,* 311 F.Supp. 1063 (W.D.Mo.1969) (conviction of private detective for wiretapping in violation of federal law overturned upon a showing that federal agents were not prosecuted for similar violations), commented on as follows in 55 Minn.L.Rev. 1234, 1243 (1971): "Implicit in the *Robinson* decision is the belief that presence of an invidious motive for prosecution is not required for a finding of discriminatory enforcement. The absence of a proper justification for not fully enforcing the statute makes any partial enforcement discriminatory. Though this seems to expand *Yick Wo,* it is probably justified."

4. *Selective enforcement vs. full enforcement.* Is the prosecutor's *failure* to exercise any discretion objectionable? In *State v. Pettitt,* 609 P.2d 1364 (Wash.1980), the defendant, after his conviction for taking a motor vehicle without permission, was charged under the habitual criminal statute pursuant to the prosecutor's "mandatory policy of filing habitual criminal complaints against all defendants with three or more prior felonies," as he had prior convictions for taking a motor vehicle without permission, second degree burglary, and unauthorized use of a vehicle. The defendant argued that "a policy which prevents the prosecutor from considering mitigating factors is a failure to exercise discretion, which may, as in this case, result in an unfair and arbitrary result." The court agreed:

"In the present case, the prosecutor (now former prosecutor) admitted that he relied on the record alone in deciding to file the habitual criminal information. He testified that he did not consider any mitigating circumstances in reaching his decision, and that he could imagine no situation which would provide for an exception to the mandatory policy.

"In our view, this fixed formula which requires a particular action *in every case* upon the happening of a specific series of events constitutes an abuse of the discretionary power lodged in the prosecuting attorney."

However, a dissenting judge objected:

"The statute makes it clear that every person who falls into the ambit of the statute *shall* be sentenced to life imprisonment. This statute is mandatory and requires that the prosecutor file a supplemental information charging each such person with being a habitual criminal. It does not say that certain persons may be charged and others may not, and it provides no standards for the exercise of prosecutorial discretion. Here the prosecutor followed the mandate of the statute."

5. *Problems of proof.* (a) *Wayte* says the defendant must "show both that the passive enforcement system had a discriminatory effect and that it was motivated by a discriminatory purpose." Compare Givelber, *The Application of Equal Protection Principles to Selective Enforcement of the Criminal Law,* 1973 U.Ill.L.F. 88, 106: "Rather than requiring a defendant to prove the prosecutor's knowledge and motivation in

a. See *A.B.A. Standards,* p. 887 supra, at § 3–2.5(b).

order to establish a denial of equal protection, a court should hold that the burden of going forward shifts to the state once the defendant proves that only a few of the knowable violators of a law have been prosecuted or that the group prosecuted for violating a law differs from the group not prosecuted in characteristics irrelevant to law enforcement purposes. Only after the state explains what has produced the unequal treatment can the court determine whether the selective enforcement results from the application of unjustifiable or arbitrary enforcement criteria."

(b) Courts are generally reluctant to require prosecutors to testify concerning their enforcement policies, even when this might be the only way defendant could establish his claim. See, e.g., *United States v. Kelly,* 556 F.2d 257 (5th Cir.1977), holding that when defendant, a former customs officer, was charged with illegal eavesdropping and he alleged that the Justice Department prosecuted such crimes by customs agents but not by drug agents the trial judge properly refused to allow defendant to subpoena the United States Attorney "without some demonstration by Kelly that his complaint might have merit."

(c) Under what circumstances should the defendant alleging discriminatory enforcement be able to gain access to the prosecution's records in an attempt to prove those allegations? Consider, for example, *United States v. Ahmad,* 347 F.Supp. 912 (M.D.Pa.1972), aff'd sub nom. *United States v. Berrigan,* 482 F.2d 171 (3d Cir. 1973), concerning the much-publicized prosecution and conviction of Philip Berrigan and Elizabeth McAlister for smuggling letters in and out of Lewisburg Federal Prison. The defendants alleged that they were prosecuted not for their criminal conduct but because of their opposition to the Viet Nam war and their dedication to civil disobedience as a means of bringing it to an end, a motive the court acknowledged would constitute a denial of equal protection if substantiated. The court quashed defense subpoenas for the prosecution's file in the instant case and for interdepartmental memoranda of the Justice Department and Bureau of Prisons containing legal memoranda, advisory opinions and prosecutorial recommendations and decisions pertaining to other prison-smuggling violations, holding that before the defendants would be allowed access to those materials they would have to "present evidence from which at least an inference of improper standards can be drawn. * * * It is clear that through these subpoenas defendants are attempting to circumvent a long-accepted intolerance toward judicial inquisition into the process whereby prosecutorial decisions are formulated." Compare *United States v. Berrios,* 501 F.2d 1207 (2d Cir.1974), concluding that "notwithstanding the apparent weakness of Berrios' claim," the trial judge did not abuse his discretion in requiring the government to turn over to him for *in camera* inspection the prosecutor's letter to his superior seeking authorization to prosecute Berrios.

(d) Considering n. 10 in *Wayte,* may the statistical method used by the Supreme Court in jury discrimination cases, see p. 1275 infra, be employed to shift the burden to the state? Consider *Butler v. Cooper,* 554 F.2d 645 (4th Cir.1977), a class action to enjoin selective enforcement of the liquor laws. The plaintiffs showed that one-third of the city population was black but that 84% of the persons arrested for violation of the liquor laws were black. The majority held the district court properly granted defendants' motion for summary judgment, as this did not show an affirmative policy of racial discrimination. Butzner, J., dissenting, asserted that plaintiffs' allegation of racially motivated enforcement plus the statistics, for which the defendants offered no explanation, were sufficient to require an evidentiary hearing.

6. *Remedies: injunction; pretrial motion to dismiss; defense at trial.* One remedy for discriminatory enforcement is injunctive

relief, although "such relief must be regarded as an extraordinary rather than a usual remedy. * * * This attitude has manifested itself in certain restrictions that limit the occasions when equitable relief will be afforded. The first restriction is the requirement that there be a threat of immediate and irreparable injury to property [as where unequal enforcement of a Sunday blue law results in the loss of sales]. The second condition, which is applied less frequently, is that the party suing for injunctive relief have clean hands." Comment, supra, at 1133–34.

If the issue of discriminatory enforcement is raised in the context of criminal proceedings, some courts permit the issue to go to the jury as a defense, while others deal with the issue upon a pretrial motion to dismiss the prosecution. Which is preferable?

PEOPLE v. WALKER

200 N.E.2d 779 (N.Y.1964).

MEMORANDUM. The judgment of conviction should be reversed and a new trial ordered. The prosecution of defendant for violations of the Multiple Dwelling Law, Consol.Laws, c. 61–A, came closely in sequence upon the exposure by her of corrupt practices in the Department of Buildings. She contends that the prosecution was the result of an intentional discrimination which deprived her of the constitutional right to equal protection of the laws. She was unduly restricted on the trial in her attempts to prove this contention. Latitude should be allowed in this complex area of proof. We do not hold that defendant has demonstrated intentional discrimination in her prosecution. We rule, merely, that she should have a fair opportunity to establish it on her trial. * * *

BURKE, JUDGE (dissenting). If the constitutional defense of unequal protection of the laws were maintainable solely upon a showing of bad motive on the part of those responsible for the placing of the violations of which appellant is admittedly guilty, then I would concur for reversal. This, however, is not the law; nor does the court say it is. Since the legislation under which appellant has been convicted is itself valid, and since appellant is admittedly guilty of the violations, the defense of unequal protection is established only upon a showing of both bad motive in the subject case and nonenforcement as to others similarly situated * * *. The el ement of uneven enforcement is of the very essence and substance of the constitutional claim. The violations are not hypertechnical nor have they fallen into a sort of desuetude. The violations, among which are the creation of an additional room by a partition, an additional class B room out of a vestibule, and the maintenance of a defective sprinkler valve, are, in my experience, commonly enforced in New York City. In any event they should not be assumed to be dead letters in the total absence of evidence to that effect.

The fact that the trial court was apparently prepared to exclude any evidence other than that bearing directly on guilt or innocence does not excuse appellant from offering to prove all of the elements of her defense. Concededly, all her offers of proof went solely to the point of bad motive in her individual case. Sympathetic as we may be toward appellant's unfortunate position as the result of what she alleges were numerous bribe solicitations by Building Department officials, we have no license to play fast and loose with the elements of so volatile a doctrine as equal protection of the laws. If the statutory requirements to which appellant was held were generally enforced, then there was no infringement of her constitutional right when she was prosecuted for their violation—no matter how contemptible may have been the motives of those who enforced the law. Were the law otherwise all enforcement proceedings could be turned into subjective expeditions into motive without the stabilizing, objectively verifiable, element of an unequal pattern of enforcement. No one has a constitutional right to random enforcement of the law. No one has a constitutional right to sincere enforcement of the law. The right is to equal enforcement of the law. All of the cases dealing with this question have required such a showing * * *. Appellant, after all, has the burden of proof of all the elements of this defense and if in fact the violation of which she is guilty were not enforced against others similarly situated it would not be difficult to so prove. Building Department records are amenable to subpoena and the Building Department officials who testified could have been questioned as to the pattern of enforcement of the relevant regulations. None of this was done. According to the respondent, this omission was calculated because it would have shown that the rigorous inspection to which appellant's building was subjected was the result of an established policy of reinspecting all buildings previously inspected by an official under suspicion of misconduct—as was the case with appellant's building. Whether this is true or not is a question essential to appellant's defense and one which she ought to have pursued at the trial in order to now make her constitutional argument. Not having done so, she is without remedy in this court. I would affirm.[a]

Notes and Questions

1. Should intentional or purposeful discrimination existing within a scheme of general or random enforcement be considered a violation of the equal protection clause? Consider Recent Case, 78 Harv.L. Rev. 884, 885–86 (1965): "Once it is recognized that the equal protection clause requires each state to enact and enforce its laws in an impartial manner, it follows that Miss Walker should be given the opportunity to prove that even though there was general or random enforcement of the statute in question she would not have been prosecuted but for the purposeful discrimination on the part of the borough superintendent. For example, assume that the superintendent has a list of 1,000 known violators and reasonably exercises his discretion to enforce the law selectively by prosecuting every other person on the list, namely, even numbers. If Miss Walker's name is 149th on the list and the superintendent admits deviating from his selective enforcement formula in order to vent his personal prejudice against her, she has been deprived of equal protection of the laws and should be permitted to quash the prosecution."

Compare Note, 50 Cornell L.Q. 309, 315 (1965): "While a prosecutor does have the obligation to act in good faith in performing his duty, he ought not to be obligated to forego prosecuting a violator whom he believes to be guilty, merely because of some personal feeling or antagonism he has toward that violator. A contrary rule might in fact result in discrimination against other violators." Would such an extension of the equal protection guarantee "be anomalous to criminal law as it is known today, for regardless of the motives of the prosecutor, the policy reasons which led to the enactment of the penal statute are being carried out, since society is still being protected from forbidden conduct"? Recent Decision, 39 St. John's L.Rev. 145, 149 (1964). And what of the point that "even if it can be proved that the prosecution might have been improperly motivated, it will be exceedingly difficult to prove that the defendant would not have been selected for prosecution in the normal course of events"? Recent Decision, 51 Va.L.Rev. 499, 507 (1965).

a. Defendant Walker finally prevailed, but the decision in her favor was in part based upon more traditional notions of equal protection, in that "the manner of prosecution was not the same as that used in the case of other property owners similarly situated" because "the time allowed to defendant for correction of alleged housing violations was so unreasonably short as to make correction an impossibility and criminal conviction a certainty." *People v. Walker,* 271 N.Y.S.2d 447 (1966).

2. In LENSKE v. UNITED STATES, 383 F.2d 20 (9th Cir.1967), defendant's conviction for tax fraud was reversed because of the speculative and uncertain manipulation at trial of figures concerning calculation of depreciation. JUDGE MADDEN, in an additional separate opinion, noted that a special agent and a revenue agent had devoted their full time for two and one-half years to this case and had recommended prosecution in a report which emphasized that Lenske was thought to be a communist.

"I regard what I have recited above as a scandal of the first magnitude in the administration of the tax laws of the United States. It discloses nothing less than a witch-hunt, a crusade by the key agent of the United States in this prosecution, to rid our society of unorthodox thinkers and actors by using federal income tax laws and federal courts to put them in the penitentiary. No court should become an accessory to such a project.

"When the Special Agent's report came in to his superiors, with his naive disclosure at the very beginning of his report that he placed high among the reasons why Lenske should be criminally prosecuted for income tax evasion Lenske's being a left-wing lawyer and having unorthodox political and social ideas, his superiors should have immediately removed him from the case and discarded every judgment which was contained in his recommendation."

Does this mean that Lenske should not have been prosecuted even if the case, in the eyes of the agent's superiors, seemed an appropriate one for prosecution? Does it make any difference how Lenske came to be investigated in the first place? Compare *United States v. Bourque,* 541 F.2d 290 (1st Cir.1976), where defendant alleged that his prosecution for wilful failure to file corporate income tax returns was brought about because of a dispute between him and the IRS District Director of Intelligence on a personal matter. The court held that even if this were so, defendant was entitled to no relief because he failed to show that "prosecutions are normally not instituted for the offenses with which he was charged." [b]

3. DIXON v. DISTRICT OF COLUMBIA, 394 F.2d 966 (D.C.Cir.1968), involved a black defendant stopped by two white police officers for alleged traffic violations. He was neither charged nor ticketed at that time, and two days later the defendant—a retired detective sergeant—filed a complaint with the police department concerning the conduct of the officers. Shortly thereafter defendant and the Corporation Counsel's office entered into a tacit agreement: defendant would proceed no further with his complaint and the government would not prosecute the traffic charges. Later, defendant did file a formal complaint with the D.C. Council on Human Relations, and after he refused to withdraw the complaint he was charged and convicted for the two traffic offenses. The Court of Appeals reversed; CHIEF JUDGE BAZELON had this to say:

"Of course prosecutors have broad discretion to press or drop charges. But there are limits. If, for example, the Government had legitimately determined not to prosecute appellant and had then reversed its position solely because he filed a complaint, this would clearly violate the first amendment. The Government may not prosecute for the purpose of deterring people from exercising their right to protest official misconduct and petition for redress of grievances. Moreover, a prosecution under such circumstances would be barred by the equal protection clause since the Government employs an impermissible classification when it punishes those who complain against police misconduct and excuses those who do not.

b. Reconsider, in this connection, the views of Prof. Freedman in fn. d at p. 889 supra.

"Appellant's case, however, is more complicated. The record indicates that the Government's initial decision not to prosecute was based on appellant's tentative agreement not to proceed with his complaint. It would therefore be naive to say that the Government made a legitimate decision not to prosecute and then reversed it solely because appellant decided to complain. On the contrary, it may be that the Government should have prosecuted Dixon and that its failure to do so stemmed from an illegitimate desire to protect the two police officers. And if the Government should have prosecuted Dixon in the first place, there is arguably no reason why it should be barred from prosecuting him now.

"But I believe reason is to be found in the need to prevent the type of agreement which was attempted in this case. * * *

"The major evil of these agreements is not that charges are sometimes dropped against people who probably should be prosecuted. Much more important, these agreements suppress complaints against police misconduct which should be thoroughly aired in a free society. And they tempt the prosecutor to trump up charges for use in bargaining for suppression of the complaint. The danger of concocted charges is particularly great because complaints against the police usually arise in connection with arrests for extremely vague offenses such as disorderly conduct or resisting arrest.

"Courts may not become the 'enforcers' of these odious agreements. We must therefore bar prosecutions which are brought because the defendant refused to promise or reneged on a promise not to file a complaint against the police. Prosecutors will then have no incentive to offer or make such agreements."

JUDGE BAZELON then observed that there is some controversy as to whether federal courts can use their supervisory power to grant immunity from prosecution because of government misconduct, but he concluded that they could. He relied heavily on the federal entrapment cases to support this conclusion.

4. MacDONALD v. MUSICK, 425 F.2d 373 (9th Cir.1970), a federal habeas corpus action concerning a state conviction, involved these facts: MacDonald was arrested and charged with driving while intoxicated, but at the time set for trial the prosecutor moved to dismiss the charge. The trial judge asked MacDonald if he would stipulate that there was probable cause for his arrest, but MacDonald declined, and the prosecutor then withdrew the motion. Later the prosecutor moved to amend the charge by adding a second count charging MacDonald with resisting arrest, and after argument on the motion it was granted by the court. MacDonald was acquitted on the drunk driving charge but was found guilty of resisting arrest. In support of the motion for leave to amend, the prosecutor said:

"Normally, a defendant will stipulate to probable cause, and there is only one reason, let's face it, for that stipulation, so that the defendant cannot sue the police department. This particular defendant would not stipulate to probable cause, which made it obvious, at least, there was an inference drawn that perhaps here is a defendant that does have in mind suing the police department. * * *

"It seems to me that it is the duty of the Deputy District Attorney, in addition to prosecuting criminals, to protect the police officers, and in so protecting the police officers, it seems to me, after evaluating the facts, any Deputy District Attorney worth his salt would have at that point included any offense, obviously, in the report on which the defendant could have been convicted."

Said the federal court, per DUNIWAY, J.:

"We strongly disagree. It is no part of the proper duty of a prosecutor to use a criminal prosecution to forestall a civil proceeding by the defendant against policemen, even where the civil case arises from the events that are also the basis for the criminal charge. We do not mean that the prosecutor cannot present such a criminal charge. What he cannot do is condition a voluntary dismissal of a charge upon a stipulation by the defendant that is designed to forestall the latter's civil case. The situation is made no better by the fact that here the record indicates that it was the court that asked MacDonald whether he would stipulate. Rather, it makes it worse. It brings the court to the aid of the prosecutor in coercing the defendant into agreeing to what amounts to a forfeiture of his civil rights. Nor can the prosecutor, because of failure to obtain the demanded stipulation, then introduce another charge in the hope of defeating the possible civil action of the defendant.

"The impropriety of the prosecutor's conduct requires little exposition. In California, extortion is defined as 'the obtaining of property from another, * * * induced by a wrongful use of * * * fear, or under color of official right.' There is no doubt that a cause of action for personal injuries is property. * * *

"The Canons of Ethics have long prohibited misuse of the criminal process by an attorney to gain advantage for his client in a civil case. A.B.A., *Code of Professional Responsibility*, 1969, provides in section DR 7–105, p. 88: '(A) A lawyer shall not present, participate in presenting, or threaten to present criminal charges solely to obtain an advantage in a civil matter.' In this respect, we can see no difference between public prosecutors and other lawyers. * * * In such a case as this, if the policemen were sued, the public entity employing the policemen would be obliged, upon their request, to defend them or at least to pay any judgment against them or to indemnify them."

JUDGE KILKENNY dissented: "It is my firm belief that those in charge of prosecution of criminal actions have a duty to protect, if probable cause exists, arresting officers from both state or federal civil actions. * * * Appellant had his day in court and was found guilty of resisting arrest. The fact that he was acquitted on the original charge does not signify that there was no probable cause for the arrest. It merely means that the state failed to prove guilt beyond a reasonable doubt."

5. Compare HOINES v. BARNEY'S CLUB, INC., 620 P.2d 628 (Cal.1980), concluding "that the time-honored practice of discharging misdemeanants on condition of a release of civil liability or stipulation of probable cause for arrest, does not contravene public policy when the prosecutor acts in the interests of justice." *MacDonald* was distinguished as a case involving "improper motivations" and "coercive tactics," and the instant case was said to involve "no coercive conduct" and "no improper motivations" in that "the motivating concerns for the release and dismissal were plaintiff's welfare as a future candidate for admission to the California State Bar, the state's lack of a keen interest in pursuing a jury trial on a misdemeanor charge [of disturbing the peace] although there was probable cause therefor, and fairness to other concerned parties [defendant club and its agents, who made the arrest] who had acted on such probable cause." The court likened what had occurred in the instant case to legitimate plea bargaining:

"The net effect of both a release-dismissal and a plea bargaining transaction is to relieve the state of prosecuting while imposing upon the accused some lesser disability than he might otherwise anticipate. In the plea bargaining transaction the accused is subjected to a known but lesser criminal sanction which he has elected to accept under the circumstances. In the release-dismissal transaction the accused escapes criminal sanctions altogether but is subjected to a civil disability which he has elected to accept under the circumstances. In neither case is there any compulsion preventing the accused from standing his ground and asserting his right to be free from all disabilities, both criminal and civil.

"There is one obvious but not fundamental difference between the two transactions. Because a release-dismissal transaction normally concerns itself with lesser acts of criminal conduct, the state may reasonably elect to forego the imposition of any criminal proceedings or sanctions. However, in doing so it must protect those who—because the charges are to be dismissed—might be improperly exposed to claims of civil liabilities due to their involvement in apprehending the accused. In requiring a release from the accused—but only by his free and voluntary election—the state accomplishes both the imposition of the bargained-for disability and protection of those it reasonably deems to be innocently involved. This, however, is not a significant departure from what is achieved in a plea bargaining transaction." [c]

UNITED STATES v. ELLIOTT

266 F.Supp. 318 (S.D.N.Y.1967).

COOPER, DISTRICT JUDGE. Defendants are under indictment for allegedly violating 18 U.S.C. § 956, which provides:

(a) If two or more persons within the jurisdiction of the United States conspire to injure or destroy specific property situated within a foreign country and belonging to a foreign government or to any political subdivision thereof with which the United States is at peace, or any railroad, canal, bridge, or other public utility so situated, and if one or more such persons commits an act within the jurisdiction of the United States to effect the object of the conspiracy, each of the parties to the conspiracy shall be fined not more than $5,000 or imprisoned not more than three years or both. * * *

Defendants are charged with conspiring in the United States to destroy a railroad bridge in the Republic of Zambia and committing several acts in furtherance of that conspiracy within the United States; that the destruction of this bridge would effectively halt the supply of Zambian copper on the world market; and that defendants expected to profit economically from the ensuing copper shortage. * * *

Defendant, contending that the statute is being selectively applied against him, urges this additional reason in support of his motion to dismiss the indictment. He points to the statute's apparent nonuse since its inception despite what he considers to be its frequent violation, and cites recent events in North Korea, Cuba, the Dominican Republic and North Vietnam. * * *

Defendant contends that the apparent absence of any prosecution under the statute since its promulgation in 1917 renders it void because of desuetude. We do not agree.

Desuetude is a civil law doctrine rendering a statute abrogated by reason of its long and continued non-use. It is not part of English jurisprudence, although it is recognized in the law of Scotland.

Its status in American law is unclear. One commentator has concluded that there are no means under American law by which a validly enacted statute can be rendered ineffective by non-use. 1 Sutherland, *Statutory Construction* § 2034 (Horach Ed.1943). Recent commentators, however, have found some vitality to the doctrine. * * *

We find little analytical aid in merely applying, or refusing to apply, the rubric of desuetude. The problem must be approached in terms of that fundamental fairness owed to the particular defendant that is the heart of due process. An analysis of the problems posed to this defendant by

c. For a critical assessment of other cases of this genre, see Trowbridge, *Restraining the Prosecutor: Restrictions on Threatening Prosecutions for Civil Ends,* 37 Me.L.Rev. 41 (1985).

this allegedly desuetudinal statute demonstrates the statute's continued vitality.

Defendant's contentions to the contrary, we are not faced here with the enforcement of either a basically obsolete or an empty law whose function has long since passed. We are not here concerned with a law forbidding the sale of candy cigarettes, or prohibiting kite flying, or banning the exhibition of films depicting a felony. The function of the statute before us—"* * * to punish acts of interference with the foreign relations * * * of the United States" (40 Stat. 217 (1917))—is as vibrantly vital today as when it was passed. Indisputably, defendant is not being punished by the letter of a rule whose reason has long since passed.

In some situations a desuetudinal statute could prevent serious problems of fair notice. However, this statute does not penalize conduct which, through a long period of non-enforcement, has acquired the status of customary usage, nor has opprobrium for the act been suddenly revived. Conspiring to destroy a bridge is not, and never has been, permitted by community mores. Defendant would have to know his act was wrong and if consummated a crime in Zambia. His surprise at finding the conspiracy an offense against the United States is naive in the extreme and clearly affords no defense.

A desuetudinal statute also contains the potential for abuse that rests in any overbroad administrative discretion; its selective enforcement raises equal protection problems analogous to the *Yick Wo* doctrine. However, defendant, as we have already noted, has adduced not a scintilla of evidence even indicating that the government singled him out, by applying an unconstitutional standard, for punishment. Defendant, in short, consequently must establish that mere non-use of a statute deprives it of life. In the absence of some specific objection (such as indicated above), we hold that non-use alone does not abrogate a statute.

Notes and Questions

Is it ever improper for the prosecutor to bring prosecution for violation of a statute which has long been unenforced? Does it make any difference why the statute was disregarded for so long, or why the prosecutor now has decided in favor of prosecution? On objection by the defendant, should the court inquire into such matters? Consider the following views:

1. *People ex rel. Poole v. Hesterburg,* 89 N.Y.S. 498 (1904). "The Anglo-Saxon sheds statutes which grow obsolete and obnoxious the same as a snake sheds his skin. He has seldom bothered to repeal them as every one acquainted with the history of laws very well knows. No citizen any longer makes a complaint under them [or observes them], and thus they become dead letter laws. It is not the business of the police to revive them. They are not employed and paid by the citizens for any such purpose."

2. In *John R. Thompson Co. v. District of Columbia,* 203 F.2d 579 (D.C.Cir.1953), the court, although holding a criminal statute on refusal to serve a Negro unenforceable on other grounds, added: "But we think it appropriate to comment, in this connection, that the enactments having lain unenforced for 78 years, in the face of a custom of race disassociation in the District, the decision of the municipal authorities to enforce them now, by the prosecution of the instant case, was, in effect, a decision legislative in character. That is to say, it was a determination that the enactments reflect a social policy which is now correct, although it was not correct—else the enactments would have been enforced—heretofore. Such a decision were better left, we think, to the Congress." On review, in *District of Columbia v. John R. Thompson Co.,* 346 U.S. 100, 73 S.Ct. 1007, 97 L.Ed. 1480 (1953), the Supreme Court disagreed: "The repeal of laws is as much a legislative function as their enactment. * * * Cases of hardship are put where criminal laws so long in disuse as to

be no longer known to exist are enforced against innocent parties. But that condition does not bear on the continuing validity of the law; it is only an ameliorating factor in enforcement."

3. In *Poe v. Ullman,* 367 U.S. 497, 81 S.Ct. 1752, 6 L.Ed.2d 989 (1961), the Court dismissed appeals from the refusal of a state court to declare the Connecticut statute outlawing the use of contraceptives unconstitutional. Said Justice Frankfurter, speaking for four members of the Court: "Neither counsel nor our own researches have discovered any other attempt [except for one test case in 1940] to enforce the prohibition of distribution or use of contraceptive devices by criminal process. * * * The undeviating policy of nullification by Connecticut of its anti-contraceptive laws throughout all the long years that they have been on the statute books bespeaks more than prosecutorial paralysis. What was said in another context is relevant here. 'Deeply embedded traditional ways of carrying out state policy * * *'—or not carrying it out—'are often tougher and truer law than the dead words of the written text.' "

4. Bickel, *The Supreme Court—Foreword,* 75 Harv.L.Rev. 40, 63 (1961): "The unenforced statute is not, in the normal way, a continuing reflection of the balance of political pressures. When it is resurrected and enforced, it represents the *ad hoc* decision of the prosecutor, unrelated to anything that may realistically be taken as present legislative policy. To be sure, consistent future enforcement will restore the political situation to normal, and reopen channels to legislative reconsideration. But of such a consistent course there is no assurance after seventy-five years of nonenforcement, and for the individual the first prosecution has all the vices of an *ad hoc* official decision."

5. Bonfield, *The Abrogation of Penal Statutes by Nonenforcement,* 49 Iowa L.Rev. 389, 415–16 (1964): "The depth of the American commitment to the abrogation of enacted law by desuetude is perhaps best revealed by analogy to the due-process fair-notice or fair-warning cases. Where both the community and its law-enforcement agencies have notoriously ignored an enactment for an unduly protracted period, it should be constitutionally impermissible to suddenly prosecute its violation because the act's proscriptions have disappeared from the legal consciousness of the body politic. The statute has neither been obeyed nor applied for such an extended period that ample justification has long existed for the public's feeling that the act has lost the force of binding law."

6. Compare the situation in which enforcement officials advise the defendant that his contemplated conduct is not criminal and thereafter prosecute him for the conduct, as in *Cox v. Louisiana,* discussed in fn. a at p. 481 supra, and consider Justice Clark's interpretation of *Cox* in his dissent to the effect that at most the police consented to the violation, which should not be a defense. *Model Penal Code* § 2.04 provides:

"(3) A belief that conduct does not legally constitute an offense is a defense to a prosecution for that offense based upon such conduct when: * * * (b) he acts in reasonable reliance upon an official statement of the law, afterward determined to be invalid or erroneous, contained in (i) a statute or other enactment; (ii) a judicial decision, opinion or judgment; (iii) an administrative order or grant of permission; or (iv) an official interpretation of the public officer or body charged by law with responsibility for the interpretation, administration or enforcement of the law defining the offense."

Should it make any difference whether the prosecutor says that the contemplated conduct is not covered by the law or that it is covered by the law but that it is not his policy to prosecute for such conduct?

III. THE DIVERSION DECISION [a]

1. In *Shade v. Pennsylvania Dep't of Transportation,* 394 F.Supp. 1237 (M.D.Pa. 1975), the plaintiffs requested the court to declare unconstitutional the Accelerated Rehabilitation Disposition (ARD) program, a pretrial diversion program embodied in Pa.R.Crim.P. 175 through 185, because the rules granted to the prosecutor the discretion to refuse to ask for ARD and instead to insist on prosecution of any particular defendant. The court declined to do so, reasoning:

"In the instant case the ARD program leaves intact the traditional principle that the prosecuting attorney should have the discretion to choose which crimes he wishes to prosecute. Even in the absence of the ARD program, the district attorney in his discretion could always *nolle pros* a criminal charge or enter into a plea bargain with a defendant. Thus ARD is merely one of several discretionary methods for disposition of criminal charges. The criminal law is not a computerized system and discretion—e.g., whether or not to arrest, indict, release, prosecute, dismiss, plea bargain, or accept a plea of guilty in a given case—is a necessary and inherent part of the criminal justice system." [b]

2. If, as stated in *Shade,* diversion is an aspect of the prosecutor's discretion, then to what extent are the prosecutor's diversion decisions subject to court review? Consider the applicability in this context of the separation of powers doctrine invoked in *Inmates of Attica,* p. 896 supra, and the equal protection challenge discussed in *Wayte,* p. 901 supra. Consider also:

(a) *State v. Leonardis,* 375 A.2d 607 (N.J.1977): Noting that pretrial diversion was adopted in the state by the supreme court pursuant to its rule-making power, conferred by the state constitution, the court concluded that the "authority to engage in rule making also includes the power to interpret and enforce court rules." Thus, "our rule-making power must be held to include the power to order the diversion of a defendant * * * where either the prosecutor or the program director arbitrarily fails to follow the guidelines in refusing to consent to diversion. Conversely, where the program director or the prosecutor would subvert the goals of the program by approving diversion, meaningful judicial review must also be cognizable." [c]

(b) *United States v. Smith,* 354 A.2d 510 (D.C.App.1976): After defendant was charged with the misdemeanor of marijuana possession, he moved to dismiss on the ground that criminal penalties for such conduct constitutes cruel and unusual punishment. The trial judge granted the motion, but this motion was reversed on appeal. Defendant then sought diversion pursuant to the prosecutor's program whereunder young people without prior records accused of minor misdemeanors not involving force or violence were ordinarily diverted. The prosecutor declined

a. For further discussion of some of the legal issues which can arise in this context, see Skoler, *Protecting the Rights of Defendants in Pretrial Intervention Programs,* 10 Crim.L.Bull. 473 (1974). For a recommended statutory scheme for diversion, see *Model Pre-Arraignment Code* §§ 320.5–320.9.

b. What then if the program *does* limit the prosecutor's discretion? In *State v. Greenlee,* 620 P.2d 1132 (Kan.1980), where the program was adopted by legislation which listed diversion criteria for prosecutors to apply, the court concluded the resulting limitation on the prosecutor's discretion did not violate the separation of powers doctrine, as the statute "does not * * * destroy or unreasonably restrict" that discretion. The court added that if such a statute had specifically provided the courts were to administer the program, or if the program had been adopted by rule of court, it would be clear that the setting of standards would not encroach on the executive power because then "a judicial function" would be involved.

c. Compare *Cleveland v. State,* 417 So.2d 653 (Fla.1982) (because statutory pretrial diversion program "requires consent of the administrator of the program, victim, judge, and state attorney, but fails to provide for *any* form of review," "the pretrial diversion decision of the state attorney is prosecutorial in nature and, thus, is not subject to judicial review").

because it was his policy to deny such treatment to defendants who had chosen to litigate any issues in their case. The trial court found this objectionable and therefore dismissed the charges. On appeal, the court first distinguished this diversion program from that in New Jersey because the former "owes its existence and operation solely to prosecutorial discretion," and then concluded:

"We have no quarrel with the trial court's ruling that a policy intended to deter defendants from exercising their legal rights cannot be tolerated in the name of prosecutorial discretion. We disagree, however, with the court's finding that the defendant has made an adequate showing that the policy questioned here has any such objective or effect. The record makes clear that if a defendant applies for, is accepted into the program, and successfully completes the requisite activities, charges are dropped without his having to go to court, and no conviction or criminal record results.

"The beneficiary of such a disposition of charges against him can scarcely be said to be deterred from exercising his right to defend himself, for, by dismissing such charges, the government has done away with any reason for him to do so. Should the prosecutor deny first offender treatment to a defendant, the latter is in no way barred from then invoking his legal rights and defenses in any manner he chooses. An accused is not prejudiced, therefore, by any official policy that no issues be litigated while his application for diversionary treatment is pending.

"* * * If it is permissible, in plea bargaining, to induce a defendant to plead guilty and waive his right to trial, *a fortiori* no substantial constitutional question is presented when a prosecutor offers to drop all charges provided the accused conforms to certain conditions, including, *inter alia,* foregoing the filing of any motions or pleas in defense."

(c) *Morse v. Municipal Court,* 529 P.2d 46 (Cal.1974): By statute, certain defendants charged with drug offenses could be diverted upon their consent. Defendant, charged with possession of marijuana, moved to suppress the evidence on Fourth Amendment grounds, and only after that motion was denied did he consent to diversion. In the course of rejecting the prosecutor's contention that the consent was untimely, the court commented: "As a practical matter, the People's insistence upon a deferral of suppression motions requires that a defendant choose between potential diversion and the possibility of an immediate dismissal of charges. His opportunity to test the strength of the evidence against him *at the outset* of the case is entirely lost if he elects diversion. Although no loss of constitutional rights thereby occurs in view of the defendant's ability to move to suppress at any later resumption of criminal proceedings by reason of a failure to complete successfully a drug treatment program, such a choice may tend to discourage defendants from consenting to consideration for diversion. As in the case of petitioner, defendants may be wont to try for even a remote chance of dismissal by virtue of the exclusionary rule in lieu of immediately committing themselves to the restrictions imposed by required participation in a rehabilitation program."

3. If the defendant and prosecutor agree to diversion, is the prosecutor free to renege for any reason? Consider:

(a) *United States v. Bethea,* 483 F.2d 1024 (4th Cir.1973): Defendant claimed that his prosecution for failure to report for induction breached an agreement with the United States attorney, who said he would seek dismissal of the case if defendant submitted himself for induction. Defendant did submit, but the Army refused to induct him upon moral grounds. As to defendant's reliance upon *Santobello v. New York,* p. 1201 infra, the court responded: "The concern of *Santobello* was to protect a defendant who by pleading guilty has surrendered valuable constitutional rights in exchange for the prosecution's assurances. That concern has no application to the facts of this case. Appellant's submission for induction surrendered none of the rights protected by *Santobello.* In the context of this case, Bethea's conduct was at most only a factor to be considered by the prosecutor in deciding whether or not to prosecute, a decision not reviewable here." [d]

(b) *United States v. Garcia,* 519 F.2d 1343 (9th Cir.1975): Defendant, arrested for selling marijuana to undercover agents, entered into a "deferred prosecution" agreement that within 90 days he would "attempt" to present the agents with a dealer in drugs who might, "in the estimation of Agents of DEA," be "capable of making" a sale of such drugs. The government agreed that if defendant did so, no charges would be sought on the previous sale, and that otherwise the government could seek an indictment within 150 days. The defendant failed to produce a dealer, but the indictment was sought only after the 150 days had expired. The court deemed *Santobello* to be controlling, as "by entering into the deferred prosecution agreement, Garcia waived his valuable right to a speedy trial." [e]

4. If diversion status is to be terminated, what procedures should (or must) be followed? Consider *N.D.A.A. National Prosecution Standards* 153–54 (1977):

"The procedural safeguards required of a termination have not been firmly established, but would seem to be analogous to procedures required for parole and probation revocation hearings. The standards established for this in *Morrissey v. Brewer* [p. 88 supra] include:

a. written notice of violation;

b. disclosure of evidence against the offender;

c. opportunity to be heard and present opposing evidence;

d. right to confront and cross-examine witnesses;

e. 'neutral and detached' hearing body; [f] and

d. Compare *People v. Reagan,* 235 N.W.2d 581 (Mich.1975). Defendant, charged with assault to do great bodily harm, entered into an agreement with the prosecutor that if he passed a state police polygraph exam his prosecution would be dismissed. He passed the test and the charge was dropped, but the prosecutor later doubted the results in view of the compelling circumstantial evidence of defendant's criminal involvement. He consulted with a psychiatrist who advised that with respect to such crimes a schizophrenic nature will sometimes distort polygraph results and that therefore truth serum should be used. The prosecutor then notified defendant that the agreement would be honored only if defendant submitted to serum testing. Defendant refused, the prosecutor refiled the charge, and defendant was convicted. On appeal, the court noted that defendant "had much to gain and relatively little to lose by subjecting himself to the polygraph," but, notwithstanding the people's contention "that the bargain offered defendant was a 'gift-type' bargain which lacked the consideration necessary to make it binding," concluded "the analogy to contract law is inappropriate. * * * It was within the power of the prosecution to enter into this agreement. We therefore reject the contention that the agreement per se is against public policy * * *. In our view, a pledge of public faith in this instance gave force to an unwise agreement which became binding."

e. Compare *United States v. Gogarty,* 533 F.2d 93 (2d Cir.1976): "The appellant failed to live up to his obligation and this agreement, unlike the agreement in *Garcia,* supra, contained no time limit on the government's right to re-prosecute the defendant in the event of noncompliance. One who fails to carry out his part of the bargain cannot invoke the agreement against the government."

f. "[T]he revocation function would presumably be exercised by the prosecutor's office or program personnel. A 'neutral' hearing officer is required. The program staff members who have gathered the facts upon which the decision to bring the termination proceeding is made, and have made the decision to apply for termination, would not meet the required impartiality standard. The Court has recognized that prior involvement in some aspect of a case will not necessarily bar a welfare official from acting as a decision-maker, but that official should not, however, have participated in making the determination under review. If the same guarantee could be made in a hearing conducted by the prosecutor's office or staff personnel, then it would arguably meet existing due process standards."

f. a written statement by the factfinders as to the reasons for revocation."

IV. SELECTION OF THE CHARGE

UNITED STATES v. BATCHELDER

442 U.S. 114, 99 S.Ct. 2198, 60 L.Ed.2d 755 (1979).

MR. JUSTICE MARSHALL delivered the opinion of the Court.

At issue in this case are two overlapping provisions of the Omnibus Crime Control and Safe Streets Act of 1968 (the Omnibus Act). Both prohibit convicted felons from receiving firearms, but each authorizes different maximum penalties. We must determine whether a defendant convicted of the offense carrying the greater penalty may be sentenced only under the more lenient provision when his conduct violates both statutes.

Respondent, a previously convicted felon, was found guilty of receiving a firearm that had traveled in interstate commerce, in violation of 18 U.S.C. § 922(h).[2] The District Court sentenced him under 18 U.S.C. § 924(a) to five years' imprisonment, the maximum term authorized for violation of § 922(h).

The Court of Appeals affirmed the conviction but, by a divided vote, remanded for resentencing. The majority recognized that respondent had been indicted and convicted under § 922(h) and that § 924(a) permits five years' imprisonment for such violations. However, noting that the substantive elements of § 922(h) and 18 U.S.C.App. § 1202(a) are identical as applied to a convicted felon who unlawfully receives a firearm, the court interpreted the Omnibus Act to allow no more than the two-year maximum sentence provided by § 1202(a).[4] * * *

This Court has previously noted the partial redundancy of §§ 922(h) and 1202(a), both as to the conduct they proscribe and the individuals they reach. However, we find nothing in the language structure or legislative history of the Omnibus Act to suggest that because of this overlap, a defendant convicted under § 922(h) may be imprisoned for no more than the maximum term specified in § 1202(a). As we read the Act, each substantive statute, in conjunction with its own sentencing provision, operates independently of the other. * * *

In resolving the statutory question, the majority below expressed "serious doubts about the constitutionality of two statutes that provide different penalties for identical conduct." Specifically, the court suggested that the statutes might (1) be void for vagueness, (2) implicate "due process

Perlman & Jaszi, *Legal Issues in Addict Diversion* 123 (1975).

2. In pertinent part, 18 U.S.C. § 922(h) provides:

"It shall be unlawful for any person—

"(1) who is under indictment for, or who has been convicted in any court of, a crime punishable by imprisonment for a term exceeding one year;

"(2) who is a fugitive from justice;

"(3) who is an unlawful user of or addicted to marihuana or any depressant or stimulant drug * * * or narcotic drug * * *; or

"(4) who has been adjudicated as a mental defective or who has been committed to any mental institution;

"to receive any firearm or ammunition which has been shipped or transported in interstate or foreign commerce."

4. Section 1202(a) states:

"Any person who—

"(1) has been convicted by a court of the United States or of a State or any political subdivision thereof of a felony, or

"(2) has been discharged from the Armed Forces under dishonorable conditions, or

"(3) has been adjudged by a court of the United States or of a State or any political subdivision thereof of being mentally incompetent, or

"(4) having been a citizen of the United States has renounced his citizenship, or

"(5) being an alien is illegally or unlawfully in the United States,

"and who receives, possesses, or transports in commerce or affecting commerce, after the date of enactment of this Act, any firearm shall be fined not more than $10,000 or imprisoned for not more than two years, or both." 18 U.S.C. App. § 1202(a).

and equal protection interest[s] in avoiding excessive prosecutorial discretion and in obtaining equal justice," and (3) constitute an impermissible delegation of congressional authority. We find no constitutional infirmities.

It is a fundamental tenet of due process that "[n]o one may be required at peril of life, liberty or property to speculate as to the meaning of penal statutes." A criminal statute is therefore invalid if it "fails to give a person of ordinary intelligence fair notice that his contemplated conduct is forbidden." So too, vague sentencing provisions may pose constitutional questions if they do not state with sufficient clarity the consequences of violating a given criminal statute.

The provisions in issue here, however, unambiguously specify the activity proscribed and the penalties available upon conviction. That this particular conduct may violate both Titles does not detract from the notice afforded by each. Although the statutes create uncertainty as to which crime may be charged and therefore what penalties may be imposed, they do so to no greater extent than would a single statute authorizing various alternative punishments. So long as overlapping criminal provisions clearly define the conduct prohibited and the punishment authorized, the notice requirements of the Due Process Clause are satisfied.

This Court has long recognized that when an act violates more than one criminal statute, the Government may prosecute under either so long as it does not discriminate against any class of defendants. Whether to prosecute and what charge to file or bring before a grand jury are decisions that generally rest in the prosecutor's discretion.

The Court of Appeals acknowledged this "settled rule" allowing prosecutorial choice. Nevertheless, relying on the dissenting opinion in *Berra v. United States,* 351 U.S. 131, 76 S.Ct. 685, 100 L.Ed. 1013 (1956),[8] the court distinguished overlapping statutes with identical standards of proof from provisions that vary in some particular. In the court's view, when two statutes prohibit "exactly the same conduct," the prosecutor's "selection of which of two penalties to apply" would be "unfettered." Because such prosecutorial discretion could produce "unequal justice," the court expressed doubt that this form of legislative redundancy was constitutional. We find this analysis factually and legally unsound.

Contrary to the Court of Appeals' assertions, a prosecutor's discretion to choose between §§ 922(h) and 1202(a) is not "unfettered." Selectivity in the enforcement of criminal laws is, of course, subject to constitutional constraints.[9] And a decision to proceed under § 922(h) does not empower the Government to predetermine ultimate criminal sanctions. Rather, it merely enables the sentencing judge to impose a longer prison sentence than § 1202(a) would permit and precludes him from imposing the greater fine authorized by § 1202(a). More importantly, there is no appreciable difference between the discretion a prosecutor exercises when deciding whether to charge under one of two statutes with different elements and the discretion he exercises when choosing one of two statutes with identical elements.

8. *Berra* involved two tax evasion statutes, which the Court interpreted as proscribing identical conduct. The defendant, who was charged and convicted under the felony provision, argued that the jury should have been instructed on the misdemeanor offense as well. The Court rejected this contention and refused to consider whether the defendant's sentence was invalid because in excess of the maximum authorized by the misdemeanor statute. The dissent urged that permitting the prosecutor to control whether a particular act would be punished as a misdemeanor or a felony raised "serious constitutional questions."

9. The Equal Protection Clause prohibits selective enforcement "based upon an unjustifiable standard such as race, religion, or other arbitrary classification." *Oyler v. Boles,* 368 U.S. 448, 456, 82 S.Ct. 501, 506, 7 L.Ed.2d 446 (1962). Respondent does not allege that his prosecution was motivated by improper considerations.

In the former situation, once he determines that the proof will support conviction under either statute, his decision is indistinguishable from the one he faces in the latter context. The prosecutor may be influenced by the penalties available upon conviction, but this fact standing alone does not give rise to a violation of the Equal Protection or Due Process Clauses. Just as a defendant has no constitutional right to elect which of two applicable federal statutes shall be the basis of his indictment and prosecution neither is he entitled to choose the penalty scheme under which he will be sentenced.

Approaching the problem of prosecutorial discretion from a slightly different perspective, the Court of Appeals postulated that the statutes might impermissibly delegate to the Executive Branch the legislature's responsibility to fix criminal penalties. We do not agree. The provisions at issue plainly demarcate the range of penalties that prosecutors and judges may seek and impose. In light of that specificity, the power that Congress has delegated to those officials is no broader than the authority they routinely exercise in enforcing the criminal laws. Having informed the courts, prosecutors and defendants of the permissible punishment alternatives available under each Title, Congress has fulfilled its duty.

Accordingly, the judgment of the Court of Appeals is reversed.

Notes and Questions

1. Similarly, in HUTCHERSON v. UNITED STATES, 345 F.2d 964 (D.C. Cir.1965), the court rejected defendant's contention that he had been denied due process because he was indicted and convicted under federal statutes (providing that a third-time narcotics offender is to receive a fine of up to $20,000 and imprisonment from 10 to 40 years, without possibility of probation or suspension of sentence) rather than identical D.C. statutes (providing multiple offenders are punishable by a fine of $500 to $5,000 and/or imprisonment up to 10 years, with suspension of sentence and probation possible). BAZELON, C.J., dissenting in part, objected:

"The choice between felony and misdemeanor in *Berra* did not have as serious consequences as the choice involved in the instant case. On conviction for the felony charge in *Berra,* the trial judge could have imposed the penalties provided by the misdemeanor statute if he was convinced that the prosecutor was mistaken in charging a felony. Here, however, prosecution under Federal rather than District narcotics law precluded any sentence less than ten years. No correction of a prosecutorial 'mistake' would be possible. When the prosecutor 'chooses' a mandatory minimum sentence, he makes a sentencing decision, without either sentencing information or expertise in sentencing. * * *

"Recent instructions from the Attorney General relating to prosecutorial decisions in narcotic cases suggest that the United States Attorney does have certain administrative guidelines for his choice. Thus Title 2, § 86.2–86.3 of the United States Attorney's Manual provides:

" 'The principal object of enforcement is * * * to prosecute the importers, dealers and traffickers * * *. The emphasis should be on prosecutions of the sellers or purveyors, particularly those who deal with minors, *and not the mere addict possessors.* * * * [C]riminal prosecutions of [addicts] in some instances may be justified so as *to compel an addict to undergo complete [rehabilitative] treatment.* * * * *[P]rosecutions for such minor offenses which are considered to be local in character may well be and often are left to the state or local authorities.* Not falling within such minor category are cases against persons, whether addicts or not, who engage in the importation or transportation or are in possession of these drugs under circumstances reasonably indicating that the drugs were intended for use in the illegal traffic. * * *

" 'In prosecutions for *serious* offenses by *traffickers* * * * *two* counts may be charged, one under the internal revenue laws and the other under [21 U.S.C. § 174].' [Emphasis supplied.] * * *

"These instructions may provide a suitable framework for structuring prosecutorial choice. The reference in the first instructions above to 'minor offenses which are considered to be local in character' suggests use of the 'local' or District statute in the absence of special circumstances. * * *

"I think it would have been open to defendant to attempt to show abuse of prosecutorial discretion on a pretrial motion to dismiss the indictment."

2. Is Judge Bazelon suggesting that *Hutcherson* should prevail if he shows the charging decision was not in accordance with the guidelines in the United States Attorney's Manual? Is it relevant that the Manual states: "This Manual provides only internal Department of Justice guidance. It is not intended to, does not, and may not be relied upon to create any rights, substantive or procedural, enforceable at law by any party in any matter civil or criminal. Nor are any limitations hereby placed on otherwise lawful litigative prerogatives of the Department of Justice." [a]

3. A somewhat different situation is that in which the prosecutor "revises" his charge selection upward following the exercise of some right by the defendant, as in BLACKLEDGE v. PERRY, 417 U.S. 21, 94 S.Ct. 2098, 40 L.Ed.2d 628 (1974). After Perry's conviction of misdemeanor assault in district court (for which he received a sentence of 6 months), he exercised his right under state law to obtain a trial de novo in the superior court. The applicable statute provided that in such a situation the slate is wiped clean, the prior conviction is annulled, and the prosecution and defense begin anew in the superior court. Prior to Perry's appearance in superior court, the prosecutor obtained an indictment, based on the same conduct for which Perry had been tried, charging him with the felony of assault with a deadly weapon with intent to kill. Perry pleaded guilty [b] to that charge and was sentenced to a term of 5–7 years. Relying upon *North Carolina v. Pearce,* p. 1434 infra (holding that due process prohibits a judge from imposing a more severe sentence for the purpose of discouraging defendants from exercising their statutory right to appeal), Perry later claimed that the felony charge deprived him of due process. The Court, per STEWART, J., agreed:

"The lesson that emerges from *Pearce* [and its progeny] is that the Due Process Clause is not offended by all possibilities of increased punishment upon retrial after appeal, but only by those that pose a realistic likelihood of 'vindictiveness.' Unlike the circumstances presented by those cases, however, in the situation here the central figure is not the judge or the jury, but the prosecutor. The question is whether the opportunities for vindictiveness in this situation are such as to impel the conclusion that due process of law requires a rule analogous to that of the *Pearce* case. We conclude that the answer must be in the affirmative.

"A prosecutor clearly has a considerable stake in discouraging convicted misdemeanants from appealing and thus obtaining a trial *de novo* in the Superior Court, since such an appeal will clearly require increased expenditures of prosecutorial resources before the defendant's conviction becomes final, and may even result in a formerly convicted defendant going free. And, if the prosecutor has the means readily at hand to discourage such

a. Quoted in Beck, *The Administrative Law of Criminal Prosecution: The Development of Prosecutorial Policy,* 27 Am.U.L.Rev. 310, 314 n. 10 (1978).

b. The Court held that the guilty plea did not bar Perry from later raising the due process claim. See p. 1252 infra.

appeals—by 'upping the ante' through a felony indictment whenever a convicted misdemeanant pursues his statutory appellate remedy—the State can insure that only the most hardy defendants will brave the hazards of a *de novo* trial.

"There is, of course, no evidence that the prosecutor in this case acted in bad faith or maliciously in seeking a felony indictment against Perry. The rationale of our judgment in the *Pearce* case, however, was not grounded upon the proposition that actual retaliatory motivation must inevitably exist. Rather, we emphasized that 'since the fear of such vindictiveness may unconstitutionally deter a defendant's exercise of the right to appeal his first conviction, due process also requires that a defendant be freed of apprehension of such a retaliatory motivation on the part of the sentencing judge.' We think it clear that the same considerations apply here. A person convicted of an offense is entitled to pursue his statutory right to a trial *de novo,* without apprehension that the State will retaliate by substituting a more serious charge for the original one thus subjecting him to a significantly increased potential period of incarceration.[c]

"Due process of law requires that such a potential for vindictiveness must not enter into North Carolina's two-tiered appellate process. We hold, therefore, that it was not constitutionally permissible for the State to respond to Perry's invocation of his statutory right to appeal by bringing a more serious charge against him at the trial *de novo.*[7]"

REHNQUIST, J., dissenting, objected: "The prosecutor here elected to proceed initially in the state district court where felony charges could not be prosecuted for reasons which may well have been unrelated to whether he believed respondent was guilty of and could be convicted of the felony with which he was later charged. Both prosecutor and defendant stand to benefit from an initial prosecution in the District Court, the prosecutor at least from its less burdensome procedures and the defendant from the opportunity for an initial acquittal and the limited penalties. With the countervailing reasons for proceeding only on the misdemeanor charge in the District Court no longer applicable once the defendant has invoked his statutory right to a trial *de novo,* a prosecutor need not be vindictive to seek to indict and convict a defendant of the more serious of the two crimes of which he believes him guilty."

4. Goodwin was charged with several misdemeanor and petty offenses, including assault, and his case was assigned to a

c. In *Thigpen v. Roberts,* 468 U.S. 27, 104 S.Ct. 2916, 82 L.Ed.2d 23 (1984), the relevant facts were essentially identical to those in *Blackledge* except that the first trial was the responsibility of the county prosecutor while the indictment and trial on the felony was the responsibility of the district attorney. The Court noted: "It might be argued that if two different prosecutors are involved, a presumption of vindictiveness, which arises in part from assumptions about the individual's personal stake in the proceedings, is inappropriate. On the other hand, to the extent the presumption reflects 'institutional pressure that * * * might * * * subconsciously motivate a vindictive prosecutorial * * * response to a defendant's exercise of his right to obtain a retrial of a decided question,' it does not hinge on the continued involvement of a particular individual. A district attorney burdened with the retrial of an already-convicted defendant might be no less vindictive because he did not bring the initial prosecution." But the Court then found it unnecessary to "determine the correct rule when two independent prosecutors are involved," for here the county prosecutor participated fully in the later proceedings, as was his statutory duty, and thus "the addition of the district attorney to the prosecutorial team changes little."

7. This would clearly be a different case if the State had shown that it was impossible to proceed on the more serious charge at the outset, as in *Diaz v. United States,* 223 U.S. 442, 32 S.Ct. 250, 56 L.Ed. 500 (1912). In that case the defendant was originally tried and convicted for assault and battery. Subsequent to the original trial, the assault victim died, and the defendant was then tried and convicted for homicide. Obviously, it would not have been possible for the authorities in *Diaz* to have originally proceeded against the defendant on the more serious charge, since the crime of homicide was not complete until after the victim's death.

Department of Justice attorney detailed temporarily to try such cases before a magistrate and who did not have authority to seek indictments or try felony cases. Goodwin indicated a desire for jury trial, not then available in a trial before a magistrate, so the case was transferred to the district court, where an assistant U.S. Attorney obtained a four-count indictment charging Goodwin with a felony count of forcibly assaulting a federal officer and three related counts. After his conviction of the felony count and one misdemeanor count, Goodwin sought to set aside the verdict on the ground of prosecutorial vindictiveness; the district court denied relief, but the court of appeals reversed on the ground that *Blackledge* entitled Goodwin to such relief even though "the prosecutor did not act with actual vindictiveness." In UNITED STATES v. GOODWIN, 457 U.S. 368, 102 S.Ct. 2485, 73 L.Ed.2d 74 (1982), the Court, per STEVENS, J., disagreed:

"There is good reason to be cautious before adopting an inflexible presumption of prosecutorial vindictiveness in a pretrial setting. In the course of preparing a case for trial, the prosecutor may uncover additional information that suggests a basis for further prosecution or he simply may come to realize that information possessed by the State has a broader significance. At this stage of the proceedings, the prosecutor's assessment of the proper extent of prosecution may not have crystallized. In contrast, once a trial begins—and certainly by the time a conviction has been obtained—it is much more likely that the State has discovered and assessed all of the information against an accused and has made a determination, on the basis of that information, of the extent to which he should be prosecuted. Thus, a change in the charging decision made after an initial trial is completed is much more likely to be improperly motivated than is a pretrial decision.

"In addition, a defendant before trial is expected to invoke procedural rights that inevitably impose some 'burden' on the prosecutor. Defense counsel routinely file pretrial motions to suppress evidence; to challenge the sufficiency and form of an indictment; to plead an affirmative defense; to request psychiatric services; to obtain access to Government files; to be tried by jury. It is unrealistic to assume that a prosecutor's probable response to such motions is to seek to penalize and to deter. The invocation of procedural rights is an integral part of the adversary process in which our criminal justice system operates.

"Thus, the timing of the prosecutor's action in this case suggests that a presumption of vindictiveness is not warranted. A prosecutor should remain free before trial to exercise the broad discretion entrusted to him to determine the extent of the societal interest in prosecution. An initial decision should not freeze future conduct. As we made clear in *Bordenkircher* [*v. Hayes,* p. 1185 infra], the initial charges filed by a prosecutor may not reflect the extent to which an individual is legitimately subject to prosecution.

"The nature of the right asserted by the respondent confirms that a presumption of vindictiveness is not warranted in this case. After initially expressing an interest in plea negotiation, respondent decided not to plead guilty and requested a trial by jury in District Court. In doing so, he forced the Government to bear the burdens and uncertainty of a trial. This Court in *Bordenkircher* made clear that the mere fact that a defendant refuses to plead guilty and forces the Government to prove its case is insufficient to warrant a presumption that subsequent changes in the charging decision are unjustified. Respondent argues that such a presumption is warranted in this case, however, because he not only requested a trial—he requested a trial by jury.

"We cannot agree. The distinction between a bench trial and a jury trial does not compel a special presumption of prosecutorial vindictiveness whenever additional charges are brought after a jury is demanded. To be sure, a jury trial is more burdensome than a bench trial. The defendant may challenge the selection of the venire; the jury itself must be impaneled; witnesses and arguments must be prepared more carefully to avoid the danger of a mistrial. These matters are much less significant, however, than the facts that before either a jury or a judge the State must present its full case against the accused and the defendant is entitled to offer a full defense. As compared to the complete trial *de novo* at issue in *Blackledge* a jury trial—as opposed to a bench trial—does not require duplicative expenditures of prosecutorial resources before a final judgment may be obtained. Moreover, unlike the trial judge in *Pearce,* no party is asked 'to do over what it thought it had already done correctly.' A prosecutor has no 'personal stake' in a bench trial and thus no reason to engage in 'self-vindication' upon a defendant's request for a jury trial. Perhaps most importantly, the institutional bias against the retrial of a decided question that supported the decisions in *Pearce* and *Blackledge* simply has no counterpart in this case.

"There is an opportunity for vindictiveness, [but] a mere opportunity for vindictiveness is insufficient to justify the imposition of a prophylactic rule. As *Blackledge* makes clear, 'the Due Process Clause is not offended by all possibilities of increased punishment * * * but only by those that pose a realistic likelihood of "vindictiveness." ' The possibility that a prosecutor would respond to a defendant's pretrial demand for a jury trial by bringing charges not in the public interest that could be explained only as penalty imposed on the defendant is so *unlikely* that a presumption of vindictiveness certainly is not warranted.

"In declining to apply a presumption of vindictiveness, we of course do not foreclose the possibility that a defendant in an appropriate case might prove objectively that the prosecutor's charging decision was motivated by a desire to punish him for doing something that the law plainly allowed him to do."

BLACKMUN, J., concurring in the judgment, found "no support in our prior cases for any distinction between pretrial and post-trial vindictiveness," but concluded there had been a permissible adjustment of the charges "based on 'objective information concerning identifiable conduct on the part of the defendant occurring after the time of the original' charging decision."[d]

BRENNAN, J., joined by Marshall, J., dissenting, objected:

"The Court suggests that the distinction between a bench trial and a jury trial is unimportant in this context. Such a suggestion is demonstrably fallacious. Experienced criminal practitioners, for both prosecution and defense, know that a jury trial entails far more prosecutorial work than a bench trial. Defense challenges to the potential-juror array, *voir dire* examination of potential jurors, and suppression hearings all take up a prosecutor's time before a jury trial, adding to his scheduling difficulties and caseload. More care in the preparation of his requested instructions, of his witnesses, and of his own remarks is necessary in order to avoid mistrial or reversible error. And there is always the specter of the 'irrational' acquittal by a jury that is unreviewable on ap-

d. In support he referred to footnote 2 of the majority opinion, reading: "By affidavit, the Assistant United States Attorney later set forth his reasons for this action: (1) he considered respondent's conduct on the date in question to be a serious violation of law, (2) Goodwin had a lengthy history of violent crime, (3) the prosecutor considered respondent's conduct to be related to major narcotics transactions, (4) the prosecutor believed that respondent had committed perjury at his preliminary hearing, and (5) Goodwin had failed to appear for trial as originally scheduled. The Government attorney stated that his decision to seek a felony indictment was not motivated in any way by Goodwin's request for a jury trial in District Court."

peal. Thus it is simply inconceivable that a criminal defendant's election to be tried by jury would be a matter of indifference to his prosecutor. On the contrary, the prosecutor would almost always prefer that the defendant waive such a 'troublesome' right. And if the defendant refuses to do so, the prosecutor's subsequent elevation of the charges against the defendant manifestly poses a realistic likelihood of vindictiveness."

5. In a situation where *Blackledge* does apply, may a prosecutor escalate the charge only in the particular situation described in footnote 7 of that case? Of what significance is it that the Court has more recently stated in *Thigpen* that "the *Blackledge* presumption is rebuttable" [e] and in *Goodwin* that it "could be overcome by objective evidence justifying the prosecutor's action" [f]? Of what significance is *Wasman v. United States,* p. 1438 infra? There, a four-Justice plurality asserted that both *Pearce* and *Blackledge* involve only a presumption of vindictiveness and that "where the presumption applies, the sentencing authority or the prosecutor must rebut the presumption that an increased sentence or charge resulted from vindictiveness." Five members of the Court declined to join that part of the opinion because, as Justice Powell put it, the *Pearce-Blackledge* presumption "is not simply concerned with actual vindictiveness, but also was intended to protect against reasonable apprehension of vindictiveness that could deter a defendant" from exercising his rights.

6. Does *Blackledge* or *Goodwin* apply when the prosecutor escalates the charges following a mistrial granted on defendant's motion because of the jury's inability to agree on a verdict? Compare *United States v. Mays,* 738 F.2d 1188 (11th Cir.1984); with *Murphy v. State,* 453 N.E.2d 219 (Ind.1983).

e. A footnote observation which, however, cites back to footnote 7 of *Blackledge.*

f. A footnote observation which, however, is followed by quotation of footnote 7 of *Blackledge.*

Chapter 14

THE PRELIMINARY HEARING

SECTION 1. THE FUNCTION(S) OF THE PRELIMINARY HEARING

I. SCREENING

> "The object or purpose of the preliminary [hearing] is to prevent hasty, malicious, improvident, and oppressive prosecutions, to protect the person charged from open and public accusations of crime, to avoid both for the defendant and the public the expense of a public trial, and to save the defendant from the humiliation and anxiety involved in public prosecution, and to discover whether or not there are substantial grounds upon which a prosecution may be based."

Rosenberry, J., in *Thies v. State,* 178 Wis. 98, 103, 189 N.W. 539, 541 (1922).

The "screening" objective described by Justice Rosenberry is universally recognized as the primary function of the preliminary hearing. Indeed, most courts recognize it as the only valid objective of the preliminary hearing, and view the other functions discussed below (i.e., discovery, perpetuation of testimony, etc.) as merely incidental attributes of the screening process. The objectives of the screening process are well stated in *Thies.* Today, courts also stress two other functions of effective screening at the preliminary hearing: (1) it ensures that the defendant who has been unjustifiably charged will be promptly released from custody or, if he made bail, from the conditions of the bail; and (2) it results in the lowering of excessive charges and thereby serves as a primary safeguard against the prosecutorial practice of "overcharging" in anticipation of plea negotiations.

The effectiveness of the preliminary hearing in performing its screening role is a matter of considerable dispute. As in the case of the grand jury (see pp. 977–81 infra), commentators and courts have offered arguments and statistics on both sides. Fruitful evaluation of their conclusions is made especially difficult, however, by substantial variations in the hearing's structure and operation from one jurisdiction to another (and sometimes, as to operation, from one county to another in the same jurisdiction).[a] Studies of the prelim-

a. See Emerson and Ames, *The Role of the Grand Jury and the Preliminary Hearing in Pretrial Screening* (1984) [hereinafter cited as Emerson and Ames] (criticizing comparisons of grand jury and preliminary hearing screening "as if they represented a single 'ideal' or 'typical' proceeding," and noting that the operation of both screening devices "varies dramatically from jurisdiction to jurisdiction, depending upon state laws and rules as well as local norms and customs").

Most helpful studies of preliminary hearings in particular state jurisdictions are found in: Graham and Letwin, *The Preliminary Hearing in Los Angeles: Some Field Findings and Legal Policy Observations,* 18 U.C.L.A.L.Rev. 635, 916 (1971) [hereinafter cited as Graham and Letwin]; Katz, et al., *Justice Is The Crime* (1972); Miller, *Prosecution: The Decision to Charge a Suspect with a Crime* (1969) [hereinafter cited as Miller]; Emerson and Ames; Gilboy, *Prosecutors' Discretionary* inary hearing in different jurisdictions (see fn. a supra) have produced, for example, quite disparate statistics on preliminary hearing dispositions. The percentage of dismissals to the total number of hearings has ranged from less than 2% to more than 30%, and only slightly less substantial differences are reported as to hearings in which the magistrate binds the case over for trial but reduces the level of the charge.

What factors might contribute to such substantial variations in the percentages of dismissals and reductions? Consider the following potential differences in legal standards and local practices, all of which have been cited as arguably having a bearing on the frequency of dismissals and reductions in a particular jurisdiction: (1) whether prosecutorial screening before the case reaches the preliminary hearing stage is extensive (as in jurisdictions where 30–50% of the cases presented by the police do not result in the filing of charges) or is largely limited to exceptional cases; (2) whether prosecutors are assigned horizontally to cases (with different prosecutors responsible for initial screening, preliminary hearing presentation, and trial) or vertically (with the same prosecutor responsible for the case from initial presentation to final disposition); (3) whether the prosecutor most often bypasses the preliminary hearing by taking the case directly to the grand jury (so that preliminary hearings are used in only a small group of cases) or only infrequently utilizes the bypass procedure (see Notes 6–8, pp. 946–48 infra); (4) whether the use of the bypass procedure is tied to the strength of the particular case (see Note 8, p. 947 infra); (5) the qualifications of the magistrates conducting the hearing (ranging from the lay justice of the peace to the full-time lawyer/judge); (6) the extent of the magistrate's caseload, which may range from 2–3 preliminary hearings per day to 10–20 hearings per day; (7) whether the caseload at the trial level necessarily precludes trial of all cases which could justifiably be boundover (thereby encouraging the magistrate to reduce charges in cases more appropriately disposed of at the misdemeanor level); (8) whether cases are settled by plea bargains prior to the preliminary hearing stage or plea bargaining begins and cases are settled largely after the case reaches the trial level court; (9) whether defense counsel regularly insist upon a preliminary hearing even in open and shut cases (largely to obtain discovery) or usually waive the hearing in such cases (see p. 940 infra); (10) whether the evidentiary standard governing the magistrate's decision to bindover is essentially the probable cause standard applied on the issuance of a warrant or a standard comparable to that imposed by a trial judge in determining whether there is sufficient evidence to send a case to the jury (see § 3 infra); (11) whether the prosecutor must meet the bindover standard through evidence that would be admissible at trial or may rely instead on hearsay and other evidence generally inadmissible at trial (see § 4 infra); (12) whether the magistrate has the same leeway as a trial court factfinder in judging credibility (see Note 6, p. 956 infra); (13) whether the scope of defense presentations is limited—e.g., whether the defense may establish affirmative defenses, and whether the leeway granted the defense in cross-examining prosecution witnesses and presenting defense witnesses generally approximates, or is considerably narrower than, that granted at trial (see § 4 infra); (14) whether the prosecution, even though not required to do so in order to satisfy the bindover standard follows the practice of presenting all of its key witnesses, or instead seeks to limit defense discovery and reduce the burden on its witnesses by introducing just enough evidence to meet the bindover

Use of the Grand Jury to Initiate and Reinitiate Prosecution, 1984 A.B.F.Res.J. 2 [hereinafter cited as Gilboy].

standard (which in some jurisdictions allows it to rely entirely on the testimony of the investigating officer) [b]; (15) whether the practical impact of a magistrate's order of dismissal is to end the case or the prosecutor frequently reinitiates prosecution without additional evidence by either taking the case to the grand jury or refiling when another judge is sitting as preliminary hearing magistrate (see Note 8, p. 957 infra).

II. DISCOVERY

> "Although the primary purpose served by the federal preliminary examination is to insure that there is 'probable cause,' * * * in practice this hearing may provide the defense with the most valuable discovery technique available to him." Weinstein, D.J. in *United States ex rel. Wheeler v. Flood,* 269 F.Supp. 194, 198 (E.D.N.Y.1967).

In meeting the evidentiary standard for a bindover, the prosecutor will necessarily provide the defense with some discovery of the prosecution's case. The defendant may obtain even more discovery by cross-examining the prosecution's witnesses at the hearing and by subpoenaing other potential trial witnesses to testify as defense witnesses at the hearing. The extent of the discovery obtained in this manner will depend upon several factors, including the following: (1) whether the prosecution can rely entirely on hearsay reports and thereby sharply limit the number of witnesses it presents (see Note 2, p. 960 infra); (2) whether, even assuming hearsay cannot be used, the bindover standard may be satisfied by the presentation of a minimal amount of testimony on each element of the offense (see Note 1, p. 953 infra); (3) whether, notwithstanding the ease with which the standard is met, the prosecutor still follows a general practice of presenting most of his case (see fn. b supra); (4) whether the defendant is limited, both in cross-examination and in the presentation of witnesses, to direct rebuttal of material presented by the prosecution (see Note 1, p. 963 infra, and Note 2, p. 966 infra); (5) whether the defendant is willing to bear the tactical costs that may be incurred in utilizing his subpoena and cross-examination authority for discovery purposes.[c]

In many jurisdictions, these factors combine to provide preliminary hearing discovery that is of quite limited use. Consider, for example, the following assessment of the discovery available in preliminary hearings in federal courts: "The kind of discovery that [defendant] gets at such a hearing is not the discovery to prepare his defense for trial, but it is the kind of discovery in which he is confronted with his accuser and informed of what he is charged with, and given some indication as to the strength of the Government's case. This is the kind of discovery that allows him to make decisions as to his plea, not as to how he will present evi-

b. Studies indicate that prosecutors in most jurisdictions follow the latter practice, see e.g., Miller, and Gilboy; but at least one leading prosecutor's office (Los Angeles) follows the former practice, see Graham and Letwin.

c. Consider in this connection, Amsterdam, *Trial Manual for the Defense of Criminal Cases* § 139 (4th ed. 1984): "Frequently, counsel may find that s/he is working at cross-purposes in seeking to discover and impeach simultaneously. S/he will obviously have to accommodate these objectives with an eye to which objective is more important * * *. If counsel vigorously cross-examines the witness, in an effort to get a contradiction or concession on record, the witness will normally dig in and give a minimum of information in an effort to save his or her testimonial position; and more than likely s/he will be uncooperative if counsel thereafter attempts to interview the witness prior to trial. On the other hand, if counsel engages the witness in routine examination, amiable and ranging, counsel may be able to pick up many clues for investigation and for planning of his defense." There may be even greater costs in seeking discovery by subpoenaing a potential state witness not called by the prosecution. The magistrate may refuse to permit the defendant to treat the witness as adverse on direct examination and allow the prosecution to lead the witness on cross-examination. Also, the defendant runs the risk of preserving damaging testimony that might not otherwise be available at trial. See id. at § 141. See also Note 1, p. 963 infra, and Note 3, p. 966 infra.

dence at trial, and how he will combat the Government's case." Senate Hearings on the Federal Magistrate's Act (1967) (testimony of Professor Dash).[d] The importance of such limited discovery to the defendant will depend in part on the alternatives available for obtaining the same or even broader discovery and the comparative costs of these alternatives. When the prior statements of prospective witnesses (including the arresting officer's report) is readily available under state discovery rules, the discovery potential of the preliminary hearing may be relatively unimportant. Where, on the other hand, state law and practice provide very little pretrial discovery, the preliminary hearing may serve as the primary discovery device under local practice. Also, even though state law provides extensive discovery, if that discovery is not available until after the critical time for plea settlements has passed, the preliminary hearing may still serve as the primary discovery vehicle for the substantial percentage of cases resolved by guilty pleas.

III. FUTURE IMPEACHMENT

> "[T]he skilled interrogation of witnesses [at the preliminary examination] by an experienced lawyer can fashion a vital impeachment tool for use in cross-examination of the State's witnesses at the trial." Brennan, J., in *Coleman v. Alabama,* 399 U.S. 1, 90 S.Ct. 1999, 26 L.Ed.2d 387 (1970).

Extensive cross-examination of prosecution witnesses at the preliminary hearing may be of value to the defense even though there is little likelihood of successfully challenging the prosecution's showing of probable cause and little to be gained by way of discovery. As Justice Brennan suggests, the skillful extraction of statements from a witness at the preliminary hearing may provide a solid foundation for effective cross-examination of that witness at trial. In many instances, witnesses are more likely to make damaging admissions or contradictory statements at the preliminary hearing because they are less thoroughly briefed for that proceeding than they are for trial. Also, with respect to some witnesses, the more they say before trial, the more likely that there will be some inconsistency between their trial testimony and their previous statements. Arguably, such inconsistencies may have a more damaging impact upon the witness' credibility when the inconsistency is with preliminary hearing testimony, as opposed to prior statements given to the police, since the preliminary hearing testimony was given under oath in a judicial setting. Of course, cross-examination designed to lay the foundation for future impeachment carries with it certain dangers for the defense. If the cross-examination focuses too much on potential weaknesses in the witness' testimony, it may educate the witness as to these weaknesses. The witness may "rehabilitate himself for the trial and state that at the hearing he was confused, but that everything is now clear in his mind." Bailey and Rothblatt, *Successful Techniques For Criminal Trials* § 25 (1971). If the witness is one who otherwise might "soften" his view of the facts as time passes and his emotional involvement les-

d. During these hearings on the Federal Magistrate's Act (see p. 944 infra), several witnesses urged that discovery should be recognized as a basic objective of the preliminary hearing and that preliminary hearing procedure should be modified accordingly (e.g., hearsay testimony generally should not be allowed, more extensive cross-examination should be permitted, and the prosecutor should not be able to bypass the preliminary hearing, see Note 4, p. 944 infra). This view was rejected by the Senate Judiciary Committee in its report on the Magistrate's Act (S.Rep. No. 371, 90th Cong., 1st Sess.):

> "[We are] of the opinion that the problem of discovery should be treated separately from that of the preliminary hearing. The preliminary hearing does not present an ideal opportunity for discovery. * * * Because its fundamental purpose is to prevent unjustified restraints of liberty, the preliminary examination should be held within a short time after an accused is first arrested. Discovery, on the other hand, can most usefully take place at a later stage, much closer to trial, when the evidence is more nearly complete and defense counsel is better prepared."

sens, extensive cross-examination at the preliminary hearing may only harden his position and make him less able to retreat to a more friendly position.[e] Finally, if the witness becomes unavailable at trial, the defense counsel may find that he has perpetuated testimony more damaging than that which would have existed without the cross-examination. See pt. IV below.

IV. THE "PERPETUATION OF TESTIMONY"

> "The function of perpetuating testimony should be of substantial concern to the prosecutor * * * because of the ever present possibility that an important witness may prove unavailable to testify at trial." Graham and Letwin, 925.

Preliminary hearing testimony traditionally has been admitted at trial as substantive evidence, under the "prior testimony" exception to the hearsay rule, where the witness is currently unavailable to testify. Thus, the hearing perpetuates the testimony of witnesses, ensuring that it may be used even if the witness should die, disappear, or otherwise become unavailable to testify.[f] While the Supreme Court has stated that a major advantage of the hearing for the defense is its availability to "preserve testimony favorable to the accused of a witness who does not appear at the trial," *Coleman v. Alabama* at p. 943 infra, the hearing is not commonly used by the defense for this purpose. See, e.g., Graham and Letwin, 658, 925. For various reasons (see Note 1, p. 965 infra), the defense rarely will have its own witnesses testify at the preliminary hearing. Accordingly, the perpetuation of testimony is of practical significance primarily as it relates to prosecution witnesses, and the possibility of perpetuation tends to be viewed by the defense as a negative feature of the hearing.[g]

The admission of the preliminary hearing testimony of a prosecution witness who is unavailable at trial (and therefore is not subject to trial cross-examination) must be reconciled with the defendant's Sixth Amendment right of confrontation. CALIFORNIA v. GREEN, 399 U.S. 149, 90 S.Ct. 1930, 26 L.Ed.2d 489 (1970), established the basic guidelines for admitting such testimony consistent with defendant's Sixth Amendment right. The Court there

e. If the witness should retreat to such a position, the prosecution may be able to use the more favorable preliminary hearing testimony to impeach its own witness. Moreover, in some jurisdictions, the inconsistent preliminary hearing testimony may be used as substantive evidence (i.e., not merely for impeachment), even though the witness testifies at trial and refutes his earlier testimony. See *California v. Green*, infra.

f. See Fed.R.Evid. 804(a) setting forth the traditional grounds of unavailability: " 'Unavailability as a witness' includes situations in which the declarant: (1) is exempted by ruling of the court on the ground of privilege from testifying concerning the subject matter of his statement; or (2) persists in refusing to testify concerning the subject matter of his statement despite an order of the court to do so; or (3) testifies to a lack of memory of the subject matter of his statement; or (4) is unable to be present or to testify at the hearing because of death or then existing physical or mental illness or infirmity; or (5) is absent from the hearing and the proponent of his statement has been unable to procure his attendance * * * by process or other reasonable means. * * *" It should be noted, in connection with the 5th ground, that persons located outside the trial jurisdiction will not necessarily be "unavailable." If his whereabouts are known, a witness located in another state ordinarily may be subjected to compulsory process under the Uniform Act to Secure The Attendance of Witnesses From Without A State In Criminal Proceedings 11 U.L.A. 2 (1974). See *State v. Kim*, 519 P.2d 1241 (Hawaii 1974) (showing of unavailability requires an attempt to use the Uniform Act where available).

g. If the prosecution has good reason to believe that the witness will be unavailable at trial, the witness' testimony can be preserved by use of deposition. See fn. f, p. 1124 infra. The preliminary hearing offers the advantage of perpetuating the testimony of witnesses who unexpectedly become unavailable as well as eliminating the burden of establishing likely unavailability to the court's satisfaction where a deposition would be available. Perpetuating the witness' testimony is also seen by some prosecutors as a useful tool in discouraging witness intimidation. See Emerson and Ames, 141–42.

upheld the constitutionality of admitting preliminary hearing testimony over a defense objection that it should not be admissible where the prosecution witness was "unavailable" solely because of a loss of memory. The defendant in *Green* had been charged with furnishing marijuana to a minor, Porter. When Porter was called to testify, he was evasive and uncooperative on the stand, claiming a lapse of memory. The prosecution then introduced two prior statements of Porter, including his preliminary hearing testimony, "to prove the truth of the matter asserted in the statements." The state court held that admission of these statements as substantive evidence, although authorized by a California statute, violated defendant's right to confrontation. The Supreme Court reversed, 7–1. The majority opinion, per WHITE, J., held that if Porter was subject to cross-examination at trial as to his prior statements, then the Confrontation Clause was not violated by admission of those statements as substantive evidence. The Court noted, however, that there was a question as to whether Porter was subject to effective cross-examination at trial in light of his lapse of memory. It accordingly went on to consider the admissibility of the preliminary hearing testimony on the assumption that Porter was, in effect, an "unavailable" witness at trial:

"We also think that Porter's preliminary hearing testimony was admissible as far as the Constitution is concerned wholly apart from the question of whether respondent had an effective opportunity for confrontation at the subsequent trial. For Porter's statement at the preliminary hearing had already been given under circumstances closely approximating those that surround the typical trial. Porter was under oath; respondent was represented by counsel—the same counsel in fact who later represented him at the trial; respondent had every opportunity to cross-examine Porter as to his statement; and the proceedings were conducted before a judicial tribunal, equipped to provide a judicial record of the hearings. * * *

"This Court long ago held that admitting the prior testimony of any unavailable witness does not violate the Confrontation Clause. *Mattox v. United States,* 156 U.S. 237, 15 S.Ct. 337, 39 L.Ed. 409 (1895). That case involved testimony given at the defendant's first trial by a witness who had died by the time of the second trial, but we do not find the instant preliminary hearing significantly different from an actual trial to warrant distinguishing the two cases for purposes of the Confrontation Clause. Indeed, we indicated as much in *Pointer v. Texas,* where we noted that '[t]he case before us would be quite a different one had Phillips' statement been taken at a full-fledged hearing at which petitioner had been represented by counsel who had been given a complete and adequate opportunity to cross examine.' [h] And in *Barber v. Page,* 390 U.S. 719, 88 S.Ct. 1318, 20 L.Ed.2d 255 (1968), although noting that the preliminary hearing is ordinarily a less searching exploration into the merits of a case than a trial, we recognized that 'there may be some justification for holding that the opportunity for cross-examination of a witness at a preliminary hearing satisfies the demands of the confrontation clause where the witness is shown to be actually unavailable. * * *' In the present case respondent's counsel does not appear to have been significantly limited in any way in the scope or nature of his cross-examination of the witness Porter at the preliminary hearing. If Porter had died or was otherwise unavailable, the Confron-

h. In *Pointer,* 380 U.S. 400, 85 S.Ct. 1065, 13 L.Ed.2d 923 (1965), the state failed to appoint counsel to assist the indigent defendant at the preliminary hearing, but subsequently used at trial the preliminary hearing testimony of a witness who was no longer available to testify. The Supreme Court held that this use violated the defendant's Sixth Amendment rights, since the witness' statement had been given without "adequate opportunity for cross-examination" by the defense.) See also *Coleman v. Alabama,* p. 943 infra, on the defendant's right to appointed counsel at the hearing.

tation Clause would not have been violated by admitting his testimony given at the preliminary hearing—the right of cross-examination then afforded provides substantial compliance with the purposes behind the confrontation requirement, as long as the declarant's inability to give live testimony is in no way the fault of the State. * * * As in the case where the witness is physically unproducible, the State here has made every effort to introduce its evidence through the live testimony of the witness; it produced Porter at trial, swore him as a witness, and tendered him for cross-examination. Whether Porter then testified in a manner consistent or inconsistent with his preliminary hearing testimony, claimed a loss of memory, claimed his privilege against compulsory self-incrimination, or simply refused to answer, nothing in the Confrontation Clause prohibited the State from also relying on his prior testimony to prove its case against Green."

JUSTICE BRENNAN, dissenting, argued that the admission of a witness' preliminary hearing statement as substantive evidence violated the accused's right of confrontation "when the witness claims to be unable to remember the events with which the statement dealt." The dissent stressed the suspicious nature of unavailability due to a lapse in memory, but also commented upon practical limitations presented in obtaining satisfactory cross-examination at a preliminary hearing. On the latter point, the dissent noted:

"[T]he purposes of the Confrontation Clause cannot be satisfied by a face-to-face encounter at the preliminary hearing. Cross-examination at the hearing pales beside that which takes place at trial. This is so for a number of reasons. First, as noted, the objective of the hearing is to establish the presence or absence of probable cause, not guilt or innocence proved beyond a reasonable doubt; thus, if evidence suffices to establish probable cause, defense counsel has little reason at the preliminary hearing to show that it does not conclusively establish guilt—or, at least, he had little reason before today's decision. Second, neither defense nor prosecution is eager before trial to disclose its case by extensive examination at the preliminary hearing; thorough questioning of a prosecution witness by defense counsel may easily amount to a grant of gratis discovery to the state. Third, the schedules of neither court nor counsel can easily accommodate lengthy preliminary hearings. Fourth, even were the judge and lawyers not concerned that the proceedings be brief, the defense and prosecution have generally had inadequate time before the hearing to prepare for extensive examination. * * * It appears, then, that in terms of the purposes of the Confrontation Clause, an equation of face-to-face encounter at the preliminary hearing with confrontation at trial must rest largely on the fact that the witness testified at the hearing under oath, subject to the penalty for perjury and in a courtroom atmosphere. These factors are not insignificant, but by themselves they fall far short of satisfying the demands of constitutional confrontation. Moreover, the atmosphere and stakes are different in the two proceedings. In the hurried, somewhat *pro forma* context of the average preliminary hearing, a witness may be more careless in his testimony than in the more measured and searching atmosphere of a trial. Similarly, a man willing to perjure himself when the consequences are simply that the accused will stand trial may be less willing to do so when his lies may condemn the defendant to loss of liberty. In short, it ignores reality to assume that the purposes of the Confrontation Clause are met during a preliminary hearing. * * *"

OHIO v. ROBERTS, 448 U.S. 56, 100 S.Ct. 2531, 65 L.Ed.2d 597 (1980), commented further upon the scope of *Green.* The Court there held that *Green* permitted admission of preliminary hearing testimony of an unavailable prosecution witness who had been called by the defense at the preliminary hearing, but had been examined, in effect, as a hostile witness. While defense counsel had not formally asked that the witness be declared hostile and that he be allowed to cross-examine her, his questioning had been the functional equivalent of cross-examination. The Court noted that counsel, in his "direct examination," had challenged the witness' perception of events and her veracity, and had not been limited "in any way" in this line of questioning. The end result was, as in *Green,* a "substantial compliance with the purposes behind the confrontation requirement." The Court added that, in light of the facts before it, there was no need to determine whether *Green* applied where a defense counsel had not actually engaged in extensive questioning of the witness. Referring to first paragraph from *Green* quoted at p. 937 supra, the majority noted:

"This passage and others in the *Green* opinion suggest that the opportunity to cross-examine at the preliminary hearing—even absent actual cross-examination—satisfies the Confrontation Clause. Yet the record showed, and the Court recognized, that defense counsel in fact had cross-examined Porter at the earlier proceeding. Thus, Mr. Justice Brennan, writing in dissent, could conclude only that '[p]erhaps' 'the mere opportunity for face-to-face encounter [is] sufficient.' 399 U.S. at 200, n. 8. We need not decide whether the Supreme Court of Ohio correctly dismissed statements in *Green* suggesting that the mere opportunity to cross-examine rendered the prior testimony admissible. See Westen, *The Future of Confrontation,* 77 Mich.L.Rev. 1185, 1211 (1979) (issue is 'truly difficult to resolve under conventional theories of confrontation'). Nor need we decide whether *de minimus* questioning is sufficient, for defense counsel in this case tested [the currently unavailable witness'] testimony with the equivalent of significant cross-examination." [i]

V. OTHER FUNCTIONS

In a particular jurisdiction the preliminary hearing may be utilized to serve other incidental functions besides discovery, preparation for trial cross-examination, and the perpetuation of testimony. Thus, in some jurisdictions, the preliminary hearing is viewed as an important opportunity for gaining reduction of bail or other terms of pretrial release. This is particularly true where bail is set at the initial appearance largely on the basis of a schedule tied to the offense charged, and the preliminary hearing provides the magistrate with his first extensive examination of the facts of the individual case.

The preliminary hearing also may serve as an integral part of the plea bargaining process, particularly where negotiations have been undertaken prior to the hearing. The hearing may then operate as a valuable "educational process" for the defendant who is not persuaded by his counsel's opinion that the prosecution has such a strong case that a negotiated plea is in the defendant's best interest. In other jurisdictions, the preliminary hearing may serve as an occasion for the initiation of plea bargaining. In some jurisdictions, the hearing may also provide the initial point at which the constitutional validity of the acquisition of certain prosecution evidence may be challenged, and may offer sufficient advantages over the motion to suppress that defense counsel will insist upon

i. Lower courts have generally held that unless the defense was limited by "unusual circumstances," the opportunity for cross-examination provided in the typical preliminary hearing will be sufficient to meet the standards of *Green.* See e.g., *People v. Haywood,* 376 N.E.2d 328 (Ill.App. 1978) (defense was not denied an adequate opportunity where the magistrate barred various defense questions as designed to obtain discovery, but the cross-examination still went beyond the scope of the direct examination); *People v. Wittebort,* 265 N.W.2d 404 (Mich.App.1978) (where defense counsel's failure to cross-examine the witness was explainable by the likelihood that cross-examination would have been "counter-productive," rather than by the alleged incompetency of counsel appointed just before the hearing started, the trial court did not abuse its discretion in admitting the preliminary hearing testimony).

a preliminary examination for this purpose even though he knows that the prosecution has sufficient additional evidence to meet the bindover standard. See Note 3 at p. 962 infra.

VI. WAIVER OF THE PRELIMINARY HEARING

Defense waiver. The potential values of the preliminary hearing to the defense might suggest that waiver of the hearing would be rare. In fact, waivers by the defense exceed fifty percent in a substantial number of jurisdictions which provide quite extensive preliminary hearings. See Katz, 46–47. What explains such a high rate of defense waivers? Commentators have pointed to a variety of factors that may influence the waiver rate in a particular jurisdiction. These factors include: (1) the availability of alternative screening and discovery devices; (2) the inadequacy of the payment schedule of appointed counsel for representation at a preliminary hearing; (3) a prosecution practice of offering significant concessions to defendants who waive their preliminary hearings; and (4) the "habit, tradition, and conventional wisdom" of the local bar. See Graham and Letwin, 923.

Practice manuals generally urge defense counsel not to waive a preliminary hearing unless the hearing presents a substantial danger to the defense that outweighs its value. Amsterdam, p. 934 supra, cites five circumstances in which such a danger may exist: (1) an essential prosecution witness is able to testify at the preliminary hearing but may well be unavailable at trial; (2) a complainant is likely to "mellow" with time if he is not required at this point to put his testimony "on the record"; (3) the preliminary hearing may add to adverse publicity that will make it difficult to obtain a fair trial;[j] (4) the preliminary hearing will call the prosecutor's attention to a curable defect in the prosecution's case that otherwise would not be noticed until trial, when it would be too late to correct it; and (5) the preliminary hearing will alert the prosecutor to the fact that the defendant is undercharged. Id. at § 137.

Prosecution waiver. In most jurisdictions, the prosecutor has a right to insist upon the preliminary hearing even though the defendant desires to waive the hearing. See, e.g., Cal.Pen.Code, § 860. The prosecutor's right is based on the premise that the state has an interest, independent of the defendant, in "determining whether or not there is sufficient probable cause." *People v. Wilcox,* 6 N.W.2d 518 (Mich. 1942). See also *Van Buren v. United States,* 36 F. 77, 82 (D.Ind.1888) ("an immediate development of the evidence and testimony is sometimes essential to the ends of justice, and it would be strange indeed if the laws are so framed * * * as to deny the government this important power"). In at least one jurisdiction, prosecutors usually will not accept a defense waiver. See Graham and Letwin, 647. More commonly, the prosecutor will only insist upon a hearing where (1) there appears to be a need to perpetuate testimony because a particular witness is likely to become unavailable, or (2) a particular witness is "shaky" and there would be some value in placing him under oath at this point.

SECTION 2. THE DEFENDANT'S RIGHT TO A PRELIMINARY HEARING

1. *Independent screening and the federal constitution. Hurtado v. California,* discussed at p. 975 infra, was the first in a series of cases considering the contention that the federal constitution requires a pretrial screening of the prosecution's proposed charge by a neutral agency to ensure that there is adequate evidentiary support for the charge. In *Hurtado,* the defendant argued that the Fourteenth Amendment due process clause required such screening

j. On the capacity of the magistrate to close the preliminary hearing, see pp. 1321–31 infra.

by a grand jury through the incorporation of the Fifth Amendment requirement that felony prosecutions be instituted only by grand jury indictment. For reasons discussed at p. 975 infra, the Court rejected defendant's contention. It held that the Fifth Amendment guarantee of prosecution by indictment was *not* a fundamental right applicable to the states through the due process requirements of the Fourteenth Amendment.

The California procedure challenged in *Hurtado* provided for charging by prosecutor's information, rather than by indictment, but it also required a magistrate's initial determination that probable cause existed, made at what was essentially a preliminary hearing. It therefore was not clear from *Hurtado* whether due process permitted a state to dispense with all forms of independent screening or just screening by a grand jury. Although there traditionally had been no screening procedure for misdemeanor offenses, felony prosecutions commonly had required either an indictment or a magistrate's preliminary hearing bindover. In *Lem Woon v. Oregon,* 229 U.S. 586, 33 S.Ct. 783, 57 L.Ed. 1340 (1913), the elimination of all screening procedures was squarely presented by an Oregon procedure permitting direct filing of an information without "any examination, or commitment by a magistrate * * * or any verification other than [the prosecutor's] official oath." A unanimous Court held that the Oregon procedure did not violate due process. Justice Pitney's opinion for the Court relied primarily upon the reasoning of *Hurtado.* It rejected as "untenable" an attempt to distinguish *Hurtado* on the ground that the California procedure upheld there required an initial finding of probable cause by the magistrate. The *Lem Woon* opinion noted: "[T]his court has * * * held [that] the 'due process of law' clause does not require the State to adopt the institution and procedure of a grand jury, [and] we are unable to see upon what theory it can be held that an examination or the opportunity for one, prior to the formal accusation by the district attorney, is obligatory upon the States."

In *Gerstein v. Pugh,* discussed at p. 306 supra, the Court also rejected the contention that a preliminary hearing was required by the Fourth Amendment. The Court there held that the Fourth Amendment "requires a judicial determination of probable cause as a prerequisite to extended restraint following arrest," but added that such determination may be made ex parte as where the judge issues an arrest warrant. Justice Stewart, in a concurring opinion, asked why the Constitution "extends less procedural protection" to an arrested person who might not gain his release prior to trial than to defendants in civil cases, held to be constitutionally entitled to a pretrial hearing to the plaintiff's temporary seizure of their property to secure any future judgment. (See fn. d at p. 307 supra). Justice Powell, speaking for the Court, responded (see n. 27 at p. 307 supra) that the "historical basis of the probable cause requirement is quite different from the relatively recent application of variable procedural due process in debtor-creditor disputes," and that the Fourth Amendment had always been thought "to define the 'process that is due' for seizure of person or property in criminal cases."

The *Gerstein* Court specifically reaffirmed *Lem Woon,* noting that

> In holding that the prosecutor's assessment of probable cause is not sufficient alone to justify restraint on liberty pending trial, we do not imply that the accused is entitled to judicial oversight or review of the decision to prosecute. Instead, we adhere to the Court's prior holding that a judicial hearing is not prerequisite to prosecution by information. * * * *Lem Woon v. Oregon.*

Neither Justice Powell nor Justice Stewart thought it necessary to explain why the concept of variable procedural due process that had been applied in the civil cases did not also protect the criminal defendant from the significant burdens imposed upon him apart from the seizure of his person (i.e., the burdens of accusation and litigation), and therefore require some form of independent screening apart from any Fourth Amendment concerns. Cf. LaFave and Israel, § 1.6 ("minimizing the risk of erroneous accusation" constitutes one of the basic goals of the criminal justice process). Did the absence of any due process right to independent screening to protect against an unfounded imposition of those burdens rest, by analogy to *Gerstein*'s Fourth Amendment reasoning, on the premise that the Fifth and Sixth Amendments prescribe all the process that is due the defendant—a process that *Gerstein* characterized as "an elaborate system, unique in jurisprudence, designed to safeguard the rights of those accused of crime"? Did the absence of a due process right to an independent screening follow from the historically accepted practice in misdemeanor cases, where American jurisdictions traditionally have provided no such screening (apart from the ex parte probable cause determination required by *Gerstein* where the defendant is arrested)? [a]

2. *The need for independent screening.* All American jurisdictions today provide for some form of independent screening of the prosecution's decision to charge in felony cases. Although a few jurisdictions provide for direct filing, they include some procedure for magistrate review in that process. See Note 7 infra. In the remaining jurisdictions, the felony defendant is entitled to screening by preliminary hearing or grand jury. Is there a need for some sort of independent screening? Emerson and Ames, at p. 4, summarize the reasoning of those who find independent screening largely unnecessary:

"Some observers claim that screening decisions made by individual prosecutors may be more effective in weeding out unfounded charges than either the preliminary hearing or the grand jury, since prosecutors generally apply a more stringent standard. Prosecutors often evaluate cases using a likelihood of conviction standard, whereas the magistrate and grand jury are generally charged with determining probable cause. Furthermore, these observers contend that prosecutors have little to gain from prosecuting weak cases and that the expense and negative public opinion associated with losing such cases are themselves sufficient barriers to prevent possible abuse. Those who hold this view often play down the role of the grand jury and preliminary hearing on other grounds as well. An oft-cited argument is that, since the trial is designed to safeguard the rights of the accused, there is little need for such safeguards at the preliminary hearing or grand jury stage. The fear is that expanding the nature and scope of these proceedings would turn them into mini-trials or allow the accused to be tried twice."

Proponents of independent screening procedures argue that such procedures are needed to guard against the prosecutor who overestimates the strength of his case. They also reject the contention that a prosecutor would not press charges on evidence that he or she knows would be insufficient to convict. Gilboy, at p. 6–7, cites several of the reasons advanced as to why a prosecutor would do exactly that: "[First], there might be public pressures to vigorously prosecute particular individuals of certain crimes. Or the prosecutor's office might have a strong interest in prosecuting individuals with a history of criminal activity. In some cases, despite the

a. Commenting upon the impracticability of requiring an adversary pretrial hearing to vindicate defendant's Fourth Amendment rights, the *Gerstein* Court noted: "Criminal justice is already overburdened, by the volume of cases and the complexities of our system. The processing of misdemeanors, in particular, and the early stages of prosecution generally are marked by delays that can seriously affect the quality of justice. A constitutional doctrine requiring adversary hearings for all persons detained pending trial could exacerbate the problem of pretrial delay."

unlikelihood of a conviction, continued prosecution might occur because prosecutors are more interested in the sanctions generated by the pretrial process itself, such as the defendant's loss of freedom, or 'public damage to the indictee's reputation,' than with any ultimate objective of obtaining a conviction. Finally, the possibility of subsequent conviction through plea bargaining might also encourage proceeding to the grand jury for indictment in cases with insufficient evidence to convict at trial.[23]"

3. *The preliminary hearing as a "critical stage."* While a state is not required constitutionally to grant defendant a preliminary hearing, COLEMAN v. ALABAMA, 399 U.S. 1, 90 S.Ct. 1999, 26 L.Ed.2d 387 (1970), holds that the Sixth Amendment right to counsel applies to such a hearing where granted under state law. In *Coleman,* a divided Court (7–2) held that the Sixth Amendment rights of an indigent defendant were violated by the state's failure to appoint counsel to assist him in a preliminary hearing provided under state law prior to indictment. Applying the "critical stage" standard (see p. 100 supra), the Court concluded that the presence of counsel at the preliminary hearing was "necessary to preserve the defendant's basic right to a fair trial as affected by his right meaningfully to cross-examine the witnesses against him and to have effective assistance of counsel at the trial itself." The Court rejected the contention that the lack of counsel would have no bearing on the defendant's trial since state law prohibited the prosecution from using at trial "anything that occurred" at a hearing involving an unrepresented defendant.[b] It stressed that counsel could take various steps at the preliminary hearing "to protect the indigent accused against an erroneous or improper prosecution":

"Plainly the guiding hand of counsel at the preliminary hearing is essential to protect the indigent accused against an erroneous or improper prosecution. First, the lawyer's skilled examination and cross-examination of witnesses may expose fatal weaknesses in the State's case that may lead the magistrate to refuse to bind the accused over. Second, in any event, the skilled interrogation of witnesses by an experienced lawyer can fashion a vital impeachment tool for use in cross-examination of the State's witnesses at the trial, or preserve testimony favorable to the accused of a witness who does not appear at the trial. Third, trained counsel can more effectively discover the case the State has against his client and make possible the preparation of a proper defense to meet that case at the trial. Fourth, counsel can also be influential at the preliminary hearing in making effective arguments for the accused on such matters as the necessity for an early psychiatric examination or bail. The inability of the indigent accused on his own to realize these advantages of a lawyer's assistance compels the conclusion that the Alabama preliminary hearing is a 'critical stage' of the State's criminal process at

23. This is not implausible given various descriptions of prosecutors' plea bargaining practices. One national study has suggested that prosecutors at early stages of the process may fail to terminate prosecution where it is questionable whether the state could actually prove its case. Some prosecutors see nothing improper in convicting [via a guilty plea] a person they believe is factually guilty even though the state may be unable with its evidence to secure a conviction; others view the legal guilt requirements as not applying to pleas of guilty—presumably a defendant willing to plead guilty agrees in effect to forego the trial's formal requirements of proof; still others argue that even the weakest case may result in a jury conviction. * * * Generally speaking, given prosecutors' keen interest in a conviction, they not only may offer concessions to procure a guilty plea from a defendant not otherwise likely to be convicted, but may make a weak case the object of *intensified* plea bargaining.

b. The dissenting opinions of Chief Justice Burger and Justice Stewart argued that this provision successfully negated any impact on the trial process that would require appointment of counsel at the preliminary hearing. Justice Stewart also stressed that there had been no showing by the defendants of "any affirmative advantage they would have enjoyed at the trial if they had a lawyer at their preliminary hearing."

which the accused is 'as much entitled to such aid [of counsel] * * * as at the trial itself.' *Powell v. Alabama.*"

4. *Preliminary hearings in the federal system.* The basic federal statutory provision on the defendant's right to a preliminary hearing is contained in the Federal Magistrate's Act, 18 U.S.C. § 3060. See also Fed.R.Crim.P. 5(c) (largely duplicating that provision). Section 3060 and Rule 5(c) initially state that "a defendant is entitled to a preliminary examination, unless waived, when charged with any offense, other than a petty offense, which is to be tried by a judge of the district court." Both provisions then set the time periods for the hearing ("within a reasonable time but in any event not later than 10 days following the initial appearance if the defendant is in custody" and 20 days if not in custody). Finally, they both include a critical proviso, set forth in Rule 5(c) as follows:

> provided, however, that the preliminary hearing shall not be held if the defendant is indicted * * * before the date set for the preliminary examination.

The above proviso restates the position that federal courts had reached under earlier versions of the Federal Rule that made no reference to the impact of intervening indictments. In a long line of decisions, the federal courts had held that the issuance of an indictment rendered "moot" the defendant's statutory right to a preliminary hearing. As stated in *Sciortino v. Zampano,* 385 F.2d 132 (2d Cir.1967): "The return of an indictment, which establishes probable cause, eliminates the need for a preliminary examination. * * * A post-indictment preliminary examination would be an empty ritual, as the government's burden of showing probable cause would be met merely by offering the indictment. Even if the [magistrate] disagreed with the grand jury, he could not undermine the authority of its finding."

In many federal districts, the impact of the proviso has been to eliminate virtually all preliminary hearings. Where a grand jury sits daily and can promptly dispose of submitted cases, the U.S. Attorney may regularly moot scheduled preliminary hearings by obtaining prior indictments. Various U.S. Attorneys have been able to perfect this practice to the point where there are no more than one or two preliminary hearings for every hundred felonies processed. In other districts, it is more difficult to obtain indictments within the time limits prescribed in Rule 5(c) and preliminary hearings are mooted only in a small portion of all cases.

5. If a federal preliminary hearing is held and the U.S. Attorney decides that it is "going badly," may he terminate the hearing by obtaining an indictment? Consider UNITED STATES v. QUINN, 357 F.Supp. 1348 (N.D.Ga.1973). In *Quinn,* an F.B.I. agent testifying at the preliminary hearing referred to his "field notes." When defense counsel asked to inspect the notes, the magistrate granted a continuance of several days, apparently to permit the agent to delete any irrelevant material prior to the inspection. Before the proceeding was recommenced, a federal grand jury issued an indictment. When the preliminary hearing was then cancelled, defense moved to quash the indictment and reopen the hearing. In rejecting that motion the District Court, per EDENFIELD, J., noted:

"[D]efendant cites 18 U.S.C. § 3060(e), which in relevant part states: 'No preliminary examination * * * shall be required to be accorded an arrested person . . . if at any time subsequent to the initial appearance of such persons before a judge or magistrate and *prior to the date fixed for the preliminary examination pursuant to subsections (b) and (c) an indictment is returned.* . . . ' (Emphasis added). Defendant argues that since the indictment was returned after the preliminary hearing had begun, by the terms of the statute, and under the substantially similar language of [Federal] Rule 5(c), defendant was entitled to have the preliminary examination proceed. In addition, defendant cites three cases from the District of Columbia Circuit which hold generally that the denial of a timely requested preliminary examination, or defects in a preliminary examination, are not excused by an intervening grand jury indictment. [See *Blue v. United States,* 342 F.2d 894 (D.C.Cir.1964); *Ross v. Sirica* (p. 972 infra); *United States v. Pollard,* 335 F.Supp. 868 (D.D.C.1971)]. Particularly noted is *United States v. Pollard,* where as a condition to the government's conduct of a lineup, the examining magistrate required the government to provide defense counsel with any prior descriptions given to the police or to the government by each witness who would be present at the lineup. Not wishing to comply with a ruling which it considered an undesirable precedent, the government immediately entered a *nolle prosequi* and obtained a grand jury indictment of defendant some two months later. The court found in the face of allegations that the government deliberately misled defense counsel into believing that the case was not being presented to the grand jury, that an 'already scheduled preliminary hearing should not be barred where, as here, the indictment does not intervene in the normal course of events, but rather is the result of unilateral action of the Government, solely for its own benefit, and accompanied by indicia of vexatiousness.'

"Without passing on whether the government's conduct in the present case was 'vexatious,' the court is in sympathy with the notion that the government ought not to be allowed to freely abandon its prosecution in a preliminary examination the moment that an unfavorable ruling is made or an adverse result seems imminent. Such a practice does nothing to encourage respect for law, creating as it does a feeling that the search for probable cause in a preliminary examination amounts to no more than a game in which the government can never lose, regardless of what the evidence reveals. Nevertheless, while this court may object to how the game is played, in the present case no substantive rights of the defendant have been lost, and consistent with the strong weight of authority, contrary to the cited cases in the District of Columbia Circuit, defendant's motions must be denied.

"In *United States v. Coley,* 441 F.2d 1299 (5th Cir.1971) defendant Coley [raised a similar objection which was denied by the Court of Appeals for this Circuit]. * * * [A]t Coley's preliminary examination, prior to indictment, a government witness refused to answer questions propounded by defendant's counsel. 'Though advised by the United States Commissioner that he must reply or risk dismissal of the case, the witness continued to refuse. The commissioner then dismissed the charges against Coley. Subsequently, however, a grand jury indicted Coley for the same offense.' * * * Coley maintained that 'he had a substantial right to cross-examine witnesses at the preliminary hearing and that the commissioner's failure to enforce this right denied him due process.' The Court of Appeals, in affirming the district [court's denial of a motion to quash the indictment], replied to this argument that 'the primary function of a preliminary hearing is not to expedite discovery. The purpose of such a hearing is to ascertain whether or not there is probable cause to warrant detention of the accused pending a grand jury hearing.' There is no constitutional right to a preliminary hearing, and '[i]n the instant case, the distinction between an aborted preliminary hearing and no hearing is one without a difference.' In *Coley* the court had before it the relevant provisions of 18 U.S.C. § 3060(e). * * * From this decision it seems clear that the magistrate in the present case had no power to compel the FBI agent to disclose his notes to defendant's counsel, as long as the government was willing to accept a dismissal of the charges against defendant. * * * Therefore, under the court's decision in *Coley,* which controls the case at bar, both defendant's motions to quash the indictment and to reopen the preliminary examination must be denied."

Compare with *Quinn, Coleman v. Burnett,* described in Note 3 at p. 971 infra. In light of *Coleman,* would the District of Columbia Circuit adhere to the position taken in *Pollard* and order some post-indictment relief, if not the dismissal of the indictment?

6. *Indictment states.* Approximately one-third of the states have provisions similar to the Fifth Amendment requiring prosecutions by indictment for all felonies (see p. 975 infra). All of these "indictment states" also have statutes or court rules granting the defendant a right to a preliminary hearing within a specified period after his arrest. However, all but a few indictment states further provide that the hearing shall not be held if the prosecutor obtains an indictment prior to the scheduled date of the hearing.

While prosecutors in indictment states thus have the legal authority to "moot" almost all preliminary hearings, that practice is not nearly as prevalent in those states as it is in the federal courts. In many judicial districts in indictment states, regularly mooting preliminary hearings would not be feasible since the grand jury's caseload is too heavy to permit prompt consideration of charges prior to the scheduled preliminary hearing. In other districts, although grand jury review could be obtained shortly after an arrest, preliminary hearings generally are not mooted because they are viewed as performing various functions that would not be served by even the most prompt grand jury review.[c] In very few districts, however, will preliminary hearings be uniformly provided to all felony defendants. Even though a district may not moot as a regular practice, there usually will be a special class of cases in which, for reasons cited in Note 8 infra, the prosecutor prefers to go directly to the grand jury, thereby bypassing the preliminary hearing.

7. *Information states.* Approximately two-thirds of the states permit felony prosecutions to be brought by either information or indictment. Because of their heavy use of the information alternative, these states are commonly described as "information states." A few information states permit the direct filing of an information without a preliminary hearing. Those jurisdictions add special requirements to the filing process to ensure that the information is supported by probable cause. Thus, one state requires that the direct filing be accepted by the magistrate, who reviews affidavits accompanying the information to determine that probable cause exists. See Mont.Rev.Code § 95–1301. In another, the defendant, after obtaining complete discovery of the prosecution's evidence, may move for dismissal on the ground that there is insufficient evidence to proceed. See *State v. Florence,* 239 N.W.2d 892 (Minn.1976).[d]

c. While the use of both the preliminary hearing and grand jury has been criticized as "wasteful," prosecutors in indictment jurisdictions may find that the benefits of the preliminary hearing offset the costs of that procedure, even though the grand jury will also be reviewing the case. They may, for example, conclude that the hearing more than "pays for itself" by providing better trial preparation or promoting defense pleas of guilty. In a jurisdiction in which the grand jury can rely upon hearsay evidence, the additional time consumed in presenting a case to the grand jury may be insubstantial, as the prosecutor will present there largely a summary of the preliminary hearing testimony. It is also probable that some districts continue regularly to utilize the preliminary hearing as a result of a practice developed when the grand jury was not readily available. Cf. Emerson and Ames, 142 (concluding that, in the jurisdiction studied, "local norms and historical practices * * * have a more important relationship to, and effect on, the relative advantages of the grand jury and the preliminary hearing than do formal laws and rules").

d. This type of procedure is supported in the Uniform Rules of Criminal Procedure. See also Anderson, *The Preliminary Hearing—Better Alternatives or More of the Same?,* 35 Mo.L.Rev. 281 (1970). Proponents of such an alternative procedure argue that it would: (1) avoid the confusion that flows from the use of the preliminary hearing to perform sometimes inconsistent functions;

In the remaining information states, an information can be filed only if there has been either a preliminary hearing bindover by the magistrate or the waiver of the hearing. In a few of these states, the prosecutor may not seek to bypass the preliminary hearing by taking the case directly to the grand jury and obtaining an indictment. In these states, the issuance of the indictment is followed by a preliminary hearing at which the magistrate makes an independent determination of probable cause. See e.g., *People v. Duncan,* 201 N.W.2d 629 (Mich.1972). In all of the other information states without direct filing, the preliminary hearing can be mooted by using the indictment process. In general, prosecutors in these information states make infrequent use of the grand jury alternative. In some districts, the preliminary hearing is never mooted and in others the percentage of cases taken to the grand jury rarely exceeds 5%. There are some districts in certain information states, however, where the prosecutor will prefer the indictment to the information and preliminary hearings will not be available in the vast majority of felony prosecutions.

8. *Prosecutorial choice.* In a district in which grand jury review is available without delay and felony cases commonly are taken directly to the grand jury, bypassing the preliminary hearing, what factors would lead a prosecutor not to moot the preliminary hearing in a particular case? Available studies (see fn. a, p. 932 supra) indicate that prosecutors look to a variety of factors in making that decision. Those include: (1) the need to perpetuate testimony for possible use at trial; (2) putting the witness to the test of testifying in public where there is some doubt as to whether the witness is willing to testify; (3) promoting the victim's interest in pursuing the matter by presenting it in a public forum; (4) gaining the defense perspective as to the events involved (e.g., through defense cross-examination) where there is some uncertainty as to what actually happened; (5) gaining a further identification of the suspect by having the witness make that identification at the hearing; (6) promoting public confidence in a sensitive prosecutorial decision by having the evidence presented in a public forum and the decision to proceed ratified by a magistrate (or, if the case is likely to be dismissed, by showing that the dismissal stemmed from deficiencies in the testimony of witnesses rather than any favoritism on the part of the prosecutor). In some districts, prosecutors will look to these factors on a case-by-case basis. In others the prosecutor will classify certain types of cases as especially appropriate for preliminary hearing review. Thus, the prosecutor may follow a regular practice of not bypassing the preliminary hearing in all cases alleging police brutality (looking to the 6th factor noted above), all assault cases involving acquaintances (looking to the 3rd and 4th factors), or all cases involving transient witnesses (looking to the 1st factor).

In a district in which the common practice is to have a preliminary hearing followed by the filing of an information (in an information state) or an indictment (in an indictment state), what factors might lead a prosecutor to bypass the preliminary hearing by promptly obtaining an indictment? Critics of the bypass procedure, arguing that the grand jury is by far the "easier" screening procedure, suggest that a prosecutor is likely to bypass the preliminary hearing where the prosecution evidence is weak, but available studies do not support that contention. See e.g., Gilboy, 8–9, 31–34; Emerson and Ames, 67–72, 108–113, 146–149. Those studies suggest that bypassing, where that is not the usual practice, can generally be attributed to one of the following special prosecutorial interests: (1) the need for the grand

(2) permit the different functions to be performed at times more appropriate for each, rather than at the single time required for the preliminary hearing; and (3) avoid the needless expenditure of the magistrate's time on functions (e.g., discovery) in which a court need not be involved.

jury's investigative authority (in which case, grand jury screening is an incidental attribute of the grand jury process); (2) the "buffer" provided by sharing with community participants the responsibility for proceeding or not proceeding in a controversial case; (3) where the prosecutor is uncertain as to the appropriate disposition in a particular sensitive situation, the desire to obtain a sense of community viewpoint; (4) the desire to gain a lay person's reaction to the credibility of a particular witness; (5) the desire to save time where the preliminary hearing would be protracted due to the number of exhibits or witnesses or the number of separate hearings that would have to be held for separate defendants; (6) the desire to speed up the process where the defendant requested one or more continuances at the preliminary hearing; (7) the desire to preclude the defense discovery inherent in a preliminary hearing, particularly where a key witness is an informer whose identity should be shielded until trial; (8) where the magistrate is likely to allow extensive cross-examination, the desire to avoid "generating a lot of paper" (i.e., the transcript of preliminary hearing testimony) that can be used to impeach a witness at trial; (9) the desire to limit the number of times that a particular complainant (e.g., a victim of a sex offense) will be required to give testimony in public; and (10) the desire to avoid a confrontation with a particularly contentious defense attorney. Here again, some prosecutors look to such factors on a case-by-case basis, while others regularly bypass the preliminary hearing in certain classes of cases (e.g., all sex offenses).

9. *Equal protection.* Is an equal protection problem presented by the prosecutor's decision to bypass the preliminary hearing in some cases but not in others? In HAWKINS v. SUPERIOR COURT, 586 P.2d 916 (1978), the California Supreme Court held that the bypass procedure violated the California constitution's equal protection clause and held that a defendant whose case was taken directly to the grand jury was therefore entitled to a post-indictment preliminary hearing. The majority opinion, per MOSK, J., initially noted the "considerable disparity" in the rights afforded a defendant charged by indictment rather than by information: "The defendant accused by information 'immediately becomes entitled to an impressive array of procedural rights, including a preliminary hearing before a neutral and legally knowledgeable magistrate, representation by retained or appointed counsel, the confrontation and cross-examination of hostile witnesses, and the opportunity to personally appear and affirmatively present exculpatory evidence'; in vivid contrast, the indictment procedure omits all the above safeguards * * *." These differences, the majority continued, could not be discounted on the ground that the preliminary hearing and grand jury review simply constitute alternative procedures for determining whether probable cause exists. The value of the preliminary hearing, the majority noted, extends beyond probable cause screening. As the United States Supreme Court noted in *Coleman v. Alabama* [p. 943 supra], the preliminary hearing also gives the defense other advantages, such as pretrial discovery. Moreover, there was a substantial difference in the quality of the probable cause screening in the two proceedings. While the grand jury supposedly stands "as a buffer between the state and the individual," the "fiction of grand jury independence" was demonstrated by studies showing that grand juries "virtually always assent to the recommendation of the prosecuting attorney." (See also Note 2, p. 980 infra).

Having concluded that there was a substantial difference between information charging and indictment charging, the *Hawkins* majority then turned to the significance of that difference under equal protection doctrine: "Under the traditional two-tier test of equal protection, a discriminatory legislative classification that impairs fundamental rights will be subjected to strict scrutiny by the courts, and the state will be required to bear the heavy burden of proving not only that it has a compelling interest which justifies the classification but also that the discrimination is necessary to promote that interest. For the reasons stated [above], the denial of a postindictment preliminary hearing deprives the defendant of 'such fundamental rights as counsel, confrontation, the right to personally appear, the right to a hearing before a judicial officer, and the right to be free from unwarranted prosecution. These guarantees are expressly or impliedly grounded in both the state and federal Constitutions and must by any test be deemed "fundamental."' The Attorney General fails to discharge his burden of proof under this test. His sole attempt to do so is to list in his brief a few tactical advantages gained by the prosecutor who chooses to use the indictment procedure.[6] But none of these reasons amounts to a constitutionally 'compelling' state interest that justifies depriving an indicted defendant of the above-discussed fundamental rights guaranteed to him in a preliminary hearing. Nor, indeed, does the Attorney General make any effort to show that this discrimination is constitutionally 'necessary' to preserve any such advantages. We conclude that the denial of a post-indictment preliminary hearing deprived defendants herein of equal protection of the laws guaranteed by article I, section 7, of the California Constitution."

Richardson, J., dissenting in *Hawkins,* acknowledged that there were "necessarily inherent" differences between prosecution by indictment and prosecution by information following a preliminary hearing bindover, but he concluded that those differences simply "do not rise to the level of unconstitutional deprivations of equal protection." In this connection, the dissent also noted that: (1) though the preliminary examination might provide the defense with added discovery, there were ample other avenues for discovery available to all defendants under California law; and (2) the court could not assume, contrary to its own prior statements and the state constitution's authorization of prosecution by indictment, that the grand jury lacked the independence to make a fair determination of probable cause.

10. In *State v. Clark,* 630 P.2d 810 (Or.1981), the Oregon Supreme Court "agreed with * * * *Hawkins* that preliminary hearing * * * offers important advantages over prosecution upon an indictment without a preliminary hearing," but refused "to follow the *Hawkins* court to the conclusion that this difference * * * necessarily represents a denial of equal protection of the laws, regardless of showing which defendants receive one or the other procedure."[e] Bypassing a preliminary hearing would violate Oregon's constitutional equivalent of the equal protection clause (requiring that "privileges and immunities * * * equally belong to all citizens") only if that action resulted in

6. The Attorney General notes: "A prosecutor may proceed by indictment for valid reasons: the prospective defendant cannot be found; witnesses may fear testifying in court; the case may have potential for prejudicial pretrial publicity; publicity may jeopardize a continuing investigation; a preliminary examination may involve prolonged delay because of the number of defendants or the complexity of the case."

e. The Court reasoned (per Linde, J.): "*Hawkins* reached this conclusion in 'classification' terms, by defining as two classes those who are indicted and those who are charged by information. But we think this is an example of the 'circular' use of the concept of 'class' * * *. The distinction to be tested is the use or nonuse of preliminary hearings. The 'classes' said to fail the test of equal protection are the 'class' of those defendants who receive preliminary hearings (because charged by information) and the 'class' of those who do not (because indicted). But these defendants do not exist as categories or as classes with distinguishing characteristics before and apart from a prosecutor's decision how to charge one, or some, or all defendants. Aside from the manner in which the decision is made, defendants charged under either procedure are 'classes' only as an effect of the dual procedural scheme itself. * * * Each of the two procedures, however, is expressly authorized by the constitution itself. Properly administered, each satisfies the fourteenth amendment."

an "unjustified differentiation among classes of citizens." In *State v. Freeland,* 667 P.2d 509 (Or.1983), the Oregon Court explained what would constitute such an "unjustified differentiation." It noted that "a constitutional claim for equal treatment is made out when the accused shows that preliminary hearings are offered or denied to individual defendants, or to social, geographic, or other classes of defendants * * * purely haphazardly or otherwise on terms that have no satisfactory explanation." In light of this standard, a coherent and systematic policy bypassing preliminary hearings in all cases of a certain type (e.g., all homicide cases) would be acceptable, but the choice of indictment over preliminary hearing cannot be based on "such day-by-day logistical circumstances as the readiness of the prosecutor or the coincidence of an empty courtroom or a crowded hearing calendar." Dissenting in *Freeland,* Jones, J., acknowledged that the standards announced by the majority served a "desirable goal," [f] but argued that imposing those standards as a constitutional mandate was without support in past precedent, including cases that had applied the equal protection clause to a variety of other exercises of prosecutorial discretion (e.g., the decision to charge).

11. As noted in the *Freeland* dissent, the *Hawkins* ruling has been rejected by all of the state and federal courts that have considered the issue since *Hawkins* (prior to *Hawkins,* equal protection arguments had been rejected also by several other courts). Although those cases do not specifically consider the narrower limitation imposed in *Clark* and *Freeland,* the reasoning of most of those opinions suggest that they would reject the Oregon Court's analysis as well. In large part, they have argued that the differences between preliminary hearing and grand jury screening are not significant for constitutional purposes. See e.g., *Whittington v. State,* 680 S.W.2d 505 (Tex.App.1984) ("Loss of the right to an examining trial does not offend any state or federal constitutional provision since the return of the true bill of indictment serves the identical purpose that an examining trial serves * * *. No 'due process' or 'equal protection' rights are involved").

SECTION 3. THE BINDOVER DETERMINATION

RIDEOUT v. SUPERIOR COURT

432 P.2d 197 (Cal.1967).

BURKE, JUSTICE. * * *

Following a preliminary hearing on the charge [unlawful transportation of marijuana], the committing magistrate held petitioners to answer. The information was filed, and a motion to set it aside on the ground they were committed without probable cause (Pen.Code, § 995) was denied. Petitioners thereafter filed the instant petition for prohibition based on the same ground (Pen.Code, § 999a).

The sole witness for the People at the preliminary hearing was Police Officer Bernard Hazen, who testified to the following effect:

About 1 p.m. on January 5, 1967, Officer Hazen observed a car being driven with a defective license plate light. He flashed his red light to direct the car to stop and pulled over behind it. The driver emerged without being asked to do so,

f. The dissent noted in this regard: "I believe the goal of the majority opinion is desirable. * * * Defendants charged by information and scheduled for preliminary hearings will not be indicted at the last moment leaving prosecution and defense witnesses in uncertainty as to when and where they are to testify. It will relieve the confusion of defendants being told their case has been dismissed at a preliminary hearing, only to be arrested and often jailed because of an indictment handed down days later. It will help defense counsel in scheduling appearances and relieve counsel of the need to prepare for a hearing that never occurs. However, all of this can be corrected by needed and proper legislation or constitutional amendment. I dissent because it is not the role of this court to take two perfectly valid and constitutional methods of charging approved by a mandate of the people and warp legal reasoning to obtain a desired result."

met the officer in front of the police car, and identified himself as George Oliver.

The officer walked over to the car Oliver had been driving to check its registration and to obtain identification from the passengers. One Lopez was sitting on the front seat, and *petitioners* were on the *back seat.* The officer ascertained that the car was registered to Oliver's father. While checking the registration, the officer noticed several speakers and stereo tapes inside the car. Since he had information that such items had been stolen, he asked permission to search the car and Oliver replied, "Go right ahead." [2]

On the floor in front of the back seat the officer observed a matchbook folded in "a circular formation." He recognized it as a "crutch," a device "used to hold the used end of marijuana cigarettes." There were no burn marks on the "crutch," but the officer presumed it had been used because matchbooks ordinarily are not folded in that manner. The officer looked into the "well" of the car behind the back seat where a convertible top folds down and saw "in plain view" a Tareyton cigarette package, which appeared to contain marijuana. (It was stipulated that the substance was marijuana.) The officer asked Oliver whom the package belonged to, and Oliver "did not state." No marijuana odor was detected in the car.

Evidence that will justify a prosecution need not be sufficient to support a conviction. "Probable cause is shown if a man of ordinary caution or prudence would be led to believe and conscientiously entertain a strong suspicion of the guilt of the accused." * * * An information will not be set aside or a prosecution thereon prohibited if there is some rational ground for assuming the possibility that an offense has been committed and the accused is guilty of it. A reviewing court may not substitute its judgment as to the weight of the evidence for that of the magistrate, and, if there is some evidence to support the information, the court will not inquire into its sufficiency. Every legitimate inference that may be drawn from the evidence must be drawn in favor of the information.

A defendant who has joint or exclusive possession of narcotics in a moving vehicle may be found guilty of unlawful transportation of narcotics. Knowledge by the defendant of both the presence of the drug and its narcotic character is essential to establish unlawful transportation, sale, or possession of narcotics. * * * [But] such knowledge may be shown by circumstantial evidence. * * * [F]rom the recited evidence the magistrate could reasonably have inferred that petitioners had possession of the marijuana and knowledge of its presence since they were the ones in closest proximity to the place where it was found, the place apparently was accessible to them, and they had an opportunity to deposit the marijuana there when the police directed the car in which they were riding to pull over. Likewise an inference of their knowledge of the narcotic character of the marijuana is warranted by the evidence of the presence of the "crutch" on the floor in front of the back seat where petitioners were sitting and the secretion of the marijuana in an ordinary package of cigarettes.

Petitioners rely upon *People v. Redrick,* 359 P.2d 255 (Cal.1961), and *People v. Jackson,* 18 Cal.Rptr. 214 (App.1961), neither of which involved the question of probable cause. The cited cases, which affirmed judgments of conviction of possession of narcotics, state that "proof of opportunity of access to a place where narcotics are found, without more, will not support a finding of unlawful possession." In the present case, however, the question is not whether the evidence will support a finding but whether there is probable cause, and here petitioners not only had an

2. Oliver denied having given permission to search. The credibility of witnesses at the preliminary hearing is, of course, a question of fact within the province of the committing magistrate to determine.

opportunity of access to the place where the marijuana was found, but they were the ones in closest proximity to that place and the "crutch" was at their feet. * * * The * * * peremptory writ is denied.

TRAYNOR, C.J., and MCCOMB and MOSK, JJ., concur.

PETERS, JUSTICE (dissenting). * * *

The writ of prohibition should issue if at the preliminary no evidence is introduced sufficient to establish probable cause that the accused committed the charged crime. That means that there must be some evidence upon which men of ordinary caution and prudence might believe the accused to be guilty. * * * In essence, the test is was there " 'some evidence' which, if unexplained would warrant a conviction by a trial jury." *Dong Haw v. Superior Court,* 183 P.2d 724 (Cal.App.1947). This means that there must be some evidence in regard to each element of the crime, and in narcotic cases this refers primarily to the element of scienter. * * * The crime charged in the instant case * * * has two scienter elements: the accused must know he possessed the drug and know it was narcotic in nature. There is no evidence of either element in this case. * * *

It has been held that knowledge of possession may be inferred when the narcotic is found in the accused's shirt pocket or hidden in the mattress of his bed. Knowledge of the narcotic nature of a substance possessed can, of course, also be implied, as where police observe a suspect suspiciously throwing away a cigarette and the man denies he had a "joint" (a term only one experienced with marijuana would be expected to use). The owner of a car or a tenant of a room may be reasonably supposed to know what is in his car, or room, or on his person. Thus, it may be implied that such a person had control or possession of substances found in his car, room or on his person. Thus, in the instant case, there may be enough evidence to hold the driver of the car, Oliver, for trial, since he had dominion and control of the car where the marijuana was found.

But Oliver is not before us. Only the two passengers sitting in the back seat of the car are involved. As to them there is a complete lack of evidence from which knowledge that there was marijuana in the car could be implied. The majority seek to imply such knowledge from the fact that had they looked at the floorboard near their feet they would have seen a rolled up matchbook of a type sometimes used, according to the evidence, as a marijuana "crutch." This "crutch" was not burned nor did it contain any marijuana. Nor was there any smell of marijuana in the car. Nor was there any evidence petitioners knew it was there. It is doubtful if an average man would recognize such a matchbook as a marijuana "crutch," and there is no reason offered why petitioners should be charged with such knowledge. But even if they recognize the matchbook as a marijuana "crutch" it does not follow that they knew marijuana was in the car. We are told by the majority that petitioners were in close proximity to the marijuana. But of what significance is proximity if there is no evidence of knowledge? Moreover, if petitioners had turned around on the back seat of the car and looked into the "well" into which the convertible top folded, there in plain sight they would have seen what appeared to be an ordinary package of Tareyton cigarettes. There was absolutely nothing to indicate that the package contained marijuana, and there were no suspicious circumstances.

The majority, in refusing prohibition, rely upon mere surmise and conjecture. There is no rational or reasonable basis for any such suspicion. This is one of those extreme cases in which prohibition should issue. As we were told * * * in *Greenberg v. Superior Court,* 121 P.2d 713 (Cal. 1946), we are obliged to uphold "the right of a person to be free from prosecution for crime unless there is some rational ground for assuming the possibility that he is guilty." Otherwise, as the same case points out, an unjustly accused defendant suffers unreasonable expense, delay, inconvenience and the shame of a trial. Unless prohibition issues in the instant case the important rights recognized in *Greenberg* will have been nullified.

TOBRINER and SULLIVAN, JJ., concur.

Notes and Questions

1. *The applicable standard.* To what extent does the disagreement between the majority and dissenting opinions in *Rideout* rest upon differences in the "probable cause" standard each applies? The majority opinion defines "probable cause" in much the same terms used by the courts in describing the Fourth Amendment test for an arrest. See Ch. 5, § 3, especially pp. 285–88. The dissent speaks of probable cause, but states that that standard refers, "in essence," to what is commonly described as a "prima facie case" or "directed acquittal" standard (whether there is " 'some evidence' which, if unexplained, would warrant a conviction by a trial jury"). Are the two standards substantially different in their requirements? Most commentators assume that they are and that the prima facie case standard is much more stringent. See LaFave and Israel, § 14.3(a).

2. The "prima facie case" standard is most commonly cited as the standard applicable to grand jury proceedings. See Note 10, p. 984 infra. The *Dong Haw* case, from which the *Rideout* dissent quotes the standard, involved the review of the sufficiency of the evidence before a grand jury. The California statutory provision on grand jury indictments also refers to the prima facie case standard. See Cal. Pen. Code § 939.8 (grand jury shall indict when the evidence before it, "if unexplained or contradicted, would, in its judgment, warrant a conviction by a trial jury"). In contrast, the California provision on preliminary hearing bindovers refers to a finding of "sufficient cause" [interpreted as "probable cause"] to believe the defendant committed the crime charged. See Cal.Pen. Code § 872. Various other jurisdictions also have grand jury provisions that refer to the prima facie case standard and preliminary hearing provisions that refer to the probable cause standard. See, e.g., Alaska R.Crim.P. 5.1(g), 6(q). May this distinction in the phrasing of the two standards be explained as merely reflecting different ways of expressing the same degree of probability, adjusted to the non-adversarial procedures of the grand jury (where only the prosecution presents evidence) and the adversarial procedures of the preliminary hearing? See 61 Cal.Op. Atty.Gen. 441, 457 (1978) (reaching that conclusion, in light of legislative history, and describing both standards as requiring "evidence which leads an ordinary person to entertain a strong suspicion of the guilt of the accused"). Assuming (as most commentators do) that the different phrasing establish different degrees of probability, why would the state direct a grand jury to apply a more stringent standard than the magistrate?

3. Appellate decisions frequently are unclear as to what standard of probable cause applies at a preliminary hearing. Quite often, the opinions merely note that the magistrate need not be convinced of guilt beyond a reasonable doubt. Where courts have made an effort to define probable cause, most have equated it to the probable cause standard applied under the Fourth Amendment. See, e.g., *People v. Stout,* 424 P.2d 704 (Cal.1967) (applying "approximately the same" standard as that for issuance of an arrest warrant).[a] Others

a. When describing the traditional bindover standard as "similar" to the probable cause standard for arrest warrants, courts often add that the proof required to establish probable cause for an arrest warrant and to support a bindover will be somewhat different. See *Goldsmith v. United States,* 277 F.2d 335 (D.C.Cir. 1960). The preliminary hearing, because of its adversary nature necessarily lends a different shading to the probable cause standard than a have suggested that it requires a somewhat higher standard without precisely defining that standard. See, e.g., *State v. Berby*, 260 N.W.2d 798 (Wis.1978) ("probable cause" required for a bindover is "greater than that required for * * * an arrest warrant, but guilt beyond a reasonable doubt need not be proven"). A few have found the closest analogy to be the directed acquittal standard. See, e.g., *Myers v. Commonwealth*, 298 N.E.2d 819, 823 (Mass.1973) ("probable cause to bindover is somewhat analogous in function to the trial court's ruling on a motion for directed verdict as to whether there is sufficient evidence to send the case to the jury" and should not be "equated * * * with probable cause for arrest or search").

4. Several commentators have argued that the prima facie case standard is the more appropriate bindover standard, and that standard is recommended in the A.L.I.'s *Model Pre-Arraignment Code* (1975). Is the prima facie case standard consistent with appropriate timing requirements for a preliminary hearing? Compare the following views:

(a) Staff Comments, *Proposed New York Criminal Procedure Law* § 90.60 (1969): "Comparing New York's (former 'prima facie case') standard with those of many other jurisdictions, it will be found that New York requires much more in the way of proof to hold a person for a grand jury than do the laws of many other states and the federal law. This does not, in practice, really benefit a defendant, but rather leads to confusion and corner-cutting. Very often there may be sufficient evidence for the issuance of a warrant of arrest or for an arrest without a warrant, but not enough evidence for a prima facie case. This may cause an arrested person to be held for a considerable time while the case is being investigated so that a complaint which spells out a prima facie case can be prepared. * * * The felony hearing is, basically, a first screening of the charge; its function is neither to accuse nor to try the defendant. These steps will come later. Meanwhile, the defendant's main interest is in obtaining his release from custody. A most important function of the felony hearing, after the decision has been made to hold the defendant for the grand jury, is to determine whether he should be released and if so, under what conditions. * * * One objective of the procedure proposed here is to promote promptness of the hearing as a matter of practice as well as requiring such promptness as a matter of law. This, it is anticipated, will be accomplished by the provision * * * that there shall be a holding for a grand jury '[I]f there is reasonable cause to believe that the defendant committed a felony.' * * * In effect, if the evidence was sufficient for the issuance of a warrant of arrest or for an arrest without a warrant—all other things being equal—it should be sufficient to hold a person for the action of the grand jury."

(b) Graham and Letwin, 691–692: [I]f the evidence is such that a jury would not be *permitted* to convict, then it is difficult to justify not disposing of the case at the preliminary hearing stage. The assumption might be that the prosecution is entitled to hold the defendant on a lesser standard while it hunts for additional evidence. This rule may have been supportable in the middle of the last century when

magistrate's ex parte issuance of a warrant. Indeed, it has been suggested that the differences are so great that little is gained by comparing the bindover standard to the arrest warrant standard. The comparison is said to provide only a general description of the "character of the belief or the degree of certainty that the evidence must adduce" which is of limited value in determining whether a bindover is justified. Graham and Letwin, 696. The authors were speaking with reference to the California preliminary hearing, commonly described as a "mini-trial" type hearing (i.e., the rules of evidence are applicable, defense is given substantial leeway in cross-examination and presenting evidence, and the magistrate may judge credibility). Does the comparison of the bindover standard to the arrest standard provide greater direction where the preliminary hearing is a much less expansive proceeding (e.g., where the prosecution can rely entirely on hearsay evidence)?

the police were not as sophisticated as they are today and when it may have been easier to flee to avoid prosecution. Today, however, unless the statute of limitations is about to run, it is difficult to defend binding over the defendant while the police search for evidence that will support a conviction. As a practical matter, in most cases police investigation ceases once the complaint has been issued. The prosecutor wants to have the defendant held, not so that the police have time to find more evidence of guilt, but in order that incarceration, the costs of defense, the risk of conviction and other pressures will lead the defendant to plead guilty."

5. *Matching cases.* Commentators have noted that it often is difficult to reconcile appellate decisions on the evidence needed to support a preliminary hearing bindover. In some jurisdictions, decisions seem to rest more on special aspects of the particular case than on any overriding notion of the quantum of evidence needed to establish probable cause. Consider *People v. McChristian,* 54 Cal.Rptr. 324 (Cal.App. 1966) as compared to *Rideout.* In *McChristian,* an officer who was an expert narcotics investigator had received information from other officers and reliable informants regarding defendant's "activity with narcotics." The officer was acquainted with the defendant and approached him on the street one afternoon. When defendant spoke to him, the officer concluded that he had something in his mouth. The officer grabbed the defendant by the throat, forcing him to open his mouth. The officer saw six to nine multicolored balloons in defendant's mouth, but before the officer could grab the balloons, the defendant broke his grip and ran away. The next day several officers saw the defendant with a handful of balloons as they entered his home (apparently to make an arrest), but defendant disappeared in the direction of the bathroom and the balloons were gone by the time the officers reached him. Defendant was charged with unlawful possession of heroin. At the preliminary examination two narcotics experts testified that they had recovered similar balloons on "hundreds" of prior occasions and most of the balloons had contained heroin. It was also noted that persons suspected of possessing heroin often placed the balloons in their mouths as a common method of transportation. In addition, the officers testified that defendant had told them that he had been preparing a "small fix."

The appellate court found the evidence insufficient to support a bindover. The defendant's admission was inadmissible unless the state first established the corpus delicti and the evidence on that point was too "speculative" and "conjectural." The experts had stated only that "most," but not all of the balloons examined on past occasions had contained heroin. Defendant's efforts to destroy the balloons did not necessarily establish that any substance therein was a narcotic; the practice of selling "phony" narcotics, for example, was recognized by state statutes prohibiting such activities.

Can *Rideout* and *McChristian* possibly be reconciled? Is the probability that McChristian's balloons contained narcotics substantially less than the probability that Rideout had deposited or assisted in depositing the Tareyton cigarette package in the well, knowing it contained marijuana? Might the two cases be reconciled on the ground that they were concerned with the sufficiency of the evidence as to different issues, *McChristian* as to whether a crime was committed and *Rideout* as to the identity of the guilty party? Consider in this connection the wording of the Cal.Pen. Code § 872, which directs the magistrate to bindover if "it appears from the examination that a public offense has been committed, and there is sufficient cause to believe the defendant guilty thereof." Note that this provision uses the phrase "sufficient cause" (interpreted as "probable cause") only when it refers to the magistrate's belief as to defendant's guilt.

Michigan cases applying a similarly worded provision (Mich.Comp.L. § 766.13) suggest that it requires a prima facie case as to the crime and traditional probable cause as to the defendant's guilt. See *People v. Paille # 2*, 178 N.W.2d 465, 468 (Mich.1970). Is there any reason why a state would want to require a higher standard of proof as to the offense than as to the accused's connection with the offense? Compare Fed.R.Crim.P. 5.1 (requiring "probable cause to believe that an offense has been committed and that the defendant committed it").

Can *Rideout* and *McChristian* be reconciled by reference to differences in the likelihood that the prosecution might furnish further evidence at trial? In *Rideout*, the prosecution conceivably could furnish substantial additional evidence that would establish the elements of the offense (e.g., the testimony of Lopez), but there appeared to be little likelihood that the prosecution could furnish "better evidence" at trial in *McChristian*. Is the potential for production of additional evidence an appropriate factor to consider under the traditional probable cause standard? If not, does this suggest that the magistrate's review will extend beyond traditional probable cause where that standard appears inadequate to serve the ultimate objective of excluding those cases that the prosecutor clearly will not be able to sustain at trial? Consider Graham and Letwin, 694, noting that "it is insufficient to seek an understanding of the nature of magisterial screening through definitions of the verbal screening formula." More useful, the authors suggest, is an appreciation of the precise nature of the screening function assigned to the preliminary hearing in the particular jurisdiction, particularly as that function relates to previous and subsequent screening procedures.

6. *Weighing credibility.* As pointed out in fn. 2 of *Rideout*, California permits the magistrate to weigh the credibility of the witnesses. Similar statements are found in other jurisdictions. See, e.g., *People v. Paille # 2*, Note 5 supra. Consider, however, *Hunter v. District Court*, 543 P.2d 1265 (Colo.1975), arguing that cases recognizing the magistrate's authority to judge credibility commonly also indicate that such authority is rather limited. Thus, *Hunter* notes, one court restricted the inquiry into credibility to judging "the plausibility of the story and not general trustworthiness," another held that magistrate can resolve conflicts in testimony "only where the evidence is overwhelming," and still another stressed that the magistrate must not usurp the role of the trial jury in determining the "weight to be accorded the testimony of witnesses." In *Hunter*, the court held that the magistrate could consider credibility "only when, as a matter of law, the testimony is implausible or incredible. When there is a mere conflict in the testimony, a question of fact exists for the jury, and the [magistrate] must draw the inference favorable to the prosecution."

The majority opinion in *Hunter*, supra, suggests that the degree of authority given to the magistrate to judge credibility follows in large part from other aspects of preliminary hearing procedure. In refusing to follow California decisions granting the magistrate extensive authority in judging credibility, the *Hunter* majority stressed the more limited role of the Colorado preliminary hearing:

"The preliminary hearing in Colorado under Crim.P. 7(h) is not a mini-trial, but rather is limited to the purpose of determining whether there is probable cause to believe that a crime was committed and that the defendant committed it. * * * It focuses upon a probable cause determination, rather than a consideration of the probability of conviction at the ensuing trial. See Note, 83 Yale L.J. 771 (1974) [contrasting the prima facie case standard]. * * * In light of its limited purpose, evidentiary and procedural rules in the preliminary hearing in Colorado are relaxed [e.g., hearsay evidence may be used]. * * * [T]he California cases

* * * hold that a judge in a preliminary hearing is always at liberty 'to weigh the evidence, resolve conflicts and give or withhold credence to particular witnesses.' * * * The preliminary hearing in California is a 'mini-trial,' emphasizing the probability of conviction at trial on admissible evidence. In such a situation, California's *Jones* decision properly allows the judge to act as a trier of fact. In Colorado, however, the preliminary hearing is not a 'mini-trial,' and the judge in such a role is not a trier of fact. Rather, his function is solely to determine the existence or absence of probable cause."[b]

7. *Magistrate "nullification."* Is it permissible for the magistrate to consider factors other than the technical sufficiency of the evidence—e.g., the likelihood that the jury will not convict because of sympathy for the defendant or disagreement with the substantive law; or the availability of civil remedies that the magistrate views as more appropriate for resolving disputes of this type? Where the prosecution is to proceed by information, should the magistrate assume essentially the same role as the grand jury in considering such factors? Cf. Note 9, p. 984 infra. Consider Miller, 93: "Formal law generally denies this form of discretion to judges but it nevertheless exists because of limitations imposed by formal law on the ability of the prosecution or anyone else to seek review of a * * * dismissal based on non-evidence-sufficiency considerations."

8. *Consequences of a dismissal.* A dismissal at a preliminary hearing is appealable in many of those states that have recently expanded their general provisions on prosecution appeals. See, e.g., *State v. Antes,* 246 N.W.2d 671 (Wis.1976). However, more traditional state provisions authorizing prosecution appeals do not encompass preliminary hearing dismissals; they provide for appeals from orders dismissing indictments or informations, but not complaints. See Note 2, p. 1456 infra. Here, appellate review of a dismissal might be obtained by application for a writ of mandamus, but that remedy ordinarily is available only if the magistrate's refusal to bindover constitutes a "gross abuse" of discretion. See, e.g., *People v. Paille # 2,* Note 5 supra.

In most jurisdictions, whether or not appellate review is available, a prosecutor will look to alternative procedures to obtain a "reversal" of a dismissal. If a grand jury is available, he may present the case directly to the grand jury. In all but a few jurisdictions, the grand jury may indict notwithstanding the magistrate's refusal to bindover and the defendant may be rearrested on the indictment. See LaFave and Israel, § 14.3(c).[c] Where a grand jury is not available, the prosecutor may refile the

b. Consider, however, the view of Erickson, J., dissenting in *Hunter:* "The preliminary hearing, under the majority decision, amounts to an *ex parte* proceeding where the defendant's attempt to explain his position is reduced to a meaningless gesture. Criminal charges, in the future, are to be bound over on the basis of a wooden comparison between the testimony of the prosecution's witness and the elements of the crime. Such a procedure undermines the true function of the preliminary hearing which is to weed out the cases which should never have been filed."

Studies suggest that magistrates hesitate to resolve conflicts in testimony even in jurisdictions, like California, granting the magistrate extensive authority to weigh credibility. See, e.g., Graham and Letwin, 702–12, noting that magistrates in Los Angeles were reluctant to exercise that authority, preferring to "leave the credibility of the witness * * * for the trial jury." Miller, 102–105, found, in a study of Detroit practice, that the two factors that most frequently led to dismissals were (1) uncertain identification by key eyewitnesses, and (2) the reluctance of the complaining witness in testifying against the accused. Could the same factors provide the basis for dismissals in the jurisdictions (e.g., Colorado) which place more substantial limits upon the magistrate's authority to weigh credibility?

c. Although this route may be legally permissible, there may be various considerations that advise against its use even though the prosecutor is convinced that a grand jury would indict. In some judicial districts, local courts may frown upon the practice. If the prosecutor uses the grand jury to reinitiate prosecution in all but the clearly exceptional case, the reinitiated cases may be treated by the courts as highly suspect. In other districts, prosecutors do not hesitate to take a dismissed case to the grand jury if they conclude that the case is strong, the offense sericomplaint and attempt to obtain a bindover at a subsequent preliminary hearing (possibly before a different magistrate). Since the preliminary hearing dismissal is prior to the attachment of jeopardy, there is no constitutional bar against reinstituting proceedings. See *United States ex rel. Rutz v. Levy,* 268 U.S. 390, 45 S.Ct. 516, 69 L.Ed. 1010 (1925). Several state courts have maintained that refiling undermines the magistrate's authority and should not be permitted unless the prosecution offers substantial "new evidence." See, e.g., *Jones v. State,* 481 P.2d 169 (Okla.Cr.App.1971); *Wittke v. State ex rel. Smith,* 259 N.W.2d 515 (Wis.1977). The majority, however, reject that position and permit refiling on the same evidence, absent proof that the prosecutor's purpose is to harass the defendant. See e.g., *State v. Fahey,* 275 N.W.2d 870 (S.D.1979). In refusing to place any substantial limits on refiling, courts have emphasized that review of an improper dismissal might otherwise not be available since the prosecution has no right to direct appeal. See, e.g., *State v. Thomas,* 529 S.W.2d 379, 382 (Mo.1975). In turn, the legislature's refusal to provide for appellate review may have been influenced by the lack of "finality" of a dismissal order due to the prosecutor's ability to refile. Compare *State v. Fahey,* supra; with *State v. Antes,* supra. The end result has been described as an "awkward and unjustified setoff of two irrational rules," Graham and Letwin, 731.

Where state law permits refiling only with "new evidence," what additional evidence should satisfy that requirement? Should "new evidence" be limited to evidence which was not "known to the state at the time of the first preliminary hearing or which could [not] easily have been acquired at that time"? See *Jones v. State,* supra (imposing such a limitation). In upholding the prosecution's right to refile, courts frequently noted that prosecutors have a natural reluctance to disclose all available evidence at a preliminary hearing, and the prosecutor's misjudgment as to the evidence needed should not immunize the defendant from further prosecution. But consider *Harper v. District Court,* 484 P.2d 891 (Okla.Cr.App.1971) (suggesting that the prosecutor who misjudges the evidence need not refile, but may simply seek a continuance for the purpose of presenting additional available evidence in the initial hearing).

9. *Consequences of a bindover.* In all but a few jurisdictions, the grand jury is in no way limited by a bindover. It may refuse to indict despite the bindover or may indict for a lesser or higher offense, depending upon the evidence presented to it. Once the grand jury indicts, the indictment serves as the basis for defendant's continued detention and the bindover itself is no longer subject to challenge. Where prosecution is by information, on the other hand, the bindover will largely control the subsequent charges.[d] The defendant may then challenge the information on the ground that the evidence supporting the bindover was insufficient. This is usually done by a motion to dismiss or quash the information (which often must be presented prior to pleading to the information). See, e.g., Cal.Pen.Code § 995 (noted in *Rideout*). Courts review-

ous, and the magistrate simply made an error. See Gilboy, 43–67 (but also noting that in many such cases the prosecutor went to the grand jury with additional evidence).

d. In several states, the prosecutor commonly may ignore a bindover on a lesser charge since his information is not strictly limited by the bindover order. These states require only that the defendant be charged with "the offense for which he is held to answer or any other offense disclosed by the evidence at the [preliminary hearing]." Mont.Rev.Code § 95–1302. Thus, the prosecutor may charge the higher offense and place the burden on the defendant to challenge the information as not supported by the evidence presented at the preliminary hearing. Note, however, *Jones v. Superior Court,* 483 P.2d 1241 (Cal.1971), holding that a similar California provision did not authorize charging a higher offense necessarily rejected by the magistrate's factual conclusions, although it did authorize charging the higher offense to challenge the magistrate's legal conclusions as to the necessary elements of that offense.

ing a bindover decision often stress, as in *Rideout,* that they may not substitute their judgment for that of the magistrate who saw and heard the testimony. Indeed, it is sometimes stated that the magistrate's decision will only be overturned when there has been a "clear abuse of discretion." *People v. Paille # 2,* supra. Accordingly the magistrate's decision (ordinarily not supported by opinion or finding of facts) is most likely to be reversed when a misinterpretation of substantive law (or perhaps, oversight) resulted in a total absence of proof on a particular element of the offense. On occasion, however, bindover decisions also are rejected on the ground that, "without attempting to reconcile conflicts or judge the credibility of witnesses," the inferences drawn from the evidence were not sufficient to support a probable cause finding. See, e.g., *People v. McChristian,* Note 5 supra.

10. *Review following trial.* Assume that a magistrate binds over on a record that clearly fails to establish probable cause, and the prosecution follows with an information based on that bindover. A timely challenge at the trial court level is rejected, and an interlocutory appeal is unavailable. See Note 1, p. 1448 infra. The defendant then is tried and convicted. On appeal, the defendant again raises the improper bindover issue. Should the subsequent conviction, based upon ample evidence at trial, render this issue moot? Cf. Note 14 at p. 1006 infra. In some jurisdictions, a proper bindover is viewed as a jurisdictional prerequisite to the filing of the information, and, accordingly, a new trial is required if the bindover was not supported by sufficient evidence. See *People v. Martinovich,* 170 N.W.2d 899 (Mich. 1969). Others hold that the magistrate's error in binding over and the trial court's error in failing to quash the information are "cured where sufficient evidence to convict is adduced at trial." *State v. Franklin,* 234 N.W.2d 610 (Neb.1975) (noting that this position may make the trial court's ruling "essentially unreviewable," but is needed "to avoid the evils of delay, proliferation of litigation, and piecemeal review").

SECTION 4. PRELIMINARY HEARING PROCEDURES

I. APPLICATION OF THE RULES OF EVIDENCE

1. *Variations in state law.* While all jurisdictions require magistrates to recognize testimonial privileges, jurisdictions vary considerably in their application of the other rules of evidence at preliminary hearings. See LaFave and Israel, § 14.4(a). Several states require full application of the rules of evidence, i.e., the magistrate may receive only evidence normally admissible at trial. These jurisdictions will not reject a bindover, however, simply because the magistrate relied erroneously on incompetent evidence. If the reviewing court concludes that there was sufficient competent evidence before the magistrate to sustain a finding of probable cause, the bindover will be upheld notwithstanding the magistrate's error. But see Graham and Letwin, p. 747 (criticizing this standard of review as reflecting the "attitude that the magistrate's assessment of evidence counts for little in the charging process"). Cf. Note 12 at p. 1005 infra.

Most jurisdictions hold the rules of evidence to be "largely applicable" to the preliminary hearings, but allow the magistrate to consider certain types of inadmissible evidence. In some of these jurisdictions, the exceptions are recognized by statute or court rule and are fairly limited. See, e.g., Tenn.R.Crim.P. 5.1(a) (excepting a limited class of hearsay). In other jurisdictions, the appellate courts simply have adopted a general guideline that the rules of evidence need not be applied "as rigidly as in trials." *Magill v. Miller,* 455 P.2d 715 (Okla.Cr.App.1969). See, e.g., Mo.R.Crim.P. 23.03 ("so far as is practicable, the preliminary hearing shall be conducted in the same manner as the trial").

Under such a standard, most rules of evidence ordinarily must be applied, but various exceptions may be allowed, depending upon the nature of the particular case. See, e.g., *Delay v. Brainard,* 156 N.W.2d 14 (Neb.1968) (magistrate may admit confession with less corroborative evidence than would be required at trial); Miller, p. 95 (describing Wisconsin decisions requiring the magistrate to adhere to "trial rule of relevancy" while permitting deviations from the "best evidence" rule).

Finally, a few jurisdictions apparently grant the magistrate complete discretion to ignore the traditional rules of evidence. In these jurisdictions, the magistrate may "consider the evidence presented without regard to whether the evidence may or may not be admissible if and when the case reaches the trial stage." *Schramm v. State,* 366 A.2d 1185, 1192 (Del.1976). See also Fed.R.Evid. 1101(d)(3) ("rules, other than with respect to privileges, do not apply in * * * preliminary examinations in criminal cases"); Fed.R.Crim.P. 5.1(a). However, Professor Miller's study suggests that even in such jurisdictions, magistrates will follow most of the rules of evidence. See Miller, 95–96. In those jurisdictions in which magistrates are not held to a full application of the rules of evidence (i.e., both those holding those rules to be "largely applicable" and those allowing complete magistrate discretion), the two classes of otherwise inadmissible evidence most frequently considered by magistrates are hearsay evidence and unconstitutionally seized evidence. The factors that have led this group of all but a handful of states to accept at least some forms of hearsay and to direct magistrates to ignore constitutional exclusionary objections are discussed below.

2. *Hearsay.* The arguments for and against the application of the hearsay rule are illustrated by the debate over the treatment of that issue in the Federal Rules. See generally, Commentary to the Proposed Amendment of Rule 5.1, 48 F.R.D. 553, 569 (1970); *Washington v. Clemmer,* 339 F.2d 715 (D.C.Cir.1964); Weinberg and Weinberg, *The Congressional Invitation to Avoid the Preliminary Hearing,* 67 Mich.L. Rev. 1361, 1396–99 (1969). Those supporting the admission of hearsay argued: (1) that hearsay will often provide a reliable basis for decision; (2) under the Federal Magistrates Act, part-time magistrates need not be lawyers, and laymen simply are not equipped to cope with the hearsay rule and the various exceptions thereto; (3) many witnesses would be even more reluctant to assist police if they were required to make two court appearances, first at the preliminary examination and then at trial; (4) in many instances, the witness' testimony does not relate to a matter really in dispute and it can be summarized quite briefly by an investigating officer (e.g., as in the Dyer Act case, where the owner of the stolen vehicle usually can furnish testimony only as to the fact that his car disappeared); (5) the federal grand jury, which will make the final charging decision, can indict solely on the basis of hearsay (see Ch. 15, § 3); (6) requiring a more strict evidentiary standard for preliminary hearings would only encourage prosecutors to bypass the preliminary hearing by taking cases directly to the grand jury; (7) a magistrate can issue a warrant based on hearsay attributed to a reliable informant, and the probable cause standard at a preliminary hearing should approximate that for issuance of an arrest warrant.

Those arguing against the admission of hearsay maintained that a bindover must be based on admissible evidence if the accused is to be protected against the unwarranted ordeal of a trial where the prosecution lacks the evidence needed to obtain a conviction. They rejected the contention that hearsay provides a sufficient basis to make a reliable assessment of the likely strength of the prosecution's case at trial. Indeed, they argued, this assumption was inconsistent with the recognized right of the defense to challenge the prosecution's case at the preliminary hearing through cross-examination. See Fed.R. Crim.P. 5.1(a). Since both sides would be represented by counsel, and most magistrates were lawyers, application of the hearsay rule should present no greater difficulty than application of other rules of evidence. The burden placed on witnesses would not be excessive, especially since they need not appear before the grand jury. Indeed, the acceptability of hearsay at other screening proceedings made it especially important that hearsay not be allowed at the preliminary hearing.

Federal Rule 5.1(a), as adopted, provides that "the finding of probable cause may be based upon hearsay evidence in whole or in part." Many other jurisdictions also acknowledge that there is a place for hearsay at the preliminary hearing, but seek to impose some limits on its use. Consider, e.g., *People ex rel. Van Meveren v. District Court,* 195 Colo. 1, 575 P.2d 405 (1978) (prosecution may not rely entirely on hearsay where the witness furnishing the hearsay is "so unfamiliar with the case that an effective cross-examination could not be afforded the defendant"); Iowa R.Crim.P. 2(4)(b) ("probable cause shall be based upon substantial evidence, which may be hearsay in whole or in part, provided there is a substantial basis for believing the source of the hearsay to be credible and for believing that there is a factual basis for the information furnished"); *Waugh v. State,* 564 S.W.2d 654 (Tenn. 1978) (hearsay will not be admissible except for "documentary proof of ownership and written reports of expert witnesses"); Ariz.R.Crim.P. 5.4(c) (hearsay acceptable only in the form of written reports of experts, documentary evidence where there is a substantial basis for believing a foundation for its admission will be available at trial, and "the testimony of a witness concerning the declaration of another * * * where there is reasonable ground to believe the declarant will be personally available for trial"). Are these "compromise positions" preferable to the standard of the Federal Rule? If so, which is the most appropriate? [a]

a. In those jurisdictions in which the matter is left entirely in the prosecutor's discretion, there may be considerable variation in the latitude that individual magistrates will allow a prosecutor in using hearsay. See Gilboy, 20. A judge who is "strict" in this regard might take the following position: hearsay will generally be allowed as to "secondary matters" (e.g., cause of death, chain of possession as to physical evidence), but not as to a lay witness' statement. Ibid. Asked why he took such a strict position (and other judges did not), a judge interviewed in the Gilboy study offered the following explanation: "[Some judges believe] that if a police officer comes in and testifies that Jane Jones said that John Smith committed rape, that if the judge believes the police officer, that this is sufficient for probable cause. I cannot buy that. I want to hear from the witness's lips what the police officer is telling. I've heard 3,000 murder cases and 2,000 rapes. I want to look at the witnesses and observe them testifying like at trial and decide whether to give weight or credibility to that witness's testimony. [Some judges believe] the state's attorney would never prosecute someone unless there were sufficient evidence. I don't start with that premise. Just because the police have arrested someone and the prosecutor has decided to file charges doesn't mean that there is sufficient evidence. That's a presumption of guilt. A person coming into preliminary hearing court, they're still innocent until proven guilty. * * * You cannot cross-examine an officer adequately on what happened to Jane Jones the night before. For example, I had a murder case where I made [the state] bring the complaining witness in. The complaining witness testified on direct that he saw two defendants. One of them in the alley had given a gun to the second, who then shot the deceased. That would have been the only statement offered in testimony if the police officer had been the only one to testify. But on cross-examination the complaining witness admitted he was so far away and it was so dark that all he saw was a piece of metal being given from one defendant to the other. He assumed it was a gun. He jumped behind the partition. He heard two sounds that sounded like gun shots and when he got up he saw the deceased. If he had never testified, we never would have gotten that story."

The judge quoted above sat in the single Branch Court to which all homicide and sex-related offenses were presented in Chicago. Would the judge's explanation apply with equal force to all other types of felonies? Notwithstanding the judge's position, the Cook County prosecutor's office did attempt to introduce its witnesses' statements through the hearsay testimony of the investigating officer in those cases where the witnesses were not at the preliminary

3. *Unconstitutionally obtained evidence.* To what extent does the application of constitutional exclusionary rules at a preliminary hearing raise considerations that are substantially different from those presented by the application of other rules of evidence? A substantial majority of the states, including many which require a general adherence to the rules of evidence, do not recognize exclusionary rule objections at the preliminary hearing. On the other hand, several states either specifically require or permit magistrates to exclude unconstitutionally obtained evidence. In a few of those states, defendants are authorized to make a suppression motion at the preliminary hearing. In others, the defendant may raise an exclusionary rule objection if the prosecutor seeks to use at the hearing evidence that appears to have been obtained in a manner that may have been unconstitutional. Consider also *State v. Mitchell,* 329 N.E.2d 682 (Ohio 1975) (directing magistrate to exclude evidence which "clearly" was obtained unconstitutionally, but to admit and accord "lesser weight" to evidence of "doubtful constitutional validity"). In most of the above jurisdictions, the magistrate's ruling ordinarily is binding only as to the preliminary hearing—i.e., the exclusion or admission of the evidence at trial will depend upon the outcome of a suppression motion made to the trial court, rather than the magistrate's determination.

The basic argument advanced in favor of applying the exclusionary rule at the preliminary hearing is the same as that advanced in support of applying other evidentiary rules—that reliance upon evidence inadmissible at trial is inconsistent with the screening function of the preliminary hearing. Arguments advanced in response rest largely on what the Federal Rules Advisory Committee described as consideration of "administrative necessity and the efficient administration of justice." 48 F.R.D. at 572. The Advisory Committee stressed, for example, that "allowing objections * * * on the ground that evidence had been illegally obtained would require two determinations of admissibility, one before the United States magistrate and one in the district court." The dual determination noted by the Advisory Committee has been criticized as both wasteful and unfair in its application. The defendant able to make an initial objection at the preliminary hearing, it is argued, would be given a valuable "dry run" in presenting his constitutional claim, but that advantage would not be available where the prosecution presented its case without using the evidence subject to challenge or simply bypassed the preliminary hearing. See also Federal Rules Advisory Committee, 48 F.R.D. at 572 (suggesting that allowance of a preliminary hearing objection would further encourage prosecutors to take cases directly to the grand jury). In jurisdictions where the preliminary hearing is held promptly after the arrest, courts also have noted that it is an "inappropriate forum in which to try the important issues raised in * * * motions to suppress" because neither side will have had "a sufficient opportunity to investigate and prepare [its] case" prior to the hearing. *People ex rel. Pierce v. Thomas,* 334 N.Y.S.2d 666 (1972).

II. THE DEFENDANT'S RIGHT OF CROSS-EXAMINATION

All jurisdictions grant the defense a right to cross-examine those witnesses presented by the prosecution at the preliminary hearing. See, e.g., Fed.R.Crim.P. 5.1(a). This right is based on local law (usually a statute or court rule) since the Supreme Court has long held that cross-examination at a preliminary hearing is not required by the confrontation clause of the Sixth Amendment. See *Goldsby v. United States,* 160 U.S. 70, 16 S.Ct. 216, 40 L.Ed.

hearing for tactical or other reasons, and when that attempt failed (and resulted in dismissal), often reinitiated the prosecution by taking it directly to the grand jury. See Gilboy, pp. 54–57.

343 (1895). In most jurisdictions, the right to cross-examine at the preliminary hearing is not quite as extensive as the right to cross-examine at trial. Fairly typical is the standard set forth in *People v. Horton*, 358 N.E.2d 1121 (Ill.1976): "It [cross-examination] may not extend beyond the scope of direct examination and such further interrogation as is directed to show interest, bias, prejudice or motive of the witness to the extent that these factors are relevant to the question of probable cause." In restricting cross-examination at the preliminary hearing, magistrates must commonly cite two grounds: (1) that the defendant is attempting improperly to use cross-examination as a pretrial discovery device, and (2) that further cross-examination is unnecessary since it would only raise issues of credibility more appropriately left to the trial jury. As indicated in the notes that follow, states vary considerably in their treatment of each of these grounds.

1. *Discovery and cross-examination.* Almost all jurisdictions have recognized the magistrate's authority to cut off cross-examination which appears to be aimed primarily at obtaining discovery. They differ, however, in the leeway granted to the magistrate to determine whether cross-examination is being used primarily to obtain discovery rather than to refute the prosecution's showing of probable cause.[a] Consider, for example, the following cases:

(a) *Coleman v. Burnett*, 477 F.2d 1187 (D.C.Cir.1973). Defendant was charged with assaulting a jailer while a prisoner in a cellblock. In cross-examining the jailer, the defense was permitted "considerable latitude," but was barred from asking questions concerning (1) disparaging remarks assertedly directed to cellblock personnel by prisoners other than the defendant, (2) the extent of the jailer's injuries, and (3) the jailer's knowledge of injuries suffered by the defendant. On appeal, defense counsel argued that the questions were not directed at discovery but at showing that the jailer had initiated the assault as a result of provocative remarks of other prisoners, that the defendant had been injured far more severely than the jailer, and that the "assault charge was brought as a subterfuge for the [jailer's] own conduct." The Court of Appeals responded: "Cross-examination at a preliminary hearing, like the hearing itself, is confined by the principle that a probe into probable cause is the end and aim of the proceeding, and the line between refutation of probable cause and discovery into the prosecution's case ofttimes is thin. Here counsel's purpose in propounding the questions which the presiding judge excluded was unquestionably blurred by the fact that counsel frequently appeared to be off on an impermissible quest for discovery. At no time prior to the rulings complained of did counsel delineate for the judge's edification the factual thesis he was seeking to promote. Only as the hearing neared its close, and after the rulings had been made, did counsel broach anything remotely similar to the defensive theory now explained on appeal. Our reading of the hearing record leaves us with the conviction that the presiding judge, when ruling on counsel's questions, could hardly divine what counsel had in mind. Therefore, we cannot say that he committed error in barring responses to inquiries that seemed unrelated to the task of evaluating probable cause."

(b) In *Wilson v. State*, 208 N.W.2d 134 (Wis.1973), the victim's wife identified the defendant at the preliminary hearing as the man who shot her husband. On cross-examination, she acknowledged that she

a Differing views of the relationship between discovery and effective cross-examination also are reflected in the rules governing defendant's access to prior recorded statements of preliminary hearing witnesses possessed by the prosecution. Several jurisdictions grant the defense access to those statements for possible use in impeaching the witnesses. Others hold, however, that disclosure of those statements is part of the pretrial or trial discovery process and access will not be granted until the time provided for such discovery.

had given a description of the assailant to the police. Defense counsel was not allowed to question her, however, as to the details of that description or her subsequent identification of the defendant at a lineup. In holding that the magistrate erred in treating those questions as aimed primarily at discovery, the Wisconsin court noted: "There is a point where attacks on credibility become discovery. That point is crossed when one delves into general trustworthiness of the witness, as opposed to plausibility of the story. Because all that need be established for a bindover is probable cause, all that is needed is a believable account of the defendant's commission of a felony. Applying this standard to the case now before this court, defense counsel should have been allowed to cross-examine the state's witness on her prior description of the man who shot her husband. * * * [T]he question propounded did not merely go to the witness's general trustworthiness, but also to the plausibility of her description of the defendant, upon which the finding of probable cause rested."

(c) In *People ex rel. Pierce v. Thomas,* 334 N.Y.S.2d 666 (Sup.Ct.1972), the complaining witness identified the defendants at the preliminary hearing as the persons who had robbed him while he was riding a subway train. On cross-examination, defense counsel elicited the complainant's acknowledgment that he had never seen the defendants prior to the three-minute long incident. Counsel was not allowed to ask, however, whether other persons had been present at the time or whether the complainant had ever recovered his possessions. In sustaining the magistrate's refusal to permit such questions, the trial court noted that the "hearing is not intended as a pre-trial discovery device nor is it a substitute for the trial itself." While defense counsel's questions would be permitted at trial, they were "beyond the scope of the hearing." See also *United States v. Hinkle,* 307 F.Supp. 117 (D.D.C.1969) (upholding the magistrate's rejection of cross-examination designed to obtain from a police officer the names of persons interviewed at the scene of an assault).

Of course, the magistrate may have the authority to curtail cross-examination, yet prefer not to exercise that power. Many magistrates regularly permit the type of questioning advanced in *Coleman, Hinkle,* and *Pierce,* provided the cross-examination is fairly brief. See, e.g., Graham and Letwin, 922. Thus, even in jurisdictions which take the narrowest view of permissible cross-examination, many lawyers regularly use the cross-examination for obvious discovery purposes. Note, however, fn. c at p. 934 supra, discussing the possible tactical costs of using the cross-examination for that purpose.

2. *Cross-examination and the magistrate's judgment of credibility.* At what point may a magistrate appropriately refuse to allow cross-examination on the ground that the direct testimony clearly establishes probable cause and therefore "nothing that cross-examination might reveal is likely to change the result"? While magistrates in most jurisdictions commonly follow such a practice, it has not been subjected to extensive scrutiny by higher courts. See, e.g., *People v. Bonner,* 229 N.E.2d 527 (Ill. 1967) (simply noting, in dictum, that the magistrate "may terminate the proceedings once probable cause is established"). The few courts that have considered and upheld the practice have emphasized either that (1) the magistrate has only limited authority to judge credibility or (2) the magistrate, as the finder of fact, may conclude that cross-examination along a certain path would not influence his judgment. Does the first ground suggest that a magistrate given extensive authority to judge credibility under state law (see Note 6, p. 956 supra) should not be able to bar relevant cross-examination even though the prosecution witness' testimony appears to be clearly sufficient to establish probable cause? See *Myers v. Commonwealth,* Note 4, p. 966 infra. Does the second ground suggest that a magistrate should

not have authority in any jurisdiction to bar cross-examination until he has at least seen the direction that it would take? See, e.g., *People v. Staton,* 406 N.Y.S.2d 242 (Crim.Ct.1978) (curtailing cross-examination after the magistrate concluded it was designed to show only the complainant's animosity toward the defendant and therefore would serve no "useful purpose" in making a judgment as to probable cause).

3. *The perpetuation of testimony.* As noted at p. 936 supra, the preliminary hearing testimony of a witness unavailable at trial may be admitted as substantive evidence at trial, but only if the defense had an adequate opportunity to cross-examine the witness at the preliminary hearing. When would the restriction of cross-examination on the grounds considered in Notes 1–2 supra deprive the defendant of that opportunity? Consider in this regard, the restrictions imposed in *Coleman,* Note 1 supra, *Pierce,* Note 1 supra, and *Altman,* Note 5, p. 967 infra. Should a magistrate refuse to restrict cross-examination, notwithstanding a valid prosecution objection based on the grounds discussed in those cases, in order to ensure that the preliminary hearing testimony will be preserved for possible trial use? See *State v. Faafiti,* 513 P.2d 697 (Hawaii 1973) (urging magistrates, in the light of *California v. Green,* p. 936 supra, "to permit the counsel for the defendant to examine fully and thoroughly witnesses at all preliminary hearings").

III. THE RIGHT TO PRESENT DEFENSE WITNESSES

1. *Use of defense witnesses.* Most jurisdictions recognize, specifically or by implication, a right of the defendant to present his own witnesses at the preliminary hearing. See, e.g., Fed.R.Crim.P. 5.1(a) (defendant "may introduce evidence on his own behalf"); Pa.R.Crim.P. 141(c)(3) (defendant may "call witnesses on his own behalf other than witnesses to his good reputation only"). In a few states, however, defense witnesses (other than the defendant himself) may be called only with the permission of the magistrate. See, e.g., N.Y.Crim.P.Law § 180.60(7). Cf. Ariz.R.Crim.P. 5.3(a) (magistrate may reject proposed defense presentation if he concludes it would be "insufficient to rebut" the prosecution's evidence).

The defense practice appears to be much the same, however, whether state law grants a right to call witnesses or leaves the matter to the magistrate's discretion. Defense counsel generally operate on the principle that defense witnesses should not be presented unless the case is quite exceptional. In many hearings, defense counsel's primary objectives are to obtain discovery and to establish a basis for the impeachment of the prosecution's witnesses at trial. Presenting defense witnesses ordinarily will not help in achieving either of these objectives. See also fn. c, p. 934 supra (citing risks involved in the defense tactic of calling adverse witnesses who were not subpoenaed by the prosecution in order to gain discovery). In other hearings, counsel also may seek to vigorously challenge the prosecution's showing of probable cause, but even then, the usual approach is to rely entirely on cross-examination of prosecution witnesses. Unless the credibility of prosecution witnesses has been shaken substantially on cross-examination, the contrary testimony of defense witnesses is likely to be treated by the magistrate as simply presenting a credibility conflict that should be resolved by the fact-finder at trial. See Note 6, p. 956 supra. Moreover, by presenting the defense witness at the preliminary hearing, the defendant runs the risk of making that witness' testimony less effective at trial. Just as the defense may use its cross-examination of prosecution witnesses to gain discovery and to prepare for future impeachment, the prosecution may use its cross-examination of the defense witnesses to achieve the same goals. Whatever value defense witnesses may have in defeating the prosecution's probable cause showing must be balanced against the tactical advantages given the prosecution if the case should go to trial.

2. *Limitations.* Jurisdictions granting the defendant a right to present his own witnesses commonly permit magistrates to limit that right on grounds similar to those applied to limit the right of cross-examination. Thus, the magistrate may refuse a defense request to subpoena a witness because (1) defense counsel is seeking primarily to obtain discovery from the witness, (2) the magistrate believes that probable cause is established by the prosecution's testimony and the defense witness' testimony would not offset the prosecution's showing, or (3) the testimony of the witness would relate only to an affirmative defense not cognizable at the preliminary hearing. Each of these limitations is discussed below.

3. When does a defense request that the magistrate subpoena a particular witness suggest an ulterior purpose of gaining discovery rather than challenging the prosecution's showing of probable cause. Consider *Desper v. State,* 318 S.E.2d 437 (W.Va.1984) (where prosecution presented only one witness, the robbery victim, who testified that he had given a written statement to the police, the magistrate erred in rejecting as an attempt to gain discovery the defense request to call the investigating officer; the officer's testimony as to the witness' initial identification of the defendant from police photographs and to the witness' written statement could have been relevant to challenging probable cause, and the magistrate "could have exercised his discretion to ensure that the scope of the officer's testimony remained within permissible grounds"); *Williams v. Virginia,* 160 S.E.2d 781 (Va.1968) (defense counsel could not call witnesses in order to gain information relating to the circumstances under which defendant had confessed); *State v. Knudson,* 187 N.W.2d 321 (Wis.1971) (magistrate properly denied defense request to call mother of victim of alleged child molesting when there was "every indication that the purpose of the defense was to fish for elements of the state's case"; moreover, even if the mother's testimony would reveal that the victim had made prior statements inconsistent with her current testimony, that current testimony had been "sufficient in the mind of the magistrate" and "credibility" was an issue "for the trial").

4. At what point may the magistrate cut off the development of a defense on the ground that further testimony would not be helpful? Consider *State v. Knudson,* Note 3 supra. Compare MYERS v. COMMONWEALTH, 298 N.E.2d 819 (Mass.1973). There, at the preliminary hearing on a rape charge, only the complaining witness testified for the prosecution. When defense counsel questioned her about her alleged belief in witchcraft, the magistrate terminated the preliminary hearing, noting that he had "heard enough testimony to find probable cause." Defense counsel stated that he wished to complete the cross-examination and introduce evidence, including a psychiatric evaluation of the complaining witness. On review prior to trial, the appellate court ordered that a new preliminary hearing be held:

"The Commonwealth argues that once a prima facie showing of probable cause has been made by prosecution testimony, the examining magistrate can end the hearing before the defendant's attorney has had an opportunity to make a complete cross-examination of the prosecution witness or to present an affirmative defense. We fail to see how such a limited procedure could possibly effectuate the hearing's primary function of screening out cases that should not go to trial. To require such minimal proof of probable cause would render the hearing, in many instances, an empty ritual with a foregone conclusion. * * * The primary function of the probable cause hearing of screening out 'an erroneous or improper prosecution,' *Coleman v. Alabama* [p. 943 supra] can only be effectuated by an adversary hearing where the defendant is given a meaningful opportunity to challenge the credibility of the prosecution's witnesses and to raise any affirmative defences he may have. * * * The facts of the instant case provide an excellent illustration of this point. The only witness at the petitioner's probable cause hearing was the complaining witness who repeated her accusation that the petitioner had raped her. If the petitioner had been afforded his statutory rights, he would have introduced testimony challenging the complaining witness's credibility and supporting his defence of a consensual sexual relationship. The examining magistrate could not have possibly made an informed judgment on the question of whether there was sufficient credible evidence of the defendant's guilt to support a bind over until he had considered all of this evidence.

"In some cases, the evidence introduced in behalf of the defendant will do no more than raise a conflict which can best be resolved by a jury at the actual trial where the Commonwealth must prove the defendant's guilt beyond a reasonable doubt. But, in other cases, the evidence elicited by defence counsel on cross-examination or from the testimony of defence witnesses or from other evidence may lead the examining magistrate to disbelieve the prosecution's witnesses and discharge the defendant for lack of probable cause. * * * Regardless of whether the petitioner's evidence in the instant case would have been sufficient to overcome the prosecution's case for probable cause, he had a statutory right to have the judge consider it before making his decision. * * *

"The Commonwealth argues * * * that granting defendants inflexible statutory rights to cross-examine witnesses against them and to present testimony in their own behalf would transform the preliminary hearing into a full-blown trial with disastrous results to a criminal justice system that is already overburdened. However, past experience indicates that trial strategy usually prevents such a result as both the prosecution and the defence wish to withhold as much of their case as possible. Normally defence counsel will be more concerned at the preliminary hearing with exploring rather than destroying the prosecution's case. * * * [D]efense tactics usually mitigate against putting the defendant on the stand or presenting exculpatory evidence at the preliminary hearing unless defence counsel believes his evidence is compelling enough to overcome the prosecution's case."

5. The states are divided as to the defendant's right to present at the preliminary hearing what are commonly characterized as "affirmative defenses"—i.e., defenses which acknowledge commission of the criminal act but rely upon a justification that relieves the actor of liability. Two cases reflecting the opposing viewpoints on this issue (and on cross-examination relating to affirmative defenses) are *State v. Altman,* 482 P.2d 460 (Ariz.1971) and *Jennings v. Superior Court,* 428 P.2d 304 (Cal.1967). Both involved an attempt by defense counsel to develop an entrapment defense through cross-examination of prosecution witnesses and direct examination of defense witnesses. *Altman* upheld the magistrate's refusal to permit the defendant to raise the entrapment defense. The court emphasized the limited function of the preliminary hearing: "[E]ntrapment is an affirmative defense to be resolved at trial. * * * A preliminary examination is not a substitute for trial. * * * The issue of innocence or guilt is not before the magistrate. * * * The full and complete exploration of all facets of the case is reserved for trial and is not the function of a preliminary examination."

In *Jennings,* the court also stressed the role of the preliminary hearing, but reached an opposite conclusion: "[T]he People share a misconception * * * that as long as the prosecution's evidence showed probable cause to hold petitioner to answer it was irrelevant at that [preliminary hearing] stage 'whether the man was, in fact, framed' (quoting the magistrate).

If this view were correct, of course, any cross-examination or testimony on behalf of the defendant would become superfluous. To accept the People's argument would be in effect to erase [Penal Code] sections 865 and 866 [providing that defendant may cross-examine witnesses and present his own witnesses] from the books and reduce the preliminary hearing to an ex parte proceeding at which the defendant's presence would be a meaningless gesture. * * * 'The purpose of the preliminary hearing is to weed out groundless or unsupported charges of grave offenses, and to relieve the accused of the degradation and expense of a criminal trial.' * * * To effectuate this constitutional and statutory purpose the defendant must be permitted, if he chooses, to elicit testimony or introduce evidence tending to overcome the prosecution's case or establish an affirmative defense."

The *Altman* analysis apparently rests on the premise that defense development of an affirmative defense is useless since the magistrate cannot refuse to bindover on the basis of such a defense. The magistrate, under this analysis, is not allowed to weigh the proof of an affirmative defense against the prosecution's proof and refuse to bindover where the evidence supporting the affirmative defense appears more persuasive. Why should the magistrate not be allowed to make this choice when he is permitted to choose between evidence of a non-affirmative defense and the prosecution's proof? Consider in this connection, Note 6, p. 956 supra, discussing the magistrate's authority to judge the credibility of witnesses. If the magistrate is allowed to consider an affirmative defense, as in *Jennings,* what standard of proof should he apply in judging affirmative defenses as to which the defendant would carry the burden of proof at trial?

Some commentators have suggested that the prohibition against the presentation of affirmative defenses may relate to the prosecution's inability to fully prepare its response to such a defense during the short time available prior to the preliminary hearing. See Miller, at 99. Isn't it likely, however, that the prosecutor will have more difficulty in preparing to respond to some non-affirmative defenses (e.g., alibi) then to some affirmative defenses (e.g., self-defense)? Where state law requires the defendant to provide advance notice if he intends to raise a particular defense at trial (e.g., alibi, see p. 1138 infra), should a similar notice requirement be imposed as a prerequisite to raising that defense at the preliminary hearing?

IV. CHALLENGING PROCEDURAL RULINGS

1. *Pretrial objections to the information.* Assume that a magistrate makes an improper procedural ruling at a preliminary hearing. The magistrate subsequently binds over, and the defendant moves to dismiss the ensuing information, arguing that the magistrate's procedural error rendered the bindover invalid. Should defendants be required to show that, if not for the improper ruling, the magistrate would not have bound over? *Jennings v. Superior Court,* p. 967 supra, holds that the defendant need not make such a showing where the magistrate's ruling deprived the defendant of a "substantial right," such as his right to cross-examine or to present witnesses. Finding reversible error in the denial of cross-examination relating to an entrapment offense, the court rejected the prosecution's contention that the error was not prejudicial because the prosecution's evidence would still have been sufficient for a bindover. The crucial issue, the court indicated, was whether the defendant was denied a "fair hearing." If so, he was entitled to relief "without further showing." The court acknowledged that not every improper curtailment of cross-examination would be viewed as denying the defendant a fair hearing, "since the [subject] matter may be too unimportant or there may be no prejudice or the questions may involve issues which can be brought up at a more appropriate time."

However, "where the subject of the cross-examination concerns the matter at issue, there can be no doubt that the refusal to permit such question results in a denial of a fair hearing." Is the *Jennings* analysis consistent with the standard commonly applied to the magistrate's erroneous admission of incompetent evidence—the standard that the bindover will nevertheless be upheld if there was sufficient competent evidence to support a probable cause finding? See Note 1, p. 959 supra.

2. *Subsequent indictment.* Assume that a magistrate improperly curtails cross-examination or denies a request to present a defense witness, but an indictment is issued before the magistrate's ruling can be challenged in the trial court. Has the defendant lost his right to relief even though the magistrate's ruling clearly resulted in an erroneous bindover? The traditional rule—followed in all but a few jurisdictions—is that all "defects" in the preliminary hearing are "cured by the subsequent indictment." This rule is based on the rationale that "once an indictment [has] been approved, the preliminary proceedings are not subject to either direct or collateral attack because the defendant has been afforded an independent determination that a prima facie case exists." *Commonwealth v. Gordon,* 385 A.2d 1013 (Pa. Super.1978). See also Note 5, p. — supra, discussing the application of basically the same rationale to the termination of an ongoing hearing. But note the position taken in *Coleman v. Burnett,* Note 6 infra. In a jurisdiction in which a bindover is promptly followed by indictment, what procedures will be available to ensure that there is sufficient trial court and appellate court review of magistrate rulings to provide adequate development of the law? May the defendant seek a stay of the grand jury proceedings so that he may obtain review of the magistrate's ruling prior to issuance of the indictment?

3. *Review after conviction.* Assume that the magistrate erroneously restricts defendant's right to cross-examination or to present evidence at a preliminary hearing. The magistrate subsequently binds over and an information is filed. Defense challenges the information as based on a defective preliminary hearing, but the trial court erroneously finds that the magistrate's rulings were proper. Interlocutory review is not available, and defendant's next opportunity to raise the issue is on appeal following conviction. Should the conviction then be viewed as having rendered harmless the magistrate's error—at least in the absence of a showing by defense counsel of actual prejudice at trial? See *People v. Marshall,* 365 N.E.2d 1122 (Ill.App.1977) (no prejudice in curtailment of cross-examination at preliminary hearing where there was extensive cross-examination at trial); *Jennings v. Superior Court,* p. 967 supra (noting that a magistrate's errors relating to the admissibility of evidence "may be found to have been cured" if correct rulings are thereafter made at the trial); *Wilson v. State,* p. 963 supra (restriction of confrontation at a preliminary hearing was harmless error where defense counsel did not seek to raise the same point by cross-examination at trial).

Compare with the above cases *Mascarenas v. State,* 458 P.2d 789 (N.M.1969), holding that the improper restriction of cross-examination amounted, in effect, to a "denial of a preliminary examination"; accordingly, since state law required a preliminary hearing as a prerequisite to "holding any person on an information," the trial court was "without jurisdiction" and the subsequent conviction was invalid. See also *People v. Walker,* 189 N.W.2d 234 (Mich.1971) (since state law required a proper bindover as a prerequisite to filing an information, conviction must be reversed where trial judge erroneously denied defendant's motion to quash the information on the ground that the bindover was based on unconstitutionally seized evidence; jurisdictional error could not be cured by introduction of sufficient evidence at trial to show that the seizure was constitutional since such evidence had not been presented at the preliminary hearing.

V. THE SIGNIFICANCE OF COLEMAN

1. In COLEMAN v. ALABAMA, 399 U.S. 1, 90 S.Ct. 1999, 26 L.Ed.2d 387 (1970), the Supreme Court held, for reasons discussed in Note 3, p. 943 supra, that the state had violated the indigent defendant's Sixth Amendment right to counsel when it failed to appoint counsel to assist him at the preliminary hearing. The state argued that even if the defendant's right to counsel had been violated, there had been no prejudice since the preliminary hearing had no bearing on defendant's subsequent indictment and conviction. It stressed that the trial court had adhered to the ruling of *Pointer v. Texas* [p. 937 supra], which "bars the admission of testimony given at a pre-trial proceeding where the accused did not have the benefit of cross-examination by and through counsel." Speaking for the majority, Justice BRENNAN responded to this argument in Part III of his opinion:

"The trial transcript indicates that the prohibition against use by the State at trial of anything that occurred at the preliminary hearing was scrupulously observed. But on the record it cannot be said whether or not petitioners were otherwise prejudiced by the absence of counsel at the preliminary hearing. That inquiry in the first instance should more properly be made by the Alabama courts. The test to be applied is whether the denial of counsel at the preliminary hearing was harmless error under *Chapman v. California* [p. 796 supra]. We accordingly vacate the petitioners' convictions and remand the case to the Alabama courts for such proceedings not inconsistent with this opinion as they may deem appropriate to determine whether such denial of counsel was harmless error, and therefore whether the convictions should be reinstated or a new trial ordered."

Justices Harlan and White, each writing separate opinions, also commented on the appropriate relief. Justice HARLAN noted: "I consider the scope of the Court's remand too broad and amorphous. I do not think that reversal of these convictions, for lack of counsel at the preliminary hearing, should follow unless petitioners are able to show on remand that they have been prejudiced in their defense at trial, in that favorable testimony that might otherwise have been preserved was irretrievably lost by virtue of not having counsel to help present an affirmative case at the preliminary hearing."

Justice WHITE expressed a somewhat similar view: "I would expect the application of the harmless-error standard on remand to produce results approximating those contemplated by Mr. Justice Harlan's separately stated views. Whether denying petitioner counsel at the preliminary hearing was harmless beyond a reasonable doubt depends upon an assessment of those factors which made the denial error. But that assessment cannot ignore the fact that petitioner has been tried and found guilty by a jury. The possibility that counsel would have detected preclusive flaws in the State's probable cause showing is for all practical purposes mooted by the trial where the State produced evidence satisfying the jury of the petitioner's guilt beyond a reasonable doubt. Also, it would be wholly speculative in this case to assume either (1) that the State's witnesses at the trial testified inconsistently with what their testimony would have been if petitioner had had counsel to cross-examine them at the preliminary hearing, or (2) that counsel, had he been present at the hearing, would have known so much more about the State's case than he actually did when he went to trial that the result of the trial might have been different. So too it seems extremely unlikely that matters related to bail * * * would ever raise reasonable doubts about the integrity of the trial. There remains the possibility, as Mr. Justice Harlan suggests, that important testimony of witnesses unavailable at the trial could have been preserved had counsel been present to cross-examine opposing witnesses or to examine witnesses for the defense."

2. Since all states now provide appointed counsel at preliminary hearing, appellate courts rarely have need today to determine whether a denial of counsel at the preliminary hearing constituted harmless error. Those courts that have considered the issue generally have followed the analysis of Mr. Justice White. See, e.g., *Moses v. Helgemoe,* 562 F.2d 62 (1st Cir. 1976) (denial of counsel was harmless error where defense obtained discovery through other means and testimony at trial was along the lines anticipated by defense counsel; the court would not accept "speculation" that the complaining witness would have given inconsistent testimony at the preliminary hearing and that any inconsistency would have been "so significant as to have laid the ground for an impeachment which could have changed the final result").

3. Does *Coleman* have any bearing on the treatment of a magistrate's erroneous ruling restricting the defendant's right to cross-examine or present witnesses? Consider COLEMAN v. BURNETT, 477 F.2d 1187 (D.C.Cir.1973). Defendant Dancis was charged with two violations of the Marijuana Tax Act. At the preliminary hearing, the magistrate denied defense counsel's request for a subpoena requiring the attendance of an unnamed undercover agent, who apparently was the sole available eyewitness to the marijuana transactions allegedly involving the defendant. The magistrate found probable cause on the basis of the hearsay testimony of the undercover agent's supervisor, and the defendant was indicted shortly thereafter. The defendant then sought, along with two other defendants, "declaratory judgments that the preliminary hearings were defective, writs of mandamus reopening them, and an injunction restraining pendente lite, presentation of their cases for grand jury consideration." The district court dismissed the action, and the defendant then obtained appellate review on application for a writ of mandamus.

The Court of Appeals (per ROBINSON, J.), initially determined that the magistrate's ruling was contrary to former Rule 5(c), now Rule 5.1, permitting the accused to "introduce evidence on his own behalf." It suggested, moreover, that more than a violation of the Federal Rules was involved: "These provisions of the Rules * * * are now reinforced by the holding in *Coleman v. Alabama* that the Sixth Amendment secures for the accused the assistance of counsel at a preliminary hearing * * *. Among counsel's potential contributions, the Supreme Court stated, is 'skilled examination . . . of witnesses [which] may expose fatal weaknesses in the [prosecution's] case that may lead the magistrate to refuse to bind the accused over.' * * * If the accused's counsel is reduced to a state of impotence in the discharge of this responsibility, it is evident that the accused is deprived of the very benefit which the Sixth Amendment's boon of counsel was designed to confer. So, an accused is normally entitled to subpoenas compelling the attendance at his preliminary hearing of witnesses whose testimony promises appreciable assistance on the issue of probable cause."

The Court of Appeals then turned to the question as "how the [magistrate's] mistake should be corrected." It first considered "whether the indictment returned against Dancis forecloses rectification of the error." It noted that the indictment "itself establishes probable cause," and a long line of cases therefore had held that a defendant "is not entitled to a preliminary hearing where he is indicted before a hearing is held." Dancis' case, however, was "markedly different" because he was given a hearing at which he was denied his right to examine a witness on his own behalf. The nature of that violation, the court concluded, "keeps Dancis in court despite the post-hearing rendition of the accused," and entitles him to appropriate remedial action. In reaching this conclusion, the court relied on *Coleman v. Alabama,* and a series of earlier D.C. Circuit cases that had been rejected in several other federal circuits (see Note 5, p. 944 supra). The court reasoned:

"Where in terms of the requirements of the Rules, a preliminary hearing is defective, the accused is obviously entitled to a reopening of the hearing to enable remediation of the defect if that can be done before a grand jury acts in the matter. * * * [W]e have not hesitated to direct a supplemental preliminary hearing on demonstration that at the original hearing the accused did not get his just due. * * * We have, moreover, adhered to the view that such a deprivation can be remedied by a reopening of the hearing even after return of an indictment. The indictment bars relitigation of the question of probable cause, of course, but the fact remains that save for disrespect of the accused's rights he would have enlarged his insight into the Government's case against him—as a byproduct of efforts pro and con on probable cause in the course of the Government's submission. * * * [Accordingly, we] * * * held [in *Ross v. Sirica,* 380 F.2d 557 (D.C.Cir.1967)] that the hearing should be reopened to afford the accused an opportunity to retrieve the part which has been lost. * * *

"Since our development of this prophylactic doctrine, however, the Federal Magistrate Act was adopted, and the question becomes whether the Act has set the doctrine for naught. * * * The Act specifies in Section 303(e) that '[n]o preliminary examination . . . shall be required to be accorded an arrested person . . . if at any time subsequent to the initial appearance of such person before a judge or magistrate and prior to the date fixed for the preliminary examination . . . an indictment is returned. . . . ' We need not ponder whether the Act erects a barrier to a post-indictment pretrial reopening of a preliminary hearing which is seriously defective under the criteria specified in the Rules. To be sure, the remedy we provided in *Ross v. Sirica,* in circumstances comparable to those here, was a remand to the magistrate for a supplemental hearing. But *Ross,* like other decisions in its day, rested on the theory that discovery was as much a function of the preliminary hearing as an investigation into probable cause to bind the accused for further prosecution. The Act was passed after *Ross* was decided, and whether or not it imposed an absolute ban on reopenings of preliminary hearings, it certainly destroyed discovery as a reason for ordering a reopening.

"Even more importantly *Ross* predated not only the Act but also the Supreme Court's decision in *Coleman v. Alabama,* and *Coleman* introduced an element of the remedy problem which this court has not hitherto had occasion to consider. * * * In *Coleman,* the Court could not determine from the record whether the absence of counsel from the accused's preliminary hearing actually worked prejudice at his trial, so it vacated the conviction and remanded the case to the Alabama courts for an inquiry on that score. * * * [*Coleman*] charts the route to be traveled when the error is judicially detected only after conviction. But that is not Dancis' situation, for while he has been indicted he has not yet been tried. * * * We think, [however], that the problem of remediation arising pretrial, no less than when it emerges after conviction, is one to be addressed by the [trial] court itself. * * *

"The concern is that the accused may suffer prejudice at his forthcoming trial by the infringement of his rights at the hearing, and avoidance of prejudice is the function and duty of the judge himself. * * * We perceive no reason why, in the circumstances presented, the problem at hand cannot be fully accommodated within the framework of the criminal prosecution pending against Dancis. The judge who is to preside at Dancis' trial is amply equipped to dissipate whatever risk of prejudice was bred by Dancis' inability to call the undercover officer as a witness at his preliminary hearing. * * * The indictment against Dancis named the undercover agent, and it may well be that he testified before the grand jury. If so, the trial judge might consider making the agent's grand jury testimony available to defense counsel. Alternatively, since after indictment the Government no longer has had an interest in keeping the agent's identity secret, and obviously will have to produce him as a witness at trial, a voluntary interview may be indicated. If need be, the judge might set appropriate bounds for an interview and arrange for the agent's participation herein. It may be that, by consent of the parties and approval of the judge, a deposition by written interrogatories to the agent would suffice as an expedient. Without any effort to exhaust the possibilities, we make these observations simply as suggestions of procedures calculated to safeguard Dancis against prejudice consistently with an orderly and expeditious progression of the case to trial."

4. Does *Coleman v. Burnett* convert *Coleman v. Alabama* into a decision which requires a jurisdiction, if it does provide a preliminary hearing, to also provide defendant with a right to extensively cross-examine prosecution witnesses and to present witnesses on his own behalf? See *United States v. King,* 482 F.2d 768 (D.C.Cir. 1973) (describing *Coleman v. Burnett* as holding that "denial of a right to call a witness whose testimony is material to the issue of probable cause is not only a contravention of Rule 5.1, but also a deprivation which reaches constitutional magnitude by its infringement of the Sixth Amendment guarantee"). Under this view, does *Coleman v. Alabama* invalidate the various restrictions upon cross-examination and witness presentation that were discussed at pp. 962–65 supra? Does it require that the *Chapman* harmless error standard be applied in determining whether a patently improper preliminary hearing restriction upon cross-examination or defense presentation of witnesses requires reversal of a subsequent conviction? Most courts have viewed *Coleman v. Alabama* as having "no application" to preliminary hearing procedures apart from the appointment of counsel. See, e.g., *People v. Marshall,* 365 N.E.2d 1122 (Ill.App.1977).

5. Relying upon nonconstitutional grounds, *Desper v. State,* Note 3, p. 966 supra, followed *Coleman v. Burnett* in prescribing the appropriate post-indictment relief for a magistrate's error in refusing to allow the defendant to subpoena a relevant witness at a preliminary hearing. See also *Scott v. State,* 359 So.2d 1355 (Miss.1978) (where the trial court found that the magistrate had improperly barred one question on cross-examination of the prosecutrix at the preliminary hearing, it ordered the prosecutrix to meet privately with defense counsel for the purpose of answering that question). Does such an approach create an arbitrary distinction between the defendant who obtains no preliminary hearing due to a prior indictment and the defendant who, notwithstanding an intervening indictment, is given some relief for discovery opportunities lost through a defective hearing? Cf. *People v. Jackson,* 266 N.Y.S. 2d 481 (Sup.Ct.1965).

Chapter 15

GRAND JURY REVIEW [a]

SECTION 1. THE ROLE OF GRAND JURY REVIEW

I. PROSECUTION BY INDICTMENT: FEDERAL AND STATE REQUIREMENTS

In Chapter 10, we discussed the investigative function of the grand jury. In this Chapter, we are concerned with another major function of the grand jury, commonly characterized as its "shielding," "buffer," or "screening" function. The standard judicial description of this function was set forth in *Wood v. Georgia,* 370 U.S. 375, 390, 82 S.Ct. 1364, 1373, 8 L.Ed.2d 569, 580 (1962):

> "Historically, this body [the grand jury] has been regarded as a primary security to the innocent against hasty, malicious and oppressive persecution; it serves the invaluable function in our society of standing between the accuser and the accused, whether the latter be an individual, minority group, or other, to determine whether a charge is founded upon reason or was dictated by an intimidating power or by malice and personal ill will."

As we noted in Chapter 10, the grand jury originally was established to assist the Crown in reporting crimes, but it was its eventual development as a shield against arbitrary prosecutions by the Crown that led to its recognition in the federal constitution. The Fifth Amendment provides that, except in certain military cases, "no person shall be held to answer for a capital, or otherwise infamous crime, unless on a presentment or indictment of a Grand Jury." [b] By preventing prosecution except upon agreement of the grand jury (expressed through its indictment), the Fifth Amendment guarantees to persons charged by the federal government the benefit of a grand jury review of that charge. Of course, the amendment is limited to "infamous crimes," but, as interpreted by the Supreme Court, this phrase includes all federal felony prosecutions. See LaFave and Israel, § 15.1(a). In misdemeanor prosecutions, where the amend-

a. Several bibliographies, as well as various other materials on grand jury review can be found in *Hearings on H.R. 94 Before the Subcomm. on Immigration, Citizenship, and International Law of the House Comm. on the Judiciary,* 95th Cong., 1st Sess. (1977) (hereinafter cited as House Hearings). The most recent major study of grand jury screening is Emerson and Ames, *The Role of the Grand Jury and the Preliminary Hearing in Pretrial Screening* (1984) (hereinafter cited as Emerson and Ames), which also includes an extensive list of references.

b. Although the Fifth Amendment refers to prosecution by "presentment" as well as "indictment," federal law now provides only for use of the indictment. See Fed.R.Crim.P. 7. Historically, a presentment was a formal charge similar to an indictment except that it was prepared by the grand jury on its own initiative. Grand jury reports, discussed at p. 700 supra, sometimes are described today as "presentments," but the constitution quite clearly referred to the traditional presentment. See *United States v. Cox,* 342 F.2d 167 (5th Cir.1965).

ment does not apply, federal law permits the prosecutor to proceed either by indictment or information. See Fed.R.Crim.P. 7(a).

At the time of the adoption of the Fifth Amendment, all of the states also required that felony prosecutions be brought by indictment. Today, however, only about one-third of the states make a grand jury indictment mandatory for the prosecution of all felonies (although several additional states require an indictment for capital offenses). The remaining states permit prosecution either by indictment or information at the option of the prosecutor. Given that choice, prosecutors in these states regularly have chosen the information alternative for the vast majority of their prosecutions, and these states therefore are commonly described as "information" jurisdictions. See LaFave and Israel, § 15.1(b) (listing the various "information" and "indictment" states).

The movement away from compulsory prosecution by indictment began with Michigan's adoption of the information alternative in 1859, and several states (including California) soon followed Michigan's lead. As expected, such a revolutionary change in the processing of felony cases did not go unchallenged. Its constitutionality reached the Supreme Court in HURTADO v. CALIFORNIA, 110 U.S. 516, 4 S.Ct. 111, 28 L.Ed. 232 (1884). The Court there sustained a California first degree murder conviction in which prosecution had been initiated by information rather than indictment. *Hurtado* was one of the first rulings interpreting the Fourteenth Amendment due process clause, and Justice Matthews' opinion for the majority stressed the need for a flexible interpretation of the clause. Due process, Justice Matthews noted, should impose on the states only those "fundamental principles of liberty and justice which lie at the base of all our civil political institutions" and should emphasize the "substance" of those principles rather than their "forms and modes of attainment." The opinion concluded:

"Tried by these principles, we are unable to say that the substitution for a presentment or indictment by a grand jury of the proceeding by information, after examination and commitment by a magistrate, certifying to the probable guilt of the defendant, with the right on his part to the aid of counsel, and to the cross-examination of the witnesses produced for the prosecution, is not due process of law. It is, as we have seen, an ancient proceeding at common law, which might include every case of an offence of less grade than a felony, except misprision of treason; and in every circumstance of its administration, as authorized by the statute of California, it carefully considers and guards the substantial interest of the prisoner. It is merely a preliminary proceeding and can result in no final judgment, except as the consequence of a regular judicial trial, conducted precisely as in cases of indictments."

Justice Harlan's dissenting opinion stressed the history of the grand jury in English and American law and the recognition of the grand jury in the federal constitution. The dissent also stressed the need for screening by representatives of the community rather than by a magistrate, who will "hold office at the will of the government or at the will of the voters." The majority position in *Hurtado* has been reaffirmed in several subsequent cases. See, e.g., *Gaines v. Washington,* 277 U.S. 81, 48 S.Ct. 468, 72 L.Ed. 793 (1928); *Gerstein v. Pugh,* Note 1, p. 940 supra.

II. THE USE OF GRAND JURY INDICTMENTS

1. *Indictment jurisdictions: the use of waiver.* While the Fifth Amendment and the various state constitutional provisions requiring grand jury indictments do not mention the possibility of waiver, courts have almost uniformly held that these provisions do not preclude acceptance of a defense waiver. The New York Court of

Appeals once suggested that the New York constitutional provision requiring grand jury indictments established a jurisdictional prerequisite, see *Simonson v. Cahn,* 261 N.E.2d 246 (N.Y.1970), but the generally accepted view is that indictment provisions confer a "personal privilege" upon the defendant that can be made subject to waiver in much the same manner as other constitutional "privileges" (e.g., the right to jury trial). See *King v. State,* 473 S.W.2d 43 (Tex.Crim.App. 1971). Several courts have suggested, however, that since waiver of indictment was not permitted at common law, it should be accepted only if authorized by statute. Most indictment jurisdictions now have statutes or court rules allowing knowing and voluntary waivers, with the effect of the waiver being to permit the prosecution to proceed by information. A few permit waiver in all cases; several, like Federal Rule 6(b), permit waiver in all but capital cases; and a few restrict the availability of waivers to certain types of non-capital cases. Several states, however, continue to follow the common law rule and will not recognize waiver in any felony case. LaFave and Israel, § 15.1(d).

2. The rate of waivers varies substantially among indictment jurisdictions. During the 1960's, indictments were waived in federal courts in approximately 25% of all felony cases, but more recent figures show a waiver rate of less than 5%. Although state waiver rates tend not to be as high as the former federal rates, they readily may fall within the 10–15% range. What considerations lead the defense to agree to a waiver? Consider LaFave and Israel, § 15.1(d):

"Waivers are most frequently made where the defendant pleads guilty, and many such waivers are probably part of a plea bargain arrangement. Where defendant intends to go to trial, defense counsel often advise against waiver, although not because they anticipate that the grand jury will refuse to indict. Prosecution by indictment may offer the defense a potential procedural advantage since pleading defects in an indictment cannot be cured as readily by amendment as similar defects in an information. Also, if the jurisdiction precludes the use of hearsay before the grand jury, key witnesses will have to testify before the grand jury and that testimony ordinarily will be available for impeachment use at trial. On the other hand, there are situations in which a waiver will be to the advantage of the defense. In some instances, the defense may be concerned that the prosecutor will gain valuable preparation for trial in presenting the witnesses before the grand jury. Defendant also has an incentive to waive if he is in jail or would otherwise be inconvenienced by delay and his case cannot promptly be presented to the grand jury. Some defense counsel also prefer that charges be presented by information because they believe that trial jurors, contrary to the court's instructions, do give weight to the fact that another group of lay persons reviewed the case and issued an indictment."

3. *Information jurisdictions.* Prosecutors in information states retain the option to proceed by indictment, and the use of that alternative varies from jurisdiction to jurisdiction and from one judicial district to another in the same jurisdiction. See e.g., Emerson and Ames (study of two major districts in Arizona, with one using the indictment in 12% of its cases and the other 74%). Where the prosecutor has need for the grand jury's investigative authority, at least those charges developed through grand jury investigations will be brought by indictment. In several information states, however, prosecutors in most districts have found no need for grand jury investigations and prosecutions by indictment are viewed as a matter of "ancient history." In many other jurisdictions, grand jury indictments are regularly used, but in only a small percentage of felony prosecutions (e.g., 1–5%). The regular practice is to proceed by information and the indictment alternative is uti-

lized only where the grand jury's investigative authority is needed or there is some special reason (e.g., bypassing a preliminary hearing) for taking the case to the grand jury. See Note 8, p. 947 supra (discussing the reasons why a prosecutor in an information state might take a particular case to the grand jury). Finally, in several information states, the tradition in at least a few districts is to present most felony cases to the grand jury.

III. EVALUATING THE GRAND JURY'S PERFORMANCE

1. *The debate.* Are the indictment states merely "being stubborn" in refusing to offer their prosecutors the option of proceeding by information? Did the information states fail to go "far enough" when they retained an option of proceeding by indictment, rather than requiring that an information be used in all cases? Both questions are hotly debated today as they have been for over a century. While many of the arguments advanced are the same as those put forth by Bentham and other early critics of grand jury screening, others reflect subsequent changes in the criminal justice process, such as the emergence of the full-time, professional prosecutor, the heavy reliance on negotiated guilty pleas, and the general pressures of extremely heavy caseloads.

Current critics of the grand jury tend to fall into three groups. First, there are those who view grand jury review as essentially worthless. The grand jury, as they see it, is merely a "rubber stamp" for the prosecutor. Thus, the California Supreme Court noted in *Hawkins v. Superior Court,* 586 P.2d 916 (Cal.1978):

> "The grand jury is independent only in the sense that it is not formally attached to the prosecutor's office; though legally free to vote as they please, grand jurors virtually always assent to the recommendations of the prosecuting attorney, a fact borne out by available statistical and survey data. * * * The pervasive prosecutorial influence reflected in such statistics has led an impressive array of commentators to endorse the sentiment expressed by United States District Judge William Campbell, a former prosecutor: 'Today, the grand jury is the total captive of the prosecutor who, if he is candid, will concede that he can indict anybody, at any time, for almost anything before any grand jury.' "

Critics in this category view the grand jury as a totally ineffective screening device and see no hope for making it an even minimally effective source for independent review. The basic problem, as they see it, lies not in any particular aspects of grand jury practice (e.g., in the reliance on hearsay testimony), but in the basic structure of the grand jury process. A process which is non-adversary, which forces the jurors to rely on the prosecutor's investigative resources and legal advice,[a] and which allows the prosecutor to establish a close rapport with the grand jury,[b] will inevitably produce a screening agency that serves as no more than the "prosecutor's puppet." Accordingly, critics in this group would go beyond the position currently

a. See fn. a, p. 702 supra. A noteable exception to the prosecutor's role of primary legal advisor to the grand jury is found in Hawaii, which requires an "independent counsel appointed by law to advise the members of the grand jury regarding matters brought before it." Hawaii Const. Art. 1, § 11. See *State v. Kahlbaun,* 638 P.2d 309 (Hawaii 1981) (independent counsel need not be present throughout the grand jury proceeding, but must be in close proximity and readily available for consultation).

b. Consider, e.g., the advice offered to prosecutors in Coffey, *Preliminary Hearings and Presentation to the Grand Jury* in The Prosecutor's Deskbook (Healy and Manak, eds. 1971): "A proper relationship starts off with a personal knowledge or acquaintance of grand jurors by the district attorney. Try to get to know your grand jurors as early as possible. * * * [L]et them know you. Let them feel that they are personally acquainted with you, and hope that you can develop this acquaintance in a manner which will develop their admiration and respect for you both professionally and as a fellow human being."

taken in information states. They would preserve the grand jury for investigative purposes, but the prosecutor would not have an option to proceed by indictment. In every case, the prosecution would be required to proceed by information, combined with the preliminary hearing or other screening procedure that is attached to the information process. See *Hawkins,* Note 9, p. 948 supra.

A second group of critics of the grand jury favor the position currently taken by most information states. These critics view the grand jury as a minimally adequate screening agency, but contend that it usually is less effective and less efficient than the preliminary hearing. They reject the concept of having both a grand jury review and a preliminary hearing as requiring useless duplication. Accordingly, they argue that all states should give the prosecutor the option to proceed by information, and prosecutors then should regularly use that option, reserving the grand jury alternative for exceptional cases.

Critics in this second category maintain that the preliminary hearing, because it is an adversary proceeding, ordinarily will provide better protection against unwarranted prosecutions than a grand jury, even if one assumes the grand jury exercises its judgment independently of the prosecutor. These critics also stress the preliminary hearing's value as an open screening procedure, as opposed to the secret grand jury proceeding. This feature is particularly important today, they say, when so many cases are resolved by guilty plea rather than by trial. Finally, they argue, the preliminary hearing is preferable simply because it is more efficient. Empaneling and servicing a grand jury is costly in terms of space, manpower, and money. The grand jury also adds to the delay in processing cases since grand juries, particularly in rural areas, are not as readily available as magistrates. The critics also point to the "intricacies and complexities" of grand jury law, claiming that they spawn "uncertainty and additional litigation" and increase the likelihood of successful challenges based on "reasons unrelated to innocence." "In short," this second group of critics note, "any benefits to be derived from a requirement that all offenses be charged by grand jury indictment are * * * outweighed by the probability that the indictment process will be ineffective as a screening device, by the cost of the proceeding, and by the procedural intricacies involved." See N.A.C. Standards, *The Courts* 75 (1973). Use of the grand jury process is only justified, they argue, where the grand jury must review the evidence in any event in the course of a lengthy investigation or the nature of the case makes lay participation in screening especially valuable.

A third group of critics contend that the grand jury can be a satisfactory screening alternative, but that it needs substantial reform to curb prosecutorial power and prevent unworthy prosecutions. They call primarily for the following reforms (already in place in at least some jurisdictions): (1) requiring the court to fully inform the grand jurors of their independent authority and to impress upon them their obligations to screen out unworthy prosecutions; (2) giving the target the right to testify before the grand jury; (3) requiring the prosecutor to present all available exculpatory evidence; (4) forbidding the prosecutor's use of evidence which would be constitutionally inadmissible at trial; (5) prohibiting the use of hearsay testimony to support an indictment, except under narrowly defined circumstances; and (6) providing for a post-indictment pretrial hearing at which a judge or magistrate will review the transcript to ensure that there were no significant procedural violations and that the indictment was supported by sufficient evidence.[c]

c. Initially proposed in Arenella, *Reforming the Federal Grand Jury and the State Preliminary Hearing to Prevent Conviction Without Adjudication,* 78 Mich.L.Rev. 463 (1980), these reforms were subsequently adopted by the A.B.A. See A.B.A. *Grand Jury Policy and Model Act* (2d ed.

Supporters of the grand jury maintain that it is an extremely effective screening agency as it currently exists.[d] They note that, in most indictment jurisdictions, only a very small percentage of indictments result in trial dismissals for lack of substantial evidence. Most cases result in guilty pleas and those cases that go to trial rarely fail to survive a motion to dismiss. See e.g., Sullivan and Nachman, fn. d supra (citing a federal conviction rate of 85–90%). Supporters also argue that the grand jury is a better screening agency than the preliminary hearing. First, it brings a layman's sense of reality to the evaluation of the circumstances surrounding the alleged offense.[e] Second, its strength lies exactly where screening is most needed—in those cases where special factors, e.g., the involvement of politics or racial animosity, are likely to result in unjust accusations. The magistrate, they note, is restricted in his judgment of credibility (see Note 6, p. 956 supra), while the grand jury can act very much like a trial jury. Lay participation permits the grand jury to evaluate the prosecution's case in light of community notions of justice and fairness. Indeed, the grand jury has a recognized authority to disregard legally sufficient evidence and indict for a lesser offense or refuse to indict altogether. Only the grand jury, they argue, can act effectively to leaven the rigidity of the law.[f] (Critics respond

1982); Arenella, *Reforming the State Grand Jury System: A Model Grand Jury Act,* 13 Rutgers L.J. 1 (1981); Emerson and Day, *Grand Jury Reform: A Review of Key Issues* (1983).

d. Not all supporters take this position. See e.g., Sullivan and Nachman, *If It Ain't Broke, Don't Fix It: Why the Grand Jury's Accusatory Function Should Not Be Changed,* 75 J.Crim.L. & Criminology 1047 (1984), acknowledging that the grand jury is dominated by the prosecutor, but contending that the federal system does not need a better screening agency. The authors conclude that "the best safeguard against grand jury abuse" lies in the selection of able and fair prosecutors and internal controls within the prosecutor's office (e.g., the internal review process for indictment decisions employed in various U.S. Attorneys' offices).

e. Although critics contend that the grand jurors tend to "just sit there, like a bump on a log," the best available study found that jurors not infrequently asked questions of witnesses in the two districts studied. See Emerson and Ames, 100–06. Witnesses were questioned by grand jurors in 66% of the cases reviewed, although the median number of questions per witness was less than 3. In a case involving a breaking and entering into the home of a former model who allegedly walked by her windows in "varying stages of undress," the jurors "repeatedly questioned the testifying officer [for a high count of 29 questions] to determine whether police had explored the possibility that the victim had enticed the defendant into her house." See also Carp, p. 982 infra. ("The more bizarre, infamous, or salacious the case, the greater the likelihood that it will be among the small percentage of cases in which the grand jury carefully performs the investigation"). In the two counties studied in the Emerson and Ames report, the jurors put their questions directly to the witnesses. In some jurisdictions, prosecutors commonly request that they be allowed to screen the questions to ensure that they are "proper in form and content." LaFave and Israel, § 8.4(b). The Emerson and Ames study also noted occasional questions directed to the prosecutor concerning case strategy (e.g., "why was this witness used to present this evidence"), but the prosecutors responded by "pointing out the options open to the grand jury" while "declining to explain the strategy."

f. Indeed, supporters argue that the grand jury, because it operates in secrecy and gains a better perspective of prosecutorial policy, is a far more effective body in this regard than the petit jury, which is most likely to nullify only where the crime is petty or the extenuating circumstances substantial. Does the following case, described in Emerson and Ames, at p. 106, support that view: "One case involved a charge of theft by embezzlement against a 16-year-old (at the time of the crime) employee who failed to deposit one day's receipts consisting of an estimated $500 in cash and a small number of checks. At the time of the investigation, the father of the suspect told police she was out of state in a special disciplinary school. No further [action] was taken for a year until the victim notified police that the suspect was back in town and had approached the victim with an offer of restitution. When questioned by police, the suspect admitted committing the crime. The jurors asked 13 questions of the witness including specifics on the discovery of the theft; the status of the suspect as an adult or a juvenile; the nature of the school she attended; reasons for the long delay; and reasons that the offer of restitution was rejected. The witness was excused, and the grand jury asked nine legal questions focusing on the distinction between adults and juveniles and the issue of delay. One series of questions was aimed at determining why there was an additional delay of over six months between the suspect's return to the state and the filing of charges. * * * After closing with more questions * * *, the grand jury retired to deliberate. They announced their decision to end the inquiry without an indictment."

that instances of nullification are rare, and that many of the most famous cases of grand jury nullification may have involved little more than political favoritism.)

Supporters of mandatory grand jury review also reject the contention that grand jury screening is more costly than preliminary hearing screening. This may have been true in the past, they note, but it no longer is true, especially in those jurisdictions in which the modern preliminary hearing is virtually a mini-trial. Studies suggest that routine grand jury cases involve substantially less time than the routine preliminary hearing,[g] and there is no parallel in the grand jury process to the extensive preliminary hearings in some celebrated cases that have lasted several weeks and cost the state over $100,000. While the grand jury proceeding must bear the cost of the jurors, the preliminary hearing adds the cost of a magistrate and the defense counsel for the indigent defendant. So too, with defense counsel frequently seeking continuances, the preliminary hearing is likely to result in greater delay. Supporters contend that difficulties in scheduling a prompt grand jury review should arise only in rural areas, and appropriate provisions for waiver and bail should substantially alleviate the consequences of those delays. Supporters also argue that minor reforms could eliminate the legal intricacies that may cause inexperienced prosecutors difficulties in using the grand jury. They suggest, moreover, that the opportunities for highly technical defense challenges to the information process now are at least equal to those for challenging indictments.

Finally, supporters contend that grand jury review clearly comes out ahead when the symbolic impact of the information and indictment processes are compared. What the grand jury loses through a non-adversary, secret proceeding is more than offset by its inclusion of community representatives in the screening process. Participation of laymen contributes to public confidence in the system and thereby justifies grand jury review even in cases that are "open and shut." Supporters note that, in a system where most cases do not go to trial, it is especially important that "private citizens" are given an "active role" in the "front lines" of the criminal justice process.

2. *Statistics.* As suggested above, both proponents and critics of the grand jury often seek support for their positions in the available statistics relating to grand jury performance. See, e.g., *Hawkins v. Superior Court,* supra. The most commonly cited statistic is the percentage of cases in which the grand jury refuses to indict. That figure varies considerably, however, among different jurisdictions. The National Advisory Commission reported "no-bill" rates in major cities in indictment jurisdictions that ranged from 20% to less than 2%. See N.A.C. Standards, supra, at 75. Critics of the grand jury frequently point to the federal system where the return of a "no-bill" is almost a rare event. See Sullivan and Nachman, fn. d supra (in 1984, federal grand jurors returned 17,419 indictments and 68 "no true bills"). Supporters of the grand jury system respond that the low rate of no-bills merely reflects careful prosecutorial screening in anticipation of mandatory grand jury review. See, e.g., *In re Dymo Industries, Inc.,* 300 F.Supp. 532, 535 (N.D.Cal.1969) ("the very existence of the grand jury process serves as a deterrent against unwarranted accusations by the prosecuting agency"). They also point to the experience in New York, where

g. See e.g., Emerson and Ames, 51–54, 94 (median number of pages of testimony per case was 4 in county regularly using the grand jury; median for preliminary hearings was 28 in county regularly using that process, with more than half of those pages occupied by defense cross-examination). Critics of grand jury screening contend that the very brevity of the process in many districts, with testimony heard and indictments issued in less than 10 minutes, suggests the inadequacy of grand jury screening. Supporters respond that it suggests only that most cases are "open-and-shut."

grand juries receive a more complete presentation of available evidence (see pp. 1005–06 infra). Over the years, New York grand juries have refused to indict in approximately 10% of the cases presented to them and have reduced to misdemeanors an almost equal percentage of cases. This substantial screening rate exists, supporters emphasize, in a jurisdiction in which defendants commonly are entitled to a preliminary hearing prior to grand jury review. See House Hearings, 525. Critics note, however, that New York prosecutors sometimes present to grand juries cases in which they desire to reduce or drop charges. See N.Y.Crim.P.Law § 190.55(2)(a) (following a preliminary hearing bindover or waiver, case must be submitted to the grand jury). They suggest that the New York figures may be deceiving since the no-bills and reductions reflect, in part, cases in which the grand jury is merely following the prosecutor's recommendation. See generally Note, 2 Colum.J.L. & Soc.Prob. 88, 99 (1966).[h]

IV. VARIATIONS IN GRAND JURY SCREENING

Both supporters and critics commonly characterize grand jury screening as if its processes were uniform throughout the country. While the fundamental elements of a non-adversarial, secret proceeding are common to all grand juries, both information and indictment jurisdictions vary considerably in their treatment of other, less basic aspects of the grand jury's structure and procedures. Many of these variations relate to features that are designed to strengthen the grand jury's independence and to make the grand jury an effective screening agency. The most significant of these features are described below. To what extent are the differences in any one or more of the features likely to have a significant bearing on the quality of grand jury review?

1. *Selection procedure.* In most jurisdictions, grand jurors are drawn from the same constituency, and selected in the same manner, as the array of petit jurors. The federal system and the majority of the states use what is commonly described as a "random selection system." Jurors are selected at random from a list containing an extensive cross-section of the community, usually a voter-registration list. See p. 1269 infra (describing the Federal Jury Selection Act). A substantial group of states, however, continue to use a "key man" or "discretionary" selection system. This system may have one or two layers of discretion. In some jurisdictions, the "key persons" (usually civic leaders) will provide a list of nominees and the grand jurors will be randomly selected from that list. In others, the judge or jury commissioners also exercise discretion in selecting jurors from the list of nominees.

Both selection systems, to meet constitutional requirements, seek representation reflecting a cross-section of the community. However, the discretionary system tends to focus on persons who have been

h. The only major study that sought to determine the degree of disagreement between prosecutors and grand juries over a wide range of jurisdictions was the study conducted by Wayne Morse in the early 1930's. See Morse, *A Survey of The Grand Jury Systems,* 10 Or.L.Rev. 101, 295 (1931). This widely cited study covered 162 prosecutors from 21 states, with special emphasis on Ohio, Illinois, and New York. Out of 6,453 cases in which prosecutors expressed their own preferences as to disposition, the grand jury disagreed in 348, approximately 5%. Morse concluded, based on his study, that grand juries basically were "a fifth wheel in the administration of criminal justice." In a widely cited response, Professor Dession concluded that the Morse study proved very little. See Dession, *From Indictment to Information—Implications of The Shift,* 40 Yale L.J. 163, 178–79 (1932). Dession argued that most cases are "open and shut," and "in cases of this group, there could scarcely be many disagreements between prosecutor and grand jury as to *probable cause.*" The "reputation of the grand juries as indicting agencies should be made or broken," he noted, in the "small minority group" of cases that were not "open and shut." The Morse study, however, did not indicate what percentage of cases fell within this minority group or how that percentage compared to the 5% rate of disagreement between prosecutors and grand juries.

active in the community or have otherwise distinguished themselves in business, religious or social organizations. As a result, it also tends to have more jurors from the "upper social and economic elements of society" than a grand jury selected at random from a voter registration list.[a] See Carp, *The Harris County Grand Jury—A Case Study,* 12 Houston L.Rev. 90 (1974). In such a grand jury more likely to be an effective screening agency? See Id. (discretionary system produces jurors of the "intelligence and social efficacy [needed] to demand full due process from hardened, work-weary district attorneys"). Consider, however, Note 3 at p. 986 infra (discussing the constitutional difficulties that may be raised by a discretionary system).

2. *Size.* At common law, grand juries were composed of 23 jurors (a number selected as twice the size of the petit jury, with one juror being dropped to preclude ties). All but a handful of jurisdictions now permit somewhat smaller grand juries. Fed.R.Crim.P. 6(a), for example, requires a grand jury of "not less than 16 nor more than 23 members." (As a matter of practice, federal grand juries are impaneled with at least 19 jurors so replacements will not be necessary if a few jurors are forced to leave during the lengthy term. See House Hearings, 231). Many states impose a roughly similar size requirement. Several, however, use grand juries that are the same size as petit juries (12) or are even smaller (e.g., 7). Is the larger grand jury likely to be a more effective screening agency? Consider House Hearings, 51 (the grand jury "must be larger than the petit jury for it to be representative and fair" for there is "no opportunity for * * * the accused to screen or voir dire the grand jury for prejudice").

3. *Vote required to indict.* While no jurisdiction requires a unanimous vote to indict (compare Note 4, p. 1262 infra, discussing petit juries), the states vary considerably as to the percentage of jurors that must support an indictment. All require at least a bare majority. In jurisdictions with a minimum and maximum size, the number required for indictment commonly is set at a bare majority of the maximum size, which may constitute a much higher proportion when the jury drops down to minimum size. See, e.g., Fed.R.Crim.P. 6 (16–23 jurors, with 12 affirmative votes for indictment). Several states require a 3/4 vote, and a few have even higher requirements. See, e.g., Ohio R.Crim.P. 6(F) (7 of 9). Is a majority vote sufficient to provide efficient screening? See Carp, supra (divided votes were quite common in the juries surveyed for only one group of offenses, victimless sex crimes); Emerson and Ames, 105 (vote unanimous in 90% of the cases sampled).

4. *Grand jury term.* Grand jury terms usually are longer than petit jury terms, but they vary considerably. While some jurisdictions call grand jurors for a term of only a few months and bar an extension beyond several months, others have juries that often serve a full year and may be extended even longer. See e.g., Fed.R. Crim.P. 6(g)(18 month limit). Does a longer term make it more or less likely that the grand jury will be an effective screening agency? Consider Carp, supra (as the grand jury term progressed, fewer cases were discussed among the jurors and there were fewer divided votes).

5. *Evidentiary restrictions.* Some jurisdictions limit the grand jury to consideration of evidence that would be admissible at trial; others permit consideration of

a. Because of the longer grand jury term (see Note 4 infra), states using a random selection system tend to be more lenient in excusing prospective grand jurors than prospective petit jurors. Where excuses are granted so readily that only "volunteers" remain, the composition of the grand jury selected under a random selection system may be quite similar to that of a grand jury selected under a discretionary selection system. See VanDyke, *The Grand Jury: Representative or Elite?,* 28 Hastings L.J. 37 (1976).

certain types of inadmissible evidence; and still others permit the grand jury to rely entirely on inadmissible evidence (e.g., hearsay). See section 3 of this Chapter, discussing the different positions on evidentiary restrictions and their possible impact upon grand jury screening.

6. *Control over the evidence presented.* States vary in allocation of legal authority to determine what evidence will be presented before the grand jury. While grand juries commonly rely on the prosecutor's judgment, the prosecutor may actually have little or no legal authority to control the evidence presented. Some states do give the prosecutor the right to insist that the grand jury consider any evidence he desires to present, but others give the jury the right to refuse to hear that evidence (or to exclude the prosecutor while the jurors question the witness). See LaFave and Israel, § 8.4(b). In almost all jurisdictions, the grand jury may have subpoenas issued for additional evidence, not presented by the prosecutor, which it believes relevant to the case. Indeed, in some jurisdictions, the grand jury is under a statutory obligation to order production of additional evidence when it has "reason to believe" that the evidence will "explain away" the charge. See Cal. Pen.Code § 939.7. That obligation has been held, moreover, to require the prosecutor to inform the grand jury of exculpatory evidence known to him. See Note 10, p. 1003 infra. Finally, ultimate authority to control the evidence presented may rest with the court, since the prosecutor and grand jury must rely on the court's subpeona authority. See N.Y.Crim.P.Law § 190.50(3) (noting the court's authority to override the grand jury directive that the prosecutor present additional witnesses); *People v. Sears,* 273 N.E.2d 380 (Ill. 1971) (court may insist that grand jury receive certain evidence, but "the preservation of the historic independence of the grand jury * * * requires that such supervisory power be exercised only when failure to do so will effect a deprivation of due process or result in a miscarriage of justice").

7. *Testimony by a prospective defendant.* In almost all jurisdictions, the prospective defendant who knows that the grand jury is considering his case may communicate with the jury by letter, setting forth any relevant information in an objective fashion. See House Hearings, 1325 (noting, however, the careful line that must be drawn to avoid liability for attempting improperly to influence the grand jury). While the prospective defendant may also request the opportunity to testify, the grand jury may freely deny that request in most jurisdictions. See, e.g., Ky.R.Crim. P. 5.08. Several states, however, give the prospective defendant a right to testify if he so desires. See, e.g., N.Y.Crim.P.Law § 190.50(5)(a). For quite diverse views on the importance of such a right in avoiding inappropriate prosecutions, see House Hearings, 716, 1376–77, 1582–83. If the right is to be provided, should the prosecutor be required to give advance notice to persons who are potential defendants so they can exercise the right? See Id.

8. *Charge on jury authority.* Jurisdictions vary in their requirements as to what the jurors must be told as to their legal authority. For example, while jurors are told that the prosecutor will serve as their legal advisor, the precise scope of that role may not be defined. Jurors may not be told that the prosecutor's legal advice is limited to issues of law regarding the grand jury's authority, not matters of "opinion" as to the bearing of particular evidence. See Note 1, p. 1007 infra. They may not be told that even as to issues of law, they may seek additional legal advice from the presiding judge, whose legal opinions will prevail over any contrary advice from the prosecutor. Neither are they necessarily informed of their right to override the prosecutor's tactical advice concerning the calling and interrogation of witnesses. Several jurisdictions, however, require that the judge's charge explain all aspects of the grand jury's authority, in-

cluding the limited role of the prosecutor as legal advisor. See, e.g., Colo.Rev.Stat. § 16–5–204(3). See also *Federal Handbook for Grand Jurors* (1980) (describing for jurors both the history and importance of the grand jury's independent review function).

9. *Grand jury nullification.* One power of the grand jury not mentioned in grand jury statutes is the grand jury's authority to "nullify" the law—i.e., to refuse to indict notwithstanding the presence of sufficient evidence. Still, contrary to the prevailing view applicable to petit juries (see Note, 6, p. 1264 infra), many judges inform the grand jury that it "may even refuse to indict, although its attention is called to a clear violation, * * * when prosecution without mercy would result in a miscarriage of justice." *Charge to A Grand Jury* (Fletcher, J.), 18 F.R.D. 211, 214 (1955). Other judges, probably the majority, make no mention of the right to nullify. See, Federal Handbook, supra (including Model Charge).

10. *Standard for indictment.* In many states, the grand jury is directed to indict if it finds "probable cause" to believe that the accused has committed a crime. In others, however, it is directed to indict "when all the evidence taken together, if unexplained or uncontradicted, would warrant a conviction of the defendant." Since the trial jury would convict only if convinced of the accused's guilt beyond reasonable doubt, it generally is assumed that this "prima facie case" standard imposes a substantially more rigorous test than the traditional "probable cause" test. See Note 2 at p. 953 supra. Consider, however, LaFave and Israel, § 15.2(b) (where the charging court follows the common practice of simply quoting the prima facie standard language, without explaining the degree of proof needed to "warrant a conviction," the greater rigor of that test is likely to be lost on the jurors). See also Emerson and Ames, 107 (probable cause explained by charging judge as "more than fifty-fifty").

11. *Grand jury secrecy.* While grand jury secrecy requirements are designed in part to strengthen the grand jury's investigative function (see Note 4, p. 698 supra), they also are designed "to protect the independence of the grand jury" in its screening function. See *Posey v. United States,* 416 F.2d 545, 557 (5th Cir.1969). Indeed, the grand jury's duty to receive evidence in secret was inspired by a famous English case in which the prosecution sought to pressure the grand jury into indicting by presenting its evidence in public. See Schwartz, *Demythologizing the Historic Role of the Grand Jury,* 10 Am.Crim. L.Rev. 701 (1972) (describing the *Earl of Shaftesbury* case). Traditional secrecy requirements were designed to protect the grand jury's independence in three respects. First, individual jurors were ensured that their votes would not be revealed. This continues to be the case as both deliberations and individual votes remain beyond the pale of discovery even where there has been an indictment. See Fed.R.Crim.P. 6(e). Second, by keeping from the suspect his target status, secrecy requirements were designed to "insure the utmost freedom to the grand jury in its deliberations, and to prevent persons subject to indictment or their friends from importuning the grand jury." *United States v. Procter & Gamble Co.,* Note 4, p. 698 supra. Since most jurisdictions today do not swear witnesses to secrecy, these witnesses may lawfully warn the target or inform the press of the subject under investigation. Of course, criminal penalties for obstruction may still deter any improper contacts by the targets or their friends, but the witness' public disclosure can result in media attention and other forms of public pressure. Finally, common law secrecy requirements afforded the grand jury the protection of making its decision without the public ever knowing precisely what evidence was before the grand jury. This protection was always somewhat limited in those cases in which an indictment was issued since at least some of the same

evidence would be produced at trial (although not identified as grand jury evidence). Today, however, disclosure is far greater. Many jurisdictions require that grand jury testimony be transcribed, and transcription is fairly common in the remaining jurisdictions, which leave the decision to transcribe in the prosecutor's discretion. In several jurisdictions, the entire transcript is made available to the defendant following his indictment. See Note 13, p. 1006 infra. In the others, the defendant ordinarily can gain disclosure of the grand jury testimony of those witnesses who testify at trial. See fn. e, p. 1123 infra.

Where an indictment is not issued, the grand jury can feel fairly confident that the transcription of the evidence before it will not be disclosed (although witnesses may still make public what they told the grand jury). Disclosure may be ordered by the court to assist litigants in a civil case, but only upon a special showing of need. See fn. b, p. 698 supra. A disappointed prosecutor, bound by the oath of secrecy, certainly cannot make public the grand jury transcript in the hope of stirring public opposition to the grand jury. On the other hand, secrecy provisions in some jurisdictions are not sufficiently broad to keep the prosecutor from disclosing a fair amount about the case. See LaFave and Israel, § 8.5.

12. *Resubmission.* In the absence of a statutory directive to the contrary, the prosecutor may resubmit to another grand jury a case in which a previous grand jury had returned a no-bill. See *United States v. Thompson,* 251 U.S. 407, 40 S.Ct. 289, 64 L.Ed. 333 (1920), rejecting court control over resubmissions: "The power and duty of the grand jury to investigate is original * * * and is not therefore dependent for its exertion upon the approval or disapproval of the court; [it] * * * is continuous [in nature] and is therefore not exhausted or limited by adverse action taken by a [previous] grand jury or by its failure to act." However, several states have provisions requiring court approval for resubmission. Some permit resubmission only upon a court finding "that the prosecutor has discovered additional evidence." Colo.Rev.Stat. § 16–5–204(4)(e). Cf. Note 8, p. 457 supra (discussing preliminary hearing resubmissions).

SECTION 2. CHALLENGES TO GRAND JURY COMPOSITION

1. *Timing of the objection.* Most jurisdictions allow for a defense motion to dismiss an indictment based on the illegal composition of the grand jury provided that motion is made before trial. See e.g., Fed.R.Crim.P. 12(6)(F) (applicable to all objections "based on defects in the institution of the prosecution"). Several jurisdictions do not permit such an objection, however, if the defendant could have challenged the grand jury's composition prior to indictment. They provide for a pre-indictment challenge by a defendant who has been "held to answer" (i.e., a defendant whose case has been boundover for grand jury review) and bar a subsequent motion to dismiss if such a defendant had a reasonable opportunity to present the pre-indictment challenge. A reasonable opportunity is assumed to have existed where, at the time of the bindover, defendant had reason to know that the grand jury would not consider his case for several days, during which he might have filed his challenge. See LaFave and Israel, § 15.3(a). See also 28 U.S.C. § 1867(a) (objections based on the Federal Jury Selection Act must be made "within 7 days after the defendant discovered or could have discovered by the exercise of diligence, the grounds therefor"). Insofar as they govern challenges based upon constitutional grounds, might such restrictive timing requirements be viewed as imposing an unconstitutional burden on the defendant's right to a fairly selected grand jury? Compare in this connection, *Michel v. Louisiana,* 350 U.S. 91, 76 S.Ct. 158, 100 L.Ed. 83 (1955) and *Reece v. Georgia,* 350 U.S. 85, 76 S.Ct. 167, 100 L.Ed. 77

(1955). In *Michel,* the Court held valid "on its face" a state rule requiring that objections be raised within 3 days after the end of the grand jury's term (or before trial, if it came earlier) even though some defendants would have to raise their objections within 3 days after their indictment. On the facts of the case before it, the defendant had "a reasonable opportunity" to present his claim and the state therefore could refuse to consider his tardy motion, which was made 7 days after both the expiration of the grand jury term and the appointment of his counsel. *Reece* held invalid the application of a state law requiring that objections to the grand jury's composition be raised before indictment. In *Reece,* defendant had not been provided with counsel until the day after indictment, and counsel had moved to quash the indictment 6 days after their appointment. Consider also *Poret v. Louisiana,* 350 U.S. 91, 76 S.Ct. 158, 100 L.Ed. 83 (1955) (due process was not violated by application of the Louisiana rule noted in *Michel* to a defendant who had been a fugitive from justice over the period during which the motion should have been made).

2. *Racial discrimination.* The Supreme Court has long held that the Fourteenth Amendment's prohibition against racial discrimination applies to the selection of grand jurors as well as petit jurors. See *Ex parte Virginia,* 100 U.S. 339, 25 L.Ed. 676 (1880). While a state need not provide for grand jury review, that factor cannot excuse its denial of equal protection in the use of such review. See *Rose v. Mitchell,* p. 992 infra, at fn. 7. The standards applied in determining whether the selection of grand jurors violates equal protection are the same as those applied to the selection of the petit jury array. Indeed, several of the cases cited in the discussion of those standards at Note 4, p. 1275 infra, involved allegations of grand jury discrimination. See, e.g., *Castaneda v. Partida,* p. 1275 infra.

3. *Cross-section violations.* In *Taylor v. Louisiana,* reprinted at p. 1269 infra, the Supreme Court held that a jury selection system which discriminated against women violated the defendant's Sixth Amendment right to be tried by a jury drawn from a "fair cross-section of the community." Though *Taylor* was based on the Sixth Amendment, which specifically requires an "impartial jury," lower courts generally assumed that the "fair cross-section" requirement also applied to the grand jury. Was this a correct assumption? *Hobby v. United States,* described in Note 4 infra, suggests that it was. The Court there, without any extensive analysis of the issue, indicated that the same cross-sectional requirements apply to the grand jury as apply to the petit jury. In the course of measuring the impact of discrimination in the selection of the grand jury foreman, Chief Justice Burger's opinion proceeded from the premise that the selection of the grand jury panel must be in accord with "the representational due process values expressed in *Peters v. Kiff*" [a federal predecessor to *Taylor*]. Those values were described as requiring that "no 'large and identifiable segment of the community, [be] excluded from jury service.'" See also LaFave and Israel, § 15.3(c) (Supp): "While *Hobby* was a federal case, and the Court did note that the federal grand jury was 'a creature of the Constitution,' the discussion of cross-section values referred to due process interests rather than the Fifth Amendment's grand jury provision. Those interests apparently would be equally applicable to state grand juries, just as other due process values have been held applicable to both state and federal grand juries, even though, under *Hurtado* [p. 975 supra], due process does not require the state to provide grand jury review."

Should the states be given more leeway in the application of the cross-section requirement to grand juries? In particular, should a selection system be constitutional, notwithstanding decreased selection from some cognizable groups, if it is designed to produce jurors who (1) are more likely to have the "intelligence and social efficacy" arguably needed to exercise independent judgment in the grand jury setting (see Note 1, p. 981 supra) or (2) are less likely to suffer hardship from the longer grand jury term (see Note 4, p. 982 supra)? Lower courts have differed somewhat in their willingness to give consideration to the special role of the grand jury as compared to the petit jury. Consider, e.g., *Quadra v. Superior Court,* 403 F.Supp. 486 (N.D.Cal.1975) (though the grand jury in question only conducted investigations and did not issue indictments, "same stringent constitutional standards should apply"); *Adler v. State,* 594 P.2d 725 (Nev.1979) (selection system that relied entirely on volunteers did not violate fair cross-section requirement; "exclusion of persons not willing to serve operates without regard to race, sex, status, or ethnic background"); *United States ex rel. Chestnut v. Criminal Court,* 442 F.2d 611 (2d Cir.1971) (upholding a grand jury selection process which (1) relied on jurors who were invited rather than summoned to serve, (2) required that jurors be between the ages of 35 and 65, (3) excluded welfare recipients, and (4) included, but statistically underrepresented, certain ethnic and economic groups).

4. *Grand jury foreman.* A jury composition problem unique to the grand jury is presented in the selection of the foreman. Unlike the petit jury foreman, the grand jury foreman is appointed by the court. In *Rose v. Mitchell,* discussed at Note 8 infra, the Court "assume[d] without deciding that discrimination with regard to the selection of only the foreman requires that a subsequent conviction be set aside, just as if the discrimination proved had tainted the selection of the entire grand jury venire." Subsequent to *Rose,* the lower courts were presented with a spate of allegations of discrimination based on substantial statistical disparities between the percentages of minority foremen and minority grand jurors. The lower courts generally concluded that racial discrimination in the selection of the foreman rendered the indictment process constitutionally invalid and therefore required reversal of a conviction. See e.g., *United States v. Perez-Hernandez,* 672 F.2d 1380 (11th Cir.1982). At the same time, however, they almost invariably found insufficient proof of discrimination, as statistical disparities were held to be offset by evidence that judges had looked to factors others than race, such as managerial and leadership experience, in appointing foremen. However, HOBBY v. UNITED STATES, 468 U.S. 339, 104 S.Ct. 3093, 82 L.Ed.2d 260 (1984), cast new light on the issue.

The defendant in *Hobby* contended that the district court had erred in refusing to sustain a pretrial motion to dismiss that had alleged purposeful discrimination against blacks and women in the selection of a federal grand jury foreman. Since defendant was a white male, he had based his challenge on due process grounds rather than on equal protection grounds. (See Note 4, p. 1275 infra). The Supreme Court majority held that, assuming arguendo that racial and gender discrimination had entered into the selection of the foreman, "such discrimination does not warrant the reversal of a conviction of, and the dismissal of the indictment against, a white male bringing a claim under the due process clause."

Chief Justice BURGER'S opinion for the Court in *Hobby* initially cited two factors that would render the issue left open in *Rose* relevant to only a few jurisdictions. In *Rose,* it was noted, the state grand jury foreman was not a member of the randomly selected grand jury panel, but a person added to that panel by judicial appointment. Accordingly, discrimination in his selection affected the overall composition of the body of jurors voting on the indictment. In the federal system (and in most state systems), in contrast, the foreman was appointed from among the randomly selected panel members; no juror derived his authority to sit on the grand jury from a discriminatory selection process. Also, in *Rose*. the state law gave the foreman substantial powers that might be used to influence the substance of the indictment (e.g., the authority to issue subpoenas for witnesses). In the federal system (and most state systems), the grand jury foreman was confined to a largely ministerial role. Accordingly, as the majority saw it, discrimination in the selection of the federal grand jury foreman did not deprive the defendant of constitutionally protected "representational due process values" in the jury's composition, nor did it result in fundamental unfairness in the jurors' consideration of the indictment. There thus was "no basis upon which to reverse petitioner's conviction or dismiss the indictment." Granting such relief simply to deter discrimination, the Court added, was inappropriate even for the exercise of its supervisory powers over the federal judicial process. It was "fully satisfied" that district judges, on their own initiative, would "see to it that no citizen is excluded from consideration on account of race, color, religion, sex, national origin or economic status." [a]

In distinguishing *Rose,* Chief Justice Burger also stressed the due process grounding of the claim presented in *Hobby.* That claim, he noted, was distinguishable from the equal protection claim brought by the two black defendants in *Rose.* "As members of the class allegedly excluded from service as the grand jury foreman, the *Rose* defendants had suffered the injuries of stigmatization and prejudice associated with racial discrimination." Why should such injuries have a bearing on the remedy of dismissal of the indictment? Was the Chief Justice here adopting a philosophy more in line with Justice Marshall's dissent (see fn. a supra)? Or was he suggesting that such injuries might have a bearing upon the fairness of the criminal justice process in evaluating the case against the minority defendant? See LaFave and Israel, § 15.3 (Supp.): "When a court has discriminated against a juror on the basis of his race, that may suggest that the same prejudice has been carried over by the court (and, perhaps, even by the grand jury which witnessed the discrimination) in its treatment of the defendant."

5. *Statutory violations.* Most jurisdictions recognize certain statutory violations in selection procedures that will require dismissal of the indictment, though they fall short of constitutional error. Ordinarily, however, the statutory violations must be so significant as to create a substantial possibility of prejudice, if not "actual prejudice." See, e.g., 28 U.S.C. 1867(a) (requiring a "substantial failure to comply" with statutory procedures). A challenge can also be brought on the seating of a juror who did not meet the statutory prerequisites for jury service (e.g., was not a citizen). However, dismissal will be granted only if, after deducting the number of the jurors not legally qualified, the number of votes supporting the indictment does not meet the statutory prerequisite. See, e.g., Fed.R.Crim.P. 6(b)(2).

6. *Pre-indictment publicity.* Does the federal constitution prohibit indictment by a grand jury that may have been "prejudiced" against the defendant as a result of adverse pre-indictment publicity? Cf. Ch. 23, § 1 (discussing the impact of pretrial publicity on the selection of petit jurors). In *Beck v. Washington,* 369 U.S. 541, 82 S.Ct. 955, 8 L.Ed.2d 98 (1962), a

a. Dissenting in *Hobby,* Marshall, J. (joined by Brennan and Stevens, JJ.) argued that the Court had erred "in its assessment of (1) the dimension of the injury to the criminal justice system caused by discrimination in the selection of grand jury foreman, (2) the dimensions of the injury to an individual defendant, and (3) the relative social costs that would likely be imposed by dismissing petitioner's indictment compared to the costs that are likely to be exacted by the Court's resolution of this case." Justice Marshall stressed the "established principle of this Court's jurisprudence * * * that the injury caused by race and sex discrimination in the formation of the grand jury and petit jury is measured not only in terms of the actual prejudice caused to individual defendants, but also in terms of injury done to public confidence in the integrity of the judicial process."

divided Court found it unnecessary to determine whether a state violated due process in accepting an indictment issued by a grand jury allegedly prejudiced by adverse publicity. The petitioner in *Beck* "did not contend that any particular grand juror was prejudiced or biased," but argued "that the judge impaneling the grand jury had breached his duty to ascertain * * * whether any [grand] prospective juror had been influenced by the adverse publicity and that this error had been compounded by his failure to adequately instruct the grand jury concerning bias and prejudice." The plurality opinion rejected this claim. The presiding judge had informed the grand jury of the subject of the investigation (possible crimes committed by officers of the Teamsters Union) and had asked whether they were conscious of any prejudice in the matter. Three jurors who acknowledged possible prejudice were excused, as were three others who had been members of unions affiliated with the Teamsters Union. The judge did not admonish the grand jurors to disregard previous news reports, but "[t]aking the instructions as a whole, they made manifest that the jurors were to sift the charges by careful investigation, interrogation of witnesses, and examinations of records, not by newspaper stories." The plurality concluded: "[E]ven if due process would require a state to furnish an unbiased body once it resorted to grand jury procedure—a question upon which we do not remotely intimate any view—we have concluded that Washington, so far as is shown by the record, did so in this case."

Most lower courts have assumed that the issue left open in *Beck* would be answered in the negative. Many take the position that prejudicial pre-indictment publicity cannot justify the dismissal of an indictment "since the lack of impartiality of a grand jury is not a ground for dismissal." *Jones v. State,* 385 N.E.2d 426 (Ind.1979). They rely basically on the rationale advanced by various lower courts in rejecting other types of bias challenges (see Note 6 infra):

"The basic theory of the functions of a grand jury, does not require that grand jurors should be impartial and unbiased. In this respect, their position is entirely different from that of petit jurors. The Sixth Amendment to the Constitution of the United States expressly provides that the trial jury in a criminal case must be 'impartial.' No such requirement in respect to grand juries is found in the Fifth Amendment, which contains the guaranty against prosecutions for infamous crimes unless on a presentment or indictment of a grand jury. It is hardly necessary to be reminded that each of these Amendments was adopted at the same time as a part of the group consisting of the first ten Amendments. A grand jury does not pass on the guilt or innocence of the defendant, but merely determines whether he should be brought to trial. It is purely an accusatory body. This review can be demonstrated by the fact that a grand jury may undertake an investigation on its own initiative, or at the behest of one of its members. In such event, the grand juror who instigated the proceeding that may result in an indictment, obviously can hardly be deemed to be impartial, but he is not disqualified for that reason." *United States v. Knowles,* 147 F.Supp. 19, 21 (D.D.C. 1957).

Other courts rejecting challenges based on pre-indictment publicity stress the administrative difficulties that would be presented by recognition of such a challenge. See Note, 39 U.Chi.L.Rev. 761, 776 (1972). While voir dire by defense counsel commonly is used to determine the impact of pretrial publicity upon prospective trial jurors, defense voir dire is not feasible in the non-adversary grand jury proceeding. A judicial inquiry into possible juror bias, such as that conducted in *Beck,* ordinarily also is not feasible; the court usually charges the grand jury only at the start of its term and is not familiar with all of the cases it will consider during the term. But consider *State v. Haberski,* 449 A.2d 373 (Me.1982) (although defendant brought the publicity to the attention of the presiding judge before the case was presented to the grand jury, that judge did not commit error in refusing to examine the jurors in camera).

Consider also the argument advanced in *People ex rel. Sears v. Romiti,* 277 N.E.2d 705, 710–11 (Ill.1971): "The adverse effect of prejudicial publicity upon the trial of a defendant can be eliminated or alleviated by transferring the case for trial in another county. This remedy is unavailable, however, in the case of pre-indictment publicity, for an indictment must be returned by a grand jury of the county in which the alleged offense occurred. To permit such an attack upon an indictment would tend to immunize persons involved in events upon which the news media concentrated their attention." See also LaFave and Israel, § 15.3(e) ("courts [also] stress that the 'taint' of any preindictment publicity that may have been 'inherently prejudicial' will be purged by the deliberations of an untainted petit jury").

Accepting the premise that due process requires the state to furnish an unbiased grand jury, several federal courts have suggested that an indictment could be dismissed on the basis of prejudicial pretrial publicity in an appropriate case. However, those courts have also concluded that it is inappropriate in the grand jury setting to apply the concept of "inherently prejudicial publicity," which sometimes is used to presume petit juror bias. See ch. 23, § 1. To support a dismissal, the defendant must show "actual bias" on the part of the seated jurors. How would a defendant make such a showing? Consider LaFave and Israel, § 15.3(e): "Since defendant has no right to voir dire the grand jurors and access to the grand jury transcript is both difficult to obtain and not very likely to reveal juror bias, this required showing has been aptly characterized as rendering preindictment publicity claims almost 'inevitably doomed as a matter of law,'" quoting *United States v. Sweig,* 316 F.Supp. 1148 (S.D.N.Y.1970). In *Sweig,* supra, the court suggested that dismissal without such a showing might be based on a "prosecutorial misconduct" theory (see Note 6, p. 1010 infra) where the adverse publicity was generated by the government.

7. *Personal bias.* In his dissent in *Beck v. Washington,* Note 6 supra, Justice Douglas asked: "Could we possibly sustain a conviction obtained in either a state or federal court where the grand jury that brought the charge was composed of the accused's political enemies?" Due process, Justice Douglas suggested, would surely require that the conviction be reversed on the basis of grand jury bias. Several federal courts, however, have held an indictment may not be challenged on the ground that a grand juror lacked impartiality due to some special interest or knowledge about the case. In adopting Federal Rule 6(b), the Supreme Court rejected a preliminary draft proposal to allow an objection to a grand juror "on the ground that * * * a state of mind exists on his part which may prevent him from acting impartially." 1943 Preliminary Draft, Rule 7(b)(1). Decisions rejecting bias objections often rely upon the rejection of that proposal as well as the rationale of *Knowles,* quoted in Note 6 supra.

A few federal courts have suggested that bias objections can be recognized under the Fed.R. 6(b) provision permitting a challenge to an "unqualified" juror. The requirement that grand jurors be unbiased, they note, follows from the language and reasoning of various Supreme Court decisions, particularly the equal protection decisions barring racial discrimination in the grand jury selection process (see Note 2 supra). As Justice Douglas noted in his *Beck* dissent, the "systematic exclusion of Negroes from grand jury service" was barred because it "infects the accusatory process * * * [with] unfairness" in much the same way as juror bias infects the process. See also *Costello v. United States,* p. 993 infra, where the Court referred to the validity on its face of "an indictment returned by a legally constituted and *unbiased* grand jury" (emphasis added). But see *Hopkins v. State,* 329 A.2d 738 (Md.App.1974): "Mr. Justice Douglas' interpretation of [the racial discrimination cases] * * * overlooks the fact that it is the manner of selection—as opposed to the mental attitude of those selected—that violates the equal protection * * * [clause]. Exclusion of Negroes from panels is not indicative of the mental attitude of white persons actually selected * * *."

A substantial minority of the states recognize at least limited bias objections, usually on the basis of statutory provisions specifically authorizing such objections. In several states, those provisions refer only to persons having a specific relationship to the case. See, e.g., N.M.Stat. § 31–6–3 ("witness against the person indicted"); Tenn.R.Crim.P. 6(c)(1) ("prosecutor," victim, or related to the victim "by blood or marriage within the sixth degree"). Other states, however, authorize challenges to any juror whose "state of mind prevent[s] him from acting impartially." Minn.R.Crim. 18.02(1). In practice, however, such provisions may allow successful challenges only where the juror had some special relationship to the victim, the target, or a key witness.[b] In such jurisdictions, the presiding judge will call the jurors' attention to the bias qualification and request that they contact him if they have doubts as to their ability to act impartially in a particular case. They may also be told that "bias" for this purpose requires a mind closed as to the particular case, not simply a "strong feeling" about the type of crime. See *State v. Salazar,* 557 P.2d 552 (Ariz.App.1976). Unless a juror informs the judge of some difficulties, has a special relationship to one of the parties,[c] or has previously made a public statement that reveals a closed mind, it will be most difficult for the defendant to establish challengable bias. See LaFave and Israel, § 8.5(a) (noting the usual prohibition against requiring jurors to reveal their deliberations); *State v. Warren,* 312 A.2d 535 (Me.1973) ("to initiate a possible invasion of the traditional secrecy and independence of a grand jury by allowing a post-indictment voir dire" would require a preliminary showing of likely prejudice). Consider also, *United States v. Waldbaum,* 593 F.Supp. 967 (E.D.N.Y.1984) (court might be willing to presume prejudice where juror's interest suggested a "potential for substantial emotional involvement, adversely affecting impartiality" but such a showing had not been made by a survey showing that a substantial percentage of the grand jurors may have been shoppers who used the double coupons that defendant supermarket chains allegedly had conspired to eliminate).

8. *Post-conviction review.* Assume that a defendant makes a timely objection to the grand jury's composition on a ground recognized under the federal constitution or state law. Assume also that the objection is improperly denied by the trial judge, interlocutory appeal is unavailable, and the

b. Note, however, that in at least one situation, the grand jurors themselves may be witnesses to the crime for which they indict. See *People v. Ward,* 323 N.Y.S.2d 316 (App.Div.1971), rejecting the argument that due process precluded a grand jury from indicting a person for contempt committed before the same grand jury. Compare *In re Murchison,* 349 U.S. 133, 75 S.Ct. 623, 99 L.Ed. 942 (1955), holding unconstitutional a state procedure permitting the same judge who served as a "one-man grand jury" (see Note 7, p. 700 supra) to hold a person in contempt based upon his grand jury testimony before that judge.

c. Such persons commonly will be excused by the judge (usually upon recommendation of the prosecutor) even in those jurisdictions that do not recognize bias objections to grand jurors. See, e.g., *United States v. Maine Lobster Co.,* 160 F.Supp. 122 (D.Me.1957), where the prosecutor brought to the court's attention the need to excuse a lobster fisherman serving on a grand jury investigating an alleged dealer conspiracy to limit prices paid to fishermen. But cf. *Hopkins v. State,* supra, (upholding an indictment by a grand jury which included a police officer), which cited as currently valid authority a series of nineteenth century cases holding persons "not disqualified to serve" though they were relatives of the accused or the victim.

case goes to trial. On appeal from a subsequent conviction, should the illegality in the grand jury's composition now be viewed as a harmless error? In *Cassell v. Texas,* 339 U.S. 282, 70 S.Ct. 629, 94 L.Ed. 839 (1950), Justice Jackson, dissenting, argued that racial discrimination in the selection of the grand jury should constitute harmless error where the defendant had been convicted by a fairly selected petit jury. The majority rejected that contention without discussion and reversed on the basis of grand jury discrimination alone. In ROSE v. MITCHELL, 443 U.S. 545, 99 S.Ct. 2993, 61 L.Ed.2d 739 (1979), the majority found Justice Jackson's contention worthy of discussion, but it was again rejected. Disagreeing with the majority, Justice STEWART, joined by Justice Rehnquist, argued that "the time had come to acknowledge that Justice Jackson's [position in *Cassell*] is unanswerable." Justice Stewart stressed that "any possible prejudice" to the defendant "disappears when a constitutionally valid trial jury later finds him guilty beyond a reasonable doubt." Justice Stewart acknowledged that other interests also are "implicated" by discrimination in the selection of the grand jury (e.g., "the compelling constitutional interest of our Nation in eliminating all forms of racial discrimination"), but he contended that those interests could be "fully vindicated" by means other than setting aside valid criminal convictions (e.g., civil actions and pretrial defense objections). In response to Justice Stewart's argument, Justice BLACKMUN'S opinion for the Court (joined in this part by Justices Brennan, White, Marshall and Stevens) noted:

"This Court, of course, consistently has rejected this argument. * * * We decline now to depart from this long-standing consistent practice, and we adhere to the Court's previous decisions. Discrimination on account of race was the primary evil at which the Amendments adopted after the War Between the States, including the Fourteenth Amendment, were aimed. * * * Discrimination on the basis of race, odious in all aspects, is especially pernicious in the administration of justice. Selection of members of a grand jury because they are of one race and not another destroys the appearance of justice and thereby casts doubt on the integrity of the judicial process. The exclusion from grand jury service of Negroes, or any group otherwise qualified to serve, impairs the confidence of the public in the administration of justice. As this Court repeatedly has emphasized, such discrimination 'not only violates our Constitution and the laws enacted under it but is at war with our basic concepts of a democratic society and a representative government.' * * * Because discrimination on the basis of race in the selection of members of a grand jury thus strikes at the fundamental values of our judicial system and our society as a whole, the Court has recognized that a criminal defendant's right to equal protection of the laws has been denied when he is indicted by a grand jury from which members of a racial group purposefully have been excluded. For this same reason, the Court also has reversed the conviction and ordered the indictment quashed in such cases without inquiry into whether the defendant was prejudiced in fact by the discrimination at the grand jury stage. * * * We do not deny that there are costs associated with this approach. But the remedy here is in many ways less drastic than in situations where other constitutional rights have been violated. In the case of a Fourth or Fifth Amendment violation, the violation often results in the suppression of evidence that is highly probative on the issue of guilt. Here, however, reversal does not render a defendant 'immune from prosecution,' nor is a subsequent reindictment and reprosecution 'barred altogether.' * * * In any event, we believe such costs as do exist are out-weighed by the strong policy the Court consistently has recognized of combatting racial discrimination in the administration of justice. And regardless of the fact that alternative remedies remain to vindicate the rights of those members of the class denied the chance to serve on grand juries, the fact is that permitting challenges to unconstitutional state action by defendants has been, and is, the main avenue by which Fourteenth Amendment rights are vindicated in this context."

SECTION 3. CHALLENGES TO THE EVIDENCE BEFORE THE GRAND JURY

COSTELLO v. UNITED STATES

350 U.S. 359, 76 S.Ct. 406, 100 L.Ed. 397 (1956).

MR. JUSTICE BLACK delivered the opinion of the Court.

We granted certiorari in this case to consider a single question: "May a defendant be required to stand trial and a conviction be sustained where only hearsay evidence was presented to the grand jury which indicted him?"

Petitioner, Frank Costello, was indicted for wilfully attempting to evade payment of income taxes due the United States for the years 1947, 1948 and 1949. The charge was that petitioner falsely and fraudulently reported less income than he and his wife actually received during the taxable years in question. Petitioner promptly filed a motion for inspection of the minutes of the grand jury and for a dismissal of the indictment. His motion was based on an affidavit stating that he was firmly convinced there could have been no legal or competent evidence before the grand jury which indicted him since he had reported all his income and paid all taxes due. The motion was denied. At the trial which followed the Government offered evidence designed to show increases in Costello's net worth in an attempt to prove that he had received more income during the years in question than he had reported. To establish its case the Government called and examined 144 witnesses and introduced 368 exhibits. All of the testimony and documents related to business transactions and expenditures by petitioner and his wife. The prosecution concluded its case by calling three government agents. Their investigations had produced the evidence used against petitioner at the trial. They were allowed to summarize the vast amount of evidence already heard and to introduce computations showing, if correct, that petitioner and his wife had received far greater income than they had reported. We have held such summarizations admissible in a "net worth" case like this.

Counsel for petitioner asked each government witness at the trial whether he had appeared before the grand jury which returned the indictment. This cross-examination developed the fact that the three investigating officers had been the only witnesses before the grand jury. After the Government concluded its case, petitioner again moved to dismiss the indictment on the ground that the only evidence before the grand jury was "hearsay," since the three officers had no first-hand knowledge of the transactions upon which their computations were based. Nevertheless the trial court again refused to dismiss the indictment, and petitioner was convicted. The Court of Appeals affirmed. * * * Petitioner here urges: (1) that an indictment based solely on hearsay evidence violates that part of the Fifth Amendment providing that "No person shall be held to answer for a capital, or otherwise infamous crime, unless on a presentment or indictment of a Grand Jury * * *." and (2) that if the Fifth Amendment does not invalidate an indictment based solely on hearsay we should now lay down such a rule for the guidance of federal courts. * * * [N]either the Fifth Amendment nor any other constitutional provision prescribes the kind of evidence upon which grand juries must act. The grand jury is an English institution, brought to this country by the early colonists and incorporated in the Constitution by the Founders. There is every reason to believe that our constitutional grand jury was intended to operate substantially like its English progenitor. The basic purpose of the English grand jury was to provide a fair method for instituting criminal proceedings against persons believed to have committed crimes. Grand jurors were selected from the body of the people and their work was not hampered by rigid procedural or evidential rules. In fact, grand jurors could act on their own knowledge and were free to make their presentments or indictments on such information as they deemed satisfactory. Despite its broad power to institute criminal proceedings the grand jury grew in popular favor with the years. It acquired an independence in England free from control by the Crown or judges. Its adoption in our Constitution as the sole method for preferring charges in serious criminal cases shows the high place it held as an instrument of justice. And in this country as in England of old the grand jury has convened as a body of laymen, free from technical rules, acting in secret, pledged to indict no one because of prejudice and to free no one because of special favor. As late as 1927 an English historian could say that English grand juries were still free to act on their own knowledge if they pleased to do so. And in 1852 Mr. Justice Nelson on circuit could say "No case has been cited, nor have we been able to find any, furnishing an authority for looking into and revising the judgment of the grand jury upon the evidence, for the purpose of determining whether or not the finding was founded upon sufficient proof * * *." *United States v. Reed,* 27 Fed. Cas. 727, 738 [1852].

In *Holt v. United States,* 218 U.S. 245, 31 S.Ct. 2, 54 L.Ed. 1021 [1910], this Court had to decide whether an indictment should be quashed because supported in part by incompetent evidence. Aside from the incompetent evidence "there was very little evidence against the accused." The Court refused to hold that such an indictment should be quashed, pointing out that "The abuses of criminal practice would be enhanced if indictments could be upset on such a ground." The same thing is true where as here all the evidence before the grand jury was in the nature of "hearsay." If indictments were to be held open to challenge on the ground that there was inadequate or incompetent evidence before the grand jury, the resulting delay would be great indeed. The result of such a rule would be that before trial on the merits a defendant could always insist on a kind of preliminary trial to determine the competency and adequacy of the evidence before the grand jury. This is not required by the Fifth Amendment. An indictment returned by a legally constituted and unbiased grand jury, like an information drawn by the prosecutor, if valid on its face, is enough to call for trial of the charge on the merits. The Fifth Amendment requires nothing more.

Petitioner urges that this Court should exercise its power to supervise the administration of justice in federal courts and establish a rule permitting defendants to challenge indictments on the ground that they are not supported by adequate or competent evidence. No persuasive reasons are advanced for establishing such a rule. It would run counter to the whole history of the grand jury institution, in which laymen conduct their inquiries unfettered by technical rules. Neither justice nor the concept of a fair trial requires such a change. In a trial on the merits, defendants are entitled to a strict observance of all the rules designed to bring about a fair verdict. Defendants are not entitled, however, to a rule which would result in interminable delay but add nothing to the assurance of a fair trial. Affirmed.

MR. JUSTICE CLARK and MR. JUSTICE HARLAN took no part in the consideration or decision of this case.

MR. JUSTICE BURTON, concurring.

I agree with the denial of the motion to quash the indictment. In my view, however, this case does not justify the breadth of the declarations made by the Court. I assume that this Court would not preclude an examination of grand jury action to ascertain the existence of bias or prejudice in an indictment. Likewise, it seems to me that if it is shown that the grand jury had before it no substantial or rationally persuasive evidence upon which to base its indictment, that indictment should be quashed. To hold a person to answer to such an empty indictment for a capital or otherwise infamous federal crime robs the Fifth Amendment of much of its protective value to the private citizen.

Here, as in *Holt,* substantial and rationally persuasive evidence apparently was presented to the grand jury. * * * At the trial, with preliminary testimony laying the foundation for it, the same testimony constituted an important part of the competent evidence upon which the conviction was obtained. To sustain this indictment under the above circumstances is well enough, but I agree with Judge Learned Hand that "if it appeared that no evidence had been offered that rationally established the facts, the indictment ought to be quashed; because then the grand jury would have in substance abdicated." 221 F.2d 668, 677 [1955]. * * *

NOTES ON EVIDENTIARY CHALLENGES

A. THE RATIONALE OF COSTELLO

1. *The relevance of history.* To what extent should the traditional practices of the grand jury, as developed by the time of the Constitution's adoption, control the Court's interpretation of the Fifth Amendment? Commentators have argued that the grand jury today operates in such a substantially different setting than the grand jury of the late eighteenth century that fulfillment of its screening role now requires the "judiciary * * * to take more positive action to ensure that the grand jury functions effectively." Johnston, *The Grand Jury—Prosecutorial Abuse of the Indictment Process,* 65 J.Crim.L. & Criminology 157 (1974). While the late eighteenth century grand jury surely considered evidence that would be inadmissible at trial, it did not have the assistance of a legally trained prosecutor. Cases were presented by the sheriff, his clerk, or a justice of the peace, and even that officer was not necessarily present when the evidence was heard. See generally House Hearings, 57, 68–69 (statement of Professor Scott). With the development of the office of the modern prosecutor, it is argued, there is less room for grand jury independence and a greater capacity in the grand jury, assisted by its legal advisor, to distinguish between admissible and inadmissible evidence. Thus, it is noted, as early as 1872, Justice Field, in his charge to a grand jury, directed it to receive "only legal evidence, to the exclusion of mere reports." *Charge to Grand Jury,* 30 F.Cas. 992, 993 (C.C.D.Cal.1872). See House Hearings, 647, 648–53 (statement of Professor Friedman). Do these changes in the structure of grand jury review undercut Justice Black's reliance upon history in *Costello?* [a]

2. *Costello's unstated premises.* Commentators have suggested three different premises which may underlie the *Costello* ruling. Although not made explicit in Justice Black's opinion, these premises, it is argued, furnish the strongest support for the Court's ruling. The three premises, each offering a different view of the grand jury's screening function, are summarized below. Does *Costello* necessarily rest on any of the three?

a. Justice Black also notes that grand jurors traditionally "could act on their own knowledge." This authority, critics argue, has considerably less significance as applied to modern grand juries. While grand jurors may utilize their personal knowledge in initiating an investigation, they lack the familiarity with events in their local district that would permit them to indict on the basis of personal knowledge. Several jurisdictions now provide that a grand juror with sufficient information to give evidence relating to a crime must be sworn like any other witness.

(1) *Costello,* it is argued, reflects the view that the grand jury's primary goal is to protect the innocent against standing trial, not to protect those who simply are not likely to be convicted. Under this view, since the grand jury should be concerned with the probability of the suspect's factual guilt, rather than the probability of his conviction, whether or not the prosecution's evidence would be admissible at trial is basically irrelevant. See also Goldstein, *The State and the Accused: Balance of Advantage in Criminal Procedure,* 69 Yale L.J. 1149, 1171–72 (1960) (*Costello* 's analysis rests on the assumption that the "accused will get his fair, 'judicial,' hearing at his trial"). But see Arenella, Note 8 infra (*Costello* errs in assuming that the trial will protect "the system's legal guilt requirements" since most cases are disposed of by a guilty plea, which may be accepted without regard to whether the person could be convicted at trial).

(2) *Costello,* it is argued, rests on the premise that prosecutors are most unlikely to seek indictments in cases in which they have substantial incompetent evidence, but not enough competent evidence to convict at trial. Prosecutors are characterized as too busy and too concerned about their "batting averages" to seek indictments where they do not have a good chance of success at trial. Frankel and Naftalis, *The Grand Jury: An Institution on Trial* 25–26 (1977).[b] Where a prosecutor seeks an indictment on the basis of hearsay, he almost certainly will have the live testimony available at trial. Though he may have overestimated the persuasiveness of that testimony, it still should be sufficient to establish probable cause. *Costello,* accordingly, recognized that requiring the prosecutor to present the actual trial witnesses before the grand jury would be a largely wasted effort. Proponents of this view acknowledge that occasionally prosecutorial vindictiveness will produce an indictment lacking sufficient evidentiary support, but they maintain that the grand jury generally should be able to screen those cases, based on obvious gaps in the prosecution's case or the unjust nature of the charges, without regard to the competency of the evidence presented.

(3) *Costello,* it is argued, rests on the premise that the grand jury must be allowed to consider material that would not be admissible at trial if it is to be able to review the prosecutor's decision apart from its legal merits. A grand jury must have the capacity to seek out information, beyond the crime itself, that relates to the same factors the prosecution will consider in deciding whether to charge. Yet, much of this information (e.g., the accused's prior record) would be inadmissible at trial. If the Court had held the *Costello* indictment invalid because it rested on incompetent evidence, that ruling, it is argued, would have opened the door to challenges to almost any indictment by a grand jury that sought to consider the complete picture. Cf. Woodward and Ahrens, *The Iowa Grand Jury,* 26 Drake L.Rev. 241 (1976).

3. *Administrative burdens.* Several commentators have suggested that the *Costello* ruling was influenced primarily by the Court's assumption that a substantial burden would be imposed on the federal judiciary if evidentiary challenges to indictments were allowed. The commentators note, in particular, Justice Black's comments upon the "resulting delay" and the likelihood of "a kind of preliminary trial" in every case (see p. 994 supra). Were

b. But compare Arenella, Note 8 infra, arguing that, vindictiveness aside, prosecutors have various incentives to prosecute with insufficient evidence, such as possibly inducing a guilty plea or gaining a tactical advantage by joining a marginal participant as a co-defendant. See also Note 2, p. 943 supra, at n. 23. But consider Sullivan and Nachman, p. 979 supra (grand jury "reforms" that would impose significant administrative burdens [see Note 3 infra] should be based on actual rather than hypothetical abuses, and there is absolutely no evidence suggesting that federal prosecutors are in fact seeking to indict unconvictable defendants to gain guilty pleas or any other advantage).

there other potential administrative difficulties that might have influenced the Court? If the Court had permitted evidentiary challenges, would it also have had to require that grand jury testimony be recorded? States that recognize evidentiary challenges uniformly require some form of recording. At the time of *Costello,* the decision to record was left to the discretion of the U.S. Attorney and many proceedings were not recorded. It was not until 1979 that Fed. Rule 6(e) was amended to require a recording in all proceedings.

Would the adoption of the position advanced by the defense in *Costello* also have required that the defendant be given access to the grand jury transcript? In *Costello,* the defendant first learned of the hearsay nature of the grand jury evidence at trial, but obtaining such information at trial is doubtful in many cases and, in any event, would hardly facilitate a timely objection. Those states that permit evidentiary challenges generally provide for post-indictment disclosure of the grand jury transcript to the defendant. See Note 13, p. 1006 infra. Since most of these states also grant liberal pretrial discovery of the prior recorded statements of prosecution witnesses, disclosure of the grand jury testimony is largely consistent with the general pattern of discovery otherwise available in the jurisdiction. In the federal courts, on the other hand, disclosure of grand jury testimony would undermine general discovery standards since prior recorded statements, including grand jury testimony, are not available to the defendant until the witness testifies at trial. See Note 1, p. 1120 supra.

Would recognition of an evidentiary challenge to an indictment also require separation of the grand jury's investigatory and screening functions? As noted in Chapter 10, grand juries are directed to track down "every available clue," including "tips" and "rumors," and this obviously includes incompetent evidence. *United States v. Dionisio* at p. 717 supra. To ensure that the grand jury's indictment was not challenged because it considered such evidence in the course of its investigation, would the prosecutor be well advised to first complete his investigation before one grand jury, and then present to a separate, indicting grand jury only that testimony developed through the investigation that would be admissible at trial? [c]

What weight, if any, should be given to the administrative burdens noted above? As Note 12, p. 1005 infra, points out, many states recognize challenges to the competency of the evidence before the grand jury, and they apparently do not find these burdens intolerable. Admittedly, most of these states ordinarily prosecute by information, but several are indictment jurisdictions. Is there any reason why the administrative burdens would pose greater difficulties in the federal system than in these other indictment jurisdictions? Does the weight given to administrative difficulties depend, in the end, upon one's view of the importance of grand jury screening? Commentators favoring evidentiary challenges frequently quote Judge Frank's remark in *In re Fried,* 161 F.2d 453, 458–59 (2d Cir.1947) (concurring):

> "[A] wrongful indictment is no laughing matter; often it works a grievous irreparable injury to the person indicted. The stigma cannot be easily erased. In the public mind, the blot on a man's escutcheon, resulting from such a public accusation of wrongdoing, is seldom

c. Some commentators also have questioned the prosecutor's capacity to ensure that only competent evidence will be presented to the grand jury. They note that the rules of evidence are designed for an adversary system in which the opponent objects and the judge rules on that objection. Before the grand jury, there is "nobody to object" and the judge is not readily available to rule on debatable issues. See Frankel and Naftalis, supra. Proponents of evidentiary challenges respond that occasional prosecutor errors will not be fatal, since the indictment would still be sustained if the grand jury also heard sufficient admissible evidence to support the charge. See Note 12, p. 1005 infra.

wiped out by a subsequent judgment of not guilty. Frequently, the public remembers the accusation, and still suspects guilt, even after an acquittal."

Is *Costello* inconsistent with Judge Frank's view of the significance of an unfounded indictment?

4. *Supervisory power.* If the Court had concluded in *Costello* that extensive reliance upon hearsay was inappropriate, but not so clearly inconsistent with the historical function of the grand jury as to constitute a Fifth Amendment violation, could it have prohibited that practice in the "exercise [of] its power to supervise the administration of justice in federal courts" (see p. 994 supra)? Several lower courts have suggested that the judiciary has a broader authority over the prosecutor's grand jury practices than over other pretrial prosecutorial practices since the grand jury is an "arm of the court." See, e.g., the cases cited in Note 7 infra, and *United States v. Serubo,* p. 1008 infra. But compare *United States v. Chanen,* 549 F.2d 1306, 1312 (9th Cir.1977) (reversing a district court ruling quashing an indictment because the U.S. Attorney, instead of calling available witnesses to testify, had simply read to the indicting grand jury the testimony of those witnesses before an earlier grand jury):

"Even if the action here falls short of the conduct which the courts have held in other instances to require dismissal of the indictment, defendants argue that the district court has a discretionary supervisory power to dismiss the indictment where the court determines that the procedures used by the prosecution to secure the indictment were fundamentally unfair. Accordingly, they argue, the dismissal in this case must be sustained unless it amounts to an abuse of discretion. We believe that the defendants' view of the trial court's discretion is not wholly correct. * * * [G]iven the constitutionally-based independence of each of the three actors—court, prosecutor and grand jury—we believe a court may not exercise its 'supervisory power' in a way which encroaches on the prerogatives of the other two unless there is a clear basis in fact and law for doing so. If the district courts were not required to meet such a standard, their 'supervisory power' could readily prove subversive of the doctrine of separation of powers." (Consider also the comments of Professor Beale at Note 5, p. 705 supra).

B. THE SCOPE OF COSTELLO

5. *Unconstitutionally obtained evidence.* In three post-*Costello* decisions, the Supreme Court indicated quite clearly, albeit in dictum, that the *Costello* rationale also barred a challenge to an indictment issued on the basis of unconstitutionally obtained evidence. See LaFave and Israel, § 15.4(a). The latest of those cases, *United States v. Calandra,* discussed at p. 723 supra, held that a grand jury witness could not refuse to answer questions based on information obtained through an unconstitutional search. In the course of explaining its ruling the Court noted: "The grand jury's sources of information are widely drawn and the validity of an indictment is not affected by the character of the evidence considered. Thus, an indictment valid on its face is not subject to challenge on the ground that the grand jury acted on the basis of inadequate or incompetent evidence, *Costello v. United States;* or even on the basis of information obtained in violation of a defendant's Fifth Amendment privilege against self-incrimination."

Could the Court readily have distinguished a challenge based on grand jury consideration of unconstitutionally obtained evidence from the challenge rejected in *Costello?* Commentators have suggested that the former challenge should have been distinguished because: (1) *Costello* was concerned only with the impact of the Fifth Amendment's indictment provision, while the challenge to the use of unconstitutionally obtained evidence also required consideration of those constitutional provisions violated in obtaining such evidence; (2) while hearsay evidence may be transformed into admissible evidence by the introduction of live testimony at trial, unconstitutionally obtained evidence cannot be transformed into admissible evidence; and (3) a challenge to an indictment based on unconstitutionally obtained evidence will not add substantially to pretrial proceedings since the legality of the acquisition of such evidence would otherwise be raised in a pretrial suppression motion. Are these arguments persuasive? See Federal Rules Advisory Committee, Commentary to Proposed Rule 7, 77 F.R.D. 520 (1978) (arguing that permitting challenges based on the purported use of illegally seized evidence "would result in substantial delays without any appreciable benefits in terms of deterrence of illegal practices"). Compare *Reaves v. State,* 250 S.E.2d 376 (Ga.1978) (accepting indictments based on at least certain types of hearsay, but requiring dismissal of indictments returned wholly on illegally seized evidence).[d] Consider also U.S. Attorneys' Manual §§ 9–11.331–332 (directing prosecutors not to present to the grand jury "for use against a person whose constitutional rights clearly have been violated evidence which the prosecutor personally knows was obtained as a direct result of a constitutional violation," but stating as to hearsay that its use is permissible where it provides the grand jury "a substantial basis for voting upon the indictment" and the presentation is "in keeping with the professional obligations of the attorney for the government").

6. *No evidence.* Prior to *Costello,* numerous federal courts had stated that an indictment would be quashed if there was a clear showing that the grand jury received absolutely no evidence relating to a necessary element of the crime charged. Does *Costello* bar a challenge on that ground? Goldstein, Note 1 supra, argued that the *Costello* majority's failure to incorporate the "narrower" reasoning of Justice Burton's concurring opinion indicated that the grand jury was now "its own judge" of "the amount" as well as "the quality" of the evidence "require[d] for indictment." See also the quotation from *Calandra,* Note 5 supra, noting that an indictment is not subject to challenge "on the basis of *inadequate* or incompetent evidence." (Emphasis added). Several lower courts, relying on *Costello,* have refused to consider claims that there was no "probative evidence, either hearsay or direct, upon which to base the indictments." See, e.g., *United States v. Cruz,* 478 F.2d 408 (5th Cir.1973).

On the other hand, other lower courts, influenced by Justice Burton's separate opinion, have indicated that a "no evidence" objection is still cognizable. *United States v. Romero,* 585 F.2d 391 (9th Cir. 1978). However, these courts also suggest that the defendant, to be successful, must establish on his own, without any right to inspect the grand jury transcript, that the evidence was totally deficient. But note *United States v. O'Shea,* 447 F.Supp. 330 (S.D.Fla.1978) (court itself inspected the transcript and dismissed the indictment because it was "not supported by any evidence, competent or otherwise, to establish a prima facie case"). Cf. *United States v. Hodge,* 496 F.2d 87 (5th Cir. 1974) (while *Costello* permits a government agent to give sworn testimony as to

d. A few federal courts have suggested that an indictment may be quashed, notwithstanding *Costello,* where the grand jury compelled the defendant to give testimony in violation of his self-incrimination privilege and then indicted him on the basis of that testimony. LaFave and Israel, § 15.4(a). Such cases are said to be distinguishable from *Costello* and its progeny because the dismissal is designed to remedy grand jury misconduct rather than the reliance upon incompetent evidence. See Note 8 infra. Relying on a similar rationale, the Second Circuit has held that an indictment also will be dismissed where the indicting grand jury had before it the immunized testimony of the defendant. See *United States v. Tantalo,* 680 F.2d 903 (2d Cir.1982). But compare *United States v. Zielezinski,* 740 F.2d 727 (9th Cir.1984) (indictment would not be dismissed if the government could establish that the indictment rested on sources independent of the immunized testimony).

statements made by others, total reliance upon "informal unsworn hearsay from the mouth of the prosecutor * * * is interdicted by the Fifth Amendment"). Consider also fn. a, p. 995 supra.

7. *Hearsay.* After *Costello,* are there any situations in which the prosecution's use of hearsay before the grand jury will justify dismissal of an indictment? Several federal courts have relied upon their supervisory power to prohibit particular uses of hearsay and have enforced these prohibitions by dismissing indictments. The Court of Appeals for the Second Circuit has recognized the most extensive restrictions on the use of hearsay, although it has not gone as far as suggested by a district court opinion it once praised. In UNITED STATES v. ARCURI, 282 F.Supp. 347 (E.D.N.Y.1968), the district court (per Weinstein, J.), announced that, in the future, "a timely motion to dismiss * * * will be granted without a showing of prejudice to the defendant if it is clear that hearsay alone was deliberately relied upon when better evidence was readily available for presentation to the grand jury." In support of this prospective ruling, the court both distinguished *Costello* and stressed deficiencies in hearsay presentations. With respect to *Costello* it noted: "There is no reason to believe that the Supreme Court in *Costello* intended to encourage the practice before grand juries of deliberately relying solely on the testimony of witnesses without any personal knowledge when better evidence is readily at hand. Rather, *Costello,* seems to have been designed to avoid technical failures of indictments because hearsay or other inadmissible evidence was used either inadvertently or because nothing more probative was immediately available."

Turning to the deficiencies in hearsay presentations, the *Arcuri* opinion stressed two shortcomings: "First, [relying on hearsay] habituates the grand jury to rely upon 'evidence' which appears smooth, well integrated and consistent in all respects. * * * [G]rand jurors do not hear cases with the rough edges that result from the often halting, inconsistent and incomplete testimony of honest observers of events. Thus, they are unable to distinguish between prosecutions which are strong and those which are relatively weak. * * * The second reason the practice is undesirable is that it prevents the defendant from utilizing grand jury testimony in cross-examining witnesses who will testify at the trial. * * * When a government witness testifies, and defense counsel seeks his grand jury testimony for use in cross-examination, he is met with the answer that the witness did not testify before the grand jury. Taken with the concurrent prosecution tactic of avoiding preliminary hearings [see Note 4, p. 944 supra], the net effect is to cut the defendant off from material which should be available to him as a partial substitute for discovery proceedings."

In affirming the lower court ruling in *Arcuri,* the Court of Appeals for the Second Circuit took note of the "penetrating opinion" of the district court that had "analyzed the vices" of regular reliance upon hearsay. See *United States v. Arcuri,* 405 F.2d 691, 693 (2d Cir.1968). However, in UNITED STATES v. ESTEPA, 471 F.2d 1132 (2d Cir.1972), the first case actually dismissing an indictment for use of hearsay, the court (per Friendly, J.) relied on narrower grounds. In that case the only witness testifying before the grand jury was a police officer whose observations of the narcotics transactions in question was "both limited and remote." The officer testified about the transactions "at length and in detail," without indicating that he was basing his testimony not on his own observations, but on information received from other officers who had participated in the transactions. Those officers apparently had been available to testify, but had not been called by the prosecution. Under these circumstances, the court concluded, the trial court should have sustained defendant's pretrial motion to dismiss the indictment and its failure to do so required reversal of the subsequent conviction. The court reasoned:

"We have not gone so far as to apply to grand juries the proposal in the American Law Institute's *Model Code of Pre-Arraignment Procedure* §§ 330.4(4) and 340.5 (Tent. Draft No. 5, 1972), that hearsay may be received at a preliminary hearing or by a grand jury only 'if the court determines that it would impose an unreasonable burden on one of the parties or on a witness to require that the primary source of the evidence be produced at the hearing, and if the witness furnishes information bearing on the informant's reliability and, as far as possible, the means by which the information was obtained,' although * * * we do not believe *Costello v. United States* would prevent this exercise of our supervisory powers should we deem it wise. But we have insisted that, even though '[t]here is no affirmative duty to tell the grand jury in *haec verba* that it is listening to hearsay,' the grand jury must not be 'misled into thinking it is getting eye-witness testimony from the agent whereas it is actually being given an account whose hearsay nature is concealed. . . . ' *United States v. Leibowitz,* 420 F.2d 39, 42 (2d Cir.1969). That was what happened here. * * *

"The many opinions in which we have affirmed convictions despite the Government's needless reliance on hearsay before the grand jury show how loathe we have been to open up a new road for attacking convictions on grounds unrelated to the merits. We have been willing to allow ample, many doubtless think too ample, latitude in the needless use of hearsay, subject to only two provisos—that the prosecutor does not deceive grand jurors as to 'the shoddy merchandise they are getting so they can seek something better if they wish,' or that the case does not involve 'a high probability that with eye-witness rather than hearsay testimony the grand jury would not have indicted.' *United States v. Leibowitz,* supra. * * * Here the Assistant United States Attorney, whether wittingly or unwittingly—we prefer to think the latter, clearly violated the first of these provisos."

The *Estepa* standards have had a mixed reception from other federal courts. At least one district court arguably has gone beyond *Estepa* to apply a standard similar to that suggested in *Arcuri.* See *United States v. Gallo,* 394 F.Supp. 310 (D.Conn. 1975).[e] Other courts appear to have accepted a modified version of *Estepa.* They apparently would dismiss an indictment "where (1) non-hearsay evidence is readily available; (2) the grand jury is misled into believing it was hearing direct testimony rather than hearsay; *and* (3) there is high probability that had the grand jury heard the eye witness it would not have indicted." *United States v. Wander,* 601 F.2d 1251 (3d Cir.1979) (emphasis added). See also *United States v. Barone,* 584 F.2d 118 (6th Cir.1978) (court did not foreclose possibility of an abuse "so egregious as to warrant intervention," but it was "not inclined to adopt the position of the second circuit in *Estepa*").

In 1978, the Federal Rules Advisory Committee put forth for comment a proposed amendment to Federal Rule 7 that apparently was designed to override both *Estepa* and *Arcuri.* The proposed amendment provided: "An indictment may not

e. In *Gallo,* the indicting grand jury was presented with a transcript of testimony given before an earlier grand jury and told that an earlier indictment, dismissed for technical defects, had been based on that testimony as well as an officer's corroborating testimony and identification of records. In dismissing the second indictment, the district court noted that the prosecutor should have: (1) alerted the grand jury as to the hearsay quality of the evidence it was considering; (2) informed the grand jurors that the key witness (Buckley) was available for live testimony in case they wanted to evaluate his credibility for themselves; (3) informed the grand jurors that Buckley's recorded testimony included his acknowledgment that he had lied in an earlier portion of his testimony (citing *Basurto,* Note 9 infra); and (4) presented the second grand jury with the police officer's corroborating testimony and the gambling records that had been presented to the first grand jury.

be dismissed on the ground that the evidence before the grand jury was not sufficient or competent." 77 F.R.D. 520 (1978). The commentary to the proposal described the district court opinion in *Arcuri* and the Second Circuit's opinions in *Estepa* and *Leibowitz* as having made undesirable "inroads" upon the "broad rule" of *Costello.* It noted: "The concerns expressed in *Arcuri, Leibowitz* and *Estepa* are not without merit. However, the degree of scrutiny of the grand jury proceedings which would be required to establish the existence of the special circumstances noted in those cases would, as noted in *Costello,* 'result in interminable delay but add nothing to the assurance of a fair trial.' A wide ranging inquiry would often be needed to establish whether better evidence was available for presentation to the grand jury or whether the grand jury would have reached a different result if eyewitness testimony had been available." 77 F.R.D. at 523.

8. *Hearsay and prosecutorial misconduct.* The relationship of *Costello* to indictment dismissals based upon prosecutorial misconduct before the grand jury is explained as follows in LaFave and Israel, § 15.4(b): *Costello* has never been thought to bar the authority of federal courts to 'preserve the integrity of the judicial process' by dismissing indictments that are the product of 'flagrantly abusive prosecutorial conduct' before the grand jury. Indeed, support for exercising that authority is found in *Costello* 's caveat that an indictment must be returned by 'an unbiased grand jury.' Abusive prosecutorial practices, such as insults and insinuations directed against the target, are seen as inconsistent with this requirement since they 'serve no other purpose than calculated prejudice.' While historical tradition allows the grand jury to consider all types of evidence, it does not allow the prosecutor to attempt to pressure the jurors into issuing an indictment. * * * Allowing challenges based on prosecutorial misconduct is also viewed as presenting far less substantial administrative costs than allowing challenges to the sufficiency or competency of the evidence before the grand jury. An objection limited to prosecutorial misconduct is not available to all defendants as would be a general evidentiary challenge. Nor does it require the automatic disclosure of the grand jury minutes to the defendant. * * * [E]vidence of misconduct can come from other sources (e.g., the witness who was harassed by the prosecutor)".

To what extent can the hearsay rulings described in Note 7 supra be grounded on a "misconduct exception" to *Costello?* Consider Arenella, *Reforming the Federal Grand Jury and the State Preliminary Hearing to Prevent Conviction Without Adjudication,* 78 Mich.L.Rev. 463 (1980), commenting upon *Estepa,* (Note 7 supra), *Gallo* (fn. f supra), *Channen* (Note 4 supra) and *Basurto* (Note 9 infra):

"Federal courts often use the [prosecutorial misconduct] doctrine to circumvent *Costello* and dismiss indictments when they are convinced that the prosecutor's presentation of evidence has produced a miscarriage of justice. Defining such a miscarriage in this setting depends largely upon the particular court's view of the grand jury's screening functions. * * * Courts which assume that the grand jury should screen factual guilt will find misconduct only in those rare cases where the prosecutor deliberately biases the grand jury's determination of factual guilt by flagrantly abusive conduct. * * * Courts which assume that the grand jury should receive sufficient evidence to assess the likelihood of conviction will find misconduct when the prosecutor precludes the grand jury from *personally* assessing the credibility of an important government witness whose veracity is in doubt. * * * [D]espite its label, the courts have used the prosecutorial misconduct doctrine in many cases to determine whether the prosecutor's evidentiary presentation impaired the grand jury's screening functions."

9. *Perjured testimony.* Relying upon the Supreme Court's perjured testimony cases (see fn. 8, p. 1150 infra), which found due process violations in the prosecution's knowing use of perjured testimony at trial, the Ninth Circuit in *United States v. Basurto,* 497 F.2d 781 (9th Cir.1974), concluded that a defendant was also denied due process where forced to stand trial on an indictment obtained through the prosecutor's knowing use of perjured testimony. Later circuit court decisions questioned whether the Supreme Court's due process rulings could appropriately be carried over to the grand jury setting, considering the limited role of the grand jury and the availability of the trial "to correct errors before the grand jury, such as perjured testimony." *United States v. Udziela,* 671 F.2d 995 (7th Cir.1982). However, those courts held that, in the exercise of their supervisory power, an indictment would be dismissed where it had been obtained through "deliberate introduction of perjured testimony" that was "material" to the issue before the grand jury. Ibid. As to what constitutes "materiality," the courts have varied, although they clearly require a more substantial likelihood of prejudicial impact than the Supreme Court rulings on the use of perjured testimony at trial. In general, "they appear to insist, at a minimum that the district court conclude that the evidence before the grand jury would have been insufficient to sustain an indictment without the perjured testimony." LaFave and Israel, § 15.4(b). Is the application of even this narrow standard of materiality reconcilable with *Costello?* If so, would application of the more expansive trial standard of materiality (i.e., viewing the perjured testimony as material if there was "any reasonable likelihood" it may have affected the grand jury's judgment) be equally reconcilable?

The perjured testimony "exception" to *Costello* is often justified by reference to the prosecutor's "misconduct" in using the perjured testimony. In light of this rationale, should the exception be applicable to a situation in which the prosecutor did not know but should have known that his witness was testifying falsely? See LaFave and Israel, § 15.4(b) (noting a division in the lower court rulings). In *Basurto,* the prosecutor first learned that the testimony of a critical witness had been perjured after the indictment was issued, but before the case went to trial. The Ninth Circuit held that the subsequent conviction should be overturned because the prosecutor failed to go back to the grand jury, although he informed the defense of that perjury and also brought it to the attention of the trial court. Was that ruling consistent with a "misconduct" rationale? Compare Rehnquist, J., denying a stay in *Bracy v. United States,* 435 U.S. 1301, 98 S.Ct. 1171, 55 L.Ed.2d 489 (1978) (suggesting that dismissal of an indictment because the prosecutor failed to inform the grand jury of subsequently discovered perjured testimony would be inconsistent with *Costello*).

10. *Exculpatory evidence.* In 1975, a state court decision *Johnson v. Superior Court,* 539 P.2d 792 (Cal.1975), attracted considerable attention when it dismissed an indictment because the prosecutor had failed to inform the grand jury of known exculpatory evidence. In that case, a magistrate had refused to bindover at a preliminary hearing after the defendant testified that (1) one of his alleged associates in a narcotics transaction had grossly exaggerated his role and (2) his limited participation had been part of a plan to furnish information to a local prosecutor in connection with a plea bargain on another charge. Not satisfied with the magistrate's decision, the prosecutor took the case to the grand jury. Only the arresting officers gave grand jury testimony, and the grand jury was not informed of defendant's preliminary hearing testimony. (Indeed, the prosecutor conveyed to the jurors "the false impression that Johnson would refuse to testify if called"). In holding the indictment invalid, the California Supreme Court relied upon a California statute requiring the grand jury to consider "evi-

dence within its reach which will explain away the charge." See Note 6, p. 983 supra. It reasoned that this requirement imposed a related duty on the prosecutor to inform the grand jury of known exculpatory evidence.

Though there is no similar federal statute, *Johnson* sparked a reexamination of earlier federal precedent holding that the prosecutor had no duty to present exculpatory evidence to the grand jury. Relying on *Costello* and the non-adversarial nature of the grand jury process, several federal courts have held that the *Johnson* ruling has no relevance to the federal system: "A federal prosecutor is not obligated to present exculpatory evidence to the grand jury," and his failure to do so does not subject an indictment to attack. *United States v. Adamo,* 742 F.2d 927 (6th Cir. 1984). Other federal courts, however, have held, or stated in dictum, that an indictment will be dismissed where the prosecutor failed to present before the grand jury known evidence that was both exculpatory and material. See LaFave and Israel, § 15.4(d). This position is squared with *Costello* by reliance upon a prosecutorial misconduct rationale. The prosecutor's failure to produce exculpatory evidence is said to "destroy the existence of an independent and informed grand jury" and thereby contradict *Costello* 's assumption of an unbiased grand jury. *United States v. Gold,* 470 F.Supp. 1336 (N.D.Ill.1979). The failure to present exculpatory is viewed in this regard as a form of deception, comparable to the knowing use of perjured testimony or the misrepresentation of hearsay as eyewitness testimony. Some courts, looking to Supreme Court rulings that have found due process violations in the prosecutor's failure to disclose exculpatory evidence at trial [see Ch. 20, § 3], have argued that an analogous obligation of "fairness" is constitutionally imposed at the pretrial stage. See *United States v. Dorfman,* 532 F.Supp. 1118 (N.D. Ill.1981). Do such rationales simply reflect a lower court refusal to accept "the breadth of the *Costello* ruling"? LaFave and Israel, § 15.4(b).

Johnson spoke of the prosecutor's duty to present to the grand jury evidence "reasonably tending to negate guilt," but the federal courts recognizing an exculpatory evidence challenge to an indictment have adopted somewhat narrower definitions of material exculpatory evidence. They have spoken of an obligation to present only evidence which "clearly negates the target's guilt" or which "might reasonably be expected to lead the jury not to indict." See *United States v. Dorfman,* supra; *United States v. Ciambrone,* 601 F.2d 616 (2d Cir. 1979). Under these standards, would a federal court quash the indictment in the fact situation presented in *Johnson?* Did that case present anything more than a "self-serving statement of the target" which was "contradicted by the prosecution's evidence"? Federal courts have held that the prosecutor is under no obligation to present such evidence even if it directly negates the defendant's guilt. LaFave and Israel, § 15.4(d).

Do the narrower standards of materiality applied by the federal courts meet what have been described as the "practical" objections to extending a prosecutorial duty to disclose exculpatory evidence to the grand jury? Critics have noted that such an obligation imposes substantially greater burdens upon the prosecutor than the disclosure obligation imposed at trial because (1) the prosecutor at the grand jury stage ordinarily does not have the advantage of defense motions identifying those items that the defense views as potentially exculpatory (although targets will occasionally request that the prosecutor present certain evidence to the grand jury), and (2) at such an early stage in the development of the case, both the possible charges and likely defenses are often uncertain, making it especially difficult for the prosecutor to determine what weight might be given to evidence that could be viewed as exculpatory. The U.S. Attorneys' Manual, § 9–11.334 provides: "[W]hen a prosecutor conducting a grand jury inquiry is personally aware of substantial evidence which directly negates the guilt of the subject of the investigation, the prosecutor must present or otherwise disclose such evidence to the grand jury before seeking an indictment against such a person."

C. COSTELLO AND THE STATES

11. *States following Costello.* A majority of the states, including most of the "indictment states," follow the basic position of *Costello.* In these states, an indictment ordinarily is not subject to challenge because the grand jury relied on evidence that would not be admissible at trial. Though several of the states in this group have statutory provisions directing the grand jury to receive only such evidence "as might be given at trial," those provisions have been held to be "admonitory in character only, not mandatory." See *State v. McDonald,* 361 P.2d 1001 (Or.1961). States following *Costello* do not necessarily refuse to consider all evidentiary challenges to indictments. Some have suggested that an indictment will be dismissed if there was "no evidence" before the grand jury or no witness "competent to testify." Relying on a misconduct rationale, several have indicated that they will dismiss an indictment if the grand jury violated the defendant's privilege against self-incrimination by forcing the accused to testify, the prosecutor made knowing use of perjured testimony, or the prosecutor failed to make the grand jury aware of significant exculpatory evidence. See LaFave and Israel, § 15.4(c), (d).

12. *States rejecting Costello.* Several indictment states and a somewhat larger group of information states (approximately a dozen in all) allow challenges to the sufficiency and competency of the evidence underlying an indictment. See LaFave and Israel, § 15.4(c). Some do so by statutory command, but others have adopted this position solely through judicial decision. The reasoning of *Costello,* it is argued, is acceptable only "if the institution of the grand jury is viewed as an anachronism." If the grand jury is to "protect * * * the innocent against oppression and unjust prosecution," a defendant "with substantial grounds for having an indictment dismissed should not be compelled to go to trial to prove the insufficiency." *State v. Parks,* 437 P.2d 642 (Alaska 1968) (Rabinowitz, J., concurring).

Jurisdictions rejecting *Costello* uniformly insist that the trial court act with caution in reviewing the sufficiency of the evidence before the grand jury. They stress that "every legitimate inference that may be drawn from the evidence must be drawn in favor of the indictment," and note that "probable cause * * * may be based on 'slight' or even marginal evidence." *State v. Freedle,* 620 P.2d 740 (Hawaii App. 1980). As a result, most of the successful sufficiency challenges arise from the prosecution's failure to offer any competent evidence on a particular element of the crime charged. A few of these jurisdictions direct the grand jury to consider only evidence that would be admissible at trial. The others generally apply the rules of evidence, but permit consideration of either limited types of hearsay (such as scientific reports) or a broader range of hearsay (tied to the burden that would be imposed in presenting direct testimony). In all of the non-*Costello* jurisdictions, the presentation of inadmissible evidence is not necessarily fatal. The indictment ordinarily will be sustained if, after excluding the inadmissible evidence, there remains sufficient admissible evidence to support the charge. However, where the inadmissible evidence was so prejudicial as to necessarily have influenced the grand jury, the indictment will be dismissed notwithstanding otherwise sufficient legal evidence. So too, prosecutorial misconduct in the presentation of evidence (e.g., the knowing use of perjured testimony or the failure to present significant exculpatory evidence) may justify a reversal even though the remaining evidence would otherwise pass a sufficiency challenge. See e.g., *Frink v. State,* 597 P.2d 154 (Alaska 1979).

13. *Inspection of grand jury transcripts.* Almost all of the jurisdictions which permit challenges to the competency and sufficiency of the grand jury evidence (i.e., the jurisdictions described in Note 12 supra) grant the defendant an automatic right to inspect the transcript of the grand jury testimony. In *Burkholder v. State,* 491 P.2d 754 (Alaska 1971), the court concluded that the right to inspect was essential "to give meaning" to the right to challenge the indictment. The court rejected as unsatisfactory a state provision, similar to Fed.R.Crim.P. 6(e)(2)(C)(ii), that allowed disclosure only "upon a showing that grounds may exist for a motion to dismiss the indictment." The difficulty with such a rule, it noted, was "that so far as the sufficiency of the indictment is concerned, * * * it is only by being able to have access to the grand jury proceedings without any prior showing that a defendant can know whether the indictment is subject to dismissal." In supporting automatic disclosure, *Burkholder* stressed that such post-indictment disclosure did not undermine any of the five justifications commonly advanced in support of grand jury secrecy (see p. 699 supra). Is that necessarily true?

Compare with *Burkholder,* the position adopted in New York. In connection with a motion to dismiss an indictment as based on insufficient legal evidence, the defendant may move for inspection of the transcript. However, the inspection initially is conducted *in camera* by the court, and further inspection by the defense may be denied if the court "determines there is not reasonable cause to believe that the evidence before the grand jury may have been legally insufficient." N.Y.Crim.P. Law § 210.30(4). Does New York's initial restriction of the inspection to *in camera* review impose a significant limit upon the challenge to the indictment? Compare *Ivey v. State,* 420 P.2d 853 (Nev.1966), rejecting *in camera* inspection on the grounds, inter alia, that (1) defendant's "right to know what evidence was formally received by the grand jury" is an important aspect of his right not to be indicted without probable cause, and (2) the court needs the "assistance of counsel for both sides if it is to judge wisely."

14. *Harmless error and reversal on appeal.* In several states recognizing evidentiary challenges to the indictment, a defendant may readily obtain interlocutory appellate review of the trial judge's rejection of a motion to dismiss. See, e.g., *Loucious v. Sheriff, Clark County,* 575 P.2d 598 (Nev. 1978) (challenge by writ of habeas corpus, with appeal permitted from an adverse ruling); *Johnson v. Superior Court,* Note 10 supra (allowing writ of prohibition, see p. 1455 infra). In other jurisdictions, however, interlocutory appellate review generally is not available (see ch. 26, § 2), and a trial judge's adverse ruling ordinarily comes before the appellate court as part of the appeal following conviction. At this point, should any insufficiency in the evidence before the grand jury be viewed as harmless error since the trial jury found sufficient evidence to convict? Cf. Note 8, p. 991 supra (discussing post-conviction appellate review of grand jury composition claims). Most state decisions apparently assume that a conviction will be reversed automatically if the trial judge erred in failing to grant the dismissal motion. See also *United States v. Estepa,* Note 7 supra (suggesting reversal following conviction was necessary to deter future prosecutorial misuse of hearsay). But compare N.Y. Crim.P.Law § 210.30(6) (validity of an order denying a motion to dismiss or to inspect the grand jury transcript is "not reviewable upon an appeal from an ensuing judgment of conviction based upon legally sufficient trial evidence").

SECTION 4. CHALLENGES TO GRAND JURY PROCEDURES

1. *Prosecutor misconduct.* I *A.B.A. Standards* § 3–3.5 provides that the prosecu-

tor, in serving as legal adviser to the grand jury "should give due deference to its status as an independent legal body" and "should not make statements or arguments in an effort to influence grand jury action in a manner which would be impermissible at trial before a petit jury." Are the A.B.A. Standards too rigid in prohibiting comments intended to influence the grand jury "which would be impermissible at trial before a petit jury"? Is it inappropriate for the prosecutor, even in response to grand juror requests for "detailed background information" about witnesses, to describe particular witness as "con-men," or "members of organized crime"? See House Hearings, 845. Consider Woodward and Ahrens, p. 996 supra, at 279–80: "The prosecutor's role before the grand jury cannot be isolated from or evaluated properly without reference to the kind of evidence and information the grand jury can legally receive and employ. * * * [I]f the grand jury is competent to evaluate and cope with prejudice, opinion and even 'off the street' rumor from other sources, it is difficult to see how the prosecutor is a particularly dangerous source of information. * * * Experience with grand juries will ultimately teach a prosecutor that they are usually interested in background information, [and the] character of witnesses and suspects."

Accepting the basic thrust of the A.B.A. Standards, courts have characterized as "misconduct" various acts of prosecutors before the grand jury, including the following: (1) expressing a personal view as to motive of the witness in testifying, *State v. Joao,* 491 P.2d 1089 (Hawaii 1971); (2) asking a witness who is a prospective defendant questions about irrelevant personal matters in an effort to "discredit and impugn her in the eyes of the jurors," *United States v. DiGrazia,* 213 F.Supp. 232 (N.D.Ill.1963); (3) noting that the accused had relied upon his self-incrimination privilege in a prior investigation, *Johnson v. Superior Court,* p. 1003 supra; (4) inviting the jurors, through unfounded references in questions put to witnesses, to "associate the defendants with a disfavored criminal class [Cosa Nostra leaders]," *United States v. Serubo,* Note 3 infra; (5) informing the grand jurors that the target had sought to plea bargain, *United States v. Griffith,* Note 3 infra; (6) appealing to the grand jurors' personal pride, *State v. Good,* 460 P.2d 662 (Ariz.App.1969); and (7) "appear[ing] as a witness before the grand jury, [and] then fail[ing] to withdraw as one of the Government's presenting attorneys," *United States v. Birdman,* 602 F.2d 547 (3d Cir.1979).

Under what circumstances, if any should such prosecutorial misconduct justify dismissal of an indictment?[a] Should there have to be a clear indication of likely prejudice? If so, should the court look primarily to the weight of the evidence before the grand jury, or should certain types of misconduct be viewed as "inherently prejudicial"? What weight, if any should be given to the prosecutor's purpose—i.e., in particular, whether his action was intended to appeal to juror prejudice or to prod a reluctant jury into voting for indictment?

2. In *State v. Fisher,* 271 A.2d 24 (Super.1970), the court rejected the defense contention that pretrial discovery of the prosecutor's "off the record" comments to the jurors was necessary to determine whether there had been "misconduct" in the return of the indictment. The court noted: " 'Misconduct' bears only on the question of probable cause or lack of it, and for that one must look to the testimony which was heard. * * * As-

a. See LaFave and Israel, § 15.5(b): "Many jurisdictions hold that prosecutorial misconduct will justify a dismissal only when that misconduct reaches the level of a constitutional violation. This limitation often stems from the interpretation of a statute that lists various grounds for challenging an indictment, but does not include prosecutorial misconduct. * * * Other jurisdictions recognize an inherent supervisory power to dismiss for misconduct that does not itself violate due process."

sume that an overzealous prosecutor was 'out to get' a particular accused; assume that he told a grand jury that they should indict, no matter what; * * * those considerations have no effect on the basic inquiry, which is whether, on the testimony before it, the grand jury had probable cause to return the indictment it did."

Compare with *Fisher, State v. Hart,* 354 A.2d 679 (N.J.Super.App.Div.1976), granting a motion to dismiss based on a prosecutor's improper comment. Shortly after the grand jury voted not to indict, one of the grand jurors asked the prosecutor what he thought of their decision? The prosecutor responded that he thought the jury "was wrong" because the explanation given by the defendant "was a complete lie." Learning of the prosecutor's statement, the presiding judge advised the jury that "the prosecutor's opinion was not binding on it and that it should act independently." The jury then decided to reconsider the case and voted to indict. In quashing the indictment, the appellate court noted: "[W]e find the assistant prosecutor's actions impinged upon the independence of the grand jury and improperly influenced its determination. Once a 'no' bill was voted, he should have refused to answer the inquiry of any of the grand jurors. Nor are we able to say the assignment judge's supplemental charge cured the defect. It would be pure speculation to attempt to gauge its effect on the grand jury."

Hart was distinguished in *State v. Schamberg,* 370 A.2d 482 (N.J.Super.App.Div.1977). In the course of examining a grand jury witness, the prosecutor noted: "I have reason to believe that you just perjured yourself." The grand jury subsequently indicted the witness for perjury. The court noted its disapproval of "the form of [the prosecutor's] comment," but refused to quash the indictment. Unlike the prosecutor's statement in *Hart,* the comment here "was not addressed to the grand jury, nor was it intended to direct the grand jury to indict." It reflected only the "culmination of efforts * * * to give the witness the opportunity to change his testimony." The court concluded: "Unless the prosecutor's misconduct before a grand jury is extreme and clearly infringes upon the jury's decision-making function, it should not be utilized as a stepping stone to dismissal of an indictment."

3. What weight should be given to the fact that the prosecutorial misconduct in the particular case appears to be an isolated incident or the latest in a series of incidents brought to the attention of the court? Consider the positions taken by the Third and Sixth Circuits.

(a) In *United States v. Serubo,* 604 F.2d 807 (3d Cir.1979), the Third Circuit, after noting that this was the latest in a series of cases involving forensic misconduct before the grand jury, suggested that the time had come for a prophylactic dismissal.[b] The court (per Gibbons, J.) noted:

"[D]ismissal of the indictment may be proper even where no actual prejudice has been shown, if there is evidence that the challenged activity was something other than an isolated incident unmotivated by sinister ends, or that the type of misconduct challenged has become 'entrenched and flagrant' in the circuit. * * * We recognize that dismissal of an indictment

b. The prosecutor, in his presentation before the first grand jury, had: (1) attempted to associate the defendants, without evidentiary basis, with organized crime; (2) referred to loansharking charges against alleged associates of the defendants without noting that the charges had resulted in acquittal; (3) impugned the testimony of a witness who failed to link the defendants with organized crime; and (4) "hectored other uncooperative witnesses for their failure to comply with unrelated federal laws." However, the indictment before the court had been issued by a second grand jury, which may not have had before it the transcript of the proceedings of the first grand jury. The case accordingly was remanded, but the Third Circuit noted the indictment should be quashed if the indicting grand jury had been "infected" by the misconduct before the first grand jury.

may impose important costs upon the prosecution and the public. At a minimum, the government will be required to present its evidence to a grand jury unaffected by bias or prejudice. But the costs of continued unchecked prosecutorial misconduct are also substantial. This is particularly so before the grand jury, where the prosecutor operates without the check of a judge or a trained legal adversary, and virtually immune from public scrutiny. The prosecutor's abuse of his special relationship to the grand jury poses an enormous risk to defendants as well. For while in theory a trial provides the defendant with a full opportunity to contest and disprove the charges against him, in practice, the handing up of an indictment will often have a devastating personal and professional impact that a later dismissal or acquittal can never undo. * * * We suspect that dismissal of an indictment may be virtually the only effective way to encourage compliance with these ethical standards, and to protect defendants from abuse of the grand jury process. Certainly the constant flow of cases to this court involving prosecutorial misconduct before petit juries demonstrates that judicial 'tongue clicking' and adjurations as to the 'better practice' are likely to have little impact on the problem."

(b) In *United States v. Griffith,* 756 F.2d 1244 (6th Cir.1985), the prosecutor informed the grand jury, in the course of a rambling discourse on the events of the last week, that: (1) the target had somehow learned that his brother had testified before the grand jury and had assaulted and threatened him, (2) the target had subsequently been charged with obstruction of justice, and the magistrate had even denied bail, which was "as rare an occurrence in the federal system as you are going to find"; (3) the target subsequently had expressed an interest in plea bargaining, but had been told that there absolutely would be no deal for probation; (4) the source of the grand jury leak was unknown, but it could have been bribery or even the planting of a bug. The Sixth Circuit (per Martin, J.) condemned the prosecutor's comments as "outrageous," but also concluded that dismissal of the indictment was not warranted:

"In this Circuit, the law is clear that a court may not order dismissal of an indictment under its supervisory power unless the defendant demonstrates that 'prosecutorial misconduct is a long-standing or common problem in grand jury proceedings in [the] district.' *United States v. Nembhard,* 676 F.2d 193 (6th Cir.1982). In addition to demonstrating long-standing prosecutorial misconduct, a defendant who seeks dismissal of an indictment also must show that he was prejudiced by the prosecutor's actions. *United States v. Nembhard.* It has been argued that a defendant who seeks dismissal under the court's supervisory power need not show actual prejudice. The rationale for this view is that the court should strive to preserve societal values—deterrence of official misconduct and preservation of the appearance of fairness—regardless of whether the misconduct results in prejudice to the defendant. We * * * rejected that view in *Nembhard.* We held that prejudice must be shown before we will use a constitutional basis or our supervisory power to dismiss an indictment for prosecutorial misconduct. * * *

"[Defendant] Reynolds has shown neither long-standing abuse of the grand jury nor actual prejudice. Reynolds offered no proof to the district court that prosecutors in the Eastern District of Michigan have a history of abusing the grand jury process. Reynolds offered no proof that [prosecutor] Leibson has a history of such abuse. * * * The record also fails to show that Reynolds was prejudiced by Leibson's remarks. Although the remarks surely were inflammatory, they occurred nearly eleven months before the prosecutor requested indictments. Reynolds points to no subsequent remarks that reinforced the incident in the jurors' minds. Indeed, the grand jury heard witnesses testify that Reynolds ultimately was acquitted on the obstruction charge. Further, Reynolds has never claimed that the evidence presented to the grand jury was insufficient to support the indictment."

4. How does a defendant challenging an indictment establish that there was prosecutorial misconduct? The best source usually is the transcript of the grand jury proceedings. However, some states do not require transcriptions. Moreover, in many jurisdictions that do require transcriptions, the transcription need not include discussions between the prosecutor and the jury (i.e., only testimony is transcribed). Where a complete transcription is available, the defendant will not gain automatic access to that transcript unless the jurisdiction is one of those non-*Costello* states cited in Note 13, p. 1006 supra. In other jurisdictions, as under Federal Rule 6(e)(C)(i), the defendant ordinarily will have to make a preliminary showing before the court will either permit defense inspection or conduct an *in camera* examination. See, e.g., *Beatrice Foods Co. v. United States,* 312 F.2d 29 (8th Cir.1963). But see *United States v. Singer,* 660 F.2d 1295 (8th Cir.1981) (district court has discretion to examine the transcript *in camera* even if the requisite showing is not made). Where the misconduct occurred while a witness was present, the witness' affidavit usually will be sufficient. If only the jurors and the prosecutor were present, the defense counsel will face a much more difficult task. In most jurisdictions, secrecy requirements prohibit grand jurors from discussing the proceedings with defense counsel, except with the permission of the court, and they will not be allowed to testify to what occurred during the proceedings. See, e.g., *People ex rel. Sears v. Romiti,* 277 N.E.2d 705 (Ill.1971) (refusing to accept juror affidavits alleging improper statements by the prosecutor).

5. *Erroneous legal advice.* Whether the legal advice comes from the prosecutor or the judge, it can be so clearly erroneous and so likely to have influenced the jury as to require dismissal of the indictment. See LaFave and Israel, § 15.5(c). Since the judge ordinarily gives only general instructions, dismissal on the basis of the judge's charge is unlikely absent comments that go substantially beyond the charging function. See, e.g., *LeGrande v. Commonwealth,* 494 S.W.2d 726 (Ky.1973) (where the judge informed the jury of "his personal knowledge and opinion concerning the prevalence of gambling in the community," his charge "warrants criticism as giving some indication of overzealous advocacy," but falls short of the direction to indict that would require dismissal). Erroneous legal advice of the prosecutor is most likely to justify dismissal where the prosecutor misstated a critical element of the offense, particularly where the misstatement was used by the prosecutor to cut off a relevant line of inquiry suggested by one or more jurors. However, indictments have also been dismissed for omissions that were sufficiently glaring (e.g., where the prosecutor failed to take even the minimal step of reading the relevant statute to the grand jury). Courts keep in mind that, unlike the trial judge who can rely upon counsel to call his attention to omissions in the jury instructions, the prosecutor before the grand jury is entirely on his own.

6. *Secrecy violations.* See LaFave and Israel, § 15.5(f): "Establishing that the prosecutor violated secrecy requirements is often difficult, but courts discussing alleged violations have emphatically condemned such disclosures and even insisted upon internal safeguards to prevent possible violations. Nevertheless, they also have suggested that even the most flagrant violation—a purposeful leak to the press—would not justify dismissing an indictment since the violation in itself would not create a reasonable likelihood of prejudice [as to the issuance of the indictment]. * * * Any potential trial prejudice can be met through voir dire, change of venue, and similar remedies." Consider, however, *United States v. Kilpatrick,* 594

F.Supp. 1324 (D.Colo.1984), where the court (Kane, J.) relied upon secrecy violations as an independent basis for dismissal, apart from various other actions also said to require dismissal. The secrecy violations consisted primarily of dissemination of information concerning the investigation to customers of the targets, the sharing of grand jury information with a government witness, improper disclosure to government personnel, and the imposing of a secrecy obligation on two witnesses. The court concluded that the violations worked to the government's tactical advantage, that they were "intentional or reckless and systematic," and that the sanction of contempt was "insufficient." But consider, *United States v. Anderson*, 778 F.2d 602 (10th Cir.1985) (rejecting a roughly similar ruling by the same district court).

7. *Juror misfeasance.* Should an indictment be dismissed upon a showing that, although the requisite number of jurors voted for indictment, less than that number heard all of the evidence presented to the grand jury? *State ex rel. McCann v. Thompson,* 144 F.2d 604 (2d Cir.1944), the leading case on the issue, answered in the negative. The court reasoned that the defendant had no cause to complain; the absentee juror heard enough evidence to convince him to vote for an indictment and the evidence he missed most likely would only have added to the case against the defendant. With some federal courts now recognizing a prosecutorial obligation to present exculpatory evidence under some circumstances (see Note 10, p. 1003 supra), should the conclusion reached in *Thompson* be reexamined? See *United States v. Leverage Funding Systems,* 637 F.2d 645 (9th Cir.1980) (*Thompson* reaffirmed; "a grand juror can * * * fulfill his or her constitutional role of determining whether the prosecution has presented a prima facie case even if he or she was absent during the presentation of exculpatory evidence"); *United States v. Lang,* 644 F.2d 1232 (7th Cir.1981) (adding that lengthy investigations would be disrupted if at least 12 jurors had to have heard all the evidence themselves; under current practices, when jurors are forced to withdraw during an ongoing investigation, the grand jury takes on replacement jurors without starting anew).

8. *Unauthorized presence.* Grand jury secrecy provisions commonly provide that no person other than the grand jurors may be present during their deliberations and only the jurors, the witness, the prosecutor, and supporting personnel (e.g., stenographer) may be present while testimony is being heard. See, e.g., Fed.R.Crim. P. 6(d). Should an indictment be dismissed because an unauthorized person was present in violation of the jurisdiction's secrecy provision? All jurisdictions agree that an unauthorized presence may justify dismissal, but they are divided as to whether dismissal will be required in the absence of a showing of likely prejudice or actual prejudice.

The Federal courts (and most state courts) treat unauthorized presence as a per se ground for dismissal requiring no showing of prejudice. Exceptions may be made for technical infractions (e.g., a messenger inadvertently wandered into the grand jury room and was quickly dispatched) but not for sustained violations. See e.g., *United States v. Mechanik,* 735 F.2d 136 (4th Cir.1984), cert. granted, ___ U.S. ___, 105 S.Ct. 3476, 87 L.Ed.2d 612 (1985) (two agents testified together before the grand jury); *United States v. Pignatiello,* 582 F.Supp. 251 (D.Colo. 1984) (S.E.C. attorney had failed to qualify as special assistant to U.S. Attorney and therefore her presence was unlawful under Rule 6). Can the adoption of a per se approach—requiring no showing as to how the unauthorized presence might have affected the grand jury's decision to indict—be squared with *Costello* or the cases discussed in Notes 1–6 supra?

Chapter 16

THE CHARGING INSTRUMENT

SECTION 1. THE DEVELOPMENT OF MODERN PLEADING REQUIREMENTS [a]

I. THE LIBERALIZATION OF PLEADING REQUIREMENTS

As first developed in the common law system, the accusatory pleading was a quite simple document. In the early fourteenth century, it was sufficient to allege that "A stole an ox," "B burgled a house," or "C slew a man." Over the next few centuries, however, as the criminal law grew more complex and defendants were allowed to use counsel to challenge indictments, English courts came to demand that the pleading contain a full statement of the facts and legal theory underlying the charge. Indictments were lengthy, highly detailed, and filled with technical jargon. Pleading requirements for particular crimes often paralleled in their complexity and formalism the special civil pleadings required for the different forms of action. An indictment charging an assault, for example, had to include the phrase "*vi et armis*," and a murder charge had to describe not only the means used but also the nature and extent of the wound inflicted.

American courts inherited the complex, formalistic, and often confusing pleading requirements of the eighteenth century common law, and they did not hesitate to require strict adherence to those requirements. Indictments were not infrequently quashed for the most picayune errors in form. Moreover, defects in an indictment were not waived by defendant's failure to raise his objection before trial; most defects could be challenged for the first time after conviction, usually by a motion in arrest of judgment. As a result, courts were often overturning convictions fully supported by the evidence simply because the underlying indictment was inartfully drawn or awkwardly worded. A conviction could also be reversed because the evidence at trial varied from the facts alleged in the indictment. Here too, the courts generally were strict, except for a variance as to the date of the offense. Thus, an early Delaware decision reversed a conviction under an indictment alleging the theft of a "pair of shoes" because the evidence established that both of the shoes stolen were for the right foot and therefore did not constitute a pair.

While the formalism and detail mandated by the common law pleading rules were designed in part to provide notice to the accused, they clearly went beyond what was needed to provide notice alone. Indeed, it has been suggested that the "common law indictment, replete with archaic terminology and ritualistic formulae, was a

a. The discussion in this section is largely derived from LaFave and Israel, § 19.2(a), and supporting citations can be found there.

lengthy and tortuous document, which * * * served more to mystify than to inform the defendant." As Sir James Stephen observed, a major function of the "strictness and technicality" in indictments was to guard against "looseness in the legal definitions of crimes." At a time when "the concepts and definitions of offenses took form largely through the experience of administration and without the aid of definitive statutes," the requirement that the offense be stated according to a particular formula, specifying in detail each element of the crime, was seen as providing assurance both that the grand jury understood what was necessary to establish an offense and that the courts did not engage in unanticipated extensions of the substance of the offense. Courts in later years suggested that perhaps an equally significant function of the complex common law requirements was to supply the judiciary with grounds that were readily available for reversing convictions in "hard cases." As one court put it: "When stealing a handkerchief worth £ I was punished by death, and there were nearly 200 different capital offenses; it was to the credit of humanity that technicalities could be invoked in order to prevent the cruelty of a strict and literal enforcement of the law."

By the mid-1800's, with the increasing codification of the substantive criminal law and the reduction in the number of capital offenses, many courts no longer insisted upon strict adherence to the technical rules of pleading. The former practice, it was noted, had in many cases permitted "public justice" to be evaded and "let loose upon society" the "most dangerous malefactors." These courts would "no longer permit the guilty man to escape punishment by averring that he cannot comprehend * * * what is palpable and evident to the common sense of everybody else." Many courts did not share this philosophy, however, and still others moved slowly in departing from common law precedents. As a result, legislative reform was deemed necessary. In general, the new legislation was directed at relaxing specific common law requirements. Thus, it was provided that a murder indictment need not allege the manner or means of causing death, that there was no need to specify the denomination or species of money taken in a theft, and that the absence of specified phrases, such as "with force and arms," did not render an indictment invalid. More general provisions stated that variances would not be fatal unless they were "material," and that indictments should not "be deemed insufficient * * * by reason of any defect or imperfection in form only, which shall not tend to the prejudice of the defendant." Since the common law pleading requirements had been carried over from indictments to informations, the new legislation was made applicable to both informations and indictments.

The judicial response to the new legislation was mixed. Although most jurisdictions had adopted some form of pleading reform by the turn of the century, courts in many states continued to insist that offenses be charged with technical accuracy and nicety of language. In 1907, the Missouri Supreme Court reversed a conviction on appeal because the indictment charged that the offense was against the "peace and dignity of State," having left out the necessary word "the" before "State." A few years later, the Illinois Supreme Court set aside a larceny conviction because the indictment stated that the property was stolen from the "American Express Company, an association" and thereby failed to aver "ownership in any person, firm, corporation, or other entity that * * * [could] be the owner of property." The legislative response to these and similar decisions was the enactment of broader pleading reform legislation. The most widely adopted measures in this second round of legislative liberalization of pleading requirements centered upon three interrelated reforms: (1) a single simplified pleading standard; (2) official forms for the most commonly prosecuted crimes; and (3) an expanded waiver rule.[b] These reforms, which had been instituted at an earlier point in many states, were incorporated in the Federal Rules of Criminal Procedure, which became effective in 1946. Today, they are found in almost all jurisdictions, with many states having provisions that are almost a verbatim copy of the Federal Rules provisions. In addition, many jurisdictions also adopted measures requiring a less stringent approach to variances.

Federal Rule 7(c) sets forth the most common formulation of a simplified pleading standard: "The indictment or information shall be a plain, concise, and definite written statement of the essential facts constituting the offense charged." This standard offered several advantages over the provisions adopted in the first wave of pleading reforms. Many of those provisions dealt either with a specific common law pleading requirement or a particular crime. Rule 7(c), on the other hand, established a single standard, applicable to the pleading of all crimes and all elements of the pleading. Moreover, that standard had behind it the basic thrust of an already achieved reform since it was a rough counterpart of the standard that reformers had previously used in mandating simplified pleadings in civil cases. Thus, looking to that civil reform, a court could readily conclude that Rule 7(c) required that a pleading do no more than "set forth, in factual terms, the elements of the offense sought to be charged."

Supporting the basic thrust of the Rule 7(c) standard were the official forms. That Rule 7(c) did not mandate all of the detail found in the common law pleading was apparent from its reference to a "concise" statement of the "essential" facts. On the other hand, the Rule 7(c) standard also rejected the truncated short-form pleading of "A murdered B," that several states had adopted (see fn. b supra). Exactly how little detail was needed obviously would vary with the offense, but the official forms provided useful illustrations of what the reformers had in mind. The Federal Rules include forms for 11 different crimes. In many states, forms were adopted for a much larger group of offenses. In addition to providing the prosecutor with a safe path for pleading the listed offenses, the forms served to "illustrate the simplicity of statement which the Rules were designed to achieve." Thus, Federal Rule Form 1, for the offense of murder in the first degree of a federal officer, stated:

> On or about the ______ day of ______, in the ______ District of ______, John Doe with premeditation and by means of shooting murdered John Roe, who was then an officer of the Federal Bureau of Investigation of the Department of Justice engaged in the performance of his official duties.[c]

b. Another legislative avenue to the liberalization of pleading requirements was the authorization of "short-form" pleadings. The authorizing statute would specify the particular language to be used in alleging the most common criminal offenses. That language would present an extremely truncated description of the criminal conduct. A murder pleading, for example, would allege only that "A.B. murdered C.D." If the defendant wanted more information, he was entitled to a "bill of particulars setting up specifically the nature of the offense charged." The theory underlying the short-form pleading was that the pleading would be immune from attack (assuming the specified language was followed) and the defendant would receive his notice through the bill of particulars. At one time, more than a dozen states had authorized some form of short-form pleading, but prosecutors in many of those jurisdictions were hesitant to use the short-forms, perhaps due to concern that the delegation of so much of the basic allegation to the prosecutor's bill of particulars was inconsistent with the concept of grand jury screening (constitutionally guaranteed in many of those states by provisions similar to the Fifth Amendment). The end result was that the short-form legislation was eventually discarded in several of the states. Today, short form pleadings are regularly used in only a handful of states.

c. In 1983, the Federal Forms were abrogated as "unnecessary." Most jurisdictions, however, continue to retain official forms.

The third element of the second round of pleading reforms was the use of an expansive waiver doctrine that forced most pleading objections to be raised before trial. Federal Rule 12, for example, provides that several specified defense claims must be raised before trial, with the failure to do so constituting a "waiver thereof." Subsection (b) of Rule 12 includes among these claims: "Defenses and objections based on defects in the indictment or information (other than it fails to show jurisdiction in the court or to charge an offense which objections shall be noticed by the court at any time during the pendency of the proceedings)." This provision was designed to restrict the defense tactic of "sandbagging" that was available in many jurisdictions under common law pleading. Under the old practice, counsel would often forego raising a pleading defect before trial. Assuming that counsel did not need further notice, the only benefit obtained from a successful pretrial objection was some degree of delay while the prosecution obtained a perfected charging instrument. On the other hand, if counsel simply bypassed the pretrial objection and the case went to trial and ended in a conviction, counsel could then raise the defect in the pleading on a motion in arrest of judgment and obtain a new trial. Federal Rule 12 eliminated this tactic as to all objections except the failure to show jurisdiction or to charge an offense. While those objections could be raised for the first time at any point in the proceeding, any lesser objection to the pleadings would be lost if not raised before trial.

While the requirement of a pretrial objection hopefully would reduce the number of convictions that were reversed due to pleading defects,[d] it did not respond to the problem of convictions reversed due to a variance between the allegations contained in a proper pleading and the proof introduced at trial. Many states, seeking to preclude application of the rather strict common law view of variance, adopted legislation permitting the pleading to be amended at trial to conform to the proof (thereby "curing" the variance), provided the defendant was not prejudiced by the amendment. The Federal Rules did not include such a provision as to indictments, although it did allow liberal amendment of an information. The Supreme Court had adopted a very strict rule on amendments of the indictment that had constitutional underpinnings. See Note 5, p. 1033 infra. Moreover, it was thought that the simplified pleading permitted under Rule 7(c) would in itself reduce the likelihood that variances would occur. Since the pleading need not include a detailed description of the circumstances of the offense, there was less factual specificity from which the proof could vary. The Rule also allowed the prosecution to allege that the offense was committed by "one or more specified means." Thus, if the prosecution was uncertain as to whether its proof would establish that the offense was committed in one manner or another, it need not make a choice and hope that its proof would support that particular alternative. Similarly, where an offense encompassed more than one mental element or result, the Federal Rules (and most states) permitted pleadings that, in effect, set forth the various possibilities as alternatives.

The effectiveness of pleading reforms such as those contained in the Federal Rules depended upon the receptiveness of the courts. The standards applied were not so precise as to preclude a court from

d. Of course, requiring that an objection to a pleading error be raised before trial does not preclude the possibility that a conviction will be reversed on appeal due to that error. The trial court may reject the defendant's pretrial objection and an appellate court may hold that that ruling was erroneous. However, if the prosecution has any doubt as to the validity of its pleading (and as to any trial court ruling upholding that pleading), it can always avoid the possibility of a reversal on appeal by substituting a new pleading that meets the objection raised in defendant's pretrial objection. The requirement of a pretrial objection at least ensures that the prosecutor will have the opportunity to decide whether to run that risk. See also Note 8, p. 1026 infra.

retaining much of the common law approach to pleadings, at least where a specific official form was not applicable. The federal courts generally were most willing to interpret the Rules in light of the spirit of the reform movement. Most state courts followed a similar approach. A few, however, continued to adhere to a policy of requiring technical preciseness of language and substantial detail in description, though hardly rivaling their common law predecessors in this regard.[e]

II. THE FUNCTIONS OF MODERN PLEADING REQUIREMENTS [a]

1. Courts frequently note that under modern pleading standards, the accusatory instrument must be tested by the basic functions that a pleading should fulfill rather than by technical pleading requirements. Although those functions are described somewhat differently by different courts, basically five different functions have been cited. These are: (1) providing protection against twice being put in jeopardy; (2) providing notice; (3) facilitating judicial review of the legal sufficiency of the prosecution's case; (4) providing a formal basis for the judgment; and (5) keeping the prosecution within the charge issued by the grand jury. The first four of these functions are said to apply to all charging instruments (basically the "complaint" or "information" in the misdemeanor case and the "information" or "indictment" in the felony case). The fifth, by its very nature, is confined to the indictment.

2. *The double jeopardy function.* The pleading's double jeopardy function—commonly formulated as a requirement that the pleading charge an offense with sufficient specificity so that the defendant can plead the double jeopardy bar to a subsequent prosecution for the same offense—was viewed as a major objective of the pleading at common law. Both commentators and courts have questioned whether it has much significance in an era of complete transcription of court proceedings. A defendant raising a double jeopardy objection no longer need rely solely on the charging instrument in his previous prosecution to establish that he is twice being tried for the same offense, but can look to the record of his trial or the showing of a factual basis accompanying his guilty plea. Accordingly, it is argued, "protection against successive prosecutions for the same offense * * * [should] not require of an accusation any more completeness than the notice function demands." Scott, *Fairness in Accusation of Crime,* 41 Minn.L. Rev. 509 (1957).

3. *Providing notice.* The notice function of the pleading is often characterized as the primary function served by modern pleading requirements. It is a function that the Supreme Court has described as constitutionally mandated by the defendant's Sixth Amendment right "to be informed of the nature and cause of the accusation." The major question asked as to this function is not whether it serves a needed end, but rather what its scope should be.

That the pleading should give the defendant "factual notice" is well accepted. The primary disagreement here concerns the amount of detail that must be provided

e. Perhaps the foremost adherent to such a policy is the Texas Court of Criminal Appeals. The decisions of that court are reviewed in Dix, *Texas Charging Instrument Law: Recent Developments and the Continuing Need for Reform,* 35 Baylor L.Rev. 689 (1983). Although various current decisions of that court could readily be placed alongside the rulings that predated the pleading reforms of the early 1900's, *Ex parte Warnell,* 606 S.W.2d 923 (Tex.Crim.App.1980) (en banc) may be the prime example. That case held that an indictment charging the defendant with burglary suffered from a "fundamental defect" (thereby justifying postconviction relief, notwithstanding a failure to object to the indictment prior to conviction) because the indictment failed to allege in its conclusion, as required by the Texas Constitution, that the offense was committed "against the peace and dignity of the state."

a. The discussion in this section is largely derived from LaFave and Israel, § 19.2(b), (c) and supporting citations can be found there.

to adequately serve this function. Is it sufficient to identify the event that is the basis for the charge or must the pleading also describe in detail each of the factual elements that will be proven to establish liability? In charging the crime of theft by deception, for example, is it sufficient to state when and where the alleged misrepresentation took place, or must the charging instrument also specify which of defendant's representations were false and, perhaps, why they were factually incorrect? Should it matter, in this regard, whether or not the same information may be obtained by the defendant through a bill of particulars? What if the same information will be presented, albeit in a less focused form, in the course of the defendant's pretrial discovery of the evidence that the prosecutor intends to introduce at trial? What if the same information already has been presented in the preliminary hearing (or would have been presented had defendant not waived his right to a preliminary hearing)? These and other "notice issues" are commonly presented in the course of determining whether the charging instrument contains sufficient factual specificity in alleging particular elements of an offense.

Another aspect of the required notice might be informing the defendant of the prosecution's basic legal theory. Such notice arguably is provided through the traditional pleading requirement that the "facts alleged establish all of the essential elements of the offense." There is disagreement, however, as to whether this "essential elements" requirement is properly grounded on the notice function or on other pleading functions. Some would contend that the notice function is limited to informing the defendant of the essential fact situation that the prosecution will establish, and that that function can readily be fulfilled without including the facts underlying each and every element of the offense. They see the essential elements requirement as an aspect of the "judicial review" function or the "formal basis" function of the pleading. Still, cases holding pleadings inadequate for failing to meet the essential elements requirement frequently refer to the need to provide the defendant with adequate notice.

4. *The "judicial review" function.* The judicial review function has been described by the Supreme Court as "inform[ing] the [trial] court of the facts alleged, so that it may be decided whether they are sufficient in law to support a conviction, if one should be had." Although this function is mentioned less frequently than the "notice" and "double jeopardy" functions, commentators have suggested that it may be the primary function underlying the requirement that the pleading contain allegations establishing all essential elements of the offense. This requirement ensures that the pleading will be sufficient to allow a pretrial testing, on a motion to dismiss, of the prosecution's view of the legal elements of the offense. Such testing is said to be especially important as to elements not fully set forth in the language of the statute. Consider, for example, a situation in which the statute does not refer to a mens rea element, and there is some question as to the level of mens rea required. By insisting that the prosecution include a specific mens rea allegation in the charging instrument, the essential elements requirement facilitates a pretrial determination as to what mens rea is required. Such a determination may save an unnecessary trial (as where the court holds that a higher mens rea is required and the prosecution lacks evidence to establish that mens rea), will allow the prosecution to gain appellate review if the court adopts an adverse interpretation of the law,[b] and should at least establish a

b. Almost all jurisdictions allow prosecution appeal from a pretrial dismissal based on a failure to charge any offense. See Note 2, p. 1456 infra. On the other hand, a ruling on the content of the offense adverse to the prosecution is not likely to be appealable if made after the trial has started, since jeopardy has then attached, common legal framework that can guide both sides in making their factual presentations.

5. *Providing a formal basis for the judgment.* Several commentators have contended that neither the judicial review nor the notice function fully explain the rigorous application of the essential elements requirement by many courts. They note that convictions have been reversed on appeal due to a charging instrument's failure to allege an essential element of the offense even though that element was clearly proven at trial, there was no objection to the charging instrument's deficiency prior to the conviction, and there was no hint of defense surprise since the element not alleged was clearly set forth in the statute defining the offense or in previous judicial rulings. Such appellate rulings—commonly accompanied by judicial statements that a pleading which fails to charge an offense is "fundamentally defective," rendering "void ab initio" any subsequent conviction—are viewed by the commentators as pointing to the continuing vitality of a pleading function only infrequently acknowledged in judicial opinions. At common law, the foremost function of the pleading was to provide a formal basis for the judgment of conviction. This function was said to require that the charging instrument set forth "everything necessary for a complete case on paper." Without such a pleading, there was no assurance that the trial court had not exceeded its authority in imposing a conviction for a particular offense and in setting punishment under that conviction. While modern pleading requirements hardly require the same degree of completeness as the common law, pleading rules still insist, it is argued, that the pleading sustain the exercise of judicial authority by alleging all of the basic elements of the offense for which punishment was imposed. Some commentators see the continued use of the pleading to serve such a function as inconsistent with the thrust of modern pleading reforms, arguing that it places a premium on the "form" of the pleading rather than the "substance of the defendant's rights." They attribute the retention of this pleading function largely to some mystical notion of "jurisdiction," rather than to any legitimate pleading need.[c]

6. *The grand jury function.* In those jurisdictions that require prosecution by indictment, modern pleading requirements may also be assigned the function of ensuring that the prosecution stays within the confines of the offense charged by the grand jury. Thus, pleading requirements may demand that the indictment contain "sufficient factual particularity to ensure that the prosecution will not fill in elements of its case with facts other than those considered by the grand jury." *United States v. Abrams,* 539 F.Supp. 378 (S.D.N.Y.1982). Here again, however, as with the double jeopardy function, courts and commentators have questioned the continuing importance of the pleading in serving this function.[d] The availability of transcribed grand jury proceedings is

and an acquittal flowing from that ruling bars prosecution appeal. See Chapter 24, section 2.

c. See Dix, p. 1016 supra, where the author describes the Texas courts' "jurisdictional" characterization of the essential elements requirement as "reflect[ing] a strongly held but undeveloped view of the requirement as being virtually beyond logical dispute." An early treatise writer, he notes, described this view as " 'originating in natural reason and abiding in abstract justice'; [u]nless a defendant stands before a court charged with all acts necessary to justify a particular punishment, infliction of a punishment—apparently despite proof of those facts—overturns 'fundamental justice.' " Professor Dix responds that a "reasoned analysis suggests no convincing reason why a trial court's jurisdiction should depend upon pleading specificity. If a charging instrument adequately establishes that the state is seeking an opportunity to prove an accused person guilty of an offense, that should suffice. In the trial process, the state must provide the accused with adequate notice and prove the accused's guilt beyond a reasonable doubt. If this is done, it simply makes no sense to regard the court as without jurisdiction and the proceeding a nullity because of some perceived inadequacy of the charging instrument."

d. Consider, e.g., *People v. Iannone,* 384 N.E.2d 656 (N.Y.1978): "[T]he development of said to have substantially diminished the importance of the indictment in assessing whether the prosecutor has departed from the basic offense found by the grand jury.[e]

SECTION 2. THE APPLICATION OF MODERN PLEADING REQUIREMENTS

RUSSELL v. UNITED STATES

369 U.S. 749, 82 S.Ct. 1038, 8 L.Ed.2d 240 (1962).

MR. JUSTICE STEWART delivered the opinion of the Court.

Each of the petitioners was convicted [of violating 2 U.S.C. § 192 by] refusing to answer certain questions when summoned before a congressional subcommittee. In each case the indictment returned by the grand jury failed to identify the subject under congressional subcommittee inquiry at the time the witness was interrogated. [Each indictment stated that the particular defendant was summoned before a subcommittee on a particular date, that the subcommittee was conducting hearings pursuant to House Resolution 5 (authorizing the House Committee on Un-American Activities to conduct investigations of "un-American propaganda activities in the United States" and "all other questions in relation thereto that would aid Congress in any necessary remedial legislation"), that the defendant refused to answer certain questions (which were set forth verbatim), and that these questions "were pertinent to the question then under inquiry"]. In each case a motion was filed to quash the indictment before trial upon the ground that the indictment failed to state the subject under investigation at the time of the subcommittee's interrogation of the defendant. In each case the motion was denied. * * *

In enacting the criminal statute under which these petitioners were convicted Congress invoked the aid of the federal judicial system in protecting itself against contumacious conduct. The obvious consequence, as the Court has repeatedly emphasized, was to confer upon the federal courts the duty to accord a person prosecuted for this statutory offense every safeguard which the law accords in all other federal criminal cases. *Sinclair v. United States,* 279 U.S. 263, 49 S.Ct. 268, 73 L.Ed. 692 [(1929)].

modern discovery rules in criminal cases has diminished the significance of the indictment's function as a provider of information. The importance of the indictment as an instrument for effectuating other objectives traditionally obtained through the indictment has also lessened. For example, the need to utilize the indictment as the means of resolving any double jeopardy inquiry has been considerably alleviated by the modern practice of maintaining full records of criminal proceedings which may be considered by subsequent courts. Similarly, the function of the indictment as the vehicle for assuring that the crime for which the defendant is tried is the one for which he was indicted by the grand jury is of less significance due to the practicability of using sources extraneous to the indictment should a challenge be made on those grounds. In short, careful consideration of the realities of criminal practice in New York leads ineluctably to the conclusion that the basic essential function of an indictment qua document is simply to notify the defendant of the crime of which he stands indicted."

e. Indeed, the attempt to perform this function through either pleading requirements or a review of the grand jury transcript may be questioned. See, e.g., Dix, p. 1016 supra, at 694: "Implementing the accused's right to grand jury protection by insisting upon certain characteristics of the charging instrument accomplishes its goal only at significant collateral costs. Whether the increase in such protection is worth the cost paid must be a major consideration in charging instrument law. In addressing this question, and particularly in assessing the importance of the right to grand jury protection, it may be useful to consider the weight given to this interest in other procedural contexts. Assuring defendants of grand jury protection has not been regarded as sufficient to warrant giving them the right to challenge an indictment on the basis of evidence insufficiency. The need for grand jury secrecy and avoidance of frequent and time-consuming inquiries into grand jury proceedings are regarded as overriding any value such attacks might have in assuring that defendants are charged only on the basis of adequate information. [See Ch. 15, § 2]. * * * If the right to adequate grand jury consideration is to be weighed more heavily when it is offered in support of charging instrument claims, that distinction clearly requires justification."

Recognizing this elementary concept, the *Sinclair* case established several propositions which provide a relevant starting point here. First, there can be criminality under the statute only if the question which the witness refused to answer pertained to a subject then under investigation by the congressional body which summoned him. * * * Secondly, because the defendant is presumed to be innocent, it is "incumbent upon the United States to plead and show that the question [he refused to answer] pertained to some matter under investigation." Finally, *Sinclair* held that the question of pertinency is one for determination by the court as a matter of law.

* * * The crucial importance of determining the issue of pertinency is reflected in many cases which have come here since *Sinclair.* Our decisions have pointed out that the obvious first step in determining whether the questions asked were pertinent to the subject under inquiry is to ascertain what that subject was. Identification of the subject under inquiry is also an essential preliminary to the determination of a host of other issues which typically arise in prosecutions under the statute. * * * To be sure, the fact that difficulties and doubts have beset the federal courts in trying to ascertain the subject under inquiry could hardly justify, in the abstract, a requirement that indictments under the statute contain averments which would simplify the courts' task. * * * [But] the repeated appearance in prosecutions under a particular criminal statute of the same critical and difficult question, which could be obviated by a simple averment in the indictment, invites inquiry into the purposes and functions which a grand jury indictment is intended to serve. * * *

As we have elsewhere noted, "this Court has, in recent years, upheld many convictions in the face of questions concerning the sufficiency of the charging papers. Convictions are no longer reversed because of minor and technical deficiencies which did not prejudice the accused. This has been a salutary development in the criminal law." *Smith v. United States,* 360 U.S. 1, 79 S.Ct. 991, 3 L.Ed.2d 1041 [(1959)]. "But," as the *Smith* opinion went on to point out, "the substantial safeguards to those charged with serious crimes cannot be eradicated under the guise of technical departures from the rules." Resolution of the issue presented in the cases before us thus ultimately depends upon the nature of "the substantial safeguards" to a criminal defendant which an indictment is designed to provide. * * *

In a number of cases the Court has emphasized two of the protections which an indictment is intended to guarantee, reflected by two of the criteria by which the sufficiency of an indictment is to be measured. These criteria are, first, whether the indictment "contains the elements of the offense intended to be charged, 'and sufficiently apprises the defendant of what he must be prepared to meet,'" and, secondly, "in case any other proceedings are taken against him for a similar offense whether the record shows with accuracy to what extent he may plead a former acquittal or conviction." * * *

Without doubt the second of these preliminary criteria was sufficiently met by the indictments in these cases. Since the indictments set out not only the times and places of the hearings at which the petitioners refused to testify, but also specified the precise questions which they then and there refused to answer, it can hardly be doubted that the petitioners would be fully protected from again being put in jeopardy for the same offense, particularly when it is remembered that they could rely upon other parts of the present record in the event that future proceedings should be taken against them. * * * The vice of these indictments, rather, is that they failed to satisfy the first essential criterion by which the sufficiency of an indictment is to be tested, i.e., that they failed to sufficiently apprise the defendant "of what he must be prepared to meet." * * * [T]he very core of criminality under 2 U.S.C. § 192, is pertinency to the subject under inquiry of the questions which the defendant refused to answer. * * * Where guilt depends so crucially upon such a specific identification of fact, our cases have uniformly held that an indictment must do more than simply repeat the language of the criminal statute.

"It is an elementary principle of criminal pleading, that where the definition of an offence, whether it be at common law or by statute, 'includes generic terms, it is not sufficient that the indictment shall charge the offence in the same generic terms as in the definition; but it must state the species,—it must descend to particulars.'" *United States v. Cruikshank,* 92 U.S. 542, 23 L.Ed. 588 [(1876)]. An indictment not framed to apprise the defendant "with reasonable certainty, of the nature of the accusation against him * * * is defective, although it may follow the language of this statute." *United States v. Simmons,* 96 U.S. 360, 24 L.Ed. 819 [(1878)]. * * * That these basic principles of fundamental fairness retain their full vitality under modern concepts of pleading, and specifically under Rule 7(c) of the Federal Rules of Criminal Procedure, is illustrated by many recent federal decisions.

The vice which inheres in the failure of an indictment under 2 U.S.C. § 192, to identify the subject under inquiry is thus the violation of the basic principle "that the accused must be apprised by the indictment, with reasonable certainty, of the nature of the accusation against him, * * *." *United States v. Simmons,* supra. A cryptic form of indictment in cases of this kind requires the defendant to go to trial with the chief issue undefined. It enables his conviction to rest on one point and the affirmance of the conviction to rest on another. It gives the prosecution free hand on appeal to fill in the gaps of proof by surmise or conjecture. The Court has had occasion before now to condemn just such a practice in a quite different factual setting. *Cole v. Arkansas,* 333 U.S. 196, 68 S.Ct. 514, 92 L.Ed. 644 [(1948)].[a] And the unfairness and uncertainty which have characteristically infected criminal proceedings under this statute which were based upon indictments which failed to specify the subject under inquiry are illustrated by the cases in this Court already discussed. The same uncertainty and unfairness are underscored by the records of the cases now before us. A single example will suffice to illustrate the point.

In No. 12, *Price v. United States,* the petitioner refused to answer a number of questions put to him by [subcommittee]. * * * At the beginning of the hearing in question, the Chairman and other subcommittee members made widely meandering statements purporting to identify the subject under inquiry. It was said that * * * the investigation was of "such attempt as may be disclosed on the part of the Communist Party . . . to influence or to subvert the American Press." It was also said that "we are simply investigating communism wherever we find it." In dealing with a witness who testified shortly before Price, counsel for the subcommittee emphatically denied that it was the subcommittee's purpose "to investigate Communist infiltration of the press and other forms of communication." But when Price was called to testify before the subcommittee no one offered even to attempt to inform him of what subject the subcommittee did have under inquiry. At the trial the Government took the position that the subject under inquiry had been Communist activities generally. The district judge before whom the case was tried found that "the questions put were pertinent to the matter under inquiry" without indicating what he though the subject under inquiry was. The Court of Appeals, in

a. *Cole* held that a state supreme court violated due process when it affirmed the conviction of defendants charged and tried for one offense on the ground that they had actually committed another offense, which was "separate, distinct, and substantially different."

affirming the conviction, likewise omitted to state what it thought the subject under inquiry had been. In this Court the Government contends that the subject under inquiry at the time the petitioner was called to testify was "Communist activity in news media." It is difficult to imagine a case in which an indictment's insufficiency resulted so clearly in the indictment's failure to fulfill its primary office—to inform the defendant of the nature of the accusation against him. * * *

It has long been recognized that there is an important corollary purpose to be served by the requirement that an indictment set out "the specific offence, coming under the general description," with which the defendant is charged. This purpose, as defined in *United States v. Cruikshank,* is "to inform the court of the facts alleged, so that it may decide whether they are sufficient in law to support a conviction, if one should be had." This criterion is of the greatest relevance here, in the light of the difficulties and uncertainties with which the federal trial and reviewing courts have had to deal in cases arising under 2 U.S.C. § 192, to which reference has already been made.

Viewed in this context, the rule is designed not alone for the protection of the defendant, but for the benefit of the prosecution as well, by making it possible for courts called upon to pass on the validity of convictions under the statute to bring an enlightened judgment to that task.

It is argued that any deficiency in the indictments in these cases could have been cured by bills of particulars. But it is a settled rule that a bill of particulars cannot save an invalid indictment. * * *

When Congress provided that no one could be prosecuted under 2 U.S.C. § 192, except upon an indictment, Congress made the basic decision that only a grand jury could determine whether a person should be held to answer in a criminal trial for refusing to give testimony pertinent to a question under congressional committee inquiry. A grand jury, in order to make that ultimate determination, must necessarily determine what the question under inquiry was. To allow the prosecutor, or the court, to make a subsequent guess as to what was in the minds of the grand jury at the time they returned the indictment would deprive the defendant of a basic protection which the guaranty of the intervention of a grand jury was designed to secure. For a defendant could then be convicted on the basis of facts not found by, and perhaps not even presented to, the grand jury which indicted him. * * * This underlying principle is reflected by the settled rule in the federal courts that an indictment may not be amended except by resubmission to the grand jury, unless the change is merely a matter of form. *Ex parte Bain* [p. 1033 infra].

For these reasons we conclude that an indictment under 2 U.S.C. § 192, 2 U.S.C.A. § 192 must state the question under congressional committee inquiry as found by the grand jury. * * *

MR. JUSTICE FRANKFURTER and MR. JUSTICE WHITE took no part in the decision of these cases.

MR. JUSTICE HARLAN, whom MR. JUSTICE CLARK joins, dissenting. * * *

The reasons given by the Court for its sudden holding, which unless confined to contempt of Congress cases bids fair to throw the federal courts back to an era of criminal pleading from which it was thought they had finally emerged, are novel and unconvincing. It is first argued that an allegation of "pertinency" in the statutory terms will not do, because that element is at "the very core of criminality" under § 192. * * * To me it seems quite clear that even under * * * cases decided long before Rule 7(c) came into being, the "pertinency" allegations of the present indictments would have been deemed sufficient. I think there can be no doubt about the matter after Rule 7(c).

In *United States v. Debrow,* [346 U.S. 374, 74 S.Ct. 113, 98 L.Ed. 92 (1953)], the Court in [upholding a perjury indictment which failed to allege either the name or authority of the person who administered the oath] * * * said: "The charges of the indictments followed substantially the wording of the statute, which embodies all the elements of the crime, and such charges clearly informed the defendants of that with which they were accused, * * * It is inconceivable to us how the defendants could possibly be misled as to the offense with which they stood charged. *The sufficiency of the indictment is not a question of whether it could have been more definite and certain.* If the defendants wanted more definite information as to the name of the person who administered the oath to them they could have obtained it by requesting a bill of particulars. Rule 7(f), F.R.Crim.Proc." (Emphasis supplied.)

It is likewise "inconceivable" to me how the indictments in the present cases can be deemed insufficient to advise these petitioners of the nature of the charge they would have to meet. * * * The subject matter of the investigations had been stated to the petitioners at the time of their appearances before the committees. And the committee transcripts of the hearings were presumably in their possession and, if not, were of course available to them. * * *

The Court says that its holding is needed to prevent the Government from switching on appeal, to the prejudice of the defendants to a different theory of pertinency from that on which the conviction may have rested. There are several good answers to this. To the extent that this fear relates to the subject under investigation, the Government cannot of course travel outside the confines of the trial record, of which the defendant has full knowledge. If what is meant is that the Government may not modify on appeal its "trial" view of the "connective reasoning" relied on to establish the germaneness of the questions asked to the subject matter of the inquiry, surely it would be free to do so, this aspect of pertinency being simply a matter of law. * * * Moreover the Court does not find these indictments deficient because they failed to allege the "connective reasoning." * * *

Referring to certain language in the *Cruikshank* case, the Court suggests that the present holding is supported by a further "important corollary purpose" which an indictment is intended to serve: to make "it possible for courts called upon to pass on the validity of convictions under the statute to bring an enlightened judgment to that task." But whether or not the Government has established its case on "pertinency" is something that must be determined on the record made at the trial, not upon the allegations of the indictment. There is no such thing as a motion for summary judgment in a criminal case. While appellate courts might be spared some of the tedium of going through these § 192 records were the allegations of indictments to spell out the "pertinency" facts, the Court elsewhere in its opinion recognizes that the issue at hand can hardly be judged in terms of whether fuller indictments "would simplify the courts' task."

The final point made by the Court is perhaps the most novel of all. It is said that a statement of the subject under inquiry is necessary in the indictment in order to fend against the possibility that a defendant may be convicted on a theory of pertinency based upon a subject under investigation different from that which may have been found by the grand jury. * * * This proposition is * * * certainly unsound on principle. In the last analysis it would mean that a prosecutor could not safely introduce or advocate at a trial evidence or theories, however relevant to the crime charged in the indictment, which he had not presented to the grand jury. If the Court's reasoning in this part of its opinion is sound, I can see no escape from the conclusion that a defendant convicted on a lesser included offense, not alleged by the grand jury in an indictment for the greater offense, would have a good plea in arrest of judgment.

In conclusion, I realize that one in dissent is sometimes prone to overdraw the impact of a decision with which he does not agree. Yet I am unable to rid myself of the view that the reversal of these convictions on such insubstantial grounds will serve to encourage recalcitrance to legitimate congressional inquiry, stemming from the belief that a refusal to answer may somehow be requited in this Court. And it is not apparent how the seeds which this decision plants in other fields of criminal pleading can well be prevented from sprouting. * * *

Notes and Questions

1. *The scope of Russell.* Is the key to *Russell* the special factual setting of that case? Dix, p. 1016 supra, notes that "the result in *Russell*—and the rhetoric supporting it—must be attributed in part at least to the committee whose questions the defendant refused to answer."

2. Is the specificity required in *Russell* largely the product of the special role of the pertinency requirement under 2 U.S.C. § 192? Compare with *Russell* the ruling in *United States v. Crippen,* 579 F.2d 340 (5th Cir.1978), as to the allegation of materiality in a perjury charge. The indictment there, charging the offense of making false statements before a grand jury, set forth the questions asked defendant and his answers (all concerning the alteration of odometer readings) and simply alleged that they were "material" to the grand jury's investigation "to determine whether violations of the Disclosure of Automobile Information Laws and other statutes of the United States had been committed." At trial, materiality was established on the theory that the offense under investigation was the use of new car stickers on used cars, and that alteration of the odometer (though not itself criminal) was "essential to the success of the suspected plan." Responding to the defendant's objection that the indictment failed to "include the factual basis for the allegation of materiality," the Fifth Circuit noted: "It is not necessary for an indictment to * * * allege in detail the factual proof that will be relied upon to support the charge. * * * That information, if essential to the defense, can be obtained by a motion for a bill of particulars. * * * To adopt the rule in false swearing cases that the full predicate for the charge be set forth in the indictment, in addition to the allegations of the essential elements of the offense, would be tantamount to requiring that such supporting evidence be alleged in indictments charging all other federal offenses."

3. *United States v. Crippen,* supra, did not discuss *Russell,* but other courts that have looked to *Russell* for guidance as to the specificity required in charging other offenses have drawn from it somewhat varying lessons. See e.g., *United States v. Winchester,* 407 F.Supp. 261 (D.Del.1975) (allegation that defendant knowingly submitted specified false purchase orders to HUD was insufficient since the order form contained numerous factual statements; to meet the " 'sufficient appraisal' requirement" of *Russell,* the indictment should have alleged which statements were viewed as false); *United States v. Bernstein,* 533 F.2d 775 (2d Cir.1976) (indictment alleging submission of false statements to FHA need not identify the specific false statements within the specified mortgage application forms; *Russell* referred to an element at the very core of criminality under the statute and the core here "is not the substance of the false statements but rather that knowing falsehoods were submitted"); *United States v. Curtis,* 506 F.2d 985 (10th Cir.1974) (indictment alleging mail fraud through "false and fictitious representations about the services of a computer matching service for single persons" did not sufficiently identify the

scheme to defraud to satisfy the "principles explicated and applied by *Russell*").

4. Would *Russell* have been decided differently if the prosecution there had been by information rather than indictment? Consider *United States v. Thomas,* 444 F.2d 919 (D.C.Cir.1971). The court there held that an indictment was insufficient in charging the felony offense of burglary since it alleged that defendant entered a dwelling "with intent to commit a criminal offense therein" but failed to identify the particular offense that defendant intended to commit upon entry. However, the court also found that the same language was sufficient to charge the lesser included misdemeanor offense of unlawful entry. Since that crime was not an "infamous" crime, defendant did not have a right to "the protections of a grand jury indictment" and the charge could be tested without reference to whether it "reveals that all the essential elements * * * were presented to the grand jury." Looking only to whether the pleading "informed appellant of the charges against him with sufficient particularity to allow him to prepare his defense," the indictment was sufficient to "place him on notice that he was charged with making an entry which was, by definition, without lawful authority," though it did not specify his unlawful purpose. But cf. *United States v. Fischetti,* 450 F.2d 34 (5th Cir.1971) (where the government has the option of bringing a misdemeanor charge by information, but elects to proceed by indictment, it is "bound by the principles governing indictments").

5. Does *Russell* establish a constitutional standard for the requisite specificity of a charging instrument in a criminal case? In *Choung v. California,* 320 F.Supp. 625 (E.D.Cal.1970), the court, relying heavily on *Russell,* held that a state defendant had been denied due process when a misdemeanor complaint charged, in the language of the governing California statute, that he entered upon school grounds "without lawful business therein" and "by his presence and acts" interfered with the peaceful conduct of the activities of the school. Under a state interpretation of the "without-lawful-business" clause, defendant would not have violated the statute unless he entered the school grounds for a purpose prohibited by another statute or regulation. The court concluded that the complaint, by failing to aver which statute or regulation ("among a potentially infinite number") the petitioner had intended to violate, left the prosecution, as in *Russell,* "free to roam at large—to shift its theory of criminality so as to take advantage of each passing vicissitude of the trial and appeal." Accordingly, the court held, the complaint failed to meet the constitutional minimum as to adequate notice.

6. *State cases.* The specificity required in setting forth the elements of a crime varies from state to state, from crime to crime, and from one element of the same crime to another. See LaFave and Israel, § 19.2(d). In general, the courts tend to insist upon greater specificity where the crime encompasses more factual variations. Thus, when charging false pretences, the prosecutor often will be required to specify which of the defendant's alleged representations were false. On the other hand, in charging a simple assault, it is usually sufficient to identify who was assaulted and when and where the assault occurred. As to almost every significant element of an offense, however, there is likely to be at least one jurisdiction that requires more or less specificity than the general rule.[a] See, e.g., *City of Tulsa v. Haley,* 554 P.2d 102

a. Perhaps the one standard that comes closest to gaining universal acceptance is the standard holding that "time and place * * * [do not] require considerable specificity because they ordinarily do not involve proof of an element of the crime." LaFave and Israel, § 19.2(d). Thus, "the time allegation can refer to the event as having occurred 'on or about a certain date' and within reasonable limits, proof of a date before or after that specified will be sufficient, provided it is within the statute of limitations." Ibid (also noting, however, that adherence to a specific time will be required where the date of the offense is material). Is the special allowance made for alle-

(Okla.Crim.App.1976) (simply alleging that defendant "assaulted" a specified person is insufficient: the defendant must know what "acts he must be prepared to meet" and this required indicating the method of assault—"did [he] strike the complainants with his fist, kick them, push or shove them down, or what?").

7. *The bill of particulars.* The function of the bill of particulars is to provide defendant with information about the details of the charge against him if this is necessary to the "preparation of his defense, and the avoidance of prejudicial surprise" at the trial. See LaFave and Israel, § 19.2(f). The exact relationship of the bill to the pleadings is not always clear. As noted in *Russell,* the bill does not cure an "invalid indictment." Yet its availability is frequently mentioned in cases holding an indictment not so vague as to be defective. See, e.g., *United States v. Debrow* (quoted in the *Russell* dissent).

Apart from the special requirements of short form pleading (see fn. b, p. 1014 supra), whether to grant or deny a request for a bill of particulars lies in the discretion of the trial court. Moreover, appellate courts will pay considerable deference to the trial courts in their exercise of that discretion. Although appellate courts frequently offer general guidelines for the use of the bill, those guidelines tend to provide only limited assistance in ruling on a particular request. For example, the directive that the bill should be used to protect the defendant against "prejudicial surprise," combined with the traditional assumption that the defendant is innocent and "has no knowledge of the facts charged," could be read literally to require disclosure of almost every alleged fact that defendant will have to meet at trial; yet even those trial judges most liberal in allowing a bill of particulars will stop far short of requiring such complete disclosure. So too, though it is commonly said that a bill of particulars "may not call for evidentiary matters," courts commonly order disclosure of information (e.g., the names of alleged coconspirators) that will identify the source of the government's evidence, if not set forth the evidence itself. The end result, as courts and commentators have noted, is a group of rulings on the bill of particulars that tend to be highly individualized and both permit and disallow requests for a wide-range of particulars.

8. *Prosecution strategy.* Where the defense raises a pretrial objection to the charging instrument alleging that it lacks sufficient specificity (as the defense did in *Russell* and in the cases cited in the Notes 2–3 supra), why doesn't the prosecution either provide that specificity by amendment or offer to do so by a bill of particulars? Consider in this connection the Notes at p. 1032 infra on the permissible scope of amendments and the Notes at p. 1039 infra on the problems presented by an evidentiary variance at trial. Does it make sense from the prosecution's perspective to keep the allegations of specifics in a charging instrument to a minimum? Consider Dix, p. 1016 supra, at 714 (discussing the strategy applicable to the initial pleading): "If sufficient specificity is provided [clearly] to survive a motion to quash, a prosecutor increases the risk that a fatal variance will develop at trial. This risk may prove to have been assumed unnecessarily. Given the uncertainty in regard to the degree of specificity required, the prosecutor may, in retrospect, find that he misconstrued what was required. Or, it may later develop that defense counsel would not have moved to quash the charging instrument, so that even the specificity demanded by the abstract law was not necessary in the particular case. On the other hand, if the instrument is drafted only to avoid fundamental deficiency, and defense counsel does move to quash, the limits on amendment will often mean that

gations of time and place, which dates back to the common law, an historical idiosyncracy or a logical product of pleading functions and practical necessity?

the state will have to reindict the defendant. This may or may not be burdensome, depending upon a variety of considerations. * * * Some delay, of course, is inevitable, and the delay may be substantial; in certain localities, reindictment may require waiting a substantial period until a new grand jury is empaneled. What effect delay will have is quite variable."

9. What bearing, if any, should *Russell* have upon the requirement that the pleading allege the essential elements of the crime? Consider *United States v. Keith,* infra.

UNITED STATES v. KEITH

605 F.2d 462 (9th Cir.1979).

HUG, CIRCUIT JUDGE:

Appellant Robert Keith, a Navajo Indian, was indicted on the charge of involuntary manslaughter within the confines of the Navajo Indian Reservation, in violation of 18 U.S.C. §§ 1153 and 1112. Before trial, Keith moved to dismiss the indictment for failure to allege two essential elements of the offense charged. After oral argument, the trial judge denied the motion. Keith was convicted after a jury trial. Keith argues that his conviction should be reversed on the ground that the district court erred in denying the motion. We agree with his argument and reverse.

Keith was charged under § 1112 with involuntary manslaughter after the automobile he was driving collided with another vehicle, killing the driver. Section 1112 provides in pertinent part:

> (a) Manslaughter is the unlawful killing of a human being without malice. It is of two kinds: (1) *Voluntary*—Upon a sudden quarrel or heat of passion; (2) *Involuntary*—In the commission of an unlawful act not amounting to a felony, or in the commission in an unlawful manner, or without due caution and circumspection, of a lawful act which might produce death.

The indictment tracked the language of § 1112 in charging that Keith operated his vehicle "without due caution and circumspection."[1]

Keith contends that two essential elements of the offense of involuntary manslaughter under § 1112 are that: (1) the defendant committed with gross negligence the action causing death; and (2) the defendant had actual knowledge that his conduct was a threat to the lives of others, or had knowledge of such circumstances as would have made reasonably foreseeable to him the peril to which his acts might subject others. He argues that the indictment failed to allege these two elements because the indictment alleged only that he operated his automobile "without due caution and circumspection." He reasons that the phrase "without due caution and circumspection" connotes simple negligence sufficient for civil liability, but not gross negligence.

Keith is correct in his contention that the two elements he cites are essential for an involuntary manslaughter conviction under § 1112. In *United States v. Pardee,* 368 F.2d 368 (4th Cir.1966), the court held that jury instructions concerning an alleged § 1112 offense were insufficient because they failed to advise that the Government must prove: (1) that the defendant acted with "gross negligence," defined as "wanton or reckless disregard for human life;" and (2) that the defendant had actual knowledge that his conduct was a threat to the lives of others, * * * or had knowledge of such circumstances as could reasonably be said to have made foreseeable to him the peril to which his

1. The indictment was worded as follows:

On or about June 15, 1978, in the District of Arizona, and within the confines of the Navajo Indian Reservation, Indian country, ROBERT KEITH, an Indian, did unlawfully kill Harold Leroy Taggart, a non-Indian, in the commission of a lawful act which might produce death, that is, the operation of an automobile by the said ROBERT KEITH, without due caution and circumspection. In violation of Title 18, United States Code, Sections 1153 and 1112.

acts might subject others. The indictment under which Keith was charged did not contain [these] elements of the offense charged.

The failure of an indictment to detail each element of the charged offense generally constitutes a fatal defect. *United States v. King,* 587 F.2d 956 (9th Cir.1978). The failure of the indictment to charge two essential elements could not be cured by the trial court by amendment or through jury instructions. The Supreme Court has stated: "The very purpose of the requirement that a man be indicted by grand jury is to limit his jeopardy to offenses charged by a group of his fellow citizens acting independently of either prosecution attorney or judge." *Russell v. United States.* To allow a prosecutor or court to make a subsequent guess as to what was in the minds of the grand jury at the time they returned the indictment would deprive the defendant of a basic protection that the grand jury was designed to secure, because a defendant could then be convicted on the basis of facts not found by, and perhaps not even presented to, the grand jury that indicted him. *Russell.* * * * The grand jury may well [not] have believed that § 1112 requires proof of those [two] elements.

The Government raises a number of objections to Keith's argument, but none of them is convincing. The Government contends that the indictment is sufficient because it tracks the language of § 1112. The Government's contention is incorrect. Although an indictment tracking the language of a statute is usually adequate because statutes usually include all the elements of a crime, an indictment is inadequate when it fails to allege an essential element of the offense even when it tracks the language of the statute. *United States v. Morrison* [Note 4, p. 1030 infra].

The Government appears to argue that Keith was not prejudiced by the language of the indictment because he did not request a bill of particulars. This argument is meritless. A bill of particulars cannot save an invalid indictment. *Russell v. United States.*

The Government notes that vagueness may not be imputed to a statute if judicial explication makes a statute clear so that fair notice is afforded. *United States v. Broncheau,* 597 F.2d 1260, 1263 (9th Cir. 1979). The Government argues that § 1112 and the indictment that tracked the language of § 1112 are not vague because numerous decisions have construed the phrase "without due caution and circumspection" to mean gross negligence. *Broncheau* is distinguishable. In *Broncheau,* the court noted that the term "Indian," which the appellant attacked as vague, as judicially developed from 1845 to the present, "has a meaning sufficiently precise for a man of average intelligence to 'reasonably understand that his contemplated conduct is proscribed.'" The phrase "without due caution and circumspection," however, has not been consistently defined by judicial decision to include the knowledge requirement of § 1112. Moreover, in *Broncheau,* the appellant admitted that he was an enrolled Indian and never suggested that he did not understand the term "Indian" as it applied to him. Here, in contrast, Keith made a timely motion to dismiss the indictment for the reason he argues on appeal. Keith's conviction for involuntary manslaughter is reversed.

MERRILL, CIRCUIT JUDGE, dissenting:

* * * A distinction must be made between two different situations: (1) Where judicial or decisional gloss adds new elements to a crime; (2) Where the gloss does no more than define the meaning of an element set forth in the statute. In the former case the newly added elements must be included in an indictment. In the latter case no new element has been added. The element set forth in the statute which has been judicially defined takes on the meaning given to it by the judicial definition. In this sense the statutory lan-

guage has become a term of art. When it is used in an indictment it carries with it the judicial definition. This is the case here. Gross negligence and foreseeability of harm are not required *in addition to* a lack of due caution and circumspection. They *constitute* that lack. Absent gross negligence and foreseeability of harm there is no such lack, and the *statutory* element has not been established.

In such a case the jury must, of course, be instructed as to the meaning of the language used in the statute just as it must be instructed as to the meaning of any element as statutorily expressed. Here the trial jury was so instructed. Since the necessary elements for involuntary manslaughter were detailed in the indictment, we should also assume that the grand jury received appropriate instructions as to the meaning of language used in the indictment, and that when it found a lack of due caution and circumspection the jurors understood what that language meant.

To require that an indictment not only contain the elements of a crime but also precisely set forth the definition judicially given to the statutory language could start an interminable definitional process and render every indictment subject, after the fact, to objections now required to be made before the fact as to jury instructions. Here, it could be argued that gross negligence would in turn have to be defined. If "wanton disregard" is used in defining it, it could be argued that the term also would have to be defined. I would affirm.

Notes and Questions

1. How would the *Keith* court have ruled on the challenge presented in UNITED STATES v. DIXON, 596 F.2d 178 (7th Cir.1979)? Defendant there, an inmate of a federal correctional institution, was apprehended with a sharpened table knife. He was charged with violation of 18 U.S.C. § 1792 in an indictment that cited that provision and tracked its language. Section 1792 makes it a crime for one to "convey * * * from place to place within [a federal correctional institution] a weapon or other thing designed to kill or injure an officer or inmate." Prior to trial, defendant challenged the indictment "for failing to allege the essential element of intent." The district court, in denying the motion, ruled that knowledge was an element of the crime, but need not be alleged in the indictment. On appeal, the Seventh Circuit affirmed. The court (per FAIRCHILD, C.J.) reasoned:

"The statute * * * does not explicitly require that such conveyance be done with knowledge, but it has been held that, notwithstanding the silence of the statute, 'obviously criminal intent is an essential element.' * * * Dixon does not really contend that he was misled or otherwise prejudiced by the lack of allegation that in conveying the knife he knew that he was doing so. He does argue, with neat logic, that since the general rule would require intent, if spelled out in the statute as an element of the offense, to be spelled out in the indictment, and since the courts interpret this statute to require knowledge or intent as an element, knowledge or intent must be spelled out in the indictment. He argues that in the absence of an explicit allegation of knowledge or intent in the indictment, the grand jury may well not have determined that there was probable cause to believe defendant acted knowingly.

"We do not agree. Conceivably, of course, an individual could carry an object into, or from place to place within, a prison without knowing that he was carrying a weapon or other thing designed to kill or injure. Courts have deemed it obvious, however, that Congress did not intend to constitute such unknowing carriage a felony. The very obviousness of that view leads to the conclusion that an indictment using the words of the statute sufficiently charges the offense, including the doing of the act with knowledge. It is sufficient to enable the defendant to defend, to avoid further prosecution, and to demonstrate that the grand jury performed its responsibility."

2. Where the statutory definition of an offense includes a particular element and the charging instrument fails to specifically refer to that element, that omission will often constitute a fatal defect. Yet courts have noted that the failure to plead an element in the precise statutory terms is not essential, provided the words or facts contained in the indictment "necessarily or fairly import" the allegation of that element. Where the defense moved to dismiss prior to trial, giving the prosecution the opportunity to correct its pleading, courts may insist that the allegation "by implication" be fairly obvious. Illustrative of cases meeting and failing to meet that standard are found in a series of First Circuit cases. See *Hughes v. United States,* 338 F.2d 651 (1st Cir.1964) (indictment charging defendants with "unlawfully" removing merchandise while it was in customs' custody failed to allege requisite mens rea element; use of word "unlawfully" does not necessarily suggest defendants acted "knowingly"); *Portnoy v. United States,* 316 F.2d 486 (1st Cir.1963) (indictment charging assault against a federal official, when it alleged that the assault was committed by defendant "on account of [the victim's] official duties," necessarily implied that defendant had the requisite knowledge that his victim was an official); *United States v. McLennan,* 672 F.2d 239 (1st Cir.1982) (that principal acted "willfully" in jumping bail was implicit in other allegations of the indictment, which stated that principal failed to appear "after having been ordered to do so," that his failure constituted a violation of 18 U.S.C. § 3150 [a], that the district court entered a "default," and that defendant as an accomplice acted "in order to hinder and prevent [principal's] apprehension"; the indictment fell "somewhere between" *Hughes* and *Portnoy,* but was closer to *"Portnoy"*).

3. *Failure to timely object.* As noted at p. 1015 supra, a critical element of the modern pleading reforms was the adoption of a rule that pleading objections generally would be lost if not raised before trial. That rule, however, does not apply to a "failure to charge an offense." See, e.g., Fed.R.Crim.P. 12(b). Such a deficiency ordinarily can be raised for the first time after conviction (usually by a motion for arrest of judgment) or on appeal. See e.g., *State v. Shofler,* 687 P.2d 29 (Kan. App.1984) (defect is jurisdictional and even where not raised by defense, appellate court has "a duty to address the issue on its own motion"). Indeed, in some jurisdictions, the issue also may be raised on collateral attack (e.g., by a writ of habeas corpus), after the time for appeal has passed. See Dix, p. 1016 supra (describing the Texas decisions).

4. Appellate courts generally agree that, where the failure to charge objection was not raised before trial, the charging instrument "should be construed liberally in favor of its sufficiency." *United States v. Norman,* 391 F.2d 212 (6th Cir.1968). Still, facing a particular deficiency, there is considerable variation in their willingness to stretch the language of the pleading to find therein the necessary element. See e.g., *United States v. Mixon,* 374 F.2d 20 (6th Cir.1967) (failure to allege that defendants charged with heroin distribution conspiracy knew that the heroin had been imported unlawfully was not fatal where the indictment referred to the statutory provision specifically requiring such knowledge); *United States v. Morrison,* 536

a. In determining whether a particular element is alleged "by implication," what weight should be given to the indictment's citation to a statute which specifically refers to that element? In *McLennan,* the court noted the general rule was that "statutory citations cannot normally supply the missing element," but added that "when considering whether an indictment for being an accessory sufficiently describes the underlying offense, common sense suggests that such a citation should not be entirely ignored where, as here, it so plainly reinforces what is implicit in the text."

F.2d 286 (9th Cir.1976) (indictment alleging that a postal employee "did convert * * * without authorization of law" certain postal moneys was insufficient; criminal intent is an element of the offense and its presence is not implicit in the allegation of a "conversion"). Some state courts tend to insist upon an almost literal reading, holding against the indictment all but the clearest inferences to be drawn from its language. See e.g., *Ex parte Seaton,* 580 S.W.2d 593 (Tex.Crim.App.1979) (where the statute prohibited the taking of a credit card without the permission of "the person for whose benefit the credit card was issued," indictment was defective in alleging that the defendant knowingly took a credit card from the person of Linda Lusk "without the consent of said Linda Lusk" because it did not allege that Linda Lusk was the person for whom the card was issued).

5. Appellate courts frequently note that the lack of specificity does not in itself result in a failure to charge an offense and therefore a deficiency in specificity is waived by the defendant's failure to raise that objection before trial. See e.g., *United States v. Varkonyi,* 645 F.2d 453 (5th Cir.1981) (defendant could raise for the first time on appeal objection to indictment charging forcible interference with a federal official insofar as he claims that the charge failed to identify the victim as a federal official, but not insofar as he claims that the allegation of "forcibly interfering" failed to specify how he interfered with the performance of an official duty). Here again, however, there exists considerable variation from jurisdiction to jurisdiction as to what will be viewed as a specificity deficiency as opposed to a failure to charge an essential element. See e.g., *United States v. Thomas,* Note 4, p. 1025 supra (where indictment charged a breaking and entry into a dwelling "with an intent to commit a criminal offense therein," the failure to identify that ulterior crime resulted in a failure to charge the offense of burglary, permitting a first time objection on appeal); *State v. Batson,* 580 P.2d 1066 (Or.App.1978) (failure to allege ulterior crime is a specificity deficiency and cannot be raised for first time on appeal). Consider also *State v. Waters,* 436 So.2d 66 (Fla.1983) (burglary indictment need not specify ulterior crime provided it alleges an intent to commit an offense).

6. *Defense strategy.* Professor Dix notes that challenging a defect in the charge prior to trial will often give the defendant a very limited tactical advantage: "[I]n most cases, it [the defect] will be easily remedied by the prosecution and little will be accomplished—from the defense perspective—other than to briefly delay the proceedings." Dix, p. 1016 supra, at 713. Where the defect results in a failure to charge an offense, the better strategy may be to delay the objection until after a verdict is reached. If the jury acquits, that will end the case, and if it should convict, the defendant will have available an objection that will require a new trial. Of course, where the defect falls short of a failure to charge an offense, it ordinarily will be lost if not raised. Here, defense counsel's "most effective strategy is to cause the defect to create reversible [trial court] error: while a motion to quash may be made, that motion might be drafted so as to preserve the [objection] * * * but not to effectively call the defect to the trial judge's attention. Further, defense counsel can forego rigorous pursuit of the motion in the trial court." Ibid. Do either of the above strategies give rise to ethical problems? Professor Dix notes:

"Whether these tactical decisions create ethical problems for defense lawyers is problematic. In 1956, the [Texas] Bar Committee on the Canons of Ethics voted 5-to-4 that a defense lawyer could properly proceed to trial on a defective indictment without raising the matter. Some of the majority's discussion suggests that counsel's duty to the client demanded that this be done. This position is, of course, consistent with the traditional notion that defense counsel has an ethical duty to present even adverse law to the court, but has no duty to call the court's attention to facts adverse to counsel's position. On the other hand, despite the committee's opinion, failing to raise a fundamental defect may be inconsistent with at least the spirit of defense counsel's possible ethical responsibility to avoid activity that serves only to delay the proceeding. The committee's evaluation may have assumed that, * * * if a fundamental defect was identified after jeopardy attached, the trial court's disposition of the case would preclude further prosecution. It is now clear, however, that * * * the most that a defendant is entitled to is a [new trial]. [See Ch. 24, § 3]. Perhaps, in light of this, nondisclosure serves only to delay the proceedings and therefore is ethically inappropriate. On the other hand, any ethical prohibition against delay may apply only to affirmative conduct. So construed, of course, it would not address defense counsel's passive failure to call a charging instrument defect to the trial judge's attention.

"Intentionally raising a nonfundamental defect in such a manner as to maximize the chance of reversible error presents much the same issue. Conceptually, this method of proceeding pursues no legitimate objective other than delaying the proceedings by requiring retrial. If this is determined to be conceptually objectionable, however, there may be few practical ramifications that follow. It is seldom possible to establish with any confidence that defense lawyer's sole objective in drafting and pursuing a motion to quash is to establish reversible error. Voluntary compliance is the only way in which compliance with a bar upon such conduct could be effective." Id. at 713–14.

THE PERMISSIBLE SCOPE OF AMENDMENTS

1. *Amendments to the information.* LaFave and Israel, § 19.2(g), describes the majority position as follows: "The prevailing standard governing the amendment of the information is set forth in Federal Rule 7(e):

> The court may permit an information to be amended at any time before verdict or finding if no additional or different offense is charged and if substantial rights of the defendant are not prejudiced.

Many states have amendment provisions with identical language, and most of the others have provisions that are similar in substance. The element of prejudice to the 'substantial rights of the defendant' is usually interpreted as requiring some showing of surprise which will interfere with the defendant's presentation at trial. Since such prejudice may be avoided before trial by granting an appropriate continuance, an amendment made before trial is unlikely to be held to have injured the substantial rights of the defendant where a continuance was granted or none was requested. Amendments made during trial will cause more difficulty, but may be accepted where they did not introduce any new material that changed the basic identity of the offense.

"Apart from the matter of surprise, most jurisdictions will also bar amendments that allege a new offense. This limitation does not apply to an amendment that perfects a defective information by adding an essential element of the crime or by changing the manner in which a crime was committed. It does, however, bar a shift to an offense that requires proof of different elements. Thus, an information charging robbery could not be amended to charge a separate offense of using force in the course of immediate flight after having committed a theft. One might ask why such a change should be prohibited in the absence of some indication that the defendant might be prejudiced in the preparation of his defense. The answer may lie in the assumption that a change in the offense necessarily raises a substantial possibility of prejudice, but that assumption often is dubious where the basic transaction identified in the original charge remains the same. Perhaps, the real concern is the bypassing of a preliminary hearing bindover. Thus, the California provision bars the amendment of an information 'so as to charge an offense not shown by the evidence taken at the preliminary examination.' "

2. What constitutes a shift to a new offense under the above standard? Where an information charged that a murder was committed with "malice aforethought, deliberation, and premeditation," is the offense changed by an amendment to charge felony murder committed in the perpetration of a burglary? See *State v. Foy,* 607 P.2d 481 (Kan.1980) (amendment permissible). Where the original information charges the defendant with rape of a person less than 12 (rape requiring sexual intercourse), can the court allow an amendment to charge sexual abuse as to the same victim (that offense requiring the touching of private parts for the purpose of gratifying sexual desire)? See *State v. Amerson,* 661 S.W.2d 852 (Mo.App.1983) (sexual abuse requires an additional mental element, and therefore is not a lesser included charge; the amendment rendered the defendant's subsequent conviction a "nullity" since an amendment charging a different offense "rises to the denial of due process of law").

3. Not all jurisdictions follow an amendment policy as liberal as that provided in Federal Rule 7(e). A substantial group of states adhere to the formulation that amendments are permitted as to "form," but not as to "substance." Although some states apply this distinction to allow roughly the same type of amendments that would be permitted under Rule 7(e), others construe it to allow a considerably narrower range of amendments. In these jurisdictions, an amendment that falls short of changing the basic offense charged can nevertheless readily be characterized as one of substance. Amendments are said to fall in that category if they alter or supply "essential facts that must be proved to make the act complained of a crime." *Brown v. State,* 400 A.2d 1133 (Md.1979). Thus, apart from any question of surprise, jurisdictions following a form/substance distinction are likely to bar an amendment that substantially alters the description of the criminal act, the mens rea accompanying that act, or the consequences of that act. See e.g., *Brown v. State,* supra (prohibiting amendment that changed the original allegation that defendant defrauded an automobile dealer of a dollar amount to an allegation that he defrauded the dealer of an automobile worth that amount); *Gullet v. State,* 116 N.E.2d 234 (Ind.1953) (disallowing amendment to change the name of the owner of a stolen vehicle); *State v. Green,* 605 P.2d 746 (Or.App.1980) (amendment could not add the ulterior crime in a burglary charge).

4. *Amendments to indictments.* Most jurisdictions treat the amendment of an indictment no differently than the amendment of an information. Either a Rule 7(e) type standard is applied to both informations and indictments or a substance/form standard is applied to both. However, the federal courts and several states draw a sharp distinction between amendments of indictments and informations, allow considerably less latitude for the indictment amendments. Indeed, some of these jurisdictions are commonly said to follow "the historic rule that an indictment may not be amended." None actually go so far as to adhere to the early common law prohibition that barred even amendments to cure misnomers, but they do follow what is sometimes described as the "rule of *Ex parte Bain.*" *Bain* and the Supreme Court cases discussing *Bain* are set forth below.

5. EX PARTE BAIN, 121 U.S. 1, 7 S.Ct. 781, 30 L.Ed. 849 (1887), involved a habeas corpus challenge to a conviction based on an amended indictment. The original indictment charged the defendant with having made a false statement in a bank report "with intent to deceive the

Comptroller of the Currency and the agent appointed to examine the affairs of said [bank]." The trial court initially sustained a demurrer to the indictment. That court apparently read the cited statute as making it an offense only to deceive the agent appointed to examine the bank records. Under the common law pleading standards the indictment therefore was fatally defective since it alleged as an offense an alternative action (deceiving the Comptroller) that was not a crime. To cure this defect, the trial court allowed the government to amend the indictment by striking the reference to the Comptroller. In an unanimous opinion, the Supreme Court, concluded that the amendment was impermissible, depriving the trial court of the power to proceed and therefore requiring habeas relief. Speaking for the Court, MILLER, J., noted:

"The learned judge who presided in the Circuit Court at the time the change was made in this indictment, says that the court allowed the words 'Comptroller of the Currency and' to be stricken out as surplusage,[a] * * *. He goes on to argue that the grand jury would have found the indictment without this language. But it is not for the court to say whether they would or not. The party can only be tried upon the indictment as found by such grand jury, and especially upon all its language found in the charging part of that instrument. While it may seem to the court, with its better instructed mind in regard to what the statute requires to be found as to the intent to deceive, that it was neither necessary nor reasonable that the grand jury should attach importance to the fact that it was the Comptroller who was to be deceived, yet it is not impossible nor very improbable that the grand jury looked mainly to that officer as the party whom the prisoner intended to deceive by a report which was made upon his requisition and returned directly to him. * * * How can the court say that there may not have been more than one of the jurors who found this indictment, who was satisfied that the false report was made to deceive the Comptroller, but was not convinced that it was made to deceive anybody else? And how can it be said that, with these words stricken out, it is the indictment which was found by the grand jury? If it lies within the province of a court to change the charging part of an indictment to suit its own notions of what it ought to have been, or what the grand jury would probably have made it if their attention had been called to suggested changes, the great importance which the common law attaches to an indictment by a grand jury, as a prerequisite to a prisoner's trial for a crime, and without which the Constitution says 'no person shall be held to answer,' may be frittered away until its value is almost destroyed."

6. In STIRONE v. UNITED STATES, 361 U.S. 212, 80 S.Ct. 270, 4 L.Ed.2d 252 (1960), the Court relied on *Bain* in concluding that the government could not accomplish through a variance between proof and charge what it could not achieve through an amendment. The indictment there, brought under the Hobbs Act, charged defendant with extortion affecting interstate commerce through wrongful use of a threatened labor dispute. The dispute was directed against Rider, a Pennsylvania supplier of ready-mixed concrete used in the construction of a Pennsylvania steel processing plant. The indictment alleged that Stirone's activities had obstructed the interstate flow of sand shipments into Rider's concrete plant. At trial, over defense objection, the judge admitted evidence concerning (and instructed the jury that their verdict could rest upon) Stirone's

a. While Federal Rule 7(d) today provides for the striking of surplusage, it uses that term with a different point of reference. Rule 7(d) is aimed at inflammatory and prejudicial language that is irrelevant to the description of the events alleged in the indictment. Accordingly, it provides only for the striking of surplusage on motion of the defendant (who arguably could be viewed as thereby waiving his right not to have the indictment amended).

interference with interstate commerce by preventing shipments that the steel plant would have made had it been built on time. A unanimous court, per BLACK, J., found this variance "fatal":

"We agree with the Court of Appeals that Rider's dependence on shipments of sand from outside Pennsylvania to carry on his ready-mixed concrete business entitled him to the Hobbs Act's protection. * * * Whether prospective steel shipments from the new steel mills would be enough, alone, to bring this transaction under the Act is a more difficult question. We need not decide this, however, since we agree with the dissenting judges in the Court of Appeals that it was error to submit that question to the jury and that the error cannot be dismissed as merely an insignificant variance between allegation and proof and thus harmless error as in *Berger v. United States* [Note 2, p. 1039 infra]. The crime charged here is a felony and the Fifth Amendment requires that prosecution be begun by indictment.

"Ever since *Ex parte Bain* was decided in 1887, it has been the rule that after an indictment has been returned its charges may not be broadened through amendment except by the grand jury itself. * * * The *Bain* case, which has never been disapproved, stands for the rule that a court cannot permit a defendant to be tried on charges that are not made in the indictment against him. Yet the court did permit that in this case. * * * The grand jury which found this indictment was satisfied to charge that Stirone's conduct interfered with interstate importation of sand. But neither this nor any other court can know that the grand jury would have been willing to charge that Stirone's conduct would interfere with interstate exportation of steel from a mill later to be built with Rider's concrete. * * * Although the trial court did not permit a formal amendment of the indictment, the effect of what it did was the same. And the addition charging interference with steel exports here is neither trivial, useless, nor innocuous. * * *

"[T]here are two essential elements of a Hobbs Act crime: interference with commerce, and extortion. Both elements have to be charged. Neither is surplusage and neither can be treated as surplusage. The charge that interstate commerce is affected is critical since the Federal Government's jurisdiction of this crime rests only on that interference. It follows that when only one particular kind of commerce is charged to have been burdened a conviction must rest on that charge and not another, even though it be assumed that under an indictment drawn in general terms a conviction might rest upon a showing that commerce of one kind or another had been burdened."

7. In 1985, in *United States v. Miller* (set forth below), the Supreme Court reexamined *Bain* in light of *Stirone* and other Supreme Court precedent. How much of *Bain* remains in light of *Miller?* Assume for example that the amendments presented in the cases discussed in Notes 2 and 3 supra were before federal courts as amendments to an indictment. Would those amendments be acceptable under *Miller,* assuming also that there was no concern as to notice?

UNITED STATES v. MILLER

___ U.S. ___, 105 S.Ct. 1811, 85 L.Ed.2d 99 (1985).

JUSTICE MARSHALL delivered the opinion of the Court.

The issue presented is whether the Fifth Amendment's grand jury guarantee is violated when a defendant is tried under an indictment that alleges a certain fraudulent scheme but is convicted based on trial proof that supports only a significantly narrower and more limited, though included, fraudulent scheme. * * *

[A federal grand jury indicted defendant for several violations of the mail fraud statute, 18 U.S.C. § 1341. The indictment alleged that defendant had defrauded an insurance company by both arranging for a burglary at his place of business and by lying to the insurer as to the value of the loss. The trial proof, however, concerned only the latter allegation, and the government moved to strike that part of the indictment that alleged prior knowledge of the burglary. The defense opposed the proposed amendment, urging that the entire indictment be submitted to the jury. This was done and the jury found defendant guilty. Defendant then appealed on the ground that the trial proof had fatally varied from the scheme alleged in the indictment. Relying on *Bain* and *Stirone,* the Third Circuit sustained that challenge. That court noted: "It is quite possible that the grand jury would have been unwilling or unable to return an indictment based solely on Miller's exaggeration of the amount of his claimed loss even though it had concluded that an indictment could be returned based on the overall scheme involving a use of the mail caused by Miller's knowing consent to the burglary."]

* * * Miller's indictment properly alleged violations of 18 U.S.C. § 1341, and it fully and clearly set forth a number of ways in which the acts alleged constituted violations. The facts proved at trial clearly conformed to one of the theories of the offense contained within that indictment, for the indictment gave Miller clear notice that he would have to defend against an allegation that he "well knew that the amount of copper claimed to have been taken during the alleged burglary was grossly inflated for the purpose of fraudulently obtaining $150,000 from Aetna Insurance Company." Competent defense counsel certainly should have been on notice that the offense was charged and would need to be defended against. Accordingly, there can be no showing here that Miller was prejudicially surprised at trial by the absence of proof concerning his alleged complicity in the burglary; nor can there be a showing that the variance prejudiced the fairness of respondent's trial in any other way. Compare *Kotteakos v. United States* [fn. b, p. 1039 infra]. See also *Berger v. United States* [Note 2, p. 1039 infra]. The indictment was also sufficient to allow Miller to plead it in the future as a bar to subsequent prosecutions. Therefore, none of these "notice" related concerns—which of course are among the important concerns underlying the requirement that criminal charges be set out in an indictment—would support the result of the Court of Appeals. See *Russell v. United States.* The Court of Appeals did not disagree, but instead argued that Miller had been prejudiced in his right to be free from a trial for any offense other than that alleged in the grand jury's indictment. It reasoned that a grand jury's willingness to indict an individual for participation in a broad criminal plan does not establish that the same grand jury would have indicted the individual for participating in a substantially narrower, even if wholly included, criminal plan. * * *

The government correctly argues that the Court of Appeals' result conflicts with a number of this Court's prior decisions interpreting the Fifth Amendment's grand jury Clause. The Court has long recognized that an indictment may charge numerous offenses or the commission of any one offense in several ways. As long as the crime and the elements of the offense that sustain the conviction are fully and clearly set out in the indictment, the right to a grand jury is not normally violated by the fact that the indictment alleges more crimes or other means of committing the same crime. * * *

A review of prior cases allowing conviction to stand in the face of variances between the indictment and proof makes the Court of Appeals' error clear. Convictions generally have been sustained as long as the proof upon which they are based corresponds to an offense that was clearly set out in the indictment. A part of the indictment unnecessary to and independent from the allegations of the offense proved may normally be treated as "a useless averment" that "may be ignored." *Ford v. United States,* 273 U.S. 593, 47 S.Ct. 531, 71 L.Ed. 793 (1927). In *Ford,* for example, an indictment charged a defendant with conspiring to import liquor in violation of various federal laws and in violation of a treaty. "The validity of the indictment [was] attacked . . . because it charge[d] that the conspiracy was to violate the treaty, although the treaty create[d] no offense against the law of the United States." Although the grand jury had included the treaty allegation as part of the indictment, this Court upheld the conviction because "that part of the indictment [was] merely surplusage and may be rejected."

This treatment of allegations independent of and unnecessary to the offense on which a conviction ultimately rests has not been confined to allegations that, like those in *Ford,* would have had no legal relevance if proved. In *Salinger v. United States,* [272 U.S. 542, 47 S.Ct. 173, 71 L.Ed. 398 (1926),] for example, the Court was presented with facts quite similar to the instant case. A grand jury charged Salinger with mail fraud in an indictment containing several counts, "[a]ll relat[ing] to the same scheme to defraud, but each charg[ing] a distinct use of the mail for the purpose of executing the scheme." As was the case with Miller, Salinger's "scheme to defraud as set forth in the indictment . . . comprehended several relatively distinct plans for fleecing intended victims." Because the evidence only sustained the charge as to one of the plans, the trial judge withdrew from the jury those portions of the indictment that related to all other plans. Salinger argued then, just as Miller argues now, that the variance between the broad allegations in the indictment and the narrower proof at trial violated his right to have had a grand jury screen any alleged offenses upon which he might be convicted at trial. This Court unanimously rejected Salinger's argument on the ground that the offense proved was fully contained within the indictment. Nothing had been added to the indictment which, in the Court's view, "remained just as it was returned by the grand jury." * * * The result reached by the Court of Appeals thus conflicts with the results reached by this Court in such cases as *Salinger* and *Ford.* * * *

The Court of Appeals principally relied on this Court's decision in *Stirone v. United States* to support its conclusion that the Fifth Amendment's grand jury right is violated by a conviction for a criminal plan narrower than, but fully included within, the plan set forth in the indictment. *Stirone,* however, stands for a very different proposition. In *Stirone* the offense proved at trial was not fully contained in the indictment, for trial evidence had "amended" the indictment by *broadening* the possible bases for conviction from that which appeared in the indictment. *Stirone* was thus wholly unlike [*Ford* and *Salinger*] * * * and unlike respondent's case, all of which involve trial evidence that narrowed the indictment's charges without adding any new offenses. As the *Stirone* Court said, the issue was "whether [Stirone] was convicted of an offense *not charged in the indictment.*" (Emphasis added). * * *

The one decision of this Court that does offer some support to the Court of Appeals' result is *Ex parte Bain,* for there the Court treated as an unconstitutional "amendment" the deletion from an indictment of allegations that would not have been necessary to prove the offense. * * * [The indictment there charged *Bain*] with intent to deceive the *Comptroller of the Currency and* the agent appointed to examine the affairs of said [banking] association. . . . The relevant statute made it a criminal offense to file " 'any false entry in any book, report, or statement . . . with intent . . . to deceive . . . any agent appointed to examine the affairs of any such association . . . .' " Thus under the terms of the statute, there was no need to charge Bain with intending to deceive "the Comptroller of the Currency." * * * Under later cases, such as *Ford* and *Salinger,* the presence of such surplusage in the indictment would not invalidate a conviction as long as the necessary intent was also alleged and proved. But in *Bain* the trial court sustained Bain's demurrer to the indictment * * * [and then] granted a motion by the Government "that the indictment be amended by striking out the words *'the Comptroller of the Currency and.'* " This Court granted a writ of habeas corpus on the ground that Bain's Fifth Amendment right to stand trial only on an indictment returned by a grand jury had been violated. The opinion reasoned that a court could not, consistent with the Fifth Amendment, assume that the narrower indictment would have been returned by the grand jury that returned the broader one.

Bain may best be understood in terms of two distinct propositions. Most generally, *Bain* stands for the proposition that a conviction cannot stand if based on an offense that is different from that alleged in the grand jury's indictment. But more specifically, *Bain* can support the proposition that the striking out of parts of an indictment invalidates the whole of the indictment, for a court cannot speculate as to whether the grand jury had meant for any remaining offense to stand independently, even if that remaining offense clearly was included in the original text. Under this latter proposition, the narrowing of an indictment is no different from the adding of a new allegation that had never been considered by the grand jury; both are treated as "amendments" that alter the nature of the offense charged. In evaluating the relevance of *Bain* to the instant case, it is necessary to examine these two aspects of *Bain* separately, for the Court has treated these two propositions quite differently in the years since *Bain.*

The proposition that a defendant cannot be convicted of an offense different from that which was included in the indictment * * * has been reaffirmed in a number of subsequent cases. See, e.g., *United States v. Norris,* 281 U.S. 619, 50 S.Ct. 424, 74 L.Ed. 1076 (1930) (citing *Bain* for the rule that "nothing can be added to an indictment without the concurrence of the grand jury by which the bill was found"). The most important reaffirmation, of course, was *Stirone.* * * * See also *Russell v. United States* (citing *Bain* for the "settled rule in the federal courts that an indictment may not be amended except by resubmission to the grand jury, unless the change is merely a matter of form").

But this aspect of *Bain* gives no support to Miller in this case, for the offense that formed the basis of Miller's conviction was clearly and fully set out in the indictment. Miller must instead rest on the second, and more specific, proposition found in *Bain,* that a narrowing of the indictment constitutes an amendment that renders the indictment void. As is clear from [our previous] discussion of * * * [*Ford* and *Salinger*], this second proposition did not long survive *Bain.* Indeed, when defendants have sought to rely on *Bain* for this point, this Court has limited or distinguished the case, sustaining convictions where courts had withdrawn or ignored independent and unnecessary allegations in the indictments. Modern criminal law has generally accepted that an indictment will support each offense contained within it. To the extent *Bain* stands for the proposition that it constitutes an unconstitutional amendment to drop from an indictment those allegations that are unnecessary to an offense that is clearly contained within it, that case has simply not survived. To avoid further confusion, we now explicitly reject that proposition. * * *

In light of the foregoing, the proper disposition of this case is clear. The variance complained of added nothing new to the grand jury's indictment and constituted no broadening. As in *Salinger* and *Ford,* what was removed from the case was in no way essential to the offense on which the jury convicted. We therefore disagree with the Court of Appeals on the issue of whether Miller has shown any compromise of his right to be tried only on offenses for which a grand jury has returned an indictment. No such compromise has been shown. The judgment of the Court of Appeals is accordingly reversed.

JUSTICE POWELL took no part in the consideration or decision of this case.

THE SCOPE OF PERMISSIBLE VARIANCES

1. *The procedural setting.* "A variance arises when the proof offered at trial departs from the allegations in the indictment or information. The defendant objecting to a variance states, in effect: 'The state may have offered evidence sufficient to establish a crime, but it is not the crime alleged in its accusatory pleading and I therefore am entitled to an acquittal.' On occasion, the state has introduced evidence covering all the allegations in its pleading and the variance relates to evidence establishing an additional theory of liability. The defense objection then is to the instruction to the jury that would permit it to consider this additional theory of liability or to the introduction of the additional evidence. Very often, the prosecution, recognizing the existence of a variance, will seek to amend the pleading to conform to the evidence. If this is permitted, the issue raised on appeal will be whether the amendment was properly allowed. Where there was no amendment (either because the trial judge viewed it as unnecessary or because the issue was not raised below), the defendant will argue that the submission of his case to the jury on the basis of the variance constituted revisible error." LaFave and Israel, § 19.2(h).

2. *The Berger standard.* The source of the prevailing standard for judging the scope of permissible variance is the frequently cited statement of Justice Sutherland in *Berger v. United States,* 295 U.S. 78, 55 S.Ct. 629, 79 L.Ed. 1314 (1935):

> The true inquiry, * * * is not whether there has been a variance in proof, but whether there has been such a variance as to "affect the substantial rights" of the accused.[a] The general rule that allegations and proof must correspond is based upon the obvious requirements (1) that the accused shall be definitely informed as to the charges against him, so that he may be enabled to present his defense and not be taken by surprise by the evidence offered at the trial; and (2) that he may be protected against another prosecution for the offense.

In light of this statement, most states hold that a "variance requires reversal of a conviction only when it deprives the defendant of a right to fair notice or leaves him open to a risk of double jeopardy." LaFave and Israel, § 19.2(h).[b]

3. In applying the notice element of the *Berger* standard, courts look to the record to determine whether it suggests "a possibility that the defendant may have been misled or embarrassed in the preparation or presentation of his defense." *Marshall v. State,* 381 So.2d 276 (Fla.App.

a. The reference was to the federal harmless error statute which directs an appellate or trial court, on challenge to a conviction, to "give judgment * * * without regard to technical errors, defects, or exceptions which do not affect the substantial rights of the parties." See Chapter 11, section 2, and Note 7, p. 1465 infra.

b. The first prong of this standard is often more broadly stated as whether the defendant suffered "actual prejudice at trial." Although notice is the primary concern in determining whether the defendant suffered such prejudice, *Berger* itself recognized that a variance could also cause prejudice where it resulted in the introduction of evidence that would not otherwise have been admissible against defendant. The defendant in *Berger* objected to the additional evidence that had been introduced at his trial because the government charged a single larger conspiracy rather than the two smaller conspiracies its proof sustained, but the Court found that the "incompetent" evidence thereby admitted was not prejudicial under the facts of that case. In *Kotteakos v. United States,* 328 U.S. 750, 66 S.Ct. 1239, 90 L.Ed. 1557 (1946), it found otherwise where thirteen parties were jointly tried, and as to all but one, the variance resulted in the jury having before it evidence of additional conspiracies which had no bearing on the individual defendant's liability.

1980). A failure to object to the variance at trial is generally viewed as a waiver of a claim of prejudice, and an eleventh hour objection is taken as strong evidence belying any such claim. If the defendant was previously aware of the prosecution's proof as a result of pretrial discovery or a preliminary hearing, that factor also will weigh against a finding of prejudice. The court will also look to the relationship of the variance to the defense presented by the defendant. Thus, variances as to factors that ordinarily are not part of the material elements of the crime (e.g., time and place) are viewed as unlikely to prejudice a defendant whose defense centered on challenging the government's proof as to one of those material elements.

4. What additional restrictions should the double jeopardy prong of the *Berger* standard add to scope of permissible variances? Consider LaFave and Israel, § 19.2(h): "The possibility of actual prejudice at trial is put aside when courts test a variance against the risk of exposing the defendant to double jeopardy. The only element considered here is the extent to which the variance alters the scope of the charge. Indeed, a challenge based on this ground may be raised by a defendant who failed to object to the variance at trial. Applying this double jeopardy test, courts have held fatal variances that establish a crime different than that charged in the original pleading, variances that establish the same crime but against a different victim, and variances that establish the same crime against the same victim but through the use of substantially different means. Whether these rulings can be justified as necessary to protect the defendant against the risk of double jeopardy is debatable. Not all of the variances held to be fatal have been sufficiently broad to establish a separate offense for the purpose of double jeopardy. Moreover, the protection against double jeopardy no longer rests on the pleading alone. If any future prosecution were attempted, the defendant could resort to the full record of the first trial to bar a prosecution on the same offense as was established by the variance."

5. *The constructive amendment limitation.* Relying on *Stirone,* Note 6, p. 1034 supra, some jurisdictions characterize as a separate limitation on permissible variances the standard applied in determining the permissible scope of an amendment to the charging instrument. Insofar as the amendment standard looks to notice (see Note 1, p. 1032 supra), it will largely duplicate the first prong of the *Berger* standard. Insofar as it also prohibits the allegation of a new offense (see Note 2, p. 1033 supra), it arguably will not go beyond the double jeopardy prong of *Berger.* But where the jurisdiction follows *Bain* in restricting permissible amendments to an indictment, even as *Bain* is limited by *Miller,* the end result may be a limitation upon variances somewhat more stringent than that imposed by *Berger's* double jeopardy prong. Consider, for example, the variance found to be fatal in *Stirone.* Would that variance have been acceptable under the double jeopardy prong of *Berger?*

6. In several jurisdictions that follow a "form/substance" distinction as to allowable amendments and view broadly what constitutes a change of substance, permissible variances are exceptionally narrow. Thus, one such jurisdiction holds that the prosecution's proof must adhere to any allegation of the indictment "which is not impertinent or foreign to the cause * * * though a prosecution for the same offense might [have] been supported without such allegation." *State v. Brooks,* 462 S.W.2d 491 (Tenn.1970) (where defendant was charged with robbery "by use of a deadly weapon; to wit * * * a pistol," evidence that defendant used a 22 caliber rifle constituted a "material variance"); *Wilson v. State,* 292 S.W.2d 188 (Tenn.1956) (proof of theft of bronze rollers constitutes a fatal variance from indictment charging theft of brass rollers).

7. *Pleading to avoid variances.* Does the combination of a state requirement of substantial specificity in pleading and a prohibition against significant variance in proof place the prosecutor on the "horns of a dilemma"? Assume, for example, that in a homicide case, the available evidence indicates that death probably was caused by blows inflicted by the defendant, but there is additional evidence suggesting that death may have been caused by the exposure of the deceased to the elements following the assault. Moreover, assume that further evidence may become available at trial that will furnish greater support for exposure as the cause of death. See *State v. Lusk,* 452 S.W.2d 219 (Mo.1970). To avoid the possibility of a variance, the prosecutor may prefer that the charge simply state that defendant "caused" the death of the deceased. But what if the state law requires greater specificity in pleading the manner in which death was caused? May the prosecutor utilize alternative allegations as to this element of the offense? Some courts have rejected alternative allegations as failing to fully inform the defendant of the charge against him. See, e.g., *Shreveport v. Bryson,* 33 So.2d 60 (La.1947) (rejecting allegation of reckless driving by driving under the influence of "intoxicating liquor or drugs"). But other courts have approved disjunctive pleading—at least where the alternatives are not extensive. See, e.g., *Commonwealth v. Schuler,* 43 A.2d 646 (Pa.Super.1945) (driving under influence of "intoxicating liquor or a narcotic or habit forming drug").

8. *Variance acquittals and reprosecutions.* Assume that an indictment alleges one means of committing an offense against a particular victim, and the court therefore excludes evidence showing that the offense was committed by another means. As a result, the jury acquits the defendant. Does double jeopardy bar reprosecution based upon the second means? Consider, for example, *State v. Brooks* [Note 7 supra], where the indictment charged armed robbery by use of a pistol, and evidence at trial indicated that defendants had used a rifle. Following Tennessee's "strict common law rule" on variance, the trial court excluded that evidence, and directed the jury, upon the prosecution's request, to "acquit the defendants * * * in view of that error in the indictment." The prosecution then filed a new indictment, identical to the former charge except that the weapon used was described as "22 caliber rifle," and defendants were convicted. The Tennessee Supreme Court upheld the conviction against a double jeopardy challenge on the ground that the second prosecution was for a "separate offense" since the "evidence necessary to support the second indictment would [not] have been sufficient to procure a legal conviction upon the first [indictment]." In *State v. Duncan,* 462 S.W.2d 491 (Tenn.1971), a companion case presented by Brooks' codefendant, the United States Supreme Court originally granted certiorari to consider the double jeopardy issue, but then dismissed the writ on the ground that that issue was "so interrelated with [state] rules of criminal pleading * * *, the constitutionality of which is not at issue, as not to warrant the exercise of certiorari jurisdiction." *Duncan v. Tennessee,* 405 U.S. 127, 92 S.Ct. 785, 31 L.Ed.2d 86 (1972). Three justices dissented from the dismissal of the writ. The dissent, per Brennan, J., noted: "Whatever relevance [Tennessee's 'different evidence'] doctrine may have in determining a variance between indictment and proof within a single trial, it certainly does not comport with the double jeopardy standards of the Fifth and Fourteenth Amendments. * * * It may be that the prosecution in this case did not have available to it a ready means * * * of amending the first indictment and thus had no choice but to end the trial and begin again. If so, its remedy lies in changing Tennessee's criminal procedure, not in denying petitioner the constitutional protection to which he is entitled." Consider also *Brown v. Ohio,* p. 1064 supra, and *Illinois v. Sommerville,* p. 1380 infra.

Chapter 17

THE LOCATION OF THE PROSECUTION

TRAVIS v. UNITED STATES

364 U.S. 631, 81 S.Ct. 358, 5 L.Ed.2d 340 (1961).

MR. JUSTICE DOUGLAS delivered the opinion of the Court.

In this case petitioner was charged on four counts of an indictment with the making and filing of false non-Communist affidavits required by § 9(h) of the National Labor Relations Act.[2] The indictment charged that the affidavits were false writings or documents made and executed in Colorado and filed in Washington, D.C., with the National Labor Relations Board.

Before the * * * petitioner moved to dismiss the indictment on the ground that venue was improperly laid in Colorado. The District Court denied the motion. * * * It is solely to this issue [of venue] that we address ourselves.

It is agreed that the affidavits were executed by petitioner as a union officer in Colorado and mailed there to the Board in Washington, D.C., where they were received and filed. The prosecution contends—and it was held below—that the offense was begun in Colorado and completed in the District of Columbia. In that view venue was properly laid in Colorado by virtue of 18 U.S.C. § 3237(a), which provides:

"Except as otherwise expressly provided by enactment of Congress, any offense against the United States begun in one district and completed in another * * * may be inquired of and prosecuted in any district in which such offense was begun * * * or completed."

We start with the provision of Art. III, § 2 of the Constitution that criminal trials "shall be held in the State where the said crimes shall have been committed," a safeguard reinforced by the command of the Sixth Amendment that the criminal trial shall be before an impartial jury of "the State and district wherein the crime shall have been committed." We start also with the assumption that Colorado, the residence of petitioner, might offer conveniences and advantages to him which a trial in the District of Columbia might lack. We are also aware that venue provi-

2. This section, which was [later] repealed provided: "No investigation shall be made by the Board of any question * * * raised by a labor organization * * * and no complaint shall be issued pursuant to a charge made by a labor organization * * * *unless there is on file with the Board an affidavit* executed contemporaneously or within the preceding twelve-month period by each officer of such labor organization that he is not a member of the Communist Party or affiliated with such party * * *. The provisions of section 35A of the Criminal Code shall be applicable in respect to such affidavits." Section 35(A) * * * is now covered * * * by 18 U.S.C. § 1001, which provides: "Whoever, *in any matter within the jurisdiction of any department or agency of the United States,* knowingly and willfully * * * makes any false, fictitious or fraudulent statements or representations, or makes or uses any false writing or document * * * shall be fined not more than $10,000 or imprisoned not more than five years, or both." (Italics added).

sions in Acts of Congress should not be so freely construed as to give the Government the choice of "a tribunal favorable" to it. *United States v. Johnson* [Note 1(a), p. 1045 infra]. We therefore begin our inquiry from the premise that questions of venue are more than matters of mere procedure. "They raise deep issues of public policy in the light of which legislation must be construed." *United States v. Johnson.*

Where various duties are imposed, some to be performed at a distant place, others at home, the Court has allowed the prosecution to fix the former as the venue of trial. *Johnston v. United States* [Note 1(b), p. 1045 infra]. The use of agencies of interstate commerce enables Congress to place venue in any district where the particular agency was used. *Armour Packing Co. v. United States,* 209 U.S. 56, 28 S.Ct. 428, 52 L.Ed. 681 [1908]. "The constitutional requirement is as to the locality of the offense, and not the personal presence of the offender." Id. * * * The decisions are discrete, each looking to the nature of the crime charged. * * *

Section 9(h) of the National Labor Relations Act, with which we are concerned, did not require union officers to file non-Communist affidavits. If it had, the whole process of filing, including the use of the mails, might logically be construed to constitute the offense. But this statutory design is different. It requires that the Board shall make no investigation nor issue any complaint in the matters described in § 9(h) "unless there is on file with the Board" a non-Communist affidavit of each union officer. The filings are conditions precedent to a union's use of the Board's procedures. The false statement statute, under which the prosecution is brought, penalizes him who knowingly makes any "false" statement "in any matter within the jurisdiction of any department or agency of the United States." There would seem to be no offense, unless petitioner completed the filing in the District of Columbia. The statute demanded that the affidavits be on file with the Board before it could extend help to the union; the forms prescribed by the Board required the filing in the District of Columbia; the indictment charged that petitioner filed the affidavits there. The words of the Act—"unless there is on file with the Board"—suggest to us that the filing must be completed before there is a "matter within the jurisdiction" of the Board within the meaning of the false statement statute. * * *

The Government admits that the filing is necessary to the "occurrence" of the offense but it argues, that the offense has its "beginning" in Colorado, because it was there that "the defendant had irrevocably set in motion and placed beyond his control the train of events which would normally result (and here did result) in the consummation of the offense." We do not agree with this analysis. Venue should not be made to depend on the chance use of the mails, when Congress has so carefully indicated the *locus* of the crime. After mailing, the affidavit might have been lost; petitioner himself might have recalled it. Multiple venue in general requires crimes consisting of "distinct parts" or involving "a continuously moving act." *United States v. Lombardo,* 241 U.S. 73, 77, 36 S.Ct. 508, 509, 510, 60 L.Ed. 897 [1916]. When a place is explicitly designated where a paper must be filed, a prosecution for failure to file lies only at that place. Id. * * *

We think that is the correct view when 18 U.S.C. § 3237 is read in light of the constitutional requirements and the explicit provision of § 9(h). The *locus* of the offense has been carefully specified; and only the single act of having a false statement at a specified place is penalized. The rationale of *United States v. Lombardo,* supra, a case involving a failure to file, is therefore equally applicable here. We conclude that venue lay only in the District of Columbia. * * *

Reversed.

MR. JUSTICE HARLAN, whom MR. JUSTICE FRANKFURTER and MR. JUSTICE CLARK join, dissenting. * * *

If this crime may properly be viewed as having been begun in the district of Colorado and completed in the district of the District of Columbia, then venue may be laid in either district under 18 U.S.C. § 3237(a). Whether that is the proper view of this offense is an issue on which the authorties in this Court are at best inconclusive. * * * *United States v. Lombardo,* which the Court considers particularly significant, is not controlling, since in that case the offense charged was the *failure* to file with the Commissioner General of Immigration certain information concerning an alien woman whom the defendant was harboring for purposes of prostitution. In such a charge it is difficult to see how the defendant does anything at all except at the place where he fails to file. But cf. *United States v. Cores,* [Note 1(c), p. 1045 infra]. In contrast, the false affidavit in the present case first came into existence in Colorado, having been made and sworn to there. * * *

In these circumstances, the proper course to follow appears to me to be to determine the appropriate venue "from the nature of the crime alleged and the location of the act or acts constituting it," *United States v. Anderson,* 328 U.S. 699, 66 S.Ct. 1213, 90 L.Ed. 1529 [1946], and that determination should take into account that " * * * [t]he provision for trial in the vicinity of the crime is a safeguard against the unfairness and hardship involved when an accused is prosecuted in a remote place. Provided its language permits, the Act in question should be given that construction which will respect such consideration." *United States v. Cores,* supra.

In this kind of case, prosecution in the district in which the affidavit was executed, most often I would suppose the place where the union offices are located, is more likely to respect the basic policy of the Sixth Amendment than would a prosecution in the district where the affidavit was filed. The witnesses and relevant circumstances surrounding the contested issues in such cases more probably will be found in the district of the execution of the affidavit than at the place of filing which, as in this instance will often be for the defendant "a remote place," *United States v. Cores,* supra—that is the District of Columbia where the headquarters of the National Labor Relations Board are located in the case of officers of international unions, or elsewhere throughout the country where the Board has branch offices in the case of local union officers. * * *

This is not to say that venue *must* be limited to the place of execution of the affidavit, but only that there is no lack of consonance with the underlying policy of the Sixth Amendment in permitting venue to be laid there if the elements of the crime allow. * * * [T]he Court considers the essence of the crime to be the filing of the affidavit, and until that is accomplished it holds that the crime is not even begun. But since it is 18 U.S.C. § 1001, which defines the offense, § 9(h) only supplying the requisite jurisdiction of the agency of the United States, and since by § 1001 the offense consists of *falsifying* a material fact, *making* a false statement, or *making* or using any false writing or document, it seems eminently reasonable to consider that the offense is at least definitively begun at the place where the false affidavit is actually made, sworn and subscribed. * * * It is of course true that the offense is not completed until the affidavit is filed with the Board, but I do not think it adds anything to say, as the Court does, that until such time as the affidavit is filed with the Board there is no matter "within the jurisdiction of any department or agency of the United States." The fact that the filing completes the offense by giving the Board jurisdiction over the matter does not, in my view, detract from the conclusion that the offense was begun when and where the affidavit was executed. Indeed this would seem to be the very type of situation contemplated by 18 U.S.C. § 3237(a). * * *

Notes and Questions

1. *Supreme Court precedent.* Prior to *Travis,* Justice Douglas had dissented in three cases (all noted in the *Travis* opinions) in which the Court also was sharply divided on the venue issue:

(a) In UNITED STATES v. JOHNSON, 323 U.S. 273, 65 S.Ct. 249, 89 L.Ed. 236 (1944), the Court split 5–4 over appropriate venue for a charge of "using" the mails for the purpose of "sending" dentures into another state in violation of the Federal Denture Act. The government argued that venue was proper in the receiving state (Delaware), while the defendant claimed that he could only be tried in his home district of Chicago, from which the dentures had been mailed. The majority found that the crucial element of the offense was the act of "sending," and therefore venue could only lie in Chicago since the offense was completed there. Although the majority recognized Congress' right to specifically provide for broader venue, it considered its interpretation of the statute "more consistent" with the "underlying spirit of the constitutional concern for trial in the vicinage." Where legislative history leaves the issue open, a court should, it noted, prefer an interpretation that avoids (1) placing upon the defendant "the serious hardship of defending prosecutions in places remote from home (including the accused's difficulties, financial and otherwise * * * of marshalling his witness)" and (2) creating the "appearance of abuses * * * in the selection of what may be deemed a tribunal favorable to the prosecution." The four dissenting judges (including Justice Douglas) sharply rejected this analysis: "The Court misapprehends the purpose of the Constitutional provisions. We understand them to assure a trial in the place where the crime is committed and not to be concerned with the domicile of the criminal nor with his familiarity with the environment of the place of trial."

(b) In JOHNSTON v. UNITED STATES, 351 U.S. 215, 76 S.Ct. 739, 100 L.Ed. 1097 (1956), the Court split 6–3 in holding that persons charged with failure to report to hospitals for civilian work, as ordered by their local draft boards, could be prosecuted only in the district where the hospitals were located rather than their home districts in which their boards were located. The majority opinion by Justice Reed (who had dissented in *Johnson*) noted that the "requirement of venue states the public policy that fixes the situs of the trial in the vicinage of the crime rather than the residence of the accused," and the crime here was a failure to perform a duty at the location of the hospital. The dissent, written by Justice Douglas, argued that it would be preferable to "read the statute with an eye to history and try the offenders at home where our forefathers thought that normally men would receive their fairest trial." The basic element of the crime, the dissent contended, was the failure to obey the draft board's order, which occurred when the registrant "refus[ed] to budge from his home town."

(c) In UNITED STATES v. CORES, 356 U.S. 405, 78 S.Ct. 875, 2 L.Ed.2d 873 (1958), the Court divided 6–3 in holding that venue for the prosecution of an alien seaman for remaining in the United States beyond the time permitted under his landing permit lay in any district where he "willfully remains after the permit expires." In finding that the crime was of a "continuing nature" and therefore within § 3237(a), the majority noted that its conclusion would permit the accused under Rule 21(b) to seek transfer to the district of his residence while a contrary view would limit venue to the district in which he was present at the time his permit expired.[a] In dissent, Justice Douglas ar-

a. At that time, Federal Rule 21 permitted transfer only to districts where venue was originally permissible under 18 U.S.C. § 3237(a). Rule 21 was subsequently amended to permit transfer to any district. See fn. b infra. As to the possible impact of this change on the Court's gued that crime was "committed" only in the latter district.

Do the rulings in *Johnson, Johnston, Cores,* and *Travis* reflect a consistent approach in determining where venue lies? Is a consistent approach reflected in Justice Douglas' dissents in *Johnson, Johnston,* and *Cores* and his majority opinion in *Travis*?

Commentators note that in some instances the definition of a criminal offense will clearly indicate what action or result must occur before the offense is "begun" or "completed." For many other offenses, however, the statutory language affords ample flexibility to adopt that construction of the offense which will best serve the underlying policy objective of the venue provision—"insur[ing] a fair trial for persons accused of crime." Kershen, *Vicinage,* 29 Okla.L.Rev. 801, 808 (1976). In such cases, they note, at least three conflicting guidelines have been advanced as to what construction will most appropriately serve that policy objective:

(1) One position maintains that liberal provisions for change of venue provide adequate protection against forcing defendants to defend in an inconvenient forum.[b] Accordingly, venue provisions should be broadly construed so that a conviction following a fair trial will not be reversed simply on the ground that the prosecutor selected the wrong district.[c]

(2) Another viewpoint would place greater emphasis on the defendant's home district. Supporters of this position, acknowledge that the draftsmen of Article III, § 2 chose the place of the commission of the crime, rather than the place of the accused's residence, as the appropriate test for venue, but they note that that test was selected primarily because it "accorded with the concept of jurisdiction held * * * in the late eighteenth century," and everyone assumed "that the place of commission of the crime and the place of residence would almost always be identical." Kershen, *Vicinage,* 30 Okla.L.Rev. 1, 22 (1977). Under this guideline, where the structure of the offense reasonably permits the court to conclude that it was committed in part in the home district, that interpretation should be adopted.

(3) A third view would stress limiting the prosecutor's discretion to choose where the prosecution will be initiated. Under this view, where possible, the court should treat an offense as non-continuing, thereby permitting venue only in a single district. This policy, it is argued, would be consistent with the assumption of the constitutional draftsmen that the crime almost invariably would be committed at a single place, that at which the accused was located when the major element of the offense occurred. It also could lead to selection of that district which would provide the

later venue rulings, see Barber, *Venue in Federal Criminal Cases: A Plea for Return to Principle,* 42 Tex.L.Rev. 39 (1963).

b. Fed.R.Crim.P. 21 is a typical venue change provision. Subsection (a), providing for transfer where "there exists * * * so great a prejudice against the defendant that he cannot obtain a fair and impartial trial," has application primarily to situations involving pretrial publicity. See Chapter 23. Subsection (b) permits transfer "for the convenience of parties and witnesses, and in the interest of justice." The decision to transfer under this provision lies in the discretion of the district judge and will necessarily rest on a weighing of the particular facts of each case. See Wright, *Federal Practice and Procedure (Criminal)* § 344 (2d ed., 1982). For a list of factors that a court might consider in exercising that discretion, see *Platt v. Minnesota Mining & Mfg. Co.,* 376 U.S. 240, 84 S.Ct. 769, 11 L.Ed.2d 674 (1964) (citing, inter alia, the location of the defendant, witnesses, and the "events likely to be in issue," the "expense to the parties," and the "docket condition of each district or division involved").

c. Cf. Barber, fn. a supra, at 46–47, criticizing *Travis:* "The mechanical approach of the Court * * * prevented conviction of defendants whose only complaint was the government's attempt to prosecute in a forum convenient to defendants. However, earnestly the defendant in *Travis* * * * urged his 'venue rights,' * * * his chief complaint was conviction, not conviction in a forum favorable to the government."

most appropriate group of jurors,[d] rather than allow the prosecution an option which would permit it to chose that district likely to produce the more favorable jury for the prosecution.

To what extent, if any, do the majority and dissenting opinions in *Johnson, Johnston, Cores,* and *Travis* reflect the application of these guidelines? Does the Supreme Court precedent clearly favor (or clearly reject) any one of these guidelines?

2. *The scope of Travis.* What, if anything, might *Travis* bode for future applications of § 3237(a)? Can the offense of issuing a false certificate of deposit be viewed as begun in a district in which the certificate is signed in blank although it is filled in elsewhere? See *Simpson v. United States,* 229 F. 940 (9th Cir.1916) (accepting that view). Where defendant, while abroad, mailed a package of marijuana to his home in Virginia, was venue on a charge of smuggling limited to the location at which the package entered the country (California) or could prosecution also be brought in Virginia? See *United States v. Lember,* 319 F.Supp. 249 (E.D.Va. 1970) (only place of entry). Where a case is pending in one district and the defendant visits a witness who lives in another district and there seeks by threats to keep the witness from testifying, can a prosecution under 18 U.S.C. § 1512 (prohibiting the purposeful intimidation of a witness) be brought in the district in which the case is pending? See *United States v. Moore,* 582 F.Supp. 1575 (D.D.C.1984) (noting a split among the circuits).

Consider, Abrams, *Conspiracy and Multi-Venue in Federal Criminal Prosecutions: The Crime Committed Formula,* 9 U.C.L.A.L.Rev. 751, 782–83 (1962): "* * * Justice Douglas drew a razor-thin distinction between a case in which union officers were *required* to file non-Communist affidavits and the instant case in which section 9(h) only made the fact that such an affidavit was 'on file with the Board' a condition precedent to a union's use of certain Board procedures. * * * The distinction is difficult to comprehend. It is not clear why the fact that under the statutory scheme there would be no offense until filing in the District was completed meant that the offense could not be 'begun' elsewhere. * * * Whatever the soundness of the distinction, it is clear from Justice Douglas' emphasis on the particular statutory context that the Court could, if it so desired, easily distinguish future cases * * *." See also *United States v. Ruehup,* 333 F.2d 641 (7th Cir.1964) (limiting *Travis* to "the statute there involved," and holding that a defendant charged with "making a false statement for the purpose of influencing an agency of the Farm Credit Administration" could be tried in the district in which the statement was prepared and mailed); *Moore's Federal Practice* § 18.02[1], fn. 22 (2d ed. 1979) (violations of 18 U.S.C. § 1001 "usually involve a continuing offense").

3. *Use of the mails.* Following *Johnson,* Note 1(a) supra, Congress added a second paragraph to § 3237(a) providing that: "Any offense involving the use of the mails, or transportation in interstate or

d. See Kershen, supra, at 158: "Once the relationship between the concept of the locality of the crime and the jurors of the vicinage, preserved by the sixth amendment, is recalled, it becomes clear that the place at which a crime is said to have been committed cannot be determined unless it is seen whether affiliating circumstances exist between the particular crime being located and the citizens who are being considered as the potential petit jurors for that particular crime. Hence, to determine the place at which a particular crime was committed, the following questions must be posed. Who are the citizens possessing, or likely to possess, the greatest amount of relevant information about the characters of the victim, defendant, witnesses, the incident itself, and the setting in which the incident occurred, that will insure the greatest likelihood that the truth about the crime will be found? Who are the citizens possessing a significant substantive law concern that their sense of justice be expressed in the interpretation of the law which will emerge in a general verdict? Who are the citizens possessing a significant sovereign concern as to whether the jury will intervene between the accused and the prosecution through a verdict of acquittal"?

foreign commerce, is a continuing offense and, except as otherwise expressly provided by enactment of Congress, may be inquired of and prosecuted in any district from, through, or into which such commerce or mail matter moves." Why wasn't this provision viewed as controlling in *Travis?* Consider *Moore's,* Note 2 supra, at § 18.03[1]: "The amendment embraces crimes where use of the mails or interstate transportation is an element of the offense. It does not apply, for example, to a prosecution under 18 U.S.C. § 1001 where the mails are incidentally used to deliver a false statement." Can the latter conclusion be derived from the *Travis* majority's statement that "venue should not be made to depend on the chance use of the mails, when Congress has so carefully indicated the locus of the crime"?

4. *Conspiracy venue.* Perhaps the most extensive choice of venue arises in conspiracy cases. The prosecutor there may initiate prosecution on the conspiracy charge in any district in which any act in furtherance of the conspiracy was committed by any of the conspirators, even though the defendant himself was not present in that district. See Abrams, Note 2 supra, for a detailed analysis of venue in such cases. See also *Hyde v. United States,* 225 U.S. 347, 385, 32 S.Ct. 793, 808, 56 L.Ed. 1114, 1137 (1912) (dissenting opinion) for Justice Holmes' famous criticism of this rule. To what extent should the conspiracy venue also permit broader venue for substantive offenses committed in furtherance of the conspiracy? Consider UNITED STATES v. WALDEN, 464 F.2d 1015 (4th Cir.1972):

"All ten defendants were indicted for conspiracy to commit larceny of a federally insured bank in violation of 18 U.S.C. § 2113(a) * * *. The remaining counts of the 13-count indictment charged various defendants with violations of 18 U.S.C. § 2113 (entering a bank to rob it) * * *. However, in counts 2, 3, 5, 6, 8, 10 and 13, the banks that the defendants were accused of entering were located in states other than South Carolina. * * * [T]he propriety of venue in the District of South Carolina for trial of all defendants for the crime of conspiracy * * * is not questioned. *Hyde v. United States* * * *. However, it is the position of the government * * * that the venue for trial on those counts of the indictment which alleged the unlawful entry of banks located in other districts [also] may properly be laid in the District of South Carolina. We disagree.

"The government * * * [relies] upon the doctrine that an accessory may be tried where his accessorial acts took place. * * * Assuming, without deciding, that conspiratorial acts within the context of this case may be equated with accessorial acts, we nevertheless disagree. That an accessory operating in South Carolina may be tried with his principal at the place of unlawful bank entry in Tennessee does not establish the converse. There is no rule of law authorizing the principal to be tried with his accessory where the accessory's acts took place. The government insists, however, that for purposes of venue the individual defendants charged in the substantive counts are in theory being charged as accessories operating within the State of South Carolina and not as principals in the making of unlawful entry into banks in other states. If we accept the argument, we would have, with respect to these substantive counts, the conceptual difficulty of a bank robbery or unlawful entry being perpetrated entirely by accessories in South Carolina without the assistance of principals at place of entry. * * * [W]here all persons charged as accessories for purposes of obtaining venue at the place where the crime was planned (South Carolina) are physically present and actively engaged in unlawful entry of a bank in another jurisdiction, we think it would distort both the substantive criminal law and the law of criminal venue to allow prosecution for the substantive offense of unlawful entry at the place (South Carolina) where the crime was planned. * * * It makes sense to bring an accessory to the place of trial of his principal; it is nonsense to reverse the procedure and serves no purpose of which we are aware except to further facilitate the prosecution of conspiracy cases and to combine such a prosecution with the prosecution of substantive offenses. * * * "

5. *State venue provisions.* State venue provisions tend to follow the federal pattern. Venue normally lies in the county in which the crime was "committed," with multi-venue possible where the crime is viewed as "begun" in one county and "completed" in another. In determining where an offense was "begun" or "completed," state courts have faced problems very much similar to those considered by the federal courts under § 18 U.S.C. 3237(a). As with the federal courts, their conclusions have varied. Thus, where a defendant planned a homicide in one county, inflicted the fatal injury in another county, and the victim died in still a third county, different state courts have suggested that venue would lie in all 3 counties, in the second and third counties only, and in the second county only. See Annot., 73 A.L.R.3d 907 (1976). States sometimes also have provisions authorizing prosecutions of a certain type of crime in a district other than that in which the offense occurred (e.g., a provision allowing all offenses committed by an escaped prisoner to be prosecuted in the district of the prison from which he escaped). But see Blume, *The Place of the Trial of Criminal Cases,* 43 Mich.L.Rev. 59 (1944) (noting limitations imposed by many state constitutional provisions).

6. *Jurisdictional limitations.* Issues similar to those presented in establishing venue also may arise in determining the scope of state penal legislation. State authority over criminal offenses generally is tied to the territorial theory: a state has power to make conduct or the result of conduct a crime if the conduct or result occurs within its territorial limits.[e] At common law this principle was thought to establish a single situs for any one crime. In general that situs would be "the place of the act (or omission) if the crime is defined only in these terms, and the place of a certain result if the definition of the crime includes such a result. This means, for example, that murder (for instance, where the killing is accomplished by shooting or mailing poisoned candy across state lines) is committed at the place where the fatal force impinges upon the body of the victim (the place where the bullet strikes or the poison is consumed), rather than where the fatal force is initiated by the defendant's act (where he fires the bullet or mails the poison) or where the victim dies. Bigamy is committed where the illegal marriage ceremony takes place, not where the parties thereafter cohabit." LaFave and Israel, § 16.2(c).

Although retaining the basic principle of territorial jurisdiction, many states have departed from the common law concept of a single situs by adopting statutes that include as a basis for jurisdiction local conduct or results other than the one particular act or result that the common law considered vital for the determination of situs. Thus, a state statute will authorize prosecution within the state based upon the commission of "any act within the state, in execution or part execution of [a criminal] intent, which culminates in the commission of a crime * * * without the state." Cal.Pen. Code § 778(a). See e.g., *People v. Buffum,* 256 P.2d 317 (Cal. 1953) (holding that "the acts done within the state [must] amount to an attempt"); *Smith v. State,* 697 P.2d 113 (Nev.1985) (although defendant's acts within the state generally must amount to an attempt, and

e. Federal criminal jurisdiction is not limited by the territorial principle, and frequently has been extended to activities occurring entirely outside national boundaries. See Blakesley, *A Conceptual Framework for Extradition and Jurisdiction Over Extraterritorial Crimes,* 1984 Utah L.Rev. 685.

the kidnapping of the victim in Nevada did not in itself constitute an attempt to commit the sexual assault and murder that occurred in California, the act of kidnapping was such a substantial and integral part of the overall criminal plan as to establish Nevada's jurisdiction over the aggravated offense); *Bright v. State,* 490 A.2d 564 (Del.1985) (where the state statute bases jurisdiction upon the commission of any element of the offense within the state, the state could have jurisdiction over a rape even though sexual penetration occurred in a neighboring state; victim was initially kidnapped in Delaware and that act furnished the coercion element of rape). So too, statutes also extend state jurisdiction to offenses "commenced without the State, [but] consummated within its boundaries by a defendant, himself outside the State, through the intervention of an innocent or guilty agent or any other means proceeding directly from said defendant." See, e.g., Cal.Pen. Code § 778; N.Y.Crim.P.Law § 20.20(2)(a) (jurisdiction extends to all "result offenses" where the "result occurred within the State"). The determination as to whether an offense was consummated within the state will often depend upon the court's view of the substantive elements of the offense. See, e.g., *People v. McGowan,* 14 P.2d 1036 (Cal.App.1932) (under continuing trespass theory, larceny is committed in state to which stolen goods are carried); *State v. Hickle,* 268 N.W.2d 826 (S.D.1978) (statute making it a crime to commit theft outside the state and to bring or be found with the property within the state punishes the act of bringing the property into the state, not the original theft, and therefore is subject to the state's penal authority); *State v. Klein,* 484 P.2d 455 (Wash.App.1971) (criminal non-support is committed where children are located, though defendant may have resided in another state).[f]

f. Of course, even though the state has territorial jurisdiction, it also must be able to obtain custody over the person located outside the state who committed a crime that falls within its jurisdiction. Ordinarily, that custody will be obtained through the extradition process. See 18 U.S.C. § 3182 (Federal Extradition Act) and the Uniform Criminal Extradition Act, 11 U.L.A. 59 (1974). Under both the uniform and federal extradition laws, the decision to extradite lies initially with the governor of the asylum state, and his decision not to extradite is not subject to judicial review. See *South Dakota v. Brown,* 576 P.2d 473 (Cal.1978). If extradition is ordered, only limited grounds are available for challenging that order in the asylum state. See *Michigan v. Doran,* p. 308 supra; LaFave and Israel, § 3.1(j). See also Note 2, p. 1096 supra.

Chapter 18

THE SCOPE OF THE PROSECUTION: JOINDER AND SEVERANCE OF OFFENSES AND DEFENDANTS

SECTION 1. JOINDER AND SEVERANCE OF OFFENSES

Fed.R.Crim.P. 8(a) allows joinder for trial of offenses "of the same or similar character," as do statutes or rules in many states. These provisions allow joinder even though the several offenses were not part of a single scheme or plan and were committed at different times and places.

Commentators have often criticized similar offense joinder. Because the offenses are distinct, each requiring its own evidence and witnesses, it is argued that there is no appreciable saving of time by joinder. Moreover, the joinder may confuse the jury and may result in the jury regarding one offense as corroborative of the other when, in fact, no such corroboration exists.[a] But a defendant may sometimes view joinder as preferable to being called upon to defend himself in a number of trials. Moreover, similar offense joinder may facilitate concurrent sentencing, to the defendant's advantage.

Fed.R.Crim.P. 8(a) also allows joinder of offenses "based on the same act or transaction or on two or more acts or transactions connected together or constituting parts of a common scheme or plan," as do many state provisions. In these jurisdictions, joinder is clearly allowed for offenses arising out of the same conduct (as where a defendant causes more than one death by reckless operation of a vehicle), offenses within a close time-space sequence (as with the killing of several people with successive shots from a gun, or burglary and the crime committed within), and offenses which are part of a single scheme, even if considerable time passes between them.

CROSS v. UNITED STATES

335 F.2d 987 (D.C.Cir.1964).

BAZELON, CHIEF JUDGE.

In a joint indictment, appellants were charged in Count I with robbery of a church rectory on February 23, 1962, and in Count II with robbery of a tourist home on May 2, 1962. Both appellants filed pretrial motions for severance of the counts. The motions were denied. The jury returned verdicts of guilty on Count I and not guilty on Count II. Appellants' chief contention on these appeals is that

a. These considerations prompted one court to hold that such joinder is permissible only if there is "such a high correlation in the details of the crimes that proof that the defendant committed one makes it very unlikely that anyone else but the defendant committed the others." *Commonwealth v. Morris,* 425 A.2d 715 (Pa.1981).

the District Court erred in refusing to sever the counts for trial. * * *

Prejudice may develop when an accused wishes to testify on one but not the other of two joined offenses which are clearly distinct in time, place and evidence. His decision whether to testify will reflect a balancing of several factors with respect to each count: the evidence against him, the availability of defense evidence other than his testimony, the plausibility and substantiality of his testimony, the possible effects of demeanor, impeachment, and cross-examination.[3] But if the two charges are joined for trial, it is not possible for him to weigh these factors separately as to each count.[4] If he testifies on one count, he runs the risk that any adverse effects will influence the jury's consideration of the other count. Thus he bears the risk on both counts, although he may benefit on only one. Moreover, a defendant's silence on one count would be damaging in the face of his express denial of the other. Thus he may be coerced into testifying on the count upon which he wished to remain silent.[5] It is not necessary to decide whether this invades his constitutional right to remain silent, since we think it constitutes prejudice within the meaning of [Fed.R.Crim.P.] 14.

In the present case the appellants did not specify at trial the counts upon which they wished to remain silent and why. It does appear that, when the trial court asked Cross whether he wished to testify in his own behalf, Cross answered: "Which case, Your Honor?" During the extended colloquy which followed, Cross repeatedly tried, without his counsel's assistance, to elaborate upon his objections to the joinder. But the court seems to have precluded this by insisting that the issue of joinder had been determined in the pre-trial denial of severance and by demanding a categorical answer to its original query. Thereafter the court applied the same ruling to Jackson.

An examination of Cross' testimony on both counts supports his claim in this court that he wished to testify on Count II and remain silent on Count I. His testimony on Count II was that he was a victim and not a cohort of the armed robbers who entered the tourist home behind him. This testimony, which met the Government's case directly, was so convincing that the jury believed it despite the prosecutor's efforts at cross-examination and impeachment. On Count I, however, his denial was plainly evasive and unconvincing. He testified that he had been drinking heavily and did not know his whereabouts at the time of the church robbery. On cross-examination he was open to questioning concerning his generally tawdry way of life and his prior convictions.

Thus it would appear that Cross had ample reason not to testify on Count I and would not have done so if that count had

3. "When he takes the stand in his own behalf, he does so as any other witness, and within the limits of the appropriate rules he may be cross-examined as to the facts in issue. He may be examined for the purpose of impeaching his credibility. His failure to deny or explain evidence of incriminating circumstances of which he may have knowledge may be the basis of adverse inference, and the jury may be so instructed. His waiver is not partial; having once cast aside the cloak of immunity, he may not resume it at will, whenever cross-examination may be inconvenient or embarrassing." *Raffel v. United States,* 271 U.S. 494, 46 S.Ct. 566, 70 L.Ed. 1054 (1926) (citations omitted).

4. "The safeguards against self-incrimination are for the benefit of those who do not wish to become witnesses in their own behalf and not for those who do." *Raffel v. United States,* supra fn. 3. But joinder may place the defendant in both categories at once.

5. The Supreme Court said in *Adamson v. California,* [p. 39 supra]:

"When evidence is before a jury that threatens conviction, it does not seem unfair to require him to choose between leaving the adverse evidence unexplained and subjecting himself to impeachment through disclosure of former crimes."

However, a defendant tried for two offenses faces a much more difficult situation: (1) his silence on one count does not prevent impeachment; (2) an inference from his silence on one count is encouraged by his lack of silence on the other. * * *

been tried separately. In a separate trial of that count the jury would not have heard his admissions of prior convictions and unsavory activities; nor would he have been under duress to offer dubious testimony on that count in order to avoid the damaging implication of testifying on only one of the two joined counts. Since the joinder embarrassed and confounded Cross in making his defense, the joinder was prejudicial within the meaning of Rule 14.

We do not agree with the Government that under *Dunaway v. United States,* 205 F.2d 23 (D.C.Cir.1953), this prejudice must be deemed cured by the acquittal on Count II. In that case three counts of housebreaking and two counts of larceny had been tried together. The trial court directed acquittals on the larceny counts, and the jury acquitted the defendant on one of the housebreaking counts. On appeal, we questioned whether "the jury acquittal, considered either alone or with the directed acquittals of larceny, disposes of the claim of prejudice due to the consolidation." But since it appeared that Dunaway "had a fair choice to take the stand or not uninfluenced to any significant degree by the consolidation," we affirmed the conviction on the ground that no prejudice could be shown. In the present case we think our discussion of the proceedings below shows that Cross had no such "fair choice" and that the resulting prejudice on Count I was not cured by the acquittal on Count II.

* * * The judgments[a] on Count I are vacated and the cases are remanded to the District Court for a new trial on that count. * * *

BASTIAN, CIRCUIT JUDGE (dissenting).

* * *

In the instant case, the trial judge specifically charged the jury:

> "Each of these two counts must be considered separately against each defendant on the sworn testimony before you in this case."

He then accurately, fairly and in some detail summarized for the jury the evidence and contentions of the parties with regard to each defendant on each count of the indictment.

Moreover, a typewritten form was given to the jury on which to record its verdict. The form set out the name of each defendant, and required a separate notation by the jury as to its decision on each of the two counts relating to that defendant; hence the verdict form was a constant reminder to the jury during its deliberations that each count was to be considered separately as to each defendant.

In these several ways the jury was apprised of its responsibility to consider each count and defendant separately. * * *

That the jury acquitted the defendants on one count while convicting on the other demonstrates that it did, in fact, consider the evidence as it related to each count separately. * * *

DREW v. UNITED STATES

331 F.2d 85 (D.C.Cir.1964).

MCGOWAN, CIRCUIT JUDGE.

This is an appeal from a conviction in the District Court on one count of robbery and one count of attempted robbery * * *. Appellant moved, both before and at the commencement of trial, to compel separate trials of the two charges; and, after verdict, he moved for a new trial because of prejudice asserted to have occurred in, and by reason of, the joint trial. The failure to grant this relief is said on this appeal to be a source of reversible error. * * *

a. In an omitted portion of the opinion, the court concluded that although codefendant Jackson's claim was not so clearly substantiated by the record, it "would be unjust and illogical to separate the two cases and uphold the judgment as to one defendant and reverse it as to the other."

The justification for a liberal rule on joinder of offenses appears to be the economy of a single trial. The argument against joinder is that the defendant may be prejudiced for one or more of the following reasons: (1) he may become embarrassed or confounded in presenting separate defenses; (2) the jury may use the evidence of one of the crimes charged to infer a criminal disposition on the part of the defendant from which is found his guilt of the other crime or crimes charged; or (3) the jury may cumulate the evidence of the various crimes charged and find guilt when, if considered separately, it would not so find. A less tangible, but perhaps equally persuasive, element of prejudice may reside in a latent feeling of hostility engendered by the charging of several crimes as distinct from only one. Thus, in any given case the court must weigh prejudice to the defendant caused by the joinder against the obviously important considerations of economy and expedition in judicial administration. * * *

It is a principle of long standing in our law that evidence of one crime is inadmissible to prove *disposition* to commit crime, from which the jury may infer that the defendant committed the crime charged. Since the likelihood that juries will make such an improper inference is high, courts presume prejudice and exclude evidence of other crimes unless that evidence can be admitted for some substantial, legitimate purpose. The same dangers appear to exist when two crimes are joined for trial, and the same principles of prophylaxis are applicable.

Evidence of other crimes is admissible when relevant to (1) motive, (2) intent, (3) the absence of mistake or accident, (4) a common scheme or plan embracing the commission of two or more crimes so related to each other that proof of the one tends to establish the other, and (5) the identity of the person charged with the commission of the crime on trial. When the evidence is relevant and important to one of these five issues, it is generally conceded that the prejudicial effect may be outweighed by the probative value.

If, then, under the rules relating to other crimes, the evidence of each of the crimes on trial would be admissible in a separate trial for the other, the possibility of "criminal propensity" prejudice would be in no way enlarged by the fact of joinder. When, for example, the two crimes arose out of a continuing transaction or the same set of events, the evidence would be independently admissible in separate trials. Similarly, if the facts surrounding the two or more crimes on trial show that there is a reasonable probability that the same person committed both crimes due to the concurrence of unusual and distinctive facts relating to the manner in which the crimes were committed, the evidence of one would be admissible in the trial of the other to prove identity. In such cases the prejudice that might result from the jury's hearing the evidence of the other crime in a joint trial would be no different from that possible in separate trials.

The federal courts, including our own, have, however, found no prejudicial effect from joinder when the evidence of each crime is simple and distinct, even though such evidence might not have been admissible in separate trials under the rules just discussed. This rests upon the assumption that, with a proper charge, the jury can easily keep such evidence separate in their deliberations and, therefore, the danger of the jury's cumulating the evidence is substantially reduced. * * *

Turning now to the case at hand, a detailed exposition of the facts is necessary. The robbery, committed at a neighborhood store belonging to High's Dairy Products Corp., occurred on July 27, 1962. The sales clerk testified that a Negro male, wearing sunglasses, entered the store. After a short delay the clerk approached the customer and asked if she could help him. He replied: "This is a holdup; I want your money, all of it."

When the witness hesitated, he said: "Get it," and pulled a gun part of the way out of his pocket. She gave him the money, and he proceeded to leave the store as another customer entered.

The attempted robbery occurred at a different High's neighborhood store on August 13, 1962 (some two and one-half weeks after the robbery). The sales clerk testified as follows: While she was alone in the store a Negro male entered the store dressed in a coat, cap, and sunglasses. When she asked to help him, he asked for a bag of peanuts. She asked whether he wanted the five or ten cent size, and he replied "five." He then said: "Give me all the money," and she replied: "If you want it, come and get it." He repeated himself several times, and each time she repeated her statement. Finally he said: "You are not going to give me that money?" and she replied negatively. At that point a customer entered the store, and appellant left hastily. The clerk testified that she was not threatened in any way. The police apprehended appellant in the vicinity of the store some twenty-five minutes later and returned to the store where the sales clerk identified him as the person who had attempted to rob her.

These facts do not show such a close similarity in the manner of committing the crimes as would make them admissible in separate trials.[a] * * *

Nor did the two offenses arise out of the same transaction, series of transactions, or continuing state of affairs so that the evidence could have come in under the fourth exception stated above. In short, we cannot find absence of prejudice on the ground that the evidence would have been admissible in separate trials.

This is not the end of the matter, however. We must still determine whether this case falls within the "simple and distinct" test * * *. As pointed out above, the very essence of this rule is that the evidence be such that the jury is unlikely to be confused by it or misuse it. It is not mere conjecture to say that the jury may have been confused in this case. A perusal of the record shows that witnesses' responses at times indicated confusion as to which crime counsel were referring to in their questions; the two crimes were repeatedly referred to as of the same order; and the prosecutor in his summation not unnaturally lumped the two together on occasion in his discussion of the evidence. These lapses do not appear to have been purposeful, but lack of improper motivation does not lessen their impact on the jury. If separate crimes are to be tried together—and we are not to be understood as intimating any conclusion that this can never, as a practical matter, be successfully undertaken—both court and counsel must recognize that they are assuming a difficult task the performance of which calls for a vigilant precision in speech and action far beyond that required in the ordinary trial. The confusion here was probably the result of the superficial similarity of the two crimes and the way in which they were committed. On this record, we cannot say that the jury probably was not confused or probably did not misuse the evidence * * *.

For these reasons we find that there was prejudice in the joinder and the court below should have granted separate trials. The conviction is reversed and the case is remanded.

a. The court noted that the "essential similarity" between the two crimes was that both were committed against High stores by a Negro wearing sunglasses, which would not be "sufficient to support a finding of reasonable probability that the two offenses were committed by the same person," particularly in view of the other facts: (1) in the robbery, the clerk was threatened with a gun at the first sign of noncompliance, while in the attempted robbery there was no such threat of violence; (2) High stores, usually staffed with one or two female clerks, "are particularly vulnerable to this kind of crime"; and (3) the circumstances of the two crimes "fit into an obvious tactical pattern which would suggest itself to almost anyone disposed to commit a depredation of this sort."

Notes and Questions

1. Note, 74 Yale L.J. 553, 560 (1965), asserts that because it will often be difficult for the trial judge to apply the *Drew* and *Cross* standards in advance of trial, the "only escape from this dilemma of how and when to apply *Cross* and *Drew* without vitiating the standards of prejudice evolved in those cases is the abolition of joinder of similar offenses under Rule 8." Is that so?

2. Does *Cross* apply to cases in which the offenses are joined for trial because they were "connected together" in their commission, or are such cases different in that the defendant must "claim a desire to testify on specific separable offenses, but also he must argue that had there been separate trials *ab initio* the order of prosecution would have been favorable to his theory of prejudice"? See Note, supra, at 561. Does *Drew* apply to cases in which the offenses are joined because they were "connected together" in their commission? What if the defendant is charged with (1) extortion and (2) having lied to the grand jury in denying his receipt of the extortion money, and he moves for severance on the ground that he will be prejudiced as to the first count if the jury is informed, by the second count, that the grand jury disbelieved his testimony when he denied committing the extortion? See *United States v. Pacente,* 490 F.2d 661 (7th Cir.1973), rev'd en banc, 503 F.2d 543 (1974).

3. Upon a motion for severance of offenses, the usual inquiry is whether, in view of the number of offenses charged and the complexity of the evidence to be offered, the trier of fact will be able to distinguish the evidence and apply the law intelligently as to each offense. If the motion is denied by the trial judge, on appeal this decision is reviewed under an abuse-of-discretion standard. There are four doctrines which are commonly relied upon by appellate courts to support a finding that the defendant was not prejudiced by the joinder: (a) that the jury is capable of following the judge's instructions to ignore certain evidence or to consider certain evidence only as to some of the charges; (b) that if the jury has acquitted the defendant on any count this shows that the jury has been selective and thus must have kept the evidence separate; (c) that the defendant has no ground for complaint if he was convicted of the several counts but received concurrent sentencing; (d) that any prejudice from the joinder is cured by overwhelming evidence of guilt. Are they convincing? [b]

SECTION 2. FAILURE TO JOIN RELATED OFFENSES

ASHE v. SWENSON

397 U.S. 436, 90 S.Ct. 1189, 25 L.Ed.2d 469 (1970).

MR. JUSTICE STEWART delivered the opinion of the Court. * * *

Sometime in the early hours of the morning of January 10, 1960, six men were engaged in a poker game in the basement of the home of John Gladson at Lee's Summit, Missouri. Suddenly three or four masked men, armed with a shotgun and pistols, broke into the basement and robbed each of the poker players of money and various articles of personal property. The robbers—and it has never been clear whether there were three or four of them—then fled in a car belonging to one of the victims of the robbery. Shortly thereafter the stolen car was discovered in a field, and later that morning three men were arrested by a state trooper while they were walking on a highway not far from where the abandoned car had

b. Consider Penrod & Tanford, *Reducing Biases in Joined Criminal Offenses* (1985), based upon the decisions of experimental jurors who watched videotaped trials, which concludes that (i) joinder of offenses in a single trial increases the likelihood that the defendant will be convicted; (ii) the similarity between the offenses or between the evidence on each of the offenses is relatively unimportant in producing this result; and (iii) even "strong" jury instructions have "no effect whatsoever" in reducing the prejudice.

been found. The petitioner was arrested by another officer some distance away.

The four were subsequently charged with seven separate offenses—the armed robbery of each of the six poker players and the theft of the car. In May 1960 the petitioner went to trial on the charge of robbing Donald Knight, one of the participants in the poker game. At the trial the State called Knight and three of his fellow poker players as prosecution witnesses. Each of them described the circumstances of the holdup and itemized his own individual losses. The proof that an armed robbery had occurred and that personal property had been taken from Knight as well as from each of the others was unassailable. The testimony of the four victims in this regard was consistent both internally and with that of the others. But the State's evidence that the petitioner had been one of the robbers was weak. Two of the witnesses thought that there had been only three robbers altogether, and could not identify the petitioner as one of them. Another of the victims, who was the petitioner's uncle by marriage, said that at the "patrol station" he had positively identified each of the other three men accused of the holdup, but could say only that the petitioner's voice "sounded very much like" that of one of the robbers. The fourth participant in the poker game did identify the petitioner, but only by his "size and height, and his actions."

The cross-examination of these witnesses was brief, and it was aimed primarily at exposing the weakness of their identification testimony. Defense counsel made no attempt to question their testimony regarding the holdup itself or their claims as to their losses. Knight testified without contradiction that the robbers had stolen from him his watch, $250 in cash, and about $500 in checks. His billfold, which had been found by the police in the possession of one of the three other men accused of the robbery, was admitted in evidence. The defense offered no testimony and waived final argument.

The trial judge instructed the jury that if it found that the petitioner was one of the participants in the armed robbery, the theft of "any money" from Knight would sustain a conviction. He also instructed the jury that if the petitioner was one of the robbers, he was guilty under the law even if he had not personally robbed Knight. The jury—though not instructed to elaborate upon its verdict—found the petitioner "not guilty due to insufficient evidence."

Six weeks later the petitioner was brought to trial again, this time for the robbery of another participant in the poker game, a man named Roberts. The petitioner filed a motion to dismiss, based on his previous acquittal. The motion was overruled, and the second trial began. The witnesses were for the most part the same, though this time their testimony was substantially stronger on the issue of the petitioner's identity. For example, two witnesses who at the first trial had been wholly unable to identify the petitioner as one of the robbers, now testified that his features, size, and mannerisms matched those of one of their assailants. Another witness who before had identified the petitioner only by his size and actions now also remembered him by the unusual sound of his voice. The State further refined its case at the second trial by declining to call one of the participants in the poker game whose identification testimony at the first trial had been conspicuously negative. The case went to the jury on instructions virtually identical to those given at the first trial. This time the jury found the petitioner guilty, and he was sentenced to a 35-year term in the state penitentiary.

* * *

"Collateral estoppel" is an awkward phrase, but it stands for an extremely important principle in our adversary system of justice. It means simply that when an issue of ultimate fact has once been determined by a valid and final judgment, that issue cannot again be litigated between the same parties in any future lawsuit. Although first developed in civil litigation, collateral estoppel has been an established rule of federal criminal law at least since this Court's decision more than 50 years ago in *United States v. Oppenheimer,* 242 U.S. 85, 37 S.Ct. 68, 61 L.Ed. 161 [1916]. As Mr. Justice Holmes put the matter in that case, "It cannot be that the safeguards of the person, so often and so rightly mentioned with solemn reverence, are less than those that protect from a liability in debt." As a rule of federal law, therefore, "[i]t is much too late to suggest that this principle is not fully applicable to a former judgment in a criminal case, either because of lack of 'mutuality' or because the judgment may reflect only a belief that the Government had not met the higher burden of proof exacted in such cases for the Government's evidence as a whole although not necessarily as to every link in the chain."

The federal decisions have made clear that the rule of collateral estoppel in criminal cases is not to be applied with the hypertechnical and archaic approach of a 19th century pleading book, but with realism and rationality. Where a previous judgment of acquittal was based upon a general verdict, as is usually the case, this approach requires a court to "examine the record of a prior proceeding, taking into account the pleadings, evidence, charge, and other relevant matter, and conclude whether a rational jury could have grounded its verdict upon an issue other than that which the defendant seeks to foreclose from consideration." The inquiry "must be set in a practical frame, and viewed with an eye to all the circumstances of the proceedings." Any test more technically restrictive would, of course, simply amount to a rejection of the rule of collateral estoppel in criminal proceedings, at least in every case where the first judgment was based upon a general verdict of acquittal.

Straightforward application of the federal rule to the present case can lead to but one conclusion. For the record is utterly devoid of any indication that the first jury could rationally have found that an armed robbery had not occurred, or that Knight had not been a victim of that robbery. The single rationally conceivable issue in dispute before the jury was whether the petitioner had been one of the robbers. And the jury by its verdict found that he had not. The federal rule of law, therefore, would make a second prosecution for the robbery of Roberts wholly impermissible.

The ultimate question to be determined, then, in the light of *Benton v. Maryland,*[a] is whether this established rule of federal law is embodied in the Fifth Amendment guarantee against double jeopardy. We do not hesitate to hold that it is. For whatever else that constitutional guarantee may embrace, it surely protects a man who has been acquitted from having to "run the gantlet" a second time.

The question is not whether Missouri could validly charge the petitioner with six separate offenses for the robbery of the six poker players. It is not whether he could have received a total of six punishments if he had been convicted in a single trial of robbing the six victims. It is simply whether, after a jury determined by its verdict that the petitioner was not one of the robbers, the State could constitutionally hale him before a new jury to litigate that issue again. * * *

In this case the State in its brief has frankly conceded that following the petitioner's acquittal, it treated the first trial as no more than a dry run for the second prosecution: "No doubt the prosecutor felt the state had a provable case on the first charge and, when he lost, he did what every good attorney would do—he refined his presentation in light of the turn of events at the first trial." But this is pre-

a. P. 39 supra, holding that the Fifth Amendment guarantee against double jeopardy is enforceable against the States through the Fourteenth Amendment.

cisely what the constitutional guarantee forbids. * * *

Reversed and remanded.

MR. JUSTICE BRENNAN, whom MR. JUSTICE DOUGLAS and MR. JUSTICE MARSHALL join, concurring.

I agree that the Double Jeopardy Clause incorporates collateral estoppel as a constitutional requirement and therefore join the Court's opinion. However, even if the rule of collateral estoppel had been inapplicable to the facts of this case, it is my view that the Double Jeopardy Clause nevertheless bars the prosecution of petitioner a second time for armed robbery. * * *

The Double Jeopardy Clause is a guarantee "that the State with all its resources and power [shall] not be allowed to make repeated attempts to convict an individual for an alleged offense, thereby subjecting him to embarrassment, expense and ordeal and compelling him to live in a continuing state of anxiety and insecurity * * *." This guarantee is expressed as a prohibition against multiple prosecutions for the "same offence." Although the phrase "same offence" appeared in most of the early common-law articulations of the double jeopardy principle, questions of its precise meaning rarely arose prior to the 18th century, and by the time the Bill of Rights was adopted it had not been authoritatively defined.

When the common law did finally attempt a definition, it adopted the "same evidence" test, which provided little protection from multiple prosecution:

> "Unless the first indictment were such as the prisoner might have been convicted upon by proof of the facts contained in the second indictment, an acquittal on the first indictment can be no bar to the second."

The "same evidence" test of "same offence" was soon followed by a majority of American jurisdictions, but its deficiencies are obvious. It does not enforce but virtually annuls the constitutional guarantee. For example, where a single criminal episode involves several victims, under the "same evidence" test a separate prosecution may be brought as to each. The "same evidence" test permits multiple prosecutions where a single transaction is divisible into chronologically discrete crimes. Even a single criminal act may lead to multiple prosecutions if it is viewed from the perspectives of different statutes. Given the tendency of modern criminal legislation to divide the phases of a criminal transaction into numerous separate crimes, the opportunities for multiple prosecutions for an essentially unitary criminal episode are frightening. And given our tradition of virtually unreviewable prosecutorial discretion concerning the initiation and scope of a criminal prosecution, the potentialities for abuse inherent in the "same evidence" test are simply intolerable.

The "same evidence" test is not constitutionally required. It was first expounded *after* the adoption of the Fifth Amendment, and * * * has never been squarely held by this Court to be the required construction of the constitutional phrase "same offence" in a case involving multiple trials. * * *

In my view, the Double Jeopardy Clause requires the prosecution, except in most limited circumstances,[7] to join at one trial all the charges against a defendant which grow out of a single criminal act, occurrence, episode, or transaction. This "same transaction" test of "same offence" not only enforces the ancient prohibition against vexatious multiple prosecutions embodied in the Double Jeopardy Clause,

7. For example, where a crime is not completed or not discovered, despite diligence on the part of the police, until after the commencement of a prosecution for other crimes arising from the same transaction, an exception to the "same transaction" rule should be made to permit a separate prosecution. Another exception would be necessary if no single court had jurisdiction of all the alleged crimes. * * *

but responds as well to the increasingly widespread recognition that the consolidation in one lawsuit of all issues arising out of a single transaction or occurrence best promotes justice, economy, and convenience. * * *

The present case highlights the hazards of abuse of the criminal process inherent in the "same evidence" test and demonstrates the necessity for the "same transaction" test. * * * Since Missouri has offered no justification for not trying the other informations at [the first] trial, it is reasonable to infer that the other informations were held in reserve to be tried if the State failed to obtain a conviction on the charge of robbing Knight. Indeed, the State virtually concedes as much since it argues that the "same evidence" test is consistent with such an exercise of prosecutorial discretion. * * *

The prosecution plainly organized its case for the second trial to provide the links missing in the chain of identification evidence that was offered at the first trial. McClendon, who was an unhelpful witness at the first trial was not called at the second trial. The hesitant and uncertain evidence of Gladson and Roberts at the first trial became detailed, positive, and expansive at the second trial. One must experience a sense of uneasiness with any double jeopardy standard that would allow the State this second chance to plug up the holes in its case. The constitutional protection against double jeopardy is empty of meaning if the State may make "repeated attempts" to touch up its case by forcing the accused to "run the gantlet" as many times as there are victims of a single episode. * * *

MR. CHIEF JUSTICE BURGER, dissenting.

The Fifth Amendment to the Constitution of the United States provides in part: "nor shall any person be subject for the same offense to be twice put in jeopardy of life or limb * * *." Nothing in the language and none of the gloss previously placed on this provision of the Fifth Amendment remotely justifies the treatment which the Court today accords to the collateral estoppel doctrine. * * *

The collateral estoppel concept—originally a product only of civil litigation—is a strange mutant as it is transformed to control this criminal case. In civil cases the doctrine was justified as conserving judicial resources as well as those of the parties to the actions and additionally as providing the finality needed to plan for the future. It ordinarily applies to parties on each side of the litigation who have the same interest as or who are identical with the parties in the initial litigation. Here the complainant in the second trial is not the same as in the first even though the State is a party in both cases. Very properly, in criminal cases, finality and conservation of private, public, and judicial resources are lesser values than in civil litigation. Also, courts which have applied the collateral concept to criminal actions would certainly not apply it to *both* parties, as is true in civil cases, i.e., here, if Ashe had been convicted at the first trial, presumably no court would then hold that he was thereby foreclosed from litigating the identification issue at the second trial. * * * [b]

[T]he majority's analysis of the facts completely disregards the confusion injected into the case by the robbery of Mrs. Gladson.[c] To me, if we are to psychoanalyze the jury, the evidence adduced at the first trial could more reasonably be construed as indicating that Ashe had been at

b. In *Simpson v. Florida,* 403 U.S. 384, 91 S.Ct. 1801, 29 L.Ed.2d 549 (1971), the Court, noting that "mutuality" is not an ingredient of the *Ashe* rule, held that defendant's conviction at his first trial (reversed on appeal for failure to instruct the jury on a lesser included offense) did not estop him from claiming that the state failed to prove his identity at the second trial.

c. Earlier in his opinion, the Chief Justice notes certain facts not stated in the opinion of the Court: "During the same period in which the men were being robbed in the basement, one man entered Mrs. Gladson's bedroom three floors above, ripped out the telephone there, tied her with the telephone cord, and removed the wedding ring from her finger. * * * Mrs. Gladson the Gladson home with the other three men but was not one of those involved in the basement robbery. Certainly, the evidence at the first trial was equivocal as to whether there were three or four robbers, whether the man who robbed Mrs. Gladson was one of the three who robbed the six male victims, and whether a man other than the three had robbed Mrs. Gladson. Then, since the jury could have thought that the "acting together" instruction given by the trial court in both trials only applied to the actual taking from the six card players, and not to Mrs. Gladson, the jury could well have acquitted Ashe but yet believed that he was present in the Gladson home. On the other hand, the evidence adduced at the second trial resolved issues other than identity which may have troubled the first jury. If believed, that evidence indicated that a fourth robber, Johnson, not Ashe, was with Mrs. Gladson when Ashe, Larson, and Brown were robbing the male victims. Johnson did go to the basement where the male victims were located, but only after the other three had already taken the stolen items and when the robbers were preparing for their departure in a car to be stolen from Roberts.[d]

Accordingly, even the facts in this case, which the Court's opinion considers to "lead to but one conclusion," are susceptible to an interpretation that the first jury did not base its acquittal on the identity ground which the Court finds so compelling. The Court bases its holding on sheer "guesswork," which should have no place particularly in our review of state convictions by way of habeas corpus. * * *

Notes and Questions

1. Schaefer, *Unresolved Issues in the Law of Double Jeopardy: Waller and Ashe,* 58 Calif.L.Rev. 391, 394 (1970): "Because the prosecution is required to prove every element of the crime beyond a reasonable doubt, the court's instructions usually offer the jury several theories upon which the defendant may be acquitted. Collateral estoppel is therefore of limited value because it is not often possible to determine with precision how the judge or jury has decided any particular issue." Is the solution to utilize special verdicts in criminal cases? See *Heald v. Mullaney,* p. 1372 infra.

2. Note, 69 Mich.L.Rev. 762, 771 (1971): "Furthermore, the general verdict places a defendant in a most troublesome dilemma. He must either put a very few of his defenses in issue, thereby assuring a collateral-estoppel effect in any future proceedings, but at the same time risking a conviction by not putting his other valid defenses in issue; or he must put all the defenses he has before the jury, thereby better shielding himself against a conviction, but unfortunately destroying the possibility of any future collateral-estoppel effect on all of the issues raised by these defenses."

3. What result under *Ashe* in the following circumstances?

(a) Defendant was charged with first-degree murder. The prosecution's theory was that defendant was guilty under the statute making any killing in the commission or attempted commission of rape first-degree murder. The evidence showed that the defendant, who had been drinking, opened the door of a parked car in which he saw a woman, and announced, "I want a piece of ass and I don't care who

did not testify [at the first trial] because she was ill on the day of trial. * * * [At the second trial,] she said that she was able to identify the robber by his voice, and that he was Johnson, not Ashe."

d. In *Harris v. Washington,* 404 U.S. 55, 92 S.Ct. 183, 30 L.Ed.2d 212 (1971), the state court held *Ashe* inapplicable where the issue of identity had not been "fully litigated" at the first trial because the trial judge had excluded evidence on grounds having "no bearing on the quality of the evidence." The Supreme Court reversed, holding that "the constitutional guarantee applies, irrespective of whether the jury considered all relevant evidence, and irrespective of the good faith of the State in bringing successive prosecutions."

knows it." The woman's husband raised up from the back seat and stepped out of the car, at which point the defendant shot and killed him. The defendant then raped the woman. The jury returned a verdict of guilty of manslaughter. Defendant has now been charged with rape. See *People v. Noth,* 33 Mich.App. 18, 189 N.W.2d 779 (1971).[e]

(b) Defendant, a postal employee, was charged with stealing a letter from the mails. At trial, a postal inspector testified that he saw the defendant take an envelope from an employees' mail box in the post office and that a search of her person uncovered three marked quarters which had been placed in the envelope. The defendant testified that she had not taken the letter and that she had procured the three quarters from a dollar-changing machine. Following defendant's acquittal, she was charged with perjury in the mail theft trial. The government is prepared to prove that there was not time for the defendant to get to the dollar-changing machine between the time she was observed taking the envelope and the time of the search, and also that she could not have obtained the marked quarters from the machine because it does not recycle coins deposited in the machine by other users. See *United States v. Nash,* 447 F.2d 1382 (4th Cir.1971).

(c) Defendant at his first trial was convicted of conspiracy but acquitted of having lied to the grand jury when he denied any knowledge of the conspiracy and of not reporting the conspiracy income on his tax return. The conspiracy conviction was reversed on appeal because of improper admission of evidence at trial. On remand for a new trial, defendant moved to dismiss the conspiracy charge. See *United States v. Price,* 750 F.2d 363 (5th Cir. 1985).

(d) Defendant was acquitted of a federal charge that he willfully and knowingly, with intent to defraud, smuggled jewels into the United States. The federal government has now instituted civil forfeiture proceedings with respect to the same jewels, under which the government must prove that the property was brought into the United States without the required declaration. See *One Lot Emerald Cut Stones and One Ring v. United States,* 409 U.S. 232, 93 S.Ct. 489, 34 L.Ed.2d 438 (1972).

(e) Defendant was charged with exhibiting an obscene motion picture. Earlier, a different defendant had been acquitted for another showing of the same film because the motion picture was not found to be obscene. See *People v. Seltzer,* 101 Cal. Rptr. 260 (App.1972); Note, 46 So.Cal. L.Rev. 922 (1973).

e. Compare *Turner v. Arkansas,* 407 U.S. 366, 92 S.Ct. 2096, 32 L.Ed.2d 798 (1972), where, some time after petitioner, his brother, Yates and another played poker, Yates was robbed and murdered. Turner was charged with murder on a felony-murder theory and acquitted, after which he was charged with the robbery which the state concedes arose out of the same facts and circumstances. Under the Arkansas statutory provisions on joinder of offenses, these two charges could not have been joined together for trial. The Court, per curiam, ruled: "The jury was instructed that it must find petitioner guilty of first degree murder if it found that he had killed the decedent Yates either with premeditation or unintentionally during the course of a robbery. The jury's verdict thus necessarily means that it found petitioner not guilty of the killing. The State's theory, however, is that the jury might have believed that petitioner and his brother robbed Yates but that this brother actually committed the murder. This theory is belied by the actual instructions given the jury. The trial judge charged that:

> 'An accessory is one who stands by, aids, abets, or assists * * * the perpetration of the crime * * *.
>
> 'All persons being present, aiding and abetting, or ready and consenting to aid and abet, in any felony, shall be deemed principal offenders, and indicted or informed against, and punished as such.'

Had the jury found petitioner present at the crime scene, it would have been obligated to return a verdict of guilty of murder even if it believed that he had not actually pulled the trigger. The only logical conclusion is that the jury found him not present at the scene of the murder and robbery, a finding which negates the possibility of a constitutionally valid conviction for the robbery of Yates."

4. What if, in *Noth,* the defendant had entered a guilty plea to manslaughter? Consider *Ohio v. Johnson,* 467 U.S. 493, 104 S.Ct. 2536, 81 L.Ed.2d 425 (1984), where defendant, charged with both murder and manslaughter based on the same killing and robbery and theft based on the same taking, entered a guilty plea over the state's objection to manslaughter and theft. In a footnote the Court asserted: "Respondent also argues that prosecution on the remaining charges is barred by the principles of collateral estoppel enunciated by this Court in *Ashe v. Swenson.* Even if the two were mutually exclusive crimes, the taking of a guilty plea is not the same as an adjudication on the merits after full trial, such as took place in *Ashe v. Swenson.* Moreover, in a case such as this, where the State has made no effort to prosecute the charges seriatim, the considerations of double jeopardy protection implicit in the application of collateral estoppel are inapplicable."

5. Phillips was tried for robbery of a federally insured bank. In response to a question from the jury, the court instructed that Phillips could not be convicted unless the jury believed he was one of those in the bank; the court also gave instructions on the "lesser included offense" of possessing what were known to be the proceeds of the robbery. Ten minutes later the jury returned a verdict of guilty of the lesser offense, which the court later set aside on the ground it was not included in the indictment. Phillips was then prosecuted for the possession offense, and evidence of his presence in the bank was admitted to prove his knowledge that the funds he received were stolen. In *Phillips v. United States,* 502 F.2d 227 (4th Cir.1974), his conviction was reversed on the authority of *Ashe.* Craven, J., dissenting, gave "two independent reasons why collateral estoppel should not apply in this case.

"First, Phillips' acquittal of bank robbery was only an implicit acquittal, arising by operation of law from the verdict of guilt on a lesser included offense. I would hold that such an implicit acquittal cannot be the basis for collateral estoppel because it leaves doubt whether the jury has made any factual determination in favor of the accused. * * *

"Second, * * * I would not allow its use to restrict proof on retrial of the *lesser* charge. Retrial in cases like this one harbors none of the prosecutorial abuses that supplied the rationale of *Ashe* * * *."

Are these reasons sound? Is there yet a third reason, namely, that the defendant's presence in the bank was, in the second prosecution, an "evidentiary" fact rather than an "ultimate" fact (i.e., presence did not have to be proved in the second trial, showing presence was merely of evidentiary value on the knowledge element)? See *State v. Sefton,* 485 A.2d 284 (N.H.1984), and compare *Wingate v. Wainwright,* 464 F.2d 209 (5th Cir.1972), holding it makes no difference "whether the relitigated issue is one of 'ultimate' fact or merely an 'evidentiary' fact in the second prosecution."

6. In UNITED STATES ex rel. DiGIANGIEMO v. REGAN, 528 F.2d 1262 (2d Cir.1975), the court (per Friendly, J.) considered the question whether the granting of a motion to suppress evidence bars introduction of that evidence in a subsequent trial. After noting that *Ashe* was not applicable because it was tied to the double jeopardy clause and jeopardy has not yet attached when the pretrial motion was granted, the court questioned "how far due process, unaided by the double jeopardy clause, requires a state to apply collateral estoppel in favor of a criminal defendant." On this point, it noted:

"A hypothetical case may help in the consideration of this problem. Defendant X is the subject of two indictments in two counties, one for bank robbery, the other for having stolen an automobile to be used as the getaway car. He pleads not guilty to both charges and notifies the state that he proposes to prove an alibi, which will exonerate him of both offenses, and for which he has strong support. The state's reliance will be on weak identification evidence and a confession to both crimes. The bank robbery charge is to be tried first. X moves to suppress the confession on a number of grounds—use of physical violence; deprivation of food, water, and rest; promises of immunity, etc. Both sides recognize that determination of the motion will very likely decide the case. After a hearing of several days, a judge suppresses the confession. The state elects not to exercise a right to appeal, drops the bank robbery indictment, and indicates its intention to press the stolen car indictment. X moves again to suppress the confession. The state insists on a hearing, saying it has new evidence to rebut X's claims. Does due process permit it to be given one?

"We think not. * * * [A]s has been said, '[t]he weight of the harassment factor is considerably increased in the criminal law,' because of the disparity usually prevailing in resources between the state and the defendant and the strain of a second prosecution even if not for the identical offense. If the hypothetical be altered so that the ruling on suppression of the confession had come in the course of a trial for bank robbery in which X was acquitted, *Ashe v. Swenson* seemingly would prevent relitigation of the admissibility of the confession in a subsequent trial for stealing the getaway car; it would appear bizarre that the more orderly procedure of trying the suppression issue before X was put in jeopardy should lead to a result less favorable to him. Assuming that the state has had an opportunity for a full hearing on suppression and at least one appeal as of right, we think due process would forbid relitigation of the issue determined adversely to it, although not, of course, the prosecution of X for auto theft on the basis of other evidence.

"Unless Fourth Amendment cases are to be treated differently * * *, it would follow that if DiGiangiemo had moved the Nassau County Court to suppress the chisel and screwdriver found in the trunk of Galante's car, due process would have required that the motion be granted."

What if the state had no right to appeal from the earlier ruling? What if the state could have appealed but did not because the motion was granted pursuant to a charge thought to be so minor as not to justify the cost of an appeal? What if the state does not want to put in "new evidence to rebut X's claims," but only desires reconsideration of the legal significance of the facts earlier established? What if physical evidence suppressed in the trial of X is offered in the later trial of Y, and Y, with standing to object, claims the earlier ruling is controlling? See LaFave, § 11.2(g).

BROWN v. OHIO

432 U.S. 161, 97 S.Ct. 2221, 53 L.Ed.2d 187 (1977).

MR. JUSTICE POWELL delivered the opinion of the Court. * * *

On November 29, 1973, the petitioner, Nathaniel Brown, stole a 1965 Chevrolet from a parking lot in East Cleveland, Ohio. Nine days later, on December 8, 1973, Brown was caught driving the car in Wickliffe, Ohio. The Wickliffe police charged him with "joyriding" * * *. The complaint charged that "on or about December 8, 1973, * * * Nathaniel H. Brown did unlawfully and purposely take, drive or operate a certain motor vehicle to wit; a 1965 Chevrolet * * * without the consent of the owner one Gloria Ingram * * *." Brown pled guilty to this charge and was sentenced to 30 days in jail and a $100 fine.

Upon his release from jail on January 8, 1974, Brown was returned to East Cleveland to face further charges, and on February 5 he was indicted by the Cuyahoga County grand jury. The indictment was in two counts, the first charging the theft of the car "on or about the 29th day of November 1973," * * * and the second charging joyriding on the same date * * *. A bill of particulars filed by the prosecuting attorney specified that

> "on or about the 29th day of November, 1973, * * * Nathaniel Brown unlawfully did steal a Chevrolet motor vehicle, and take, drive or operate such vehicle without the consent of the owner, Gloria Ingram * * *."

Brown objected to both counts of the indictment on the basis of former jeopardy.

On March 18, 1974, at a pretrial hearing in the Cuyahoga County Court of Common Pleas, Brown pled guilty to the auto theft charge on the understanding that the court would consider his claim of former jeopardy on a motion to withdraw the plea. Upon submission of the motion, the court overruled Brown's double jeopardy objections. The court sentenced Brown to six months in jail but suspended the sentence and placed Brown on probation for one year.

The Ohio Court of Appeals affirmed. * * *

The Double Jeopardy Clause of the Fifth Amendment, applicable to the States through the Fourteenth, provides that no person shall "be subject for the same offence to be twice put in jeopardy of life or limb." It has long been understood that separate statutory crimes need not be identical—either in constituent elements or in actual proof—in order to be the same within the meaning of the constitutional prohibition. The principal question in this case is whether auto theft and joyriding, a greater and lesser included offense under Ohio law, constitute the "same offense" under the Double Jeopardy Clause. * * *

The established test for determining whether two offenses are sufficiently distinguishable to permit the imposition of cumulative punishment was stated in *Blockburger v. United States,* 284 U.S. 299, 304, 52 S.Ct. 180, 182, 76 L.Ed. 306 (1932):

> "The applicable rule is that where the same act or transaction constitutes a violation of two distinct statutory provisions, the test to be applied to determine whether there are two offenses or only one, is whether each provision requires proof of an additional fact which the other does not. * * *"
>
> * * *

If two offenses are the same under this test for purposes of barring consecutive sentences at a single trial, they necessarily will be the same for purposes of barring successive prosecutions. Where the judge is forbidden to impose cumulative punishment for two crimes at the end of a single proceeding, the prosecutor is forbidden to strive for the same result in successive proceedings.

* * * Here the Ohio Court of Appeals has authoritatively defined the elements of the two Ohio crimes: joyriding consists of taking or operating a vehicle without the owner's consent, and auto theft consists of joyriding with the intent permanently to deprive the owner of possession. Joyriding is the lesser included offense. The prosecutor who has established joyriding need only prove the requisite intent in order to establish auto theft; the prosecutor who has established auto theft necessarily has established joyriding as well.

Applying the *Blockburger* test, we agree with the Ohio Court of Appeals that joyriding and auto theft, as defined by the court, constitute "the same statutory offense" within the meaning of the Double Jeopardy Clause. * * *

This conclusion merely restates what has been this Court's understanding of the Double Jeopardy Clause at least since * * * 1889 [, when] the Court endorsed the rule that

> "where * * * a person has been tried and convicted for a crime which has various incidents included in it, he cannot be a second time tried for one of

those incidents without being twice put in jeopardy for the same offense."

Although in this formulation the conviction of the greater precedes the conviction of the lesser, the opinion makes it clear that the sequence is immaterial. * * * Whatever the sequence may be, the Fifth Amendment forbids successive prosecution and cumulative punishment for a greater and lesser included offense.[7]

After correctly holding that joyriding and auto theft are the same offense under the Double Jeopardy Clause, the Ohio Court of Appeals nevertheless concluded that Nathaniel Brown could be convicted of both crimes because the charges against him focused on different parts of his 9-day joyride.[a] We hold a different view. The Double Jeopardy Clause is not such a fragile guarantee that prosecutors can avoid its limitations by the simple expedient of dividing a single crime into a series of temporal or spatial units. The applicable Ohio statutes, as written and as construed in this case, make the theft and operation of a single car a single offense. Although the Wickliffe and East Cleveland authorities may have had different perspectives on Brown's offense, it was still only one offense under Ohio law.[8] Accordingly, the specification of different dates in the two charges on which Brown was convicted cannot alter the fact that he was placed twice in jeopardy for the same offense in violation of the Fifth and Fourteenth Amendments.

Reversed.

MR. JUSTICE BRENNAN, with whom MR. JUSTICE MARSHALL joins, concurring.

I join the Court's opinion, but in any event would reverse on the ground, not addressed by the Court, that the State did not prosecute petitioner in a single proceeding. I adhere to the view that the Double Jeopardy Clause of the Fifth Amendment, applied to the States through the Fourteenth Amendment, requires the prosecution in one proceeding, except in extremely limited circumstances not present here, of "all the charges against a defendant that grow out of single criminal act, occurrence, episode, or transaction." In my view the Court's suggestion that the Ohio Legislature might be free to make joyriding a separate and distinct offense for each day a motor vehicle is operated without the owner's consent would not affect the applicability of the single transaction test. Though under some circumstances a legislature may divide a continuing course of conduct into discrete offenses, I would nevertheless hold that all charges growing out of conduct constituting a "single criminal act, occurrence, episode, or transaction" must be tried in a single proceeding.

MR. JUSTICE BLACKMUN, with whom THE CHIEF JUSTICE and MR. JUSTICE REHNQUIST join, dissenting. * * *

Nine days elapsed between the two incidents that are the basis of petitioner's convictions. During that time the automobile moved from East Cleveland to Wickliffe. It strains credulity to believe that petitioner was operating the vehicle every minute of those nine days. A time must have come when he stopped driving the car. When he operated it again nine days later

7. An exception may exist where the State is unable to proceed on the more serious charge at the outset because the additional facts necessary to sustain that charge have not occurred or have not been discovered despite the exercise of due diligence.

a. The Ohio court stated: "The two prosecutions are based on two separate acts of the appellant, one which occurred on November 29th and one which occurred on December 8th. Since appellant has not shown that both prosecutions are based on the same act or transaction, the second prosecution is not barred by the double jeopardy clause."

8. We would have a different case if the Ohio Legislature had provided that joyriding is a separate offense for each day in which a motor vehicle is operated without the owner's consent. We also would have a different case if in sustaining Brown's second conviction the Ohio courts had construed the joyriding statute to have that effect. We then would have to decide whether the state courts' construction, applied retroactively in this case, was such "an unforeseeable judicial enlargement of a criminal statute" as to violate due process. See *Bouie v. City of Columbia*, 378 U.S. 347, 353, 84 S.Ct. 1697, 1702, 12 L.Ed.2d 894 (1964).

in a different community, the Ohio courts could properly find, consistently with the Double Jeopardy Clause, that the acts were sufficiently distinct to justify a second prosecution. Only if the Clause requires the Ohio courts to hold that the allowable unit of prosecution is the course of conduct would the Court's result here be correct. On the facts of this case, no such requirement should be inferred, and the state courts should be free to construe Ohio's statute as they did.

This Court, I fear, gives undeserved emphasis to the Ohio Court of Appeals' passing observation that the Ohio misdemeanor of joyriding is an element of the Ohio felony of auto theft. That observation was merely a preliminary statement, indicating that the theft and any simultaneous unlawful operation were one and the same. But the Ohio Court of Appeals then went on flatly to hold that such simultaneity was not present here. Thus, it seems to me, the Ohio courts did precisely what this Court, in its n. 8, professes to say they did not do. * * *

Notes and Questions

1. Contrary to what is intimated in *Brown,* the Court later held with respect to cumulative *sentencing* that the *Blockburger* rule is not a constitutional limitation but merely a device for determining an otherwise uncertain legislative intent. In *Missouri v. Hunter,* 459 U.S. 359, 103 S.Ct. 673, 74 L.Ed.2d 535 (1983), upholding defendant's conviction and sentencing in a single trial for both armed criminal action and the lesser included offense of first degree robbery, the Court stated: "Where, as here, a legislature specifically authorizes cumulative punishment under two statutes, regardless of whether those two statutes proscribe the 'same' conduct under *Blockburger,* a court's task of statutory construction is at an end and the prosecutor may seek and the trial court or jury may impose cumulative punishment under such statutes in a single trial." Can *Brown* and *Hunter* be reconciled, or are Marshall and Stevens, JJ., dissenting, correct in saying that the phrase "the same offence" should not be interpreted "to mean one thing for purposes of the prohibition against multiple prosecutions and something else for purposes of the prohibition against multiple punishments"?

2. In ILLINOIS v. VITALE, 447 U.S. 410, 100 S.Ct. 2260, 65 L.Ed.2d 222 (1980), an auto driven by Vitale, a juvenile, struck two small children, causing their death. A month later, he was convicted of failing to reduce speed to avoid an accident and was fined $15. The next day, a petition for adjudication of wardship was filed in juvenile court charging Vitale with two counts of involuntary manslaughter. The appellate court held that the manslaughter prosecution was barred by the state compulsory joinder statute, but the state supreme court affirmed for the "more compelling reason" that such prosecution was barred by the double jeopardy clause. The Supreme Court, per WHITE, J., concluded:

"If, as a matter of Illinois law, a careless failure to slow is always a necessary element of manslaughter by automobile, then the two offenses are the 'same' under *Blockburger* and Vitale's trial on the latter charge would constitute double jeopardy under *Brown v. Ohio.* In any event, it may be that to sustain its manslaughter case the State may find it necessary to prove a failure to slow or to rely on conduct necessarily involving such failure; it may concede as much prior to trial. In that case, because Vitale has already been convicted for conduct that is a necessary element of the more serious crime for which he has been charged, his claim of double jeopardy would be substantial under *Brown* and our later decision in *Harris v. Oklahoma.*[b]

b. 433 U.S. 682, 97 S.Ct. 2912, 53 L.Ed.2d 1054 (1977), where petitioner was convicted of felony murder on proof that his companion shot and killed a clerk during a robbery of a store by the two men. Though proof of the underlying felony of robbery with firearms was necessary for the felony murder conviction, petitioner was thereafter tried and convicted on a charge of that felony.

"Because of our doubts about the relationship under Illinois law between the crimes of manslaughter and a careless failure to reduce speed to avoid an accident, and because the reckless act or acts the State will rely on to prove manslaughter are still unknown, we vacate the judgment of the Illinois Supreme Court and remand the case to that court for further proceedings not inconsistent with this opinion."

STEVENS, J., joined by Brennan, Stewart and Marshall, JJ., dissenting, asserted there were "two separate reasons, each of which is sufficient in itself, for affirming the judgment of the Illinois Supreme Court. First, after applying the test set forth in *Brown v. Ohio,* the Illinois Supreme Court made a finding that failing to reduce speed to avoid a collision is a lesser included offense of reckless homicide as a matter of state law. This Court clearly has a duty to respect that finding. Second, even if the dissenting members of the Illinois Supreme Court were correct in their view that, as a matter of state law, the traffic offense is not necessarily a lesser included offense in every reckless homicide prosecution, the Double Jeopardy Clause bars the homicide prosecution under the particular facts of this case. For, even if the State intended to rely on evidence other than respondent's failure to reduce speed to establish the element of reckless driving necessary for a homicide conviction, the prosecutor's failure to apprise the respondent and the court of such a theory at some point in the lengthy proceedings on the double jeopardy issue should bar the second trial in this case."

3. GARRETT v. UNITED STATES, ___ U.S. ___, 105 S.Ct. 2407, 85 L.Ed.2d 764 (1985), involved these facts: Two months after pleading guilty to a federal charge of importing marijuana off the coast of Washington, defendant was indicted in a Florida federal court for several offenses, including that of engaging in a continuing criminal enterprise. That crime requires proof of three or more successive violations of a specified type within a specified period of time, and at trial the government's proof in that respect included the importation offense to which defendant had earlier pleaded guilty. Defendant claimed that his conviction of engaging in a continuing criminal enterprise violated *Brown,* in that the importation charge was a "lesser included offense" of the continuing criminal enterprise offense. REHNQUIST, J., for the plurality, assuming but not deciding that this latter characterization was correct, concluded that the case nonetheless fell outside *Brown* because "the continuing criminal enterprise charged against Garrett in Florida had not been completed at the time that he was indicted in Washington":

"Were we to sustain Garrett's claim, the Government would have been able to proceed against him in either one of only two ways. It would have to have withheld the Washington charges, alleging crimes committed in October 1979 and August 1980, from the grand jury which indicted Garrett in March 1981, until it was prepared to present to a grand jury the continuing criminal enterprise charges which were alleged to have been, and found by a jury to be, continuing on each of those dates; or it would have to have submitted the continuing criminal enterprise charge to the Washington grand jury in March 1981, even though the indictment ultimately returned against Garrett on that charge alleged that the enterprise had continued until July 1981. We do not think that the Double Jeopardy Clause may be employed to force the Government's hand in this manner, however we were to resolve Garrett's lesser-included-offense argument. One who insists that the music stop and the piper be paid at a particular point must at least have stopped dancing himself before he may seek such an accounting."

The Supreme Court, per curiam, reversed. "When, as here, conviction for a greater crime, murder, cannot be had without conviction for the lesser crime, robbery with firearms, the Double Jeopardy Clause bars prosecution for the lesser crime after conviction for the greater one."

The plurality deemed it irrelevant "whether the Government could in March 1981 have successfully indicted and prosecuted Garrett for a different continuing criminal enterprise—one ending in March 1981," explaining that a determination of that question is not "required at the behest of one who at the time the first indictment is returned is continuing to engage in other conduct found criminal by the jury which tried the second indictment." STEVENS, J., joined by Brennan and Marshall, JJ., dissenting, objected that the instant case did not come within the fn. 7 exception in *Brown* because, while the government alleged that the enterprise continued to the date of the Florida indictment, all the facts necessary to prove a continuing criminal enterprise charge had occurred before the Washington indictment was returned. The other participating member of the Court,[c] O'CONNOR, J., concurring, found "merit to this position" of the dissenters, but reached "a different conclusion upon balancing the interests protected by the Double Jeopardy Clause," including the desirability of allowing the government to decide prosecution is warranted whenever "the defendant continues unlawful conduct after the time the Government prosecutes him for a predicate offense."

4. In JEFFERS v. UNITED STATES, 432 U.S. 137, 97 S.Ct. 2207, 53 L.Ed.2d 168 (1977), two indictments were returned against petitioner: the first charged him and nine others under 21 U.S.C. § 846 with conspiracy to distribute drugs; the second charged him with violation of 21 U.S.C. § 848, which prohibits conducting a continuing criminal enterprise to violate the drug laws. The government filed a motion to join the charges for trial, but petitioner objected, pointing out that "much of the evidence in the conspiracy trial would not inculpate petitioner and would therefore be inadmissible against him in the continuing criminal enterprise trial." The court denied the government's motion, and trial on the § 846 charge commenced. Petitioner later moved to dismiss the § 848 charge on double jeopardy grounds, but that motion was denied, and petitioner was separately convicted of both offenses.

BLACKMUN, J., announced the judgment of the Court in an opinion in which the Chief Justice and Powell and Rehnquist, JJ., joined.[d] He first assumed, "*arguendo,* that * * * § 846 is a lesser included offense of § 848," and then continued:

"If the defendant expressly asks for separate trials on the greater and the lesser offenses, or, in connection with his opposition to trial together, fails to raise the issue that one offense might be a lesser included offense of the other, [an] exception to the *Brown* rule emerges. * * * [A]lthough a defendant is normally entitled to have charges on a greater and a lesser offense resolved in one proceeding, there is no violation of the Double Jeopardy Clause when he elects to have the two offenses tried separately and persuades the trial court to honor his election.[20]

c. Powell, J., took no part in the decision.

d. White, J., concurred as to the issue here considered.

20. The considerations relating to the propriety of a second trial obviously would be much different if any action by the Government contributed to the separate prosecutions on the lesser and greater charges. No hint of that is present in the case before us, since the Government affirmatively sought trial on the two indictments together.

Unlike the dissenters, we are unwilling to attach any significance to the fact that the grand jury elected to return two indictments against petitioner for the two statutory offenses. As the Court of Appeals' opinion made clear, before this case it was by no means settled law that § 846 was a lesser included offense of § 848. Even now, it has not been necessary to settle that issue definitively. If the position reasonably could have been taken that the two statutes described different offenses, it is difficult to ascribe any improper motive to the act of requesting two separate indictments. Furthermore, as noted supra, it was the Government itself that requested a joint trial on the two indictments, which also indicates that no sinister purpose was behind the formal method of proceeding.

"In this case, trial together of the conspiracy and continuing criminal enterprise charges could have taken place without undue prejudice to petitioner's Sixth Amendment right to a fair trial.[21] If the two charges had been tried in one proceeding, it appears that petitioner would have been entitled to a lesser included offense instruction. If such an instruction had been denied on the ground that § 846 was not a lesser included offense of § 848, petitioner could have preserved his point by proper objection. Nevertheless, petitioner did not adopt that course. Instead, he was solely responsible for the successive prosecutions for the conspiracy offense and the continuing criminal enterprise offense. Under the circumstances, we hold that his action deprived him of any right that he might have had against consecutive trials."

STEVENS, J., joined by Brennan, Stewart, and Marshall, JJ., dissented: "The defendant surely cannot be held responsible for the fact that two separate indictments were returned,[2] or for the fact that other defendants were named in the earlier indictment, or for the fact that the Government elected to proceed to trial first on the lesser charge.[3] The other defendants had valid objections to the Government's motion to consolidate the two cases for trial.[4] Most trial lawyers will be startled to learn that a rather routine joint opposition to that motion to consolidate has resulted in the loss of what this Court used to regard as 'a vital safeguard in our society, one that was clearly won and one that should continue to be highly valued.' "

5. In *Ciucci v. Illinois,* 356 U.S. 571, 78 S.Ct. 839, 2 L.Ed.2d 983 (1958), petitioner was charged in four separate indictments with murdering by separate gunshots his wife and three children on the same occasion. In two successive trials, petitioner was convicted of murdering his wife and one child, but the jury fixed the penalty at 20 years and 45 years imprisonment, respectively. Newspaper reports which were not a part of the record indicated that the prosecutor was determined to prosecute petitioner until a death sentence was obtained. The third trial resulted in a death sentence. In a per curiam opinion, five members of the Court affirmed "upon the record as it stands," although two of them indicated that "the matters set forth in the aforementioned newspaper articles might, if established, require a ruling that fundamental unfairness existed here." Three dissenters concluded that petitioner had been denied

21. Petitioner argues that a finding of waiver is inconsistent with the decision in *Simmons v. United States* [p. 781 supra], where the Court held that a defendant could not be required to surrender his Fifth Amendment privilege against compulsory self-incrimination in order to assert an arguably valid Fourth Amendment claim. In petitioner's case, however, the alleged Hobson's choice between asserting the Sixth Amendment fair trial right and asserting the Fifth Amendment double jeopardy claim is illusory. Had petitioner asked for a Rule 14 severance from the other defendants, the case might be different. In that event, he would have given the court an opportunity to ensure that prejudicial evidence relating only to other defendants would not have been introduced in his trial. Assuming that a valid Fifth Amendment point was in the background, due to the relationship between §§ 846 and 848, petitioner could have had no complaint about a trial of the two charges together. No such motion, however, was made. Under the circumstances of this case, therefore, no dilemma akin to that in *Simmons* arose.

2. The plurality implies that the result in this case would be different "if any action by the Government contributed to the separate prosecutions on the lesser and greater charges." I wonder how the grand jury happened to return two separate indictments.

3. The Government retained the alternative of trying petitioner on both charges at once, while trying the other defendants separately for conspiracy. The prosecutor never attempted this course, and defense counsel—not having had an opportunity to read today's plurality opinion—had no reason to believe he had a duty to suggest it. Until today it has never been the function of the defense to give legal advice to the prosecutor.

4. When the Government attempted to obtain a joint trial on all the charges against all the defendants, the attorney representing all the defendants resisted the Government motion. He did so largely because of the possible prejudice to petitioner's codefendants, and gave relatively little emphasis to arguments relating to petitioner alone.

due process because each of the first two trials had "in effect" been trials "for the murder of all four victims for the gruesome details of each of the four deaths were introduced into evidence," while Justice Black dissented on the ground that the Fourteenth Amendment bars a state from placing a defendant twice in jeopardy for the same offense. Which conduct is more offensive, the successive trials in *Ashe* and *Brown* or those in *Ciucci?* Should it make any difference what the prosecutor's purpose was?

6. Several state courts have adopted the same transaction standard advanced by Justice Brennan. Is this position sound? Consider *State v. Conrad,* 243 So.2d 174 (Fla.App.1971): "The absurdity of the 'same transaction' standard can be easily illustrated. Assume that one breaks and enters a building to commit larceny of an automobile, does thereafter in fact steal the automobile and drive away, killing the night watchman in the process, and two blocks away runs a red light which brings about his arrest by the municipal police. Could it be said with any logic that a plea of guilty to breaking and entering would bar a subsequent prosecution for murder? If so, presumably a plea of guilty to the traffic offense would likewise, since all arise out of the 'same transaction.' "

Does this mean that some intermediate position is desirable? What of Ill.Rev. Stat. ch. 38, § 3–3(b), mandating joinder only if the offenses "are based on the same act"? Or N.Y.Crim.P.Law § 40.20(2)(b), which permits successive prosecutions where "the offenses * * * [contain] an element which is not an element of the other, and the statutory provisions defining such offenses are designed to prevent very different kinds of harm or evil"?

Are there, in any event, other limits which are necessary to meet the concerns of the court in *Conrad?* What, for example, of the additional requirement in the above Illinois statute that "the several offenses are known to the proper prosecuting officer at the time of commencing the prosecution and are within the jurisdiction of a single court"?

SECTION 3. JOINDER AND SEVERANCE OF DEFENDANTS

Fed.R.Crim.P. 8(b) provides that "two or more defendants may be charged in the same indictment or information if they are alleged to have participated in the same act or transaction or in the same series of acts or transactions constituting an offense or offenses." Some states have identical provisions, while others utilize similar language. These rules and statutes are intended to promote economy and efficiency and to avoid a multiplicity of trials.[a]

One common joinder situation is that in which the several defendants are connected by virtue of a charged conspiracy relationship, as where the joined defendants are all charged in a conspiracy count and some or all are also charged with substantive offenses alleged to have been committed in furtherance of the conspiracy. Joinder of multiple conspiracies is permissible if they are sufficiently related, which is not shown merely by a slight membership overlap. Even absent a conspiracy count, defendants may be joined when their acts were part of a common plan (e.g., individual acts of income tax evasion related to joint gambling activities) or were so closely connected in respect to time, place and occasion that it would be difficult to separate the proof of one charge from proof of the other (e.g., negligent homicide charges against several drivers involved in same accident).

Although a few states still grant defendants an absolute right to separate trials,[b]

a. Whether joint trials actually have these benefits has been seriously questioned. See Dawson, *Joint Trials of Defendants in Criminal Cases: An Analysis of Efficiencies and Prejudices,* 77 Mich.L.Rev. 1379, 1381–97 (1979).

b. One of these states is Vermont. There it has been found that granting defendants an absolute right of severance does not mean many more trials. "In a vast majority of the cases, an initial conviction has induced the awaiting codefendants in most jurisdictions joined defendants may obtain a severance only by a showing of prejudice flowing from the joinder.

SCHAFFER v. UNITED STATES

362 U.S. 511, 80 S.Ct. 945, 4 L.Ed.2d 921 (1960).

MR. JUSTICE CLARK delivered the opinion of the Court. * * *

The indictment charged transportation in interstate commerce of goods known to have been stolen and having a value in excess of $5,000. It contained three substantive counts. Count 1 charged the two Schaffers (petitioners in No. 111) and the three Stracuzzas (defendants below, who either pleaded guilty or had the charges against them *nolle prossed* at trial) with transporting stolen ladies' and children's wearing apparel from New York to Pennsylvania. Count 2 charged petitioner Marco and the Stracuzzas with a similar movement of stolen goods from New York to West Virginia. Count 3 charged petitioner Karp and the Stracuzzas with like shipments from New York to Massachusetts. The fourth and final count of the indictment charged all of these parties with a conspiracy to commit the substantive offenses charged in the first three counts. The petitioners here were tried on the indictment simultaneously in a single trial. On motion of petitioners for acquittal at the close of the Government's case, the court dismissed the conspiracy count for failure of proof. This motion was denied, however, as to the substantive counts, the court finding that no prejudice would result from the joint trial. Upon submission of the substantive counts to the jury on a detailed charge, each petitioner was found guilty and thereafter fined and sentenced to prison. * * *

It is admitted that the three Stracuzzas were the common center of the scheme to transport the stolen goods. The four petitioners here participated in some steps of the transactions in the stolen goods, although each was involved with separate interstate shipments. The separate substantive charges of the indictment employed almost identical language and alleged violations of the same criminal statute during the same period and in the same manner. This made proof of the over-all operation of the scheme competent as to all counts. The variations in the proof related to the specific shipments proven against each petitioner. This proof was related to each petitioner separately and proven as to each by different witnesses. It included entirely separate invoices and other exhibits, all of which were first clearly identified as applying only to a specific petitioner and were so received and shown to the jury under painstaking instructions to that effect. In short, the proof was carefully compartmentalized as to each petitioner. The propriety of the joinder prior to the failure of proof of conspiracy was not assailed. When the Government rested, however, the petitioners filed their motion for dismissal and it was sustained as to the conspiracy count. The petitioners then pressed for acquittal on the remaining counts, and the court decided that the evidence was sufficient on the substantive counts. The case was submitted to the jury on each of these counts, and under a charge which was characterized by petitioners' counsel as being "extremely fair." This charge meticulously set out separately the evidence as to each of the petitioners and admonished the jury that they were "not to take into consideration any proof against one defendant and apply it by inference or otherwise to any other defendant."

Petitioners contend that prejudice would nevertheless be implicit in a continuation of the joint trial after dismissal of the conspiracy count. They say that the result-

to negotiate a plea." Langrock, *Joint Trials: A Short Lesson from Little Vermont,* 9 Crim.L.Bull. 612 (1973). An intermediate position is that in Minn.R.Crim.P. 17.03, which reverses the usual presumption that jointly charged defendants should be jointly tried by placing the burden of justifying a joint trial upon the party wishing it, usually the prosecutor.

ing prejudice could not be cured by any cautionary instructions, and that therefore the trial judge was left with no discretion. Petitioners overlook, however, that the joinder was authorized under Rule 8(b) [c] and that subsequent severance was controlled by Rule 14, which provides for separate trials where "it appears that a defendant * * * is prejudiced * * * by such joinder for trial * * *." It appears that not only was no prejudice shown, but both the trial court and the Court of Appeals affirmatively found that none was present. We cannot say to the contrary on this record. Nor can we fashion a hard-and-fast formula that, when a conspiracy count fails, joinder is error as a matter of law. We do emphasize, however, that, in such a situation, the trial judge has a continuing duty at all stages of the trial to grant a severance if prejudice does appear. And where, as here, the charge which originally justified joinder turns out to lack the support of sufficient evidence, a trial judge should be particularly sensitive to the possibility of such prejudice. However, the petitioners here not only failed to show any prejudice that would call Rule 14 into operation but even failed to request a new trial. Instead they relied entirely on their motions for acquittal. Moreover, the judge was acutely aware of the possibility of prejudice and was strict in his charge—not only as to the testimony the jury was not to consider, but also as to that evidence which was available in the consideration of the guilt of each petitioner separately under the respective substantive counts. The terms of Rule 8(b) having been met and no prejudice under Rule 14 having been shown, there was no misjoinder. * * *

MR. JUSTICE DOUGLAS, with whom THE CHIEF JUSTICE, MR. JUSTICE BLACK, and MR. JUSTICE BRENNAN concur, dissenting. * * *

[O]nce it becomes apparent during the trial that the defendants have not participated "in the same series" of transactions, it would make a mockery of Rule 8(b) to hold that the allegation alone, now known to be false, is enough to continue the joint trial.

The Court in *Kotteakos v. United States,* 328 U.S. 750, 66 S.Ct. 1239, 90 L.Ed. 1557 (1946), disapproved the joinder for trial of eight or more conspiracies related in kind "when the only nexus among them lies in the fact that one man participated in all." Guilt with us remains personal. "The dangers of transference of guilt from one to another across the line separating conspiracies, subconsciously or otherwise, are so great," said the Court in the *Kotteakos* case, "that no one really can say prejudice to substantial right has not taken place." A like danger of such transference existed in the present case. It is not enough to say that evidence of the guilt of each of the present petitioners may have been clear. Reasons for severance are founded on the principle that evidence against one person may not be used against a codefendant whose crime is unrelated to the others. Instructions can be given the jury and admonitions can be made explicit that the line between the various defendants must be kept separate. The district judge conscientiously made that effort here. But where, as here, there is no nexus between the several crimes, the mounting proof of the guilt of one is likely to affect another. There is no sure way to protect against it except by separate trials, especially where, as here, the several defendants, though unconnected, commit the crimes charged by dealing with one person, one house, one establishment. By

c. Compare *United States v. Lane,* 735 F.2d 799 (5th Cir.1984), cert. granted, ___ U.S. ___, 105 S.Ct. 1167, 84 L.Ed.2d 318 (1985), involving *mis*joinder in violation of Rule 8(b) in that the indictment did not even allege an overarching conspiracy or a single scheme involving the several defendants. The court concluded such joinder "is inherently prejudicial," so that the granting of a severance motion "is mandatory and not discretionary with the district court." But *United States v. Hatcher,* 680 F.2d 438 (6th Cir.1982), in contrast to *Lane,* held that on appeal the harmless error rule could be applied (albeit "with great caution") to misjoinder of defendants.

a joint trial of such separate offenses, a subtle bond is likely to be created between the several defendants though they have never met nor acted in unison; prejudice within the meaning of Rule 14 is implicit.

This is unlike the case where the conspiracy count and the substantive counts are submitted to the jury, the verdict being not guilty of conspiracy but guilty on the other counts. There is then no escape from the quandary in which defendants find themselves. Once the conspiracy is supported by evidence, it presents issues for the jury to decide. What may motivate a particular jury in returning a verdict of not guilty on the conspiracy count may never be known. * * *

Notes and Questions

1. Is the *Schaffer* rule unsound because it "may have the effect of encouraging an unscrupulous prosecutor to frame a baseless conspiracy count in order that several defendants, accused of similar but unrelated offenses, may be tried together"? Note, 42 N.Y.U.L.Rev. 513, 518 (1967). Or, is the dissent's position unsound because it "could militate against the very result that the argument seeks to achieve," in "that a trial judge, faced with a rigid rule requiring severance as a matter of law and consequent time consuming multiple trials, might be extremely reluctant to dismiss the charge upon which joinder is founded." Note, 45 Minn.L.Rev. 1066, 1073 (1961).

2. Does the question presented in *Schaffer* call for a different conclusion in light of the *Bruton* decision, following?

BRUTON v. UNITED STATES

391 U.S. 123, 88 S.Ct. 1620, 20 L.Ed.2d 476 (1968).

MR. JUSTICE BRENNAN delivered the opinion of the Court.

This case presents the question, last considered in *Delli Paoli v. United States,* 352 U.S. 232, 77 S.Ct. 294, 1 L.Ed.2d 278 (1957), whether the conviction of a defendant at a joint trial should be set aside although the jury was instructed that a codefendant's confession inculpating the defendant had to be disregarded in determining his guilt or innocence. * * *

The basic premise of *Delli Paoli* was that it is "reasonably possible for the jury to follow" sufficiently clear instructions to disregard the confessor's extrajudicial statement that his codefendant participated with him in committing the crime. If it were true that the jury disregarded the reference to the codefendant, no question would arise under the Confrontation Clause, because by hypothesis the case is treated as if the confessor made no statement inculpating the nonconfessor. But since *Delli Paoli* was decided this Court has effectively repudiated its basic premise. Before discussing this, we pause to observe that in *Pointer v. Texas,* 380 U.S. 400, 85 S.Ct. 1065, 13 L.Ed.2d 923 (1965), we confirmed "that the right of cross-examination is included in the right of an accused in a criminal case to confront the witnesses against him" secured by the Sixth Amendment * * *.

Delli Paoli assumed that this encroachment on the right to confrontation could be avoided by the instruction to the jury to disregard the inadmissible hearsay evidence. But, as we have said, that assumption has since been effectively repudiated. True, the repudiation was not in the context of the admission of a confession inculpating a codefendant but in the context of a New York rule which submitted to the jury the question of the voluntariness of the confession itself. *Jackson v. Denno* [see p. 842 supra]. Nonetheless the message of *Jackson* for *Delli Paoli* was clear. We there held that a defendant is constitutionally entitled to have at least the trial judge first determine whether a confession was made voluntarily before submitting it to the jury for an assessment of its credibility. More specifically, we expressly rejected the proposition that a jury, when determining the confessor's guilt, could be relied on to ignore his confession of guilt should they find the confession involuntary. * * *

The significance of *Jackson* for *Delli Paoli* was suggested by Chief Justice Traynor in *People v. Aranda,* 63 Cal.2d 518, 407 P.2d 265 (1965):

"Although *Jackson* was directly concerned with obviating any risk that a jury might rely on an unconstitutionally obtained confession in determining the defendant's guilt, its logic extends to obviating the risks that the jury may rely on any inadmissible statements. If it is a denial of due process to rely on a jury's presumed ability to disregard an involuntary confession, it may also be a denial of due process to rely on a jury's presumed ability to disregard a codefendant's confession implicating another defendant when it is determining that defendant's guilt or innocence.

"Indeed, the latter task may be an even more difficult one for the jury to perform than the former. Under the New York procedure, which *Jackson* held violated due process, the jury was only required to disregard a confession it found to be involuntary. If it made such a finding, then the confession was presumably out of the case. In joint trials, however, when the admissible confession of one defendant inculpates another defendant, the confession is never deleted from the case and the jury is expected to perform the overwhelming task of considering it in determining the guilt or innocence of the declarant and then of ignoring it in determining the guilt or innocence of any codefendants of the declarant. A jury cannot 'segregate evidence into separate intellectual boxes.' * * * It cannot determine that a confession is true insofar as it admits that A has committed criminal acts with B and at the same time effectively ignore the inevitable conclusion that B has committed those same criminal acts with A." * * *

Finally, the reason advanced by the majority in *Delli Paoli* was to tie the result to maintenance of the jury system. "Unless we proceed on the basis that the jury will follow the court's instructions where those instructions are clear and the circumstances are such that the jury can reasonably be expected to follow them, the jury system makes little sense." * * * We agree that there are many circumstances in which this reliance is justified. Not every admission of inadmissible hearsay or other evidence can be considered to be reversible error unavoidable through limiting instructions; instances occur in almost every trial where inadmissible evidence creeps in, usually inadvertently. * * * It is not unreasonable to conclude that in many such cases the jury can and will follow the trial judge's instructions to disregard such information. Nevertheless, as was recognized in *Jackson v. Denno,* supra, there are some contexts in which the risk that the jury will not, or cannot, follow instructions is so great and the consequences of failure so vital to the defendant, that the practical and human limitations of the jury system cannot be ignored. * * * Such a context is presented here, where the powerfully incriminating extrajudicial statements of a codefendant, who stands accused side-by-side with the defendant, are deliberately spread before the jury in a joint trial. Not only are the incriminations devastating to the defendant but their credibility is inevitably suspect, a fact recognized when accomplices do take the stand and the jury is instructed to weigh their testimony carefully given the recognized motivation to shift blame onto others. The unreliability of such evidence is intolerably compounded when the alleged accomplice, as here, does not testify and cannot be tested by cross-examination. It was against such threats to a fair trial that the Confrontation Clause was directed. * * *

MR. JUSTICE WHITE, dissenting. * * *

The situation in this case is very different. Here we deal with a codefendant's confession which is admitted only against the codefendant and with a firm instruction to the jury to disregard it in determining the defendant's guilt or innocence.

That confession cannot compare with the defendant's own confession in evidentiary value. * * * Whereas the defendant's own confession possesses greater reliability and evidentiary value than ordinary hearsay, the codefendant's confession implicating the defendant is intrinsically much less reliable.

The defendant's own confession may not be used against him if coerced, not because it is untrue but to protect other constitutional values. The jury may have great difficulty understanding such a rule and following an instruction to disregard the confession. In contrast, the codefendant's admissions cannot enter into the determination of the defendant's guilt or innocence because they are unreliable. This the jury can be told and can understand. * * *

The rule which the Court announces today will severely limit the circumstances in which defendants may be tried together for a crime which they are both charged with committing. Unquestionably, joint trials are more economical and minimize the burden on witnesses, prosecutors and courts. They also avoid delays in bringing those accused of crime to trial. This much the Court concedes. It is also worth saying that separate trials are apt to have varying consequences for legally indistinguishable defendants. The unfairness of this is confirmed by the common prosecutorial experience of seeing codefendants who are tried separately strenuously jockeying for position with regard to who should be the first to be tried. * * *

Notes and Questions

1. In NELSON v. O'NEIL, 402 U.S. 622, 91 S.Ct. 1723, 29 L.Ed.2d 222 (1971), O'Neil and Runnels were charged with kidnapping, robbery and vehicle theft, and at their joint trial defended by offering mutually dependent alibis. A police officer testified that Runnels had confessed to the crimes, implicating O'Neil as his confederate, and this testimony was admitted on instructions that the jury should consider it only against Runnels. Runnels took the stand, denied making the confession, and asserted that the substance of the purported confession was false. Both defendants were convicted, but O'Neil, relying upon *Bruton,* successfully sought relief by federal habeas corpus. The Court of Appeals affirmed, relying upon a quotation in *Bruton* that "effective confrontation * * * was possible only if [the witness] affirmed the statement as his." The Supreme Court, per STEWART, J., reversed:

"Had Runnels in this case 'affirmed the statement as his,' the respondent would certainly have been in far worse straits than those in which he found himself when Runnels testified as he did. For then counsel for the respondent could only have attempted to show through cross-examination that Runnels had confessed to a crime he had not committed, or, slightly more plausibly, that those parts of the confession implicating the respondent were fabricated. This would, moreover, have required an abandonment of the joint alibi defense, and the production of a new explanation for the respondent's presence with Runnels in the white Cadillac at the time of their arrest. To be sure, Runnels might have 'affirmed the statement' but denied its truthfulness, claiming, for example, that it had been coerced, or made as part of a plea bargain. But cross-examination by the respondent's counsel would have been futile in that event as well. For once Runnels had testified that the statement was false, it could hardly have profited the respondent for his counsel through cross-examination to try to shake that testimony. If the jury were to believe that the statement was false as to Runnels, they could hardly conclude that it was not false as to the respondent as well.

"The short of the matter is that, given a joint trial and a common defense, Runnels' testimony respecting his alleged out-of-court statement was more favorable to the respondent than any that cross-examination by counsel could possibly have produced, had Runnels 'affirmed the statement as his.' It would be unrealistic in the extreme in the circumstances here presented to hold that the respondent was denied either the opportunity or the benefit of full and effective cross-examination of Runnels.

"We conclude that where a codefendant takes the stand in his own defense, denies making an alleged out-of-court statement implicating the defendant, and proceeds to testify favorably to the defendant concerning the underlying facts, the defendant has been denied no rights protected by the Sixth and Fourteenth Amendments."

Justices Brennan, Douglas, and Marshall dissented, arguing that *Bruton* compels the conclusion "that the Federal Constitution forbids the States from assuming that juries can follow instructions which tell them to wipe their minds of highly damaging, incriminating admissions of one defendant which simultaneously incriminate another defendant whose guilt or innocence the jury is told to decide."

2. Respondents Randolph, Pickens and Hamilton, together with the two Wood brothers, were jointly tried and convicted of murder committed during a poker-game robbery. The state's case against the three respondents, none of whom took the stand, rested primarily on their oral confessions, as one of the Wood brothers did the shooting while the others were not present and the other Wood brother gathered up the money after entering with other persons whom a bystander could not positively identify. These confessions, imperfectly redacted so that it was apparent each one implicated the other respondents, were admitted on instructions that each confession could be used only against the defendant who gave it. The state supreme court affirmed on the ground that *Bruton* is not violated when there are "interlocking inculpatory confessions," but on federal habeas corpus the Court of Appeals ruled otherwise. The Supreme Court granted certiorari to resolve the conflict on that issue existing in both the state and federal courts.

In PARKER v. RANDOLPH, 442 U.S. 62, 99 S.Ct. 2132, 60 L.Ed.2d 713 (1979), REHNQUIST, J., concluded in the plurality opinion: [a] "The prejudicial impact of a codefendant's confession upon an incriminated defendant who has, insofar as the jury is concerned, maintained his innocence from the beginning is simply too great in such cases to be cured by a limiting instruction. The same cannot be said, however, when the defendant's own confession—'probably the most probative and damaging evidence that can be admitted against him,'—is properly introduced at trial. The defendant is 'the most knowledgeable and unimpeachable source of information about his past conduct,' and one can scarcely imagine evidence more damaging to his defense than his own admission of guilt. Thus, the incriminating statements of a codefendant will seldom, if ever, be of the 'devastating' character referred to in *Bruton* when the incriminated defendant has admitted his own guilt. The right protected by *Bruton*—the 'constitutional right of cross-examination,'—has far less practical value to a defendant who has confessed to the crime than to one who has consistently maintained his innocence. Successfully impeaching a codefendant's confession on cross-examination would likely yield small advantage to the defendant whose own admission of guilt stands before the jury unchallenged. Nor does the natural 'motivation to shift blame onto others,' recognized by the *Bruton* Court to render the incriminating statements of codefendants 'inevitably suspect,' require application of the *Bruton* rule when the incriminated defendant has corroborat-

a. Joined by Stewart and White, JJ., and the Chief Justice. Powell, J., took no part in the case.

ed his codefendant's statements by heaping blame onto himself."

BLACKMUN, J., although concurring in the judgment by reliance upon the harmless error rule of *Harrington v. California,* p. 798 supra, emphasized he would not "depart from the traditional harmless error analysis * * * in interlocking confession cases. The fact that confessions may interlock to some degree does not ensure, as a *per se* matter, that their admission will not prejudice a defendant so substantially that a limiting instruction will not be curative. The two confessions may interlock in part only. Or they may cover only a portion of the events in issue at the trial. Although two interlocking confessions may not be internally inconsistent, one may go far beyond the other in implicating the confessor's codefendant. In such circumstances, the admission of the confession of the codefendant who does not take the stand could very well serve to prejudice the defendant who is incriminated by the confession, notwithstanding that the defendant's own confession is, to an extent, interlocking. I fully recognize that in most interlocking confession cases, any error in admitting the confession of a nontestifying codefendant will be harmless beyond a reasonable doubt. Even so, I would not adopt a rigid *per se* rule that forecloses a court from weighing all the circumstances in order to determine whether the defendant in fact was unfairly prejudiced by the admission of even an interlocking confession."

STEVENS, J., joined by Brennan and Marshall, JJ., dissenting, after concluding that "the concurrent findings of the District Court and the Court of Appeals that the error here was not harmless preclude this Court from reaching a different result on this kind of issue," objected that the plurality opinion rested upon two erroneous assumptions: "First, it assumes that the jury's ability to disregard a codefendant's inadmissible and highly prejudicial confession is invariably increased by the existence of a corroborating statement by the defendant. Second, it assumes that all unchallenged confessions by a defendant are equally reliable. Aside from two quotations from the dissent in *Bruton,* however, the plurality supports these assumptions with nothing more than the force of its own assertions. But the infinite variability of inculpatory statements (whether made by defendants or codefendants), and of their likely effect on juries, makes those assertions untenable." By way of illustration, the dissenters put a hypothetical case in which the prosecutor's case against X and Y, neither of whom take the stand at their joint trial for assassinating a public figure, consists of 8 items of circumstantial evidence insufficient to support a conviction, a taped television interview with Y describing in detail how he and X planned and executed the crime, and the testimony of a drinking partner, a former cellmate, or a divorced spouse of X who vaguely recalls X saying that he had been with Y at the approximate time of the killing.

Are the confessions "interlocking" where, in a felony-murder case, all confessions admit participation in the felony but differ as to who did the killing? See *Tamilio v. Fogg,* 713 F.2d 18 (2d Cir. 1983).

3. In TENNESSEE v. STREET, ___ U.S. ___, 105 S.Ct. 2078, 85 L.Ed.2d 425 (1985), Street testified at trial that his confession to murder and burglary had been coerced by the sheriff reading to him the prior confession of severed co-defendant Peele and then directing Street to say the same thing. Peele's confession was then admitted in rebuttal to show the several differences in the two confessions. The Court, per CHIEF JUSTICE BURGER, after concluding that use of Peele's confession for this "legitimate, nonhearsay purpose" itself "raises no Confrontation Clause concerns," noted that the "only similarity to *Bruton* is that Peele's statement, like the codefendant's confession in *Bruton,* could have been misused by the jury." But in the present context the Court concluded that the trial court's limit-

ing instruction (that Peele's confession was to be considered "for the purpose of rebuttal only") constituted an "appropriate way to limit the jury's use of that evidence in a manner consistent with the Confrontation Clause." This was because here, "unlike the situation in *Bruton,* there were no alternatives that would have both assured the integrity of the trial's truthseeking function and eliminated the risk of the jury's improper use of evidence." The already-granted severance did not solve the problem, and redaction of Peele's confession "would have made it more difficult for the jury to evaluate" Street's claim that his confession was a coerced imitation of Peele's.

4. *In re Hill,* 458 P.2d 449 (Cal.1969), held that "the Sixth Amendment right to confrontation is intended to give to defendants in criminal cases the right to cross-examine as to statements made by the witness *at the time the witness makes those statements,*" so that *Bruton* applies even when the confessing co-defendant "took the stand and testified consistently with his prior extra-judicial statements." However, that position was rejected in *California v. Green,* [p. 936 supra] upholding a California statute which permitted the admission of a witness' prior inconsistent statement to prove the truth of the matter asserted therein, whether or not the defense had an opportunity for cross-examination when it was made. After noting that "there is little difference as far as the Constitution is concerned" between that situation and *Bruton,* the Court held that "the Confrontation Clause does not require excluding from evidence the prior statements of a witness who concedes making the statements, and who may be asked to defend or otherwise explain the inconsistency between his prior and his present version of the events in question, thus opening himself to full cross-examination at trial as to both stories."

What then, in a *Bruton* -type situation, of a case in which the confessing co-defendant does *not* take the stand at trial, but did testify in earlier proceedings (e.g., on a motion to suppress his confession) at which the other defendants could have cross-examined him concerning the confession, as in *People v. Moll,* 256 N.E.2d 185 (N.Y.1970)? Consider that in the *Green* case, the Supreme Court also held that a witness' "preliminary hearing testimony was admissible as far as the Constitution is concerned wholly apart from the question of whether respondent had an effective opportunity for confrontation at the subsequent trial," in that his "statement at the preliminary hearing had already been given under circumstances closely approximating those that surround the typical trial."

5. When is a reference to a codefendant in a confession "incriminating" so as to bring *Bruton* into play? What if *A* gives a confession in which he admits robbing a bank, as charged, and his confession merely states that *B,* also so charged, was present in the bank at the time of the robbery? Does it make any difference whether *B* 's defense is alibi or that he was present but not involved? Or, what if *A* 's confession never mentions *B* at all, but contains significant "linkage evidence," that is, facts which connect *B* with the crime when considered with other evidence admitted at trial? See *United States v. Wilkinson,* 754 F.2d 1427 (2d Cir.1985).

6. As to the "viable alternatives" referred to in *Bruton,* consider *A.B.A. Standards* § 13–3.2(a): "When a defendant moves for severance because an out-of-court statement of a codefendant makes reference to, but is not admissible against, the moving defendant, the court should determine whether the prosecution intends to offer the statement in evidence as part of its case in chief. If so, the court should require the prosecuting attorney to elect one of the following courses: (i) a joint trial at which the statement is not admitted into evidence; (ii) a joint trial at which the statement is admitted into evidence only after all references to the moving defendant have been deleted, provided that, as

deleted, the statement will not prejudice the moving defendant; [b] or (iii) severance of the moving defendant." [c]

7. Should the defendant who *made* the confession ever have something to say about how the confession is edited for the benefit of the codefendant named in the confession? About whether a mistrial should be declared as to *him* in order to avoid a *Bruton* problem?

8. Compare with *Bruton* the situation in which some other type of evidence (e.g., of a prior conviction) is admissible against one defendant but not another joined defendant. In *United States v. Figueroa,* 618 F.2d 934 (2d Cir.1980), the Court found the *Bruton* analogy less than compelling, for "[u]nlike a *Bruton* confession, prior act evidence is not so inevitably prejudicial to co-defendants that the worth of limiting instructions can be totally discounted." Thus: "When evidence is offered against one defendant in a joint trial, determination of admissibility against that defendant resolves only the Rule 403 balancing [d] as to him, i.e., that the probative value of the evidence in *his* "case" is not substantially outweighed by unfair prejudice to *him.* But if the evidence creates a significant risk of prejudice to the codefendants, a further issue arises as to whether the evidence is admissible *in a joint trial,* even though limited by cautionary instructions to the "case" of a single defendant. That issue can be considered either as a question of admissibility of evidence or severance. If the justification for a joint trial is outweighed by the prejudice to the co-defendants, the trial court can confront the prosecutor with the choice of foregoing either the evidence or the joint trial."

9. Other grounds upon which defendants sometimes obtain severances are: (a) because the number of defendants or the complexity of the evidence as to the several defendants is such that the trier of fact probably will be unable to distinguish the evidence and apply the law intelligently as to the charges against each defendant; (b) because the several defendants have antagonistic defenses; and (c) because it would otherwise be impossible to call a codefendant as a witness. As to (b), it is often required that the defenses be "irreconcilable," in the sense that belief of one compels disbelief of the other. *United States v. McClure,* 734 F.2d 484 (10th Cir.1984). As to (c), "the defendant must show that he would call the codefendant at a severed trial, that the codefendant would in fact testify, and that the testimony would be favorable to the moving defendant." *United States v. Vigil,* 561 F.2d 1316 (9th Cir.1977). Compare Westen, *The Compulsory Process Clause,* 73 Mich.L.Rev. 73, 143 (1974), arguing that "once the defendant shows that his co-defendant may be able to exculpate him—either by showing that the co-defendant has already exculpated him out of court or by reference to the nature of the offense—and that joinder 'could' tend to silence the witness, the burden should shift to the government to demonstrate that joinder would have no such effect." Cf. Note 14(b), p. 1358 infra.

10. *De Luna v. United States,* 308 F.2d 140 (5th Cir.1962), involved these facts: de Luna and Gomez, after denial of a severance motion, were jointly tried on a narcotics charge. They were the occupants of a moving car from which police had seen Gomez throw a package of narcotics. Gomez testified that he was inno-

b. Merely replacing the moving defendant's name with an X, a blank, or the phrase "another person" will not suffice. *Sims v. State,* 358 N.E.2d 746 (Ind.1977).

c. Yet another alternative is a joint trial utilizing a separate jury for each defendant, with each jury hearing only that evidence admissible against the defendant as to whom it is to render a verdict. See *State v. Corsi,* 430 A.2d 210 (N.J. 1981). Is this a sound solution? What problems are created by this procedure?

d. The reference is to Fed.R.Evid. 403, which provides: "Although relevant, evidence may be excluded if its probative value is substantially outweighed by the danger of unfair prejudice, confusion of the issues, or misleading the jury, or by considerations of undue delay, waste of time, or needless presentation of cumulative evidence."

cent, explaining that de Luna had thrown the package to him and told him to throw it out the window when the police approached. De Luna did not testify, but his lawyer argued that Gomez had the package at all times. Gomez's attorney commented on de Luna's failure to take the stand. Gomez was acquitted; de Luna was found guilty. On appeal, de Luna's conviction was reversed because of the violation of his privilege against self incrimination. Two members of the court went on to say that under these circumstances the proper result below would have been to permit the comment and then grant a severance. Gomez's "attorneys should be free to draw all rational inferences from the failure of a co-defendant to testify, just as an attorney is free to comment on the effect of any interested party's failure to produce material evidence in his possession or to call witnesses who have knowledge of pertinent facts."

Is the analogy an apt one? Given the analysis in *Griffin v. California,* p. 1360 infra, what "rational inferences" may be drawn from de Luna's failure to testify? What if Gomez's attorney had merely called attention to the fact that his client had taken the stand?

Chapter 19

THE RIGHT TO A "SPEEDY TRIAL"—AND TO "SPEEDY DISPOSITION" AT OTHER STEPS IN THE CRIMINAL PROCESS

SECTION 1. CONSTITUTIONAL AND STATUTORY PROVISIONS [a]

BARKER v. WINGO

407 U.S. 514, 92 S.Ct. 2182, 33 L.Ed.2d 101 (1972).

MR. JUSTICE POWELL delivered the opinion of the Court.

Although a speedy trial is guaranteed the accused by the Sixth Amendment to the Constitution, this Court has dealt with that right on infrequent occasions. The Court's opinion in *Klopfer v. North Carolina,* 386 U.S. 213, 87 S.Ct. 988, 18 L.Ed.2d 1 (1967), established that the right to speedy trial is "fundamental" and is imposed by the Due Process Clause of the Fourteenth Amendment on the States. [I]n none of these cases have we attempted to set out the criteria by which the speedy trial right is to be judged. This case compels us to make such an attempt.

On July 20, 1958, in Christian County, Kentucky, an elderly couple was beaten to death by intruders wielding an iron tire tool. Two suspects, Silas Manning and Willie Barker, the petitioner, were arrested shortly thereafter. The grand jury indicted them on September 15. Counsel was appointed on September 17, and Barker's trial was set for October 21. The Commonwealth had a stronger case against Manning, and it believed that Barker could not be convicted unless Manning testified against him. Manning was naturally unwilling to incriminate himself. Accordingly, on October 23, the day Silas Manning was brought to trial, the Commonwealth sought and obtained the first of what was to be a series of 16 continuances of Barker's trial. Barker made no objection. By first convicting Manning, the Commonwealth would remove possible problems of self-incrimination and would be able to assure his testimony against Barker.

The Commonwealth encountered more than a few difficulties in its prosecution of Manning. The first trial ended in a hung jury. A second trial resulted in a conviction, but the Kentucky Court of Appeals reversed because of the admission of evidence obtained by an illegal search. At his third trial, Manning was again convict-

a. See Misner, *Speedy Trial: Federal and State Practice* (1983); Joseph, *Speedy Trial Rights in Application,* 48 Fordham L.Rev. 611 (1980).

ed, and the Court of Appeals again reversed because the trial court had not granted a change of venue. A fourth trial resulted in a hung jury. Finally, after five trials, Manning was convicted, in March 1962, of murdering one victim, and after a sixth trial, in December 1962, he was convicted of murdering the other.

The Christian County Circuit Court holds three terms each year—in February, June, and September. Barker's initial trial was to take place in the September term of 1958. The first continuance postponed it until the February 1959 term. The second continuance was granted for one month only. Every term thereafter for as long as the Manning prosecutions were in process, the Commonwealth routinely moved to continue Barker's case to the next term. When the case was continued from the June 1959 term until the following September, Barker, having spent 10 months in jail, obtained his release by posting a $5,000 bond. He thereafter remained free in the community until his trial. Barker made no objection, through his counsel, to the first 11 continuances.

When on February 12, 1962, the Commonwealth moved for the twelfth time to continue the case until the following term, Barker's counsel filed a motion to dismiss the indictment. The motion to dismiss was denied two weeks later, and the State's motion for a continuance was granted. The State was granted further continuances in June 1962 and September 1962, to which Barker did not object.

In February 1963, the first term of court following Manning's final conviction, the Commonwealth moved to set Barker's trial for March 19. But on the day scheduled for trial, it again moved for a continuance until the June term. It gave as its reason the illness of the ex-sheriff who was the chief investigating officer in the case. To this continuance, Barker objected unsuccessfully.

The witness was still unable to testify in June, and the trial, which had been set for June 19, was continued again until the September term over Barker's objection. This time the court announced that the case would be dismissed for lack of prosecution if it were not tried during the next term. The final trial date was set for October 9, 1963. On that date, Barker again moved to dismiss the indictment, and this time specified that his right to a speedy trial had been violated. The motion was denied; the trial commenced with Manning as the chief prosecution witness; Barker was convicted and given a life sentence.

Barker appealed his conviction to the Kentucky Court of Appeals, relying in part on his speedy trial claim. The court affirmed. In February 1970 Barker petitioned for habeas corpus in the United States District Court for the Western District of Kentucky. Although the District Court rejected the petition without holding a hearing, the Court granted petitioner leave to appeal *in forma pauperis* and a certificate of probable cause to appeal. On appeal, the Court of Appeals for the Sixth Circuit affirmed the District Court. * * * We granted Barker's petition for certiorari.

The right to a speedy trial is generically different from any of the other rights enshrined in the Constitution for the protection of the accused. In addition to the general concern that all accused persons be treated according to decent and fair procedures, there is a societal interest in providing a speedy trial which exists separate from and at times in opposition to the interests of the accused. The inability of courts to provide a prompt trial has contributed to a large backlog of cases in urban courts which, among other things, enables defendants to negotiate more effectively for pleas of guilty to lesser offenses and otherwise manipulate the system. In addition, persons released on bond for lengthy periods awaiting trial have an opportunity to commit other crimes. It must be of little comfort to the residents of Christian County, Kentucky, to know that Barker was at large on bail for over four years while accused of a vicious and brutal murder of which he was ultimately convicted. Moreover, the longer an accused is free awaiting trial, the more tempting becomes his opportunity to jump bail and escape. Finally, delay between arrest and punishment may have a detrimental effect on rehabilitation.

If an accused cannot make bail, he is generally confined, as was Barker for 10 months, in a local jail. This contributes to the overcrowding and generally deplorable state of those institutions. Lengthy exposure to these conditions "has a destructive effect on human character and makes the rehabilitation of the individual offender much more difficult." At times the result may even be violent rioting. Finally, lengthy pretrial detention is costly. The cost of maintaining a prisoner in jail varies from $3 to $9 per day, and this amounts to millions across the Nation. In addition, society loses wages which might have been earned, and it must often support families of incarcerated breadwinners.

A second difference between the right to speedy trial and the accused's other constitutional rights is that deprivation of the right may work to the accused's advantage. Delay is not an uncommon defense tactic. As the time between the commission of the crime and trial lengthens, witnesses may become unavailable or their memories may fade. If the witnesses support the prosecution, its case will be weakened, sometimes seriously so. And it is the prosecution which carries the burden of proof. Thus, unlike the right to counsel or the right to be free from compelled self-incrimination, deprivation of the right to speedy trial does not *per se* prejudice the accused's ability to defend himself.

Finally, and perhaps most importantly, the right to speedy trial is a more vague concept than other procedural rights. It is, for example, impossible to determine with precision when the right has been denied. We cannot definitely say how long is too long in a system where justice is supposed to be swift but deliberate. As a consequence, there is no fixed point in the criminal process when the State can put the defendant to the choice of either exercising or waiving the right to a speedy trial. If, for example, the State moves for a 60-day continuance, granting that continuance is not a violation of the right to speedy trial unless the circumstances of the case are such that further delay would endanger the values the right protects. It is impossible to do more than generalize about when those circumstances exist. There is nothing comparable to the point in the process when a defendant exercises or waives his right to counsel or his right to a jury trial. * * *

The amorphous quality of the right also leads to the unsatisfactorily severe remedy of dismissal of the indictment when the right has been deprived. This is indeed a serious consequence because it means that a defendant who may be guilty of a serious crime will go free, without having been tried. Such a remedy is more serious than an exclusionary rule or a reversal for a new trial, but it is the only possible remedy.

Perhaps because the speedy trial right is so slippery, two rigid approaches are urged upon us as ways of eliminating some of the uncertainty which courts experience in protecting the right. The first suggestion is that we hold that the Constitution requires a criminal defendant to be offered a trial within a specified time period. The result of such a ruling would have the virtue of clarifying when the right is infringed and of simplifying courts' application of it. Recognizing this, some legislatures have enacted laws, and some courts have adopted procedural rules which more narrowly define the right. * * *

But such a result would require this Court to engage in legislative or rulemaking activity, rather than in the adjudicative process to which we should confine our efforts. We do not establish procedural rules for the States, except when mandated by the Constitution. We find no constitutional basis for holding that the speedy trial right can be quantified into a specified number of days or months. The States, of course, are free to prescribe a reasonable period consistent with constitutional standards, but our approach must be less precise.

The second suggested alternative would restrict consideration of the right to those cases in which the accused has demanded a speedy trial. Most States have recognized what is loosely referred to as the "demand rule," although eight States reject it. It is not clear, however, precisely what is meant by that term. Although every Federal Court of Appeals that has considered the question has endorsed some kind of demand rule, some have regarded the rule within the concept of waiver, whereas others have viewed it as a factor to be weighed in assessing whether there has been a deprivation of the speedy trial right. We shall refer to the former approach as the demand-waiver doctrine. The demand-waiver doctrine provides that a defendant waives any consideration of his right to speedy trial for any period prior to which he has not demanded a trial. Under this rigid approach, a prior demand is a necessary condition to the consideration of the speedy trial right. This essentially was the approach the Sixth Circuit took below.

Such an approach, by presuming waiver of a fundamental right from inaction, is inconsistent with this Court's pronouncements on waiver of constitutional rights. The Court has defined waiver as "an intentional relinquishment or abandonment of a known right or privilege." Courts should "indulge every reasonable presumption against waiver," and they should "not presume acquiescence in the loss of fundamental rights." * * *

In excepting the right to speedy trial from the rule of waiver we have applied to other fundamental rights, courts that have applied the demand-waiver rule have relied on the assumption that delay usually works for the benefit of the accused and on the absence of any readily ascertainable time in the criminal process for a defendant to be given the choice of exercising or waiving his right. But it is not necessarily true that delay benefits the defendant. There are cases in which delay appreciably harms the defendant's ability to defend himself. Moreover, a defendant confined to jail prior to trial is obviously disadvantaged by delay as is a defendant released on bail but unable to lead a normal life because of community suspicion and his own anxiety.

The nature of the speedy-trial right does make it impossible to pinpoint a precise time in the process when the right must be asserted or waived, but that fact does not argue for placing the burden of protecting the right solely on defendants. A defendant has no duty to bring himself to trial; the State has that duty as well as the duty of insuring that the trial is consistent with due process. Moreover, for the reasons earlier expressed, society has a particular interest in bringing swift prosecutions, and society's representatives are the ones who should protect that interest.

It is also noteworthy that such a rigid view of the demand rule places defense counsel in an awkward position. Unless he demands a trial early and often, he is in danger of frustrating his client's right. If counsel is willing to tolerate some delay because he finds it reasonable and helpful in preparing his own case, he may be unable to obtain a speedy trial for his client at the end of that time. Since under the demand-waiver rule no time runs until the demand is made, the government will have whatever time is otherwise reasonable to bring the defendant to trial after a demand has been made. Thus, if the first demand is made three months after arrest in a jurisdiction which prescribes a six months rule, the prosecution will have a total of nine months—which may be wholly unreasonable under the circumstances. The result in practice is likely to be either an automatic, *pro forma* demand made immediately after appointment of counsel or delays which, but for the demand-waiver rule, would not be tolerated. Such a result is not consistent with the interests of defendants, society, or the Constitution.

We reject, therefore, the rule that a defendant who fails to demand a speedy trial forever waives his right. This does not mean, however, that the defendant has no responsibility to assert his right. We think the better rule is that the defendant's assertion of or failure to assert his right to a speedy trial is one of the factors to be considered in an inquiry into the deprivation of the right. Such a formulation avoids the rigidities of the demand-waiver rule and the resulting possible unfairness in its application. It allows the trial court to exercise a judicial discretion based on the circumstances, including due consideration of any applicable formal procedural rule. It would permit, for example, a court to attach a different weight to a situation in which the defendant knowingly fails to object from a situation in which his attorney acquiesces in long delay without adequately informing his client or from a situation in which no counsel is appointed. It would also allow a court to weigh the frequency and force of the objections as opposed to attaching significant weight to a purely *pro forma* objection.

In ruling that a defendant has some responsibility to assert a speedy-trial claim, we do not depart from our holdings in other cases concerning the waiver of fundamental rights, in which we have placed the entire responsibility on the prosecution to show that the claimed waiver was knowingly and voluntarily made. Such cases have involved rights which must be exercised or waived at a specific time or under clearly identifiable circumstances, such as the rights to plead not guilty, to demand a jury trial, to exercise the privilege against self incrimination, and to have the assistance of counsel. We have shown above that the right to a speedy trial is unique in its uncertainty as to when and under what circumstances it must be asserted or may be deemed waived. But the rule we announce today, which comports with constitutional principles, places the primary burden on the courts and the prosecutors to assure that cases are brought to trial. We hardly need add that if delay is attributable to the defendant, then his waiver may be given effect under standard waiver doctrine, the demand rule aside.

We, therefore, reject both of the inflexible approaches—the fixed time period because it goes further than the Constitution requires; the demand-waiver rule because it is insensitive to a right which we have deemed fundamental. The approach we accept is a balancing test, in which the conduct of both the prosecution and the defendant are weighed.

A balancing test necessarily compels courts to approach speedy-trial cases on an *ad hoc* basis. We can do little more than identify some of the factors which courts should assess in determining whether a particular defendant has been deprived of his right. Though some might express them in different ways, we identify four such factors: Length of delay, the reason for the delay, the defendant's assertion of his right, and prejudice to the defendant.

The length of the delay is to some extent a triggering mechanism. Until there is some delay which is presumptively prejudicial, there is no necessity for inquiry into the other factors that go into the balance. Nevertheless, because of the imprecision of the right to speedy trial, the length of delay that will provoke such an inquiry is necessarily dependent upon the peculiar circumstances of the case. To take but one example, the delay that can be tolerated for an ordinary street crime is considerably less than for a serious, complex conspiracy charge.

Closely related to length of delay is the reason the government assigns to justify the delay. Here, too, different weights should be assigned to different reasons. A deliberate attempt to delay the trial in order to hamper the defense should be weighed heavily against the government. A more neutral reason such as negligence or overcrowded courts should be weighed less heavily but nevertheless should be considered since the ultimate responsibility for such circumstances must rest with the government rather than with the defendant. Finally, a valid reason, such as a missing witness, should serve to justify appropriate delay.

We have already discussed the third factor, the defendant's responsibility to assert his right. Whether and how a defendant asserts his right is closely related to the other factors we have mentioned. The strength of his efforts will be affected by the length of the delay, to some extent by the reason for the delay, and most particularly by the personal prejudice, which is not always readily identifiable, that he experiences. The more serious the deprivation, the more likely a defendant is to complain. The defendant's assertion of his speedy trial right, then, is entitled to strong evidentiary weight in determining whether the right is being deprived. We emphasize that failure to assert the right will make it difficult for a defendant to prove that he was denied a speedy trial.

A fourth factor is prejudice to the defendant. Prejudice, of course, should be assessed in the light of the interests of defendants which the speedy trial right was designed to protect. This Court has identified three such interests: (i) to prevent oppressive pretrial incarceration; (ii) to minimize anxiety and concern of the accused; and (iii) to limit the possibility that the defense will be impaired. Of these, the most serious is the last, because the inability of a defendant adequately to prepare his case skews the fairness of the entire system. If witnesses die or disappear during a delay, the prejudice is obvious. There is also prejudice if defense witnesses are unable to recall accurately events of the distant past. Loss of memory, however, is not always reflected in the record because what has been forgotten can rarely be shown.

We have discussed previously the societal disadvantages of lengthy pretrial incarceration, but obviously the disadvantages for the accused who cannot obtain his release are even more serious. The time spent in jail awaiting trial has a detrimental impact on the individual. It often means loss of a job; it disrupts family life; and it enforces idleness. Most jails offer little or no recreational or rehabilitative programs. The time spent in jail is simply dead time. Moreover, if a defendant is locked up, he is hindered in his ability to gather evidence, contact witnesses, or otherwise prepare his defense. Imposing those consequences on anyone who has not yet been convicted is serious. It is especially unfortunate to impose them on those persons who are ultimately found to be innocent. Finally, even if an accused is not incarcerated prior to trial, he is still disadvantaged by restraints on his liberty and by living under a cloud of anxiety, suspicion, and often hostility.

We regard none of the four factors identified above as either a necessary or sufficient condition to the finding of a deprivation of the right of speedy trial. Rather, they are related factors and must be considered together with such other circumstances as may be relevant. In sum, these factors have no talismanic qualities; courts must still engage in a difficult and sensitive balancing process. But, because we are dealing with a fundamental right of the accused, this process must be carried out with full recognition that the accused's interest in a speedy trial is specifically affirmed in the Constitution.

The difficulty of the task of balancing these factors is illustrated by this case, which we consider to be close. It is clear that the length of delay between arrest and trial—well over five years—was extraordinary. Only seven months of that period can be attributed to a strong excuse, the illness of the ex-sheriff who was in charge of the investigation. Perhaps some delay would have been permissible under ordinary circumstances, so that Manning could be utilized as a witness in Barker's trial, but more than four years was too long a period, particularly since a good part of that period was attributable to the Commonwealth's failure or inability to try Manning under circumstances that comported with due process.

Two counter-balancing factors, however, outweigh these deficiencies. The first is that prejudice was minimal. Of course, Barker was prejudiced to some extent by living for over four years under a cloud of suspicion and anxiety. Moreover, although he was released on bond for most of the period, he did spend 10 months in jail before trial. But there is no claim that any of Barker's witnesses died or otherwise became unavailable owing to the delay. The trial transcript indicates only two very minor lapses of memory—one on the part of a prosecution witness—which were in no way significant to the outcome.

More important than the absence of serious prejudice, is the fact that Barker did not want a speedy trial. Counsel was appointed for Barker immediately after his indictment and represented him throughout the period. No question is raised as to the competency of such counsel. Despite the fact that counsel had notice of the motions for continuances, the record shows no action whatever taken between October 21, 1958, and February 12, 1962, that could be construed as the assertion of the speedy-trial right. On the latter date, in response to another motion for continuance, Barker moved to dismiss the indictment. The record does not show on what ground this motion was based, although it is clear that no alternative motion was made for an immediate trial. Instead the record strongly suggests that while he hoped to take advantage of the delay in which he had acquiesed, and thereby obtain a dismissal of the charges, he definitely did not want to be tried. Counsel conceded as much at oral argument:

> "Your honor, I would concede that Willie Mae Barker—probably—I don't know this for a fact—probably did not want to be tried. I don't think any man wants to be tried. And I don't consider this a liability on his behalf. I don't blame him."

The probable reason for Barker's attitude was that he was gambling on Manning's acquittal. The evidence was not terribly strong against Manning, as the reversals and hung juries suggest, and Barker undoubtedly thought that if Manning were acquitted, he would never be tried. Counsel also conceded this:

> "Now, it's true that the reason for this delay was the Commonwealth of Kentucky's desire to secure the testimony of the accomplice, Silas Manning. And it's true that if Silas Manning were never convicted, Willie Mae Barker would never have been convicted. We concede this."

That Barker was gambling on Manning's acquittal is also suggested by his failure, following the *pro forma* motion to dismiss filed in February 1962, to object to the Commonwealth's next two motions for continuances. Indeed, it was not until March 1963, after Manning's convictions were final, that Barker, having lost his gamble, began to object to further continuances. At that time, the Commonwealth's excuse was the illness of the ex-sheriff, which Barker has conceded justified the further delay.

We do not hold that there may never be a situation in which an indictment may be dismissed on speedy-trial grounds where the defendant has failed to object to continuances. There may be a situation in which the defendant was represented by incompetent counsel, was severely prejudiced, or even cases in which the continuances were granted *ex parte.* But barring extraordinary circumstances, we would be reluctant indeed to rule that a defendant was denied this constitutional right on a record that strongly indicates, as does this one, that the defendant did not want a speedy trial. We hold, therefore, that Barker was not deprived of his due process right to a speedy trial. * * * [b]

NOTES ON THE CONSTITUTIONAL AND STATUTORY RIGHT TO SPEEDY TRIAL

1. *The Barker balancing test.* Consider Uviller, *Barker v. Wingo: Speedy Trial Gets a Fast Shuffle,* 72 Colum.L.Rev. 1376, 1399–1400 (1972): "[T]o the extent that Powell's superficial examination represents the authoritative doctrine of a substantial majority, if not the entire Court, it is disappointing in several important aspects. First, he slights the importance of the length of delay. By treating it only as a threshold 'triggering' factor, he ignores the difference between a six-week hiatus and a five-year wait. Second, the Court radically bends the doctrine of waiver, looking not to the overt, express relinquishment normally insisted upon, but rather probing the subjective disposition and attitude of the supposed beneficiary. True desire becomes the test, and appellate counsel's concessions the proof of relinquishment. On the valid assumption that many defendants do not share the state's eagerness for trial, the Court concludes that they are not entitled to it. Having no obligation to promote speed, the passive defendant is nonetheless taxed for his reluctance. Third, Powell unduly disparages the inchoate aspects of prejudice, virtually insisting upon proof by the accused of actual demonstrable harm to his case. * * * Finally, the Court blandly indicates unwarranted acceptance of all but the most unfair reasons for state delay. * * *

"Most importantly, however, the Court in its pronouncements and in their application to the facts before it seems to arrive at a distorted formula for the interplay of the elements of the speedy trial guarantee. It runs something like this: notwithstanding the lapse of a substantial period of time to which the accused did not affirmatively consent, he is not denied a speedy trial if the court determines as a fact that he did not really want to be sooner tried, and he fails to demonstrate concretely some actual and significant deterioration of his defensive case suffered by reason of the delay. With all due deference, it is here submitted that a formulation more closely harmonious with traditional concepts and prior insights from other quarters, might be shaped thus: absent an explicit and competent waiver for the period in question, the accused is denied his right to a speedy trial by the passage of an unreasonable period of time without a demonstration by the state of good and sufficient reason or necessity therefor; and further, prejudice presumptively increases with the length of elapsed time, imposing upon the state the increasing burden of proving the delay harmless by reasons more particular and persuasive than convenience, negligence, or the hope of tactical advantage."

2. *Federal statute.* The Speedy Trial Act of 1974, set out in Supp.App. B, establishes specific time limits within which

b. White, J., joined by Brennan, J., concurring, emphasized that the crowded dockets could not justify an unreasonable delay in providing a trial: "[F]or those who desire an early trial, * * * [the defendant's interests] should prevail if the only countervailing considerations offered by the State are those connected with crowded dockets and prosecutorial case loads. A defendant desiring a speedy trial, therefore, should have it within some reasonable time; and only special circumstances presenting a more pressing public need with respect to the case itself should suffice to justify delay. * * * Of course, cases will differ among themselves as to the allowable time between charge and trial so as to permit prosecution and defense adequately to prepare their case. But unreasonable delay in run-of-the-mill criminal cases cannot be justified by simply asserting that the public resources provided by the State's criminal justice system are limited and that each case must await its turn."

On the impact of *Barker,* see Rudstein, *Right to Speedy Trial: Barker v. Wingo in the Lower Courts,* 1975 U.Ill.L.F. 11.

the trial and certain other steps must commence in a federal prosecution.[c] Much criticism has been directed toward this legislation.[d]

3. *Speedy trial in the states; constitution vs. statute.* Although the Sixth Amendment right to a speedy trial was not applied to the states until *Klopfer,* all state constitutions also provide such a guarantee. An overwhelming majority of the states have enacted statutes setting forth the time within which a defendant must be tried following the date he was arrested, held to answer, committed, or indicted, and it is these statutes which have received principal attention. If a statutory violation is found, there is seldom any inquiry into the alleged constitutional denial; and if the statute has not been violated, it is typically assumed that the constitutional provision has been satisfied.

4. *Excuses for delay.* Speedy trial statutes declare that trial must commence within a fixed period—expressed in days, months, or terms of courts—following some prior event, such as arrest, indictment, or holding to answer, but also recognize that certain periods of time are not to be counted in determining whether this time has run. A majority of jurisdictions merely provide for additional time upon a showing of "good cause," while some statutes enumerate some of the more common legitimate reasons for delay. See, e.g., the excluded periods in § 3161(h) of the Speedy Trial Act of 1974. Because of the excluded periods, a substantial number of cases will not come to trial within the period specified in the statute.

5. *Waiver by counsel. Townsend v. Superior Court,* 543 P.2d 619 (Cal.1975), involved these facts, as summarized in the dissent: "In the instant situation, defendant faced a charge of possession of narcotics. Because of his indigence the court appointed the public defender to represent him. Defendant remained incarcerated following arraignment. He continuously claimed his [statutory] right to be tried within 60 days and vociferously refused to consent to any continuances. Nevertheless, his counsel, the public defender, requested a number of such continuances; these requests for more time, entered over defendant's objections, did not emanate from the complexity of defendant's case or from misconduct of defendant but from the public defender's own heavy case load. Although he was in no way responsible for, and did not acquiesce in, the delay, defendant was compelled to wait in jail for over 100 days following arraignment without being brought to trial."

The majority declared that while counsel could not waive the defendant's fundamental Sixth Amendment right to speedy trial "over his client's objection," the same was not true of the statutory right, which "cannot properly be termed 'fundamental' in the foregoing sense and therefore beyond counsel's primary control." Though counsel may not "effectively waive his client's rights where the record reveals that the latter was the victim of inadequate representation," the court concluded this

c. Guidelines for administering the Act appear at 106 F.R.D. 271 (1985). For an empirical study of experience under the Act, see Bridges, *The Speedy Trial Act of 1974: Effect on Delays in Federal Criminal Litigation,* 73 J.Crim.L. & C. 50 (1982).

d. See, e.g., Frase, *The Speedy Trial Act of 1974,* 43 U.Chi.L.Rev. 667, 669–70 (1976) ("The Act * * * contains numerous unresolved policy issues, ambiguities, and drafting errors"); Hansen & Reed, *The Speedy Trial Act of 1974 in Constitutional Perspective,* 47 Miss.L.J. 365, 419–20 (1976) ("Unless additional manpower and resources are provided, the Act will become an albatross around the neck of the federal criminal justice system"); Kozinski, *That Can of Worms: The Speedy Trial Act,* 62 A.B.A.J. 862, 864 (1976) ("an obtuse and complicated statute—it remains to be seen whether the depletion of judicial resources required to implement the Speedy Trial Act will not have an effect on the disposition of criminal trials quite opposite to that contemplated by its framers"). Compare Steinberg, *Right to Speedy Trial: The Constitutional Right and Its Applicability to the Speedy Trial Act of 1974,* 66 J.Crim.L. & C. 229, 230 (1975) ("a highly commendable piece of legislation").

was not such a case because "[i]nadequacy of time for defense counsel to prepare for trial, and calendar conflicts of court and defense counsel account for the delay involved." Tobriner, J., dissenting, objected:

"Assuming, however, that a counsel generally does have authority, incident to the power to control trial tactics, to decide that the complexity of a defendant's case or the need for investigation warrants a waiver of the statutory speedy trial provision, it does not follow that the waiver in the instant case was proper. Here, defendant's defense was not so 'complex and myriad' that counsel needed additional time to prepare effectively for trial. If the delay had resulted from such circumstances, then there would be some justification for the majority's characterization of the case as a conflict between defendant's right to a speedy trial and his right to effective counsel. Here, however, the delay ensued simply because the defense counsel was overburdened with *other* cases which took precedence over that of the defendant.

"If an affluent defendant chooses to employ a counsel who is involved in many other cases, then the courts, quite appropriately, can require the defendant to wait until his selected counsel is ready for trial; if the delay is unacceptable to the defendant, he can always engage another, less burdened attorney. The indigent defendant, however, can exercise no such option."

6. *Consequences of denial of speedy trial.* In *United States v. Strunk,* 467 F.2d 969 (7th Cir.1972), the court after finding the defendant was denied a speedy trial under *Barker* while serving a sentence in the state prison, concluded: "The remedy for a violation of this constitutional right has traditionally been the dismissal of the indictment or the vacation of the sentence. Perhaps the severity of that remedy has caused courts to be extremely hesitant in finding a failure to afford a speedy trial. Be that as it may, we know of no reason why less drastic relief may not be granted in appropriate cases. Here no question is raised about the sufficiency of evidence showing defendant's guilt, and, as we have said, he makes no claim of having been prejudiced in presenting his defense. In these circumstances, the vacation of the sentence and a dismissal of the indictment would seem inappropriate. Rather, we think the proper remedy is to remand the case to the district court with direction to enter an order instructing the Attorney General to credit the defendant with the period of time elapsing between the return of the indictment and the date of the arraignment. Fed.R.Crim.P. 35 provides that the district court may correct an illegal sentence at any time. We choose to treat the sentence here imposed as illegal to the extent of the delay we have characterized as unreasonable."

The Supreme Court did not agree. In an opinion for a unanimous Court, *Strunk v. United States,* 412 U.S. 434, 93 S.Ct. 2260, 27 L.Ed.2d 56 (1973), Burger, C.J., noted that delay in a situation such as this "may subject the accused to an emotional stress" and that as a result "the prospect of rehabilitation may also be affected," and concluded: "In light of the policies which underlie the right to a speedy trial, dismissal must remain, as *Barker* noted, 'the only possible remedy.' "

As to the prosecution's failure to comply with statutory speedy trial provisions, consider Note, 57 Colum.L.Rev. 846, 859–60 (1957): "Three different positions have been taken on the effect of statutory dismissal for want of prosecution. One group of states treats it as a bar to another prosecution for the same offense, while another group does not. The third position is that such a dismissal prevents subsequent prosecutions for the same charge if it is a misdemeanor, but not if it is a felony. This last view is based on unequivocal statutory language, while statutes are far less clear in states adopting the first two positions. In resolving this ambiguity, courts have relied on either of the two opposing policy considerations. Those barring subsequent prosecutions stress the importance of speedy trial and the need for a potent sanction to enforce it. The opposing view emphasizes the need for effective prosecution of criminal cases. It demands clear legislative intent before barring prosecutions of any offense on the ground that not to do so would require the court to bar subsequent prosecutions of even the most serious offenses."

Under § 3162(a) of the Speedy Trial Act of 1974, Supp.App. B, the sanction is dismissal "with or without prejudice," depending upon the court's assessment of various factors, including those listed in the statute. Is this a sensible approach? How should trial judges go about making that judgment? Consider Steinberg, *Dismissal With or Without Prejudice Under the Speedy Trial Act: A Proposed Interpretation,* 68 J.Crim.L. & C. 1, 14 (1977), asserting that "only by a vigorous judicial application of the remedy of dismissal with prejudice will the prosecution be deterred from noncompliance with the time limits." But see *United States v. Brown,* 770 F.2d 241 (1st Cir.1985) (there is no presumption in favor of dismissal with prejudice, and thus trial judge's choice of that alternative is reviewable on appeal only under the "normal abuse of discretion standard").

7. *Interlocutory appeal.* If a defendant's pretrial motion to dismiss on speedy trial grounds is denied, he need not be allowed an interlocutory appeal to fully protect his rights under *Barker v. Wingo,* as it "is the delay before trial, not the trial itself, that offends against the constitutional guarantee of a speedy trial." See *United States v. MacDonald,* discussed at p. 1104 infra.

8. *When does the time begin to run?* Under state speedy trial statutes, the time usually runs from the date the defendant first appears in court following his arrest, except that it typically runs from the date of the formal charge if it precedes arrest. As to the constitutional right to speedy trial, only the delay following arrest or formal charge (whichever comes first) is taken into account. See *United States v. Lovasco,* p. 1098 infra.

NOTES ON THE PUBLIC INTEREST IN SPEEDY TRIAL

1. Consider the remarks of Professor Herman Goldstein in National Conference on Bail and Criminal Justice, *Proceedings and Interim Report,* 152–53 (1965), commenting upon what Justice Powell described in *Barker* as the "societal interest in providing a speedy trial":

"A case which illustrates * * * the need for more expeditious handling of our court cases—is that involving a Chicago subject—Anthony Massari. Massari was released from the Illinois State Penitentiary upon completion of a three-year term for burglary and armed robbery in 1961. On July 8, 1963, Massari was apprehended in the act of committing a burglary. He was indicted and released on bail totaling $7,500. On August 24, 1963, while free on bail, the subject was apprehended in the commission of a second burglary and was found to have in his possession the proceeds of still another burglary committed earlier in the day. He was indicted on two counts of burglary and released on $4,500 bail. The subject was again arrested on November 18, 1963, when he was found to be in possession of a loaded firearm and burglary tools. On January 16, 1964, he was arrested in the act of committing a burglary and found to have the proceeds of two other burglaries in his possession. He was indicted the following day and released on $15,000 bail, only to be arrested on the same afternoon while committing still another burglary for which he was indicted and bail set at $5,000. Subsequently, he was arrested on February 8, 1964, with release on bail set at $10,000; again on February 21, 1964, with release on bail of $5,000; and again on March 5, 1964, when bail was set at $5,000.

"On April 24, 1964, when Massari went to trial, he had been arrested nine times in the period from July 8, 1963, to March 5, 1964, indicted on ten counts and was free on $48,500 in bail. He entered a guilty plea to the 10 indictments and was sentenced from five to 15 years in the penitentiary on each count—the sentence to run concurrently.

"The pattern in the Massari case is often repeated. The offender launches himself on a cycle. He commits more crimes in order to acquire more money in order to meet larger amounts of bail and the accumulation of attorney's fees. He often becomes more daring in the types of crimes he commits and is more likely to use force as his concern for the eventual consequences of his actions decreases."

2. "Continuances may compromise the fairness of criminal proceedings if a delayed trial has a different, and less just, outcome from a speedy one. Witnesses may die. Their memories may fade. Their testimony may become more vulnerable to cross-examination. They may be 'worn out' by repeated trips to court and refuse to appear again, or become less cooperative. A cynic, or a vigilant law enforcement officer, would add that opportunity for intimidating witnesses or bribing officials increase as a function of time. Although these consequences of delay can disadvantage either the prosecution or the defense, observers insist that 'staleness' is far more likely to injure the prosecution which is responsible for the production of most witnesses and has the burden of proving guilt beyond a reasonable doubt. Thus a prosecutor, aware that his case is growing weaker with the passage of time, may be forced to consent to a reduction of the charge or to end prosecution altogether. To those critical of the court system, 'lost convictions' are the most significant cost of continuances." Project, 35 U.Chi.L.Rev. 259, 261–62 (1968).

3. What steps are appropriate to protect the public interest in the speedy disposition of criminal cases? Compare *Giacalone v. Lucas,* 445 F.2d 1238 (6th Cir. 1971) (taking into account "the public interest in the prompt and efficient administration of justice," trial judge's denial of a continuance was not an abuse of discretion where defendant's counsel was hospitalized but his associate was available and prepared to try the case); and *Commonwealth v. Scott,* 277 N.E.2d 483 (Mass. 1971) (in view of public right "that criminal complaints or indictments be tried and disposed of with reasonable dispatch," defendant was properly denied option of insisting upon change of counsel on date set for trial); with *Moore v. Jamieson,* 306 A.2d 283 (Pa.1973) (court rule providing that attorney who represents 10 defendants whose indictments are more than a year old may not enter appearance in any additional criminal cases is unconstitutional; some limits on free choice of counsel by defendants and upon counsel's practice are justified to prevent scheduling conflicts which cause delay, but this rule is overbroad because it fails to take account of whether it is counsel's fault that his cases are over a year old).

SECTION 2. THE IMPRISONED DEFENDANT

SMITH v. HOOEY

393 U.S. 374, 89 S.Ct. 575, 21 L.Ed.2d 607 (1969).

MR. JUSTICE STEWART delivered the opinion of the Court. * * *

In 1960 the petitioner was indicted in Harris County, Texas, upon a charge of theft. He was then, and still is, a prisoner in the federal penitentiary at Leavenworth, Kansas.[2] Shortly after the state charge was filed against him, the petitioner mailed

2. On May 5, 1960, the sheriff of Harris County notified the warden at Leavenworth that a warrant for the petitioner's arrest was outstanding, and asked for notice of "the minimum release date." That date is apparently January 6, 1970.

a letter to the Texas trial court requesting a speedy trial. In reply, he was notified that "he would be afforded a trial within two weeks of any date [he] might specify at which he could be present." Thereafter, for the next six years, the petitioner, "by various letters, and more formal so-called 'motions,'" continued periodically to ask that he be brought to trial. Beyond the response already alluded to, the State took no steps to obtain the petitioner's appearance in the Harris County trial court. Finally, in 1967, the petitioner filed in that court a verified motion to dismiss the charge against him for want of prosecution. No action was taken on the motion.

The petitioner then brought a mandamus proceeding in the Supreme Court of Texas, asking for an order to show cause why the pending charge should not be dismissed. Mandamus was refused. * * *

There can be no doubt that if the petitioner in the present case had been at large for a six-year period following his indictment, and had repeatedly demanded that he be brought to trial, the State would have been under a constitutional duty to try him. And Texas concedes that if during that period he had been confined in a Texas prison for some other state offense, its obligation would have been no less. But the Texas Supreme Court has held that because petitioner is, in fact, confined in a federal prison, the State is totally absolved from any duty at all under the constitutional guarantee. We cannot agree.

[T]his constitutional guarantee has universally been thought essential to protect at least three basic demands of criminal justice in the Anglo-American legal system: "[1] to prevent undue and oppressive incarceration prior to trial, [2] to minimize anxiety and concern accompanying public accusation and [3] to limit the possibilities that long delay will impair the ability of an accused to defend himself." These demands are both aggravated and compounded in the case of an accused who is imprisoned by another jurisdiction.

At first blush it might appear that a man already in prison under a lawful sentence is hardly in a position to suffer from "undue and oppressive incarceration prior to trial." But the fact is that delay in bringing such a person to trial on a pending charge may ultimately result in as much oppression as is suffered by one who is jailed without bail upon an untried charge. First, the possibility that the defendant already in prison might receive a sentence at least partially concurrent with the one he is serving may be forever lost if trial of the pending charge is postponed. Secondly, under procedures now widely practiced, the duration of his present imprisonment may be increased, and the conditions under which he must serve his sentence greatly worsened, by the pendency of another criminal charge outstanding against him.

And while it might be argued that a person already in prison would be less likely than others to be affected by "anxiety and concern accompanying public accusation," there is reason to believe that an outstanding untried charge (of which even a convict may, of course, be innocent) can have fully as depressive an effect upon a prisoner as upon a person who is at large. * * * In the opinion of the former Director of the Federal Bureau of Prisons,

"[I]t is in their effect upon the prisoner and our attempts to rehabilitate him that detainers are most corrosive. The strain of having to serve a sentence with the uncertain prospect of being taken into the custody of another state at the conclusion interferes with the prisoner's ability to take maximum advantage of his institutional opportunities. His anxiety and depression may leave him with little inclination towards self-improvement."

Finally, it is self-evident that "the possibilities that long delay will impair the ability of an accused to defend himself" are markedly increased when the accused is incarcerated in another jurisdiction. Confined in a prison, perhaps far from the place where the offense covered by the outstanding charge allegedly took place, his ability to confer with potential defense witnesses, or even to keep track of their whereabouts, is obviously impaired. And, while "evidence and witnesses disappear, memories fade, and events lose their perspective," a man isolated in prison is powerless to exert his own investigative efforts to mitigate these erosive effects of the passage of time.

Despite all these considerations, the Texas Supreme Court has said that the State is under no duty even to attempt to bring a man in the petitioner's position to trial, because "[t]he question is one of power and authority and is in no way dependent upon how or in what manner the federal sovereignty may proceed in a discretionary way under the doctrine of comity." [11] Yet Texas concedes that if it did make an effort to secure a federal prisoner's appearance, he would, in fact, "be produced for trial in the state court." This is fully confirmed by the brief that the Solicitor General has filed in the present case:

"[T]he Bureau of Prisons would doubtless have made the prisoner available if a writ of habeas corpus *ad prosequendum* had been issued by the state court. It does not appear, however, that the State at any point sought to initiate that procedure in this case."[13]

In view of these realities, we think the Texas court was mistaken in allowing doctrinaire concepts of "power" and "authority" to submerge the practical demands of the constitutional right to a speedy trial. Indeed, the rationale upon which the Texas Supreme Court based its denial of relief in this case was wholly undercut last Term in *Barber v. Page,* 390 U.S. 719, 88 S.Ct. 1318, 20 L.Ed.2d 255 [1968]. In that case we dealt with another Sixth Amendment guarantee—the right of confrontation. In holding that Oklahoma could not excuse its failure to produce a prosecution witness simply because he was in a federal prison outside the State, we said: * * *

11. *Cooper v. State,* 400 S.W.2d 890, 892 [1966]. The only other basis suggested by the Texas Supreme Court for its denial of relief in *Cooper* was the expense that would be involved in bringing a federal prisoner to trial, the court noting that a directive of the Federal Bureau of Prisons provided that "satisfactory arrangements for payment of expenses [must be] made before the prisoner is actually removed to the place of trial." But the expense involved in effectuating an occasional writ of habeas corpus *ad prosequendum* would hardly be comparable to what is required to implement other constitutional rights, e.g., the appointment of counsel for every indigent defendant. *Gideon v. Wainwright* [p. 61 supra]. And custodial as well as transportation expenses would also be incurred if the State brought the petitioner to trial after his federal sentence had run. If the petitioner is, as the State maintains, not an indigent, there is nothing to prevent a fair assessment of necessary expenses against him. Finally, the short and perhaps the best answer to any objection based upon expense was given by the Supreme Court of Wisconsin in a case much like the present one: "We will not put a price tag upon constitutional rights." *State ex rel. Fredenberg v. Byrne,* 20 Wis. 2d 504, 512, 123 N.W.2d 305, 310 [1963].

13. That brief also states:

"It is the policy of the United States Bureau of Prisons to encourage the expeditious disposition of prosecutions in state courts against federal prisoners. The normal procedure under which production is effected is pursuant to a writ *ad prosequendum* from the state court. Almost invariably, the United States has complied with such writs and extended its cooperation to the state authorities. The Bureau of Prisons informs us that removals are normally made by United States marshals, with the expenses borne by the state authorities. In some instances, to mitigate the cost to the State, the Bureau of Prisons has removed an inmate to a federal facility close to the site of prosecution. In a relatively small number of instances, prisoners have been produced pursuant to 18 U.S.C. § 4085, which provides in part:

"Whenever any federal prisoner has been indicted, informed against, or convicted of a felony in a court of record of any State or the District of Columbia, the Attorney General shall, if he finds it in the public interest to do so, upon the request of the Governor or the executive authority thereof, and upon the presentation of a certified copy of such indictment, information or judgment of conviction, cause such a person, prior to his release, to be transferred to a penal or correctional institution within such State or District."

"The Court of Appeals majority appears to have reasoned that because the State would have had to request an exercise of discretion on the part of federal authorities, it was under no obligation to make any such request. Yet as Judge Aldrich, sitting by designation, pointed out in dissent below, 'the possibility of a refusal is not the equivalent of asking and receiving a rebuff.' In short, a witness is not 'unavailable' for purposes of the foregoing exception to the confrontation requirement unless the prosecutorial authorities have made a good-faith effort to obtain his presence at trial. The State made no such effort here, and, so far as this record reveals, the sole reason why Woods was not present to testify in person was because the State did not attempt to seek his presence. The right of confrontation may not be dispensed with so lightly."

By a parity of reasoning we hold today that the Sixth Amendment right to a speedy trial may not be dispensed with so lightly either. Upon the petitioner's demand, Texas had a constitutional duty to make a diligent, good-faith effort to bring him before the Harris County court for trial. * * * [a]

Notes and Questions

1. *Detainers and their use.* A detainer, or hold order, may be filed by a prosecutor, court, police chief or any other official empowered to take persons into custody, and it need not be supported by an indictment or information. A detainer notifies the incarcerating authorities that the prisoner is wanted, and requests that the authorities desiring custody be forewarned of the prisoner's release date so they can arrange to pick him up at the institution. Filing a detainer is an informal process; it does not bind the requesting authority to act (and roughly one-half are never acted upon), nor does it bind the incarcerating authorities to hold the prisoner, although this is usually done as a matter of comity between sovereigns.

The existence of a detainer may have several adverse effects upon the prisoner. He may, for that reason, be held under maximum security or be denied opportunities open to other prisoners, such as transfer to a minimum security area, the privilege of being a trusty, or assignment to a job involving a degree of trust. The detainer makes the prisoner's future uncertain, and thus renders more difficult the formulation of an effective rehabilitation program. Many parole boards will not consider parole for a prisoner who has a detainer lodged against him, although some jurisdictions are now using the parole-to-detainer device, which allows release of the detainee while he serves another sentence or answers other charges.[a]

2. *Provisions on transfer of custody for trial.* (a) *intrastate.* The Uniform Mandatory Disposition of Detainer Act, 11 U.L.A. 328 (1974) adopted in seven states, provides that custodial officials must advise prisoners of detainers lodged against them, and establishes procedures whereby the prisoner may demand trial. Upon receipt of such a request, the charge must be tried within a fixed period of time or it is thereafter barred. Several other states have adopted similar provisions.

(b) *interstate.* The Uniform Criminal Extradition Act, 11 U.L.A. 59 (1974), adopted in almost all states, provides in § 5: "When it is desired to have returned to this state a person charged in this state with a crime, and such person is imprisoned or is held under criminal proceedings then pending against him in another state, the Governor of this state may agree with the Executive Authority of such other state for the extradition of such person before the conclusion of such proceedings or his term of sentence in such other state, upon condition that such person be returned to such other state at the expense

a. The separate opinions of Black, White, and Harlan, JJ., have been omitted.

a. See Abramson, *Criminal Detainers* (1979).

of this state as soon as the prosecution in this state is terminated." In addition, virtually all states have adopted the Interstate Agreement on Detainers, which appears at 11 U.L.A. 323 (1974). Under this Compact, the prisoner against whom a detainer has been filed must be promptly notified of that fact and of his right to demand trial, and if he demands trial then trial must be had within 180 days thereafter. Problems of extradition are avoided, as the incarcerating state, by adopting the Compact, agrees to surrender temporary custody, and the prisoner automatically waives extradition by requesting trial. If trial is not had within 180 days and good cause for delay is not shown, the charges are dismissed with prejudice.

(c) *federal prisoner, state charge.* See 18 U.S.C. § 4085, quoted in fn. 13 of *Smith v. Hooey.*

3. In light of *Smith v. Hooey,* just how should the right of speedy trial for those in prison be defined? What are the relevant considerations, in addition to the three "basic demands" listed by the Court? Consider:

(a) *detainer or no detainer.* Is the important thing whether a detainer has been filed? *A.B.A. Standards,* § 12–3.1 provides that "if the prosecuting attorney knows that a person charged with a criminal offense is serving a term of imprisonment in a penal institution of that or another jurisdiction, he or she must promptly: (i) undertake to obtain the presence of the prisoner for trial; or (ii) cause a detainer to be filed with the official having custody of the prisoner and request the official to so advise the prisoner and to advise the prisoner of his or her right to demand trial." The commentary to this section notes that "[s]uch a requirement is appropriate, for otherwise the prisoner's right to speedy trial could be circumvented by delay on the part of the prosecutor in lodging a detainer against the prisoner." Under the Interstate Agreement, the prosecutor may refrain from lodging a detainer and thereby not give rise to the situation whereby the prisoner may demand trial.

(b) *prosecutor's knowledge of prisoner's whereabouts.* The *A.B.A. Standards* provision quoted above is limited to those cases in which the prosecutor knows of the prisoner's whereabouts. Should there be such a limitation? "[T]he extensive national system of reporting wanted persons and convicts gives the jurisdiction access to knowledge of convicts' whereabouts. A flat rule that the jurisdiction has constructive notice at the time the accused begins serving his sentence would properly put the burden of improving this system on the jurisdictions which have the power to modify it. If the right to speedy trial began only when the accusing jurisdiction had actual notice, the defendant would face the almost impossible task of refuting the state's claim that it had no knowledge of his whereabouts." Note, 77 Yale L.J. 767, 777 (1968).

(c) *lack of demand by prisoner.* The prisoner need not demand trial to "trigger" his right to a speedy trial if he has not been adequately apprised of the fact that charges are outstanding against him. But, what if the prisoner knows he may demand trial but does not do so? It has been argued that even under these circumstances the prosecutor should be obliged to seek the prisoner's presence for trial, though such a change "would deny prisoners an opportunity to gamble that detainers may be lifted and charges dropped prior to expiration of their terms. But it is not clear that they should have this opportunity, and its loss would seem a small price to pay for the preservation of speedy trial without reliance on the prisoner's own efforts * * *." Comment, 31 U.Chi.L. Rev. 535, 554–55 (1964).

(d) *refusal of incarcerating jurisdiction to transfer prisoner.* Even in those states which prior to *Smith v. Hooey* had ruled that the prosecutor must attempt (at least upon the prisoner's demand) to bring the prisoner back from another jurisdiction, it was accepted that the prisoner's right to a speedy trial is not violated if such an attempt is made but the incarcerating jurisdiction refuses to transfer the prisoner. See, e.g., *People v. South,* 10 P.2d 109 (Cal. App.1932). Why should this be so? It has been argued that a contrary rule would "provide an incentive for the incarcerating jurisdiction to yield temporary custody of the defendant. Refusal will no longer mean simply a delayed trial in the requesting jurisdiction; it will mean dismissal of the charges. A refusing jurisdiction will have to fear retaliatory refusals in the future by the requesting jurisdiction." Note, 77 Yale L.J. 767, 778–79 (1968).

(e) *negligence or oversight by incarcerating officials.* Who should bear the burden of negligence or oversight by officials of the incarcerating state, as where a prosecutor in another jurisdiction has filed a detainer, but the warden fails to call it to the attention of the prisoner or else receives the prisoner's demand for trial but fails to send it back to the prosecutor? See, e.g., *Rhodes v. Schoen,* 574 F.2d 968 (8th Cir. 1978).

4. As to the availability of federal habeas corpus for a prisoner in state *A* against whom a detainer has been lodged by state *B,* see *Braden v. 30th Judicial Circuit Court,* 410 U.S. 484, 93 S.Ct. 1123, 35 L.Ed.2d 443 (1973), and Note 3, p. 1469 infra.

SECTION 3. THE RIGHT TO OTHER SPEEDY DISPOSITION

UNITED STATES v. LOVASCO

431 U.S. 783, 97 S.Ct. 2044, 52 L.Ed.2d 752 (1977).

MR. JUSTICE MARSHALL delivered the opinion of the Court. * * *

On March 6, 1975, respondent was indicted for possessing eight firearms stolen from the United States mail, and for dealing in firearms without a license. The offenses were alleged to have occurred between July 25 and August 31, 1973, more than 18 months before the indictment was filed. Respondent moved to dismiss the indictment due to the delay.

The District Court conducted a hearing on respondent's motion at which the respondent sought to prove that the delay was unnecessary and that it had prejudiced his defense. In an effort to establish the former proposition, respondent presented a Postal Inspector's report on his investigation that was prepared one month after the crimes were committed, and a stipulation concerning the post-report progress of the probe. The report stated, in brief, that within the first month of the investigation respondent had admitted to Government agents that he had possessed and then sold five of the stolen guns, and that the agents had developed strong evidence linking respondent to the remaining three weapons.[1] The report also stated, however, that the agents had been unable to confirm or refute respondent's claim that he had found the guns in his car when he returned to it after visiting his son, a mail handler, at work. The stipulation into which the Assistant United States Attorney entered indicated that little additional information concerning the crimes was uncovered in the 17 months following the preparation of the Inspector's report.

To establish prejudice to the defense, respondent testified that he had lost the testimony of two material witnesses due to the delay. The first witness, Tom Stewart, died more than a year after the alleged crimes occurred. At the hearing respondent claimed that Stewart had been his

1. The report indicated that the person to whom respondent admitted selling five guns had told Government agents that respondent had actually sold him eight guns which he, in turn, had sold to one Martin Koehnken. The report also indicated that Koehnken had sold three of these guns to undercover federal agents and that a search of his house had uncovered four others. Finally the report stated that the eighth gun was sold by one David Northdruft to Government agents, and that Northdruft claimed Koehnken had sold him the gun.

At the hearing on the motion to dismiss, respondent for the first time admitted that he had possessed and sold eight guns.

source for two or three of the guns. The second witness, respondent's brother, died in April 1974, nine months after the crimes were completed. Respondent testified that his brother was present when respondent called Stewart to secure the guns, and witnessed all of respondent's sales. Respondent did not state how the witnesses would have aided the defense had they been willing to testify.[4]

The Government made no systematic effort in the District Court to explain its long delay. The Assistant United States Attorney did expressly disagree, however, with defense counsel's suggestion that the investigation had ended after the Postal Inspector's Report was prepared. The prosecutor also stated that it was the Government's theory that respondent's son, who had access to the mail at the railroad terminal from which the guns were "possibly stolen," was responsible for the thefts. Finally, the prosecutor elicited somewhat cryptic testimony from the Postal Inspector indicating that the case "as to these particular weapons involves other individuals"; that information had been presented to a grand jury "in regard to this case other than . . . [on] the day of the indictment itself"; and that he had spoken to the prosecutors about the case on four or five occasions.

Following the hearing, the District Court filed a brief opinion and order. The court found that by October 2, 1973, the date of the postal inspector's report, "The Government had all the information relating to defendant's alleged commission of the offense charged against him," and that the 17-month delay before the case was presented to the grand jury "had not been explained or justified" and was "unnecessary and unreasonable." The Court also found that "[a]s a result of the delay defendant has been prejudiced by reason of the death of Tom Stewart, a material witness on his behalf." Accordingly, the court dismissed the indictment.

The Government appealed to the United States Court of Appeals for the Eighth Circuit. In its brief the Government explained the months of inaction by stating:

> "[T]here was a legitimate Government interest in keeping the investigation open in the instant case. The defendant's son worked for the Terminal Railroad and had access to mail. It was the Government's position that the son was responsible for the theft and therefore further investigation to establish this fact was important.
>
> ". . . Although the investigation did not continue on a full time basis, there was contact between the United States Attorney's office and the Postal Inspector's office throughout . . . and certain matters were brought before a Federal Grand Jury prior to the determination that the case should be presented for indictment . . . ."

The Court of Appeals accepted the Government's representation as to the motivation for the delay, but a majority of the court nevertheless affirmed the District Court's finding that the Government's actions were "unjustified, unnecessary, and unreasonable." The majority also found that respondent had established that his defense had been impaired by the loss of Stewart's testimony because it understood respondent to contend that "were Stewart's testimony available it would support [respondent's] claim that he did not know that the guns were stolen from the United States mails." * * *

We granted certiorari, and now reverse.[7]

4. Respondent admitted that he had not mentioned Stewart to the Postal Inspector when he was questioned about his source of the guns. He explained that this was because Stewart "was a bad tomato" and "was liable to take a shot at me if I told [on] him." Respondent also conceded that he did not mention either his brother's or Stewart's illness or death to the Postal Inspector on the several occasions in which respondent called the Inspector to inquire about the status of the probe.

7. In addition to challenging the Court of Appeals' holding on the constitutional issue, the

In *United States v. Marion,* 404 U.S. 307, 92 S.Ct. 455, 30 L.Ed.2d 468 (1971), this Court considered the significance, for constitutional purposes, of a lengthy preindictment delay. We held that as far as the Speedy Trial Clause of the Sixth Amendment is concerned, such delay is wholly irrelevant, since our analysis of the language, history, and purposes of the Clause persuaded us that only "a formal indictment or information or else the actual restraints imposed by arrest and holding to answer a criminal charge . . . engage the particular protections" of that provision. We went on to note that statutes of limitations, which provide predictable, legislatively enacted limits on prosecutorial delay, provide "the primary guarantee, against bringing overly stale criminal charges." [a] But we did acknowledge that the "statute of limitations does not fully define [defendants'] rights with respect to the events occurring prior to indictment," and that the Due Process Clause has a limited role to play in protecting against oppressive delay.

Respondent seems to argue that due process bars prosecution whenever a defendant suffers prejudice as a result of preindictment delay. To support that proposition respondent relies on the concluding sentence of the Court's opinion in *Marion* where, in remanding the case, we stated that "[e]vents of the trial may demonstrate actual prejudice, but at the present time appellees' due process claims are speculative and premature." But the quoted sentence establishes only that proof of actual prejudice makes a due process claim concrete and ripe for adjudication, not that it makes the claim automatically valid. Indeed, two pages earlier in the opinion we expressly rejected the argument respondent advances here:

> "[W]e need not . . . determine when and in what circumstances actual prejudice resulting from preaccusation delay requires the dismissal of the prosecution. Actual prejudice to the defense of a criminal case may result from the shortest and most necessary delay; and no one suggests that every delay-caused detriment to a defendant's case should abort a criminal prosecution."

Thus *Marion* makes clear that proof of prejudice is generally a necessary but not sufficient element of a due process claim, and that the due process inquiry must consider the reasons for the delay as well as the prejudice to the accused.

United States argues that the District Court should have deferred action on the motion to dismiss until after trial, at which time it could have assessed any prejudice to the respondent in light of the events at trial. This argument, however, was not raised in the District Court or in the Court of Appeals. Absent exceptional circumstances, we will not review it here. * * *

a. The statute of limitations, in contrast to the speedy trial time limitations, runs from the date the offense is committed (or, in a few states, from the date the offense is discovered) to the date prosecution is commenced (in some states this means the date an indictment or information is filed, in others the date a warrant of arrest is issued). The typical statute specifies situations in which time is not counted against the period of limitation, such as when the defendant is out of the state or is away from his usual residence for the purpose of avoiding prosecution. "There are several reasons for the imposition of time limitations: First, and foremost, is the desirability that prosecutions be based upon reasonably fresh evidence. With the passage of time memories fade, witnesses die or leave the area, and physical evidence becomes more difficult to obtain, identify, or preserve. In short, possibility of erroneous conviction is minimized when prosecution is prompt. Second, if the actor long refrains from further criminal activity, the likelihood increases that he has reformed, diminishing the necessity for imposition of the criminal sanction. If he has repeated his criminal behavior, he can be prosecuted for recent offenses committed within the period of limitation. Hence, the need for protecting society against the perpetrator of a particular offense becomes less compelling as the years pass. Third, after a protracted period the retributive impulse which may have existed in the community is likely to yield to a sense of compassion aroused by the prosecution for an offense long forgotten. Fourth, it is desirable to reduce the possibility of blackmail based on a threat to prosecute or to disclose evidence to enforcement officials. Finally, statutes of limitations 'promote repose by giving security and stability to human affairs.'" *Model Penal Code* § 1.06, Comment (1985).

The Court of Appeals found that the sole reason for the delay here was "a hope on the part of the Government that others might be discovered who may have participated in the theft . . . ." It concluded that this hope did not justify the delay, and therefore affirmed the dismissal of the indictment. But the Due Process Clause does not permit courts to abort criminal prosecutions simply because they disagree with a prosecutor's judgment as to when to seek an indictment. Judges are not free, in defining "due process," to impose on law enforcement officials our "personal and private notions" of fairness and to "disregard the limits that bind judges in their judicial function." Our task is more circumscribed. We are to determine only whether the actions complained of—here, compelling respondent to stand trial after the Government delayed indictment to investigate further—violates those "fundamental conceptions of justice which lie at the base of our civil and political institutions," and which define "the community's sense of fair play and decency."

It requires no extended argument to establish that prosecutors do not deviate from "fundamental conceptions of justice" when they defer seeking indictments until they have probable cause to believe an accused is guilty; indeed it is unprofessional conduct for a prosecutor to recommend an indictment on less than probable cause. It should be equally obvious that prosecutors are under no duty to file charges as soon as probable cause exists but before they are satisfied they will be able to establish the suspect's guilt beyond a reasonable doubt. To impose such a duty "would have a deleterious effect both upon the rights of the accused and upon the ability of society to protect itself." From the perspective of potential defendants, requiring prosecutions to commence when probable cause is established is undesirable because it would increase the likelihood of unwarranted charges being filed, and would add to the time during which defendants stand accused but untried. * * * From the perspective of law enforcement officials, a requirement of immediate prosecution upon probable cause is equally unacceptable because it could make obtaining proof of guilt beyond a reasonable doubt impossible by causing potentially fruitful sources of information to evaporate before they are fully exploited. And from the standpoint of the courts, such a requirement is unwise because it would cause scarce resources to be consumed on cases that prove to be insubstantial, or that involve only some of the responsible parties or some of the criminal acts.[12] Thus, no one's interests would be well served by compelling prosecutors to initiate prosecutions as soon as they are legally entitled to do so.

It might be argued that once the Government has assembled sufficient evidence to prove guilt beyond a reasonable doubt, it should be constitutionally required to file charges promptly, even if its investigation of the entire criminal transaction is not complete. Adopting such a rule, however, would have many of the same consequences as adopting a rule requiring immediate prosecution upon probable cause.

First, compelling a prosecutor to file public charges as soon as the requisite proof has been developed against one participant on one charge would cause numerous problems in those cases in which a criminal transaction involves more than one person or more than one illegal act. In some instances, an immediate arrest or indictment would impair the prosecutor's ability to continue his investigation, thereby preventing society from bringing lawbreakers to justice. In other cases, the prosecutor would be able to obtain additional indictments despite an early prosecution, but the necessary result would be multiple trials involving a single set of

12. Defendants also would be adversely affected by trials involving less than all of the criminal acts for which they are responsible, since they likely would be subjected to multiple trials growing out of the same transaction or occurrence.

facts. Such trials place needless burdens on defendants, law enforcement officials, and courts.

Second, insisting on immediate prosecution once sufficient evidence is developed to obtain a conviction would pressure prosecutors into resolving doubtful cases in favor of early—and possibly unwarranted—prosecutions. The determination of when the evidence available to the prosecution is sufficient to obtain a conviction is seldom clear-cut, and reasonable persons often will reach conflicting conclusions. In the instant case, for example, since respondent admitted possessing at least five of the firearms, the primary factual issue in dispute was whether respondent knew the guns were stolen as required by 18 U.S.C. § 1708. Not surprisingly, the Postal Inspector's report contained no direct evidence bearing on this issue. The decision whether to prosecute, therefore, required a necessarily subjective evaluation of the strength of the circumstantial evidence available and the credibility of respondent's denial. Even if a prosecutor concluded that the case was weak and further investigation appropriate, he would have no assurance that a reviewing court would agree. To avoid the risk that a subsequent indictment would be dismissed for preindictment delay, the prosecutor might feel constrained to file premature charges with all the disadvantages that entails.[14]

Finally, requiring the Government to make charging decisions immediately upon assembling evidence sufficient to establish guilt would preclude the Government from giving full consideration to the desirability of not prosecuting in particular cases. The decision to file criminal charges, with the awesome consequences it entails, requires consideration of a wide range of factors in addition to the strength of the Government's case, in order to determine whether prosecution would be in the public interest. Prosecutors often need more information than proof of a suspect's guilt, therefore, before deciding whether to seek an indictment. Again the instant case provides a useful illustration. Although proof of the identity of the mail thieves was not necessary to convict respondent of the possessory crimes with which he was charged, it might have been crucial in assessing respondent's culpability, as distinguished from his legal guilt. If, for example, further investigation were to show that respondent had no role in or advance knowledge of the theft and simply agreed, out of paternal loyalty, to help his son dispose of the guns once respondent discovered his son had stolen them, the United States Attorney might have decided not to prosecute, especially since at the time of the crime respondent was over 60 years old and had no prior criminal record.[16] Requiring prosecution once the evidence of guilt is clear, however, could prevent a prosecutor from awaiting the information necessary for such a decision.

We would be most reluctant to adopt a rule which would have these consequences absent a clear constitutional command to do so. We can find no such command in the Due Process Clause of the Fifth Amendment. In our view, investigative delay is fundamentally unlike delay undertaken by the Government solely "to gain tactical advantage over the accused," precisely because investigative delay is not so one-sided.[17] Rather than deviating from

14. In addition, if courts were required to decide in every case when the prosecution should have commenced, it would be necessary for them to trace the day-by-day progress of each investigation. Maintaining daily records would impose an administrative burden on prosecutors, and reviewing them would place an even greater burden on the courts.

16. Of course, in this case further investigation proved unavailing and the United States Attorney ultimately decided to prosecute based solely on the Inspector's report. But this fortuity cannot transform an otherwise permissible delay into an impermissible one.

17. In *Marion* we noted with approval that the Government conceded that a "tactical" delay would violate the Due Process Clause. The Government renews that concession here, and expands it somewhat by stating that "A due process violation might also be made out upon a showing elementary standards of "fair play and decency," a prosecutor abides by them if he refuses to seek indictments until he is completely satisfied that he should prosecute and will be able promptly to establish guilt beyond a reasonable doubt. Penalizing prosecutors who defer action for these reasons would subordinate the goal of "orderly expedition" to that of "mere speed." This the Due Process Clause does not require. We therefore hold that to prosecute a defendant following investigative delay does not deprive him of due process, even if his defense might have been somewhat prejudiced by the lapse of time.

In the present case, the Court of Appeals stated that the only reason the Government postponed action was to await the results of additional investigation. Although there is, unfortunately, no evidence concerning the reasons for the delay in the record, the court's "finding" is supported by the prosecutor's implicit representation to the District Court, and explicit representation to the Court of Appeals, that the investigation continued during the time that the Government deferred taking action against respondent. The finding is, moreover, buttressed by the Government's repeated assertions in their Petition for Certiorari, their Brief, and their oral argument in this Court, "that the delay was caused by the Government's efforts to identify persons in addition to respondent who may have participated in the offenses." We must assume that these statements by counsel have been made in good faith. In light of this explanation, it follows that compelling respondent to stand trial would not be fundamentally unfair. The Court of Appeals therefore erred in affirming the District Court's decision dismissing the indictment.

In *Marion* we conceded that we could not determine in the abstract the circumstances in which preaccusation delay would require dismissing prosecutions. More than five years later, that statement remains true. Indeed, in the intervening years so few defendants have established that they were prejudiced by delay that neither this Court nor any lower court has had a sustained opportunity to consider the constitutional significance of various reasons for delay.[19] We therefore leave to the lower courts, in the first instance, the task of applying the settled principles of due process that we have discussed to the particular circumstances of individual cases. We simply hold that in this case the lower courts erred in dismissing the indictment.[b]

of prosecutorial delay incurred in reckless disregard of circumstances, known to the prosecution, suggesting that there existed an appreciable risk that delay would impair the ability to mount an effective defense." As the Government notes, however, there is no evidence of recklessness here.

19. Professor Amsterdam has catalogued some of the noninvestigative reasons for delay:

"[P]roof of the offense may depend upon the testimony of an undercover informer who maintains his 'cover' for a period of time before surfacing to file charges against one or more persons with whom he has dealt while disguised. . . . [I]f there is more than one possible charge against a suspect, some of them may be held back pending the disposition of others in order to avoid the burden upon the prosecutor's office of handling charges that may turn out to be unnecessary to obtain the degree of punishment that the prosecutor seeks. There are many other motives for delay, of course, including sinister ones, such as a desire to postpone the beginning of defense investigation or the wish to hold a 'club' over the defendant.

"Additional reasons for delay may be partly or completely beyond the control of the prosecuting authorities. Offenses may not be immediately reported; investigation may not immediately identify the offender; an identified offender may not be immediately apprehendable. . . . [A]n indictment may be delayed for weeks or even months until the impaneling of the next grand jury. It is customary to think of these delays as natural and inevitable . . . but various prosecutorial decisions—such as the assignment of manpower and priorities among investigations of known offenses—may also affect the length of such delays." Amsterdam, *Speedy Criminal Trial: Rights and Remedies,* 27 Stan.L.Rev. 525, 527–528 (1975).

b. Stevens, J., dissenting, agreed with the foregoing principles, but concluded the majority had erred in not deciding the case on the record made in the district court, wherein the government's delay was unexplained.

Notes and Questions

1. *Marion* was also relied upon in UNITED STATES v. MacDONALD, 456 U.S. 1, 102 S.Ct. 1497, 71 L.Ed.2d 696 (1982), holding that the time between dismissal of military charges and the subsequent indictment on civilian charges may not be considered in determining whether the delay in bringing the defendant to trial violated his Sixth Amendment right to speedy trial. BURGER, C.J., stated for the Court:

"Once charges are dismissed, the speedy trial guarantee is no longer applicable.[8] At that point, the formerly accused is, at most, in the same position as any other subject of a criminal investigation. Certainly the knowledge of an ongoing criminal investigation will cause stress, discomfort and perhaps a certain disruption in normal life. This is true whether or not charges have been filed and then dismissed. This was true in *Marion,* where the defendants had been subjected to a lengthy investigation which received considerable press attention. But with no charges outstanding, personal liberty is certainly not impaired to the same degree as it is after arrest while charges are pending. After the charges against him have been dismissed, 'a citizen suffers no restraints on his liberty and is [no longer] the subject of public accusation: his situation does not compare with that of a defendant who has been arrested and held to answer.' *United States v. Marion.* Following dismissal of charges, any restraint on liberty, disruption of employment, strain on financial resources, and exposure to public obloquy, stress and anxiety is no greater than it is upon anyone openly subject to a criminal investigation."

Four members of the Court[c] found that conclusion to be "inconsistent with the language and policies of the Speedy Trial Clause and with this Court's decisions," such as *Klopfer,* said to teach "that the anxiety suffered by an accused person, even after the initial prosecution has terminated and after he has been discharged from custody, warrants application of the speedy trial protection." They added that the majority's conclusion was "also senseless" because "[a]ny legitimate government reason for delay during the period between prosecutions can, indeed must, be weighed when a court determines whether the defendant's speedy trial right has been violated. No purpose is served by simply ignoring that period for speedy trial purposes."

2. In *People v. Lawson,* 367 N.E.2d 1244 (Ill.1977), decided a few days before *Lovasco,* the court stated:

"Although the various cases vary on the manner of the determination of prejudice due to preindictment delay, we agree that a delicate judgment by the trial court is necessitated, whether engaged in before, during, or after trial. Where there has been a delay between an alleged crime and indictment or arrest or accusation, the defendant must come forward with a clear showing of actual *and* substantial prejudice. Mere assertion of inability to recall is insufficient. If the accused satisfies the trial court that he or she has been substantially prejudiced by the delay, then the burden shifts to the State to show the reasonableness, if not the necessity, of the delay.

8. *Klopfer v. North Carolina* [p. 1082 supra], is not to the contrary. There, under an unusual state procedure, a prosecutor was able to suspend proceedings on an indictment indefinitely. The prosecutor could activate the charges at any time and have the case restored for trial, "without further order" of the court. The charges against the defendant were thus never dismissed or discharged in any real sense so the speedy trial guarantee continued to apply.

c. Marshall, J., joined by Brennan and Blackmun, JJ., dissenting, took a different view of the scope of the Sixth Amendment speedy trial protection and then, applying the four factors from *Barker,* concluded that MacDonald's speedy trial rights were violated. Stevens, J., concurring, agreed with the dissenters' scope analysis but disagreed with their application of the *Barker* factors.

"If this two-step process ascertains both substantial prejudice and reasonableness of a delay, then the court must make a determination based upon a balancing of the interests of the defendant and the public. Factors the court should consider, among others, are the length of the delay and the seriousness of the crime."

The supplemental opinion on denial of rehearing states in part: "The State, in its petition for rehearing, suggests that *Lovasco* establishes a more restrictive standard for the determination of a due process violation, the result of prejudice from preindictment delay, than does our decision in this case. We do not read *Lovasco* quite so narrowly. The State apparently believes prejudice and unreasonableness of the delay are two elements which must be proved by the defendant to establish a due process claim. We, of course, do not require that—nor does *Lovasco.*"

3. In *United States v. Moran,* 759 F.2d 777 (9th Cir.1985), the court stated:

"The government asserts that certain language from *United States v. Marion* and *Lovasco* * * * requires that the defendant prove either intentional or reckless conduct on the part of the government. We reject this contention. The language from these two cases merely acknowledges governmental concessions that intentional or reckless conduct would or might be considered violations of the due process clause if actual prejudice had been shown. The *Lovasco* court did not set out intent or recklessness as required standards of fault. * * *

"The determination of whether a preindictment delay has violated due process is essentially decided under a balancing test, and we do not find that intent or reckless behavior by the government is an essential ingredient in the mix. If mere negligent conduct by the prosecutors is asserted, then obviously the delay and/or prejudice suffered by the defendant will have to be greater than that in cases where recklessness or intentional governmental conduct is alleged."

Looking to the facts of the particular case, the *Moran* court held the district judge had erred in dismissing certain charges. The court expressed doubt as to whether defendant had met his "heavy burden to prove that a pre-indictment delay caused actual prejudice." Defendant showed that five of his witnesses had died or were now out of the country, but the court said it was a "close question" whether this was sufficient, as "protection from lost testimony generally falls solely within the ambit of the statute of limitations." But the court grounded its reversal on the fact that defendant had not met his burden of making "some showing of government culpability."

4. As to what other steps in the criminal process should the defendant have a constitutional right to speedy disposition? What about a right to "speedy judgment" when a criminal case is tried before a judge? See *Campodonico v. United States,* 222 F.2d 310 (9th Cir.1955). To "speedy sentencing"? See *People v. Drake,* 462 N.E.2d 376 (N.Y.1984) To a "speedy appeal"? See *State v. Hall,* 487 A.2d 166 (Vt.1984). To a "speedy probation revocation proceeding"? See *Fariss v. Tipps,* 463 S.W.2d 176 (Tex.1971). To a "speedy parole revocation proceeding"? See *Morrissey v. Brewer,* p. 88 supra, and compare *Moody v. Daggett,* 429 U.S. 78, 97 S.Ct. 274, 50 L.Ed.2d 236 (1976), where the Court, per Burger, C.J., held that a federal parolee imprisoned for a crime committed while on parole was not constitutionally entitled to a prompt parole revocation hearing when a parole violator warrant was issued and lodged with the institution of his confinement but not served on him. The Court stressed that his present confinement did not derive from the warrant, that the warrant did not diminish his opportunity for parole on the intervening sentence, and that it would be more appropriate to hold the revocation hearing at the expiration of the interven-

ing sentence because at that time a more relevant and accurate prediction of the parolee's ability to live at large in a law-abiding way can be made. Stevens and Brennan, JJ., dissenting, concluded that the reasoning of *Smith v. Hooey,* p. 1093 supra, dictated a contrary result.

5. United States Customs officials seized $8,850 in currency from the claimant as she entered the country, but the government delayed for 18 months the filing of a civil proceeding for forfeiture of the money. When the claimant asserted that this delay violated her Fifth Amendment right against deprivation of property without due process, the government responded that this issue should be resolved under the *Lovasco* due process standard and not the *Barker* criminal trial standard. But in *United States v. Eight Thousand Eight Hundred and Fifty Dollars,* 461 U.S. 555, 103 S.Ct. 2005, 76 L.Ed.2d 143 (1983), the Court, per O'Connor, J., concluded that *Barker* provided "a more apt analogy." The Court reasoned that a person who "has been entirely deprived of the use of the property" seized is in a situation more comparable to the charged defendant who "no longer retains his complete liberty" than to the uncharged suspect who "retains his liberty." Applying the *Barker* balancing test to the relevant facts, the Court then concluded there had been no constitutional violation.[d]

d. Stevens, J., dissenting, argued that "a rule that allows the Government to dispossess a citizen of her property for more than 18 months without her consent and without a hearing is a flagrant violation of the Fifth Amendment."

Part Four

THE ADVERSARY SYSTEM AND THE DETERMINATION OF GUILT

Analysis

Chapter 20

DISCOVERY AND DISCLOSURE

SECTION 1. PRETRIAL DISCOVERY BY THE DEFENSE

I. THE GREAT DEBATE

During the 1930's and 1940's, courts and legislatures dramatically altered the pretrial discovery process in civil cases. By providing for depositions, interrogatories, requests for admissions, and the compulsory production of documents and other tangible items, they gave each side in a civil case pretrial access to almost all relevant information possessed by the opposing party. The success of this liberalization of civil discovery naturally led legislatures and courts to consider similarly expanding pretrial discovery in criminal cases. There followed during the 50's and 60's one of the classic debates in the field of criminal procedure. Since prosecution discovery from the defense was thought to be largely prohibited by the defendant's privilege against self-incrimination, the focus of the debate was primarily upon liberalizing defense discovery from the prosecution. Today the issues raised in that discovery debate have been largely resolved in each jurisdiction by court rules or statutes providing either limited or expansive defense discovery. An understanding of the policy considerations raised in the debate remains of critical significance however, as those considerations furnish an important guidepost to the interpretation of current discovery provisions. Indeed those policy considerations are cited not only in opinions interpreting defense discovery provisions, but also in opinions interpreting provisions governing prosecution discovery from the defense. See, e.g., *People v. District Court,* 531 P.2d 626 (Colo.1975). Two of the foremost entries in the discovery debate of the 50's and 60's are set forth below. For others, see the citations in LaFave and Israel, § 19.3(a).

VANDERBILT, C.J.—MAJORITY OPINION IN STATE v. TUNE [a]

98 A.2d 881 (N.J.1953).

Defendant argues that in keeping with the modern trend toward liberal discovery in civil proceedings we should grant him the unqualified right to an inspection of all papers and other documents in the possession of the State * * *. With this we cannot agree. Such an argument completely ignores the fundamental difference between civil and criminal proceedings. In any judicial proceedings, civil or criminal, the purpose of broad discovery is "to

a. Defendant, charged with murder, moved for pretrial discovery of his 14-page confession and any signed statements of others persons relating to the crime. The trial court granted discovery of the confession, but denied discovery of all other statements. A divided (4–3) New Jersey Supreme Court (per Vanderbilt, C.J.) reversed the order granting discovery of the confession, and affirmed that denying discovery of other statements. The dissent, by Justice Brennan, would have affirmed the trial judge's order "in its entirety."

promote the fullest possible presentation of the facts, *minimize opportunities for falsification of evidence,* and eliminate the vestiges of trial by combat," 60 Yale L.J. 626 (emphasis supplied). "Liberal procedures for discovery in preparation for trial are essential to any modern judicial system in which the search for truth in aid of justice is paramount and in which concealment and surprise are not to be tolerated." *Lang v. Morgan's Home Equipment,* 78 A.2d 705 (N.J.1951). However, such liberal fact-finding procedures are not to be used blindly where the result would be to defeat the ends of justice. In criminal proceedings long experience has taught the courts that often discovery will lead not to honest fact-finding, but on the contrary to perjury and the suppression of evidence. Thus the criminal who is aware of the whole case against him will often procure perjured testimony in order to set up a false defense.[b] Another result of full discovery would be that the criminal defendant who is informed of the names of all of the State's witnesses may take steps to bribe or frighten them into giving perjured testimony or into absenting themselves so that they are unavailable to testify. Moreover, many witnesses, if they know that the defendant will have knowledge of their names prior to trial, will be reluctant to come forward with information during the investigation of the crime. * * * All these dangers are more inherent in criminal proceedings where the defendant has much more at stake, often his own life, than in civil proceedings. * * *

In considering the problem it must be remembered that in view of the defendant's constitutional and statutory protections against self-incrimination, the State has no right whatsoever to demand an inspection of any of his documents or to take his deposition, or to submit interrogatories to him. * * * Except for its right to demand particulars from the defendants as to any alibi on which he intends to rely, Rule 2:5–7, the State is completely at the mercy of the defendant who can produce surprise evidence at the trial, can take the stand or not as he wishes, and generally can introduce any sort of unforeseeable evidence he desires in his own defense. To allow him to discover the prosecutor's whole case against him would be to make the prosecutor's task almost insurmountable.[c] * * * In *U.S. v. Garsson,* 291 F. 646, 649 (D.C.S.D.

b. See LaFave and Israel, § 19.3(a): "Opponents of liberal discovery * * * acknowledge that many defendants who desire to fabricate a defense will do so whether or not they are given discovery, but they contend that the danger lies in the improved quality of perjury that comes with discovery. If a defendant is aware of the state's evidence, he can carefully tailor his testimony, both to minimize conflict with the prosecution's evidence and to take advantage of the weakest point in the prosecution's evidence. For example, if a dishonest defendant learns through pretrial discovery that the prosecution can place him at the scene of the crime, he will switch his fabricated defense from alibi to a defense consistent with his presence at the scene. If he learns that the prosecution's witness saw him flee from the scene, he will know better than to testify that he was just taking a leisurely stroll. Of course, since the defendant does not testify until after the state has presented its case in chief, he will obtain some advance notice even without pretrial discovery. But pretrial defense discovery gives him far more time to skillfully plan his fabrication and thereby makes it more likely that the fabrication will be successful."

c. Consider also Flannery, *The Prosecutor's Case Against Liberal Discovery,* 33 F.R.D. 74 (1963): "A civil trial is a search for the truth by both sides. But is a criminal trial a search for the truth? As far as the Government is concerned, it certainly is, for the Government prosecutor has just as great a duty to protect the innocent as he has to prosecute the guilty. The defense lawyer, however, has no duty to reveal the truth. * * * The defense lawyer, for instance, may know that the defendant has given a completely voluntary, truthful confession; but he has a duty to suppress the truth by moving to bar the confession from evidence if there has been a short but unnecessary delay in taking the defendant before a committing magistrate. * * * There is therefore, a vast difference between a civil and criminal case in that a civil case is a search for the truth and there can be a mutual exchange of information so that the truth may be ascertained, whereas in a criminal case involving a guilty defendant, there is a one-sided search for the truth and there can be no equal exchange of information due to the very nature of the proceedings."

N.Y.1923), Judge Learned Hand in his opinion for the court stated:

"Under our criminal procedure the accused has every advantage. While the prosecution is held rigidly to the charge, he need not disclose the barest outline of his defense. He is immune from question or comment on his silence; he cannot be convicted when there is the least fair doubt in the minds of any one of the twelve. Why in addition he should in advance have the whole evidence against him to pick over at his leisure, and make his defense, fairly or foully, I have never been able to see. * * * Our dangers do not lie in too little tenderness to the accused. Our procedure has been always haunted by the ghost of the innocent man convicted. It is an unreal dream. What we need to fear is the archaic formalism and watery sentiment that obstructs, delays, and defeats the prosecution of crime." [d]

JUSTICE WILLIAM J. BRENNAN, JR.—THE CRIMINAL PROSECUTION: SPORTING EVENT OR QUEST FOR TRUTH?

1963 Wash.U.L.Q. 279, 285–88, 290–94.

I submit that we must rethink our opposition to allowing the accused criminal discovery, certainly if we are to continue to maintain that our system of criminal justice, if not favoring the accused, at least keeps the scales evenly balanced in his contest with the state. Are the scales really evenly balanced? Who are our criminal defendants? Are they people having relatives with resources capable of helping in their defense? By and large, the so-called "white collar" criminal probably does have the resources and friends to aid him in his defense. Justice is indeed well served when prosecution and defense are fairly evenly matched. But is this the situation for the vast majority of our "blue collar" defendants? Judges know that the largest percentage of these people are indigent. To put it another way, these offenders, the largest number by far of the total of all offenders, come from that section of society where conditions result in the largest crime rate. It is here also that the mentally retarded are found. * * *

Do not these less privileged of our society present the particular problem that without resources to prepare a defense, they often don't have an adequate defense? * * * Criminal discovery would be one tool whereby they would have a better chance to meet on more equal terms what the state, at its leisure and without real concern for expense, gathers to convict them.

And what of the task society puts on the shoulders of assigned counsel? * * * [W]e deny him both financial help to prepare a defense and the discovery, which if not the best, might at least provide a substitute. Moreover, the court-appointed lawyer in a criminal case usually comes to the case late, after the state has gathered

d. Judge Hand's assessment of the "balance of advantage" is sharply challenged in Abraham Goldstein's classic article, *The State and the Accused: Balance of Advantage in Criminal Procedure,* 69 Yale L.J. 1149 (1960). Professor Goldstein reasoned that (1) the protection of the reasonable doubt standard had been undercut by its "removal" from the "legal test of the sufficiency of the evidence" applied by the judge in determining whether a case could go to the jury [see Note 1, p. 1369 infra]; (2) that the movement toward looseness in pleading, the allowance of substantial variance in proof, and the unavailability of substantial pretrial discovery deprived the defense of the effective notice needed to permit it to be as able as the prosecutor to "make the most of the facts potentially at [its] disposal or of legal research"; (3) that the state, through the police investigatory authority (especially its capacity to interrogate the accused "up to the point of coercion") and the grand jury's subpoena authority, had a capacity for pretrial discovery far greater than that of the accused; and (4) that the Hand view "grossly exaggerated" the significance of the defendant's privilege of silence at trial since defendant is "under the utmost pressure to take the stand to rebut the inference of guilt which will likely be drawn by the jury" if he should remain silent, and the prosecution's use at trial of defendant's statements obtained through police interrogation commonly creates still further pressure to "take the stand."

its evidence against the accused. * * * [Counsel] must do what he can within the limited time usually allowed him before trial, often long after the trail has grown cold. He must deal with an accused whose obvious interest in self-justification complicates his lawyer's task of finding the true facts. Even if he can learn the names of witnesses against his client, those witnesses have already talked to the state's investigators and more frequently than not have been warned not to talk with anyone representing the accused. * * *

What assigned counsel obviously needs to discharge the heavy responsibility we give him is at least the opportunity to do what the state does when the trial is fresh, namely, seek corroboration of the accused's story, or lack of it, from external facts, through avenues of inquiry opened by what the state has learned. The implication in the argument against discovery is that the accused is guilty, so that not only may he not complain of the use against him even of his confession, or to its use as a source of leads to make the case against him as ironclad as possible, but that he really has no complaint that his counsel is denied access to the same materials to aid him better to develop the whole truth. In other words, the state may eat its cake and have it too. To that degree, does not the denial of all discovery set aside the presumption of innocence—is not such denial blind to the superlatively important public interest in the acquittal of the innocent? To shackle counsel so that he cannot effectively seek out the truth and afford the accused the representation which is not his privilege but his absolute right seems seriously to imperil the bedrock presumption of innocence.

And might not expanded discovery benefit the prosecution as well as the accused? If sharpening of the issues, exposure of untenable arguments and more efficient marshaling of the evidence result from discovery, doesn't the prosecution profit? For if voluntary disclosure to defense counsel often results in guilty pleas because defense counsel becomes convinced of the hopelessness of the client's cause, should not a rule authorizing criminal discovery in every case result in even more dispositions without trial?

The beneficial results claimed for statutes of an increasing number of states, which require an accused to give the prosecution pre-trial notice of an alibi or insanity defense, include not only preventing surprise at the trial but also aiding more effective preparation for trial. What justifies our being so sure then that according criminal discovery to the accused will benefit only the accused at the expense of the state?

But rigid opposition to pre-trial criminal discovery for the accused still persists. I don't think the reasons for this resistance have been better expressed than they were in *State v. Tune* * * *. Plainly enough, each of [Chief Justice Vanderbilt's] reasons has a persuasive appeal. But are their merits so clear? * * *

* * * I cannot be persuaded that the old hobgoblin perjury, invariably raised with every suggested change in procedure to make easier the discovery of the truth, supports the case against criminal discovery. I should think rather that its complete fallacy has been starkly exposed through the extensive and analogous experience in civil causes where liberal discovery has been allowed and perjury has not been fostered. Indeed, this experience has suggested that liberal discovery, far from abetting, actually deters perjury and fabrication.[a] * * * In any event, as has

a. See also LaFave and Israel, § 19.3(a): "Proponents of expansive discovery * * * reject the [contention] that there necessarily is a greater incentive for perjury in criminal cases, noting that civil cases too often involve substantial stakes. To assume that criminal defendants are more likely to be dishonest is to ignore, they argue, the presumption that the defendant is innocent. They also stress that the prosecution, though it cannot depose the defendant—a procedure that in civil cases is said to limit the opportunity for perjury by permitting either side to been said, "The true safeguard against perjury is not to refuse to permit any inquiry at all, for that will eliminate the true as well as the false, but the inquiry should be so conducted as to separate and distinguish the one from the other where both are present." We must remember that society's interest is equally that the innocent shall not suffer and not alone that the guilty shall not escape. * * *

Besides, isn't there a suggestion in the argument, and a rather slanderous one, that the criminal defense bar cannot be trusted? After all, isn't it the defense attorney and not the accused himself who will have access to the state's materials? Whatever justification there may be for the assumption that the desperate accused will try anything to escape his fate, the notion that his lawyer can't wait to conspire with him to that end hardly comports with the foundation of trust and ethics which underlies our professional honor system.[b]

The second argument is that an accused, knowing the names of witnesses against him, may see to it that they are silenced before the trial. Of course, there have been instances where this has happened. * * * Where that possibility may appear, a trial judge's discretion affords an ample safeguard. Dangers and other abuses of this kind are clearly a matter of legitimate concern—they argue however not for wholesale prohibition of criminal discovery but only for circumspection and for appropriate sanctions tailored to dealing with apprehended abuses in the particular case.

The third objection—that our constitutional privilege against self-incrimination prevents discovery being a two-way street—is admittedly more troublesome. * * * But is this premise really sound? Is the privilege against self-incrimination in fact a barrier to state discovery of the accused? * * * [Justice Brennan here noted that the privilege had not prevented the state from commonly obtaining substantial information from the defendant through the process of interrogation.] And even apart from discovery of this sort, what of the investigatory paraphernalia important to the preparation of criminal evidence which is, as of course it should be, available to law officers? Laboratories, skilled investigators, experts in all areas are an essential part of the equipment of every agency which would boast of being abreast of the modern techniques for the detection and prevention of crime. All of us are gratified that our agencies are so equipped, and would not want to strip their resources. But I suggest it overstates the fact to say that we don't need to extend criminal discovery procedures to the accused because the scales are already distorted in his favor by the privilege against self-incrimination and the fact that the state has the burden of proving his guilt beyond a reasonable doubt. * * *[c]

immediately 'freeze' his opponent's story—can use various other devices (e.g., police interrogation) to 'pin down' the defendant."

b. But see *United States v. Louis Carreau, Inc.*, 42 F.R.D. 408, 415 (S.D.N.Y.1967) (Mansfield, J.): "It is ingenuous to suggest that the risk of a defendant's 'tailoring' his trial testimony * * * is minimal for the reason that defendant's attorney can be relied upon to protect against fabrication * * *. His attorney is rarely a witness to the events in issue. * * * While the attorney may, in the sanctity of his own office, cross-examine his client closely, in the last analysis he has little alternative but to leave to the jury the issue of credibility of his client's latest story." Consider also the discussion of counsel's obligations in dealing with client perjury at p. 161 supra.

c. Consider also, LaFave and Israel, § 19.3(a): "If the privilege against self-incrimination creates a discovery imbalance in favor of the defense, that imbalance, supporters of liberal discovery argue, is consistent with the intent of the framers; the defendant should not be denied a procedure essential to the establishment of the truth in an attempt to offset a protection granted by the Constitution. Proponents also reject the contention that discovery can appropriately be denied the defendant because he has other 'advantages' in the criminal justice process. This position, they argue, looks at the process as a sporting contest and ignores the need to take

Notes and Questions

1. To what extent does the strength of the arguments advanced for and against defense discovery vary with the nature of the evidence the defendant seeks to discover? As discussed in the Notes starting at p. 1114 infra, jurisdictions often tend to be far more receptive to granting discovery of certain items (e.g., defendant's confession or scientific reports) than others (e.g., statements of witnesses). Do these distinctions follow from an analysis of the considerations discussed by Justices Vanderbilt and Brennan, such as the potential for defense misuse and the unavailability of reciprocal prosecution discovery?

2. Has there been a substantial change in the "balance of advantage" with respect to prosecution and defense discovery since Justices Vanderbilt and Brennan wrote? Does *Miranda* undercut the contention that the prosecution can gain considerable "informal" discovery from the defendant himself? Do the recent cases interpreting self-incrimination restrictions on formal prosecution discovery from the defense (see Section 2 infra) provide the prosecution with considerably more discovery than Justice Vanderbilt assumed? Does the greater reliance upon public defenders to represent the indigent, and provisions allowing court appointed lawyers investigative and other assistance (see p. — supra), place the indigent defendant in a better position to offset the investigatory advantages of the state that were stressed by Justice Brennan?

3. In the years since Justices Vanderbilt and Brennan wrote, a substantial number of states have adopted broad defense discovery provisions. Proponents of discovery argue that the experience of these states clearly contradicts the contention of Justice Vanderbilt and others that liberalization would lead to widespread perjury and witness intimidation. The proponents note that these "liberal discovery" jurisdictions have not experienced a higher acquittal rate nor have they had more prosecutions for perjury or attempts to tamper with witnesses. How conclusive is such data? Opponents of broad discovery contend that the criminal justice system is so overloaded that it necessarily will accommodate any change in the adversary balance through the exercise of discretion in the charging and plea bargaining process. Prosecutors may be willing, for example, to make greater plea bargaining concessions to offset the defense advantage of expansive discovery, and cases of suspected defense perjury or witness intimidation may be responded to with higher sentences for the convicted defendant rather than separate charges. More significant than the statistics, they argue, is the "common sense" impression of many prosecutors that increased discovery has and will lead to increased perjury and intimidation.

4. To what extent should a legislature or court, in prescribing the allowable scope of pretrial discovery, take into consideration alternative procedures for obtaining discovery? While the preliminary hearing is the most obvious alternative procedure, other procedures such as the motion to suppress, the bill of particulars, the bail hearing, and the pretrial conference (see Fed.R.Crim.P. 17.1) also may be used to obtain discovery. Is it inappropriate to give consideration to these alternatives because they are not designed basically as discovery devices? Proponents of liberal discovery provisions argue that a major advantage of such provisions is that they remove the incentive of the defense to manipulate other procedures to achieve a discovery objective those procedures were not designed to fill. If alternative procedures are considered, must provision be made for cases in which those procedures are not available (e.g., where the prosecution bypasses the preliminary hearing by gaining a prior grand jury indictment)?[a]

every precaution to ensure that the innocent are not convicted."

a. Consider also LaFave and Israel, § 19.3(a), discussing another aspect of the "alternative

5. Does the relationship of defense discovery to the defendant's effective presentation of a defense at trial, as discussed by Justice Brennan, suggest a constitutional grounding for defense discovery? Commentators have argued that such a foundation can be found in the Sixth Amendment right to effective counsel or the due process guarantee of a fair trial, but the Supreme Court has not been convinced. The Court has recognized a constitutional obligation of the prosecution to disclose exculpatory evidence (see Section 3 infra), but has rejected the suggestion that the defendant has a right to discover before trial the evidence (basically adverse) that the prosecution intends to introduce at trial. The Court has noted, for example, that while it may be the "better practice" to grant to the defendant pretrial discovery of his confession where the prosecution intends to use it at trial, the failure to follow that practice does not violate due process. *Cicenia v. La Gay,* 357 U.S. 504, 78 S.Ct. 1297, 2 L.Ed.2d 1523 (1958). It also has held that a jurisdiction does not violate due process when it fails to grant pretrial disclosure as to other material relevant to defense preparation but not exculpatory. See *Moore v. Illinois,* 408 U.S. 786, 92 S.Ct. 2562, 33 L.Ed.2d 706 (1972) (prior recorded statement of witness); *Weatherford v. Bursey,* 429 U.S. 545, 97 S.Ct. 837, 51 L.Ed.2d 30 (1977) (failure to inform defendant that an associate was an undercover agent and would testify for the prosecution at trial). State courts, however, have occasionally found that the prosecution's failure to disclose before trial certain critical portions of its evidence deprived the defendant of an adequate opportunity to prepare to meet the government's case and therefore violated due process. See e.g., *Gilchrist v. Commonwealth,* 317 S.E.2d 784 (Va.1984) (failure to furnish key autopsy report until chief medical examiner testified at trial); *Wynne v. State,* 676 S.W.2d 650 (Tex.App.1984) (defense was furnished with report of one of the state's experts on the insanity issue only shortly before that expert was prepared to testify and never received the report of the other expert).

II. THE CURRENT STATUS OF DEFENSE DISCOVERY

STATE VARIATIONS: AN OVERVIEW

1. "*Common law jurisdictions.*" In approximately 10 states, pretrial discovery by the defense is governed almost entirely by judicially developed standards. Although these jurisdictions may have an occasional statute governing one or two narrow aspects of defense discovery, they treat discovery basically as a "common law" subject. None, however, adhere to the early

means" argument: "[I]n some jurisdictions, prosecutors have adopted an 'open file' policy that gives the defense greater access to certain types of material than would be available under even the most liberal discovery statutes. Where such extensive 'informal discovery' is widely available, it adds an extra dimension to the traditional discovery debate. Opponents of expansive discovery requirements commonly argue that informal discovery practices serve all legitimate needs of the defense while avoiding most of the dangers [and time consuming procedures] that may accompany formal discovery requirements. Under an informal discovery practice, the prosecutor readily can deny discovery where there is substantial likelihood that the defendant will use it to fabricate a defense or to intimidate witnesses. Similarly, where the prosecutor is concerned that discovery will upset the balance of the adversary system, he can condition his offer of discovery on the defendant's willingness to reciprocate. The end result, it is argued, is a system that is preferable to formal discovery requirements, at least where prosecutors are acting in an even-handed manner. Proponents of expansive discovery requirements respond that discovery is too significant to be left to the discretion of the prosecutor. The 'ultimate responsibility' for the fairness of the trial process lies with the court, and therefore, they argue, the court also must bear the 'responsibility for the exercise of judgment as to the merit of the grounds for withholding disclosure in a particular case.' Too often, it is contended, the availability of informal discovery varies with the particular assistant prosecutor * * * [or the reputation of defense counsel]. Proponents of expansive defense discovery also contend that prosecutors who insist upon full reciprocity in granting informal discovery are seeking to circumvent the defendant's privilege against self-incrimination."

common law rulings which held that courts lacked authority to order pretrial discovery in the absence of legislative authorization. All recognize a trial court's discretionary authority to require pretrial discovery as an exercise of its inherent powers to control the trial process. In general, this authority is held to extend to the pretrial disclosure of a variety of items, including: (1) recorded statements made by the defendant to the police; (2) scientific reports of prosecution experts; (3) documents, photographs and tangible items that the prosecutor intends to use in evidence; (4) the names of prospective prosecution witnesses; and (5) recorded statements of those witnesses. The "common law jurisdictions" vary, however, in the leeway they grant to the trial court in the exercise of its discretion. Appellate guidelines governing discovery differ substantially from jurisdiction to jurisdiction in their characterization of the "sound exercise of discretion."

A typical "common law" guideline favoring discovery will hold that there is a general presumption in favor of discovery and that the failure to grant discovery will constitute an abuse of discretion unless the prosecution can establish a "paramount interest in nondisclosure." *Bernard v. State,* 230 N.E.2d 536 (Ind.1967). That interest might be found in a realistic threat of witness intimidation, see, e.g., *People v. Lopez,* 384 P.2d 16 (Cal.1963), or, perhaps, in the fact that the defense request constitutes no more than a "fishing expedition" seeking to obtain "all information which has been obtained by the People in their investigation of the crime," see e.g., *People v. Cooper,* 349 P.2d 964 (Cal.1960). In common law jurisdictions less favorable to defense discovery, the guideline might hold that a defense request for discovery ordinarily should be granted only where the defense has established a "particularized need" for pretrial disclosure. Such a standard commonly requires the defense to show (1) that pretrial disclosure of the requested item will be especially helpful to the defense and (2) that the defense has no other means of obtaining the requested information. Particularized need for a listing of res gestae witnesses might be established, for example, where the defense states that (1) it is considering relying upon an insanity defense and the defense psychiatrist therefore has a need to interview persons who observed the defendant when he committed the criminal act, and (2) that defendant lacks the capacity to identify those persons.

2. *Discovery rules and statutes.* In contrast to the common law jurisdictions, roughly forty states and the federal judicial system have adopted statutes or court rules that govern most aspects of defense discovery. Although these provisions vary in content, they tend to be similar in structure. Those sections applicable to defense discovery (the same statutes or court rules commonly also deal with prosecution discovery) will: (1) specify those items that are subject to disclosure as a matter of right or at the discretion of the trial court [see, e.g., Fed.R. 16(a)(1)]; (2) specify items that are not subject to disclosure [see, e.g., Fed.R. 16(a)(2)]; (3) establish a procedure for the presentation of defense requests and prosecution responses thereto [see, e.g., Fed.R. 16(d) [a]]; (4) establish a continuing prosecution obligation to disclose discoverable material obtained by the prosecution after its initial submission [see, e.g., Fed.R. 16(c)]; (5) provide for the issuance of protective orders restricting or denying otherwise required discovery upon an adequate prose-

a. Most provisions are designed to operate without the filing of a court motion. A defense request is sufficient to impose upon the prosecution a duty to respond unless the prosecution challenges the request as outside the scope of the jurisdiction's discovery provision. In some jurisdictions, the prosecution has an automatic obligation to disclose certain items without regard to any defense request. Several jurisdictions utilize an "omnibus hearing" procedure which allows for an initial stage of informal discovery followed by a single proceeding at which all discovery issues are resolved and all pretrial motions are raised. See LaFave and Israel, § 19.3(b).

cutorial showing [see, e.g., Fed.R. 16(d)(1)]; and (6) authorize the trial court to impose various sanctions or remedies where there has been a failure to comply with a discovery order [see, e.g., Fed.R. 16(d)(2)].

3. *Coverage of discovery provisions.* While each jurisdiction's discovery provision will to some extent be unique, the provisions generally tend to follow one of four basic models in their basic coverage. Those models are:

(1) *The 1966 version of Federal Rule 16.* Provisions following this model grant the trial court discretion to order discovery of the following items where within the prosecutor's possession or control: (1) "written or recorded statements made by the defendant" (including his recorded grand jury testimony, if any); (2) results and reports of physical or mental examinations and of scientific tests of experiments; and (3) relevant documents and other "tangible objects." The statutes or court rules in this group also specifically prohibit the trial court from ordering pretrial discovery of "internal government documents" and statements made by prosecution witnesses.

(2) *The 1975 version of Federal Rule 16.* Subject only to a protective order provision, these statutes or court rules provide for mandatory disclosure of the following items where within the prosecutor's possession or control: (1) written or recorded statements (including grand jury testimony) of the defendant and, in some states, of any codefendant; (2) the substance of any oral statement of the defendant (and, in some states, of a codefendant) that the prosecution intends to use at trial; (3) the defendant's prior criminal record; (4) relevant documents and other tangible objects; (5) results and reports of physical or mental examinations and of scientific tests or experiments. As in category (1), the provisions in this group prohibit court-ordered disclosure of prosecution witnesses' statements or internal memoranda. In some states, the court is given discretionary authority to order disclosure of the prosecution witnesses' names.

(3) *An expanded version of Federal Rule 16.* Subject to a protective order provision, these statutes or court rules initially encompass the same items of mandatory disclosure as the provisions in category (2) (although some add mandatory disclosure of witnesses names). Unlike the Federal Rule 16 provisions, however, they do not prohibit disclosure of witness statements or internal memoranda. Items falling outside the mandatory disclosure requirement may be discovered at the discretion of the court, although the court may not order disclosure of material classified as attorney work product.

(4) *The 1970 version of the A.B.A. standards.*[b] Subject to a protective order provision, these statutes or court rules provide for mandatory disclosure of all of the items included in the provisions patterned after Federal Rule 16 (see category 2 above) plus the following items: (1) names and addresses of all prospective prosecution witnesses; (2) the written or recorded statements of those witnesses, including their grand jury testimony; (3) the criminal record, if any, of those witnesses; and (4) written or recorded statements and the substance of any oral statements of a codefendant in a joint trial. These mandatory disclosure provisions are limited only by exceptions for work product, protection of a non-witness informant under the informer's privilege, and protection of national security secrets. The court also is given discretion, subject to these limitations, to

b. *A.B.A. Standards Relating to Discovery and Procedure Before Trial* (Approved Draft 1970). The A.B.A. standards were revised in 1978 to provide open-file discovery. II A.B.A. Standards § 11–2.1 ("upon request of the defense, the prosecuting attorney shall disclose to defense counsel all of the material and information within the prosecutor's possession and control"). However, state provisions following the A.B.A. standards continue to rely upon the original version rather than the 1978 revision.

provide for discovery of additional material upon a showing of materiality.

4. *Discretionary disclosure.* Do provisions for discretionary disclosure, even where supplemented by appellate court guidelines such as those described in Note 1 supra, necessarily result in substantial variations dependent upon the viewpoint of the particular trial judge? Consider *People v. Green,* 371 N.Y.S.2d 271 (Crim. Ct.1975), commenting upon the application of a New York provision allowing discretionary disclosure of non-exempt items beyond those specified in earlier sections as automatically discoverable: "Some courts grant disclosure of almost any item requested by the defendant, others have so strictly construed Article 240 as to disallow discovery for all material other than that expressly enumerated under subdivisions 1 and 2 * * *, and still other courts have adopted an eclectic approach, depending on the circumstances of the case and the personal philosophy of the particular trial judge involved. Consequently, the result has frequently been an utter lack of consistency in the practice relating to pretrial disclosure."

Is there any reason why standards governing discovery should give the trial judge more precise directives than the standards governing other aspects of pretrial or trial procedure? Consider Fletcher, *Pretrial Discovery in State Criminal Cases,* 12 Stan.L.Rev. 293 (1960) (noting that discovery rulings are ordinarily subject to appellate review only upon appeal from a conviction and "since it is difficult * * * to show prejudice resulting from the denial of discovery, the obstacles in the path of reversal are formidable").

5. To what extent do protective order provisions limit mandatory disclosure requirements? Federal Rule 16(d)'s provision simply notes that a protective order "deny[ing], restrict[ing] or deferr[ing]" otherwise automatic discovery shall be issued "upon sufficient showing." State provisions often limit protective orders to restricting or deferring discovery and list the type of interests that may justify issuance of such an order. See e.g., N.J.R. Crim.P. 3:13–3 ("protection of witnesses and others from physical harm, threats of harm, bribes, economic reprisals and other intimidation; maintenance of * * * secrecy regarding informants * * *; protection of confidential relationships and privileges recognized by law; any other relevant consideration"). The burden of establishing a need for a protective order rests, of course, on the government as the party seeking that order. Its showing ordinarily may be made in camera on the theory that the protective order would be valueless if the government, to obtain the order, had to disclose to the defense that information which the government seeks to protect under the order. If the court enters the order, the record of the government's showing is sealed and made available for review on appeal.

6. *Items "within the control of the prosecution."* Discovery provisions commonly extend only to those discoverable items "within the prosecutor's possession or control." But compare Rule 16(a)(1)(A) (including statements "the existence of which is known, or by due diligence may become known, to the attorney for the government"). What should be viewed as within the prosecutor's control? It clearly encompasses the police department working with the prosecutor in the particular case, but should it extend to "any * * * prosecutorial or law enforcement office" of the particular state. See *State v. Coney,* 294 So. 2d 82 (Fla.1973) (criminal records "within the actual or constructive possession of the prosecutor" included data obtainable from the F.B.I.); *State v. Edmaiston,* 679 S.W.2d 360 (Mo.App.1984) (discovery rule violated by nondisclosure of basic investigative file prepared by police in another city who had also investigated the incident, notwithstanding that file was not known to the prosecutors until an officer of that department appeared to testify at trial). Consider also *State v. Brown,* 552

S.W.2d 383 (Tenn.1977) (defendant entitled to discovery of state hospital's medical records on prosecution witness). But compare *United States v. Trevino,* 556 F.2d 1265 (5th Cir.1977) (presentence report in the possession of the probation department of the court is not within the control of the prosecution).

STATE VARIATIONS: SPECIFIC ITEMS

1. *Defendant's prior recorded statement.* Federal Rule 16 and all but a handful of state discovery provisions require the prosecution to allow the defense to inspect and copy prior recorded statements made by the defendant. In states where discovery rests in the discretion of the trial court, appellate guidelines often suggest that discovery of defendant's prior recorded statement should be almost automatic. Why is there such strong support for discovery of this item? Consider the following arguments: (1) the precise wording of defendant's statement is especially important to defense counsel in preparing for trial or in determining whether a guilty plea is advisable; (2) disclosure here does not pose a substantial threat of successful perjury since the defendant may be impeached effectively by reference to his statement; (3) disclosure of defendant's statement does not create a reciprocity problem since the state obviously gained discovery from the defendant in obtaining the statement from him originally; and (4) if disclosure is not granted directly, the defendant will simply use the motion to suppress as an indirect discovery device.

What constitutes a prior recorded statement of defendant? Consider LaFave and Israel, § 19.3(c): "It clearly encompasses statements written, signed, or otherwise approved by the defendant and all verbatim recordings (e.g., tapes), whether recorded with or without defendant's knowledge. Because of the special status of grand jury secrecy, most jurisdictions have added provisions specifically noting that defendant's grand jury testimony also is included. [See e.g., Fed.R. 16(a)(1)]. Courts have disagreed, however, as to whether a written summary of a defendant's comments (prepared either by the person to whom he spoke or a third party who overheard or received a substantial account of his comments) constitutes a recorded statement. Some would include almost any written description of defendant's comments, others only a summary that captures the substance of defendant's comments, and still others would seem to require a substantially verbatim recording."

2. *Defendant's oral statements.* Where discovery provisions require disclosure of the substance of defendant's oral statements, there may be no need to determine whether a particular summary of defendant's comments constitutes a prior recorded statement. Provisions requiring disclosure of oral statements are not as common, however, as provisions requiring disclosure of prior recorded statements. Moreover, they tend to be narrower in scope. Only a handful of jurisdictions require pretrial disclosure of all oral statements of the defendant known to the prosecution. Most provisions on defendant's oral statements require disclosure only of those statements the prosecution "intends to offer in evidence at the trial." Federal Rule 16(a)(1)(A) adds the limitation that the statements have been made "in response to interrogation by any person known to the defendant to be a government agent." Why are such limitations imposed upon the right to discover the substance of defendant's oral statements when similar limitations are not imposed on discovery of defendant's prior recorded statements?

3. *Codefendants' statements.* Approximately half of the states require disclosure of a codefendant's statement under at least some circumstances. Several have provisions requiring the disclosure of recorded or oral statements of codefendants without limitation. Others restrict such disclosure to cases in which the codefendants will be jointly tried, or to statements which the

prosecution intends to use at trial. In many of these jurisdictions, the codefendant's statement would not otherwise be discoverable since they do not generally provide for discovery of the statements of all possible witnesses to the offense (see Note 1, p. 1120 infra). Why are codefendants' statements given this special treatment? Consider Rezneck, *The New Federal Rules of Criminal Procedure,* 54 Geo. L.J. 1276 (1966) arguing that codefendants' statements should be discoverable because such statements: "(1) * * * are potentially important to defense counsel in preparing to meet the government's case and developing evidence on defendant's behalf; (2) * * * aid defense counsel in deciding whether to make a severance motion and in assisting the judicial determination of such a motion; (3) * * * mitigate the well-known proclivities of some criminal defendants not to give their own lawyers a truthful account of the actions." Do these grounds justify special treatment of the codefendant's statement in all of the situations covered by the statutes cited above?

4. *Scientific reports.* Federal Rule 16 and a substantial majority of the state discovery provisions make mandatory the disclosure of various reports of medical and physical examinations, scientific tests, and experiments. Most jurisdictions encompass all such reports that are "made in connection with the particular case." A few require that the reports be intended for use by the government at trial, while several follow the federal formula of requiring that the reports be either "material to the preparation of the defense or * * * intended for use by the government as evidence in chief at the trial." Fed.R.Crim.P. 16(a)(1)(D). Mandatory disclosure of scientific reports is justified on the following grounds: "Once the report is prepared, the scientific expert's position is not readily influenced, and therefore disclosure presents little danger of prompting perjury or intimidation. Disclosure is also justified on the ground that 'it lessens the imbalance which may result from the State's early and complete investigation in contrast to [defendant's] * * * late and limited investigation.' It is further noted that 'this sort of evidence is practically impossible for the adversary to test or rebut at trial without an adversary opportunity to examine it closely.'" LaFave and Israel, § 19.3(d).

5. *Documents and tangible objects.* Jurisdictions that require mandatory disclosure of scientific tests ordinarily also require mandatory disclosure of documents and tangible objects. Provisions requiring disclosure of documents and tangible objects generally apply to items "which the prosecution will use at trial or which were obtained from or purportedly belong to the defendant." Federal Rule 16 and various state provisions also include a third category of documents and objects, those "which are material to the preparation of the defense." [a] Fed.R.Crim.P. 16(a)(1)(D). Document and tangible object pro-

a. When relying on a standard of this type, the defendant commonly will have to make some specific showing of likely materiality. Courts vary, however, as to the substantiality of that showing. Compare *State ex rel. Dean v. City Court,* 680 P.2d 211 (Ariz.App.1984) (city police department's internal affairs records were subject to in camera inspection and possible disclosure based on defense contention that arresting officer had a well known reputation for being dishonest in his testimony); *Taylor v. State,* 324 S.E.2d 788 (Ga.App.1984) (defense request for drunk driving reports of arresting officer for the month of defendant's arrest, which defense requested for the purpose of "raising an issue as to [his] credibility," was properly denied; there was no showing of the relevance of "any specific report," which suggested that defendant was engaged in a "fishing expedition").

In some situations, relevant documents in the possession of agencies other than the prosecutor may be obtained through provisions like the Federal Freedom of Information Act. See *United States v. Wahlin,* 384 F.Supp. 43 (W.D.Wis.1974) (defendant charged with tax evasion could obtain under the federal act copies of IRS private letter rulings to other taxpayers allegedly finding no tax liability under similar circumstances). The Freedom of Information Act applies to records of various federal agencies, including many involved in criminal investigations (e.g., the F.B.I. and visions are most frequently used to obtain disclosure of such items as physical evidence taken from the defendant, photographs of the scene of the crime, and financial records the government intends to use in establishing a white collar crime. Here, as with scientific reports, discovery is often justified on the ground that it poses no substantial threat of perjury and an inspection in advance of the trial will often be necessary to challenge the evidence at trial.

6. *Witness lists.* State provisions patterned after the ABA Standards generally require the prosecution to provide the defense with "the names and addresses of persons whom the State intends to call as witnesses." [b] A few states with ABA-type provisions have a broader standard requiring the prosecutor to list the names and addresses of all persons "known by the government to have knowledge of relevant facts" without regard to whether they will be called as witnesses. Several additional jurisdictions have pleading provisions requiring that the names of witnesses be endorsed upon the information or indictment. When these jurisdictions are added to those with discovery provisions, approximately half of the states can be said generally to require pretrial disclosure of the names of the prosecution's witnesses. In the remaining jurisdictions, discovery of the names of witnesses ordinarily lies in the discretion of the trial.

In many of those jurisdictions where witness list discovery is discretionary, trial courts will order such discovery only in "extraordinary circumstances." LaFave and Israel, § 19.3(f) contend that this position "is based only partly on the need to protect against possible intimidation of witnesses." Noting that a "strong presumption" against granting disclosure is applied even where surrounding circumstances suggest almost no likelihood that defendant "will intimidate or otherwise improperly influence witnesses," they suggest that these courts "apparently are concerned that the adoption of a policy which sought to distinguish [* * * situations presenting a realistic threat of defense misuse], but thereby allowed disclosure in a substantial number of cases, would inevitably reinforce the natural reluctance of many persons to offer to testify at trial." Is this a legitimate ground for refusing to require disclosure? Various federal prosecutors relied largely on such reasoning in opposing a 1974 proposed amendment to Federal Rule 16 (approved by the Supreme Court but eventually rejected by Congress) that would have required the government to provide defendants with witness lists unless it established grounds for a protective order. They noted that (1) gaining victim/witness cooperation was one of the most difficult tasks facing law enforcement, (2) that many of these persons, with or without justification in the particular case, were fearful of retaliation or harassment, and (3) that protective orders could not screen out all cases of likely intimidation or provide assurance to witnesses in general. See Note 3, p. 1121 infra (relating to defense interviews of witnesses).

THE SPECIAL PROBLEMS OF WITNESS STATEMENTS AND POLICE REPORTS

1. Undoubtedly the most controversial item of potential defense discovery is the prior recorded statement of the prosecution witness. Approximately a third of the states require pretrial disclosure of a witness' statements, subject to a protective order where appropriate and to a "work product" exemption [a]; approximately a

other units of the Justice Department). However, the Act includes a substantial exemption for "investigatory records." See 5 U.S.C. § 552(b)(7).

b. This obligation commonly applies only to those witnesses that the prosecution intends to present in building its case-in-chief. In some jurisdictions, however, the prosecution also must list rebuttal witnesses when it can anticipate who they will be.

a. As with witness lists (see Note 6 above), a few of these provisions go beyond the statements of prosecution witnesses alone and require disclothird allow a trial court to order such disclosure at its discretion, but most of those jurisdictions also tend to frown upon such discovery, reserving it for the most exceptional cases; approximately a third of the states and the federal system specifically prohibit pretrial discovery of witness statements. Jurisdictions in the latter category ordinarily include in their discovery rules a specific prohibition similar to that found in Federal Rule 16(a)(2). The federal provision states that Rule 16 "does not authorize the discovery or inspection of * * * statements made by government witnesses or prospective government witnesses except as provided in 18 U.S.C. § 3500." The cited exception is to the Jencks Act (18 U.S.C. 3500), which was designed to ensure that prior recorded statements of witnesses are available for impeachment use, but not subject to pretrial discovery. The Jencks Act provides that after a government witness testifies on direct examination, the government shall make available his prior recorded statement insofar as that statement relates to the subject matter of the defendant's testimony,[b] but it also adds:

> [N]o statement * * * in the possession of the United States which was made by a Government witness or prospective Government witness (other than the defendant) shall be the subject of subpoena, discovery, or inspection until said witness has testified on direct examination in the trial of the case.[c]

2. Although the reluctance of many jurisdictions to grant pretrial discovery of a witness' prior recorded statement is based in part on the same concern for possible witness intimidation that led those jurisdictions to sharply restrict or deny the disclosure of witness lists, other concerns obviously have also played a substantial role. Discovery of witness statements is sharply restricted or prohibited altogether in several jurisdictions in which witness lists are automatically discoverable. So too, in many jurisdictions in which witness lists may be discovered at the discretion of the court, discovery of witness statements is barred or subjected to a more stringent discretionary standard. Is the more restrictive treatment of witness statements justified on any or all of the following grounds: (1) disclosure of such statements is more likely to facilitate defense perjury than disclosure of any other aspect of the prosecution's case; (2) the defendant's alternative means for preparation, assuming defendant is given a witness list, are more adequate as to witness testimony than as to other items (e.g., scientific reports) of potential discovery; (3) disclosure of witness statements tends to undermine the adversary system by giving the defense the benefit of the litigation analysis of the prosecution; and (4) requiring disclosure of a witness' recorded statement will only lead the prosecution to "commit to memory rather than [to] paper or other record" what the witness has told it? See Louisell, *Criminal Discovery: Dilemma Real or Apparent,* 49 Cal.L.Rev. 56 (1961) (largely rejecting each of these grounds, but noting the need for protective orders and work product provisions to respond to the 1st and 3rd grounds). Consider also Notes 3–4 infra.

3. Denial of defense discovery of a witness' prior recorded statement has been justified on the ground that it is in the defendant's best interest to pursue his in-

sure of the statements of all persons "known by the government to have knowledge of relevant facts." See e.g., Alaska R.Crim.P. 16(b)(1)(i).

b. While many states have similar provisions, others do not provide for automatic disclosure at trial, limiting such disclosure to situations in which the defense can establish the likely usefulness of the statement in impeaching the witness. See LaFave and Israel, § 19.3(g).

c. Notwithstanding this language, some federal courts, to avoid the delays generated by repeated recesses needed to permit defense counsel to study the prior statement before undertaking cross-examination, will require disclosure on the evening before the witness testifies or shortly before the trial begins. But see, *United States v. Algie,* 667 F.2d 569 (6th Cir.1982) (district court cannot order earlier disclosure over prosecution's objection).

vestigation by interviewing witnesses rather than by relying on statements obtained by police. The need to discourage defense counsel from "riding the coattails" of the prosecution explains, it is argued, why a jurisdiction will grant automatic disclosure of witness lists yet deny discovery of witness statements. Cf. Feldman, *The Work Product Rule in Criminal Practice and Procedure,* 50 U.Cinn.L.Rev. 495 (1981) ("empirical studies demonstrate that routine discovery of witness statements can encourage lazy defense attorneys to obtain a free ride on their opponents' diligence"). Responding to this coattails contention, proponents of automatic pretrial disclosure of witness statements argue that: (1) witnesses often either refuse to talk to defense counsel or insist upon very limited interviews;[d] (2) because an interview will not come nearly as promptly after the event as the initial police investigation, the defense has a need to examine the witness' statement to the police even if the witness is now willing to cooperate fully with the defense counsel; (3) because the statement and the interview are not completely overlapping sources of information, diligent defense counsel will seek to interview witnesses even if the defense is given discovery of their statements; and (4) if lack of diligence is a significant problem in defense work, the answer lies not in limiting discovery but in the training and selection of defense counsel.

4. *The "work product" exemption.* The work product doctrine is designed to protect the adversary process by exempting from discovery certain materials that reflect the thought processes of the adversaries. The doctrine's objective is to give counsel free rein in his analysis of the case without concern that that analysis will be disclosed to his opponent and used to his opponent's advantage. Several commentators have argued that a work product exemption is inappropriate as applied to criminal defense discovery since the prosecutor is not simply an adversary, but has a duty to "see that justice is done." There is no reason, it is argued, for a prosecutor to keep his analysis to himself simply because it may be of assistance to the other side. Both courts and legislatures, however, have consistently rejected this position, noting that the criminal trial is still largely an adversary process. See, e.g., *United States v. Nobles,* 422 U.S. 225, 95 S.Ct. 2160, 45 L.Ed.2d 141 (1975) (work product doctrine is needed in criminal cases to "assure the thorough preparation and presentation of each side of the case").

The primary disputes concerning application of the work product doctrine in criminal cases have related to the appropriate scope of the doctrine. In civil cases, the doctrine originally was held to grant a qualified exemption from discovery to those materials prepared in connection with prospective litigation that reflected "an attorney's mental impressions, conclusions, opinions, or legal theories." *Hickman v. Taylor,* 329 U.S. 495, 67 S.Ct. 385, 91 L.Ed. 451 (1947). However, as the Supreme Court noted in *Nobles,* supra, the doctrine is "an intensely practical one, grounded on the realities of litigation in our adversary system," and "one of those

d. Courts have consistently held that the prosecution and police cannot advise or direct witnesses not to cooperate with defense counsel. On the other hand, they have also stated that, since "the witness is free to decide whether to grant or refuse an interview, * * * it is not improper for the government to inform the witness of that right." *United States v. White,* 454 F.2d 435 (7th Cir.1971). But compare *A.B.A. Standards Relating to the Prosecution* 78 (1971) (counsel should also advise witness that "it is in the interests of justice that the witness make himself available for interviews by [opposing] counsel"). If the witness refuses to be interviewed, the court will not direct the witness to cooperate. Indeed, such a directive is usually viewed as inappropriate even where the prosecutor previously directed the witness not to cooperate. See *Commonwealth v. St. Pierre,* 387 N.E.2d 1135 (Mass.1979) (proper remedy is to have the judge "bring the witness before him, and to have him explain in some detail, on the record, the basis and dimensions of the principle [that witnesses belong to neither side], and then to make sure that [defense] counsel was given access to the witnesses on neutral ground without any overshadowing influence").

realities is that attorneys often must rely on assistance of the investigators." Accordingly, the civil work product doctrine has been extended in most jurisdictions to include material prepared by investigators or other agents of counsel, provided that material reflects their "mental impressions, conclusions, opinions, or legal theories." See, e.g., Fed.R.Civ.P. 26(b)(3). Does it follow that the work product doctrine should be extended in criminal cases to reports prepared by police officers? Compare II A.B.A. Standards § 11–2.6 (1978) (limited to material containing the "opinions, theories, or conclusions of the prosecuting attorney or members of the prosecutor's legal staff"); Vt.R.Crim.P. 16(d)(1) (disclosure "shall not be required of * * * records, correspondence, reports, or memoranda to the extent that they contain the mental impressions, conclusions, opinions, or legal theories of * * * agents of the prosecution, including investigators and police officers").

Assuming that the work product doctrine applies to material prepared by police officers, does it follow that the defense should face an absolute bar against discovery of the prior recorded statements of prosecution witnesses? Advocates of such a bar argue that most recorded statements are given in response to police questioning, and therefore commonly reflect, in part, the mental impression of the investigating officer. They see provisions prohibiting the disclosure of witness' statements as doing no more than excluding from discovery a class of materials that generally would be exempted in any event under a broad work product doctrine. See e.g., *Thigpen v. State,* 355 So.2d 392 (Ala.Cr.App.1977). Proponents of defense discovery respond that the absolute bar can hardly be compared to a case by case application of the work product doctrine, which is all that is needed to protect the adversary process. Most often, they note, the recorded statement will consist of little more than the witness' narrative of events in response to an open-ended question (e.g., "What happened?"). On occasion, the officer's questions may reflect some aspect of his theories or analysis, or his non-verbatim written summary of the witness' comments may do the same, but such material, it is argued, can often be deleted. Where the structure of the statement makes that impossible, there should still be the possibility, they argue, of balancing the defendant's need for discovery against the prosecutor's interest in protecting work product. As developed in civil cases, the work product doctrine traditionally has created a "qualified exemption" from discovery, subject to the opposing party's superior need for disclosure.

5. *The "recorded statement" limitation.* Provisions requiring mandatory pretrial disclosure of recorded statements of prosecution witnesses vary in their definition of a "recorded statement." Some borrow from the Jencks Act definition of "statements" which includes only (1) written statements "made and signed or otherwise adopted or approved" by the witness, (2) recordings that are a "substantially verbatim recital of an oral statement * * * and recorded contemporaneously with the making of such oral statement" and (3) "a statement, however taken or recorded, or a transcription thereof, if any, made by said witness to a grand jury." [e] 18 U.S.C. § 3500(e). Other provisions encompass all "written and recorded statements and

e. At one time, many jurisdictions imposed more stringent restrictions upon the discovery of a witness' grand jury testimony on the ground that every breach of grand jury secrecy tended to undermine the effectiveness of the grand jury in future investigations. Cf. fn. b, p. 698 supra. Today, discovery provisions commonly treat grand jury testimony no differently than other recorded statements given by witnesses. It is subject to pretrial discovery in most states that generally grant disclosure of prior recorded statements. Indeed, in those jurisdictions that give the defendant a right to review the grand jury transcript for the purposes of presenting a challenge to grand jury procedures [see Note 13, p. 1006 supra], the defendant may have access to a witness' grand jury testimony where he would not be able to gain discovery of that witness' other recorded statements. See LaFave and Israel, § 8.5(f).

existing memoranda reporting or summarizing part or all of the oral statements." Mo.R.Crim.P. 25.03(A)(1). Which is the better approach? Consider *A.B.A. Standards Relating to Discovery and Procedure Before Trial* 62–63 (1970):

"A substantial majority of the Committee rejects the much litigated restrictive definition of 'statements' in the Jencks Act. It has been said that the definition of this term must be restricted to substantially verbatim statements, for otherwise it would be grossly unfair to allow an attorney to confront a witness on cross-examination with reports of his utterances which are neither substantially his own words nor approved or adopted by him. The minority [of the Committee] believes that the kind of harassment of witnesses which such cross-examination might produce would tend to discourage potential witnesses from coming forward to cooperate with law enforcement authorities. The Committee majority is of the view, however, that both fairness and the system's stated objectives require that the defense have the benefit of written and recorded statements of prospective witnesses in whatever form they have been preserved. This policy would, moreover, tend to discourage the practice engaged in by some law enforcement officers of destroying original notes, after transforming them into secondary transcriptions, in order to avoid the rigors of cross-examination based upon materials. * * * It should be noted that the problem [under the Jencks Act] is primarily how the statements of a witness which are not substantially verbatim can be used in cross-examination at a hearing or trial, not how defense counsel can make use of them before trial or plea. * * * The kinds of records which may have to be disclosed [to provide effective pretrial discovery] include interview notes, however fragmentary, and even if they are merely 'jottings' to aid the prosecutor."

6. *Discovery depositions.* In civil cases, a party ordinarily cannot gain discovery of the statements that the opposing party has obtained in the course of interviewing its witnesses, but those witnesses can be deposed. While depositions are generally available in criminal cases for the purpose of preserving the testimony of witnesses who are likely to be unavailable at trial, only a handful of jurisdictions authorize the use of depositions for discovery purposes.[f] In general, those same jurisdictions also allow discovery of the recorded statements of prosecution witnesses. If the discovery deposition is available, what justification exists for also granting automatic pretrial disclosure of witness statements? Cf. Note 3 supra. If a choice must be made between the two procedures, which should be viewed as the primary means of discovery? Consider the commentary in depositions in the *A.B.A. Standards Relating to Discovery and Procedure Before Trial* 87–88 (1970) (which provided for automatic discovery of a witness' statements, but left the utilization of depositions to the discretion

f. LaFave and Israel, § 19.3(k). The typical statute or court rule governing depositions authorizes the trial court to order that a person be deposed upon a showing that the person is a "material witness" and "is likely not to be able to attend the trial." A fair number of provisions use a somewhat more flexible standard (designed to ensure that the deposition will be available to the prosecution to "freeze" the testimony of those government witnesses who might well be subjected to intimidation), but those provisions still look to preserving testimony rather than discovery. See e.g., Fed.R.Crim.P. 15(a) ("whenever due to the exceptional circumstances of the case, it is in the interest of justice that the testimony of a prospective witness of a party be taken and preserved for trial"). The discovery deposition, as developed in civil cases and allowed in a small group of states in criminal cases, is not limited as to persons who may be deposed and does not require the prior approval of the court (i.e., the deposition is taken simply upon notification to the deponent and the prosecutor). In addition to the states with this type of discovery deposition, a few states allow discovery depositions in criminal cases upon a special showing of need. See e.g., Ariz.R.Crim.P. 15.3(a) (must show that deponent's testimony is "material to the case" or "necessary adequately to prepare a defense," that deponent was "not a witness at the preliminary hearing," and that "he will not cooperate in granting a personal interview").

of the court upon a showing of "materiality" and "reasonableness"):

"That the defendant should have the *right* to take depositions in a criminal case for discovery purposes was seriously considered by the Advisory Committee but was rejected by a majority as a minimum standard. Although such a right is granted in civil cases in many jurisdictions, there are different considerations in the criminal process. First, there is no inherent limitation of cost on the conduct of unnecessary depositions, because in many cases the cost of the defense must be borne by the state; and it would be manifestly unfair to grant the right only to defendants who are able to finance their own defense. Second, if stated as a right, the need to take depositions might be construed as part of the adequacy of representation required by the constitutional right to counsel. Third, the imposition on civilian witnesses may discourage their coming forward in criminal cases. And, finally, underlying the importance of these considerations is the belief that depositions in addition to the disclosures otherwise required by these standards will not be necessary in most criminal cases. Under its responsibilities in bringing a criminal case, the prosecution will ordinarily possess written statements or transcripts of testimony of potential witnesses of such completeness that additional interrogation by the defense attorney, prior to trial, will be of only marginal value in most cases. Moreover, anything of which the prosecution has knowledge, in addition to the statements, which may tend to negate the guilt of the accused must also be disclosed."

In an early study of one of the first states to use discovery depositions, the author concluded that discovery depositions were not being used for "blind fishing expeditions," that depositions were probably utilized in less than 8% of all cases, and that many practitioners thought the availability of depositions reduced the need for trials. Langrock, *Vermont's Experiment in Criminal Discovery,* 53 A.B.A.J. 732 (1967). Do these conclusions necessarily undercut the conclusion of the A.B.A. Advisory Committee? Should the availability of discovery depositions also be influenced by the availability of a grand jury procedure that may be used by the prosecutor to compel testimony and the availability of a preliminary hearing that may be used as a makeshift deposition procedure by both parties? Cf. Ariz.R. Crim.P. 15.3(a) (fn. f supra); Unif.R. Crim.P. 431, 432 (proposing elimination of both the grand jury and the preliminary hearing and substituting reliance upon extensive use of depositions by both sides, including a precharge investigatory deposition available to the prosecutor).

7. *Police reports.* Where a police report contains a sufficiently detailed description of a statement given to the police by a defendant, codefendant, or prosecution witness to constitute a recorded statement of that person, that portion of the report will fall within the jurisdiction's discovery rule governing such recorded statements. So too, an abridged description may be subject to discovery when state law encompasses summaries of oral statements of such persons. The critical issue with respect to police reports is whether there should be pretrial discovery of additional information that would not fall under the provisions governing recorded or oral statements. This would include the officer's comments on his own observations (where the officer is not himself a prosecution witness) and references to conversations with persons who are not defendants, codefendants, or prosecution witnesses. That portion of the report might fit, however, under several other discovery provisions, including: (1) provisions for discovery of documents "which are material to the preparation of the defense"; (2) provisions requiring disclosure of statements of persons having knowledge of relevant facts (see fn. a supra); and (3) provisions authorizing discretionary disclosure of "relevant material and information" not otherwise specified in the discovery rule. The

Federal Rules and approximately twenty states specifically exempt police reports and similar documents from discovery under such provisions. LaFave and Israel, § 19.3(h). Thus, Federal Rule 16(a)(2) provides that except as authorized under provisions for disclosure of defendant's statements, criminal records, and scientific reports, Rule 16 "does not authorize the discovery or inspection of reports, memoranda, or other internal government documents made by the attorney for the government or other internal government agents in connection with the investigation or prosecution of the case."

What justifies the special treatment of police reports in the jurisdictions noted above? Can it be argued that such reports automatically constitute work product? See *Cooks v. State,* 276 So.2d 634 (Ala.Cr. App.1973). In jurisdictions without specific provisions exempting police reports, a report otherwise subject to discovery may still be exempt under a work product provision (assuming that provision encompasses material prepared by the police as well as the prosecutor's legal staff), but each report will be examined to determine whether the officer's description of his investigation does reflect his "mental impressions, conclusions, opinions or legal theories." See Vt.R.Crim.P. 16(d)(1). Can it be argued that the exemption of police-report from discovery is needed to ensure that there will not be disclosure of information relating to specific investigations or investigative procedures that might be useful to those engaged in crime? Cf. Fla.R.Crim.P. 3.220(a)(1)(ii) ("if the court determines *in camera* proceedings * * * that any police report contains irrelevant, sensitive information or information interrelated with other crimes or criminal activities and [that] disclosure * * * may seriously impair law enforcement or jeopardize the investigation of such other crimes or activities, the court may prohibit or partially restrict with disclosure"). Can the exemption of police reports be justified as a means of discouraging "red herring defenses" in which the defense counsel seeks to shift the focus of the case from the weight of the evidence against the defendant to a trial of the thoroughness of the police investigation?

DISCOVERY SANCTIONS

STATE v. QUINTAL

479 A.2d 117 (R.I.1984).

MURRAY, JUSTICE.

This is an appeal by the state from an order by the trial justice dismissing the indictment against the defendant. The dismissal resulted from the state's failure to comply with a court order compelling it to produce certain medical records pertaining to the complaining witness. We affirm the decision of the trial justice and hold that the trial justice did not abuse his discretion in dismissing the indictment.

On August 3, 1981, defendant was secretly indicted by a Newport County Grand Jury on four counts of third-degree sexual assault. At defendant's September 21, 1981 arraignment, defense counsel filed a request for discovery and inspection pursuant to Rule 16. The state's response to this request, filed on October 5, 1981, included the Summary Note of Dr. Richard Palumbo, a psychologist who examined the complaining witness in connection with the reported sexual assaults.

Subsequently, defense counsel filed a motion to compel more responsive answers to the September 21, 1981 request—specifically, defense counsel requested complete medical reports pertaining to the mental health and gynecological history of the complaining witness. This motion was granted by the trial justice on November 9, 1981, and the state was ordered to furnish to defendant the mental records and psychological history of the complaining witness, the physician's report of the gynecological examination, the witness's diary, and tape recordings of conversations between her and defendant. On January 8, 1982, defense counsel filed a motion to dismiss the indictment on the ground that the state had failed to comply with the discovery order.

The motion to dismiss was heard on June 25, 1982. In the period between the filing of the motion and the trial justice's consideration thereof, the state provided defendant with various records relating to the complaining witness's medical history. One of these was Dr. Palumbo's Summary Note, which had previously been furnished to defendant; two others made reference to additional medical records that were never produced. The trial justice treated defendant's motion to dismiss as a motion to compel production and granted it.

The state subsequently produced some records but did not completely satisfy the orders of November 9, 1981, and June 25, 1982. At a pretrial conference on November 23, 1982, the trial justice ordered the state to produce the psychiatric records requested by defense counsel. A conditional sixty-day order was entered specifying that if the state failed to comply with the court's command, the case would automatically be dismissed with prejudice. This was agreed upon by defense counsel and the representative from the Office of the Attorney General, and the order was entered on November 30, 1982, setting January 24, 1983, as the deadline for compliance.

The Attorney General's office apparently overlooked or ignored the order since no records were furnished to defendant by the January 24, 1983 deadline. On January 26, 1983, in the presence of an attorney from the Attorney General's office, defense counsel made an oral motion for dismissal in the Newport County Superior Court based on the state's failure to comply with the November 23, 1982 order. The trial justice granted the motion and ordered the case dismissed, but the dismissal was stayed pending a hearing on the state's motion to vacate the January 26 order of dismissal. On April 5, 1983, after extensive argument by both the Attorney General's office and defense counsel, the state's motion to vacate was denied. * * *

"The imposition of any of the sanctions listed in Rule 16(i) is a matter addressed to the sound discretion of the trial justice." *State v. Sciarra,* R.I., 448 A.2d 1215 (1982). The exercise of such discretion demands a consideration of what is " 'right and equitable under all of the circumstances and the law.' " *State v. Sciarra.* Although Rule 16(i) provides specifically for various sanctions for noncompliance, a trial justice is clearly free, within the bounds of sound discretion, to enter any order he or she deems most appropriate.[1] We will not disturb a trial judge's action in this regard absent a clear showing that the trial justice abused his or her discretion.

The state has failed to establish any abuse of discretion by the trial justice. Rule 16(i) allows a trial justice to enter an order compelling discovery, to grant a continuance to a party prejudiced by the untimely disclosure of discoverable material, or to exclude evidence not properly disclosed. In the present case, a previous order compelling discovery was not adequately complied with by the state. Since the case had not reached trial and since the records requested by defense counsel were never produced, a continuance was certainly not the proper sanction for the state's noncompliance. Finally, the records sought by defense counsel may well have contained exculpatory evidence, and thus the interests of justice, and the interests of

1. Rule 16(i) of the Superior Court Rules of Criminal Procedure provides as follows: "If at any time during the course of the proceedings it is brought to the attention of the court that a party has failed to comply with this rule or with an order issued pursuant to this rule, it may order such party to provide the discovery or inspection, grant a continuance, or prohibit the party from introducing in evidence the material which or testimony of a witness whose identity or statement were not disclosed, or it may enter such other order as it deems appropriate."

defendant in particular, did not call for exclusion of any nondisclosed records. None of the sanctions specifically provided for in Rule 16(i) could possibly have neutralized the prejudice suffered by defendant, especially in light of the state's persistent refusal to comply with the court-ordered discovery. Accordingly, the trial justice availed himself of the Rule 16(i) provision authorizing a trial justice to enter any such order he or she deems appropriate. It is within the trial justice's discretion to impose a sanction for noncompliance with a criminal discovery order in light of the attendant circumstances of a given case.[2] * * *

The state argues that any noncompliance with the November 23, 1982 order was inadvertent and that this fact should somehow affect our analysis. It does not. As we have stated before, "[I]t would be unfair to allow the state the tactical advantage of surprise gained by violating, *whether intentionally or unintentionally,* the rules of discovery." (Emphasis added.) *State v. Darcy,* 442 A.2d 900 [(R.I.1977)]. * * *

The state cites *United States v. Hemmer,* 729 F.2d 10 (1st Cir.1984) in support of the proposition that, to prevail on a motion to dismiss grounded on the government's failure to comply with a Rule 16 discovery order, a criminal defendant must establish that he has been prejudiced by such noncompliance. We do not disagree. However, *Hemmer* involved *late* state disclosure of requested materials. The defendant in *Hemmer* never requested a continuance and thus could not establish that he was prejudiced by the late disclosure. In the present case, *no* disclosure was made at all, and thus the state's noncompliance robbed defendant of the very tools needed to establish the requisite prejudice.

We hold that the trial justice did not abuse his discretion in dismissing the indictment because of the state's noncompliance with the Rule 16 discovery order. * * * [T]he state's appeal is denied and dismissed, the order of dismissal entered below is hereby affirmed, and the case is remanded to the Superior Court.

Notes and Questions

1. *United States v. Hemmer,* distinguished by the *Quintal* court, involved the more frequently presented question of what remedy should be imposed when the government at trial introduces evidence (in *Hemmer,* a scientific report) that should have been previously disclosed to the defendant under the jurisdiction's pretrial discovery rule.[a] Here too, appellate courts note that the trial judge must be given "broad latitude" in the choice of sanction, but they also have advanced (and sometimes rigorously enforced) various guidelines for the exercise of that authority. Those guidelines are summarized in LaFave and Israel, § 19.3(j):

"The preferred remedy, at least where the prosecutor acted in good faith, is to order immediate compliance and offer the

2. In addition, it is important to note that the state agreed to the sixty-day conditional order of dismissal during the pretrial conference of November 23, 1982. Although there is some disagreement over whether the state actually understood that order to call for dismissal with prejudice, we find most credible the remarks of the trial justice * * * to the effect that all parties agreed to and understood the potential effect of the conditional order.

a. See LaFave and Israel, § 19.3(j): "Perhaps no defense claim relating to discovery is more frequently raised on appeal than the claim that the trial court failed to utilize the proper remedy when the defendant discovered shortly before or during trial that the prosecution had breached a discovery order. The claim usually relates to the prosecution's presentation of a witness who was not endorsed on its witness list or its introduction into evidence of a previously undisclosed statement of the defendant or a scientific report. On occasion, it will be based upon the late disclosure of discoverable material that was not used as prosecution evidence, but which might have been helpful to the defense, if disclosed earlier, in developing its own case or in impeaching a prosecution witness. The usual defense complaint is that the trial court should have excluded evidence or declared a mistrial as opposed to granting some lesser remedy, such as simply ordering immediate disclosure, or combining such disclosure with a brief continuance."

defendant a continuance so that he can take advantage of the delayed discovery. Thus, where the non-compliance consists of the failure to have previously endorsed a prosecution witness, the trial court is advised to allow the witness to testify, but first grant the defendant sufficient time to interview the witness. Similarly, where defendant's complaint relates to the state's failure to make timely disclosure of the existence of some item that defendant might want to offer in evidence, the trial court is advised to grant a continuance sufficient to permit the defendant to obtain that evidence. * * * [Appellate courts] also recognize that * * * there are [certain] cases in which a continuance will not eliminate potential prejudice. Such situations arise primarily where disclosure is first made during trial and the defendant has already committed himself to a line of defense that he would not have presented if he had previously been aware of the evidence now offered by the prosecution. In such situations, the exclusion of the evidence or the declaration of a mistrial may be necessary. However, * * * [c]onsistent with their advice to trial courts to give serious consideration to granting a continuance, appellate courts also frequently warn against the unnecessary exclusion of evidence. The trial court, it is noted, 'should seek to apply sanctions that affect the evidence at trial and the merits of the case as little as possible.' Where possible, sanctions should not have 'adverse effects on the rights of the parties, rather than on the offending attorneys themselves' * * *. Some courts have suggested, however, that preclusion (or even dismissal) is an especially appropriate sanction where the prosecutor has acted in bad faith. Others suggest that, even then, exclusion is not desirable unless needed to remedy apparent prejudice; the more appropriate sanction is holding the prosecutor in contempt. A sanction should 'not be regarded as a bonus awarded without regard to its need in furtherance of fair trial rights.' "

2. Was the trial court's ruling in *Quintal* consistent with the basic thrust of the above guidelines? If not, is a different appraoch applicable because, as the Rhode Island Supreme Court stressed, "no disclosure was made at all, and thus the state's noncompliance robbed the defendant of the very tools needed to establish the requisite prejudice." Could the trial court have provided these "tools" by holding the prosecutor in charge of the case in civil contempt until there was full compliance with its order? Were there other interests of the defendant Quintal, beyond his right to discovery, that might justify the imposition of a sanction of dismissal with prejudice? While the prosecutor's noncompliance caused considerable delay, would that delay amount to a violation of defendant's statutory or constitutional rights to a speedy trial? See Ch. 19, § 1. Did the conditional sixty-day order of November 30th create in defendant an enforceable expectation that the burdens of accusation and litigation would end if the January 24th deadline passed without full disclosure by the prosecution? Cf. Note 3, p. 922 supra and Note 8, p. 1204 infra (discussing the enforcement of prosecutorial promises not to prosecute).

3. When the government's failure to provide required discovery is first uncovered after the trial is completed and the defendant convicted, the issue before the appellate or trial court is somewhat different. Even though there has been a discovery violation that would require some remedy at trial, that violation will not necessarily require that the defendant be granted a new trial at which proper discovery can be provided. Whether a new trial is needed is said to depend upon "the extent of the Government's culpability for failure to make disclosable material available to the defense, on the one hand, weighed against the amount of prejudice to the defense which resulted on the other." *United States v. Miranda,* 526 F.2d 1319, 1324 (2d Cir.1975). See also *State v. Burkhalter,* 735 F.2d 1327 (11th Cir.

1984) (court should consider five factors: "(1) the amount of prejudice that resulted from the failure to disclose; (2) the reason for nondisclosure; (3) the extent to which the harm caused by nondisclosure was mitigated by subsequent events; (4) the weight of the properly admitted evidence supporting the defendant's guilt; and (5) other relevant factors arising out of the circumstances of the case").

4. What if the prosecutor's failure to disclose stems from the loss or destruction of discoverable material? It generally is recognized that the prosecution's duty to disclose carries with it an obligation to preserve discoverable material within the government's possession. See *Brown v. United States,* 372 A.2d 557 (D.C.App. 1977). Most authorities also agree that a "pragmatic balancing approach" must be applied to determine whether the loss of discoverable material requires the exclusion of related prosecution evidence or even dismissal of the charges. As the Second Circuit noted, see *United States v. Miranda,* Note 3 supra: "[T]he appropriateness or extent of sanctions in such situations depends upon a case-by-case assessment of the government's culpability for the loss, together with a realistic appraisal of its significance when viewed in light of its nature, its bearing upon critical issues in the case, and the strength of the government's untainted proof." The *Miranda* court concluded that sanctions there were not required for the loss of the tape recording of a conversation between defendant and an informant. The court stressed that (1) the loss was inadvertent, (2) it was "more likely" that the recording would have supported the government's version of the conversation than the "somewhat incredible version" testified to by the defendant, (3) the defense counsel had "made the most" of the loss of the tape in his argument to the jury, and (4) the case against the defendant "was a strong one." Consider also Note 7, p. 1162 infra (discussing the due process standard applicable where the list or destroyed evidence had an apparent exculpatory value).

In *United States v. Bryant,* 439 F.2d 642 (D.C.Cir.1971), the court applied the balancing test noted above, but suggested that in the future the government would bear a much heavier burden in avoiding sanctions for the loss of discoverable material. The court noted:

> [W]e hold that sanctions for nondisclosure based on loss of evidence will be invoked in the future unless the Government can show that it has promulgated, enforced and attempted in good faith to follow rigorous and systematic procedures designed to preserve all discoverable evidence gathered in the course of a criminal investigation. The burden, of course, is on the Government to make this showing. Negligent failure to comply with the required procedures will provide no excuse.

Other federal courts appear to have rejected the proposed prophylactic standard of *Bryant.* See LaFave and Israel, § 19.3(j). Indeed, *Miranda,* supra, questioned whether the D.C. Circuit itself had subsequently applied that standard. Does *Quintal* go beyond the *Bryant* standard?

SECTION 2. DISCOVERY BY THE PROSECUTION

WILLIAMS v. FLORIDA

399 U.S. 78, 90 S.Ct. 1893, 26 L.Ed.2d 446 (1970).

MR. JUSTICE WHITE delivered the opinion of the Court.

Prior to his trial for robbery in the State of Florida, petitioner filed a "Motion for a Protective Order," seeking to be excused from the requirements of Rule 1.200 [now Rule 3.200] of the Florida Rules of Criminal Procedure. That rule requires a defendant, on written demand of the prosecuting attorney, to give notice in advance of trial if the defendant intends to claim an alibi, and to furnish the prosecuting attorney with information as to the place he claims to have been and with the names and addresses of the alibi witnesses he intends to use. In his motion petitioner openly declared his intent to claim an alibi, but objected to the further disclosure requirements on the ground that the Rule "compels the defendant in a criminal case to be a witness against himself" in violation of his Fifth and Fourteenth Amendment rights. The motion was denied. Petitioner also filed a pretrial motion to impanel a 12-man jury instead of the six-man jury provided by Florida law in all but capital cases. [See p. 1260 infra].

Florida's notice-of-alibi rule is in essence a requirement that a defendant submit to a limited form of pretrial discovery by the State whenever he intends to rely at trial on the defense of alibi. In exchange for the defendant's disclosure of the witnesses he proposes to use to establish that defense, the State in turn is required to notify the defendant of any witnesses it proposes to offer in rebuttal to that defense. Both sides are under a continuing duty promptly to disclose the names and addresses of additional witnesses bearing on the alibi as they become available. The threatened sanction for failure to comply is the exclusion at trial of the defendant's alibi evidence—except for his own testimony—or, in the case of the State, the exclusion of the State's evidence offered in rebuttal to the alibi.

In this case, following the denial of his Motion for a Protective Order, petitioner complied with the alibi rule and gave the State the name and address of one Mary Scotty. Mrs. Scotty was summoned to the office of the State Attorney on the morning of the trial, where she gave pretrial testimony. At the trial itself, Mrs. Scotty, petitioner and petitioner's wife all testified that the three of them had been in Mrs. Scotty's apartment during the time of the robbery. On two occasions during cross-examination of Mrs. Scotty, the prosecuting attorney confronted her with her earlier deposition in which she had given dates and times which in some respects did not correspond with the dates and times given at trial. Mrs. Scotty adhered to her trial story, insisting that she had been mistaken in her earlier testimony. The State also offered in rebuttal the testimony of one of the officers investigating the robbery who claimed that Mrs. Scotty had asked him for directions on the afternoon in question during the time when she claimed to have been in her apartment with petitioner and his wife.

We need not linger over the suggestion that the discovery permitted the State against petitioner in this case deprived him of "due process" or a "fair trial." Florida law provides for liberal discovery by the defendant against the State, and the notice-of-alibi rule is itself carefully hedged with reciprocal duties requiring state disclosure to the defendant. Given the ease with which an alibi can be fabricated, the State's interest in protecting itself against an eleventh hour defense is both obvious and legitimate. Reflecting this interest, notice-of-alibi provisions, dating at least from 1927, are now in existence in a substantial number of States. The adversary system of trial is hardly an end to itself; it is not yet a poker game in which players enjoy an absolute right always to conceal their cards until played. We find ample room in that system, at least as far as "due process" is concerned, for the instant Florida rule, which is designed to enhance the search for truth in the criminal trial by insuring both the defendant and the State ample opportunity to investigate certain facts crucial to the determination of guilt or innocence.

Petitioner's major contention is that he was "compelled to be a witness against himself" contrary to the commands of the Fifth and Fourteenth Amendments because the notice-of-alibi rule required him to give the State the name and address of Mrs. Scotty in advance of trial and thus to furnish the State with information useful in convicting him. No pretrial statement of petitioner was introduced at trial; but armed with Mrs. Scotty's name and address and the knowledge that she was to be petitioner's alibi witness, the State was able to take her deposition in advance of trial and to find rebuttal testimony. Also, requiring him to reveal the elements of his defense is claimed to have interfered with his right to wait until after the State had presented its case to decide how to defend against it. We conclude, however, as has apparently every other court which has considered the issue, that the privilege against self-incrimination is not violated by a requirement that the defendant give notice of an alibi defense and disclose his alibi witnesses.[14]

The defendant in a criminal trial is frequently forced to testify himself and to call other witnesses in an effort to reduce the risk of conviction. When he presents his witnesses, he must reveal their identity and submit them to cross-examination which in itself may prove incriminating or which may furnish the State with leads to incriminating rebuttal evidence. That the defendant faces such a dilemma demanding a choice between complete silence and presenting a defense has never been thought an invasion of the privilege against compelled self-incrimination. The pressures generated by the State's evidence may be severe but they do not vitiate the defendant's choice to present an alibi defense and witnesses to prove it, even though the attempted defense ends in catastrophe for the defendant. However "testimonial" and "incriminating" the alibi defense proves to be, it cannot be considered "compelled" within the meaning of the Fifth and Fourteenth Amendments.

Very similar constraints operate on the defendant when the State requires pretrial notice of alibi and the naming of alibi witnesses. Nothing in such a rule requires the defendant to rely on an alibi or prevents him from abandoning the defense; these matters are left to his unfettered choice. That choice must be made, but the pressures which bear on his pretrial decision are of the same nature as those which would induce him to call alibi witnesses at the trial: the force of historical fact beyond both his and the State's control and the strength of the State's case built on these facts. Response to that kind of pressure by offering evidence or testimony is not compelled self-incrimination transgressing the Fifth and Fourteenth Amendments.

In the case before us, the notice-of-alibi rule by itself in no way affected petitioner's crucial decision to call alibi witnesses or added to the legitimate pressures leading to that course of action. At most, the rule only compelled petitioner to accelerate the timing of his disclosure, forcing him to divulge at an earlier date information which the petitioner from the beginning planned to divulge at trial. Nothing in the Fifth Amendment privilege entitles a defendant as a matter of constitutional right to await the end of the State's case before announcing the nature of his defense, any more than it entitles him to await the jury's verdict on the State's case-in-chief before deciding whether or not to take the stand himself.

Petitioner concedes that absent the notice-of-alibi rule the Constitution would raise no bar to the court's granting the State a continuance at trial on the grounds of surprise as soon as the alibi witness is called. Nor would there be self-incrimination problems if, during that continuance, the State was permitted to do precisely what it did here prior to trial: to depose the witness and find rebuttal evidence. But if so utilizing a continuance is permissible under the Fifth and Fourteenth Amendments, then surely the same result may be accomplished through pretrial dis-

14. We emphasize that this case does not involve the question of the validity of the threatened sanction, had petitioner chosen not to comply with the notice-of-alibi rule. Whether and to what extent a State can enforce discovery rules against a defendant who fails to comply, by excluding relevant, probative evidence is a question raising Sixth Amendment issues which we have no occasion to explore. It is enough that no such penalty was exacted here.

covery, as it was here, avoiding the necessity of a disrupted trial.[17] We decline to hold that the privilege against compulsory self-incrimination guarantees the defendant the right to surprise the state with an alibi defense.

MR. CHIEF JUSTICE BURGER, concurring.

I join fully in Mr. Justice White's opinion for the Court. I see an added benefit to the alibi notice rule in that it will serve important functions by way of disposing of cases without trial in appropriate circumstances—a matter of considerable importance when courts, prosecution offices and legal aid and defender agencies are vastly overworked. [The Chief Justice noted that a prosecutor receiving the names of alibi witnesses in advance of trial often would be able to determine whether an alibi defense was "reliable and unimpeachable" or "contrived and fabricated." The former determination "would very likely lead to dismissal of the charges," while the latter could lead to a defense decision to plead guilty. In either instance, the Chief Justice noted, "the ends of justice will have been served and the processes expedited."]

MR. JUSTICE BLACK, with whom MR. JUSTICE DOUGLAS joins, dissenting.

* * * Although this case itself involves only a notice-of-alibi provision, it is clear that the decision means that a State can require a defendant to disclose in advance of trial any and all information he might possibly use to defend himself at trial. This decision, in my view, is a radical and dangerous departure from the historical and constitutionally guaranteed right of a defendant in a criminal case to remain completely silent, requiring the State to prove its case without any assistance of any kind from the defendant himself.

The core of the majority's decision is an assumption that compelling a defendant to give notice of an alibi defense before a trial is no different from requiring a defendant, after the State has produced the evidence against him at trial, to plead alibi before the jury retires to consider the case. * * * [But] when a defendant is required to indicate whether he might plead alibi in advance of trial, he faces a vastly different decision than that faced by one who can wait until the State has presented the case against him before making up his mind. Before trial the defendant knows only what the State's case *might* be. Before trial there is no such thing as the "strength of the State's case," there is only a range of possible cases. At that time there is no certainty as to what kind of case the State will ultimately be able to prove at trial. Therefore any appraisal of the desirability of pleading alibi will be beset with guesswork and gambling far greater than that accompanying the decision at the trial itself. * * * Clearly the pressures on defendants to plead an alibi created by this procedure are not only quite different than the pressures operating at the trial itself, but are in fact significantly greater. Contrary to the majority's assertion, the pretrial decision cannot be analyzed as simply a matter of "timing," influenced by the same factors operating at the trial itself.

The Court apparently also assumes that a defendant who has given the required notice can abandon his alibi without hurting himself. Such an assumption is implicit in and necessary for the majority's argument that the pretrial decision is no different than that at the trial itself. I, however, cannot so lightly assume that pretrial notice will have no adverse effects on a defendant who later decides to forego such a defense. Necessarily the defendant will have given the prosecutor the names of persons who may have some knowledge about the defendant himself or his activi-

17. It might also be argued that the "testimonial" disclosures protected by the Fifth Amendment include only statements relating to the historical facts of the crime, not statements relating solely to what a defendant proposes to do at trial.

ties. Necessarily the prosecutor will have every incentive to question these persons fully, and in doing so he may discover new leads or evidence. Undoubtedly there will be situations in which the State will seek to use such information—information it would probably never have obtained but for the defendant's coerced cooperation.

It is unnecessary for me, however, to engage in any such intellectual gymnastics concerning the practical effects of the notice-of-alibi procedure, because the Fifth Amendment itself clearly provides that "[n]o person * * * shall be compelled in any criminal case to be a witness against himself." If words are to be given their plain and obvious meaning, that provision, in my opinion, states that a criminal defendant cannot be required to give evidence, testimony, or any other assistance to the State to aid it in convicting him of crime. The Florida notice-of-alibi rule in my opinion is a patent violation of that constitutional provision because it requires a defendant to disclose information to the State so that the State can use that information to destroy him. * * *

It is no answer to this argument to suggest that the Fifth Amendment as so interpreted would give the defendant an unfair element of surprise, turning a trial into a "poker game" or "sporting contest," for that tactical advantage to the defendant is inherent in the type of trial required by our Bill of Rights. The Framers were well aware of the awesome investigative and prosecutorial powers of government and it was in order to limit those powers that they spelled out in detail in the Constitution the procedure to be followed in criminal trials. * * * The defendant, under our Constitution, need not do anything at all to defend himself, and certainly he cannot be required to help convict himself. Rather he has an absolute, unqualified right to compel the State to investigate its own case, find its own witnesses, prove its own facts, and convince the jury through its own resources. Throughout the process the defendant has a fundamental right to remain silent, in effect challenging the State at every point to "Prove it!" * * *

This constitutional right to remain absolutely silent cannot be avoided by superficially attractive analogies to any so-called "compulsion" inherent in the trial itself which may lead a defendant to put on evidence in his own defense. Obviously the Constitution contemplates that a defendant can be "compelled" to stand trial, and obviously there will be times when the trial process itself will require the defendant to do something in order to try to avoid a conviction. But nothing in the Constitution permits the State to add to the natural consequences of a trial and compel the defendant in advance of trial to participate in any way in the State's attempt to condemn him. * * *

On the surface this case involves only a notice-of-alibi provision, but in effect the decision opens the way for a profound change in one of the most important traditional safeguards of a criminal defendant. The rationale of today's decision is in no way limited to alibi defenses, or any other type or classification of evidence. The theory advanced goes at least so far as to permit the State to obtain under threat of sanction complete disclosure by the defendant in advance of trial of all evidence, testimony and tactics he plans to use at that trial. In each case the justification will be that the rule affects only the "timing" of the disclosure, and not the substantive decision itself.

* * * [I]n spite of the history of oppression that produced the Bill of Rights and the strong reluctance of our governments to compel a criminal defendant to assist in his own conviction, the Court today reaches out to embrace and sanctify at the first opportunity a most dangerous departure from the Constitution and the traditional safeguards afforded persons accused of crime. I cannot accept such a result and must express my most emphatic disagreement and dissent.

Notes and Questions

1. *The scope of the Williams dissent.* In *Scott v. State,* 519 P.2d 774 (Alaska 1974), the court noted that it was "persuaded" by Justice Black's dissent in *Williams* to read the self-incrimination clause of the Alaska constitution "more broadly" than *Williams* interpreted the federal clause. However, the court did not strike down all elements of the lower court's alibi-notice order. It held unconstitutional the requirements that the defendant list his alibi witnesses and specify the "alternative location where he claims to have been," but sustained the requirement that the defendant note in advance his intent to rely upon an alibi defense. The court reasoned that that notice alone would not disclose the "substance of [the] defense theory" (as would the alternative location) or "any weaknesses or inconsistencies therein" (as would the witness list), and it therefore was "difficult to conceive" how it could possibly "provide the state with another 'link' in its chain of evidence." Would the rationale of Justice Black's dissent in *Williams* have required the rejection of the notice requirement?

2. *The rationale of Williams.* The reach of the "accelerated disclosure" rationale advanced in *Williams* has been a subject of considerable dispute, at least among commentators. See LaFave and Israel, § 19.4(b). The commentators agree that accelerated disclosure may give the prosecution several benefits, but disagree as to whether the *Williams* rationale upholds the State's right to insist upon all of those benefits.

Accelerated disclosure is seen as giving the prosecution at least four possible benefits it would not receive if the defendant were allowed to delay disclosing the nature of his evidence until he was ready to introduce it at trial. First, accelerated disclosure may provide the prosecution with information that will lead it to other evidence useful in presenting its case-in-chief. Admittedly, the same information often would subsequently become available to the prosecution during trial, when the defendant utilized that information in his defense, but the prosecutor frequently can make more effective use of the information when it is received before trial, with more time to develop leads. More significantly, there are instances in which the information revealed under accelerated disclosure would not later become available because the defendant eventually would find that he did not have to use it at trial—e.g., where the prosecution was unable to establish a sufficient case-in-chief based on its own sources or where the defendant decided to rely on a different defense at trial. Second, the prosecution similarly may obtain information through accelerated disclosure that will lead it to evidence establishing defendant's involvement in unrelated offenses. Here again, this could be information it might not have eventually received at trial. Third, the accelerated disclosure may provide the prosecution with information useful in developing a rebuttal to the defendant's defense.[a] Of course, the prosecution eventually would receive this information when the defense was presented at trial, but it would often be much more difficult for the prosecution to make effective use of the information at that point (particularly in a jurisdiction in which trial judges frown on granting continuances). Finally, accelerated disclosure, by indicating the direction the defense is likely to take, permits the prosecution to husband its resources and thereby to do a better job in presenting both its case-in-chief and its rebuttal to the defense.

a. A somewhat related contention is that accelerated disclosure may make it more difficult for the defendant to present his defense because proposed defense witnesses may be intimidated by police inquiries conducted in the course of the prosecution's development of its rebuttal evidence. Cf. Vt.R.Crim.P. 16.1(c) (defense must disclose witnesses it intends to use at trial, but such witnesses thereafter may be interviewed by the government only in the presence of defense counsel).

While *Williams* clearly indicates that the Fifth Amendment does not bar an accelerated disclosure which provides the prosecution with the third and fourth advantages above, does the same follow for the first and second? To what extent did the *Williams* majority view the Florida alibi-notice provision as likely to give the prosecution such advantages? Assume that a defendant in a particular case could show that the alibi witnesses he would list could assist the state in developing its case-in-chief or could furnish incriminating information concerning another offense. Does *Williams* hold that the defendant lacks a valid self-incrimination objection in such a case? Compare Van Kessel, *Prosecutorial Discovery and the Privilege Against Self-Incrimination: Accommodation or Capitulation,* 4 Hast.L.Q. 855 (1977) (*Williams* did not address "the issue of whether pretrial disclosures that support the prosecutor's case-in-chief may be compelled," but was concerned with the use of the disclosed information for "impeachment and rebuttal purposes only"); Nakell, *Criminal Discovery for the Defense and Prosecution: The Developing Constitutional Considerations,* 50 N.C.L.Rev. 437 (1972) (*Williams'* analysis may be based on the assumption that alibi evidence ordinarily does not include "incriminating information"); Westen, *Order of Proof: An Accused's Right to Control The Timing and Sequence of Evidence in His Defense,* 66 Cal.L.Rev. 935, 947–959, 981 (1978) (*Williams* appears to rest on a rationale that is not limited by the nature of the defense evidence disclosed—the rationale that, "as long as a defendant has substantial pretrial discovery of the prosecution's case," enabling him "to gain almost as much knowledge of the state's case before trial as he eventually would have at trial," the "incremental increase in pressures * * * due to acceleration of his disclosure decision" are not of "sufficient magnitude to violate the privilege against self-incrimination"); Blumenson, *Constitutional Limitations on Prosecutorial Discovery,* 18 Harv.C.R.–C.L.L.Rev. 122 (1983) ("Justice White's reasoning on the Fifth Amendment applies equally to a rule requiring a defendant who intends to testify to answer pretrial interrogatories about her testimony: truth seeking would be enhanced by advancing the 'timing' of disclosure").

3. Does BROOKS v. TENNESSEE, described in Note 5 at p. 1364 infra, provide any assistance in determining the scope of the *Williams* rationale? In *Brooks,* a divided Supreme Court held unconstitutional a state rule that a defendant, if he desired to testify in his own defense, had to do so before any other defense witnesses gave testimony. The majority found that rule imposed an unjustifiable burden upon defendant's constitutional right not to testify since he was being forced to decide whether or not to testify before he could evaluate the strength of the testimony of his other witnesses. The Court acknowledged that the state had an interest in ensuring that a defendant not shape his testimony to conform to that of the defense witnesses testifying before him (an interest accomplished as to other witnesses by their sequestration prior to testifying). It concluded, however, that barring defendant's later testimony if he does not testify as the first defense witness "is not a constitutionally permissible means of insuring his honesty." The majority in *Brooks* did not refer to *Williams,* but the dissent cited *Williams,* among other cases, in arguing that the burden imposed upon the defendant was no worse than analogous burdens accepted in past cases.

Is *Brooks* inconsistent with the interpretation of the Fifth Amendment advanced in *Williams?* Several commentators have reached that conclusion. See Westen, Note 2 supra (arguing that *Williams'* reasoning applied "with equal force" to *Brooks,* and that the *Brooks* result must be justified by reference to a defendant's constitutional right to control the order of his proof). Clinton, *The Right To Present A Defense,* 9 Ind.L.Rev. 713, 775 (1976) (*Brooks* necessarily rejects the "*Williams* holding that the *timing* of defense disclosure did not raise fifth amendment questions"). Lapides, *Cross-Currents In Prosecutorial Discovery,* 7 S.F.L.Rev. 216, 228 (1973) (the choices imposed upon the defendants in the two cases were "basically indistinguishable," each defendant being required to "relinquish" his "right to remain silent" before he had had an opportunity to fully evaluate all of the evidence in the case). Could the Court have distinguished *Williams* on the ground that the defendant there, unlike the defendant in *Brooks,* was able to make his decision with almost as much information as he would have had later since Florida's liberal discovery provisions permitted him to "know everything about the prosecution's case before he was required to decide whether he was going to put on an alibi"? See Amsterdam, *A Selective Survey of Supreme Court Decisions in Criminal Law and Procedure,* 9 Crim.L.Bull. 389, 405 (1973). Might the Court have distinguished *Brooks* on the ground that the defendant there was being asked to reveal "potential evidence" (i.e., evidence which, at the time, he was not certain that he wanted to use), while *Williams* required disclosure of evidence that the defendant there had already decided to use at trial? See Blumenson, Note 2 supra (arguing that the defendant in *Brooks* was being forced to do more than make the accelerated disclosure required in *Williams,* as he was required to make an accelerated decision as to use of evidence at trial). Is it significant that *Brooks* related to defendant's own testimony? See fn. c, p. 1365 infra.

4. *Reciprocal discovery.* In WARDIUS v. OREGON, 412 U.S. 470, 93 S.Ct. 2208, 37 L.Ed.2d 82 (1973), a unanimous Court held unconstitutional a state alibi-notice provision which made no provision for reciprocal discovery. The Court noted (per MARSHALL, J.):

"We hold that the Due Process Clause of the Fourteenth Amendment forbids enforcement of alibi rules unless reciprocal discovery rights are given to criminal defendants. * * * [A]lthough the Due Process Clause has little to say regarding the amount of discovery which the parties must be afforded, but cf. *Brady v. Maryland* [p. 1146 infra], it does speak to the balance of forces between the accused and his accuser. The *Williams* court was therefore careful to note that 'Florida law provides for liberal discovery by the defendant against the State, and the notice-of-alibi rule is itself carefully hedged with reciprocal duties requiring state disclosure to the defendant.' The same cannot be said of Oregon law. As the State conceded at oral argument, Oregon grants no discovery rights to criminal defendants, and, indeed, does not even provide defendants with bills of particulars. More significantly, Oregon, unlike Florida, has no provision which requires the State to reveal the names and addresses of witnesses it plans to use to refute an alibi defense.

"We do not suggest that the Due Process Clause of its own force requires Oregon to adopt such provisions. But we do hold that in the absence of a strong showing of state interests to the contrary, discovery must be a two-way street. The State may not insist that trials be run as a 'search for truth' so far as defense witnesses are concerned, while maintaining 'poker game' secrecy for its own witnesses. It is fundamentally unfair to require a defendant to divulge the details of his own case while at the same time subjecting him to the hazard of surprise concerning refutation of the very pieces of evidence which he disclosed to the State."

How far does *Wardius* extend the requirement of reciprocal discovery? Does it require the state to provide the defendant with extensive discovery apart from the discovery of its rebuttal to the alibi defense? Justice Traynor of California, who first developed the accelerated disclosure rationale, described it as holding that a defendant could fairly "be required to make his decision * * * before trial *if he is given discovery of the prosecution's case before trial,*" see Traynor, *Ground Lost and*

Found in Criminal Discovery, 39 N.Y.U.L. Rev. 228 (1964) (emphasis added). Does *Wardius* combine with *Williams* to insist upon that discovery prerequisite, thereby guaranteeing defendant extensive discovery of the prosecution's case-in-chief? See Nakell, Note 2 supra. Or does *Wardius* reflect a concern only with maintaining the traditional "balance of advantage" between defense and prosecution and therefore require only that the prosecution provide equivalent discovery as to the alibi itself? See Westen, Note 2 supra. Cf. *People v. Fields,* 322 N.E.2d 33 (Ill.1974) (concluding that extensive defense discovery, modeled after the A.B.A. Standards, was not sufficient to uphold an alibi statute which failed to provide also for the disclosure of the prosecution's rebuttal witnesses on the alibi defense).

5. *Insanity notice requirements.* Over half of the states require the defendant to give advance notice if he intends to rely upon a defense of insanity or to introduce expert testimony that he lacked the requisite mens rea for the offense charged due to mental disease or defect. See LaFave and Israel, § 19.4(c). Most require only that such a defense be noted and that the defendant submit to a psychiatric exam by a court appointed expert.[b] Several, however, also require the defendant to list all expert witnesses to be called in support of his defense. Are such provisions distinguishable from the alibi-notice provision upheld in *Williams* because insanity is a defense of "confession and avoidance whereby alibi involves only an avoidance" (i.e., insanity is a defense through which the defendant "confesses to committing the criminal act")? See *Radford v. Stewart,* 320 F.Supp. 826 (D.Mont.1970), aff'd, 472 F.2d 1161 (9th Cir.1973) (rejecting a defense attempt to distinguish *Williams* on those grounds). Nakell, Note 2 supra, suggests that *Williams* should be viewed as upholding advance notice requirements only for "affirmative defenses"—i.e., defenses in which "the burden of going forward with the evidence is on the defendant" and the defense "establishes facts other than those occurring at the time and place of the crime to affect inferentially the determination of what did then and there take place." Would an advance notice requirement as to a mental illness defense, including the listing of expert witnesses, be acceptable under such a standard?

6. *Notice as to defenses beyond alibi and insanity.* Several states require the defendant to state in advance of trial the general nature of the defense he intends to raise at trial. See LaFave and Israel, § 19.4(e). Typical examples of the types of defenses to be listed are entrapment, duress, intoxication, claim of authority, justifiable use of force, and lack of mens rea. As with the alibi defense in *Williams,* the defendant is not bound to raise the listed defense at trial, and the prosecution cannot use against the defense its failure to do so. Does *Williams* necessarily sustain the constitutionality of such provisions? Consider Van Kessel, Note 2 supra, suggesting that *Williams* might be limited to defenses that "generally are easy to fabricate, difficult to rebut or disprove, and available to the defense as a last minute surprise weapon, often shifting the focus of the trial to a single narrow issue." The author suggests that alibi and claims of "physical or mental incapacity, such as impotency, insanity, and diminished capacity" share "most of these characteristics," but defenses involving "excuse or justification, such as self-defense, duress, mistake, or accident" generally do not. The latter defenses, it is argued, are "usually apparent from the facts" and "rarely [are] difficult to contest."

b. Jurisdictions commonly prohibit use of the defendant's statements during the compelled psychiatric exam for any purpose other than determining his mental condition, although not all jurisdictions view that prohibition as automatically eliminating self-incrimination difficulties. See *Blaisdell v. Commonwealth,* 364 N.E.2d 191 (Mass.1977); *United States v. Byers,* 740 F.2d 1104 (D.C.Cir.1984).

7. *Witness lists.* Approximately fifteen states, including several with defense-notice provisions, require the defendant to disclose before trial the names and addresses of those persons he expects to call as defense witnesses. See LaFave and Israel, § 19.4(f). In all of these jurisdictions, the defendant is entitled to a similar listing of prosecution witnesses. A few additional states give the court discretion to order the defendant to produce such a list when the state has been required to list its witnesses. Does the breadth of witness-list disclosure present a "self-incrimination problem not as readily answered by an accelerated disclosure analysis [as the problem presented in *Williams*]"? Ibid.

In *Prudhomme v. Superior Court,* 466 P.2d 673 (Cal.1970), the California Supreme Court struck down a trial court's discovery order in a murder case which included reciprocal disclosure of witnesses. Although the California Court had earlier accepted an accelerated disclosure analysis in upholding the pretrial disclosure of a scientific report that defendant intended to introduce at trial, it concluded that that precedent could not justify a wholesale listing of witnesses. The court reasoned: "It is apparent that the principle element in determining whether a particular demand for discovery should be allowed is not simply whether * * * defendant intends to introduce or rely upon the evidence at trial, but whether disclosure thereof conceivably might lighten the prosecution's burden of proving its case-in-chief. * * * [T]he order herein is not limited to any particular defense or category of witnesses from which a court could attempt to determine its incriminatory effect. It requires no great effort or imagination to conceive of a variety of situations wherein the disclosure of the expected testimony of defense witnesses, or even their names and addresses, could easily provide an essential link in a chain of evidence underlying the prosecution's case-in-chief. For example, if a defendant in a murder case intended to call witness A to testify that defendant killed in self-defense, pretrial disclosure of that information could provide the prosecution with its sole eyewitness to defendant's homicide."

Although *Prudhomme* was decided before *Williams, Allen v. Superior Court,* 557 P.2d 65 (Cal.1976), reaffirmed *Prudhomme* as an interpretation of the California constitution. In this connection, the majority opinion noted that while "no decisions of the United States Supreme Court [are] in direct conflict with *Prudhomme,*" the "trend of the federal higher court's decisions [citing *Williams* and *United States v. Nobles,* p. 1141 infra] is not wholly consistent with our interpretation of the privilege against self-incrimination." In what respect might *Williams* be viewed as "not wholly consistent" with *Prudhomme?* Consider *People v. District Court,* 531 P.2d 626 (Colo.1975) (a post-*Williams* ruling upholding as constitutional on its face a court rule permitting discovery of defense theories and names of supporting witnesses to be used at trial, but noting that the rule might be unconstitutional as applied in a particular case if the requested disclosure "seeks information which might serve as an unconstitutional link in a chain of evidence tending to establish the accused's guilt of a criminal offense"). Compare, however, *State ex rel. Keller v. Criminal Court,* 317 N.E.2d 433 (Ind.1974), upholding, on the basis of *Williams* and *Wardius,* a court order requiring "substantially full pretrial discovery by both the prosecutor and defendant," including "the names and last known addresses of persons [defendant] intends to call as witnesses." The court noted, inter alia: "The defendant is not testifying when he gives the names of witnesses who may testify. * * * When we consider that it is well-established that the State has a right to fingerprint the defendant, to photograph him, to examine him physically, to take samples of blood, hair and other like materials from his body, and to secure samples of his handwriting, it can scarcely be argued that to ask for a list of witnesses he expects to produce at the trial is an invasion of his constitutional right against self-incrimination." Consider also fn. 17 of *Williams.*

8. *Defense disclosure of documents, scientific reports, and tangible objects.* Various discovery provisions provide for pretrial disclosure by the defense of documents, tangible items, and scientific reports that it intends to introduce at trial. Some, like Fed.R. Crim.P. 16(b)(1)(A), (B), apply only if the defendant requested production of similar items from the prosecution. Others require automatic disclosure of such items by both the prosecutor and the defense. Do such provisions raise a less or more substantial constitutional issue than the alibi-notice provision upheld in *Williams?* The Advisory Committee Note to the original version of the Federal Rules provision stressed the special need for pretrial disclosure of this type of evidence: "While the government normally has resources adequate to secure the information necessary for trial, there are some situations in which mutual disclosure would appear necessary to prevent the defendant from obtaining an unfair advantage. For example, in cases where both prosecution and defense have employed experts to make psychiatric examinations, it seems as important for the government to study the opinions of the experts to be called by the defendant in order to prepare for trial as it does for the defendant to study those of the government's witnesses. Or in cases (such as antitrust cases) in which the defendant is well represented and well financed, mutual disclosure so far as consistent with the privilege against self-incrimination would seem as appropriate as in civil cases." 39 F.R.D. 69, 177 (1966).

9. *Conditional discovery.* Assuming arguendo that required defense disclosure of any of the items discussed in Notes 2–8 supra would be unconstitutional, would that constitutional barrier be overcome by conditioning the disclosure on a defendant's exercise of a statutory right to discover similar material from the prosecution? Many jurisdictions requiring the defense to disclose witness lists, documents, or scientific reports condition that obligation on an initial defense request for disclosure of the same type of item from the prosecutor. See, e.g., Fed.R.Crim.P. 16(b)(1)(A), (B). The Nebraska provision specifically notes, in authorizing such conditional disclosure, that a defendant requesting discovery from the prosecution "shall be deemed to have waived his privilege of self-incrimination" for the purposes of that provision. Neb.Stat. § 29–1916(2). Is such a "waiver" invalid on the ground that "an option [i.e., discovery from the prosecution] which exacts a 'penalty' upon the exercise of the privilege against self-incrimination violates the Fifth Amendment"? *United States v. Fratello,* 44 F.R.D. 444, 447 (S.D.N.Y.1968) (raising, but not deciding the issue). Pulaski, *Extending the Disclosure Requirements of the Jencks Act to Defendants: Constitutional and Non-Constitutional Considerations,* 64 Iowa L.Rev. 1 (1978), argues that the Supreme Court has upheld state procedures that present defendants with choices which impose more substantial burdens on the exercise of their self-incrimination privilege. Thus, in *Crampton v. Ohio,* 402 U.S. 183, 91 S.Ct. 1454, 28 L.Ed.2d 711 (1971), the state was allowed to insist upon a "unitary" trial procedure in capital cases, which forced the defendant "to submit to cross-examination on the question of guilt in order to take advantage of whatever constitutional right he might enjoy to speak before the jury regarding sentence." Ibid. See also the cases upholding plea bargaining, discussed in Ch. 21, § 2.

DISCLOSURE OF MATERIALS THAT DEFENSE DOES NOT INTEND TO USE AT TRIAL

1. *Pretrial disclosure of witness statements: Self-incrimination objections.* About half of the states requiring the defense to list its witnesses also require the defense to disclose those prior recorded statements of

such witnesses that are in its possession. In all of these jurisdictions, the defendant has a right to receive from the prosecution the prior recorded statements of its witnesses. Self-incrimination objections to reciprocal pretrial disclosure of the prior recorded statements of defense witness have been rejected by several courts. See LaFave and Israel, § 19.4(g). Those courts have relied largely on the Supreme Court's discussion of the reach of the privilege in UNITED STATES v. NOBLES, 422 U.S. 225, 95 S.Ct. 2160, 45 L.Ed.2d 141 (1975), a case involving trial rather than pretrial disclosure.

In *Nobles,* defense counsel asked two key prosecution witnesses about statements they allegedly had made to a defense investigator. Those statements indicated that the witnesses' recollection of the bank robber had been considerably less clear than their current testimony suggested. One witness denied making the alleged statement and the other claimed it was inaccurate. Defense counsel later called the investigator as a defense witness for the purpose of testifying as to the statements. The trial judge then granted the prosecutor the right to inspect those portions of the investigator's report relating to the witnesses' statements for the purpose of cross-examining the investigator. When defense counsel stated that he would not produce the report, the court ruled that the investigator would not be allowed to testify about the witnesses' statements. On appeal following conviction, the Court of Appeals held that the trial court's disclosure order had violated the Fifth Amendment. The Supreme Court, per POWELL, J., reversed:

"The Court of Appeals concluded that the Fifth Amendment renders criminal discovery 'basically a one-way street.' Like many generalizations in constitutional law, this one is too broad. The relationship between the accused's Fifth Amendment rights and the prosecution's ability to discover materials at trial must be identified in a more discriminating manner. The Fifth Amendment privilege against compulsory self-incrimination is an 'intimate and personal one,' which protects 'a private inner sanctum of individual feeling and thought and proscribes state intrusion to extract self-condemnation.' *Couch v. United States* [p. 757 supra]. As we noted in *Couch,* the 'privilege is a *personal* privilege: it adheres basically to the person, not to information that may incriminate him.'

"In this instance disclosure of the relevant portions of the defense investigator's report would not impinge on the fundamental values protected by the Fifth Amendment. The court's order was limited to statements allegedly made by third parties who were available as witnesses to both the prosecution and the defense. Respondent did not prepare the report, and there is no suggestion that the portions subject to the disclosure order reflected any information that he conveyed to the investigator. The fact that these statements of third parties were elicited by a defense investigator on respondent's behalf does not convert them into respondent's personal communications. Requiring their production from the investigator therefore would not in any sense compel respondent to be a witness against himself or extort communications from him." [a]

a. Following *Nobles,* Fed.R.Crim.P. 26.2 was adopted. That Rule provides for what is in effect reciprocal Jencks Act disclosure [see p. 1121 supra] of the prior recorded statements of all witnesses except the defendant. As under the Jencks Act, the witness' statement is made available to the opposing party at trial, after the witness has testified, insofar as the statement "relates to the subject matter concerning which the witness has testified."

Relying on its state constitution, the California Supreme Court held unconstitutional a provision similar to Rule 26.2 as applied to defense witnesses. *In re Misener,* 698 P.2d 637 (Cal.1985). The California court held that its *Prudhomme* analysis [see Note 7, p. 1139 supra] was not limited to disclosures that might assist the prosecution in carrying its burden of proof as to its "case in chief," but extended also to disclosures that "might conceivably lighten the burden which the

2. Does *Nobles'* analysis carry over to the pretrial disclosure of a witness' statements? Consider LaFave and Israel, § 19.4(g): "Assuming that the witness' prior recorded statement does not reflect information obtained from the defendant, *Nobles* holds that its production does not require the defendant to make a testimonial declaration and therefore is not protected by his privilege against self-incrimination. *Fisher v. United States* [p. 757 supra], denying a taxpayer's self-incrimination objection to a subpoena requiring the production of workpapers prepared by his accountant, reinforces this conclusion. While the defendant may be acknowledging the existence of the witness' recorded statement, the witness himself serves as the primary source for its authentication. Of course, *Nobles* involved production at trial, rather than pretrial disclosure. But if the production does not involve defendant's own communication (in contrast, for example, to the listing of defense witnesses, which would ordinarily be based on information supplied by defendant himself), the privilege would not apply no matter when disclosure is required. Once the pretrial identification of the witness is sustained under *Williams,* the production of the statements of those witnesses may be justified under *Nobles.*"

3. *Disclosure of witness statements: Work product exemption.* The defendant in *Nobles* objected to the court order there on the basis of the work product doctrine, as well as the self-incrimination clause, and the Court's treatment of that aspect of his claim has generally been viewed as more favorable to those opposing pretrial disclosure of a defense witness' statement. The Court in *Nobles* noted initially that defendant was correct in assuming that the work product doctrine would be applied in the federal courts to criminal as well as civil cases. The Court also indicated that the defendant was correct in assuming that the doctrine was not simply limited to reports prepared by counsel, but could also apply to a report written by a defense investigator. The "realities of litigation in our adversary system," it noted, make it "necessary that the doctrine protect material prepared by agents for the attorney as well as those prepared by the attorney himself." Defendant's work product claim ultimately failed, however, because of waiver. The protection of the doctrine had been waived as to that portion of the investigator's report covered by the investigator's testimony when the defense elected to have him testify.

Since the waiver analysis of *Nobles* would not be applicable to pretrial disclosure, several courts have read *Nobles* as essentially prohibiting on work product grounds the required pretrial disclosure of prior recorded statements of defense witnesses. See e.g., *Spears v. State,* 403 N.E.2d 828 (Ind.1980). Would such an absolute bar be consistent with the analysis of work product applied to defense discovery of the recorded statements of prosecution witnesses? See Note 4, p. 1122 supra. What if that statement was no more than a verbatim recording of the witness' narrative in response to an open ended question of the defense lawyer or investigator? In a jurisdiction in which work product is limited to material prepared by the "prosecuting attorney and members of his legal staff" and therefore does not encompass

prosecution bears in bringing about a conviction of the accused" (here, by assisting the prosecution in its impeachment of defense witnesses). "The rationale in *Nobles,*" the court noted, had "failed to consider the aspect of the privilege against self-incrimination that requires the prosecution to carry the burden of convicting a defendant." Moreover, *Noble's* reasoning was flawed in its assumption that disclosure of defense witnesses' statements did not relate to the communications of the defendant himself: "[A]s allegedly occurred in the present case, a witness' statements to a defense attorney may be inextricably intertwined with the defendant's own statements. A defense attorney often finds witnesses through the defendant, and interviews those witnesses using information given to him by the defendant. Thus, even if the privilege against self-incrimination were to be limited to the defendant's own statements, it could be violated by a discovery order demanding witness statements made to the defense attorney or his agent."

statements taken by the police, should it also be held not to apply to statements taken by defense investigators? Commentators have suggested that pretrial disclosure of witness statements goes beyond the question of how a state will define work product. Requiring the pretrial disclosure of any written reports of the defense team, they argue, may infringe upon the defendant's right to the effective assistance of counsel; a defense counsel aware that a written report will be available to the prosecution may either decide not to have the witnesses interviewed or not to have their statements recorded. See Allis, *Limitations on Prosecutorial Discovery of the Defense Cases in Federal Courts: The Shield of Confidentiality,* 50 S.Cal.L.Rev. 461 (1977). But consider *Commonwealth v. Brinkley,* 480 A.2d 980 (Pa.1984) (similar view of work product should be taken as to both prosecution and defense, not including as to either a substantially verbatim recording of a witness' narrative); *Commonwealth v. Paszko,* 461 N.E.2d 222 (Mass.1984) (state was not required to adopt the broader view of work product accepted in *Nobles;* reciprocal discovery of investigator's reports describing witness statements not barred by work product).

4. *Disclosure of scientific reports.* Some state provisions governing prosecution discovery of scientific reports in the possession of the defendant are sufficiently broad to encompass all reports made in connection with the particular case, without regard to whether the defendant intends to rely upon the particular report or the expert who prepared the report. See e.g., N.J.R.Crim.P. 3:13–3(b). Does the defendant's privilege against self-incrimination protect against pretrial discovery of a report which defendant does not intend to use because it is not favorable to the defense? Is the short answer to such a claim that, under *Nobles,* the self-incrimination clause cannot apply since the defendant himself is not being asked to testify (assuming that the expert's report is not based on information furnished by the defendant). See e.g., *Gipson v. State,* 609 P.2d 1038 (Alaska 1980) (compelled disclosure of defense expert's ballistics test did not violate defendant's self-incrimination privilege because the report was not "testimonial" as to defendant, but disclosure was barred as unauthorized under state discovery rule). Should it matter "whether the prosecution was well aware of the existence of the report, so the defendant was not being asked 'whether there had been any scientific test conducted' and if so who conducted them"? LaFave and Israel, § 19.4(i) (suggesting that discovery which in effect force defendant to answer such questions though his act of production would be questionable under *Fisher* and *Doe,* pp. 757, 764 supra).

Does the Sixth Amendment bar pretrial discovery of an expert's report that the defense does not intend to use at trial? Consider *State v. Mingo,* 392 A.2d 590 (N.J.1978). The defendant, charged with robbery, requested that the state allow the defense's handwriting experts to examine a note written by the robber. The court conditioned that disclosure on the state having access to the resulting reports, and the prosecution, after reviewing one report, called the expert to testify on behalf of the state. On appeal, the court rejected the contention that the discovery order violated the work product privilege as codified in N.J.R.Crim.P. 3:13–3(c) (barring discovery of "internal reports, memoranda, or documents" prepared by defense agents). The report of the handwriting expert did not fall "within the intent of the foregoing delineation of work product as its constitute[d] a species of evidence admissible under some circumstances whereas true work product is [nonevidential]." Nevertheless, the discovery order did violate the defendant's right to effective assistance of counsel (although the other evidence introduced at trial rendered that violation harmless). To safeguard that right, the court noted, it was essential to afford counsel "the maximum freedom to seek the guidance of expert advice in assessing the soundness and advisability of offering a particular defense without the fear that any unfavorable material so obtained can be used against his client. * * * Reliance upon the confidentiality of an expert's advise itself is a crucial aspect of a defense attorney's ability to consult with and advise his client. If the confidentiality of that advice cannot be anticipated, the attorney might well forego seeking such assistance, to the consequent detriment of his client's cause."

SANCTIONS FOR DEFENSE VIOLATIONS OF DISCOVERY ORDERS

1. Provisions authorizing the imposition of sanctions for defense violations of its discovery obligations commonly refer to the same wide range of sanctions as may be imposed upon the prosecution for its failure to meet discovery obligations. They typically authorize the trial court, at its discretion, to utilize such sanctions as ordering immediate disclosure, granting a continuance, excluding evidence, and holding the responsible party in contempt. As noted in the discussion of sanctions imposed upon the prosecutor [see Note 1, p. 1128 supra], many courts view with disfavor the exclusion of evidence, particularly where the discovery violation was not a product of bad faith. As applied to the defendant, does that presumption against exclusion have a constitutional grounding? Although the Supreme Court left open the issue in *Williams* [see fn. 14, p. 1132 supra] and again in *Wardius,* a long line of lower court cases have held that defendant's Sixth Amendment right to compulsory process does not bar the exclusion of defense evidence where defendant has failed to meet valid pretrial discovery obligations. See LaFave and Israel, § 19.4(j). The courts have stressed that the Sixth Amendment right is not absolute, but can be subjected to procedural requirements reasonably supported by a substantial state interest. Thus, it is noted, in *United States v. Nobles,* the Supreme Court not only upheld the trial court's order requiring defense counsel to allow inspection of the investigator's report, but also sustained the trial court's further ruling excluding the investigator's testimony after the defense counsel refused to permit inspection. The Sixth Amendment, the Court noted there, "does not confer the right to present testimony free from the legitimate demands of the adversary system." Adherence to a reciprocal discovery system, the lower courts reason, is also one of the "legitimate demands of the adversary system." [a] The varied objectives underlying reciprocal discovery provide a compelling state interest for achieving effective enforcement, including the use of the sanction of exclusion where it serves that purpose. After all, the courts frequently note, the discovery requirements "do not prevent a defendant from compelling the attendance of witnesses," but only impose "reasonable conditions for their presentation." *State v. Smith,* 543 P.2d 834 (N.M.App.1975).

2. While accepting the constitutionality of the exclusion sanction, lower courts agree that the Sixth Amendment forbids an automatic use of the sanction. At a minimum, it is noted, there must be a showing either that the defense counsel acted in bad faith or that the discovery violation resulted in some prejudice to the prosecution. See e.g., *United States ex rel. Robinson v. McGinnis,* 593 F.Supp. 175 (D.Ill.1984), aff'd, 753 F.2d 1078 (7th Cir.1985). Must there also be a showing that exclusion is the "least drastic means" available—that the prejudice cannot other-

a. Consider, however, *United States v. Davis,* 639 F.2d 239 (5th Cir.1981), reading *Nobles* as holding only that it is appropriate to exclude evidence where the defense failed to comply with a court order designed to ensure the integrity of that evidence (thus *Nobles* excluded the investigator's testimony because the violated order was needed to permit full cross-examination of the investigator). The state's interest in "preventing surprise," *Davis* noted, did not meet that test, and it therefore was not constitutionally permissible to exclude defense evidence "solely as a sanction for the failure of a criminal defendant to comply with a discovery rule."

wise be cured and that bad faith violations cannot be deterred by other sanctions? See Clinton, *The Right to Present a Defense: An Emergent Constitutional Guarantee in Criminal Trials,* 9 Ind.L.Rev. 713 (1976). Or should the standard be no different than that applied to the forfeiture of constitutional claims by defendants who fail to comply with state procedural requirements for raising various constitutional claims. See Note, 51 U.Chi.L.Rev. 254 (1984) (preclusion should be tested no differently than the forfeiture of a search and seizure objection by failing to make a pretrial motion to suppress). In examining the validity of such procedural forfeitures, the focus is upon whether the procedural requirement serves a legitimate state interest, not whether the state could possibly have achieved that objective in the particular case without imposing a forfeiture. See e.g., *Wainwright v. Sykes,* p. 1506 infra; *Michel v. Louisiana,* p. 985 supra.

Assuming a less drastic means test is to be applied, as several courts have suggested, will exclusion ever be an appropriate sanction? Will not contempt necessarily constitute a more effective remedy for intentional violations? Will not either (1) granting the prosecution a continuance for the purpose of obtaining evidence to counter defense evidence not previously disclosed, or (2) allowing the prosecution to urge the jury to consider the defendant's discovery violation in evaluating evidence not previously disclosed, constitute remedies equal to exclusion in responding to potential prejudice? Consider, however, *State v. Mai,* 656 P.2d 315 (Or.1982) (standard allowing exclusion only where "no lesser sanction" would suffice was met where defense counsel purposefully failed to present a witness list, the trial court ordered that the witness be made available for a prosecution interview, but counsel directed the witness to answer no questions); *State v. Lindsey,* 284 N.W.2d 368 (Minn.1979) (although preclusion was a remedy "not lightly invoked," its use was justified where defense had disclosed the names of only 2 of its 8 witnesses, it was "too late in the trial to grant a continuance," and the court had excluded the testimony only of those unlisted witnesses as to whom the prosecution presented the strongest claim of surprise); *Taliaferro v. State,* 456 A.2d 29 (Md.1983) (a 1½ day continuance might be sufficient to check the background of the unlisted alibi witnesses, but it would hardly give the state time to find rebuttal witnesses; if a continuance is always viewed as a less drastic alternative, the threat of a significant sanction will be lost).

3. Most discovery provisions limit the exclusion sanction to the testimony of persons other than defendant himself. See, e.g., Fed.R.Crim.P. 12.1(d). Are the applicable considerations substantially different where a defendant is kept from providing alibi testimony because he did not list himself as an alibi witness? Consider *Alicea v. Gagnon,* 675 F.2d 913 (7th Cir. 1982). Holding unconstitutional the preclusion of defendant's alibi testimony, the court there noted that the surprise element was less substantial as to defendant's testimony; since the prosecution had to prove the defendant's presence during the crime as an essential element of the crime, it should be in a "formidable position to refute defendant's unexpected alibi testimony." An alibi introduced by the defendant's testimony alone also was less likely to be believed, but if it should raise a reasonable doubt, a continuance for further investigation was possible.

SECTION 3. THE PROSECUTION'S CONSTITUTIONAL DUTY TO DISCLOSE

UNITED STATES v. BAGLEY

___ U.S. ___, 105 S.Ct. 3375, 87 L.Ed.2d 481 (1985).

JUSTICE BLACKMUN announced the judgment of the Court and delivered an opinion of the Court except as to Part III.

In *Brady v. Maryland,* 373 U.S. 83, 83 S.Ct. 1194, 10 L.Ed.2d 215 (1963), this Court held that "the suppression by the prosecution of evidence favorable to an accused upon request violates due process where the evidence is material either to guilt or punishment." The issue in the present case concerns the standard of materiality to be applied in determining whether a conviction should be reversed because the prosecutor failed to disclose requested evidence that could have been used to impeach Government witnesses.

I

In October 1977, respondent Hughes Anderson Bagley was indicted in the Western District of Washington on 15 charges of violating federal narcotics and firearms statutes. On November 18, 24 days before trial, respondent filed a discovery motion. The sixth paragraph of that motion requested:

> "The names and addresses of witnesses that the government intends to call at trial. Also the prior criminal records of witnesses, and any deals, promises or inducements made to witnesses in exchange for their testimony."

The Government's two principal witnesses at the trial were James F. O'Connor and Donald E. Mitchell. O'Connor and Mitchell were state law-enforcement officers employed by the Milwaukee Railroad as private security guards. Between April and June 1977, they assisted the federal Bureau of Alcohol, Tobacco and Firearms (ATF) in conducting an undercover investigation of respondent.

The Government's response to the discovery motion did not disclose that any "deals, promises or inducements" had been made to O'Connor or Mitchell. In apparent reply to a request in the motion's ninth paragraph for "[c]opies of all Jencks Act material," the Government produced a series of affidavits that O'Connor and Mitchell had signed between April 12 and May 4, 1977, while the undercover investigation was in progress. These affidavits recounted in detail the undercover dealings that O'Connor and Mitchell were having at the time with respondent. Each affidavit concluded with the statement, "I made this statement freely and voluntarily without any threats or rewards, or promises of reward having been made to me in return for it."

Respondent waived his right to a jury trial and was tried before the court in December 1977. At the trial, O'Connor and Mitchell testified about both the firearms and the narcotics charges. On December 23, the court found respondent guilty on the narcotics charges, but not guilty on the firearms charges.

In mid-1980, respondent filed requests for information pursuant to the Freedom of Information Act and to the Privacy Act of 1974, 5 U.S.C. §§ 552 and 552a. [See fn. a, p. 1119 supra]. He received in response copies of ATF form contracts that O'Connor and Mitchell had signed on May 3, 1977. Each form was entitled "Contract for Purchase of Information and Payment of Lump Sum Therefor." The printed portion of the form stated that the vendor "will provide" information to ATF and that "upon receipt of such information by the Regional Director, Bureau of Alcohol, Tobacco and Firearms, or his representative, and upon the accomplishment of the objective sought to be obtained by the use of such information to the satisfaction of said Regional Director, the United States will pay to said vendor a sum commensurate with services and information rendered." Each form contained the following typewritten description of services:

> "That he will provide information regarding T–I and other violations committed by Hughes A. Bagley, Jr.; that he will purchase evidence for ATF; that he will cut [*sic*] in an undercover capacity for ATF; that he will assist ATF in gathering of evidence and testify against the violator in federal court."

The figure "$300.00" was handwritten in each form on a line entitled "Sum to Be Paid to Vendor."

Because these contracts had not been disclosed to respondent in response to his pretrial discovery motion,[4] respondent moved under 28 U.S.C. § 2255 to vacate his sentence. He alleged that the Government's failure to disclose the contracts, which he could have used to impeach O'Connor and Mitchell, violated his right to due process under *Brady v. Maryland, supra.*

The motion came before the same District Judge who had presided at respondent's bench trial. An evidentiary hearing was held before a Magistrate. The Magistrate found that the printed form contracts were blank when O'Connor and Mitchell signed them and were not signed by an ATF representative until after the trial. He also found that on January 4, 1978, following the trial and decision in respondent's case, ATF made payments of $300 to both O'Connor and Mitchell pursuant to the contracts. Although the ATF case agent who dealt with O'Connor and Mitchell testified that these payments were compensation for expenses, the Magistrate found that this characterization was not borne out by the record. * * * The District Court adopted each of the Magistrate's findings except for the last one to the effect that "[n]either O'Connor nor Mitchell expected to receive the payment of $300 or any payment from the United States for their testimony." Instead, the court found that it was "probable" that O'Connor and Mitchell expected to receive compensation, in addition to their expenses, for their assistance, "though perhaps not for their testimony." The District Court also expressly rejected, the Magistrate's conclusion, that "the United States did not withhold, during pretrial discovery, information as to any 'deals, promises or inducements' to these witnesses." The District Court found beyond a reasonable doubt, however, that had the existence of the agreements been disclosed to it during trial, the disclosure would have had no effect upon its finding that the Government had proved beyond a reasonable doubt that respondent was guilty of the offenses for which he had been convicted. The District Court reasoned: Almost all of the testimony of both witnesses was devoted to the firearms charges in the indictment. Respondent, however, was acquitted on those charges. The testimony of O'Connor and Mitchell concerning the narcotics charges was relatively very brief. On cross-examination, respondent's counsel did not seek to discredit their testimony as to the facts of distribution but rather sought to show that the controlled substances in question came from supplies that had been prescribed for respondent's personal use. The answers of O'Connor and Mitchell to this line of cross-examination tended to be favorable to respondent. Thus, the claimed impeachment evidence would not have been helpful to respondent and would not have affected the outcome of the trial. Accordingly, the District Court denied respondent's motion to vacate his sentence.

The United States Court of Appeals for the Ninth Circuit reversed. * * * [It] apparently based its reversal, on the theory that the Government's failure to disclose the requested *Brady* information that respondent could have used to conduct an effective cross-examination impaired respondent's right to confront adverse witnesses. The court noted: "In *Davis v. Alaska,* . . . the Supreme Court held that the denial of the 'right of *effective* cross-examination' was ' "constitutional error of the first magnitude" ' requiring automatic reversal." 719 F.2d, at 1464 (quoting *Davis v. Alaska,* 415 U.S. 308, 318, 94 S.Ct. 1105, 1111, 39 L.Ed.2d 347 (1974)) (emphasis added by Court of Ap-

4. The Assistant United States Attorney who prosecuted respondent stated in stipulated testimony that he had not known that the contracts existed and that he would have furnished them to respondent had he known of them.

peals). In the last sentence of its opinion, the Court of Appeals concluded: "we hold that the government's failure to provide requested *Brady* information to Bagley so that he could effectively cross-examine two important government witnesses requires an automatic reversal." * * *

II

The holding in *Brady v. Maryland* requires disclosure only of evidence that is both favorable to the accused and "material either to guilt or punishment." The Court explained in *United States v. Agurs,* 427 U.S. 97, 96 S.Ct. 2392, 2397, 49 L.Ed.2d 342 (1976): "A fair analysis of the holding in *Brady* indicates that implicit in the requirement of materiality is a concern that the suppressed evidence might have affected the outcome of the trial." The evidence suppressed in *Brady* would have been admissible only on the issue of punishment and not on the issue of guilt, and therefore could have affected only Brady's sentence and not his conviction. Accordingly, the Court affirmed the lower court's restriction of Brady's new trial to the issue of punishment.[a]

The *Brady* rule is based on the requirement of due process. Its purpose is not to displace the adversary system as the primary means by which truth is uncovered, but to ensure that a miscarriage of justice does not occur.[6] Thus, the prosecutor is not required to deliver his entire file to defense counsel,[7] but only to disclose evidence favorable to the accused that, if suppressed, would deprive the defendant of a fair trial. * * * As *Agurs* noted: "For unless the omission deprived the defendant of a fair trial, there was no constitutional violation requiring that the verdict be set aside; and absent a constitutional violation, there was no breach of the prosecutor's constitutional duty to disclose. . . . " *United States v. Agurs.*

In *Brady* and *Agurs,* the prosecutor failed to disclose exculpatory evidence. In the present case, the prosecutor failed to disclose evidence that the defense might have used to impeach the Government's witnesses by showing bias or interest. Im-

a. The defendant Brady and a companion, Boblit, had been found guilty of felony murder and sentenced to death. Prior to Brady's separate trial, his counsel had asked the prosecutor to allow him to examine all of the statements that Boblit had given to the police. Counsel was shown several of Boblit's statements, but for some unexplained reason failed to receive one statement in which Boblit admitted that he had done the actual killing. At trial, defendant admitted his participation in the crime, but claimed that he had not himself killed the victim. Defense counsel stressed this claim in his closing argument, asking the jury to show leniency and not impose the death penalty. Following defendant's conviction, defense counsel learned of the undisclosed statement and sought a new trial based on this newly discovered evidence. The Supreme Court affirmed a state court ruling granting a new trial as to the issue of punishment alone. Whether or not defendant himself killed the victim had no bearing on his liability for the homicide, and Boblit's statement therefore would not have been admissible in evidence on that issue. On the other hand, the statement could have been used to support defendant's plea for leniency as to punishment, and the prosecution's failure to disclose the statement had deprived Brady of a fair hearing on that issue. In refusing a new trial on the issue of guilt, the Court noted that it would not adopt a "sporting theory of justice" which assumed that the jury would have disregarded a trial judge's directive that Boblit's statement could be considered in assessing punishment but not in determining guilt.

6. By requiring the prosecutor to assist the defense in making its case, the *Brady* rule represents a limited departure from a pure adversary model. The Court has recognized, however, that the prosecutor's role transcends that of an adversary: he "is the representative not of an ordinary party to a controversy, but of a sovereignty . . . whose interest . . . in a criminal prosecution is not that it shall win a case, but that justice shall be done." *Berger v. United States,* 295 U.S. 78, 55 S.Ct. 629, 79 L.Ed. 1314 (1935).

7. * * * An interpretation of *Brady* to create a broad, constitutionally required right of discovery "would entirely alter the character and balance of our present systems of criminal justice." *Giles v. Maryland,* 386 U.S. 66, 117, 87 S.Ct. 793, 818, 17 L.Ed.2d 737 (1967) (dissenting opinion). Furthermore, a rule that the prosecutor commits error by any failure to disclose evidence favorable to the accused, no matter how insignificant, would impose an impossible burden on the prosecutor and would undermine the interest in the finality of judgments.

peachment evidence, however, as well as exculpatory evidence, falls within the *Brady* rule. Such evidence is "evidence favorable to an accused," *Brady,* so that, if disclosed and used effectively, it may make the difference between conviction and acquittal. Cf. *Napue v. Illinois* [fn. 8 infra] ("The jury's estimate of the truthfulness and reliability of a given witness may well be determinative of guilt or innocence, and it is upon such subtle factors as the possible interest of the witness in testifying falsely that a defendant's life or liberty may depend").

The Court of Appeals treated impeachment evidence as constitutionally different from exculpatory evidence. According to that court, failure to disclose impeachment evidence is "even more egregious" than failure to disclose exculpatory evidence "because it threatens the defendant's right to confront adverse witnesses." Relying on *Davis v. Alaska* [p. 1348 infra], the Court of Appeals held that the Government's failure to disclose requested impeachment evidence that the defense could use to conduct an effective cross-examination of important prosecution witnesses constitutes " 'constitutional error of the first magnitude' " requiring automatic reversal. 719 F.2d, at 1464 (quoting *Davis*).

This Court has rejected any such distinction between impeachment evidence and exculpatory evidence. In *Giglio v. United States,* [405 U.S. 150, 92 S.Ct. 763, 31 L.Ed.2d 104 (1972),] the Government failed to disclose impeachment evidence similar to the evidence at issue in the present case, that is, a promise made to the key government witness that he would not be prosecuted if he testified for the Government.[b] This Court said:

> "When the 'reliability of a given witness may well be determinative of guilt or innocence,' nondisclosure of evidence affecting credibility falls within the general rule [of *Brady*]. We do not, however, automatically require a new trial whenever 'a combing of the prosecutors' files after the trial has disclosed evidence possibly useful to the defense but not likely to have changed the verdict . . . .' A finding of materiality of the evidence is required under *Brady* . . . . A new trial is required if 'the false testimony could . . . in any reasonable likelihood have affected the judgment of the jury . . . .' "

Thus, the Court of Appeals' holding is inconsistent with our precedents.

Moreover, the court's reliance on *Davis v. Alaska* for its "automatic reversal" rule is misplaced. In *Davis,* the defense sought to cross-examine a crucial prosecution witness concerning his probationary status as a juvenile delinquent. * * * Pursuant to a state rule of procedure and a state statute making juvenile adjudications inadmissible, the trial judge prohibited the defense from conducting the cross-examination. This Court reversed the defendant's conviction, ruling that the direct restriction on the scope of cross-examination denied the defendant "the right of effective cross-examination which " 'would be constitutional error of the first magnitude and no amount of showing of want of prejudice would cure it.' " The present case, in contrast, does not involve any direct restriction on the scope of cross-examination. The defense was free to cross-examine the

b. In *Giglio,* the defense counsel "vigorously cross-examined [a key witness] seeking to discredit his testimony by revealing possible agreements or arrangements for prosecutorial leniency." The witness denied the existence of such agreements, and in his summation, the government attorney stated that the witness "received no promises that he would not be indicted." In fact, a promise had been made by another government attorney, but the trial attorney had been unaware of that discussion. The Court held that the nondisclosure of the promise was the responsibility of the government, and the failure of the original attorney to inform his superiors of the promise was no excuse: "The prosecutor's office is an entity and as such it is the spokesman for the Government. A promise made by one attorney must be attributed for these purposes to the Government."

witnesses on any relevant subject, including possible bias or interest resulting from inducements made by the Government. The constitutional error, if any, in this case was the Government's failure to assist the defense by disclosing information that might have been helpful in conducting the cross-examination. As discussed above, such suppression of evidence amounts to a constitutional violation only if it deprives the defendant of a fair trial. Consistent with "our overriding concern with the justice of the finding of guilt," *United States v. Agurs,* a constitutional error occurs, and the conviction must be reversed, only if the evidence is material in the sense that its suppression undermines confidence in the outcome of the trial.

III

It remains to determine the standard of materiality applicable to the nondisclosed evidence at issue in this case. Our starting point is the framework for evaluating the materiality of *Brady* evidence established in *United States v. Agurs.* The Court in *Agurs* distinguished three situations involving the discovery, after trial, of information favorable to the accused that had been known to the prosecution but unknown to the defense. The first situation was the prosecutor's knowing use of perjured testimony or, equivalently, the prosecutor's knowing failure to disclose that testimony used to convict the defendant was false. The Court noted the well-established rule that "a conviction obtained by the knowing use of prejured testimony is fundamentally unfair, and must be set aside if there is any reasonable likelihood that the false testimony could have affected the judgment of the jury." 427 U.S., at 103, 96 S.Ct., at 2397.[8] Although this rule is stated in terms that treat the knowing use of perjured testimony as error subject to harmless-error review,[9] it may as easily be stated as a materiality standard under which the fact that testimony is perjured is

8. In fact, the *Brady* rule has its roots in a series of cases dealing with convictions based on the prosecution's knowing use of perjured testimony. In *Mooney v. Holohan,* 294 U.S. 103, 55 S.Ct. 340, 79 L.Ed. 791 (1935), the Court established the rule that the knowing use by a state prosecutor of perjured testimony to obtain a conviction and the deliberate suppression of evidence that would have impeached and refuted the testimony constitutes a denial of due process. The Court reasoned that "a deliberate deception of court and jury by the presentation of testimony known to be perjured" is inconsistent with "the rudimentary demands of justice." The Court reaffirmed this principle in broader terms in *Pyle v. Kansas,* 317 U.S. 213, 63 S.Ct. 177, 87 L.Ed. 214 (1942), where it held that allegations that the prosecutor had deliberately suppressed evidence favorable to the accused and had knowingly used perjured testimony were sufficient to charge a due process violation. The Court again reaffirmed this principle in *Napue v. Illinois,* 360 U.S. 264, 79 S.Ct. 1173, 3 L.Ed.2d 1217 (1959). In *Napue,* the principal witness for the prosecution falsely testified that he had been promised no consideration for his testimony. The Court held that the knowing use of false testimony to obtain a conviction violates due process regardless of whether the prosecutor solicited the false testimony or merely allowed it to go uncorrected when it appeared. The Court explained that the principle that a State may not knowingly use false testimony to obtain a conviction—even false testimony that goes only to the credibility of the witness—is "implicit in any concept of ordered liberty." Finally, the Court held that it was not bound by the state court's determination that the false testimony "could not in any reasonable likelihood have affected the judgment of the jury." The Court conducted its own independent examination of the record and concluded that the false testimony "may have had an effect on the outcome of the trial." Accordingly, the Court reversed the judgment of conviction.

9. The rule that a conviction obtained by the knowing use of perjured testimony must be set aside if there is any reasonable likelihood that the false testimony could have affected the jury's verdict derives from *Napue v. Illinois.* See n. 8. *Napue* antedated *Chapman v. California* [p. 796 supra], where the "harmless beyond a reasonable doubt" standard was established. The Court in *Chapman* noted that there was little, if any, difference between a rule formulated, as in *Napue,* in terms of " 'whether there is a reasonable possibility that the evidence complained of might have contributed to the conviction,' " and a rule " 'requiring the beneficiary of a constitutional error to prove beyond a reasonable doubt that the error complained of did not contribute to the verdict obtained.' " It is therefore clear, as indeed petitioner concedes, that this Court's precedents indicate that the standard of review applicable to the knowing use of perjured testimony is equivalent to the *Chapman* harmless-error standard.

considered material unless failure to disclose it would be harmless beyond a reasonable doubt. The Court in *Agurs* justified this standard of materiality on the ground that the knowing use of perjured testimony involves prosecutorial misconduct and, more importantly, involves "a corruption of the truth-seeking function of the trial process."

At the other extreme is the situation in *Agurs* itself, where the defendant does not make a *Brady* request and the prosecutor fails to disclose certain evidence favorable to the accused. The Court rejected a harmless-error rule in that situation, because under that rule every nondisclosure is treated as error, thus imposing on the prosecutor a constitutional duty to deliver his entire file to defense counsel.[10] At the same time, the Court rejected a standard that would require the defendant to demonstrate that the evidence if disclosed probably would have resulted in acquittal.[c] The Court reasoned: "If the standard applied to the usual motion for a new trial based on newly discovered evidence were the same when the evidence was in the State's possession as when it was found in a neutral source, there would be no special significance to the prosecutor's obligation to serve the cause of justice." The standard of materiality applicable in the absence of a specific *Brady* request is therefore stricter than the harmless-error standard but more lenient to the defense than the newly discovered evidence standard.[d]

10. This is true only if the nondisclosure is treated as error subject to harmless-error review, and not if the nondisclosure is treated as error only if the evidence is material under a not-"harmless beyond a reasonable doubt" standard.

c. The reference here was to what *Agurs* described as the "Rule 33 Standard"—the test applied to a motion for a new trial based on newly discovered evidence. That standard typically requires that the defendant establish (1) that the failure to learn of the evidence previously was due to no lack of diligence, (2) that the evidence is material, not merely "cumulative or impeaching," and (3) that the evidence "will probably produce an acquittal." See Wright, *Federal Practice and Procedure (Criminal)* § 557 (1912). A somewhat different standard is sometimes applied where the after-discovered evidence reveals witness perjury at trial. Compare *Larrison v. United States,* 24 F.2d 82 (7th Cir.1928) (question is whether without the perjured testimony "the jury might have reached a different conclusion"); with *United States v. Stofsky,* 527 F.2d 237 (2d Cir.1975) (usual Rule 33 standard applied).

d. The defendant in *Agurs* had been convicted of the second degree murder of James Sewell. Although the defense had not offered any evidence, it had argued that self-defense was apparent from several facts brought out in the prosecution's evidence. It was shown there that the defendant had screamed for help, that Sewell was on top of her when the help arrived, and that Sewell possessed two knives, which indicated that he was a violence-prone person. In rejecting the self-defense claim, the jury apparently concluded that it was inconsistent with other factors suggesting that defendant initiated the attack and then sought help only when Sewell resisted (the evidence established, for example, that Sewell had been repeatedly stabbed, while defendant was unscathed). Three months after the conviction, defense counsel sought a new trial, alleging that he had recently discovered that Sewell had a prior criminal record, with convictions for assault and the possession of a deadly weapon. That record would have been admissible at trial to show that Sewell was violence-prone, and defense counsel claimed that the prosecution's failure to bring it to the attention of the defense constituted a *Brady* violation. The defense counsel had not requested disclosure of the record (and indeed, the Court, in a footnote, rejected the contention that this omission constituted ineffectiveness of counsel).

The trial court rejected defendant's *Brady* claim on the ground that (1) Sewell's criminal record would shed no light on his character that was not already apparent from the uncontradicted evidence (particularly his possession of two knives) and (2) the jury had ample justification for rejecting the self-defense claim. A divided Supreme Court affirmed the trial court's ruling. The majority, per Stevens, J., reasoned that in this type of case, not involving a "pretrial request for specific evidence" (in contrast to *Brady* itself) the appropriate standard for judging materiality, was whether "the omitted evidence creates a reasonable doubt that did not otherwise exist." Applying this standard, it concluded that there had been no constitutional violation: "[S]ince after considering it in the context of the entire record the trial judge remained convinced of respondent's guilt beyond a reasonable doubt, and since we are satisfied that his firsthand appraisal of the record was thorough and entirely reasonable, we hold that the prosecutor's failure to tender Sewell's [arrest] record to the defense did not deprive respondent of a fair trial as guaranteed by the Due Process Clause of the Fifth Amendment."

The third situation identified by the Court in *Agurs* is where the defense makes a specific request and the prosecutor fails to disclose responsive evidence. The Court did not define the standard of materiality applicable in this situation, but suggested that the standard might be more lenient to the defense than in the situation in which the defense makes no request or only a general request. The Court also noted: "When the prosecutor receives a specific and relevant request, the failure to make any response is seldom, if ever, excusable."

The Court has relied on and reformulated the *Agurs* standard for the materiality of undisclosed evidence in two subsequent cases arising outside the *Brady* context. In neither case did the Court's discussion of the *Agurs* standard distinguish among the three situations described in *Agurs.* In *United States v. Valenzuela-Bernal* [p. 1351 infra], the Court held that due process is violated when testimony is made unavailable to the defense by Government deportation of witnesses "only if there is a reasonable likelihood that the testimony could have affected the judgment of the trier of fact." And in *Strickland v. Washington,* [p. 143 supra], the Court held that a new trial must be granted when evidence is not introduced because of the incompetence of counsel only if "there is a reasonable probability that, but for counsel's unprofessional errors, the result of the proceeding would have been different." The *Strickland* Court defined a "reasonable probability" as "a probability sufficient to undermine confidence in the outcome."

We find the *Strickland* formulation of the *Agurs* test for materiality sufficiently flexible to cover the "no request," "general request," and "specific request" cases of prosecutorial failure to disclose evidence favorable to the accused: The evidence is material only if there is a reasonable probability that, had the evidence been disclosed to the defense, the result of the proceeding would have been different. A "reasonable probability" is a probability sufficient to undermine confidence in the outcome.

The Government suggests that a materiality standard more favorable to the defendant reasonably might be adopted in specific request cases. The Government notes that an incomplete response to a specific request not only deprives the defense of certain evidence, but has the effect of representing to the defense that the evidence does not exist. In reliance on this misleading representation, the defense might abandon lines of independent investigation, defenses, or trial strategies that it otherwise would have pursued.

We agree that the prosecutor's failure to respond fully to a *Brady* request may impair the adversary process in this manner. And the more specifically the defense requests certain evidence, thus putting the prosecutor on notice of its value, the more reasonable it is for the defense to assume from the nondisclosure that the evidence does not exist, and to make pretrial and trial decisions on the basis of this assumption. This possibility of impairment does not necessitate a different standard of materiality, however, for under the *Strickland* formulation the reviewing court may consider directly any adverse effect that the prosecutor's failure to respond might have had on the preparation or presentation of the defendant's case. The reviewing court should assess the possibility that such effect might have occurred in light of the totality of the circumstances and with an awareness of the difficulty of reconstructing in a post-trial proceeding the course that the defense and the trial would have taken had the defense not been misled by the prosecutor's incomplete response.

In the present case, we think that there is a significant likelihood that the prosecutor's response to respondent's discovery motion misleadingly induced defense counsel to believe that O'Connor and Mitchell could not be impeached on the basis of bias or interest arising from inducements offered by the Government.

Defense counsel asked the prosecutor to disclose any inducements that had been made to witnesses, and the prosecutor failed to disclose that the possibility of a reward had been held out to O'Connor and Mitchell if the information they supplied led to "the accomplishment of the objective sought to be obtained . . . to the satisfaction of [the Government]." This possibility of a reward gave O'Connor and Mitchell a direct, personal stake in respondent's conviction. The fact that the stake was not guaranteed through a promise or binding contract, but was expressly contingent on the Government's satisfaction with the end result, served only to strengthen any incentive to testify falsely in order to secure a conviction. Moreover, the prosecutor disclosed affidavits that stated that O'Connor and Mitchell received no promises of reward in return for providing information in the affidavits implicating respondent in criminal activity. In fact, O'Connor and Mitchell signed the last of these affidavits the very day after they signed the ATF contracts. While petitioner is technically correct that the blank contracts did not constitute a "promise of reward," the natural effect of these affidavits would be misleadingly to induce defense counsel to believe that O'Connor and Mitchell provided the information in the affidavits, and ultimately their testimony at trial recounting the same information, without any "inducements."

The District Court, nonetheless, found beyond a reasonable doubt that, had the information that the Government held out the possibility of reward to its witnesses been disclosed, the result of the criminal prosecution would not have been different. If this finding were sustained by the Court of Appeals, the information would be immaterial even under the standard of materiality applicable to the prosecutor's knowing use of perjured testimony. Although the express holding of the Court of Appeals was that the nondisclosure in this case required automatic reversal, the Court of Appeals also stated that it "disagreed" with the District Court's finding of harmless error. In particular, the Court of Appeals appears to have disagreed with the factual premise on which this finding expressly was based. The District Court reasoned that O'Connor's and Mitchell's testimony was exculpatory on the narcotics charges. The Court of Appeals, however, concluded, after reviewing the record, that O'Connor's and Mitchell's testimony was in fact inculpatory on those charges. Accordingly, we reverse the judgment of the Court of Appeals and remand the case to that court for a determination whether there is a reasonable probability that, had the inducement offered by the Government to O'Connor and Mitchell been disclosed to the defense, the result of the trial would have been different.

JUSTICE POWELL took no part in the decision of this case.

JUSTICE WHITE, with whom THE CHIEF JUSTICE and JUSTICE REHNQUIST join, concurring in part and concurring in the judgment.

I agree with the Court that respondent is not entitled to have his conviction overturned unless he can show that the evidence withheld by the Government was "material," and I therefore join Parts I and II of the Court's opinion. I also agree with Justice Blackmun that for purposes of this inquiry, "evidence is material only if there is a reasonable probability that, had the evidence been disclosed to the defense, the result of the proceeding would have been different." As the Justice correctly observes, this standard is "sufficiently flexible" to cover all instances of prosecutorial failure to disclose evidence favorable to the accused. Given the flexibility of the standard and the inherently factbound nature of the cases to which it will be applied, however, I see no reason to attempt to elaborate on the relevance to the inquiry of the specificity of the defense's request for disclosure, either generally or with respect to this case. I would hold simply that the proper standard is one of reasonable probability and that the Court of Appeals' failure to apply this standard necessitates reversal. I therefore concur in the judgment.

JUSTICE MARSHALL, with whom JUSTICE BRENNAN joins, dissenting.

The Court today chooses to reverse and remand the case for application of its newly stated standard to the facts of this case. While I believe that the evidence at issue here, which remained undisclosed despite a particular request, undoubtedly was material under the Court's standard, I also have serious doubts whether the Court's definition of the constitutional right at issue adequately takes account of the interests this Court sought to protect in its decision in *Brady v. Maryland.*

I begin from the fundamental premise, which hardly bears repeating, that "[t]he purpose of a trial is as much the acquittal of an innocent person as it is the conviction of a guilty one." When evidence favorable to the defendant is known to exist, disclosure only enhances the quest for truth; it takes no direct toll on that inquiry. Moreover, the existence of any small piece of evidence favorable to the defense may, in a particular case, create just the doubt that prevents the jury from returning a verdict of guilty. The private whys and wherefores of jury deliberations pose an impenetrable barrier to our ability to know just which piece of information might make, or might have made, a difference.

* * * We have long recognized that, within the limit of the State's ability to identify so-called exculpatory information, the State's concern for a fair verdict precludes it from withholding from the defense evidence favorable to the defendant's case in the prosecutor's files. * * * This recognition no doubt stems in part from the frequently considerable imbalance in resources between most criminal defendants and most prosecutors' offices. Many, perhaps most, criminal defendants in the United States are represented by appointed counsel, who often are paid minimal wages and operate on shoestring budgets. In addition, unlike police, defense counsel generally is not present at the scene of the crime, or at the time of arrest, but instead comes into the case late. Moreover, unlike the Government, defense counsel is not in the position to make deals with witnesses to gain evidence. Thus, an inexperienced, unskilled, or unaggressive attorney often is unable to amass the factual support necessary to a reasonable defense. When favorable evidence is in the hands of the prosecutor but not disclosed, the result may well be that the defendant is deprived of a fair chance before the trier of fact, and the trier of fact is deprived of the ingredients necessary to a fair decision. This grim reality, of course, poses a direct challenge to the traditional model of the adversary criminal process, and perhaps because this reality so directly questions the fairness of our longstanding processes, change has been cautious and halting. Thus, the Court has not gone the full road and expressly required that the State provide to the defendant access to the prosecutor's complete files, or investigators who will assure that the defendant has an opportunity to discover every existing piece of helpful evidence. But cf. *Ake v. Oklahoma* [p. 102 supra]. Instead, in acknowledgment of the fact that important interests are served when potentially favorable evidence is disclosed, the Court has fashioned a compromise, requiring that the prosecution identify and disclose to the defendant favorable material that it possesses. This requirement is but a small, albeit important; step toward equality of justice.[3]

3. Indeed, this Court's recent decision stating a stringent standard for demonstrating ineffective assistance of counsel makes an effective *Brady* right even more crucial. Without a real guarantee of effective counsel, the relative abilities of the state and the defendant become even more skewed, and the need for a minimal guarantee of access to potentially favorable information becomes significantly greater. See *Strickland v. Washington* [p. 143 supra].

Brady v. Maryland, of course, established this requirement of disclosure as a fundamental element of a fair trial by holding that a defendant was denied due process if he was not given access to favorable evidence that is material either to guilt or punishment. Since *Brady* was decided, this Court has struggled, in a series of decisions, to define how best to effectuate the right recognized. To my mind, the *Brady* decision, the reasoning that underlay it, and the fundamental interest in a fair trial, combine to give the criminal defendant the right to receive from the prosecutor, and the prosecutor the affirmative duty to turn over to the defendant, *all* information known to the government that might reasonably be considered favorable to the defendant's case. Formulation of this right, and imposition of this duty, are "the essence of due process of law. It is the State that tries a man, and it is the State that must insure that the trial is fair." * * * If that right is denied, or if that duty is shirked, however, I believe a reviewing court should not automatically reverse but instead should apply the harmless error test the Court has developed for instances of error affecting constitutional rights. See *Chapman v. California* [p. 796 supra].

My view is based in significant part on the reality of criminal practice and on the consequently inadequate protection to the defendant that a different rule would offer. * * * At the trial level, the duty of the state to effectuate *Brady* devolves into the duty of the prosecutor; the dual role that the prosecutor must play poses a serious obstacle to implementing *Brady.* The prosecutor is by trade, if not necessity, a zealous advocate. He is a trained attorney who must aggressively seek convictions in court on behalf of a victimized public. At the same time, as a representative of the State, he must place foremost in his hierarchy of interests the determination of truth. Thus, for purposes of *Brady,* the prosecutor must abandon his role as an advocate and pore through his files, as objectively as possible, to identify the material that could undermine his case. Given this obviously unharmonious role, it is not surprising that these advocates oftentimes overlook or downplay potentially favorable evidence, often in cases in which there is no doubt that the failure to disclose was a result of absolute good faith. Indeed, one need only think of the Fourth Amendment's requirement of a neutral intermediary, who tests the strength of the policeman-advocate's facts, to recognize the curious status *Brady* imposes on a prosecutor. * * *

The prosecutor surely greets the moment at which he must turn over *Brady* material with little enthusiasm. In perusing his files, he must make the often difficult decision as to whether evidence is favorable, and must decide on which side to err when faced with doubt. In his role as advocate, the answers are clear. In his role as representative of the State, the answers should be equally clear, and often to the contrary. Evidence that is of doubtful worth in the eyes of the prosecutor could be of inestimable value to the defense, and might make the difference to the trier of fact.

Once the prosecutor suspects that certain information might have favorable implications for the defense, either because it is potentially exculpatory or relevant to credibility, I see no reason why he should not be required to disclose it. After all, favorable evidence indisputably enhances the truth-seeking process at trial. And it is the job of the defense, not the prosecution, to decide whether and in what way to use arguably favorable evidence. In addition, to require disclosure of all evidence that might reasonably be considered favorable to the defendant would have the precautionary effect of assuring that no information of potential consequence is mistakenly overlooked. By requiring full disclosure of favorable evidence in this way, courts could begin to assure that a possibly dispositive piece of information is not withheld from the trier of fact by a prosecutor who is torn between the two roles he must play. A clear rule of this kind, coupled with a presumption in favor of disclosure, also would facilitate the prosecutor's admittedly difficult task by removing a substantial amount of unguided discretion. * * *

The Court, however, offers a complex alternative. It defines the right not by reference to the possible usefulness of the particular evidence in preparing and presenting the case, but retrospectively, by reference to the likely effect the evidence will have on the outcome of the trial. Thus, the Court holds that due process does not require the prosecutor to turn over evidence unless the evidence is "material," and the Court states that evidence is "material" "only if there is a reasonable probability that, had the evidence been disclosed to the defense, the result of the proceeding would have been different." Although this looks like a post-trial standard of review, see, e.g., *Strickland v. Washington*, it is not. Instead, the Court relies on this review standard to define the contours of the defendant's constitutional right to certain material prior to trial. By adhering to the view articulated in *United States v. Agurs*—that there is no constitutional duty to disclose evidence unless nondisclosure would have a certain impact on the trial—the Court permits prosecutors to withhold with impunity large amounts of undeniably favorable evidence, and it imposes on prosecutors the burden to identify and disclose evidence pursuant to a pretrial standard that virtually defies definition.

* * * Besides legitimizing the nondisclosure of clearly favorable evidence, the standard set out by the Court also asks the prosecutor to predict what effect various pieces of evidence will have on the trial. He must evaluate his case and the case of the defendant—of which he presumably knows very little—and perform the impossible task of deciding whether a certain piece of information will have a significant impact on the trial, bearing in mind that a defendant will later shoulder the heavy burden of proving how it would have affected the outcome. At best, this standard places on the prosecutor a responsibility to speculate, at times without foundation, since the prosecutor will not normally know what strategy the defense will pursue or what evidence the defense will find useful. At worst, the standard invites a prosecutor, whose interests are conflicting, to gamble, to play the odds, and to take a chance that evidence will later turn out not to have been potentially dispositive. * * *

* * * The State's interest in nondisclosure at trial is minimal, and should therefore yield to the readily apparent benefit that full disclosure would convey to the search for truth. After trial, however, the benefits of disclosure may at times be tempered by the State's legitimate desire to avoid retrial when error has been harmless. However, in making the determination of harmlessness, I would apply our normal constitutional error test and reverse unless it is clear beyond a reasonable doubt that the withheld evidence would not have affected the outcome of the trial. See *Chapman v. California*.[6]

Any rule other than automatic reversal, of course, dilutes the *Brady* right to some extent and offers the prosecutor an incentive not to turn over all information. In practical effect, it might be argued, there is little difference between the rule I propose—that a prosecutor must disclose all favorable evidence in his files, subject to harmless error review—and the rule the Court adopts—that the prosecutor must disclose only the favorable information

6. In a case of deliberate prosecutorial misconduct, automatic reversal might well be proper. Certain kinds of constitutional error so infect the system of justice as to require reversal in all cases, such as discrimination in jury selection. A deliberate effort of the prosecutor to undermine the search for truth clearly is in the category of offenses anathema to our most basic vision of the role of the State in the criminal process.

that might affect the outcome of the trial. According to this argument, if a constitutional right to all favorable evidence leads to reversal only when the withheld evidence might have affected the outcome of the trial, the result will be the same as with a constitutional right only to evidence that will affect the trial outcome. See Capra, *Access to Exculpatory Evidence: Avoiding the Agurs Problems of Prosecutorial Discretion and Retrospective Review*, 53 Ford.L.Rev. 391, 409–410, n. 117 (1984). For several reasons, however, I disagree. First, I have faith that a prosecutor would treat a rule requiring disclosure of all information of a certain kind differently from a rule requiring disclosure only of some of that information. Second, persistent or egregious failure to comply with the constitutional duty could lead to disciplinary actions by the courts. Third, the standard of harmlessness I adopt is more protective of the defendant than that chosen by the Court, placing the burden on the prosecutor, rather than the defendant, to prove the harmlessness of his actions. It would be a foolish prosecutor who gambled too glibly with that standard of review. * * *

JUSTICE STEVENS, dissenting.

This case involves a straightforward application of the rule announced in *Brady v. Maryland,* a case involving nondisclosure of material evidence by the prosecution in response to a specific request from the defense. I agree that the Court of Appeals misdescribed that rule, but I respectfully dissent from the Court's unwarranted decision to rewrite the rule itself. * * *

The two situations in which the [*Brady*] rule applies are those demonstrating the prosecution's knowing use of perjured testimony, exemplified by *Mooney v. Holohan,* and the prosecution's suppression of favorable evidence specifically requested by the defendant, exemplified by *Brady* itself. In both situations, the prosecution's deliberate nondisclosure constitutes constitutional error—the conviction must be set aside if the suppressed or perjured evidence was "material" [e] and there was "any reasonable likelihood" that it "could have affected" the outcome of the trial. *United States v. Agurs.* * * * The combination of willful prosecutorial suppression of evidence and, "more importantly," the potential "corruption of the truth seeking function of the trial process" requires that result. *Agurs.* * * *

The question in *Agurs* was whether the *Brady* rule should be *extended,* to cover a case in which there had been neither perjury nor a specific request—that is, whether the prosecution has some constitutional duty to search its files and disclose automatically, or in response to a general request, all evidence that "might have helped the defense, or might have affected the outcome." Such evidence would, of course, be covered by the *Brady* formulation if it were specifically requested. We noted in *Agurs,* however, that because there had been no specific defense request for the later-discovered evidence, there was no notice to the prosecution that the defense did not already have that evidence or that it considered the evidence to be of particular value. Consequently, we stated that in the absence of a request the prosecution has a constitutional duty to volunteer only "obviously exculpatory evidence." Because this constitutional duty to disclose is *different* from the duty described in *Brady,* it is not surprising that we developed a different standard of materiality in the *Agurs* context. * * * But the *Brady* rule itself unquestionably applies to this case, because the Government

e. At a later point in his dissent, Justice Stevens noted that he viewed "materiality" as strictly an "evidentiary concept." The dissent noted: "The Court's approach stretches the concept of 'materiality' beyond any recognizable scope, transforming it from merely an evidentiary concept as used in *Brady* and *Agurs,* which required that material evidence be admissible and probative of guilt or innocence in the context of a specific request, into a result-focused standard that seems to include an independent weight in favor of affirming convictions despite evidentiary suppression."

failed to disclose favorable evidence that was clearly responsive to the defendant's specific request. Bagley's conviction therefore must be set aside if the suppressed evidence was "material"—and it obviously was, and if there is "any reasonable likelihood" that it could have affected the judgment of the trier of fact.

Moreover, the Court's analysis reduces the significance of deliberate prosecutorial suppression of potentially exculpatory evidence to that merely of one of numerous factors that "may" be considered by a reviewing court. [Citing Justice Blackmun's discussion at p. 1152 supra of the appropriate consideration of a lack of response to a specific request]. This is not faithful to our statement in *Agurs* that "[w]hen the prosecutor receives a specific and relevant request, the failure to make any response is seldom, if ever, excusable." Such suppression is far more serious than mere nondisclosure of evidence in which the defense has expressed no particular interest. A reviewing court should attach great significance to silence in the face of a specific request, when responsive evidence is later shown to have been in the Government's possession. Such silence actively misleads in the same way as would an affirmative representation that exculpatory evidence does not exist when, in fact, it does (*i.e.*, perjury)—indeed, the two situations are aptly described as "sides of a single coin." Babcock, *Fair Play: Evidence Favorable to An Accused and Effective Assistance of Counsel*, 34 Stan.L.Rev. 1133 (1982).

Accordingly, although I agree that the judgment of the Court of Appeals should be vacated and that the case should be remanded for further proceedings, I disagree with the Court's statement of the correct standard to be applied.

Notes and Questions

1. *Brady and the false testimony cases.* Is there a distinction in the rationales underlying the perjured testimony cases and the nondisclosure cases that justifies imposing a less strict standard of materiality in nondisclosure cases, whether or not it involved a specific request? The *Brady* opinion described the due process ruling of that case as a logical extension of the perjured testimony cases. In describing the relationship between the two lines of cases, *Brady* noted: "We now hold that the suppression by the prosecution of evidence favorable to an accused upon request violates due process where the evidence is material either to guilt or to punishment, irrespective of the good faith or bad faith of the prosecution. The principle of *Mooney v. Holohan* [fn. 8, p. 1150 supra] is not punishment of society for misdeeds of a prosecutor but avoidance of an unfair trial to the accused." Not all found this analysis satisfactory, at least as it described *Mooney.* Consider Westen, *The Compulsory Process Clause,* 73 Mich.L.Rev. 71, 121–23 (1974): "The original suppression cases, starting with *Mooney v. Holohan,* * * * did not purport to create affirmative rights in the accused, but to condemn deliberate misconduct by the prosecutor. * * * The Court would have done better [in *Brady*] to acknowledge that it was dealing with two separate principles. By obscuring the fact that *Mooney* involved deliberate misconduct, the Court disparaged the theme of deterrence that proved useful in the past and would prove useful again in the future." Has *Bagley,* in treating the knowing use of perjured testimony as subject to a harmless error standard of materiality (see p. 1150 supra), "restored" the *Mooney-Napue* line of cases to the "deliberate misconduct" theme that Professor Westen found there?

Assuming that there is an element of deliberate misconduct in the knowing use of perjured testimony that is not found even in nondisclosure cases involving specific requests, can that distinction survive the later perjured testimony which have gone substantially beyond the intentional use of perjured testimony? Consider, e.g., *State v. Harris,* 498 F.2d 1164 (3d Cir.

1974), offering the following description of the prosecution's constitutional obligation to correct the testimony of its witnesses:

> "Regardless of the lack of intent to lie on the part of the witness, *Giglio* and *Napue* require that the prosecutor apprise the court when he knows that his witness is giving testimony that is substantially misleading. This is not to say that the prosecutor must play the role of defense counsel, and ferret out ambiguities in his witness' responses on cross-examination. However, when it should be obvious to the Government that the witness' answer, although made in good faith, is untrue, the Government's obligation to correct that statement is as compelling as it is in a situation where the Government knows that the witness is intentionally committing perjury." [a]

2. *The nature of Brady material.* Does *Brady* encompass information that clearly is favorable to the defense, but could not be used as evidence at trial (e.g., the hearsay report of an informant that some other person was commonly rumored to have committed the crime)? Three different positions have been suggested by the lower courts. See Note, 69 J.Crim.L. & C. 197, 207–11 (1978) (collecting cases). Some maintain that *Brady* applies only to material that would be admissible at trial. Others view admissibility as a crucial factor but would extend *Brady* to inadmissible material that could readily lead the defense to the discovery of admissible evidence. Finally, other courts appear to view admissibility as an irrelevant factor; they apparently would apply *Brady* to information that is not admissible and is most unlikely to produce admissible evidence, provided the information could have some other use (e.g., in developing strategy). Do the several opinions in *Bagley* suggest a Court majority clearly favoring one or the other of these positions? What of the following comment in *Agurs?* After noting that "the proper standard of materiality must reflect our overriding concern with the justice of the finding of guilt," the *Agurs* majority added in its footnote 20:

> "It has been argued that the standard should focus on the impact of the undisclosed evidence on the defendant's ability to prepare for trial, rather than the materiality of the evidence to the issue of guilt or innocence. * * * Such a standard would be unacceptable for determining the materiality of what has been generally recognized as '*Brady* material' for two reasons. First, that standard would necessarily encompass incriminating evidence as well as exculpatory evidence, since knowledge of the prosecutor's entire case would always be useful in planning the defense. Second, such an approach would primarily involve an analysis of the adequacy of the notice given to the defendant by the State, and it has always been the Court's view that the notice component of due process refers to the charge rather than the evidentiary support for the charge."

a. What constitutes an answer so misleading as to be deemed subject to such an obligation to correct? Consider, e.g., *Giles v. Maryland,* 386 U.S. 66, 87 S.Ct. 793, 17 L.Ed.2d 737 (1967). The defendants there were charged with the rape of a young girl after coming upon her and a male companion parked in a car in a secluded, heavily wooded area. The defendants claimed the girl had consented after noting that "she had relations with 16 or 17 boys that week and two or three more wouldn't make a difference." On cross examination, her male companion was asked whether he had taken the girl to the wooded area to have sexual relations. He answered "No," that they had intended to go swimming. In a statement previously given to the police, the companion had stated that he and the girl had sexual relations shortly before the defendant arrived on the scene. The Court majority concluded that there had not been a *Mooney* violation, although the case was remanded on other grounds. Justice Harlan, in an opinion for four justices, noted that the companion's answer was "an adequate response to the precise question asked," and was consistent with his statement to the police, which described what had happened rather than the couple's reason for visiting the area. Three justices sharply questioned this analysis, suggesting that the prosecutor had allowed several key witnesses, including the companion, to conceal from the jury evidence of the girl's promiscuity.

3. *Specific requests.* Insofar as it remains relevant after *Bagley* whether the defense made a "specific request" for exculpatory material, what distinguishes a "specific request" from a "general request"? *Agurs* characterized a general request as "really giv[ing] the prosecutor no better notice than no request," and offered only one illustration of such a request (where defendant asks for "all *Brady* material"). Lower courts have varied in their classification of requests as specific or general. Consider, for example, the ruling in *Chaney v. Brown,* 730 F.2d 1334 (10th Cir.1984), and Chief Justice Burger's comments on that ruling in dissenting from the Supreme Court's denial of certiorari. The defendant there, charged with a murder arising from a kidnapping, submitted a pretrial request for disclosure of "statements of all persons who have been interviewed by . . . any governmental agency in connection with the subject matter of this case." Following his trial, conviction, and sentence to death, defendant discovered four recorded witness statements to the F.B.I. that had not been disclosed.[b] Three suggested that the kidnap victim had been seen with another person shortly before the kidnapping and another lent support to other evidence at trial that the telephone caller, demanding a ransom from the victim's husband, had stated there were four kidnappers. The Tenth Circuit, in a pre-*Bagley* ruling, held that there had been a *Brady* violation with respect to the sentencing phase of the case. The Court noted initially that a more strict standard of materiality was applicable to "specific request" cases, and the request here fell in that category. That request "gave the prosecutor 'notice of exactly what the defendant required' * * * and was formulated in terms as specific as possible in the circumstances." The Tenth Circuit concluded that the undisclosed evidence "might have affected" the jury's decision to impose capital punishment since it suggested, contrary to the prosecutor claim that the defendant acted alone, that there might have been accomplices and one of those persons might have been the actual killer.

Chief Justice BURGER (joined by White and Rehnquist, JJ.), in dissenting from the denial of certiorari, BROWN v. CHANEY, ___ U.S. ___, 105 S.Ct. 601, 83 L.Ed.2d 710 (1984) argued that the Tenth Circuit's characterization of the request in *Chaney* as a specific request "conflicted sharply" with the "common-sense" approach to the general/specific distinction adopted by other courts. Describing those cases, he noted:

"They have found 'specific' only those requests that give notice 'of the defendant['s] interest in a *particular* piece of evidence.' *Commonwealth v. Jackson,* 445 N.E.2d 1033 (Mass.1983) (emphasis added). Nor is it a 'specific' request to seek statements of all persons who have been interviewed by the State but who are not expected to be called as witnesses. *Thompson v. Missouri,* 724 F.2d 1314 (CA8 1984). Similarly, a request for written statements taken from any witnesses subsequent to the murder is 'general.' *United States ex rel. Moore v. Brierton,* 560 F.2d 288 (CA7 1977). * * * [The Tenth Circuit justifies its 'broad' view of specific requests] by focusing on what heretofore has been an imponderable—the defendant's ability to phrase the request more precise-

b. Although a state prosecution, the defense request clearly encompassed statements possessed by the F.B.I., and a subsequent court order directing disclosure of all exculpatory evidence referred specifically to F.B.I. materials. Lower courts have regularly held that the prosecutor's *Brady* obligation extends to material within the files of the various investigative agencies participating in the case. See 34 A.L.R.3d 16 (collecting cases); Carlson, *False or Suppressed Evidence: Why a Need for the Prosecutorial Tie?,* 1969 Duke L.J. 1171 (arguing for broad coverage since "governmental action is present and equally harmful whether local or remote law enforcement officers suppress material evidence"). But consider *United States v. Diecidue,* 448 F.Supp. 1011 (M.D.Fla. 1978) (United States Attorney could not be charged with knowledge possessed by a state investigative agency, even though that agency participated in a "joint task force" with the F.B.I., where federal and state prosecutors depended almost exclusively on their own agencies in presenting their cases).

ly. This Court has suggested that the critical distinction does not derive from the defendant's ability to frame a more detailed request. * * * In *Agurs* it did not matter whether the withheld information was available elsewhere; this would suggest that neither does it matter whether the request was 'as specific as possible.' "

4. *Timing of the disclosure.* Though *Brady* itself involved a request for pretrial disclosure, lower courts agree that the "*Brady* principal" does not impose a general requirement of pretrial disclosure of exculpatory material. As one court has noted, "*Brady* is not a discovery rule, but a rule of fairness and minimum prosecutorial obligation." *United States v. Beasley,* 576 F.2d 626 (5th Cir.1978). Due process, it is said, requires only that disclosure of exculpatory material be made in sufficient time to permit defendant to make effective use of that material. See *United States v. Campagnuolo,* 592 F.2d 852 (5th Cir. 1979). The lower courts acknowledge that this standard occasionally will require pretrial disclosure. See, e.g., *United States v. Gleason,* 265 F.Supp. 880 (S.D.N.Y. 1967) (citing as an illustration, a case in which the "prosecutor knows of witnesses potentially useful to the defense, does not intend to call such witnesses himself, and knows—or should reasonably be expected to suppose—that his knowledge is not shared by the defense"); *Schwartzmiller v. Winters,* 576 P.2d 1052 (Idaho 1978) (disclosure at trial of victim's perjury and subornation of perjury at the preliminary hearing was too late to satisfy *Brady* since defendant lacked "adequate time * * * to prepare a defense based on the victim's lack of veracity"). Lower courts also agree, however, that disclosure at trial ordinarily will be adequate to satisfy the prosecutor's due process obligation. If disclosure is made at trial, the burden rests with the defendant to establish that the "lateness of that disclosure so prejudiced [defendant's] preparation or presentation of his defense that he was prevented from receiving his constitutionally guaranteed fair trial." *United States v. Shelton,* 588 F.2d 1242, 1247 (9th Cir.1978). Moreover, if the defendant failed to request a continuance when disclosure was first made at trial, that failure often will be viewed as automatically negating any claim of actual prejudice. See *Gorham v. Wainwright,* 588 F.2d 178 (5th Cir.1979).

5. *Pretrial in camera hearings.* As a matter of practice, *Brady* disclosures often are made before trial. In jurisdiction with ABA-type discovery provisions, those provisions often require disclosure of exculpatory material as part of pretrial discovery. See Note 2, p. 1116 supra. Even without such a provision, if the defense counsel makes a pretrial request for the disclosure of specific evidence, the prosecutor ordinarily will respond affirmatively if the requested evidence is thought to be exculpatory. This practice is consistent with the recommendation of numerous courts that "the prosecutor disclose *Brady* material as soon as possible, preferably pretrial." If the prosecutor refuses to respond affirmatively to a pretrial request for disclosure on the ground that material requested does not fall within *Brady,* the defense may ask the trial court to examine the material in camera and to order disclosure if the court concludes that it is exculpatory. How should a court respond to such a request?

As noted in LaFave and Israel, § 19.5(e), most courts "have been extremely reluctant to undertake a pretrial review of a *Brady* request. In support of this position, it is noted: (1) 'the judge is ordinarily less oriented to the facts of the case and possible defenses than is the prosecuting attorney'; (2) 'requiring the judge to review prosecution files for information useful to the defendant casts the judge in a defense advocate's role'; and (3) in camera inspection can become a 'ponderous, time-consuming task if utilized in every case merely on demand.' These courts ordinarily will not provide in camera inspection unless the request is limited to no more than a few items of evidence and the defendant can show some basis for believing that the material may be favorable to the defense." Compare with this majority viewpoint, the arguments advanced in favor of automatic in camera review in Capra, p. 1157 supra. The author argues that in camera review is necessary because "good faith and integrity do not and cannot guarantee an objective review of the file by the prosecutor," who is necessarily an advocate. Requiring that the defendant make a preliminary showing of materiality is "too limited" because the defendant cannot be expected to prove materiality "in the dark." While the trial judge is not as familiar with the case as the prosecuting attorney, "a judge who knows only the general outlines of a case is likely to determine reliably and objectively whether information * * * is favorable or relevant to a logical defense to the charge." In making that decision, the judge would act as an independent adjudicator stepping between the prosecutor and the defendant in much the same manner as the magistrate who reviews a warrant application. Finally, while the process might be time consuming, "the actual burdens, when compared with the burdens imposed by the *Aqurs* system [through appellate review and retrials where *Brady* violations did occur], may not be so great."

6. *Duty to assist the defense in obtaining exculpatory material.* In several jurisdictions, local discovery provisions grant the defense the right to conduct its own scientific tests of physical evidence obtained by the prosecution. Might *Brady* impose a constitutional obligation upon the prosecution to permit such tests? Several courts have held that it does where the defendant can establish a reasonable basis for believing that the test results may be both "favorable" and "material." See *State v. Koennecke,* 545 P.2d 127 (Or.1976). Consider also *Warren v. State,* 288 So.2d 826 (Ala.1973) (where the charge is possession of an alleged narcotic substance, content of the substance is so critical that the defendant must be allowed independent testing). Compare *People v. Bell,* 253 N.W.2d 726 (Mich.1977) (independent scientific examination of alleged narcotic substance is not required by due process where the defendant is afforded "full opportunity of cross-examination" of the prosecution's expert).

Although lower courts frequently have noted that a defendant has "no constitutional right to a lineup," *Evans v. Superior Court,* 522 P.2d 681 (Cal.1974), held that due process requires the prosecution to honor a defense request for a lineup where "eyewitness identification is shown to be in material issue and there exists a reasonable likelihood of a mistaken identification which a lineup would tend to resolve." The *Evans* opinion reasoned: "Because the People are in a position to compel a lineup and utilize what favorable evidence is derived therefrom, fairness requires that the accused be given a reciprocal right to discover and utilize contrary evidence. See *Wardius v. Oregon.*" Does *Wardius,* discussed at p. 1137 supra, establish a constitutional grounding apart from *Brady* for a prosecution responsibility to permit the defense to conduct its own testing of physical evidence obtained from the defendant? See also Note 7, p. 665 supra.

7. *Lost or destroyed material.* The Supreme Court considered the due process implications of the government's failure to preserve relevant evidence in CALIFORNIA v. TROMBETTA, 467 U.S. 479, 104 S.Ct. 2528, 81 L.Ed.2d 413 (1984). Defendants there, after being stopped in unrelated incidents on suspicion of drunken driving, submitted to Intoxilyzer (breath-analysis) tests. Each registered a blood-alcohol concentration sufficient to be presumed to be intoxicated. Although it was technically feasible to preserve the samples of the defendant's breath, the arresting officers, following their ordinary practice, failed to utilize that procedure. Prior to trial, defendants moved to suppress the Intoxilyzer test results on the ground that the failure to preserve the breath samples restricted their opportunity to impeach the test results. Those motions were denied, but a state appellate court

reversed, holding that due process required the arresting officers to preserve the samples. A unanimous Supreme Court disagreed. MARSHALL, J., in the opinion for the Court, reasoned:

"We have * * * never squarely addressed the Government's duty to take affirmative steps to preserve evidence on behalf of criminal defendants. The absence of doctrinal development in this area reflects, in part, the difficulty of developing rules to deal with evidence destroyed through prosecutorial neglect or oversight. Whenever potentially exculpatory evidence is permanently lost, courts face the treacherous task of divining the import of materials whose contents is unknown and, very often, disputed. Moreover, fashioning remedies for the illegal destruction of evidence can pose troubling choices. In nondisclosure cases, a court can grant the defendant a new trial at which the previously suppressed evidence may be introduced. But, when evidence has been destroyed in violation of the Constitution, the court must choose between barring further prosecution or suppressing—as the California Court of Appeal did in this case—the State's most probative evidence.

"One case in which we have discussed due process constraints on the Government's failure to preserve potentially exculpatory evidence is *Killian v. United States,* 368 U.S. 231, 82 S.Ct. 302, 7 L.Ed. 2d 256 (1961). In *Killian,* the petitioner had been convicted of giving false testimony in violation of 18 U.S.C. § 1001. A key element of the Government's case was an investigatory report prepared by the F.B.I. The Solicitor General conceded that, prior to petitioner's trial, the F.B.I. agents who prepared the investigatory report destroyed the preliminary notes they had made while interviewing witnesses. The petitioner argued that these notes would have been helpful to his defense and that the agents had violated the Due Process Clause by destroying this exculpatory evidence. While not denying that the notes might have contributed to the petitioner's defense, the Court ruled that their destruction did not rise to the level of constitutional violation. * * *

"In many respects the instant case is reminiscent of *Killian.* To the extent that respondents' breath samples came into the possession of California authorities, it was for the limited purpose of providing raw data to the Intoxilyzer. The evidence to be presented at trial was not the breath itself but rather the Intoxilyzer results obtained from the breath samples. As the petitioner in *Killian* wanted the agents' notes in order to impeach their final reports, respondents here seek the breath samples in order to challenge incriminating tests results produced with the Intoxilyzer.

"Given our precedents in this area, we cannot agree with the California Court of Appeal that the State's failure to retain breath samples for respondents constitutes a violation of the Federal Constitution. To begin with, California authorities in this case did not destroy respondents' breath samples in a calculated effort to circumvent the disclosure requirements established by *Brady v. Maryland* and its progeny. In failing to preserve breath samples for respondents, the officers here were acting 'in good faith and in accord with their normal practices.' *Killian.* The record contains no allegation of official animus towards respondents or of a conscious effort to suppress exculpatory evidence.

"More importantly, California's policy of not preserving breath samples is without constitutional defect. Whatever duty the Constitution imposes on the States to preserve evidence, that duty must be limited to evidence that might be expected to play a significant role in the suspect's defense. To meet this standard of constitutional materiality, see *United States v. Agurs,* evidence must both possess an exculpatory value that was apparent before the evidence was destroyed, and also be of such a nature that the defendant would be unable to obtain comparable evidence by other reasonably available means. Neither of these conditions is met on the facts of this case.

"Although the preservation of breath samples might conceivably have contributed to respondents' defenses, a dispassionate review of the Intoxilyzer and the California testing procedures can only lead one to conclude that the chances are extremely low that preserved samples would have been exculpatory. The accuracy of the Intoxilyzer has been reviewed and certified by the California Department of Health. * * * In all but a tiny fraction of cases, preserved breath samples would simply confirm the Intoxilyzer's determination that the defendant had a high level of blood-alcohol concentration at the time of the test. * * * Even if one were to assume that the Intoxilyzer results in this case were inaccurate and that breath samples might therefore have been exculpatory, it does not follow that respondents were without alternative means of demonstrating their innocence. Respondents have identified only a limited number of ways in which an Intoxilyzer might malfunction: faulty calibration, extraneous interference with machine measurements, and operator error. * * * [They] were perfectly capable of raising these issues without resort to preserved breath samples."

SECTION 4. THE DEFENSE COUNSEL'S RESPONSIBILITIES

MORRELL v. STATE

575 P.2d 1200 (Alaska, 1978).

RABINOWITZ, JUSTICE. * * *

[Morrell was charged with kidnapping and various counts of forcible rape. At Morrell's request, a friend (Wagner) cleaned out one of Morrell's vehicles and came upon a legal pad on which had been written what appeared to be a kidnapping plan. Wagner arranged a meeting with the public defender (Cline), who had been appointed to represent Morrell, and asked the public defender to take possession of the legal pad, which he did. When asked about the pad, Morrell told Cline that the plan had been sketched in response to a television report of an earlier kidnapping. Cline then sought the advice of the Alaska Bar Association's Ethics Committee. The Committee advised him to return the pad to Wagner, to explain to Wagner the law on concealment of evidence, and to withdraw from the case if it appeared to him that a violation of ethical rules would occur. Cline returned the pad to Wagner, and withdrew from the case as soon as he contacted his client.

[At a subsequent suppression hearing, Cline testified that he helped Wagner arrange the transfer of the pad to the police, but that he did so only after it became clear that Wagner intended to turn the evidence over to the police. Wagner, on the other hand, testified that it had been Cline's idea to contact the police. Cline testified that, although he gave Wagner a copy of the statute governing concealment of evidence, he did not discuss the statute's meaning or applicability and he refused to give Wagner advice intended either to encourage or discourage his transmission of the pad to the police. Morrell argued that Cline's actions deprived him of his right to effective assistance of counsel and that the evidence therefore should be suppressed. The trial court rejected the suppression motion and admitted the pad into evidence. On appeal from his subsequent conviction, the Alaska Supreme Court unanimously rejected Morrell's contention.]

As Morrell notes, authority in this area is surprisingly sparse. The existing authority seems to indicate, however, that a criminal defense attorney has an obligation to turn over to the prosecution physical evidence which comes into his possession, especially where the evidence comes into the attorney's possession through acts of a third party who is neither a client of the attorney nor an agent of a client. After turning over such evidence, an attorney may have either a right or a duty to remain silent as to the circumstances under which he obtained such evidence, but Morrell presents no authority which establishes that a criminal defendant whose attorney chooses to testify regarding to these matters is denied effective assistance of counsel.

Most of the decisions which discuss the situation in question involve bar disciplinary proceedings or contempt proceedings against the attorney for refusing to answer questions or to turn over evidence. In *State v. Olwell,* 394 P.2d 681 (Wash.1964), an order holding an attorney in contempt was reversed. The attorney had refused to comply with a subpoena duces tecum or answer questions at a coroner's inquest concerning a knife owned by a client. The Washington Supreme Court assumed for purposes of its decision that the attorney had obtained the knife in question as a result of a confidential communication with his client. The court stated that if the evidence had been obtained from a third party with whom no attorney-client relationship existed, communications concerning the knife would not be privileged.

The court in *Olwell* held that incriminating objects delivered to a criminal defense attorney by his client may be withheld by the attorney for a reasonable time to help the attorney prepare his case, and then they must be given to the prosecution. In addition, the court held that in order to protect the attorney-client relationship, the prosecution must not reveal the source of such evidence in the presence of the jury when it is introduced at trial. In discussing the scope of this limited privilege, the court stated that to be protected as a privileged communication at all, the objects obtained by the attorney must have been delivered to the attorney by the client or have been acquired as a direct result of information communicated by the client and not merely have been obtained by the attorney while acting in that capacity for the client. In short, the *Olwell* rule requires a criminal defense attorney to turn over to the prosecution physical evidence that the attorney obtains from his client. This rule requires the defense attorney to avoid giving to investigating or prosecuting authorities any information concerning the source of the evidence or the manner in which it was obtained. Finally, if the evidence is obtained from a non-client third party who is not acting as the client's agent, even the privilege to refuse to testify concerning the manner in which the evidence was obtained is inapplicable.

Also of significance is *In re Ryder,* 263 F.Supp. 360 (E.D.Va.1967), *aff'd* 381 F.2d 713 (4th Cir.1967). *Ryder* involved a proceeding to determine whether an attorney should be suspended or disbarred. The attorney had taken possession from his client of stolen money and a sawed-off shotgun, knowing that the money was stolen and that the gun had been used in an armed robbery. The attorney intended to retain the property until after his client's trial and then to return the money to its rightful owner. The client in *Ryder* [originally] had put the money and the gun in his safe deposit box. The attorney, knowing that the money in the box was marked and disbelieving his client's story about how the client had acquired the money, went to the bank to transfer the money to his own safe deposit box. Upon opening the client's box, the attorney discovered the shotgun and transferred both the money and the gun to his own box. The court stated in dicta that the attorney's state of mind when he transferred the evidence demonstrated sufficient knowledge to fall within the statute prohibiting knowing concealment of stolen property.

The court in *Ryder* suspended the attorney, holding that his actions did not fall within the protection of the attorney-client privilege. The court noted, however, that neither the client nor his attorney could be compelled to produce merely evidentiary articles, as opposed to fruits or instrumentalities of the crime. This dictum was based on the notion that such merely evidentiary articles could not even be seized in a legal search; and, therefore, their production could not be compelled. The rule that mere evidence may not be seized in a lawful search has since been disapproved. *Warden v. Hayden* [p. 253 supra]. Therefore, we think that no distinction should be drawn in the privilege context between physical evidence obtained by a criminal defense attorney which is "mere evidence" of a client's crime and that which may be said to be either a fruit or an instrumentality of the crime. * * *

From the foregoing cases emerges the rule that a criminal defense attorney must turn over to the prosecution real evidence that the attorney obtains from his client. Further, if the evidence is obtained from a non-client third party who is not acting for the client, then the privilege to refuse to testify concerning the manner in which the evidence was obtained is inapplicable. We think the foregoing rules are sound, and we apply them in reaching our resolution of the effective assistance-of-counsel issue in the case at bar.

Morrell correctly cites cases which establish that misprision statutes are generally interpreted to require an affirmative act of concealment in addition to a failure to disclose a crime to the authorities. See *United States v. Daddano,* 432 F.2d 1119 (7th Cir.1970). However, the cases disciplining attorneys for failing to turn over evidence or upholding denials of motions to suppress evidence turned over by attorneys do not rest alone on the notion that an attorney who does not turn over such evidence may be guilty of a crime. The cases cited are also based on the proposition that it would constitute unethical conduct for an attorney—an officer of the court—to knowingly fail to reveal relevant evidence in a criminal case.

We believe that Cline would have been obligated to see that the evidence reached the prosecutor in this case even if he had obtained the evidence from Morrell. His obligation was even clearer because he acquired the evidence from Wagner, who made the decision to turn the evidence over to Cline without consulting Morrell and therefore was not acting as Morrell's agent.

Since Cline was obligated to see that the evidence reached the prosecutor, Morrell cannot have been deprived of effective assistance of counsel by Cline's decision to return the evidence to Wagner. Further, Cline's efforts to aid Wagner's transfer of the evidence to the police appear to have been within the scope of Cline's obligation. Cline could have properly turned the evidence over to the police himself and would have been obliged to do so if Wagner had refused to accept the return of the evidence.[17]

One additional aspect of this issue remains for discussion. As was noted earlier, the Ethics Committee of the Alaska Bar Association gave Cline an advisory opinion as to what to do with the questioned legal pad. The opinion advised Cline to return the subject papers to Wagner, to explain to Wagner the law on concealment of evidence,[18] and to withdraw from the case if it later became obvious to Cline that a violation of ethical rules would result from his continued representation of Morrell.

17. The only remaining question is whether Cline's testimony concerning the Wagner incident was within the attorney-client privilege and, if it was, whether the testimony deprived Morrell of his rights to effective assistance of counsel and to a fair trial. While the *Olwell* rule might have imposed a duty on Cline to remain silent as to these matters if Cline had obtained the evidence from Morrell, the acquisition of incriminating evidence from a non-client third party who is not acting as a client's agent falls outside the attorney-client privilege. Cline could not have claimed that the attorney-client privilege precluded him from testifying as to his acquisition of the evidence from Wagner. Therefore, Morrell cannot have been deprived of effective assistance of counsel by Cline's testimony.

18. AS 11.30.315 provides: *Destroying, altering or concealing evidence.* A person who wilfully destroys, alters or conceals evidence concerning the commission of a crime or evidence which is being sought for production during an investigation, inquiry or trial, with the intent to prevent the evidence from being discovered or produced, is guilty of a misdemeanor * * *.

On June 6, 1977, the Board of Governors of the Alaska Bar Association adopted Ethics Opinion 76–7 which embodied the advice the Ethics Committee had earlier given Cline. The opinion also stated, however, that Cline would be ethically obligated not to reveal the existence of the physical evidence "unless required to do so by statute." The Bar Association declined to render an opinion as to the applicability of AS 11.30.315 or other state law.

We think Cline followed the advice of the Bar Association in relation to his dealings with Wagner. * * * Assuming Ethics Opinion 76–7 is a correct statement of the law, whether Cline rendered effective counsel then turns on whether he could reasonably have concluded that AS 11.30.315 required him to reveal the existence of the evidence. Otherwise, the opinion states that he had an ethical obligation not to reveal the evidence. AS 11.30.315 makes it a crime to wilfully destroy, alter or conceal evidence concerning the commission of a crime or evidence which is being sought for production during an investigation, inquiry or trial, with the intent to prevent the evidence from being discovered or produced. While statutes which address the concealing of evidence are generally construed to require an affirmative act of concealment in addition to the failure to disclose information to the authorities, taking possession of evidence from a non-client third party and holding the evidence in a place not accessible to investigating authorities would seem to fall within the statute's ambit. Thus, we have concluded that Cline breached no ethical obligation to his client which may have rendered his legal services to Morrell ineffective. * * *

Notes and Questions

1. Consider also, NEW YORK STATE BAR ASSOCIATION COMMITTEE ON PROFESSIONAL ETHICS, OPINION NO. 479 (BELGE), N.Y.L.J., March 7, 1978, at 24, 22 Cr.L.Rptr. 2537 (1978):

"The allegations on which our opinion was based may be summarized as follows:

"A client charged with homicide tells his lawyer during the course of representation that he had previously killed two other persons in homicides totally unrelated to that for which he has been indicted. The lawyer makes a record of his client's conversation containing this incriminating information. At the lawyer's request, the client also informs him of the location of the corpses, which was indicated on a diagram. Following such disclosure, the lawyer goes to this location, discovers the bodies and photographs them. Before doing so he moves parts of a body which had been dismembered to bring it within range of his camera. No attempt is made to conceal either body in any way.

"At a later date, the lawyer destroys the photographs, the record of his conversation with his client and the diagram of the location of the bodies. He does not disclose to the authorities or to anyone else any of the information so obtained. Thereafter, during discussions with the District Attorney concerning the crime charged in the indictment, the lawyer, in discussing the possibility of an appropriate plea disposition, suggests that he is in a position to provide information concerning two unsolved murders still under investigation by the authorities. * * *

"The questions raised are complex and difficult. Legal issues, upon which we do not pass, may be inextricably interwoven with ethical considerations. Illegal conduct involving moral turpitude is per se unethical. DR 1–102(A)(3).[a]

"1. The lawyer's failure to disclose his knowledge of the two unrelated homicides was not improper, assuming, as the facts

a. The Committee's references to Disciplinary Rules (DR), Ethical Considerations (EC) and Canons are to the *A.B.A., Code of Professional Responsibility* (1969). The A.B.A. subsequently replaced the *Model Code* with its *Model Rules of Professional Conduct* (1983). While several states given us indicate, that the information came to the lawyer during the course of his employment. Furthermore, the requirements of Canon 4 that 'a lawyer should preserve the confidences and secrets of a client,' and of EC 4–1 and DR 4–101(B), would have been violated if such disclosure had been made.[b] * * * Proper representation of a client calls for full disclosure by the client to his lawyer of all possibly relevant facts, even though such facts may reveal the client's commission of prior crimes. To encourage full disclosure, the client must be assured of confidentiality, a requirement embodied by law in the attorney-client privilege and broadly incorporated into Canon 4 of the Code and the EC's and DR's thereunder. * * *

"Narrow and limited exceptions to the rule of confidentiality have been incorporated in DR 4–101(C) and DR 7–102(B), the most important of which relate to information involving the intention of the client to commit a crime in the future or the course of the lawyer's representation of the client, or where the client consents following full disclosure. None of the specified narrow exceptions appear to apply to the situation here presented.[c] * * * [I]f a lawyer were compelled to reveal information inculpating a client, the lawyer would, in effect, become his client's adversary in violation of the mandate of EC 4–5 and DR 4–101(B).

"Thus, the lawyer was under an injunction not to disclose to the authorities his knowledge of the two prior murders, and was duty-bound not to reveal to the authorities the location of the bodies. The lawyer's knowledge with respect to the location of the bodies was obtained solely from the client in confidence and in secret. Without the client's revelation in secret and in confidence, he would not have been in a position to assist the authorities

have adopted the *Model Rules*, the disciplinary standards in the vast majority of states continue to follow the *Model Code* (with occasional variation in particular states).

DR 1–102(A)(3) provides: "A lawyer shall not * * * engage in illegal conduct involving moral turpitude." Model Rule 8.4(b) states that "it is professional misconduct for a lawyer to * * * commit a criminal act that reflects adversely on the lawyer's honesty, trustworthiness or fitness as a lawyer in other respects."

b. DR 4–101 provides:

(A) "Confidence" refers to information protected by the attorney-client privilege under applicable law, and "secret" refers to other information gained in the professional relationship that the client has requested be held inviolate or the disclosure of which would be embarrassing or would be likely to be detrimental to the client.

(B) Except when permitted under DR 4–101(C), a lawyer shall not knowingly:

(1) Reveal a confidence or secret of his client.

* * *

(C) A lawyer may reveal: * * *

(2) Confidences or secrets when permitted under Disciplinary Rules or required by law or court order.

(3) The intention of his client to commit a crime and the information necessary to prevent the crime.

EC 4–1 stresses the value of the lawyer's general obligation to preserve the confidences and secrets of a client, noting that "a client must feel free to discuss whatever he wishes with his lawyer and a lawyer must be equally free to obtain information beyond that volunteered by his client."

Model Rule 1.6 provides that a "lawyer shall not reveal information relating to representation of a client unless the client consents after consultation except * * * (1) to prevent the client from committing a criminal act that the lawyer believes is likely to result in imminent death or substantial bodily harm." The Commentary to Rule 1.6 states: "[A] lawyer may be obligated or permitted by other provisions of law to give information about a client. Whether another provision of law supersedes Rule 1.6 is a matter of interpretation beyond the scope of these Rules, but a presumption should exist against such a supersession."

c. As to the DR 4–101(C) exceptions, see fn. b supra. DR 7–102(B) relates to fraud committed upon a person or tribunal (e.g., through the use of perjured testimony, see p. 1340 infra). In another portion of its opinion, the Committee referred to another "exception" to the "rule of confidentiality" that it viewed as not applicable to this case. It noted: "Similar exceptions exist where a lawyer 'knowingly . . . takes possession of and secrets the fruits or instrumentalities of a crime' with intent to prevent their use as evidence. *In re Ryder* [p. 1165 supra]. Cf. *State v. Olwell* [p. 1165 supra]."

in this regard. Thus, his personal knowledge is a link solidly welded to the chain of privileged communications and, without the client's express permission, must not be disclosed. The relationship between lawyer and client is in many respects like that between priest and penitent. Both lawyer and priest are bound by the bond of silence.

"2. A lawyer's obligation to hold a client's confidences and secrets inviolate extends beyond information imparted orally and embraces written material from the client 'coming into existence merely as a communication to the attorney.' See 8 *Wigmore on Evidence* § 2307 * * *. Similarly, written material prepared by the client for his lawyer is a form of written communication and falls within the attorney-client privilege. Such documents are not instruments or fruits of the crime, which under certain circumstances the lawyer might be obliged to turn over to authorities. See, e.g., *State v. Olwell* [p. 1165 supra]. Accordingly, neither the lawyer nor his client was obliged to reveal an incriminating diagram, whether prepared by the client for his lawyer or by the lawyer on the basis of information gained by him during the course of the client's representation. * * *

"3. This Committee does not pass upon the legality of alleged conduct, but if such conduct is illegal, it would of course be unethical, with rare exceptions of inadvertent violations involving no moral turpitude. Thus, any tampering, concealment or destruction of physical evidence in violation of N.Y.Penal Law § 215.40 would also be violative of the code. Even in the absence of any violation of law and in the absence of an intention on the part of the lawyer to tamper, conceal or destroy evidence, there could be an appearance of impropriety in violation of Canon 8 in moving a part of one of the bodies.[d] Such conduct should be avoided to prevent even the appearance that there might have been an intent to tamper with or suppress evidence.

"4. There is no ethical impropriety in the lawyer's discussing with the District Attorney the possibility of an appropriate plea disposition, provided that the lawyer had the express consent of his client before making such disclosure. Plea bargaining is an accepted part of our criminal procedures today. A lawyer engaged or attempting to engage in it with his client's consent would be properly serving his client. Thus, the lawyer's suggestion to the District Attorney that he might be in a position to assist the authorities in resolving open cases during such a discussion would appear to involve no violation of proper professional standards. One can conceive of a variety of circumstances in which such a disclosure might be helpful to a client. For example, the disclosure of the client's commission of prior crimes of violence might very well establish the client's need for confinement for medical treatment rather than imprisonment."[e]

d. Canon 8 provides: "A lawyer should assist in improving the legal system."

e. The *Belge* case is discussed in Freedman, *Lawyers' Ethics in An Adversary System* 1–8 (1975); Hazard and Hodes, *The Law of Lawyering* 109–111 (1985). Attorney Belge was indicted for failing to report a death that had occurred without medical attendance. The indictment subsequently was dismissed on the ground that the attorney-client privilege relieved the defendant of any obligation he might otherwise have under the New York Public Health Law. See *People v. Belge*, 372 N.Y.S.2d 798 (1975), aff'd, 376 N.Y.S.2d 771 (1975), aff'd, 359 N.E.2d 377 (N.Y.1976). However, the trial court also noted: "If the grand jury had returned an indictment charging Mr. Belge with obstruction of justice under a proper statute, the work of this court would have been more difficult than it is."

Because of the "extraordinary circumstances" confronting Mr. Belge and his associate, the trial court awarded them fees beyond the normal statutory maximum for acting as appointed counsel. See *Application of Armani*, 371 N.Y.S.2d 563 (Co. Ct.1975). Public reaction to the attorneys' behavior generally was adverse; both received threatening calls, and their law practices suffered considerably. See *Lawyer-Client Privilege Gets Severe Test*, 64 A.B.A.J. 644 (1978).

2. Note, 47 U.Cinn.L.Rev. 431 (1978), after analyzing the *Morrell* and *Belge* cases, concludes that they "highlight the confused authority" which provides "few guidelines" for the practicing attorney. Do you agree? In light of *Belge* and *Morrell,* what are counsel's professional responsibilities in the following cases:

(a) Defendant places on his counsel's desk a handgun and informs counsel that this was the gun used in the robbery with which he has been charged. Counsel informs the defendant that counsel is under obligation to turn the weapon over to the police.[f] The client then responds by returning the gun to his pocket and announcing that, no matter what counsel advises, he intends to drop the gun in the lake. Counsel makes no report to the police.

(b) Assume the same initial facts as above except that defendant responds by picking up the gun, wiping off the fingerprints and again presenting it to the lawyer.

3. Does the ruling in *People v. Meredith,* 631 P.2d 46 (Cal.1981) follow from *Morrell* and *Belge?* In response to counsel's warning that he needed to be "fully acquainted with the facts to avoid being 'sandbagged' by the prosecution," defendant told counsel that he had thrown in a barrel behind his house a wallet that he had picked up at the scene of the robbery-murder. Counsel then sent his investigator to that location, where the wallet was found and taken to counsel. When counsel found within the wallet identification indicating that it belonged to the victim of the crime, he turned the wallet and its contents over to the detective investigating the case. At trial, the wallet was introduced, and the investigator was required to testify, over defense objection, as to the location at which he found the wallet. On appeal, the court initially noted that "defendant concedes, and we agree that the wallet itself was admissible in evidence." It then turned to the challenge to the investigator's testimony as violating the attorney-client privilege. Since the investigator was acting on information furnished by the client to the counsel (and through counsel to the investigator), the privilege would apply to facts observed by the investigator "as a direct result of the [client's] confidential communication" [citing *Olwell* and *Belge*]. However, where "the defense, by removing or altering evidence, interferes with the prosecution's opportunity to discover that evidence," the privilege no longer applies. Such interference would be automatically assumed in all cases of removal without regard to the probability that the prosecution would in fact have found the evidence if it had been left in place. As a result, where counsel makes the "tactical choice" to "remove the evidence to examine or test it," rather than to leave it in place, counsel (or the investigator acting at his direction) can be required to testify as to the location at which he found the evidence. At the same time, "in offering the evidence, the prosecution should present the information in a manner which avoids revealing the content of the attorney-client communications or the original source of the information."

4. Statutes prohibiting the destruction of evidence vary as to the precise point in the process at which such action becomes criminal. Some prohibit intentional destruction of evidence only if that evidence is pertinent to an ongoing criminal proceeding; others prohibit intentional destruction when there is an ongoing investigation; many prohibit intentional destruction when the actor believes that "an official proceeding or investigation is

f. Consider Hazard and Hodes, fn. e supra: "If the client is told what the law is, he may demand the gun back and dispose of it himself. An especially quick-witted client might demand the gun back, wipe off any lingering fingerprints, and present it to the lawyer again! But if he is not told, the basic principle that a lawyer must always consult with a client and keep him informed about legal consequences is compromised. (See Rules 1.2(a), 1.2(e), and 1.4)."

pending or about to be instituted" (Model Penal Code § 241.7); and several "make destruction of real evidence a criminal offense if done with intent to prevent its production in a trial or other legal proceeding regardless of the time of the act." Note, 88 Yale L.J. 1665 (1979) (also arguing that "the failure of the Code of Professional Responsibility to prohibit an attorney from advising his client to destroy documents unless the act is illegal undermines the [adversary system's] commitment to the equalization of parties").

Chapter 21

COERCED, INDUCED AND NEGOTIATED GUILTY PLEAS; PROFESSIONAL RESPONSIBILITY

SECTION 1. SOME VIEWS OF NEGOTIATED PLEAS

A. INTRODUCTION

1. "The American criminal justice system has been transformed by plea bargaining. The traditional model of the criminal process provides for an impartial trier of fact to determine guilt after a formal adversarial trial and then for a judge to select a penalty appropriate for the offender from a range specified by the legislature. In practice, however, the locus of the criminal process has shifted largely from trial to plea bargaining. In the vast majority of cases, guilt and the applicable range of sentences are determined through informal negotiations between the prosecutor and the defense attorney." [a]

2. "There is a broad range of plea arrangements currently used by prosecutors. The three most common are the sentence recommendation, the plea to a lesser included offense, and the dismissal of charges in an indictment, information, or other charging paper.[7]

"Under the sentence recommendation practice, the prosecuting attorney promises that he will recommend to the court a sentence favorable to the defendant, will not seek the maximum penalty, or will refrain from making any recommendations. Most often the sentence recommendation involves a promise by the prosecutor to suggest to the trial judge a mutually satisfactory term of years as the appropriate punishment in return for a defendant's guilty plea. In order for the practice to have any value to defendants and prosecutors there must be a reasonable expectation of judicial acceptance of the recommendations. Where there is a judicial practice of following recommendations, the promise of a recommended sentence

a. Note, 90 Harv.L.Rev. 569 (1977). As to the percentage of cases determined by guilty pleas, see p. 12 supra; Finkelstein, *A Statistical Analysis of Guilty Plea Practices in the Federal Courts,* 89 Harv.L.Rev. 293 (1975). See also Notes 22 and 23 at pp. 1183–85 infra as to the practice in those jurisdictions that have abolished or sharply restricted "plea bargaining."

7. Many other types of agreements are made with defendants to induce a plea. These include promises not to prosecute codefendants, promises to arrange for the defendant or a codefendant to be incarcerated in a particular prison, promises to have the defendant or a codefendant tried in the juvenile court, recommendations for presentence investigations, recommendations for concurrent sentences, and agreements not to oppose probation. Promises of immunity by the prosecutor can also be used to induce guilty pleas. Immunity can be promised with respect to some crimes in order to obtain a plea on another crime. Technically, immunity promises could come within the scope of a promise to dismiss charges in an indictment, but often the immunity relates to crimes not yet charged.

can be tantamount to a promise of a definite term. But each defendant who pleads guilty in reliance on a prosecutor's promise to recommend a specific sentence takes the risk that in his particular case the judge will not follow the suggestion in imposing sentence. In addition, many defendants may enter into agreements with prosecutors to avoid imposition of the maximum sentence, but, unless they are informed of actual sentencing patterns, may needlessly bargain away their right to trial since sentences often fall considerably below the maximums provided by the legislatures.

"In some jurisdictions the prosecutor may recommend that the court accept a guilty plea to a lesser offense included in the offense actually charged. The court's permission to plead to a lesser included offense is usually required, and in some jurisdictions the prosecutor must file reasons for recommending the lesser plea. * * *

"The prosecutor may also offer to dismiss certain criminal allegations in the charging papers in order to induce a defendant to plead guilty to the remaining charges. This procedure calls for the defendant to plead guilty to the charges agreed upon and for the prosecutor, at the time set aside by the court for dismissals, to move for dismissal of the remaining charges. The court's approval is usually required for the dismissal of any charges, and ordinarily charges are dismissed as a matter of course.

"The charge dismissal practice developed as a possible plea bargaining tool because of the multiplicity of crimes which often arise out of a single incident. However, an apparently advantageous bargain may actually be specious because of the tendency of many courts to sentence concurrently, or to suspend sentence on all but one or two of the multiple and similar charges arising out of the same incident." [b]

3. Although the practice of plea bargaining is a longstanding one, only in recent times has it been openly discussed and assessed in the legal literature and the public press.[c] E.g., compare the President's Commission on Law Enforcement and Administration of Justice, *The Challenge of Crime in a Free Society* (1967), approving of plea bargaining within certain defined limits; with this National Advisory Commission on Criminal Justice Standards and Goals proposal:

"As soon as possible, * * * negotiations between prosecutors and defendants—either personally or through their attorneys—concerning concessions to be made in return for guilty pleas should be prohibited. In the event that the prosecution makes a recommendation as to sentence, it should not be affected by the willingness of the defendant to plead guilty to some or all of the offenses with which he is charged. A plea of guilty should not be considered by the court in determining the sentence to be imposed." [d]

4. Courts were for many years reluctant to even acknowledge the existence of plea bargaining, but this is no longer the case. The Supreme Court has upheld the practice as necessary and proper,[e] as have the lower courts. Illustrative is *People v. Selikoff,* 318 N.E.2d 784 (N.Y.1974):

"Throughout history the punishment to be imposed upon wrongdoers has been subject to negotiation. Plea negotiation, in some form, has existed in this country since at least 1804. Even in England, where there are no public prosecutors, no

b. Note, 112 U.Pa.L.Rev. 865–68 (1964). Reprinted with permission of the publisher; copyright © 1964 by the University of Pennsylvania.

c. See the books and articles cited in J. Markowitz, *Plea Bargaining: An Annotated Bibliography* (1978); Matheny, *A Bibliography on Plea Bargaining,* 13 Law & Soc.Rev. 661 (1979).

d. *N.A.C. Standards, The Courts* § 3.1.

e. E.g., *Bordenkircher v. Hayes,* p. 1185 infra; *Santobello v. New York,* p. 1201 infra. The Supreme Court's first extended discussion of plea bargaining came in *Brady v. United States,* decided in 1970. See fn. a at p. 1187 infra.

inflexible sentencing standards, and considerably less pressure on the trial courts, a limited form of plea negotiation seems to be developing. Moreover, convictions upon guilty pleas, pleas probably to lesser crimes, have been high since 1839 both in rural, where there is little trial court congestion, and in urban areas, where there is much congestion. History and perspective suggest, then, that plea negotiation is not caused solely, or even largely, by overcrowded dockets. This is not to say, however, that plea negotiation is not acutely essential to relieve court calendar congestion, as indeed it is. In budget-starved urban criminal courts, the negotiated plea literally staves off collapse of the law enforcement system, not just as to the courts but also to local detention facilities.

"Plea negotiations, of course, serve many other needs. They relieve the prosecution and the defense too, for that matter, from 'the inevitable risks and uncertainties of trial'. The negotiation process which results in a guilty plea telescopes the judicial process and the necessarily protracted intervals involved in charge, trial, and sentence, and even appeals, hopefully starting the offender on the road to possible rehabilitation. The process also serves significant goals of law enforcement by permitting an exchange of leniency for information and assistance.

"Perhaps most important, plea negotiation serves the ends of justice. It enables the court to impose 'individualized' sentences, an accepted ideal in criminology, by avoiding mandatory, harsh sentences adapted to a class of crime or a group of offenders but inappropriate, and even Draconian, if applied to the individual before the court.[f] Obviously no two defendants are quite alike even if they have committed, in legal definition, identical offenses. The negotiation process often brings to light mitigating circumstances unknown when the defendant was charged."

B. ADMINISTRATIVE CONVENIENCE

5. It is commonly assumed that the system can function only if a high percentage of cases are disposed of by guilty plea and that this will happen only if concessions are granted to induce pleas. As Chief Justice Burger has commented:

"It is an elementary fact, historically and statistically, that the system of courts—the number of judges, prosecutors, and of courtrooms—has been based on the premise that approximately 90 per cent of all defendants will plead guilty, leaving only 10 per cent, more or less, to be tried. But that premise may no longer be a reliable yardstick of our needs.

"Changes in the law that are part of what we lawyers call the 'revolution in criminal justice,' which began as far back as the 1930's have brought this about. Anyone who questions these changes must recognize that until recently criminal law was the neglected stepchild of the law.

"The consequences of what might seem on its face a small percentage change in the rate of guilty pleas can be tremendous. A reduction from 90 per cent to 80 per cent in guilty pleas requires the assignment of twice the judicial manpower and facilities—judges, court reporters, bailiffs, clerks, jurors and courtrooms. A reduction to 70 per cent trebles this demand." [g]

f. Consider, in this connection, the current trend toward "reform" of sentencing by reducing or eliminating sentencing discretion, as by (i) restricting or eliminating the powers of parole boards, (ii) adopting "fixed" sentencing schemes, whereunder the statutes specify the exact penalty that will follow conviction of each offense, or (iii) adopting "presumptive" sentencing, whereunder statutes specify the "normal" sentence for each offense and allow limited departures only in atypical cases. As noted in Alschuler, *Sentencing Reform and Prosecutorial Power: A Critique of Recent Proposals for "Fixed" and "Presumptive" Sentencing,* 126 U.Pa.L.Rev. 550, 551 (1978), "this sort of reform is likely to produce its antithesis," namely, greater reliance on plea bargaining.

g. Address at the American Bar Association Annual Convention, N.Y. Times, August 11, 1970, p. 24, col. 4.

6. "[T]he most pernicious of the myths with which the apologists for plea bargaining have surrounded the process [is] the notion that, absent a radical restructuring of the criminal justice system, plea bargaining will remain a 'practical necessity.' Contrary to this widespread belief, the best estimate is that fewer than 350,000 people are charged with felonies each year in the United States, and if society were to provide each of them with the kind of trial that, say, $1,000 could buy, the total cost of $350 million would be about one-fourteenth of Lockheed's cost overrun on the C5–A aircraft.

"The prospect of multiplying current criminal-court resources several times over may seem unthinkable until one realizes how limited these resources are. The situation in my own jurisdiction, however, seems typical. (Those familiar with criminal courts elsewhere can make their own rough calculations.) In Travis County, Texas, a county of more than 250,000 people, one judge hears felony cases full-time, and another hears felony cases part-time. To multiply these resources five times, or ten, or fifteen would require no more than the building and staffing of a single new courthouse, a task that might be almost as difficult as the building and staffing of a new hospital or a new high school. If the need were in the area of medicine or education, however, responsible citizens would at least talk about meeting it. They would not insist that 'practical necessity' required bargaining with patients to 'waive' their operations or with students to 'waive' their classes." [h]

7. But, it has been questioned whether an end to plea bargaining would significantly increase the burdens on the criminal justice system. For one thing, it has been noted that the existence of plea bargaining is itself responsible for much delay; to get a better plea, "defense attorneys commonly devise strategies whose only utility lies in the threat they pose to the court's and the prosecutor's time." [i] For another, it has been asserted that an end to bargaining would not necessarily mean more trials, for "if prosecutors and defense attorneys were convinced that plea bargaining would not occur, the charges filed by prosecutors would correspond more closely to what the prosecutor reasonably thinks he can and should get as a result. * * * If the defendant and his attorney agree that this is the likely result—as the Commission believes will more often be the case than under existing practice—they can and should enter a plea of guilty." [j]

h. Alschuler, *Book Review,* 12 Crim.L.Bull. 629, 632 (1976). Compare: "It is easy to minimize administrative convenience and need. Simply increase the staff of prosecutors, judges, defense counsel, and probation officers if the present complement is insufficient to handle the task, it is said. Even if the money were readily available, it would still not be clear that we could call upon sufficient numbers of competent personnel. A lowering of standards in order to man the store adequately may well result in poorer justice. It may also divert both funds and personnel from other segments of the criminal process, such as corrections work, where they are arguably more needed." Enker, *Perspectives on Plea Bargaining,* in Task Force Report: The Courts 108, 112.

i. Alschuler, *The Prosecutor's Role in Plea Bargaining,* 36 U.Chi.L.Rev. 50, 56 (1968). These tactics, he explains, include routine jury demands even when there is no desire for a trial of any kind, repeated requests for continuances, and a host of pretrial motions.

j. *N.A.C. Standards,* fn. d supra, at 47. In Berger, *The Case Against Plea Bargaining,* 62 A.B.A.J. 621, 623, 624 (1976), the county attorney of Maricopa County, Arizona, reports:

"Approximately five years ago we adopted a policy of not plea bargaining charges of sale of narcotics, sale of drugs, and sale of marijuana. This was an experimental program to see if a ban on plea bargaining would cause an increase in cases taken to trial. We found that this ban did not cause a rise in the number of trials. It resulted in defendants pleading guilty to the charges, and in many cases there were fewer trials. A review of the figures show that this policy has become so successful that the great majority of defendants in narcotic sales cases now plead guilty to the charge without going to trial. This has helped alleviate case backlog rather than cause it."

C. ACCURATE AND FAIR RESULTS

8. "[T]he disposition of cases in a plea-bargaining system tends to be governed to an unacceptable degree by tactical factors, such as court and prosecutor workload, or the aggressiveness of the lawyers, or their personal relationships, or by mechanical factors, such as standard reductions of charge or sentence offered routinely in all cases to speed and encourage negotiation. These factors are irrelevant to the correctional needs of the defendant or the requirements of law enforcement and, to the extent that they determine the case, they prevent the criminal process from dealing effectively with the essential problem of reducing the likelihood that the offender will commit further offenses.

"The consequence of these vices is likely to be increased fear that the innocent will be convicted, that serious offenders will escape with undeserved leniency, and that a sense of hucksterism and venality pervades the halls of justice." [k]

9. "[T]he practice of bargaining hardest when the case is weakest leads to grossly disparate treatment for identical offenders—assuming, for the moment, that they are offenders. Chicago defense attorney J. Eugene Pincham comments, 'When a prosecutor has a dead-bang case, he is likely to come up with an impossible offer like thirty to fifty years. When the case has a hole in it, however, the prosecutor may scale the offer all the way down to probation. The prosecutors' goal is to get something from every defendant, and the correctional treatment the defendant may require is the last thing on their minds.'

"A prosecutor's sentencing decisions may therefore be made on nonpenological grounds for tactical as well as administrative reasons. So long as prosecutors believe that their interest lies in securing as many convictions as possible, this characteristic would seem inherent in the guilty-plea system. There is, however, a more serious criticism of the prosecutors' plea-bargaining practices. It is that the greatest pressures to plead guilty are brought to bear on defendants who may be innocent. The universal rule is that the sentence differential between guilty-plea and trial defendants increases in direct proportion to the likelihood of acquittal." [l]

10. "Maximization of adjudication by trial may actually result in more inaccurate verdicts. So long as trials are the exception rather than the rule and are limited, by and large, to cases in which the defense offers a substantial basis for contesting the prosecutor's allegations, the defendant's presumption of innocence and the requirement of proof beyond a reasonable doubt are likely to remain meaningful to a jury. The very fact that the defendant contests the charges impresses upon the jurors the seriousness of their deliberations and the need to keep an open mind about the evidence and to approach the testimony of accusing witnesses with critical care and perhaps even a degree of skepticism. If contest becomes routine, jurors may likely direct their skepticism at the defense. Prosecutors too readily apply the overall,

k. Rosett, *The Negotiated Guilty Plea,* 374 Annals 70, 72–73 (1967). Consider also the following remarks before the Association of the Bar of the City of New York by Police Commissioner Patrick V. Murphy, N.Y. Times, March 24, 1972, p. 39, col. 2: "Last year we made 94,042 felony arrests, an increase of 165 per cent over a ten-year period. You ask what happened to last year's 94,000 felony arrests? Exactly 552 of them went to trial, 552 out of 94,000. The rest of them were disposed of. Disposed of means dismissed outright, reduced to misdemeanors via plea-bargaining, reduced to much lesser felonies via plea-bargaining. No doubt certain of the honest, dedicated policemen who made these 94,000 arrests last year came to the belief that conscientious police work is a waste of time, a waste of effort and a waste of devotion." Compare Vera Institute of Justice, *Felony Arrests: Their Prosecution and Disposition in New York's City Courts* 134 (1977), which arrived "at a different conclusion: Where crimes are serious, evidence is strong, and victims are willing to prosecute, felons with previous criminal histories end up with relatively heavy sentences."

l. Alschuler, fn. i supra, at 60–61.

and overwhelming, statistical probability of guilt to individual cases; we do not want jurors to do the same. It makes some sense, then, to screen out those cases where there is no real dispute and encourage their disposition by plea, leaving for trial to the extent possible only those cases where there exists a real basis for dispute.[m] * * *

"The possibility that innocent defendants might be induced to plead guilty in order to avoid the possibility of a harsh sentence should they be convicted after trial is obviously cause for concern. Because of the emotional potential of the problem, it is easy to overstate. The truth is that we just do not know how common such a situation is. * * *

"Still, perhaps the problem can be put in a better perspective. In the first place, trials, too, may not always result in truthful or accurate verdicts. It is interesting to note that disposition by trial and by negotiated plea are similar in that in neither instance do we have any relatively accurate idea of the incidence of mistaken judgments. On one level, then, the significant question is not how many innocent people are induced to plead guilty but is there a significant likelihood that innocent people who would be (or have a fair chance of being) acquitted at trial might be induced to plead guilty?

"Further, concern over the possibility that a negotiated plea can result in an erroneous judgment of conviction assumes a frame of reference by which the accuracy of the judgment is to be evaluated. It assumes an objective truth existing in a realm of objective historical fact which it is the sole function of our process to discover. Some, but by no means all, criminal cases fit this image. For example, this is a relatively accurate description of the issues at stake in a case in which the defendant asserts a defense of mistaken identity. If all other issues were eliminated from the case, there would still exist a world of objective historical fact in which the accused did or did not perpetrate the act at issue. And if he did not, a negotiated guilty plea would represent an erroneous judgment. In this instance, then, the issue suggested is the comparative likelihood of such erroneous decisions as between trial and negotiation.

"But not all criminal cases fit the above picture. * * * Much criminal adjudication concerns the passing of value judgments on the accused's conduct as is obvious where negligence, recklessness, reasonable apprehension of attack, use of unnecessary force, and the like are at issue. Although intent is thought of as a question of fact, it too can represent a judgment of degrees of fault, for example, in cases where the issue is whether the defendants entertained intent to defraud or intent to kill. In many of these cases, objective truth is more ambiguous, if it exists at all. Such truth exists only as it emerges from the fact-determining process, and accuracy in this context really means relative equality of results as between defendants similarly situated and relative congruence between the formal verdict and our understanding of society's less formally expressed evaluation of such conduct.

"The negotiated plea can, then, be an accurate process in this sense. So long as the judgment of experienced counsel as to the likely jury result is the key element

m. Compare Griffiths, *Ideology in Criminal Procedure, or a Third Model of the Criminal Process,* 79 Yale L.J. 359, 397–98 (1970), suggesting "a process which includes a trial (perhaps a shorter and neater trial) for *every* defendant":

"Current discussions of guilty pleas and plea bargaining contain no consideration of the possibility that trials themselves might be good for defendants and for society. [They] are concerned only with the relationship of trials and pleas to the end of the process—punishment of the guilty. But if a trial can be seen as a goal in itself—a lesson in legal procedure, dignity, fairness and justice, for the public and for the accused (whether he is convicted or acquitted)—we would not want to lose its potential for good by encouraging short-circuits. Because of the constraints imposed by our ideology about criminal procedure, speculation in this direction has been almost entirely neglected."

entering into the bargain, substantial congruence is likely to result. Once we recognize that what lends rationality to the factfinding process in these instances lies not in an attempt to discover objective truth but in the devising of a process to express intelligent judgment, there is no inherent reason why plea negotiation need be regarded any the less rational or intelligent in its results.

"Indeed, it may be that in some instances plea negotiation leads to more 'intelligent' results. A jury can be left with the extreme alternatives of guilty of a crime of the highest degree or not guilty of any crime, with no room for any intermediate judgment. And this is likely to occur in just those cases where an intermediate judgment is the fairest and most 'accurate' (or most congruent).

"Clearly, the line between responsibility and irresponsibility due to insanity is not as sharp as the alternatives posed to a jury would suggest. It may be that such a dividing line exists in some world of objective reality and that the ambiguity arises from the difficulties of accurate factfinding. It is more realistic, however, to view responsibility as a matter of degree at best only roughly expressed in the law's categories of first and second degree murder, manslaughter, etc. The very visibility of the trial process may be one factor that prevents us from offering the jury this compromise in order to preserve the symbolism of uniform rules evenly applied. The low visibility of the negotiated plea allows this compromise which may be more rational and congruent than the result we are likely to arrive at after a trial. While the desire to protect the symbolism of legality and the concern over lay compromises may warrant limiting the jury to extreme alternative, it does not follow that to allow the defendant to choose such a compromise is an irrational or even a less rational procedure." [n]

11. "Advocates of the process assert that plea negotiations add flexibility to the criminal justice system and permit avoidance of unjustifiably harsh provisions of substantive law. * * *

"But it is by no means clear that negotiation over plea is essential to performance of this function, if it is agreed that the function is a legitimate one. A prosecutor can accomplish the same result by care in his selection of initial charge. To the extent that greater flexibility is desired, it should be made available as a matter of formal law, either by changes in the definitions of substantive crimes or by a modification of dispositional alternatives available to sentencing courts." [o]

D. THE PROBLEM OF DISPARITY

12. Should the fact the defendant pleaded guilty actually have any bearing on the sentence he receives? If defendants who plead guilty receive leniency, does it not necessarily follow that defendants who go to trial are being dealt with too harshly? Consider *People v. Snow,* 194 N.W.2d 314 (Mich.1972), where the defendant, tried and convicted by a jury of prison escape, received a sentence of 2 to 5 years, but on appeal showed that of 234 prison escape cases in the county over a 26-month period, 207 pled guilty and (except in 5 cases where aggravated circumstances were present) received minimum

n. Enker, fn. h supra, at 112–14. Compare Griffiths, supra fn. m, at 398–99: "[T]here are social interests in criminal cases which cannot be left to the parties to submerge in pleas of guilty. * * * Consider, for example, the insanity defense. So long as the criminal process is a struggle between hostile forces, the insanity defense and the policies it represents will often be submerged in pleas of guilty. But it seems hardly conceivable that whatever is at stake in the insanity defense should be left to defendants and prosecutors to negotiate away—particularly, although not exclusively, because the defendants concerned can hardly be regarded as fully competent to do so. * * * [I]f some persons are not to be regarded as responsible, but are to be treated (or left alone) upon another basis, we cannot ultimately regard it as desirable that they pull themselves up into functional responsibility by the bootstraps of a guilty plea."

o. *N.A.C. Standards,* fn. d supra, at 47.

sentences of 1½ years or less, while 13 were tried by a jury and (except in 1 case in which the defendant entered a guilty plea during the trial) received sentences of 2 years or more, and 1 was tried by the court and received a 1½ year minimum. The court concluded that because "in the usual escape case a minimum sentence of 1½ years has been deemed appropriate by the sentencing judge" and "examination of the record in this case fails to reveal a single fact that would place this defendant in a different category," the case should be remanded for resentencing.

13. Sometimes this disparity is explained in terms of factors which are believed to warrant greater severity for many defendants who elect to stand trial. One survey of federal judges revealed these reasons why a defendant convicted at trial may receive a more severe sentence than a defendant who entered a guilty plea: (1) because the judge is convinced the defendant committed perjury in the course of his defense[p]; (2) because the defendant presented a frivolous defense; (3) because the brutal circumstances of the crime are more vividly portrayed if there is a trial.[q]

14. *A.B.A. Standards* § 14–1.8, on the other hand, explains the disparity in terms of factors which are likely to call for leniency when a plea of guilty is entered:

"(a) The fact that a defendant has entered a plea of guilty or nolo contendere should not, by itself alone, be considered by the court as a mitigating factor in imposing sentence. It is proper for the court to grant charge and sentence concessions to defendants who enter a plea of guilty or nolo contendere when consistent with the protection of the public, the gravity of the offense, and the needs of the defendant, and when there is substantial evidence to establish that:

"(i) the defendant is genuinely contrite and has shown a willingness to assume responsibility for his or her conduct;

"(ii) the concessions will make possible alternative correctional measures which are better adapted to achieving protective, deterrent, or other purposes of correctional treatment, or will prevent undue harm to the defendant from the form of conviction;

"(iii) the defendant, by making public trial unnecessary, has demonstrated genuine consideration for the victims of his or her criminal activity, by desiring either to make restitution or to prevent unseemly public scrutiny or embarrassment to them;[r] or

p. Consider *United States v. Grayson,* 438 U.S. 41, 98 S.Ct. 2610, 57 L.Ed.2d 582 (1978). Because the trial judge, in explaining the sentence, stated to the defendant it was his "view that your defense was a complete fabrication without the slightest merit whatsoever," the court of appeals held that defendant must be resentenced, but the Supreme Court, per the Chief Justice, disagreed. As for defendant's constitutional argument that the sentence constituted punishment for the crime of perjury for which he had not been indicted, tried or convicted, the Court responded "that it is proper—indeed, even necessary for the rational exercise of discretion—to consider the defendant's whole person and personality, as manifested by his conduct at trial and his testimony under oath, for whatever light those may shed on the sentencing decision." As for defendant's claim that permitting consideration of perjury will "chill" defendants in exercising their right to testify on their own behalf, the Court answered that the "right guaranteed by law to a defendant is narrowly the right to testify truthfully in accordance with the oath," so that if "the sentencing judge's consideration of defendants' untruthfulness in testifying has any chilling effect on a defendant's decision to testify falsely, that effect is entirely permissible."

q. Comment, 66 Yale L.J. 204, 211–19 (1966).

r. On the other hand, are there cases in which the public interest is best served by *not* having the case disposed of by a guilty plea? Consider Newman & Nemoyer, *Issues of Propriety in Negotiated Justice,* 47 Denver L.J. 367, 398–99 (1970): "Where public figures are involved, either as perpetrators or victims, there often is a demand for more information, while rumors and suspicions that there is 'more than meets the eye' abound. For example, the guilty plea of Senator Edward Kennedy to the traffic charge following his automobile accident in which a young girl was killed was viewed by many Americans as an inadequate termination of the case. In fact, the pressure for further explanation was so great that the Senator went on national television to "(iv) the defendant has given or offered cooperation when such cooperation has resulted or may result in the successful prosecution of other offenders engaged in equally serious or more serious criminal conduct.[s]

"(b) The court should not impose upon a defendant any sentence in excess of that which would be justified by any of the protective, deterrent, or other purposes of the criminal law because the defendant has chosen to require the prosecution to prove guilt at trial rather than to enter a plea of guilty or nolo contendere."[t]

15. In *Scott v. United States,* 419 F.2d 264 (D.C.Cir.1969), Chief Judge Bazelon commented: "[T]here may be circumstances under which the prosecutor may bargain with the defendant without raising the constitutional question of whether the exercise of the right to trial can be made costly. When there is substantial uncertainty concerning the likely outcome of a trial, 'each side is interested in limiting these inherent litigation risks.' The prosecutor may be willing to accept a plea of guilty on a lesser charge rather than chance an acquittal on the more serious. The accused may be similarly willing to acknowledge his guilt of the lesser charge rather than risk conviction on the more serious, or to accept the promise of a lighter sentence to escape the possibility of conviction after trial and a heavier sentence.

"Superficially it may seem that even in such a case the defendant who insists upon a trial and is found guilty pays a price for the exercise of his right when he receives a longer sentence than his less venturesome counterpart who pleads guilty. In a sense he has. But the critical distinction is that the price he has paid is not one imposed by the state to discourage others from a

explain his position. Much the same situation applies to the apparently negotiated guilty plea entered by James Earl Ray in connection with the murder of Dr. Martin Luther King. Here again, the sparse information contained in the charge and the monosyllabic guilty plea hardly satisfied those who are more concerned about the full details of the murder of a notable public figure."

s. In *Roberts v. United States,* 445 U.S. 552, 100 S.Ct. 1358, 63 L.Ed.2d 622 (1980), the Court held that the district court properly considered, as one factor in imposing consecutive sentences on a petitioner who had pleaded guilty to two counts of using a telephone to facilitate the distribution of heroin, petitioner's refusal to cooperate with government officials investigating a related criminal conspiracy to distribute heroin in which he was a confessed participant. Citing this provision in the ABA Standards, the majority expressed "doubt that a principled distinction may be drawn between 'enhancing' the punishment imposed upon the petitioner and denying him the 'leniency' he claims would be appropriate if he had cooperated." Marshall, J., dissenting, objected that such "a distinction has been recognized," and concluded that the enhancement of petitioner's sentence as approved by the majority "represented an improper involvement of the judicial office in the prosecutorial function."

t. The commentary to this standard explains two significant deletions from the first edition as follows:

"Original subparagraph (a)(i) has been deleted. This provision authorized concessions to the defendant when the plea 'aided in ensuring the prompt and certain application of correctional measures. . . .' But unless defendants plead just before or during trial, all defendants who plead contribute to the imposition against them of 'prompt and certain . . . correctional measures.' This fact alone, however, is not believed sufficient to justify lesser punishment. A defendant who pleads early in a criminal proceeding may do so for a variety of reasons (e.g., to escape pretrial confinement or to take advantage of an attractive plea offer). Such a defendant may be totally unreceptive to the 'correctional measures' sought to be 'promptly' and 'certainly' imposed against the defendant.

"Original subparagraph (a)(vi) has also been deleted. This provision sanctioned the granting of concessions to defendants who, by virtue of their pleas, 'aided in avoiding delay (including delay due to crowded dockets) in the disposition of other cases and thereby . . . increased the probability of prompt and certain application of correctional measures to other offenders.' Although congestion in criminal court calendars in many parts of the country remains a significant problem, these standards no longer express the view that it is permissible to grant charge and sentence concessions to defendants solely for the purpose of processing cases through the system. The solution for crowded criminal dockets is the availability of sufficient personnel and other resources, so that prompt trials can be readily given to all defendants who want them."

similar exercise of their rights, but rather one encountered by those who gamble and lose. After the fact, the defendant who pleads innocent and is convicted receives a heavier sentence. But, by the same token, the defendant who pleads innocent and is acquitted receives no sentence. To the extent that the bargain struck reflects only the uncertainty of conviction before trial, the 'expected sentence before trial'—length of sentence discounted by probability of conviction—is the same for those who decide to plead guilty and those who hope for acquittal but risk conviction by going to trial.

"In determining who has or has not 'paid a price,' it is essential to reason clearly concerning what class of defendants are being compared with what other class of defendants for what purpose and at what point in time. The danger presented by plea bargaining is that defendants deciding upon a plea will be deterred from exercising their right to a trial. The relevant vantage point is thus before trial, and the relevant comparison is between the expectations of those who decide to insist upon a trial and those who decide to eliminate the risk of trial by pleading guilty. If the sentence expectations of those two classes at that time are the same, then there will be no chilling effect upon exercise of the right to trial, and it is accurate to say that no 'price' has been placed upon exercise of the right.

"To determine the expectations of those defendants who insist upon a trial, we must consider the probability of conviction as well as the sentences received by those who plead innocent and are later convicted. The argument that the defendant who receives a heavier sentence after trial has 'paid a price' because he receives a heavier sentence than the defendant who is acquitted (and goes free) or pleads guilty (and receives a shorter sentence on the same or a reduced charge) errs on two counts: (1) the comparison is made at the wrong time—after trial, when the uncertainty of litigation has passed, rather than before trial—and (2) the comparison is made between the wrong categories of defendants—the class of defendants convicted after trial versus the class of defendants who plead guilty or are acquitted rather than the class of defendants who exercise their right to trial versus the class of defendants who do not."

16. Should there instead be a "standard discount" in all cases to avoid the evils of unequal bargaining and excessive leniency previously noted? Consider the proposal that bargaining occur only at a pre-plea conference before a judge who, upon consideration of a presentence report and other facts provided by the parties, "would order two alternative dispositions of the defendant's case": (1) the sentence the defendant would receive after trial and conviction; and (2) the sentence the defendant would receive if he pleads guilty, "determined by a *specific discount rate.* This rate would be uniform for all defendants within a given jurisdiction and would embody the median plea concession necessary to induce an administratively acceptable volume of guilty pleas in that jurisdiction." If the defendant did not plead guilty, he would be tried by another judge, who could not impose a higher sentence than alternative (1) above.[u]

17. Assuming the Bazelon theory in *Scott* is valid, does it make any difference *why* there is a "substantial uncertainty concerning the likely outcome of a trial"? Consider the following variations on a case

u. Note, 82 Yale L.J. 286 (1972), contending that this model would improve plea bargaining in the following ways: (1) it would curb the prosecutor's opportunity to abuse his charging power; (2) it would stress the systematic use of sentencing information and criteria as the measure of plea concessions; (3) illegally obtained evidence would not influence the disposition (as motions to suppress could be ruled upon at the hearing); (4) it would discourage tactics wasteful of judicial time and resources which are undertaken in an effort to gain a better bargaining position; (5) the defendant would know specifically the risks of standing trial and the benefits of a guilty plea; and (6) it would tend to equalize the tactical positions of affluent and indigent defendants.

in which the defendant and an accomplice have been charged with robbery and burglary after allegedly breaking into a house, threatening a babysitter with a gun, and taking a substantial amount of money and valuables: (1) The defendant's accomplice, after making a full, substantiated confession implicating the defendant, flees the jurisdiction and cannot be found, and without his testimony the state has insufficient evidence to establish a prima facie case. (2) The only evidence the state can produce is the babysitter's identification, but it is undisputed that she saw the robbers only briefly in poor light and that she originally gave the police a rather sketchy description. (3) Same as variation 2, except that the defendant confesses, giving a full account of the crime with details only the perpetrator could know, but the confession is inadmissible because obtained in violation of *Miranda.* (4) Two hours after the robbery, police find the stolen goods and the gun in the defendant's apartment, but there is about a 60% chance that the evidence will be excluded because obtained in violation of the Fourth Amendment.[v]

E. OTHER ATTRIBUTES AND CONSEQUENCES

18. "Several factors enhance the prosecutor's bargaining position when the defendant is in custody. If the prosecutor believes that the defendant has already been incarcerated for a sufficient period of time and is willing to recommend a 'time-in' sentence, the defendant will invariably agree to plead guilty to obtain immediate freedom. Even if the prosecutor does not agree to a 'time-in' sentence, an incarcerated defendant, frightened and demoralized by the prospect of an indefinite period of confinement, may be willing to enter a plea and accept a fixed period of imprisonment. Finally, in a 'jail room' case, the prosecutor deals almost exclusively with an assistant voluntary defender. Because the defender will probably work with the prosecutor again and will be interested in maintaining a good relationship, he may often be highly receptive to guilty plea negotiations."[w]

19. "[T]he criminal practitioner's role in the plea-bargain-basement-forum is far more that of the striving-to-be-liked jolly salesman than that of the professional man. He is the sycophantic pleader who knows prosecutors and judges, and who is familiar with their aversions and their weaknesses, and who has skillfully developed the art of delay so that he can get before the right judge and the right prosecutor at the right time to get the right plea. What need is there for Darrow-like understanding of the motivations of crime and of potentials for rehabilitation when certain judges and certain prosecutors will take set 'markdown' on certain charges as a matter of course? Too often the criminal lawyer in New York's big-City practice today needs courthouse 'racing forms', not lawbooks."[x]

20. "What makes inmates most cynical about their preprison experience is the plea-bargaining system. * * * Even though an inmate may receive the benefit

v. See White, *A Proposal for Reform of the Plea Bargaining Process,* 119 U.Pa.L.Rev. 439, 458–62 (1971), for consideration of what the prosecutor should do in each of these situations.

w. White, fn. v supra, at 445. Compare Comment, 50 Texas L.Rev. 60, 61 (1971), which "advances the premise that the pressures toward cooperation are equally strong when a private attorney provides the defense. Political considerations remain. Fee limitations necessitate abbreviated defenses, just as do inadequate budgets for a public agency. Expanding caseloads maintain their constant pressure. Participants still desire a pleasant working environment. With cooperation no one has to work quite so hard. A lawyer's concern with preserving his relationships within the criminal justice system may assume greater importance than his more transitory interest in his client. His tendency may be to place long-run objectives ahead of short-run obligations. He may also be able to rationalize that although an occasional client must suffer, his clients as a whole benefit from his standing in the system. These are the same attitudes that threaten the autonomy of a public defender office."

x. Kuh, *Plea Copping,* 24 N.Y.Co. Bar Bull. 160, 164–65 (1966–67).

of a shorter sentence, the plea-bargaining system is characterized by deception and hypocrisy which divorce the inmate from the reality of his crime. * * * The Hughes Committee (the Joint Legislative Committee on Crime) made a study of prisoner attitudes towards plea bargaining * * * and found that almost 90 percent of the inmates surveyed had been solicited to enter a plea bargain. Most were bitter, believing that they did not receive effective legal representation or that the judge did not keep the state's promise of a sentence which had induced them to enter guilty pleas.

"As the Hughes Committee observed, the large segment of the prison population who believe they have been 'victimized' by the courts or bar 'are not likely to accept the efforts of another institution of society, the correctional system, in redirecting their attitudes.' The Hughes Committee warned that no program of rehabilitation can be effective on a 'prisoner who is convinced in his own mind that he is in prison because he is the victim of a mindless, undirected, and corrupt system of justice.' " [y]

F. More on the Consequences of Prohibiting Plea Bargaining

21. "[T]hough it might be possible to proscribe 'explicit plea bargaining' (that is, explicit negotiation between prosecutor, defense attorney, and judge), it would be impossible to proscribe what we might call 'implicit plea bargaining.' By implicit plea bargaining I mean * * * that there is agreement among all court actors that most guilty defendants should plead guilty and be rewarded for their plea. Thus, even if formal negotiations were verboten, the expectation that guilty defendants should plead would remain. All criminal court actors would recognize 'implicitly' that the defendant who pleads receives a reward and that the defendant who goes to trial does not. Perhaps those working in the system would have to learn to tolerate a bit more uncertainty because of the proscription against formal agreements, but I would guess that not too much time would elapse before the implicit rewards became well known, and defense attorneys could then make 'good guesses' as to what sentence the defendant would receive.

"Furthermore, I would hypothesize that even with these 'good guesses' the system would be unstable. Defendants would not be satisfied to place complete faith in their attorneys' guesses and would continue to press for specific agreements regarding charge and sentence reduction. And I think after the initial ballyhoo surrounding the 'abolition of plea bargaining' abates, the defense attorney's efforts to arrange more explicit deals would meet with success." [z]

22. In 1975, the Attorney General of Alaska forbid all prosecutors in that state from engaging in plea negotiations, reducing or dropping charges in exchange for guilty pleas, and making sentence recommendations to the court. An empirical study [a] of the effects of that policy concluded: (a) That "explicit sentencing bargaining * * * practically disappeared," and that when charge bargaining now occurs "it usually involves dropping one or more counts from multiple-count indictments, typical in prosecutions for forgeries, bad checks, and drug sales." (b) That "experienced defense counsel who have developed good working relations with individual district attorneys sometimes report success at negotiations," while "[l]ess experienced defense counsel, particularly younger members of the public defender's staff, report that plea bargaining is virtually nonexistent in their practices." (c) That some lawyers "are simply refusing private

y. N.Y.State Special Commission on Attica, *Attica* 30–31 (1972). See also Casper, *Criminal Justice, The Consumer Perspective* 3–54 (1972).

z. Heumann, *Plea Bargaining* 157–58 (1977).

a. Summarized in Rubenstein & White, *Plea Bargaining: Can Alaska Live Without It?*, 62 Judicature 266 (1978).

criminal business because clients cannot afford the fees, or because the attorney honestly believes that the actual benefits of his service are not likely to be worth what he must charge to prepare a competent defense," which has "led to the claim that the no-plea-bargaining policy has had its strongest negative impact on middle-class defendants who can neither afford high-priced legal talent nor qualify for representation by the public defender." (d) That some judges, until the practice was expressly proscribed by a state supreme court decision, "circumvented the ban on plea bargaining and made the prosecutor irrelevant through direct dealings with defense counsel." (e) That though "the rate of trials did increase substantially, the projected on-slaught never materialized." (f) That the policy "produced a strong, if selective, effect on sentence severity. Violent criminals, who always got stiff treatment, did not fare any worse. The ones who received harsher punishment were the relatively minor property offenders, the drug offenders, and those who wrote bad checks, embezzled, or committed credit-card offenses." (g) That defendants "who go to trial, other factors being equal, appear to serve more time than those who plead guilty. Multiple regression analysis of length of sentences given after guilty pleas compared with those imposed after trial show that for violent and fraud crimes, sentences are significantly longer after trials. The disparity is greater in violent crimes, where sentences after trial are 445 per cent longer than those given after pleas. For fraud crimes, trial sentences are 334 per cent longer. No such plea/trial 'differential' appears in property crimes, and there were too few trials for drug crimes in the two years to make a valid analysis." Has the Alaska experiment been a success or a failure?

23. The experience in Philadelphia and Pittsburgh, where the practice is not to plea bargain but instead to bargain for jury waivers, suggests that "a proposition about criminal justice reform that may seem too simple to be true may be true in fact. Without elaborate planning, scholarly studies, and additional funding, one effective way to prohibit plea bargaining would be just to prohibit it. Confronted with an immediate and unqualified prohibition, the criminal justice system's powerful mechanisms of bureaucratic adjustment would * * * match resources to caseloads, not by continuing to provide costly trials to the few while inducing the many to plead guilty, but by affording simpler trials to all who wished to be heard. Moreover, courts whose fears of administrative overload have led them to invoke disingenuous concepts of waiver in support of plea bargaining could invoke the same theories in support of less sweeping waivers by defendants—waivers that could bring an operational trial system into existence without additional resources. In short, if a legislature were to prohibit the exchange of concessions for pleas of guilty without forbidding official concessions for waivers of the right to jury trial, the invisible hand that sometimes is thought to make plea bargaining inevitable could continue its disturbing work. The differing resource limitations of various jurisdictions would be reflected, however, not in varying guilty plea rates or in differing concessions offered for pleas of guilty, but in forms and procedures of the nonjury trials that most defendants would be induced to accept." [b]

Would this be a better system, or just a different one? Consider: "Jury waiver concessions differ from guilty plea concessions in three striking ways. First, and most importantly, the defendant who waives a jury retains most of his significant adversary trial rights. Thus, although from the state's perspective the jury waiver concession has the same justification and most of the same advantages as does a guilty plea concession, the jury waiver con-

b. Alschuler, *Implementing the Criminal Defendant's Right to Trial: Alternatives to the Plea Bargaining System,* 50 U.Chi.L.Rev. 931, 1042–43 (1983).

cession entails far fewer dangers for the accused. Second, because the defendant who waives a jury gives up much less than does one who pleads guilty, the concession needed to induce the jury waiver will necessarily be smaller than that needed to induce a guilty plea in the same case. Third, jury waiver concessions are much less likely than guilty plea concessions to vary in attractiveness as the probability of acquittal changes from case to case; thus, the risk that excessive concessions may elude judicial control and endanger the innocent defendant is in practice much less serious than in the case of plea bargaining."[c]

SECTION 2. REJECTED, KEPT AND BROKEN BARGAINS; UNREALIZED EXPECTATIONS

BORDENKIRCHER v. HAYES

434 U.S. 357, 98 S.Ct. 663, 54 L.Ed.2d 604 (1978).

MR. JUSTICE STEWART delivered the opinion of the Court. * * *

[Paul Hayes was indicted in Fayette County, Ky., on a charge of uttering a forged instrument in the amount of $88.30, punishable by two to 10 years in prison. Hayes and his retained counsel met with the prosecutor who offered to recommend a sentence of five years if Hayes would plead guilty and added that if Hayes did not plead guilty he would seek an indictment under the Kentucky Habitual Criminal Act, which would subject Hayes to a mandatory sentence of life imprisonment by reason of his two prior felony convictions. Hayes chose not to plead guilty, and the prosecutor did obtain such an indictment. A jury found Hayes guilty on the principal charge of uttering a forged instrument and, in a separate proceeding, further found that he had twice before been convicted of felonies. As required by the habitual offender statute, he was sentenced to a life term in the penitentiary. The Kentucky Court of Appeals rejected Hayes' constitutional objections to the enhanced sentence, and on Hayes' petition for a federal writ of habeas corpus the district court agreed that there had been no constitutional violation in the sentence or the indictment procedure. The Court of Appeals for the Sixth Circuit reversed on the ground that the prosecutor's conduct had violated the principles of *Blackledge v. Perry*, p. 927 supra, which "protect defendants from the vindictive exercise of a prosecutor's discretion."]

It may be helpful to clarify at the outset the nature of the issue in this case. While the prosecutor did not actually obtain the recidivist indictment until after the plea conferences had ended, his intention to do so was clearly put forth at the outset of the plea negotiations. Hayes was thus fully informed of the true terms of the offer when he made his decision to plead not guilty. This is not a situation, therefore, where the prosecutor without notice brought an additional and more serious charge after plea negotiations relating only to the original indictment had ended with the defendant's insistence on pleading not guilty. As a practical matter, in short, this case would be no different if the grand jury had indicted Hayes as a recidivist from the outset, and the prosecutor had offered to drop that charge as part of the plea bargain.

The Court of Appeals nonetheless drew a distinction between "concessions relating to prosecution under an existing indictment," and threats to bring more severe charges not contained in the original indictment—a line it thought necessary in order to establish a prophylactic rule to guard against the evil of prosecutorial vindictiveness.[6] Quite apart from this chron-

c. Schulhofer, *Is Plea Bargaining Inevitable?*, 97 Harv.L.Rev. 1037, 1092–93 (1984).

6. "Although a prosecutor may in the course of plea negotiations offer a defendant concessions relating to prosecution under an existing indictment * * * he may not threaten a defendant with the consequences that more severe charges may be brought if he insists on going to trial. When a prosecutor obtains an indictment less severe than the facts known to him at the time

ological distinction, however, the Court of Appeals found that the prosecutor had acted vindictively in the present case since he had conceded that the indictment was influenced by his desire to induce a guilty plea. The ultimate conclusion of the Court of Appeals thus seems to have been that a prosecutor acts vindictively and in violation of due process of law whenever his charging decision is influenced by what he hopes to gain in the course of plea bargaining negotiations.

We have recently had occasion to observe that "[w]hatever might be the situation in an ideal world, the fact is that the guilty plea and the often concomitant plea bargain are important components of this country's criminal justice system. Properly administered, they can benefit all concerned." *Blackledge v. Allison* [p. 1242 infra]. The open acknowledgment of this previously clandestine practice has led this Court to recognize the importance of counsel during plea negotiations, *Brady v. United States* [p. 1191 infra], the need for a public record indicating that a plea was knowingly and voluntarily made, *Boykin v. Alabama* [p. 1234 infra], and the requirement that a prosecutor's plea bargaining promise must be kept, *Santobello v. New York* [p. 1201 infra]. The decision of the Court of Appeals in the present case, however, did not deal with considerations such as these, but held that the substance of the plea offer itself violated the limitations imposed by the Due Process Clause of the Fourteenth Amendment. For the reasons that follow, we have concluded that the Court of Appeals was mistaken in so ruling.

This Court held in *North Carolina v. Pearce* [p. 1434 infra], that the Due Process Clause of the Fourteenth Amendment "requires that vindictiveness against a defendant for having successfully attacked his first conviction must play no part in the sentence he receives after a new trial." The same principle was later applied to prohibit a prosecutor from reindicting a convicted misdemeanant on a felony charge after the defendant had invoked an appellate remedy, since in this situation there was also a "realistic likelihood of 'vindictiveness.'" *Blackledge v. Perry.*

In those cases the Court was dealing with the State's unilateral imposition of a penalty upon a defendant who had chosen to exercise a legal right to attack his original conviction—a situation "very different from the give-and-take negotiation common in plea bargaining between the prosecution and the defense, which arguably possess relatively equal bargaining power." The Court has emphasized that the due process violation in cases such as *Pearce* and *Perry* lay not in the possibility that a defendant might be deterred from the exercise of a legal right, see *Colten v. Kentucky* [p. 1442 infra]; *Chaffin v. Stynchombe* [p. 1443 infra], but rather in the danger that the State might be retaliating against the accused for lawfully attacking his conviction. See *Blackledge v. Perry.*

To punish a person because he has done what the law plainly allows him to do is a due process violation of the most basic sort, see *North Carolina v. Pearce* (opinion of Black, J.), and for an agent of the State to pursue a course of action whose objective is to penalize a person's reliance on his legal rights is "patently unconstitutional." *Chaffin v. Stynchcombe.* But in the "give-and-take" of plea bargaining, there is no such element of punishment or retaliation so long as the accused is free to accept or reject the prosecution's offer.

Plea bargaining flows from "the mutuality of advantage" to defendants and prosecutors, each with his own reasons for want-

might permit, he makes a discretionary determination that the interests of the state are served by not seeking more serious charges. * * * Accordingly, if after plea negotiations fail, he then procures an indictment charging a more serious crime, a strong inference is created that the only reason for the more serious charges is vindictiveness. Under these circumstances, the prosecutor should be required to justify his action."

ing to avoid trial. *Brady v. United States* [a] [p. 1191 infra]. Defendants advised by competent counsel and protected by other procedural safeguards are presumptively capable of intelligent choice in response to prosecutorial persuasion, and unlikely to be driven to false self-condemnation. Indeed, acceptance of the basic legitimacy of plea bargaining necessarily implies rejection of any notion that a guilty plea is involuntary in a constitutional sense simply because it is the end result of the bargaining process. By hypothesis, the plea may have been induced by promises of a recommendation of a lenient sentence or a reduction of charges, and thus by fear of the possibility of a greater penalty upon conviction after a trial. See A.B.A. Standards, *Pleas of Guilty* § 3.1 (1968).[b]

While confronting a defendant with the risk of more severe punishment clearly may have a "discouraging effect on the defendant's assertion of his trial rights, the imposition of these difficult choices [is] an inevitable"—and permissible—"attribute of any legitimate system which tolerates and encourages the negotiation of pleas." *Chaffin v. Stynchcombe.* It follows that, by tolerating and encouraging the negotiation of pleas, this Court has necessarily accepted as constitutionally legitimate the simple reality that the prosecutor's interest at the bargaining table is to persuade the defendant to forego his right to plead not guilty.

It is not disputed here that Hayes was properly chargeable under the recidivist statute, since he had in fact been convicted of two previous felonies. In our system, so long as the prosecutor has probable

a. Although *Brady* did not involve a plea bargaining situation, see Note 1 at p. 1242 infra, the Court analogized the plea involved there to a plea obtained through plea bargaining, and then commented generally on the validity of a plea produced by the "mutuality of advantage" that flows from a negotiated plea: "We decline to hold * * * that a guilty plea is compelled and invalid under the Fifth Amendment whenever motivated by the defendant's desire to accept the certainty or probability of a lesser penalty rather than face a wider range of possibilities extending from acquittal to conviction and a higher penalty authorized by law for the crime charged. * * * [B]oth the state and the defendant often find it advantageous to preclude the possibility of the maximum penalty authorized by law. For a defendant who sees slight possibility of acquittal, the advantages of pleading guilty and limiting the probable penalty are obvious—his exposure is reduced, the correctional processes can begin immediately, and the practical burdens of a trial are eliminated. For the State there are also advantages—the more promptly imposed punishment after an admission of guilt may more effectively attain the objectives of punishment; and with the avoidance of trial, scarce judicial and prosecutorial resources are conserved for those cases in which there is a substantial issue of the defendant's guilt or in which there is substantial doubt that the State can sustain its burden of proof. It is this mutuality of advantage which perhaps explains the fact that at present well over three-fourths of the criminal convictions in this country rest on pleas of guilty, a great many of them no doubt motivated at least in part by the hope or assurance of a lesser penalty than might be imposed if there were a guilty verdict after a trial to judge or jury."

b. Now § 14–3.1 in the second edition, which as revised reads:

"(a) The prosecuting attorney may engage in plea discussions with counsel for the defendant for the purpose of reaching a plea agreement. Where the defendant has waived counsel pursuant to these standards, the prosecuting attorney may engage in plea discussions with the defendant. Ordinarily a verbatim record should be made and preserved for all such discussions.

"(b) The prosecuting attorney, in reaching a plea agreement, may agree to one or more of the following, as dictated by the circumstances of the individual case:

"(i) to make or not to oppose favorable recommendations as to the sentence which should be imposed if the defendant enters a plea of guilty or nolo contendere;

"(ii) to dismiss, to seek to dismiss, or not to oppose dismissal of the offense charged if the defendant enters a plea of guilty or nolo contendere to another offense reasonably related to defendant's conduct; or

"(iii) to dismiss, to seek to dismiss, or not to oppose dismissal of other charges or potential charges against the defendant if the defendant enters a plea of guilty or nolo contendere.

"(c) Similarly situated defendants should be afforded equal plea agreement opportunities.

"(d) The prosecuting attorney should make every effort to remain advised of the attitudes and sentiments of victims and law enforcement officials before reaching a plea agreement."

cause to believe that the accused committed an offense defined by statute, the decision whether or not to prosecute, and what charge to file or bring before a grand jury, generally rests entirely in his discretion.[8] Within the limits set by the legislature's constitutionally valid definition of chargeable offenses, "the conscious exercise of some selectivity in enforcement is not in itself a federal constitutional violation" so long as "the selection was [not] deliberately based upon an unjustifiable standard such as race, religion, or other arbitrary classification." To hold that the prosecutor's desire to induce a guilty plea is an "unjustifiable standard," which, like race or religion, may play no part in his charging decision, would contradict the very premises that underlie the concept of plea bargaining itself. Moreover, a rigid constitutional rule that would prohibit a prosecutor from acting forthrightly in his dealings with the defense could only invite unhealthy subterfuge that would drive the practice of plea bargaining back into the shadows from which it has so recently emerged.

There is no doubt that the breadth of discretion that our country's legal system vests in prosecuting attorneys carries with it the potential for both individual and institutional abuse. And broad though that discretion may be, there are undoubtedly constitutional limits upon its exercise. We hold only that the course of conduct engaged in by the prosecutor in this case, which no more than openly presented the defendant with the unpleasant alternatives of foregoing trial or facing charges on which he was plainly subject to prosecution, did not violate the Due Process Clause of the Fourteenth Amendment.

Accordingly, the judgment of the Court of Appeals is

Reversed.

MR. JUSTICE BLACKMUN, with whom MR. JUSTICE BRENNAN and MR. JUSTICE MARSHALL, join dissenting.

I feel that the Court, although purporting to rule narrowly (that is, on "the course of conduct engaged in by the prosecutor in this case"), is departing from, or at least restricting, the principles established in *North Carolina v. Pearce,* and in *Blackledge v. Perry.* If those decisions are sound and if those principles are salutary, as I must assume they are, they require, in my view, an affirmance, not a reversal, of the judgment of the Court of Appeals in the present case.

In *Pearce,* as indeed the Court notes, it was held that "vindictiveness against a defendant for having successfully attacked his first conviction must play no part in the sentence he receives after a new trial." Accordingly, if on the new trial, the sentence the defendant receives from the court is greater than that imposed after the first trial, it must be explained by reasons "based upon objective information concerning identifiable conduct on the part of the defendant occurring after the time of the original sentencing proceeding," other than his having pursued the appeal or collateral remedy. * * *

Then later, in *Perry,* the Court applied the same principle to prosecutorial conduct where there was a "realistic likelihood of 'vindictiveness.' " It held that the requirement of Fourteenth Amendment due process prevented a prosecutor's reindictment of a convicted misdemeanant on a felony charge after the defendant had exercised his right to appeal the misdemeanor conviction and thus to obtain a trial *de novo.* It noted the prosecution's "considerable stake" in discouraging the appeal.

The Court now says, however, that this concern with vindictiveness is of no import in the present case, despite the difference

8. This case does not involve the constitutional implications of a prosecutor's offer during plea bargaining of adverse or lenient treatment for some person *other* than the accused, which might pose a greater danger of inducing a false guilty plea by skewing the assessment of the risks a defendant must consider.

between five years in prison and a life sentence, because we are here concerned with plea bargaining where there is give-and-take negotiation, and where, it is said, "there is no such element of punishment or retaliation so long as the accused is free to accept or reject the prosecution's offer." Yet in this case vindictiveness is present to the same extent as it was thought to be in *Pearce* and in *Perry;* the prosecutor here admitted that the sole reason for the new indictment was to discourage the respondent from exercising his right to a trial.[1] Even had such an admission not been made, when plea negotiations, conducted in the face of the less serious charge under the first indictment, fail, charging by a second indictment a more serious crime for the same conduct creates "a strong inference" of vindictiveness. As then Judge McCree aptly observed, in writing for a unanimous panel of the Sixth Circuit, the prosecutor initially "makes a discretionary determination that the interests of the state are served by not seeking more serious charges." I therefore do not understand why, as in *Pearce,* due process does not require that the prosecution justify its action on some basis other than discouraging respondent from the exercise of his right to a trial.

Prosecutorial vindictiveness, it seems to me, in the present narrow context, is the fact against which the Due Process Clause ought to protect. I perceive little difference between vindictiveness after what the Court describes as the exercise of a "legal right to attack his original conviction," and vindictiveness in the "give-and-take negotiation common in plea bargaining." Prosecutorial vindictiveness in any context is still prosecutorial vindictiveness. The Due Process Clause should protect an accused against it, however it asserts itself. The Court of Appeals rightly so held, and I would affirm the judgment.

It might be argued that it really makes little difference how this case, now that it is here, is decided. The Court's holding gives plea bargaining full sway despite vindictiveness. A contrary result, however, merely would prompt the aggressive prosecutor to bring the greater charge initially in every case, and only thereafter to bargain. The consequences to the accused would still be adverse, for then he would bargain against a greater charge, face the likelihood of increased bail, and run the risk that the court would be less inclined to accept a bargain plea. Nonetheless, it is far preferable to hold the prosecution to the charge it was originally content to bring and to justify in the eyes of its public.[2]

MR. JUSTICE POWELL, dissenting.

Although I agree with much of the Court's opinion, I am not satisfied that the

1. In *Brady v. United States,* where the Court as a premise accepted plea bargaining as a legitimate practice, it nevertheless observed:

"We here make no reference to the situation where the prosecutor or judge, or both, deliberately employ their charging and sentencing powers to induce a particular defendant to tender a plea of guilty."

2. That prosecutors, without saying so, may sometimes bring charges more serious than they think appropriate for the ultimate disposition of a case, in order to gain bargaining leverage with a defendant, does not add support to today's decision, for this Court, in its approval of the advantages to be gained from plea negotiations, has never openly sanctioned such deliberate overcharging or taken such a cynical view of the bargaining process. Normally, of course, it is impossible to show that this is what the prosecutor is doing, and the courts necessarily have deferred to the prosecutor's exercise of discretion in initial charging decisions.

Even if overcharging is to be sanctioned, there are strong reasons of fairness why the charges should be presented at the beginning of the bargaining process, rather than as a filliped threat at the end. First, it means that a prosecutor is required to reach a charging decision without any knowledge of the particular defendant's willingness to plead guilty; hence the defendant who truly believes himself to be innocent, and wishes for that reason to go to trial, is not likely to be subject to quite such a devastating gamble since the prosecutor has fixed the incentives for the average case.

Second, it is healthful to keep charging practices visible to the general public, so that political bodies can judge whether the policy being followed is a fair one. Visibility is enhanced if the prosecutor is required to lay his cards on the result in this case is just or that the conduct of the plea bargaining met the requirements of due process.

Respondent was charged with the uttering of a single forged check in the amount of $88.30. Under Kentucky law, this offense was punishable by a prison term of from two to 10 years, apparently without regard to the amount of the forgery. During the course of plea bargaining, the prosecutor offered respondent a sentence of five years in consideration of a guilty plea. I observe, at this point, that five years in prison for the offense charged hardly could be characterized as a generous offer. * * *

The prosecutor's initial assessment of respondent's case led him to forego an indictment under the habitual criminal statute. The circumstances of respondent's prior convictions are relevant to this assessment and to my view of the case. Respondent was 17 years old when he committed his first offense. He was charged with rape but pled guilty to the lesser included offense of "detaining a female." One of the other participants in the incident was sentenced to life imprisonment. Respondent was sent not to prison but to a reformatory where he served five years. Respondent's second offense was robbery. This time he was found guilty by a jury and was sentenced to five years in prison, but he was placed on probation and served no time. Although respondent's prior convictions brought him within the terms of the Habitual Criminal Act, the offenses themselves did not result in imprisonment; yet the addition of a conviction on a charge involving $88.30 subjected respondent to a mandatory sentence of imprisonment for life. Persons convicted of rape and murder often are not punished so severely.

No explanation appears in the record for the prosecutor's decision to escalate the charge against respondent other than respondent's refusal to plead guilty. The prosecutor has conceded that his purpose was to discourage respondent's assertion of constitutional rights, and the majority accepts this characterization of events.

It seems to me that the question to be asked under the circumstances is whether the prosecutor reasonably might have charged respondent under the Habitual Criminal Act in the first place. The deference that courts properly accord the exercise of a prosecutor's discretion perhaps would foreclose judicial criticism if the prosecutor originally had sought an indictment under that act, as unreasonable as it would have seemed.[2] But here the prosecutor evidently made a reasonable, responsible judgment not to subject an individual to a mandatory life sentence when his only

table with an indictment of public record at the beginning of the bargaining process, rather than making use of unrecorded verbal warnings of more serious indictments yet to come.

Finally, I would question whether it is fair to pressure defendants to plead guilty by threat of reindictment on an enhanced charge for the same conduct when the defendant has no way of knowing whether the prosecutor would indeed be entitled to bring him to trial on the enhanced charge. Here, though there is no dispute that respondent met the then current definition of a habitual offender under Kentucky law, it is conceivable that a properly instructed Kentucky grand jury, in response to the same considerations that ultimately moved the Kentucky Legislature to amend the habitual offender statute, would have refused to subject respondent to such an onerous penalty for his forgery charge. There is no indication in the record that, once the new indictment was obtained, respondent was given another chance to plead guilty to the forged check charge in exchange for a five year sentence.

2. The majority suggests that this case cannot be distinguished from the case where the prosecutor initially obtains an indictment under an enhancement statute and later agrees to drop the enhancement charge in exchange for a guilty plea. I would agree that these two situations would be alike *only if* it were assumed that the hypothetical prosecutor's decision to charge under the enhancement statute was occasioned not by consideration of the public interest but by a strategy to discourage the defendant from exercising his constitutional rights. In theory, I would condemn both practices. In practice, the hypothetical situation is largely unreviewable. The majority's view confuses the propriety of a particular exercise of prosecutorial discretion with its unreviewability. In the instant case, however, we have no problem of proof.

new offense had societal implications as limited as those accompanying the uttering of a single $88 forged check and when the circumstances of his prior convictions confirmed the inappropriateness of applying the habitual criminal statute. I think it may be inferred that the prosecutor himself deemed it unreasonable and not in the public interest to put this defendant in jeopardy of a sentence of life imprisonment.

There may be situations in which a prosecutor would be fully justified in seeking a fresh indictment for a more serious offense. The most plausible justification might be that it would have been reasonable and in the public interest initially to have charged the defendant with the greater offense. In most cases a court could not know why the harsher indictment was sought, and an inquiry into the prosecutor's motive would neither be indicated nor likely to be fruitful. In those cases, I would agree with the majority that the situation would not differ materially from one in which the higher charge was brought at the outset.

But this is not such a case. Here, any inquiry into the prosecutor's purpose is made unnecessary by his candid acknowledgement that he threatened to procure and in fact procured the habitual criminal indictment because of respondent's insistence on exercising his constitutional rights. We have stated in unequivocal terms, in discussing *United States v. Jackson* [fn. c infra], and *North Carolina v. Pearce,* that "*Jackson* and *Pearce* are clear and subsequent cases have not diluted their force: if the only objective of a state practice is to discourage the assertion of constitutional rights it is 'patently unconstitutional.'" *Chaffin v. Stynchcombe.* And in *Brady v. United States,* we drew a distinction between the situation there approved and the "situation where the prosecutor or judge, or both, deliberately employ their charging and sentencing powers to induce a particular defendant to tender a plea of guilty."

The plea-bargaining process, as recognized by this Court, is essential to the functioning of the criminal-justice system. It normally affords genuine benefits to defendants as well as to society. And if the system is to work effectively, prosecutors must be accorded the widest discretion, within constitutional limits, in conducting bargaining. This is especially true when a defendant is represented by counsel and presumably is fully advised of his rights. Only in the most exceptional case should a court conclude that the scales of the bargaining are so unevenly balanced as to arouse suspicion. In this case, the prosecutor's actions denied respondent due process because their admitted purpose was to discourage and then to penalize with unique severity his exercise of constitutional rights. Implementation of a strategy calculated solely to deter the exercise of constitutional rights is not a constitutionally permissible exercise of discretion. I would affirm the opinion of the Court of Appeals on the facts of this case.

Notes and Questions

1. BRADY v. UNITED STATES, 397 U.S. 742, 90 S.Ct. 1463, 25 L.Ed.2d 747 (1970), involved these facts: In 1959, Brady was charged with kidnapping in violation of 18 U.S.C. § 1201(a), which could result in a maximum penalty of death if the jury verdict should so recommend. Brady elected to plead not guilty, but upon learning that a codefendant would plead guilty and be available to testify against him, he changed his plea to guilty. He was sentenced to 50 years imprisonment, later reduced to 30. Eight years later Brady unsuccessfully challenged his plea in the district court and the court of appeals. The Supreme Court granted certiorari to consider whether Brady's plea was invalid in light of the Court's intervening decision in *United States v. Jackson,* 390 U.S. 570, 88 S.Ct. 1209, 20 L.Ed.2d 138 (1968), holding the death penalty provi-

sion of § 1201(a) unconstitutional.[c] The Court, per WHITE, J., held:

"Plainly, it seems to us, *Jackson* ruled neither that all pleas of guilty encouraged by the fear of a possible death sentence are involuntary pleas nor that such encouraged pleas are invalid whether involuntary or not. *Jackson* prohibits the imposition of the death penalty under § 1201(a), but that decision neither fashioned a new standard for judging the validity of guilty pleas nor mandated a new application of the test theretofore fashioned by courts and since reiterated that guilty pleas are valid if both 'voluntary' and 'intelligent.' * * *

"The standard as to the voluntariness of guilty pleas must be essentially that defined by Judge Tuttle of the Fifth Circuit Court of Appeals:

> '[A] plea of guilty entered by one fully aware of the direct consequences, including the actual value of any commitments made to him by the court, prosecutor, or his own counsel, must stand unless induced by threats (or promises to discontinue improper harassment), misrepresentation (including unfulfilled or unfulfillable promises), or perhaps by promises that are by their nature improper as having no proper relationship to the prosecutor's business (e.g. bribes).' [13]

Under this standard, a plea of guilty is not invalid merely because entered to avoid the possibility of a death penalty.

"The record before us also supports the conclusion that Brady's plea was intelligently made. He was advised by competent counsel, he was made aware of the nature of the charge against him, and there was nothing to indicate that he was incompetent or otherwise not in control of his mental faculties; once his confederate had pleaded guilty and became available to testify, he chose to plead guilty, perhaps to ensure that he would face no more than life imprisonment or a term of years. Brady was aware of precisely what he was doing when he admitted that he had kidnaped the victim and had not released her unharmed."

As for Brady's objection that his attorney had advised him the jury could impose the death penalty, which, as later held in *Jackson,* was not the case, the Court declared:

"Often the decision to plead guilty is heavily influenced by the defendant's appraisal of the prosecution's case against him and by the apparent likelihood of securing leniency should a guilty plea be offered and accepted. Considerations like these frequently present imponderable questions for which there are no certain answers; judgments may be made which in the light of later events seem improvident, although they were perfectly sensible at the time. The rule that a plea must be intelligently made to be valid does not require that a plea be vulnerable to later attack if the defendant did not correctly

c. As explained in *Brady:*

"In *Jackson,* the defendants were indicted under § 1201(a). The District Court dismissed the § 1201(a) count of the indictment, holding the statute unconstitutional because it permitted imposition of the death sentence only upon a jury's recommendation and thereby made the risk of death the price of a jury trial. This Court held the statute valid, except for the death penalty provision; with respect to the latter, the Court agreed with the trial court 'that the death penalty provision * * * imposes an impermissible burden upon the exercise of a constitutional right * * *.' The problem was to determine 'whether the Constitution permits the establishment of such a death penalty, applicable only to those defendants who assert the right to contest their guilt before a jury.' The inevitable effect of the provision was said to be to discourage assertion of the Fifth Amendment right not to plead guilty and to deter exercise of the Sixth Amendment right to demand a jury trial. Because the legitimate goal of limiting the death penalty to cases in which a jury recommends it could be achieved without penalizing those defendants who plead not guilty and elect a jury trial, the death penalty provision 'needlessly penalize[d] the assertion of a constitutional right,' and was therefore unconstitutional."

13. *Shelton v. United States,* 246 F.2d 571 (5th Cir.1957) (en banc), rev'd on confession of error on other grounds, 356 U.S. 26, 78 S.Ct. 563, 2 L.Ed.2d 579 (1958).

assess every relevant factor entering into his decision. A defendant is not entitled to withdraw his plea merely because he discovers long after the plea has been accepted that his calculus misapprehended the quality of the State's case or the likely penalties attached to alternative courses of action. More particularly, absent misrepresentation or other impermissible conduct by state agents, cf. *Von Moltke v. Gillies,* 332 U.S. 708, 68 S.Ct. 316, 92 L.Ed. 309 (1948), a voluntary plea of guilty intelligently made in the light of the then applicable law does not become vulnerable because later judicial decisions indicate that the plea rested on a faulty premise. A plea of guilty triggered by the expectations of a competently counseled defendant that the State will have a strong case against him is not subject to later attack because the defendant's lawyer correctly advised him with respect to the then existing law as to possible penalties but later pronouncements of the courts, as in this case, hold that the maximum penalty for the crime in question was less than was reasonably assumed at the time the plea was entered." [d]

2. In CORBITT v. NEW JERSEY, 439 U.S. 212, 99 S.Ct. 492, 58 L.Ed.2d 466 (1978), defendant was tried and convicted of first degree murder and sentenced to the mandatory punishment of life imprisonment. Had he entered a plea of non vult or nolo contendere,[e] then by state law the punishment would have been "either imprisonment for life or the same as that imposed upon a conviction of murder in the second degree," i.e., a term of not more than 30 years. Though the defendant claimed that this scheme was unconstitutional under *Jackson,* the Supreme Court, per WHITE, J., did not agree. The Court first concluded that there was "no difference of constitutional significance between *Bordenkircher* and this case," while there were "substantial differences between this case and *Jackson* " in that the instant case (i) did not involve the death penalty and (ii) did not involve a scheme whereby the maximum penalty was reserved exclusively for those who insisted on a jury trial. The Court then continued:

"The New Jersey Supreme Court observed that the 'encouragement of guilty defendants not to contest their guilt is at the very heart of an effective plea negotiation program.' Its conclusion was that in this light there were substantial benefits to the State in providing the opportunity for lesser punishment and that the statutory pattern could not be deemed a needless or arbitrary burden on the defendant's constitutional rights within the meaning of *Jackson v. United States.*

"We are in essential agreement with the New Jersey Supreme Court. Had Corbitt tendered a plea and had it been accepted and a term of years less than life imposed, this would simply have recognized the fact that there had been a plea and that in sentencing it is constitutionally permissible to take that fact into account. The States and the Federal Government are free to abolish guilty pleas and plea bargaining; but absent such action, as the Constitution

d. Brennan, J., joined by Douglas and Marshall, JJ., concurred in the result in *Brady* but dissented in the companion case of *Parker v. North Carolina,* 397 U.S. 790, 90 S.Ct. 1458, 25 L.Ed.2d 785 (1970), involving a guilty plea to first-degree burglary entered at a time when North Carolina law permitted imposition of the death penalty for this offense only following a not guilty plea and trial. They objected that "those who resisted the pressures identified in *Jackson* and after a jury trial were sentenced to death receive relief, but those who succumbed to the same pressures and were induced to surrender their constitutional rights are left without any remedy at all. Where the penalty scheme failed to produce its unconstitutional effect, the intended victims obtain relief; where it succeeded, the real victims have none." They then concluded that reversal was required in *Parker* because the "North Carolina courts have consistently taken the position that *United States v. Jackson* has no applicability to the former North Carolina capital punishment scheme," but not in *Brady,* for while "Brady was aware he faced a possible death sentence, there is no evidence that this factor alone played a significant role in his decision to enter a guilty plea."

e. On the nature of such pleas, see Note 1 at p. 1228 infra.

has been construed in our cases, it is not forbidden to extend a proper degree of leniency in return for guilty pleas. New Jersey has done no more than that.

"We discern no element of retaliation or vindictiveness against Corbitt for going to trial. There is no suggestion that he was subjected to unwarranted charges. Nor does this record indicate that he was being punished for exercising a constitutional right. Indeed, insofar as this record reveals, Corbitt may have tendered a plea and it was refused. There is no doubt that those homicide defendants who are willing to plead *non vult* may be treated more leniently than those who go to trial, but withholding the possibility of leniency from the latter cannot be equated with impermissible punishment as long as our cases sustaining plea bargaining remain undisturbed. Those cases, as we have said, unequivocally recognize the constitutional propriety of extending leniency in exchange for a plea of guilty and of not extending leniency to those who have not demonstrated those attributes on which leniency is based.[14]

"Finally, we are unconvinced that the New Jersey statutory pattern exerts such a powerful influence to coerce inaccurate guilty pleas that it should be deemed constitutionally suspect. There is no suggestion here that Corbitt was not well counseled or that he misunderstood the choices that were placed before him. Here, as in *Bordenkircher,* the State did not trespass on the defendant's rights 'so long as the accused [was] free to accept or [refuse the choice presented to him by the state]', that is, to go to trial and face the risk of life imprisonment or to seek acceptance of a *non vult* plea and the imposition of the lesser penalty authorized by law.[15]"

STEWART, J., though concurring in the judgment, disagreed with the majority's statement that there was "no difference of constitutional significance between *Bordenkircher* and this case": "It seems to me that there is a vast difference between the settlement of litigation through negoti-

14. The dissent appears to question any system that subjects the defendant who stands trial to a substantial risk of greater punishment than the defendant who pleads guilty. But in the next breath, the dissent appears to embrace plea bargaining, although the plea-bargaining systems operating in a majority of the jurisdictions throughout the country inherently extend to defendants who plead guilty the probability or the certainty of leniency that will not be available if they go to trial.

The dissent asserts that the attack here is on the statutory scheme rather than upon the system of plea bargaining, which is said to individualize defendants and does not mandate a different standard of punishment depending solely on whether or not a plea is entered. The distinction is without substance for the purposes of this case. In the first place, plea bargaining by state prosecutors operates by virtue of state law, here by virtue of the formal rules of the Supreme Court of New Jersey. That system permits a proper amount of leniency in return for pleas, leniency that is denied if one goes to trial. In this sense, the standard of punishment is necessarily different for those who plead and for those who go to trial. For those who plead, that fact itself is a consideration in sentencing, a consideration that is not present when one is found guilty by a jury. Second, under the New Jersey statutes, pleas may be rejected even if tendered; there must, for example, be a factual basis for the plea. Even if a plea is accepted, there is discretion to impose life imprisonment. The statute leaves much to the judge and to the prosecutor and does not mandate lesser punishment for those pleading *non vult* than is imposed on those who go to trial. It is also true that under normal circumstances, juries in New Jersey may find a defendant guilty of second-degree murder rather than first.

Third, we cannot hold that a prosecutor may charge a person with a crime carrying a mandatory punishment and secure a valid conviction, despite his power to offer leniency to those who plead—including dismissal of the mandatory count in return for a plea—and yet hold that the legislature may not openly provide for the possibility of leniency in return for a plea. This is particularly true where it is contemplated that plea bargaining will in any event go forward within the limits set by the legislature.

15. We do not suggest that every conceivable statutory sentencing structure, plea-bargaining system or particular plea bargain would be constitutional. We hold only that a State may make due allowance for pleas in their sentencing decisions and that New Jersey has not exceeded its powers in this respect by its statutory provision extending the possibility of leniency to those who plead guilty in homicide cases.

ation between counsel for the parties, and a state statute such as is involved in the present case. While a prosecuting attorney, acting as an advocate, necessarily must be able to settle an adversary criminal lawsuit through plea bargaining with his adversary a state legislature has a quite different function to perform. Could a state legislature provided that the penalty for every criminal offense to which a defendant pleads guilty is to be one-half the penalty to be imposed upon a defendant convicted of the same offense after a not guilty plea? I would suppose that such legislation would be clearly unconstitutional under *United States v. Jackson.*"

STEVENS, J., joined by BRENNAN and MARSHALL, JJ., dissented:

"Nor is this statutory scheme the equivalent of a plea bargain negotiated between defense counsel and the prosecutor. While such bargains serve a state interest in common with § 2A:113, they do so without penalizing the defendant's assertion of his legal rights. In the bargaining process, individual factors relevant to the particular case may be considered by the prosecutor in charging and by the trial judge in sentencing, regardless of the defendant's plea; the process does not mandate a different standard of punishment depending solely on whether or not a plea is entered.

"Of even greater importance is the fact that a defendant who refuses a plea bargain will not be punished for his constitutionally protected recalcitrance; whatever punishment he receives will be for his conduct in committing the offense or offenses the State has proved at trial. In contrast, a defendant who faces a more severe range of statutory penalties simply because he has insisted on a trial, is subjected to punishment not only for the crime the State has proved, but also for the 'offense' of entering a 'false' not guilty plea." [f]

3. Under *Hayes, Brady,* and *Corbitt,* what is the status of a plea entered because of a prosecutor's assertion that if the defendant pleads guilty his wife or fiancee will not be prosecuted? Consider *United States v. Nuckols,* 606 F.2d 566 (5th Cir. 1979) ("if an accused elects to sacrifice himself for such motives, that is his choice"). What about a plea which is accepted on the condition that the defendant not appeal? Compare *People v. Stevenson,* 231 N.W.2d 476 (Mich.App.1975) ("the right to appeal [is] non-negotiable in the instance of plea-based convictions"); with *United States ex rel. Amuso v. LaVallee,* 291 F.Supp. 383 (E.D.N.Y.1968) (a proper "method of making a plea agreement enforceable"); and consider *State v. Gibson,* 348 A.2d 769 (N.J.1975) (plea not inherently coercive, but defendant still free to appeal, in which case state is relieved of its part of the bargain).

4. Are there some promises which, even if kept, promise so much that they constitute an excessive and unjustified pressure upon the defendant? Consider Kuh, *Plea Copping,* 24 N.Y.Co.Bar Bull. 160, 164 (1966–67): "[T]he defendant who faced a mandatory minimum of ten years in State prison, and a possibility of thirty years, and who is offered the alternative of a misdemeanor plea and sentence, has an awful lot of thinking to do, *regardless of whether he is guilty or whether he truly believes that his guilt can be proven,* before he turns it down. * * * When conviction may spell long term tragedy, and pleading guilty carries with it relatively inconsequential punishment, the bait for waiving rights is flavorful." But, "since the factual distinction between good and bad inducements involves a difficult evaluation of the subjective state of mind of the defendant at the time of the plea," Comment, 32

f. For criticism of Corbitt, see Abrams, *Systemic Coercion: Unconstitutional Conditions in the Criminal Law,* 72 J.Crim.L. & C. 128, 158–62 (1981); Clarke, *Plea Bargaining and Trial Penalties: When May the State Legitimately Require Criminal Defendants to Surrender Their Trial Rights,* 55 Ind.L.J. 71, 89 (1979).

U.Chi.L.Rev. 167, 177 (1964), should the good be separated from the bad by a subjective or objective test?

5. As to the requirement (as stated in *Brady*) that the defendant know "the actual value of any commitments made to him," consider *Dillon v. United States,* 307 F.2d 445 (9th Cir.1962), where the prosecutor promised to recommend a lenient sentence if the judge asked for a recommendation. Because the prosecutor knew that the judge never asked for a recommendation, the court found the prosecutor's bargain "wholly illusory." [g] It has been noted that many bargains are "hollow in value"; the prosecutor, for example, may promise to recommend probation in a type of case where probation is routinely granted. Newman, *Conviction: The Determination of Guilt or Innocence Without Trial* 98 (Remington ed., 1966). Should such a plea be subject to attack on the ground that the defendant did not know the actual value of the prosecutor's commitment?

Consider *People v. Marsh,* 679 P.2d 1033 (Cal.1984), where the bargain involved dropping an existing charge, in which the court concluded defendant could not raise an "illusory bargain" issue based on his claim there was insufficient evidence to support the dropped charge. The court stated that "defendant makes the unwarranted assumption that a nolo or guilty plea is invalid unless made for a consideration which would support a contract. If that were the law a defendant could not 'plead to the sheet,' simply in the hope that the court will show leniency. In any event, defendant got exactly what he bargained for—dismissal of the simple kidnapping charge. There was no condition that the charge not be vulnerable to a motion to dismiss * * *—a motion which, incidentally, was never made."

6. Can the defendant know the value of the prosecutor's commitment without knowing the strength of the prosecution's case? Reconsider *Scott v. United States,* p. 1180 supra, and see Comment, 119 U.Pa. L.Rev. 527 (1971), arguing for broad pre-plea discovery on the ground that "a defendant can assess the likelihood of conviction at trial only if he first secures and evaluates relevant evidence held by the prosecutor." Consider, in this regard, the material in chapter 20, particularly § 1, pt. I, and § 3.

7. Should the defendant be free to initiate and participate in plea discussions without having his statements used against him at trial if he does not plead guilty? Does it make any difference to whom the statements were made? Consider Fed.R. Crim.P. 11(e)(6), which in its present form is intended to foreclose results such as in *United States v. Herman,* 544 F.2d 791 (5th Cir.1977) (defendant in custody of two postal inspectors during continuance of removal hearing instigated conversation with them and at some point said he would plead guilty to armed robbery if the murder charge was dropped, but inspector then explained they were not "in position to make any deals in this regard"; held, defendant's statements inadmissible under earlier version of rule 11(e)(6) because he made them "during the course of a conversation in which he sought concessions from the government in return for a guilty plea"). Is the change objectionable because it "fails to provide protection for defendants who plea bargain under the reasonable belief that the agent has bargaining authority," as asserted in Note, 70 Geo.L.J. 315, 344 (1981)?

Compare the situation as to the admissibility of a withdrawn plea, discussed at p. 1239 infra, and also that in *Hutto v. Ross,* 429 U.S. 28, 97 S.Ct. 202, 50 L.Ed.2d 194 (1976), where the Court, per curiam, reversed the holding of the court of ap-

g. See also *United States v. Maggio,* 514 F.2d 80 (5th Cir.1975), holding that if it is the policy of a particular trial judge never to accept sentence recommendations from the prosecutor, he "shall tell this to the defendant" who tenders a guilty plea.

peals that defendant's confession, given subsequent to a negotiated plea agreement from which the defendant later withdrew, was involuntary because it would not have been made "but for the plea bargaining." Noting that "causation in that sense has never been the test of voluntariness," the Court concluded: "The existence of the bargain may well have entered into respondent's decision to give a statement, but counsel made it clear to respondent that he could enforce the terms of the plea bargain whether or not he confessed. The confession thus does not appear to have been the result of 'any direct or implied promises' or any coercion on the part of the prosecution, and was not involuntary." In passing the Court observed that the case did not "involve the admissibility in criminal trials of statements made during the plea negotiation process."

Should the prosecutor's statements in the course of plea discussions be admissible in defendant's favor? Consider *United States v. Verdoorn,* 528 F.2d 103 (8th Cir. 1976), holding that the trial judge properly refused to permit the defendants to put into evidence at their trial the fact the prosecution had attempted to plea bargain with them, as "meaningful dialogue between the parties would, as a practical matter, be impossible if either party had to assume the risk that plea offers would be admissible in evidence."

NOTES ON JUDICIAL INVOLVEMENT IN PLEA BARGAINING

1. Alschuler, *The Trial Judge's Role in Plea Bargaining, Part I,* 76 Colum.L.Rev. 1059, 1133–34 (1976), describes *People v. Dennis,* 328 N.E.2d 135 (Ill.App.1975): "A defense attorney testified in a post-conviction proceeding that a Chicago trial judge had offered to sentence his client to a term of two-to-four years if the client would plead guilty. The prosecutor recalled the pretrial conference somewhat differently and testified that the judge had proposed a sentence of two-to-six years in exchange for the defendant's plea. Whatever the trial judge's offer, however, the defendant declined it; and following his conviction by a jury, the judge sentenced him to a term of 40-to-80 years. The appellate court noted that, because the trial judge had been advised of the state's evidence and of the defendant's prior criminal record during the pretrial conference, the sentence that he imposed almost certainly did not reflect circumstances of which he had been unaware at the time of his offer. The court concluded that a ' "reasonable inference" of constitutional deprivation may be drawn where a great disparity exists between the sentence offered at a pretrial conference to which the trial judge was a participant and one imposed at the conclusion of a jury trial.' Accordingly, it exercised its authority under Illinois Supreme Court Rules to reduce the defendant's sentence. The court did not, however, reduce the sentence to the two-to-four or the two-to-six year term that the defendant would have served if he had pleaded guilty. Rather, it reduced the sentence to six-to-eighteen years 'in the interests of justice.' The court's rule thus seemed to be that a defendant may be penalized for exercising his right to trial by a sentence three times more severe than that he could have secured by pleading guilty, but not by a sentence twenty times more severe."

2. In light of *Bordenkircher v. Hayes,* p. 1185 supra, how would the Supreme Court have dealt with *Dennis?* Cf. *Longval v. Meachum,* 693 F.2d 236 (1st Cir.1982) (where "the trial court, sua sponte, informed the defendant that if he did not follow its advise to bargain and plead, it 'might be disposed to impose a substantial sentence' if the jury convicted him," and defendant did not follow that advice and received sentence of 40–50 years upon conviction, while co-defendant who pleaded guilty received 3 years, there a "reasonable apprehension of vindictiveness" under *Blackledge v. Perry,* p. 927 supra, and a "reasonable likelihood of vindictiveness"

under *United States v. Goodwin,* p. 929 supra, so that defendant entitled to relief on habeas corpus).

3. In UNITED STATES ex rel. ELKSNIS v. GILLIGAN, 256 F.Supp. 244 (S.D.N.Y.1966), the defendant, charged with second degree murder, and his attorney conferred with the judge in chambers. The judge assured the defendant that if he pleaded guilty to first degree manslaughter the sentence would not exceed 10 years. Soon thereafter the defendant so pleaded in open court, but a few weeks later the judge imposed a sentence of 17½ to 35 years. After exhausting his state remedies, defendant challenged his plea in federal court. The court, WEINFELD, J., concluded that the plea could not stand because the judge had failed to adhere to his promise, and then continued:

"The unequal positions of the judge and the accused, one with the power to commit to prison and the other deeply concerned to avoid prison, at once raise a question of fundamental fairness. When a judge becomes a participant in plea bargaining he brings to bear the full force and majesty of his office. His awesome power to impose a substantially longer or even maximum sentence in excess of that proposed is present whether referred to or not. A defendant needs no reminder that if he rejects the proposal, stands upon his right to trial and is convicted, he faces a significantly longer sentence. One facing a prison term, whether of longer or shorter duration, is easily influenced to accept what appears the more preferable choice. Intentionally or otherwise, and no matter how well motivated the judge may be, the accused is subjected to a subtle but powerful influence. A guilty plea predicated upon a judge's promise of a definite sentence by its very nature does not qualify as a free and voluntary act. The plea is so interlaced with the promise that the one cannot be separated from the other; remove the promise and the basis for the plea falls.

"A judge's prime responsibility is to maintain the integrity of the judicial system; to see that due process of law, equal protection of the laws and the basic safeguards of a fair trial are upheld. The judge stands as the symbol of evenhanded justice, and none can seriously question that if this central figure in the administration of justice promises an accused that upon a plea of guilty a fixed sentence will follow, his commitment has an all-pervasive and compelling influence in inducing the accused to yield his right to trial. A plea entered upon a bargain agreement between a judge and an accused cannot be squared with due process requirements of the Fourteenth Amendment. * * *

"It may well be, as has been suggested, that voluntary, as distinguished from coercive, bargaining between the prosecutor and the defendant has been sanctioned by propriety and practice—in some measure they deal at arm's length. But this is quite different from approbation of plea bargaining between the judge and the accused, where the disparity of positions is extremely marked. * * *

"Finally, a bargain agreement between a judge and a defendant, however free from any calculated purpose to induce a plea, has no place in a system of justice. It impairs the judge's objectivity in passing upon the voluntariness of the plea when offered. As a party to the arrangement upon which the plea is based, he is hardly in a position to discharge his function of deciding the validity of the plea—a function not satisfied by routine inquiry, but only, as the Supreme Court has stressed, by 'a penetrating and comprehensive examination of all the circumstances under which such a plea is tendered.' "

4. Is the court in *Elksnis* correct in saying that even if the promise had been kept the plea would be involuntary because a product of bargaining between defendant and judge? Were the circumstances in *Elksnis* more coercive than when the bargaining takes place between defen-

dant and prosecutor? Compare Recent Developments, 19 Stan.L.Rev. 1082, 1086 (1967), arguing that because "the prosecutor has many means not available to the judge of putting pressure upon the defendant * * * the 'disparity of position,' in terms of power over the accused, may be even greater between prosecutor and defendant than between judge and defendant."

In *United States ex rel. Rosa v. Follette,* 395 F.2d 721 (2d Cir.1968), holding that "the participation of the trial judge in plea discussions does not *in itself* render the plea involuntary," the court reasoned: "We cannot blind ourselves to the fact that 'it is not at all unusual for the prosecutor to predict the sentence with a high degree of accuracy and to communicate this prediction to the defendant.' * * * And, every defense attorney plays the prophet as best he can. In the instant case, Rosa was fortunate in being given the security of the Judge's beneficence by learning immediately what most defendants are tortured over, can only hope for and anticipate—that the trial judge will follow the prosecutor's recommendation." Consider also *Brown v. Peyton,* 435 F.2d 1352 (4th Cir.1970), contending that the quotation from *Shelton* appearing in *Brady v. United States* at p. 1192 supra "can only contemplate plea bargaining in which the judge has participated." Is this a fair reading of *Brady?*

5. Are there other reasons for keeping the trial judge out of the bargaining process? Consider Recent Developments, 19 Stan.L.Rev. at 1089: "Another valid reason for distinguishing judicial from prosecutorial bargaining relates to the prestige and dignity of the judicial system. Judge Weinfeld noted that judicial bargaining involves the prestige of the judicial office, but he saw this problem only as part of the question of judicial coercion of the defendant. There is, however, a need both to protect the dignity of the judge per se—he should not be an advocate, but rather a symbol of even-handed justice—and to preserve respect for the entire legal process. Toleration of a procedure which leads defendants to think of the judge as just one more official to be 'bought off' is clearly not conducive to respect for the law."

6. Compare Lambros, J., *Plea Bargaining and the Sentencing Process,* 53 F.R.D. 509, 514–18 (1972): "[T]here are also several reasons in support of [judicial] participation in plea discussions. For one, * * * the plea itself becomes * * * a more meaningful and informed plea in two respects. Judicial participation in plea discussions inevitably causes the prosecutor to open his file and to freely discuss the strength of his case. As a consequence, defense counsel receives information which would not otherwise be discoverable. From this full disclosure of the prosecutor's case, defendant and defense counsel are better able to evaluate all the factual issues and the risk factors involved. * * * It is also more meaningful and informed as a result of discussions as to the sentencing alternatives. From my experience, I have discerned that the prosecutor and defense counsel do not have a workable knowledge as to the wide array of sentencing possibilities. * * *

"Another reason is that judicial involvement in plea discussions would expedite litigation and in turn, reduce the backlog of cases. Experience has shown that defendants and defense counsel are inclined to undergo the full ritual of technical and procedural machinery. [A]n inevitable plea of guilty which is usually entered in the vast majority of cases is postponed for many months and in many instances, many years, creating a logjam in the criminal docket. This logjam is largely prompted by the sense of uncertainty as to ultimate disposition which preoccupies an accused and his counsel. * * * Judicial involvement in plea discussions tends to remove this cloak of uncertainty and in turn, prompts the timely entering of a plea of guilty.

"Judicial involvement in plea discussions would provide the judge a vehicle through which he could acquire additional information so as to supplement the report of the Probation Department. * * * Although he should rely upon the Probation Department, nonetheless, the judge must make his own observations, inquiry, and analysis of the defendant and of the offense committed. This cannot be accomplished by the brief confrontations between the judge and the defendant and defense counsel at the time the plea of guilty is entered nor at the time of sentencing."

7. Precisely how should judicial involvement in the plea bargaining process be limited? Is it best to provide that the judge shall not "participate" in plea discussions, as in Fed.R.Crim.P. 11(e)(1), or that the judge shall not "initiate" plea discussions, as in Ill.Sup.Ct.R. 402(d)(1)? Consider *A.B.A. Standards* § 14–3.3(c): "When the parties are unable to reach a plea agreement, if the defendant's counsel and prosecutor agree, they may request to meet with the judge in order to discuss a plea agreement. If the judge agrees to meet with the parties, the judge shall serve as a moderator in listening to their respective presentations concerning appropriate charge or sentence concessions. Following the presentation of the parties, the judge may indicate what charge or sentence concessions would be acceptable or whether the judge wishes to have a preplea report before rendering a decision. The parties may thereupon decide among themselves, outside of the presence of the court, whether to accept or reject the plea agreement tendered by the court."

If, under the A.B.A. procedure, the defendant is permitted to withdraw his guilty plea, should the trial judge recuse himself? Ill.Sup.Ct.R. 402(d)(3) so provides.[a] Does this permit judge-shopping and offer-shopping? See Alschuler, supra, at 1111–12.

8. On the other hand, does Fed.R.Crim.P. 11(e), by permitting the reaching of an agreement as to a specific sentence and its communication to the judge, who can either concur and accept the plea agreement or else reject the plea agreement, involve the judge too much? Compare *State v. Evans,* 234 N.W.2d 199 (Neb.1975) (defendant may only bargain for prosecutor's recommendation, and trial judge may not permit withdrawal of plea because he gives sentence higher than was recommended); *United States v. Green,* 1 M.J. 453 (U.S.C.M.A.1976) (the judge must announce his sentence before inquiring into what sentence limits were contemplated in the plea bargain).

9. Whatever the judge's role otherwise in the plea negotiation process, should the defendant be able to bargain with the judge over the prosecutor's objection? Consider *United States v. Werker,* 535 F.2d 198 (2d Cir.1976) (where prosecutor not prepared to offer sentence concessions, it improper for trial judge to reveal to defendant in advance of his guilty plea what the sentence would be on a plea of guilty);[b] *State v. Carlson,* 555 P.2d 269 (Alaska, 1976) (where prosecutor not willing to

a. Compare *United States v. Gallington,* 488 F.2d 637 (8th Cir.1973) (where judge rejected plea bargain on ground that contemplated 10-year sentence was inadequate, he may then excuse himself from further involvement in the case and should give serious consideration to doing so, but judge in this case did not abuse his discretion in electing to preside over jury trial of defendant); *United States v. Walker,* 473 F.2d 136 (D.C.Cir. 1972) (no prejudicial error in trial judge's failure to withdraw from a nonjury case in which he had learned of defendant's prior offer to plead guilty, but "it would be better if he exercised his prerogative to recuse himself or to insist upon a jury trial").

b. Compare Uviller, *Pleading Guilty: A Critique of Four Models,* 41 Law & Contemp.Prob. 102, 116–17 (1977), criticizing *Werker* and asking: "When a trial judge has informed himself of the defendant's background and the circumstances of his crime, when he has formed at least a tentative decision on the appropriate sentence, and even (according to some) when the sentence concession is not contingent on the plea but would be followed even if the defendant elected to be tried, what interests of the defendant are protected by bargain down to a reduced charge, the court may not accept a plea of guilty to a reduced charge).[c]

SANTOBELLO v. NEW YORK

404 U.S. 257, 92 S.Ct. 495, 30 L.Ed.2d 427 (1971).

MR. CHIEF JUSTICE BURGER delivered the opinion of the Court.

[After negotiations with the prosecutor, petitioner withdrew his previous not-guilty plea to two felony counts and pleaded guilty to a lesser-included offense, the prosecutor having agreed to make no recommendation as to sentence. At petitioner's appearance for sentencing many months later a new prosecutor recommended the maximum sentence, which the judge (who stated that he was uninfluenced by that recommendation) imposed. Petitioner attempted unsuccessfully to withdraw his guilty plea, and his conviction was affirmed on appeal.]

* * * The disposition of criminal charges by agreement between the prosecutor and the accused, sometimes loosely called "plea bargaining," is an essential component of the administration of justice. Properly administered, it is to be encouraged. If every criminal charge were subjected to a full-scale trial, the States and the Federal Government would need to multiply by many times the number of judges and court facilities.

Disposition of charges after plea discussions is not only an essential part of the process but a highly desirable part for many reasons. It leads to prompt and largely final disposition of most criminal cases; it avoids much of the corrosive impact of enforced idleness during pretrial confinement for those who are denied release pending trial; it protects the public from those accused persons who are prone to continue criminal conduct even while on pretrial release; and, by shortening the time between charge and disposition, it enhances whatever may be the rehabilitative prospects of the guilty when they are ultimately imprisoned. * * *

This phase of the process of criminal justice, and the adjudicative element inherent in accepting a plea of guilty, must be attended by safeguards to insure the defendant what is reasonably due in the circumstances. Those circumstances will vary, but a constant factor is that when a plea rests in any significant degree on a promise or agreement of the prosecutor, so that it can be said to be part of the inducement or consideration, such promise must be fulfilled. * * *

We need not reach the question whether the sentencing judge would or would not have been influenced had he known all the details of the negotiations for the plea. He stated that the prosecutor's recommendation did not influence him and we have no reason to doubt that. Nevertheless, we conclude that the interests of justice and appropriate recognition of the duties of the prosecution in relation to promises made in the negotiation of pleas of guilty will be best served by remanding the case to the state courts for further consideration. The ultimate relief to which petitioner is entitled we leave to the discretion of the state court, which is in a better position to decide whether the circumstances of this case require only that there be specific performance of the agreement on the plea, in which case petitioner should be resentenced by a different judge, or whether, in the view of the state court, the circumstances require granting the relief sought by petitioner, i.e., the opportunity to withdraw his plea of guilty.[2] * * *

prohibiting the judge from communicating this information to him?"

c. As for the power of the judge to refuse to reduce the charge notwithstanding the prosecutor's bargain to do so, see *United States v. Ammidown*, p. 1223 infra.

2. If the state court decides to allow withdrawal of the plea, the petitioner will, of course, plead anew to the original charge on two felony counts.

MR. JUSTICE DOUGLAS, concurring.

* * *

I join the opinion of the Court and favor a constitutional rule for this as well as for other pending or oncoming cases. Where the "plea bargain" is not kept by the prosecutor, the sentence must be vacated and the state court will decide in light of the circumstances of each case whether due process requires (a) that there be specific performance of the plea bargain or (b) that the defendant be given the option to go to trial on the original charges. One alternative may do justice in one case, and the other in a different case. In choosing a remedy, however, a court ought to accord a defendant's preference considerable, if not controlling, weight inasmuch as the fundamental rights flouted by a prosecutor's breach of a plea bargain are those of the defendant, not of the State.

MR. JUSTICE MARSHALL, with whom MR. JUSTICE BRENNAN and MR. JUSTICE STEWART join, concurring in part and dissenting in part.

* * * When a prosecutor breaks the bargain, he undercuts the basis for the waiver of constitutional rights implicit in the plea. This, it seems to me, provides the defendant ample justification for rescinding the plea. Where a promise is "unfulfilled," *Brady v. United States* [p. 1191 supra] specifically denies that the plea "must stand." Of course, where the prosecutor has broken the plea agreement, it may be appropriate to permit the defendant to enforce the plea bargain. But that is not the remedy sought here.* Rather, it seems to me that a breach of the plea bargain provides ample reason to permit the plea to be vacated.

It is worth noting that in the ordinary case where a motion to vacate is made prior to sentencing, the government has taken no action in reliance on the previously entered guilty plea and would suffer no harm from the plea's withdrawal. More pointedly, here the State claims no such harm beyond disappointed expectations about the plea itself. At least where the government itself has broken the plea bargain, this disappointment cannot bar petitioner from withdrawing his guilty plea and reclaiming his right to a trial.

I would remand the case with instructions that the plea be vacated and petitioner given an opportunity to replead to the original charges in the indictment.

Notes and Questions

1. Exactly what constitutes a broken bargain—or, at least, deserves to be treated in the same way as the broken bargain in *Santobello?* For example, if the prosecutor agrees to recommend or not oppose the defendant's request for a particular sentence, and he then performs as promised but the court does not give such a sentence, is the defendant then entitled to relief? There is a split of authority at the state level. Which is the better view? What is the result under Fed.R.Crim.P. 11(e)?

2. Sometimes it is difficult to determine just what the dimensions of the bargain were. Illustrative is *United States v. Alessi,* 544 F.2d 1139 (2d Cir.1976), where a plea bargain between the defendant and a federal strike force attorney operating in the Eastern District of New York was that if defendant would plead guilty to a charge of conspiracy to violate the narcotics laws, "then, in return for his plea, overt acts in furtherance of this conspiracy would not give rise to subsequent individual prosecutions." Defendant entered his plea of guilty, but was later charged in the Southern District of New York with a heroin sale connected with the same conspiratorial organization. The

* Mr. Justice Douglas, although joining the Court's opinion (apparently because he thinks the remedy should be chosen by the state court), concludes that the state court "ought to accord a defendant's preference considerable, if not controlling, weight." Thus, a majority of the Court appears to believe that in cases like these, when the defendant seeks to vacate the plea, that relief should generally be granted. [Ed. note: there were two vacancies on the Court at the time.]

court held this prosecution could be undertaken, as "it was not in the contemplation of either side that anyone outside of the Eastern District U.S. Attorney or Strike Force Offices was bound."

3. If the plea bargain is that the prosecutor will seek a certain disposition, how hard must he try? In UNITED STATES v. BENCHIMOL, ___ U.S. ___, 105 S.Ct. 2103, 85 L.Ed.2d 462 (1985), defendant entered a plea of guilty in exchange for the prosecutor's promise to recommend probation with restitution. At the sentencing hearing, defense counsel informed the court of that fact (correcting the presentence report statement that the government "would stand silent"), the prosecutor merely commented that defense counsel's statement was "an accurate representation," and the court then sentenced defendant to six years. The court of appeals held the government had breached the bargain because it "made no effort to explain its reasons for agreeing to recommend a lenient sentence but rather left an impression with the court of less-than-enthusiastic support for leniency." But the Supreme Court disagreed, concluding "it was error for the Court of Appeals to imply as a matter of law a term which the parties themselves did not agree upon." The Court emphasized that the instant case was unlike *United States v. Brown,* 500 F.2d 375 (4th Cir.1974), where "the Government attorney appearing personally in court at the time of the plea bargain expressed personal reservations about the agreement to which the Government had committed itself," and also that the government had not made an express commitment either to make the recommendation enthusiastically or to state reasons for it.

4. If, on the other hand, the plea bargain was that the prosecutor would not recommend a sentence or would not oppose defendant's recommendations, it may be claimed that the prosecutor did too much. Compare *United States v. Miller,* 565 F.2d 1273 (3d Cir.1977) (where prosecutor promised to make no recommendation, bargain not violated by his comments at sentencing hearing concerning defendant's lack of cooperation); with *United States v. Crusco,* 536 F.2d 21 (3d Cir.1976) (where prosecutor promised to take no position on the sentence, he was precluded from making any response to argument made by defense counsel at sentencing hearing). Consider also *Brooks v. United States,* 708 F.2d 1280 (7th Cir. 1983) (prosecutor's promise to make no recommendation not violated by his opposition to defendant's later Fed.R.Crim.P. 35(b) motion for reduction of sentence imposed), criticized in Comment, 52 U.Chi.L.Rev. 751, 771 (1985): "If a plea agreement does not, either upon its face or upon the admission of extrinsic evidence, show the parties' shared expectations, the court must apply a gap-filling presumption to cover the omitted term. The gap-filling term that satisfies the constitutional requisite for a guilty plea is one that accords with a defendant's reasonable expectations, not with the intentions of the prosecutor."

5. If a defendant charged with armed robbery (punishable by an indeterminate term with a 5-year minimum) pleads guilty to robbery (punishable by imprisonment from 1 to 20 years) as a result of plea negotiations, is the bargain broken if the judge receives and considers, at the time of sentencing, evidence that the defendant was armed? Does it make a difference whether or not the judge imposed a sentence with more than a 5-year minimum? See *People v. Fields,* 291 N.E.2d 258 (Ill. App.1972). Or, if the bargain is that the defendant will plead guilty to one count if other counts are dismissed, is the bargain broken if the judge receives and considers evidence on the other counts at the time of sentencing, or if the parole board receives such evidence in determining defendant's parole eligibility? See *United States ex rel. Goldberg v. Warden,* 622 F.2d 60 (3d Cir. 1980).

6. Should deception by the defendant or changed circumstances relieve the prosecutor of his commitments? Consider

Hamlin v. Barrett, 335 So.2d 898 (Miss. 1976) (though bargain was for probation, defendant concealed from prosecutor and court fact he had a prior robbery conviction in another state, which by state law made him ineligible for probation without some imprisonment, and thus defendant may be sentenced to imprisonment); *State v. Pascall,* 358 N.E.2d 1368 (Ohio App. 1972) (bargain was that prosecutor would recommend probation, but there was an implied promise by defendant that the circumstances will remain substantially the same, and thus prosecutor excused from fulfilling promise where in interim defendant convicted of burglary and armed robbery); *State v. Segarra,* 388 So.2d 1017 (Fla.1980) (where defendant entered plea pursuant to agreement that his sentence would not exceed 5 years and he then placed on probation but probation later revoked for violation of condition, sentence of 15 years then imposed lawful, as the "events which bring about a revocation open a new chapter in which the court ought to be able to mete out any punishment within the limits prescribed for the crime").

7. Thomas was charged with atrocious assault and battery, assault with intent to rob, and robbery of Murray. As a result of plea bargaining, Thomas pleaded guilty on October 27, 1969, to the first charge on the understanding that the prosecutor, at the appropriate time, would dismiss the remaining counts. On January 23, 1970, Murray died from the wounds inflicted by Thomas. On the prosecutor's motion, the court dismissed the two other counts on September 15, 1970. On October 29, 1970, Thomas was charged with murder. If Thomas were now tried on the felony-murder theory that the death occurred during the commission of a robbery, would this constitute a broken bargain? See *State v. Thomas,* 276 A.2d 391 (N.J. Super.1971) (prosecution on this theory barred by collateral estoppel rule of *Ashe v. Swenson,* p. 1056 supra). What if the robbery count had been dismissed *before* Murray died?

8. If, as in *Santobello,* the defendant seeks to withdraw his plea because of nonperformance of the bargain, should the prosecution always (or, under some circumstances) be able to bar withdrawal by now performing as promised? On the other hand, what if the defendant in *Santobello* had asked for specific performance of the bargain? Should he be entitled to this remedy, or can the prosecution insist that he be limited to the remedy of plea withdrawal? Compare *Jordan v. Commonwealth,* 225 S.E.2d 661 (Va.1976) (defendant agreed to plead guilty to assault charge if burglary charge not brought, after his plea burglary charge was brought because of public criticism; held, defendant entitled to specific performance); with *People v. Young,* 367 N.E.2d 976 (Ill. App.1977) (even if defendant correct in assertion that trial judge promised probation, he wrong in asserting "that the remedy for such claimed unfulfilled promises is specific performance"). May these cases be reconciled on the ground, as stated in *Davis v. State,* 308 So.2d 27 (Fla.1975), that *Santobello* "requires specific performance by a prosecutor of a promise on which a defendant relied," but not "that plea discussions can be specifically enforced against a court"? Or, is the point that specific performance is required when the defendant "cannot be restored to his former position," as stated in *Brooks v. Narick,* 243 S.E.2d 841 (W.Va.1978) (as part of bargain, defendant had already spent 60 days in custody for diagnostic study).

Consider Westen & Westin, *A Constitutional Law of Remedies for Broken Plea Bargains,* 66 Calif.L.Rev. 471, 500, 512, 513 (1978), concluding: (1) that a constitutional right of specific performance cannot be based on the requirement that pleas be "voluntary," as "the subsequent failure of the inducement cannot have any effect on the desirability of the inducement at the time the defendant accepts it"; (2) that such a constitutional right cannot be based on the requirement that pleas be "intelligent," as that interest is protected "by vacating the plea"; and (3) that therefore "*Santobello* can be understood as extending constitutional protection to the personal expectations created in defendants by plea agreements with the state." Why should the Constitution protect those expectations? If it should, does this "constitutional law of contracts" extend to *all* (i.e., even illegal) promises?

9. Is the prosecutor free to withdraw his offer at any time prior to defendant's entry of a guilty plea in reliance thereon? Not if there has been other detrimental reliance by the defendant. "Providing information to government authorities, testifying for the government, confessing guilt, returning stolen property, making monetary restitution, failing to file a motion to have charges presented to a grand jury, submitting to a lie detector test and waiving certain procedural guarantees have all been held to constitute acts made in detrimental reliance upon a prosecutor's breached promises." Note, 58 N.C.L. Rev. 599, 606–07 (1980).

Going well beyond that position is *Cooper v. United States,* 594 F.2d 12 (4th Cir. 1979), holding that unless the prosecutor's plea proposal is properly conditioned it may be enforceable by a defendant who, prior to the prosecutor's withdrawal of the offer, had neither entered a guilty plea nor relied to his detriment on the bargain. The court declared that there were "two distinct sources" for such a ruling: (1) the Sixth Amendment right to effective assistance of counsel, involved here because to "the extent that the government attempts through defendant's counsel to change or retract positions earlier communicated, a defendant's confidence in his counsel's capability and professional responsibility * * * are necessarily jeopardized and the effectiveness of counsel's assistance easily compromised"; and (2) a due process right to enforcement of the plea proposal "on the basis alone of expectations reasonably formed in reliance upon the honor of the government in making and abiding by its proposals" where, as here, the offer was unambiguous and not unreasonable and was promptly assented to by the defendant and no "extenuating circumstances affecting the propriety of the proposal" intervened.

A unanimous Supreme Court rejected the *Cooper* approach in MABRY v. JOHNSON, 467 U.S. 504, 104 S.Ct. 2543, 81 L.Ed.2d 437 (1984). As for the right to counsel argument, the Court stated it failed "to see how an accused could reasonably attribute the prosecutor's change of heart to his counsel any more than he could have blamed counsel had the trial judge chosen to reject the agreed-upon recommendation, or, for that matter, had he gone to trial and been convicted." Moreover, where, as in the instant case, there had been no detrimental reliance by the defendant, there was no due process violation either. When his agreement to accept the prosecution's offer of a 21-year concurrent sentence for a murder plea resulted in that offer being withdrawn as "a mistake" and replaced by an offer of a 21-year consecutive sentence, the defendant accepted the second offer after the trial began. Noting that this plea "was in no sense induced by the prosecutor's withdrawn offer," the Court concluded that defendant's "inability to enforce the prosecutor's offer is without constitutional significance" because that offer "did not impair the voluntariness or intelligence of his guilty plea." As for the prosecutor's possible negligence or culpability in making and withdrawing the first offer, the Court deemed that irrelevant because the due process clause "is not a code of ethics for prosecutors" but is concerned "with the manner in which persons are deprived of their liberty."

10. In *Santobello,* the Court said that if the plea was withdrawn the two felony counts could be reinstated. Compare *People v. McMiller,* 208 N.W.2d 451 (Mich. 1973), where defendant, charged with

murder, pled guilty to manslaughter and then successfully appealed that conviction, only to be charged and convicted of murder thereafter, and the court held "that upon the acceptance of a plea of guilty, as a matter of policy, the state may not thereafter charge a higher offense arising out of the same transaction":

"We recognize that a prosecutor's willingness to allow an accused person to plead to a lesser offense is generally predicated on the assumption that the accused will, upon acceptance of a plea of guilty, stand convicted and will be sentenced for the lesser offense. We also recognize that the rule we adopt means that a successful appeal from a plea-based conviction for a lesser offense defeats that legitimate expectation, deprives the prosecutor of leverage he otherwise would have in further plea bargaining upon reprosecution, may well, therefore, burden the prosecutor with the need to prove his case at a trial and at the same time limits the people to a conviction less than the proofs may justify.

"We balance these considerations against the danger that reprosecuting on higher charges those who successfully appeal from plea-based convictions and imposition of sentence based on the higher charge, will cause convicted persons to forego legitimate appeals and thereby encourage a return to practices which the carefully worked out guilty-plea procedures are designed to obviate. * * *

"By agreeing to a plea to a lesser offense the prosecutor thereby vouches that the ends of justice will be served by accepting a plea of guilty to that offense. We perceive, therefore, even in the relatively few cases where defendants will succeed on appeal in setting aside a guilty-plea-based conviction, no erosion of law enforcement in the rule we adopt."

Is the *McMiller* rule constitutionally required in light of *Green v. United States* and *Price v. Georgia,* at p. 1424 infra, or in light of *Blackledge v. Perry* and *North Carolina v. Pearce,* see Note 8 at p. 1444 infra? Is the answer to be found in *Bordenkircher v. Hayes,* p. 1185 supra? Compare *McMiller* with the prevailing view, as expressed in *United States ex rel. Williams v. McMann,* 436 F.2d 103 (2d Cir.1970):

"For us to hold that one in William's position may not be tried and sentenced upon the charge originally brought would encourage gamesmanship of a most offensive nature. Defendants would be rewarded for prevailing upon the prosecutor to accept a reduced charge and to recommend a lighter punishment in return for a guilty plea, when the defendant intended at the time he entered that plea to attack it at some future date. Although there is no suggestion in the record that Williams attempted this gambit, one way in which it might be achieved would be to plead guilty after a bargain has been struck with the prosecutor on the lesser charge and sentence. But, if the court after reading the defendant's probation report imposed a sentence higher than contemplated, the 'unbargained-for' longer sentence would then trigger proceedings to vacate the plea. Indeed, any reason the defendant could conceive for setting aside his plea and sentence would lose him little. If the defendant's argument were to prevail, then a trial on the lesser charge only could result. The defendant would thus run no risks by this maneuver for his trial could end in acquittal, but if he should be convicted, he urges he could not receive a sentence greater than that imposed on the guilty plea to the lesser offense. This is nothing more than a 'heads-I-win-tails-you-lose gamble. To frustrate this strategy, prosecutors would be restrained from entering plea bargains, thereby adding further to the staggering burdens of our criminal courts, and judges would become more rigid in exercising their discretion in favor of permitting withdrawal of a guilty plea. This would hardly enhance the administration of criminal justice." [a]

a. Considering the "gambit" mentioned in *Williams,* should it make any difference which side is trying to escape from the terms of the original agreement? In that case, it was the

11. What then if the defendant does *not* challenge the plea but instead, in a post-plea setting, fails to carry out one of the terms of the bargain? In *Brown v. State,* 367 So.2d 616 (Fla.1979), where the defendant, charged with first degree murder, entered a negotiated plea to second degree murder on the condition that he aid the state in the prosecution of his accomplice but thereafter refused to testify, the plea was then vacated and defendant was convicted of first degree murder. The court reasoned that such a result was consistent with the Supreme Court's mutuality of advantage theory of plea bargaining, expressed in *Brady v. United States,* p. 1191 supra, and that it did not constitute a violation of the defendant's double jeopardy protection. There had been no "prosecutorial or judicial overreaching," and the defendant's failure to cooperate as agreed nullified the plea just as a "prosecution is nullified by the affirmative act of a defendant, such as a motion for a mistrial or an appeal of a conviction."

UNITED STATES ex rel. THURMOND v. MANCUSI

275 F.Supp. 508 (E.D.N.Y.1967).

WEINSTEIN, DISTRICT JUDGE.

Petitioner pled guilty to the felony of attempting to sell six marijuana cigarettes. A first offender, he was sentenced in March of 1964 by the County Court, Nassau County, to a term of two and one-half to five years imprisonment. He did not appeal but commenced serving his sentence at once. After unsuccessfully seeking a writ of coram nobis in the state courts, petitioner now seeks release from Attica State Prison through a writ of habeas corpus from this Court. * * *

According to petitioner's testimony at the coram nobis hearing—testimony which was disputed in part—petitioner consistently maintained his innocence. His attorney strongly urged him on several occasions to change his plea. Petitioner testified that he was told by defense counsel that "they have a pretty tough case against you" and that "you are facing 7½ to 15 years." Petitioner steadfastly refused to plead guilty, insisting that he was going to "fight it."

Petitioner further testified that immediately before his trial started he saw his attorney talking with the Assistant District Attorney and overheard the latter say, "if your man doesn't want to cooperate, I can prosecute him to the fullest extent of the law. I can see he gets lots of time [but] if your man cooperates with me, it will go easy on him." When the conversation ended, petitioner claimed that he was told by his attorney that since he had a clean record, the Assistant District Attorney would recommend a suspended sentence if he pled guilty to an attempted sale. Petitioner still refused to change his plea.

The trial then began and one witness (the person to whom petitioner allegedly sold the marijuana) testified. Again, petitioner was urged by his attorney to plead guilty to an attempt. Finally, petitioner testified, after being assured that he would not go to prison, he agreed. The subsequent proceedings in the courtroom, as revealed by the full transcript, were as follows:

THE CLERK: Is there an application?

state which reneged on the sentence agreement, thereby prompting the defendant to move for withdrawal of his plea. Should the defendant be able to enforce the original bargain in that situation, but not where he is attempting to get something less than he originally agreed to? As to the latter situation, see *Stewart v. Cupp,* 506 P.2d 503 (Or.App.1973) (where defendant pleaded guilty to two counts in exchange for dismissal of two other counts, prosecutor cannot reinstate one of dismissed charges after defendant successfully challenged the constitutionality of the statute underlying one of his guilty pleas), and consider also *United States v. Hallam,* 472 F.2d 168 (9th Cir.1973) (where defendant, charged with felony, negotiated plea to misdemeanor on condition felony charge be dismissed, government cannot have agreement rescinded on ground that the misdemeanor charge is defective and might be challenged by defendant as soon as statute of limitations has run on the felony). Or, what if the defendant pleaded guilty to a nonexistent offense or to a related offense which includes an element that does not correspond to the actual facts? See Comment, 62 Calif.L.Rev. 258, 292 (1974).

MR. FARRELL: Application at this time, I would like to withdraw the plea of not guilty and enter a plea of guilty to attempted felonious sale of narcotics under count number one in full satisfaction of the indictment.

MR. CESTARO: Your Honor, this is acceptable to our office. May the record indicate that no promises or representations have been made concerning punishment.

THE COURT: Eliot [sic] Thurmond, do you understand what is being done?

THE DEFENDANT: Yes, sir.

THE COURT: Do you understand that you are withdrawing your plea of not guilty?

THE DEFENDANT: Yes, sir.

THE COURT: To feloniously selling a narcotic drug and you are entering a plea of guilty to attempted selling of a narcotic drug?

THE DEFENDANT: Yes, sir.

THE COURT: That is your wish?

THE DEFENDANT: Yes, sir. * * *

Petitioner claims not to have heard the District Attorney's statement that no promise had been made. As he put it, "I was upset and a little confused." The court's questions could reasonably be construed as inquiring only if defendant knew he was pleading guilty.

On the day of sentencing, petitioner's attorney, apparently assuming that sentence would be suspended, allegedly told his client, "when this is over, be sure to keep your nose clean. Stay out of trouble."

At the time of sentencing there was no inquiry with respect to the plea. Petitioner's record was characterized as "not good" by the court without indicating the basis for this conclusion. (Petitioner, it will be recalled, was a first offender.) Petitioner was sentenced to two and one-half to five years in jail. His attorney remained mute during the sentencing. Petitioner testified:

> "I was bewildered. I looked around and all I could see was [my lawyer's] back going out the door * * * I was confused. The man [court officer] grabbed me by the arm and took me out."

A few days thereafter, having been allegedly deserted by his attorney, petitioner wrote a letter to the sentencing judge from the Nassau County jail stating that he had been told by his lawyer that he would receive a suspended sentence and asking the court to investigate. * * *

In reply petitioner received a letter from the Chief Law Assistant of the Nassau County Court informing him that nothing could be done. * * *

In order to determine whether a guilty plea was made voluntarily, a two step inquiry is necessary. First, we must decide whether improper promises or threats were made by a state official to induce the plea. This finding requires a determination of what observable physical events and conversations took place—in a sense, an "objective" matter. Second, if we find that there was no such official threat or promise, we must decide whether the defendant believed such a promise or threat had been made and whether his belief "induced" the plea. The finding and standard in this second stage can be characterized as "subjective" since an inquiry into the individual defendant's state of mind is involved. * * *

This Court is bound by the clear finding in the state court, following the coram nobis hearing, that no promise was made by the District Attorney and that there was none to be broken. * * *

If, at the time he pled guilty, the defendant believed that a coercive promise or threat had been made by either the court or the prosecutor, though in fact no such promise or threat had been made, and his plea was induced by this belief, it is an involuntary and void plea. This conclusion necessarily follows from the fact that voluntariness connotes a state of mind of an actor. If the actor—i.e., the defendant—believes that a promise has been made, the effect on his state of mind is exactly the same as if such a promise had in fact been made. Thus, any test of whether a person acts voluntarily is necessarily "subjective". * * *

Although not, perhaps, of constitutional significance, we should not ignore the fact that it is as embittering to a defendant—and as destructive of possible rehabilitation—for him to falsely conclude that he was misled as it is for him to reach that conclusion correctly. Certainly, no procedure can prevent many defendants from believing that they were unfairly treated. Whatever the circumstances, many of them, brooding in their cells, will ultimately be convinced of their own purity and the impropriety of society in dealing with them. But it is not too much to expect that society will so design its criminal procedures as to satisfy itself that it has done all that it can reasonably do to be fair to the defendant and to permit the defendant to make his decision in a voluntary and uncoerced way.

A guilty plea induced by a mistaken belief that a binding plea agreement had been made is invalid even if it is the defendant's own attorney who is responsible for the defendant's mistaken belief. * * *

A clearcut statement by defense counsel that the District Attorney has made a promise, or an ambiguous remark to which the defendant gives the same meaning, has much the same psychological effect on the defendant as a promise by the District Attorney. The effect may be greater since the defendant is likely to place more trust in his own attorney than in a member of the prosecutor's staff. The statements of an attorney may even support a finding that he acted so improperly that, for constitutional purposes, defendant was denied the right of effective counsel.

It cannot always be assumed that the presence of counsel automatically insures that the defendant has not been misled into pleading guilty. Recent writings suggest that there are instances where defense counsel have considered their own rather than their clients' interest in disposing of a case by a guilty plea rather than by a long trial. Indeed, it would be especially incongruous to impute the knowledge of counsel to his client in cases in which the latter claims that it was his own attorney who misled him.

There is little merit in the state's contention that a subjective test of what the defendant believed rather than what a district attorney or judge told him is too difficult to apply. The state of a man's mind, like most other issues of fact, is decided on the basis of reasonable inferences drawn from the known surrounding facts and circumstances. * * * While a prisoner may proclaim that his prior state of mind negated the voluntariness of his plea, if it was unreasonable for him to entertain such a belief, faith in his veracity will be shattered. "[R]easonableness goes to the credibility of the accused as a matter of evidence."

Moreover, there are very practical procedural answers to the contention that a subjective test is too difficult to administer. Candor, a full record and a bona fide attempt by the trial court "to verify that the defendant's plea is the result of an intelligent and knowing choice" should not be overly burdensome.

If the inquiry is made properly in the first instance, there will be no need for extensive post-conviction hearings such as have been required in this case. Such hearings are difficult not only because of the passage of time and attenuation of evidence, but because the court cannot accept at face value the defendant's statement of what was in his mind. At the time the plea is taken, the defendant's statement of why he is pleading can be accepted and acted upon. * * *

In this case, the trial court did not conduct an inquiry to determine whether petitioner's plea was voluntary. There was no "penetrating and comprehensive examination of all the circumstances under which such a plea is tendered". * * *

Judicial notice of tensions surrounding acceptance of pleas makes it impossible to decide without a hearing that defendant understood the significance of the District Attorney's statement for the record that no promise was made. But even if the defendant did hear and did comprehend, his failure to challenge when his attorney stood mute is not conclusive evidence of acquiescence. * * *

In view of the circumstances of this case and the fact that defendant immediately wrote a letter to the court stating that he had only pled guilty because he had been told he would receive a suspended sentence, there can be no assumption that the plea was valid. * * *

The hearing before this Court will determine whether the petitioner believed at the time he pled guilty that coercive threats or promises had been made by the state to induce his plea. * * *

FOLLOWING HEARING

The following constitutes the Court's findings of fact and conclusions of law based upon the documents submitted by the state in its return and supplemental returns, argument by counsel, and testimony and exhibits at the evidentiary hearing: * * *

(5) It is probable that petitioner had no belief that if he pled guilty he was assured of a suspended sentence. Petitioner's own witnesses testified to this effect. His uncle stated that petitioner had said that "he was pleading guilty because his lawyer had told him that he would probably get a suspended sentence." Another uncle, speaking of the same conversation, testified that petitioner had said, "I think I will get a suspended sentence." It is highly probable that petitioner believed that a suspended sentence was likely. It is highly probable that petitioner was surprised by the sentence. The Court finds that at the time he pled guilty petitioner did not believe that the state, any of its representatives, or his own trial counsel, promised a suspended sentence or any kind of specific sentence if he pled guilty.

[Judge Weinstein then found that petitioner had been denied his right to appeal, and the judgment of conviction was vacated on that ground.]

Notes and Questions

1. Those cases in which a defendant, after pleading guilty, received a sentence greater than that he subjectively expected are not all of a kind. One situation is that in which the defendant had no belief that there was a plea bargain, but yet expected a lesser sentence because of what his attorney said. Such a case is *Wellnitz v. Page,* 420 F.2d 935 (10th Cir.1970), where the court stated that "an attorney may offer his client a prediction, based upon his experience or instinct, of the sentence possibilities the accused should weigh in determining upon a plea. An erroneous sentence estimate by defense counsel does not render a plea involuntary. And a defendant's erroneous expectation, based on his attorney's erroneous estimate, likewise does not render a plea involuntary."

2. Another situation is that in which the defendant is specifically but erroneously advised by his counsel that there exists a plea bargain including a particular commitment. Such a case is *Ex parte Griffin,* 679 S.W.2d 15 (Tex.Crim.App.1984), holding that "a plea of guilty is invalid if it is induced by defense counsel's direct misrepresentation that the State has made a concession which in fact was not part of the plea agreement." The court explained: "While this is not a broken bargain under *Santobello v. New York,* it is nevertheless clear that applicant's plea was not knowing and intelligent under the

standard of *Brady v. United States,*" p. 1191 supra.

3. What then of a case which falls somewhere between these two, in that the defense attorney did not specifically state that there was a plea agreement but the defendant claims that he interpreted the attorney's remarks as meaning there was one? In *United States ex rel. LaFay v. Fritz,* 455 F.2d 297 (2d Cir.1972), district judge Weinstein applied his *Thurmond* subjective test to another set of facts and concluded that, while no promises had actually been made by the prosecutor or court, the petitioner was entitled to relief because he believed the judge had promised a maximum of five years as a consequence of his counsel's observation that counsel had "an indication or an intimation" that "the Judge thought that five years was an adequate minimum sentence." But the court of appeals reversed, relying on *Welnitz* and opining that the *Thurmond* subjective test "would seem to be contrary to the law of this circuit." Is this a satisfactory resolution of the matter? Is the point, as *LaFay* was later construed in *United States ex rel. Curtis v. Zelker,* 466 F.2d 1092 (2d Cir. 1972), that "a defendant's mistaken subjective impressions gained from conference with his legal counsel, in the absence of substantial objective proof showing that they were reasonably justified, do not provide sufficient grounds upon which to set aside his guilty plea"?

4. As indicated in *Thurmond,* if the defendant's belief is based upon representations by his own counsel, the court may find that the defendant did not have the effective assistance of counsel. Such a result was reached in *State v. Tunender,* 157 N.W.2d 165 (Neb.1968), where defendant (who received a sentence of 18 months) testified his attorney promised him probation outright, and his attorney's "versions of the odds stated to defendant climbed from possibility to strong chance to probability." Questioning of counsel at the post-conviction hearing produced the following: "Q. * * * Did you, or did you not, say it was all cut and dried? Did you make that statement in those * * * particular words? * * * A. I may have probably said something to that effect; of course your words of 'Cut and dried' are more or less strong talk."

Does this constitute ineffective assistance of counsel sufficient for relief under the two-part test of *Strickland v. Washington,* p. 143 supra? Cf. *Hill v. Lockhart,* p. 1250 infra. Does such a holding, as urged in a *Tunender* dissent, present the risk that "the fear of a tarnished professional reputation may become more compelling than the best interests of the indigent defendant"? Is it true, as claimed by another of the dissenting justices, that the same criticism made against the original attorney "may well be made of the second attorney who, after much effort, succeeds in getting the original judgment of conviction set aside, and upon a retrial not only sees his client again convicted but also facing a longer period of incarceration than he was subject to in the first instance"?

5. Enker, in *Task Force Report: The Courts* at 111, notes: "One further type of plea bargain merits attention. This may be called the 'tacit bargain.' In this instance, there are no formal or explicit negotiations between the defense and the prosecution. Defendant, aware of an established practice in the court to show leniency to defendants who plead guilty, pleads guilty to the charges in the expectation that he will be so treated. This expectation is almost invariably satisfied without the need to enter into any negotiations or make any explicit promises."

6. It is improper for the trial judge to make known the "established practice," such as by announcing in open court that a certain defendant's sentence would have been lower had he pleaded guilty? Consider the position of Chief Judge Bazelon in *Scott v. United States,* p. 1180 supra:

"In this case the trial judge did not bargain with the defendant. Indeed he did not even point out that he might be more lenient with a defendant who pleaded guilty until after trial. But in so stating at the sentencing hearing he announced to all future defendants the guidelines in his court room. We cannot approve of these guidelines for the same reasons that we could not condone actual plea bargaining by a trial judge. The policy announced by the trial judge may not endanger his actual impartiality at trials as much as his participation in plea bargaining sessions might. And we certainly do not criticize the impartiality displayed by the experienced trial judge in this case. But we cannot ignore the impact of such a policy on the appearance of justice to criminal defendants and their ability to choose wisely between a plea of guilty and an exercise of their right to trial.

"In recognizing that an announced policy of differential sentencing presents some of the same dangers as conventional plea bargaining, we do not, as the concurring opinion suggests, equate the two practices. Overt plea bargaining by a trial judge places direct and immediate pressure upon the defendant to forego his right to a trial. An announced policy of differential sentencing which distinguishes between defendants who demand a trial and those who do not presents an inducement to plead guilty which may be less coercive in the individual case, but which nevertheless must affect the decision to exercise the constitutional right to a trial."

SECTION 3. PROFESSIONAL RESPONSIBILITY; THE ROLE OF PROSECUTOR AND DEFENSE COUNSEL

In ANDERSON v. NORTH CAROLINA, 221 F.Supp. 930 (W.D.N.C.1963), a federal habeas corpus proceeding, the following facts were established by an evidentiary hearing: Counsel was appointed for Anderson when he was indicted for the capital crime of rape; Anderson appeared with counsel at arraignment and entered a plea of not guilty at 11:30 a.m. on December 14, 1961; that afternoon, the Solicitor and members of his staff talked with Anderson in jail in the absence of his counsel but with counsel's consent; the Solicitor indicated to Anderson that he would face the probability of a death sentence unless he agreed to plead guilty to the lesser offense of assault with intent to rape, in which case he could not be imprisoned more than 15 years and in all probability would receive a sentence of 2 to 3 or 3 to 5 years; at 4:30 p.m. the same day Anderson appeared in court again and entered a plea to the lesser offense, answering in the affirmative to the court's inquiry as to whether the plea was entered "freely and voluntarily, knowing the probability is you will get an extended prison term"; defense counsel then addressed the court asking for leniency, but the court sentenced Anderson to a term of 12–15 years. CRAVEN, C.J. held:

"The right to counsel is not merely a matter of form. It can be waived by the defendant—but not by his counsel. It is, therefore, irrelevant that counsel may have consented for the Solicitor to conduct—in counsel's absence—what amounted to a pre-trial conference with the prisoner in jail. Unquestionably, the most important part of the proceedings against Anderson occurred in jail—when his counsel was not present to advise him. It was at that time and place that the decision was made to plead guilty to the lesser felony. Otherwise, he would not have been returned to the courtroom—for the jury had long since gone, and his trial had been set for the next term. What happened in the courtroom was to merely make a formal record of a decision arrived at upstairs in jail in a conference between the Solicitor and the defendant. Counsel's presence at the sentencing (he was sent for by the Solicitor) does not give it validity. The most he could have done was to ratify a decision previously made. More than this is implicit in the right to counsel: petitioner was entitled to have counsel aid and help him *in making the decision.* * * *

"The constitutional validity of the time-honored compromise plea is assumed for purposes of this opinion. But, a compromise necessarily involves negotiation, and here Anderson was without the assistance of his lawyer in negotiating the compromise with the Solicitor. * * *

"Unquestionably petitioner Anderson could not bargain on equal terms with the Solicitor. The conference in the jail was inherently unfair, and the agreement made there infects all subsequent proceedings.

"It is idle to speculate whether petitioner's counsel could have, if present, worked out a better deal with the Solicitor. The point is Anderson was entitled to have him *try.* For lack of effective counsel at a 'critical' stage of the proceedings against him, those proceedings are constitutionally defective." [a]

Notes and Questions

1. Compare *People v. Bowman,* 239 N.E.2d 433 (Ill.1968), where an indigent defendant was charged with burglary. Appointed counsel appeared with defendant at the preliminary hearing and indicated defendant did not waive grand jury indictment. Later that day, defendant participated in negotiations directly with the county sheriff, who assured defendant that if he entered a plea of guilty the three burglary charges pending in other counties would be dropped and the prosecution would recommend a sentence of three to five years. Defendant said he "wanted to plead and get it over with," so he was taken into court the next day. In the interim, the sheriff attempted to contact defendant's attorney, but was unsuccessful because the attorney was out of town. In court, defendant waived indictment and pleaded guilty; the court took note of the fact that defendant's counsel was not present, and permitted defendant to proceed only after defendant stated three times that he wished to plead without his attorney. The defendant's plea was accepted, and he thereafter received a sentence of three to five years. On appeal, the court characterized the issue as involving "the correlative right of the accused to proceed *pro se* if he freely and understandingly chooses to do so," and then found that defendant had made such a choice.

Did the majority correctly state the issue, or is Justice Schaefer, dissenting, correct in saying that the issue is "whether the defendant was denied the effective assistance of counsel when the sheriff, in the absence of the defendant's attorney and without notice to him, engaged in plea negotiations with the defendant"? Is this case distinguishable from *Anderson* in that, as the majority pointed out, "[c]onsidering the presence of a confession as to the validity of which no substantial challenge is made, a prior record of two burglary convictions, the pending escape charge and the burglary charges in the three adjoining counties, it is difficult to envision prosecution agreement to any arrangement more advantageous to petitioner"?

2. Waiver of counsel by a guilty plea defendant must meet the standards for an "intelligent and competent" waiver described at p. 121 supra. What weight should be given to defendant's expressed desire to plead guilty in determining whether his waiver of counsel was valid? Where defendant was informed of the charge against him and told of his right to appointed counsel, does his reply that he desires to plead guilty establish a valid waiver? See *People v. Dunn,* 158 N.W.2d 404 (Mich.1968) (waiver of counsel need not be in "express form" and expression

a. *A.B.A. Code of Prof. Resp.* D.R. 7–104 reads: "(A) During the course of his representation of a client a lawyer shall not: (1) Communicate or cause another to communicate on the subject of the representation with a party he knows to be represented by a lawyer in that matter unless he has the prior consent of the lawyer representing such other party or is authorized by law to do so. (2) Give advice to a person who is not represented by a lawyer, other than the advice to secure counsel, if the interests of such person are or have a reasonable possibility of being in conflict with the interests of his client."

of desire to plead guilty sufficient). But compare, *Von Moltke v. Gilies,* discussed at p. 121 supra. Even if the defendant is told of all of the factors relating to the charge required by *Von Moltke,* and he expressly waives counsel, is that satisfactory if he is not also told what counsel might accomplish through plea negotiations even if there is no trial?

3. A few states do not permit felony defendants to plead guilty without counsel. Consider Note, 112 U.Pa.L.Rev. 865, 889 (1964): "One can seriously question whether a defendant who pleads guilty should ever be permitted to waive counsel. The need for an attorney may be more dramatically perceived in the trial context, but at least in that situation there may be some tactical advantage for a defendant to be unrepresented—the court and the jury may be more sympathetically disposed toward a layman contending with an accomplished legal expert. In the guilty plea context, however, there is nothing for a defendant to gain by being unrepresented—in fact, the very decision to plead guilty and waive the right to trial requires an evaluation of the prosecution's case, something at which a layman is inept. The right to an attorney interested in protecting the interests of the defendant is such a substantial factor in the guilty plea procedure that it is difficult to imagine a situation that would warrant a finding of an informed waiver of that right." Does *Faretta v. California,* p. 122 supra, require a different assessment?

NOTES ON THE PROFESSIONAL RESPONSIBILITY OF DEFENSE COUNSEL

1. Consider the following excerpts from the *A.B.A. Code of Prof. Resp.* Ethical Consideration 7–7 provides in part: "A defense lawyer in a criminal case has the duty to advise his client fully on whether a particular plea to a charge appears to be desirable, * * * but it is for the client to decide what plea should be entered." Ethical Consideration 7–9 reads in part: "A lawyer should advise his client of the possible effect of each legal alternative. A lawyer should bring to bear upon this decision-making process the fullness of his experience as well as his objective viewpoint. * * * He may emphasize the possibility of harsh consequence that might result from assertion of legally permissible positions."

2. In *McLaughlin v. Royster,* 346 F.Supp. 297 (E.D.Va.1972), the court observed: "It appears to this Court that the primary foundation upon which rests the rule that a voluntary guilty plea is not subject to attack is that a defendant entering such a plea does so assisted and informed by adequate counsel. The constitutional requirement is not satisfied upon a perfunctory appearance by counsel who does nothing whatever before or during trial to advise a client or to protect his rights except to acquiesce with the client's wishes. Perfunctory or hand-holding representation is simply not consistent with the right to counsel. A client's professed desire to plead guilty is not the end of an attorney's responsibility. When a defendant convicts himself in open court the Constitution recognizes that the critical stage of adjudication has proceeded for the most part outside the courtroom. That process contemplates the pursuit by counsel of factual and legal theories in order to reach a conclusion as to whether a contest would best serve the attorney's client's interest. In short, effective representation when a guilty plea is contemplated to a great extent entails affirmative action on the part of counsel."

Compare *Wilson v. State,* 291 N.E.2d 570 (Ind.App.1973), where the court, in response to a guilty plea defendant's claim that his counsel did not investigate the facts or interview witnesses, concluded that such failures did not constitute incompetence, as counsel represented "his client as he was directed" in that defendant told counsel "he wanted to get off with the least amount he could."

3. Stolen property was found in an illegal search of Heirens' residence, and as a result of a "truth serum" illegally given to him he confessed to several burglaries and three murders, with which he was then charged. His attorneys, employed by his parents, investigated the case and concluded an insanity defense would not likely succeed and that there was some chance Heirens could get the death penalty. The attorneys and parents, to whom Heirens had admitted the murders, agreed that the best course was plea discussions. The prosecutor said that if Heirens would plead guilty and make a complete confession to the murders, he would recommend concurrent life sentences. After his attorneys and parents met with him, Heirens agreed to this disposition, and he thereafter pleaded guilty to the three murders and to 26 additional charges of various burglaries, robberies and assaults. Then, as reported in *People v. Heirens,* 122 N.E.2d 231 (Ill.1954):

"Prior to the pronouncement of sentence the prosecutor and the principal defense attorney addressed the court. The State's Attorney in his remarks acknowledged the 'co-operative assistance' of defense counsel and observed: 'The small likelihood of a successful murder prosecution of William Heirens early prompted the State's Attorney's office to seek out and obtain the co-operative help of defense counsel and, through them, that of their client. * * * Without the aid of the defense we would to this day have no answer for the death of Josephine Ross. Without their aid, to this day a great and sincere public doubt might remain as to the guilt of William Heirens in the killing of Suzanne Degnan and Frances Brown'. Petitioner's attorney then proceeded to state to the court the reasons which impelled him and his cocounsel to adopt the course they followed. He remarked in part: 'I have no memory of any case, certainly not in my time at the bar, when counsel on both sides were so perplexed as to the mental status of an individual and the causes which motivated him to do certain acts. In those cases we both sought psychiatrists in the hope that they might aid us. I must confess that at this time there exists in my mind many doubts as to this defendant's mental capacity for crime; and I believe doubt must exist in our minds as to just what the relation of cause and effect was, and how he could, in a manner so devoid of feeling, do the acts here charged and upon which the plea has been guilty. On acquiring knowledge, your Honor, of the facts we were further notified at a later date of his mental condition. We were collectively agreed that any thought on the part of the State to cause this man to forfeit his life would be unjust. It would be unfair. By the same token we were collectively agreed that any course on our part which would assist in having him returned to society would be equally unfair.' "

In later post-conviction proceedings, Heirens claimed his attorneys had not given him effective assistance because "their recommendation to plead guilty was made from motives of public duty as well as those of duty to their client." The court rejected this contention and asserted that although Heirens "was young, emotionally unstable and unusually susceptible to suggestions, he was of normal intelligence and able to make his own decisions."

4. In *United States v. Rogers,* 289 F.Supp. 726 (D.Conn.1968), the defendant was charged under three federal statutes for a single alleged sale of narcotics. Defendant told his retained counsel that he was innocent of the crimes charged and that he had two witnesses who could testify he did not make the sale, but admitted that he was a convicted felon and that the two witnesses were narcotic addicts. Counsel received a bill of particulars indicating that the alleged sale was made to a named government agent at a specified time and place. Thereafter, counsel learned that the government would be willing to dismiss the two counts which carried a mandatory minimum sentence of

five years if defendant would plead guilty to the count which carried a two year minimum. Counsel so advised the defendant, and despite the defendant's consistent protestations of innocence recommended that it was in defendant's best interest to plead guilty because the government agent's testimony would be given great credibility while the testimony of defendant and his two friends would not be believed. The attorney added that the decision was up to the defendant. Defendant entered a plea of guilty as recommended, but prior to sentencing (and just after learning that the government agent had been arrested for counterfeiting) he moved to withdraw the plea. Judge Timbers, in ruling for the defendant, observed:

"Trial counsel doubtless believed that he was acting in the best interest of his client in recommending a guilty plea. A plea bargain had been struck. It was reasonable to assume that a jury would more likely believe a government agent than a convicted felon and narcotics addicts. But to this Court it appears utterly unreasonable for counsel to recommend a guilty plea to a defendant without first cautioning him that, no matter what, he should not plead guilty unless he believed himself guilty. Most certainly such a recommendation should not be made when the defendant in the past has maintained his innocence and has stated that he has two witnesses whom counsel has not attempted to interview. It may well have been trial counsel's opinion that even if defendant were innocent he would still be convicted. Such a view is not only cynical but unwarranted. Innocent men in the past have been convicted; but such instances have been so rare and our judicial system has so many safeguards that no lawyer worthy of his profession justifiably may assume that an innocent person will be convicted."

Assuming *Rogers* to be a case in which the defendant was innocent but there was a strong probability of conviction, and *Heirens* to be a case in which the defendant was guilty but (as acknowledged by the state's attorney) there was a "small likelihood" of conviction, who acted more "unethically," Rogers' attorney or Heirens' attorneys? Reconsider *Rogers* in light of *North Carolina v. Alford,* p. 1235 infra; and compare *Williams v. State,* 349 N.W.2d 58 (S.D.1984), where the defendant claimed he had received ineffective assistance of counsel because his attorney influenced him to enter into a plea bargain despite his protestations of innocence: "From his study of police records and interviews, counsel apparently concluded that a conviction was likely, and despite appellant's protestations of innocence. We are not convinced that counsel's perception of the acquittal odds was incorrect. Having formed such a conclusion, defense counsel committed no error in telling this to his client and recommending that he plead guilty in the hope of lenient sentence."

5. In *People v. Whitfield,* 239 N.E.2d 850 (Ill.1968), where defendant was charged with murder, the state's attorney advised defense counsel that he would accept a plea of guilty to manslaughter and recommend probation. Defense counsel "thought he could win the case," so he did not advise defendant of this offer and later told the state's attorney that his client would not plead guilty. Defendant was convicted and received a sentence of 14 to 18 years. On appeal, the court reversed:

"A defendant has * * * the right to decide whether to plead not guilty. These rights and others go beyond trial strategy. [See Note 3, p. 131 supra]. It follows logically that if a defendant has the right to make a decision to plead not guilty, he also has the right to make the decision to plead guilty. Due process demands this protection." [a]

a. Consider also *United States ex rel. Simon v. Murphy,* 349 F.Supp. 818 (E.D.Pa.1972), holding that where defendant's attorney agreed to represent her on a contingent fee basis, with the balance to be paid out of life insurance proceeds which the defendant could receive only if she was

Does it follow logically? Would it make any difference if the defendant had previously insisted upon his innocence, and counsel believes that if he learned of the offer he would unwisely decide to plead guilty? Or, what if defense counsel believes that the prosecutor is being unduly lenient, contrary to the best interests of his client? Consider Enker, in *Task Force Report, The Courts* at 111: "[D]efense counsel, perhaps in part because of legitimate skepticism over the availability of meaningful correctional treatment and of doubts as to the fairness of such programs, seem to regard their duty to the client solely in terms of obtaining for him as lenient a sentence as possible. Perhaps a broader view of the lawyer's role should include within the counseling function the duty to attempt to make the client aware of the fact that he has a problem and of his need for some correctional program. Thus far, however, lawyers have preferred to avoid the welfare implications of their role as counselors and the conflicts this role would create and to limit their role to getting the client 'as good a deal' as they can."

6. Does it follow from *Whitfield* that defense counsel always (or, sometimes) has an obligation to sound out the prosecutor as to what concessions would be granted in exchange for a plea of guilty by his client? In *United States ex rel. Tillman v. Alldredge,* 350 F.Supp. 189 (E.D.Pa.1972), petitioner, convicted after a plea of not guilty and sentenced to a mandatory minimum of five years for a narcotics sale, contended that "he was denied the effective assistance of counsel by his attorney's failure to explore the possibility of * * * a plea bargain." The court responded:

"An attorney is in a sensitive area, and he must carefully weigh a number of considerations, when he broaches the subject of a guilty plea to a client who asserts that he is innocent. The subject has been very recently considered in American Bar Association's Project on Standards for Criminal Justice. In Part VI of the Approved Draft of Standards Relating to the Prosecution Function and the Defense Function, the Committee proposed the following guidelines:

" '6.1 Duty to explore disposition without trial

* * *

" '(b) When the lawyer concludes, on the basis of full investigation and study, that under controlling law and the evidence, a conviction is probable, he should so advise the accused and seek his consent to engage in plea discussions with the prosecutor, if such appears desirable.

" '(c) Ordinarily the lawyer should secure his client's consent before engaging in plea discussions with the prosecutor.'

"Trial counsel's testimony at the hearing before me made it quite clear that Tillman, apparently insisting that he was innocent of all charges, 'didn't wish to plead guilty to anything.' Since it is Tillman's burden to establish ineffective assistance of counsel, it was incumbent on him to present evidence that trial counsel was aware, before trial, of facts and circumstances indicating that a conviction was probable. An effort by the court to elicit such evidence was thwarted by Tillman's present counsel. * * *

"In the absence of evidence as to what Tillman might have told his trial attorney about his involvement in the charges, all that appears is Tillman's apparent insistence to trial counsel that he was innocent and that he 'didn't wish to plead guilty to anything.' Under such circumstances I cannot say that counsel's failure to suggest to Tillman that he should consider entering a guilty plea constituted ineffective assistance of counsel. Petitioner's present

acquitted of the charge of killing her husband, and counsel did not communicate a tendered plea bargain to her, the contingent fee arrangement created a conflict of interest to the prejudice of the defendant, notwithstanding the fact that she relied upon a self-defense claim throughout the trial.

counsel has cited no case authority for the proposition he urges, and in the absence of such authority, I am not prepared to hold that an attorney who fails to explore the possibility of a plea bargain on behalf of a client who insists that he is innocent, has represented his client ineffectively."

Would the result have been different if Tillman had made a showing that his trial counsel knew that conviction was probable? If there had been no such showing, but Tillman had not asserted that he did not wish to plead guilty? Consider the fact that in the second edition of the *A.B.A. Standards* the language quoted above has been replaced by the following, now designated § 4–6.1(b): "A lawyer may engage in plea discussions with the prosecutor, although ordinarily the client's consent to engage in such discussions should be obtained in advance. Under no circumstances should a lawyer recommend to a defendant acceptance of a plea unless a full investigation and study of the case has been completed, including an analysis of controlling law and the evidence likely to be introduced at trial."

7. Attorney Hardin was appointed to represent both Brown and Ruffin, who were charged with participating in the same felony-murder. At separate trials they were convicted and sentenced to death. Hardin had negotiated with the prosecutor concerning a plea bargain for Brown which would have required Brown to testify against Ruffin, but for some reason the agreement collapsed. In *Ruffin v. Kemp,* 767 F.2d 748 (11th Cir.1985), the court held that Ruffin had established (i) actual conflict of interest and (ii) a resulting adverse effect upon his attorney's performance, as required by *Strickland v. Washington,* p. 143 supra, so as to be entitled to relief on habeas corpus. "While Hardin was negotiating for a plea bargain for Brown, having offered Brown's testimony against Ruffin, he could not at the same time effectively negotiate a plea bargain for Ruffin and offer Ruffin's testimony against Brown as part of the deal." Because "actual prejudice need not be shown" in a conflict of interest situation, as compared to other ineffective assistance of counsel claims, the court added, it sufficed that "the evidence in this case does establish that the prosecutor was open to plea bargain negotiations"; Ruffin need not "show that the prosecutor probably would have accepted such a plea bargain on Ruffin's behalf."

8. Defense counsel may influence a guilty plea by a particular defendant because it would be to the advantage of another defendant also being represented by him. See, e.g., *United States v. Truglio,* 493 F.2d 574 (4th Cir.1974) (where Truglio was charged with four others and attorney Pietranton, representing all five defendants, successfully urged Truglio to plead guilty in conformance with a deal worked out with the prosecutor concerning all defendants, Truglio was denied effective assistance of counsel, as it "is quite understandable that having obtained what he considered to be a favorable bargain for all of the defendants Pietranton would be somewhat more than reluctant to see the bargain collapse in its entirety by Truglio's insistence that the trial continue"); *Commonwealth v. Breaker,* 318 A.2d 354 (Pa.1974) (where one Mangold was arrested while committing a burglary and thereafter confessed to several other burglaries and implicated others, including Breaker, in the hope of favorable treatment, and Mangold's attorney represented Breaker when he pleaded guilty, there was a sufficient "possibility of harm" that the plea cannot stand, as "to build a record of cooperation, Mangold's attorney would necessarily desire as many guilty pleas as possible to be entered").

NEWMAN v. UNITED STATES

127 U.S.App.D.C. 263, 382 F.2d 479 (1967).

BURGER, CIRCUIT JUDGE: * * *

Appellant and one Anderson were indicted for housebreaking and petty larceny. Negotiations between Anderson's counsel and an Assistant United States Attorney led to Anderson's being allowed to plead guilty to misdemeanors of petty larceny and attempted housebreaking. The United States Attorney declined to consent to the same plea for Appellant. The essence of Appellant's claim on appeal is that the United States Attorney's conduct denied him due process, "equal standing" and equal protection. * * *

The issue in this Court, of course, must be resolved on the basis of the constitutional powers of the Executive. Few subjects are less adapted to judicial review than the exercise by the Executive of his discretion in deciding when and whether to institute criminal proceedings, or what precise charge shall be made, or whether to dismiss a proceeding once brought.

The United States Attorney, under the direction and control of the Attorney General, is the attorney for the Executive, charged with faithful execution of the laws, protection of the interests of the United States, and prosecution of offenses against the United States. As such, he must have broad discretion. * * *

An attorney for the United States, as any other attorney, however, appears in a dual role. He is at once an officer of the court and the agent and attorney for a client; in the first capacity he is responsible to the Court for the manner of his conduct of a case, i.e., his demeanor, deportment and ethical conduct; but in his second capacity, as agent and attorney for the Executive, he is responsible to his principal and the courts have no power over the exercise of his discretion or his motives as they relate to the execution of his duty within the framework of his professional employment. * * *

To say that the United States Attorney must literally treat every offense and every offender alike is to delegate him an impossible task; of course this concept would negate discretion. Myriad factors can enter into the prosecutor's decision. Two persons may have committed what is precisely the same legal offense but the prosecutor is not compelled by law, duty or tradition to treat them the same as to charges. On the contrary, he is expected to exercise discretion and common sense to the end that if, for example, one is a young first offender and the other older, with a criminal record, or one played a lesser and the other a dominant role, one the instigator and the other a follower, the prosecutor can and should take such factors into account; no court has any jurisdiction to inquire into or review his decision.

It is assumed that the United States Attorney will perform his duties and exercise his powers consistent with his oaths; and while this discretion is subject to abuse or misuse just as is judicial discretion, deviations from his duty as an agent of the Executive are to be dealt with by his superiors.

The remedy lies ultimately within the establishment where power and discretion reside. The President has abundant supervisory and disciplinary powers—including summary dismissal—to deal with misconduct of his subordinates; it is not the function of the judiciary to review the exercise of executive discretion whether it be that of the President himself or those to whom he has delegated certain of his powers.[9]

Affirmed.

BAZELON, CHIEF JUDGE (concurring in affirmance): * * * Appellant made no attempt to establish the reasons for the different treatment, and so it is impossible for him to maintain that the difference was

9. The concurring opinion would reserve judicial power to review "irrational" decisions of the prosecutor. We do our assigned task of appellate review best if we stay within our own limits, recognizing that we are neither omnipotent so as to have our mandates run without limit, nor omniscient so as to be able to direct all branches of government. The Constitution places on the Executive the duty to see that the "laws are faithfully executed" and the responsibility must reside with that power.

irrational or otherwise unconstitutional. Therefore, I join the majority in holding that the Assistant United States Attorney did not act unconstitutionally in this case. I have not considered any of the other statements in the majority opinion because they go very far beyond the necessities of this frivolous case.

Notes and Questions

1. Compare Alschuler, *The Prosecutor's Role in Plea Bargaining,* 36 U.Chi.L.Rev. 50, 105 (1968): "This argument reaches what should be an empirical conclusion by pulling on the bootstraps of a legal theory. Even as a matter of theory, moreover, the argument seems unsound. It leaps from the prosecutor's traditional power to exercise a unilateral discretion to the conclusion that he may also engage in bilateral exchanges: he may trade his unilateral discretion for a defendant's waiver of his constitutional rights. Under traditional law, prosecutors are usually trusted to evaluate the extent of the public interest in particular prosecutions, but they usually have nothing to gain by agreeing to a lenient disposition for a particular defendant. In plea negotiations, however, prosecutors gain something of value for deciding that a certain punishment is adequate, and there may therefore be greater reason for mistrust."

2. Is the court in *Newman* saying it will *never* review a prosecutor's plea bargaining policies? What, for example, would the court have done if Newman had established that he and Anderson played the same role in the crime and that their backgrounds were essentially the same? Should equal protection issues which arise in this context be viewed any differently than those which arise out of the prosecutor's charging policies, discussed at p. 933 supra? See *United States v. Bell,* 506 F.2d 207 (D.C.Cir.1974).[a]

3. A more common problem may be that the prosecutor will offer equally lenient bargains to defendants whose situations are only superficially similar, contrary to the public interest. There is a "possibility of inadequate knowledge of the facts, either as to the crime itself or the defendant's background, on the part of the prosecutor who negotiates the guilty plea. Under the pressure of a heavy, time-consuming caseload, the prosecutor may easily be seduced at an early stage of the proceedings, before such facts are more fully developed, by the offer of a quick guilty plea in exchange for a light sentence, only to discover too late that the offense, or the offender, was far more serious than originally thought." Enker, in *Task Force Report, The Courts* at 110–11. What is the solution to this problem?

4. To what extent should the prosecutor's willingness to bargain be contingent upon the views of the crime victim? Consider the federal Victim and Witness Protection Act of 1982, which provides that "the victim of a serious crime, or in the case of a minor child or a homicide, the family of the victim, shall be consulted by the attorney for the Government in order to obtain the views of the victim or family about the disposition of any Federal criminal case brought as a result of such crime, including the views of the victim or family about * * * plea negotiations." Section 6(a)(5) of the Act, in note to 18 U.S.C. § 1512. This, it has been suggested, may mean that the prosecutor is "obligated to consult the victim and to transmit the victim's views to the court, especially if they differ from the prosecution's. If the prosecutor does not do so, the court may decide that its discretion encompasses hearing the victim's views and even permitting him to appear at the hearing on the dismissal or guilty plea. In short, although the statute does not explicitly confer upon the victim a right to a hearing at

a. Consider also *Complaint of Rook,* 556 P.2d 1351 (Or.1976), upholding the disciplining of a prosecutor who refused to plea bargain with defendants, as long as they were represented by certain attorneys, on the same basis as previously offered another defendant.

such stages, the trial judge, at the request of the victim, probably may compel the prosecutor to do his duty under the statute." A. Goldstein, *The Victim and Prosecutorial Discretion: The Federal Victim and Witness Protection Act of 1982*, 47 Law & Contemp.Prob. 225, 232–33 (1984).[b]

5. Is it "unethical" for the prosecutor to bluff about the strength of his case during plea negotiations? Consider Alschuler, supra, at 66–67:

"It is especially difficult to check the prosecutor's bluff when he resorts to deliberate misrepresentation in an effort to sustain it. A Houston defense attorney recalls a case in which negotiations had broken down. Suddenly the prosecutor offered to recommend an award of probation if the defendant would plead guilty.

"The defense attorney, who had attempted unsuccessfully to locate the prosecuting witness for more than a year, thought that he knew what lay behind the prosecutor's offer. He replied, 'So you can't find your witness. I'll take probation when I see her in the courtroom.'

"The prosecutor answered, 'If she has to come in, we'll try the case. But I had her served yesterday, and you can check the return if you like.'

"The defense attorney checked, and it was as the prosecutor had reported. But the defense attorney was not Little Red Riding Hood; he suspected that the process server had been made a party to the bluff and had filed a fraudulent return. He therefore refused the prosecutor's offer, and the case was dismissed.

"Cases of missing or reluctant witnesses are not the only situations in which prosecutors may resort to bluffing. A Philadelphia prosecutor says, 'I would never tell a defense attorney that the red material on the defendant's undershorts was someone's blood when I knew the material was paint.[c] But I have sometimes misrepresented the facts in an effort to induce the compromise of constitutional defenses. In plea bargaining, the rule is *caveat emptor*, lawyer.' "

Defense attorneys also engage in bluffing at the plea negotiation stage. Are the responsibilities of the prosecutor in this regard different than those of the defense counsel?[d] Compare their responsibilities as to disclosure before trial, dealt with in Chapter 20 of this Book.

6. Fambo was charged with two counts of possession of an explosive substance with intent to use the same unlawfully, based upon alleged possession of a tube of dynamite on Nov. 29 and Dec. 1. After plea negotiations, those charges were dropped when Fambo pleaded guilty to the lesser offense of possessing an incendiary device. It later came to light that the prosecutor had known that prior to the second possession police had removed the dynamite from the tube and replaced it with sawdust, and on habeas corpus Fambo claimed this invalidated his plea. Applying *United States v. Agurs*, p. 1148 supra, the court in *Fambo v. Smith*, 433 F.Supp. 590 (W.D.N.Y.1977), aff'd, 565 F.2d 233 (2d Cir.1977) decided the prosecutor had acted improperly. "In order to maintain the integrity of the plea bargaining process and to assure that a guilty plea entered by a defendant is done so voluntari-

b. Consider also Ind.Code Ann. § 35–5–6–1.5(a), declaring that a prosecutor who recommends a plea bargain to the court must first "(1) Inform the victim that he has entered into discussions with defense counsel or the court concerning a recommendation; (2) Inform the victim of the contents of the recommendation before it is filed; and (3) Notify the victim so that he might be present, when the court considers the recommendation."

c. The reference is to *Miller v. Pate*, 386 U.S. 1, 87 S.Ct. 785, 17 L.Ed.2d 690 (1967) (prosecutor's misrepresentation resulted in denial of due process). See also Note 1, p. 1158 supra.

d. Or, are some forms of "bluffing" improper on both sides? *A.B.A. Stanrdards* § 3–4.1(c) provides: "It is unprofessional conduct for a prosecutor knowingly to make false statements or representations in the course of plea discussions with defense counsel or the accused." *A.B.A. Standards* § 4–6.2 reads: "It is unprofessional conduct for a lawyer knowingly to make false statements concerning the evidence in the course of plea discussions with the prosecutor."

ly, knowingly and intelligently, a prosecutor has a duty, during the course of plea bargaining, to disclose to the defendant evidence that is as clearly exculpatory of certain elements of the crime charged as is the contested evidence in this case." But the court then concluded this was harmless error, as Fambo could have been convicted on the first count and of an attempt with respect to the second count (both more serious offenses than the one to which he pleaded), and "there was thus sufficient mutuality of advantage to support this bargain."

7. Jones was charged with first degree robbery and related offenses arising out of the robbery of Rodriguez. After plea negotiations, Jones pleaded guilty to third degree robbery in full satisfaction of the indictment, but he later moved to withdraw his plea on the ground the prosecutor had failed to disclose that Rodriguez had died. In affirming denial of the motion, the court in *People v. Jones,* 375 N.E.2d 41 (N.Y.1978), after first concluding that *Agurs* was not controlling because the death of a witness was not "evidence," reasoned:

"Counsel cite no reported case, nor has our independent research disclosed any, in which judicial attention has been focused on the failure of a prosecutor before trial or during plea negotiations to disclose nonevidentiary information pertinent to the tactical aspects of a defendant's determination not to proceed to trial. No particularized rule can or need be laid down; some comments may usefully be assayed, however. At the threshold we assume that, notwithstanding that the responsibilities of a prosecutor for fairness and open-dealing are of a higher magnitude than those of a private litigant, no prosecutor is obliged to share his appraisal of the weaknesses of his own case (as opposed to specific exculpatory evidence) with defense counsel. * * * At the other extreme it is equally clear that the courts will allow a defendant to withdraw a guilty plea when the prosecution has either coerced him by threats or persuaded him by affirmative deceit to enter a guilty plea. All the reported instances of deceitful persuasion appear to have involved positive misstatement or misrepresentations; none has considered the effect to be accorded silence only. Consistent with legal principles recognized elsewhere in our jurisprudence, it would seem that silence should give rise to legal consequences only if it may be concluded that the one who was silent was under an affirmative duty to speak. Whether and to what extent the courts, in the absence of statute or possible rule of court would impose such an affirmative duty on a prosecutor would necessarily be dependent on the circumstances of the individual case. Thus, we do not decide what the rule might be where in the course of plea negotiation a particular defendant staunchly and plausibly maintains his innocence but states explicitly and creditably that as a matter of balanced judgment in the light of the apparent strength of the People's proof he wishes to interpose a negotiated plea to reduced charges to avoid the risk of a more severe sentence likely to attend conviction after trial; failure of the prosecutor to reveal the death of a critical complaining witness might then call for a vacatur of the plea. Silence in such circumstances might arguably be held to be so subversive of the criminal justice process as to offend due process. * * *

"Turning then to the present case, we hold that there was no obligation on the part of the prosecutor to reveal to defense counsel that Rodriguez had died, prior to acceptance of defendant's plea of guilty. Defendant does not protest his innocence; on the contrary he testified to the factual basis for the charge to which he pleaded. While the prosecutor failed to inform defense counsel of Rodriguez' death, there is no claim of affirmative misrepresentation. And, it is critical, the failure to disclose did not involve exculpatory evidence. We perceive no reason to depart from the principle that a fairly and voluntarily negotiated plea is the equivalent of a conviction after trial."

Compare *Model Pre-Arraignment Code* § 320.3(1), providing that before any plea agreement "the prosecutor shall disclose to the defendant sufficient information within his knowledge to enable the defendant to make an informed assessment of the likely outcome upon a trial of the case."

If, as in *Newman,* the courts will not intervene on behalf of a defendant, does it follow that intervention in the public interest is likewise inappropriate? Consider:

UNITED STATES v. AMMIDOWN

497 F.2d 615 (D.C.Cir.1973).

LEVENTHAL, CIRCUIT JUDGE.

* * *

In a case of extraordinary notoriety, Robert L. Ammidown was charged with first degree murder and conspiracy to commit murder in the death of his wife. Ammidown admitted that a month previous he arranged to have her murdered at a parking garage of a Virginia department store. At the last minute he changed his mind, because he did not want his son, who was to accompany his mother on that day, to witness the murder. Subsequently, according to his written confession, Ammidown and an associate, Richard Anthony Lee, devised a plan whereby Lee would abduct Mrs. Ammidown and by threat to her life extort a sum of money to be used by Ammidown and Lee to make the down payment for a club on the Eastern Shore of Maryland. The plan called for Ammidown to take his wife to dinner at the Flagship Restaurant in Southwest Washington. After dinner, as they were departing from the Flagship, Lee would halt Ammidown's car at a specified intersection near the restaurant.

And so it was done. In due course, and at the prearranged spot, Lee jumped into Ammidown's car and directed him to drive to the East Capitol Street Bridge, where Lee dragged Mrs. Ammidown from the car and raped her, as planned, to impress Mrs. Ammidown "with the seriousness of the threat."

What then happened was that Lee killed Mrs. Ammidown. Ammidown did not confess to complicity in the murder.

Just prior to trial, the United States Attorney and Ammidown entered into this agreement: Ammidown would plead guilty to second degree murder, and the first degree murder charge would be dismissed. There was no agreement for the prosecutor to recommend sentence less than the maximum, life imprisonment. Ammidown, then aged 49, had no possibility of being even considered for parole for 15 years. Ammidown agreed to testify in the grand jury proceedings and impending trial of Lee, a much younger man, who was believed by the prosecution to be involved in another murder.

The trial judge, however, refused to approve the agreement and accept the lesser plea. With full understanding of the prosecutor's concern with the importance of Ammidown's agreement in connection with its successful prosecution of Lee, the court nonetheless decided that under Rule 11 of the Federal Rules of Criminal Procedure it had the discretion to refuse the plea when it found that the crime was so heinous and the evidence of guilt so overwhelming that the public interest would be ill-served by a judgment of second degree murder, which it referred to as a "tap on the wrist." Appellant then pleaded not guilty to first degree and second degree murder; at trial he was convicted of first degree murder and felony murder and sentenced to two terms of life imprisonment, to run consecutively.

Appellant now asserts that the failure of the trial court to accept his proffered plea of guilty to second degree murder constituted reversible error, and asks this court to remand with instructions to enter a judgment of second degree murder.

* * *

By its terms, Rule 11 deals with the moment when the accused stands before the judge to enter his plea. Although the rule provides that a trial court "may refuse to accept a plea of guilty," it fails to delineate the circumstance under which it may do so. * * *

The element in a plea bargain of dismissal of the charge of the greater offense leads us to consider Rule 48(a) of the Federal Rules of Criminal Procedure, which requires the prosecutor to obtain leave of court in order to terminate a prosecution by dismissal of an indictment. Rule 48(a) does not apply as such to the case at bar, but study of the judicial role in dismissals illuminates our course. As proposed by the Advisory Committee this provision would have adopted the common law rule that the power of the prosecutor to enter a nolle prosequi in a criminal case was unrestricted, and added only the requirement, prevalent in state practice, that the prosecutor state his reasons for seeking dismissals. However, when this rule was promulgated by the Supreme Court in 1944, it substituted the requirement that dismissal be obtained only by leave of court. The Supreme Court did not state reasons for its action. The primary concern, at least as discerned by subsequent decisions of other federal courts, was that of protecting a defendant from harassment, through a prosecutor's charging, dismissing without having placed a defendant in jeopardy, and commencing another prosecution at a different time or place deemed more favorable to the prosecution. * * *

A distinctly different situation is presented when the defendant concurs in the dismissal but the court is concerned whether the action sufficiently protects the public. As to this, while there is a paucity of authority, some principles do emerge. First, Rule 48(a)'s requirement of judicial leave, theretofore known in state practice, gives the court a role in dismissals following indictment. Second, in the exercise of its responsibility, the court will not be content with a mere conclusory statement by the prosecutor that dismissal is in the public interest, but will require a statement of reasons and underlying factual basis. Third, the court does not have primary responsibility, but rather the role of guarding against abuse of prosecutorial discretion. The rule contemplates exposure of the reasons for dismissal "in order to prevent abuse of the uncontrolled power of dismissal previously enjoyed by prosecutors," and in pursuance of this purpose "to gain the Court's favorable discretion, it should be satisfied that the reasons advanced for the proposed dismissal are substantial." * * *

The third element of a plea bargain involving a plea to a lesser included offense, and indeed the most frequent motive behind it, is to circumscribe the judge's discretion in pronouncing sentence. The negotiated plea reduces the upper and lower limits of the range of sentence available to the judge. It is axiomatic that, within the limits imposed by the legislature, imposition of sentence is a matter for discretion of the trial judge. The prosecutor has no role beyond the advisory, and even that is frowned on in the District Court for the District of Columbia. We hesitate to say, therefore, that the United States Attorney and the defendant can by plea manipulate this traditional power of the judge without any recourse by the judge permitting him to forestall gross abuses of prosecutorial discretion.

We have identified that both the District Judge and the United States Attorney have roles in the plea bargaining process. What is required is an effort to harmonize their responsibilities, and to suggest a standard for determining when judicial intervention may be proper.

We start with the presumption that the determination of the United States Attorney is to be followed in the overwhelming number of cases. He alone is in a position to evaluate the government's prosecution resources and the number of cases it is able to prosecute.

Where vigorous prosecution of one case threatens to undermine successful prosecution of another, it has traditionally been the prosecutor who determines which case will be pressed to conclusion, and his decision has been given great deference by the courts.

On the other hand, we do not think Rule 48(a) intends the trial court to serve merely as a rubber stamp for the prosecutor's decision. We agree that "the judge should be satisfied that the agreement adequately protects the public interest".

We now state what, in our view, are the appropriate doctrines governing trial judges in considering whether to deny approval either to dismissals of cases outright or to the diluted dismissal—a guilty plea to a lesser included offense.

First, the trial judge must provide a reasoned exercise of discretion in order to justify a departure from the course agreed on by the prosecution and defense. This is not a matter of absolute judicial prerogative. The authority has been granted to the judge to assure protection of the public interest, and this in turn involves one or more of the following components: (a) fairness to the defense, such as protection against harassment; (b) fairness to the prosecution interest, as in avoiding a disposition that does not serve due and legitimate prosecutorial interest; (c) protection of the sentencing authority reserved to the judge. The judge's statement or opinion must identify the particular interest that leads him to require an unwilling defendant and prosecution to go to trial.

We now turn to the content of these components, and begin by passing any discussion of fairness to the defense, since it is not directly involved in the case at bar and it has already been identified in the precedents referred to earlier in this opinion. As to fairness to the prosecution interest, here we have a matter in which the primary responsibility, obviously, is that of the prosecuting attorney. The District Court cannot disapprove of his action on the ground of incompatibility with prosecutive responsibility unless the judge is in effect ruling that the prosecutor has abused his discretion. The requirement of judicial approval entitles the judge to obtain and evaluate the prosecutor's reasons. That much, indeed, was proposed by the Advisory Committee, and the Supreme Court's amendment obviously did not curtail the proposed authority of the judge. The judge may withhold approval if he finds that the prosecutor has failed to give consideration to factors that must be given consideration in the public interest, factors such as the deterrent aspects of the criminal law. However, trial judges are not free to withhold approval of guilty pleas on this basis merely because their conception of the public interest differs from that of the prosecuting attorney. The question is not what the judge would do if he were the prosecuting attorney, but whether he can say that the action of the prosecuting attorney is such a departure from sound prosecutorial principle as to mark it an abuse of prosecutorial discretion.

In like vein, we note that a judge is free to condemn the prosecutor's agreement as a trespass on judicial authority only in a blatant and extreme case. In ordinary circumstances, the change in grading of an offense presents no question of the kind of action that is reserved for the judiciary.

Applying these tests to the case at bar, we find the record establishes beyond all doubt that the United States Attorney considered, indeed agonized over, the public interest and concluded that it was best served by assuring a successful prosecution of Lee—"a young man . . . a killer." The Assistant United States Attorney presented this to the court unequivocally:

> We have spent night after night trying to resolve this thing. We have talked with the homicide officers. We have had them to our office. We have pulled the file of Richard Anthony Lee. Your

Honor, we are scared to death that unless there is a successful way to prosecute this man—he is a young man. We believe he is a killer. We believe that somewhere in this city right now there is someone who because he will not be prosecuted will die one day in say the next ten years. We believe that Mr. Ammidown pleading to second degree murder—that the sentence in that case will neutralize him. We have no fear of him now. We are afraid of what Richard Anthony Lee might do.

Your Honor, we have one obligation. And that is the same obligation that your Honor has, and that is for the public. I prosecute for the Government—for the public—for the people of this city.

The trial judge was not free to disapprove this assessment by the prosecutor without both stating his reasons and determining that the prosecutor abused his discretion. Neither of these elements appears in the case at bar. The trial judge provided no statement of reasons, and such colloquy as appears indicates that the Judge assumed that the correct test was what the judge independently considered best in the public interest.

When we come to the possible ground of intrusion on the sentencing function of the trial judge, we have a consideration that is interdependent of the other. That is to say, a dropping of an offense that might be taken as an intrusion on the judicial function if it were not shown to be related to a prosecutorial purpose takes on an entirely different coloration if it is explained to the judge that there was a prosecutorial purpose, an insufficiency of evidence, a doubt as to the admissibility of certain evidence under exclusionary rules, a need for evidence to bring another felon to justice, or other similar consideration.

Because the trial judge did not provide a statement of reasons based on intrusion on the sentencing authority of the judge, it would be necessary to remand in any event. At the time the judge took the action appealed from, first degree murder was punishable by death, and second degree murder by a maximum of life imprisonment. We need not consider what kind of remand we might have provided if that kind of sentencing disparity were in effect at the present time. For the Supreme Court's decision in *Furman v. Georgia,* 408 U.S. 238, 92 S.Ct. 2726, 33 L.Ed.2d 346 (1972), has established the unavailability of the death sentence for appellant. We are required to accompany our reversal for lack of requisite findings with a disposition in the interest of justice that takes into account current conditions.

The situation as it stands today is such that we cannot conceive that if the trial judge were required to provide a current reassessment of the problem in the light of the standards set forth in this opinion, he could justify his rejection of the first degree murder reversal and of the second degree murder plea as reflecting a sentence disparity so blatant as to constitute an intrusion upon the judicial domain. The life sentence is mandatory on a conviction for first degree murder, and discretionary with the court on a conviction for murder in the second degree. Parole is available after a minimum of 20 years in the case of first degree murder, and after a minimum of 15 years in the case of murder in the second degree. The difference is insufficient by itself to warrant judicial rejection of a properly bargained plea of guilty to murder in the second degree on the ground of undue interference with the sentencing domain of the judiciary.[a]

* * *

a. On a petition for reconsideration, amicus argued that this premise was undercut by the fact "that the trial judge could rightly consider, in the exercise of his sentencing discretion, that the consecutive life sentences, for premeditated murder (on the first count) and for felony murder (on the second count) resulted in a minimum term of 40 years (20 plus 20) before parole could be granted by the executive officials involved, as contrasted with 15 years for a single sentence on

For the reasons stated, the judgment and sentence on a conviction of murder in the first degree is vacated and the case remanded with instructions to accept appellant's plea of guilty to second degree murder.

Notes and Questions

1. The trial judge later elaborated upon his reasons in J. Sirica, *To Set the Record Straight* 42–43 (1979): "Prior to his trial, the husband claimed that the accomplice had been blackmailing him by threatening to disclose his extramarital affair and that the murder was then planned to get the money to buy off the accomplice. In his own defense, the accomplice said that he did know the husband but had not conspired to murder the wife. The prosecutors wanted to let the husband plead guilty to a reduced charge in exchange for his testimony against the accomplice, who would then likely be convicted of premeditated murder and, at a minimum, spend the rest of his life in jail. I rejected the plea bargain, however, relying upon the legal axiom of 'equal justice under law.' The law states that conspirators are culpable in like degree even if one goes further in carrying out the conspiracy than the other. The two men were equally responsible for this brutal killing, in my view. And another problem was also on my mind. The husband was white; the accomplice was black. I shuddered to think what might be the reaction of Washington's large black community if the white man who planned his own wife's death was let off with a fifteen-year-to-life term while the black man might have to pay with his life. In separate trials each was convicted of first-degree murder. On appeal, my rejection of the husband's guilty plea was overturned and the case was remanded to me to accept a second-degree plea. I sentenced him to the maximum jail term for second-degree murder.

"In mid-June, 1972, I was faced with sentencing the accomplice, and I wasn't getting much sleep thinking about it. I have always had mixed feelings about capital punishment, but the facts in this case were so disgusting, so horrible, that it seemed made for the death sentence. Still, having the power to take a person's life is an awful thing. On the weekend of June 17, it weighed very heavily on my mind.* "

2. As reflected by *United States v. Jackson,* 563 F.2d 1145 (4th Cir.1977), the positions of the prosecutor and judge are quite different when sentencing bargaining rather than charge bargaining is involved. In that case, a plea agreement was reached whereby the defendant agreed to plead guilty to the charge of operating a lottery and the prosecutor agreed to recommend a sentence of one year. At arraignment, the trial judge made it clear that he would give no consideration to the recommendation in the plea agreement, but after a recess the defendant entered a plea of guilty anyway and later received a 3-year sentence. On appeal, the court found "Jackson's challenge of his guilty plea solely on the ground that the district court arbitrarily declined to consider any plea bargain to be without merit." The legislative history of rule 11, the court noted, made it clear that "each individual judge is free to decide whether, and to what degree, he will entertain plea bargains, and his refusal to consider any plea bargaining whatsoever will not vitiate a guilty plea which has otherwise been knowingly and voluntarily entered."

3. Some have argued that to distinguish between charge bargains and sentence bargains in determining the range of

second degree murder." In a supplemental opinion, Judge Leventhal responded that this argument rested upon a false premise, as "a defendant committing a single homicide cannot be given consecutive sentences for both first degree murder and another crime of homicide."

* On June 22, I sentenced the accomplice to death. But he was never executed. Later that year, the Supreme Court invalidated the kinds of death-penalty statutes under which he had been sentenced. He is now serving a life sentence.

the judge's discretion in deciding whether the contemplated concessions should be granted assumes a difference which does not exist. Alschuler, *The Trial Judge's Role in Plea Bargaining, Part I,* 76 Colum.L.Rev. 1059, 1074 (1976), asserts: "From the defendant's perspective, the primary significance of the charge-reduction process plainly lies in its effect on the sentence that he will receive. The basic commodity that prosecutors offer defendants in exchange for their pleas remains the same in a system of charge-reduction bargaining as in a system of sentence recommendation bargaining."

SECTION 4. RECEIVING THE DEFENDANT'S PLEA; PLEA WITHDRAWAL

I. PLEADING ALTERNATIVES

1. When the defendant is called upon to enter his plea at arraignment; he may enter a plea of (1) not guilty, (2) guilty, (3) not guilty by reason of insanity (in a few jurisdictions where such a plea is a prerequisite to the presentation of an insanity defense at trial); or (4) nolo contendere (in the federal system and about half of the states). A plea of nolo contendere—sometimes referred to as a plea of non vult contendere or of non vult—is simply a device by which the defendant may assert that he does not want to contest the issue of guilt or innocence. Such a plea may not be entered as a matter of right, but only with the consent of the court, and it is generally the practice of courts not to consent to a nolo contendere plea unless the prosecutor concurs.

2. Although some minor variations are to be found from jurisdiction to jurisdiction, in most states which permit a plea of nolo contendere it has the following significance: (1) Unlike a plea of guilty or a conviction following a plea of not guilty, a plea of nolo contendere may not be put into evidence in a subsequent civil action as proof of the fact that the defendant committed the offense to which he entered the plea. (2) When a nolo contendere plea has been accepted, the defendant may be given the same sentence as if he had pleaded guilty. (3) Judgment following entry of a nolo contendere plea is a conviction, and may be admitted as such in other proceedings (e.g., to apply multiple offender penalty provisions, to deny or revoke a license because of conviction, or to claim double jeopardy in a subsequent prosecution). See Note, 44 S.Cal.L.Rev. 737 (1971).

3. "While it is in the discretion of the Court to reject or accept such a plea, no criteria have been established to guide the Court in the exercise of this discretion." *United States v. Bagliore,* 182 F.Supp. 714 (E.D.N.Y.1960). What should the criteria be? Consider *United States v. David E. Thompson, Inc.,* 621 F.2d 1147 (1st Cir. 1980), holding the district court did not abuse its discretion in rejecting a nolo plea in a criminal antitrust action where entry of the plea would have deprived the victims of the antitrust conspiracy of a significant opportunity in subsequent civil actions to benefit from the government's efforts. Should a court not accept a nolo contendere plea "unless the situation is an extraordinary one" because to do otherwise would "breed contempt for law enforcement"? *United States v. Chin Doong Art,* 193 F.Supp. 820 (E.D.N.Y.1961). In terms of the defendant's rehabilitation, is it sometimes wise to insist that the defendant either acknowledge his guilt by a plea of guilty or else go to trial?

4. The concern herein is with what procedures are to be followed when the defendant tenders a plea of guilty. Those required in the federal system are set out in Fed.R.Crim.P. 11, which should be examined at this point. State provisions are not always this elaborate. In examining the material which follows, consider: (i) what procedures are (or should be) constitutionally required; and (ii) what other procedures, even if not constitutionally required, are desirable.

II. DETERMINING VOLUNTARINESS OF GUILTY PLEA AND COMPETENCY OF DEFENDANT

1. When the legitimacy of plea bargaining was in doubt, the general practice was not to reveal in court that a bargain had been struck. Thus, when the trial judge asked the defendant if his plea was the result of any promises, he would respond in the negative even when everyone in the courtroom knew otherwise. Most jurisdictions have now moved away from this charade, so that the voluntariness inquiry includes a determination of whether a plea agreement has been reached and, if so, what it is. See, e.g., Fed.R.Crim.P. 11(d) & (e).

2. The defendant may sometimes complain because the judge was overly concerned about the voluntariness requirement, as in *United States v. Martinez,* 486 F.2d 15 (5th Cir.1973) where the defendant was indicted for (i) conspiracy to import marijuana, (ii) actual importation, (iii) possession of same with intent to distribute, and (iv) assaulting a federal officer. Martinez tendered a plea to the second count as a result of an agreement with the prosecution that the other counts would then be dismissed. Upon inquiry into the voluntariness of the plea, the judge learned that Martinez' waiver of his *Miranda* rights had been obtained by a promise that nothing would happen to him, and thus declined the plea as involuntary notwithstanding counsel's efforts to persuade him that the government possessed sufficient evidence to convict independently of Martinez' statement. Martinez was then tried and convicted of all four counts. On appeal, the court viewed "the action of the district court as contrary to both the spirit and the purpose of Rule 11," in that he rejected a guilty plea which was not "involuntary in the sense of Rule 11" merely "because of the possibility of later collateral attack on the judgment to be entered upon the plea." Thus, the court vacated the convictions on all but the second count.

3. An inquiry into the mental competency of a defendant who has tendered a guilty plea is not routinely undertaken. However, a trial court is constitutionally compelled to hold a hearing, sua sponte, at any time that substantial evidence appears that a criminal defendant is incompetent to enter a guilty plea. The prevailing view is "that the degree of competence required to plead guilty is the same as that required to stand trial." *United States ex rel. Heral v. Franzen,* 667 F.2d 633 (7th Cir.1981). But in *Sieling v. Eyman,* 478 F.2d 211 (9th Cir.1973), criticized in Note, 1974 Duke L.J. 149 (1974), the court held it will not suffice that the defendant was earlier found competent to stand trial, for one may be competent to stand trial but yet not competent to plead guilty, as in the latter instance one is incompetent "if a mental illness has substantially impaired his ability to make a reasoned choice among the alternatives presented to him and to understand the nature of the consequences of his plea."

4. Mark Chapman, accused of killing John Lennon, entered a guilty plea to murder just before jury selection was to begin. Chapman's plea was against the advice of his attorneys, who maintained he was "delusional and psychotic" and hoped to show that a mental aberration had prevented him from knowing or understanding what he had done. Before the plea was accepted, the following colloquy took place between Chapman and prosecutor Sullivan:

"MR. SULLIVAN: This is your own decision?

"MR. CHAPMAN: It is my decision and God's decision.

"MR. SULLIVAN: When you say it's God's decision, and I ask it advisedly since certain representations have been made to me by Mr. Marks, did you hear any voices actually in your ears?

"MR. CHAPMAN: Any audible voices?

"MR. SULLIVAN: Any audible voices.

"MR. CHAPMAN: No, sir.

"MR. SULLIVAN: Before you made this decision, did you indulge in any prayer?

"MR. CHAPMAN: Yes, there were a number of prayers.

"MR. SULLIVAN: After you prayed, did you come to the realization that you understand to come from God that you should plead guilty?

"MR. CHAPMAN: Yes, it was his directive, command.

"MR. SULLIVAN: Is that a realization you came to within yourself, inspired perhaps by God?

"MR. CHAPMAN: No, I felt it was God telling me to plead guilty, and then probing with my own decision whether to do what God wanted me to do or whether to do what I wanted to do, I decided to follow God's directive.

"MR. SULLIVAN: Would you say at this time that this plea is a result of your own free will?

"MR. CHAPMAN: Yes."

N.Y. Times, June 23, 1981, at 1, col. 3.

III. DETERMINING GUILTY PLEA IS UNDERSTANDINGLY MADE

1. *The charge.* Defendant, 19 years old and substantially below average intelligence, was indicted for first degree murder. His attorneys unsuccessfully sought to have the charge reduced to manslaughter, but were only able to induce the prosecutor to reduce to second degree murder in exchange for defendant's plea of guilty. The attorneys did not tell defendant that the new charge included intent to kill as a required element, nor was any reference made to this element at the time of defendant's plea. At sentencing, the defendant's lawyers explained his version of the offense, particularly noting that he "meant no harm to the lady" when he entered her room with a knife, but this was disputed by the prosecutor. The defendant later obtained relief via federal habeas corpus, and in HENDERSON v. MORGAN, 426 U.S. 637, 96 S.Ct. 2253, 49 L.Ed.2d 108 (1976), the Court, per STEVENS, J., affirmed:

"We assume, as petitioner argues, that the prosecutor had overwhelming evidence of guilt available. We also accept petitioner's characterization of the competence of respondent's counsel and of the wisdom of their advice to plead guilty to a charge of second-degree murder. Nevertheless, such a plea cannot support a judgment of guilt unless it was voluntary in a constitutional sense. And clearly the plea could not be voluntary in the sense that it constituted an intelligent admission that he committed the offense unless the defendant received 'real notice of the true nature of the charge against him, the first and most universally recognized requirement of due process.' *Smith v. O'Grady,* 312 U.S. 329, 334, 61 S.Ct. 572, 574, 85 L.Ed. 859.

"The charge of second-degree murder was never formally made. Had it been made, it necessarily would have included a charge that respondent's assault was 'committed with a design to effect the death of the person killed.' That element of the offense might have been proved by the objective evidence even if respondent's actual state of mind was consistent with innocence or manslaughter. But even if such a design to effect death would almost inevitably have been inferred from evidence that respondent repeatedly stabbed Mrs. Francisco, it is nevertheless also true that a jury would not have been required to draw that inference. The jury would have been entitled to accept defense counsel's appraisal of the incident as involving only manslaughter in the first degree. Therefore, an admission by respondent that he killed Mrs. Francisco does not necessarily also admit that he was guilty of second-degree murder.

"There is nothing in this record that can serve as a substitute for either a finding after trial, or a voluntary admission, that respondent had the requisite intent. Defense counsel did not purport to stipulate to that fact; they did not explain to him that his plea would be an admission of that fact; and he made no factual statement or admission necessarily implying that he had such intent. In these circumstances it is impossible to conclude that his plea to the unexplained charge of second-degree murder was voluntary.

"Petitioner argues that affirmance of the Court of Appeals will invite countless collateral attacks on judgments entered on pleas of guilty, since frequently the record will not contain a complete enumeration of the elements of the offense to which an accused person pleads guilty.[18] We think petitioner's fears are exaggerated.

"Normally the record contains either an explanation of the charge by the trial judge, or at least a representation by defense counsel that the nature of the offense has been explained to the accused. Moreover, even without such an express representation, it may be appropriate to presume that in most cases defense counsel routinely explain the nature of the offense in sufficient detail to give the accused notice of what he is being asked to admit. This case is unique because the trial judge found as a fact that the element of intent was not explained to respondent. Moreover, respondent's unusually low mental capacity provides a reasonable explanation for counsel's oversight; it also forecloses the conclusion that the error was harmless beyond a reasonable doubt, for it lends at least a modicum of credibility to defense counsel's appraisal of the homicide as a manslaughter rather than a murder."

REHNQUIST, J., joined by THE CHIEF JUSTICE, dissenting, argued that at least before *McCarthy v. United States,* p. 1239 infra, which should not be applied retroactively to this case, "where the defendant is counselled, there was no requirement that every element of the offense be explained to or admitted by the defendant," so that "the only remaining issue is whether he was 'properly advised.'" Under *Brady v. United States,* p. 1191 supra, and *McMann v. Richardson,* p. 1244 infra, this "depends upon the sort of advice reasonably competent counsel would have been expected to give him." Because defendant told his attorneys that he had stabbed the victim "many times," this "suggests that experienced counsel would not consider the 'design to effect death' issue to be in serious dispute."

WHITE, J., joined by STEWART, BLACKMUN, and POWELL, JJ., concurring, responded: "Either a new constitutional rule is being established in *this* case—in which event we will have to address at some future time the question whether this rule is retroactive—or, as I believe to be true, this case rests on the long-accepted principle that a guilty plea must provide a trustworthy basis for believing that the defendant is in fact guilty." [a]

What constitutes a "critical element" under fn. 18 of *Henderson?* Consider, e.g., *Ramirez v. People,* 682 P.2d 1181 (Colo. 1984) (meaning of "attempt" should be explained, as it "not a crime that is readily understandable to a person of ordinary intelligence"). Is explanation unnecessary if, as commonly assumed, e.g., *Commonwealth v. Begin,* 474 N.E.2d 1120 (Mass. 1985), defendant's statements to the court indicate the presence of the unexplained elements?

Is the judge's responsibility different if the defendant is not represented by counsel? Consider *Else v. State,* 555 P.2d 1210 (Alaska, 1976), holding that a trial court

18. "There is no need in this case to decide whether notice of the true nature, or substance, of a charge always requires a description of every element of the offense; we assume it does not. Nevertheless, intent is such a critical element of the offense of second-degree murder that notice of that element is required."

a. See also *Marshall v. Lonberger,* p. 1527 infra.

must advise an unrepresented defendant of the elements contained in the wording of the applicable statute and also elements created by judicial construction. Thus, in advising defendant of the elements of a charge of assault with a deadly weapon, the court was required as a matter of due process to inform the defendant that the phrase "dangerous weapon" had been construed so that he would not be guilty if the gun was unloaded and not used as a bludgeon.

2. *The sentence.* Kelleher, charged in New York with attempted murder, rejected a pretrial offer of 6 to 18 years if he pleaded guilty, but later entered a guilty plea after the trial was under way. The judge told him he faced "a very big sentence * * * a very stiff sentence," but did not state what the maximum and minimum terms were. Kelleher received a sentence of 7–21 years. After a federal district court denied relief on habeas corpus, Kelleher appealed, relying upon *United States ex rel. Leeson v. Damon,* 496 F.2d 718 (2d Cir.1974); and *United States ex rel. Hill v. Ternullo,* 510 F.2d 844 (2d Cir.1975). In Kelleher v. Henderson, 531 F.2d 78 (2d Cir.1976), the court affirmed, reasoning: "In [*Leeson*], petitioner had been erroneously informed by his counsel that under state law he faced 'at most' a maximum term of 1.3 to 2.6 years. Because of his youth, however, petitioner could have received and in fact did receive a five-year reformatory term. Petitioner had not been advised by either his attorney or the court of the latter possibility. A panel of this court reversed a denial of the writ, Judge Hays dissenting. We pointed out that 'the undisputed proof' was that

> the defendant entered his plea in ignorance of what the maximum possible sentence was, believing it to be substantially less than that which the court was authorized to impose and which, indeed, it did impose.

"In [*Hill*], a state prisoner claimed that his guilty plea 'was tainted by a misunderstanding, fostered by counsel, of the sentence consequences of the plea.' There was a dispute over 'the petitioner's understanding of the sentence consequences when he pleaded guilty,' and so a panel of this court remanded for an evidentiary hearing. Although the opinion emphasizes the 'erroneous legal advice' and the 'misstatement [by counsel] of easily accessible fact,' the court did say:

> If [the district court] finds that the petitioner's plea was made without understanding of the minimum or maximum sentence possibilities, the district court must issue the writ or grant other appropriate relief. . . .

"Although the broad language in these cases unquestionably supports appellant's legal position, we do not believe that we are required to reverse Judge Werker. * * * In both *Leeson* and *Hill,* the state defendant actually received misinformation regarding the maximum sentence faced. In such a case, perhaps it can be assumed that accurate information would have affected a defendant's decision to plead guilty. In this case, however, there is no indication at all that appellant would have acted differently if he had been told of the possibility of a 25-year sentence. He had already been offered, and had rejected, a sentence of six to 18 years, he had heard the overwhelming evidence against him, he then initiated the guilty plea himself so that there is no problem of policing an arguably coercive plea bargaining process and he had been advised he would get a 'stiff sentence,' which actually turned out to be seven to 21 years, only slightly heavier than that previously offered. Under the circumstances, we agree with Judge Werker that 'it would be incredible to conclude that petitioner would not have plead guilty had he known that he faced a maximum of twenty-five years.' " [b]

b. Is this reasoning more persuasive when the defendant has pleaded guilty in exchange for a specific sentence? See *People v. Hartman,* 285 N.E.2d 600 (Ill.App.1972), holding that failure of the judge to advise the defendant of the statutory maximum and minimum, as required by court

Does the constitutional issue turn upon whether the defendant was represented by counsel? In *Von Moltke v. Gillies,* 332 U.S. 708, 68 S.Ct. 316, 92 L.Ed. 309 (1948), where defendant—charged with a capital offense—waived counsel and then entered a plea of guilty, the opinion of the Court (joined in by only four Justices) asserted that there was no intelligent and understanding waiver of the constitutional right to *counsel* because "such waiver must be made with an apprehension of the nature of the charges, the statutory offenses included within them, the range of allowable punishments thereunder, possible defenses to the charges and circumstances in mitigation thereof, and all other facts essential to a broad understanding of the whole matter."

When a person convicted of the crime charged is by law ineligible for probation or parole, should the defendant be so advised before his guilty plea is accepted? "While some cases have expressed the view that eligibility and ineligibility for parole involve merely matters of 'legislative grace' rather than matters of right, and are therefore not 'consequences' of a guilty plea, other cases have rejected this view and have expressed the view that (1) the average defendant assumes that he will be eligible for parole, and (2) if a defendant, upon conviction for a particular crime, will be ineligible for parole, such a complete denial of the opportunity for him to be paroled is an inseparable part of the punishment for his crime, directly affects the duration of his incarceration, and is thus a 'consequence' of his guilty plea" Annot., 8 A.L.R.Fed. 760, 763 (1971).

3. *Collateral consequences.* Note, 112 U.Pa.L.Rev. 865, 875–76 (1964): "Courts have not considered it necessary to inform the defendant of possible collateral consequences when such consequences result from subsequent criminal convictions of the defendant or do not relate directly to the charge to which the defendant pleads guilty. There is no obligation to inform a defendant that the conviction of the present crime will be considered under a multiple offender law if he should be convicted of another crime. Similarly, there is no obligation to tell a defendant that in the event of any subsequent convictions the present conviction could be considered in determining whether to give a lenient or severe penalty on the subsequent conviction, or that society generally discriminates against convicted offenders. Nor need a court inform a defendant that conviction can mean deportation, court martial from the armed services, loss of the right to vote, or loss of the right to operate a business licensed by the state. It also does not seem that the defendant must know what rehabilitation programs will be available to him."

When is a consequence only "collateral"? For example, as to the consequence of deportation, does it make any difference whether deportation upon conviction of the crime charged is mandatory rather than discretionary? See the dissenting opinion in *Vizcarra-Delgadillo v. United States,* 395 F.2d 70 (9th Cir.1968). If conviction will result in revocation of the defendant's driver's license, must the defendant be so advised by the judge? See *Moore v. Hinton,* 513 F.2d 781 (5th Cir. 1975). If the defendant is presently on parole, must the judge advise him that his parole could be revoked on the basis of his guilty plea? See *Watts v. Brewer,* 340 F.Supp. 378 (S.D.Iowa 1972).

In *Cuthrell v. Director, Patuxent Institution,* 475 F.2d 1364 (4th Cir.1973), the court held that a state defendant was not constitutionally entitled to be advised, before his plea of guilty, that he might be given an indeterminate sentence to Patuxent, a therapeutic institution for defective delinquents, because (1) that sentence did not automatically result from the plea, but resulted from a subsequent civil hearing, and (2) commitment to Patuxent was for

rule, was not reversible error because the defendant "knew precisely what would happen to him so far as sentence for this offense."

treatment rather than punishment. Both reasons are criticized in Note, 31 Wash. & Lee L.Rev. 236 (1974).

4. *Rights waived by plea.* After Wilkins' trial for first degree murder had commenced, he entered a guilty plea to second degree murder and was sentenced to a term of 50 years. Though the trial judge had determined that the plea was voluntary and had warned defendant that he could be sentenced to life imprisonment, Wilkins sought relief via federal habeas corpus. In WILKINS v. ERICKSON, 505 F.2d 761 (9th Cir.1974), the court stated:

"Wilkins relies upon *Boykin v. Alabama,* [395 U.S. 238, 89 S.Ct. 1709, 23 L.Ed.2d 274 (1969).] He contends that since he was not personally advised by the trial judge on entry of his plea that by pleading guilty he was waiving (1) his privilege against self-incrimination, (2) his right to trial by jury, and (3) his right to confront his accusers; that he was unaware of the consequences, and that his plea, therefore, was not voluntarily and intelligently made. Wilkins further argues that the failure of the trial judge to articulate these three rights on the record resulted in a 'silent' record which cannot be supplemented by a post-conviction evidentiary hearing. Accordingly, he wants the opportunity to re-plead.

"Wilkins relies on the following language from *Boykin:*

> 'We cannot presume a waiver of these three important federal rights from a silent record.
>
> 'What is at stake for an accused facing death or imprisonment demands the utmost solicitude of which courts are capable in canvassing the matter with the accused to make sure he has a full understanding of what a plea connotes and of its consequence. When the judge discharges that function, he leaves a record adequate for any review that may be later sought.'

"The district court's decision, however, is supported by Supreme Court decisions subsequent to *Boykin* and several circuits. The rigid interpretation of *Boykin* urged by Wilkins has not been adopted by the Supreme Court in subsequent decisions on voluntariness of guilty pleas. In *Brady v. United States,* the Court citing *Boykin,* upheld a guilty plea as voluntary and intelligent even though defendant had not been specifically advised of the three rights discussed in *Boykin.* The *Brady* Court clarified *Boykin* by stating, '[t]he new element added in *Boykin* was the requirement that the record must affirmatively disclose that a defendant who pleaded guilty entered his plea understandingly and voluntarily.' In *North Carolina v. Alford,* the Court stated that in determining the validity of guilty pleas the 'standard was and remains whether the plea represents a voluntary and intelligent choice among the alternative courses of action open to the defendant.' Specific articulation of the *Boykin* rights is not the sine qua non of a valid guilty plea.

" * * * Accordingly, we hold that *Boykin* does not require specific articulation of the above mentioned three rights in a state proceeding." [c]

IV. DETERMINING FACTUAL BASIS OF GUILTY PLEA

1. The Advisory Committee Note to Fed.R.Crim.P. 11(f) reads in part: "The

c. Several other courts have reached the same conclusion. Compare *People v. Jaworski,* 194 N.W.2d 868 (Mich.1972): "While it may be true, as the majority of the Court of Appeals reasoned, that '*Boykin* is devoid of any specific language stating that in order to have a valid waiver of the three federal constitutional rights involved when a plea of guilty is entered the three rights must be specifically enumerated and specifically waived,' in our opinion both Justice Douglas' language and his logic require that the defendant must be informed of these three rights, for without knowledge he cannot understandingly waive those rights." Noting that the appeal was brought by the same attorney who represented the defendant at the time of the guilty plea, the court also expressed concern over defense counsel's responsibility to see that the defendant's plea is properly made.

court should satisfy itself, by inquiry of the defendant or the attorney for the government, or by examining the presentence report, or otherwise, that the conduct which the defendant admits constitutes the offense charged or an offense included therein to which the defendant has pleaded guilty. Such inquiry should, e.g., protect a defendant who is in the position of pleading voluntarily with an understanding of the nature of the charge but without realizing that his conduct does not actually fall within the charge." [d] Several states have adopted a similar requirement.

Compare *Model Pre-Arraignment Code* § 350.4(3): "Unless there has been a prior judicial determination upon a preliminary hearing that there exists reasonable cause * * *, the court shall not enter judgment upon a plea of guilty without first making inquiry to satisfy itself that such reasonable cause exists." Is this a less demanding or more demanding standard than rule 11? Under that approach, should there be any need for inquiry if the defendant waived his right to a preliminary hearing? Consider Uviller, *Pleading Guilty: A Critique of Four Models,* 41 Law & Contem.Prob. 102, 124–25 (1977), asserting that "where means for challenging the adequacy of the accusation are provided by the law of the jurisdiction, * * * I do not think justice demands that the pleading court assure itself of the bona fides of a charge which [a counseled] defendant has freely accepted as valid."

2. In NORTH CAROLINA v. ALFORD, 400 U.S. 25, 91 S.Ct. 160, 27 L.Ed.2d 162 (1970), Alford was indicted for first-degree murder, a capital offense. His appointed counsel questioned witnesses the defendant said would substantiate his claim of innocence, but these witnesses instead gave statements that strongly indicated his guilt. The attorney recommended a plea of guilty, but left the final decision to Alford. Alford thereafter pleaded guilty to second-degree murder, following which the trial court received a summary of the state's case, indicating that Alford had taken a gun from his house with the stated intention of killing the victim and had later returned with the declaration that he had carried out the killing. Alford then took the stand and testified that he had not committed the murder but that he was pleading guilty because he faced the threat of the death penalty if he did not do so.[e] When the defendant persisted in his plea, it was accepted by the trial court. The Supreme Court, per JUSTICE WHITE, relied upon *Brady v. United States,* p. 1191 supra, in concluding that Alford's desire to avoid the death penalty did not necessarily

d. For example, *Gilbert v. United States,* 466 F.2d 533 (5th Cir.1972), where the defendant pleaded guilty to four counts of interstate transportation of stolen money orders, but, had the judge not failed to determine the factual basis, he would have learned that there was only one crossing of state lines and thus only one violation of the statute; held, it not sufficient to now vacate the sentence on all but one count, as "the number of crimes charged and the maximum punishment to which he was exposed might well have influenced defendant's decision to plead guilty rather than stand trial."

e. Alford's testimony is set out as follows in footnote 2 of the Court's opinion:

"* * * I pleaded guilty on second degree murder because they said there is too much evidence, but I ain't shot no man, but I take the fault for the other man. We never had an argument in our life and I just pleaded guilty because they said if I didn't they would gas me for it, and that is all."

In response to questions from his attorney, Alford affirmed that he had consulted several times with his attorney and with members of his family and had been informed of his rights if he chose to plead not guilty. Alford then reaffirmed his decision to plead guilty to second-degree murder:

"Q. [by Alford's attorney]. And you authorized me to tender a plea of guilty to second degree murder before the Court?

"A. Yes, sir.

"Q. And in doing that, that you have again affirmed your decision on that point?

"A. Well, I'm still pleading that you all got me to plead guilty. I plead the other way, circumstantial evidence; that the jury will prosecute me on—on the second. You told me to plead guilty, right. I don't—I'm not guilty but I plead guilty."

make his guilty plea involuntary, and then proceeded to consider the significance of Alford's denial of guilt:

"State and lower federal courts are divided upon whether a guilty plea can be accepted when it is accompanied by protestations of innocence and hence contains only a waiver of trial but no admission of guilt. Some courts, giving expression to the principle that '[o]ur law only authorizes a conviction where guilt is shown,' require that trial judges reject such pleas. But others have concluded that they should not 'force any defense on a defendant in a criminal case,' particularly when advancement of the defense might 'end in disaster * * *.' They have argued that, since 'guilt, or the degree of guilt, is at times uncertain and elusive * * * [a]n accused, though believing in or entertaining doubts respecting his innocence, might reasonably conclude a jury would be convinced of his guilt and that he would fare better in the sentence by pleading guilty * * *.' [7]

"This Court has not confronted this precise issue, but prior decisions do yield relevant principles. In *Lynch v. Overholser,* 369 U.S. 705, 82 S.Ct. 1063, 8 L.Ed.2d 211 (1962), the defendant Lynch, who had been charged in the Municipal Court of the District of Columbia with drawing and negotiating bad checks, a misdemeanor punishable by a maximum of one year in jail, sought to enter a plea of guilty, but the trial judge refused to accept the plea since a psychiatric report in the judge's possession indicated that Lynch had been suffering from a manic depressive psychosis, at the time of the crime charged, and hence might have been not guilty by reason of insanity. Although at the subsequent trial Lynch did not rely on the insanity defense, he was found not guilty by reason of insanity and committed for an indeterminate period to a mental institution. On habeas corpus, the Court ordered his release, construing the congressional legislation seemingly authorizing the commitment as not reaching a case where the accused preferred a guilty plea to a plea of insanity. The Court expressly refused to rule that Lynch had an absolute right to have his guilty plea accepted, but inferred that there would have been no constitutional error had his plea been accepted even though evidence before the judge indicated that there was a valid defense.

"The issue in *Hudson v. United States,* 272 U.S. 451, 47 S.Ct. 127, 71 L.Ed. 347 (1926), was whether a federal court has power to impose a prison sentence after accepting a plea of *nolo contendere,* a plea by which a defendant does not expressly admit his guilt, but nonetheless waives his right to a trial and authorizes the court for purposes of the case to treat him as if he were guilty. The Court held that a trial court does have such power * * *. Implicit in the *nolo contendere* cases is a recognition that the Constitution does not bar imposition of a prison sentence upon an accused who is unwilling expressly to admit his guilt but who, faced with grim alternatives, is willing to waive his trial and accept the sentence.[f]

"These cases would be directly in point if Alford had simply insisted on his plea but refused to admit the crime. The fact that his plea was denominated a plea of guilty rather than a plea of *nolo contendere* is of no constitutional significance with respect to the issue now before us, for the Constitution is concerned with the practical consequences, not the formal categorizations of state law. Thus, while most pleas of guilty consist of both a waiver of

7. A third approach has been to decline to rule definitively that a trial judge must either accept or reject an otherwise valid plea containing a protestation of innocence, but to leave that decision to his sound discretion. See *Maxwell v. United States,* 368 F.2d 735, 738–739 (CA9 1966).

f. On the other hand, it was held in *United States v. Cepeda Penes,* 577 F.2d 754 (1st Cir. 1978), that a federal judge does not abuse his discretion in refusing a nolo plea for which no factual basis was shown, "for acceptance of a nolo plea is solely a matter of grace."

trial and an express admission of guilt, the latter element is not a constitutional requisite to the imposition of criminal penalty. An individual accused of crime may voluntarily, knowingly, and understandingly consent to the imposition of a prison sentence even if he is unwilling or unable to admit his participation in the acts constituting the crime.

"Nor can we perceive any material difference between a plea which refuses to admit commission of the criminal act and a plea containing a protestation of innocence when, as in the instant case, a defendant intelligently concludes that his interests require entry of a guilty plea and the record before the judge contains strong evidence of actual guilt. Here the State had a strong case of first-degree murder against Alford. Whether he realized or disbelieved his guilt, he insisted on his plea because in his view he had absolutely nothing to gain by a trial and much to gain by pleading. Because of the overwhelming evidence against him, a trial was precisely what neither Alford nor his attorney desired. Confronted with the choice between a trial for first-degree murder, on the one hand, and a plea of guilty to second-degree murder, on the other, Alford quite reasonably chose the latter and thereby limited the maximum penalty to a 30-year term. When his plea is viewed in light of the evidence against him, which substantially negated his claim of innocence and which further provided a means by which the judge could test whether the plea was being intelligently entered, its validity cannot be seriously questioned. In view of the strong factual basis for the plea demonstrated by the State and Alford's clearly expressed desire to enter it despite his professed belief in his innocence, we hold that the trial judge did not commit constitutional error in accepting it.[11]"

Justices Brennan, Douglas, and Marshall, dissenting, concluded that Alford's guilty plea was not voluntary "without reaching the question whether due process permits the entry of judgment upon a plea of guilty accompanied by a contemporaneous denial of acts constituting the crime."

3. Exactly what is the factual basis standard in an *Alford* situation? Consider Uviller, supra, at 126: "While it probably overruns the mark to declare that in order to convict the defendant on his plea, the trial judge must find his guilt beyond a reasonable doubt (as due process requires at trial), one might choose the 'clear and convincing' standard as the most appropriate to the purpose."

4. While footnote 11 in *Alford* states that the trial judge would likewise not commit constitutional error in rejecting the plea, it also indicates that the scope of a federal judge's discretion to do so under rule 11 is another matter. In *United States v. Gaskins,* 485 F.2d 1046 (D.C.Cir.1973), where the defendant was convicted of first degree burglary after the judge refused to accept a bargained plea to unlawful entry because the defendant equivocated about his guilt, the court held that "it is an abuse of discretion to refuse a guilty plea solely because the defendant does not admit the alleged facts of the crime" when there is "strong factual evidence implicating defendant," as the "entry of such a plea of guilty in such a situation is not contrary to the interests of justice."

Alschuler, *The Defense Attorney's Role in Plea Bargaining,* 84 Yale L.J. 1179, 1301 (1975), is critical of fn. 11 in *Alford:* "Under *Alford,* the choice is not the defendant's but the court's, and a court's discre-

11. Our holding does not mean that a trial judge must accept every constitutionally valid guilty plea merely because a defendant wishes so to plead. A criminal defendant does not have an absolute right under the Constitution to have his guilty plea accepted by the court, although the States may by statute or otherwise confer such a right. Likewise, the States may bar their courts from accepting guilty pleas from any defendants who assert their innocence. Cf. Fed.Rule Crim. Proc. 11, which gives a trial judge discretion to "refuse to accept a plea of guilty * * *." We need not now delineate the scope of that discretion.

tion to refuse an *Alford* plea is apparently subject to no restrictions and no standards. This result is, of course, consistent with the Supreme Court's reluctance to view the problem of the 'innocent' defendant as a problem of constitutional law and with the Court's willingness to tolerate a variety of approaches among the various states. The practical effect, however, is to create a system in which defendants have no rights and trial courts can do no wrong. Despite the Supreme Court's suggestion that upholding a defendant's choice of plea serves important 'human values,' this choice can apparently be denied on the basis of judicial whim."

5. Not infrequently, a factual basis for the plea will be lacking in the sense that the facts will show that the defendant committed a different crime and that the offense to which the plea is offered is not even a logical included offense of the crime committed. For example, in a jurisdiction with an offense of breaking and entering in the nighttime (a nonprobationable offense with a 15-year maximum) and an offense of breaking and entering in the daytime (a probationable offense with a 5-year maximum), a bargained plea to the latter offense may be tendered although the facts show that the crime occurred at midnight. Newman, *Conviction: The Determination of Guilt or Innocence Without Trial* 99–104 (Remington, ed., 1966). Should the judge accept the plea under these circumstances? What then should the result be in *People v. Foster,* 225 N.E.2d 200 (N.Y.1967), where defendant was originally charged with manslaughter in the first degree, but was allowed to plead guilty to attempted manslaughter in the second degree. On appeal, defendant argued that because manslaughter in the first and second degree are homicides committed "without a design to effect death" and an attempt is "an act done with intent to commit a crime," his plea could not stand because attempted manslaughter is logically and legally impossible.

V. PLEA WITHDRAWAL GENERALLY

1. One means commonly employed in an effort to "undo" a guilty plea is a motion to the trial court to withdraw the plea.[g] Fed.R.Crim.P. 32(d) permits such a motion only before sentencing, but there is considerable variation in state practice. Some allow the motion only before sentencing or before judgment, but many (following the *former* federal approach) allow the motion thereafter as well. If the time for presenting a withdrawal motion has passed, the plea might be challenged by a timely appeal (limited to issues reflected by the record at arraignment and sentencing) or by collateral attack (typically limited to constitutional violations or other serious violations of law).

2. The federal standard for presentence withdrawal motions, derived from dictum in *Kercheval v. United States,* 274 U.S. 220, 47 S.Ct. 582, 71 L.Ed. 1009 (1927), is "any fair and just reason"; it is commonly used at the state level as well for presentence motions. As for later motions, the states typically utilize some higher standard, such as "miscarriage of justice" or "manifest injustice." As explained in *State v. Olish,* 266 S.E.2d 134 (W.Va.1980):

"The basis for the distinction between these two rules is three-fold. First, once sentence is imposed, the defendant is more likely to view the plea bargain as a tactical mistake and therefore wish to have it set aside. Second, at the time the sentence is imposed, other portions of the plea bargain agreement will often be performed by the prosecutor, such as the dismissal of additional charges or the return or destruction of physical evidence, all of which may be difficult to undo if the defendant later attacks his guilty plea. Finally, a higher

g. On plea withdrawal because the judge learns he cannot go along with a plea agreement which he earlier concurred in, see Note 7, p. 1200 supra.

post-sentence standard for withdrawal is required by the settled policy of giving finality to criminal sentences which result from a voluntary and properly counseled guilty plea."

3. Though the higher test has different meanings in different states, it is commonly treated as equivalent to the grounds for relief upon collateral attack in a post-conviction proceeding. As for the lower "fair and just reason" test, it has received different interpretations. Compare *United States v. Savage,* 561 F.2d 554 (4th Cir.1977) (any desire to withdraw the plea before sentence suffices so long as the prosecution fails to establish that it would be prejudiced by the withdrawal); with *United States v. Saft,* 558 F.2d 1073 (2d Cir. 1977) (there is no occasion to inquire into the matter of prejudice unless the defendant first shows good reason for being allowed to withdraw his plea). Though there remains variation at the state level, *Saft* now prevails in the federal courts. As explained in *United States v. Barker,* 514 F.2d 208 (D.C.Cir.1975): "Were withdrawal automatic in every case where the defendant decided to alter his tactics and present his theory of the case to the jury, the guilty plea would become a mere gesture, a temporary and meaningless formality reversible at the defendant's whim. In fact, however, a guilty plea is no such trifle, but 'a grave and solemn act,' which is 'accepted only with care and discernment.' "

4. Should a withdrawn plea be admissible against the defendant at his subsequent trial? Some jurisdictions earlier ruled in the affirmative on the ground that the plea is a fact inconsistent with the defendant's claim of innocence, but the modern cases have consistently adopted the view that the withdrawal of the plea adjudicates the impropriety of its prior reception and thus forbids any subsequent evidentiary use of it.[h]

h. Compare the situation as to the admissibility of a tendered guilty plea, discussed in Note 7, p. 1196 supra.

VI. SIGNIFICANCE OF NONCOMPLIANCE WITH REQUIREMENTS FOR RECEIVING GUILTY PLEA

1. In McCARTHY v. UNITED STATES, 394 U.S. 459, 89 S.Ct. 1166, 22 L.Ed.2d 418 (1969), the trial judge failed to address the defendant personally and determine that his plea was made voluntarily and with an understanding of the nature of the charge, as required by Rule 11. The Court, per Chief Justice WARREN, rejected the government's contention that under such circumstances the government should still be allowed to prove that the defendant in fact pleaded voluntarily and with an understanding of the charge:

"From the defendant's perspective, the efficacy of shifting the burden of proof to the Government at a later voluntariness hearing is questionable. In meeting its burden, the Government will undoubtedly rely upon the defendant's statement that he desired to plead guilty and frequently a statement that the plea was not induced by any threats or promises. This prima facie case for voluntariness is likely to be treated as irrebuttable in cases such as this one, where the defendant's reply is limited to his own plaintive allegations that he did not understand the nature of the charge and therefore failed to assert a valid defense or to limit his guilty plea only to a lesser included offense. No matter how true these allegations may be, rarely, if ever, can a defendant corroborate them in a post-plea voluntariness hearing. * * *

"We thus conclude that prejudice inheres in a failure to comply with Rule 11, for noncompliance deprives the defendant of the Rule's procedural safeguards, which are designed to facilitate a more accurate determination of the voluntariness of his plea. Our holding that a defendant whose plea has been accepted in violation of Rule

11 should be afforded the opportunity to plead anew not only will insure that every accused is afforded those procedural safeguards, but also will help reduce the great waste of judicial resources required to process the frivolous attacks on guilty plea convictions that are encouraged, and are more difficult to dispose of, when the original record is inadequate."

2. In UNITED STATES v. TIMMRECK, 441 U.S. 780, 99 S.Ct. 2085, 60 L.Ed.2d 634 (1979), the trial judge explained to the defendant who tendered a guilty plea that he could receive a sentence of 15 years imprisonment and a $25,000 fine, but failed to describe the mandatory special parole term of at least 3 years. The judge then accepted the plea and sentenced defendant to 10 years imprisonment, plus a special parole term of 5 years and a fine of $5,000. The defendant raised no objection to the sentence at the time, and did not take an appeal. About two years later, defendant collaterally attacked his plea in a 28 U.S.C. § 2255 proceeding on the ground that the judge had violated Rule 11 by not informing him of the mandatory special parole term. The district court concluded the Rule 11 violation did not entitle defendant to § 2255 relief because he had not suffered any prejudice, inasmuch as his sentence was within the maximum described to him when the plea was accepted. But the Court of Appeals held that "a Rule 11 violation is per se prejudicial" and thus a basis for relief via § 2255. STEVENS, J., relying upon the limits on § 2255 relief set out in *Hill v. United States,* 368 U.S. 424, 82 S.Ct. 468, 7 L.Ed.2d 417 (1962), stated for a unanimous Court:

"The reasoning in *Hill* is equally applicable to a formal violation of Rule 11. Such a violation is neither constitutional nor jurisdictional: the 1966 amendment to Rule 11 obviously could not amend the Constitution or limit the jurisdiction of the federal courts. Nor can any claim reasonably be made that the error here resulted in a 'complete miscarriage of justice' or in a proceeding 'inconsistent with the rudimentary demands of fair procedure.' Respondent does not argue that he was actually unaware of the special parole term or that, if he had been properly advised by the trial judge, he would not have pleaded guilty. His only claim is of a technical violation of the rule. That claim could have been raised on direct appeal, see *McCarthy v. United States,* but was not. * * *

"Indeed, if anything, this case may be a stronger one for foreclosing collateral relief than the *Hill* case. For the concern with finality served by the limitation on collateral attack has special force with respect to convictions based on guilty pleas.

> 'Every inroad on the concept of finality undermines confidence in the integrity of our procedures; and, by increasing the volume of judicial work, inevitably delays and impairs the orderly administration of justice. The impact is greatest when new grounds for setting aside guilty pleas are approved because the vast majority of criminal convictions result from such pleas. Moreover, the concern that unfair procedures may have resulted in the conviction of an innocent defendant is only rarely raised by a petition to set aside a guilty plea.' *United States v. Smith,* 440 F.2d 521 (1971) (Stevens, J., dissenting).

"As in *Hill,* we find it unnecessary to consider whether § 2255 relief would be available if a violation of Rule 11 occurred in the context of other aggravating circumstances. 'We decide only that such collateral relief is not available when all that is shown is a failure to comply with the formal requirements of the Rule.' "

3. It was disputed whether *McCarthy* and *Timmreck* meant that any "technical violation" of Rule 11 required reversal on direct appeal? In *United States v. Dayton,* 604 F.2d 931 (5th Cir.1979). Gee, J., for the majority, concluded that "a failure by the trial court to address any one or more of the rule's three core concerns [absence

of coercion, understanding of the accusation, and knowledge of the direct consequences] as occurred in *McCarthy* requires automatic reversal," but that in the case of "fallings off from the post-*McCarthy* elaborations of Rule 11" the harmless error doctrine applies, as Rule 11 "is now at such a level of complexity as to render letter-perfect compliance with each of its many provisions very difficult indeed." Brown, C.J., concurring, found "the Court's breakdown into old and new components of the Rule unpersuasive" and would instead "reserve use of harmless error for situations in which the failure to comply with Rule 11 is merely a technical departure from the Rule or in which there has been substantial compliance with the demands of Rule 11." The four dissenters concluded that "*Timmreck* clearly stands for the proposition that *McCarthy* continues to command what it mandated on the day it was decided: strait compliance with all procedures demanded by Rule 11." Fed.R.Crim.P. 11(h) was added thereafter.

4. State courts are not in complete agreement as to the significance of noncompliance with state provisions similar to Federal Rule 11. However, most of the recent cases follow the *Timmreck* approach.

5. *Boykin v. Alabama,* p. 1234 supra, concerned a defendant who had pleaded guilty in state court to five armed robbery indictments and thereafter received the death penalty. At arraignment, "so far as the record shows, the judge asked no questions of petitioner concerning his plea, and petitioner did not address the court." The Supreme Court reversed, concluding that it "was error, plain on the face of the record, for the trial judge to accept petitioner's guilty plea without an affirmative showing that it was intelligent and voluntary."

But in *North Carolina v. Alford,* p. 1235 supra, the Court noted in footnote 3: "At the state court hearing on post-conviction relief, the testimony confirmed that Alford has been fully informed by his attorney as to his rights on a plea of not guilty and as to the consequences of a plea of guilty. Since the record in this case affirmatively indicates that Alford was aware of the consequences of his plea of guilty and of the rights waived by the plea, no issues of substance under *Boykin v. Alabama* would be presented even if that case was held applicable to the events here in question."

This means that if a state defendant challenges his plea by federal habeas corpus, "all that the Constitution and *Boykin* require is that this Court be able to conclude that the record as it now exists, including the transcript, if any, made at the plea session, the record made at the state habeas corpus proceeding and the record made before this Court, conclusively establish that the guilty pleas of petitioner were in fact freely, voluntarily, and knowingly entered." *Walker v. Caldwell,* 335 F.Supp. 308 (M.D.Ga.1971).

VII. SIGNIFICANCE OF COMPLIANCE WITH REQUIREMENTS FOR RECEIVING GUILTY PLEA

1. Is the "logical converse" of *McCarthy* and *Boykin* that if the trial judge does have the defendant indicate for the record that his plea is voluntary and with knowledge of the charge and the consequences, then the defendant may not thereafter challenge his plea as being involuntary and unknowing? In *Fontaine v. United States,* 411 U.S. 213, 93 S.Ct. 1461, 36 L.Ed.2d 169 (1973), it was held that upon a federal defendant's motion under 28 U.S.C. § 2255 to vacate his sentence on the grounds that his plea of guilty had been induced by a combination of fear, coercive police tactics, and illness (including mental illness), a hearing was required "on this record" notwithstanding full compliance with Federal Rule 11, as § 2255 calls for a hearing unless "the motion and the files and records of the case conclusively show that the prisoner is entitled to no relief"; the objective of Rule 11 "is to flush out and resolve all such issues, but like any

procedural mechanism, its exercise is neither always perfect nor uniformly invulnerable to subsequent challenge calling for an opportunity to prove the allegations."

2. Allison was indicted in North Carolina for breaking and entering, attempted safe robbery and possession of burglary tools, after which he entered a plea of guilty to the second charge. In accordance with procedures then used in the state, the judge in taking the plea read from a printed form 13 questions, each of which Allison answered in the manner required for acceptance of the plea. He responded in the affirmative to the question, "Do you understand that upon your plea of guilty you could be imprisoned for as much as minimum [sic] of 10 years to life?"; and no to the question, "Has the Solicitor, or your lawyer, or any policeman, law officer or anyone else made any promises or threats to you to influence you to plead guilty in this case?" The only record of the proceedings was the executed form. The judge accepted the plea and at a later unrecorded sentencing hearing sentenced Allison to 17–21 years in prison. After exhausting his state remedies, Allison sought relief via federal habeas corpus. In his petition, he alleged that his attorney had told him an agreement had been reached with the prosecutor and judge whereby if he pleaded guilty he would get only 10 years, and that his attorney had cautioned him he should nonetheless answer the questions of the judge as he did. The district court denied the petition on the ground that the form "conclusively shows" no constitutional violation and thus met the standard of *Fontaine,* but the court of appeals reversed. In BLACKLEDGE v. ALLISON, 431 U.S. 63, 97 S.Ct. 1621, 52 L.Ed.2d 136 (1977), the Court, per STEWART, J., affirmed. After noting the several benefits of negotiated pleas and that they "can be secured * * * only if dispositions by guilty plea are accorded a great measure of finality," he continued:

"The allegations in this case were not in themselves so 'vague [or] conclusory,' as to warrant dismissal for that reason alone. Allison alleged as a ground for relief that his plea was induced by an unkept promise. But he did not stop there. He proceeded to elaborate upon this claim with specific factual allegations. The petition indicated exactly what the terms of the promise were; when, where, and by whom the promise had been made; and the identity of one witness to its communication. The critical question is whether these allegations, when viewed against the record of the plea hearing, were so 'palpably incredible,' so 'patently frivolous or false', as to warrant summary dismissal. In the light of the nature of the record of the proceeding at which the guilty plea was accepted, and of the ambiguous status of the process of plea bargaining at the time the guilty plea was made, we conclude that Allison's petition should not have been summarily dismissed.

"Only recently has plea bargaining become a visible practice accepted as a legitimate component in the administration of criminal justice. For decades it was a *sub rosa* process shrouded in secrecy and deliberately concealed by participating defendants, defense lawyers, prosecutors, and even judges. Indeed, it was not until our decision in *Santobello v. New York* [p. 1201 supra], that lingering doubts about the legitimacy of the practice were finally dispelled.

"Allison was arraigned a mere 37 days after the *Santobello* decision was announced, under a North Carolina procedure that had not been modified in light of *Santobello* or earlier decisions of this Court recognizing the process of plea bargaining. That procedure itself reflected the atmosphere of secrecy which then characterized plea bargaining generally. No transcript of the proceeding was made. The only record was a standard printed form. There is no way of knowing whether the trial judge in any way deviated from or supplemented the text of the form. The record is silent as to what statements Allison, his lawyer, or the prosecutor might have made regarding promised sentencing concessions. And there is no record at all of the sentencing hearing three days later, at which one of the participants might well have made a statement shedding light upon the veracity of the allegations Allison later advanced.

"The litany of form questions followed by the trial judge at arraignment nowhere indicated to Allison (or indeed to the lawyers involved) that plea bargaining was a legitimate practice that could be freely disclosed in open court. Neither lawyer was asked to disclose any agreement that had been reached, or sentencing recommendation that had been promised. The process thus did nothing to dispel a defendant's belief that any bargain struck must remain concealed—a belief here allegedly reinforced by the admonition of Allison's lawyer himself that disclosure could jeopardize the agreement. Rather than challenging counsel's contention at oral argument in this Court that 'at that time in North Carolina plea bargains were never disclosed in response to such a question on such a form,' counsel for the State conceded at oral argument that '[t]he form was a minimal inquiry.'

"Although '[l]ogically the general inquiry should elicit information about plea bargaining, * * * it seldom has in the past.' Advisory Committee Note to 1974 Amendment of Fed.Rule Crim.Proc. 11. Particularly if, as Allison alleged, he was advised by counsel to conceal any plea bargain, his denial that any promises had been made might have been a courtroom ritual more sham than real. We thus cannot conclude that the allegations in Allison's habeas corpus petition, when measured against the 'record' of the arraignment, were so 'patently false or frivolous' as to warrant summary dismissal.

"North Carolina has recently undertaken major revisions of its plea bargaining procedures in part to prevent the very kind of problem now before us. Plea bargaining is expressly legitimate. N.C. Gen.Stat. § 15A–1021, & Official Commentary (1975). The judge is directed to advise the defendant that courts have approved plea bargaining and he may thus admit to any promises without fear of jeopardizing an advantageous agreement or prejudicing himself in the judge's eyes. Specific inquiry about whether a plea bargain has been struck is then made not only of the defendant, but also of his counsel and the prosecutor. N.C.Gen.Stat. § 15A–1023(a), (c) (1975). Finally, the entire proceeding is to be transcribed verbatim. Id., § 15A–1026, as amended, ibid. (Int.Supp.1976).

"Had these commendable procedures been followed in the present case, Allison's petition would have been cast in a very different light. The careful explication of the legitimacy of plea bargaining, the questioning of both lawyers, and the verbatim record of their answers at the guilty plea proceedings would almost surely have shown whether any bargain did exist and, if so, insured that it was not ignored. But the salutary reforms recently implemented by North Carolina highlight even more sharply the deficiencies in the record before the District Court in the present case.

"This is not to say that every set of allegations not on its face without merit entitles a habeas corpus petitioner to an evidentiary hearing. As in civil cases generally, there exists a procedure whose purpose is to test whether facially adequate allegations have sufficient basis in fact to warrant plenary presentation of evidence. That procedure is, of course, the motion for summary judgment. Upon remand the Warden will be free to make such a motion, supporting it with whatever proof he wishes to attach. If he chooses to do so, Allison will then be required either to produce some contrary proof indicating that there is a genuine issue of fact to be resolved by the District Court or to explain his inability to provide such proof."

3. Are more elaborate procedures along the lines of present federal Rule 11 sufficient to foreclose a later attack upon a guilty plea? Note, 86 Yale L.J. 1395, 1410, 1421 (1977), concludes that this comprehensive hearing "can succeed in eliminating later hearings when attacks are made on the knowing and intelligent character of a plea," but "cannot eliminate the need for post conviction hearings when attacks are directed at events that transpired outside the Rule 11 hearing," such as when it is claimed a plea was influenced by secret government promises, as "any government coercion powerful enough to induce a defendant to plead guilty and thus consent to immediate conviction would surely be powerful enough to obtain untruthful answers to questions about the plea." Compare *Richardson v. United States,* 577 F.2d 447 (8th Cir.1978), concluding that where the defendant sought § 2255 relief on the ground that his guilty plea was induced by an unkept promise of the prosecutor that he would receive not more than 7 years, but the rule 11 record indicated defendant had said no promises had been made about his sentence, no hearing was required because "Richardson has offered no plausible excuse for his statements denying the existence of a promise as to the length of his sentence.".

4. Is there any way to take a guilty plea which will completely immunize it from subsequent attack? What of the procedures mandated in *Bryan v. United States,* 492 F.2d 775 (5th Cir.1974): "The court shall state that plea agreements are permissible and that the defendant and all counsel have a duty to disclose the existence and details of any agreement which relates to the plea tendered. Specific inquiry shall be made as to the existence of such an agreement before a plea is accepted. The defendant shall be placed under oath." Cf. *United States v. Stassi,* 583 F.2d 122 (3d Cir.1978) (defendant's conviction of making false statements under oath, based on fact his statements under oath at rule 11 hearing were inconsistent with those made at subsequent § 2255 proceeding to vacate plea, affirmed notwithstanding defendant's argument that "there was a widespread practice of ' "routine lying" under oath at Rule 11 colloquies' "). Compare Note, 46 Fordham L.Rev. 1242, 1260 (1978): "When a defendant routinely affirms, at a rule 11 inquiry, that his guilty plea was not the result of any threats or promises, the fact that he was under oath at the time should not be used categorically to deter him from later presenting a meritorious claim that his previous assertion was not true." Does this mean another inquiry is needed later? Consider *Model Pre-Arraignment Code* § 350.6: "The court after pronouncing the sentence of a defendant who has pleaded guilty or nolo contendere shall inquire of the defendant personally whether the sentence pronounced violates any agreement or understanding the defendant had with respect to the sentence."

SECTION 5. THE EFFECT OF A GUILTY PLEA: MORE ON THE EFFECTIVE ASSISTANCE OF COUNSEL AND THE WAIVER (OR FORFEITURE) OF RIGHTS

McMANN v. RICHARDSON

397 U.S. 759, 90 S.Ct. 1441, 25 L.Ed.2d 763 (1970).

MR. JUSTICE WHITE delivered the opinion of the Court. * * *

The core of the Court of Appeals' holding is the proposition that if in a collateral proceeding a guilty plea is shown to have been triggered by a coerced confession—if there would have been no plea had there been no confession—the plea is vulnerable at least in cases coming from New York where the guilty plea was taken prior to *Jackson v. Denno,* [p. 842 supra]. We are unable to agree with the Court of Appeals in this proposition. * * *

For present purposes, we put aside those cases where the defendant has his own reasons for pleading guilty wholly aside from the strength of the case against him as well as those cases where the defendant, although he would have gone to trial had he thought the State could not prove its case, is motivated by evidence against him independent of the confession. In these cases, as the Court of Appeals recognized, the confession, even if coerced, is not a sufficient factor in the plea to justify relief. Neither do we have before us the uncounselled defendant, see *Pennsylvania ex rel. Herman v. Claudy*, 350 U.S. 116, 76 S.Ct. 223, 100 L.Ed. 126 (1956), nor the situation where the circumstances that coerced the confession have abiding impact and also taint the plea. Cf. *Chambers v. Florida*, 309 U.S. 227, 60 S.Ct. 472, 84 L.Ed. 716 (1940). It is not disputed that in such cases a guilty plea is properly open to challenge.[12]

The issue on which we differ with the Court of Appeals arises in those situations involving the counselled defendant who allegedly would put the State to its proof if there was a substantial enough chance of acquittal, who would do so except for a prior confession which might be offered against him, and who because of the confession decides to plead guilty to save himself the expense and agony of a trial and perhaps also to minimize the penalty which might be imposed. After conviction on such a plea, is a defendant entitled to a hearing, and to relief if his factual claims are accepted, when his petition for habeas corpus alleges that his confession was in fact coerced and that it motivated his plea? We think not if he alleges and proves no more than this.

Since we are dealing with a defendant who deems his confession crucial to the State's case against him and who would go to trial if he thought his chances of acquittal were good, his decision to plead guilty or not turns on whether he thinks the law will allow his confession to be used against him. For the defendant who considers his confession involuntary and hence unusable against him at a trial, tendering a plea of guilty would seem a most improbable alternative. * * * [A] guilty plea in such circumstances is nothing less than a refusal to present his federal claims to the state court in the first instance—a choice by the defendant to take the benefits, if any, of a plea of guilty and then to pursue his coerced confession claim in collateral proceedings. Surely later allegations that the confession rendered his plea involuntary would appear incredible, and whether his plain bypass of state remedies was an intelligent act depends on whether he was so incompetently advised by counsel concerning the forum in which he should first present his federal claim that the Constitution will afford him another chance to plead.

A more credible explanation for a plea of guilty by a defendant who would go to trial except for his prior confession is his prediction that the law will permit his admissions to be used against him by the trier of fact. At least the probability of the State's being permitted to use the confession as evidence is sufficient to convince him that the State's case is too strong to contest and that a plea of guilty is the most advantageous course. Nothing in this train of events suggests that the defendant's plea, as distinguished from his confession, is an involuntary act. His later petition for collateral relief asserting that a *coerced* confession induced his plea is at most a claim that the admissibility of his confession was mistakenly assessed and that since he was erroneously advised, either under the then applicable law or un-

12. *Pennsylvania ex rel. Herman v. Claudy*, involved a plea of guilty made by a defendant without assistance of counsel. *Herman* did not hold that a plea of guilty, offered by a defendant assisted by competent counsel, is invalid whenever induced by the prosecution's possession of a coerced confession. Likewise, *Chambers v. Florida* does not support the position taken by the Court of Appeals in these cases. In *Chambers* the voluntariness of the confessions was properly considered by this Court both because the alleged coercion producing the confessions appeared to carry over to taint the guilty pleas and because the convictions were based on the confessions as well as the guilty pleas.

der the law later announced, his plea was an unintelligent and voidable act. The Constitution, however, does not render pleas of guilty so vulnerable.

As we said in *Brady v. United States* [p. 1191 supra], the decision to plead guilty before the evidence is in frequently involves the making of difficult judgments. All the pertinent facts normally cannot be known unless witnesses are examined and cross-examined in court. Even then the truth will often be in dispute. In the face of unavoidable uncertainty, the defendant and his counsel must make their best judgment as to the weight of the State's case. Counsel must predict how the facts, as he understands them, would be viewed by a court. If proved, would those facts convince a judge or jury of the defendant's guilt? On those facts would evidence seized without a warrant be admissible? Would the trier of fact on those facts find a confession voluntary and admissible? Questions like these cannot be answered with certitude; yet a decision to plead guilty must necessarily rest upon counsel's answers, uncertain as they may be. Waiving trial entails the inherent risk that the good-faith evaluations of a reasonably competent attorney will turn out to be mistaken either as to the facts or as to what a court's judgment might be on given facts.

That a guilty plea must be intelligently made is not a requirement that all advice offered by the defendant's lawyer withstand retrospective examination in a post-conviction hearing. Courts and judges continue to have serious differences among themselves on the admissibility of evidence, both with respect to the proper standard by which the facts are to be judged and with respect to the application of that standard to particular facts. That this Court might hold a defendant's confession inadmissible in evidence, possibly by a divided vote, hardly justifies a conclusion that the defendant's attorney was incompetent or ineffective when he thought the admissibility of the confession sufficiently probable to advise a plea of guilty.[a]

In our view a defendant's plea of guilty based on reasonably competent advice is an intelligent plea not open to attack on the grounds that counsel may have misjudged the admissibility of the defendant's confession. Whether a plea of guilty is unintelligent and therefore vulnerable when motivated by a confession erroneously thought admissible in evidence depends as an initial matter not on whether a court would retrospectively consider counsel's advice to be right or wrong, but on whether that advice was within the range of competence demanded of attorneys in criminal cases. On the one hand, uncertainty is inherent in predicting court decisions; but on the other hand defendants facing felony charges are entitled to the effective assistance of competent counsel. Beyond this we think the matter, for the most part, should be left to the good sense and discretion of the trial courts with the admonition that if the right to counsel guaranteed by the Constitution is to serve its purpose, defendants cannot be left to the mercies of incompetent counsel, and that judges should strive to maintain proper standards of performance by attorneys who are representing defendants in criminal cases in their courts.

We hold, therefore, that a defendant who alleges that he pleaded guilty because of a prior coerced confession is not, without more, entitled to a hearing on his petition for habeas corpus. Nor do we deem the situation substantially different where the defendant's plea was entered

a. In the companion case of *Parker v. North Carolina*, p. 1193 supra, where the defendant told his attorney that his pre-*Miranda* confession after overnight detention "had not been prompted by threats or promises and that he had not been frightened when he made the statement to the police," and "counsel apparently deemed the confession admissible and his advice to plead guilty was followed by his client," the Court applied *Richardson* and concluded that the advice Parker received "was well within the range of competence required of attorneys representing defendants in criminal cases."

prior to *Jackson v. Denno* [holding unconstitutional the New York procedure which required the trial judge, when a confession was offered and a prima facie case of voluntariness established, to submit the issue to the jury without himself finally resolving disputed issues of fact and determining whether or not the confession was voluntary, and overruling *Stein v. New York,* 346 U.S. 156, 73 S.Ct. 1077, 97 L.Ed. 1522 (1953), which had approved the New York practice].

Whether a guilty plea was entered before or after *Jackson v. Denno,* the question of the validity of the plea remains the same: was the plea a voluntary and intelligent act of the defendant? * * * For the respondents in these cases successfully to claim relief based on *Jackson v. Denno,* each must demonstrate gross error on the part of counsel when he recommended that the defendant plead guilty instead of going to trial and challenging the New York procedures for determining the admissibility of confessions. Such showing cannot be made, for precisely this challenge was presented to the New York courts and to this Court in *Stein,* and in 1953 this Court found no constitutional infirmity in the New York procedures for dealing with coerced confession claims. Counsel for these respondents cannot be faulted for not anticipating *Jackson v. Denno* or for considering the New York procedures to be as valid as the four dissenters in that case thought them to be.

We are unimpressed with the argument that because the decision in *Jackson* has been applied retroactively to defendants who had previously gone to trial, the defendant whose confession allegedly caused him to plead guilty prior to *Jackson* is also entitled to a hearing on the voluntariness of his confession and to a trial if his admissions are held to have been coerced. A conviction after trial in which a coerced confession is introduced rests in part on the coerced confession, a constitutionally unacceptable basis for conviction. It is that conviction and the confession on which it rests which the defendant later attacks in collateral proceedings. The defendant who pleads guilty is in a different posture. He is convicted on his counseled admission in open court that he committed the crime charged against him. The prior confession is not the basis for the judgment, has never been offered in evidence at a trial, and may never be offered in evidence. Whether or not the advice the defendant received in the pre-*Jackson* era would have been different had *Jackson* then been the law has no bearing on the accuracy of the defendant's admission that he committed the crime. * * *

JUSTICE BRENNAN, with whom JUSTICES DOUGLAS and MARSHALL join, dissenting. * * *

As I understand the Court's opinion, there are basically three reasons why the Court rejects the contention that the *Jackson-Denno* defect may unconstitutionally infect the pleading process. The first is the highly formalistic notion that the guilty plea, and not the antecedent confession, is the basis of the judgments against respondents. Of course this is true in the technical sense that the guilty plea is *always* the legal basis of a judgment of conviction entered thereon. However, this argument hardly disposes adequately of the contention that the plea in turn was at least partially induced, and therefore is tainted, by the fact that no constitutionally adequate procedures existed to test the validity of a highly prejudicial and allegedly coerced confession. * * *

Secondly, the Court views the entry of the guilty pleas as waiver of objections to the allegedly coerced confession. For the reasons previously stated, I do not believe that the pleas were legally voluntary if respondents' allegations are proved. Nor were the pleas the relinquishment of a *known* right, for it was only when *Stein v. New York* was overruled by *Jackson v. Denno* that it became clear that the New York procedure was constitutionally inadequate. Thus there is no sense in which respondents deliberately by-passed or "waived" state procedures constitutionally adequate to adjudicate their coerced confession claims.

Finally, the Court takes the position, in effect, that the defect in the *Stein*-approved New York procedure was not very great—that the procedure was only a little bit unconstitutional—and hence that it is too speculative to inquire whether the difference between the pre-*Jackson* and post-*Jackson* procedures would, in a particular case, alter the advice given by counsel concerning the desirability of a plea. If, indeed, the deficiency in the pre-*Jackson* procedure was not very great, then it is difficult to understand why we found it necessary to invalidate the procedure and, particularly, why it was imperative to apply the *Jackson* decision retroactively. * * *

Despite the disclaimers to the contrary, what is essentially involved * * * is nothing less than the determination of the Court to preserve the sanctity of virtually all judgments obtained by means of guilty pleas. There is no other adequate explanation for the surprising notion of partial retroactivity which the Court today propounds. * * *

Notes and Questions

1. Does *McMann* suggest that the procedures for receiving guilty pleas need to be expanded? Consider the proposal of Judge Bazelon, dissenting in *United States v. Simpson,* 475 F.2d 934 (D.C.Cir.1973): "If constitutional waiver standards are to be judicially enforceable, there must be some external check on the quality of counsel's assistance in the plea bargaining process. In fairness to the defendant and the courts, that check should occur at the stage of the proceeding when the burden of showing a knowing and voluntary waiver is on the Government. I would require that trial judges determine that the defendant's decision to plead guilty is a properly informed choice by including in the record a showing that counsel has made 'an independent examination of the facts, circumstances, pleadings and laws involved and then [offered the defendant] his informed opinion as to what plea should be entered.' Developing precise contours for this requirement might take some experience with actual cases, but we could well begin by requiring that the attorney indicate, orally or in writing, the extent and results of his investigation of the facts of the case and a concise breakdown of his steps in its preparation."

2. In TOLLETT v. HENDERSON, 411 U.S. 258, 93 S.Ct. 1602, 36 L.Ed.2d 235 (1973), the Court, per REHNQUIST, J., relying upon *Brady, Parker,* and *McMann,* held that a defendant who pleaded guilty to murder on advice of counsel is not entitled to federal collateral relief merely on proof that, unknown to defendant and his counsel, the indicting grand jury was unconstitutionally selected:

"There are no doubt factual and legal differences between respondent's present assertion of the claim of discriminatory selection of the members of a grand jury, and the assertion of the constitutional claims by the prisoners in the *Brady* trilogy. In the latter cases, the facts giving rise to the constitutional claims were generally known to the defendants and their attorneys prior to the entry of the guilty pleas, and the issue in this Court turned on the adequacy of the attorneys' advice in evaluating those facts as a part of the recommendation to plead guilty. In the instant case, the facts relating to the selection of the Davidson County grand jury in 1948 were found by the District Court and the Court of Appeals to have been unknown to both respondent and his attorney. If the issue were to be cast solely in terms of 'waiver,' the Court of Appeals was undoubtedly correct in concluding that there had been no such waiver here. But just as the guilty pleas in the *Brady* trilogy were found to foreclose direct inquiry into the merits of claimed antecedent constitutional violations there, we conclude that respondent's guilty plea here alike forecloses independent inquiry into the claim of discrimination in the selection of the grand jury. * * *

"A guilty plea, voluntarily and intelligently entered, may not be vacated because the defendant was not advised of every conceivable constitutional plea in abatement he might have to the charge, no matter how peripheral such a plea might be to the normal focus of counsel's in quiry. And just as it is not sufficient for the criminal defendant seeking to set aside such a plea to show that his counsel in retrospect may not have correctly appraised the constitutional significance of certain historical facts, *McMann,* it is likewise not sufficient that he show that if counsel had pursued a certain factual inquiry such a pursuit would have uncovered a possible constitutional infirmity in the proceedings.

"The principal value of counsel to the accused in a criminal prosecution often lies not in counsel's ability to recite a list of possible defenses in the abstract, nor in his ability, if time permitted, to amass a large quantum of factual data and inform the defendant of it. Counsel's concern is the faithful representation of the interest of his client, and such representation frequently involves highly practical considerations as well as specialized knowledge of the law. Often the interests of the accused are not advanced by challenges that would only delay the inevitable date of prosecution, or by contesting all guilt. A prospect of plea bargaining, the expectation or hope of a lesser sentence, or the convincing nature of the evidence against the accused are considerations that might well suggest the advisability of a guilty plea without elaborate consideration of whether pleas in abatement, such as unconstitutional grand jury selection procedures, might be factually supported.

"In order to obtain his release on federal habeas under these circumstances, respondent must not only establish the unconstitutional discrimination in selection of grand jurors. He must also establish that his attorney's advice to plead guilty without having made inquiry into the composition of the grand jury rendered that advice outside the 'range of competence demanded of attorneys in criminal cases.' "

MARSHALL, J., joined by DOUGLAS and BRENNAN, JJ., dissented: "The Court today extends the holdings of the 'guilty plea' trilogy without reference to the rationale by which those cases were reconciled with the requirements of the Constitution, that a plea is a waiver of constitutional rights only where the defendant has been informed of those rights and decides not to invoke them in order to gain some advantage.[b]

"In the end, the Court seems to adopt a concept of professional responsibility that I cannot accept. It would let an attorney 'advance' the interests of his client without even informing himself about the facts underlying a constitutional challenge so that he might inform the client about the way in which, in the attorney's professional judgment, the course he is taking in fact advances those interests. 'Faithful representation of the interest of his client', means, I believe, that an attorney must consult with the client fully on matters of constitutional magnitude. Without such consultation, the representation of criminal defendants becomes only another method of manipulating persons in situations

b. Justice Marshall noted elsewhere that "that decision must be made by the defendant, for we would not let an attorney bargain away his client's rights," to which he appended the following footnote:

"Some of this Court's decisions suggest that an attorney's decision, in which the defendant does not participate, not to raise a constitutional objection may sometimes preclude successful reliance on the constitutional claim. [See Note 3, p. 1503 infra.] If such a rule is to be squarely adopted by this Court, it should be limited narrowly to situations in which practical realities bar consultation, as often may happen during the course of trial."

where their control over their lives is precisely what is at stake.

"If plea bargaining is to be constitutionally acceptable, it must rest upon personal choices made by defendants informed about possible alternatives; at least, they should know what options are open to them. In this case, Henderson might have secured a sentence shorter than 99 years by requiring the State to defend the constitutionality of its procedures for selecting grand juries. As is clear from this record, such a defense could not have succeeded, and the embarrassment of attempting a defense might well have led the prosecution to offer a more favorable bargain.[3] I find nothing in the opinion of the Court that persuades me that Henderson's attorney acted 'within the range of competence demanded of attorneys in criminal cases,' *McMann v. Richardson,* because he did not consult with his client on a matter about which consultation is required.

"Petitioner suggests, however, that Henderson's attorney *may* have considered the possibility of challenging the indictment but rejected that course because he *believed* that the grand jury was in fact selected by procedures that conformed to constitutional requirements. There is only the barest support in the record for this contention, and the District Judge explicitly found that no objection was made by counsel 'quite simply, because the possibility never occurred to him.' But even if petitioner's suggestion were correct, it would not advance his cause. For then, as Judge Celebrezze aptly put it, the attorney's decision would have been 'grossly inadequate in light of the clearly established constitutional law of the period.' " [c]

3. In HILL v. LOCKHART, ___ U.S. ___, 106 S.Ct. 366, 88 L.Ed.2d 203 (1985), the Court, per POWELL, J., held "that the two-part *Strickland v. Washington* [p. —— supra] test applies to challenges to guilty pleas based on ineffective assistance of counsel. In the context of guilty pleas, the first half of the *Strickland v. Washington* test is nothing more than a restatement of the standard of attorney competence already set forth in *Tollett v. Henderson* and *McMann v. Richardson.* The second, or 'prejudice,' requirement, on the other

3. Even if the State successfully defended its procedures in a preliminary attack, or if it decided to institute proceedings anew by convening a new grand jury, Henderson would have secured time in which to prepare a better defense and in which passions over his offense might subside, so that a plea of not guilty might have been more attractive to him.

c. The dissenters went on to note that Henderson was indicted in a county which was 25% black but which had not had a single black on a grand jury, and that blacks were specifically identified on the lists from which members of the grand jury were chosen, and then observed:

"Two points about these facts must be emphasized. First, the law was clear in 1948 that it was extremely difficult for a State to establish that it did not unconstitutionally exclude Negroes from service on the grand jury if no Negroes in fact served and a method of selection was used that brought to the attention of the persons selecting the grand jury the race of potential grand jurors. It was therefore relatively easy to assess whether, if an attorney could present that kind of evidence, a constitutional challenge to the indictment was likely to succeed. Thus, making the decision to challenge the grand jury is different from making the decision to challenge a confession as coerced or a search as unreasonable. The latter decision, as the Court emphasized in *McMann v. Richardson,* often turns upon predictions about how certain facts will be viewed by a court attempting to apply largely unstructured tests of reasonableness or voluntariness under all the circumstances. I would therefore accord less weight to the fact that an attorney must make professional judgments in cases like this one than in cases like *McMann,* in line with the difference in the ease with which such judgments can confidently be made.

"Second, it takes almost no inquiry at all to determine whether any Negroes had served on local grand juries and whether racial designations appeared on the lists from which grand jurors were chosen. In its quest to establish a general rule applicable to all cases of challenges to the composition of grand juries, the Court disregards this fact. Instead, it characterizes the problem as involving 'amass[ing] a large quantum of factual data' and 'elaborate consideration of whether pleas in abatement . . . might be factually supported.' Whatever might be the situation in other cases, the facts in this case show that no large amounts of data or elaborate consideration is involved. That is enough to demonstrate the fallacy of the Court's attempt to define a broad general rule. I would adhere to tests that turn on the facts of each case."

hand, focuses on whether counsel's constitutionally ineffective performance affected the outcome of the plea process. In other words, in order to satisfy the 'prejudice' requirement, the defendant must show that there is a reasonable probability that, but for counsel's errors, he would not have pleaded guilty and would have insisted on going to trial.

"In many guilty plea cases, the 'prejudice' inquiry will closely resemble the inquiry engaged in by courts reviewing ineffective assistance challenges to convictions obtained through a trial. For example, where the alleged error of counsel is a failure to investigate or discover potentially exculpatory evidence, the determination whether the error 'prejudiced' the defendant by causing him to plead guilty rather than go to trial will depend on the likelihood that discovery of the evidence would have led counsel to change his recommendation as to the plea. This assessment, in turn, will depend in large part on a prediction whether the evidence likely would have changed the outcome of a trial. Similarly, where the alleged error of counsel is a failure to advise the defendant of a potential affirmative defense to the crime charged, the resolution of the 'prejudice' inquiry will depend largely on whether the affirmative defense likely would have succeeded at trial. See, e.g., *Evans v. Meyer,* 742 F.2d 371, 375 ([7th Cir.] 1984) ('It is inconceivable to us . . . that [the defendant] would have gone to trial on a defense of intoxication, or that if he had done so he either would have been acquitted or, if convicted, would nevertheless have been given a shorter sentence than he actually received'). As we explained in *Strickland v. Washington,* these predictions of the outcome at a possible trial, where necessary, should be made objectively, without regard for the 'idiosyncrasies of the particular decisionmaker.'

"In the present case the claimed error of counsel is erroneous advice as to eligibility for parole under the sentence agreed to in the plea bargain. We find it unnecessary to determine whether there may be circumstances under which erroneous advice by counsel as to parole eligibility may be deemed constitutionally ineffective assistance of counsel, because in the present case we conclude that petitioner's allegations are insufficient to satisfy the *Strickland v. Washington* requirement of 'prejudice.' Petitioner did not allege in his habeas petition that, had counsel correctly informed him about his parole eligibility date, he would have pleaded not guilty and insisted on going to trial. He alleged no special circumstances that might support the conclusion that he placed particular emphasis on his parole eligibility in deciding whether or not to plead guilty. Indeed, petitioner's mistaken belief that he would become eligible for parole after serving one-third of his sentence would seem to have affected not only his calculation of the time he likely would serve if sentenced pursuant to the proposed plea agreement, but also his calculation of the time he likely would serve if he went to trial and were convicted."

4. In MENNA v. NEW YORK, 423 U.S. 61, 96 S.Ct. 241, 46 L.Ed.2d 195 (1975), the Court, per curiam, held that the defendant's previously asserted claim that his indictment should be dismissed as in violation of the double jeopardy clause was not thereafter "waived" by his counseled plea of guilty to the charge. The Court observed in footnote 2:

"Neither *Tollett v. Henderson* nor our earlier cases on which it relied, *e.g., Brady v. United States* and *McMann v. Richardson,* stand for the proposition that counseled guilty pleas inevitably 'waive' all antecedent constitutional violations. If they did so hold, the New York Court of Appeals might be correct. However in *Tollett* we emphasized that waiver was not the basic ingredient of this line of cases. The point of these cases is that a counseled plea of guilty is an admission of factual guilt so reliable that, where voluntary and intelligent, it *quite validly* removes the issue of factual guilt from the case. In most cases, factual guilt is a sufficient basis for the State's imposition of punishment. A guilty plea, therefore, simply renders irrelevant those constitutional violations not logically inconsistent with the valid establishment of factual guilt and which do not stand in the way of conviction if factual guilt is validly established. Here, however, the claim is that the State may not convict petitioner no matter how validly his factual guilt is established. The guilty plea, therefore does not bar the claim.

"We do not hold that a double jeopardy claim may never be waived. We simply hold that a plea of guilty to a charge does not waive a claim that—judged on its face—the charge is one which the State may not constitutionally prosecute."

5. Consider also BLACKLEDGE v. PERRY, p. 927 supra. Following his conviction of misdemeanor assault in the district court, Perry asserted his statutory right to trial de novo in the superior court, which prompted the prosecutor to escalate the charge to felony assault. After ruling that "such a potential for vindictiveness" violated due process, the Court held Perry was not precluded from raising the claim by his guilty plea to the felony charge: "While the petitioner's reliance upon the *Tollett* opinion is understandable, there is a fundamental distinction between this case and that one. Although the underlying claims presented in *Tollett* and the *Brady* trilogy were of constitutional dimension, none went to the very power of the State to bring the defendant into court to answer the charge brought against him. The defendants in *McMann v. Richardson,* for example, could surely have been brought to trial without the use of the allegedly coerced confessions, and even a tainted indictment of the sort alleged in *Tollett* could have been 'cured' through a new indictment by a properly selected grand jury. In the case at hand, by contrast, the nature of the underlying constitutional infirmity is markedly different. * * * Unlike the defendant in *Tollett,* Perry is not complaining of 'antecedent constitutional violations' or of a 'deprivation of constitutional rights that occurred prior to the entry of the guilty plea.' Rather, the right that he asserts and that we today accept is the right not to be hailed into court at all upon the felony charge. The very initiation of the proceedings against him in the Superior Court thus operated to deny him due process of law."

Justice Rehnquist's dissent, joined by Justice Powell, disagreed: "I believe this case is governed by cases culminating in *Tollett v. Henderson.* In that case the state no doubt lacked power to bring Henderson to trial without a valid grand jury indictment; yet that constitutional disability was held by us to be merged in the guilty plea. I do not see why a constitutional claim the consequences of which make it the identical twin of double jeopardy may not, like double jeopardy, be waived by the person for whose benefit it is accorded. * * * Since the great majority of criminal cases are resolved by plea bargaining, defendants as a class have at least as great an interest in the finality of voluntary guilty pleas as do prosecutors. If that finality may be swept aside with the ease exhibited by the Court's approach today, prosecutors will have a reduced incentive to bargain, to the detriment of the many defendants for whom plea bargaining offers the only hope for ameliorating the consequences to them of a serious criminal charge."

6. Consider Westen, *Away From Waiver: A Rationale for the Forfeiture of Constitutional Rights in Criminal Procedure,* 75 Mich. L.Rev. 1214, 1223, 1234–35 (1977)[d]: "There are several problems with the *Menna* footnote. The most serious objection, which I shall discuss in greater detail later, is that there is no constitutional justification for such a rule. The more immediate

d. Reprinted with permission of the publisher; copyright © 1977 by the Michigan Law Review Association.

problem, however, is that the *Menna* footnote is inconsistent with the Court's own cases. In *Tollett,* for example, the defendant was asserting a claim that was independent of his factual guilt: the right of the accused to be charged by a process that is free from racial discrimination is a right that exists without regard to whether the defendant himself is guilty; even if he is guilty, he can challenge his conviction on the ground that other defendants who are similarly situated except for their racial background are not being prosecuted. Thus, by the standard of *Menna,* the defendant in *Tollett* should have been permitted to assert his defense of equal protection; yet the Court there held that he had forfeited the defense by pleading guilty. * * *

"This brings us to the real issue in *Menna.* We must assume that the Court did not decide that a guilty plea is nothing but an admission of factual guilt under state law, because it had no jurisdiction to do so; nor did it decide that a guilty plea is an admission of factual guilt as an empirical matter, because that is simply not true. Rather, in deciding that the guilty plea in *Menna* operated as a forfeiture only of defenses relating to factual guilt, the Court made a *constitutional* judgment: it held that insofar as state law provided for the forfeiture of a defense not relating to factual guilt, i.e., defenses relating to 'legal' guilt, the state law of forfeiture was unconstitutional. Thus, *Menna* stands for the proposition that for purposes of forfeiture, the states have constitutional authority to treat a guilty plea *as if* it is an admission of factual guilt, but not *as if* it is an admission of legal guilt.

"But the above merely restates, rather than justifies, the rule in *Menna.* The truly important questions remain to be answered. Why does the Constitution permit a state to treat a guilty plea as if it were a conclusive admission of factual guilt, contrary to our experience? Conversely, why does the Constitution forbid a state from treating a guilty plea as if it were also an admission of 'legal guilt?' If these 'legal' defenses can be waived (and the Court assumes they can), why does the Constitution prohibit a state from treating a guilty plea as if it were a final admission of legal guilt? Are the constitutional defenses relating to legal guilt more important than those relating to factual guilt? Is the defense of double jeopardy more important than the privilege against self-incrimination? These are the questions that must be answered if we are to assume that *Menna* is to be taken seriously as a new rule of forfeiture. If (as I suspect) there is no satisfactory answer, then we must assume that, unlike the distinction between 'curable' and 'incurable' defenses [see *Blackledge v. Perry*],[e] there is no constitu-

e. As to this distinction, the author notes: "[T]he rule in *Blackledge* might be designed to identify those cases in which to set aside a conviction based on a guilty plea places the state in no worse a position with respect to its ability to obtain a valid conviction against the defendant at trial than it occupied before entry of the plea. The state, which has a general interest in the finality of all convictions, has a particularly great interest in the finality of convictions based on guilty pleas. If a conviction based on a trial is later set aside, the state faces the difficult task of proving again that the defendant is guilty beyond a reasonable doubt. The task is difficult because it is *never* easy to sustain such a burden of proof, and the task becomes more difficult as the time period between the alleged criminal act and trial lengthens. Yet the state at least has the advantage of having once prepared its case for trial and of having preserved much, if not all, of its evidence in a form that is admissible at trial. On the other hand, if a guilty plea is later set aside, the state is in a much worse position vis-a-vis the defendant with respect to its ability to prove him guilty beyond a reasonable doubt. The state typically does not prepare cases terminating in a guilty plea as thoroughly as those destined for trial. Even if it prepares a guilty plea case as thoroughly, it does not preserve the case in a form that is readily admissible against the defendant should he now choose to go to trial. * * *

The rule in *Blackledge* is ideally suited to further this interest in the finality of guilty pleas. It holds that a defendant is not permitted to challenge a guilty plea because of a constitutional error that is 'curable' since, even where an error can be cured, the entry of the plea itself may have impaired the state's ability thereafter to prove the defendant guilty at trial. * * * Con-tional justification for the distinction between defenses relating to 'factual guilt' and defenses relating to 'legal guilt.' "

7. Under *McMann, Tollett, Menna* and *Blackledge,* what result where, "although a defendant has some reason to believe that he has been denied a speedy trial in violation of the sixth amendment, he nonetheless decides to plead guilty. The judge informs the defendant at his arraignment that, by pleading guilty, he will be waiving his privilege against self-incrimination and his rights to trial by jury and to confront witnesses against him. The judge also informs him that, by pleading guilty, he will also waive any speedy trial defense he might otherwise have. The defendant, after consulting with his attorney, enters a plea of guilty and receives the maximum sentence provided by law for the offense charged. Six months later, after consulting with new counsel, the defendant decides to attack his conviction on the ground that he was denied a speedy trial in violation of the sixth amendment. The prosecution opposes the motion on the ground that the defendant deliberately and freely waived his sixth amendment defense." Westen, supra, at 1255. Would it make any difference if the plea was a result of negotiations whereby the prosecutor also agreed to drop another, more serious charge as to which there was clearly no speedy trial defense? See Westen, supra, at 1256–57.

8. In HARING v. PROSISE, 462 U.S. 306, 103 S.Ct. 2368, 76 L.Ed.2d 595 (1983), the respondent, who earlier entered a guilty plea to a state charge of manufacturing a controlled substance, brought a damage action under 42 U.S.C. § 1983 in federal court against the officers who made the allegedly illegal search uncovering evidence of that offense. In rejecting the officers' contention that respondent's suit was barred because his guilty plea amounted to a waiver of the Fourth Amendment claim, a unanimous Court, per MARSHALL, J., declared:

"Under our past decisions, * * * a guilty plea results in the defendant's loss of any meaningful opportunity he might otherwise have had to challenge the admissibility of evidence obtained in violation of the Fourth Amendment. It does not follow, however, that a guilty plea is a 'waiver' of antecedent Fourth Amendment claims that may be given effect outside the confines of the criminal proceeding. The defendant's rights under the Fourth Amendment are not among the trial rights that he necessarily waives when he knowingly and voluntarily pleads guilty. Moreover, our decisions provide no support for petitioners' waiver theory for the simple reason that these decisions did not rest on any principle of waiver. The cases relied on by petitioners all involved challenges to the validity of a state criminal conviction. Our decisions in *Tollett* and the cases that followed simply recognized that when a defendant is convicted pursuant to his guilty plea rather than a trial, the validity of that conviction cannot be affected by an alleged Fourth Amendment violation because the conviction does not rest in any way on evidence that may have been improperly seized. State law treats a guilty plea as 'a break in the chain of events [that] preceded it in the criminal process,' *Tollett v. Henderson.* Therefore, the conclusion that a Fourth Amendment claim ordinarily may not be raised in a habeas proceeding following a plea of guilty does not rest on any notion of waiver, but rests on the simple fact that the claim is irrelevant to the constitutional validity of the conviction."

9. N.Y.Crim.P.Law § 710.70 provides that "an order finally denying a motion to suppress evidence [allegedly obtained unlawfully by a search, eavesdropping, inter-

versely a defendant is permitted to challenge a guilty plea because of a constitutional error that is incurable. In this case, the state is in precisely the same position after the entry of the guilty plea as it occupied before hand with respect to its ability to prove the defendant guilty at trial, because the error would always have prevented it from obtaining a valid conviction at trial."

rogation, or identification procedures] may be reviewed upon an appeal from an ensuing judgment of conviction notwithstanding the fact that such judgment is entered upon a plea of guilty." See also Fed.R. Crim.P. 11(a). Are these desirable provisions? Consider *United States v. Cox,* 464 F.2d 937 (6th Cir.1972) ("the disadvantages in terms of the internal consistency of our criminal process, the accuracy of appellate review, and conflict with the hoary doctrine of avoiding constitutional questions if possible, far outweigh the putative gains"). What effect do such provisions have upon plea bargaining?

If, in the absence of such a provision, the defendant pleads guilty but expressly reserves his right to appeal from the prior overruling of his motion to suppress, what courses of action are open to the appellate court? See *United States v. Cox,* supra.

10. *Uniform R.Crim.P.* 444(d) provides that the plea "bars an appeal based upon any nonjurisdictional defect in the proceedings, but an order denying (1) a pretrial motion to suppress evidence, or (2) any pretrial motion which, if granted, would be dispositive of the case, may be reviewed on appeal from an ensuing judgment of conviction." But a proviso in rule 443(a) says that "the parties may agree that the defendant will plead on [the condition that] the defendant will not seek appellate review, as permitted under Rule 444(d), of an order denying a pretrial motion." Compare *People v. White,* 298 N.E.2d 659 (N.Y.1973), holding defendant's guilty plea was coerced where one of the conditions of the prosecutor's offer of a plea to a lesser offense was that the defendant withdraw his outstanding motion to dismiss for want of a speedy trial; and consider *People v. Esajerre,* 323 N.E.2d 175 (N.Y.1974), holding that *White* does not require invalidation of a plea to a lesser offense conditioned upon the defendant's withdrawal of his motion to suppress narcotics.

11. In LEFKOWITZ v. NEWSOME, 420 U.S. 283, 95 S.Ct. 886, 43 L.Ed.2d 196 (1975), the Court considered "the question of a defendant's right to file a federal habeas corpus petition challenging the lawfulness of a search or the voluntariness of a confession or presenting other constitutional claims when a State provides for appellate review of those issues after a guilty plea." A majority of the Court, per STEWART, J., concluded that Newsome, who was such a defendant, was not foreclosed from seeking that relief in light of the fact that his "plea carried with it the guarantee that judicial review of his constitutional claim would continue to be available to him": "*Tollett v. Henderson* [is] simply inapposite. Newsome has satisfied all the prerequisites for invoking the habeas corpus jurisdiction of the federal courts. He is no less entitled to federal review of his constitutional claim than is any other defendant who raises his claim in a timely fashion, in accordance with state procedure, and who pursues his claim through all available levels of state appellate review.

"Denying Newsome the right to file a federal habeas corpus petition raising his claim of an unconstitutional seizure would not only deprive him of a federal forum despite the fact that he has satisfied all the requirements for invoking federal habeas corpus jurisdiction; it would also frustrate the State's policy in providing for postguilty plea appellate review of pretrial motions to suppress. * * *

"To deny federal habeas corpus relief to those in Newsome's position would make New York's law a trap for the unwary. On the other hand, it is safe to predict that those New York defendants who knew that federal habeas corpus would be foreclosed would again be dissuaded from pleading guilty and instead would insist on a trial solely to preserve the right to an ultimate federal forum in which to litigate their constitutional claims. Such a result would eviscerate New York's commendable efforts to relieve the problem of congested criminal trial calendars in a manner that does not diminish the opportunity for the assertion of rights guaranteed by the Constitution."

WHITE, J., joined by the Chief Justice and Rehnquist, J., dissenting, objected that the issue was whether a state, by adopting a statute such as that found in New York, "thereby creates a *federal* constitutional right to set aside the guilty plea where none would have existed otherwise." They answered in the negative, reasoning: (1) that under *Tollett* "federal constitutional principles simply preclude the setting aside of a state conviction by a federal court where the defendant's guilt has been conclusively established by a voluntary and intelligent plea of guilty"; (2) that "since the applicable law in this case is federal, it is for us, and not the New York State Legislature, to say whether Fourth Amendment claims such as those involved here will or will not be waived by a guilty plea"; and (3) that there "is no reason for the Court to decide the case one way for New York's benefit, when New York is arguing strenuously that we should decide the case the other way." [f]

f. In a separate dissent by Powell, J., joined by the Chief Justice and Rehnquist, J., it was also argued that relief should generally be unavailable on federal habeas corpus with respect to Fourth Amendment claims by state prisoners, a position later adopted by a majority of the Court in *Stone v. Powell*, p. 1480 infra.

Chapter 22

TRIAL BY JURY

SECTION 1. RIGHT TO JURY TRIAL; WAIVER

In DUNCAN v. LOUISIANA, 391 U.S. 145, 88 S.Ct. 1444, 20 L.Ed.2d 491 (1968), the Court concluded that "trial by jury in criminal cases is fundamental to the American scheme of justice," and thus held "that the Fourteenth Amendment guarantees a right of jury trial in all criminal cases which—were they to be tried in a federal court—would come within the Sixth Amendment's guarantee." In support, WHITE, J., reasoned:

"The guarantees of jury trial in the Federal and State Constitutions reflect a profound judgment about the way in which law should be enforced and justice administered. A right to jury trial is granted to criminal defendants in order to prevent oppression by the Government. Those who wrote our constitutions knew from history and experience that it was necessary to protect against unfounded criminal charges brought to eliminate enemies and against judges too responsive to the voice of higher authority. The framers of the constitutions strove to create an independent judiciary but insisted upon further protection against arbitrary action. Providing an accused with the right to be tried by a jury of his peers gave him an inestimable safeguard against the corrupt or overzealous prosecutor and against the complaint, biased, or eccentric judge. If the defendant preferred the common-sense judgment of a jury to the more tutored but perhaps less sympathetic reaction of the single judge, he was to have it. Beyond this, the jury trial provisions in the Federal and State Constitutions reflect a fundamental decision about the exercise of official power—a reluctance to entrust plenary powers over the life and liberty of the citizen to one judge or to a group of judges. Fear of unchecked power, so typical of our State and Federal Governments in other respects, found expression in the criminal law in this insistence upon community participation in the determination of guilt or innocence. The deep commitment of the Nation to the right of jury trial in serious criminal cases as a defense against arbitrary law enforcement qualifies for protection under the Due Process Clause of the Fourteenth Amendment, and must therefore be respected by the States.

"Of course jury trial has 'its weaknesses and the potential for misuse,' *Singer v. United States* [p. 1267 infra]. We are aware of the long debate, especially in this century, among those who write about the administration of justice, as to the wisdom of permitting untrained laymen to determine the facts in civil and criminal proceedings. Although the debate has been intense, with powerful voices on either side, most of the controversy has centered on the jury in civil cases. Indeed, some of the severest critics of civil juries acknowledge that the arguments for criminal juries are much stronger. In addition, at the heart of the dispute have been express or implicit assertions that juries are incapable of adequately understanding evidence or determining issues of fact, and that they are unpredictable, quixotic, and little better than a roll of dice. Yet, the most recent and exhaustive study of the jury in criminal cases concluded that juries do understand the evidence and come to sound conclusions in most of the cases presented to them and that when juries differ with the result at which the judge would have arrived, it is usually because they are serving some of the very purposes for which they were created and for which they are now employed.[26]"

HARLAN, J., joined by Stewart, J., dissenting because they could "see no reason why this Court should reverse the conviction of appellant, absent any suggestion that his particular trial was in fact unfair," had this to say about the jury:

"The jury is of course not without virtues. It affords ordinary citizens a valuable opportunity to participate in a process of government, an experience fostering, one hopes, a respect for law. It eases the burden on judges by enabling them to share a part of their sometimes awesome responsibility. A jury may, at times, afford a higher justice by refusing to enforce harsh laws (although it necessarily does so haphazardly, raising the questions whether arbitrary enforcement of harsh laws is better than total enforcement, and whether the jury system is to be defended on the ground that jurors sometimes disobey their oaths). And the jury may, or may not, contribute desirably to the willingness of the general public to accept criminal judgments as just.

"It can hardly be gainsaid, however, that the principal original virtue of the jury trial—the limitations a jury imposes on a tyrannous judiciary—has largely disappeared. We no longer live in a medieval or colonial society. Judges enforce laws enacted by democratic decision, not by regal fiat. They are elected by the people or appointed by the people's elected officials, and are responsible not to a distant monarch alone but to reviewing courts, including this one.

"The jury system can also be said to have some inherent defects, which are multiplied by the emergence of the criminal law from the relative simplicity that existed when the jury system was devised. It is a cumbersome process, not only imposing great cost in time and money on both the State and the jurors themselves, but also contributing to delay in the machinery of justice. Untrained jurors are presumably less adept at reaching accurate conclusions of fact than judges, particularly if the issues are many or complex. And it is argued by some that trial by jury, far from increasing public respect for law, impairs it: the average man, it is said, reacts favorably neither to the notion that matters he knows to be complex are being decided by other average men, nor to the way the jury system distorts the process of adjudication."

NOTES ON THE DIMENSIONS OF THE RIGHT TO JURY TRIAL

1. *Petty offenses.* In *Duncan,* the Court noted that "there is a category of petty crimes or offenses which is not subject to the Sixth Amendment jury trial provisions and should not be subject to the Fourteenth Amendment jury trial requirement here applied to the States," but did not have occasion to "settle in this case the exact location of the line between petty offenses and serious crimes." But in BALDWIN v. NEW YORK, 399 U.S. 66, 90 S.Ct. 1886, 26 L.Ed.2d 437 (1970), where appellant had been denied a jury trial when convicted of a misdemeanor punishable by imprisonment up to one

26. Kalven & Zeisel, *The American Jury* (1966).

year, a 5–3 majority held that "no offense can be deemed 'petty' for purposes of the right to trial by jury where imprisonment for more than six months is authorized." The principal opinion was by JUSTICE WHITE, who recalled that "in the federal system, as we noted in *Duncan,* petty offenses have been defined as those punishable by no more than six months in prison and a $500 fine. And, with a few exceptions, crimes triable without a jury in the American States since the late 18th century were also generally punishable by no more than a six-month prison term." Justice White noted that when *Duncan* was decided only three states denied jury trial for a crime punishable by imprisonment for longer than six months and that, in response to *Duncan,* the number had been reduced to one: "In the entire Nation, New York City alone denies an accused the right to interpose between himself and a possible prison term of over six months, the common sense judgment of a jury of his peers. * * * This near-uniform judgment of the Nation furnishes us with the only objective criterion by which a line could ever be drawn—on the basis of the possible penalty alone—between offenses which are and which are not regarded as 'serious' for purposes of trial by jury." [a]

In *United States v. Sanchez-Meza,* 547 F.2d 461 (9th Cir.1976), the court concluded *Baldwin* did not hold that the maximum potential sentence was the sole criterion, and that consequently the Supreme Court had left undisturbed *District of Columbia v. Clawans,* 300 U.S. 617, 57 S.Ct. 660, 81 L.Ed. 843 (1937), and *District of Columbia v. Colts,* 282 U.S. 63, 51 S.Ct. 52, 75 L.Ed. 177 (1930). The court went on to hold that the defendant, charged with conspiring to elude an examination by immigration officers by making false and misleading representations (punishable by 6 months imprisonment), was entitled to a jury trial under *Clawans* and *Colts,* "first, because the crime with which he was charged was an indictable and serious offense at common law, and second, because the crime itself is morally offensive and *malum in se.*"

2. *Contempt.* The "petty offense" distinction is also important in criminal contempt cases, although in such cases the penalty actually imposed will govern if the legislature has made no judgment about the maximum penalty. See *Dyke v. Taylor Implement Mfg. Co.,* 391 U.S. 216, 88 S.Ct. 1472, 20 L.Ed.2d 538 (1968) (jury trial not required where maximum sentence authorized by statute is 10 days in jail and a $50 fine); *Bloom v. Illinois,* 391 U.S. 194, 88 S.Ct. 1477, 20 L.Ed.2d 522 (1968) (no statutory limits; denial of requested jury trial to defendant sentenced to imprisonment for 24 months constitutional error); *Frank v. United States,* 395 U.S. 147, 89 S.Ct. 1503, 23 L.Ed.2d 162 (1969) (where petitioner convicted of criminal contempt without jury and received suspended sentence and probation for 3 years, and government conceded that he could receive not more than 6 months if he violated the terms of probation, this a petty offense, as in "noncontempt cases, Congress has not viewed the possibility of five years' probation as onerous enough to make an otherwise petty offense 'serious' ").

In CODISPOTI v. PENNSYLVANIA, 418 U.S. 506, 94 S.Ct. 2687, 41 L.Ed.2d 912 (1974), the Court, per White, J., held that in the case of post-verdict adjudications of various acts of contempt committed during trial, the Sixth Amendment requires a jury trial if the sentences imposed aggregate more than six months, even

a. Brennan and Marshall, JJ., joined the White opinion. Black and Douglas, JJ., concurring, would have held that every criminal defendant is entitled to jury trial, whether the offense charged is "petty" or "serious." Burger, C.J., dissenting, could "see no reason why an infinitely complex entity such as New York City should be barred from deciding that misdemeanors can be punished with up to 365 days' confinement without a jury trial while in less urban areas another body politic would fix a six-month maximum for offenses tried without a jury." Harlan and Stewart, JJ., dissented on the basis of their *Duncan* dissent.

though no sentence for more than six months was imposed for any one act of contempt. "Notwithstanding respondent's characterization of the proceeding [as involving "separate offenses" each of which "was necessarily a petty offense triable without a jury"], the salient fact remains that the contempts arose from a single trial, were charged by a single judge and were tried in a single proceeding." [b]

In MUNIZ v. HOFFMAN, 422 U.S. 454, 95 S.Ct. 2178, 45 L.Ed.2d 319 (1975), a labor union contended it was entitled to a jury trial in a criminal contempt proceeding for violating temporary injunctions, which resulted in the imposition of a fine of $10,000 on the union. The Court, per WHITE, J., after finding no statutory right to jury trial in such circumstances, considered the union's contention "that when a fine of this magnitude is imposed a contempt cannot be considered a petty offense": "Under [18 U.S.C. § 1(3)], petty offenses are defined as those crimes '[a] penalty for which does not exceed imprisonment for a period of six months or a fine of no more than $500, or both.' But in referring to that definition, the Court accorded it no talismanic significance; and we cannot accept the proposition that a contempt must be considered a serious crime under all circumstances where the punishment is a fine of more than $500, unaccompanied by imprisonment. It is one thing to hold that deprivation of an individual's liberty beyond a six-month term should not be imposed without the protections of a jury trial, but it is quite another to suggest that, regardless of the circumstances, a jury is required where any fine greater than $500 is contemplated. From the standpoint of determining the seriousness of the risk and the extent of the possible deprivation faced by a contemnor, imprisonment and fines are intrinsically different. It is not difficult to grasp the proposition that six months in jail is a serious matter for any individual, but it is not tenable to argue that the possibility of a $501 fine would be considered a serious risk to a large corporation or labor union. [W]e cannot say that the fine of $10,000 imposed on Local 70 in this case was a deprivation of such magnitude that a jury should have been interposed to guard against bias or mistake. This union, the Government suggests, collects dues from some 13,000 persons; and although the fine is not insubstantial, it is not of such magnitude that the union was deprived of whatever right to jury trial it might have under the Sixth Amendment." [c]

3. *Size.* In WILLIAMS v. FLORIDA, 399 U.S. 78, 90 S.Ct. 1893, 26 L.Ed.2d 446 (1970), the Court held "that respondent's refusal to impanel more than the six members provided for by Florida law [in petitioner's trial for robbery] did not violate petitioner's Sixth Amendment rights as applied to the States through the Fourteenth." Unable "to divine precisely what the word 'jury' imported to the Framers," WHITE, J., turned to the relationship of the 12-man requirement "to the purposes of the jury trial."

"The purpose of the jury trial, as we noted in *Duncan,* is to prevent oppression by the Government. * * * Given this purpose, the essential feature of a jury

b. Marshall, J., concurring, declined to join that part of the Court's opinion "which suggests that the trial judge in a situation such as we have here could impose an unlimited number of separate, consecutive six-month sentences upon a defendant 'for separate contemptuous acts during the trial,' so long as the judge convicts and punishes summarily upon the occurrence of each contemptuous act." Blackmun, J., joined by three other members of the Court, dissented, arguing that *Bloom* should not be extended to a case of direct contempt, as there is no "role a jury is to perform" where "the contempt took place in open court and the incident and all its details are fully preserved on the trial record" and the "judge, not the jury, will impose the sentence."

c. Four members of the Court dissented on the ground that 18 U.S.C. § 3692 afforded a right to jury trial, but only one of the four (Douglas, J.) also argued that "the Constitution deprives us of the power to grant or withhold trial by jury depending upon our assessment of the substantiality of the penalty."

obviously lies in the interposition between the accused and his accuser of the common-sense judgment of a group of laymen, and in the community participation and shared responsibility which results from that group's determination of guilt or innocence. The performance of this role is not a function of the particular number of the body which makes up the jury. To be sure, the number should probably be large enough to promote group deliberation, free from outside attempts at intimidation, and to provide a fair possibility for obtaining a representative cross section of the community. But we find little reason to think that these goals are in any meaningful sense less likely to be achieved when the jury numbers six, than when it numbers 12—particularly if the requirement of unanimity is retained. And, certainly the reliability of the jury as a fact-finder hardly seems likely to be a function of its size.

"It might be suggested that the 12-man jury gives a defendant a greater advantage since he has more 'chances' of finding a juror who will insist on acquittal and thus prevent conviction. But the advantage might just as easily belong to the State, which also needs only one juror out of twelve insisting on guilt to prevent acquittal.[47] What few experiments have occurred—usually in the civil area—indicate that there is no discernible difference between the results reached by the two different-sized juries. In short, neither currently available evidence nor theory[49] suggests that the 12-man jury is necessarily more advantageous to the defendant than a jury composed of fewer members.

"Similarly, while in theory the number of viewpoints represented on a randomly selected jury ought to increase as the size of the jury increases, in practice the difference between the 12-man and the six-man jury in terms of the cross section of the community represented seems likely to be negligible. Even the 12-man jury cannot insure representation of every distinct voice in the community, particularly given the use of the peremptory challenge. As long as arbitrary exclusions of a particular class from the jury rolls are forbidden, the concern that the cross section will be significantly diminished if the jury is decreased in size from 12 to six seems an unrealistic one."[d]

In *Ballew v. Georgia,* 435 U.S. 223, 98 S.Ct. 1029, 55 L.Ed.2d 234 (1978), a unanimous Court held that petitioner's trial before a 5-member jury deprived him of his constitutional right to jury trial. Looking to recent scholarly writings on the subject, Justice Blackmun found that "they raise significant questions about the wisdom and constitutionality of a reduction below six." Specifically, he relied on empirical data which "suggest that progressively smaller juries are less likely to foster effective group deliberation," "raise doubts about the accuracy of the results achieved by smaller and smaller panels," "suggest that the verdicts of jury deliberation in criminal cases will vary as juries become smaller, and that the variance

47. It is true, of course, that the "hung jury" might be thought to result in a minimal advantage for the defendant, who remains unconvicted and who enjoys the prospect that the prosecution will eventually be dropped if subsequent juries also "hang." Thus a 100-man jury would undoubtedly be more favorable for defendants than a 12-man jury. But when the comparison is between 12 and six, the odds of continually "hanging" the jury seem slight, and the numerical difference in the number needed to convict seems unlikely to inhere perceptibly to the advantage of either side.

49. Studies of the operative factors contributing to small group deliberation and decision-making suggest that jurors in the minority on the first ballot are likely to be influenced by the proportional size of the majority aligned against them. * * *

d. Harlan, Stewart, Black, and Douglas, JJ., concurred in the result. Blackmun, J., took no part in the case. Marshall, J., dissenting, adhered "to the decision of the Court in *Thompson v. Utah* [170 U.S. 343, 18 S.Ct. 620, 42 L.Ed. 1061 (1898)] that the jury guaranteed by the Sixth Amendment consists 'of twelve persons, neither more nor less.'"

amounts to an imbalance to the detriment of one side, the defense," and show that "the opportunity for meaningful and appropriate [minority group] representation does decrease with the size of the panels." Although the Court did "not pretend to discern a clear line between six members and five," the data was deemed to justify the conclusion that "any further reduction" in jury size "attains constitutional significance," especially in light of the fact that there is "no significant state advantage in reducing the number of jurors from six to five." [e]

4. *Unanimity.* In APODACA v. OREGON, 406 U.S. 404, 92 S.Ct. 1628, 32 L.Ed.2d 184 (1972), petitioners, convicted of felonies by 11–1 and 10–2 votes, unsuccessfully challenged a state constitutional provision which permits 10 members of a jury to render guilty verdicts in noncapital cases. WHITE, J., joined by Burger, C.J., and Blackmun and Rehnquist, JJ., announced the judgment, ruling that the sixth amendment, made applicable to the states by the fourteenth, does not require jury unanimity.[f]

After finding the "legislative history" of the sixth amendment inconclusive, White, J., observed: "Our inquiry must focus upon the function served by the jury in contemporary society. As we said in *Duncan,* the purpose of trial by jury is to prevent oppression by the Government by providing a 'safeguard against the corrupt or overzealous prosecutor and against the complaint, biased or eccentric judge.' 'Given this purpose, the essential feature of a jury obviously lies in the interposition between the accused and his accuser of the commonsense judgment of a group of laymen * * *.' A requirement of unanimity, however, does not materially contribute to the exercise of this commonsense judgment. As we said in *Williams,* a jury will come to such a judgment as long as it consists of a group of laymen representative of a cross section of the community who have the duty and the opportunity to deliberate, free from outside attempts at intimidation, on the question of a defendant's guilt. In terms of this function we perceive no difference between juries required to act unanimously and those permitted to convict or acquit by votes of 10 to two or 11 to one. Requiring unanimity would obviously produce hung juries in some situations where nonunanimous juries will convict or acquit. But in either case, the interest of the defendant in hav-

e. Stevens, J., joined the Blackmun opinion. White, J., concurred in the judgment. Powell, J., joined by the Chief Justice and Rehnquist, J., concurred in the judgment but expressed "reservations as to the wisdom—as well as the necessity—of Mr. Justice Blackmun's heavy reliance on numerology derived from statistical studies." Brennan, J., joined by Stewart and Marshall, JJ., joined the Blackmun opinion "insofar as it holds that the Sixth and Fourteenth Amendments require juries in criminal trials to contain more than five persons."

f. In the companion case of *Johnson v. Louisiana,* 406 U.S. 356, 92 S.Ct. 1620, 32 L.Ed.2d 152 (1972), a 5–4 majority of the Court, per White, J., upheld a 9–3 robbery conviction against due process and equal protection challenges. Since the case was tried before *Duncan,* appellant conceded that the sixth amendment was not applicable to his case. Rather, he argued that (1) in order to give substance to the "proof beyond a reasonable doubt" standard required by the fourteenth amendment, jury verdicts in state criminal cases must be unanimous; and (2) state law requiring unanimous verdicts in five-man jury cases (for minor offenses) and in twelve-man jury cases (for capital offenses), but permitting 9–3 convictions in other cases violates equal protection. As for (1), the Court observed that "nine jurors—a substantial majority of the jury—were convinced by the evidence. [D]isagreement of three jurors does not alone establish reasonable doubt, particularly when such a heavy majority of the jury, after having considered the dissenters' views, remains convinced of guilt." As for (2), the Court "perceive[d] nothing unconstitutional or invidiously discriminatory * * * in a State's insisting that its burden of proof be carried with more jurors where more serious crimes or more severe punishments are at issue. * * * As to the crimes triable by a five-man jury, if appellant's position is that it is easier to convince nine of 12 jurors than to convince all of five, he is simply challenging the judgment of the Louisiana legislature. That body obviously intended to vary the difficulty of proving guilt with the gravity of the offense and the severity of the punishment. We remain unconvinced * * * that this legislative judgment was defective in any constitutional sense."

ing the judgment of his peers interposed between himself and the officers of the State who prosecute and judge him is equally well served." [g]

Blackmun, J., joined Justice White's opinions in *Apodaca* and *Johnson* (fn. f supra), but in a brief concurring opinion did "not hesitate to say" that "a 7–5 standard, rather than a 9–3 or 75% minimum, would afford me great difficulty. As Mr. Justice White points out in *Johnson,* 'a substantial majority of the jury' are to be convinced. That is all that is before us in each of these cases." [h]

Powell, J., concurring, rejected the premise that "all of the elements of jury trial within the meaning of the Sixth Amendment are necessarily embodied in or incorporated into the Due Process Clause of the Fourteenth," and thus deemed *Apodaca* not inconsistent with the Court's long-standing presumption "that unanimous verdicts are essential in federal jury trials."

DOUGLAS, J., joined by Brennan and Marshall, JJ., dissented:

"The diminution of verdict reliability flows from the fact that nonunanimous juries need not debate and deliberate as fully as must unanimous juries. As soon as the requisite majority is attained, further consideration is not required either by Oregon or by Louisiana even though the dissident jurors might, if given the chance, be able to convince the majority. Such persuasion does in fact occasionally occur in States where the unanimous requirement applies: 'In roughly one case in ten, the minority eventually succeeds in reversing an initial majority, and these may be cases of special importance.' [4] * * *

"It is said that there is no evidence that majority jurors will refuse to listen to dissenters whose votes are unneeded for conviction. Yet human experience teaches that polite and academic conversation is no substitute for the earnest and robust argument necessary to reach unanimity. * * *

"Moreover, even where an initial majority wins the dissent over to its side, the ultimate result in unanimous jury States may nonetheless reflect the reservations of uncertain jurors. I refer to many compromise verdicts on lesser-included offenses and lesser sentences. * * *

"The new rule also has an impact on cases in which a unanimous jury would have neither voted to acquit nor to convict, but would have deadlocked. In unanimous jury States, this occurs about 5.6% of the time. Of these deadlocked juries, Kalven and Zeisel say that 56% contain either one, two, or three dissenters. In these latter cases, the majorities favor the prosecution 44% (of the 56%) but the defendant only 12% (of the 56%). Thus, by eliminating these deadlocks, Louisiana wins 44 cases for every 12 that it

g. The plurality opinion also rejected the contentions that (1) a sixth amendment "jury trial" should be held to require unanimity in order to effectuate the "reasonable doubt" standard and (2) unanimity is a necessary precondition for effective application of the requirement that jury panels reflect a cross section of the community. As for (1), the reasonable doubt standard developed separately from both the jury trial and the unanimous verdict. The contention is rooted, in effect, in due process and has been rejected in *Johnson v. Louisiana,* fn. f supra. As for (2), the Court rejected the assumption that "minority groups, even when they are represented on a jury, will not adequately represent the viewpoint of those groups simply because they may be outvoted in the final result. They will be present during all deliberations, and their views will be heard."

h. But consider Stewart, J., joined by Brennan and Marshall, JJ., dissenting in *Johnson:* "[N]otwithstanding Mr. Justice Blackmun's disclaimer, there is nothing in the reasoning of the Court's opinion that would stop it from approving verdicts by 8–4 or even 7–5." Consider, too, Douglas, J., joined by Brennan and Marshall, JJ., dissenting in *Johnson* and *Apodaca:* "Would the Court relax the standard of reasonable doubt still further by resorting to eight to four verdicts or even a majority rule? Moreover, in light of today's holdings and that of *Williams,* in the future would it invalidate three to two or even two to one convictions?"

4. Kalven & Zeisel, *The American Jury* 490 (1966). See also *The American Jury: Notes For an English Controversy,* 48 Chi.Bar Rec. 195 (1967).

loses, obtaining in this band of outcomes a substantially more favorable conviction ratio (3.67) than the unanimous jury ratio of slightly less than two guilty verdicts for every acquittal. By eliminating the one and two dissenting juror cases, Oregon does even better, gaining 4.25 convictions for every acquittal." [i]

In *Burch v. Louisiana,* 441 U.S. 130, 99 S.Ct. 1623, 60 L.Ed.2d 96 (1979), a unanimous Court struck down a provision that misdemeanors punishable by more than 6 months "shall be tried before a jury of six persons, five of whom must concur to render a verdict." Rehnquist, J., for the Court, stressed "that lines must be drawn somewhere if the substance of the jury trial right is to be preserved"; that the "near-uniform judgment of the Nation," reflected by the fact only two states allow nonunanimous verdicts by 6-member juries, "provides a useful guide in delimiting the line between those jury practices that are constitutionally permissible and those that are not"; and that claims nonunanimous 6-person juries save considerable time "are speculative, at best."

5. *Trial de novo.* At issue in LUDWIG v. MASSACHUSETTS, 427 U.S. 618, 96 S.Ct. 2781, 49 L.Ed.2d 732 (1976), was a "two-tier" system of trial courts in which there was a right to jury trial only at the second tier, available after a conviction upon a trial without a jury at the first tier. The opinion of the Court, delivered by Blackmun, J., concluded: (a) that the right to jury trial was not unconstitutionally burdened by the cost of an additional trial, as a defendant may reach the second tier by "admitting sufficient findings of fact" and thus "need not pursue, in any real sense, a defense at the lower tier"; (b) that the right to jury trial was not unconstitutionally burdened by the danger of a harsher sentence at the second tier, in light of *North Carolina v. Pearce,* p. 1434 infra, and *Colten v. Kentucky,* p. 1442 infra, and (c) that it was not established that the right to jury trial was unconstitutionally burdened by the psychological and physical hardships of two trials, as appellant "has not presented any evidence to show that there is a greater delay in obtaining a jury in Massachusetts than there would be if the Commonwealth abandoned its two-tier system." Reconsideration of *Callan v. Wilson,* 127 U.S. 540, 8 S.Ct. 1301, 32 L.Ed. 223 (1888), holding invalid a two-tier system in the District of Columbia that provided for jury trial only at the second tier, was deemed unnecessary for two reasons: (1) *Callan* also rested upon Art. III, § 2, cl. 3 of the Constitution, which is not applicable to the states; and (2) under the D.C. system it was necessary for the defendant to be "fully tried" in the first tier.[j]

6. *Jury nullification.* In *Duncan,* the Court observed that the framers of the federal and state constitutions believed that if "the defendant preferred the common-sense judgment of a jury to the more tutored but perhaps less sympathetic reaction of the single judge, he was to have it." Consider, in this connection, UNITED STATES v. DOUGHERTY, 473 F.2d 1113 (D.C.Cir.1972), growing out of convictions of the so-called "D.C. Nine" for their unconsented entry into Dow Chemical Company offices and destruction of property therein. Rejecting appellants'

i. Separate dissenting opinions were also written by Brennan, Stewart, and Marshall, JJ.

j. Powell, J., concurred on the basis of his opinion in *Apodaca.* Stevens, J., joined by Brennan, Stewart, and Marshall, JJ., dissenting, objected that "[a]ll of the legitimate benefits of the two-tier system could be obtained by giving the defendant the right to waive the first-tier trial completely," and found the burden in the Massachusetts system "significant" because: (a) for various reasons a "second trial of the same case is never the same as the first"; (b) the choice "between admitting the truth and also the prima facie sufficiency of the evidence the defendant considers false or misleading, on the one hand, or insisting on a full nonjury trial, on the other, is not an insignificant price to pay for the exercise of a constitutional right"; and (c) the first trial may have a significant impact notwithstanding the right to immediate appeal, as it may tarnish the defendant's reputation, have an impact upon the judge in the second trial, and may be known by the jurors in the second trial.

claim that they were entitled to have the jury informed of its power to "nullify" the law, JUDGE LEVENTHAL, joined by Adams, J., on this issue, maintained:

"The way the jury operates may be radically altered if there is alteration in the way it is told to operate. The jury knows well enough that its prerogative is not limited to the choices articulated in the formal instructions of the court. The jury gets its understanding as to the arrangements in the legal system from more than one voice. There is the formal communication from the judge. There is the informal communication from the total culture—literature (novel, drama, film, and television); current comment (newspapers, magazines and television); conversation; and, of course, history and tradition. The totality of input generally convey adequately enough the idea of prerogative, of freedom in an occasional case to depart from what the judge says. Even indicators that would on their face seem too weak to notice—like the fact that the judge tells the jury it must acquit (in case of reasonable doubt) but never tells the jury in so many words that it must convict—are a meaningful part of the jury's total input. Law is a system, and it is also a language, with secondary meanings that may be unrecorded yet are part of its life.

"When the legal system relegates the information of the jury's prerogative to an essentially informal input, it is not being duplicitous, chargeable with chicane and intent to deceive. The limitation to informal input is, rather, a governor to avoid excess: the prerogative is reserved for the exceptional case, and the judge's instruction is retained as a generally effective constraint. We 'recognize a constraint as obligatory upon us when we require not merely reason to defend our rule departures, but damn good reason.' The practicalities of men, machinery and rules point up the danger of articulating discretion to depart from a rule, that the breach will be more often and casually invoked. We cannot gainsay that occasionally jurors uninstructed as to the prerogative may feel themselves compelled to the point of rigidity. The danger of the excess rigidity that may now occasionally exist is not as great as the danger of removing the boundaries of constraint provided by the announced rules.

" * * * To assign the role of mini-legislature to the various petit juries, who must hang if not unanimous, exposes criminal law and administration to paralysis, and to a deadlock that betrays rather than furthers the assumptions of viable democracy.

"Moreover, to compel a juror involuntarily assigned to jury duty to assume the burdens of mini-legislator or judge, as is implicit in the doctrine of nullification, is to put untoward strains on the jury system. It is one thing for a juror to know that the law condemns, but he has a factual power of lenity. To tell him expressly of a nullification prerogative, however, is to inform him, in effect, that it is he who fashions the rule that condemns. That is an overwhelming responsibility, an extreme burden for the jurors' psyche. And it is not inappropriate to add that a juror called upon for an involuntary public service is entitled to the protection, when he takes action that he knows is right, but also knows is unpopular, either in the community at large or in his own particular grouping, that he can fairly put it to friends and neighbors that he was merely following the instructions of the court. * * *

"What makes for health as an occasional medicine would be disastrous as a daily diet. The fact that there is widespread existence of the jury's prerogative, and approval of its existence as a 'necessary counter to case-hardened judges and arbitrary prosecutors,' does not establish as an imperative that the jury must be informed by the judge of that power. On the contrary, it is pragmatically useful to structure instructions in such ways that the jury must feel strongly about the values involved in the case, so strongly that it must itself identify the case as establishing a call of high conscience, and must independently initiate and undertake an act in contravention of the established instructions. This requirement of independent jury conception confines the happening of the lawless jury to the occasional instance that does not violate, and viewed as an exception may even enhance, the over-all normative effect of the rule of law. An explicit instruction to a jury conveys an implied approval that runs the risk of degrading the legal structure requisite for true freedom, for an ordered liberty that protects against anarchy as well as tyranny."

Dissenting on the jury nullification issue, CHIEF JUDGE BAZELON observed:

"The Court reasons that * * * the spontaneous and unsolicited act of nullification is * * * less likely, on the whole, to reflect bias and a perverse sense of values than the act of nullification carried out by a jury carefully instructed on its power and responsibility.

"It seems substantially more plausible to me to assume that the very opposite is true. The juror motivated by prejudice seems to me more likely to make spontaneous use of the power to nullify, and more likely to disregard the judge's exposition of the normally controlling legal standards. The conscientious juror, who could make a careful effort to consider the blameworthiness of the defendant's action in light of prevailing community values, is the one most likely to obey the judge's admonition that the jury enforce strict principles of law. * * *

"My own view rests on the premise that nullification can and should serve an important function in the criminal process. * * * The doctrine permits the jury to bring to bear on the criminal process a sense of fairness and particularized justice. The drafters of legal rules cannot anticipate and take account of every case where a defendant's conduct is 'unlawful' but not blameworthy, any more than they can draw a bold line to mark the boundary between an accident and negligence. It is the jury—as spokesman for the community's sense of values—that must explore that subtle and elusive boundary. * * *

"I do not see any reason to assume that jurors will make rampantly abusive use of their power. * * * If a jury refuses to apply strictly the controlling principles of law, it may—in conflict with values shared by the larger community—convict a defendant because of prejudice against him, or acquit a defendant because of sympathy for him and prejudice against his victim. Our fear of unjust conviction is plainly understandable. But it is hard for me to see how a nullification instruction could enhance the likelihood of that result. The instruction would speak in terms of acquittal, not conviction, and it would provide no comfort to a juror determined to convict a defendant in defiance of the law or the facts of the case. * * *

"As for the problem of unjust acquittal, it is important to recognize the strong internal check that constrains the jury's willingness to acquit. Where defendants seem dangerous, juries are unlikely to exercise their nullification power, whether or not an explicit instruction is offered."

Does it follow that defense counsel may not even argue for nullification, as concluded in *United States v. Trujillo,* 714 F.2d 102 (11th Cir.1983), or is permitting argument but not instruction the best compromise, as concluded in *State v. Mayo,* 480 A.2d 85 (N.H.1984)?

7. *Fact or law.* At defendant's trial for interstate transportation of a falsely made security, the judge instructed the jury that the Gold Certificate Contract which defendant allegedly transported was a "security" within the meaning of the applicable statute as a matter of law. On appeal, defendant claimed this infringed upon his constitutional right to jury trial, but the court in *United States v. Johnson,* 700 F.2d 163 (5th Cir.1983), disagreed. The majority reasoned that the judge was simply applying

the statutory definition of what a "security" is to the document in this case, a matter of law rather than an issue of fact because that definition "requires no * * * adoption of factual evidence. * * * It is the nature of the document itself which is at issue, not what may or may not have happened to it." Rubin, J., dissenting, objected that the "issue before us is neither the distinction between 'fact' or 'law' questions nor the correctness of characterizing a particular question as one or the other. It is the respective province of judge and jury in a criminal trial." He continued: "In criminal cases, the court simply may not direct a verdict on any disputed issue. The inquiry is not 'when does the definition of security, normally a question of law, become so intimately connected with the facts of a criminal case that a jury's resolution is necessary in order to comply with the Sixth Amendment?' [as the majority states.] The real question is: when may the judge in a criminal case take a disputed issue from the jury and decide it himself? My answer is categorical: never." On rehearing en banc, 718 F.2d 1317 (5th Cir.1983), the Rubin position prevailed.

8. *Sentencing.* As stated in *Spaziano v. Florida,* 468 U.S. 447, 104 S.Ct. 3154, 82 L.Ed.2d 340 (1984), the Sixth Amendment "never has been thought to guarantee a right to a jury determination" of "the appropriate punishment to be imposed on an individual." The Court there held that this was so even as to the death penalty, and that consequently there was no constitutional prohibition upon a sentencing scheme which allowed a trial judge to override a jury's recommendation of a life sentence instead of the death penalty. In response to the claim that because "the jury serves as the voice of the community, the jury is in the best position to decide whether a particular crime is so heinous that the community's response must be death," the Court, per Blackmun, J., declared that the "community's voice is heard at least as clearly in the legislature when the death penalty is authorized and the particular circumstances in which death is appropriate are defined." [k]

9. *Waiver.* In SINGER v. UNITED STATES, 380 U.S. 24, 85 S.Ct. 783, 13 L.Ed.2d 630 (1965), petitioner, convicted by a jury of 29 counts of mail fraud, challenged Fed.R.Crim.P. 23(a), which provides a defendant may waive a jury trial only "with the approval of the court and the consent of the government," because the government had declined to consent in his case. The Court, per WARREN, C.J., concluded:

"The ability to waive a constitutional right does not ordinarily carry with it the right to insist upon the opposite of that right. For example, although a defendant can, under some circumstances, waive his constitutional right to a public trial, he has no absolute right to compel a private trial, * * * although he can waive his right to be tried in the State and district where the crime was committed, he cannot in all cases compel transfer of the case to another district, * * * and although he can waive his right to be confronted by the witnesses against him, it has never been seriously suggested that he can thereby compel the Government to try the case by stipulation. * * *

"Trial by jury has been established by the Constitution as the 'normal and * * * preferable mode of disposing of

k. Stevens, J., joined by Brennan and Marshall, JJ., dissenting in part, concluded: "The same consideration that supports a constitutional entitlement to a trial by a jury rather than a judge at the guilt or innocence stage—the right to have an authentic representative of the community apply its lay perspective to the determination that must precede a deprivation of liberty—applies with special force to the determination that must precede a deprivation of life. In many respects capital sentencing resembles a trial on the question of guilt, involving as it does a prescribed burden of proof of given elements through the adversarial process. But more important than its procedural aspects, the life-or-death decision in capital cases depends upon its link to community values for its moral and constitutional legitimacy."

issues of fact in criminal cases.' As with any mode that might be devised to determine guilt, trial by jury has its weaknesses and the potential for misuse. However, the mode itself has been surrounded with safeguards to make it as fair as possible—for example, venue can be changed when there is a well-grounded fear of jury prejudice, Rule 21(a) of the Federal Rules of Criminal Procedure, and prospective jurors are subject to *voir dire* examination, to challenge for cause, and to peremptory challenge, Rule 24(a) and (b).

"In light of the Constitution's emphasis on jury trial, we find it difficult to understand how the petitioner can submit the bald proposition that to compel a defendant in a criminal case to undergo a jury trial against his will is contrary to his right to a fair trial or to due process. A defendant's only constitutional right concerning the method of trial is to an impartial trial by jury. We find no constitutional impediment to conditioning a waiver of this right on the consent of the prosecuting attorney and the trial judge when, if either refuses to consent, the result is simply that the defendant is subject to an impartial trial by jury—the very thing that the Constitution guarantees him. The Constitution recognizes an adversary system as the proper method of determining guilt, and the Government, as a litigant, has a legitimate interest in seeing that cases in which it believes a conviction is warranted are tried before the tribunal which the Constitution regards as most likely to produce a fair result. * * *

"In upholding the validity of Rule 23(a), we reiterate the sentiment expressed in *Berger v. United States,* 295 U.S. 78, 88, 55 S.Ct. 629, 633, 79 L.Ed. 1314 [1935], that the government attorney in a criminal prosecution is not an ordinary party to a controversy, but a 'servant of the law' with a 'twofold aim * * * that guilt shall not escape or innocence suffer.' * * * Because of this confidence in the integrity of the federal prosecutor, Rule 23(a) does not require that the Government articulate its reasons for demanding a jury trial at the time it refuses to consent to a defendant's proffered waiver. Nor should we assume that federal prosecutors would demand a jury trial for an ignoble purpose. We need not determine in this case whether there might be some circumstances where a defendant's reasons for wanting to be tried by a judge alone are so compelling that the Government's insistence on trial by jury would result in the denial to a defendant of an impartial trial. Petitioner argues that there might arise situations where 'passion, prejudice * * * public feeling' or some other factor may render impossible or unlikely an impartial trial by jury. However, since petitioner gave no reason for wanting to forgo jury trial other than to save time, this is not such a case, and petitioner does not claim that it is."

In what respect does the prosecution have "a legitimate interest" in jury trial? If both the defendant and the prosecutor agree to trial without a jury, does the trial judge have "a legitimate interest" in nonetheless requiring jury trial? Are there "circumstances where a defendant's reasons for wanting to be tried by a judge alone are so compelling that the Government's insistence on trial by jury would result in the denial to a defendant of an impartial trial"? What if the defendant has a prior murder conviction which would be admitted for purposes of impeachment were he to take the stand, as in *United States v. Kramer,* 355 F.2d 891 (7th Cir.1966)? Or, what of a request for trial without jury because of substantial pretrial publicity about the case?

An empirical study determined that jury waiver was largely a matter of regional custom, although the nature of the offense charged is also an important consideration in practice. Jury waivers are low for such crimes as murder, manslaughter, rape and robbery, and high for such offenses as carrying concealed weapons, larceny, auto theft, and drug law violations. This study also revealed a high correlation between jury waiver and jury leniency; juries are more lenient than judges as to those offenses for which jury trial is least often waived. Kalven & Zeisel, *The American Jury* ch. 2 (1966).

Why do defendants often waive jury trial? "Paramount is the expectation of a lesser sentence if the conviction comes in a bench trial rather than from a jury, just as the plea of guilty carries a lesser sentence than the verdict of guilty. The defendant who does not want to wholly deprive himself of the possibility of an acquittal, but wants to assure a modicum of leniency in case of conviction, might be moved to waive the jury. There is some modest evidence that jury waiver may accomplish this." Id. at 26–27.

SECTION 2. JURY SELECTION

The purpose of the *Federal Jury Selection and Service Act of 1968,* 28 U.S.C. § 1861 et seq., reprinted in Supp.App. B, is to ensure that juries are "selected at random from a fair cross section of the communities in the district or division wherein the court convenes" and that "no citizen shall be excluded from service as a grand or petit juror in the district courts of the United States on account of race, color, religion, sex, national origin, or economic status." Each district court is required to devise and place into operation a written plan for jury selection, which "shall specify whether the names of prospective jurors shall be selected from the voter registration lists or the lists of actual voters of the political subdivision within the district or division. The plan shall prescribe some other source or sources of names in addition to voter lists where necessary to foster the policy and protect the rights" set forth above.

Largely as a result of changes adopted in recent years, most states now follow similar procedures in an effort to select jurors at random from some standardized list. Lists of voters are most commonly used, although some states instead or in addition utilize other lists, such as a local census, the tax rolls, city directories, telephone books, and drivers' license lists. But about a third of the states still utilize the key-man system, under which political and civic leaders (the "key men") are asked for suggestions of prospective jurors. They usually recommend persons they know, so that the list of prospective jurors is unlikely to be representative of the community.

Many of those whose names are drawn for state jury service seek to be excused, and in many states excuses are rather readily granted. Persons are most commonly excused because of economic hardship, poor health, advanced age, a need to care for small children, or the distance they live from the courthouse. In addition, state jury selection statutes typically list those persons who are disqualified from serving as jurors (e.g., those not of voting age, not residents of the jurisdiction some minimum time, unable to read and write English, or with a felony conviction) and those who are exempted from jury service because of their occupation (e.g., doctors, teachers, clergy). For a description of the selection process in each state, see Van Dyke, *Jury Selection Procedures* 258–62 (1977); on the practical aspects, see Ginger, *Jury Selection in Civil and Criminal Trials* (1984).

TAYLOR v. LOUISIANA

419 U.S. 522, 95 S.Ct. 692, 42 L.Ed.2d 690 (1975).

MR. JUSTICE WHITE delivered the opinion of the Court.

When this case was tried, Art. VII, § 41, of the Louisiana Constitution, and Art. 402 of the Louisiana Code of Criminal Procedure provided that a woman should not be selected for jury service unless she had previously filed a written declaration of her desire to be subject to jury service. The constitutionality of these provisions is the issue in this case. * * *

The Louisiana jury selection system does not disqualify women from jury service, but in operation its conceded systematic impact is that only a very few women, grossly disproportionate to the number of eligible women in the community, are called for jury service.[a] In this case, no women were on the venire from which the petit jury was drawn. The issue we have, therefore, is whether a jury selection system which operates to exclude from jury service an identifiable class of citizens constituting 53% of eligible jurors in the community comports with the Sixth and Fourteenth Amendments.

The State first insists that Taylor, a male, has no standing to object to the exclusion of women from his jury. But Taylor's claim is that he was constitutionally entitled to a jury drawn from a venire constituting a fair cross section of the community and that the jury that tried him was not such a jury by reason of the exclusion of women. Taylor was not a member of the excluded class; but there is no rule that claims such as Taylor presents may be made only by those defendants who are members of the group excluded from jury service. In *Peters v. Kiff,* 407 U.S. 493, 92 S.Ct. 2163, 33 L.Ed.2d 83 (1972), the defendant, a white man, challenged his conviction on the ground that Negroes had been systematically excluded from jury service. Six Members of the Court agreed that petitioner was entitled to present the issue and concluded that he had been deprived of his federal rights. Taylor, in the case before us, was similarly entitled to tender and have adjudicated the claim that the exclusion of women from jury service deprived him of the kind of fact finder to which he was constitutionally entitled.

The background against which this case must be decided includes our holding in *Duncan v. Louisiana* [p. 1257 supra], that the Sixth Amendment's provision for jury trial is made binding on the States by virtue of the Fourteenth Amendment. Our inquiry is whether the presence of a fair cross section of the community on venires, panels or lists from which petit juries are drawn is essential to the fulfillment of the Sixth Amendment's guarantee of an impartial jury trial in criminal prosecutions. * * *

The unmistakable import of this Court's opinions, at least since 1941, and not repudiated by intervening decisions, is that the selection of a petit jury from a representative cross section of the community is an essential component of the Sixth Amendment right to a jury trial. * * *

We accept the fair cross section requirement as fundamental to the jury trial guaranteed by the Sixth Amendment and are convinced that the requirement has solid foundation. The purpose of a jury is to guard against the exercise of arbitrary power—to make available the commonsense judgment of the community as a hedge against the overzealous or mistaken prosecutor and in preference to the professional or perhaps overconditioned or biased response of a judge. This prophylactic vehicle is not provided if the jury pool is made up of only special segments of the populace or if large, distinctive groups are excluded from the pool. Community participation in the administration of the criminal law, moreover, is not only consistent with our democratic heritage but is also critical to public confidence in the fairness of the criminal justice system. Restricting jury service to only special groups or excluding identifiable segments playing major roles in the community cannot be squared with the constitutional concept of jury trial. * * *

We are also persuaded that the fair cross section requirement is violated by the systematic exclusion of women, who in the judicial district involved here amounted to 53% of the citizens eligible for jury service. This conclusion necessarily entails the judgment that women are sufficiently

a. It was stipulated that no more than 10% of the persons on the jury wheel were women, that only 12 females were among the 1,800 persons drawn to fill petit jury venires, and that this discrepancy was the result of the operation of the challenged provisions.

numerous and distinct from men that if they are systematically eliminated from jury panels, the Sixth Amendment's fair cross section requirement cannot be satisfied. This very matter was debated in *Ballard v. United States,* 329 U.S. 187, 67 S.Ct. 261, 91 L.Ed. 181 (1946). Positing the fair cross-section rule—there said to be a statutory one—the Court concluded that the systematic exclusion of women was unacceptable. The dissenting view that an all-male panel drawn from various groups in the community would be as truly representative as if women were included, was firmly rejected:

> "The thought is that the factors which tend to influence the action of women are the same as those which influence the action of men—personality, background, economic status—and not sex. Yet it is not enough to say that women when sitting as jurors neither act nor tend to act as a class. Men likewise do not act as a class. But, if the shoe were on the other foot, who would claim that a jury was truly representative of the community if all men were intentionally and systematically excluded from the panel? The truth is that the two sexes are not fungible; a community made up exclusively of one is different from a community composed of both; the subtle interplay of influence one on the other is among the imponderables. To insulate the courtroom from either may not in a given case make an iota of difference. Yet a flavor, a distinct quality is lost if either sex is excluded. The exclusion of one may indeed make the jury less representative of the community than would be true if an economic or racial group were excluded."

In this respect, we agree with the Court in *Ballard:* If the fair cross-section rule is to govern the selection of juries, as we have concluded it must, women cannot be systematically excluded from jury panels from which petit juries are drawn. This conclusion is consistent with the current judgment of the country, now evidenced by legislative or constitutional provisions in every State and at the federal level qualifying women for jury service.

There remains the argument that women as a class serve a distinctive role in society and that jury service would so substantially interfere with that function that the State has ample justification for excluding women from service unless they volunteer, even though the result is that almost all jurors are men. It is true that *Hoyt v. Florida,* 368 U.S. 57, 82 S.Ct. 159, 7 L.Ed. 2d 118 (1961), held that such a system did not deny due process of law or equal protection of the laws because there was a sufficiently rational basis for such an exemption. But *Hoyt* did not involve a defendant's Sixth Amendment right to a jury drawn from a fair cross section of the community and the prospect of depriving him of that right if women as a class are systematically excluded. The right to a proper jury cannot be overcome on merely rational grounds. There must be weightier reasons if a distinctive class representing 53% of the eligible jurors is for all practical purposes to be excluded from jury service. No such basis has been tendered here.

The States are free to grant exemptions from jury service to individuals in case of special hardship or incapacity and to those engaged in particular occupations the uninterrupted performance of which is critical to the community's welfare. It would not appear that such exemptions would pose substantial threats that the remaining pool of jurors would not be representative of the community. A system excluding all women, however, is a wholly different matter. It is untenable to suggest these days that it would be a special hardship for each and every woman to perform jury service or that society cannot spare *any* women from their present duties. This may be the case with many, and it may be burdensome to sort out those who should serve. But that task is performed in the case of men, and the administrative convenience in dealing with women as a class is insufficient justification for diluting the quality of community judgment represented by the jury in criminal trials. * * *

Our holding does not augur or authorize the fashioning of detailed jury selection codes by federal courts. The fair cross section principle must have much leeway in application. The States remain free to prescribe relevant qualifications for their jurors and to provide reasonable exemptions so long as it may be fairly said that the jury lists or panels are representative of the community. * * *

It should also be emphasized that in holding that petit juries must be drawn from a source fairly representative of the community we impose no requirement that petit juries actually chosen must mirror the community and reflect the various distinctive groups in the population. Defendants are not entitled to a jury of any particular composition; but the jury wheels, pools of names, panels or venires from which juries are drawn must not systematically exclude distinctive groups in the community and thereby fail to be reasonably representative thereof. * * *

Reversed and remanded.

MR. CHIEF JUSTICE BURGER concurred in the result.

MR. JUSTICE REHNQUIST, dissenting. * * *

I cannot conceive that today's decision is necessary to guard against oppressive or arbitrary law enforcement, or to prevent miscarriages of justice and to assure fair trials. Especially is this so when the criminal defendant involved makes no claims of prejudice or bias. The Court does accord some slight attention to justifying its ruling in terms of the basis on which the right to jury trial was read into the Fourteenth Amendment. It concludes that the jury is not effective, as a prophylaxis against arbitrary prosecutorial and judicial power, if the "jury pool is made up of only special segments of the populace or if large, distinctive groups are excluded from the pool." It fails, however, to provide any satisfactory explanation of the mechanism by which the Louisiana system undermines the prophylactic role of the jury, either in general or in this case. The best it can do is to posit "a flavor, a distinct quality," which allegedly is lost if either sex is excluded. However, this "flavor" is not of such importance that the Constitution is offended if any given petit jury is not so enriched. This smacks more of mysticism than of law. The Court does not even purport to practice its mysticism in a consistent fashion—presumably doctors, lawyers, and other groups, whose frequent exemption from jury service is endorsed by the majority, also offer qualities as distinct and important as those at issue here. * * *

Notes and Questions

1. In DUREN V. MISSOURI, 439 U.S. 357, 99 S.Ct. 664, 58 L.Ed.2d 579 (1979), the defendant established (1) that 54% of the adult inhabitants of the county were women, (2) that only 15% of the persons placed on venires were women, and (3) that any woman could decline jury service (a) by claiming an exemption in response to a prominent notice on a jury-selection questionnaire, (b) by returning the summons for jury duty as indicated on the summons, or (c) by simply not reporting for jury duty. The Court, per White, J., held that the defendant had made out "a prima facie fair-cross-section violation" (by showing "(1) that the group alleged to be excluded is a 'distinctive' group in the community; (2) that the representation of this group in venires from which juries are selected is not fair and reasonable in relation to the number of such persons in the community; and (3) that this under-representation is due to systematic exclusion of the group in the jury selection process") and that the state had not carried its "burden of justifying this infringement by showing attainment of a fair cross section to be incompatible with a significant state interest." Recognizing "that a State may have an important interest in assuring

that those members of the family responsible for the care of children are available to do so," Justice White suggested that an exemption "appropriately tailored to this interest would * * * survive a fair-cross-section challenge."

Rehnquist, J., dissenting, expressed the fear "that today's decision will cause States to abandon not only gender-based but also occupation-based classifications for purposes of jury service. Doctors and nurses, though virtually irreplaceable in smaller communities, may ultimately be held by the Court to bring their own 'flavor' or 'indescribable something' to a jury venire."

2. *The cross-section requirement.* In light of *Taylor,* what groups may be excluded from jury service? Consider:

(a) *The young.* In *Barber v. Ponte,* 772 F.2d 982 (1st Cir.1985), concerning underrepresentation by those 18–34 years of age, apparently as a consequence of using a key man system of jury selection, the panel concluded such persons constituted a "distinctive group" within the meaning of *Duren.* The panel emphasized that "many sociologists contend that young people do comprise a class with distinctive values, outlooks, manners, roles, and behavior patterns," and that one study "showed greater differences of opinion by age than by race or gender in such matters as: the inference of guilt from silence; the presumption of innocence; the predisposition of the young to break the law; and the performance and prerogatives of the police." But on rehearing en banc, that ruling was reversed. The court stated that the "essence of a distinctive group is that its members share specific common characteristics," and that the record in the instant case contained no "evidence that the attitudes and thinking of, say, 30 year olds have more in common with 18 year olds than they do with 40 year olds, or for that matter, going to the other end of the scale, that 18 year olds have more in common with 28 year olds than with 16 year olds." Moreover, said the court, in *Duren* the Supreme Court "wanted to give heightened scrutiny to groups needing special protection, not to all groups generally." But the court then cautioned: "That is not to say, however, that if a classification were *specifically* and *systematically excluded* from jury duty the same standard would be used as here, where defendant simply relies on a statistical disparity in the venires to challenge its constitutionality. If certain people are specifically and systematically excluded from jury duty, then the jury-administering authority would have created its own group." One dissenter objected: "The holding that young adults are not a cognizable group and, therefore, need not be included in the jury pool to make it a reasonable cross section of the community, but cannot be overtly excluded is inherently contradictory." Is it? [b]

(b) *The old.* In *State v. Brewer,* 247 N.W.2d 205 (Iowa 1977), the court upheld a statutory provision making ineligible all persons over 65: "The State has a rational basis for its special exclusion of persons over 65. Defendant has not shown the excluded class has any special perspective not attainable from the balance of the community."

(c) *Persons not registered to vote.* If persons are not excluded from voter registration lists by invidiously discriminatory laws, customs, or practices, is it then per-

b. In *Hamling v. United States,* 418 U.S. 87, 94 S.Ct. 2887, 41 L.Ed.2d 590 (1974) the Court, per Rehnquist, J., held that even assuming "the young are an identifiable group entitled to a group-based protection under our prior cases," a prima facie case of discrimination was not made out upon a showing that the master jury wheel had not been refilled for nearly four years, so that the youngest potential juror was at least 24, and that the petitioner's motion for a continuance until after a forthcoming refilling was denied. "[I]f the jury wheel is not discriminatory when completely updated at the time of each refilling, a prohibited 'purposeful discrimination' does not arise near the end of the period simply because the young and other persons have belatedly become eligible for jury service by becoming registered voters."

missible to rely solely upon those lists as a source of jurors, or is this objectionable on the ground that it tends to exclude the "politically alienated" and others who do not avail themselves of the opportunity to register? See, e.g., *United States v. Lewis,* 472 F.2d 252 (3d Cir.1973), rejecting this objection to the use of voter lists.[c]

(d) *Aliens.* The federal requirement of citizenship was upheld in *United States v. Gordon-Nikkar,* 518 F.2d 972 (5th Cir. 1975). Though the defendants were of Cuban origin and were tried in Miami, where 30% of the population were resident aliens, the court concluded there was "a compelling interest 'in ensuring that persons who serve as jurors are personally committed to the proper application and enforcement of the laws of the United States.' "

(e) *Persons in the professions.* In *United States v. Arnett,* 342 F.Supp. 1255 (D.Mass. 1970), the juror selection process was challenged on the ground that ministers, doctors, dentists, pharmacists, nurses, teachers, lawyers and sole proprietors of businesses could be excused upon request. The court responded: "The excuses reflect a rational accommodation between the community's need for jurors and its needs for uninterrupted religious, medical, teaching and like services. If persons of professional background be regarded as a cognizable group, that group is adequately represented by persons from disciplines which are not made a basis for excuse from jury duty."

3. *"Fair and reasonable" representation.* In *State v. McCarthy,* 496 A.2d 513 (Conn. 1985), defendant showed that of the 12,351 persons called for jury duty in the county over two and a half years only 1.9% had Hispanic surnames, that the federal census indicated there should have been 3.75%, and that utilizing "statistical decision theory" this disparity would not have occurred randomly. The state conceded that Hispanics were a "distinctive" group under *Duren,* but the court held defendant had failed to establish the second *Duren* factor. The court deemd the statistical decision theory (discussed in *Castaneda v. Partida,* Note 4 infra) "to be more relevant to the issue of discrimination posed in an equal protection challenge to jury composition than to the question of whether the jury pool reflects adequately the diversity of the community from which it is selected." By contrast, "best suited to a fair cross section claim" is "the substantial impact test," which "allows the courts to reject challenges when the challenged practices did not significantly alter the composition of the typical * * * petit jury."[d] The court next concluded there had been no such impact here, for if the 225 missing Hispanics were in the 12,351 potential juror pool, which if divided into juries of six (used in cases such as defendant's) would have served 2,000 potential juries, "one more Hispanic would have been available for selection on only one out of nine juries. * * * The decision of the six must be unanimous [, but e]ven taking this into account, however, we cannot conclude that the underrepresentation of Hispanics in the jury venires of Fairfield county was so substantial as to violate the defendant's due process right to a jury

c. Compare *United States v. Burkett,* 342 F.Supp. 1264 (D.Mass.1972), where Judge Wyzanski observed: "A jury selection system which is fundamentally based upon voters' registration lists in a state in which no one is required to register for voting, and in which it is obvious to anyone who scans the voters' registration lists that the black, those of Oriental origin, those with Spanish surnames, women, young persons, and poor and deprived persons generally tend not to register to vote, in proportions related to their number in the citizenry, and it is obvious to anyone who scans the lists of jurors actually serving that affluent and educated citizens are a smaller percentage of the jurors serving than their percentage in the citizenry, is a jury system which raises constitutional problems of serious import."

d. Quoting Beale, *Integrating Statistical Evidence and Legal Theory to Challenge the Selection of Grand and Petit Jurors,* 46 Law & Contemp. Probs. 269, 275 (1983).

representing a fair cross section of the community."

4. *Racial discrimination.* Fourteenth Amendment equal protection challenges to state jury selection procedures prevailed long before the Sixth Amendment right to jury trial was applied to the states. In *Strauder v. West Virginia,* 100 U.S. 303, 25 L.Ed. 664 (1880), it was held that for a state to try a black defendant before a jury from which all members of his race had been excluded by statute is a denial of equal protection, and in *Neal v. Delaware,* 103 U.S. 370, 26 L.Ed. 567 (1881), the principle was extended to the discriminatory administration of ostensibly fair jury selection laws to achieve the same result.

Strauder and *Neal* had a limited impact for several years because the defendant was required to show a definite purpose to discriminate by jury officials; the state action was presumed constitutional and the lower court findings were presumed to be true unless the defendant proved the contrary. But in *Norris v. Alabama,* 294 U.S. 587, 55 S.Ct. 579, 79 L.Ed. 1074 (1935), the Court held that a defendant in a criminal case could make out a prima facie case of discrimination by showing (a) the existence of a substantial number of blacks in the community, and (b) their total or virtual exclusion from jury service. The burden then shifts to the state to prove that the exclusion did not flow from discrimination. *Avery v. Georgia,* 345 U.S. 559, 73 S.Ct. 891, 97 L.Ed. 1244 (1953). This burden cannot be met merely by testimony by the jury commissioner that he did not intend to discriminate, *Eubanks v. Louisiana,* 356 U.S. 584, 78 S.Ct. 970, 2 L.Ed. 2d 991 (1958), or that he did not know any qualified blacks. *Hill v. Texas,* 316 U.S. 400, 62 S.Ct. 1159, 86 L.Ed. 1559 (1942).

A statute requiring jury commissioners to select for jury service those persons who are "generally reported to be honest and intelligent * * * and * * * esteemed in the community for their integrity, good character and sound judgment" is not unconstitutional on its face, for such a statute—to be found in many states—is "devoid of any mention of race," has "antecedents * * * of ancient vintage, and there is no suggestion that the law was originally adopted or subsequently carried forward for the purpose of fostering racial discrimination." *Carter v. Jury Comm. of Greene County,* 396 U.S. 320, 90 S.Ct. 518, 24 L.Ed.2d 549 (1970). However, a prima facie case of discrimination may be made out by showing that the substantial disparity between minority group members in the population and on the jury list "originated, at least in part, at the one point in the selection process where the jury commissioners invoked their subjective judgment rather than objective criteria." *Turner v. Fouche,* 396 U.S. 346, 90 S.Ct. 532, 24 L.Ed.2d 567 (1970).

In *Castaneda v. Partida,* 430 U.S. 482, 97 S.Ct. 1272, 51 L.Ed.2d 498 (1977), in a 5–4 decision, the Court, per Blackmun, J., held that a showing that the population of the county was 79.1% Mexican-American, but that over an 11-year period only 39% of the persons summoned for grand jury service were Mexican-American, established a prima facie case of discrimination, which was unrebutted absent evidence that racially neutral qualifications for grand jurors resulted in the lower proportion of Mexican-Americans. The dissenters objected that especially because the case "involves neither tokenism nor absolute exclusion," "*eligible* population statistics, not gross population figures, provide the relevant starting point" for proving a prima facie case of discrimination. The dissenters stressed that the respondent had the burden of proving "discriminatory intent" because "in a state case in which the challenge is to the grand jury, only the Fourteenth Amendment applies, and the defendant has the burden of proving a violation of the Equal Protection Clause." By contrast, they noted, under the Fifth Amendment right to a federal grand jury and the Sixth Amendment right to a federal and state petit jury, a defendant has a right to a body "that reflects a fair cross-section of the community," which means that then he "need only show that the jury selection procedure 'systematically exclude[s] distinctive groups in the community and thereby fail[s] to be reasonably representative thereof.' "

5. *Vicinage.* In *People v. Jones,* 510 P.2d 705 (Cal.1973), Jones resided in the 77th Street Precinct (73% black) of Los Angeles, where the three sales of marijuana with which he was charged occurred. Because of a shortage of judges and courtrooms, it was ordered that crimes committed in the 77th Street Precinct not be tried in the Central District (31% black), where the precinct was located, but rather in the Southwest District (7% black), which did not draw jurors from the 77th Street Precinct. Held: "Although a jury drawn either from an entire county wherein the crime was committed or from that portion of a county wherein the crime was committed will satisfy the constitutional requirement of 'an impartial jury of the State and district wherein the crime shall have been committed' (U.S.Const., 6th Amend.) a jury drawn from only a portion of a county, exclusive of the place of the commission of the crime, will not satisfy the requirement."

However, the prevailing view of the Sixth Amendment vicinage (geographical location of jurors) requirement is that it "prohibits courts only from obtaining petit jurors from beyond the boundaries of two large units, the state and the federal judicial district," and does not bar excluding residents of portions of those units—even those residing in the immediate vicinity of the crime. *Zicarelli v. Gray,* 543 F.2d 466 (3d Cir.1976).[e] Might the *Jones* result be explained in terms of the *Taylor* cross-section requirement? Cf. *People v. Taylor,* 350 N.E.2d 600 (N.Y.1976), holding that trial of a defendant by jurors drawn from a county other than that in which the crime was committed did not violate the cross section requirement where there was "no significant disparity in the racial, ethnic or sexual composition" of the population of the two counties.

6. *Challenge to the array.* Constitutional objections to the manner in which prospective jurors were selected are made by a challenge to the array, sometimes referred to as a motion to quash the venire or panel. Such a challenge may also be made on the ground that the state law requirements for jury selection were not followed. However, although statutes often purport to allow challenge "on the ground that the jurors were not selected or drawn according to law," the prevailing view is that there must be a "material departure" from the statutory requirements. The timing of challenges to the array is usually governed by provisions similar to Fed.R. Crim.P. 12(b) or 28 U.S.C. 1867. Cf. Note 1 at p. 985 supra.

HAMER v. UNITED STATES

259 F.2d 274 (9th Cir.1958).

BARNES, CIRCUIT JUDGE. * * *

[On appeal, defendant, who had been convicted for fraudulently importing narcotic drugs and facilitating the sale thereof, claimed a deprivation of the right to jury trial for three reasons: (1) she was denied a list of the names and addresses of prospective jurors in advance of trial; (2) her counsel was not allowed to question prospective jurors directly during the *voir dire* examination; and (3) the prosecutor, at the *voir dire,* used a jury book setting out how prospective jurors acted or voted while on previous juries.]

Congress, in its wisdom, has seen fit to require that there be given advance notice, by service of jury lists, to defense counsel in certain classes of cases—primarily, treason and capital offenses. 18 U.S.C. § 3432. This statute has never been held

e. See Kershen, *Vicinage,* 30 Okla.L.Rev. 1 (1977).

applicable to non-capital offenses. * * *

The very fact that Congress has seen fit to require the furnishing of the list of prospective jurors to defendants in the more serious capital offense cases alone, and not in the cases involving other lesser offenses, indicates that it found no necessity for such a rule in the lesser types of cases.

Appellant's remedy then, if any exists, is from the hands of Congress, not from the courts. The courts now are following the congressional intent and purpose.

The cases to which we have referred above do not discuss whether there a personal voir dire by defense counsel was allowed. But there also exists a line of cases determining that there is no constitutional right to a personal voir dire of the jury. * * * The holding of these cases has been embodied in rule 24(a) of the Federal Rules of Criminal Procedure. These cases, however, do not discuss whether there was a view of the jury lists before trial.

Considered separately, both these rules seem sound and not violative of a defendant's constitutional rights. But the point which appellant here raises is that there is a denial of the right to an impartial jury, and thereby a fair jury trial, when *both* these requests are denied. Upon this question neither side has cited authorities.

A short answer might be that if there is no error separately, then there can be none when the two are combined. Provided that the selection of the jury when viewed as a whole is fair and impartial, such a test would comport with the Supreme Court's view of the basic premise of the due process clauses of the Fifth and Fourteenth Amendments of the Constitution. However we are not dealing with a claimed violation of the due process clause, but rather there is raised a specific denial of other constitutional safeguards. * * *

We find the voir dire examination permitted and undertaken here by the trial judge was adequate and fair to insure defendant the unbiased selection of an impartial jury to which he was entitled. The trial court advised counsel that if he had any additional voir dire questions, he could request the court to ask them. No such request was made. When the court asked if there were anything further on the issue of challenges for cause, defendant's counsel stated, "Nothing further." We hold the voir dire examination in this case was sufficient.

We have examined the jury book used by government counsel.[7] The use of "jury books" showing how members of a jury panel voted on previous juries has long existed in our courts. It has been praised and criticized; attacked and defended. Many an experienced trial lawyer will insist that knowing how a juror votes on one case will not give the slightest indication how he or she would vote on another, even if it is the same kind of case. If the

7. It lists some two hundred and fifty or three hundred jurors, one on each loose-leaf page. Of one juror it said: "This Juror very poor.—held up jury for 4 hours 11–1." On each of the other eleven jurors who had sat with this juror there appeared the notation that they had sat on this same jury that R______ had held up for four hours. (These were the "twelve times" referred to by the court below that a reference had been made in the book to an individual juror's action in the jury room.) A second juror "caused the jury to be hung several hours." The address and business, or the spouse's business, and the age of most jurors were given; how long they had lived in Southern California; their former place of residence; number of children, etc.

One juror was characterized as inattentive, another as having a hard time staying awake during later stages of trial; another juror listened carefully; "this juror slept during trial—was excused by the Court;" this juror was attentive to instructions; one was characterized as a strong juror for the government, another as "too sympathetic to boys in handcuffs;" another as an outstanding juror (after voting four times for conviction in government cases).

All other comments in the book had to do with juries as a whole—"excellent jury;" "good attentive jury;" "verdict in less than 20 min.;" "took 4 hours on simple case;" etc., "good jury, quick verdict."

facts differ, it is a different case, and different pressures, feelings, and sympathies come into being. And, of course, facts do differ in each narcotics case; in each tax case; each personal injury case; and each case of any "type" or "kind."

Whether the United States District Attorney's staff in any district keeps a "jury book" or not (written or mental), whether it keeps a black-list of the few "sympathetic jurors," or a white list of the few "hanging jurors," cannot be considered error per se. Any group of attorneys associated together for any reason, who are constantly engaged in the trial of cases, will discuss and communicate as much information and knowledge as they possibly can to each other. Defense counsel, though perhaps not with the same enthusiasm, will discuss and relay information about jurors—"good" or "bad," as they may appear to interested partisans * * *.

But, says appellant, the list here was more than mere reputation. It contains references to how the jurors voted. It must be conceded that with respect to the reference to two jurors having "held up" a jury for "four" or "several" hours, such notation purports to pass along information as to what happened within a jury room.

Again, as any jury trial lawyer knows, it is almost impossible to prevent eleven jurors who have been held from a decision for several hours by *one* who saw the matter the other way, from publicly expressing their displeasure or disgust. The proverbial request by the foreman of the hung jury "for eleven dinners and a bale of hay" is well known to all.

If counsel for this defendant had tried cases before some of the jurors on this panel and had received information or come to any conclusions with respect to their individual intelligence, attentiveness, or sympathetic attitude, he would have felt he was negligent toward his client's interest had he not utilized his knowledge, or his intuition, to his client's best advantage.

We are not impressed with the argument that under any and all circumstances, and irrespective of what may be in a jury book, its use should be declared to deprive a defendant of a fair jury trial. To carry such a theory to its ultimate and ridiculous conclusion, no defendant could be prosecuted by a government attorney who had more information about how jurors on that panel had voted, in other cases, than his own counsel had. If defense counsel chosen was trying his first case before that panel, must the government hire a lawyer who likewise has tried no cases before that same jury panel? Is a defendant, in the name of his constitutional rights, entitled to be prosecuted by a government prosecutor with no more experience than his own counsel, or vice versa? If so, how is such experience to be measured? If the government lawyer is a tyro, must a defendant replace his more experienced defense counsel? Such a proposed rule would break down law enforcement in this country. It cannot be seriously considered. Perfect equality in counsel can never be achieved, any more than there can be two judges, or groups of judges, with precisely similar competence. * * *

Notes and Questions

1. 28 U.S.C. § 1867(f), giving defendant access to "papers used by the jury commission or clerk in connection with the jury selection process," has been characterized as granting defendant "essentially an unqualified right to inspect jury lists." *Test v. United States,* 420 U.S. 28, 95 S.Ct. 749, 42 L.Ed.2d 786 (1975). But the statute applies to a challenge to the entire panel, and thus is inapplicable where the list is desired only for the purposes of the voir dire.

On the state level, some states have expressly provided for defendants to obtain jury lists in all criminal cases, while others have limited the right to capital cases or felonies. In those jurisdictions without such legislation, it is usually held that a defendant has no right to a list of the panel, although there are cases holding that a defendant, upon timely motion, is entitled to the list even in the absence of statute.

Consider also the "anonymous jury" situation, in which the names of the jurors and their addresses and places of employment are withheld in advance of trial *and* during jury selection as well. See, e.g., *United States v. Thomas,* 757 F.2d 1359 (2d Cir.1985) ("there must be, first, strong reason to believe that the jury needs protection and, second, reasonable precaution must be taken to minimize the effect that such a decision might have on the jurors' opinions of the defendants").

2. Fed.R.Crim.P. 24(a) gives the court discretion to either conduct the examination itself or permit counsel to do so. This is the rule in 13 states; 20 give the attorney primary control of the questioning; and 17 provide for the judge to begin the questioning and for attorneys to then ask additional questions. Which procedure is best?

3. Two important functions of the voir dire are (i) to elicit information which would establish a basis for challenges for cause; and (ii) to acquire information to afford an intelligent exercise of peremptory challenges. A third, which many would not view as legitimate, is said to be that of "indoctrinating the potential jurors on the merits of the case and developing rapport." Comment, 70 Calif.L.Rev. 708, 714 (1982).

4. Is it permissible for the prosecution to send police officers out to interview the prospective jurors about their backgrounds and views on certain issues, as in *Commonwealth v. Smith,* 215 N.E.2d 897 (Mass. 1966)? To have an FBI investigation of members of the venire conducted, as in *United States v. Falange,* 426 F.2d 930 (2d Cir.1970)? To question members of the panel about their votes in previous cases? *A.B.A. Code of Prof. Resp.* D.R. 7–108 provides: "(A) Before the trial of a case a lawyer connected therewith shall not communicate with or cause another to communicate with anyone he knows to be a member of the venire from which the jury will be selected for the trial of the case. * * * (E) A lawyer shall not conduct or cause, by financial support or otherwise, another to conduct a vexatious or harassing investigation of either a venireman or a juror."

5. "In all but a few jurisdictions, discovery of juror information by either the prosecution or defense is not allowed. Typically, the cases find the defense seeking discovery of juror information sifted from police records or compiled by a government agency and employed by the prosecution. Judges have held almost uniformly that the prosecution need not reveal this information, although the courts consistently have failed to articulate any convincing rationale for this position." Note, 49 So.Cal.L.Rev. 597, 602–03 (1976). But see *People v. Murtishaw,* 631 P.2d 446 (Cal.1981) (trial courts "have the discretion to permit a defendant, who lacks funds to investigate prospective jurors, to inspect prosecution jury records and investigations"); *Losavio v. Mayber,* 496 P.2d 1032 (Colo.1972) (where prosecutor obtained information from police files on prospective jurors, defense attorney entitled to the same information; the "requirements of fundamental fairness and justice dictate no less"); *People v. Aldridge,* 209 N.W.2d 796 (Mich.App.1973) (same result; court adds that this "doctrine of fairness does not mean that defendants are permitted to seek disclosure of the prosecutor's dossier while preserving the secrecy of their own investigative report upon prospective jurors").[a]

a. Consider also *United States v. Kyle,* 469 F.2d 547 (D.C.Cir.1972), where the prosecutor failed to disclose that several prospective jurors (three of whom ultimately served on the jury which convicted the defendant) had been members of a jury which two days earlier had been berated by another trial judge for returning a verdict of acquittal of which he would be "ashamed" and for showing too little concern for the "crime situation." The court observed:

6. In some recent trials, social science techniques have been employed in jury selection. The first step is to survey randomly as large a sample as possible of the population from which the jury will be selected. The researchers attempt to discern attitudes relevant to the issues in the particular forthcoming trial. Data from the survey is fed into a computer with socioeconomic background characteristics (e.g., religion, age, sex, occupation) in order to identify those characteristics which would identify a favorable and unfavorable juror. The questions asked on voir dire are geared to ascertaining those characteristics found to be associated with favorable or unfavorable attitudes. Instead or in addition, the jury panel may be observed in court and rated by psychologists or psychiatrists on authoritarianism scales or by kinesiologists in terms of body language.

"At this stage in its development, the cost of the new techniques is so great that only the very rich, or those famous enough to secure donated time and money, are able to afford them. * * *

"So far the new juror investigative techniques have been used exclusively by defendants in trials with strong political overtones. However, prosecutors will no doubt begin to utilize the techniques as well, if only to counterbalance the effect of studies done for defendants. The impact of prosecutorial use of these techniques could be profound; state and federal governments have not only the resources to employ social scientists and computers necessary to utilize the new techniques, but they have also a wealth of specific juror information unavailable to the defense. Furthermore, the effectiveness of the techniques in selecting favorably biased juries will be a strong incentive for prosecutors to employ the techniques in all important trials regardless of whether the defense has conducted a study of its own." Note, 49 So.Cal.L.Rev. 597, 606–07 (1976).

Is this a cause for concern? Saks, *The Limits of Scientific Jury Selection: Ethical and Empirical,* 17 Jurimetrics J. 3, 4 (1976), warns: "If the outcome of a trial can be manipulated simply by impaneling jurors designated acceptable by social scientists, then trial by jury may cease to function satisfactorily and, ultimately, may be abandoned." What, then, should be done?

7. Most jurisdictions have provided by statute or court rule for the selection of extra jurors during protracted trials. Under the more common alternate juror (or substituted juror) approach, one or more persons specifically identified as alternates are chosen in advance of trial. If a regular juror is discharged prior to the time the jury retires (or, in a few jurisdictions, prior to the time of verdict), an alternate juror is then designated to take his place. Under the additional juror (or eliminated juror) approach, more than 12 jurors are selected in advance of trial, and if a juror must be discharged during the trial nothing more is done at that time. If more than 12 jurors remain at the time the jury is to retire, the 12 who shall determine the case are selected by lot. Does either of these approaches have an advantage over the other?

8. What should be done when a juror must be excused after jury deliberations

"Ordinarily there would be no basis for a duty to disclose material pertaining to public aspects of a juror's service, for example voting record in other cases, and relative experience or inexperience, but when there has been a prior governmental impetus affecting a juror's prior service, and it is of a nature likely to escape the attention even of reasonably diligent appointed counsel, considerations of basic fairness may generate a duty to disclose."

However, the court affirmed, noting that the prosecutor's failure to disclose was not unreasonable or in bad faith and that the jurors would not have been automatically disqualified because of the prior incident. Bazelon, J., dissenting, emphasized that the prosecutor's "action deprived the trial judge of the ability to rule on a question that goes to the heart of the fairness of the appellant's trial" and that "even if these jurors would not be subject to automatic disqualification, they could have been peremptorily challenged by the defense."

have commenced? (The prevailing rule is that a juror may be replaced by an alternate only up to the time that the jury retires for their deliberations.) Consider Fed.R.Crim.P. 23(b); *United States v. Phillips,* 664 F.2d 971 (5th Cir.1981) (replacement of juror after deliberations began not a violation of the Sixth Amendment right to jury trial, and, given fact the court "sequestered the alternate during the preliminary jury deliberations, carefully questioned each juror individually about whether he or she could and would start the deliberations anew, and pointedly instructed the jury to begin its deliberations anew," not a prejudicial violation of Fed. R.Crim.P. 24(c)); and *Johnson v. Duckworth,* 650 F.2d 122 (7th Cir.1981) (constitutional to have alternate in jury room as observer from outset, as it not "the sort of invasion of the jury's privacy that will tend to stifle the jury's debate").

NOTES ON CHALLENGES FOR CAUSE AND VOIR DIRE EXAMINATION

1. Statutes setting forth the permissible grounds for challenge for cause typically cover such specific situations as where the prospective juror has previously served as a juror on some related matter, where he has been or will be a witness against the defendant, and where he is related in some degree to the defendant or others involved in the case. A more general ground for challenge is often stated in these terms:

"That the juror has a state of mind in reference to the cause or to the defendant or to the person alleged to have been injured by the offense charged, or to the person on whose complaint the prosecution was instituted, which will prevent him from acting with impartiality; but the formation of an opinion or impression regarding the guilt or innocence of the defendant shall not of itself be sufficient ground of challenge to a juror, if he declares, and the court is satisfied, that he can render an impartial verdict according to the evidence."

2. In *Dennis v. United States,* 339 U.S. 162, 70 S.Ct. 519, 94 L.Ed. 734 (1950), a 5–2 majority of the Court, per Minton, J., held that in a case to which the federal government is a party, its employees are not challengeable for cause solely by reason of their employment. The Court also rejected the argument that the failure to sustain the challenge denied petitioner an "impartial jury" under the "special circumstances of this case"—a prosecution of a Communist for contempt of the House Un-American Activities Committee, where the government's interest was said to be "the vindication of a direct affront, as distinguished from its role in an ordinary prosecution"; and where, because of an alleged "aura of surveillance and intimidation" said to exist because of a "Loyalty Order," government employees "would be hesitant to vote for acquittal because such action might be interpreted as 'sympathetic association' with Communism." *Dennis* continues to be followed. See, e.g., *United States v. Boyd,* 446 F.2d 1267 (5th Cir.1971) (must show actual bias of government employee in theft from government case).

3. As for employment by a nongovernmental victim of the crime charged, compare the following cases in which the prospective juror was employed at the bank robbed, albeit at a branch other than where the robbery occurred: *United States v. Brown,* 644 F.2d 101 (2d Cir.1981) (not excusable for cause; court unwilling "to institute a series of presumptions of implied bias in other employment relationships"); *United States v. Allsup,* 566 F.2d 68 (9th Cir.1977) ("The employment relationship coupled with a reasonable apprehension of violence by bank robbers leads us to believe that bias of those who work for the bank should be presumed"). Should bias also be presumed because of a prospective juror's membership in a certain group? For example, may a member of the Ku Klux Klan sit on a jury in a case involving a black defendant?

4. The implied bias vs. actual bias issue may also arise in a post-trial setting. In SMITH v. PHILLIPS, 455 U.S. 209, 102 S.Ct. 940, 71 L.Ed.2d 78 (1982), where the prosecutor failed to disclose his mid-trial discovery that one of the jurors had just made application to the District Attorney's Office for employment as an investigator, the majority rejected the defendant's argument that "the law must impute bias to jurors in [such a] position" because "a court cannot possibly ascertain the impartiality of a juror by relying solely upon the testimony of the juror in question." The Court, per Rehnquist, J., relying upon such cases as *Dennis,* concluded "that due process does not require a new trial every time a juror has been placed in a potentially compromising situation" and that consequently the defendant would have to show actual bias in order to prevail. O'Connor, J., concurring on the understanding "that the opinion does not foreclose the use of 'implied bias' in appropriate circumstances," asserted that "there are some extreme situations that would justify a finding of implied bias. Some examples might include a revelation that the juror is an actual employee of the prosecuting agency, that the juror is a close relative of one of the participants in the trial or the criminal transaction, or that the juror was a witness or somehow involved in the criminal transaction. Whether or not the state proceedings resulted in a finding of 'no bias,' the Sixth Amendment right to an impartial jury should not allow a verdict to stand under such circumstances." Marshall, J., joined by Brennan and Stevens, JJ., dissenting, concluded "that in cases like this one, where the probability of bias is very high, and where the evidence adduced at a hearing can offer little assurance that prejudice does not exist, the juror should be deemed biased as a matter of law," because the "right to a trial by an impartial jury is too important, and the threat to that right too great, to justify rigid insistence on actual proof of bias."

5. In *Witherspoon v. Illinois,* 391 U.S. 510, 88 S.Ct. 1770, 20 L.Ed.2d 776 (1968), the Court, per Stewart, J., held "that a sentence of death cannot be carried out if the jury that imposed or recommended it was chosen by excluding veniremen for cause simply because they voiced general objections to the death penalty or expressed conscientious or religious scruples against its infliction." In so doing, "the State crossed the line of neutrality" and "produced a jury uncommonly willing to condemn a man to die." *Witherspoon* appeared to permit exclusion only if the prospective juror made it "unmistakably clear" that he would "automatically vote against the imposition of capital punishment." But in *Adams v. Texas,* 448 U.S. 38, 100 S.Ct. 2521, 65 L.Ed.2d 581 (1980), it was said a juror could be challenged for his views about capital punishment if "those views should prevent or substantially impair the performance of his duties as a juror in accordance with his instructions and his oath." [a]

In WAINWRIGHT v. WITT, ___ U.S. ___, 105 S.Ct. 844, 83 L.Ed.2d 841 (1985), the Court, per REHNQUIST, J., opted for the *Adams* formulation. "*Witherspoon* is not grounded in the Eighth Amendment's prohibition against cruel and unusual punishment, but in the Sixth Amendment. Here, as elsewhere, the quest is for jurors who will conscientiously apply the law and find the facts. That is what an 'impartial' jury consists of, and we

a. Though *Witherspoon* involved a procedure for selecting juries in capital cases where the jury did the sentencing and had complete discretion as to whether the death penalty should be imposed, *Adams* held the rule of that case also applies when the jury considered punishment in a subsequent penalty proceeding at which the jury is only permitted to answer certain questions about the presence of statutorily-defined aggravated circumstances which, if present, mandate a sentence of death by the judge. The Court stressed that jurors "will characteristically know that affirmative answers to the questions will result in the automatic imposition of the death penalty" and will "unavoidably exercise a range of judgment and discretion while remaining true to their instructions and their oaths."

do not think, simply because a defendant is being tried for a capital crime, that he is entitled to a legal presumption or standard that allows jurors to be seated who quite likely will be biased in his favor.

"* * * We note that, in addition to dispensing with *Witherspoon's* reference to 'automatic' decisionmaking, this standard likewise does not require that a juror's bias be proved with 'unmistakable clarity.' This is because determinations of juror bias cannot be reduced to question-and-answer sessions which obtain results in the manner of a catechism. What common sense should have realized experience has proved: many veniremen simply cannot be asked enough questions to reach the point where their bias has been made 'unmistakably clear'; these veniremen may not know how they will react when faced with imposing the death sentence, or may be unable to articulate, or may wish to hide their true feelings. Despite this lack of clarity in the printed record, however, there will be situations where the trial judge is left with the definite impression that a prospective juror would be unable to faithfully and impartially apply the law."

BRENNAN and MARSHALL, JJ., dissenting, questioned the majority's assumption that the standard otherwise used to determine juror bias was applicable in the *Witherspoon* context. "The very nature of a *Witherspoon* challenge illuminates the difference. In typical cases involving an allegation of juror bias unrelated to death penalty scruples, the convicted defendant challenges the *inclusion* of particular jurors. In a *Witherspoon* case the convicted defendant challenges the *exclusion* of particular jurors. If, as the Court suggests, the only interest at stake in a *Witherspoon* case is the equivalent right of the defendant and the State to impartial individual jurors, then the entire thrust of the *Witherspoon* inquiry makes no sense. To be relevant to the right the Court claims is at stake, the inquiry would have to focus on whether the individual jurors who replaced the excluded prospective jurors were impartial; if so, then no harm would result from the exclusion of particular prospective jurors, whatever the reason for the exclusion."

6. The Court in *Witherspoon* rejected the petitioner's additional contention that his conviction should also be reversed because "such a jury, unlike one chosen at random from a cross-section of the community, must necessarily be biased in favor of conviction." The Court found it could not conclude, "either on the basis of the record now before us or as a matter of judicial notice, that the exclusion of jurors opposed to capital punishment results in an unrepresentative jury on the issue of guilt or substantially increases the risk of conviction."

In *Keeten v. Garrison,* 742 F.2d 129 (4th Cir.1984), the court overturned the district court's ruling, based on statistical studies presented to it, that (i) jurors excluded under *Witherspoon* are a distinctive group in the community and their exclusion violates the Sixth Amendment requirement under *Taylor v. Louisiana,* p. 1269 supra, that jurors be drawn from a fair cross-section of the community; and (ii) such exclusion creates a conviction prone jury in violation of the due process clause. On the first point, the court of appeals reasoned that the Sixth Amendment right "does not include the right to be tried by jurors who are unable or unwilling to follow the law and the instructions of the trial judge in a capital case. The state as well as the defendant has legitimate and vital interests at stake at both the guilt and penalty stages of a capital case." As for the second point, the court responded: "The fact that a death-qualified jury may be more conviction prone than one which includes jurors strongly opposed to the death penalty does not demonstrate which jury is impartial. Rather, '[i]t indicates only that a death-qualified jury might favor the prosecution and that a nondeath-qualified jury might favor the defendant.' "

Compare *Grigsby v. Mabry,* 758 F.2d 226 (8th Cir.1985), cert. granted, ___ U.S.

___, 106 S.Ct. 59, 88 L.Ed.2d 48 (1985), where, after reviewing the empirical evidence relied upon by the district court in making the factual finding that death-qualified juries are more prone to convict, the court held that a conviction rendered by such a jury violates the defendant's Sixth and Fourteenth Amendment rights to an impartial jury: "The question is not whether a jury would be biased one way or the other, but whether an impartial jury can exist when a distinct group in the community is excluded by systematically challenging them for cause."

7. HAM v. SOUTH CAROLINA, 409 U.S. 524, 93 S.Ct. 848, 35 L.Ed.2d 46 (1973), concerned a black, bearded civil rights worker who was convicted of possession of marijuana. During his voir dire examination of prospective jurors, the trial judge asked general questions as to bias, prejudice, or partiality,[b] but declined to ask more specific questions tendered by defense counsel which sought to elicit any possible prejudice against the defendant because of his race or his beard. The Court, per REHNQUIST, J., held: "Since one of the purposes of the Due Process Clause of the Fourteenth Amendment is to insure [the] 'essential demands of fairness,' and since a principal purpose of the adoption of the Fourteenth Amendment was to prohibit the States from invidiously discriminating on the basis of race, we think that the Fourteenth Amendment required the judge in this case to interrogate the jurors upon the subject of racial prejudice. * * * [T]he trial judge was not required to put the question in any particular form, or to ask any particular number of questions on the subject, simply because requested to do so by petitioner. * * * In this context either of the brief, general questions urged by the petitioner[c] would appear sufficient to focus the attention of prospective jurors to any racial prejudice they might entertain.

"The third of petitioner's proposed questions was addressed to the fact that he wore a beard. While we cannot say that prejudice against people with beards might not have been harbored by one or more of the potential jurors in this case, this is the beginning and not the end of the inquiry as to whether the Fourteenth Amendment required the trial judge to interrogate the prospective jurors about such possible prejudice. Given the traditionally broad discretion accorded to the trial judge in conducting *voir dire,* and our inability to constitutionally distinguish possible prejudice against beards from a host of other possible similar prejudices, we do not believe the petitioner's constitutional rights were violated when the trial judge refused to put this question. The inquiry as to racial prejudice derives its constitutional stature * * * from a principal purpose as well as from the language of those who adopted the Fourteenth Amendment. The trial judge's refusal to inquire as to particular bias against beards, after his inquiries as to bias in general, does not reach the level of a constitutional violation."[d]

8. In *Ristaino v. Ross,* 424 U.S. 589, 96 S.Ct. 1017, 47 L.Ed.2d 258 (1976), the Court, per Powell, J., concluded that "*Ham* did not announce a requirement of universal applicability." The Court did "not agree with the Court of Appeals that the need to question veniremen specifically about racial prejudice also rose to con-

b. The three questions asked were, in substance, the following:

"1. Have you formed or expressed any opinion as to the guilt or innocence of the defendant, Gene Ham?

"2. Are you conscious of any bias or prejudice for or against him?

"3. Can you give the State and the defendant a fair and impartial trial?"

c. They were:

"1. Would you fairly try this case on the basis of the evidence and disregarding the defendant's race?

"2. You have no prejudice against negroes? Against black people? You would not be influenced by the use of the term 'black'?"

d. Douglas and Marshall, JJ., dissented.

stitutional dimensions in this case.[9] The mere fact that the victim of the crimes alleged [armed robbery, assault with a dangerous weapon, and assault with intent to murder] was a white man and the defendants were Negroes was less likely to distort the trial than were the special factors involved in *Ham.* The victim's status as a security officer, also relied upon by the Court of Appeals, was cited by respective defense counsel primarily as a separate source of prejudice, not as an aggravating racial factor, and the trial judge dealt with it by his question about law-enforcement affiliations. The circumstances thus did not suggest a significant likelihood that racial prejudice might infect Ross' trial. This was made clear to the trial judge when Ross was unable to support his motion concerning *voir dire* by pointing to racial factors such as existed in *Ham* or others of comparable significance. In these circumstances, the trial judge acted within the Constitution in determining that the demands of due process could be satisfied by his more generalized but thorough inquiry into the impartiality of the veniremen." [e]

9. In *Dukes v. Waitkevitch,* 536 F.2d 469 (1st Cir.1976), the court held that where a black man was accused of participation in a gang rape of several white women, the trial court did not commit constitutional error in refusing to inquire into racial prejudice on voir dire: "While interracial rape may be a classic category of racial prejudice, the prejudice inheres in the identity of the parties and not in the specific issues." Is this a correct interpretation of *Ross?*

10. As for the more demanding standard in federal trials, referred to in footnote 9 of *Ristaino,* the 4-man plurality opinion by White, J., in *Rosales-Lopez v. United States,* 451 U.S. 182, 101 S.Ct. 1629, 68 L.Ed.2d 22 (1981), concluded "it is usually best to allow the defendant to resolve this conflict by making the determination of whether or not he would prefer to have the inquiry into racial or ethnic prejudice pursued. Failure to honor his request, however, will only be reversible error where the circumstances of the case indicate that there is a reasonable possibility that racial or ethnic prejudice might have influenced the jury." That opinion added "that federal courts must make such an inquiry when requested by a defendant accused of a violent crime and where the defendant and the victim are members of different racial or ethnic groups," in that such a situation falls within "the 'reasonable possibility standard' articulated above," but two concurring justices objected to this "*per se* rule" out of "fear that its use of the term 'violent crime' and the term 'different racial or ethnic groups' is apt to spawn new litigation over the meaning of these terms." The Court concluded the above test was not met in the instant case where defendant, of Mexican descent, was charged with aiding members of his own ethnic group gain illegal entry into the United States.

11. Edward Bennett Williams suggests in 17 Student L.J. 24 (1971) "that we eliminate once and for all what I regard as the shameful process that has wasted 12 weeks and more in selecting a jury for several cases that have attracted national attention. I suggest that this is the judicial

9. "Although we hold that *voir dire* questioning directed to racial prejudice was not constitutionally required, the wiser course generally is to propound appropriate questions designed to identify racial prejudice if requested by the defendant. Under our supervisory power we would have required as much of a federal court faced with the circumstances here. * * *"

e. Consider also *Turner v. Bass,* 753 F.2d 342 (4th Cir.1985), cert. granted, ___ U.S. ___, 105 S.Ct. 2319, 85 L.Ed.2d 838 (1985) (absent showing of "special circumstances," black defendant accused of killing white victim not entitled to have jurors questioned on racial prejudice, and "special circumstances" not shown by fact that death penalty sought or by statistics purporting to show that historically the death penalty has been imposed in a racially discriminatory manner in that county).

counterpart of the legislative filibuster. It is time that we put an end to it. There is no case, I suggest to you, that should require more than a day of jury selection. * * * I have never taken more than a day in any case to get a jury, and I have never lost a case because I didn't have time enough for jury selection."

Compare the comments of Marshall, J., concurring in *Press-Enterprise Co. v. Superior Court,* p. 1328 infra:

"Also, I feel compelled to note my strong disagreement with the Court's gratuitous comments concerning the length of *voir dire* proceedings in this and other cases. The Court's opinion states that

> 'We cannot fail to observe that a *voir dire* process of such length [six weeks], in and of itself undermines public confidence in the courts and the legal profession. The process is to ensure a fair impartial jury, not a favorable one. Judges, not advocates, must control that process to make sure privileges are not so abused. Properly conducted it is inconceivable that the process could extend over such a period. We note, however, that in response to questions counsel stated that it is not unknown in California courts for jury selection to extend six months.'

The question whether the *voir dire* proceedings in this case extended for too long a period is not before this Court. Nor surprisingly, therefore, we know few of the facts that would be required to venture a confident ruling on that question. Some of the circumstances of which we are aware, however, cast considerable doubt on the majority's judgment. Albert Greenwood Brown, Jr. was accused of an interracial sexual attack and murder. Given the history and continuing legacy of racism in our country, that fact alone should suggest that a greater than usual amount of inquiry may have been needed in order to obtain a fair and impartial jury in this case. I find it not at all 'inconceivable' that the *voir dire* process could have legitimately extended over six weeks."

12. "Many courts, however, will not allow questions pertaining to rules of law. It is often claimed that such questions are improperly used to indoctrinate the jurors. Another reason advanced for excluding this method of voir dire is that the questions are too time consuming and are unnecessary when the same subject matter is covered in the judge's final instructions to the jury." Gold, *Voir Dire: Questioning Prospective Jurors on Their Willingness to Follow the Law,* 60 Ind.L.J. 163, 164 (1984). But see *People v. Zehr,* 469 N.E.2d 1062 (Ill.1984) ("essential to the qualification of jurors in a criminal case is that they know that a defendant is presumed innocent, that he is not required to offer any evidence in his own behalf, that he must be proved guilty beyond a reasonable doubt, and that his failure to testify in his own behalf cannot be held against him").

McCRAY v. ABRAMS

750 F.2d 1113 (2d Cir.1984).

KEARSE, CIRCUIT JUDGE:

[Michael McCray, a black, was prosecuted in New York for robbery of Phillip Roberts, a white art student. His first trial before a jury of nine whites and three blacks ended in a hung jury. Nine jurors voted to convict and three to acquit; either two or three of the latter were black. During jury selection for retrial, after the prosecutor had used 11 of her peremptory challenges and had thereby excluded 7 blacks and one Hispanic, McCray moved that the prosecutor be called upon to testify as to why she had excluded the persons she did. The judge denied the motion, explaining that excusing a juror of the same race as the defendant on the ground of perceived group affinity is "a time honored basis for the exercise of peremptory challenges." McCray was convicted by an all-white jury, and his conviction was affirmed on appeal. McCray's habeas petition in federal district court alleged: "The prosecution's use of peremptory challenges to exclude all minority members (7 blacks, 1 Hispanic) drawn for the jury panel on the basis of race violates the Sixth Amendment right to trial by an impartial jury and the Equal Protection Clause of the Fourteenth Amendment." The district court agreed, and the state then appealed.]

II. Equal Protection and Swain v. Alabama

We begin with a review of *Swain v. Alabama,* 380 U.S. 202, 85 S.Ct. 824, 13 L.Ed.2d 759 (1965), which is the only United States Supreme Court decision thus far to address directly the constitutional validity of the use of peremptory jury challenges to discriminate on the basis of race. Although much criticized, *Swain* has led most courts to reject all constitutional challenges to the prosecutor's alleged discriminatory use of peremptories.

A. *Swain v. Alabama*

Swain was a black defendant convicted by an all-white jury of the rape of a white woman. In his case, the trial jury venire had included eight blacks, two of whom were exempt; the prosecution used its peremptory challenges to remove the other six. Swain also showed that in the county in which he was tried, there had not since 1950 "been a Negro on a petit jury in either a civil or criminal case * * * and that in criminal cases prosecutors ha[d] consistently and systematically exercised their strikes to prevent any and all Negroes on petit jury venires from serving on the petit jury itself." Invoking a long line of cases that had held that "a State's purposeful or deliberate denial to Negroes on account of race of participation as jurors in the administration of justice violates the Equal Protection Clause," Swain contended, *inter alia,* that the prosecution's use of its peremptory challenges constituted invidious discrimination in the selection of jurors, in violation of his rights under the Equal Protection Clause. The Supreme Court disagreed.

In Part II of its opinion, the Court discussed at some length the history and purposes of the peremptory challenge. The Court noted the persistent use of peremptories in American trials and the prevailing view that they are a necessary part of a trial by jury, for they allow the challenge of a person thought to be less than fair and impartial but for whom cause to strike cannot be shown, and permit the removal of a person who may have been offended by a probing voir dire. The Court stated that "[t]he essential nature of the peremptory challenge is that it is one exercised without a reason stated, without inquiry and without being subject to the court's control," and that " 'it is, as Blackstone says, an arbitrary and capricious right; and it must be exercised with full freedom, or it fails of its full purpose.' "

Given the nature and the history of the peremptory challenge, the Court found merit in the proposition that the system, "in and of itself, provides justification for striking any group of otherwise qualified jurors in any given case, whether they be Negroes, Catholics, accountants or those with blue eyes." The Court concluded that "we cannot hold that the striking of Negroes in a particular case is a denial of equal protection of the laws."

> In the light of the purpose of the peremptory system and the function it serves in a pluralistic society in connection with the institution of jury trial, *we cannot hold that the Constitution requires an examination of the prosecutor's reasons for the exercise of his challenges in any given case.* The presumption in any particular case must be that the prosecutor is using the State's challenges to obtain a fair and impartial jury to try the case before the court. *The presumption is not overcome and the prosecutor therefore subjected to examination by allegations that in the case at hand all Negroes were removed from the jury or that they were removed because they were Negroes.* Any other result, we think, would establish a rule wholly at odds

with the peremptory challenge system as we know it.

The Court went on to say, in Part III of its opinion, that a defendant could require judicial inquiry into the prosecutor's use of peremptory challenges if he could show that

> the prosecutor in a county, in case after case, whatever the circumstances, whatever the crime and whoever the defendant or the victim may be, is responsible for the removal of Negroes who have been selected as qualified jurors by the jury commissioners and who have survived challenges for cause, with the result that no Negroes ever serve on petit juries * * *. If the State has not seen fit to leave a single Negro on any jury in a criminal case, the presumption protecting the prosecutor may well be overcome. Such proof might support a reasonable inference that Negroes are excluded from juries for reasons wholly unrelated to the outcome of the particular case on trial and that the peremptory system is being used to deny the Negro the same right and opportunity to participate in the administration of justice enjoyed by the white population. These ends the peremptory challenge is not designed to facilitate or justify.

The Court found, however, that Swain had not met this standard of proof.

B. Mission Impossible

Not surprisingly, almost no other defendants in the nearly two decades since the *Swain* decision have met this standard of proof either. * * *

As Justice Marshall noted in his dissent to the denial of McCray's petition for certiorari, "[i]n the nearly two decades since it was decided, *Swain* has been the subject of almost universal and often scathing criticism." Many of these commentaries have been critical, in our view rightly, of the nearly impossible task set for the defendant in Part III of the *Swain* opinion, *i.e.,* to show that in all cases, in all circumstances, whoever the victim, whoever the defendant, blacks were excluded from juries without cause.

We disagree as well with some of the fundamental premises found in Part II of *Swain.* For example, the Court's statement that there was no violation of equal protection because blacks and whites "are alike subject to being challenged without cause" ignores practice. In most communities a majority of those eligible for jury duty are white; and as a practical matter, the prosecution does not peremptorily excuse whites simply because they are whites. Thus, although the implication in Part III of *Swain,* is that "the Negro [should have] the same right and opportunity to participate in the administration of justice enjoyed by the white population," we think the assumption of Part II that that right is not violated simply because both blacks and whites are "subject to" being peremptorily excluded is fanciful.

More importantly, *Swain's* basic premise furthers the erosion of that right. The *Swain* Court found it permissible for a prosecutor to eliminate all blacks in any given case simply because they are blacks, because the "presumption * * * must be that the prosecutor is using the State's challenges to obtain a fair and impartial jury * * *." * * * Yet, it is fallacious to assume that all persons sharing an attribute of skin color, or of gender or ethnic origin, *etc.,* will *ipso facto* be partial to others sharing that attribute. Thus, in jury selection contexts other than those involving peremptory challenges, the Court has rejected the notion that a particular racial or ethnic group will make determinations solely on the basis of their group affiliation. In *Ristaino v. Ross,* for example, the Court ruled that "[t]he mere fact that the victim of the crimes alleged was a white man and the defendants were Negroes" did not give the defendant a constitutional right even to cause a voir dire question relating specifically to racial prejudice to be asked in addition to the usual questions as to general bias. * * *

According to *Swain,* however, there is no type of case in which blacks *qua* blacks may not be summarily eliminated on the presumption that the prosecutor is merely seeking a "fair and impartial jury." The premise of *Swain* and the rarity of wholesale challenges to white venirepersons thus serve only to limit artificially the opportunity of blacks for participation in our system of justice, and to perpetuate an invidious proposition of racial inferiority that has been outlawed in virtually every area of public affairs—in employment, in education, in housing, in property rights. How unfortunate that the invidious proposition has been allowed to flourish in the administration of justice.

C. State Court Developments

In light of the near impossibility experienced by defendants in attempting to meet the requirements set by *Swain,* a small number of state courts have fashioned standards based on their state constitutions to guarantee to the defendant a trial before a jury that has not had cognizable groups eliminated by the discriminatory acts of the prosecutor. In most instances, the state court was influenced by the fact that at the time *Swain* was decided, the Supreme Court had not yet ruled that the guarantee of the Sixth Amendment of trial by an impartial jury was binding on the states through incorporation into the Due Process Clause of the Fourteenth Amendment. * * *

D. Applicability of Swain's Equal Protection Analysis to the Present Case

In light of (a) the criticisms of *Swain,* (b) the developments in Sixth Amendment doctrine since the decision of *Swain,* (c) the state court developments curtailing the use of peremptory challenges on a discriminatory basis, and (d) the intimations in the opinions joined by five Justices in connection with the denial of McCray's petition for certiorari that the time is drawing near for a reconsideration of *Swain,*[a] both McCray and the State urge us to rule that *Swain* is no longer good law. While the assaults on *Swain* are not without considerable force, we are constrained to note that, on the question of the vulnerability of the prosecution's use of peremptory challenges to attack under the Equal Protection Clause, *Swain* is clear, direct, and unequivocal. It states that a defendant may not mount a successful equal protection challenge to the prosecution's racially discriminatory use of its peremptory challenges solely on the basis of the prosecution's acts in a single case. Since McCray's contentions rest solely on the State's use of its peremptories in his own case, he does not meet the requirements set by *Swain.* We therefore decline to rest our decision in this case on equal protection principles. * * *

III. The Sixth Amendment

* * *

A. The Development of Sixth Amendment Doctrine As Applicable to the States

In a long sequence of cases, the Supreme Court has faced such questions as whether the Sixth Amendment permitted the exclusion of blacks, women, and conscientious objectors from jury panels; whether jury verdicts of guilty could be less than unanimous; and whether juries could consist of groups smaller than the traditional twelve. The answers to these questions have varied, but the touchstone of each analysis has been whether the practice in question deprived the defendant of the possibility of a jury that represented a cross section of the community. * * *[b]

a. More recently, the Court has granted certiorari in another case in which *Swain* was relied upon to deny relief to a defendant in whose case blacks on panel were removed by the prosecutor's use of his peremptory challenges. *Batson v. Kentucky,* ___ U.S. ___, 105 S.Ct. 2111, 85 L.Ed.2d 476 (1985).

b. The court at this point discussed *Williams v. Florida,* p. 1260 supra; *Ballew v. Georgia,* p.

B. The Import of the Sixth Amendment for the Final Phase of the Jury Selection Process

The jury selection process obviously does not end with the assembling of the venire, and it is the final phase of the process, the actual selection of the petit jury, with which we are concerned here. Although, as discussed in Part II above, a few courts and commentators have concluded that peremptory challenges exercised at this stage may properly be subjected to the cross-section requirement, a far larger body of case authority has developed in support of the proposition that the cross-section requirement of the Sixth Amendment does not extend to this final phase and thus has no applicability to the prosecution's exercise of its peremptory challenges. The latter rulings are said to be mandated by the fact that most of the Supreme Court decisions invalidating the exclusion of cognizable groups in the jury selection process have focused on the selection of the venire rather than the selection of the petit jury, and by the Court's statement in *Taylor v. Louisiana* that there is no requirement that the petit jury actually reflect a cross section of the community.

We agree entirely with the proposition that the defendant has no right to a petit jury of any particular composition. The random drawing of petit jurors from the venire is by its very nature inconsistent with any guarantee of a particular resulting composition. But we disagree with the conclusion of those courts that have reasoned that the lack of such a guarantee means that the Sixth Amendment has no implications for the process of selecting the petit jury from the venire. We think such a conclusion is belied by the Supreme Court's repeated emphasis on the cross-section requirement of the Sixth Amendment and the fundamental value judgments underlying that requirement.

We begin by analyzing the goal of the guarantee that the venire itself represent a fair cross section of the community. The venire *qua* venire is a body that, assuredly, gives service to the community by standing ready to serve on a petit jury if called upon to do so; but it is a group that takes no action and makes no decisions. No defendant has ever been tried before a venire; the venire is not the body that deliberates in the jury room; no defendant has ever been found guilty by a venire. If there is a Sixth Amendment requirement that the venire represent a fair cross section of the community, it must logically be because it is important that the defendant have the chance that the petit jury will be similarly constituted. The necessary implication is that the Sixth Amendment guarantees the defendant that possibility. It guarantees not that the possibility will ripen into actuality, but only the fair and undistorted chance that it will. We thus agree that the Sixth Amendment does not require any action to ensure that the representative character of the venire be carried over to the petit jury; we think the Amendment simply prohibits the state's systematic elimination of the possibility of such a carry-over.

Our conclusion that the Sixth Amendment guarantees the defendant the possibility of a cross-sectional petit jury is supported by, for example, *Ballew v. Georgia*, in which there was no suggestion that the venire was improper. The Court held that the calling of only five persons from even a valid venire to form the petit jury was inconsistent with the Sixth Amendment, in part because so small a group had an unreasonably low possibility of comprising a cross section of the community. The state was not permitted to deal with the valid venire in a way that so limited the possibility that a fair cross section might be drawn.

We find even clearer support for the proposition that the process of selecting a

1261 supra; *Apodaca v. Oregon*, p. 1262 supra; *Witherspoon v. Illinois*, p. 1282 supra; *Taylor v. Louisiana*, p. 1269 supra; *Duren v. Missouri*, p. 1272 supra; and related cases.

jury from a proper venire is subject to constitutional scrutiny in *Witherspoon v. Illinois* which focused squarely on the challenge stage of the proceedings. There was no implication that those who objected to the death penalty were excluded from the venire; the venire was validly constituted. The statute that was invalidated was one that permitted the state to challenge for cause any venireperson who opposed the death penalty, and thus to eliminate such persons as a group in the very last phase of the jury selection process. *Witherspoon* is thus irreconcilable with the notion that the challenge stage of jury selection is not subject to constitutional scrutiny. If the only constitutional requirement were that there be a fair cross section on the venire, with no concern for what followed, the challenges for cause in *Witherspoon* would have escaped review.
* * *

In sum, the conclusion we draw from the Supreme Court cases is that whatever the nature of the state statute or practice may be (e.g., granting exemptions from jury service as in *Duren,* or adjusting the size of the petit jury as in *Ballew,* or defining "cause" to challenge as in *Witherspoon,* or departing from the traditional requirement of unanimity as in *Apodaca*), and whatever the stage of the selection process that is subjected to that statute or practice (e.g., selection of the venire as in *Taylor,* or selection of the petit jury as in *Witherspoon,* or the operations of the petit jury as in *Apodaca*), the state is not permitted by the Sixth Amendment to restrict unreasonably the possibility that the petit jury will comprise a fair cross section of the community.

C. Peremptory Challenges and the Proper Scope of the Court's Focus

We turn next to the questions of whether and on what basis peremptory challenges, as contrasted with challenges for cause, may be subjected to scrutiny under the Sixth Amendment. As noted above, some believe that *Swain* immunized peremptory challenges from all constitutional scrutiny, and indeed, it appears that *Swain's* extensive review of the history of the peremptory challenge system and its conclusions as to the importance of that system in American jury trials have created a myth that peremptory challenges are sacrosanct. We believe the proper view is that they are not.

First, as the review in *Swain* makes clear, the peremptory challenge is not rooted in the Constitution; it existed at common law, and it is now a creature of rule and statute. But it is not provided for in the Constitution of the United States, nor in any state constitution that we know of. It is an important right; it may be an invaluable right in certain circumstances; but it is not a right of constitutional dimension. As a matter of sound jurisprudence, therefore, when a defendant has made a prima facie showing that the prosecution's use of its peremptories conflicts with a fundamental right that is protected by the Sixth Amendment, it is the inscrutability of the peremptory challenge that must yield, not the constitutional right.

Nor does *Swain* stand for the proposition that the peremptory challenge is beyond scrutiny even under the Equal Protection Clause. Part III of the *Swain* opinion, although dictum, set forth the circumstances that a defendant would have to show in order to subject the prosecution's use of peremptories to inquiry by the court. Although the standards set by *Swain* have proven to be practically impossible to meet, they were nevertheless enunciated. Plainly, therefore, even the *Swain* Court did not believe that peremptory challenges are immune from remedial judicial action should the defendant make a prima facie showing that they conflict with a constitutional right.

Finally, we see no meaningful distinction, for Sixth Amendment purposes, between a state's exclusion of identifiable groups from the petit jury by means of a statute or practice, as in *Witherspoon,* and the exclusion of such groups by means of the systematic action of the prosecutor, who is an agent of the state. The latter is equally state action and should be equally subject to scrutiny. Indeed, one of the rationales for according any right to a jury trial is that it provides "a hedge against the overzealous or mistaken prosecutor." *Taylor v. Louisiana.* Plainly the hedge is blighted if the prosecutor is allowed arbitrarily to remove entire segments of the panel and thereby destroy any possibility that the jury may represent a fair cross section of the community.

For purposes of determining what a defendant must show in order to establish a prima facie case of a prosecutor's use of peremptory challenges in violation of the Sixth Amendment, we think the principal difference between *Swain's* equal protection analysis and proper analysis under the Sixth Amendment lies in the appropriate scope of the court's focus. The Sixth Amendment provides that the right of the accused to trial by an impartial jury shall exist in "*all* criminal prosecutions." (Emphasis added.) Thus, that Amendment protects each defendant who is to stand trial, not simply the last in a sequence of defendants to suffer the deprivation of an impartial jury. Accordingly, we construe the Sixth Amendment's provision to require the court to decide each case on the basis of the acts or practices complained of in that very case, and not to require the defendant to show, as *Swain* requires for an equal protection claim, that those acts or practices have had undesirable effects in case after case. We confess that we are not sure why the Equal Protection Clause should protect only the last of a number of defendants to be subjected to discrimination, but we are sure that it is not sound to extend that proposition to the interpretation of a constitutional provision that is expressly directed to "all" criminal prosecutions.

Accordingly, we conclude that a defendant may appropriately subject to scrutiny under the Sixth Amendment the prosecution's use of its peremptory challenges on the basis of its actions in his own particular case.

D. Impermissible Exclusions Under the Sixth Amendment

In addition to the Sixth Amendment's conception of the ideal jury as one that represents a cross section of the community, several principles provide guidance for determining whether an allegation of the systematic peremptory exclusion of blacks and Hispanics from the petit jury states a claim under the Amendment. First, the goal of jury selection is to assure that each juror is free from bias. By this we mean that he or she is likely to be able to decide the case solely on the basis of the evidence before the jury. Further, the notions that all persons who share an attribute, such as the same skin color, will *ipso facto* view matters in the same way, and that minority groups are less able than whites to decide the case solely on the basis of the evidence, are both fallacious and pernicious.

* * *

Accordingly, we conclude that the Sixth Amendment's guarantee of trial by an impartial jury allows the prosecution to exercise its peremptory challenges to excuse jurors to whom, on the basis of their personal history or behavior, some bias may be imputed; but it forbids the exercise of such challenges to excuse jurors solely on the basis of their racial affiliation.

IV. Procedures Under the Sixth Amendment

* * * We conclude that in order to establish a prima facie violation of his right to the possibility of a fair cross section in the petit jury, the defendant must show that in his case, (1) the group alleged to be excluded is a cognizable group in the community, and (2) there is a substantial likelihood that the challenges leading to this exclusion have been made on the basis of the individual venirepersons' group affiliation rather than because of any indication of a possible inability to decide the

case on the basis of the evidence presented.

If the defendant establishes such a prima facie case, " ' "the burden of proof shifts to the State to rebut the presumption of unconstitutional action by showing that permissible racially neutral selection criteria and procedures have produced the monochromatic result." ' "

In order to rebut the defendant's showing, the prosecutor need not show a reason rising to the level of cause. There are any number of bases on which a party may believe, not unreasonably, that a prospective juror may have some slight bias that would not support a challenge for cause but that would make excusing him or her desirable. Such reasons, if they appear to be genuine, should be accepted by the court, which will bear the responsibility of assessing the genuineness of the prosecutor's response and of being alert to reasons that are pretextual. See, e.g., *People v. Hall,* 35 Cal.3d 161, 197 Cal.Rptr. 71, 75, 672 P.2d 854, 858 (1983) (en banc) (reasons proffered by prosecutor for peremptorily excusing blacks were equally applicable to whites not excused; *held,* defendant's prima facie showing not rebutted). If the court determines that the prosecution's presentation is inadequate to rebut the defendant's proof, the court should declare a mistrial and a new jury should be selected from a new panel. * * *

V. Application of Sixth Amendment Analysis to the Present Case

Application of the foregoing principles to the present case poses two questions: first, whether McCray established a prima facie case; and second, whether the State is entitled to a hearing at which it may present evidence to rebut that case. We answer both questions in the affirmative.

The district court correctly ruled that McCray had made a prima facie showing that the prosecutor exercised the State's peremptory challenges to exclude black and Hispanic jurors on the basis of their group affiliation. McCray's trial counsel objected during the voir dire and detailed the prosecutor's use of the State's challenges, which up to that point had eliminated all of the blacks and Hispanics drawn. He identified several minority venirepersons who were excused despite having proffered no discernible reason to believe that they would not be unbiased jurors, and one black who was excused despite having had an experience that one might think would make him identify more with a complaining witness than with a defendant. McCray's showing was ample to shift to the State the burden of coming forward with some reason other than group affiliation for the challenges.

We are not persuaded to the contrary view by the State's argument that one black venireperson was eventually seated as a jury alternate. Questions of possible tokenism aside, we note that the selection of that alternate did not occur until after McCray had challenged the prosecutor's use of eight of the State's eleven peremptories to rid the jury of all the blacks and Hispanics called to that point. McCray had established his prima facie case at the time of his first objection to the prosecutor's actions. The trial court should have inquired into the prosecutor's reasons for the use of the State's peremptories against the minority members of the venire and, in the absence of a response showing permissible reasons, a mistrial should have been ordered and the jury selection process begun afresh.

The question that remains is whether the record that now exists warranted the district court's conditional granting of the writ without further proceedings. [On this point, the court ruled that "the district court itself should have held a hearing on the State's proffer of rebutting evidence," as the state's failure to do so in the state court could well have been because "the State believed there was no immediate urgency to come forward with a factual showing in light of the uncertainty that the federal constitutional contentions advanced by McCray, which had theretofore been rejected by virtually every other court to consider them, would be accepted, and the fact that McCray himself had requested, if those contentions were accepted, that a hearing be held."]

MESKILL, CIRCUIT JUDGE, dissenting:

* * *

The weight of authority against the majority's *Swain*/Sixth Amendment analysis exists for good reason: the Sixth Amendment cases are not inconsistent with *Swain.* Like *Swain,* the Sixth Amendment decisions that involve exclusion of prospective jurors focus on systematic exclusion. *See, e.g., Witherspoon v. Illinois* (state may not challenge for *cause* potential jurors opposed to death penalty; possibly due process rather than Sixth Amendment grounds); *Taylor v. Louisiana* ("women cannot be systematically excluded from jury panels from which petit juries are drawn"); *Duren v. Missouri* (the "systematic exclusion of women that results in jury venires averaging less than 15% female violates the Constitution's fair-cross-section requirement"). * * *

Even if we could decide this case in a vacuum, removed from the precedent against the majority's approach, there are a number of practical factors that militate against the majority's decision. First, the majority gives far too little weight to the peremptory challenge's long history as a tool used to ensure an impartial jury. An attorney who uses her challenges to exclude from the jury members of the same race, religion, sex, occupation, class or ethnic background as her opponent's client is not invidiously discriminating against members of that group. Rather, the attorney is trying to ensure that her client faces a jury that at least will be unbiased and at best will be receptive to her view of the case. We must remember that at the same time the defense counsel, who may well have more challenges, is engaged in the same process. The result of this adversarial system should be an impartial jury. * * *

* * * the actual issue in this case is not whether a prosecutor may systematically exclude members of some group from sitting on juries but whether a prosecutor may use peremptory challenges to exclude individual members of a group because she believes that *in that particular case* they *may* be biased in favor of members of the defendant's group. A competent prosecutor will only strike a member of the defendant's group in situations where she believes the possibility of that individual having a group bias—even if very small—is greater than the possibility of some other prospective juror having a bias. Where the group based assumption against members of the defendant's group is outweighed by some other assumption, the prosecutor will turn to the other assumptions; for instance, if a black college student is being tried in a draft registration case, the prosecutor may prefer to challenge a white social worker rather than a black veteran. By banning the use of such assumptions, the majority has severely limited the effectiveness of the peremptory challenge.

In addition, the majority fails to confront the obvious implication of its ruling for defense attorneys. As the Seventh Circuit recently recognized, "[i]t would be hard to argue that only a defendant should be allowed to challenge racially motivated peremptory challenges * * *. As it cannot be right to believe that racial discrimination is wrong only when it harms a criminal defendant, and not when it harms the law abiding community represented by the prosecutor * * *." * *

The majority also fails to confront the virtual limitlessness of its Sixth Amendment analysis. For example, in any given community, people opposed to the death penalty may be a "distinctive group" and thus under the majority's analysis they may not be peremptorily challenged. It also appears that men, women, old people, young people, laborers, professionals, Democrats, Republicans, etc. are distinctive groups. Therefore, no group based assumptions may be used to eliminate any member of these groups. Such a change is not simply "a modification of the way in which the peremptory challenge system works." It effectively eliminates the peremptory challenge for all but the most frivolous reasons (people who wear gray, smile, or wear contact lenses). * * *

NOTES ON PEREMPTORY CHALLENGES

1. At common law the defendant was entitled to 35 peremptory challenges, but most states have now provided for a lesser number, usually 20 for offenses punishable by death or life imprisonment, 10 for other felonies, and 3 for misdemeanors. Most states give the prosecution a number of peremptory challenges equal to those granted the defendant, but some give a lesser number (seldom below half those granted the defendant). Where several defendants are to be tried together, the common law rule was that each defendant has as many challenges as he would have if tried alone, but several states now provide otherwise by statute or rule of court.

2. The prevailing practice is for the prosecutor to call and examine 12 veniremen, exercise his challenges for cause and such peremptory challenges as he then wishes to use, replace those excused with others, and then tender a group of 12 to the defendant. The defendant then follows a similar procedure with this group and tenders a jury of 12 back to the prosecutor, and they continue on in this manner until both parties have exhausted their challenges or indicated their satisfaction with the jury. By contrast, under the struck jury system jurors are first examined and challenged for cause by both sides, excused jurors are replaced on the panel, and the examination of replacements continues until a panel of qualified jurors is presented. The size of the panel at this time is 12 plus the number of peremptory strikes allowed all parties. The parties then proceed to exercise their peremptories in some order which will result in all exhausting their strikes at approximately the same time. Which system is preferable?

3. What kinds of individuals would you, as prosecutor, eliminate by use of your peremptories? As defense counsel? There is considerable lore on the subject. It is often said that, from the defendant's point of view: (a) it is better to have roundfaced, jovial-looking persons than underweight and delicate types: (b) it is better to have persons of Italian, Irish, Jewish, Latin American and South European extraction than those of British, Scandinavian or German extraction, as the latter are presumably more law-abiding and conservative; (c) women jurors are desirable if the defendant or defense counsel is a handsome male or if the principal witness against the defendant is a woman, but not if the defendant is a woman; (d) it is better to have new jurors than experienced jurors; and (e) salesmen, actors, artists and writers are preferred, as they are more prone to forgive indiscretions, while bankers, members of management and salaried white-collar workers are undesirable, as they have been trained to give or take orders and thus expect everyone to toe the line. Rothblatt, *Techniques for Jury Selection,* 2 Crim.L.Bull. 14 (No. 4, 1966).

4. Can (should) the defendant's use of peremptories be limited as the prosecutor's were in *McCray?* Consider *Commonwealth v. Hutchinson,* 481 N.E.2d 188 (Mass. 1985) (defendant, charged with murder of 4-year-old child, not denied her right to impartial jury when judge, upon ascertaining a pattern of the defense challenging female prospective jurors, barred further use of peremptories solely on the basis of sex).

NOTES ON CHALLENGING THE JUDGE

1. The defendant has a right to an impartial judge; see, e.g., *Ward v. Village of Monroeville,* 409 U.S. 57, 93 S.Ct. 80, 34 L.Ed.2d 267 (1972) (where mayor before whom defendant was compelled to stand trial for traffic offenses was responsible for village finances, and mayor's court through fines, forfeitures, costs and fees provided a substantial portion of the village funds, petitioner was denied trial before a disinterested and impartial judicial officer as guaranteed by due process clause); *Tumey v. Ohio,* 273 U.S. 510, 47 S.Ct. 437, 71 L.Ed. 749 (1927) (same result where mayor, in addition to his regular salary, received fees and costs levied by him against violators).[a]

2. It is not objectionable that the trial judge was involved in some prior proceedings in the case. As noted in *Withrow v. Larkin,* 421 U.S. 35, 95 S.Ct. 1456, 43 L.Ed.2d 712 (1975): "Judges repeatedly issue arrest warrants on the basis that there is probable cause to believe that a crime has been committed and that the person named in the warrant has committed it. Judges also preside at preliminary hearings where they must decide whether the evidence is sufficient to hold a defendant for trial. Neither of these pretrial involvements has been thought to raise any constitutional barrier against the judge presiding over the criminal trial and, if the trial is without a jury, against making the necessary determination of guilt or innocence."

3. Trial judges, like jurors, are subject to challenge for "cause." Grounds for challenge generally are set forth in a statute or court rule, and usually include (1) a family relationship to the defendant, counsel, or the victim of the crime; (2) being a material witness; and (3) a general ground of "bias."[b] In some jurisdictions, determination of the challenge for cause may be made by the judge being challenged. Counsel generally are most hesitant to file such motions on grounds of general bias. Even absent actual bias, a judge as a matter of judicial ethics has a responsibility to recuse himself under certain circumstances, including "whenever the judge believes his or her impartiality can reasonably be questioned." I *A.B.A. Standards* § 6–1.7.

a. The issue often arises in the context of contempt proceedings. In *Mayberry v. Pennsylvania,* 400 U.S. 455, 91 S.Ct. 499, 27 L.Ed.2d 532 (1971), a criminal defendant repeatedly insulted and vilified the trial judge during the trial. After the trial ended and before sentence was imposed, the judge pronounced defendant guilty of criminal contempt and sentenced him to a total of from 11 to 22 years for 11 contempts. The Supreme Court, per Douglas, J., vacated the judgment of contempt. As the separate acts or outbursts occurred, the trial judge "could with propriety, have instantly acted, holding [defendant] in contempt, or excluding him from the courtroom." Where, however, the trial judge does not act when the contempt is committed, but waits until the end of the trial, due process requires that "another judge, not bearing the sting of these slanderous remarks, and having the impersonal authority of the law," sit in judgment on defendant's conduct.

In *Taylor v. Hayes,* 418 U.S. 488, 94 S.Ct. 2697, 41 L.Ed.2d 897 (1974), the Court, per White, J., held that another judge should have been substituted for the trial judge for the purpose of finally disposing of the contempt charges against a defense attorney where the record showed that "marked personal feelings were present on both sides" and that marks of "unseemly conduct [had] left personal stings."

See also *Johnson v. Mississippi,* 403 U.S. 212, 91 S.Ct. 1778, 29 L.Ed.2d 423 (1971), a per curiam decision holding that where the contemptuous conduct in court was not directly witnessed by the judge and no immediate action was taken by the judge, the hearing should take place before another judge because the trial judge "immediately prior to the adjudication of contempt was a defendant in one of petitioner's civil rights suits and a losing party at that."

b. 28 U.S.C. § 144 requires "personal bias or prejudice," to be distinguished from "judicial bias" in the sense of the judge favoring a particular legal principle, which is not a ground for challenge. Drawing the distinction is sometimes difficult. See, e.g., *United States v. Thompson,* 483 F.2d 527 (3d Cir.1973) (affidavit reciting that judge said it his policy to sentence selective service violators to no less than 30 months imprisonment sufficient to require disqualification; dissent argues majority in error in holding that "the bias is personal, as opposed to judicial, in nature").

4. Several states also grant the defendant a single peremptory challenge of the trial judge. In others, the initial challenge made in the form of a motion alleging prejudice automatically results in the substitution of another judge. In still others, the defendant may file a conclusory affidavit of prejudice. Which procedure is best? Should the prosecution have a like right?

Chapter 23

"TRIAL BY NEWSPAPER"—AND TELEVISION

SECTION 1. PRETRIAL PUBLICITY AND JURY SELECTION [a]

1. IRVIN v. DOWD, 366 U.S. 717, 81 S.Ct. 1639, 6 L.Ed.2d 751 (1961) marked the first time the Supreme Court struck down a state conviction solely on the ground of prejudicial pretrial publicity. Six murders were committed in Vanderburgh County, Indiana. Shortly after petitioner was arrested, the county prosecutor and local police officials issued press releases, which were intensively publicized. Headline stories announced that petitioner had confessed to the six murders and to twenty-four burglaries (the *modus operandi* of these crimes was compared to that of the murders and the similarity noted). Reports that petitioner had offered to plead guilty if promised a ninety-nine-year sentence, but that the prosecutor was determined to secure the death penalty, were widely circulated. In many of the newspaper stories petitioner was described as the "confessed slayer of six," a parole violator and fraudulent-check artist. Petitioner sought a change of venue, which was granted, but to an adjoining county. His request that venue be changed to a further removed county was denied. Some 370 prospective jurors, or almost ninety percent of those examined on the point, "entertained some opinion as to guilt—ranging in intensity from mere suspicion to absolute certainty." The Court, per Justice CLARK, observed:

"In essence the right to jury trial guarantees to the criminally accused a fair trial by a panel of impartial, 'indifferent' jurors. * * * 'The theory of the law is that a juror who has formed an opinion cannot be impartial.' It is not required, however, that the jurors be totally ignorant of the facts and issues involved. In these days of swift, widespread and diverse methods of communication, an important case can be expected to arouse the interest of the public in the vicinity, and scarcely any of those best qualified to serve as jurors will not have formed some impression or opinion as to the merits of the case. * * * It is sufficient if the juror can lay aside his impression or opinion and render a verdict based on the evidence presented in court.

"The adoption of such a rule, however, 'cannot foreclose inquiry as to whether, in a given case, the application of that rule works a deprivation of the prisoner's life or liberty without due process.' The test is 'whether the nature and strength of the opinion formed are such as in law neces-

a. On the impact of pre-charge publicity upon the selection of the grand jury, see Note 6, p. 988 supra. Throughout this Chapter, reference will be made to two editions of the A.B.A. Standards, *Fair Trial and Free Press.* The first edition will be cited as *A.B.A. Standards* (1968) and the 2d edition, approved in 1978, as *A.B.A. Standards.*

sarily * * * raise the presumption of partiality. * * * The affirmative issue is upon the challenger. Unless he shows the actual existence of such an opinion in the mind of the juror as will raise the presumption of partiality, the juror need not necessarily be set aside.' * * *

"It is true that the presiding judge personally examined those members of the jury panel whom petitioner, having no more peremptory challenges, insisted should be excused for cause, and that each indicated that notwithstanding his opinion he could render an impartial verdict. But as Chief Justice Hughes observed: 'Impartiality is not a technical conception. It is a state of mind. For the ascertainment of the mental attitude * * * the Constitution lays down no particular tests * * *.'

"Here the 'pattern of deep and bitter prejudice' shown to be present throughout the community * * * was clearly reflected in the sum total of the voir dire examination of a majority of the jurors finally placed in the jury box. Eight out of the 12 thought petitioner was guilty. With such an opinion permeating their minds, it would be difficult to say that each could exclude this preconception of guilt from his deliberations. The influence that lurks in an opinion once formed is so persistent that it unconsciously fights detachment from the mental processes of the average man. * * * Where one's life is at stake—and accounting for the frailities of human nature—we can only say that in the light of the circumstances here the finding of impartiality does not meet constitutional standards. Two-thirds of the jurors had an opinion that petitioner was guilty and were familiar with the material facts and circumstances involved, including the fact that other murders were attributed to him, some going so far as to say that it would take evidence to overcome their belief. * * * No doubt each juror was sincere when he said that he would be fair and impartial to petitioner, but psychological impact requiring such a declaration before one's fellows is often its father. Where so many, so many times, admitted prejudice, such a statement of impartiality can be given little weight."

2. Compare *Irvin* with MURPHY v. FLORIDA, 421 U.S. 794, 95 S.Ct. 2031, 44 L.Ed.2d 589 (1975): Petitioner, generally referred to in the media as "Murph the Surf," had first made himself notorious for his part in the 1964 theft of the Star of India sapphire. In 1969 he was convicted on one count of murder in another county and later that year pled guilty to one count of a federal indictment involving stolen securities. These events and the January 1968 robbery of a Miami Beach home, which led to the instant conviction in the summer of 1970, received extensive press coverage. The Court, per MARSHALL, J., held that petitioner had not been denied a fair trial:

"[*Irvin*] cannot be made to stand for the proposition that juror exposure to information about a state defendant's prior convictions or to news accounts of the crime with which he is charged alone presumptively deprives the defendant of due process. * * * Qualified jurors need not [be] totally ignorant of the facts and issues involved [quoting from *Irvin*]. At the same time, the juror's assurances that he is equal to the task cannot be dispositive of the accused's rights, and it remains open to the defendant to demonstrate 'the actual existence of such an opinion in the mind of the juror as will raise the presumption of partiality.' *Irvin.*

"The *voir dire* in this case indicates no such hostility to petitioner by the jurors who served in his trial as to suggest a partiality that could not be laid aside. * * *. In the entire *voir dire* transcript * * * only one colloquy [supports] even a colorable claim of partiality by a juror. In response to a leading and hypothetical question, presupposing [an extensive] presentation of evidence against petitioner and his failure to put on any defense,[b] one juror conceded that his prior impression of petitioner [e.g., the knowledge that he was a convicted murderer] would dispose him to convict. We cannot attach great significance to this statement, however, in light of the leading nature of counsel's questions and the juror's other testimony indicating that he had no deep impression of petitioner at all. * * *

"Even these indicia of impartiality might be disregarded in a case where the general atmosphere in the community or courtroom is sufficiently inflammatory, but the circumstances surrounding petitioner's trial are not at all of that variety. [T]he news articles concerning petitioner had appeared almost entirely during [a 13-month period ending] seven months before the jury in this case was selected. They were, moreover, largely factual in nature.

"The length to which the trial court must go in order to select jurors who appear to be impartial is another factor relevant in evaluating those jurors' assurances of impartiality. In a community where most veniremen will admit to a disqualifying prejudice, the reliability of the others' protestations may be drawn into question; for it is then more probable that they are part of a community deeply hostile to the accused, and more likely that they may unwittingly have been influenced by it. In *Irvin,* for example, the Court noted that 90% of those examined on the point were inclined to believe in the accused's guilt, and the court had excused for this cause 268 of the 430 veniremen. In the present case, by contrast, 20 of the 78 persons questioned were excused because they indicated an opinion as to petitioner's guilt. This may indeed be 20 more than would occur in the trial of a totally obscure person, but it by no means suggests a community with sentiment so poisoned against petitioner as to impeach the indifference of jurors who displayed no animus of their own."

Dissenting Justice BRENNAN maintained that "*Irvin* requires reversal of this conviction. * * * The risk that taint of widespread publicity regarding [petitioner's] criminal background, known to all members of the jury, infected the jury's deliberations is apparent, the trial court made no attempt to prevent discussion of the case or petitioner's previous criminal exploits among the prospective jurors [or to insulate the jurors from media coverage of the case], and one juror freely admitted that he was predisposed to convict petitioner. * * * It is of no moment that several jurors ultimately testified that they would try to exclude from their deliberations their knowledge of petitioner's past misdeeds and of his community reputation. *Irvin* held in like circumstances that little weight could be attached to such self-serving protestations.

"[This] is a plain case, from a review of the entire *voir dire,* where 'the extent and nature of the publicity had caused such a buildup of prejudice that excluding the preconception of guilt from the deliberations would be too difficult for the jury to be honestly found impartial.' [T]he denial of a change of venue was therefore prejudicial error * * *."[c]

3. *Irvin* was distinguished in PATTON v. YOUNT, 467 U.S. 1025, 104 S.Ct. 2885, 81 L.Ed.2d 847 (1984), which arose as follows: In 1966, Yount was convicted of murdering one of his high school students, but his conviction was reversed because based on statements obtained in violation of *Miranda*. Before and during the extensive *voir dire* that occurred at his 1970 retrial (in the same courtroom before the same judge who had presided at

b. As it turned out, at his trial petitioner chose not to take the stand and offered no evidence.

c. Burger, C.J., who concurred in the judgment of the Court, shared the dissent's view that the trial judge was "woefully remiss," but, although he "would not hesitate to [reverse] in the exercise of our supervisory powers, were this a federal case," agreed with the Court that the circumstances of petitioner's case "did not rise to the level" of a due process violation.

the first trial), Yount moved for a change of venue, arguing that the widespread dissemination of prejudicial information could not be eradicated from the minds of potential jurors. The trial court denied the motions, and also a motion for a new trial after Yount was again convicted of first-degree murder.

In 1981, Yount sought federal habeas corpus relief, claiming that his conviction had been obtained in violation of his right to a fair trial by an impartial jury. Relying primarily on the analysis in *Irvin,* the U.S. Court of Appeals for the Third Circuit granted relief. After independently examining the publicity surrounding the second trial and the *voir dire* testimony, the Third Circuit concluded that "despite their assurance of impartiality, the jurors could not set aside their opinions and render a verdict based solely on the evidence presented." The court pointed out that all but two of 163 veniremen questioned about the case had heard of it and that 126 or 77 percent admitted they would carry an opinion into the jury box—a higher percentage than in *Irvin.* Moreover, eight of the fourteen jurors and alternates actually seated admitted that at some time they had formed an opinion as to Yount's guilt. A 6–2 majority, per POWELL, J., reversed: [a]

"[The *Irvin* Court] noted [that] the trial court's findings of impartiality might be overturned only for 'manifest error.' [The court below] did not address this aspect of the *Irvin* decision [and it] failed to give adequate weight to other significant circumstances in this case. [T]he extensive adverse publicity and the community's sense of outrage were at their height prior to Yount's first trial in 1966. The jury selection for Yount's second trial, at issue here, did not occur until four years later, at a time when prejudicial publicity was greatly diminished and community sentiment had softened. In these circumstances, [the] trial court did not commit manifest error in finding that the jury as a whole was impartial.

"[The court] below thought that the fact that the great majority of veniremen 'remembered the case' showed that time had not served 'to erase highly unfavorable publicity from the memory of the community.' This conclusion, without more, is essentially irrelevant. The relevant question is not whether the community remembered the case, but whether the jurors at Yount's trial had such fixed opinions that they could not judge impartially the guilt of the defendant. *Irvin.* * * * [I]t is clear that the passage of time between a first and a second trial can be a highly relevant fact. In the circumstances of this case, we hold that it clearly rebuts any presumption of partiality or prejudice that existed at the time of the initial trial. There was fair, even abundant, support for the trial court's findings that between the two trials of this case there had been 'practically no publicity given to this matter through the news media,' and that there had not been 'any great effect created by any publicity.' "

The Court also rejected Yount's contention that one juror and two alternates were erroneously seated over his challenge for cause. The partiality of an individual juror is a question of "historical fact," "not one of mixed law and fact." Thus, the presumption of correctness due a state court's factual finding applies. The ambiguity in the testimony of the challenged jurors, concluded the Court, "is insufficient to overcome the presumption of correctness owed to the trial court's findings."

Dissenting Justice STEVENS, joined by Brennan, J., maintained that "the record clearly establishes that the case was still a 'cause celebre' in the [county in which it was retried] in 1970": The jury selection took ten days. Of the 163 veniremen who were questioned, all but two had read or heard about the case. "Of the 121 dismissed for cause, 96 testified that they

a. Marshall, J., took no part in the case.

had firm opinions that could not be changed regardless of what evidence might be presented. Twenty-one others testified that they could only change their opinion if Yount could convince them to do so. In addition, there were nine veniremen who were unsuccessfully challenged for cause who also testified that they had opinions that they could change only if Yount could convince them to do so."

The "totality of circumstances" convinced the dissenters that "the trial judge committed manifest error in determining that the jury as a whole was impartial. The trial judge's comment that there was little talk in public about the second trial is plainly inconsistent with the evidence adduced during the *voir dire.* Similarly, the trial court's statement that 'there was practically no publicity given to this matter through the news media * * *' simply ignores at least 55 front-page articles that are in the record. [The] trial judge's 'practically no publicity' statement also ignores the first-trial details within the news stories, [such as] Yount's confessions, testimony and conviction of rape—all of which were outside the evidence presented at the second trial. Under these circumstances, I do not believe that the jury was capable of deciding the case solely on the evidence before it."

As for Yount's claim that juror Hrin was erroneously seated over his challenge for cause, the dissent maintained that "whether a juror has a disqualifying opinion is a mixed question of law and fact.[b] * * * *Reynolds v. United States,* 98 U.S. 145, 25 L.Ed. 244 (1879) and *Irvin* teach that the question whether a juror has an opinion that disqualifies is a mixed one of law and fact. Therefore, one cannot apply the presumption of correctness found in 28 U.S.C. § 2254(d) because the statutory language by definition applies only to the factual determinations of state courts. Applying the proper analytical framework, I believe that Hrin's testimony clearly raised a presumption of partiality. Therefore, the trial judge committed manifest error by improperly impaneling Hrin."

4. Consider in light of the previously discussed cases, I *A.B.A. Standards* § 8–3.5:

Standard 8–3.5. Selecting the jury

The following standards govern the selection of a jury in those criminal cases in which questions of possible prejudice are raised.

(a) If there is a substantial possibility that individual jurors will be ineligible to serve because of exposure to potentially prejudicial material, the examination of each juror with respect to exposure shall take place outside the presence of other chosen and prospective jurors. An accurate record of this examination shall be kept by court reporter or tape recording whenever possible. The questioning shall be conducted for the purpose of determining what the prospective juror has read and heard about the case and how any exposure has affected that person's attitude toward the trial, not to convince the prospective juror that an inability to cast aside any preconceptions would be a dereliction of duty.

(b) Both the degree of exposure and the prospective juror's testimony as to state of mind are relevant to the determination of acceptability. A prospective juror testifying to an inability to overcome preconceptions shall be subject to challenge for cause no matter how slight the exposure. If the prospective juror remembers information that will be developed in the course of the trial, or that may be inadmissible but does not create a substantial risk of im-

b. Moreover, argued the dissent, "even if we regard the relevant rulings as findings of fact, Hrin's testimony clearly is sufficient to overcome the presumption of correctness due a state court's factual findings under § 2254(d). * * * Hrin not only indicated that he had a previous opinion as to Yount's guilt or innocence, but that he required evidence produced at trial to dispel that opinion. Further, he stated—pursuant to the prosecution's questioning—that '[i]t would be rather difficult [to] answer' whether he could enter the jury box presuming Yount's innocence."

pairing judgment, that person's acceptability shall turn on the credibility of testimony as to impartiality. If the formation of an opinion is admitted, the prospective juror shall be subject to challenge for cause unless the examination shows unequivocally the capacity to be impartial. A prospective juror who has been exposed to and remembers reports of highly significant information, such as the existence or contents of a confession, or other incriminating matters that may be inadmissible in evidence, or substantial amounts of inflammatory material, shall be subject to challenge for cause without regard to the prospective juror's testimony as to state of mind.

(c) Whenever there is a substantial likelihood that, due to pretrial publicity, the regularly allotted number of peremptory challenges is inadequate, the court shall permit additional challenges to the extent necessary for the impaneling of an impartial jury.

(d) Whenever it is determined that potentially prejudicial news coverage of a given criminal matter has been intense and has been concentrated in a given locality in a state (or federal district), the court shall have authority in jurisdictions where permissible to draw jurors from other localities in that state (or district).

5. Assume that a state adopts Standard 8–3.5. Should it then be willing to rely on jury selection procedures as the basic means of avoiding prejudice from pretrial publicity in all but the most exceptional cases? The commentary to 8–3.5 cautions against such an approach:

"Wigmore's excessive faith in voir dire now seems outmoded: Voir dire, in his view, was 'beyond doubt the greatest legal engine ever invented for the discovery of truth.' Today, judges, legal commentators, and social scientists are considerably more guarded about its effectiveness. This caution is attributable to at least three distinct but closely related factors: (1) inadequate understanding of the way pretrial publicity influences the thought processes of prospective jurors; (2) the tendency among a significant number of prospective jurors to underplay the importance of exposure to prejudicial publicity and to exaggerate their ability to be impartial; and (3) persistent concern about the ability of attorneys and trial judges to discern bias, particularly at the subconscious level, even when the prospective juror is being completely candid. * * *

Of the available procedures to promote trial fairness to the accused, voir dire is typically the most relied upon because of its manageability and relatively low cost. One need only give cursory consideration to the difficulty and expense associated with continuance, change of venue, and the use of foreign venires to understand the trial judge's perspective.[6] Yet from the defendant's perspective, this preference carries serious risks. The acceptable margin of error in the jury selection process is small indeed. Given the current state of the art, success or failure depends on fluid combination of elements: common sense, intuition, and luck. While the dynamics within the jury generally prove sufficient to blunt the undetected biases of individual jurors in the ordinary criminal case, the reverse process, an intensification of predispositions, might occur when a jury determines guilt or innocence in an atmosphere saturated with prejudicial publicity. The thrust here is not to make an argument against the value of voir dire, but rather to note its deficiencies when employed as the primary, sometimes exclusive, means of protecting the accused's right to a fair trial."

6. The A.B.A. Commentary to the first edition of § 8–3.5 notes: "It is not unthinkable that under such a standard, in a particularly notorious case in which substantial amounts of inflammatory or other-

6. The difficulties associated with these procedural measures should not overshadow the fact that a searching voir dire can impose significant costs as well. Levit et al., *Expediting Voir Dire: An Empirical Study,* 44 S.Cal.L.Rev. 916, 923, fn. 28 (1971).

wise prejudicial material have been disseminated, an acceptable jury could not be impaneled. Perhaps this is not too great a price to pay to make the rights of all those subjected to the criminal process more secure. But a far better resolution * * * that would render such an occurrence virtually impossible, would be the adoption of the standards recommended in this section in conjunction with the restrictions [on release of publicity, etc.] proposed in the remainder of this report." *A.B.A. Standards* (1968), 135. Consider in this connection the following cases:

(a) The *Seale-Huggins* case: After the murder-kidnapping case of Bobby Seale and Ericka Huggins ended in a hung jury, Connecticut Superior Court Judge Mulvey dismissed all charges against them, concluding that an unbiased jury could not be selected "without superhuman efforts—efforts which this court, the state and these defendants should not be called upon either to make or to endure." N.Y. Times, May 26, 1971, p. 1, col. 3. Judge Mulvey observed, inter alia, that some 1000 prospective jurors had been screened, over a four month voir dire, to get the jury for the first trial, and that chances of drawing a new panel this year were "practically nil." See also Ginger, *Jury Selection in Civil and Criminal Cases* § 7.65 (1984).

(b) *People v. Speck,* 41 Ill.2d 177, 242 N.E.2d 208 (1968), where defendant was charged with the murder of eight young women in their townhouse residence in Chicago. "Because of the violence of the crimes and the number of the victims the slayings received wide publicity on a nation-wide scale for a period of about two weeks commencing with the date of the crime and continuing through the arrest and indictment of the defendant." The case was moved to Peoria county upon defendant's motion, but a subsequent motion for another change of venue was denied. The court found that the Peoria county papers had given the case front page attention for about a week, including articles on the slayings, defendant's arrest, his criminal record, a report that his fingerprints were found in the house, a report that the sole survivor had identified him, and a report that defendant would claim insanity. (At trial, the state did rely on fingerprints found at scene and eyewitness identification by the survivor; prior to trial, defendant was found competent to stand trial). The Illinois Supreme Court found that the trial court had not erred in refusing to grant a further change of venue. It noted that all communities in the state had been served by the major wire services and any such community would have been subjected to the same publicity as Peoria. "We must bear in mind," it noted, "that the defendant had to be tried in some community in Illinois." The courts also noted that the trial judge had properly accepted the testimony of the 12 jurors finally selected that, although all of them had read some of the sensational newspaper publicity (which had been published several months before), they had no preconceived notions of the defendant's guilt which would prevent their rendering a fair and impartial verdict. The court viewed the dismissal of 250–300 prospective jurors, because of a preconceived belief in defendant's guilt,[e] as evidence of the care which the trial court exercised in assuring that defendant had a fair and impartial jury (defendant maintained that excusing so many jurors for cause demonstrated that the degree of prejudice in the county was so great that defendant could not receive a fair trial). It also assigned significance to the fact that defendant exercised less than half of his 160 peremptory

e. In *Speck,* the first four jurors chosen had to be sequestered five weeks until the last four were finally selected. The trial judge denied reporters access to transcripts of the *voir dire* and forbid them to report the questions and answers on *voir dire,* or the names of the jurors. The Supreme Court of Illinois ordered that reporting of all proceedings in open court be permitted, but upheld the ban on reporting jurors' names until they were either excused or sworn. See Taylor, *Two Studies in Constitutional Interpretation* 127, 137–38 (1969).

challenges. [Note, however, fn. c, p. 1308 infra].

(c) *United States v. Faul,* 748 F.2d 1204 (8th Cir.1984), where defendants were charged with the murder of two U.S. Marshals. The court sustained the refusal to grant defendants' motion for a change of venue, holding that the case did not fall "within the category of cases wherein the publicity so pervaded the proceedings as to give rise to a presumption of prejudice against the defendant. See, e.g., *Sheppard; Estes; Rideau.* * * * [W]hile 50% of the prospective jurors questioned did indicate partiality, only 27% attributed their inability to be impartial to the media's coverage of the case. In *Murphy* * * * [d]espite the fact that 26%—20 of 78—of the venirepersons were prejudiced against the defendant, the Court held this 'by no means suggests a community with sentiment so poisoned against petitioner as to impeach the indifference of jurors who displayed no animus of their own.' Here, 39 of 78 eligible jurors were excluded as potentially being partial. We do not believe that the number of venirepersons excluded for being partial gives rise to the conclusions the [defendants] assert. * * *

"The district court took several steps to insure the impartiality of the jurors actually selected. One hundred fourteen venirepersons were selected in this case, a substantially larger jury pool than is utilized in most cases. Additionally, the defendants were granted 16 peremptory challenges as opposed to the normal 10. Furthermore the trial judge took great care during the *voir dire* proceedings to ensure that an impartial jury was selected. * * *

"We cannot say that the pretrial publicity was so extensive or that the examination of the prospective jurors revealed such prejudice, that the Court erred in accepting the selected jurors' assurance of impartiality."

(d) If Lee Harvey Oswald had been brought to trial on the assassination of President Kennedy, could an acceptable jury have been impaneled? See *Report of the President's Commission on the Assassination of President Kennedy* 94–99 (Assoc. Press ed. 1964) (the Warren Report); Griswold, *Responsibility of the Legal Profession,* Sat.Rev., Oct. 24, 1964, p. 21; and Jaffe, *Trial by Newspaper,* 40 N.Y.U.L.Rev. 504 (1965) (symposium on Warren Commission Report).

(e) If former president Richard Nixon had been charged with participation in the "Watergate conspiracy," could an acceptable jury have been impaneled? Compare *Counsel's Memorandum on Behalf of Richard Nixon,* reprinted in the 1980 Supplement to Modern Criminal Procedure (4th ed.) at p. 359 (arguing that the nationwide publicity, including widely circulated statements by Congressmen expressing their opinion that Mr. Nixon was guilty, had deprived him of any opportunity to obtain a fair trial); Watergate Special Prosecution Force, *Report* 128–29 (1975) (Special Prosecutor Jaworski "concluded that any prosecution of the former President might require a nine-month to one-year delay * * * to allow existing and foreseeable pre-trial publicity to dissipate," but selection of an impartial jury was possible); *United States v. Haldeman,* 559 F.2d 31, 59–71 (D.C.Cir.1976) (upholding the jury selection process in the Watergate conspiracy trial; the court stressed that the judge did not accept jurors simply on their "subjective assurances" that they could be impartial, but also relied on their demeanor and "objective information relating to how closely they had followed Watergate and their sources of information").

Consider also Seidman, *The Trial and Execution of Bruno Richard Hauptmann: Still Another Case That "Will Not Die,"* 66 Geo. L.J. 1, 17–29 (1977) (discussing the jury selection in various other highly publicized cases).

SECTION 2. CHANGE OF VENUE

1. Consider Note, 42 Notre Dame Law. 925, 941–42 (1967):

"[W]here the prejudicial publicity is widespread, or of the kind likely to follow a defendant wherever he goes, change of venue is an impotent protective device. On the other hand, when the prejudicial publicity is rooted in circumstances peculiar to a particular community and draws its strength from only those circumstances, removal is indeed a most effective protective device. An examination of the cases reveals that more often than not, removal is an inherently effective protective device. Thus, writers in the field are correct in concluding that courts have failed to use venue change to its fullest possible extent in promoting the ends of justice.

"The reasons that explain this judicial hesitancy are several. Removal is capable of working an extreme dislocation in the administration of criminal justice. It is expensive and generally inconvenient, and it has excellent potential as a dilatory tactic. Further, it amounts to an admission that justice cannot be done in the forum in which the motion is made, which is a severe blow to people who pride themselves in their ability to be fair to their fellows. Finally, removal runs counter to the tradition that the administration of criminal law is primarily the concern of the community in which the crime is committed."

2. RIDEAU v. LOUISIANA, 373 U.S. 723, 83 S.Ct. 1417, 10 L.Ed.2d 663 (1963), grew out of the following facts: Some two months before petitioner's trial began and some two weeks before he was arraigned on charges of robbery, kidnapping and murder, a local TV station broadcast three different times in the space of three days a twenty-minute film of petitioner, flanked by the sheriff and two state troopers, admitting in detail the commission of the various offenses in response to leading questions by the sheriff. The parish had a population of approximately 150,000. The estimated audiences included 24,000 people on the first T.V. showing, 53,000 on the second, and 29,000 on the third. Appointed counsel moved for a change of venue, which was denied. Defendant was subsequently convicted and sentenced to death. Three members of the jury had stated on voir dire that they had seen the broadcast on at least one occasion. A 7–2 majority, per STEWART, J., reversed:

"[I]t was a denial of due process of law to refuse the request for a change of venue, after the people of [the] Parish had been exposed repeatedly and in depth to the spectacle of Rideau personally confessing in detail to the crimes with which he was later to be charged. For anyone who has ever watched television the conclusion cannot be avoided that this spectacle, to the tens of thousands of people who saw and heard it, in a very real sense *was* Rideau's trial—at which he pleaded guilty to murder. Any subsequent court proceedings in a community so pervasively exposed to such a spectacle could be but a hollow formality.

"[W]e do not hesitate to hold, without pausing to examine a particularized transcript of the *voir dire* examination of the members of the jury, that due process of law in this case required a trial before a jury drawn from a community of people who had not seen and heard Rideau's 'interview.' "

The author of the *Irvin* opinion, Justice CLARK, joined by Justice Harlan, dissented: "[The majority has failed to establish] any substantial nexus between the televised 'interview' and petitioner's trial, which occurred almost two months later. Unless the adverse publicity is shown by the record to have fatally infected the trial, there is simply no basis for the Court's inference that the publicity, epitomized by the televised interview, called up some informal and illicit analogy to *res judicata,* making petitioner's trial a meaningless formality. * * *

"The most crucial evidence [in this case] relates to the composition of the 12-man jury. Of the 12 members of the panel only three had seen the televised interview which had been shown almost two months before the trial. The petitioner does not assert, and the record does not show, that these three testified to holding opinions of petitioner's guilt. They did testify, however, that they 'could lay aside any opinion, give the defendant the presumption of innocence as provided by law, base their decision solely upon the evidence, and apply the law as given by the court.' * * * The determination of impartiality, in which demeanor plays such an important part, is particularly within the province of the trial judge. And when the jurors testify that they can discount the influence of external factors and meet the standard imposed by the Fourteenth Amendment, that assurance is not lightly to be discarded. When the circumstances are unusually compelling, as in *Irvin,* the assurances may be discarded, but 'it is not asking too much that the burden of showing essential unfairness be sustained by him who claims such injustice and seeks to have the result set aside * * *.' "

3. Does *Rideau* indicate that a change in venue was constitutionally required in that case without regard to the actual composition of the jury? For example, would the venue change have been required if all twelve of the jurors had stated that they had not seen nor heard about the televised "interview"? What if the truth of their statements was supported by reasonable grounds—e.g. several had been out of town at the time, others never read the papers or watched television. Note the Court's reference to a trial "in a community so pervasively exposed." Does *Rideau* reflect concern about community pressure being applied to the jurors, no matter who they are? Or is the court concerned that any 12 jurors having no knowledge of the televised "spectacle" are unlikely to reflect a cross-section of the community? To what extent is *Rideau* limited by the nature of the pretrial publicity in that case? Would a similar approach have been taken if the "interview" had been published in a newspaper with a large circulation? What if, instead of the "interview," the broadcast had contained only a summary of the evidence (aside from the confession) in the possession of local authorities? [a]

4. Consider, in light of *Rideau,* I *A.B.A. Standards* § 8–3.3:

Standard 8–3.3. Change of venue or continuance

The following standards govern the consideration and disposition of a motion in a criminal case for change of venue or continuance based on a claim of threatened interference with the right to a fair trial.

(a) Except as federal or state constitutional or statutory provisions otherwise require, a change of venue or continuance may be granted on motion of either the prosecution or the defense.[b]

(b) In addition to the testimony or affidavits of individuals in the community, which shall not be required as a condi-

a. It remains common practice after *Rideau* for trial courts to refuse to rule on a request for a change of venue until after an attempt has been made to select an impartial jury. If the court is convinced, as a result of voir dire, that a jury cannot be selected, then the change of venue is granted. However, if the court believes that an impartial jury has been selected, then the motion is denied. See Note, 42 Notre Dame, supra; *United States v. Haldeman,* p. 1305 supra. Similarly, on appeal following a conviction, the appellate court ordinarily will not reverse based on a failure to order a change of venue if it appears that the jury selected met the constitutional standards of *Irvin.* See, e.g., *People v. Speck,* p. 1304 supra; *United States v. Haldeman,* p. 1305 supra. But note *A.B.A. Standards,* § 8–3.3(d), Note 4 infra.

b. If the prosecution is granted a change of venue because of pretrial publicity adverse to the prosecution's case—e.g., adverse information concerning the complaining witness that could not be used by defense counsel for impeachment—would this interfere with the defendant's constitutional right to a jury trial? See Note 5, p. 1276 supra. While many jurisdictions have provisions authorizing either side to seek a change of venue, others refer only to motions made by the defense. Compare Note 1, p. 1281 supra.

tion to the granting of a motion for change of venue or continuance, qualified public opinion surveys shall be admissible as well as other materials having probative value.

(c) A motion for change of venue or continuance shall be granted whenever it is determined that, because of the dissemination of potentially prejudicial material, there is a substantial likelihood that, in the absence of such relief, a fair trial by an impartial jury cannot be had. This determination may be based on such evidence as qualified public opinion surveys or opinion testimony offered by individuals, or on the court's own evaluation of the nature, frequency, and timing of the material involved. A showing of actual prejudice shall not be required.

(d) If a motion for change of venue or continuance is made prior to the impaneling of the jury, the court may defer ruling until the completion of voir dire. The fact that a jury satisfying prevailing standards of acceptability has been selected shall not be controlling if the record shows that the criterion for the granting of relief set forth in paragraph (c) has been met.[c]

(e) It shall not be a ground for denial of a change of venue that one such change has already been granted. The claim that the venue should have been changed or a continuance granted shall not be considered to have been waived by the waiver of the right to trial by jury or by the failure to exercise all available peremptory challenges.

5. In GROPPI v. WISCONSIN, 400 U.S. 505, 91 S.Ct. 490, 27 L.Ed.2d 571 (1971), appellant, charged with the misdemeanor of resisting arrest, moved for a change of venue on grounds of local community prejudice or, in the alternative, that he be permitted to prove the nature and extent of the prejudice and its effect on his right to an impartial jury trial. The trial judge denied the motion solely on the ground that state law did not permit a change of venue in misdemeanor cases. The state supreme court affirmed the conviction. The Court reversed, per STEWART, J., holding that a state law which categorically prevents a change of venue, regardless of the extent of local prejudice against the defendant, solely because the crime charged is a misdemeanor, violates the right to trial by an impartial jury: "It is doubtless true, as the [state supreme court observed], that community prejudice is not often aroused against a man accused only of a misdemeanor. But under the Constitution a defendant must be given an opportunity to show that a change of venue *is* required in *his* case." [a]

c. *Maine v. Superior Court,* 438 P.2d 372 (Cal. 1968), held that mandamus lies to gain appellate review prior to trial of the denial of a defense motion for change of venue. The court, per Mosk, J., was not impressed with the argument that petitioners retained an adequate remedy in that the trial court denied their motion without prejudice to its renewal if the voir dire examination of prospective jurors indicated that a venue change was warranted:

"Experience shows * * * that trial courts are often reluctant to order a venue change after a jury has been empaneled. Defense counsel, moreover, is placed in an unnecessarily awkward position: unless he exhausts all his peremptory challenges he cannot claim on appeal, in the absence of a specific showing of prejudice, that the jury was not impartial. Yet, convinced that he must go to trial because his motion for a venue change was at first denied and in all likelihood will not ultimately prevail, he may fail to use every peremptory challenge, sensing that the jurors he has examined may be comparatively less biased than others who might be seated were his peremptory challenges exhausted. * * * In an antagonistic atmosphere 'there will remain the problem of obtaining accurate answers on voir dire—is the juror consciously or subconsciously harboring prejudice against the accused resulting from widespread news coverage in the community'? We can only conclude that the naked right to renew the motion for change of venue is not an adequate remedy at law to require denial of a mandamus petition. * * *"

For a general discussion of the use of mandamus to obtain review of the denial of a pretrial motion, see Note 9, p. 1453 infra.

a. Blackmun, J., joined by Burger, C.J., concurred in the result, stressing that the remand to the state supreme court "does not *necessarily* mean a new trial for Father Groppi," only an "opportunity" to demonstrate prejudice and the likelihood of an unfair trial.

Dissenting Justice Black maintained that "it simply cannot be said" that the right to trial

6. *Use of Imported Juries.* When there is a substantial likelihood that the public has been infected by prejudicial publicity, instead of moving the case out of the county would "a more simple and less costly expedient" be to import a jury venire from outside the county and, if necessary, to sequester the selected jury during the course of the trial? If a jury were impanelled in another county and "imported," would only the jurors "be inconvenienced—as jurors generally are in any event—compared to the venue change difficulty of moving the defendant, prosecutor, defense counsel, security officers, records and exhibits"? See Mosk, J., concurring in *Williams v. Superior Court,* 668 P.2d 799, 806–07 (Cal.1983); Mosk, J., dissenting in *Odle v. Superior Court,* 654 P.2d 225, 242 (Cal.1982). See *Use of Imported Juries Gains in Popularity,* 68 A.B.A.J. 668 (1982) (discussion of states that have adopted practice of importing juries instead of changing venue).

SECTION 3. CONDUCT OF THE TRIAL

A. Conduct of Reporters in and Near the Courtroom

Many defendants have protested that their rights to a fair trial have been abridged by the media, but SHEPPARD v. MAXWELL, 384 U.S. 333, 86 S.Ct. 1507, 16 L.Ed.2d 600 (1966) is probably the most notorious "trial by newspaper" case of all. The Court, per CLARK, J. (only Black, J., dissenting), agreed with the "finding" of the Ohio Supreme Court that the atmosphere of the defendant's murder trial was that of a " 'Roman holiday' for the news media." During the entire nine weeks of trial, the courtroom was jammed with reporters, and their movements in and out of the courtroom "often caused so much confusion that, despite the loudspeaker installed in the courtroom, it was difficult for the witnesses and counsel to be heard." And in the corridors outside the courtroom, "there was a host of photographers and television personnel," who photographed witnesses, counsel, and jurors as they entered and left the courtroom. Throughout the trial, there was a deluge of publicity, much of which contained information that was never offered in evidence, yet the jurors were never sequestered until the trial was over and they had begun their deliberations.

Viewing the "totality of the circumstances" of the case, the Court concluded that defendant had been denied a fair trial. And it put the primary blame for the release of leads, information and gossip to the press [a] and for the lack of courtroom decorum on the trial judge. He could "easily" have prevented the "carnival atmosphere at the trial" "since the courtroom and courthouse premises" are subject to his control. For example, he should have provided privacy for the jury; insulated the witnesses from the media, instead of allowing them to be interviewed at will; limited the number of reporters in the courtroom and prohibited the reporters from handling and photographing trial exhibits during recesses. No one "coming under the jurisdiction of the court should be permitted to frustrate its function."

The Court recognized that "there is nothing that proscribes the press from reporting events that transpire in the courtroom. But where there is a reasonable likelihood that prejudicial news prior to trial will prevent a fair trial, the judge should continue the case until the threat abates, or transfer it to another county not so permeated with publicity. In addition, sequestration of the jury was something the judge should have raised sua sponte with counsel. If publicity during the proceedings threatens the fairness of the trial, a new trial should be ordered. But we must remember that reversals are but palliatives; the cure lies in those remedial

before an impartial jury "must necessarily include a right to change of venue."

a. See p. 1314 infra.

measures that will prevent the prejudice at its inception."

However, the Court reiterated its extreme reluctance "to place any direct limitations on the freedom traditionally exercised by the news media for '[w]hat transpires in the courtroom is public property.' The press does not simply publish information about trials but guards against the miscarriage of justice by subjecting the police, prosecutors, and judicial processes to extensive public scrutiny and criticism." [b]

B. Broadcasting, Photographing and Televising Courtroom Proceedings

In 1937, largely in response to the notorious media coverage of the 1935 trial of Bruno Hauptmann for the Lindbergh baby kidnapping, the American Bar Association adopted Judicial Canon 35 (carried forward as canon 3A(1)), banning all photographic and broadcast coverage of courtroom proceedings. In 1952 that provision was amended to proscribe television coverage as well. But the 1970s saw widespread state court experimentation with television coverage of criminal proceedings. And in *Chandler v. Florida* (1981), infra, the Court held there was no *per se* constitutional bar to such television coverage. In 1982, when the absolute ban on TV coverage had been effectively repudiated by more than 30 states, the A.B.A. reversed its long-standing policy by adopting new canon 3A(1) and new Standard 8–3, infra, authorizing the broadcasting, televising and photographing of courtroom proceedings under certain conditions and subject to certain limitations and guidelines.

The televising of criminal trials has been before the Supreme Court on two occasions, first in 1965, then in 1981. The Court's responses have been very different.

1. In ESTES v. TEXAS, 381 U.S. 532, 85 S.Ct. 1628, 14 L.Ed.2d 543 (1965), the Court held that the defendant had been denied due process as a result of the televising of his trial and certain pretrial hearings. Defendant was a well known financier and his prosecution received considerable publicity. Pretrial hearings to determine whether the trial should be televised were themselves televised live (with commercials inserted during pauses in the proceedings). Four persons later selected as jurors had seen or heard part of these telecasts or related radio broadcasts. During the trial, the television cameras were located in a special booth at the rear of the courtroom. They were "noiseless cameras," and floodlights and flash bulbs were not allowed, but the cameras were clearly visible to all participants. Live telecasting was not permitted during the presentation of evidence, but those proceedings were recorded for subsequent showings. The closing arguments of counsel were televised live. (The defense attorney objected to being photographed, so the cameras focused on others while he was speaking and his arguments were relayed to the television audience by an announcer).

Writing for a 5–4 majority (which included Harlan, J., who concurred "subject to the reservations" discussed infra), Justice CLARK recognized that due process deprivations usually require "a showing of identifiable prejudice to the accused," but concluded that this was one of those times when "a procedure employed by the State involves such a probability that prejudice will result that it is deemed inherently lacking in due process."

"[E]xperience teaches that there are numerous situations in which [the use of television] might cause actual unfairness—

b. On retrial for the same offense, Sheppard was acquitted. N.Y. Times, Nov. 17, 1966, p. 1, col. 7.

some so subtle as to defy detection by the accused or control by the judge." [a]

In his special concurrence, Justice HARLAN rejected the broad sweep of Clark's opinion, but concluded that "at least as to a notorious criminal trial such as this one, the considerations against allowing television in the courtroom so far outweigh the countervailing factors advanced in its support as to require a holding that what was done in this case infringed the fundamental right to a fair trial assured by [due process]."

Justice STEWART, joined by Black, Brennan and White, JJ., thought that, "at least in the present state of the art," TV coverage of courtroom proceedings was "an extremely unwise policy." But he was "unable to escalate this personal view into a *per se* constitutional rule." Nor was he able to find, "on the specific record of this case, that the circumstances attending the limited televising of the petitioner's trial resulted in the denial of any [of his constitutional rights.]"

"The suggestion that there are limits upon the public right to know what goes on in the courts," wrote Stewart, "causes me deep concern. The idea of imposing upon any medium of communication the burden of justifying its presence is contrary to where I had always thought the presumption must lie in the area of First Amendment freedoms.

2. CHANDLER v. FLORIDA, 449 U.S. 560, 101 S.Ct. 802, 66 L.Ed.2d 740 (1981), per BURGER, C.J., held that subject to certain safeguards a state may permit electronic media and still photography coverage of public criminal proceedings over the objection of the accused. The Court concluded that "*Estes* did not announce a constitutional rule that all photographic or broadcast coverage of criminal trials is inherently a denial of due process" and it declined to promulgate "such a per se rule":

"Whatever may be the 'mischievous potentialities [of broadcast coverage] for intruding upon the detached atmosphere which should always surround the judicial process,' *Estes,* at present no one has been able to present empirical data sufficient to establish that the mere presence of the broadcast media inherently has an adverse impact on that process. The appellants have offered nothing to demonstrate that their trial was subtly tainted by broadcast coverage—let alone that all broadcast trials would be so tainted.

"Where, as here, we cannot say that a denial of due process automatically results from activity authorized by a state, the admonition of Justice Brandeis, dissenting in *New State Ice Co. v. Liebmann,* 285 U.S. 262, 52 S.Ct. 371, 76 L.Ed. 747 (1932), is relevant:

" '* * * It is one of the happy incidents of the federal system that a single courageous state may, if its citizens choose, serve as a laboratory; and try novel social and economic experiments without risk to the rest of the country. This Court has the power to prevent an experiment * * * [but] in the exercise of this high power, we must be ever on our guard, lest we erect our prejudices into legal principles. * * * '

"This concept of federalism, echoed by the states favoring Florida's experiment, must guide our decision. * * *"

Chandler arose as follows: After evaluating the results of its earlier state pilot programs permitting electronic coverage of all judicial proceedings and studying the experience of other states which allowed electronic coverage of trials, the Florida Supreme Court promulgated a revised

a. Justice Clark then discussed how the awareness that they are being televised distracts jurors; how the medium "will often" impair the quality of the testimony in criminal cases—some witnesses may be "demoralized and frightened," others "cocky and given to overstatement"—how the presence of television is a "form of mental—if not physical—harassment" of the defendant; and how television coverage puts additional responsibilities on the trial judge.

Canon 3A(7) of the Florida Code of Judicial Conduct, which provides:

"Subject at all times to the authority of the presiding judge to (i) control the conduct of proceedings before the court, (ii) ensure decorum and prevent distractions, and (iii) ensure fair administration of justice in the pending cause, electronic media and still photography coverage of public judicial proceedings in the appellate and trial courts of this state shall be allowed in accordance with standards of conduct and technology promulgated by the Supreme Court of Florida."

Implementing guidelines specify in detail the kind of electronic equipment to be used and the manner of its use (e.g., only one TV camera and only one camera technician is allowed, equipment may not be moved during trial, artificial lighting is prohibited, the jury may not be filmed, audio recording of conferences between lawyers, between parties and counsel, or at the bench is forbidden). Moreover, as the U.S. Supreme Court noted, these guidelines give the judge "discretionary power to forbid coverage whenever satisfied that coverage may have a deleterious effect on the paramount right of the defendant to a fair trial. The Florida Supreme Court has the right to revise these rules as experience dictates, or indeed to bar all broadcast coverage [in] courtrooms."

The trial of appellants, Miami Beach police officers charged, inter alia, with conspiracy to commit burglary and grand larceny, attracted considerable media attention. A TV camera was in place for one entire afternoon, during which the prosecution's chief witness testified. "Only two minutes and fifty-five seconds of the trial below were broadcast—and those depicted only the prosecution's side of the case." After the jury returned a guilty verdict on all counts, appellants moved for a new trial on the ground that the television coverage had denied them a fair and impartial trial, but "[n]o evidence of specific prejudice was tendered."

In upholding appellants' conviction and the constitutionality of the challenged canon, the U.S. Supreme Court deemed it "important to note that in promulgating the revised Canon 3A(7), the Florida Supreme Court pointedly rejected any state or federal constitutional right of access on the part of photographers or the broadcast media to televise or electronically record and thereafter disseminate court proceedings [and] predicated [the canon] upon its supervisory authority over the Florida courts * * *. Hence, we have before us only the limited question of the Florida Supreme Court's authority to promulgate the canon for the trial of cases in Florida courts."

Although there was no dissent in *Chandler,*[a] two concurring Justices sharply disputed the Court's reading of *Estes.* "I believe now," wrote concurring Justice STEWART, "as I believed in dissent then, that *Estes* announced a per se rule that the Fourteenth Amendment 'prohibits all television cameras from a state courtroom whenever a criminal trial is in progress.' Accordingly, rather than join what seems to me a wholly unsuccessful effort to distinguish that decision, I would now flatly overrule it. * * * The constitutional violation perceived by the *Estes* Court did not * * * stem from physical disruption that might one day disappear with technological advances in television equipment. The violation inhered, rather, in the hypothesis that the mere presence of cameras and recording devices might have an effect on the trial participants prejudicial to the accused."

In a separate concurring opinion, "for the reasons stated by Justice Stewart," Justice WHITE also maintained that "*Estes* must be overruled to affirm the judgment below. * * * The Florida rule has no exception for the sensational or widely

a. Stevens, J., took no part in the decision of the case.

publicized case. Absent a showing of specific prejudice, any kind of case may be televised as long as the rule is otherwise complied with. Thus, even if the present case is precisely the kind of case referred to in Justice Harlan's concurrence in *Estes* ['criminal trials of great notoriety'], the Florida rule overrides the defendant's objections. The majority opinion does not find it necessary to deal with appellants' contention that because their case attracted substantial publicity, specific prejudice need not be shown. By affirming the judgment below, which sustained the rule, the majority indicates that not even the narrower reading of *Estes* will any longer be authoritative."

3. *Are first amendment interests at stake when cameras are excluded from the courtroom?* Consider Ares, *Chandler v. Florida: Television, Criminal Trials, and Due Process,* 1981 Sup.Ct.Rev. 157, 159–60, 177: "The note that dominates the *Chandler* opinion is that [despite the very real risks that television coverage of a trial may compromise the defendant's right to a fair trial], notions of federalism required the states to be allowed to experiment. This deference to the states which rings so harmoniously to ears tuned to rejecting claims of 'substantive due process' seems strangely jolting when offered as a response to a claim that a state's criminal procedure has violated due process. The recitation of Justice Brandeis's familiar statement of federalism [hardly] seems an adequate justification.

"The feeling of unease one gets upon reading the opinion may stem from the almost total absence of any discussion of the First Amendment values that necessarily lie beneath the surface of the case. One would think that only interests at least similar to those protected by the First Amendment would justify running the risks of prejudice to the defendant that the Court acknowledged are created whenever trials are televised. * * *

"When and if [the claim that the first amendment requires television access to trials] is faced directly, it is hard to see how television can be treated as constitutionally different from other forms of the press. [Given the decision in *Chandler* that televising trials does not inherently violate due process] and the powerful role television plays in disseminating information to the public, there do not seem to be any grounds on which television can be denied the same rights of access that *Richmond Newspapers* [p. 1322 infra] upholds for the public and the print press."

4. Consider, in light of *Sheppard* and *Chandler,* I *A.B.A. Standards* §§ 8–3.___; 8–3.6:

Standard 8–3.___. Broadcasting, Televising, Recording and Photographing Courtroom Proceedings

A judge should prohibit broadcasting, televising, recording, or photographing in courtrooms and areas immediately adjacent thereto during sessions of court, or recesses between sessions, except that under rules prescribed by a supervising appellate court or other appropriate authority, a judge may authorize broadcasting, televising, recording and photographing of judicial proceedings in courtrooms and areas immediately adjacent thereto consistent with the right to a fair trial and subject to express conditions, limitations, and guidelines which allow such coverage in a manner that will be unobtrusive, will not distract or otherwise adversely affect witnesses or other trial participants, and will not otherwise interfere with the administration of justice. * * *

Standard 8–3.6. Conduct of the trial

The following standards govern the conduct of a criminal trial when problems relating to the dissemination of potentially prejudicial materials are raised.

(a) Whenever appropriate, in view of the notoriety of a case or the number or conduct of news media representatives present at any judicial proceeding, the

court shall ensure the preservation of decorum by instructing those representatives and others as to the permissible use of the courtroom and other facilities of the court, the assignment of seats to news media representatives on an equitable basis, and other matters that may affect the conduct of the proceeding.

(b) Sequestration shall be ordered only if it is determined that the case is of such notoriety or the issues are of such a nature that, in the absence of sequestration, there is a substantial likelihood that highly prejudicial matters will come to the attention of the jurors. Either party may move for sequestration of the jury at the beginning of the trial or at any time during the course of the trial, and, in appropriate circumstances, the court may order sequestration on its own motion. Whenever sequestration is ordered, the court, in advising the jury of the decision, shall not disclose which party requested it. As an alternative to sequestration in cases where there is a significant threat of juror intimidation during or after the trial, the court may consider an order withholding public disclosure of jurors' names and addresses as long as that information is not otherwise required by law to be a matter of public record.

(c) Whenever appropriate, in light of the issues in the case or the notoriety of the case, the court shall instruct jurors and court personnel and shall caution parties and witnesses not to make extrajudicial statements relating to the case or the issues in the case for dissemination by any means of public communication during the course of the trial. The court may also order sequestration of witnesses, prior to their appearance, when it appears likely that in the absence of sequestration they will be exposed to extrajudicial reports that may influence their testimony. * * *

(f) If it is determined that material disseminated during the trial goes beyond the record on which the case is to be submitted to the jury and raises serious questions of possible prejudice, the court may on its own motion or shall on the motion of either party question each juror, out of the presence of the others, about exposure to that material. The examination shall take place in the presence of counsel, and an accurate record of the examination shall be kept. The standard for excusing a juror who is challenged on the basis of such exposure shall be the same as the standard of acceptability recommended in standard 8–3.5(b) [p. 1302 supra] except that a juror who has seen or heard reports of potentially prejudicial material shall be excused if reference to the material in question at the trial itself would have required a mistrial to be declared.

SECTION 4. PREVENTING PREJUDICIAL PUBLICITY

A. Restricting Public Statements

1. In *Sheppard v. Maxwell,* supra, in discussing the various ways by which the trial judge could have exercised his "power to control the publicity about the trial," the Court asserted:

"[T]he trial court might well have proscribed extra-judicial statements by any lawyer, party, witness, or court official which divulged prejudicial matters, such as the refusal of Sheppard to submit to interrogation or take any lie detector tests; any statement made by Sheppard to officials; the identity of prospective witnesses or their probable testimony; any belief in guilt or innocence; or like statements concerning the merits of the case. * * * Being advised of the great public interest in the case, the mass coverage of the press, and the potential prejudicial impact of publicity, the court could also have requested the appropriate city and county officials to promulgate a regulation with respect to dissemination of information about the case by their employees."

2. Consider Rule 3.6 of the *A.B.A. Model Rules of Professional Conduct* (1983), which provides:

RULE 3.6 TRIAL PUBLICITY

(a) A lawyer shall not make an extrajudicial statement that a reasonable person would expect to be disseminated by means of public communication if the lawyer knows or reasonably should know that it will have a substantial likelihood of materially prejudicing an adjudicative proceeding.

(b) A statement referred to in paragraph (a) ordinarily is likely to have such an effect when it refers to a civil matter triable to a jury, a criminal matter, or any other proceeding that could result in incarceration, and the statement relates to:

(1) the character, credibility, reputation or criminal record of a party, suspect in a criminal investigation or witness, or the identity of a witness, or the expected testimony of a party or witness;

(2) in a criminal case or proceeding that could result in incarceration, the possibility of a plea of guilty to the offense or the existence or contents of any confession, admission, or statement given by a defendant or suspect or that person's refusal or failure to make a statement;

(3) the performance or results of any examination or test or the refusal or failure of a person to submit to an examination or test, or the identity or nature of physical evidence expected to be presented;

(4) any opinion as to the guilt or innocence of a defendant or suspect in a criminal case or proceeding that could result in incarceration;

(5) information the lawyer knows or reasonably should know is likely to be inadmissible as evidence in a trial and would if disclosed create a substantial risk of prejudicing an impartial trial; or

(6) the fact that a defendant has been charged with a crime, unless there is included therein a statement explaining that the charge is merely an accusation and that the defendant is presumed innocent until and unless proven guilty.

(c) Notwithstanding paragraphs (a) and (b) (1–5), a lawyer involved in the investigation or litigation of a matter may state without elaboration:

(1) the general nature of the claim or defense;

(2) the information contained in a public record;

(3) that an investigation of the matter is in progress, including the general scope of the investigation, the offense or claim or defense involved and, except when prohibited by law, the identity of the persons involved;

(4) the scheduling or result of any step in litigation;

(5) a request for assistance in obtaining evidence and information necessary thereto;

(6) a warning of danger concerning the behavior of a person involved, when there is reason to believe that there exists the likelihood of substantial harm to an individual or to the public interest; and

(7) in a criminal case:

(i) the identity, residence, occupation and family status of the accused;

(ii) if the accused has not been apprehended, information necessary to aid in apprehension of that person;

(iii) the fact, time and place of arrest; and

(iv) the identity of investigating and arresting officers or agencies and the length of the investigation.

Comment

It is difficult to strike a balance between protecting the right to a fair trial and safeguarding the right of free expression. Preserving the right to a fair trial necessarily entails some curtailment of the information that may be disseminated about a party prior to trial, particularly where trial by jury is involved. If there were no such limits, the result would be the practical nullification of the protective effect of the rules of forensic decorum and the exclusionary rules of evidence. On the other hand, there are vital social interests served by the free dissemination of information about events having legal consequences and about legal proceedings themselves. The public has a right to know about threats to its safety and measures aimed at assuring its security. It also has a legitimate interest in the conduct of judicial proceedings, particularly in matters of general public concern. Furthermore, the subject matter of legal proceedings is often of direct significance in debate and deliberation over questions of public policy. * * *

3. *What standard is needed to protect the First Amendment interests of attorneys?* Note that Model Rule 3.6(a) prohibits public statements that a lawyer knows or should know will have "*a substantial likelihood* of materially prejudicing an adjudicative proceeding" (emphasis added). Rule 7–107(D) of the *A.B.A. Code of Professional Responsibility* (1978) and Standard 1.1 of the *first edition* of the A.B.A. Standards on Fair Trial and Free Press similarly prohibit a lawyer from making public statements when there is a "*reasonable likelihood*" that such statements would interfere with a fair trial or otherwise prejudice the due administration of justice (emphasis added).

However, in light of such decisions as *Chicago Council of Lawyers v. Bauer,* 522 F.2d 242 (7th Cir.1975) (the "reasonable likelihood" formula is "overbroad"; only lawyer comments that "pose a 'serious and imminent threat' of interference with the fair administration of justice can be constitutionally proscribed"), the original A.B.A. Standard was changed so that it now reads (8–1.1): "A lawyer shall not release or authorize the release of information or opinion for dissemination by any means of public communication if such dissemination would pose *a clear and present danger* to the fairness of the trial." (Emphasis added). According to the commentary to present Standard 8–1.1, "[a]s a first amendment formulation, [the] serious and imminent threat standard [used in *Chicago Council of Lawyers*] is substantively indistinguishable from clear and present danger."

Hirschkop v. Snead, 594 F.2d 356 (4th Cir.1979), holds that the "reasonable likelihood" test satisfies the First Amendment, relying heavily on language in *Sheppard:* "[The *Sheppard* Court] stated that 'where there is a reasonable likelihood the prejudicial news' would prevent a fair trial, the judge should take remedial action or grant a new trial. * * * If remedial action is required on the basis of a reasonable likelihood test, * * * the rules for the avoidance of the harm must be considered under the same test. Implicitly, if not explicitly, the Supreme Court must have approved the reasonable likelihood standard for the application of the preventive rules."

4. *Should restrictions on public statements apply to defense counsel to the same extent that they apply to the prosecutor?* For the view that Model Rule 3.6, supra, when applied to criminal defense attorneys, "operates to reduce the flow of information about the administration of justice in a manner which fails to meet applicable constitutional standards"; is "insufficiently precise, and no empirical evidence exists on which to support a nexus between defense attorney publicity and interference with jury impartiality," see Swift, *Model Rule 3.6: An Unconstitutional Regulation of Defense Attorney Trial Publicity,* 64 B.U.L.Rev. 1003, 1006 (1984). For the view generally that defense counsel has a greater need than the prosecutor to comment about a criminal case (e.g., to vindicate his client's reputation, to obtain funds to pay for the litigation, and to offset the impact of an arrest, publication of an indictment and other comments on the prosecution side), see A. Friendly & R. Goldfarb, *Crime and Publicity* 135–36 (1967); Swift, *Restraints on Defense Publicity in Criminal Jury Cases,* 1984 Utah L.Rev. 45, 80–84. but, counters *A.B.A. Standards* § 1.1 (1968) (Commentary), "it

is hard to see how the prosecution can be expected to remain silent in the face of a defense crusade in the media" and continual debate about the merits of the case is likely to aggravate the prejudice to the defendant.

5. *Statements by other participants.* Consider *A.B.A. Standards* § 8–3.6(c), reprinted at p. 1314 supra. The commentary to that standard notes: "Even though complete forbearance from extrajudicial statements may be desirable generally, no binding instructions on parties and witnesses should be authorized under paragraph (c). Once parties and witnesses in a criminal case are outside the courtroom, they have the full prerogatives of any private citizen to question, criticize, or condemn the actions of government even though they may be swept up in its processes at the time." The commentary stresses that the witnesses and "parties" (i.e., defendants) do not "stand in a continuing relationship to the court" and are not "performing a fact-finding function." Does it therefore follow that the court lacks authority to issue a binding order prohibiting witnesses (including the defendant) from discussing their testimony for public dissemination prior to trial? Consider again the comment in *Sheppard* on prohibiting extrajudicial remarks.

A.B.A. Standards § 8–2.1 recommends that police departments adopt regulations largely similar in content to rules restricting lawyers as to matters that may and may not be included in public statements from the commencement of the investigation until the completion of the trial. This has sometimes been done (as to, e.g., the FB1, see 28 C.F.R. § 50.2), but such self-regulation is often lacking. See Isaacson, *Fair Trial and Free Press: An Opportunity for Coexistence,* 29 Stan.L.Rev. 561, 568–69 (1977).

B. Restraining the Media From Reporting

Consider NEBRASKA PRESS ASS'N v. STUART, 427 U.S. 539, 96 S.Ct. 2791, 49 L.Ed. 683 (1976): In anticipation of the trial of Simants for a mass murder which had attracted widespread news coverage, the county court banned everyone in attendance from, inter alia, releasing or authorizing for publication "any testimony given or evidence adduced." Simants' preliminary hearing (open to the public) was held the same day, subject to the restrictive order. Simants was bound over for trial. Respondent Nebraska state trial judge then entered an order which, as modified by the state supreme court, restrained the media from reporting any confessions or incriminating statements made by Simants to law enforcement officers or third parties (except members of the press), and from reporting other facts "strongly implicative" of the defendant. The order expired by its own terms when the jury was impaneled. The Court, per Burger, C.J., struck down the state court order:

"To the extent that the order prohibited the reporting of evidence adduced at the open preliminary hearing, it plainly violated settled principles: '[T]here is nothing that proscribes the press from reporting events that transpire in the courtroom.' *Sheppard.* [O]nce a public hearing had been held, what transpired there could not be subject to prior restraint."

To the extent that the order prohibited publication "based on information gained from other sources," it also failed because the state had not met the heavy burden imposed as a condition to securing a prior restraint.[a] On this point, the court reasoned:

"[P]retrial publicity—even pervasive, adverse publicity—does not inevitably lead to an unfair trial. The capacity of the jury

a. The Court also noted that the portion of the order regarding "implicative" information was "too vague and too broad" to survive the scrutiny imposed on restraints on First Amendment rights.

eventually impaneled to decide the case fairly is influenced by the tone and extent of the publicity, which is in part, and often in large part, shaped by what attorneys, police and other officials do to precipitate news coverage. [T]he measures a judge takes or fails to take to mitigate the effects of pretrial publicity—the measures described in *Sheppard*—may well determine whether the defendant receives a trial consistent [with] due process. * * *

"[The] Court has interpreted [first amendment] guarantees to afford special protection against orders that prohibit the publication or broadcast of particular information or commentary—orders that impose [a] 'prior' restraint on speech. None of our decided cases on prior restraint involved restrictive orders entered to protect a defendant's right to a fair and impartial jury, but [they] have a common thread relevant to this case. * * *

"The thread running through [*Near v. Minnesota,* 283 U.S. 697, 51 S.Ct. 625, 75 L.Ed. 1357 (1931) and *New York Times Co. v. United States* (Pentagon Papers), 403 U.S. 713, 91 S.Ct. 2140, 29 L.Ed.2d 822 (1971)] is that prior restraints on speech and publication are the most serious and the least tolerable infringement on First Amendment rights. A criminal penalty or a judgment in a defamation case is subject to the whole panoply of protections afforded by deferring the impact of the judgment until all avenues of appellate review have been exhausted. [But] a prior restraint [has] an immediate and irreversible sanction. If it can be said that a threat of criminal or civil sanctions after publication 'chills' speech, prior restraint 'freezes' it at least for the time. * * *

"We turn now to the record in this case to determine whether, as Learned Hand put it, 'the gravity of the "evil," discounted by its improbability, justifies such invasion of free speech as is necessary to avoid the danger,' *Dennis v. United States,* 183 F.2d 201, 212 (2d Cir.1950), aff'd. To do so, we must examine the evidence before the trial judge when the order was entered to determine (a) the nature and extent of pretrial news coverage; (b) whether other measures would be likely to mitigate the effects of unrestrained pretrial publicity; (c) how effectively a restraining order would operate to prevent the threatened danger. The precise terms of the restraining order are also important. We must then consider whether the record supports the entry of a prior restraint on publication, one of the most extraordinary remedies known to our jurisprudence."

As to (a), although the trial judge was justified in concluding there would be extensive pretrial publicity concerning this case, he "found only 'a clear and present danger that pretrial publicity *could* impinge upon the defendant's right to a fair trial.' [Emphasis added by the Court]. His conclusion as to the impact of such publicity on prospective jurors was of necessity speculative, dealing as he was with factors unknown and unknowable."

"[As to (b)], [w]e find little in the record that goes [to] determining whether measures short of an order restraining all publication would have insured the defendant a fair trial. * * * Most of the alternatives to prior restraint of publication in these circumstances were discussed with obvious approval in *Sheppard:* (a) change of trial venue to a place less exposed to the intense publicity that seemed imminent in Lincoln County; (b) postponement of the trial to allow public attention to subside; (c) searching questioning of prospective jurors, * * * [and] (d) the use of emphatic and clear instructions on the sworn duty of each juror to decide the issues only on evidence presented in open court. * * *

* * * There is no finding that alternative measures would not have protected Simants' rights, and the Nebraska Supreme Court did no more than imply that such measures might not be adequate. Moreover, the record is lacking in evidence to support such a finding."

As to (c), in view of such practical problems as the limited territorial jurisdiction of the trial court issuing the order, the difficulties of predicting what information "will in fact undermine the impartiality of jurors," the problem of drafting an order that will "effectively keep prejudicial information from prospective jurors," and that the events "took place in a community of only 850 people"—throughout which, "it is reasonable to assume," rumors that "could well be more damaging than reasonably accurate news accounts" would "travel swiftly by word of mouth"—"it is far from clear that prior restraint on publication would have protected Simants' rights."

"[It] is significant that when this Court has reversed a state conviction because of prejudicial publicity, it has carefully noted that some course of action short of prior restraint would have made a critical difference. However difficult it may be, we need not rule out the possibility of showing the kind of threat to fair trial rights that would possess the requisite degree of certainty to justify restraint. * * * [We] reaffirm that the guarantees of freedom of expression are not an absolute prohibition under all circumstances, but the barriers to prior restraint remain high and the presumption against its use continues intact. We hold that, with respect to the order entered in this case [the] heavy burden imposed as a condition to securing a prior restraint was not met * * *."

Concurring, BRENNAN, J., joined by Stewart and Marshall, JJ., would hold that "resort to prior restraints on the freedom of the press is a constitutionally impermissible method for enforcing [the right to a fair trial by a jury]; judges have at their disposal a broad spectrum of devices for ensuring that fundamental fairness is accorded the accused without necessitating so drastic an incursion on the equally fundamental and salutary constitutional mandate that discussion of public affairs in a free society cannot depend on the preliminary grace of judicial censors."

"Commentary and reporting on the criminal justice system," emphasized Brennan, "is at the core of First Amendment values, for the operation and integrity of that system is of crucial import to citizens concerned with the administration of Government. Secrecy of judicial action can only breed ignorance and distrust of courts and suspicion concerning the competence and impartiality of judges; free and robust reporting, criticism, and debate can contribute to public understanding of the rule of law and to comprehension of the functioning of the entire criminal justice system, as well as improve the quality of that system by subjecting it to the cleansing effects of exposure and public accountability."

Although they joined the Court's opinion, WHITE and POWELL, JJ., also filed brief concurring opinions. White, J., expressed "grave doubts" that these types of restrictive orders "would ever be justifiable." Powell, J., "emphasize[d] the unique burden" resting upon one who "undertakes to show the necessity for prior restraint on pretrial publicity." In his judgment a prior restraint "requires a showing that (i) there is a clear threat to the fairness of trial, (ii) such a threat is posed by the actual publicity to be restrained, and (iii) no less restrictive alternatives are available. Notwithstanding such a showing, a restraint may not issue unless it also is shown that previous publicity or publicity from unrestrained sources will not render the restraint inefficacious. [A]ny restraint must comply with the standards of specificity always required in the First Amendment context."

STEVENS, J., also wrote a brief separate opinion, concurring in the judgment. For the reasons articulated by Brennan, J., he "agree[d] that the judiciary is capable of protecting the defendant's right to a fair trial without enjoining the press from publishing information in the public domain, and that it may not do so." But he reserved judgment, until further argument, on "[w]hether the same absolute protection would apply no matter how shabby or illegal the means by which the information is obtained, no matter how serious an intrusion on privacy might be involved, no matter how demonstrably false the information might be, no matter how prejudicial it might be to the interests of innocent persons, and no matter how perverse the motivation for publishing it." He indicated that "if ever required to face the issue squarely" he "may well accept [Brennan, J.'s] ultimate conclusion." [b]

Notes and Questions

1. *Why the prior restraint reliance?* Does "the reasoning used by all of the justices, premised solely on the traditional aversion to prior restraints, insufficiently" protect the press? Sack, *Principle and Nebraska Press Association v. Stuart,* 29 Stan.L. Rev. 411 (1977). Would the *Nebraska Press* order have been "equally objectionable" if "framed as a statutory sanction punishing publication after it had occurred"? Id. at 415. See also Barnett, *The Puzzle of Prior Restraint,* 29 Stan.L.Rev. 539, 542–44, 560 (1977).

2. *Future press restraints.* Was *Nebraska Press* a strong case for restraint? Is it "difficult to believe that any other case will provide an exception to the rule against prior restraints in fair trial/free press cases"? Goodale, *The Press Ungagged: The Practical Effect on Gag Order Litigation of Nebraska Press Association v. Stuart,* 29 Stan.L.Rev. 497, 504 (1977).

3. *Application to non-press defendants.* Should *Nebraska Press* standards apply to court orders preventing prosecutors, witnesses, potential witnesses, jurors, defendants, or defense attorneys from talking to the press about the case? Should different standards apply to each category—e.g. do defendants and defense attorneys deserve as much protection as the press? See Freedman & Starwood, *Prior Restraints on Freedom of Expression by Defendants and Defense Attorneys: Ratio Decidendi v. Obiter Dictum,* 29 Stan.L.Rev. 607 (1977).

4. *Confidentiality and privacy:* A series of cases has rebuffed state efforts to protect confidentially or privacy by prohibiting publication: *Cox Broadcasting Corp. v. Cohn,* 420 U.S. 469, 95 S.Ct. 1029, 43 L.Ed.2d 328 (1975) (state could not impose civil liability for public dissemination of the name of rape victim derived from public court documents); *Oklahoma Pub. Co. v. District Court,* 430 U.S. 308, 97 S.Ct. 1045, 51 L.Ed.2d 355 (1977) (pretrial order enjoining press from publishing name or picture of 11-year-old boy accused of murder invalid when reporters had been lawfully present at a prior public hearing and had photographed him en route from the courthouse); *Landmark Communications, Inc. v. Virginia,* 435 U.S. 829, 98 S.Ct. 1535, 56 L.Ed.2d 1 (1978) (statute making it a crime to divulge information regarding confidential judicial tenure proceedings invalid as applied to nonparticipant in the proceedings, at least when the information had been lawfully acquired); *Smith v. Daily Mail Pub. Co.,* 443 U.S. 97, 99 S.Ct. 2667, 61 L.Ed.2d 399 (1979) (statute making it a crime for newspapers (but not broadcasters) to publish the name of any youth charged as a juvenile offender invalid as applied to information lawfully acquired from private sources). But cf. *Seattle Times Co. v. Rhinehart,* 467 U.S. 20, 104 S.Ct. 2199, 81 L.Ed.2d 17 (1984) (order enjoining newspaper from disseminating information acquired as a litigant in pretrial discovery valid so long as order is entered on a showing of good cause and does not restrict the dissemination of the information if gained from other sources).

b. For background on *Nebraska Press,* see F. Friendly & Elliot, *The Constitution: That Delicate Balance* 148–58 (1984).

C. Closing the Proceedings

The question presented in GANNETT CO., INC. v. DEPASQUALE, 443 U.S. 368, 99 S.Ct. 2898, 61 L.Ed.2d 608 (1979), was "whether members of the public have an independent constitutional right to insist upon access to a pretrial judicial proceeding, even though the accused, the prosecutor and the trial judge all have agreed to the closure of that proceeding in order to assure a fair trial." All of the Justices agreed that the problem was distinguishable from that in *Nebraska Press* because the issue here was "not one of prior restraint on the press [but] of *access* to a judicial proceeding."

Two murder defendants moved to suppress allegedly involuntary confessions. Their attorneys moved to exclude the public and press from the suppression hearing in order to assure their clients a fair trial. The prosecutor did not oppose this motion, which was granted. Although the trial judge viewed the press as having a First Amendment right of access to the pretrial hearing, he concluded—after finding that an open suppression hearing posed a "reasonable probability of prejudice to these defendants"—that the press' interest was outweighed in this case by the defendants' right to a fair trial. The New York Court of Appeals upheld the closure order, deeming the presumptive openness of criminal proceedings overcome in this case because of the danger that defendants might not receive a fair trial.

A 5–4 majority, per STEWART, J., affirmed. The Court recognized that "there is a strong societal interest in public trials." But recognition of an "independent public interest" in a defendant's Sixth Amendment "right to [a] public trial" is "a far cry [from] the creation of a constitutional right on the part of the public. * * * [O]ur adversary system of criminal justice is premised upon the proposition that the public interest is fully protected by the participants in the litigation," who had agreed to the closure order.

After concluding that the Sixth Amendment guarantee of a public trial is for the benefit of the defendant alone, the Court quickly disposed of the claim of a First Amendment "right of access": [E]ven assuming, arguendo, that [the First Amendment] may guarantee such access in some situations, a question we do not decide, this putative right was given all appropriate deference by the trial court in the present case."

"Because of the importance of the public's having accurate information concerning the operation of its criminal justice system," POWELL, J., concurring, "would hold explicitly" that the press had a First Amendment right to be present at the pretrial suppression hearing, but he recognized that the right was not absolute. The appropriate question for a trial court considering a closure motion at a pretrial suppression hearing "is whether a fair trial for the defendant is likely to be jeopardized by publicity, if members of the press and public are present and free to report prejudicial evidence that will not be presented to the jury." Since, in Powell's view, the trial court had applied a standard similar to the one he proposed, "the procedure followed by the trial court fully comported with that required by the Constitution." [a]

BLACKMUN, J., joined by Brennan, White and Marshall, dissented. As had

a. Burger, C.J., joined the Court's opinion, but wrote separately "to emphasize [that] a hearing on a motion before trial to suppress evidence is not a *trial;* it is a *pretrial* hearing."

Rehnquist, J., joined the Court's opinion, but wrote separately to emphasize that "[t]he Court today holds, without qualification, that 'members of the public have no constitutional right under the Sixth and Fourteenth Amendments to attend criminal trials.' * * * [T]his Court emphatically has rejected the proposition advanced in Justice Powell's concurring opinion that the First Amendment is some sort of constitutional 'sunshine law' that requires notice, an opportunity to be heard and substantial reasons before a governmental proceeding may be closed to the public and press."

Justice Stewart, the dissent focused primarily on the public trial provision of the Sixth Amendment. It found "no basis" in the language and history of the Sixth Amendment for "the inference that the accused may compel a private proceeding simply by waiving [the right to a public trial]." Fourteenth Amendment Due Process, insofar as it incorporates the Sixth Amendment public trial provision, maintained the dissent, "prohibits the States from excluding the public from a proceeding within the ambit of the Sixth Amendment's guarantee without affording full and fair consideration to the public's interests in maintaining an open proceeding." And this is so "notwithstanding the fact it is the accused who seeks to close the trial."

The dissent also concluded that "a pretrial suppression hearing is the close equivalent of the trial on the merits for purposes of applying the public trial provision of the Sixth Amendment." For "[u]nlike almost any other proceeding apart from the trial itself, the suppression hearing implicates all the policies that require that the trial be public."

Justice Blackmun acknowledged that the trial judge entered the exclusion order "because of his apparent concern for the fair-trial rights of the defendants and his suspicion that those rights would be threatened if the hearing were public," but, on the record, could not conclude, as a matter of law, "that there was a sufficient showing to establish the strict and inescapable necessity that supports an exclusion order. The circumstances also would not have justified a holding by the trial court that there was substantial probability that alternatives to closure would not have sufficed to protect the rights of the accused."

RICHMOND NEWSPAPERS, INC. v. VIRGINIA, 448 U.S. 555, 100 S.Ct. 2814, 65 L.Ed.2d 973 (1980), marked the first time the Court was asked to decide "whether a criminal trial itself may be closed to the public upon the unopposed request of a defendant, without any demonstration that closure is required to protect the defendant's superior right to a fair trial, or that some other overriding consideration requires closure." The case arose as follows:

At the commencement of his fourth trial on a murder charge (his first conviction having been reversed and two subsequent retrials having ended in mistrials), defendant moved, without objection by the prosecutor or two reporters present, that the trial be closed to the public—defense counsel stating that he did not "want any information being shuffled back and forth when we have a recess as [to] who testified to what." The trial judge granted the motion, stating that "the statute gives me that power specifically." He presumably referred to Virginia Code § 19.2–266, providing that in all criminal trials "the court may, in its discretion, exclude [any] persons whose presence would impair the conduct of a fair trial, provided that the [defendant's right] to a public trial shall not be violated." Later the same day the trial court granted appellants' request for a hearing on a motion to vacate the closure order. At the closed hearing, appellants observed that prior to the entry of its closure order the court had failed to make any evidentiary findings or to consider any other, less drastic measures to ensure a fair trial. Defendant stated that he "didn't want information to leak out," be published by the media, perhaps inaccurately, and then be seen by the jurors. Noting inter alia that "having people in the Courtroom is distracting to the jury" and that if "the rights of the defendant are infringed in any way [and if his closure motion] doesn't completely override all rights of everyone else, then I'm inclined to go along with" the defendant, the court denied the motion to vacate the closure order. Defendant was subsequently found not guilty.

The Court held that the First Amendment gave the public and the press a right of access to criminal trials, but there was no opinion of the Court. BURGER, C.J., announced the judgment of the Court and delivered an opinion joined by White and Stevens, JJ.:

"[U]nbroken, uncontradicted history * * * [compels us] to conclude that a presumption of openness inheres in the very nature of a criminal trial under our system of criminal justice. * * *

"The Bill of Rights was enacted against the backdrop of the long history of trials being presumptively open. [In] guaranteeing freedoms such as those of speech and press, the First Amendment can be read as protecting the right of everyone to attend trials so as to give meaning to those explicit guarantees. * * *

"[It] is not crucial whether we describe this right to attend criminal trials to hear, see, and communicate observations concerning them as a 'right of access,' or a 'right to gather information,' for we have recognized that 'without some protection for seeking out the news, freedom of the press could be eviscerated.' *Branzburg v. Hayes,* 408 U.S. 665, 92 S.Ct. 2646, 33 L.Ed.2d 626 (1972). The explicit, guaranteed rights to speak and to publish concerning what takes place at a trial would lose much meaning if access to observe the trial could, as it was here, be foreclosed arbitrarily. * * *

"We hold that the right to attend criminal trials is implicit in the guarantees of the First Amendment; without the freedom to attend such trials, which people have exercised for centuries, important aspects of freedom of speech and 'of the press could be eviscerated.'

"[In the present case,] the trial court made no findings to support closure; no inquiry was made as to whether alternative solutions [such as sequestration of the jurors] would have met the need to ensure fairness; there was no recognition of any right under the Constitution for the public or press to attend the trial. * * * Absent an overriding interest articulated in findings, the trial of a criminal case must be open to the public."

Concurring Justice BRENNAN, joined by Marshall, J., observed:

"[T]he First Amendment embodies more than a commitment to free expression and communicative interchange for their own sakes; it has a *structural* role to play in securing and fostering our republican system of self-government. Implicit in this structural role is not only "the principle that debate on public issues should be uninhibited, robust, and wide-open," but the antecedent assumption that valuable public debate—as well as other civic behavior—must be informed. The structural model links the First Amendment to that process of communication necessary for a democracy to survive, and thus entails solicitude not only for communication itself, but for the indispensable conditions of meaningful communication.

"[This Court has] persistently defended the public character of the trial process. *In re Oliver,* 333 U.S. 257, 68 S.Ct. 499, 92 L.Ed. 682 (1948), established that [fourteenth amendment due process] forbids closed criminal trials [and] acknowledged that open trials are indispensable to First Amendment political and religious freedoms.

"By the same token, a special solicitude for the public character of judicial proceedings is evident in the Court's rulings upholding the right to report about the administration of justice. While these decisions are impelled by the classic protections afforded by the First Amendment to pure communication, they are also bottomed upon a keen appreciation of the structural interest served in opening the judicial system to public inspection. * * *

"Public access is essential [if] trial adjudication is to achieve the objective of maintaining public confidence in the administration of justice. But the trial [also] plays a pivotal role in the entire judicial process, and, by extension, in our form of government. Under our system, judges are not mere umpires, but, in their own sphere, lawmakers—a coordinate branch of *government.* [Thus], so far as the trial is the mechanism for judicial factfinding, as well as the initial forum for legal decision-making, it is a genuine governmental proceeding.

"[More] importantly, public access to trials acts as an important check, akin in purpose to the other checks and balances that infuse our system of government. 'The knowledge that every criminal trial is subject to contemporaneous review in the forum of public opinion is an effective restraint on possible abuse of judicial power,' *Oliver*—an abuse that, in many cases, would have ramifications beyond the impact upon the parties before the court. * * *

"Popular attendance at trials, in sum, substantially furthers the particular public purposes of that critical judicial proceeding.[22] In that sense, public access is an indispensable element of the trial process itself. Trial access, therefore, assumes structural importance in our 'government of laws.'

"[R]esolution of First Amendment public access claims in individual cases must be strongly influenced by the weight of historical practice and by an assessment of the specific structural value of public access in the circumstances. With regard to the case at hand, our ingrained tradition of public trials and the importance of public access to the broader purposes of the trial process, tip the balance strongly toward the rule that trials be open.[23] What countervailing interests might be sufficiently compelling to reverse this presumption of openness need not concern us now,[24] for the statute at stake here authorizes trial closures at the unfettered discretion of the judge and parties.[25] [Thus it] violates the First and Fourteenth Amendments".[a]

GLOBE NEWSPAPER CO. v. SUPERIOR COURT, 457 U.S. 596, 102 S.Ct. 2613, 73 L.Ed.2d 248 (1982) struck down a Massachusetts statute (§ 16A) which, as construed by the state's highest court, re-

22. In advancing these purposes, the availability of a trial transcript is no substitute for a public presence at the trial itself. As any experienced appellate judge can attest, the "cold" record is a very imperfect reproduction of events that transpire in the courtroom. * * *

23. The presumption of public trials is, of course, not at all incompatible with reasonable restrictions imposed upon courtroom behavior in the interests of decorum. Thus, when engaging in interchanges at the bench, the trial judge is not required to allow public or press intrusion upon the huddle. Nor does this opinion intimate that judges are restricted in their ability to conduct conferences in chambers, inasmuch as such conferences are distinct from trial proceedings.

24. For example, national security concerns about confidentiality may sometimes warrant closures during sensitive portions of trial proceedings, such as testimony about state secrets.

25. Significantly, closing a trial lacks even the justification for barring the door to pretrial hearings: the necessity of preventing dissemination of suppressible prejudicial evidence to the public before the jury pool has become, in a practical sense, finite and subject to sequestration.

a. Blackmun, J., concurred in the judgments, noting that "the Court's ultimate ruling in *Gannett,* with such clarification as is provided by the opinions in this case today, apparently is now to the effect that there is no *Sixth* Amendment right on the part of the public—or the press—to an open hearing on a motion to suppress." He continued to believe that *Gannett* was in error, but "with the Sixth Amendment set to one side in this case," he was "driven to conclude, as a secondary position, that the First Amendment must provide some measure of protection for public access to the trial."

Stevens, J., concurred in the judgment, calling *Richmond Newspapers* "a watershed case. Until today the Court has accorded virtually absolute protection to the dissemination of information or ideas, but never before has it squarely held that the acquisition of newsworthy matter is entitled to any constitutional protection whatever."

Justice Stewart and White also wrote separate concurring opinions. Powell, J., took no part in the consideration or decision of the case, but recall his concurring opinion in *Gannett.*

Rehnquist, J., dissented. As he viewed the matter, the issue is "not whether the 'right' to freedom of the press * * * overrides the defendant's 'right' to fair trial, [but] whether any provision in the Constitution may fairly be read to prohibit what the [trial court] did in this case." He was "unable to find any such prohibition" in the Constitution.

quired trial judges, at rape and other sex-offense trials involving an alleged victim under the age of 18, to exclude the press and general public from the courtroom under all circumstances during the testimony of that victim. The Supreme Judicial Court of Massachusetts "did not think 'that *Richmond Newspapers* require[d] the invalidation of the requirement, given the statute's narrow scope in an area of traditional sensitivity to the needs of victims.'" The Court, per BRENNAN, J., disagreed:

"Although the right of access to criminal trials is of constitutional stature, it is not absolute. But the circumstances under which the press and public can be barred from a criminal trial are limited; the State's justification in denying access must be a weighty one. Where, as in the present case, the State attempts to deny the right of access in order to inhibit the disclosure of sensitive information, it must be shown that the denial is necessitated by a compelling governmental interest, and is narrowly tailored to serve that interest. * * *

"The state interests asserted to support § 16A [are] reducible to two: the protection of minor victims of sex crimes from further trauma and embarrassment; and the encouragement of such victims to come forward and testify in a truthful and credible manner. We consider these interests in turn.

"We agree [that] the first interest—safeguarding the physical and psychological well-being of a minor [19]—is a compelling one. But as compelling as that interest is, it does not justify a *mandatory*-closure rule, for it is clear that the circumstances of the particular case may affect the significance of the interest. A trial court can determine on a case-by-case basis whether closure is necessary to protect the welfare of a minor victim.[20] Among the factors to be weighed are the minor victim's age, psychological maturity, and understanding, the nature of the crime, the desires of the victim, and the interests of parents and relatives. Section 16A, in contrast, requires closure even if the victim does not seek the exclusion of the press and general public, and would not suffer injury by their presence.[22] In the case before us, for example, the names of the minor victim were already in the public record, and the record indicates that the victims may have been willing to testify despite the presence of the press. If the trial court had been permitted to exercise its discretion, closure might well have been deemed unnecessary. In short, § 16A cannot be viewed as a narrowly tailored means of accommodating the State's asserted interest: That interest could be served just as well by requiring the trial court to determine on a case-by-case basis whether the State's legitimate concern for the well-being of the minor victim necessitates closure. Such an approach ensures that the constitutional right of the press and public to gain access to criminal trials will not be restricted except where necessary to protect the State's interest.[25]

19. It is important to note that in the context of § 16A, the measure of the State's interest lies not in the extent to which minor victims are injured by testifying, but rather in the incremental injury suffered by testifying *in the presence of the press and the general public.*

20. Indeed, the plurality opinion in *Richmond Newspapers* suggested that individualized determinations are *always* required before the right of access may be denied: "Absent an overriding interest *articulated in findings,* the trial of a criminal case must be open to the public." [Emphasis added by the *Globe Newspaper* Court.]

22. It appears that while other States have statutory or constitutional provisions that would *allow* a trial judge to close a criminal sex-offense trial during the testimony of a minor victim, no other State has a *mandatory* provision excluding both the press and general public during such testimony. Of course, we intimate no view regarding the constitutionality of these state statutes.

25. Of course, for a case-by-case approach to be meaningful, representatives of the press and general public "must be given an opportunity to be heard on the question of their exclusion." *Gannett* (Powell, J., concurring). This does not mean, however, that for purposes of this inquiry the court cannot protect the minor victim by denying these representatives the opportunity to

"Nor can § 16A be justified on the basis of the Commonwealth's second asserted interest—the encouragement of minor victims of sex crimes to come forward and provide accurate testimony. The Commonwealth has offered no empirical support for the claim that the rule of automatic closure contained in § 16A will lead to an increase in the number of minor sex victims coming forward and cooperating with state authorities. Not only is the claim speculative in empirical terms, but it is also open to serious question as a matter of logic and common sense. Although § 16A bars the press and general public from the courtroom during the testimony of minor sex victims, the press is not denied access to the transcript, court personnel, or any other possible source that could provide an account of the minor victim's testimony. Thus § 16A cannot prevent the press from publicizing the substance of a minor victim's testimony, as well as his or her identity. If the Commonwealth's interest in encouraging minor victims to come forward depends on keeping such matters secret, § 16A hardly advances that interest in an effective manner. And even if § 16A effectively advanced the State's interest, it is doubtful that the interest would be sufficient to overcome the constitutional attack, for that same interest could be relied on to support an array of mandatory-closure rules designed to encourage victims to come forward: Surely it cannot be suggested that minor victims of sex crimes are the *only* crime victims who, because of publicity attendant to criminal trials, are reluctant to come forward and testify. The State's argument based on this interest therefore proves too much, and runs contrary to the very foundation of the right of access recognized in *Richmond Newspapers:* namely, 'that a presumption of openness inheres in the very nature of a criminal trial under our system of justice.' (plurality opinion).

"For the foregoing reasons, we hold that § 16A, as construed by the Massachusetts Supreme Judicial Court, violates the First Amendment to the Constitution.[27] " [a]

Dissenting Chief Justice BURGER, joined by Rehnquist, J., protested: "Historically our Society has gone to great lengths to protect minors *charged* with crime, particularly by prohibiting the release of the names of offenders, barring the press and public from juvenile proceedings, and sealing the records of those proceedings. Yet today the Court holds unconstitutional a state statute designed to protect not the *accused,* but the minor *victims* of sex crimes. In doing so, it advances a disturbing paradox. Although states are permitted, for example, to mandate the closure of all proceedings in order to protect a 17-year-old charged with rape, they are not permitted to require the closing of part of criminal proceedings in order to protect an innocent child who has been raped or otherwise sexually abused.

"* * * The Court apparently believes that the statute does not prevent any significant trauma, embarrassment or humiliation on the part of the victim simply be-

confront or cross-examine the victim, or by denying them access to sensitive details concerning the victim and the victim's future testimony. Such discretion is consistent with the traditional authority of trial judges to conduct in camera conferences. Without such trial court discretion, a State's interest in safeguarding the welfare of the minor victim, determined in an individual case to merit some form of closure, would be defeated before it could ever be brought to bear.

27. We emphasize that our holding is a narrow one: that a rule of mandatory closure respecting the testimony of minor sex victims is constitutionally infirm. In individual cases, and under appropriate circumstances, the First Amendment does not necessarily stand as a bar to the exclusion from the courtroom of the press and general public during the testimony of minor sex-offense victims. But a mandatory rule, requiring no particularized determinations in individual cases, is unconstitutional.

a. Concurring Justice O'Connor "interpret[ed] neither *Richmond Newspapers* nor the Court's decision to carry any implications outside the context of criminal trials," but concurred in the judgment because this case "does involve a criminal trial" and "[m]oreover [a] statute mandating automatic exclusion of the public from certain testimony."

cause the press is not prevented from discovering and publicizing both the identity of the victim and the substance of the victim's testimony. Section 16A is intended not to preserve confidentiality, but to prevent the risk of severe psychological damage caused by having to relate the details of the crime in front of a crowd which inevitably will include voyeuristic strangers.[6] In most states, that crowd may be expanded to include a live television audience, with reruns on the evening news. That ordeal could be difficult for an adult; to a child, the experience can be devastating and leave permanent scars. * * *

"There is, of course, 'a presumption of openness [that] inheres in the very nature of a criminal trial under our system of justice.' But we have consistently emphasized that this presumption is not absolute or irrebuttable. [The] Massachusetts statute has a relatively minor incidental impact on First Amendment rights and gives effect to the overriding state interest in protecting child rape victims." [b]

Notes and Questions

1. *Is the electronic media sure, or likely, to follow the print media?* Does the Chief Justice seem to be saying in his *Globe Newspaper* dissent that where the First Amendment requires *the print media* to be present, the electronic media are sure, or at least likely, to follow? To what extent, if at all, does *Chandler v. Florida* support such a view? Need (should) the electronic media's "right of access" be as extensive as that of the print reporters? See Ares, *Chandler v. Florida: Television, Criminal Trials and Due Process,* 1981 Sup.Ct.Rev. 157, 181–82.

2. *Right of access to juvenile delinquency proceedings.* After *Richmond Newspapers* and *Globe,* can the states still mandate the closure of all juvenile delinquency proceedings? To what extent do the Court's reasons for extending a public right of access to criminal trials apply to juvenile proceedings as well? If even the compelling state interest asserted in *Globe* did not justify a *mandatory*-closure rule during the testimony of a minor witness in a sex-offense case, can laws *mandating* the exclusion of the public from juvenile proceedings survive First Amendment challenge?

Stressing the need to distinguish the interest in withholding the identity of the juvenile offender from the public at large and the interest in preserving a confidential atmosphere in the juvenile proceeding itself, Note, *The Public Right of Access to Juvenile Delinquency Hearings,* 81 Mich.L. Rev. 1540 (1983), concludes that a public right of access to juvenile delinquency hearings should be recognized but that admission of the public to such hearings should be conditioned on the promise not to disclose the identity of the accused juvenile? Would such a "conditional" right of access pass constitutional muster?

3. *Right of access to "rape shield" evidentiary hearings.* What are *Globe's* implications for "rape shield" hearings? In recent years most states have enacted "rape shield" laws designed to control or even prohibit the use of evidence respecting the rape complainant's previous sexual conduct. In order to use such evidence as the law does not entirely bar, a typical "rape shield" statute requires the defendant to

6. As one commentator put it, "Especially in cases involving minors, the courts stress the serious embarrassment and shame of the victim who is forced to testify to sexual acts or whose intimate life is revealed in detail before a crowd of the idly curious." V. Berger, *Man's Trial, Woman's Tribulation: Rape Cases in the Courtroom,* 77 Colum.L.Rev. 1, 88 (1977). The victim's interest in avoiding the humiliation of testifying in open court is thus quite separate from any interest in preventing the public from learning of the crime. It is ironic that the Court emphasizes the failure of the Commonwealth to seal the trial transcript and bar disclosure of the victim's identity. The Court implies that a state law more severely encroaching upon the interests of the press and public would be upheld.

b. Justice Stevens dissented separately on procedural grounds.

make a written motion offering proof of relevance. If the court finds the offer sufficient, it holds a hearing away from the jury to decide whether the proposed material satisfies the applicable standard. Some laws posit an in camera hearing before trial, others a hearing during trial prior to the proof's admission. See V. Berger, *Man's Trial, Woman's Tribulation: Rape Cases in the Courtroom,* 77 Colum.L.Rev. 1, 32–39 (1977). After *Globe,* would the Supreme Court sustain a *mandatory*-closure rule for rape shield evidentiary hearings? How significant is it that the victim's prior sexual history will *often* be less central to the case than the victim's version of the claimed attack, the admissibility of a confession or other issues? What if a particular case is the rare case where the admissibility of the victim's prior sexual conduct is, or appears to be, critically important? Should there not at least be a finding on this issue? See Kamisar, *Globe Newspaper: The Court Balks at Mandatory Closure Rules—Even for Specific Testimony,* in Choper, Kamisar & Tribe, *The Supreme Court: Trends and Developments, 1981–82* at 121, 136–38 (1983).

PRESS–ENTERPRISE CO. v. SUPERIOR COURT, 464 U.S. 501, 104 S.Ct. 819, 78 L.Ed.2d 629 (1984), per BURGER, C.J., held, without dissent, that "the guarantees of open public proceedings in criminal trials cover proceedings for the *voir dire* examination of potential jurors." The case arose as follows: Before the *voir dire* examination of prospective jurors began at a trial for the rape and murder of a teenage girl, petitioner moved that the *voir dire* be open to the public and the press. The state objected, arguing that if the press were present, juror responses would lack the candor necessary to assure a fair trial. The trial judge agreed and permitted petitioner to attend the "general" but not the "individual" *voir dire* proceedings. All but approximately three days of the six-week *voir dire* were thus closed to the public. After the jury was empaneled, petitioner moved for release of the complete transcript of the *voir dire* proceedings, but both defense counsel and the prosecutor maintained that release of the transcript would violate the jurors' right to privacy. After defendant had been convicted and sentenced to death, the court denied petitioner's second application for release of the *voir dire* transcript. Petitioner then sought unsuccessfully in the state courts to compel release of the transcript and to vacate the order closing the *voir dire* proceedings. The Court vacated the judgment of the state supreme court. The historical evidence "reveals that, since the development of trial by jury, the process of selection of jurors has presumptively been a public process with exceptions only for good cause shown"; "[t]he presumption of openness may be overcome only by an overriding interest based on findings that closure is essential to preserve higher values and is narrowly tailored to serve that interest"; and the presumption of openness had not been rebutted in this case:

"Although three days of *voir dire* in this case were open to the public, *six weeks* of the proceedings were closed, and media requests for the transcript were denied. The Superior Court asserted two interests in support of its closure order and orders denying a transcript: the right of the defendant to a fair trial, and the right to privacy of the prospective jurors. [The court's] conclusion that Sixth Amendment and privacy interests were sufficient to warrant prolonged closure was unsupported by findings showing that an open proceeding in fact threatened those interests; hence it is not possible to conclude that closure was warranted. Even with findings adequate to support closure, the trial court's orders denying access to *voir dire* testimony failed to consider whether alternatives were available to protect the interests of the prospective jurors that the trial court's orders sought to guard. Absent consideration of alternatives to closure, the trial court could not constitutionally close the *voir dire.*" [a]

In WALLER v. GEORGIA, 467 U.S. 39, 104 S.Ct. 2210, 81 L.Ed.2d 31 (1984), the Court held unanimously, per POWELL, J., that the accused's Sixth Amendment right to a public trial extends to a pretrial suppression hearing; that under the Sixth Amendment any closure of a suppression hearing over the objections of the accused must meet the [First Amendment] tests set out in *Press-Enterprise* and its predecessors"; and that, applying these tests, "the closure of the entire suppression hearing plainly was unjustified." Petitioners were indicted for violating state gambling laws. Prior to trial they moved to suppress wiretap evidence. On the state's motion, and over petitioner's objections, the trial court closed the entire suppression hearing (which lasted seven days), finding that insofar as the wiretap evidence related to alleged offenders not then on trial, the evidence would be tainted and could not be used in future prosecutions. The state supreme court ruled that the trial court had properly balanced petitioners' rights to a public hearing against the privacy rights of others under state law and the Sixth Amendment. The U.S. Supreme Court reversed, holding that the trial court had failed to give proper weight to Sixth Amendment concerns:

"[Although the analysis in recent open trial cases] has proceeded largely under the First Amendment, [there] can be little doubt that the explicit Sixth Amendment right of the accused is no less protective of a public trial than the implicit First Amendment right of the press and public. The central aim of a criminal proceeding must be to try the accused fairly, and '[o]ur cases have uniformly recognized the public-trial guarantee as one created for the benefit of the defendant.'

"[The aims and interests of a public trial] are no less pressing in a hearing to suppress evidence. As several of the individual opinions in *Gannett* recognized, suppression hearings often are as important as the trial itself. [In] *Gannett,* as in many

a. Blackmun, J., agreed that the trial judge had erred in closing the *voir dire* proceedings and in refusing to release a transcript of that proceeding "without appropriate specific findings that nondisclosure was necessitated by a compelling governmental interest and was narrowly tailored to serve that interest," but wrote separately "to emphasize my understanding that the Court does not decide, nor does this case require it to address, the asserted 'right to privacy of the prospective jurors.'" He voiced concern that "recognition of a juror's privacy 'right' would unnecessarily complicate the lives of trial judges attempting to conduct a *voir dire* proceeding."

Stevens, J., joined the opinion of the Court, but pointed out in a separate opinion: "If the defendant had advanced a claim that his Sixth Amendment right to a public trial was violated by the closure of the *voir dire,* it would be important to determine whether the selection of the jury was a part of the 'trial' within the meaning of that Amendment. But the distinction between trials and other official proceedings is not necessarily dispositive, or even important, in evaluating the First Amendment issues. [The] focus commanded by the First Amendment makes it appropriate to emphasize the fact that the underpinning of our holding today is not simply the interest in effective judicial administration; the First Amendment's concerns are much broader."

Marshall, J., concurring in the judgment, agreed with the result reached by the Court but wrote separately "to stress that the constitutional rights of the public and press to access to all aspects of criminal trials are not diminished in cases in which 'deeply personal matters' are likely to be elicited in *voir dire* proceedings. Indeed, the policies underlying those rights are most severely jeopardized when courts conceal from the public sensitive information that bears upon the ability of jurors impartially to weigh the evidence presented to them. Therefore, prior to issuing a closure order, a trial court should be obliged to show that the order in question constitutes *the least restrictive means available* for protecting compelling state interests. In those cases where a closure order is imposed, the constitutionally preferable method for reconciling the First Amendment interests of the public and press with the legitimate privacy interests of jurors and the interests of defendants in fair trials is to redact transcripts in such a way as to preserve the anonymity of jurors while disclosing the substance of their responses. Only in the most extraordinary circumstances can the substance of a juror's response to questioning at *voir dire* be permanently excluded from the salutary scrutiny of the public and the press."

cases, the suppression hearing was the *only* trial, because the defendants thereafter [pled guilty].[a]

"In addition, a suppression hearing often resembles a bench trial [and the] outcome frequently depends on a resolution of factual matters. The need for an open [suppression hearing] may be particularly strong [because a] challenge to the seizure of evidence frequently attacks the conduct of police and prosecutor. [The] public in general also has a strong interest in exposing substantial allegations of police misconduct to the salutary effects of public scrutiny. In sum, we hold that under the Sixth Amendment any closure of a suppression hearing over the objections of the accused must meet the tests set out in *Press-Enterprise* and its predecessors.

"* * * Under *Press-Enterprise,* the party seeking to close the hearing must advance an overriding interest that is likely to be prejudiced, the closure must be no broader than necessary to protect that interest, the trial court must consider reasonable alternatives to closing the proceeding, and it must make findings adequate to support the closure. In this case, the only evidence about which the prosecutor expressed concern was the information derived from the wiretaps; he argued that unnecessary 'publication' would render the taps inadmissible under the Georgia wiretap statute. The Georgia Supreme Court advanced the more general, but essentially identical, interest in protecting the privacy of persons not before the court. Under certain circumstances, these interests may well justify closing portions of a suppression hearing to the public.

"Here, however, the State's proffer was not specific as to whose privacy interests might be infringed, how they would be infringed, what portions of the tapes might infringe them, and what portion of the evidence consisted of the tapes. As a result, the trial court's findings were broad and general, and did not purport to justify closure of the entire hearing. The court did not consider alternatives to immediate closure of the entire hearing: directing the government to provide more detail about its need for closure, in camera if necessary, and closing only those parts of the hearing that jeopardized the interests advanced. As it turned out, of course, the closure was far more extensive than necessary. The tapes lasted only two-and-one-half hours of the seven-day hearing, and few of them mentioned or involved parties not then before the court."

San Jose Mercury News v. Municipal Court, 638 P.2d 655 (Cal.1982), upheld a provision of the state criminal code (§ 868) *mandating* closure of the preliminary examination of criminal defendants upon the defendant's request. The court noted, inter alia, that preliminary hearings, unlike trials, were traditionally private at common law. The California legislature then amended § 868 so that it now *permits* closure of the preliminary hearing "upon the request of the defendant *and* a finding by the magistrate that exclusion of the public is *necessary* in order to protect the defendant's right to a fair and impartial trial" (emphasis added).

Press-Enterprise Co. v. Superior Court, 691 P.2d 1026 (Cal.1984), cert. granted, ___ U.S. ___, 106 S.Ct. 224, 88 L.Ed.2d 223

a. Consider *United States v. Criden,* 675 F.2d 550 (3d Cir.1982), a case growing out of the prosecution of several "Abscam" defendants, holding that "the same societal interests and structural arguments that mandated a first amendment right of access to criminal trials in *Richmond Newspapers* apply with equal force to pretrial criminal proceedings" and thus "the public has a first amendment right of access to pretrial suppression, due process, and entrapment hearings." The Third Circuit recognized that at common law the public had no right to attend pretrial criminal proceedings, but thought it "clear that the relative importance of pretrial procedure to that of trial has grown immensely in the last two hundred years." Moreover, the court found "no counterpart at common law to the modern suppression hearing." See also *Application of The Herald Co.,* 734 F.2d 93 (2d Cir.1984); United States v. Brooklier, 685 F.2d 1162 (9th Cir.1982).

(1985), interpreted "necessary" to mean "a reasonable likelihood of substantial prejudice which would impinge upon the right to a fair trial" and upheld the statute as so construed. The court maintained that neither the U.S. Supreme Court decisions in *Globe Newspapers* nor in *Press Enterprise* "warrants repudiation of the conclusion in *San Jose Mercury-News* that the First Amendment does not provide a right of access to preliminary hearings." Both U.S. Supreme Court cases, said the California Supreme Court, "were concerned with the right of access to trials rather than preliminary hearings." And "the main concern asserted in both cases to justify closure was not prejudice to the defendant but the interests of others, i.e., the privacy rights of prospective jurors and the physical and psychological well-being of minor sex victims."

But consider *State v. Williams,* 459 A.2d 641 (N.J.1983) and *Kearns-Tribune Corporation v. Lewis,* 685 P.2d 515 (Utah 1984), both concluding that the reasons supporting the First Amendment right of public access to criminal *trials* apply equally to *preliminary hearings* (although the exceptions that justify closure may occur more frequently with preliminary hearings than with trials).

Chapter 24

THE CRIMINAL TRIAL

SECTION 1. THE ADVERSARY SYSTEM: SOME DIFFERENT PERSPECTIVES

Many, if not most, industrialized countries have a two-tier system of adjudication for serious charges. At the higher level is its "complicated" system of adjudication, designed for those who claim to be innocent, that provides for the full development of relevant evidence and affords the defendant a panoply of rights and protective procedures. At the lower level is a simplified or summary proceeding designed for defendants who do not seriously contest the charges brought against them. Under this procedure, the defendant "waives most or all of his rights, [f]actfinding is reduced to a minimum, and proceedings are swift, convenient, and inexpensive." Weigand, *Continental Cures for American Ailments: European Criminal Procedure as a Model for Law Reform*, 2 Crime and Justice 405 (Morris and Tonry, eds. 1980). In the United States, the higher-tier procedure is the trial (especially the jury trial), while the guilty plea is the simplified or lower-tier procedure.[a] Those who have looked for major flaws in the American criminal justice process have concentrated on adjudication by guilty plea, stressing particularly the evils of plea bargaining. See Ch. 21, § 5. In large part, the American trial has been accepted as basically sound in concept, although some would argue that it is somewhat too complex and costly and many would acknowledge the need for some fine tuning. A small group of commentators, however, have challenged the basic structure of the trial and the adversary system on which it

a. In countries with basically inquisitorial systems and countries with more pronouncedly "mixed" systems (e.g., Japan), conviction for at least a serious offense ordinarily requires more than an admission of guilt. A finding of guilt must be based on a trial, whether or not the defendant contests his guilt. However, trials in those countries usually can readily be separated into higher-tier "complicated" proceedings, used where defendant contests his guilt, and lower-tier "simplified" proceedings, used where the defendant admits his guilt. In some countries, the formal structure of the trial may differ depending upon whether the defendant does or does not contest his guilt, but even if the formal structure remains constant, the substance of the two types of trials will be quite distinct. In the uncontested trial, the evidence introduced is likely to consist largely of the defendant's confession and the testimony of one or two witnesses, with the defense waiving its right to require the prosecution to strictly adhere to the rules of evidence. If the defendant does produce evidence, it is likely to relate only to question of sentencing. The result is an abbreviated hearing, substantially less costly and time consuming than the more complex proceeding applied in contested cases. See Goldstein and Marcus, *The Myth of Judicial Supervision in Three "Inquisitorial" Systems: France, Italy, and Germany*, 87 Yale L.J. 240, 264–269 (1977). But see Weigand, supra at 411 (noting a recent German study finding that "average trial of a confessing defendant took about 50 minutes, whereas trial time increased [only] to about 70 minutes where there was no confession"). See also Hughes, *Pleas Without Bargains*, 33 Rutgers L.Rev. 753 (1981); Langbein and Weinreb, *Continental Criminal Procedure: Myth and Reality*, 87 Yale L.J. 1549 (1978).

is founded. Several comparativists have asked whether the criminal justice system on the whole might not be fairer and more efficient if it adopted some of the inquisitorial elements found in the systems of continental Europe. A major aspect of the question they pose is whether the adversary trial as we know it sufficiently ensures accurate factfinding. Of course, all acknowledge that the trial involves far more than a search for the truth, as reflected by such procedural guarantees as the self-incrimination prohibition. Yet accurate factfinding certainly is a major goal of the process, especially insofar as it precludes the conviction of the innocent. See e.g., *Ake v. Oklahoma,* p. 102 supra (the "private interest in the accuracy of a criminal proceeding * * * is almost uniquely compelling"). The excerpts that follow are taken from two of the leading articles questioning the effectiveness of the adversary trial in providing an accurate factfinding process.

MIRJAN DAMASKA—PRESENTATION OF EVIDENCE AND FACTFINDING PRECISION

123 U.Pa.L.Rev. 1083, 1091–95 (1975).

For at least a century a debate has been raging about the relative advantages of the adversary and nonadversary presentation of evidence as tools in the quest for the truth. * * * In our age, so enamored of scientific methodology and so desirous of replacing "soft" by "hard" data, the question arises: can at last some themes of the debate be translated into a form susceptible of empirical analysis?[b] * * *

As I am interested in the problem of which of the two described arrangements [the adversary and nonadversary "modes of developing evidence"] leads to more accurate factual findings, the insights offered by experimental psychology become valuable. And it is just one of many melancholy facts unraveled by this relatively young discipline that all interrogation techniques exert some distorting influences. It is true that we operate tolerably well with rough approximations of what scientists would demand of factfinding precision, and that the psychological pitfalls of the interrogation process can easily be exaggerated. Even so, in their most diluted form, psychological caveats contain sobering messages of humility vis-a-vis our sometimes revered and often overrated techniques of using witnesses. * * *

Let me first allude to a number of problems with the nonadversary mode of developing testimonial evidence. It will be recalled that the judge must have some prior knowledge of the case in order to become an effective interrogator at trial. But his necessary prior knowledge is, at the same time, a considerable shortcoming from the epistemological point of view. Being somewhat familiar with the case, the judge inevitably forms certain tentative hypotheses about the reality he is called upon to reconstruct. More or less imperceptibly, these preconceptions influence the kinds of questions he addresses to witnesses. More importantly, there is an ever-present danger that the judge will be more receptive to information conforming to his hypotheses than to that which clashes with them. Although the resulting dangers to accurate decisionmaking are somewhat decreased by the fact that judges are usually aware of this distorting psychological mechanism, the shortcomings of this arrangement cannot be entirely eliminated.

b. The author later notes, however, that even if experimentation should prove conclusively that "one manner of presenting evidence leads to more precise factual findings than another," the "significance of such empirical datum" will be limited: "As the criminal process is not an untrammeled exercise in cognition, it does not take much imagination to realize that from the standpoint of other important values, an epistemologically inferior technique may on the whole be preferable. Preoccupation with the rationality of one component can be irrational when judged from the point of view of the entire scheme."

Consider now the adversary manner of developing evidence. It is designed in such a way that the art of suspended judgment can be practiced for a much longer period of time by the adjudicators. They are not driven by the duty to lead an inquiry into forming early tentative theories about the facts of the case. This is, of course, an advantage of the adversary mode. There may be yet another one, although it is much less certain in terms of experimental witness psychology. It is possible that an interrogator "hostile" to the witness may be in a better position to bring out potential conscious or unconscious distortion mechanisms inherent in his testimony (e.g., inaccurate perception, faulty memory images, mystifications, etc.).

But all this is only part of the story: there are important cognitive costs of the adversary arrangements. As this darker view of the cathedral is seldom illuminated, let us explore various epistemological pitfalls that lie in the tactical wake of letting two adversaries control the development of evidence at trial. I do not propose here to start the reader on an extended tour of experimental psychology relevant to problems of the rival use of evidentiary sources. It is enough for my limited purposes to call attention to a few of the most salient shortcomings of this arrangement, assuming, at all times, that the parties are not engaging in unethical practices.

It may be in the narrow interest of only one party, or in the common interest of both, that some items of information which the witness possesses do not reach the adjudicator—even though their relevancy in the quest for the truth is beyond dispute. Evidence unsupportive of one's case has no function in the adversary litigation process, nor do matters which the parties decide to leave out of the disputation. And, as the witness is limited to answering relatively narrow and precise questions, much information may effectively be kept away from the decisionmaker who presumably is responsible for finding the truth within the limits of the charge. Accordingly, the factual basis for the decision may be incomplete.

But there are much more important costs of the development of evidence through rival use of informational sources. The damage to testimony inflicted by the preparation of witnesses is very serious. Parties can hardly be expected to interview the potential witnesses in relatively detached ways that minimize the damage of interrogation to memory images. During the sessions devoted to "coaching," the future witness is likely to try to adapt himself to expectations mirrored in the interviewer's onesided attitude. As a consequence, gaps in his memory may even unconsciously be filled out by what he thinks accords with the lawyer's expectations and are in tune with his thesis. Later, in court, these additions to memory images may appear to the witness himself as accurate reproductions of his original perceptions. Another important cost accompanies the cross-examination technique, which, with its challenge to the credibility of witnesses, is a two-edged sword. As Judge Frankel has noted, it is "to a considerable degree . . . like other potent weapons, equally lethal for heroes and villains." [See p. 1337 infra]. Even with the best of intentions on the cross-examiner's part, reliable testimony may easily be made to look debatable, and clear information may become obfuscated.

Finally, observe the procedural position of the passive decisionmaker. It is old hat in experimental psychology that people display different cognitive needs; they try to reach knowledge and understanding along different paths. It therefore stands to reason that decisionmakers may sometimes require a different method of presentation than that of the clash of two onesided versions, and that, at a psychologically crucial point, they would sometimes like to ask a specific question of a witness, which in their passivity they cannot do.

Even this brief digression into experimental psychology clearly shows that it is treacherous to make definitive pronouncements about which of the two manners of presenting evidence is a more effective tool in the search for the truth. Speculation about these problems is made even more intractable because the narrow epistemological problem involved can hardly ever be totally separated from a cluster of attitudes and values comprising the larger legal culture. * * * [c]

MARVIN E. FRANKEL—THE SEARCH FOR THE TRUTH: AN UMPIREAL VIEW

123 U.Pa.L.Rev. 1031, 1032–40, 1052–59 (1975). Reprinted with the permission of the author; copyright © 1975 by Marvin E. Frankel; this article is reprinted, as revised, in Frankel, *Partisan Justice* (1980), published by Hill and Wang, a division of Farrar, Straus, & Giroux, Inc.

My theme, to be elaborated at some length, is that our adversary system rates truth too low among the values that institutions of justice are meant to serve. * * * [d]

c. See fn. b supra. Consider also Arnold, *Symbols of Government* (1935), discussing the symbolic significance of the criminal trial: "When a great government treats the lowliest of criminals as an equal antagonist, strips itself of the executive power which it possesses, and submits the case to twelve ordinary men, allowing the judge only the authority of an umpire, we have a gesture of recognition of the dignity of the individual which has an extraordinary dramatic appeal. Its claim is on our emotions, rather than our common sense. We feel that our conception of human equality needs this concrete institution to give it reality."

There are those, however, who claim that a "hard look" at the reality of today's trial largely destroys the symbolism that Arnold found in the adversary process. See e.g., Jackson, *Law and Disorder* 78–81 (1984):

"In theory, the criminal court consists of five actors: the judge, a disinterested manager and arbiter, concerned primarily that justice be done; the prosecutor, pursuing the accusatory case but interested primarily in discovery of truth and delivery of justice; the defendant, charged with a crime but presumed by all except the prosecutor to be innocent; the defense attorney, who without compromise represents the accused in adversary fashion; and the jury, which without bias hears the evidence, weighs the facts, and decides on the legal guilt or innocence of the accused. [But] the real people who fill these theoretical roles almost never act that way.

"The last thing in the world prosecutors or defense lawyers want is a totally unbiased jury; both fight very hard during *voir dire* * * * to have at least some people in the jury box predisposed to their client or cause. * * * Few judges are accused by attorneys or prosecutors of total objectivity, which is why both attorneys and prosecutors work hard at "judge shopping"—managing a case so it will or will not appear before a specific judge. * * * Prosecutors, with rare exceptions, are concerned with winning, not with justice. * * * Most criminal justice lawyers work as partners with the court and the prosecutors, not as unequivocal representatives of the defendants. The defendants come and go, but the attorney's relationships with the other officers of the court continue for years. An individual case is an opportunity for another mutual accommodation. New observers and new defendants in criminal courts are often startled the first time they realize that during brief recesses the defense attorneys chat not with the clients but with the prosecutors. * * *

"The spectacular trials that get great press coverage—Angela Davis, John Mitchell, the Chicago 7, T. Cullen Davis, Charles Manson, Wayne Williams, Claus von Bulow—take considerable time. Motions are made and remade. Jurors are carefully considered, and selected or rejected. Witnesses are qualified or disqualified in lengthy *Wade* hearings. The legitimacy of evidence is questioned. There are a lot of witnesses, many pieces of evidence. The transcripts are thick and the appeals, if necessary, are long and complex. Most trials are nothing like that; as far as most defendants are concerned, those trials are closer to movieland than real life."

d. At another point in the article, the author (a former federal judge) notes that he does not mean "to question the presumption of innocence or the prosecution's burden of proof beyond a reasonable doubt": "In any particular case, because we are unwilling to incur more than a minimal risk of convicting the innocent, these bedrock principles must prevail. The statistical fact remains that the preponderant majority of those brought to trial did substantially what they are charged with. While we undoubtedly convict some innocent people, a truth horrifying to confront, we also acquit a far larger number who are guilty, a fact we bear with much more equanimity. One reason we bear it so well is our awareness that in the last analysis truth is not the only goal."

This is a topic on which our profession has practiced some self-deception. We proclaim to each other and to the world that the clash of adversaries is a powerful means for hammering out the truth. Sometimes, less guardedly, we say it is "best calculated to getting out all the facts . . . ." That the adversary technique is useful within limits none will doubt. That it is "best" we should all doubt if we were able to be objective about the question. Despite our untested statements of self-congratulation, we know that others searching after facts—in history, geography, medicine, whatever—do not emulate our adversary system. We know that most countries of the world seek justice by different routes. What is much more to the point, we know that many of the rules and devices of adversary litigation as we conduct it are not geared for, but are often aptly suited to defeat, the development of the truth.

We are unlikely ever to know how effectively the adversary technique would work toward truth if that were the objective of the contestants. Employed by interested parties, the process often achieves truth only as a convenience, a byproduct, or an accidental approximation. The business of the advocate, simply stated, is to win if possible without violating the law. (The phrase "if possible" is meant to modify what precedes it, but the danger of slippage is well known.) His is not the search for truth as such. To put that thought more exactly, the truth and victory are mutually incompatible for some considerable percentage of the attorneys trying cases at any given time. * * *

Whatever doctrine teaches, it is a fact of interest here that most criminal defense counsel are not at all bent upon full disclosure of the truth. To a lesser degree, but stemming from the same ethos, we know how fiercely prosecutors have resisted disclosure, how often they have winked at police lapses, how mixed has been their enthusiasm for the principle that they must seek justice, not merely convictions. While the patterns of civil cases are different, and variable, we may say that it is the rare case in which either side yearns to have the witnesses, or anyone, give *the whole truth.* And our techniques for developing evidence feature devices for blocking and limiting such unqualified revelations.

The devices are too familiar to warrant more than a fleeting reminder. To begin with, we leave most of the investigatory work to paid partisans, which is scarcely a guarantee of thorough and detached exploration. Our courts wait passively for what the parties will present, almost never knowing—often not suspecting—what the parties have chosen not to present. The ethical standards governing counsel command loyalty and zeal for the client, but no positive obligation at all to the truth. Counsel must not knowingly break the law or commit or countenance fraud. Within these unconfining limits, advocates freely employ time-honored tricks and strategems to block or distort the truth.

As a matter of strict logic, in the run of cases where there are flatly contradictory assertions about matters of fact, one side must be correct, the other wrong. Where the question is "Did the defendant pass a red light?" or "Does the plaintiff have a scarred retina?" or "Was the accused warned of the reasons why anyone of sound mind would keep quiet and did he then proceed nevertheless like a suicidal idiot to destroy himself by talking?" the "facts" are, or were, one way or the other. To be sure, honest people may honestly differ, and we mere lawyers cannot—actually, must not—set ourselves up as judges of the facts. That is the great release from effective ethical inhibitions. We are not to pass judgment, but only to marshal our skills to present and test the witnesses and other evidence—the skills being to make the most of these for our side and the least for the opposition. What will out, we sometimes tell ourselves and often tell others, is the truth. And, if worse comes to worst, in the end who really knows what is truth?

There is much in this of cant, hypocrisy, and convenient overlooking. As people, we know or powerfully suspect a good deal more than we are prepared as lawyers to admit or explore further. The clearest cases are those in which the advocate has been informed directly by a competent client, or has learned from evidence too clear to admit of genuine doubt, that the client's position rests upon falsehood. It is not possible to be certain, but I believe from recollection and conversation such cases are far from rare. Much more numerous are the cases in which we manage as counsel to avoid too much knowledge. The sharp eye of the cynical lawyer becomes at strategic moments a demurely averted and filmy gaze. It may be agreeable not to listen to the client's tape recordings of vital conversations that may contain embarrassments for the ultimate goal of vindicating the client. Unfettered by the clear prohibitions actual "knowledge" of the truth might impose, lawyers may be effective and exuberant in employing the familar skills: techniques that make a witness look unreliable although the look stems only from counsel's artifice, cunning questions that stop short of discomfiting revelations, complaisant experts for whom some shopping may have been necessary. The credo that frees counsel for such arts is not a doctrine of truth-seeking.

The litigator's devices, let us be clear, have utility in testing dishonest witnesses, ferreting out falsehoods, and thus exposing the truth. But to a considerable degree these devices are like other potent weapons, equally lethal for heroes and villains. It is worth stressing, therefore, that the gladiator using the weapons in the courtroom is not primarily crusading after truth, but seeking to win. If this is banal, it is also overlooked too much and, in any event, basic to my thesis. * * *

* * * Having argued that we are too much committed to contentiousness as a good in itself and too little devoted to truth, I proceed to some prescriptions of a general nature for remedying these flaws. Simply stated, these prescriptions are that we should: (1) modify (not abandon) the adversary ideal; (2) make truth a paramount objective; and (3) impose upon the contestants a duty to pursue that objective.[e]

A. Modifying the Adversary Ideal

We should begin, as a concerted professional task, to question the premise that adversariness is ultimately and invariably good. For most of us trained in American law, the superiority of the adversary process over any other is too plain to doubt or examine. The certainty is shared by people who are in other respects widely separated on the ideological spectrum. The august *Code of Professional Responsibility,* as has been mentioned, proclaims, in order, the "*Duty of the Lawyer to a Client,*" then the "*Duty of the Lawyer to the Adversary System of Justice.*" There is no announced "Duty to the Truth" or "Duty to the Community." Public interest lawyers, while they otherwise test the law's bounds, profess a basic commitment "to the adversary system itself" as the means of giving "everyone affected by corporate and bureaucratic decisions . . . a voice in those decisions . . . ." We may note similarly the earnest and idealistic scholar who brought the fury of the (not necessarily consistent) establishment upon himself when he wrote, reflecting upon experience as devoted defense counsel for poor peo-

e. The author previously had rejected two other possible prescriptions: "Two means for controlling adversary excesses in the trial process are intervention by the judge and better training and regulation of counsel. Both have been proposed, and attempted to some extent. The second method is receiving serious attention today, with high and persuasive sponsorship. Neither of the two approaches, at least as they have been formulated thus far, contemplates any basic changes in the existing standards and procedures. For this central reason, neither seems to me to hold much promise. * * *"

ple, that as an advocate you must (a) try to destroy a witness "whom you know to be telling the truth," (b) "put a witness on the stand when you know he will commit perjury," and (c) "give your client legal advice when you have reason to believe that the knowledge you give him will tempt him to commit perjury." [58] The "policies" he found to justify these views, included, as the first and most fundamental, the maintenance of "an adversary system based upon the presupposition that the most effective means of determining truth is to present to a judge and jury a clash between proponents of conflicting views." [f]

Our commitment to the adversary or "accusatorial" mode is buttressed by a co-

58. Freedman, *Professional Responsibility of the Criminal Defense Lawyer: The Three Hardest Questions,* 64 Mich.L.Rev. 1469 (1966).

[Professor Freedman originally presented his conclusions at a trial institute in Washington, D.C., where certain local judges responded by filing a complaint (later dismissed) with the Bar Grievance Committee. Professor Freedman then set forth his position at greater length in the Michigan Law Review article cited above. As part of the same symposium, Professor Noonan, in *The Purposes of Advocacy and the Limits of Confidentiality,* 64 Mich.L.Rev. 1485 (1966), suggested that Professor Freedman's position followed from a "battle model" of the trial rather than the more appropriate view that a "trial is * * * a process 'within which man's capacity for impartial judgment can attain its fullest realization,' and the function of the advocate is to assist the trier of fact in making this impartial judgment."]

f. Professor Freedman, both in his article cited supra and his later book, *Lawyers' Ethics in an Adversary System* (1975), contends that defense counsel, to be an effective advocate, must have "full knowledge of every pertinent fact" and can gain such disclosure from the defendant only by promising complete confidentiality. Faced with a client who then insists on giving perjured testimony, notwithstanding counsel's attempt to dissuade him, the defense counsel must respect that pledge of confidentiality. Accordingly, Professor Freedman argues, the counsel's obligation is to "proceed in the normal fashion in presenting the testimony and arguing the case to the jury." *Lawyers' Ethics,* supra, at 31. Any attempt to withdraw would only lead the client to lie to his next attorney, and any attempt to treat the prejured testimony in a special manner (e.g., having the defendant testify without direct examination by counsel or reference to his testimony in closing argument) would only signal the jury that defendant's own counsel has "turned his back" on the defendant at the "most critical point in the trial."

Professor Freedman finds a similar obligation on the part of counsel to seek through cross-examination to challenge the testimony of a prosecution witness even though counsel knows that testimony is truthful and accurate. He rejects the contention that this obligation can be justified on grounds separate from those that govern the counsel's obligation with respect to perjured testimony. Some commentators have suggested that the duty to cross-examine follows from the function of the advocate to use "all the legitimate tools available to test the truth of the prosecutor's case" and therefore differs from the knowing presentation of perjured testimony. See *Lawyers' Ethics,* supra, at 44–45 (citing the comments of Chief Justice Burger in a panel discussion on professional responsibility). Professor Freedman responds that there is no difference in "practical effect" in the two situations: "In both cases, the lawyer participates in misleading the finder of fact. In the case of the perjured witness, the attorney asks only nonleading questions, while in the case of impeachment, the lawyer takes an active, aggressive role, using professional training and skills." The duty to "destroy the truthful witness," he concludes, also arises from the need to fully preserve the pledge of confidentiality made to the client.

In his initial article, Professor Freedman argued that basically the same consideration supported his third conclusion, that counsel had an obligation to provide the client legal advice even though there was reason to believe that the client would use that advice to construct a false defense (i.e., that the client would shape his testimony to fit the legal excuses for his conduct noted in counsel's advice). In *Lawyers' Ethics,* however, Professor Freedman modified his analysis of that "most difficult" question of professional responsibility. He concluded: "In interviewing, therefore, the attorney must take into account the practical psychological realities of the situation. That means, at least at the earlier stages of eliciting the client's story, that the attorney should assume a skeptical attitude, and that the attorney should give the client legal advice that might help in drawing out useful information that the client, consciously or unconsciously, might be withholding. To that extent * * *, I adhere to my earlier position that there are situations in which it may be proper for the attorney to give the client legal advice even though the attorney has reason to believe that the advice may induce the client to commit perjury. There does come a point, however, where nothing less than 'brute rationalization' can purport to justify a conclusion that the lawyer is seeking in good faith to elicit truth, rather than actively participating in the creation of perjury [which is beyond counsel's role as 'an advocate in an adversary system']."

rollary certainty that other, alien systems are inferior. We contrast our form of criminal procedure with the "inquisitorial" system, conjuring up visions of torture, secrecy, and dictatorial government. Confident of our superiority, we do not bother to find out how others work. It is not common knowledge among us that purely inquisitorial systems exist scarcely anywhere; that elements of our adversary approach exist probably everywhere; and that the evolving procedures of criminal justice, in Europe and elsewhere, are better described as "mixed" than as strictly accusatorial or strictly inquisitorial.

In considering the possibility of change, we must open our minds to the variants and alternatives employed by other communities that also aspire to civilization. Without voting firmly, I raise the question whether the virginally ignorant judge is always to be preferred to one with an investigative file. We should be prepared to inquire whether our arts of examining and cross-examining, often geared to preventing excessive outpourings of facts, are inescapably preferable to safeguarded interrogation by an informed judicial officer. It is permissible to keep asking, because nobody has satisfactorily answered, why our present system of confessions in the police station versus no confessions at all is better than an open and orderly procedure of having a judicial official question suspects.

If the mention of such a question has not exhausted your tolerance, consider whether our study of foreign alternatives might suggest means for easing the unending tension surrounding the privilege against self-incrimination as it frequently operates in criminal trials. It would be prudent at least to study closely whether our criminal defendant, privileged to stay suspiciously absent from the stand or to testify subject to a perjury prosecution or "impeachment" by prior crimes, is surely better off than the European defendant who cannot escape questioning both before and at trial, though he may refuse to answer, but is free to tell his story without either the oath or the impeachment pretext for using his criminal record against him. Whether or not the defendant is better off, the question remains open whether the balance we have struck is the best possible.

To propose only one other topic for illustration, we need to study whether our elaborate struggles over discovery, especially in criminal cases, may be incurable symptoms of pathology inherent in our rigid insistence that the parties control the evidence until it is all "prepared" and packaged for competitive manipulation at the eventual continuous trial. Central in the debates on discovery is the concern of the ungenerous that the evidence may be tainted or alchemized between the time it is discovered and the time it is produced or countered at the trial. The concern, though the debaters report it in differing degrees, is well founded. It is significant enough to warrant our exploring alternative arrangements abroad where investigation "freezes" the evidence (that is, preserves usable depositions and other forms of relatively contemporaneous evidence) for use at trial, thus serving both to inhibit spoilage and to avoid pitfalls and surprises that may defeat justice. * * *

B. Making Truth the Paramount Objective

* * * This topic heading contains for me the most debatable and the least thoroughly considered of the thoughts offered here. It is a brief suggestion for a revolution, but with no apparatus of doctrine or program. * * * Apart from our image, we have had to reckon for ourselves in the dark hours with the knowledge that "selling" our stories rather than striving for the truth cannot always seem, because it is not, such noble work as befits the practitioner of a learned profession. The struggle to win, with its powerful pressures to subordinate the love of truth, is often only incidentally, or coincidentally, if at all, a service to the public interest. * * *

Professional standards that placed truth above the client's interests would raise more perplexing questions. The privilege for client's confidences might come in for reexamination and possible modification. We have all been trained to know without question that the privilege is indispensable for effective representation. The client must know his confidences are safe so that he can tell all and thus have fully knowledgeable advice. We may want to ask, nevertheless, whether it would be an excessive price for the client to be stuck with the truth rather than having counsel allied with him for concealment and distortion. The full development of this thought is beyond my studies to date. Its implications may be unacceptable. I urge only that it is among the premises in need of examination. * * *

C. A Duty to Pursue the Truth

The rules of professional responsibility should compel disclosures of material facts and forbid material omissions rather than merely proscribe positive frauds. This final suggestion is meant to implement the broad and general proposition that precedes it. In an effort to be still more specific, I submit a draft of a new disciplinary rule that would supplement or in large measure displace existing disciplinary rule 7–102 of the *Code of Professional Responsibility*.[69] The draft says:

(1) In his representation of a client, unless prevented from doing so by a privilege reasonably believed to apply, a lawyer shall:

(a) Report to the court and opposing counsel the existence of relevant evidence or witnesses where the lawyer does not intend to offer such evidence or witnesses.[g]

(b) Prevent, or when prevention has proved unsuccessful, report to the court and opposing counsel the making of any untrue statement by client or witness or any omission to state a material fact necessary in order to make statements made, in the light of the circumstances under which they were made, not misleading.[h]

(c) Question witnesses with a purpose and design to elicit the whole truth, including particularly supplementary and qualifying matters that render evidence already given more accurate, intelligible, or fair than it otherwise would be.

(2) In the construction and application of the rules in subdivision (1), a

69. The affected portions of DR 7–102 are:

(A) In his representation of a client, a lawyer shall not: * * *

(3) Conceal or knowingly fail to disclose that which he is required by law to reveal.

(4) Knowingly use perjured testimony or false evidence.

(5) Knowingly make a false statement of law or fact.

(6) Participate in the creation or preservation of evidence when he knows or it is obvious that the evidence is false.

(7) Counsel or assist his client in conduct that the lawyer knows to be illegal or fraudulent.

(B) A lawyer who receives information clearly establishing that:

(1) His client has, in the course of the representation, perpetrated a fraud upon a person or tribunal shall promptly call upon his client to rectify the same, and if his client refuses or is unable to do so, he shall reveal the fraud to the affected person or tribunal [except when the information is protected as a privileged communication]. [The bracketed material was added in 1974, see Freedman at p. 1414 infra].

(2) A person other than his client has perpetrated a fraud upon a tribunal shall promptly reveal the fraud to the tribunal.

g. See Ch. 20, §§ 3, 4.

h. See *Whiteside v. Scurr,* p. 161 supra; MacCarthy and Mejia, *The Perjurious Client Question: Putting Criminal Defense Lawyers Between a Rock and a Hard Place,* 75 J.Crim.L. & Criminology, 1197 (1984) (analyzing *A.B.A. Model R. Prof. Cond.*, and concluding that the Model Rules "build more forcefully than does the Code toward requiring disclosure of client perjury," but the Rules commentary at the same time "provides a coherent, constitutional basis for excluding the criminal defense attorney from the duty to reveal intended or actual perjury by his own client").

lawyer will be held to possess knowledge he actually has or, in the exercise of reasonable diligence, should have.

Key words in the draft, namely, in (1)(b), have been plagiarized, of course, from the Securities and Exchange Commission's rule 10b–5. That should serve not only for respectability; it should also answer, at least to some extent, the complaint that the draft would impose impossibly stringent standards. The morals we have evolved for business clients cannot be deemed unattainable by the legal profession. * * * [i]

SECTION 2. PRESENCE OF THE DEFENDANT

ILLINOIS v. ALLEN

397 U.S. 337, 90 S.Ct. 1057, 25 L.Ed.2d 353 (1970).

MR. JUSTICE BLACK delivered the opinion of the Court.

[Allen was convicted by an Illinois jury of armed robbery and was sentenced to a term of 10 to 30 years. Before trial, the judge acceded to Allen's wish to conduct his own defense, although court-appointed counsel would "sit in and protect the record." During the *voir dire* examination, Allen "started to argue with the judge in a most abusive and disrespectful manner" when the judge directed him to confine his questioning to matters relating to the prospective juror's qualifications. The judge then asked appointed counsel to proceed with the examination, upon which Allen continued to talk and concluded his remarks by saying to the judge, "When I go out for lunchtime, you're going to be a corpse here." The judge then warned Allen that he would be removed from the courtroom if there was another outbreak of that sort. Allen continued to talk back, saying, "There's not going to be no trial, either. I'm going to sit here and you're going to talk and you can bring your shackles out and straight jacket and put them on me and tape my mouth, but it will do no good because there's not going to be no trial." After more abusive remarks, the judge ordered the trial to proceed in Allen's absence. After a noon recess, the judge permitted Allen to return to the courtroom with the warning that he could remain only so long as he behaved himself. Shortly thereafter, Allen spoke out again, saying, "There is going to be no proceeding. I'm going to start talking all through the trial. There's not going to be no trial like this." The judge again ordered Allen removed, and he remained out of the courtroom during the presentation of the State's case-in-chief except when brought in for purposes of identification. Thereafter, Allen was permitted to return to the courtroom upon his promise to conduct himself properly, and he remained for the rest of the trial, principally his defense, which was conducted by his appointed counsel. Allen's conviction was affirmed by the Supreme Court of Illinois, and on federal habeas corpus the district court found no constitutional violation and declined to issue the writ. The court of appeals reversed.]

The Court of Appeals felt that the defendant's Sixth Amendment right to be

i. Responses to Judge Frankel's critique of the adversary system varied. Some commentators concluded that Judge Frankel failed to give sufficient weight to the effectiveness of the adversary process in protecting the innocent or to other values (e.g., respecting the dignity of the individual). Others agreed that the adversary system failed in practice to sufficiently pursue the truth, but argued that the fault was with lawyer excesses rather than the design of the system. Still others agreed that structural changes were needed to ensure that the factfinder had before it all relevant facts, but argued that those changes should come in areas other than a redefinition of the lawyer-client relationship (e.g., in changing evidentiary rules or expanding the role of the judge). For a sampling of these various viewpoints, see Freedman, *Judge Frankel's Search for Truth,* 123 U.Pa.L.Rev. 1060 (1975); Uviller, *The Advocate, the Truth and Judicial Hackles,* 123 U.Pa.L.Rev. 1067 (1975); Pye, *The Role of Counsel in the Suppression of Truth,* 1978 Duke L.J. 921; Prizzi, *Judge Frankel and the Adversary System,* 52 Colo.L.Rev. 357 (1981); Alschuler, *The Search for Truth Continued, the Privilege Retained,* 54 Colo.L.Rev. 67 (1982) (responding to Judge Frankel's later article at 54 Colo.L.Rev. 51).

present at his own trial was so "absolute" that, no matter how unruly or disruptive the defendant's conduct might be, he could never be held to have lost that right so long as he continued to insist upon it, as Allen clearly did. * * * We cannot agree that the Sixth Amendment, the cases upon which the Court of Appeals relied, or any other cases of this Court so handicap a trial judge in conducting a criminal trial. * * * We accept instead the statement of Mr. Justice Cardozo who, speaking for the Court in *Snyder v. Massachusetts,* 291 U.S. 97, 106, 54 S.Ct. 330, 332, 78 L.Ed. 674 (1934), said: "No doubt the privilege [of personally confronting witnesses] may be lost by consent or at times even by misconduct." Although mindful that courts must indulge every reasonable presumption against the loss of constitutional rights, *Johnson v. Zerbst* [p. 121 supra], we explicitly hold today that a defendant can lose his right to be present at trial if, after he has been warned by the judge that he will be removed if he continues his disruptive behavior, he nevertheless insists on conducting himself in a manner so disorderly, disruptive, and disrespectful of the court that his trial cannot be carried on with him in the courtroom. Once lost, the right to be present can, of course, be reclaimed as soon as the defendant is willing to conduct himself consistently with the decorum and respect inherent in the concept of courts and judicial proceedings.

It is essential to the proper administration of criminal justice that dignity, order, and decorum be the hallmarks of all court proceedings in our country. The flagrant disregard in the courtroom of elementary standards of proper conduct should not and cannot be tolerated. We believe trial judges confronted with disruptive, contumacious, stubbornly defiant defendants must be given sufficient discretion to meet the circumstances of each case. No one formula for maintaining the appropriate courtroom atmosphere will be best in all situations. We think there are at least three constitutionally permissible ways for a trial judge to handle an obstreperous defendant like Allen: (1) bind and gag him, thereby keeping him present; (2) cite him for contempt; (3) take him out of the courtroom until he promises to conduct himself properly.

Trying a defendant for a crime while he sits bound and gagged before the judge and jury would to an extent comply with that part of the Sixth Amendment's purposes that accords the defendant an opportunity to confront the witnesses at the trial. But even to contemplate such a technique, much less see it, arouses a feeling that no person should be tried while shackled and gagged except as a last resort. Not only is it possible that the sight of shackles and gags might have a significant effect on the jury's feelings about the defendant, but the use of this technique is itself something of an affront to the very dignity and decorum of judicial proceedings that the judge is seeking to uphold. Moreover, one of the defendant's primary advantages of being present at the trial, his ability to communicate with his counsel, is greatly reduced when the defendant is in a condition of total physical restraint. It is in part because of these inherent disadvantages and limitations in this method of dealing with disorderly defendants that we decline to hold with the Court of Appeals that a defendant cannot under any possible circumstances be deprived of his right to be present at trial. However, in some situations which we need not attempt to foresee, binding and gagging might possibly be the fairest and most reasonable way to handle a defendant who acts as Allen did here.

In a footnote the Court of Appeals suggested the possible availability of contempt of court as a remedy to make Allen behave in his robbery trial, and it is true that citing or threatening to cite a contumacious defendant for criminal contempt might in itself be sufficient to make a defendant stop interrupting a trial. If so, the problem would be solved easily, and the defendant could remain in the courtroom. Of course, if the defendant is determined to prevent *any* trial, then a court in attempting to try the defendant for contempt is still confronted with the identical dilemma that the Illinois court faced in this case. And criminal contempt has obvious limitations as a sanction when the defendant is charged with a crime so serious that a very severe sentence such as death or life imprisonment is likely to be imposed. In such a case the defendant might not be affected by a mere contempt sentence when he ultimately faces a far more serious sanction. Nevertheless, the contempt remedy should be borne in mind by a judge in the circumstances of this case.

Another aspect of the contempt remedy is the judge's power, when exercised consistently with state and federal law, to imprison an unruly defendant such as Allen for civil contempt and discontinue the trial until such time as the defendant promises to behave himself. This procedure is consistent with the defendant's right to be present at trial, and yet it avoids the serious shortcomings of the use of shackles and gags. It must be recognized, however, that a defendant might conceivably, as a matter of calculated strategy, elect to spend a prolonged period in confinement for contempt in the hope that adverse witnesses might be unavailable after a lapse of time. A court must guard against allowing a defendant to profit from his own wrong in this way.

The trial court in this case decided under the circumstances to remove the defendant from the courtroom and to continue his trial in his absence until and unless he promised to conduct himself in a manner befitting an American courtroom. As we said earlier, we find nothing unconstitutional about this procedure. Allen's behavior was clearly of such an extreme and aggravated nature as to justify either his removal from the courtroom or his total physical restraint. Prior to his removal he was repeatedly warned by the trial judge that he would be removed from the courtroom if he persisted in his unruly conduct, and, as Judge Hastings observed in his dissenting opinion, the record demonstrates that Allen would not have been at all dissuaded by the trial judge's use of his criminal contempt powers. Allen was constantly informed that he could return to the trial when he would agree to conduct himself in an orderly manner. Under these circumstances we hold that Allen lost his right guaranteed by the Sixth and Fourteenth Amendments to be present throughout his trial. * * *

The judgment of the Court of Appeals is reversed.

MR. JUSTICE BRENNAN, concurring. * * *

I would add only that when a defendant is excluded from his trial, the court should make reasonable efforts to enable him to communicate with his attorney and, if possible, to keep apprised of the progress of his trial. Once the court has removed the contumacious defendant, it is not weakness to mitigate the disadvantages of his expulsion as far as technologically possible in the circumstances.[a]

Notes and Questions

1. Compare the situation in which the defendant absents himself during the trial. In *Taylor v. United States,* 414 U.S. 17, 94 S.Ct. 194, 38 L.Ed.2d 174 (1973), the Court, per curiam, rejected the defendant's contention that "his mere voluntary absence from the trial cannot be construed as an effective waiver * * * unless it is demonstrated that he knew or had been expressly warned by the trial court not only that he had a right to be present but also that the trial would continue in his absence and thereby effectively foreclose his right to testify and to confront personally the witnesses against him." The

a. Douglas, J., in a separate opinion, concluded the Court "should reverse the case for staleness of the record and affirm the denial of relief by the District Court."

Court noted: "It is wholly incredible to suggest that petitioner, who was at liberty on bail, had attended the opening session of his trial, and had a duty to be present at the trial, entertained any doubts about his right to be present at every stage of his trial. It seems equally incredible to us, as it did to the Court of Appeals, 'that a defendant who flees from a courtroom in the midst of a trial—where judge, jury, witnesses and lawyers are present and ready to continue—would not know that as a consequence the trial could continue in his absence.' "

2. May the same be said when the defendant is not even present at the commencement of the trial? Consider UNITED STATES v. TORTORA, 464 F.2d 1202 (2d Cir.1972), concerning the trial of Santoro and four others for engaging in loansharking:

"On the facts on this case, there were no constitutional constraints against the trial judge's proceeding with the trial even though Santoro failed to appear on August 16. Santoro had pleaded not guilty to the indictment on January 8, 1971. Released on $20,000 bail, he then appeared before Judge Pollack on April 15, 1971, when the case was called for trial, and also on August 10, 1971, the date the court had set as the most convenient for this multiple-defendant trial. Santoro was present in open court when Judge Pollack continued the case until August 16. Indeed, at 11:30 P.M. on the evening of August 15, Santoro called his attorney to arrange for a ride to court the following morning. Thus it is clear beyond peradventure that Santoro had been adequately apprised that he was to appear in court on August 16 and that his trial would commence on that day. No justification, either to the district court or on appeal, has been offered for his absence. Having had every opportunity to present his defense, Santoro cannot now complain of his failure actively to participate therein or of the trial having proceeded without him. Accordingly, we hold that his conviction complied with all the requisites of the Constitution.[6]

"It is obviously desirable that a defendant be present at his own trial. We do not here lay down a general rule that, in every case in which the defendant is voluntarily absent at the empanelment of the jury and the taking of evidence, the trial judge should proceed with the trial. We only hold that this is within the discretion of the trial judge, to be utilized only in circumstances as extraordinary as those before us. Indeed, we would add that this discretion should be exercised only when the public interest clearly outweighs that of the voluntarily absent defendant. Whether the trial will proceed will depend upon the trial judge's determination of a complex of issues. He must weigh the likelihood that the trial could soon take place with the defendant present; the difficulty of rescheduling, particularly in multiple-defendant trials; the burden on the Government in having to undertake two trials, again particularly in multiple-defendant trials where the evidence against the defendants is often overlapping and more than one trial might keep the Government's witnesses in substantial jeopardy.[7]

"We hold that the trial judge was well within his discretion in refusing to adjourn the trial on August 16 or to sever Santoro's trial from that of the other defendants. As a result of the difficulty of coordinating the defense attorneys' conflicting schedules and the unsubstantiated claims of physical ailments made by two other defendants, numerous delays had already occurred in this multiple-defendant trial. The Govern-

6. Similarly, Santoro's conviction complies with the requisites of Rule 43 of the Federal Rules of Criminal Procedure. The rule is no more than a restatement of the defendant's constitutional rights, see Advisory Committee Note ("the rule is a restatement of existing laws"), and its protections can be waived by the defendant's conduct.

7. It is difficult for us to conceive of any case where the exercise of this discretion would be appropriate other than a multiple-defendant case.

ment's case rested almost exclusively on the testimony of one witness who had already been threatened on numerous occasions by the appellants. Extensive delays would almost certainly have accompanied any adjournment and the Government's main witness would have continued to be in potential danger until his testimony was completed. Severance would have added substantially to the burden on the Government and its witnesses, necessitating two trials in the place of one: it would have been an unwarranted delay in the expeditious administration of justice. Moreover, the danger to the Government's witness would have continued until that indefinite time in the future when the witness's testimony in the second trial would have been completed."

3. In *Rushen v. Spain* (further described at Note 7, p. 1529 infra), a juror in a state homicide trial twice went to the judge's chambers to tell him of her personal acquaintance with the victim of an earlier murder about which impeachment testimony had been received. The Court, assuming without deciding that the defendant's constitutional right to presence was implicated in such circumstances, concluded: "There is scarcely a lengthy trial in which one or more jurors does not have occasion to speak to the trial judge about something, whether it relates to a matter of personal comfort or to some aspect of the trial. The lower federal courts' conclusion that an unrecorded *ex parte* communication between trial judge and juror can never be harmless error ignores these day-to-day realities of courtroom life and undermines society's interest in the administration of criminal justice."

In *United States v. Gagnon,* ___ U.S. ___, 105 S.Ct. 1482, 84 L.Ed.2d 486 (1985), the judge at the request of counsel for one of the defendants met with a juror in chambers to ensure that this juror was not prejudiced as a result of the juror's expressed concern about defendant's conduct in making sketches of the jurors during trial. A transcript was made of the in camera proceeding, and no objection was made by any of the defendants to the procedure, which was announced to them and their counsel in advance in open court. Noting that the defendants "could have done nothing had they been at the conference, nor would they have gained anything by attending," the Court held that the "Fifth Amendment does not require that all the parties be present when the judge inquires into such a minor occurrence." Citing *Taylor v. United States,* p. 1343 supra, in support, the Court then held the defendants had waived their rule 43 right to be present at every "stage of the trial" by their "total failure to assert their rights to attend the conference."

4. In *United States v. Fitzpatrick,* 437 F.2d 19 (2d Cir.1970), at the commencement of trial defense counsel moved to waive defendant's right to be present, but the motion was denied. On appeal, the defendant claimed this was reversible error. "This contention finds no support either in Rule 43 or in the case law. Rule 43 * * * does not give a defendant a right to absent himself from the courtroom, especially when his identification is the focal point of his trial."

SECTION 3. THE PRESENTATION OF EVIDENCE

1. *The opening statements.* Prior to the presentation of evidence, both sides may present opening statements. "The purpose of the opening statement is narrow and limited to a brief statement of the issues and an outline of what counsel believes he can support with competent and admissible evidence." *A.B.A. Standards Relating To The Prosecution Function and the Defense Function,* 119 (1971). In all jurisdictions, the prosecutor presents the initial opening statement. In some states, if the defense chooses to make an opening statement, it must do so immediately after the prosecution has completed its statement. In other jurisdictions, the defense may reserve giving its opening statement until after the close of the prosecutor's case.

Strategies differ on whether and when the defense should present its opening statement. There is an advantage in speaking immediately after the prosecution so as to offset the thrust of its statement, but there is also concern that the defense should not commit itself to the tack that it will take until it has seen the prosecution's case.

Since the opening statements are not to be argumentative, prohibitions against expressions of opinion, potentially inflammatory remarks, and the injection of irrelevant issues tend to be more strictly enforced in opening statements than closing statements. See Note 3, p. 1368 infra. On the other hand, as noted in N.D.A.A., *National Prosecution Standards* 248 (1977), a prosecutor's "overzealous and harmful assertions in an opening statement" usually will be viewed as "cured" by an appropriate "court admonition and instructions to the jury to disregard." In exceptional cases, however, a prosecutor's remarks have been so inflammatory, or the judge's response so inadequate, that appellate reversals have been granted. See LaFave and Israel, § 23.3(a).[a]

2. The most common appellate challenge to a prosecutor's opening statement is that it referred to evidence that subsequently was not admitted at trial. The opening statement may not refer to particular evidence "unless there is a good faith and reasonable basis for believing that such evidence will be tendered and admitted in evidence." I *A.B.A. Standards* § 3–5.5. What precautions must a prosecutor take to ensure that he meets this standard? If the prosecutor has referred to evidence that never was produced, what action should the trial court take? Consider, for example, the following case. Prior to trial, defense counsel warns the prosecutor that an alleged accomplice, who already has pled guilty, will invoke his privilege against self-incrimination if called as a prosecution witness. The prosecutor checks with the police officer in charge of the case, and the officer states that the accomplice will testify. The accomplice's probation officer and a close relative express a similar opinion. The prosecutor accordingly includes a brief summary of the accomplice's anticipated testimony in his opening statement. The accomplice does not testify, however, because he announces, when called, that he will invoke the privilege. The judge, in charging the jury, includes only the standard instruction that the jury "must not regard any statements made by counsel * * * concerning the facts * * * as evidence." See *Frazier v. Cupp,* 394 U.S. 731, 89 S.Ct. 1420, 22 L.Ed.2d 684 (1969) (finding no constitutional violation under roughly similar facts, though noting that a "more specific limiting instruction might have been desirable, but none was requested").

3. *The presentation of the prosecution's case.* In presenting its case-in-chief, the prosecution must offer sufficient evidence on each element of the crime to establish guilt beyond a reasonable doubt. See Note 1, p. 1369 infra. If the defense raises an affirmative defense through cross-examination of the prosecution's witnesses, the prosecution also may respond to that defense in its case-in-chief. (Where the defense first raises an affirmative defense during its presentation of evidence, the prosecution will respond in its rebuttal). The evidence introduced by the prosecution must, of course, be admissible under the rules of evidence.

a. Appellate courts rarely have the opportunity to consider the propriety of opening (or closing) statements by defense counsel. If the defendant is acquitted, the prosecution may not appeal. See Ch. 26, § 3. On a defense appeal from a conviction, the court is concerned only with prosecution errors—although an inappropriate closing statement by the defense may be a factor considered in determining whether the response of the prosecutor also was inappropriate. See Note 3, p. 1368 infra. If the trial court views a defense statement as so inappropriate as to require a mistrial, the validity of the mistrial will be subject to appellate review (under a double jeopardy claim) if the defendant is retried and convicted. While the appropriateness of the defense counsel's statement may be assessed at this point, that assessment often is clouded by other factors relevant to the double jeopardy claim. See, *Oregon v. Kennedy,* p. 1395 infra.

Should the prosecution have the right to introduce evidence on an element of the crime even though the defense desires to stipulate facts that would establish that element? The defense commonly will offer to stipulate where the prosecution's evidence is potentially prejudicial and is not inconsistent with the defense's intended presentation. Thus, where the defense in a murder case is relying on an alibi defense, it may be willing to stipulate to the fact of death in order to avoid gruesome photographs and medical testimony. See, e.g., *People v. Nicholls,* 245 N.E.2d 771 (Ill. 1969). Ordinarily the prosecution is not required to accept such a stipulation. Forcing acceptance of the stipulation, it is argued, deprives the prosecution of the "persuasiveness and forcefulness" of its evidence and may interfere with the "coherence" of its presentation. *People v. McClellan,* 457 P.2d 871 (Cal.1969). Nevertheless, courts also note that the trial judge has discretion to require acceptance of the stipulation in exceptional cases. See *United States v. Brinklow,* 560 F.2d 1008 (10th Cir.1977).

4. In several jurisdictions, the prosecution has an obligation to present all available eyewitnesses to the crime (sometimes called "res gestae" witnesses). In most jurisdictions, however, the prosecution is not obligated to call any particular witness. If the prosecutor fails to call an available witness whose testimony would clearly be relevant (e.g., the victim of the crime),[b] the defense may request a "missing witness" instruction. That instruction informs the jury that a party's failure to produce an available, material witness "may give rise to an inference that [the witness'] testimony would be unfavorable" to that party. See Devitt and Blackmar, *Federal Jury Practice and Instructions* § 17.19 (3d ed. 1977). The instruction is only available, however, where production of the witness is "peculiarly within the power" of one of the parties. Thus, if the prosecutor fails to produce an eyewitness and that witness is "equally available" to the defense through the use of its subpoena power, a missing witness instruction will not be given. See id.; *Shurman v. United States,* 233 F.2d 272 (5th Cir.1956) (where informer was known to defendant and was readily located in jail, he was equally available to the defense, and the trial court properly refused a missing witness instruction). If a key witness is "unavailable", the prosecution may request that the jury be so informed and directed not to draw any inferences from the witness' absence. See *Bowles v. United States,* 439 F.2d 536 (D.C.Cir.1970). See also fn. f, p. 936 supra (on the nature of "unavailability").

5. As noted in I *A.B.A. Standards* § 3–5.7(c), the prosecutor may not "call a witness who the prosecutor knows will claim a valid privilege * * * for the purpose of impressing upon the jury the fact of the claim of privilege." Violation of this prohibition may result in reversible error notwithstanding a judicial direction to the jury to ignore the claim of the privilege. See, e.g., *San Fratello v. United States,* 340 F.2d 560 (5th Cir.1965). Note, however, *Namet v. United States,* 373 U.S. 179, 83 S.Ct. 1151, 10 L.Ed.2d 278 (1963) (reversible error is not invariably committed when a witness claims the privilege in the presence of the jury; consideration must be given to such factors as the extent of prosecutorial misconduct, the relationship of the witness to the defendant, and the instructions of the court).

6. *Defendant's right of cross-examination.* All jurisdictions recognize both a defense and prosecution right to cross-examine the opposing party's witnesses. State law varies somewhat in defining the permissible scope of cross-examination, particularly as to questions that extend beyond the subject matter of the direct testimony and as

b. While the victim's reluctance to testify may be considered by the prosecutor in deciding whether to press charges, the victim must testify (or face contempt sanctions) if subpoenaed. It is no excuse, for example, that the victim is fearful of retaliation. See *People v. Carradine,* 287 N.E.2d 670 (Ill.1972).

to matters that may be raised in an attempt to impeach the witness. The permissible scope of cross-examination by the defense, however, may be taken beyond state law by federal constitutional requirements. The Sixth Amendment's confrontation clause has long been held to encompass a right of cross-examination. See *Pointer v. Texas,* p. 41 supra (collecting the earlier precedents). Accordingly, any state restriction upon the scope of cross-examination must be tested against that constitutional right. In *Smith v. Illinois,* 390 U.S. 129, 88 S.Ct. 748, 19 L.Ed.2d 956 (1968), and *Davis v. Alaska,* 415 U.S. 308, 94 S.Ct. 1105, 39 L.Ed.2d 347 (1974), state restrictions failed that test.[c]

In *Smith,* supra, the state's key witness was an informer who testified that he had purchased heroin from the defendant. The informer identified himself by reference to an alias, and defense questions as to his "correct name" and address were rejected as irrelevant by the trial court. The Supreme Court held that the trial court's ruling violated defendant's constitutional right of confrontation. Justice Stewart's opinion for the Court noted: "[W]hen the credibility of a witness is in issue, the very starting point in 'exposing falsehood and bringing out the truth' through cross-examination must necessarily be to ask the witness who he is and where he lives. The witness' name and address open countless avenues of in-court examination and out-of-court investigation. * * * 'It is the essence of a fair trial that reasonable latitude be given the cross-examiner, even though he is unable to state to the court what facts a reasonable cross-examination might develop. * * * To say that prejudice can be established only by showing that the cross-examination, if pursued, would necessarily have brought out facts tending to discredit the testimony in chief, is to deny a substantial right and withdraw one of the safeguards essential to a fair trial.' "

In *Davis,* supra, an important state witness in a burglary case was a juvenile (Green), who was on juvenile court probation. Prior to trial, the prosecutor requested a protective order barring cross-examination relating to Green's juvenile record. The defense opposed, noting its intention to show that Green was biased by the fear that his probation would be revoked if he did not testify favorably for the prosecution. The trial court granted the protective order, relying on a state statutory provision designed to protect the confidentiality of juvenile court records. The Supreme Court reversed. The Court, per Burger, C.J., noted: "The claim is made that the State has an important interest in protecting the anonymity of juvenile offenders and that this interest outweighs any competing interest this petitioner might have in cross-examining Green about his being on probation. * * * We do not and need not challenge the State's interest as a matter of its own policy in the administration of criminal justice to seek to preserve the anonymity of a juvenile offender. Here, however, petitioner sought to introduce evidence of Green's probation for the purpose of suggesting that Green was biased and, therefore, that his testimony was either not to be believed in his identification of petitioner or at least very carefully considered in that light. Serious damage to the strength of the State's case would have been a real possibility had petitioner been allowed to pursue this line of inquiry. In this setting we conclude that the right of confrontation is paramount to the State's policy of protecting a juvenile offender. Whatever temporary embarrassment might result to Green or his family by disclosure of his juvenile

c. *Smith* and *Davis* both were concerned with defense cross-examination of prosecution witnesses. Consider *Chambers v. Mississippi,* p. 1355 infra, as to the defendant's right to "cross-examine" a witness that he has called. Although *Chambers* discussed defendant's right to challenge a hostile defense witness as a right derived from the Sixth Amendment's confrontation clause, some commentators argue that it is more appropriately derived from the Sixth Amendment's compulsory process clause. See Westen, fn. d infra, at 601–13. Compare Graham, *The Confrontation Clause, the Hearsay Rule, and the Forgetful Witness,* 56 Tex.L.Rev. 151, 192 (1978).

record—if the prosecution insisted on using him to make its case—is out-weighed by petitioner's right to probe into the influence of possible bias in the testimony of a crucial identification witness." [d]

7. *Confrontation and the prosecution's use of hearsay.* The defendant's Sixth Amendment right of confrontation also limits the prosecution's use of statements of persons who do not testify at trial and therefore cannot be cross-examined. Such statements, when offered for their truth, ordinarily constitute hearsay and are admissible under local rules of evidence only when they fall within a recognized hearsay exception. The Court has stressed, however, that the crucial question under the confrontation clause is not compliance with common law hearsay rules, but fulfillment of the "mission of the confrontation clause to advance the accuracy of the truth determining process * * * by assuring that the trier of fact has a satisfactory basis for evaluating the truth of a prior statement." *California v. Green,* p. 936 supra. Hearsay exceptions will be acceptable only when they take into account this underlying function of cross-examination and rely on an acceptable substitute that provides a satisfactory "indicia of reliability." Id.

In OHIO v. ROBERTS, described at p. 938 supra, the Court summarized the limitations imposed upon the admission of hearsay under this functional analysis of the confrontation clause. The majority there noted:

"The Confrontation Clause operates in two separate ways to restrict the range of admissible hearsay. First, in conformance with the Framers' preference for face-to-face accusation, the Sixth Amendment establishes a rule of necessity. In the usual case (including cases where prior cross-examination has occurred), the prosecution must either produce or demonstrate the unavailability of the declarant whose statement it wishes to use against the defendant. See *Mancusi v. Stubbs; Barber v. Page.*[e] See also *California v. Green* [p. 936 supra].[7]

d. Do *Smith* and *Davis* add up to "the proposition that the defendant's right of cross-examination—like his right to be present at trial [see *Illinois v. Allen,* p. 1341 supra]—can be overcome, if at all, only for compelling reasons"? Westen, *Confrontation and Compulsory Process: A Unified Theory of Evidence for Criminal Cases,* 91 Harv.L.Rev. 567, 580–81 (1978).

Although some commentators assumed that the confrontation clause also might require the prosecution to disclose to the defense at least certain material that might be used in impeaching prosecution witnesses, *United States v. Bagley,* discussed at p. 1145 supra, held that any such constitutional obligation of the prosecution was governed by the due process standard of *Brady v. Maryland.*

e. Traditional grounds for unavailability are listed in Fed.R.Evid. 804(a), set forth in fn. f, p. 936 supra. *Mancusi v. Stubbs,* 408 U.S. 204, 92 S.Ct. 2308, 33 L.Ed.2d 293 (1972), held that permanent transfer to a foreign country was sufficient to establish unavailability, while *Barber v. Page,* 390 U.S. 719, 88 S.Ct. 1318, 20 L.Ed.2d 255 (1968), concluded that imprisonment in a federal prison was not sufficient where the state had made no effort to secure the prisoner's appearance through the cooperation of federal authorities. In *Roberts,* the Court divided as to the sufficiency of the prosecution's showing of unavailability. The majority held that the showing was sufficient where the witness' mother testified that (1) her daughter had left home, saying she was going to Tucson, over a year ago, (2) shortly thereafter a San Francisco social worker had contacted the mother concerning a welfare claim the daughter had filed there, (3) through the social worker, the mother had been able to reach the daughter once by phone, and (4) when the daughter last called, several months ago, she said that she "was travelling," but did not reveal her whereabouts. The majority concluded that the prosecutor "did not breach its duty of good-faith effort" by failing to go beyond the parents in seeking to locate the witness. The dissent (Brennan, J., joined by Marshall and Stevens, JJ.) argued that the "prosecution's mere speculation about the difficulty of locating [the missing witness] cannot relieve it of the obligation to find her" and the witness therefore could not be deemed unavailable where the prosecution had done "nothing whatsoever" except issue subpoenas in her name at her parents' address even after they knew she was no longer living there. The dissent suggested that "a skilled investigator armed with this information [from the mother] (and any additional facts not brought out through the voir dire [of the mother]) might have discovered [the witness'] whereabouts with reasonable efforts."

7. A demonstration of unavailability, however, is not always required. In *Dutton v. Evans,* 400 U.S. 74, 91 S.Ct. 210, 27 L.Ed.2d 213 (1970), for example, the Court found the utility of trial confrontation so remote that it did not require

"The second aspect operates once a witness is shown to be unavailable. Reflecting its underlying purpose to augment accuracy in the fact-finding process by ensuring the defendant an effective means to test adverse evidence, the Clause countenances only hearsay marked with such trustworthiness that 'there is no material departure from the reason of the general rule.' The principle recently was formulated in *Mancusi v. Stubbs:*

> 'The focus of the Court's concern has been to insure that there "are indicia of reliability which have been widely viewed as determinative of whether a statement may be placed before the jury though there is no confrontation of the declarant," *Dutton v. Evans,* and to "afford the trier of fact a satisfactory basis for evaluating the truth of the prior statement." *California v. Green.* It is clear from these statements, and from numerous prior decisions of this Court, that even though the witness be unavailable his prior testimony must bear some of these "indicia of reliability." 408 U.S., at 213, 92 S.Ct., at 2513.

"The Court has applied this 'indicia of reliability' requirement principally by concluding that certain hearsay exceptions rest upon such solid foundations that admission of virtually any evidence within them comports with the 'substance of the constitutional protection.' This reflects the truism that 'hearsay rules and the Confrontation Clause are generally designed to protect similar values,' *California v. Green,* and 'stem from the same roots.' *Dutton v. Evans.* It also responds to the need for certainty in the workaday world of conducting criminal trials.

"In sum, when a hearsay declarant is not present for cross-examination at trial, the Confrontation Clause normally requires a showing that he is unavailable. Even then, his statement is admissible only if it bears adequate 'indicia of reliability.' Reliability can be inferred without more in a case where the evidence falls within a firmly rooted hearsay exception. In other cases, the evidence must be excluded, at least absent a showing of particularized guarantees of trustworthiness."

8. *The defendant's right to obtain witnesses.* All jurisdictions have statutes or court rules authorizing defense use of the court's subpoena power to compel the attendance of witnesses at trial. Fed.R.Crim.P. 17 is a typical provision. Subsection (a) directs the clerk to issue a subpoena "signed and sealed but otherwise in blank" upon request of the defense. If the defendant is indigent (i.e., "financially unable to pay the witness fee"), subsection (b) directs that the subpoena be issued upon an ex parte showing that the "presence of the witness is necessary to an adequate defense." Lower courts have held that, in light of defendant's "Sixth Amendment right to compulsory process" and his "Fifth Amendment right not to be subject to disabilities * * * because of financial status," the "word 'necessary' must be read to mean [only] relevant, material, and

the prosecution to produce a seemingly available witness.

[In *Dutton,* defendant Evans was indicted for murder and tried separately from his alleged accomplice, Williams. The prosecution presented a strong case, including another accomplice who testified under an immunity grant and described the killings by Evans in detail. Another prosecution witness (Shaw) testified that when he asked Williams how he made out at arraignment, Williams responded, "If it hadn't been for that dirty son-of-a-bitch Alex Evans, we wouldn't be in this now." This testimony was admitted under the Georgia version of the co-conspirators exception to the hearsay rule, which permits introduction of a co-conspirator's statement even if it was made during the concealment phase of the conspiracy. Justice Stewart's plurality opinion, concluded that the Sixth Amendment right to confrontation was not violated. The plurality opinion apparently assumed that Williams was an available witness, noting that Evans' counsel had himself acknowledged that he could have called Williams but did not do so because "this course was not in the best interest of his client." The plurality opinion reasoned that Evans exercised fully his right to cross-examine witness Shaw as to whether he actually heard Williams make the alleged statement, and that Evans' inability to cross-examine Williams was not significant under the circumstances.]

useful to an adequate defense." *United States v. Barker,* 553 F.2d 1013, 1020 (6th Cir.1977). In several states, indigent defendants have the right to subpoena a certain number of witnesses at government expense without making any showing of materiality. See, e.g., Mont.Rev.Code § 95–1801(b) (6 witnesses). On the other hand, other jurisdictions are more restrictive than the federal courts in dealing with indigent defendants. A few require a more substantial showing of need while others require the showing to be made in an open proceeding that may be attended by the prosecutor. See Westen, *Compulsory Process II,* 74 Mich.L.Rev. 191, 251–76 (1975) (discussing the constitutionality of these and other restrictions upon the indigent's access to the court's subpoena authority). In a state case, a defendant who seeks to compel the attendance of a witness located in another state also must show that the witness is "material and necessary." See the Uniform Act to Secure the Attendance of Witnesses From Without A State in Criminal Proceedings § 2, 11 U.L.A. 2 (1974).

9. The defendant's Sixth Amendment right to compulsory process may not be satisfied by simply issuing process at the defendant's request. The state also has a responsibility not to take actions that undermine the defendant's use of the subpoena authority. Consider, e.g., *Webb v. Texas,* 409 U.S. 95, 93 S.Ct. 351, 34 L.Ed.2d 330 (1972). The defendant's sole witness had an extensive criminal record and currently was serving a prison sentence. Before the witness took the stand, the trial judge, on his own initiative, warned him against committing perjury. The judge told the witness that if he told the truth, he would be "all right," but if he lied, he could "get into real trouble." The judge warned that he would "personally see" that any lies were brought to the attention of the grand jury. A conviction for perjury, the judge added "is probably going to mean several years" and "will be held against you * * * when you're up for parole." The judge also noted that the witness "didn't owe anybody anything to testify." After hearing these remarks and the judge's comment to defense counsel that the witness could "decline to testify," the witness refused to give testimony. The Supreme Court reversed the defendant's conviction on due process grounds (although it quoted extensively from a leading compulsory process case, *Washington v. Texas,* Note 12 infra). "In the circumstances of this case," the Court concluded, the judge's remarks violated defendant's right to a fair trial. The judge's admonition had been cast in "unnecessarily strong terms" and "effectively drove the witness off the stand." [f]

In UNITED STATES v. VALENZUELA–BERNAL, 458 U.S. 858, 102 S.Ct. 3440, 73 L.Ed.2d 1193 (1982), the Supreme Court reversed a Ninth Circuit ruling that the principles underlying *Webb* barred a government practice of prompt deportations of smuggled aliens that resulted in the aliens being shipped back to Mexico before counsel for the defendant charged with the smuggling even had an opportunity to interview them. The majority, per REHNQUIST, J., noted that the Court of Appeals had failed to give sufficient weight to the government's "manifold responsibilities" in immigration cases. Those responsibilities included not only the enforcement of the criminal law, but

f. Consider also Clinton, *The Right to Present A Defense: An Emergent Constitutional Guarantee in Criminal Trials,* 9 Ind.L.Rev. 711, 848 (1976): "Although the *Webb* case dealt only with judicial admonitions * * *, other cases hold that prosecutorial efforts to harass or discourage defense witnesses also constitute a denial of the right to present a defense. Such prosecutorial efforts have been known to include not only perjury admonitions, but also direct threats of prosecution or arrest for testifying for the defense. Of course, the right guaranteed the accused is not violated merely because the court or prosecutor has interjected a single discouraging comment. The cases properly suggest that the accused must demonstrate that he was in fact denied the witness' testimony or that the witness changed his testimony as a result of harassment or discouragement."

also the faithful execution of congressional policy favoring prompt deportation of illegal aliens and the avoidance of unnecessary financial and physical burdens involved in prolonged detentions, as well as the "human cost" to the detained witness-alien. In light of these additional responsibilities, the majority noted, the Government's decision to deport was "not to be judged by standards which might be appropriate if the Government's only responsibility were to prosecute criminal offenses." Accordingly, appropriate analogies were to be found in decisions such as *Brady v. Maryland* [p. 1146 supra], and *Roviaro v. United States* [Note 10 infra], all of which required a showing as to the materiality and favorable nature of lost evidence in establishing a constitutional violation. The majority concluded:

"To summarize, the responsibility of the Executive Branch faithfully to execute the immigration policy adopted by Congress justifies the prompt deportation of illegal-alien witnesses upon the Executive's good-faith determination that they possess no evidence favorable to the defendant in a criminal prosecution. The mere fact that the Government deports such witnesses is not sufficient to establish a violation of the Compulsory Process Clause of the Sixth Amendment or the Due Process Clause of the Fifth Amendment. A violation of these provisions requires some showing that the evidence lost would be both material and favorable to the defense. * * * Sanctions may be imposed on the Government for deporting witnesses only if the criminal defendant makes a plausible showing that the testimony of the deported witnesses would have been material and favorable to his defense, in ways not merely cumulative to the testimony of available witnesses. * * * In making such a determination, courts should afford some leeway for the fact that the defendant necessarily proffers a description of the material evidence rather than the evidence itself. Because determinations of materiality are often best made in light of all of the evidence adduced at trial, judges may wish to defer ruling on motions until after the presentation of evidence." [g]

In dissent, Justice BRENNAN, joined by Marshall, J., contended that the Government should be required to follow the procedure adopted in the Southern District of California, which "represents a practical and sensitive accommodation between a criminal defendant's constitutional rights under the Compulsory Process Clause and the Government's policy of prompt deportation of illegal aliens." Under that procedure, "illegal-alien eyewitnesses are held in custody for a short period of time—about ten days—after appointment of counsel for the criminal defendant." During that period, defense counsel may interview the witnesses, and determine whether they can provide "testimony material to the defense." A magistrate would then hold a material witness bail review hearing, pursuant to 18 USC § 3149, with the witness being immediately deported if neither the prosecution nor defense could show materiality. Since the Government, in contrast with this procedure, had adopted in this case "a wholly

g. In a brief opinion, concurring in the judgment of the Court, Justice Blackmun noted that "at least a 'plausible theory' of how the testimony of the deported witness would be helpful to the defense must be offered, [but] none was advanced here." Also concurring in the judgment, Justice O'Connor noted her concern that the standard announced by the Court "may not protect adequately the interests of the prosecution and the defense in a fair trial and may encourage litigation over whether the defendant has made a 'plausible showing.'" She suggested that the Court, in the exercise of its supervisory power, should impose a requirement of brief detention of potential alien witnesses so as to permit defense interviews. With this procedure, roughly similar to that described by the dissent, the "deportation of alien witnesses without affording the defense an opportunity to interview them" would be only an "occasional event." In that exceptional case, Justice O'Connor noted, she "agree[d] with the Court that sanctions should be available against the Government if defendant sets forth some plausible theory explaining how the deported witnesses would have provided material evidence that was not simply cumulative of evidence readily available to the defendant."

unilateral procedure," the defendant should not be required to demonstrate materiality.

10. Does the prosecution have an obligation to assist the defendant in finding potential defense witnesses? Consider ROVIARO v. UNITED STATES, 353 U.S. 53, 77 S.Ct. 623, 1 L.Ed.2d 639 (1957). Defendant was charged with (1) an illegal sale of heroin to "John Doe," and (2) illegal transportation of heroin. Before trial, defendant moved for a bill of particulars listing, inter alia, Doe's name and address. The motion was denied on the ground that Doe was an informer and his identity was privileged. At trial, the court again rejected defense attempts, through cross-examination, to learn Doe's identity. The government itself did not call Doe, but relied entirely on the testimony of two investigative officers. The first officer (Durham) had Doe under surveillance on the night of the alleged transaction. He testified that Doe picked up the defendant on a street corner and drove to another location where the defendant left the car, picked up a package near a tree, gave the package to Doe, and walked away. The second officer (Bryson), who was hidden in the trunk of Doe's car, testified that he heard defendant discuss with Doe the proposed transfer of the package (which contained narcotics). The Supreme Court reversed the defendant's conviction in the exercise of its supervisory power. Justice BURTON's opinion for the (6–1) majority noted:

"Petitioner contends that the trial court erred in upholding the right of the Government to withhold the identity of John Doe. He argues that Doe was an active participant in the illegal activity charged and that, therefore, the Government could not withhold his identity, his whereabouts, and whether he was alive or dead at the time of trial. The Government does not defend the nondisclosure of Doe's identity with respect to Count 1, which charged a sale of heroin to John Doe, but it attempts to sustain the judgment on the basis of the conviction on Count 2, charging illegal transportation of narcotics. It argues that the conviction on Count 2 may properly be upheld since the identity of the informer, in the circumstances of this case, has no real bearing on that charge and is therefore privileged.

"What is usually referred to as the informer's privilege is in reality the Government's privilege to withhold from disclosure the identity of persons who furnish information of violations of law to officers charged with enforcement of that law. The purpose of the privilege is the furtherance and protection of the public interest in effective law enforcement. The privilege recognizes the obligation of citizens to communicate their knowledge of the commission of crimes to law-enforcement officials and, by preserving their anonymity, encourages them to perform that obligation. * * * [But] [w]here the disclosure of an informer's identity, or of the contents of his communication, is relevant and helpful to the defense of an accused, or is essential to a fair determination of a cause, the privilege must give way. In these situations the trial court may require disclosure and, if the Government withholds the information, dismiss the action. * * *

"We believe that no fixed rule with respect to disclosure is justifiable. The problem is one that calls for balancing the public interest in protecting the flow of information against the individual's right to prepare his defense. Whether a proper balance renders nondisclosure erroneous must depend on the particular circumstances of each case, taking into consideration the crime charged, the possible defenses, the possible significance of the informer's testimony, and other relevant factors. The materiality of John Doe's possible testimony must be determined by reference to the offense charged in Count 2 and the evidence relating to that count. * * * While John Doe is not expressly mentioned, this charge, when viewed in connection with the evidence introduced at the trial, is so closely related to John Doe as to make his identity and testimony highly material. * * *

"The circumstances of this case demonstrate that John Doe's possible testimony was highly relevant and might have been helpful to the defense. So far as petitioner knew, he and John Doe were alone and unobserved during the crucial occurrence for which he was indicted. Unless petitioner waived his constitutional right not to take the stand in his own defense, John Doe was his one material witness. Petitioner's opportunity to cross-examine Police Officer Bryson and Federal Narcotics Agent Durham was hardly a substitute for an opportunity to examine the man who had been nearest to him and took part in the transaction. Doe had helped to set up the criminal occurrence and had played a prominent part in it. His testimony might have disclosed an entrapment. He might have thrown doubt upon petitioner's identity or on the identity of the package. He was the only witness who might have testified to petitioner's possible lack of knowledge of the contents of the package that he 'transported' from the tree to John Doe's car. The desirability of calling John Doe as a witness, or at least interviewing him in preparation for trial, was a matter for the accused rather than the Government to decide.

"Finally, the Government's use against petitioner of his conversation with John Doe while riding in Doe's car particularly emphasizes the unfairness of the nondisclosure in this case. The only person, other than petitioner himself, who could controvert, explain or amplify Bryson's report of this important conversation was John Doe. Contradiction or amplification might have borne upon petitioner's knowledge of the contents of the package or might have tended to show an entrapment.

"This is a case where the Government's informer was the sole participant, other than the accused, in the transaction charged. The informer was the only witness in a position to amplify or contradict the testimony of government witnesses. Moreover, a government witness testified that Doe denied knowing petitioner or ever having seen him before. We conclude that, under these circumstances, the trial court committed prejudicial error in permitting the Government to withhold the identity of its undercover employee in the face of repeated demands by the accused for his disclosure." [h]

11. Although *Roviaro* was based on the Court's supervisory jurisdiction over federal courts, both lower courts and commentators have viewed the Court's "reasoning and language" as "suggest[ing] that the decision was constitutionally compelled." Westen, *The Compulsory Process Clause,* 73 Mich.L.Rev. 71, 165 (1974). Can *Roviaro* 's reasoning be extended to establish a Sixth Amendment grounding for a defense right to a lineup? See Note 6, p. 1162 supra. Might it require a modification of state practice governing pretrial disclosure? The *Roviaro* opinion noted that, since Doe's crucial role on count 1 was apparent from the face of the charge, the trial court there erred in denying the bill of particulars as well as in refusing to require disclosure at trial. Compare Note 7, p. 1026 supra. See also Ch. 20, § 3.

12. *The defendant's right to a witness' testimony.* Consider WASHINGTON v. TEXAS, 388 U.S. 14, 87 S.Ct. 1920, 18 L.Ed.2d 1019 (1967). Defendant Washington was charged with a murder that arose out of a confrontation at a friend's

h. Lower courts generally have required disclosure, upon defense request, of eyewitness informants to the crime even though the police witnesses were also present and in the same position as the informant. In most of these cases, the eyewitness informant was also a participant in the illegal transaction. But see *United States v. Roberts,* 388 F.2d 646 (2d Cir.1968) (informant was present, but did not participate in the narcotics sale). On the other hand, the lower courts consistently have held that disclosure is not required where the informant merely provided information concerning the offense (e.g., informed police of the location of contraband). LaFave and Israel, § 23.3(e).

house. Defendant testified that his alleged accomplice (Fuller) had the gun, that he had tried to persuade Fuller to leave, and that he was withdrawing from the scene when he heard the shooting. He then offered Fuller (who had already been convicted) as a defense witness, noting that Fuller would testify that he acted on his own in firing the fatal shot. Fuller was not permitted to testify because a Texas statute rendered accomplices incompetent to testify for one another, although there was no bar to their testifying for the state. The Supreme Court unanimously reversed defendant's conviction, with eight justices finding a violation of defendant's Sixth Amendment right to compulsory process. (Justice Harlan concurred on due process grounds). The opinion for the Court (per WARREN, C.J.) initially rejected the contention that the Sixth Amendment had no relevance since the state had not refused to subpoena Fuller, but had simply refused to permit him to testify under a local rule of evidence. Turning to the history of the Sixth Amendment, the Court noted that a primary purpose of the Amendment was to reaffirm the common law's repudiation of its earlier rule that rendered incompetent all witnesses for the defense in felony cases. The Sixth Amendment was designed to guarantee the defendant's right "to put his witnesses on the stand, as well as the right to compel their attendance in court." In light of this history, the Court continued, the state's refusal to permit Fuller to testify was invalid:

"[I]t could hardly be argued that a State would not violate the [compulsory process] clause if it made all defense testimony inadmissible as a matter of procedural law. It is difficult to see how the Constitution is any less violated by arbitrary rules that prevent whole categories of defense witnesses from testifying on the basis of a priori categories that presume them unworthy of belief. The rule disqualifying an alleged accomplice from testifying on behalf of the defendant cannot even be defended on the ground that it rationally sets apart a group of persons who are particularly likely to commit perjury. The absurdity of the rule is amply demonstrated by the exceptions that have been made to it. For example, the accused accomplice may be called by the prosecution to testify against the defendant. Common sense would suggest that he often has a greater interest in lying in favor of the prosecution rather than against it, especially if he is still awaiting his own trial or sentencing. To think that criminals will lie to save their fellows but not to obtain favors from the prosecution for themselves is indeed to clothe the criminal class with more nobility than one might expect to find in the public at large. * * *

"We hold that the petitioner in this case was denied his right to have compulsory process for obtaining witnesses in his favor because the State arbitrarily denied him the right to put on the stand a witness who was physically and mentally capable of testifying to events that he had personally observed and whose testimony would have been relevant and material to the defense.[21] The Framers of the Constitution did not intend to commit the futile act of giving to a defendant the right to secure the attendance of witnesses whose testimony he had no right to use."

13. Consider also CHAMBERS v. MISSISSIPPI, 410 U.S. 284, 93 S.Ct. 1038, 35 L.Ed.2d 297 (1973). *Chambers* arose from what has been described as a "bizarre, yet compelling, set of facts." See Clinton, fn. f supra. A police officer, Liberty, was killed during an incident in

21. Nothing in this opinion should be construed as disapproving testimonial privileges, such as the privilege against self-incrimination or the lawyer-client or husband-wife privilege, which are based on entirely different considerations from those underlying the common-law disqualifications for interest. Nor do we deal in this case with nonarbitrary state rules that disqualify as witnesses persons who, because of mental infirmity or infancy, are incapable of observing events or testifying about them.

which a group of 20–25 men tried to prevent an arrest. Before Liberty died, he took deliberate aim and fired into an alley from which the fatal shots had been fired. His shot hit Chambers, who later was charged with Liberty's homicide. The state's case against Chambers rested primarily on the fact that Liberty had deliberately fired at Chambers and on the testimony of two police officers. One officer testified that he saw Chambers shoot Liberty; the other testified that he could not see whether Chambers had a gun, but he did see Chambers "break his arm down" shortly before the shots were fired.

In his defense, Chambers sought to introduce evidence relating to the guilt of McDonald, who also had been present at the scene. McDonald allegedly had told several persons that he had killed Liberty and had given Chambers attorney a sworn confession, which he later repudiated. At the trial, one defense witness testified that he saw McDonald shoot Liberty, and another testified that he saw McDonald with a gun in his hand. Chambers also sought to have testify three witnesses to whom McDonald allegedly had admitted his guilt. Their testimony as to McDonald's confession was barred on the ground that it constituted hearsay. Chambers also called McDonald to the stand, and had his sworn confession admitted in evidence. On cross-examination by the state, McDonald noted his prior repudiation of the confession, professed his innocence, and offered an alibi. Defense counsel then asked to be allowed to examine McDonald under the "adverse witness exception" to the rule that a party may not impeach his own witness. That request was denied. McDonald did not fall within the exception, the state court noted, because "[n]owhere did he point the finger at Chambers."

A nearly unanimous (8–1) Supreme Court reversed Chambers' conviction. The Court relied on due process rather than Sixth Amendment grounds, arguably because of jurisdictional reservations relating to Chambers' presentation of his claims in the state proceedings. See Westen, fn. d supra, at 607. Justice POWELL's opinion for the Court stressed the combined impact of the refusal to permit examination of McDonald as an adverse witness and the exclusion of the testimony of those persons to whom McDonald made oral confessions. The opinion noted:

[P]etitioner's request to cross-examine McDonald was denied on the basis of a Mississippi common-law rule that a party may not impeach his own witness. The rule rests on the presumption—without regard to the circumstances of the particular case—that a party who calls a witness 'vouches for his credibility.' Although the historical origins of the 'voucher' rule are uncertain, it appears to be a remnant of primitive English trial practice in which 'oath-takers' or 'compurgators' were called to stand behind a particular party's position in any controversy. Their assertions were strictly partisan and, quite unlike witnesses in criminal trials today, their role bore little relation to the impartial ascertainment of the facts.

"Whatever validity the 'voucher' rule may have once enjoyed, and apart from whatever usefulness it retains today in the civil trial process, it bears little present relationship to the realities of the criminal process. It might have been logical for the early common law to require a party to vouch for the credibility of witnesses he brought before the jury to affirm his veracity. Having selected them especially for that purpose, the party might reasonably be expected to stand firmly behind their testimony. But in modern criminal trials, defendants are rarely able to select their witnesses: they must take them where they find them. Moreover, as applied in this case, the 'voucher' rule's impact was doubly harmful to Chambers' efforts to develop his defense. Not only was he precluded from cross-examining McDonald, but, as the State conceded at oral argument, he was also restricted in the scope of his direct examination by the rule's corollary requirement that the party calling the witness is bound by anything he might say. * * *

"In this Court, Mississippi has not sought to defend the rule or explain its underlying rationale. Nor has it contended that its rule should override the accused's right of confrontation. Instead, it argues that there is no incompatability between the rule and Chambers' rights because no right of confrontation exists unless the testifying witness is 'adverse' to the accused. The State's brief asserts that the 'right of confrontation applies to witnesses "*against*" an accused.' * * * [This] argument that McDonald's testimony was not 'adverse' to, or 'against,' Chambers is not convincing. The State's proof at trial excluded the theory that more than one person participated in the shooting of Liberty. To the extent that McDonald's sworn confession tended to incriminate him, it tended also to exculpate Chambers. And, in the circumstances of this case, McDonald's retraction inculpated Chambers to the same extent that it exculpated McDonald. * * * The availability of the right to confront and to cross-examine those who give damaging testimony against the accused has never been held to depend on whether the witness was initially put on the stand by the accused or by the State. We reject the notion that a right of such substance in the criminal process may be governed by that technicality or by any narrow and unrealistic definition of the word 'against.' The 'voucher' rule, as applied in this case, plainly interfered with Chambers' right to defend against the State's charges.

"We need not decide, however, whether this error alone would occasion reversal since Chambers' claimed denial of due process rests on the ultimate impact of that error when viewed in conjunction with the trial court's refusal to permit him to call other witnesses. The trial court refused to allow him to introduce the testimony of Hardin, Turner, and Carter. Each would have testified to the statements purportedly made by McDonald, on three separate occasions shortly after the crime, naming himself as the murderer. The State Supreme Court approved the exclusion of this evidence on the ground that it was hearsay.

"The hearsay rule, which has long been recognized and respected by virtually every State, is based on experience and grounded in the notion that untrustworthy evidence should not be presented to the triers of fact. * * * A number of exceptions have developed over the years to allow admission of hearsay statements made under circumstances that tend to assure reliability and thereby compensate for the absence of the oath and opportunity for cross-examination. Among the most prevalent of these exceptions is the one applicable to declarations against interest—an exception founded on the assumption that a person is unlikely to fabricate a statement against his own interest at the time it is made. Mississippi recognizes this exception but applies it only to declarations against pecuniary interest. It recognizes no such exception for declarations, like McDonald's in this case, that are against the penal interest of the declarant.

"This materialistic limitation on the declaration-against-interest hearsay exception appears to be accepted by most States in their criminal trial processes, although a number of States have discarded it. * * * Exclusion, where the limitation prevails, is usually premised on the view that admission would lead to the frequent presentation of perjured testimony to the jury. It is believed that confessions of criminal activity are often motivated by extraneous considerations and, therefore, are not as inherently reliable as statements against pecuniary or proprietary interest. While that rationale has been the subject of considerable scholarly criticism, we need not decide in this case whether, under other circumstances, it might serve some valid state purpose by excluding untrustworthy testimony.

"The hearsay statements involved in this case were originally made and subsequently offered at trial under circumstances that provided considerable assurance of their reliability. First, each of McDonald's confessions was made spontaneously to a close acquaintance shortly after the murder had occurred. Second, each one was corroborated by some other evidence in the case—McDonald's sworn confession, the testimony of an eye-witness to the shooting, the testimony that McDonald was seen with a gun immediately after the shooting, and proof of his prior ownership of a .22-caliber revolver and subsequent purchase of a new weapon. The sheer number of independent confessions provided additional corroboration for each. Third, whatever may be the parameters of the penal-interest rationale, each confession here was in a very real sense self-incriminatory and unquestionably against interest. McDonald stood to benefit nothing by disclosing his role in the shooting to any of his three friends and he must have been aware of the possibility that disclosure would lead to criminal prosecution. Indeed, after telling Turner of his involvement, he subsequently urged Turner not to 'mess him up.' Finally, if there was any question about the truthfulness of the extrajudicial statements, McDonald was present in the courtroom and was under oath. He could have been cross-examined by the State, and his demeanor and responses weighed by the jury. * * *

"We conclude that the exclusion of this critical evidence, coupled with the State's refusal to permit Chambers to cross-examine McDonald, denied him a trial in accord with traditional and fundamental standards of due process. In reaching this judgment, we establish no new principles of constitutional law. Nor does our holding signal any diminution in the respect traditionally accorded to the States in the establishment and implementation of their own criminal trial rules and procedures. Rather, we hold quite simply that under the facts and circumstances of this case the rulings of the trial court deprived Chambers of a fair trial."

14. In light of *Chambers* and *Washington,* is there a constitutional violation in any of the cases described below?

(a) The defendant was arrested by two department store detectives for shoplifting. At trial, the prosecution called one of the detectives and a store clerk, but not the other detective who had actually signed the complaint. Defendant then called the other detective, but he confirmed the testimony of his colleague. Defendant was barred from further examination designed to bring out the fact that the detective had told a somewhat different story when interviewed by defendant's father (a retired lawyer). The trial court noted that state law permitted a defendant to impeach "his own witness" with a prior inconsistent statement "only if the prior statement is either sworn or subscribed." See *Lipinski v. New York,* 557 F.2d 289 (2d Cir.1977) (finding no constitutional violation in light of the limited role that further impeachment would have played, and the New York, prohibition against use of the statement as substantive evidence). Cf. *United States v. Nobles,* p. 1141 supra.

(b) Defendant, charged with murder, claimed that Smith had committed the crime. Both defendant and a defense witness testified that Smith had admitted committing the crime in their presence. The district court refused, however, to permit the defendant to call Smith after it was ascertained that Smith would invoke his privilege against self-incrimination. The court also barred defense counsel from informing the jury that Smith had invoked the privilege. Defendant did not request an instruction informing the jury that Smith was not available to testify. See *Bowles v. United States,* 439 F.2d 536 (D.C. Cir.1970) (no error found). Compare *Stewart v. State,* 355 So.2d 94 (Miss.1978) (trial court should have permitted witness to be called where he would have answered some questions, even though he would have invoked the privilege as to most questions). Cf. Note 5 supra.

(c) At the start of the trial, the court invoked the "witness rule," requiring that witnesses be sequestered prior to their testimony. A defense witness who arrived late missed the instruction, and, unknown to counsel, remained in the courtroom while part of the prosecution's evidence was presented. The witness then was prevented from testifying because he had violated the witness rule. See *Braswell v. Wainwright,* 463 F.2d 1148 (5th Cir.1972) (under these circumstances, preclusion sanction violated defendant's Sixth Amendment right to compulsory process). See also *United States v. Kiliyan,* 456 F.2d 555 (8th Cir.1972) (preclusion of wife's testimony upheld where she remained in the courtroom though well aware of the "witness rule").

15. Consider LaFave and Israel, § 23.3(f): "In *Washington v. Texas,* the Supreme Court noted that the decision should not be construed 'as disapproving testimonial privileges, such as the privilege against self-incrimination.' This would suggest, as a great many courts have held, that there is no general right of a criminal defendant to have use immunity granted to a witness so that the witness can testify on the defendant's behalf. No such right has been found in the compulsory process clause, for it 'gives the defendant the right to bring his witness to court and have the witness's non-privileged testimony heard, but does not carry with it the additional right to displace a proper claim of privilege, including the privilege against self-incrimination. . . . While the prosecutor may prevent or discourage a defense witness from testifying, . . . it is difficult to see how the Sixth Amendment of its own force places upon either the prosecutor or the court any affirmative obligation to secure testimony from a defense witness by replacing the protection of the self-incrimination privilege with a grant of use immunity.' A 'more plausible basis for defense witness immunity' is the requirement of basic fairness emanating from the due process clause. * * * Several courts have suggested that in a case where the government relies on the testimony of witnesses who have received a grant of immunity, it then may have an obligation, as a matter of fundamental fairness, to grant use immunity for defense witnesses as well. In response, it is argued that 'in the context of criminal investigation and criminal trials, where accuser and accused have inherently different roles, with entirely different powers and rights, equalization is not a sound principle on which to extend any particular procedural device.' Another type of due process argument is that denial of defense witness immunity may in some circumstances thwart the search for the truth. Under *Brady v. Maryland,* the government as a general rule is obligated to divulge exculpatory evidence. It does not necessarily follow, [however], that the government is required to assist the defense in extracting evidence from others or that all lawful privileges must give way to the search for the truth."

Commentators and some courts have suggested that the crucial concern in the witness-immunity situation is not the protection of the witness' self-incrimination privilege, for the grant of use/derivative-use immunity leaves the witness "in no better or worse legal position than before," but the impact upon the government's ability to subsequently prosecute the witness. Can a court appropriately balance on a case-by-case basis the government's interest in a possibly lost prosecution against the defendant's interest in testimony that might establish his innocence? See Garth, J., concurring in *United States v. Herman,* 589 F.2d 1191 (3d Cir.1978). Can it at least seek to determine whether the government's refusal to grant the witness immunity stems from the "deliberate intention of distorting the fact finding process" as opposed to a prosecution interest in a possible subsequent prosecution? See *Government of the Virgin Islands v. Smith,* 615 F.2d 964 (3d Cir.1980). Compare

United States v. Turkish, 623 F.2d 769 (2d Cir.1980) (asserting that such an inquiry would "propel a trial court into uncharted waters," but leaving open the possibility of a different approach where the prosecutor "cannot or prefers not to present any claim that the witness is a potential defendant" and the defense "demonstrates that the witness's testimony will clearly be material, exculpatory, and not cumulative").

SECTION 4. THE DEFENDANT'S RIGHT TO REMAIN SILENT

GRIFFIN v. CALIFORNIA

380 U.S. 609, 85 S.Ct. 1229, 14 L.Ed.2d 106 (1965).

MR. JUSTICE DOUGLAS delivered the opinion of the Court.

Petitioner was convicted of murder in the first degree after a jury trial in the California court. He did not testify at the trial on the issue of guilt, though he did testify at the separate trial on the issue of penalty. The trial court instructed the jury on the issue of guilt, stating that a defendant has a constitutional right not to testify. But it told the jury: [2]

> "As to any evidence or facts against him which the defendant can reasonably be expected to deny or explain because of facts within his knowledge, if he does not testify or if, though he does testify, he fails to deny or explain such evidence, the jury may take that failure into consideration as tending to indicate the truth of such evidence and as indicating that among the inferences that may be reasonably drawn therefrom those unfavorable to the defendant are the more probable."

It added, however, that no such inference could be drawn as to evidence respecting which he had no knowledge. It stated that failure of a defendant to deny or explain the evidence of which he had knowledge does not create a presumption of guilt nor by itself warrant an inference of guilt nor relieve the prosecution of any of its burden of proof.

Petitioner had been seen with the deceased the evening of her death, the evidence placing him with her in the alley where her body was found. The prosecutor made much of the failure of petitioner to testify:

> "The defendant certainly knows whether Essie Mae had this beat up appearance at the time he left her apartment and went down the alley with her.
>
> "What kind of a man is it that would want to have sex with a woman that beat up if she was beat up at the time he left?
>
> "He would know that. He would know how she got down the alley. He would know how the blood got on the bottom of the concrete steps. He would know how long he was with her in that box. He would know how her wig got off. He would know whether he beat her or mistreated her. He would know whether he walked away from that place cool as a cucumber when he saw Mr. Villasenor because he was conscious of his own guilt and wanted to get away from that damaged or injured woman.
>
> "These things he has not seen fit to take the stand and deny or explain.
>
> "And in the whole world, if anybody would know, this defendant would know.
>
> "Essie Mae is dead, she can't tell you her side of the story. The defendant won't."

The death penalty was imposed and the California Supreme Court affirmed. The case is here on a petition for a writ of certiorari which we granted to consider the single question whether comment on

2. Article I, § 13, of the California Constitution provides in part:

"* * * in any criminal case, whether the defendant testifies or not, his failure to explain or to deny by his testimony any evidence or facts in the case against him may be commented upon by the court and by counsel, and may be considered by the court or the jury."

the failure to testify violated the Self-Incrimination Clause of the Fifth Amendment which we made applicable to the States by the Fourteenth in *Malloy v. Hogan,* 378 U.S. 1, 84 S.Ct. 1489, 12 L.Ed. 2d 653 (1964), decided after the Supreme Court of California had affirmed the present conviction.[3]

If this were a federal trial, reversible error would have been committed. *Wilson v. United States,* 149 U.S. 60, 13 S.Ct. 765, 37 L.Ed. 650 [1893] so holds. It is said, however, that the *Wilson* decision rested not on the Fifth Amendment, but on an Act of Congress. 18 U.S.C. § 3481. That indeed is the fact, as the opinion of the Court in the *Wilson* case states. * * * But that is the beginning, not the end of our inquiry. The question remains whether, statute or not, the comment rule, approved by California, violates the Fifth Amendment.

We think it does. It is in substance a rule of evidence that allows the State the privilege of tendering to the jury for its consideration the failure of the accused to testify. No formal offer of proof is made as in other situations; but the prosecutor's comment and the court's acquiescence are the equivalent of an offer of evidence and its acceptance. The Court in the *Wilson* case stated:

> "* * * the Act was framed with a due regard also to those who might prefer to rely upon the presumption of innocence which the law gives to every one, and not wish to be witnesses. It is not every one who can safely venture on the witness stand, though entirely innocent of the charge against him. Excessive timidity, nervousness when facing others and attempting to explain transactions of a suspicious character, and offenses charged against him, will often confuse and embarrass him to such a degree as to increase rather than remove prejudices against him. It is not every one, however honest, who would therefore willingly be placed on the witness stand. The statute, in tenderness to the weakness of those who from the causes mentioned might refuse to ask to be witnesses, particularly when they may have been in some degree compromised by their association with others, declares that the failure of a defendant in a criminal action to request to be a witness shall not create any presumption against him."

If the words "Fifth Amendment" are substituted for "Act" and for "statute" the spirit of the Self-Incrimination Clause is reflected. For comment on the refusal to testify is a remnant of the "inquisitorial system of criminal justice" which the Fifth Amendment outlaws. It is a penalty imposed by courts for exercising a constitutional privilege. It cuts down on the privilege by making its assertion costly. It is said, however, that the inference of guilt for failure to testify as to facts peculiarly within the accused's knowledge is in any event natural and irresistible, and that comment on the failure does not magnify that inference into a penalty for asserting a constitutional privilege. What the jury may infer given no help from the court is one thing. What they may infer when the court solemnizes the silence of the accused into evidence against him is quite another. * * *

We said in *Malloy v. Hogan* that "the same standards must determine whether an accused's silence in either a federal or state proceeding is justified." We take that in its literal sense and hold that the Fifth Amendment, in its direct application to the federal government and its bearing on the States by reason of the Fourteenth Amendment, forbids either comment by the pros-

3. The California Supreme Court later held that its "comment" rule squared with *Malloy v. Hogan.* The overwhelming consensus of the States, however, is opposed to allowing comment on the defendant's failure to testify. The legislatures or courts of 44 States have recognized that such comment is in light of the privilege against self-incrimination, "an unwarrantable line of argument." * * *

ecution on the accused's silence or instructions by the court that such silence is evidence of guilt.[6]

Reversed.[a]

MR. JUSTICE STEWART, with whom MR. JUSTICE WHITE joins, dissenting. * * *

We must determine whether the petitioner has been "compelled to be a witness against himself." Compulsion is the focus of the inquiry. Certainly, if any compulsion be detected in the California procedure, it is of a dramatically different and less palpable nature than that involved in the procedures which historically gave rise to the Fifth Amendment guarantee. When a suspect was brought before the Court of High Commission or the Star Chamber, he was commanded to answer whatever was asked of him, and subjected to a far-reaching and deeply probing inquiry in an effort to ferret out some unknown and frequently unsuspected crime. He declined to answer on pain of incarceration, banishment, or mutilation. And if he spoke falsely, he was subject to further punishment. Faced with this formidable array of alternatives, his decision to speak was unquestionably coerced.

Those were the lurid realities which lay behind enactment of the Fifth Amendment, a far cry from the subject matter of the case before us. I think that the Court in this case stretches the concept of compulsion beyond all reasonable bounds, and that whatever compulsion may exist derives from the defendant's choice not to testify, not from any comment by court or counsel. In support of its conclusion that the California procedure does compel the accused to testify, the Court has only this to say: "It is a penalty imposed by courts for exercising a constitutional privilege. It cuts down on the privilege by making its assertion costly." Exactly what the penalty imposed consists of is not clear. It is not, as I understand the problem, that the jury becomes aware that the defendant has chosen not to testify in his own defense, for the jury will, of course, realize this quite evident fact, even though the choice goes unmentioned. Since comment by counsel and the court does not compel testimony by creating such an awareness, the Court must be saying that the California constitutional provision places some other compulsion upon the defendant to incriminate himself, some compulsion which the Court does not describe and which I cannot readily perceive.

It is not at all apparent to me, on any realistic view of the trial process, that a defendant will be at more of a disadvantage under the California practice than he would be in a court which permitted no comment at all on his failure to take the witness stand. How can it be said that the inferences drawn by a jury will be more detrimental to a defendant under the limiting and carefully controlling language of the instruction here involved than would result if the jury were left to roam at large with only their untutored instincts to guide them, to draw from the defendant's silence broad inferences of guilt? * * *

Moreover, no one can say where the balance of advantage might lie as a result of the attorneys' discussion of the matter. No doubt the prosecution's argument will seek to encourage the drawing of inferences unfavorable to the defendant. However, the defendant's counsel equally has an opportunity to explain the various other reasons why a defendant may not wish to take the stand, and thus rebut the natural if uneducated assumption that it is because the defendant cannot truthfully deny the accusations made. * * *

The California rule allowing comment by counsel and instruction by the judge on

6. We reserve decision on whether an accused can require, as in *Bruno v. United States*, 308 U.S. 287, 60 S.Ct. 198, 84 L.Ed. 257 [1939], that the jury be instructed that his silence must be disregarded.

a. The Chief Justice took no part in the decision of the case. Harlan, J., concurred "with great reluctance."

the defendant's failure to take the stand is hardly an idiosyncratic aberration. The Model Code of Evidence, and Uniform Rules of Evidence both sanction the use of such procedures. The practice had been endorsed by resolution of the American Bar Association and the American Law Institute, and has the support of the weight of scholarly opinion. * * *

Notes and Questions

1. Compare the views of Justice Schaefer, *The Suspect and Society* 70–71 (1967): "[U]ndue emphasis upon the accusatorial aspects of our system has an embarrassingly parochial quality. Most nations of the world do not rely upon a system that is wholly accusatorial, nor do they go to the other extreme. Instead they require that the silence of an accused be noted for consideration in the ultimate determination of guilt or innocence. They neither require that he take an oath nor do they employ contempt as a sanction for his failure to answer. These rules seem to me to follow natural assumptions. The silence of the accused is noted and taken into account because of the strength of the inference of guilt that flows from his failure to respond; the refusal to administer an oath to the accused, or to force him to answer, reflects spiritual and physical aspects of the law of self-preservation invoked by John Lilburn before the Star Chamber. The epithet "inquisitorial" evokes the image of historic abuses that are not relevant to an obligation to respond to orderly inquiry."

2. The question on which *Griffin* reserved decision in footnote 6 was finally reached in *Carter v. Kentucky,* 450 U.S. 288, 101 S.Ct. 1112, 67 L.Ed.2d 241 (1981), where the Court, per Stewart, J., concluded:

"The *Griffin* case stands for the proposition that a defendant must pay no court-imposed price for the exercise of his constitutional privilege not to testify. The penalty was exacted in *Griffin* by adverse comment on the defendant's silence; the penalty may be just as severe when there is no adverse comment, but when the jury is left to roam at large with only its untutored instincts to guide it, to draw from the defendant's silence broad inferences of guilt. Even without adverse comment, the members of a jury, unless instructed otherwise, may well draw adverse inferences from a defendant's silence. * * *

"A trial judge has a powerful tool at his disposal to protect the constitutional privilege—the jury instruction—and he has an affirmative constitutional obligation to use that tool when a defendant seeks its employment. No judge can prevent jurors from speculating about why a defendant stands mute in the face of a criminal accusation, but a judge can, and must, if requested to do so, use the unique power of the jury instruction to reduce that speculation to a minimum.[21]" [b]

Rehnquist, J., dissenting, objected "that the Court's decision allows a criminal defendant in a state proceeding virtually to take from the trial judge any control over the instructions to be given to the jury."

3. In LAKESIDE v. OREGON, 435 U.S. 333, 98 S.Ct. 1091, 55 L.Ed.2d 319 (1978), the petitioner argued "that this protective instruction becomes constitutionally impermissible when given over

21. The importance of a no-inference instruction is underscored by a recent national public opinion survey conducted for the National Center for State Courts, revealing that 37% of those interviewed believed that it is the responsibility of the accused to prove his innocence. 64 ABAJ 653 (1978).

b. In *James v. Kentucky,* 466 U.S. 341, 104 S.Ct. 1830, 80 L.Ed.2d 346 (1984), the Court held that, notwithstanding an ambiguous distinction in state law between "admonitions" and "instructions," defense counsel's request for an admonition to the jury on defendant's right to remain silent was sufficient to invoke the protections of *Carter.* In declining to characterize counsel's action as a request for an oral rather than a written statement to the jury, the Court stated, with respect to both the *Carter* and *Lakeside* holdings, that the Constitution "does not afford the defendant the right to dictate, inconsistent with state practice, *how* the jury is to be told."

the defendant's objection" because it "is like 'waving a red flag in front of the jury.'" The Court, per Stewart, J., concluded:

"The petitioner's argument would require indulgence in two very doubtful assumptions: First, that the jurors have not noticed that the defendant did not testify and will not, therefore, draw adverse inferences on their own. Second, that the jurors will totally disregard the instruction, and affirmatively give weight to what they have been told not to consider at all. Federal constitutional law cannot rest on speculative assumptions so dubious as these."

As for petitioner's argument that the instruction infringed upon his constitutional right to the effective assistance of counsel, the Court found "it falls of its own weight once the petitioner's primary argument has been rejected. * * * To hold otherwise would mean that the constitutional right to counsel would be implicated in almost every wholly permissible ruling of a trial judge, if it is made over the objection of the defendant's lawyer."

Stevens and Marshall, JJ., dissenting, objected:

"It is unrealistic to assume that instructions on the right to silence always have a benign effect. At times the instruction will make the defendant's silence costly indeed. So long as *Griffin* is good law, the State must have a strong reason for ignoring the defendant's request that the instruction not be given. Remarkably, the Court fails to identify any reason for overriding the defendant's choice.[8]"

4. In *Lockett v. Ohio,* 438 U.S. 586, 98 S.Ct. 2954, 57 L.Ed.2d 973 (1978), where the prosecutor repeatedly referred to the state's evidence as "unrefuted" and "uncontradicted," the Court held this did not violate the Constitution because it "added nothing to the impression that had already been created by Lockett's refusal to testify after the jury had been promised a defense by her lawyer and told that Lockett would take the stand." What would the result have been if the defense attorney had not made those statements? Should the prosecutor have more leeway to talk about the defendant's failure to take the stand if defense counsel has attempted to turn the defendant's failure to his advantage, such as by arguing to the jury that since defendant had pleaded not guilty he presumably would have denied his guilt if he had testified?

5. In BROOKS v. TENNESSEE, 406 U.S. 605, 92 S.Ct. 1891, 32 L.Ed.2d 358 (1972), petitioner questioned the constitutionality of a statute which required that a criminal defendant "desiring to testify shall do so before any other testimony for the defense is heard," a rule related to the ancient practice of sequestering prospective witnesses in order to prevent their being influenced by other testimony in the case. The Court, per BRENNAN, J., held: (a) That the statute "violates an accused's constitutional right to remain silent," as a defendant "cannot be absolutely certain that his witnesses will testify as expected or that they will be effective on the stand" and thus "may not know at the close of the State's case whether his own testimony will be necessary or even helpful to his cause."

8. How far the Court deviates from the course charted in *Griffin* may be seen by comparing its reasoning to the analysis in an earlier case that followed *Griffin* more faithfully. In *Brooks v. Tennessee* [Note 5 infra] state law required the defendant to be the first defense witness if he wanted to testify at all. Since defendants may not be sequestered like other witnesses, this rule was the only way to prevent opportunistic defendants from shading their testimony to match that of other defense witnesses. Despite the substantial state interest in avoiding perjury, this Court struck down the rule, relying on *Griffin.* The *Brooks* court thought that a defendant who planned to take the stand only if his case was weak, but who could not judge its weakness in advance, might be unnecessarily compelled to testify under the Tennessee law. In *Brooks,* the State had a good reason for its action; here the State has none. In *Brooks,* the compulsive force of the rule was speculative at best; here it is direct and plain. If today we are true to *Griffin,* as the Court asserts, then *Brooks* was surely wrong.

"Pressuring the defendant to take the stand, by foreclosing later testimony if he refuses, is not a constitutionally permissible means of ensuring his honesty. It fails to take into account the very real and legitimate concerns that might motivate a defendant to exercise his right of silence. And it may compel even a wholly truthful defendant, who might otherwise decline to testify for legitimate reasons, to subject himself to impeachment and cross-examination at a time when the strength of his other evidence is not yet clear." (b) That the statute constitutes "an infringement on the defendant's right of due process," as "by requiring the accused and his lawyer to make [the choice of whether to testify] without an opportunity to evaluate the actual worth of their evidence," the accused is "thereby deprived of the 'guiding hand of counsel' in the timing of this critical element of his defense." THE CHIEF JUSTICE, joined by Blackmun and Rehnquist, JJ., dissenting, argued that there was no violation of the right to remain silent in that the defendant was not confronted with a choice any more difficult than that approved by the Court in *Williams v. Florida*, p. 1130 supra; and that there was no due process violation because counsel may "be restricted by ordinary rules of evidence and procedure in presenting an accused's defense" even "if it might be more advantageous to present it in some other way," as illustrated by the rule forbidding counsel from asking leading questions of the defendant.[c]

SECTION 5. CLOSING ARGUMENTS

ALBERT W. ALSCHULER—COURTROOM MISCONDUCT BY PROSECUTORS AND TRIAL JUDGES

50 Tex.L.Rev. 629, 633–36 (1972).

The courts have fairly well delineated the basic outlines of a few forms of prosecutorial misconduct. * * * Thus a prosecutor may not comment on the failure of the defendant to testify; he may not assert facts which have not been presented in evidence; he may not suggest that evidence exists which he has been unable to introduce; he may not express his personal belief in the defendant's guilt; he may not, at least in noncapital cases, discuss the possibility of pardon or parole; nor may he argue that erroneous convictions can always be reversed on appeal. When it comes to what are commonly the most

c. See also Note 3, p. 1136 supra; Westen, *Order of Proof: An Accused's Right to Control the Timing and Sequence of Evidence in His Defense*, 66 Cal.L.Rev. 935 (1978) (arguing that *Brooks* is inconsistent with *Williams* as a Fifth Amendment case, but that *Brooks* could have been based on a Sixth Amendment right of the defendant to control the order of his presentation of proof). In comparing *Brooks* to *Williams*, Westen, supra, rejects the contention that *Brooks* involved a "heavier burden" for the defendant because the "preclusion sanction" involved in *Brooks* applied to the defendant's own testimony while the sanction involved in *Williams* applied only to the testimony of other witnesses. The author notes: "The trouble with this argument is that it rests on the questionable premise that the right of a defendant to call himself as a witness for the defense is more important—and its loss, therefore, more 'burdensome'—than the right of a defendant to call third persons as witnesses in his defense. This assumption finds no support in either the realities of trial litigation or in the history of constitutional procedure. When a defendant testifies on his own behalf, his credibility is regularly discounted by the factfinder for reasons of self-interest; moreover, in many cases, his credibility is further impeached by evidence of prior crimes. As a result, although the defendant may be an important witness for the defense, his value can hardly be said to exceed the total value of all other witnesses for the defense. This assessment is also reflected in the history of the sixth amendment. Thus, while the framers of the sixth amendment made specific provision for the production and presentation of third persons as witnesses for the defense, they made no mention of the right of the defendant to testify as a witness for the defense. Indeed, far from having a constitutional right to testify on their own behalf, federal defendants until 1878 were *prohibited* from testifying in their own defense. It is significant that as late as 1961 the Supreme Court was still reluctant to grant that a defendant had a constitutional right to testify on his own behalf, and it was not until 1975, and then only in dictum, that the Court was prepared to recognize the right." 66 Cal.L.Rev. at 952–53. But cf. *Geders v. United States*, p. 144 supra.

disruptive forms of prosecutorial misbehavior, however—abuse and insult, inflammatory argument, and appeals to prejudice—specific judicial standards are usually lacking. A starting point for the courts is often the statement of the American Bar Association's Code of Professional Responsibility, "The responsibility of a public prosecutor differs from that of the usual advocate; his duty is to seek justice, not merely to convict." Or a court may begin with Mr. Justice Sutherland's classic opinion in *Berger v. United States,* 295 U.S. 78, 88, 55 S.Ct. 629, 633, 79 L.Ed. 655 (1935):

> The United States Attorney is the representative not of an ordinary party to a controversy, but of a sovereignty whose obligation to govern impartially is as compelling as its obligation to govern at all; and whose interest, therefore, in a criminal prosecution is not that it shall win a case, but that justice shall be done. As such, he is in a peculiar and very definite sense the servant of the law, the twofold aim of which is that guilt shall not escape or innocence suffer. He may prosecute with earnestness and vigor—indeed, he should do so. But, while he may strike hard blows, he is not at liberty to strike foul ones. It is as much his duty to refrain from improper methods calculated to produce a wrongful conviction as it is to use every legitimate means to bring about a just one.

Eloquent as they are, statements at this level of generality do not solve cases. They are instead invoked ceremoniously when an appellate court decides, on more detailed grounds, to reverse a conviction for prosecutorial misconduct. Nor do these statements seem inconsistent with the "boilerplate" on the other side. Even before its decision in *Berger,* the Supreme Court, in *Dunlop v. United States,* 165 U.S. 486, 498, 17 S.Ct. 375, 379, 41 L.Ed. 799 (1897), had provided some quotable language that could be employed whenever an appellate court decided to disregard an instance of prosecutorial misconduct:

> There is no doubt that, in the heat of argument, counsel do occasionally make remarks that are not justified by the testimony, and which are, or may be, prejudicial to the accused. . . . If every remark made by counsel outside of the testimony were grounds for a reversal, comparatively few verdicts would stand, since in the ardor of advocacy, and in the excitement of trial, even the most experienced counsel are occasionally carried away by this temptation.

The tone of other judicial statements seems to depart even further from the ideal of impartiality suggested by the Code of Professional Responsibility and the *Berger* opinion. For example, the Ninth Circuit observed in 1945 [*Ballard v. United States,* 152 F.2d 941, 943 (9th Cir.1945), rev'd on other grounds 329 U.S. 187, 67 S.Ct. 261, 91 L.Ed. 181 (1946)]:

> It is our opinion that if the conduct of the prosecution in argument in this case constitutes error, then, the prosecution in every case is limited to a listless, vigorless summation of fact in Chesterfieldian politeness. Gone are the days of the great advocates whose logic glowed and flowed with the heat of forensics! Gone, except for counsel for the defense.

As general as this rhetoric on both sides seems to be, it does raise the basic problem of the attitude with which a prosecutor should approach his courtroom tasks. Should he really be a man for all seasons, "both an advocate, determined to convict the defendant, and a representative of the state, safeguarding the rights of all"? Or should he follow the line suggested by Whitney North Seymour Jr. and act as a quasi-judicial officer in deciding whether to prosecute and then, once the trial begins, as a zealous champion who leaves the judging to the judges? My own answer to these questions is admittedly extreme: The prosecutor should not think of oratory as part of his job at all. He should avoid the "glow and flow of the heat of forensics" and should, in fact, strive for more "Chesterfieldian politeness." The prosecutor should forego not only appeals to prejudice, but any deliberate appeal to emotion.

Notes and Questions

1. Assuming that a prosecutor takes to heart Professor Alschuler's suggestion that the prosecution should "strive for more 'Chesterfieldian politeness,' " what portion of the following advice on closing argument, offered in Vance, *Final Argument in Criminal Cases* in The Prosecutor's Deskbook 487 (Healy and Manak, eds. 1971), should be ignored or modified? Under the heading of "Refutation of Defense Counsel's Argument," District Attorney Vance notes:

"[Y]ou must prevent the jury from going on a 'wild goose chase' by pointing out that these matters are extraneous, immaterial, and have no real bearing on the issue to be decided. Then refute his best points in a cursory manner and advise that it will become more apparent later on in the address and in the overall picture that these facts cannot stand. Before getting into the refutations point by point, you may want to say something similar to this:

> Counsel has stood before you and talked at length and perhaps in desperation on the so-called fallacies of our case. Although the answer to most of his argument is obvious and most of his points are weak and without foundation, it is out of an abundance of precaution in representing the law abiding people of this county that I feel compelled to answer these assertions. And I want you to know that it is in the spirit of wanting to be overly thorough and abundantly fair that I answer counsel and certainly not due to any great merit of his position that I proceed.

[Then], in refuting his argument the following items should be mentioned in weakening his position, that the defendant's contentions are based on, (a) the testimony of the defendant who has the most to lose, (b) the testimony of his witnesses who are all ex-convicts, (c) the testimony of his wife who will have to support his five kids if he goes to the penitentiary, etc.[a] * * * A polite intimation relating to your advocate's pecu-

a. Should the prosecutor in this regard follow the advice offered in a leading manual on closing argument for the defense, Cohen, *How to Win Criminal Cases by Establishing A Reasonable Doubt* 818–19 (1970):

"A mere recital of the evidence is not recommended. * * * For example: One of the peoples' witnesses has testified and identified your client as the perpetrator of the crime. The witness has a past record and is not of good moral character. You will not be doing your client justice by using the following language—'The last witness was Sam Brooks. Mr. Brooks testified that he observed my client pass a package of heroin and get $8 in exchange. And then you heard cross-examination about this man's record. We have shown you that he has been convicted on three prior occasions; that he lives in sin and that his past is a sordid one. We have destroyed his credibility and therefore we submit to you that this man is unworthy of belief. When you evaluate his testimony, consider his background, his record, his morals and then determine whether he is worthy of belief.'

"To be more effective and highlight your cross-examination of this witness in an interesting, colorful and logical method, you might use the following technique—'And then, ladies and gentlemen, they brought a man by the name of Sam Brooks and asked you to believe his testimony. Now, I can't blame the D.A. for calling Mr. Brooks. He doesn't choose his witnesses; he must work with whomever he has. Let's look at and analyze the type of man whom you folks are asked to believe. Here is the man, ladies and gentlemen, Sam Brooks—a man who quit school at age 14—a man who has never earned an honest dollar in his life—a man, who by his own admission, has been convicted of larceny. This is the man you are expected to believe so as to convict my client—a man convicted of assault, convicted of rape. Here is the man, ladies and gentlemen—Sam Brooks. Inspect his background—ask yourself, are we going to convict somebody upon the testimony of this type of individual? Sam Brooks—he lives with many women, he gambles, he drinks, he exemplifies the underworld and destroys everything that is decent. Are you twelve people, sitting in this jury, about to say that you are going to accept the testimony of this degenerate. I don't think so. I don't believe that any reasonable people, such as you, are going to believe what this man told you. This is the man—Sam Brooks, an addict, a gigolo, liarities might help the cause here, such as referring to (a) the man with the 'pearl complexion and the Budweiser belly,' (b) or the man who 'was unable to say the Lord's Prayer without reading from his notes,' (c) or the man who had Abel slaying Cain,' (d) or the man who can't remember the testimony of the witnesses, etc."

2. As suggested by Professor Alschuler, some of the basic prohibitions applicable to closing arguments are fairly specific while others are stated in quite general terms. However, even those that "are fairly well delineated" may present considerable difficulty in application. Consider, for example, the following illustrations, all drawn from the very extensive review of appellate precedents in Vess, *Walking a Tightrope: A Survey of Limitations on the Prosecutor's Closing Argument,* 64 J.Crim.L. & Criminology 22 (1973) (hereinafter cited as Vess).[b] In applying the prohibition against expressions of personal belief as to the truthfulness of a witness' testimony, one court sustained the prosecutor's comment that there was not "one bit of conduct" on the part of his witnesses that rang with anything but truth, while another rejected a prosecutor's statement that the chief government witness was a government employee and therefore eminently credible. Similarly, one court upheld the prosecutor's characterization of a defense witness as "shifty," while another held improper the prosecutor's statement that a defense witness was such a scoundrel that he had to be watched. See Vess, 45–46.

One of the most troublesome limitations upon closing argument is the prohibition against "injecting issues broader than the guilt or innocence of the accused." I. *A.B.A. Standards,* § 3–5.8(c). As Vess notes, it usually is proper for the prosecutor "to dwell upon the end results of the crime and to urge a fearless administration of the criminal law." Courts also have accepted arguments that a conviction would deter others from committing similar crimes, but such arguments come close to exceeding permissible limits. Thus, they have held it improper to assert that a guilty verdict would relieve community fears or would serve as a good example for the young people in the community. Courts have also condemned appeals to jurors as taxpayers or as members of a particular element of the community. See Vess, 49–51.

3. In determining whether to reverse a conviction on the basis of an improper closing argument, an appellate court will consider a variety of factors besides the propriety of the prosecutor's statement. Those factors most frequently cited as relevant include: (1) whether the prosecutor's remarks were invited or provoked by the improper comments of the defense;[c] (2) whether defense counsel made a timely objection to the prosecutor's comments;

a criminal. Believe him and you believe in everything that's bad and rotten in the world. It's unfortunate that the D.A. of this county must rely upon Sam Brooks; but as I said, he is stuck with him. You folks are not. You folks have a choice to believe or disbelieve. I show you Sam Brooks and ask you to use your common sense, your logic, your reasoning. Is this man worthy of being believed? Of course not.' "

b. See also, Gershman, *Prosecutorial Misconduct,* Ch. 10 (1985) Since appellate review of defense's closing argument is quire rare (see fn. a, p. 1346 supra), the articles on closing arguments almost always concentrate on the prosecutor's closing argument. It should be noted, however, that the same basic limitations apply to defense arguments. See, e.g, I. *A.B.A. Standards.* §§ 3–5.8, 4–7.8.

c. See *United States v. Young,* ___ U.S. ___, 105 S.Ct. 1038, 84 L.Ed.2d 1 (1985). *Young* rejected the contention that, because two wrongs do not make a right, an improper prosecution argument should as readily require a reversal even though made in response to an improper defense argument. The Court stressed that the appropriate response to an improper defense argument is a prosecution objection, accompanied by a "request that the [trial] court give a timely warning [to defense counsel] and curative instructions to the jury." However, because a "criminal conviction is not to be lightly overturned on the basis of a prosecutor's comments alone," even though the prosecutor did not respond in the correct manner, the reviewing court cannot avoid evaluating the prosecutor's improper, responsive comments in light of "opening salvo" of defense counsel. Recognition of the concept of an "invited response" is

(3) whether the trial judge had taken appropriate corrective action, such as instructing the jury to disregard the improper remarks; (4) whether the improper comments were only isolated or brief episodes in an otherwise proper argument; (5) whether the improper summation was combined with other trial errors; and (6) whether there was overwhelming evidence of guilt.

4. The Supreme Court has held that a prejudicial closing argument may reach the level of a federal constitutional violation, but only if the argument "so infect[s] the trial with unfairness as to make the resulting conviction a denial of due process." See *Donelly v. DeChristoforo,* 416 U.S. 637, 643, 94 S.Ct. 1868, 40 L.Ed.2d 431 (1974). *Donnelly* held that there had not been a constitutional violation where the prosecutor stated: "They [the defendant and his counsel] said that they hope that you find him not guilty. I quite frankly think that they hope you find him guilty of something a little less than first-degree murder." The Court of Appeals had found a due process violation on the ground that the jury might have taken the prosecutor's remark as indicating that the defendant had been willing to plead guilty to a lesser charge. A codefendant had pleaded guilty to a lesser charge at the close of the evidence and the jury had been aware of that fact. Three justices argued that the lower court's conclusion was not manifestly erroneous and therefore should be affirmed. The majority concluded, however, that the inference drawn by the lower court was unacceptable. The Court stressed that the prosecutor's statement was highly ambiguous and constituted "but one moment in an extended trial." It also noted that the trial court had clearly admonished the jury to disregard the prosecutor's statement and to base its decision solely on the evidence before it. The majority distinguished *Griffin v. California,* supra, noting that *Donnelly* was "not a case in which * * * the prosecutor's remarks so prejudiced a specific right, such as the privilege against compulsory self-incrimination, as to amount to a denial of that right."

SECTION 6. SUBMITTING THE CASE TO THE JURY

1. *Motion for judgment of acquittal.* The trial judge may not direct a verdict of guilty no matter how conclusive the evidence in the case may be.[a] But in the overwhelming majority of jurisdictions, the trial judge—either upon his own motion or the motion of the defendant—may take the case from the jury because the evidence is insufficient to sustain a conviction. Such a motion, most commonly known as a motion for a directed verdict, is appropriate after the conclusion of the prosecution's case or at the close of all the evidence.

What test should the trial judge apply in deciding whether to take the case from the jury? The prevailing view is that "the criminal defendant is entitled to an acquittal if reasonable men could not conclude on the evidence taken in the light most favorable to the prosecution that guilt has been proved beyond a reasonable doubt." Comment, 24 U.Chi.L.Rev. 561, 562 (1957), citing cases from each jurisdiction following this view. However, a small and waning number of courts have taken the position that submission of a case to the jury is improper unless the *only* conclusion which the evidence permits is that of guilt beyond a reasonable doubt—that is, a

not intended to give prosecutors a "license to make otherwise improper arguments," but simply reflects the task of reviewing court, which is to determine whether the prosecutor's comments, "taken in context, unfairly prejudiced the defendant."

a. However, the court is "permitted to withhold the defense of not guilty by reason of mental disease or defect, like other defenses, from the consideration of the jury when there is no evidence presented or there is insufficient evidence to present a jury question on the defense." *State v. Leach,* 370 N.W.2d 240 (Wis.1985).

motion for acquittal must be granted when a conclusion of guilt beyond a reasonable doubt is not the only reasonable conclusion possible. Is this a better test, on the ground that when reasonable men may disagree, then it follows that there is a reasonable doubt? Or, on the ground that "if a reasonable jury could properly find innocence on a given set of facts, it is wrong to refuse to acquit solely because another reasonable jury might properly reach a conclusion of guilt on the same facts"? Id. at 566.

If the defendant's motion for acquittal at the close of the prosecution's case is denied, the defendant then must make a tactical decision as to whether to introduce any evidence. If he declines to do so, he then preserves his right to appeal from the denial of the motion for acquittal, but if he introduces evidence he then may merely move for acquittal again at the close of all the evidence, at which time the court may consider evidence damaging to the defendant which may have come out (most likely on cross-examination) during presentation of the defendant's case. Appeal is possible only as to denial of the second motion. Should this be so? That is, does the notion that an erroneous denial of the motion for acquittal at the conclusion of the prosecution's case may be cured by subsequent developments come perilously close to compelling the defendant to incriminate himself?

If a defendant moves for acquittal at the end of the government's case, would it be proper for the trial judge to reserve decision on the motion until the close of all the evidence? To permit the government to reopen its case? If the defendant's motion is made at the close of all the evidence, would it be proper for the trial judge to reserve decision on the motion, submit the case to the jury, and decide the motion either before the jury returns a verdict or after it returns a verdict of guilty or is discharged without having returned a verdict?

2. *Instructions to the jury.* Before the jury retires for deliberations, the judge gives instructions regarding the law of the case. In a typical case, these instructions will cover such matters as the province of court and jury, the presumption of innocence [b] and the burden of proof, various evidentiary problems (e.g., on determining the weight to be given to a confession; on the significance of flight, concealment or other circumstantial evidence), a definition of the offense or offenses charged, additional clarification of the critical elements of these offenses (e.g., intent, possession), any defenses which are properly in the case, and the procedures to be followed in the jury room.

Before the time for instruction of the jury, the judge will ask the parties to submit in writing their requests for instructions. It is commonly required that a copy be furnished the other parties. It is often recognized that the court may direct counsel to prepare instructions on a certain point; it is particularly appropriate that this be so in criminal cases because of the special responsibility of the trial judge to ensure that certain essential instructions are given whether or not they are requested. In some jurisdictions the preparation of jury instructions has been simplified somewhat by the development of so-called "pattern instructions," a set of approved, published instructions which are to be used whenever applicable. Pattern jury instructions have been praised for their accuracy, saving of time, impartiality, intel-

b. In *Kentucky v. Whorton,* 441 U.S. 786, 99 S.Ct. 2088, 60 L.Ed.2d 640 (1979), the Court, 6–3, held that "the failure to give a requested instruction on the presumption of innocence does not in and of itself violate the Constitution." The majority stressed that *Taylor v. Kentucky,* 436 U.S. 478, 98 S.Ct. 1930, 56 L.Ed.2d 468 (1978), reversing a conviction where the trial judge refused to give such an instruction, "focused on the failure to give the instruction as it related to the overall fairness of the trial considered in its entirety." In *Taylor,* the trial judge's instructions were Spartan, the prosecutor improperly referred to the indictment and otherwise made remarks of dubious propriety, and the evidence against the defendant was weak.

ligibility and uniformity, but sometimes have been criticized as tending to be too abstract and general because they were prepared for continued use without the facts of any particular case in mind.[c]

After all requested instructions have been submitted, a conference on jury instructions is held. At this conference, counsel will have an opportunity to object to any instruction tendered by another party or prepared at the direction of the court. The court will advise counsel what instructions will be given so that counsel may structure their closing arguments accordingly. Generally, it may be said that points not raised at the conference on instructions are waived: a party usually may not raise on appeal the failure to give an instruction unless he tendered it, nor may he raise on appeal the giving of an instruction unless he objected thereto and stated distinctly the grounds of his objection.

There are, however, instances in which the doctrine of waiver will not be applied. The federal courts and most state courts have taken the position that in a criminal case the trial judge has a responsibility to ensure that certain essential instructions are given. Certain basic instructions essential to a fair determination of the case by the jury (e.g., burden of proof, elements of the offense charged) must be given, and the notion of waiver will not be employed to bar reversal if a defendant has been convicted in the absence of these instructions. One troublesome question has been whether an instruction on a lesser offense is of this kind. That is, if defendant is on trial for murder and the evidence develops in such a way that the jury could also be given a voluntary manslaughter instruction, should it be reversible error for the judge not to do so in the absence of a request for such an instruction from the defendant? Does the absence of a request reflect a tactical decision by the defense to go for all or nothing, by which the defendant should be bound? Or, is it the responsibility of the judge to send all verdict possibilities to the jury, without regard to what the parties would prefer?

3. *Summary and comment on the evidence.* "A jury trial in which the judge is deprived of the right to comment on the evidence and to express his opinion on the facts * * * is not the jury trial which we inherited." *Patton v. United States,* 281 U.S. 276, 288, 50 S.Ct. 253, 254, 74 L.Ed. 854 (1930). But, while the federal courts have retained this power, in the overwhelming majority of states this function of the trial judge was taken from him by constitutional provision, statute, or judicial decision. Presently, about 20 states allow neither comment nor summary, a slightly smaller number are said to allow summary only, while the rest allow both summary and comment on the evidence. In about half of the states included in the intermediate position, the trial judge has in fact been so limited that he has little if any authority to summarize the evidence.

SECTION 7. DELIBERATIONS AND VERDICT

I. UNANIMOUS VERDICTS

1. Reconsider Note 4 at p. 1262 supra.

2. In *United States v. Gipson,* 553 F.2d 453 (5th Cir.1977), the defendant was charged with violating 18 U.S.C. § 2313, which provides: "Whoever receives, conceals, stores, barters, sells or disposes of any motor vehicle or aircraft moving as, or which is a part of, or which constitutes interstate or foreign commerce, knowing the same to have been stolen, shall be fined not more than $5,000 or imprisoned not more than five years or both." The trial judge instructed the jury that "[i]f each of you is satisfied beyond any reason-

c. As reported in 2 Justice Assistance News 6 (June-July 1981); a two-year federally-funded study utilizing 1,000 volunteer jurors concluded that "the average juror may understand only about 50 percent of the instructions on the law presented by a judge prior to deliberations on a defendant's guilt or innocence."

able doubt that he did any one of those acts charged, and did it with the requisite state of mind, then there would be a unanimous verdict, * * * even though there may have been disagreement within the jury as to whether it was receiving or storing or what." On appeal, the court reversed: "These six acts fall into two distinct conceptual groupings; the first consisting of receiving, concealing, and storing, and the second comprised of bartering, selling, and disposing. Within each grouping, the acts are sufficiently analogous to permit a jury finding of the actus reus element of the offense to be deemed 'unanimous' despite differences among the jurors as to which of the intragroup acts the defendant committed. This is so for two reasons. First, the acts within each grouping are not conceptually distinct. The single act of keeping a vehicle in a certain place may constitute both concealing and storing; or the single act of marketing a vehicle may simultaneously constitute bartering, selling, and disposing. Second, distinguishing among the acts within each grouping presents characterization problems. One juror may view a defendant's actions in housing a stolen vehicle as receiving, while another juror may conclude that the same actions constitute concealing or storing. Similar definitional problems would likely confront a jury faced with the task of choosing among the terms bartering, selling, and disposing for the proper label for a defendant's actions.

"On the other hand, the two conceptual groupings are sufficiently different so that a jury finding of the actus reus element of the offense would not be 'unanimous' if some of the jurors thought the defendant committed only an act in the first conceptual grouping while others believed he committed an act only in the second."

3. Comment, 91 Harv.L.Rev. 499 (1977), observes: "Such 'patchwork' guilty verdicts have been held to meet state jury unanimity requirements by the majority of state courts which have considered the question." See, e.g., *People v. Failla,* 414 P.2d 39 (Cal.1966) (where defendant charged with burglary by entering building with intent to steal or to commit a felony, jurors need not agree what felony defendant intended to commit).

4. Is *Gipson* sound? If so, is it correct to say it is "binding upon the states"? Comment, supra, at 505. Would "the policies supporting the *Gipson* decision * * * require the same result even if the statute simply contained a general prohibition on 'trafficking' in stolen vehicles, instead of the more specific division into six acts"? Id. at 501.

II. SPECIAL VERDICTS

1. Comment, supra, at 503, observes that, as compared with jury instructions requiring unanimity as to every element, special verdicts and special interrogatories "are undoubtedly more effective in protecting *Gipson* rights."

2. At Heald's trial for being an accessory before the fact to an armed robbery, a question arose as to whether his proximity in the getaway car made him a principal because of constructive presence. The trial judge told the jury it must acquit if it found him to be a principal, and then told the jury to make two special findings in the event of a not guilty verdict: (i) whether it found the defendant not guilty "only because he was constructively present at the scene of the crime"; and (ii) whether the finding was "based upon the fact that the State failed to prove the elements of the crime of accessory before the fact beyond a reasonable doubt." Heald was convicted, and on his appeal from a denial of his petition for a writ of habeas corpus in federal district court, the court in HEALD v. MULLANEY, 505 F.2d 1241 (1st Cir.1974), concluded:

"Heald argues that any use of special verdicts and special questions in criminal cases is so alien to the Anglo-American tradition of trial by jury as to deny due process of law under the fourteenth amendment. He says that to require a jury to particularize or explain its general verdict of 'guilty' or 'not guilty' must inevitably undermine its independence. The instant case is said to be especially bad because a special finding was required only in the event of a 'not guilty' verdict. * * *

"This circuit's views on special questions in a federal criminal case are set forth in *United States v. Spock,* 416 F.2d 165 (1st Cir.1969). We held that there was a danger that such questions would 'catechize' a reluctant juror away from an acquittal towards a seemingly more 'logical' conviction. Yet

> 'the jury, as the conscience of the community, must be permitted to look at more than logic. . . . If it were otherwise there would be no more reason why a verdict should not be directed against a defendant in a criminal case than in a civil one. The constitutional guarantees of due process and trial by jury require that a criminal defendant be afforded the full protection of a jury unfettered, directly or indirectly.'

Spock is in accord with general disapproval of special questions and verdicts in federal criminal cases. * * * There is precedent, however, even within the federal judicial system for a limited use of special jury findings, usually in connection with sentence: a jury could be asked to determine whether the death penalty is to be imposed or whether the value of stolen property was more or less than $100.

"The states generally decline to permit special verdicts and questions in criminal proceedings, although there are exceptions. See e.g., *State v. Ellis,* 262 N.C. 446, 137 S.E.2d 840 (1964) (separate verdicts on issues of paternity, non-support, and guilt utilized in criminal bastardy proceedings).

"Viewed against this background we do not believe that a mechanical *per se* rule of unconstitutionality is warranted for all special questions in criminal cases. In *Spock* we were exercising our supervisory powers and, therefore, did not have to reach constitutional ground. To be sure, *Spock* condemned special questions in terms of their effect upon the independence of juries, a ground going to the institutional integrity of juries and having plain constitutional implications. We have little doubt that, in general, the use of special questions and verdicts in any criminal proceeding, state or federal, is suspect not only as a matter of sound judicial policy but of due process as well.

"We know, however, that special questions have been permitted for some very limited purposes even in federal criminal proceedings. We cannot say that every specialized use that may emerge under state procedures and statutes necessarily violates the due process clause. Some usages may be exempt from the dangers described in *Spock;* for example, certain questions may plainly lack any capacity to catechize, color or coerce the jury's decision making.

"In any event, our function is not to draw global rules for all seasons but to examine the fairness and propriety of the actual procedures to which Heald was exposed. Upon doing so, we are satisfied that the two special questions were harmless and that Heald received a trial before an impartial jury whose independence was not placed in jeopardy.

"It must be borne in mind that the two questions were merely designed to record whether an acquittal—had there been one—was based on the usual considerations (*viz.,* that guilt had not been proven), or whether it was based on a further defense-sponsored theory that if Heald was also a principal, he could not be convicted as an accessory. The latter theory was, it turned out, erroneous. Paradoxically, it made Heald's chances better the deeper his criminal involvement. By presenting that mistaken theory to the jury, the judge enlarged Heald's chances for acquittal, and it is difficult to see how the jury's consideration of questions designed only to distinguish between the alternate grounds of acquittal could have done him harm. Neither question called for an answer leading towards a verdict of guilt. The jury remained at all times free to acquit for the usual reasons; and the requirement that it label such an acquittal by saying 'Yes' to the question whether the state had failed to prove its case, does not, in this context, seem a significant burden."

III. INCONSISTENT VERDICTS

1. In *United States v. Maybury,* 274 F.2d 899 (2d Cir.1960), a 2–1 majority of the court, per Friendly, J., rejected the government's argument that the rule laid down in *Dunn v. United States,* 284 U.S. 390, 52 S.Ct. 189, 76 L.Ed. 356 (1932), upholding jury verdicts in criminal cases despite inconsistency as between counts, applies when a criminal case has been tried to a judge. "The vogue for repetitious multiple count indictments," noted the court, "may well produce an increase in seemingly inconsistent jury verdicts, where in fact the jury is using its power to prevent the punishment from getting too far out of line with the crime. * * * Ignoring inconsistency in a jury's disposition of the counts of a criminal indictment may * * * be deemed a price for securing the unanimous verdict that the Sixth Amendment requires * * * and for interposing 'the voice of the country' against the possibly excessive zeal of prosecutors. * * * None of these considerations is fairly applicable to the trial of a criminal case before a judge. * * * We do not believe we would enhance respect for law or for the courts by recognizing for a judge the same right to indulge in 'vagaries' in the disposition of criminal charges that, for historic reasons, has been granted the jury."

2. When the Second Circuit later reached the *Maybury* result as a constitutional matter in a habeas corpus case involving a state prisoner who objected to the apparent inconsistency within the trial judge's verdict finding him guilty and his accomplice not guilty, the Supreme Court reversed in HARRIS v. RIVERA, 454 U.S. 339, 102 S.Ct. 460, 70 L.Ed.2d 530 (1981):

"Inconsistency in a verdict is not a sufficient reason for setting it aside. We have so held with respect to inconsistency between verdicts on separate charges against one defendant, *Dunn v. United States,* and also with respect to verdicts that treat codefendants in a joint trial inconsistently, *United States v. Dotterweich,* 320 U.S. 277, 279, 64 S.Ct. 134, 135, 88 L.Ed. 48 (1943). Those cases, however, involved jury trials; as the Court of Appeals correctly recognized, both of those opinions stressed the unreviewable power of a jury to return a verdict of not guilty for impermissible reasons. It is argued that a different rule should be applied to cases in which a judge is the factfinder.

"Although *Dunn* and *Dotterweich* preclude a holding that inconsistency in a verdict is intolerable in itself, inconsistency nevertheless might constitute evidence of arbitrariness that would undermine confidence in the quality of the judge's conclusion. In this case, the Court of Appeals suggested the possibility that the trial judge might have relied on impermissible considerations such as the fact that neither respondent nor his wife testified, or knowledge of adverse information not contained in the record. Undeniably, these possibilities exist, but they also would have existed if Robinson had been convicted or if he had been tried separately. In bench trials, judges routinely hear inadmissible evidence that they are presumed to ignore when making decisions. It is equally routine for them to instruct juries that no adverse inference may be drawn from a defendant's failure to testify; surely we must presume that they follow their own instructions when they are acting as factfinders. We are not persuaded that an apparent inconsistency in a trial judge's verdict gives rise to an inference of irregularity in his finding of guilt that is sufficiently strong to overcome the well-established presumption that the judge adhered to basic rules of procedure.

"Other explanations for an apparent inconsistency are far more likely. Most apparent is the likelihood that the judge's actual observation of everything that transpired in the courtroom created some doubt about the guilt of one defendant that he might or might not be able to articulate in a convincing manner. In this case, if the judge was convinced beyond a reasonable doubt that respondent and his wife were both guilty, it would be most unfortunate if a concern about the plausibility of a lingering doubt about Robinson should cause him to decide to convict all three rather than to try to articulate the basis for his doubt.

"It is also possible that the judge may have made an error of law and erroneously assumed, for example, that Robinson should not be found guilty without evidence that he was to share in the proceeds of the larceny. There is no reason—and surely no constitutional requirement—that such an error pertaining to the case against Robinson should redound to the benefit of respondent.

"Even the unlikely possibility that the acquittal is the product of a lenity that judges are free to exercise at the time of sentencing but generally are forbidden to exercise when ruling on guilt or innocence, would not create a constitutional violation. We are aware of nothing in the Federal Constitution that would prevent a State from empowering its judges to render verdicts of acquittal whenever they are convinced that no sentence should be imposed for reasons that are unrelated to guilt or innocence. The Constitution does not prohibit state judges from being excessively lenient."

3. Most state courts have followed the rule in *Dunn,* but a substantial minority have taken the position that such inconsistency is reversible error. Is it true that "an enlightened jurisprudence should not thus permit the jailing of accused persons on a record exhibiting verdicts in which a jury simultaneously says 'yes' and 'no' in answer to a single critical question"? *United States v. Vastine,* 363 F.2d 853, 855 (3d Cir.1966) (Hastie, J., concurring). Is that approach more harmful because then "the Government would be entitled to have the jury warned that an acquittal on some counts might undermine a guilty verdict on others—almost the opposite of the standard instruction"? *United States v. Carbone,* 378 F.2d 420 (2d Cir.1967).

4. A unanimous Court reaffirmed the *Dunn* rule in *United States v. Powell,* 469 U.S. 57, 105 S.Ct. 471, 83 L.Ed.2d 461 (1984), rejecting in the process the claim that *Dunn* had been undercut by *Ashe v. Swenson,* p. 1056 supra: "The problem is that the same jury reached inconsistent results; once that is established principles of collateral estoppel—which are predicated on the assumption that the jury acted rationally and found certain facts in reaching its verdict—are no longer useful."

IV. THE DEADLOCKED JURY

1. In *Allen v. United States,* 164 U.S. 492, 17 S.Ct. 154, 41 L.Ed. 528 (1896), the Court held that the trial judge had not committed error in giving the jury a supplemental instruction, when it returned during its deliberations, that "in a large proportion of cases absolute certainty could not be expected; that, although the verdict must be the verdict of each individual juror, and not a mere acquiescence in the conclusion of his fellows, yet they should examine the question submitted with candor, and with a proper regard and deference to the opinions of each other; that it was their duty to decide the case if they could conscientiously do so; that they should listen, with a disposition to be convinced, to each other's arguments; that, if much the larger number were for conviction, a dissenting juror should consider whether his doubt was a reasonable one which made no impression upon the minds of so many men, equally honest, equally

intelligent with himself. If, upon the other hand, the majority were for acquittal, the minority ought to ask themselves whether they might not reasonably doubt the correctness of a judgment which was not concurred in by the majority."

Although this kind of instruction, commonly referred to as the "*Allen* charge" or "dynamite charge," has frequently been used over the years in state and federal courts, recently a number of appellate courts have disapproved of the charge.[a] Though "most courts in turning away from *Allen* have done so on other than constitutional grounds," arguments have been made that the *Allen* charge violates due process because "(1) it defeats the unanimity rule, (2) it does violence to the 'beyond a reasonable doubt' standard, (3) the jury does not remain impartial, and (4) the jury is instructed to consider matters extraneous to the guilt or innocence of the accused." Marcus, *The Allen Instruction in Criminal Cases,* 43 Mo.L.Rev. 613, 627–28 (1978).

2. Although the rule was to the contrary at early common law, the modern rule is that the trial judge has discretionary power to discharge the jury in any criminal trial without the consent of either party when, after sufficient and reasonable time for deliberation, the jury cannot agree on a verdict. However, the court may abuse its discretion in discharging the jury too quickly, which will bar a second trial of the defendant unless he consented to the discharge. On what basis should it be determined whether the trial judge discharged the jury too quickly?

3. It is the general view that the court may send the jury back for additional deliberations even though the jury has indicated once, twice, or several times that it cannot agree or even after the jury has requested that it be discharged. However, the court may not require or threaten to require the jury to deliberate for an unreasonable length of time or for unreasonable intervals. Should the judge be allowed to tell the jury how much longer they will be required to deliberate? To ascertain the numerical division within the jury before sending it back for further deliberations?

V. THE RULE AGAINST JURORS IMPEACHING THEIR VERDICTS vs. THE RIGHT OF CONFRONTATION

1. In *Parker v. Gladden,* 385 U.S. 363, 87 S.Ct. 468, 17 L.Ed.2d 420 (1966), a bailiff assigned to shepherd a sequestered jury in a state trial told them that defendant was guilty and that if there were any errors in reaching a verdict of guilty, the Supreme Court would correct it. Finding that the bailiff had, in a sense, become a witness against the defendant in violation of his right, under the Sixth and Fourteenth Amendments, to "be confronted

a. These courts have usually recommended that trial judges instead conform to the more guarded charge proposed in *A.B.A. Standards* § 15–4.4, which provides:

"(a) Before the jury retires for deliberation, the court may give an instruction which informs the jury:

"(i) that in order to return a verdict, each juror must agree thereto;

"(ii) that jurors have a duty to consult with one another and to deliberate with a view to reaching an agreement, if it can be done without violence to individual judgment;

"(iii) that each juror must decide the case for himself or herself, but only after an impartial consideration of the evidence with the other jurors;

"(iv) that in the course of deliberations, a juror should not hesitate to reexamine his or her own views and change an opinion if the juror is convinced it is erroneous; and

"(v) that no juror should surrender his or her honest conviction as to the weight or effect of the evidence solely because of the opinion of the other jurors, or for the mere purpose of returning a verdict.

"(b) If it appears to the court that the jury has been unable to agree, the court may require the jury to continue their deliberations and may give or repeat an instruction as provided in subsection (a). The court shall not require or threaten to require the jury to deliberate for an unreasonable length of time or for unreasonable intervals."

with the witnesses against him," the Supreme Court reversed the conviction.

2. *Parker* led the New York Court of Appeals, in PEOPLE v. DeLUCIA, 229 N.E.2d 211 (N.Y.1967), to re-examine the applicability of the long familiar rule that "jurors may not impeach their own duly rendered verdict by statements or testimony averring their own misconduct within or without the jury room" to circumstances such as those present in the instant case, where several jurors not only made an unauthorized visit to the scene of the alleged crime, but actually re-enacted the alleged crime. A majority of the court, per KEATING, J., observed that "where, as in the case of statements regarding juryroom deliberations, every verdict might be rendered suspect, and jurors might become subjected to continuous posttrial harassment, the public policy reasons for holding such statements inadmissible must *ordinarily* override public injustice to a defendant, for here our jury system itself is at stake." (Emphasis added.) On the other hand, "statements concerning *outside influences* on a jury, occurring less frequently and more susceptible to adequate proof, should be admissible to show that the defendant was prejudiced, for here the danger to our jury system is minimal compared with the more easily proven prejudice to the defendant." (Emphasis added.) In the instant case, concluded the majority, the several jurors who went to the scene and re-enacted the alleged crime became, "to use the reasoning of the Supreme Court in *Parker,* * * * unsworn witnesses against the defendants in direct contravention of their right, under the Sixth Amendment, 'to be confronted with the witnesses' against them." [b]

Dissenting Judge VAN VOORHIS, joined by Scileppi and Bergan, JJ., insisted that the reasons for the rule against jurors impeaching their own verdicts "apply equally to receiving affidavits or testimony of jurors to impeach their verdict by showing that they visited the scene of a crime or place of a disputed transaction as they do to discussion in the jury room. Each equally opens the way to sinister and ulterior attempts by corrupt defeated litigants to impugn adverse verdicts by unscrupulous methods. * * * All of the decisions, for the rule and against it, appear to be agreed that jurors cannot be questioned concerning faulty reasoning which may have produced a verdict, but where is the line to be drawn between defective reasoning and extraneous factors, among which the cases against the rule generally combine compromise verdicts, personal experiences or expert knowledge of jurors, biases for or against particular kinds of people more or less resembling parties to the action, viewing the place of the transaction, and a multitude of other 'extraneous factors' which are to be distinguished from and contrasted with what is merely 'wrong reasoning.' The court calendars, it seems to me, are congested enough as it is without opening all of these post-verdict fields of investigation and litigation."

3. What should the result be if *all* the jurors had participated in the unauthorized view? Consider that in *Snyder v. Massachusetts,* 291 U.S. 97, 54 S.Ct. 330, 78 L.Ed. 674 (1934), the Court (with four Justices dissenting) held that a view was not a "witness," and hence the defendant had

b. Consider Fed.R.Evid. 606(b), which provides:

"*Inquiry into validity of verdict or indictment.* Upon an inquiry into the validity of a verdict or indictment, a juror may not testify as to any matter or statement occurring during the course of the jury's deliberations or to the effect of anything upon his or any other juror's mind or emotions as influencing him to assent to or dissent from the verdict or indictment or concerning his mental processes in connection therewith, except that a juror may testify on the question whether extraneous prejudicial information was improperly brought to the jury's attention or whether any outside influence was improperly brought to bear upon any juror. Nor may his affidavit or evidence of any statement by him concerning a matter about which he would be precluded from testifying be received for these purposes."

no right to attend, at least when his counsel was permitted to attend. If the view is not a witness and some of the jurors have not served as witnesses to the others, then on what basis could it be argued that the defendant was denied his right to confrontation?

4. Impeachment of a jury's verdict must be distinguished from polling the jury, a procedure of common law origin whereby each juror is separately asked whether the verdict reported by the foreman is his verdict. The purpose of the poll is to determine "before it is too late, whether the jury's verdict reflects the conscience of each of the jurors or whether it was brought about through the coercion or dominion of one of them by some of his fellow jurors or resulted from sheer mental or physical exhaustion of a juror." *Commonwealth v. Martin,* 109 A.2d 325 (Pa.1954). In most jurisdictions the jury must be polled upon the timely request of any party, although a few states have adopted the view that whether to allow a poll on request is within the sound discretion of the trial judge. There is no constitutional right to poll the jury, and thus the court need not advise the defendant of such right and waiver may be inferred from the defendant's silence. Absent any request, the court may poll the jury on its own motion.

The typical state provision is that if there is not concurrence by all of the jurors, then "the jury must be sent out for further deliberation," while Fed.R.Crim.P. 31(d) provides that the court may either direct the jury to retire for further deliberations or discharge the jury. Which is the better approach? Should the defendant be allowed to demand a mistrial?

VI. POST-VERDICT MOTIONS

1. *Motion for judgment of acquittal.* A motion for judgment of acquittal may be made following a guilty verdict, just as it may be made prior to the submission of the case to the jury. See Note 1, p. 1369 supra. When made after the verdict, it is sometimes referred to as a motion for an acquittal "n.o.v." While some jurisdictions permit the post-verdict motion to be made only as a renewal of an earlier motion, most permit the post-verdict motion even if an earlier motion was not made. See, e.g., Fed.R.Crim.P. 29(c). The motion challenges the sufficiency of the evidence, and the court applies the same standard as in a pre-verdict motion. See Note 1, p. 1369 supra. But Rezneck, *The New Federal Rules of Criminal Procedure,* 54 Geo. L.J. 1276, 1313 (1966), advises counsel against deferring the motion "in view of the impact a guilty verdict is likely to have on the court's determination of the motion".

2. *Motion for a new trial (on grounds other than new evidence).* The motion for new trial may be based on a broad range of issues. In some jurisdictions, the governing rule or statute lists specific grounds, but the list usually includes a "catch-all" provision, e.g., that the "verdict is contrary to law and evidence." In other jurisdictions, the only statutory standard is that the new trial be "in the interest of justice," e.g., Fed.R.Crim.P. 33. A new trial motion often will raise a wide variety of alleged trial errors, such as the admission of improper evidence, variance between the indictment and proof, or improper joinder. Ordinarily, of course, these grounds will not be considered if the defendant failed to raise them at the appropriate time during the trial. In some jurisdictions, the defense must present in the new trial motion all objections that he intends to raise on appeal. Requiring a new trial motion as a prerequisite for appellate review is intended "to allow a trial court some opportunity to review and correct its own errors and, thereby, in some instances avoid the extra travail and expense of an appeal." *Graham v. State,* 249 N.E.2d 25 (Ind.1969).

Frequently, a motion for new trial will accompany a motion for judgment of acquittal since it provides an alternative device for challenging the sufficiency of the evidence. The motion for new trial gives the judge far broader authority in reviewing the evidence. Wright, § 553, observes: "On a motion for judgment of acquittal, the court is required to approach the evidence from a standpoint most favorable to the government, and to assume the truth of the evidence offered by the prosecution. If on this basis there is substantial evidence justifying an inference of guilt, the motion for acquittal must be denied. On a motion for new trial, however, * * * the court * * * may weigh the evidence and consider the credibility of witnesses. If the court reaches the conclusion that the verdict is contrary to the weight of the evidence and that a miscarriage of justice may have resulted, the verdict may be set aside and a new trial granted. It has been said that on such a motion, the court sits as a thirteenth juror * * * [although] the discretion of the court * * * should be exercised with caution and * * * a new trial [granted] only in exceptional cases in which the evidence preponderates heavily against the verdict."

3. *Motion in arrest of judgment.* The scope of the motion in arrest of judgment generally is rather narrow. In the federal courts, for example, it extends only to (1) a lack of jurisdiction over the offense charged or (2) failure of the indictment to charge an offense. Fed.R.Crim.P. 34. These are the same defects that Rule 12(b)(2) says "shall be noticed by the court at any time during the pendency of the proceedings." See Note 3, p. 1030 supra. In some jurisdictions, the motion may also extend to a limited number of other issues, e.g., double jeopardy.

4. *Newly discovered evidence.* The requirements for a motion for a new trial based on newly discovered evidence were discussed in connection with *Bagley.* See fn. c, p. 1151 supra. Ordinarily, the time period for making a motion based on newly discovered evidence is substantially longer than that for the ordinary new trial motion. See, e.g., Fed.R.Crim.P. 33 (2 years as opposed to 7 days).

Chapter 25

REPROSECUTION AND THE BAN AGAINST DOUBLE JEOPARDY [a]

SECTION 1. REPROSECUTION AFTER A MISTRIAL

ILLINOIS v. SOMERVILLE

410 U.S. 458, 93 S.Ct. 1066, 35 L.Ed.2d 425 (1973).

MR. JUSTICE REHNQUIST delivered the opinion of the Court.

We must here decide whether declaration of a mistrial over the defendant's objection, because the trial court concluded that the indictment was insufficient to charge a crime, necessarily prevents a State from subsequently trying the defendant under a valid indictment. We hold that the mistrial met the "manifest necessity" requirement of our cases, since the trial court could reasonably have concluded that the "ends of public justice" would be defeated by having allowed the trial to continue. Therefore the Double Jeopardy Clause of the Fifth Amendment, made applicable to the States through the Due Process Clause of the Fourteenth Amendment, did not bar trial under a valid indictment.

On March 19, 1964, respondent was indicted by an Illinois grand jury for the crime of theft. The case was called for trial and a jury impaneled and sworn on November 1, 1965. The following day, before any evidence had been presented, the prosecuting attorney realized that the indictment was fatally deficient under Illinois law because it did not allege that

a. The double jeopardy clause states that no person shall "be subject for the same offence to be twice put in jeopardy of life or limb." Accordingly, the first question to be asked in testing a second prosecution against the double jeopardy bar is whether it is for the "same offense" as the original prosecution. That question is not raised in the materials that follow because, except for the cases presented in section 4, the materials presented in this chapter deal with reprosecutions brought under the same charge and under the same statute (and therefore clearly for the same offense). As to when different charges under separate statutes constitute prosecution for the "same offense," see Ch. 18, § 2 (also discussing the collateral estoppel limitations upon separate prosecutions for different offenses).

While the Fifth Amendment refers to twice placing a person in jeopardy of "life or limb," it was early held that the clause applies to all "crimes," not just those punishable by capital or corporal punishment. See LaFave and Israel, § 24.1(b). *Benton v. Maryland,* 395 U.S. 784, 89 S.Ct. 2056, 23 L.Ed.2d 707 (1969), held that the Fifth Amendment's double jeopardy prohibition was fully applicable to the states (see Ch. 2, § 1), and since *Benton,* the Court has far more frequently faced double jeopardy issues. In *United States v. DiFrancesco,* 449 U.S. 117, 101 S.Ct. 426, 66 L.Ed.2d 328 (1980), Justice Blackmun, citing 21 double jeopardy cases decided by the Court over the previous decade, acknowledged that application of the double jeopardy bar "has not proved to be facile or routine," as demonstrated by various "changes in direction or in emphasis" found in those cases. The *DiFrancesco* opinion offers a brief summary of the "general principles [that] emerge from the Court's double jeopardy decisions." A more extensive review is presented in LaFave and Israel, §§ 24.1–24.4 (also citing various secondary sources).

respondent intended to permanently deprive the owner of his property. Under the applicable Illinois criminal statute, such intent is a necessary element of the crime of theft, and failure to allege intent renders the indictment insufficient to charge a crime. But * * * Illinois further provides that only formal defects, of which this was not one, may be cured by amendment. The combined operation of these rules of Illinois procedure and substantive law meant that the defect in the indictment was "jurisdictional"; it could not be waived by the defendant's failure to object, and could be asserted on appeal or in a post-conviction proceeding to overturn a final judgment of conviction.

Faced with this situation, the Illinois trial court concluded that further proceedings under this defective indictment would be useless and granted the State's motion for a mistrial. On November 3, the grand jury handed down a second indictment alleging the requisite intent. Respondent was arraigned two weeks after the first trial was aborted, raised a claim of double jeopardy which was overruled, and the second trial commenced shortly thereafter. The jury returned a verdict of guilty, sentence was imposed, and the Illinois courts upheld the conviction. Respondent then sought federal habeas corpus * * *. The Seventh Circuit affirmed the denial of habeas corpus prior to our decision in *United States v. Jorn,* 400 U.S. 470, 91 S.Ct. 547, 27 L.Ed.2d 543 (1971). The respondent's petition for certiorari was granted, and the case remanded for reconsideration in light of *Jorn* and *Downum v. United States,* 372 U.S. 734, 83 S.Ct. 1033, 10 L.Ed.2d 100 (1963). On remand, the Seventh Circuit held that respondent's petition for habeas corpus should have been granted because * * * jeopardy had attached when the jury was impaneled and sworn and a declaration of mistrial over respondent's objection precluded a retrial under a valid indictment. For the reasons stated below, we reverse that judgment.

The fountainhead decision construing the Double Jeopardy Clause in the context of a declaration of a mistrial over a defendant's objection is *United States v. Perez,* 9 Wheat. (22 U.S.) 579 (1824). Mr. Justice Story, writing for a unanimous Court, set forth the standards for determining whether a retrial, following a declaration of a mistrial over a defendant's objection, constitutes double jeopardy * * *. In holding that the failure of the jury to agree on a verdict of either acquittal or conviction did not bar retrial of the defendant, Mr. Justice Story wrote:

> We think, that in all cases of this nature, the law has invested Courts of justice with the authority to discharge a jury from giving any verdict, whenever, in their opinion, taking all the circumstances into consideration, there is a manifest necessity for the act, or the ends of public justice would otherwise be defeated. They are to exercise a sound discretion on the subject; and it is impossible to define all the circumstances, which would render it proper to interfere. * * *

This formulation, consistently adhered to by this Court in subsequent decisions, abjures the application of any mechanical formula by which to judge the propriety of declaring a mistrial in the varying and often unique situations arising during the course of a criminal trial. The broad discretion reserved to the trial judge in such circumstances has been consistently reiterated in decisions of this Court. * * * In reviewing the propriety of the trial judge's exercise of his discretion, this Court following the counsel of Mr. Justice Story, has scrutinized the action to determine whether, in the context of that particular trial, the declaration of a mistrial was dictated by "manifest necessity" or the "ends of public justice." [b]

b. In *Arizona v. Washington,* p. 1389 infra, the Court added the following comments on the meaning of the *Perez* "manifest necessity" standard: "The words 'manifest necessity' appropri-

In *United States v. Perez,* * * * this Court held that "manifest necessity" justified the discharge of juries unable to reach verdicts, and therefore the Double Jeopardy Clause did not bar retrial. In *Simmons v. United States,* 142 U.S. 148, 12 S.Ct. 171, 35 L.Ed. 968 (1891), a trial judge dismissed the jury, over defendant's objection, because one of the jurors had been acquainted with the defendant, and therefore was probably prejudiced against the Government; this Court held that the trial judge properly exercised his power "to prevent defeat of the ends of justice." In *Thompson v. United States,* 155 U.S. 271, 15 S.Ct. 73, 39 L.Ed. 146 (1894), a mistrial was declared after the trial judge learned that one of the jurors was disqualified, he having been a member of the grand jury that indicted the defendant. Similarly, in *Lovato v. New Mexico,* 242 U.S. 199, 37 S.Ct. 107, 61 L.Ed. 244 (1916), the defendant demurred to indictment, his demurrer was overruled and a jury sworn. The district attorney, realizing that the defendant had not pleaded to the indictment after the demurrer had been overruled, moved for the discharge of the jury and arraignment of the defendant for pleading; the jury was discharged, the defendant pleaded not guilty, the same jury was again impaneled, and a verdict of guilty rendered. In both of those cases this Court held that the Double Jeopardy Clause did not bar reprosecution.

While virtually all of the cases turn on the particular facts and thus escape meaningful categorization, it is possible to distill from them a general approach, premised on the "public justice" policy enunciated in *United States v. Perez,* to situations such as that presented by this case. A trial judge properly exercises his discretion to declare a mistrial if an impartial verdict cannot be reached, or if a verdict of conviction could be reached but would have to be reversed on appeal due to an obvious procedural error in the trial. If an error would make reversal on appeal a certainty, it would not serve "the ends of public justice" to require that the Government proceed with its proof, when, if it succeeded before the jury, it would automatically be stripped of that success by an appellate court. This was substantially the situation in both *Thompson v. United States* and *Lovato v. New Mexico.* While the declaration of a mistrial on the basis of a rule or a defective procedure that lent itself to prosecutorial manipulation would involve an entirely different question, cf. *Downum v. United States,* such was not the situation in the above cases or in the instant case.

In *Downum,* the defendant was charged with six counts of mail theft and forging and uttering stolen checks. A jury was selected and sworn in the morning, and instructed to return that afternoon. When the jury returned, the Government moved for the discharge of the jury on the ground that a key prosecution witness, for two of the six counts against defendant, was not present. The prosecution knew, prior to the selection and swearing of the jury, that this witness could not be found and had not been served with a subpoena. The trial judge discharged the jury over the defendant's motions to dismiss two counts for failure to prosecute and to continue the other four. This Court, in reversing the convictions on the ground of double jeopardy, emphasized that "[e]ach case must turn on its own facts," and held that the second prosecution constituted double jeopardy, because the absence of the witness and the reason therefor did not there justify, in terms of "manifest necessity," the declaration of a mistrial.

In *United States v. Jorn,* the Government called a taxpayer witness in a prosecution for willfully assisting in the preparation of fraudulent income tax returns. Prior to

ately characterize the magnitude of the prosecutor's burden [in justifying the mistrial]. * * * [But] it is manifest that the key word 'necessity' cannot be interpreted literally; instead, contrary to the teaching of Webster, we assume that there are degrees of necessity and we require a 'high degree' before concluding that a mistrial is appropriate."

his testimony, defense counsel suggested he be warned of his constitutional right against compulsory self-incrimination. The trial judge warned him of his rights, and the witness stated that he was willing to testify and that the IRS agent who first contacted him warned him of his rights. The trial judge, however, did not believe the witness' declaration that the IRS had so warned him, and refused to allow him to testify until after he had consulted with an attorney. After learning from the Government that the remaining four witnesses were "similarly situated," and after surmising that they too had not been properly informed of their rights, the trial judge declared a mistrial to give the witnesses the opportunity to consult with attorneys. In sustaining a plea in bar of double jeopardy * * *, the plurality opinion of the Court, emphasizing the importance to the defendant of proceeding before the first jury sworn, concluded:

> It is apparent from the record that no consideration was given to the possibility of a trial continuance; indeed, the trial judge acted so abruptly in discharging the jury that, had the prosecutor been disposed to suggest a continuance, or the defendant to object to the discharge of the jury, there would have been no opportunity to do so. When one examines the circumstances surrounding the discharge of this jury, it seems abundantly apparent that the trial judge made no effort to exercise a sound discretion to assure that, taking all the circumstances into account, there was a manifest necessity for the *sua sponte* declaration of this mistrial. *United States v. Perez.* Therefore, we must conclude that in the circumstances of this case, appellee's reprosecution would violate the double jeopardy provision of the Fifth Amendment.

* * * [R]espondent argues that our decision in *United States v. Jorn,* which respondent interprets as narrowly limiting the circumstances in which a mistrial is manifestly necessary, requires affirmance. Emphasizing the "Valued right to have his trial completed by a particular tribunal," *United States v. Jorn,* quoting *Wade v. Hunter,* respondent contends that the circumstances did not justify depriving him of that right. * * * We believe that in light of the State's established rules of criminal procedure the trial judge's declaration of a mistrial was not an abuse of discretion. Since this Court's decision in *Benton v. Maryland* [fn. a supra], federal courts will be confronted with such claims that arise in large measure from the often diverse procedural rules existing in the 50 States. Federal courts should not be quick to conclude that simply because a state procedure does not conform to the corresponding federal statute or rule, it does not serve a legitimate state policy. * * *

In the instant case, the trial judge terminated the proceeding because a defect was found to exist in the indictment that was, as a matter of Illinois law, not curable by amendment. The Illinois courts have held that even after a judgment of conviction has become final, the defendant may be released on habeas corpus, because the defect in the indictment deprives the trial court of "jurisdiction." The rule prohibiting the amendment of all but formal defects in indictments is designed to implement the State's policy of preserving the right of each defendant to insist that a criminal prosecution against him be commenced by the action of a grand jury. The trial judge was faced with a situation similar to those in *Simmons, Lovato,* and *Thompson,* in which a procedural defect might or would preclude the public from either obtaining an impartial verdict or keeping a verdict of conviction if its evidence persuaded the jury. If a mistrial were constitutionally unavailable in situations such as this, the State's policy could only be implemented by conducting a second trial after verdict and reversal on appeal, thus wasting time, energy, and money for all concerned. Here the trial judge's action was a rational determination designed to implement a legitimate state policy, with no suggestion that the implementation of that policy in this manner could be manipulated so as to prejudice the defendant. This situation is thus unlike *Downum,* where the mistrial entailed not only a delay for the defendant, but also operated as a post-jeopardy continuance to allow the prosecution an opportunity to strengthen its case. Here the delay was minimal, and the mistrial was, under Illinois law, the only way in which a defect in the indictment could be corrected. Given the established standard of discretion set forth in *Perez, Gori,* and *Hunter,* we cannot say that the declaration of a mistrial was not required by "manifest necessity" and the "ends of public justice." * * *

The determination by the trial court to abort a criminal proceeding where jeopardy has attached is not one to be lightly undertaken, since the interest of the defendant in having his fate determined by the jury first impaneled is itself a weighty one. *United States v. Jorn.* Nor will the lack of demonstrable additional prejudice preclude the defendant's invocation of the double jeopardy bar in the absence of some important countervailing interest of proper judicial administration. Ibid. But where the declaration of a mistrial implements a reasonable state policy and aborts a proceeding that at best would have produced a verdict that could have been upset at will by one of the parties, the defendant's interest in proceeding to verdict is outweighed by the competing and equally legitimate demand for public justice. Reversed.

MR. JUSTICE WHITE, with whom MR. JUSTICE DOUGLAS and MR. JUSTICE BRENNAN join, dissenting.

* * * Despite the generality of the *Perez* standard, some guidelines have evolved from past cases, as this Court has reviewed the exercise of trial court discretion in a variety of circumstances. *Jorn* and *Downum,* for example, make it abundantly clear that trial courts should have constantly in mind the purposes of the Double Jeopardy Clause to protect the defendant from continued exposure to embarrassment, anxiety, expense, and restrictions on his liberty, as well as to preserve his "valued right to have his trial completed by a particular tribunal." * * * Although the exact extent of the emotional and physical harm suffered by Somerville during the period between his first and second trial is open to debate, it cannot be gainsaid that Somerville lost "his option to go to the first jury and, perhaps, end the dispute then and there with an acquittal." *United States v. Jorn.* * * * There was not, in this case any more than in *Downum* and *Jorn,* "manifest necessity" for the loss of that right.

The majority recognizes that "the interest of the defendant in having his fate determined by the jury first impaneled is itself a weighty one," but finds that interest outweighed by the State's desire to avoid "conducting a second trial after verdict and reversal on appeal [on the basis of a defective indictment], thus wasting time, energy, and money for all concerned." The majority finds paramount the interest of the State in "keeping a verdict of conviction if its evidence persuaded the jury." Such analysis, however, completely ignores the possibility that the defendant might be acquitted by the initial jury. It is, after all, that possibility—the chance to "end the dispute then and there with an acquittal,"—that makes the right to a trial before a particular tribunal of importance to a defendant. * * *

Apparently the majority finds "manifest necessity" for a mistrial and the retrial of the defendant in "the State's policy of preserving the right of each defendant to insist that a criminal prosecution against him be commenced by the action of a grand jury" and the implementation of that policy in the absence from Illinois procedural rules of any procedure for the amendment of indictments. Conceding the reasonableness of such a policy, it must be remembered that the inability to amend an indictment does not come into play, and a mistrial is not necessitated, unless an error on the part of the State in the framing of the indictment is committed. Only when the indictment is defective—only when the State has failed to properly execute its responsibility to frame a proper indictment—does the State's procedural framework necessitate a mistrial.

Although recognizing that "a criminal trial is, even in the best of circumstances, a complicated affair to manage," *id.,* the Court has not thought prosecutorial error sufficient excuse for not applying the Double Jeopardy Clause. In *Jorn,* for instance, the Court declared that "unquestionably an important factor to be considered is the need to hold litigants on both sides to standards of responsible professional conduct in the clash of an adversary criminal process" and cautioned, "the trial judge must recognize that lack of preparedness by the Government . . . directly implicates policies underpinning both the double jeopardy provision and the speedy trial guarantee." Id. Here, the prosecutorial error, not the independent operation of a state procedural rule, necessitated the mistrial. Judged by the standards of *Downum* and *Jorn* I cannot find, in the words of the majority, an "important countervailing interest of proper judicial administration" in this case; I cannot find "manifest necessity" for a mistrial to compensate for prosecutorial mistake. * * *

MR. JUSTICE MARSHALL, dissenting.

* * * A fair reading of [*Jorn* and *Downum*] shows how the balance should properly be struck here. The first element to be considered is the necessity for declaring a mistrial. That I take to mean consideration of the alternatives available to the judge confronted with a situation in the midst of trial that seems to require correction. In *Downum,* for example, * * * because the [missing] witness was essential to presentation of only two of the six counts * * * there was no necessity to declare a mistrial as to all six. Similarly, in *Jorn,* * * * the alternative of interrupting the trial briefly so that the witnesses might consult with attorneys was available but not invoked.

A superficial examination of this case might suggest that there were no alternatives except to proceed where "reversal on appeal [would be] a certainty." (Majority opinion, supra). * * * The majority treats it as unquestionably clear that the failure to allege that intent in the indictment made the indictment fatally defective. And indeed, since the time of trial Illinois courts have so held. * * * But the answer was not so clear when the trial judge made his decision. The Illinois Code of Criminal Procedure had just recently been amended to require that an indictment name the offense and the statutory provision alleged to have been violated, and that it set forth the nature and elements of the offense charged. Ill.Rev. Stat. ch. 38, § 111–3(a) (1963). The indictment here was sufficiently detailed to meet the federal requirement that the indictment "contains the elements of the offense intended to be charged, 'and sufficiently apprises the defendant of what he must be prepared to meet.' " *Hagner v. United States,* 285 U.S. 427, 52 S.Ct. 417, 76 L.Ed. 861 (1932); see also *Russell v. United States* [p. 1019 supra].

Had the Illinois courts been made aware of the substantial constitutional questions raised by rigid application of an archaic mode of reading indictments, they might well have refused to hold that the defect in the indictment here was jurisdictional and nonwaivable. Conscientious state trial judges certainly must attempt to anticipate the course of interpretation of state law. But they must also contribute to that course by pointing out the constitutional implications of alternative interpretations. * * * Thus, [the trial judge] could have proceeded to try the case on the first indictment, risking reversal as any trial judge does when making rulings of law, but with no guarantee of reversal.

If the only alternative to declaring a mistrial did require the trial judge to ignore the tenor of previous state decisional law though, perhaps declaring a mistrial would have been a manifest necessity. But there obviously was another alternative. The trial judge could have continued the trial. The majority suggests that this would have been a useless charade. But to a defendant, forcing the Government to proceed with its proof would almost certainly not be useless. The Government might not persuade the jury of the defendant's guilt. * * *

Once it is shown that alternatives to the declaration of a mistrial existed, as they did here, we must consider whether the reasons which led to the declaration were sufficient, in light of those alternatives, to overcome the defendant's interest in trying the case to the jury. * * * Here again the majority mischaracterizes the state policy at stake here. What is involved is not, as the majority says, "the right of each defendant to insist that a criminal prosecution against him be commenced by the action of a grand jury." Rather, the interest is in making the defect in the indictment here jurisdictional and not waivable by a defendant. Ordinarily, a defect in jurisdiction means that one institution has invaded the proper province of another. Such defects are not waivable because the State has an interest in preserving the allocation of competence between those institutions. Here, for example, the petty jury would invade the province of the grand jury if it returned a verdict of guilty on an improper indictment. However, allocation of jurisdiction is most important when one continuing body acts in the area of competence reserved to another continuing body. While it may be desirable to keep a single petty jury from invading the province of a single grand jury, surely that interest is not so substantial as to outweigh the "defendant's valued right to have his trial completed by a particular tribunal." * * *

I believe that *Downum* and *Jorn* are controlling.[2] As in those cases, the trial judge here did not pursue an available alternative, and the reason which led him to declare a mistrial was prosecutorial negligence, a reason that this Court found insufficient in *Downum.*[c]

Notes and Questions

1. *When jeopardy attaches.* Under the rule traditionally applied in federal courts, jeopardy attaches in jury trials when the jury is "empaneled and sworn" and attaches in bench trials when the "first witness is sworn." *Somerville* apparently assumed that the federal rule was constitutionally mandated and therefore applied to state as well as federal cases. That assumption was challenged, unsuccessfully, in CRIST v. BRETZ, 437 U.S. 28, 98 S.Ct. 2156, 57

2. So far I have read *Jorn* and *Downum* as restrictively as they can be fairly read. But those cases, I believe, should be read more expansively. They show to me that "manifest necessity" cannot be created by errors on the part of the prosecutor or judge; it must arise from some source outside their control. *Wade v. Hunter,* was clearly such a case. So were the cases that the majority says involved situations where "an impartial verdict cannot be reached." In those cases, a juror or the jury as a whole, uncontrolled by the judge or prosecutor, prevented the trial from proceeding to a verdict. *United States v. Perez; Simmons v. United States; Thompson v. United States.*

c. At an earlier point in Justice Marshall's dissent, a footnote on *Downum* stated: "*Downum* may perhaps be read as stating a prophylactic rule. While the evil to be avoided is the intentional manipulation by the prosecutor of the availability of his witnesses, it may be extremely difficult to secure a determination of intentional manipulation. Proof will inevitably be hard to come by. And the relations between judges and prosecutors in many places may make judges reluctant to find intentional manipulation. Thus, a general rule that the absence of crucial prosecution witnesses is not a reason for declaring a mistrial is necessary. Although the abuses of misdrawing indictments are less apparent than those of manipulating the availability of witnesses, I believe that, even if *Downum* is based on the foregoing analysis—an analysis which appears nowhere in the opinion—a similar prophylactic rule is desirable here. For example, in this case the State gained two weeks to strengthen a weak case. This is far longer than the two-day delay in *Downum,* * * *."

L.Ed.2d 24 (1978). In that case a mistrial had been granted, on grounds conceded not to constitute manifest necessity, after the jury had been sworn but before the first witness had been sworn. The state courts upheld a reprosecution on the basis of a state rule that jeopardy did not attach until the first witness was sworn in either jury or bench trials. In seeking to support the constitutionality of its rule, the state argued that the contrary federal standard was "no more than an arbitrarily chosen rule of convenience, similar in its lack of constitutional status to the federal requirement of an unanimous verdict of 12 jurors." Rejecting the state's contention, the majority opinion (per STEWART, J.) stressed the historic development of the double jeopardy bar. The Court noted that the Fifth Amendment guarantee originally was viewed as applicable only after the trial had been completed and a judgment of conviction or acquittal had been entered. Under this view, the double jeopardy bar served only a function "akin to that served by the doctrines of *res judicata* and collateral estoppel—to preserve the finality of judgment." However, the English common law, from which the double jeopardy clause was derived, also reflected "a strong tradition that, once bonded together, a jury should not be discharged until it had completed its solemn task of announcing a verdict." This tradition was treated as an aspect of double jeopardy in *Perez,* and it soon became an integral part of "double jeopardy jurisprudence." Thus, the Court concluded, "regardless of its historic origin," the defendant's "valued right to have his trial completed before a particular tribunal" had become an essential element of the constitutional guarantee. It followed, the Court reasoned, that the "federal rule that jeopardy attaches when the jury is empanelled and sworn" similarly had become part of that guarantee: "[T]he federal rule * * * reflects and protects the defendant's interest in retaining a chosen jury. We cannot hold that this rule, so grounded, is only at the periphery of double jeopardy concerns. Those concerns—the finality of judgments, the minimization of harassing exposure to the harrowing experiences of a criminal trial, and the valued right to continue with the chosen jury—have combined to produce the federal law that in a jury trial jeopardy attaches when the jury is empaneled and sworn. We agree with the Court of Appeals that the time when jeopardy attaches in a jury trial 'serves as the lynchpin for all double jeopardy jurisprudence.' "

Justice BLACKMUN wrote a separate concurrence. He stressed that more than the defendant's right "to have his trial completed by a particular tribunal" was at stake. If only that right were considered, jeopardy might attach at the very beginning of the jury selection process, rather than the swearing of the jury. Consideration also must be given, he noted, to the other interests of the defendant noted in the majority opinion. "I would," he concluded, "bring all these interests into focus * * * at the point where the jury is sworn because it is then and there that the defendant's interest in the jury reaches its highest plateau, because the opportunity for prosecutorial overreaching thereafter increases substantially and because stress and possible embarrassment for the defendant from then on is sustained."

Justice POWELL, joined by the Chief Justice and Justice Rehnquist, dissented. Justice Powell contended that "neither history nor doctrinal reasoning" supported the view that the double jeopardy guarantee was designed to protect the defendant's interest in retaining the selected and sworn jury because that jury might be "favorably inclined toward his cause." That type of interest was not protected for bench trials, he noted, since a case could readily be reassigned from one judge to another before jeopardy attached with the start of the trial. The "one event" that should bring the defendant's interest in a particular tribunal within the constitutional guarantee, the dissent concluded, was the "beginning of the fact finder's work" through the "hearing of evidence."

2. *The scope of the Somerville dissents.* Can the rationale of the *Somerville* dissents be squared with the *Simmons, Thompson,* and *Lovato* cases cited by the majority at p. 1382 supra? Are those cases less readily characterized as presenting situations in which the mistrials were "occasioned by official error"? [d] Was there less justification for denying those defendants their "opportunity to go to the first jury, and, perhaps, end[ing] the dispute then and there with an acquittal"? There is no indication that the trial judges in either *Thompson* or *Simmons* considered the possibility of proceeding with eleven jurors. Would the analysis offered in either or both of the *Somerville* dissents require consideration of that alternative before declaring a mistrial in a juror disqualification case? What if the failure to consider that alternative was based on precedent in the jurisdiction suggesting that a jury of less than 12 lacked authority to render a competent verdict (a position once favored, but commonly rejected today)? What if the applicable local law allowed continuation of the case with an 11-person jury only upon agreement of both parties and the judge, and the prosecutor or judge refused to agree. See, e.g., *People v. Loving,* 136 Cal.Rptr. 851 (Cal.App.1977) (where juror failed to appear and state insisted on its right to 12-person jury, mistrial was appropriate though defendant sought to complete the trial with 11 jurors). Compare *Hutchens v. District Court,* 423 P.2d 474 (Okla.Crim.App.1967) (mistrial inappropriate where it was discovered that one of the jurors was the mother-in-law of a deputy sheriff, but the state refused to proceed with an 11-person jury for no "cogent or compelling reason").

3. *Reconciling Somerville and Downum.* As Justice Marshall notes, the prosecutor in *Downum* could have proceeded to trial and could have obtained a valid conviction on four counts without the missing witness. Can *Downum* therefore appropriately be distinguished from *Somerville* as a case in which the available alternatives to a mistrial were less costly to the "ends of public justice" than the alternatives available in *Somerville* ? If not, can the two cases be distinguished on the ground that the prosecutor's error in *Downum,* unlike that in *Somerville,* "lent itself to prosecutorial manipulation" (p. 1382 supra)? Consider Schulhofer, *Jeopardy and Mistrials,* 125 U.Pa.L.Rev. 449, 469–70 (1977): "In neither case was the difficulty likely to be injected deliberately so that the prosecution would have an escape hatch if its case

d. While there appeared to be clear error in *Lovato,* although arguably more on the part of the trial court than the prosecutor, the responsibility for not discovering the grounds for juror disqualification in *Simmons* and *Thompson* apparently rested elsewhere. In *Simmons,* the juror had apparently lied on voir dire when asked whether he was acquainted with the defendant. In *Thompson,* the Court's opinion offered no explanation of how a grand juror happened to be seated as a petit juror, but the jury selection system probably was designed to prevent that from happening. Compare in this connection, *Brindle v. State,* 187 S.E.2d 310 (Ga.App.1972), holding that a retrial was barred under a state double jeopardy standard requiring "absolute moral or physical necessity" to justify a mistrial. The trial court there had declared a mistrial after it was first discovered in the midst of the trial that a juror was the second cousin of the defendant—a disqualification under local law. The juror stated that she had held up her hand in reply to a standard voir dire question concerning juror relationship to the participants, but the trial judge noted "that he did not see her raise her hand and * * * the district attorney was seated with his back to her [at the time]." The appellate court held that the mistrial, declared over the defendant's objection, was not justified since the prosecutor's failure to object during voir dire constituted an implied waiver of the juror's disqualification.

Assuming that there is neither prosecutorial nor judicial error, would that end the matter for the *Somerville* dissenters? Would Justice Marshall, for example, uphold the ruling in *United States ex rel. Clauser v. McCevers,* 731 F.2d 423 (9th Cir.1984) (mistrial justified by manifest discovery when testimony received at trial indicated that, through no fault of the prosecutor, false testimony had been presented before the indicting grand jury and the trial court concluded, without objection by the defense, that any conviction based on that indictment could not be upheld on appeal)?

should go badly. If anything, the difficulty in *Downum* was less susceptible to prosecutorial manipulation: a prosecutor might hope for conviction on a technically defective indictment, but he or she scarcely could expect to convict without the witnesses essential to prove the case." Compare Israel, *Criminal Procedure, The Burger Court, and The Legacy of the Warren Court,* 75 Mich.L.Rev. 1319, 1353 (1977): "In *Downum,* the prosecution's error was in an area [obtaining additional witnesses] where the potential existed for manipulation * * *; indeed the mistrial was granted for the very purpose of granting the prosecution 'an opportunity to strengthen its case,' 410 U.S. at 469. * * * While the actual error in *Downum* was not the product of manipulation, [if] the Court [were to] accept that type of error as a basis for a mistrial, it might be difficult to distinguish those cases that actually did involve manipulation." Consider also *Arizona v. Washington,* Note 4 infra: "The strictest scrutiny is appropriate when the basis for the mistrial is the unavailability of critical prosecution evidence or when there is reason to believe that the prosecutor is using the superior resources of the State to harass or to achieve a tactical advantage over the accused." [e]

4. *Arizona v. Washington.* The leading post-*Somerville* decision applying the *Perez* standard is ARIZONA v. WASHINGTON, 434 U.S. 497, 98 S.Ct. 824, 54 L.Ed.2d 717 (1978). In that case, defense counsel, in his opening statement, told the jury that they would learn through defense testimony that the prosecutor had suppressed exculpatory evidence at a previous trial and this "misconduct" had caused the Arizona Supreme Court to grant a new trial in the case. The prosecutor then moved for a mistrial, arguing that defense counsel's statement was clearly improper, that it had prejudiced the jury, and that "the prejudice could not be repaired by any cautionary instruction." The defense counsel disagreed on all points, and the trial court took the motion under advisement. The court expressed concern that an erroneous mistrial might bar reprosecution, but eventually granted a mistrial after the defense counsel was unable to present any legal support for his contention that his opening statement had been proper. In issuing his ruling, the trial judge did not expressly note that there was "manifest necessity" nor expressly state that he had considered alternatives to the mistrial order. Defendant's double jeopardy objection to his subsequent reprosecution was rejected by the state courts, but it was

e. In light of this statement and the *Downum* ruling, how much room is available to the trial judge to grant a mistrial for the purpose of allowing the prosecution to gain the testimony of a missing witness. Consider in this regard the following cases: *Davis v. State,* 318 S.E.2d 202 (Ga.App.1984) (mistrial justified when essential prosecution witness, for whom runaway warrant previously had been issued, left unsecured juvenile shelter in which she was to have remained overnight pending resumption of trial the following morning); *State v. Connery,* 679 P.2d 1266 (Nev.1984) (manifest necessity warranted mistrial where witness became unavailable due to attempted suicide during the period between the empanelment of the jury and the scheduled start of trial); *State v. Messier,* 686 P.2d 272 (N.M.App. 1984) (manifest necessity justified mistrial where videotape of child victim's testimony proved to be inaudible and child was unavailable to testify in person because of illness and potential emotional harm that might result; while it was "arguable" that the prosecutor should have previously checked the tape, "in this age of advanced technology," he was not "derelict" in "failing to do so").

Would it matter whether, if in *Downum* or any of the other missing witness cases, the case had been tried to the judge and the same judge was available to rehear the case after the missing witness became available? Consider *Belveal v. Rambo,* 487 P.2d 714 (Okla.Crim.App.1971), holding that double jeopardy barred continuation of a bench trial where the trial judge granted a two week continuance, on the prosecution's request, after the court had ruled that the preliminary hearing testimony of a missing witness was not admissible because the state had not exercised due diligence to secure the witness. *Belveal* was overruled "regarding the application of double jeopardy" in *State ex rel. Fallis v. Vestrem,* 527 P.2d 195 (Okla.Crim.App.1974), where the court concluded that defendant's speedy trial interests constituted the proper basis for limiting the grant of a continuance.

upheld by the lower federal courts on a federal habeas corpus challenge. Those courts apparently did not consider whether manifest necessity actually existed, but held that the state trial court had committed constitutional error in failing to make either a specific finding that manifest necessity existed or a specific finding that alternatives to a mistrial were inadequate. A divided Supreme Court (6–3) reversed.

The Supreme Court majority held that the lower courts had erred in insisting on explicit findings as to the presence of manifest necessity. In this case the basis for the trial judge's ruling was "adequately disclosed by the record," which included "an extensive argument of counsel prior to the judge's ruling." Where the trial record provides "sufficient justification" for the mistrial ruling, the "state judge's mistrial declaration is not subject to [constitutional] attack * * * simply because he failed to find 'manifest necessity' in those words or to articulate on the record all the factors which informed the deliberate exercise of his discretion."

Justice White, in a dissenting opinion, argued that the Court, having found that the lower federal courts applied an improper legal standard, should simply remand the case for a factual determination as to whether the justification for the mistrial was sufficient to meet the manifest necessity standard. The remaining justices concluded, however, that a remand was unnecessary. They went on to make their own determination as to whether the record established the requisite "high degree of necessity" (see fn. b supra). The majority, per STEVENS, J., initially noted that, in making certain types of mistrial determinations, trial judges must be given "broad discretion" in deciding "whether or not 'manifest necessity' justifies a discharge of the jury." The classic illustration of such a determination, it noted, was the trial judge's decision as to whether to discharge or require further deliberations from a "hung jury." [f] The majority concluded that, "along the spectrum of trial problems which may warrant a mistrial and which vary in their amenability to appellate scrutiny, the difficulty which led to the mistrial in this case also falls in an area where the trial judge's determination is entitled to special respect." The majority opinion reasoned:

"We * * * start from the premise that defense counsel's comment was improper and may have affected the impartiality of the jury. We recognize that the extent of the possible bias cannot be measured, and that the District Court was quite correct in believing that some trial judges might have proceeded with the trial after giving the jury appropriate cautionary instructions. In a strict, literal sense, the mistrial was not 'necessary.' Nevertheless, the overriding interest in the evenhanded administration of justice requires

f. The *Washington* Court noted that, "in this situation, there are compelling reasons for allowing the trial judge to exercise broad discretion." If trial judges were deterred by stringent appellate review from discharging juries "unable to reach a verdict after protracted * * * deliberations," the end result could be jury verdicts "result[ing] from pressures inherent in the situation rather than the considered judgment of all of the jurors," as well as the encouragement of judges to "employ coercive means to break the apparent deadlock." While appellate courts accordingly have given great deference to the trial judge's decision to discharge an apparently deadlocked jury, they have also emphasized that that deference is not without limits. See e.g., *United States v. Horn*, 583 F.2d 1124 (10th Cir.1978) (retrial barred where jury initially deadlocked after only 3½ hours of deliberation, judge delivered further charge and requested that the jury continue its deliberations, and then, after only 1 hour of further deliberation and without "communication" from the jurors, summarily terminated the trial).

Does there come "a breaking point" at which a series of properly declared mistrials due to hung juries becomes so oppressive as to bar reprosecution? See *Ex parte Anderson*, 457 So.2d 446 (Ala. 1984) (reviewing the cases and concluding that while such a breaking point may exist, it did not come after only 3 hung juries). Consider also Findlater, *Retrial After a Hung Jury: The Double Jeopardy Problem*, 129 U.Pa.L.Rev. 701 (1981) (sharply questioning the logic, in light of underlying double jeopardy policies, of allowing retrials in hung jury cases).

that we accord the highest degree of respect to the trial judge's evaluation of the likelihood that the impartiality of one or more jurors may have been affected by the improper comment. The consistent course of decision in this Court in cases involving possible juror bias supports this conclusion. * * * [The Court here discusses *Simmons v. United States* and *Thompson v. United States,* described in *Somerville* [p. 1382 supra]. * * *

"An improper opening statement unquestionably tends to frustrate the public interest in having a just judgment reached by an impartial tribunal. Indeed, such statements create a risk, often not present in the individual juror bias situation, that the entire panel may be tainted. The trial judge, of course, may instruct the jury to disregard the improper comment. In extreme cases, he may discipline counsel, or even remove him from the trial as he did in *United States v. Dinitz* [p. 1397 infra]. Those actions, however, will not necessarily remove the risk of bias that may be created by improper argument. Unless unscrupulous defense counsel are to be allowed an unfair advantage, the trial judge must have the power to declare a mistrial in appropriate cases. The interest in orderly, impartial procedure would be impaired if he were deterred from exercising that power by a concern that anytime a reviewing court disagreed with his assessment of the trial situation a retrial would automatically be barred. The adoption of a stringent standard of appellate review in this area, therefore, would seriously impede the trial judge in the proper performance of his 'duty, in order to protect the integrity of the trial, to take prompt and affirmative action to stop . . . professional misconduct.' Id.

"There are compelling institutional considerations militating in favor of appellate deference to the trial judge's evaluation of the significance of possible juror bias. He has seen and heard the jurors during their *voir dire* examination. He is the judge most familiar with the evidence and the background of the case on trial. He has listened to the tone of the argument as it was delivered and has observed the apparent reaction of the jurors. In short, he is far more 'conversant with the factors relevant to the determination' than any reviewing court can possibly be.

"Our conclusion that a trial judge's decision to declare a mistrial based on his assessment of the prejudicial impact of improper argument is entitled to great deference does not, of course, end the inquiry. * * * The trial judge * * * 'must always temper the decision whether or not to abort the trial by considering the importance to the defendant of being able, once and for all, to conclude his confrontation with society through the verdict of a tribunal he might believe to be favorably disposed to his fate.' *United States v. Jorn.* In order to ensure that this interest is adequately protected, reviewing courts have an obligation to satisfy themselves that, in the words of Mr. Justice Story, the trial judge exercised 'sound discretion' in declaring a mistrial. Thus, if a trial judge acts irrationally or irresponsibly, cf. *United States v. Jorn,* supra, his action cannot be condoned. But our review of this record indicates that this was not such a case. * * * We are * * * persuaded by the record that the trial judge acted responsibly and deliberately, and accorded careful consideration to respondent's interest in having the trial concluded in a single proceeding. Since he exercised 'sound discretion' in handling the sensitive problem of possible juror bias created by the improper comment of defense counsel, the mistrial order is supported by the 'high degree' of necessity which is required in a case of this kind.[35] "

35. Two considerations, while not determinative, add support to this conclusion. First, crowded calendars throughout the Nation impose a constant pressure on our judges to finish the business at hand. Generally, they have an interest in having the trial completed as promptly as possible, an interest which frequently parallels the constitutionally protected interest of the ac-

Dissenting Justice MARSHALL, joined by Justice Brennan, disagreed with the majority's conclusion. Justice Marshall noted, however, that his "disagreement with the majority" was a "narrow one." Justice Marshall noted: "I [do not] quarrel with the proposition that reviewing courts must accord substantial deference to a trial judge's determination that the prejudicial impact of an improper opening statement is so great as to leave no alternative but a mistrial to secure the ends of public justice. Where I part ways from the Court is in its assumption that an 'assessment of the prejudicial impact of improper argument,' sufficient to support the need for a mistrial may be implied from this record."

Justice Marshall stressed that the improper remarks of the defense counsel "occupied only one page of a long opening statement" and did not produce an immediate objection from the prosecutor, although he had vigorously interrupted the opening statement on other points. Justice Marshall also noted that the anticipated length of the trial made it "not unlikely that, had the jury been appropriately instructed * * *, any prejudice would have dissipated before deliberations were to begin." Under these circumstances, the dissent reasoned, the "necessity for a mistrial was not manifest on the record" and the Court therefore should insist that the record otherwise "makes clear" that the trial court applied the correct standard.

5. *The status of Gori.* In *Gori v. United States,* 367 U.S. 364, 81 S.Ct. 1523, 6 L.Ed.2d 901 (1961), the trial judge, "on his own motion and with neither approval nor objection by counsel," declared a mistrial during the government's direct examination of its fourth witness. The trial judge apparently had believed that the prosecutor's questioning "presaged inquiry calculated to inform the jury of other crimes by the accused" and had declared the mistrial "to forestall" that prejudice. A divided Supreme Court (5–4) held that reprosecution was not barred by double jeopardy. The majority viewed the mistrial order as "neither apparently justified nor clearly erroneous" and emphasized the need for granting the trial judge leeway in the exercise of his discretion. The majority concluded: "We are unwilling, where it clearly appears that a mistrial has been granted in the sole interest of the defendant, to hold that its necessary consequence is to bar all retrial." Following *Jorn* [p. 1381 supra], several commentators and lower courts suggested that *Gori* was no longer a viable precedent. The dissenters in *Jorn* had contended that the decision there was "flatly inconsistent" with *Gori,* and the plurality opinion in *Jorn* had rejected the government's argument, based on *Gori,* that an erroneous mistrial ruling should bar a retrial whenever the ruling benefited the defendant.

Has *Washington* now revived the viability of *Gori* through its recognition of the "great deference" that must be granted a trial judge's declaration of a mistrial where that decision was based on the judge's evaluation of the possible creation of jury bias? Consider Schulhofer, Note 3 supra, suggesting that such deference is not appropriate where an improper comment may have created bias against the defendant. In such a case, it is argued, defense counsel is in a far better position to determine whether a mistrial is in the best interests of the defendant and a mistrial therefore should not be granted unless the defendant prefers the mistrial over other alternatives. But compare *United States ex rel. Stewart v. Hewitt,* 517 F.2d 993 (3d Cir.1975) (suggesting that the need to preserve the "appearance of impartiality" justifies granting a mistrial even though the event precipitating the mistrial creates potential prejudice primarily for the defendant and the defendant would prefer to complete the trial; *Stewart* found that the

cused in having the trial concluded by a particular tribunal. Second, respondent does not attempt to demonstrate specific prejudice from the mistrial ruling, other than the harm which always accompanies retrial.

"ends of public justice" justified granting a mistrial over defendant's expressed wishes when the court discovered that the tip-staff servicing the jurors was the father of the homicide victim); *State v. Montalbano,* 326 S.E.2d 634 (N.C.App.1985) (where the judge observed the chief investigating officer violating the judge's cautionary instructions by speaking to two jurors, the judge acted "reasonably within his discretion" in sua sponte declaring a mistrial even though the conversation related only to the jurors' time schedule; the trial judge "sought to protect the defendant" and to sustain both "his credibility" and "public confidence in the jury verdict"). Of course, even if the deference noted in *Washington* applies equally when the potential bias would work against the defendant, that deference would not be due where (unlike *Washington*) the record indicates that the judge could not have given any consideration to alternatives. See Holleman, *Mistrials and the Double Jeopardy Clause,* 14 Ga.L.Rev. 45 (1980). But consider *Abdi v. Georgia,* 744 F.2d 1500 (11th Cir.1984) (an immediate sua sponte declaration of a mistrial does not necessarily evidence "an abrupt or precipitous decision that failed to consider the alternatives").

6. *Lower court cases.* Professor Schulhofer, Note 3 supra, after reviewing nearly 200 appellate court decisions decided after *Somerville,* concluded that "little consensus exists among the courts regarding either the factors that should be analyzed or the result that should be reached in recurring factual contexts." Do the cases that follow evidence such a disarray or do they suggest meaningful distinctions drawn in accordance with the general analysis suggested by Supreme Court precedent?

(a) During the third day of a murder trial, defendant suffered a collapsed lung which required his hospitalization for an estimated 7 to 10 days. Defense counsel requested that a continuance be granted and that the jury, which had been sequestered, be allowed to go home. The prosecutor took no position on the defense proposal, but did suggest that a mistrial would not create double jeopardy problems. The trial court discharged the jury "on its own motion," with the judge noting: "I don't think I have any alternative [in] fairness to both the respondent and the state." See *Dunkerley v. Hogan,* 579 F.2d 141 (2d Cir.1978) (divided court holding the mistrial was not justified under *Perez* standard since the record suggested no reason why the continuance requested by the defense would not have been a "feasible and practical solution"). Compare *In re Dunkerley,* 376 A.2d 43 (Vt.1977) (reaching an opposite conclusion on the same facts, but considering, as the primary alternative to the mistrial, the continuation of the trial with the defendant waiving his right to be present, another proposal that had been offered by defense counsel).

(b) When defense counsel's opening statement challenged the credibility of the complaining witness by reference to previous complaints she had filed that had resulted in no criminal charges, the prosecutor informed the court that he would be required to take the stand to refute the suggestion that the district attorney's office had found those earlier complaints lacking in credibility. The defense objected both to the prosecutor's being allowed to testify and to the declaration of a mistrial to permit him to testify. After determining that the prosecutor could not be allowed to testify and continue with the trial, and that no other prosecutor familiar with the case was available to try the case, the trial court granted the prosecutor's motion for a mistrial. See *State v. Duckett,* 358 N.W.2d 300 (Wis.App.1984) (giving deference to the trial judge's discretion, the mistrial was justified by manifest necessity; the mistrial was not prompted by a "deficiency in the state's evidence," but an unexpected turn of events that presented the "ethical dilemma involved in assuming the dual roles of advocate and witness"). Compare *Douglas v. United States,* 488 A.2d

121 (D.C.App.1985) (once it was determined at trial that a conflict existed between defense counsel and defendant—by virtue of a grievance, currently under investigation, filed by defendant against counsel on the basis of his earlier handling of the case—the court should not have declared a mistrial over defense objection without first exploring the alternative of obtaining defendant's voluntary and intelligent waiver of his right to conflict-free counsel).

(c) After the defendant had completed his testimony, defense counsel, in the presence of the jury, offered to have the defendant respond to any questions that the jury might wish to ask him. The court then excused the jury and asked defense counsel why the court had not been told in advance that the defense wanted to follow such an unusual procedure. Defense counsel stated that the procedure had been used elsewhere and he considered it appropriate. The judge then held that the procedure was improper, noted that defense counsel's announcement had "contaminated" the jury, and declared a mistrial. *Strawn v. State ex rel. Anderberg,* 332 So.2d 601 (Fla.1976) (mistrial justified under *Perez:* while "there well may have been better ways, after meditation, to dispose of the crisis, * * * we are unable to say that [the judge's] decision was an abuse of discretion"). Compare *People v. Johnson,* 396 Mich. 424, 240 N.W.2d 729 (1976) (where defense counsel inadvertently inquired of police officer whether the defendant had asked to take a lie detector test, mistrial was not justified by manifest necessity; mere mention of a polygraph test does not constitute reversible error but may be cured by appropriate instructions to the jury).

7. Several commentators have suggested that the *Perez* standard, as applied, requires that a variety of factors be balanced in determining the propriety of a mistrial. Among the factors cited as relevant to this decision are: (1) the source of the difficulty that led to the mistrial—i.e., whether the difficulty was the product of the actions of the prosecutor, defense counsel, trial judge, or events over which the participants lacked control; (2) whether the difficulty could have been intentionally created or manipulated for the purpose of giving the prosecution an opportunity to strengthen its case; (3) whether the possible prejudice or other legal complication created by the difficulty could be "cured" by some alternative action that would preserve the fairness of the trial; (4) whether the record indicates that the trial judge considered such alternatives; (5) whether any conviction resulting from the trial would inevitably be subject to reversal on appeal; (6) whether the trial judge acted during the "heat of a trial confrontation"; (7) whether the trial judge's determination rested on an evaluation of the demeanor of the participants, the "atmosphere" of the trial, or any other factors that similarly are not amenable to strict appellate review; (8) whether the trial judge granted the mistrial solely for the purpose of protecting the defendant against possible prejudice; (9) whether the evidence presented by the prosecution prior to the mistrial suggested a weakness in the prosecution's case (e.g., a witness had failed to testify as anticipated); (10) whether the jurors had heard enough of the case to formulate some tentative opinions; (11) whether the case had proceeded so far as to give the prosecution a substantial preview of the defense's tactics and evidence; and (12) whether the composition of the jury was unusual and not likely to be repeated. To what extent does the *Perez* standard, as interpreted by the Supreme Court, support consideration of each of these factors? To what extent does it suggest specific weights that should be assigned to particular factors?

8. *Defense "consent" to the mistrial.* In the cases discussed above, the mistrial was declared over the objection of the defendant or without giving the defendant an opportunity to take a position on the mistrial. To what extent should the applica-

ble double jeopardy standard be different where the defendant either requested the mistrial or expressly acquiesced in the court's suggestion that a mistrial be declared? The materials that follow deal with this issue as well as others relating to a defense consent to a mistrial.

OREGON v. KENNEDY

456 U.S. 667, 102 S.Ct. 2083, 72 L.Ed.2d 416 (1982).

JUSTICE REHNQUIST delivered the opinion of the Court.

* * * Respondent was charged with the theft of an oriental rug. During his first trial, the State called an expert witness on the subject of Middle Eastern rugs to testify as to the value and the identity of the rug in question. On cross-examination, respondent's attorney apparently attempted to establish bias on the part of the expert witness by asking him whether he had filed a criminal complaint against respondent. The witness eventually acknowledged this fact, but explained that no action had been taken on his complaint. On redirect examination, the prosecutor sought to elicit the reasons why the witness had filed a complaint against respondent, but the trial court sustained a series of objections to this line of inquiry.[1] The following colloquy then ensued:

> "Prosecutor: Have you ever done business with the Kennedys?
>
> "Witness: No, I have not.
>
> "Prosecutor: Is that because he is a crook?"

The trial court then granted respondent's motion for a mistrial.

When the State later sought to retry respondent, he moved to dismiss the charges because of double jeopardy. After a hearing at which the prosecutor testified, the trial court found as a fact that "it was not the intention of the prosecutor in this case to cause a mistrial." On the basis of this finding, the trial court held that double jeopardy principles did not bar retrial, and respondent was then tried and convicted.

Respondent then successfully appealed to the Oregon Court of Appeals, which sustained his double jeopardy claim. * * * The Court of Appeals accepted the trial court's finding that it was not the intent of the prosecutor to cause a mistrial. Nevertheless, the court held that retrial was barred because the prosecutor's conduct in this case constituted what it viewed as "overreaching." Although the prosecutor intended to rehabilitate the witness, the Court of Appeals expressed the view that the question was in fact "a direct personal attack on the general character of the defendant." This personal attack left respondent with a "Hobson's choice—either to accept a necessarily prejudiced jury, or to move for a mistrial and face the process of being retried at a later time." * * *

Where the trial is terminated over the objection of the defendant, the classical test for lifting the double jeopardy bar to a second trial is the "manifest necessity" standard first enunciated in Justice Story's opinion for the Court in *United States v. Perez.* * * * The "manifest necessity" standard provides sufficient protection to the defendant's interests in having his case finally decided by the jury first selected while at the same time maintaining "the public's interest in fair trials designed to end in just judgments." *Wade v. Hunter* [p. 1383 supra]. But in the case of a mistrial declared at the behest of the defendant, quite different principles come into play. Here the defendant himself has elected to terminate the proceedings against him, and the "manifest necessity" standard has no place in the application of the Double Jeopardy Clause. *United States*

1. The Court of Appeals later explained that respondent's "objections were not well taken, and the judge's rulings were probably wrong." 49 Or. App. 415, 417, 619 P.2d 948, 949 (1980).

v. Dinitz, [424 U.S. 600, 96 S.Ct. 1075, 47 L.Ed.2d 267 (1976)].[a] * * *

Our cases, however, have indicated that even where the defendant moves for a mistrial, there is a narrow exception to the rule that the Double Jeopardy Clause is no bar to retrial. See, e.g., *United States v. Dinitz.* The circumstances under which respondent's first trial was terminated require us to delineate the bounds of that exception more fully than we have in previous cases.

Since one of the principal threads making up the protection embodied in the Double Jeopardy Clause is the right of the defendant to have his trial completed before the first jury empaneled to try him, it may be wondered as a matter of original inquiry why the defendant's election to terminate the first trial by his own motion should not be deemed a renunciation of that right for all purposes. We have recognized, however, that there would be great difficulty in applying such a rule where the prosecutor's actions giving rise to the motion for mistrial were done "in order to goad the [defendant] into requesting a mistrial." *United States v. Dinitz.* In such a case, the defendant's valued

a. Explaining this position, the Court in *Dinitz* noted:

"Different considerations obtain, however, when the mistrial has been declared at the defendant's request. The reasons for the distinction were discussed in the plurality opinion in the *Jorn* case [p. 1382 supra]:

> 'If that right to go to a particular tribunal is valued, it is because, independent of the threat of bad-faith conduct by judge or prosecutor, the defendant has a significant interest in the decision whether or not to take the case from the jury when circumstances occur which might be thought to warrant a declaration of mistrial. Thus, where circumstances develop not attributable to prosecutorial or judicial overreaching, a motion by the defendant for mistrial is ordinarily assumed to remove any barrier to reprosecution, even if the defendant's motion is necessitated by prosecutorial or judicial error. * * *'

"The distinction between mistrials declared by the court *sua sponte* and mistrials granted at the defendant's request or with his consent is wholly consistent with the protections of the Double Jeopardy Clause. Even when judicial or prosecutorial error prejudices a defendant's prospects of securing an acquittal, he may nonetheless desire 'to go to the first jury and, perhaps, end the dispute then and there with an acquittal.' *United States v. Jorn,* supra. Our prior decisions recognize the defendant's right to pursue this course in the absence of circumstances of manifest necessity requiring a *sua sponte* judicial declaration of mistrial. But it is evident that when judicial or prosecutorial error seriously prejudices a defendant, he may have little interest in completing the trial and obtaining a verdict from the first jury. The defendant may reasonably conclude that a continuation of the tainted proceeding would result in a conviction followed by a lengthy appeal and, if a reversal is secured, by a second prosecution. In such circumstances, a defendant's mistrial request has objectives not unlike the interests served by the Double Jeopardy Clause—the avoidance of the anxiety, expense, and delay occasioned by multiple prosecutions.

"The Court of Appeals viewed the doctrine that permits a retrial following a mistrial sought by the defendant as resting on a waiver theory. The court concluded, therefore, that 'something more substantial than a Hobson's choice' is required before a defendant can 'be said to have relinquished voluntarily his right to proceed before the first jury.' * * * But traditional waiver concepts have little relevance where the defendant must determine whether or not to request or consent to a mistrial in response to judicial or prosecutorial error. See *United States v. Jorn,* supra. In such circumstances, the defendant generally does face a 'Hobson's choice' between giving up his first jury and continuing a trial tainted by prejudicial, judicial or prosecutorial error. The important consideration, for purposes of the Double Jeopardy Clause, is that the defendant retains primary control over the course to be followed in the event of such error."

Speaking to the waiver analogy, the *Dinitz* opinion added in a footnote: "The respondent characterizes a defendant's mistrial motion as a waiver of 'his right not to be placed twice in jeopardy' and argues that to be valid the waiver must meet the knowing, intelligent, and voluntary standard set forth in *Johnson v. Zerbst* [p. 121 supra]. This approach erroneously treats the defendant's interest in going forward before the first jury as a constitutional right comparable to the right to counsel. It fails to recognize that the protection against the burden of multiple prosecutions underlying the constitutional prohibition against double jeopardy may be served by a mistrial declaration and the concomitant relinquishment of the opportunity to obtain a verdict from the first jury. This Court has implicitly rejected the contention that the permissibility of a retrial following a mistrial or a reversal of a conviction on appeal depends on a knowing, voluntary, and intelligent waiver of a constitutional right. * * *"

right to complete his trial before the first jury would be a hollow shell if the inevitable motion for mistrial were held to prevent a later invocation of the bar of double jeopardy in all circumstances. But the precise phrasing of the circumstances which *will* allow a defendant to interpose the defense of double jeopardy to a second prosecution where the first has terminated on his own motion for a mistrial have been stated with less than crystal clarity in our cases which deal with this area of the law. * * * The language [of *Dinitz* at points] would seem to broaden the test from one of *intent* to provoke a motion for a mistrial to a more generalized standard of "bad faith conduct" or "harassment" on the part of the judge or prosecutor. It was upon this language that the Oregon Court of Appeals apparently relied in concluding that the prosecutor's colloquy with the expert witness in this case amount to "overreaching."

The difficulty with the more general standards which would permit a broader exception than one merely based on intent is that they offer virtually no standards for their application. Every act on the part of a rational prosecutor during a trial is designed to "prejudice" the defendant by placing before the judge or jury evidence leading to a finding of his guilt. Given the complexity of the rules of evidence, it will be a rare trial of any complexity in which some proffered evidence by the prosecutor or by the defendant's attorney will not be found objectionable by the trial court. Most such objections are undoubtedly curable by simply refusing to allow the proffered evidence to be admitted, or in the case of a particular line of inquiry taken by counsel with a witness, by an admonition to desist from a particular line of inquiry.

More serious infractions on the part of the prosecutor may provoke a motion for mistrial on the part of the defendant, and may in the view of the trial court warrant the granting of such a motion. The "overreaching" standard applied by the court below and urged today by Justice Stevens, however, would add another classification of prosecutorial error, one requiring dismissal of the indictment, but without supplying any standard by which to assess that error.[5]

By contrast, a standard that examines the intent of the prosecutor, though certainly not entirely free from practical difficulties, is a manageable standard to apply. It merely calls for the court to make a finding of fact. Inferring the existence or nonexistence of intent from objective facts and circumstances is a familiar process in our criminal justice system. When it is remembered that resolution of double jeopardy questions by state trial courts are reviewable not only within the state court system, but in the federal court system on habeas corpus as well, the desirability of an easily applied principle is apparent.

Prosecutorial conduct that might be viewed as harassment or overreaching, even if sufficient to justify a mistrial on defendant's motion, therefore, does not bar retrial absent intent on the part of the prosecutor to subvert the protections afforded by the Double Jeopardy Clause. A defendant's motion for a mistrial constitutes "a deliberate election on his part to forgo his valued right to have his guilt or innocence determined before the first trier of fact." *United States v. Scott* [p. 1403 infra]. Where prosecutorial error even of a degree sufficient to warrant a mistrial has

5. "If the Court were to hold, as would Justice Stevens, that such a determination requires an assessment of the facts and circumstances but without explaining how such an assessment ought to proceed, the Court would offer little guidance to the federal and state courts that must apply our decisions. Justice Stevens disagrees with this decision below because his reaction to a cold record is different from that of the Oregon Court of Appeals. The Court of Appeals found 'overreaching'; Justice Stevens finds none. Neither articulates a basis for reaching their respective conclusions which can be applied to other factual situations. We are loath to adopt such an essentially standardless rule."

occurred, "[t]he important consideration, for purposes of the Double Jeopardy Clause, is that the defendant retain primary control over the course to be followed in the event of such error." *United States v. Dinitz.* Only where the governmental conduct in question is intended to "goad" the defendant into moving for a mistrial may a defendant raise the bar of double jeopardy to a second trial after having succeeded in aborting the first on his own motion.

Were we to embrace the broad and somewhat amorphous standard adopted by the Oregon Court of Appeals, we are not sure that criminal defendants as a class would be aided. Knowing that the granting of the defendant's motion for mistrial would all but inevitably bring with it an attempt to bar a second trial on grounds of double jeopardy, the judge presiding over the first trial might well be more loath to grant a defendant's motion for mistrial. If a mistrial were in fact warranted under the applicable law, of course, the defendant could in many instances successfully appeal a judgment of conviction on the same grounds that he urged a mistrial, and the Double Jeopardy Clause would present no bar to retrial.[7] But some of the advantages secured to him by the Double Jeopardy Clause—the freedom from extended anxiety, and the necessity to confront the government's case only once—would be to a large extent lost in the process of trial to verdict, reversal on appeal, and subsequent retrial.

* * * We do not by this opinion lay down a flat rule that where a defendant in a criminal trial successfully moves for a mistrial, he may not thereafter invoke the bar of double jeopardy against a second trial. But we do hold that the circumstances under which such a defendant may invoke the bar of double jeopardy in a second effort to try him are limited to those cases in which the conduct giving rise to the successful motion for a mistrial was intended to provoke the defendant into moving for a mistrial. Since the Oregon trial court found, and the Oregon Court of Appeals accepted, that the prosecutorial conduct culminating in the termination of the first trial in this case was not so intended by the prosecutor, that is the end of the matter for purposes of the Double Jeopardy Clause of the Fifth Amendment to the United States Constitution. * * *

JUSTICE BRENNAN, with whom JUSTICE MARSHALL joins, concurring in the judgment.

I concur in the judgment and join in the opinion of Justice Stevens. However, it should be noted that nothing in the holding of the Court today prevents the state courts, on remand, from concluding that respondent's retrial would violate the pro-

7. Justice Stevens' concurring opinion [at fn. 22] criticizes the suggestion that the broader rule he espouses would make it less likely the judges would grant a motion for mistrial than if the narrower rule prevailed. * * * Tested by the * * * assumption that the courts would be applying the all encompassing standard denominated "overreaching," which he espouses, we do not find his criticisms persuasive. If appellate courts and trial courts alike in this branch of the law of double jeopardy were applying a rule of "black letter law" to a pre-determined set of facts, it might be true that an appellate court would inevitably reach the conclusion that reprosecution should be barred in a number of cases where the trial court had actually denied the motion for mistrial. But there are two reasons why such a hypothesis is inapplicable here. First, the rule espoused by Justice Stevens is anything but a rule of "black letter law." We are admonished that "it is unnecessary and unwise to attempt to identify all the factors that might inform the Court's judgment." Second, appellant courts have traditionally given weight to a trial court's assessment as to the necessity for a mistrial in deciding questions of double jeopardy. * * * It seems entirely reasonable to expect, therefore, that appellate judges will continue to defer to the judgment of trial judges who are 'on the scene' in this area, and that they will not inexorably reach the same conclusion on a cold record at the appellate stage that they might if any one of them had been sitting as a trial judge. And a trial judge trying to faithfully apply the amorphous standard enunciated by Justice Stevens could surely be forgiven if in cases he regarded as extremely close he resolved the doubt in favor of continuing a trial to its conclusion rather than aborting it.

vision of the Oregon Constitution that prohibits double jeopardy * * *.

JUSTICE POWELL, concurring.

I join the Court's opinion holding that the *intention* of a prosecutor determines whether his conduct, viewed by the defendant and the court as justifying a mistrial, bars a retrial of the defendant under the Double Jeopardy Clause. Because "subjective" intent often may be unknowable, I emphasize that a court—in considering a double jeopardy motion—should rely primarily upon the objective facts and circumstances of the particular case.

In the present case the mistrial arose from the prosecutor's conduct in pursuing a line of redirect examination of a key witness. The Oregon Court of Appeals identified a single question as constituting "overreaching" so serious as to bar a retrial. Yet, there are few vigorously contested lawsuits—whether criminal or civil—in which improper questions are not asked. Our system *is* adversarial and vigorous advocacy is encouraged.

Nevertheless, this would have been a close case for me if there had been substantial factual evidence of intent beyond the question itself. Here, however, other relevant facts and circumstances strongly support the view that prosecutorial intent to cause a mistrial was absent. First, there was no sequence of overreaching prior to the single prejudicial question. Moreover, it is evident from a colloquy between counsel and the court, out of the presence of the jury, that the prosecutor not only resisted, but also was surprised by, the defendant's motion for a mistrial. Finally, at the hearing on respondent's double jeopardy motion, the prosecutor testified—and the trial found as a fact and the appellate court agreed—that there was no " 'intention . . . to cause a mistrial.' " In view of these circumstances, the Double Jeopardy Clause provides no bar to retrial.

JUSTICE STEVENS, with whom JUSTICE BRENNAN, JUSTICE MARSHALL, and JUSTICE BLACKMUN join, concurring in the judgment.

* * * The rationale for the exception to the general rule permitting retrial after a mistrial declared with the defendant's consent is illustrated by the situation in which the prosecutor commits prejudicial error with the intent to provoke a mistrial. In this situation the defendant's choice to continue the tainted proceeding or to abort the proceeding and begin anew is inadequate to protect his double jeopardy interests. For, absent a bar to reprosecution, the defendant would simply play into the prosecutor's hands by moving for a mistrial. The defendant's other option—to continue the tainted proceeding—would be no option at all if, as we might expect given the prosecutor's intent, the prosecutorial error has virtually guaranteed conviction. There is no room in the balance of competing interests for this type of manipulation of the mistrial device. Or to put it another way, whereas we tolerate some incidental infringement upon a defendant's double jeopardy interests for the sake of society's interest in obtaining a verdict of guilt or innocence, when the prosecutor seeks to obtain an advantage by intentionally subverting double jeopardy interests, the balance invariably tips in favor of a bar to reprosecution.

Today the Court once again recognizes that the exception properly encompasses the situation in which the prosecutor commits prejudicial error with the intent to provoke a mistrial. But the Court reaches out to limit the exception to that one situation, rejecting the previous recognition that prosecutorial overreaching or harassment is also within the exception.[22]

22. The Court offers two reasons for cutting back on the exception. First, the Court states that "[t]he difficulty with the more general standards which would permit a broader exception than one merely based on intent is that they offer virtually no standards for their application." As I indicate in the text, however, some generality in the formula is a virtue and, in any event, meaningful and principled standards can be developed on a case-by-case basis that will not inhibit legiti-

Even if I agreed that the balance of competing interests tipped in favor of a bar to reprosecution only in the situation in which the prosecutor intended to provoke a mistrial, I would not subscribe to a standard that conditioned such a bar on the determination that the prosecutor harbored such intent when he committed prejudicial error. It is almost inconceivable that a defendant could prove that the prosecutor's deliberate misconduct was motivated by an intent to provoke a mistrial instead of an intent simply to prejudice the defendant. The defendant must shoulder a strong burden to establish a bar to reprosecution when he has consented to the mistrial, but the Court's subjective intent standard would eviscerate the exception.

A broader objection to the Court's limitation of the exception is that the rationale for the exception extends beyond the situation in which the prosecutor intends to provoke a mistrial. There are other situations in which the defendant's double jeopardy interests outweigh society's interest in obtaining a judgment on the merits even though the defendant has moved for a mistrial. For example, a prosecutor may be interested in putting the defendant through the embarrassment, expense, and ordeal of criminal proceedings even if he cannot obtain a conviction. In such a case, with the purpose of harassing the defendant the prosecutor may commit repeated prejudicial errors and be indifferent between a mistrial or mistrials and an unsustainable conviction or convictions. Another example is when the prosecutor seeks to inject enough unfair prejudice into the trial to ensure a conviction but not so much as to cause a reversal of that conviction. This kind of overreaching would not be covered by the Court's standard because, by hypothesis, the prosecutor's intent is to obtain a conviction, not to provoke a mistrial. Yet the defendant's choice—to continue the tainted proceeding or to abort it and begin anew—can be just as "hollow" in this situation as when the prosecutor intends to provoke a mistrial.

To invoke the exception for overreaching, a court need not divine the exact motivation for the prosecutorial error. It is sufficient that the court is persuaded that egregious prosecutorial misconduct has rendered unmeaningful the defendant's choice to continue or to abort the proceeding. It is unnecessary and unwise to attempt to identify all the factors that might inform the court's judgment, but several considerations follow from the rationale for recognizing the exception. First, because the exception is justified by the intolerance of intentional manipulation of the defendant's double jeopardy interests, a finding of deliberate misconduct normally would be a prerequisite to a reprosecution bar. Second, because the defendant's option to abort the proceeding after prosecutorial misconduct would retain real meaning for the defendant in any case in which the trial was going badly for him, normally a required finding would be that the prosecutorial error virtually eliminated, or at least substantially reduced, the probability of acquittal in a proceeding that was going badly for the government. It should be apparent from these observations that only in a rare and compelling case will a mistri-

mate prosecution practices. Moreover, the general standards could hardly be more difficult to apply than the Court's subjective intent standard.

* * *

Second, the Court is "not sure that criminal defendants as a class would be aided" by a broader exception. If a mistrial will more frequently constitute a bar to reprosecution, the Court supposes that trial judges will tend to refuse the defendant's mistrial motion and permit the error to be corrected on appeal of the conviction, in which event there would be no bar to reprosecution. This reasoning is premised on the assumption that an appellate court that concluded not only that the defendant's mistrial motion should have been granted but also that the prosecutor intended to provoke a mistrial would not be obligated to bar reprosecution as well as reverse the conviction. The assumption is "irrational." *Commonwealth v. Potter,* 478 Pa. 251, 386 A.2d 918 (1978) (Roberts, J.) (Pomeroy, J.).

al declared at the request of the defendant or with his consent bar a retrial.

No one case, of course, is a proper vehicle for identifying the limits of the exception. The Court repeatedly has shunned inflexible standards in applying the comparable "manifest necessity" exception to the general rule that a defendant is entitled to go to final judgment before the initial tribunal. The value of the overreaching standard, like "[t]he value of the [manifest necessity standard,] thus lies in [its] capacity for informed application under widely different circumstances without injury to defendants or to the public interest." *Wade v. Hunter.* The inexactitude of the standard used to protect defendants in the exceptional case surely should not concern the Court any more than the equally ill-defined formula used to protect prosecutors in the exceptional case. * * *

* * * The isolated prosecutorial error [here] occurred early in the trial, too early to determine whether the case was going badly for the prosecution. If anyone was being harassed at that time, it was the prosecutor who was frustrated by improper defense objections in her attempt to rehabilitate her witness. The gist of the comment that the respondent was a "crook" could fairly have been elicited from the witness, since defense counsel injected the respondent's past alleged improprieties into the trial by questioning the witness about his bias towards the defendant. The comment therefore could not have injected the kind of prejudice that would render unmeaningful the defendant's option to proceed with the trial. Because the present case quite clearly does not come within the recognized exception, I join the Court's judgment.

Notes and Questions

1. On remand, the Oregon Supreme Court, though affirming defendant's conviction, did adopt, under the Oregon Constitution, a broader exception to the "defense-request" rule than that announced in *Kennedy.* The Oregon Court ruled that, even though defendant moved for the mistrial, retrial would be barred "when improper official conduct is so prejudicial to the defendant that it cannot be cured by means short of a mistrial, and if the official knows that the conduct is improper and prejudicial and either intends or is indifferent to the resulting mistrial or reversal." *State v. Kennedy,* 666 P.2d 1316 (Or. 1983). Other state courts also have adopted standards more protective than that required by *Kennedy.* See, e.g., *Commonwealth v. Murchison,* 465 N.E.2d 256 (Mass.1984) (retrial barred where prosecutor's misconduct either meets *Kennedy* standard or results in "such irremediable harm that a fair trial * * * is no longer possible)."

To what extent do the above standards meet (or exacerbate) the objections raised by Justice Rehnquist to the standard advanced by Justice Stevens in *Kennedy?* Does the adoption of a broader standard than that adopted in *Kennedy* require a jurisdiction to also reconsider the consequences of an appellate reversal of a conviction based upon prosecutorial error? As noted by the *Kennedy* majority (see n. 7), the traditional rule governing such appellate reversals (the *Ball* rule) allows a retrial no matter how flagrant the prosecutorial error that requires a reversal? See Notes 1–3 at pp. 1417–19 infra. It has been argued that the mistrial and appellate reversal cases are invariably linked and that any standard adopted for precluding a retrial in the defense-request mistrial cases should be carried over to bar retrial following an appellate reversal. See Gershman, *Prosecutorial Misconduct § 11.8* (1985); Ponsoldt, *When Guilt Should Be Irrelevant: Government Overreaching as a Bar to Reprosecution Under the Double Jeopardy Clause After Oregon v. Kennedy,* 69 Cornell L.Rev. 76 (1983) (also arguing that adequate protection of "defendant's right to be free from harassment" requires prohibiting a retrial where a mistrial granted upon defense motion or an appellate reversal was occasioned by prosecutorial or judicial error "sufficient in magnitude and clarity" to constitute a "plain error" under Federal Rule 52, which requires an error so " 'serious and manifest' that it affects the very integrity of the trial process").

2. Does it follow from *Kennedy* that the burden of persuasion as to whether the prosecutor intended to provoke a mistrial lies with the defense? See Note, 82 Mich. L.Rev. 365 (1983) (noting that, as to factual issues presented in other double jeopardy contexts, most courts place the burden on the defendant, but arguing that both "practical and constitutional considerations" mandate that the burden be placed on the government).

3. What factors should be considered by the trial court in determining the prosecutor's intention? Should the error have to be one that is clear under prevailing law? Must there have been some indication that the prosecution's case was weaker than the prosecutor might have anticipated before trial? Consider *State v. Catch The Bear,* 352 N.W.2d 637 (S.D.1984) (trial court finding of intentionally provoked mistrial was clearly erroneous where pretrial in limine ruling prohibited reference to defendant's prearrest silence and prosecutorial error in opening statement consisted of reference to post-arrest silence, prosecutor strenuously argued that his opening statement was legally permissible, the error occurred before the prosecution has any basis for gauging the jury's reaction to its case, and the trial judge initially believed that the error was negligent rather than intentional).

4. Does *Kennedy*'s emphasis on the prosecutor's intention produce a standard that is "practically impossible" to establish, "short of an outright admission" by the prosecutor, and that therefore completely fails to deter prosecutorial misconduct? See Gershman, *The Burger Court and Prosecutorial Misconduct,* 21 Crim.L.Bull. 217 (1985). Does Justice Powell's concurring opinion provide a satisfactory answer to this concern? What of the following comments in *State v. Catch the Bear* (Note 3 supra): "[W]e in no sense approve of the actions or comments of the state's attorney; they were clearly mistaken and prejudicial to the defendant in this case. As such, they are not to be countenanced by the courts of this jurisdiction. In this regard, however, we wish to make clear that the granting of a mistrial with prejudice is an inappropriate manner of punishing a negligent state's attorney. The primary concern of the criminal justice system is to provide a fair and proper forum for the trial of defendants accused of serious crimes such as this one. An erring state's attorney can be disciplined in ways which do not infringe upon this concern and yet guarantee a fair trial for the accused."

5. As the Court noted in *Dinitz* (fn. a supra), the rule announced there makes the *Perez* standard inapplicable to mistrials "granted at the defendant's request or *with his consent*" (emphasis added). Should the defense be viewed as having "consented" to the mistrial where the trial court informed defense counsel that it was considering ordering a mistrial and defendant counsel failed to object? Consider *Anderson v. United States,* 481 A.2d 1299 (D.C. App.1984) (consent implicit where defense raised issue of prejudice and, when offered opportunity to comment, neither objected to mistrial nor suggested other alternative). Note, however, Schulhofer, p. 1388 supra, criticizing the "readiness of many courts to engraft upon the consent doctrine notions of tacit consent or constructive consent that expand the concept far beyond its justifiable limits." As a practice pointer for defense counsel, it has been suggested that: "In any case in which the court proposes a mistrial *sua sponte,* counsel should take the position that he does not actively oppose the mistrial but should insist that the accused may not again be placed in jeopardy for the same offense." Annot., 77 A.L.R.3d 1143, 1152 (1977). Would following this tactic

thereby avoid application of the consent doctrine?

6. In LEE v. UNITED STATES, 432 U.S. 23, 97 S.Ct. 2141, 53 L.Ed.2d 80 (1977), the Supreme Court considered the bearing upon the *Dinitz* "consent doctrine" of defendant's timing in raising an objection. The defendant there had been charged by information with theft and had elected a bench trial. After the prosecutor's opening statement, defense counsel moved to dismiss the information on the ground that it did not allege specific intent. The trial court tentatively denied the motion subject to further study. At the close of the two hour trial, the judge took a fifteen minute recess. When the judge returned from the recess, he noted that the defendant's guilt had been established beyond a reasonable doubt; however, he had concluded that the information was indeed insufficient, and the motion to dismiss would be granted. The Supreme Court, per POWELL, J., held that the reprosecution was not barred by double jeopardy.

The *Lee* Court first concluded that the dismissal order had been the functional equivalent of a declaration of a mistrial. The dismissal had been based on the insufficiency of the information, rather than any insufficiency of the evidence, and therefore was granted in apparent contemplation of a second trial. The Court then found that the dismissal order was subject to the rule applied to mistrials granted at defendant's request. Rejecting petitioner's attempt to distinguish *Dinitz,* Justice POWELL noted:

"[Petitioner] contends (i) that he should never have had to undergo the first trial because the court was made aware of the defective information before jeopardy had attached; and (ii) that once the court had determined to hear evidence despite the defective charge, he was entitled to have the trial proceed to a formal finding of guilt or innocence. The Government responds that petitioner had only himself to blame in both respects. By the last-minute timing of his motion to dismiss, he virtually invited the court to interrupt the proceedings before formalizing a finding on the merits. We think that the Government had the better of the argument on both points under the principles explained in our decision in *United States v. Dinitz.* * * * "

Justice Brennan, in a concurring opinion, emphasized that "an entirely different case would be presented if the petitioner had afforded the trial judge ample opportunity to rule on his motion prior to trial, and the court, in failing to take advantage of this opportunity [had] permitted the attachment of jeopardy before ordering dismissal of the indictment." Justice Marshall dissented. He argued that the "petitioner was needlessly placed in jeopardy" since the judge could just as easily have recessed the case for 15 minutes before trial and determined at that point that the information was invalid.

SECTION 2. REPROSECUTION FOLLOWING AN ACQUITTAL

UNITED STATES v. SCOTT

437 U.S. 82, 98 S.Ct. 2187, 57 L.Ed.2d 65 (1978).

MR. JUSTICE REHNQUIST delivered the opinion of the Court.

On March 5, 1975, respondent, a member of the police force in Muskegon, Mich., was charged * * * with distribution of various narcotics. Both before his trial in the United States District Court and twice during the trial, respondent moved to dismiss the two counts of the indictment which concerned transactions that took place during the preceding September, on the ground that his defense had been prejudiced by preindictment delay. At the close of all the evidence, the court granted respondent's motion. Although the court did not explain its reasons for dismissing the second count, it explicitly concluded that respondent had "presented sufficient proof of prejudice with respect to the first count." * * *

The Government sought to appeal the dismissals of the first two counts to the United States Court of Appeals for the Sixth Circuit. That court, relying on our opinion in *United States v. Jenkins,* 420 U.S. 358, 95 S.Ct. 1006, 43 L.Ed.2d 250 (1975), concluded that any further prosecution of respondent was barred by the Double Jeopardy Clause of the Fifth Amendment, and therefore dismissed the appeal. The Government has sought review in this Court only with regard to the dismissal of the first count. We granted certiorari to give further consideration to the applicability of the Double Jeopardy Clause to Government appeals from orders granting defense motions to terminate a trial before verdict. We now reverse.

I

The problem presented by this case could not have arisen during the first century of this Court's existence. The Court has long taken the view that the United States has no right of appeal in a criminal case, absent explicit statutory authority. Such authority was not provided until the enactment of the Criminal Appeals Act, Act of Mar. 2, 1907, which permitted the United States to seek a writ of error in this Court from any decision dismissing an indictment on the basis of "the invalidity, or construction of the statute upon which the indictment is founded." Our consideration of Government appeals over the ensuing years ordinarily focused upon the intricacies of the Act and its amendments. In 1971, however, Congress adopted the current language of the Act, permitting Government appeals from any decision dismissing an indictment, "except that no appeal shall lie where the Double Jeopardy Clause of the United States Constitution prohibits further prosecution." 18 U.S.C. § 3731. * * *

In our first encounter with the new statute, we concluded "that Congress intended to remove all statutory barriers to Government appeals and to allow appeals whenever the Constitution would permit." *United States v. Wilson,* 420 U.S. 332, 95 S.Ct. 1013, 43 L.Ed.2d 232 (1975). A detailed canvass of the history of the double jeopardy principles in [*Wilson*] * * * led us to conclude that the Double Jeopardy Clause was primarily "directed at the threat of multiple prosecutions," and posed no bar to Government appeals "where those appeals would not require a new trial." We accordingly held in *Jenkins,* that, whether or not a dismissal of an indictment after jeopardy had attached amounted to an acquittal on the merits, the Government had no right to appeal, because "further proceedings of some sort, devoted to the resolution of factual issues going to the elements of the offense charged, would have been required upon reversal and remand." [a]

If *Jenkins* is a correct statement of the law, the judgment of the Court of Appeals relying on that decision, as it was bound to do, would in all likelihood have to be affirmed. Yet, though our assessment of the history and meaning of the Double Jeopardy Clause in *Wilson, Jenkins,* and *Serfass v. United States,* 420 U.S. 377, 95 S.Ct. 1055, 43 L.Ed.2d 265 (1975), occurred only three Terms ago, our vastly increased exposure to the various facets of the Double Jeopardy Clause has now con-

a. In *Wilson,* after the jury returned a verdict of guilty, the trial court reconsidered an earlier motion and dismissed the indictment on due process grounds. The Supreme Court stressed that an appellate court reversal of the dismissal would not require a new trial since the appellate court could simply reinstate the jury's verdict. See Note 8, p. 1416 infra. In *Jenkins,* the dismissal was issued by the trial judge, sitting in a bench trial, before the judge reached a verdict. The trial judge's dismissal order was based on his interpretation of the substantive law, but the judge had not indicated what result he would have reached as the finder of fact if a contrary interpretation had been adopted. Thus, if the trial judge's order were reversed, further resolution of the facts relating to the elements of the offense would be required. The *Jenkins* opinion stressed this consequence of reversal rather than the grounding of the trial court's ruling.

vinced us that *Jenkins* was wrongly decided. It placed an unwarrantedly great emphasis on the defendant's right to have his guilt decided by the first jury empaneled to try him so as to include those cases where the defendant himself seeks to terminate the trial before verdict on grounds unrelated to factual guilt or innocence. We have therefore decided to overrule *Jenkins,* and thus to reverse the judgment of the Court of Appeals in this case.

II

* * * At the time the Fifth Amendment was adopted, its principles were easily applied, since most criminal prosecutions proceeded to final judgment, and neither the United States nor the defendant had any right to appeal an adverse verdict. The verdict in such a case was unquestionably final, and could be raised in bar against any further prosecution for the same offense.

* * * It was not until 1889 that Congress permitted criminal defendants to seek a writ of error in this Court, and then only in capital cases. Only then did it become necessary for this Court to deal with the issues presented by the challenge of verdicts on appeal. And, in the very first case presenting the issues, *United States v. Ball,* 163 U.S. 662, 16 S.Ct. 1192, 41 L.Ed. 300 (1896), the Court established principles that have been adhered to ever since. Three persons had been tried together for murder; two were convicted, the other acquitted. This Court reversed the convictions, finding the indictment fatally defective, whereupon all three defendants were tried again. This time all three were convicted and they again sought review here. This Court held that the Double Jeopardy Clause precluded further prosecution of the defendant who had been *acquitted* at the original trial but that it posed no such bar to the prosecution of those defendants who had been *convicted* in the earlier proceeding.

* * * These then, at least, are two venerable principles of double jeopardy jurisprudence. The successful appeal of a judgment of conviction, on any ground other than the insufficiency of the evidence to support the verdict, *Burks v. United States* [p. 1419 infra], poses no bar to further prosecution on the same charge. A judgment of acquittal, whether based on a jury verdict of not guilty or on a ruling by the court that the evidence is insufficient to convict, may not be appealed and terminates the prosecution when a second trial would be necessitated by a reversal.[7] What may seem superficially to be a disparity in the rules governing a defendant's liability to be tried again is explainable by reference to the underlying purposes of the Double Jeopardy Clause. * * * [T]he law attaches particular significance to an acquittal. To permit a second trial after an acquittal, however mistaken the acquittal may have been, would present an unacceptably high risk that the Government, with its vastly superior resources, might wear down the defendant so that "even though innocent, he may be found guilty." *Green v. United States* [p. 1424 infra]. On the other hand, to require a criminal defendant to stand trial again after he has successfully invoked a statutory right of appeal to upset his first conviction is not an act of governmental oppression of the sort against which the Double Jeopardy Clause was intended to protect. * * *

7. In *Jenkins* we had assumed that a judgment of acquittal could be appealed where no retrial would be needed on remand: "When this principle is applied to the situation where the jury returns a verdict of guilt but the trial court thereafter enters a judgment of acquittal an appeal is permitted. In that situation a conclusion by an appellate court that the judgment of acquittal was improper does not require a criminal defendant to submit to a second trial; the error can be corrected on remand by the entry of a judgment on the verdict." 420 U.S., at 365, 95 S.Ct. at 1011. Despite the Court's heavy emphasis on the finality of an acquittal in *Martin Linen* [p. 1416 infra] and *Sanabria v. United States* [p. 1411 infra], neither decision explicitly repudiates this assumption.

III

Although the primary purpose of the Double Jeopardy Clause was to protect the integrity of a final judgment, this Court has also developed a body of law guarding the separate but related interest of a defendant in avoiding multiple prosecutions even where no final determination of guilt or innocence has been made. Such interests may be involved in two different situations: the first, in which the trial judge declares a mistrial; the second, in which the trial judge terminates the proceedings favorably to the defendant on a basis not related to factual guilt or innocence.

* * * In passing on the propriety of a declaration of mistrial granted at the behest of the prosecutor or on the court's own motion, this Court has [applied the *Perez* standard of manifest necessity]. * * * In our recent decision in *Arizona v. Washington,* we reviewed this Court's attempts to give content to the term "manifest necessity," * * * and we noted that the trial court's discretion must be exercised with a careful regard for the interests first described in *United States v. Perez.* * * * Where, on the other hand, a *defendant* successfully seeks to avoid his trial prior to its conclusion by a motion for mistrial, the Double Jeopardy Clause is not offended by a second prosecution. * * * Such a motion by the defendant is deemed to be a deliberate election on his part to forego his valued right to have his guilt or innocence determined before the first trier of fact. *United States v. Dinitz* [p. 1395 supra]. * * *

We turn now to the relationship between the Double Jeopardy Clause and reprosecution of a defendant who has successfully obtained not a mistrial, but a termination of the trial in his favor before any determination of factual guilt or innocence. Unlike the typical mistrial, the granting of a motion such as this obviously contemplates that the proceedings will terminate then and there in favor of the defendant. The prosecution, if it wishes to reinstate the proceedings in the face of such a ruling, ordinarily must seek reversal of the decision of the trial court. * * * *Jenkins* held that, regardless of the character of the midtrial termination, appeal was barred if "further proceedings of some sort, devoted to the resolution of factual issues going to the elements of the offense charged, would have been required upon reversal and remand." However, only last term, in *Lee v. United States* [p. 1403 supra], the Government was permitted to institute a second prosecution after a midtrial dismissal of an indictment. The Court found the circumstances presented by that case "functionally indistinguishable from a declaration of a mistrial." Thus, *Lee* demonstrated that, at least in some cases, the dismissal of an indictment may be treated on the same basis as the declaration of a mistrial. * * * [O]ur growing experience with Government appeals convinces us that we must reexamine the rationale of *Jenkins* in light of *Lee* and other recent expositions of the Double Jeopardy Clause.

IV

Our decision in *Jenkins* was based upon our perceptions of the underlying purposes of the Double Jeopardy Clause:

> "The underlying idea, one that is deeply ingrained in at least the Anglo-American system of jurisprudence is that the State with all its resources and power should not be allowed to make repeated attempts to convict an individual for an alleged offense, thereby subjecting him to embarrassment, expense and ordeal and compelling him to live in a continuing state of anxiety and insecurity * * *." *Jenkins,* quoting *Green v. United States* [p. 1424 infra].

Upon fuller consideration, we are now of the view that this language from *Green,* while entirely appropriate in the circumstances of that opinion, is not a principle which can be expanded to include situations in which the defendant is responsible for the second prosecution. It is quite true that the Government with all its resources and power should not be allowed to make repeated attempts to convict an individual for an alleged offense. This truth is expressed in the three common-law pleas of *autrefois acquit, autrefois convict,* and pardon, which lie at the core of the area protected by the Double Jeopardy Clause. As we have recognized in cases from *Ball* to *Sanabria v. United States* [p. 1411 infra], a defendant once acquitted may not be again subjected to trial without violating the Double Jeopardy Clause.

But that situation is obviously a far cry from the present case, where the Government was quite willing to continue with its production of evidence to show the defendant guilty before the jury first empaneled to try him, but the defendant elected to seek termination of the trial on grounds unrelated to guilt or innocence. This is scarcely a picture of an all-powerful state relentlessly pursuing a defendant who had either been found not guilty or who had at least insisted on having the issue of guilt submitted to the first trier of fact. It is instead a picture of a defendant who chooses to avoid conviction and imprisonment, not because of his assertion that the Government has failed to make out a case against him, but because of a legal claim that the Government's case against him must fail even though it might satisfy the trier of fact that he was guilty beyond a reasonable doubt.

We have previously noted that "the trial judge's characterization of his own action cannot control the classification of the action." *United States v. Jorn.* * * * [A] defendant is acquitted only when "the ruling of the judge, whatever its label, actually represents a resolution [in the defendant's favor], correct or not, of some or all of the factual elements of the offense charged," *United States v. Martin Linen Supply* [p. 1416 infra]. Where the court, before the jury returns a verdict, enters a judgment of acquittal pursuant to Fed.Rule Crim.Proc. 29, appeal will be barred only when "it is plain that the District Court * * * evaluated the Government's evidence and determined that it was legally insufficient to support a conviction." Id.

Our opinion in *Burks* [p. 1419 infra] necessarily holds that there has been a "failure of proof" requiring an acquittal when the Government does not submit sufficient evidence to rebut a defendant's essentially factual defense of insanity, though it may otherwise be entitled to have its case submitted to the jury. The defense of insanity, like the defense of entrapment, arises from "the notion that Congress could not have intended criminal punishment for a defendant who has committed all the elements of a proscribed offense," *United States v. Russell* [p. 493 supra], where other facts established to the satisfaction of the trier of fact provide a legally adequate justification for otherwise criminal acts. Such a factual finding *does* "necessarily establish the criminal defendant's lack of criminal culpability," post, (Brennan, J., dissenting), under the existing law; the fact that "the acquittal may result from erroneous evidentiary rulings or erroneous interpretations of governing legal principles," ibid., affects the accuracy of that determination, but it does not alter its essential character. By contrast, the dismissal of an indictment for preindictment delay represents a legal judgment that a defendant, although criminally culpable, may not be punished because of a supposed constitutional violation. * * *

[I]n the present case, [defendant] successfully avoided a submission of the first count of the indictment [to the jury] by persuading the trial court to dismiss it on a basis which did not depend on guilt or innocence. He was thus neither acquitted nor convicted, because he himself successfully undertook to persuade the trial court not to submit the issue of guilt or innocence to the jury which had been empaneled to try him. * * * [Defendant] has not been "deprived" of his valued right to go to the first jury; only the public has been deprived of its valued right to "one complete opportunity to convict those who have violated its laws." *Arizona v. Washington.* No interest protected by the Double Jeopardy Clause is invaded when the Government is allowed to appeal and seek reversal of such a midtrial termination of the proceedings in a manner favorable to the defendant.[13]

It is obvious from what we have said that we believe we pressed too far in *Jenkins,* the concept of the "defendant's valued right to have his trial completed by a particular tribunal." We now conclude that where the defendant himself seeks to have the trial terminated without any submission to either judge or jury as to his guilt or innocence, an appeal by the Government from his successful effort to do so is not barred by 18 U.S.C. § 3731.

MR. JUSTICE BRENNAN, with whom MR. JUSTICE WHITE, MR. JUSTICE MARSHALL, and MR. JUSTICE STEVENS join, dissenting.

* * * While the Double Jeopardy Clause often has the effect of protecting the accused's interest in the finality of particular favorable determinations, this is not its objective. For the Clause often permits Government appeals from final judgments favorable to the accused. See *United States v. Wilson* (whether or not final judgment was an acquittal, Government may appeal if reversal would not necessitate a retrial). The purpose of the Clause, which the Court today fails sufficiently to appreciate, is to protect the accused against the agony and risks attendant upon undergoing more than one criminal trial for any single offense. See ibid. * * * Society's "willingness to limit the Government to a single criminal proceeding to vindicate its very vital interest in enforcement of criminal laws" bespeaks society's recognition of the gross unfairness of requiring the accused to undergo the strain and agony of more than one trial for any single offense. *United States v. Jorn.* Accordingly, the policies of the Double Jeopardy Clause mandate that the Government be afforded but one complete opportunity to convict an accused and that when the first proceeding terminates in a final judgment favorable to the defendant any retrial be barred. The rule as to acquittals can only be understood as simply an application of this larger principle.

Judgments of acquittal normally result from jury or bench verdicts of not guilty. In such cases, the acquittal represents the factfinder's conclusion that, under the controlling legal principles, the evidence does not establish that the defendant can be convicted of the offense charged in the indictment. But the judgment does not necessarily establish the criminal defendant's lack of criminal culpability; the acquittal may result from erroneous evidentiary rulings or erroneous interpretations of governing legal principles induced by the defense. Yet the Double Jeopardy Clause bars a second trial. * * * The reason is not that the first trial established the defendant's factual innocence, but rather that the second trial would present all the untoward consequences the Clause was designed to prevent. Government would

13. We should point out that it is entirely possible for a trial court to reconcile the public interest in the Government's right to appeal from an erroneous conclusion of law, with the defendant's interest in avoiding a second prosecution. In *Wilson,* supra, the court permitted the case to go to the jury, which returned a verdict of guilty, but it subsequently dismissed the indictment for preindictment delay on the basis of evidence adduced at trial. Most recently in *United States v. Ceccolini,* 435 U.S. 268, 98 S.Ct. 1054, 55 L.Ed.2d 268 (1978), we described similar action with approval: "The District Court had sensibly first made its finding on the factual question of guilt or innocence, and then ruled on the motion to suppress; a reversal of these rulings would require no further proceedings in the District Court, but merely a reinstatement of the finding of guilt."

We of course do not suggest that a midtrial dismissal of a prosecution, in response to a defense motion on grounds unrelated to guilt or innocence, is necessarily improper. Such rulings may be necessary to terminate proceedings marred by fundamental error. But where a defendant prevails on such a motion, he takes the risk that an appellate court will reverse the trial court.

be allowed to seek to persuade a second trier of fact of the defendant's guilt, to strengthen any weaknesses in its first presentation, and to subject the defendant to the expense and anxiety of a second trial.

* * * The whole premise for today's retreat from *Jenkins* * * * is the Court's new theory that a criminal defendant who seeks to avoid conviction on a "ground unrelated to factual innocence" somehow stands on a different constitutional footing than a defendant whose participation in his criminal trial creates a situation in which a judgment of acquittal has to be entered. This premise is simply untenable. * * * [T]he reasons that bar a retrial following an acquittal are equally applicable to a final judgment entered on a ground "unrelated to factual innocence." The heavy personal strain of the second trial is the same in either case. So too is the risk that, though innocent, the defendant may be found guilty at a second trial. If the appeal is allowed in either situation, the Government will, following any reversal, not only obtain the benefit of the favorable appellate ruling but also be permitted to shore up any other weak points of its case and obtain all the other advantages at the second trial that the Double Jeopardy Clause was designed to forbid.

Moreover, the Government's interest in retrying a defendant simply cannot vary depending on the ground of the final termination in the accused's favor. I reject as plainly erroneous the Court's suggestion that final judgments not based on innocence deprive the public of "its valued right to 'one complete opportunity to convict those who have violated its laws,'" quoting *Arizona v. Washington*,[6] and therefore differ from "true acquittals." The Government has the same "complete opportunity" in either situation by virtue of its participation as an adversary at the criminal trial.

Equally significant, the distinction between the two is at best purely formal. Many acquittals are the consequence of rulings of law made on the accused's motion that are not related to the question of his factual guilt or innocence: e.g., a ruling on the law respecting the scope of the offense or excluding reliable evidence. *Sanabria v. United States* [Note 2, p. 1411 infra] illustrates the point. * * *

Here the legal ruling that the Court characterizes as unrelated to the defendant's factual guilt itself terminated the prosecution with prejudice. In *Sanabria*, after the District Court rendered the two erroneous rulings that excluded most of the relevant evidence of defendant's guilt, it remained for the trial court to take the pro forma step of granting the defendant's motion for a judgment of acquittal. Surely, this difference between the cases should not possess constitutional significance. By holding that it does, the Court suggests that the present case would have been decided differently if the trial court had remedied the due process violation by excluding all the government's evidence on count one and then entering an acquittal pursuant to Rule 29.

* * * A critical feature of today's holding appears to be the Court's definition of acquittal [p. 1407 supra] as "a resolution [in the defendant's favor], correct or not, of some or all of the factual elements of the offense charged," * * *. The language quoted from *Martin Linen Supply Co.*, was tied to the particular issue in that case and was never intended to serve as an all encompassing definition of acquittal for all purposes. Rather, *Martin Linen Supply* referred generally to "acquittal" as "a legal determi-

6. Similarly unpersuasive is the Court's suggestion that its holding is supported by the well-recognized rules that a criminal defendant may twice be tried for the same offense if he either successfully moved for a mistrial at the first trial, see *Lee*, supra; *United States v. Dinitz*, supra, or succeeded in having a conviction set aside on a ground other than the insufficiency of the evidence. See *United States v. Ball*, supra. What distinguishes these situations, of course, is that neither involved a final judgment entered for the accused and that in both the Government could not be said to have had a complete opportunity to convict the accused.

nation on the basis of facts adduced at trial relating to the general issue of the case," and this is the accepted definition. This * * * traditional definition of "acquittal" obviously is responsive to the values protected by the Double Jeopardy Clause. * * *

But I will not dwell further on this point. As the Court opinion itself demonstrates, what is perhaps as important as the actual definition is how it is applied. The pertinent question, thus, is one the Court never addresses: why, for purposes of its new definition of "acquittal," is not the fact *vel non* of preindictment delay one of the "factual elements of the offense charged"? The Court plainly cannot answer that preindictment delay is not referred to in the statutory definition of the offense charged in count one, for it states that dismissals based on the defenses of insanity and entrapment—neither of which is bound up with the statutory definition of federal crimes—will constitute "acquittals." How can decisions based on the trial evidence that a defendant is "not guilty by reason of insanity" or "not guilty by reason of entrapment" erect a double jeopardy bar, and a decision—equally based on evaluation of the trial evidence—that the defendant is "not guilty by reason of pre-accusation delay" not also prohibit further prosecution? * * * Ironically, it seems likely that, when all is said and done, there will be few instances indeed in which defenses can be deemed unrelated to factual innocence. If so, today's decision may be limited to disfavored doctrines like preaccusation delay. See generally *United States v. Lovasco* [p. 1098 supra]. * * *

Notes and Questions

1. *The function of the "acquittal rule".* Professor Westen has challenged the explanations offered by both the majority and dissenting opinions in *Scott* as to the interests underlying the rule barring a retrial after an acquittal. See Westen and Drubel, *Towards a General Theory of Double Jeopardy,* 1978 Sup.Ct.Rev. 81; Westen, *The Three Faces of Double Jeopardy: Reflections on Governmental Appeals of Criminal Sentences,* 78 Mich. L.Rev. 1001 (1980). As for the defendant's interest in avoiding the burdens and tactical disadvantages of a second trial (stressed in Justice Brennan's dissent), Professor Westen notes that those interests have been rejected as a basis for establishing an absolute bar to retrial "in every other area of double jeopardy." Thus, he notes, "the state may retry a defendant following mistrials declared over his objection, mistrials declared because of hung juries, and convictions reversed on appeal," and, absent a showing of governmental action "solely for the purpose of improving upon its case, shopping for a more favorable trier of fact, or harassing the defendant," it "may do so even though the state itself is partly at fault." Since the defendant in such cases is equally subject to the expense and anxiety of the second trial, to the tactical disadvantages of having disclosed his case to the prosecution, and to the possibility that the government will be able to shore up any weak points in its case, the rule prohibiting retrials following acquittals must rest, says Professor Westen, on other concerns. He rejects, however, the suggestion of the *Scott* majority that retrials following acquittals are barred because they pose "an unacceptably high risk" of resulting in the conviction of an innocent defendant. This rationale, he argues, would have to rest on the assumption that the defendant who has been acquitted, even in a trial flawed by error, is more likely to be innocent than the defendant forced to face a retrial after a mistrial, after a conviction reversed on appeal, or after a dismissal based on non-acquittal grounds (such as that involved in *Scott*). Such an assumption is said to be inconsistent with an acquittal rule so absolute as to bar retrial "even where the acquittals are known to be egregiously erroneous" [quoting *Fong Foo v. United States,* 369 U.S. 141, 82 S.Ct. 671, 7 L.Ed.2d 629 (1962)]. The only sound grounding for the absolute prohibition of

retrials following acquittals, Professor Westen argues, is the need to protect the "jury's prerogative to acquit against the evidence"—an interest that distinguishes the acquittal situation because only there does the possibility exist that the jury has exercised that prerogative.

In *United States v. DiFrancesco* (p. 1427 infra), the Court cited both the *Scott* majority's analysis [see p. 1405 supra, quoting *Green*] and Professor Westen's jury nullification thesis in explaining the acquittal rule. Do both rationales have equal applicability to acquittals entered by a trial court based on its assessment of the credibility or weight of the evidence? Does either rationale justify applying the acquittal rule to a judicial finding of insufficient evidence to convict where that finding rests on the trial judge's erroneous view of the content of the substantive law? Consider in this connection, *Sanabria v. United States,* discussed in Note 2 infra.

2. *Sanabria.* SANABRIA v. UNITED STATES, 437 U.S. 54, 98 S.Ct. 2170, 57 L.Ed.2d 43 (1978), was aptly described by Justice Blackmun as "an odd and an unusual [case], factually and procedurally." [b] The defendant in *Sanabria* was one of eleven persons charged with participation in an "illegal gambling business" in violation of 18 U.S.C. § 1955. Under that provision a gambling business violates federal law only if it also violates the law of the state in which the business is located. The single-count indictment in *Sanabria* charged that the defendants' gambling business involved wagers on a numbers pool and on horse racing in violation of Section 17 of a Massachusetts statute. The government's evidence tied Sanabria to the numbers operation, but not to the horsebetting. At the close of the government's case, defense counsel moved for a judgment of acquittal on the ground that Section 17 of the Massachusetts statute did not prohibit numbers betting since it applied only to betting in "games of competition," such as horse racing. The motion initially was denied, but then was reconsidered after the defendant rested his case. The trial court agreed that Section 17 did not encompass the numbers operation. Another provision of the Massachusetts statute, Section 7, did make numbers betting illegal, but the government could not rely on that provision since it was not cited in the indictment. Accordingly, the court ruled, all of the evidence relating to the numbers operation had to be excluded. The court then granted the requested judgment of acquittal on the ground that there was no evidence tying the defendant to the horsebetting activities.

The government subsequently sought to appeal under 18 U.S.C. § 3731. It conceded that there was insufficient evidence of Sanabria's involvement with horsebetting, but requested that a new trial be ordered on the portion of the indictment relating to numbers betting. The government contended that the trial court had erred twice in dealing with the numbers operation. First the failure of the indictment to allege violation of Section 7 of the Massachusetts statute, in addition to violation of Section 17, was harmless error and should not have barred consideration of the numbers betting as violating Massachusetts law. Second, even if it were assumed that the numbers operation could not be used to establish the illegality of the gambling business, Sanabria's participation in the numbers operation was still relevant since the federal statute would hold liable a person who participated in a lawful portion of a combined gambling venture that was unlawful due to another portion, the horse racing. On review before the Supreme Court, the Court assumed that the

b. The description is taken from Justice Blackmun's dissent in *Sanabria,* joined by Justice Rehnquist. Justice Blackmun also contended that *Sanabria,* because of its unusual setting would "afford little guidance as precedent in the Court's continuous struggle to create order and understanding out of the confusion of the lengthening list of its decisions on the Double Jeopardy."

trial court had erred on both grounds. It held the trial court's order nevertheless was not appealable.

The opinion for the Court, per MARSHALL, J., initially noted that "when a defendant has been acquitted at trial, he may not be retried on the same offense, even if the legal rulings underlying the acquittal were erroneous." The government, the opinion further noted, did not take issue with this principle, as it conceded the unreviewability of "the acquittal for insufficient evidence on what it refers to as the horsebetting theory of liability." The government contended, however, that its "numbers theory of liability" was "dismissed from the count before the judgment of acquittal was entered and therefore that petitioner was not acquitted of the numbers theory." The Court rejected this contention on two grounds: (1) the indictment had contained a single count, charging a single violation, and the acquittal therefore covered both theories of liability; and (2) even if the numbers theory was viewed as dismissed separately, a retrial on that theory would nevertheless be barred since there was only a single offense—participation in any aspect of the gambling enterprise—and the acquittal on the horsebetting necessarily constituted a final judgment as to the entire offense, see *Brown v. Ohio,* p. 1064 supra. In connection with the first point, the opinion stressed the structure of the lower court's ruling:

"With regard to the one count that was in fact charged, as to which petitioner has been at least formally acquitted, we are not persuaded that it is correct to characterize the trial court's action as a 'dismissal' of a discrete portion of the count. * * * [We] assume that the trial court's interpretation of the indictment was erroneous. But not every erroneous interpretation of an indictment for purposes of deciding what evidence is admissible can be regarded as a 'dismissal.' Here the District Court did not find that the count failed to charge a necessary element of the offense, cf. *Lee v. United States* [p. 1403 supra]; rather, it found the indictment's description of the offense too narrow to warrant the admission of certain evidence. To this extent, we believe the ruling below is properly to be characterized as an erroneous evidentiary ruling, which led to an acquittal [on the entire count] for insufficient evidence. That judgment of acquittal, however erroneous, bars further prosecution on any aspect of the count and hence bars appellate review of the trial court's error."

3. *Sanabria* has been criticized as failing to recognize that a judicial ruling framed as an "acquittal," where based solely on the trial court's view of the substantive law (as opposed to an assessment of evidentiary credibility) is just as readily subject to appellate review without disturbing factual findings relating to the defendant's factual innocence as the trial court's ruling in *Scott.* Cooper, *Government Criminal Appeals,* 81 F.R.D. 539 (1979). If the Supreme Court in *Sanabria* had accepted this criticism and treated the trial judge's order as similar to a *Scott*-type dismissal, would this simply have suggested to defense counsel that the better procedure would be to concentrate on favorable jury instructions rather than a judicial "acquittal"? If the judge in *Sanabria* had let the case go to the jury and had charged the jury that defendant could be held liable only if he participated in the horsebetting, the jury presumably would have acquitted (since there was no evidence tying the defendant to horsebetting) and that acquittal clearly would have barred reprosecution.

4. Cooper, Note 3 supra, suggests that the combination of *Sanabria* and *Lee* [Note 6, p. 1403 supra] may mean "that the trial court has discretion to control the double jeopardy consequences of its ruling by choosing the form employed." The author notes that the trial court often will have a choice between framing its order as an "acquittal" based on the prosecution's failure to prove all of the elements of the offense or as a "dismissal" for the failure

of the indictment to charge all the elements of the offense. When the former form is used, *Sanabria* establishes that the government may not appeal even though the trial court's decision is based on a mistaken interpretation of the necessary elements of the offense. When the latter form is used, *Lee* suggests that double jeopardy does not bar an appeal if a mistrial would be permitted under the same circumstances. Professor Cooper concludes: "Although it is troubling that trial judges should be left with discretion to determine whether their legal rulings should be free from appellate review, procedural punctilio at least has the advantage of helping the defendant to know whether further proceedings may be possible."

Under precisely what circumstances will the trial court have the discretion noted by Professor Cooper? Could the trial judge in *Santabello,* for example, have altered his ruling to frame it as a dismissal of the indictment for failure to charge an offense? Can defense counsel control the application of the double jeopardy bar by adopting the following tactic: (1) refusing to challenge an indictment for its failure to include a particular element; (2) hope that the state does not introduce any evidence on that element, but if it does, then insist that the evidence be excluded since the element was not noted in the indictment (see the discussion of variances at p. 1039 supra); and (3) if the evidence has not been introduced in the state's case-in-chief, then seek an acquittal on the ground that the prosecution had failed to establish the missing element? See also Note 6 infra.

5. Do the trial court rulings in the following cases constitute "acquittals" in light of *Scott* and *Sanabria?*

(a) In *United States v. Maker,* 751 F.2d 614 (3d Cir.1984), the indictment charged defendants with a single scheme to defraud in connection with insurance claims arising out of two motor-vehicle accidents. In its opening statement to the jury, the government indicated its intention to introduce transcripts of separate sworn statements made by each of the defendants. The judge then examined the transcripts, and concluded therefrom that the government would not be able to establish the single scheme alleged in the indictment. This conclusion was based on the court's mistaken assumption that proof of a single scheme required proof that fraud as to both accidents had been planned in advance of the first accident. Based on that conclusion, the trial court severed the trial as to both accidents, as requested by the defendants. After the trial continued as to the first accident only, counsel for the defense brought to the court's attention an appellate opinion holding that a defendant could not be tried for multiple schemes to defraud under an indictment charging a single scheme. The trial judge thereupon dismissed the indictment. The Third Circuit subsequently held that an appeal (and retrial following the ensuing appellate reversal) was not barred by double jeopardy. The district court ruling, the court noted, had not "resolved in Maker's favor 'an essential element of the offense charged.'" The government's appeal would be barred "only if the district court's determination about the elements of a single scheme conviction is correct" and that determination was in fact erroneous.

(b) In *United States v. Moore,* 613 F.2d 1029 (D.C.Cir.1979), defendant, charged with making false declarations before a grand jury, waived his right to a jury trial and the case was submitted to the court for a decision on the sole issue of materiality. After the government had presented the testimony of the grand jury foreman bearing on the materiality issue, defense counsel raised an additional defense, contending that defendant's subsequent statements brought the case within the purview of the statutory provision barring prosecution of recanting witnesses. Agreeing with that contention, the court asked the government whether it would allow the defendant to reappear before the grand jury for the purpose of testifying anew. When the government stated it was not willing to do so, the court dismissed the indictment. The D.C. Circuit held that the ruling below was not an acquittal under *Scott.* The court reasoned: "Recantation, * * * is not a defense bearing on guilt or innocence, nor, by the same token, a defense such that its assertion may not be appealed without implicating the Double Jeopardy Clause. Unlike insanity or entrapment, recantation does not excuse a defendant because it makes him any less guilty, or justifies his otherwise criminal conduct. Rather, statutory recantation erects a barrier that permits escape from prosecution, despite guilt, in the interest of encouraging corrected testimony." Consider also *Wilkett v. United States,* 655 F.2d 1007 (10th Cir.1981) (no acquittal under *Scott* where trial was terminated because the government "failed to prove an element which is more procedural than substantive, namely venue").

6. *The timing of the defense objection.* In *Serfass v. United States,* Note 7 infra, the Court reserved judgment as the appropriate treatment of a midtrial ruling terminating the prosecution where the defendant could have raised the underlying objection prior to the attachment of jeopardy but failed to do so. *Lee v. United States,* Note 6, p. 1403 supra, considered a similar problem in the context of a midtrial dismissal order that was the functional equivalent of declaring a mistrial. In *Sanabria,* the government relied on the combination of *Lee* and *Serfass* to argue that the trial court's ruling, even if viewed as an acquittal, should not bar retrial because of Sanabria's failure to make a pretrial objection to the government's theory that the offense could be established by reference to the gambling organization's numbers activities. It was only after the government had completed its case that the defendant raised his basic contention that the numbers operation was not prohibited under section 17 of the state statute and therefore the government's case was limited to the horsebetting activities. Since a pretrial objection would have allowed the government to seek an amendment of the indictment to refer to section 7 (encompassing numbers betting), this delay, argued the government, amounted to a "waiver" of the defendant's subsequent double jeopardy objection. The Court, over the objection of two dissenters, rejected the government's theory:

"[*Serfass* spoke] of a defendant who is afforded an opportunity to obtain a determination of a legal defense prior to trial and nevertheless knowingly allows himself to be placed in jeopardy before raising the defense. * * * Unlike questions of whether an indictment states an offense, a statute is unconstitutional, or conduct set forth in an indictment violates the statute, what proof may be presented in support of a valid indictment and the sufficiency of that proof are not 'legal defenses' required to be or even capable of being resolved before trial. In all of the former instances, a ruling in the defendant's favor completely precludes conviction, at least on that indictment. Here, even if the numbers language had been struck before trial, there was no 'legal' reason why petitioner could not have been convicted on this indictment [through the horsebetting], as were his 10 codefendants."

7. *The timing of the court's ruling.* Are all rulings relating to the insufficiency of the evidence necessarily acquittals for the purpose of the *Scott* ruling? Consider the following pre-*Scott* rulings:

(a) In SERFASS v. UNITED STATES, 420 U.S. 377, 95 S.Ct. 1055, 43 L.Ed.2d 265 (1975), petitioner was indicted for willful failure to submit to military induction. Petitioner pleaded not guilty and demanded a jury trial. Petitioner then filed a motion to dismiss the indictment, contending that the induction order was invalid because the local selective service board had not given proper consideration to a post-induction claim of conscientious objector status. The district court, after a hearing on defendant's motion, requested and received the defendant's selective service file. The court then granted the motion to dismiss, noting that it was relying on facts "derived from petitioner's affidavit, from his selective service file, and from the oral stipulation of counsel at the argument 'that the information [petitioner] * * * submitted to the board establish[ed] a prima facie case for conscientious objector status * * *.'" The government appealed this ruling, and the Court of Appeals, after rejecting petitioner's objection to the appeal, reversed and remanded the case for trial. With only Justice Douglas dissenting, the Supreme Court, per BURGER, C.J., affirmed:

"* * * Under our cases jeopardy had not yet attached when the District Court granted petitioner's motion to dismiss the indictment. Petitioner was not then, nor has he ever been, 'put to trial before the trier of facts.' The proceedings were initiated by his motion to dismiss the indictment. Petitioner had not waived his right to a jury trial, and, of course a jury trial could not be waived by him without the consent of the Government and of the court. Fed.Rule Crim.Proc. 23(a). In such circumstances, the District Court was without power to make any determination regarding petitioner's guilt or innocence. * * *

"Petitioner acknowledges that 'formal or technical jeopardy had not attached' at the time the District Court ruled on his motion to dismiss the indictment. However, he argues that because that ruling was based on 'evidentiary facts outside of the indictment, which facts would constitute a defense on the merits at trial,' it was the 'functional equivalent of an acquittal on the merits' and 'constructively jeopardy had attached.' * * * [P]etitioner argues that the Court has admonished against the use of 'technicalities' in interpreting the Double Jeopardy Clause, and he contends that the normal rule as to the attachment of jeopardy is merely a presumption which is rebuttable in cases where an analysis of the respective interests of the Government and the accused indicates that the policies of the Double Jeopardy Clause would be frustrated by further prosecution. * * *

"[This] Court has consistently adhered to the view that jeopardy does not attach until a defendant is 'put to trial before the trier of facts, whether the trier be a jury or a judge.' This is by no means a mere technicality, nor is it a 'rigid mechanical' rule. It is, of course, like most legal rules, an attempt to impart content to an abstraction. When a criminal prosecution is terminated prior to trial, an accused is often spared much of the expense, delay, strain, and embarrassment which attend a trial. Although an accused may raise defenses or objections before trial which are 'capable of determination without the trial of the general issue,' Fed.Rule Crim.Proc. 12(b)(1), and although he must raise certain other defenses or objections before trial, Fed.Rule Crim.Proc. 12(b)(2), in neither case is he 'subjected to the hazards of trial and possible conviction.' Moreover, in neither case would an appeal by the United States 'allow the prosecutor to seek to persuade a second trier of fact of the defendant's guilt after having failed with the first.' *United States v. Wilson.* Both the history of the Double Jeopardy Clause and its terms demonstrate that it does not come into play until a proceeding begins before a trier 'having jurisdiction to try the question of the guilt or innocence of the accused.' *Kepner v. United States.*"

(b) Consider also UNITED STATES v. SANFORD, 429 U.S. 14, 97 S.Ct. 20, 50 L.Ed.2d 17 (1976). Defendant was charged with the federal offense of illegal hunting in a national park. His initial trial resulted in a hung jury, and the trial court declared a mistrial. Four months later, prior to a scheduled retrial, the trial court dismissed the indictment on the ground that the government had "consented to the activities which formed the basis of the indictment." That ruling apparently was based on information brought out during the initial trial. (The government's case was based upon defendant's service as an outfitter and guide for two hunters who were actually undercover agents). The government's appeal from the dismissal of the indictment was dismissed by the court of appeals as barred by double jeopardy. The Supreme Court reversed summarily, with Justices Brennan and Marshall, in dissent, noting that the case should have been set for oral argument. The per curiam opinion for the majority noted initially that a retrial following the initial mistrial was not barred by double jeopardy under the *Perez* rule. The opinion then concluded that the appeal should be governed by *Serfass* since the appeal was from a dismissal issued prior to a permissible retrial.

(c) Compare with *Sanford,* UNITED STATES v. MARTIN LINEN SUPPLY, 430 U.S. 564, 97 S.Ct. 1349, 51 L.Ed.2d 642 (1977). A "hopelessly deadlocked" jury was discharged when unable to agree upon a verdict at the defendant corporation's criminal contempt trial. Defendant then made a motion for judgments of acquittal on each count pursuant to Fed.R. Crim.P. 29(c). That rule authorizes such a motion to be made within seven days after the jury is discharged. The trial court granted the motion and the government then sought to appeal pursuant to 18 U.S.C. § 3731. The Supreme Court, with Chief Justice Burger dissenting, held that the double jeopardy clause barred the government's appeal. Justice Brennan's opinion for the Court noted: "There can be no question that the judgments of acquittal entered here by the District Court were 'acquittals' in substance as well as form. The District Court plainly granted the Rule 29(c) motion on the view that the Government had not proved facts constituting criminal contempt. * * * Since Rule 29 merely replaces the directed-verdict mechanism * * *, and accords the federal trial judge greater flexibility in timing his judgment of acquittal, no persuasive basis exists for construing the rule as weakening the trial court's binding authority for purposes of double jeopardy."

8. *Post-conviction rulings.* Assume that the defendant is tried before a jury and found guilty. The trial judge then reconsiders a motion for a judgment of acquittal and concludes that, notwithstanding the jury verdict, the testimony of the chief prosecution witness was so inherently incredible that no reasonable person could find defendant guilty beyond a reasonable doubt. The trial judge then enters a judgment of acquittal notwithstanding the jury's verdict, as allowed under state law. See Note 1, p. 1378 supra. Would a prosecution appeal from that order place the defendant in double jeopardy? Consider footnote 7 of the Court's opinion in *Scott.* The statement from *Jenkins* cited in footnote 7 was based upon an analysis offered in UNITED STATES v. WILSON, 420 U.S. 332, 95 S.Ct. 1013, 43 L.Ed.2d 232 (1975), described below.

In *Wilson,* after the jury returned a verdict of guilty, the trial court reconsidered an earlier motion and dismissed the indictment on the ground that the government's preindictment delay had resulted in a denial of due process. In sustaining the government's appeal from that order, the Court found no need to determine "whether the ruling in Wilson's favor was actually an 'acquittal.'" (Compare *Scott*). It concluded that the appeal was not barred by the double jeopardy clause since the defendant would not be exposed to multiple trials. JUSTICE MARSHALL'S opinion for the Court noted:

"[W]here there is no threat of either multiple punishment or successive prosecutions, the Double Jeopardy Clause is not offended. In various situations where appellate review would not subject the defendant to a second trial, this Court has held that an order favoring the defendant could constitutionally be appealed by the Government. Since the 1907 Criminal Appeals Act, for example, the Government has been permitted without serious constitutional challenge to appeal from orders arresting judgment after a verdict has been entered against the defendant. Since reversal on appeal would merely reinstate the jury's verdict, review of such an order does not offend the policy against multiple prosecution.

"* * * Although review of any ruling of law discharging a defendant obviously enhances the likelihood of conviction and subjects him to continuing expense and anxiety, a defendant has no legitimate claim to benefit from an error of law when that error could be corrected without subjecting him to a second trial before a second trier of fact. * * * Respondent contends that *United States v. Ball* [p. 1405 supra] * * * stand[s] for the proposition that the key to invoking double jeopardy protection is not whether the defendant might be subjected to multiple trials, but whether he can point to a prior verdict or judgment of acquittal. In *Ball,* however, the Court explained that review of the verdict of acquittal was barred primarily because it would expose the defendant to the risk of a second trial after the finder of fact had ruled in his favor in the first. * * *" [c]

SECTION 3. REPROSECUTION FOLLOWING A CONVICTION

I. THE GENERAL RULE

1. *The Ball rule.* As noted in *Scott* (see p. 1405 supra), *United States v. Ball* recognized an exception to the general double jeopardy prohibition against reprosecuting a person for an offense for which he already has been convicted. That exception, as it now stands, holds that the double jeopardy clause does not bar reprosecution where the convicted defendant has managed through appeal or other procedure to set aside his conviction on grounds other than the insufficiency of the evidence. *Ball* itself held that double jeopardy did not bar a reprosecution following reversal of a conviction on appeal. Later decisions reached a similar conclusion as to reprosecution following a trial judge's ruling setting aside the conviction or following a habeas corpus ruling that the conviction was invalid. See, e.g., *United States v. Tateo,* 377 U.S. 463, 84 S.Ct. 1587, 12 L.Ed.2d 448 (1964). *Burks v. United States,* p. 1419 infra, held that reprosecution is barred, however, if the conviction was set aside on the ground that the evidence was insufficient to support a conviction.

2. *The rationale of the rule.* Although the "*Ball* rule" is a "well-established part of our constitutional jurisprudence," *Tateo,* some uncertainty exists as to the doctrinal basis for the rule. *Ball* itself offered little more than a statement of the rule, disposing of defendant's double jeopardy objection, as *Scott* notes, "almost peremptorily." *Trono v. United States,* 199 U.S. 521, 26 S.Ct. 121, 50 L.Ed. 292 (1905), suggested that the defendant, by successfully appealing his erroneous conviction, had waived any double jeopardy objection to a subsequent retrial. Another theory, suggested in Justice Holmes' dissent in *Kepner v. United States,* 195 U.S. 100, 24 S.Ct. 797, 49 L.Ed. 114 (1904), contended that the jeopardy of the first trial continued through the appeal and into the subsequent retrial. Under this theory, the prosecution was viewed as continuing until the defendant had a fair trial, free from reversible error, so a retrial following an appellate reversal was simply a continuation of the original trial and the original jeopardy.

c. Justice Douglas, joined by Justice Brennan dissented. The dissenters contended that the cases prohibiting appeal from an acquittal should apply because the trial court's ruling was "based in part on the evidence adduced at the trial," and therefore was "part and parcel of the process of weighing the Government's evidentiary case."

Relying upon *Wilson,* lower court decisions have upheld appeals from judgments of acquittal based on the insufficiency of the government's evidence (including an evaluation of the strength of testimony) where those acquittals were entered after the jury had returned a guilty verdict. See, LaFave and Israel, § 24.3. Supreme Court rulings have not gone beyond the situation cited in footnote 13 of *Scott* (i.e., rulings allowing government appeals from post-guilty verdict orders reconsidering and granting defense suppression motions).

Today, the Court considers the "most reasonable" justification for the *Ball* rule (see *Burks v. United States,* infra) that which was advanced by Justice Harlan in *United States v. Tateo,* supra:

"While different theories have been advanced to support the permissibility of retrial, of greater importance than the conceptual abstractions employed to explain the *Ball* principle are the implications of that principle for the sound administration of justice. Corresponding to the right of an accused to be given a fair trial is the societal interest in punishing one whose guilt is clear after he has obtained such a trial. It would be a high price indeed for society to pay were every accused granted immunity from punishment because of any defect sufficient to constitute reversible error in the proceedings leading to conviction. From the standpoint of a defendant, it is at least doubtful that appellate courts would be as zealous as they now are in protecting against the effects of improprieties at the trial or pretrial stage if they knew that reversal of a conviction would put the accused irrevocably beyond the reach of further prosecution. In reality, therefore, the practice of retrial serves defendants' rights as well as society's interest."

Compare the position taken by Judge M. Fleming in *The Price of Perfect Justice,* 58 Judicature 340, 344 (1975). Discussing changes in procedure that would help to reduce delay in the administration of the criminal justice process, Judge Fleming noted: "My third suggestion is that a defendant be tried only once to judgment. If on appeal after judgment of conviction the trial is found substantially defective or unfair the judgment should be reversed and the defendant go free. If defects are found in the trial but the defects have not substantially influenced the result, the judgment should stand and become immune from further judicial examination. The occasional mistakes and mishaps discovered after judgment can be cured through executive action and the pardoning power without infringing upon the integrity of the court's judgment. This proposal may sound revolutionary, but it is actually a return to first principles. The English have always had a system of only one trial to final judgment. * * * [I]t was not until 1896 in the case of *United States v. Ball* that multiple trials were sanctioned in the federal courts. One trial would certainly sharpen the responsibility of everyone connected with a criminal cause, trial judge, counsel, witnesses, appellate court, to whom the seriousness of what they were doing would be brought home by realization of its finality."

3. *Relation to the mistrial rules.* Under the standard applied to mistrials, a prosecution error causing a mistrial may, depending upon the circumstances, bar further prosecution. Under the *Ball* rule, on the other hand, if a mistrial is not declared and the same error results in a conviction reversed on appeal, reprosecution will never be prohibited. The explanation traditionally given for the different consequences is that "in the * * * [*Ball*] situation the defendant has not been deprived of his option to go to the first jury and, perhaps, end the dispute then and there with an acquittal." *United States v. Jorn,* supra. See also, *United States v. Tateo,* supra (Goldberg, J. dissenting), noting that there is a substantial constitutional difference between receiving "a jury trial, albeit not the error-free jury trial to which by law the defendant is entitled" and being deprived entirely of "the valued right to have the original jury consider [the] case."

How far does the above explanation carry? In *Kennedy,* p. 1395 supra, the Court noted that defendant would be protected against reprosecution, notwithstanding his request for a mistrial, where prosecutorial misconduct was intended to goad the defendant into moving for a mistrial. Assume that, in such a situation, the trial court denies the mistrial request, the defendant is convicted, and that conviction is reversed on appeal. Should reprosecution be barred in light of the improper prosecutorial purpose? Lower courts have acknowledged that "there is some support in logic" to prohibiting a retrial when the appellate reversal is based on prosecutorial misconduct that was aimed at intentionally goading a defendant into moving for a mistrial. See *United States v. Opager,* 616 F.2d 231 (5th Cir.1980); LaFave and Israel, § 24.4(a). Does *Kennedy,* in its footnote 7, open the door for the development of such an exception to the *Ball* rule? See also, Note 1, p. 1401 supra.

II. EVIDENTIARY INSUFFICIENCY

1. *The Burks limitation.* In BURKS v. UNITED STATES, 437 U.S. 1, 98 S.Ct. 2141, 57 L.Ed.2d 1 (1978), the Court held that the *Ball* rule did not apply where the appellate reversal was based on the insufficiency of the evidence at trial to sustain a guilty verdict. The Court of Appeals there reversed defendant's conviction on the ground that the government's evidence was insufficient to rebut defendant's proof that he was insane, but it then remanded the case with the suggestion that a retrial would be permissible. The Supreme Court held the remand invalid on the ground that a retrial would be inconsistent with the double jeopardy prohibition. The opinion for a unanimous Court, per Chief Justice BURGER, initially noted that the appellate court's ruling logically should stand in the same position as a trial court acquittal:

"It is unquestionably true that the Court of Appeals' decision 'represent[ed] a resolution, correct or not, of some or all of the factual elements of the offense charged.' *United States v. Martin Linen Supply Co.* By deciding that the government had failed to come forward with sufficient proof of petitioner's capacity to be responsible for criminal acts, the court was clearly saying that Burks' criminal culpability had not been established. If the District Court had so held in the first instance, as the reviewing court said it should have done, a judgment of acquittal would have been entered and, of course, petitioner could not be retried for the same offense. Consequently, as Mr. Justice Douglas correctly perceived in *Sapir v. United States,* it should make no difference that the reviewing court, rather than the trial court, determined the evidence to be insufficient." [a]

The *Burks* opinion then rejected several earlier decisions that had misconstrued *Ball* as allowing a retrial in a case such as *Burks. Ball,* the Court noted, was limited to the separate problem of a reversal based upon a trial error:

"[R]eversal for trial error, as distinguished from evidentiary insufficiency does not constitute a decision to the effect that the government has failed to prove its case. As such, it implies nothing with respect to the guilt or innocence of the defendant. Rather, it is a determination that a defendant has been convicted through a judicial process which is defective in some fundamental respect, * * *. When this occurs, the accused has a strong interest in obtaining a fair readjudication of his guilt free from error, just as society maintains a valid concern for insuring that the guilty are punished. The same cannot be said when a defendant's conviction has been overturned due to a failure of proof at trial, in which case the prosecution cannot complain of prejudice,

a. The Court noted, in this regard, that a lower federal court could appropriately make such a ruling only "where the prosecution's failure is clear." The function of a trial or appellate judge in determining whether the trial evidence was sufficient to support a guilty verdict was quite limited: "Even the trial court, which has heard the testimony of witnesses firsthand, is not to weigh the evidence or assess the credibility of witnesses when it judges the merits of a motion for acquittal. The prevailing rule has long been that a district judge is to submit a case to the jury if the evidence and inferences therefrom most favorable to the prosecution would warrant the jury finding the defendant guilty beyond a reasonable doubt. Obviously a federal appellate court applies no higher a standard; rather it must sustain the verdict if there is substantial evidence, viewed in the light most favorable to the Government, to uphold the jury's decision."

for it has been given one fair opportunity to offer whatever proof it could assemble."

2. *The prosecutor's fair opportunity.* Should it "make no difference that the reviewing court, rather than the trial court, determined the evidence to be insufficient"? *Burks,* supra. Might the two situations be distinguished on the basis of likely differences in the prosecution's opportunity to correct its case? Where a defendant moves for a judgment of acquittal at trial, arguing that the prosecution has failed to introduce any evidence on a necessary element of the crime, the trial court often has discretion to permit the prosecution to reopen its case so as to introduce evidence on the missing element. Where the particular aspect of insufficiency is first raised before the appellate court, on the other hand, the prosecution has no opportunity to correct its error even though it may be obvious that the missing evidence could have been supplied if the prosecution had been made aware of this problem. Cf. *Sumpter v. DeGroote,* 552 F.2d 1206 (7th Cir.1977) (involving a state prostitution conviction reversed on appeal because the prosecution neglected to present any evidence that the defendant was a female, which was an element of the crime).[b]

3. In describing the appellate court's ruling on the insufficiency of the evidence, the Supreme Court in *Burks* noted: "There is no claim in this case that the trial court committed error by excluding prosecution evidence, which, if received, would have rebutted any claim of evidentiary insufficiency." This statement has been taken as suggesting that a reprosecution might not be barred where the insufficiency of the government's evidence would have been "cured" by evidence erroneously excluded by the trial court. Could such a holding be squared with the premise of *Burks* that an appellate court's ruling as to insufficiency should stand in the same position as a trial court's acquittal? Cf. *Sanabria v. United States,* Note 2, p. 1411 supra (where an erroneous exclusion order led to a trial court acquittal and thereby barred further prosecution). Consider, however, *State v. Boone,* 393 A.2d 1361 (Md.1978), noting that *Burks* also stressed that the prosecution there had been given "one fair opportunity to offer whatever proof it could assemble." The court in *Boone* concluded it could not "conceive" that "the rationale of *Burks* " would be applied to prohibit a retrial where the insufficiency was really the product of a judicial error in excluding evidence rather than a "failure attributable to the prosecution to prove its case."

4. In *Greene v. Massey,* 437 U.S. 19, 98 S.Ct. 2151, 57 L.Ed.2d 15 (1978), the Court again indicated that *Burks* might not apply to all appellate reversals based on the insufficiency of trial evidence. The Court found that a state appellate opinion was too ambiguous to determine whether the appellate reversal there was governed by *Burks.* One possible reading of the state court opinion was that the trial judge had erred in admitting certain hearsay evidence and, with that evidence discounted, there remained insufficient evidence to permit the jury to convict. Remanding the case for further inquiry, the Supreme Court noted that it was not willing "to express an opinion as to the double jeopardy implications of a retrial ordered on such grounds." In *State v. Boone,* Note 3, supra, the Maryland court concluded that

b. Of course, not all trial court rulings of evidentiary insufficiency involve situations in which the prosecution would have an opportunity to correct its case. A challenge to the sufficiency of the evidence may also be presented to the trial court in a post-verdict motion. See e.g., Fed.R. Crim.P. 29(c). Could a state, in an effort to ensure that the prosecutor has some notice at trial of any alleged evidentiary deficiency, provide that challenges to the sufficiency of the evidence will not be considered unless originally made before the case was sent to the jury? On appeal, federal courts frequently state that the sufficiency of the evidence will not be considered unless an objection was timely raised below, but an obvious insufficiency is likely to be viewed as "plain error" requiring reversal even though there was no trial objection.

the rationale of *Burks* should not bar retrial in this situation left open in *Greene.* The court reasoned that the prosecution in such a case would not have been given "one fair opportunity" to offer its proof: "The prosecution, * * * in proving its case is entitled to rely upon the correctness of the rulings of the court and proceed accordingly. * * * Were it otherwise, the State, to be secure, would have to consider every ruling by the court on the evidence to be erroneous and marshall and offer every bit of relevant and competent evidence. The practical consequences of this would seriously affect the orderly administration of justice, if for no other reason, because of the time which would be required to prepare for trial and try the case." But compare *Commonwealth v. Funches,* 397 N.E.2d 1097 (Mass.1979) (retrial impermissible: state had opportunity "to offer whatever proof it could assemble, and had the trial court made the correct ruling on suppression, a favorable ruling on defendants' motion for directed verdicts would have been required as a matter of law").

5. *The thirteenth-juror reversal.* In TIBBS v. FLORIDA, 457 U.S. 31, 102 S.Ct. 2211, 72 L.Ed.2d 652 (1982), a divided Court (5–4) held that *Burks* did not apply to a thirteenth-juror appellate reversal—i.e., a reversal based on the weight of the evidence rather than the sufficiency of the evidence. The majority, per O'Connor, J., stressed that an appellate reversal based on the weight of the evidence does not rest on the premise that an acquittal was the only proper verdict the jury could have reached. Instead, the appellate court simply expresses its disagreement with the jury's resolution of the conflicting testimony. Just as a deadlocked jury does not result in an acquittal barring retrial, an appellate court's disagreement, as the "thirteenth juror," with the trial jurors' weighing of the evidence also does not require the special deference accorded verdicts of acquittal. The majority characterized the reversal based on the weight of the evidence as designed primarily to "give the defendant a second chance." It rejected, in this connection, the suggestion of the dissenters that such a reversal necessarily required the prosecution to produce additional evidence to sustain a conviction on retrial. "The weight of the evidence rule," the majority noted, "often derives from a mandate to act in the interests of justice," and while "reversal of a first conviction based on sharply conflicting testimony may serve the interests of justice, reversal of a second conviction based on the same evidence may not."

The majority also rejected the contention that drawing a distinction between the weight and the sufficiency of the evidence would be "unworkable" and would "undermine *Burks* by encouraging appellate judges to base reversals on the weight, rather than the sufficiency, of the evidence." The majority noted the "demonstrated ability" of trial and appellate courts to draw that distinction, as reflected in their common practice.[c] It noted also that a reversal on the weight of the evidence was permissible constitutionally only after the reviewing court has first found, consistent with federal due process standards, that there was sufficient evidence to persuade a rational factfinder of guilt beyond a reasonable doubt. The majority concluded that this due process standard, "together with our belief that state appellate

c. In *Hudson v. Louisiana,* 450 U.S. 40, 101 S.Ct. 970, 67 L.Ed.2d 30 (1981), a unanimous Court held that *Burks* barred a retrial where a trial judge granted a new trial following conviction on the ground that there "certainly [was] not evidence beyond a reasonable doubt, to sustain the verdict." Although the trial court ruling was made on a motion for a new trial, the record did not support the state's contention that the trial judge granted the new trial acting only as a "thirteenth juror." The Court also rejected the further contention that *Burks* was inapplicable because the trial court had found that there was some evidence of guilt, although not enough to support the conviction. The reasoning of *Burks* was not limited, the Court noted, to insufficiency rulings based on a total lack of evidence.

judges faithfully honor their obligations to enforce applicable state and federal laws, persuades us that today's ruling will not undermine *Burks.*"

The dissenting opinion of White, J. (joined by Brennan, Marshall, and Blackmun, J.J.) contended that the crucial distinction for double jeopardy purposes should be whether a reversal is based on "evidentiary grounds" or on "procedural grounds." Only in the later case, it noted, can the "State proceed to retrial without offending the deeply ingrained principle that 'the State with all its resources and power should not be allowed to make repeated attempts to convict an individual for an alleged offense.'" Where the reversal is due to a "failure of proof," with "the State [having] received a 'fair opportunity to offer whatever proof it could assemble,'" it should be immaterial that "proof fails on state law, rather than federal law."

6. *Continuing proceedings.* The implications of *Burks* were explored further in JUSTICES OF BOSTON MUNICIPAL COURT v. LYDON, 466 U.S. 294, 104 S.Ct. 1805, 80 L.Ed.2d 311 (1984) and RICHARDSON v. UNITED STATES, 468 U.S. 317, 104 S.Ct. 3081, 82 L.Ed.2d 242 (1984).

In *Justices of Boston Municipal Court,* the defendant had a choice between a bench trial before the municipal court, which carried with it an absolute right to a trial de novo, or a jury trial before the same court, which was subject to the usual appellate review on the record. He chose the bench trial, and after conviction, requested a trial de novo. Before that trial commenced, however, he moved for dismissal of the charges in the second-tier court on the ground that the first-tier conviction had not been supported by sufficient evidence to establish guilt beyond a reasonable doubt. The state courts held that he was not entitled to consideration of that claim, his only avenue for relief being the trial de novo. The Supreme Court concluded that this position did not result in a second trial in violation of double jeopardy.

Justice White's opinion for the Court found the state's limitation of review of the first-tier conviction to a trial de novo was consistent with both the reasoning and holding in *Burks.* The Court had there "recognized the danger of 'affording the prosecution another opportunity to supply evidence which it failed to muster in the first proceeding,'" but the "defendant's right to obtain de novo review without alleging error * * * ameliorate[d] * * * [that] concern." The two-tier system did not undercut the prosecution's incentive to put forth its strongest case in the bench trial, since the failure to do so could result in an acquittal there that would end all proceedings. The burden of the trial de novo, even if necessitated by an erroneous initial conviction, was hardly oppressive in light of the various advantages that the two-tier system afforded the defendant as compared to the usual system of appeal. Finally, if the defendant subsequently was erroneously convicted on the basis of insufficient evidence at the trial de novo, which had continued the jeopardy of the first trial, he could then rely on *Burks* to gain an appellate reversal that would preclude a new trial.

Justice Brennan, joined by Justice Marshall, concurred separately. Justice Brennan criticized the majority opinion for invoking the concept of continuing jeopardy without analyzing the "relationship between the circumstances at issue and the policies underlying the Double Jeopardy Clause." Ordinarily, Justice Brennan argued, the conviction entered by the first-tier judge would have all the earmarks of the termination of the initial jeopardy, thereby prohibiting a retrial under the *Burks* rule if the evidence at that first proceeding was insufficient to support the conviction. In this case, however, the defendant elected to proceed under the two-tier system, knowing from the outset that his first trial would not be irrevocable.

This knowledge, combined with the "strategic advantage gained by a defendant who chooses the two-tier system," reduced the pressure and burdens of litigation to the point where the ending of the first-tier proceeding did not terminate the jeopardy initiated with that proceeding.[d]

In *Richardson v. United States,* supra, the Court held that where a mistrial was declared following a hung jury, *Burks* did not bar a new trial, regardless of the possible insufficiency of the evidence at that first trial. Petitioner in *Richardson* had moved unsuccessfully for a judgment of directed acquittal prior to the mistrial, and he argued that the appellate court was bound to review the denial of that motion and bar a retrial if the trial judge had erred in failing to direct an acquittal. Speaking for the majority, REHNQUIST, J., concluded that petitioner was reading more into *Burks* than the ruling there could sustain. He reasoned:

"Our decision in *Burks* did not extend beyond the procedural setting in which it arose. * * * It has been established for 160 years, since the opinion of Justice Story in *United States v. Perez,* that a failure of the jury to agree on a verdict was an instance of 'manifest necessity' which permitted a trial judge to terminate the first trial and retry the defendant, because 'the ends of public justice would otherwise be defeated.' * * * We are entirely unwilling to uproot this settled line of cases by extending the reasoning of *Burks,* which arose out of an appellate finding of insufficiency of evidence to convict following a jury verdict of guilty, to a situation where the jury is unable to agree on a verdict. * * *

"We think that the principles governing our decision in *Burks,* and the principles governing our decisions in the hung jury cases, are readily reconciled when we recognize that the protection of the Double Jeopardy Clause by its terms applies only if there has been some event, such as an acquittal, which terminates the original jeopardy. See *Justices of Boston Municipal Court v. Lydon.* Since jeopardy attached here when the jury was sworn, petitioner's argument necessarily assumes that the judicial declaration of a mistrial was an event which terminated jeopardy in his case and which allowed him to assert a valid claim of double jeopardy. But this proposition is irreconcilable with cases such as *Perez,* and we hold on the authority of these cases that the failure of the jury to reach a verdict is not an event which terminates jeopardy. * * * The Government, like the defendant, is entitled to resolution of the case by verdict from the jury, and jeopardy does not terminate when the jury is discharged because it is unable to agree. Regardless of the sufficiency of the evidence at petitioner's first trial, he has no valid double jeopardy claim to prevent his retrial."

Relying on his separate concurrence in *Justices of Boston Municipal Court,* Justice Brennan, joined by Justice Marshall, accused the Court of again relying "on a formalistic concept of continuing jeopardy." Under the Court's position, "a defendant who is constitutionally *entitled to an acquittal* but who fails to receive one—because he happens to be tried before an irrational or lawless factfinder or because his jury cannot agree on a verdict—is worse off than a defendant tried before a factfinder who demands constitutionally

d. Disagreeing in part with both the majority and Justice Brennan, Justice Stevens also concurred separately. He argued that a defendant erroneously convicted at the first-tier trial on the basis of insufficient evidence was denied due process. However, *Burks* did not bar his retrial in the absence of a judicial ruling that the evidence was insufficient. If the state refused to afford defendant an opportunity to gain such a ruling, he could turn to the federal habeas court, but habeas review prior to the trial de novo would be premature. In *Berry v. Commonwealth,* 473 N.E. 2d 1115 (Mass.1985), the highest state court concluded that a trial de novo was barred under state double jeopardy doctrine where the evidence before the first-tier court was not supported by sufficient evidence.

sufficient evidence. Indeed, he is worse off than a *guilty* defendant who is acquitted due to mistakes of fact or law." Such a "paradoxical result," Justice Brennan argued, could hardly be squared with the fundamental principle underlying *Burks* — that "double jeopardy precludes a retrial where the state has failed as a matter of law despite a fair opportunity to do so."

III. CONVICTIONS AND IMPLIED ACQUITTALS

1. In GREEN v. UNITED STATES, 355 U.S. 184, 78 S.Ct. 221, 2 L.Ed.2d 199 (1957), the defendant was charged with first degree murder, and the jury was informed that they could find him guilty either of first degree murder or of the lesser included offense of second degree murder. The jury returned a verdict of guilty on the second degree murder charge, saying nothing as to the first degree murder charge. Green appealed his second degree murder conviction, and the appellate court reversed on the basis of a trial error. He was then retried on the original first degree murder charge. The second jury convicted him of first degree murder, but a divided (5–4) Supreme Court reversed, holding that double jeopardy barred conviction on that charge. The majority opinion, by BLACK, J., noted:

"Green was in direct peril of being convicted and punished for first degree murder at his first trial. He was forced to run the gantlet once on that charge and the jury refused to convict him. When given the choice between finding him guilty of either first or second degree murder it chose the latter. In this situation the great majority of cases in this country have regarded the jury's verdict as an implicit acquittal on the charge of first degree murder. But the result in this case need not rest alone on the assumption, which we believe legitimate, that the jury for one reason or another acquitted Green of murder in the first degree. For here, the jury was dismissed without returning any express verdict on that charge and without Green's consent. Yet it was given a full opportunity to return a verdict and no extraordinary circumstances appeared which prevented it from doing so. Therefore it seems clear, under established principles of former jeopardy, that Green's jeopardy for first degree murder came to an end when the jury was discharged so that he could not be retried for that offense. *Wade v. Hunter* [p. 1383 supra]. In brief, we believe this case can be treated no differently, for purposes of former jeopardy, than if the jury had returned a verdict which expressly read: 'We find the defendant not guilty of murder in the first degree but guilty of murder in the second degree.' "

2. Assume that on Green's second prosecution for first degree murder, the jury had found him guilty of second degree murder—i.e., reached the same verdict as the first jury. Must that conviction be reversed on the authority of *Green? Price v. Georgia,* 398 U.S. 323, 90 S.Ct. 1757, 26 L.Ed.2d 300 (1970), held *Green* applicable in such a situation: "Although the petitioner was not convicted of the greater charge on retrial whereas Green was, the risk of conviction on the greater charge was the same in both cases, and the Double Jeopardy Clause of the Fifth Amendment is written in terms of potential or risk of trial and conviction, not punishment. * * * To be charged and to be subjected to a second trial for first-degree murder is an ordeal not to be viewed lightly. Further, and perhaps of more importance, we cannot determine whether or not the murder charge against petitioner induced the jury to find him guilty of the less serious offense of voluntary manslaughter rather than to continue to debate his innocence."

3. What decisions fall within the *Green* ruling? Consider *United States ex rel. Jackson v. Follette,* 462 F.2d 1041 (2d Cir. 1972), where the defendant was charged with first degree murder on two grounds, premeditated murder and felony murder,

each of which carried potentially different punishments. Without objection by the defendant, the jury was told that if it returned a verdict on one ground, it was to remain silent on the other. Under these circumstances, the appellate court held, the jury's finding of guilt on the basis of premeditated murder did not indicate that it had rejected the felony murder theory, and it could not be said that the jury had been given "the full opportunity to return a verdict" on a separate offense. Accordingly, defendant's reprosecution on both theories was permissible following the appellate reversal of defendant's original conviction.

4. It is generally accepted that the implied acquittal rationale of *Green* does not apply to the acceptance of a guilty plea—i.e., the acceptance of a guilty plea to a lesser charge does not constitute "an inferential finding of not guilty" to a higher charge. *Commonwealth v. Therrien,* 269 N.E.2d 687 (Mass.1971). This conclusion follows both from the nature of the determination made by the court in accepting a guilty plea to a lesser charge (see Ch. 21, § 4) and the fact that "the defendant has not really been in jeopardy as to the higher charge, as unlike the jury in *Green,* the judge receiving the plea could not have convicted the defendant of [that charge]." LaFave and Israel, § 24.4(c). With no implied acquittal, if the defendant should overturn his guilty plea to the lesser charge, double jeopardy does not bar prosecution on the higher charge—although other limitations may bear on use of that charge (see, Note 10, p. 1205 supra, and Note 5, p. 1441 infra). Indeed, under some circumstances, the defendant may plead guilty to a lesser included offense and the prosecution on the higher charge may continue to trial. See *Ohio v. Johnson,* p. 1063 supra.

IV. RESENTENCING

1. *Sentencing and the Ball rule.* In NORTH CAROLINA v. PEARCE, 395 U.S. 711, 89 S.Ct. 2072, 23 L.Ed.2d 656 (1969), the Court considered two related issues concerning the sentence that can be imposed where a defendant has been reprosecuted after his original conviction was overturned. *Pearce* involved two defendants who had successfully challenged their original convictions and had then been reprosecuted and again convicted, as permitted under *Ball.* The first issue considered by the Court was "whether in computing the new sentence, the Constitution requires that credit must be given for that part of the original sentence already served." A unanimous Court held that a denial of credit for time served under the first sentence violated the double jeopardy "protect[ion] against multiple punishment's for the same offense." [e] STEWART, J., speaking for the Court, reasoned:

"We think it is clear that this basic constitutional guarantee is violated when punishment already exacted for an offense is not fully 'credited' in imposing sentence upon a new conviction for the same offense. The constitutional violation is flagrantly apparent in a case involving the imposition of a maximum sentence after reconviction. Suppose, for example, in a jurisdiction where the maximum allowable sentence for larceny is 10 years' imprisonment, a man succeeds in getting his larceny conviction set aside after serving three years in prison. If, upon reconviction, he is given a 10-year sentence, then, quite clearly, he will have received multiple punishments for the same offense, for he will have been compelled to serve separate prison terms of three years and 10 years, although the maximum single punishment for the offense is 10 years' imprisonment. Though not so dramatically evident, the same principle obviously holds true whenever punishment already endured is not

e. As to the nature of that protection, see the discussion of *Ex parte Lange* in *United States v. DiFrancesco,* p. 1427 infra, and Note 1, p. 1067 supra.

fully subtracted from any new sentence imposed."

2. The second issue presented in *Pearce* was whether, assuming credit is given for time served, the trial judge may impose a longer sentence on reconviction than was imposed following the original conviction. The defendants challenged the imposition of a longer sentence following reprosecution as violating three constitutional guarantees—double jeopardy, equal protection, and due process. The equal protection and due process arguments are considered in that portion of the *Pearce* opinion reprinted at p. 1434 infra. (The Court rejected the equal protection argument, but held that due process did bar a longer sentence under certain circumstances). The Court was divided (6–3) on the defendants' double jeopardy claim, with the majority rejecting that claim on the basis of *Ball.* Speaking for the majority, STEWART, J., noted:

"At least since 1896, when *United States v. Ball* was decided, it has been settled that this constitutional guarantee imposes no limitations whatever upon the power to *retry* a defendant who has succeeded in getting his first conviction set aside. * * * And at least since 1919, when *Stroud v. United States,* 251 U.S. 15, 40 S.Ct. 50, 64 L.Ed. 103 (1919), was decided, it has been settled that a corollary of the power to retry a defendant is the power, upon the defendant's reconviction, to impose whatever sentence may be legally authorized, whether or not it is greater than the sentence imposed after the first conviction.[16] * * *

"Although the rationale for this 'well-established part of our constitutional jurisprudence' has been variously verbalized, it rests ultimately upon the premise that the original conviction has, at the defendant's behest, been wholly nullified and the slate wiped clean. As to whatever punishment has actually been suffered under the first conviction, that premise is, of course, an unmitigated fiction, as we have recognized in Part I of this opinion [holding that credit must be given for time served under the first conviction]. But, so far as the conviction itself goes, and that part of the sentence that has not yet been served, it is no more than a simple statement of fact to say that the slate has been wiped clean. The conviction has been set aside and the unexpired portion of the original sentence will never be served. A new trial may result in an acquittal. But if it does result in a conviction, we cannot say that the constitutional guarantee against double jeopardy of its own weight restricts the imposition of an otherwise lawful single punishment for the offense in question. To hold to the contrary would be to cast doubt upon the whole validity of the basic principle enunciated in *United States v. Ball,* and upon the unbroken line of decisions that have followed that principle for almost 75 years. We think those decisions are entirely sound, and we decline to depart from the concept they reflect."

Justice Douglas (joined by Justice Marshall) and Justice Harlan wrote separate dissents on the double jeopardy claim. Both viewed the claim as controlled by the rationale of the *Green* decision. Thus, JUSTICE DOUGLAS reasoned:

"The theory of double jeopardy is that a person need run the gantlet only once. The gantlet is the risk of the range of punishment which the State or Federal Government imposes for that particular conduct. It may be a year to 25 years, or 20 years to life, or death. He risks the maximum permissible punishment when

16. In *Stroud* the defendant was convicted of first-degree murder and sentenced to life imprisonment. After reversal of this conviction, the defendant was retried, reconvicted of the same offense, and sentenced to death. This Court upheld the conviction against the defendant's claim that his constitutional right not to be twice put in jeopardy had been violated. * * * The Court's decision in *Green v. United States,* is of no applicability to the present problem. The *Green* decision was based upon the double jeopardy provision's guarantee against retrial for an offense of which the defendant was acquitted.

first tried. That risk having been faced once need not be faced again. And the fact that he takes an appeal does not waive his constitutional defense of former jeopardy to a second prosecution. *Green v. United States.* * * * It is argued that that case is different because * * * [*Green* involved] two different crimes with different punishments provided by statute for each one. That, however, is a matter of semantics. 'It is immaterial to the basic purpose of the constitutional provision against double jeopardy whether the Legislature divides a crime into different degrees carrying different punishments or allows the court or jury to fix different punishments for the same crime.' *People v. Henderson,* 386 P.2d 677, 686 (Cal.1963) (Traynor, J.)."

3. *Sentencing appeals.* The Organized Crime Control Act authorizes the imposition of an increased sentence upon a convicted "dangerous offender" and grants the government the right, under specified conditions, to gain appellate review of that sentence. In UNITED STATES v. DI FRANCESCO, 449 U.S. 117, 101 S.Ct. 426, 66 L.Ed.2d 328 (1980), a divided Court upheld the constitutionality of the Act's provision (§ 3576) authorizing appellate review of a dangerous offender sentence. In that case, the trial judge had concluded that the defendant fell within the Act's dangerous offender definition and imposed an additional sentence, but had that sentence run concurrently with the sentence for the underlying offense. The government appealed, arguing that the use of a concurrent dangerous offender sentence constituted an abuse of sentencing discretion since it added only one year to the length of the defendant's incarceration. Speaking for the Court, BLACKMUN, J., reasoned:

"This Court's decisions in the sentencing area clearly establish that a sentence does not have the qualities of constitutional finality that attend an acquittal. In *Bozza v. United States,* 330 U.S. 160, 67 S.Ct. 645, 91 L.Ed. 818 (1947), the defendant was convicted of a crime carrying a mandatory minimum sentence of fine and imprisonment. The trial court, however, sentenced the defendant only to imprisonment. Later on the same day, the judge recalled the defendant and imposed both fine and imprisonment. This Court held that there was no double jeopardy. 'The Constitution does not require that sentencing should be a game in which a wrong move by the judge means immunity for the prisoner.' * * * And in *North Carolina v. Pearce,* the Court held that there was no absolute constitutional bar to the imposition of a more severe sentence on reconviction after the defendant's successful appeal of the original judgment of conviction. * * * If any rule of finality had applied to the pronouncement of a sentence, the original sentence in *Pearce* would have served as a ceiling on the one imposed at retrial. While *Pearce* dealt with the imposition of a new sentence after retrial rather than, as here, after appeal, that difference is no more than a 'conceptual nicety.' *North Carolina v. Pearce.*

"* * * We have noted above the basic design of the double jeopardy provision, that is, as a bar against repeated attempts to convict, with consequent subjection of the defendant to embarrassment, expense, anxiety, and insecurity, and the possibility that he may be found guilty even though innocent. These considerations, however, have no significant application to the prosecution's statutorily granted right to review a sentence. This limited appeal does not involve a retrial or approximate the ordeal of a trial on the basic issue of guilt or innocence. Under § 3576, the appeal is to be taken promptly and is essentially on the record of the sentencing court.[f] The defendant, of course, is charged with knowledge of the

f. At a later point in its opinion, the Court noted: "The federal statute specifies that the [appellate court] may increase the sentence only if the trial court has abused its discretion or employed unlawful procedures or made clearly statute and its appeal provisions, and has no expectation of finality in his sentence until the appeal is concluded or the time to appeal has expired.

"We turn to the question whether the increase of a sentence on review under § 3576 constitutes multiple punishment in violation of the Double Jeopardy Clause. The Court of Appeals found that it did. This conclusion appears to be attributable primarily to that court's extending to an appeal this Court's dictum in *United States v. Benz,* 282 U.S. 304, 51 S.Ct. 113, 75 L.Ed. 354 (1931), to the effect that the federal practice of barring an increase in sentence by the trial court after service of the sentence has begun is constitutionally based. * * * But the dictum's source, *Ex parte Lange,* [85 U.S. (18 Wall.) 163, 21 L.Ed. 872 (1873),] states no such principle. In *Lange* the trial court erroneously imposed both imprisonment and fine, even though it was authorized by statute to impose only one or the other of these two punishments. Lange had paid the fine and served five days in prison. The trial court then resentenced him to a year's imprisonment. The fine having been paid and the defendant having suffered one of the alternative punishments, 'the power of the court to punish further was gone.' The Court also observed that to impose a year's imprisonment (the maximum) after five days had been served was to punish twice for the same offense. The holding in *Lange,* and thus the dictum in *Benz,* are not susceptible of general application. We confine the dictum in *Benz* to *Lange's* specific context. Although it might be argued that the defendant perceives the length of his sentence as finally determined when he begins to serve it, and that the trial judge should be prohibited from thereafter increasing the sentence, that argument has no force where, as in the dangerous special offender statute, Congress has specifically provided that the sentence is subject to appeal. Under such circumstances there can be no expectation of finality in the original sentence. * * *"[g]

Dissenting in *DiFrancesco,* Justice Brennan (joined by Justices White, Marshall, and Stevens) stressed that: (1) the "Court repeatedly [had] said [e.g., in *United States v. Benz*] that sentences may not be increased after imposition without violating the double jeopardy prohibition against multiple punishments"; (2) there is "an analytical similarity of a verdict of acquittal and an imposition of sentence" [cf., the *Pearce* dissents]; and (3) the increased anxiety to which the defendant was subjected by a sentencing appeal was not distinguishable from the anxiety borne in a reprosecution, as reflected by the fact that "most defendants are more concerned with how much time they must spend in prison than with whether their record shows a conviction."

4. *Capital sentencing.* Compare with *Pearce* and *DiFrancesco,* BULLINGTON v. MISSOURI, 451 U.S. 430, 101 S.Ct. 1852, 68 L.Ed.2d 270 (1981). A divided (5–4) Court there held that a state could

erroneous findings. The appellate court thus is empowered to correct only a legal error."

g. *United States v. Jones,* 722 F.2d 632 (11th Cir.1983), concluded that *DiFrancesco*'s general discussion of double jeopardy values in the sentencing context logically suggested certain guidelines for allowable resentencing during the same term of court. The defendant in *Jones* had initially been sentenced to a split sentence, and he immediately thereafter reported to his probation officer. A week later, the sentencing judge, after discovering that he had misunderstood certain facts, through no fault of the defendant, raised that sentence by requiring a straight jail term. In making that modification, the trial judge concluded that the defendant had not yet begun to serve his sentence, but the Eleventh Circuit ruled that the defendant started to serve the sentence as soon as he was subjected to the "restrictive conditions" imposed thereunder. At that point, the court reasoned, the defendant had "legitimate expectations as to the length of his sentence," and since *DiFrancesco* had characterized the protection of such expectations as a primary concern of the double jeopardy clause, the subsequent increase in his sentence was invalid. The court noted that the result would be otherwise if a defendant intentionally deceived the sentencing authority or otherwise acted so as to make his expectations less than legitimate.

not seek the death penalty on a retrial where the original jury had decided against imposing capital punishment following a trial-type sentencing procedure. The majority per Blackmun, J., noted that, under Missouri law, the jury determination as to capital punishment involved application of specific factual standards, relating to the presence of aggravating and mitigating factors, following an extensive trial-type hearing in which the prosecution bore the burden of proof beyond a reasonable doubt. The original jury's determination not to impose capital punishment was therefore comparable to a trial acquittal as to the issue of the death penalty, rather than to the traditional sentencing determination. While *DiFrancesco* also involved a separate sentencing hearing, appellate review there was "on the record of the sentencing court," and did not involve giving the government "the opportunity to convince a second factfinder of its view of the acts." Moreover, the choice presented to the federal judge in *DiFrancesco* was far broader than that given to the jury here, which had "only two choices—life or death." Finally, the government's burden of proof in *DiFrancesco* as to special offender status was only by a preponderance of the evidence, rather than the reasonable doubt standard applicable under the Missouri procedure. *Stroud v. United States* [n. 16, p. 1426 supra] would not be extended to "this very different situation."

The four *Bullington* dissenters, including three justices who had joined the majority in *DiFrancesco,* argued that the rationale of *Stroud, Pearce,* and *DiFrancesco* was controlling. The dissenters argued that the ordeal of the defendant here in being subjected to a second sentencing determination was no different than that of the defendants in those cases. The dissent also argued that the crucial factor was not the different sentencing procedures, as the majority suggested, but the difference between sentencing and trial decisions. "The sentencer's function," the dissent noted, "is not to discover a fact, but to mete out just desserts as he sees them." [h]

SECTION 4. REPROSECUTION BY A DIFFERENT SOVEREIGN

In BARTKUS v. ILLINOIS, 359 U.S. 121, 79 S.Ct. 676, 3 L.Ed.2d 684 (1959), the defendant initially was tried and acquitted in federal court for robbery of a federally insured bank. He then was tried and convicted in the state court for the same bank robbery under the general robbery provision of the state criminal code. A divided Supreme Court upheld the state conviction on the basis of a long line of decisions rejecting constitutional challenges to successive state and federal prosecutions even though based on the same conduct. Those decisions had been grounded on the "two sovereigns" or "dual sovereignty" doctrine set forth in Justice Grier's opinion in *Moore v. Illinois,* 55 U.S. (14 How.) 13, 14 L.Ed. 306 (1852):

> "Every citizen of the United States is also a citizen of a State or territory. He may be said to owe allegiance to two sovereigns, and may be liable to punishment for an infraction of the laws of either. The same act may be an offence or transgression of the laws of both. * * * That either or both may (if they see fit) punish such an offender, cannot be doubted. Yet it cannot be truly averred that the offender has been twice punished for the same offence; but only that by one act he has committed two offences, for each of which he is justly punishable."

The Supreme Court majority in *Bartkus* found no justification for rejecting this

h. Relying on *Bullington, Arizona v. Rumsey,* 467 U.S. 203, 104 S.Ct. 2305, 81 L.Ed.2d 164 (1984), held that Arizona's capital sentencing procedure, in which the trial judge must follow exacting guidelines in choosing between the death penalty and life imprisonment, also is comparable to a trial for double jeopardy purposes, and therefore the state could not sentence the defendant to death after an appellate court set aside the life sentence originally imposed by the trial judge, who had misinterpreted the capital punishment statute in defendant's favor.

well established doctrine. Justice FRANKFURTER's opinion for the Court noted:

"With this body of precedent as irrefutable evidence that state and federal courts have for years refused to bar a second trial even though there had been a prior trial by another government for a similar offense, it would be disregard of a long unbroken, unquestioned course of impressive adjudication for the Court now to rule that due process compels such a bar. A practical justification for rejecting such a reading of due process also commends itself in aid of this interpretation of the Fourteenth Amendment. In *Screws v. United States,* 325 U.S. 91, 89 L.Ed. 1495, 65 S.Ct. 1031 (1945) defendants were tried and convicted in a federal court under federal statutes with maximum sentences of a year and two years respectively.[a] But the state crime there involved was a capital offense. Were the federal prosecution of a comparatively minor offense to prevent state prosecution of so grave an infraction of state law, the result would be a shocking and untoward deprivation of the historic right and obligation of the States to maintain peace and order within their confines. It would be in derogation of our federal system to displace the reserved power of States over state offenses by reason of prosecution of minor federal offenses by federal authorities beyond the control of the States. * * * Time has not lessened the concern of the Founders in devising a federal system which would likewise be a safeguard against arbitrary government. The greatest self-restraint is necessary when that federal system yields results with which a court is in little sympathy. * * * "

A dissenting opinion by Justice Black, joined by Chief Justice Warren and Justice Douglas, rejected the precedents cited by the majority, and argued alternatively that the majority had gone beyond the leading prior decision in upholding here "a state conviction of a defendant who had been *acquitted* of the same offense in the federal courts." The dissent placed primary emphasis on the "long established" principle against using "governmental power to try people twice for the same conduct." It found no justification for ignoring that "ancient safeguard" in "the name of federalism."

The *Bartkus* order of prosecutions was reversed in the companion case of ABBATE v. UNITED STATES, 359 U.S. 187, 79 S.Ct. 666, 3 L.Ed.2d 729 (1959). The petitioners there conspired to dynamite telephone company facilities. They originally were indicted in a state court for conspiring to destroy the property of another in violation of state law. Upon pleading guilty, each was sentenced to three months imprisonment. Thereafter, based upon the same conspiracy, they were prosecuted in a district court for the federal offense of conspiring to destroy communication facilities "operated or controlled by the United States," and they were convicted. Reaffirming a prior decision (*United States v. Lanza*), a 6–3 majority, per Brennan, J., held that the federal prosecution did not violate the double jeopardy bar. Justice Brennan's opinion reiterated the fears voiced in earlier cases that "if the States are free to prosecute criminal acts violating their laws, and the resultant state prosecutions bar federal prosecutions based on the same acts, federal law enforcement must necessarily be hindered."

Notes and Questions

1. In *Murphy v. Waterfront Comm'n,* described at p. 738 supra, the Court rejected the contention that the "dual sovereignty" doctrine limited the scope of the constitutional privilege against self-incrimination. In light of *Murphy* and *Benton v. Maryland* (holding the Fifth Amendment double jeopardy bar applicable to the states via the Fourteenth Amendment), several com-

a. In *Screws,* the defendant, a sheriff, was prosecuted under the federal Civil Rights Act for the denial of the due process rights of a Negro prisoner by purposely beating the prisoner to death.

mentators suggested that the Supreme Court might be inclined to overrule *Bartkus* and *Abbate.* However, subsequent decisions have shown no such inclination. Thus, in *United States v. Wheeler,* 435 U.S. 313, 98 S.Ct. 1079, 55 L.Ed.2d 303 (1978), the Court relied heavily on *Bartkus* and *Abbate* in holding that the double jeopardy clause did not prohibit a federal criminal prosecution of an Indian who had been convicted of a lesser included offense in a tribal court. A unanimous Court held that the separate sovereignty concept, as recognized in *Bartkus* and *Abbate,* applied equally to Indian tribes that had retained their "sovereign power to punish tribal offenders." So too, in *Heath v. Alabama,* ___ U.S. ___, 106 S.Ct. 433, 88 L.Ed.2d 387 (1985), the Court held that the dual sovereignty doctrine permits two states to maintain successive prosecutions of a defendant for the same harm (a murder) that involved actions in both states. The Court rejected the defendant's contention that the dual sovereignty principle should be restricted "to cases in which two governmental entities hav[e] concurrent jurisdiction and pursu[e] quite different interests," noting that such a "balancing of interest approach" had been rejected in *Abbate.* Relying on that approach, Justice Marshall (joined by Justice Brennan) argued in dissent that the states had similar interests and therefore were in a situation quite different from the "unique relationship between the Federal Government and the States."

2. Shortly after *Abbate,* Attorney General Rogers issued a memorandum to U.S. Attorneys containing the following directive: "It is our duty to observe not only the rulings of the Court but the spirit of the rulings as well. In effect, the Court said [in *Abbate*] that although the rule of the *Lanza* case [upholding a federal prosecution following a state prosecution] is sound law, enforcement officers should use care in applying it. * * * [Accordingly,] no federal case should be tried when there has already been a state prosecution for substantially the same act or acts without * * * [the approval of an Assistant Attorney General after consultation with the Attorney General]." N.Y.Times, April 6, 1959, p. 1, col. 4, p. 19, cols. 1, 2. This policy was noted by the Supreme Court in *Petite v. United States,* 361 U.S. 529, 80 S.Ct. 450, 4 L.Ed.2d 490 (1960), and it subsequently has been described as the *Petite* policy. It has served as the basis for dismissing indictments and vacating convictions, on the government's motion, in numerous cases in which federal prosecutions were inadvertently initiated after state prosecutions. See, e.g., *Petite v. United States,* supra. Indeed, in *Rinaldi v. United States,* 434 U.S. 22, 98 S.Ct. 81, 54 L.Ed.2d 207 (1977), the Court held that it was an abuse of discretion for a district court to refuse to vacate a conviction where such action was requested by the government on the ground that it had violated its *Petite* policy. On the other hand, the defendant may not obtain a dismissal of an indictment, over the objection of the government, simply because the United States Attorney failed to obtain prior approval of an Assistant Attorney General as required by *Petite.* See *United States v. King,* 590 F.2d 253 (8th Cir. 1978).

3. Today, over half the states would prohibit state prosecution following federal prosecution in the situation presented in *Bartkus.* In a few of these states, appellate decisions have held that state constitutional provisions bar such a state prosecution. See LaFave and Israel, § 24.5(b). Most, however, rely on statutes that specifically prohibit state prosecution for offenses that relate to a previous federal prosecution. Those statutes vary in scope. Some prohibit a state prosecution based on the "same act or omission" as the federal prosecution, some prohibit a state prosecution unless that prosecution and the federal prosecution each require proof of a fact not required by the other, and a few bar state prosecutions based on the "same transaction" as the federal prosecution.

State courts applying these different standards have produced decisions that do not always reflect the comparative breadth or narrowness of the state standard. Consider, e.g., the following rulings: *Journey v. State,* 521 S.W.2d 210 (Ark.1975) (under a statute prohibiting prosecution for state offenses "committed in the same course of conduct" and of the "same character" as the federal offense, defendant's acquittal on federal charges of transporting stolen property across state lines did not bar state prosecution for possession of stolen property; defendant could have been innocent of transporting the property yet still guilty of possessing it); *Epps v. Commonwealth,* 216 S.E.2d 64 (Va.1975) (where defendant had been acquitted of the federal offense of aggravated bank robbery—prohibiting robbery "of an insured bank under the aggravated circumstances of jeopardizing the life of 'any person' in the course of the robbery"—state prosecution for attempted murder of the bank guard was permissible under statute prohibiting state prosecution for the "same act" as federal prosecution); *Commonwealth v. Grazier,* 393 A.2d 335 (Pa.1978) (under "interest-analysis" standard prescribed by state constitutional decision, state prosecution for arson was prohibited following acquittal on a federal mail fraud charge which had been based on an alleged scheme to defraud insurers in connection with the alleged arson of a hotel; where the basic difference between the state and federal provisions is a jurisdictional element—use of the mails—the federal and state interests will both be viewed as directed at the same underlying wrongdoing).

4. In WALLER v. FLORIDA, 397 U.S. 387, 90 S.Ct. 1184, 25 L.Ed.2d 435 (1970), a unanimous court rejected the extension of *Bartkus* to successive municipal and state prosecutions. Petitioner had removed a canvas mural which was affixed to a wall inside the city hall and had carried it through the streets until, after a scuffle with the police, it was recovered in a damaged condition. After being convicted of violating two city ordinances (destruction of city property, disorderly breach of the peace), he was convicted of the felony of grand larceny in violation of state law. On the basis of the state court's view that the felony charge was based on the "same acts" as the city ordinance violations and on the state court's "assumption that the ordinance violations were included offenses of the felony charge," the Court held, per Chief Justice Burger, that the second trial violated the double jeopardy prohibition. *Bartkus* and *Abbate* were distinguished on the ground that cities and states are not "separate sovereignties"; rather, cities, counties, and other political subdivisions of states are "subordinate governmental instrumentalities created by the State to assist in the carrying out of state governmental functions."

Although the Court in *Waller* did not specify what standard would be used in determining whether an ordinance violation and state statute prohibit the same offense, lower courts have assumed that the standard traditionally applied to prosecutions under separate state statutes (see *Brown v. Ohio,* p. 1064 supra) also applies here. In *Waller,* on remand, the state court held that the ordinance violation there was not in fact a lesser included offense of the felony charge. See *Waller v. State,* 270 So.2d 26 (Fla.App.1972). Lower courts have also held that the *Waller* ruling is subject to a "subsequent events exception" (cf. n. 7, p. 1066 supra), applicable to situations in which the state offense was not fully consummated when the ordinance prosecution was brought [e.g., where the assault victim subsequently died], and to a "collusion exception," applicable to situations in which the ordinance conviction was procured by collusion between the offender and city officials for the purpose of protecting the offender against more serious state charges. See LaFave and Israel, § 24.5(c).

Part Five

APPEALS, POST-CONVICTION REVIEW

Analysis

Chapter 26

APPEALS

SECTION 1. THE DEFENDANT'S RIGHT TO APPEAL

1. *A constitutional right to appeal?* In *McKane v. Durston,* 153 U.S. 684, 14 S.Ct. 913, 38 L.Ed. 867 (1894), the Supreme Court noted, in dictum, that "a review by an appellate court of the final judgment in a criminal case, however grave the offense of which the accused is convicted, was not at common law and is not now a necessary element of due process." Although there have been numerous changes in constitutional criminal procedure since *McKane* was decided, the Court has never questioned the *McKane* dictum. Indeed, opinions dealing with questions that relate to appellate review of criminal convictions not infrequently start off by citing *McKane* and noting that "a state is not required by the Federal Constitution to provide * * * a right of appeal." *Griffin v. Illinois,* p. 105 supra. See also, *Ross v. Moffitt,* p. 112 supra; *Jones v. Barnes,* p. 176 supra. However, the Court is unlikely ever to face a case in which it must decide whether the *McKane* dictum should be converted to a holding. All jurisdictions, for some years now, have provided convicted defendants with an avenue for obtaining appellate review. In those jurisdictions with intermediate appellate courts, review is provided as a matter of right, while jurisdictions with a single tier of appellate courts commonly provide for review at the discretion of the appellate court (usually through a writ of certiorari). See pp. 15, 31–32 supra.

Does it matter whether defendant's opportunity for appellate review is treated as having a statutory rather than a constitutional grounding, assuming that no state is likely to withdraw that right? As noted in Chapter Three, *Griffin v. Illinois,* p. 105 supra, holds that once a state grants defendants a right to appellate review, it cannot condition that right in a manner that violates the indigent's right to equal protection. *Douglas v. California,* p. 108 supra, further holds that the equal protection guarantee requires that the state provide the indigent defendant with the assistance of counsel in presenting his first appeal granted as a matter of statutory right. *Evitts v. Lucey,* p. 119 supra, guarantees to a defendant the effective assistance of counsel on such an appeal, whether that counsel is appointed or retained. Would defendants be afforded any broader rights with respect to the appellate process if their opportunity to obtain at least one level of appellate review was viewed as constitutionally guaranteed? Consider in this connection the due process protection of the statutory right of appeal as provided in *North Carolina v. Pearce,* set forth below.

NORTH CAROLINA v. PEARCE

395 U.S. 711, 89 S.Ct. 2073, 23 L.Ed.2d 656 (1969).

[As noted at p. 1425 supra, this case presented two issues relating to the sentence that could be imposed upon a defendant's reconviction after his original conviction had been set aside. The Court's discussion of the first issue presented—whether credit must be given for time served under the original sentence—is reprinted at p. 1425 supra. With respect to the second question—whether the trial court could impose a more severe sentence than that originally imposed—the two defendants in *Pearce* [a] raised double jeopardy, equal protection, and due process claims. The Court's disposition of their double jeopardy claim is discussed in Note 2, p. 1426 supra. We reprint here those parts of the majority, concurring, and dissenting opinions that deal with defendants' equal protection and due process claims.]

MR. JUSTICE STEWART delivered the opinion of the Court.

* * * [Defendants'] other argument advanced in support of the proposition that the Constitution absolutely forbids the imposition of a more severe sentence upon retrial is grounded upon the Equal Protection Clause. The theory advanced is that, since convicts who do not seek new trials cannot have their sentences increased, it creates an invidious classification to impose that risk only upon those who succeed in getting their original convictions set aside. The argument, while not lacking in ingenuity, cannot withstand close examination. In the first place, we deal here, not with increases in existing sentences, but with the imposition of wholly new sentences after wholly new trials. Putting that conceptual nicety to one side, however, the problem before us simply cannot be rationally dealt with in terms of "classifications." A man who is retried after his first conviction has been set aside may be acquitted. If convicted, he may receive a shorter sentence, he may receive the same sentence, or he may receive a longer sentence than the one originally imposed. The result may depend upon a particular combination of infinite variables peculiar to each individual trial. It simply cannot be said that a State has invidiously "classified" those who successfully seek new trials, any more than that the State has invidiously "classified" those prisoners whose convictions are not set aside by denying the members of that group the opportunity to be acquitted. To fit the problem of this case into an equal protection framework is a task too Procrustean to be rationally accomplished.

We hold, therefore, that neither the double jeopardy provision nor the Equal Protection Clause imposes an absolute bar to a more severe sentence upon reconviction. A trial judge is not constitutionally precluded, in other words, from imposing a new sentence, whether greater or less than the original sentence, in the light of events subsequent to the first trial that may have thrown new light upon the defendant's "life, health, habits, conduct and mental and moral propensities." *Williams v. New York,* 337 U.S. 241, 69 S.Ct. 1079, 93 L.Ed. 1337 (1949). Such information may come to the judge's attention from evidence adduced at the second trial itself, from a new presentence investigation, from the defendant's prison record, or possibly from other sources. The freedom of a sentencing judge to consider the defendant's conduct subsequent to the first conviction in imposing new sentence is no more than consonant with the principle, fully approved in *Williams,* that a State may adopt the "prevalent modern philoso-

a. The Court in *Pearce* had before it two separate cases. In No. 413, defendant Pearce had been convicted of assault with intent to commit rape and sentenced to a prison term of 12 to 15 years. After the conviction was set aside in a post-conviction proceeding, he was reprosecuted and convicted of the same offence. The judge then sentenced him to 15 years imprisonment less seven years already served. In No. 418, defendant Rice had pleaded guilty to four separate charges of second degree burglary, and had been sentenced to prison terms totaling 10 years. The pleas were set aside in a post-conviction proceeding on the ground that defendant had not been accorded his right to counsel. He was then retried on three of the charges, convicted and sentenced to an aggregate prison term of 25 years.

phy of penology that the punishment should fit the offender and not merely the crime."

To say that there exists no absolute constitutional bar to the imposition of a more severe sentence upon retrial is not, however, to end the inquiry. There remains for consideration the impact of the Due Process Clause of the Fourteenth Amendment.

It can hardly be doubted that it would be a flagrant violation of the Fourteenth Amendment for a state trial court to follow an announced practice of imposing a heavier sentence upon every reconvicted defendant for the explicit purpose of punishing the defendant for his having succeeded in getting his original conviction set aside. Where, as in each of the cases before us, the original conviction has been set aside because of a constitutional error, the imposition of such a punishment, "penalizing those who choose to exercise" constitutional rights, "would be patently unconstitutional." *United States v. Jackson,* [p. 1191 supra]. And the very threat inherent in the existence of such a punitive policy would, with respect to those still in prison, serve to "chill the exercise of basic constitutional rights." See also *Griffin v. California,* [p. 1360 supra]. But even if the first conviction has been set aside for nonconstitutional error, the imposition of a penalty upon the defendant for having successfully pursued a statutory right of appeal or collateral remedy would be no less a violation of due process of law. * * * A court is "without right to * * * put a price on an appeal. A defendant's exercise of a right of appeal must be free and unfettered. * * * [I]t is unfair to use the great power given to the court to determine sentence to place a defendant in the dilemma of making an unfree choice." *Worcester v. Commissioner of Internal Revenue,* 370 F.2d 713 (1st Cir.1966). "This Court has never held that the States are required to establish avenues of appellate review, but it is now fundamental that, once established, these avenues must be kept free of unreasoned distinctions that can only impede open and equal access to the courts." *Griffin v. Illinois* [p. 105 supra].

Due process of law, then, requires that vindictiveness against a defendant for having successfully attacked his first conviction must play no part in the sentence he receives after a new trial. And since the fear of such vindictiveness may unconstitutionally deter a defendant's exercise of the right to appeal or collaterally attack his first conviction, due process also requires that a defendant be freed of apprehension of such a retaliatory motivation on the part of the sentencing judge.[20]

In order to assure the absence of such a motivation, we have concluded that whenever a judge imposes a more severe sentence upon a defendant after a new trial, the reasons for his doing so must affirmatively appear. Those reasons must be based upon objective information concerning identifiable conduct on the part of the defendant occurring after the time of the original sentencing proceeding. And the factual data upon which the increased sentence is based must be made part of the record, so that the constitutional legitimacy of the increased sentence may be fully reviewed on appeal.

We dispose of the two cases before us in the light of these conclusions. In No. 418, United States District Court Judge Johnson noted that "the State of Alabama offers no evidence attempting to justify the increase in Rice's original sentences * * *." He * * * found that "the conclusion is inescapable that the State of Alabama is punishing petitioner Rice for his having exercised his post-conviction right of review . . . ." In No. 413 the situation is not so dramatically clear. Nonetheless, the fact remains that neither

20. The existence of a retaliatory motivation would, of course, be extremely difficult to prove in any individual case. But data have been collected to show that increased sentences on reconviction are far from rare. See Note, 1965 Duke L.J. 395. * * *

at the time the increased sentence was imposed upon Pearce, nor at any stage in this habeas corpus proceeding, has the State offered any reason or justification for that sentence beyond the naked power to impose it. We conclude that in each of the cases before us, the judgment should be affirmed.

MR. JUSTICE WHITE, concurring in part.

I join the Court's opinion except that in my view * * * [it] should authorize an increased sentence on retrial based on any objective, identifiable factual data not known to the trial judge at the time of the original sentencing proceeding.

MR. JUSTICE BLACK, concurring in part and dissenting in part.

* * * I agree with the Court's rejection of respondents' claims that the increased sentences violate the Double Jeopardy and Equal Protection Clauses of the Constitution. * * *

The Court goes on, however, to hold that it would be a flagrant violation of due process for a "state trial court to follow an announced practice of imposing a heavier sentence upon every reconvicted defendant for the explicit purpose of punishing the defendant for his having succeeded in getting his original conviction set aside." * * * I also agree that it would violate the Constitution for any judge to impose a higher penalty on a defendant solely because he had taken a legally permissible appeal. On this basis there is a plausible argument for upholding the judgment in No. 418. * * * But this provides no basis for affirming the judgment of the Court of Appeals in No. 413, the case involving respondent Pearce. For in that case there is not a line of evidence to support the slightest inference that the trial judge wanted or intended to punish Pearce for seeking postconviction relief. Indeed the record shows that this trial judge meticulously computed the time Pearce had served in jail in order to give him full credit for that time.

The Court justifies affirming the release of Pearce in this language:

> "In order to assure the absence of such a motivation, we have concluded that whenever a judge imposes a more severe sentence upon a defendant after a new trial, the reasons for his doing so must affirmatively appear. Those reasons must be based upon objective information concerning identifiable conduct on the part of the defendant occurring after the time of the original sentencing proceeding. And the factual data upon which the increased sentence is based must be made part of the record, so that the constitutional legitimacy of the increased sentence may be fully reviewed on appeal."

Of course nothing in the Due Process Clause grants this Court any such power as it is using here. Punishment based on the impermissible motivation described by the Court is, as I have said, clearly unconstitutional, and courts must of course set aside the punishment if they find, by the normal judicial process of fact-finding, that such a motivation exists. But, beyond this, the courts are not vested with any general power to prescribe particular devices "[i]n order to assure the absence of such a motivation." Numerous different mechanisms could be thought of, any one of which would serve this function. Yet the Court does not explain why the particular detailed procedure spelled out in this case is *constitutionally* required, while other remedial devices are not. This is pure legislation if there ever was legislation.

* * * Apart from this, the possibility that judicial action will be prompted by impermissible motives is a particularly poor reason for holding that detailed rules of procedure are constitutionally binding in every state and federal prosecution. The danger of improper motivation is of course ever present. A judge *might* impose a specially severe penalty solely because of a defendant's race, religion, or political views. He *might* impose a special-

ly severe penalty because a defendant exercised his right to counsel, or insisted on a trial by jury, or even because the defendant refused to admit his guilt and insisted on any particular kind of trial. In all these instances any additional punishment would of course be * * * flagrantly unconstitutional. But it has never previously been suggested by this Court that "[i]n order to assure the absence of such a motivation," this Court could, as a matter of constitutional law, direct all trial judges to spell out in detail their reasons for setting a particular sentence, making their reasons "affirmatively appear," and basing these reasons on "objective information concerning identifiable conduct." Nor has this Court ever previously suggested in connection with sentencing that "the factual data * * * must be made part of the record." * * * There are many perfectly legitimate reasons that a judge might have for imposing a higher sentence. For instance, take the case of respondent Rice. Without a lawyer, he pleaded guilty to four charges of burglary and received a sentence of only 10 years. Although not shown by the record, what happened is not difficult to see. It is common knowledge that prosecutors frequently trade with defendants and agree to recommend low sentences in return for pleas of guilty. Judges frequently accept such agreements without carefully scrutinizing the record of the defendant. One needs little imagination to infer that Rice's original sentence was the result of precisely such a practice. This explains both the first 10-year sentence and the fact that, after a full trial and examination of the entire record, the trial judge concluded that a 25-year sentence was called for. The Court's opinion today will—unfortunately, I think, for defendants—throw stumbling blocks in the way of their making similar beneficial agreements in the future. Moreover, the Court's opinion may hereafter cause judges to impose heavier sentences on defendants in order to preserve their lawfully authorized discretion should defendants win reversals of their original convictions. * * * [b]

Notes and Questions

1. *The prophylactic remedy of Pearce.* In *Michigan v. Payne,* 412 U.S. 47, 93 S.Ct. 1966, 36 L.Ed.2d 736 (1973), the Court stated that that portion of the *Pearce* ruling requiring the sentencing court to set forth the reasons for imposing a higher sentence on retrial following an appeal, and restricting those reasons to certain types of factual data, would not be applied retroactively. Those requirements constituted a "prophylactic limitation," designed to serve a "protective role" against vindictiveness, and therefore gained nothing through retroactive application. The Court noted, however, that the other aspect of the *Pearce* ruling—the prohibition against "retaliatory motivation" in resentencing—was a "basic due process protection" which would be "available equally to defendants resentenced before and after the date of the [*Pearce*] decision."

2. Different perspectives on the content and role of *Pearce*'s prophylactic requirements were reflected in the several opinions in WASMAN v. UNITED STATES, 468 U.S. 559, 104 S.Ct. 3217, 82 L.Ed.2d 424 (1984). The petitioner there, following his conviction for knowingly and wilfully making false statements in a passport application, was sentenced to two years imprisonment, with all but six months suspended in favor of three years probation. At the time of that sentence, there was pending against petitioner an unrelated charge for mail fraud. When the government informed the sentencing judge of that charge, he noted that he always considered prior convictions when sentencing, but he would not give weight to charges not yet tried. The petitioner

b. The dissenting opinions of Justices Douglas and Harlan, relying on the defendants' double jeopardy claim, are noted at p. 1426 supra. Justice Douglas' opinion, joined by Justice Marshall, did note "agree[ment] with the Court as to the reach of due process."

subsequently obtained a reversal of his passport conviction, with the case remanded for a new trial. In the interim between the original sentence and the reversal, a charge of possession of counterfeit certificates of deposit had been substituted for the mail fraud charge, and petitioner had pleaded nolo contendere to that lesser charge. Petitioner was retried on the passport charge before the same judge who had conducted the original trial. Following his conviction, the judge again sentenced petitioner to two years imprisonment, but this time refused to suspend any portion of that sentence. The judge noted that he was now taking into consideration the interim conviction, which previously had been only a pending charge. The Supreme Court unanimously rejected petitioner's contention that the sentencing judge had violated the requirements of *Pearce.* However, CHIEF JUSTICE BURGER'S opinion for the Court did not gain majority support for its full discussion of *Pearce.* While five justices joined Parts III–A and III–C of the opinion, only three (White, Rehnquist, and O'Connor, J.J.) joined Parts II–B and III–B.

In Part II–B of his opinion, the Chief Justice reviewed the various Supreme Court cases that had considered possible application of "a presumption of vindictiveness of the kind imposed in *Pearce.*" Although a similar presumption had been adopted in *Blackledge v. Perry* [p. 927 supra], the Court had been "chary about extending" the *Pearce* approach, as evidenced by the rulings in *Colten v. Kentucky* [p. 1442 infra]; *Chaffin v. Stynchcombe* [p. 1443 infra]; *Bordenkircher v. Hayes* [p. 1185 supra]; and *United States v. Goodwin* [p. 929 supra]. The Chief Justice then added:

"If it was not clear from the Court's holding in *Pearce,* it is clear from our subsequent cases applying *Pearce* that due process does not in any sense forbid enhanced sentences or charges, but only enhancement motivated by *actual vindictiveness* toward the defendant for having exercised guaranteed rights. In *Pearce* and in *Blackledge,* the Court 'presumed' that the increased sentence and charge were the products of actual vindictiveness aroused by the defendants' appeals. It held that the defendants' right to due process was violated not because the sentence and charge were enhanced, but because there was no evidence introduced to rebut the presumption that actual vindictiveness was behind the increases; in other words, by operation of law, the increases were deemed motivated by vindictiveness. In *Colten, Chaffin, Bordenkircher,* and *Goodwin,* on the other hand—where the presumption was held not to apply—we made clear that a due process violation could be established only by proof of actual vindictiveness. In sum, where the presumption applies, the sentencing authority or the prosecutor must rebut the presumption that an increased sentence or charge resulted from vindictiveness; where the presumption does not apply, the defendant must affirmatively prove actual vindictiveness."

In Part III of his opinion, the Chief Justice turned to application of the "*Pearce* presumption" to the case before the Court. Part III–A set forth the petitioner's basic contention:

"Here, petitioner in effect received a greater sentence of confinement following retrial than he had originally received. This was sufficient to engage the presumption of *Pearce.* In sharp contrast to *Pearce* and *Blackledge,* however, the trial judge here carefully explained his reasons for imposing the greater sentence. * * * Petitioner does not charge that the judge was vindictive. Rather, he argues that any consideration of his intervening conviction was foreclosed by the plain language of *Pearce.* Petitioner points to the passage in *Pearce* stating that the reasons posited by a court for increasing a defendant's sentence on retrial 'must be based upon objective information concerning identifiable *conduct* on the part of the defendant occurring *after* the time of the original sentencing proceeding' (emphasis added). His contention is that the 'conduct' for which he was convicted, *i.e.,* possession of counterfeit certificates of deposit, occurred prior to the time of his original sentencing proceeding and thus could not be considered by the trial judge.

Responding to the petitioner's contention, the Chief Justice initially noted in Part III–A that "*Pearce* is not without its ambiguities." In contrast to the passage cited by petitioner, there was the additional passage (see p. 1435 supra) discussing *Williams v. New York,* which spoke to "*events* subsequent to the first trial that may have thrown new light upon defendant's 'life, health, habits, conduct and mental and moral propensities.' " The Chief Justice also noted, in segment B of Part III of his opinion (a segment not joined by the majority), that another ambiguity was suggested by the separate opinions of Justices Douglas and Black in *Pearce.* Those opinions were viewed as suggesting that "the Court did not intend to confine the sentencing authority's consideration to 'conduct' occurring subsequent to the first sentencing proceeding," but also allowed consideration of "information that had been developed after the initial trial" (quoting Douglas, J.). Indeed, it was noted, Justice Black "did not refer to a temporal limitation on the information that could be considered."

Having noted these ambiguities, the Chief Justice then added the following comments in Part III–C of the opinion (which had majority support):

"We find it unnecessary, however, to reconcile these apparent ambiguities. In the two cases before the Court in *Pearce* there was no asserted explanation or justification for the heightened sentence. This case, on the other hand, squarely presents the question of the scope of information that may be relied upon by a sentencing authority to justify an increased sentence after retrial.

"We conclude that any language in *Pearce* suggesting that an intervening conviction for an offense committed prior to the original sentencing may not be considered upon sentencing after retrial, is inconsistent with the *Pearce* opinion as a whole. There is no logical support for a distinction between 'events' and 'conduct' of the defendant occurring after the initial sentencing insofar as the kind of information that may be relied upon to show a nonvindictive motive is concerned. This is clear from *Williams v. New York,* 337 U.S. 241, 69 S.Ct. 1079, 93 L.Ed. 1337 (1949), which provides that the underlying philosophy of modern sentencing is to take into account the person as well as the crime by considering 'information concerning every aspect of a defendant's life.'

"Even without a limitation on the type of factual information that may be considered, the requirement that the sentencing authority or prosecutor detail the reasons for an increased sentence or charge enables appellate courts to ensure that a nonvindictive rationale supports the increase. A contrary conclusion would result in the needless exclusion of relevant sentencing information from the very authority in whom the sentencing power is vested. The response of the Court of Appeals to petitioner's argument was entirely correct: 'No reason exists for applying a phrase in the *Pearce* guidelines to circumstances bearing no relation to the purpose of those guidelines.' 700 F.2d, at 668."

Justice POWELL, joined by Blackmun, J., filed a separate concurring opinion, noting he did not join Parts II–B and III–B of the Chief Justice's opinion. "This case," Justice Powell stated "involves a straight forward application of the Court's holding in *North Carolina v. Pearce.*" As noted in the Chief Justice's opinion, the *Pearce* opinion had referred to "events" subsequent to the first trial. Any attempt to restrict the *Pearce* ruling to "conduct" alone would "exalt words above substance." Justice Powell concluded: "The *Pearce* presumption is not simply concerned with actual vindictiveness, but also was intended to protect against reasonable apprehension of vindictiveness that could deter a defendant from appealing a first conviction. Both of these concerns are fully met in this case. It would be difficult to think of an event or occurrence more relevant to the determination of a proper sentence than a criminal conviction obtained in the interim between an original sentencing and a sentencing following retrial."

Justicc BRENNAN, joined by Marshall, J., concurred in the judgment, noting that he did so "substantially for the reasons expressed by Justice Powell in his separate opinion." Justice STEVENS, concurring in the judgment, stated that he was unable to join the Chief Justice's opinion because "it interprets *North Carolina v. Pearce* as resting entirely on a concern with the actual vindictiveness of the sentencing judge and does not identify the interest in protecting the defendant against the reasonable apprehension of vindictiveness that might deter him from prosecuting a meritorious appeal." Justice Stevens added that, "like Justice Brennan, Justice Marshall, Justice Blackmun, and Justice Powell," he would "decide this case on the ground that affirmance of a prior conviction after the initial sentencing constitutes the type of intervening event that may be considered by a trial judge as a ground for enhancing a sentence after a successful appeal."

3. If the Court were to accept Chief Justice Burger's view of *Pearce,* what would be necessary to rebut what the Chief Justice describes as the "presumption" of vindictiveness? Would it be sufficient to show that the second sentence was imposed by a new judge who had no knowledge of the previous sentence? Would a higher sentence be justified where the sentencing court relies upon new information establishing that defendant played a larger role in the crime, or that the crime itself caused greater harm than was suggested in the first proceeding? Lower courts, sharing the view of *Pearce* advanced in Justice Powell's opinion in *Wasman,* generally have held that such factors cannot justify a higher sentence or retrial. See LaFave and Israel, § 26.1(c). They insist upon some "intervening conduct or event" that reflect adversely on defendant's character. See *United States v. Whitley,* 759 F.2d 327 (4th Cir.1985).

4. Is there any reason why the defendant's "intervening conduct" justifying a higher sentence should not include his giving testimony at the second trial that the trial judge views as clearly false? The Supreme Court has held that a trial court convinced that a defendant has committed perjury may weigh that factor against him in sentencing. See *United States v. Grayson,* p. 1179 supra. But it has been suggested that allowing the sentencing court to rely on such a factor in the *Pearce* context opens the door to "the masked vindictiveness which *Pearce* sought to prohibit by its prophylactic rule." LaFave and Israel, § 26.1(c). Does the answer lie in the relationship of the testimony at the second trial to that at the first trial? Consider *United States v. Saletko,* 452 F.2d 193, 199 (7th Cir.1971) ("defendant's allegation * * *, even if perjurious, constituted no new fact upon which a more severe sentence could be predicated since that same testimony was given at the first trial"; to justify an increased sentence, there must be substantial false testimony not offered at the first trial). But compare *United States v. Gambert,* 433 F.2d 321, 323 (4th Cir.1970) ("testimony of the defendant at his second trial which revealed 'inconsistencies and incredible explanations not before the previous sentencing court' does not constitute 'identifiable conduct' of the type contemplated by *Pearce*).

5. *Vacated guilty pleas.* One of the two cases before the Court in *Pearce* (that of defendant Rice, see fn. a supra) involved a higher sentence imposed following a vacated guilty plea. Although the Court did not distinguish that factual setting in discussing its prophylactic requirements, it did note that the federal habeas court had specifically found that the state judge acted vindictively in imposing the substantially

higher sentence following Rice's trial and reconviction. Lower courts have generally held that, absent specific circumstances suggesting actual vindictiveness (as were found as to defendant Rice), the judge imposing a higher sentence for the same charge following a vacated guilty plea may justify that sentence under *Pearce* by simply noting that defendant lost the sentencing advantages of a guilty plea when he chose to go to trial his second time around. See e.g., *Sweetwine v. State,* 398 A.2d 1262 (Md.App.1979) (defendant "with his initial plea of guilty, brought 'leniency' and then stopped payment on the check"). Could the higher sentence in such a situation also be justified on the ground that the judge trying the case has a better view of the circumstances surrounding the crime than the judge who takes a guilty plea on a "cold record"? See *State v. Stubbendick,* 329 N.W.2d 399 (Wis.1983) (relying in part on that ground). Consider also the cases discussed at Note 10, p. 1205 supra.

Since *Pearce* dealt with resentencing for the same offense, lower courts have generally held that *Pearce's* prophylactic requirement does not apply to the situation in which defendant gained a reduction of charges in return for a guilty plea, successfully overturned that plea, then went to trial on the original higher charge, and received a higher sentence following his conviction on that charge. See e.g., *United States ex rel. Williams v. McMann,* 436 F.2d 103 (2d Cir.1970) (the "fact that the [second] sentence was imposed upon conviction for a more serious crime * * * [is a] complete and obvious explanation for the longer sentence; we see no need to demand the type of justification ordered in *Pearce*"). Is this situation sufficiently distinguishable from that presented in defendant Rice's case to hold *Pearce's* prophylactic limitation inapplicable, or does it reflect a lower court view that *Pearce* overlooked the special considerations applicable to vacated guilty pleas (perhaps because of the special circumstances of Rice's case) and accordingly should not be extended beyond the situation there presented of resentencing on the same charge? See *United States v. Cunningham,* 529 F.2d 884 (6th Cir.1976) (noting that "the language in *Pearce* concerning the permissible basis for an increased sentence was directed to the retrial situation and not to the process of sentencing after the withdrawal of a plea of guilty" and suggesting that *Pearce's* prophylactic limitation should not apply to plea withdrawal cases even where the sentencing was on the same charge).

6. *Trial de novo.* In COLTEN v. KENTUCKY, 407 U.S. 104, 92 S.Ct. 1953, 32 L.Ed.2d 584 (1972), a divided Court (7–2) held that the *Pearce* requirement did not apply to sentences imposed on a trial *de novo* "appeal" of a misdemeanor conviction. The defendant there was charged with disorderly conduct for refusing to obey an officer's order that he leave a congested roadside where a fellow political demonstrator was being ticketed for a traffic offense. After the defendant had been tried, convicted, and fined $10 by a minor county court, he exercised his right to "appeal" by obtaining a trial *de novo* before a court of general criminal jurisdiction. The judge of that court, following defendant's new trial and conviction, fined defendant $50. The Supreme Court, per Justice WHITE, noted:

"Our view of the Kentucky two-tier system of administering criminal justice * * * does not lead us to believe, and there is nothing in the record or presented in the briefs to show, that the hazard of being penalized for seeking a new trial, which underlay the holding of *Pearce,* also inheres in the *de novo* trial arrangement. Nor are we convinced that defendants convicted in Kentucky's inferior courts would be deterred from seeking a second trial out of fear of judicial vindictiveness. The possibility of vindictiveness, found to exist in *Pearce,* is not inherent in the Kentucky two-tier system.

"We note first the obvious: that the court which conducted Colten's trial and imposed the final sentence was not the court with whose work Colten was sufficiently dissatisfied to seek a different result on appeal; and it is not the court that is asked to do over what it thought it had already done correctly. Nor is the *de novo* court even asked to find error in another court's work. Rather, the Kentucky court in which Colten had the unrestricted right to have a new trial was merely asked to accord the same trial, under the same rules and procedures, available to defendants whose cases are begun in that court in the first instance. It would also appear that, however understandably a court of general jurisdiction might feel that the defendant who has had a due process trial ought to be satisfied with it, the *de novo* court in the two-tier system is much more likely to reflect the attitude of the Kentucky Court of Appeals in this case when it stated that 'the inferior courts are not designed or equipped to conduct error-free trials, or to insure full recognition of constitutional freedoms. They are courts of convenience, to provide speedy and inexpensive means of disposition of charges of minor offenses.' We see no reason, and none is offered, to assume that the *de novo* court will deal any more strictly with those who insist on a trial in the superior court after conviction in the Quarterly Court than it would with those defendants whose cases are filed originally in the superior court and who choose to put the State to its proof in a trial subject to constitutional guarantees. * * *

Mr. Justice MARSHALL, dissenting, responded: "[T]he Court faults the appellant for failing to present evidence that the danger of vindictiveness is as great here as in the precise context presented in *Pearce.* But *Pearce* did not rest on evidence that most trial judges are hostile to defendants who obtain a new trial after appeal. *Pearce* was based, rather, on the recognition that whenever a defendant is tried twice for the same offence, there is inherent in the situation the danger of vindictive sentencing the second time around, and that this danger will deter some defendants from seeking a second trial. This danger, with its deterrent effect, is exactly the same even though the second trial takes place in a different court from the first. Certainly a defendant has good reason to fear that his case will not be well received by a second court after he rejects a disposition as favorable as the sentence originally imposed in this case. * * * The core problem is the second trial. In both cases we have a second full and complete trial. *Pearce* should control."

7. *Jury sentencing.* Building upon *Colten,* the Court held in CHAFFIN v. STYNCHCOMBE, 412 U.S. 17, 93 S.Ct. 1977, 36 L.Ed.2d 714 (1973), that *Pearce's* prophylactic rule also would not be applied to jury sentencing. A closely divided Court concluded that, unlike the situation in *Pearce,* the potential for vindictive sentencing by a jury was "*de minimus* in a properly controlled retrial." Powell, J., speaking for the majority, noted initially that the jury imposing the sentence in the second trial would not know of the earlier sentence. While it probably would be aware that there had been an earlier trial, it would not know whether that trial had been on the same charge or whether it had resulted in a conviction or a mistrial. Second, as was true in *Colten,* "the second sentence is not meted out by the same judicial authority" that had its earlier proceeding reversed on appeal. The jury has no personal stake in the earlier proceeding, and it "is unlikely to be sensitive to the institutional interests that might occasion higher sentences by a judge desirous of discouraging what he regards as meritless appeals." [c] Responding to the dissent, the *Chaffin* majority also rejected the

c. The dissenters in *Chaffin,* also argued that even though the jury might have no interest in vindictive sentencing, the prosecutor had such an interest and he could have a substantial influence on the ultimate sentence. Thus, it was argued, as "punishment for a successful appeal," the prosecutor could convince the jury to impose a higher sentence than he had sought in the contention that applying *Pearce* to judge sentencing, but not to jury sentencing, placed an unconstitutional burden on the defendant's right to jury trial. It was true that the defendant who chose trial by jury (and thereby jury sentencing) opened the door to a more severe second sentence, a result that *Pearce* ordinarily would bar if he chose a bench trial. But this distinction in the possible consequence of selecting a jury over a bench trial did not impose the kind of "needless burden" held invalid in other cases. See e.g., *United States v. Jackson* (p. 1191 supra). Here, the distinction flowed from a legitimate state policy that favored unfettered jury sentencing, with each jury allowed to make its own determination based on its personal assessment of the evidence before it.

8. *Limitations upon the prosecutor's charging authority.* Reconsider *Blackledge v. Perry,* described at Note 3, p. 927 supra. Although *Blackledge* involved the bringing of a higher charge in a trial de novo, the reasoning there has generally been viewed as equally applicable to the bringing of a higher charge following a successful challenge to a conviction. In *Blackledge,* however, the Court did not suggest that the higher charge could be justified on grounds that would justify a higher sentence under *Pearce.* Should such grounds be available at least in the case of a higher charge brought after a successful challenge to a conviction? If so, where a defendant was charged initially with a single offense arising out of a particular transaction, was convicted of that offense, and subsequently successfully challenged that conviction on appeal, can the prosecution, consistent with *Blackledge,* now present additional charges on the basis of "intervening evidence * * * of which the government was excusably unaware at the time of the first indictment"? See *United States v. Jamison,* 505 F.2d 407 (D.C.Cir.1974) (so holding); *United States v. Johnson,* 537 F.2d 1170 (4th Cir.1976) (suggesting the proper test may be whether the prosecutor had been aware of the new evidence in sufficient time to seek a superseding indictment prior to the original conviction). Consider also *Hardwick v. Doolittle,* 558 F.2d 292, 301 (5th Cir.1977) ("other explanations which would negate vindictiveness could include mistake or oversight in the initial action, a different approach to prosecutorial duty by the successor prosecutor, or public demand for prosecution on the additional crimes allegedly committed").

SECTION 2. DEFENSE APPEALS AND THE FINAL ORDER REQUIREMENT

FLANAGAN v. UNITED STATES

465 U.S. 259, 104 S.Ct. 1051, 79 L.Ed.2d 288 (1984).

JUSTICE O'CONNOR delivered the opinion of the Court.

In *Firestone Tire & Rubber Co. v. Risjord,* 449 U.S. 368, 101 S.Ct. 669, 66 L.Ed.2d 571 (1981), the Court held that a pretrial denial of a motion to disqualify counsel in a civil case is not appealable prior to trial under 28 U.S.C. § 1291 as a final collateral order. The Court reversed the questions of the immediate appealability of pretrial denials of disqualification motions in criminal cases and of pretrial grants of disqualification motions in both criminal and civil cases. We decide today that a District Court's pretrial disqualification of defense counsel in a criminal prosecution is not immediately appealable under 28 U.S.C. § 1291.

[Petitioners, four Philadelphia police officers, were indicted by a federal grand jury

original trial. The *Chaffin* majority responded that it might be a "desirable precaution" for the prosecutor to seek the same sentence in both trials, as had been done in the case before it. In any event, the majority continued, given the various strategical considerations that influence the prosecutor's decision to seek a particular sentence, and considering "the bar against informing the jury of the facts of prior conviction and sentence," the "possibility that a harsher sentence will be obtained through prosecutorial malice seems remote."

for conspiring to deprive citizens of their civil rights and for committing substantive civil rights offenses. Prior to the return of the indictment, petitioners had retained the Sprague and Rubenstein law firm to act as joint counsel. They continued with the joint representation after the indictment, although the indictment did not make the same allegations against each of them. After three of the petitioners moved to sever, and all moved to dismiss the conspiracy count (arguing that the asserted differences in their activities alleged in the substantive courts negated the existence of a conspiracy), the government moved to disqualify the Sprague and Rubenstein firm from joint representation. See Fed.R.Crim.P. 44(c) and pp. 170–74 supra. That motion was granted and the Court of Appeals affirmed. That court held that the disqualification order was appealable under 28 U.S.C. § 1291, which allows appeals only from "final decisions" of district courts. It relied on the so-called "collateral order exception" of *Cohen v. Beneficial Industrial Loan Corp.* (see fn. a infra).]

"Finality as a condition of review is an historic characteristic of federal appellate procedure." *Cobbledick v. United States,* 309 U.S. 323, 60 S.Ct. 540, 84 L.Ed. 783 (1940). Thus, the jurisdictional statute applicable to this case limits the jurisdiction of the Courts of Appeals to appeals from "final decisions of the district court." 28 U.S.C. § 1291. This final judgment rule requires "that a party must ordinarily raise all claims of error in a single appeal following final judgment on the merits." *Firestone Tire & Rubber Co. v. Risjord.* In a criminal case the rule prohibits appellate review until conviction and imposition of sentence. *Berman v. United States,* 302 U.S. 211, 58 S.Ct. 164, 82 L.Ed. 204 (1937).

The final judgment rule serves several important interests. It helps preserve the respect due trial judges by minimizing appellate-court interference with the numerous decisions they must make in the prejudgment stages of litigation. It reduces the ability of litigants to harass opponents and to clog the courts through a succession of costly and time-consuming appeals. It is crucial to the efficient administration of justice. For these reasons, "[t]his Court has long held that the policy of Congress embodied in [section 1291] is inimical to piecemeal appellate review of trial court decisions which do not terminate the litigation. . . ." *United States v. Hollywood Motor Car Co.,* 458 U.S. 263, 102 S.Ct. 3081, 73 L.Ed.2d 754 (1982).

The Court has also long held that "this policy is at its strongest in the field of criminal law." Ibid. More than 40 years ago the Court noted that the reasons for the final judgment rule are "especially compelling in the administration of criminal justice." *Cobbledick v. United States.* Promptness in bringing a criminal case to trial has become increasingly important as crime has increased, court dockets have swelled, and detention facilities have become overcrowded.

As the Sixth Amendment's guarantee of a Speedy Trial indicates, the accused may have a strong interest in speedy resolution of the charges against him. In addition, "there is a societal interest in providing a speedy trial which exists separate from, and at times in opposition to, the interests of the accused." *Barker v. Wingo* [p. 1082 supra]. As time passes, the prosecution's ability to meet its burden of proof may greatly diminish: evidence and witnesses may disappear, and testimony becomes more easily impeachable as the events recounted become more remote. Delay increases the cost of pretrial detention and extends "the period during which defendants released on bail may commit other crimes." *United States v. MacDonald,* 435 U.S. 850, 98 S.Ct. 1547, 56 L.Ed.2d 18 (1978). Delay between arrest and punishment prolongs public anxiety over community safety if a person accused of a serious crime is free on bail. It may also adversely affect the prospects for rehabilitation. Finally, when a crime is committed against a community, the community has a strong collective psychological and moral interest in swiftly bringing the person responsible to justice. Prompt acquittal of a person wrongly accused, which forces prosecutorial investigation to continue, is as important as prompt conviction and sentence of a person rightly accused. Crime inflicts a wound on the community, and that wound may not begin to heal until criminal proceedings have come to an end.

The importance of the final judgment rule has led the Court to permit departures from the rule "only when observance of it would practically defeat the right to any review at all." *Cobbledick v. United States.* The Court has allowed a departure only for the "limited category of cases falling within the 'collateral order' exception delineated in *Cohen [v. Beneficial Industrial Loan Corporation].*" [a] *United States v. Hollywood Motor Car Co.,* supra, 458 U.S., at 265, 102 S.Ct., at 3081. To come within this "narrow exception," a trial court order must, at a minimum, meet three conditions. First, it "must conclusively determine the disputed question"; second, it must "resolve an important issue completely separate from the merits of the action"; third, it must "be effectively unreviewable on appeal from a final judgment." *Coopers & Lybrand v. Livesay,* 437 U.S. 463, 468, 98 S.Ct. 2454, 2457, 57 L.Ed.2d 351 (1978).

Because of the compelling interest in prompt trials, the Court has interpreted the requirements of the collateral-order exception to the final judgment rule with the utmost strictness in criminal cases. The Court has found only three types of pretrial orders in criminal prosecutions to meet the requirements. Each type involves " 'an asserted right the legal and practical value of which would be destroyed if it were not vindicated before trial.' " An order denying a motion to reduce bail may be reviewed before trial. The issue is finally resolved and is independent of the issues to be tried, and the order becomes moot if review awaits conviction and sentence. *Stack v. Boyle,* 342 U.S. 1, 72 S.Ct. 1, 96 L.Ed. 3 (1951). Orders denying motions to dismiss an indictment on double jeopardy or Speech or Debate grounds are likewise immediately appealable. Such orders finally resolve issues that are separate from guilt or innocence, and appellate review must occur before trial to be fully effective. The right guaranteed by the Double Jeopardy Clause is more than the right not to be convicted in a second prosecution for an offense: it is the right not to be "placed in jeopardy"—that is, not to be tried for the offense. *Abney v. United States,* 431 U.S. 651, 97 S.Ct. 2034, 52 L.Ed.2d 651 (1977). Similarly, the right guaranteed by the Speech or Debate Clause is more than the right not to be convicted for certain legislative activities: it is the right not to "be questioned" about them—that is, not to be tried for them. *Helstoski v. Meanor,* 442 U.S. 500, 99 S.Ct. 2445, 61 L.Ed.2d 30 (1979). Refusals to dismiss an indictment for violation of the Double Jeopardy Clause or of the Speech or Debate Clause, like denials of bail reduction, are truly final and collateral, and the asserted rights in all three cases would be irretrievably lost if review were postponed until trial is complete.

An order disqualifying counsel lacks the critical characteristics that make orders denying bail reduction or refusing to dismiss

a. In *Cohen,* 337 U.S. 541, 69 S.Ct. 1221, 93 L.Ed. 1528 (1949), the defendant in a stockholder's derivative suit sought to appeal a district court ruling refusing to direct the plaintiffs to post a security bond as would be required if state law governed. The Supreme Court held that the district court's ruling was immediately appealable under 28 U.S.C. § 1291, noting that the concept of a "final decision" was not limited to final judgments that fully terminated litigation but could also include certain orders collateral to the basic litigation. The Court stressed that the district court's ruling had fully disposed of the question of the applicability of the state security statute, that the district court's ruling was not one that "would be merged in the final judgment," and that the decision involved an important right that would be "lost, probably irreparable" if review had to await the final judgment terminating the litigation.

on double jeopardy or Speech or Debate grounds immediately appealable. Unlike a request for bail reduction, a constitutional objection to counsel's disqualification is in no danger of becoming moot upon conviction and sentence. Moreover, it cannot be said that the right petitioners assert, whether based on the Due Process Clause of the Fifth Amendment or on the Assistance of Counsel Clause of the Sixth Amendment, is a right not to be tried. Double jeopardy and Speech or Debate rights are *sui generis* in this regard. Rather, just as the speedy trial right is merely a right not to be convicted at an excessively delayed trial, *United States v. MacDonald,* the asserted right not to have joint counsel disqualified is, like virtually all rights of criminal defendants, merely a right not to be convicted in certain circumstances. Unlike a double jeopardy or Speech or Debate claim, petitioners' claim "would be largely satisfied by an acquittal resulting from the prosecution's failure to carry its burden of proof." Ibid. See also *United States v. Hollywood Motor Car Co.,* (vindictive prosecution right fully protected by post-conviction review). "Bearing the discomfiture and cost of a prosecution for crime even by an innocent person is one of the painful obligations of citizenship." *Cobbledick v. United States,* supra.

A disqualification order thus is not analogous to any of the three types of interlocutory orders that this Court has found immediately appealable in criminal cases. * * * Nor does petitioners' jurisdictional assertion gain support from a direct inquiry into whether a disqualification order satisfies the three *Coopers & Lybrand* conditions. This is so regardless of the nature of the right to joint representation claimed by petitioners.[4]

Petitioners correctly concede that post-conviction review of a disqualification order is fully effective to the extent that the asserted right to counsel of one's choice is like, for example, the Sixth Amendment right to represent oneself. Obtaining reversal for violation of such a right does not require a showing of prejudice to the defense, since the right reflects constitutional protection of the defendant's free choice independent of concern for the objective fairness of the proceeding. See *McKaskle v. Wiggins* [p. 127 supra]. Similarly, post-conviction review is concededly effective to the extent that petitioners' asserted right is like the Sixth Amendment rights violated when a trial court denies appointment of counsel altogether, see *Gideon v. Wainwright* [p. 77 supra], or denies counsel's request to be replaced because of a conflict of interest, see *Holloway v. Arkansas* [p. 166 supra]. No showing of prejudice need be made to obtain reversal in these circumstances because prejudice to the defense is presumed. In sum, as petitioners concede, if establishing a violation of their asserted right requires no showing of prejudice to their defense, a pretrial order violating the right does not meet the third condition for coverage by the collateral order exception: it is not "effectively unreviewable on appeal from a final judgment."

If, on the other hand, petitioners' asserted right is one that is not violated absent some specifically demonstrated prejudice to the defense, a disqualification order still falls outside the coverage of the collateral order exception. We need not consider, however, whether the third *Coopers & Lybrand* condition is satisfied—that is, whether post-conviction review is plainly ineffective. It is sufficient to note that the second *Coopers & Lybrand* condition—that the order be truly collateral—is not satisfied if petitioners' asserted right is one requiring prejudice to the defense for its violation.

On this assumption, a disqualification order, though final, is not independent of the issues to be tried. Its validity cannot

4. We need not and do not express any view on the nature or existence of that right.

be adequately reviewed until trial is complete. The effect of the disqualification on the defense, and hence whether the asserted right has been violated, cannot be fairly assessed until the substance of the prosecution's and defendant's cases is known. In this respect the right claimed by petitioners is analogous to the speedy trial right. In *United States v. MacDonald,* the Court concluded that because impairment of the defense is an important factor in judging whether a speedy trial violation has occurred, a denial of a motion to dismiss on speedy trial grounds is not separable from the issues at trial. The same conclusion applies to a disqualification order if prejudice to the defense is a necessary element of petitioners' claim. In these circumstances, the second *Coopers & Lybrand* condition for immediate appealability as a collateral order is not satisfied: the disqualification order does not resolve an "issue completely separate from the merits of the action." See supra, at 1055.

In short, whether or not petitioners' claim requires a showing of prejudice, a disqualification order does not qualify as an immediately appealable collateral order in a straightforward application of the necessary conditions laid down in prior cases. Further, petitioners' claim does not justify expanding the small class of criminal case orders covered by the collateral order exception to the final judgment rule—either by eliminating any of the *Coopers & Lybrand* conditions or by interpreting them less strictly than the Court's cases have done. The costs of such expansion are great, and the potential rewards are small.

Unlike an appeal of a bail decision, see *Stack v. Boyle,* an appeal of a disqualification order interrupts the trial. In criminal cases such interruption exacts a presumptively prohibitive price. Moreover, an appellate court's reversal of a disqualification order would not result in dismissal of the prosecution. The prosecution would continue, though only after long delay. The potential rewards of an immediate appeal are thus even smaller than they were in *United States v. MacDonald,* and in *United States v. Hollywood Motor Car Co.,* where the Court rejected claims of immediate appealability for orders denying motions to dismiss on speedy trial and vindictive prosecution grounds even though reversal of the orders would have led to dismissal of all or some charges. See also *Roche v. Evaporated Milk Ass'n,* 319 U.S. 21, 63 S.Ct. 938, 87 L.Ed. 1185 (1943) (no pretrial review of order denying motion to dismiss indictment for lack of jurisdiction); *Heike v. United States,* 217 U.S. 423, 30 S.Ct. 539, 54 L.Ed. 821 (1910) (no pretrial review of order rejecting claim of statutory immunity from prosecution). Here, a delayed trial is a certain result of interlocutory appellate review. Allowing immediate appeal of a disqualification order thus, would severely undermine the policies behind the final judgment rule. * * *

Notes and Questions

1. *Statutory exceptions.* The *Flanagan* case presented an issue relating to disqualification on which the lower federal courts were divided. See Note 8, p. 173 supra. Congress in 1958 had adopted a statute designed to allow appeals from interlocutory orders raising such issues (upon district court certification that the issue presented is a "controlling question" as to which there is "substantial ground for difference of opinion"), but that statute was specifically limited to "civil actions." 28 U.S.C. § 1292(b). See *In re April 1977 Grand Jury Subpoenas (General Motors),* 584 F.2d 1366 (6th Cir.1978) (divided court holding that a grand jury proceeding is not a "civil action" under this provision). Many states have similarly recognized a need to allow appeals from certain interlocutory orders, but have not limited their statutory exceptions to civil cases. They have either extended provisions like 28 U.S.C. § 1292(b) to criminal cases or simply provide for interlocutory appeal by leave of the appellate court, without re-

quiring certification by the trial judge.[a] The latter provisions commonly identify as relevant considerations to the granting of interlocutory review such factors as the need to "clarify an issue of general importance in the administration of justice" or to "protect the petitioner from substantial or irreparable injury." LaFave and Israel, § 26.2(a). Typical of the case in which discretionary review might be granted to protect against "irreparable injury" is that in which defendant challenges a discovery order that would require him to disclose information useful to the prosecution. The theory here is that, once the disclosure is made, it would be most difficult to remove the taint from the prosecution's case if it were later determined on appeal that the discovery order violated defendant's rights. See *Beckman v. Commonwealth,* 388 N.E.2d 678 (Mass.1979).

2. What are the advantages to defendant of interlocutory review (assuming it is available under state law)? Consider Amsterdam, *Trial Manual for the Defense of Criminal Cases* § 314 (4th ed. 1984) (noting the advantage gained by a defendant where liberal use of the extraordinary writs permits him to obtain interlocutory review): "[On] matters such as trial delay, discovery, change of venue, and the right to state-paid investigative facilities or other aids, counsel * * * will frequently come to an appellate court in a more favorable posture before trial than after. After trial, * * * the case may come before appellate judges on a record that reeks of the defendant's guilt. * * * Furthermore, particular claims may be made more persuasive, their equities more visible, at the pretrial stage. In reviewing the denial of a defendant's request for discovery after verdict, the appellate court will have the benefit of hindsight, and may say that, in light of the developments at trial, the defendant does not seem to have been hurt by not knowing whatever s/he was denied the right to know in preparing his or her defense. On an application for a prerogative writ before trial, the appellate judges know no more about the case than does defense counsel, and they are therefore put somewhat in counsel's place and can see counsel's preparatory predicament. * * * Finally, interlocutory review proceedings may be a headache for the prosecutor. S/he is probably going to have to go up on appeal after conviction in any event, so s/he has no reason to capitulate on close questions which the trial court decides in favor of the prosecution. The burden of opposing an interlocutory mandamus, on the other hand, may seem to the prosecutor incommensurate with the harm of giving the defendant what defense counsel wants."

3. *The special qualities of double jeopardy claims.* The *Flanagan* opinion characterizes the double jeopardy and speech and debate rights as "*sui generis* " in their provision of a right not to be tried, which justifies allowing immediate appeal of a lower court ruling allegedly denying such a right. Although state courts generally read their "final decision" provisions in much the same way as the Supreme Court reads § 1291, the *Abney* distinction has been viewed as questionable by some state courts. See e.g., *People ex rel. Mosley v. Carey,* 387 N.E.2d 325 (Ill.1979) (refusing to follow *Abney* under a provision allowing appeals only from "final judg-

a. IV *A.B.A. Standards* § 21–1.3, recommends adoption of a § 1292(b)-type certification procedure for criminal cases. The standards also recommend that "interlocutory review, in the discretion of the appellate court," be made available "to review trial court decisions denying claims of procedural rights that concern the competence of the trial court." Claims falling within this category would include "lack of jurisdiction, improper place of trial, and vitiating flaws in the selection process for the petit jury or the grand jury."

Apart from any § 1292(b)-type provision or discretionary interlocutory review provision that a particular state may have, appellate review at the state level generally is restricted to review of "final judgments" or "final orders" under statutory provisions that tend to be interpreted in much the same way as 28 U.S.C. § 1291. See LaFave and Israel, § 26.2.

ments"). On the other hand, other state courts have questioned whether a state's failure to grant a right to immediate appeal from a denial of a double jeopardy claim is constitutionally acceptable. *Abney,* they note, stated that the protection afforded by the double jeopardy clause "would be significantly undermined if appellate review of double jeopardy claims were postponed until after conviction." These courts therefore suggest that the state, as part of its constitutional obligation to effectively enforce the double jeopardy bar, must provide for an immediate appeal from the trial court's denial of a nonfrivolous double jeopardy objection. See LaFave and Israel, § 26.2(c) (citing cases both advancing and rejecting this view of *Abney*).

4. Assuming that the function of the double jeopardy right requires its special treatment under § 1291, does it follow that the due process prohibition against vindictive prosecution does not fall in the same category, or are there other qualities of that prohibition, as it relates to the consequences of allowing immediate appellate review, that led the Court to distinguish it from the double jeopardy and speech and debate claims? In UNITED STATES v. HOLLYWOOD MOTOR CAR, p. 1445 supra, the Court acknowledged that there was language in the leading vindictiveness case, *Blackledge v. Perry* [p. 927 supra], "suggesting that the defendant possessed a 'right not to be haled into court at all' " upon a vindictive charge. But that language, it noted, was used in a case where it was clear that an "adequate means of vindicating the right of the accused" would have been post-conviction relief granting defendant a new trial "free of vindictiveness" (i.e., a new trial de novo on the original misdemeanor charge). Of course, when the vindictiveness related to the total prosecution, rather than the charging of a higher offense, a successful claim would not result in a new trial but "dismissal of charges altogether." Even here, *Hollywood* reasoned, as in *MacDonald* (the speedy trial case), "proceeding with the trial does not cause or compound the deprivation already suffered," as the vindictiveness claim rests on a "right whose remedy requires the dismissal of charges" rather than a "right not be tried."

Justice Blackmun's dissent in *Hollywood,* joined by Justices Brennan and Marshall, argued that the issue presented was more complex than the Court's opinion suggested, and it should not have been resolved by a summary per curiam reversal. The dissent noted that unlike the speedy trial claim presented in *MacDonald,* "an allegation that the prosecutor impermissibly increased the charges in response to the defendant's exercise of a legal right may be evaluated before trial, for all the facts relevant to such a claim are fully available." Also, unlike *MacDonald,* where the critical delay offending the constitutional guarantee was the "delay before trial, not the trial itself," [b] here it could be argued that the right sought to be vindicated was one "not to be tried." Post-conviction review might not "suffice to remedy the chilling effect the vindictive prosecution is designed to prevent."

5. Are there some double jeopardy claims that should be treated differently than others for the purpose of allowing an immediate appeal? RICHARDSON v. UNITED STATES, 468 U.S. 317, 104 S.Ct. 3081, 82 L.Ed.2d 242 (1984), raised that issue in the case of a defendant who sought to raise before his second trial a double jeopardy contention based on the alleged insufficiency of the evidence at his first trial. Defendant contended that his motion for directed acquittal should have

b. *MacDonald* also cited one other factor in distinguishing *Abney.* The Court noted that, unlike a double jeopardy claim, which requires an initial showing of prior jeopardy, there was "nothing about a speedy trial claim which inherently limits the availability of the claim." If a right to immediate appeal were recognized, "any defendant" could move for dismissal on speedy trial grounds and then proceed to delay his trial by appealing the denial of that motion.

been granted at his first trial and therefore his second trial on the same charge (following a hung jury) constituted a double jeopardy violation under the *Burks* rationale [see p. 1419 supra]. The Supreme Court eventually held that the petitioner's double jeopardy claim was without merit even if the government's case at the first trial had been insufficient (see p. 1423 supra), but it first concluded that *Abney* sustained the immediate appeal of the trial court ruling denying that claim. REHNQUIST, J., speaking for the Court, reasoned:

"The Government contends, * * * that the double jeopardy claim raised by petitioner in this case does not meet the three-part test of the *Cohen* case. It argues that resolution of the double jeopardy claim inevitably involves evaluation of the sufficiency of the evidence against petitioner at the first trial, and therefore the claim is not completely collateral to the merits of the charge against petitioner. To dispose of petitioner's double jeopardy claim, the reviewing court would have to conclude that the evidence introduced at the first trial on these counts was insufficient as a matter of law to convict petitioner. This canvassing of the record would be indistinguishable from an assessment of the sufficiency of the evidence that would be reviewed after a judgment of conviction, and, of course, would go to the heart of the Government's case on the merits. The Government * * * therefore [is] of the view that petitioner's double jeopardy claim may be only reviewed following a final judgment of conviction after a second trial.

"All of this may be conceded, and yet we think that the collateral-order doctrine applied in *Abney* should not be read so narrowly as to bar from interlocutory review the type of double jeopardy claim asserted here. Petitioner seeks review of the sufficiency of the evidence at his first trial, not to reverse a judgment entered on that evidence, but as a necessary component of his separate claim of double jeopardy. * * * The Government understandably expresses concern that interlocutory appeals of this nature may disrupt the administration of criminal justice. But allowing appeals such as this is completely consistent with the Court's admonition in *Cohen* that the words 'final decision' in § 1291 should have a 'practical rather than a technical construction.' Petitioner's first trial had ended and his second trial had been rescheduled before he asserted his double jeopardy claim to bar retrial. There was thus no effort to interrupt or delay proceedings * * *. Moreover, we have indicated that the appealability of a double jeopardy claim depends upon its being at least 'colorable,' *MacDonald,* and that 'frivolous claims of former jeopardy' may be weeded out by summary procedures, *Abney.*" [c]

6. *Independent proceedings.* Certain proceedings though related to an ongoing or contemplated criminal prosecution may be viewed as sufficiently separate from that prosecution so that an order terminating the proceeding is itself a final decision and therefore immediately appealable. This ordinarily is the case, for example, when a third party seeks relief relating to an ongoing prosecution (e.g., where a newspaper challenges a closure order, or an unindicted co-conspirator challenges the denial of his request to strike his name from the indictment). The proceeding is less likely to be viewed as independent, however, when it involves a potential or actual defendant who has sought relief that would have a direct bearing on an ongoing or contemplated prosecution. Two situa-

c. Several circuits have held that, where the district court finds no "colorable foundation" for defendant's double jeopardy claim and makes written findings to support that determination, it may proceed to trial on schedule, notwithstanding the defendant's filing of a notice of appeal; the appeal will then be placed on an expedited calendar, but if defendant filed that appeal only shortly before the scheduled trial, he may be forced to go to trial before the appeal is heard. See LaFave and Israel, § 26.2(c).

tions that commonly pose that issue are the pre-charge challenge to an illegal search and the contempt proceeding.

7. *Pre-charge challenges to searches.* In DiBELLA v. UNITED STATES, 369 U.S. 121, 82 S.Ct. 654, 7 L.Ed.2d 614 (1962), a unanimous Court held nonappealable the denial of a motion to suppress that had been filed by the petitioner before he was indicted but after he was arrested. The Court reasoned that the ruling on the suppression motion was not "fairly severable from the context of a larger litigation process" since the disposition of that motion, whether made before or after the indictment, would "necessarily determine the conduct of the eventual trial." Justice Frankfurter's opinion for the Court concluded: "We hold, accordingly, that the mere circumstance of a pre-indictment motion does not transmute the ensuing evidentiary ruling into an independent proceeding begetting finality even for purposes of appealability. * * * When at the time of ruling there is outstanding a complaint, or a detention or release on bail following arrest, or an arraignment, information, or indictment—in each such case the order on a suppression motion must be treated as 'but a step in the criminal case preliminary to the trial thereof.' *Cogen v. United States* * * *. Only if the motion is solely for return of property and is in no way tied to a criminal prosecution *in esse* against the movant can the proceedings be regarded as independent."

The last sentence of *DiBella* quoted above indicates that a challenge to a search will be viewed as an independent proceeding where the petitioner moved "solely for the return of [the seized] property" and that motion was "in no way tied to a criminal prosecution in esse." This point was reiterated in *United States v. Ryan,* 402 U.S. 530, 91 S.Ct. 1580, 29 L.Ed.2d 85 (1971), where the Court noted that refusing to permit review under such circumstances "would mean that the Government might indefinitely retain the property without any opportunity for the movant to assert on appeal his right to possession." Lower courts have experienced difficulty, however, in applying both of the elements that *DiBella* viewed as needed to characterize a pre-charge challenge as an independent proceeding. Federal Rule 41(e), as amended in 1972, included a suppression remedy within the motion for a return of illegally seized property, so it is no longer possible to have a motion "solely" for the return of property. This change has led the courts to seek to determine whether the "primary purpose" of a particular Rule 41(e) motion truly is to obtain the return of property, a quest that has produced a variety of different approaches. Even if the motion passes this test, it will not be viewed as an independent proceeding if there is a criminal prosecution "in esse," and here again there has been considerable disagreement. While many courts hold the prosecution is not in being until charges are filed, others deem it sufficient that there is an ongoing investigatory proceeding, such as a grand jury investigation. See LaFave and Israel, § 26.2(d).

8. *Contempt proceedings.* The Supreme Court has long held that a lower court's rejection of a witness' objection to a subpoena or to some other order in an ongoing criminal proceeding does not in itself constitute a final order. To gain appellate review, the witness must refuse to comply and be held in contempt. The justification for this requirement was succinctly stated in *United States v. Ryan,* Note 7, supra: "[W]e have consistently held that the necessity for expedition in the administration of the criminal law justifies putting one who seeks to resist the production of desired information to a choice between compliance with a trial court's order to produce prior to any review of that order, and resistance to that order with the concomitant possibility of an adjudication of contempt if his claims are rejected on appeal." [d]

d. See also *In the Matter of Klein,* 776 F.2d 628 (7th Cir.1985) where it is noted that the requirement that the subject stand in contempt "ensures that people raise only those claims that are sufficiently serious that they are willing to make a sacrifice to obtain appellate review. Self-

The contempt prerequisite has been carried over to the grand jury setting, where the Court has noted that "it is no less important to safeguard against undue interruption of the inquiry instituted by a grand jury than to protect from delay the progress of the trial after an indictment has been found." *Cobbledick v. United States,* 309 U.S. 323, 60 S.Ct. 540, 84 L.Ed. 783 (1940). The witness who stands in contempt overrides this concern because, as the *Cobbledick* opinion also noted, "not to allow interruption [here] * * * would forever preclude review of the witness' claim, for his alternatives are to abandon the claim or languish in jail."

The grand jury witness who stands in contempt and seeks appellate review may be a prospective defendant, but that status does not take away his opportunity to immediately appeal the contempt sanction imposed against him. Should the same opportunity be afforded to an actual defendant who refuses to comply with an order of the trial court (e.g., a discovery order) and stands in contempt? Here a case from the early 1900's suggests that the contempt proceeding will be viewed as an independent proceeding if the contempt judgment is criminal, but not if it is civil. See *Doyle v. London Guarantee & Accident Company,* 204 U.S. 599, 27 S.Ct. 313, 51 L.Ed. 641 (1907). This distinction would deny the defendant an opportunity for immediate appeal in most cases, since the contempt sanction used to gain compliance with a court order in an ongoing proceeding ordinarily is civil rather than criminal. The *Doyle* case has stood without Supreme Court reaffirmation during a period in which there has been some restructuring of the contempt rule in other contexts, and commentators have questioned its continuing vatality. See e.g., Andre, *The Final Judgment Rule and Party Appeals of Civil Contempt Orders: Time for a Change,* 55 N.Y.U.L.Rev. 1041 (1980). Does it continue to make sense as applied to criminal cases on the ground that the defendant need not disobey the order and stand in contempt; he can instead comply and then argue on any later appeal from a conviction that the erroneous order requires a new trial. See LaFave and Israel, § 26.2(f) (but also noting that this remedy may not be satisfactory where the court's order affects "interests that go beyond obtaining a fair trial," as where the defendant claims that he is being required to disclose privileged matters).

9. *Review by writ.* Under some circumstances, appellate review of interlocutory orders may be obtained in the federal system through the extraordinary writ procedure authorized by 18 U.S.C. § 1651(a), the All Writs Act. That Act empowers appellate courts to issue writs (e.g., mandamus or prohibition) where "necessary or appropriate in aid of their respective jurisdictions and agreeable to the usages and principles of law." Federal courts have repeatedly stated that these writs may not be employed as a "mere substitute for appeal" and therefore should

interest cuts down dramatically on the number of appeals taken to obtain delay. When people may appeal any order enforcing a subpoena, it is easy to oppose every subpoena and make broad claims."

Klein involved an application of the "*Perlman* exception" to the requirement that the party stand in contempt. That exception allows an appeal where the subpoena is directed to a third party who holds the documents and the challenge comes from the owner of the documents. Thus in *Perlman v. United States,* 247 U.S. 7, 38 S.Ct. 417, 62 L.Ed. 950 (1918), Perlman was allowed to appeal the denial of his challenge to a court order directing the clerk of the court to produce certain documents in which Perlman claimed a continuing interest. Since the subpoena was not directed to Perlman, he could not himself refuse to comply and stand in contempt, and he could hardly expect the clerk of the court to take such action on his behalf. The issue presented in *Klein* was whether the *Perlman* exception applies as to a client's challenge to a subpoena directing his lawyer to produce documents in the lawyer's possession. *Klein* held that it did, but other courts have concluded that the special relationship between lawyer and client makes *Perlman* inapplicable. They argue that the lawyer should be expected to stand in civil contempt, especially since courts ordinarily will stay the contempt sanction pending the appeal when the contemnor is counsel and the objection to the subpoena is not frivolous. See LaFave and Israel, § 26.2(f).

be limited to "extraordinary" cases. The Supreme Court has emphasized the extraordinary nature of the writs in the guidelines it has set forth for their issuance. See, e.g., *Kerr v. United States District Court,* 426 U.S. 394, 96 S.Ct. 2119, 48 L.Ed.2d 725 (1976):

"[T]he writ [of mandamus] 'has traditionally been used in the federal courts only to confine an inferior court to a lawful exercise of its prescribed jurisdiction or to compel it to exercise its authority when it is its duty to do so.' *Will v. United States,* 389 U.S. [90], 88 S.Ct. [269, 19 L.Ed.2d 305] (1967). And, while we have not limited the use of mandamus by an unduly narrow and technical understanding of what constitutes a matter of 'jurisdiction,' the fact still remains that 'only exceptional circumstances amounting to a judicial "usurpation of power" will justify the invocation of this extraordinary remedy.' *Will v. United States.*[e] * * * As a means of implementing the rule that the writ will issue only in extraordinary circumstances, we have set forth various conditions for its issuance. Among these are that the party seeking issuance of the writ have no other adequate means to attain the relief he desires, and that he satisfy 'the burden of showing that [his] right to issuance of the writ is clear and indisputable.' *Will v. United States.* Moreover, it is important to remember that issuance of the writ is in large part a matter of discretion with the court to which the petition is addressed."

Lower federal courts, consistent with the Supreme Court guidelines, frequently speak of the writs as "extraordinary remedies," to be "sparingly used" as needed to avoid an "irreparable harm." Still, writs have issued to review a wide range of lower court orders, including orders directing defendants to appear in a lineup, prohibiting comments to the press, denying a request for a jury trial, refusing to permit out-state counsel to appear pro hoc vice, and limiting permissible discovery. See Wright, Miller, Cooper, and Gressman, *Federal Practice and Procedure,* § 3936 (1977) (collecting cases). Each opinion has stressed, however, the special circumstances of the particular case. Thus, in *United States v. Hughes,* 413 F.2d 1244 (5th Cir.1969), vacated as moot, 397 U.S. 93, 90 S.Ct. 817, 25 L.Ed.2d 77 (1970), granting mandamus to review a discovery order, the court emphasized that both sides urged review, that the ruling below presented a "basic" issue as to the extent of district court power under a newly adopted federal rule, that district court rulings within the circuit were in conflict on that issue, and that prompt resolution of the issue could avoid possible reversal of trials that were certain to be "lengthy and expensive."[f]

Many state courts view the writs as encompassing a much narrower range of objections than the lower federal courts. See

e. But consider Cooper, *Extraordinary Writ Practice in Criminal Cases: Analogies for the Military Courts,* 98 F.R.D. 593 (1983), suggesting that the scope of writ has been extended far beyond "jurisdictional" issues or the correction of flagrant abuses of authority. Professor Cooper notes: "[C]ourts of appeals have slowly evolved a practice known as supervisory or advisory mandamus. Appeals writs are used to resolve questions that seem important, and likely to avoid timely or effective determination in the ordinary processes of appeal. * * * The writs have become an extraordinary appeal process, and one that is not so very far out of the ordinary at that."

f. Consider, in this connection, the comments of Wright, Miller, Cooper, and Gressman, supra, speaking to the use of mandamus in the review of discovery orders: "The great advantage of mandamus in this area is not only that it is discretionary, but that it can be adapted much more easily to provide review of questions that are important either intrinsically or because of general impact, without simultaneously opening the door to review of similar questions in all future cases. The best use of mandamus is to seize upon single cases to answer questions that have repeatedly troubled district courts. It would be difficult indeed to accomplish the same goal by ruling that the discovery ruling was final only for the case chosen to answer the question."

LaFave and Israel, § 26.4(b) (noting jurisdictions adhering to the "traditional" view that mandamus is available only to compel action "ministerial" in nature and prohibition available only to "bar orders that the lower court lacked authority to issue under any set of circumstances"). Other states take a position similar to that adopted by the federal courts, and still others permit quite liberal use of the writs. Where the writs are liberally used, the end result may be a situation quite similar to that found in jurisdictions providing for appellate review of interlocutory orders at the discretion of the appellate court. Consider, for example, the experience in California, where the appellate courts have reviewed through defense writ applications an almost unlimited range of trial court orders, including the denial of defense motions to obtain broader pretrial discovery, to authorize a hypnotic examination of the defendant, to change venue to a community less saturated by publicity, to dismiss an indictment where the prosecutor failed to present exculpatory evidence to the grand jury, to appoint a requested attorney as defense counsel, to place defendant in a statutorily prescribed diversion program, and to exclude from consideration in a pending prosecution a prior conviction obtained without an effective waiver of counsel. LaFave and Israel, § 26.4(d). The "common thread" woven through these cases, the California Supreme Court has noted, is "the responsiveness of appellate tribunals when initiative is required to protect a defendant's right to a fair trial," recognizing that "the burden, expense and delay involved in a trial" may often render "an appeal from an eventual judgment an inadequate remedy." *Maine v. Superior Court,* 438 P.2d 372 (Cal.1968).

SECTION 3. PROSECUTION APPEALS

1. *The need for specific legislative authorization.* In *United States v. Sanges,* 144 U.S. 310, 12 S.Ct. 609, 36 L.Ed. 445 (1892), the government sought to gain appellate review of a district court order that had quashed an indictment on constitutional grounds. The government argued that the appeal was authorized under the predecessor of 28 U.S.C. § 1291; the district court's order was clearly a "final decision," and the statute on circuit court jurisdiction authorized an appeal from a final decision "in any case" involving the construction of the federal constitution. The Supreme Court rejected the government's argument, noting that the statute had to be read in light of the common law. The Court noted that it was "settled by an overwhelming weight of American authority, that the State has no right to sue out a writ of error upon a judgment in favor of the defendant in a criminal case, except under and in accordance with express statutes." This well established position reflected the policy that

> the defendant, having been once put upon his trial and discharged by the court, is not to be again vexed for the same cause, unless the legislature, acting within its constitutional authority, has made express provision for a review of the judgment at the instance of the government.

Since the provision relied upon by the government said "nothing as to the party by whom the writ of error may be brought," it would not be presumed that Congress intended "to make so serious and far-reaching an innovation in the criminal jurisprudence of the United States" as to allow an appeal by the government.

Although *Sanges* was decided before the turn of the century, the philosophy expressed there continues to prevail in both federal and state courts. See, e.g., *Arizona v. Manypenny,* 451 U.S. 232, 101 S.Ct. 1657, 68 L.Ed.2d 58 (1981), where the Court noted that the "presumption that the prosecutor lacks appellate authority absent express legislative authorization" reflects "an abiding concern to check the Federal Government's possible misuse of its enormous prosecutorial power. By insisting that Congress speak with a clear voice when extending to the Executive a right to expand criminal prosecutions, *Sanges* and its subsequent applications have placed the responsibility * * * in the democratically elected legislature where it belongs."

2. *Statutory provisions and double jeopardy limitations.* Except for Texas, all United States jurisdictions now have provisions allowing prosecution appeals from at least a limited class of orders in criminal cases. Some, like the Federal Criminal Appeals Act of 1970 (18 U.S.C. § 3731, Supp. App. B), reflect the policy of allowing prosecution appeals from all final orders except where "the double jeopardy clause * * * prohibits further prosecution." [a] However, unless the statutory language clearly evidences such intent, the courts will not turn first to double jeopardy concerns in determining whether the appeal should be allowed. Where the statutory language refers to appeals from specific types of orders (e.g., an "order arresting judgment"), the court, guided by the *Sanges* philosophy, will first ascertain whether the ruling in question squarely fits within the specified category.

In many jurisdictions, the statutory limitations upon government appeals are such that allowable appeals rarely pose any significant double jeopardy issues. Indeed those limitations are often far narrower than what would be available within the outer limits of the double jeopardy prohibition. Several states, for example, allow appeals only from pretrial dismissals of indictments (or counts of an indictment). These jurisdictions do not allow government appeals from dismissals issued during trial even though double jeopardy would not bar an appellate reversal and subsequent new trial in such a situation (see e.g., *United States v. Scott,* p. 1403 supra). Similarly, other states allow post-verdict appeals only from an order "arresting judgment." Such provisions encompass certain orders setting aside a guilty verdict but not others. They would include the post-verdict dismissal based on some ground unrelated to factual innocence (e.g., lack of jurisdiction), but not a judgment of acquittal entered notwithstanding the jury verdict. Supreme Court precedent suggests that appellate review of all such post-verdict orders is consistent with double jeopardy since a reversal requires no more than reinstating the jury's verdict of guilt. See Note 8, p. 1416 supra. Is there any reason apart from double jeopardy concerns for distinguishing between orders "arresting judgment" and other post-verdict orders, or distinguishing between pretrial dismissals and mid-trial dismissals?

3. *Appeals from interlocutory orders.* Consider LaFave and Israel, § 26.4(b): "As noted previously, a defendant has no right to appeal an adverse interlocutory order, though some states do allow discretionary appeals from interlocutory orders issued before trial. Of course, if the defendant is convicted, he can gain review of the adverse ruling on the appeal from his conviction. The prosecution, however, is in a quite different position. If it is not allowed an immediate appeal from an adverse interlocutory ruling, there will be no opportunity for later appellate review. An erroneous interlocutory ruling may result in the prosecution losing its case at trial, but the acquittal of the defendant will end the matter since the double jeopardy prohibition then bars further prosecution. For some jurisdictions, this circumstance justifies providing the prosecution with a substantially broader opportunity for appeals from pretrial interlocutory orders than is given to the defendant. For others, the defendant's interest in the 'swift resolution of his case' and the con-

a. Several states also permit a "moot appeal" where double jeopardy would bar a retrial following an appellate reversal. The prosecution may appeal from an acquittal but that appeal will present issues solely for determining the law for future cases, the appellate court lacking any power to upset the judgment of acquittal. See LaFave and Israel, § 26.3(a).

cern that the prosecution not be able to 'wear down the defendant' are more important considerations."

Jurisdictions generally allowing prosecution appeals from interlocutory orders do so in a variety of ways, although they all limit such appeals to pretrial rulings (with the exception of the post-verdict new trial order, discussed in Note 5 infra). In some states, provisions allowing discretionary appellate review of pretrial interlocutory orders (see Note 1, p. 1448 supra) are extended to the prosecution as well as the defense. In others, the prosecution is given a right to appeal a series of specified pretrial rulings that do not constitute final orders (e.g., the granting of a change of venue). Several grant the prosecution a right of appellate review for any pretrial interlocutory ruling where it is shown that the interlocutory ruling will have a "reasonable likelihood of causing either serious impairment to or termination of the prosecution." See LaFave and Israel, § 26.3(b) (further describing the various provisions). Once one concludes that the state's interest in being able to present its case in accordance with a correct interpretation of law justifies imposing upon the defendant some delay in the disposition of the charges against him, does it follow that one or the other of these approaches to providing prosecution appeals from interlocutory orders is clearly preferable? Should any provision for prosecution appeal from an adverse interlocutory order necessarily carry with it a requirement that defendant be free on his personal recognizance while the appeal is pending? See IV *A.B.A. Standards* § 21–1–4(c) ("defendant should be released unless there is cogent evidence that the defendant will not abide by the judgment of the appellate court").

4. *Pretrial suppression orders.* Even those jurisdictions, such as the federal, that generally restrict the government to appeals from final orders commonly recognize one exception—the order granting a pretrial motion to suppress evidence. A suppression order is generally held not to fall within provisions authorizing government appeals from a "final judgment" or a "dismissal of an indictment" since it does not formally terminate the prosecution. However, the federal system and over half of the states have adopted provisions specifically authorizing appeals from suppression orders. Such provisions have been supported on two grounds. First, the practical effect of the granting of a motion to suppress often is to terminate the case since the prosecution, lacking sufficient additional evidence, will be required to request dismissal of the indictment. Second, the rules relating to searches and seizures and other police practices that lead to suppression motions frequently are uncertain, and law enforcement officials should be entitled to base their policies on the rulings of the highest court; if appellate review of an adverse decision on a police practice is not available, the police can obtain a higher court ruling only by persisting in the challenged practice until they obtain a favorable decision from a different lower court, which would then be appealed to the higher court by the defendant.

In accord with the first argument noted above, some jurisdictions limit prosecution appeals of suppression orders to cases in which the excluded evidence constitutes "substantial proof of the charge pending against the defendant." See 18 U.S.C. § 3731. In accord with the second ground, many provisions are limited to suppression orders based on the illegal acquisition of evidence. Others, like 18 U.S.C. § 3731, speak generally of orders "suppressing or excluding evidence." These provisions have been held applicable to a broad range of pretrial orders. Thus, the state was allowed under such a provision to appeal a court order directing it to disclose psychiatric reports pertaining to its witnesses where the sanction for failing to disclose was the exclusion of the testimony of those witnesses. *People v. Phipps,* 413 N.E.2d 1277 (Ill.1980). Similarly, although the defense was not obligated to use an *in limine* motion to challenge the reliability of certain scientific tests, where it used such a motion and the trial court held that the tests would not be admissible, the prosecution was allowed to appeal that pretrial ruling. *State v. Tate,* 265 S.E.2d 223 (N.C.1980). Indeed, it has been suggested that the prosecution can utilize these provisions to gain appellate review of a wide range of orders that otherwise would be made at trial and subsumed in an acquittal. Where the prosecution can foresee difficulties in gaining admission of crucial evidence, it is to its advantage to obtain a pretrial ruling so that an adverse decision can be appealed as a suppression order.[b] The Supreme Court upheld an appeal developed through this tactic in *United States v. Helstoski,* 442 U.S. 477, 99 S.Ct. 2432, 61 L.Ed.2d 12 (1979), although the basic evidentiary issue presented there was prompted by a related defense objection.

5. *Post-verdict new trial orders.* A substantial number of jurisdictions, though generally not allowing prosecution appeals from interlocutory orders, do provide for prosecution appeals from orders setting aside a conviction and granting the defendant a new trial. Allowance of appeals from such orders is supported on two related grounds: (1) the new trial order has been preceded by a guilty verdict, and that verdict indicates that, apart from the alleged error on which the new trial was ordered, the defendant should stand convicted; and (2) the defendant, having already received a prompt trial, opens the door to delay in any second trial by challenging the result in that first trial (in much the same way, it is argued, as a defense appeal to an intermediate appellate court opens the door to the delay resulting when the government then appeals an adverse decision of that court to a higher appellate court). Responding to both contentions, those opposing the appealability of new trial orders point not only to the general considerations opposing appeals of interlocutory orders but also to what they characterize as an undeserved "bonus" received by the prosecution due to the trial court's indecision. Most often, they note, the new trial order is based on the reconsideration of a defense contention raised during trial and originally rejected by the trial court; if that objection had originally been sustained, the prosecutor would not have been able to appeal that ruling, and it should not be allowed to do so now.

6. *Review by writ.* Prosecutors may also seek to utilize the extraordinary writs to gain review of interlocutory or final orders that are not included within statutory provisions allowing prosecution appeals, but courts tend to be very wary of the use of the writs in such situations. The Supreme Court's often cited opinion in WILL v. UNITED STATES, 389 U.S. 90, 88 S.Ct. 269, 19 L.Ed.2d 305 (1967), reflects the prevailing view in most jurisdictions. The

b. Allowing the prosecution to "force the issue" in this matter has been justified as necessary to offset a defense tactic of delaying an objection until after jeopardy has attached and therefore cutting off the prosecution's statutory right to appeal an adverse suppression ruling. That tactic generally is not available to the defense where the suppression is based on the illegal acquisition of evidence. All but a few jurisdictions require that such an objection be presented before trial. While most also allow the trial court at least limited discretion to entertain a defense motion to suppress made during trial, one factor clearly to be considered in determining whether to exercise that discretion is the impact of the timing of the motion on the state's right to appeal. Recognizing that there are cases in which the surrounding circumstances nevertheless justify allowing an otherwise untimely suppression motion (e.g., where defendant lacked a reasonable opportunity to present the motion before trial), Illinois has sought to safeguard the interests of both defendant and prosecution by directing the trial judge who grants an untimely mid-trial motion to order a mistrial when the state desires to appeal. See Ill.Rev.Stat. ch. 28 § 114–12(c). The mandatory mistrial has been justified as an appropriate condition that the state may impose upon the defendant who presents a mid-trial motion (at least where the state itself is not responsible for the defendant's failure to present the motion before trial). With the defendant's motion viewed, in effect, as requesting the mistrial, reprosecution following a successful prosecution appeal is held not to be barred by double jeopardy. See Ch. 25, § 1.

district court in *Will* had ordered the government to provide a bill of particulars disclosing information concerning oral statements of the defendants that the government intended to use at trial. At the time, the Federal Rule on defense discovery did not encompass oral statements, and the government sought and obtained a writ of mandamus from the Seventh Circuit. Reversing that ruling, Chief Justice WARREN'S opinion for the Court initially cited the traditional formulas designed to limit the writ to cases involving "clear and undisputable" claims of jurisdictional excesses. It then turned to what it described as the "additional considerations" presented by application of the writ to a criminal case. The Chief Justice noted:

"All our jurisprudence is strongly colored by the notion that appellate review should be postponed, except in certain narrowly defined circumstances, until after final judgment has been rendered by the trial court. This general policy against piecemeal appeals takes on added weight in criminal cases, where the defendant is entitled to a speedy resolution of the charges against him. Moreover, 'in the federal jurisprudence, at least, appeals by the Government in criminal cases are something unusual, exceptional, not favored,' at least in part because they always threaten to offend the policies behind the double-jeopardy prohibition. Government appeal in the federal courts have thus been limited by Congress to narrow categories of orders terminating the prosecution, see 18 U.S.C. § 3731, and the Criminal Appeals Act is strictly construed against the Government's right of appeal.[c] Mandamus, of course, may never be employed as a substitute for appeal in derogation of these clear policies. Nor is the case against permitting the writ to be used as a substitute for interlocutory appeal 'made less compelling * * * by the fact that the Government has no later right to appeal.' This is not to say that mandamus may never be used to review procedural orders in criminal cases. It has been invoked successfully where the action of the trial court totally deprived the Government of its right to initiate a prosecution, *Ex parte United States,* and where the court overreached its judicial power to deny the Government the rightful fruits of a valid conviction, *Ex parte United States.*[d] But this Court has never approved the use of the writ to review an interlocutory procedural order in a criminal case which did not have the effect of a dismissal. We need not decide under what circumstances, if any, such a use of mandamus would be appropriate. It is enough to note that we approach the decision in this case with an awareness of the constitutional precepts that a man is entitled to a speedy trial and that he may not be placed twice in jeopardy for the same offense."

Relying on what has been described as "the flavor of the Chief Justice's opinion," some federal appellate courts have suggested that the use of the writs by the prosecution should be carefully tied to "the distinction between 'jurisdiction' and 'power' on the one hand, and 'error,' however substantial on the other." *In re United States,* 598 F.2d 233 (D.C.Cir.1979). Many state courts take a similar view. They hold that the writ will be available only when the lower court "acted in excess of its jurisdiction"—i.e., where it issued an order that it had no authority to issue under any circumstances or failed to issue an order that it had no discretion under any circumstances not to issue—and even then, only if the "need for review [by writ] outweighs the risk of harassment of

c. *Will* was decided prior to the expansion of the Criminal Appeals Act in 1970, which allows government appeals of final orders to the limits of the double jeopardy prohibition on reprosecution. See Note 2 supra.

d. In *Ex parte United States,* 287 U.S. 241, 53 S.Ct. 129, 77 L.Ed. 283 (1932), mandamus was issued to correct the refusal of a lower court to issue a bench warrant for the arrest of a defendant indicted by a grand jury. In *Ex parte United States,* 242 U.S. 27, 37 S.Ct. 72, 61 L.Ed. 129 (1916), the writ was issued to set aside an unauthorized order that would have suspended permanently the execution of a sentence.

the accused." *People v. Superior Court of Lassen County,* 596 P.2d 691 (Cal.1979). Included in this group are jurisdictions (e.g., California) which make liberal use of the writs on behalf of the defense, but see the prosecution's similar use of the writ as conflicting with the "substantive limitation" legislatively imposed on the authority of the state through statutes restricting the prosecution's right to appeal. See LaFave and Israel, § 26.4(e).

On the other side, relying on other language in *Will,*[e] and noting the greater flexibility suggested by double jeopardy rulings since *Will,*[f] a few federal appellate courts have allowed prosecution use of the writs to correct gross abuses of discretion or gain a prompt decision on a legal question of general significance. This view, also shared by a number of state courts, is illustrated by the Second Circuit's ruling in *United States v. Newman,* 549 F.2d 240 (2d Cir.1977). The district judge there, after a statistical analysis of the use of peremptory challenges in prior cases, upheld a defense motion that the prosecution's exercise of its peremptory challenge against four black veniremen be struck as "an act of invidious discrimination." The judge further ordered that the United States Attorney keep statistics on the exclusion of blacks from jury panels and make them available thereafter to the federal public defender. The Second Circuit concluded that the case presented "exceptional circumstances" calling for the issuance of a writ, in the exercise of its "supervisory powers," striking both district court orders. The "district court's findings of fact and conclusions of law * * * were in error," constituted an "abrupt departure from the statutes and rules," and would have "an immediate and continuing detrimental impact on the administration of criminal justice in the district."

SECTION 4. THE SCOPE OF APPELLATE REVIEW

1. *Moot cases.* An appellate court will not review the trial court's decision in a case, civil or criminal, where the litigation has become "moot." In criminal cases, the litigation traditionally was viewed as having become moot when the sentence imposed by the trial court was fully satisfied—i.e., when the defendant had paid his fine and served the full period of imprisonment or probation.[a] While some jurisdictions still adhere to this view, most have recognized at least some significant depar-

e. In denying relief, the Court in *Will* noted that the government has contended that the district court's ruling reflected a "pattern of manifest noncompliance" with the Federal Rules' provisions limiting discovery, but the record before the Court included no showing of the general practices of Judge Will or other judges of the district. The Court added "in passing" that earlier cases allowing supervisory use of the writ [see fn. e, p. 1454 supra] had all involved civil proceedings. In light of the skimpy record, there was no need at this time to decide whether the context of a criminal case "imposes a more stringent standard" for use of the writ "as a means of policing compliance with the procedural rules." In its final paragraph the Court stated further that it was not prepared to say "what might be the proper decision upon a more complete record, supplemented by the findings and conclusions of the Court of Appeals."

f. Consider, e.g., *United States v. Scott,* p. 1403 supra, and *United States v. Wilson,* p. 1416 supra. Lower courts have also noted that *Will*'s reference to defendant's speedy trial interest must be viewed in light of the procedural setting of that case. In certain settings (as with challenges to dismissals entered after defendant was tried and convicted or challenges to rulings relating to precharge investigatory proceedings), the impact of the delay may not be as great as in the setting that *Will* had before it.

a. Even under this view, a fully satisfied sentence may not always render the case moot. If the state law provides for remittance of a fine paid on an invalid conviction, the possibility of gaining that remedy may prevent the appeal from becoming moot. Similarly, where the defendant had no alternative but to immediately comply with the sentence (e.g., a stay of incarceration pending appeal is not available) and delays in the appellate process preclude review until after the sentence is satisfied, the state may be estopped from treating the case as moot. See e.g., *Sibron v. New York,* infra, where the Supreme Court held that it would not allow the state, through a combination of "inevitable delays" in its court system and a statutory prohibition against bail pending appeal, to effectively "cut off federal review" of a criminal conviction.

tures from the "fully satisfied sentence" standard. Several jurisdictions have gone so far as to hold that a criminal case never becomes moot since the defendant retains an interest in removing the "stigma of guilt" even after his sentence has been served. The federal courts and most states have refused to go that far, but they have held that a fully satisfied sentence does not render a case moot if the defendant is still subject to collateral legal consequences as a result of his conviction. Courts taking a narrow view of the collateral consequences doctrine require the defendant to show that a particular adverse collateral consequence is likely to be applied to him (e.g., that he is in a licensed profession and the conviction will result in the loss of his license). This reading of the doctrine was rejected for the federal courts in SIBRON v. NEW YORK, 392 U.S. 40, 88 S.Ct. 1889, 20 L.Ed.2d 917 (1968). Chief Justice WARREN'S opinion for the Court there noted:

"[I]n *Pollard v. United States* * * *, [we] abandoned all inquiry into the actual existence of specific collateral consequences and in effect presumed that they existed. * * * The Court thus acknowledged the obvious fact of life that most criminal convictions do in fact entail adverse collateral legal consequences. The mere 'possibility' that this will be the case is enough to preserve a criminal case from ending 'ignominiously in the limbo of mootness.'

"This case certainly meets that test for survival. Without pausing to canvass the possibilities in detail, we note that New York expressly provides by statute that Sibron's conviction may be used to impeach his character should he choose to put it in issue at any future criminal trial, and that it must be submitted to a trial judge for his consideration in sentencing should Sibron again be convicted of a crime. There are doubtless other collateral consequences. Moreover, we see no relevance in the fact that Sibron is a multiple offender. * * * A judge or jury faced with a question of character, like a sentencing judge, may be inclined to forgive or at least discount a limited number of minor transgressions, particularly if they occurred at some time in the relatively distant past. It is impossible for this Court to say at what point the number of convictions on a man's record renders his reputation irredeemable. And even if we believed that an individual had reached that point, it would be impossible for us to say that he had no interest in beginning the process of redemption with the particular case sought to be adjudicated. We cannot foretell what opportunities might present themselves in the future for the removal of other convictions from an individual's record.

"The question of the validity of a criminal conviction can arise in many contexts, and the sooner the issue is fully litigated the better for all concerned. It is always preferable to litigate a matter when it is directly and principally in dispute, rather than in a proceeding where it is collateral to the central controversy. Moreover, litigation is better conducted when the dispute is fresh and additional facts may, if necessary, be taken without a substantial risk that witnesses will die or memories fade. And it is far better to eliminate the source of a potential legal disability than to require the citizen to suffer the possibly unjustified consequences of the disability itself for an indefinite period of time before he can secure adjudication of the State's right to impose it on the basis of some past action."

2. Does *Sibron* 's view of the collateral legal consequences doctrine basically eliminate mootness in criminal cases? See Note, 82 Harv.L.Rev. 63, 297–98 (1968) (suggesting that, in light of the wide range of disabilities imposed in the various states, there will always be some state in which a legal disability might exist). The lower federal courts have occasionally dismissed appeals as moot, but those cases may be explained by the defendant's emphasis on the extra-legal consequences of the chal-

lenged confession. See e.g., *Cancino v. Craven,* 511 F.2d 1371 (9th Cir.1975) (holding moot an attorney's appeal from a criminal contempt conviction, where he claimed that the conviction, resulting in a $50 fine, would have an adverse impact upon his "future for political office"). The Supreme Court itself found a case to be moot in a post-*Sibron* ruling, although the challenge there did not go to the conviction itself. In *Lane v. Williams,* 455 U.S. 624, 102 S.Ct. 1322, 71 L.Ed.2d 508 (1982), the petitioner, reincarcerated for a parole violation, brought a habeas corpus action challenging his special parole but not the underlying conviction. By the time his habeas challenge reached the appellate courts, petitioner's parole term expired and he was released from custody. Holding his challenge moot, the Supreme Court majority reasoned that the parole violation simply did not carry with it sufficient collateral legal consequences. There was no automatic loss of civil rights or other significant statutory disabilities such as commonly attached to a conviction. At most, the Court noted, "certain non-statutory consequences may occur; employment prospects or the sentence imposed in a future proceeding could be affected." Moreover, these were discretionary decisions in which the employer or sentencing judge would look to the underlying conduct, not simply whether the parole term was declared void. In dissent, Justice Marshall contended that the Court was departing from the rationale of *Sibron,* which did not require the "actual existence of specific collateral consequences."

3. *The concurrent sentence doctrine.* Prior to *Sibron,* federal appellate courts traditionally followed the rule that, where defendant was sentenced to equal concurrent sentences on different counts of an indictment, the court would not consider challenges to the remaining counts once conviction on any one count was found to be valid. In *Benton v. Maryland,* 395 U.S. 784, 89 S.Ct. 2056, 23 L.Ed.2d 707 (1969), the Supreme Court held that, in light of its *Sibron* ruling, the concurrent sentence doctrine could no longer be justified on mootness grounds. The defendant had an obvious interest in challenging all of the counts on which he was convicted because separate collateral consequences could flow from each. The Court recognized the possibility, however, that the concurrent sentence doctrine might continue to be employed as a "rule of judicial convenience."

Since *Benton,* several state courts, and at least one federal circuit, have rejected the concurrent sentence doctrine. See *United States v. DeBright,* 730 F.2d 1255 (9th Cir. 1984). Most appellate courts, however, continue to apply the doctrine on a discretionary basis. See LaFave and Israel, § 26.5(b) (noting the various standards courts use in determining whether to utilize the doctrine). Where the doctrine is applied and one or more counts are not reviewed, some courts will vacate the judgments on those counts to ensure that the defendant does not suffer any collateral consequences from those convictions. If the government at some later date should desire to utilize those convictions, it can request reinstatement (which would then be accompanied by appellate review). See *United States v. Butera,* 677 F.2d 1376 (11th Cir.1982). But see *United States v. DeBright,* supra (criticizing this practice as (1) violating the principle of separation of powers, (2) failing to give sufficient weight to the government's and public's interest in "retaining the unreviewed convictions," and (3) presenting "substantial practical difficulties").

4. *Issues not properly raised.* Perhaps no justification for limiting the scope of appellate review is more frequently cited than the so-called "raise-or-waive" doctrine.[b] Simply put, this doctrine holds that, with

b. The description of the rule as one of "waiver," rather than "forfeiture" has been sharply criticized. See e.g., Wangerin, *"Plain Error" and "Fundamental Fairness": Toward a Definition of Exceptions to the Rules of Procedural Default,* 29 DePaul L.Rev. 753, 757–58 (1980) (waiver sugsome exceptions (see e.g., Notes 5 and 6 infra), appellate courts will not consider a defense allegation of error that was not properly raised and preserved at trial. What constitutes the proper presentation of a claim at the trial level will vary with the nature of the objection and the procedural idiosyncrasies of the particular jurisdiction. Timing requirements, for example, may require that the objection be made before indictment (e.g., challenge to a preliminary hearing bindover), before trial (e.g., suppression of illegally seized evidence), or contemporaneous with the error (e.g., improper cross-examination). While a single objection may be sufficient for some errors, others may have to be raised at different stages in the proceeding. Indeed, in some jurisdictions, the trial court must be given the opportunity to correct itself as to all alleged errors through a motion for new trial that again raises those errors. See Note 2, p. 1378 supra. Why is it that the failure to adhere to these and other rules relating to the timing and form of trial objections results in the loss of appellate review? Consider the answer of *State v. Applegate*, 591 P.2d 371 (Or.App.1979):

"There are many rationales for the raise-or-waive rule: that it is a necessary corollary of our adversary system in which issues are framed by the litigants and presented to a court; that fairness to all parties requires a litigant to advance his contentions at a time when there is an opportunity to respond to them factually, if his opponent chooses to; that the rule promotes efficient trial proceedings; that reversing for error not preserved permits the losing side to second-guess its tactical decisions after they do not produce the desired result; and that there is something unseemly about telling a lower court it was wrong when it never was presented with the opportunity to be right. The principal rationale, however, is judicial economy. There are two components to judicial economy: (1) if the losing side can obtain an appellate reversal because of error not objected to, the parties and public are put to the expense of retrial that could have been avoided had an objection been made; and (2) if an issue had been raised in the trial court, it could have been resolved there, and the parties and public would be spared the expense of appeal."

5. *Exceptions.* It follows from the reasoning of *Applegate* that certain procedural settings may justify appellate consideration of trial errors even not properly presented below. The clearest case is that in which the defendant did not have a reasonable opportunity to raise his claim within the time limit prescribed by the state's procedural requirement. Indeed, the refusal to consider a claim based on a procedural rule that arbitrarily imposes an impossible time limit may in itself constitute a violation of due process. See e.g., *Reece v. Georgia,* 350 U.S. 85, 76 S.Ct. 167, 100 L.Ed. 77 (1955) (state requirement that defendant challenge the grand jury composition prior to indictment held invalid as applied to indigent defendant not provided with counsel until the day after indictment). Similarly, appellate courts may also consider objections not raised at trial where an intervening ruling established the grounds for the objection and counsel's failure to raise the issue was understandable in light of the controlling precedent at the time of trial.

Is it consistent with *Applegate*'s explanation of the rule to consider an issue where the defense has no excuse for not raising it below but there is a "strong possibility of reoccurrence," *State v. Dreske,* 276 N.W. 2d 324 (Wis.App.1979), or the "issue is one of public policy or of broad * * * concern," *State v. Junkin,* 599 P.2d 244 (Ariz.App.1979)? Should an appellate court also be willing to consider a claim not properly raised below when that claim

gests an "intentional relinquishment of a known right," while forfeiture occurs "either inadvertently or intentionally"). Most courts speak of the rule as one of waiver, but some refer to it as a rule of "forfeiture" or "default."

will be open to postconviction review? Several state courts have held that, since habeas corpus would often be available to raise constitutional claims even though not presented at trial, an appellate court should ordinarily consider any constitutional issue raised on appeal, without regard to whether it was raised below, provided the record is sufficient to permit a determination of the issue. At least one has limited its review to the conditions that would excuse a procedural default for habeas review (see Ch. 25, § 2), but others will apparently consider on appeal any substantial first-time constitutional challenge, with little or no consideration as to why the issue was not presented below, provided there is no need for an evidentiary hearing. See LaFave and Israel, § 26.5(c).

Is there anything in the *Applegate* explanation of the raise-or-waive rule that would explain why appellate courts will consider first-time challenges that raise "jurisdictional" questions? This exception to the rule is universally recognized, and, in some instances, incorporated in statutes or court rules governing trial and appellate procedure. See e.g., Fed.R.Crim.P. 12(b) (indictment's failure "to show jurisdiction in the court or to charge an offense * * * shall be noticed by the court at any time during the pendency of the proceedings"). However, courts here tend to utilize a narrower and somewhat more traditional definition of a jurisdictional defect than in other areas where jurisdictional claims have been given separate treatment (see e.g., Note 5, p. 1252 supra, and Note 2, p. 1478 infra). Consider LaFave and Israel, § 26.5(c): "A challenge to subject matter jurisdiction clearly may be raised for the first time on appeal, and many courts will also consider on a similar basis an allegation that the offense occurred outside the territorial jurisdiction of the state. Courts generally are reluctant, however, to include within the jurisdictional category objections to other elements of the proceedings. Thus, defects in the indictment process generally cannot be presented for the first time on appeal, although the complete absence of an indictment might be treated differently. While several appellate courts allow a first-time challenge to the constitutionality of the statute on which the prosecution is based, most hold that such an objection is not jurisdictional and therefore cannot be raised unless it fits within some other exception to the raise-or-waive rule. Similarly, although some jurisdictions treat a double jeopardy claim as a 'quasi-jurisdictional' defect that can be raised for the first time on appeal, most deny it that status."

6. *Plain error.* All but a few jurisdictions recognize the authority of an appellate court to reverse on the basis of a plain error even though that error was not properly raised and preserved at the trial level. In most jurisdictions, the doctrine extends to all types of errors provided they are "plain errors or defects affecting substantial rights," Fed.R.Crim.P. 52(b), but some states by judicial interpretation or statute limit the doctrine's application to a specified class of errors (e.g., constitutional violations). What raises an error to the level of a "plain error"? The essence of the application of the doctrine has been admirably captured by Professor Wright in his description of the federal court rulings:

> Courts have endeavored to put a gloss on the rule by defining the kind of error for which they can reverse under Rule 52(b). Thus it is said that "plain error" means "error both obvious and substantial," or "serious and manifest errors," or "seriously prejudicial error," or "grave errors which seriously affect substantial rights of the accused." Perhaps these attempts to define "plain error" do not harm, but it is doubtful whether they are of much help. The sounder perception is that whether an appellate court should take notice of an error not raised below must be made on the facts of the particular case, and there are no "hard and fast classifications in either

the application of the principle or the use of a descriptive title." Indeed the cases give the distinct impression that "plain error" is a concept appellate courts find impossible to define, save that they know it when they see it. Wright, *Federal Practice and Procedure (Criminal)* § 856 (2d ed., 1982).

Consistent with Professor Wright's analysis, opinions frequently stress that "no talismanic method exists for determining plain error," and that each case must be examined on its own facts. There are, however, certain factors which clearly have a positive influence on the application of the doctrine. The more closely balanced the evidence, for example, the greater the likelihood that an error otherwise not viewed as sufficiently patent or fundamental will meet the standard. Courts also acknowledge that errors of constitutional magnitude will be noticed more freely under the plain error doctrine than violations of most statutes or common law standards. Various rulings also suggest that the doctrine is more likely to be applied where there might be a good reason for the lack of objection below, or where the error could not have been remedied by the trial judge even if called to his attention. On the other side, the doctrine is less likely to be applied where the error could have been readily corrected by an objection at trial, or where such an objection might have led the government to introduce additional evidence on the issue. See LaFave and Israel, § 26.6(d).

7. *Harmless error.* As was seen in Chapter 11, Section 2, an appellate court's finding that there was a constitutional violation at the trial level does not necessarily require reversal of a defendant's conviction. With some exceptions, constitutional violations are subject to the harmless error standard of *Chapman v. California* [p. 796 supra]. Under that standard, a conviction will be affirmed, notwithstanding a constitutional error in the proceedings leading to that conviction, if the appellate court is convinced "beyond a reasonable doubt that the error complained of did not contribute to the verdict obtained." The federal system and all 50 states also have harmless error rules applicable to non-constitutional violations. Indeed, most of the states have a statute or court rule similar to Fed.Rule 52(a), which provides that "any error, defect, irregularity, or variance which does not affect substantial rights should be disregarded."

Courts vary in the standards applied in determining whether a non-constitutional error affects the "substantial rights of the accused." For those "rights that might loosely be described as concerned with the structure of the proceeding, the question becomes one of whether the error was merely a technical violation or took from the defendant the substantive protection of the right, * * * [with] a violation of the substance of the right automatically requiring a new trial. * * * This mode of analysis is applied to errors relating to such matters as jury selection, pleadings, venue, and the acceptance of guilty pleas." LaFave and Israel, § 26.6(a). Where the error relates to the presentation of evidence or the standards applied in evaluating evidence (e.g., errors as to the admissibility of evidence, cross-examination, discovery, jury instructions, and argument by the prosecutor), the focus is upon the likely impact of the error upon the jury's evaluation of the case. It is here that the greatest diversity is found, with development of standards aptly characterized by one commentator as reflecting a history "of innovation and regression, of instability and uncertainty" that cannot be explained in terms of any "evolving progression of jurisprudential theories." Saltzburg, *The Harm of Harmless Error,* 59 Va.L.Rev. 988 (1973).

A few states apply to evidence-related non-constitutional errors basically the same standard applied to constitutional errors of this type—reversal is required unless the appellate court is convinced "beyond a reasonable doubt" that there is no "reasonable probability" that the error contributed to the verdict. *Commonwealth v. Story,* 383 A.2d 155 (Pa.1978). Many more apply the standard of *Kotteakos v. United States,* 328 U.S. 750, 66 S.Ct. 1239, 90 L.Ed. 1557 (1946):

> If, when all is said and done, the conviction is sure that the error did not influence the jury, or had but very slight effect, the verdict and the judgment should stand * * *. But if one cannot say, with fair assurance, after pondering all that happened without stripping the erroneous action from the whole, that the judgment was not substantially swayed by the error, it is impossible to conclude that substantial rights were not affected.

To what extent is this standard "less stringent" (i.e., more readily allowing the error to be deemed harmless) than the standard of *Chapman?* What of state court standards that require a "fair assurance" that the judgment of the jury was not "substantially swayed" by the error, the lack of any "reasonable possibility" that the error "might have contributed to the conviction," or a "high probability" that the error did not contribute to the judgment? LaFave and Israel, § 26.6(b).

Do the standards set forth above do any more than "set the stage for the harmless error inquiry"? *Commonwealth v. Story,* supra. Does it follow from the selection of one standard or another that the prosecutor or the defendant bears the burden of convincing the appellate court that the error did or did not have an impact upon the jury's verdict? Compare *Chapman* at p. 797 supra. Is the allocation of that burden a critical issue in any event? See Traynor, *The Riddle of Harmless Error* 25–26 (1970) (suggesting that the allocation of that burden is largely meaningless since the appellate court is limited to the record before it).

Do the different standards as to the likely impact of the error indicate what weight should be given to the presence of overwhelming evidence of guilt? Should the appellate court ask whether the error was likely to have influenced a reasonable juror based solely on the nature of the error, without regard to the strength of the evidence properly before that juror? See LaFave and Israel, § 26.6(b) (appellate courts "generally have not been receptive" to this approach). Should the standard as to the likely impact be measured by reference to whether the jury would have reached a different result in a trial without the error? Should it be measured by asking "whether the properly admitted evidence of guilt is so overwhelming and the prejudicial effect of the error is so insignificant by comparison" that the appellate court can say, with the requisite degree of certainty, that the error could not have "contributed to the verdict"? *Commonwealth v. Story,* supra. In what types of cases will these distinctions in approach be significant? Consider LaFave and Israel, § 26.6(b): "[C]ertain types of jury charging errors ordinarily should not be viewed as harmless if the true test is influence on the judgment actually rendered rather than what the jury would have decided without the error. When, for example, a judge erroneously tells the jury that proof of a certain element is not needed to establish an offense, it must be assumed that the jury relied upon that direction. This should preclude a finding of harmlessness even though, if it had been properly charged, the jury most likely would have found that element to be present."

Chapter 27

HABEAS CORPUS AND RELATED COLLATERAL REMEDIES [a]

INTRODUCTION

1. *The nature of collateral remedies.* What avenues, if any, are available to a convicted defendant for challenging his conviction after all opportunities for appellate review are exhausted? The answer varies from one jurisdiction to another, but all jurisdictions recognize at least one procedure that will permit a post-appeal challenge to a conviction on at least a few grounds. Such post-appeal procedures are commonly described as "collateral remedies," although that description may often be attributed more to their heritage than their current form. The current collateral remedies are derived in large part from the common law writs of habeas corpus and coram nobis. The common law habeas proceeding presented a truly collateral attack upon the conviction. It was a separate civil action in which a defendant-petitioner challenged his continued detention and, through that custody challenge, attacked the conviction on which his detention was based. Because the relief sought was the release from custody, the habeas petition was filed in that court having jurisdiction over the official holding the petitioner in custody (e.g., the prison warden), rather than the court of conviction. The writ of coram nobis directly attacked the conviction and was sought in the court of conviction, but it also was commonly viewed as an independent civil action. Today, jurisdictions commonly rely on statutory collateral remedies which, even where they refer to habeas corpus or coram nobis, almost invariably have modified the common law remedy. While some of these statutory proceedings are viewed as independent civil actions, many are considered part of the original criminal case, paralleling a post-appeal motion for a new trial. Thus, the designation of a post-appeal remedy as "collateral" tends today to mean simply that the remedy "provide[s] an avenue for upsetting judgments [of conviction] that have become otherwise final." *Mackey v. United States,* 401 U.S. 667, 91 S.Ct. 1160, 28 L.Ed.2d 404 (1971).

2. *The range of state collateral remedies.* Although state collateral remedies are quite diverse, they can be divided roughly into four groups: (1) the writ of habeas corpus; (2) the writ of coram nobis; (3) statutory provisions modeled after 28 U.S.C. § 2255; and (4) the Uniform Post-Conviction Procedure Act.

The common law writ of habeas corpus is a broad remedy insofar as it allows challenges to a wide range of detentions

a. See Popper, *Post-Conviction Remedies* (1978); Yackle, *Postconviction Remedies* (1981) (hereinafter cited as Yackle); Wilkes, *Federal and State Postconviction Remedies and Relief* (1983) (hereinafter cited as Wilkes).

incident to civil and criminal proceedings,[b] but it is a fairly narrow remedy insofar as it allows a collateral attack upon a conviction. Since the writ presents a challenge to detention, it initially requires that the convicted defendant be in custody. In some jurisdictions, this makes the writ only a "prisoner's remedy" (i.e., custody exists only if the defendant is incarcerated), although other jurisdictions view convicted defendants who are on probation or parole as also sufficiently "in custody" to use the writ. In addition to its custody requirement, the habeas remedy is limited by the range of defects in a conviction that are cognizable via a challenge to detention. The habeas court traditionally was viewed as having the authority to release a person detained under a criminal conviction only where the trial court lacked jurisdiction to impose that conviction. While some jurisdictions have rejected this limitation and others have adopted a broad view of jurisdictional defects (cf. Note 2, p. 1478 infra), still others continue to recognize only claims that clearly go the jurisdiction of the trial court. See Wilkes, 216–17.

The writ of coram nobis was initially developed at a time when a trial court could not correct its own errors after judgment was entered and the appellate court could consider only alleged mistakes of law. Applicable to civil as well as criminal cases, the writ of coram nobis authorized the trial court to correct after judgment errors of fact that would have prevented entry of that judgment, provided those errors could not readily have come to the trial court's attention at the time of trial. As applied to criminal cases, the writ was used to raise claims that were not apparent from the face of the record and understandably not raised at trial (e.g., that the uncounseled defendant was insane at the time of trial or that defendant had entered a guilty plea out of fear of mob violence). The range of cognizable claims is somewhat broader today in many jurisdictions, but the writ is still generally limited to claims that rest on facts dehors the record. Unlike the habeas remedy, it is available to convicted defendants without regard to whether they remain "in custody." See Yackle, 40–61.

The statutory remedy of 28 U.S.C. § 2255 (Supp., App. B) was adopted by Congress in 1948 as the major collateral remedy for persons challenging federal convictions. It was designed to provide a remedy "exactly commensurate with that which had been previously available by habeas corpus," *United States v. Hayman,* 342 U.S. 205, 72 S.Ct. 263, 96 L.Ed. 232 (1952), while using a substantially simplified procedure. The primary procedural reform was to provide for the challenge to be brought in the court of conviction rather than the court of current detention. This was an especially significant change in the federal system since federal prisoners were often incarcerated in prisons located far from the district of their conviction. Following the congressional lead, several states adopted collateral remedies modeled after § 2255. Although the § 2255 remedy had the same scope as the federal habeas corpus writ, the federal courts had expanded upon the common law writ. The federal writ encompassed a greater range of claims and took a more liberal view of what constituted custody. The state provisions modeled after § 2255

b. In the civil context, the writ is used to challenge custody in such varied settings as civil commitments, child custody proceedings, and military conscription. In the criminal context, the writ was originally used to challenge pretrial detention (see fn. b, p. 1471 infra) and it is still so used in many jurisdictions. Thus, in some jurisdictions, it remains the primary vehicle for raising the following objections: (1) an arrestee's claim that he is being detained without prompt presentment before a magistrate as required by state law; (2) a defendant's claim that he has been denied the right to be released on nonexcessive bail; (3) a defendant's claim that he is being denied the right to a speedy trial; and (4) an arrestee's claim that he is being detained for extradition pursuant to an invalid extradition request. In many jurisdictions, reliance upon the writ is no longer needed to raise such issues as they may be presented by a motion requesting appropriate relief filed with the trial court of general jurisdiction.

adopted these federal standards and therefore provided a remedy that went substantially beyond what they previously had allowed under the common law remedy. In large part, they continue to follow § 2255 precedent (which, in turn, follows the precedent under §§ 2241–2254, discussed at Note 3 infra).

The Uniform Post-Conviction Procedure Act, originally proposed in 1966 and revised in 1980, has served as a model for roughly a dozen states. See 11 U.L.A. 216 (1985 Supp.). It is a substantially broader remedy than even the § 2255-type provision. Unlike § 2255 and the writ of habeas corpus, it is not limited by a custody requirement. It also encompasses the broadest range of claims, including: (1) all constitutional violations; (2) jurisdictional defects; (3) the presentation of material evidence, not previously heard, that justifies vacating the judgment "in the interest of justice"; (4) a "significant change in substantive or procedural law" that is to be applied retroactively; and (5) any other objection recognized as a proper subject of collateral attack under any common law or statutory remedy recognized in the jurisdiction.

3. *The federal habeas remedy for state prisoners.* In 1867, Congress expanded the scope of the federal habeas remedy by making it available to "any person restrained of his or her liberty in violation of the constitution." Prior to that point, the statutory authorization for federal court issuance of the writ referred only to persons held in custody by the federal government, but the new language clearly encompassed as well persons held in custody by the state. The current version of the 1867 Act, containing the same coverage, is found in 28 U.S.C. §§ 2241–2254, with the § 2254 specifically directed at habeas petitions presented by persons held in state custody (see Supp., App. B). These sections present what is undoubtedly the most significant of all collateral remedies. It is the only remedy that extends nationwide to persons held in custody by all of the states. The number of petitions filed under the federal writ (7,000–8,000 per year) far outstrips the number filed under any individual state's collateral remedy or under § 2255. Moreover, the decisions interpreting the federal habeas remedy have an important bearing on those other remedies. Those rulings are carried over in large part to § 2255 because that provision was intended to give federal prisons a remedy parallel in scope to the federal habeas writ.[c] The federal habeas rulings are often followed as well by the states that employ the habeas writ or a § 2255-type provision as their primary collateral remedy. See LaFave and Israel, § 27.11.

The three sections that follow focus on the identification of those claims upon which relief will be granted in a federal habeas proceeding and the role of the habeas court in ruling on such claims. A cognizable claim is not the only prerequisite, however, for obtaining habeas relief. Two of the more significant additional pre-

c. The § 2255 remedy, although its scope is "exactly commensurate" with that of the habeas writ (see *Hayman*, p. 1468 supra), does present issues as to scope that are not likely to arise in challenges to state convictions. In particular, while both § 2255 and § 2241 refer to persons being held in custody in violation of the laws of the United States, state prisoners rarely can point to a federal statute as a basis for upsetting their conviction. Federal prisoners, on the other hand, prosecuted under federal law and tried under a procedure prescribed by federal law, will much more readily raise such claims. Thus, the scope of the writ as to non-constitutional claims has been resolved largely in § 2255 proceedings. In large part, the Supreme Court has held that non-constitutional claims are cognizable only when "the claimed error constituted a fundamental defect which inherently results in a complete miscarriage of justice." *United States v. Addonizio,* 442 U.S. 178, 99 S.Ct. 2235, 60 L.Ed.2d 805 (1979).

Decisions dealing with the scope of the federal habeas remedy as to constitutional claims tend to be carried over directly to § 2255. However, certain procedural aspects of the federal habeas remedy are molded in light of federalism concerns not applicable to § 2255 proceedings, and the habeas decisions based on those concerns may not be carried over to the § 2255 setting. See LaFave and Israel, § 27.10.

requisites come from the statutory requirements of "custody" and "exhaustion."

Federal habeas relief is available only to the petitioner who is "in custody." The writ is an "extraordinary remedy [directed at] the extraordinary restraints of custodial situations." See LaFave and Israel, § 27.8(a). The Supreme Court has held that the concept of custody for this purpose is not limited to incarceration. It encompasses as well the restraints commonly associated with parole, probation, or even release on personal recognizance pending habeas review of a conviction. *Hensleyt v. Municipal Court,* 411 U.S. 345, 93 S.Ct. 1571, 36 L.Ed.2d 294 (1973). Indeed, when a person is incarcerated under the first of two consecutive sentences, he is sufficiently in custody to attack the second sentence that he has not yet begun to serve. See *Peyton v. Rowe,* 391 U.S. 54, 88 S.Ct. 1549, 20 L.Ed.2d 426 (1968). This can be done even though the second sentence is to be served in another state, at least where that state has filed a detainer. See LaFave and Israel, § 27.8(e). Thus, custody does not pose a substantial barrier to the use of the habeas remedy except where the petitioner has fully served his sentence and faces only collateral consequences. Compare Note 1, p. 1460 supra (discussing mootness).

The exhaustion requirement, currently set forth in § 2254(b), requires that the petitioner give the state courts an adequate opportunity to first rule on his claim, provided a state procedure for gaining review is still open to him. It is viewed as an attribute of the "equitable nature" of habeas relief. The Supreme Court has held that the requirement mandates that the state have been given only one opportunity; the defendant need not return to the state courts simply because they will allow a person to repeatedly assert the same claim. See LaFave and Israel, § 27.7. But if that one presentation did not squarely put the issue to the state courts, and a state remedy is still available, the petitioner ordinarily will be required to use that remedy again. In sum, exhaustion is not a requirement that permanently precludes habeas review, but it may delay review. See Yackle, § 55. Compare the doctrine of procedural forfeiture discussed in § 2 infra.

SECTION 1. ISSUES COGNIZABLE

FAY v. NOIA

372 U.S. 391, 83 S.Ct. 822, 9 L.Ed.2d 837 (1963).

MR. JUSTICE BRENNAN delivered the opinion of the Court.

[The facts of *Fay* are set forth at p. 1497 infra. At issue was the appropriate disposition of the habeas petition of a state prisoner (Noia) raising a coerced confession claim that he had failed to fully present in his state proceedings (by failing to file a state appeal). The Supreme Court previously had held in *Brown v. Allen,* 344 U.S. 443, 73 S.Ct. 397, 97 L.Ed. 469 (1953), that a coerced confession claim was cognizable in a habeas proceeding—i.e., a state prisoner was entitled to habeas corpus relief under § 2241 et seq. if his conviction had been based upon a coerced confession. The additional question presented in *Fay* was whether habeas relief was unavailable there due to Noia's procedural forfeiture under state law by failing to raise his claim on appeal. The majority's discussion of that issue is reprinted in Section 2 of this Chapter at p. 1497 infra. Before reaching that issue, however, the majority opinion discussed at length the general range of claims that should be cognizable in a habeas proceeding.[a] Excerpts from that portion of the majority opinion are set forth below.]

a. Although *Brown* arguably had gone beyond past precedents in holding that a coerced confession claim was cognizable under habeas corpus, Justice Reed's opinion in *Brown* had concentrated primarily on other issues presented in that case. The majority opinion in *Fay* may have been responding in part to criticism of this aspect of the *Brown* opinion.

We do well to bear in mind the extraordinary prestige of the Great Writ, *habeas corpus ad subjiciendum,* in Anglo-American jurisprudence * * *. Received into our own law in the colonial period, given explicit recognition in the Federal Constitution, Art. I, § 9, cl. 2, incorporated in the first grant of federal court jurisdiction, Act of September 24, 1789, habeas corpus was early confirmed by Chief Justice John Marshall to be a "great constitutional privilege." * * * Although in form the Great Writ is simply a mode of procedure, its history is inextricably intertwined with the growth of fundamental rights of personal liberty. For its function has been to provide a prompt and efficacious remedy for whatever society deems to be intolerable restraints. Its root principle is that in a civilized society, government must always be accountable to the judiciary for a man's imprisonment: if the imprisonment cannot be shown to conform with fundamental requirements of law, the individual is entitled to his immediate release. Thus, there is nothing novel in the fact that today habeas corpus in the federal courts provides a mode for the redress of denials of due process of law. Vindication of due process is precisely its historic office. * * *

History refutes the notion that until recently the writ was available only in a very narrow class of lawless imprisonments. [Relying primarily on *Bushell's Case,* 124 Eng.Rep. 1006 (1670), Justice Brennan concluded that English common law recognized habeas corpus as a remedy that went beyond an "inquiry into the jurisdiction, in a narrow sense, of the committing court." In *Bushell's Case,* habeas relief was granted to jurors who were held in contempt after they returned a verdict of not guilty in the trial of William Penn. The decision of the court there was characterized as resting "on the plain denial of due process, violative of Magna Charta," rather than a theory that the committing court lacked jurisdiction to commit persons for contempt.[b]] * * *

Thus, at the time that the Suspension Clause was written into our Federal Constitution and the first Judiciary Act was passed conferring habeas corpus jurisdiction upon the federal judiciary, there was respectable common-law authority for the proposition that habeas was available to remedy any kind of governmental restraint contrary to fundamental law. In this connection it is significant that neither the Constitution nor the Judiciary Act anywhere defines the writ, although the Act does intimate, 1 Stat. 82, that its issuance is to be "agreeable to the principles and usages of law"—the common law, presumably. We need not pause to consider

b. This view of *Bushell's Case* was subsequently criticized by several commentators. See e.g., Oaks, *Legal History in The High Court—Habeas Corpus,* 64 Mich.L.Rev. 401 (1966). As they note, the characterization of habeas corpus as the Great Writ—the "procedural underpinning" of the Magna Charta—came about through its use during the seventeenth century to challenge arbitrary detentions by the Crown that lacked judicial authorization. It was to further implement this use of the writ that Parliament, not long after the decision in *Bushell's Case,* enacted the famed Habeas Corpus Act of 1679. While instituting procedural reforms that would reenforce judicial authority to release those illegally arrested and detained by Royal officials, the 1679 Act also clearly reflected a commonly accepted restriction on the writ's use in specifically excluding from the Act's coverage persons confined as a result of criminal conviction. The inclusion of this restriction is said to evidence the prevailing view of *Bushell's Case* as a significant but nonetheless narrow ruling. *Bushell's Case* involved a commitment for contempt, which was not an ordinary conviction. Moreover, it did not present a broadly based challenge that claimed to question the basic procedures underlying a conviction. It was consistent with the traditional right of the convicted person, both before and after *Bushell's Case* and the 1679 Act, to challenge the jurisdiction of the trial court. In sum, it is argued, *Bushell's Case* did not alter the basic function of the writ. In both England and the colonies, it has "won its place as the most important safeguard of personal liberty," not as applied to convicted persons, but "when employed against the Crown and its officers * * * to elicit the cause for an individual's imprisonment and to ensure that he was released, admitted to bail, or promptly tried." Oaks, *Habeas Corpus in the States—1776–1865,* 32 U.Chi.L.Rev. 243 (1965).

whether it was the Framers' understanding that congressional refusal to permit the federal courts to accord the writ its full common-law scope as we have described it might constitute an unconstitutional suspension of the privilege of the writ. There have been some intimations of support for such a proposition in decisions of this Court. * * * But at all events it would appear that the Constitution invites, if it does not compel, * * * a generous construction of the power of the federal courts to dispense the writ conformably with common-law practice.

The early decision of this Court in *Ex parte Watkins,* 28 U.S. (3 Pet.) 193, 7 L.Ed. 650 [1830], which held that the judgment of a federal court of competent jurisdiction could not be impeached on habeas, seemed to have viewed the power more narrowly. But *Watkins* may have been compelled by factors, affecting peculiarly * * * this Court [in issuing a writ in its original jurisdiction], which are not generally applicable to federal habeas corpus powers. * * * But even as to this Court's power, the life of the principles advanced in *Watkins* was relatively brief. In *Ex parte Lange,* 85 U.S. (18 Wall.) 163, 21 L.Ed. 872 [1873], again a case of direct application to this Court for the writ, the Court ordered the release of one duly convicted in a Federal Circuit Court. The trial judge, after initially imposing upon the defendant a sentence in excess of the legal maximum, had attempted to correct the error by resentencing him. The Court held this double-sentencing procedure unconstitutional, on the ground of double jeopardy, and while conceding that the Circuit Court had a general competence in criminal cases, reasoned that it had no jurisdiction to render a patently lawless judgment. This marked a return to the common-law principle that restraints contrary to fundamental law, by whatever authority imposed, could be redressed by writ of habeas corpus. The principle was clearly * * * [reaffirmed] a few years after the *Lange* decision * * * in *Ex parte Siebold,* 100 U.S. 371, 376–377, 25 L.Ed. 717 (1879) [upholding a challenge by a prisoner convicted under an unconstitutional statute]. The course of decisions of this Court from *Lange* and *Siebold* to the present makes plain that restraints contrary to our fundamental law, the Constitution, may be challenged on federal habeas corpus even though imposed pursuant to the conviction of a federal court of competent jurisdiction. * * *

It now remains to consider this principle in the application to the present case. It was settled in *Brown v. Allen,* supra, that the use of a coerced confession in a state criminal trial could be challenged in a federal habeas corpus proceeding. Yet actually the principle had been foreshadowed much earlier—indeed, in the very first case in which this Court reversed a state conviction [on direct review] on the ground that coerced confessions had been used in evidence. "The complaint is . . . of a wrong so fundamental that it made the whole proceeding a mere pretense of a trial and rendered the conviction and sentence wholly void. . . . [A]nd the proceeding thus vitiated could be challenged in any appropriate manner." *Brown v. Mississippi,* 297 U.S. 278, 56 S.Ct. 461, 465, 80 L.Ed. 682 [1936]. Under the conditions of modern society, Noia's imprisonment, under a conviction procured by a confession held by the Court of Appeals to have been coerced, and which the State here concedes was obtained in violation of the Fourteenth Amendment, is no less intolerable than was Bushell's under the conditions of a very different society; and habeas corpus is no less the appropriate remedy.

But, it is argued, a different result is compelled by the exigencies of federalism, which played no role in *Bushell's Case.* We can appraise this argument only in light of the historical accommodation that has been worked out between the state and federal courts respecting the administration of federal habeas corpus. Our starting point is the Judiciary Act of February 5, 1867, which first extended federal habeas corpus to state prisoners generally, and which survives, except for some changes in wording in the present statutory codification. Although the Act of 1867, like its English and American predecessors, nowhere defines habeas corpus, its expansive language and imperative tone, viewed against the background of post-Civil War efforts in Congress to deal severely with the States of the former Confederacy, would seem to make inescapable the conclusion that Congress was enlarging the habeas remedy as previously understood, not only in extending its coverage to state prisoners, but also in making its procedures more efficacious. In 1867, Congress was anticipating resistance to its Reconstruction measures and planning the implementation of the post-war constitutional Amendments. Debated and enacted at the very peak of the Radical Republicans' power * * *, the Act of 1867 seems plainly to have been designed to furnish a method additional to and independent of direct Supreme Court review of state court decisions for the vindication of the new constitutional guarantees. * * * [A] remedy almost in the nature of *removal* from the state to the federal courts of state prisoners' constitutional contentions seems to have been envisaged. * * *

In thus extending the habeas corpus power of the federal courts evidently to what was conceived to be its constitutional limit, the Act of February 5, 1867, clearly enough portended difficult problems concerning the relationship of the state and federal courts in the area of criminal administration. Such problems were not slow to mature. * * * [I]n *Ex parte Royall,* 117 U.S. 241, 6 S.Ct. 734, 29 L.Ed. 868 [1886], a case in which habeas had been sought in advance of trial, * * * [this] Court held that even in such a case the federal courts had the *power* to discharge a state prisoner * * * but that ordinarily the federal court should stay its hand on habeas pending completion of the state court proceedings. This qualification plainly stemmed from considerations of comity rather than power, and envisaged only the postponement, not the relinquishment, of federal habeas corpus jurisdiction * * *.

The reasoning of *Ex parte Royall* and its progeny suggested that after the state courts had decided the federal question on the merits against the habeas petitioner, he could return to the federal court on habeas and there relitigate the question, else a rule of timing would become a rule circumscribing the power of the federal courts on habeas, in defiance of unmistakable congressional intent. And so this Court has consistently held, save only in *Frank v. Mangum,* 237 U.S. 309, 35 S.Ct. 582, 59 L.Ed. 969 [1915]. In that case, the State Supreme Court had rejected on the merits petitioner's contention of mob domination at his trial, and this Court held that habeas would not lie because the State had afforded petitioner corrective process [on appeal before the State Supreme Court] * * *. The majority's position in *Frank,* however, was substantially repudiated in *Moore v. Dempsey,* 261 U.S. 86, 43 S.Ct. 265, 67 L.Ed. 543 [1923], a case almost identical in all pertinent respects to *Frank.* Mr. Justice Holmes, writing for the Court in *Moore* (he had written the dissenting opinion in *Frank*), said: "if in fact a trial is dominated by a mob so that there is an actual interference with the course of justice, there is a departure from due process of law; . . . [if] the State Courts failed to correct the wrong, . . . perfection in the machinery for correction . . . can [not] prevent this Court from securing to the petitioners their constitutional rights." It was settled in *Moore,* restoring what evidently had been the assumption until *Frank,* that the state courts' view of the merits was not entitled to conclusive weight. We have not deviated from that position. * * * "The State court cannot have the last say when it, though on fair consideration and what procedurally may be deemed fairness, may have misconceived a federal constitutional right." 344 U.S., as 508, 73 S.Ct., at 446 (opinion of Mr. Justice Frankfurter in *Brown v. Allen*). * * * [c]

In KAUFMAN v. UNITED STATES, 394 U.S. 217, 89 S.Ct. 1068, 22 L.Ed.2d 227 (1969), the opinion for the Court (per Brennan, J.) rejected the government's contention that *Fay v. Noia's* analysis of the range of issues cognizable under habeas corpus did not apply to section 2255 petitions of federal prisoners. *Kaufman* held that "the claim of a federal prisoner that he was convicted on evidence obtained in an unconstitutional search and seizure is cognizable in a post-conviction proceeding under 28 U.S.C. § 2255." In reaching this conclusion, the majority opinion noted:

"Our decisions leave no doubt that the federal habeas remedy extends to state prisoners alleging that unconstitutionally obtained evidence was admitted against them at trial. The Government argues, however, that federal post-conviction relief should not be available to federal prisoners in as broad a range of cases as that cognizable when presented by state prisoners. Support for this proposition is drawn from the fact that considerations which this Court in *Fay v. Noia* deemed justifications for affording a federal forum to state prisoners—e.g., the necessity that federal courts have the "last say" with respect to questions of federal law, the inadequacy of state procedures to raise and preserve federal claims, the concern that state judges may be unsympathetic to federally created rights, the institutional constraints on the exercise of this Court's certiorari jurisdiction to review state convictions—do not obtain with respect to federal prisoners. Thus, we are told that the federal prisoner, having already had his day in federal court, stands in a different position with regard to federal collateral remedies than does the state prisoner. Conceding this distinction, we are unable to understand why it should lead us to restrict completely or severely access by federal prisoners with illegal search and seizure claims to federal collateral remedies, while placing no similar restriction on access by state prisoners.

"The opportunity to assert federal rights in a federal forum is clearly not the sole justification for federal post-conviction relief, otherwise there would be no need to make such relief available to federal prisoners at all. The provision of federal collateral remedies rests more fundamentally upon a recognition that adequate protection of constitutional rights relating to the criminal trial process requires the continuing availability of a mechanism for relief. This is no less true for federal prisoners than it is for state prisoners."

In SCHNECKLOTH v. BUSTAMONTE, 412 U.S. 218, 93 S.Ct. 2041, 36 L.Ed.2d 854 (1973), the majority found it unnecessary to consider the state's contention that *Kaufman* should be overruled. [Compare *Stone v. Powell*, p. 1480 infra]. However, JUSTICE POWELL, joined by the Chief Justice and Justice Rehnquist, wrote a concurring opinion supporting that position. Justice Powell's

c. Dissenting opinions were written by Justice Harlan (joined by Justices Clark and Stewart) and by Justice Clark. Both dissenting opinions focused on the majority's treatment of the procedural forfeiture issue presented in *Fay*, see p. 1501 infra. However, Justice Harlan's dissent, in discussing the scope of the habeas corpus remedy, did differ with the majority's view of the Court's earlier decisions, particularly *Moore v. Dempsey*. Relying on an analysis advanced in Bator, *Finality in Criminal Law and Federal Habeas Corpus for State Prisoners*, 76 Harv.L.Rev. 441 (1963), Justice Harlan concluded: "Prior to *Brown v. Allen*," * * * habeas corpus would not lie for a prisoner who was in custody pursuant to a state judgment of conviction by a court of competent jurisdiction if he had been given an adequate opportunity to obtain full and fair consideration of his federal claim in the state courts." *Brown* had "substantially expanded the scope of inquiry on an application for federal habeas corpus" by holding cognizable a constitutional trial error that could be "fully considered" under available state procedures.

analysis in part extended beyond the issue of habeas corpus consideration of Fourth Amendment claims. In its discussion of the historic function of habeas corpus and the "costs" of habeas corpus review of state convictions, Justice Powell's opinion suggested that habeas relief should be available only where the petitioner's claim related to the determination of the defendant's factual guilt.

Justice Powell's discussion of the historic function of the writ initially rejected "*Fay v. Noia's* version of the writ's historic function" as resting upon a "revisionist view" of history. Relying particularly upon studies by Professors Bator and Oaks, (see fns. b and c supra), Justice Powell noted that: (1) at the time of the adoption of the constitution, "a court disposing of a habeas petition could not go behind the conviction for any purpose other than to verify the formal jurisdiction of the committing court," and (2) "there is no evidence that Congress intended [the Habeas Corpus Act of 1867] to jettison the respect theretofore shown by a reviewing court for prior judgments by a court of proper jurisdiction." The concurring opinion acknowledged that "much had transpired" in the subsequent interpretation of the Habeas Corpus Act. No one would now suggest, Justice Powell noted, "that this Court be imprisoned by every particular of habeas corpus as it existed in the late 18th or 19th centuries." On the other hand, the historical scope of the writ did point in a direction that suggested an appropriate limit upon the constitutional claims that should be cognizable in a habeas petition. That limit and its relation to history were described as follows:

"The historical evidence demonstrates that the purposes of the writ, at the time of the adoption of the Constitution, were tempered by a due regard for the finality of the judgment of the committing court. This regard was maintained substantially intact when Congress, in the Habeas Act of 1867, first extended federal habeas review to the delicate interrelations of our dual court systems. Recent decisions, however, have tended to depreciate the importance of the finality of prior judgments in criminal cases. See *Kaufman v. United States; Sanders v. United States* [p. 1525 infra]; *Fay v. Noia.* This trend may be a justifiable evolution of the use of habeas corpus where the one in state custody raises a constitutional claim bearing on his innocence. But the justification for disregarding the historic scope and function of the writ is measurably less apparent in the typical Fourth Amendment claim asserted on collateral attack. In this latter case, a convicted defendant is most often asking society to redetermine a matter with no bearing at all on the basic justice of his incarceration.

"I am aware that history reveals no exact tie of the writ of habeas corpus to a constitutional claim relating to innocence or guilt. Traditionally, the writ was unavailable even for many constitutional pleas grounded on a claimant's innocence, while many contemporary proponents of expanded employment of the writ would permit its issuance for one whose deserved confinement was never in doubt. We are now faced, however, with the task of accommodating the historic respect for the finality of the judgment of a committing court with recent Court expansions of the role of the writ. This accommodation can best be achieved, with due regard to all of the values implicated, by recourse to the central reason for habeas corpus: the affording of means, through an extraordinary writ, of redressing an *unjust* incarceration."

Justice Powell also suggested that limiting the habeas remedy to claims "relating to guilt or innocence" was supported by an examination of "the costs" of federal habeas review, as measured "in terms of [its] serious intrusions on other societal values." His concurring opinion noted:

"[O]ther values have been subordinated [by expanded habeas corpus review] * * *. They include (i) the most effective utilization of limited judicial resources, (ii) the necessity of finality in criminal trials, (iii) the minimization of friction between our federal and state systems of justice, and (iv) the maintenance of the constitutional balance upon which the doctrine of federalism is founded.

"When raised on federal habeas, a claim generally has been considered by two or more tiers of state courts. It is the solemn duty of these courts, no less than federal ones, to safeguard personal liberties and consider federal claims in accord with federal law. The task which federal courts are asked to perform on habeas is thus most often one that has or should have been done before. The presumption that 'if a job can be well done once, it should not be done twice' is sound and one calculated to utilize best 'the intellectual, moral, and political resources involved in the legal system.' Those resources are limited but demand on them constantly increases. There is an insistent call on federal courts both in civil actions, many novel and complex, which affect intimately the lives of great numbers of people and in original criminal trials and appeals which deserve our most careful attention. To the extent the federal courts are required to reexamine claims on collateral attack, they deprive primary litigants of their prompt availability and mature reflection. * * *

"The present scope of federal habeas corpus also has worked to defeat the interest of society in a rational point of termination for criminal litigation. Professor Amsterdam has identified some of the finality interests at stake in collateral proceedings:

> 'They involved (a) duplication of judicial effort; (b) delay in setting the criminal proceeding at rest; (c) inconvenience and possibly danger in transporting a prisoner to the sentencing court for hearing; (d) postponed litigation of fact, hence litigation which will often be less reliable in reproducing the facts (i) respecting the postconviction claim itself and (ii) reflecting the issue of guilt if the collateral attack succeeds in a form which allows a retrial. . . . ' Amsterdam, *Search, Seizure, and Section 2255,* 112 U.Pa.L.Rev. 378, 383–384 (1964).

No effective judicial system can afford to concede the continuing theoretical possibility that there is error in every trial and that every incarceration is unfounded. At some point the law must convey to those in custody that a wrong has been committed, that consequent punishment has been imposed, that one should no longer look back with the view to resurrecting every imaginable basis for further litigation but rather should look forward to rehabilitation and to becoming a constructive citizen. * * *

"Finally, the present scope of habeas corpus tends to undermine the values inherent in our federal system of government. To the extent that every state criminal judgment is to be subject indefinitely to broad and repetitive federal oversight, we render the actions of state courts a serious disrespect in derogation of the constitutional balance between the two systems. The present expansive scope of federal habeas review has prompted no small friction between state and federal judiciaries. Justice Paul C. Reardon of the Massachusetts Supreme Judicial Court and then President of the National Center for State Courts, in identifying problems between the two systems noted bluntly that 'the first, without question, is the effect of federal habeas corpus proceedings on State courts.' He spoke of the 'humiliation of review from the full bench of the highest State appellate court to a single United States District judge.' Such broad federal habeas powers encourage in his view the 'growing denigration of the State courts and their functions in the public mind.' * * *

"This case involves only a relatively narrow aspect of the appropriate reach of habeas corpus. The specific issue before us, and the only one that need be decided at this time, is the extent to which a state prisoner may obtain federal habeas corpus review of a Fourth Amendment claim. Whatever may be formulated as a more comprehensive answer to the important broader issues (whether by clarifying legislation or in subsequent decisions), Mr. Justice Black has suggested what seems to me to be the appropriate threshold requirement in a case of this kind:

> '. . . I would always require that the convicted defendant raise the kind of constitutional claim that casts some shadow of a doubt on his guilt.' *Kaufman v. United States,* (dissenting opinion).

In a perceptive analysis, Judge Henry J. Friendly expressed a similar view. He would draw the line against habeas corpus review in the absence of a 'colorable claim of innocence':

> '. . . with a few important exceptions, convictions should be subject to collateral attack only when the prisoner supplements his constitution plea with a colorable claim of innocence.' " [23]

Notes and Questions

1. *Departures from history.* Can one reconcile Justice Brennan's view that Congress' extension of the federal writ to state prisoners in 1867 was designed to provide federal court vindication of the rights provided in its "Reconstruction measures" (see p. 1473 supra) and the view of Justice Powell that the writ had previously been limited in challenging convictions to claims going to the jurisdiction of the committing court. Consider LaFave and Israel, § 27.2 (state attempts to enforce laws contrary to the Thirteenth Amendment and the Civil Rights Act would be subject to habeas challenge even under Justice Powell's view since the unconstitutionality of the statute underlying a conviction had come to be viewed—see *Siebold,* p. 1472 supra—as a "jurisdictional defect"). Compare Peller, *In Defense of Federal Habeas Corpus Relitigation,* 16 Harv.Civ.Rts.-Civ.Lib.L.Rev. 579 (1982) (Congress' object was to give the federal courts superintending control over the state criminal justice systems, utilizing the broad habeas review authority that had been exercised previously by lower federal courts in federal prisoner cases; the Supreme Court's narrower rulings prior to 1867 only reflected the Court's desire not to undercut congressional legislation that sharply restricted its appellate review of federal convictions). See also Saltzburg, *Habeas Corpus: The Supreme Court and Congress,* 44 Ohio St.L.Rev. 367 (1983) (noting that the 1867 Act was marked by little debate and no clear indication of congressional goals).[a]

23. Friendly, *Is Innocence Irrelevant? Collateral Attack on Criminal Judgments,* 38 U.Chi.L. Rev. 142 (1970). Judge Friendly's thesis, as he develops it, would encompass collateral attack broadly both within the federal system and with respect to federal habeas for state prisoners. Subject to the exceptions carefully delineated in his article, Judge Friendly would apply the criterion of a "colorable showing of innocence" to any collateral attack of a conviction, including claims under the Fifth and Sixth as well as the Fourth Amendments. Id., at 151–157. In this case we need not consider anything other than the Fourth Amendment claims.

a. Consider also LaFave and Israel, § 27.2 at n. 27: "[A]nother argument currently advanced in favor of the Court's refusal to view the writ as requiring relief for all constitutional errors under all circumstances rests on the narrower scope of the constitutional rights available to state defendants at the time the 1867 Act was adopted. Even if it is assumed that the Congress that adopted the 1867 Act and the Congress that incorporated the substance of that Act in the 1948 revision of the habeas corpus provisions both intended that it apply to all constitutional restrictions applicable to state proceedings at the time, it does not follow, it is argued, that either Congress would anticipate use of the writ as to the broad array of constitutional regulations applicable to the state criminal justice process today. Read in light of the scope of constitutional law as it stood at the time, the writ should be limited, it is argued, to 'cases that truly involve fundamental unfairness.' See Stevens, J., concurring in *Rose v. Lundy* [Note 4, p. 1515 infra]. But see Olsen, *Judicial Proposals to Limit the Jurisdictional Scope of Federal Post-Conviction Habeas Corpus Consideration of the Claims of State Prisoners,* 31 Buffalo L.Rev. 301, 304, 325–26 (1982) (no indication that Congress intended to 'freeze' constitutional coverage)."

2. If habeas corpus relief for convicted defendants had historically been tied to a jurisdictional touchstone, when did the Court begin to depart from that limitation? Was the "concept of jurisdiction * * * subjected to considerable strain" (Harlan, J., in *Fay*) in the early decisions of *Siebold* and *Ex parte Lange* (p. 1472 supra)? Did the Court depart from the jurisdictional limitation when, in *Frank v. Mangum* (p. 1473 supra), it looked to whether the defendant had been given "an adequate opportunity in state court to raise his constitutional claim" (Powell, J., in *Schneckloth*)? Consider also the Court's reasoning in *Johnson v. Zerbst,* 304 U.S. 458, 58 S.Ct. 1019, 82 L.Ed. 1461 (1938). *Johnson* held that a Sixth Amendment claim—the denial of appointed counsel for an indigent defendant—was an appropriate habeas corpus claim. The Court noted: "Since the Sixth Amendment constitutionally entitles one charged with crime to the assistance of counsel, compliance with this constitutional mandate is an essential jurisdiction prerequisite to a federal court's authority to deprive an accused of his * * * liberty. * * * A court's jurisdiction at the beginning of trial may be lost 'in the course of the proceedings' due to failure to complete the court—as the Sixth Amendment requires—by providing counsel for an accused who is unable to obtain counsel. * * * The judgment of conviction pronounced by a court without jurisdiction is void and one imprisoned thereunder may obtain release by habeas corpus." Judge Friendly suggests that *Frank v. Mangum,* and *Moore v. Dempsey* (see p. 1473 supra) easily "can be fitted under the [jurisdiction] rubric" as interpreted in *Johnson,* but that *Brown v. Allen* cannot be fitted under that "rubric." See Friendly, p. 1477 supra. Compare Amsterdam, p. 1476 supra, suggesting that the concept of a jurisdictional defect "blew balloon thin and burst in *Johnson v. Zerbst.*" [b]

Assuming that habeas corpus relief no longer need be tied to jurisdictional claims, would it be appropriate to adopt a standard defining cognizable claims that would not necessarily include all jurisdictional defects? Would that be the result if the Court adopted a standard limiting habeas consideration to "the kind of constitutional claim that casts some shadow of a doubt on guilt" (Black, J., dissenting in *Kaufman*)? Consider, in this connection, *Blackledge v. Perry,* p. 1252 supra.

3. *The burden of habeas petitions.* Considerable disagreement exists as to the extent of the burden that habeas corpus petitions have imposed on the criminal justice system. Various commentators (including several federal judges), pointing to the large number of annual habeas filings (see Note 3, p. 1469 supra), argue that such petitions impose a heavy burden on federal courts and are a major factor contributing to the current backlog of cases. Other commentators contend that the burden is greatly overstated. They claim that the petitions require a much smaller portion of the courts' time than the typical civil case because (1) only a small portion require evidentiary hearings, and (2) the initial evaluation of the petitions, including hearings, may be delegated to magistrates.[c]

b. See also *Waley v. Johnston,* 316 U.S. 101, 62 S.Ct. 964, 86 L.Ed. 1302 (1946), discarding the jurisdictional touchstone in holding that petitioner "could * * * by habeas corpus attack his sentence on the ground that his guilty plea was coerced." The Court noted that petitioner's claim was based on "facts * * * dehors the record and their effect on the judgment was not open to consideration and review on appeal. In such circumstances, the use of the writ * * * to test the constitutional validity of a conviction is not restricted to these cases where the judgment of conviction is void for want of jurisdiction of the trial court to render it. It extends also to those exceptional cases where the conviction has been in disregard of constitutional rights of the accused, and where the writ is the only effective means of preserving his rights [citing *Moore v. Dempsey*]."

c. Under 28 U.S.C. § 636 a judge may designate a magistrate "to conduct hearings, including evidentiary hearings, and to submit to a judge of the court proposed findings of fact and recommendations for the disposition of * * * applications for posttrial relief made by individuals con-

But cf. Friendly, p. 1477 supra (noting that "the ability of the Federal courts to dispense with evidentiary hearings * * * is due in considerable measure to *state* post-conviction hearings," and the burden of such state hearings must be considered in evaluating the impact of federal habeas corpus upon the total criminal justice system).[d]

4. *The need for finality.* How significant are the finality interests noted by Justice Powell? Some commentators have suggested that decisions like *Brown v. Allen* and *Fay v. Noia* have unduly undermined a sense of "repose [that] is a psychological necessity in a secure and active society"—i.e., that the decisions have deprived the judicial system of a well established point at which it may be assumed "we have tried hard enough and thus [we] may take it that justice has been done." Bator, p. 1474 supra. Instead, they argue, such decisions may have catered to a "perpetual and unreasoned anxiety that there is a possibility that an error may have been committed in any case." Id. Compare, however, Lay, *Modern Administrative Proposals for Federal Habeas,* 21 DePaul L.Rev. 701, 709–10 (1972): "Sober reflection upon why we have devised a system which allows a continual questioning of its processes discloses that our purpose is not so much to remove the discomforting doubt or to achieve the ultimate assurance, as it is to give safeguard to rights not readily visible or easily acknowledged. We would not send two astronauts to the moon without providing them with at least three or four back-up systems. Should we send literally thousands of men to prison with even less reserves? * * * [W]ith knowledge of our fallibility and a realization of past errors, we can hardly insure our confidence by creating an irrevocable end to the guilt-determining process."

5. Not unexpectedly, there also has been considerable dispute as to the impact of a "lack of finality" upon the prisoner's efforts toward rehabilitation. While some commentators have suggested that the potential for "endless litigation" may have an adverse effect upon the prisoner's outlook, as suggested by Justice Powell, others have suggested that "the availability of collateral relief is [itself] a very wholesome kind of therapy." Freund, *Symposium on Habeas Corpus,* 9 Utah L.Rev. 27, 30 (1964). Consider also H. Schwartz, *Retroactivity, Reliability and Due Process,* 33 U.Chi.L.Rev. 719, 744 (1966), ("We currently know too little about and do too little for prisoner education and deterrence to warrant firm judgments that liberal habeas corpus impairs these objectives"); Michael, *The "New" Federalism and the Burger Court's Deference to the States in Federal Habeas Proceedings,* 64 Iowa L.Rev. 233, 254 (1979) (with the § 2254 court rules now placing a "laches" limitation upon delayed petitions and an "abuse of writ" limitation upon repeat petitions [see Note 7, p. 1524 infra], "the injury to the policy of finality

victed of criminal offenses." If objections are made to the magistrate's proposed findings, the district judge must make a "de novo determination" as to those findings.

d. Unfortunately, the best available statistical analysis of the judicial effort devoted to habeas petitions is now somewhat dated. See Shapiro, *Federal Habeas Corpus: A Study in Massachusetts,* 87 Harv.L.Rev. 321 (1973). Looking to the practice in a single judicial district, it concluded that: (1) the percentage of cases involving some sort of evidentiary hearing (38% in the district studied) is fairly substantial, notwithstanding some seemingly contrary statistics; most hearings, however, do not last more than a day; (2) while a substantial number of petitions are dismissed summarily, those cases often involve a significant investment of time; (3) a considerable portion of the function of screening petitions is delegated to federal magistrates; (4) there is considerable variation in the time devoted by different judges to reviewing petitions; (5) counsel are frequently utilized and probably do save the court time in considering petitions, but they are not an effective agency in preventing the filing of frivolous petitions; and (6) the Administrative Office is "realistic" in assigning to habeas corpus petitions a time study weight "less than the median for all types of cases, [but] far from the bottom of the list." The study also supports the usual estimate that petitioners are successful in obtaining some form of relief (discharge or a new hearing) in less than 5 percent of the cases filed.

* * * is not appreciably greater than that caused by direct Supreme Court appellate review").

6. *Relations between federal and state courts.* To what extent has the "expansive scope of federal habeas review" strained the institutional relationship between federal and state courts and diminished the "sense of responsibility" of state judges. Compare with the statement of Justice Reardon quoted in *Schneckloth,* Chisum, *In Defense of Modern Federal Habeas Corpus for State Prisoners,* 21 De Paul L.Rev. 682, 693 (1972). The author there contends that habeas corpus review is a most unlikely source of resentment among state trial judges since "the chances that a state trial-level judge will see an individual convicted in his court obtain federal habeas relief are minuscule." The author acknowledges that there is "widespread resentment against federal intrusion," but he argues that the real source of that resentment is the Supreme Court's decisions expanding the rights of defendants and overriding state procedures. Consider also Cover and Aleinikoff, *Dialectical Federalism: Habeas Corpus and the Court,* 86 Yale L.J. 1035 (1977) (noting the opportunities provided by habeas corpus for promoting a dialogue between state and federal courts as to constitutional issues not yet resolved by the Supreme Court).[e]

7. *Congressional proposals.* Since *Brown v. Allen,* various proposals have been introduced in Congress to limit the scope of federal habeas corpus. Those legislative proposals originally sought to overrule *Brown* and *Fay,* but subsequent proposals also added the limitations suggested in Justice Powell's concurring opinion in *Schneckloth.* The only changes that gained passage, however, were those relating to state court findings of fact (see Note 4, p. 1326 infra). What weight, if any, should be given to this legislative inaction? Consider Justice Rehnquist's comment in *Wainwright v. Sykes,* p. 1506 infra, that the Court's habeas decisions have illustrated an "historic willingness to overturn or modify its earlier views on the scope of the writ, even where the statutory language authorizing judicial action has remained unchanged." See also *Stone v. Powell,* infra.

STONE v. POWELL

428 U.S. 465, 96 S.Ct. 3037, 49 L.Ed.2d 1067 (1976).

MR. JUSTICE POWELL delivered the opinion of the Court.

Respondents in these cases were convicted of criminal offenses in state courts, and their convictions were affirmed on appeal. The prosecution in each case relied upon evidence obtained by searches and seizures alleged by respondents to have been unlawful. Each respondent subsequently sought relief in a federal district court by filing a petition for a writ of federal habeas corpus * * * [against petitioners, their respective wardens]. The question presented is whether a federal court should consider, in ruling on a petition for habeas corpus relief filed by a state prisoner, a claim that evidence obtained by an unconstitutional search or seizure was introduced at his trial, when he has previously been afforded an opportunity for full and fair litigation of his claim in the state courts. The issue is of considerable importance to the administration of criminal justice.

I

We summarize first the relevant facts and procedural history of these cases. [Respondent Powell, convicted of murder in 1968, had challenged under the Fourth Amendment the admissibility of the murder weapon, which had been obtained through a search incident to his arrest for

e. Insofar as the strained relationship noted by Justice Powell stems from the capacity of a single federal district court judge to reject a state appellate court decision, might the best response be a congressional alteration of the structure of habeas procedure? Several commentators have urged that habeas consideration of state convictions be shifted to the federal appellate courts. See, e.g., Carrington, Meador, and Rosenberg, *Justice on Appeal* 115–116 (1976).

vagrancy. The California courts had rejected his claim, with the appellate court holding that any error had been harmless under the standard of *Chapman v. California* (p. 796 supra). On habeas review, the federal district court upheld the search, but the Ninth Circuit reversed on the ground that the ordinance was unconstitutionally vague.[a] In the second case before the Court, involving respondent Rice, the defendant had also been convicted of murder. Defendant was alleged to have been a co-conspirator in the planting of a booby trap that killed a policeman purposefully lured to the scene of the trap. After obtaining a warrant for the arrest of Peak, a member of the National Committee to Combat Fascism, the police went to Rice's home, believing he might have hidden Peak. When there was no response to their repeated knocking (although the lights and television were on), they guarded the house while other officers obtained a search warrant. Entering pursuant to that warrant, they discovered explosives and related materials that were introduced in evidence at Rice's trial. The Nebraska courts rejected Rice's Fourth Amendment objection, but the federal district court granted relief on the ground that affidavit supporting the search warrant failed to meet the standards of *Spinelli v. United States* (p. 261 supra). That court also rejected the state's alternative contention that the search could be justified without a warrant under an exigent circumstances rationale.]

II

[Justice Powell's opinion here reviewed the "expansion" of the scope of the writ of habeas corpus in Supreme Court rulings. The opinion advanced essentially the same view of this development as in the concurring opinion in *Schneckloth,* see p. 1474 supra].

During the period in which the substantive scope of the writ was expanded, the Court did not consider whether exceptions to full review might exist with respect to particular categories of constitutional claims.[11] Prior to the Court's decision in *Kaufman v. United States,* however, a substantial majority of the federal courts of appeals had concluded that collateral review of search-and-seizure claims was inappropriate on motions filed by federal prisoners under 28 U.S.C. § 2255 * * * *Kaufman* rejected this [position] and held that search and seizure claims are cognizable in § 2255 proceedings. The Court noted that "the federal habeas remedy extends to state prisoners alleging that unconstitutionally obtained evidence was admitted against them at trial," and concluded, as a matter of statutory construction, that there was no basis for restricting "access by federal prisoners with illegal search-and-seizure claims to federal collateral remedies, while placing no similar restriction on access by state prisoners." Although in recent years the view has been expressed that the Court should reexamine the substantive scope of federal habeas jurisdiction and limit collateral review of search-and-seizure claims "solely to the question of whether the petitioner was provided with a fair opportunity to raise and have adjudicated the question in state courts," *Schneckloth v. Bustamonte,* the Court without discussion or consideration of the issue, has continued to accept jurisdiction in cases raising such claims.

The discussion in *Kaufman* of the scope of federal habeas corpus rests on the view

a. Compare the position later taken by the Supreme Court in *Michigan v. DeFillippo,* Note 6, p. 229 supra.

11. In construing broadly the power of a federal district court to consider constitutional claims presented in a petition for writ of habeas corpus, the Court in *Fay* also reaffirmed the equitable nature of the writ, noting that "[d]iscretion is implicit in the statutory command that the judge * * * 'dispose of the matter as law and justice require,' 28 U.S.C. § 2243." More recently, in *Francis v. Henderson* [p. 1505 infra], we emphasized: "This Court has long recognized that in some circumstances considerations of comity and concerns for the orderly administration of criminal justice require a federal court to forego the exercise of its habeas corpus power. See *Fay v. Noia.*"

that the effectuation of the Fourth Amendment, as applied to the States through the Fourteenth Amendment, requires the granting of habeas corpus relief when a prisoner has been convicted in state court on the basis of evidence obtained in an illegal search or seizure since those Amendments were held in *Mapp v. Ohio* [p. 210 supra], to require exclusion of such evidence at trial and reversal of conviction upon direct review. Until this case we have not had occasion fully to consider the validity of this view. Upon examination, we conclude, in light of the nature and purpose of the Fourth Amendment exclusionary rule, that this view is unjustified.[16] We hold, therefore, that where the State has provided an opportunity for full and fair litigation of a Fourth Amendment claim, the Constitution does not require that a state prisoner be granted federal habeas corpus relief on the ground that evidence obtained in an unconstitutional search or seizure was introduced at his trial.

III

* * * The exclusionary rule * * * [is] a judicially created means of effectuating the rights secured by the Fourth Amendment. * * * The primary justification for the exclusionary rule * * * is the deterrence of police conduct that violates Fourth Amendment rights.[b] Post-*Mapp* decisions have established that the rule is not a personal constitutional right. Is is not calculated to redress the injury to the privacy of the victim of the search or seizure, for any "[r]eparation comes too late." *Linkletter v. Walker* [p. 49 supra].

* * * [D]espite the broad deterrent purpose of the exclusionary rule, it has never been interpreted to proscribe the introduction of illegally seized evidence in all proceedings or against all persons. As in the case of any remedial device, "the application of the rule has been restricted to those areas where its remedial objectives are thought most efficaciously served." *United States v. Calandra* [p. 230 supra]. Thus, our refusal to extend the exclusionary rule to grand jury proceedings was based on a balancing of the potential injury to the historic role and function of the grand jury by such extension against the potential contribution to the effectuation of the Fourth Amendment through deterrence of police misconduct. * * * The same pragmatic analysis of the exclusionary rule's usefulness in a particular context was evident earlier in *Walder v. United States* [p. 828 supra], where the Court permitted the Government to use unlawfully seized evidence to impeach the credibility of a defendant who had testified broadly in his own defense. The Court held, in effect, that the interests safeguarded by the exclusionary rule in that context were outweighed by the need to prevent perjury and to assure the integrity of the trial process. * * *

The balancing process at work in these cases also finds expression in the standing requirement. Standing to invoke the exclusionary rule has been found to exist only when the Government attempts to use illegally obtained evidence to incriminate the victim of the illegal search. The standing requirement is premised on the

16. The issue in *Kaufman* was the scope of § 2255. Our decision today rejects the dictum in *Kaufman* concerning the applicability of the exclusionary rule in federal habeas corpus review of state court decisions pursuant to § 2254. To the extent the application of the exclusionary rule in *Kaufman* did not rely upon the supervisory role of this Court over the lower federal courts, cf. *Elkins v. United States* [p. 212 supra], the rationale for its application in that context is also rejected.

b. The majority opinion also discussed the role of the "imperative of judicial integrity" as a justification for the exclusionary rule. It concluded: "While courts * * * must ever be concerned with preserving the integrity of the judicial process, this concern has limited force as a justification for the exclusion of highly probative evidence. The force of this justification becomes minimal where federal habeas corpus relief is sought by a prisoner who previously has been afforded the opportunity for full and fair consideration of his search-and-seizure claim at trial and on direct review."

view that the "additional benefits of extending the rule" to defendants other than the victim of the search or seizure are outweighed by the "further encroachment upon the public interest in prosecuting those accused of crime and having them acquitted or convicted on the basis of all the evidence which exposes the truth." *Alderman v. United States* [p. 778 supra].

IV

We turn now to the specific question presented by these cases. Respondents allege violations of Fourth Amendment rights guaranteed them through the Fourteenth Amendment. The question is whether state prisoners—who have been afforded the opportunity for full and fair consideration of their reliance upon the exclusionary rule with respect to seized evidence by the state courts at trial and on direct review—may invoke their claim again on federal habeas corpus review. The answer is to be found by weighing the utility of the exclusionary rule against the costs of extending it to collateral review of Fourth Amendment claims.

The costs of applying the exclusionary rule even at trial and on direct review are well known: the focus of the trial, and the attention of the participants therein, is diverted from the ultimate question of guilt or innocence that should be the central concern in a criminal proceeding. Moreover, the physical evidence sought to be excluded is typically reliable and often the most probative information bearing on the guilt or innocence of the defendant. As Mr. Justice Black emphasized in his dissent in *Kaufman:*

> "A claim of illegal search and seizure under the Fourth Amendment is crucially different from many other constitutional rights; ordinarily the evidence seized can in no way have been rendered untrustworthy by the means of its seizure and indeed often this evidence alone establishes beyond virtually any shadow of a doubt that the defendant is guilty."

Application of the rule thus deflects the truthfinding process and often frees the guilty. The disparity in particular cases between the error committed by the police officer and the windfall afforded a guilty defendant by application of the rule is contrary to the idea of proportionality that is essential to the concept of justice. Thus, although the rule is thought to deter unlawful police activity in part through the nurturing of respect for Fourth Amendment values, if applied indiscriminately it may well have the opposite effect of generating disrespect for the law and administration of justice. These long-recognized costs of the rule persist when a criminal conviction is sought to be overturned on collateral review on the ground that a search-and-seizure claim was erroneously rejected by two or more tiers of state courts.[31]

Evidence obtained by police officers in violation of the Fourth Amendment is excluded at trial in the hope that the frequency of future violations will decrease. Despite the absence of supportive empiri-

31. Resort to habeas corpus, especially for purposes other than to assure that no innocent person suffers an unconstitutional loss of liberty, results in serious intrusions on values important to our system of government. They include "(i) the most effective utilization of limited judicial resources, (ii) the necessity of finality in criminal trials, (iii) the minimization of friction between our federal and state systems of justice, and (iv) the maintenance of the constitutional balance upon which the doctrine of federalism is founded." *Schneckloth v. Bustamonte,* supra (Powell, J., concurring). See also *Kaufman v. United States,* supra (Black, J., dissenting).

We nevertheless afford broad habeas corpus relief, recognizing the need in a free society for an additional safeguard against compelling an innocent man to suffer an unconstitutional loss of liberty. The Court in *Fay v. Noia,* supra, described habeas corpus as a remedy for "whatever society deems to be intolerable restraints," and recognized that those to whom the writ should be granted "are persons whom society has grievously wronged." But in the case of a typical Fourth Amendment claim, asserted on collateral attack, a convicted defendant is usually asking society to redetermine an issue that has no bearing on the basic justice of his incarceration.

cal evidence, we have assumed that the immediate effect of exclusion will be to discourage law enforcement officials from violating the Fourth Amendment by removing the incentive to disregard it. More importantly, over the long term, this demonstration that our society attaches serious consequences to violation of constitutional rights is thought to encourage those who formulate law enforcement policies, and the officers who implement them, to incorporate Fourth Amendment ideals into their value system.

We adhere to the view that these considerations support the implementation of the exclusionary rule at trial and its enforcement on direct appeal of state court convictions. But the additional contribution, if any, of the consideration of search-and-seizure claims of state prisoners on collateral review is small in relation to the costs. To be sure, each case in which such claim is considered may add marginally to an awareness of the values protected by the Fourth Amendment. There is no reason to believe, however, that the overall educative effect of the exclusionary rule would be appreciably diminished if search-and-seizure claims could not be raised in federal habeas corpus review of state convictions. Nor is there reason to assume that any specific disincentive already created by the risk of exclusion of evidence at trial or the reversal of convictions on direct review would be enhanced if there were the further risk that a conviction obtained in state court and affirmed on direct review might be overturned in collateral proceedings often occurring years after the incarceration of the defendant. The view that the deterrence of Fourth Amendment violations would be furthered rests on the dubious assumption that law enforcement authorities would fear that federal habeas review might reveal flaws in a search or seizure that went undetected at trial and on appeal.[35] Even if one rationally could assume that some additional incremental deterrent effect would be present in isolated cases, the resulting advance of the legitimate goal of furthering Fourth Amendment rights would be outweighed by the acknowledged costs to other values vital to a rational system of criminal justice.

In sum, we conclude that where the State has provided an opportunity for full and fair litigation of a Fourth Amendment claim, a state prisoner may not be granted federal habeas corpus relief on the ground that evidence obtained in an unconstitutional search or seizure was introduced at his trial.[37] In this context the contribution

35. The policy arguments that respondents marshal in support of the view that federal habeas corpus review is necessary to effectuate the Fourth Amendment stem from a basic mistrust of the state courts as fair and competent forums for the adjudication of federal constitutional rights. The argument is that state courts cannot be trusted to effectuate Fourth Amendment values through fair application of the rule, and the oversight jurisdiction of this Court on certiorari is an inadequate safeguard. The principal rationale for this view emphasizes the broad differences in the respective institutional setting within which federal judges and state judges operate. Despite differences in institutional environment and the unsympathetic attitude to federal constitutional claims of some state judges in years past, we are unwilling to assume that there now exists a general lack of appropriate sensitivity to constitutional rights in the trial and appellate courts of the several States. State courts, like federal courts, have a constitutional obligation to safeguard personal liberties and to uphold federal law. *Martin v. Hunter's Lessee,* [14 U.S.] 1 Wheat. 304, 4 L.Ed. 97 (1816). Moreover, the argument that federal judges are more expert in applying federal constitutional law is especially unpersuasive in the context of search-and-seizure claims, since they are dealt with on a daily basis by trial level judges in both systems. In sum, there is "no intrinsic reason why the fact that a man is a federal judge should make him more competent, or conscientious, or learned with respect to the [consideration of Fourth Amendment claims] than his neighbor in the state courthouse." Bator [fn. c, p. 1474 supra].

37. The dissent characterizes the Court's opinion as laying the groundwork for a "drastic withdrawal of federal habeas jurisdiction, if not for all grounds * * *, then at least [for many] * * *." It refers variously to our opinion as a "novel reinterpretation of the habeas statute," as a "harbinger of future eviscerations of the habeas statutes," as "rewrit[ing] Congress' jurisdictional statutes * * * and [barring] access to federal courts by state prisoners with constitutional claims distasteful to a majority" of the Court, and of the exclusionary rule, if any, to the effectuation of the Fourth Amendment is minimal and the substantial societal costs of application of the rule persist with special force.

MR. CHIEF JUSTICE BURGER, concurring.

I concur in the Court's opinion. By way of dictum, and somewhat hesitantly, the Court notes that the holding in this case leaves undisturbed the exclusionary rule as applied to criminal trials. For reasons stated in my dissent in *Bivens v. Six Unknown Named Federal Agents,* it seems clear to me that the exclusionary rule has been operative long enough to demonstrate its flaws. The time has come to modify its reach, even if it is retained for a small and limited category of cases. * * * [See Note 5, p. 228 supra].

MR. JUSTICE BRENNAN, with whom MR. JUSTICE MARSHALL concurs, dissenting.

* * * The Court, assuming without deciding that respondents were convicted on the basis of unconstitutionally obtained evidence erroneously admitted against them by the state trial courts, acknowledges that respondents had the right to obtain a reversal of their convictions on appeal in the state courts or on certiorari to this Court.[c] * * * The Court, however, simply ignores the settled principle that for purposes of adjudicating constitutional claims Congress, which has the power to do so under Art. III of the Constitution, has effectively cast the district courts sitting in habeas in the role of surrogate Supreme Courts.

* * * [B]y conceding that today's "decision does not mean that the federal [district] court lacks jurisdiction over [respondents'] claim[s]," ante, at n. 37, the Court admits that respondents have sufficiently alleged that they are "in custody in violation of the Constitution" within the meaning of § 2254 and that there is no "constitutional" rationale for today's holding. * * * Therefore, the real ground of today's decision—a ground that is par-

as a "denigration of constitutional guarantees [that] must appall citizens taught to expect judicial respect" of constitutional rights.

With all respect, the hyperbole of the dissenting opinion is misdirected. Our decision today is *not* concerned with the scope of the habeas corpus statute as authority for litigating constitutional claims generally. We do reaffirm that the exclusionary rule is a judicially created remedy rather than a personal constitutional right, and we emphasize the minimal utility of the rule when sought to be applied to Fourth Amendment claims in a habeas corpus proceeding. * * *. In sum, we hold only that a federal court need not apply the exclusionary rule on habeas review of a Fourth Amendment claim absent a showing that the state prisoner was denied an opportunity for a full and fair litigation of that claim at trial and on direct review. Our decision does not mean that the federal court lacks jurisdiction over such a claim, but only that the application of the rule is limited to cases in which there has been both such a showing and a Fourth Amendment violation.

c. Justice Brennan had earlier raised the question of whether the Court majority was actually saying that the federal habeas court did not have before it a constitutional violation. Speaking to this point he noted: "[I]t escapes me as to what logic can support the assertion that the defendant's unconstitutional confinement obtains during the process of direct review, no matter how long that process takes, but that the unconstitutionality then suddenly dissipates at the moment the claim is asserted in a collateral attack on the conviction. The only conceivable rationale upon which the Court's 'constitutional' thesis might rest is the statement that 'the [exclusionary] rule is not a personal constitutional right. . . . Instead, "the rule is a judicially created remedy designed to safeguard Fourth Amendment rights generally through its deterrent effect,"' ante, at [p. 1482]. Although my dissent in *Calandra* [p. 230 supra] rejected * * * the premise that an individual has no constitutional right to have unconstitutionally seized evidence excluded from all use by the government, I need not dispute that point here. For today's holding is not logically defensible even under *Calandra.* However the Court reinterprets *Mapp,* * * * the prevailing constitutional *rule* is that unconstitutionally seized evidence *cannot be admitted* in the criminal trial of a person whose federal constitutional rights were violated by the search or seizure. The erroneous admission of such evidence is a violation of the Federal Constitution—*Mapp* inexorably means at least this much * * *—and an accused against whom such evidence is admitted has been convicted in derogation of rights mandated by, and is 'in custody in violation of,' the Constitution of the United States."

ticularly troubling in light of its portent for habeas jurisdiction generally—is the Court's novel reinterpretation of the habeas statutes; this would read the statutes as requiring the District Courts routinely to deny habeas relief to prisoners "in custody in violation of the Constitution or laws of the United States" as a matter of judicial "discretion"—a "discretion" judicially manufactured today contrary to the express statutory language—because such claims are "different in kind" from other constitutional violations in that they "do not 'impugn the integrity of the fact-finding process,'" and because application of such constitutional strictures "often frees the guilty." Much in the Court's opinion suggests that a construction of the habeas statutes to deny relief for non-"guilt-related" constitutional violations, based on this Court's vague notions of comity and federalism, is the actual premise for today's decision, and although the Court attempts to bury its underlying premises in footnotes, those premises mark this case as a harbinger of future eviscerations of the habeas statutes that plainly does violence to congressional power to frame the statutory contours of habeas jurisdiction. [The dissent here quotes from footnotes 31 and 35 of the majority opinion.]

* * * If today's decision were only that erroneous state court resolution of Fourth Amendment claims did not render the defendant's resultant confinement "in violation of the Constitution," these pronouncements would have been wholly irrelevant and unnecessary. I am therefore justified in apprehending that the groundwork is being laid today for a drastic withdrawal of federal habeas jurisdiction, if not for all grounds of alleged unconstitutional detention, then at least for claims—for example, of double jeopardy, entrapment, self-incrimination, *Miranda* violations, and use of invalid identification procedures—that this Court later decides are not "guilt-related."

* * * Without even paying the slightest deference to principles of *stare decisis* or acknowledging Congress' failure for two decades to alter the habeas statutes in light of our interpretation of congressional intent to render all federal constitutional contentions cognizable on habeas, the Court today rewrites Congress' jurisdictional statutes as heretofore construed and bars access to federal courts by state prisoners with constitutional claims distasteful to a majority of my Brethren. But even ignoring principles of *stare decisis* dictating that Congress is the appropriate vehicle for embarking on such a fundamental shift in the jurisdiction of the federal courts, I can find no adequate justification elucidated by the Court for concluding that habeas relief for all federal constitutional claims is no longer compelled under the reasoning of *Brown, Fay,* and *Kaufman.*

* * * The procedural safeguards mandated in the Framers' Constitution are not admonitions to be tolerated only to the extent they serve functional purposes that ensure that the "guilty" are punished and the "innocent" freed; rather, every guarantee enshrined in the Constitution, our basic charter and the guarantor of our most precious liberties, is by it endowed with an independent vitality and value, and this Court is not free to curtail those constitutional guarantees even to punish the most obviously guilty. Particular constitutional rights that do not affect the fairness of factfinding procedures cannot for that reason be denied at the trial itself. What possible justification then can there be for denying vindication of such rights on federal habeas when state courts do deny those rights at trial? To sanction disrespect and disregard for the Constitution in the name of protecting society from lawbreakers is to make the government itself lawless and to subvert those values upon which our ultimate freedom and liberty depend. * * *

* * * Enforcement of federal constitutional rights that redress constitutional violations directed against the "guilty" is a particular function of *federal* habeas review, lest judges trying the "morally unworthy"

be tempted not to execute the supreme law of the land. State judges popularly elected may have difficulty resisting popular pressures not experienced by federal judges given lifetime tenure designed to immunize them from such influences, and the federal habeas statutes reflect the Congressional judgment that such detached federal review is a salutary safeguard against *any* detention of an individual "in violation of the Constitution or laws of the United States."

Federal courts have the duty to carry out the congressionally assigned responsibility to shoulder the ultimate burden of adjudging whether detentions violate federal law, and today's decision substantially abnegates that duty. The Court does not, because it cannot, dispute that institutional constraints totally preclude any possibility that this Court can adequately oversee whether state courts have properly applied federal law, and does not controvert the fact that federal habeas jurisdiction is partially designed to ameliorate that inadequacy. Thus, although I fully agree that state courts "have a constitutional obligation to safeguard personal liberties and to uphold federal law," and that there is no "general lack of appropriate sensitivity to constitutional rights in the trial and appellate courts of the several States," ante, at n. 35, I cannot agree that it follows that, as the Court today holds, federal court determination of almost all Fourth Amendment claims of state prisoners should be barred and that state court resolution of those issues should be insulated from the federal review Congress intended. * * *

If proof of the necessity of the federal habeas jurisdiction were required, the disposition by the state courts of the underlying Fourth Amendment issues presented by these cases supplies it. In [the Powell case], respondent was arrested pursuant to a statute which obviously is unconstitutional under *Papachristou v. City of Jacksonville,* 405 U.S. 156, 92 S.Ct. 839, 31 L.Ed.2d 110 (1972). * * * Without elaborating on the various arguments buttressing this result, * * * I would note only that the ordinance, due to the Court's failure to address its constitutionality today, remains in full force and effect, thereby affirmatively encouraging further Fourth Amendment violations. * * *

Even more violative of constitutional safeguards is the manner in which the Nebraska courts dealt with the merits in respondent Rice's case. [Justice Brennan here noted that the "thorough and thoughtful" opinion of the district court established that the search warrant used by the Omaha police was based on a "clearly deficient" affidavit and that "no extant exception to the warrant requirement" otherwise justified the search. "Yet," the dissent continued, "the Nebraska Supreme Court upheld the search on the alternative and patently untenable ground that there is no Fourth Amendment violation if a defective warrant is supplemented *at a suppression hearing* by facts that theoretically could have been, but were not presented to the issuing magistrate." This rationale, Justice Brennan noted, was clearly contrary to the basic principle of magistrate review established in numerous prior opinions of the Supreme Court.[d] The "Nebraska Supreme Court's distortion of the Fourth Amendment in an emotionally charged case" clearly illustrated "the general potential for erroneous state-court adjudication of Fourth Amendment claims."]

MR. JUSTICE WHITE, dissenting.

For many of the reasons stated by MR. JUSTICE BRENNAN, I cannot agree that the writ of habeas corpus should be any less available to those convicted of state crimes where they allege Fourth Amend-

d. The majority opinion stated, in a footnote, that the Nebraska Supreme Court had found the affidavit sufficient on its face but had also referred to additional information that had not been before the magistrate. The majority opinion noted that the state's argument that it could "supplement the affidavit" with such additional information was "a contention that we have several times rejected and need not reach here again."

ment violations than where other constitutional issues are presented to the federal court. Under the amendments to the habeas corpus statute, which were adopted after *Fay v. Noia,* and represented an effort by Congress to lend a modicum of finality to state criminal judgments, I cannot distinguish between Fourth Amendment and other constitutional issues.

Suppose, for example, that two confederates in crime, Smith and Jones, are tried separately for a state crime and convicted on the very same evidence, including evidence seized incident to their arrest allegedly made without probable cause. Their constitutional claims are fully aired, rejected and preserved on appeal. Their convictions are affirmed by the State's highest court. Smith, the first to be tried, does not petition for certiorari, or does so but his petition is denied. Jones, whose conviction was considerably later, is more successful. His petition for certiorari is granted and his conviction reversed because this Court, without making any new rule of law, simply concludes that on the undisputed facts the arrests were made without probable cause and the challenged evidence was therefore seized in violation of the Fourth Amendment. The State must either retry Jones or release him, necessarily because he is deemed in custody in violation of the Constitution. It turns out that without the evidence illegally seized, the State has no case; and Jones goes free. Smith then files his petition for habeas corpus. He makes no claim that he did not have a full and fair hearing in the state courts, but asserts that his Fourth Amendment claim had been erroneously decided and that he is being held in violation of the Federal Constitution. He cites this Court's decision in Jones' case to satisfy any burden placed on him by § 2254 to demonstrate that the state court was in error. Unless the Court's reservation, in its present opinion, of those situations where the defendant has not had a full and fair hearing in the state courts is intended to encompass all those circumstances under which a state criminal judgment may be re-examined under § 2254—in which event the opinion is essentially meaningless and the judgment erroneous—Smith's petition would be dismissed, and he would spend his life in prison while his colleague is a free man. I cannot believe that Congress intended this result.

* * * I would affirm the judgments of the Courts of Appeals as being acceptable applications of the exclusionary rule applicable in state criminal trials by virtue of *Mapp v. Ohio,* supra. I feel constrained to say, however, that I would join four or more other Justices in substantially limiting the reach of the exclusionary rule as presently administered under the Fourth Amendment in federal and state criminal trials. * * *

Notes and Questions

1. *Federal vs. state judges.* Are there any "intrinsic reasons" why state judges may be less effective in protecting a defendant's Fourth Amendment rights than federal judges considering habeas corpus applications? Commentators who disagree with Justice Powell's conclusion (see fn. 35 supra) cite various "institutional distinctions" between state and federal courts. As suggested by Justice Brennan, they cite the additional pressure placed on judges who must seek reelection as opposed to judges who have lifetime tenure. This distinction does not apply to all state judges, however, since several states also utilize lifetime appointments and many others utilize the Missouri plan, which requires only an uncontested (i.e., retention/rejection) election. Greater stress is placed on the possibility that "the state judge's allegiance to the Constitution may be weakened by his proximity to the state's enforcement of its criminal law." Developments. *Federal Habeas Corpus,* 83 Harv.L.Rev. 1038, 1061 (1970).[a] Still others point to "psychologi-

a. A related argument distinguishes between the function of the trial court and the habeas court, arguing that there is a need for a separate review of constitutional questions by a court that is not so closely tied to the "inquiry into guilt or innocence." "The momentum of the trial process cal and attitudinal characteristics." See, e.g., Neuborne, *The Myth of Parity,* 90 Harv.L.Rev. 1105, 1124–25 (1977), arguing that "federal district judges [are] more likely to enforce constitutional rights vigorously" (at least as compared to state trial judges) because: (1) "an elite tradition animates the federal judiciary, instilling elan and a sense of mission in federal judges * * * as heirs of a tradition of constitutional enforcement"; (2) "federal judges often display an enhanced sense of bureaucratic receptivity to the pronouncements of the Supreme Court's interpretation of the federal constitution"; and (3) "the scope of federal jurisdiction, even taking account of that over federal crimes and habeas corpus, is such that federal judges are insulated from the more cynicism-breeding dimensions of constitutional law." See also Cover and Aleinikoff, p. 1480 supra (federal courts tend to reflect a "utopian perspective" while state courts tend to reflect a "pragmatic perspective"). But cf. Israel, *Criminal Procedure, The Burger Court, and The Legacy of the Warren Court,* 75 Mich.L.Rev. 1319, 1407 (1977) (noting the high reversal rates on search and seizure issues for several state appellate courts, and concluding that, even before *Stone,* a state trial judge with "an inclination to ignore the Fourth Amendment" was more likely to be deterred by the prospect of reversal by a state appellate court than reversal by a federal habeas court). Does the capacity of state courts to fairly adjudicate federal constitutional claims vary with the nature of the claim, so that state courts may be less effective in protecting certain constitutional rights than they are in protecting Fourth Amendment rights? See *Rose v. Mitchell,* Note 3, p. 1493 infra (making such a distinction).

2. *Supreme Court review of state decisions.* What influence should *Stone* have upon the Supreme Court's exercise of its certiorari authority? In *Mincey v. Arizona,* described at p. 321 supra, Justice Marshall, joined by Justice Brennan, commented on what he viewed as "the additional responsibilities placed on this Court in the wake of *Stone*": "[W]e will often be faced with a Hobson's choice in cases of less than national significance that could formerly have been left to the lower federal courts: either to deny certiorari and thereby let stand divergent state and federal decisions with regard to Fourth Amendment rights; or to grant certiorari and thereby add to our calendar, which many believe is already overcrowded, cases that might better have been resolved elsewhere. In view of this problem and others, I hope that the Court will at some point reconsider the wisdom of *Stone v. Powell.*"

3. *The "opportunity for full and fair litigation" exception.* What view of habeas jurisdiction underlies the "full and fair litigation" exception recognized in *Stone*? Consider Seidman, *Factual Guilt and the Burger Court: An Examination of Continuity and Change in Criminal Procedure,* 80 Colum.L.Rev. 436, 456–459 (1980):

"The insistence upon an opportunity for a full and fair hearing becomes comprehensible only when one realizes that the Court has attempted to respond with one stroke to two fundamentally inconsistent arguments often marshalled in criticism of the Warren Court's expansion of habeas jurisdiction.[b] * * * The first argu-

and the trial judge's focus upon the central issue of the accused's guilt or innocence," it is argued, "tend to divert attention from ancillary questions relating to constitutional guarantees," while habeas corpus review provides a "dispassionate second look focused exclusively on adjudication of constitutional issues." Developments, supra, at p. 1488.

b. The author had previously noted: "[T]he [full and fair hearing] qualification is not easily comprehensible even if one reads *Stone,* as I have suggested, as resting on a judgment regarding the utility of the exclusionary rule in different contexts. Since the state court's putative denial of an opportunity for a fair hearing occurs after the fourth amendment violation has taken place, it is hard to see how that denial has any impact at all on the deterrent efficacy of the rule. To be sure, if a state had a consistent *policy* of declining to enforce the rule on direct review, that policy might seriously detract from the rule's deterrent impact and so necessitate federal intervention. But the *Stone* Court nowhere suggests that a defendant must demonstrate such a policy to ment, stated most forcefully in a seminal article by Judge Friendly [p. 1473 supra], is that habeas corpus relief should be reserved for those cases in which the petitioner asserts a colorable claim of factual innocence. The argument is premised on the assumptions that the basic goal of the criminal justice system is to separate the guilty from the innocent and that the flood of habeas petitions raising claims that are not guilt-related is interfering with the realization of that goal. * * * A wholly separate argument in favor of less expansive habeas jurisdiction, associated with the writings of Professor Bator [p. 1474 supra], is that habeas relief for state prisoners should be geared to only those instances where the state's own mechanism for adjudicating the claims presented in the habeas petition has been inadequate. Thus, a state's faulty procedures trigger a need for federal intervention regardless of the ultimate 'correctness' of the state's decision. Indeed, whereas Judge Friendly wishes to limit habeas *to* questions of ultimate fact, Professor Bator wishes to limit habeas *because* questions of ultimate fact are ultimately unanswerable. * * * For Judge Friendly, the petitioner's factual guilt or innocence is crucial; for Professor Bator, it is unknowable and, therefore, in the end, irrelevant. * * * The result in *Stone* seems confused because the Court has coupled Judge Friendly's rhetoric with Professor Bator's test for finality. The 'full and fair hearing' qualification is a direct outgrowth of Professor Bator's insistence that the central role for habeas corpus is not to assure that federal questions are correctly decided, but to assure that they are decided by procedures calculated to reach a correct decision."

4. What constitutes "an opportunity for full and fair litigation of a Fourth Amendment claim"? Lower courts applying this standard have generally agreed that a two step inquiry is required: (1) whether the state procedural mechanism is satisfactory in the abstract, and (2) whether there was a failure of the mechanism in the individual case. Since state procedures for raising Fourth Amendment claims tend to be very much like the suppression motion procedure followed in the federal courts, a finding of inadequacy is most likely to come under the second inquiry. See, e.g., *Boyd v. Mintz,* 631 F.2d 247 (3d Cir.1980) (petitioner did not receive adequate opportunity when his counsel was appointed one day before the expiration of the time period for presenting a suppression motion and the trial court applied an unwritten local rule mandating a written application in denying counsel's oral request for an extension); *Riley v. Gray,* 674 F.2d 522 (6th Cir.1982) (petitioner was denied an adequate opportunity where a state appellate court sustained the motion to suppress on the ground that a recent decision had eliminated the concept of automatic standing, but then failed to remand the case so as to allow a surprised petitioner [the standing issue had not been raised by the state] to establish his standing under the newly adopted decision).

5. Should a state court's adoption of a clearly erroneous interpretation of the Fourth Amendment constitute a denial of the required opportunity? Lower courts generally have answered in the negative. See LaFave and Israel, § 27.3(d). They note that the *Stone* Court did not suggest that defendant Rice had been denied the required opportunity, notwithstanding Justice Brennan's characterization of the Nebraska Supreme Court's ruling as relying on a "patently untenable ground." They also reason that allowing the *Stone* exception to be based on any form of substantive error would render *Stone* "a nullity, since petitioners would routinely allege the necessary error." Halpern, *Federal Habeas Corpus and the Mapp Exclusionary Rule After Stone v. Powell,* 82 Colum.L.Rev.

justify habeas review. Taken at face value, the Court seems to be saying that the mere isolated failure of the state court to provide an opportunity for a hearing in the defendant's case is sufficient to support federal habeas intervention."

1 (1982). But consider *Gamble v. Oklahoma,* 583 F.2d 1161 (10th Cir.1978). Petitioner there claimed that his incriminating statements to the police had been the fruit of an illegal arrest. Although petitioner brought to the state courts' attention the recent decision of the Supreme Court in *Brown v. Illinois,* p. 805 supra, that decision was not cited by the state courts in rejecting petitioner's claim. The last appellate court opinion simply noted that the claim was without merit since *Miranda* warnings automatically eliminated the taint of the illegal arrest. The federal habeas court concluded that the state courts had simply ignored *Brown* and the defendant therefore had been denied "full and fair consideration" of his claim: "The [*Stone* standard] contemplates recognition and at least colorable application of the correct Fourth Amendment constitutional standard. Thus, a federal court is not precluded from considering Fourth Amendment claims in habeas corpus proceedings where the state court wilfully refuses to apply the correct and controlling constitutional standards." The *Gamble* court also noted that it could "foresee the possibility that the correct federal standard could be applied, but in a manner so unconscionable as to deny a defendant the opportunity for *full* and *fair* litigation."

6. Does the "opportunity exception" apply where the state procedure was fair, but the Fourth Amendment claim was not considered by the state courts because defense counsel negligently failed to present that claim? Under *Wainwright v. Sykes,* discussed at p. 1506 infra, a procedural default does not bar review of a constitutional claim if petitioner can establish "cause and prejudice." Should the same standard apply to Fourth Amendment issues, with a procedural default sufficiently excusable and sufficiently harmful to meet *Sykes'* "cause and prejudice" standard treated as constituting a denial of an opportunity for full and fair litigation? Consider *O'Berry v. Wainwright,* 546 F.2d 1204 (5th Cir.1977) (court divided, with the majority suggesting that the key is solely the opportunity provided by state law). If error by counsel would constitute "cause and prejudice" only when it reaches the level of constitutional incompetency of counsel (see Note 4, p. 1523 infra), will it matter whether "*Stone* preempts the normal habeas rule on procedural defaults and looks only to the adequacy of the state's corrective process, or whether it incorporates the current default standard in assessing the opportunity provided the petitioner, the result is likely to be the same"? LaFave and Israel, § 27.3(d). See Strazzella, *Ineffective Assistance of Counsel Claims: New Uses, New Problems,* 19 Ariz.L.Rev. 443, 480–81 (1977) (suggesting that, under one view of *Stone,* constitutional ineffectiveness of counsel may be taken to have deprived a defendant of the "opportunity" required by *Stone*); *Sallie v. North Carolina,* 587 F.2d 636 (4th Cir.1978) (suggesting that incompetency of counsel is a separate issue, apart from the opportunity required by *Stone,* and relief can be granted on an incompetency claim based solely on counsel's failure to challenge an obviously unconstitutional search; a concurring judge objected, however, that this approach would have the "effect of sweeping aside *Stone*"). But note *LiPuma v. Commissioner,* 560 F.2d 84, 93 (2d Cir.1977) (suggesting that, where defendant's ineffective assistance claim is based on counsel's failure to raise a timely motion to suppress, *Stone* bars consideration of that claim because the state has provided "an opportunity for full and fair litigation" and an "alleged Fourth Amendment violation" lies "at the heart of the case").

ON EXTENDING STONE TO OTHER CLAIMS

1. *Other non-cognizable claims.* Following *Stone v. Powell,* there was considerable speculation as to whether constitutional claims other than Fourth Amendment claims also would be viewed as not cognizable under federal habeas corpus (provid-

ed the state had provided an "opportunity for full and fair litigation" of the claim). Some commentators noted that Justice Powell's *Stone* opinion differed from his *Schneckloth* concurring opinion in placing greater emphasis upon the special aspects of the exclusionary rule and less emphasis upon the general function and costs of federal habeas review. This difference, they suggested, might lead the Court to limit *Stone* to Fourth Amendment claims. Other commentators agreed that the *Stone* rationale was fairly narrow, but concluded that it should also encompass other constitutional claims based upon a "prophylactic remedy" concept, such as *Miranda* violations. Still other commentators speculated, however, that the *Stone* decision would be extended to all "non-jurisdictional" claims that did not relate to the possible innocence of the defendant. What do the following Supreme Court rulings suggest as to the likely extension of *Stone?*

2. *Evidentiary insufficiency.* In JACKSON v. VIRGINIA, 443 U.S. 307, 99 S.Ct. 2781, 61 L.Ed.2d 560 (1979), the question presented, as stated by the Court, was "what standard [should] be applied in a federal habeas corpus proceeding when the claim is made that a person has been convicted in a state court upon insufficient evidence." The lower federal courts had held that a due process violation was established only if the trial record was "wholly devoid of any relevant evidence of a crucial element of the offense charged." This "no-evidence standard" was derived from *Thompson v. Louisville,* 362 U.S. 199, 80 S.Ct. 624, 4 L.Ed.2d 654 (1960), which held that a conviction totally devoid of evidentiary support constituted an "arbitrary deprivation of liberty." However, in a later case, *In re Winship,* 397 U.S. 358, 90 S.Ct. 1068, 25 L.Ed.2d 368 (1970), the Supreme Court had noted that a state must require its factfinders in criminal cases to apply the traditional evidentiary standard of proof beyond a reasonable doubt. A 5–3 majority in *Jackson* concluded that *Winship* also required appellate courts and federal habeas courts to apply the reasonable doubt standard in their review of the sufficiency of the trial evidence. In reaching that conclusion, the majority rejected the contention that requiring a habeas court to apply the *Winship* standard would be inconsistent with the analysis of *Stone v. Powell.* On this point, the majority opinion, per STEWART, J., noted:

"[T]he respondent has urged that any departure from the *Thompson* test in federal habeas corpus proceedings will expand the number of meritless claims brought to the federal courts, will duplicate the work of the state appellate courts, will disserve the societal interest in the finality of state criminal proceedings, and will increase friction between the federal and state judiciaries. In sum, counsel for the State urges that this type of constitutional claim should be deemed to fall within the limit on federal habeas corpus jurisdiction identified in *Stone v. Powell,* with respect to Fourth Amendment claims. We disagree.

"First, the burden that is likely to follow from acceptance of the *Winship* standard has, we think, been exaggerated. Federal court challenges to the evidentiary support for state convictions have since *Thompson* been dealt with under § 2254. A more stringent standard will expand the contours of this type of claim, but will not create an entirely new class of cases cognizable on federal habeas corpus. Furthermore, most meritorious challenges to constitutional sufficiency of the evidence undoubtedly will be recognized in the state courts, and, if the state courts have fully considered the issue of sufficiency, the task of a federal habeas court should not be difficult. And this type of claim can almost always be judged on the written record without need for an evidentiary hearing in the federal court.

"Second, the problems of finality and federal-state comity arise whenever a state prisoner invokes the jurisdiction of a federal court to redress an alleged constitutional violation. * * * Although state appellate review undoubtedly will serve in the vast majority of cases to vindicate the due process protection that follows from *Winship,* the same could also be said of the vast majority of other federal constitutional rights that may be implicated in a state criminal trial. It is the occasional abuse that the federal writ of habeas corpus stands ready to correct. * * * The constitutional issue presented in this case is far different from the kind of issue that was the subject of the Court's decision in *Stone v. Powell,* supra. The question whether a defendant has been convicted upon inadequate evidence is central to the basic question of guilt or innocence."

In response to the majority's arguments, STEVENS, J. (joined by Burger, C.J., and Rehnquist, J.) contended that the standard of review required by the majority would be "seriously harmful to both the State and Federal Judiciaries"—"undermin[ing] the morale and esteem of the State Judiciary" and "impos[ing] countless additional hours of unproductive labor on federal judges and their assistants." Moreover, Justice Stevens noted, the majority's standard would not "significantly reduce the risk of * * * erroneous convictions," for there was no "appreciable risk that a factfinding made by a jury beyond a reasonable doubt, and twice reviewed by a trial judge on directed verdict and post-trial motions and by one or more levels of [state] appellate courts on direct appeal, as well as by two federal courts under the *Thompson* 'no evidence' rule, is likely to be erroneous." The *Stone* case, Justice Stevens argued, was clearly relevant:

"In the past, collateral review of state proceedings has been justified largely on the grounds (1) that federal judges have special expertise in the federal issues that regularly arise in habeas corpus proceeding, and (2) that they are less susceptible than state judges to political pressures against applying constitutional rules to overturn convictions. But neither of these justifications has any force in the present context. State judges are more familiar with the elements of state offenses than are federal judges and should be better able to evaluate sufficiency claims. Moreover, of all decisions overturning convictions, the least likely to be unpopular and thus to distort state decisionmaking processes are ones based on the inadequacy of the evidence. Indeed, once federal courts were divested of authority to second-guess state courts on Fourth Amendment issues, which are far more likely to generate politically motivated state-court decisions, see *Stone v. Powell,* a like result in this case would seem to be a fortiori."

3. *Discrimination in grand jury composition.* In ROSE v. MITCHELL, 443 U.S. 545, 99 S.Ct. 2993, 61 L.Ed.2d 739 (1979), a divided Court held that the petitioners there, state prisoners convicted of murder, had failed to establish racial discrimination in the selection of the foreman of the grand jury that indicted them. Seven of the Justices also considered the related question as to whether the petitioners' claim was properly cognizable on habeas corpus. Justice Blackmun's opinion for the Court, joined in this part by Justices Brennan, White, Marshall, and Stevens, held that the claim was cognizable. Justice Powell, joined by Justice Rehnquist, disagreed. Justice BLACKMUN noted:

"The State makes the additional argument that the decision in *Stone v. Powell* should be extended so as to foreclose a grant of federal habeas corpus relief to a state prisoner on the ground of discrimination in the selection of the grand jury. Mr. Justice Powell, dissenting in *Castaneda v. Partida,* [p. 1275 supra], joined by The Chief Justice and Mr. Justice Rehnquist, and at least inferentially by Mr. Justice Stewart, specifically observed that a 'strong case may be made that claims of grand jury discrimination are not cognizable on federal habeas corpus after *Stone v. Powell.*' In this connection, Mr. Justice Powell noted that a claim by a convicted prisoner of grand jury discrimination goes only to the 'moot determination by the grand jury that there was sufficient cause to proceed to trial [and not to any] flaw in the trial itself.' He concluded that, as in *Stone,* 'the incremental benefit of extending habeas corpus as a means of correcting unconstitutional grand jury selection procedures might be viewed as "outweighed by acknowledged costs to other values vital to a rational system of justice."' The State echoes these arguments. * * *

"In *Stone v. Powell,* * * * the Court made it clear that it was confining its ruling to cases involving the judicially created exclusionary rule, which had minimal utility when applied in a habeas corpus proceeding. * * * Mindful of this limited reach of *Stone,* we conclude that a claim of discrimination in the selection of the grand jury differs so fundamentally from application on habeas of the Fourth Amendment exclusionary rule that the reasoning of *Stone v. Powell* should not be extended to foreclose habeas review of such claims in federal court.

"In the first place, claims such as those pressed by respondents in this case concern allegations that the trial court itself violated the Fourteenth Amendment in the operation of the grand jury system. In most such cases, as in this one, this same trial court will be the court that initially must decide the merits of such a claim, finding facts and applying the law to those facts. This leads us to doubt that claims that the operation of the grand jury system violates the Fourteenth Amendment in general will receive the type of full and fair hearing deemed essential to the holding of *Stone.* In Fourth Amendment cases, courts are called upon to evaluate the actions of the police in seizing evidence, and this Court believed that State courts were as capable of performing this task as federal habeas courts. See *Stone* at n. 35. But claims that the state judiciary itself has purposely violated the Equal Protection Clause are different. There is a need in such cases to ensure that an independent means of obtaining review by a federal court is available on a broader basis than review only by this Court will permit. A federal forum must be available if a full and fair hearing of such claims is to be had.

"Beyond this, there are fundamental differences between the claim here at issue and the claim at issue in *Stone v. Powell.* Allegations of grand jury discrimination involve charges that state officials are violating the direct command of the Fourteenth Amendment, * * *. Since the first days after adoption of the Amendment, the Court has recognized that by its direct operation the Equal Protection Clause forbids the States to discriminate in the selection of members of a grand jury. This contrasts with the situation in *Stone,* where the Court considered application of 'a judicially created remedy rather than a personal constitutional right.' Indeed, whereas the Fourteenth Amendment by its terms always has been directly applicable to the States, the Fourth Amendment and its attendant exclusionary rule only recently have been applied fully to the States. In this context, the federalism concerns that motivated the Court to adopt the rule of *Stone v. Powell* are not present. Federal courts have granted relief to state prisoners upon proof of the proscribed discrimination for nearly a century. See, e.g., *Virginia v. Rives,* 100 U.S. 313, 25 L.Ed. 667 (1880). * * *

"Further, *Stone* rested to a large extent on the Court's perception that the exclusionary rule is of minimal value when applied in a federal habeas proceeding. The Court there found that the deterrent value of the exclusionary rule was not enhanced by the possibility that a 'conviction obtained in state court and affirmed on direct review might be overturned in collateral proceedings often occurring years after the incarceration of the defendant.' Nor did the Court believe that the 'overall educative effect of the exclusionary rule would be appreciably diminished if search-and-seizure claims could not be raised in federal habeas review of state convictions.' And it could not find any basis to say that federal review would reveal flaws in the search or seizure that had gone undetected at trial or on appeal. Ibid. In these circumstances, the Court concluded that the benefits of applying the Fourth Amendment exclusionary rule on federal habeas did not outweigh the costs associated with it.

"None of this reasoning has force here. Federal habeas review is necessary to ensure that constitutional defects in the state judiciary's grand jury selection procedure are not overlooked by the very state judges who operate that system. There is strong reason to believe that federal review would indeed reveal flaws not appreciated by state judges perhaps too close to the day-to-day operation of their system to be able properly to evaluate claims that the system is defective. The educative and deterrent effect of federal review is likely to be great, since the state officials who operate the system, judges or employees of the judiciary, may be expected to take note of a federal court's determination that their procedures are unconstitutional and must be changed. * * * It is also true that the concern with judicial integrity, deprecated by the Court in *Stone* in the context of habeas review of exclusionary rule issues, is of much greater concern in grand jury discrimination cases. The claim that the court has discriminated on the basis of race in a given case brings the integrity of the judicial system into direct question. The force of this justification for extending federal habeas review cannot be said to be minimal where allegations of improper judicial conduct are made.

" * * * [One] is tempted to exaggerate the costs associated with quashing an indictment returned by an improperly constituted grand jury. In fact, the costs associated with quashing an indictment are significantly less than those associated with suppressing evidence. Evidence suppressed under the Fourth Amendment may not be used by the State in any new trial, though it be highly probative on the issue of guilt. In contrast, after a federal court quashes an indictment, the State remains free to use at a second trial any and all evidence it employed at the first proceeding. A prisoner who is guilty in fact is less likely to go free, therefore, than in cases involving the exclusionary rule. Providing federal habeas corpus relief is, as a consequence, less of an intrusion on the State's system of criminal justice than was the case in *Stone.*

"Finally, we note that the constitutional interests that a federal court adjudicating a claim on habeas of grand jury discrimination seeks to vindicate are substantially more compelling than those at issue in *Stone.* As noted above, discrimination on account of race in the administration of justice strikes at the core concerns of the Fourteenth Amendment and at fundamental values of our society and our legal system. Where discrimination that is 'at war with our basic concepts of a democratic society and a representative government,' *Smith v. Texas,* 311 U.S. [128,] 130, 61 S.Ct. [164,] 165 (1940), infects the legal system, the strong interest in making available federal habeas corpus relief outweighs the costs associated with such relief."

Justice POWELL, responding to the majority, relied largely on the analysis advanced in his concurring opinion in *Schneckloth v. Bustamonte.* He expressed strong disagreement with the claim that no serious "federalism concerns" were presented by the majority's ruling. While federal courts had reviewed state grand jury claims over the years, the earlier cases involved either review on direct appeal or habeas review where the challenge went to the selection of the petit jury as well as the grand jury. Justice Powell also characterized as "wholly unacceptable" the suggestion that "state judges cannot be trusted to rule fairly" on grand jury discrimination claims. Trial judges, he noted, often are "called upon to rule on the validity of their own judicial and administrative actions." Briefly summarizing his criticism, Justice Powell noted:

"Preventing discrimination in the selection of grand juries * * * is a goal of high priority in our system. But the question is not simply, as the Court seems to think, whether the goal and the interests it serves are important. Habeas corpus is not a general writ meant to promote the social good or vindicate all societal interests of even the highest priority. The question rather is whether this ancient writ, developed by the law to serve a precise and particular purpose, properly may be employed for the furthering of the general societal goal of grand jury integrity. For the provision of indictment by grand jury does not protect innocent defendants from unjust convictions. Rather, it helps to assure that innocent persons will not be made unjustly to stand trial at all. Once a defendant is found guilty beyond a reasonable doubt by a fairly drawn petit jury, following a fair trial, he hardly can claim that it was unjust to have made him stand trial. Because the need to protect the innocent from incarceration is not implicated in cases such as this, the writ of habeas corpus is not an appropriate remedy. Other remedies can be, and have been, provided to protect society's interest in eliminating racial discrimination in the selection of those who are to serve on grand juries."

4. *Confessions.* In *Wainwright v. Sykes,* p. 1506 infra, the Court held that petitioner was barred by a procedural default from presenting a claimed *Miranda* violation, but a footnote in Justice Rehnquist's opinion added:

> [The State] does not argue, and we do not pause to consider, whether a bare allegation of a *Miranda* violation, without accompanying assertions going to the actual voluntariness or reliability of the confession, is a proper subject for consideration on federal habeas review, where there has been a full and fair opportunity to raise the argument in the state proceedings. See *Stone v. Powell.*

In *Brewer v. Williams,* [p. 626 supra] the Court held that the Sixth Amendment ruling of *Massiah v. United States* barred use of a confession obtained from an accused without a proper waiver of his right to counsel. Chief Justice Burger, in a wide-ranging dissent, suggested that *Stone* should be extended to such Sixth Amendment violations where the evidence was reliable and probative of guilt. Justice Powell, in a concurring opinion, noted that it was not appropriate to consider the applicability of *Stone* because that issue had not been considered by the lower court or presented by counsel. He added that "many Fifth and Sixth Amendment claims arise in the context of challenges to the fairness of a trial or the integrity of the factfinding process," but others "more closely parallel claims under the Fourth Amendment." In *Nix v. Williams (Williams II),* p. 810 supra, the Court again noted that there was no need to decide whether "*Stone v. Powell* should be extended to bar federal habeas review of Williams' Sixth Amendment claim." In *Cardwell v. Taylor,* 461 U.S. 571, 103 S.Ct. 2015, 76 L.Ed.2d 333 (1983), the Court summarily reversed a Ninth Circuit ruling recognizing a habeas challenge to the admissibility of a confession based upon *Dunaway v. New York* (p. 385 supra, excluding a confession as the fruit of an illegal arrest). While noting that the ruling below was contrary to *Stone,* the Court also pointed out that the habeas court was free to consider whether "the statements were involuntary, and therefore obtained in violation of the Fifth Amendment."[a]

a. In *White v. Finkbeiner,* 687 F.2d 885 (7th Cir.1982), vac'd on other grounds, 465 U.S. 1075, 104 S.Ct. 1433, 79 L.Ed.2d 756 (1984), the court offered two grounds for refusing to extend the *Stone* rationale to *Miranda* violations. First, the *Miranda* rule, unlike the *Mapp* exclusionary rule, effectuates a significant policy beyond the deterrence of police misconduct, as it also seeks to uphold the adversarial nature of the criminal justice system. Second, eliminating federal habeas jurisdiction over *Miranda* claims would not reduce the habeas caseload of the federal district courts, which was one of the underlying purposes of *Stone.* If petitioners were barred

5. In a substantial group of post-*Stone* cases that came to the federal courts via habeas corpus, the Supreme Court ruled on the merits of the petitioner's claim without any mention of *Stone.* Included were claims related to double jeopardy, incompetency of counsel, juror bias, consideration of testimony that arguably violated defendant's Fifth and Sixth Amendment rights (e.g., the misuse of testimony derived from a court-ordered psychiatric exam), the employment of a photo identification procedure alleged to be so suggestive as to violate due process, and due process violations in the revocation of probation. See LaFave and Israel, § 27.3(c). In light of the cases in which the Court specifically held open the possible extension of *Stone* (see Note 4 supra), should it be assumed that the above claims clearly pose no difficulties under *Stone?* If so, what do these rulings suggest about the possible extension of *Stone?* Consider also the post-*Stone* rulings discussed in sections 2 and 3 infra. Note, in particular, the opinions of Justice Stevens in *Rose v. Lundy* (Note 4, p. 1515 infra) and *Wainwright v. Sykes* (p. 1510 infra).

SECTION 2. CLAIMS FORECLOSED BY PROCEDURAL DEFAULTS

FAY v. NOIA

372 U.S. 391, 83 S.Ct. 822, 9 L.Ed.2d 837 (1963).

MR. JUSTICE BRENNAN delivered the opinion of the Court.

* * * Noia was convicted in 1942 with Santo Caminito and Frank Bonino * * * of a felony murder. * * * The sole evidence against each defendant was his signed confession. Caminito and Bonino, but not Noia, appealed their convictions to the Appellate Division of the New York Supreme Court. These appeals were unsuccessful, but subsequent legal proceedings resulted in the releases of Caminito and Bonino on findings that their confessions had been coerced and their convictions therefore procured in violation of the Fourteenth Amendment. Although it has been stipulated that the coercive nature of Noia's confession was also established, the United States District Court held in Noia's federal habeas corpus proceeding that because of his failure to appeal he must be denied relief under the provision of 28 U.S.C. § 2254 whereby "an application for writ of habeas corpus . . . shall not be granted unless it appears the applicant has exhausted remedies available in the courts of the State . . . ." The Court of Appeals reversed, one judge dissenting, and ordered that Noia's conviction be set aside and that he be discharged from custody unless given a new trial forthwith. * * *

* * * We affirm the judgment of the Court of Appeals but reach that court's result by a different course of reasoning. We hold: (1) Federal courts have *power* under the federal habeas statute to grant relief despite the applicant's failure to have pursued a state remedy not available to him at the time he applies; the doctrine under which state procedural defaults are held to constitute an adequate and independent state law ground barring direct Supreme Court review is not to be extended to limit the power granted the federal courts under the federal habeas statute. (2) Noia's failure to appeal was not a failure to exhaust "the remedies available in the courts of the State" as required by § 2254; that requirement refers only to a failure to exhaust state remedies still open

from challenging the admission of their statements under *Miranda,* they could still resort to the claim that the confession was involuntary, an issue clearly cognizable under habeas review. Does *Cardwell* in any way detract from the weight of the second ground? Consider also Schulhofer, *Confessions and the Court,* 79 Mich.L. Rev. 865 (1981): "Ironically, the extension of *Stone* to *Miranda* claims would not even remove the *Miranda* issue from the case, except in a purely theoretical sense: the habeas court still would have to determine whether the interrogated suspect had been warned of his rights, because such warnings are recognized as an important factor in due process analysis of the totality of the circumstances."

to the applicant at the time he files his application for habeas corpus in the federal court. (3) Noia's failure to appeal cannot under the circumstances be deemed an intelligent and understanding waiver of his right to appeal such as to justify the withholding of federal habeas corpus relief. * * *

[Parts I and II of the majority opinion, discussing the range of issues cognizable on a habeas petition, are reprinted at p. 1470 supra].

III.

We have reviewed the development of habeas corpus at some length because the question of the instant case has obvious importance to the proper accommodation of a great constitutional privilege and the requirements of the federal system. Our survey discloses nothing to suggest that the Federal District Court lacked the *power* to order Noia discharged because of a procedural forfeiture he may have incurred under state law. * * * At the time the privilege of the writ was written into the Federal Constitution it was settled that the writ lay to test any restraint contrary to fundamental law, which in England stemmed ultimately from Magna Charta but in this country was embodied in the written Constitution. Congress in 1867 sought to provide a federal forum for state prisoners having constitutional defenses by extending the habeas corpus powers of the federal courts to their constitutional maximum. Obedient to this purpose, we have consistently held that federal court jurisdiction is conferred by the allegation of an unconstitutional restraint and is not defeated by anything that may occur in the state court proceedings. State procedural rules plainly must yield to this overriding federal policy.

A number of arguments are advanced against this conclusion. One, which concedes the breadth of federal habeas power, is that a state prisoner who forfeits his opportunity to vindicate federal defenses in the state court has been given all the process that is constitutionally due him, and hence is not restrained contrary to the Constitution. But this wholly misconceives the scope of due process of law, which comprehends not only the right to be heard but also a number of explicit procedural rights—for example, the right not to be convicted upon evidence which includes one's coerced confession—drawn from the Bill of Rights. * * *

A variant of this argument is that if the state court declines to entertain a federal defense because of a procedural default, then the prisoner's custody is actually due to the default rather than to the underlying constitutional infringement, so that he is not in custody in violation of federal law. But this ignores the important difference between rights and particular remedies. * * * A defendant by committing a procedural default may be debarred from challenging his conviction in the state courts even on federal constitutional grounds. But a forfeiture of remedies does not legitimize the unconstitutional conduct by which his conviction was procured. * * *

It is a familiar principle that this Court will decline to review state court judgments which rest on independent and adequate state grounds, notwithstanding the co-presence of federal grounds. * * * *Murdock v. Memphis,* 87 U.S. (20 Wall.) 590, 22 L.Ed. 429 [1874]. * * * Thus, a default such as Noia's, if deemed adequate and independent (a question on which we intimate no view), would cut off review by this Court of the state coram nobis proceeding in which the New York Court of Appeals refused him relief. It is contended that it follows from this that the remedy of federal habeas corpus is likewise cut off.

The fatal weakness of this contention is its failure to recognize that the adequate state-ground rule is a function of the limitations of *appellate* review. * * * [T]he *Murdock* case is devoted to demonstrating the Court's lack of jurisdiction on direct review to decide questions of state law in cases also raising federal questions. It followed from this holding that if the state question was dispositive of the case, the Court could not decide the federal question. The federal question was moot; nothing turned on its resolution.

But while our appellate function is concerned only with the judgments or decrees of state courts, the habeas corpus jurisdiction of the lower federal courts is not so confined. The jurisdictional prerequisite is not the judgment of a state court but detention *simpliciter.* The entire course of decisions in this Court elaborating the rule of exhaustion of state remedies is wholly incompatible with the proposition that a state court *judgment* is required to confer federal habeas jurisdiction. And the broad power of the federal courts under 28 U.S.C. § 2243 summarily to hear the application and to "determine the facts, and dispose of the matter as law and justice require," is hardly characteristic of an appellate jurisdiction. Habeas lies to enforce the right of personal liberty; when that right is denied and a person confined, the federal court has the power to release him. Indeed, it has no other power; it cannot revise the state court judgment; it can act only on the body of the petitioner.

To be sure, this may not be the entire answer to the contention that the adequate state-ground principle should apply to the federal courts on habeas corpus as well as to the Supreme Court on direct review of state judgments. * * * For the federal courts to refuse to give effect in habeas proceedings to state procedural defaults might conceivably have some effect upon the States' regulation of their criminal procedures. * * * [However, the] state's interest in an airtight system of forfeitures is of a different order from that, vindicated in *Murdock,* in the autonomy of state law within the proper sphere of its substantive regulation.

* * * A practical appraisal of the state interest here involved plainly does not justify the federal courts' enforcing on habeas corpus a doctrine of forfeitures under the guise of applying the adequate state-ground rule. We fully grant that the exigencies of federalism warrant a limitation whereby the federal judge has the discretion to deny relief to one who has deliberately sought to subvert or evade the orderly adjudication of his federal defenses in the state courts. Surely no stricter rule is a realistic necessity. A man under conviction for crime has an obvious inducement to do his very best to keep his state remedies open, and not stake his all on the outcome of a federal habeas proceeding which, in many respects, may be less advantageous to him than a state court proceeding. And if because of inadvertence or neglect he runs afoul of a state procedural requirement, and thereby forfeits his state remedies, appellate and collateral, as well as direct review thereof in this Court, those consequences should be sufficient to vindicate the State's valid interest in orderly procedure.

* * * For these several reasons we reject as unsound in principle, as well as not supported in authority, the suggestion that the federal courts are without power to grant habeas relief to an applicant whose federal claims would not be heard on direct review in this Court because of a procedural default furnishing an adequate and independent ground of state decision. * * *

IV.

Although we hold that the jurisdiction of the federal courts on habeas corpus is not affected by procedural defaults incurred by the applicant during the state court proceedings, we recognize a limited discretion in the federal judge to deny relief to an applicant under certain circumstances. Discretion is implicit in the statutory command that the judge, after granting the writ and holding a hearing of appropriate scope, "dispose of the matter as law and justice require," 28 U.S.C. § 2243; and discretion was the flexible concept employed by the federal courts in developing the exhaustion rule. Furthermore, habeas corpus has traditionally been regarded as governed by equitable principles. * * * Among them is the principle that a suitor's conduct in relation to the matter at hand may disentitle him to the relief he seeks. Narrowly circumscribed, in conformity to the historical role of the writ of habeas corpus as an effective and imperative remedy for detentions contrary to fundamental law, the principle is unexceptionable. We therefore hold that the federal habeas judge may in his discretion deny relief to an applicant who has deliberately bypassed the orderly procedure of the state courts and in so doing has forfeited his state court remedies.

But we wish to make very clear that this grant of discretion is not to be interpreted as a permission to introduce legal fictions into federal habeas corpus. The classic definition of waiver enunciated in *Johnson v. Zerbst,* 304 U.S. 458, 464, 58 S.Ct. 1019, 1023, 82 L.Ed. 1461 [1938]—"An intentional relinquishment or abandonment of a known right or privilege"—furnishes the controlling standard. If a habeas applicant, after consultation with competent counsel or otherwise, understandingly and knowingly forewent the privilege of seeking to vindicate his federal claims in the state courts, whether for strategic, tactical, or any other reasons that can fairly be described as the deliberate bypassing of state procedures, then it is open to the federal court on habeas to deny him all relief if the state courts refused to entertain his federal claims on the merits—though of course only after the federal court has satisfied itself, by holding a hearing or by some other means, of the facts bearing upon the applicant's default. * * * At all events we wish it clearly understood that the standard here put forth depends on the considered choice of the petitioner.[44] * * * A choice made by counsel not participated in by the petitioner does not automatically bar relief. Nor does a state court's finding of waiver bar independent determination of the question by the federal courts on habeas, for waiver affecting federal rights is a federal question. * * *

The application of the standard we have adumbrated to the facts of the instant case is not difficult. Under no reasonable view can the State's version of Noia's reason for not appealing support an inference of deliberate bypassing of the state court system. For Noia to have appealed in 1942 would have been to run a substantial risk of electrocution. His was the grisly choice whether to sit content with life imprisonment or to travel the uncertain avenue of appeal which, if successful, might well have led to a retrial and death sentence. * * * He declined to play Russian roulette in this fashion. This was a choice by Noia not to appeal, but under the circumstances it cannot realistically be deemed a merely tactical or strategic litigation step, or in any way a deliberate circumvention of state procedures. This is not to say that in every case where a heavier penalty, even the death penalty, is a risk incurred by taking an appeal or otherwise foregoing a procedural right, waiver as we have defined it cannot be found. Each case must stand on its facts. In the instant case, the language of the judge in sentencing Noia made the risk that Noia, if reconvicted, would be sentenced to death, palpable and indeed unusually acute.[a]

44. To the extent that any decisions of this Court may be read to suggest a standard of discretion in federal habeas corpus proceedings different from what we lay down today, such decisions shall be deemed overruled to the extent of any inconsistency.

a. [Footnote 3, by the Court, here transposed] * * * The District Court held a hearing limited to an inquiry into the facts surrounding Noia's failure to appeal but made no findings as to Noia's reasons. Noia and the lawyer who defended him at his trial testified. Noia said that while aware of his right to appeal, he did not appeal because he did not wish to saddle his family with an additional financial burden and had no funds of his own. The gist of the lawyer's testimony was that Noia was also motivated not to appeal by fear that if successful he might get the death

It should be unnecessary to repeat what so often has been said and what so plainly is the case: that the availability of the Great Writ of habeas corpus in the federal courts for persons in the custody of the States offends no legitimate state interest in the enforcement of criminal justice or procedure. * * * Surely no fair-minded person will contend that those who have been deprived of their liberty without due process of law ought nevertheless to languish in prison. Noia, no less than his codefendants Caminito and Bonino, is conceded to have been the victim of unconstitutional state action. Noia's case stands on its own; but surely no just and humane legal system can tolerate a result whereby a Caminito and a Bonino are at liberty because their confessions were found to have been coerced yet a Noia, whose confession was also coerced, remains in jail for life. For such anomalies, such affronts to the conscience of a civilized society habeas corpus is predestined by its historical role in the struggle for personal liberty to be the ultimate remedy. If the States withhold effective remedy, the federal courts have the power and the duty to provide it. Habeas corpus is one of the precious heritages of Anglo-American civilization. We do no more today than confirm its continuing efficacy.

MR. JUSTICE HARLAN, whom MR. JUSTICE CLARK and MR. JUSTICE STEWART join, dissenting.

I dissent from the Court's opinion and judgment for the reason that the federal courts have no *power*, statutory or constitutional, to release the respondent Noia from state detention. This is because his custody by New York does not violate any federal right, since it is pursuant to a conviction whose validity rests upon an adequate and independent state ground which the federal courts are required to respect.

[Justice Harlan's opinion first reviewed the previous Supreme Court decisions determining the scope of the writ. See fn. c at p. 1501 supra. Justice Harlan noted, in particular, that even though the Court extended the range of cognizable issues in *Brown v. Allen,* it ruled in a companion case, *Daniels v. Allen,* that habeas relief was not available where the state "decision to detain [the petitioner] rested not on the determination of a federal claim but rather on an adequate non-federal ground which would have barred direct review [by the Supreme Court]." [b] Taking into consideration the total course of the Court's decisions, including *Daniels,* Justice Harlan concluded that the majority's ruling in *Noia* "finds virtually no support in more than a century of this Court's experience"].

[Justice Harlan's opinion then discussed the rationale underlying the "rule that an adequate and independent state ground bars Supreme Court review of the state court decision." He noted that where the state decision rests on an adequate state ground, a ruling by the Supreme Court on the federal question alone would constitute an advisory opinion, forbidden by

sentence if convicted on a retrial. The trial judge, not bound to accept the jury's recommendation of a life sentence, had said when sentencing him, "I have thought seriously about rejecting the recommendation of the jury in your case, Noia, because I feel that if the jury knew who you were and what you were and your background as a robber, they would not have made a recommendation. But you have got a good lawyer, that is my wife. The last thing she told me this morning is to give you a chance." Noia's confession included an admission that he was the one who had actually shot the victim.

b. Justice Harlan noted, however, that he did not necessarily support the finding that an adequate nonfederal ground existed in *Daniels.* The trial court there had given the defendant 60 days within which to file an appeal. Defense counsel hand delivered the appeal papers on the 61st day, which was the day on which the papers would have arrived if mailed on the 60th day as permitted by the trial court's order. The state court nevertheless held that the appeal was not timely and refused to consider it. The Supreme Court divided (6–3) in finding that the petitioner's detention rested on an adequate state ground. Justice Frankfurter's dissent stressed that the state did not have a statutorily fixed period for taking an appeal.

Article III, since the state ground would still cover the disposition of the case. See *Murdock* (p. 1498 supra). This same constitutional limitation on federal court authority, he noted, also applied to the federal habeas court. That court was "constitutionally [no] more free than the Supreme Court on direct review to 'ignore' the adequate state ground."]

Of course, as the majority states, a judgment is not a "jurisdictional prerequisite" to a habeas corpus application * * * but that is wholly irrelevant. The point is that if the applicant is detained *pursuant* to a judgment, termination of the detention necessarily nullifies the judgment. * * * In habeas as on direct review, ordering the prisoner's release invalidates the judgment of conviction and renders ineffective the state rule relied upon to sustain that judgment. Try as the majority does to turn habeas corpus into a roving commission of inquiry into every possible invasion of the applicant's civil rights that may ever have occurred, it cannot divorce the writ from a judgment of conviction if that judgment is the basis of the detention. * * *

It [therefore] is the adequacy, or fairness, of the state ground that should be the controlling question in this case. New York asserts that a claim of the kind involved here must be raised on timely appeal if it is to be preserved, and contends that in permitting an appeal it has provided a reasonable opportunity for the claim to be made. * * * Under the circumstances here—particularly the fact that Noia was represented by counsel whose competence is not challenged—is this a reasonable ground for barring collateral assertion of the federal claim? Certainly the State has a vital interest in requiring that appeals be taken on the basis of facts known at the time, since the first assertion of a claim many years later might otherwise require release long after it was feasible to hold a new trial. And although in *Daniels v. Allen* [fn. b supra] it might have been argued that the State's refusal to entertain an appeal actually received on time amounted to an evasion of the federal claim, no such argument can be made here, since no appeal was *ever* sought. * * *

* * * I recognize that Noia's predicament may well be thought one that strongly calls for correction. But the proper course to that end lies with the New York Governor's powers of executive clemency, not with the federal courts. Since Noia is detained pursuant to a state judgment whose validity rests on an adequate and independent state ground, the judgment below should be reversed.

Notes and Questions

1. *The significance of Fay. Fay v. Noia* has frequently been characterized as one of the "landmark" decisions of the "Warren Court." See Gibbons, *Waiver: Habeas Corpus Jurisdiction,* 2 Seton H.L.Rev. 291 (1971). It has been so characterized not only because of its ruling relating to "procedural forfeitures," but also because of its possible impact upon other areas of the law. Thus, *Fay v. Noia* has been cited as a major factor contributing to the Court's development of the doctrine of non-retroactive application of certain decisions adopting expanded interpretations of constitutional guarantees. See Ch. 2, § 3. Gibbons, supra, suggests that *Fay's* expansion of habeas corpus jurisdiction may have contributed as well to the development of the doctrine of "harmless constitutional error." See Ch. 11, § 2. *Fay's* adoption of a deliberate bypass standard commonly also is credited with having delayed the development of more stringent constitutional standards relating to the adequacy of counsel, since it permitted the habeas court to focus on the merits of the defendant's claim rather than the inadequacy of counsel in failing to present that claim in the state proceedings. See Meador, *The Impact of Federal Habeas Corpus on State Trial Procedures,* 52 Va.L.Rev. 286 (1966) (suggesting that *Fay* represented "the Supreme Court's indirect way of get-

ting at the problem of ineffective representation of criminal defendants").

The significance of the *Fay* bypass standard may lie primarily in past developments; its future application in habeas proceedings may be quite limited. See Note 3, p. 1514 infra. Indeed, in *Wainwright v. Sykes,* infra, the majority "leaves for another day" consideration of the continuing significance of *Fay* even as to the particular procedural omission—the failure to appeal—presented on the facts of *Fay.* See n. 12 at p. 1507 infra. Yet, even if the deliberate bypass standard eventually is rejected *in toto* by the Supreme Court, it might retain considerable significance for state post-conviction remedies. The *Fay* deliberate bypass standard remains a most widely used state standard for determining whether a failure to comply with procedural requirements in the original state proceedings will bar a state collateral attack. See LaFave and Israel, § 27.11(c) (discussing the Uniform Post-Conviction Procedure Act).

2. *"Deliberate bypass" versus "waiver."* Does *Fay* suggest a deliberate bypass will exist only when there has been a "true waiver" under the *Johnson v. Zerbst* standard, i.e., the "intentional relinquishment * * * of a known right"? If so, how would one explain the district court's discretion to exercise jurisdiction and grant relief even when there has been a deliberate bypass (i.e., waiver)? If there has been a waiver, can the petitioner's custody still be viewed as being "in violation of the Constitution"? Consider *A.B.A. Standards, Relating to Post-Conviction Remedies* 36 (1968), noting with respect to a waiver: "Where a right was understood and intelligently relinquished, the right is never violated and a claim that the defendant has been unlawfully deprived of that right, no matter when made, is unmeritorious." The A.B.A. commentary distinguishes, however, between a "valid waiver" and an "abuse of process" (defined as "deliberately and inexcusably" failing to utilize available procedures to raise a claim). See Id. at 85–89. As applied to trial rights, this distinction apparently rests on the view that a waiver requires an intent to permanently relinquish a claim, while a deliberate bypass requires an intent only to relinquish a particular opportunity to raise a claim—i.e., the defendant may have every intent of raising the claim at a later point. Under this view, all waivers would constitute a deliberate bypass, but not all deliberate bypasses would encompass a waiver. Is the discussion in part IV of the majority opinion in *Fay* consistent with this distinction? Consider also Rosenberg, *Jettisoning Fay v. Noia,* 62 Minn.L.Rev. 341, 349 (1978).

Does *Warden v. Hayden,* 387 U.S. 294, 87 S.Ct. 1642, 18 L.Ed.2d 782 (1967) shed any light on the relationship between the concepts of "waiver" and "deliberate bypass"? The Court there held that the deliberate bypass rule of *Fay* did not apply where the state court had been willing to entertain petitioner's claim despite his deliberate bypass. D. Currie, *Federal Courts, Cases and Materials* 177 (1968), suggests that the *Warden* ruling may make "good sense * * * as a corollary of deference to state procedural interests," but questions its relevance to any view of a deliberate bypass as a form of "waiver of a federal right." Note, however, the limited scope of *Warden* suggested in *Curry v. Wilson,* 405 F.2d 110 (9th Cir.1968). The majority there, per Duniway, J., held that, although state court consideration of petitioner's claim on the merits barred reliance on the deliberate bypass rule, the federal district court might still dismiss a habeas petition where counsel's bypass also constituted an "affirmative waiver" of the constitutional objection.

3. *The "considered choice of the petitioner."* Although *Fay* states that the deliberate bypass standard "depends on the considered choice of petitioner" (p. 1500 supra), subsequent Supreme Court decisions, as well as lower court rulings, have recognized that a counsel's decision not to raise a particular constitutional claim at trial may

constitute a deliberate bypass even though defendant did not participate in that decision. See Note 3, p. 131 supra, and *Wainwright v. Sykes,* p. 1509 infra, at n. 14. Thus the decisions described in Notes 4–6 infra, dealing with the lack of an objection at trial, are concerned primarily with the "choice" made by counsel rather than by the defendant.

4. *Relinquishment of a known right.* Should the failure to raise a claim in the original proceedings constitute a deliberate bypass if counsel was not aware of the strength of that claim? Lower courts generally refused to find a deliberate bypass where counsel failed to object to a practice that was accepted "under the applicable law of the time" but then was held invalid in a subsequent decision that overruled or went substantially beyond prior precedent. They reasoned that one cannot "knowingly relinquish a constitutional right when the right was unknown at the time." *Ledbetter v. Warden,* 368 F.2d 490 (4th Cir. 1966). Where defense counsel had an arguable constitutional objection under the current state of the law, but still failed to present that objection, some courts sought to distinguish between the case in which counsel was totally unaware of the basis for that objection and the case in which counsel mistakenly underestimated its persuasiveness. See *Kuhl v. United States,* 370 F.2d 20 (9th Cir.1966) (search and seizure objection abandoned by defense counsel was deliberately bypassed even though the abandonment may have been a product of counsel's "mistake of law" in believing that the objection probably would fail on the standing issue). Compare *Pineda v. Craven,* 424 F.2d 369 (9th Cir.1970) (search and seizure objection was not deliberately bypassed where counsel was unaware of the *Aguilar* decision; "there is nothing strategic or tactical about ignorance, and neither a deliberate bypass nor a waiver could be based on such evidence").

5. *Voluntary relinquishment. Fay* is generally viewed as a case involving a "knowing" but "involuntary" failure to utilize state court remedies. See Note, 39 N.Y. U.L.Rev. 78, 87 (1964). Can the finding of involuntariness in *Fay* properly be limited by the special facts of that case—particularly the trial judge's comments in passing sentence? (Even so, would *North Carolina v. Pearce,* p. 1434 supra, now eliminate the basis for finding an involuntary relinquishment even in a fact situation identical to that in *Fay?*) *Whitus v. Balkcom,* 333 F.2d 496 (5th Cir.1964), is commonly cited as the "classic" case of an "involuntary" relinquishment of a constitutional objection. The court there found that defendant's failure to object to racial discrimination in jury selection did not constitute a deliberate bypass where defense counsel had reasonably feared that presenting that objection "would have filled the air with such hostility that an acquittal would almost have been impossible." Relying upon *Fay,* the court concluded that there was no voluntary relinquishment of rights where defendant was confronted by such a "grisly choice." (Cf. *Fay* at p. 1500 supra).

6. *Establishing a deliberate bypass.* In determining whether a deliberate bypass occurred, lower courts often relied heavily upon the "suggestions of the record" as to counsel's possible strategy in failing to raise or fully litigate an issue. Thus, where an objection was raised at trial, but the constitutional ground was not as clearly stated as required by state law, they ordinarily found that there was no deliberate bypass. On the other hand, where defense counsel made no objection to the admission of illegally obtained evidence or other practice subject to constitutional attack, but instead made affirmative use of such evidence or practice in presenting a defense, they generally concluded that there had been a deliberate bypass. Where the record did not point in one direction or another, but the absence of an objection could conceivably have been supported by a possible defense strategy, the lower courts divided. Many assumed

a tactical decision had been made, shifting to the defense the burden to show otherwise. Moreover, they saw no need for a hearing if all the defense could produce on its side was the testimony of counsel "as to why he did what he did, or failed to do what he did not do." *Kuhl v. United States,* Note 4 supra (noting that such a procedure "places counsel in the unenviable position where, if he can recall his reasons and they are good, he is hurting his former client, and if he can't recall his reasons or they are bad, or even not very good, he is impugning his professional competence"). Other courts, however, "were more receptive to hearings, to placing the burden on the state, and to finding that defaults were not deliberate bypasses." LaFave and Israel, § 27.4(c).

7. *The development of the "cause and prejudice" standard.* DAVIS v. UNITED STATES, 411 U.S. 233, 93 S.Ct. 1577, 36 L.Ed.2d 216 (1973), presented a § 2255 motion of a federal prisoner, filed three years after his trial, in which he claimed that there had been racial discrimination in the selection of the grand jury. Davis argued that his failure to raise that claim at trial should be judged under the deliberate bypass standard, which had been held after *Fay* to apply to § 2255 proceedings as well as federal habeas proceedings. See e.g., *Kaufman v. United States,* p. 1474 supra. Treating the question as one of statutory interpretation, the Supreme Court rejected Davis' contention. The Court noted that if Davis' case had come before it on direct review, it would have been decided under Federal Rule 12(b). That Rule provided that the failure to raise before trial a defect in the institution of the prosecution, such as grand jury discrimination, would "constitute a waiver, but the court for cause shown may grant relief from the waiver." The Court found it "inconceivable" that Congress, having foreclosed such a claim from review in the initial proceeding, meant to nonetheless allow it to be presented on collateral attack. Accordingly, the Rule 12(b) standard was held to apply under § 2255 as well as in the original proceeding. This meant that the petitioner could have his claim considered only if his failure to object was justified by "cause shown." The Court concluded that the district court had not abused its discretion in holding that such a showing of cause had not been made. Indeed, Davis had offered "no plausible explanation for his failure to timely make objection." The district court also had properly considered the absence of any showing of prejudice in reaching its conclusion. While racial discrimination in the selection of the grand jury was presumed to be prejudicial where a timely objection was made, a petitioner attempting to fall within the Rule 12(b) exception for "cause shown" would have to establish "actual prejudice."

Three years after *Davis,* FRANCIS v. HENDERSON, 425 U.S. 536, 96 S.Ct. 1708, 48 L.Ed.2d 149 (1976), presented to the Court a case almost identical to *Davis* except that the petitioner was a state prisoner seeking federal habeas review. A state statute required objections to the grand jury's composition to be raised before trial and the petitioner had failed to object, resulting in a procedural default. Without mentioning the deliberate bypass standard, the Court held that the standard announced in *Davis*—now described as requiring a showing of "cause" and "actual prejudice"—was applicable. The state requirement of a pretrial objection, the Court noted, served many of the same salutory purposes as Rule 12(b):

> If its time limits are followed, inquiry into an alleged defect may be concluded and, if necessary, cured before the court, the witnesses and the parties have gone to the burden and expense of a trial. If defendants were allowed to flout its time limitations, on the other hand, there would be little incentive to comply with its terms when a successful attack might simply result in a new indictment prior to trial.

"Surely," the Court concluded, "considerations of comity and federalism require that * * * [habeas courts] give no less effect to the same clear interests when asked to overturn state convictions."

Dissenting in *Francis,* Justice Brennan foresaw the eventual demise of the deliberate bypass standard, but several commentators suggested that the *Francis* ruling was limited by the special attributes of the grand jury discrimination claim—an objection as to which there was a decided tactical advantage in postponing the challenge if it were later available. *Wainwright v. Sykes,* infra, proved that Justice Brennan was the better prophet.

WAINWRIGHT v. SYKES

433 U.S. 72, 97 S.Ct. 2497, 53 L.Ed.2d 594 (1977).

MR. JUSTICE REHNQUIST delivered the opinion of the Court.

[Respondent Sykes presented a habeas corpus challenge based upon a *Miranda* claim that he had not raised in his state trial. At Sykes' trial (for murder) the prosecution introduced into evidence an incriminating statement that Sykes had given to the police after having been warned of his *Miranda* rights. Although Sykes later claimed in his habeas challenge that he had not understood the *Miranda* warnings and the statement therefore was involuntary, neither he nor his counsel raised that claim prior to trial or during the trial. The applicable state procedural rule (Fla. R.Crim.P. 3.190) required that such claims be raised by a pretrial motion to suppress, but it also granted the trial court discretion to entertain a later objection at trial. Sykes also failed to raise his *Miranda* claim on appeal, but even if that had been done, the Florida appellate courts would not have considered the issue since Sykes had not complied with Fla.R.Crim.P. 3.190. On petition for habeas corpus, the state argued that Sykes' violation of the state's procedural rule, which the federal court characterized as a "contemporaneous objection" standard, barred consideration of the merits of petitioner's claim. The federal Court of Appeals rejected that contention, relying on *Fay v. Noia.*]

* * * The simple legal question before the Court calls for a construction of the language of 28 U.S.C. § 2254(a), which provides that the federal courts shall entertain an application for a writ of habeas corpus "in behalf of a person in custody pursuant to the judgment of a state court only on the ground that he is in custody in violation of the Constitution or laws or treaties of the United States." But, to put it mildly, we do not write on a clean slate in construing this statutory provision. * * * For more than a century since the 1867 amendment, this Court has grappled with the relationship between the classical common-law writ of habeas corpus and the remedy provided in 28 U.S.C. § 2254. Sharp division within the Court has been manifested on more than one aspect of the perplexing problems which have been litigated in this connection.

[The Court here discussed Supreme Court decisions dealing with several major issues relating to the scope of the writ. Its discussion stressed in particular the movement in the decisions dealing with the range of cognizable claims, tracing that movement from *Ex parte Watkins* through *Stone v. Powell.* That movement and similar developments in the treatment of other issues (e.g., the scope of "custody") were cited as "illustrat[ing] this Court's historical willingness to overturn or modify its earlier views of the scope of the writ, even where the statutory language authorizing judicial action has remained unchanged." With this precedent in mind, the Court then turned to the issue before it—which it described as determining when "an adequate and independent state ground [will] bar consideration of otherwise cognizable federal issues on federal habeas review."]

* * * [I]t is a well-established principle of federalism that a state decision resting on an adequate foundation of state substantive law is immune from review in

the federal courts. * * * The area of controversy which has developed has concerned the reviewability of federal claims which the state court has declined to pass on because not presented in the manner prescribed by its *procedural* rules. The adequacy of such an independent state procedural ground to prevent federal habeas review of the underlying federal issue has been treated very differently than where the state-law ground is substantive. The pertinent decisions marking the Court's somewhat tortuous efforts to deal with this problem are: *Daniels v. Allen* [fn. b, p. 1501 supra]; *Fay v. Noia; Davis v. United States;* and *Francis v. Henderson.* [The Court here noted the specific holdings in each of these cases]. * * *

To the extent that the dicta of *Fay v. Noia* may be thought to have laid down an all-inclusive rule rendering state timely objection rules ineffective to bar review of underlying federal claims in federal habeas proceedings—absent a "knowing waiver" or a "deliberate bypass" of the right to so object—its effect was limited by *Francis,* which applied a different rule and barred a habeas challenge to the makeup of a grand jury. Petitioner Wainwright in this case urges that we further confine its effect by applying the principle enunciated in *Francis* to a claimed error in the admission of a defendant's confession. * * * [The] Florida procedure [here] did, consistently with the United States Constitution, require that respondent's confession be challenged at trial or not at all, and thus his failure to timely object to its admission amounted to an independent and adequate state procedural ground which would have prevented direct review here. We thus come to the crux of this case. Shall the rule of *Francis v. Henderson,* supra, barring federal habeas review absent a showing of "cause" and "prejudice" attendant to a state procedural waiver, be applied to a waived objection to the admission of a confession at trial? [11] We answer that question in the affirmative.

As earlier noted in the opinion, since *Brown v. Allen* [p. 1470 supra], it has been the rule that the federal habeas petitioner who claims he is detained pursuant to a final judgment of a state court in violation of the United States Constitution is entitled to have the federal habeas court make its own independent determination of his federal claim, without being bound by the determination on the merits of that claim reached in the state proceedings. This rule of *Brown v. Allen* is in no way changed by our holding today. Rather, we deal only with contentions of federal law which were *not* resolved on the merits in the state proceeding due to respondent's failure to raise them there as required by state procedure. We leave open for resolution in future decisions the precise definition of the "cause"-and-"prejudice" standard, and note here only that it is narrower than the standard set forth in dicta in *Fay v. Noia,* which would make federal habeas review generally available to state convicts absent a knowing and deliberate waiver of the federal constitutional contention. It is the sweeping language of *Fay v. Noia,* going far beyond the facts of the case eliciting it, which we today reject.[12]

11. Petitioner does not argue, and we do not pause to consider, whether a bare allegation of a *Miranda* violation, without accompanying assertions going to the actual voluntariness or reliability of the confession, is a proper subject for consideration on federal habeas review, where there has been a full and fair opportunity to raise the argument in the state proceeding. See *Stone v. Powell.* We do not address the merits of that question because of our resolution of the case on alternative grounds.

12. We have no occasion today to consider the *Fay* rule as applied to the facts there confronting the Court. Whether the *Francis* rule should preclude federal habeas review of claims not made in accordance with state procedure where the criminal defendant has surrendered, other than for reasons of tactical advantage, the right to have all of his claims of trial error considered by a state appellate court, we leave for another day.

The Court in *Fay* stated its knowing-and-deliberate-waiver rule in language which applied not only to the waiver of the right to appeal, but to failures to raise individual substantive objections in the state trial. Then, with a single sentence in a footnote, the Court swept aside all decisions of

The reasons for our rejection of it are several. The contemporaneous-objection rule itself is by no means peculiar to Florida, and deserves greater respect than *Fay* gives it, both for the fact that it is employed by a coordinate jurisdiction within the federal system and for the many interests which it serves in its own right. A contemporaneous objection enables the record to be made with respect to the constitutional claim when the recollections of witnesses are freshest, not years later in a federal habeas proceeding. It enables the judge who observed the demeanor of those witnesses to make the factual determinations necessary for properly deciding the federal constitutional question. While the 1966 amendment to § 2254 [see Note 4, p. 1526 infra] requires deference to be given to such determinations made by state courts, the determinations themselves are less apt to be made in the first instance if there is no contemporaneous objection to the admission of the evidence on federal constitutional grounds.

A contemporaneous-objection rule may lead to the exclusion of the evidence objected to, thereby making a major contribution to finality in criminal litigation. Without the evidence claimed to be vulnerable on federal constitutional grounds, the jury may acquit the defendant, and that will be the end of the case; or it may nonetheless convict the defendant, and he will have one less federal constitutional claim to assert in his federal habeas petition. If the state trial judge admits the evidence in question after a full hearing, the federal habeas court pursuant to the 1966 amendment to § 2254 will gain significant guidance from the state ruling in this regard. Subtler considerations as well militate in favor of honoring a state contemporaneous-objection rule. An objection on the spot may force the prosecution to take a hard look at its hole card, and even if the prosecutor thinks that the state trial judge will admit the evidence he must contemplate the possibility of reversal by the state appellate courts or the ultimate issuance of a federal writ of habeas corpus based on the impropriety of the state court's rejection of the federal constitutional claim.

We think that the rule of *Fay v. Noia,* broadly stated, may encourage "sandbagging" on the part of defense lawyers, who may take their chances on a verdict of not guilty in a state trial court with the intent to raise their constitutional claims in a federal habeas court if their initial gamble does not pay off. The refusal of federal habeas courts to honor contemporaneous-objection rules may also make state courts themselves less stringent in their enforcement. Under the rule of *Fay v. Noia,* state appellate courts know that a federal constitutional issue raised for the first time in the proceeding before them may well be decided in any event by a federal *habeas* tribunal. Thus, their choice is between addressing the issue notwithstanding the petitioner's failure to timely object, or else face the prospect that the federal habeas court will decide the questions without the benefit of their views.

The failure of the federal habeas courts generally to require compliance with a contemporaneous-objection rule tends to detract from the perception of the trial of a criminal case in state court as a decisive and portentous event. A defendant has been accused of a serious crime, and this is the time and place set for him to be tried by a jury of his peers and found either guilty or not guilty by that jury. To the greatest extent possible all issues which bear on this charge should be determined in this proceeding: the accused is in the courtroom, the jury is in the box, the judge is on the bench, and the witnesses, having been subpoenaed and duly sworn, await their turn to testify. Society's resources have been concentrated at that

this Court "to the extent that [they] may be read to suggest a standard of discretion in federal habeas corpus proceedings different from what we lay down today . . . ." See *Fay* at n. 44 [p. 1500 supra]. We do not choose to paint with a similarly broad brush here.

time and place in order to decide, within the limits of human fallibility, the question of guilt or innocence of one of its citizens. Any procedural rule which encourages the result that those proceedings be as free of error as possible is thoroughly desirable, and the contemporaneous-objection rule surely falls within this classification.

We believe the adoption of the *Francis* rule in this situation will have the salutary effect of making the state trial on the merits the "main event," so to speak, rather than a "tryout on the road" for what will later be the determinative federal habeas hearing. There is nothing in the Constitution or in the language of § 2254 which requires that the state trial on the issue of guilt or innocence be devoted largely to the testimony of fact witnesses directed to the elements of the state crime, while only later will there occur in a federal habeas hearing a full airing of the federal constitutional claims which were not raised in the state proceedings. If a criminal defendant thinks that an action of the state trial court is about to deprive him of a federal constitutional right there is every reason for his following state procedure in making known his objection.

The "cause"-and-"prejudice" exception of the *Francis* rule will afford an adequate guarantee, we think, that the rule will not prevent a federal habeas court from adjudicating for the first time the federal constitutional claim of a defendant who in the absence of such an adjudication will be the victim of a miscarriage of justice. Whatever precise content may be given those terms by later cases, we feel confident in holding without further elaboration that they do not exist here. Respondent has advanced no explanation whatever for his failure to object at trial,[14] and, as the proceeding unfolded, the trial judge is certainly not to be faulted for failing to question the admission of the confession himself. The other evidence of guilt presented at trial, moreover, was substantial to a degree that would negate any possibility of actual prejudice resulting to the respondent from the admission of his inculpatory statement.

We accordingly conclude that the judgment of the Court of Appeals for the Fifth Circuit must be reversed, and the cause remanded * * * with instructions to dismiss respondent's petition for a writ of habeas corpus.

MR. CHIEF JUSTICE BURGER, concurring.

I concur fully in the judgment and in the Court's opinion. I write separately to emphasize one point which, to me, seems of critical importance to this case. In my view, the "deliberate bypass" standard enunciated in *Fay v. Noia* was never designed for, and is inapplicable to, errors—even of constitutional dimension—alleged to have been committed during trial.

In *Fay v. Noia,* the Court applied the "deliberate bypass" standard to a case where the critical procedural decision—whether to take a criminal appeal—was entrusted to a convicted defendant. Although Noia, the habeas petitioner, was represented by counsel, he himself had to make the decision whether to appeal or not; the role of the attorney was limited to giving advice and counsel. In giving content to the new deliberate-bypass standard, *Fay* looked to the Court's decision in *Johnson v. Zerbst,* a case where the defendant had been called upon to make the decision whether to request representation by counsel in his federal criminal trial [see p. 121

14. In *Henry v. Mississippi,* 379 U.S. [443], 85 S.Ct. [564, 13 L.Ed.2d 408 (1965)], the Court noted that decisions of counsel relating to trial strategy, even when made without the consultation of the defendant, would bar direct federal review of claims thereby forgone, except where "the circumstances are exceptional." Last term in *Estelle v. Williams,* [425 U.S. 501, 96 S.Ct. 1691, 48 L.Ed.2d 126 (1976),] the Court reiterated the burden on a defendant to be bound by the trial judgments of his lawyer: "Under our adversary system, once a defendant has the assistance of counsel the vast array of trial decisions, strategic and tactical, which must be made before and during trial rests with the accused and his attorney."

supra]. Because in both *Fay* and *Zerbst,* important rights hung in the balance of the *defendant's own decision,* the Court required that a waiver impairing such rights be a knowing and intelligent decision by the defendant himself. * * *

The touchstone of *Fay* and *Zerbst,* then, is the exercise of volition by the defendant himself with respect to his own federal constitutional rights. In contrast, the claim in the case before us relates to events during the trial itself. * * * Once counsel is appointed, the day-to-day conduct of the defense rests with the attorney. He, not the client, has the immediate—and ultimate—responsibility of deciding if and when to object, which witnesses, if any, to call, and what defenses to develop. Not only do these decisions rest with the attorney, but such decisions must, as a practical matter, be made without consulting the client.[1] The trial process simply does not permit the type of frequent and protracted interruptions which would be necessary if it were required that clients give knowing and intelligent approval to each of the myriad tactical decisions as a trial proceeds.[2]

Since trial decisions are of necessity entrusted to the accused's attorney, the *Fay-Zerbst* standard of "knowing and intelligent waiver" is simply inapplicable. The dissent in this case, written by the author of *Fay v. Noia,* implicitly recognizes as much. According to the dissent, *Fay* imposes the knowing-and-intelligent-waiver standard "where possible" during the course of the trial. [See p. 1513 infra]. In an extraordinary modification of *Fay,* Mr. Justice Brennan would now require "that the lawyer actually exercis[e] his expertise and judgment in his client's service, and with his client's knowing and intelligent participation *where possible*"; he does not intimate what guidelines would be used to decide when or under what circumstances this would actually be "possible." (Emphasis supplied.) What had always been thought the standard governing the *accused's* waiver of his own constitutional rights the dissent would change, in the trial setting, into a standard of conduct imposed upon the defendant's *attorney.* This vague "standard" would be unmanageable to the point of impossibility. * * *

MR. JUSTICE STEVENS, concurring.

Although the Court's decision today may be read as a significant departure from the "deliberate bypass" standard announced in *Fay v. Noia,* I am persuaded that the holding is consistent with the way other federal courts have actually been applying *Fay.* The notion that a client must always consent to a tactical decision not to assert a constitutional objection to a proffer of evidence has always seemed unrealistic to me. Conversely, if the constitutional issue is sufficiently grave, even an express waiver by the defendant himself may sometimes be excused.[3] Matters such as the competence of counsel, the procedural context in which the asserted waiver occurred, the character of the constitutional right at stake, and the overall fairness of the entire proceeding, may be more significant than the language of the test the Court purports to apply. I therefore believe the Court has wisely refrained from attempting to give precise content to its "cause" and "prejudice" exception to the rule of *Francis v. Henderson.*

In this case I agree with the Court's holding that collateral attack on the state-

1. Only such basic decisions as whether to plead guilty, waive a jury, or testify in one's own behalf are ultimately for the accused to make. See *ABA Report on Standards Relating to the Prosecution Function and Defense Function § 5.2,* pp. 237–238 (Approved Draft 1971).

2. One is left to wonder what use there would have been to an objection to a confession corroborated by witnesses who heard Sykes freely admit the killing at the scene within minutes after the shooting.

3. The test announced in *Fay* was not actually applied in that case. The Court held that habeas relief was available notwithstanding the client's participation in the waiver decision, and notwithstanding the fact that the decision was made on a tactical basis. * * *

court judgment should not be allowed. The record persuades me that competent trial counsel could well have made a deliberate decision not to object to the admission of the respondent's in-custody statement. That statement was consistent, in many respects, with the respondent's trial testimony. It even had some positive value, since it portrayed the respondent as having acted in response to provocation, which might have influenced the jury to return a verdict on a lesser charge. To the extent that it was damaging, the primary harm would have resulted from its effect in impeaching the trial testimony, but it would have been admissible for impeachment in any event, *Harris v. New York* [p. 828 supra]. Counsel may well have preferred to have the statement admitted without objection when it was first offered rather than making an objection which, at best, could have been only temporarily successful.

Moreover, since the police fully complied with *Miranda,* the deterrent purpose of the *Miranda* rule is inapplicable to this case. Finally, there is clearly no basis for claiming that the trial violated any standard of fundamental fairness. Accordingly, no matter how the rule is phrased, this case is plainly not one in which a collateral attack should be allowed. I therefore join the opinion of the Court.

MR. JUSTICE WHITE, concurring in the judgment.

Under the Court's cases a state conviction will survive challenge in federal habeas corpus not only when there has been a deliberate bypass within the meaning of *Fay v. Noia,* but also when the alleged constitutional error is harmless beyond a reasonable doubt within the intendment of *Harrington v. California* [p. 798 supra] and similar cases. * * * It is thus of some moment to me that the Court makes its own assessment of the record and itself declares that the evidence of guilt in this case is sufficient to "negate any possibility of actual prejudice resulting to the respondent from the admission of his inculpatory statement." [p. 1509 supra]. This appears to be tantamount to a finding of harmless error under the *Harrington* standard and is itself sufficient to foreclose the writ and to warrant reversal of the judgment. * * *

MR. JUSTICE BRENNAN, with whom MR. JUSTICE MARSHALL joins, dissenting.

Over the course of the last decade, the deliberate-bypass standard announced in *Fay v. Noia,* has played a central role in efforts by the federal judiciary to accommodate the constitutional rights of the individual with the States' interests in the integrity of their judicial procedural regimes. The Court today decides that this standard should no longer apply with respect to procedural defaults occurring during the trial of a criminal defendant. In its place, the Court adopts the two-part "cause"-and-"prejudice" test originally developed in *Davis v. United States,* and *Francis v. Henderson.* As was true with these earlier cases, however, today's decision makes no effort to provide concrete guidance as to the content of those terms. More particularly, left unanswered is the thorny question that must be recognized to be central to a realistic rationalization of this area of law: How should the federal habeas court treat a procedural default in a state court that is attributable purely and simply to the error or negligence of a defendant's trial counsel? Because this key issue remains unresolved, I shall attempt in this opinion a re-examination of the policies that should inform—and in *Fay* did inform—the selection of the standard governing the availability of federal habeas corpus jurisdiction in the face of an intervening procedural default in the state court.

I begin with the threshold question: What is the meaning and import of a procedural default? If it could be assumed that a procedural default more often than not is the product of a defendant's conscious refusal to abide by the duly constituted, legitimate processes of the state courts, then I might agree that a regime of collateral review weighted in favor of a State's procedural rules would be warranted. *Fay,* however, recognized that such rarely is the case; and therein lies *Fay*'s basic unwillingness to embrace a view of habeas jurisdiction that results in "an airtight system of [procedural] forfeitures."

This, of course, is not to deny that there are times when the failure to heed a state procedural requirement stems from an intentional decision to avoid the presentation of constitutional claims to the state forum. *Fay* was not insensitive to this possibility. Indeed, the very purpose of its bypass test is to detect and enforce such intentional procedural forfeitures of outstanding constitutionally based claims. * * * For this reason, the Court's assertion that it "think[s]" that the *Fay* rule encourages intentional "sandbagging" on the part of the defense lawyers is without basis; certainly the Court points to no cases or commentary arising during the past 15 years of actual use of the *Fay* test to support this criticism. Rather, a consistent reading of case law demonstrates that the bypass formula has provided a workable vehicle for protecting the integrity of state rules in those instances when such protection would be both meaningful and just. * * *

In brief then, any realistic system of federal habeas corpus jurisdiction must be premised on the reality that the ordinary procedural default is born of the inadvertence, negligence, inexperience, or incompetence of trial counsel. The case under consideration today is typical. The Court makes no effort to identify a tactical motive for the failure of Sykes' attorney to challenge the admissibility or reliability of a highly inculpatory statement. While my Brother Stevens finds a possible tactical advantage, I agree with the Court of Appeals that this reading is most implausible: "We can find no possible advantage which the defense might have gained, or thought they might gain, from the failure to conform with Florida Criminal Procedure Rule 3.190(i)." * * * [A]ny realistic reading of the record demonstrates that we are faced here with a lawyer's simple error. * * *

What are the interests that Sykes can assert in preserving the availability of federal collateral relief in the face of his inadvertent state procedural default? Two are paramount. As is true with any federal habeas applicant, Sykes seeks access to the federal court for the determination of the validity of his federal constitutional claim. Since at least *Brown v. Allen,* it has been recognized that the "fair effect [of] the habeas corpus jurisdiction as enacted by Congress" entitles a state prisoner to such federal review. * * * But federal review is not the full measure of Sykes' interest, for there is another of even greater immediacy: assuring that his constitutional claims can be addressed to *some* court. For the obvious consequence of barring Sykes from the federal courthouse is to insulate Florida's alleged constitutional violation from any and all judicial review because of a lawyer's mistake. From the standpoint of the habeas petitioner, it is a harsh rule indeed that denies him "any review at all where the state has granted none," *Daniels v. Allen* (Black, J., dissenting)—particularly when he would have enjoyed both state and federal consideration had his attorney not erred.

* * * Florida, of course, can point to a variety of legitimate interests in seeking allegiance to its reasonable procedural requirements, the contemporaneous-objection rule included. As *Fay* recognized, a trial, like any organized activity, must conform to coherent process, and "there must be sanctions for the flouting of such procedure." The strict enforcement of procedural defaults, therefore, may be seen as a means of deterring any tendency on the part of the defense to slight the state forum, to deny state judges their due opportunity for playing a meaningful role in the evolving task of constitutional adjudica-

tion, or to mock the needed finality of criminal trials. All of these interests are referred to by the Court in various forms.[11]

The question remains, however, whether any of these policies or interests are efficiently and fairly served by enforcing both intentional and inadvertent defaults pursuant to the identical stringent standard. I remain convinced that when one pierces the surface justifications for a harsher rule posited by the Court, no standard stricter than *Fay* 's deliberate-bypass test is realistically defensible. Punishing a lawyer's unintentional errors by closing the federal courthouse door to his client is both a senseless and misdirected method of deterring the slighting of state rules. It is senseless because unplanned and unintentional action of any kind generally is not subject to deterrence; and, to the extent that it is hoped that a threatened sanction addressed to the defense will induce greater care and caution on the part of trial lawyers, thereby forestalling negligent conduct or error, the potential loss of all valuable state remedies would be sufficient to this end. And it is a misdirected sanction because even if the penalization of incompetence or carelessness will encourage more thorough legal training and trial preparation, the habeas applicant, as opposed to his lawyer, hardly is the proper recipient of such a penalty. Especially with fundamental constitutional rights at stake, no fictional relationship of principal-agent or the like can justify holding the criminal defendant accountable for the naked errors of his attorney. This is especially true when so many indigent defendants are without any realistic choice in selecting who ultimately represents them at trial. Indeed, if responsibility for error must be apportioned between the parties, it is the State, through its attorney's admissions and certification policies, that is more fairly held to blame for the fact that practicing lawyers too often are ill-prepared or ill-equipped to act carefully and knowledgeably when faced with decisions governed by state procedural requirements. * * * In short, I believe that the demands of our criminal justice system warrant visiting the mistakes of a trial attorney on the head of a habeas corpus applicant only when we are convinced that the lawyer actually exercised his expertise and judgment in his client's service, and with his client's knowing and intelligent participation where possible. This, of course, is the precise system of habeas review established by *Fay v. Noia.* * * *

One final consideration deserves mention. Although the standards recently have been relaxed in various jurisdictions, it is accurate to assert that most courts, this one included, traditionally have resisted any realistic inquiry into the competency of trial counsel. * * * If the scope of habeas jurisdiction previously governed by *Fay v. Noia* is to be redefined so as to enforce the errors and neglect of lawyers with unnecessary and unjust rigor, the time may come when conscientious and fairminded federal and state courts, in adhering to the teaching of *Johnson v. Zerbst,* will have to reconsider whether they can continue to indulge the comfortable fiction that all lawyers are skilled or even competent craftsmen in representing the fundamental rights of their clients.

11. In my view, the strongest plausible argument for strict enforcement of a contemporaneous-objection rule is one that the Court barely relies on at all: the possibility that the failure of timely objection to the admissibility of evidence may foreclose the making of a fresh record and thereby prejudice the prosecution in later litigation involving that evidence. There may be force to this contention, but it rests on the premise that the State in fact has suffered actual prejudice because of a procedural lapse. Florida demonstrates no such injury here. Sykes' trial occurred in June 1972. He subsequently filed his petition for a writ of habeas corpus in April 1973, thereby apprising Florida of his constitutional objection. There is no basis in the record for concluding that lost evidence or other form of prejudice, see, e.g., *Barker v. Wingo* [p. 1082 supra], arising during this 10½-month interval effectively forestalls Florida's defense of the Fifth Amendment claim or the reprosecution of Sykes should his constitutional challenge prevail.

Notes and Questions

1. *State excused defaults.* Should *Sykes* alter the rule of *Warden v. Hayden,* Note 2 at p. 1503 supra, that even a deliberate bypass will not bar habeas corpus consideration of a constitutional claim where the state courts ignored that bypass and considered the claim on its merits? Post-*Sykes* rulings have continued to apply this "excused default" doctrine. See, e.g., *County Court of Ulster County v. Allen,* 442 U.S. 140, 99 S.Ct. 2213, 60 L.Ed.2d 777 (1979), where the Court noted: "[T]he 'adequate state ground exception' to habeas corpus jurisdiction * * * [is designed] to accord appropriate respect to the sovereignty of the States in our federal system, * * * but if neither the state legislature nor the state courts indicate that a federal constitutional claim is barred by some state procedural rule, a federal court implies no disrespect for the state by entertaining the claim." See also Note, 83 Mich.L.Rev. 1393 (1985) (discussing the application of the excused default doctrine to state decisions based on alternative grounds).

Should a procedural default bar review where the state court had authority to excuse the default but refused to do so? In *Sykes,* for example, the state rule required that the motion to suppress be raised before trial, but it also permitted the trial court in its discretion to consider a motion made at trial. If the defendant had raised his objection at trial and the trial court had refused to exercise its discretion to excuse the lack of a pretrial motion, would the *Francis* standard apply? On direct review, the Supreme Court has noted that a state ruling based on a procedural default will not constitute an adequate state ground if the state court had discretion to excuse such defaults and exercised that discretion against considering federal claims but in favor of considering "kindred [state] issues." *Wolfe v. North Carolina,* 364 U.S. 177, 80 S.Ct. 1482, 4 L.Ed.2d 1650 (1960). Hill, *The Forfeiture of Constitutional Rights in Criminal Cases,* 78 Colum.L.Rev. 1050 (1978), argues that a federal habeas court should have the same authority to reject a procedural default based on such a discriminatory exercise of state court discretion. The author suggests, moreover, that the federal courts, on direct review or on habeas corpus, should have the authority to reject a procedural default if, without regard to discrimination, the state court violated its own standards in failing to excuse the default.

2. *The adequate state ground standard.* Did *Francis-Sykes* restore the concept that state court reliance upon an adequate state ground precludes federal habeas corpus relief? Is the "cause and prejudice" exception simply another way of describing a case in which a state's forfeiture rule does not constitute an adequate state procedural ground because it fails to serve a "legitimate state interest"? See Hill, supra (*Sykes* will produce same standard for habeas and direct review, but that standard will be far more rigorous in judging the adequacy of a state procedure requirement than the ready acceptance found in earlier habeas and direct review cases, such as *Daniel v. Allen,* fn. b, p. 1501 supra). Consider, however, Seidman, p. 1489 supra, at 465–67: "The subsequent controversy and confusion surrounding the deliberate bypass test have caused some commentators to forget that the most important and innovative holding in *Fay* was that a habeas court had the statutory and constitutional power to reach federal questions despite a state procedural default. Nothing in *Estelle, Francis,* or *Wainwright* casts the slightest doubt on this central teaching of *Fay.* Indeed, the Burger Court has gone out of its way to embrace it."

3. *The proper place of the deliberate bypass standard.* In what situations, if any, should a lower court continue to apply the deliberate bypass standard, as opposed to the *Francis-Sykes* standard, to a state's procedural forfeiture of a constitutional claim? Does the deliberate bypass standard still apply to: (1) the forfeiture of claims as to which

personal participation by the defendant is necessary for a valid waiver (see n. 1 of Chief Justice Burger's opinion); (2) the forfeiture of claims as to which there would be no reason for a tactically-motivated default since the claim, if successful, would bar conviction (e.g., a double jeopardy or speedy trial claim); (3) the forfeiture of "jurisdictional defects"; or (4) only forfeitures based upon the defendant's failure to appeal? [a] Where a particular type of claim can be raised on habeas notwithstanding a guilty plea (see Notes 4–6, pp. 1251–54 supra), should not the same claim also be subject to habeas review where the defendant went to trial—even if there was a deliberate bypass? See LaFave and Israel, § 27.4. Are certain claims (e.g., the unconstitutionality of the substantive offense) basically "non-waivable"?

4. *Justice Stevens' approach.* Along with his concurring opinion in *Sykes,* consider Justice Stevens' dissent in *Rose v. Lundy,* 455 U.S. 509, 102 S.Ct. 1198, 71 L.Ed.2d 379 (1982), where the majority held that the exhaustion rule (see Note 3, p. 1469 supra) precluded consideration of a habeas petition if any of the several claims raised could still be presented for initial consideration on the merits in the state courts. Arguing that a distinction should be drawn according to the nature of the exhausted and unexhausted claims, Justice Stevens noted:

"In my opinion claims of constitutional error are not fungible. There are at least four types. The one most frequently encountered is a claim that attaches a constitutional label to a set of facts that does not disclose a violation of any constitutional right. In my opinion, each of the four claims asserted in this case falls in that category. The second class includes constitutional violations that are not of sufficient import in a particular case to justify reversal even on direct appeal, when the evidence is still fresh and a fair retrial could be promptly conducted. *Chapman v. California* [p. 796 supra]. A third category includes errors that are important enough to require reversal on direct appeal but do not reveal the kind of fundamental unfairness to the accused that will support a collateral attack on a final judgment. See e.g., *Stone v. Powell.*[8] The fourth category includes those errors that are so fundamental that they infect the validity of the underlying judgment itself, or the integrity of the process by which that judgment was obtained. This category cannot be defined precisely; concepts of 'fundamental fairness' are not frozen in

a. One major ground cited in support of the *Francis* standard—that it will limit the frequency with which the federal habeas court will be required to conduct evidentiary hearings—arguably would distinguish cases such as *Fay* where the petitioner failed only to raise his claim on appeal. Where a cognizable claim was not raised at trial, the federal habeas court ordinarily must hold such a hearing to rule upon the claim. On the other hand, where the claim was litigated at trial, but then not appealed, an evidentiary hearing is not necessary since the federal court may rely upon the fact-findings of the trial court. See § 3 infra. Consider also the distinction noted by Rehnquist, J., concurring in *Mullaney v. Wilbur,* 421 U.S. 684, 95 S.Ct. 1881, 44 L.Ed.2d 508 (1975) ("It is one thing to fail to utilize the appeal process to cure a defect which already inheres in a judgment of conviction, but it is quite another to forego making an objection or exception which might prevent the error from ever occurring").

8. In my opinion a claim generally belongs in this category if the purpose and significance of the constitutional rule is such that the Court enforces it prospectively but not retroactively, cf. *Linkletter v. Walker* [p. 49 supra], or if the probable significance of the claim is belied by the fact that otherwise competent defense counsel did not raise a timely objection, cf. *Wainwright v. Sykes.* I recognize the apparent incongruity in suggesting that there is a class of constitutional error—not constitutionally harmless—that does not render a criminal proceeding fundamentally unfair. It may be argued, with considerable force, that a rule of procedure that is not necessary to ensure fundamental fairness is not worthy of constitutional status. The fact that such a category of constitutional error exists, however, is demonstrated by the jurisprudence of this Court concerning the retroactive application of newly recognized constitutional rights. * * * In ruling that a constitutional principle is not to be applied retroactively, the Court implicitly suggests that the right is not necessary to ensure the integrity of the underlying judgment; the Court certainly would not allow claims of such magnitude to remain unremedied.

time. But the kind of error that falls in this category is best illustrated by recalling the classic grounds for the issuance of a writ of habeas corpus—that the proceeding was dominated by mob violence; that the prosecutor knowingly made use of perjured testimony; or that the conviction was based on a confession extorted from the defendant by brutal methods. Errors of this kind justify collateral relief no matter how long a judgment may have been final and even though they may not have been preserved properly in the original trial. * * *

"In recent years federal judges at times have lost sight of the true office of the great writ of habeas corpus. It is quite unlike the common law writ of error that enabled a higher court to correct errors committed by a *nisi prius* tribunal in the trial of civil or criminal cases by ordering further proceedings whenever trial error was detected. The writ of habeas corpus is a fundamental guarantee of liberty. * * * The doctrine of non-retroactivity, the emerging 'cause and prejudice' doctrine, and today's 'total exhaustion' rule are examples of judicial lawmaking that might well have been avoided by confining the availability of habeas corpus relief to cases that truly involve fundamental unfairness."

APPLYING THE "CAUSE AND PREJUDICE" STANDARD

1. In ENGLE v. ISAAC, 456 U.S. 107, 102 S.Ct. 1558, 71 L.Ed.2d 783 (1982), the three respondents had raised claims of self-defense in their Ohio trials. For many years Ohio law required the defendant to carry the burden of proving self-defense by a preponderance of the evidence. In each of the defendants' trials, the jury was instructed in accordance with the traditional rule. None of the defendants objected to this instruction. A recently enacted Ohio Criminal Code stated in § 2901.05 that the prosecution bore the burden of proof, with defendants carrying the "burden of going forward" on affirmative defenses. It was apparently assumed, however, that this provision did not alter the traditional Ohio rule.

Two of the defendants presented state appeals in which they again failed to challenge the instruction. Prior to the appeal of the third, the Ohio Supreme Court held, in *State v. Robinson,* that Ohio Criminal Code § 2901.05 placed only the burden of production, but not the burden of persuasion, on a defendant. Respondent Isaac relied on the *Robinson* case on his appeal, but the Ohio appellate court rejected his challenge because Isaac had failed to object to the jury instructions during trial as required by Ohio R.Crim.P. 30. The three respondents subsequently filed habeas petitions in the federal district court. These petitions raised two claims: (1) that § 2901.05 implicitly designated the absence of self-defense as an element of the crime in its treatment of affirmative defenses, and due process therefore required the prosecution to prove absence of self-defense beyond a reasonable doubt, and (2) without regard to § 2901.05, Ohio could not constitutionally shift the burden of proof to the defense since self-defense negated the mental elements of purposeful or knowing behavior required for each of the crimes charged against respondents. The federal district courts dismissed respondents' petitions, but the Court of Appeals reversed. It held that *Wainwright v. Sykes* did not bar review, since cause and prejudice existed, and the jury instructions had violated due process.

The Supreme Court majority, per O'CONNOR, J., initially noted that respondent's first claim was completely without merit as a constitutional issue. Respondent's second claim did state a "colorable constitutional claim" under several Supreme Court decisions, including *In re Winship* [p. 1492 supra], *Mullaney v. Wilbur,* 421 U.S. 684, 95 S.Ct. 1881, 44 L.Ed.2d 508 (1975) and *Patterson v. New York,* 432 U.S. 197, 97 S.Ct. 2319, 53 L.Ed.2d 281 (1977). That claim, however, was foreclosed from review by the "principles articulated in *Wainwright v. Sykes.*" As to the application of those principles, the Court noted:

"The writ of habeas corpus indisputably holds an honored position in our jurisprudence. Tracing its roots deep into English common law, it claims a place in Article I of our Constitution. Today, as in prior centuries, the writ is a bulwark against convictions that violate 'fundamental fairness.' *Wainwright v. Sykes,* supra (Stevens, J., concurring).

"We have always recognized, however, that the Great Writ entails significant costs. Collateral review of a conviction extends the ordeal of trial for both society and the accused. As Justice Harlan once observed, '[b]oth the individual criminal defendant and society have an interest in insuring that there will at some point be the certainty that comes with an end to litigation, and that attention will ultimately be focused not on whether a conviction was free from error but rather on whether the prisoner can be restored to a useful place in the community.' *Sanders v. United States.* * * * Liberal allowance of the writ, moreover, degrades the prominence of the trial itself. * * * Our Constitution and law surround the trial with a multitude of protections for the accused. Rather than enhancing these safeguards, ready availability of habeas corpus may diminish their sanctity by suggesting to the trial participants that there may be no need to adhere to those safeguards during the trial itself.

"We must also acknowledge that writs of habeas corpus frequently cost society the right to punish admitted offenders. Passage of time, erosion of memory, and dispersion of witnesses may render retrial difficult, even impossible. While a habeas writ may, in theory, entitle the defendant only to retrial, in practice it may reward the accused with complete freedom from prosecution.

"Finally, the Great Writ imposes special costs on our federal system. The States possess primary authority for defining and enforcing the criminal law. In criminal trials they also hold the initial responsibility for vindicating constitutional rights. Federal intrusions into state criminal trials frustrate both the States' sovereign power to punish offenders and their good faith attempts to honor constitutional rights. See *Schneckloth v. Bustamonte* (Powell, J., concurring).

"In *Wainwright v. Sykes,* we recognized that these costs are particularly high when a trial default has barred a prisoner from obtaining adjudication of his constitutional claim in the state courts. In that situation, the trial court has had no opportunity to correct the defect and avoid problematic retrials. The defendant's counsel, for whatever reasons, has detracted from the trial's significance by neglecting to raise a claim in that forum. The state appellate courts have not had a chance to mend their own fences and avoid federal intrusion. Issuance of habeas writ, finally, exacts an extra charge by undercutting the State's ability to enforce its procedural rules. These considerations supported our *Sykes* ruling that, when a procedural default bars state litigation of a constitutional claim, a state prisoner may not obtain federal habeas relief absent a showing of cause and actual prejudice.

"Respondents urge that we should limit *Sykes* to cases in which the constitutional error, did not affect the truthfinding function of the trial. In *Sykes* itself, for example, the prisoner alleged that the State had violated the rights guaranteed by *Miranda v. Arizona.* While this defect was serious, it did not affect the determination of guilt at trial.

"We do not believe, however, that the principles of *Sykes* lend themselves to this limitation. The costs outlined above do not depend upon the type of claim raised by the prisoner. While the nature of a constitutional claim may affect the calculation of cause and actual prejudice, it does not alter the need to make that threshold showing. We reaffirm, therefore, that any prisoner bringing a constitutional claim to the federal courthouse after a state procedural default must demonstrate cause and actual prejudice before obtaining relief.

"Respondents seek cause for their defaults in two circumstances. First, they urge that they could not have known at the time of their trials that the Due Process Clause addresses the burden of proving affirmative defenses. Second, they contend that any objection to Ohio's self-defense instruction would have been futile since Ohio had long required criminal defendants to bear the burden of proving this affirmative defense.

"We note at the outset that the futility of presenting an objection to the state courts cannot alone constitute cause for a failure to object at trial. If a defendant perceives a constitutional claim and believes it may find favor in the federal courts, he may not bypass the state courts simply because he thinks they will be unsympathetic to the claim. Even a state court that has previously rejected a constitutional argument may decide, upon reflection, that the contention is valid. Allowing criminal defendants to deprive the state courts of this opportunity would contradict the principles supporting *Sykes.*

"Respondents' claim, however, is not simply one of futility. They further allege that, at the time they were tried, they could not know that Ohio's self-defense instructions raised constitutional questions. A criminal defendant, they urge, may not waive constitutional objections unknown at the time of trial.

"We need not decide whether the novelty of a constitutional claim ever establishes cause for failure to object.[a] We might hesitate to adopt a rule that would require trial counsel either to exercise extraordinary vision or to object to every aspect of the proceedings in the hope that some aspect might mask a latent constitutional claim. On the other hand, later discovery of a constitutional defect unknown at the time of trial does not invariably render the original trial fundamentally unfair. These concerns, however, need not detain us here since respondents' claims were far from unknown at the time of their trials.

"*In re Winship,* decided four-and-one half years before the first of respondents' trials, laid the basis for their constitutional claim. * * * During the five years following this decision, dozens of defendants relied upon this language to challenge the constitutionality of rules requiring them to bear a burden of proof.[b] In most of these cases, the defendants' claims countered well-established principles of law. Nevertheless, numerous courts agreed that the Due Process Clause requires the prosecution to bear the burden of disproving certain affirmative defenses. In light of this activity, we cannot say that respondents lacked the tools to construct their constitutional claim.

"We do not suggest that every astute counsel would have relied upon *Winship* to assert the unconstitutionality of a rule saddling criminal defendants with the burden of proving an affirmative defense. Every trial presents a myriad of possible claims. Counsel might have overlooked or chosen to omit respondents' due process argument while pursuing other avenues of defense. We have long recognized, however, that the Constitution guarantees criminal defendants only a fair trial and a competent attorney. It does

a. But see Note 6 infra, discussing the Court's later ruling on that issue.

b. The Court here cited as examples, 22 state and federal cases in which defendants challenged burden of proof allocations on a variety of issues, including insanity, alibi, intoxication, and self-defense. In a subsequent footnote, the Court added that "several commentators also perceived that *Winship* might alter traditional burdens of proof for affirmative defenses." Finally, the Court's ruling in *Mullaney*, decided three months before respondent Isaac's trial, had relied upon *Winship* to hold unconstitutional a state's placement of the burden of proving provocation on a homicide defendant.

not insure that defense counsel will recognize and raise every conceivable constitutional claim. Where the basis of a constitutional claim is available, and other defense counsel have perceived and litigated that claim, the demands of comity and finality counsel against labelling alleged unawareness of the objection as cause for a procedural default.

"Respondents, finally, urge that we should replace or supplement the cause-and-prejudice standard with a plain-error inquiry. We rejected this argument when pressed by a federal prisoner, see *United States v. Frady* [Note 2 infra], and find it no more compelling here. The federal courts apply a plain-error rule for direct review of federal convictions. Fed.Rule Crim.Proc. 52(b). Federal habeas challenges to state convictions, however, entail greater finality problems and special comity concerns. We remain convinced that the burden of justifying federal habeas relief for state prisoners is 'greater than the showing required to establish plain error on direct appeal.' *United States v. Frady.*

"Contrary to respondents' assertion, moreover, a plain-error standard is unnecessary to correct miscarriages of justice. The terms 'cause' and 'actual prejudice' are not rigid concepts; they take their meaning from the principles of comity and finality discussed above. In appropriate cases those principles must yield to the imperative of a fundamentally unjust incarceration. Since we are confident that victims of a fundamental miscarriage of justice will meet the cause-and-prejudice standard, we declined to adopt the more vague inquiry suggested by the words 'plain error.' " [c]

JUSTICE BRENNAN, joined by Justice Marshall, dissented. Justice Brennan contended that, "in purporting to give content to the 'cause' standard * * *, the Court defines cause in a way supported neither by *Sykes* nor by common sense." The dissent noted:

"According to the Court, 'cause' is *not* demonstrated when the Court 'cannot say that [habeas petitioners] lacked the tools to construct their constitutional claim,' however primitive those tools were and thus however inchoate the claim was when petitioners were in the state courts. The Court concludes, after several pages of tortuous reasoning, that respondents in the present cases did indeed have 'the tools' to make their constitutional claims. This conclusion is reached by the sheerest inference: It is based on citations to other cases in other jurisdictions, where other defendants raised other claims assertedly similar to those that respondents 'could' have raised. To hold the present respondents to such a high standard of foresight is tantamount to a complete rejection of the notion that there is a point before which a claim is so inchoate that there is adequate 'cause' for the failure to raise it. In thus rejecting inchoateness as 'cause,' the Court overlooks the fact that none of the rationales used in *Sykes* to justify adoption of the cause-and-prejudice standard can justify today's definition of 'cause.'

"*Sykes* adopted the cause-and-prejudice standard in order to accord 'greater respect' to state contemporaneous-objection rules than was assertedly given by *Fay v. Noia,* supra. The Court then offered a number of reasons why contemporaneous-objection rules should be given such greater respect:

c. Justice Blackmun concurred in the result, without opinion. Justice Stevens concurred in part and dissented in part, expressing a position similar to that noted in his opinion in *Rose v. Lundy* [Note 4, p. 1515 supra]. Justice Stevens contended that the Court's "preoccupation with procedural hurdles is more likely to complicate than to simplify the processing of habeas corpus petitions by federal judges." The crucial issue, as he saw it, was that "neither of the respondents' claims justified a collateral attack on their convictions." Respondents' second claim was no more "plausible" than the first claim and should have been rejected in the same manner as the first claim.

"(1) 'A contemporaneous objection enables the record to be made with respect to the constitutional claim when the recollections of witnesses are freshest, not a year later in a federal habeas proceeding.'

"(2) A contemporaneous objection 'enables the judge who observed the demeanor of those witnesses to make the factual determinations necessary for properly deciding the federal constitutional question.'

"(3) 'A contemporaneous-objection rule may lead to the exclusion of evidence objected to, thereby making a major contribution to finality in criminal litigation.'

"(4) The *Fay v. Noia* rule 'may encourage "sandbagging" on the part of defense lawyers, who may take their chances on a verdict of not guilty in a state trial court with the intent to raise their constitutional claims in a federal habeas court if their initial gamble does not pay off.'

"(5) A contemporaneous objection rule 'encourages the result that [criminal trials] be as free of error as possible.'

"None of these rationales has any force in the present case. The first three reasons are valid, if at all, only in the particular context of objections to the admission of evidence, such as were at issue in *Sykes.* As for the 'sandbagging' rationale, dutifully repeated by today's Court, that was fully answered in my *Sykes* dissent: That argument still 'offends common sense,' and does not become less offensive by sententious repetition. And the final reason—relied on again today—is plainly irrelevant to a case involving inchoate constitutional claims. Such claims are *ex hypothesis* so embryonic that only the extraordinarily foresighted criminal defendant will raise them. It is completely implausible to expect that the raising of such claims will predictably—or even occasionally—make trials more 'free of error.'

"* * * The Court concedes, that *Sykes* itself involved the violation of the habeas petitioner's *Miranda* rights, and that although 'this defect was serious, it did not affect the determination of guilt at trial.' But despite the fact that the present cases admittedly do involve a defect affecting the determination of guilt, the Court refuses to limit *Sykes* and thus bars federal review. * * * In so holding, the Court ignores the manifest differences between claims that affect the truth-finding function of the trial and claims that do not. The Court proclaimed in *Stone v. Powell* [that] 'the ultimate question of guilt or innocence * * * should be the central concern in a criminal proceeding.' * * * In my view, the *Sykes* standard is misguided and insupportable in any context. But if it is to be suffered to exist at all, it should be limited to the arguable peripheries of the trial process: It should not be allowed to insulate from all judicial review all violations of the most fundamental rights of the accused."

2. In UNITED STATES v. FRADY, 456 U.S. 152, 102 S.Ct. 1584, 71 L.Ed.2d 816 (1982), the Court had before it a § 2255 challenge to respondent's 1963 conviction for a homicide committed in Washington, D.C. Respondent argued that the Court of Appeals, in cases decided after his trial and appeal, had disapproved of instructions identical to those used in his case. As determined by those later rulings, the triai court improperly equated intent with malice by stating that "a wrongful act * * * intentionally done * * * is therefore done with malice aforethought." The trial court also erred in incorrectly instructing the jury as to a presumption of malice attaching to the use of a weapon. Respondent contended that these instructions "compelled the jury to presume malice and thereby wrongfully eliminated any possibility of a manslaughter verdict, since manslaughter was defined as culpable homicide without malice."

The district court denied the § 2255 motion, stating that respondent should have challenged the jury instructions on appeal, or in one of his many earlier motions. The Court of Appeals reversed. It held that the applicable standard for review was the Federal Rule 52(b) "plain error" standard rather than the "cause and actual prejudice" standard of *Wainwright v. Sykes.* The Court of Appeals concluded that the challenged instructions were plainly erroneous and remanded the case for a new trial or a reduction of the conviction to manslaughter. The Supreme Court majority, per O'CONNOR, J., rejected this analysis. The majority reasoned:

"Nineteen years after his crime, Frady now complains he was convicted by a jury erroneously instructed on the meaning of malice. At trial, however, Frady did not object to the instructions, nor did he raise the issue on direct appeal. Rule 30 of the Federal Rules of Criminal Procedure declares in pertinent part that: 'No party may assign as error any portion of the charge or omission therefrom unless he objects thereto before the jury retires to consider its verdict, stating distinctly the matter to which he objects and the grounds of his objection.' Rule 52(b), however, somewhat tempers the severity of Rule 30. It grants the Courts of Appeals the latitude to correct particularly egregious errors on appeal regardless of a defendant's trial default: 'Plain errors or defects affecting substantial rights may be noticed although they were not brought to the attention of the court.'

"Rule 52(b) was intended to afford a means for the prompt redress of miscarriages of justice. By its terms, recourse may be had to the rule only on appeal from a trial infected with error so 'plain' the trial judge and the prosecutor were derelict in countenancing it, even absent the defendant's timely assistance in detecting it. The rule thus reflects a careful balancing of our need to encourage all trial participants to seek a fair and accurate trial the first time around against our insistence that obvious injustice be promptly redressed.

"Because it was intended for use on direct appeal, however, the 'plain error' standard is out of place when a prisoner launches a collateral attack against a criminal conviction after society's legitimate interest in the finality of the judgment has been perfected by the expiration of the time allowed for direct review or by the affirmance of the conviction on appeal. * * * By adopting the same standard of review for § 2255 motions as would be applied on direct appeal, the Court of Appeals accorded no significance whatever to the existence of a final judgment perfected by appeal. Once the defendant's chance to appeal has been waived or exhausted, however, we are entitled to presume he stands fairly and finally convicted, especially when, as here, he already has had a fair opportunity to present his federal claims to a federal forum. Our trial and appellate procedures are not so unreliable that we may not afford their completed operation any binding effect beyond the next in a series of endless post-conviction collateral attacks. To the contrary, a final judgment commands respect. * * *

"We believe the proper standard for review of Frady's motion is the 'cause and actual prejudice' standard enunciated in *Davis v. United States,* and later confirmed and extended in *Francis v. Henderson,* and *Wainwright v. Sykes.* Under this standard, to obtain collateral relief based on trial errors to which no contemporaneous objection was made, a convicted defendant must show both (1) 'cause' excusing his double procedural default, and (2) 'actual prejudice' resulting from the errors of which he complains. In applying this dual standard to the case before us, we find it unnecessary to determine whether Frady has shown cause, because we are confident he suffered no actual prejudice of a degree sufficient to justify collateral relief nineteen years after his crime.

"In considering the prejudice, if any, occasioned by the erroneous jury instructions used at Frady's trial, we note that in *Wainwright v. Sykes* we refrained from giving 'precise content' to the term 'prejudice,' expressly leaving to future cases further elaboration of the significance of that term. While the import of the term in other situations thus remains an open question, our past decisions nevertheless eliminate any doubt about its meaning for a defendant who has failed to object to jury instructions at trial.

"Recently, for example, Justice Stevens, in his opinion without dissent in *Henderson v. Kibbe,* 431 U.S. 145, 97 S.Ct. 1730, 52 L.Ed.2d 203 (1977), summarized the degree of prejudice we have required a prisoner to show before obtaining collateral relief for errors in the jury charge as 'whether the ailing instruction by itself so infected the entire trial that the resulting conviction violates due process,' not merely whether 'the instruction is undesirable, erroneous, or even universally condemned.' We reaffirm this formulation, which requires that the degree of prejudice resulting from instruction error be evaluated in the total context of the events at trial. * * *

"We now apply these established standards to Frady's case. * * * Frady bases his claim that he was prejudiced on his assertion that the jury was not given an adequate opportunity to consider a manslaughter verdict * * * [for killing without malice]. According to Frady, the trial court's erroneous instructions relieved the Government of the burden of proving malice, an element of the crime of murder.

"* * * At the outset, we emphasize that this would be a different case had Frady brought before the District Court affirmative evidence indicating that he had been convicted wrongly of a crime of which he was innocent. But Frady, it must be remembered, did not assert at trial that he and Richard Gordon beat Thomas Bennett to death without malice. Instead, Frady claimed he had nothing whatever to do with the crime. The evidence, however, was overwhelming, and Frady promptly abandoned that theory on appeal. Since that time, Frady has never presented colorable evidence, even from his own testimony, indicating such justification, mitigation, or excuse that would reduce his crime from murder to manslaughter.

"Indeed, the evidence in the record compels the conclusion that there was, as the dissenters from the denial of a rehearing en banc below put it, 'malice aplenty.' Frady and Gordon twice reconnoitered their victim's house on the afternoon and evening of the murder. Just before the killing, they were overheard in a conversation suggesting that they 'were assassins hired by George Bennett to do away with his brother.' They brought gloves to the scene of the murder which they discarded during their flight from the police, and the murder weapon bore no fingerprints. Finally, there was the unspeakable brutality of the killing itself.

"Indeed, the evidence of malice was strong enough that the 10 judges closest to the case—the trial judge and the nine judges who 17 years ago decided Frady's appeal en banc—were at that time *unanimous* in finding the record at least sufficient to sustain a conviction for second-degree murder—a killing with malice. Nine of the 10 judges went further, finding the evidence sufficient to sustain the jury's verdict that Frady not only killed with malice, but with premeditated and deliberate intent.

"We conclude that the strong uncontradicted evidence of malice in the record, coupled with Frady's utter failure to come forward with a colorable claim that he acted without malice, disposes of his contention that he suffered such actual prejudice that reversal of his conviction 19 years later could be justified. We perceive no risk of a fundamental miscarriage of justice in this case.

"Should any doubt remain, our examination of the jury instructions shows no substantial likelihood that the same jury that found Frady guilty of first-degree murder would have concluded, if only the malice instructions had been better framed, that his crime was only manslaughter. The jury, after all, did not merely find Frady guilty of second-degree murder, which requires only malice. It found Frady guilty of first-degree—deliberate and premeditated—murder. * * *

"In sum, Frady has fallen far short of meeting his burden of showing that he has suffered the degree of actual prejudice necessary to overcome society's justified interests in the finality of criminal judgments. Therefore, the judgment of the Court of Appeals is reversed, and the case is remanded for further proceedings consistent with this opinion."

Chief Justice BURGER and Justice MARSHALL took no part in the case. Justice STEVENS concurring, noted that his view "of the relevance of the cause for counsel's failure to object to the jury instruction is significantly different from the Courts'", citing his separate opinions in *Wainwright v. Sykes, Rose v. Lundy* and *Engle v. Isaac.* He nevertheless joined the Court's opinion "because it properly focused on the character of the prejudice to determine whether collateral relief is appropriate."

Justice BLACKMUN concurred in the judgment, though disagreeing with the Court's conclusion that the Rule 52(b) standard was inapplicable. He concluded that the Court of Appeals had "erred in holding that respondent was entitled to relief under Rule 52(b)." Respondent had simply failed, he noted, to demonstrate that the erroneous jury instructions "so infected the entire trial that the resulting conviction violates due process." JUSTICE BRENNAN, dissenting, also argued that the Rule 52(b) standard was applicable to § 2255 proceedings. He characterized the majority ruling as "further step" in the Court's "progressive emasculation of collateral review of criminal convictions."

3. Prior to *Isaac,* several lower courts had held that counsel's ignorance or inadvertence in failing to raise a constitutional claim could constitute "cause" even where such negligence failed in itself to amount to a Sixth Amendment violation. The Fourth Circuit has continued to adhere to this position. See *Carrier v. Hutto,* 724 F.2d 396 (4th Cir.1983), affirmed en banc, 754 F.2d 520 (4th Cir.1985). Looking to *Sykes'* criticism of *Noia*'s bypass rule as possibly encouraging "sandbagging," that court has reasoned that "attorney error short of wholesale ineffectiveness of counsel can constitute * * * 'cause,' provided that the act or omission resulting in procedural default emanated from ignorance or inadvertence, rather than deliberate strategy." Ibid. Can this position be squared with the reasoning of Justice O'Connor's opinion in *Isaac?* See Marcus, *Federal Habeas Corpus After State Default: A Definition of Cause and Prejudice,* 53 Fordham L.Rev. 663 (1985) (*Isaac* may be read either as "establishing the fungibility of 'overlooking' and choosing" or as simply concluding that an "allegation" of unawareness as to an "issue in the public domain" would be "difficult to credit and therefore is insufficient"); Yackle (1983 Supp.) § 86 (*Isaac* opinion was "closely groomed to the consolidated cases at bar"). But compare Guttenberg, *Federal Habeas Corpus, Constitutional Rights and Procedural Forfeiture,* 12 Hofstra L.Rev. 617 (1984) (criticizing *Isaac,* but reading it broadly).

4. After *Sykes,* various commentators suggested that prisoners thereafter would seek to "outflank the Court's attempt to limit habeas review" by presenting incompetency of counsel claims, even where "the only basis of ineffectiveness is counsel's failure to object." Tague, *Federal Habeas Corpus and Ineffective Representation of Counsel: The Supreme Court Has Work To Do,* 31 Stan.L.Rev. 1 (1978). With the Supreme Court's subsequent insistence upon a showing of prejudice as an element of establishing incompetency, see *Strickland v. Washington,* p. 143 supra, does the petitioner have any easier route in framing his

challenge as an incompetency claim? On the other hand, where the petitioner seeks to establish "cause" by reference to counsel's negligence, must he necessarily establish a degree of negligence that meets the *Strickland* standard for incompetence? Consider LaFave and Israel, § 27.4 (1986 Supp.) (citing the last paragraph of Justice O'Connor's *Isaac* opinion quoted at p. 1519 supra, the authors suggest "a sufficiently strong showing of 'actual prejudice,' perhaps establishing a likelihood of factual innocence," may lead to the conclusion that a counsel's error falling short of ineffectiveness constituted "cause" [d]); Batey, *Federal Habeas Corpus and the Death Penalty: "Finality With A Capital F,"* 36 Fla.L.Rev. 252 (1984) (unique status of death penalty should be an appropriate consideration under the *Sykes* standard).

5. What, if anything, does the Court's opinion in *Frady* add to the definition of prejudice? In particular, what is the significance of the Court's reference to the nineteen year period since the trial and Frady's failure to make a colorable showing of innocence during that period. Does *Frady* suggest that, "at least as to claims that are guilt related, the requisite likelihood that the error influenced the outcome will be measured in light of the available proof of innocence contained in both the trial record and subsequent proceedings"? LaFave and Israel, § 27.4(e).

6. In *Reed v. Ross,* 468 U.S. 1, 104 S.Ct. 2901, 82 L.Ed.2d 1 (1984), the Court answered the "novel-question" issue left open in *Isaac* (see p. 1518 supra, at fn. a). A divided Court there held that the failure to raise a claim "so novel that its legal basis [was] not reasonably available" did not "seriously implicate any of the concerns that might otherwise require deference to a state's procedural bar" and therefore should not preclude habeas review. Justice Brennan's opinion for the Court reasoned: "Just as it is reasonable to assume that a competent lawyer will fail to perceive the possibility of raising such a claim, it is also reasonable to assume that a court will similarly fail to appreciate the claim. * * * Despite the fact that a constitutional concept may ultimately enjoy general acceptance, * * * when the concept is in its embryonic stage, it will, by hypothesis, be rejected by most courts. Consequently, a rule requiring a defendant to raise a truly novel issue is not likely to serve any functional purpose. * * * In addition, if we were to hold that the novelty of a constitutional question does not give rise to cause for counsel's failure to raise it, we might actually disrupt state-court proceedings by encouraging defense counsel to include any and all remotely plausible constitutional claims that could, some day, gain recognition." [e]

7. Under what circumstances should a petitioner's failure to raise a particular claim

d. The authors note that "*Riner v. Owens,* 764 F.2d 1253 (7th Cir.1985), is one case that arguably might fit this mold, although the court [there] did not describe it as such." In *Riner,* defense counsel objected to testimony concerning a statement made by petitioner's codefendant, but did not further object when the trial court issued a cautionary instruction rather than the severance required under *Bruton v. United States* [see p. 1074 supra]. On habeas review, the Seventh Circuit found obvious "actual prejudice" in that the codefendant's statement "was the only evidence before the jury of the petitioner's involvement in aiding and abetting the burglary and murder." "Cause" was found for the default at trial by virtue of the fact that petitioner's trial counsel also represented the codefendant (although the court did not suggest that the joint representation presented an actual conflict rendering counsel incompetent under the Sixth Amendment). "Cause" for the failure to raise the *Bruton* issue on direct appeal was found in the fact that the same counsel represented defendant at trial and on appeal.

e. In dissent, Rehnquist, J. (joined by Chief Justice Burger and Justices Blackmun and O'Connor) found that the claim petitioner was now raising had not been novel at the time of his trial. The dissenters also suggested that the novelty of the claim did not necessarily work in petitioner's favor. A claim that almost certainly would have been rejected by the courts when petitioner was tried, even though it later gained general acceptance, might well not be the type of claim that should be open on habeas review, for "the more 'novel' a claimed constitutional right, the more unlikely that a violation of that claimed right undercut the fundamental fairness of the trial."

in his first habeas petition preclude consideration of that claim in a subsequent petition? In *Sanders v. United States,* 373 U.S. 1, 83 S.Ct. 1068, 10 L.Ed.2d 148 (1963), the Court held that such a ground must be considered unless there had been an "abuse of writ." As to what constituted such an abuse, the Court noted simply that the principles developed in *Fay v. Noia* "govern equally here." When Congress reframed the successive application provision of § 2244(b) in 1966, it included a reference to the abuse-of-writ doctrine. In noting that the habeas court need not entertain a successive application unless it alleges a new ground, the section added the proviso that the court be "satisfied that the applicant has not in the earlier application deliberately withheld the newly asserted ground or otherwise abused the writ." Rule 9(b) of the § 2254 Rules also refers to the doctrine. It states that the habeas court may dismiss the application if it finds "the failure of the petitioner to assert those grounds [referring to "new and different grounds"] in a prior petition constituted an abuse of writ." In light of *Sykes,* would one expect the Court to now construe these provisions as imposing a "cause and prejudice" standard rather than a deliberate bypass standard? See LaFave and Israel, § 27.5 (noting that the abuse of writ doctrine, unlike the standard developed in *Sykes,* was looking to an action taken when the petitioner was without the assistance of counsel, see pp. 92–95 supra).

SECTION 3. THE SPECIAL STATUS OF STATE FACTFINDING

1. One of the issues presented in *Brown v. Allen,* 344 U.S. 443, 73 S.Ct. 397, 97 L.Ed. 469 (1953), was the appropriate scope of federal habeas review of a cognizable claim that had been treated in the state courts. There were two majority opinions in *Brown* due to a split on other questions, but the Court was in agreement as to basic scope of habeas review. Initially, the federal habeas court was to "independently apply the correct constitutional standard to the historical facts underlying * * * [the] claim, no matter how fairly and completely the claim has been litigated in the state courts." Both opinions added, however, that the federal habeas court could, in most circumstances, rely upon the state court's findings of historical fact rather than conduct its own independent factfinding. Thus, Justice Frankfurter summarized the district judge's role as follows:

> [I]t may appear that the issue turns on basic facts and that the facts (in the sense of a recital of external events and the credibility of their narrators) have been tried and adjudicated against the applicant. Unless a vital flaw be found in the process of ascertaining such facts in the State court, the District Judge may accept their determination in the State proceeding and deny the application. On the other hand, State adjudication of questions of law cannot, under the habeas corpus statute, be accepted as binding. It is precisely these questions that the federal judge is commanded to decide.

2. Consider LaFave and Israel, § 27.6(a): "Neither majority opinion in *Brown* explained exactly why the 'final say' given the federal habeas court permitted it to accept the state court's determination of historic facts in contrast to the independent judgment it required as to the legal consequences of those facts. There was nothing in § 2243, the provision on evidentiary hearings, that suggested such a distinction between factual and legal determinations, and one might have argued that the protection of a federal claim in a federal forum required independent assessment of the facts as well as the law. The distinction has been justified, however, on several grounds. It has been argued that there is less need for independent federal factfinding because 'the guilt determining momentum and judicial loyalty to state institutional interests are not as likely to influence the accuracy of a state judge's factfinding process as they are to impair his application of constitutional standards.' Arguably also, any value that federal pro-

cedures and federal judges would bring to the accuracy of the factfinding process is more than offset by the timing advantage of the state court hearing, as compared to a federal habeas hearing typically held long after the events in question occurred. Finally, it is generally agreed that independent federal factfinding exacerbates many of the costs of habeas review, extending substantially the call on scarce judicial resources and increasing the friction between state and federal courts."

3. In *Townsend v. Sain,* 372 U.S. 293, 83 S.Ct. 745, 9 L.Ed.2d 770 (1963), the Court sought to add flesh to Justice Frankfurter's suggestion in *Brown* that an evidentiary hearing (and independent factfinding) was needed where there was a "vital flaw" in the state factfinding process. While a district court always had discretion to hold an independent hearing, it would be required to do so, *Townsend* stated, under the following six circumstances: "(1) the merits of the factual dispute were not resolved in the state hearing; (2) the state factual determination is not fairly supported by the record as a whole; (3) the factfinding procedure employed by the state court was not adequate to afford a full and fair hearing; (4) there is a substantial allegation of newly discovered evidence; (5) the material facts were not adequately developed at the state court hearing; or (6) for any reason it appears that the state trier of fact did not afford the habeas applicant a full and fair hearing."

4. In 1966, Congress responded to *Townsend* by adding subsections (d)–(f) to 28 U.S.C. § 2254 (see Supp., App. B). The key provision was the lengthy and complex subsection (d). That provision can be broken down into three segments. The first segment describes the type of state finding to which the provision applies—"a determination after a hearing on the merits of a factual dispute made by a state court of competent jurisdiction * * *, evidenced by a written finding, written opinion, or other reliable and adequate written indicia." The second segment provides that the finding "shall be presumed to be correct," unless the habeas court finds that one of eight conditions (largely taken from the *Townsend* list) are present.[a] The third segment indicates the consequences of the presumption of correctness. It provides that in an evidentiary hearing, upon "due proof" of a state factfinding subject to subsection (d) and not exempted by any of the conditions (1)–(8), the "burden shall rest upon the applicant to establish by convincing evidence that the factual determination by the State court was erroneous."

In *Sumner v. Mata,* 449 U.S. 539, 101 S.Ct. 764, 66 L.Ed.2d 722 (1981), the Court gave notice that the lower courts were to take seriously § 2254(d)'s presumption of correctness. *Sumner* rejected the contention that it should be assumed that a federal habeas court reaching a contrary factual determination, without explanation, had properly relied upon one of the § 2254(d) exceptions rendering the presumption inapplicable. "In order to ensure that this mandate of Congress is

a. See LaFave and Israel, § 27.6: "Although § 2254(d) has been described by lower courts as 'in the main codifying *Townsend,*' it actually rejects certain assumptions implicit in *Townsend,* though incorporating other aspects of that ruling. The immediate focus of *Townsend* was on those circumstances that required an evidentiary hearing. Section 2254(d), on the other hand, does not speak directly to when a hearing must be held; its focus is on the burden of proof applicable at that hearing. However, by implication, it would suggest that a hearing be held where there is a factual dispute and the state court findings are not entitled to the presumption of correctness under one of the eight exceptions noted in the statute. In this regard, it would seem to reinforce, if not codify, *Townsend*'s six circumstances. The eight exceptions specified in § 2254(d) are not identical to those six circumstances, but the differences are not particularly significant. * * * *Townsend* [also] held that the habeas court had discretion to hold an evidentiary hearing even where its guidelines did not mandate a hearing. Section 2254(d) does not directly affect that authority. However, it was also the apparent assumption of *Townsend* that the habeas court, at a discretionary hearing, could make a completely independent determination of the historical facts. Here § 2254 does state otherwise."

followed," a federal habeas court would be required to "include in its opinion granting the writ the reasoning which led it to conclude that any of the first seven factors were present, or the reasoning which led it to conclude that the state finding was 'not fairly supported by the record' [the 8th factor]." This responsibility, the Court added, would not be fulfilled by mere " 'boiler plate language,' " but required a specific listing of findings similar to that required of a judge in a bench trial under Rule 52 of the Civil Rules.

5. Under § 2254(d)(8), a state court's factual finding is not entitled to the presumption of correctness if it is not "fairly supported by the record." Some argue that this standard gives the habeas court ample leeway to reject state court findings that it views as incorrect, but MARSHALL v. LONBERGER, 459 U.S. 422, 103 S.Ct. 843, 74 L.Ed.2d 646 (1983), might suggest otherwise. At respondent's trial for murder in Ohio, the prosecution sought to prove a prior conviction for attempted murder, one of the statutory "specifications" that allowed imposition of the death penalty. The prosecution accordingly sought to admit into evidence respondent's plea of guilty to a 4 count Illinois indictment charging aggravated battery and attempted murder and the transcript of the hearing at which the plea was received. At that guilty plea hearing, respondent had been asked if he had committed aggravated battery "and did on the same date attempt on Dorothy Maxwell with a knife," and he replied by saying, "Yes, sir." Respondent objected that this evidence did not establish a proper conviction for attempted murder, claiming that he had not been aware at the time that he was pleading guilty to that offense. The Ohio trial court held an evidentiary hearing and concluded that the plea to the attempted murder charge had been made intelligently and voluntarily. The prosecution's evidence was admitted and respondent was subsequently convicted and sentenced to death, although that sentence was later reduced to life imprisonment by a state appellate court.

On his subsequent federal habeas petition, the Court of Appeals upheld respondent's claim, reasoning that the guilty plea had been invalid since respondent had not known that his plea was to an attempted murder charge. The Court of Appeals noted that the respondent had so testified at the Ohio trial court's hearing, that the trial court had made no express finding concerning respondent's credibility, and that the prosecution had not introduced contrary evidence. The state court's finding therefore was not "fairly supported" by the record and should be rejected under 28 U.S.C. § 2254(d)(8).

The Supreme Court, in a 5–4 decision, reversed. The Court rejected the dissent's challenge to the use of the prior conviction at the trial stage, relying on *Spencer v. Texas,* 385 U.S. 554, 87 S.Ct. 648, 17 L.Ed.2d 606 (1967). Turning to the voluntariness of the plea supporting that conviction, the Court noted that, as stated in *Henderson v. Morgan* (p. 1230 supra), even without an express statement of all of the charges by the guilty plea judge, it was appropriate to assume that a counseled defendant ordinarily was made aware of the nature of the offense to which he entered his plea. Applying this standard, the factual determination of the Ohio court in this case could not be said to be without "fair support" in the record. The Court of Appeals, in ruling to the contrary, had failed to appreciate the full impact of *Sumner.* Describing that failure, the majority (per REHNQUIST, J.) noted:

"The Court of Appeals' reliance on respondent's testimony * * * and the fact that 'the state produced no contrary evidence,' is quite wide of the mark for purposes of deciding whether factual findings are fairly supported by the record. 28 U.S.C. § 2254(d) gives federal habeas courts no license to redetermine credibility of witnesses whose demeanor has been observed by the state trial court, but not by them.[b] * * * While disbelief of respondent's testimony may not form the basis for any affirmative findings by the state trial court on issues with respect to which the state bore the burden of proof, it certainly negates any inferences favorable to respondent such as those drawn by the Court of Appeals, based on his testimony before the Ohio trial court. Thus, the factual conclusions which the federal habeas courts were bound to respect in assessing respondent's constitutional claims were the contents of the Illinois court records, the finding of the Ohio trial court that respondent was 'an intelligent individual, well experienced in the criminal processes and well represented in all stages of the proceedings by competent and capable counsel in Illinois,' and the similar conclusion of the Ohio Court of Appeals, and the inferences fairly deducible from these facts. These records and findings show, with respect to the attempted murder charge, that it was one of the four counts contained in the Cook County indictment returned against respondent. The 'conviction certificate' recites that at the time respondent pleaded guilty, he was duly advised by the court of the consequences of pleading guilty, and nonetheless adhered to his plea. The transcript, as appears from its face and as found by the Ohio Court of Appeals, shows that respondent answered affirmatively that he was pleading guilty, *inter alia,* to the offense of 'attempt on Dorothy Maxwell, with a knife * * *.' Respondent's attorney, in his presence, stipulated that the indictment was 'both sufficient in law and in fact to sustain a finding of guilty on the charges involving [respondent].' * * *

"Under *Henderson,* respondent must be presumed to have been informed, either by his lawyers or at one of the presentencing proceedings, of the charges on which he was indicted. Given this knowledge of the indictment and the fact that the indictment contained no other attempt charges, respondent could only have understood the judge's reference to 'attempt on Dorothy Maxwell, with a knife' as a reference to the indictment's charge of attempt to kill."

6. The Supreme Court has frequently noted that § 2254(d) applies only to a determination of "historic fact" as opposed to "a mixed determination of law and fact that requires the application of legal principles to the historical facts." In *Cuyler v. Sullivan* (p. 165 supra), there was unanimous agreement that the determination of the state court that counsel had not undertaken the multiple representation of three codefendants was outside the reach of § 2254(d). The state court's findings as to the role counsel played in the defense of petitioner and his codefendants related to historic fact, but the holding that this did not constitute legally representing all three involved a legal conclusion, "open to review on collateral attack in a federal court." See also *Strickland v. Washington's* comments on § 2254(d) at p. 150 supra. Later cases, however, found the distinction between a historic fact and an application of legal principles more difficult to apply. The division in the first and second set of rulings in SUMNER v. MATA is illustrative.[c]

b. See also *Maggio v. Fulford,* 462 U.S. 111, 103 S.Ct. 2261, 76 L.Ed.2d 794 (1983). In *Fulford,* the federal habeas court had relied heavily on the trial testimony of a psychiatrist who suggested that the petitioner "had paranoid delusions" and therefore was not competent to stand trial. The state court had rejected this testimony in concluding, based on its own observations of the defendant, that he was "cognizant of everything around him" and his eleventh-hour motion for a competency commission was simply a "subterfuge." The Supreme Court majority concluded that the habeas court's ruling could not be sustained if the § 2254(d) standard of proof applied. It noted that the federal court "erroneously substituted its own judgment as to the credibility of witnesses for that of the Louisiana courts—a prerogative which 28 U.S.C. § 2254 does not allow."

c. 449 U.S. 539, 101 S.Ct. 764, 66 L.Ed.2d 722 (1981) (*Mata I*); review following remand 455

Mata involved a challenge to a pretrial photo-identification. In upholding the admissibility of that identification, the state court had held that there was no showing that the witnesses had been "influenced" by the investigating officer, that the witnesses had an "adequate opportunity" to view the crime, and that their initial descriptions of the assailant were "accurate." The habeas court, holding the photo-identification impermissibly suggestive, concluded that the circumstances surrounding the witnesses' observation of the crime were suspect, the witnesses had failed to give sufficiently detailed initial descriptions, and "considerable pressure" had been brought to bear on them. In *Mata I* (discussed in note 4 supra) the Supreme Court remanded the case to the habeas court for an explanation as to why it had not relied on § 2254(d). The habeas court responded that the section did not apply since its rulings dealt with a mixed question of fact and law. Justice Brennan (joined by Justice Marshall) had dissented in *Mata I* on exactly that ground. He had argued that whether a "person's opportunity to view a crime is 'adequate' for constitutional purposes" was a legal question. Legal issues were also involved, in his view, in the habeas court's determination that the action of the state officials had been coercive and in its characterization of the initial descriptions as not sufficiently detailed to dispel doubts about the photographic procedure.

Reviewing the case again, the Supreme Court held (6–3) in *Mata II* that the lower court had erred in concluding that § 2254(d) was inapplicable. The majority reasoned:

"We agree with the * * * [lower court] that the ultimate question as to the constitutionality of the pretrial identification procedures used in this case is a mixed question of law and fact that is not governed by § 2254. In deciding this question, the federal court may give different weight to the facts as found by the state court and may reach a different conclusion in light of the legal standard. But the questions of fact that underlie this ultimate conclusion are governed by the statutory presumption as our earlier opinion made clear. Thus, whether the witnesses in this case had an opportunity to observe the crime or were too distracted; whether the witnesses gave a detailed, accurate description; and whether the witnesses were under pressure from prison officials or others are all questions of fact as to which the statutory presumption applies."

Is it significant that the Court's description of the "factual issues" differs somewhat from Justice Brennan's earlier description of the "legal issues"? The Court, for example, refers to the question of whether the witnesses had "an opportunity" to view the crime rather than whether that opportunity was "adequate." The habeas court had concluded that the witnesses "quite likely" were distracted while observing the crime, thus apparently disagreeing with the state court's finding as to their behavior at that time. If the habeas court had reasoned that, even accepting the state court's conclusion as to the witness' capacity to observe, the opportunity to observe was insufficient to offset the suggestive quality of the photo-display, would that finding have been categorized as involving an application of legal analysis to historic fact? Consider the cases discussed in Note 7 infra.

7. In *Rushen v. Spain,* 464 U.S. 114, 104 S.Ct. 453, 78 L.Ed.2d 267 (1983), the issue before the Court was whether, assuming an ex parte communication between judge and juror violated defendant's rights (see p. 1345 supra), that error could be viewed as harmless. The majority reasoned that, while application of the harmless error standard was a question of law, the underlying factual finding of the state

U.S. 591, 102 S.Ct. 1303, 71 L.Ed.2d 480 (1982) (*Mata II*).

court that the ex parte communication had no bearing on the juror's impartiality was entitled to § 2254(d)'s presumption of correctness. That finding, the Court noted, was amply supported by a record that included the juror's repeated statement that the incident discussed in the ex parte communication had not affected her impartiality. In dissent, Justice Marshall was willing to accept arguendo that "the question of whether a juror is biased is a matter of historical fact," but concluded that the state court's findings were not "fairly supported by the record." In a separate dissent, Justice Blackmun suggested that Justice Marshall's analysis supported adoption of a "conclusive presumption of bias" under the facts of the case, which required an application of legal principles beyond the reach of § 2254(d).

Relying on *Rushen, Patton v. Yount,* 467 U.S. 1025, 104 S.Ct. 2885, 81 L.Ed.2d 847 (1984), held that, while § 2254(d) did not encompass a state court's finding as to whether prejudicial publicity had made a fair trial impossible, it did apply to the trial judge's finding, based on a juror's responses on voir dire, that the individual juror was not biased. The question of the "partiality of an individual juror," the Court noted,

> is plainly one of historical fact: did a juror swear that he could set aside any opinion he might hold and decide the case, and should the juror's protestation of impartiality have been believed. There are good reasons to apply the statutory presumption of correctness to these questions. First, the determination has been made only after an often extended voir dire proceeding * * *. Second, the determination is one of credibility and therefore largely one of demeanor.

In dissent, Justice Stevens, joined by Brennan, J., argued that "whether a juror has a disqualifying opinion is a mixed question of law and fact," since a court is necessarily "called upon to determine whether the nature and strength of the opinion formed are such as in law necessarily to raise a presumption of partiality." [d]

8. In MILLER v. FENTON, ___ U.S. ___, 106 S.Ct. 445, 88 L.Ed.2d 405 (1985), the lower court, after reviewing the Supreme Court's recent decisions under § 2254(d), concluded that the § 2254(d) presumption applied to a state court's finding as to the voluntariness of a confession, provided the state court had applied the "proper legal test." The Supreme Court reversed, with only Justice Rehnquist dissenting. Speaking for the Court, Justice O'CONNOR reasoned:

"The Court of Appeals recognized that treating the voluntariness of a confession as an issue of fact was difficult to square with 'fifty years of caselaw' in this Court. It believed, however, that this substantial body of contrary precedent was not controlling in light of our more recent decisions addressing the scope of the § 2254(d) presumption of correctness. See *Wainwright v. Witt* [fn. d supra]; *Patton v. Yount* [Note 7 supra]; *Rushen v. Spain* [Note 7 supra]; *Maggio v. Fulford* [fn. b supra]; *Marshall v. Lonberger* [Note 5 supra]. We acknowledge that the Court has not charted an entirely clear course in this area. We reject, however, the Court of Appeals' conclusion that these case-specific holdings tacitly overturned the longstanding rule that the voluntariness of a confession is a matter for independent federal determination.

"In the § 2254(d) context, as elsewhere, the appropriate methodology for distinguishing questions of fact from questions of law has been, to say the least,

d. Consider also *Wainwright v. Witt,* ___ U.S. ___, 105 S.Ct. 844, 83 L.Ed.2d 841 (1985), where the Court, after rejecting the lower court's conclusion that a "strict legal standard" applied to the exclusion of a juror opposed to capital punishment (see p. 1282 supra), concluded § 2254(d) applied to the state trial court's finding that the particular juror's opposition to capital punishment would substantially impair her ability to comply with the court's instruction.

elusive. A few principles, however, are by now well established. For example, that an issue involves an inquiry into state of mind is not at all inconsistent with treating it as a question of fact. See, e.g., *Maggio v. Fulford.* Equally clearly, an issue does not lose its factual character merely because its resolution is dispositive of the ultimate constitutional question. * * * But beyond these elemental propositions, negative in form, the Court has yet to arrive at a rule or principle that will unerringly distinguish a factual finding from a legal conclusion. * * *

"Perhaps much of the difficulty in this area stems from the practical truth that the decision to label an issue a 'question of law,' a 'question of fact,' or a 'mixed question of law and fact' is sometimes as much a matter of allocation as it is of analysis. See Monaghan, *Constitutional Fact Review,* 85 Colum.L.Rev. 229, 237 (1985). At least in those instances in which Congress has not spoken and in which the issue falls somewhere between a pristine legal standard and a simple historical fact, the fact/law distinction at times has turned on a determination that, as a matter of the sound administration of justice, one judicial actor is better positioned than another to decide the issue in question. Where, for example, as with proof of actual malice in First Amendment libel cases, the relevant legal principle can be given meaning only through its application to the particular circumstances of a case, the Court has been reluctant to give the trier of fact's conclusions presumptive force and, in so doing, strip a federal appellate court of its primary function as an expositor of law. * * * Similarly, on rare occasions in years past the Court has justified independent federal or appellate review as a means of compensating for 'perceived shortcomings of the trier of fact by way of bias or some other factor . . . .' [The Court here cited a series of earlier coerced confession cases.] In contrast, other considerations often suggest the appropriateness of resolving close questions concerning the status of an issue as one of 'law' or 'fact' in favor of extending deference to the trial court. When, for example, the issue involves the credibility of witnesses and therefore turns largely on an evaluation of demeanor, there are compelling and familiar justifications for leaving the process of applying law to fact to the trial court and according its determinations presumptive weight. *Patton v. Yount,* and *Wainwright v. Witt,* are illustrative. * * *

"For several reasons we think that it would be inappropriate to abandon the Court's longstanding position that the ultimate question of the admissibility of a confession merits treatment as a legal inquiry requiring plenary federal review. We note at the outset that we do not write on a clean slate. 'Very weighty considerations underlie the principle that courts should not lightly overrule past decisions.' * * * Moreover, as previously noted, Congress patterned § 2254(d) after *Townsend v. Sain,* a case that clearly assumed that the voluntariness of a confession was an issue for independent federal determination. Thus, not only are *stare decisis* concerns compelling, but, unlike in *Marshall v. Lonberger, Rushen v. Spain,* or any of our other recent § 2254(d) cases, in the confession context we have the benefit of some congressional guidance in resolving whether the disputed issue falls outside of the scope of the § 2254(d) presumption. * * * We reiterate our confidence that state judges, no less than their federal counterparts, will properly discharge their duty to protect the constitutional rights of criminal defendants. We note only that in the confession context, independent federal review has traditionally played an important parallel role in protecting the rights at stake when the prosecution secures a conviction through the defendant's own admissions."

*

Index

References are to Pages

References are to Pages

†